Introduction

The Ethiopian Bible, known for its unique canon of 88 books, is one of the oldest and most comprehensive collections of sacred scripture in the world. Revered within the Ethiopian Orthodox Tewahido Church, this Bible encompasses a rich tapestry of texts that have shaped the spiritual and cultural landscape of Ethiopia for centuries. Notably, it includes several ancient writings, such as the Book of Enoch and the Book of Jubilees, which offer valuable insights into the historical and theological context of early Judaism and Christianity. These texts reflect the deeply rooted spiritual tradition of Ethiopia, a country that has played a pivotal role in the history of Christianity since its earliest centuries.

The Ethiopian Orthodox Tewahido Church holds the Bible not only as a source of divine revelation but also as the foundation of its faith and practice. Central to the identity of the Church is its unwavering commitment to the unity of divine and human natures in Christ, a belief encapsulated in the term "Tewahido," meaning "made one" or "united." This theological perspective influences the Church's approach to scripture, emphasizing the interconnectedness of the sacred texts with the lived experience of faith, worship, and moral reflection. The Ethiopian Bible is thus a guide to understanding the mysteries of God and a means of fostering deeper communion with Him.

The Bible's contents are deeply integrated into the liturgical life of the Ethiopian Orthodox Tewahido Church, which is known for its rich and vibrant worship traditions. Many of its passages are recited or chanted in the ancient Ge'ez language during services, underscoring the Bible's role as both a spiritual guide and a cultural treasure. The Ethiopian Bible is also used extensively in teaching and catechesis, helping the faithful to understand their faith and apply its principles to daily life. Its stories, prayers, and teachings serve as a source of inspiration and guidance, encouraging believers to cultivate a life of holiness and compassion.

The compilation of the Ethiopian Bible of 88 Books reflects the collective efforts of a community deeply devoted to preserving and honoring its sacred heritage. Drawing on centuries of scriptural scholarship and tradition, this version embodies the Church's commitment to maintaining the integrity and depth of its theological legacy. Through careful preservation and meticulous transmission, the Ethiopian Orthodox Tewahido Church has ensured that this sacred text continues to speak to the hearts and minds of believers across generations. The Ethiopian Bible also reflects the Church's profound respect for its ancient Jewish roots, as seen in its inclusion of texts such as the Book of Jubilees and the Book of Enoch, which expand upon the narratives of the Hebrew Bible with intricate details and theological insights. These writings, alongside the rest of the canon, reveal a deep continuity between the faith of Israel and the message of Christ, affirming the Church's belief in the fulfillment of the Old Testament prophecies in the New Testament.

In the Ethiopian Orthodox Tewahido tradition, scripture is not only a source of knowledge but also a pathway to spiritual transformation. Believers are encouraged to meditate on the teachings of the Bible, allowing its divine wisdom to shape their thoughts, words, and actions. The Bible is seen as a living text, offering guidance for every aspect of life and drawing individuals closer to the mystery of God's love and grace.

In sharing the Ethiopian Bible of 88 Books, we do so with a deep sense of reverence and responsibility, mindful of the rich heritage it represents. This compilation stands as a testament to the enduring faith of the Ethiopian Orthodox Tewahido Church and its commitment to preserving the sacred traditions that have nourished its people for centuries. It is our hope that readers will engage with these texts in a spirit of openness and respect, finding within them a source of spiritual inspiration and a deeper appreciation for the rich tapestry of Ethiopian Christianity.

Copyright Notice © 2025

All rights reserved. This publication contains selections from the Ethiopian Bible, a collection that includes texts in the public domain. The introductory sections, contextual commentary, and any supplementary materials have been authored specifically for this work and are protected under copyright. No part of this publication may be reproduced, distributed, or transmitted in any form or by any means, whether electronic, mechanical, photocopying, recording, or any other information storage and retrieval system, without prior written permission from the publisher. Brief quotations may be used in reviews or academic works, provided proper credit is given and the use complies with copyright law.

Disclaimer

This book is a curated presentation of the Ethiopian Bible's 88 books, designed to provide an accessible format for study, reflection, and worship. The scriptural texts themselves remain unaltered, preserving their original content and significance. The introductory and concluding sections, as well as contextual commentaries, have been added by the author to enhance the reader's understanding and appreciation of these ancient writings. These additions are not part of the original sacred texts but are intended to offer historical, theological, and spiritual insights that complement them. The author emphasizes that these sections should not be interpreted as altering the meaning or authority of the scriptures.

While every effort has been made to ensure the accuracy and faithfulness of the content, translations, and accompanying commentary, readers are encouraged to approach the texts with the reverence and respect they deserve, mindful of their profound spiritual and cultural heritage.

Limitation of Liability

The author and publisher disclaim all liability for any damages, losses, or consequences resulting from the use of this book. This publication is provided "as is," without any express or implied warranties regarding its suitability for a particular purpose or its completeness. While great care has been taken to preserve the integrity of the texts and provide thoughtful commentary, the publisher is not responsible for any interpretations, outcomes, or actions derived from its use.

This book is a labor of respect and devotion to the Ethiopian Bible and its enduring influence. It is offered as a resource for individuals seeking to engage with its profound teachings, historical depth, and spiritual insights. Readers are encouraged to seek further understanding through prayer, study, and consultation with qualified **religious and historical experts where necessary.**

Introduction to the Author

This book is the culmination of an extensive and thoughtful effort to provide an invaluable resource for understanding the Ethiopian Bible, one of the most ancient and complete collections of sacred scripture in existence. Drawing from years of dedicated research and collaboration with experts in theology, biblical studies, and EthiopianChristian tradition, the author has carefully

curated this work to illuminate the profound historical, theological, and spiritual significance of these sacred texts. The Ethiopian Bible stands apart with its unique canon, including numerous books not found in other Christian Bibles. With meticulous care, the author has ensured that this presentation is both engaging and informative, reflecting the depth and richness of Ethiopian Christianity. Special attention has been given to the historical and cultural context of the texts, highlighting the central role of the Ethiopian Orthodox Tewahido Church in preserving early Christian writings and traditions.

This book has been crafted to guide readers through the expansive canon of the Ethiopian Bible, offering a clear understanding of its diverse books and the apocryphal texts that have played a pivotal role in shaping Ethiopian Christian faith and practice. Every effort has been made to respect the sacred and historical importance of these writings while making them accessible to modern readers who seek a deeper connection to this ancient tradition.

Grounded in scholarly research and a deep reverence for the Ethiopian Christian heritage, this work serves as a bridge between the past and the present. It offers a unique opportunity for readers to explore the Ethiopian Bible's contributions to global Christianity and to discover its enduring spiritual relevance. The author's dedication to preserving the integrity of these sacred texts while offering insights into their significance reflects a heartfelt commitment to sharing their wisdom with a worldwide audience.

Table Of Content

1 – Genesis 6
2 – Exodus 31
3 – Leviticus 47
4 – Numbers 61
5 – Deuteronomy 81
6 – Joshua 99
7 – Judges 111
8 – Ruth 120
9 – 1 Samuel 122
10 – 2 Samuel 135
11 – 1 king 144
12 – 2 Kings 159
13 – 1 Chronicles 172
14 – 2 Chronicles 186
15 – Ezra 202
16 – Nehemiah 206
17 – Esther 213
18 – Job 216
19 – Psalms 232
20 – Proverbs 265
21 – Ecclestiates 275
22 – Song of Solomon 279
23 – Isahia 280
24 – Jeremiah 303
25 – Lamentations 329
26 – Ezekiel 331
27 – Daniel 351
28 – Hosea 355
29 – Joel 358
30 – Amos 359
31 – Obadiah 361
32 – Jonah 361
33 – Micah 362
34 – Nahum 363
35 – Habakuk 364
36 – Zaphaniah 365
37 – Haggai 366
38 – Zechariah 366
39 – Malachi 369
40 – Mathew 370
41 – Mark 384
42 – Luke 391
43 – John 401
44 – Acts 411
45 – Romans 423
46 – 1 Corinthians 428
47 – 2 Corinthians 432
48 – Galatians 435
49 – Ephasians 436
50 – Philipians 438
51 – Colossians 439
52 – 1 Thessalonians 440
53 – 2 Thessolonians 441
54 – 1 Timmothy 442
55 – 2 Timothy 443
56 – 2 Titus 444
57 - 2 Philemon 444
58 – Hebrews 445
59 – 1 Peter 449
60 – 2 Peter 450
61 – James 451
62 – 1 John 452
63 – 2 John 453

64 – 3 John	454
65 – Jude	454
66 – Revelation	454
67 – Tobit	459
68 – Judith	462
69 – Letter of Jeremiah	466
70 – The Prayer of Azariah	467
71 – Esdaras	467
72 – Wisdom of Solomon	472
73 – The First Book of Maccabees	479
74 – The Second Book of Maccabees	488
75 – The Third book of Maccabees	494
76 – The Book oF Enoch	496
77 – The First Epistle of Clement to the Corinthians	505
78 – 1 Baruch	511
79 – 2 Baruch	511
80 – The book of Sirach, or Ecclesiasticus	511
81 – Jubilees	524
82 – Bel and the Dragon	544
83 – Prayer of Manasseh	545
84 – Psalm 151	545
85 – The Song of the Three Holy Children	545
86 – First Testament of Abraham	546
87 – The History of Susanna	547
88 – The Shepherd of Hermas	547
The Complete Audio File	549

1 – Genesis
Chapter 1
1. In the start, God created the heavens and the earth. (Heavens: the sky or universe; earth: the planet) 2. The earth was formless, empty, and darkness covered the deep waters. The Spirit of the Lord relocated over the waters. (Formless: without form; deep waters: primordial waters) 3. God said, "Let there be light," and light seemed there. (Light: seen illumination) 4. God saw that the light was good, and He separated it from the darkness. (Separated: divided) 5. God called the light "Day" and the darkness "Night." There was evening, and there was morning—the first day. (Night: sunset; morning: dawn) 6. God said, "Let there be a firmament in the midst of the waters, and let it divide the waters from the waters." (Firmament: expanse, sky) 7. God made the firmament and separated the waters beneath it from the waters above it. And it was so. (Waters beneath: oceans; waters above: clouds) 8. God called the firmament "Heaven." And the evening and the morning marked the second day. (Heaven: sky or heavens) 9. God said, "Let the waters beneath the heaven be gathered into one place, and let the dry land appear." And it was so. (Dry land: earth) 10. God called the dry land "Earth," and the gathered waters He called "Seas." And God saw that it was good. (Earth: land; Seas: oceans) 11. Then God said, "Let the earth bring forth grass, plants that yield seeds, and trees that bear fruit, with seeds inside, each according to its kind." And it was so. (Yield: produce; seeds: reproductive units) 12. The earth brought forth grass, seed-bearing plants, and trees that bore fruit with seeds in it, each according to its kind. And God saw that it was good. (Seeds: contained in the fruit) 13. The evening and the morning marked the third day. 14. God said, "Let there be lights in the firmament of the heaven to divide day from night, and let them serve as signs for seasons, days, and years." (Lights: stars, celestial bodies; seasons: times of the year) 15. "Let them shine upon the earth." And it was so. (Shine: illuminate) 16. God made two great lights: the greater light to rule the day, and the lesser light to rule the night. He also made the stars. (Greater light: sun; lesser light: moon) 17. God set them in the firmament of the heavens to give light upon the earth, (Firmament: sky) 18. to rule over the day and night, and to divide light from darkness. And God saw that it was good. (Rule: govern; divide: separate) 19. The evening and the morning marked the fourth day. 20. God said, "Let the waters bring forth creatures that live and move, and let birds fly above the earth across the sky." 21. God created great sea creatures and every living thing that moves in the waters, each according to its kind, and every bird according to its kind. And God saw that it was good. (Sea creatures: marine animals; kinds: species) 22. God blessed them, saying, "Be fruitful, multiply, fill the seas, and let birds multiply on the earth." (Blessed: empowered; multiply: reproduce) 23. The evening and the morning marked the fifth day. (Evening: sunset; morning: dawn) 24. God said, "Let the earth bring forth living creatures according to their kinds: cattle, creeping things, and wild beasts of the earth, each according to its kind." And it was so. (Living creatures: animals; creeping things: small creatures) 25. God made the wild beasts according to their kinds, the livestock according to their kinds, and everything that creeps on the earth according to its kind. And God saw that it was good. (Kinds: species) 26. Then God said, "Let us make man in Our image, according to Our likeness, and let them have dominion over the fish of the sea, the birds of the air, the cattle, and all the earth, and every living thing that moves on the earth." (Us: plural reference; dominion: rule or authority) 27. So God created man in His own image; in the image of God He created him; male and female He created them. (Image: likeness) 28. God blessed them and said, "Be fruitful, multiply, fill the earth, and subdue it. Have dominion over the fish of the sea, the birds of the air, and every living thing that moves on the earth." (Subdue: bring under control) 29. Then God said, "I have given you every plant that produces seeds on the earth, and every tree with fruit that contains seeds. They will be your food." (Plants: flora; seeds: reproductive units) 30. "And to every beast of the earth, every bird of the air, and every creature that moves on the ground, I have given every green plant for food." And it was so. (Beast: wild animal; green plant: vegetation) 31. God saw everything He had made, and indeed, it was very good. The evening and the morning marked the sixth day. (Good: perfect, complete)

Chapter 2
1. Hence, the heavens and the earth were finished, along with their entire host. (Host: all living beings) 2. On the seventh day, God completed His work that He had performed, and He rested on the seventh day from all His work. (Completed: finished; rested: ceased from labor) 3. God blessed the seventh day and made it holy, because on it He rested from all His work of creation. (Holy: set aside) 4. These are the generations of the heavens and the earth after they had been created, on the day when the Lord God made the earth and the heavens. (Generations: origins or records) 5. Every plant of the field had not yet appeared on the earth, and every herb had not yet grown. For the Lord God had not caused it to rain on the earth, and there was no man to till the ground. (Till: cultivate) 6. But a mist rose from the earth and watered the whole surface of the ground. (Mist: vapor) 7. The Lord God formed man from the dust of the earth and breathed into his nostrils the breath of life, and man became a living being. (Living being: soul, living creature) 8. The Lord God planted a garden in Eden, to the east, and placed the man He had formed there. (Garden: paradise) 9. Out of the ground, the Lord God made every tree grow that was pleasant to the sight and good for food. Also, in the midst of the garden, He planted the tree of life, and the tree of the knowledge of good and evil. (Pleasant: beautiful; knowledge of good and evil: moral discernment) 10. A river flowed out of Eden to water the garden, and from there it divided into four branches. (Divided: separated) 11. The name of the first river is Pison; it winds through the whole land of Havilah, where there is gold. (Pison: river name; Havilah: region) 12. The gold of that land is good, and there is also bdellium and onyx stone. (Bdellium: resin from a tree; onyx: gemstone) 13. The second river is Gihon; it flows around the whole land of Cush. (Gihon: river name; Cush: ancient region, likely in Africa) 14. The third river is Hiddekel; it flows toward the east of Assyria. The fourth river is the Euphrates. (Hiddekel: Tigris River; Assyria: ancient empire) 15. The Lord God took the man and placed him in the garden of Eden to cultivate it and keep it. (Cultivate: tend to) 16. The Lord God commanded the man, "You may freely eat from every tree in the garden, (Freely: without limit) 17. but of the tree of the knowledge of good and evil, you shall not eat from it; for in the day that you eat from it, you will surely die." (Knowledge of good and evil: moral awareness; surely die: face certain death) 18. The Lord God said, "It is not good for man to be alone; I will make a helper suitable for him." (Helper: partner; suitable: fit for him) 19. Out of the ground, the Lord God formed every animal of the field and every bird of the air and brought them to Adam to see what he would call them. Whatever Adam called each living creature, that was its name. (Brought: presented; living creature: animal) 20. Adam gave names to all the cattle, the birds of the air, and every animal of the field; but for Adam, no suitable helper was found. (Suitable: corresponding) 21. So the Lord God caused a deep sleep to fall upon Adam, and he slept. He took one of his ribs and closed up the place with flesh. (Deep sleep: unconscious sleep) 22. Then the rib that the Lord God had taken from the man, He made into a woman and brought her to the man. 23. Adam said, "This is now bone of my bones, and flesh of my flesh. She shall be called Woman, because she was taken out of Man." (Bone of my bones: part of me; woman: from man) 24. Therefore, a man shall leave his father and mother and be united to his wife, and they shall become one flesh. (United: cleave; one flesh: a unified bond) 25. The

man and his wife were both naked, and they were not ashamed. (Naked: without clothing; not ashamed: unembarrassed)

Chapter 3

1. Now, the serpent was more cunning than any of the wild animals the Lord God had made. He asked the woman, "Did God really say you cannot eat from any tree in the garden?" (Cunning: foxy) 2. The woman answered the serpent, "We can eat the fruit from the trees in the garden, (Answered: responded) 3. but about the fruit from the tree in the middle of the garden, God said, 'You shall not eat from it, nor touch it, or you will die.'" (You will die: face death) 4. The serpent told the woman, "You will not die, (You will not die: no death will come) 5. for God knows that when you eat from it, your eyes will be opened, and you will become like God, knowing good and evil." (Knowing good and evil: moral discernment) 6. When the woman saw that the tree was good for food, pleasing to the eyes, and desirable for gaining wisdom, she took some of its fruit and ate it. She also gave some to her husband, who was with her, and he ate it. (Desirable: attractive) 7. Then their eyes were opened, and they realized they were naked; so they sewed fig leaves together and made themselves loincloths. 8. They heard the sound of the Lord God walking in the garden during the cool of the day, and Adam and his wife hid themselves from the Lord God among the trees. (Hid: concealed themselves) 9. But the Lord God called to Adam and asked, "Where are you?" 10. He answered, "I heard You in the garden, and I was afraid because I was naked, so I hid myself." (Hid: concealed) 11. And God asked, "Who told you that you were naked? Have you eaten from the tree I commanded you not to eat from?" (Commanded: instructed) 12. The man answered, "The woman You put here with me—she gave me some fruit from the tree, and I ate it." (Answered: replied) 13. Then the Lord God said to the woman, "What have you done?" The woman said, "The serpent deceived me, and I ate." (Deceived: misled) 14. So the Lord God said to the serpent, "Because you have done this, you are cursed more than all cattle and wild animals. You will crawl on your belly and eat dust all the days of your life." (Cursed: condemned) 15. "I will put enmity between you and the woman, and between your offspring and hers; he will crush your head, and you will strike his heel." (Offspring: descendants; crush: defeat) 16. To the woman, He said, "I will greatly increase your pain in childbirth; with pain, you will bring forth children. Your desire will be for your husband, and he will rule over you." (Pain: suffering; desire: longing) 17. To Adam, He said, "Because you listened to your wife and ate from the tree I commanded you not to eat from, cursed is the ground because of you. In painful toil, you will eat from it all the days of your life. (Toil: hard work) 18. It will produce thorns and thistles for you, and you will eat the plants of the field." (Thorns: prickly plants) 19. "By the sweat of your brow, you will eat food until you return to the ground, for from it you were taken; for dust you are, and to dust you will return." (Sweat of your brow: through hard labor) 20. Adam named his wife Eve because she would become the mother of all the living. (Eve: life-giver) 21. The Lord God made garments of skin for Adam and his wife and clothed them. (Garments: clothing) 22. And the Lord God said, "Behold, the man has become like one of us, knowing good and evil. Now, lest he take also from the tree of life, and eat and live forever," (Like one of Us: having divine knowledge) 23. So the Lord God expelled him from the garden of Eden to work the ground from which he had been taken. (Expelled: sent away) 24. After that, He drove the man out, and He placed cherubim on the east of the garden of Eden, along with a flaming sword that turned in every direction to guard the way to the tree of life. (Cherubim: angelic beings; flaming sword: symbol of divine protection)

Chapter 4

1. Adam had relations with Eve, his wife, and he conceived and gave birth to Cain. She said, "I have acquired a man with the help of the LORD." (Acquired: gotten) 2. Later, she gave birth to his brother Abel. Abel became a shepherd, while Cain worked the soil. (Shepherd: flock caretaker) 3. At the end of days, Cain brought an offering from the produce of the land to the LORD. (At the end of days: as time passed) 4. Abel, likewise, brought an offering of the firstborn of his flock and their fat portions. The LORD accepted Abel and his offering, (Firstborn: firstlings) 5. but He did not accept Cain and his offering. Cain became very angry, and his face fell. (Angry: wroth) 6. The LORD asked Cain, "Why are you angry? Why has your face fallen?" (Face fallen: expression changed) 7. "If you do what is right, will you not be accepted? But if you do not, sin is crouching at your door; it desires to control you, but you must rule over it." (Accepted: have the excellency; desires: is subject) 8. Cain said to Abel, "Let's go out into the field." While they were there, Cain attacked Abel and killed him. (Attacked: rose up against) 9. Then the LORD asked Cain, "Where is your brother Abel?" Cain answered, "I don't know. Am I my brother's keeper?" (Keeper: caretaker) 10. The LORD said, "What have you done? Your brother's blood is crying out to Me from the ground." (Crying out: speaks from) 11. "Now you are cursed from the earth, which has opened its mouth to receive your brother's blood from your hand. (Cursed: condemned) 12. When you work the soil, it will no longer yield good crops for you. You will be a restless wanderer on the earth." (Restless wanderer: fugitive and vagabond) 13. Cain said to the LORD, "My punishment is more than I can bear! (Punishment: iniquity) 14. Today you have driven me from the land, and I will be hidden from Your presence. I will be a fugitive and a wanderer, and anyone who finds me will kill me." (Hidden: far from You) 15. The LORD said to him, "Not so! Anyone who kills Cain will suffer vengeance seven times over." Then the LORD put a mark on Cain to protect him from being killed. (Mark: protective sign) 16. So Cain left the LORD's presence and settled in the land of Nod, east of Eden. (Nod: wandering) 17. Cain had relations with his wife, and she became pregnant and gave birth to Enoch. Cain built a city and named it after his son, Enoch. (Enoch: meaning "dedicated") 18. Enoch became the father of Irad, and Irad became the father of Mehujael, Mehujael became the father of Methusael, and Methusael became the father of Lamech. (Lamech: meaning "strong") 19. Lamech married two wives: the name of one was Adah, and the other's name was Zillah. (Married: took) 20. Adah gave birth to Jabal; he was the father of those who live in tents and raise livestock. (Jabal: father of herders) 21. His brother's name was Jubal; he was the father of all who play the harp and flute. (Jubal: father of musicians) 22. Zillah also had a son, Tubal-Cain, who forged all kinds of tools out of bronze and iron. His sister was Naamah. (Tubal-Cain: maker of tools) 23. Lamech said to his wives, "Adah and Zillah, listen to my voice; wives of Lamech, hear my words: I have killed a man for wounding me, a young man for hurting me." (Voice: speech; listen: heed) 24. "If Cain is avenged seven times, then Lamech seventy-seven times." (Seventy-seven times: in many instances) 25. Adam had relations with his wife again, and she gave birth to a son and named him Seth, saying, "God has appointed another child in place of Abel, since Cain killed him." (Appointed: given) 26. Seth also had a son, and he named him Enosh. At that time, people began to call on the name of the LORD. (Enosh: meaning "man"; call on: invoke)

Chapter 5

1. This is the account of the descendants of Adam. When God created man, He made him in His very own likeness. (Likeness: resemblance) 2. He created them male and lady, blessed them, and referred to as their name Adam after they have been created. (Call: Adam, which means "man") 3. Adam lived 130 years, after which fathered a son in his own likeness, according to his image. He named him Seth. (Likeness: resemblance) 4. After Seth's start, Adam lived 800 greater years and had other little children. (Little children: different offspring) 5. In total, Adam lived 930 years, after which he died. (Died: passed away) 6. Seth lived 105 years and fathered Enos. (Enos: Hebrew for "guy") 7. After Enos became born, Seth lived some other 807 years and had other little kids. (other little children: greater kids) 8. Seth lived 912 years in general, after which he died.

9. Enos lived 90 years and fathered Cainan. (Cainan: Hebrew for "possession") 10. After Cainan's birth, Enos lived another 815 years and had different little kids. (little kids: extra children) 11. Enos lived 905 years in overall, after which he died. 12. Cainan live d 70 years and fathered Mahalaleel. (Mahalaleel: Hebrew for "reward of God") 13. After Mahalaleel turned into born, Cainan lived other 840 years and had other little kids. (little children: extra offspring) 14. Cainan lived 910 years in general, after which he died. 15. Mahalaleel lived sixty five years and fathered Jared. (Jared: Hebrew for "descent") 16. After Jared became born, Mahalaleel lived every other 830 years and had other little children. (Sons and daughters: extra kids) 17. Mahalaleel lived 895 years in general, and then he died. (Died: handed away) 18. Jared lived 162 years and fathered Enoch. (Enoch: Hebrew for "devoted") 19. After Enoch turned into born, Jared lived any other 800 years and had other little kids. (Little kids: more children)20. Jared lived 962 years in total, after which he died. (died: passed away) 21. Enoch lived 65 years and fathered Methuselah. (Methuselah: Hebrew for "guy of the spear") 22. After Methuselah changed into born, Enoch walked intently with God for three hundred years, and had other little children. (Walked closely: lived in fellowship with) 23. Enoch lived 365 years in total. (Died: did now not die, was taken through God) 24. Enoch walked with God; then he changed into no more, due to the fact God took him away. (Was taken: eliminated without loss of life) 25. Methuselah lived 187 years and fathered Lamech. (Lamech: Hebrew for "effective") 26. After Lamech changed into born, Methuselah lived another 782 years and had different sons and daughters. (little kids: extra offspring) 27. Methuselah lived 969 years in general, and then he died. (died: handed away) 28. Lamech lived 182 years and fathered a son. (son: Noah, that means "relaxation" or "consolation") 29. Lamech named him Noah, announcing, "This one will bring us comfort from our paintings and from the painful hard work of our fingers, because of the floor which the LORD has cursed." (Noah: meaning "rest" or "consolation") 30. After Noah's delivery, Lamech lived some other 595 years and had different little kids. (little children: extra offspring) 31. Lamech lived 777 years in total, after which he died. (died: surpassed away) 32. when Noah became 500 years old, he became the daddy of Shem, Ham, and Japheth. (Shem, Ham, Japheth: Noah's sons)

Chapter 6
1. As mankind started out to multiply on earth, and daughters have been born to them, (multiply: increase in range) 2. the sons of God noticed that the daughters of fellows have been lovely, and they chose better halves for themselves from all they favored. (Sons of God: divine beings, probable angels) 3. The LORD said, "My Spirit shall no longer remain with man forever, for he is likewise flesh; his days may be limited to one hundred twenty years." (Flesh: mortal nature, restricted lifespan) 4. There had been giants on earth in the ones days, or even in a while, when the sons of God had family members with the daughters of fellows, and that they bore youngsters to them. those youngsters became effective guys of vintage, men of renown. (Giants: Nephilim, often described as amazing or fallen ones) 5. The LORD noticed how excellent the wickedness of mankind had grown to be on this planet, and that each inclination of the thoughts of his heart changed into most effective evil all of the time. (Wickedness: moral corruption, evil goals) 6. The LORD regretted that He had made man on the earth, and His coronary heart became deeply. (Regretted: felt sorrow) 7. So the LORD said, "I can wipe mankind, whom I have created, from the face of the earth—guys and animals, creatures that circulate alongside the ground, and birds of the air—for I regret that I have made them." (wipe: smash, do away with) 8. however Noah observed favor within the eyes of the LORD. (Favor: grace, kindness) 9. this is the account of Noah: Noah was a righteous man, innocent most of the people of his time, and he walked faithfully with God. (Righteous: just, morally upright)10. Noah had three sons: Shem, Ham, and Japheth. (Sons: the 3 who survived the flood) 11. Now the earth was corrupt in God's sight, and the earth became packed with violence. (Corrupt: morally degraded, wicked) 12. God saw how corrupt the earth had turn out to be, for all of the humans on this planet had corrupted their methods. (Corrupted: deviated from God's approaches) 13. So God stated to Noah, "The end of every body has come earlier than me, for the earth is filled with violence because of them. i'm going to ruin them along with the earth." (End: the very last judgment on the earth) 14. Make yourself an ark of cypress wooden; make rooms in it and coat it with pitch interior and out. (Ark: a massive boat; cypress wooden: a durable cloth) 15. this is how you're to build it: The ark is to be 450 toes lengthy, 75 toes extensive, and forty five ft. excessive. (Duration, width, height: measurements for the ark) 16. Make a roof for the ark and finish it to a cubit underneath the roof. Placed a door within the side of the ark and make lower, middle, and upper decks. (roof: pinnacle cover; cubit: a unit of size) 17. i am going to bring floodwaters on the earth to break all life underneath the heavens, each creature that has the breath of lifestyles in it. Everything on the planet will perish. (Floodwaters: an extremely good deluge) 18. However i can establish My covenant with you, and you'll enter the ark—you and your sons and your spouse and your sons' wives with you. (Covenant: a binding settlement or promise) 19. you're to convey into the ark two of all residing creatures, male and female, to keep them alive with you. (Living creatures: all forms of animals) 20. two of every sort of fowl, of each kind of animal, and of each kind of creature that movements alongside the floor will come to you to be kept alive. (Creature: any dwelling aspect, which includes bugs) 21. you are to take each form of meals this is to be eaten and store it away as meals for you and for them. (Meals: provisions for the adventure) 22. Noah did the whole lot just as God commanded him. (Obeyed: accompanied God's instructions)

Chapter 7
1. Then the LORD said to Noah, "Come into the ark, you and your entire household, for I have found you righteous in this generation." (Righteous: morally upright, favored by God) 2. Take with you seven pairs of every kind of clean animal, male and female, and one pair of every kind of unclean animal, male and female. (Clean animals: suitable for sacrifice; unclean: animals considered impure) 3. Likewise, take seven pairs of every kind of bird, male and female, to keep their species alive on the earth. (Seven pairs: ensuring survival of species) 4. In seven days, I will send rain on the earth for forty days and forty nights, and I will wipe out every living thing that I have made from the face of the earth. (Wipe out: destroy entirely) 5. Noah did everything the LORD commanded him. (Obeyed: fully followed God's instructions) 6. Noah was six hundred years old when the floodwaters came upon the earth. (Noah's age: indicating the great age before the flood) 7. Noah, his sons, his wife, and his sons' wives entered the ark to escape the waters of the flood. (Entered: boarded the ark to survive) 8. Of clean and unclean animals, birds, and all creatures that move along the ground, (take every kind: animals of all sorts were included) 9. Two of each kind, male and female, came to Noah and entered the ark, just as God had commanded him. (Two of every kind: symbolic of preservation) 10. And after seven days, the floodwaters came upon the earth. (After seven days: the flood began as promised) 11. On the seventeenth day of the second month of Noah's six hundredth year, the fountains of the deep burst open, and the floodgates of the heavens were opened. (Fountains of the deep: waters from beneath the earth, floodgates: celestial windows opened) 12. It rained on the earth for forty days and forty nights. 13. On the very day Noah, along with his sons Shem, Ham, and Japheth, and his wife, and the three wives of his sons, entered the ark, (the family: Noah's family entering for safety) 14. they and every kind of animal—wild beasts, cattle, creeping things, and every kind of bird— (kind: species or category of living creatures) 15. came in pairs, male and female, to Noah and entered the ark. (Pair: ensuring survival) 16. The animals that entered, male and female of every living thing,

went in as God had commanded Noah; and the LORD shut him in. (LORD shut him in: God closed the door, securing Noah's safety) **17.** For forty days the floodwaters increased, lifting the ark high above the earth. (Floodwaters increased: the waters continued rising) **18.** The waters surged and became more powerful on the earth, and the ark floated on the surface. (Surged: overflowed, rose dramatically) **19.** The waters became so mighty that all the high mountains under the heavens were covered. (high mountains: even the highest peaks were submerged) **20.** The waters rose by more than fifteen cubits, and the mountains were covered. (covered: the earth's surface was submerged by floodwaters) **21.** Every living thing that moved on the earth—birds, livestock, wild animals, and all creatures that swarmed over the earth—died. (Swarmed: creatures moving over the ground) **22.** Everything on dry land that had the breath of life in its nostrils died. (Breath of life: vital spirit that sustains life) **23.** Every living thing was wiped out, and only Noah and those with him in the ark remained alive. (wiped out: destroyed from the earth) **24.** The waters flooded the earth for one hundred and fifty days. (Flooded: the deluge continued for a lengthy period)

Chapter 8

1. Then God remembered Noah, and all the animals and creatures that were with him in the ark. God sent a wind to blow across the earth, and the waters began to recede. (God remembered: God turned His attention to Noah's situation) **2.** The fountains of the deep and the windows of heaven were closed, and the rain from the sky stopped. (Fountains of the deep: the waters from beneath the earth) **3.** Gradually, the waters began to retreat from the earth. After one hundred and fifty days, the waters had significantly decreased. (Gradually: waters returned slowly and steadily) **4.** On the seventeenth day of the seventh month, the ark came to rest on the mountains of Ararat. (Ararat: a mountain range in modern-day Turkey) **5.** The waters continued to diminish until the tenth month. On the first day of the tenth month, the peaks of the mountains became visible. (Peaks visible: the earth's surface began to reemerge) **6.** After forty days, Noah opened the window he had made in the ark. (Window: an opening for ventilation) **7.** He sent out a raven, which flew back and forth until the waters had dried up from the earth. (Back and forth: the raven searched but found no dry land) **8.** Next, he sent out a dove to see if the waters had receded from the surface of the ground. (Dove: a symbol of peace and hope) **9.** The dove could not find a place to rest, as the waters still covered the earth. So, she returned to Noah in the ark, and he took her in. (took her in: brought her back into the ark) **10.** After waiting another seven days, Noah sent the dove out again. (Waiting seven days: giving more time for the waters to recede) **11.** In the evening, the dove returned with an olive leaf in her beak. Noah knew then that the waters had receded from the earth. (Olive leaf: a sign of renewal and peace) **12.** Noah waited another seven days and sent the dove out again, but this time she did not return. (no return: the dove found a place to rest) **13.** In the six hundred and first year of Noah's life, on the first day of the first month, the earth was completely dry. Noah removed the covering of the ark and saw that the ground was dry. (Earth dry: signifying the end of the flood) **14.** By the twenty-seventh day of the second month, the earth was fully dried. (Full dryness: the earth had completely dried out) **15.** Then God spoke to Noah, saying, (God speaks: God's command to leave the ark) **16.** "Go out of the ark, you, your wife, your sons, and your sons' wives with you. (Leave the ark: a command to repopulate the earth) **17.** Bring out with you every living thing that is with you—birds, animals, and every creeping thing—that they may multiply on the earth and be fruitful, and fill the earth." (Multiply: God's command for creation to flourish again) **18.** So Noah, his sons, his wife, and his sons' wives left the ark. (Noah and family: they exited the ark together) **19.** Every animal, every creeping thing, and every bird, according to their kinds, went out of the ark. (Kinds: categories or species of living creatures) **20.** Then Noah built an altar to the LORD and offered burnt offerings of every clean animal and clean bird on it. (Burnt offerings: acts of worship and gratitude to God) **21.** The LORD smelled the pleasing aroma and said in His heart, "Never again will I curse the ground because of man, even though every inclination of his heart is evil from childhood. And never again will I destroy all living creatures, as I have done." (Pleasing aroma: the scent of the sacrifice pleased God) **22.** "As long as the earth endures, seedtime and harvest, cold and heat, summer and winter, day and night will never cease." (Earth's stability: God's promise of the seasons and natural order continuing)

Chapter 9

1. God blessed Noah and his sons, saying to them, "Be fruitful, increase in number, and fill the earth. (Blessing: God's command to repopulate the earth) **2.** The fear and awe of you will fall on all creatures—beasts of the earth, birds of the sky, every creature that moves on the ground, and all the fish in the sea. They are now under your authority. (Fear and awe: creation is placed under humanity's dominion) **3.** Everything that lives and moves will be food for you. Just as I gave you the green plants, now I give you everything to eat. (Provision: God grants humanity all living creatures as food) **4.** But you must not eat meat that still has its lifeblood in it. (Lifeblood: the sanctity of life is emphasized) **5.** I will demand an account for the lifeblood of every living thing. From each animal, I will require an accounting, and from each human being, too, I will demand an accounting for the life of another human. (Accountability: God establishes responsibility for life) **6.** "Whoever takes a human life will have their blood taken by humans. For in the image of God, God made mankind." (Justice: the sanctity of human life is affirmed) **7.** "But you, be fruitful and multiply; increase in number and spread out across the earth." (Multiplying: God's ongoing command for humanity to spread and prosper) **8.** Then God said to Noah and his sons, (God speaks: the establishment of a covenant) **9.** "I now make my covenant with you and your descendants after you, (the covenant is extended to Noah's family and their descendants) **10.** And with every living creature that was with you— the birds, the livestock, and all the wild animals, all that came out of the ark with you. (Inclusive: the covenant includes all of creation) **11.** "I establish my covenant with you: Never again will a flood destroy all life; there will never again be a flood to wipe out the earth." (Perpetual promise: God promises no more global floods) **12.** And God said, "This is the sign of the covenant I am making between me and you, and all living creatures with you, a covenant for all generations to come: (sign: the covenant will endure across all generations) **13.** I have set my rainbow in the clouds, and it will serve as the sign of the covenant between me and the earth. (Rainbow: a visible reminder of God's promise) **14.** "Whenever I bring clouds over the earth and the rainbow appears in the clouds, (appearance of the rainbow: the sign's purpose) **15.** I will remember my covenant with you and all living creatures of every kind. Never again will the waters become a flood to destroy all life. (God's reminder: the rainbow will prompt God's remembrance) **16.** "Whenever the rainbow appears in the clouds, I will see it and remember the everlasting covenant between God and all living creatures of every kind on the earth." (Everlasting: God's covenant is eternal) **17.** So God said to Noah, "This is the sign of the covenant I have established between me and all life on the earth." (God confirms: the rainbow is the covenant's sign) **18.** The sons of Noah who came out of the ark were Shem, Ham, and Japheth. (Ham was the father of Canaan.) (Lineage: Noah's sons and the reference to Canaan) **19.** These were the three sons of Noah, and from them came the people who were scattered over the whole earth. (Dispersal: humanity spread out from Noah's sons) **20.** Noah, a man of the soil, planted a vineyard. (Noah's labor: his connection to the earth continues) **21.** When he drank some of its wine, he became drunk and lay uncovered in his tent. **22.** Ham, the father of Canaan, saw his father's nakedness and told his two brothers outside. (Ham's sin: a shameful act) **23.** But Shem and Japheth took a garment, laid it across their shoulders, and walked in backward to cover their father's naked body. They turned their faces the other way so as not to see their father's nakedness. (Shem and Japheth's respect: they covered their father without looking) **24.** When Noah awoke from his wine and found out what his youngest son had done to him, (Noah's realization: he awoke to the shameful act) **25.** he said, "Cursed be Canaan! The lowest of slaves will he be to his brothers." (Noah's curse: Canaan is cursed because of Ham's actions) **26.** He also said, "Praise be to the LORD, the God of Shem! May Canaan be the slave of Shem (Shem blessed for his respect and piety) **27.** May God extend Japheth's territory; may Japheth live in the tents of Shem, and may Canaan be the slave of Japheth." (Japheth's blessing: Japheth is also favored, and Canaan is cursed further) **28.** After the flood, Noah lived 350 years. (Noah's long life: his life continued after the flood) **29.** Noah lived a total of 950 years, and then he died. (Death of Noah: marking the end of Noah's long life)

Chapter 10

1. This is the genealogy of Noah's sons—Shem, Ham, and Japheth—who had children after the flood. (A record of Noah's descendants after the flood) **2.** Japheth's sons were Gomer, Magog, Madai, Javan, Tubal, Meshek, and Tiras. (Japheth's descendants, ancestors of European and some Asian peoples) **3.** Gomer's children were Ashkenaz, Riphath, and Togarmah. (Tribes from the Caucasus, Europe, and Central Asia) **4.** Javan's descendants were Elishah, Tarshish, the Kittites, and the Rodanites. (Mediterranean peoples, including Greeks and maritime traders) **5.** These groups, spreading out across the earth, became the maritime peoples, each with its own language. (Seafaring nations, speaking different languages) **6.** The sons of Ham were Cush, Egypt, Put, and Canaan. (Ham's descendants, ancestors of African and some Middle Eastern nations) **7.** Cush had five sons: Seba, Havilah, Sabtah, Raamah, and Sabteka. Raamah's sons were Sheba and Dedan. (African and Arabian tribes) **8.** Cush was the father of Nimrod, a powerful leader on earth. (Nimrod: a mighty hunter and early empire-builder) **9.** He was a great hunter, respected by God, which is why people say, "Like Nimrod, a mighty hunter before the LORD." (Nimrod: Known for his strength and power) **10.** His kingdom began in Babylon, Uruk, Akkad, and Kalneh, in the region of Shinar. (Babylon, Uruk, Akkad: Ancient Mesopotamian cities in modern-day Iraq) **11.** From there, Nimrod moved into Assyria and established the cities of Nineveh, Rehoboth Ir, Calah, **12.** and Resen, which lay between Nineveh and Calah, becoming a major city. (Nineveh: Capital of Assyria; Rehoboth Ir, Calah, and Resen: important Assyrian cities) **13.** Egypt's descendants included the Ludites, Anamites, Lehabites, Naphtuhites, **14.** Pathrusites, Kasluhites (from whom the Philistines came), and Caphtorites. (Philistines: Ancient people who lived on the coastal region of Canaan) **15.** Canaan's children were Sidon (his firstborn), the Hittites, **16.** the Jebusites, the Amorites, the Girgashites, **17.** the Hivites, the Arkites, the Sinites, **18.** the Arvadites, the Zemarites, and the Hamathites. The Canaanites later spread out. (Canaanites: Tribes of the ancient Near East; later settled in Canaan) **19.** Canaan's land extended from Sidon, near Gerar, as far as Gaza, and toward Sodom, Gomorrah, Admah, Zeboyim, and Lasha. (Sodom and Gomorrah: Famous cities destroyed for their wickedness) **20.** These are the sons of Ham, organized by their clans, languages, territories, and nations. **21.** Sons were also born to Shem, the older brother of Japheth. Shem was the ancestor of all the descendants of Eber. (Shem: Ancestor of the Semitic people, including the Hebrews) **22.** Shem's children were Elam, Ashur, Arphaxad, Lud, and Aram. (Elam: Ancient region in southwestern Iran; Ashur: Assyrian ancestors; Arphaxad: Ancestor of the Hebrews) **23.** Aram's sons were Uz, Hul, Gether, and Meshek. (Aram: Region of Syria; Uz: Possible location near Edom) **24.** Arphaxad was the father of Shelah, and Shelah was the father of Eber. (Shelah and Eber: Ancestors in the Semitic line leading to the Hebrews) **25.** Eber had two sons: One was named Peleg, because during his time, the earth was divided; his brother was named Joktan. (Peleg: His time marked a major geographical division; Joktan: Ancestor of various Arabian tribes) **26.** Joktan had many children: Almodad, Sheleph, Hazarmaveth, Jerah, **27.** Hadoram, Uzal, Diklah, **28.** Obal, Abimael, Sheba, **29.** Ophir, Havilah, and Jobab. These were the sons of Joktan. (Joktan's sons: Tribes in Arabia and the eastern regions) **30.** The territory where they lived stretched from Mesha to Sephar, in the eastern hill country. (Mesha and Sephar: Locations in Arabian Peninsula) **31.** These are the sons of Shem, grouped by their clans, languages, territories, and nations. **32.** These are the families of Noah's sons, who spread out across the earth after the flood. (The nations of the earth descended from Noah's three sons)

Chapter 11

1. The whole world spoke one language and shared the same words. (Unified language) **2.** As the people moved east, they discovered a plain in Shinar and settled there. (Shinar: Region in Mesopotamia, later associated with Babylon) **3.** They said to each other, "Let's make bricks and bake them thoroughly." They used brick instead of stone and tar for mortar. (Brick and tar: Materials for building; a shift from natural stone to man-made materials) **4.** "Let's build a city with a tower that reaches the heavens, so we can make a name for ourselves. Otherwise, we will be scattered across the earth." (Ambition: The desire to remain united and create a legacy) **5.** The LORD came down to see the city and the tower the people were building. (God observes their prideful actions) **6.** The LORD said, "If as one people speaking the same language, they have begun this, nothing they plan will be impossible. (Unity: The power of shared language and purpose) **7.** Come, let us confuse their language so they won't understand each other." (Divine intervention: God decides to confuse their speech) **8.** So the LORD scattered them from their across the earth, and they stopped building the city. (Dispersal: The people were scattered to prevent further unity) **9.** That is why it was called Babel, because there the LORD confused the language of the world. From there, the LORD scattered them across the earth. (Babel: Derived from "balal" meaning to confuse) **10.** This is the family line of Shem: After the flood, when Shem was 100 years old, he became the father of Arphaxad. (Shem: Father of Arphaxad, a key ancestor in the biblical line) **11.** After Arphaxad's birth, Shem lived 500 more years and had other sons and daughters. (Shem's descendants) **12.** When Arphaxad was 35, he became the father of Shelah. (Arphaxad: Father of Shelah, continuing the lineage) **13.** After Shelah's birth, Arphaxad lived 403 more years and had other sons and daughters. (Arphaxad's extended family) **14.** When Shelah was 30, he became the father of Eber. (Shelah: Father of Eber, whose descendants played a major role in the Bible) **15.** After Eber's birth, Shelah lived 403 more years and had other sons and daughters. (Eber: Ancestor of the Hebrews) **16.** When Eber was 34, he became the father of Peleg. (Eber: Father of Peleg, during whose time the earth was divided) **17.** After Peleg's birth, Eber lived 430 more years and had other sons and daughters. (Peleg: His name means "division," marking a significant event in the world) **18.** When Peleg was 30, he became the father of Reu. (Peleg: Father of Reu) **19.** After Reu's birth, Peleg lived 209 more years and had other sons and daughters. (Reu: Descendant of Peleg) **20.** When Reu was 32, he became the father of Serug. (Reu: Father of Serug) **21.** After Serug's birth, Reu lived 207 more years and had other sons and daughters. (Serug: Ancestor of Nahor) **22.** When Serug was 30, he became the father of Nahor. (Serug: Father of Nahor) **23.** After Nahor's birth, Serug lived 200 more years and had other sons and daughters. (Nahor: Father of Terah) **24.** When Nahor was 29, he became the father of Terah. (Nahor: The father of Terah, Abraham's father) **25.** After Terah's birth, Nahor lived 119 more years and had other sons and daughters. (Terah: Father of Abram) **26.** After living 70 years, Terah became the father of Abram, Nahor, and Haran. (Terah: Father of Abram, the key figure in the covenant with God) **27.** This is the account of Terah's family: Terah had three sons: Abram, Nahor, and Haran. Haran was the father of Lot. (Lot: Nephew of Abram, son of

Haran) **28.** While Terah was still alive, Haran died in Ur of the Chaldeans, his birthplace. (Ur of the Chaldeans: A city in ancient Mesopotamia) **29.** Abram and Nahor married. Abram's wife was Sarai, and Nahor's wife was Milkah, who was the daughter of Haran. (Sarai: Abram's wife; Milkah: Nahor's wife, daughter of Haran) **30.** Sarai was barren and could not have children. (Sarai: Initially childless, which plays a significant role in the narrative) **31.** Terah took his son Abram, his grandson Lot (son of Haran), and his daughter-in-law Sarai, and set out from Ur of the Chaldeans to go to Canaan, but they settled in Harran. (Harran: A city in Mesopotamia where they temporarily stopped) **32.** Terah lived 205 years and died in Harran. (Terah: Died in Harran, ending his journey)

Chapter 12

1. The LORD told Abram, "Leave your country, your people, and your father's household, and go to the land I will show you. (God's command: Abram is told to leave his homeland and family for an unknown land) **2.** "I will make you into a great nation, bless you, and make your name great. You will be a blessing. (Promise of greatness: God promises Abram descendants and blessings) **3.** "I will bless those who bless you, and curse those who curse you; and all the families of the earth will be blessed through you." (Universal blessing: All nations will be blessed through Abram's descendants) **4.** So Abram went as the LORD had commanded him, and Lot went with him. Abram was seventy-five years old when he left Harran. (Abram obeys: At 75, Abram begins his journey to the Promised Land) **5.** He took his wife Sarai, his nephew Lot, all their possessions, and the people they had acquired in Harran, and they set out for Canaan. They arrived in Canaan. (The journey begins: Abram departs with his family and wealth, reaching Canaan) **6.** Abram traveled through the land to the oak of Moreh at Shechem. At that time, the Canaanites were in the land. (Shechem: The place where Abram arrives in Canaan, home to the Canaanites) **7.** The LORD appeared to Abram and said, "To your offspring, I will give this land." So he built an altar to the LORD, who had appeared to him. (God's promise: The land of Canaan is promised to Abram's descendants, and he worships) **8.** From there, Abram moved to the east of Bethel, pitching his tent with Bethel on the west and Ai on the east. He built an altar to the LORD and called on His name. (Bethel and Ai: Abram worships God between these two locations in Canaan) **9.** Then Abram journeyed on toward the Negev. (Negev: A southern region in Canaan where Abram continues his journey) **10.** There was a famine in the land, so Abram went to Egypt to stay for a while, as the famine was severe. (Famine: Abram is forced to go to Egypt due to a severe food shortage) **11.** As he approached Egypt, Abram said to his wife Sarai, "I know how beautiful you are. (Abram's fear: He worries about Sarai's beauty causing trouble in Egypt) **12.** "When the Egyptians see you, they will say, 'This is his wife.' Then they will kill me but let you live. (Fear for his life: Abram fears the Egyptians will kill him to take Sarai) **13.** "Say you are my sister, so that I will be treated well for your sake and my life will be spared because of you." (Deception: Abram asks Sarai to pretend she is his sister to protect himself) **14.** When Abram entered Egypt, the Egyptians saw that Sarai was very beautiful. (Sarai's beauty: The Egyptians notice Sarai's striking appearance) **15.** Pharaoh's officials praised her to him, and she was taken into Pharaoh's palace. (Pharaoh's interest: Sarai is taken to Pharaoh's palace after being admired) **16.** Pharaoh treated Abram well for her sake, and Abram acquired sheep, cattle, donkeys, servants, and camels. (Reward: Abram receives wealth from Pharaoh in exchange for Sarai's presence) **17.** But the LORD inflicted serious diseases on Pharaoh and his household because of Sarai, Abram's wife. (Divine intervention: God sends plagues to Pharaoh's household to protect Sarai) **18.** So Pharaoh summoned Abram and asked, "What have you done to me? Why didn't you tell me she was your wife? (Pharaoh's anger: Pharaoh rebukes Abram for his deception) **19.** "Why did you say, 'She is my sister,' so that I took her to be my wife? Now here's your wife. Take her and go!" (Pharaoh's command: Pharaoh demands that Abram leave Egypt with his wife) **20.** Pharaoh gave orders to his men to send Abram away, along with his wife and all his possessions. (Departure: Abram and his family are sent away from Egypt with all their wealth).

Chapter 13

1. After leaving Egypt, Abram journeyed toward the Negev with his wife and everything he owned, accompanied by Lot. (Abram, his family, and Lot travel back from Egypt) **2.** Abram had acquired great wealth, including livestock, silver, and gold. (Abram became very prosperous) **3.** He moved through the Negev and traveled to Bethel, to the area between Bethel and Ai, where he had camped before. (Abram returns to the place between Bethel and Ai where he had previously settled) **4.** there, he had built an altar and called on the name of the LORD. (Abram resumes worshiping at the altar) **5.** Lot, who was traveling with Abram, also owned flocks, herds, and tents. (Lot had livestock as well) **6.** But the land was not large enough to support both of them, because their possessions had grown too vast for them to remain together. (The land couldn't support both due to their expanding wealth) **7.** Disagreements arose between Abram's herders and Lot's. Additionally, the Canaanites and Perizzites were living in the land at that time. (Strife emerges between the herders; the land is inhabited by Canaanites and Perizzites) **8.** Abram said to Lot, "Let's not have any disputes between us or between our herders, because we are family. (Abram calls for peace, emphasizing their family connection) **9.** "The whole land is before you. Let's separate. If you go left, I will go right, and if you go right, I will go left." (Abram offers Lot the first choice of land) **10.** Lot looked around and saw that the entire plain of the Jordan, toward Zoar, was well watered, like the garden of the LORD, or like the land of Egypt. (This was before the LORD destroyed Sodom and Gomorrah.) (Lot chooses the fertile Jordan plain, unaware of the future destruction of Sodom) **11.** Lot chose the entire plain of the Jordan and moved toward the east, and the two men parted ways. (Lot selects the fertile Jordan valley, and they separate) **12.** Abram settled in the land of Canaan, while Lot chose to live near the cities of the plain, pitching his tents near Sodom. **13.** The people of Sodom were exceedingly wicked and sinful against the LORD. (Sodom's residents are notorious for their wickedness) **14.** After Lot had separated from him, the LORD spoke to Abram, saying, "Lift up your eyes from where you are and look in all directions: north, south, east, and west. (God speaks to Abram after their separation) **15.** "All the land that you see, I will give to you and your descendants forever. (God promises Abram the land for his descendants) **16.** "Your offspring will be as numerous as the dust of the earth. If anyone could count the dust, they could count your descendants. (Descendants will be countless like the dust of the earth) **17.** "Walk the length and breadth of the land, for I am giving it to you." (God invites Abram to explore the land he will inherit) **18.** So Abram moved his tents and settled near the oak trees of Mamre at Hebron, where he built an altar to the LORD. (Abram settles at Mamre near Hebron and worships God)

Chapter 14

1. When Amraphel was king of Shinar, Arioch of Ellasar, Kedorlaomer of Elam, and Tidal of Goyim, (Names of the four kings) **2.** These kings fought against Bera of Sodom, Birsha of Gomorrah, Shinab of Admah, Shemeber of Zeboyim, and the king of Bela (Zoar). (The five kings of the plain) **3.** The five kings formed an alliance in the Valley of Siddim (the Dead Sea Valley). (They prepare for battle in the valley) **4.** For twelve years, they had been ruled by Kedorlaomer, but in the thirteenth year, they rebelled. (The five kings rebel against their overlord) **5.** In the fourteenth year, Kedorlaomer and his allies defeated the Rephaites in Ashteroth Karnaim, the Zuzites in Ham, and the Emites in Shaveh Kiriathaim, (Kedorlaomer's campaign continues) **6.** and the Horites in the hill country of Seir, as far as El Paran, near the desert. (Defeating more nations) **7.** They then turned back and attacked En Mishpat (Kadesh), conquering the Amalekites and the Amorites in Hazezon Tamar. (Kedorlaomer's forces conquer more regions) **8.** The king of Sodom, Gomorrah, Admah, Zeboyim, and Bela (Zoar) mustered their armies in the Valley of Siddim, (The five kings assemble for battle) **9.** against Kedorlaomer, Tidal, Amraphel, and Arioch — four kings against five. (The battle is four against five) **10.** The Valley of Siddim was full of tar pits, and when Sodom and Gomorrah's kings fled, some men fell into them, and the rest ran to the hills. (The valley's tar pits cause chaos during the flight) **11.** The four kings took all the goods and food of Sodom and Gomorrah and left. (The invaders plunder the cities) **12.** They also captured Lot and his possessions, for he was living in Sodom. (Lot is taken captive) **13.** A survivor came and told Abram the Hebrew, who lived near the oak groves of Mamre the Amorite, Eshkol, and Aner, his allies. (A messenger reports to Abram) **14.** When Abram learned that Lot had been captured, he called his 318 trained men and pursued them as far as Dan. (Abram prepares to rescue Lot) **15.** During the night, Abram divided his forces and attacked, routing them as far as Hobah, north of Damascus. (Abram divides his men to attack at night) **16.** He recovered all the goods, and brought back Lot, his possessions, and the other people taken. (Abram rescues Lot and others) **17.** After returning from defeating Kedorlaomer and his allies, the king of Sodom met Abram in the Valley of Shaveh (the King's Valley). (The king of Sodom meets Abram post-victory) **18.** Melchizedek, king of Salem, brought out bread and wine; he was priest of God Most High. (Melchizedek offers gifts and blessings) **19.** He blessed Abram, saying, "Blessed be Abram by God Most High, Creator of heaven and earth. (Melchizedek blesses Abram, recognizing God's supremacy) **20.** And praise be to God Most High, who gave you victory over your enemies." Abram gave him a tenth of everything. (Abram gives Melchizedek a tithe) **21.** The king of Sodom said to Abram, "Give me the people, and keep the goods for yourself." (The king of Sodom offers Abram the spoils) **22.** But Abram replied, "I have sworn to the LORD, God Most High, Creator of heaven and earth, (Abram swears an oath to God) **23.** that I will take nothing from you, not even a thread or sandal strap, so you can't say, 'I made Abram rich.' (Abram refuses the spoils to avoid any claim on his wealth) **24.** I will take only what my men have eaten and the share for my allies, Aner, Eshkol, and Mamre. Let them have their share." (Abram accepts only what's owed to his men and allies)

Chapter 15

1. After this, the phrase of the LORD came to Abram in a vision: "Do now not be afraid, Abram. I am your shield, your very great reward." (God reassures Abram of His protection and praise) **2.** But Abram answered, "Sovereign LORD, what can you give me since I remain childless, and the one who will inherit my property is Eliezer of Damascus?" (Abram expresses concern about having no children) **3.** He continued, "You have given me no children, so a servant in my household will be my heir." (Abram acknowledges his lack of children) **4.** Then the word of the LORD came to him: "This man will not be your heir, but a son from your own flesh and blood will be your heir." (God promises Abram a biological son as his heir) **5.** God took him outside and said, "Look up at the sky and count the stars— if you can. So shall your offspring be." (God uses the stars to demonstrate the number of Abram's descendants) **6.** Abram believed the LORD, and He credited it to him as righteousness. (Abram's faith is counted as righteousness) **7.** He also said to him, "I am the LORD, who brought you out of Ur of the Chaldeans to give you this land to possess." (God reminds Abram of His past actions in delivering him) **8.** Abram asked, "Sovereign LORD, how can I know that I will gain possession of it?" (Abram seeks assurance of God's promise regarding the land) **9.** So the LORD answered, "Bring me a heifer, a goat, and a ram, each three years old, along with a dove and a young pigeon." (God instructs Abram to prepare an offering) **10.** Abram brought all these to Him, cut them in two, and arranged the halves opposite each other; the birds, however, he did not cut in half. (Abram follows the ritual to prepare the sacrifice) **11.** Then birds of prey came down on the carcasses, but Abram drove them away. (Abram protects the sacrifice from scavengers) **12.** As the sun was setting, Abram fell into a deep sleep, and a thick and dreadful darkness came over him. (Abram experiences a deep sleep and ominous darkness) **13.** Then the LORD said to him, "Know for certain that your descendants will be strangers in a land not their own, and they will be enslaved and mistreated for 400 years. (God reveals the future slavery of Abram's descendants in Egypt) **14.** "But I will punish the nation they serve as slaves, and afterward, they will come out with great possessions. (God promises to judge their oppressors and bless the Israelites) **15.** "As for you, you will go to your ancestors in peace and be buried at a good old age. (God assures Abram of a peaceful death in his old age) **16.** "In the fourth generation, your descendants will return here, for the sin of the Amorites has not yet reached its full measure." (God's plan includes the eventual return of Abram's descendants to the land after the Amorites' sin is complete) **17.** When the sun had set and darkness had fallen, a smoking firepot with a blazing torch appeared and passed between the pieces. (A symbolic act of God's presence and covenant affirmation) **18.** On that day, the LORD made a covenant with Abram and said, "To your descendants, I give this land, from the Wadi of Egypt to the great river, the Euphrates— (God establishes the covenant with Abram concerning the land) **19.** The land of the Kenites, Kenizzites, Kadmonites, **20.** Hittites, Perizzites, Rephaites, **21.** Amorites, Canaanites, Girgashites, and Jebusites." (The boundaries of the Promised Land are described)

Chapter 16

1. Sarai, Abram's wife, had not borne him any children, but she had an Egyptian servant named Hagar. (Hagar: Sarai's Egyptian maidservant) **2.** Sarai said to Abram, "The LORD has prevented me from having children. Take my servant and sleep with her; perhaps I can build a family through her." Abram agreed to Sarai's plan. (Sarai's plan: Sarai suggests using Hagar as a surrogate) **3.** After ten years in Canaan, Sarai took her Egyptian servant Hagar and gave her to Abram as his wife. (Canaan: The land promised to Abram by God) **4.** Abram slept with Hagar, and she became pregnant. When Hagar realized she was pregnant, she began to look down on Sarai. (Pregnancy: Hagar's pride after becoming pregnant) **5.** Sarai said to Abram, "You are responsible for the wrong I am suffering. I gave my servant to you, and now she despises me. May the LORD judge between us?" (Conflict: Sarai blames Abram for the tension) **6.** Abram responded, "She is your servant; do as you please." Sarai mistreated Hagar, and Hagar fled. (Abram's response: He gives Sarai control over Hagar) **7.** The angel of the LORD found Hagar by a spring in the desert, near the road to Shur. (Shur: A desert region, likely near Egypt) **8.** The angel asked, "Hagar, Sarai's servant, where have you come from and where are you going?" Hagar replied, "I'm running away from my mistress Sarai." (Hagar's flight: Hagar flees due to mistreatment) **9.** The angel of the LORD said, "Return to your mistress and submit to her." (Angel's command: Hagar is instructed to go back to Sarai) **10.** The angel also promised, "I will increase your descendants so much that they will be too numerous to count." (Promise: God's blessing of numerous descendants) **11.** The angel continued, "You are pregnant and will bear a son. Name him Ishmael, because the LORD has heard of your misery." (Ishmael: meaning "God hears") **12.** "He will be a wild man, like a donkey, and his hand will be against everyone, and everyone's hand will be against him. He will live in hostility toward all his relatives." (Ishmael's future: Describes his tough nature and conflicts) **13.** Hagar gave this name to the LORD: "You are the God who sees me," for she said, "I have now seen the One who sees me." (God's recognition: Hagar acknowledges God's presence and care) **14.** That is why the well was called Beer Lahai Roi. It is still there, between Kadesh and Bered. (Beer Lahai Roi: meaning "the well of the Living One who sees me") **15.** Hagar gave birth to a son for Abram, and Abram named him Ishmael. (Birth of Ishmael: Hagar gives birth to Abram's son, as

promised) **16.** Abram was eighty-six years old when Hagar gave birth to Ishmael. (Abram's age: Abram is 86 at the time of Ishmael's birth)
Chapter 17
1. while Abram was ninety-9 years vintage, the LORD regarded to him and stated, "i am God Almighty; walk before Me with integrity and be innocent." (God Almighty: God's name, indicating ideal power) **2.** "Then i'm able to set up my covenant with you and substantially multiply your descendants." (Covenant: A binding promise between God and Abram) **3.** Abram fell facedown, and God spoke to him, announcing, (Fell facedown: A signal of reverence and submission) **4.** "That is my covenant with you: you may be the father of many nations." (Father of many countries: God promises Abram descendants that will become countries) **5.** "You'll now not be called Abram; your call might be Abraham, for i have made you the father of many nations." (Abram to Abraham: God changes Abram's name to mirror his new function) **6.** "I'm able to make you relatively fruitful; nations will come from you, and kings will descend from you." (Tremendously fruitful: Promising terrific prosperity and influence) **7.** "i will establish my everlasting covenant among me and you, and your descendants when you, to be your God and the God of your descendants." (Eternal covenant: A perpetual promise that extends to Abraham's descendants) **8.** "The entire land of Canaan, wherein you currently live as a foreigner, may be an eternal ownership for you and your descendants, and i might be their God." (Canaan: The Promised Land to Abram's descendants) **9.** God then stated to Abraham, "As for you, you ought to hold My covenant, along with your descendants, for all generations to come." (Preserve My covenant: The obligation to uphold God's command) **10.** "this is the covenant you and your descendants are to hold: every male amongst you must be circumcised." (Circumcision: A bodily sign of the covenant) **11.** "You need to go through circumcision, so as to function a sign of the covenant between me and also you." (sign of the covenant: Circumcision as a mark of the connection with God) **12.** "each male, 8 days antique and older, need to be circumcised, such as the ones born to your family or sold from foreigners, even supposing they're now not your direct descendants." (family individuals: consists of both organic and non-organic individuals of the family) **13.** "Whether or not born to your household or offered with cash, they ought to be circumcised. This may be My eternal covenant for your flesh." (Eternal covenant in your flesh: Circumcision as a perpetual sign) **14.** "Any male who isn't circumcised could be cut off from his people; he has damaged My covenant." (Reduce off: Being excluded from the network due to disobedience) **15.** God also stated to Abraham, "As for Sarai, your wife, you are to now not name her Sarai; her name can be Sarah." (Sarai to Sarah: God adjustments Sarah's name to signify her new role) **16.** "I'm able to bless her and give you a son through her. She could be the mother of nations; kings of peoples will come from her." (Sarah's blessing: God guarantees Sarah will bear a son, and countries will emerge from her) **17.** Abraham fell facedown; he laughed to himself and said, "Will a son be born to someone who's a hundred years old? Will Sarah endure a child at 90?" (Abraham's disbelief: Abraham laughs on the impossibility of getting a baby at his antique age) **18.** And Abraham stated to God, "If only Ishmael might stay beneath Your blessing!" (Ishmael: Abraham's son by Hagar, his request for Ishmael's blessing) **19.** God stated, "sure, but your wife Sarah will undergo you a son, and you will call him Isaac. i'm able to set up my covenant with him as an everlasting covenant for his descendants." (Isaac: The son who can be the key inheritor to the covenant) **20.** "As for Ishmael, I've heard your plea. i will bless him, make him fruitful, and multiply him significantly. He may be the daddy of twelve rulers, and I'm able to make him right into a tremendous state." (Ishmael's blessing: God guarantees to bless Ishmael and his descendants) **21.** "but My covenant could be hooked up with Isaac, whom Sarah will bear to you through this time subsequent 12 months." (Isaac's position: Isaac, no longer Ishmael, might be the child of the covenant) **22.** After speaking with Abraham, God ascended from him. (God's departure: After handing over His message, God leaves Abraham) **23.** On that identical day, Abraham took his son Ishmael, and all the men in his household—those born or sold—and circumcised them, as God had commanded. **24.** Abraham turned into ninety-nine years antique when he became circumcised, (Abraham's age: Abraham's circumcision at 99 years vintage) **25.** And his son Ishmael changed into 13. (Ishmael's age: Ishmael is thirteen when circumcised) **26.** Abraham and his son Ishmael were each circumcised on the same day. (Same day: both father and son circumcised at the equal day) **27.** Every male in Abraham's family, including the ones born or sold, become circumcised together with him. (Family circumcision: All adult males in Abraham's household followed the covenant command)
Chapter 18
1. The LORD regarded to Abraham near the large bushes of Mamre, while he was sitting at the entrance of his tent in the course of the heat of the day. (Mamre: a place close to Hebron wherein Abraham camped) **2.** Abraham looked up and saw 3 men standing nearby. When he saw them, he quickly ran to satisfy them from the entrance of his tent and bowed low to the ground. (3 men: The LORD and angels inside the form of fellows) **3.** He said, "If I have located prefer to your sight, my lord, please do no longer pass by your servant. (Determined favor: Abraham seeks to reveal hospitality to his visitors) **4.** Let me convey you some water to wash your feet, and rest underneath this tree. (Wash your feet: A common gesture of hospitality in ancient instances) **5.** I can get you something to eat in order that you may be refreshed before continuing on your way, now that you have come to your servant." "Very well," they replied, "Do as you have said." (Be refreshed: Abraham desires to offer those meals and relaxation) **6.** Abraham moved quickly into the tent to Sarah and said, "Quick, take three seahs of the greatest flour, knead it, and bake some bread." (Seahs: A measure of grain, approximately 7.5 liters) **7.** Then he ran to the herd, chose a soft calf, and gave it to a servant, who quickly organized it. (Tender calf: A choice animal for a unique meal) **8.** He introduced curds and milk, along with the prepared calf, and set these earlier than them. When they ate, Abraham stood close by underneath a tree. (Curds and milk: A common dish in the ancient world) **9.** "Where is your wife Sarah?" they asked. "She is inside the tent," he replied. (Sarah: Abraham's wife) **10.** One of them said, "I can actually go back to you this time next year, and your wife Sarah could have a son." Sarah turned into listening at the entrance of the tent, which was in the back of him. (Promise of a son: The divine promise of Isaac's birth) **11.** Abraham and Sarah were very old, and Sarah was past the age of childbearing. (Beyond the age of childbearing: Sarah was 90 years old) **12.** So Sarah laughed to herself, wondering, "After I'm wiped out and my lord is old, will I now have this satisfaction?" (Sarah's doubt: Sarah's laughter reflects disbelief at the promise) **13.** Then the LORD said to Abraham, "Why did Sarah snicker and say, 'Will I surely have a infant, now that I am antique?' (The LORD's reaction: God questions Sarah's disbelief) **14.** Is something too difficult for the LORD? I'm able to return to you at the appointed time next year, and Sarah may have a son." (Nothing is too difficult: God affirms His strength to accomplish the impossible) **15.** Sarah became afraid, so she denied guffawing, announcing, "I did now not snicker." But He responded, "Sure, you probably did giggle." (Sarah's denial: She tries to hide her disbelief, however God knew her coronary heart) **16.** When the men got up to leave, they appeared closer to Sodom, and Abraham walked along with them to send them on their way. (Sodom: The town wherein Lot lived, soon to be destroyed) **17.** The LORD said, "Shall I disguise from Abraham what I'm about to do? (Shall I hide: God contemplates revealing His plans to Abraham) **18.** Abraham will really become a splendid and effective state, and all nations on earth might be blessed through him. (Blessing thru Abraham: A reference to God's promise to Abraham's descendants) **19.** For I've chosen him,

so that he will direct his children and his family after him to keep the way of the LORD by doing what's right and simply, so that the LORD will bring about for Abraham what He has promised him." (Right and just: Abraham's position in guiding his descendants to follow God's commandments) **20.** Then the LORD said, "The outcry against Sodom and Gomorrah is so great and their sin so grievous, (Sodom and Gomorrah: Towns recognized for wickedness) **21.** that I can go down and see if what they've done is as terrible as the outcry that has reached Me. If not, I'll know." (Go down and see: God personally investigates the situation) **22.** The men turned away and went in the direction of Sodom, but Abraham remained standing before the LORD. (Abraham stays: Abraham remains in dialogue with God) **23.** Abraham approached God and said, "Will you destroy the righteous with the wicked? (Abraham pleads: He intercedes for Sodom, wondering God's justice) **24.** What if there are fifty righteous people within the city? Will you truly destroy it and not spare the region for the sake of the fifty righteous in it? (Fifty righteous: Abraham's first plea) **25.** Far be it from you to do one of these thing—to kill the righteous with the wicked, treating the righteous and the wicked alike. Far be it from you! Will not the Judge of all of the earth do right?" (The Judge of all of the earth: Abraham appeals to God's justice) **26.** The LORD answered, "If I find fifty righteous people in the city of Sodom, I will spare the whole area for their sake." (God's settlement: God is willing to spare Sodom if fifty righteous people are found) **27.** Then Abraham spoke again: "Now that I've been so bold as to speak to the Lord, even though I am nothing but dust and ashes, (Boldness in prayer: Abraham humbly keeps pleading) **28.** what if the number of the righteous is five less than fifty? Will you destroy the whole city for lack of five people?" The LORD responded, "If I find forty-five there, I will not destroy it." (Forty-five righteous: Abraham negotiates with God) **29.** Once again Abraham spoke, "What if only forty are found there?" The LORD answered, "For the sake of forty, I will not do it." (Forty righteous: Abraham continues his appeal) **30.** Then he said, "May the LORD not be angry, but let me speak. What if only thirty can be found there?" He replied, "I will not destroy it if I find thirty there." (Thirty righteous: Abraham keeps his intercession) **31.** Abraham said, "Now that I've been so bold as to speak to the Lord, what if only twenty may be found there?" The LORD answered, "For the sake of twenty, I will not destroy it." (Twenty righteous: Abraham presses further) **32.** Then he said, "May the LORD not be angry, but let me speak just yet again. What if only ten can be found there?" The LORD replied, "For the sake of ten, I will not destroy it." (Ten righteous: Abraham's final plea) **33.** When the LORD had finished speaking with Abraham, He left, and Abraham returned home. (God departs: God concludes His communication with Abraham)

Chapter 19

1. That night, two angels arrived in Sodom, and Lot became sitting on the metropolis gate. When he noticed them, he stood and bowed together with his face to the floor. (Sodom: an historical town destroyed by God for its wickedness) **2.** He said, "My lords, please come to my residence, live the night time, and wash your toes. Within the morning, you could depart in your manner." But they responded, "No, we are able to spend the night within the square." (Lords: a term of respect, often used for men of authority) **3.** Lot advised them, and they grew to become towards his house. He prepared a meal for them, baking unleavened bread, and that they ate. (Unleavened bread: bread made without yeast, often eaten all through Passover) **4.** Before they went to bed, the guys of Sodom, old and young, from all parts of the city, surrounded Lot's house. **5.** They called, "Wherein are the guys who got here to you? Bring them out so we will have family members with them." (Family members: relating to immoral sexual acts) **6.** Lot went out of doors, shutting the door in the back of him. **7.** He stated, "Please, my brothers, do no longer act so wickedly." **8.** "I have daughters who have by no means been with a person. Let me deliver them out to you, and do as you want, however do not anything to those guys, for they've come beneath my roof's protection." **9.** They replied, "Get out of the manner! You got here right here to live, and now you act as a choose. We'll deal with you worse than them." And they pressed in opposition to Lot, trying to interrupt down the door. **10.** The angels pulled Lot internal and shut the door. **11.** They struck the men outside with blindness, so they couldn't locate the door. **12.** The angels stated, "Do you've got everyone else here? Sons-in-law, sons, daughters, or each person? Take them out of this vicinity!" **13.** "We're approximately to destroy this metropolis, for its outcry has reached the Lord. He despatched us to ruin it." **14.** Lot went to his sons-in-law and said, "Hurry, the Lord will break the metropolis!" But they notion he became joking. **15.** At sunrise, the angels urged Lot, "Hurry, take your spouse and daughters, or you'll be swept away inside the city's punishment." **16.** At the same time, while Lot hesitated, the angels took his own family by way of the hand, showing mercy, and led them appropriately out. **17.** Once outside, one angel said, "Run on your life! Don't look again or stop anywhere in the plain. Escape to the mountains, otherwise you'll be destroyed." (Plain: a flat vicinity of land) **18.** Lot said, "Please, no, my lords! **19.** You have shown mercy via saving my existence, however I cannot escape to the mountains, or I'd die. **20.** Look, there's a small town nearby. Let me flee there and my life could be spared." **21.** The angel spoke back, "I'm able to furnish your request. I'm able to now not wreck that metropolis." **22.** "Hurry, get away there, for I cannot do anything until you arrive." That metropolis changed into referred to as Zoar. (Zoar: a small metropolis near Sodom) **23.** The solar had risen when Lot entered Zoar. **24.** Then the Lord rained burning sulfur on Sodom and Gomorrah, destroying them with hearth from the sky. (Gomorrah: a neighboring town to Sodom, additionally destroyed for sin) **25.** He destroyed the cities, the plain, and all the inhabitants, with the whole thing that grew on the land. **26.** However Lot's spouse seemed again and have become a pillar of salt. (Pillar of salt: a metaphor for permanent judgment) **27.** Early the next morning, Abraham went to the area wherein he had stood earlier than the Lord. **28.** He regarded in the direction of Sodom and Gomorrah, and saw smoke rising like smoke from a furnace. **29.** When God destroyed the towns, He remembered Abraham and sent Lot out before the destruction, because Lot had lived there. **30.** Lot and his daughters left Zoar and went to the mountains, afraid to stay there. They lived in a cave. **31.** The older daughter said to the younger, "Our father is vintage, and there's no man here to marry us, as is the custom. **32.** Let's make him drink wine, and we'll sleep with him to keep our own family line." **33.** So they made him drink wine, and the older daughter slept with him. He did no longer know while she lay down or were given up. **34.** Tomorrow, the older daughter stated, "Let's make him drink wine again, and also you sleep with him to preserve our own family line." **35.** They made him drink wine again, and the more youthful daughter slept with him. He did now not know while she lay down or were given up. **36.** Each of Lot's daughters became pregnant through their father. **37.** The older daughter gave beginning to a son and named him Moab. He's the daddy of the Moabites these days. (Moabites: descendants of Moab, a humans residing east of Israel) **38.** The younger daughter had a son and named him Ben-Ammi. He is the daddy of the Ammonites nowadays. (Ammonites: descendants of Ben-Ammi, a human beings dwelling east of Israel)

Chapter 20

1. Abraham journeyed from there toward the southern region and lived between Kadesh and Shur, settling for a time in Gerar. (Gerar was a Philistine city, and Abraham had moved further south from Canaan) **2.** Abraham said of Sarah, his wife, "She is my sister," and so Abimelech, the king of Gerar, sent for her and took her. (Abraham again used the half-truth about Sarah being his sister to protect himself) **3.** But God came to Abimelech in a dream one night and said, "You are as good as dead because of the woman you have taken; she is another man's wife." (God intervenes directly to protect Sarah) 4. But Abimelech had not yet touched her, and he asked, "Lord, will You kill an innocent nation?" (Abimelech's concern shows his integrity in not committing the sin of adultery) 5. "Did he not tell me, 'She is my sister,' and did she not herself say, 'He is my brother'? I have done this with a clear conscience and innocent hands." (Abimelech defends his actions, claiming that he acted in good faith) 6. God replied to him in the dream, "Yes, I know you did this with a clear conscience, and I have kept you from sinning against Me. That is why I did not let you touch her." (God's intervention prevents sin and protects Sarah from harm) 7. "Now return the woman to her husband, for he is a prophet, and he will pray for you, and you will live. But if you do not return her, know that you will surely die, you and all who belong to you." (God gives a stern warning to Abimelech, urging him to restore Sarah) 8. Early the next morning, Abimelech called together all his servants and told them everything that had happened. The men were terrified. (Abimelech's honesty and fear of God led to an immediate response to the warning) 9. Abimelech then summoned Abraham and asked him, "What have you done to us? What wrong have I committed against you, that you would bring such a great sin upon me and my kingdom? You have done things to me that should never be done." (Abimelech is upset, as Abraham's actions have endangered his kingdom) 10. He asked Abraham, "What were you thinking when you did this?" (Abimelech seeks an explanation for Abraham's actions) 11. Abraham answered, "Because I thought, 'Surely there is no fear of God in this place, and they will kill me because of my wife.'" (Abraham justifies his lie, fearing for his life in a foreign land) 12. "Besides, she is indeed my sister; she is the daughter of my father, but not the daughter of my mother, and she became my wife." (Abraham clarifies that Sarah is his half-sister, though his deception still stands) 13. "And when God caused me to wander from my father's house, I said to her, 'this is your kindness to me: wherever we go, say of me, 'He is my brother.'" (Abraham explains the agreement he and Sarah had made as they journeyed) 14. Abimelech took sheep, cattle, male and female servants, and gave them to Abraham, and he returned Sarah, his wife, to him. (Abimelech's restitution includes wealth and a full return of Sarah) 15. Abimelech said, "The land is before you. Live wherever it pleases you." (Abimelech offers Abraham the freedom to settle wherever he chooses, showing his respect and desire to make amends) 16. To Sarah he said, "I have given your brother a thousand pieces of silver. This is to compensate for any offense against you; it will be a covering for your honor before everyone in your household." Thus, she was vindicated. (Abimelech gives a large sum to Sarah as a form of reconciliation) 17. Abraham prayed to God, and God healed Abimelech, his wife, and his female servants, so that they could bear children. (Abraham's prayer results in divine healing for Abimelech's household, ending the infertility caused by God's judgment) 18. For the LORD had closed up every womb in Abimelech's household because of Sarah, Abraham's wife. (God's direct action had prevented any children from being born in Abimelech's house, as a consequence of his taking Sarah)

Chapter 21
1. The LORD visited Sarah as He had promised, and did for her as He had spoken. (God's promise to Sarah fulfilled) 2. Sarah conceived and bore Abraham a son in his old age, at the set time God had promised. (Isaac's birth in God's timing) 3. Abraham named his son Isaac, the child Sarah bore him. (Isaac's name given) 4. Abraham circumcised Isaac when he was eight days old, as God commanded. (Abraham obeys God's covenant) 5. Abraham was 100 years old when Isaac was born. (Abraham's age at Isaac's birth) 6. Sarah said, "God has made me laugh, and all who hear will laugh with me." (Sarah's joy at Isaac's birth) 7. She said, "Who would have said that Sarah would nurse children? For I have borne a son in my old age." (Sarah marvels at having a child) 8. The child grew and was weaned, and Abraham held a great feast on the day Isaac was weaned. (Isaac's weaning celebrated) 9. Sarah saw Ishmael, the son of Hagar, mocking Isaac. (Ishmael mocks Isaac) 10. Sarah told Abraham, "Cast out the bondwoman and her son; he shall not inherit with Isaac." (Sarah demands Hagar and Ishmael be sent away) 11. This was distressing to Abraham because of his son. (Abraham grieved over the situation) 12. But God told Abraham, "Do not let it distress you; listen to Sarah, for Isaac's descendants will be named." (God affirms Isaac's role) 13. "I will also make a nation of the son of the bondwoman, because he is your seed." (God promises a blessing to Ishmael) 14. Abraham gave Hagar bread and water, sent her and Ishmael away, and they wandered in the wilderness of Beer-sheba. (Hagar and Ishmael sent away) 15. The water ran out, and she placed the child under a shrub. (Water runs out in the wilderness) 16. She went a short distance away, not wanting to see the child die, and wept. (Hagar in despair) 17. God heard the boy's cry, and the angel called to Hagar, saying, "Do not fear; God has heard the boy where he is." (God comforts Hagar) 18. "Lift up the boy and hold him, for I will make him a great nation." (God promises to bless Ishmael) 19. God opened her eyes, and she saw a well of water, filled her bottle, and gave the boy drink. (God provides water) 20. God was with the boy, who grew up, lived in the wilderness, and became an archer. (Ishmael's life and skills) 21. He lived in Paran, and his mother found him a wife from Egypt. (Ishmael marries an Egyptian woman) 22. At that time, Abimelech and Phicol, his army commander, spoke to Abraham, saying, "God is with you in all you do." (Abimelech acknowledges God's favor) 23. "Swear to me you will not deal falsely with me or my descendants, but treat me as I have treated you." (Abimelech asks for a treaty) 24. Abraham agreed, saying, "I will swear." (Abraham agrees to the oath) 25. Abraham reproved Abimelech over a well that his servants had taken. (Abraham addresses the well dispute) 26. Abimelech said, "I didn't know who did this; you didn't tell me until now." (Abimelech denies knowing about it) 27. Abraham gave sheep and oxen to Abimelech, and they made a covenant. (A covenant is made) 28. Abraham set apart seven ewe lambs. (Seven lambs set aside) 29. Abimelech asked, "What do these seven lambs mean?" (Abimelech inquires about the lambs) 30. Abraham replied, "These seven lambs are a witness that I dug this well." (The lambs confirm Abraham's ownership of the well) 31. The place was called Beer-sheba because they swore an oath there. (Beer-sheba means "Well of the Oath") 32. They made a covenant at Beer-sheba, and Abimelech and Phicol returned to the Philistines. (The covenant is sealed) 33. Abraham planted a tamarisk tree at Beer-sheba, called on the LORD, the Everlasting God. (Abraham worships God) 34. Abraham stayed in the land of the Philistines for many days. (Abraham dwells in the Philistine land)

Chapter 22
1. After these events, God tested Abraham and called to him, "Abraham!" And Abraham replied, "Here I am." (God tests Abraham) 2. God said, "Take your son, your only son Isaac, whom you love, and go to the land of Moriah. Offer him there as a burnt offering on one of the mountains I will show you." (God's command to sacrifice Isaac) 3. Abraham rose early the next morning, saddled his donkey, took two young men and Isaac, cut the wood for the burnt offering, and set out for the place God had instructed. (Abraham prepares for the journey) 4. On the third day, Abraham looked up and saw the place in the distance. (The place of sacrifice seen) 5. Abraham told his servants, "Stay here with the donkey; the boy and I will go on ahead to worship, and then we will return to you." (Abraham tells his servants to wait) 6. Abraham placed the wood for the offering on Isaac's back, took the fire and the knife, and the two of them walked on together. (Isaac carries the wood) 7. Isaac said to Abraham, "Father?" Abraham replied, "Here I am, my son." Isaac asked, "We have the fire and the wood, but where is the lamb for the offering?" (Isaac questions Abraham) 8. Abraham answered, "God will provide the lamb for the burnt offering, my son." And they continued walking together. (Abraham's faith in God's provision) 9. When they reached

the place God had indicated, Abraham built an altar, arranged the wood, and bound Isaac, placing him on the altar. (The altar is prepared) **10.** Abraham took the knife to sacrifice Isaac. (Abraham prepares to obey) **11.** But the angel of the LORD called to him from heaven, "Abraham, Abraham!" Abraham answered, "Here I am." (God intervenes) **12.** The angel said, "Do not harm the boy or do anything to him, for now I know that you fear God because you have not withheld your son, your only son, from me." (God's test passed) **13.** Abraham looked up and saw a ram caught in a thicket by its horns. He went, took the ram, and offered it as a burnt offering in place of Isaac. (The ram is provided) **14.** Abraham called the place Jehovah-jireh (The LORD will provide). To this day, it is said, "On the mount of the LORD, it will be provided." (The name of the place) **15.** The angel of the LORD called to Abraham a second time from heaven. (God speaks again to Abraham) **16.** The angel said, "I swear by myself, declares the LORD, that because you have done this and have not withheld your son, your only son," (God swears a blessing) **17.** "I will bless you and multiply your descendants as the stars of the sky and the sand on the seashore. Your descendants will possess the gates of their enemies. (God's promise of blessings and descendants) **18.** "Through your offspring, all nations on earth will be blessed, because you have obeyed my voice." (The blessing to all nations) **19.** Abraham returned to his servants, and they went back together to Beer-sheba, where Abraham settled. (Abraham returns to Beer-sheba) **20.** Sometime later, Abraham was told, "Milcah has borne children to your brother Nahor:" (Abraham learns of Nahor's family) **21.** Huz, his firstborn, and Buz, his brother, and Kemuel the father of Aram, (Nahor's children) **22.** And Chesed, Hazo, Pildash, Jidlaph, and Bethuel. (Additional children of Nahor) **23.** Bethuel fathered Rebekah; these eight children Milcah bore to Nahor, Abraham's brother. (Rebekah born to Nahor) **24.** Nahor's concubine, Reumah, also had children: Tebah, Gaham, Thahash, and Maachah. (Nahor's concubine and her children)

Chapter 23

1. Sarah lived to the age of 127; these were the years of her life. (Sarah's lifespan) **2.** She passed away in Kirjath-arba, also known as Hebron, in the land of Canaan. Abraham came to mourn her and weep for her. (Sarah's death and location) **3.** Abraham rose from his mourning and spoke to the Hittite people, saying, 4. "I am a foreigner and a visitor among you. Please give me a piece of land where I can bury my deceased wife, so that I may lay her to rest away from my sight." (Abraham requests a burial plot) **5.** The Hittites responded to Abraham, saying, (The Hittites respond respectfully) **6.** "Listen to us, sir. You are a respected leader among us. Choose any of our tombs for your dead, none of us will deny you a burial place." (Hittites offer their tombs) **7.** Abraham rose and bowed to the people of the land, the Hittites, in appreciation. (Abraham shows respect) **8.** He then spoke to them, saying, "If you agree to let me bury my dead here, please ask Ephron, the son of Zohar, to sell me the cave of Machpelah at the end of his field. I will pay him the full price for it, so it may become my permanent burial place." (Abraham specifically requests the cave of Machpelah) **9.** Ephron, who lived among the Hittites, answered Abraham in front of the city elders at the city gate, saying, (Ephron responds publicly) **10.** "No, my lord, listen to me. I will give you the field and the cave in it freely, before the people here. Bury your dead in peace." (Ephron offers the land as a gift) **11.** Abraham bowed before the people of the land in gratitude. (Abraham expresses humility) **12.** Then Abraham spoke to Ephron in front of everyone, saying, "If you are willing to give me the land, please hear me out: I will pay you for the field. Take the payment, and I will bury my deceased wife there." (Abraham insists on paying) **13.** Ephron replied to Abraham, saying, (Ephron sets a price) **14.** "Sir, please listen to me. The land is worth 400 shekels of silver. What does that matter between us? Go ahead and bury your dead." (Ephron offers a price) **15.** Abraham agreed to the price Ephron had set, and in front of the Hittites, he paid the 400 shekels of silver. (Abraham accepts and pays the amount) **16.** Abraham weighed out 400 shekels of silver, the standard price for merchants, and handed it over to Ephron in the presence of the people. (The transaction is made public) **17.** So, the field of Ephron, located in Machpelah near Mamre, along with its cave and all the surrounding trees, became Abraham's possession as a burial site. (The land is officially Abraham's) **18.** This was done in front of the Hittites, witnessed by all those who entered the city gate. (The deal is finalized publicly) **19.** Afterward, Abraham buried his wife Sarah in the cave of the field of Machpelah, facing Mamre, which is Hebron, in the land of Canaan. (Sarah's burial place) **20.** Thus, the field and cave were legally transferred to Abraham as his permanent burial site, in the presence of the Hittites. (Final transfer of ownership)

Chapter 24

1. Abraham was old and advanced in years, and the Lord had blessed him in every way. (Abraham's old age and God's blessings on him) **2.** He called his chief servant, the one in charge of all he owned, and said, "Place your hand under my thigh, (A gesture for making a solemn vow in ancient times) **3.** "I swear to you by the Lord, the God of heaven and earth that you will not take a wife for my son from the Canaanites, among whom I live. (Canaanites: the local inhabitants of the land where Abraham lived) **4.** "Go instead to my homeland, to my relatives, and find a wife for my son Isaac." (Isaac: Abraham's son, to be married) **5.** The servant replied, "But what if the woman is unwilling to come back with me? Should I then take your son back to the land from which you came?" (The servant's concern about the woman not agreeing to come) **6.** Abraham answered, "Be careful not to take my son back there. (Abraham's strong command not to take Isaac away from the Promised Land) **7.** "The Lord, the God of heaven, who took me from my father's house and promised this land to my descendants, will send His angel ahead of you, and you will find a wife for Isaac there. (The Lord's promise of guidance to the servant) **8.** "If the woman refuses to follow you, then you will be freed from this oath, but never bring my son back there." (The oath is conditional on the woman's willingness) **9.** The servant swore to Abraham regarding this matter. (Servant takes the oath) **10.** The servant took ten of his master's camels and left, carrying all the goods of his master with him. He traveled to the city of Nahor in Mesopotamia. (Mesopotamia: an ancient region where Abraham's family lived) **11.** At evening, when women typically came to draw water, he made the camels kneel by the well. (The time when women usually gathered water) **12.** He prayed, "Lord God of my master Abraham, grant me success today and show kindness to my master. (The servant prays for God's help in finding the right wife for Isaac) **13.** "I am standing here by the well, and the daughters of the town are coming to draw water. (The servant's observation of the women coming to the well) **14.** "Let the girl to whom I ask for a drink, and who offers to water my camels too, be the one you've chosen for Isaac. Then I will know you have shown kindness to my master." (The servant's test for God's choice of wife for Isaac) **15.** Before he finished speaking, Rebekah, who was the daughter of Bethuel (son of Nahor and Milcah), came out with her water jar on her shoulder. (Rebekah is introduced as the daughter of Bethuel, Abraham's relative) **16.** She was very beautiful, a virgin whom no man had ever known. She went down to the well, filled her jar, and came back up. (Rebekah's physical description as a virgin) **17.** The servant ran to her and asked, "Please give me a little water from your jar." (The servant's request for water) **18.** She said, "Drink, my lord," and quickly lowered her jar, giving him a drink. (Rebekah's hospitality) **19.** After he had finished drinking, she said, "I will draw water for your camels too, until they've had enough." (Rebekah offers to water the camels) **20.** She emptied her jar into the trough and ran back to the well to draw water, doing this until all the camels had drunk their fill. (Rebekah works hard to water all the camels) **21.** The servant watched her in silence, wondering whether the Lord had made his journey successful. (The servant observes in silence, hoping for confirmation from God) **22.** When the camels had finished drinking, the servant took a gold earring weighing half a shekel and two gold bracelets weighing ten shekels, and gave them to her. (Jewelry as gifts to Rebekah) **23.** He asked, "Whose daughter are you? Is there room in your father's house for us to stay?" (Servant asks Rebekah her family background) **24.** She replied, "I am the daughter of Bethuel, the son of Nahor and Milcah." (Rebekah confirms her family lineage, connecting her to Abraham's relatives) **25.** She added, "We have plenty of straw and feed, and room for you to stay." (Rebekah offers hospitality for the servant and his men) **26.** The servant bowed and worshipped the Lord, (Servant praises God for guiding him) **27.** Saying, "Praise be to the Lord, the God of my master Abraham, who has not forsaken His kindness and faithfulness to my master. He led me on the right path to the family of my master's relatives." (The servant praises God for leading him to the right family) **28.** Rebekah ran to tell her family what had happened. (Rebekah shares the news with her family) **29.** Rebekah had a brother named Laban, who hurried to the well when he saw the gifts and heard Rebekah's story. (Laban, Rebekah's brother, is introduced) **30.** When Laban saw the earring and bracelets, and heard his sister's account, he went to the man standing by the camels and said, "Come, you are blessed of the Lord! Why stand outside? I've prepared a place for you and the camels." (Laban invites the servant inside, recognizing the Lord's blessing) **31.** The servant entered the house, and Laban gave the camels straw and feed, and water to wash the servant's and his men's feet. (The hospitality extended to the servant and his men) **32.** Food was set before the servant, but he said, "I will not eat until I've told you why I'm here." (The servant prioritizes his mission over eating) **33.** "I am Abraham's servant," he explained. (The servant introduces himself) **34.** "The Lord has greatly blessed my master, and he has become wealthy with flocks, silver, gold, and servants. (Abraham's wealth and success) **35.** "Sarah, my master's wife, bore him a son in her old age, and to him he has given everything he owns. (Isaac, Abraham's son, inheriting everything) **36.** "My master made me swear that I would not take a wife for his son from the Canaanites but from his own family. (Abraham's instructions to the servant) **37.** "I asked my master, 'What if the woman will not come?' (Servant's concerns about the woman refusing) **38.** "He told me, 'The Lord will send His angel with you and make your journey successful. You will find a wife for Isaac from my kin.'" (The Lord's assurance of success) **39.** "If they refuse, then I will be free from my oath." (The servant clarifies the condition of the oath) **40.** "I came today to this well and prayed, asking God to show me the right woman for Isaac." (The servant explains his prayer) **41.** "When a virgin comes to draw water, I asked her to give me a drink, and if she also offers to water my camels, let that be the sign that she's the one the Lord has chosen." (The servant recounts the specific prayer) **42.** "Before I even finished speaking, Rebekah came out, and she did exactly as I had prayed." (The servant recognizes God's answer) **43.** "I asked her whose daughter she was, and when she told me, I gave her the earrings and bracelets." (The confirmation of Rebekah's identity and gifts given) **44.** "I worshipped the Lord and thanked Him for leading me to the right place." (The servant's gratitude) **45.** "Now, if you are willing to do what is right and kind for my master, tell me; if not, I'll go elsewhere." (The servant asks for the family's consent) **46.** Laban and Bethuel answered, "This comes from the Lord, we cannot say anything bad or good. (Laban and Bethuel agree that it's God's will) **47.** "Rebekah is here, take her and let her become Isaac's wife, as the Lord has spoken." (They consent to Rebekah's marriage to Isaac) **48.** The servant bowed to the ground in worship, thanking the Lord. (The servant's worship of God) **49.** He then gave Rebekah valuable gifts and also gave precious items to her family. (The servant gives more gifts) **50.** After eating and drinking, the servant and his men stayed the night. In the morning, he asked to leave for his master. (The servant prepares to leave) **51.** Rebekah's family asked her to stay for ten more days, but the servant insisted, "Do not delay me, for the Lord has made my journey successful; let me go." (The servant urges urgency) **52.** They called Rebekah and asked her, "Will you go with this man?" (Rebekah is asked to make her decision) **53.** She answered, "I will go." (Rebekah agrees to the journey) **54.** They sent her off with her nurse, the servant, and his men. (Rebekah's departure) **55.** They blessed Rebekah, saying, "You are our sister, may you become the mother of thousands and your descendants possess the gates of their enemies." (A blessing for Rebekah's future) **56.** Rebekah and her maids mounted the camels and followed the servant on his journey. (Rebekah begins her journey to Isaac) **57.** Isaac was returning from the well Lahai-roi, and as evening came, he went out to meditate in the field. (Isaac is introduced and found meditating) **58.** When he looked up, he saw camels approaching. (Isaac sees the camels approaching) **59.** Rebekah, seeing Isaac, got off her camel and... (Rebekah first sees Isaac) **60.** They blessed Rebekah and said to her, "Our sister, may you become the mother of thousands and tens of thousands; may your descendants possess the gates of those who hate them." (The family blesses Rebekah with a prophecy of fertility and strength for her descendants) **61.** Rebekah and her maids got on the camels and followed the servant. So the servant took Rebekah and went on his way. (Rebekah leaves with the servant, beginning the journey to Isaac) **62.** Isaac had just come from the Negev and was living in the region of Beer-lahai-roi. (Isaac's location and where he had been) **63.** One evening, Isaac went out to meditate in the field, and as he looked up, he saw camels approaching. (Isaac is in the field, perhaps reflecting or praying, when he spots the camels carrying Rebekah) **64.** Rebekah also looked up, and when she saw Isaac, she got down from her camel. (Rebekah notices Isaac and dismounts in preparation to meet him) **65.** She asked the servant, "Who is that man walking in the field to meet us?" The servant replied, "He is my master." So she took her veil and covered herself. (Rebekah inquires about Isaac, and upon learning it is him, she covers herself as was customary for a woman preparing to meet her future husband) **66.** The servant told Isaac all the things he had done. (The servant recounts the entire journey and the successful fulfillment of Abraham's mission) **67.** Isaac brought Rebekah into the tent of his mother Sarah, and he married her. He loved her, and Isaac was comforted after his mother's death. (Isaac marries Rebekah and finds solace in her companionship after losing his mother)

Chapter 25

1. Abraham took another wife, and her name was Keturah (2nd spouse of Abraham). **2.** She bore him Zimran, Jokshan, Medan, Midian, Ishbak, and Shuah. **3.** Jokshan fathered Sheba and Dedan. The descendants of Dedan were Asshurim, Letushim, and Leummim. **4.** The sons of Midian were Ephah, Epher, Hanoch, Abida, and Eldaah. These were the children of Keturah. **5.** Abraham gave all his possessions to Isaac, his son (the heir). **6.** But to the sons of his concubines, Abraham gave gifts, and sent them far away from Isaac, his son, while he was still alive, to the east (the lands to the east of Canaan). **7.** These are the years of Abraham's life: he lived 175 years. **8.** Then Abraham passed away at a ripe old age, an elderly man full of years, and was gathered to his ancestors (died peacefully). **9.** Isaac and Ishmael, his sons, buried him in the cave of Machpelah, in the field of Ephron, son of Zohar the Hittite, near Mamre (a burial site near Hebron). **10.** This field was purchased by Abraham from the Hittites. There Abraham and Sarah, his wife, were buried. **11.** After Abraham's death, God blessed his son Isaac, who lived near the well Lahai-roi (a well in the desert). **12.** These are the generations of Ishmael, Abraham's son, whom Hagar, the Egyptian servant of Sarah, bore to Abraham: **13.** The names of Ishmael's sons, by their tribes and generations, were: Nebajoth (Ishmael's firstborn), Kedar, Adbeel, Mibsam, **14.** Mishma, Dumah, Massa, **15.** Hadar, Tema, Jetur, Naphish, and Kedemah. **16.** These were the sons of Ishmael, and they lived in towns and camps; twelve tribal chiefs, each with their own nations. **17.** Ishmael lived 137 years. He died and was gathered to his people (passed away). **18.** His descendants lived from Havilah to Shur, which is east of Egypt, toward Assyria. He died in the presence of all his brothers (in the wilderness). **19.** These are the generations of Isaac, son of Abraham: Abraham was the father of Isaac. **20.** Isaac was 40 years old when he married Rebekah, daughter of Bethuel the Aramean from Paddan Aram, and sister of Laban the Aramean. **21.** Isaac prayed to the Lord on behalf of his wife, because she was barren. The Lord answered his prayer, and his wife Rebekah conceived. **22.** But the children struggled inside her, and she said, "Why is this happening to me?" So she went to inquire of the Lord. **23.** The Lord said to her, "Two nations are in your womb, and two peoples will be separated from your body. One will be stronger than the other, and the older will serve the younger." **24.** When her time came to give birth, there were twin boys in her womb. **25.** The first came out red, his whole body like a hairy garment, and they named him Esau (meaning "hairy"). **26.** After this, his brother came out, grasping Esau's heel, and he was named Jacob (meaning "supplanter" or "heel-grabber"). Isaac was sixty years old when Rebekah gave birth to them. **27.** The boys grew up, and Esau became a skillful hunter, a man of the field, while Jacob was a quiet man, staying in the tents (a man of the house). **28.** Isaac loved Esau because he enjoyed eating the wild game Esau brought home, but Rebekah loved Jacob. **29.** One day Jacob was cooking some stew, and Esau came in from the field, famished. **30.** Esau said to Jacob, "Let me eat some of that red stew, for I am exhausted." (That is why he was also called Edom, which means "red.") **31.** Jacob responded, "First, sell me your birthright." **32.** Esau said, "Look, I am about to die. What good is my birthright to me?" **33.** Jacob said, "Swear to me first." So Esau swore an oath to him, selling his birthright to Jacob. **34.** Then Jacob gave Esau bread and lentil stew. Esau ate and drank, then got up and left. So Esau despised his birthright (rejected his inheritance).

Chapter 26

1. There was a famine in the land, besides the earlier famine during Abraham's time. Isaac went to Abimelech, the Philistine king, in Gerar. (Gerar: A Philistine city) **2.** The Lord appeared to Isaac and said, "Do not go to Egypt. Stay in the land I will show you." (Egypt: A neighboring land, often seen as a place of refuge in times of famine) **3.** "Live here and I will bless you. To you and your descendants, I give these lands, fulfilling the promise made to your father Abraham." (Promise to Abraham: A covenant made by God with Isaac's father) **4.** "I will make your descendants like the stars, and give them all these lands. Through your offspring, all nations will be blessed." (Stars: Referring to the vast number of Isaac's descendants) **5.** "This is because Abraham obeyed My commands, laws, and instructions." (Abraham's obedience: Referring to Abraham's faithfulness to God's laws) **6.** So Isaac stayed in Gerar. (Gerar: A Philistine city) **7.** The men of the place asked about his wife, and he said, "She is my sister," because he feared they might kill him for Rebekah, who was beautiful. (Rebekah: Isaac's wife, noted for her beauty) **8.** After a long time, King Abimelech saw Isaac and Rebekah showing affection. (Abimelech: A Philistine king, possibly a title for successive rulers) **9.** Abimelech called Isaac and said, "She is your wife! Why did you say she is your sister?" Isaac said, "I feared I might be killed because of her." (Deception: Isaac's fear caused him to lie about his relationship) **10.** Abimelech said, "What have you done? Someone could have taken her, and you would have brought guilt upon us." (Guilt: A transgression that would have affected the entire community) **11.** Abimelech warned his people, saying, "Anyone who touches this man or his wife will be put to death." (Decree: A royal command to protect Isaac and Rebekah) **12.** Isaac sowed in that land and reaped a hundredfold in the same year, for the Lord blessed him. (Hundredfold: A bountiful harvest, representing God's favor) **13.** Isaac became wealthy and continued to prosper. (Prosperity: Isaac's wealth grew significantly as a sign of God's blessing) **14.** He had flocks, herds, and many servants, which caused the Philistines to envy him. (Flocks and herds: Symbols of wealth in ancient times) **15.** The Philistines filled the wells Abraham had dug with earth after his death. (Wells: Vital sources of water, which the Philistines destroyed) **16.** Abimelech told Isaac, "Leave us, for you have become too powerful." (Powerful: Isaac's increasing wealth and influence) **17.** Isaac moved and settled in the Valley of Gerar. (Valley of Gerar: A region where Isaac chose to live) **18.** Isaac reopened the wells his father had dug, which the Philistines had stopped up, and renamed them after his father. (Reopened wells: Isaac reclaimed his father's legacy by re-digging wells) **19.** Isaac's servants dug in the valley and found a well of fresh water. (Fresh water: A valuable resource in the desert) **20.** The herders of Gerar quarreled with Isaac's herders, saying, "This water is ours!" Isaac named it Esek, because they quarreled over it. (Esek: Means "contention" or "strife" in Hebrew) **21.** They dug another well, but they quarreled over that too, so Isaac called it Sitnah. (Sitnah: Means "enmity" or "hostility" in Hebrew) **22.** Isaac moved again and dug another well. This time, there was no dispute, so he called it Rehoboth, saying, "Now the Lord has made room for us." (Rehoboth: Means "room" or "space" in Hebrew, symbolizing peace) **23.** Isaac then went to Beersheba. (Beersheba: A city of significance in the southern part of Canaan) **24.** That night, the Lord appeared to him and said, "I am the God of your father Abraham. Do not fear, for I am with you. I will bless you and multiply your descendants for Abraham's sake." (God of Abraham: Refers to the covenant God made with Isaac's father) **25.** Isaac built an altar and called upon the name of the Lord. He pitched his tent, and his servants dug a well. (Altar: A place of worship and sacrifice to God) **26.** Abimelech came to Isaac from Gerar, with Ahuzzath and Phichol, his officials. (Ahuzzath and Phichol: Abimelech's advisors, likely military and political figures) **27.** Isaac asked, "Why have you come to me, since you sent me away?" (Hostility: Isaac questioned the motivation behind their visit) **28.** They said, "We clearly see that the Lord is with you. Let's make a covenant, so that there will be no harm between us, as we have not harmed you." (Covenant: A formal agreement to establish peace) **29.** Isaac prepared a feast, and they ate and drank together. (Feast: A shared meal to seal their covenant) **30.** The next morning, they swore an oath to each other. Isaac sent them away, and they left in peace. (Oath: A solemn promise to honor the peace agreement) **31.** That same day, Isaac's servants came to him, saying, "We have found water in the well." (Discovery: The well provided water, a sign of God's ongoing blessing) **32.** Isaac named the well Shebah, and the city was called Beersheba, which means "well of the oath." (Shebah/Beersheba: The name reflects the covenant made with Abimelech) **33.** When Esau was forty years old, he married Judith, daughter of Beeri the Hittite, and Basemath, daughter of Elon the Hittite. (Esau's marriages: Esau married outside the covenant family, to the grief of his parents) **34.** These marriages caused great distress to Isaac and Rebekah. (Distress: Esau's choice of wives created emotional hardship for his parents)

Chapter 27

1. As Isaac grew old and his sight dimmed, he called for Esau, his older son, and said, "My son." Esau replied, "Here I am." (Isaac: The patriarch of the family) **2.** Isaac then said, "I am old, and I do not know when I will die." (Isaac's age: Reflecting his declining health) **3.** "Take your weapons, your bow, and go to the field to hunt game for me. **4.** Make the tasty dish I love and bring it to me, so that I may eat and bless you before I die." (Blessing: A paternal prayer for the son's future) **5.** Rebekah overheard Isaac's conversation with Esau, and Esau went out to hunt. (Rebekah: Isaac's wife, who was listening) **6.** Rebekah then spoke to Jacob, her son, saying, "I heard your father tell Esau, **7.** 'Prepare me game and make me a meal so that I may bless you before I die.'" (Jacob: Isaac and Rebekah's younger son) **8.** "Now, my son, listen to me and do what I command. **9.** Go to the flock and bring me two choice goats, and I will prepare them as your father loves." (Flock: The group of sheep or goats) **10.** "Then take the food to your father, that he may eat and bless you before he dies."

(Blessing: A ceremonial act that involved a prayer for prosperity) **11.** Jacob said to Rebekah, "Esau is hairy, and I am smooth-skinned. **12.** Perhaps my father will feel me and think I am deceiving him, bringing a curse upon myself instead of a blessing." (Deceiving: Jacob's fear of being caught in a lie) **13.** Rebekah assured him, "Let any curse fall on me, my son. Just obey me, and go get the goats." (Cursed: A reversal of blessing, a fear of divine punishment) **14.** Jacob went to the flock, brought two goats, and his mother prepared them as Isaac liked. (Goats: The animals used to make the dish Isaac loved) **15.** Rebekah took Esau's best clothes and put them on Jacob, her younger son. **16.** She also covered his hands and neck with goat skins to imitate Esau's hair. (Esau's clothes: Used to deceive Isaac into thinking Jacob was Esau) **17.** She gave Jacob the food and bread she had prepared to take to Isaac. (Bread: A staple food item) **18.** Jacob went to his father and said, "My father." Isaac replied, "Here I am, who are you, my son?" (Isaac's recognition: Isaac is trying to identify who is speaking) **19.** Jacob said, "I am Esau, your firstborn. I've done as you asked, so rise and eat my game, that you may bless me." (Game: The wild animals that Esau hunted) **20.** Isaac wondered, "How did you find it so quickly, my son?" Jacob answered, "The Lord your God brought it to me." (God's role: Jacob invoked divine assistance to justify his speed) **21.** Isaac told Jacob, "Come closer so I can feel you and know if you are really Esau." (Isaac's doubt: He wants to confirm Jacob's identity by touch) **22.** Jacob approached, and Isaac felt him, saying, "The voice is Jacob's, but the hands are Esau's." (Voice: The key identifying factor for Isaac) **23.** Isaac didn't recognize him because his hands were hairy like Esau's, so he blessed him. (Hairy hands: Isaac relied on touch to identify his son) **24.** Isaac asked, "Are you truly my son Esau?" Jacob replied, "I am." (Jacob's deception: He continued his ruse) **25.** Isaac said, "Bring it to me, and I will eat, so that my soul may bless you." Jacob brought it to him, and Isaac ate; he also drank wine. (Wine: A drink served with meals, possibly as a ritual part of blessing) **26.** Isaac then said, "Come near and kiss me, my son." (Kiss: A traditional gesture of affection and final confirmation) **27.** Jacob kissed Isaac, and Isaac smelled his clothes, blessing him and saying: "The scent of my son is like the field the Lord has blessed." (Blessing: Isaac's prophetic prayer over Jacob) **28.** "May God give you the dew of heaven and the richness of the earth, abundance of grain and wine. **29.** May nations serve you, and peoples bow down to you. Be master over your brothers, and let your mother's sons bow to you. Cursed be those who curse you, and blessed be those who bless you." (Blessing: A royal and prosperous future for Jacob) **30.** As soon as Isaac finished blessing Jacob and he left, Esau returned from his hunt. (Esau's return: The moment of realization for Isaac) **31.** Esau made a meal and brought it to his father, saying, "Let my father rise and eat, so that you may bless me." (Esau's meal: His offering for Isaac's blessing) **32.** Isaac asked, "Who are you?" Esau replied, "I am your firstborn, Esau." (Isaac's confusion: He is shocked and confused by the situation) **33.** Isaac trembled violently and said, "Who then hunted game and brought it to me? I ate it all before you came, and I have blessed him, and indeed he will be blessed." (Trembled: Isaac's shock and realization of the deception) **34.** Esau let out a bitter cry and said, "Bless me too, my father!" (Esau's grief: His desperation to receive a blessing) **35.** Isaac replied, "Your brother came deceitfully and took your blessing." (Deceit: Isaac recognizes Jacob's trickery) **36.** Esau said, "Isn't he rightly named Jacob? He has deceived me twice—he took my birthright, and now my blessing." (Jacob's name: "Jacob" means "supplanter" or "deceiver") **37.** Isaac responded, "I have made him your master and given him all his brothers as servants, with grain and wine. What can I do for you?" (Master: Jacob's elevated status after the blessing) **38.** Esau pleaded, "Do you only have one blessing, Father? Bless me too." Esau wept aloud. (Esau's plea: His deep sorrow at losing the blessing) **39.** Isaac replied, "Your dwelling will be away from the earth's richness and from the dew of heaven. **40.** By your sword you will live, and you will serve your brother. But when you grow restless, you will break his yoke from your neck." (Esau's destiny: A life of struggle and eventual independence) **41.** Esau hated Jacob because of the blessing Isaac had given him, and he planned to kill Jacob after their father's death. (Hatred: Esau's desire for revenge) **42.** Rebekah heard Esau's words and called Jacob, saying, "Esau plans to kill you, so flee to my brother Laban in Haran. **43.** Stay there a while until Esau's anger subsides. **44.** When he forgets what you have done, I will send for you. Why should I lose you both in one day?" (Laban: Rebekah's brother, to whom Jacob would flee) **45.** Rebekah then spoke to Isaac, saying, **46.** "I am weary of my life because of the Hittite women. If Jacob marries one of them, what good is my life?" (Hittite women: Canaanite women who displeased Isaac and Rebekah)

Chapter 28

1. Isaac called Jacob, blessed him, and instructed him, "Do not marry a Canaanite woman. **2.** Go to Padan Aram, to the house of Bethuel, your mother's father, and take a wife from there, from the daughters of Laban, your mother's brother. **3.** May God Almighty bless you, make you fruitful, and multiply you, so that you may become a community of nations. **4.** May He give you the blessing of Abraham, to you and your descendants, so that you may inherit the land where you are a stranger, which God gave to Abraham." (Padan Aram: A region northeast of Canaan, where Isaac's family originated) **5.** Isaac sent Jacob away, and he traveled to Padan Aram to Laban, son of Bethuel the Aramean, Rebekah's brother, the mother of Jacob and Esau. **6.** When Esau realized that Isaac had blessed Jacob and sent him to Padan Aram to find a wife, **7.** and that Jacob had obeyed his parents and gone to Padan Aram, **8.** Esau also saw that his Canaanite wives did not please his father Isaac. **9.** So Esau went to Ishmael, the son of Abraham, and took Mahalath, the daughter of Ishmael, and sister of Nebajoth, as another wife, in addition to his other wives. (Ishmael: Isaac's half-brother, Abraham's son by Hagar) **10.** Jacob left Beersheba and set out toward Haran. **11.** When he reached a certain place, he spent the night there because the sun had set. He took one of the stones from that place and placed it under his head to sleep. **12.** He dreamed, and behold, a ladder was set up on the earth, and its top reached to heaven; the angels of God were ascending and descending on it. (Ladder: A symbolic vision, often interpreted as a connection between heaven and earth) **13.** And the Lord stood above it and said, "I am the Lord, the God of Abraham your father and the God of Isaac; the land on which you lie I will give to you and your descendants. **14.** Your descendants will be like the dust of the earth. You will spread out to the west, east, north, and south, and through you and your offspring, all the families of the earth will be blessed. **15.** I am with you, and I will protect you wherever you go. I will bring you back to this land, for I will not leave you until I have fulfilled what I have promised you." (The Promise: God's covenant with Jacob, continuing Abraham's blessing) **16.** When Jacob awoke from his sleep, he said, "Surely the Lord is in this place, and I didn't realize it." **17.** He was afraid and said, "How awesome is this place! This is none other than the house of God, and this is the gate of heaven!" (House of God: Jacob's recognition of the sacredness of the place, later named Bethel) **18.** Early the next morning, Jacob took the stone he had placed under his head, set it up as a pillar, and poured oil on top of it. **19.** He called the place Bethel, though the city had previously been named Luz. (Bethel: "House of God," the name Jacob gave to the place after his vision) **20.** Then Jacob made a vow, saying, "If God will be with me and protect me on this journey, and provide me with food and clothing, **21.** So that I return to my father's house in peace, then the Lord will be my God. **22.** And this stone I have set up as a pillar will be God's house, and of all that You give me, I will surely give a tenth to You." (Vow: Jacob promises to honor God with a tithe if His promises are fulfilled)

Chapter 29

1. Jacob continued his journey and arrived in the land of the people from the East. **2.** He saw a well in the field, and there were three flocks of sheep resting by it. The sheep were watered from this well. A large stone covered the well's opening. **3.** The flocks would gather there, and the stone would be rolled away from the well's mouth to water the sheep, then it would be put back in place. **4.** Jacob asked the shepherds, "Where are you from?" They replied, "We are from Haran." (Haran is an ancient city in Mesopotamia, known as the birthplace of Abraham.) **5.** Jacob then asked, "Do you know Laban, the son of Nahor?" (Nahor was Abraham's brother.) They answered, "We know him." **6.** Jacob asked, "Is he well?" They replied, "He is well, and here comes his daughter Rachel with the sheep." (Rachel was the younger daughter of Laban.) **7.** Jacob said, "It is still early; it's not time to gather the sheep. Water them, and then take them to pasture." **8.** They replied, "We cannot do that until all the flocks have arrived, and we have rolled away the stone from the well's mouth. Only then can we water the sheep." **9.** While Jacob was still talking with them, Rachel came with her father's sheep, as she was a shepherdess. **10.** When Jacob saw Rachel, the daughter of Laban, his mother's brother, he rolled the stone away from the well's mouth and watered Laban's flock. **11.** Jacob then kissed Rachel, and overwhelmed with emotion, he wept aloud. **12.** Jacob told Rachel that he was her relative, the son of Rebekah. (Rebekah was her father Laban's sister.) She ran to tell her father. **13.** When Laban heard the news about Jacob, his sister's son, he ran to meet him, embraced him, kissed him, and brought him to his home, where Jacob explained everything. **14.** Laban said, "You are my own flesh and blood," and Jacob stayed with him for a month. **15.** After some time, Laban said to Jacob, "Since you are my relative, you shouldn't work for me for nothing. Tell me what your wages should be." **16.** Laban had two daughters: Leah, the elder, and Rachel, the younger. **17.** Leah had delicate eyes (possibly referring to soft or weak eyes), but Rachel was beautiful, both in form and appearance. **18.** Jacob loved Rachel and said, "I will serve you for seven years if you will give me Rachel, your younger daughter, as my wife." **19.** Laban agreed, saying, "It's better that I give her to you than to another man. Stay with me." **20.** Jacob worked for seven years for Rachel, but they seemed like just a few days because of his deep love for her. **21.** After the seven years, Jacob said to Laban, "Give me my wife, for my time is fulfilled, and I want to marry her." **22.** Laban gathered all the men of the place and prepared a feast. **23.** In the evening, Laban took his daughter Leah and brought her to Jacob, and he slept with her. **24.** Laban gave his maidservant Zilpah to Leah as her maid. **25.** When morning came, Jacob realized that it was Leah, not Rachel. He confronted Laban, saying, "Why have you deceived me? Didn't I work for Rachel?" **26.** Laban responded, "In our country, we do not give the younger daughter before the older one." **27.** "Finish the week of the wedding feast, and then I will give you Rachel, in exchange for another seven years of work." **28.** Jacob agreed, completed Leah's bridal week, and then Laban gave him Rachel as his wife. **29.** Laban also gave Rachel his maidservant Bilhah to be her maid. **30.** Jacob loved Rachel more than Leah, and he worked another seven years for Laban. **31.** When the Lord saw that Leah was unloved, He opened her womb, but Rachel remained childless. **32.** Leah conceived and bore a son, and named him Reuben (Reuben means "see, a son"), saying, "The Lord has looked on my affliction. Now my husband will love me." **33.** She conceived again and bore another son, saying, "Because the Lord has heard that I am unloved, He has given me another son." She named him Simeon (Simeon means "heard"). **34.** Leah conceived once more and bore another son, saying, "Now my husband will be attached to me, because I have borne him three sons." She named him Levi (Levi means "joined"). **35.** She conceived again and bore another son, saying, "This time I will praise the Lord." She named him Judah (Judah means "praise"), and then she stopped bearing children.

Chapter 30

1. When Rachel saw that she bore Jacob no kids, she became jealous of her sister and said to Jacob, "Give me children, otherwise I die!" **2.** Jacob became angry with Rachel and said, "Am I in the place of God, who has withheld from you the fruit of the womb?" **3.** Rachel answered, "Here is my maid Bilhah (Rachel's servant), go to her, and she will bear a child on my behalf, that I may also have children through her." **4.** So Rachel gave Bilhah her maid as a wife to Jacob, and Jacob went in to her. **5.** Bilhah conceived and bore Jacob a son. **6.** Then Rachel said, "God has judged my case; He has also heard my voice and given me a son." Therefore, she named him Dan (Dan means "judge"). **7.** Bilhah, Rachel's maid, conceived again and bore another son for Jacob. **8.** Rachel said, "With great wrestlings, I have wrestled with my sister, and indeed I have prevailed." So she named him Naphtali (Naphtali means "wrestling"). **9.** When Leah saw that she had stopped bearing children, she gave her maid Zilpah (Leah's servant) to Jacob as a wife. **10.** Zilpah, Leah's maid, bore Jacob a son. **11.** Leah said, "A troop comes!" So she named him Gad (Gad means "troop" or "fortune"). **12.** Zilpah bore Jacob a second son. **13.** Leah said, "I am happy, for the daughters will call me blessed." So she named him Asher (Asher means "happy" or "blessed"). **14.** During the wheat harvest, Reuben (Leah's firstborn) found mandrakes (a type of plant believed to have fertility-boosting properties) in the field and brought them to his mother Leah. Rachel said to Leah, "Please give me some of your son's mandrakes." **15.** Leah responded, "Is it a small matter that you have taken away my husband? Would you take my son's mandrakes also?" Rachel replied, "I will let Jacob lie with you tonight for your son's mandrakes." **16.** When Jacob came in from the field that evening, Leah went out to meet him and said, "You must come in to me, for I have hired you with my son's mandrakes." And he lay with her that night. **17.** God listened to Leah, and she conceived and bore Jacob a fifth son. **18.** Leah said, "God has given me my wages because I gave my maid to my husband." So she named him Issachar (Issachar means "wages"). **19.** Leah conceived again and bore Jacob a sixth son. **20.** Leah said, "God has endowed me with a good endowment; now my husband will dwell with me, because I have borne him six sons." So she named him Zebulun (Zebulun means "dwelling"). **21.** Later, Leah bore a daughter and named her Dinah (Dinah means "judgment" or "vindication"). **22.** Then God remembered Rachel, and God listened to her and opened her womb. **23.** She conceived and bore a son and said, "God has taken away my reproach." **24.** She named him Joseph (Joseph means "may he add"), saying, "The Lord shall add to me another son." **25.** After Rachel bore Joseph, Jacob said to Laban, "Send me away, that I may go to my own place and to my country. **26.** Give me my wives and children for whom I have served you, and let me go, for you know how faithfully I have served you." **27.** Laban said to him, "Please stay, if I have found favor in your eyes, for I have learned by experience that the Lord has blessed me for your sake." **28.** Laban continued, "Name your wages, and I will give it." **29.** Jacob replied, "You know how I have served you and how your livestock has prospered under my care. **30.** When I arrived, your flock was small, but it has increased greatly, and the Lord has blessed you since my coming. Now, when will I provide for my own family?" **31.** Laban asked, "What shall I give you?" Jacob answered, "You don't need to give me anything. But if you will do this one thing for me, I will continue to tend your flocks: **32.** Let me go through all your flock today and remove every speckled and spotted sheep, every brown lamb, and every spotted or speckled goat. These will be my wages. **33.** So my honesty will be evident in the future, when you come to check my wages: any sheep or goats that are not speckled or spotted, or not brown among the lambs, will be considered stolen by me." **34.** Laban agreed, "Oh, that it were according to your word!" **35.** That day, Laban removed all the speckled and spotted male goats, all the speckled and spotted female goats, everyone with white markings, and all the brown lambs, and gave them to his sons. **36.** Then he put a three-day journey between himself and Jacob, while Jacob tended the rest of Laban's flock. **37.** Jacob took fresh branches from poplar, almond, and chestnut trees, peeled white strips in them, exposing the white beneath. **38.** He set the peeled rods in front of the watering troughs, where the flocks came to drink, so that they would conceive when they came to drink. **39.** The flocks conceived in front of the rods, and they brought forth streaked, speckled, and spotted young. **40.** Jacob separated the lambs, and made the flocks face toward the streaked and the brown ones in Laban's flock. His own flocks he separated, not mixing them with Laban's flocks. **41.** Whenever the stronger livestock conceived, Jacob placed the rods before their eyes in the troughs, so that they would conceive near the rods. **42.** But when the weaker livestock conceived, he did not put the rods in front of them. So the feebler animals became Laban's, and the stronger ones became Jacob's. **43.** As a result, Jacob became exceedingly prosperous, with large flocks, male and female servants, camels, and donkeys.

Chapter 31

1 Jacob heard the words of Laban's sons, saying, "Jacob has taken all that belonged to our father, and from what was our father's, he has acquired this wealth." (Laban's sons: Accusation against Jacob) **2** Jacob noticed that Laban's attitude toward him was no longer favorable, as it had been before. (Laban's changing attitude) **3** Then the Lord spoke to Jacob, saying, "Return to the land of your fathers and to your family, and I will be with you." (God's command to return) **4** So Jacob called Rachel and Leah to the field where his flocks were, **5** and said to them, "I see that your father's attitude is no longer favorable toward me, but the God of my father has been with me. **6** You know how I have served your father with all my strength. **7** Yet your father has deceived me and changed my wages ten times, but God did not allow him to harm me. **8** If he said, 'The speckled shall be your wages,' then all the flocks bore speckled. And if he said, 'The streaked shall be your wages,' then all the flocks bore streaked. (Jacob's faithful service) **9** So God has taken away your father's livestock and given them to me. **10** At the time the flocks conceived, I looked up and saw in a dream that the rams which mated with the flocks were streaked, speckled, and spotted. **11** Then the Angel of God spoke to me in a dream, saying, "Jacob." And I replied, "Here I am." **12** The angel said, "Look up and see, all the rams which leap on the flocks are streaked, speckled, and spotted; for I have seen all that Laban is doing to you. **13** I am the God of Bethel, where you anointed a pillar and made a vow to Me. Now arise, leave this land, and return to the land of your family." (Bethel: The place of Jacob's dream and vow) **14** Then Rachel and Leah answered, "Do we still have any share or inheritance in our father's house? **15** Are we not regarded as strangers by him? For he has sold us and completely consumed our money. (Rachel and Leah's concerns) **16** All the wealth that God has taken from our father is really ours and our children's; now do whatever God has told you." (Rachel and Leah's agreement) **17** So Jacob arose, put his sons and wives on camels, **18** and took all his livestock and possessions that he had acquired in Padan Aram to go to his father Isaac in the land of Canaan. (Padan Aram: Jacob's previous home) **19** Now, while Laban was away shearing his sheep, Rachel stole her father's household idols. (Household idols: Idols used for worship or inheritance) **20** Jacob deceived Laban the Syrian by not telling him he was leaving. (Laban: "The Syrian" refers to his origin) **21** So Jacob fled with all that he had. He crossed the river and headed toward the mountains of Gilead. (Gilead: Region east of the Jordan River) **22** On the third day, Laban was told that Jacob had fled. **23** Laban took his relatives with him and pursued Jacob for seven days, overtaking him in the mountains of Gilead. **24** But God appeared to Laban in a dream that night, warning him, "Be careful not to say anything to Jacob, either good or bad." (God's warning to Laban) **25** Laban caught up with Jacob. Now Jacob had pitched his tent in the mountains, and Laban, with his relatives, pitched in the mountains of Gilead. **26** Laban said to Jacob, "What have you done, that you've deceived me and carried off my daughters like captives taken with the sword? **27** Why did you flee secretly and steal away from me? You didn't even let me kiss my daughters and grandchildren. You have acted foolishly. **28** I could harm you, but last night the God of your father spoke to me, saying, 'Be careful not to say anything to Jacob, either good or bad.' **29** You have gone because you long for your father's house, but why have you stolen my gods?" (Laban's accusation: Idols are stolen) **30** Jacob answered, "I was afraid because I thought you might take your daughters from me by force. **31** If you find anyone who has your gods, let that person die. In the presence of our relatives, point out what is yours, and take it." Jacob did not know that Rachel had stolen them. (Rachel's theft) **32** So Laban searched Jacob's tent, then Leah's, and finally the two maidservants' tents, but he didn't find them. He then went into Rachel's tent. **33** Now Rachel had taken the idols, put them in the camel's saddle, and sat on them. Laban searched the tent, but found nothing. **34** She said to her father, "Don't be angry that I cannot rise before you, for the way of women is with me." He searched but found no idols. (Rachel's excuse) **35** Then Jacob became angry and rebuked Laban. He said, "What is my offense? What is my sin, that you have pursued me so fiercely? **36** After searching all my things, what of yours have you found? Set it before my relatives and yours, and let them judge between us. **37** These 20 years I have been with you; your ewes and goats have not miscarried, and I have not eaten your rams. **38** I have never brought you anything torn by wild animals; I have borne the loss myself. You have demanded it from me, whether stolen by day or by night. **39** It was like this for me: In the day the heat consumed me, and the frost at night, and sleep fled from my eyes. **40** I have been in your house 20 years, serving you for your two daughters and for your flocks, and you changed my wages ten times. **41** If the God of my father, the God of Abraham, and the Fear of Isaac had not been with me, you would have sent me away empty-handed. But God has seen my misery and the labor of my hands, and rebuked you last night." (God's intervention) **42** Laban answered, "These daughters are mine, and these children are mine, and this flock is mine. All you see is mine. But what can I do today to these daughters or their children? **43** Come, let us make a covenant, you and I, and let it be a witness between us." (Laban's challenge) **44** So Jacob took a stone and set it up as a pillar. **45** Then Jacob said to his relatives, "Gather stones." And they took stones, made a heap, and ate there by the heap. (Covenant ceremony) **46** Laban called it Jegar Sahadutha, but Jacob called it Galeed. (Jegar Sahadutha: "Heap of Witness"; Galeed: "Witness heap") **47** Laban said, "This heap is a witness between you and me today." Therefore, it was called Galeed, **48** and also Mizpah, for he said, "May the Lord watch between us when we are absent from each other. **49** If you afflict my daughters, or take other wives, although no one is with us—see, God is a witness between you and me!" (Mizpah: "Watchtower") **50** Laban said to Jacob, "Here is this heap and pillar I have placed between you and me. **51** This heap is a witness, and this pillar is a witness, that I will not pass beyond this heap and pillar to harm you, and you will not pass beyond them to harm me. **52** The God of Abraham and Nahor, the God of their father, judge between us." And Jacob swore by the Fear of his father Isaac. (God of Abraham and Nahor) **53** Then Jacob offered a sacrifice on the mountain and called his relatives to eat bread. They ate and spent the night on the mountain. **54** Early the next morning, Laban kissed his daughters and grandchildren, and blessed them. **55** Then he departed and returned to his home. (Laban's departure)

Chapter 32

1. So Jacob continued his journey, and God's angels met him along the way. **2.** When Jacob saw them, he said, "This must be God's camp," and named the place Mahanaim (Two camps). **3.** Jacob sent messengers ahead to his brother Esau, who lived in Seir, the region of Edom (Seir: mountainous region). **4.** He instructed them to say: "Your servant Jacob says: I have lived with Laban, my uncle, and stayed there until now (Laban: Jacob's uncle). **5.** I have oxen, donkeys, flocks, and servants. I am sending this to seek your favor, my lord." **6.** The messengers returned with the news: "Esau is coming to meet you, and he has 400 men with him (Esau's army)." **7.** Jacob was very afraid and distressed. He divided his people, flocks, herds, and camels into two groups. **8.** He thought, "If Esau attacks one group and defeats it, the other group will have a chance to escape (Strategic division)." **9.** Jacob prayed, "God of my father Abraham and Isaac, You who told me, 'Return to your homeland, and I will do you good,' **10.** I am unworthy of all the kindness and faithfulness You have shown me, Your servant. When I crossed the Jordan with only my staff, I now have two groups of people (Referring to past blessings). **11.** Rescue me from my brother Esau's hand, for I fear he will harm me and the women and children. **12.** But You promised, 'I will surely bless you and make your descendants as numerous as the sands on the seashore' (God's promise)." **13.** That night, Jacob took a generous gift for his brother Esau: **14.** 200 female goats, 20 male goats, 200 ewes, 20 rams, **15.** 30 camels with their young, 40 cows, 10 bulls, 20 female donkeys, and 10 foals (Large offering). **16.** He placed them in the care of his servants, in separate groups, and instructed them, "Go ahead of me, and leave space between each group." **17.** To the first group, he said: "When Esau my brother meets you and asks, 'Who do you belong to, and where are you going? Whose animals are these ahead of you?' **18.** You are to say, 'They belong to your servant Jacob. They are a gift sent to my lord Esau, and Jacob himself is behind us.'" **19.** He gave similar instructions to the second and third groups, and to everyone following the herds, saying, **20.** "This is what you will say to Esau when you meet him: 'Your servant Jacob is behind us.'" Jacob thought, "I will try to pacify him with the gift in front of me, and afterward, I will face him. Perhaps he will accept me (Gift to appease)." **21.** The gift passed on ahead of Jacob, but he stayed that night in the camp. **22.** That night, Jacob got up, took his two wives, his two female servants, and his eleven sons, and crossed the ford of Jabbok (Jabbok River). **23.** He sent them across the stream, along with all his possessions (Strategic separation). **24.** Jacob was left alone, and a man wrestled with him until daybreak (Divine figure). **25.** When the man saw he could not overpower Jacob, he touched the socket of Jacob's hip, and it was dislocated as they wrestled. **26.** The man said, "Let me go, for it is nearly dawn." But Jacob replied, "I will not let You go unless You bless me!" (Jacob's determination). **27.** The man asked, "What is your name?" Jacob answered, "Jacob." **28.** The man said, "Your name will no longer be Jacob, but Israel, because you have fought with both God and men, and have prevailed (Israel: 'He struggles with God')." **29.** Jacob asked, "Please tell me Your name." But the man replied, "Why do you ask about My name?" And there He blessed him. **30.** Jacob named the place Peniel, saying, "I have seen God face to face, and yet my life has been spared (Peniel: 'Face of God')." **31.** As Jacob passed Peniel, the sun rose, and he limped because of the injury to his hip (Permanent limp). **32.** Therefore, the Israelites do not eat the tendon attached to the socket of the hip, because the man touched the socket of Jacob's hip near the tendon (Cultural practice).

Chapter 33

1. Now Jacob lifted his eyes and looked, and there, Esau was coming, accompanied by 400 men. So he divided the children among Leah, Rachel, and the two maidservants. **2.** He placed the maidservants and their children in front, Leah and her children behind, and Rachel and Joseph last. **3.** Then he went ahead of them and bowed to the ground seven times as he approached his brother. **4.** But Esau ran to meet him, embraced him, threw his arms around his neck, kissed him, and they both wept. **5.** Esau then looked up and saw the women and children, asking, "Who are these with you?" Jacob replied, "The children whom God has graciously given to your servant." **6.** The maidservants came forward with their children, and they bowed down. **7.** Leah came forward with her children, and they bowed down. Then Joseph and Rachel came forward, and they bowed down. **8.** Esau asked, "What is the meaning of all these groups I met?" Jacob answered, "These are to find favor in the sight of my lord." **9.** But Esau replied, "I have plenty, my brother; keep what you have for yourself." **10.** Jacob insisted, "No, please, if I have found favor in your eyes, accept my gift. I have seen your face as if I have seen the face of God, and you were pleased with me. **11.** Please accept the blessing I have brought you, for God has been gracious to me, and I have enough." So Esau accepted it. **12.** Esau then said, "Let us travel on together, and I will go ahead of you." **13.** But Jacob replied, "My lord knows that the children are tender, and the nursing flocks are with me. If they are driven hard for even one day, all the flocks will die. **14.** Please let my lord go on ahead of his servant, and I will move at a pace that is comfortable for the children and the flocks, until I reach my lord in Seir." **15.** Esau said, "Let me leave some of my men with you." But Jacob answered, "Why do that? Let me find favor in the sight of my lord." **16.** So Esau returned to his way to Seir that day. **17.** Jacob, however, journeyed to Succoth, built himself a house, and made shelters for his livestock. Therefore, the place was called Succoth (Succoth: "booths"). **18.** Jacob then arrived safely at the city of Shechem, in the land of Canaan, after coming from Padan Aram. He set up camp in front of the city (Shechem: City in Canaan). **19.** He bought a piece of land where he had pitched his tent from the sons of Hamor, Shechem's father, for one hundred pieces of silver (Hamor: Father of Shechem). **20.** There he set up an altar and called it El Elohe Israel (El Elohe Israel: "God, the God of Israel").

Chapter 34

1. Dinah, the daughter of Leah, went out to visit the daughters of the land. (Leah: Jacob's first spouse) **2.** Shechem, the son of Hamor the Hivite, noticed her, took her, slept together with her, and dishonored her. (Hamor: a Hivite prince; Hivite: a Canaanite institution) **3.** Shechem became deeply interested in Dinah, loved her, and spoke kindly to her. (Attracted: emotionally related) **4.** Shechem spoke to his father Hamor, saying, "Get me this woman as my wife." (Spoke: communicated) **5.** When Jacob heard that Shechem had defiled his daughter, he remained silent due to the fact his sons had been away. (Defiled: violated or dishonored) **6.** Hamor, Shechem's father, went to speak with Jacob. (Hamor: a Canaanite prince) **7.** Jacob's sons returned, heard of the problem, and were deeply distressed and angry over Shechem's act against their sister. (Disgraceful: shameful) **8.** Hamor spoke to them, announcing, "My son Shechem longs in your daughter. Please supply her to him as a spouse." (Longs for: deeply goals) **9.** "Make marriages with us, provide your daughters to us, and take ours for yourselves." (Marriages: union or trade) **10.** "You can settle right here and change in the land, for it is large enough for anybody." (Settle: stay and establish a domestic) **11.** Shechem stated to Jacob and his sons, "Let me discover want in your sight. Something you ask, I can supply." (Prefer: approval or kindness) **12.** "Ask for any dowry or gift, and I'm able to give as a whole lot as you call for. Just give me the younger girl as a spouse." (Dowry: a present given to the groom's own family) **13.** Jacob's sons spoke back deceitfully because Shechem had defiled their sister. (Deceitfully: dishonestly) **14.** "We can't provide our sister to a person uncircumcised, for that might be a disgrace to us." (Uncircumcised: someone now not circumcised, a Jewish custom) **15.** "But, we are able to agree if each male amongst you is circumcised." (Circumcised: the removal of the foreskin as a spiritual practice) **16.** "Then we will supply our daughters to you, and we can take yours, and live as one humans." (Live as one humans: shape an alliance or union) **17.** "But if you do now not agree, we are able to take our daughter and go away." (Agree: consent) **18.** Hamor and Shechem have been thrilled with the idea. (Pleased: satisfied) **19.** Shechem quickly agreed, because he turned into delighted with Dinah and more honorable than his father's household. (Honorable: respectable) **20.** Hamor and Shechem spoke to the guys in their town, announcing, (Shechem: Hamor's son) **21.** "Those men are peaceful. Let them settle and trade within the land, for it is huge enough. Let us take their daughters as other halves and give ours to them." (Non-violent: no longer opposed) **22.** "However on one condition: each male among us should be circumcised, just as they're." (Condition: requirement) **23.** "Will not their livestock, belongings, and the whole lot they own be ours? Let us agree, and they may stay amongst us." (Cattle: animals raised for farming) **24.** All the men of the metropolis agreed, and every male changed into circumcised. (Agreed: consented) **25.** Three days later, while the men have been nevertheless in ache from the circumcision, Simeon and Levi, Dinah's brothers, attacked the city and killed all of the men. (Attacked: assaulted) **26.** They killed Hamor and Shechem, took Dinah from Shechem's house, and left. (Swords: weapons) **27.** Jacob's sons raided the town, looting it due to the shame achieved to their sister. (Raided: attacked) **28.** They took all of the cattle, wealth, better halves, children, and plundered everything inside the metropolis and fields. (Plundered: seized goods) **29.** Jacob said to Simeon and Levi, "You've made me a stench a number of the Canaanites and Perizzites, and they may wreck us. I could be worn out, and so will my family." (Stench: shame) **30.** They replied, "Ought to he treat our sister like a prostitute?" (Prostitute: a girl accomplishing sexual acts for cash)

Chapter 35

1. Then God spoke to Jacob, saying, "Get up, go to Bethel and settle there; build an altar to God, who appeared to you when you fled from your brother Esau." (God's command to Jacob) **2.** Jacob said to his household and all who were with him, "Get rid of the foreign gods among you, purify yourselves, and change your clothes." (Jacob's instructions to his family) **3.** "Then let us go to Bethel, where I will build an altar to God, who answered me in my distress and has been with me on my journey." (Jacob's reason for returning to Bethel) **4.** They gave Jacob their foreign gods and earrings, which he buried under the terebinth tree near Shechem. (The removal of idols) **5.** As they traveled, God struck the cities around them with fear, so they did not pursue Jacob's sons. (God's protection during their journey) **6.** Jacob arrived at Luz, also called Bethel, in Canaan, with all his people. (Jacob and his family reach Bethel) **7.** He built an altar there and named the place El Bethel, because God appeared to him when he fled from Esau. (The naming of the altar and place) **8.** Deborah, Rebekah's nurse, died and was buried near Bethel, under the terebinth tree. The place was called Allon Bachuth, meaning "oak of weeping." (Deborah's death and burial) **9.** After Jacob returned from Padan Aram, God appeared to him again and blessed him. (God reappears to Jacob) **10.** God said, "Your name is Jacob, but you will now be called Israel." So He named him Israel. (The renaming of Jacob to Israel) **11.** God said, "I am God Almighty. Be fruitful and multiply; nations and kings will come from you." (God's blessing and promise to Jacob) **12.** "The land I gave to Abraham and Isaac, I give to you and your descendants." (Promise of land to Jacob and his descendants) **13.** Then God ascended from him at the place where He had spoken. (God's departure after the blessing) **14.** Jacob set up a stone pillar where God had spoken to him, and poured a drink offering and oil on it. (Jacob's memorial to God) **15.** Jacob named the place Bethel, where God had spoken to him. (The renaming of the location) **16.** They traveled from Bethel, and when they were near Ephrath, Rachel went into labor and had a difficult delivery. (Rachel's childbirth) **17.** As she struggled, the midwife said, "Do not fear; you will have this son too." (Midwife's reassurance) **18.** As her soul departed (for she died), she named him Ben-Oni, but his father named him Benjamin. (Rachel's death and the naming of her son) **19.** So Rachel died and was buried on the way to Ephrath, which is Bethlehem. (Rachel's burial place) **20.** Jacob set up a pillar over her grave, which still stands today as Rachel's grave. (The memorial at Rachel's grave) **21.** Then Israel journeyed and pitched his tent beyond the tower of Eder. (Israel's movement to a new location) **22.** While living in that area, Reuben slept with Bilhah, his father's concubine, and Israel heard about it. The sons of Jacob were twelve: (Reuben's sin with Bilhah) **23.** The sons of Leah were Reuben (Jacob's firstborn), Simeon, Levi, Judah, Issachar, and Zebulun; (The sons of Leah) **24.** The sons of Rachel were Joseph and Benjamin; (The sons of Rachel) **25.** The sons of Bilhah, Rachel's maidservant, were Dan and Naphtali; (The sons of Bilhah) **26.** The sons of Zilpah, Leah's maidservant, were Gad and Asher. These were the sons of Jacob, born to him in Padan Aram. (The sons of Zilpah) **27.** Jacob came to his father Isaac at Mamre, or Kiriath Arba (Hebron), where Abraham and Isaac had lived. (Jacob returns to Isaac's home) **28.** Isaac lived to 180 years old. (Isaac's age at death) **29.** Isaac died, was gathered to his people, and was buried by his sons Esau and Jacob. (Isaac's death and burial)

Chapter 36

1. This is the account of Esau, who is also known as Edom. (Edom is another name for Esau.) **2.** Esau married wives from the daughters of Canaan: Adah, daughter of Elon the Hittite, Aholibamah, daughter of Anah, who was the daughter of Zibeon the Hivite, **3.** and Basemath, daughter of Ishmael and sister of Nebajoth. (Esau's Canaanite wives.) **4.** Adah bore Eliphaz, while Basemath bore Reuel. (Esau's sons from Adah and Basemath.) **5.** Aholibamah bore three sons to Esau: Jeush, Jaalam, and Korah. These are the children Esau had in Canaan. (Esau's children from Aholibamah.) **6.** Esau gathered all his family—wives, children, servants, livestock, and possessions—and moved away from his brother Jacob's territory. (Esau moves away to avoid conflict with Jacob.) **7.** Their wealth and livestock were too abundant for them to live together, and the land could not support them both. (The land was too small for both families and their flocks.) **8.** Thus, Esau settled in the hill country of Seir, which is also called Edom. (Esau settles in Seir, known as Edom.) **9.** This is the genealogy of Esau, the patriarch of the Edomites who settled in Seir. (Esau's descendants in Edom are now listed.) **10.** Esau's sons were: Eliphaz, son of Adah, and Reuel, son of Basemath, his wives. (The names of Esau's sons: Eliphaz and Reuel.) **11.** Eliphaz's sons were Teman, Omar, Zepho, Gatam, and Kenaz. (Children of Eliphaz.) **12.** Timna, a concubine of Eliphaz, bore him Amalek. These are the descendants of Adah, Esau's wife. (Timna, Eliphaz's concubine, bore Amalek.) **13.** Reuel's children were Nahath, Zerah, Shammah, and Mizzah. These were the sons of Basemath, Esau's wife. (The children of Reuel, Esau's son by Basemath.) **14.** Aholibamah, another of Esau's wives, daughter of Anah and granddaughter of Zibeon, bore Esau three sons: Jeush, Jaalam, and Korah. (Aholibamah's children by Esau.) **15.** These were the chiefs among Esau's descendants: the sons of Eliphaz, Esau's firstborn, were Chief Teman, Chief Omar, Chief Zepho, Chief Kenaz, **16.** Chief Korah, Chief Gatam, and Chief Amalek. These chiefs of Eliphaz were from the land of Edom, the sons of Adah. (The leading figures from Eliphaz's line in Edom.) **17.** The sons of Reuel, Esau's son, were Chief Nahath, Chief Zerah, Chief Shammah, and Chief Mizzah. These were the chiefs of Reuel in Edom, the children of Basemath. (The chiefs descended from Reuel.) **18.** The sons of Aholibamah, Esau's wife, were: Chief Jeush, Chief Jaalam, and Chief Korah. These chiefs were descendants of Aholibamah, daughter of Anah. (The chiefs descended from Aholibamah.) **19.** These are the descendants of Esau, who is also called Edom, and their chiefs. (Summary of Esau's descendants and their leadership.) **20.** The descendants of Seir the Horite, the original inhabitants of the land, were: Lotan, Shobal, Zibeon, Anah, **21.** Dishon, Ezer, and Dishan. These were the chiefs of the Horites, the sons of Seir, who lived in Edom. (The Horites, the ancient inhabitants of Seir.) **22.** Lotan's children were Hori and Hemam. Timna was Lotan's sister. (Lotan's children and his sister, Timna.) **23.** The children of Shobal were Alvan, Manahath, Ebal, Shepho, and Onam. (Shobal's children.) **24.** The sons of Zibeon were Ajah and Anah. It was Anah who discovered the water in the wilderness while tending his father's donkeys. (Anah's discovery of water while pasturing donkeys.) **25.** Anah's children were Dishon and Aholibamah. (Anah's children, including his daughter Aholibamah.) **26.** The sons of Dishon were Hemdan, Eshban, Ithran, and Cheran. (Dishon's children.) **27.** The sons of Ezer were Bilhan, Zaavan, and Akan. (Ezer's children.) **28.** The sons of Dishan were Uz and Aran. (Dishan's children.) **29.** These were the chiefs of the Horites: Chief Lotan, Chief Shobal, Chief Zibeon, Chief Anah, **30.** Chief Dishon, Chief Ezer, and Chief Dishan. These were the Horite chiefs in the land of Seir. (A list of the Horite chiefs in Seir.) **31.** Before Israel had kings, these were the kings who ruled in Edom: (The kings of Edom before Israel had its monarchy.) **32.** Bela, son of Beor, was the first king of Edom, and his city was called Dinhabah. (Bela, the first king, ruled from Dinhabah.) **33.** After Bela's death, Jobab, son of Zerah from Bozrah, became king. (Jobab succeeded Bela.) **34.** Following Jobab's death, Husham from the Temanites became king. (Husham succeeded Jobab.) **35.** When Husham passed away, Hadad, son of Bedad, who had struck down the Midianites in the fields of Moab, became king. His city was called Avith. (Hadad, famous for his victory over the Midianites, succeeded Husham.) **36.** After Hadad's death, Samlah of Masrekah became the next ruler. (Samlah succeeded Hadad.) **37.** When Samlah died, Saul of Rehoboth-by-the-River took his place as king. (Saul succeeded Samlah.) **38.** After Saul died, Baal-Hanan, son of Achbor, became king. (Baal-Hanan succeeded Saul.) **39.** When Baal-Hanan died, Hadar became king. His city was called Pau, and his wife was Mehetabel, daughter of Matred, granddaughter of Mezahab. (Hadar succeeded Baal-Hanan, and his wife's lineage is described.) **40.** These are the names of the chiefs of Esau, according to their families and regions: Chief Timnah, Chief Alvah, Chief Jetheth, **41.** Chief Aholibamah, Chief Elah, Chief Pinon, **42.** Chief Kenaz, Chief Teman, Chief Mibzar, **43.** Chief Magdiel, and Chief Iram. These were the chiefs of Edom, in the land they inherited. Esau was the father of the Edomites. (A final list of Edomite chiefs and their territories.)

Chapter 37

1. Jacob settled in the land of Canaan, where his father had lived as a foreigner. **2.** This is the account of Jacob's family. When Joseph was seventeen, he tended sheep with his brothers, the sons of Bilhah and Zilpah, and brought a bad report to his father about them. **3.** Israel loved Joseph more than his other sons because he had him in his old age, so he made him a richly ornamented coat. **4.** When his brothers saw this, they became jealous and could not speak kindly to him. **5.** Joseph had a dream, and when he shared it, his brothers hated him even more. **6.** He said to them, "Listen to my dream: **7.** We were binding sheaves in the field, and my sheaf stood upright, while yours gathered around it and bowed down to mine." **8.** His brothers said, "Will you reign over us?" They hated him even more because of his dream. **9.** Then Joseph had another dream, and told his brothers, "The sun, the moon, and eleven stars were bowing down to me." **10.** He shared it with his father and brothers, and his father rebuked him. "Will your mother, brothers, and I really bow down to you?" he asked. **11.** His brothers were jealous, but his father kept the matter in mind. **12.** His brothers went to graze their father's flocks near Shechem. **13.** Israel said to Joseph, "Your brothers are grazing near Shechem. Go check on them." Joseph replied, "Here I am." **14.** Israel told him to see if all was well and bring back word. So Joseph went to Shechem, **15.** where a man found him wandering and asked, "What are you looking for?" **16.** "I'm looking for my brothers. Can you tell me where they are grazing?" **17.** The man replied, "They've moved on. I heard them say, 'Let's go to Dothan.'" So Joseph went after them and found them at Dothan. (Dothan: a place where Joseph's brothers were) **18.** When they saw him in the distance, they plotted to kill him. **19.** "Here comes the dreamer!" they said. **20.** "Let's kill him and throw him into a cistern, then say a wild animal devoured him. We'll see what happens to his dreams!" **21.** When Reuben heard this, he tried to rescue him. "Let's not take his life," he said. **22.** "Don't shed blood. Throw him into this cistern and don't harm him," Reuben suggested, planning to rescue him later. **23.** When Joseph reached them, they stripped him of his coat and threw him into the empty cistern. **24.** While sitting down to eat, they saw a caravan of Ishmaelites coming from Gilead, with camels carrying spices, balm, and myrrh, heading to Egypt. **25.** Judah said, "What do we gain by killing him? Let's sell him to the Ishmaelites and not harm him—after all, he's our brother." His brothers agreed. **26.** So they sold Joseph to the Ishmaelites for twenty shekels of silver, and they took him to Egypt. (Ishmaelites: descendants of Ishmael, son of Abraham) **27.** When Reuben returned and found Joseph gone, he tore his clothes. **28.** He went back to his brothers and said, "The boy is gone! What will I do now?" **29.** They took Joseph's coat, slaughtered a goat, and dipped it in the blood. **30.** They brought the coat to their father, saying, "We found this. Is it your son's coat?" **31.** Jacob recognized it and said, "It's my son's coat! A wild animal has devoured him. Joseph has been torn to pieces." **32.** Then Jacob tore his clothes, put on sackcloth, and mourned for his son for many days. (Sackcloth: a rough garment worn in mourning) **33.** His sons and daughters tried to comfort him, but he refused. "I will mourn until I join my son in the grave," he said. And he wept. **34.** Meanwhile, the Midianites sold Joseph in Egypt to Potiphar, one of Pharaoh's officials, the captain of the guard. (Potiphar: an Egyptian official) **35.** All his sons and daughters came to comfort him, but he refused to be comforted. "No," he said, "I will continue to mourn until I join my son in the grave." So his father wept for him. **36.** Meanwhile, the Midianites sold Joseph in Egypt to Potiphar, one of Pharaoh's officials, the captain of the guard. (Potiphar: an Egyptian official)

Chapter 38

1. At that point, Judah separated from his brothers and visited Hirah, a man from Adullam. (Adullam: a town in Judah) **2.** Judah saw a Canaanite woman named Shua, married her, and had family members together with her. (Canaanite: a set of historical peoples) **3.** She conceived and bore a son, whom Judah named Er. (Er: Judah's firstborn) **4.** She bore some other son, naming him Onan. (Onan: Judah's 2nd son) **5.** She had yet every other son, named Shelah, born at Chezib. **6.** Judah took a wife for Er, his firstborn, named Tamar. (Tamar: wife of Er, daughter-in-law of Judah) **7.** However, Er changed into wicked within the Lord's sight, and the Lord took his life. (Depraved: immoral) **8.** Judah advised Onan, "Go in to your brother's spouse, marry her, and have a baby for your brother." (Move in to: have family members with) **9.** Onan knew the kid could now not be his, so he spilled his seed at the floor to keep away from giving his brother an heir. (Spilled his seed: a euphemism for contraceptive motion) **10.** What Onan did was wicked, and the Lord took his life as well. (Wicked: sinful) **11.** Judah informed Tamar to stay as a widow in her father's residence till Shelah grew up, fearing he might die like his brothers. (Widow: a woman whose husband has died) **12.** After a while, Judah's wife died, and he went to Timnah with his pal Hirah to visit the sheep shearers. (Timnah: a metropolis in Judah) **13.** Tamar found out that Judah was going to Timnah to shear his sheep. (Shear: to reduce wool from sheep) **14.** She took off her widow's garments, veiled herself, and sat at the entrance to Enaim, since Shelah had grown but had not been given to her as a husband. (Enaim: an area near Timnah) **15.** Judah noticed her and thought she turned into a prostitute due to the fact her face turned into covered. (Prostitute: a girl who sells sexual services) **16.** He approached her and stated, "Let me sleep with you." She spoke back, "What is going to you provide me?" (Sleep with: have family members) **17.** He provided a younger goat from his flock, and she or he requested for a pledge till it became despatched. (Pledge: a guarantee) **18.** He gave her his signet, cord, and team of workers. They slept together, and she or he have become pregnant. (Signet: a personal seal) **19.** Later on, she left and put on her widow's garments again. (Widow's clothes: worn after a husband's demise) **20.** Judah sent the younger goat by using Hirah to retrieve his pledge, however he couldn't find her. (Hirah: Judah's friend) **21.** Judah requested the men of the vicinity, "Where is the prostitute by way of the roadside?" They said, "There was no prostitute here." (Prostitute: a woman presenting sexual offerings) **22.** Judah returned to Hirah and said, "I couldn't discover her, and the men said there was no prostitute here." (Again: came again) **23.** Judah said, "Let her hold them, or we are able to be shamed. I sent the goat, but couldn't discover her." (Shamed: dishonored) **24.** Three months later, Judah turned into told, "Tamar has acted like a prostitute and is pregnant." Judah stated, "Let her be burned." (Burned: an execution method) **25.** When she turned into introduced out, Tamar sent a message: "I am pregnant by the person who owns these objects. Please understand whose they are." (Signet, twine, body of workers: Judah's objects) **26.** Judah recognized them and stated, "She is more righteous than I, because I didn't deliver her to Shelah." He did no longer sleep along with her again. (Righteous: morally proper) **27.** When it became time for her to provide delivery, she observed she turned into sporting twins. (Twins: kids born on the same time) **28.** One baby caught out his hand, and the midwife tied a scarlet thread, announcing, "This one came out first." (Scarlet thread: a crimson thread marking the firstborn) **29.** However, as he drew his hand lower back, his brother came out. She exclaimed, "What a breakthrough! This one could be named Perez." (Perez: "breach" or "breaking thru") **30.** Then his brother, with the scarlet thread, came out. His call changed into Zerah. (Zerah: "brightness" or "shining")

Chapter 39

1. Joseph had been taken to Egypt, and Potiphar, an Egyptian officer and the captain of Pharaoh's guard, bought him from the Ishmaelites who had brought him there. (Potiphar: an Egyptian official; Ishmaelites: descendants of Ishmael, traders from the east) **2.** The Lord was with Joseph, and he became a prosperous man, serving in the house of his Egyptian master. (Success: prosperity and favor granted by God) **3.** Potiphar noticed that the Lord was with Joseph and that God made all his work prosper. (Prosper: to succeed or thrive in one's work or life) **4.** Joseph found favor in Potiphar's eyes and served him, and Potiphar made him overseer of his household, putting everything under Joseph's care. (Overseer: one who supervises or manages) **5.** From that time, the Lord blessed Potiphar's house because of Joseph, and the blessing extended to all he had, in both his house and his fields. (Blessing: divine favor that brings prosperity and success) **6.** Potiphar trusted Joseph with everything and didn't concern himself with anything except the food he ate. Now Joseph was well-built and handsome. (Well-built: physically strong; Handsome: good in appearance) **7.** After some time, Potiphar's wife took notice of Joseph and said, "Come to bed with me." (Longing eyes: desiring or lusting after someone) **8.** But Joseph refused, saying, "My master trusts me completely and has given me charge over everything in his house. (Full charge: complete responsibility or authority) **9.** There's no one greater than I in this house, and he has withheld nothing from me except you, because you are his wife. How could I do such a wicked thing and sin against God?" (Withheld: kept back or denied) **10.** She persisted day after day, but Joseph did not listen to her or even stay near her. (Lying with her: engaging in sexual activity) **11.** One day, when Joseph entered the house to do his work and none of the men were around, **12.** she caught him by his garment and said, "Come to bed with me!" But he left his garment in her hand and fled outside. (Garment: his clothing; Fled: ran away quickly) **13.** When she saw that Joseph had left his garment and fled, **14.** she called the servants and said, "Look, this Hebrew slave you brought us tried to mock us. He came in to sleep with me, but I screamed loudly." (Hebrew slave: referring to Joseph's ethnicity; Mock us: insult or belittle us) **15.** "When I screamed, he left his garment with me and ran outside." (Scream: cry out loudly in protest) **16.** She kept his garment until her husband came home. (Garment kept: used as proof of the accusation) **17.** She told him, "The Hebrew servant you brought here came in to mock me. **18.** But as soon as I screamed, he left his garment and ran away." (Screamed: to call for help, accusing him) **19.** Potiphar became angry when he heard his wife's accusation. **20.** He took Joseph and put him in prison, where the king's prisoners were kept, and Joseph remained there. (King's prisoners: prisoners who had been under Pharaoh's authority) **21.** But the Lord was with Joseph, showing him kindness and granting him favor in the eyes of the prison warden. (Kindness: divine favor; Warden: the person in charge of the prison) **22.** The warden put Joseph in charge of all the prisoners, and Joseph oversaw everything that was done in the prison. (In charge: Joseph was given authority over other prisoners) **23.** The warden didn't worry about anything under Joseph's care, because the Lord was with him, and whatever Joseph did, the Lord made it prosper. (Prosper: to succeed or flourish under God's blessing)

Chapter 40

1. After these events, the butler and the baker of Pharaoh, the king of Egypt, offended their master, Pharaoh. (Butler: wine servant; Baker: bread servant) **2.** Pharaoh grew angry with his two officers, the chief butler and the chief baker. (Officers: Pharaoh's high-ranking servants) **3.** He placed them in custody in the house of the captain of the guard, in the prison where Joseph was held. (Captain of the guard: chief jailer) **4.** The captain of the guard entrusted Joseph with the responsibility of serving them, so they were confined for a time. (Entrusted: gave responsibility) **5.** Both the butler and baker, confined in prison, had dreams on the same night, and each dream had its own meaning. (Dreams: symbolic visions) **6.** Joseph came to them the next morning, noticed their sad expressions, and asked, "Why do you look so troubled today?" (Troubled: unhappy or anxious) **7.** They answered, "We each had a dream, but there is no one to interpret it." Joseph replied, "Do not interpretations belong to God? Tell them to me." (Interpretations: meanings of dreams) **8.** The chief butler began by telling Joseph his dream: "In my dream, a vine was before me. (Vine: grape plant, symbolizing growth) **9.** There were three branches on the vine. As they budded, blossoms appeared, and the grapes ripened. (Bud: to start growing; Blossoms: flowers; Ripened: fully developed) **10.** I held Pharaoh's cup in my hand, pressed the grapes into it, and placed the cup in Pharaoh's hand." (Cup: vessel for drinking) **11.** Joseph said, "The dream's meaning is this: The three branches represent three days. (Meaning: Joseph explains the symbolism) **12.** In three days, Pharaoh will restore you to your position, and you will once again serve him by handing him his cup." (Restore: return to your position) **13.** "But when things go well for you, remember me. Please show me kindness by mentioning me to Pharaoh, and have me released from this prison." (Kindness: favor; Released: set free) **14.** "I was forcibly taken from the land of the Hebrews, and I've done nothing to deserve being put in this dungeon." (Hebrews: descendants of Abraham) **15.** Seeing that Joseph's interpretation was favorable, the chief baker told his dream: "In my dream, I had three white baskets on my head. (Baskets: containers for food) **16.** The top basket was filled with baked goods for Pharaoh, but the birds were eating them from the basket on my head." (Baked goods: food items; Birds: symbolizing destruction) **17.** Joseph replied, "Here's the interpretation: The three baskets represent three days. (Interpretation: Joseph explains further) **18.** In three days, Pharaoh will remove your head and hang you on a tree, and the birds will devour your flesh." (Hang: execution by hanging; Devour: consume completely) **19.** On the third day, which was Pharaoh's birthday, he held a feast for all his officials, and he lifted up the chief butler and chief baker among his servants. (Birthday: the day of Pharaoh's celebration) **20.** Pharaoh restored the chief butler to his position, placing the cup back in Pharaoh's hand. (Restored: returned to position) **21.** But Pharaoh hanged the chief baker, just as Joseph had predicted. (Hanged: executed by hanging) **22.** However, the chief butler forgot about Joseph and did not mention him to Pharaoh. (Forgot: failed to remember) **23.** Yet the chief butler did not remember Joseph, but forgot him.

Chapter 41

1. Two full years passed, and Pharaoh had a dream while standing by the river. (Full years: two complete years passed) **2.** Seven healthy, fat cows emerged from the river and grazed in the meadow. (Healthy: well-fed and strong; Grazed: ate grass) **3.** Then, seven thin, sickly cows came up after them and stood beside the healthy cows on the riverbank. (Thin and sickly: weak and emaciated) **4.** The thin cows ate the seven healthy ones. Pharaoh woke up. (Ate up: consumed; Woke up: from his dream) **5.** He fell back asleep and had another dream. Seven plump, ripe heads of grain grew on one stalk. (Heads of grain: ears of corn or wheat) **6.** Then, seven thin heads, scorched by the east wind, appeared after them. (Scorched: dried out by heat) **7.** The thin heads devoured the plump ones. Pharaoh woke up, realizing it was only a dream. (Devoured: consumed completely) **8.** In the morning, Pharaoh was troubled and called for all Egypt's magicians and wise men to interpret his dreams, but none could. (Troubled: distressed; Magicians: dream interpreters) **9.** Then, the chief butler remembered his mistakes and spoke to Pharaoh. (Faults: his past mistakes) **10.** "When Pharaoh became angry with us, he put me and the chief baker in the custody of the captain of the guard, **11.** We each had a dream one night, with distinct meanings. **12.** A young Hebrew man, a servant of the captain of the guard, was with us. We told him our dreams, and he interpreted them for us. (Hebrew: a member of the Israelite people) **13.** And exactly as he interpreted, it happened: I was restored to my position, and the chief baker was hanged." (Restored: returned to his former position) **14.** Pharaoh summoned Joseph and quickly brought him out of prison. He shaved, changed his clothes, and came to Pharaoh. (Shaved: prepared himself for Pharaoh's presence) **15.** Pharaoh said to Joseph, "I had a dream, and no one can interpret it. I've heard you can interpret dreams." (Interpret: explain the meaning) **16.** Joseph replied, "It's not me, but God who will give Pharaoh an answer of peace." (Answer of peace: a favorable interpretation) **17.** Pharaoh described his dream: "I stood on the riverbank, **18.** Suddenly, seven healthy cows came up from the river and fed in the meadow. (Fed: grazed on the grass) **19.** Then, seven ugly, gaunt cows came up after them, so thin I've never seen their like in all Egypt. (Gaunt: thin and weak) **20.** The thin cows ate the healthy ones. Afterward, they looked as bad as before. I woke up. (Ate: consumed; Woke up: from his sleep) **21.** I also saw seven heads of grain, full and good, growing on one stalk. (Heads of grain: ears of corn) **22.** Then seven withered, thin heads, scorched by the east wind, sprang up after them. (Withered: dried up) **23.** The thin heads devoured the full heads. I told this to the magicians, but no one could explain it to me." (Devoured: consumed completely) **24.** Joseph said to Pharaoh, "The dreams are one and the same. God has shown Pharaoh what He is about to do: (One and the same: identical in meaning) **25.** The seven good cows are seven years, and the seven good heads of grain are seven years. The dreams are one. (Good cows and good grain: symbols of abundance) **26.** The seven thin, ugly cows are seven years, and the seven empty, scorched heads are seven years of famine. (Blighted: damaged by heat) **27.** God is revealing to Pharaoh: Seven years of plenty are coming to Egypt, **28.** But after them, seven years of famine will come, making the abundance forgotten, and the famine will devastate the land. (Famine: lack of food) **29.** The abundance won't be remembered because the famine will be so severe it will ruin the land. (Severe: intense or extreme) **30.** The dream was repeated twice because God has firmly decided it, and He will soon bring it to pass. (Firmly decided: certain to happen) **31.** Pharaoh should seek out a wise and discerning man and appoint him over Egypt. (Discerning: able to judge wisely) **32.** Let Pharaoh appoint officers to collect one-fifth of the produce during the seven years of abundance, (One-fifth: 20% of the harvest) **33.** And store the food in the cities under Pharaoh's authority to reserve it for the seven years of famine. (Reserve: saved for future use) **34.** This will prevent the land from perishing during the famine. (Perishing: being destroyed) **35.** Pharaoh and his servants found Joseph's advice good. (Servants: Pharaoh's advisors) **36.** Pharaoh asked his servants, "Can we find anyone like this, a man in whom is the Spirit of God?" (Spirit of God: divine wisdom) **37.** Pharaoh said to Joseph, "Since God has shown you all this, there is no one as wise and discerning as you. (Discerning: able to understand and judge) **38.** You will be over my house, and all my people will obey your commands. Only in regard to the throne will I be greater than you." (Throne: Pharaoh's position as ruler) **39.** Pharaoh told Joseph, "I'm appointing you over all the land of Egypt." (Appointing: placing in charge) **40.** Pharaoh took his signet ring off and put it on Joseph's hand, dressed him in fine linen, and placed a gold chain around his neck. (Signet ring: symbol of authority) **41.** He made Joseph ride in the second chariot, and they shouted, "Bow the knee!" Thus, Joseph became second in command over Egypt. (Second chariot: next in authority) **42.** Pharaoh said to Joseph, "I am Pharaoh, and without your consent, no one will lift a hand or foot in all Egypt." (Consent: permission) **43.** Pharaoh gave Joseph the name Zaphnath-Paaneah and gave him Asenath, daughter of Poti-Pherah, priest of On, as his wife. (Zaphnath-Paaneah: Joseph's new name; Asenath: Joseph's wife) **44.** Joseph went out over all the land of Egypt. (Out over: traveled across Egypt) **45.** Joseph was thirty years old when he began serving Pharaoh, and he traveled throughout Egypt. (Thirty years: his age when appointed) **46.** During the seven years of abundance, the land produced plentifully. (Abundance: a time of great plenty) **47.** Joseph gathered all the food during those years and stored it in the cities. He collected grain from the fields surrounding each city. (Stored: kept for future use) **48.** He gathered so much grain that it was like the sand of the sea, too much to measure. (Beyond measure: countless) **49.** Before the famine came, Joseph had two sons by Asenath, daughter of Poti-Pherah, priest of On. (On: a city in Egypt) **50.** Joseph named his first son Manasseh, meaning, "God has made me forget my hardship and my father's house." (Manasseh: "to forget") **51.** He named his second son Ephraim, meaning, "God has made me fruitful in the land of my affliction." (Ephraim: "fruitful") **52.** After seven years of abundance, **53.** The seven years of famine began, just as Joseph had predicted. The famine spread to every land, but Egypt had food. (Famine: a period of food scarcity) **54.** When the people of Egypt cried to Pharaoh for food, he told them, "Go to Joseph; do whatever he tells you." (Cried out: asked for help) **55.** The famine was severe, and Joseph opened the storehouses, selling grain to the Egyptians. (Storehouses: places where grain was stored) **56.** The famine grew so severe that people from all nations came to buy grain from Joseph in Egypt. (All countries: nations affected by the famine) **57.** So all countries came to Joseph in Egypt to buy grain, because the famine was severe in all lands.

Chapter 42
1. When Jacob noticed that there was grain in Egypt, he said to his sons, "Why do you look at one another?" (Grain: Egypt has food) **2.** He said, "I have heard that there is grain in Egypt; go there and buy for us, so we can also live and not die." (live: avoid hunger) **3.** So Joseph's ten brothers went to Egypt to buy grain. (Ten brothers: except for Benjamin) **4.** But Jacob did not send Benjamin with them, for he said, "Lest some calamity befall him." (Feared harm: concern for Benjamin's safety) **5.** The sons of Israel went to buy grain, for there was famine in Canaan. (Famine: severe food shortage) **6.** Now Joseph was governor over Egypt, and it was he who sold grain. His brothers came and bowed down before him. (Bowed: fulfilling Joseph's dreams) **7.** Joseph recognized his brothers, but acted as a stranger and spoke roughly to them, saying, "Where do you come from?" They answered, "From Canaan to buy food." (roughly: questioning them) **8.** Joseph recognized them, but they did not recognize him. (Didn't recognize: Joseph changed) **9.** Then Joseph remembered the dreams he had dreamed about them and said, "You are spies! You've come to see the nakedness of the land!" (Spies: accusing them) **10.** They replied, "No, my lord, your servants have come to buy food. (sincere men: denying accusation) **11.** We are all one man's sons; we are honest men; your servants are not spies." (sincere men: further defense) **12.** He said, "No, you have come to see the nakedness of the land." (Spies: repeating accusation) **13.** They said, "Your servants are twelve brothers, the sons of one man

in Canaan; the youngest is with our father, and one is no more." (One is no more: Joseph is thought dead) **14.** But Joseph said, "It is as I spoke to you: you are spies! (test: continuing the accusation) **15.** By this you will be tested: by Pharaoh's life, you shall not leave unless your youngest brother comes here." (test: sending one to bring Benjamin) **16.** Send one of you to bring your brother, and the rest of you will be kept in prison to test whether your words are true; otherwise, by Pharaoh's life, you are spies!" (prison: testing honesty) **17.** So he put them all in prison for three days. (prison: a way to test them) **18.** On the third day, Joseph said, "Do this and live, for I fear God: (fear God: showing his reverence) **19.** If you are honest men, let one of your brothers stay here in prison, but the rest of you go and take grain to your families. (honest men: second test) **20.** And bring your youngest brother to me, so your words may be verified, and you will not die." And they did so. (Verification: proof of honesty) **21.** Then they said to each other, "We are truly guilty concerning our brother, for we saw the anguish of his soul when he pleaded with us, and we would not listen; therefore, this distress has come upon us." (guilty: regret over Joseph) **22.** Reuben answered, "Did I not tell you not to sin against the boy? But you would not listen. Now his blood is required of us." (Reuben: regrets not stopping them) **23.** They didn't know that Joseph understood them, for he spoke through an interpreter. (Interpreter: Joseph's language barrier) **24.** He turned away from them and wept. Then he returned and talked with them, taking Simeon from them and binding him before their eyes. (Wept: emotional reaction) **25.** Joseph commanded that their sacks be filled with grain, that each man's money be returned, and that provisions be given for the journey. And it was done. (back money: secretly giving back their payment) **26.** They loaded their donkeys with grain and departed. (Departed: leaving with supplies) **27.** At the encampment, one of them opened his sack to give his donkey feed and saw his money inside the mouth of the sack. (money found: confusion and fear) **28.** He said to his brothers, "My money has been returned; it's in my sack!" And their hearts sank, and they were afraid, saying, "What is this that God has done to us?" (fear: confused by the money return) **29.** They returned to their father Jacob in Canaan and told him all that had happened. (return: telling Jacob the details) **30.** "The man who is lord of the land spoke roughly to us and accused us of being spies. (Spies: accusation Joseph made) **31.** But we said, 'We are honest men, not spies.' (Denial: claiming innocence) **32.** We are twelve brothers, sons of our father; one is no more, and the youngest is with our father in Canaan.'" (family: explaining their story) **33.** "Then the man, the lord of the country, said to us, 'By this I will know that you are honest men: leave one brother here with me, take food to your families, and go. (test: bring Benjamin to prove honesty) **34.** And bring your youngest brother to me; then I will know that you are not spies, but honest men. I will give you your brother, and you may trade in the land.'" (proof: honesty test) **35.** As they emptied their sacks, every man found his money in his sack, and when they and their father saw the money, they were afraid. (money: a second surprise) **36.** And Jacob their father said, "You have bereaved me: Joseph is no more, Simeon is no more, and you want to take Benjamin. All these things are against me." (Jacob's sorrow: fearing further loss) **37.** Then Reuben spoke to his father, saying, "Kill my two sons if I do not bring him back to you; put him in my hands, and I will bring him back." (Reuben's vow: drastic guarantee) **38.** But Jacob answered, "My son shall not go with you, for his brother is dead, and he is left alone. If any calamity befalls him on the way, you will bring my gray hair down to the grave in sorrow." (gray hair: Jacob's refusal due to fear).

Chapter 43
1. There has been an extreme famine in the land. (Famine: massive food scarcity) **2.** While the grain they brought from Egypt was finished, their father said to them, "Go back and buy more food." (Grain: harvested crop) **3.** But Judah said, "The man warned us, 'You will not see my face again unless your brother is with you.'" (Judah: one of Jacob's sons) **4.** "If you send our brother with us, we will go and buy food." (Brother: Benjamin, the youngest son) **5.** "But if you don't send him, we won't go. The man said, 'You will not see my face until your brother is with you.'" **6.** Israel said, "Why did you tell the man you had another brother?" (Israel: Jacob, the father) **7.** They answered, "The man asked us about our family, 'Is your father still alive? Do you have another brother?' We answered him honestly. How could we know he would say, 'Bring your brother here'?" **8.** Then Judah said, "Send the boy with me, and we will go, so we may live and not die—both we and our children." (Boy: Benjamin) **9.** "I can guarantee his safety. If I do not bring him back to you, let me bear the blame forever." (guarantee: promise to take responsibility) **10.** "If we hadn't delayed, we could have gone and returned twice by now." (delayed: taken too long) **11.** Then Israel said, "If it must be, then do this: Take the best products of the land and a gift for the man—balm, honey, spices, myrrh, pistachios, and almonds." (Balm: fragrant resin; Myrrh: used in perfumes) **12.** "Take double the money with you, and return the money that was put back into your sacks. Perhaps it was a mistake." (Double: times the amount) **13.** "Take your brother also, and go back to the man." (Brother: Benjamin) **14.** "May God Almighty grant you mercy before the man, so he will release your brother and Benjamin. If I am bereaved, I am bereaved!" (God Almighty: a title for God emphasizing His power) **15.** So the men took the gift, Benjamin, and double the money, and set off for Egypt, where they stood before Joseph. (gift: present) **16.** When Joseph saw Benjamin with them, he told his steward, "Take them to my house, slaughter an animal, and prepare a meal. They will dine with me at noon." (Steward: manager of the house) **17.** The steward did as Joseph instructed and brought the men to Joseph's house. **18.** The men were afraid, thinking, "We're being brought here because of the money in our sacks. He will attack us and make us slaves, along with our donkeys." (Donkeys: animals used for transportation) **19.** So as they approached the steward, they spoke to him at the entrance: **20.** "Sir, we came the first time to buy food, **21.** and when we opened our sacks at the campsite, every man found his money in full in the mouth of his sack. We've brought it back, **22.** and we've brought additional money to buy more food. We don't know who put the money in our sacks." (Campsite: temporary stopping place) **23.** He replied, "Peace to you! Don't be afraid. Your God and the God of your father must have put treasure in your sacks. I had your money." Then he brought Simeon out to them. (Treasure: precious objects) **24.** The steward took the men into Joseph's house, gave them water to wash their feet, and provided feed for their donkeys. (Feed: food for animals) **25.** They prepared the gift for Joseph's arrival at noon, because they knew they would dine with him. **26.** When Joseph came home, they presented the gift and bowed to him to the ground. (Bowed down: act of respect) **27.** He asked them, "How is your father, the old man you spoke about? Is he still alive?" (old man: reference to their father Jacob) **28.** They answered, "Your servant, our father, is well; he is still alive." And they bowed their heads and prostrated themselves. (Prostrated: laid flat in reverence) **29.** Then Joseph saw Benjamin, his mother's son. He asked, "Is this your younger brother, the one you spoke about?" And he said, "May God be gracious to you, my son." (younger brother: Benjamin) **30.** Joseph's heart went out to him, and he hurried out because he was so moved that he wanted to weep. He went to his private room and wept there. (heart went out: deep compassion) **31.** After washing his face, he came out and controlled himself. "Serve the food," he ordered. **32.** They ate separately—Joseph by himself, his brothers by themselves, and the Egyptians by themselves—for it was an abomination for Egyptians to eat with Hebrews. (Abomination: something considered forbidden) **33.** The men were seated by age, from the oldest to the youngest, and they looked at each other in astonishment. (Firstborn: oldest son) **34.** When portions were served from Joseph's table, Benjamin's portion was

five times as much as any of theirs. And they drank and were merry with him. (Merry: happy)

Chapter 44
1. And he commanded the steward, "Fill the men's sacks with food as much as they can carry, and put each man's money in the mouth of his sack." (steward: house manager) 2. "Also put my silver cup in the youngest's sack, along with his grain money." He did as Joseph commanded. (silver cup: special drinking vessel) 3. At dawn, the men were sent away with their donkeys. (donkeys: animals for carrying) 4. When they had left the city, and were not far off, Joseph said to his steward, "Follow the men. When you catch up with them, say, 'Why have you repaid evil for good?'" (catch up: overtake) 5. "Is this not the cup my lord drinks from, and with which he practices divination? You have done wrong." (divination: seeking knowledge of the future) 6. The steward caught up with them and said the same words. (caught up: overtook) 7. They replied, "Why does my lord say such things? We would never do such a thing!" (never: we would not) 8. "Look, we brought back the money we found in our sacks from Canaan. How could we steal silver or gold from your lord's house?" (Canaan: land promised to Israel's descendants) 9. "Whoever is found with it, let him die, and we will be your slaves." (slaves: servants) 10. He said, "Let it be as you say. He with whom it is found shall be my slave, and you shall be innocent." (innocent: blameless) 11. Each man quickly lowered his sack, and opened it. (quickly: speedily) 12. He searched, starting with the oldest, and found the cup in Benjamin's sack. (oldest: firstborn son) 13. They tore their clothes, loaded their donkeys, and returned to the city. (tore: ripped in distress) 14. Judah and his brothers came to Joseph's house, and they bowed before him. (Judah: one of Jacob's sons) 15. Joseph said, "What is this deed you've done? Did you not know I can practice divination?" (divination: seeking supernatural knowledge) 16. Judah answered, "What can we say to our lord? God has revealed our guilt; we are your slaves, both we and the one with the cup." (revealed: shown, guilt: sin) 17. But Joseph said, "Far be it from me. The man with the cup shall be my slave, but you go up in peace to your father." (far be it from me: it's not right) 18. Judah came near and said, "Please let me speak. Do not be angry with me, for you are like Pharaoh. (Pharaoh: Egyptian king) 19. "My lord asked, 'Do you have a father or a brother?'" (father: Jacob, patriarch) 20. "We told you, 'We have a father, an old man, and a young son of his old age. His brother is dead, and he is the only one left. His father loves him.'" (young son: Benjamin) 21. "Then you said, 'Bring him to me, that I may see him.'" (see: look upon) 22. "We said, 'The boy cannot leave his father, for if he does, his father will die.'" (boy: Benjamin) 23. "But you said, 'Unless your youngest brother comes, you shall not see my face again.'" (youngest: Benjamin) 24. "When we returned to our father, we told him your words." (returned: came back) 25. "Our father said, 'Go back and buy us food.'" (buy: purchase) 26. "But we said, 'We cannot go unless our youngest brother is with us, for we cannot see the man's face without him.'" (face: presence) 27. "Our father said, 'You know I had two sons; 28. one went from me, and I said, 'He is surely torn to pieces.' I have not seen him since." (torn to pieces: presumed dead) 29. "But if you take this one, and harm comes to him, you will bring my gray hair down to the grave in sorrow." (harm: injury, gray hair: sign of old age) 30. "If I return without the boy, my father's life is bound up with his; he will die." (bound up: deeply connected) 31. "When he sees that the boy is missing, he will die, and we will bring our father's gray hair down in sorrow." (gray hair: symbol of aging) 32. "I promised my father that if I didn't return the boy, I would bear the blame forever." (blame: responsibility for failure) 33. "Let me stay as your slave instead of the boy, and let him return with his brothers." (instead: in place of) 34. "How can I return to my father without the boy, for fear of seeing the harm that would come to him?" (harm: distress, fear: dread)

Chapter 45
1. Joseph couldn't control himself any longer, and he cried, "Make everyone leave!" No one stayed with him as he revealed himself to his brothers. (monitor: make known) 2. He wept loudly, and the Egyptians, including Pharaoh's family, heard him. (Pharaoh's family: the king's own family and servants) 3. Joseph said to his brothers, "I am Joseph; is my father still alive?" But they were too greatly surprised to answer, for they were terrified. (terrified: afraid) 4. Then Joseph said, "Come closer to me." So they came closer, and he said, "I am Joseph, your brother, whom you sold into Egypt." (sold: trafficked) 5. "Do not be distressed or angry with yourselves for selling me here, for God sent me ahead of you to preserve life." (distressed: upset) 6. "There has been a famine in the land for two years, and five more years remain without plowing or harvesting." (plowing: preparing land for crops) 7. "God sent me before you to ensure your survival, and to provide you with a great deliverance." (deliver: save) 8. "It was not you who sent me here, but God. He has made me a father to Pharaoh, lord of all his house, and ruler over Egypt." (father: adviser) 9. "Hurry, go to my father and say, 'Joseph says: God has made me lord of all Egypt; come to me quickly.'" (lord: ruler) 10. "You will live in the land of Goshen, near me, you and your children, your flocks, and all that you have." (Goshen: fertile land in Egypt) 11. "I will provide for you there, so that you and your family do not suffer during the remaining years of famine." (suffer: experience hardship) 12. "You will see with your own eyes, and Benjamin's, that it is my mouth speaking to you." (Benjamin: Joseph's brother) 13. "Tell my father about all my glory in Egypt and everything you have seen. Hurry and bring him back here." (glory: honor, achievements) 14. Then Joseph embraced Benjamin and wept; Benjamin also cried on his neck. (embraced: hugged) 15. He kissed all his brothers and wept over them, and afterward, they spoke with him. (spoke: conversed) 16. Word spread through Pharaoh's house, saying, "Joseph's brothers have come." Pharaoh and his servants were thrilled. (thrilled: happy) 17. Pharaoh told Joseph, "Tell your brothers: 'Load your animals and return to Canaan. (animals: livestock) 18. Bring your father and families and come to me. I will provide you with the best of Egypt, and you will enjoy the wealth of the land.'" (wealth: abundance) 19. "Also, take carts from Egypt for your children and wives; bring your father back with you." (carts: wagons) 20. "Do not worry about your possessions, for the best of Egypt will be yours." (possessions: belongings) 21. The sons of Israel did as Pharaoh commanded; Joseph gave them carts and provisions for the journey. (provisions: supplies) 22. He gave each of them new clothes, but to Benjamin, he gave three hundred pieces of silver and five changes of clothes. (new clothes: changes of garments) 23. He sent ten donkeys loaded with Egypt's finest goods and ten female donkeys loaded with grain, bread, and provisions for their journey. (goods: items) 24. Joseph sent his brothers away with these gifts and told them, "Do not quarrel on the way." (quarrel: argue) 25. They left Egypt and returned to Canaan to their father, Jacob. (Canaan: the land of Israel) 26. They told him, "Joseph is still alive, and he is the ruler of all Egypt." Jacob was stunned and did not believe them. (stunned: shocked) 27. But after they explained everything Joseph had said, and showed him the carts Joseph had sent, Jacob's spirit revived. (revived: was renewed) 28. Then Israel said, "It's enough. Joseph is alive! I will go and see him before I die." (Israel: Jacob, his new name)

Chapter 46
1. Israel set out with everything he had, arriving at Beersheba, where he offered sacrifices to the God of his father Isaac. (Beersheba: a city in southern Canaan) 2. That night, God spoke to Israel in a vision, calling, "Jacob, Jacob!" He answered, "Here I am." (Vision: a divine revelation) 3. God said, "I am the God of your father. Do not fear to go down to Egypt, for I will make you a great nation there." (Egypt: land of exile) 4. "I will go with you to Egypt and bring you back. Joseph will be there to close your eyes." (Close your eyes: a metaphor for death) 5. Jacob left Beersheba, and his sons helped him

settle into the carts Pharaoh had sent. (Carts: transport vehicles) 6. They took their herds and possessions and traveled to Egypt, with Jacob and his entire family. (Herds: flocks of animals) 7. His sons, grandsons, daughters, granddaughters, and all his descendants went with him. (Descendants: children and their offspring) 8. Here are the names of Israel's children who went to Egypt: Reuben, Jacob's firstborn. (Firstborn: eldest son) 9. The sons of Reuben were Hanoch, Pallu, Hezron, and Carmi. (Reuben: Jacob's first son) 10. The sons of Simeon were Jemuel, Jamin, Ohad, Jachin, Zohar, and Shaul, the son of a Canaanite woman. (Simeon: second son of Jacob) 11. The sons of Levi were Gershon, Kohath, and Merari. (Levi: third son of Jacob) 12. The sons of Judah were Er, Onan, Shelah, Perez, and Zerah (Er and Onan died in Canaan). The sons of Perez were Hezron and Hamul. (Judah: fourth son of Jacob) 13. The sons of Issachar were Tola, Puvah, Job, and Shimron. (Issachar: fifth son of Jacob) 14. The sons of Zebulun were Sered, Elon, and Jahleel. (Zebulun: sixth son of Jacob) 15. These were the sons of Leah, whom she bore to Jacob in Paddan Aram, including Dinah. All were thirty-three. (Leah: Jacob's first wife, Paddan Aram: region near Haran) 16. The sons of Gad were Ziphion, Haggi, Shuni, Ezbon, Eri, Arodi, and Areli. (Gad: seventh son of Jacob) 17. The sons of Asher were Jimnah, Ishuah, Isui, Beriah, and their sister Serah. The sons of Beriah were Heber and Malchiel. (Asher: eighth son of Jacob) 18. These were the sons of Zilpah, whom Laban gave to Leah. She bore these sons to Jacob: sixteen in total. (Zilpah: Leah's maidservant, bore children for Jacob) 19. The children of Rachel, Jacob's wife, were Joseph and Benjamin. (Rachel: Jacob's beloved wife) 20. In Egypt, Joseph had two sons: Manasseh and Ephraim, whom Asenath, the daughter of Poti-Pherah, priest of On, bore to him. (Asenath: Joseph's Egyptian wife, On: Egyptian city) 21. The sons of Benjamin were Belah, Becher, Ashbel, Gera, Naaman, Ehi, Rosh, Muppim, Huppim, and Ard. (Benjamin: youngest son of Jacob) 22. These were the children of Rachel, born to Jacob: fourteen people in total. (Rachel's children: Joseph and Benjamin) 23. The son of Dan was Hushim. (Dan: one of Jacob's sons, Hushim: his only son) 24. The sons of Naphtali were Jahzeel, Guni, Jezer, and Shillem. (Naphtali: son of Jacob, Naphtali's sons: four) 25. These were the children of Bilhah, whom Laban gave to Rachel. She bore these sons to Jacob: seven in total. (Bilhah: Rachel's maidservant) 26. All those who came with Jacob to Egypt, excluding his sons' wives, numbered sixty-six. (Sixty-six: total family members) 27. Joseph's sons born in Egypt were two. Thus, the total number of Jacob's family in Egypt was seventy. (Seventy: total count including Joseph's sons) 28. Jacob sent Judah ahead to Joseph to guide him to Goshen. (Judah: fourth son of Jacob, Goshen: fertile land in Egypt) 29. Joseph made ready his chariot and went to Goshen to meet his father Israel. He embraced him, weeping for a long time. (Chariot: royal carriage, Goshen: land for settlement) 30. Israel said, "Now I can die, for I have seen your face and know you are alive." (Israel: Jacob's name after his spiritual transformation) 31. Joseph then told his brothers and his father's household, "I will go to Pharaoh and tell him, 'My brothers and family from Canaan have come to me.'" (Pharaoh: Egyptian king) 32. "They are shepherds, for they have lived with livestock all their lives, bringing their flocks and herds." (Shepherds: herders of sheep and cattle) 33. "When Pharaoh asks, 'What is your occupation?' (Pharaoh: ruler of Egypt) 34. say, 'We have been shepherds, both we and our ancestors, so we may settle in Goshen, for Egyptians despise shepherds.'" (Goshen: region for pasture, despise: regard with disdain)

Chapter 47

1. Joseph went to Pharaoh and said, "My father and my brothers, their flocks, herds, and all they own have come from Canaan, and they are now in Goshen." (Goshen: fertile land in Egypt) 2. Joseph selected five of his brothers and presented them to Pharaoh. 3. Pharaoh asked his brothers, "What is your profession?" They replied, "We are shepherds, as were our ancestors." (Shepherds: herders of farm animals) 4. They added, "We've come to live in Egypt because there is no pasture for our flocks in Canaan due to the famine. Please let us settle in Goshen." (Famine: severe food scarcity) 5. Pharaoh said to Joseph, "Your father and brothers have come to you." (Pharaoh: king of Egypt) 6. "The land of Egypt is before you. Let your family settle in the best land, Goshen. If any of them are capable men, make them overseers of my cattle." (Goshen: the best land) 7. Joseph brought his father Jacob before Pharaoh, and Jacob blessed Pharaoh. (Blessed: offered well-wishes) 8. Pharaoh asked Jacob, "How old are you?" (Pharaoh: ruler of Egypt) 9. Jacob answered, "I have lived 130 years, but my life has been short and full of complications compared to my ancestors." (Pilgrimage: the journey of life) 10. Jacob blessed Pharaoh again, then left his presence. (Blessed: gave a prayer of good fortune) 11. Joseph settled his family in the land of Goshen, giving them the best part of the land, as Pharaoh had ordered. (Rameses: a district in Egypt) 12. Joseph provided food for his family, giving them enough according to their numbers. (Provisions: food and supplies) 13. There was no food anywhere, for the famine was severe, causing both Egypt and Canaan to suffer. (Languished: weakened or suffered) 14. Joseph collected all the money from Egypt and Canaan for grain, bringing it into Pharaoh's treasury. (Treasury: an area where wealth is stored) 15. When the money ran out, the Egyptians came to Joseph, asking for food. "Why should we die before you? The money is gone," they said. (Ran out: money was spent) 16. Joseph replied, "Bring your livestock, and I will trade bread for them if your money is gone." (Livestock: animals like horses and cattle) 17. They brought their animals to Joseph, who gave them bread in exchange for their horses, cattle, and donkeys, feeding them throughout the year. (Herds: groups of animals) 18. When the year ended, the Egyptians returned, saying, "We have no money or livestock left. There's only our land and ourselves. Why should we perish before you? Buy us and our land for bread, and we will serve Pharaoh." (Land: property used for cultivation) 19. "Give us seed so we may plant and live, and our land will not become desolate." (Seed: for planting crops) 20. Joseph bought all the land in Egypt for Pharaoh, as every Egyptian had to sell their land due to the famine. Thus, the land became Pharaoh's. (Desolate: abandoned or unproductive) 21. The people were relocated to cities across Egypt. (Relocated: moved to new places) 22. However, Pharaoh did not buy the priests' land, as they had an allocated portion from Pharaoh and ate from it. (Priests: religious leaders of Egypt) 23. Joseph told the people, "I have bought you and your land for Pharaoh. Here is seed for you, so you can plant your land." (Seed: plants to be cultivated) 24. "In the harvest, give one-fifth of your crops to Pharaoh. Four-fifths will be yours to keep, for food and seed for future planting." (One-fifth: 20% of crops) 25. They replied, "You have saved our lives; we will be Pharaoh's servants." (Servants: people in service to Pharaoh) 26. Joseph established a law that Pharaoh would receive one-fifth of the produce, except for the priests' land. (Law: a rule or regulation) 27. Israel lived in Goshen, prospered, and grew exceedingly in number. (Goshen: fertile area for settlement) 28. Jacob lived in Egypt for seventeen years, reaching the age of 147 years. (Seventeen years: time spent in Egypt) 29. As Jacob neared death, he called for Joseph, asking him, "If I have found favor in your sight, swear that you will bury me with my ancestors in Canaan." (Favor: kindness or goodwill) 30. "Don't bury me in Egypt, but take me back to bury me with my fathers." Joseph agreed. (Ancestors: family members from past generations) 31. Jacob asked Joseph to swear an oath, and Joseph swore it. Then Jacob bowed in reverence at the top of his bed. (Swear: make a solemn promise)

Chapter 48

1. After these events, Joseph was told, "Your father is ill," so he took his sons, Manasseh and Ephraim, with him. (Unwell: in poor health) 2. When Jacob was told, "Joseph is coming to see you," he gathered his strength and sat up in bed. (Gathered strength: regained enough power) 3. Jacob said to Joseph, "God Almighty appeared to me at Luz

in Canaan and blessed me." (God Almighty: a name for God emphasizing His power) **4.** He said, "I will make you fruitful and multiply your descendants. I will create a great kingdom from you, and this land will be an everlasting possession to your descendants." (Fruitful: rich or productive) **5.** "Your sons, Ephraim and Manasseh, who were born to you in Egypt before I came here, are now mine. They will be treated as Reuben and Simeon, my own sons." (Reuben and Simeon: Jacob's first and second sons) **6.** "Any children you have after them will be yours, but they will inherit under the names of their brothers." (Inheritance: the right to receive family property) **7.** "As for me, when I was on my way from Padan, Rachel died near Ephrath in Canaan. I buried her there on the way to Ephrath, which is also called Bethlehem." (Bethlehem: the city where Rachel was buried) **8.** When Jacob saw Joseph's sons, he asked, "Who are these?" (Saw: recognized or identified) **9.** Joseph answered, "These are my sons, whom God has given me here." Jacob replied, "Bring them to me so I may bless them." (Bless: speak good things or favor someone) **10.** Jacob's eyesight was poor because of his old age, and he couldn't see clearly. Joseph brought his sons toward him, and Jacob kissed and embraced them. (Eyesight: the ability to see) **11.** Israel said to Joseph, "I never expected to see your face again, but now God has also allowed me to see your children!" (Allowed: permitted or granted) **12.** Joseph moved the boys from his knees, bowed his face to the ground before his father. (Knees: his lap or lower body) **13.** Joseph placed Ephraim at his father's right hand and Manasseh at his left, bringing them closer for the blessing. (Right hand: the favored position) **14.** Israel stretched out his right hand and placed it on Ephraim's head, though he was the younger. His left hand was placed on Manasseh's head, though Manasseh was the firstborn. He did this intentionally, knowing that Manasseh was the elder. (Intentionally: deliberately, with purpose) **15.** Then Jacob blessed Joseph, saying: "The God before whom my ancestors, Abraham and Isaac, walked, the God who has provided for me throughout my life, **16.** the Angel who has rescued me from all harm, bless these boys. May my name and the names of Abraham and Isaac be upon them, and may they grow into a great nation in the earth." (Angel: a messenger or divine being) **17.** When Joseph saw that his father placed his right hand on Ephraim's head, he was displeased. He reached out to move his father's hand from Ephraim's head to Manasseh's. (Displeased: unhappy or dissatisfied) **18.** Joseph said, "No, father, this is the firstborn. Please place your right hand on his head." (Firstborn: the eldest child) **19.** But Jacob refused and said, "I know, my son, I know. Manasseh may become a great nation, but his younger brother will be even greater, and his descendants will become a multitude of nations." (Multitude: a large group of people or things) **20.** So Jacob blessed them that day, saying, "Israel will bless by saying, 'May God make you like Ephraim and Manasseh.'" And he placed Ephraim before Manasseh. (Bless: give a prayer of favor) **21.** Then Israel said to Joseph, "I am about to die, but God will be with you and will bring you back to the land of your ancestors." (Bring back: return to) **22.** "Moreover, I have given you one portion above your brothers, which I took from the Amorites with my sword and bow." (Amorites: a group of ancient people who lived in Canaan).

Chapter 49
1. Jacob known as his sons collectively and said, "Come near, so I will tell you what is going to show up to you in the future. **2.** "Collect together, pay attention, sons of Jacob, and take note of your father Israel. **3.** "Reuben, you are my firstborn, the power of my energy, the primary sign of my might, the honour of my dignity and the satisfaction of my power. **4.** "But you are risky like water, and you'll now not be extremely good. You defiled my mattress when you went up to it; you dishonored it. **5.** "Simeon and Levi are brothers; their home is complete of violence. **6.** "Let my soul now not be a part of their plans, and let my honor not be attached to their actions. Of their anger, they killed a man, and of their rage, they maimed an ox. **7.** "Cursed be their anger, for it's far violent; and their wrath, for it's miles cruel! I'm able to scatter them a number of the tribes of Israel and divide them among the humans. **8.** "Judah, you may be praised through your brothers. Your hand can be at the neck of your enemies, and your father's kids will bow right down to you. **9.** "Judah is a lion's cub; like a lion, you will rise up. You crouch, you lie down like a lion, and who will disturb him? **10.** "The scepter will now not depart from Judah, nor the ruler's workforce from among his ft, until Shiloh comes, and to Him will the humans obey." (Shiloh: a title referring to a messianic discern) **11.** "He ties his donkey to the vine, and his colt to the selection vine; he washes his garments in wine, and his garments within the blood of grapes." (Symbolizes abundance and prosperity) **12.** "His eyes are darker than wine, and his tooth whiter than milk." (Symbolizing electricity and vitality) **13.** "Zebulun will live near the seashore, and he may be a haven for ships. His borders could be near Sidon." (Sidon: a Phoenician metropolis) **14.** "Issachar is a sturdy donkey, resting among burdens. **15.** "He noticed that rest changed into true, and the land turned into satisfactory; he regularly occurring the paintings and became a servant. **16.** "Dan might be a decide for his people, like some other tribe of Israel. **17.** "Dan may be like a serpent by means of the street, a viper by using the direction, biting the pony's heels, so the rider falls backward. **18.** "I search for your salvation, O Lord!" (Salvation: deliverance or rescue) **19.** "Gad might be attacked by way of a group, but in the long run, he'll succeed. **20.** "Asher's bread can be rich, and he will offer royal delicacies. **21.** "Naphtali is a speedy deer, speaking beautiful phrases. **22.** "Joseph is a fruitful vine, a fruitful vine near a nicely; his branches climb over the wall." (Symbolizing boom and prosperity) **23.** "The archers have attacked him, and that they have hated him. **24.** "But his bow remained regular, and the hands of his palms have been bolstered by means of the hands of the amazing God of Jacob, the Shepherd, the Stone of Israel. **25.** "Via the God of your father, who will help you, and by means of the Almighty, who will bless you with advantages from above, blessings from the deep underneath, advantages from the breasts and the womb. **26.** "The advantages of your father are greater than the advantages of my ancestors, surpassing the boundaries of the eternal hills. They may rest on the top of Joseph and at the crown of the only set other than his brothers. **27.** "Benjamin is a fierce wolf; within the morning he's going to devour the prey, and at night he'll divide the smash. **28.** "These are the twelve tribes of Israel, and that is what their father stated to them. He blessed every one in all them, giving each a particular blessing. **29.** Then Jacob advised his sons, "I am approximately to be amassed to my humans. Bury me with my ancestors inside the cave of Ephron the Hittite, **30.** Within the cave in the area of Machpelah, near Mamre, in Canaan. Abraham bought this area from Ephron the Hittite as a burial website." **31.** "There Abraham and Sarah, his spouse, have been buried. There Isaac and Rebekah, his spouse, were buried, and that I buried Leah there too." **32.** "The sector and the cave had been purchased from the Hittites." **33.** After giving his very last commands, Jacob lay down, drew up his feet into the mattress, and breathed his closing, becoming a member of his ancestors. (Breathed his final: died)

Chapter 50
1. Joseph fell on his father's face, weeping and kissing him. **2.** He gave commands to the Egyptian physicians to embalm his father, and in order that they embalmed Israel. (Embalm: keep body) **3.** Forty days have been required for embalming, as this turned into the standard period in Egypt. The Egyptians mourned for him for seventy days. (Mourned: expressed grief) **4.** When the days of mourning had been complete, Joseph spoke to Pharaoh's household, saying, "If I have determined want in your sight, please ask Pharaoh to grant me permission to bury my father, as I swore to him, **5.** 'I'm about to die; bury me within the grave I prepared for myself in Canaan.' Please let me go and bury him, and then I can return." **6.** Pharaoh answered, "Go and bury your father as you have sworn." (Sworn: made a

solemn promise) **7.** So Joseph went to bury his father, and with him went all Pharaoh's servants, the elders of Pharaoh's family, and all the elders of Egypt, **8.** along with Joseph's family, his brothers, and his father's family. They left only their children, flocks, and herds in Goshen. **9.** Chariots and horsemen followed them, creating a very large procession. (Horsemen: soldiers on horseback) **10.** When they reached the threshing floor of Atad, beyond the Jordan River, they mourned with a great and solemn lamentation. They mourned for seven days. (Threshing floor: place in which grain is separated from husks) **11.** The Canaanites saw the mourning at Atad and said, "This is a deep mourning by the Egyptians." Therefore, the place was referred to as Abel Mizraim, which means "Mourning of Egypt," and it is beyond the Jordan. (Abel Mizraim: "Mourning of Egypt") **12.** Joseph's sons did exactly as he had commanded them. **13.** They carried his body to Canaan and buried him in the cave of the field of Machpelah, near Mamre, which Abraham had bought from Ephron the Hittite as a burial site. (Machpelah: burial cave) **14.** After burying his father, Joseph returned to Egypt, along with his brothers and all who had accompanied him for the burial. **15.** When Joseph's brothers saw that their father was dead, they said, "Perhaps Joseph will now hate us and pay off us for all the evil we did to him." **16.** So they sent a message to Joseph, saying, "Before your father died, he commanded, **17.** 'Say to Joseph: "I beg you, forgive the wrongdoings of your brothers and their sin, for they dealt with you badly." Please forgive the trespass of your brothers, the servants of the God of your father.'" Joseph wept when they spoke to him. (Trespass: wrongful act) **18.** His brothers went to him, fell down before him, and said, "We are your servants." (Servants: those in submission) **19.** Joseph said to them, "Do not be afraid. Am I in the position of God? (Position of God: position of judgment) **20.** You meant to harm me, but God meant it for good, to bring about the salvation of many people, as is happening today. (Salvation: deliverance or rescue) **21.** So do not be afraid; I will provide for you and your children." He comforted them and spoke kindly to them. **22.** Joseph remained in Egypt, along with his father's family. He lived to be 110 years old. **23.** Joseph saw the children of Ephraim to the third generation. The children of Machir, the son of Manasseh, were also brought up on Joseph's knees. (Knees: image of care and nurturing) **24.** Joseph said to his brothers, "I am about to die, but God will surely visit you and bring you out of this land to the land He promised to Abraham, Isaac, and Jacob." (Visit you: come to help) **25.** Then Joseph made the Israelites swear an oath, saying, "God will surely visit you, and when He does, you must carry my bones up from here." (Oath: solemn promise) **26.** So Joseph died at the age of 110. They embalmed him, and his body was placed in a coffin in Egypt. (Coffin: container for burial).

2 – Exodus
Chapter 1

1. These are the names of the sons of Israel who went to Egypt, each with their family alongside Jacob. (sons: male descendants) **2.** Reuben, Simeon, Levi, and Judah, **3.** Issachar, Zebulun, and Benjamin, **4.** Dan, Naphtali, Gad, and Asher. **5.** The total number of Jacob's descendants who came to Egypt was seventy, and Joseph had already been in Egypt. (descendants: children, grandchildren, and their children) **6.** Joseph passed away, along with all his brothers and that entire generation. (generation: all the people born in a given time period) **7.** The descendants of Israel grew strong, became numerous, and spread widely, filling the land with their people. (descendants: children and their offspring, numerous: many) **8.** Then, a new king arose over Egypt who did not recognize Joseph. (arose: appeared, recognize: acknowledge) **9.** He said to his people, "The Israelites have become too numerous and powerful for us." (numerous: many, powerful: strong) **10.** Let's act carefully to prevent them from growing too strong, for if war breaks out, they might ally with our enemies and fight against us, causing us to lose the land." (ally: join forces, break out: start suddenly) **11.** So, they appointed taskmasters to oppress the Israelites with heavy labor, forcing them to build the store cities of Pithom and Raamses for Pharaoh. (appointed: assigned, taskmasters: supervisors, oppress: treat harshly) **12.** However, the more they were oppressed, the more they multiplied and spread and the Egyptians became afraid of them. (oppressed: treated unfairly, multiplied: increased in number) **13.** The Egyptians made their lives miserable with severe labor. (Miserable: very unhappy, severe: very harsh) **14.** They forced them to work in brickmaking, mortar, and every type of fieldwork, with harsh conditions in all their labor. (Mortar: a mixture used to bind bricks, harsh: very difficult) **15.** Pharaoh spoke to the Hebrew midwives, whose names were Shiphrah and Puah. (Midwives: women who assist in childbirth) **16.** He told them, "When you help the Hebrew women give birth and see that it is a boy, kill him; if it is a girl, let her live." (birth: delivery of a baby) **17.** But the midwives feared God and did not obey the king's orders; they allowed the boys to live. (feared: respected greatly, obey: follow orders) **18.** Pharaoh called for the midwives and asked, "Why have you done this? Why have you let the boys live?" (called for: summoned, let: allowed) **19.** The midwives replied, "The Hebrew women are strong and give birth before we even get to them." (Replied: answered, strong: healthy) **20.** Because the midwives feared God, He treated them well, and the Israelites continued to grow and become very numerous. (treated: dealt with, continued: kept going) **21.** Because the midwives feared God, He blessed them with families of their own. (blessed: gave favor to) **22.** Finally, Pharaoh commanded all his people, "Every Hebrew boy born must be thrown into the river, but every girl should be allowed to live." (commanded: ordered, allowed: permitted)

Chapter 2

1. A man from the tribe of Levi married a Levite woman. (Levi: descendants of Levi) **2.** She became pregnant and gave birth to a son. Seeing he was beautiful, she hid him for three months. **3.** When she could no longer hide him, she placed him in a basket made of bulrushes, sealed it with tar, and set it by the river. (Bulrushes: water plants; Tar: sticky substance) **4.** His family watched from a distance to see what would happen. **5.** Pharaoh's daughter came to bathe in the river and saw the basket. She sent her maid to fetch it. (Pharaoh's daughter: daughter of the king of Egypt) **6.** Opening it, she saw the baby crying and took pity on him, saying, "This is one of the Hebrew children." **7.** His sister asked, "Shall I find a Hebrew woman to nurse him?" **8.** Pharaoh's daughter replied, "Go," and the girl brought the child's mother. **9.** Pharaoh's daughter said, "Take this child and nurse him for me, and I will pay you." The woman took him and nursed him. **10.** When the child grew, she brought him to Pharaoh's daughter, who adopted him as her own son. She named him Moses, saying, "I drew him out of the water." **11.** When Moses grew up, he went to see his people and noticed their suffering. He saw an Egyptian beating a Hebrew, one of his own people. **12.** Looking around and seeing no one, he killed the Egyptian and hid him in the sand. **13.** The next day, he saw two Hebrews fighting and asked the aggressor, "Why are you striking your fellow Hebrew?" **14.** The man replied, "Who made you ruler and judge over us? Are you going to kill me like you did the Egyptian?" Moses feared, thinking, "This is known." **15.** When Pharaoh heard of it, he sought to kill Moses, so Moses fled to Midian and sat by a well. (Midian: region east of Egypt) **16.** The priest of Midian had seven daughters who came to draw water for their father's flock. (Priest of Midian: religious leader in Midian; Flock: group of sheep) **17.** Some shepherds drove them away, but Moses defended them and watered their flock. (Shepherds: herdsman) **18.** When they returned, their father asked, "Why have you come back so soon?" **19.** They answered, "An Egyptian rescued us from the shepherds, and he even drew water for us." (Egyptian: man from Egypt) **20.** He asked, "Where is he? Why did you leave him? Invite him to eat." **21.** Moses agreed to stay, and the priest gave him his daughter Zipporah as wife. (Zipporah: Moses wife) **22.** She bore a son, and Moses named him Gershom, saying, "I have been a stranger in a foreign land." (Gershom: "a foreigner there") **23.** After some time, the king of Egypt died, and the Israelites groaned under their slavery and cried out to God. (King of Egypt: Pharaoh; Israelites: people of Israel; Slavery: bondage) **24.** God heard their cries and remembered His covenant with Abraham, Isaac, and Jacob. (Covenant: promise; Abraham, Isaac, Jacob: patriarchs of Israel) **25.** God looked on the Israelites and was concerned for them.

Chapter 3

1. Moses was tending the flock of his father-in-law, Jethro, the clerk of Midian. He led the lamb to the far side of the nature and came to Horeb, the mountain where God had revealed Himself. (Jethro was Moses' father-in-law; Midian was a region in northwest Arabia; Horeb, also known as Mount Sinai, is where God met Moses.) **2.** The Angel of the Lord appeared to him in a honey of fire from the middle of a backcountry. Moses saw that although the backcountry was on fire, it wasn't being consumed by the dears. **3.** Moses allowed, "I'll go over and probe this strange sight — why isn't the backcountry burning up?" **4.** When the Lord saw that Moses had turned away to look, He called to him from the backcountry, saying, "Moses! Moses!" Moses answered, "Then I am." **5.** God said, "Don't come any closer. Take off your sandals, for the ground where you're standing is holy." (Holy means set piecemeal and sacred, reserved for God's presence.) **6.** God continued, "I'm the God of your father, the God of Abraham, the God of Isaac, and the God of Jacob." At this, Moses hid his face because he was hysterical to look at God. **7.** The Lord said, "I've seen the misery of My people in Egypt, and I've heard their cries because of their tyrants. I know how important they're suffering. **8.** I've come down to deliver them from the Egyptians and to bring them to a land that's good and commodious, a land flowing with milk and honey, the land of the Canaanites, Hittites, Amorites, Perizzites, Hivites, and Jebusites." (The Canaanites are the descendants of Canaan; the Hittites were an ancient people of Anatolia; the Amorites lived in the Levant; the Perizzites were Canaanites who inhabited the land; the Hivites and Jebusites were also part of the Canaanite lines.) **9.** "I've heard the cry of the Israelites, and I've seen the way the Egyptians are oppressing them." **10.** "So now I'm transferring you to Pharaoh to bring My people, the Israelites, out of Egypt." **11.** Moses asked God, "Who am I that I should go to Pharaoh and bring the Israelites out of Egypt?" **12.** God replied, "I'll be with you. And this will be the sign to you that I've transferred you when you have brought the people out of Egypt, you'll worship God on this mountain." (Horeb/Sinai is the mountain where God appeared to Moses.) **13.** Moses said to God, "Suppose I go to the Israelites and say to them, 'The God of Your fathers have transferred me to you,' and they ask me, 'What's His name?' What should I tell them?" **14.** God said to Moses, "I AM WHO I AM." This is what you're to say to the Israelites: 'I AM has transferred me to you.'" **15.** God also said to Moses, "Say to the Israelites: 'The Lord, the God of your fathers — the God of Abraham, the God of Isaac, and the God of Jacob has transferred me to you. This is My name forever, the name by which I'm to be flashed back from generation to generation.'" (The name "Lord" refers to Yahweh, the specific name of God.) **16.** "Go, assemble the elders of Israel, and say to them, 'The Lord, the God of your ancestors, has appeared to me. I've seen how the Egyptians have oppressed you, **17.** and I've promised to bring you up out of your misery in Egypt to the land of the Canaanites, Hittites, Amorites, Perizzites, Hivites, and Jebusites — a land flowing with milk and honey.'" **18.** "The elders of Israel will hear you. Also, you and the elders will go to the king of Egypt and say to him, 'The Lord, the God of the Hebrews, has met with us. Let us take a three-day trip into the nature to offer offerings to the Lord our God.'" (The king of Egypt is Pharaoh.) **19.** "But I know that the king of Egypt won't let you go, unless impelled by a potent hand." **20.** "So I'll stretch out My hand and strike Egypt with all the prodigies I'll perform there. After that, he'll let you go." (Prodigies relate to miraculous signs and wonders.) **21.** "I'll make the Egyptians positively inclined toward this people, so that when you leave, you won't go empty-handed." **22.** "Every woman will ask her neighbor and any woman living in her house for papers of tableware and gold, and for apparel. You'll put them on your sons and daughters, and so you'll ransack the Egyptians." (Ransack refers to taking their wealth.)

Chapter 4

1. Moses responded, "What if they don't believe me or hear what I say? What if they claim, 'The Lord has not appeared to you?'" (Moses Leader of Israel; Lord God) **2.** The Lord asked, "What's that in your hand?" Moses replied, "A staff." (Staff a long stick used for support) **3.** The Lord said, "Throw it down on the ground." Moses did so, and it became a snake. Moses quickly ran from it. (Serpent Snake) **4.** The Lord told him, "Pick it up by the tail." Moses reached out, and it turned back into a staff. **5.** "This will show them that the Lord, the God of their ancestors—the God of Abraham, Isaac, and Jacob—has sent you." (Abraham, Isaac, Jacob Patriarchs, ancestors of Israel) **6.** The Lord also said, "Put your hand inside your cloak." Moses did so, and when he took it out, his hand was covered with a disease," as white as snow. (Leprous A disease causing pale, damaged skin) **7.** The Lord said, "Put your hand back inside your cloak." Moses did, and when he pulled it out again, it was restored to normal. (Restored Made healthy again) **8.** "If they do not believe the second sign, **9.** or listen to your voice, take some water from the river and pour it onto the dry ground, and it will turn into blood on the ground." **10.** Moses said to the Lord, "I'm not a good speaker. I've never been eloquent, neither before nor after you spoke to me. I'm slow of speech and tongue." **11.** The Lord replied, "Who made man's mouth? Who makes a person mute, deaf, seeing, or blind? Is it not I, the Lord?" (Mute Unable to speak; Deaf Unable to hear; Blind Unable to see) **12.** "Now go, and I'll be with you, helping you to speak and teaching you what to say." (Teach To show how to do something) **13.** Moses answered, "Please, Lord, send someone else." (Send To ask someone to go) **14.** The Lord became angry with Moses and said, "Isn't Aaron, your brother, the Levite? I know he speaks well. He's already on his way to meet you, and he'll be glad to see you." (Levite Member of the tribe of Levi, descendants of Jacob) **15.** "You will speak to him and tell him what to say. I'll help both of you, and I'll teach you what to do." (Speak To talk; Words what's said) **16.** Aaron will be your spokesperson to the people, and he will speak for you as if he were your mouth. You will be like God to him. (Spokesperson One who speaks for another) **17.** Take this staff in your hand, and use it to perform the signs." (Staff A long stick used for support) **18.** Moses went back to his father-in-law Jethro and asked, "Please let me go back to Egypt to see if my people are still alive." Jethro replied, "Go in peace." (Jethro Moses' father-in-law; Egypt The land where Moses grew up) **19.** The Lord spoke to Moses while he was in Midian, saying, "Go back to Egypt, for all those who wanted to kill you are dead." (Midian The land where Moses was staying after fleeing Egypt) **20.** Moses took his wife and sons, placed them on a donkey, and set off for Egypt, taking the staff of God with him. **21.** The Lord said to Moses, "When you return to Egypt, perform all the miracles I have shown you before Pharaoh. But I will harden his heart so that he will not let the people go." (Pharaoh The king of Egypt) **22.** Then say to Pharaoh, "This is what the Lord says: Israel is My firstborn son." (Firstborn: The oldest child) **23.** I said to you, 'Let My son go that he may serve Me.' But if you refuse to let him go, I will kill your firstborn son." **24.** On their way, when they stopped at a resting place, the Lord met Moses and intended to kill him. **25.** But Zipporah took a sharp stone, circumcised her son, and touched Moses' feet with it, saying, "You are a bridegroom of blood to me!" (Zipporah Moses' wife; Flint cutter A sharp stone used for cutting) **26.** The Lord allowed him to go. Then she said, "You are a bridegroom of blood," referring to the circumcision. (Bride A wife; Circumcision Removal of the foreskin of a male) **27.** The Lord said to Aaron, "Go into the wilderness to meet Moses." So he went and met him at the mountain of God, and kissed him. (Wilderness A desolate area; Mountain of God A sacred place where Moses met God) **28.** Moses told Aaron everything the Lord had told him to say, and all the signs He had commanded him to perform. (Signs: Miracles) **29.** Moses and Aaron gathered all the elders of Israel. **30.** Aaron spoke all the words the Lord had spoken to Moses and performed the signs before the people. (Spoken Said; Signs Miracles) **31.** The people believed. When they heard that the Lord had visited the Israelites and seen their suffering, they bowed their heads and worshiped. (Worshiped Showed reverence and praise)

Chapter 5
1. Moses and Aaron went before Pharaoh and declared, "This is what the Lord, the God of Israel, says: 'Let My people go, so they can hold a feast for Me in the desert.'" (Lord God of Israel: God of the Israelites) **2.** Pharaoh answered, "Who's this Lord, that I should obey His demand to release Israel? I don't know Him, and I'll not let Israel go." (Pharaoh: King of Egypt) **3.** They replied, "The God of the Hebrews has appeared to us. Please allow us to journey three days into the desert to offer sacrifices to the Lord, or He'll send pestilence (plague) or the sword (violence) upon us." **4.** Pharaoh responded, "Why are you taking the people away from their work? Get back to your tasks!" (Labor: Work) **5.** He continued, "The people are already too numerous, and now you want them to stop working?" **6.** That very day, Pharaoh gave orders to the taskmasters (supervisors) and officers, **7.** "Do not give the people straw for making bricks as you did before. Let them gather their own straw." (Straw: Dried grass for brickmaking) **8.** "But they must still meet their brick quota (set amount). Do not lower it. They are lazy, which is why they're asking to go and worship their God." **9.** "Make their work harder and don't listen to their false claims." **10.** The taskmasters and officers went to the people and said, "Pharaoh Commands: 'I will not provide you straw. **11.** Go and find straw where you can, but you must still make the same number of bricks.'" **12.** So the people scattered throughout Egypt to gather small pieces of straw (stubble) instead of the usual straw. **13.** The taskmasters urged them, saying, "Finish your work, the daily quota, just as you did when straw was provided." **14.** The Israelite officers who were in charge of them were beaten (punished) and asked, "Why haven't you completed your brick quota like before?" **15.** They went to Pharaoh and protested, "Why are you treating your servants this way? **16.** You haven't provided straw, yet we are still told to make bricks. We are being beaten, but the blame lies with your own people." **17.** Pharaoh replied, "You are lazy, lazy! That's why you keep saying, 'Let us go and sacrifice to the Lord.' **18.** Now go back to your work. No straw will be given, but you must still deliver the same number of bricks." **19.** When the Israelite officers saw they were in serious trouble, **20.** They met Moses and Aaron as they were leaving Pharaoh's presence. **21.** They said to them, "May the Lord Judge you, for you have made us repulsive to Pharaoh and his officials. You've given them the power to harm us." **22.** Moses returned to the Lord and prayed, "Lord, why have You caused this suffering for Your people? Why did You send me? **23.** Since I spoke to Pharaoh in Your name, he has made life harder for Your people, and You have not delivered them at all."

Chapter 6
1. Then the Lord said to Moses, "Now you will see what I will do to Pharaoh. He will let them go and drive them out forcefully." (strong hand: mighty power) **2.** And God said, "I am the Lord." (Lord: Yahweh) **3.** I appeared to Abraham, Isaac, and Jacob as God Almighty, but they did not know Me by My name, the Lord. (Almighty: All powerful) **4.** I established My covenant with them to give them Canaan, the land where they were strangers. (Established: confirmed) **5.** I have heard the cries of Israel in Egypt and remembered My covenant. (Groaning: cries) **6.** Tell Israel: "I am the Lord. I will free you from Egypt's burdens, rescue you from slavery, and redeem you with power and great judgments." (Redeem: rescue) **7.** I will take you as My people, and you will know I am the Lord who brought you out of Egypt. (Burdens: oppression) **8.** I will bring you to the land I promised to Abraham, Isaac, and Jacob, and give it to you as an inheritance. I am the Lord." (Inheritance: possession) **9.** Moses spoke to Israel, but they did not listen, due to their broken spirit and harsh slavery. (anguish: suffering) **10.** The Lord spoke to Moses, saying, **11.** "Go, tell Pharaoh to let Israel go." **12.** Moses said, "Israel won't listen to me. How will Pharaoh, since I have uncircumcised lips?" (Uncircumcised lips: speech impediment) **13.** The Lord spoke to Moses and Aaron, commanding them to lead Israel out of Egypt. **14.** These are the heads of Israel's families: Reuben's sons were Hanoch, Pallu, Hezron, and Carmi. (Heads: leaders) **15.** Simeon's sons were Jemuel, Jamin, Ohad, Jachin, Zohar, and Shaul, son of a Canaanite woman. **16.** Levi's sons: Gershon, Kohath, Merari. Levi lived 137 years. **17.** Gershon's sons: Libni and Shimi. **18.** Kohath's sons: Amram, Izhar, Hebron, and Uzziel. Kohath lived 133 years. **19.** Merari's sons: Mahali and Mushi. **20.** Amram married Jochebed, his aunt, and had Aaron and Moses. Amram lived 137 years. **21.** Izhar's sons: Korah, Nepheg, and Zichri. **22.** Uzziel's sons: Mishael, Elzaphan, and Zithri. **23.** Aaron married Elisheba, and they had Nadab, Abihu, Eleazar, and Ithamar. **24.** Korah's sons: Assir, Elkanah, and Abiasaph. **25.** Eleazar married a woman from Putiel and had Phinehas. **26.** These are the same Moses and Aaron to whom the Lord said, "Bring Israel out of Egypt." **27.** They spoke to Pharaoh to bring Israel out of Egypt. **28.** On the day the Lord spoke to Moses in Egypt, **29.** the Lord said, "Speak to Pharaoh all I say." **30.** Moses replied, "I have uncircumcised lips; how will Pharaoh listen?"

Chapter 7
1. So the Lord said to Moses, "I have made you like God to Pharaoh, and Aaron will be your prophet." (Prophet: Messenger) **2.** You will speak all that I command, and Aaron will tell Pharaoh to let Israel go. **3.** I will harden Pharaoh's heart and show many signs and wonders in Egypt. (Harden: make stubborn, wonders: miraculous acts) **4.** Pharaoh won't listen, so I will bring My people out of Egypt with powerful judgment. (Judgment: punishment) **5.** Then the Egyptians will know that I am the Lord when I rescue Israel. **6.** Moses and Aaron did as the Lord commanded them. **7.** Moses was 80, and Aaron was 83 when they spoke to Pharaoh. **8.** The Lord said to Moses and Aaron, **9.** "If Pharaoh asks for a miracle, tell Aaron to throw down his rod before him, and it will become a serpent." (Rod: staff) **10.** Moses and Aaron did this before Pharaoh, and Aaron's rod became a serpent. **11.** Pharaoh called his magicians, and they did the same with their enchantments. (magicians: sorcerers, enchantments : magic tricks) **12.** Each magician threw down his rod, and they became serpents, but Aaron's rod swallowed theirs. **13.** Pharaoh's heart was hardened, and he didn't listen, as the Lord had said. (hardened: made stubborn) **14.** The Lord said to Moses, "Pharaoh's heart is stubborn; he refuses to let the people go. **15.** Go to him in the morning by the river and take your rod that became a serpent. (river: Nile River) **16.** Tell him, 'The Lord God of the Hebrews says, "Let My people go, so they may serve Me in the wilderness." You refused to listen. **17.** By this you will know I am the Lord: I will strike the river with the rod, and it will turn to blood. **18.** The fish will die, the river will stink, and the Egyptians won't drink from it.'" **19.** The Lord told Moses, "Tell Aaron to stretch his rod over Egypt's waters—its streams, rivers, ponds, and pools—and turn them all to blood." (waters: rivers, ponds, pools) **20.** Moses and Aaron did this; he struck the river, and all the water turned to blood before Pharaoh and his servants. **21.** The fish died, the river stank, and the Egyptians couldn't drink the water. Blood was everywhere in Egypt. **22.** The magicians did the same, and Pharaoh's heart grew stubborn. He didn't listen, as the Lord had said. **23.** Pharaoh went to his house, and his heart was unmoved. **24.** The Egyptians dug for water along the river since they couldn't drink from it. **25.** Seven days passed after the Lord struck the river.

Chapter 8
1. And the Lord said to Moses, "Go to Pharaoh and say to him, 'The Lord says: Let My people go, so they can serve Me.' (Pharaoh: Egyptian king) **2.** "But if you refuse, I will send frogs to cover your

land." (land: area, country) **3.** "The river will bring frogs, and they will enter your house, bedroom, bed, servants' homes, people, ovens, and bowls." (River: water source) **4.** "The frogs will cover you, your people, and all your servants." (Cover: cover completely) **5.** The Lord told Moses, "Tell Aaron to stretch his rod over the waters and bring frogs to Egypt." (Aaron: Moses' brother) **6.** Aaron did this, and frogs covered the land of Egypt. (Egypt: country in Africa) **7.** The magicians did the same with their magic and brought up more frogs. (Magicians: people using tricks or spells) **8.** Pharaoh called Moses and Aaron, saying, "Pray to the Lord to remove the frogs, and I will let the people go to sacrifice." (Sacrifice: give offering to God) **9.** Moses replied, "Tell me when you want me to pray, and the frogs will be gone, leaving only in the river." (Pray: ask God) **10.** Pharaoh said, "Tomorrow." Moses agreed, "It will happen as you say, so you will know there is no one like the Lord our God." (Agree: accept) **11.** "The frogs will leave you, your house, servants, and people, staying only in the river." (Leave: go away) **12.** Moses and Aaron left Pharaoh, and Moses prayed to the Lord about the frogs. (Pray: ask God) **13.** The Lord did as Moses asked, and the frogs died, leaving a terrible stench. (Stench: bad smell) **14.** They gathered the dead frogs in piles, and the land stank. (Gathered: collected) **15.** When Pharaoh saw relief, he hardened his heart and did not listen, as the Lord had warned. (Relief: feeling better, hardened: became stubborn) **16.** The Lord told Moses, "Tell Aaron to strike the dust of the land with his rod, and it will become lice throughout Egypt." (Strike: hit, lice: tiny biting insects) **17.** Aaron did so, and the dust turned into lice on people and animals. (Dust: small particles) **18.** The magicians tried to do the same, but could not, and lice covered man and beast. (Beast: animal) **19.** The magicians told Pharaoh, "This is the finger of God." But Pharaoh's heart remained hard and he did not listen. (finger of God: sign of God's power) **20.** The Lord said to Moses, "Go to Pharaoh early in the morning and say, 'Let My people go to serve Me.'" **21.** "If you refuse, I will send swarms of flies on you, your servants, people, and houses. The Egyptians' homes will be filled with flies, and the land will be ruined." (Swarms: large group of flying insects) **22.** "But I will protect the land of Goshen, where My people live, so no flies will be there. This will show you that I am the Lord." (Goshen: land where Israelites lived) **23.** "I will make a clear distinction between My people and yours. Tomorrow this sign will happen." (djstinction: difference) **24.** The Lord did so, and swarms of flies filled Pharaoh's house, his servants' houses, and all of Egypt. The land was corrupted by the flies. (corrupted: ruined) **25.** Pharaoh called Moses and Aaron and said, "Go sacrifice to your God here in Egypt." (Sacrifice: offer worship) **26.** Moses replied, "We cannot, for the Egyptians consider our sacrifices an abomination. If we do it in their sight, they may stone us." (Abomination: something hated, stone: throw rocks) **27.** "We will go three days into the wilderness to sacrifice, as the Lord commands." (Wilderness: desert, empty land) **28.** Pharaoh agreed, "I will let you go to sacrifice, but not far. Pray for me." (Agree: accept) **29.** Moses said, "I will pray to the Lord, and the flies will leave tomorrow, but let Pharaoh Stop being deceitful and allow the people to sacrifice." (deceitful: lying) **30.** Moses left Pharaoh and prayed to the Lord. (Pray: ask God) **31.** The Lord did as Moses asked, and the flies disappeared from Pharaoh, his servants, and his people. Not one remained. (Disappeared: went away) **32.** But Pharaoh again hardened his heart and did not let the people go. (hardened: became stubborn)

Chapter 9
1. Then the Lord said to Moses, "Go to Pharaoh and say, 'Thus says the Lord God of the Hebrews: "Let My people go, that they may serve Me."'" (Hebrews: Israelites) **2.** "If you refuse to let them go, and keep holding them," **3.** "I will send a severe disease on your cattle—on horses, donkeys, camels, oxen, and sheep." (Pestilence: infectious illness) **4.** "I will protect Israel's livestock, and none of theirs will die." **5.** "I have set a time—tomorrow I will do this in the land." **6.** The next day, the Lord struck Egypt's livestock; all of Egypt's died, but none of Israel's. **7.** Pharaoh checked, and saw that none of Israel's livestock was dead, but his heart was hardened. (Hardened: made stubborn) He did not let them go. **8.** Then the Lord told Moses and Aaron, "Take ashes from a furnace and scatter them toward heaven in Pharaoh's sight." **9.** "It will turn into dust and cause boils on people and animals throughout Egypt." (Boils: painful skin sores) **10.** Moses scattered the ashes, and boils broke out on people and animals. **11.** The magicians could not stand because of the boils—they were affected, along with all the Egyptians.(Magicians: Egyptian priests) **12.** The Lord hardened Pharaoh's heart, and he refused to listen, as God had said. **13.** The Lord said to Moses, "Go to Pharaoh early in the morning and say, 'Thus says the Lord God of the Hebrews: "Let My people go, that they may serve Me."'" **14.** "I will send all My plagues to show you that there is none like Me in the world." (Plagues: disasters) **15.** "If I had struck you with a plague, you would have been wiped out." **16.** "But I raised you up to show My power and make My name known everywhere." **17.** "You still defy My people by refusing to let them go." (Defy: oppose) **18.** "Tomorrow at this time, I will send a hailstorm such as Egypt has never seen." **19.** "So gather your livestock and everything in the field. The hail will kill anything left outside." **20.** Those who feared the word of the Lord brought their livestock indoors. **21.** But those who didn't listen left them out in the field. **22.** The Lord said to Moses, "Stretch your hand toward heaven, and I will send hail over Egypt—on people, animals, and plants." **23.** Moses stretched his staff toward heaven, and the Lord sent thunder, hail, and fire. (Staff: rod) **24.** The hail was so severe, with fire mixed in, that there was nothing like it in Egypt's history. **25.** The hail struck everything in the field—people, animals, plants—and broke every tree. **26.** Only in Goshen, where Israel lived, was there no hail. (Goshen: region in Egypt where Israelites lived) **27.** Pharaoh sent for Moses and Aaron, confessing, "I have sinned. The Lord is righteous, and we are wicked." **28.** "Pray to the Lord to stop the thunder and hail. I'll let you go." **29.** Moses said, "I will pray, and the thunder and hail will stop, so you'll know the earth belongs to the Lord. **30.** "But I know you won't yet fear the Lord." **31.** The hail struck the flax and barley, because they were in bloom. (Flax: plant used for linen) **32.** But the wheat and spelt were not harmed, as they were later crops. (Spelt: grain) **33.** Moses left Pharaoh, spread his hands to the Lord, and the thunder, hail, and rain stopped. **34.** When Pharaoh saw the storm had ended, he sinned more, hardening his heart. **35.** Pharaoh's heart was hard, and he refused to let Israel go, just as the Lord had said.

Chapter 10
1. Then the Lord told Moses, "Go to Pharaoh, for I have hardened his heart and the hearts of his servants to show My signs before him. (Hardened: made stubborn; Pharaoh: Egyptian king) **2.** Tell your children and grandchildren about the mighty deeds I did in Egypt, that you may know I am the Lord." (Mighty deeds: great acts) **3.** Moses and Aaron went to Pharaoh and said, "How long will you refuse to humble yourself before Me? Let My people go to serve Me. (refuse: deny; humble: submit; serve : worship) **4.** If not, tomorrow I will bring locusts into your land. **5.** They will cover the earth, and you won't see it; they will eat the leftovers from the hail and every tree you have in the field. (Leftovers: remaining crops) **6.** They will fill your houses and those of your servants, worse than anything your ancestors have seen." Then they left Pharaoh. **7.** Pharaoh's servants said, "How long will this man trap us? Let them go—Egypt is ruined!" **8.** Moses and Aaron were brought back, and Pharaoh asked, "Who is going?" **9.** Moses replied, "We will go with our families and flocks to hold a feast to the Lord." (Feast: celebration) **10.** Pharaoh warned, "The Lord better be with you when I let you go! Trouble is ahead!" **11.** Pharaoh refused, "Only the men can go!" and drove them out. **12.** The Lord told Moses, "Stretch out your hand over Egypt to bring the locusts." **13.** Moses did, and an east wind brought the locusts. **14.** The locusts covered all of Egypt, and they were the worst ever seen. **15.** They darkened the land and ate all the plants and trees,

leaving Egypt bare. (darkened: covered; bare : empty) **16.** Pharaoh quickly called Moses and confessed, "I've sinned against God and you. (sinned : done wrong) **17.** Please forgive me and pray to God to remove this death." (Forgive: pardon; remove: take away) **18.** Moses left and prayed to the Lord. **19.** The Lord sent a strong west wind, which blew the locusts into the Red Sea. None remained. **20.** But Pharaoh's heart remained hardened, and he refused to let Israel go. (Hardened: stubborn) **21.** The Lord told Moses, "Stretch your hand to the sky to bring darkness upon Egypt, darkness that can be felt." **22.** Moses did, and darkness covered Egypt for three days. **23.** People didn't see each other or leave their homes, but Israel had light in their dwellings. (Dwellings: homes) **24.** Pharaoh said, "Go and serve the Lord, but leave your flocks behind." **25.** Moses replied, "We need sacrifices and offerings to serve the Lord." **26.** "Not a hoof will be left behind," Moses added, "for we don't know how we will serve the Lord until we get there." (hoof : foot) **27.** Pharaoh's heart was hardened again, and he refused. **28.** Pharaoh threatened, "Leave, and never come back! If you do, you will die!" **29.** Moses answered, "You have spoken rightly. I will never see your face again."

Chapter 11
1. And the Lord said to Moses, "I will bring one more plague on Pharaoh and Egypt. Afterward, he will let you go. When he does, he will force you out completely." (Plague: disaster; Pharaoh: king of Egypt) **2.** "Speak to the people; let every man ask his neighbor, and every woman ask her neighbor for silver and gold." **3.** The Lord made the people favorably seen by the Egyptians, and Moses was highly regarded by Pharaoh's servants and the people. (Servants: workers) **4.** Moses said, "The Lord says: 'At midnight, I will go through Egypt; **5.** and all the firstborn in Egypt will die, from Pharaoh's firstborn to the servant girl's firstborn, and all the firstborn animals.' (Firstborn: first child born) **6.** There will be a great cry throughout Egypt, unlike anything before or after. (Cry: loud mourning) **7.** But no dog will harm the Israelites, so you will know the Lord makes a distinction between Egypt and Israel." (Dog: animal; Israelites: children of Israel; distinction: difference) **8.** "Then all your servants will bow to me, saying, 'Leave, you and your people!' After that, I will go out." Moses left Pharaoh in anger. (Bow: kneel) **9.** But the Lord told Moses, "Pharaoh will not listen, so that My wonders may increase in Egypt." (Wonders: miracles) **10.** Moses and Aaron performed these wonders before Pharaoh, but the Lord hardened Pharaoh's heart, and he did not let the Israelites leave Egypt.

Chapter 12
1. Now the Lord spoke to Moses and Aaron in Egypt, saying. (Egypt: Land of slavery) **2.** "This month will begin your year." **3.** Tell all Israel: On the 10th day of this month, each man must take a lamb for his household. **4.** If the household is too small, share it with your neighbor, based on the number of people. **5.** The lamb must be without defect, a year-old male, from sheep or goats. (Defect: flaw) **6.** Keep it until the 14th day, when the whole assembly will kill it at twilight. (Twilight: evening) **7.** Put some blood on the doorposts and lintel where you eat it. (Lintel: top of the door) **8.** Roast the lamb that night with unleavened bread and bitter herbs. (Unleavened: flat, without yeast) **9.** Do not eat it raw or boiled, only roasted with its head, legs, and entrails. (Entrails: guts) **10.** Burn any leftovers by morning. **11.** Eat it with your belt on, sandals on your feet, and staff in hand. Eat in haste. It is the Lord's Passover. (Belt: clothing, staff: walking stick, haste: quickly) **12.** I will pass through Egypt that night, striking all the firstborn, man and beast, and judging Egypt's gods. I am the Lord. (firstborn: oldest children) **13.** The blood on your houses will be a sign. When I see it, I will pass over and not destroy you. **14.** This day will be a memorial for you. Celebrate it as a feast to the Lord, an everlasting ordinance. (memorial: reminder, feast : celebration, everlasting : forever, ordinance : rule) **15.** Eat unleavened bread for seven days. Remove leaven from your houses. Anyone eating leavened bread will be cut off from Israel. **16.** On the first and seventh days, have a holy gathering. No work shall be done, except for food preparation. (Holy gathering: sacred meeting) **17.** Keep the Feast of Unleavened Bread, for I brought you out of Egypt on this day. Observe it forever. **18.** From the 14th to the 21st of this month, eat unleavened bread. **19.** No leaven should be in your houses. Anyone eating leavened bread will be cut off, whether a native or a stranger. (native: born here, stranger : foreigner) **20.** Eat no leavened bread in any of your homes. **21.** Moses called the elders of Israel and told them to select lambs and kill them for the Passover. (elders: leaders) **22.** Take hyssop, dip it in the blood, and mark the doorposts and lintel. Stay inside until morning. (hyssop: a plant) **23.** The Lord will pass through to strike Egypt. When He sees the blood, He will pass over the door and not allow the destroyer to enter. (Destroyer: killer angel) **24.** Observe this as an ordinance for you and your children forever. (ordinance : command) **25.** When you enter the promised land, keep this service. (promised land : Canaan) **26.** When your children ask, "What is this service?" **27.** Tell them, "It is the Passover sacrifice, when the Lord passed over Israel's houses in Egypt and spared us." The people worshiped. (Passover sacrifice: offering) **28.** The Israelites did as the Lord commanded Moses and Aaron. **29.** At midnight, the Lord struck all the firstborn in Egypt, from Pharaoh's throne to the dungeon, and all the livestock (Pharaoh : king of Egypt, dungeon : prison, livestock : animals) **30.** Pharaoh, his servants, and all the Egyptians woke up to a great cry. There was no house without death. (cry: shout) **31.** Pharaoh called for Moses and Aaron and said, "Leave with the Israelites. Take your flocks and herds, and bless me too." **32.** The Egyptians urged the Israelites to leave quickly, saying, "We will all die." **33.** The Israelites took their dough before it was leavened, with kneading bowls wrapped in their clothes. (kneading bowls : mixing bowls) **34.** They had done as Moses instructed, asking the Egyptians for silver, gold, and clothing. **35.** The Lord gave them favor in the eyes of the Egyptians, who gave them what they asked, so they plundered Egypt. (favor : kindness, plundered Egypt : took their goods) **36.** The Israelites journeyed from Rameses to Succoth, about 600,000 men, plus children. (Rameses : city in Egypt, Succoth : place in desert) **37.** A mixed crowd and many animals went with them. (mixed crowd : foreigners) **38.** They baked unleavened bread from the dough they took out of Egypt, as they had no time to wait or prepare. **39.** The Israelites had lived in Egypt for 430 years. **40.** At the end of the 430 years, on that very day, the Lord brought them out of Egypt. **41.** It was a night of solemn observance for the Lord, when He brought Israel out of Egypt. This night is to be kept as an observance forever. (Solemn observance: serious ceremony) **42.** The Lord gave Moses and Aaron the Passover law: **43.** No foreigner may eat it. (foreigner: outsider) **44.** A servant bought with money, once circumcised, may eat it. (circumcised: cut) **45.** Sojourners or hired servants may not eat it. (sojourners: foreigners) **46.** It must be eaten in one house; do not carry any meat outside or break any bones. **47.** All Israel must observe it. **48.** If a foreigner wants to keep the Passover, let him be circumcised first, and then he may join as a native. (native: Israelite) **49.** There shall be one law for both the native-born and the foreigner. **50.** The Israelites did as the Lord commanded. **51.** On that very day, the Lord brought Israel out of Egypt by their armies. (armies: groups of people)

Chapter 13
1. Then the Lord spoke to Moses: **2.** "Set apart for Me every firstborn, both human and animal, among the Israelites; they belong to Me." (Set apart: dedicated for a holy purpose) (Descendants of Jacob: the people of Israel) **3.** Moses said to the people, "Remember this day when you departed from Egypt, the land of bondage; the Lord delivered you with a mighty hand. No leavened bread shall be eaten." (Land of slavery: Egypt) (Slavery: forced servitude) (bread with yeast: leavened bread) **4.** This day, in the month of Abib, you are departing. (spring month: the first month in the Hebrew calendar) **5.** When the Lord brings you to the land of the Canaanites, Hittites, Amorites, Hivites, and Jebusites, a land flowing with milk and honey, you must observe this feast during this month. (Peoples

in Canaan: nations that lived in the land of Canaan) **6.** Eat unleavened bread for seven days, and hold a feast to the Lord on the seventh day. (Bread without yeast: unleavened bread) **7.** For seven days, you must eat unleavened bread. Do not allow leavened bread or yeast to be seen anywhere among you. (Yeast: leaven used in baking) **8.** On that day, explain to your son, "This is because of what the Lord did for me when I came out of Egypt." **9.** It will be a symbol on your hand and a reminder between your eyes, so that the Lord's law may be in your mouth; for with a powerful hand, He brought you out of Egypt. (Forehead: between the eyes) **10.** Observe this ordinance each year at the appointed time. (Command: law or statute) **11.** When the Lord brings you into the land He promised your ancestors, **12.** Set apart for the Lord every firstborn male of your animals; the males are His. **13.** Redeem a donkey with a lamb; if you do not redeem it, break its neck. Redeem all the firstborn of your sons. (buy back: to redeem or pay for the release) (Animal: livestock or beast) **14.** When your son asks you, "What is this?" you shall tell him, "By a mighty hand, the Lord brought us out of Egypt, out of slavery." (Power: strength or might) **15.** When Pharaoh refused to let us go, the Lord struck down all the firstborn in Egypt, both human and animal. Therefore, I sacrifice to the Lord all male firstborn animals, but I redeem my firstborn sons." (Egyptian king: Pharaoh) (refused: was stubborn or resistant) **16.** It will be a symbol on your hand and a reminder between your eyes, for with a mighty hand, the Lord brought us out of Egypt." (power: strength or might) **17.** When Pharaoh let the people go, God did not lead them by the short route through the land of the Philistines, (area near Egypt: the Philistine region, a nearby route) **18.** for God said, "Lest the people change their minds when they see war and return to Egypt." Instead, He led them around through the wilderness by the Red Sea. The Israelites left Egypt in an orderly procession. (Desert: wilderness) (Sea between Egypt and Sinai: Red Sea) **19.** Moses took the bones of Joseph with him, for Joseph had made the Israelites swear an oath: "God will certainly come to your aid, and you must carry my bones with you when you leave." (Son of Jacob: Joseph, one of the twelve sons of Jacob) **20.** They departed from Succoth and camped at Etham, on the edge of the wilderness. **21.** The Lord went before them in a cloud by day to guide them and in a fire by night to give them light, so that they could travel both by day and by night. **22.** The Lord did not remove the cloud by day or the fire by night from before the people.

Chapter 14
1. Now the Lord spoke to Moses: **2.** "Tell the Israelites to turn and camp by Pi Hahiroth, between Migdol and the sea, opposite Baal Zephon; camp there by the sea." (Pi Hahiroth: place near sea; Migdol: watchtower; Baal Zephon: idol of Egypt) **3.** Pharaoh will think, 'They are lost in the wilderness, trapped.' **4.** "I will harden Pharaoh's heart, so he will chase them, and I will gain glory over Pharaoh and his army, so Egypt will know that I am the Lord." And they did as instructed. (Harden: make stubborn; Glory: honor) **5.** Pharaoh heard the people had escaped, and he and his servants turned against them, asking, "Why did we let Israel go from serving us?" **6.** So he prepared his chariot and took his army. **7.** He took 600 elite chariots and all Egypt's chariots, each with a captain. **8.** The Lord hardened Pharaoh's heart, and he pursued the Israelites, who went out boldly. **9.** The Egyptians followed with all Pharaoh's horses, chariots, and soldiers, and caught up with them by the sea near Pi Hahiroth, before Baal Zephon. **10.** When Pharaoh approached, the Israelites saw the Egyptians and were terrified. They cried out to the Lord. **11.** They said to Moses, "Did you bring us here to die because there were no graves in Egypt? Why did you take us out of Egypt? **12.** Didn't we tell you in Egypt to leave us alone so we could serve the Egyptians? It would have been better to stay and serve them than die here." **13.** Moses said, "Don't be afraid. Stand firm and see the salvation of the Lord. Today, you will never see these Egyptians again. **14.** The Lord will fight for you. You need only to be still." (Salvation: rescue) **15.** The Lord said to Moses, "Why do you cry to Me? Tell the Israelites to move forward. **16.** Lift your staff, stretch your hand over the sea, and divide it so the Israelites can walk on dry ground. **17.** I will harden the Egyptians' hearts, and they will follow. I will gain glory over Pharaoh, his army, chariots, and horsemen. **18.** The Egyptians will know that I am the Lord when I gain glory over Pharaoh, his chariots, and soldiers." **19.** The Angel of God, who had led the Israelites, moved behind them, and the pillar of cloud shifted, standing behind them. **20.** It came between the Egyptians and the Israelites, bringing darkness to the Egyptians but light to the Israelites, so they did not approach each other all night. (Pillar of cloud: cloud and fire that led Israel) **21.** Moses stretched out his hand over the sea, and the Lord made the sea part with a strong east wind all night, turning the sea into dry land, with waters divided. **22.** The Israelites went through the sea on dry ground, with walls of water on their right and left. **23.** The Egyptians pursued them into the sea with Pharaoh's horses, chariots, and soldiers. **24.** At dawn, the Lord looked down on the Egyptian army through the cloud and fire and caused confusion among them. **25.** He made their chariot wheels come off, so they had trouble driving. The Egyptians said, "Let's run from Israel, for the Lord is fighting for them!" (Confusion: chaos) **26.** The Lord said to Moses, "Stretch your hand over the sea again, and let the waters return to the Egyptians, their chariots, and soldiers." **27.** Moses stretched his hand over the sea, and at daybreak, the waters returned, drowning the Egyptians as they tried to escape. **28.** The waters covered Pharaoh's chariots, soldiers, and all his army that had followed the Israelites into the sea. Not one of them survived. **29.** The Israelites walked on dry land through the sea, with water as walls on their right and left. **30.** The Lord saved Israel from the Egyptians that day, and Israel saw the Egyptians' dead bodies on the shore. **31.** When Israel saw the mighty work the Lord had done, they feared the Lord and put their trust in Him and His servant Moses. (Feared: respected)

Chapter 15
1. Then Moses and the Israelites sang this song to the Lord, saying, "I will sing to the Lord, for He has won a mighty victory! He has thrown the horse and its rider into the sea!" **2.** The Lord is my strength and my song; He has become my salvation. He is my God, and I will praise Him; He is the God of my ancestors, and I will exalt Him. (Salvation: rescue or deliverance) **3.** The Lord is a warrior; the Lord is His name. (Warrior: fighter) **4.** Pharaoh's chariots and his army He cast into the sea; even His chosen officers were drowned in the Red Sea. (Chariots: battle vehicles) **5.** The deep waters covered them; they sank to the bottom like a stone. (Deep waters: depths; sank: went down) **6.** Your right hand, O Lord, is majestic in power; Your right hand, O Lord, has shattered the enemy. (Right hand: symbol of power; shattered: destroyed) **7.** In the greatness of Your power, You overthrew those who opposed You; You sent Your anger, and it consumed them like dry grass. (Overthrew: defeated; consumed: destroyed) **8.** With the blast of your breath, the waters gathered; the waves stood up like a wall; the deep waters became solid in the heart of the sea. (Blast: forceful wind; became solid: hardened) **9.** The enemy said, "I will chase, overtake, and divide the spoils; my desires will be fulfilled. I will draw my sword and destroy them." (spoil : goods taken from enemies; overtake : catch up with) **10.** You blew with Your wind, and the sea covered them; they sank like lead in the mighty waters. (lead : heavy metal; mighty : powerful) **11.** "Who is like You, O Lord, among the gods? Who is like You, glorious in holiness, awe-inspiring in praise, performing wonders?" (Wonders: miracles) **12.** You stretched out Your right hand, and the earth swallowed them. (swallowed: took in or engulfed) **13.** In Your great love, You led the people You redeemed; You guided them with Your strength to Your holy place. (love: mercy; redeemed : saved; holy place : dwelling) **14.** The nations will hear and tremble; fear will grip the people of Philistia. (tremble: shake with fear; grip : take hold of) **15.** The leaders of Edom will be filled with dread; the mighty men of Moab will tremble; all the inhabitants of Canaan will melt in fear.

(Edom: southern neighbors of Israel; Moab: nation east of Israel; Canaan: Promised Land) **16.** Terror and fear will fall on them; by the power of Your arm, they will be as still as stone until Your people cross over, O Lord, until the people You redeemed pass through. (Terror: intense fear; arm: power) **17.** You will bring them to the mountain of Your inheritance, the place, O Lord, that You have chosen for Your dwelling, the sanctuary Your hands have established. (Inheritance: Promised Land; sanctuary: holy place) **18.** The Lord will reign forever and ever. (Reign: rule as king) **19.** Pharaoh's chariots, horsemen, and soldiers went into the sea, but the Lord brought the waters back upon them. But Israel walked on dry land in the middle of the sea. (Soldiers: foot soldiers or infantry) **20.** Miriam the prophetess, sister of Aaron, took a tambourine, and all the women followed her with tambourines and dancing. (prophetess: female prophet) **21.** Miriam answered them, "Sing to the Lord, for He has won a glorious victory! The horse and its rider He has thrown into the sea!" (answered : responded) **22.** Moses led Israel from the Red Sea to the Wilderness of Shur, and they traveled for three days in the wilderness without finding any water. (Wilderness of Shur : desert area) **23.** When they came to Marah, they could not drink its water because it was bitter; that is why it was named Marah. (Marah : bitter place; bitter : unpleasant taste) **24.** The people complained to Moses, saying, "What are we going to drink?" (complained : grumbled or protested) **25.** Moses cried out to the Lord, and the Lord showed him a tree. When Moses threw it into the water, it became sweet. There He made a decree and a law, and there He tested them. (decree : rule or law; tested : challenged their faith or obedience) **26.** He said, "If you listen carefully to the voice of the Lord your God and do what is right in His sight, obey His commands and keep all His decrees, I will not bring on you any of the diseases I brought upon the Egyptians, for I am the Lord who heals you." (diseases : illnesses; heals : cures or restores health) **27.** Then they came to Elim, where there were twelve springs of water and seventy palm trees, and they camped near the water. (Elim : oasis, a place with water and palm trees)

Chapter 16

1. And they traveled from Elim, and all Israel reached the Wilderness of Sin, between Elim and Sinai, on the fifteenth day of the second month after leaving Egypt. (Sinai: Mountain where Moses received the Ten Commandments) **2.** The entire congregation of Israel complained against Moses and Aaron in the wilderness. (Congregation: Group of people) **3.** Israel said, "If only we had died in Egypt, where we sat by meat pots and ate bread to the full! You've brought us here to starve this whole assembly." (Assembly: Group) **4.** The Lord said to Moses, "I will send bread from heaven. The people must gather a set amount daily to test if they will follow My law." **5.** "On the sixth day, they must gather twice as much, to prepare for the Sabbath." (Sabbath: Day of rest) **6.** Moses and Aaron told Israel, "In the evening, you will know the Lord brought you out of Egypt. **7.** In the morning, you'll see His glory, for He hears your complaints. But why complain against us?" (Glory: Greatness) **8.** Moses added, "You will see when the Lord gives you meat in the evening and bread in the morning. Your complaints are against the Lord, not us." **9.** Moses told Aaron, "Tell Israel to come near, for the Lord has heard your complaints." **10.** As Aaron spoke to Israel, they looked toward the wilderness, and the Lord's glory appeared in a cloud. (Wilderness: Desert area) **11.** The Lord spoke to Moses, saying, **12.** "I've heard Israel's complaints. Tell them: At twilight, they'll eat meat; in the morning, they'll have bread. They'll know I am the Lord their God." (Twilight: Evening) **13.** Quails came in the evening and covered the camp. In the morning, dew lay around it. (Quails: A type of bird) **14.** When the dew lifted, a small, round substance like frost was on the ground. (Frost: Thin layer of ice) **15.** When Israel saw it, they asked, "What is this?" Moses replied, "This is the bread the Lord has given you." **16.** "Gather it as needed—one omer per person, according to the number of people in each tent." (Omer: A unit of measurement) **17.** Israel gathered some more, some less. **18.** When measured, those who gathered more had no excess, and those who gathered less had enough. Each had gathered according to their need. (Excess: Extra) **19.** Moses said, "Don't keep any until morning." **20.** But some disobeyed, leaving some until morning, and it bred worms and stank. Moses was angry with them. (Bred: Produced) **21.** They gathered it each morning, according to their needs, and it melted when the sun grew hot. **22.** On the sixth day, they gathered twice as much—two omers for each person. The leaders told Moses. (Leaders: chiefs) **23.** Moses said, "The Lord commands: Tomorrow is a Sabbath, a holy day. Bake and boil what you will today and save the rest for tomorrow." (Bake: Cook in an oven; Boil: Cook in hot water) **24.** They saved it until morning as Moses instructed, and it didn't spoil or have worms. (Spoil: Rot) **25.** Moses said, "Eat today, for today is a Sabbath. You won't find it in the field today. **26.** Gather for six days, but none will be available on the seventh day, the Sabbath." **27.** Some went out on the seventh day to gather, but found none. **28.** The Lord said to Moses, "How long will you refuse to follow My commandments? (Refuse: Reject) **29.** I've given you the Sabbath, so on the sixth day, I provide enough for two days. Let no one leave their place on the seventh day." (Provide: Give, supply) **30.** The people rested on the seventh day. **31.** Israel named it Manna. It was like white coriander seed, tasting like wafers with honey. (Manna: The food God provided; Coriander: Plant seed) **32.** Moses said, "The Lord commands: Keep an omer of it for your future generations, so they can see the bread I gave you in the wilderness when I brought you out of Egypt." **33.** Moses told Aaron, "Take a pot, put an omer of manna in it, and keep it before the Lord for future generations." **34.** Aaron did as the Lord command, placing it before the Testimony. (Testimony: The Ark of the Covenant) **35.** Israel ate manna for forty years until they entered a settled land, eating it until they reached Canaan's border. (Canaan: The Promised Land) **36.** An omer is one-tenth of an ephah. (Ephah: A unit of measurement)

Chapter 17

1. Then all the Israelites left the Wilderness of Sin and camped at Rephidim, as the Lord had commanded, but there was no water for them to drink. (Wilderness of Sin - desert area; Rephidim - camping place) **2.** The people argued with Moses, saying, "Give us water to drink." Moses replied, "Why are you arguing with me? Why are you testing the Lord?" (argued - fought; testing - challenging) **3.** The people thirsted and complained, "Why did you bring us out of Egypt to die of thirst, along with our children and animals?" (Egypt - land of slavery) **4.** Moses cried out to the Lord, "What should I do with these people? They are ready to stone me!" (Cried out - prayed; stone - hurt) **5.** The Lord told Moses, "Go ahead of the people with some elders of Israel. Take your staff—the one you used to strike the river—and go. (Elders - leaders) **6.** I will stand before you on the rock at Horeb; strike the rock, and water will flow for the people to drink." Moses did this in front of the elders. (Rock - large stone; Horeb - mountain) **7.** He named the place Massah and Meribah, because the Israelites argued and tested the Lord, asking, "Is the Lord with us or not?" **8.** Then Amalek came and fought against Israel at Rephidim. (Amalek - enemy tribe) **9.** Moses said to Joshua, "Choose some men and fight Amalek. Tomorrow I will stand on the hill with the staff of God." (Hill - high ground) **10.** Joshua fought Amalek as Moses had said, while Moses, Aaron, and Hur went up the hill. (Aaron - Moses' brother; Hur - Moses' helper) **11.** As long as Moses held up his hand, Israel won; but when he lowered his hand, Amalek won. **12.** Moses' hands grew tired, so they brought him a stone to sit on, and Aaron and Hur supported his hands, one on each side, until sunset. **13.** Joshua defeated Amalek and his army with the sword. **14.** The Lord told Moses, "Write this down as a reminder in the book and tell Joshua that I will completely erase the memory of Amalek from the earth." (Erase - destroy) **15.** Moses built an altar and named it "The-Lord-Is-My-Banner." (Altar - place of worship) **16.** He said, "The Lord has sworn to be at war with Amalek from generation to generation." (Sworn - promised)

Chapter 18

1. And Jethro, priest of Midian, and Moses' father-in-law, heard what God had done for Moses and Israel—how the Lord brought Israel out of Egypt. (Midian: a region) **2.** Jethro took Zipporah, Moses' wife, whom he had sent back, **3.** With her two sons: one named Gershom (meaning "stranger" in a foreign land), **4.** And the other named Eliezer (meaning "God helped me, saving me from Pharaoh's sword"). **5.** Jethro came to Moses in the wilderness, where he was camped near God's mountain, with his wife and sons. (God's mountain: Mount Sinai) **6.** Jethro told Moses, "I'm coming to you with your wife and sons." **7.** Moses went to meet him, bowed, and kissed him. They greeted each other, and then entered the tent. **8.** Moses shared all that the Lord had done for Israel, including the hardships and how God had delivered them. **9.** Jethro rejoiced for all the good God had done, rescuing Israel from Egypt. **10.** Jethro said, "Blessed is the Lord, who saved you from Egypt and Pharaoh, and rescued the people from their oppression." **11.** "Now I know the Lord is greater than all gods; in the very thing they boasted, He proved superior." **12.** Jethro offered a burnt offering and other sacrifices to God. (Burnt offering: sacrifice) Aaron and the elders of Israel joined Moses and Jethro to eat before God. (Aaron: Moses' brother) **13.** The next day, Moses sat to judge the people, who stood before him from morning to evening. **14.** Jethro saw this and asked, "Why do you alone sit, with all the people standing before you all day?" **15.** Moses replied, "The people come to me for guidance from God. **16.** When they have disputes, I judge between them and teach God's laws." **17.** Jethro said, "What you're doing isn't good. **18.** You and the people will wear yourselves out—this is too much for you to handle alone. **19.** Listen to my advice, and God will be with you: represent the people before God, bringing their problems to Him. **20.** Teach them God's laws and show them how to live and what work to do. **21.** Choose capable men who fear God, are honest, and hate bribes, to be leaders of thousands, hundreds, fifties, and tens. **22.** Let them judge smaller matters; bring the hard cases to you. This will make your work easier, as they'll share the burden. **23.** If you follow this advice, and God commands it, you will be able to endure, and the people will be at peace." **24.** Moses listened to Jethro's advice and did everything he suggested. **25.** Moses chose capable men from all Israel and made them leaders: rulers of thousands, hundreds, fifties, and tens. **26.** They judged the people at all times, bringing the difficult cases to Moses, but handling the smaller matters themselves. **27.** Moses sent Jethro away, and he returned to his own land.

Chapter 19

1. In the third month after Israel left Egypt, they arrived at the Wilderness of Sinai on the same day. (Wilderness of Sinai: desert area near mountain) **2.** They had left Rephidim and camped in the wilderness, near the mountain. (Rephidim: camping place) **3.** Moses went up to God, and the Lord called to him, saying, "Say this to the house of Jacob and the Israelites: **4.** 'You saw what I did to the Egyptians and how I carried you on eagles' wings and brought you to Me. (eagles' wings: helped you greatly) **5.** Now, if you obey My voice and keep My covenant, you will be a special treasure to Me above all nations; for all the earth is Mine. (Covenant: agreement) **6.** You will be a kingdom of priests and a holy nation.' These are the words you will speak to Israel." (Priests: servants of God, holy: set apart) **7.** Moses called the elders and told them all the Lord's commands. (Elders: leaders) **8.** The people responded, "We will do everything the Lord has spoken." Moses took their response to the Lord. **9.** The Lord said, "I will come to you in a thick cloud, so the people will hear and believe you forever." Moses relayed the message. (Thick cloud: dense fog) **10.** The Lord told Moses, "Go to the people and consecrate them today and tomorrow. Let them wash their clothes. (Consecrate: make holy) **11.** They must be ready by the third day, for on that day the Lord will come down on Mount Sinai for all to see. (Mount Sinai: mountain) **12.** Set boundaries around the mountain, saying, 'Be careful not to approach or touch the mountain. Anyone who does will die. (Boundaries: limits) **13.** They must not be touched, but will be stoned or shot with an arrow, whether man or beast; they will not survive. When the trumpet sounds long, the people may come near the mountain.'" (Stoned: killed by rocks, beast: animal) **14.** Moses went down, sanctified the people, and they washed their clothes. (Sanctified: made holy) **15.** He told them, "Be ready by the third day and avoid contact with your wives." (Contact with your wives: no sexual relations) **16.** On the third day, there were thunder, lightning, a thick cloud on the mountain, and a loud trumpet blast that made everyone tremble. (Thunder: loud sounds, lightning: flashes of light) **17.** Moses led the people to the mountain to meet God, and they stood at its base. **18.** Mount Sinai was covered in smoke because the Lord descended in fire. The smoke rose like a furnace, and the mountain trembled. (Mount Sinai: mountain, fire: fire came down, trembled: shook) **19.** As the trumpet blast grew louder, Moses spoke, and God answered him with a voice. **20.** The Lord came down to the top of Mount Sinai and called Moses up. Moses went up. **21.** The Lord said, "Warn the people not to break through and gaze at Me, or many will die. (break through: try to cross, gaze: look) **22.** Also, let the priests consecrate themselves, or I will break out against them. (Priests: servants of God, consecrate: make holy, break out: punish) **23.** Moses replied, "The people cannot come up to mount Sinai; You told us to set boundaries and consecrate it." (Mount Sinai: mountain, consecrate: make holy) **24.** The Lord said, "Go down and then bring Aaron up with you. But the priests and people must not break through, or I will break out against them." (Break out: punish) **25.** Moses went down and told the people.

Chapter 20

1. God spoke all these words, saying: **2.** "I am the Lord your God, who brought you out of Egypt, from a life of slavery. (Bondage: captivity, oppression) **3.** You must have no other gods besides Me. **4.** Do not make for yourselves an idol or any image of things in the sky, on the earth, or in the waters beneath. (idol: false god; water below: seas, oceans) **5.** Do not bow to or worship them, for I, the Lord your God, am a jealous God, punishing the children for the sins of their parents to the third and fourth generations of those who reject Me, (possessive: protective, demanding loyalty; paying back: punishing) **6.** but showing mercy to thousands of generations of those who love Me and obey My commands. (kindness: compassion, favor) **7.** You shall not misuse the name of the Lord your God. (Empty or disrespectful use: using God's name carelessly or falsely; guiltless: innocent, blameless) **8.** Remember the Sabbath day and keep it holy. (set apart for rest: dedicated for spiritual rest) **9.** Work for six days and do all your duties, **10.** but the seventh day is the Sabbath of the Lord your God. On that day, do not work—neither you, your children, your servants, your animals, nor any foreigners within your borders. (Strangers: foreigners, outsiders) **11.** For in six days the Lord created the heavens, the earth, the sea, and everything in them, and rested on the seventh day. That is why the Lord blessed the Sabbath and made it sacred. **12.** Honor your father and mother so that you may live long in the land the Lord is giving you. **13.** You shall not murder. **14.** You shall not commit adultery. (cheating: unfaithfulness in marriage) **15.** You shall not steal. **16.** You shall not give false testimony against your neighbor. (lie: speak untruths) **17.** You shall not covet your neighbor's house, wife, servants, animals, or anything else that belongs to your neighbor. (Desire wrongly: wanting what belongs to someone else) **18.** All the people witnessed the thunder, lightning, the sound of the trumpet, and the mountain smoking, and they were afraid, standing at a distance. (Mount Sinai: the mountain where God appeared to Moses and the Israelites) **19.** They said to Moses, "You speak to us, and we will listen, but do not let God speak to us, or we will die." **20.** Moses replied to the people, "Do not be afraid; God has come to test you, and to make sure His reverence remains before you so that you do not sin." (Try: test, examine) **21.** The people stood far off, but Moses went near the thick cloud where God was. (Cloud: symbol of God's presence) **22.** The Lord said to Moses, "Tell the Israelites: 'You have seen that I have spoken to you from heaven. **23.** Do not make gods of silver or gold to be with Me. **24.** You shall build an altar of earth for Me, and offer your burnt offerings and peace offerings, your sheep and oxen. Wherever I record My name, I will come to you and bless you. (Soil: dirt, earth) **25.** If you build an altar of stone, do not use cut stones; if you do, you have desecrated it. (Cut or carved: shaped by tools; desecrate: make unholy, violate) **26.** Do not make steps to My altar, so that your nakedness is not exposed." (Exposure: nakedness, vulnerability)

Chapter 21

1. "These are the laws you must present to them: **2.** if you buy a Hebrew servant, he serves six years; in the seventh, he is free with no payment. (Hebrew: Jewish person) **3.** If he comes alone, he leaves alone; if married, his wife leaves with him. **4.** If his master gave him a wife and she bore children, they belong to the master, and he leaves alone. **5.** But if he says, 'I love my master, wife, and children; I won't go free,' **6.** His master must bring him to the judges, pierce his ear, and he will serve forever. (Judges: legal authorities) **7.** If a man sells his daughter as a slave, she doesn't go free like male slaves. **8.** If her master doesn't like her, he must let her be redeemed; he cannot sell her to foreigners. (Redeemed: bought back) **9.** If he gives her to his son, she is treated as a daughter. **10.** If he marries another, he must not reduce her food, clothing, or rights. **11.** If he fails, she goes free without payment. **12.** Anyone who kills another must be put to death. **13.** But if it wasn't intentional, and God allowed it, a refuge city will be provided. (Refuge city: safe place to flee) **14.** If someone kills with premeditation, even at the altar, they must be put to death. (Premeditation: planning) **15.** Anyone who strikes their parents must be put to death. **16.** Kidnappers or those selling a person must be put to death. **17.** Anyone who curses their parents must be put to death. **18.** If men fight and one injures the other, but he recovers, **19.** The attacker is cleared but must pay for lost time and medical care. **20.** If a master beats a servant to death, he will be punished. **21.** If the servant survives a day or two, no punishment, as he is property. **22.** If men fight and harm a pregnant woman, causing premature birth but no injury, **23.** The offender must pay as the husband demands, and the judges decide. **24.** But if there's harm, then life for life, **25.** Eye for eye, tooth for tooth, hand for hand, foot for foot, **26.** Burn for burn, wound for wound, stripe for stripe. **27.** If a master injures his servant's eye, he must free him. **28.** If a servant's tooth is knocked out, he must be freed. **29.** If an ox kills a person, it must be stoned, and the owner is not punished. **30.** But if the ox had been known to gore and was not confined, both the ox and the owner are stoned. (Gore: attack with its horn) **31.** If money is required for the owner's life, he must pay what is set. **32.** If the ox kills a servant, the owner must pay 30 shekels of silver, and the ox is stoned. (Shekel: ancient currency) **33.** If a man digs a pit and doesn't cover it, and an animal falls in, **34.** The pit owner must pay for the animal but keep the carcass. (Carcass: body) **35.** If one ox kills another, the owners sell both and divide the money. **36.** But if the ox had a history of goring and wasn't contained, the owner must pay ox for ox. (Goring: past attacks)

Chapter 22

1. If a man steals an ox or a sheep, and kills or sells it, he must restore five oxen for one ox, and four sheep for one sheep. **2.** If the thief is caught breaking in and is struck so that he dies, there is no guilt for his death. **3.** If it happens after sunrise, there is guilt for his bloodshed. He must repay fully; if he has nothing, he shall be sold for his theft. **4.** If the stolen animal (ox, donkey, or sheep) is found alive in his hand, he must restore double. **5.** If a man lets his animal graze in another's field or vineyard, he must repay from the best of his own crops. **6.** If a fire breaks out and consumes crops or a field, the one who started the fire must make full restitution. **7.** If a man gives money or goods to a neighbor to keep, and they are stolen, the thief must repay double if found. **8.** If the thief is not found, the homeowner must appear before the judges to see if he took the goods. **9.** For any trespass, whether it involves an ox, donkey, sheep, clothing, or lost property, the issue shall be brought before the judges; the guilty party must repay double. **10.** If a man gives a neighbor a donkey, ox, sheep, or any animal to keep, and it dies, is injured, or goes missing without witnesses, **11.** Both must swear an oath that no theft occurred; the owner shall accept the oath and not demand repayment. **12.** If it is stolen, the one who kept it must repay the owner. **13.** If it is torn by a beast, he must bring the remains as proof, and no restitution is required. **14.** If a man borrows an item and it is damaged or dies while the owner is not present, he must repay. **15.** If the owner is present, no repayment is necessary; if it was rented, no repayment is due. **16.** If a man seduces an unmarried virgin and sleeps with her, he must pay the bride-price and marry her. **17.** If her father refuses to give her to him, the man must pay the bride-price for virgins. **18.** You shall not allow a sorceress to live. (Sorceress: female witch or magic worker) **19.** Anyone who has sexual relations with an animal must be put to death. **20.** Anyone who sacrifices to any god except the Lord must be destroyed. (Lord: God of Israel) **21.** Do not mistreat or oppress a stranger, for you were strangers in Egypt. (Egypt: land of captivity for Israel) **22.** Do not afflict a widow or an orphan. (Widow: woman whose husband has died; orphan: child without parents) **23.** If you afflict them and they cry out to Me, I will hear their cry; **24.** My anger will burn, and I will kill you with the sword; your wives will be widows, and your children will be fatherless. **25.** If you lend money to the poor among you, do not charge interest. (Interest: extra payment for borrowing money) **26.** If you take your neighbor's garment as a pledge, return it before sunset. (Pledge: something given as security for a loan)**27.** It is his only covering, his garment for warmth. If he cries to Me, I will hear, for I am gracious. **28.** Do not revile God, nor curse a ruler of your people. (revile: speak disrespectfully) **29.** Do not delay offering the first of your produce or juice. The firstborn of your sons you shall give to Me. (produce: crops, fruits) **30.** Do the same with your oxen and sheep; let them stay with their mother for seven days, then give them to Me. **31.** You shall be holy to Me; do not eat meat torn by beasts; throw it to the dogs. (beasts : wild animals)

Chapter 23

1. "Do not spread false reports. Do not join the wicked to be an unjust witness. **2.** Do not follow the crowd to do evil, or pervert justice in a dispute. (Pervert: twist) **3.** Do not show favoritism to the poor in a legal matter. **4.** If you find your enemy's ox or donkey lost, return it to him. **5.** If you see your enemy's donkey struggling, help him. **6.** Do not distort justice for the poor in their dispute. (Distort: change unfairly) **7.** Stay away from false matters; do not kill the innocent. I will not acquit the guilty. (Acquit: declare innocent) **8.** Do not take bribes, as they blind judgment and corrupt the righteous. (Corrupt: change wrongly) **9.** Do not oppress strangers, for you know their hearts, having been strangers in Egypt. (Oppress: treat unfairly) **10.** "Work the land for six years and gather its produce, **11.** But in the seventh year, let it rest so the poor may eat, and wild animals may feed on what remains. Do the same with your vineyard and olive grove. **12.** Work for six days; on the seventh day, rest, so that your animals and servants may also rest. **13.** be careful to follow all I have said, and do not mention other gods. **14.** "Hold three feasts a year for Me: **15.** The Feast of Unleavened Bread (eat unleavened bread for seven days in the month of Abib, when you left Egypt; do not appear before Me empty-handed), **16.** the Feast of Harvest (celebrate the firstfruits of your labor), and the Feast of Ingathering (at year's end, when you gather your crops). **17.** Three times a year, all your men must appear before Me, the Lord. **18.** Do not offer My sacrifice with leavened bread, and do not keep the fat of My sacrifice until morning. (Leavened: yeast) **19.** Bring the first of your crops into the house of the Lord. Do not boil a young goat in its mother's milk. **20.** "I will send an Angel to guide you to the place I have prepared. **21.** Obey Him and do not provoke Him, for He will not forgive your sins; My name is in Him. (Provoke: anger) **22.** If you obey Him and follow My commands, I will be an enemy to your enemies. **23.** My Angel will lead you to defeat the Amorites, Hittites, Perizzites, Canaanites, Hivites, and Jebusites; and I will destroy them. **24.** Do not worship their gods, nor follow their ways; destroy their idols and pillars. **25.** Serve the Lord, and He will bless your food and water, and remove sickness from you. **26.** No one will miscarry or be barren, and I will fulfill your lifespan. (Miscarry: lose pregnancy, barren: unable to have children, fulfill: complete) **27.** I will send fear before you, causing confusion among your enemies, and they will flee from you. **28.** I will send hornets to drive out the Hivites, Canaanites, and Hittites. **29.** I will not drive them all out in one year, or the land will become desolate. (Desolate: empty) **30.** Little by little, I will drive them out as you grow in number and inherit the land. (Inherit: take possession of) **31.** I will set your borders from the Red Sea to the Philistine Sea and from the desert to the Euphrates River. (Borders: boundaries, Euphrates River: major river in the Middle East) You will conquer the land and drive out its inhabitants. **32.** Do not make covenants with them or their gods. (Covenants: agreements) **33.** Do not let them stay in your land, or they will lead you to sin by serving their gods. It will be a trap for you. (trap: snare)

Chapter 24
1. The Lord said to Moses, "Come up to Me, you, Aaron, Nadab, Abihu, and seventy of Israel's elders, and worship from a distance." (Worship: show reverence) **2.** Only Moses is to come near; the others must stay behind, and the people should not approach. **3.** Moses told the people all the Lord's commands and laws, and they replied with one voice, "We will do everything the Lord has commanded." (Laws: rules) **4.** Moses wrote down all the Lord's instructions, and then built an altar at the base of the mountain, along with twelve pillars representing the twelve tribes of Israel. (Altar: a place for offerings) **5.** He sent young men of Israel to offer burnt and peace offerings of oxen to the Lord. (Offerings: gifts to God) **6.** Moses took half the blood, placing it in bowls, and sprinkled the other half on the altar. (Basins: bowls) **7.** Moses read aloud the Book of the Covenant to the people, and they responded, "We will do everything the Lord has commanded." (Covenant: agreement) **8.** Moses sprinkled the blood on the people, declaring, "This is the blood of the covenant that the Lord has made with you, based on these words." **9.** Moses, Aaron, Nadab, Abihu, and seventy elders ascended the mountain, **10.** And they saw the God of Israel. Under His feet was a pavement of sapphire, as clear as the sky. (Sapphire: precious blue stone) **11.** He did not strike down the leaders of Israel, and they ate and drank in His presence. (Leaders: elders) **12.** The Lord spoke to Moses, saying, "Come up to the mountain and remain there. I will give you stone tablets with the law and commands to teach the people." (Tablets: stone plates) **13.** Moses, accompanied by his assistant Joshua, went up the mountain of God. (Joshua: Moses' helper) **14.** Moses instructed the elders, "Stay here until we return. Aaron and Hur are with you, and they can help with any issues." (Hur: a leader) **15.** Moses ascended, and a cloud covered the mountain. **16.** The Lord's glory rested on Mount Sinai, and the cloud covered it for six days. On the seventh day, the Lord called Moses from the cloud. (Glory: God's presence) (Sinai: mountain where Moses met God) **17.** The appearance of the Lord's glory was like a consuming fire on the mountaintop, visible to all the people of Israel. (Fire: burning light) **18.** Moses entered the cloud and climbed the mountain, where he stayed for forty days and forty nights. (Cloud: God's presence)

Chapter 25
1. Then the Lord spoke to Moses: **2.** "Tell the Israelites to bring an offering. Take My offering from those who give willingly. **3.** The offering is to include: gold, silver, and bronze; **4.** blue, purple, and scarlet yarn, fine linen, and goats' hair; **5.** ram skins dyed red, badger skins, and acacia wood; **6.** oil for the light, spices for anointing oil, and sweet incense; **7.** onyx stones and stones for the ephod and breastplate. **8.** Let them build Me a sanctuary, so I can dwell among them. **9.** Make it according to the pattern I show you for the tabernacle and its furnishings. **10.** "Make an ark of acacia wood: 2½ cubits long, 1½ cubits wide, and 1½ cubits high. (Ark: chest) **11.** Overlay it with pure gold inside and out, and make a gold molding around it. **12.** Cast four gold rings and put them at the four corners—two on each side. **13.** Make poles of acacia wood and cover them with gold. **14.** Insert the poles into the rings, so the ark can be carried. **15.** The poles must stay in the rings and never be removed. **16.** Place the Testimony inside the ark. (Testimony: law) **17.** "Make a mercy seat of pure gold: 2½ cubits long, 1½ cubit wide. (Mercy seat : cover) **18.** Make two cherubim of hammered gold, one at each end of the mercy seat. (cherubim: angel-like figures) **19.** The cherubim should be of one piece with the mercy seat, at both ends. **20.** The cherubim must spread their wings over the mercy seat, facing each other. **21.** Place the mercy seat on top of the ark, and put the Testimony inside it. **22.** There I will meet with you and speak to you from above the mercy seat, between the cherubim, about My commands to Israel. **23.** "Make a table of acacia wood: 2 cubits long, 1 cubit wide, and 1½ cubits high. (table : altar) **24.** Overlay it with pure gold and make a gold molding around it. **25.** Make a frame of a handbreadth around it, and a gold molding for the frame. (frame: border) **26.** Make four gold rings and place them on the four corners of the table. **27.** The rings should be close to the frame, for the poles to carry the table. **28.** Make poles of acacia wood and overlay them with gold, so the table can be carried. **29.** Make its dishes, pans, pitchers, and bowls for pouring, all of pure gold. **30.** Always place the showbread on the table before Me. (showbread : bread for offering) **31.** "Make a lampstand of pure gold, hammered into one piece. Its shaft, branches, bowls, knobs, and flowers should all be one piece. (lampstand : candlestick) **32.** Six branches will come out: three on one side, and three on the other. **33.** Each branch will have three almond-shaped bowls, with a knob and flower. **34.** The lampstand itself will have four almond-shaped bowls with knobs and flowers. **35.** There will be a knob under each pair of branches, in total six knobs. **36.** The knobs and branches will be of one piece, all hammered from pure gold. **37.** Make seven lamps, and arrange them to shine in front of the lampstand. **38.** Make wick-trimmers and trays of pure gold. (wick-trimmers : scissors for wicks) **39.** The entire lampstand, with all its utensils, will weigh a talent of pure gold. (talent: a unit of weight) **40.** Make them according to the pattern shown to you on the mountain. (mountain: Mount Sinai)

Chapter 26
1. "Make the tabernacle with ten curtains of fine linen, and blue, purple, and scarlet thread, woven with cherubim designs." (Cherubim: angelic beings, designs: patterns) **2.** "Each curtain shall be 28 cubits long and 4 cubits wide; all curtains shall be the same size." (Cubits: unit of length) **3.** "Join five curtains together, and the other five in the same way." **4.** "Make blue loops on the edge of one set, and do the same on the other set." **5.** "Make 50 loops on the edge of one curtain, and 50 loops on the edge of the other set, to clasp them together." (Clasped: fastened) **6.** "Make 50 gold clasps to fasten the curtains, so that they form one tabernacle." (Clasps: fasteners, tabernacle: sacred tent) **7.** "Make curtains of goats' hair to cover the tabernacle; 11 curtains in total." (Goats' hair: coarse fabric) **8.** "Each curtain shall be 30 cubits long and 4 cubits wide; all curtains will be the same size." **9.** "Join five curtains together, and six curtains together, folding the sixth over the front of the tent." **10.** "Make 50 loops on the edge of the outer curtain in one set, and 50 loops on the other set." **11.** "Make 50 bronze clasps to fasten the curtains, so that they form one tent." (Bronze: a metal alloy) **12.** "The remaining half curtain shall hang over the back of the tabernacle." **13.** "One cubit on each side of the remaining curtain shall hang over the sides of the tabernacle." (Cubit: unit of length) **14.** "Make a covering of red

ram skins for the tent, and a covering of badger skins above that." (Badger: animal skin) **15.** "Make boards of acacia wood for the tabernacle, standing upright." (Acacia: a type of tree) **16.** "Each board shall be 10 cubits long and 1.5 cubits wide." **17.** "Each board shall have two tenons to bind them together." (Tenons: projecting parts of wood for joining) **18.** "Make 20 boards for the south side of the tabernacle." (south side: one of the four sides of the tabernacle) **19.** "Make 40 silver sockets for the 20 boards, two sockets under each board." (Sockets: base holders)**20.** "For the north side, make 20 boards with 40 silver sockets, two under each board." (North side: one of the four sides of the tabernacle)**21.** "For the far side of the tabernacle, to the west, make six boards." (West: direction toward the setting sun)**22.** "Make two boards for the back corners of the tabernacle." **23.** "They shall be joined at the bottom and top with one ring, for both corners." (Ring: circular connector)**24.** "There shall be eight boards with 16 silver sockets, two sockets under each board." **25.** "Make five bars of acacia wood for the boards on one side of the tabernacle." (bars: horizontal rods) **26.** "Make five bars for the boards on the other side, and five bars for the west side." (west side: direction toward the setting sun) **27.** "The middle bar shall pass through the boards from end to end." **28.** "Overlay the boards with gold, and make gold rings to hold the bars, overlaying the bars with gold." (Overlay: cover with a layer) **29.** "Raise up the tabernacle according to the pattern shown on the mountain." (mountain: refers to Mount Sinai, the place where Moses received instructions) **30.** "Make a veil of blue, purple, and scarlet thread, with cherubim designs." **31.** "Hang it on four acacia pillars, overlaid with gold, with gold hooks on four silver sockets." (pillars: upright supports) **32.** "Hang the veil from the clasps, and bring the Ark of the Testimony behind it. The veil will separate the Holy from the Most Holy." (Ark of the Testimony: sacred chest containing the Ten Commandments) **33.** "Place the mercy seat on the Ark of the Testimony, in the Most Holy Place." (mercy seat: covering of the Ark, symbolizing God's presence) **34.** "Set the table outside the veil, and place the lampstand across from the table, on the south side." (south side: one of the four sides of the tabernacle) **35.** "Make a screen for the door of the tabernacle, woven with blue, purple, and scarlet thread." **36.** "Make five pillars of acacia wood for the screen, overlay them with gold, and cast five bronze sockets for them." (acacia: type of wood, bronze: alloy of copper and tin) **37.** "Place the screen on the pillars, and overlay them with gold; the hooks shall be gold, and the sockets bronze."

Chapter 27
1. "Make an altar of acacia wood, five cubits long and wide—square in shape—and three cubits high. (Cubits: measurement, acacia: type of wood) **2.** Create four horns at its corners, one piece with the altar, and overlay it with bronze. (Horns: projections overlay: cover) **3.** Make pans for ashes, shovels, basins, forks, and fire pans, all of bronze. (Pans: containers, basins: shallow bowls) **4.** Make a bronze grate for it, with four rings at the corners. (Grate: metal framework) **5.** Place the grate under the altar rim, midway up. (Rim: edge) **6.** Make poles of acacia wood and overlay them with bronze. (Poles: long rods) **7.** Insert the poles into the rings and use them to carry the altar. (Insert: put in) **8.** Construct it hollow with boards, as shown to you on the mountain. (Hollow: empty inside, boards: flat pieces of wood) **9.** "Build the court of the tabernacle with hangings of fine linen, one hundred cubits long on the south side. (Court: open area, hangings: fabric walls) **10.** The twenty pillars and sockets will be bronze, with silver hooks and bands. (Pillars: supporting posts, sockets: bases)**11.** Similarly, on the north side, one hundred cubits of hangings, twenty pillars with bronze sockets, and silver hooks and bands. (North side: one direction of the tabernacle)**12.** On the west side, fifty cubits of hangings, with ten pillars and ten sockets. (West side: one direction of the tabernacle)**13.** On the east side, also fifty cubits. (east side: one direction of the tabernacle) **14.** The hangings by the gate will be fifteen cubits, with three pillars and three sockets. (Gate: entrance) **15.** The opposite side will also have fifteen cubits, with three pillars and three sockets. **16.** "The gate screen will be twenty cubits long, woven with blue, purple, and scarlet thread, and fine linen, made by a weaver. It will have four pillars and four sockets. (Screen: fabric barrier, woven: interlaced threads) **17.** All the pillars around the court will have silver bands, silver hooks, and bronze sockets. (Bands: rings, hooks: metal fasteners)**18.** The court will be one hundred cubits long, fifty cubits wide, and five cubits high, made of fine linen with bronze sockets. (Court: open space) **19.** All the utensils of the tabernacle, including pegs for the tabernacle and court, will be bronze. (Utensils: tools, pegs: stakes to hold things)**20.** "Command the Israelites to bring pure olive oil for the light, to keep the lamp burning continuously. (olive oil: oil from olives, continuously: without stopping) **21.** Aaron and his sons will tend it from evening to morning, outside the veil in the Tabernacle, as a permanent ordinance for Israel." (Veil: curtain separating the holy areas, tend: care for, ordinance: rule)

Chapter 28
1. "Take Aaron, your brother, and his sons from Israel, to serve as priests: Aaron and his sons Nadab, Abihu, Eleazar, and Ithamar. **2.** Make holy garments for Aaron for glory and beauty. (Glory: greatness; beauty: attractiveness) **3.** Tell all skilled artisans, filled with wisdom, to make Aaron's garments to consecrate him as priest. (Artisans: craftsmen; wisdom: knowledge; consecrate: set apart as sacred) **4.** They shall make a breastplate, ephod, robe, tunic, turban, and sash for Aaron and his sons, for priestly service. (Breastplate: chest piece; ephod: sacred vestment; turban: head covering) **5.** Use gold, blue, purple, scarlet thread, and fine linen. (Linen: thin, woven fabric) **6.** The ephod shall be made of these materials, skillfully worked. (Skillfully worked: crafted) **7.** It will have two shoulder straps joined at the edges. **8.** The ephod's band shall be made of the same materials. (Band: belt) **9.** Take two onyx stones and engrave the names of Israel's sons on them. (Onyx: precious stones; engrave: carve) **10.** Six names on one stone, six on the other, in birth order. **11.** Engrave them like signet engravings, and set them in gold. (Signet: seal) **12.** Place the stones on the ephod's shoulders as memorials, so Aaron can carry the names before the Lord. (Memorials: reminders) **13.** Make gold settings for the stones. (Settings: frames) **14.** Make two pure gold chains like braided cords and attach them to the settings. (Chains: links) **15.** Make the breastplate of judgment, woven like the ephod, with the same materials. (Breastplate: chest piece; judgment: decision-making) **16.** It shall be square, a span in length and width. (Square: having equal sides) **17.** Set four rows of stones: sardius, topaz, and emerald in the first row; **18.** turquoise, sapphire, and diamond in the second; **19.** Jacinth, agate, and amethyst in the third; **20.** Beryl, onyx, and jasper in the fourth, all in gold settings. (sardius: ruby; turquoise: blue-green stone; sapphire: blue stone; jacinth: purple stone; agate: multicolored stone; amethyst: purple stone; beryl: green stone; onyx: striped stone; jasper: multicolored stone) **21.** The stones shall bear the names of Israel's twelve tribes, like signet engravings. (Tribes: family groups; signet: seal) **22.** Make braided gold chains for the breastplate. (Braided: woven) **23.** Make two rings of gold for the breastplate, one at each end. **24.** Attach the two gold braided chains to the rings. **25.** Attach the other ends of the chains to the ephod's shoulder straps. **26.** Make two more gold rings, placing them on the inner edge of the breastplate. **27.** Make two gold rings for the shoulder straps, near the front seams. **28.** Bind the breastplate to the ephod with a blue cord, ensuring it doesn't come loose. (Bind: tie; cord: string) **29.** Aaron shall carry the names on the breastplate over his heart, as a memorial before the Lord. (Memorial: reminder) **30.** Place the Urim and Thummim in the breastplate to guide Aaron in judgment. (Urim and Thummim: objects for divine decision) **31.** Make the robe of the ephod entirely blue. **32.** The robe shall have a head opening, reinforced to prevent tearing. **33.** Attach blue, purple, and scarlet pomegranates to the robe's hem, with golden bells

between. (Pomegranates: fruit-shaped designs) **34.** Alternate golden bells and pomegranates around the hem. **35.** The bells will be heard when Aaron enters the holy place, so he won't die. (Holy place: sanctuary) **36.** Make a pure gold plate, engraved with "HOLINESS TO THE LORD." **37.** Attach it to a blue cord, and place it on Aaron's turban. (Turban: headband) **38.** It shall be on his forehead so Aaron can bear the iniquity of Israel's holy offerings and be accepted before the Lord. (Iniquity: sin) **39.** Weave a fine linen tunic, turban, and sash. **40.** For Aaron's sons, make tunics, sashes, and hats for glory and beauty. (Glory: greatness; beauty: attractiveness) **41.** Dress Aaron and his sons, anoint and consecrate them to serve as priests. (Anoint: set apart with oil; consecrate: make sacred) **42.** Make linen trousers to cover their nakedness, from waist to thighs. (Nakedness: private parts) **43.** These shall be worn by Aaron and his sons when they enter the tabernacle or altar, to prevent sin and death. This law is permanent for them and their descendants. (Tabernacle: holy tent; permanent: forever)

Chapter 29

1. "This is what you shall do to consecrate them for serving Me as priests: Take one young bull and two flawless rams," (consecrate: set apart) **2.** "And unleavened bread, unleavened cakes mixed with oil, and unleavened wafers anointed with oil (make them from wheat flour)." **3.** "Put them in one basket with the bull and two rams." **4.** "Bring Aaron and his sons to the tabernacle's entrance and wash them with water." (Tabernacle: meeting place) **5.** "Dress Aaron in the tunic, ephod robe, ephod, and breastplate, and fasten the woven band of the ephod around him." (Ephod: priestly garment) **6.** "Place the turban on his head and the holy crown on it." (Turban: headpiece) **7.** "Pour anointing oil on Aaron's head and anoint him." (Anoint: set apart for holy use) **8.** "Dress his sons in tunics." **9.** "Belt Aaron and his sons with sashes and put hats on them. The priesthood will be theirs forever. Consecrate them." (Consecrate: make holy) **10.** "Bring the bull to the tabernacle entrance, and Aaron and his sons shall lay their hands on its head." **11.** "Slay the bull before the Lord at the tabernacle entrance." (slay: kill) **12.** "Place some of the bull's blood on the altar's horns and pour the rest beside the altar's base." **13.** "Take the fat covering the intestines, the liver's fat, and the kidneys' fat, and burn them on the altar." **14.** "Burn the bull's flesh, skin, and offal outside the camp; it is a sin offering." (Offal: waste parts) **15.** "Take one ram, and Aaron and his sons shall lay their hands on its head." **16.** "Slay the ram; sprinkle its blood around the altar." **17.** "Cut the ram into pieces, wash its intestines and legs, and then place them with its pieces and head." **18.** "Burn the whole ram on the altar. It is a burnt offering, a pleasing aroma to the Lord." **19.** "Take the other ram, and Aaron and his sons shall lay their hands on its head." **20.** "Kill the ram and place some blood on Aaron and his sons' right ear tips, right thumbs, and right big toes, and sprinkle blood around the altar." **21.** "Take some altar blood and anointing oil; sprinkle it on Aaron, his garments, and his sons, consecrating them." (Consecrating: making holy) **22.** "Take the fat of the ram, the fat tail, liver, kidneys, right thigh, one loaf, one oil cake, and one wafer from the unleavened bread," (right thigh: portion for consecration) **23.** "Place them in Aaron and his sons' hands, and wave them before the Lord." **24.** "Take them back and burn them on the altar as a burnt offering, a sweet aroma to the Lord." **25.** "Take the breast of the ram of Aaron's consecration and wave it before the Lord; it shall be your portion." **26.** "Consecrate the breast and thigh from the ram of consecration for Aaron and his sons." (Consecrate: set apart) **27.** "It shall be a heave offering for Aaron and his sons from the children of Israel, from their peace offerings." (Heave offering: offering lifted up) **28.** "Aaron's holy garments will be passed to his sons after him to be consecrated in them." (Consecrated: set apart) **29.** "The son who becomes priest will wear them for seven days when entering the tabernacle to minister." (Tabernacle: meeting place) **30.** "Boil the consecration ram's flesh in the holy place." (Holy place: sacred area) **31.** "Aaron and his sons shall eat the ram's flesh and bread at the tabernacle entrance." **32.** "They shall eat what consecrated them, but no outsider may eat them, for they are holy." **33.** "If any remains until morning, burn it; it must not be eaten as it is holy." **34.** "Follow all these instructions for seven days to consecrate Aaron and his sons." (Consecrate: make holy) **35.** "Offer a bull every day as a sin offering for atonement, cleansing and anointing the altar to sanctify it." (Atonement: payment for sin) **36.** "Make atonement for the altar for seven days, and it will be most holy." **37.** "Whatever touches the altar must be holy." **38.** "Offer two lambs, one each day, continually." **39.** "Offer one lamb in the morning and the other at twilight." **40.** "With the morning lamb, offer one-tenth ephah of flour, a fourth hin of oil, and a fourth hin of wine." (Ephah: measure, hin: measure) **41.** "Offer the evening lamb with the same grain and drink offering, a sweet aroma to the Lord." **42.** "This continual burnt offering is for all generations at the tabernacle entrance, where I will meet you." (tabernacle: meeting place) **43.** "There I will meet the Israelites, and the tabernacle will be sanctified by My glory." (sanctified: made holy) **44.** "I will consecrate the tabernacle and altar, and Aaron and his sons will minister to Me as priests." (consecrate: set apart, minister: serve) **45.** "I will dwell among the Israelites and be their God." (dwell: live) **46.** "They shall know that I am the Lord their God, who brought them out of Egypt to dwell among them. I am the Lord their God." (Egypt: land of slavery)

Chapter 30

1. "You shall make an altar to burn incense on; it shall be made of acacia wood. (Acacia wood – wood from a tree) **2.** Its length and width shall each be one cubit, and its height shall be two cubits. Its horns shall be part of the altar. (Cubit – a unit of measurement, about 18 inches) **3.** Cover its top, sides, and horns with pure gold, and make a gold molding around it. (Molding – a decorative edge) **4.** Make two gold rings for it under the molding on both sides; these will hold the poles. (Poles – long rods used to carry the altar) **5.** Make the poles of acacia wood, covered with gold. (Acacia wood – wood from a tree) **6.** Place the altar before the veil, in front of the ark of the Testimony, where I will meet with you. (Ark of the Testimony – the chest containing the tablets of the law; veil – curtain separating areas in the temple) **7.** Aaron shall burn sweet incense on it every morning, when he tends the lamps. (Aaron – brother of Moses, high priest) **8.** He shall also burn incense at twilight, a perpetual offering to the Lord. (Twilight – the time just before night) **9.** Do not offer strange incense, burnt offerings, grain offerings, or drink offerings on it. (Strange incense – incense not prescribed by God) **10.** Aaron shall make atonement on its horns once a year with the blood of the sin offering; it is most holy to the Lord. (Atonement – reconciliation for sins) **11.** Then the Lord spoke to Moses, saying: (Moses – leader of Israel) **12.** "When you take a census of Israel, every man shall give a ransom to the Lord to avoid a plague. (Census – a count of people; plague – a deadly disease) **13.** Each person shall give half a shekel (about 10 grams), as an offering to the Lord. (Shekel – a unit of currency, about 10 grams of silver) **14.** Those aged 20 and above shall give this offering. (Aged 20 and above – those who are 20 years old or older) **15.** The rich shall not give more, nor the poor less, than half a shekel for atonement. (Atonement – reconciliation for sins) **16.** Use the atonement money for the service of the tabernacle, as a memorial to the Lord. (Tabernacle – a portable sanctuary or tent of meeting) **17.** Then the Lord spoke to Moses, saying: (Moses – leader of Israel) **18.** "Make a bronze laver (basin) with a bronze base for washing, and place it between the tabernacle and the altar. (Laver – a large basin for washing) **19.** Aaron and his sons shall wash their hands and feet in it. (Aaron – brother of Moses, high priest) **20.** When entering the tabernacle or approaching the altar, they must wash to avoid death. (Tabernacle – a portable sanctuary or tent of meeting) **21.** This shall be a lasting statute for them and their descendants. (Statute – a law or rule) **22.** The Lord spoke to Moses, saying: (Moses – leader of Israel) **23.** "Take 500 shekels of myrrh, 250 shekels of cinnamon, 250 shekels of cane, **24.** And 500 shekels of cassia, along with a hin (about 5 liters) of olive oil. (Myrrh – a resin used in perfumes; Cinnamon – a spice; Cassia – a spice similar to cinnamon) **25.** Make holy anointing oil from these, as an ointment according to the perfumer's craft. (Anointing **oil** – oil used to consecrate or make things holy) **26.** Use it to anoint the tabernacle, the ark of the Testimony, (Ark of the Testimony – the chest containing the tablets of the law) **27.** The table and its utensils, the lampstand and its utensils, and the altar of incense; (Table – the table for showbread in the tabernacle; Lampstand – a stand for the sacred lamps) **28.** the altar of burnt offering, its utensils, and the laver with its base. (Laver – a large basin for washing) **29.** Consecrate them, so they may be most holy. Whatever touches them shall be holy. (Consecrate – to make something sacred or holy) **30.** Anoint Aaron and his sons to consecrate them as priests. (Aaron – brother of Moses, high priest) **31.** This anointing oil shall be holy to you for all generations. (Anointing oil – oil used to consecrate or make things holy) **32.** It shall not be poured on ordinary people or made in a similar way. It is holy and must be treated as holy. (Ordinary people – anyone not set apart for holy purposes) **33.** Anyone who makes or uses it improperly shall be cut off from the people. (Cut off – to be excluded or cast out) **34.** The Lord said to Moses: "Take sweet spices—stacte, onycha, galbanum, and frankincense—in equal amounts. (Stacte – a gum resin; Onycha – a spice from a shell; Galbanum – a resin used in incense) **35.** Make compound incense, according to the perfumer's craft, salted, pure, and holy. (Compound incense – incense mixed from different ingredients) **36.** Grind some fine, and place it before the Testimony in the tabernacle where I will meet you. It shall be most holy. (Tabernacle – a portable sanctuary or tent of meeting; Testimony – the tablets of the law in the ark) **37.** Do not make incense like it for yourselves. It is holy to the Lord. (Incense – aromatic substance burned for fragrance) **38.** Whoever makes it for personal use shall be cut off from the people. (Cut off – to be excluded or cast out)

Chapter 31

1. The Lord spoke to Moses, saying, **2.** "I've chosen Bezalel, the son of Uri, the son of Hur, from the lineage of Judah. (Bezalel, a professed handworker) **3.** I've filled him with the Spirit of God, giving him wisdom, understanding, knowledge, and all kinds of artificer. (Artificer skill in work) **4.** He'll be suitable to design and produce cultural pieces, working with gold, tableware, and citation, **5.** Cutting precious monuments for setting, sculpturing wood, and making all kinds of cultural creations. (Artificer skill in work) **6.** I've also appointed Aholiab, the son of Ahisamach, from the lineage of Dan, to help him. I've filled the hearts of all the professed workers with wisdom so that they can produce everything I've commanded you, **7.** the temple, the ark of the Testimony, the mercy seat, and all the temple's furnishings— **8.** the table and its accessories, the pure gold lampstand with all its corridor, the balcony of incense, **9.** The balcony of burnt immolations and its tools, and the laver with its base— (laver, large receptacle for washing) **10.** The clerkly garments, the holy blankets for Aaron the clerk, and the garments for his sons, to serve as preachers, **11.** As well as the anointing oil painting and the sweet incense for the holy place. Everything will be made according to My commands." **12.** Also, the Lord spoke to Moses, saying, **13.** "Tell the Israelites: You must observe My Sabbaths, as it'll be a sign between you and Me for all generations, so that you'll know that I'm the Lord who makes you holy. (Makes you holy, sanctifies you) **14.** You shall keep the Sabbath, for it's holy to you. Anyone who violates it shall be put to death; anyone who works on it shall be cut off from their people. **15.** Work may be done for six days, but the seventh day is the Sabbath of rest, holy to the Lord. Whoever does any work on the Sabbath day must be put to death. **16.** The Israelites must keep the Sabbath, observing it as a lasting covenant. (Lasting covenant, ongoing agreement) **17.** It'll be a sign ever between Me and the people of Israel, for in six days the Lord made the welkin and the earth, and on the seventh day He rested and was refreshed.'" **18.** When God finished speaking with Moses on Mount Sinai, (Mount Sinai, the mountain where God gave Moses the law) He gave Moses two gravestone tablets, the tablets of the Testimony, written by the cutlet of God.

Chapter 32

1. Now when the people saw that Moses delayed, they gathered to Aaron and said, "Make us gods to lead us; we don't know what happened to Moses." **2.** Aaron said, "Take off the gold earrings from your wives, sons, and daughters, and bring them to me." **3.** The people took off the gold earrings and gave them to Aaron. **4.** Aaron melted the gold, shaped it, and made a calf. They said, "This is your god, Israel, who brought you out of Egypt!" **5.** Aaron built an altar before it and proclaimed, "Tomorrow is a feast to the Lord." **6.** The next day, they offered burnt offerings, ate, drank, and danced. **7.** The Lord told Moses, "Go down! Your people have corrupted themselves." **8.** They quickly turned from My commands, made a calf, worshiped it, and sacrificed to it, saying, 'This is your god, Israel, who brought you out of Egypt!' **9.** The Lord said, "I see this people; they are stubborn (stiff-necked: proud, rebellious)." **10.** "Let Me be, that My anger may burn and consume them, and I will make you a great nation." **11.** Moses pleaded, "Lord, why should Your anger burn against Your people, whom You rescued with great power (strength: might)?" **12.** "Why should the Egyptians say, 'He brought them out to kill them in the mountains (Sinai: the mountain where Moses received God's laws)?' Turn from Your wrath and spare them." **13.** "Remember Abraham, Isaac, and Israel (Jacob: ancestor of Israel - God's chosen people), Your servants, to whom You promised to multiply their descendants and give them this land forever." **14.** The Lord relented and did not bring the disaster He had planned. **15.** Moses went down with the tablets, written on both sides, the work of God. **16.** The tablets were engraved (carved: cut into) by God. **17.** Joshua heard the noise and said to Moses, "It sounds like war!" **18.** Moses replied, "It's not victory or defeat, but the sound of singing." **19.** When Moses saw the calf and the dancing, his anger burned. He threw down the tablets and broke them at the foot of the mountain (Sinai: the mountain where Moses received God's laws). **20.** He burned the calf, ground it to powder, scattered it in the water, and made the people drink it. **21.** Moses asked Aaron, "What did this people do to you to bring such a great sin on them?" **22.** Aaron said, "Don't be angry! You know they are prone (tend: likely) to evil." **23.** They told me to make gods since they didn't know what happened to Moses. **24.** I told them to give me their gold. I threw it in the fire, and the calf came out." **25.** Moses saw the people were out of control (unrestrained: not under control), for Aaron had allowed it, causing shame among their enemies. **26.** Moses stood at the camp's entrance and said, "Who is on the Lord's side? Come to me." The Levites (tribe of Israel: descendants of Levi, one of the twelve tribes of Israel) gathered. **27.** He said, "The Lord commands: 'Take your swords, go through the camp, and kill those who have sinned.'" **28.** The Levites obeyed, and about 3,000 men died that day. **29.** Moses said, "Consecrate yourselves (set yourselves apart: dedicate yourselves) to the Lord today, so He will bless you, since you opposed your own brothers." **30.** The next day, Moses said, "You've sinned greatly. I will go to the Lord and try to atone (make up: reconcile) for your sin." **31.** Moses returned to the Lord and said, "These people have sinned and made a golden god. **32.** If You will forgive them, fine, but if not, erase me from Your book." **33.** The Lord replied, "Whoever sins against Me, I will erase from My book." **34.** Now go, lead the people, and My Angel (messenger of God: a divine being sent to carry out God's will) will go before you. But I will punish them for their sin when I visit." **35.** The Lord sent a plague on the people because of the calf Aaron made.

Chapter 33

1. Then the Lord said to Moses, "Go up with the people you brought out of Egypt to the land I promised to Abraham, Isaac, and Jacob, saying, 'I will give it to your descendants.' " **2.** "I will send My Angel before you and drive out the Canaanites, Amorites, Hittites, Perizzites, Hivites, and Jebusites. **3.** Go to a land flowing with milk and honey, but I will not go with you, for you are a stubborn people, and I might destroy you on the way." (Stubborn: stiff-necked, unyielding) **4.** When the people heard this, they mourned, and no one wore their jewelry. (Mourned: grieved) **5.** The Lord told Moses, "Tell Israel, 'You are a stubborn people. I could destroy you instantly, so take off your jewelry so I can decide what to do with you.'" **6.** So the Israelites removed their jewelry at Mount Horeb. (Mount Horeb: mountain where Moses received the Ten Commandments) **7.** Moses set up his tent outside the camp, calling it the Tabernacle of Meeting. Anyone seeking the Lord went out to the tabernacle. **8.** Whenever Moses went to the tabernacle, the people stood at their tent doors and watched him until he entered. **9.** When Moses entered, the cloud descended and stood at the tabernacle's door, and the Lord spoke with Moses. (Cloud: God's presence) **10.** The people saw the cloud at the tabernacle, and they worshiped at their tent doors. **11.** The Lord spoke to Moses face to face, as a friend. Moses would return to camp, but Joshua, the young servant, stayed at the tabernacle. **12.** Moses said, "You told me to lead this people, but You haven't told me who You will send with me. You've said I've found favor in Your sight." **13.** "If I've found favor, show me Your way so I may know You and find more grace. Remember, these are Your people." (Favor: grace)**14.** The Lord said, "My Presence will go with you, and I will give you rest." **15.** Moses replied, "If You don't go with us, don't bring us up from here." **16.** "How will anyone know that You and Your people have found favor, unless You go with us? We'll be different from all the people on earth." (Different: set apart) **17.** The Lord replied, "I will do what you've asked because I know you by name and you have found favor." **18.** Moses said, "Please, show me Your glory." (Glory: full greatness)**19.** The Lord answered, "I will make all My goodness pass before you and proclaim My name. I will be gracious to whom I choose and compassionate to whom I choose." (Gracious: kind, compassionate: merciful)**20.** "But you cannot see My face, for no one can see Me and live." **21.** The Lord said, "There is a place near Me where you can stand on the rock." **22.** "When My glory passes, I will put you in a crack in the rock and cover you with My hand until I pass." (Crack: cleft) **23.** "Then I will remove My hand, and you will see My back, but not My face."

Chapter 34
1. And the Lord said to Moses, "Cut two stone tablets like the first, and I will write on them the words from the tablets you broke. **2.** Be ready in the morning; come up to Mount Sinai and present yourself to Me at the top. (Mount Sinai: mountain where Moses received the Ten Commandments) **3.** No one shall come with you, nor should anyone be seen on the mountain; neither flocks nor herds should graze nearby." **4.** Moses cut two stone tablets like the first, rose early, and went up to Mount Sinai with the tablets. **5.** The Lord descended in a cloud and stood with him, and proclaimed His name. (cloud: sign of God's presence) **6.** The Lord passed by and proclaimed, "The Lord, the merciful and gracious God, slow to anger, abundant in goodness and truth, **7.** keeping mercy for thousands, forgiving sin, but not clearing the guilty, visiting the iniquity of the fathers on their children to the third and fourth generations." (Iniquity: wrongdoing) **8.** Moses quickly bowed his head to the ground and worshiped. **9.** "If I have found favor, let my Lord go with us, for we are stubborn people. Pardon our sin and take us as your people." (Favor: kindness) (stubborn: stiff-necked) **10.** "I make a covenant. I will perform wonders before all your people, never seen before, and all will know My work among you. It will be amazing." (Covenant: promise)**11.** "I am driving out the Amorite, Canaanite, Hittite, Perizzite, Hivite, and Jebusite before you. (Amorite, Canaanite, Hittite, Perizzite, Hivite, Jebusite: nations in the Promised Land)**12.** Be careful not to make a covenant with the people of the land; it could trap you." **13.** "Destroy their altars, break their sacred stones, and cut down their Asherah poles. (Asherah poles: idols)**14.** Do not worship other gods; the Lord, whose name is Jealous, is a jealous God. **15.** Do not make covenants with them; they may lead you to worship their gods, eat sacrifices, or intermarry." **16.** "Do not allow your sons and daughters to marry theirs, lest they turn your children to idolatry." **17.** "Do not make idols for yourselves." **18.** "Keep the Feast of Unleavened Bread. Eat unleavened bread for seven days, as I commanded, in the month of Abib, when you came out of Egypt." (Abib: the month of the Exodus)**19.** "All firstborns are Mine, both human and animal, including the firstborn of your livestock." **20.** "Redeem the firstborn donkey with a lamb, or break its neck. Redeem your firstborn sons. None shall come before Me empty-handed." (redeem: buy back) **21.** "Work for six days, but rest on the seventh, even during planting and harvest." **22.** "Observe the Feast of Weeks and the Feast of Ingathering at year's end." (Feast of Weeks: harvest festival; Feast of Ingathering: final harvest festival) **23.** "Three times a year all your men must appear before the Lord, the God of Israel." **24.** "I will drive out nations before you, enlarge your borders, and no one will covet your land when you appear before Me three times a year." **25.** "Do not offer My sacrifice with leaven, nor leave the Passover sacrifice until morning." (Leaven: yeast) **26.** "Bring the first fruits of your land to My house. Do not boil a young goat in its mother's milk." **27.** Then the Lord said to Moses, "Write these words, for by them I have made a covenant with you and Israel." (covenant: promise) **28.** Moses stayed with the Lord for 40 days and nights, neither eating nor drinking, and wrote the words of the covenant—the Ten Commandments. **29.** When Moses came down from the mountain with the tablets, his face shone, but he didn't realize it. **30.** When Aaron and the Israelites saw Moses' shining face, they were afraid to come near him. **31.** Moses called to them, and Aaron and the leaders of the congregation came to him, and Moses spoke to them. **32.** Then all the Israelites came near, and Moses gave them the Lord's commandments from Mount Sinai. (Mount Sinai: mountain of God's revelation) **33.** After speaking with them, Moses put a veil over his face. **34.** Whenever he went before the Lord, he took the veil off; when he came out, he spoke to the people whatever the Lord had commanded. **35.** When the people saw Moses' shining face, he would put the veil back on until he went in to speak with God again.

Chapter 35
1. Then Moses gathered the Israelites and said, "These are the Lord's commands for you: **2.** Work for six days, but the seventh is a holy day, a Sabbath to the Lord. Anyone who works on it must die. **3.** Do not light a fire in your homes on the Sabbath." (Sabbath: day of rest) **4.** Moses spoke to the people, saying, "This is what the Lord has commanded: **5.** 'Take an offering for the Lord. Anyone with a willing heart should bring gold, silver, and bronze; **6.** blue, purple, and scarlet thread, fine linen, and goats' hair; **7.** Ram skins dyed red, badger skins, and acacia wood; **8.** oil for the light, spices for the anointing oil and incense; **9.** onyx stones and stones for the ephod and breastplate." (Ephod: priest's garment; breastplate: part of priest's attire) **10.** 'All skilled workers among you should make what the Lord has commanded: **11.** the tabernacle, its tent, covering, clasps, boards, bars, pillars, and sockets; (tabernacle: portable sanctuary) **12.** the ark with its poles, mercy seat, and veil; (ark: chest for sacred items; mercy seat: cover for the ark; veil: curtain) **13.** the table with its poles, utensils, and showbread; (showbread: sacred loaves of bread) **14.** the lampstand with its utensils, lamps, and oil for the light; **15.** the incense altar with its poles, anointing oil, incense, and screen at the entrance of the tabernacle; (screen: curtain) **16.** the burnt offering altar with its bronze grating, poles, utensils, and the laver with its base; (laver: basin) **17.** the court's hangings, pillars, sockets, and screen at the gate; **18.** the pegs of the tabernacle and court, with cords; **19.** the garments for ministry, including holy garments for Aaron and his sons to serve as priests.' (Garments for priests)**20.** The congregation of Israel left Moses'

presence. **21.** All whose hearts were stirred and spirits willing brought offerings for the tabernacle, its service, and the holy garments. **22.** Both men and women, as many as were willing, brought gold jewelry—earrings, nose rings, rings, and necklaces—every man who offered gold to the Lord. **23.** Those with blue, purple, and scarlet thread, fine linen, goats' hair, ram skins, and badger skins brought them. **24.** Those with silver or bronze offerings brought them, as well as anyone with acacia wood for the service. (acacia: a type of tree) **25.** All women skilled in spinning brought the yarn they had spun—blue, purple, and scarlet thread, and fine linen. **26.** Some women whose hearts were wise spun goats' hair yarn. (wise: skilled) **27.** The rulers brought onyx stones, stones for the ephod and breastplate, **28.** spices, and oil for the light, anointing oil, and incense. **29.** The Israelites brought freewill offerings—men and women whose hearts were willing to contribute to the work the Lord had commanded. **30.** Moses said to the Israelites, "The Lord has called Bezalel son of Uri, son of Hur, from the tribe of Judah; (Judah: one of the 12 tribes of Israel) **31.** He has filled him with the Spirit of God, giving him wisdom, understanding, knowledge, and skill in all craftsmanship, **32.** to make artistic designs in gold, silver, and bronze, **33.** to cut jewels for setting, carve wood, and work in all artistic craftsmanship. **34.** He has also given him the ability to teach, along with Aholiab, son of Ahisamach, from the tribe of Dan. (Dan: one of the 12 tribes of Israel) **35.** The Lord has filled them with skill to do all kinds of engraving, designing, and weaving work in blue, purple, scarlet, and fine linen—those skilled in all types of artistic creation."

Chapter 36
1. "Bezalel, Aholiab, and every skilled worker whom the Lord has given wisdom and understanding to do all the work for the sanctuary shall follow the Lord's commands." (Wisdom: knowledge, understanding: insight) **2.** Then Moses called Bezalel, Aholiab, and all the skilled workers whose hearts the Lord had moved to do the work. (Moved: stirred) **3.** They received from Moses all the offerings brought by the Israelites for the sanctuary's work, and continued bringing freewill offerings every morning. (Freewill: voluntary, offerings: gifts) **4.** All the craftsmen doing the sanctuary work came, each from the task he was working on, **5.** And said to Moses, "The people bring more than enough for the work the Lord commanded us to do." (More than enough: more than needed) **6.** So Moses gave an order, and it was proclaimed throughout the camp, "Let neither man nor woman do any more work for the sanctuary offering." And the people stopped bringing. (Proclaimed: announced, sanctuary: holy place) **7.** For the material was sufficient for all the work to be done—indeed, too much. (Sufficient: enough) **8.** All the skilled workers made ten curtains of fine linen, with blue, purple, and scarlet thread, designed with cherubim. (Cherubim: angelic beings) **9.** Each curtain was 28 cubits long and 4 cubits wide; all the curtains were the same size. (Cubits: unit of length) **10.** He joined five curtains together and the other five curtains similarly. **11.** He made loops of blue yarn on the edge of one set of curtains, and likewise on the outer edge of the second set. (Yarn: thread) **12.** He made 50 loops on one curtain and 50 loops on the edge of the other curtain, to hold them together. **13.** He made 50 gold clasps, to couple the curtains together, making one tabernacle. (Clasps: fasteners, tabernacle : sacred tent) **14.** He made curtains of goats' hair for the tent over the tabernacle; eleven curtains in total. **15.** Each curtain was 30 cubits long and 4 cubits wide; all the curtains were the same size. (Cubits: measurement) **16.** He joined five curtains by themselves and six curtains by themselves. **17.** He made 50 loops on the outer edge of the first set, and 50 loops on the edge of the second set. **18.** He made 50 bronze clasps to couple the curtains together, making one tent. (Bronze: metal) **19.** He made a covering for the tent of ram skins dyed red, and above it a covering of badger skins. (ram : male sheep, dyed : colored) **20.** For the tabernacle, he made boards of acacia wood, standing upright. (acacia : type of wood) **21.** Each board was 10 cubits long and 1.5 cubits wide. (Cubits: unit of length) **22.** Each board had two tenons for binding them together. Thus, he made all the boards of the tabernacle. (Tenons: projecting pieces for joining) **23.** He made 20 boards for the south side of the tabernacle. **24.** He made 40 silver sockets, two for each board to hold them in place. (sockets : bases) **25.** For the north side, he made 20 boards, and 40 silver sockets, two for each board. **26.** For the west side, he made 6 boards. **27.** He made two boards for the two back corners of the tabernacle. **28.** These were coupled at the bottom and at the top by one ring, making them one. **29.** There were 8 boards, with 16 silver sockets, two under each board. **30.** He made 5 acacia wood bars: five for the boards on one side of the tabernacle, **31.** five bars for the boards on the other side, and five bars for the west side of the tabernacle. **32.** He made a middle bar to pass through the boards from one end to the other. **33.** He overlaid the boards with gold, made gold rings to hold the bars, and overlaid the bars with gold. **34.** He made a veil of blue, purple, and scarlet thread, with fine woven linen, worked with cherubim designs. (cherubim : angelic figures) **35.** He made four pillars of acacia wood, overlaid them with gold, and made gold hooks for them; and he cast four silver sockets for them. (hooks: fasteners, acacia : tree) **36.** He also made a screen for the tabernacle door, made of blue, purple, and scarlet thread, with fine woven linen, made by a weaver, **37.** and its five pillars with hooks, overlaid with gold, and five bronze sockets for the pillars. (bronze : metal) **38.** And he overlaid their capitals and their rings with gold, but their five sockets were bronze. (capitals : tops of pillars)

Chapter 37
1. Bezalel crafted the ark from acacia wood, measuring 2.5 cubits in length, 1.5 cubits in width, and 1.5 cubits in height. (Ark: sacred chest, Cubits: units of length) **2.** He covered it entirely with pure gold, both inside and out, and placed a gold border around it. (Molding: decorative border) **3.** Four gold rings were cast for it, two on each side at the corners. (Cast: shaped by pouring into a mold) **4.** He made poles from acacia wood and covered them in gold. **5.** The poles were placed into the rings for carrying the ark. **6.** The mercy seat was made of pure gold, with the same dimensions as the ark's top: 2.5 cubits long and 1.5 cubits wide. (Mercy seat: lid of the ark) **7.** He shaped two cherubim from hammered gold, forming them as one piece at each end of the mercy seat. (Cherubim: angel-like beings) **8.** One cherub was placed at each end, forming a single piece with the mercy seat. **9.** The cherubim spread their wings above the mercy seat, facing each other, with their faces directed toward it. **10.** Bezalel made the table from acacia wood, measuring 2 cubits in length, 1 cubit in width, and 1.5 cubits in height. **11.** It was overlaid with pure gold, and a gold molding was placed around it. **12.** A gold frame, one handbreadth wide, was added around the table, with a gold border for the frame. (Handbreadth: width of a hand) **13.** Four gold rings were cast and placed at the four corners of the table's legs. **14.** The rings were positioned near the frame to hold the poles for carrying the table. **15.** The carrying poles were made of acacia wood, overlaid with gold. **16.** Bezalel crafted gold utensils for the table, including dishes, cups, bowls, and pitchers for pouring. **17.** The lampstand was made entirely of pure gold, shaped by hammering. The shaft, branches, bowls, knobs, and flowers were all made from a single piece. (Hammered work: shaped by pounding metal) **18.** The lampstand had six branches: three on each side. **19.** Each branch had three almond-blossom-shaped bowls, with a knob and a flower. (Almond blossom: flower shape) **20.** The main lampstand also had four bowls shaped like almond blossoms, each with a knob and a flower. **21.** A knob was placed under each pair of branches. **22.** All knobs and branches were made from a single hammered piece of pure gold. **23.** He made seven lamps, wick-trimmers, and trays, all from pure gold. (Wick-trimmers: tools for adjusting the wicks in lamps) **24.** The entire lampstand, along with its accessories, weighed a talent of pure gold. (Talent: weight unit) **25.** The incense altar was made from acacia wood, measuring a cubit in length and width, and

2 cubits in height. Its horns were formed from the same piece as the altar. (Horns: projections at the corners) **26.** It was overlaid with pure gold, covering the top, sides, and horns, and a gold border was added. **27.** Two gold rings were made under the molding at the corners to hold the poles for carrying the altar. **28.** The carrying poles were made of acacia wood, overlaid with gold. **29.** Bezalel also created the holy anointing oil and pure incense, crafted from sweet spices, as a perfumer would prepare. (Perfumer: someone who creates scents)

Chapter 38

1. He made the altar of burnt offering from acacia wood; it was five cubits long, five cubits wide (square), and three cubits high. (Altar: a raised structure for sacrifices) **2.** He made horns on its four corners, all one piece with it, and overlaid it with bronze. (Horns: projections) **3.** He made the altar's utensils: pans, shovels, basins, forks, and firepans—all of bronze. (Utensils: tools) **4.** He made a bronze grate for the altar, placed halfway from the bottom, under its rim. (Grate: a metal grid) **5.** He cast four bronze rings at the four corners of the grate for poles. **6.** He made poles from acacia wood and overlaid them with bronze. (Acacia: a type of wood) **7.** He put the poles into the rings to carry the altar, which was hollow with boards. (Hollow: empty inside) **8.** He made the laver (bowl) of bronze with its base from the bronze mirrors of the women who served at the tabernacle entrance. (Laver: a large basin for washing; mirrors: reflective metal) **9.** He made the court on the south side, with fine linen hangings, 100 cubits long. (Court: the open area around the tabernacle; linen: cloth made from flax) **10.** There were 20 pillars and 20 bronze sockets; their hooks and bands were silver. (Pillars: tall supports; sockets: bases) **11.** On the north side, the hangings were the same length, with 20 pillars, 20 bronze sockets, and silver hooks and bands. **12.** The west side had 50-cubit hangings, with 10 pillars and 10 bronze sockets; the hooks and bands were silver. (West: direction) **13.** The east side had 50-cubit hangings. **14.** One side of the gate had 15-cubit hangings, with three pillars and three sockets. **15.** The other side of the gate was the same, with 15-cubit hangings, three pillars, and three sockets. **16.** All the court's hangings were fine woven linen. **17.** The pillars' sockets were bronze, their hooks and bands were silver, and the capitals were overlaid with silver; all court pillars had silver bands. (Capitals: top parts of the pillars) **18.** The gate's screen was made of blue, purple, and scarlet thread with fine linen, 20 cubits long and 5 cubits high. (Scarlet: deep red) **19.** It had four pillars with bronze sockets, silver hooks, and silver capitals and bands. **20.** All the pegs for the tabernacle and court were bronze. (Pegs: stakes to hold the structure) **21.** This is the inventory of the tabernacle, counted by Moses' command for the Levites' service, by Ithamar, son of Aaron. (Ithamar: Aaron's son) **22.** Bezalel, son of Uri, from Judah, made everything God commanded Moses. (Bezalel: artist and craftsman; Judah: a tribe) **23.** Aholiab, son of Ahisamach from Dan, helped, a skilled engraver, designer, and weaver of blue, purple, and scarlet thread, and fine linen. (Aholiab: craftsman; Dan: a tribe) **24.** The gold used in the holy place work was 29 talents and 730 shekels, according to the sanctuary shekel. (Talents: units of weight) **25.** The silver from those numbered in the congregation was 100 talents and 1,775 shekels, according to the sanctuary shekel. **26.** A bekah (half shekel) for each person over 20 year's old, totaling 603,550 men. (bekah: small coin) **27.** From the 100 talents of silver, he made the sanctuary's sockets and the veil's bases—100 sockets, one talent each. **28.** From the 1,775 shekels, he made hooks for the pillars, overlaid the capitals, and made bands for them. **29.** The bronze offering was 70 talents and 2,400 shekels. **30.** He used it to make the tabernacle's door sockets, the bronze altar, its grating, and all its utensils, **31.** Plus the sockets around the court, the gate bases, and all the pegs for the tabernacle and court.

Chapter 39

1. They made garments for service from blue, purple, and scarlet thread, and holy garments for Aaron, as the Lord had commanded Moses. (Garments for service: clothes used for sacred duties) **2.** The ephod was made of gold, blue, purple, scarlet thread, and fine linen. (Ephod: a sacred garment worn by priests) **3.** They beat gold into thin sheets and cut it into threads to work it with the threads into designs. (Beat: hammered, sheets: flat pieces) **4.** They made shoulder straps to attach it together at its edges. **5.** The woven band of the ephod was made of the same materials, as the Lord had commanded. **6.** They set onyx stones in gold settings, engraved with the names of the sons of Israel. (Onyx: a type of stone) **7.** The stones were placed on the ephod's shoulders as a memorial for the sons of Israel, as commanded. (Memorial: reminder) **8.** They made the breastplate like the ephod, of gold, blue, purple, scarlet thread, and fine linen. **9.** The breastplate was square, doubled; its length and width were a span. (Span: distance between thumb and little finger) **10.** Four rows of stones were set: sardius, topaz, and emerald in the first row; **11.** Turquoise, sapphire, and diamond in the second; **12.** Jacinth, agate, and amethyst in the third; **13.** Beryl, onyx, and jasper in the fourth, all in gold settings. **14.** Twelve stones, one for each tribe, engraved with their names like a signet. (Signet: seal or stamp) **15.** They made braided chains of pure gold for the breastplate. **16.** Two gold settings and rings were placed on the breastplate's ends. **17.** The chains were fastened into the rings. **18.** The chains were connected to the ephod's shoulder straps at the front. **19.** Two gold rings were placed on the breastplate's edge, on the inward side of the ephod. **20.** Two more rings were placed on the shoulder straps near the front, above the woven band. **21.** They bound the breastplate to the ephod with a blue cord, so it wouldn't come loose, as the Lord commanded. (Bound: tied) **22.** The robe of the ephod was made entirely of blue woven fabric. **23.** There was an opening in the robe's center, with a woven binding to prevent tearing. (binding : edge covering) **24.** On the robe's hem, they made pomegranates of blue, purple, scarlet, and fine linen. (hem : the edge of the robe) **25.** They made bells of pure gold and placed them between the pomegranates. **26.** Bells and pomegranates alternated around the hem to minister in, as commanded. (minister : serve) **27.** They made fine linen tunics for Aaron and his sons. **28.** They made a turban, hats, and trousers of fine linen. **29.** A sash of fine linen with blue, purple, and scarlet thread was also made, as commanded. (sash : belt) **30.** They made the holy crown of pure gold, inscribed "HOLINESS TO THE LORD." (holy crown : a sacred headpiece) **31.** They tied a blue cord to the crown and fastened it above the turban, as commanded. **32.** All the work of the tabernacle was completed. The Israelites did everything as the Lord commanded. (tabernacle : sacred tent for worship) **33.** They brought the tabernacle to Moses: the tent, furnishings, clasps, boards, bars, pillars, sockets; **34.** coverings of ram skins dyed red, badger skins, and the veil; **35.** the ark of the Testimony with poles, and the mercy seat; (ark : sacred chest, mercy seat : cover) **36.** the table with its utensils and showbread; (showbread : bread for sacred offerings) **37.** the gold lampstand with lamps and oil; **38.** the gold altar, anointing oil, incense, and the door screen; **39.** the bronze altar with its grate, poles, and utensils; the laver with its base; (laver : large wash basin) **40.** the court's hangings, pillars, sockets, screen for the gate, cords, and pegs; all the utensils for the tabernacle service; (court : outer area of the tabernacle) **41.** the garments of ministry for the holy place, for Aaron and his sons as priests. (garments of ministry : priestly clothing) **42.** The Israelites did everything as the Lord commanded Moses. **43.** Moses inspected the work and saw they had done it as commanded. He blessed them.

Chapter 40

1. Then the Lord spoke to Moses, saying: **2.** "On the first day of the first month, set up the tabernacle of the meeting tent. (place of worship) **3.** Place the ark of the Testimony in it, and separate it with the veil. (Sacred chest, curtain) **4.** Bring in the table and arrange its items; light the lampstand. (Seven lamps) **5.** Set the gold altar for incense before the ark, and hang the screen at the tabernacle door. (Entrance curtain) **6.** Place the burnt offering altar before the tabernacle door. (Sacrifice altar) **7.** Put the laver between the tabernacle and altar, and fill it with water.**8.** Set up the court around it, and hang the gate screen. (Outer area, entrance curtain) **9.** Anoint the tabernacle and all its contents, making them holy. (Pour oil on)**10.** Anoint the altar and its tools, consecrating them as most holy. (Making holy) **11.** Anoint the laver and its base, consecrating them. (stand) **12.** Bring Aaron and his sons to the tabernacle door and wash them with water. **13.** Dress Aaron in holy garments, anoint and consecrate him as priest. (Priestly clothes) **14.** Dress Aaron's sons in tunics. (Robes) **15.** Anoint them as you did Aaron, making them priests for an everlasting priesthood. **16.** Moses did all as the Lord command him. **17.** On the first day of the second year, the tabernacle was set up. **18.** Moses set up the tabernacle, secured its sockets, and set its boards, bars, and pillars. (Foundation, supporting posts)**19.** He spread the tent over the tabernacle and placed the covering on it, as instructed. **20.** He placed the Testimony in the ark, inserted the poles, and put the mercy seat on top. (Stone tablets, carrying rods, cover) **21.** Moses brought the ark into the tabernacle, hung the veil, and separated the ark, as commanded. (Curtain) **22.** He placed the table on the north side, outside the veil, **23.** And arranged the bread on it before the Lord. **24.** He placed the lampstand opposite the table, on the south side, **25.** and lit the lamps before the Lord, as commanded. **26.** He placed the gold altar in front of the veil, **27.** and burned incense on it, as commanded. (sweet-smelling smoke) **28.** He hung the screen at the tabernacle door. (Entrance) **29.** He placed the burnt offering altar at the door and offered sacrifices. (Burnt offerings)**30.** He set the laver between the tabernacle and altar, filling it with water for washing. (Wash basin)**31.** Moses, Aaron, and his sons washed their hands and feet there. **32.** They washed whenever entering the tabernacle or approaching the altar. **33.** He set up the court and hung the screen at the gate. Moses completed the work. (Outer area)**34.** The cloud covered the tabernacle, and the Lord's glory filled it. (Divine presence)**35.** Moses could not enter the tabernacle because the cloud rested on it. **36.** Whenever the cloud lifted, the Israelites moved on. (Descendants of Jacob)**37.** If the cloud did not lift, they stayed until it did. **38.** The cloud was above the tabernacle by day and fire by night, visible to all Israel during their journeys.

3 – Leviticus
Chapter 1

1. The LORD called to Moses from the tabernacle and spoke to him (tabernacle: sacred tent of worship). **2.** "Tell the Israelites: When anyone brings an offering to the LORD, it should be from the cattle, herd, or flock (offering: gift to God; herd/flock: groups of animals). **3.** If the offering is a burnt sacrifice from the herd, it should be a male without defect, offered freely at the entrance of the tabernacle, before the LORD (burnt sacrifice: offering burned entirely; defect: imperfection or flaw). **4.** He shall place his hand on the offering's head, and it will be accepted on his behalf to make atonement (atonement: act of making up for sin). **5.** He shall kill the bull, and Aaron's sons, the priests, shall sprinkle its blood around the altar at the entrance of the tabernacle (sprinkle: scatter small drops). **6.** The burnt offering shall then be skinned and cut into pieces (skinned: remove the hide or outer covering). **7.** Aaron's sons, the priests, shall put fire on the altar and arrange wood on it (altar: structure for offering sacrifices). **8.** They shall place the parts, head, and fat on the wood over the fire on the altar. **9.** The insides and legs shall be washed with water, and the priest shall burn everything on the altar as a burnt offering, a pleasing aroma to the LORD (pleasing aroma: scent that is pleasing to God). **10.** If the offering is from the flock, a sheep or goat, it should also be a male without defect. **11.** It shall be killed on the north side of the altar before the LORD, and its blood sprinkled around the altar by the priests. **12.** The offering shall be cut into pieces, with its head and fat, and arranged on the wood over the fire on the altar. **13.** The insides and legs shall be washed with water, and the priest shall burn all on the altar as a burnt offering, a pleasing aroma to the LORD. **14.** If the offering is a bird, it should be a turtledove or young pigeon (turtledove: a small dove; pigeon: type of bird). **15.** The priest shall bring it to the altar, wring off its head, and burn it on the altar, draining its blood on the side (wring off: twist or pull off). **16.** The crop and feathers shall be removed and placed on the east side of the altar with the ashes (crop: part of the bird's throat used to store food). **17.** The bird shall be torn open by its wings but not completely split, then burned on the altar over the wood. It is a burnt offering, a pleasing aroma to the LORD (pleasing aroma: scent that is pleasing to God).

Chapter 2

1. When offering a meat offering to the LORD, it must be fine flour, with oil poured on it and frankincense added. (Fine flour: finely ground wheat; Frankincense: aromatic resin burned for fragrance) **2.** Bring it to the priests, who will take a handful of flour, oil, and frankincense to burn as a memorial on the altar, a pleasing offering to the LORD. (Memorial: a portion set aside as a remembrance) **3.** The remaining meat offering belongs to Aaron and his sons, as it is most holy among the offerings to the LORD made by fire. (Holy: sacred, set apart) **4.** If baked in an oven, the meat offering should be unleavened cakes of fine flour mixed with oil or unleavened wafers anointed with oil. (Unleavened: without yeast; Wafers: thin, flat cakes) **5.** If cooked in a pan, the meat offering must be fine flour, unleavened, and mixed with oil. (Pan: a flat, shallow cooking vessel) **6.** Divide it into pieces, pour oil on it, and it will be a meat offering. (Divide: separate into portions) **7.** If fried in a pan, it must be made with fine flour and oil. (Fried: cooked in hot oil) **8.** Present the meat offering to the LORD; the priest will bring it to the altar. (Present: to bring before or offer) **9.** The priest will take a portion and burn it as a memorial offering, a pleasing aroma to the LORD. (Aroma: a pleasant scent or fragrance) **10.** The remaining meat offering belongs to Aaron and his sons, as it is most holy among the offerings made by fire to the LORD. (Offering: a gift or sacrifice given to God) **11.** No meat offering should contain leaven or honey; these are not to be burned in any offering made by fire. (Leaven: yeast, which causes dough to rise; Honey: sweet, viscous substance) **12.** The first fruits offering should be presented to the LORD, but not burned on the altar as a sweet aroma. (First fruits: the initial produce of the harvest) **13.** Every meat offering must be seasoned with salt, and the salt of God's covenant must never be missing from the offering. (Seasoned: flavored or treated with spices; Covenant: an agreement or promise) **14.** If offering firstfruits as a meat offering, bring dried green ears of corn or corn beaten from full ears. (Ears of corn: the part of the plant that holds the kernels) **15.** Add oil and frankincense to it; this is a meat offering. (Frankincense: aromatic resin burned for fragrance) **16.** The priest will burn part of the corn, oil, and frankincense as a fire offering to the LORD. (Burn: to consume by fire).

Chapter 3

1. If the offering is a peace sacrifice from the herd, whether male or female, it must be without blemish and presented before the LORD. (Blemish: flaw or imperfection) **2.** He shall lay his hand on the offering's head and kill it at the tabernacle door; Aaron's sons will sprinkle the blood around the altar. (Tabernacle: the sacred tent for worship) **3.** He will offer the fat covering the inner parts and all the fat on the inner organs as a fire offering to the LORD. **4.** He will also offer the two kidneys and the fat on them, near the flanks, and the caul over the liver with the kidneys. (Caul: a membrane over the liver) **5.** Aaron's sons will burn it on the altar, on the burnt sacrifice over the wood and fire, a pleasing offering to the LORD. (Burnt sacrifice: an offering completely consumed by fire) **6.** If the peace offering is from the flock, whether male or female, it must be without blemish. **7.** If offering a lamb, it must be presented before the LORD. **8.** He will lay his hand on the lamb's head and kill it before the tabernacle; Aaron's sons will sprinkle the blood around the altar. **9.** He will offer the fat and the whole rump, removing it near the backbone, and all the fat covering the inner organs. **10.** He will also offer the two kidneys, the fat on them near the flanks, and the caul over the liver with the kidneys. **11.** The priest will burn it on the altar; it is the food of the fire offering to the LORD. **12.** If the offering is a goat, it must be presented before the LORD. **13.** He will lay his hand on the goat's head and kill it before the tabernacle; Aaron's sons will sprinkle the blood around the altar. **14.** He will offer the fat covering the inner parts and all the fat on the inner organs. **15.** He will also offer the two kidneys and the fat on them, near the flanks, and the caul over the liver with the kidneys. **16.** The priest will burn it on the altar; it is the food of the fire offering, a pleasing aroma; all the fat is the LORD's. **17.** This will be a perpetual statute for all generations, prohibiting the consumption of fat and blood. (Perpetual: lasting forever).

Chapter 4

1. And the LORD spoke to Moses, saying, **2.** "Speak to the children of Israel, saying, 'If anyone sins unintentionally by breaking any of the LORD's commandments, doing something that should not be done, and does any of these things, (Unintentionally: without knowledge or intent; Commandments: instructions from God) **3.** if the anointed priest sins and causes the people to become guilty, he must bring a flawless young bull to the LORD as a sin offering for the sin he has committed. (Anointed: chosen for a special purpose; Flawless: without any defect) **4.** He will bring the bull to the entrance of the tabernacle of meeting, place his hand on its head, and kill the bull before the LORD. (Tabernacle of meeting: a sacred place where God's presence was believed to dwell) **5.** The anointed priest will take some of the bull's blood and bring it to the tabernacle of meeting. **6.** The priest will dip his finger in the blood and sprinkle it seven times before the LORD, in front of the veil of the sanctuary. (Sprinkle: to scatter small drops or particles; Veil: a curtain or screen separating the holy space) **7.** The priest will put some of the blood on the horns of the altar of incense before the LORD, which is in the tabernacle of meeting, and pour all the blood at the base of the altar of burnt offering, at the door of the tabernacle of meeting. (Horns: projections or raised parts of the altar) **8.** The priest will take all the fat from the bull for the sin offering, including the fat that covers the inner organs and the fat on the inner organs, **9.** The two kidneys, the fat near them, and the fat around the liver, and remove them. (Kidneys: organs that filter waste from the blood; Liver: organ that processes nutrients and toxins) **10.** As it was done with the peace offering, the priest will burn them on the altar of burnt offering. (Peace offering: a sacrifice offered as a sign of thankfulness or peace with God) **11.** But the bull's skin, flesh, head, legs, internal organs, and waste **12.** The entire bull—will be taken outside the camp to a clean place where the ashes are dumped, and it will be burned on a wood fire where the ashes are poured out. (Ashes: remains after burning) **13.** If the whole congregation of Israel sins unintentionally, and the matter is hidden from them, and they do something against any of the LORD's commandments, becoming guilty, **14.** When their sin becomes known, the congregation will offer a young bull for the sin and bring it before the tabernacle of meeting. (Congregation: a group of people gathered together, often for worship) **15.** The elders of the congregation will place their hands on the bull's head before the LORD, and the bull will be slaughtered before the LORD. (Elders: respected leaders of the community) **16.** The anointed priest will take some of the bull's blood to the tabernacle of meeting. **17.** The priest will dip his finger in the blood and sprinkle it seven times before the LORD, in front of the veil. **18.** The priest will put some of the blood on the horns of the altar before the LORD, which is in the tabernacle of meeting, and pour the rest of the blood at the base of the altar of burnt offering at the door of the tabernacle of meeting. (Altar: a structure used for sacrifices and offerings) **19.** He will take all the fat from the bull and burn it on the altar. **20.** The priest will do with this bull as he did with the sin offering bull, and by this, the priest will make atonement for them, and their sin will be forgiven. (Atonement: the process of making amends for wrongdoing). **21.** He shall take the bull outside the camp and burn it as he did the first one; it is a sin offering for the community. (Community: a group of people gathered together) **22.** If a leader sins by unknowingly breaking any of the LORD's commandments that should not be done, and becomes guilty, **23.** Or if his sin becomes known to him, he shall offer a male goat, free from defects, as his sin offering. (Leader: a person in a position of authority) **24.** He will place his hand on the goat's head and slaughter it at the location where burnt offerings are killed, before the LORD; it is a sin offering. (Burnt offering: an offering completely consumed by fire) **25.** The priest will take some of the goat's blood with his finger and place it on the horns of the altar of burnt offerings. He will then pour out the remaining blood at the base of the altar. **26.** He will burn all the fat on the altar, as is done with the fat from peace offerings. The priest will make atonement for him regarding his sin, and his sin will be forgiven. (Atonement: the act of making amends or reconciliation for sin) **27.** If any member of the community unknowingly breaks any of the LORD's commandments that should not be done and becomes guilty, **28.** or if their sin becomes known to them, they shall offer a female goat, without defects, as their sin offering. (Community member: a regular person within the community) **29.** They will lay their hand on the goat's head and slaughter it at the place where the burnt offerings are killed. **30.** The priest will take some of its blood with his finger, place it on the horns of the altar of burnt offering, and pour out all the remaining blood at the base of the altar. **31.** He will remove all the fat, just as the fat from the peace offerings is removed, and the priest will burn it on the altar, creating a pleasing aroma to the LORD. The priest will make atonement for them, and their sin will be forgiven. (Pleasing aroma: a sacrifice that is accepted by God) **32.** If someone brings a lamb as a sin offering, it must be a female without defects. **33.** They will lay their hand on the lamb's head and slaughter it in the same place as the burnt offering. **34.** The priest will take some of the lamb's blood with his finger, place it on the horns of the altar of burnt offerings, and pour out all the remaining blood at the base of the altar. **35.** He will remove all the fat, just as the fat of the lamb is removed from the peace offerings, and the priest will burn it on the altar as an offering made by fire to the LORD. The priest will make atonement for their sin, and it will be forgiven. (Peace offerings: voluntary offerings made to express gratitude or seek favor).

Chapter 5

1. If someone sins and hears a swear word or takes an oath, and is a witness, whether they saw or knew about it, but do not speak up, they will bear the consequences of their sin. (Swear word: a statement or oath made with strong language; Witness: someone who has seen or knows about something) **2.** If someone touches anything unclean, like the dead body of an unclean animal, or the dead body of an unclean livestock, or the dead body of unclean creeping creatures, and is unaware of it, they shall be unclean and guilty. (Unclean: ritually impure or defiled) **3.** Or if they touch something unclean related to a person, like any form of impurity or defilement a person may have, and do not realize it, but later recognize it, they will be guilty. (Defilement: the state of being contaminated or impure) **4.** Or if someone makes a vow to do evil or to do good, or makes an oath regarding something, but later realizes that they were unaware of the vow, they shall be guilty in one of these ways. (Vow: a serious promise or pledge) **5.** When they realize their guilt in one of these things, they must confess their sin. (Confess: admit or declare) **6.** They shall bring a trespass offering to the LORD for the sin they have committed, a female lamb or goat from the flock, for a sin offering, and the priest will make atonement for them for their sin. (Trespass offering: a sacrifice made to make amends for sin) **7.** If they cannot afford a lamb, they shall bring two turtledoves or two young pigeons to the LORD; one for a sin offering and the other for a burnt offering. (Turtledoves: a small bird, often used in sacrifices) **8.** They shall bring these to the priest, who will offer the one for the sin offering first, wring off its head without dividing it. (Wring off: to twist or pull the head off) **9.** The priest will sprinkle the blood of the sin offering on the side of the altar, and the remaining blood will be poured at the base of the altar; this is the sin offering. (Sprinkle: to scatter drops of liquid). **10.** The second bird will be offered as a burnt offering, following the prescribed method, and the priest will make atonement for the person for their sin, and it will be forgiven. (Burnt offering: a sacrifice completely consumed by fire) **11.** If they cannot bring two turtledoves or two pigeons, they shall bring a tenth of an ephah of fine flour for a sin offering, but without oil or frankincense, for it is a sin offering. (Ephah: a unit of measurement for grain). **12.** They shall bring it to the priest, who will take a handful as a memorial portion and burn it on the altar, as a fire offering to the LORD; it is a sin offering. (Memorial portion: a small amount kept to remember the offering) **13.** The priest will make atonement for the person for their sin, and it will be forgiven; the rest will be the priest's, as part of a grain offering. (Grain offering: an offering made of fine flour) **14.** The LORD spoke to Moses, saying, (Moses: the leader and prophet of Israel) **15.** If someone commits a trespass and sins through ignorance in relation to the holy things of the LORD, they must bring a ram without blemish from the flock, valued in silver shekels according to the sanctuary's standard, as a trespass offering. (Trespass: a violation or sin) **16.** They shall make restitution for the harm they have done to the holy things and add a fifth of its value to it, giving it to the priest. The priest will make atonement for them with the ram, and it will be forgiven. (Restitution: compensation or payment for loss) **17.** If someone sins and commits any forbidden act by the commandments of the LORD, even if they were unaware, they will still be guilty and must bear the consequences of their sin. (Forbidden: not allowed by law) **18.** They shall bring a ram without blemish from the flock, valued according to the standard, for a trespass offering to the priest. The priest will make atonement for them for their ignorance, and it will be forgiven. (Blemish: a flaw or defect) **19.** This is a trespass offering, and they have certainly trespassed against the LORD. (Trespassed: committed an offense against).

Chapter 6
1. The LORD spoke to Moses, saying, **2.** If anyone sins and wrongs the LORD by lying to their neighbor about something entrusted to them, or in any agreement or transaction, or if they take something by force, or deceive their neighbor, (Deceive: to mislead or trick someone) **3.** Or if they find something that was lost and lie about it, or falsely swear about any of these things, they have sinned. (Swear: make a false promise or statement under oath) **4.** Therefore, because they are guilty of sin, they must restore what they took by force, or what they deceived their neighbor to get, or any item that was entrusted to them, or anything they found and lied about. (Restore: return something to its rightful owner) **5.** They must return the item in full, plus an additional one-fifth of its value, and give it to the rightful owner on the day they bring their trespass offering. (Trespass offering: a sacrifice made for wrongdoing) **6.** They must then bring a ram, without blemish, from their flock, and present it to the priest as a trespass offering, according to the prescribed value. (Blemish: a physical flaw or imperfection) **7.** The priest will make atonement for them before the LORD, and they will be forgiven for the sin they have committed. (Atonement: making peace or reconciliation) **8.** Then the LORD spoke again to Moses, saying, **9.** Instruct Aaron and his sons, telling them that this is the law for the burnt offering. It is to burn on the altar all night until morning, and the fire on the altar must keep burning. (Burnt offering: an offering completely consumed by fire) **10.** The priest shall wear linen clothing, including linen pants, and gather the ashes from the burnt offering. He shall place them beside the altar. (Linen: a fabric made from flax) **11.** Afterward, he shall change his clothes; take the ashes outside the camp to a clean place. (Ashes: the remains after something has been burned) **12.** The fire on the altar must always be kept burning; it shall not go out. Each morning, the priest will add wood and arrange the burnt offering on it, burning the fat from the peace offerings on the fire. (Peace offerings: sacrifices made to express thanks or fellowship) **13.** The fire must never go out; it is to burn continually on the altar. (Continually: without interruption) **14.** This is the law for the grain offering: Aaron's sons will offer it before the LORD at the altar. (Grain offering: an offering of fine flour, oil, and incense). **15.** The priest shall take a handful of the grain offering, with its oil and all the frankincense, and burn it on the altar as a sweet aroma to the LORD. (Frankincense: a type of incense used in offerings) **16.** The remaining portion of the grain offering shall be eaten by Aaron and his sons, with unleavened bread, in a holy place, within the courtyard of the tabernacle. (Unleavened: bread made without yeast) **17.** It must not be baked with yeast, as it is their portion from the offerings made by fire to the LORD. It is considered most holy, just like the sin offering and the trespass offering. (Yeast: a substance that causes dough to rise). **18.** Only the males among Aaron's descendants shall eat of it; it is an eternal statute for all generations, and anyone who touches it shall be holy. (Statute: an established rule or law; Eternal: lasting forever) **19.** The LORD also spoke to Moses, saying, **20.** This is the offering that Aaron and his sons shall present to the LORD on the day of their anointing: a tenth of an ephah of fine flour for a perpetual (ongoing) grain offering, with half in the morning and half at night. (Anointing: the act of consecrating or setting someone apart for a special purpose) **21.** It shall be prepared with oil in a pan. Once baked, the priest shall bring it to the altar and offer the baked pieces as a sweet aroma to the LORD. (Aroma: a pleasant smell) **22.** The priest who is anointed in Aaron's place shall offer it as a lasting ordinance to the LORD, and it shall be completely burned. (Ordinance: a command or regulation) **23.** Every grain offering for the priest must be entirely burned; it is not to be eaten. **24.** The LORD spoke to Moses again, saying, **25.** Instruct Aaron and his sons, saying, this is the law for the sin offering: The sin offering is to be killed in the same place as the burnt offering, before the LORD. It is most holy. (Sin offering: a sacrifice made to atone for sins) **26.** The priest who offers it for sin shall eat it in a holy place, within the tabernacle courtyard. (Tabernacle: a portable sanctuary or tent used for worship) **27.** Anything that touches the flesh of the sin offering shall be considered holy, and any garment that has blood sprinkled on it must be washed in a holy place. (Holy: set apart for God) **28.** If it is cooked in an earthen pot, it must be broken, but if it is cooked in a bronze pot, it must be scrubbed and rinsed with water. (Earthen: made of clay; Rinsed: washed lightly) **29.** Only the males among the priests are allowed to eat it, as it is most holy. **30.** No sin offering, whose blood is brought into the tabernacle for reconciliation in the holy place, is to be eaten; it must be burned in the fire. (Reconciliation: restoring peace or favor).

Chapter 7
1. This is the law regarding the trespass offering: it is considered most holy. (Most holy: set apart for a sacred purpose) **2.** The trespass offering must be slaughtered in the same place as the burnt offering, and its blood is to be sprinkled around the altar. (Altar: a structure for offerings or sacrifices) **3.** All of its fat must be offered, including the tail, the fat covering the internal organs. (Rump: the back part of an animal) **4.** The two kidneys, the fat on them near the flanks, and the lobe of fat above the liver along with the kidneys. (Flanks: sides of the body) **5.** The priest will burn these parts on the altar as a fire offering to the LORD; it is a trespass offering. (Offering: something given as a religious sacrifice) **6.** Any male among the priests may eat of it; it must be eaten in the holy place because it is most holy. (Holy place: sacred space designated for worship) **7.** The law for the trespass offering is the same as for the sin offering: there is one rule for both, and the priest who makes atonement for it will receive it. (Atonement: reconciliation or forgiveness) **8.** The priest who offers a person's burnt offering will have the skin of the burnt offering for

himself. **9.** All the grain offerings that are baked in the oven, prepared in a pan, or cooked on a griddle belong to the priest who offers them. (Griddle: a flat cooking surface) **10.** Any grain offering that is mixed with oil or is dry will be shared equally among the sons of Aaron. (Sons of Aaron: the descendants of Aaron, the first high priest) **11.** This is the law for the sacrifice of peace offerings that one offers to the LORD. **12.** If the offering is for thanksgiving, it must include unleavened cakes mixed with oil, unleavened wafers coated with oil, and cakes made of fine flour fried in oil. (Unleavened: bread made without yeast) **13.** In addition to the cakes, leavened bread must also be offered as part of the thanksgiving peace offering. (Leavened: bread with yeast) **14.** One portion of the entire offering is to be set aside as a heave offering to the LORD and it will belong to the priest who sprinkles the blood of the peace offerings. (Heave offering: a portion lifted up and presented to God) **15.** The meat of the thanksgiving peace offering must be eaten on the same day it is offered; none of it should be left until the morning. **16.** If the offering is a vow or voluntary offering, it should be eaten on the same day; any remaining meat may be eaten the next day. (Vow: a solemn promise or pledge) **17.** Any leftover meat on the third day must be burned with fire. **18.** If any of the meat from the peace offering is eaten on the third day, it will not be accepted, and the person who eats it will be guilty. It will be an abomination, and anyone who eats it will bear the consequences. (Abomination: something that is hated or detestable) **19.** Meat that touches anything unclean should not be eaten; it must be burned. Clean meat, however, can be eaten. (Unclean: ritually impure) **20.** Anyone who eats the meat of a peace offering while being unclean will be cut off from their people. (Cut off: excluded, or banished) **21.** Anyone who touches anything unclean, like the uncleanness of a person or an unclean animal, and then eats the meat of the peace offering will be cut off from their people. **22.** The LORD spoke to Moses and said, **23.** "Tell the people of Israel: You shall not eat any fat from oxen, sheep, or goats. **24.** The fat of an animal that dies on its own or is torn by wild animals can be used for other purposes, but you must not eat it. (wild animals: animals that kill for food in the wild) **25.** Anyone who eats the fat from an animal offered as a fire offering to the LORD will be cut off from their people. **26.** You shall not eat any blood, whether from birds or animals, in any of your homes. (Blood: the vital fluid in the body) **27.** Anyone who eats blood will be cut off from their people. (Cut off: excluded, or banished) **28.** The LORD spoke to Moses and said, **29.** "Tell the people of Israel: If someone offers a peace offering to the LORD, they must bring part of it as a gift to the LORD. **30.** They must bring it with their own hands, including the fat and the breast, which will be waved as a wave offering before the LORD. (Wave offering: an offering presented by lifting it up) **31.** The priest will burn the fat on the altar, but the breast will belong to Aaron and his sons. **32.** The right thigh shall be given to the priest as a heave offering from the peace offerings. (Heave offering: a portion lifted up and presented to God) **33.** The priest who offers the blood and fat of the peace offerings will receive the right thigh as their portion. **34.** The wave breast and heave shoulder are taken from the Israelites' peace offerings and given to Aaron and his sons as a permanent statute. (Statute: a rule or law) **35.** This is the portion for the anointing of Aaron and his sons from the offerings made by fire to the LORD, on the day they were anointed to serve as priests. (Anointing: the act of consecrating someone to a sacred office) **36.** These offerings were commanded by the LORD to be given to them by the Israelites on the day they were anointed, as a statute for all generations. **37.** This is the law for the burnt offering, the grain offering, the sin offering, the trespass offering, the consecrations, and the peace offerings. **38.** The LORD commanded Moses on Mount Sinai when He told the Israelites to bring their offerings to the LORD in the wilderness of Sinai. (Mount Sinai: the mountain where Moses received the Ten Commandments, wilderness of Sinai: the desert region where the Israelites camped after leaving Egypt).

Chapter 8

1. The LORD spoke to Moses, saying, **2.** "Take Aaron and his sons along with him, along with the priestly garments, the anointing oil, a young bull for the sin offering, two rams, and a basket of unleavened bread." (Anointing oil: oil used to consecrate or set apart; sin offering: offering to remove sin) **3.** "Gather all the people at the entrance of the tabernacle of meeting." (Tabernacle of meeting: the place of worship) **4.** Moses followed the LORD's instructions, and the congregation gathered at the entrance of the tabernacle. **5.** Moses said to the people, "This is what the LORD has commanded to be done." **6.** Moses brought Aaron and his sons, and washed them with water. **7.** He dressed Aaron in the tunic, fastened the belt around him, clothed him with the robe, put the ephod on him, and secured the special belt of the ephod around him. (Ephod: special priestly garment) **8.** He placed the breastplate on him, and placed the Urim and Thummim in the breastplate. (Breastplate: piece of clothing worn by priests; Urim and Thummim: objects used for making decisions) **9.** He put the mitre on Aaron's head and attached the golden plate, the holy crown to the front of the mitre, as the LORD instructed Moses. (mitre: head covering; holy crown: a holy symbol) **10.** Moses took the anointing oil and anointed the tabernacle and everything in it, setting it apart as holy. (Anointing oil: oil used for consecration; consecrate: to make holy or set apart) **11.** He sprinkled some of the oil on the altar seven times, anointed the altar and its utensils, including the basin and its base, to consecrate them. (altar: place of sacrifice; basin: container for water) **12.** Moses poured the anointing oil on Aaron's head and anointed him to set him apart for service to God. (Anointed: consecrated for service) **13.** Moses brought Aaron's sons, clothed them with tunics, fastened belts around them, and placed head coverings on them, as the LORD commanded. **14.** Moses presented the bull for the sin offering, and Aaron and his sons laid their hands on its head. (sin offering: offering for forgiveness) **15.** Moses slaughtered it, took the blood and applied it to the horns of the altar all around with his finger, purifying the altar. He poured the remaining blood at the base of the altar to consecrate it and make atonement for it. (Atonement: reconciliation) **16.** He took all the fat from the internal organs, the lobe of fat above the liver, the two kidneys with their fat, and burned them on the altar. (Fat: fatty tissue) **17.** The rest of the bull—its hide, flesh, and waste—Moses burned with fire outside the camp, as the LORD had commanded him. (Hide: skin; waste: excrement) **18.** Moses brought the ram for the burnt offering, and Aaron and his sons laid their hands on its head. **19.** Moses slaughtered it, sprinkled its blood around the altar. **20.** He cut the ram into pieces, and Moses burned the head, pieces, and fat on the altar. **21.** Moses washed the inner parts and legs of the ram with water, then burned the entire animal on the altar as a burnt offering, a pleasing aroma to the LORD, as the LORD commanded (burnt offering: complete burnt sacrifice; pleasing aroma: pleasing scent to God). **22.** Moses brought the second ram, the ram for consecration, and Aaron and his sons placed their hands on its head (consecration: setting apart as holy). **23.** Moses killed it and put some of its blood on Aaron's right ear, right thumb, and right big toe. **24.** He then brought Aaron's sons forward and put blood on their right ears, thumbs, and big toes. Moses also sprinkled blood around the altar (sprinkled: scattered drops of liquid). **25.** Moses took the fat, the tail, the fat covering the inner organs, the liver's lobe, the kidneys and their fat, and the right thigh (fat covering: fatty layer around organs). **26.** From the basket of unleavened bread before the LORD, he took one unleavened cake, one cake of oiled bread, and one wafer, placing them on top of the fat and the right thigh (unleavened: without yeast or leaven). **27.** He placed all these items in the hands of Aaron and his sons, who presented them as a wave offering before the LORD (wave offering: lifted or waved gift). **28.** Moses then took these items from their hands and burned them on the altar with the burnt offering, as a pleasing aroma. This was an offering made by fire to the LORD (altar:

place of worship sacrifice). **29.** Moses took the breast and presented it as a wave offering before the LORD. This was Moses' share of the ram of consecration, as the LORD had commanded him (share: priest's portion of offering). **30.** Moses sprinkled some of the anointing oil and blood from the altar on Aaron and his sons, and on their garments, consecrating them and their garments (anointing: pouring oil as blessing). **31.** Moses instructed Aaron and his sons to cook the meat at the entrance of the Tent of Meeting and eat it with the bread from the basket of consecrations, as he commanded, saying Aaron and his sons should eat it (Tent of Meeting: holy meeting tent). **32.** Any remaining meat or bread was to be burned (burned: destroyed completely by fire). **33.** They were not to leave the entrance of the Tent of Meeting for seven days, until their consecration period was completed, for the LORD was consecrating them (entrance: doorway or place to enter). **34.** What was done on this day was commanded by the LORD to make atonement for them (atonement: making things right with God). **35.** They were to stay at the entrance of the Tent of Meeting day and night for seven days and follow the LORD's instructions, so they would not die, as commanded (instructions: detailed guidance given). **36.** Aaron and his sons did everything the LORD had commanded through Moses (commanded: given authoritative instruction).

Chapter 9
1. On the eighth day, Moses called for Aaron, his sons, and the leaders of Israel to gather together. (Leaders: those in authority) **2.** Moses instructed Aaron, "Take a young calf to offer as a sin offering and a ram for the burnt offering, both flawless, and present them to the LORD." (Sin offering: sacrifice to atone for sin, burnt offering: offering entirely burned) **3.** To the Israelites, Moses said, "Bring a goat as a sin offering, and a calf and lamb, both one year old and without defect, as burnt offerings." (Without defect: flawless) **4.** He also instructed them to bring a bull and a ram for peace offerings to be sacrificed before the LORD, along with a grain offering mixed with oil, because today the LORD will make His presence known to you. (Peace offerings: sacrifices made to thank or seek favor from God, grain offering: offering made of grain and oil) **5.** The people brought everything Moses had commanded them to the entrance of the Tabernacle, and the entire congregation gathered there before the LORD. (Tabernacle: the sacred tent where worship took place, congregation: the group of people gathered for worship) **6.** Moses told them, "This is what the LORD has commanded you to do so that His glory will be revealed to you." (Glory: God's visible presence) **7.** Moses then instructed Aaron, "Go to the altar, offer your sin offering and burnt offering, make atonement for yourself and the people, and offer the people's sacrifices to make atonement for them, just as the LORD has commanded." (Atonement: making amends for sin) **8.** Aaron went to the altar, sacrificed the calf of the sin offering for himself, and followed the ritual as instructed. (Ritual: prescribed procedure for worship) **9.** Aaron's sons brought the blood to him, and he dipped his finger in the blood, placing it on the horns of the altar, and then poured out the rest of the blood at the altar's base. (Horns: the raised corners of the altar, base: the bottom part of the altar) **10.** He burned the fat, the kidneys, and the lobe above the liver of the sin offering on the altar, as the LORD had instructed Moses. (Fat: the fatty portions of the animal, kidneys: internal organs, lobe above the liver: part of the liver) **11.** The remaining flesh and the hide were burned outside the camp. (hide: the skin of the animal, camp: the area where the Israelites were camped) **12.** Aaron sacrificed the burnt offering, and his sons presented the blood to him, which he sprinkled around the altar. (Sprinkled: scattered) **13.** They brought the burnt offering with its pieces and head, and he burned them all on the altar. (Pieces: parts of the offering) **14.** He washed the internal organs and legs, and burned them on top of the burnt offering on the altar. (Internal organs: the insides of the animal) **15.** Aaron then presented the people's offering, took the goat for the sin offering, killed it, and offered it as a sin offering just as he had done with the first. (Offering: sacrifice presented to God) **16.** He presented the burnt offering, offering it according to the proper procedure. (Procedure: prescribed method) **17.** He brought the grain offering, took a handful, and burned it on the altar, in addition to the morning's burnt offering. (Grain offering: offering made from grains like flour) **18.** Aaron sacrificed the bull and the ram for the peace offerings, and his sons presented the blood, which he sprinkled around the altar. (Bull: male cow, ram: male sheep) **19.** He took the fat from the bull and ram, including the tail, the fat covering the internal organs, the kidneys, and the lobe above the liver. (Tail: the rear part of the animal) **20.** He placed the fat on the breasts and burned it on the altar. (Breasts: chest portion of the animal) **21.** Aaron waved the breasts and the right shoulder before the LORD as a wave offering, as Moses had instructed. (Wave offering: offering lifted to God) **22.** Aaron then raised his hand toward the people, blessed them, and came down from the altar after offering the sin, burnt, and peace offerings. (Blessed: pronounced God's favor upon) **23.** Moses and Aaron went into the Tabernacle, came out, and blessed the people. Then the glory of the LORD appeared to all the people. (Glory: God's presence made visible) **24.** A fire came out from the LORD and consumed the burnt offering and fat on the altar. When the people saw this, they shouted in amazement and fell to the ground in worship. (Consumed: completely burned up, worship: reverence or praise to God).

Chapter 10
1. Nadab and Abihu, sons of Aaron, offered unauthorized fire before the LORD, which He had not commanded. (Unauthorized fire: fire not approved by God) **2.** Fire came from the LORD and consumed them, and they died before Him. (Consumed: burned up) **3.** Moses told Aaron; "This is what the LORD meant when He said, 'I will be honored by those who approach Me.'" Aaron remained silent. (Honored: praised) **4.** Moses called Mishael and Elzaphan, sons of Aaron's uncle, and told them to carry the bodies of Nadab and Abihu out of the camp. (Uncle: relative) **5.** They followed Moses' instructions and carried the bodies out in their tunics. (Tunics: simple garments) **6.** Moses instructed Aaron, Eleazar, and Ithamar not to mourn publicly, so God's wrath wouldn't fall on the people. Let the rest of Israel mourn. (Wrath: anger) **7.** "Stay inside the Tabernacle, or you will die, as the LORD's anointing oil is on you." They obeyed Moses. (Tabernacle: sacred tent, anointing oil: holy oil used in rituals) **8.** The LORD spoke to Aaron, saying, (spoke: communicated directly) **9.** "You and your sons must not drink wine or strong drink when entering the Tabernacle or you will die. This is a lasting law for your generations." (strong drink: alcohol) **10.** "This law is to help you distinguish between holy and common, clean and unclean." (distinguish: tell apart, holy: sacred) **11.** "Teach Israel all the laws I gave them through Moses." (laws: commandments) **12.** Moses told Aaron and his sons to eat the remaining meat offering without leaven near the altar, as it is most holy. (Meat offering: offering of flour and oil) **13.** "Eat it in a holy place, as it is your share of the LORD's offerings, as commanded." (Share: portion) **14.** "Eat the wave breast and heave shoulder in a clean place, for they are your due from the peace offerings." (Wave breast: offering part lifted before God, heave shoulder: offering part raised before God) **15.** "These parts, along with the fat, will be yours by a lasting ordinance, as the LORD commanded." (Ordinance: rule) **16.** Moses was angry when he found the sin offering had been burned, and questioned Eleazar and Ithamar. (Sin offering: offering for sin) **17.** "Why didn't you eat the sin offering in the holy place? It was given to bear the people's sin and atone for them." (Atoned: reconciled) **18.** "The blood was not brought into the holy place; you should have eaten it there as I commanded." (Blood: symbol of sacrifice) **19.** Aaron replied, "Today, we've offered sacrifices to the LORD. If I had eaten the sin offering, would it have been accepted?" (Accepted: pleasing to God) **20.** Moses agreed with Aaron's explanation and was content. (Content: satisfied)

Chapter 11

1. The LORD spoke to Moses and Aaron, saying, **2.** "Tell the children of Israel: These are the animals you may eat from those on the earth." **3.** "Any animal with a divided hoof, that is cloven-footed, and chews the cud, among the beasts, you may eat." **4.** "But do not eat the camel, which chews the cud but does not have a divided hoof; it is unclean to you." (Unclean: ritually impure) **5.** "The coney, which chews the cud but does not have a divided hoof, is also unclean to you." (Coney: a small animal like a rabbit) **6.** "The hare, which chews the cud but does not have a divided hoof, is unclean to you." (Hare: a type of rabbit) **7.** "The pig, though it has a divided hoof, does not chew the cud; it is unclean to you." (Pig: swine) **8.** "Do not eat their meat or touch their carcasses; they are unclean to you." (Carcass: dead body) **9.** "Of all creatures in the waters, you may eat those with fins and scales." (Fins and scales: parts of fish) **10.** "Anything in the waters that does not have fins and scales is an abomination to you." (Abomination: detestable) **11.** "Such creatures are an abomination; do not eat their flesh, and avoid touching their dead bodies." **12.** "Anything in the waters without fins and scales is an abomination to you." **13.** "Among birds, these are an abomination and should not be eaten: the eagle, ossifrage, and osprey," (ossifrage: a bird of prey, osprey: a fish-eating bird) **14.** "The vulture, the kite, and every kind of raven," (kite: a bird of prey) **15.** "The owl, night hawk, cuckoo, and hawk of all kinds," (night hawk: a type of bird, cuckoo: a bird with a distinctive call) **16.** "The little owl, the cormorant, and the great owl," (cormorant: a type of water bird) **17.** "The swan, pelican, and gier eagle," (gier eagle: a type of eagle) **18.** "The stork, the heron of its kind, the lapwing, and the bat." (Lapwing: a bird, bat: a flying mammal) **19.** "All birds that crawl on four legs are an abomination to you." (Crawl: move on all fours) **20.** "You may eat every flying insect that walks on four legs but has legs above its feet for leaping." **21.** "These insects may be eaten: locusts, bald locusts, beetles, and grasshoppers." (Bald locusts: a type of locust) **22.** "But all other flying insects with four feet are an abomination to you." **23.** "Anyone who touches the carcass of these creatures will be unclean until evening." (Carcass: dead body) **24.** "If someone carries part of their carcass, they must wash their clothes and be unclean until evening." **25.** "The carcasses of animals that have divided hooves but do not chew the cud are unclean to you; anyone who touches them will be unclean." **26.** "Animals that walk on their paws are unclean to you; anyone who touches their carcass will be unclean until evening." (Paws: feet of certain animals) **27.** "Whoever carries their carcass must wash their clothes and be unclean until evening." **28.** "The weasel, the mouse, the tortoise, the ferret, the chameleon, the lizard, the snail, and the mole are unclean to you." (Tortoise: a type of turtle) **29.** "Anyone who touches the dead body of these creatures will be unclean until evening." **30.** "Any object that their carcass falls on will be unclean, whether it's wood, cloth, leather, or sack. It must be washed in water and will remain unclean until evening." (Object: item) **31.** "If their carcass falls into an earthen vessel, it must be broken." (Earthen vessel: pottery) **32.** "Any food or drink in a vessel that has touched their carcass will be unclean." **33.** "Anything touched by their carcass, like ovens or cooking pots must be destroyed because they are unclean." **34.** "However, a spring or a well with water will remain clean, but anything that touches their carcass will be unclean." **35.** "If their carcass falls on seeds to be sown, they are clean. **36.** "But if water is added to the seed and part of their carcass falls on it, it will be unclean." **37.** "If any clean animal dies, anyone who touches its carcass will be unclean until evening." **38.** "If someone eats the carcass, they must wash their clothes and be unclean until evening." **39.** "Every creeping thing that crawls on the earth is an abomination and should not be eaten." (Creeping thing: insect or small animal) **40.** "Anything that goes on its belly, on four legs, or with more feet among creeping things should not be eaten, as it is an abomination." **41.** "Do not make yourselves unclean with these creeping things; avoid them to keep yourselves holy." **42.** "I am the LORD your God; sanctify yourselves and be holy, as I am holy. Do not defile yourselves with these creeping things." **43.** "I am the LORD who brought you out of Egypt to be your God; therefore, be holy, for I am holy." **44.** "This is the law concerning animals, birds, creatures of the sea, and creeping things." **45.** "These laws distinguish between clean and unclean, and what may or may not be eaten." **46.** "This is the law for the animals, birds, creatures that move in the water, and all creatures that creep on the earth." **47.** "To make a distinction between the unclean and the clean, and between animals that may be eaten and those that may not."

Chapter 12

1. The LORD instructed Moses, saying, **2.** "Tell the people of Israel, 'If a woman gives birth to a son, she will be considered unclean for seven days, just as she is during her regular time of impurity.'" (Impurity: ceremonial uncleanliness) **3.** "On the eighth day, the baby boy will undergo circumcision." (Circumcision: the removal of the foreskin) **4.** "After that, she will continue her purification for thirty-three more days, and she must avoid anything sacred or entering the holy place until her purification period is complete." (Purification: cleansing, sacred: holy) **5.** "But if she has a daughter, she will be unclean for two weeks, just like her time of impurity, and will remain in purification for sixty-six days." (Impurity: ceremonial uncleanliness) **6.** "Once her purification period ends, whether for a son or a daughter, she must bring a one-year-old lamb for a burnt offering and a young pigeon or turtledove for a sin offering to the entrance of the Tabernacle and present them to the priest." (Tabernacle: holy tent) **7.** "The priest will offer them to the LORD, and this will make her clean from her blood. This is the rule for women after childbirth, whether for a son or a daughter." (Make clean: purify, blood: symbol of impurity) **8.** "If she cannot afford a lamb, she may bring two turtledoves or two pigeons—one for the burnt offering and one for the sin offering. The priest will make atonement for her, and she will be clean." (Atonement: reconciliation, turtledoves: small birds)

Chapter 13

1. The LORD spoke to Moses and Aaron, saying: **2.** If someone has a swelling, scab, or bright spot on their skin that might be leprosy, they must be brought to Aaron the priest or one of his sons. (Leprosy: serious skin disease) **3.** The priest will examine the sore. If the hair in the sore has turned white and it looks deeper than the skin, it is leprosy. The priest will declare them unclean. (Unclean: impure) **4.** If the bright spot is white but not deeper than the skin and the hair hasn't turned white, the priest will isolate the person for seven days. (Isolate: separate) **5.** On the seventh day, the priest will examine them again. If the sore hasn't changed or spread, they will be isolated for another seven days. **6.** If, on the seventh day, the sore is fading and hasn't spread, the priest will declare them clean. It is only a scab. They must wash their clothes and will be clean. (Scab: small crusted sore) **7.** But if the scab spreads after they were examined, they must go back to the priest. **8.** If the priest sees that it has spread, they will declare the person unclean—it is leprosy. **9.** When someone has leprosy, they must be brought to the priest. **10.** If the sore is white, has turned the hair white, and there is raw flesh in it, **11.** it is an advanced leprosy. The priest will declare them unclean without isolating them. (Raw flesh: open wound) **12.** If the disease spreads and covers their whole body, **13.** And their skin has turned completely white; the priest will declare them clean. **14.** But if raw flesh appears, they are unclean. **15.** The priest will examine the raw flesh and declare them unclean because raw flesh indicates leprosy. (Indicates: shows or suggests) **16.** If the raw flesh heals and turns white, they must return to the priest. **17.** If the priest sees that the sore has turned white, they are clean. **18.** If someone had a boil that healed, **19.** but leaves a white or reddish spot, they must show it to the priest. (Boil: swelling filled with pus) **20.** If it appears deeper than the skin and the hair in it has turned white, the priest will declare it leprosy. **21.** If it is not deeper than the skin and has no white hair, the priest will isolate them for seven days. **22.** If it spreads, they are unclean. **23.** But if it stays the same, it is just a boil scar, and they are clean. (Scar: mark left after a wound heals) **24.** If someone has a burn and it leaves a white or reddish spot, **25.** The priest will examine it. If the hair has turned white and it looks deeper than the skin, it is leprosy. **26.** If it is not deeper than the skin and has no white hair, they will be isolated for seven days. **27.** If it spreads, they are unclean. **28.** If it doesn't spread and looks lighter, it is just an inflammation from the burn, and they are clean. (Inflammation: redness and swelling) **29.** If a man or woman has a sore on their head or beard, **30.** And it appears deeper than the skin with thin yellow hair; the priest will declare them unclean. **31.** If it is not deeper than the skin and has no black hair, they will be isolated for seven days. **32.** On the seventh day, if it hasn't spread, they must shave the area around the sore but not the sore itself. They will be isolated for another seven days. **33.** If the sore hasn't spread by the end of this time, they are clean and must wash their clothes. **34.** But if it spreads, they are unclean. **35.** If the sore grows after cleansing, **36.** And it spreads; the priest will declare them unclean. **37.** If the sore doesn't grow and black hair appears, the person is healed and clean. (Black hair: healthy, normal hair) **38.** If someone has bright white spots on their skin, **39.** and they are pale and dull, it is a harmless skin condition. They are clean. (dull: lacking brightness or color) **40.** A man who loses his hair is bald but still clean. **41.** If hair falls out at the front of his head, he is forehead bald but still clean. **42.** If a reddish-white sore appears on his bald head or forehead, it is leprosy. **43.** The priest will examine it, and if it looks like leprosy, **44.** they will declare the person unclean. **45.** A person with leprosy must tear their clothes, keep their hair unkempt, cover their mouth, and shout, "Unclean!" **46.** They must live outside the camp while they are unclean. (unkempt: untidy or messy) **47.** If a garment of wool, linen, or leather develops greenish or reddish spots, **48.** it must be shown to the priest. **49.** If the spot spreads, it is leprosy in the garment. **50.** The priest will isolate the item for seven days. **51.** If the spot spreads, the garment must be burned. **52.** If it hasn't spread, the item will be washed and isolated for another seven days. **53.** If the spot fades, the garment is clean after washing. **54.** But if the spot remains, the item must be burned. **55.** If the priest examines the item after washing and the spot hasn't changed color or spread, it is unclean and must be burned, whether it's damaged on the inside or outside. **56.** If the priest finds the spot has faded after washing, the affected part must be cut out of the garment, leather, or fabric. **57.** But if the spot reappears on the item, it is a spreading disease, and the item must be burned. **58.** If the spot disappears after washing, the item must be washed again, and it will be clean. **59.** This is the law concerning leprosy in garments of any material to determine if they are clean or unclean.

Chapter 14

1. The LORD spoke to Moses, saying: **2.** "This is the law for the cleansing of a leper: He must be brought to the priest. **3.** The priest shall go outside the camp and examine him. If the leprosy is healed, **4.** the priest will command two clean birds, cedar wood, scarlet, and hyssop for the cleansing. (Cedar wood: a type of tree used in rituals, scarlet: red-colored fabric, hyssop: a plant used in purification rites) **5.** One bird is to be killed over running water in an earthen vessel. (Earthen vessel: a container made of clay or pottery) **6.** The living bird, cedar wood, scarlet, and hyssop are to be dipped in the blood of the dead bird, **7.** And the priest will sprinkle the leper seven times, declaring him clean. Then the living bird will be released into the field. **8.** The cleansed person must wash his clothes, shave off all his hair, and wash himself in water, then stay outside his tent for seven days. **9.** On the seventh day, he must shave off all his hair, wash his clothes, and bathe, becoming clean. **10.** On the eighth day, he will bring two unblemished lambs, one ewe lamb, fine flour, and oil. (Unblemished: without defect) **11.** The priest will present the offerings before the LORD at the tabernacle entrance. (Tabernacle: a portable sanctuary or place of worship) **12.** He will take one lamb for a guilt offering and the log of oil, and wave them as a wave offering. (Guilt offering: a sacrifice made to atone for sin, wave offering: ritual waving of a sacrifice as a sign of dedication) **13.** The lamb will be slain in the holy place, where sin and burnt offerings are made, as it is most holy. (Holy place: a sacred or consecrated area) **14.** The priest will take some blood from the guilt offering and put it on the tip of the leper's right ear, right thumb, and right big toe. **15.** The priest will pour oil into his left palm, **16.** Dip his right finger in the oil, and sprinkle it seven times before the LORD. **17.** The priest will put the remaining oil on the leper's ear, thumb, and toe, over the blood of the guilt offering. **18.** The remaining oil will be poured on the leper's head for atonement. (Atonement: the act of making amends for sin) **19.** The priest will offer the sin offering for atonement, and then offer the burnt offering. **20.** The priest will offer both the burnt and grain offerings on the altar and make atonement, and the leper will be clean. **21.** If the person is poor and cannot afford all this, he shall bring one lamb for the guilt offering, fine flour with oil, a log of oil, **22.** And two turtledoves or pigeons, one for a sin offering and one for a burnt offering. (Turtledoves: a type of small bird used in sacrifices) **23.** He will bring these to the priest on the eighth day at the tabernacle entrance. **24.** The priest will wave the guilt offering lamb and oil before the LORD. **25.** The lamb will be slaughtered, and some of its blood will be applied to the leper's ear, thumb, and toe. **26.** The priest will pour the oil into his left hand, **27.** sprinkle it seven times before the LORD, **28.** and apply it to the leper's ear, thumb, and toe, over the blood of the guilt offering. **29.** The rest of the oil will be poured on the leper's head for atonement. **30.** The priest will offer the turtledoves or pigeons, with the grain offering, for atonement. **31.** This is the law for the leper who cannot afford the full offering. **32.** This law applies to all types of leprosy, whether on a person, garment, or house, **33.** or for other skin conditions like scabs or spots. (scabs: crusts that form over healing sores) **34.** "When you enter the land of Canaan and I send a leprous plague on a house, **35.** the owner must tell the priest, saying, 'It seems there is a plague in my house.' (plague: a widespread disease or affliction) **36.** The priest will order the house to be emptied before inspecting the plague, so nothing inside becomes unclean. **37.** He will examine the house, and if the plague is in the walls, with greenish or reddish marks, **38.** the priest will shut the house for seven days. **39.** On the seventh day, the priest will inspect it again. If the plague has spread, **40.** the priest will have the stones with the plague removed and cast outside the city into an unclean place. **41.** He will scrape the house inside and dispose of the dust in an unclean place outside the city. **42.** Then new stones will be placed, and the house will be re-plastered. (re-plastered: re-covered with a new layer of plaster) **43.** If the plague returns after the house is re-plastered, **44.** it is a persistent leprosy, and the house will be declared unclean. (persistent: continuing or enduring) **45.** The house will be torn down, and the materials will be taken outside the city to an unclean place. **46.** Anyone who enters the house while it is shut up will be unclean until evening. **47.** Anyone who sleeps or eats in the house must wash their clothes. **48.** If the priest finds that the plague has not spread after the house is re-plastered, **49.** he will declare it clean and perform a cleansing ceremony with two birds, cedar wood, scarlet, and hyssop. **50.** One bird will be killed in an earthen vessel over running water, **51.** and the priest will dip the cedar wood, hyssop, scarlet, and living bird in the blood of the slain bird, **52.** sprinkling the house seven times. **53.** The priest will cleanse the house with the blood, water, living bird, cedar wood, hyssop, and scarlet, **54.** and release the living bird into the field. The house will then be clean. **55.** This is the law for cleansing a house with leprosy, **56.** for a person's leprosy, or for any skin conditions like scabs or spots, **57.** to determine when something is clean or unclean. This is the law of leprosy."

Chapter 15

1. The LORD spoke to Moses and Aaron, saying: **2.** "Tell the Israelites: When a man has a discharge from his body, he is unclean because of it. **3.** Whether the discharge continues or stops, it makes him unclean. **4.** Any bed or chair he sits on is unclean. **5.** Anyone who touches his bed must wash their clothes, bathe, and remain unclean until evening. **6.** Anyone who sits on what he sat on must wash their clothes, bathe, and remain unclean until evening. **7.** Anyone who touches the body of someone with the issue must wash their clothes, bathe, and remain unclean until evening. **8.** If the person with the issue spits on someone clean, the person must wash their clothes, bathe, and remain unclean until evening. **9.** Any saddle the person with the issue rides is unclean. **10.** Anyone who touches anything under him is unclean until evening. Anyone who carries these items must wash their clothes, bathe, and remain unclean until evening. **11.** Anyone who touches someone with the issue and has not washed their hands must wash their clothes, bathe, and remain unclean until evening. **12.** Any clay vessel the person touches must be broken, and any wooden vessel must be washed. (clay vessel: pottery or ceramic container) **13.** When the person with the issue is healed, he must count seven days for cleansing, wash his clothes, and bathe in running water to be clean. (running water: flowing water, such as from a stream or river) **14.** On the eighth day, he must bring two turtledoves or two young pigeons to the priest at the entrance of the tabernacle, (turtledoves: a type of small bird used in rituals, pigeons: another type of bird used in sacrifices, tabernacle: a portable sanctuary or place of worship) **15.** and the priest will offer one as a sin offering and the other as a burnt offering, making atonement for him before the LORD. (sin offering: a sacrifice to atone for sin, burnt offering: a sacrifice completely burned as an offering to God, atonement: reconciliation or making amends for sin) **16.** If a man has a discharge of semen, he must wash his body and remain unclean until evening. (Semen: male reproductive fluid) **17.** Any clothing or skin touched by semen must be washed and remain unclean until evening. **18.** If a man has intercourse with a woman, they both must bathe and remain unclean until evening. (intercourse: sexual relations) **19.** If a woman has a discharge of blood, she must be set apart for seven days; anyone who touches her will be unclean until evening. (set apart: separated for a period of time due to ritual impurity) **20.** Anything she lies on or sits on during her period is unclean. (period: monthly menstruation) **21.** Anyone who touches her bed must wash their clothes, bathe, and remain unclean until evening. **22.** Anyone who touches anything she sat on must wash their clothes, bathe, and remain unclean until evening. **23.** If the discharge is on her bed or chair, the person who touches it will be unclean until evening. **24.** If a man lies with her during her period, he will be unclean for seven days, and the bed he lies on will be unclean. **25.** If a woman has a discharge of blood beyond her period, her discharge will be treated as the same uncleanness as her period, and she will be unclean. **26.** Any bed she lies on or chair she sits on will be unclean, just like during her period. **27.** Anyone who touches these things will be unclean and must wash their clothes, bathe, and remain unclean until evening. **28.** If she is cleansed of her discharge, she must count seven days, and then she will be clean. **29.** On the eighth day, she must bring two turtledoves or two young pigeons to the priest at the tabernacle entrance. **30.** The priest will offer one as a sin offering and the other as a burnt offering, making atonement for her before the LORD for her uncleanness. **31.** This is how you will separate the Israelites from their uncleanness, so they do not die in their impurity when they defile the tabernacle. (defile: to make something unclean or impure) **32.** This is the law for anyone with a discharge, for anyone whose seed goes from him, and for anyone with a discharge of blood. (seed: semen, discharge: the flow of bodily fluids) **33.** This law applies to both men and women, and to anyone who has relations with an unclean person. (relations: sexual intercourse)

Chapter 16

1. After the death of Aaron's two sons, when they offered unauthorized fire before the LORD and died, (unauthorized fire: fire that was not commanded by God) **2.** the LORD told Moses to instruct Aaron that he should not come into the Holy Place whenever he wants, but only in the right way, or he will die. God will appear in the cloud above the mercy seat on the ark. (Holy Place: the inner sanctuary of the tabernacle, mercy seat: the gold-covered lid of the Ark of the Covenant where God's presence would appear) **3.** When Aaron enters the holy place, he must bring a young bull for a sin offering and a ram for a burnt offering. **4.** He must wear holy linen garments: a linen coat, breeches, a linen girdle, and a linen turban. He must wash himself and put these on. (linen: a fabric made from the flax plant, breeches: pants or trousers) **5.** He must take two goats from the people of Israel for a sin offering and one ram for a burnt offering. **6.** Aaron must offer the bull as a sin offering for himself, to make atonement for himself and his family. (atonement: reconciliation or making amends for sin) **7.** He must present the two goats at the door of the tabernacle, **8.** then cast lots over the goats: one lot for the LORD, the other for the scapegoat. (lots: a casting of lots is a way to determine a decision, often by chance or by drawing names; scapegoat: a goat symbolically burdened with the sins of the people, then sent away) **9.** The goat chosen for the LORD will be offered as a sin offering, **10.** and the scapegoat will be sent alive into the wilderness to carry away the sins of the people. (wilderness: an uninhabited or desolate area) **11.** Aaron will bring the bull and make atonement for himself and his house by killing the bull. **12.** Then he must take a censer full of burning coals and incense into the Holy Place, (censer: a container used to hold incense) **13.** and put the incense on the fire, so that the cloud of incense will cover the mercy seat and keep him from dying. **14.** He must take the bull's blood and sprinkle it on the mercy seat seven times, **15.** then kill the goat for the people's sin offering and bring its blood into the Holy Place, sprinkling it on the mercy seat as he did with the bull's blood. **16.** This will make atonement for the holy place, because of the uncleanness and sins of Israel. (uncleanness: ritual impurity) **17.** No one is allowed to be in the tabernacle while Aaron is making atonement, until he finishes for himself, his family, and all the people of Israel. **18.** Afterward, he will go to the altar before the LORD and make atonement for it, sprinkling the blood of the bull and goat on the horns of the altar. (horns: the projections or corners of the altar) **19.** He will cleanse and consecrate the altar, (consecrate: to dedicate or set apart for holy use) **20.** and once the atonement for the sanctuary, tabernacle, and altar is complete, he will bring the live goat. **21.** Aaron will lay both hands on the scapegoat's head and confess all the sins of Israel, placing them on the goat, then send it into the wilderness with a fit man. (fit man: a man who is chosen to lead the scapegoat into the wilderness) **22.** The scapegoat will carry all the sins of the people into an uninhabited land and be released. (uninhabited land: a place with no inhabitants, like a wilderness) **23.** Aaron will then return to the tabernacle, remove his linen garments, and leave them there. **24.** He will wash himself in the holy place, put on his regular clothes, and offer the burnt offerings for himself and the people, making atonement. **25.** The fat of the sin offering will be burned on the altar. **26.** The person who released the scapegoat will wash their clothes and bathe before returning to the camp. **27.** The bull and goat whose blood was taken into the Holy Place must be carried outside the camp and burned, including their flesh, skins, and dung. (dung: animal waste) **28.** The person who burns them must wash their clothes and bathe before returning to the camp. **29.** This will be a lasting ordinance for you: On the tenth day of the seventh month, you will humble yourselves and do no work, whether you are an Israelite or a foreigner. (ordinance: a law or commandment, humble yourselves: to practice humility or repentance) **30.** On this day, the priest will make atonement for you, cleansing you from all your sins before the LORD. **31.** It will be a Sabbath of rest, a day to humble yourselves, forever. (Sabbath: a day of rest, typically the seventh day of the week, a day set apart for worship) **32.** The priest who is anointed and consecrated to serve in his father's place will make the atonement, wearing the holy linen garments. (anointed: consecrated or chosen for a special purpose) **33.** He will make atonement for the sanctuary, the tabernacle, the altar, the priests, and all the people. **34.** This is a lasting statute: Atonement will be made once a year for Israel's sins. And Aaron did as the LORD commanded Moses. (statute: a permanent law or rule).

Chapter 17
1. The LORD spoke to Moses, saying, **2.** "Tell Aaron, his sons, and all the people of Israel this message: **3.** 'Any person in Israel who slaughters an ox, sheep, or goat within the camp or outside the camp, **4.** but does not bring it to the entrance of the tabernacle to offer it to the LORD, will be considered guilty of shedding blood and will be cut off from their people. (shed blood: killed) **5.** The Israelites are to bring their sacrifices to the LORD at the entrance of the tabernacle, and offer them as peace offerings. (peace offerings: gifts) **6.** The priest will then sprinkle the blood on the altar and burn the fat as a pleasing aroma to the LORD. (sprinkle: scatter, fat: tissue, aroma: scent) **7.** From now on, they must not offer sacrifices to demons, as they have done in the past. This will be a permanent rule for them. (demons: spirits, permanent: lasting) **8.** If anyone from Israel or from among the foreigners living among you offers a burnt offering, **9.** but does not bring it to the entrance of the tabernacle, they will be cut off from the community. (burnt offering: sacrifice, community: group) **10.** If anyone eats blood, I will turn against them and remove them from the people of Israel. (turn against: oppose, remove: exclude) **11.** The life of all creatures is in the blood, and I have given it to you on the altar to make atonement for your souls. It is the blood that makes atonement. (atonement: forgiveness, souls: lives) **12.** Therefore, I command that none of you, whether an Israelite or a foreigner living among you, is to eat blood. (foreigner: non-Israelite, living among you: resident) **13.** Anyone who hunts and kills an animal or bird that can be eaten must pour out its blood and cover it with dirt. (cover: bury) **14.** The blood is the life of the creature, and this is why I have told the Israelites: Do not eat the blood of any living creature. Anyone who eats blood will be cut off. (creature: living thing) **15.** Anyone who eats an animal that has died naturally or was torn by wild animals, whether they are an Israelite or a foreigner, must wash their clothes and bathe in water. They will be unclean until evening, and then they will be clean. (unclean: impure) **16.** But if they do not wash their clothes or bathe their bodies, they will bear their guilt." (bear their guilt: carry their sin)

Chapter 18
1. The LORD spoke to Moses, saying, **2.** "Speak to the Israelites and tell them, 'I am the LORD your God. **3.** Do not follow the practices of Egypt, where you used to live, nor the practices of Canaan, to which I am bringing you. Do not follow their customs. (customs = traditions) **4.** You must follow my laws and carefully observe my decrees. I am the LORD your God. (observe = watch over, decrees = orders) **5.** Keep my statutes and my judgments; anyone who does them will live by them. I am the LORD. (statutes = rules, judgments = decisions) **6.** No one is to have sexual relations with close family members. I am the LORD. **7.** Do not dishonor your father's nakedness by having relations with your mother; she is your mother, and you must not uncover her nakedness. (dishonor = shame, nakedness = private parts) **8.** Do not have relations with your father's wife, as she is your father's nakedness. **9.** Do not have relations with your sister, whether she is the daughter of your father or of your mother, whether born at home or abroad. (abroad = outside the home) **10.** Do not have relations with your granddaughter, whether the daughter of your son or of your daughter; this is your own nakedness. (nakedness = private parts) **11.** Do not have relations with the daughter of your father's wife, as she is your sister. **12.** Do not have relations with your father's sister; she is your father's relative. **13.** Do not have relations with your mother's sister, for she is your mother's relative. **14.** Do not have relations with your father's brother, and do not approach his wife; she is your aunt. **15.** Do not have relations with your daughter-in-law; she is your son's wife. **16.** Do not have relations with your brother's wife, as this is your brother's nakedness. (nakedness = private parts) **17.** Do not have relations with both a woman and her daughter, nor take her granddaughter, whether from a son or daughter, to have relations with her; they are close relatives, and it is wickedness. (wickedness = evil) **18.** Do not take your sister-in-law as a wife, to cause rivalry and to uncover her nakedness while your other wife is still alive. (rivalry = competition, nakedness = private parts) **19.** Do not approach a woman to have relations with her during her menstrual period, when she is unclean. (unclean = impure) **20.** Do not have relations with your neighbor's wife, defiling yourself with her. (defiling = polluting) **21.** Do not sacrifice your children to Molech, nor profane the name of your God. I am the LORD. (profane = dishonor) **22.** Do not engage in homosexual relations, as it is an abomination. (abomination = disgusting act) **23.** Do not have sexual relations with any animal, nor should any woman approach an animal to have relations with it. This is perversion. (perversion = corruption) **24.** Do not defile yourselves by doing any of these things; for by committing such acts, the nations I am driving out before you have become defiled. (defile = contaminate) **25.** The land itself has become defiled, and I will bring its punishment upon it. The land will vomit out its inhabitants. (punishment = consequence, vomit out = reject) **26.** But you must keep my decrees and my laws and not commit any of these abominations, neither the natives nor the foreigners living among you. (decrees = orders, natives = locals, foreigners = outsiders) **27.** For all these abominations have been committed by the people who lived in the land before you, and the land has become defiled. (abominations = disgusting acts, defiled = polluted) **28.** If you defile the land, it will vomit you out, as it vomited out the nations before you. (defile = contaminate, vomit out = reject) **29.** Anyone who commits any of these abominations will be cut off from their people. (abominations = disgusting acts, cut off = removed) **30.** Keep my ordinances and do not commit any of these abominable practices which were done before you, so that you do not defile yourselves. I am the LORD your God. (ordinances = rules, abominable = horrible, defile = pollute)

Chapter 19
1. The Lord spoke to Moses, saying: **2.** "Tell all the people of Israel, 'Be holy, because I, the Lord your God, am holy. (holy: pure, set apart) **3.** Honor your father and mother, and keep my Sabbaths. I am the Lord your God. (honor: respect, keep: observe) **4.** Do not turn to idols or make molten gods for yourselves. I am the Lord your God. (molten: melted, idols: false gods) **5.** If you offer a peace offering to the Lord, offer it willingly. (willingly: voluntarily) **6.** It must be eaten the same day you offer it, or the next day. If anything remains until the third day, it must be burned. (remains: leftover) **7.** If you eat it on the third day, it will be unclean and will not be accepted. (unclean: impure, accepted: approved) **8.** Anyone who eats it will be guilty because they have profaned the sacred offering of the Lord. That person will be cut off from the people. (guilty: responsible, profaned: disrespected, cut off: excluded) **9.** When you harvest the crops of your land, do not harvest the corners of your field, and do not gather the leftover grain. (harvest: collect, leftover: remaining) **10.** Do not glean your vineyard or gather every grape. Leave them for the poor and the foreigner. I am the Lord your God. (glean: gather, foreigner: outsider) **11.** Do not steal, lie, or deceive one another. (steal: take, deceive: trick) **12.** Do not swear falsely by my name, and do not profane the name of your God. I am the Lord. (swear falsely: make false oaths, profane: disrespect) **13.** Do not defraud or rob your neighbor. Pay a worker their wages before the sun sets. (defraud: cheat, rob: steal) **14.** Do not curse the deaf or put a stumbling block in front of the blind. Fear your God. I am the Lord. (stumbling block: obstacle) **15.** Do not be unfair in judgment. Do not show favoritism

to the poor or respect the mighty. Judge your neighbor fairly. (unfair: biased, favoritism: preference) **16.** Do not spread false rumors or slander among your people. Do not stand by when your neighbor's life is at risk. I am the Lord. (false rumors: lies, slander: defamation, stand by: ignore) **17.** Do not harbor hatred in your heart. Rebuke your neighbor openly to prevent sin. (harbor: hold, rebuke: correct, prevent: stop) **18.** Do not seek revenge or bear a grudge, but love your neighbor as yourself. I am the Lord. (revenge: payback, grudge: resentment) **19.** Keep my statutes. Do not crossbreed your animals or plant mixed seeds. Do not wear clothing made of two different materials. (statutes: laws, crossbreed: mix, materials: fabrics) **20.** If a man has relations with a female slave who is promised to another man, and she has not been set free or redeemed, she shall be scourged. They will not be put to death, for she is not free. (relations: sex, promised: betrothed, redeemed: freed, scourged: punished) **21.** The man shall bring a guilt offering to the Lord at the tabernacle. A ram for a guilt offering shall be offered. (guilt offering: sin offering, ram: male sheep, tabernacle: tent of meeting) **22.** The priest will make atonement with the ram for the man's sin, and the sin will be forgiven. (atonement: reconciliation, forgiven: pardoned) **23.** When you enter the land and plant fruit trees, count the fruit as uncircumcised for three years. It is not to be eaten. (uncircumcised: unclean) **24.** In the fourth year, the fruit shall be holy, a praise offering to the Lord. (holy: set apart, praise offering: offering of thanks) **25.** In the fifth year, you may eat the fruit, and it will increase your harvest. I am the Lord your God. (increase: multiply) **26.** Do not eat meat with blood still in it. Do not practice sorcery or witchcraft. (sorcery: magic, witchcraft: occult practices) **27.** Do not shave the sides of your head or trim your beard. (shave: cut, trim: shorten) **28.** Do not make cuts on your body for the dead, nor tattoo yourselves. I am the Lord. (cuts: marks, tattoo: body art) **29.** Do not prostitute your daughter, causing her to become a prostitute, or the land will fall into wickedness. (prostitute: sell sex, wickedness: sin) **30.** Keep my Sabbaths and respect my sanctuary. I am the Lord. (sanctuary: holy place) **31.** Do not consult mediums or spiritists, or you will be defiled by them. I am the Lord your God. (mediums: fortune-tellers, spiritists: those who communicate with spirits, defiled: made impure) **32.** Stand in honor of the elderly and fear your God. I am the Lord. (stand in honor: respect, fear: reverence) **33.** If a foreigner lives among you, do not mistreat them. (mistreat: harm) **34.** Treat the foreigner as one of your own people, and love them as yourself. For you were foreigners in Egypt. I am the Lord your God. (own people: fellow citizens) **35.** Do not cheat in measurements, weight, or volume. (measurements: dimensions, volume: quantity) **36.** Use honest scales, weights, and measures. I am the Lord your God, who brought you out of Egypt. (honest: fair, scales: weighing instruments) **37.** Therefore, keep all my statutes and judgments, and follow them. I am the Lord." (statutes: laws, judgments: decrees, follow: obey)

Chapter 20

1. And the LORD spoke to Moses, saying: **2.** Tell the children of Israel: Anyone, whether Israelite or foreigner, who gives his child to Molech, must be put to death. The people shall stone him. (Foreigner: outsider, stone: throw stones at) **3.** I will set my face against him and cut him off from his people for defiling my sanctuary and profaning my name. (Face: turn against, cut off: remove, defiling: desecrating, profaning: disrespecting) **4.** If the people ignore the man when he offers his child to Molech and do not kill him, (ignore: disregard) **5.** I will turn my face against him and his family, and all who follow his example in worshiping Molech. (Turn: direct, example: pattern) **6.** Anyone who seeks out spirits or wizards will be cut off from among their people. (Seeks out: consults, wizards: sorcerers) **7.** Sanctify yourselves, and be holy, for I am the LORD your God. (Sanctify: purify, holy: set apart) **8.** Keep my statutes and follow them; I am the LORD who sanctifies you. (Statutes: laws, follow: obey, sanctifies: makes holy) **9.** Anyone who curses their father or mother must be put to death; their blood is on them. (curses: insults) **10.** The man who commits adultery with another's wife, both the adulterer and the adulteress, must be put to death. (Commits: has, adulterer: male cheater, adulteress: female cheater) **11.** The man who sleeps with his father's wife, uncovering his father's nakedness, must die, as must she. (sleeps with: has relations with, uncovering: exposing, nakedness: private parts) **12.** If a man lies with his daughter-in-law, both shall die; they have committed wickedness. (Lies with: has relations with, wickedness: evil) **13.** If a man sleeps with another man as he would with a woman, both have committed an abomination and must die. (Sleeps with: has relations with, abomination: sin) **14.** If a man marries both a woman and her mother, they shall be burned with fire for their wickedness. (Wickedness: evil) **15.** If a man lies with a beast, both the man and the beast must die. (Lies with: have relations with, beast: animal) **16.** If a woman approaches a beast and lies with it, both the woman and the beast must die. (approaches: comes near, lies with: has relations with) **17.** If a man sleeps with his sister, he has uncovered her nakedness, and they must be cut off from their people. (Sleeps with: has relations with, uncovered: exposed, nakedness: private parts) **18.** If a man sleeps with a woman during her menstrual period, both are cut off from their people. (sleeps with: has relations with, menstrual period: monthly cycle) **19.** Do not uncover the nakedness of your aunts, for they are your near kin. (uncover: expose, nakedness: private parts, kin: relatives) **20.** If a man lies with his uncle's wife, they shall bear their sin and die childless. (lies with: has relations with, bear: carry, childless: without children) **21.** If a man marries his brother's wife, it is unclear, and they will be childless. (unclean: sinful, childless: without children) **22.** Keep all my statutes and judgments, or the land will expel you. (statutes: laws, judgments: decrees, expel: force out) **23.** Do not follow the customs of the nations I am driving out, for they committed these sins and I abhorred them. (Follow: imitate, customs: practices, abhorred: hated) **24.** You will inherit their land, a land flowing with milk and honey. I am the LORD your God, who has separated you from other people. (Inherit: receive, flowing: abundant, separated: set apart) **25.** Distinguish between clean and unclean animals, and do not defile yourselves with unclean creatures. (Distinguish: separate, defile: pollute, creatures: animals) **26.** Be holy to me, for I am holy and have set you apart as my people. (Holy: set apart, set apart: chosen) **27.** Anyone with a familiar spirit or who practices witchcraft must be put to death; they shall be stoned with stones. (Familiar spirit: medium, witchcraft: sorcery, stoned: executed by stones).

Chapter 21

1. The LORD said to Moses, Speak to the priests, the sons of Aaron: No one among them should become unclean by contact with the dead, except for close family members. (unclean: impure, contact: touching) **2.** A priest may become unclean for his mother, father, son, daughter, or brother. (unclean: impure) **3.** He may also become unclean for his unmarried sister who is close to him. (unmarried: single) **4.** However, as a leader among his people, a priest should not make himself unclean in such a way that would dishonor his role. (Leader: guide, dishonor: disgrace, role: position) **5.** Priests must not shave their heads, trim their beards, or cut their bodies. (Shave: clip, trim: shorten, bodies: skin) **6.** They must be holy to God and not dishonor His name, as they offer the LORD's offerings and the bread of God. (holy: sacred, dishonor: defile, offerings: sacrifices) **7.** They must not marry a woman who is immoral or divorced, because they are holy to God. (Immoral: unchaste, divorced: separated) **8.** They are to be sanctified, for they offer the bread of God. They must remain holy, for I, the LORD, am holy. (sanctified: consecrated, remain: stay) **9.** If a priest's daughter becomes immoral, she dishonors her father and must be burned with fire. (Dishonors: disgraces) **10.** The high priest, who has been anointed with oil and consecrated to wear the special garments, must not uncover his head or tear his clothes. (Anointed: set apart, consecrated: dedicated, garments: clothing) **11.** He must not go near a dead body, even for his father or mother, and he must not leave the sanctuary, because the anointing oil of God is upon him. (Sanctuary: holy place, anointing: consecrating) **12.** The high priest must not profane the sanctuary, for I am the LORD. (Profane: desecrate, sanctuary: holy place) **13.** He must marry a virgin. (virgin: unmarried woman) **14.** He must not marry a widow, divorced woman, immoral woman, or harlot. He should marry a virgin from his own people. (Widow: bereaved woman, immoral: unchaste, harlot: prostitute) **15.** He must not dishonor his descendants, for I, the LORD, sanctify him. (Dishonor: disgrace, descendants: children) **16.** The LORD spoke to Moses: **17.** Speak to Aaron and tell him that any of his descendants with a physical defect may not approach to offer the bread of God. (Defect: flaw, approach: come near) **18.** Any man with a defect, such as being blind, lame, or having a flat nose, may not approach. (Defect: imperfection, lame: crippled, flat nose: deformed nose) **19.** This includes those with broken feet or hands, a crooked back, dwarfism, or defects in their eyes, skin diseases, or broken genitals. (Dwarfism: short stature, genitals: private parts) **20.** No man with a defect from Aaron's descendants shall come near to offer the LORD's offerings. (Offerings: sacrifices) **21.** However, such a man may eat the holy offerings. (holy: sacred, offerings: sacrifices) **22.** He can eat the bread of God, both the most holy and holy offerings, but he may not go into the inner sanctuary or approach the altar. (inner sanctuary: most holy place, altar: place of sacrifice) **23.** He should not profane the sanctuaries, for I, the LORD, sanctify them. (profane: desecrate, sanctuaries: holy places) **24.** Moses communicated these instructions to Aaron, his sons, and all the Israelites. (Communicated: conveyed, instructions: commands)

Chapter 22

1. And the LORD spoke to Moses, saying: **2.** Tell Aaron and his sons to separate themselves from the holy offerings of the Israelites, so they do not profane my holy name in the things they dedicate to me. I am the LORD. (separate: set apart, profane: disrespect) **3.** If anyone among your descendants is unclean and touches the holy offerings, they shall be cut off from my presence. (descendants: children, unclean: impure, cut off: removed) **4.** A priest with a skin disease or a bodily discharge must not eat of the holy offerings until he is clean. Anyone who touches a dead body, has an issue, or comes in contact with anything unclean is unclean. (skin disease: leprosy, bodily discharge: flow, issue: affliction) **5.** Those who touch creeping things or have other sources of uncleanness shall be unclean until evening, and they must wash before eating the holy offerings. (creeping things: insects, sources: causes, wash: cleanse) **6.** After sundown, they are clean and may eat the offerings, for it is their food. (sundown: sunset, clean: pure) **7.** They must not eat the meat of animals that die of themselves or are torn by beasts. I am the LORD. (torn: mauled) **8.** They must observe my ordinances to avoid sin and death if they profane them. I, the LORD, sanctify them. (observe: follow, ordinances: laws, avoid: prevent, profane: desecrate, sanctify: make holy) **9.** No foreigner shall eat the holy offerings, nor shall a hired servant or a priest's sojourner. (foreigner: outsider, hired servant: laborer, sojourner: temporary resident) **10.** Only those who belong to the priest's household, including those bought with money, may eat the holy offerings. (household: family, bought: purchased) **11.** A priest's daughter may eat the holy offerings if she returns to her father's house, but not if she marries a stranger. (returns: comes back, stranger: foreigner) **12.** If a priest's daughter is widowed or divorced and has no children, she may return to her father's house and eat the holy offerings, but a stranger may not. (widowed: lost her husband, divorced: separated, stranger: foreigner) **13.** If someone eats a holy offering unintentionally, they must pay a penalty of a fifth of the offering's value, plus the offering. (unintentionally: by mistake, penalty: fine, value: worth) **14.** The holy offerings must not be profaned, nor should those who eat them bear the guilt of their sin. I, the LORD, sanctify them. (profaned: desecrated, bear: carry, guilt: blame, sanctify: make holy) **17.** And the LORD spoke to Moses, saying: **18.** Speak to Aaron, his sons, and all the Israelites, and say: Anyone in Israel or a foreigner among them who offers an offering to the LORD, (foreigner: outsider) **19.** Must offer a male without defect, from the cattle, sheep, or goats. (defect: flaw) **20.** Do not offer anything with a blemish, for it will not be accepted. (blemish: imperfection, accepted: approved) **21.** Peace offerings made to fulfill a vow must be perfect to be accepted; there must be no defects. (vow: promise, perfect: flawless) **22.** Do not offer blind, broken, maimed, or diseased animals, nor anything with scabs or sores as a burnt offering to the LORD. (blind: sightless, broken: damaged, maimed: injured, diseased: sick, scabs: crusts, sores: wounds) **23.** You may offer an animal with a defect for a freewill offering, but not for a vow. (defect: flaw, freewill offering: voluntary gift, vow: promise) **24.** Do not offer bruised, crushed, broken, or cut animals, nor offer any of these in your land. (bruised: wounded, crushed: smashed, broken: damaged, cut: severed) **25.** Do not offer any animals with blemishes from a foreigner, for they are corrupt and not acceptable to you. (blemishes: imperfections, corrupt: spoiled, acceptable: approved) **26.** And the LORD spoke to Moses, saying: **27.** When a bull, sheep, or goat is born, it shall remain with its mother for seven days. On the eighth day, it may be accepted as a burnt offering. (remain: stay, accepted: approved) **28.** Do not kill both the mother and her young in the same day. (kill: slaughter) **29.** When offering a thanksgiving sacrifice, offer it as a freewill offering. (thanksgiving: gratitude, freewill offering: voluntary gift) **30.** It must be eaten the same day; nothing shall remain until morning. I am the LORD. (same: exact, remain: stay) **31.** Therefore, keep my commandments and follow them. I am the LORD. (keep: obey, commandments: laws, follow: observe) **32.** Do not profane my holy name, but I will be sanctified among the Israelites. I am the LORD who sanctifies you. (profane: dishonor, sanctified: set apart) **33.** I brought you out of Egypt to be your God. I am the LORD. (brought: delivered, Egypt: land of slavery).

Chapter 23

1. The Lord spoke to Moses, saying, **2.** "Tell the Israelites: 'These are the appointed festivals of the Lord, sacred gatherings you are to declare. (Convocations: Gatherings or assemblies) **3.** For six days you may work, but the seventh day is a Sabbath, a day of rest, a holy assembly. You must not work on that day; it is the Lord's Sabbath observed in all your homes. (Sabbath: A day of rest; Convocation: A gathering or assembly) **4.** These are the Lord's appointed feasts, sacred gatherings that you are to announce at their designated times. **5.** The Lord's Passover is to be celebrated on the fourteenth day of the first month, at twilight. (Twilight: The time between day and night) **6.** The next day, the fifteenth day of the same month, begins the Feast of Unleavened Bread. You will eat unleavened bread for seven days. (Unleavened: Without yeast) **7.** On the first day of the feast, hold a holy assembly and refrain from all regular work. (Customary: Usual or regular) **8.** For seven days, offer fire offerings to the Lord. The seventh day is a holy assembly, and no regular work should be done.' **9.** The Lord spoke to Moses, saying, **10.** "Say to the Israelites: 'When you enter the land I will give you and begin to harvest its crops, bring a sheaf of the firstfruits to the priest. (Sheaf: A bundle; Firstfruits: The first harvested crops) **11.** The priest will wave the sheaf before the Lord so it can be accepted on your behalf. This will take place on the day after the Sabbath. **12.** On that day, you must offer a one-year-old male lamb, without defect, as a burnt offering to the Lord. (Blemish: A flaw or imperfection) **13.** The accompanying grain offering shall be two-tenths of an ephah of fine flour mixed with oil, presented as a fire offering with a pleasing aroma, along with a drink offering of one-quarter hin of wine. (Ephah: A measure of grain; Hin: A measure of liquid) **14.** You must not eat any bread or fresh grain from your harvest until you have presented this offering to your God. This is a permanent law for all generations, wherever you live. (Statute: A law or command) **15.** From the day after the Sabbath, when you bring the sheaf of the wave offering, count seven weeks—complete the seven full weeks. **16.** Then, count fifty days from the day after the seventh Sabbath and offer a new grain offering to the Lord. **17.** Bring two loaves of fine flour, baked with yeast, as your firstfruits to the Lord. (Wave loaves: Loaves of bread presented as an offering; Leaven: Yeast) **18.** Along with the bread, present seven one-year-old lambs without defect, one young bull, and two rams. They are to be a burnt offering to the Lord, along with their grain and drink offerings, made by fire, with a pleasing aroma. **19.** You must also offer one goat as a sin offering and two male lambs as a peace offering. (Kid: A young goat) **20.** The priest will wave these offerings, together with the bread of the firstfruits, before the Lord. They will be holy to the Lord and set apart for the priest. **21.** Announce this day as a holy assembly and do no regular work. It is a lasting ordinance for all generations, wherever you live. **22.** When you harvest the crops of your land, do not harvest all the way to the edges of your fields, nor gather the leftover grain. Leave them for the poor and the foreigner. I am the Lord your God.' (Gleanings: Leftover crops collected after harvest; Stranger: A foreigner or outsider) **23.** The Lord spoke to Moses, saying, **24.** "Say to the Israelites: 'On the first day of the seventh month, observe a Sabbath of rest, a remembrance marked by the blowing of trumpets, a holy assembly. (Sabbath-rest: A day of rest; Memorial: A reminder or commemoration) **25.** Do no regular work, but present a fire offering to the Lord.' **26.** The Lord spoke to Moses, saying, **27.** "On the tenth day of the seventh month, observe the Day of Atonement. It is a holy assembly, and you must humble yourselves and present a fire offering to the Lord. (Atonement: The act of making amends for wrongs; Afflict: To humble or deny) **28.** Do no work on that day, for it is the Day of Atonement, meant to make atonement for you before the Lord. **29.** Anyone who does not humble themselves on that day will be cut off from their people. (Afflicted: Involved in self-denial or sorrow) **30.** Anyone who works on that day will be removed from among the people. **31.** Do no work on that day. It is a permanent law for all generations, wherever you live. **32.** It is a Sabbath of solemn rest, and you must humble yourselves. From evening to evening, celebrate the Sabbath on the ninth day of the month." **33.** The Lord spoke to Moses, saying, **34.** "Say to the Israelites: 'On the fifteenth day of the seventh month, the Feast of Tabernacles begins. It will last for seven days in honor of the Lord. (Tabernacles: Temporary shelters or booths) **35.** On the first day, hold a holy assembly and do no regular work. **36.** For seven days, present fire offerings to the Lord. On the eighth day, hold a holy assembly and offer a fire offering to the Lord. It will be a sacred gathering; do no regular work. (Sacred: Holy or set apart) **37.** These are the appointed feasts of the Lord, which you are to declare as holy assemblies. They include fire offerings to the Lord—burnt offerings, grain offerings, sacrifices, and drink offerings—each on its appointed day, **38.** in addition to the Lord's Sabbaths, your gifts, vows, and freewill offerings. **39.** On the fifteenth day of the seventh month, when you have gathered the crops of the land, celebrate the Feast of the Lord for seven days. The first day will be a Sabbath-rest, and the eighth day will also be a Sabbath-rest. **40.** On the first day, take the fruit of beautiful trees, branches of palm trees, boughs of leafy trees, and willows from the brook. Rejoice before the Lord for seven days. (Boughs: Branches; Willows of the brook: A type of tree grown near water) **41.** Celebrate this feast to the Lord for seven days each year. It is a lasting ordinance, to be celebrated in the seventh month. **42.** Live in temporary shelters (booths) for seven days. All native-born Israelites must live in booths, (Dwell: Live) **43.** so that your descendants will know that I made the Israelites live in booths when I brought them out of Egypt. I am the Lord your God.' **44.** So Moses declared to the Israelites the appointed feasts of the Lord."

Chapter 24
1. The LORD spoke to Moses and said, **2.** "Instruct the people of Israel to bring you pure olive oil, pressed, to keep the lamps burning continually." **3.** "Outside the curtain of the testimony, in the tabernacle, Aaron will keep the lamps in order from evening to morning before the LORD. This is a permanent law for all generations." (testimony: sacred place, permanent law: everlasting ordinance) **4.** "He is to arrange the lamps on the pure lampstand in front of the LORD at all times." (lampstand: candelabrum) **5.** "You will take fine flour and bake twelve loaves of bread. Each loaf should be made from two-tenths of an ephah of flour." (loaves: cakes, ephah: dry measure) **6.** "Place them in two rows, six in each row, on the pure table in front of the LORD." (place: set, rows: lines, pure: consecrated) **7.** "Put pure frankincense on each row of bread, so that it becomes an offering to the LORD, a memorial." (frankincense: incense, memorial: reminder, offering: sacrifice) **8.** "Every Sabbath, you will arrange the bread before the LORD, as a lasting covenant with the people of Israel." (lasting covenant: eternal agreement) **9.** "The bread belongs to Aaron and his sons, and they will eat it in the holy place. It is most holy, a part of the fire offerings to the LORD, and a statute that lasts forever." (fire offerings: burnt sacrifices, statute: law) **10.** "An Israelite woman's son, whose father was Egyptian, had a dispute with a man of Israel in the camp." (dispute: argument, camp: encampment) **11.** "The son of the Israelite woman blasphemed the name of the LORD and cursed. They brought him to Moses, and his mother's name was Shelomith, the daughter of Dibri, from the tribe of Dan." (blasphemed: disrespected, cursed: swore) **12.** "They kept him in custody until the LORD's will could be revealed." (custody: detention, will: decision) **13.** The LORD spoke to Moses, saying, **14.** "Take the one who has cursed outside the camp, and let all those who heard him place their hands on his head. Then the whole assembly will stone him." (stone: execute by stoning) **15.** "Tell the people of Israel, 'Anyone who curses God must bear the consequences.'" (consequences: punishment) **16.** "Anyone who blasphemes the name of the LORD must be put to death. The entire congregation shall stone him, whether a native or a foreigner. Anyone who blasphemes the name of the LORD shall be put to death." (blasphemes: disrespects, native: citizen) **17.** "Anyone who kills a person must be put to death." (kills: murders) **18.** "Anyone who kills an animal must make restitution, animal for animal." (restitution: compensation) **19.** "If a person injures another, as they have done, so it will be done to them:" (injures: harms) **20.** "Fracture for fracture, eye for eye, tooth for tooth. The injury caused by one person should be paid back in kind." (fracture: break, injury: harm) **21.** "Anyone who kills an animal shall make restitution, but anyone who kills a person shall be put to death." (make restitution: repay, put to death: executed) **22.** "There will be one law for both the foreigner and the native-born. For I am the LORD your God." (foreigner: outsider, native-born: citizen) **23.** Moses spoke to the people of Israel, and they took the man who had cursed outside the camp and stoned him, as the LORD commanded Moses. (stoned: executed by stoning).

Chapter 25
1. "The LORD spoke to Moses on Mount Sinai, saying:" **2.** "Speak to the people of Israel and tell them: When you enter the land I am giving you, the land must observe a sabbath rest to the LORD." (observe: keep, sabbath rest: rest day) **3.** "For six years, you shall sow your fields, prune your vineyards, and gather their produce." (sow: plant, produce: crops) **4.** "But in the seventh year, the land must rest. Do not sow your fields or prune your vineyards." (rest: lie fallow) **5.** "Do not harvest what grows on its own, and do not pick the untended grapes. It is a year of rest for the land." (harvest: gather, untended: unharvested) **6.** "The rest of the land will provide food for you, your servants, your maids, your hired workers, and for the foreigners living among you." (provide: supply, hired workers: employees) **7.** "It will also provide food for your animals and the wild beasts in the land. All of it will be for food." (beasts: animals) **8.** "You shall count seven sabbatical years, seven times seven years, making forty-nine years." (sabbatical: rest) **9.** "On the tenth day of the seventh month, the Day of Atonement, sound the trumpet

throughout the land." (atonement: reconciliation) **10.** "Consecrate the fiftieth year and proclaim liberty throughout the land to all its inhabitants. It will be a Jubilee year for you, and everyone will return to their land and family." (consecrate: sanctify, liberty: freedom) **11.** "In the fiftieth year, do not sow or harvest what grows on its own, nor pick the untended grapes. It is a holy year for you, and you will eat from the land's produce." (holy: sacred) **12.** "In the Jubilee year, every person will return to their property." (Jubilee: year of restoration, property: land) **13.** "If you sell anything to your neighbor or buy from them, do not cheat one another." (cheat: deceive) **14.** "When buying from your neighbor, the price should reflect the number of years until the Jubilee, and you should adjust the price based on the years of crops remaining." (adjust: change, crops: harvests) **15.** "If there are many years left, the price should be higher; if there are few years left, the price should be lower." (higher: greater, lower: smaller) **16.** "Do not oppress one another; fear God, for I am the LORD your God." (oppose: mistreat, fear: respect) **17.** "Follow my statutes, obey my judgments, and keep my commands, and you will live safely in the land." (statutes: laws, judgments: decrees, safely: securely) **18.** "The land will produce its fruit, and you will have plenty to eat and live in safety." (produce: yield, plenty: abundance) **19.** "If you ask, 'What will we eat in the seventh year if we do not sow or gather crops?' I will bless you in the sixth year, and it will produce enough for three years." (bless: provide for) **20.** "You will sow in the eighth year, but will still eat the produce from the sixth year until the ninth year, when the new crops come in." (sow: plant, produce: crops) **21.** "The land must not be sold permanently, because the land is mine. You are strangers and residents with me." (permanently: forever, strangers: outsiders) **22.** "In all the land you possess, you shall allow for the redemption of the land." (redemption: recovery) **23.** "If your brother becomes poor and sells some of his land, his nearest relative may redeem it." (redeem: buy back) **24.** "If there is no one to redeem it and the man is able, he may redeem the land himself." (redeem: buy back) **25.** "He should calculate the years since the sale and pay back the difference to the buyer, so that the land can return to him." (calculate: figure, difference: remaining amount) **26.** "If he cannot redeem it, the land will stay with the buyer until the Jubilee year, when it will be returned to the original owner." (stay: remain, returned: restored) **27.** "If a man sells a house in a walled city, he can redeem it within a year after the sale." (redeem: buy back) **28.** "If it is not redeemed within a full year, the house becomes the permanent property of the buyer and will not be returned in the Jubilee." (permanent: lasting, property: possession) **29.** "If a man sells a house in a village that is not surrounded by a wall, it may be redeemed, and it will be returned in the Jubilee year." (redeemed: bought back) **30.** "But houses in walled cities are not to be returned in the Jubilee year. Once sold, they remain the permanent property of the buyer." (permanent: lasting) **31.** "However, houses in villages without walls are treated as open fields and can be redeemed in the Jubilee year." (redeemed: bought back) **32.** "The Levites may redeem their houses in any city they own at any time." (redeem: buy back) **33.** "If a man buys a house from a Levite, it must be returned to him in the Jubilee year. The Levites' houses in their cities are their permanent possession." (permanent: lasting, possession: property) **34.** "But the field around their cities, which is their property, must not be sold. It is their perpetual possession." (perpetual: never-ending, possession: property) **35.** "If your brother becomes poor and is unable to support himself, you must help him, even if he is a foreigner or a traveler. Let him live with you." (support: provide for) **36.** "Do not charge him interest or make a profit from him. Fear God, so that your brother may live with you." (profit: extra gain) **37.** "Do not lend him money with interest, or sell him food at a profit." (interest: extra charge, profit: extra gain) **38.** "I am the LORD your God, who brought you out of Egypt to give you the land of Canaan, and to be your God." (brought: led) **39.** "If a man from your community becomes poor and sells himself to you, do not make him work as a slave." (slave: servant) **40.** "He shall be treated as a hired worker or a temporary resident. He will serve you until the year of Jubilee." (hired worker: employee, temporary resident: sojourner) **41.** "In the Jubilee year, he and his children shall be set free, and they will return to their family and the land of their ancestors." (set free: released) **42.** "For the Israelites are my servants, whom I brought out of Egypt. They must not be sold as slaves." (servants: workers) **43.** "Do not treat them harshly, but fear your God." (harshly: cruelly) **44.** "Your slaves and slave women, whom you acquire from the nations around you, may be inherited by your children after you. They may become your property." (acquire: obtain, slave women: female servants) **45.** "You may also acquire slaves from the foreigners who live among you, and from their families born in your land. These will be your property." (acquire: obtain) **46.** "You may keep them as a possession for your children after you, and they will serve you forever. But you must not treat your fellow Israelites harshly." (possession: property, serve: work) **47.** "If a foreigner or temporary resident becomes wealthy, and your brother becomes poor and sells himself to them or to a member of their family, you may redeem him." (redeem: buy back) **48.** "After he has been sold, his close relative may redeem him. Or if he is able, he may redeem himself." (redeem: buy back) **49.** "The price for his redemption will be based on how many years are left until the Jubilee. The amount will be like that of a hired worker." (redemption: buying back, hired worker: employee) **50.** "If many years remain, the cost of redemption will be higher. If only a few years remain, the price will be lower." (redemption: buying back) **51.** "If the man is not redeemed during those years, he and his children will go free in the Jubilee year." (redeemed: bought back) **52.** "For the Israelites are my servants. I brought them out of Egypt to be their God, so they must not be sold as slaves." (servants: workers) **53.** "Do not treat him with severity, but as a hired worker, or as a guest among you." (severity: harshness) **54.** "If he is not redeemed in these years, then he and his children will be released in the Jubilee year." (redeemed: bought back, released: freed) **55.** "For the Israelites are my servants, whom I brought out of Egypt. I am the LORD your God." (servants: workers, brought: led)

Chapter 26

1. "Do not make idols or carved images, or set up any stone images in your land to worship them. I am the LORD your God." (idols: false gods, carved: sculpted, images: statues) **2.** "Observe my Sabbaths and honor my sanctuary. I am the LORD." (Observe: keep, Sabbaths: rest days, honor: respect, sanctuary: holy place) **3.** "If you obey my laws, follow my commands, and live according to them," (obey: listen to, laws: rules, commands: instructions) **4.** "I will send rain at the proper time, and the land will yield its produce. The trees will bear their fruit." (proper: right, yield: produce, produce: crops) **5.** "Your harvests will last until the next planting season, and you will have enough food. You will live securely in your land." (harvests: crops, planting: sowing, securely: safely) **6.** "I will bring peace to your land, and you will be able to rest without fear. I will remove harmful animals, and there will be no war in your land." (peace: harmony, harmful: dangerous) **7.** "You will defeat your enemies, and they will fall before you by the sword." (defeat: overcome, sword: weapon) **8.** "Five of you will chase a hundred, and a hundred of you will chase ten thousand. Your enemies will fall before you." (chase: pursue, fall: collapse) **9.** "I will look favorably on you, multiply you, and keep my covenant with you." (favorably: kindly, multiply: increase, covenant: agreement) **10.** "You will eat the crops from previous years, and there will be enough for the new harvest." (crops: produce, harvest: yield) **11.** "I will set my presence among you, and I will not reject you." (presence: dwelling, reject: refuse) **12.** "I will walk among you, be your God, and you will be my people." (walk: live, people: followers) **13.** "I am the LORD your God, who brought you out of Egypt so you would no longer be slaves. I broke the yoke of your bondage and set you free." (slaves: servants, yoke: burden, bondage:

oppression, set free: liberated) **14.** "But if you do not listen to me and refuse to obey my commands," (refuse: reject, obey: follow) **15.** "If you despise my laws and break my covenant," (despise: hate, break: violate) **16.** "Then I will bring terror, diseases, and fever that will drain your energy and cause grief. Your crops will be taken by your enemies." (terror: fear, diseases: illnesses, grief: sorrow, crops: produce) **17.** "I will turn against you, and you will be defeated by those who hate you. You will flee even when no one is chasing you." (defeated: overcome, flee: run) **18.** "If you still do not listen, I will punish you seven times more for your sins." (punish: correct) **19.** "I will break your pride and make your skies like iron and your land like bronze." (pride: arrogance) **20.** "Your strength will be wasted, and the land will not yield crops. The trees will not bear fruit." (strength: energy, yield: produce, bear fruit: grow) **21.** "If you continue to oppose me, I will increase your punishments seven times more according to your sins." (oppose: resist, increase: multiply) **22.** "I will send wild animals among you that will harm your children, destroy your livestock, and reduce your numbers. Your roads will be deserted." (wild: dangerous, harm: hurt, livestock: animals, deserted: empty) **23.** "If you remain unrepentant and continue to oppose me," (unrepentant: unchanged, oppose: resist) **24.** "Then I will oppose you and punish you seven times more for your sins." (oppose: resist, punish: correct) **25.** "I will bring a sword upon you to avenge the breaking of my covenant. When you gather in your cities, I will send plagues, and you will be handed over to your enemies." (avenge: seek revenge, plagues: diseases, handed over: surrendered) **26.** "When I break your food supply, ten women will bake your bread in one oven. They will give you bread by weight, and you will eat but not be satisfied." (supply: provision, weight: measure) **27.** "If you do not listen to me but continue to oppose me," (oppose: resist) **28.** "Then I will punish you in anger and chastise you seven times more for your sins." (punish: correct, chastise: rebuke, anger: wrath) **29.** "You will eat the flesh of your sons and daughters." (flesh: meat) **30.** "I will destroy your places of worship, cut down your idols, and throw your dead bodies on top of your idols. I will reject you." (destroy: demolish, places of worship: temples, idols: statues) **31.** "I will make your cities desolate, destroy your temples, and refuse to accept your offerings." (desolate: empty, temples: holy places, offerings: sacrifices) **32.** "I will bring your land to ruin, and the nations living there will be shocked." (ruin: destruction, shocked: astonished) **33.** "I will scatter you among the nations and bring the sword after you. Your land will be desolate, and your cities will be in ruins." (scatter: disperse, desolate: empty, ruins: wreckage) **34.** "Then the land will rest and enjoy its Sabbaths while it lies desolate. You will be in your enemies' land, and the land will rest." (rest: relax, Sabbaths: rest days) **35.** "As long as the land remains desolate, it will rest, for it did not observe the Sabbaths while you were living in it." (remains: stays, observe: keep) **36.** "Those of you who remain will feel faint and fearful in the land of your enemies. The sound of a rustling leaf will make them flee, and they will run as if fleeing from a sword." (faint: weak, rustling: shaking, flee: run) **37.** "They will stumble over one another, as though running from a sword, even when no one is chasing them. You will have no strength to stand before your enemies." (stumble: trip, flee: run, strength: power) **38.** "You will perish among the nations, and the land of your enemies will consume you." (perish: die, consume: devour) **39.** "Those of you who remain will waste away in the lands of your enemies because of their sins, and the sins of their ancestors will also weigh them down." (waste away: weaken, weigh down: burden) **40.** "If they confess their sins and the sins of their ancestors, and acknowledge their rebellion against me," (confess: admit, rebellion: defiance) **41.** "And if they humble their hearts and accept the punishment for their sins," (humble: lower, punishment: correction) **42.** "Then I will remember my covenant with Jacob, Isaac, and Abraham, and I will remember the land." (covenant: agreement) **43.** "The land will be abandoned by them and will rest while it lies desolate without them. They will accept the punishment for their sins because they despised my laws and abhorred my statutes." (abandoned: deserted, despised: hated, abhorred: loathed) **44.** "Yet, even in the land of their enemies, I will not cast them away or completely destroy them. I will not break my covenant with them, for I am the LORD their God." (cast away: reject, completely: entirely, destroy: ruin) **45.** "But I will remember the covenant I made with their ancestors, whom I brought out of Egypt in the sight of the nations, to be their God. I am the LORD." (ancestors: forefathers, brought out: freed) **46.** "These are the laws, decrees, and instructions the LORD gave to the Israelites at Mount Sinai through Moses." (laws: rules, decrees: commands, instructions: directions)

Chapter 27

1. The Lord spoke to Moses. **2.** Tell the Israelites that if someone makes a special vow, the value of the person will be set by your estimation. (vow: promise, estimation: assessment) **3.** For a man aged 20-60, the value is 50 shekels of silver. **4.** For a woman, the value is 30 shekels. **5.** For a boy aged 5-20, the value is 20 shekels; for a girl, 10 shekels. **6.** For a child aged 1 month to 5 years, a boy is worth 5 shekels, and a girl is worth 3 shekels. **7.** For a person aged 60 and above, a man is worth 15 shekels, and a woman 10 shekels. (if you're setting values: value: worth, shekels: silver coins) **8.** If someone is too poor to meet the set value, they should present themselves to the priest, who will adjust the value based on their ability. (adjust: modify, ability: means) **9.** If someone dedicates an animal as an offering to the Lord, it is holy. (dedicates: consecrates, offering: gift, holy: sacred) **10.** It must not be swapped for another; if swapped, both animals become holy. (swapped: exchanged) **11.** If it's an unclean animal, the owner must present it to the priest for valuation. (unclean: impure, valuation: assessment) **12.** The priest will assess whether it is good or bad and set the value accordingly. (assess: evaluate, accordingly: appropriately) **13.** If the owner wants to redeem it, they must add a fifth of its value to the price. (redeem: buy back, fifth: 20%, price: cost) **14.** If a person sanctifies their house, the priest will assess its value, good or bad. (sanctifies: dedicates, value: worth) **15.** If they want to redeem the house, they must add a fifth of its value. (redeem: buy back) **16.** If someone sanctifies part of their field, its value depends on the type of seed, for example, 50 shekels for an homer of barley seed. (depends: is based, seed: crops, homer: measurement, barley: type of grain) **17.** If the field is sanctified in the Year of Jubilee, it is valued based on the jubilee year. (sanctified: dedicated, Jubilee: special year, valued: assessed) **18.** If someone sanctifies their field after the Jubilee, the priest will calculate its value based on the remaining years until the Jubilee and reduce the value accordingly. (sanctifies: dedicates, calculate: determine, remaining: leftover, reduce: lower, accordingly: appropriately) **19.** If the person wants to redeem the field, they must add a fifth of its value, and it will be secured for them. (redeem: buy back, fifth: 20%, secured: protected) **20.** If they don't redeem the field or sell it to someone else, it cannot be redeemed. (redeem: recover, sell: transfer) **21.** The field will be holy in the Jubilee and belong to the priests. (holy: sacred, Jubilee: special year, belong: revert) **22.** If someone sanctifies a field they bought, not part of their own land, (sanctifies: dedicates, bought: purchased, part: portion) **23.** The priest will assess its value based on the years until the Jubilee, and it will be given as a holy offering to the Lord. (assess: evaluate, value: worth, offering: gift, given: presented) **24.** In the Jubilee, the field will return to its original owner. (return: revert, original: former) **25.** All valuations should be made according to the shekel of the sanctuary, which is 20 gerahs. (valuations: assessments, shekel: unit of currency, sanctuary: holy place, gerahs: smaller unit) **26.** The firstborn of animals belongs to the Lord; it cannot be sanctified. (firstborn: eldest, belongs: is dedicated, sanctified: consecrated) **27.** If it's an unclean animal, it may be redeemed for its value, adding a fifth of its worth. If not redeemed, it is sold at the estimated value. (unclean: impure, redeemed: bought back, worth: value, estimated: appraised) **28.** No devoted item, whether a person, animal, or field, can be sold or redeemed; it is entirely holy to the Lord. (devoted: consecrated, sold: transferred, redeemed: recovered, entirely: completely) **29.** A devoted person must be put to death; they cannot be redeemed. (devoted: consecrated, put to death: executed, redeemed: bought back) **30.** A tenth of the land's produce, whether grain or fruit, belongs to the Lord and is holy. (tenth: 10%, produce: harvest, grain: cereal crops, fruit: produce) **31.** If a person redeems part of their tithe, they must add a fifth of its value. (redeems: buys back, tithe: 10% offering, part: portion, value: worth) **32.** The tithe of livestock, whether cattle or sheep, is also holy to the Lord, and a tenth must be given. (tithe: 10% offering, livestock: animals, cattle: cows, sheep: wooly animals) **33.** The owner must not check if it's good or bad, and if they exchange it, both the original and the replacement are holy and cannot be redeemed. (check: examine, exchange: swap, original: initial, replacement: substitute) **34.** These are the commandments the Lord gave Moses for the Israelites at Mount Sinai. (commandments: instructions, gave: delivered, Israelites: people of Israel, Sinai: mountain).

4 – Numbers
Chapter 1

1. The LORD spoke to Moses in the Tabernacle, in the wilderness of Sinai, on the first day of the second month of the second year after the Israelites had left Egypt. He said: (Tabernacle: Sacred tent; Wilderness: Desert) **2.** "Take a census of all the people of Israel, organizing them by their tribes and families, and record the name of every man individually. (Census: Population count; Tribes: Family groups) **3.** You and Aaron are to count all the men of Israel who are twenty years or older and able to serve in the army, based on their tribal divisions. (Tribal divisions: Groups by families; Army: Military service) **4.** A leader from each tribe, who is the head of his family, will assist you. (Leader: Chief; Head: Leader) **5.** Here are the names of the men who will help you: from Reuben, Elizur son of Shedeur; **6.** from Simeon, Shelumiel son of Zurishaddai; (Simeon: Tribe; Shelumiel: Name) **7.** from Judah, Nahshon son of Amminadab **8.** from Issachar, Nethanel son of Zuar; **9.** from Zebulun, Eliab son of Helon; **10.** from the sons of Joseph: from Ephraim, Elishama son of Ammihud; and from Manasseh, Gamaliel son of Pedahzur; (Joseph: Patriarch; Ephraim: Tribe; Manasseh: Tribe) **11.** from Benjamin, Abidan son of Gideoni; (Benjamin: Tribe; Abidan: Name) **12.** from Dan, Ahiezer son of Ammishaddai **13.** from Asher, Pagiel son of Okran; (Asher: Tribe; Pagiel: Name) **14.** from Gad, Eliasaph son of Deuel; **15.** from Naphtali, Ahira son of Enan." (Naphtali: Tribe; Ahira: Name) **16.** These are the men chosen from the community, the leaders of their families. They were the heads of the Israelite clans. (Chosen: Selected; Leaders: Chiefs) **17.** Moses and Aaron gathered these men, whose names were given to them, (Gathered: Assembled; Names: Identifiers) **18.** and called the whole community together on the first day of the second month. The people recorded their family lineage by their tribes, and all men twenty years or older were listed by name, one by one, (Community: Group; Lineage: Ancestry) **19.** as the LORD had commanded Moses. So, Moses took the count in the wilderness of Sinai: (Commanded: Instructed; Wilderness: Desert) **20.** From the descendants of Reuben, the firstborn son of Israel: every man twenty years or older, able to serve in the army, was listed by name, according to the records of their families. (Reuben: Tribe; Able: Capable) **21.** The total number from the tribe of Reuben was 46,500. From the descendants of Simeon: all the men twenty years or older who could serve in the army were listed by name, based on the records of their families. (Simeon: Tribe; Serve: Fight) **23.** The total number from the tribe of Simeon was 59,300. (Total: Sum; Tribe: Family group) **24.** From the descendants of Gad: all the men twenty years or older who were fit for military service were listed according to their family records. **25.** The total number from the tribe of Gad was 45,650. (Tribe: Family group) **26.** From the descendants of Judah: all the men twenty years or older, capable of military service, were listed according to their clan records. **27.** The total number from the tribe of Judah was 74,600. (Tribe: Family group) **28.** From the descendants of Issachar: all the men twenty years or older who were able to serve in the army were listed according to their family records. (Issachar: Tribe; Able: Capable) **29.** The total number from the tribe of Issachar was 54,400. (Total: Sum; Tribe: Family group) **30.** From the descendants of Zebulun: all the men twenty years or older who could serve in the army were listed according to their family records. (Zebulun: Tribe; Serve: Fight) **31.** The total number from the tribe of Zebulun was 57,400. **32.** From the sons of Joseph: From the descendants of Ephraim: All the men twenty years old or older who could serve in the army were listed by name, according to their clans and families. **33.** The total number from the tribe of Ephraim was 40,500. **34.** From the descendants of Manasseh: All the men twenty years old or older who could serve in the army were listed by name, according to their clans and families. **35.** The total number from the tribe of Manasseh was 32,200. **36.** From the descendants of Benjamin: All the men twenty years old or older who could serve in the army were listed by name, according to their clans and families. **37.** The total number from the tribe of Benjamin was 35,400. **38.** From the descendants of Dan: All the men twenty years old or older who could serve in the army were listed by name, according to their clans and families. (Dan: Tribe; Army: Military service) **39.** The total number from the tribe of Dan was 62,700. **40.** From the descendants of Asher: All the men twenty years old or older who could serve in the army were listed by name, according to their clans and families. (Asher: Tribe; Army: Military service). **41.** The total number from the tribe of Asher was 41,500. . **42.** From the descendants of Naphtali: All the men twenty years old or older who could serve in the army were listed by name, according to their clans and families. **43.** The total number from the tribe of Naphtali was 53,400. . **44.** These were the men counted by Moses and Aaron, along with the twelve leaders of Israel, each representing his family. (Leaders: Chiefs; Representing: Standing for) **45.** All the Israelites aged twenty years or older, who were able to serve in Israel's army, were counted by their families. (Israelites: Descendants; Army: Military service). **46.** The total number was 603,550. **47.** However, the tribe of Levi was not included in this count. (Levi: Tribe). **48.** The LORD had commanded Moses, (LORD: God) **49.** "Do not count the tribe of Levi or include them in the census of the other Israelites. (Levi: Tribe). **50.** Instead, appoint the Levites to be responsible for the care of the tabernacle of the covenant law—over all its furnishings and everything that belongs to it. They are to carry the tabernacle and all its furnishings, take care of it, and set up camp around it. (Levites: Tribe; Tabernacle: Sacred tent). **51.** Whenever the tabernacle is to move, the Levites must take it down. When the tabernacle is to be set up, the Levites will do it. Anyone else who comes near it must be put to death. (Tabernacle: Sacred tent; Put to death: Execute) **52.** The Israelites will set up their camps by divisions, each group in their designated area under their standard. (Divisions: Groups; Standard: Flag). **53.** The Levites, however, will set up their camp around the tabernacle of the covenant law so that my anger will not fall upon the Israelite community. The Levites will be responsible for the care of the tabernacle of the covenant law." (Tabernacle: Sacred tent; Covenant: Agreement). **54.** The Israelites did everything just as the LORD commanded Moses. (Commanded: Ordered).

Chapter 2

1. The LORD gave instructions to Moses and Aaron, saying (Instructions: Commands) **2.** "The Israelites are to set up camp around the temple, each group under their flag, with their families gathered together." (Tabernacle: Tent of meeting; Group: Division) **3.** On the east side, facing the daylight, the lineage of Judah will chamber under their banner, led by Nahshon, son of Amminadab. (Banner: Flag; Nahshon: Leader of Judah) **4.** Judah's camp will correspond of 74,600 men. **5.** The lineage of Issachar will chamber coming to them, with Nethanel son of Zuar as their leader. (Issachar: Tribe) **6.** Issachar's division will number 54,400 men. **7.** Beside them, the lineage of Zebulun will chamber, led by Eliab son of Helon. (Beside: Next to) **8.** Zebulun's camp will have 57,400 men. **9.** The total number for Judah's camp, including all its divisions, will be 186,400 men. They will march first. (Total: Sum; March: Begin the trip) **10.** On the south side, the lineage of Reuben will chamber under their flag, with Elizur son of Shedeur as their leader. (Reuben: Tribe; Flag: Banner). **11.** Reuben's camp will have 46,500 men. . **12.** The lineage of Simeon will chamber coming to Reuben, led by Shelumiel son of Zurishaddai. (Simeon: Tribe). **13.** Simeon's camp will correspond of 59,300 men. (Camp: Group of dogfaces). **14.** The lineage of Gad will chamber beside Simeon, with Eliasaph son of Deuel as their leader. (Gad: Tribe). **15.** Gad's camp will have 45,650 men. **16.** The total number for Reuben's camp, including all its divisions, will be 151,450 men. They will march second. (Total: Sum; March: Depart) **17.** The temple and the Levites will be positioned in the middle of the camps. They will travel in the same order as they chamber, each group staying in its designated place. (Levites: Priestly lineage). **18.** To the west, the lineage of Ephraim will chamber under their banner, led by Elishama son of Ammihud. (Ephraim: Tribe). **19.** Ephraim's camp will have 40,500 men. **20.** The lineage of Manasseh will chamber beside Ephraim, with Gamaliel son of Pedahzur as their leader. (Manasseh: Tribe). **21.** Manasseh's camp will number 32,200 men. . **22.** The lineage of Benjamin will chamber coming to Manasseh, led by Abidan son of Gideoni. (Benjamin: Tribe) **23.** Benjamin's camp will have 35,400 men. . **24.** The total number for Ephraim's camp, including all its divisions, will be 108,100 men. They will march third. (Total: Sum; March: Depart) **25.** On the north side, the lineage of Dan will chamber under their banner, with Ahiezer son of Ammishaddai as their leader. (Dan: Tribe). **26.** Dan's camp will have 62,700 men. . **27.** The lineage of Asher will chamber coming to Dan, led by Pagiel son of Okran. (Asher: Tribe) **28.** Asher's camp will number 41,500 men. **29.** The lineage of Naphtali will chamber beside Asher, with Ahira son of Enan as their leader. (Naphtali: Tribe). **30.** Naphtali's camp will have 53,400 men. . **31.** The total number for Dan's camp, including all its divisions, will be 157,600 men. They will march last. (Total: Sum; March: Depart) **32.** These are the total figures of the Israelites, organized by their families. All the men in the camps, by their divisions, total 603,550. (Total: Sum; Divisions: Groups). **33.** The Levites weren't included in this count, as the LORD had commanded Moses. (Levites: Priestly lineage). **34.** The Israelites followed all the instructions given by the LORD to Moses, setting up camp and marching in the order He commanded, each group by its family and lineage. (Instructions: Commands; Group: Division).

Chapter 3

1. This is the account of Aaron and Moses when the LORD spoke to Moses at Mount Sinai. (Account: Record) **2.** Aaron's sons were Nadab (the firstborn), Abihu, Eleazar, and Ithamar. (Firstborn: Eldest son) **3.** These were the names of Aaron's sons, the blessed priests, chosen to serve as priests. (Consecrated: Set apart as sacred) **4.** Nadab and Abihu failed before the LORD when they offered unauthorized fire before Him in the Desert of Sinai. They had no sons, so Eleazar and Ithamar served as priests during Aaron's continuance. (Unauthorized: Not allowed; Duties: Arrears) **5.** The LORD said to Moses. (Said: Commanded) **6.** "Bring the lineage of Levi and present them to Aaron the clerk to help him." (Help: Assist) **7.** They are to serve him and the entire community at the roof of meeting, minding for the tabernacle. (Tabernacle: Sacred tent) **8.** They will take care of the tabernacle's furnishings and fulfill the Israelites' scores related to it. (Furnishings: Sacred particulars) **9.** Assign the Levites to Aaron and his sons; they are fully devoted to him. (Devoted: Committed) **10.** Appoint Aaron and his sons as priests, and anyone else who approaches the sanctuary should be put to death." (Sanctuary: Holy area) **11.** The LORD also said to Moses. (Said: Commanded) **12.** "I have taken the Levites from among the Israelites to replace the firstborn of every Israelite woman. The Levites are Mine." (Mine: Belong to Me) **13.** For every firstborn belongs to Me. When I struck down the firstborn in Egypt, I sanctified every firstborn in Israel, whether mortal or beast, to be Mine. I am the LORD." (Sanctified: Made holy) **14.** The LORD spoke to Moses in the desert of Sinai, saying. (Saying: Commanding) **15.** "Count the Levites by their families and clans. Count every virile one month old or aged." (Count: Take a tally) **16.** So Moses counted them as the LORD commanded. (Counted: Recorded) **17.** These were the names of the sons of Levi: Gershon, Kohath, and Merari. (Names: Lineages) **18.** The Gershonite clans were Libni and Shimei. (Clans: Services) **19.** The Kohathite clans were Amram, Izhar, Hebron, and Uzziel. (Clans: Family groups) **20.** The Merarite clans were Mahli and Mushi. These were the Levite families. (Families: Lineages) **21.** To Gershon belonged the clans of the Libnites and Shimeites; these were the Gershonite clans. (Clans: Family groups) **22.** The number of males one month old or older was 7,500. (Males: Men or boys) **23.** The Gershonite clans were to camp on the west side of the tabernacle. (West side: Direction of the evening) **24.** The leader of the Gershonite families was Eliasaph, son of Lael. (Leader: Chief) **25.** The Gershonites were responsible for the care of the tabernacle's roof, coverings, and the curtain at its entrance, (Coverings: Protective materials) **26.** the yard's curtains and the curtain at the entrance, as well as the ropes and all related items. (Ropes: Strong cords) **27.** To Kohath belonged the clans of the Amramites, Izharites, Hebronites, and Uzzielites. (Clans: Family groups) **28.** The number of males one month old or older was 8,600. The Kohathites were responsible for the care of the sanctuary. (Sanctuary: Holy place) **29.** The Kohathite clans were to camp on the south side of the tabernacle. (South side: Opposite of north) **30.** The leader of the Kohathite families was Elizaphan, son of Uzziel. (Leader: Chief) **31.** They cared for the ark, table, lampstand, altars, and other sacred items used in the tabernacle. (Sacred: Holy) **32.** Eleazar, son of Aaron, was the chief of the Levites, in charge of the sanctuary. (Chief: Highest-ranking). **33.** To Merari belonged the clans of the Mahlites and Mushites. The number of males one month or older was 6,200. (Clans: Subdivisions). **34.** The leader of the Merarite families was Zuriel, son of Abihail. They camped on the north side. (Leader: Chief). **35.** The Merarites were responsible for the frames of the tabernacle, its crossbars, posts, and bases, and all related items, (Frames: Structural supports) **36.** Including the posts of the courtyard with their bases, tent pegs, and ropes. (Tent pegs: Stakes to secure the tent). **37.** Moses, Aaron, and his sons camped east of the tabernacle, in front of the tent of meeting. They were responsible for the sanctuary. Anyone else approaching the sanctuary was to be put to death. (Sanctuary: Holy area). **38.** The total number of Levites counted was 22,000, as commanded by the LORD. **39.** The LORD said to Moses: (Said: Commanded) **40.** "Count all the firstborn Israelite males, one month or older, and list their names. (Firstborn: Eldest son). **41.** Take the Levites for Me in place of the firstborn of the Israelites, and the Levites' livestock for the Israelites' livestock. I am the LORD." (Livestock: Domesticated animals). **42.** So Moses counted all the firstborn of the Israelites, as commanded. (Counted: Recorded). **43.** The total number of firstborn males one month or older was 22,273. **44.** The LORD also said to Moses: (Said: Commanded) **45.** "Take the Levites in place of all the firstborn of Israel, and the Levites' livestock in place of theirs. The Levites are Mine. I am the LORD." (Mine: Belonging to Me) **46.** To redeem the 273 firstborn Israelites exceeding the Levites' number, (Redeem: Buy back) **47.** collect five shekels for each, according to the sanctuary shekel, which weighs twenty gerahs. (Shekel: Ancient currency). **48.** Give the redemption money to Aaron and his sons." (Redemption: Payment to free). **49.** So Moses collected the redemption money from those exceeding the Levites' number. (Collected: Gathered) **50.** Moses collected 1,365 shekels of silver from the firstborn of Israel, according to the sanctuary shekel. (Silver: Precious metal). **51.** Moses gave the redemption money to Aaron and his sons, as commanded by the LORD. (Gave: Delivered).

Chapter 4
1. The LORD spoke to Moses and Aaron, announcing, **2.** "Take a census of the Kohathite department of the Levites by way of their clans and households. (Census: count) **3.** Count all the men between the ages of thirty and fifty who are to serve in the work at the tent of meeting. (Tent of meeting: sacred place of worship) **4.** "This is the work of the Kohathites at the tent of meeting: the care of the most holy things. (Holy: sacred) **5.** When the camp is to move, Aaron and his sons shall go in, take down the shielding curtain, and cover the ark of the covenant law with it. (Shielding curtain: protective cover) **6.** Then they shall cover the curtain with a durable leather, spread a solid blue cloth over that, and put the poles in place. (Durable: strong) **7.** "Over the table of the Presence they are to spread a blue cloth and place the plates, dishes, bowls, and jars for drink offerings on it; the bread that is continually there shall remain on it. **8.** They are to cover them with a scarlet cloth, place a durable leather covering over that, and put the poles in place. (Scarlet: red) **9.** "They are to take a blue cloth and cover the lampstand for light, along with its lamps, wick trimmers, trays, and all its jars of olive oil. (Lampstand: holder for lamps) **10.** Then they shall wrap it and all its accessories in a covering of durable leather and place it on a carrying frame. (Carrying frame: transport structure) **11.** "Over the gold altar they are to spread a blue cloth, cover it with durable leather, and put the poles in place. (Altar: place of sacrifice) **12.** "They are to take all the articles used for ministering in the sanctuary, wrap them in a blue cloth, cover them with durable leather, and place them on a carrying frame. (Ministering: serving) **13.** "They are to remove the ashes from the bronze altar and spread a purple cloth over it. (Bronze: made of copper and tin) **14.** Then they shall place all the utensils used for ministering at the altar on it, including the firepans, meat forks, shovels, and sprinkling bowls. Over it they are to spread a covering of durable leather and put the poles in place. (Firepans: containers for burning incense) **15.** "After Aaron and his sons have finished covering the holy furnishings and all the holy articles, and when the camp is ready to move, only then shall the Kohathites come and carry them. But they must not touch the holy things, or they will die. The Kohathites are to carry these things that are in the tent of meeting. (Furnishings: furniture or items) **16.** "Eleazar son of Aaron, the priest, shall have charge of the oil for the light, the fragrant incense, the regular grain offering, and the anointing oil. He shall be in charge of the entire tabernacle and everything in it, including its holy furnishings and articles." (Charge: responsibility) **17.** The LORD spoke to Moses and Aaron, saying, **18.** "See that the Kohathite tribal clans are not destroyed among the Levites. (Tribal: related to a tribe) **19.** So that they may live and not die when they come near the most holy things, do this for them: Aaron and his sons shall go into the sanctuary and assign to each man his work and what he is to carry. (Sanctuary: holy place) **20.** But the Kohathites must not go in to look at the holy things, even for a moment, or they will die. (Look: gaze) **21.** The LORD spoke to Moses, saying, (LORD: God) **22.** "Take a census also of the Gershonites by their families and clans. (Gershonites: descendants of Gershon) **23.** Count all the men between the ages of thirty and fifty who come to serve in the work at the tent of meeting. (Tent of meeting: place of worship) **24.** "This is the service of the Gershonite clans in their carrying and other work: (Service: work) **25.** They are to carry the curtains of the tabernacle, that is, the tent of meeting, its covering, and its outer covering of durable leather, the curtains for the entrance to the tent of meeting, (Tabernacle: portable sanctuary) **26.** the curtains of the courtyard surrounding the tabernacle and the altar, the curtain for the entrance to the courtyard, the ropes, and all the equipment used in the service of the tent. The Gershonites are to do all that is needed with these things. (Courtyard: outdoor area) **27.** All their service, whether carrying or doing other work, is to be done under the direction of Aaron and his sons. You shall assign to them as their responsibility all that they are to carry. (Direction: guidance) **28.** This is the service of the Gershonite clans at the tent of meeting. Their duties are under the direction of Ithamar son of Aaron, the priest. (Duties: tasks) **29.** "Count the Merarites by their clans and families. (Merarites: descendants of Merari) **30.** Count all the men between the ages of thirty and fifty who come to serve in the work at the tent of meeting. (Tent of meeting: sacred space) **31.** As part of all their service at the tent, they are to carry the frames of the tabernacle, its crossbars, posts, and bases, (Frames: supports) **32.** as well as the posts of the surrounding courtyard with their bases, tent pegs, ropes, and all their equipment and everything related to their use. Assign to each man the specific things he is to carry. (Tent pegs: stakes) **33.** This is the service of the Merarite clans as they work at the tent of meeting under the direction of Ithamar son of Aaron, the priest." (Merarite: a member of Merari's descendants) **34.** Moses, Aaron, and the leaders of the community counted the Kohathites by their clans and families. (Leaders: heads of the community) **35.** All the men between the ages of thirty and fifty who came to serve in the work at the tent of meeting, (Tent of meeting: place of worship) **36.** counted by clans, were 2,750. (Clans: groups of families) **37.** This was the total of all those in the Kohathite clans who served at the tent of meeting. Moses and Aaron counted them according to the LORD's command through Moses. **38.** The Gershonites were counted by their clans and families. (Gershonites: descendants of Gershon) **39.** All the men between the ages of thirty and fifty who came to serve in the work at the tent of meeting, (Tent of meeting: sacred tent) **40.** counted by their clans and families, were 2,630. (Clans: families) **41.** This was the total of those in the Gershonite clans who served at the tent of meeting. Moses and Aaron counted them according to the LORD's command. **42.** The Merarites were counted by their clans and families. (Merarites: descendants of Merari) **43.** All the men between the ages of thirty and fifty who came to serve in the work at the tent of meeting, (Tent of meeting: the worship space) **44.** counted by their clans, were 3,200. (Clans: families) **45.** This was the total of those in the Merarite clans. Moses and Aaron counted them according to the LORD's command through Moses. **46.** So Moses, Aaron, and the leaders of Israel counted all the Levites by their clans and families. (Levites: descendants of Levi, priestly tribe) **47.** All the men between the ages of thirty and fifty who came to do the work of serving and carrying the tent of meeting (Tent of meeting: the sacred worship space) **48.** numbered 8,580. (Numbered: counted) **49.** At the LORD's command through Moses, each was assigned his work and told what to carry. Thus they were counted, as the LORD commanded Moses. (Assigned: given tasks)

Chapter 5
1. The LORD spoke to Moses, **2.** "Instruct the Israelites to send away anyone with a skin disease, bodily discharge, or who is ceremonially unclean due to contact with a dead body. (Skin disease: leprosy, Discharge: bodily flow, Ceremonially unclean: religiously impure) **3.** Send both men and women outside the camp so that they do not defile the camp where I dwell among them." (Defile: pollute, Dwell: live) **4.** The Israelites followed these instructions and sent the people outside the camp as the LORD had commanded Moses. (Followed: obeyed, Instructions: commands) **5.** Then the LORD spoke to Moses again, **6.** "Tell the Israelites: 'If someone wrongs another and violates their trust, they are guilty of sin against the LORD, (Wrongs: harms, Violates: betrays) **7.** and must confess their sin. They must make full restitution, adding one-fifth of the value, and give it to the person they wronged. (Confess: admit, Restitution: compensation) **8.** If the person wronged has no family member to receive restitution, the compensation goes to the LORD and is given to the priest, along with a ram for atonement. (Atonement: forgiveness, Ram: male sheep) **9.** All sacred offerings brought by the Israelites to a priest will belong to that priest. (Sacred: holy, Offerings: gifts) **10.** Sacred things belong to

their owners, but anything given to the priest will be the priest's property." (Property: possession) **11.** The LORD spoke again to Moses, saying, **12.** "Tell the Israelites: 'If a man's wife becomes unfaithful and is suspected of adultery, (Unfaithful: betrays, Adultery: cheating) **13.** and another man has had relations with her, but her husband does not know for sure and no one has witnessed the act— (Relations: sex, Witnessed: seen) **14.** and if the husband becomes jealous and suspects his wife of impurity, or if he is just suspicious even though she may be innocent— (Jealous: suspicious, Impurity: uncleanness) **15.** then he must bring his wife to the priest, along with a grain offering made of one-tenth of an ephah of barley flour. He must not put oil or incense on it, for it is a grain offering for jealousy, meant to remind of wrongdoing. (Grain offering: flour gift, Jealousy: suspicion) **16.** "The priest shall have her stand before the LORD. (Stand: present) **17.** He shall take holy water in a clay pot and mix in dust from the tabernacle floor. (Holy: sacred, Tabernacle: sanctuary) **18.** After presenting her to the LORD, the priest will loosen her hair and place the jealousy offering in her hands, while holding the bitter water that carries a curse. (Loosen: untie, Bitter water: cursed water) **19.** The priest shall put the woman under an oath, saying, "If you have been faithful to your husband and have not gone astray, may this bitter water cause you no harm. (Oath: vow, Faithful: loyal) **20.** But if you have been unfaithful and have had relations with another man, this curse will cause harm to you. (Unfaithful: cheating, Curse: harm) **21.** The priest will invoke this curse: 'May the LORD cause you to suffer, making your abdomen swell and your womb miscarry, (Invoke: call upon, Suffer: feel pain) **22.** as the curse takes effect. May this bitter water enter you, causing your body to react and your womb to lose the child.' The woman will answer, 'Amen. So be it.' (React: respond) **23.** The priest shall write down these curses on a scroll and wash them into the bitter water. (Scroll: paper, Wash: dissolve) **24.** Then he will make the woman drink the bitter water, which will bring the curse into her body. (Drink: consume, Bring: cause) **25.** The priest shall take the grain offering from her hands, wave it before the LORD, and place it on the altar. (Wave: move, Altar: sacred table) **26.** He will burn a portion of the offering as a memorial on the altar, then have the woman drink the water. (Burn: set on fire, Memorial: reminder) **27.** If she is guilty of unfaithfulness, the water will cause her body to react, and she will suffer the effects of the curse: her abdomen will swell, her womb will miscarry, and she will become a curse among her people. (Miscarry: lose child) **28.** But if she has not been unfaithful, she will be declared innocent and will be able to have children. (Declared: proclaimed, Innocent: not guilty) **29.** This is the procedure for handling jealousy when a woman is suspected of being unfaithful or when a man feels jealousy because of his suspicions. (Procedure: process, Suspected: thought guilty) **30.** The priest will apply this entire law to the woman, standing her before the LORD. (Apply: follow, Law: rule) **31.** The husband will be free from guilt, but the woman will face the consequences of her sin.'" (Free: innocent, Consequences: results)

Chapter 6

1. The LORD spoke to Moses, saying: **2.** "Tell the Israelites that when a man or woman decides to dedicate themselves as a Nazarite, they must separate themselves to the LORD. **3.** They must refrain from drinking wine, strong drinks, vinegar made from wine, or vinegar made from strong drinks. They must not consume any form of grape juice or even eat fresh or dried grapes. (Refrain: avoid) **4.** During their vow, they must avoid everything made from the vine, from the seeds to the skins. **5.** For the entire time of their vow, no razor is to touch their head. They must allow their hair to grow long as a symbol of their dedication until their vow is completed. (Razor: sharp tool for shaving; Symbol: representation) **6.** Throughout the vow, they are forbidden from coming into contact with any dead body. **7.** They must not make themselves unclean, even if a close family member— father, mother, brother, or sister—dies, because they are consecrated to God. (Unclean: ritually impure; Consecrated: dedicated to a sacred purpose) **8.** During the entire period of their vow, they remain holy to the LORD. (Holy: set apart for sacred use) **9.** If, by accident, someone dies near them, and they have defiled their vow, they must shave their head on the day of purification, which happens on the seventh day. **10.** On the eighth day, they must bring two turtle doves or two young pigeons to the priest at the entrance of the Tabernacle. (Turtle doves: small sacrificial birds) **11.** The priest will offer one bird as a sin offering and the other as a burnt offering to make atonement for their sin in contact with the dead, and he will cleanse their head. (Atonement: reconciliation; Burnt offering: a sacrifice entirely burned) **12.** They must then dedicate the rest of their vow days to the LORD and bring a lamb as a trespass offering. However, the previous days of their vow are lost, as their dedication was broken. (Trespass: a sin) **13.** This is the law for the Nazarite when their vow is complete: they must come to the entrance of the Tabernacle. **14.** They will offer their sacrifices to the LORD: a perfect lamb for a burnt offering, a flawless ewe lamb for a sin offering, and a ram without blemish for a peace offering. (Flawless: perfect) **15.** They must also bring a basket of unleavened bread, including cakes made with fine flour and oil, along with wafers of unleavened bread anointed with oil, as well as their meat and drink offerings. (Unleavened: made without yeast) **16.** The priest will present these offerings before the LORD, performing the sin and burnt offerings. **17.** The priest will offer the ram as the peace offering, accompanied by the basket of unleavened bread, and also offer the meat and drink offerings. **18.** The Nazarite will shave their hair at the entrance of the Tabernacle, and burn it under the peace offering sacrifice. **19.** The priest will take the cooked shoulder of the ram, an unleavened cake, and a wafer, and place them in the hands of the Nazarite after their hair is shaved. **20.** The priest will wave these offerings before the LORD, as a holy offering for the priest, alongside the wave breast and heave shoulder. After this, the Nazarite may drink wine. (Wave offering: ritual movement; Heave shoulder: an offering lifted and moved) **21.** This is the law of the Nazarite, including their vow and offerings to the LORD. They must fulfill everything according to the vow they made. (Vow: a solemn promise) **22.** The LORD spoke to Moses, saying: **23.** "Tell Aaron and his sons this: 'This is how you are to bless the Israelites: **24.** May the LORD bless and protect you. **25.** May the LORD make His face shine upon you and show you mercy. **26.** May the LORD lift His face toward you and give you peace.' (Mercy: kindness) **27.** They will put My name on the Israelites, and I will bless them."

Chapter 7

1. When Moses had completed setting up the Tabernacle, anointing it, and consecrating it, along with all its instruments, including the altar and its vessels, he sanctified them as well. (Consecrating means setting apart for holy use.) **2.** The leaders of Israel, the heads of their families, and the princes of the tribes, who were in charge of the census, brought their offerings. (The princes were leaders over the tribes.) **3.** They brought before the Lord six covered wagons and twelve oxen—two wagons and four oxen for each of the tribes, and each prince brought one ox. They presented these offerings at the Tabernacle. (A "wain" is an old term for a wagon used for transport.) **4.** The Lord spoke to Moses and said, **5.** "Accept the offerings from the princes, for they will be used in the service of the Tabernacle, and give them to the Levites, distributing them according to their specific duties." (Levites were the tribe assigned to assist with worship and the Tabernacle duties.) **6.** Moses accepted the wagons and oxen from the princes and gave them to the Levites. **7.** He gave two wagons and four oxen to the Gershonites (the descendants of Gershon), according to their responsibilities in the service of the Tabernacle. (Gershonites were responsible for the Tabernacle's coverings.) **8.** He gave four wagons and eight oxen to the Merarites (the descendants of Merari), according to their duties, under the leadership of Ithamar, the son of Aaron the priest. (Merarites were responsible for the structure of the Tabernacle.) **9.** However, he did not give any wagons to the Kohathites (the descendants of Kohath), because their duty was to carry the sacred objects of the Tabernacle on their shoulders. (Kohathites were responsible for carrying the holy items, such as the Ark.) **10.** On the day the altar was consecrated and anointed, the princes brought their offerings for the altar. (The altar is where sacrifices were offered.) **11.** The Lord instructed Moses, "Each prince will bring their offering on their designated day for the dedication of the altar." **12.** The first offering was brought by Nahshon, son of Amminadab, the prince of Judah, on the first day. (Judah was one of the tribes of Israel.) **13.** Nahshon's offering consisted of one silver platter weighing 130 shekels, one silver bowl weighing 70 shekels, both filled with fine flour mixed with oil for a grain offering. **14.** He also brought one gold spoon weighing 10 shekels, filled with incense. **15.** For the burnt offering, he brought one young bull, one ram, and one lamb of the first year. (Burnt offering means the whole animal is burned in the fire as an offering to God.) **16.** For the sin offering, he brought one goat. **17.** And for the peace offerings, he brought two oxen, five rams, five male goats, and five lambs of the first year. This was the offering of Nahshon, the prince of Judah. **18.** On the second day, Nethaneel, son of Zuar, the prince of Issachar, made his offering. (Issachar was another tribe of Israel.) **19.** Nethaneel's offering included one silver platter weighing 130 shekels, one silver bowl weighing 70 shekels, both filled with fine flour mixed with oil for a grain offering. **20.** He also brought one gold spoon weighing 10 shekels, full of incense. **21.** For the burnt offering, he brought one young bull, one ram, and one lamb of the first year. **22.** For the sin offering, he brought one goat. **23.** For the peace offerings, he brought two oxen, five rams, five male goats, and five lambs of the first year. This was the offering of Nethaneel, the prince of Issachar. **24.** On the third day, Eliab, son of Helon, the prince of Zebulun, offered his gifts. **25.** Eliab's offering included one silver platter weighing 130 shekels, one silver bowl weighing 70 shekels, both filled with fine flour mixed with oil for a grain offering. **26.** He also brought one gold spoon weighing 10 shekels, filled with incense. **27.** For the burnt offering, he brought one young bull, one ram, and one lamb of the first year. **28.** For the sin offering, he brought one goat. **29.** For the peace offerings, he brought two oxen, five rams, five male goats, and five lambs of the first year. This was the offering of Eliab, the prince of Zebulun. **30.** On the fourth day, Elizur, son of Shedeur, the prince of Reuben, offered his gifts. **31.** Elizur's offering consisted of one silver platter weighing 130 shekels, one silver bowl weighing 70 shekels, both filled with fine flour mixed with oil for a grain offering. **32.** He also brought one gold spoon weighing 10 shekels, filled with incense. **33.** For the burnt offering, he brought one young bull, one ram, and one lamb of the first year. **34.** For the sin offering, he brought one goat. **35.** For the peace offerings, he brought two oxen, five rams, five male goats, and five lambs of the first year. This was the offering of Elizur, the prince of Reuben. **36.** On the fifth day, Shelumiel, son of Zurishaddai, the prince of Simeon, offered his gifts. **37.** Shelumiel's offering consisted of one silver platter weighing 130 shekels, one silver bowl weighing 70 shekels, both filled with fine flour mixed with oil for a grain offering. **38.** He also brought one gold spoon weighing 10 shekels, filled with incense. **39.** For the burnt offering, he brought one young bull, one ram, and one lamb of the first year. **40.** For the sin offering, he brought one goat. **41.** For the peace offerings, he brought two oxen, five rams, five male goats, and five lambs of the first year. This was the offering of Shelumiel, the prince of Simeon. **42.** On the sixth day, Eliasaph, son of Deuel, the prince of Gad, offered his gifts. **43.** Eliasaph's offering consisted of one silver platter weighing 130 shekels, one silver bowl weighing 70 shekels, both filled with fine flour mixed with oil for a grain offering. **44.** He also brought one gold spoon weighing 10 shekels, filled with incense. **45.** For the burnt offering, he brought one young bull, one ram, and one lamb of the first year. **46.** For the sin offering, he brought one goat. **47.** For the peace offerings, he brought two oxen, five rams, five male goats, and five lambs of the first year. This was the offering of Eliasaph, the prince of Gad. **48.** On the seventh day, Elishama, son of Ammihud, the prince of Ephraim, offered his gifts. **49.** Elishama's offering consisted of one silver platter weighing 130 shekels, one silver bowl weighing 70 shekels, both filled with fine flour mixed with oil for a grain offering. **50.** He also brought one gold spoon weighing 10 shekels, filled with incense. **51.** For the burnt offering, he brought one young bull, one ram, and one lamb of the first year. **52.** For the sin offering, he brought one goat. **53.** For the peace offerings, he brought two oxen, five rams, five male goats, and five lambs of the first year. This was the offering of Elishama, the prince of Ephraim. **54.** On the eighth day, Gamaliel, son of Pedahzur, the prince of Manasseh, offered his gifts. **55.** Gamaliel's offering consisted of one silver platter weighing 130 shekels, one silver bowl weighing 70 shekels, both filled with fine flour mixed with oil for a grain offering. **56.** He also brought one gold spoon weighing 10 shekels, filled with incense. **57.** For the burnt offering, he brought one young bull, one ram, and one lamb of the first year. **58.** For the sin offering, he brought one goat. **59.** For the peace offerings, he brought two oxen, five rams, five male goats, and five lambs of the first year. This was the offering of Gamaliel, the prince of Manasseh. **60.** On the ninth day, Abidan, son of Gideoni, the prince of Benjamin, offered his gifts. **61.** Abidan's offering consisted of one silver platter weighing 130 shekels, one silver bowl weighing 70 shekels, both filled with fine flour mixed with oil for a grain offering. **62.** He also brought one gold spoon weighing 10 shekels, filled with incense. **63.** For the burnt offering, he brought one young bull, one ram, and one lamb of the first year. **64.** For the sin offering, he brought one goat. **65.** For the peace offerings, he brought two oxen, five rams, five male goats, and five lambs of the first year. This was the offering of Abidan, the prince of Benjamin. **66.** On the tenth day, Ahiezer, son of Ammishaddai, the prince of Dan, offered his gifts. **67.** Ahiezer's offering consisted of one silver platter weighing 130 shekels, one silver bowl weighing 70 shekels, both filled with fine flour mixed with oil for a grain offering. **68.** He also brought one gold spoon weighing 10 shekels, filled with incense. **69.** For the burnt offering, he brought one young bull, one ram, and one lamb of the first year. **70.** For the sin offering, he brought one goat. **71.** For the peace offerings, he brought two oxen, five rams, five male goats, and five lambs of the first year. This was the offering of Ahiezer, the prince of Dan. **72.** On the eleventh day, Pagiel, son of Ocran, the prince of Asher, offered his gifts. **73.** Pagiel's offering consisted of one silver platter weighing 130 shekels, one silver bowl weighing 70 shekels, both filled with fine flour mixed with oil for a grain offering. **74.** He also brought one gold spoon weighing 10 shekels, filled with incense. **75.** For the burnt offering, he brought one young bull, one ram, and one lamb of the first year. **76.** For the sin offering, he brought one goat. **77.** For the peace offerings, he brought two oxen, five rams, five male goats, and five lambs of the first year. This was the offering of Pagiel, the prince of Asher. **78.** On the twelfth day, Ahira, son of Enan, the prince of Naphtali, offered his gifts. **79.** Ahira's offering consisted of one silver platter weighing 130 shekels, one silver bowl weighing 70 shekels, both filled with fine flour mixed with oil for a grain offering. **80.** He also brought one gold spoon weighing 10 shekels, filled with incense. **81.** For the burnt offering, he brought one young bull, one ram, and one lamb of the first year. **82.** For the sin offering, he brought one goat. **83.** For the peace offerings, he brought two oxen, five rams, five male goats, and five lambs of the first year. This was the offering of Ahira, the prince of Naphtali. **84.** This was the dedication of the altar when it was anointed, by the twelve princes of Israel, each bringing their offerings: twelve silver platters, twelve silver bowls, and twelve gold spoons filled with incense. **85.** Each silver platter weighed 130 shekels, each silver bowl 70 shekels. In total, the silver weighed 2,400 shekels. **86.** The twelve gold spoons weighed 10 shekels each, totaling 120 shekels of gold. **87.** The twelve bullocks for the burnt offering, the twelve rams, the twelve lambs of the first year, and their grain offerings, along with twelve goats for sin offerings were all provided. **88.** Additionally, the peace offerings included twenty-four oxen, sixty rams, sixty male goats, and sixty lambs of the first year. This was the dedication of the altar after it had been anointed. **89.** When Moses entered the Tabernacle to speak with the Lord, he heard God's voice speaking from above the mercy seat on the Ark of the Covenant, between the two cherubim. (Cherubim are angelic beings)

Chapter 8

1. The LORD instructed Moses: **2.** "Tell Aaron, 'When you arrange the lamps, ensure that all seven light up the area in front of the lampstand.'" (lampstand : lamp holder) **3.** Aaron followed this command and arranged the lamps to face forward on the lampstand, as the LORD had instructed Moses. (lampstand : lamp holder) **4.** This is how the lampstand was crafted: It was made of hammered gold, from its base to its top, including its blossoms. It was designed exactly according to the pattern the LORD showed Moses. (hammered gold : beaten gold) **5.** The LORD spoke to Moses: **6.** "Take the Levites (tribe for service) from the Israelites and ceremonially cleanse them. (Levites : tribe of Levi) **7.** To purify them, sprinkle the water of cleansing on them, have them shave their entire bodies, and wash their clothes. In this way, they will purify themselves. (water of cleansing : purification water) **8.** Then, they are to bring a young bull along with a grain offering made of the finest flour mixed with olive oil; take a second young bull for a sin offering. (grain offering : flour offering) **9.** Bring the Levites to the front of the Tent of Meeting (place of worship), and gather the entire Israelite community. (Tent of Meeting : tabernacle) **10.** Present the Levites before the LORD, and let the Israelites lay their hands on them. (lay their hands on : symbol of blessing) **11.** Aaron is to offer the Levites before the LORD as a wave offering from the Israelites, so that they may be ready to serve the LORD. (wave offering : symbolic offering) **12.** "Next, the Levites are to place their hands on the bulls' heads—one bull for a sin offering to the LORD and the other for a burnt offering, to atone for the Levites. (sin offering : forgiveness offering) **13.** Let the Levites stand before Aaron and his sons, and present them as a wave offering to the LORD. (wave offering : symbolic offering) **14.** In this way, you will set the Levites apart from the rest of the Israelites, and they will belong to Me. (set apart : consecrate) **15.** "Once you have purified and presented the Levites as a wave offering, they will be ready to serve at the Tent of Meeting. **16.** They will be given to Me in place of the firstborn male from every Israelite woman. (firstborn : first male child) **17.** Every firstborn male, whether human or animal, is Mine. When I struck down the firstborn in Egypt, I set them apart for Myself. (struck down : killed) **18.** I have chosen the Levites to replace all the firstborn sons in Israel. (chosen : selected) **19.** From the Israelites, I have given the Levites as a gift to Aaron and his sons, to assist in the work at the Tent of Meeting and to make atonement for the people, so that no plague will come upon the Israelites when they approach the sanctuary." (atonement : reconciliation) **20.** Moses, Aaron, and the entire Israelite community did as the LORD commanded Moses. (Israelite community : God's people) **21.** The Levites purified themselves and washed their clothes. Then Aaron presented them as a wave offering before the LORD and made atonement for them to purify them. (purified : cleansed) **22.** After this, the Levites began their work at the Tent of Meeting under the direction of Aaron and his sons. They carried out their duties exactly as the LORD commanded Moses. (direction : supervision) **23.** The LORD spoke to Moses: **24.** "This is the rule for the Levites: Men who are twenty-five years old or older shall be part of the service at the Tent of Meeting. (service : religious work) **25.** But at the age of fifty, they must retire from active service and no longer perform the work. (retire : stop working) **26.** However, they may help their fellow Levites with the duties of the Tent of Meeting, but they themselves must not do the work. This is how you are to assign the responsibilities of the Levites." (assign : allocate)

Chapter 9

1. The LORD spoke to Moses in the Wilderness of Sinai (location where Israel camped after leaving Egypt) in the first month of the second year after the Exodus. He said, **2.** "Instruct the Israelites to observe the Passover (feast commemorating the Exodus) at the appointed time. **3.** Celebrate it at the designated time, at twilight on the fourteenth day of this month, following all its rules and instructions." (appointed time : set time) **4.** So Moses told the Israelites to observe the Passover, **5.** and they did so in the Wilderness of Sinai at twilight on the fourteenth day of the first month, following all that the LORD had commanded Moses. (Wilderness of Sinai : desert region) **6.** However, some individuals were unable to celebrate the Passover on that day because they were ceremonially unclean due to contact with a dead body. They came to Moses and Aaron that same day **7.** and asked Moses, "We are unclean because of a dead body, but why should we be excluded from offering the LORD's sacrifice with the rest of Israel at the appointed time?" (unclean : ritually impure) **8.** Moses replied, "Wait here while I inquire of the LORD what He commands concerning you." (inquire : seek guidance) **9.** Then the LORD spoke to Moses, **10.** "Tell the Israelites: 'If any of you or your descendants are unclean due to contact with a dead body, or if you are away on a journey, you may still celebrate the LORD's Passover. **11.** Instead, you must do it on the fourteenth day of the second month, at twilight. You are to eat the lamb, along with unleavened bread and bitter herbs. (unleavened bread : bread made without yeast; bitter herbs : herbs representing the bitterness of slavery) **12.** Do not leave any of it until morning or break any of its bones. You must follow all the instructions when observing the Passover. (instructions : detailed rules) **13.** However, if a person is clean and not on a journey but neglects to observe the Passover, that person will be cut off from their people for failing to offer the LORD's sacrifice at the appointed time. They will bear the guilt of their sin. (cut off : excluded from the community; sin : wrongdoing) **14.** "A foreigner living among you must also celebrate the Passover in the same manner, according to its rules and regulations. The same laws apply to both the foreigner and the native-born." (foreigner : non-Israelite resident) **15.** When the tabernacle (portable temple) was set up, the cloud covered it. From evening until morning, the cloud above the tabernacle appeared like fire. (tabernacle : mobile sanctuary) **16.** The cloud remained over the tabernacle, and at night it appeared as fire. (cloud : visible sign of God's presence) **17.** Whenever the cloud lifted from above the tent, the Israelites would break camp and move on. Whenever the cloud settled, the Israelites would pitch their tents. (break camp : leave camp; pitch tents : set up camp) **18.** At the LORD's command, the Israelites would move, and at His command, they would remain in camp. As long as the cloud stayed over the tabernacle, they remained in place. (command : divine instruction) **19.** When the cloud remained over the tabernacle for an extended period, the Israelites would obey the LORD and stay where they were. (obey : follow instructions) **20.** Sometimes the cloud remained over the tabernacle for only a few days. When the cloud lifted, they would move on, and when it settled, they would encamp again. (encamp : set up camp) **21.** Sometimes the cloud stayed from evening to morning, and when it lifted in the morning, they would set out. Whether it was day or night, whenever the cloud lifted, they would set out. (set out : begin moving) **22.** Whether the cloud stayed over the tabernacle for two days, a month, or a year, the Israelites would remain in camp until it lifted. When it lifted, they would continue their journey. (remain : stay in one place) **23.** At the LORD's command, they would camp, and at His command, they would set out. They followed the LORD's orders, in accordance with His instructions given through Moses. (camp : stay; set out : depart)

Chapter 10

1. The LORD spoke to Moses, saying: (Moses: Israel's leader) **2.** "Make two silver trumpets, crafted from hammered silver, to call the community together and signal when the camps are to depart. (Trumpets: Signal instruments) **3.** When both trumpets are blown, the entire community must gather at the entrance of the Tent of Meeting. (Tent of Meeting: Sacred tent) **4.** If only one trumpet is blown, the leaders of Israel's tribes are to gather before you. (Leaders: Tribal heads) **5.** The tribes camping on the east should set out when the first trumpet blast sounds. (East: Direction of Judah) **6.** The tribes to the south should depart when the second trumpet blast sounds. This will be the signal for them to move. (South: Direction of Reuben) **7.** To assemble the people, sound the trumpets, but not as a signal to depart. (Assemble: Gather people) **8.** "The sons of Aaron, the priests, will blow the trumpets. This practice is to continue as a permanent law for you and your descendants. (Aaron: First high priest) **9.** When you go into battle in your land against enemies who are oppressing you, blow the trumpets. Then, the LORD your God will remember you and deliver you from your enemies. (Battle: Armed conflict) **10.** At your times of celebration—during your appointed festivals and New Moon feasts—blow the trumpets over your offerings. They will serve as a memorial before your God. I am the LORD your God." (Feasts: Sacred celebrations) **11.** On the twentieth day of the second month of the second year, the cloud lifted from above the tabernacle of the covenant. (Tabernacle: Sacred tent) **12.** The Israelites then journeyed from the Desert of Sinai to the Desert of Paran. (Sinai: Desert location) (Paran: Desert area) **13.** They began their journey at the LORD's command through Moses. (Journey: Travel) **14.** The divisions of the camp of Judah went first, under their banner. Nahshon, son of Amminadab, led them. (Judah: Tribe of Israel) (Nahshon: Leader of Judah) **15.** Nethanel, son of Zuar, was in charge of Issachar's division. (Issachar: Tribe of Israel) **16.** and Eliab, son of Helon, led Zebulun's division. (Zebulun: Tribe of Israel) **17.** The tabernacle was taken down, and the Gershonites and Merarites set out with it. (Gershonites: Levite family) (Merarites: Levite family) **18.** The divisions of the camp of Reuben followed, under their banner. Elizur, son of Shedeur, led them. (Reuben: Tribe of Israel) **19.** Shelumiel, son of Zurishaddai, was in charge of Simeon's division. (Simeon: Tribe of Israel) **20.** and Eliasaph, son of Deuel, led Gad's division. (Gad: Tribe of Israel) **21.** Next, the Kohathites set out, carrying the most holy items. (Kohathites: Levite family) **22.** The divisions of the camp of Ephraim went next, under their banner. Elishama, son of Ammihud, led them. (Ephraim: Tribe of Israel) **23.** Gamaliel, son of Pedahzur, was in charge of Manasseh's division. (Manasseh: Tribe of Israel) **24.** and Abidan, son of Gideoni, led Benjamin's division. (Benjamin: Tribe of Israel) **25.** Lastly, the divisions of the camp of Dan, as the rear guard, set out under their banner. Ahiezer, son of Ammishaddai, led them. (Dan: Tribe of Israel) **26.** Pagiel, son of Okran, was in charge of Asher's division. (Asher: Tribe of Israel) **27.** and Ahira, son of Enan, led Naphtali's division. (Naphtali: Tribe of Israel) **28.** This was the order in which the Israelite divisions marched. (March: Organized movement) **29.** Moses spoke to Hobab, son of Reuel the Midianite, saying, "We are traveling to the place the LORD promised us. Come with us, and we will treat you well, for the LORD has spoken good things concerning Israel." (Hobab: Moses' brother-in-law) (Midianite: From Midian) **30.** Hobab replied, "No, I will return to my own land and people." (Refusal: Decline to join) **31.** Moses said, "Please don't leave us. You know the places where we should camp in the wilderness, and you can guide us." (Guide: Show the way) **32.** "If you come with us, we will share with you all the good things the LORD gives us." (Share: Offer benefits) **33.** They set out from the mountain of the LORD, traveling for three days. The Ark of the Covenant went ahead of them during these three days to guide them to a place to rest. (Ark of the Covenant: Sacred chest) **34.** The cloud of the LORD stayed over them by day as they left the camp. (Cloud: God's presence) **35.** Whenever the Ark set out, Moses would say, "Rise up, LORD! May your enemies be scattered, and may your foes flee before you." (Prayer: Plea for victory) **36.** When the Ark came to rest, he would say, "Return, LORD, to the countless thousands of Israel."

Chapter 11
1. Now the people complained about their hardships in the hearing of the LORD, and when He heard them, His anger was aroused. Then fire from the LORD burned among them and consumed some of the outskirts of the camp. (Complained: Grumbled) (Fire: Divine judgment) **2.** When the people cried out to Moses, he prayed to the LORD, and the fire died down. (Prayed: Interceded) **3.** So that place was called Taberah, because fire from the LORD had burned among them. (Taberah: Burning place) **4.** The rabble with them began to crave other food, and again the Israelites started wailing and said, "If only we had meat to eat!" (Rabble: Mixed crowd) (Crave: Desire strongly) **5.** We remember the fish we ate in Egypt at no cost—also the cucumbers, melons, leeks, onions, and garlic. (Egypt: Place of slavery) **6.** But now we have lost our appetite; we never see anything but this manna! (Manna: Heavenly bread) **7.** The manna was like coriander seed and looked like resin. (Coriander: Seed spice) (Resin: Plant sap) **8.** The people went around gathering it, and then ground it in a hand mill or crushed it in a mortar. They cooked it in a pot or made it into loaves. And it tasted like something made with olive oil. (Milled: Ground into flour) **9.** When the dew settled on the camp at night, the manna also came down. (Dew: Moisture) **10.** Moses heard the people of every family wailing at the entrance to their tents. The LORD became exceedingly angry, and Moses was troubled. (Wailing: Crying out) **11.** He asked the LORD, "Why have You brought this trouble on Your servant? What have I done to displease You that You put the burden of all these people on me?" (Burden: Heavy load) **12.** Did I conceive all these people? Did I give them birth? Why do You tell me to carry them in my arms, as a nurse carries an infant, to the land You promised on oath to their ancestors? (Nurse: Caregiver) **13.** Where can I get meat for all these people? They keep wailing to me, 'Give us meat to eat!' (Wailing: Crying out) **14.** I cannot carry all these people by myself; the burden is too heavy for me. (Burden: Overwhelming responsibility) **15.** If this is how You are going to treat me, please go ahead and kill me—if I have found favor in Your eyes—and do not let me face my own ruin. (Ruin: Destruction) **16.** The LORD said to Moses: "Bring Me seventy of Israel's elders who are known to you as leaders and officials among the people. Have them come to the Tent of Meeting, that they may stand there with you." (Elders: Tribal leaders) (Tent of Meeting: Sacred tent) **17.** I will come down and speak with you there, and I will take some of the power of the Spirit that is on you and put it on them. They will share the burden of the people with you so that you will not have to carry it alone. (Spirit: Divine presence) **18.** "Tell the people: 'Consecrate yourselves in preparation for tomorrow, when you will eat meat. The LORD heard you when you wailed, "If only we had meat to eat! We were better off in Egypt!" Now the LORD will give you meat, and you will eat it.'" (Consecrate: Make holy) **19.** You will not eat it for just one day, or two days, or five, ten, or twenty days, **20.** but for a whole month—until it comes out of your nostrils and you loathe it—because you have rejected the LORD, who is among you, and have wailed before Him, saying, "Why did we ever leave Egypt?" (Loathe: Disgust) **21.** But Moses said, "Here I am among six hundred thousand men on foot, and You say, 'I will give them meat to eat for a whole month!'" (Six hundred thousand: Large number) **22.** Would they have enough if flocks and herds were slaughtered for them? Would they have enough if all the fish in the sea were caught for them?" (Flocks: Herds of animals) **23.** The LORD answered Moses, "Is the LORD's arm too short? Now you will see whether or not what I say will come true for you." (Arm: Power) **24.** So Moses went out and told the people what the LORD had said. He brought together seventy of their elders and had them stand around the Tent. (Elders: Tribal leaders) **25.** Then the LORD came down in the cloud and spoke with him, and He took some of the power of the Spirit that was on him and put it on the seventy elders. When the Spirit rested on them,

they prophesied—but did not do so again. (Prophesied: Spoke God's message) **26.** However, two men, whose names were Eldad and Medad, had remained in the camp. They were listed among the elders, but did not go out to the Tent. Yet the Spirit also rested on them, and they prophesied in the camp. (Eldad & Medad: Two elders) **27.** A young man ran and told Moses, "Eldad and Medad are prophesying in the camp." (Prophesying: Speaking God's word) **28.** Joshua son of Nun, who had been Moses' aide since youth, spoke up and said, "Moses, my lord, stop them!" (Aide: Assistant) **29.** But Moses replied, "Are you jealous for my sake? I wish that all the LORD's people were prophets and that the LORD would put His Spirit on them!" (Jealous: Protective) **30.** Then Moses and the elders of Israel returned to the camp. (Returned: Went back) **31.** Now a wind went out from the LORD and drove quail in from the sea. It scattered them up to two cubits deep all around the camp, as far as a day's walk in any direction. (Wind: Divine power) (Quail: Birds) **32.** All that day and night and all the next day the people went out and gathered quail. No one gathered less than ten homers. Then they spread them out all around the camp. (Homer: Measurement) **33.** But while the meat was still between their teeth and before it could be consumed, the anger of the LORD burned against the people, and He struck them with a severe plague. (Plague: Divine punishment) **34.** Therefore the place was named Kibroth Hattaavah, because there they buried the people who had craved other food. (Kibroth Hattaavah: Grave of craving) **35.** From Kibroth Hattaavah the people traveled to Hazeroth and stayed there. (Hazeroth: Location in wilderness)

Chapter 12

1. Miriam and Aaron spoke against Moses because he had married a Cushite woman, as she was from Cush. (Cushite: Ethiopian) **2.** They said, "Is Moses the only one through whom the LORD has spoken? Hasn't He also spoken through us?" And the LORD heard their words. (Spoken: Communicated) **3.** (Moses was a very humble man, more so than anyone else on the earth.) (Humble: Meek, modest) **4.** The LORD immediately told Moses, Aaron, and Miriam, "Come out to the Tent of Meeting, all three of you." So they all stepped forward. (Tent of Meeting: Sacred tent) **5.** The LORD descended in a cloud pillar, stopped at the tent's entrance, and called Aaron and Miriam forward. They approached. (Pillar of Cloud: Divine sign) **6.** The LORD said, "Hear My words: When I send a prophet among you, I make Myself known to them in visions and speak to them through dreams. (Prophet: God's messenger) **7.** But My servant Moses is different; he is completely trustworthy in all My house. (Trustworthy: Loyal, faithful) **8.** With him, I speak directly and openly, not in riddles. He even sees My form. Why then did you dare to speak against My servant Moses?" (Riddles: Mysteries) **9.** The LORD's anger flared against them, and He departed. (Flared: Intensified) **10.** When the cloud lifted from above the tent, Miriam's skin turned leprous—white like snow. Aaron looked at her and saw the disease on her skin. (Leprous: Diseased, afflicted) **11.** Aaron said to Moses, "My lord, please don't hold this sin against us; we acted foolishly and sinned. (Foolishly: Recklessly) **12.** Don't let her be like a stillborn baby whose flesh is half-decayed at birth." (Stillborn: Dead at birth) **13.** Moses cried out to the LORD, saying, "God, please heal her!" (Heal: Make whole) **14.** The LORD responded, "If her father had spit in her face, wouldn't she be disgraced for seven days? Let her remain outside the camp for seven days, and then she can return." (Disgraced: Shamed, dishonored) **15.** So Miriam stayed outside the camp for seven days, and the Israelites did not travel until she was brought back. (Outside: Separated) **16.** Afterward, the people moved on from Hazeroth and camped in the wilderness of Paran. (Hazeroth: Camp location) (Paran: Desert region)

Chapter 13

1. The LORD spoke to Moses, **2.** "Send men to investigate the land of Canaan, which I am giving to the Israelites. Choose one leader from each tribe to go." (Canaan: Promised land) **3.** Following the LORD's instructions, Moses sent these leaders from the Desert of Paran. (Paran: Wilderness region) **4.** Their names were: Shammua son of Zakkur from Reuben, **5.** Shaphat son of Hori from Simeon, **6.** Caleb son of Jephunneh from Judah, **7.** Igal son of Joseph from Issachar, **8.** Hoshea son of Nun from Ephraim, **9.** Palti son of Raphu from Benjamin, **10.** Gaddiel son of Sodi from Zebulun, **11.** Gaddi son of Susi from Manasseh, a Joseph tribe, **12.** Ammiel son of Gemalli from Dan, **13.** Sethur son of Michael from Asher, **14.** Nahbi son of Vophsi from Naphtali, **15.** and Geuel son of Maki from Gad. **16.** These were the men Moses sent to scout the land, and he renamed Hoshea, son of Nun, as Joshua. (Joshua: "The LORD saves") **17.** Moses instructed them, "Travel through the Negev and then into the hill country. (Negev: Dry southern region) **18.** Examine the land—are its people strong or weak, and are their numbers small or large? **19.** Check the land they live on—is it fertile or barren? Do their towns have walls, or are they open? **20.** Look at the soil quality—is it productive? Are there trees? Bring back some of the fruit." (It was the time of the first ripe grapes.) **21.** They explored the land from the Desert of Zin to Rehob, near Lebo Hamath. (Zin: Wilderness area) **22.** Passing through the Negev, they reached Hebron, where Ahiman, Sheshai, and Talmai—the descendants of Anak—lived. (Hebron: Ancient city; Anak: Noted giants) **23.** In the Valley of Eshkol, they cut off a branch with one cluster of grapes, carried on a pole by two men, along with pomegranates and figs. (Eshkol: "Cluster") **24.** That location was named the Valley of Eshkol because of the cluster of grapes gathered there. **25.** After 40 days, they completed their exploration and returned. **26.** The men came back to Moses, Aaron, and the Israelite community at Kadesh in the Desert of Paran. They displayed the fruit of the land. (Kadesh: Holy desert camp) **27.** They reported, "We explored the land, and it truly flows with milk and honey! Here is some of its fruit. (Milk and honey: Prosperity) **28.** However, the people there are mighty, and their cities are well-fortified. We even saw Anak's descendants there." (Fortified: Strongly defended) **29.** "The Amalekites inhabit the Negev, while the Hittites, Jebusites, and Amorites dwell in the hills. The Canaanites live along the sea and near the Jordan River." (Amalekites: Hostile nomads) **30.** Caleb quieted the people before Moses, saying, "We should go up and take the land—we are capable of succeeding!" (Caleb: Courageous leader) **31.** But the other men responded, "We cannot face those people; they are stronger than us." **32.** They spread discouraging accounts, saying, "The land devours its inhabitants, and the people are enormous. **33.** We saw the Nephilim there, descendants of Anak. We felt like grasshoppers compared to them, and they likely saw us the same way." (Nephilim: Mythical giants)

Chapter 14

1. That night all of the participants of the community raised their voices and wept aloud. (Community: group; Wept: cried aloud) **2.** All of the Israelites grumbled in opposition to Moses and Aaron, and the whole assembly stated to them, "If only we had died in Egypt! Or in this wilderness!" (Grumbled: complained; Assembly: gathering) **3.** Why is the LORD bringing us to this land only to let us fall by the sword? Our wives and children will be taken as plunder. Wouldn't it be better for us to go back to Egypt?" (Plunder: loot; Sword: weapon) **4.** And they said to each other, "We should pick a leader and go back to Egypt." (Pick: choose; Leader: guide) **5.** Then Moses and Aaron fell facedown in front of the whole Israelite assembly gathered there. (Facedown: lying flat) **6.** Joshua son of Nun and Caleb son of Jephunneh, who were among those who had explored the land, tore their clothes. (Tore: ripped) **7.** And said to the whole Israelite assembly, "The land we passed through and explored is exceedingly good. (Exceedingly: very; Good: excellent) **8.** If the LORD is pleased with us, he will lead us into that land, a land flowing with milk and honey, and will give it to us. (Pleased: satisfied; Flowing: abundant) **9.** Only do not rebel against the LORD. And do not be afraid of the people of the land, because we will devour them. Their protection is gone, but the LORD is with us. Do not be afraid of them." (Rebel: resist; Devour: consume; Protection: defense) **10.** But the whole assembly talked about stoning them. Then the glory of the LORD appeared at the tent of meeting to all the Israelites. (Stoning: killing with stones; Glory: splendor) **11.** The LORD said to Moses, "How long will these people treat me with contempt? How long will they refuse to believe in me, despite all the signs I have performed among them? (Contempt: disrespect; Refuse: reject; Signs: miracles) **12.** I will strike them down with a plague and destroy them, but I will make you into a nation greater and stronger than they." (Strike: punish; Plague: disease; Destroy: ruin) **13.** Moses said to the LORD, "Then the Egyptians will hear about it! By your power you brought these people up from among them. (Egyptians: people of Egypt; Power: strength) **14.** And they will tell the inhabitants of this land about it. They have already heard that you, LORD, are with these people and that you, LORD, have been seen face to face, that your cloud stays over them, and that you go before them in a pillar of cloud by day and a pillar of fire by night. (Inhabitants: residents; Cloud: mist; Pillar: column) **15.** If you put all these people to death, leaving none alive, the nations who have heard this report about you will say, (Death: killing; Report: news) **16.** 'The LORD was not able to bring these people into the land he promised them on oath, so he slaughtered them in the wilderness.' (Slaughtered: killed) **17.** "Now may the Lord's strength be displayed, just as you have declared: (Strength: power; Displayed: shown) **18.** 'The LORD is slow to anger, abounding in love and forgiving sin and rebellion. Yet he does not leave the guilty unpunished; he punishes the children for the sin of the parents to the third and fourth generation.' (Abounding: overflowing; Rebellion: defiance) **19.** In accordance with your great love, forgive the sin of these people, just as you have pardoned them from the time they left Egypt until now." (Pardoned: forgiven; Sin: wrongdoing) **20.** The LORD replied, "I have forgiven them, as you asked. (Forgiven: pardoned; Asked: requested) **21.** Nevertheless, as surely as I live and as surely as the glory of the LORD fills the whole earth, (Surely: certainly; Glory: greatness) **22.** not one of those who saw my glory and the signs I performed in Egypt and in the wilderness but who disobeyed me and tested me ten times— (Disobeyed: defied; Tested: challenged) **23.** not one of them will ever see the land I promised on oath to their ancestors. No one who has treated me with contempt will ever see it. (Contempt: disrespect) **24.** But because my servant Caleb has a different spirit and follows me wholeheartedly, I will bring him into the land he went to, and his descendants will inherit it. (Wholeheartedly: completely loyal; Inherit: receive) **25.** Since the Amalekites and the Canaanites are living in the valleys, turn back tomorrow and set out toward the desert along the route to the Red Sea." (Valleys: low areas; Set out: begin; Route: path) **26.** The LORD said to Moses and Aaron: (Said: spoke) **27.** "How long will this wicked community grumble against me? I have heard the complaints of these grumbling Israelites. (Grumble: complain; Wicked: evil; Complaints: grievances) **28.** So tell them, 'As surely as I live, declares the LORD, I will do to you the very thing I heard you say: (Declare: announce; Heard: listened) **29.** In this wilderness your bodies will fall—every one of you twenty years old or more who was counted in the census and who has grumbled against me. (Census: population count; Grumbled: complained) **30.** Not one of you will enter the land I swore with uplifted hand to make your home, except Caleb son of Jephunneh and Joshua son of Nun. (Uplifted: raised) **31.** As for your children that you said would be taken as plunder, I will bring them in to enjoy the land you have rejected. (Plunder: loot; Reject: refuse) **32.** But as for you, your bodies will fall in this wilderness. (Fall: die) **33.** Your children will be shepherds here for forty years, suffering for your unfaithfulness, until the last of your bodies lies in the wilderness. (Shepherds: caretakers; Unfaithfulness: betrayal) **34.** For forty years—one year for each of the forty days you explored the land—you will suffer for your sins and know what it is like to have me against you.' (Suffer: endure pain; Sins: wrongdoings) **35.** I, the LORD, have spoken, and I will surely do these things to this whole wicked community, which has banded together against me. They will meet their end in this wilderness; here they will die." (Spoken: declared; Wicked: evil; Band: unite; End: death) **36.** So the men Moses had sent to explore the land, who returned and made the whole community grumble against him by spreading a bad report about it— (Explore: search; Report: news) **37.** these men who were responsible for spreading the bad report about the land were struck down and died of a plague before the LORD. (Struck down: killed; Plague: disease) **38.** Of the men who went to explore the land, only Joshua son of Nun and Caleb son of Jephunneh survived. (Survived: lived) **39.** When Moses reported this to all the Israelites, they mourned bitterly. (Mourned: grieved) **40.** Early the next morning they set out for the highest point in the hill country, saying, "Now we are ready to go up to the land the LORD promised. Surely we have sinned!" (Set out: left; Hill country: elevated land) **41.** But Moses said, "Why are you disobeying the LORD's command? This will not succeed! (Command: order) **42.** Do not go up, because the LORD is not with you. You will be defeated by your enemies, (Defeated: beaten; Enemies: opponents) **43.** for the Amalekites and the Canaanites will face you there. Because you have turned away from the LORD, he will not be with you and you will fall by the sword." (Turned away: rebelled; Fall: die) **44.** Nevertheless, in their presumption they went up toward the highest point in the hill country, though neither Moses nor the ark of the LORD's covenant moved from the camp. (Presumption: overconfidence; Ark: sacred chest) **45.** Then the Amalekites and the Canaanites who lived in that hill country came down and attacked them and beat them down all the way to Hormah. (Attacked: assaulted; Beat: defeated; Hormah: a place name)

Chapter 15

1. The LORD stated to Moses, (Moses: leader) **2.** "Talk to the Israelites and say: 'Once you enter the land I'm supplying you with as a home, (Land: territory; Domestic: living place) **3.** and present food services from the herd or flock, as an aroma attractive to the LORD—whether or not burnt offerings, sacrifices, vows, freewill offerings, or festival services— (Offerings: gifts; Aroma: fragrance; Vows: promises; Freewill: voluntary) **4.** The man or woman ought to gift a grain offering of a tenth of an ephah of the finest flour mixed with a quarter of a hin of olive oil. (Ephah: size of volume; Flour: ground wheat; Hin: liquid dimension; Olive oil: oil from olives) **5.** With each lamb for the burnt offering, prepare a quarter of a hin of wine as a drink offering. (Lamb: young sheep; Drink offering: wine poured out) **6.** "With a ram prepare a grain offering of two-tenths of an ephah of the finest flour mixed with a third of a hin of olive oil, (Ram: male sheep; Grain offering: flour offering) **7.** and a third of a hin of wine as a drink offering. (Wine: fermented grape juice) **8.** "When preparing a young bull for a burnt offering or sacrifice, bring a grain offering of three-tenths of an ephah of the finest flour mixed with half a hin of olive oil, (Bull: male cow; Grain offering: flour offering; Three-tenths: 30% of; Half: 50% of) **9.** and half of a hin of wine as a drink offering. (Wine: grape juice) **10.** This will be a food offering, an aroma appealing to the LORD. (Food offering: flour offering) **11.** Each bull or ram, each lamb or young goat, is to be prepared this way. (Prepared: made ready) **12.** Do this for each one. (Prepare: make ready) **13.** "Everyone who is native-born ought to do these things when presenting a food offering as an aroma pleasing to the LORD. (Native-born: born in the land) **14.** For the generations to come, when a foreigner presents a food offering, they must do as you do. (Foreigner: outsider) **15.** The same rules apply to both you and the foreigner. (Rules: laws) **16.** The same laws apply to everyone. (Laws: rules) **17.** The LORD said to Moses, (Said: spoke) **18.** "Talk to the Israelites and say: 'When you enter the land I'm taking you, (Land: territory) **19.** and eat the food of the land, present a portion as an offering to the LORD. (Portion: part; Food: produce) **20.** Present a loaf from the first of your ground meal. (Loaf: bread; Meal: flour)

21. Give this offering to the LORD from the first of your ground meal. (Offering: gift) **22.** "If you accidentally fail to keep any of these commands the LORD gave Moses— (Accidentally: by mistake; Fail: neglect) **23.** and if this is done without the community knowing, the whole community is to offer a young bull for a burnt offering as an aroma pleasing to the LORD, along with its grain offering, drink offering, and a male goat for a sin offering. (Community: group; Grain offering: flour offering; Sin offering: offering to atone for sin) **24.** The priest is to make atonement for the whole Israelite community, and they will be forgiven. (Atonement: reconciliation; Forgiven: pardoned) **25.** The whole Israelite community and foreigners will be forgiven, because all the people were involved. (Foreigners: outsiders; Involved: included) **26.** "But if just one person sins accidentally, that person must bring a year-old female goat for a sin offering. (Sin: wrongdoing; Accidentally: by mistake) **27.** The priest will make atonement for the one who erred, and when atonement has been made, that person will be forgiven. (Atonement: reconciliation; Erred: made a mistake) **28.** One law applies to everyone who sins accidentally. (Law: rule) **29.** "But anyone who sins defiantly blasphemes the LORD and must be cut off from the people of Israel. (Defiantly: rebelliously; Blasphemes: insults; Cut off: removed) **30.** They have despised the LORD's word and broken his commands, and their guilt remains on them. (Despised: hated; Guilt: responsibility for sin) **32.** While in the desert, a man was found gathering wood on the Sabbath. (Desert: wilderness area; Sabbath: day of rest) **33.** Those who found him brought him to Moses, Aaron, and the assembly, (Assembly: group) **34.** and they kept him in custody, because it was not clear what to do. (Custody: detention; Clear: certain) **35.** The LORD said, "The man must die. The assembly must stone him outside the camp." (Stone: kill by throwing stones) **36.** So the assembly stoned him to death, as the LORD commanded Moses. (Stoned: killed by throwing stones) **37.** The LORD said to Moses, (Said: spoke) **38.** "Speak to the Israelites and say: 'Make tassels on the corners of your garments, with a blue cord on each tassel. (Tassels: small decorative pieces; Garments: apparel; Cord: string) **39.** You will have these tassels to look at and remember all the commands of the LORD, so you will obey them and not chase after your own desires. (Lusts: desires) **40.** Then you will remember to obey all my commands and be consecrated to your God. (Consecrated: dedicated) **41.** I am the LORD your God, who brought you out of Egypt to be your God. (Brought: led; Egypt: land of slavery)

Chapter 16

1. Korah son of Izhar, the son of Kohath, the son of Levi, and sure Reubenites—Dathan and Abiram, sons of Eliab, and On son of Peleth—became insolent. (Insolent: smug) **2.** and rose up in opposition to Moses. With them have been 250 Israelite men, network leaders who had been appointed contributors of the council. (Leaders: prominent) **3.** They came as a collection to oppose Moses and Aaron and stated to them, "you have long gone too a ways! The entire community is holy, each certainly one of them, and the LORD is with them. Why then do you put yourselves above the LORD's meeting?" (Oppose: face up to) **4.** when Moses heard this, he fell facedown. (Facedown: Prostrate) **5.** Then he stated to Korah and all his fans: "inside the morning the LORD will show who belongs to him and who is holy, and he could have that man or woman come near him. the person he chooses he'll reason to come near him. (Holy: Sacred) **6.** You, Korah, and all your followers are to do this: Take censers. (Censers: bins) **7.** and the next day put burning coals and incense in them earlier than the LORD. the person the LORD chooses can be the only who is holy. You Levites have long past too far!" (Levites: priests) **8.** Moses also stated to Korah, "Now concentrate, you Levites! (concentrate: hear) **9.** Isn't it enough for you that the God of Israel has separated you from the rest of the Israelite community and brought you close to himself to do the paintings at the LORD's tabernacle and to stand before the network and minister to them? (Separated: Set-aside) **10.** He has introduced you and all of your fellow Levites close to himself, however now you are attempting to get the priesthood too. (Priesthood: Clergy) **11.** it's miles against the LORD that you and all of your followers have banded collectively. who's Aaron that you need to grumble towards him?" (Grumble: whinge) **12.** Then Moses summoned Dathan and Abiram, the sons of Eliab. but they said, "we are able to not come!" (Summoned: referred to as) **13.** Isn't it enough which you have added us up out of a land flowing with milk and honey to kill us inside the wilderness? And now you also need to lord it over us! (Lord it over: Dominate) **14.** furthermore, you haven't brought us into a land flowing with milk and honey or given us an inheritance of fields and vineyards. Do you want to deal with these guys like slaves? No, we can now not come!" (Slaves: Servants) **15.** Then Moses became very indignant and said to the LORD, "Do now not receive their providing. i've not taken a lot as a donkey from them, nor have I wronged any of them." (Wronged: Harmed) **16.** Moses said to Korah, "You and all of your fans are to appear earlier than the LORD day after today— you and that they and Aaron. (appear: gift) **17.** each man is to take his censer and placed incense in it—250 censers in all—and gift it earlier than the LORD. You and Aaron are to give your censers additionally." (gift: offer) **18.** So every of them took his censer, placed burning coals and incense in it, and stood with Moses and Aaron at the entrance to the tent of assembly. (Tent of assembly: Sanctuary) **19.** whilst Korah had accumulated all his fans in opposition to them at the doorway to the tent of assembly, the distinction of the LORD seemed to the whole assembly. (Glory: Radiance) **20.** The LORD stated to Moses and Aaron, **21.** "Separate yourselves from this meeting so i can placed an end to them straight away." (Separate: Distance) **22.** however Moses and Aaron fell facedown and cried out, "O God, the God who offers breath to all residing matters, will you be indignant with the complete meeting while best one guy sins?" (Breath: life) **23.** Then the LORD said to Moses, **24.** "Say to the assembly, 'move faraway from the tents of Korah, Dathan and Abiram.'" (assembly: Congregation) **25.** Moses were given up and went to Dathan and Abiram, and the elders of Israel followed him. (Elders: Leaders) **26.** He warned the assembly, "circulate back from the tents of these wicked guys! Do not touch whatever belonging to them, or you may be swept away due to all their sins." (wicked: Evil) **27.** so they moved faraway from the tents of Korah, Dathan and Abiram. Dathan and Abiram had pop out and were status with their wives, kids and children at the entrances to their tents. (little ones: kids) **28.** Then Moses said, "this is how you will understand that the LORD has sent me to do all these things and that it become no longer my idea: (sent: Directed) **29.** If these men die a natural death and suffer the fate of all mankind, then the LORD has now not despatched me. (natural: ordinary) **30.** however if the LORD brings approximately some thing completely new, and the earth opens its mouth and swallows them, with the whole lot that belongs to them, and they move down alive into the area of the lifeless, then you will recognise that these men have dealt with the LORD with contempt." (Realm: Underworld) **31.** As quickly as he completed pronouncing all this, the floor underneath them split aside (break up: Cracked) **32.** and the earth opened its mouth and swallowed them and their households, and all the ones associated with Korah, collectively with their possessions. (related: connected) **33.** They went down alive into the world of the dead, with the entirety they owned; the earth closed over them, and that they perished and were gone from the community. (Perished: Died) **34.** At their cries, all the Israelites around them fled, shouting, "The earth is going to swallow us too!" (Fled: Ran) **35.** And hearth came out from the LORD and consumed the 250 guys who have been offering the incense. (consumed: Destroyed) **36.** The LORD stated to Moses, **37.** "inform Eleazar son of Aaron, the priest, to put off the censers from the charred stays and scatter the coals a ways away, for the censers are holy— (Eleazar: Priest) **38.** the censers of the guys who sinned at the fee of their lives. Hammer the censers into sheets to overlay the altar, for they were offered earlier than the LORD and feature come to be holy. allow them to be a sign to the Israelites." (Overlay: cover) **39.** So Eleazar the priest accumulated the bronze censers added by way of folks who were burned to loss of life, and he had them hammered out to overlay the altar, (Bronze: metal) **40.** because the LORD directed him via Moses. This became to remind the Israelites that no person except a descendant of Aaron must come to burn incense before the LORD, or he might become like Korah and his fans. (Descendant: Offspring) **41.** tomorrow the complete Israelite network grumbled against Moses and Aaron. "you have got killed the LORD's people," they said. (Grumbled: Complained) **42.** but when the meeting amassed in opposition to Moses and Aaron and turned towards the tent of meeting, abruptly the cloud included it and the glory of the LORD seemed. (Cloud: Mist) **43.** Then Moses and Aaron went to the the front of the tent of assembly, **44.** and the LORD stated to Moses, **45.** "break out from this meeting so i will put an give up to them immediately." and that they fell facedown. (Facedown: Prostrate) **46.** Then Moses said to Aaron, "Take your censer and positioned incense in it, together with burning coals from the altar, and hurry to the assembly to make atonement for them. Wrath has pop out from the LORD; the plague has began." (Atonement: Reconciliation) **47.** So Aaron did as Moses said, and ran into the midst of the assembly. The plague had already started most of the people, however Aaron provided the incense and made atonement for them. (Midst: middle) **48.** He stood between the residing and the useless, and the plague stopped. (Plague: disorder) **49.** but 14,700 humans died from the plague, further to those who had died due to Korah. (Addition: increase) **50.** Then Aaron again to Moses at the doorway to the tent of meeting, for the plague had stopped. (front: Door)

Chapter 17
1. The LORD stated to Moses, (stated: told) **2.** "speak to the Israelites and get twelve staffs from them, one from the leader of every in their ancestral tribes. Write the call of every guy on his body of workers. (Staffs: Rods) **3.** on the body of workers of Levi write Aaron's name, for there ought to be one group of workers for the pinnacle of every ancestral tribe. (Ancestral: Tribal) **4.** location them in the tent of assembly in the front of the ark of the covenant law, where I meet with you. (Tent of meeting: Sanctuary) **5.** The personnel belonging to the person I pick will sprout, and i'm able to rid myself of this constant grumbling towards you via the Israelites." (Sprout: grow) **6.** So Moses spoke to the Israelites, and their leaders gave him twelve staffs, one for the leader of every in their ancestral tribes, and Aaron's personnel become among them. (Leaders: Chiefs) **7.** Moses placed the staffs before the LORD inside the tent of the covenant law. (Covenant: settlement) **8.** tomorrow Moses entered the tent and noticed that Aaron's body of workers, which represented the tribe of Levi, had not only sprouted but had budded, blossomed and produced almonds. (Budded: Sprouted) **9.** Then Moses introduced out all the staffs from the LORD's presence to all the Israelites. They looked at them, and every of the leaders took his very own group of workers. (looked: found) **10.** The LORD said to Moses, "positioned back Aaron's workforce in the front of the ark of the covenant law, to be kept as a sign to the rebellious. this will placed an cease to their grumbling against me, in order that they may no longer die." (Rebellious: Defiant) **11.** Moses did simply because the LORD commanded him. (Commanded: Directed) **12.** The Israelites stated to Moses, "we are able to die! we are lost, we are all misplaced! (lost: Doomed) **13.** every body who even comes near the tabernacle of the LORD will die. Are we all going to die?" (Tabernacle: Sanctuary)

Chapter 18
1. The LORD said to Aaron, "You, your sons and your family are to bear the responsibility for offenses connected with the sanctuary, and you and your sons alone are to bear the responsibility for offenses connected with the priesthood. (Offenses: Sins) **2.** Bring your fellow Levites from your ancestral tribe to join you and assist you when you and your sons minister before the tent of the covenant law. (Ancestral: Tribal) **3.** They are to be responsible to you and are to perform all the duties of the tent, but they must not go near the furnishings of the sanctuary or the altar. Otherwise both they and you will die. (Furnishings: Items) **4.** They are to join you and be responsible for the care of the tent of meeting—all the work at the tent—and no one else may come near where you are. (Care: Maintenance) **5.** "You are to be responsible for the care of the sanctuary and the altar, so that my wrath will not fall on the Israelites again. (Wrath: Anger) **6.** I myself have selected your fellow Levites from among the Israelites as a gift to you, dedicated to the LORD to do the work at the tent of meeting. (Dedicated: Devoted) **7.** But only you and your sons may serve as priests in connection with everything at the altar and inside the curtain. I am giving you the service of the priesthood as a gift. Anyone else who comes near the sanctuary is to be put to death." (Connected: Associated) **8.** Then the LORD said to Aaron, "I myself have put you in charge of the offerings presented to me; all the holy offerings the Israelites give me I give to you and your sons as your portion, your perpetual share. (Charge: Responsibility) **9.** You are to have the part of the most holy offerings that is kept from the fire. From all the gifts they bring me as most holy offerings, whether grain or sin or guilt offerings, that part belongs to you and your sons. (Grain: Cereal) **10.** Eat it as something most holy; every male shall eat it. You must regard it as holy. (Regard: Consider) **11.** "This also is yours: whatever is set aside from the gifts of all the wave offerings of the Israelites. I give this to you and your sons and daughters as your perpetual share. Everyone in your household who is ceremonially clean may eat it. (Ceremonially: Ritualistically) **12.** "I give you all the finest olive oil and all the finest new wine and grain they give the LORD as the firstfruits of their harvest. (Firstfruits: First portions) **13.** All the land's firstfruits that they bring to the LORD will be yours. Everyone in your household who is ceremonially clean may eat it. (Land's: Earth's) **14.** "Everything in Israel that is devoted to the LORD is yours. (Devoted: Dedicated) **15.** The first offspring of every womb, both human and animal, that is offered to the LORD is yours. But you must redeem every firstborn son and every firstborn male of unclean animals. (Redeem: Buy back) **16.** When they are a month old, you must redeem them at the redemption price set at five shekels of silver, according to the sanctuary shekel, which weighs twenty gerahs. (Redemption: Recovery) **17.** "But you must not redeem the firstborn of a cow, a sheep or a goat; they are holy. Splash their blood against the altar and burn their fat as a food offering, an aroma pleasing to the LORD. (Splash: Sprinkle) **18.** Their meat is to be yours, just as the breast of the wave offering and the right thigh are yours. (Wave offering: Ritual offering) **19.** Whatever is set aside from the holy offerings the Israelites present to the LORD I give to you and your sons and daughters as your perpetual share. It is an everlasting covenant of salt before the LORD for both you and your offspring." (Covenant: Agreement) **20.** The LORD said to Aaron, "You will have no inheritance in their land, nor will you have any share among them; I am your share and your inheritance among the Israelites. (Inheritance: Legacy) **21.** "I give to the Levites all the tithes in Israel as their inheritance in return for the work they do while serving at the tent of meeting. (Tithes: Offerings) **22.** From now on the Israelites must not go near the tent of meeting, or they will bear the consequences of their sin and will die. (Consequences: Penalty) **23.** It is the Levites who are to do the work at the tent of meeting and bear the responsibility for any offenses they commit against it. This is a lasting ordinance for the generations to come. They will receive no inheritance among the Israelites. (Offenses: Sins) **24.** Instead, I give to the Levites as their inheritance the tithes that the Israelites present as an offering to the LORD. That is why I said concerning them: 'They will have no inheritance among the Israelites.' " (Present: Give) **25.** The LORD said to Moses, (Said: Instructed) **26.** "Speak to the Levites and say to them: 'When you receive from the Israelites the tithe I give you as your inheritance,

you must present a tenth of that tithe as the LORD's offering. **27.** Your offering will be reckoned to you as grain from the threshing floor or juice from the winepress. (Reckoned: Counted) **28.** In this way you also will present an offering to the LORD from all the tithes you receive from the Israelites. From these tithes you must give the LORD's portion to Aaron the priest. (Portion: Share) **29.** You must present as the LORD's portion the best and holiest part of everything given to you.' (Holiest: Most sacred) **30.** "Say to the Levites: 'When you present the best part, it will be reckoned to you as the product of the threshing floor or the winepress. (Product: Produce) **31.** You and your households may eat the rest of it anywhere, for it is your wages for your work at the tent of meeting. (Wages: Payment) **32.** By presenting the best part of it you will not be guilty in this matter; then you will not defile the holy offerings of the Israelites, and you will not die.' " (Defile: Pollute)

Chapter 19

1. The LORD said to Moses and Aaron: (Said: Instructed) **2.** "This is a requirement of the law that the LORD has commanded: Tell the Israelites to bring you a red heifer without defect or blemish and that has never been under a yoke. (Heifer: Cow) **3.** Give it to Eleazar the priest; it is to be taken outside the camp and slaughtered in his presence. (Slaughtered: Killed) **4.** Then Eleazar the priest is to take some of its blood on his finger and sprinkle it seven times toward the front of the tent of meeting. (Sprinkle: Scatter) **5.** While he watches, the heifer is to be burned—its hide, flesh, blood and intestines. (Intestines: Guts) **6.** The priest is to take some cedar wood, hyssop and scarlet wool and throw them onto the burning heifer. (Cedar: Tree) **7.** After that, the priest must wash his clothes and bathe himself with water. He may then come into the camp, but he will be ceremonially unclean till evening. (Ceremonially: Ritualistically) **8.** The man who burns it must also wash his clothes and bathe with water, and he too will be unclean till evening. (Burns: Incinerates) **9.** "A man who is clean shall gather up the ashes of the heifer and put them in a ceremonially clean place outside the camp. They are to be kept by the Israelite community for use in the water of cleansing; it is for purification from sin. (Ashes: Remains) **10.** The man who gathers up the ashes of the heifer must also wash his clothes, and he too will be unclean till evening. This will be a lasting ordinance both for the Israelites and for the foreigners residing among them. (Ordinance: Law) **11.** "Whoever touches a human corpse will be unclean for seven days. (Corpse: Body) **12.** They must purify themselves with the water on the third day and on the seventh day; then they will be clean. But if they do not purify themselves on the third and seventh days, they will not be clean. (Purify: Cleanse) **13.** If they fail to purify themselves after touching a human corpse, they defile the LORD's tabernacle. They must be cut off from Israel. Because the water of cleansing has not been sprinkled on them, they are unclean; their uncleanness remains on them. (Defile: Contaminate) **14.** "This is the law that applies when a person dies in a tent: Anyone who enters the tent and anyone who is in it will be unclean for seven days, (Anyone: Person) **15.** and every open container without a lid fastened on it will be unclean. (Container: Vessel) **16.** "Anyone out in the open who touches someone who has been killed with a sword or someone who has died a natural death, or anyone who touches a human bone or a grave, will be unclean for seven days. (Grave: Tomb) **17.** "For the unclean person, put some ashes from the burned purification offering into a jar and pour fresh water over them. (Purification: Cleansing) **18.** Then a man who is ceremonially clean is to take some hyssop, dip it in the water and sprinkle the tent and all the furnishings and the people who were there. He must also sprinkle anyone who has touched a human bone or a grave or anyone who has been killed or anyone who has died a natural death. (Hyssop: Herb) **19.** The man who is clean is to sprinkle those who are unclean on the third and seventh days, and on the seventh day he is to purify them. Those who are being cleansed must wash their clothes and bathe with water, and that evening they will be clean. (Sprinkle: Douse) **20.** But if those who are unclean do not purify themselves, they must be cut off from the community, because they have defiled the sanctuary of the LORD. The water of cleansing has not been sprinkled on them, and they are unclean. (Cut off: Exiled) **21.** This is a lasting ordinance for them. "The man who sprinkles the water of cleansing must also wash his clothes, and anyone who touches the water of cleansing will be unclean till evening. (Sprinkles: Douses) **22.** Anything that an unclean person touches becomes unclean, and anyone who touches it becomes unclean till evening." (Touches: Contacts)

Chapter 20

1. In the first month, the entire Israelite community arrived at the Desert of Zin and camped at Kadesh. It was here that Miriam passed away and was buried. (Miriam: The sister of Moses and Aaron.) **2.** There was no water available for the people, and they gathered in opposition to Moses and Aaron. (Opposition: Resistance or disagreement.) **3.** They argued with Moses, saying, "If only we had died with our brothers who perished before the LORD! (Argued: To have a disagreement or fight over something.) **4.** Why did you lead the LORD's people into this wilderness, where we and our animals are doomed to die? (Doomed: Destined to fail or suffer.) **5.** Why did you bring us out of Egypt to this desolate place where there is no grain, figs, grapes, or pomegranates, and there is no water to drink?" (Desolate: Empty and barren, without life or comfort.) **6.** Moses and Aaron left the assembly and went to the entrance of the Tent of Meeting, where they fell to the ground. The glory of the LORD appeared to them. (Tent of Meeting: The portable sanctuary where the Israelites met with God.) **7.** The LORD spoke to Moses and said: **8.** "Take your staff, and you and your brother Aaron gather the people. Speak to the rock in front of them, and it will yield water. You will provide water from the rock for the people and their livestock." (Yield: To produce or give something.) **9.** So Moses took the staff from the LORD's presence, just as he was instructed. **10.** He and Aaron gathered the people in front of the rock. Moses said to them, "Listen, you rebels, must we bring you water from this rock?" (Rebels: Those who resist authority or go against established rules.) **11.** Then Moses raised his arm and struck the rock twice with his staff. Water poured out, and the people and their animals drank. (Struck: Hit forcefully.) **12.** But the LORD said to Moses and Aaron, "Because you did not trust me enough to treat me as holy in front of the Israelites, you will not bring this assembly into the land I am giving them." (Trust: Belief in the reliability, truth, or strength of something or someone.) (Holy: Sacred or set apart for God.) **13.** These are the waters of Meribah, where the Israelites quarreled with the LORD, and where He showed His holiness to them. (Meribah: The place where the Israelites disputed with Moses and God.) (Quarreled: Argued or fought.) **14.** Edom Refuses Israel's Request Moses sent messengers from Kadesh to the king of Edom, saying: "This is what your brother Israel says: You know about all the hardships that have befallen us. (Hardships: Difficult situations or challenges.) **15.** Our ancestors went down into Egypt, and we lived there for many years. The Egyptians treated us and our ancestors badly, (Ancestors: Family members from previous generations.) **16.** but when we cried out to the LORD, He heard our cry, and sent an angel who led us out of Egypt. Now we are at Kadesh, a town on the border of your land. (Cry out: To call out in distress or need.) **17.** Please allow us to pass through your territory. We will not go through your fields or vineyards, nor drink water from your wells. We will follow the King's Highway and not turn aside until we have crossed your land." (Vineyards: Areas where grapevines are grown.) (King's Highway: An ancient trade route running through Edom.) **18.** But Edom replied, "You cannot pass through our land. If you try, we will attack you with the sword." (Sword: A weapon used for cutting or thrusting.) **19.** The Israelites said, "We will stay on the main road, and if we or our animals drink any of your water, we will pay for it. We only want to pass through on foot, nothing more." (Main road:

The primary or most important road for travel.) 20. But again they responded, "You shall not pass through." And Edom came out with a large army to oppose them. (Oppose: To resist or act against something.) 21. Since Edom refused to let them pass, Israel turned away and did not try to enter their land. (Refused: Denied or rejected.) 22. The whole community of Israel moved from Kadesh and came to Mount Hor. 23. There, near the border of Edom, the LORD spoke to Moses and Aaron, saying: 24. "Aaron will be gathered to his people. He will not enter the land I am giving the Israelites, because both of you rebelled against My command at the waters of Meribah. (Gathered: Taken to be with one's ancestors or loved ones in death.) 25. Take Aaron and his son Eleazar, and bring them up to Mount Hor. 26. Remove Aaron's garments and put them on his son Eleazar, for Aaron will die there." (Garments: Clothing.) 27. Moses did as the LORD commanded. They went up to Mount Hor in full view of the community. 28. Moses removed Aaron's priestly garments and put them on his son Eleazar. Aaron died on the mountain. Then Moses and Eleazar came back down. (Priestly garments: The special clothing worn by priests in religious ceremonies.) 29. When the entire community learned that Aaron had died, they mourned for him for thirty days. (Mourned: Expressed sorrow or grief.)

Chapter 21

1. When the Canaanite king of Arad, who ruled in the Negev, heard that the Israelites were approaching on the road to Atharim, he attacked them and took some of them captive.(Negev: a desert region in southern Israel) 2. In response, Israel made a vow to the Lord: "If You give these people into our hands, we will completely destroy their cities." 3. The Lord heard Israel's plea and handed the Canaanites over to them. They destroyed them and their cities entirely, so the place was named Hormah. (Hormah: means "destruction") 4. The Israelites then traveled from Mount Hor on their way to the Red Sea, intending to go around Edom. But the people grew frustrated during the journey. 5. They complained against God and Moses, saying, "Why did you bring us out of Egypt to die in this wilderness? There is no bread, no water, and we hate this worthless food!" 6. In response, the Lord sent venomous snakes among them. The snakes bit the people, and many Israelites died. (Venomous: poisonous) 7. The people came to Moses and confessed, "We have sinned by speaking against the Lord and against you. Please pray to the Lord to take the snakes away from us." So Moses prayed for the people. 8. The Lord told Moses, "Make a bronze snake and put it on a pole. Anyone who is bitten can look at it and be healed." (Bronze: a type of metal) 9. So Moses made a bronze snake and mounted it on a pole. Whenever someone was bitten by a snake, if they looked at the bronze snake, they were healed. 10. The Israelites then moved on and camped at Oboth. 11. From Oboth, they set out and camped at Iye Abarim, a place in the wilderness facing Moab, to the east. (Iye Abarim: "ruins of the Abarim" or "wasteland of the Abarim"; Abarim: a range of mountains or region in Moab) 12. From there, they continued and camped in the Zered Valley. 13. They journeyed on from there and camped near the Arnon River, in the wilderness that stretches into the Amorite territory. The Arnon marks the boundary between Moab and the Amorites. (Arnon: a river that marks the boundary between Moab and the Amorites) 14. This is why the Book of the Wars of the Lord mentions: "Zahab in Suphah and the ravines, the Arnon 15. "and the slopes of the ravines that lead to the settlement of Ar and lie along the border of Moab." 16. From there, they traveled to Beer, the well where the Lord told Moses, "Gather the people, and I will give them water." (Beer: a well or water source) 17. Then Israel sang this song: "Spring up, O well! Sing of it!" 18. "Sing of the well that the princes dug, the nobles of the people dug, with their scepters and staffs." After that, they moved from the wilderness to Mattanah. (Scepters: staffs or symbols of royal power) 19. From Mattanah, they traveled to Nahaliel, and from Nahaliel to Bamoth. 20. From Bamoth, they camped in the valley in Moab, at the peak of Pisgah, which overlooks the wasteland. (Pisgah: a peak or mountain range in Moab) 21. Israel sent messengers to Sihon, the king of the Amorites, with the following message: 22. "Let us pass through your land. We will not turn aside into any field or vineyard or drink water from any well. We will travel along the King's Highway until we have passed through your territory." (King's Highway: an ancient trade route) 23. But Sihon refused to let Israel pass through his land. Instead, he gathered his entire army and came out to fight Israel in the wilderness. They met at Jahaz, where Sihon engaged Israel in battle. 24. Israel, however, defeated him with the sword and took over his land from the Arnon River to the Jabbok River, though they did not take land beyond the Ammonites' territory, which was well-fortified. (Jabbok: a river that forms the boundary between Israel and Ammon) 25. Israel captured all the cities of the Amorites and settled in them, including Heshbon and its surrounding towns. 26. Heshbon had been the city of Sihon, the king of the Amorites. He had fought against the previous king of Moab and taken all his land as far as the Arnon River. 27. This is why the poets say: "Come to Heshbon and let it be rebuilt; let Sihon's city be restored." 28. "Fire went out from Heshbon, a flame from the city of Sihon. It consumed Ar of Moab, the heights of Arnon." 29. "Woe to you, Moab! You are destroyed, people of Chemosh! He has given up his sons as refugees and his daughters as captives to Sihon, the king of the Amorites." (Chemosh: the god of Moab) 30. "But we have overthrown them. Heshbon's rule has been destroyed all the way to Dibon. We have leveled them as far as Nophah, extending to Medeba." (Dibon: a city of Moab; Nophah: a place mentioned in the conquest) 31. So Israel took possession of the land of the Amorites. 32. After Moses sent spies to Jazer, the Israelites captured its surrounding towns and drove out the Amorites living there. 33. Then they turned and moved along the road toward Bashan, where Og, the king of Bashan, and his whole army marched out to meet them in battle at Edrei. 34. But the Lord said to Moses, "Do not be afraid of him, for I have handed him and his entire army over to you, as well as his land. Do to him what you did to Sihon, the king of the Amorites, who reigned in Heshbon." 35. So Israel struck Og and his sons, along with his entire army, leaving no survivors. They took possession of his land.

Chapter 22

1. Then the Israelites traveled to the plains of Moab and camped along the Jordan across from Jericho. (Jericho: ancient city) 2. Now Balak, the son of Zippor, saw all that Israel had done to the Amorites, (Amorites: ancient people) 3. and Moab was terrified because there were so many people. Indeed, Moab was filled with dread because of the Israelites. (Dread: fear) 4. The Moabites said to the elders of Midian, "This horde is going to consume everything around us, like an ox consumes the grass of the field." So Balak, son of Zippor, who was king of Moab at that time, (Horde: large group) 5. sent messengers to summon Balaam, son of Beor, who was at Pethor, near the Euphrates River, in his native land. Balak said: "A people has come out of Egypt; they cover the face of the land and have settled next to me. (Pethor: ancient city; Euphrates: river) 6. Now come and put a curse on these people, because they are too powerful for me. Perhaps then I will be able to defeat them and drive them out of the land. For I know that whoever you bless is blessed, and whoever you curse is cursed." (Curse: invoke evil; bless: invoke favor) 7. The elders of Moab and Midian left, taking with them the fee for divination. When they came to Balaam, they told him what Balak had said. (Divination: fortune-telling) 8. "Spend the night here," Balaam said to them, "and I will report back to you with the answer the Lord gives me." So the Moabite officials stayed with him. (Officials: leaders) 9. God came to Balaam and asked, "Who are these men with you?" (God: supreme being) 10. Balaam said to God, "Balak, son of Zippor, king of Moab, sent me this message: (King: ruler) 11. 'A people that has come out of Egypt covers the face of the land. Now come and put a curse on them for me. Perhaps then I will be able to fight them

and drive them away.'" (Egypt: ancient nation) **12.** But God said to Balaam, "Do not go with them. You must not put a curse on those people, because they are blessed." (Blessed: favored) **13.** The next morning, Balaam got up and said to Balak's officials, "Go back to your own country, for the Lord has refused to let me go with you." (Refused: declined) **14.** So the Moabite officials returned to Balak and said, "Balaam refused to come with us." (Refused: declined) **15.** Then Balak sent other officials, more numerous and more distinguished than the first. (Distinguished: respected) **16.** They came to Balaam and said: "This is what Balak, son of Zippor, says: Do not let anything keep you from coming to me, (Keep: prevent) **17.** because I will reward you handsomely and do whatever you say. Come and put a curse on these people for me." (Reward: compensation; handsomely: generously) **18.** But Balaam answered them, "Even if Balak gave me all the silver and gold in his palace, I could not do anything great or small to go beyond the command of the Lord my God. (Silver: precious metal; gold: valuable metal) **19.** Now spend the night here so that I can find out what else the Lord will tell me." (Find out: discover) **20.** That night God came to Balaam and said, "Since these men have come to summon you, go with them, but do only what I tell you." (Summon: call) **21.** Balaam got up in the morning, saddled his donkey, and went with the Moabite officials. (Saddled: prepared a saddle) **22.** But God was very angry when he went, and the angel of the Lord stood in the road to oppose him. Balaam was riding on his donkey, and his two servants were with him. (Angry: enraged; oppose: resist) **23.** When the donkey saw the angel of the Lord standing in the road with a drawn sword in his hand, it turned off the road into a field. Balaam beat it to get it back on the road. (Drawn: unsheathed) **24.** Then the angel of the Lord stood in a narrow path through the vineyards, with walls on both sides. (Vineyards: grape fields) **25.** When the donkey saw the angel of the Lord, it pressed close to the wall, crushing Balaam's foot against it. So he beat the donkey again. (Pressed: pushed; crushing: squeezing) **26.** Then the angel of the Lord moved on ahead and stood in a narrow place where there was no room to turn, either to the right or to the left. (Narrow: tight) **27.** When the donkey saw the angel of the Lord, it lay down under Balaam, and he was angry and beat it with his staff. (Staff: rod) **28.** Then the Lord opened the donkey's mouth, and it said to Balaam, "What have I done to you to make you beat me these three times?" (Mouth: opening for speech) **29.** Balaam answered the donkey, "You have made a fool of me! If only I had a sword in my hand, I would kill you right now." (Fool: idiot) **30.** The donkey said to Balaam, "Am I not your own donkey, which you have always ridden, to this day? Have I been in the habit of doing this to you?" "No," he said. (Habit: custom) **31.** Then the Lord opened Balaam's eyes, and he saw the angel of the Lord standing in the road with his sword drawn. So he bowed low and fell facedown. (Bowed: knelt; facedown: prostrate) **32.** The angel of the Lord asked him, "Why have you beaten your donkey these three times? I have come here to oppose you because your path is a reckless one before me. (Reckless: careless) **33.** The donkey saw me and turned away from me these three times. If it had not turned away, I would certainly have killed you by now, but I would have spared it." (Spared: saved) **34.** Balaam said to the angel of the Lord, "I have sinned. I did not realize you were standing in the road to oppose me. Now if you are displeased, I will go back." (Sinned: wronged) **35.** The angel of the Lord said to Balaam, "Go with the men, but speak only what I tell you." So Balaam went with Balak's officials. (Displeased: upset) **36.** When Balak heard that Balaam was coming, he went out to meet him at the Moabite town on the Arnon border, at the edge of his territory. (Arnon: river; border: boundary) **37.** Balak said to Balaam, "Did I not send you an urgent summons? Why didn't you come to me? Am I really not able to reward you?" (Urgent: pressing) **38.** "Well, I have come to you now," Balaam replied. "But I can't say whatever I please. I must speak only what God puts in my mouth." (Pleased: want) **39.** Then Balaam went with Balak to Kiriath Huzoth. (Kiriath Huzoth: city) **40.** Balak sacrificed cattle and sheep, and gave some to Balaam and the officials who were with him. (Sacrificed: offered) **41.** The next morning, Balak took Balaam up to Bamoth Baal, and from there he could see the outskirts of the Israelite camp. (Bamoth Baal: high place; outskirts: borders)

Chapter 23

1. Balaam instructed, "Set up seven altars for me here, and sacrifice seven bulls and seven rams on them." (Altars: sacred platforms; bulls: male cattle; rams: male sheep). **2.** Balak complied, doing exactly as Balaam asked. Together, they sacrificed a bull and a ram on each altar. (Complied: agreed; sacrificed: offered in worship). **3.** Balaam then said to Balak, "Stay here with your offerings while I go and seek the LORD. I will return with whatever message He gives me." He went up to a high, barren place. (Seek: search for; barren: empty, desolate). **4.** God met Balaam there, and Balaam said, "I have set up seven altars and offered a bull and a ram on each one." (Set up: prepared; offered: sacrificed). **5.** The LORD put words into Balaam's mouth and said, "Go back to Balak and deliver this message." (Words: message; deliver: give). **6.** Balaam returned to Balak and found him standing next to his offering, surrounded by all the officials of Moab. (Officials: leaders). **7.** Balaam then proclaimed, "Balak brought me here from Aram, the king of Moab from the mountains of the east. He said, 'Come, curse Jacob for me, come, condemn Israel!'" (Proclaimed: announced; Aram: an ancient region; curse: call down misfortune; condemn: criticize). **8.** "How can I curse those whom God has not cursed? How can I denounce those whom the LORD has not condemned?" (Denounce: accuse publicly; condemned: judged negatively). **9.** "From the rocky peaks, I see them, from the heights, I behold them. I see a people set apart, who do not mingle with the other nations." (Peaks: high points; behold: look at; set apart: distinct, unique). **10.** "Who can count the dust of Jacob or even number a fraction of Israel? Let me die the death of the righteous, and let my end be like theirs!" (Righteous: just, virtuous; fraction: small part). **11.** Balak responded angrily, "What have you done to me? I brought you here to curse my enemies, and instead, you have only blessed them!" (Responded: replied; blessed: spoken favorably about). **12.** Balaam replied, "I can only speak what the LORD tells me to speak." (Replied: answered; tells: commands). **13.** Balak then said, "Come with me to another place where you will be able to see part of the people, and from there, curse them for me." (Part: portion; curse: call down misfortune). **14.** Balak took Balaam to the field of Zophim, on the top of Pisgah. There, Balaam built seven altars and sacrificed a bull and a ram on each one. (Pisgah: a mountain; Zophim: a location; field: open land). **15.** Balaam told Balak, "Stay here by your offerings while I go and meet with the LORD over there." (Stay: remain; meet: encounter). **16.** The LORD met with Balaam, putting words in his mouth and telling him, "Return to Balak and deliver this message." (Words: message). **17.** Balaam returned to Balak, finding him still standing by his offerings with the Moabite officials. Balak asked him, "What did the LORD say?" (Returned: came back; officials: leaders). **18.** Balaam delivered his message: "Rise up, Balak, and listen closely; hear me, son of Zippor." (Rise: stand up; closely: attentively). **19.** "God is not a man, that He should lie, nor a son of man, that He should change His mind. Does He speak and then not act? Does He promise and not fulfill?" (Lie: deceive; change His mind: alter His decision; fulfill: complete). **20.** "I have been commanded to bless; He has blessed, and I cannot undo it." (Blessed: favored; undo: reverse). **21.** "No harm is seen in Jacob, no misery in Israel. The LORD their God is with them; the sound of the King is among them." (Harm: misfortune; misery: suffering; sound: voice; King: God). **22.** "God brought them out of Egypt; they are as strong as a wild ox." (Brought out: delivered; ox: powerful animal). **23.** "There is no magic or sorcery against Jacob, no evil omen against Israel. People will now say, 'Look what God has done!'" (Magic: divination; sorcery: witchcraft; omen: sign). **24.** "The people rise up like a lioness; they rouse themselves like a lion that does not rest until it devours its prey and drinks the blood of its victims." (Rouse: awaken; devours: consumes; prey: hunted animal; victims: those harmed). **25.** Balak said to Balaam, "Don't curse them or bless them at all!" (Curse: speak evil of; bless: speak favorably about). **26.** Balaam responded, "Did I not tell you that I can only do what the LORD commands?" (Responded: answered; commands: instructs). **27.** Balak then said, "Let me take you to another place. Perhaps it will please God to allow you to curse them from there." (Please: satisfy; curse: call down misfortune). **28.** Balak took Balaam to the top of Peor, which overlooks the wasteland. (Wasteland: barren land). **29.** Balaam said, "Build me seven altars here, and prepare seven bulls and seven rams for me." (Altars: sacred platforms). **30.** Balak did exactly as Balaam requested, offering a bull and a ram on each altar. (Offered: sacrificed).

Chapter 24

1. When Balaam noticed that it thrilled the LORD to bless Israel, he avoided the use of divination as he had before. Rather, he turned his attention to the desert. (Divination: seeking knowledge of the future by supernatural means) **2.** As Balaam gazed upon Israel, camped tribe by tribe, the Spirit of God came upon him. (Gazed: looked; camped: settled) **3.** And he delivered his message: "This is the prophecy of Balaam son of Beor, the prophecy of the one whose vision is clear, (Vision: insight; prophecy: message from God) **4.** the prophecy of the one who hears the words of God, who sees a vision from the Almighty, who falls prostrate, and whose eyes are opened. (Prostrate: lying down in reverence; Almighty: all-powerful God) **5.** "How lovely are your tents, Jacob, your dwelling places, Israel! (Tents: homes; dwelling places: houses) **6.** "They spread out like valleys, like gardens beside a river, like aloes planted by the LORD, like cedars near the water. (Spread out: grow; aloes: fragrant trees; cedars: tall trees) **7.** "Water will flow from their buckets, and their seed will be watered abundantly. Their king will be greater than Agag; their kingdom will be exalted. (Seed: descendants; exalted: lifted up, honored) **8.** "God brought them out of Egypt; they have the strength of a wild ox. They will devour hostile nations and crush their bones; with their arrows, they will pierce them. (Devour: consume; hostile: unfriendly; pierce: penetrate) **9.** "Like a lion, they crouch and lie down; like a lioness—who dares to awaken them? May those who bless you be blessed, and those who curse you be cursed!" (Crouch: lower themselves; awaken: stir up; lioness: female lion) **10.** Balak's anger flared up at Balaam. He clapped his hands together and said, "I summoned you to curse my enemies, but you have blessed them three times. (Flared up: became very angry; clapped: struck together) **11.** "Now leave immediately and return to your home! I told you I would reward you richly, but the LORD has kept you from receiving any reward." (Immediately: right away; richly: abundantly) **12.** Balaam responded to Balak, "Did I not tell the messengers you sent to me, (Messengers: people sent with a message) **13.** 'Even though Balak gave me all the silver and gold in his palace, I could not act beyond the LORD's command, whether good or bad. I must only speak what the LORD says'? (Act: do; command: order; beyond: outside) **14.** "Now I am returning to my people, but let me warn you about what this people will do to your people in the future." (Warn: advise; future: coming days) **15.** Balaam then spoke his message: "This is the prophecy of Balaam son of Beor, the prophecy of the one whose vision is clear, (Message: statement; vision: insight) **16.** the prophecy of the one who hears the words of God, who has knowledge from the Most High, who sees a vision from the Almighty, who falls prostrate, and whose eyes are opened. (Most High: God; knowledge: understanding) **17.** "I see him, but not now; I behold him, but not near. A star will come out of Jacob; a scepter will rise from Israel. He will crush the foreheads of Moab, and the skulls of all the people of Sheth. (Behold: see; scepter: symbol of kingship; crush: destroy) **18.** "Edom will be conquered, and Seir, his enemy, will be defeated, but Israel will grow stronger. (Conquered: defeated; Seir: region of Edom; defeated: overcome) **19.** "A ruler will come from Jacob and destroy the survivors of the city." (Ruler: leader; survivors: remaining people) **20.** Balaam then saw Amalek and delivered his message: "Amalek was the first among the nations, but their end will be total destruction." (Amalek: a people from the south; destruction: complete ruin) **21.** Then he saw the Kenites and spoke his message: "Your dwelling place is secure, your nest is set in a rock; (Kenites: a nomadic tribe; dwelling: home; nest: secure place) **22.** yet you Kenites will be destroyed when Ashur takes you captive." (Destroyed: ruined; Ashur: Assyria) **23.** Balaam then spoke his message: "Alas! Who can survive when God does this? (Alas: an expression of sorrow; survive: live) **24.** "Ships will come from the coast of Cyprus; they will subdue Ashur and Eber, but they too will come to destruction." (Cyprus: an island in the Mediterranean; subdue: defeat; destruction: ruin) **25.** Balaam then rose and went home, and Balak returned to his own way. (Rose: stood up; returned: went back)

Chapter 25

1. While Israel was staying in Shittim, the men began to indulge in sexual immorality with Moabite women, (Indulge: to enjoy; Immorality: sinful behavior) **2.** who invited them to the sacrifices to their gods. The people ate the sacrificial meal and bowed down before these gods. (Sacrificial: offering; Bowed: bent forward) **3.** So Israel yoked themselves to the Baal of Peor. And the LORD's anger burned against them. (Yoked: united; Baal: a pagan god) **4.** The LORD said to Moses, "Take all the leaders of these people, kill them and expose them in broad daylight before the LORD, so that the LORD's fierce anger may turn away from Israel." (Expose: reveal; Fierce: intense) **5.** So Moses said to Israel's judges, "Each of you must put to death those of your people who have yoked themselves to the Baal of Peor." (Judges: leaders) **6.** Then an Israelite man brought into the camp a Midianite woman right before the eyes of Moses and the whole assembly of Israel while they were weeping at the entrance to the tent of meeting. (Assembly: gathering; Weeping: crying) **7.** When Phinehas son of Eleazar, the son of Aaron, the priest, saw this, he left the assembly, took a spear in his hand (Phinehas: priest; Spear: weapon) **8.** and followed the Israelite into the tent. He drove the spear into both of them, right through the Israelite man and into the woman's stomach. Then the plague against the Israelites was stopped; (Plague: epidemic) **9.** but those who died in the plague numbered 24,000. (Numbered: counted) **10.** The LORD said to Moses, **11.** "Phinehas son of Eleazar, the son of Aaron, the priest, has turned my anger away from the Israelites. Since he was as zealous for my honor among them as I am, I did not put an end to them in my zeal. (Zealous: passionate) **12.** Therefore tell him I am making my covenant of peace with him. (Covenant: agreement) **13.** He and his descendants will have a covenant of a lasting priesthood, because he was zealous for the honor of his God and made atonement for the Israelites." (Descendants: offspring; Atonement: reconciliation) **14.** The name of the Israelite who was killed with the Midianite woman was Zimri son of Salu, the leader of a Simeonite family. (Simeonite: tribe member) **15.** And the name of the Midianite woman who was put to death was Kozbi daughter of Zur, a tribal chief of a Midianite family. (Tribal: relating to a tribe; Chief: leader) **16.** The LORD said to Moses, **17.** "Treat the Midianites as enemies and kill them. (Enemies: opponents) **18.** They treated you as enemies when they deceived you in the Peor incident involving their sister Kozbi, the daughter of a Midianite leader, the woman who was killed when the plague came as a result of that incident." (Deceived: tricked; Incident: event)

Chapter 26

1. After the plague, the LORD spoke to Moses and Eleazar, Aaron's son, saying, (plague: deadly disease) **2.** "Take a census of the entire Israelite community by family—those 20 and older who can serve in the army." (census: count of people) **3.** Moses and Eleazar spoke to them on the plains of Moab, near the Jordan, across from Jericho, saying, (Moab: a region; Jericho: a city in Israel) **4.** "Take a census of all men 20 and older, as the LORD commanded Moses. These are the

Israelites who came out of Egypt: (census: count of people) **5.** The descendants of Reuben, Israel's firstborn, were: through Hanok, the Hanokite clan; through Pallu, the Palluite clan; (Reuben: first son of Israel) **6.** through Hezron, the Hezronite clan; through Karmi, the Karmite clan. **7.** These were the clans of Reuben; 43,730 were counted. (clans: family groups) **8.** The son of Pallu was Eliab, **9.** and Eliab's sons were Nemuel, Dathan, and Abiram—who rebelled with Korah and opposed Moses and Aaron. (rebellion: defiance) **10.** The earth swallowed them along with Korah, whose followers died in fire. This was a warning. (swallowed: engulfed; consumed: burned) **11.** But the line of Korah did not perish. (line: descendants) **12.** The descendants of Simeon were: through Nemuel, the Nemuelite clan; through Jamin, the Jaminite clan; through Jakin, the Jakinite clan; (Simeon: son of Israel) **13.** through Zerah, the Zerahite clan; through Shaul, the Shaulite clan. **14.** These were the clans of Simeon; 22,200 were counted. (clans: family groups) **15.** The descendants of Gad were: through Zephon, the Zephonite clan; through Haggi, the Haggite clan; through Shuni, the Shunite clan; (Gad: son of Israel) **16.** through Ozni, the Oznite clan; through Eri, the Erite clan; **17.** through Arodi, the Arodite clan; through Areli, the Arelite clan. **18.** These were the clans of Gad; 40,500 were counted. **19.** Er and Onan, sons of Judah, died in Canaan. (Judah: a son of Israel; Canaan: land in the ancient world) **20.** The descendants of Judah were: through Shelah, the Shelanite clan; through Perez, the Perezite clan; through Zerah, the Zerahite clan. (Judah: a son of Israel) **21.** The descendants of Perez were: through Hezron, the Hezronite clan; through Hamul, the Hamulite clan. **22.** These were the clans of Judah; 76,500 were counted. (clans: family groups) **23.** The descendants of Issachar were: through Tola, the Tolaite clan; through Puah, the Puite clan; (Issachar: a son of Israel) **24.** through Jashub, the Jashubite clan; through Shimron, the Shimronite clan. (Jashub: a name; Shimron: a name) **25.** These were the clans of Issachar; 64,300 were counted. **26.** The descendants of Zebulun were: through Sered, the Seredite clan; through Elon, the Elonite clan; through Jahleel, the Jahleelite clan. (Zebulun: a son of Israel) **27.** These were the clans of Zebulun; 60,500 were counted. (clans: family groups) **28.** The descendants of Joseph by their clans through Manasseh and Ephraim were: (Joseph: a son of Israel; Manasseh: son of Joseph; Ephraim: another son of Joseph) **29.** The descendants of Manasseh: through Makir, the Makirite clan (Makir fathered Gilead); through Gilead, the Gileadite clan. **30.** These were the descendants of Gilead: through Iezer, the Iezerite clan; through Helek, the Helekite clan; (Gilead: region) **31.** through Asriel, the Asrielite clan; through Shechem, the Shechemite clan; (Shechem: an ancient city) **32.** through Shemida, the Shemidaite clan; through Hepher, the Hepherite clan. **33.** (Zelophehad, son of Hepher, had no sons, only daughters: Mahlah, Noah, Hoglah, Milkah, and Tirzah.) **34.** These were the clans of Manasseh; 52,700 were counted. (clans: family groups) **35.** These were the descendants of Ephraim by their clans: through Shuthelah, the Shuthelahite clan; through Beker, the Bekerite clan; through Tahan, the Tahanite clan. (Ephraim: a son of Joseph) **36.** The descendants of Shuthelah: through Eran, the Eranite clan. **37.** These were the clans of Ephraim; 32,500 were counted. These were the descendants of Joseph. (clans: family groups) **38.** The descendants of Benjamin were: through Bela, the Belaite clan; through Ashbel, the Ashbelite clan; through Ahiram, the Ahiramite clan; (Benjamin: a son of Israel) **39.** through Shupham, the Shuphamite clan; through Hupham, the Huphamite clan. **40.** The descendants of Bela were: through Ard, the Ardite clan; through Naaman, the Naamite clan. **41.** These were the clans of Benjamin; 45,600 were counted. **42.** The descendants of Dan by their clans were: through Shuham, the Shuhamite clan. (Dan: a son of Israel) **43.** All were Shuhamite clans; 64,400 were counted. (clans: family groups) **44.** The descendants of Asher were: through Imnah, the Imnite clan; through Ishvi, the Ishvite clan; through Beriah, the Beriite clan; (Asher: a son of Israel) **45.** and through Beriah's descendants: through Heber, the Heberite clan; through Malkiel, the Malkielite clan. (Heber: a name; Malkiel: a name) **46.** (Asher had a daughter named Serah.) **47.** These were the clans of Asher; 53,400 were counted. (clans: family groups) **48.** The descendants of Naphtali were: through Jahzeel, the Jahzeelite clan; through Guni, the Gunite clan; (Naphtali: a son of Israel) **49.** through Jezer, the Jezerite clan; through Shillem, the Shillemite clan. **50.** These were the clans of Naphtali; 45,400 were counted. (clans: family groups) **51.** The total number of Israelite men was 601,730. (total: complete count) **52.** The LORD said to Moses, (LORD: a title for God) **53.** "The land must be divided among them as an inheritance, based on their numbers. (inheritance: property passed down) **54.** To larger groups, give more land; to smaller groups, give less. Each will inherit according to their numbers." (inheritance: property passed down) **55.** The land will be divided by lot. Each group's inheritance will be based on their ancestral tribe's names. (lot: a method of random selection) **56.** The inheritance will be distributed by lot among the large and small groups." (inheritance: property passed down) **57.** These were the Levites by their clans: through Gershon, the Gershonite clan; through Kohath, the Kohathite clan; through Merari, the Merarite clan. (Levites: tribe of Levi) **58.** These were the Levite clans: the Libnite, Hebronite, Mahlite, Mushite, and Korahite clans. (Kohath was the ancestor of Amram; **59.** Amram's wife was Jochebed, a descendant of Levi, born in Egypt. She bore Aaron, Moses, and their sister Miriam.) **60.** Aaron was the father of Nadab, Abihu, Eleazar, and Ithamar. (Nadab: a name; Ithamar: a name) **61.** But Nadab and Abihu died when they offered unauthorized fire before the LORD. (unauthorized: not permitted) **62.** All male Levites a month old or older numbered 23,000. They were not counted with the other Israelites because they received no inheritance. (Levites: tribe of Levi) **63.** These were the ones counted by Moses and Eleazar when they took the census in Moab, near the Jordan River, across from Jericho. (census: count of people; Eleazar: a name) **64.** Not one of those counted in the Desert of Sinai remained. (Desert of Sinai: a desert in the Middle East) **65.** The LORD had said they would die in the wilderness, leaving only Caleb and Joshua.

Chapter 27

1. The daughters of Zelophehad, son of Hepher, son of Gilead, son of Makir, son of Manasseh, from the clans of Manasseh, son of Joseph, were Mahlah, Noah, Hoglah, Milkah, and Tirzah. **2.** They came before Moses, Eleazar the priest, the leaders, and the entire assembly at the entrance to the Tent of Meeting and said, **3.** "Our father died in the wilderness. He wasn't part of Korah's rebellion, but he died for his own sin and left no sons. (rebellion: defiance) **4.** Why should our father's name disappear just because he had no sons? Give us property among his relatives." **5.** So Moses brought their case before the LORD, **6.** and the LORD said to him, **7.** "What Zelophehad's daughters are saying is right. You must give them property as an inheritance among their father's relatives and pass on their father's inheritance to them." **8.** "Tell the Israelites: 'If a man dies and leaves no son, give his inheritance to his daughter. **9.** If he has no daughter, give it to his brothers. **10.** If he has no brothers, give it to his father's brothers. **11.** If his father has no brothers, give it to the nearest relative in his clan. This law must apply to the Israelites, as I have commanded Moses.' " (inheritance: property passed down; clan: family group) **12.** Then the LORD said to Moses, "Go up to the Abarim Range and see the land I have given the Israelites. **13.** After you've seen it, you will be gathered to your people, as your brother Aaron was, **14.** for when the community rebelled at Meribah Kadesh in the Desert of Zin, both of you disobeyed my command to honor me as holy before their eyes." (Abarim Range: a mountain range; Meribah Kadesh: a place in the wilderness; Zin: a desert region) **15.** Moses said to the LORD, **16.** "May the LORD, the God who gives breath to all living things, appoint someone over this community **17.** to lead them, one who will guide them out and bring them in, so the LORD's people won't be like sheep without a shepherd." (shepherd: leader)

18. So the LORD said to Moses, "Take Joshua son of Nun, a man filled with the spirit of leadership, and lay your hand on him. **19.** Have him stand before Eleazar the priest and the whole assembly, and commission him in their presence. **20.** Give him some of your authority so the whole Israelite community will obey him. (commission: formally appoint) **21.** He will stand before Eleazar the priest, who will make decisions for him by consulting the Urim before the LORD. At his command, the community will go out, and at his command, they will come in." (Urim: a tool used by priests to seek divine guidance) **22.** Moses did as the LORD commanded him. He took Joshua, had him stand before Eleazar the priest, and the whole assembly. **23.** Then he laid his hands on him and commissioned him, as the LORD instructed through Moses.

Chapter 28

1. The LORD spoke to Moses, **2.** "Tell the Israelites: 'Ensure you gift my meals offerings at the appointed time, as a pleasing aroma to me.' **3.** Say to them: 'This is the offering you're to give: two one-year-old lambs without defect, as a daily burnt offering. **4.** Offer one lamb in the morning and the other at twilight, **5.** with a grain offering of a tenth of an ephah of fine flour mixed with a quarter of a hin of olive oil. **6.** This is the regular burnt offering at Mount Sinai, a pleasing aroma, a food offering to the LORD. **7.** The accompanying drink offering must be a quarter of a hin of fermented drink for each lamb, poured out at the sanctuary. **8.** Offer the second lamb at twilight with the same grain and drink offering as the morning. This is a food offering, a pleasing aroma to the LORD. (grain offering: an offering of fine flour mixed with oil; hin: an ancient liquid measurement) **9.** "On the Sabbath, offer one-year-old lambs without defect, with their drink and grain offerings—a tenth of an ephah of the finest flour mixed with oil. **10.** This is the burnt offering for the Sabbath, in addition to the regular burnt offering and its drink offering. (Sabbath: weekly day of rest) **11.** "On the first day of each month, offer to the LORD a burnt offering of two young bulls, one ram, and seven one-year-old male lambs, all without defect. **12.** With each bull, offer a grain offering of three-tenths of an ephah of fine flour mixed with oil; with the ram, offer two-tenths; **13.** and with each lamb, offer a tenth of an ephah of fine flour mixed with oil. This is for a burnt offering, a pleasing aroma, a food offering to the LORD. **14.** For each bull, offer half a hin of wine; for the ram, a third of a hin; and for each lamb, a quarter of a hin. This is the monthly burnt offering at each new moon. **15.** In addition to the regular burnt offering and its drink offering, offer one male goat as a sin offering to the LORD. (sin offering: offering for atonement of sin) **16.** "On the fourteenth day of the first month, hold the LORD's Passover. **17.** On the fifteenth day of this month, celebrate a festival for seven days, eating unleavened bread. **18.** On the first day, hold a sacred assembly and do no regular work. (Passover: a festival commemorating the Exodus from Egypt) **19.** Present to the LORD a burnt offering: two young bulls, one ram, and seven one-year-old male lambs, all without defect. **20.** With each bull, offer three-tenths of an ephah of fine flour mixed with oil; with the ram, two-tenths; **21.** and with each of the seven lambs, one-tenth. **22.** Include one male goat as a sin offering to make atonement for you. **23.** Offer these in addition to the regular morning burnt offering. **24.** Present the food offering every day for seven days, as a pleasing aroma to the LORD, in addition to the regular burnt offering and its drink offering. **25.** On the seventh day, hold a sacred assembly and do no regular work. (atonement: reconciliation with God) **26.** "On the day of firstfruits, when you offer new grain to the LORD during the Festival of Weeks, hold a sacred assembly and do no regular work. (firstfruits: the first produce of the harvest) **27.** Present a burnt offering of two young bulls, one ram, and seven one-year-old male lambs as a pleasing aroma to the LORD. **28.** With each bull, offer three-tenths of an ephah of fine flour mixed with oil; with the ram, two-tenths; **29.** and with each of the seven lambs, one-tenth. **30.** Include one male goat to make atonement for you. **31.** Offer these with their drink offerings, in addition to the regular burnt offering and its grain offering. Make sure the animals are without defect. (Defect: imperfection or flaw in the animals)

Chapter 29

1. "On the first day of the seventh month, hold a sacred assembly and do no regular work. It is a day to sound the trumpets. **2.** Offer a burnt offering of one young bull, one ram, and seven one-year-old male lambs, all without defect, as an aroma pleasing to the LORD. **3.** With the bull, offer a grain offering of three-tenths of an ephah of the finest flour mixed with olive oil; with the ram, offer two-tenths; **4.** and with each of the seven lambs, one-tenth. **5.** Include one male goat as a sin offering to make atonement for you. **6.** These are in addition to the monthly and daily burnt offerings with their grain and drink offerings, as specified. They are food offerings, a pleasing aroma to the LORD. (atonement: reconciliation with God; ephah: ancient measurement of dry grain; hin: liquid measure) **7.** "On the tenth day of this month, hold a sacred assembly. Deny yourselves and do no work. **8.** Present a burnt offering of one young bull, one ram, and seven one-year-old male lambs, all without defect, as an aroma pleasing to the LORD. **9.** With the bull, offer three-tenths of an ephah of the finest flour mixed with oil; with the ram, two-tenths; **10.** and with each of the seven lambs, one-tenth. **11.** Include one male goat as a sin offering, in addition to the regular burnt offering and its grain and drink offerings. (grain offering: flour mixed with oil; drink offering: liquid poured out as a ritual) **12.** "On the fifteenth day of the seventh month, hold a sacred assembly and do no regular work. Celebrate a festival to the LORD for seven days. **13.** Present a food offering of thirteen young bulls, two rams, and fourteen one-year-old male lambs, all without defect, as an aroma pleasing to the LORD. **14.** With each of the thirteen bulls, offer three-tenths of an ephah of the finest flour mixed with oil; with the two rams, two-tenths; **15.** and with each of the fourteen lambs, one-tenth. **16.** Include one male goat as a sin offering, in addition to the regular burnt offering with its grain and drink offerings. **17.** "On the second day, offer twelve young bulls, two rams, and fourteen one-year-old male lambs, all without defect. **18.** With the bulls, rams, and lambs, offer their grain and drink offerings as specified. **19.** Include one male goat as a sin offering, in addition to the regular burnt offering with its grain and drink offerings. **20.** "On the third day, offer eleven bulls, two rams, and fourteen one-year-old male lambs, all without defect. **21.** With the bulls, rams, and lambs, offer their grain and drink offerings as specified. **22.** Include one male goat as a sin offering, in addition to the regular burnt offering with its grain and drink offerings. **23.** "On the fourth day, offer ten bulls, two rams, and fourteen one-year-old male lambs, all without defect. **24.** With the bulls, rams, and lambs, offer their grain and drink offerings as specified. **25.** Include one male goat as a sin offering, in addition to the regular burnt offering with its grain and drink offerings. **26.** "On the fifth day, offer nine bulls, two rams, and fourteen one-year-old male lambs, all without defect. **27.** With the bulls, rams, and lambs, offer their grain and drink offerings as specified. **28.** Include one male goat as a sin offering, in addition to the regular burnt offering with its grain and drink offerings. **29.** "On the sixth day, offer eight bulls, two rams, and fourteen one-year-old male lambs, all without defect. **30.** With the bulls, rams, and lambs, offer their grain and drink offerings as specified. **31.** Include one male goat as a sin offering, in addition to the regular burnt offering with its grain and drink offerings. **32.** "On the seventh day, offer seven bulls, two rams, and fourteen one-year-old male lambs, all without defect. **33.** With the bulls, rams, and lambs, offer their grain and drink offerings as specified. **34.** Include one male goat as a sin offering, in addition to the regular burnt offering with its grain and drink offerings. **35.** "On the eighth day, hold a closing special assembly and do no regular work. **36.** Present a food offering of one bull, one ram, and seven one-year-old male lambs, all without defect, as an aroma pleasing to the LORD. **37.** With the bull, the ram, and the lambs, offer their grain and drink offerings as specified. **38.** Include one male goat as a sin offering, in addition to the regular burnt offering with its grain and drink offerings. **39.** "In addition to what you vow and your freewill offerings, offer these to the LORD at your appointed festivals: burnt offerings, grain offerings, drink offerings, and fellowship offerings." **40.** Moses told the Israelites all that the LORD had commanded him. (fellowship offerings: offerings shared in community or with God)

Chapter 30

1. Moses said to the heads of the tribes of Israel: "This is what the LORD commands: **2.** When a man makes a vow to the LORD or takes an oath to obligate himself by a pledge, he must not break his word but must do everything he said. (Vow: A solemn promise or commitment made to God; Pledge: A formal promise, often involving a personal obligation) **3.** "When a young woman still living in her father's household makes a vow to the LORD or obligates herself by a pledge, **4.** and her father hears about her vow or pledge but says nothing, then all her vows and pledges will stand. **5.** But if her father forbids her when he hears about it, none of her vows or pledges will stand; the LORD will release her because her father has forbidden her. (Nullify: To cancel or invalidate) **6.** "If she marries after making a vow or uttering a rash promise, (Rash promise: A hasty or thoughtless vow that may not be well-considered) **7.** and her husband hears about it but says nothing, her vows will stand. **8.** But if her husband forbids her, he nullifies the vow, and the LORD will release her. **9.** "Any vow or obligation taken by a widow or divorced woman will be binding on her. **10.** If a woman living with her husband makes a vow or pledges an oath, **11.** and her husband hears about it but says nothing, her vows will stand. **12.** But if her husband nullifies them when he hears about them, none of the vows will stand. The LORD will release her. **13.** Her husband may confirm or nullify any vow or pledge she makes. **14.** If her husband says nothing, he confirms her vows by his silence. **15.** If, however, he nullifies them later, he must bear the consequences of her wrongdoing. **16.** These are the regulations the LORD gave Moses concerning a man and his wife, and a father and his young daughter still living at home.

Chapter 31

1 The LORD spoke to Moses, **2** "Take vengeance on the Midianites for Israel. After that, you will join your ancestors." (vengeance: punishment) **3** Moses told the people, "Send men to fight the Midianites and carry out the LORD's vengeance. **4** Send a thousand men from each tribe." **5** So, twelve thousand men, one thousand from each tribe, were chosen from Israel's clans. **6** Moses sent them with Phinehas, son of Eleazar the priest, carrying sacred items and trumpets for signaling. (sacred: holy) **7** They fought Midian as the LORD commanded and killed all the men. **8** Among the dead were the five kings of Midian—Evi, Rekem, Zur, Hur, and Reba—and Balaam, son of Beor. **9** The Israelites captured the Midianite women, children, and all their herds, flocks, and possessions. (herds: livestock) **10** They destroyed the towns and camps where the Midianites had lived. **11** They took the spoils—people, animals, and goods— (spoils: items) **12** and brought them to Moses, Eleazar, and the assembly at the camp on the plains of Moab, across from Jericho. **13** Moses, Eleazar, and the leaders met them outside the camp. **14** Moses was angry with the officers—those in charge of thousands and hundreds—who returned from battle. (officers: leaders) **15** "Why have you allowed the women to live?" he asked. **16** "They followed Balaam's advice, leading Israel into sin at Peor, causing a plague among the people." (plague: disease) **17** "Now kill all the boys and every woman who has had relations with a man, (relations: sexual activity) **18** but spare the girls who have never been with a man." (spare: save) **19** "Anyone who killed or touched a dead body must stay outside the camp for seven days. Purify yourselves and the captives on the third and seventh days. (purify: cleanse) **20** Purify all clothes, leather, goat hair, and wood."**21** Eleazar told the soldiers, "This is what the LORD commands: **22** Gold, silver, bronze, iron, tin, and lead, **23** and anything that can survive fire, must be passed through fire to be purified. What cannot endure fire must be purified by water. **24** On the seventh day, wash your clothes, and you will be clean to return to camp." **25** The LORD spoke to Moses, **26** "You and Eleazar, along with the leaders, should count the people and animals captured. (count: number) **27** Divide the spoils equally between the soldiers and the rest of the community. **28** From the soldiers, set apart one of every five hundred items as tribute for the LORD—people, cattle, donkeys, or sheep. (tribute: offering) **29** Give this tribute to Eleazar the priest. **30** From the Israelites' share, set apart one of every fifty for the Levites, who care for the LORD's tabernacle." (Levites: religious workers, tabernacle: temple) **31** Moses and Eleazar did as the LORD commanded. **32** The remaining spoils were 675,000 sheep, **33** 72,000 cattle, **34** 61,000 donkeys, **35** and 32,000 women who had never had relations with a man. **36** The soldiers' share was 337,500 sheep, **37** with 675 for the LORD; **38** 36,000 cattle, with 72 for the LORD; **39** 30,500 donkeys, with 61 for the LORD; **40** 16,000 people, with 32 for the LORD. **41** Moses gave the LORD's portion to Eleazar as commanded. **42 The half belonging to the Israelites, which Moses set apart from that of the fighting men— 43** The Israelites' share—337,500 sheep, **44** 36,000 cattle, **45** 30,500 donkeys, **46** and 16,000 people— **47** was divided, and one of every fifty was given to the Levites. **48** The army leaders approached Moses **49** and said, "Not one of our soldiers is missing. **50** We've brought gold—armlets, bracelets, rings, earrings, and necklaces—as atonement for ourselves." (atonement: reparation) **51** Moses and Eleazar accepted the gold offerings. **52** The total weight of the gold from the commanders was 16,750 shekels. (shekels: weights of gold) **53** Each soldier kept his share of the plunder. (plunder: goods) **54** Moses and Eleazar presented the gold in the tent of meeting as a memorial for the Israelites before the LORD. (memorial: reminder)

Chapter 32

1. The Reubenites and Gadites, who had very big herds and flocks, noticed that the lands of Jazer and Gilead had been appropriate for livestock. (cattle: Domesticated animals raised for food, wool, or hard work) **2.** So they came to Moses, Eleazar the priest, and the leaders of the community, and said, **3.** "Ataroth, Dibon, Jazer, Nimrah, Heshbon, Elealeh, Sebam, Nebo, and Beon— (The names of towns and regions suitable for livestock) **4.** the land the LORD subdued before the Israelites—are good for livestock, and your servants have livestock. **5.** If we have found favor in your sight," they said, "let this land be given to your servants as our possession. Do not make us cross the Jordan." (favor: Approval or blessing) **6.** Moses said to the Gadites and Reubenites, "Should your fellow Israelites go to war while you stay here?" (A question challenging their commitment to the collective cause) **7.** Why do you discourage the Israelites from crossing into the land the LORD has given them? (Discourage: To dissuade or deter from action) **8.** This is what your ancestors did when I sent them from Kadesh Barnea to explore the land. (Kadesh Barnea: A place in the wilderness, from which the Israelites were sent to scout the Promised Land) **9.** When they went up to the Valley of Eshkol and saw the land, they discouraged the Israelites from entering the land the LORD had given them. (Valley of Eshkol: A region in southern Canaan where spies brought back fruit) **10.** The LORD's anger was aroused that day, and he swore this oath: **11.** 'Because they did not follow me wholeheartedly, none of those who were twenty years old or more when they came out of Egypt will see the land I promised on oath to Abraham, Isaac, and Jacob— (Wholeheartedly: With full commitment and sincerity) **12.** except Caleb son of Jephunneh the Kenizzite and Joshua son of Nun, for they followed the LORD wholeheartedly.' (Kenizzite: An ancient tribe, Caleb's ancestral line; Joshua: Moses' assistant who led Israel after him) **13.** The LORD's anger burned against Israel, and he made them wander in the desert forty years, until the entire generation of those who had done evil in his sight was gone. (Wander: To move without a fixed direction; Evil: Sinful actions against God) **14.** "And here you are, a brood of sinners, standing in the place of your ancestors and making the LORD even more angry with Israel." (Brood: A group or offspring, here implying a group of people inheriting sinful tendencies) 15. If you turn away from following him, he will again leave all these people in the desert, and you will be the cause of their destruction." (Turn away: To abandon or depart from God's will) 16. Then they came to him and said, "We would like to build pens here for our livestock and cities for our women and children." (Pens: Enclosures for animals; cities: Settlements for people) 17. But we will arm ourselves for battle and go ahead of the Israelites until we have brought them to their place. Meanwhile, our women and children will stay in fortified cities for protection from the inhabitants of the land. (Fortified: Strongly built for defense) 18. We will not return to our homes until every Israelite has received his inheritance. (Inheritance: The portion of land promised by God to each tribe) 19. We will not receive any inheritance with them across the Jordan, because our inheritance has come to us on this side of the Jordan." (East side of the Jordan: The area they had already settled, east of the river) 20. Then Moses said to them, "If you do this—if you arm yourselves before the LORD for battle (Arm: Prepare for conflict with weapons) 21. and if all of you who are armed cross the Jordan before the LORD until he has driven his enemies out before him— (Cross over: To enter into the land of Canaan; Enemies: Those opposing the Israelites) 22. then, when the land is subdued before the LORD, you may return and be free from your obligation to the LORD and to Israel. And this land will be your possession before the LORD." (Subdued: Conquered and made peaceful) 23. "But if you fail to do this, you will be sinning against the LORD; and you can be sure that your sin will find you out." (Fail: To not fulfill a promise or responsibility; Sin: Disobedience to God's commandments) 24. Build cities for your women and children, and pens for your flocks, but do what you have promised." 25. The Gadites and Reubenites said to Moses, "We your servants will do as our lord commands. 26. Our children and wives, our flocks and herds will remain here in the cities of Gilead. 27. But your servants, every man armed for battle, will cross over to fight before the LORD, just as our lord says." (Gilead: A region east of the Jordan, now designated for their inheritance) 28. Then Moses gave orders concerning them to Eleazar the priest, Joshua son of Nun, and to the family heads of the Israelite tribes. (Family heads: Leaders of the various tribes of Israel) 29. He said to them, "If the Gadites and Reubenites, every man armed for battle, cross over the Jordan with you before the LORD, then when the land is subdued before you, you must give them the land of Gilead as their possession." (Possession: The right to own or control land) 30. But if they do not cross over with you armed, they must accept their possession with you in Canaan." 31. The Gadites and Reubenites answered, "Your servants will do what the LORD has commanded. 32. We will cross over before the LORD into Canaan armed, but the property we inherit will be on this side of the Jordan." 33. Then Moses gave to the Gadites, the Reubenites, and the half-tribe of Manasseh son of Joseph the kingdom of Sihon king of the Amorites and the kingdom of Og king of Bashan—the entire land with its towns and the surrounding territory. (Amorites: A people group in Canaan; Bashan: A region east of the Jordan River) 34. The Gadites built up Dibon, Ataroth, Aroer, 35. Atroth Shophan, Jazer, Jogbehah, 36. Beth Nimrah, and Beth Haran as fortified cities, and built pens for their flocks. 37. The Reubenites rebuilt Heshbon, Elealeh, and Kiriathaim, 38. as well as Nebo and Baal Meon (these names were changed) and Sibmah. They gave names to the towns they rebuilt. (Rebuilt: Restored or re-established cities) 39. The descendants of Makir son of Manasseh went to Gilead, captured it, and drove out the Amorites who were there. (Descendants: Offspring or heirs of Makir; Captured: Took possession by force) 40. So Moses gave Gilead to the Makirites, the descendants of Manasseh, and they settled there. (Settled: Took up residence or established themselves) 41. Jair, a descendant of Manasseh, captured their settlements and called them Havvoth Jair. 42. And Nobah captured Kenath and its surrounding settlements and called it Nobah after himself. (Captured: Took control of; Settlements: Communities or villages)

Chapter 33

1. These are the stages in the Israelites' journey from Egypt, by divisions under Moses and Aaron. (Summary of the journey) 2. At the LORD's command, Moses recorded their journey by stages. (Moses follows God's instructions to document the journey) 3. They set out from Rameses on the fifteenth day of the first month, the day after the Passover. They marched out boldly in full view of the Egyptians. (Departure after Passover, in sight of the Egyptians) 4. Who were burying their firstborn, whom the LORD had struck down. The LORD had brought judgment on their gods. (Egyptians were mourning the loss of their firstborn due to God's judgment) 5. They left Rameses and camped at Sukkoth. (First stop after leaving Egypt) 6. They left Sukkoth and camped at Etham, on the edge of the desert. (Moving to the desert's edge) 7. They turned back to Pi Hahiroth, east of Baal Zephon, and camped near Migdol. (They retraced their steps to Pi Hahiroth) 8. They crossed the sea into the desert, and after three days in the Desert of Etham, they camped at Marah. (Crossing the sea and traveling to Marah) 9. They left Marah and went to Elim, where there were twelve springs and seventy palm trees, and camped there. (Arrival at the oasis of Elim) 10. They left Elim and camped by the Red Sea. (Next stop by the Red Sea) 11. They left the Red Sea and camped in the Desert of Sin. (Arrival in the Desert of Sin) 12. They left the Desert of Sin and camped at Dophkah. (Continued journey to Dophkah) 13. They left Dophkah and camped at Alush. (Next camp at Alush) 14. They left Alush and camped at Rephidim, where there was no water for the people. (Rephidim stop, no water) 15. They left Rephidim and camped in the Desert of Sinai. (Arrival at Sinai) 16. They left Sinai and camped at Kibroth Hattaavah. (Departure from Sinai to Kibroth Hattaavah) 17. They left Kibroth Hattaavah and camped at Hazeroth. (Journey continued to Hazeroth) 18. They left Hazeroth and camped at Rithmah. (Move to Rithmah) 19. They left Rithmah and camped at Rimmon Perez. (Continued to Rimmon Perez) 20. They left Rimmon Perez and camped at Libnah. (Next stop was Libnah) 21. They left Libnah and camped at Rissah. (Traveled from Libnah to Rissah) 22. They left Rissah and camped at Kehelathah. (Move to Kehelathah) 23. They left Kehelathah and camped at Mount Shepher. (Next camp at Mount Shepher) 24. They left Mount Shepher and camped at Haradah. (Continued journey to Haradah) 25. They left Haradah and camped at Makheloth. (Journey to Makheloth) 26. They left Makheloth and camped at Tahath. (Camp at Tahath) 27. They left Tahath and camped at Terah. (Next stop was Terah) 28. They left Terah and camped at Mithkah. (Traveled from Terah to Mithkah) 29. They left Mithkah and camped at Hashmonah. (Move to Hashmonah) 30. They left Hashmonah and camped at Moseroth. (Continued to Moseroth) 31. They left Moseroth and camped at Bene Jaakan. (Next camp at Bene Jaakan) 32. They left Bene Jaakan and camped at Hor Haggidgad. (Traveled to Hor Haggidgad) 33. They left Hor Haggidgad and camped at Jotbathah. (Moved to Jotbathah) 34. They left Jotbathah and camped at Abronah. (Next stop at Abronah) 35. They left Abronah and camped at Ezion Geber. (Camped at Ezion Geber) 36. They left Ezion Geber and camped at Kadesh, in the Desert of Zin. (Journey continued to Kadesh in the Desert of Zin) 37. They left Kadesh and camped at Mount Hor, on the border of Edom. (Traveled to Mount Hor on Edom's border) 38. At the LORD's command, Aaron went up Mount Hor and died on the first day of the fifth month in the fortieth year after leaving Egypt. (Aaron dies at Mount Hor after 40 years) 39. Aaron was 123 years old when he died on Mount Hor. (Aaron's age at death) 40. The Canaanite king of Arad, in the Negev of Canaan, heard the Israelites were coming. (The Canaanite king of Arad hears of their arrival) 41. They left Mount Hor and camped at Zalmonah. (Traveled to Zalmonah) 42. They left Zalmonah and camped at Punon. (Journeyed to Punon) 43. They left Punon and camped at Oboth. (Moved to

Oboth) **44.** They left Oboth and camped at Iye Abarim, on the border of Moab. (Iye Abarim on Moab's border) **45.** They left Iye Abarim and camped at Dibon Gad. (Traveled to Dibon Gad) **46.** They left Dibon Gad and camped at Almon Diblathaim. (Journey to Almon Diblathaim) **47.** They left Almon Diblathaim and camped in the mountains of Abarim, near Nebo. (Move to the Abarim mountains) **48.** They left the mountains of Abarim and camped on the plains of Moab, by the Jordan across from Jericho. (Camps on the plains of Moab near Jericho) **49.** There, on the plains of Moab, they camped from Beth Jeshimoth to Abel Shittim. (Camping along the Jordan River) **50.** The LORD said to Moses, (God speaks to Moses) **51.** "Speak to the Israelites and say: 'When you cross the Jordan into Canaan, (The Israelites are commanded to cross the Jordan) **52.** drive out all the inhabitants, destroy their idols, and demolish their high places. (Instructions to drive out the inhabitants and destroy idols) **53.** Take possession of the land, for I have given it to you. (God promises the land to them) **54.** Distribute the land by lot, with larger groups getting larger shares. Whatever falls to them will be theirs.' (Land to be divided by lot among the tribes) **55.** "But if you do not drive out the inhabitants, they will become thorns in your sides and barbs in your eyes. They will trouble you in the land you live. (Failure to drive out inhabitants will cause future trouble) **56.** And I will do to you what I plan to do to them." (God warns of consequences if they fail to obey)

Chapter 34

1. The LORD said to Moses, (God speaks to Moses) **2.** "Command the Israelites and say to them: 'When you enter Canaan, the land that will be allotted to you as an inheritance is to have these boundaries: (Instructions to Moses to set boundaries for the land of Canaan) **3.** "Your southern side will include some of the Desert of Zin along the border of Edom. Your southern boundary will start in the east from the southern end of the Dead Sea, (Description of the southern boundary, starting at the Dead Sea) **4.** cross south of Scorpion Pass, continue on to Zin and go south of Kadesh Barnea. Then it will go to Hazar Addar and over to Azmon, (Further details of the southern boundary, passing through significant locations) **5.** where it will turn, join the Wadi of Egypt and end at the Mediterranean Sea. (The boundary turns toward the Wadi of Egypt and ends at the Mediterranean) **6.** "Your western boundary will be the coast of the Mediterranean Sea. This will be your boundary on the west. (Western boundary along the Mediterranean coast) **7.** "For your northern boundary, run a line from the Mediterranean Sea to Mount Hor (Northern boundary starting from the Mediterranean to Mount Hor) **8.** and from Mount Hor to Lebo Hamath. Then the boundary will go to Zedad, (The boundary runs from Mount Hor to Zedad) **9.** continue to Ziphron and end at Hazar Enan. This will be your boundary on the north. (Continued details of the northern boundary) **10.** "For your eastern boundary, run a line from Hazar Enan to Shepham. (Eastern boundary runs from Hazar Enan to Shepham) **11.** The boundary will go down from Shepham to Riblah on the east side of Ain and continue along the slopes east of the Sea of Galilee. (Further details of the eastern boundary, passing through Riblah) **12.** Then the boundary will go down along the Jordan and end at the Dead Sea. "This will be your land, with its boundaries on every side." (The boundary completes at the Dead Sea, forming a fully enclosed land) **13.** Moses commanded the Israelites: "Assign this land by lot as an inheritance. The LORD has ordered that it be given to the nine-and-a-half tribes, (Moses instructs the Israelites to assign the land by lot to the nine and a half tribes) **14.** because the families of the tribe of Reuben, the tribe of Gad and the half-tribe of Manasseh have received their inheritance. (The two-and-a-half tribes already received their inheritance east of the Jordan) **15.** These two-and-a-half tribes have received their inheritance east of the Jordan across from Jericho, toward the sunrise." (Details of the two-and-a-half tribes' inheritance on the east side of the Jordan) **16.** The LORD said to Moses, (God speaks again to Moses) **17.** "These are the names of the men who are to assign the land for you as an inheritance: Eleazar the priest and Joshua son of Nun. (The appointed leaders for dividing the land are Eleazar and Joshua) **18.** And appoint one leader from each tribe to help assign the land. (Moses is instructed to appoint one leader from each tribe) **19.** These are their names: Caleb son of Jephunneh, from the tribe of Judah; (Caleb from Judah) **20.** Shemuel son of Ammihud, from the tribe of Simeon; (Shemuel from Simeon) **21.** Elidad son of Kislon, from the tribe of Benjamin; (Elidad from Benjamin) **22.** Bukki son of Jogli, the leader from the tribe of Dan; (Bukki from Dan) **23.** Hanniel son of Ephod, the leader from the tribe of Manasseh son of Joseph; (Hanniel from Manasseh) **24.** Kemuel son of Shiphtan, the leader from the tribe of Ephraim son of Joseph; (Kemuel from Ephraim) **25.** Elizaphan son of Parnak, the leader from the tribe of Zebulun; (Elizaphan from Zebulun) **26.** Paltiel son of Azzan, the leader from the tribe of Issachar; (Paltiel from Issachar) **27.** Ahihud son of Shelomi, the leader from the tribe of Asher; (Ahihud from Asher) **28.** Pedahel son of Ammihud, the leader from the tribe of Naphtali." (Pedahel from Naphtali) **29.** These are the men the LORD commanded to assign the inheritance to the Israelites in the land of Canaan. (List of the men appointed by God to divide the land among the Israelites)

Chapter 35

1. On the plains of Moab by the Jordan across from Jericho, the LORD said to Moses, (region and setting of the command to Moses) **2.** "Command the Israelites to present the Levites cities to live in from the inheritance the Israelites will own. And provide them pasturelands around the cities. (commands to allocate towns and pasturelands to the Levites) **3.** Then they may have towns to stay in and pasturelands for the farm animals they very own and all their different animals. (The Levites may have cities and land for their cattle) **4.** "The pasturelands across the towns which you provide the Levites will expand one thousand cubits from the town wall. (size of the pasturelands across the towns given to the Levites) **5.** Outside the city, measure two thousand cubits on the east side, two thousand at the south side, two thousand at the west, and two thousand at the north, with the city in the middle. They may have this area as pastureland for the towns. (further specification of pastureland limitations around each city) **6.** "Six of the towns you provide the Levites will be cities of refuge, to which a person who has killed a person may also flee. Further, give them forty-two other cities. (Six of the Levite cities will be towns of refuge for those who accidentally kill someone) **7.** In all you must give the Levites forty-eight cities, together with their pasturelands. (total number of towns for the Levites, including cities of refuge) **8.** The cities you give the Levites from the land the Israelites possess are to be given in proportion to the inheritance of each tribe: Take many towns from a tribe that has many, but few from one that has few." (The number of Levite towns will be proportionate to the size of each tribe's inheritance) **9.** Then the LORD said to Moses: (God speaks again to Moses) **10.** "Speak to the Israelites and say to them: 'When you cross the Jordan into Canaan, (commands to Moses to tell the Israelites about selecting cities of refuge upon entering Canaan) **11.** Select some cities to be your cities of refuge, to which a person who has killed someone accidentally may also flee. (Selection of cities of refuge for accidental killers) **12.** They will be places of refuge from the avenger, so that anyone accused of murder may not die before they stand trial before the assembly. (Purpose of the cities of refuge is to protect the accused from the avenger of blood until trial) **13.** These six cities you give will be your cities of refuge. (Affirmation of the six towns of refuge) **14.** Give three on this side of the Jordan and three in Canaan as cities of refuge. (3 cities of refuge to be placed east of the Jordan and three west of it) **15.** These six cities will be a place of refuge for Israelites and for foreigners residing among them, so that anyone who has killed another accidentally can flee there. (Cities of refuge are for both Israelites and foreigners who accidentally cause death) **16.** "If anyone strikes someone a fatal blow with an iron object, that person is a murderer; the murderer is to be put to death. (A person who kills with an iron object is guilty of murder) **17.** Or if anyone is holding a stone and strikes someone a fatal blow with it, that person is a murderer; the murderer is to be put to death. (A person who kills with a stone is guilty of murder) **18.** Or if anyone is holding a wooden object and strikes someone a fatal blow with it, that person is a murderer; the murderer is to be put to death. (A person who kills with a wooden object is guilty of murder) **19.** The avenger of blood shall put the murderer to death; when the avenger comes upon the murderer, the avenger shall put the murderer to death. (The avenger of blood is authorized to execute the murderer) **20.** If anyone with malice aforethought shoves another or throws something at them intentionally so they die (Malicious acts resulting in death are punishable by death) **21.** Or if out of enmity one person hits another with their fist so that the other dies, that person is to be put to death; that person is a murderer. The avenger of blood shall put the murderer to death when they meet. (Acts of enmity resulting in death also require the death of the perpetrator) **22.** "But if without enmity someone suddenly pushes another or throws something at them unintentionally (Accidental acts causing death are not treated as murder) **23.** Or, without seeing them, drops on them a stone heavy enough to kill them, and they die, then since that other person was not an enemy and no harm was intended, (Further clarification that unintentional deaths without malice are not murder) **24.** The assembly must judge between the accused and the avenger of blood according to these regulations. (The assembly must mediate between the accused and the avenger of blood in case of accidental deaths) **25.** The assembly must protect the one accused of murder from the avenger of blood and send the accused back to the city of refuge to which they fled. The accused must stay there until the death of the high priest, who was anointed with the holy oil. (The accused is protected in the city of refuge until the death of the high priest) **26.** "But if the accused ever goes outside the limits of the city of refuge to which they fled (If the accused leaves the city of refuge) **27.** And the avenger of blood finds them outside the city, the avenger of blood may kill the accused without being guilty of murder. (The avenger is not guilty if the accused leaves the city of refuge) **28.** The accused must stay in the city of refuge until the death of the high priest; only after the death of the high priest may they return to their own property. (The accused may only return home after the death of the high priest) **29.** "This is to have the force of law for you throughout the generations to come, wherever you live. (This law is to be observed for future generations) **30.** "Anyone who kills a person is to be put to death as a murderer only on the testimony of witnesses. But no one is to be put to death on the testimony of only one witness. (The death penalty requires multiple witnesses, not just one) **31.** "Do not accept a ransom for the life of a murderer, who deserves to die. They are to be put to death. (A murderer cannot be pardoned with a ransom) **32.** "Do not accept a ransom for anyone who has fled to a city of refuge and so allow them to go back and live on their own land before the death of the high priest. (A person who has fled to a city of refuge cannot return before the high priest dies) **33.** "Do not pollute the land where you are. Bloodshed pollutes the land, and atonement cannot be made for the land on which blood has been shed, except by the blood of the one who shed it. (Bloodshed defiles the land, and only the murderer's death can atone for it) **34.** Do not defile the land where you live and where I dwell, for I, the LORD, dwell among the Israelites." (God's presence in Israel requires that the land remain undefiled by bloodshed)

Chapter 36

1. The own family heads of Gilead, son of Makir, son of Manasseh, from the clans of Joseph, spoke before Moses and the leaders, the heads of Israelite families. (The leaders of Manasseh boost a difficulty approximately inheritance legal guidelines.) **2.** They stated, "when the LORD commanded my lord to give the land as an inheritance by way of lot, He ordered you to offer the inheritance of our brother Zelophehad to his daughters. (They remind Moses of the inheritance given to Zelophehad's daughters.) **3.** but in the event that they marry guys from other tribes, their inheritance might be taken from our ancestral inheritance and delivered to the tribe they marry into. (concern that inheritance may be lost to some other tribe if the daughters marry out of doors their tribe.) **4.** while the year of Jubilee comes, their inheritance will shift to the tribe they marry into, and it will likely be taken from our ancestors' inheritance." (Inheritance would completely skip to some other tribe at the year of Jubilee.) **5.** on the LORD's command, Moses said: "What the tribe of Joseph is announcing is right. (Moses concurs with their subject.) **6.** this is the LORD's command: Zelophehad's daughters might also marry anyone they pick, but inside their father's tribal clan. (Daughters can marry freely however need to live within their tribe to maintain inheritance.) **7.** No inheritance is to pass from one tribe to every other, for every tribe need to preserve its ancestral land. **8.** each daughter who inherits land must marry within her father's tribe, so that the inheritance remains in the tribe. (Daughters inheriting land should marry inside their father's tribe.) **9.** No inheritance can also skip among tribes; every tribe must maintain its land." (Reaffirming that land ought to stay inside the tribe.) **10.** So Zelophehad's daughters obeyed the LORD's command to Moses. (The daughters obeyed God's command.) **11.** Zelophehad's daughters—Mahlah, Tirzah, Hoglah, Milkah, and Noah—married their cousins on their father's facet. (The daughters married within their family tribe.) **12.** They married inside the clans of Manasseh son of Joseph, and their inheritance remained of their father's tribe. (Their marriages stored the inheritance within the tribe of Manasseh.) **13.** these are the instructions and guidelines the LORD gave thru Moses to the Israelites at the plains of Moab via the Jordan across from Jericho. (summary of the legal guidelines given to Israel whilst camped on the plains of Moab.)

5 – Deuteronomy

Chapter 1

1. These are the words that Moses spoke to all Israel on this side of the Jordan in the wilderness, in the plain opposite Suph, between Paran, Tophel, Laban, Hazeroth, and Dizahab. (wilderness: desert) **2.** It is an eleven-day journey from Horeb by way of Mount Seir to Kadesh Barnea. (journey: trip) **3.** Now it happened in the fortieth year, in the eleventh month, on the first day of the month, that Moses spoke to the children of Israel according to all that the Lord had commanded him to give them. **4.** This was after he defeated Sihon king of the Amorites, who lived in Heshbon, and Og king of Bashan, who lived in Ashtaroth at Edrei. (defeated: conquered) **5.** On this side of the Jordan in the land of Moab, Moses began to explain this law, saying, (explain: clarify) **6.** "The Lord our God spoke to us in Horeb, saying, 'You have stayed long enough at this mountain. (dwelt: stayed) **7.** Turn and set out on your journey, and go to the mountains of the Amorites and all the surrounding regions—in the plains, the hills, the lowlands, the southern regions, and the seacoast—to the land of the Canaanites and to Lebanon, all the way to the great Euphrates River. (lowlands: valleys) **8.** See, I have placed the land before you; go in and take possession of it, the land that the Lord swore to give to your ancestors—Abraham, Isaac, and Jacob—and their descendants after them. (possession: ownership) **9.** And at that time, I said to you, 'I am unable to bear the weight of you all by myself. (bear: support) **10.** The Lord your God has multiplied you, and now you are as numerous as the stars of heaven. (multiplied: increased) **11.** May the Lord, the God of your ancestors, make you a thousand times more numerous and bless you as He has promised! (ancestors: forefathers) **12.** But how can I carry your troubles, burdens, and disputes alone? (burdens: responsibilities) **13.** Choose wise, understanding, and knowledgeable men from your tribes, and I will set them as leaders over you. (knowledgeable: informed) **14.**

And you replied to me, saying, 'What you have said is good.' (replied: answered) **15.** So I selected wise and knowledgeable leaders from among your tribes and appointed them as heads over you, leaders of thousands, hundreds, fifties, tens, and officers for your tribes. (appointed: designated) **16.** Then I instructed your judges at that time, saying, 'Listen to the cases among your people and judge fairly between a person and their brother or any foreigner among them. (judges: officials) **17.** Show no partiality in judgment; hear both small and great cases alike. Do not be intimidated by anyone, for the judgment belongs to God. Any case too difficult for you, bring to me, and I will handle it. (partiality: favoritism) **18.** At that time, I commanded you in all the actions you should take. (commanded: ordered) **19.** So we left Horeb and went through the vast and fearful wilderness that you saw on the way to the hill country of the Amorites, just as the Lord our God commanded us. Finally, we arrived at Kadesh Barnea. (fearful: frightening) **20.** And I said to you, 'You have reached the hill country of the Amorites, which the Lord our God is giving us. (giving: providing) **21.** Look, the Lord your God has placed this land before you. Go up and take possession of it, as the Lord, the God of your ancestors, has promised you; do not be afraid or discouraged. (discouraged: disheartened) **22.** Then all of you came to me and said, 'Let us send men ahead of us to explore the land and bring back information on the route we should take and the cities we will reach.' (explore: scout) **23.** The plan pleased me, so I selected twelve men from among you, one from each tribe. (selected: chosen)

Chapter 2

1. "We turned down and traveled into the nature along the Red Sea route, as the Lord instructed me, and we circled Mount Seir for numerous days." (Seir: a mountain range) **2.** "Also the Lord spoke to me, saying, 'You've circled this mountain long enough. Now turn north.'" (Circled: moved around) **3.** "Give the people this command: 'You're about to pass through the land of your cousins, the descendants of Esau, who live in Seir. They will be hysterical of you, so be conservative.'" (Conservative: careful) **4.** "Don't provoke or engage them in conflict, for I'll not give you any of their land—not indeed a bottom of it—because I've given Mount Seir to Esau as his heritage." (Provoke: stir up; Heritage: possession) **5.** "You may buy food from them with plutocrat to eat and buy water with plutocrat to drink." (Plutocrat: wealth; Purchase: steal) **6.** "For the Lord your God has blessed all your work. He knows your trip through this vast nature. For these forty times, the Lord your God has been with you, and you have demanded nothing." (Vast: large; Demanded: didn't have) **7.** "After passing by the descendants of Esau in Seir, we moved down from the road through the desert, beyond Elath and Ezion Geber, and traveled through the nature of Moab." (Descendants: seed; Nature: desert) **8.** "Also the Lord spoke to me, saying: 'Don't provoke the people of Moab or fight them, for I'll not give you any of their land as an heritage. I've given the land of Ar to the descendants of Lot.'" (Provoke: stir up; Heritage: possession) **9.** "The Emim had lived there—a people as potent, multitudinous, and altitudinous as the Anakim." (Emim: titans) **10.** "They were titans, like the Anakim, but the Moabites call them Emim." (Moabites: people of Moab) **11.** "The Horites lived in Seir, but Esau's descendants drove them out, destroyed them, and took their land, just as Israel did with the land the Lord gave them as their heritage." (Horites: ancient people; Drove out: expelled) **12.** "The Lord said: 'Get up and cross the Valley of the Zered.' So we crossed the Valley of the Zered." (Zered: vale) **13.** "It took us thirty-eight times to travel from Kadesh Barnea to the Valley of the Zered, during which the entire generation of soldiers decomposed, just as the Lord had promised." (Generation: group of people born at the same time; Decomposed: failed) **14.** "The Lord's hand was against them, to exclude them from the camp, until they were each gone." (Exclude: spread) **15.** "When all the dogfaces had failed and were no longer among the people," **16.** "The Lord spoke to me, saying, 'Moment, you're to cross at Ar, on the border of Moab.'" (Ar: megacity; Border: boundary) **17.** "As you approach the people of Ammon, don't provoke or fight them. I'll not give you their land as an heritage, for I've given it to the descendants of Lot." (Ammon: people of Ammon; Provoke: stir up) **18.** "That land was formerly inhabited by titans; they were called Zamzummim by the Ammonites." (Inhabited: lived in; Zamzummim: titans) **19.** "A people as numerous, powerful, and tall as the Anakim. But the Lord wiped them out before you, and you took possession of their land and settled there." (Anakim: Giants) **20.** "Just as He did with the descendants of Esau, who lived in Seir, when He destroyed the Horites before them. They took possession of their land and lived there, even to this day." (Seir: A region in the mountains; Horites: An ancient people) **21.** "And the Avim, who lived in villages as far as Gaza—were destroyed by the Caphtorim, who came from Caphtor, and they took over their land and settled there." (Avim: A group of people near Gaza; Caphtorim: People from the region of Caphtor) **22.** "Rise up, take your journey, and cross over the River Arnon. Look, I have given Sihon, the Amorite king of Heshbon, and his land into your hands. Begin to take possession of it and engage him in battle." (Arnon: A river; Amorite: A people of Canaan; Heshbon: A city of the Amorites) **23.** "This day, I will begin to make the fear and dread of you fall upon all the nations under the entire heavens. They will hear reports about you and will tremble and be in anguish because of you." (Anguish: Extreme distress) **24.** "I sent messengers from the Wilderness of Kedemoth to Sihon, king of Heshbon, with words of peace, saying," (Kedemoth: A location in the wilderness) **25.** "'Let me pass through your land; I will stay on the main road, not turning aside to the right or the left.'" (Main road: The direct route) **26.** "You shall sell me food for money so that I may eat, and give me water for money so that I may drink; just let me pass through on foot," (Sell me: To provide in exchange for payment) **27.** "Just as the descendants of Esau, who live in Seir, and the Moabites, who live in Ar, did for me, until I cross the Jordan into the land the Lord our God is giving us." (Moabites: Descendants of Lot; Ar: A city in Moab) **28.** "But Sihon, king of Heshbon, refused to let us pass through, because the Lord your God had hardened his spirit and made his heart stubborn, to deliver him into your hands, as it is today." (Hardened: Made resistant to change) **29.** "And the Lord said to me, 'See, I have begun to give Sihon and his land into your hands. Begin to take possession of it, so that you may inherit his land.'" (Possess: To take control of) **30.** "Then Sihon and all his people came out to fight us at Jahaz." (Jahaz: A battle location) **31.** "And the Lord our God gave him into our hands, and we defeated him, his sons, and all his people." (Defeated: Overcame in battle) **32.** "We captured all his cities at that time, and we completely destroyed every city's inhabitants—men, women, and children. We left no survivors." (Completely destroyed: Annihilated) **33.** "We only took the livestock and plunder from the cities that we captured." (Plunder: Goods taken by force) **34.** "From Aroer, which is on the bank of the River Arnon, and from the city in the ravine, as far as Gilead, there was not one city too strong for us. The Lord our God gave all of them into our hands." (Aroer: A city by the Arnon River; Gilead: A region east of the Jordan) **35.** "Only you did not approach the land of the Ammonites, anywhere along the River Jabbok, or the cities in the mountains, or anywhere the Lord our God had forbidden us." (Ammonites: Descendants of Lot; Jabbok: A river; Forbidden: Not allowed) **36.** "Then we turned and went up the road to Bashan, and King Og of Bashan came out against us, he and all his people, to battle at Edrei." (Bashan: A region; Edrei: A battle location) **37.** "The Lord said to me, 'Do not fear him, for I have delivered him and all his people and his land into your hands. You shall do to him as you did to Sihon, king of the Amorites, who lived in Heshbon.'" (Fear: To be afraid)

Chapter 3

1. Also we turned and traveled along the road to Bashan, and Og, the king of Bashan, came out with all his people to fight against us at Edrei. (Bashan: rich land) **2.** The Lord said to me, 'Don't be hysterical of him, for I've handed over to you Og, his people, and his land. You'll deal with him as you did with Sihon, the king of the Amorites, who lived in Heshbon.' (Amorites: ancient people) **3.** So, the Lord our God gave us Og, king of Bashan, and all his people, and we fought against him until there were no survivors. **4.** We captured all his metropolises at that time. There wasn't a single megacity we didn't take—sixty metropolises in total, all in the region of Argob, the area of Og in Bashan. (Argob: rocky land) **5.** Each of these metropolises was fortified with high walls, gates, and bars, along with numerous pastoral townlets that were unfortified. (Fortified: defended) **6.** We fully destroyed them, just as we had done with Sihon, the king of Heshbon, destroying all the men, women, and children of every megacity. **7.** Still, we took the beast and the plunder from the metropolises for ourselves. (Ransack: spoil) **8.** At that time, we took the land from the two lords of the Amorites who were on this side of the Jordan River, stretching from the Arnon River to Mount Hermon. (Hermon: mountain) **9.** (The Sidonians call Mount Hermon "Sirion," and the Amorites relate to it as "Senir.") **10.** This included all the metropolises of the table, all of Gilead, and all of Bashan, reaching as far as Salcah and Edrei, the main metropolises in Og's area in Bashan. (Gilead: hilly region) **11.** Only Og, king of Bashan, was left of the last of the Rephaim (titans). His bed was made of iron—kept in Rabbah of the Ammonites—and measured nine cubits in length and four cubits in range, by the standard cubit. (Cubit: 18 elevation) **12.** This land that we held from Aroer, near the Arnon River, and half of the hill country of Gilead and its metropolises, I assigned to the Reubenites and Gadites. (Aroer: city near Moab) **13.** The rest of Gilead, along with all of Bashan, the area of Og, I gave to half of the lineage of Manasseh. (This whole region of Argob in Bashan was known as the land of the Rephaim.) (Rephaim: titans) **14.** Jair, the son of Manasseh, took the whole region of Argob as far as the borders of the Geshurites and Maachathites and named the area Bashan, calling it Havoth Jair, a name that remains to this day. (Maachathites: original lineage) **15.** I also gave Gilead to Machir. (Machir: a leader in Manasseh) **16.** To the Reubenites and Gadites, I gave the land from Gilead to the Arnon River, with the swash's middle marking the boundary, and reaching to the Jabbok River, which borders the land of the Ammonites. (Jabbok: swash) **17.** Also included was the Jordan Valley, from Chinnereth to the east side of the ocean of the Arabah (Salt Sea), below the pitches of Pisgah. (Arabah: desert vale) **18.** At that time, I commanded you, saying, 'The Lord your God has given you this land to enthrall. All your fighting men must cross over, fortified, ahead of your fellow Israelites. **19.** But your women, children, and beast (and I know you have a great deal of beast) shall stay in the metropolises I've given you, **20.** until the Lord subventions peace to your fellow Israelites as He has to you, and they too have taken possession of the land the Lord your God is giving them beyond the Jordan. Also, each of you may return to the property I've given you.' **21.** At that time, I also commanded Joshua, saying, 'You have seen all that the Lord your God has done to these two lords. The Lord will do the same to all the fiefdoms where you're going. **22.** Don't be hysterical of them, for the Lord your God Himself will fight for you.' **23.** Also I contended with the Lord at that time, saying, **24.** 'O Lord God, You have begun to show Your menial Your greatness and potent power. For what god in heaven or on earth can perform deeds and potent workshops like Yours? **25.** Please let me cross over to see the good land beyond the Jordan, the beautiful hills and Lebanon.' (Lebanon: region known for cedar trees) **26.** But the Lord was angry with me because of you, and He'd not hear. He said to me, 'Enough! Don't talk to Me presently about this matter. **27.** Go up to the top of Pisgah and look to the west, north, south, and east. View it with your own eyes, for you won't cross this Jordan. **28.** But charge Joshua, encourage him, and strengthen him, for he'll lead this people and enable them to inherit the land you see.' **29.** So we remained in the vale near Beth Peor. (Beth Peor: place east of Jordan)

Chapter 4

1 "Now, Israel, pay attention to the laws and judgments I am teaching you to follow, so that you may live and enter the land that the Lord, the God of your ancestors, is giving to you. (statutes: laws, judgments: decisions) **2** Do not add to or take away from what I am commanding you, so that you may keep the commands of the Lord your God as I am giving them to you. (commandments: rules, commands) **3** You have witnessed what the Lord did at Baal Peor, for the Lord your God destroyed everyone among you who followed the god Baal of Peor. **4** But those of you who stayed faithful to the Lord your God are all alive today. (held fast: stayed loyal) **5** I have indeed taught you laws and judgments just as the Lord my God directed me, so that you will live by them in the land you are about to enter. (judgments: decisions) **6** Keep them carefully, for this will show your wisdom and understanding to other nations, who will hear these laws and say, 'Surely this nation is wise and has great understanding.' (understanding: insight, wisdom) **7** What other nation is so blessed to have their God so close to them as the Lord our God is to us whenever we call on Him? **8** And what other nation has such righteous laws and fair judgments as this entire law that I am sharing with you today? (righteous: morally right, judgments: decisions) **9** Just be careful, and guard yourself well, so that you do not forget the things you have seen and they do not fade from your heart. Teach them to your children and grandchildren. (diligently: carefully, take heed: pay attention) **10** Especially remember the day when you stood before the Lord your God at Horeb, and the Lord said to me, 'Gather the people so they may hear My words and learn to honor Me throughout their lives, and teach these lessons to their children.' (Horeb: a mountain where God spoke to the Israelites) **11** You approached and stood at the foot of the mountain, and the mountain blazed with fire up to the heavens, with clouds and intense darkness. **12** The Lord spoke to you from the fire. You heard His words but saw no shape—only a voice. (midst: center) **13** He announced His covenant to you, the Ten Commandments, and instructed you to keep them. Then He wrote them on two stone tablets. (covenant: agreement, commandments: rules) **14** And at that time, the Lord commanded me to teach you these laws and judgments so that you would live by them in the land you are about to enter. **15** Be careful to guard yourselves, for you saw no shape when the Lord spoke to you at Horeb from the fire. **16** So do not act sinfully by making any carved image or form representing a man or woman. (corruptly: wickedly, carved image: statue or idol) **17** Do not create any likeness of animals on the earth, or of birds that fly in the air, **18** or of creatures that move on the ground, or of fish that live in the waters below. (creeps: moves) **19** Be cautious not to lift your eyes to the skies and be tempted to worship the sun, moon, or stars—all of which the Lord your God has provided for everyone under heaven. **20** But the Lord took you out of Egypt, a land of suffering, to make you His people and His special possession, as you are today. (iron furnace: symbol of oppression, inheritance: special possession) **21** The Lord was angered with me because of you and vowed that I would not cross over the Jordan or enter the good land that the Lord your God is giving to you. **22** I must die in this land and cannot cross the Jordan, but you will cross over and claim that good land. **23** So be careful not to forget the covenant of the Lord your God that He made with you, and do not make an idol of anything the Lord your God has forbidden. (covenant: agreement, carved image: idol) **24** For the Lord your God is a consuming fire and a God who is deeply loyal to His people. (jealous: protective) **25** When you have children and grandchildren and have lived in the land a long time, if you act wickedly and make idols, doing what is wrong in the eyes of the Lord your God, you will provoke Him to anger. (provoke: cause) **26** I call heaven and earth to witness this day that if you do this, you will soon perish completely from the land that you are crossing the Jordan to possess; your days in it will not be extended, but you will be utterly destroyed. (utterly: completely, prolong: extend) **27** And the Lord will disperse you among many nations, leaving only a small number among the peoples He sends you. (scatter: disperse, drive: forcefully send) **28** There, you will worship gods made by human hands—wood and stone that cannot see, hear, eat, or smell. (serve: worship, gods: idols) **29** But from there, if you search for the Lord your God with all your heart and soul, you will find Him. (seek: search, heart and soul: deepest sincerity) **30** When you are in hardship, and these warnings come upon you in the future, if you turn to the Lord and obey His commands, He will respond. (distress: hardship, latter days: future times) **31** For the Lord your God is compassionate. He will not abandon, destroy, or forget the promise to your ancestors. (merciful: compassionate, covenant: sacred promise, forsake: abandon) **32** Reflect on the days since God created humanity. Ask from one end of heaven to the other if anything like this has ever happened. (ask: consider, days that are past: former times) **33** Has any people ever heard God's voice from the fire as you have, and lived? (midst: center, live: survive) **34** Did God ever rescue a nation from another with trials, signs, wonders, war, His powerful hand, and terrifying events, like He did for you in Egypt? (mighty hand: powerful intervention, terrors: fearful events) **35** God showed you these things so you would know that He alone is Lord, and there is no other. (know: deeply understand, none other: no other deity) **36** He allowed you to hear His voice from heaven to teach you, and displayed His great fire, with His words from within it. (instruct: teach, midst: center) **37** Because He loved your ancestors, He chose their descendants and brought you out of Egypt with His presence and power. (descendants: offspring, presence: divine presence) **38** He drove out nations greater than you to bring you into their land and give it to you as an inheritance, as you see today. (driving out: expelling, inheritance: land passed down) **39** So know today and keep in your heart that the Lord is God in heaven and on earth, and there is no other. (consider: think deeply, no other: no alternative deity) **40** Therefore, obey His decrees and commandments that I give you today so that you and your children may prosper and enjoy long life in the land the Lord is giving you forever. (statutes: laws, prolong: lengthen) **41** Then Moses designated three cities east of the Jordan River, toward the sunrise, **42** where anyone who killed another unintentionally, without hatred, could flee for safety. By reaching one of these cities, they could preserve their life. (manslayer: one who kills unintentionally, flee: escape) **43** These cities were Bezer for Reuben, Ramoth for Gad, and Golan for Manasseh. (plateau: flat elevated land) **44** This is the law Moses set before the Israelites. (law: guiding rules) **45** These are the testimonies, regulations, and judgments Moses declared after their departure from Egypt, **46** while they were on the eastern side of the Jordan, in the valley near Beth Peor, in the land of Sihon, king of the Amorites, whom Moses and Israel defeated. (dwelt: lived, defeated: overcame) **47** They took possession of his land and that of Og, king of Bashan—two Amorite kings east of the Jordan, **48** from Aroer on the Arnon River to Mount Sion (Mount Hermon), **49** and all the plains east of the Jordan to the Sea of the Arabah, below the slopes of Pisgah. (Sea of the Arabah: Dead Sea, slopes: inclines)

Chapter 5

1. And Moses gathered all of Israel and said, "hear, O Israel, to the laws and rulings I proclaim moment, so that you may learn and follow them precisely. (rulings : rules and commands) **2.** The Lord our God made a covenant with us at Mount Horeb. (covenant : agreement) **3.** The Lord didn't establish this covenant with our ancestors, but with us — those alive also moment. **4.** The Lord spoke directly to you from the fire on the mountain. **5.** At that time, I stood between you and the Lord to explain His words to you, for you were hysterical of the fire and didn't approach the mountain. He said (hysterical : scarified) **6.** "I am the Lord your God, who brought you out of Egypt, from slavery." (slavery : forced labor) **7.** "You shall have no other gods before Me." **8.** "You shall not make for yourselves a graven image — any likeness of anything in the firmament over, on the earth below, or in the waters beneath the earth." (inscribed image : idol) **9.** "You shall not bow down to them or serve them, for I, the Lord your God, am a jealous God, visiting the sins of the fathers on the children to the third and fourth generations of those who hate Me," **10.** "but showing love and mercy to thousands who love Me and keep My commandments." (mercy : kindness and absolution) **11.** "You shall not misuse the name of the Lord your God, for the Lord won't leave unpunished anyone who misuses His name." (abuse : take in vain, use erroneously) **12.** "Observe the Sabbath day and keep it holy, as the Lord your God has commanded you." (observe : keep, holy : set incremental) **13.** "Six days you shall work and do all your labor," **14.** "but the seventh day is the Sabbath of the Lord your God. On it, you shall not do any work — neither you, nor your son, son, virile or womanish retainers, ox, moke, or any brutes, nor strangers within your gates, so your retainers may rest as you do." (municipality gates : megacity limits) **15.** "Flash back you were formerly slaves in Egypt, and the Lord your God brought you out with a potent hand and outstretched arm; that is why the Lord your God has commanded you to keep the Sabbath." **16.** "Honor your father and ma, as the Lord your God has commanded you, so your days may be dragged, and it may go well with you in the land the Lord is giving you." (honor : respect, dragged : dragged) **17.** "You shall not murder." (murder : kill without cause) **18.** "You shall not commit infidelity." (infidelity : unlawful relations with someone else's mate) **19.** "You shall not steal." (steal : take commodity that belongs to someone else) **20.** "You shall not give false substantiation against your neighbor." (false substantiation : tale) **21.** "You shall not covet your neighbor's woman or ask your neighbor's house, field, retainers, ox, moke, or anything that belongs to your neighbor." (covet : desire in an unhealthy way) **22.** "These words the Lord spoke to your entire assembly at the mountain, from the fire, the pall, and deep darkness, with a loud voice; He added nothing further. He wrote them on two monument tablets and gave them to me." (assembly : gathering, deep darkness : thick darkness) **23.** "When you heard the voice from the darkness, while the mountain was blazing with fire, all the heads of your lines and elders came near to me." (blazing: burning) **24.** "And you said' The Lord our God has shown us His glory and greatness, and we have heard His voice from the fire. This day we have seen that God speaks with humans, yet they still live.'" **25.** "Now, why should we die? For this great fire will consume us. However, we will die, If we hear the voice of the Lord any longer." **26.** "For who among all meat has heard the voice of the living God speaking from the fire, as we have, and still lived?" **27.** "You go near and hear to all the Lord says, also tell us everything He tells you, and we will hear and observe." **28.** "Also the Lord heard your words and said' I have heard what this people said to you. They have spoken well.'" **29.** "Oh, that their hearts would always be like this, that they would sweat Me, and keep all My commandments, so it might go well with them and their children ever!" (fear : respect and honor) **30.** "Go and tell them,' Return to your tents.'" **31.** "But you, stand also with Me, and I will tell you all the commandments, laws, and judgments to educate them, so they may follow them in the land I am giving them to retain." (judgments : opinions) **32.** "Be careful to do everything the Lord has commanded; don't turn down to the right or left." (turn down : go down) **33.** "Follow the way the Lord has commanded you, so that you may live, and it may go well with you, and you may stretch your days in the land you will retain." (entire : each, stretch : outstretch)

Chapter 6

1. "This is the command, with the laws and decrees the Lord your God has instructed me to teach you, so you may follow them in the land you're about to enter and possess." (decrees: rules or orders) **2.** "You are to fear the Lord your God by obeying all His laws and commands I give you, your children, and grandchildren, all your life, so your days may be long." (fear: respect deeply) **3.** "Listen, Israel, and be careful to follow these instructions, so it will go well with you, and you may multiply greatly, as the Lord, the God of your ancestors, promised—a land flowing with milk and honey." (multiply: increase in number) **4.** "Listen, Israel: The Lord our God, the Lord is one." (one: only one God) **5.** "You must love the Lord your God with all your heart, soul, and strength." (heart: thoughts and emotions; soul: inner being; strength: all your effort) **6.** "These commandments I give you today must be in your heart." (heart: thoughts and actions) **7.** "Teach them diligently to your children, and talk about them when at home, walking, lying down, and getting up." (diligently: carefully, consistently) **8.** "Tie them as reminders on your hands, and wear them as symbols on your foreheads." **9.** "Write them on the doorframes of your houses and on your gates." (doorframes: around doors, gates: entryways) **10.** "When the Lord your God brings you into the land He promised to your forefathers—Abraham, Isaac, and Jacob—and gives you cities you did not build," (forefathers: ancestors) **11.** "and houses full of good things you did not fill, wells you did not dig, and vineyards and olive trees you did not plant—when you have eaten and are satisfied," (vineyards: grapevine fields; olive trees: trees that produce olives) **12.** "be careful not to forget the Lord, who brought you out of Egypt, out of the land of slavery." (slavery: forced labor) **13.** "You must fear the Lord your God and serve Him, and take oaths in His name." (oaths: solemn promises) **14.** "Do not follow other gods, the gods of the peoples around you," (gods: deities worshipped by others) **15.** "for the Lord your God is a jealous God among you. His anger could flare up and destroy you from the earth." (jealous: wanting exclusive loyalty; flare up: suddenly increase; destroy: wipe out) **16.** "Do not test the Lord your God as you did at Massah." (test: challenge or doubt; Massah: place where Israelites doubted God) **17.** "Be careful to follow the Lord's commands, His testimonies, and His decrees He has given you." (testimonies: evidence of God's authority; decrees: orders, commands) **18.** "Do what is right and good in the Lord's eyes so it may go well with you, and you may enter and possess the good land the Lord promised your ancestors." (possess: take control of) **19.** "He will drive out your enemies before you, as He has spoken." (drive out: remove forcefully) **20.** "When your child asks, 'What do these laws, commands, and regulations the Lord our God gave us mean?'" (regulations: rules or principles) **21.** "Tell them: 'We were slaves of Pharaoh in Egypt, but the Lord brought us out with a mighty hand.'" (slaves: forced workers; mighty: powerful) **22.** "The Lord displayed mighty signs and wonders before us, great and terrible, against Egypt, Pharaoh, and his household." (signs: miracles of God's power; wonders: astonishing events) **23.** "He brought us out to bring us in, and give us the land He promised to our ancestors." (ancestors: forefathers, predecessors) **24.** "The Lord commanded us to obey these laws, to revere the Lord our God for our good, always, so He may preserve our lives, as He has done this day." (revere: respect deeply; preserve: keep safe) **25.** "It will be righteousness for us if we are careful to observe all these commands before the Lord our God, as He commanded us." (righteousness: being morally right; observe: follow carefully)

Chapter 7
1. When the Lord your God leads you into the land you are to possess, He will drive out many nations before you—the Hittites, Girgashites, Amorites, Canaanites, Perizzites, Hivites, and Jebusites—seven nations larger and stronger than you. (possess: own) **2.** When the Lord your God hands them over to you, you must conquer and destroy them completely. Do not make any agreements with them or show them mercy. (mercy: compassion) **3.** Do not intermarry with them; do not give your daughters to their sons or take their daughters for your sons. (intermarry: marry across groups) **4.** They will turn your children away from following Me to serve other gods, and the Lord's anger will burn against you and destroy you quickly. (aroused: provoked) **5.** You must tear down their altars, smash their sacred pillars, cut down their wooden idols, and burn their carved images. (altars: worship structures) **6.** For you are a holy people chosen by the Lord your God to be His treasured possession above all the nations on earth. (holy: sacred) **7.** The Lord did not choose you because you were numerous, for you were the smallest of all peoples. (numerous: many) **8.** Instead, it was because the Lord loves you and is keeping His promise to your ancestors. With great power, He freed you from slavery under Pharaoh, the king of Egypt. (redeemed: rescued) **9.** Know that the Lord your God is the faithful God, who keeps His covenant and shows mercy for a thousand generations to those who love Him and obey His commands. (faithful: loyal) **10.** He repays those who hate Him to their face, destroying them. He will not delay; He will repay them directly. (slack: slow) **11.** Therefore, obey the commands, laws, and decrees I am giving you today. (decrees: orders) **12.** If you carefully follow these laws, the Lord your God will keep His covenant of love with you, as He promised your ancestors. (covenant: agreement) **13.** He will love and bless you, increasing your descendants, crops, livestock, and everything in the land He swore to give your ancestors. (offspring: children) **14.** You will be more blessed than all nations. None among you or your livestock will be unable to reproduce. (barren: unable to bear offspring) **15.** The Lord will keep you from illness and will not afflict you with the dreadful diseases you knew in Egypt but will bring them upon your enemies. (afflict: harm) **16.** You must destroy all the nations the Lord delivers to you. Show them no pity, and do not worship their gods, for that will trap you. (snare: trap) **17.** If you think, "These nations are stronger than us; how can we drive them out?"— **18.** Do not be afraid. Remember what the Lord your God did to Pharaoh and all of Egypt. (dispossess: remove) **19.** Recall the miracles and mighty power that brought you out of Egypt. The Lord will do the same to every nation you fear. (wonders: miraculous acts) **20.** The Lord your God will send hornets among them until those who hide from you are destroyed. (hornet: stinging insect) **21.** Do not fear them, for the Lord your God, a great and awesome God, is with you. (awesome: inspiring fear or wonder) **22.** The Lord will drive out these nations gradually, so the wild animals will not overwhelm you. (beasts: animals) **23.** He will deliver them into your hands and defeat them until they are completely destroyed. (inflict: cause) **24.** He will hand their kings over to you, erasing their names forever. No one will stand against you until you destroy them. (deliver: hand over) **25.** Burn their idols, and do not desire the silver or gold on them, for it will trap you. Such things are hated by the Lord. (covet: strongly desire) **26.** Do not bring anything detestable into your home, or you will be destroyed with it. Reject it completely, for it is cursed. (abomination: something sinful)

Chapter 8
1. Be careful to follow all the commands I am giving you today. By doing so, you will thrive, increase in number, and take possession of the land that the Lord promised to your ancestors. (Thrive: grow successfully) **2.** Remember how the Lord your God guided you through the wilderness for forty years. He allowed you to face challenges to humble you and to test what was truly in your heart, to see if you would obey His commandments. (Humble: make you realize your dependence on Him) **3.** He humbled you by letting you experience hunger, then provided manna that neither you nor your ancestors had ever known. This was to teach you that life is not sustained by food alone, but by every word spoken by the Lord. (Manna: miraculous food) **4.** During these forty years, your clothing never wore out, and your feet never swelled. (Swelled: became enlarged) **5.** Understand in your heart that, just as a parent disciplines their child, the Lord your God also disciplines you for your benefit. (Disciplines: corrects) **6.** Therefore, obey the commandments of the Lord your God. Live in alignment with His ways and have reverence for Him. (Reverence: deep respect) **7.** The Lord your God is bringing you into a prosperous land—a place with streams, fountains, and springs that flow through valleys and hills. (Prosperous: successful) **8.** This land will have wheat, barley, grapevines, fig trees, pomegranates, olive oil, and honey—an

abundance of resources. (Abundance: plenty) **9.** It will be a land where you can eat without scarcity, where you will lack nothing. Its rocks will yield iron, and its hills will provide copper that you can mine. (Scarcity: shortage; Yield: produce) **10.** After you have eaten and are satisfied, give thanks to the Lord your God for the good land He has given you. **11.** Be careful not to forget the Lord your God by neglecting to follow His commandments, laws, and decrees that I am instructing you to keep today. (Neglecting: ignoring; Decrees: commands) **12.** Otherwise, when you have eaten and are full, and you've built comfortable homes and are living in them, **13.** and when your livestock and wealth—silver and gold—have greatly increased, along with everything you possess. (Livestock: herds) **14.** Your heart may become proud, and you might forget the Lord your God who rescued you from slavery in Egypt. (Proud: arrogant) **15.** He led you through a vast and dangerous wilderness filled with fiery serpents, scorpions, and parched land with no water. He brought water for you out of solid rock. (Vast: large; Parched: dry) **16.** He provided manna in the wilderness, food unknown to your ancestors, to humble and test you, ultimately for your benefit. (Test: examine; Ultimately: in the end) **17.** But when you are prosperous, be careful not to think in your heart, "My strength and my abilities have brought me this wealth." (Prosperous: successful) **18.** Always remember the Lord your God, for He is the one who gives you the ability to acquire wealth in order to fulfill the covenant He swore to your ancestors, which is still in effect today. (Acquire: obtain; Covenant: promise) **19.** If you forget the Lord your God and turn to worship other gods, serving them, I solemnly warn you today that you will certainly be destroyed. (Solemnly: seriously; Warn: advise) **20.** Like the nations the Lord is eliminating before you, so you will perish if you refuse to obey the voice of the Lord your God. (Eliminating: removing; Perish: be destroyed)

Chapter 9

1. "Hear, O Israel! Today you'll cross over the Jordan River and take possession of nations stronger and more numerous than you, with cities vast and fortified, reaching up to the heavens." (Jordan River: the crossing the Israelites must make) **2.** "You'll encounter a people who are large and tall, the descendants of the Anakim (a giant race), of whom you're familiar and have heard, 'Who can stand against the descendants of Anak?'" (Anakim: giants) **3.** "So now, know that the Lord your God goes before you like a consuming fire. He will destroy them and bring them down before you. You'll drive them out and destroy them quickly, as the Lord has commanded." (Consuming fire: intense fire that destroys completely) **4.** "Do not say after the Lord has driven them out before you, 'It's because of my righteousness that the Lord has brought me to possess this land.' It's because of the wickedness of these nations that the Lord is removing them for you." (Wickedness: moral wrongness) **5.** "It is not because of your righteousness or integrity that you're entering, but because of the wickedness of these nations that the Lord your God is expelling them and fulfilling His promise to your ancestors, Abraham, Isaac, and Jacob." (Integrity: honesty) **6.** "So understand this clearly: The Lord your God is not giving you this land because of your righteousness, for you are a stubborn people." (Stubborn: resistant to change) **7.** "Remember how you provoked the Lord to anger in the wilderness. From the day you left Egypt until you arrived here, you have been rebellious against the Lord." (Provoked: caused wrath) **8.** "Indeed, at Horeb, you provoked the Lord to anger, and He was furious enough to destroy you." (Furious: extremely angry) **9.** "When I went up to receive the tablets of stone, the tablets of the covenant the Lord made with you, I stayed forty days and forty nights without eating bread or drinking water." (Covenant: agreement) **10.** "Then the Lord gave me two tablets of stone, written by the finger of God. On them were all the words the Lord spoke to you on the mountain from the fire during the assembly." (Assembly: gathering) **11.** "At the end of forty days and forty nights, the Lord gave me the two tablets of stone, the tablets of the covenant." (Covenant: formal agreement) **12.** "The Lord said to me, 'Get up and go down quickly from here, for your people whom you brought out of Egypt have corrupted themselves. They have turned aside quickly from the way I commanded and made a molded image.'" (Molded image: statue) **13.** "The Lord said to me, 'I have seen this people, and they are a stubborn people.'" (Stubborn: resistant to change) **14.** "'Leave Me alone so I may destroy them and blot out their name from under heaven. I will make a nation greater and mightier than they.'" (Blot out: abolish) **15.** "I turned and came down from the mountain, and the mountain was burning with fire. The two tablets of the covenant were in my hands." (Burning: on fire) **16.** "I saw that you had sinned against the Lord your God, had made a molded calf, and had turned aside from the way the Lord had commanded you." (Calf: a young cow) **17.** "I took the tablets and threw them out of my hands, breaking them before your eyes." (Breaking: destroying) **18.** "I fell before the Lord, as I had before, for forty days and forty nights. I neither ate bread nor drank water because of your sin, which provoked Him to wrath." (Sin: wrongdoing) **19.** "I was afraid of the Lord's anger and hot displeasure, for He was about to destroy you. But the Lord listened to me at that time." (Displeasure: wrath) **20.** "The Lord was very angry with Aaron and would have destroyed him, so I prayed for him at that time." (Angry: worried) **21.** "I took your sin, the calf you made, burned it, crushed it, ground it to powder, and threw it into the brook that flowed down from the mountain." (Crushed: broken into pieces) **22.** "At Taberah, Massah, and Kibroth Hattaavah, you continued to provoke the Lord." (Taberah, Massah, Kibroth Hattaavah: places of rebellion) **23.** "When the Lord sent you from Kadesh Barnea, saying, 'Go up and take possession of the land I have given you,' you rebelled and did not trust or obey His voice." (Rebelled: defied authority) **24.** "From the day I knew you, you have been rebellious against the Lord." (Rebellious: disobedient) **25.** "I prostrated myself before the Lord for forty days and forty nights, because the Lord had said He would destroy you." (Prostrate: lying flat) **26.** "I prayed to the Lord, 'O Lord God, do not destroy Your people, Your inheritance whom You have redeemed by Your great power and brought out of Egypt with a mighty hand.'" (Redeemed: saved) **27.** "Remember Your servants, Abraham, Isaac, and Jacob; do not look upon their stubbornness or their wickedness or their sin." (Wickedness: wrong) **28.** "Otherwise, the land You brought us from might say, 'Because the Lord was not able to bring them into the land He promised them, He brought them out to kill them in the wilderness.'" (Wilderness: desolate place) **29.** "Yet they are Your people, Your inheritance, whom You brought out by Your great power and Your outstretched arm." (Outstretched arm: symbol of strength)

Chapter 10

1. "At that time, the Lord instructed me, 'Carve two stone tablets like the first ones, and come up to Me on the mountain. Also, prepare a wooden ark.'" (Ark: chest) **2.** "'I will inscribe the same words on these tablets that were written on the first ones, which you broke, and you shall place them in the ark.'" (Inscribe: engrave) **3.** So I crafted an ark from acacia wood, chiseled two stone tablets like the first ones, and carried them up the mountain. (Acacia: durable wood) **4.** "There, God wrote on the tablets the same Ten Commandments He had spoken to you earlier on the mountain from within the fire during the day of the assembly. Then He gave the tablets to me." (Commandments: laws) **5.** "Afterward, I descended from the mountain and placed the tablets inside the ark I had made, as the Lord commanded me, and they remain there to this day." (Descended: came down) **6.** (The Israelites traveled from the wells of Bene Jaakan to Moserah, where Aaron passed away and was buried. His son Eleazar succeeded him as priest.) (Priest: religious leader) **7.** "From Moserah, they journeyed to Gudgodah and then to Jotbathah, a land abundant in streams of water." (Abundant: plentiful) **8.** "At that time, the Lord set apart the tribe of Levi to carry the ark of the covenant of the Lord, to stand before Him in service, and to pronounce blessings in His name, as they continue to do today." (Covenant: agreement) **9.** "Because of this, the Levites have no share or inheritance of land among their brothers; the Lord Himself is their inheritance, as He promised them." (Inheritance: legacy) **10.** "Once again, I remained on the mountain for forty days and nights, just as before. The Lord listened to me at that time too, and He chose not to destroy you." (Remained: stayed) **11.** "Then the Lord said to me, 'Get up and lead the people onward so they can take possession of the land I promised to their ancestors.'" (Possession: ownership) **12.** "Now, Israel, what does the Lord your God ask of you but to show reverence for Him, to follow His ways, to love Him, and to serve Him with all your heart and soul?" (Reverence: respect) **13.** "Keep the Lord's commands and statutes that I give you today for your benefit." (Statutes: laws) **14.** "Look, the heavens—even the highest heavens—and the earth and everything in it belong to the Lord your God." (Heavens: skies) **15.** "Yet, out of love, He chose your ancestors and their descendants, setting you apart from all other nations, as you are today." (Descendants: offspring) **16.** "Therefore, circumcise the foreskin of your hearts, and stop being stiff-necked." (Circumcise: purify) **17.** "For the Lord your God is the supreme God and Lord over all, mighty and awe-inspiring, who is impartial and cannot be bribed." (Impartial: fair) **18.** "He ensures justice for orphans and widows and loves foreigners, providing them with food and clothing." **19.** "So you must also love foreigners, because you were once foreigners in Egypt." (Egypt: ancient land) **20.** "Fear the Lord your God, serve Him, cling to Him, and swear by His name." (Cling: hold) **21.** "He is the One you praise and your God, who has performed these great and awesome deeds that you witnessed with your own eyes." (Praise: honor) **22.** "When your ancestors went to Egypt, they were just seventy in number. Now, the Lord your God has made you as numerous as the stars in the sky." (Numerous: many)

Chapter 11
1. "Therefore, love the Lord your God, keep His commands, decrees, laws, and ordinances forever." (Decrees: formal orders, Ordinances: rules) **2.** "Understand today that I am not speaking to your children, who have not experienced or seen the discipline of the Lord your God, His greatness, mighty power, and outstretched arm." **3.** "His miracles and wonders in Egypt, to Pharaoh, the king of Egypt, and to his kingdom;" (Kingdom: territory ruled by a king) **4.** "what He did to Egypt's army, horses, and chariots—how He made the Red Sea overwhelm them as they chased you, and how the Lord destroyed them to this day;" (Overwhelm: overpower) **5.** "what He did for you in the wilderness until you reached this place;" (Wilderness: uninhabited land) **6.** "and what He did to Dathan and Abiram, sons of Eliab, son of Reuben—how the earth opened up and swallowed them, their families, tents, and possessions, right in front of all Israel." (Swallowed: consumed) **7.** "But your eyes have witnessed every great act the Lord has done." (Witnessed: seen firsthand) **8.** "Therefore, obey every command I give you today, so you may be strong, enter, and take possession of the land you are crossing over to possess." (Possess: take control of) **9.** "And that you may live long in the land the Lord promised to give your ancestors and descendants, 'a land flowing with milk and honey.'" (Descendants: children or future generations) **10.** "For the land you are about to enter and possess is not like Egypt, where you planted seeds and watered them by hand, like a vegetable garden;" (Watered by hand: watered manually) **11.** "but the land you are crossing to possess is a land of hills and valleys, which drinks water from heaven's rain;" (Rain of heaven: rain sent by God) **12.** "a land the Lord your God cares for; His eyes are always on it, from the start to the end of the year." (Cares for: provides for) **13.** "If you truly obey My commands today, to love the Lord your God and serve Him with all your heart and soul," (Serve Him: worship and obey) **14.** "then I will send rain in its season, early and latter rain, so you can gather your grain, new wine, and oil." (Early rain: rain at the start of the planting season; Latter rain: rain at the end of the growing season) **15.** "I will also provide grass for your cattle, so you will eat and be satisfied." (Cattle: livestock) **16.** "Be careful not to let your heart be deceived, turning away to serve other gods and worship them," (Deceived: misled) **17.** "or the Lord's anger will be aroused, and He will shut the heavens so there is no rain, and the land won't produce, and you will perish from the good land the Lord is giving you." (Aroused: stirred up) **18.** "Therefore, keep these words in your heart and soul, and bind them as a sign on your hands, and as reminders between your eyes." (Bind: secure or tie) **19.** "Teach them to your children, speak of them when you sit in your house, when you walk along the road, when you lie down, and when you rise." (Teach: instruct) **20.** "Write them on the doorframes of your house and on your gates," (Doorframes: frames around doors) **21.** "so your days and your children's days may be many in the land the Lord promised to give your ancestors, like the days of heaven on earth." (Many: abundant) **22.** "If you are careful to observe all these commands—to love the Lord your God, walk in all His ways, and hold fast to Him—" (Hold fast: cling) **23.** "then the Lord will drive out all these nations before you, and you will possess nations greater and mightier than yourselves." (Mightier: stronger) **24.** "Every place you walk will be yours: from the wilderness to Lebanon, from the Euphrates River to the Western Sea, your territory will extend." (Set foot: walk on) **25.** "No one will stand against you; the Lord will put fear and dread of you on the whole land, just as He promised." (Dread: great fear) **26.** "Today I set before you a blessing and a curse:" (Set before: offer) **27.** "the blessing, if you obey the commands of the Lord your God;" (Obey: follow) **28.** "and the curse, if you do not obey His commands, but turn from the path I command, worshiping other gods you have not known." (Turn away: stray) **29.** "When the Lord brings you into the land you are about to possess, you will pronounce the blessing on Mount Gerizim and the curse on Mount Ebal." (Pronounce: declare) **30.** "Are they not on the other side of the Jordan, toward the west, in the land of the Canaanites near Gilgal, by the oak trees of Moreh?" (Arabah: desert region) **31.** "For you will cross the Jordan and take possession of the land the Lord is giving you, and you will possess and live in it." (Take possession: claim) **32.** "Be careful to observe all the statutes and ordinances I set before you today." (Statutes: laws, Ordinances: decrees)

Chapter 12
1. "These are the rulings and opinions that you must follow in the land the Lord, the God of your ancestors, is giving you to retain. You must observe them all your life on earth." (rulings : rules) **2.** "You must fully destroy all the places where the nations you're expropriating worshiped their gods, on the high hills, mountains, and under every lush tree." (expropriating : removing) **3.** "Demolish their stages, break their sacred pillars, burn their rustic icons with fire, hash down their sculpted images, and abolish their names from those places." (Demolish : destroy; Sculpted : structured) **4.** "You mustn't worship the Lord your God as they worshiped their gods." (Worshiped : honored) **5.** "Rather, seek the place the Lord your God will choose, from among all your lines, to establish His name and dwelling place; and there, you must go." (Dwelling : hearthstone) **6.** "There, bring your burnt immolations, offerings, tithes, lifted-up immolations, pledged immolations, voluntary immolations, and the firstborn of your herds and flocks." (pledged : engaged) **7.** "You and your families will eat before the Lord your God and rejoice in all your work, as you and your homes enjoy the blessings the Lord has given you." (Rejoice : celebrate) **8.** "You mustn't do as we do moment — each person doing what seems right in their own eyes." (feel appear) **9.** "Because you haven't yet entered the rest and heritage the Lord is giving you." (Rest : peace; heritage : possession) **10.** "When you cross the Jordan and settle in the land the Lord is giving you, and He grants peace from all your adversaries, so you live safely," (subventions : grants; Safety : protection) **11.** "Also there will

be the place where the Lord your God chooses to make His name dwell. There, bring all I command your burnt immolations, offerings, tithes, immolations lifted up, and your special immolations to the Lord." (Dwelling : live; Oath : pledge) **12.** "And you'll rejoice before the Lord your God, you, your sons and daughters, retainers, and the Levite who lives among you, because he has no heritage with you." (Levite : clerk) **13.** "Be careful not to offer your burnt immolations anywhere you see fit;" (Fit : applicable) **14.** "But in the place the Lord chooses in one of your lines, there you must offer your burnt immolations, and do all I command you." (lines : groups) **15.** "Still, you may butcher and eat meat in your municipalities, whatever you ask, according to the blessing the Lord has given you. Both the clean and sick may eat it, whether it's a gazelle or a deer." (Slaughter : kill; Clean : pure) **16.** "But don't eat the blood; pour it out on the ground like water." (Pour : slip) **17.** "Don't eat the tithe of your grain, new wine, oil painting, the firstborn of your herds or flocks, or any of your pledged immolations, volunteer immolations, or lifted-up immolations within your gates." (Tithe : tenth) **18.** "Rather, eat them before the Lord your God in the place He chooses, you, your son, your son, your manly menial, your womanish menial, and the Levite who lives in your municipalities; and you'll rejoice before the Lord in everything you do." **19.** "Be careful not to leave the Levite as long as you live in the land." (leave : abandon) **20.** "When the Lord increases your home as He promised, and you say, 'I want to eat meat because you long for it,' you may eat as much as you ask." (home : land) **21.** "If the place the Lord chooses to put His name is too far, you may butcher from your herd or flock, as I commanded, and eat within your municipalities as much as you ask." (Herd : cattle; Flock : lamb) **22.** "You may eat it as you would a gazelle or a deer. Both the clean and sick may eat it." (Gazelle : antelope) **23.** "But don't eat the blood, for the blood is the life. Don't eat the life with the meat." (Life : substance) **24.** "Don't eat it; pour it on the ground like water." **25.** "Don't eat it so that it may go well with you and your children when you do what's right in the Lord's sight." (Go well : succeed) **26.** "But only the holy effects and pledged immolations must you take to the place the Lord chooses." (Holy : sacred) **27.** "There, offer the meat and blood of your burnt immolations on the Lord's balcony; the blood of your offerings must be poured out on the balcony, and you may eat the meat." (Stages : places of immolation) **28.** "Be sure to observe all these words I command you, so it may go well with you and your children when you do what's good and right in the Lord's sight." (observe : follow) **29.** "When the Lord cuts off the nations before you, and you displace them and settle in their land," (Cut off : destroyed; Displaced : replaced) **30.** "Be careful not to be entangled by following them, after they're destroyed. Don't interrogate about their gods, asking, 'How did these nations serve their gods? I want to do the same.'" (entangled : trapped; Inquire : ask) **31.** "Don't worship the Lord your God this way, because every despicable act the Lord hates, they've done for their gods. They indeed burn their sons and daughters in the fire to their gods." (despicable : disgusting) **32.** "Be careful to follow everything I command; don't add to it or abate from it." (Add : include; Abate : spread)

Chapter 13

1. "If a prophet or a utopian of dreams arises among you and performs a sign or wonder, **2.** and the sign or wonder happens as they prognosticated, and they say to you, 'Let us follow other gods' — gods you haven't known and let us worship them, **3.** don't hear to what that prophet or utopian says. The Lord your God is testing you to see if you truly love Him with all your heart and soul." (Testing: examining) **4.** "You must follow the Lord your God, sweat Him, observe His commands, hear to His voice, serve Him, and remain faithful to Him. **5.** That prophet or utopian of dreams must be put to death because they've encouraged you to turn down from the Lord your God, who brought you out of Egypt, out of slavery, and they tried to lead you down from the path that God has set for you. Remove similar wrong from your midst." (Evil: wickedness) **6.** "If your close family member — your mama's son, your son, your partner, or a friend who's as dear to you as your own soul — intimately entices you, saying, 'Let us serve other gods' — gods you haven't known, neither you nor your ancestors, **7.** gods of the peoples around you, whether near or far, from one end of the earth to the other, **8.** you mustn't hear to them. Don't feel sorry for them, don't spare or hide them; **9.** rather, you must kill them. Your hand should be the first to strike them, followed by the hand of the others." (Extra save) **10.** "You shall sharpen them to death because they tried to turn you down from the Lord your God, who brought you out of Egypt, out of slavery. **11.** All Israel will hear about it, be hysterical, and noway again commit similar wickedness among you." (Wickedness: sin) **12.** "If you hear that in one of your metropolises, which the Lord your God is giving you to live in, **13.** some wicked people have gone out from among you and led the citizens of that megacity to worship other gods — gods you haven't known, **14.** also you must probe, interrogate precisely, and search to confirm if it's true that such an abomination has taken place among you." (Abomination: despicable act) **15.** "If it's indeed true, you must strike down the people of that megacity with the brand, destroying everything in it, including the beast, with the brand." (Strike down: kill) **16.** "Gather all the plunder from the megacity into the middle of the road, and burn it fully with fire, along with all the plunder, as an immolation to the Lord your God. The megacity will come a mound of remains ever and will noway be rebuilt." (Ransack: stolen goods) **17.** "None of the accursed effects should remain in your possession, so that the Lord may turn down from His fierce wrathfulness and show you mercy, have compassion on you, and increase your figures, as He promised your ancestors." (Cursed: condemned; Fierce: violent) **18.** "This will be because you have adhered the voice of the Lord your God, keeping all His commandments and doing what's right in His sight." (Adhered: followed)

Chapter 14

1. "You're the descendants of the Lord your God; don't harm yourselves by making cuts on your bodies or by paring the front of your head to mourn the dead." (Mourn: express anguish) **2.** "For you're a sacred people to the Lord your God, and He has chosen you to be His treasured possession, a people set piecemeal from all the other nations on the earth." (Sacred: holy, Treasured possession: special) **3.** "You mustn't eat any sick or despicable food." (Despicable: interdicted) **4.** "These are the creatures you're permitted to eat: the ox, the lamb, and the scapegoat. **5.** You may eat the deer, the gazelle, the roe deer, the wild scapegoat, the mountain scapegoat, the antelope, and the mountain lamb. **6.** You're allowed to eat any beast that has divided hooves, with the hooves resolve into two parts, and that chews cud, similar as these." (Cud: food masticated again) **7.** "Still, among those that bite the cud or have divided hooves, these you mustn't eat: the camel, the hare, and the gemstone hyrax; they bite the cud but don't have divided hooves, so they're sick for you." (Sick: interdicted) **8.** "Also, the gormandizer is sick for you because it has divided hooves but doesn't bite cud; you shall not eat its meat or touch its corpse." (Corpse: dead body) **9.** "You may eat all fish that have fins and scales. **10.** But any fish that doesn't have fins or scales you mustn't eat; it's sick for you. **11.** All clean catcalls are admissible to eat. **12.** Still, don't eat these catcalls: the eagle, the shark, the bloodsucker, **13.** the red vampire, the falcon, and the vampire of their species; **14.** every raven of its kind; **15.** the poltroon, the owl with short cognition, the seagull, and the jingoist of their species; **16.** the little owl, the screech owl, the white owl, **17.** the jackdaw, the carnage shark, the fisherman owl, **18.** the stork, the heron of its species, and the hoopoe, along with the club." (Carrion: decaying meat) **19.** "All insects that fly are sick for you; they mustn't be eaten. **20.** You may eat any clean raspberry. **21.** Don't eat any beast that has failed naturally; you may give it to a outsider living in your city, and they may eat it, or you may vend it to a non-Israelite. For you're a holy people to the Lord your God. Don't boil a youthful scapegoat in its mama's milk." (Pustule: chef) **22**. "You shall surely give a tenth (tithe: one-tenth) of all the crops that grow in your fields each time." **23**. "You're to eat before the Lord your God, in the place He'll choose to make His name known, the tithe of your grain, new wine, and oil painting, along with the firstborn of your herds and flocks, so that you may learn to sweat (fear: reverence) the Lord your God always." **24**. "But if the trip is too long for you, and you cannot carry the tithe, or if the place where the Lord your God has chosen to put His name is too far, and the Lord your God has blessed you, **25**. also you may change it for plutocrat, take the plutocrat in your hand, and go to the place the Lord your God will choose. **26**. There, you may spend the plutocrat on anything your heart desires: cattle, lamb, wine, or any other drink, or anything differently you wish, and there you and your ménage will eat and rejoice before the Lord your God. **27**. Don't neglect the Levite (Levite: the clerical lineage) living among you, for they've no portion or heritage with you." (Levite: clerk) **28**. "At the end of every third time, you shall bring out and store the tithe of your crops from that time within your municipalities. **29**. The Levite, because he has no land or heritage with you, and the outsider, the nameless, and the widow in your municipalities, may come and eat and be satisfied, so that the Lord your God may bless you in all the work of your hands." (Nameless: orphans, Widow: woman without a hubby)

Chapter 15
1. "At the conclusion of every seven years, you must forgive any debts." (Debts: money owed) **2**. "This is how the forgiveness of debts should work: Every lender who has given money to their neighbor must cancel the debt; they should not demand it back from their neighbor or relative, as it is called the Lord's cancellation of debts." (Lender: person who lends money; Demand: request forcefully) **3**. "You may demand payment from a foreigner, but you must forgive the debts of your fellow Israelite." (Foreigner: outsider; Fellow: companion) **4**. "There should be no poverty among you, for the Lord will bless you in the land He is giving you to inherit." (Poverty: being poor; Inherit: receive as a legacy) **5**. "This will happen only if you listen to the Lord your God and carefully follow all the commandments I give you today." (Diligently: carefully; Commandments: divine laws) **6**. "The Lord will bless you as He promised, you will lend to many nations, but you will not need to borrow; you will rule over many nations, but they will not rule over you." (Lend: loan; Borrow: take temporarily) **7**. "If there is a poor person among your fellow Israelites, within any city in the land the Lord is giving you, you must not harden your heart or close your hand to your poor brother." (Harden: make unfeeling; Brother: fellow Israelite) **8**. "Instead, open your hand generously and lend him whatever he needs." (Generously: freely; Need: necessity) **9**. "Be careful not to have a wicked thought in your heart, saying, 'The seventh year, the year of debt release, is near,' and then look down on your poor brother and refuse to help him. If he cries out to the Lord against you, it will be a sin for you." (Wicked: evil; Cry out: plead loudly) **10**. "You must give to him, and your heart should not be troubled when you give, because the Lord your God will bless you in all you do." (Troubled: worried; Bless: favor) **11**. "For there will always be poor people in the land, so I command you to open your hand to your brother, to the poor and needy in your land." (Needy: poor; Command: order) **12**. "If a fellow Israelite is sold to you and works for you for six years, in the seventh year you must set them free." (Sold: bought; Set free: release) **13**. "When you release them, do not let them go empty-handed." (Release: let go; Empty-handed: without anything) **14**. "Provide them generously from your flocks, your threshing floor, and your winepress. Give them what the Lord has blessed you with." (Flocks: herds of animals; Threshing floor: place for separating grain) **15**. "Remember that you were once slaves in Egypt, and the Lord your God redeemed you; therefore, I command you to do this today." (Slaves: forced laborers; Redeemed: saved from slavery) **16**. "If they say, 'I do not want to leave you,' because they love you and your household, and are doing well with you," (Household: family; Prosper: succeed) **17**. "then take an awl and pierce their ear to the door, and they will serve you for life. Do the same with a female servant." (Awl: pointed tool; Pierce: make a hole) **18**. "Do not find it hard to set them free; for they have worked for you for six years, and they are worth twice the wages of a hired servant. Then the Lord your God will bless you." (Hired: employed; Servant: worker) **19**. "You must dedicate all the firstborn males of your herd and flock to the Lord. You shall not use the firstborn of your herd for work, nor shear the firstborn of your flock." (Dedicate: set apart; Shear: cut wool) **20**. "You and your household shall eat it before the Lord your God year by year at the place the Lord chooses." (Household: family) **21**. "But if the animal is lame, blind, or has any defect, you must not sacrifice it to the Lord." (Lame: unable to walk; Defect: flaw) **22**. "You may eat it within your own cities. Both the clean and unclean may eat it, as you would eat a deer or gazelle." (Clean: pure; Unclean: impure) **23**. "But do not eat its blood; pour it on the ground like water." (Blood: fluid in animals; Pour: spill out)

Chapter 16
1. "Observe the month of Abib, and celebrate the Passover to the Lord your God, for in that month the Lord your God brought you out of Egypt during the night. (Abib: first month of the Hebrew calendar, Passover: Jewish festival commemorating the Exodus **2**. "Sacrifice the Passover offering to the Lord your God, using animals from your flock and herd, at the place the Lord chooses to establish His name. (Sacrifice: offering, Flock: group of sheep or goats) **3**. "Do not eat leavened bread with it; for seven days eat unleavened bread, the bread of affliction, because you left Egypt in haste, remembering the day of your departure throughout your life. (Leavened: risen, Affliction: hardship) **4**. "For seven days, no leaven should be found in your territory, and none of the meat from the first day's sacrifice should remain until morning. (Leaven: yeast, Territory: land) **5**. "Do not sacrifice the Passover in your towns that the Lord your God gives you. (Sacrifice: offering, Towns: settlements) **6**. "Instead, sacrifice it at the place where the Lord your God chooses to place His name, at twilight, at sunset, when you left Egypt. (Twilight: evening, Sunset: when the sun goes down) **7**. "Roast and eat it at the place the Lord your God chooses, then return to your tents in the morning. (Roast: cook by direct heat, Tents: temporary shelters) **8**. "For six days, eat unleavened bread, and on the seventh day, hold a sacred assembly to the Lord your God, doing no work. (Sacred: holy, Assembly: gathering) **9**. "Count seven weeks from the time you begin to harvest the grain. (Weeks: seven-day periods, Harvest: gathering crops) **10**. "Then celebrate the Feast of Weeks before the Lord your God with a freewill offering, according to the blessings He has given you. (Feast: festival, Freewill: voluntary) **11**. "Rejoice before the Lord your God, you, your son, daughter, servants, Levites, foreigners, orphans, and widows, at the place where the Lord establishes His name. (Rejoice: celebrate, Levites: priestly tribe) **12**. "Remember you were once a slave in Egypt, and observe these statutes. (Slave: forced worker, Statutes: laws) **13**. "Celebrate the Feast of Tabernacles for seven days after gathering the produce from your threshing floor and winepress. (Feast: celebration, Tabernacles: temporary shelters) **14**. "Rejoice in your feast, you, your son, daughter, servants, Levites, foreigners, orphans, and widows in your towns. (Rejoice: celebrate, Feast: festival) **15**. "For seven days, keep a sacred feast to the Lord your God in the place He chooses, for He will bless you in your harvest and work, so that you may be joyful. (Sacred: holy, Harvest: crops) **16**. "Three times a year, all your men must appear before the Lord at the place He chooses: during the Feast of Unleavened Bread, the Feast of Weeks, and the Feast of Tabernacles. They shall not appear empty-handed. (Empty-handed: without a gift, Unleavened: without yeast) **17**. "Every man must give according to his ability, in proportion to the blessings the Lord has given him. (Ability: capacity, Proportion: share) **18**. "Appoint judges and officers in all your towns, as the Lord gives you, according to your tribes, to judge the people

fairly. (Judges: decision-makers, Officers: administrators) **19.** "Do not distort justice, show partiality, or accept a bribe, for it blinds the wise and twists the words of the righteous. (Distort: misrepresent, Bribe: payment for influence) **20.** "Follow what is just and right, so you may live and inherit the land the Lord is giving you. (Right: morally good, Possession: ownership) **21.** "Do not plant any tree as an idol near the altar you build for the Lord. (Idol: object of worship, Altar: place for sacrifices) **22.** "Do not set up a sacred pillar, which the Lord detests. (Sacred: holy, Pillar: stone idol)"

Chapter 17

1. "Do not offer a bull or sheep to the Lord your God if it has any flaw or imperfection, because such an offering is detestable to the Lord your God. (Detestable: greatly disliked or wrong) **2.** "If you discover within any of your towns, which the Lord your God has given you, a man or woman who has acted wickedly in the sight of the Lord by violating His covenant, (Wickedly: immorally or sinfully; Covenant: an agreement or promise) **3.** "By going and worshiping other gods, such as the sun, moon, or any of the heavenly bodies, which I did not command, (Heavenly bodies: stars, planets, or constellations) **4.** "And you hear about it, you must investigate thoroughly. If you find that it is true and that such an abomination has taken place in Israel, (Abomination: detestable action or sin) **5.** "Then you must bring that person to your gates and stone them to death with stones. (Gates: city entrances) **6.** "Anyone deserving of death must be executed based on the testimony of two or three witnesses; they should not be executed based on the testimony of one witness. (Testimony: a statement or evidence given by a witness) **7.** "The witnesses must be the first to throw stones at the person to carry out the death sentence, and then the rest of the people should join in. This is how you will remove evil from your community. (Sentence: punishment; Remove: eliminate) **8.** "If you face a difficult case that is too complex to decide—whether it involves bloodshed, disputes over guilt, or different opinions about punishment—you must go to the place where the Lord your God has chosen. (Bloodshed: murder or injury; Disputes: disagreements) **9.** "There, you will consult with the priests, the Levites, and the judge who is in office at that time. They will make a decision for you. (Consult: seek advice or information) **10.** "You must follow their decision and carefully obey all their instructions. (Instructions: orders or directions) **11.** "You are to follow the law and judgment they give you, and you should not deviate from what they tell you, whether to the right or to the left. (Deviate: move away or change direction) **12.** "If anyone acts arrogantly and refuses to listen to the priest serving before the Lord your God, or to the judge, that person must die. This is how you will eliminate wickedness from Israel. (Arrogantly: with excessive confidence or pride; Eliminate: remove) **13.** "All the people will hear about it and be afraid, and no one will act arrogantly again. (Arrogantly: with excessive confidence or pride) **14.** "When you enter the land the Lord your God is giving you and settle there, and you say, 'I want to set a king over me, like the other nations around me,' (Settle: live in a place) **15.** "You must appoint a king whom the Lord your God chooses. He must be one of your own people; you cannot appoint a foreigner to rule over you. (Appoint: choose or nominate; Foreigner: someone not from your people or nation) **16.** "The king must not accumulate many horses for himself, nor should he make the people return to Egypt to acquire more horses, for the Lord has told you, 'You must never go back that way again.' (Accumulate: gather or collect; Acquire: obtain or get) **17.** "Nor should he have many wives, or his heart will be led astray; and he must not accumulate large amounts of silver and gold for himself. (Led astray: misled or distracted) **18.** "When the king takes the throne of his kingdom, he must write a personal copy of this law in a book, from the one that is kept by the priests, the Levites. (Throne: seat of power; Levites: members of the priestly tribe) **19.** "It must be with him, and he must read it daily throughout his life, so that he may learn to fear the Lord his God and carefully follow all the laws and regulations. (Fear: respect and obey) **20.** "This way, his heart will not become proud above his fellow Israelites, nor will he turn away from the commandments to the right or to the left, and he will reign for a long time, he and his children, in the kingdom of Israel. (Proud: arrogant or haughty; Reign: rule or govern)"

Chapter 18

1. "The priests, from the tribe of Levi, shall not receive land or inheritance in Israel; they will live off the offerings made to the Lord by fire, which will be their share. (Inheritance: property passed down through generations) **2.** "Therefore, they will have no portion among their fellow Israelites; the Lord is their inheritance, as promised. (Portion: a share) **3.** "This is the priest's entitlement: those who bring sacrifices, whether a bull or sheep, shall give the priest the shoulder, cheeks, and stomach. (Entitlement: having a right) **4.** "You must give the priest the first part of your grain, wine, oil, and wool from your sheep. (Firstfruits: the first part of a harvest) **5.** "The Lord has chosen him and his descendants from all the tribes of Israel to serve in His name forever. (Descendants: future generations) **6.** "If a Levite comes from any of your towns in Israel and desires to go to the place the Lord chooses to worship, (Desires: wants strongly) **7.** "he may serve in the name of the Lord his God, just as the other Levites minister before the Lord. (Minister: serve in a religious capacity) **8.** "He will share equally in the food with his fellow Levites, excluding income from the sale of his inheritance. **9.** "When you enter the land the Lord is giving you, do not adopt the detestable practices of the nations there. (Detestable: highly offensive) **10.** "Do not allow anyone to sacrifice their son or daughter by passing them through fire, or practice witchcraft, fortune-telling, soothsaying, or sorcery, (Witchcraft: magic for evil purposes; Fortune-teller: predicts the future; Soothsayer: predicts the future; Sorcerer: practices magic) **11.** "a spell-caster, a medium, a spiritist, or anyone who calls up the dead. (Spell-caster: uses spells; Medium: communicates with spirits; Spiritist: communicates with the dead) **12.** "All who engage in these practices are detestable to the Lord, and because of these abominations, the Lord will drive these nations out before you. (Engage: participate in; Abominations: extremely offensive things) **13.** "You must remain blameless before the Lord. (Blameless: free from guilt) **14.** "The nations you will dispossess listen to fortune-tellers and diviners; but the Lord has not permitted you to do so. (Dispossess: take away; Diviners: those who predict the future) **15.** "The Lord will raise up for you a prophet like me from your people. You must listen to him, (Prophet: one who speaks for God) **16.** "just as you requested of the Lord at Horeb, when you said, 'Let us not hear the voice of the Lord or see this great fire anymore, or we will die.' (Assembly: gathering) **17.** "The Lord said: 'What they have spoken is good.' (Spoken: said) **18.** "'I will raise up a prophet like you from their fellow Israelites, and put My words in His mouth. He will tell them everything I command.' (Command: order) **19.** "'Anyone who does not listen to the words this prophet speaks in My name will be held accountable.' (Accountable: responsible) **20.** "'But the prophet who presumes to speak in My name something I have not commanded, or speaks in the name of other gods, must die.' (Presumes: assumes) **21.** "If you say, 'How can we know whether the message is from the Lord?' (Message: communication) **22.** "If a prophet speaks in the Lord's name, but what he prophesies does not come true, then the Lord has not spoken. The prophet has spoken presumptuously, and you need not fear him. (Prophesies: predicts the future; Fulfilled: completed)"

Chapter 19

1. "When the Lord your God removes the nations whose land He is giving you, and you take their place by living in their cities and houses. (Dispossesses: removes and takes over possession) **2.** "You must set apart three cities for yourself within the land the Lord your God is granting you to possess. (Designate: set apart for a specific purpose) **3.** "Prepare roads and divide your land into three regions, so that anyone who unintentionally kills someone can escape there. (Unintentionally: accidentally) **4.** "This is the rule for someone who kills another unintentionally and seeks refuge: if they did not harbor hatred toward the victim in the past. (Harbor hatred: to keep feelings of animosity or ill will) **5.** "For instance, when two people go to cut wood, and one swings an ax, but the blade slips from the handle and fatally strikes the other, they can flee to one of these cities and live. (Slips: detaches accidentally) **6.** "This is to prevent the avenger of blood, in a moment of anger, from pursuing and killing the one who caused the accidental death, even though they do not deserve to die. (Avenger: one who seeks revenge; Anger: intense displeasure or rage) **7.** "Therefore, I command you to set apart three cities for this purpose. (Command: give an authoritative order) **8.** "If the Lord your God enlarges your territory as He promised your ancestors and gives you the land He pledged to them. (Enlarges: increases in size; Ancestors: forefathers) **9.** "If you obey all His commandments to love Him and walk in His ways, then you must add three more cities to the original three. (Walk in His ways: follow His teachings and commandments) **10.** "This ensures that innocent blood is not shed in the land the Lord your God is giving you, and prevents guilt from falling on you. (Innocent: free from wrongdoing; Guilt: responsibility for wrongdoing) **11.** "But if someone harbors hatred, ambushes their neighbor, and intentionally kills them, then flees to one of these cities. (Ambushes: attacks suddenly and unexpectedly) **12.** "The elders of their city must send for the killer and hand them over to the avenger of blood to face death. (Elders: leaders or officials in authority) **13.** "Do not show pity but remove the guilt of innocent bloodshed from Israel, so that everything may go well for you. (Pity: compassion for someone; Guilt: moral or legal responsibility) **14.** "Do not move your neighbor's boundary marker set by previous generations in the land you are inheriting. (Landmark: a marker that defines property boundaries) **15.** "A single witness cannot convict someone of a crime; two or three witnesses are needed to confirm the matter. (Witness: someone who testifies about what they have seen or know) **16.** "If a false witness testifies against someone, claiming they did wrong. (False witness: someone who lies in their testimony) **17.** "Both parties must stand before the Lord to be judged by the priests and officials of that time. (Judged: evaluated and given a decision) **18.** "The judges must carefully investigate, and if the witness is found to be lying. (Carefully: thoroughly and attentively; Lying: intentionally providing false information) **19.** "Then the false witness must face the punishment they intended for the accused. This will remove evil from your community. (Punishment: penalty for wrongdoing) **20.** "When others hear about this, they will fear and avoid repeating such evil acts. (Fear: feel afraid or anxious about consequences) **21.** "Do not show pity: life for life, eye for eye, tooth for tooth, hand for hand, foot for foot. (Pity: mercy or leniency for someone)"

Chapter 20
1. "When you go into battle against your enemies and see their horses and chariots, and armies larger than yours, do not be afraid, for the Lord your God, who brought you out of Egypt, is with you. (Chariots: war vehicles; Enemies: opponents) **2.** "Before the battle begins, the priest will come forward to speak to the people. (Priest: religious leader; Battle: armed conflict) **3.** "He will say, 'Listen, Israel! Today you are about to face your enemies. Do not let your hearts grow weak; do not fear, shake, or feel terror because of them. (Faint: grow weak; Terrified: overcome with fear) **4.** "For the Lord your God goes with you to fight for you against your enemies and to give you victory. (Victory: success in battle; Fight: engage in combat) **5.** "Then the officers will address the people, saying, 'Is there anyone who has built a new house but hasn't dedicated it yet? Let him go back home so that he does not die in battle and someone else takes it.' (Dedicated: made sacred; Officers: leaders) **6.** "Also, if anyone has planted a vineyard but hasn't yet enjoyed its fruit, let him go home so that he doesn't die in battle and someone else eats it. (Vineyard: grape garden; Fruit: produce) **7.** "And if anyone is engaged to a woman but hasn't married her yet, let him go back to his home so that he doesn't die in battle and another marries her. (Betrothed: engaged; Marry: take as spouse) **8.** "The officers will also say, 'If there is anyone afraid or lacking courage, let him go home so he does not weaken the hearts of his fellow soldiers.' (Fainthearted: easily frightened; Courage: bravery) **9.** "When the officers finish addressing the people, they will appoint commanders to lead the troops. (Appoint: assign; Commanders: leaders) **10.** "When you approach a city to engage in battle, first offer it terms of peace. (Approach: come near; Peace: non-violence) **11.** "If the city agrees to peace and opens its gates to you, then all the people within it will serve you and pay you tribute. (Tribute: payment of respect; Serve: work for) **12.** "But if the city refuses your peace offer and chooses to fight, then surround and lay siege to it. (Refuses: declines; Siege: military blockade) **13.** "When the Lord your God hands the city over to you, strike down all the men with the sword. (Strike down: kill; Sword: weapon) **14.** "However, you may take the women, children, animals, and goods for yourselves, enjoying the plunder your God has given you. (Plunder: war spoils; Goods: possessions) **15.** "You should follow this rule for all cities far from you and not belonging to nearby nations. (Rule: guideline; Nations: countries or tribes) **16.** "But in the cities that the Lord your God gives you as an inheritance, do not let anything that breathes remain alive. (Inheritance: something passed down; Breathes: is alive) **17.** "You must completely destroy the Hittites, Amorites, Canaanites, Perizzites, Hivites, and Jebusites, as the Lord your God commanded you. (Destroy: eliminate; Commanded: instructed) **18.** "This is to keep them from teaching you to do detestable practices for their gods, which would lead you to sin against the Lord your God. (Detestable: offensive; Sin: wrongdoing) **19.** "When you besiege a city for a long time, do not cut down its fruit trees, as you can eat from them. Do not use these trees for the siege because they provide food. (Besiege: surround in attack; Siege: military attack) **20.** "However, you may cut down trees that don't produce food to build siege equipment against the city until it is conquered. (Conquered: defeated; Equipment: tools)"

Chapter 21
1. "If a dead body is set up lying in the open field in the land the Lord your God is giving you to enthrall, and it isn't clear who's responsible for the death, (taken: killed) **2.** also your leaders and judges must measure the distance from the body to the nearest municipalities. (elders: leaders; judges: decision-makers) **3.** The elders of the city closest to the dead person must take a cow that has noway been used for work or linked to a plow. **4.** The elders of that city will bring the cow to a vale with running water, a place that has noway been furrowed or planted, and there they will break the cow's neck. (vale: low land; furrowed: dug up) **5.** also, the preachers from the lineage of Levi shall approach, for the Lord has chosen them to serve Him and bless in His name; through their word, all dissensions will be settled. (preachers: religious leaders; Levites: lineage of preachers) **6.** The elders of the nearest city will wash their hands over the cow whose neck was broken in the vale. (wash their hands: show innocence) **7.** They will say, 'Our hands didn't exfoliate this blood, and our eyes have n't seen it be. (chalet: slip) **8.** Forgive, O Lord, Your people Israel, whom You have saved, and don't let innocent blood be criticized on Your people Israel.' And atonement will be made for the bloodshed. (atonement: conciliation) **9.** By doing what's right in the sight of the Lord, you'll remove the guilt of innocent blood from among you. (guilt: responsibility) **10.** When you go to war against your adversaries and the Lord your God gives you palm, and you take captures, (delivers them into your hand: gives you control) **11.** if you see among the internees a woman who's seductive, and you ask to take her as your woman, (desire: want) **12.** also bring her to your home. She must shave her head and trim her nails. (shave: cut off; neat: cut short) **13.** She must change her prison clothes, remain in your house, and mourn her parents for a month. After that, you may marry her. (mourn: suffer) **14.** But if you're no longer pleased with her, you must let her go free; you cannot vend her for plutocrat or

treat her cruelly, because you have lowered her. (lowered: lowered) **15.** If a man has two women, one whom he loves and one whom he does not, and both have borne him children, and the firstborn son belongs to the woman he doesn't love, (bequeaths: gives) **16.** when he divides his heritage among his sons, he cannot give the firstborn's heritage to the son of the loved woman over the true firstborn. (firstborn: oldest) **17.** rather, he must fete the son of the unloved woman as the firstborn and give him a double portion of his heritage, for he's the first sign of his father's strength; the firstborn's rights belong to him. (double portion: redundant share; right of the firstborn: heritage rights) **18.** If a man has a son who's stubborn and rebellious, and refuses to observe his parents, indeed after they've chastened him, (stubborn: unyielding) **19.** also his parents must take him to the elders of the megacity, to the gate of the megacity. (elders: elderly leaders) **20.** They will tell the elders, 'Our son is stubborn and rebellious; he refuses to hear to us. He's a gormandizer and a tippler.' (gormandizer: hog) **21.** also all the men of the megacity shall sharpen him to death with monuments. You must relieve yourselves of this wrong, and all Israel will hear of it and be hysterical. (gravestone: him to death; execute with monuments) **22.** If a man has committed a sin that deserves death and is put to death, and his body is hung on a tree, (accursed: condemned) **23.** you mustn't leave his body on the tree overnight. You must bury him the same day, so that the land the Lord your God is giving you as an heritage is n't defiled. For anyone who's hanged is under God's curse." (defiled: made impure)

Chapter 22

1. "If you see your fellow Israelite's ox or sheep wandering away, do not ignore it; instead, you must return it to your brother. (Ox: a domesticated working animal) **2.** If your brother is not nearby, or if you don't know who he is, then bring it into your own house. Keep it there until your brother comes looking for it, and then you must return it to him. (Nearby: close by) **3.** Do the same with his donkey or his clothing, or any other item of his that you find to be lost; do not ignore it, but help your brother in this way. (Donkey: a domesticated animal used for carrying loads) **4.** If you see your brother's donkey or ox fall along the road, do not ignore it. You must help him lift it up again. (Fall: collapse) **5.** "A woman must not wear clothing meant for men, nor should a man wear women's clothing, for anyone who does this is detestable to the Lord your God. (Detestable: deeply disliked) **6.** "If you happen to come across a bird's nest along your way, whether in a tree or on the ground, and the mother is sitting on the eggs or the young, do not take the mother along with the young; (Come across: find unexpectedly) **7.** you must let the mother go free, but you may take the young for yourself. Doing so will bring you prosperity and allow you to live a long life. (Prosperity: success or well-being) **8.** "When you build a new house, you must make a guardrail for your roof to prevent the guilt of bloodshed from falling upon your household if someone falls off. (Guardrail: a protective barrier) **9.** "You must not plant two types of seed in your vineyard, or else both the crop you plant and the produce of the vineyard will become unclean. (Unclean: impure or defiled) **10.** "Do not plow with an ox and a donkey together. (Plow: break up the soil) **11.** "Do not wear clothes made from mixed fabrics, such as wool and linen woven together. (Woven: interlaced) **12.** "Make tassels on the four corners of your clothing that you wear. (Tassels: decorative threads) **13.** "If a man marries a woman, and after having relations with her, dislikes her, **14.** and accuses her of disgraceful conduct, claiming, 'I married this woman, but when I approached her, I found that she was not a virgin,' (Disgraceful: dishonorable) **15.** then the woman's parents must bring the proof of her virginity before the city elders at the gate. (Proof: evidence) **16.** The father of the woman will say to the elders, 'I gave my daughter to this man in marriage, and he dislikes her. **17.** Now he has accused her of shameful behavior, saying, "I did not find her to be a virgin," but here is the proof of my daughter's virginity.' Then they will spread the cloth before the elders of the city. (Shameful: dishonorable) **18.** The elders of the city will take the man and punish him; **19.** they will fine him a hundred shekels of silver, which will be given to the woman's father, because he has publicly humiliated a virgin in Israel. The man will be required to remain married to her; he will not be allowed to divorce her. (Fine: monetary penalty; Humiliated: publicly disgraced) **20.** But if the accusation is true and no proof of the woman's virginity is found, **21.** then the woman will be brought to her father's door, and the men of the city will stone her to death. She has done a disgraceful thing by acting like a prostitute in her father's house. In this way, you will remove this evil from among you. (Prostitute: a person who engages in sexual acts for money) **22.** "If a man is found having sexual relations with a woman who is married to someone else, both the man and the woman must be put to death. You must remove this evil from Israel. (Sexual relations: intimate physical relations) **23.** "If a young woman, a virgin, is engaged to a man, and another man comes across her in the city and lies with her, **24.** both of them must be brought to the city's gate and stoned to death. The young woman will die because she did not cry for help in the city, and the man will die because he violated his neighbor's wife. In this way, you will remove this evil from among you. (Violated: wrongfully touched or harmed) **25.** "But if a man finds a betrothed young woman in the countryside and forces himself on her, only the man who committed the act will die. (Betrothed: engaged) **26.** Do not harm the young woman, for she has not sinned in this case and deserves no punishment. This situation is like when a man rises up against his neighbor and kills him. (Harm: injure) **27.** For the young woman cried out, but there was no one to rescue her. (Cry out: scream for help) **28.** "If a man finds an unmarried young woman and rapes her, and they are caught in the act, **29.** the man must pay the young woman's father fifty shekels of silver, and he must marry her. Since he has dishonored her, he cannot divorce her all his life. (Rapes: forces sexual relations upon; Dishonored: treated with disrespect) **30.** "A man must not marry his father's wife or uncover his father's nakedness. (Uncover: expose)"

Chapter 23

1. "No one who has been emasculated by injury or mutilation shall enter the Lord's assembly." (Emasculated: castrated) **2.** "A child born out of wedlock shall not enter the Lord's assembly; even to the tenth generation, none of his descendants shall join the Lord's assembly." (Illegitimate: born outside of marriage) **3.** "Neither an Ammonite nor a Moabite shall enter the Lord's assembly; even to the tenth generation, none of their descendants shall join the assembly forever." (Ammonite, Moabite: ancient people descended from Lot) **4.** "They did not provide you with food and water on your journey from Egypt and hired Balaam son of Beor from Pethor in Mesopotamia to curse you." (Balaam: a prophet, Mesopotamia: ancient region) **5.** "But the Lord your God refused to listen to Balaam and turned the curse into a blessing for you, because He loves you." (Balaam: a prophet) **6.** "You must never seek peace or prosperity from them for all time." (Prosperity: success, wealth) **7.** "Do not despise an Edomite, for he is your brother, nor an Egyptian, because you were a stranger in his land." (Edomite: descendant of Esau, Egyptian: from Egypt) **8.** "The children of the third generation born to them may enter the Lord's assembly." (Third generation: three generations removed) **9.** "When your army goes out to fight, avoid any form of wickedness." (Wickedness: evil actions) **10.** "If anyone becomes unclean due to a nocturnal event, he must leave the camp and not return." (Unclean: ritually impure) **11.** "At evening, he must wash with water and may re-enter the camp after sunset." (Re-enter: return) **12.** "You must have a designated area outside the camp for relieving yourself." (Relieve yourself: use the restroom) **13.** "Carry a tool and, when sitting outside, use it to dig a hole and cover your waste." (Tool: digging instrument) **14.** "For the Lord your God walks in your camp to protect you and deliver your enemies into your hands; your camp must be holy, so He does not turn away from you."

(Holy: sacred, pure) **15.** "You must not return a slave who has escaped to his master." (Slave: person in servitude) **16.** "He may live anywhere within your towns, in a place that seems best to him; do not oppress him." (Oppress: mistreat) **17.** "There shall be no ritual prostitution among the daughters or male shrine prostitutes among the sons of Israel." (Prostitution: selling sexual services) **18.** "You must not bring the earnings of a prostitute or the price of a dog into the Lord's house as a vow offering, as both are detestable to the Lord." (Dog: male prostitute, Detestable: repulsive) **19.** "Do not charge your fellow Israelite interest on loans of money, food, or anything you lend." (Interest: extra charge on loan) **20.** "You may charge interest to foreigners, but not to Israelites, so the Lord may bless you in everything you do in the land you possess." (Foreigners: non-Israelites) **21.** "When you make a vow to the Lord your God, do not delay in fulfilling it, for the Lord will require it, and failing to keep it is a sin." (Vow: solemn promise) **22.** "If you refrain from vowing, it is not a sin to you." (Refrain: abstain) **23.** "Whatever you have promised with your lips, keep and perform, because you voluntarily made a vow to the Lord." (Voluntarily: willingly) **24.** "When you enter your neighbor's vineyard, you may eat your fill of grapes, but do not take any with you." (Vineyard: grape farm) **25.** "When you enter your neighbor's standing grain, you may pluck the heads with your hand, but do not use a sickle." (Sickle: curved cutting tool)

Chapter 24

1. "If a man marries a woman and later finds something displeasing in her, such as a fault or uncleanliness, he must write her a divorce certificate, hand it to her, and send her away." (Uncleanliness: something morally wrong) **2.** "If she leaves his house and marries another man," **3.** "and if this second husband dislikes her, gives her a divorce certificate, and sends her away, or if he dies," (Divorce certificate: formal document ending the marriage) **4.** "then her first husband, who divorced her, cannot take her back as his wife. This would be wrong and an abomination before the Lord. You must not bring sin upon the land God is giving you." (Abomination: something sinful or detestable) **5.** "When a man marries a new wife, he is not to go to war or take on business for the first year. He is to stay home and bring joy to his wife." (Obligations: duties or responsibilities) **6.** "No one shall take a millstone, top or bottom, as collateral for a loan, because this takes away someone's means of making a living." (Millstone: large stone used for grinding grain; Collateral: something pledged for a loan) **7.** "If someone kidnaps an Israelite, treats them badly, or sells them into slavery, the kidnapper shall die. Remove this evil from your community." (Kidnapping: forcibly taking someone; Slavery: state of being forced to work without pay) **8.** "Be careful with leprosy and follow the priests' instructions. As I commanded them, follow their guidance." (Leprosy: contagious skin disease; Levites: priestly tribe of Israel) **9.** "Remember what the Lord did to Miriam when you were leaving Egypt." (Miriam: Moses' sister) **10.** "When you lend something to your brother, do not enter his house to collect his pledge." (Pledge: something given as security for a loan) **11.** "Instead, stand outside, and let the person bring the pledge out to you." **12.** "If the person is poor, do not keep the pledge overnight." (Pledge: something given as security for a loan) **13.** "Return the pledge by sundown, so they can sleep in their clothes and bless you. This will be righteousness before God." (Sundown: the time when the sun sets; Righteousness: morally right actions) **14.** "Do not oppress a poor hired servant, whether they are an Israelite or a foreigner." (Oppress: treat unfairly; Hired servant: employee) **15.** "Pay their wages daily before sundown, because they are poor and rely on the pay. If you withhold it, they may cry to the Lord, and it will be sin." (Withhold: to keep back) **16.** "Fathers should not be punished for children's sins, nor children for fathers' sins. Each is responsible for their own actions." (Punished: subjected to penalty for wrongdoing) **17.** "Do not distort justice for foreigners or orphans, and do not take a widow's cloak as collateral for a loan." (Distort: misrepresent; Widow: woman whose husband has died) **18.** "Remember you were slaves in Egypt, and the Lord redeemed you. Therefore, I command you to act with kindness and justice." (Redeemed: rescued or saved; Kindness: being considerate) **19.** "When you harvest in your field and forget a bundle, do not return for it. Leave it for the foreigner, orphan, and widow, so God may bless your work." (Orphan: child without parents) **20.** "When you gather olives, do not go back for the remaining ones. Leave them for the foreigner, orphan, and widow." (Olives: small fruits from the olive tree) **21.** "When you harvest grapes, do not go over the vines again. Leave the remaining grapes for the foreigner, orphan, and widow." (Vines: plants that produce grapes) **22.** "Remember you were slaves in Egypt, and therefore I command you to do these things." (Slaves: people forced to work without pay)

Chapter 25

1. "If there is a disagreement between two people, and they go to court, the judges will decide. They will defend the right and condemn the wrong." (Dispute: disagreement; Justify: defend as right; Condemn: declare guilty) **2.** "If the guilty person deserves beating, the judge will have him lie down and be beaten according to his crime, with a set number of lashes." (Beaten: struck as punishment; Lashes: blows with a whip) **3.** "He may receive up to forty lashes, but no more, lest the punishment exceed this, dishonoring your brother before you." (Exceed: go beyond; Humiliated: made to feel ashamed) **4.** "You shall not prevent an ox from eating while it works to separate the grain." (Muzzle: to prevent from eating) **5.** "If two brothers live together, and one dies without a son, the widow shall not marry outside the family. Her husband's brother must marry her and fulfill his duty to her." (Widow: a woman whose husband has died; Brother-in-law: the husband's brother) **6.** "The firstborn son will inherit his deceased father's name, so it is not erased from Israel." (Firstborn: first child born; Erased: wiped out) **7.** "If the brother is unwilling to marry his brother's widow, she must go to the elders and say, 'My husband's brother refuses to carry on his name; he will not fulfill his duty.'" (Elders: respected older members) **8.** "The elders will call him and speak with him. If he insists, 'I do not wish to marry her,'" (Firm: resolute) **9.** "then his brother's widow shall come before the elders, remove his sandal, spit in his face, and say, 'This happens to the man who refuses to build up his brother's family.'" (Sandal: footwear) **10.** "His name will be known as 'The house of the man whose sandal was removed.'" (House: family) **11.** "If two men fight, and the wife of one tries to help her husband by stopping the other man, and she grabs him by the genitals," (Genitals: reproductive organs) **12.** "then you must cut off her hand; show no mercy." (Mercy: compassion) **13.** "You shall not keep differing weights in your bag, one heavy, one light." (Weights: instruments for measuring weight) **14.** "You shall not have differing measures in your house, one large, one small." (Measures: tools for measuring quantity) **15.** "Use honest and accurate weights and measures, so you may live long in the land the Lord is giving you." (Honest: truthful; Accurate: correct) **16.** "All who act unjustly are an abomination to the Lord." (Abomination: something detestable; Unjustly: unfairly) **17.** "Remember what Amalek did to you as you traveled out of Egypt," (Amalek: a hostile group) **18.** "how he attacked you and struck down those who lagged behind when you were tired and weak, and showed no fear of God." (Lagging: moving slower; Weak: lacking strength) **19.** "Therefore, when the Lord gives you rest from your enemies, you must erase the memory of Amalek. You must not forget." (Grant: give; Inherit: receive as a heritage; Erase: remove)

Chapter 26

1. "When you enter the land the Lord your God is giving you as an heritage, and you take possession of it and settle there," (heritage: inheritance; settle: live) **2.** "you must take some of the first fruits of your crops, which the Lord your God is giving you, place them in a handbasket, and go to the place where the Lord your God has chosen for His name to dwell." (first fruits: crop; dwell: live) **3.** "You'll approach the clerk in those days and say, 'moment, I declare to the

Lord your God that I've arrived in the land the Lord promised our ancestors.'" (declare: advertise; ancestors: forebearers) **4.** "The clerk will take the handbasket from your hands and place it before the balcony of the Lord your God." (balcony: sacred table) **5.** "You'll say before the Lord your God 'My ancestor was a wandering Aramean, about to corrupt, and he went to Egypt and lived there, a small group; but there, he became a great, potent, and vibrant nation.'" (Aramean: ancient people; corrupt: bones; vibrant: multitudinous) **6.** "Still, the Egyptians manhandled us, oppressed us, and subordinated us to hard labor." (manhandled: harmed; oppressed: burdened; labor: work) **7.** "We cried out to the Lord, the God of our ancestors, and the Lord heard our cry, looked at our suffering, labor, and oppression." (suffering: pain; cry out: cry for help) **8.** "So the Lord brought us out of Egypt with His potent hand and outstretched arm, with great terror, and with miraculous signs and prodigies." (mighty: important; outstretched arm: strength; terror: fear) **9.** "He brought us to this place and gave us this land, a land flowing with milk and honey." (flowing: abundant) **10.** "And now, behold, I've brought the first fruits of the land You, O Lord, have given me.' Place it before the Lord your God and worship Him there." (behold: see; deification: reverence) **11.** "You should rejoice in all the good effects the Lord your God has given to you and your ménage, including the Levite and the outsider among you." (rejoice: celebrate; Levite: priestly lineage; outsider: stranger) **12.** "'When you finish setting aside the tithe of your crops in the third time, the time of tithing, and have given it to the Levite, the outsider, the orphan, and the widow, so they can eat within your city and be satisfied," (tithe: tenth; orphan: child without parents; widow: woman without hubby) **13.** "also you'll say before the Lord your God 'I've removed the holy tithe from my house and have given it to the Levite, the outsider, the orphan, and the widow, just as You commanded me; I have n't defied Your commandments, nor have I forgotten them." (holy: sacred; defied: violated) **14.** "I have n't eaten any of it while in mourning, nor have I taken any of it for a sick purpose, nor have I given any of it to the dead. I've adhered to the voice of the Lord my God, and have done all You commanded." (mourning: grieving; sick: impure) **15.** "Look down from Your holy lodging in heaven, and bless Your people Israel and the land You gave us, just as You swore to our ancestors, 'A land flowing with milk and honey.'" (holy lodging: sacred hearthstone; swore: promised) **16.** "Moment, the Lord your God commands you to follow these laws and rulings; thus, be active to observe them with all your heart and soul." (active: careful; rulings: laws) **17.** "Moment you have declared the Lord to be your God, and that you'll walk in His ways, keep His bills, commandments, and rulings, and hear to His voice." (bills: laws; commandments: directives) **18.** "Moment the Lord has declared you to be His special people, as He promised you, that you should keep all His commandments," (special: chosen; promised: assured) **19.** "and that He'll raise you up over all the nations He has made, to praise, recognize, and distinction, and that you'll be a holy people to the Lord your God, just as He has spoken." (distinction: honor; holy: sacred)

Chapter 27

1. "Now Moses, with Israel's leaders, instructed the people: 'Obey all the commandments I give you today.'" (Commandments: laws) **2.** "When you cross the Jordan into the land the Lord your God is giving you, take large stones and coat them with lime." (Lime: a white powder used for coating) **3.** "Write all the words of this law on these stones after crossing, to enter the land the Lord is giving you—a land flowing with milk and honey, as He promised your ancestors." (Flowing: abundant) **4.** "When you cross, set up these stones on Mount Ebal as I instruct, and cover them with lime." (Mount Ebal: a mountain in Israel) **5.** "There, build an altar to the Lord your God, made of stones. Do not use iron tools on them." (Altar: a structure for offerings) **6.** "Use uncut stones to build the altar, and offer burnt offerings to the Lord." (Uncut: not shaped) **7.** "You will offer peace offerings, eat, and rejoice before the Lord your God." (Peace offerings: sacrifices in gratitude) **8.** "Write clearly on these stones all the words of this law." (Clearly: in a way that is easy to understand) **9.** "Then Moses, with the priests and Levites (those set apart to serve God), spoke to Israel: 'Pay attention, O Israel, for today you have become the people of the Lord your God.'" (Levites: priests from the tribe of Levi) **10.** "Therefore, obey the voice of the Lord your God, and follow His commandments and laws I give you today." (Voice: the command given) **11.** "On the same day, Moses gave the following command:" **12.** "When you cross, these tribes will stand on Mount Gerizim to bless the people: Simeon, Levi, Judah, Issachar, Joseph, and Benjamin." (Bless: to speak favorably of) **13.** "And these tribes will stand on Mount Ebal to declare curses: Reuben, Gad, Asher, Zebulun, Dan, and Naphtali." (Curses: pronouncements of misfortune) **14.** "Then the Levites will speak loudly to all the people of Israel, saying:" (Loudly: with strength) **15.** "Cursed is the one who makes a carved or molded idol, detestable (causing hatred) to the Lord, the work of a craftsman, and sets it up in secret." And all the people will reply, "Amen!" (Idol: an image worshiped as a god) **16.** "Cursed is the one who dishonors his father or mother." And all the people will say, "Amen!" (Dishonors: shows disrespect) **17.** "Cursed is the one who moves his neighbor's boundary marker." And all the people will say, "Amen!" (Boundary: a dividing line) **18.** "Cursed is the one who causes a blind person to lose their way." And all the people will say, "Amen!" (Blind: unable to see) **19.** "Cursed is the one who denies justice to the foreigner, the orphan, or the widow." And all the people will say, "Amen!" (Denies: refuses) (Foreigner: a person from another country) **20.** "Cursed is the one who commits adultery with his father's wife, for he has dishonored his father's bed." And all the people will say, "Amen!" (Adultery: sexual relations with someone not one's spouse) **21.** "Cursed is the one who has sexual relations with an animal." And all the people will say, "Amen!" (Relations: sexual contact) **22.** "Cursed is the one who has sexual relations with his sister, whether the daughter of his father or mother." And all the people will say, "Amen!" (Sister: a female sibling) **23.** "Cursed is the one who has sexual relations with his mother-in-law." And all the people will say, "Amen!" (Mother-in-law: spouse's mother) **24.** "Cursed is the one who secretly attacks his neighbor." And all the people will say, "Amen!" (Attacks: acts of violence) **25.** "Cursed is the one who takes a bribe to kill an innocent person." And all the people will say, "Amen!" (Bribe: money or favor to influence someone) (Innocent: not guilty) **26.** "Cursed is the one who does not uphold all the words of this law by following them." And all the people will say, "Amen!" (Uphold: support)

Chapter 28

1. "If you truly hear to the Lord your God and precisely follow all His commands that I give you moment, also the Lord your God will lift you up over all the nations on the earth." (Diligently: precisely; observe: follow) **2.** "All these blessings will come upon you and catch you because you observe the voice of the Lord your God." (Catch: catch up with and overwhelm) **3.** "You'll be blessed in the megacity and blessed in the country." **4.** "Your children will be blessed, your crops will grow, and your herds and flocks will increase." (Fruit of your body: children; yield of your ground: crops; increase: growth) **5.** "Your handbasket and kneading coliseum will be blessed." (Kneading coliseum: coliseum used for mixing dough) **6.** "You'll be blessed when you enter and blessed when you leave." **7.** "The Lord will beget your adversaries who rise against you to be defeated before you; they will come at you from one direction, but flee from you in seven directions." (Catch: to be overwhelmed or outnumbered) **8.** "The Lord will bless everything you store and all that you put your hands to. He'll bless you in the land He's giving you." **9.** "The Lord will make you a holy people for Himself, as He promised, if you follow His commands and walk in His ways." (Holy: set piecemeal for God's purpose) **10.** "Also all the peoples of the earth will see that you're called by the name of the Lord, and they will be hysterical of you." **11.** "The Lord will bless you with plenitude of goods with healthy children, abundant crops, and large beast, in the land He promised your ancestors." **12.** "The Lord will open the welkin, His good storage, and shoot rain on your land in its season. He'll bless everything you do. You'll advance to numerous nations, but you won't adopt." (Storehouses: places where effects are stored) **13.** "The Lord will make you the leader, not the follower. You'll be above only, and not beneath, if you hear to the commands of the Lord your God and observe them precisely." (Head: leader; tail: follower) **14.** "You mustn't turn away from the words I command you moment, to follow other gods and serve them." **15.** "But if you don't observe the voice of the Lord your God and don't precisely follow all His commands and laws that I give you moment, all these curses will come upon you and catch you." (Curses: mischances or corrections) **16.** "You'll be cursed in the megacity and cursed in the country." **17.** "Your handbasket and kneading coliseum will be cursed." **18.** "Your children will be cursed, your crops will fail, and your beast will drop." **19.** "You'll be cursed when you enter and cursed when you leave." **20.** "The Lord will shoot upon you curses, confusion, and reproach in everything you do, until you're destroyed because of your wickedness in turning down from Him." (Confusion: complaint; reproach: rebuke) **21.** "The Lord will bring a pest upon you until He has wiped you out from the land you're about to take possession of." (Plague: deadly complaint) **22.** "The Lord will strike you with affections like fever, inflammation, and painful conditions. They will pursue you until you're destroyed." (Consumption: wasting complaint) **23.** "The skies above you'll be like citation, and the earth beneath you'll be like iron." (Citation: a essence; iron: a heavy essence) **24.** "The Lord will turn the rain in your land into dust, and it'll fall from the sky until you're destroyed." **25.** "The Lord will beget you to be defeated before your adversaries. You'll flee in seven directions, and you'll become a trouble to all the fiefdoms of the earth." **26.** "Your bodies will become food for the catcalls and creatures, and no bone will scarify them down." **27.** "The Lord will strike you with boils like those in Egypt, with excrescences, scabs, and itching that can not be cured." (Boils: painful bumps on the skin) **28.** "The Lord will strike you with madness, blindness, and confusion of mind." **29.** "You'll fish around at noon, like an eyeless man in darkness. You won't prosper in your ways. You'll be oppressed and despoiled continually, and no bone will help you." (Gropes: feel around; Despoiled: burgled) **30.** "You'll remarry (promise to marry) a woman, but another man will take her; you'll make a house, but not live in it; you'll plant a croft, but not enjoy its fruit." **31.** "Your ox will be massacred before your eyes, but you won't eat any of it. Your jackass will be taken from you, and it'll not be returned. Your lamb will be given to your adversaries, and no bone will save them for you." **32.** "Your sons and daughters will be taken by another people, and you'll long for them all day, but you'll be helpless to do anything about it." **33.** "A foreign nation you don't know will eat the fruits of your land and labor, and you'll be continually oppressed and crushed." (Oppressed: treated unfairly) **34.** "You'll go **35.** The Lord will strike you with painful, incurable boils from head to toe." (Boils: painful, swollen sores) **36.** "The Lord will send you and your king to a distant nation where you will serve gods made of wood and stone." (Forced: made to do something against your will) **37.** "You will become a disgrace, a byword, and an amazement among the nations to which the Lord will send you." (Disgrace: shame or dishonor) **38.** "You will sow much, but harvest little, for locusts will consume it." (Locusts: destructive insects) **39.** "You will plant vineyards, but not drink wine or gather grapes, for worms will destroy them." (Vineyards: fields of grapevines) **40.** "You will have olive trees, but the olives will fall, and you won't use the oil." (Olives: small fruit used to make oil) **41.** "You will have sons and daughters, but they will be taken into captivity." (Captivity: being held as a prisoner) **42.** "Locusts will devour your trees and crops." (Devour: eat up completely) **43.** "Foreigners among you will become more powerful, and you will become weaker." (Foreigners: people from other countries) **44.** "The foreigner will lend to you, but you won't lend to them. They will lead, and you will follow." (Lend: to give temporarily) **45.** "These curses will overtake you and destroy you, because you did not obey the Lord's commands." (Curses: harmful punishments) **46.** "These curses will serve as a sign and wonder to you and your descendants forever." (Sign: a symbol; Wonder: something remarkable) **47.** "Because you did not serve the Lord with joy for all His blessings," (Serve: to follow or work for) **48.** "You will serve your enemies, suffering hunger, thirst, and lack, with an iron yoke until destroyed." (Yoke: a heavy burden) **49.** "The Lord will send a fierce nation against you, whose language you don't understand." (Swift: quick) **50.** "This nation will show no respect for the elderly or pity for the young." (Pity: sympathy) **51.** "They will consume your crops and livestock until you are destroyed." (Consume: eat or use up) **52.** "They will besiege your cities, destroying your strong walls and attacking all the land the Lord gave you." (Besiege: to surround and attack) **53.** "During the siege, you will eat your own children because of the great distress your enemies cause." (Resort: turn to; Distress: extreme trouble) **54.** "The most refined man will be hostile, unwilling to help his family because of the dire need." (Refined: cultured; Hardened: emotionally tough) **55.** "He will refuse to share the flesh of his children, whom he will eat, due to the desperate circumstances." (Refuse: to reject; Desperate: urgent) **56.** "The delicate woman will eat her own children secretly because of the extreme lack of food." (Delicate: fragile) **57.** "She will even eat her placenta and children, due to the severe conditions of the siege." (Placenta: the organ nourishing a baby) **58.** "If you do not carefully follow the law and honor the Lord," (Honor: respect greatly) **59.** "The Lord will bring plagues and long-lasting sicknesses upon you and your descendants." (Plagues: widespread disasters) **60.** "He will bring back the diseases you feared in Egypt, and they will cling to you." (Cling: stick closely) **61.** "The Lord will bring every sickness not written in this book, and they will continue until you are destroyed." (Continue: to last) **62.** "You will become few in number, though once as numerous as the stars, because you did not listen to the Lord." (Numerous: many) **63.** "Just as the Lord once delighted in blessing you, He will now delight in bringing ruin upon you and removing you from the land." (Delight: great pleasure) **64.** "The Lord will scatter you among the nations, and there you will serve foreign gods made of wood and stone." (Scatter: spread widely) **65.** "You will find no rest among these nations, with constant anxiety and fear." (Turmoil: confusion) **66.** "Your life will be filled with doubt and fear, with no security." (Security: safety) **67.** "You will long for evening in the morning and morning in the evening because of your fear." (Overwhelm: to overpower) **68.** "The Lord will take you back to Egypt in ships, and there, you will be sold as slaves, but no one will buy you." (Route: a way; Slaves: people forced to work without freedom)

Chapter 29

1. "These are the terms of the covenant that the Lord commanded Moses to establish with the Israelites in the land of Moab, in addition to the covenant He made with them at Horeb." (Horeb is another name for Mount Sinai) 2. Moses gathered all of Israel and addressed them: "You have witnessed everything the Lord did in Egypt, to Pharaoh, his servants, and his entire land— 3. the tremendous trials you saw with your own eyes, the miraculous signs, and the great wonders." (Trials: tests or challenges) 4. "Yet, to this day, the Lord has not given you a heart to understand, eyes to see, or ears to hear." 5. "I led you for forty years through the wilderness. During this time, your clothes did not wear out, and your sandals did not become damaged." 6. "You did not eat bread, nor did you drink wine or any other fermented drink, so that you would know that I am the Lord your God." 7. "When you reached this place, King Sihon of Heshbon and King Og of Bashan came out to fight against us, but we defeated them." 8. "We took their land and gave it as an inheritance to the tribes of Reuben, Gad, and the half-tribe of Manasseh." (Inheritance: a right to property or possessions passed down) 9. "Therefore, obey

the terms of this covenant and follow them, so that you may prosper in all that you do." (Prosper: succeed or flourish) **10**. "Today, all of you stand before the Lord your God: your leaders, tribes, elders, officers, and all the men of Israel, **11**. as well as your children, wives, and foreigners living among you, from the one who gathers your wood to the one who draws your water—" (Foreigners: people from other nations) **12**. "in order to enter into covenant with the Lord your God and to swear the oath He makes with you today," (Swear: promise solemnly) **13**. "so that He may establish you as His people and be your God, as He promised you and swore to your ancestors, to Abraham, Isaac, and Jacob." **14**. "I am making this covenant and oath, not just with you who are here today **15**. but also with those who are not present today **16**. (for you know how we lived in Egypt and traveled through the nations you passed, **17**. and how you saw their detestable practices and idols—made of wood, stone, silver, and gold);" (Detestable: morally wrong and offensive) **18**. "so that no one among you, whether man or woman, family or tribe, will turn away from the Lord our God to serve the gods of these nations. And no root of bitterness or poison will grow among you." (Root of bitterness: something that causes pain or resentment) **19**. "It may happen that when such a person hears the words of this curse, they will think to themselves, 'I will be fine, even if I follow my own desires,' as if the sober person could be compared to the drunkard." (Sober: not drunk) **20**. "The Lord will not pardon such a person. His anger and jealousy will burn against them, and every curse written in this book will come upon them, and the Lord will erase their name from under heaven." (Pardon: forgive, Jealousy: strong desire or protectiveness) **21**. "The Lord will separate them from all the tribes of Israel, bringing hardship upon them in accordance with all the curses of the covenant written in this Book of the Law," (Hardship: difficulty or trouble) **22**. "so that future generations of your children and any foreigners who come from distant lands will ask, when they see the plagues and diseases the Lord has brought upon the land:" (Plagues: disasters or troubles) **23**. "'The whole land is burned with sulfur, salt, and desolation. It is not sown, nor does it grow, nor does any grass sprout there, like the destruction of Sodom, Gomorrah, Admah, and Zeboim, which the Lord destroyed in His anger and wrath.'" (Sulfur: a chemical element, Desolation: complete ruin or destruction, Wrath: intense anger) **24**. "All nations will ask, 'Why has the Lord done this to this land? What caused the fierceness of His great anger?'" **25**. "And the people will answer, 'Because they abandoned the covenant of the Lord, the God of their ancestors, the covenant He made with them when He brought them out of the land of Egypt; **26**. for they went and served other gods and worshiped them, gods they did not know, and gods He had not allowed them to worship." **27**. "So the anger of the Lord was kindled against this land, bringing upon it all the curses written in this book." (Kindled: set on fire) **28**. "The Lord uprooted them from their land in anger, wrath, and great fury, and He threw them into another land, as it is today." (Uprooted: removed, Fury: strong, intense anger) **29**. "The secret matters belong to the Lord our God, but those things which are revealed belong to us and to our children forever, so that we may obey all the words of this law." (Secret matters: things that are hidden or unknown, Revealed: made known)

Chapter 30

1. "When all these things happen to you—the blessings and curses I have laid out—and you reflect on them while living among the nations where the Lord your God has sent you" (scattered: dispersed), **2**. "and you return to the Lord your God, obeying His voice with all your heart and soul, you and your children, following all that I command you today" (obey: follow), **3**. "then the Lord your God will restore you from captivity, show you mercy, and bring you back from the nations where He has scattered you" (captivity: exile), **4**. "Even if banished to the farthest corners of the earth, the Lord your God will gather you from there and bring you back" (banished: sent away), **5**. "The Lord your God will return you to the land your ancestors possessed, and you will claim it as your own. He will bless you with prosperity and increase your numbers even more than your ancestors" (prosperity: abundance), **6**. "The Lord your God will change your heart and the hearts of your descendants, enabling you to love Him with all your heart and soul so that you may live" (descendants: offspring), **7**. "The Lord your God will turn these curses against your enemies—those who hate and persecute you" (persecute: mistreat), **8**. "You will again listen to the Lord's voice and carry out the commands I am giving you today" (carry out: perform), **9**. "The Lord your God will bless everything you do, including your children, livestock, and harvests of your fields. He will delight in making you prosper, just as He delighted in blessing your ancestors" (livestock: farm animals), **10**. "This will happen if you obey His voice and follow His commandments and statutes written in this Book of the Law. Turn to the Lord your God with all your heart and soul" (statutes: laws). **11**. "The commandment I am giving you today is not too difficult to understand, nor is it beyond your reach" (commandment: divine instruction), **12**. "It is not in heaven that you need to ask, 'Who will go up to heaven for us, retrieve it, and explain it so we can obey it?'" (retrieve: bring back), **13**. "Nor is it across the sea, requiring someone to say, 'Who will cross the sea for us, retrieve it, and teach it to us so we can follow it?'" (follow: obey), **14**. "Instead, the word is very close to you—it is in your mouth and heart—so you can follow it" (word: divine message), **15**. "Today I have set before you a choice: life and goodness, or death and evil" (goodness: righteousness), **16**. "I command you today to love the Lord your God, walk in His ways, and keep His commandments, laws, and judgments. By doing so, you will thrive, multiply, and be blessed in the land you are entering to possess" (possess: take ownership), **17**. "But if you turn away from Him, refuse to listen, and are drawn to worship and serve other gods" (worship: show devotion), **18**. "I am warning you today that you will surely be destroyed. Your time in the land you are crossing the Jordan to possess will be cut short" (destroyed: ruined), **19**. "Today, I call heaven and earth as witnesses that I have set before you life and death, blessings and curses. Choose life so that you and your descendants may live" (witnesses: observers), **20**. "Love the Lord your God, obey His voice, and hold tightly to Him. He is your life and the length of your days. This way, you will dwell in the land the Lord swore to give to your ancestors—Abraham, Isaac, and Jacob" (swore: vowed).

Chapter 31

1. "Also Moses went and delivered these words to all the people of Israel." (deliver: to communicate or hand over) **2**. "He said to them, 'Moment, I turn one hundred and twenty times old. I'm no longer suitable to lead you or share in your peregrinations. Also, the Lord has told me, 'You won't cross the Jordan River.'" (Jordan: a swash forming part of the boundary of the Promised Land) **3**. "The Lord your God will go ahead of you. He'll destroy the nations in your path, enabling you to take possession of their land. Joshua will lead you across the Jordan, as the Lord has declared." (oust: to take down possession or control) **4**. "The Lord will deal with these nations as He did with Sihon and Og, the Amorite lords, and their homes when He destroyed them." (Amorites: an ancient people living in Canaan) **5**. "He'll hand these nations over to you, and you must observe all the commands I've given you." (commandments: godly laws or instructions) **6**. "Be strong and valorous! Don't sweat or be anxious about them, because the Lord your God will accompany you. He'll noway leave or leave you." **7**. "Also Moses summoned Joshua and, in the presence of all Israel, encouraged him, saying, 'Be strong and stalwart, for you'll lead this people into the land the Lord promised their ancestors, and you'll insure they admit it as their heritage.'" (heritage: commodity passed down or given) **8**. "The Lord will go ahead of you and stay with you. He'll not abandon or fail you. Don't be hysterical or dismayed." **9**. "Moses wrote down the law and gave it to the preachers, the sons of Levi, who carried the Ark of the Covenant of the Lord, and also to the elders of Israel." (covenant: a solemn agreement or pledge) **10.** "Moses commanded them, 'At the end of every seven times, during the time of release, at the Feast of Tabernacles,'" (release: the cancellation of debts in the seventh time) **11.** "'When all Israel gathers to appear before the Lord at the place He chooses, read this law audibly so they can hear it.'" **12.** "'Assemble the men, women, children, and nonnatives living among you so they may hear, learn to recognize and admire the Lord your God, and faithfully follow His instructions.'" (foreigner: an outsider or someone not native to the community) **13.** "'Educate it so their children, who haven't yet learned these laws, may come to know and venerate the Lord as long as you live in the land you'll enthrall across the Jordan.'" **14.** "The Lord said to Moses, 'The time of your death is near. Call Joshua and bring him to the roof of meeting so I can commission him.' So Moses and Joshua went to the roof of meeting." (inaugurate: to formally appoint or begin) **15.** "The Lord appeared in the roof as a pillar of pall, which remained at the entrance." (pillar: an altitudinous, perpendicular structure) **16.** "The Lord said to Moses, 'Soon you'll rest with your ancestors, but these people will turn down and worship the gods of foreign nations. They will leave Me and violate the covenant I made with them.'" **17.** "'My wrathfulness will burn against them, and I'll abandon them, hiding My presence from them. They will be consumed by disasters until they say, 'These disasters have happed because our God is no longer with us.'" (disasters: great mischances or disasters) **18.** "'On that day, I'll continue to hide My face because of all the wrong they've done by turning to other gods.'" **19.** "'Thus, write down this song and educate it to the Israelites. Make them study it so it serves as a evidence for Me against them.'" (evidence: substantiation or evidence of commodity) **20.** "'When I bring them into the land flowing with milk and honey, which I promised their ancestors, and when they're full and satisfied, they will turn to false gods, worship them, and break My covenant.'" **21.** "'When disasters overwhelm them, this song will swear against them because their descendants won't forget it. I formerly know their tendencies indeed now, before I bring them into the land I promised.'" (inclination: a natural tendency or prompt to act) **22.** "So Moses wrote the song that day and tutored it to the Israelites." **23.** "Also the Lord commissioned Joshua, son of Nun, saying, 'Be strong and valorous, for you'll lead the people of Israel into the land I promised them, and I'll be with you.'" **24.** "Once Moses completed writing down all the words of the law in a book," **25.** "he instructed the Levites, who carried the Ark of the Covenant of the Lord, saying," **26.** "'Take this Book of the Law and place it beside the Ark of the Covenant of the Lord your God, where it'll serve as a substantiation against you.'" **27.** "'For I know how rebellious and stubborn you are. If you have defied the Lord while I'm still alive, how much worse will it be after my death?'" (stiff-necked: stubborn and unintentional to change) **28.** "'Assemble the elders and officers of your lines so I can address them and call upon heaven and earth as substantiations against them,'" **29.** "'I'm certain that after my death, you'll come loose, turning down from the path I commanded you. In the future, disaster will come upon you because of the wrong you do, provoking the Lord to incense with your deeds.'" (provoke: to incite or arouse) **30.** "Moses recited the entire song audibly for all the people of Israel to hear."

Chapter 32
1. "Listen, O heavens, as I speak; Hear, O earth, the words I say." (Heavens: Sky, Earth: Land) **2.** "Let my teaching fall like rain, my words like dew, like showers on plants and grass." (Teaching: Instruction, Dew: Moisture) **3.** "For I declare the name of the Lord; give greatness to our God." (Declare: Proclaim, Greatness: Majesty) **4.** "He is the Rock, His work is perfect; all His ways are just. He is a God of faithfulness, without wrongdoing; He is righteous and upright." (Perfect: Flawless, Righteous: Just) **5.** "They have corrupted themselves; they are not His children, their flaws are clear. They are a twisted, perverse generation." (Corrupted: Spoiled, Perverse: Wicked) **6.** "Is this how you repay the Lord, you foolish people? Is He not your Father, who made and established you?" (Repay: Pay back, Foolish: Unwise) **7.** "Remember the days of old, consider many generations. Ask your father, and he will tell you; your elders, and they will explain:" (Elders: Wise leaders, Generations: Successive descendants) **8.** "When the Most High divided the inheritance for the nations, He set the boundaries according to Israel." (Most High: God, Inheritance: Heritage) **9.** "For the Lord's portion is His people; Jacob is His inheritance." (Portion: Share, Inheritance: Legacy) **10.** "He found him in a desolate land, a barren wilderness. He protected and instructed him, keeping him as the apple of His eye." (Desolate: Empty, Wilderness: Uninhabited) **11.** "Like an eagle stirring its nest, hovering over its young, lifting them on its wings," (Hovering: Floating, Pinions: Wings) **12.** "So the Lord alone led him, with no foreign god." (Led: Guided, Foreign: External) **13.** "He made him ride on the heights, to feast on the fields, giving honey from the rock and oil from the flinty rock;" (Heights: Elevated, Flinty: Hard) **14.** "curds, milk from the flock, lamb's fat, rams from Bashan, goats, the best wheat; and wine, the blood of grapes." (Curds: Cheese, Bashan: Fertile region) **15.** "But Jeshurun grew fat and rebellious; you grew thick and forsook God. You despised the Rock of your salvation." (Jeshurun: Israel, Forsook: Abandoned) **16.** "They provoked Him with foreign gods, angering Him with abominations." (Provoked: Annoyed, Abominations: Detestable things) **17.** "They sacrificed to demons, not to God, to new gods their fathers did not fear." (Sacrificed: Offered, Demons: Evil spirits) **18.** "You forgot the Rock who gave you birth and the God who formed you." (Forgotten: Ignored, Formed: Created) **19.** "When the Lord saw this, He was angered because of the provocation of His children." (Angered: Mad, Provocation: Irritation) **20.** "He said, 'I will hide My face from them, and see what will become of them. They are a perverse generation, children without faith.'" (Hide: Conceal, Perverse: Corrupt) **21.** "They made Me jealous with what is not a god; I will make them jealous with a foolish nation." (Jealous: Envious, Idols: False gods) **22.** "For a fire has ignited My anger, burning to the lowest pit. It will consume the earth, and set fire to the mountains." (Ignited: Set aflame, Consume: Destroy) **23.** "I will bring disasters and use My arrows against them." (Disasters: Calamities, Arrows: Missiles) **24.** "They will be wasted with hunger, devoured by plague and destruction. I will send wild animals, and serpents' poison." (Wasted: Depleted, Serpents: Snakes) **25.** "The sword will strike outside, and terror within. It will bring down the young man and the elderly." (Sword: Weapon, Terror: Fear) **26.** "I would have destroyed them and wiped out their memory," (Destroy: Annihilate, Memory: Recollection) **27.** "if I had not feared the enemy's provocation, lest they say, 'Our hand has prevailed; it wasn't the Lord.'" (Adversaries: Enemies, Misunderstand: Misinterpret) **28.** "They are a nation without wisdom, and no understanding in them." (Devoid: Lacking, Understanding: Knowledge) **29.** "If only they were wise, and would consider their final end!" (Wise: Knowledgeable, Final end: Ultimate fate) **30.** "How could one chase a thousand, and two put ten thousand to flight, unless their Rock had sold them, and the Lord had given them up?" (Chase: Pursue, Sold: Surrendered) **31.** "For their gemstone is n't like our gemstone; indeed their adversaries would admit this." **32.** "Their vine is from Sodom and Gomorrah; their grapes are bitter, filled with bane, and their clusters full of wickedness." (Sodom and Gomorrah: Metropolises known for sin; bitterness: Bane) **33.** "Their wine is the venom of serpents and the cruel bane of cobras." (Venom: Bane) **34.** "'Is not this stored up with Me, sealed among My treasures?' **35.** "Revenge belongs to Me, and recompense; their bases will slip at the right time. Their downfall is near, and what's coming will snappily catch them." (Recompense: Price or discipline) **36.** "'The Lord will judge His people and show mercy when their strength is gone, and no bone is left, whether free or enslaved.'" **37.** "He'll ask, 'Where are their gods, the gemstone they trusted? **38.** "Who ate the fat of their offerings and drank their drink immolations? Let them rise and help you.'" (Fat: Choice parts

of a immolation; drink immolations: Liquid immolations made to God) **39.** "'Look, I'm He, and there's no other God. I bring death and life; I wound and heal; no bone can escape My power.' **40.** "'I raise My hand to heaven and declare, "As surely as I live ever, **41.** "if I edge My brand and take hold of judgment, I'll bring revenge on My adversaries and repay those who detest Me. **42.** "My arrows will be drenched in blood, and My brand will devour meat, the blood of the taken and internees, from the heads of the leaders of the adversary.'" **43.** "'Rejoice, you Heathens, with His people, for He'll retaliate the blood of His retainers and bring revenge on His adversaries. He'll give atonement for His land and His people.'" (Atonement: Conciliation for sin) **44.** "So Moses, with Joshua the son of Nun, spoke all the words of this song before the people. **45.** "After Moses finished speaking to Israel, **46.** "he said, 'Give careful attention to all the words I swear to you moment. Command your children to observe all these words of the law. **47.** "This isn't an empty thing for you; it's your life, and by following it, you'll protract your days in the land you're about to enter and retain.'" **48.** "Later that same day, the Lord spoke to Moses, saying **49.** "'Go up to the mountain of Abarim, Mount Nebo, in the land of Moab, across from Jericho. Look at the land of Canaan, which I'm giving to the Israelites. **50.** "There, you'll die on the mountain and be gathered to your people, as your family Aaron failed on Mount Hor and was gathered to his people. **51.** "This will be because you defied Me at the waters of Meribah Kadesh in the Nature of Zin, when you didn't treat Me as holy before the Israelites. **52.** "You'll see the land before you, but won't enter it, the land I'm giving to the Israelites."

Chapter 33

1. This is the blessing Moses, the servant of God, gave to Israel before his death. (blessing: divine favor; servant: one who serves God) **2.** He said: "The Lord came from Sinai, Shone on them from Seir, Radiated from Mount Paran, And appeared with thousands of holy ones; From His right hand, He gave a fiery law to them." (radiated: emitted light; fiery law: powerful, holy law) **3.** He loves the people; All His holy ones are in Your care; They sit at Your feet; Every one receives Your teachings. (holy ones: saints, set apart for God; care: protection) **4.** Moses gave us the law, A possession for the congregation of Jacob. (congregation: gathering of people; possession: inheritance) **5.** He was King in Jeshurun when the leaders gathered, All the tribes of Israel together. (Jeshurun: poetic name for Israel; gathered: assembled) **6.** "Let Reuben live, and not perish, Nor let his people be few." (perish: die or be destroyed; few: small in number) **7.** He said of Judah: "Hear, Lord, the cry of Judah, Bring him to his people; Let his hands be enough for him, And may You be a defense against his foes." (foes: enemies; defense: protection) **8.** Concerning Levi, he said: "Let Your Thummim and Urim be with Your chosen one, Whom You tested at Massah, And with whom You contended at Meribah," (Thummim: sacred objects for casting lots; Urim: used with Thummim for divination) **9.** Who said of his parents, 'I have not recognized them'; Nor did he acknowledge his brothers, Or know his own children; For they obeyed Your word and covenant. (acknowledge: recognize; covenant: agreement) **10.** They shall teach Your decrees to Jacob, And Your law to Israel. They shall offer incense and a burnt offering on Your altar. (decrees: laws or orders; incense: substance burned for fragrance) **11.** Bless his possessions, Lord, And accept his work; Strike the loins of those who rise against him, And of those who hate him, that they rise not again." (loins: lower back; strike: hit) **12.** Of Benjamin, he said: "The beloved of the Lord shall dwell in safety, Who protects him all day long; And he shall rest on His shoulders." (beloved: dearly loved; safety: protection) **13.** Of Joseph, he said: "Blessed by the Lord is his land, With the best gifts of the heavens, with the dew, And deep waters below, (gifts: blessings; dew: moisture) **14.** With the best fruits of the sun, And the finest produce of the months, (fruits: crops; produce: yield) **15.** With the choicest gifts of the ancient mountains, With the most precious things of the eternal hills, (choicest: best; eternal: lasting forever) **16.** With the best of the earth and all it contains, And the favor of Him who appeared in the burning bush. Let the blessing fall on Joseph's head, And the crown of the one set apart from his brothers." (favor: blessing; burning bush: where God spoke to Moses) **17.** His majesty is like a firstborn bull, And his horns like the horns of a wild ox; With them, he will drive the nations To the ends of the earth; They are the ten thousand of Ephraim, And the thousands of Manasseh." (majesty: greatness; horns: authority) **18.** Of Zebulun, he said: "Rejoice, Zebulun, in your going out, And Issachar in your tents! (going out: ventures; tents: homes) **19.** They will call the people to the mountain; There they will offer sacrifices of righteousness; For they shall share in the abundance of the seas And treasures hidden in the sand." (sacrifices: offerings; abundance: plenty) **20.** And of Gad, he said: "Blessed is the one who enlarges Gad; He lives like a lion, And rends (tears) the arm and crown of his head. (enlarges: strengthens; rends: tears apart) **21.** He chose the best part for himself, As a lawgiver's portion was assigned there. He came with the leaders of the people; He administered the justice of the Lord, And His judgments with Israel." (lawgiver: one who enforces the law; judgments: decisions) **22.** And of Dan, he said: "Dan is like a lion's cub; He will leap from Bashan." (cub: young lion; leap: jump) **23.** And of Naphtali, he said: "O Naphtali, satisfied with favor, And full of the blessing of the Lord, Take possession of the west and the south." (satisfied: content; favor: blessing) **24.** And of Asher, he said: "Asher is the most blessed of sons; Let him be honored by his brothers, And let him dip his foot in oil. (honored: respected; oil: symbol of abundance) **25.** Your sandals shall be iron and bronze; As your days are, so shall your strength be." (iron: strong metal; bronze: metal alloy) **26.** "There is no one like the God of Jeshurun, Who rides the heavens to help you, And in His greatness on the clouds. (rides: moves across; greatness: majesty) **27.** The eternal God is your refuge, And beneath you are His everlasting arms; He will drive out your enemies before you, And will say, 'Destroy them!' (eternal: lasting forever; refuge: shelter) **28.** Then Israel will live in safety, The fountain of Jacob alone, In a land of grain and new wine; His heavens will also drop dew." (fountain: source; dew: moisture) **29.** Blessed are you, O Israel! Who is like you, a people saved by the Lord, The shield of your help And the sword of your majesty! Your enemies will submit to you, And you will trample down their high places." (shield: protector; trample: crush)

Chapter 34

1. "Also Moses went up from the plains of Moab to Mount Nebo, to the top of Pisgah, across from Jericho. The Lord showed him all the land of Gilead to Dan." (Gilead: A region east of the Jordan River, Dan: A megacity in northern Israel) **2.** "All Naphtali, Ephraim, Manasseh, and Judah to the Western Sea," (Western Sea: The Mediterranean Sea) **3.** "The South, and the plain of Jericho, the megacity of win trees, to Zoar." (Zoar: A small megacity near the Dead Sea) **4.** "Also the Lord said, 'This is the land I swore to give Abraham, Isaac, and Jacob, saying, "I'll give it to your descendants." You have seen it, but won't cross over.'" (Swore: Made a solemn pledge) **5.** "So Moses, the menial of the Lord, failed in Moab, as the Lord had said." (Menial: One who faithfully serves God's will) **6.** "The Lord buried him in a vale in Moab, contrary Beth Peor; his grave is unknown." (Beth Peor: A place near where Moses failed) **7.** "Moses was 120 times old when he failed. His eyes were clear, and his strength undiminished." (Vigor: Strength and energy) **8.** "The Israelites mourned Moses in Moab for thirty days. When the mourning ended, they moved on." (Mourning: Expressing grief or anguish) **9.** "Joshua, son of Nun, was filled with wisdom because Moses laid hands on him; the Israelites adhered him, following the Lord's commands as Moses had instructed." (Heeded: Paid attention to or followed) **10.** "Since also, no prophet like Moses has arisen, whom the Lord knew face to face," (Face to face: A direct relationship with God) **11.** "Performing signs and wonders the Lord transferred him to do in Egypt, before Pharaoh, his retainers, and in all his land," (Signs and prodigies: Miraculous acts or events) **12.** "With potent power and great terror ahead all Israel." (Potent power: Great strength, Terror: Fear or admiration).

6 – Joshua
Chapter 1
1. After Moses, the menial of the Lord, passed down, the Lord spoke to Joshua, son of Nun, who had been his assistant, saying (assistant; helper) **2.**"Moses, My menial, has failed. Now, rise up and lead these people across the Jordan River into the land that I'm giving them — the land promised to the Israelites. (Rise up; stand up, promised; pledged) **3.** Wherever your bases walk, I've given it to you, just as I promised Moses. (Walk step upon) **4.** Your boundaries will stretch from the nature to the north, from Lebanon, all the way to the great swash Euphrates, and to the Mediterranean Sea in the west. (Boundaries borders; Euphrates swash) **5.** No bone will be suitable to repel you as long as you live. Just as I was with Moses, I'll also be with you. I'll no way abandon or leave you (oppose; abandon leave before) **6.** Be firm and valorous, for you'll be the one to distribute this land as an heritage to the people, fulfilling the pledge I made to their ancestors (establishment, strong; heritage property passed down) **7.** Only be veritably strong and bent, and precisely observe all that Moses instructed you. Don't transgress from it, so that you may succeed in everything you do.(Resolute determined; slapdash diverge) **8.** This Book of the Law shouldn't leave your mouth. Reflect on it day and night, so that you may live according to everything written in it also your trip will be prosperous, and you'll achieve your pretensions. (Reflect meditate; prosperous successful; achieve reach) **9.** Have I not commanded you to be strong and valorous? Don't sweat or be demoralized, because the Lord your God is with you wherever you go (demoralized; discouraged) **10.** Joshua also instructed the leaders of the people, saying, (Instructed; directed) **11.**" Go through the camp and tell everyone to prepare their inventories. In three days, you'll cross the Jordan River to take possession of the land that the Lord is giving you" (inventories; vittles) **12.** Also Joshua addressed the Reubenites, the Gadites, and half the lineage of Manasseh, saying, (Reubenites, Gadites, Manasseh lines of Israel) **13.**" Flash back the pledge Moses, the menial of the Lord, made to you, that the Lord your God will give you with rest and this land (Promise; assurance) **14.** Your women, children, and beast will stay in the land Moses gave you, but all your soldiers must cross the Jordan, fortified, to help your fellow Israelites (soldiers dogfaces; fellow other) **15.** You'll continue to help your sisters until the Lord grants them rest, just as He gave you also you may return to your own land and enjoy the heritage Moses gave you on the east side of the Jordan" (subventions gives; heritage property) **16.** The people replied to Joshua," We'll follow your commands and go wherever you shoot us (Follow observe) **17.** Just as we adhered Moses, we will also observe you. May the Lord your God be with you, as He was with Moses"(Adhered; followed) **18.** Anyone who refuses to hear to your orders or disobeys your commands will be put to death. Be strong and valorous" (Refuses; declines).

Chapter 2
1. Joshua, son of Nun, secretly sent two men from the Acacia Grove to scout out the land of Canaan. He told them, "Go and explore the land, especially the city of Jericho." The two men set out and arrived at the home of Rahab, a woman who worked as a prostitute, and they stayed there. (Scout; survey, worked as: was employed as) **2.** Word spread quickly to the king of Jericho, who heard, "Some men from Israel have come here tonight to secretly investigate the land." (Spread quickly: was quickly reported; investigate: examine) **3.** The king of Jericho immediately sent a message to Rahab, demanding, "Bring the men who entered your house, for they have come to search out the land." (Demanding: requesting strongly; search out: spy on) **4.** But Rahab had hidden the men. She replied, "Yes, the men did come to me, but I don't know where they are from. (Hidden: concealed) **5.** They left before the city gate closed, and I don't know where they went. If you hurry, you may catch up with them." (Hurry: go quickly) **6.** (In truth, she had taken them up to her roof and hidden them under bundles of flax that were laid out there.) (Bundes: tied groups) **7.** The king's men pursued them, following the road to the Jordan River, looking for them at the fords. After the pursuers left, the city gate was shut tight. (Pursuers: chasers; fords: shallow crossings) **8.** Before the two men rested, Rahab went up to the roof and spoke to them. (Rested: laid down) **9.** She said, "I know that the Lord has given you this land. We are terrified of you, and everyone in the land is overwhelmed by fear because of you. (Terrified: frightened; overwhelmed: shaken) **10.** We've heard how the Lord dried up the waters of the Red Sea before you when you came out of Egypt. We also know what you did to the two kings of the Amorites, Sihon and Og, whom you completely destroyed. (Dried up: parted; completely destroyed: utterly defeated) **11.** When we heard these things, our hearts sank, and no one has the courage to face you, for we know that the Lord, your God, is the true God in heaven above and on earth below. (Sank: melted; true: only; courage: bravery) **12.** Now, please swear to me by the Lord that, since I've shown you kindness, you will show kindness to my family and give me a sign of your promise. (Swear: vow; kindness: favor) **13.** Spare the lives of my father, mother, brothers, sisters, and everyone in my household, and protect us from death." (Spare: save; protect: shield) **14.** The men answered her, "If you keep our mission a secret, then we will protect you when the Lord gives us the land. Your life for ours." (Keep: hide; protect: save) **15.** She lowered them from the window by a rope, since her house was built into the city wall, and she lived in the wall itself. (Lowered: let down) **16.** Rahab told the men, "Go to the mountains so that the pursuers won't find you. Hide there for three days until the chasers have returned. After that, you can leave safely." (Mountains: hills) **17.** The men replied, "We will be free of responsibility for this oath you made us swear, (Responsibility: blame) **18.** unless, when we return to take the land, you tie a scarlet cord in the window through which you let us down. Then, bring your father, mother, brothers, and all your family into your home. (Scarlet cord: red rope) **19.** Anyone who goes outside your house will be responsible for their own death, but anyone inside with you will be safe, and we will protect them. If anyone harms them, the blame will be on us. (Responsible: liable; protect: defend; harm: injure) **20.** If you tell anyone about this plan, then we are free from the promise you made to us." (Promise: oath) **21.** Rahab answered, "Let it be as you have said." She sent them away, and they left. She tied the scarlet cord in the window as they had instructed. (Tied: fastened) **22.** The two men went into the mountains and stayed there for three days, waiting until the pursuers returned. They searched for them along the way but could not find them. (Waiting: resting) **23.** After three days, the men descended from the mountains, crossed over, and went back to Joshua, son of Nun. They told him everything that had happened. (Descended: came down; crossed over: passed) **24.** They said to Joshua, "The Lord has truly delivered the entire land into our hands. Everyone in the land is trembling with fear because of us." (Delivered: given; trembling: afraid)

Chapter 3
1. Early in the morning, Joshua and the entire community of Israel broke camp and left Acacia Grove. They traveled to the Jordan River, where they set up camp, staying there before crossing over. (Broke camp: packed up and left; Set up camp: made camp) **2.** Three days later, the leaders of Israel went through the camp and began to give instructions to the people. (Leaders: officers; Instructions: commands) **3.** They told everyone, "When you see the ark of the covenant, carried by the priests who are Levites, get ready to move. Follow it closely, (Ark of the covenant: sacred chest; Levites: priestly tribe) **4.** but make sure you keep a distance of about two thousand cubits between you and the ark. Don't approach it, so that you will know the way to go, because you haven't traveled this road before."

(Cubits: ancient unit of length) **5.** Joshua then instructed the people, "Purify yourselves, for tomorrow the Lord will perform great miracles among you." (Purify: sanctify; Miracles: wonders) **6.** Joshua spoke to the priests, saying, "Take up the ark of the covenant and lead the way before the people." The priests picked up the ark and moved ahead of the Israelites. (Lead the way: go ahead) **7.** The Lord then spoke to Joshua, saying, "Today I will begin to lift you up in front of all Israel, so they will know that just as I was with Moses, I will also be with you." (Lift you up: exalt; In front of: before) **8.** "Instruct the priests who carry the ark: 'When you reach the edge of the Jordan River, stand in the water.'" (Instruct: command) **9.** Joshua called the people together and said, "Listen to the words of the Lord your God." (Called: gathered) **10.** He continued, "This is how you will know that the living God is in your midst. He will certainly drive out the Canaanites, Hittites, Hivites, Perizzites, Girgashites, Amorites, and Jebusites before you (Living God: true and active God) **11.** The ark of the covenant of the Lord, who rules over all the earth, is going ahead of you into the Jordan" (Rules over all the earth: sovereign ruler) **12.** Now, select twelve men, one from each tribe of Israel. (Select: choose) **13.** When the priests carrying the ark of the Lord—the ruler of the earth—step into the waters of the Jordan, the waters flowing from upstream will stop, and the river will be cut off, forming a heap of water." (Cut off: halted) **14.** As soon as the people left their camp to cross the river, the priests who were carrying the ark led the way. (Left: departed; Led the way: went first) **15.** When the priests stepped into the water at the edge of the Jordan River, and the waters were still high due to the harvest season, (Still high: overflowing) **16.** the waters from upstream stopped and piled up far away, near the town of Adam, close to Zaretan. The water that flowed into the Dead Sea was completely cut off, and the people crossed over directly opposite Jericho. (Piled up: gathered; Dead Sea: Salt Sea) **17.** The priests carrying the ark of the Lord stood firm on dry ground in the middle of the river, while all the people of Israel crossed over on dry land until everyone had passed through (Stood firm: remained still).

Chapter 4
1. After all the Israelites had successfully crossed the Jordan River, the Lord spoke to Joshua, saying, (Successfully crossed: completely crossed over) **2.** "Select twelve men from among the people, one from each tribe, (Select: choose) **3.** and give them these instructions: 'Go to the riverbed and gather twelve stones from the place where the priests stood firm, right in the middle of the Jordan. Carry these stones with you and place them at your camp tonight.'" (Instructions: orders; Riverbed: dry ground where the river was) **4.** Joshua called the twelve men he had chosen from the tribes of Israel, one from each tribe, (Chosen: selected) **5.** and he said to them, "Go ahead of the ark of the Lord your God and walk into the middle of the Jordan. Each of you is to pick up a stone and carry it on your shoulder, one for each tribe of Israel. (Ahead of: before) **6.** These stones will serve as a reminder for you. When future generations ask, 'What is the meaning of these stones?' **7.** You will tell them, 'The river was stopped in front of the ark of the Lord's covenant, and when it crossed the Jordan, the waters parted. These stones will always stand as a memorial for Israel.'" (Memorial: permanent reminder) **8.** The Israelites followed Joshua's commands exactly. They took twelve stones from the Jordan and brought them to their camp, placing them there as instructed. (Followed: obeyed) **9.** Joshua also placed twelve stones in the middle of the Jordan, where the priests who carried the ark had stood. To this day, they remain in that spot. (Placed: set up; Remain: stay) **10.** The priests who carried the ark remained standing in the middle of the Jordan until everything was done as the Lord had commanded Joshua. The people quickly crossed over, as the Lord had instructed. (Quickly: hastily) **11.** Once all the people had crossed, the ark and the priests also crossed before the people. (Before: in front of) **12.** The tribes of Reuben, Gad, and half of Manasseh crossed over, fully armed, leading the way for the rest of Israel, just as Moses had ordered. (Fully armed: prepared for battle) **13.** About forty thousand soldiers, ready for battle, crossed over ahead of the others and made their way toward the plains near Jericho. (Soldiers: warriors) **14.** On that day, the Lord elevated Joshua's status in the eyes of all Israel. They held him in reverence and respected him as they had Moses throughout his lifetime. (Elevated: honored; Reverence: fear) **15.** Then the Lord instructed Joshua, saying, (Instructed: commanded) **16.** "Tell the priests who carry the ark of the covenant to come up from the Jordan." (Come up: ascend) **17.** Joshua gave the command, and the priests who had been standing in the middle of the Jordan stepped out. (Stepped out: emerged) **18.** As soon as the priests' feet touched dry ground, the waters of the Jordan returned to their place, flooding the banks as they had before. (Flooding: overflowing) **19.** On the tenth day of the first month, the people crossed over from the Jordan and camped at Gilgal, on the east side of Jericho. (Crossed over: passed over) **20.** Joshua set up the twelve stones taken from the Jordan at Gilgal, creating a lasting monument. (Monument: permanent reminder) **21.** He then spoke to the Israelites, saying, "When your children ask in the future, 'What are these stones?' (Spoke: addressed) **22.** You will tell them, 'Israel crossed the Jordan on dry land.' (Crossed: passed through) **23.** For the Lord your God dried up the waters of the Jordan before you, just as He did with the Red Sea, and we crossed over on dry ground. (Dried up: stopped) **24.** This is so that all the nations of the earth may know that the Lord's power is unmatched, and that you will always revere the Lord your God." (Unmatched: mighty)

Chapter 5
1. When the kings of the Amorites, who lived on the west side of the Jordan, and the kings of the Canaanites, who were near the coast, heard that the Lord had miraculously stopped the flow of the Jordan River for the Israelites to cross, their hearts sank. They lost all courage and resolve because of the Israelites. (Miraculously: by God's intervention; Sank: collapsed) **2.** At that time, the Lord spoke to Joshua and instructed him, "Make flint knives for yourself, and have the Israelites undergo circumcision again." (Instructed: told) **3.** So, Joshua crafted the flint knives, and performed the circumcision on the Israelites at a place called Gibeath-Haaraloth, meaning "the hill of the foreskins." (Crafted: made) **4.** The reason Joshua circumcised them was because all the men who had left Egypt, who were of military age, had died during their journey in the wilderness. (Military age: able-bodied men of fighting age) **5.** Although the Israelites who left Egypt had been circumcised, all the children born in the wilderness on the journey had not been circumcised. (Born: those born in the wilderness) **6.** For forty years, the Israelites wandered in the wilderness until all the men who had been part of the military, those who had come out of Egypt, passed away. This was because they had not obeyed the Lord's command. The Lord had sworn not to allow them to enter the promised land, the land He had promised to their ancestors, a land flowing with milk and honey. (Wandered: traveled aimlessly) **7.** Now, Joshua circumcised the sons of the men who had died in the wilderness. These new men had not been circumcised because their fathers had not circumcised them on the journey. (Sons: descendants) **8.** Once the circumcision was completed, the Israelites remained camped in place until they recovered. (Completed: finished; Recovered: healed) **9.** The Lord then spoke to Joshua and said, "Today, I have removed the disgrace of Egypt from you." Therefore, the place was named Gilgal, and it has been called that ever since. (Removed: taken away; Disgrace: shame) **10.** The Israelites camped at Gilgal and observed the Passover on the evening of the fourteenth day of the first month, on the plains near Jericho. **11.** The day after the Passover, they ate from the produce of the land, unleavened bread and roasted grain, on the very same day. (Produce: crops) **12.** The manna that had sustained them in the wilderness ceased the very day they ate from the crops of Canaan. From that point on, they ate the produce of the land of

Canaan for the rest of that year. (Sustained: nourished) **13.** While Joshua was near Jericho, he lifted his eyes and saw a man standing before him, holding a drawn sword. Joshua approached him and asked, "Are you with us, or are you with our enemies?" (Approached: went toward) **14.** The man replied, "Neither! But I am the commander of the army of the Lord, and I have come now." At this, Joshua fell on his face to the ground and worshiped him. He asked, "What message does my Lord have for His servant?" (Worshiped: bowed in reverence) **15.** The commander of the Lord's army said to Joshua, "Take off your sandals, for the place where you are standing is holy." And Joshua obeyed. (Obeyed: complied)

Chapter 6

1. Jericho was completely shut off from the Israelites. No one came in, and no one went out because the city was on high alert. (Shut off: closed or sealed) **2.** Then the Lord spoke to Joshua: "Look! I have handed Jericho, its king, and its mighty warriors over to you." (Handed over: given) **3.** You will march around the city with all your armed men. You will circle the city once each day for six days. (March around: move around) **4.** Seven priests will carry seven ram's horn trumpets ahead of the ark. On the seventh day, you will march around the city seven times, and the priests will blow the trumpets. (Carry: hold; Blow: play) **5.** When the long blast of the ram's horn sounds and you hear the trumpet, all the people will shout with a loud voice. The walls of the city will collapse, and the people will rush in straight ahead, each man going directly before him." (Collapse: fall down) **6.** So Joshua, son of Nun, called the priests together and instructed them, "Take up the ark of the covenant and let seven priests carry the seven ram's horn trumpets before it." (Instructed: told) **7.** He also told the people, "Advance and march around the city. Let those who are armed go first, ahead of the ark of the Lord." (Advance: move forward) **8.** When Joshua gave the command, the seven priests carrying the seven ram's horn trumpets moved forward, blowing the horns as the ark of the covenant followed. (Moved forward: began moving) **9.** The armed guards walked in front of the priests, and the rear guard followed the ark, while the priests kept blowing the trumpets. (Guards: soldiers; Rear guard: last group) **10.** Joshua had ordered the people, "Do not shout or make any noise. No one is to speak a word until I tell you to shout. Then you will shout." (Ordered: commanded) **11.** So the ark of the Lord circled the city, going around it once, and then they returned to camp and spent the night there. (Circled: moved around) **12.** The next morning, Joshua got up early, and the priests took the ark of the Lord. (Got up early: woke up at dawn) **13.** The seven priests with their trumpets led the procession, continuing to blow the horns as they moved forward. The armed soldiers went before them, and the rear guard followed the ark, with the priests blowing the trumpets the whole time. (Continuing: kept on) **14.** On the second day, they marched around the city once and returned to camp. They did this for six days. (Marched around: walked around) **15.** But on the seventh day, they rose at dawn and marched around the city seven times in the same manner. On that day alone, they circled the city seven times. (Rose at dawn: woke up early) **16.** The seventh time, as the priests blew the trumpets, Joshua ordered the people, "Shout! For the Lord has given you the city!" (Ordered: commanded) **17.** "The city and everything in it is devoted to the Lord for destruction, except for Rahab the prostitute, and all who are with her in her house, because she hid the messengers we sent." (Devoted to the Lord: dedicated for God's purpose) **18.** But be sure to avoid the accursed things, or you will bring destruction on yourselves. If you take any of the things devoted to destruction, you will make the camp of Israel accursed and bring trouble upon it. (Accursed things: things under God's ban; Destruction: ruin) **19.** All the silver, gold, and vessels made of bronze and iron are sacred to the Lord. They must be placed in the Lord's treasury." (Sacred: consecrated) **20.** When the people heard the trumpets and shouted, the walls of Jericho collapsed. The Israelites then surged into the city, each man advancing straight ahead, and they captured the city. (Collapsed: fell down) **21.** They utterly destroyed everything in the city: men, women, young, old, cattle, sheep, and donkeys—all were put to the sword. (Utterly destroyed: completely destroyed) **22.** However, Joshua had told the two men who had spied out the land, "Go into the prostitute's house and bring out the woman and all her family, just as you promised her." (Spy out: secretly observe) **23.** The two men who had been spies went in and brought out Rahab, her father, mother, brothers, and all her family. They brought them outside the camp of Israel. (Outside the camp: away from the camp) **24.** Then they burned the entire city, including everything in it. But they kept the silver, gold, and the bronze and iron vessels, which they put into the treasury of the Lord's house. (Burned: destroyed by fire) **25.** Joshua spared Rahab the prostitute, her family, and everything she owned, and they lived among the Israelites to this day, because she had hidden the messengers Joshua had sent to spy out Jericho. (Spared: saved) **26.** At that time, Joshua pronounced a curse, saying, "Cursed be anyone who attempts to rebuild the city of Jericho. He will lay its foundations at the cost of his firstborn, and he will set up its gates at the cost of his youngest." (Pronounced: declared) **27.** So the Lord was with Joshua, and his fame spread throughout the entire land. (Spread: became known)

Chapter 7

1. But the Israelites violated the command regarding the devoted things, for Achan, the son of Carmi, from the tribe of Judah, took some of the things devoted to destruction. This act angered the Lord, and His wrath burned against Israel. (Violated: broke; Devoted things: things set apart for destruction) **2.** Joshua then sent men from Jericho to Ai, located near Beth Aven, east of Bethel, to scout out the land. He instructed them, "Go up and assess the situation in Ai." (Scout out: explore) **3.** The men returned to Joshua and reported, "There is no need for the entire army to go up. Let about two or three thousand men attack Ai. The people there are few, and it will not be a difficult battle." (Reported: told) **4.** So about three thousand soldiers went up, but they were quickly defeated and fled before the men of Ai. (Quickly defeated: easily beaten) **5.** The men of Ai killed about thirty-six Israelites, chasing them from the city gate to the stone quarries, and striking them down on the descent. This caused the hearts of the Israelites to melt in fear, and they became like water. (Melted: were filled with fear) **6.** Then Joshua tore his clothes, fell to the ground before the ark of the Lord, and remained there until evening. The elders of Israel joined him, and they sprinkled dust on their heads in mourning. (Sprinkled dust: showed sorrow) **7.** Joshua cried out, "Alas, Lord God, why did You bring us across the Jordan to deliver us into the hands of the Amorites to destroy us? Would it have been better for us to remain on the other side of the Jordan? (Cried out: lamented) **8.** O Lord, what will I say now that Israel has turned its back to its enemies? **9.** The Canaanites and all the people of the land will hear of this and surround us. They will wipe us out, and Your name will be dishonored." (Honored: respected) **10.** But the Lord replied to Joshua, "Get up! Why are you lying on your face? **11.** Israel has sinned. They have violated My covenant by taking some of the things that were set apart for destruction. They have stolen, lied, and hidden these things among their possessions. (Violated: broken; Set apart: dedicated for destruction) **12.** Because of this, the Israelites cannot stand before their enemies. They will turn and flee unless they remove the cursed things from among them. **13.** Get up, consecrate the people, and tell them, 'Consecrate yourselves for tomorrow. The Lord, the God of Israel, says, "There is an accursed thing in your midst. You cannot stand before your enemies until you deal with it." (Consecrate: purify) **14.** Tomorrow, you will approach the Lord by tribes. The tribe the Lord selects will come forward by families, and the family the Lord chooses will come forward by households, and the household the Lord chooses will come forward man by man. **15.** The man who has taken the accursed thing will be burned with fire, along with everything he owns, because he has broken My covenant and done a disgraceful thing in Israel.'" (Accursed thing: stolen goods; Burned with fire: utterly destroyed) **16.** So Joshua got up early the next morning and brought Israel before their tribes. The tribe of Judah was selected. **17.** Joshua then brought forward the clan of Judah, and the Zerahite family was chosen. Next, the family of the Zerahites was brought forward, and Zabdi was selected. **18.** Finally, Joshua brought forward Zabdi's household, and Achan, son of Carmi, son of Zabdi, son of Zerah, from the tribe of Judah, was selected. (Selected: chosen) **19.** Joshua said to Achan, "My son, give glory to the Lord, the God of Israel, and make confession to Him. Tell me what you have done; do not hide it from me." (Make confession: admit what you did) **20.** Achan replied to Joshua, "Indeed, I have sinned against the Lord, the God of Israel. Here is what I did: **21.** When I saw among the spoils a beautiful Babylonian garment, two hundred shekels of silver, and a wedge of gold weighing fifty shekels, I coveted them and took them. They are hidden in the ground inside my tent, with the silver beneath them." (Coveted: desired) **22.** So Joshua sent messengers to Achan's tent. They found the stolen items buried there, with the silver hidden under the garments. **23.** They took the items from his tent, brought them to Joshua, and displayed them before the Lord and all Israel. (Displayed: laid out) **24.** Joshua, along with all Israel, took Achan, his family, his livestock, his tent, and everything he had, and brought them to the Valley of Achor. **25.** Joshua said to Achan, "Why have you caused trouble for us? Today the Lord will bring trouble upon you." Then all Israel stoned Achan with stones, and they burned his body and possessions with fire. (Caused trouble: brought disaster) **26.** They raised a large pile of stones over Achan, which remains there to this day. Then the Lord's anger turned away. Therefore, that place was called the Valley of Achor, which means "Valley of Trouble," to this day. (Pile of stones: heap; Turned away: ceased)

Chapter 8

1. And the LORD said unto Joshua, Fear not, neither be thou dismayed: take all the people of war with thee, and arise, go up to Ai: see, I have given into thy hand the king of Ai, and his people, and his city, and his land: (dismayed: discouraged) **2.** And thou shalt do to Ai and her king as thou didst unto Jericho and her king: only the spoil thereof, and the cattle thereof, shall ye take for a prey unto yourselves: lay thee an ambush for the city behind it (spoil: loot, prey: plunder, ambush: trap) **3.** So Joshua arose, and all the people of war, to go up against Ai: and Joshua chose out thirty thousand mighty men of valour, and sent them away by night. (valour: bravery) **4.** And he commanded them, saying, Behold, ye shall lie in wait against the city, even behind the city: go not very far from the city, but be ye already: (lie in wait: hide, ready: prepared) **5.** And I, and all the people that are with me, will approach unto the city: and it shall come to pass, when they come out against us, as at the first, that we will flee before them, (come out: attack) **6.** For they will come out after us till we have drawn them from the city; for they will say, They flee before us, as at the first: therefore we will flee before them (drawn: lured) **7.** Then ye shall rise up from the ambush, and seize upon the city: for the LORD your God will deliver it into your hand (seize: capture, ambush: hidden position) **8.** And it shall be, when ye have taken the city, that ye shall set the city on fire: according to the commandment of the LORD shall ye do. See, I have commanded you (commandment: instruction) **9.** Joshua therefore sent them forth: and they went to lie in ambush, and abode between Bethel and Ai, on the west side of Ai: but Joshua lodged that night among the people (abode: stayed, lodged: rested) **10.** And Joshua rose up early in the morning, and numbered the people, and went up, he and the elders of Israel, before the people to Ai (numbered: counted) **11.** And all the people, even the people of war that were with him, went up, and drew nigh, and came before the city, and pitched on the north side of Ai: now there was a valley between them and Ai (drew nigh: approached, pitched: set up camp) **12.** And he took about five thousand men, and set them to lie in ambush between Bethel and Ai, on the west side of the city (set: placed) **13.** And when they had set the people, even all the host that was on the north of the city, and their liers in wait on the west of the city, Joshua went that night into the midst of the valley (host: army, liers in wait: ambushers, midst: center) **14.** And it came to pass, when the king of Ai saw it, that they hasted and rose up early, and the men of the city went out against Israel to battle, he and all his people, at a time appointed, before the plain; but he wist not that there were liers in ambush against him behind the city (hasted: hurried, wist: knew, appointed: set, plain: flat area) **15.** And Joshua and all Israel made as if they were beaten before them, and fled by the way of the wilderness (made as if: pretended, wilderness: desert) **16.** And all the people that were in Ai were called together to pursue after them: and they pursued after Joshua, and were drawn away from the city (pursued: chased, drawn away: led away) **17.** And there was not a man left in Ai or Bethel, that went not out after Israel: and they left the city open, and pursued after Israel (left: remained, open: undefended) **18.** And the LORD said unto Joshua, Stretch out the spear that is in thy hand toward Ai; for I will give it into thine hand. And Joshua stretched out the spear that he had in his hand toward the city (stretch out: raise) **19.** And the ambush arose quickly out of their place, and they ran as soon as he had stretched out his hand: and they entered into the city, and took it, and hasted and set the city on fire (ambush: hidden attackers, hasted: hurried) **20.** And when the men of Ai looked behind them, they saw, and, behold, the smoke of the city ascended up to heaven, and they had no power to flee this way or that way: and the people that fled to the wilderness turned back upon the pursuers (ascended: rose, turned back: returned) **21.** And when Joshua and all Israel saw that the ambush had taken the city, and that the smoke of the city ascended, then they turned again, and slew the men of Ai (slew: killed) **22.** And the other issued out of the city against them; so they were in the midst of Israel, some on this side, and some on that side: and they smote them, so that they let none of them remain or escape (issued: came out, smote: struck, remain: survive) **23.** And the king of Ai they took alive, and brought him to Joshua (took: captured) **24.** And it came to pass, when Israel had made an end of slaying all the inhabitants of Ai in the field, in the wilderness wherein they chased them, and when they were all fallen on the edge of the sword, until they were consumed, that all the Israelites returned unto Ai, and smote it with the edge of the sword (slaying: killing, fallen: killed, edge of the sword: sword strike) **25.** And so it was, that all that fell that day, both of men and women, were twelve thousand, even all the men of Ai (fell: died) **26.** For Joshua drew not his hand back, wherewith he stretched out the spear, until he had utterly destroyed all the inhabitants of Ai (drew back: withdrew) **27.** Only the cattle and the spoil of that city Israel took for a prey unto themselves, according unto the word of the LORD which he commanded Joshua (spoil: loot, prey: plunder) **28.** And Joshua burnt Ai, and made it a heap forever, even a desolation unto this day (burnt: set on fire, heap: mound, desolation: ruin) **29.** And the king of Ai he hanged on a tree until eventide: and as soon as the sun was down, Joshua commanded that they should take his carcass down from the tree, and cast it at the entering of the gate of the city, and raise thereon a great heap of stones, that remaineth unto this day (hanged: executed, carcass: body, eventide: evening) **30.** Then Joshua built an altar unto the LORD God of Israel in mount Ebal, (altar: place of sacrifice, mount: mountain) **31.** As Moses the servant of the LORD commanded the children of Israel, as it is written in the book of the law of Moses, an altar of whole stones, over which no man hath lift up any iron: and they offered thereon burnt offerings unto the LORD, and sacrificed peace offerings (whole: uncut, burnt offerings: sacrifices by fire, peace offerings: sacrifices of thanksgiving) **32.** And he wrote there upon the stones a copy of the law of Moses, which he wrote in the presence of the children of Israel (copy: replica) **33.** And all Israel, and their elders, and officers, and their judges, stood on this side the ark and on that side before the priests the Levites, which bare the ark of the covenant of the LORD, as well the stranger, as he that was born among them; half of them over against mount Gerizim, and half of them over against mount Ebal; as Moses the servant of the LORD had commanded before, that they should bless the people of Israel (bare: carried, stranger: foreigner) **34.** And afterward he read all the words of the law, the blessings and cursings, according to all that is written in the book of the law (cursings: curses) **35.** There was not a word of all that Moses commanded, which Joshua read not before all the congregation of Israel, with the women, and the little ones, and the strangers that were conversant among them (congregation: assembly, conversant: living among).

Chapter 9
1. And it came to pass, when all the kings which were on this side Jordan, in the hills, and in the valleys, and in all the coasts of the great sea over against Lebanon, the Hittite, and the Amorite, the Canaanite, the Perizzite, the Hivite, and the Jebusite, heard thereof; (coasts: borders, over against: opposite) **2.** That they gathered themselves together, to fight with Joshua and with Israel, with one accord (accord: agreement) **3.** And when the inhabitants of Gibeon heard what Joshua had done unto Jericho and to Ai, (inhabitants: people living in) **4.** They did work wilily, and went and made as if they had been ambassadors, and took old sacks upon their asses, and wine bottles, old, and rent, and bound up; (wilily: deceitfully, ambassadors: representatives, asses: donkeys, rent: torn, bound up: tied) **5.** And old shoes and clouted upon their feet, and old garments upon them; and all the bread of their provision was dry and mouldy (clouted: patched, provision: supplies, mouldy: decayed) **6.** And they went to Joshua unto the camp at Gilgal, and said unto him, and to the men of Israel, We be come from a far country: now therefore make ye a league with us (league: agreement, treaty) **7.** And the men of Israel said unto the Hivites, Peradventure ye dwell among us; and how shall we make a league with you? (peradventure: perhaps, dwell: live) **8.** And they said unto Joshua, We are thy servants. And Joshua said unto them, Who are ye? and from whence come ye? (servants: subjects, whence: where) **9.** And they said unto him, From a very far country thy servants are come because of the name of the LORD thy God: for we have heard the fame of him, and all that he did in Egypt, (fame: reputation) **10.** And all that he did to the two kings of the Amorites, that were beyond Jordan, to Sihon king of Heshbon, and to Og king of Bashan, which was at Ashtaroth (beyond: on the other side of, kings: rulers) **11.** Wherefore our elders and all the inhabitants of our country spake to us, saying, Take victuals with you for the journey, and go to meet them, and say unto them, We are your servants: therefore now make ye a league with us (elders: leaders, victuals: food) **12.** This our bread we took hot for our provision out of our houses on the day we came forth to go unto you; but now, behold, it is dry, and it is mouldy: (mouldy: spoiled) **13.** And these bottles of wine, which we filled, were new; and, behold, they be rent: and these our garments and our shoes are become old by reason of the very long journey (bottles: containers, rent: torn, reason of: because of) **14.** And the men took of their victuals, and asked not counsel at the mouth of the LORD (counsel: guidance) **15.** And Joshua made peace with them, and made a league with them, to let them live: and the princes of the congregation sware unto them (made peace: formed an agreement, sware: promised) **16.** And it came to pass at the end of three days after they had made a league with them, that they heard that they were their neighbours, and that they dwelt among them (neighbours: nearby people, dwelt: lived) **17.** And the children of Israel journeyed, and came unto their cities on the third day. Now their cities were Gibeon, and Chephirah, and Beeroth, and Kirjath-jearim (journeyed: traveled) **18.** And the children of Israel smote them not, because the princes of the congregation had sworn unto them by the LORD God of Israel. And all the congregation murmured against the princes (smote: struck, murmured: complained) **19.** But all the princes said unto all the congregation, We have sworn unto them by the LORD of Israel: now therefore we may not touch them (sworn: pledged, touch: harm) **20.** This we will do to them; we will even let them live, lest wrath be upon us, because of the oath which we sware unto them (wrath: anger, lest: in case) **21.** And the princes said unto them, Let them live; but let them be hewers of wood and drawers of water unto all the congregation; as the princes had promised them (hewers: cutters, drawers: carriers) **22.** And Joshua called for them, and he spake unto them, saying, Wherefore have ye beguiled us, saying, We are very far from you; when ye dwell among us? (beguiled: deceived, dwell: live) **23.** Now therefore ye are cursed, and there shall none of you be freed from being bondmen, and hewers of wood and drawers of water for the house of my God (cursed: doomed, bondmen: slaves) **24.** And they answered Joshua, and said, Because it was certainly told thy servants, how that the LORD thy God commanded his servant Moses to give you all the land, and to destroy all the inhabitants of the land from before you, therefore we were sore afraid of our lives because of you, and have done this thing (certainly: assuredly, sore: greatly, inhabitants: people living in) **25.** And now, behold, we are in thine hand: as it seemeth good and right unto thee to do unto us, do (seemeth: seems) **26.** And so did he unto them, and delivered them out of the hand of the children of Israel, that they slew them not (slew: killed) **27.** And Joshua made them that day hewers of wood and drawers of water for the congregation, and for the altar of the LORD, even unto this day, in the place which he should choose (hewers: cutters, drawers: carriers).

Chapter 10
1. When Adoni-zedek, the king of Jerusalem, heard that Joshua had conquered Ai and completely destroyed it, just as he had done with Jericho and its king, and how the people of Gibeon had made peace with Israel and joined them, (completely destroyed: wiped out, joined them: became their allies) **2.** he was terrified, because Gibeon was a large city, comparable to a royal city, and its warriors were strong and mighty. (royal city: a city with significant power or importance, mighty: powerful) **3.** So, Adoni-zedek sent a message to Hoham, king of Hebron, Piram, king of Jarmuth, Japhia, king of Lachish, and Debir, king of Eglon, saying, (sent a message: called upon) **4.** "Come and help me attack Gibeon, for it has made a treaty with Joshua and the Israelites." (attack: strike, treaty: agreement) **5.** Thus, the five kings of the Amorites—kings of Jerusalem, Hebron, Jarmuth, Lachish, and Eglon—gathered their armies and went to besiege Gibeon. (besiege: surround and try to capture) **6.** The people of Gibeon sent word to Joshua at the camp in Gilgal, pleading, "Do not abandon us; come quickly and rescue us. All the kings of the Amorites are attacking us." (pleading: begging, abandon: leave) **7.** So Joshua and all the soldiers of Israel, along with their mighty warriors, traveled overnight from Gilgal to Gibeon. (mighty warriors: strong fighters, traveled overnight: journeyed all night) **8.** The Lord said to Joshua, "Do not be afraid of them, for I have already given them into your hands; not one of them will be able to stand against you." (given them into your hands: made them powerless, stand against: resist) **9.** Joshua marched through the night and arrived at the enemy forces unexpectedly. (marched: moved forward) **10.** The Lord threw the enemy into confusion, and Israel struck them down with great slaughter at Gibeon. They pursued them along the route to Beth-horon, and struck them all the way to Azekah and Makkedah. (threw into confusion: caused panic, slaughter: killing) **11.** As the enemies fled towards Beth-horon, the Lord hurled large stones from heaven upon them, killing more of them than the Israelites did with their swords. (hurled: threw, stones from heaven: hailstones) **12.** On that day, Joshua spoke to the Lord in front of Israel, saying, "Sun, stand still over Gibeon, and Moon, stop in the Valley of Ajalon." (spoke to the Lord: prayed) **13.** And the sun remained still, and the moon stopped, until Israel had avenged itself on its enemies. This event is recorded in the Book of Jasher. The sun stayed in place for a full day,

not setting. (avenged itself: took revenge, recorded: written down) **14.** There has never been a day like that, either before or since, when the Lord answered a man's request, for the Lord fought for Israel. (answered: responded to, fought for: defended) **15.** Then Joshua and the Israelites returned to their camp at Gilgal. (returned: went back) **16.** Meanwhile, the five kings fled and hid in a cave at Makkedah. (fled: ran away, hid: concealed themselves) **17.** Joshua was informed that the five kings had been found hiding in a cave. (informed: told) **18.** Joshua ordered, "Roll a large stone to cover the entrance of the cave and set guards to keep watch over it." (entrance: mouth, guards: watchmen) **19.** He then commanded the rest of the army to continue pursuing their enemies and prevent them from reaching their fortified cities, for the Lord had already delivered them into Israel's hands. (fortified: protected, delivered: handed over) **20.** After Israel had completely destroyed their enemies, the remaining survivors fled into walled cities. (destroyed: defeated, survivors: those who lived) **21.** All the people returned to Joshua's camp at Makkedah, where they were at peace, and no one spoke against Israel. (spoke against: criticized) **22.** Joshua said, "Open the cave and bring out the five kings." (bring out: take out) **23.** They did as he commanded, and brought the five kings out—those of Jerusalem, Hebron, Jarmuth, Lachish, and Eglon. (commanded: ordered) **24.** Joshua called for all the leaders of Israel and said to the captains of the army, "Come forward and place your feet on the necks of these kings." They did so. (captains: leaders, place your feet on the necks: demonstrate power over them) **25.** Joshua told them, "Do not be afraid or discouraged. Be strong and courageous, for this is what the Lord will do to all your enemies." (discouraged: disheartened) **26.** Afterward, Joshua killed the kings, hung their bodies on trees, and left them hanging until evening. (hung: crucified) **27.** At sunset, Joshua commanded that the bodies be taken down from the trees, placed back into the cave where they had been hiding, and sealed with large stones. This remains in place to this day. (seal: block off, remains: is still there) **28.** That day, Joshua captured Makkedah, defeated its king, and destroyed all its people, leaving none alive, just as he had done to Jericho. (defeated: conquered, destroyed: wiped out) **29.** Next, Joshua and the Israelites moved on to Libnah and fought against it. (moved on: went next) **30.** The Lord handed Libnah and its king over to Israel, and they defeated it, sparing no one, just as they had done to Jericho. (handed over: delivered) **31.** Then, from Libnah, Joshua and his army went to Lachish, encamped there, and fought against it. (encamped: set up camp) **32.** The Lord delivered Lachish into Israel's hands on the second day, and they struck down everyone there, just as they had done in Libnah. (delivered: handed over) **33.** Horam, the king of Gezer, came to help Lachish, but Joshua defeated him and his army, leaving no survivors. (defeated: destroyed) **34.** From Lachish, Joshua and his army traveled to Eglon and camped there, preparing to fight. (camped: set up camp) **35.** They attacked Eglon that same day, completely destroying everyone there, just as they had done to Lachish. (completely destroying: wiping out) **36.** Joshua and the Israelites then moved on to Hebron and fought against it. (moved on: traveled to) **37.** They captured it, killed the king, and destroyed all its inhabitants, just as they had done to Eglon. (captured: took, inhabitants: people) **38.** Next, Joshua and his army traveled to Debir, fought against it, and captured it. **39.** They killed everyone there, leaving no one alive, just as they had done to Hebron, and wiped out its king and cities as well. (wiped out: destroyed) **40.** Joshua defeated all the lands in the hill country, the Negev (southern region), the lowlands, and the hill country's springs, along with their kings, leaving none alive, as the Lord commanded. (hill country: elevated area, lowlands: flatter regions) **41.** He defeated everyone from Kadesh-barnea to Gaza, and all the land of Goshen to Gibeon. (defeated: conquered) **42.** Joshua took all these kings and their lands at once, because the Lord fought for Israel. (took: captured, fought for: defended) **43.** Joshua and all Israel returned to Gilgal. (returned: went back).

Chapter 11

1. When Jabin, the king of Hazor, heard about Israel's victories, he sent messages to Jobab, the king of Madon, the king of Shimron, and the king of Achshaph, (sent messages: reached out) **2.** He also contacted the kings from the northern mountain regions, the plains south of Chinneroth, the valley, and the borders of Dor to the west, (plains: flat areas, valley: lowland regions) **3.** as well as the Canaanites in the east and west, the Amorites, Hittites, Perizzites, Jebusites in the mountains, and the Hivites who lived near Hermon, in the land of Mizpeh. (Hivites: a group of people in the region, Hermon: a mountain range) **4.** They gathered together with their vast armies—so many soldiers that they were like the sand on the shore, accompanied by a large number of horses and chariots. (vast armies: huge military forces, chariots: horse-drawn vehicles used in battle) **5.** The kings assembled at the waters of Merom, ready to fight Israel. (assembled: gathered, ready to fight: prepared for battle) **6.** The Lord spoke to Joshua, saying, "Do not be afraid of them. Tomorrow, I will hand them all over to you, slain. You are to cripple their horses and burn their chariots." (cripple: hamstring, burn: destroy by fire) **7.** So, Joshua and his army moved against them at the waters of Merom unexpectedly, and they attacked the enemy forces. (unexpectedly: with surprise, attacked: launched an assault) **8.** The Lord gave the enemy into Israel's hands, and they struck them down, pursuing them as far as Great Zidon, Misrephoth-maim, and the valley of Mizpeh to the east, until no enemy soldiers remained. (struck them down: defeated them, pursuing them: chased them, no soldiers remained: wiped them out) **9.** Joshua followed the Lord's instructions: he crippled their horses and burned their chariots with fire. (followed the Lord's instructions: obeyed God's command) **10.** Then, Joshua turned back and attacked Hazor, killing its king with the sword. Hazor had been the leader of all the kingdoms in that region. (attacked: besieged, leader: ruler) **11.** The Israelites completely wiped out everyone in the city, leaving no survivors. They burned Hazor to the ground. (wiped out: destroyed, survivors: people left alive) **12.** Joshua took all the cities of the kings and their kings as well, striking them down with the sword, just as Moses, the servant of the Lord, had commanded. (striking them down: killing) **13.** However, the cities that were still fortified, Israel did not burn, except for Hazor, which Joshua destroyed by fire. (fortified: protected with walls, destroyed by fire: burned to the ground) **14.** The Israelites took the spoils from these cities, including the livestock, as their reward. They killed every living person, leaving no one alive. (took the spoils: claimed the wealth) **15.** As the Lord had commanded Moses, Moses gave instructions to Joshua, and Joshua carried out every detail without failing to do anything the Lord had commanded. (carried out: followed through) **16.** Joshua took possession of all the land—every region of the hills, the southern regions, the land of Goshen, the valleys, the plains, the mountains of Israel, and their valleys. (took possession: claimed as his own) **17.** This included the entire territory from Mount Halak, which rises toward Seir, to Baal-gad in the valley of Lebanon at the foot of Mount Hermon. Joshua defeated all their kings and struck them down. (territory: land, struck them down: killed them) **18.** Joshua waged war against these kings for a long time. (waged war: fought continually) **19.** No city made peace with Israel, except for the Hivites from Gibeon. All the others Israel took by force. (made peace: offered an agreement, took by force: conquered through battle) **20.** It was the Lord's will to harden their hearts, so they came together to fight Israel, in order that Israel might completely destroy them, without showing them mercy, as the Lord had commanded Moses. (hardening their hearts: causing them to resist, without showing them mercy: offering no grace) **21.** At that time, Joshua also cut off the Anakim from the mountains of Judah and Israel. He destroyed their cities in Hebron, Debir, Anab, and all the hill country of Judah and Israel. (cut off: wiped out) **22.** None of the Anakim remained in the land of Israel, except in Gaza, Gath, and Ashdod. (Anakim: a race of giants) **23.** Thus, Joshua took the entire land, just as the Lord had told Moses. He gave it as an inheritance to Israel, according to their tribal divisions. And the land was at rest from war. (took: conquered, inheritance: land passed down to descendants, at rest from war: there was peace)

Chapter 12
1. These are the kings of the land that the Israelites defeated and took possession of on the east side of the Jordan, from the river Arnon to Mount Hermon, and all the land in the plain to the east. (defeated: conquered, took possession of: claimed) 2. Sihon, the king of the Amorites, ruled from Heshbon. His territory stretched from Aroer on the bank of the river Arnon, to the middle of the river, half of Gilead, and all the way to the river Jabbok, which formed the border of the Ammonites. (stretched: extended) 3. His land included the plain, all the way to the Sea of Chinneroth on the east, and to the Salt Sea, eastward toward Beth-jeshimoth, and southward under Ashdoth-pisgah. (included: covered, toward: leading) 4. Og, king of Bashan, the last of the Rephaim giants, ruled in the cities of Ashtaroth and Edrei. (last of the giants: final remnant, Rephaim giants: ancient giants) 5. His kingdom extended over Mount Hermon, Salcah, and all of Bashan, reaching as far as the borders of the Geshurites and the Maachathites, and half of Gilead, which was also part of Sihon's territory. (extended: stretched) 6. Moses, the servant of the Lord, and the Israelites defeated these kings, and Moses assigned their land as an inheritance to the tribes of Reuben, Gad, and half of the tribe of Manasseh. (assigned: gave, inheritance: land) 7. These are the kings of the land that Joshua and the Israelites conquered on the west side of the Jordan, from Baal-gad in the valley of Lebanon to Mount Halak, which rises toward Seir. Joshua gave this land to the tribes of Israel as their inheritance, according to their divisions. (conquered: defeated, rises toward: ascends) 8. It covered the mountains, the valleys, the plains, the springs, the wilderness, and the southern regions, and included the Hittites, Amorites, Canaanites, Perizzites, Hivites, and Jebusites. (covered: included, regions: territories) 9. The king of Jericho: one; the king of Ai, near Bethel: one. (near Bethel: close to) 10. The king of Jerusalem: one; the king of Hebron: one. (Jerusalem: Judah's capital, Hebron: in Judah) 11. The king of Jarmuth: one; the king of Lachish: one. (Jarmuth: southern Canaan city) 12. The king of Eglon: one; the king of Gezer: one. (Eglon: near the Philistine border) 13. The king of Debir: one; the king of Geder: one. (Debir: southern Judah city) 14. The king of Hormah: one; the king of Arad: one. (Hormah: south of Judah, Arad: Canaanite city) 15. The king of Libnah: one; the king of Adullam: one. (Libnah: city in Judah, Adullam: southern Judah city) 16. The king of Makkedah: one; the king of Bethel: one. (Makkedah: southern Canaan city, Bethel: north of Jerusalem) 17. The king of Tappuah: one; the king of Hepher: one. (Tappuah: Judah hill country city) 18. The king of Aphek: one; the king of Lasharon: one. (Aphek: near Israel-Phoenicia border) 19. The king of Madon: one; the king of Hazor: one. (Madon: northern Canaan city, Hazor: major northern city) 20. The king of Shimron-meron: one; the king of Achshaph: one. (Shimron-meron: northern Canaan city, Achshaph: another northern city) 21. The king of Taanach: one; the king of Megiddo: one. (Taanach: near Jezreel, Megiddo: near Jezreel Valley) 22. The king of Kedesh: one; the king of Jokneam of Carmel: one. (Kedesh: northern Israel city, Carmel: coastal mountain region) 23. The king of Dor, on the coast of Dor: one; the king of the nations of Gilgal: one. (coast of Dor: Canaan coastal city) 24. The king of Tirzah: one; in total, there were thirty-one kings. (Tirzah: Ephraim hill country city)

Chapter 13
1. Joshua was old and well-advanced in age; and the LORD said to him, "You are old, and much land remains to be taken." (well-advanced in age: very old) 2. The land that still remains includes the territories of the Philistines and the Geshurites. (still remains: is left) 3. From Sihor, near Egypt, to the northern border of Ekron, which is part of the Canaanite land, including the five Philistine lords: Gazathites, Ashdothites, Eshkalonites, Gittites, Ekronites; and the Avites. (near Egypt: close to Egypt, part of: belongs to) 4. The southern land includes the Canaanites, and Mearah near the Sidonians, extending to Aphek, the border of the Amorites. (includes: covers) 5. The land of the Giblites, all of Lebanon, eastward, from Baal-gad under Mount Hermon to the entrance of Hamath. (eastward: to the east) 6. I will drive out all the inhabitants from the hill country of Lebanon to Misrephoth-maim, and all the Sidonians, before Israel; but divide the land by lot for Israel as I commanded you. (inhabitants: people, divide by lot: distribute) 7. Now, divide this land among the nine tribes and the half-tribe of Manasseh. (divide: allocate) 8. The Reubenites and the Gadites have already received their inheritance, which Moses gave them east of the Jordan River. (received: got) 9. The land of Reuben begins at Aroer on the river Arnon, extending to the city in the middle of the river and all the plains of Medeba to Dibon. (begins at: starts at) 10. It also includes all the cities of Sihon, king of the Amorites, who reigned in Heshbon, to the border of the Ammonites. (cities: towns, reigned: ruled) 11. The land includes Gilead, the borders of the Geshurites and Maachathites, all of Mount Hermon, and all of Bashan to Salcah. (includes: covers) 12. It also includes the kingdom of Og in Bashan, who reigned in Ashtaroth and Edrei, and who was the last of the giants; Moses defeated them and drove them out. (kingdom of Og: Og's domain, giants: ancient people) 13. However, the Israelites did not expel the Geshurites or Maachathites; they still live among Israel. (did not expel: didn't remove) 14. Only the tribe of Levi received no inheritance; the LORD God of Israel is their inheritance, as He promised. (received no inheritance: got no land) 15. Moses gave the tribe of Reuben their inheritance according to their families. (gave: assigned) 16. Their territory included Aroer on the Arnon River, the city in the middle of the river, and all the plains of Medeba to Dibon. (territory: land) 17. Heshbon, and all the cities in the plains; Dibon, Bamoth-baal, Beth-baal-meon, (in the plains: in the flat lands) 18. Jahazah, Kedemoth, Mephaath, (places: towns) 19. Kirjathaim, Sibmah, Zareth-shahar in the valley, (in the valley: within the valley) 20. Beth-peor, Ashdoth-pisgah, Beth-jeshimoth, (places: towns) 21. All the cities of the plain, all the kingdom of Sihon, king of the Amorites, whom Moses defeated, along with the princes of Midian: Evi, Rekem, Zur, Hur, and Reba, the leaders of Sihon. (kingdom of Sihon: land ruled by Sihon, defeated: conquered) 22. Balaam, the son of Beor, the soothsayer, was also killed by the Israelites with the sword. (soothsayer: diviner) 23. The border of Reuben was the Jordan River. This is their inheritance, with their cities and villages. (border: boundary, inheritance: land) 24. Moses gave the tribe of Gad their inheritance according to their families. (gave: assigned) 25. Their territory included Jazer, all the cities of Gilead, and half the land of the Ammonites, to Aroer before Rabbah. (territory: land, before: near) 26. From Heshbon to Ramath-mizpeh, Betonim; from Mahanaim to the border of Debir; (places: towns) 27. In the valley, Beth-aram, Beth-nimrah, Succoth, Zaphon, the rest of Sihon's kingdom, the Jordan, and its border, all the way to the Sea of Chinnereth on the east side of the Jordan. (rest of: remaining portion) 28. This is the inheritance of the Gadites, with their cities and villages. (inheritance: land) 29. Moses gave the half-tribe of Manasseh their inheritance by their families. (gave: assigned) 30. Their territory included Mahanaim, all of Bashan, all of Og's kingdom, and all the towns of Jair in Bashan, sixty cities. (territory: land, towns of Jair: cities of Jair) 31. Half of Gilead, Ashtaroth, and Edrei, cities in Og's kingdom, were given to Machir, son of Manasseh, and half of his descendants by their families. (cities in Og's kingdom: towns of Og) 32. These are the regions Moses distributed as inheritance in the plains of Moab, east of Jericho. (distributed: allocated) 33. But Moses did not give any inheritance to the tribe of Levi; the LORD God of Israel is their inheritance, as He promised. (no inheritance: no land, is their inheritance: becomes their portion)

Chapter 14

1. These are the lands that the Israelites inherited in Canaan, which were allocated to them by Eleazar the priest, Joshua son of Nun, and the leaders of the tribes. (inherited: received, allocated: divided) **2.** The inheritance was determined by casting lots, as the LORD had instructed through Moses, for the nine tribes and the half-tribe of Manasseh. (determined: decided, casting lots: drawing lots) **3.** Moses had already assigned land to two and a half tribes on the east side of the Jordan River, but the Levites received no land among them. (assigned: gave) **4.** The children of Joseph were split into two tribes: Manasseh and Ephraim. Therefore, the Levites received no inheritance in the land, except for cities to live in and pastureland for their animals. (split into two: became two, received: got) **5.** The Israelites followed the LORD's commands and divided the land as instructed. (followed: obeyed) **6.** Then the tribe of Judah came to Joshua in Gilgal, and Caleb son of Jephunneh, the Kenezite, spoke to him: "You remember what the LORD said to Moses concerning both you and me at Kadesh-barnea." (spoke to him: said to him, remember: recall) **7.** I was 40 years old when Moses sent me from Kadesh-barnea to spy out the land, and I reported back exactly what was in my heart. (reported back: gave a report, exactly: truthfully) **8.** However, the other men who went with me discouraged the people, causing their hearts to melt. But I fully followed the LORD my God. (discouraged: caused to fear, fully followed: wholeheartedly obeyed) **9.** On that day, Moses swore to me, saying, "The land where your feet have walked will belong to you and your descendants forever, because you followed the LORD my God wholeheartedly." (swore: promised, will belong to: will be your inheritance) **10.** Now, behold, the LORD has kept me alive for these 45 years, since the time He spoke this word to Moses while Israel wandered in the desert. And here I am today, 85 years old. (kept me alive: preserved my life, wandered: traveled) **11.** I am just as strong now as I was then when Moses sent me out. My strength remains the same for battle, both to go out and return. (remains the same: is still as strong, for battle: to fight) **12.** So, give me this mountain that the LORD promised me that day. You heard how the Anakim were there, and the cities were large and fortified. But if the LORD is with me, I will be able to drive them out, just as the LORD said." (give me: grant me, drive them out: remove them) **13.** Then Joshua blessed him and gave Caleb the son of Jephunneh the city of Hebron as his inheritance. (blessed him: honored him, granted: gave) **14.** Therefore, Hebron has belonged to Caleb son of Jephunneh, the Kenezite, as an inheritance to this day, because he wholeheartedly followed the LORD God of Israel. (belonged to: became the inheritance of, wholeheartedly: with full commitment) **15.** Previously, Hebron was called Kirjath-arba; Arba was a great man among the Anakim. And the land had peace from war. (previously: before, had peace from war: was free from battle)

Chapter 15

1. This then was the lot of the tribe of the children of Judah by their families; even to the border of Edom the wilderness of Zin southward was the uttermost part of the south coast. (Wilderness of Zin: desert region near Edom.) **2.** And their south border was from the shore of the salt sea, from the bay that looketh southward: (Salt Sea: Dead Sea.) **3.** And it went out to the south side to Maaleh-acrabbim, and passed along to Zin, and ascended up on the south side unto Kadesh-barnea, and passed along to Hezron, and went up to Adar, and fetched a compass to Karkaa: (Maaleh-acrabbim: Scorpion Pass; Kadesh-barnea: key site in Israel's wilderness journey.) **4.** From thence it passed toward Azmon, and went out unto the river of Egypt; and the goings out of that coast were at the sea: this shall be your south coast. (River of Egypt: Wadi el-Arish.) **5.** And the east border was the salt sea, even unto the end of Jordan. (Jordan River's mouth into the Dead Sea.) **6.** And their border in the north quarter was from the bay of the sea at the uttermost part of Jordan. **7.** And the border went up to Beth-hogla, and passed along by the north of Beth-arabah; and the border went up to the stone of Bohan the son of Reuben: (Beth-hogla: town near Jordan River.) **8.** And the border went up toward Debir from the valley of Achor, and so northward, looking toward Gilgal, that is before the going up to Adummim, which is on the south side of the river: and the border passed toward the waters of En-shemesh, and the goings out thereof were at En-rogel: (Debir: town formerly called Kirjath-sepher; En-shemesh: spring; En-rogel: well near Jerusalem.) **9.** And the border was drawn from the top of the hill unto the fountain of the water of Nephtoah, and went out to the cities of mount Ephron; and the border was drawn to Baalah, which is Kirjath-jearim: (Nephtoah: spring; Ephron: region; Baalah: Kirjath-jearim, a key town.) **10.** And the border compassed from Baalah westward unto mount Seir, and passed along unto the side of mount Jearim, which is Chesalon, on the north side, and went down to Beth-shemesh, and passed on to Timnah: (Mount Seir: Edom; Mount Jearim: Chesalon; Beth-shemesh and Timnah: towns in Judah.) **11.** And the border went out unto the side of Ekron northward: and the border was drawn to Shicron, and passed along to mount Baalah, and went out unto Jabneel; and the goings out of the border were at the sea. (Ekron: Philistine city; Jabneel: coastal town.) **12.** And the west border was to the great sea, and the coast thereof. This is the coast of the children of Judah round about according to their families. (Great Sea: Mediterranean Sea.) **13.** And unto Caleb the son of Jephunneh he gave a part among the children of Judah, according to the commandment of the LORD to Joshua, even the city of Arba the father of Anak, which city is Hebron. (Caleb received Hebron, a key city in southern Judah.) **14.** And Caleb drove thence the three sons of Anak, Sheshai, and Ahiman, and Talmai, the children of Anak. (Anak: giants in the Bible.) **15.** And he went up thence to the inhabitants of Debir: and the name of Debir before was Kirjath-sepher. (Debir, formerly called Kirjath-sepher, meaning "city of books.") **16.** And Caleb said, He that smiteth Kirjath-sepher, and taketh it, to him will I give Achsah my daughter to wife. (Caleb offers his daughter in marriage to the conqueror.) **17.** And Othniel the son of Kenaz, the brother of Caleb, took it: and he gave him Achsah his daughter to wife. (Othniel, Caleb's brother, conquers the city and marries Achsah.) **18.** And it came to pass, as she came unto him, that she moved him to ask of her father a field: and she lighted off her ass; and Caleb said unto her, What wouldest thou? (Achsah requests land with water sources from her father.) **19.** Who answered, Give me a blessing; for thou hast given me a south land; give me also springs of water. And he gave her the upper springs, and the nether springs. (Caleb grants her both upper and lower springs.) **20.** This is the inheritance of the tribe of the children of Judah according to their families. (Summary of Judah's inheritance.) **21.** And the uttermost cities of the tribe of the children of Judah toward the coast of Edom southward were Kabzeel, and Eder, and Jagur, (Kabzeel, Eder, and Jagur: towns near Judah's southern border.) **22.** And Kinah, and Dimonah, and Adadah, (Kinah and Dimonah: towns in the Negev.) **23.** And Kedesh, and Hazor, and Ithnan, (Kedesh: town in the Negev; Hazor: different from the northern Hazor.) **24.** Ziph, and Telem, and Bealoth, (Ziph, Telem, Bealoth: towns in Judah.) **25.** And Hazor, Hadattah, and Kerioth, and Hezron, which is Hazor, (Hazor is mentioned twice; Kerioth and Hadattah are nearby towns.) **26.** Amam, and Shema, and Moladah, (Amam, Shema, Moladah: small towns in Judah.) **27.** And Hazar-gaddah, and Heshmon, and Beth-palet, (Hazar-gaddah, Heshmon, Beth-palet: towns in the southern region.) **28.** And Hazar-shual, and Beer-sheba, and Bizjothjah, (Beer-sheba is the most famous; Hazar-shual is a village.) **29.** Baalah, and Iim, and Azem, (Baalah is also called Kirjath-jearim; Iim and Azem: smaller towns.) **30.** And Eltolad, and Chesil, and Hormah, (Eltolad and Chesil: small towns; Hormah: desert location.) **31.** And Ziklag, and Madmannah, and Sansannah, (Ziklag: a key town; Madmannah and Sansannah: villages.) **32.** And Lebaoth, and Shilhim, and Ain, and Rimmon: all the cities are twenty and nine, with their villages. (These towns are in Judah's southern and western regions.) **33.** And in the valley, Eshtaol, and Zoreah, and Ashnah, (Eshtaol, Zoreah, Ashnah: valley towns.) **34.** And Zanoah, and En-gannim, Tappuah, and Enam, (Zanoah, En-gannim, and Tappuah: towns in Judah.) **35.** Jarmuth, and Adullam, Socoh, and Azekah, (Jarmuth and Adullam: major cities; Socoh and Azekah: smaller settlements.) **36.** And Sharaim, and Adithaim, and Gederah, and Gederothaim; fourteen cities with their villages. (A group of smaller towns.) **37.** Zenan, and Hadashah, and Migdal-gad, (Zenan, Hadashah, Migdal-gad: towns in the lowlands.) **38.** And Dilean, and Mizpeh, and Joktheel, (Dilean and Mizpeh: towns; Joktheel: a location in Judah.) **39.** Lachish, and Bozkath, and Eglon, (Lachish: significant city; Bozkath and Eglon: nearby towns.) **40.** And Cabbon, and Lahmam, and Kithlish, (Cabbon and Lahmam: smaller settlements.) **41.** And Gederoth, Beth-dagon, and Naamah, and Makkedah; sixteen cities with their villages. (Beth-dagon and Makkedah: notable towns.) **42.** Libnah, and Ether, and Ashan, (Libnah: major town; Ether and Ashan: smaller settlements.) **43.** And Jiphtah, and Ashnah, and Nezib, (Jiphtah and Ashnah: villages; Nezib: a town.) **44.** And Keilah, and Achzib, and Mareshah; nine cities with their villages. (Keilah: major town; Achzib: small settlement.) **45.** Ekron, with her towns and her villages: (Ekron: major Philistine city.) **46.** From Ekron even unto the sea, all that lay near Ashdod, with their villages: (A coastal region, including Ashdod.) **47.** Ashdod with her towns and her villages, Gaza with her towns and her villages, unto the river of Egypt, and the great sea, and the border thereof: (Ashdod, Gaza: major Philistine cities.) **48.** And in the mountains, Shamir, and Jattir, and Socoh, (Shamir and Jattir: mountain towns.) **49.** And Dannah, and Kirjath-sannah, which is Debir, (Dannah and Kirjath-sannah: towns in the southern hills.) **50.** And Anab, and Eshtemoh, and Anim, (Anab, Eshtemoh, Anim: mountain cities.) **51.** And Goshen, and Holon, and Giloh; eleven cities with their villages. (Goshen, Holon, Giloh: mountain towns.) **52.** Arab, and Dumah, and Eshean, (Arab, Dumah, Eshean: towns in the wilderness.) **53.** And Janum, and Beth-tappuah, and Aphekah, (Janum and Beth-tappuah: small villages.) **54.** And Humtah, and Kirjath-arba, which is Hebron, and Zior; nine cities with their villages. (Hebron is the key city; others are nearby.) **55.** Maon, Carmel, and Ziph, and Juttah, (Maon, Carmel, Ziph: towns in the hill country.) **56.** And Jezreel, and Jokdeam, and Zanoah, (Jezreel and Jokdeam: towns.) **57.** Cain, Gibeah, and Timnah; ten cities with their villages. (Cain, Gibeah, Timnah: towns.) **58.** Halhul, Beth-zur, and Gedor, (Halhul, Beth-zur, Gedor: towns in the hills.) **59.** And Maarath, and Beth-anoth, and Eltekon; six cities with their villages. (Maarath, Beth-anoth, Eltekon: villages.) **60.** Kirjath-baal, which is Kirjath-jearim, and Rabbah; two cities with their villages. (Kirjath-baal is also Kirjath-jearim; Rabbah is a city.) **61.** In the wilderness, Beth-arabah, Middin, and Secacah, (Beth-arabah, Middin, Secacah: wilderness towns.) **62.** And Nibshan, and the city of Salt, and En-gedi; six cities with their villages. (Nibshan, Salt, En-gedi: wilderness towns; En-gedi is famous.) **63.** As for the Jebusites the inhabitants of Jerusalem, the children of Judah could not drive them out: but the Jebusites dwell with the children of Judah at Jerusalem unto this day. (Jebusites: original inhabitants of Jerusalem.)

Chapter 16

1. The allotment for the descendants of Joseph extended from the Jordan River, near Jericho, to the waters east of Jericho, and then into the wilderness that leads up to Mount Bethel. (Joseph's territory begins at Jericho, extending eastward to Mount Bethel.) **2.** From Bethel, the boundary continued to Luz, then passed through the territory of the Archites and reached Ataroth. (The border goes from Bethel to Luz, then through the Archite region to Ataroth.) **3.** The line then went westward to Japhleti's coast, along the lower Beth-horon, and reached Gezer; it ended at the Mediterranean Sea. (The western boundary runs to Gezer, meeting the sea.) **4.** Thus, the tribes of Manasseh and Ephraim, the sons of Joseph, received their inheritance. (Manasseh and Ephraim claimed their respective portions.) **5.** For Ephraim, the border began at Ataroth-addar in the east and continued to the upper Beth-horon. (Ephraim's eastern boundary stretches from Ataroth-addar to Beth-horon.) **6.** It then moved northward to Michmethah, turned east to Taanath-shiloh, and continued past it to Janohah. (The northern border reaches Michmethah, Taanath-shiloh, and Janohah.) **7.** From Janohah, it descended toward Ataroth, passed through Naarath, reached Jericho, and ended at the Jordan River. (The boundary moves south to Jericho and the Jordan.) **8.** The line then ran west from Tappuah to the river Kanah, ending at the Mediterranean. This was the Ephraimites' inheritance, according to their families. (The western boundary extends to the river Kanah, meeting the sea.) **9.** Ephraim's separate cities were spread within Manasseh's territory, with all their towns and villages. (Ephraim's cities were interspersed in Manasseh's land.) **10.** The Ephraimites did not drive out the Canaanites living in Gezer; as a result, the Canaanites remain there, serving the Ephraimites as subjects. (Ephraim failed to expel the Canaanites from Gezer, who still serve them.)

Chapter 17

1. The tribe of Manasseh, the firstborn of Joseph, received Gilead and Bashan, given to Machir, a warrior. (Manasseh's inheritance included Gilead and Bashan, given to Machir.) **2.** The rest of Manasseh's descendants received land by their families: Abiezer, Helek, Asriel, Shechem, Hepher, and Shemida. (The remaining families of Manasseh received portions of land.) **3.** Zelophehad had no sons, only daughters: Mahlah, Noah, Hoglah, Milcah, and Tirzah. (Zelophehad's daughters inherited his land.) **4.** Zelophehad's daughters requested land, and the Lord granted them inheritance. (The daughters were given land as commanded by God.) **5.** Manasseh received ten portions, plus Gilead and Bashan across the Jordan. (Manasseh gets ten portions, with extra land across the Jordan.) **6.** The daughters of Manasseh inherited with the sons; the rest received Gilead. (Manasseh's daughters shared the inheritance with his sons.) **7.** The boundary of Manasseh stretched from Asher to Michmethah, including En-tappuah. (Manasseh's territory extended to Asher and Shechem.) **8.** Manasseh had Tappuah, but Tappuah near Ephraim's border was Ephraim's. (Tappuah was shared with Ephraim.) **9.** The boundary went south to the river Kanah, with Ephraim's cities included in Manasseh's. (Manasseh's border reached the river Kanah, including Ephraim's cities.) **10.** The southern part was Ephraim's, the northern part Manasseh's, meeting at Asher and Issachar. (Manasseh's northern boundary met Ephraim's at Asher and Issachar.) **11.** Manasseh's cities included Beth-shean, Ibleam, Dor, Endor, Taanach, and Megiddo. (Manasseh had cities in Issachar and Asher, like Beth-shean and Megiddo.) **12.** Manasseh could not drive out the Canaanites; they remained in those cities. (Manasseh failed to expel the Canaanites.) **13.** When Israel grew stronger, they made the Canaanites pay tribute. (The Canaanites were put under tribute, but not driven out.) **14.** The children of Joseph asked why they got only one portion, since they were many. (Joseph's descendants requested more land due to their numbers.) **15.** Joshua told them to cut down land in the hill country if Ephraim's land was too small. (Joshua advised them to expand into the hills.) **16.** The children of Joseph said the hill country was not enough, and the Canaanites had iron chariots. (They argued the hill country was insufficient because of Canaanite chariots.) **17.** Joshua assured them they would get more land, including the mountains. (Joshua promised more land, including mountainous regions.) **18.** Despite the Canaanites' iron chariots, Joseph's descendants would drive them out. (Joshua assured them they would conquer the Canaanites, despite their chariots.)

Chapter 18

1. The entire assembly of the Israelites gathered at Shiloh and set up the Tabernacle there. The land was now subdued and under control. (Shiloh: the sacred site where the Tabernacle was placed.) **2.** Seven tribes of Israel had yet to receive their inheritance. **3.** Joshua addressed the Israelites: "How long will you hesitate to take possession of the land that the LORD, the God of your ancestors, has given you?" (Hesitate: delay in taking action) **4.** "Select three men from each tribe, and I will send them to explore the land. They will map it out according to the inheritance of each tribe, and then return to me." (Map out: survey or document) **5.** "They will divide the land into seven parts: Judah will stay in their territory in the south, and the house of Joseph will be in their territory in the north." **6.** "You will describe the land in seven parts and bring the details to me. I will cast lots for you here before the LORD our God." (Cast lots: decide by random selection) **7.** "The Levites have no inheritance among you, for the priesthood of the LORD is their portion. Also, Gad, Reuben, and half of Manasseh have received their inheritance east of the Jordan, which Moses, the servant of the LORD, gave them." (Levites: members of the priestly tribe of Israel) **8.** The men got up and left, and Joshua instructed them, saying, "Go, explore the land, make a detailed record, and return to me, so that I can cast lots for you before the LORD in Shiloh." **9.** The men traveled through the land, documenting the cities into seven sections and returned to Joshua at the camp in Shiloh. (Documenting: recording or writing down) **10.** Joshua cast lots for them at Shiloh before the LORD, dividing the land for the Israelites according to their tribes. **11.** The lot for the tribe of Benjamin came up, and their boundary ran between the territories of Judah and Joseph. **12.** The northern boundary of Benjamin's lot extended from the Jordan River, and went up to the side of Jericho on the north, ascending into the hill country to the wilderness of Beth-aven. (Jericho: an ancient city; Beth-aven: a location) **13.** From there, the boundary moved toward Luz, on the side of Luz, which is also called Bethel, and descended southward to Ataroth-adar, near the hill south of lower Beth-horon. (Luz: an ancient town; Bethel: a city in Israel) **14.** Then the boundary was drawn westward, going around the corner toward the sea from the hill in front of Beth-horon, and it ended at Kirjath-baal (which is also called Kirjath-jearim), a city of Judah. This was the western border. (Kirjath-baal/Kirjath-jearim: a city of Judah) **15.** The southern boundary began at the end of Kirjath-jearim, and the border extended westward to the spring of Nephtoah. (Nephtoah: a place near Jerusalem) **16.** The boundary descended to the mountain before the Valley of the Son of Hinnom, which is in the Valley of the Giants to the north, and then down to the Valley of Hinnom, at the side of the Jebusites, and reached En-rogel. (Hinnom: a valley; Giants: people of great size; En-rogel: a spring near Jerusalem) **17.** The border moved northward, continuing to En-shemesh, then to Geliloth, which lies opposite the ascent of Adummim, and finally down to the stone of Bohan, son of Reuben. (Geliloth: a place near Adummim) **18.** From there, it passed along to the side opposite the Arabah, northward, and descended into the Arabah. (Arabah: a desert region) **19.** The boundary then turned toward the northern side of Beth-hoglah and ended at the northern bay of the Salt Sea, at the southern end of the Jordan River. This was the southern boundary. (Beth-hoglah: a location) **20.** The Jordan River marked the eastern border of Benjamin's land. This was the inheritance of the tribe of Benjamin, according to their borders, divided by their families. **21.** The cities allocated to the tribe of Benjamin were Jericho, Beth-hoglah, Keziz Valley, (Keziz: a location) **22.** Beth-arabah, Zemaraim, and Bethel, (Zemaraim: a town) **23.** Avim, Parah, Ophrah, (Avim: a place name) **24.** Chephar-haammonai, Ophni, and Gaba; twelve cities in all, with their villages. **25.** Gibeon, Ramah, and Beeroth, (Beeroth: a town) **26.** Mizpeh, Chephirah, and Mozah, **27.** Rekem, Irpeel, and Taralah, (Rekem: a town) **28.** Zelah, Eleph, Jebusi (which is Jerusalem), Gibeath, and Kirjath; fourteen cities in total, with their villages. This was the inheritance of the tribe of Benjamin, as allotted to their families.

Chapter 19
1. The second lot was given to the tribe of Simeon, according to their families. Their inheritance was within the territory of Judah. **2.** Their inheritance included Beer-sheba, or Sheba, and Moladah, **3.** Hazar-shual, Balah, Azem, **4.** Eltolad, Bethul, and Hormah, **5.** Ziklag, Beth-marcaboth, and Hazar-susah, **6.** Beth-lebaoth, and Sharuhen; thirteen cities and their villages. (Villages: smaller settlements or communities) **7.** Ain, Remmon, Ether, and Ashan; four cities with their villages. **8.** And all the surrounding villages near these cities, up to Baalath-beer and Ramath of the south. This is the inheritance of Simeon according to their families. **9.** The inheritance of Simeon came from the portion of Judah, as Judah's territory was too large for them. Therefore, Simeon's inheritance was within Judah's territory. (Portion: a part or share of something) **10.** The third lot was given to the tribe of Zebulun, according to their families. Their border extended to Sarid. **11.** Their border went up toward the sea, including Maralah, Dabbasheth, and the river near Jokneam. **12.** It turned eastward toward the sunrise to Chisloth-tabor, then to Daberath, and up to Japhia, **13.** Then to Gittah-hepher, Ittah-kazin, and Remmon-methoar to Neah. **14.** The border turned northward to Hannathon, and the boundary ended at the valley of Jiphthah-el. (Jiphthah-el: a valley) **15.** The cities included Kattath, Nahallal, Shimron, Idalah, and Bethlehem; twelve cities in total with their villages. (Shimron: a town) **16.** This was the inheritance of Zebulun according to their families, including these cities and their villages. **17.** The fourth lot was given to the tribe of Issachar, according to their families. **18.** Their border included Jezreel, Chesulloth, and Shunem, **19.** Hapharaim, Shion, Anaharath, **20.** Rabbith, Kishion, and Abez, **21.** Remeth, En-gannim, En-haddah, and Beth-pazzez; **22.** The border extended to Tabor, Shahazimah, and Beth-shemesh, and ended at the Jordan River. Sixteen cities in total with their villages. **23.** This was the inheritance of Issachar according to their families, with their cities and villages. **24.** The fifth lot was given to the tribe of Asher, according to their families. **25.** Their border included Helkath, Hali, Beten, Achshaph, **26.** Alammelech, Amad, and Misheal; it reached Carmel to the west and Shihor-libnath; **27.** Then it turned eastward to Beth-dagon, Zebulun, and the valley of Jiphthah-el to the north side of Beth-emek, Neiel, and continued to Cabul on the left. **28.** The border also included Hebron, Rehob, Hammon, Kanah, even to great Zidon; (Zidon: an ancient Phoenician city) **29.** It turned toward Ramah, the strong city of Tyre, and then toward Hosah; the border extended to the sea, to Achzib. (Tyre: a powerful ancient city) **30.** The cities of Asher included Ummah, Aphek, and Rehob; twenty-two cities with their villages. **31.** This is the inheritance of the tribe of Asher according to their families, with their cities and villages. **32.** The sixth lot was given to the tribe of Naphtali, according to their families. **33.** Their border began at Heleph, from Allon to Zaanannim, Adami, Nekeb, and Jabneel, up to Lakum, and ended at the Jordan River. **34.** Then the border turned westward to Aznoth-tabor, and reached Hukkok, continuing to Zebulun on the south, Asher to the west, and Judah to the east. **35.** The fenced cities included Ziddim, Zer, Hammath, Rakkath, Chinnereth, **36.** Adamah, Ramah, Hazor, **37.** Kedesh, Edrei, En-hazor, **38.** Iron, Migdal-el, Horem, Beth-anath, and Beth-shemesh; nineteen cities in total with their villages. **39.** This was the inheritance of Naphtali according to their families, including their cities and villages. **40.** The seventh lot was given to the tribe of Dan, according to their families. **41.** The border of their inheritance included Zorah, Eshtaol, Ir-shemesh, **42.** Shaalabbin, Ajalon, Jethlah, **43.** Elon, Thimnathah, Ekron, **44.** Eltekeh, Gibbethon, Baalath, **45.** Jehud, Bene-berak, Gath-rimmon, **46.** Me-jarkon, Rakkon, and the border near Japho. (Japho: a location, possibly Joppa) **47.** The territory of Dan was too small for them, so they went to fight against Leshem. They conquered it, struck it with the sword, possessed it, and renamed it Dan after their father. (Leshem: an ancient city) **48.** This is the inheritance of the tribe of Dan, with their cities and villages. **49.** After the land was divided, the Israelites gave an inheritance to Joshua, son of Nun, among them. **50.** According to the LORD's command, they gave him the city he asked for, Timnath-serah in the hill country of Ephraim. He built the city and settled there. (Timnath-serah: a town Joshua requested) **51.** These were the inheritances

that Eleazar the priest, Joshua, and the leaders of Israel's families divided by lot at Shiloh before the LORD, at the entrance of the Tabernacle. They finished distributing the land. (Tabernacle: the sacred tent where God's presence dwelled)

Chapter 20

1. The LORD spoke to Joshua, saying, **2.** "Tell the Israelites to designate cities of refuge, as I instructed Moses." **3.** "These cities will be places of safety for anyone who kills someone by accident, offering protection from the avenger of blood." **4.** "When the person seeking refuge arrives at the city gate, they must explain their case to the city's elders. The elders will allow them to stay, giving them a place to live among the city's people." **5.** "If the avenger of blood comes after them, they shall not be handed over, since the death was unintentional and there was no prior hatred." **6.** "The person who flees must remain in that city until they are tried by the assembly. They shall stay there until the death of the high priest, after which they may return to their home and the city from which they fled." **7.** The cities appointed were Kedesh in Galilee, in the hill country of Naphtali; Shechem in the hill country of Ephraim; and Kirjath-arba (which is Hebron) in the hill country of Judah. (Kedesh: city in northern Israel, **Shechem**: ancient city in Ephraim, Kirjath-arba: Hebron, a major city) **8.** "On the eastern side of the Jordan, near Jericho, the cities assigned were Bezer in the wilderness of Reuben, Ramoth in Gilead from Gad, and Golan in Bashan from Manasseh." (Bezer: city in the wilderness, Ramoth: a city in Gilead, Golan: city in Bashan) **9.** "These cities were provided for the Israelites and for any foreigner residing among them, so that anyone who unintentionally kills someone can flee there and be protected from the avenger of blood, until they stand trial before the assembly." (Avenger of blood: a relative seeking justice for a murder)

Chapter 21

1. Then the leaders of the Levite families approached Eleazar the priest, Joshua son of Nun, and the tribal leaders of Israel. (Levites: tribe of Levi; Eleazar: priest; Nun: Joshua's father) **2.** They spoke to them at Shiloh in the land of Canaan, saying, "The LORD commanded through Moses to give us cities to live in, with pasturelands for our livestock." (Shiloh: a city; pasturelands: grazing areas) **3.** In response, the Israelites gave the Levites cities and their surrounding lands, as the LORD had instructed through Moses. (Instructed: commanded) **4.** The first lot was drawn for the Kohathites. The descendants of Aaron the priest, from the Levites, received 13 cities by lot from the tribes of Judah, Simeon, and Benjamin. (Kohathites: Kohath's descendants; Lot: chosen portion) **5.** The remaining Kohathites received 10 cities from the tribes of Ephraim, Dan, and half the tribe of Manasseh. (Ephraim, Dan, Manasseh: Israelite tribes) **6.** The Gershonites received 13 cities by lot from the tribes of Issachar, Asher, Naphtali, and from half the tribe of Manasseh in Bashan. (Gershonites: Gershon's descendants; Bashan: region east of Jordan) **7.** The Merarites received 12 cities from the tribes of Reuben, Gad, and Zebulun. (Merarites: Merari's descendants) **8.** The Israelites gave these cities and their surrounding lands to the Levites, following the LORD's command through Moses. (Following: according to) **9.** They gave cities from the tribes of Judah and Simeon, specifically named for the descendants of Aaron, the Kohathites, who received the first lot. (Descendants: offspring) **10.** These were the cities given to the children of Aaron, the Kohathites, from the tribe of Judah: Hebron, the city of Arba (the father of Anak), along with its surrounding pasturelands. (Hebron: city of refuge; Anak: giant ancestor) **11.** However, the fields and villages around the city were given to Caleb son of Jephunneh as his inheritance. (Caleb: leader from Judah) **12.** The cities given to the descendants of Aaron included Hebron (a city of refuge for manslayers), Libnah, Jattir, Eshtemoa, Holon, Debir, Ain, Juttah, and Beth-shemesh, totaling 9 cities from the tribes of Judah and Simeon. (Manslayers: unintentional killers) **13.** From the tribe of Benjamin, the cities given were Gibeon, Geba, Anathoth, and Almon, making 4 cities. (Benjamin: one of the tribes) **14.** In total, the priests' cities came to 13, along with their surrounding pasturelands. (Priests' cities: for Levite priests) **15.** The remaining Kohathites, who were not of the Aaronic line, received cities from the tribe of Ephraim. (Aaronic line: descendants of Aaron) **16.** These cities included Shechem (a city of refuge), Gezer, Kibzaim, and Beth-horon, making 4 cities in total. (Shechem: city of refuge) **17.** From the tribe of Dan, they received Eltekeh, Gibbethon, Aijalon, and Gath-rimmon, 4 cities in total. (Dan: one of the tribes) **18.** From half the tribe of Manasseh, they received Tanach and Gath-rimmon, 2 cities in total. (Manasseh: one of the tribes) **19.** All the cities for the Kohathites came to 10, with their surrounding pasturelands. (Pasturelands: grazing land) **20.** The Gershonites, a division of the Levites, received cities from the other half of Manasseh, including Golan in Bashan (a city of refuge) and Beesh-terah, making 2 cities. (Golan: city of refuge) **21.** From the tribe of Issachar, the Gershonites received Kishon, Dabareh, Jarmuth, and En-gannim, a total of 4 cities. (Issachar: one of the tribes) **22.** From the tribe of Asher, they received Mishal, Abdon, Helkath, and Rehob, another 4 cities. (Asher: one of the tribes) **23.** From the tribe of Naphtali, they received Kedesh in Galilee (a city of refuge), Hammoth-dor, and Kartan, a total of 3 cities. (Naphtali: one of the tribes) **24.** In total, the Gershonites received 13 cities with their surrounding pasturelands. (Pasturelands: grazing land) **25.** The Merarites, another division of the Levites, received cities from the tribe of Zebulun, including Jokneam, Kartah, Dimnah, and Nahalal, a total of 4 cities. (Zebulun: one of the tribes) **26.** From the tribe of Reuben, they received Bezer, Jahazah, Kedemoth, and Mephaath, another 4 cities. (Reuben: one of the tribes) **27.** From the tribe of Gad, they received Ramoth in Gilead (a city of refuge), Mahanaim, Heshbon, and Jazer, a total of 4 cities. (Gad: one of the tribes; Gilead: region east of Jordan) **28.** In total, the Merarites received 12 cities with their surrounding pasturelands. (Pasturelands: grazing land) **29.** The Levites received a total of 48 cities, each with its surrounding pasturelands. (Total: sum) **30.** All these cities were distributed among the Levites, ensuring that the inheritance of each family line was fulfilled. (Inheritance: property rights) **31.** The LORD gave Israel all the land He had promised to their ancestors, and they took possession of it, settling in the land. (Possession: ownership) **32.** The LORD provided peace on every side, fulfilling all His promises. Not a single enemy stood against Israel; the LORD delivered all their enemies into their hands. (Delivered: gave over) **33.** There was not a single promise the LORD made to Israel that failed; all came to pass. (Came to pass: occurred)

Chapter 22

1. Joshua called the Reubenites, Gadites, and half-tribe of Manasseh, (Reubenites: descendants of Reuben; Gadites: descendants of Gad) **2.** He said to them, "You have obeyed all that Moses, the servant of the LORD, commanded, and followed all my commands. (Obeyed: followed; commanded: instructed) **3.** You have not left your brothers, but kept the LORD's command. (Brothers: fellow Israelites) **4.** Now, the LORD has given rest to your brothers as promised. Go back to your tents and the land of your possession, which Moses gave you on the other side of the Jordan. (Rest: peace, settled life) **5.** But be very careful to follow the LORD's commands: love Him, walk in His ways, keep His commandments, and serve Him wholeheartedly. (Wholeheartedly: with full commitment) **6.** So Joshua blessed them and sent them back to their tents. (Blessed: gave good wishes) **7.** Half the tribe of Manasseh had received land in Bashan from Moses, while Joshua gave the other half land west of the Jordan. Joshua also blessed them when he sent them home. (Bashan: region east of Jordan) **8.** He told them to return with great wealth—cattle, silver, gold, brass, iron, and clothing—and to divide the spoils with their brothers. (Spoils: goods taken in battle) **9.** The Reubenites, Gadites, and half-tribe of Manasseh returned from Shiloh (in Canaan) to Gilead, to the land they had been given, according to the LORD's command through Moses. (Gilead: region east of Jordan) **10.** When they reached the Jordan River, they built a large altar near the border of Canaan. (Altar: a place for sacrifices) **11.** The Israelites heard about this and gathered at Shiloh to go to war against them. (War: battle) **12.** The whole congregation of Israel gathered at Shiloh to prepare for battle. (Congregation: group of people) **13.** The Israelites sent Phinehas, son of Eleazar the priest, to speak to the Reubenites, Gadites, and half-tribe of Manasseh in Gilead. (Phinehas: priest, son of Eleazar) **14.** With Phinehas were ten leaders, one from each tribe of Israel, all heads of their families. (Leaders: princes; Heads: leaders) **15.** They went to Gilead and questioned the tribes, asking, (Questioned: asked) **16.** "Why have you built an altar to turn away from the LORD, and rebel against Him by building an altar?" (Rebel: defy authority) **17.** "Isn't the sin of Peor enough for us? We still suffer from that sin, which caused a plague among the people." (Peor: location of a previous sin; Plague: divine punishment) **18.** "If you turn away from following the LORD today, He will be angry with all Israel tomorrow." (Turn away: reject) **19.** "If your land is unclean, come over to the LORD's land, where His tabernacle is, and live among us. Do not rebel against the LORD or build an altar beside the LORD's altar." (Unclean: ritually impure; Tabernacle: sacred tent) **20.** "Didn't Achan's sin cause all Israel to suffer, and he didn't die alone for his sin?" (**Sin**: wrongdoing) **21.** The Reubenites, Gadites, and half-tribe of Manasseh answered the leaders, saying, (Answered: replied) **22.** "The LORD, God of gods, knows the truth, and Israel will know if we have rebelled or sinned today. If so, may He punish us." (Rebelled: disobeyed; Punish: exact penalty) **23.** "If we built this altar for offerings or sacrifices, may the LORD judge us." (Judge: punish) **24.** "We built the altar not for offerings, but as a memorial. We fear that in the future, your children might ask our children, 'What do you have to do with the LORD God of Israel?'" (Memorial: a reminder; Fear: respect) **25.** "The Jordan River separates us from you; your children might tell ours that they have no share in the LORD." (Separate: divide) **26.** "So we decided to build an altar, not for offerings, but as a witness between us and you and future generations." (Witness: evidence) **27.** "We did it to show we will continue to serve the LORD with offerings and sacrifices, and that your children won't say we have no part in the LORD." (Serve: worship) **28.** "We want to say, 'Look at the altar of the LORD, which our ancestors built.' It's not for offerings, but as a reminder of our shared worship.". "God forbid that we should turn away from the LORD and build an altar for offerings beside the LORD's altar." (God forbid: may it never happen) **30.** When Phinehas and the leaders heard this explanation, they were pleased. (Pleased: satisfied) **31.** Phinehas said, "Today we see that the LORD is with us, because you have not sinned against Him. You have saved Israel from His anger." (Sinned: committed wrong) **32.** Phinehas and the leaders returned to Canaan and reported back to the Israelites. (Reported: told) **33.** The Israelites were pleased with the explanation, and they blessed God. They no longer planned to attack the Reubenites, Gadites, and Manassites. (Planned: intended) **34.** The Reubenites, Gadites, and half-tribe of Manasseh named the altar "Ed," saying, "It is a witness between us that the LORD is God." (Witness: reminder)

Chapter 23

1. A long time passed after the LORD had given Israel rest from their enemies, and Joshua grew old and advanced in age. (Rest: peace, settled life) **2.** Joshua called all Israel—elders, heads, judges, and officers—and said, "I am old and advanced in age." (Advanced: progressed; Elders: older leaders) **3.** "You have seen all that the LORD your God has done to the nations because of you; He fought for you." (Fought: battled) **4.** "I have divided the remaining nations among you as an inheritance for your tribes, from the Jordan to the Great Sea." (Inheritance: land passed down; Jordan: river marking Israel's eastern border) **5.** "The LORD your God will drive them out from before you, and you will possess their land as He promised." (Drive out: force out) **6.** "Therefore, be very strong to obey everything written in the book of the law of Moses. Do not turn from it to the right or left." (Obey: follow; Law of Moses: God's commandments) **7.** "Do not mingle with the remaining nations; do not mention their gods or swear by them, serve them, or bow to them." (Mingle: associate; Bow: show respect) **8.** "But cling to the LORD your God, as you have done until now." (Cling: hold firmly) **9.** "The LORD has driven out great and powerful nations before you, and no one has been able to stand against you." (Driven out: forced away) **10.** "One of you can chase a thousand, for the LORD fights for you, as He promised." (Chase: defeat; Fights: battles) **11.** "So be very careful to love the LORD your God." (Love: devotion) **12.** "If you turn back and join the remaining nations, make marriages with them, and become mixed, know for certain that the LORD will no longer drive out these nations from before you." (Mix: intermarry) **13.** "They will become traps, snares, whips in your sides, and thorns in your eyes, until you are destroyed from this good land." (Snares: traps; Whips: painful punishment) **14.** "Look, I am going the way of all the earth, and you know in your hearts that not one thing has failed of all the good things the LORD promised; all have come to pass." (Promised: said He would do) **15.** "But just as all the good things the LORD promised have happened, so He will bring upon you all the evil things until He has destroyed you from this good land." (Evil things: punishment) **16.** "If you break the covenant of the LORD and serve other gods, the LORD's anger will be kindled against you, and you will quickly perish from this land." (Break: disobey; Kindled: ignited, stirred up)

Chapter 24

1. Joshua gathered all the tribes of Israel at Shechem and called together the elders, leaders, judges, and officers of Israel to present themselves before God. (Shechem: an ancient city; Officers: leaders) **2.** Joshua addressed the people, saying, "This is the message of the LORD, the God of Israel: 'Long ago, your ancestors lived beyond the Euphrates River. They worshiped other gods, including Terah, the father of Abraham and Nahor.'" (Euphrates: a major river; Ancestors: forefathers) **3.** "I took your ancestor Abraham from the other side of the river and led him throughout the land of Canaan. I gave him Isaac, and to Isaac, I gave Jacob and Esau." (Other side: beyond, opposite; Led: guided) **4.** "I gave Esau the mountainous region of Seir to possess, but Jacob and his children went down to Egypt." (Mountains of Seir: the region inhabited by Esau's descendants) **5.** "I sent Moses and Aaron to Egypt, and I sent great plagues upon the land. Afterward, I brought you out." (Plagued: struck with disasters) **6.** "I led your ancestors out of Egypt, and when you came to the Red Sea, the Egyptians chased after you with their chariots and horsemen." (Chariots: battle vehicles) **7.** "When they cried out to the LORD, He caused darkness to separate you from the Egyptians, and He made the sea come upon them, drowning them. You witnessed what I did to Egypt, and you stayed in the wilderness for many years." (Darkness: a supernatural cloud barrier) **8.** "I brought you into the land of the Amorites, who lived on the other side of the Jordan River. They fought against you, but I handed them over to you, and you took possession of their land." (Amorites: a group of ancient peoples; Possession: control of land) **9.** "Then Balak, the king of Moab, rose up to fight Israel and sent for Balaam, the son of Beor, to curse you." (Waged war: fought; Curse: speak harm over) **10.** "But I did not listen to Balaam. Instead, he blessed you, and I saved you from his grasp." (Delivered: rescued) **11.** "You crossed over the Jordan River and came to Jericho, where its people, along with the Amorites, Perizzites, Canaanites, Hittites, Girgashites, Hivites, and Jebusites, fought against you. But I gave them into your hands." (Jericho: a city; Perizzites: another Canaanite group) **12.** "I sent hornets ahead of you to drive out the two kings of the Amorites, not through your own sword or bow." (Hornets: insects used as symbols of overwhelming force) **13.** "I gave you land that you did not work for, cities you did not build, and vineyards and olive groves that you did not plant, yet you enjoy the fruits of them." (Labor: work) **14.** "Now, reverently fear the LORD and serve Him wholeheartedly.

Remove the gods your ancestors worshiped beyond the river and in Egypt, and serve the LORD alone." (Sincerity: honesty; Truth: faithfulness) **15.** "But if serving the LORD doesn't seem right to you, then choose today whom you will serve—whether the gods your forefathers worshiped beyond the river, or the gods of the Amorites in whose land you now live. But as for me and my family, we will serve the LORD." (Undesirable: unappealing) **16.** The people answered, "God forbid that we should abandon the LORD and serve other gods." (Forsake: abandon) **17.** "It was the LORD our God who brought us and our ancestors out of Egypt, from the house of slavery. He performed great signs before our eyes and protected us on our journey." (Bondage: slavery) **18.** "He drove out all the nations, including the Amorites who lived in the land. Therefore, we will also serve the LORD, for He is our God." (Drive out: forced out) **19.** Joshua told the people, "You cannot serve the LORD—for He is a holy and jealous God. He will not forgive your sins and rebellion." (Holy: sacred, pure; Jealous: zealous, protective) **20.** "If you abandon the LORD and worship other gods, He will bring disaster upon you, destroying you after He has been good to you." (Disaster: ruin) **21.** The people responded, "No! We will serve the LORD." (Will: choose) **22.** Joshua said, "You are witnesses against yourselves that you have chosen to serve the LORD." And the people replied, "We are witnesses." (Witnesses: those who testify) **23.** "Now then, put away the foreign gods among you and direct your hearts to the LORD, the God of Israel." (Foreign gods: idols; Incline: direct) **24.** The people said, "We will serve the LORD our God and obey His voice." (Obey: follow) **25.** So Joshua made a covenant with the people that day, establishing decrees and laws for them at Shechem. (Covenant: formal agreement) **26.** Joshua recorded these words in the Book of the Law of God, and took a large stone and set it up under an oak tree near the sanctuary of the LORD. (Sanctuary: sacred place) **27.** Joshua said, "This stone will stand as a witness against us, for it has heard all the words the LORD has spoken to us. It will testify to ensure that you do not reject your God." (Deny: reject) **28.** Then Joshua sent the people home, each to their inherited land. (Inheritance: land allotted to them) **29.** After these events, Joshua, the servant of the LORD, passed away at the age of 110. (Servant: devoted follower) **30.** They buried him in his allotted land in Timnath-serah, in the hill country of Ephraim, north of Mount Gaash. (Timnath-serah: a location in Ephraim; Inheritance: land given to him) **31.** Israel served the LORD throughout Joshua's lifetime and during the time of the elders who outlived him, and who had witnessed all the works the LORD had done for Israel. (Outlived: lived longer than) **32.** The bones of Joseph, which the Israelites had brought from Egypt, were buried in Shechem in a plot of land Jacob had purchased from the sons of Hamor for 100 pieces of silver. This land became the inheritance of the children of Joseph. (Pieces of silver: money) **33.** Eleazar, the son of Aaron, passed away, and they buried him in a hill that belonged to his son Phinehas, in the hill country of Ephraim. (Eleazar: the priest; Phinehas: his son)

7 – Judges
Chapter 1

1. After Joshua's death, the Israelites asked the LORD, "Who will lead us in battle against the Canaanites first?" (Mizpeh: a gathering place) **2.** The LORD answered, "Judah shall go up first; I have given them victory over the land." (Judah: one of the twelve tribes of Israel) **3.** Judah then called upon his brother Simeon, saying, "Come with me to fight the Canaanites, and I will help you in your territory." Simeon agreed to join him. (Simeon: another tribe of Israel) **4.** Judah went up, and the LORD gave them victory, defeating the Canaanites and the Perizzites, killing ten thousand in Bezek. (Bezek: a location in Canaan) **5.** They found Adoni-bezek in Bezek and fought him, defeating the Canaanites and Perizzites. (Adoni-bezek: king of Bezek) **6.** Adoni-bezek fled, but they caught him, cut off his thumbs and big toes. (Thumbs and toes: symbolic of power and leadership) **7.** Adoni-bezek said, "Seventy kings with their thumbs and big toes cut off ate scraps under my table. I did as much, and now God has repaid me." They brought him to Jerusalem, where he died. (Jerusalem: a major city in Israel) **8.** The people of Judah fought against Jerusalem, captured it, struck it with the sword, and set it on fire. (Jerusalem: the city of David) **9.** Afterward, they moved to fight the Canaanites in the hill country, the south, and the valley. (Hill country: elevated land) **10.** Judah attacked the Canaanites in Hebron (formerly called Kirjath-arba) and killed Sheshai, Ahiman, and Talmai. (Hebron: a city in southern Israel) **11.** Then, they fought the people of Debir, which was once called Kirjath-sepher. (Debir: another city in Canaan) **12.** Caleb offered his daughter Achsah as a wife to whoever captured Kirjath-sepher. (Caleb: a leader from Judah) **13.** Othniel, Caleb's younger brother, captured it, and Caleb gave him Achsah as his wife. (Othniel: son of Kenaz, Caleb's brother) **14.** When Achsah came to Othniel, she urged him to ask her father for a field. She got off her donkey, and Caleb asked, "What do you want?" (Achsah: Caleb's daughter) **15.** She replied, "Give me a blessing, for you've given me land in the south. Also, give me springs of water." Caleb gave her both the upper and lower springs. (Springs: sources of water) **16.** The descendants of the Kenite (Moses' father-in-law) went up from the city of palm trees with Judah into the wilderness south of Arad, where they settled among the people. (Kenites: descendants of Moses' father-in-law) **17.** Judah and Simeon fought against Zephath, destroyed it, and renamed it Hormah. (Hormah: a city in southern Canaan) **18.** Judah captured Gaza, Askelon, and Ekron, along with their territories. (Gaza, Askelon, Ekron: cities of the Philistines) **19.** The LORD was with Judah, helping them drive out the mountain inhabitants, but they could not defeat those in the valley because they had iron chariots. (Iron chariots: advanced military technology) **20.** As Moses had promised, they gave Hebron to Caleb, and he drove out the three sons of Anak. (Anak: a group of giants) **21.** The tribe of Benjamin did not drive out the Jebusites from Jerusalem; the Jebusites remained in the city with the Benjamites. (Jebusites: ancient inhabitants of Jerusalem) **22.** The house of Joseph also went up against Bethel, and the LORD was with them. (Bethel: a sacred site in Israel) **23.** The house of Joseph sent spies to observe Bethel (formerly called Luz). (Luz: an old name for Bethel) **24.** The spies saw a man coming out of the city and asked him to show them the way into the city, promising mercy in return. (Mercy: kindness or clemency) **25.** He showed them the entrance, and they struck the city with the sword but spared the man and his family. (Struck: attacked) **26.** The man went to the Hittite territory, built a city, and named it Luz, and it still bears that name today. **27.** Manasseh did not drive out the people of Beth-shean, Taanach, Dor, Ibleam, or Megiddo and their surrounding towns; the Canaanites remained. (Beth-shean, Taanach, Dor, Ibleam, Megiddo: cities in Canaan) **28.** When Israel became strong, they made the Canaanites pay tribute but did not drive them out completely. (Tribute: payment made to a conqueror) **29.** Ephraim also did not drive out the Canaanites from Gezer, and they lived among them. (Ephraim: a tribe of Israel) **30.** Zebulun did not drive out the Canaanites from Kitron or Nahalol, so the Canaanites lived among them and became their servants. (Zebulun: a tribe of Israel) **31.** Asher failed to drive out the Canaanites from Accho, Zidon, Ahlab, Achzib, Helbah, Aphik, and Rehob. (Asher: a tribe of Israel) **32.** The people of Asher lived among the Canaanites, as they did not drive them out. (Asherites: descendants of Asher) **33.** Naphtali did not drive out the people of Beth-shemesh or Beth-anath, and the Canaanites lived among them, but they made the Canaanites pay tribute. (Naphtali: a tribe of Israel) **34.** The Amorites forced the Danites into the mountains and did not let them come down into the valley. (Danites: descendants of Dan) **35.** The Amorites lived in Mount Heres, Aijalon, and Shaalbim, but the house of Joseph was strong enough to make them pay tribute. (Aijalon: a city in the hill country) **36.** The border of the Amorites stretched from Akrabbim to the rock and upward. (Akrabbim: a region or pass in Canaan)

Chapter 2

1. Then the Angel of the Lord came from Gilgal to Bochim and said, "I brought you up from Egypt and gave you the land I promised your ancestors. I said, 'I will never break My covenant with you.' (Gilgal: a place in Israel; Bochim: a place in Israel) **2.** Do not make any agreements with the people of this land, and tear down their altars. But you have not obeyed Me. Why have you done this? **3.** Therefore, I will not drive them out before you; they will be thorns in your side, and their gods will trap you." **4.** When the Angel of the Lord spoke these words to all the Israelites, the people wept aloud. **5.** They called the place Bochim and offered sacrifices there to the Lord. **6.** After Joshua dismissed the people, the Israelites went to take possession of their land. **7.** The people served the Lord all the days of Joshua and the elders who outlived him, those who had seen the great works of the Lord. **8.** Joshua son of Nun, the servant of the Lord, died at 110 years old. (Joshua: leader of Israel) **9.** They buried him in his inheritance at Timnath Heres, in the mountains of Ephraim, north of Mount Gaash. (Timnath Heres: a town; Ephraim: a tribe of Israel; Gaash: a mountain) **10.** After that generation died, another arose who did not know the Lord or the works He had done for Israel. **11.** The Israelites did evil in the Lord's sight and served the Baals. (Baals: false gods) **12.** They forsook the Lord, who brought them out of Egypt, and followed the gods of the surrounding nations, provoking the Lord to anger. **13.** They abandoned the Lord and served Baal and the Ashtoreths. (Ashtoreths: Canaanite deities) **14.** The Lord's anger burned against Israel, so He gave them into the hands of raiders who plundered them and sold them to their enemies. They could no longer stand before their foes. **15.** Wherever they went, the Lord's hand was against them, bringing disaster as He had warned and sworn to them. They were greatly distressed. **16.** The Lord raised up judges who saved them from the hands of their raiders. **17.** Yet they did not listen to their judges; they prostituted themselves to other gods and bowed down to them. They quickly turned from the ways their ancestors followed, not obeying the Lord. **18.** When the Lord rose up judges, He was with the judge and saved them from their enemies for as long as the judge lived. The Lord had compassion on their groaning under oppression. **19.** But when the judge died, they returned to their corrupt ways and became even worse than their ancestors, following other gods and serving them. They did not abandon their evil practices. **20.** The Lord's anger was hot against Israel, and He said, "Because this nation has violated My covenant and not obeyed My voice, **21.** I will no longer drive out before them any of the nation's Joshua left when he died. **22.** I will test Israel through them, to see if they will keep the Lord's ways, as their ancestors did, or not." **23.** So the Lord left those nations, not driving them out immediately, nor delivering them into Joshua's hands.

Chapter 3

1. The Lord left these nations to test Israel, those who hadn't endured war in Canaan. (Canaan: ancient land of Israel) **2.** This was to educate the generations of Israel, especially those who didn't know war. **3.** These nations included the five Philistine lords, Canaanites, Sidonians, and Hivites who lived in Mount Lebanon, from Baal Hermon to the entrance of Hamath. (Philistine: ancient adversary of Israel; Sidonians: people from Sidon; Hamath: megacity in northern Syria) **4.** They were left to test Israel, to see if they would follow God's commands given through Moses. **5.** The Israelites lived among the Canaanites, Hittites, Amorites, Perizzites, Hivites, and Jebusites. **6.** They intermarried, taking their daughters as wives. **7.** And serving their gods. **8.** The Israelites did evil, forgetting the Lord and serving the Baals and Asherahs. (Baals: false gods; Asherahs: Canaanite goddesses) **9.** The Lord's wrathfulness burned, and He sold them to Cushan-Rishathaim, king of Mesopotamia, and they served him for eight years. (Cushan-Rishathaim: king of Mesopotamia) **10.** When they cried out, the Lord raised up Othniel, son of Kenaz, Caleb's younger brother, to deliver them. (Othniel: judge of Israel; Caleb: one of Israel's leaders) **11.** The Spirit of the Lord came upon him, and he led Israel to battle, defeating Cushan-Rishathaim. **12.** The land had peace for forty years until Othniel died. **13.** The Israelites again did evil, and the Lord strengthened Eglon, king of Moab, against them for their sin. (Moab: area east of Israel) **14.** Eglon allied with the Ammonites and Amalekites, defeated Israel, and captured the City of Palms. (Ammonites: people from Ammon; Amalekites: vagrant lineage) **15.** The Israelites served Eglon for eighteen years. **16.** When they cried out, the Lord raised up Ehud, son of Gera, a left-handed Benjamite, to deliver them. Ehud brought Israel's tribute to Eglon. (Ehud: judge of Israel; Benjamite: member of the lineage of Benjamin) **17.** Ehud made a double-edged dagger, a cubit long, and hid it on his right thigh. (Cubit: a dimension from elbow to fingertip) **18.** He presented the tribute to Eglon, who was very fat. (Eglon: king of Moab) **19.** After presenting the tribute, he sent down those who carried it. **20.** Ehud turned back near the idols at Gilgal and said to Eglon, "I have a secret message for you." Eglon ordered silence, and everyone left. Ehud went up to Eglon, who was sitting in his private chamber, and said, "I have a message from God." Eglon stood up. (Gilgal: ancient Israelite camp) **21.** Ehud reached with his left hand, took the dagger from his right thigh, and thrust it into the king's belly. **22.** The blade sank in, and the fat closed over it; Ehud left the dagger inside, and the king's bowels spilled out. **23.** Ehud left through the veranda, locked the door behind him. **24.** When Eglon's retainers came and found the doors locked, they assumed he was relieving himself in his chamber. **25.** They waited until they became embarrassed, and then opened the doors to find their king dead on the floor. **26.** Meanwhile, Ehud had escaped, passing the idols and fleeing to Seirah. (Seirah: a city in Israel) **27.** He blew a trumpet in Ephraim's mountains, and the Israelites gathered to follow him. (Ephraim: region in Israel) **28.** Ehud said, "The Lord has delivered the Moabites into your hands!" They seized the fords of the Jordan to prevent Moabites from escaping. **29.** They killed about ten thousand Moabite soldiers, all strong men; not one escaped. **30.** Moab was subdued that day, and Israel had peace for eighty years. **31.** After him, Shamgar, son of Anath, struck down six hundred Philistines with an ox goad, delivering Israel. (Shamgar: judge of Israel; Ox goad: a long stick used to drive cattle).

Chapter 4

1. After Ehud died, the Israelites did evil again in the sight of the Lord. (Ehud: a judge of Israel) **2.** So the Lord handed them over to Jabin, king of Canaan, who ruled from Hazor, and his army commander was Sisera, who lived in Harosheth Hagoyim. (Jabin: Canaanite king; Hazor: an ancient city in Canaan; Sisera: army commander) **3.** The Israelites cried out to the Lord, for Jabin had nine hundred iron chariots and oppressed them for twenty years. (Chariots: wheeled military vehicles) **4.** At that time, Deborah, a prophetess and wife of Lapidoth, was leading Israel. (Deborah: a female prophet and judge) **5.** She sat under the Palm of Deborah, between Ramah and Bethel, in the mountains of Ephraim, where the Israelites came to her for judgment. (Ramah: a city; Bethel: a religious center; Ephraim: a tribe of Israel) **6.** Deborah called Barak, son of Abinoam from Kedesh in Naphtali, and said, "Hasn't the Lord commanded you to gather troops at Mount Tabor and take ten thousand men from Naphtali and Zebulun? (Kedesh: a city in Naphtali; Mount Tabor: a mountain; Naphtali and Zebulun: tribes of Israel) **7.** I will bring Sisera, the commander of Jabin's army, to the Kishon River and give him into your hands." (Kishon River: a river in Canaan) **8.** Barak replied, "If you go with me, I will go; if not, I won't." **9.** Deborah agreed, "I will go, but the glory will not be yours, for the Lord will give Sisera to a woman." So Deborah went with Barak to Kedesh. **10.** Barak gathered men from Zebulun and Naphtali, and with ten thousand men, they went up, with Deborah leading them. **11.** Heber the Kenite, a descendant of Hobab (Moses' father-in-law), had separated from his people and pitched his tent near Zaanaim, by Kedesh. (Heber: a Kenite; Hobab: Moses' father-in-law) **12.** Sisera learned that Barak had gone to Mount Tabor. **13.** Sisera gathered his nine hundred iron chariots and his troops from Harosheth Hagoyim to the Kishon River. (Harosheth Hagoyim: a city of Canaanites) **14.** Deborah said to Barak, "Go! The Lord has given Sisera into your hands. Hasn't He already gone ahead of you?" Barak led ten thousand men down from Mount Tabor. **15.** The Lord routed Sisera, his chariots, and his army, and Sisera fled on foot. **16.** Barak pursued them to Harosheth Hagoyim, and Sisera's entire army was killed, not a man remained. **17.** Sisera fled on foot to the tent of Jael, wife of Heber the Kenite, because there was peace between Jabin, king of Hazor, and Heber's family. (Jael: Heber's wife; Hazor: an ancient Canaanite city) **18.** Jael greeted Sisera, "Come in, don't be afraid." He entered her tent, and she covered him with a blanket. **19.** He asked for water, and she gave him milk, then covered him again. **20.** Sisera told her, "Stand at the door, and if anyone asks if there's a man here, say 'No.'" **21.** Jael quietly took a tent peg and hammer, and drove the peg through his temple into the ground, killing him while he slept. **22.** When Barak came searching for Sisera, Jael showed him the body, with the peg still in his temple. **23.** That day, God defeated Jabin, king of Canaan, before the Israelites. **24.** The Israelites grew stronger against Jabin and eventually destroyed him.

Chapter 5
1. On that day, Deborah and Barak, son of Abinoam, sang this song. **2.** Praise the LORD for avenging Israel, when the people freely offered themselves. **3.** Listen, O kings; pay attention, O rulers; I, even I, will sing to the LORD, I will praise the LORD God of Israel. **4.** LORD, when You came from Seir and marched from Edom's fields, the earth shook, the skies poured, and the clouds brought rain. (Seir: a mountainous region; Edom: an ancient kingdom southeast of Israel) **5.** The mountains melted before the LORD, even Sinai before the LORD God of Israel. (Sinai: the mountain where Moses received the Ten Commandments) **6.** In the days of Shamgar, son of Anath, and Jael, the highways were deserted, and travelers took the back roads. (Shamgar: an Israelite judge; Jael: a woman who killed Sisera) **7.** The villages stopped in Israel, until I, Deborah, arose as a mother in Israel. **8.** The people chose new gods, and war broke out at the city gates. Was there a shield or spear among forty thousand in Israel? **9.** My heart is with Israel's leaders, who volunteered to fight. Bless the LORD. **10.** Speak, those who ride on white donkeys, who sit in judgment, and walk along the road. (White donkeys: a symbol of nobility or leadership) **11.** Those rescued from the archers at the water sources will praise the righteous acts of the LORD, and the people will go down to the gates. **12.** Wake up, Deborah! Wake up and sing! Arise, Barak, and lead your captives away, son of Abinoam. **13.** Then the survivors became rulers over the mighty, and the LORD gave me dominion over the strong. **14.** From Ephraim came leaders against Amalek; after you, Benjamin, with your people; from Machir came governors, and from Zebulun came those who wrote the law. (Amalek: an enemy of Israel; Machir: a clan of the tribe of Manasseh) **15.** The princes of Issachar were with Deborah, and also Barak, who was sent on foot into the valley. Reuben's divisions had deep thoughts. (Issachar: a tribe of Israel) **16.** Why did you stay among the sheepfolds, listening to the bleating of the flocks? Reuben had great concerns. **17.** Gilead stayed across the Jordan, and why did Dan remain with the ships? Asher stayed on the coast, staying by his coves. (Gilead: a region east of the Jordan; Dan: a tribe of Israel) **18.** Zebulun and Naphtali risked their lives in battle on the high ground. (Naphtali: a tribe of Israel) **19.** The kings came and fought, the kings of Canaan fought at Taanach by Megiddo's waters; they took no spoils. (Taanach: a city in Canaan; Megiddo: an ancient city) **20.** The stars fought from heaven against Sisera. **21.** The Kishon River swept them away, that ancient river, the Kishon. O my soul, you have trampled strength. (Kishon: a river in Israel) **22.** The horse hooves broke from the galloping of their mighty ones. **23.** Curse Meroz, says the angel of the LORD, curse its people for not coming to the help of the LORD against the mighty. (Meroz: a city whose people did not come to fight) **24.** Blessed above all women is Jael, wife of Heber the Kenite; she is blessed above women in the tent. (Jael: a woman who killed Sisera; Heber: a Kenite) **25.** He asked for water, and she gave him milk; she brought out cream in a noble dish. **26.** She took a tent peg and a hammer, and struck Sisera's head, piercing his temples. **27.** At her feet, he bowed, fell, and lay dead. **28.** The mother of Sisera looked out the window and cried, "Why is his chariot so late? Why do the wheels tarry?" **29.** Her wise women answered her, and she returned an answer to herself: **30.** "Are they not dividing the spoil? A young girl or two for each man, embroidered garments for Sisera, fit for the necks of the victorious." **31.** So, let all Your enemies perish, O LORD! But those who love You will be like the sun rising in its strength. And the land had peace for forty years.

Chapter 6
1. The Israelites did evil in the Lord's sight, and He gave them into the hands of Midian for seven years. (Midian: a people descended from Abraham) **2.** Midian oppressed Israel, so they hid in caves, dens, and strongholds in the mountains. (Strongholds: fortified places) **3.** Whenever Israel planted crops, the Midianites, Amalekites, and people from the East would invade. (Amalekites: descendants of Esau, East: the direction of the desert) **4.** They destroyed the crops as far as Gaza, leaving nothing—no sheep, ox, or donkey. (Gaza: a city on the Mediterranean coast) **5.** They came in vast numbers with livestock and tents, as countless as locusts, and ravaged the land. **6.** Israel became very poor due to Midian's oppression, and the Israelites cried out to the Lord. **7.** When the Israelites cried out because of Midian, **8.** the Lord sent them a prophet, saying, "I brought you up from Egypt, out of slavery, **9.** rescued you from the Egyptians and all your oppressors, drove them out, and gave you their land. **10.** I told you, 'I am the Lord your God; do not fear the gods of the Amorites, whose land you live in.' But you did not obey Me." (Amorites: ancient people of Canaan) **11.** The Angel of the Lord came and sat under the oak in Ophrah, which belonged to Joash the Abiezrite, while Gideon was threshing wheat in the winepress to hide from the Midianites. (Ophrah: a town in Israel, Joash: Gideon's father) **12.** The Angel appeared and said, "The Lord is with you, mighty warrior!" **13.** Gideon replied, "If the Lord is with us, why has all this happened? Where are His miracles? Didn't He bring us up from Egypt? Now He has abandoned us and given us to Midian." **14.** The Lord said to him, "Go with your strength, and you will save Israel from Midian. I am sending you." **15.** Gideon answered, "How can I save Israel? My clan is the weakest in Manasseh, and I am the least in my family." (Manasseh: one of the tribes of Israel) **16.** The Lord said, "I will be with you, and you will strike down Midian as one man." **17.** Gideon asked, "If I have found favor with You, give me a sign that it's You talking to me. **18.** Please stay here until I bring an offering and set it before You." The Lord said, "I will wait until you return." **19.** Gideon prepared a goat and unleavened bread, brought them under the oak, and presented them. **20.** The Angel instructed him, "Place the meat and bread on this rock and pour out the broth." Gideon did so. **21.** The Angel touched the offering with His staff, and fire sprang from the rock, consuming the meat and bread. Then the Angel vanished. **22.** Gideon realized it was the Angel of the Lord and said, "Alas, Lord! I've seen the Angel of the Lord face to face." **23.** The Lord reassured him, "Peace be with you; do not fear. You will not die." **24.** Gideon built an altar to the Lord and named it "The Lord is Peace," and it remains in Ophrah to this day. **25.** That night, the Lord instructed him, "Take your father's second bull, a seven-year-old, and destroy the altar of Baal. Cut down the idol beside it. **26.** Build an altar to the Lord on this rock, and offer the bull as a burnt sacrifice using the wood of the idol." **27.** Gideon took ten servants and did as the Lord commanded, but he did it at night because he feared his family and the townspeople. **28.** The next morning, the people saw the altar of Baal destroyed, the idol cut down, and the bull sacrificed on the new altar. **29.** They asked, "Who did this?" When they found out it was

Gideon, the son of Joash, **30.** they demanded he be brought out to die for destroying the altar of Baal and cutting down the idol. **31.** Joash replied, "Are you defending Baal? If Baal is a god, let him defend himself, since his altar has been destroyed." **32.** That day, Joash named Gideon "Jerubbaal," meaning "Let Baal contend with him," because he had destroyed Baal's altar. **33.** The Midianites, Amalekites, and people from the East gathered, crossed over, and camped in the Valley of Jezreel. (Jezreel: a valley in northern Israel) **34.** The Spirit of the Lord came upon Gideon, and he blew a trumpet to summon the Abiezrites to follow him. **35.** He sent messengers to Manasseh, Asher, Zebulun, and Naphtali, and they came to join him. **36.** Gideon said to God, "If You will save Israel by my hand as You promised, **37.** I will place a wool fleece on the threshing floor. If there is dew on the fleece but the ground is dry, I will know You will save Israel through me." **38.** It happened as he asked. The next morning, he squeezed out the fleece and wrung out a bowlful of dew. **39.** Gideon said, "Please, don't be angry with me, but let me test once more: Let the fleece be dry, but the ground be covered with dew." **40.** God did so: the fleece was dry, but the ground had dew.

Chapter 7

1. Then Jerubbaal (Gideon) and all his men rose early and camped by the well of Harod. The Midianites were to the north, near the hill of Moreh, in the valley. (Harod: well in Israel; Moreh: hill in Israel) **2.** The LORD said to Gideon, "You have too many men for me to hand the Midianites over to you. Israel might boast, 'We saved ourselves.'" (Boast: brag or show off) **3.** Proclaim to the people, "Anyone afraid may leave and return home from Mount Gilead." Twenty-two thousand left, leaving only ten thousand. (Mount Gilead: a region east of the Jordan) **4.** The LORD said, "There are still too many. Take them to the water, and I will test them. I'll tell you who should stay and who should go." (Test: to assess or judge) **5.** Gideon brought them to the water. The LORD said, "Separate those who lap water with their tongue like a dog from those who kneel to drink." (Lap: drink using the tongue) **6.** Three hundred lapped the water with their hands; the rest knelt to drink. (Kneel: bend down on the knees) **7.** The LORD told Gideon, "With these three hundred, I will save you and give the Midianites into your hands. Let the others go home." (Hands: possession or control) **8.** The men took food and trumpets, and Gideon sent the rest of Israel home, keeping only the three hundred. The Midianites lay in the valley below. (Trumpets: signaling instruments) **9.** That night, the LORD told Gideon, "Get up, go down to the camp. I've given it into your hands." (Camp: enemy's military camp) **10.** "If you're afraid, take your servant Phurah with you and listen to what they say." (Phurah: Gideon's servant) **11.** Gideon and Phurah went to the edge of the camp and overheard a soldier's dream. (Edge: outer area of the camp) **12.** The Midianites, Amalekites, and the people of the East lay in the valley, as countless as locusts, with camels as numerous as sand by the sea. (Amalekites: nomadic people; Locusts: insects that swarm in large numbers) **13.** Gideon overheard one man tell his friend, "I dreamed a barley cake rolled into the Midianite camp and struck a tent, knocking it over." (Barley: type of grain) **14.** His friend replied, "This is the sword of Gideon, son of Joash, a man of Israel. God has given Midian into his hands." (Gideon: leader of Israel) **15.** When Gideon heard the dream and its interpretation, he worshiped God, returned to the camp, and said, "Get up! The LORD has given Midian to us." (Worship: show reverence to God) **16.** He divided the three hundred men into three groups. Each had a trumpet, an empty jar, and a torch inside. (Torch: a light source) **17.** He told them, "Watch me and do the same. When I reach the edge of the camp, do as I do." (Edge: outer boundary) **18.** "When I blow the trumpet, everyone with me will blow theirs, and all will shout, 'The sword of the LORD and of Gideon!'" (Shout: cry out loudly) **19.** Gideon and his hundred men reached the camp's edge at the middle watch and blew their trumpets, breaking their jars. (Middle watch: part of the night shift, usually midnight to 3 AM) **20.** The three groups blew their trumpets, broke their jars, held the torches in their left hands and the trumpets in their right, shouting, "The sword of the LORD and of Gideon!" (Torches: light sources) **21.** Each man stood in place, and the enemy army panicked, running, crying out, and fleeing. (Panicked: filled with fear) **22.** The three hundred blew their trumpets, and the LORD caused the Midianites to turn on each other with their swords. The rest fled to Beth-shittah, Zererath, and Abel-meholah, near Tabbath. (Zererath: a place in Israel; Abel-meholah: a town) **23.** Men from Naphtali, Asher, and Manasseh gathered and pursued the Midianites. (Naphtali, Asher, Manasseh: tribes of Israel) **24.** Gideon sent messengers to Ephraim, saying, "Come and seize the waters near Beth-barah and the Jordan River." The men of Ephraim gathered and took the crossings. (Ephraim: a tribe of Israel; Beth-barah: a location) **25.** They captured two Midianite princes, Oreb and Zeeb, killed Oreb at the rock of Oreb, and Zeeb at the winepress of Zeeb. They pursued Midian and brought their heads to Gideon across the Jordan. (Oreb, Zeeb: Midianite princes; Winepress: a place for crushing grapes)

Chapter 8

1. The men of Ephraim said to Gideon, "Why did you not call us to fight the Midianites?" They argued with him sharply. (Ephraim: tribe of Israel) **2.** Gideon replied, "What have I done compared to you? Is not the leftover harvest of Ephraim better than the full harvest of Abi-ezer?" (Abi-ezer: a family of Manasseh) **3.** God handed over the leaders of Midian, Oreb and Zeeb, to you. What could I have done compared to you?" Their anger calmed when he spoke this. (Oreb and Zeeb: Midianite princes) **4.** Gideon and his 300 men crossed the Jordan, weary but still chasing the enemy. (Jordan: river in Israel) **5.** He asked the men of Succoth, "Give bread to my soldiers, for they are exhausted as I chase Zebah and Zalmunna, kings of Midian." (Succoth: town in Israel) **6.** The leaders of Succoth replied, "Are Zebah and Zalmunna already in your hands that we should give you bread?" **7.** Gideon answered, "When the Lord delivers Zebah and Zalmunna to me, I will punish you with thorns and briers of the wilderness." (Zebah and Zalmunna: Midianite kings) **8.** He went to Penuel and said the same, but the men of Penuel responded like the men of Succoth. (Penuel: town in Israel) **9.** He told them, "When I return safely, I will destroy this tower." (Tower: stronghold or fortress) **10.** Zebah and Zalmunna were at Karkor with 15,000 men, the last of the eastern armies, after 120,000 had fallen. (Karkor: a place in the desert) **11.** Gideon took the route east of Nobah and Jogbehah, and struck the unsuspecting camp. (Nobah and Jogbehah: towns near Midian) **12.** When Zebah and Zalmunna fled, Gideon captured them and defeated their entire army. **13.** Gideon, the son of Joash, returned before sunrise. **14.** He captured a young man from Succoth and asked him to identify the 77 leaders and elders of the town. **15.** Gideon confronted the men of Succoth, saying, "Here are Zebah and Zalmunna, whom you mocked. Why didn't you help us?" **16.** He took the elders, used thorns and briers, and punished the men of Succoth. (Thorns and briers: sharp plants used for punishment) **17.** He tore down the tower of Penuel and killed the men of the city. **18.** Gideon asked Zebah and Zalmunna, "What kind of men did you kill at Tabor?" They replied, "They were like you, sons of kings." (Tabor: a mountain in Israel) **19.** Gideon said, "They were my brothers, sons of my mother. If you had spared them, I would not kill you." **20.** He told his firstborn son, Jether, to kill them, but the boy was too afraid. (Jether: Gideon's son) **21.** Zebah and Zalmunna urged Gideon, "Kill us, for as you are, so is your strength." Gideon rose and killed them, taking their camels' ornaments. (Ornaments: jewelry or decorative items) **22.** The Israelites asked Gideon, "Rule over us, you and your descendants, for you saved us from Midian." **23.** Gideon answered, "I will not rule over you, nor will my son. The Lord will rule over you." **24.** Gideon asked them, "Give me the gold earrings from your spoils." (Spoils: treasures taken in war) **25.** They agreed, spreading a garment to collect the earrings. **26.** The gold earrings weighed 1,700 shekels, along with the Midianite kings' ornaments, collars, purple garments, and chains from camels. (Shekels: a unit of weight and currency) **27.** Gideon made an ephod from the gold and placed it in Ophrah, but all Israel worshiped it, causing a snare to Gideon and his family. (Ephod: a priestly garment) **28.** Midian was subdued before Israel, and the land had peace for 40 years during Gideon's life. **29.** Gideon, son of Joash, returned to his home. **30.** Gideon had 70 sons from his many wives. **31.** His concubine from Shechem also bore him a son, named Abimelech. (Shechem: a city in Israel) **32.** Gideon died at a good old age and was buried in the tomb of Joash, his father, in Ophrah. (Ophrah: a town of the Abi-ezerites) **33.** After Gideon's death, the Israelites turned to worship Baalim and made Baal-Berith their god. (Baal-Berith: a Canaanite god) **34.** The Israelites did not remember the Lord who had saved them from all their enemies. **35.** They did not show kindness to the family of Gideon, despite all the good he had done for Israel.

Chapter 9

1. Abimelech, son of Jerubbaal, went to Shechem to speak with his mother's relatives. **2.** He asked them to speak to the men of Shechem: "Is it better for seventy sons of Jerubbaal to rule over you, or just one? Remember, I am your own flesh and blood." **3.** His relatives spoke to the men of Shechem, and they decided to support Abimelech, saying, "He is our brother." **4.** They gave him seventy silver pieces from the house of Baal-Berith, which he used to hire worthless men to follow him. **5.** Abimelech went to his father's house in Ophrah and killed seventy sons of Jerubbaal on one stone, except for Jotham, the youngest, who hid. **6.** The men of Shechem and the house of Millo gathered and made Abimelech king at the pillar in Shechem. **7.** When Jotham heard, he stood on Mount Gerizim, cried out, and said, "Listen, that God may listen to you." **8.** The trees went to anoint a king, asking the olive tree, "Reign over us." **9.** The olive tree replied, "Should I give up my oil, which honors God and man, to rule over trees?" **10.** The trees asked the fig tree, "Come, reign over us." **11.** The fig tree said, "Should I forsake my sweetness and good fruit to rule over trees?" **12.** Then the trees asked the vine, "Come, reign over us." **13.** The vine said, "Should I leave my wine, which cheers both God and man, to rule over trees?" **14.** Finally, all the trees asked the bramble, "Come, reign over us." **15.** The bramble replied, "If you truly want me as king, put your trust in my shadow, or let fire come out of me and destroy the cedars of Lebanon." **16.** "If you have acted sincerely in making Abimelech king and treating Jerubbaal's house well, **17.** (For my father fought for you and delivered you from Midian), **18.** and you have killed my father's sons and made Abimelech, his servant's son, king, because he is your brother, **19.** if you have been sincere, then rejoice in Abimelech, and let him rejoice in you. **20.** But if not, let fire come from Abimelech and destroy the men of Shechem and the house of Millo, and let fire come from them and consume Abimelech." **21.** Jotham fled to Beer because he feared Abimelech. **22.** After three years of Abimelech's rule over Israel, **23.** God sent an evil spirit between Abimelech and the men of Shechem, and they betrayed him. **24.** The cruelty against the seventy sons of Jerubbaal was avenged, and their blood was laid on Abimelech, who killed them, and on the men of Shechem who helped. **25.** The men of Shechem set ambushes in the mountains and robbed anyone passing by, which was reported to Abimelech. **26.** Gaal, son of Ebed, came to Shechem, and the men of Shechem trusted him. **27.** They went to gather their vineyards, celebrated, and cursed Abimelech at their god's house. **28.** Gaal said, "Who is Abimelech, and who is Shechem that we should serve him? He is the son of Jerubbaal. Why serve him when we could serve Hamor's men?" **29.** "If I had control, I would remove Abimelech. Let him increase his army and come out." **30.** Zebul, the ruler of Shechem, became angry when he heard Gaal's words. **31.** He sent messengers to Abimelech secretly, saying, "Gaal, the son of Ebed, and his brothers have come to Shechem, and they are strengthening the city against you." **32.** "So, rise up by night, you and your men, and hide in the fields. **33.** In the morning, as soon as the sun rises, get up and attack the city. When Gaal and his men come out against you, do to them whatever you can." **34.** Abimelech and his men rose up by night and lay in ambush near Shechem in four groups. **35.** Gaal, the son of Ebed, went out and stood at the gate of the city. Abimelech and his men rose up from their hiding place. **36.** When Gaal saw them, he said to Zebul, "Look, people are coming down from the mountains!" Zebul replied, "You're seeing the shadows of the mountains as if they were men." **37.** Gaal spoke again, "No, I see people coming down from the middle of the land, and another group is coming from the plain of Meonenim." **38.** Then Zebul said to him, "Where is your boasting now, when you said, 'Who is Abimelech that we should serve him?' Isn't this the people you despised? Now go out and fight them." **39.** Gaal went out with the men of Shechem and fought against Abimelech. **40.** Abimelech chased him, and Gaal fled before him. Many were wounded, and some were even killed at the entrance of the gate. **41.** Abimelech stayed at Arumah, and Zebul drove Gaal and his brothers out of Shechem, preventing them from living there. **42.** The next day, the people went into the fields, and Abimelech was informed. **43.** He divided his men into three companies and set an ambush in the fields. When the people came out of the city, he attacked them. **44.** Abimelech and his company positioned themselves at the gate of the city, while the other two companies attacked those in the fields and killed them. **45.** Abimelech fought the city all day, took it, and killed the people inside. He destroyed the city and sowed it with salt, symbolizing its desolation. **46.** When the people in the tower of Shechem heard this, they took refuge in the stronghold of the house of the god Berith. **47.** Abimelech was told that the men of the tower of Shechem had gathered there. **48.** Abimelech went up to Mount Zalmon with all his men. He cut a branch from the trees, placed it on his shoulder, and said to his men, "Do what you have seen me do." **49.** The men followed him, each cutting a branch, and they piled the branches against the stronghold, setting it on fire. About a thousand men and women died in the fire. **50.** Abimelech then went to Thebez, camped against it, and took the city. **51.** In the city was a strong tower. The men and women of the city fled to the tower and locked themselves inside, climbing to the top. **52.** Abimelech came to the tower, fought against it, and approached the door to set it on fire. **53.** A woman threw a millstone down from the tower, hitting Abimelech on the head and cracking his skull. **54.** Abimelech quickly called his armor-bearer, saying, "Draw your sword and kill me, so people won't say a woman killed me." The armor-bearer struck him down, and he died. **55.** When the Israelites saw that Abimelech was dead, they all returned to their homes. **56.** Thus, God repaid Abimelech for the wickedness he committed against his father by killing his seventy brothers. **57.** And God also repaid the evil of the men of Shechem, bringing upon them the curse of Jotham, the son of Jerubbaal. (Jotham: the youngest son of Gideon, who pronounced the curse)

Chapter 10

1. After Abimelech, Tola, son of Puah from Issachar, arose to defend Israel and lived in Shamir, in the mountain region of Ephraim. (Shamir: A town in Ephraim, a hill country) 2. He judged Israel for 23 years, then died and was buried in Shamir. 3. After him, Jair, a Gileadite, arose and judged Israel for 22 years. (Gileadite: From the region of Gilead, east of the Jordan River) 4. Jair had 30 sons who rode 30 donkeys, and they controlled 30 cities called Havoth-jair in Gilead. (Havoth-jair: "Villages of Jair," cities named after him) 5. Jair died and was buried in Camon. (Camon: A city in Gilead) 6. The Israelites again did evil in the sight of the LORD, worshipping Baalim, Ashtaroth, and the gods of Syria, Sidon, Moab, Ammon, and the Philistines, forsaking the LORD. (Baalim: Canaanite gods; Ashtaroth: Fertility goddess) 7. The LORD's anger burned against Israel, and He handed them over to the Philistines and the Ammonites. 8. For 18 years, the Ammonites oppressed Israelites in Gilead, east of the Jordan River. (Ammonites: People from Ammon, east of Israel) 9. The Ammonites crossed the Jordan to fight against Judah, Benjamin, and Ephraim, distressing Israel greatly. (Ephraim: One of the tribes of

Israel) 10. The Israelites cried to the LORD, admitting, "We have sinned by forsaking You and serving Baalim." 11. The LORD said, "Did I not deliver you from Egypt, the Amorites, the Ammonites, and the Philistines? (Amorites: Ancient people who lived in Canaan) 12. The Zidonians, Amalekites, and Maonites oppressed you, and you cried to me, and I delivered you from them." (Zidonians: People of Sidon; Amalekites: Descendants of Esau) 13. "But you have forsaken me and served other gods. Therefore, I will not deliver you again." 14. "Cry out to the gods you have chosen; let them deliver you in your time of trouble." 15. The Israelites pleaded, "We have sinned. Do what seems right to You, but deliver us this day." 16. They removed the foreign gods and served the LORD, and His soul was grieved by Israel's suffering. 17. The Ammonites gathered in Gilead, and the Israelites assembled at Mizpeh. (Mizpeh: A gathering place in Gilead) 18. The leaders of Gilead asked, "Who will lead the fight against the Ammonites? He will be ruler over all Gilead."

Chapter 11

1. Jephthah, a mighty man of valor from Gilead, was the son of a prostitute. Gilead fathered him. (Gilead: Region east of the Jordan River) 2. Gilead's wife bore him sons, but when they grew up, they expelled Jephthah, saying, "You cannot inherit in our father's house, for you are the son of a foreign woman." 3. Jephthah fled to Tob, where a group of worthless men gathered around him. (Tob: A region near Gilead) 4. The Ammonites waged war against Israel. (Ammonites: People from Ammon, east of Israel) 5. When the Ammonites fought Israel, the elders of Gilead went to bring Jephthah from Tob. 6. They asked Jephthah to be their leader to fight the Ammonites. 7. Jephthah responded, "Did you not hate me and drive me out? Why come to me now when you're in trouble?" 8. The elders replied, "We turn to you now, to lead us against the Ammonites and become our head over Gilead." 9. Jephthah asked, "If you bring me back to fight the Ammonites and the LORD delivers them to me, will I be your leader?" 10. The elders assured him, "The LORD is our witness; we will do as you say." 11. Jephthah went with the elders, and they made him head and leader over them, speaking before the LORD at Mizpah. (Mizpah: A place of gathering in Gilead) 12. Jephthah sent messengers to the king of Ammon, asking, "Why are you attacking me?" 13. The Ammonite king replied, "Israel took my land when they came from Egypt, from Arnon to Jabbok and the Jordan. Restore my land peacefully." 14. Jephthah sent messengers again to the Ammonite king, 15. saying, "Israel did not take the land of Moab or Ammon. 16. When Israel left Egypt, they traveled through the wilderness to the Red Sea and came to Kadesh. 17. Israel sent messengers to Edom and Moab, asking to pass through, but both kings refused, so Israel stayed in Kadesh. 18. They passed through the wilderness, went around Edom and Moab, and camped near Arnon, but not within Moab, for Arnon marked Moab's boundary. (Edom: A region south of Israel; Moab: A territory east of Israel) 19. Israel sent messengers to Sihon, king of the Amorites, asking to pass through his land. (Sihon: King of the Amorites) 20. But Sihon refused and gathered his people to fight Israel at Jahaz. (Jahaz: A town near the border of Moab) 21. The LORD gave Sihon and his people into Israel's hands, and Israel defeated them, taking possession of the Amorite land. 22. Israel took all the Amorite territory from Arnon to Jabbok, and from the wilderness to the Jordan. 23. The LORD has dispossessed the Amorites before Israel. Should you now take their land? 24. Will you claim what Chemosh, your god, gives you? We will possess whatever the LORD gives us. (Chemosh: The god of the Moabites) 25. Are you any better than Balak, king of Moab? Did he ever fight Israel or contend with them, 26. when Israel lived in Heshbon and its towns for 300 years? Why didn't you recover the land then? (Heshbon: A city in the territory of the Amorites) 27. I have not wronged you, but you are wronging me by waging war against me. Let the LORD be the judge between Israel and Ammon. 28. The Ammonite king did not listen to Jephthah's words. 29. Then the Spirit of the LORD came upon Jephthah, and he passed through Gilead, Manasseh, and Mizpah of Gilead before going to fight the Ammonites. 30. Jephthah made a vow to the LORD: "If You deliver the Ammonites into my hands, 31. then whatever comes out of my house to greet me when I return in peace, I will sacrifice it to the LORD as a burnt offering." 32. Jephthah fought the Ammonites, and the LORD gave them into his hands. 33. He struck them from Aroer to Minnith, twenty cities in total, and inflicted a great slaughter. The Ammonites were subdued before Israel. 34. When Jephthah returned to his house at Mizpah, his daughter came out to greet him with timbrels and dancing. She was his only child. 35. Jephthah tore his clothes and said, "Oh no, my daughter! You have brought me low, for I have made a vow to the LORD and cannot go back." 36. She replied, "If you have made a vow to the LORD, do to me as you have said, for the LORD has given you victory over your enemies." 37. She asked for two months to mourn her virginity in the mountains with her friends. 38. Jephthah granted her request, and she went with her companions to mourn. 39. After two months, she returned, and Jephthah fulfilled his vow, and she remained a virgin. It became a custom in Israel 40. for the daughters of Israel to mourn the daughter of Jephthah, the Gileadite, four days each year. (Jephthah: A judge of Israel; Gileadite: From the region of Gilead)

Chapter 12

1. The men of Ephraim gathered and went to Jephthah, criminating him, "Why did you go to war against the Ammonites without calling us? We'll burn your house down!" (Ephraim Tribe of Israel; Ammonites People of Ammon) 2. Jephthah answered them, "I was in a fierce conflict with the Ammonites, and when I called for your help, you didn't deliver me." 3. "Seeing that you didn't come to my aid, I took matters into my own hands and went to battle. The LORD gave them into my power. Why do you now come to fight me?" 4. Jephthah gathered the Gileadites and fought the Ephraimites. They defeated Ephraim, criminating them, "You Gileadites are just runaways from Ephraim and Manasseh!" (Gilead Region east of Israel; Ephraim Tribe of Israel; Manasseh Tribe of Israel) The Gileadites controlled the crossings of the Jordan. When an Ephraimite tried to flee and was asked, "Are you from Ephraim?" If he denied, they told him to say "Shibboleth." If he said "Sibboleth," they knew he was from Ephraim and killed him. Forty-two thousand Ephraimites failed. 7. Jephthah ruled Israel for six times, also failed and was buried in one of Gilead's municipalities. (Gilead Region east of Israel) 8. After Jephthah, Ibzan of Bethlehem judged Israel. (Bethlehem A city in Judah) 9. Ibzan had thirty sons and thirty daughters, whom he transferred to marry abroad, and he brought in thirty daughters for his sons. He judged Israel for seven times. 10. Ibzan failed and was buried in Bethlehem. 11. After him, Elon, from the lineage of Zebulun, judged Israel for ten times. (Zebulun Tribe of Israel) 12. Elon failed and was buried in Aijalon, in Zebulun's region. (Aijalon Town in Zebulun) 13. After Elon, Abdon, son of Hillel, from Pirathon, judged Israel. (Pirathon Town in Ephraim) 14. Abdon had forty sons and thirty grandsons, who rode seventy burros. He ruled Israel for eight times. 15. Abdon failed and was buried in Pirathon, in Ephraim's hill country, among the Amalekites. (Amalekites vagrant people frequently in conflict with Israel)

Chapter 13

1. The Israelites again did evil in the sight of the Lord, and He gave them into the hands of the Philistines for forty years. (Philistines: ancient people, often enemies of Israel) 2. A man named Manoah from Zorah, of the Danite tribe, had a wife who was childless. (Zorah: town in the tribe of Dan) 3. The Angel of the Lord appeared to her and said, "Although you are unable to have children, you will conceive and give birth to a son." 4. "Take care not to drink wine or any intoxicating beverage, and avoid eating anything that is ceremonially unclean." 5. "You will give birth to a son, and his hair will never be cut, for he will be set apart for God from his birth. He will begin the deliverance of Israel from the Philistines." (Nazirite: someone consecrated to God with special vows) 6. The woman went

to her husband and said, "A man of God appeared to me, and His appearance was like that of an angel—truly awe-inspiring. I didn't ask where He was from, and He did not reveal His name." **7.** "He said, 'You will conceive a son. Do not drink wine or strong drink, nor eat anything unclean, for he will be a Nazirite to God from birth to death.'" **8.** Manoah prayed, "Lord, please let the man You sent return and instruct us on what we should do for the child." **9.** God heard Manoah's prayer, and the Angel of the Lord appeared again to the woman while she was in the field. Her husband was not with her. **10.** The woman ran to her husband, saying, "The man who came to me has appeared again!" **11.** Manoah followed his wife and asked the man, "Are You the one who spoke to my wife?" He answered, "I am." **12.** Manoah asked, "Let Your words come true. What will the child's life and work be?" **13.** The Angel answered, "Let the woman do all I have instructed her to do. **14.** She should not eat anything from the vine, drink wine or strong drink, or consume anything unclean. Let her follow all My commands." **15.** Manoah said, "Please stay a little longer, and allow us to prepare a young goat for You." **16.** The Angel replied, "I will not eat your food, but if you offer a burnt offering, let it be for the Lord." (Manoah did not realize He was the Angel of the Lord.) **17.** Manoah asked, "What is Your name, so that we may honor You when Your words come to pass?" **18.** The Angel replied, "Why do you ask My name, seeing that it is beyond understanding?" **19.** Manoah took the goat and grain offering and placed them on a rock as a burnt offering to the Lord. As they watched, the Lord performed a miraculous act— **20.** when the flame rose from the altar, the Angel ascended in the flame. Manoah and his wife fell to the ground in awe. **21.** After the Angel of the Lord appeared no more, Manoah realized it was the Angel of the Lord. **22.** Manoah said to his wife, "We will surely die, for we have seen God!" **23.** But his wife replied, "If the Lord had intended to kill us, He would not have accepted our offerings or shown us all these things." **24.** The woman gave birth to a son and named him Samson. The boy grew, and the Lord's blessing was upon him. **25.** The Spirit of the Lord began to move him at Mahaneh Dan, between Zorah and Eshtaol. (Mahaneh Dan: a place located between Zorah and Eshtaol)

Chapter 14
1. Samson went to Timnath and saw a woman from the Philistines. (Timnath: a town in Israel) **2.** He told his parents, "I've seen a Philistine woman in Timnath. Get her for me to marry." **3.** His parents asked, "Why not marry someone from our people?" But Samson insisted, "She is right for me." **4.** They didn't realize this was God's plan to create an opportunity against the Philistines, who ruled Israel. **5.** Samson, with his parents, went to Timnath. As they passed through the vineyards, a lion attacked him. (Vineyards: fields for growing grapes) **6.** The Spirit of the Lord empowered him, and he killed the lion with his bare hands, but didn't tell his parents. **7.** Samson talked with the woman, and he liked her. **8.** Later, he returned to marry her and saw honey in the lion's carcass. (Carcass: dead body of the lion) **9.** He ate the honey, gave some to his parents without telling them where it came from. **10.** Samson's father went to the woman, and Samson prepared a feast, as was customary. **11.** The people brought thirty companions to be with him. **12.** Samson proposed a riddle: "If you solve it in seven days, I'll give you thirty garments; if not, you owe me thirty." **13.** They agreed, "Tell us the riddle." **14.** He said, "From the eater came food, and from the strong came sweetness." They couldn't solve it. **15.** On the seventh day, they threatened Samson's wife, "Trick him into telling us, or we'll burn you and your family." **16.** She cried, "You don't love me. You gave a riddle but didn't share it with me." He replied, "I haven't told my parents; why would I tell you?" **17.** She pressed him for seven days, and on the last day, he told her. She then told the others. **18.** On the seventh day, they answered, "What's sweeter than honey? What's stronger than a lion?" Samson said, "If you hadn't tricked me, you wouldn't have solved it." **19.** The Spirit of the Lord came on Samson. He went to Ashkelon (Ashkelon: a city of the Philistines), killed thirty men, took their clothes, and gave them to those who solved the riddle. He was angry and went home. **20.** Samson's wife was given to his companion, the man who had been his friend.

Chapter 15
1. Sometime later, during the wheat harvest, Samson visited his wife with a young goat, and said, "I'll go to my wife's chamber," but her father stopped him. (Wheat harvest: season of gathering wheat) **2.** Her father said, "I thought you hated her, so I gave her to your companion. Isn't her younger sister more beautiful? Take her instead." (Companion: a friend or partner) **3.** Samson replied, "Now I will be blameless, even if I harm the Philistines." (Blameless: without fault or guilt) **4.** Samson caught three hundred foxes, tied their tails together in pairs, and placed a torch between each pair. (Foxes: wild animals, used for destruction) **5.** He set the torches on fire and released the foxes into the Philistine's fields, burning their grain, vineyards, and olive trees. (Vineyards: fields for growing grapes; Olive trees: trees producing olives) **6.** The Philistines asked, "Who did this?" They were told, "Samson, the son-in-law of the Timnite, because he took his wife and gave her to his companion." The Philistines burned her and her father alive. (Timnite: from Timnah, a town in Israel) **7.** Samson said, "Although you've done this, I will take revenge, and then I will stop." (Revenge: payback for a wrong done) **8.** Samson struck them severely, causing many deaths, and then went to live at the rock of Etam. (Etam: a rocky place in Israel) **9.** The Philistines came up and camped in Judah, spreading out at Lehi. (Lehi: a location in Judah) **10.** The men of Judah asked, "Why have you come against us?" They replied, "To capture Samson and repay him for what he did to us." (Capture: seize or arrest) **11.** Three thousand men of Judah went to Etam and said, "Don't you know the Philistines rule over us? Why have you done this?" Samson answered, "I did to them what they did to me." (Rule: authority or dominance over) **12.** They said, "We've come to bind you and hand you over to the Philistines." Samson replied, "Promise me you won't kill me." (Bind: tie or restrain) **13.** They said, "We won't kill you, but we will tie you up and give you to them." They bound him with two new ropes and brought him up from the rock. (Ropes: strong cords to bind) **14.** When Samson came to Lehi, the Philistines shouted at him. The Spirit of the Lord came upon him, and the ropes broke like burnt flax, setting him free. (Spirit of the Lord: divine strength) **15.** He found a fresh jawbone of a donkey, took it, and killed a thousand men with it. (Jawbone: bone from the jaw of an animal) **16.** Samson said, "With the jawbone of a donkey, I've piled up a thousand men." (Slain: killed in battle) **17.** After speaking, he threw the jawbone away and named the place Ramath-lehi. (Ramath-lehi: "Hill of the Jawbone") **18.** Samson became very thirsty and called on the Lord, "You gave me this great victory, but will I die of thirst and fall into the hands of the uncircumcised?" (Uncircumcised: those not circumcised, often the Philistines) **19.** God caused water to flow from the jawbone, and Samson drank, regaining his strength. He named the place En-hakkore. (En-hakkore: "The Spring of the Caller") **20.** Samson judged Israel for twenty years during the time the Philistines ruled. (Judged: served as leader and deliverer)

Chapter 16
1. Samson went to Gaza, saw a courtesan, and went to her. (Gaza: Philistine megacity) **2.** The people of Gaza learned of this, girdled him, and waited at the megacity gate all night, planning to kill him in the morning. **3.** Samson stayed until night, then tore off the megacity gates and posts, carrying them to the hill near Hebron. (Hebron: ancient megacity in Judah) **4.** Later, he fell in love with a woman in the Valley of Sorek named Delilah. (Sorek: valley in Israel) **5.** The Philistine autocrats went to Delilah and offered her 1,100 pieces of silver each if she could discover the secret of Samson's strength. **6.** Delilah asked Samson to tell her the secret of his great strength and how he could be bound. **7.** Samson replied, "If they bind me with seven fresh, undried cords, I'll be weak like any other man." **8.** The Philistines gave her the seven fresh cords, and she bound him. **9.**

While men lay in ambush in the room, Delilah told Samson the Philistines were coming. He broke the cords as if they were thread. **10.** Delilah complained that he'd mocked her and prevaricated, asking again how he could be bound. **11.** He replied, "If they bind me with new ropes that have never been used, I'll be weak like any other man." **12.** Delilah bound him with new ropes, but when she cried out that the Philistines were coming, Samson broke the ropes like thread. **13.** Delilah, frustrated, asked him again how he could be bound. He said, "If you weave the seven cinches of my hair into a loom." **14.** She wove his hair into the loom and tried to trap him, but he woke up, removed the pin, and broke free. **15.** Delilah indicted him of not loving her, saying he'd mocked her three times and refused to tell her the truth. **16.** She pressed him daily, and his soul was so vexed he nearly died. **17.** Eventually, Samson told her, "I've been a Nazarite to God since birth. If my hair is cut, I'll lose my strength and become like any other man." (Nazarite: someone devoted to God by oath) **18.** Delilah saw he'd told her everything and called for the Philistine autocrats, saying, "He has revealed everything to me." They brought money with them. **19.** She made him sleep on her lap, then called for a man to shave off the seven cinches of his hair, weakening him. **20.** Delilah cried, "The Philistines are upon you!" Samson woke up, thinking he could escape, but didn't realize the LORD had left him. **21.** The Philistines captured him, gouged out his eyes, took him to Gaza, and bound him with bronze shackles. He was put to work grinding grain in prison. **22.** His hair began to grow back after it was shaved. **23.** The Philistine autocrats gathered for a great sacrifice to their god Dagon, saying, "Our god has delivered Samson, our adversary, into our hands." (Dagon: Philistine god) **24.** The people praised Dagon, saying, "Our god has delivered our adversary, the one who destroyed our land and killed many of us." **25.** When their hearts were merry, they called for Samson to entertain them. He was brought out of prison and made sport before them, standing between the pillars. **26.** Samson asked the boy who held his hand to let him feel the pillars of the house, so he could lean on them. **27.** The house was filled with men and women, including all the lords of the Philistines. About 3,000 people were on the roof, watching Samson. **28.** Samson prayed, "O LORD God, remember me and give me strength just once more, that I may avenge the Philistines for my eyes." **29.** Samson grasped the two middle pillars, one with his right hand and the other with his left. **30.** Samson said, "Let me die with the Philistines!" He pushed with all his might, and the house collapsed on the lords and all the people inside. He killed more in his death than he had in life. **31.** His family came, took his body, and buried him between Zorah and Eshtaol, in the grave of his father Manoah. He'd judged Israel for 20 times.(Zorah city in Judah; Eshtaol city in Judah; Manoah Samson's father)

Chapter 17

1. A man named Micah lived in the hill country of Ephraim. (Ephraim: region in Israel) 2. He told his mother, "The 1,100 shekels of silver you lost and cursed, I took." His mother replied, "Blessed be you, my son, by the Lord!" 3. After returning the silver, his mother said, "I dedicated it to the Lord to make a graven image, and now I will give it back to you." 4. Micah returned the silver, and his mother gave 200 shekels to a silversmith, who made a carved and molten image. They were placed in Micah's house. 5. Micah had a sanctuary with idols, an ephod (sacred garment), and teraphim (household gods), and consecrated his son as a priest. 6. At that time, there was no king in Israel, and everyone did what seemed right in their own eyes. 7. A Levite from Bethlehem in Judah came to live in Ephraim. (Bethlehem: city in Judah) 8. The Levite traveled to find a place and arrived at Micah's house in Ephraim. 9. Micah asked, "Where are you from?" The Levite answered, "I'm from Bethlehem in Judah, looking for a place to stay." 10. Micah said, "Stay with me, be like a father and priest to me. I'll give you ten shekels of silver, clothes, and food." So the Levite agreed. 11. The Levite was happy, living with Micah like a son. 12. Micah consecrated the Levite, and he became his priest in Micah's house. 13. Micah said, "Now I know the Lord will bless me, since I have a Levite as my priest."

Chapter 18

1. In those days, Israel had no king, and the Danites were looking for land to settle in, as they hadn't yet entered their inheritance. (Danites: members of the tribe of Dan) 2. The Danites sent five strong men from Zorah and Eshtaol to scout the land. They arrived at Micah's house in Mount Ephraim and stayed there. (Zorah, Eshtaol: towns in the tribe of Dan; Ephraim: region in Israel) 3. At Micah's house, they recognized the voice of the young Levite and asked, "Who brought you here? What are you doing in this place?" 4. He answered, "Micah hired me to be his priest." 5. They asked him, "Please ask God if our trip will succeed." 6. The priest replied, "Go in peace; the Lord is with you on your way." 7. The five men traveled to Laish, where they saw the people living securely, like the Zidonians, without any ruler to trouble them. (Laish: city in northern Israel; Zidonians: people of Sidon, a Phoenician city) 8. They returned to Zorah and Eshtaol, and their people asked, "What did you find?" 9. They replied, "Let's go up and take the land. It's very good. Don't hesitate, but enter and possess it." 10. "You'll find a secure and prosperous land, with everything you need. God has given it to you." 11. Six hundred armed Danites set out from Zorah and Eshtaol. 12. They camped in Kirjath-jearim, Judah, and named the place Mahaneh-dan, meaning "Dan's camp." (Kirjath-jearim: city in Judah; Mahaneh-dan: "Dan's camp") 13. They also traveled to Mount Ephraim and arrived at Micah's house. 14. The five spies told their people, "Do you know that in these houses are idols, an ephod, and teraphim? Consider what you should do." (Ephod: sacred garment; Teraphim: household idols) 15. They turned toward Micah's house and greeted the Levite priest. 16. The six hundred armed Danites stood by the gate. 17. The spies entered the house, took the idols, ephod, and teraphim, while the priest stood at the gate. 18. They took the carved image, ephod, and teraphim, and the priest asked, "What are you doing?" 19. They told him, "Be quiet, go with us, and be a priest to our tribe. Is it better for you to serve one man or a whole tribe?" 20. The priest was pleased, took the idols, and went with them. 21. They left, placing their children, cattle, and belongings ahead of them. 22. As they left Micah's house, Micah's neighbors caught up with the Danites. 23. Micah asked, "Why have you come with such a large group?" 24. He said, "You've taken my gods and my priest, and now what do I have left?" 25. The Danites advised him, "Don't raise your voice, or angry men will attack you, and you and your family will be killed." 26. The Danites continued on, and Micah saw they were too strong for him, so he turned back home. 27. The Danites took Micah's idols and priest, attacked Laish, and burned the city with fire. (Laish: an undefended city) 28. There was no one to save them because the city was far from Sidon and had no allies. It was in a valley near Beth-rehob. They rebuilt the city and settled there. (Beth-rehob: a place near Laish) 29. They named the city Dan, after their ancestor Dan, though it was originally called Laish. 30. The Danites set up Micah's idols, and Jonathan, the son of Gershom, the son of Manasseh, and his descendants served as priests for the tribe of Dan until the land was taken into captivity. (Jonathan: descendant of Moses' father-in-law) 31. They worshiped Micah's carved image all the time the house of God was at Shiloh. (Shiloh: a religious center in ancient Israel)

Chapter 19

1. During a time when Israel had no king, a Levite man from the region of Mount Ephraim took a concubine from Bethlehem in Judah. (Levite: a member of the priestly tribe of Israel; Mount Ephraim: a mountainous region in Israel) 2. His concubine was unfaithful and left him, returning to her father's house in Bethlehem, where she stayed for four months. (Bethlehem: a town in Judah) 3. The Levite man went after her, hoping to reconcile, and took his servant and two donkeys with him. Upon arriving at her father's house, her father welcomed him with joy. (Donkeys: used as pack

animals) 4. The concubine's father kept him for three days, during which they ate, drank, and spent time together. (Concubine: a woman in a relationship with a man but not legally married to him) 5. On the fourth day, as they prepared to leave, her father invited him to eat before departing. (Morsel of bread: a small portion of food) 6. They sat and ate together, and the father urged him to stay longer and enjoy himself. (Heart be merry: to enjoy oneself) 7. When the man tried to leave again, his father-in-law persuaded him to stay another night. 8. On the fifth day, the Levite tried to leave early, but the father encouraged him to stay longer. They remained until the afternoon, eating together. 9. As the man got ready to leave, the father asked him to stay, pointing out that the day was ending and it would be better to rest there overnight. They could leave early the next day. 10. However, the man refused to stay and instead traveled on. They passed near Jebus (Jerusalem) as nightfall came, with two donkeys and the concubine with him. (Jebus: an ancient name for Jerusalem) 11. As they approached Jebus, the servant suggested they stop there for the night, but the Levite refused, saying it was a city of foreigners. 12. The Levite then told his servant they would continue to Gibeah. (Gibeah: a town in the territory of Benjamin) 13. They passed on toward Gibeah or Ramah, hoping to find a place to stay. 14. When they reached Gibeah, the sun had set, and they decided to stay there overnight. (Benjamin: the smallest tribe of Israel) 15. They entered the city and sat in the street, but no one invited them into their home for shelter. 16. As an old man from Mount Ephraim was returning home from work in the fields, he saw them and offered them lodging. (Mount Ephraim: a mountainous region in Israel) 17. The old man asked where they were headed and where they had come from. 18. The Levite explained that they were traveling from Bethlehem in Judah toward Mount Ephraim and were on their way to the house of the Lord, but no one had offered them hospitality. (House of the Lord: a reference to the place of worship) 19. He assured the man they had enough food and supplies for the journey, and they only needed a place to stay. 20. The old man welcomed them, saying he would take care of their needs, but urged them not to stay in the street. 21. The man brought them into his home, gave their donkeys food, and they washed their feet before eating and drinking. 22. While they were enjoying themselves, wicked men from the city surrounded the house, demanding the man who had entered be brought out so they could harm him. 23. The old man went outside and pleaded with them, asking them not to commit such a wicked act since the man was a guest in his home. 24. He offered his daughter and the concubine to them instead, asking them to do with them as they wished, but not to harm the man. 25. The men refused, so the Levite took his concubine and pushed her outside, where the men abused her throughout the night until morning. At dawn, they released her. 26. The woman came to the house at daybreak and collapsed on the doorstep, with her hands resting on the threshold. 27. The Levite got up the next morning, opened the door, and was shocked to find his concubine lying at the door with her hands on the threshold. 28. He told her to get up so they could continue their journey, but she didn't respond. He placed her on one of the donkeys and left. 29. When he arrived home, he took a knife, cut her body into twelve pieces, and sent the pieces throughout Israel. 30. Everyone who saw the atrocity said nothing like this had ever happened since the Israelites left Egypt. They were urged to consider the matter, seek counsel, and speak out. (Israelites: the descendants of Jacob, also called Israel)

Chapter 20

1. Then all the people of Israel gathered together as one, from Dan to Beer-sheba, including the land of Gilead, before the LORD in Mizpeh.(Mizpeh: a place of assembly for Israel) 2. The leaders of all the tribes of Israel presented themselves in God's assembly with 400,000 soldiers armed with swords. (Soldiers: warriors ready for battle) 3. (The Benjamites heard that the Israelites had gathered at Mizpeh.) Then the Israelites asked, "What was this evil act?" (Evil: morally wrong action) 4. The Levite, whose wife had been killed, replied, "I went to Gibeah in Benjamin with my concubine to stay for the night." (Gibeah: a city in the tribe of Benjamin) 5. The men of Gibeah surrounded my house at night, intending to kill me. They raped my concubine, and she died. (Raped: forced into an unlawful act) 6. I took her body, cut it into pieces, and sent the pieces throughout Israel to show the wickedness committed. (Wickedness: sinful behavior) 7. "You are all Israelites; give us your counsel and judgment." (Judgment: wise decision) 8. All the people arose as one, saying, "We will not return to our tents or homes." (Tents: temporary shelters) 9. "This is what we will do to Gibeah: we will go up and attack it by drawing lots." (Lots: a method of decision-making) 10. "We will take ten men from each hundred in Israel, one hundred from each thousand, and a thousand from every ten thousand, to gather provisions for the people, so they can carry out justice in Gibeah for the wickedness done." (Provisions: supplies for the journey) 11. So all the men of Israel gathered together against the city, united as one. (United: in agreement) 12. The tribes of Israel sent messengers through Benjamin, asking, "What is this evil among you?" (Evil: immoral act) 13. "Now, hand over the wicked men in Gibeah so we can put them to death and remove this evil from Israel." But the Benjamites refused to listen. (Wicked: morally corrupt) 14. The Benjamites gathered together in Gibeah to prepare for battle against the Israelites. (Prepared: got ready for conflict) 15. The Benjamites numbered 26,000 soldiers, besides 700 elite men from Gibeah. (Elite: specially chosen warriors) 16. Among these were 700 left-handed men who could sling stones with such precision that they never missed. (Left-handed: skilled with the left hand) 17. The Israelites, excluding Benjamin, numbered 400,000 soldiers, all skilled in war. (Skilled: experienced in combat) 18. The Israelites went up to the house of God and sought God's counsel, asking, "Who should go first to fight against Benjamin?" And the LORD said, "Let Judah go first." (Judah: one of Israel's tribes) 19. The Israelites rose early and camped against Gibeah. (Camped: set up camp) 20. The men of Israel went out to battle against Benjamin, positioning themselves for combat at Gibeah. (Positioned: arranged for battle) 21. The Benjamites came out of Gibeah and killed 22,000 Israelites that day. (Killed: destroyed in battle) 22. The Israelites encouraged themselves and reorganized their forces where they had first arranged themselves. (Reorganized: set up again) 23. (The Israelites went up and wept before the LORD until evening, asking, "Should we go again to fight against Benjamin, our brother?" And the LORD replied, "Go up against him.") (Wept: cried in sorrow) 24. The next day, the Israelites advanced toward Benjamin. (Advanced: moved forward) 25. On the second day, the Benjamites came out of Gibeah and struck down eighteen thousand Israelites, all armed men. (Gibeah: city in Benjamin) 26. Then all the Israelites went up to the house of God, wept, fasted until evening, and presented burnt offerings and peace offerings before the Lord. (House of God: the sanctuary in Israel) 27. The Israelites inquired of the Lord (for the Ark of the Covenant was there at that time), (Ark of the Covenant: sacred chest holding the tablets of the law) 28. with Phinehas, the son of Eleazar, son of Aaron, standing before it. They asked, "Should we fight the Benjamites again, or should we stop?" The Lord replied, "Go up again; tomorrow I will deliver them into your hands." (Phinehas: high priest; Aaron: Moses' brother) 29. Israel placed an ambush around Gibeah. (Gibeah: city in Benjamin) 30. On the third day, the Israelites moved out and set up their battle lines near Gibeah, as they had before. 31. The Benjamites went out and began to fight Israel, drawing them away from the city. They struck down about thirty men on the roads, one leading to the house of God and the other to Gibeah. 32. The Benjamites thought, "They are defeated again," but Israel said, "Let us flee and draw them into the open fields." 33. All Israel moved to Baal-tamar, and the ambush set by Israel came from the meadows near Gibeah. 34. Ten thousand of Israel's best soldiers attacked Gibeah, and the battle was fierce, but the Benjamites did

not realize the trap. **35.** The Lord struck the Benjamites before Israel, and Israel killed twenty-five thousand one hundred Benjamites that day. **36.** When the Benjamites saw they were losing, they thought the Israelites were retreating again, but the ambush was set to strike. **37.** The ambushers quickly attacked Gibeah and completely destroyed the city with the sword. **38.** There had been a prearranged signal between the Israelites and the ambushers: when a great column of smoke rose from the city, they knew to advance.(Ambushers: hidden troops) **39.** As the Israelites withdrew, the Benjamites began to kill about thirty Israelites, thinking they had won again. **40.** But when they saw the smoke rise from the city, they turned to see Gibeah burning with fire. **41.** The Israelites then turned and advanced on the Benjamites, who were filled with fear as they saw their defeat unfolding. **42.** The Benjamites turned to flee toward the wilderness, but Israel pursued them, cutting down those who came out from the cities. **43.** Israel surrounded the Benjamites, chasing them east of Gibeah, and trampled them with ease. **44.** That day, eighteen thousand Benjamite soldiers fell. **45.** The survivors fled to the rock of Rimmon, and Israel pursued them, killing five thousand along the roads, and two thousand more at Gidom. (Rock of Rimmon: a place of refuge) **46.** In total, twenty-five thousand Benjamites, all warriors, were killed that day. **47.** Six hundred Benjamites escaped to the rock of Rimmon, where they stayed for four months. **48.** Then Israel returned and struck down the remaining Benjamites, killing every man, woman, and child, as well as the animals, and burned all the cities they encountered.(Benjamites: members of the tribe of Benjamin)

Chapter 21

1. The Israelites had made a vow at Mizpeh, saying, "No one among us will give their daughter to a Benjaminite to wife."(Vow: solemn promise) **2.** The people gathered at the house of God, stayed there until evening, and wept before the LORD.(Wept: cried deeply) **3.** They prayed, saying, "Why has this happened in Israel? Why is there one tribe missing today?"(Missing: lost or absent) **4.** The next morning, the people rose early, built an altar, and offered burnt offerings and peace offerings.(Offerings: gifts to God) **5.** The Israelites asked, "Which tribe didn't come up to Mizpeh for the LORD?" They had made a vow that anyone who didn't come would be put to death.(Vow: promise, put to death: killed) **6.** The Israelites felt sorry for Benjamin, their brother, and said, "One tribe is cut off from Israel today."(Cut off: separated) **7.** They asked, "How can we provide wives for the remaining Benjamites, since we swore not to give them our daughters?"(Provide: give) **8.** They then asked, "Which tribe didn't come to Mizpeh?" And they found that no one from Jabesh-gilead had come.(Jabesh-gilead: a town) **9.** When they counted the people, no one from Jabesh-gilead had come.(Counted: counted the numbers) **10.** The congregation sent 12,000 of the bravest men to destroy the people of Jabesh-gilead, including women and children.(Bravest: strongest warriors) **11.** They were told to destroy every male and every woman who had been with a man.(With a man: married or had relations) **12.** They found 400 young women in Jabesh-gilead who had never been with a man, and they brought them to Shiloh.(Shiloh: a place of worship) **13.** The Israelites then sent messengers to the Benjamites at the rock of Rimmon and offered peace to them. (Messengers: those delivering messages) **14.** Benjamin came out, and the Israelites gave them wives from those they had spared from Jabesh-gilead, but there were not enough for all the Benjamites.(Spared: saved alive) **15.** The people felt sorry for Benjamin because the LORD had caused a division in Israel.(Division: separation) **16.** The elders said, "What can we do for the remaining Benjamites, since all the women of Benjamin are gone?"(Remaining: those left) **17.** They said, "There must be a way for the Benjamites to have wives so that one tribe isn't lost from Israel."(Lost: destroyed) **18.** However, they couldn't give their daughters to Benjamin, since they had sworn an oath saying, "Anyone who gives a wife to a Benjaminite is cursed."(Cursed: under a divine punishment) **19.** Then they said, "There is an annual feast to the LORD in Shiloh, north of Bethel, along the road from Bethel to Shechem, south of Lebonah."(Feast: a religious celebration) **20.** So they instructed the Benjamites, saying, "Go and hide in the vineyards.(Hide: wait secretly) **21.** When the daughters of Shiloh come out to dance, catch a wife for yourselves from them and take her back to Benjamin."(Catch: take quickly) **22.** They said, "If their fathers or brothers complain, we'll tell them, 'Please be kind to them, since we didn't give them wives, and they weren't taken in war.'"(Complain: express anger or disappointment) **23.** The Benjamites did as instructed, catching wives from the dancers, and returned to their land, rebuilding their cities and living in them. (Rebuilding: fixing up) **24.** Then the Israelites returned to their tribes and families, each to their own land. (Returned: went back) **25.** In those days, Israel had no king; everyone did what seemed right in their own eyes.(Seemed right: followed their own judgment)

8 – Ruth

Chapter 1

1. During the time when Israel was governed by judges, a famine struck the land. A man from Bethlehem in Judah decided to leave with his wife Naomi and their two sons and go to the country of Moab to live (famine: severe shortage of food, decided: making a decision). **2.** The name of the man was Elimelech, the name of his wife was Naomi, and the names of their two sons were Mahlon and Chilion. They were from the area of Ephrathah in Bethlehem, Judah. They went to live in Moab and settled there. (Bethlehem: a town in the region of Judah, known for its fertile land, Moab: a country east of Israel)**3.** After a time, Elimelech, Naomi's husband, passed away, leaving her alone with her two sons (passed away: died). **4.** Naomi's sons married women from Moab. One of them was named Orpah, and the other was named Ruth. They lived in Moab for about ten years. They lived in Moab for about ten years. **5.** Sadly, both Mahlon and Chilion also passed away, and Naomi was left alone, with neither her husband nor her sons. **6.** When Naomi heard that the Lord had blessed His people in Judah by providing food, she decided to return to her homeland, leaving Moab behind (homeland: native land). **7.** Naomi set out to go back, and her two daughters-in-law went with her. They began the journey to return to Judah (set out: started her journey). **8.** As they walked, Naomi turned to her daughters-in-law and said, "Go back to your own mothers' homes. May the Lord show you kindness, just as you have shown kindness to your dead husbands and to me (kindness: compassion and mercy). **9.** May the Lord grant that you find rest in the home of a new husband." She kissed them, and they all began to cry aloud (rest: peace and safety). **10.** Both daughters-in-law replied, "We will certainly go with you to your people in Judah." **11.** But Naomi replied, "Why do you want to go with me? Am I going to have more sons who could become your husbands? **12.** Turn back, my daughters, go home. I am too old to marry again. Even if I had hope for a future and married tonight, and even if I had sons, **13.** would you wait for them to grow up and marry you? Would you remain unmarried all that time? No, my daughters, it would be too bitter for me, for the Lord's hand has turned against me" (bitter: sorrowful) **14.** Then they all cried again. Orpah kissed her mother-in-law goodbye, but Ruth held on tightly to Naomi. **15.** Naomi said, "Look, your sister-in-law has returned to her people and her gods. Go back with her." **16.** But Ruth said, "Do not ask me to leave you, or to stop following you. Wherever you go, I will go. Wherever you stay, I will stay. Your people will be my people, and your God will be my God. **17.** Where you die, I will die, and there I will be buried. May the Lord deal with me, and even more so, if anything but death separates us." **18.** When Naomi saw that Ruth was determined to stay with her, she stopped trying to convince her to leave. **19.** So the two of them continued on their journey and arrived in Bethlehem. When they entered Bethlehem, the whole town was stirred up because of them, and the women of the town asked, "Is this Naomi?" (Bethlehem: the town of Naomi's birth). 20. But Naomi said to them, "Don't call me Naomi. Call me Mara, because the Almighty (God) has made my life very bitter (Naomi means 'pleasant' or 'joyful', Mara means 'bitter'). 21. I went away full, but the Lord has brought me back empty. Why do you call me Naomi, since the Lord has testified against me, and the Almighty has caused me to suffer?" 22. So Naomi returned to Bethlehem, accompanied by Ruth, her Moabite daughter-in-law. They returned from the country of Moab and arrived in Bethlehem just as the barley harvest was beginning (a time when the barley crops are gathered).

Chapter 2
1. Naomi had a relative on her husband's side, a wealthy and influential man from the family of Elimelech. His name was Boaz. (Kinsman: a relative; Mighty man of wealth: a man of great influence and resources; Family of Elimelech: part of Elimelech's family line) 2. Ruth, the Moabite, said to Naomi, "Let me go to the fields and gather leftover grain from whoever will show me favor." Naomi replied, "Go ahead, my daughter." (Glean: to gather leftover grain or produce after harvest; Grace/favor: kindness or mercy shown to someone) 3. So Ruth went, worked in the fields after the harvesters, and by chance ended up in a field that belonged to Boaz, who was a relative of Elimelech. 4. Just then, Boaz arrived from Bethlehem and greeted the workers, "The Lord be with you!" They replied, "The Lord bless you!" (Bethlehem: the town where Boaz lived, and the birthplace of David) 5. Boaz asked the overseer of the workers, "Who is that young woman?" (Overseer: the person in charge of supervising the workers) 6. The overseer replied, "She is the Moabite woman who came back with Naomi from Moab." (Moabitess: a woman from Moab, a neighboring nation to Israel) 7. She said, "Please let me gather grain behind the harvesters." She has been working steadily from morning until now, and only rested a short time in the shelter. 8. Boaz said to Ruth, "Listen, my daughter, don't go to gather grain in any other field. Stay here with my workers. (Hearken: listen carefully) 9. Keep your eyes on the field where they are harvesting, and follow along after the young women. I have told the men not to harm you. When you are thirsty, help yourself to the water that the men have drawn." 10. Ruth bowed down with her face to the ground and asked, "Why have I found favor in your eyes, that you notice me, a foreigner?" 11. Boaz replied, "I've heard about all that you've done for your mother-in-law since the death of your husband. You left your father and mother, and the land of your birth, and came to live among a people you didn't know before. 12. May the Lord repay you for what you have done, and may you receive a full reward from the Lord, the God of Israel, under whose wings you have come to take refuge." (Wings: a metaphor for God's protection) 13. Ruth said, "May I continue to find favor in your eyes, my lord, for you have comforted me and spoken kindly to me, though I am not one of your servants." 14. At mealtime, Boaz said to her, "Come, eat with us and dip your bread in the vinegar." So she sat with the reapers, and Boaz gave her some roasted grain to eat. She ate, was satisfied, and had some left over. (Morsel: a small piece of food; Parched corn: roasted grain) 15. When she got up to continue gathering grain, Boaz instructed his men, "Let her gather even among the bundles of grain. Don't rebuke her. (Rebuke: to criticize or shame; Handfuls of purpose: deliberately dropped extra grain) 16. Let some of the grain fall purposely for her to collect, and don't say anything to stop her." 17. So Ruth gathered grain until evening. Then she threshed what she had gathered, and it amounted to about an ephah of barley. (Ephah: a unit of measurement, roughly equivalent to 22 liters or about a bushel) 18. She took it up to the town and showed her mother-in-law what she had gleaned. She also gave her the food she had left after eating her fill. 19. Her mother-in-law asked, "Where did you glean today? Where did you work? Blessed be the man who took notice of you!" Ruth told her mother-in-law that she had worked in the field of Boaz. (Wrought: worked) 20. Naomi said to her daughter-in-law, "The Lord bless him! He has shown kindness to both the living and the dead." Then Naomi said, "That man is a relative of ours; he is one of our kinsmen-redeemers." (Kinsman-redeemer: a relative who has the responsibility to redeem a family member in need, such as marrying a widow to preserve the family line) 21. Ruth the Moabite said, "He even told me to stay with his workers until they finish all the harvest." (Moabitess: a woman from Moab, a neighboring nation) 22. Naomi replied, "It is good, my daughter, that you go with his young women, so that nothing will happen to you in another field." (Maidens: young women; Meet: encounter) 23. So Ruth stayed close to the women of Boaz and gleaned until the end of the barley and wheat harvests. And she lived with her mother-in-law. (Dwelt: lived)

Chapter 3
1. Naomi, her mother-in-law, said to her, "My daughter, shouldn't I find a secure place for you to settle, so that your life may be blessed?" (Secure place: a settled life) 2. "Isn't Boaz, with whom you worked, a close relative of ours? Tonight, he will be winnowing barley at the threshing floor." (Winnowing: separating grain; threshing floor: grain processing area) 3. "Wash yourself, anoint yourself with oil, put on your best clothes, and go down to the threshing floor. But don't reveal yourself to the man until he has finished eating and drinking." (Anoint: apply oil; Raiment: clothing) 4. "When he lies down, take note of the spot where he is resting. Then, go in, uncover his feet, and lie down there. He will tell you what to do next." (Uncover: reveal; Resting place: where he sleeps) 5. Ruth answered, "I will do everything that you have instructed me to do." (Handmaid: servant) 6. So, Ruth went down to the threshing floor and did everything her mother-in-law had told her to do. 7. After Boaz had eaten, drunk, and was in good spirits, he went to lie down at the end of the pile of barley. Ruth quietly approached, uncovered his feet, and lay down. (Merry: content; Pile of barley: grain heap) 8. At midnight, Boaz woke up, startled, and turned over. To his surprise, he found a woman lying at his feet. (Startled: surprised) 9. He asked, "Who are you?" She responded, "I am Ruth, your servant. Spread the corner of your garment over me, for you are a kinsman-redeemer." 10. Boaz blessed her and said, "May you be richly blessed by the Lord, my daughter. You have shown even greater kindness now than before, by not seeking to marry younger men, whether rich or poor." (Kindness: loyalty; Inasmuch as: since) 11. "And now, my daughter, do not be afraid. I will do for you all that you ask. All the people in this town know that you are a woman of noble character." 12. "It is true that I am a close relative, but there is one who is more closely related than I am." 13. "Stay here tonight, and in the morning, if he is willing to fulfill his duty as your kinsman-redeemer, good; let him do so. But if he refuses, as the Lord lives, I will redeem you. Lie down until morning." 14. Ruth lay at his feet until morning, but she got up before anyone could recognize her. Boaz said, "Let no one know that a woman came to the threshing floor." 15. Boaz then said, "Bring me the shawl you are wearing, and hold it out." When she did, he measured six scoops of barley and placed them in the shawl. Then she went back to the city. 16. When Ruth returned to her mother-in-law, Naomi asked, "How did it go, my daughter?" Ruth told her everything Boaz had done for her. 17. Ruth added, "He gave me these six measures of barley, saying, 'don't go back to your mother-in-law empty-handed.'" (Empty-handed: without a gift) 18. Naomi replied, "Wait, my daughter, until you see how this turns out. For the man will not rest until the matter is settled today.

Chapter 4
1. Boaz went up to the town gate and sat down. Soon, the relative Boaz had mentioned came by. Boaz called to him, "Come over here and sit down." The man turned aside and sat down. (Gate: the entrance to the city; Kinsman: a close relative) 2. Boaz then took ten of the town's elders and said, "Sit here." They sat down. (Elders: older, respected men of the town) 3. Boaz said to the relative,

"Naomi, who has returned from Moab, is selling a piece of land that belonged to our relative Elimelech. (Parcel: a piece or section of land) **4.** I wanted to let you know about it and give you the opportunity to buy it in front of the townspeople and elders. If you want to redeem it, do so. If not, tell me, because I am next in line." The man replied, "I will redeem it." (Redeem: to buy back or restore) **5.** Boaz then said, "When you buy the land from Naomi, you must also take Ruth, the widow of Mahlon, to raise up a son for his name, to keep the inheritance in the family." (Widow: a woman whose husband has died; Inheritance: property passed down through family lines) **6.** The relative said, "I cannot redeem it myself, because it might endanger my own inheritance. You redeem it for yourself, because I cannot." **7.** (Now in earlier times in Israel, this was the custom to settle such matters: a man would remove his sandal and give it to the other as a sign of agreement.) **8.** So, the relative said to Boaz, "Take it, you redeem it." He removed his sandal. **9.** Boaz said to the elders and all the people, "Today you are witnesses that I have bought all that belonged to Elimelech, as well as the property of Chilion and Mahlon, from Naomi." **10.** "I have also acquired Ruth, the Moabite widow of Mahlon, to be my wife, in order to raise up the name of the dead on his inheritance. Let his name not be erased from among his relatives or at the town gate. You are witnesses today." (Moabite: from Moab, a neighboring nation) **11.** The people and elders at the gate said, "We are witnesses. May the Lord make the woman who is entering your home like Rachel and Leah, the two who built the house of Israel. May you prosper in Ephrathah and be renowned in Bethlehem." (Renowned: famous, well-known) **12.** "May your family be like that of Perez, whom Tamar bore to Judah. May the Lord give you descendants through this young woman." (Perez: a great-grandson of Abraham; Descendants: offspring or children) **13.** So Boaz took Ruth, and she became his wife. When they were together, the Lord gave her the ability to conceive, and she gave birth to a son. **14.** The women said to Naomi, "Praise be to the Lord, who has not left you without a redeemer today, and may his name be famous in Israel." (Redeemer: a relative who restores or redeems) **15.** "He will renew your life and sustain you in your old age. Your daughter-in-law, who loves you and is better to you than seven sons, has given him birth." (Sustain: provide for; Better: more valuable or precious) **16.** Naomi took the child and laid him on her lap, and she became his nurse. (Nurse: a caregiver or guardian) **17.** The women living there gave him a name, saying, "A son has been born to Naomi." They named him Obed. He was the father of Jesse, the father of David. (Obed: meaning "worshiper" or "servant"; Jesse: father of King David) **18.** These are the descendants of Perez: Perez was the father of Hezron, (Generations: family lineage) **19.** Hezron was the father of Ram, and Ram was the father of Amminadab, (Begat: fathered) **20.** Amminadab was the father of Nahshon, and Nahshon was the father of Salmon, (Amminadab: an ancestor of King David) **21.** Salmon was the father of Boaz, and Boaz was the father of Obed, (Salmon: Boaz's father) **22.** Obed was the father of Jesse, and Jesse was the father of David. (Jesse: father of King David)

9 – 1 Samuel
Chapter 1

1. Now there was a man from Ramah in Ephraim, named Elkanah, son of Jeroham, son of Elihu, son of Tohu, son of Zuph, an Ephraimite. (Ephraimite: a person from the tribe of Ephraim) **2.** He had two wives: Hannah and Peninnah. Peninnah had children, but Hannah had none. **3.** Elkanah went yearly to Shiloh to worship and sacrifice to the Lord, where Eli's sons, Hophni and Phinehas, were priests. (Shiloh: a city in Israel; priests: religious leaders) **4.** When offering sacrifices, Elkanah gave portions to Peninnah and her children. (Portions: shares of food or offering) **5.** But to Hannah, he gave a double portion, for he loved her, though the Lord had closed her womb. (Womb: the place where a baby grows) **6.** Peninnah provoked Hannah bitterly to make her miserable, because of her childlessness. (Provoked: teased or mocked) **7.** Year after year, when they went to the house of the Lord, Peninnah taunted Hannah, who wept and wouldn't eat. (Taunted: mocked or ridiculed) **8.** Elkanah asked, "Hannah, why do you weep? Why don't you eat? Am I not better to you than ten sons?" **9.** After eating, Hannah went to the tabernacle, where Eli sat by the doorpost. (Tabernacle: a tent or dwelling place of worship) **10.** In deep sorrow, she prayed to the Lord, weeping greatly. (Sorrow: sadness) **11.** She vowed, "Lord of hosts, if You remember me and give Your servant a son, I will dedicate him to the Lord all his life, and no razor shall touch his head." (Vowed: promised; Hosts: all-powerful God; Razor: tool for cutting hair) **12.** While praying, Eli noticed her mouth moving but heard no voice. **13.** She prayed silently; only her lips moved, so Eli thought she was drunk. **14.** Eli said, "How long will you be drunk? Put away your wine!" (Drunk: intoxicated by alcohol) **15.** Hannah replied, "I am a woman of sorrowful spirit. I have not drunk wine or strong drink, but have poured out my soul before the Lord." (Sorrowful spirit: deeply sad; Strong drink: alcohol) **16.** "Do not think I am a wicked woman; I have been praying in my grief and distress." (Wicked: evil or immoral; Grief: great sorrow; Distress: suffering) **17.** Eli answered, "Go in peace, and may the God of Israel grant your request." (Grant: give or fulfill) **18.** She said, "Let your servant find favor in your sight." Then she ate, and her face was no longer sad. (Favor: approval or kindness) **19.** The next morning, they worshiped the Lord and returned home. Elkanah knew Hannah, and the Lord remembered her. (Knew: had relations with) **20.** In time, Hannah conceived and bore a son, whom she named Samuel, saying, "Because I asked the Lord for him." (Conceived: became pregnant; Samuel: name means "asked of God") **21.** Elkanah and his family went up to offer the yearly sacrifice, but **22.** Hannah stayed behind, saying to Elkanah, "I will wait until the child is weaned, then I will bring him to the Lord to stay forever." (Weaned: no longer nursing) **23.** Elkanah agreed, "Do what seems best. Let the Lord fulfill His word." So she stayed and nursed the child. (Fulfill: complete or make happen) **24.** After weaning him, she took Samuel to Shiloh, bringing three bulls, flour, and wine, and presented him to Eli. (Bulls: young cattle) **25.** They sacrificed a bull and brought Samuel to Eli. **26.** Hannah said, "I am the woman who prayed here for this child. **27.** I prayed for him, and the Lord has granted my request." (Granted: gave or fulfilled) **28.** "Therefore, I dedicate him to the Lord for his whole life." And they worshiped the Lord there. (Dedicate: set apart for service)

Chapter 2

1. And Hannah supplicated: "My heart rejoices in the Lord; my strength is exalted in Him. I smile at my adversaries, because I rejoice in Your deliverance. (Rejoices: happiness, exalted: lifted) **2.** No one is holy like the Lord; there's none besides You, nor any gemstone like our God. (Gemstone: precious stone or rare, retreat: refuge or safe place) **3.** Stop being proud; let no arrogance come from your mouth, for the Lord is the God of knowledge; by Him conduct are counted. (Arrogance: tone—significance; counted: judged) **4.** The potent curvatures are broken, and the weak are strengthened. (Curvatures: hunters stumble, potent: strong, curvatures: bending or curves) **5.** The full hire themselves for food, and the empty check to hunger. Indeed, the barren has seven children, while the mama of numerous grows weak. (Barren: childless) **6.** The Lord kills and makes alive; He brings down to the grave and raises up. (Grave: death , rises up: gives life) **7.** The Lord makes poor and rich; He brings low and lifts up. (low: humbles, lifts up: exalts) **8.** He raises the poor from the dust, lifts the beggar from the ash mound, to set them among tycoons and give them the throne of glory. For the pillars of the earth are the Lord's, and He has set the world upon them. (inherit: admit, pillars: foundations) **9.** He guards the bases of His saints, but the wicked will be silent in darkness. For by strength no man will prevail. (Saints: holy ones) **10.** The adversaries of the Lord will be shattered; He'll thunder from heaven against them. The Lord will judge the earth. He'll give strength to His king and exalt the cornucopia of His besmeared. (Besmeared: chosen one, anointed one) **11.** Also Elkanah went home to Ramah, but the child Samuel administered before the Lord under Eli. (Ramah: a megacity in Ephraim) **12.** Now Eli's sons were loose; they did not know the Lord. (Loose: dishonest) **13.** The preachers' custom was that when anyone offered a immolation, the clerk's menial would take a three-rounded chopstick and use it while the meat boiled. (Custom: a standard practice) **14.** He'd thrust it into the pot, and the clerk would take whatever came up. This was done in Shiloh with all the Israelites. (Shiloh: a megacity in Ephraim) **15.** Before burning the fat, the clerk's menial would ask for raw meat to repast, not boiled. (Fat: special corridor of the beast, the fatty portion considered sacred) **16.** Still, the menial would demand the raw meat by force, if the man offered to burn the fat first. (Demand: ask for) **17.** The sin of the youthful men was veritably great before the Lord, for people abominated offering to the Lord. (Abominated: hated, strongly rejected) **18.** But Samuel served before the Lord as a child, wearing a linen ephod. (Ephod: priestly garment) **19.** His mama made him a small mask and brought it to him each time when she and her hubby came for the monthly immolation. (Mask: covering or robe). **20.** Eli would bless Elkanah and his woman, saying: "The Lord give you children for the loan you made to the Lord." Also they went home. (Blessed: invoked God's favor) **21.** The Lord visited Hannah, and she bore three sons and two daughters. Meanwhile, Samuel grew before the Lord. (Visited: watched for, observed) **22.** Eli was veritably old, and he heard all the evil his sons did, how they slept with women at the tabernacle entrance. (Evil: wicked). **23.** He said to them: "Why do you do similar effects? I hear of your evil deeds from all the people. (Deeds: conduct, actions). **24.** No, my sons! The reports are not good. You're making the Lord's people stray. **25.** Still, God will judge him, if someone sins against another. But if someone sins against the Lord, who'll mediate for him?" But they did not hear, for the Lord was determined to kill them. (Mediate: intervene, determined: decided) **26.** Meanwhile, Samuel grew in elevation and in favor with the Lord and with men. (Elevation: height, favor: blessing). **27.** Also a man of God came to Eli, saying: "Therefore says the Lord: 'Did I not reveal Myself to your father's house when they were in Egypt? (Reveal: show, Egypt: land of Pharaoh) **28.** Did I not choose him from all the lines of Israel to be My clerk, to offer offerings and burn incense before Me? Did I not give your family all the immolations of Israel made by fire? (choose: elect, immolations: offerings) **29.** Why do you scorn My immolation and immolations, recognizing your sons further than Me, and making yourselves fat with the stylish of the immolations? (despisement: lack of respect) **30.** Thus, the Lord God of Israel says: 'I promised that your house and your father's house would walk before Me ever, but now I say: Far be it from Me; for those who recognize Me I'll recognize, and those who despise Me will be smoothly esteemed.' (recognize: honor, despise: hate) **31.** Behold, the days are coming when I'll cut off your strength and that of your father's house, so there will be no old man in your house. (cut off: end) **32.** You'll see your adversaries in My dwelling place, despite the good God does for Israel. There will be no old man in your house ever. (dwelling place: holy sanctuary) **33.** Any man of yours whom I don't cut off from My balcony will make your eyes weak and suffer your heart. Your descendants will die in the florescence of life. (cut off: spread, suffer: mourn) **34.** This will be a sign to you: In one day both your sons, Hophni and Phinehas, will die. (subscribe: warning) **35.** Also I'll raise up for Myself a faithful clerk who'll do according to My will. I'll make him a lasting house, and he'll serve before My besmeared ever. (faithful: pious, besmeared: chosen one) **36.** And all who remain in your house will come and bow before him for a piece of silver and a loaf of bread, saying, 'Please put me in one of the priestly positions, that I may eat a piece of bread.'" (serve: work)

Chapter 3

1. Samuel served the Lord under Eli's guidance. During that time, the Lord's messages were rare, and visions were infrequent. (Revelations: divine messages, Eli: priest, guide) **2.** Eli was resting in his usual place, and his eyesight had become so weak that he could no longer see. (Eli: priest, eyesight: vision) **3.** The lamp of God was still burning in the sanctuary (holy tent: place of worship), and Samuel was lying down nearby. **4.** The Lord called out to Samuel, and he answered, "Here I am!" **5.** Samuel ran to Eli and said, "You called me." But Eli replied, "I did not call you; go back and lie down." So Samuel returned to his place. **6.** The Lord called Samuel again, and he went to Eli, saying, "You called me." Eli responded, "I didn't call you, my son; go lie down again." **7.** At this point, Samuel didn't yet know the Lord, and the Lord's messages had not been revealed to him. (Revelations: divine messages) **8.** The Lord called Samuel a third time. He got up, went to Eli, and said, "You called me." Eli then realized it was the Lord calling the boy. **9.** Eli instructed Samuel, "Go and lie down. If He calls you again, say, 'Speak, Lord, for Your servant is listening.'" Samuel returned to his resting place. **10.** The Lord came and called out, "Samuel! Samuel!" Samuel replied, "Speak, for Your servant is listening." **11.** The Lord said, "I am about to do something in Israel (Israel: the nation) that will make everyone who hears it tremble." **12.** "On that day, I will carry out everything I have spoken concerning Eli's family, from beginning to end." **13.** "I warned Eli that judgment would come to his household forever because of the sins he knew about. His sons were corrupt, and he failed to restrain them." (Sin: wrongdoing, Eli: priest) **14.** "I have sworn that the guilt of Eli's family will never be atoned for by sacrifice or offering." (Sworn: promised strongly, Offering: ritual gift to God) **15.** Samuel stayed in bed until morning and then opened the doors of the Lord's house. He was afraid to tell Eli about the vision. **16.** Eli called out to Samuel, "Samuel, my son!" Samuel answered, "Here I am." **17.** Eli asked, "What did the Lord say to you? Do not hide it from me. May God deal with you harshly if you keep anything from me that He told you." **18.** Samuel told Eli everything without holding back. Eli responded, "It is the Lord; let Him do what He thinks is best." **19.** As Samuel grew up, the Lord was with him, and everything he said came to pass. (Fulfilled: came true) **20.** Everyone in Israel, from Dan (northern city) to Beersheba (southern city), knew that Samuel was established as a prophet of the Lord. **21.** The Lord continued to appear in Shiloh (town of the tabernacle) and revealed Himself to Samuel through His word.

Chapter 4

1. Samuel's message spread throughout Israel. The Israelites prepared for battle against the Philistines, setting up camp at Ebenezer, while the Philistines established their camp at Aphek. (Philistines: sea people; Ebenezer: stone of help; Aphek: Canaanite city) **2.** The Philistines arranged their forces and defeated the Israelites, killing around 4,000 men on the battlefield. **3.** Upon returning to camp, the Israelite elders questioned, "Why has the Lord allowed us to face defeat? Let us bring the ark of the covenant from Shiloh to deliver us from our enemies." (Ark of the covenant: sacred chest; Shiloh: holy city) **4.** They sent men to Shiloh to retrieve the ark of the covenant of the Lord of hosts, who is enthroned between the cherubim. Eli's sons, Hophni and Phinehas, accompanied the ark. (Lord of hosts: God of armies; Cherubim: angelic figures) **5.** When the ark arrived at the camp, the Israelites let out such a loud shout that the ground shook. **6.** Hearing the commotion, the Philistines wondered, "Why is there such loud shouting in the Hebrews' camp?" They soon realized that the ark of the Lord had entered the camp. **7.** Filled with fear, the Philistines exclaimed, "God has come into their camp! This spells disaster for us—nothing like this has happened before!" (Woe: disaster) **8.** They continued, "What chance do we have? These are the gods who struck Egypt with plagues in the wilderness!" (Plagues: disasters; Wilderness: desert) **9.** Rallying themselves, they said, "Be strong, Philistines, and fight like men! Otherwise, you'll become slaves to the

Hebrews, just as they were enslaved to you. Be brave and fight!" **10.** The Philistines fought hard and won. Israel suffered a massive defeat—thirty thousand soldiers died, and the rest fled to their homes. **11.** The ark of God was captured, and Eli's sons, Hophni and Phinehas, were killed. **12.** That same day, a man from the tribe of Benjamin ran from the battlefield to Shiloh with torn clothes and dirt on his head, signs of mourning. (Benjamin: Israelite tribe; Torn clothes and dirt: signs of mourning) **13.** Eli, worried about the ark, sat near the road watching. When the man reached the city with the news, the entire city cried out. **14.** Hearing the wailing, Eli asked, "What is all this noise about?" The man quickly approached him to deliver the news. **15.** Eli, who was ninety-eight years old and nearly blind, listened intently. **16.** The messenger said, "I have come from the battlefield today." Eli asked, "What happened, my son?" **17.** The man reported, "Israel has been defeated by the Philistines. There's been a great slaughter, your two sons, Hophni and Phinehas, are dead, and the ark of God has been taken." **18.** Upon hearing about the ark, Eli fell backward off his chair near the gate, breaking his neck. He died because he was old and heavy. Eli had led Israel as judge for forty years. (Judged: led) **19.** Eli's daughter-in-law, Phinehas' wife, was pregnant and near delivery. When she heard that the ark had been captured and that her father-in-law and husband had died, she went into labor. **20.** As she was dying, the women assisting her tried to comfort her, saying, "Do not be afraid; you've given birth to a son." But she did not reply or acknowledge them. **21.** She named the boy Ichabod, saying, "The glory has departed from Israel," because the ark was captured and her family was lost. (Ichabod: no glory; Glory: honor) **22.** She repeated, "The glory has departed from Israel, for the ark of God has been taken."

Chapter 5

1. The Philistines captured the ark of God and brought it from Ebenezer to Ashdod. (Ark: sacred chest) **2.** They placed the ark of God in the temple of Dagon, setting it beside their god. (Dagon: Philistine deity) **3.** Early the next morning, Dagon had fallen face down before the ark of the Lord. They set Dagon back in its place. (Fallen: collapsed) **4.** The following morning, Dagon was again face down, but now its head and hands were broken off at the threshold; only its torso remained. (Threshold: doorway) **5.** From that day, Dagon's priests and visitors avoided stepping on the threshold of his temple in Ashdod. (Priests: religious leaders) **6.** The Lord's hand brought devastation upon the people of Ashdod, afflicting them with tumors. (Tumors: swellings or sores) **7.** The men of Ashdod said, "The ark of Israel's God cannot stay here; His power is too severe on us and Dagon." (severe: harsh) **8.** They summoned all Philistine rulers and asked, "What should we do with the ark?" They decided to send it to Gath, and it was moved there. (Rulers: leaders) **9.** But in Gath, the Lord struck the city, causing destruction and afflicting its people, both young and old, with tumors. (Destruction: devastation) **10.** So they sent the ark to Ekron, but the Ekronites cried, "They've brought the ark here to kill us and our people!" (Ekronites: people of Ekron) **11.** The Philistine rulers gathered again, saying, "Send the ark back to Israel to stop this deadly destruction." The Lord's hand was heavy on the city. (Deadly: fatal) **12.** Those who survived were afflicted with tumors, and the city's cries reached heaven. (Afflicted: suffered)

Chapter 6

1. Now the ark of the Lord was in Philistine land for seven months. (Philistines: ancient people of the area) **2.** The Philistines called for priests and diviners, saying, "What should we do with the ark? How should we send it back?" **3.** They replied, "Do not send the ark back empty. Return it with a trespass offering, and you will be healed. Then you will understand why His hand is still upon you." (Trespass offering: penalty gift) **4.** "What should the trespass offering be?" they asked. They answered, "Five golden tumors and five golden rats, matching the number of Philistine lords, because the same plague has affected all of you and your rulers." (Tumors: growths; Rats: pests; Plague: disease) **5.** "Make images of your tumors and rats that plagues the land, and gives glory to Israel's God. Maybe He will lighten His hand from you, your gods, and your land." **6.** "Why do you harden your hearts like the Egyptians did? When God did mighty works among them, did they not let the Israelites go?" (Egyptians: people of Egypt; Israelites: descendants of Jacob) **7.** "Make a new cart, take two cows that have never been yoked, and hitch them to it. Take their calves home." (Yoked: harness; Calves: baby cows) **8.** "Place the ark on the cart and the golden items as a trespass offering beside it. Then send it off." **9.** "Watch: if it goes to Beth Shemesh, we know God has done this. If not, it was just by chance." (Beth Shemesh: a town in ancient Israel) **10.** The men did as instructed, taking the cows and placing the ark and gold items on the cart. **11.** The cows went straight toward Beth Shemesh, lowing as they went, without turning off the path. The Philistine lords followed them. **12.** The people of Beth Shemesh, harvesting wheat, saw the ark and rejoiced. **13.** The cart reached the field of Joshua in Beth Shemesh, where they stopped at a large stone. They broke the cart's wood and offered the cows as a burnt offering. (Joshua: a man in Beth Shemesh; Burnt offering: offering burned as a sacrifice) **14.** The Levites took the ark and gold items from the cart and placed them on the stone. The people offered burnt offerings and sacrifices that day. (Levites: members of the priestly tribe of Israel) **15.** The five Philistine lords saw this and returned to Ekron. (Ekron: a city of the Philistines) **16.** These were the golden tumors returned as trespass offerings: one for each Philistine city—Ashdod, Gaza, Ashkelon, Gath, and Ekron. **17.** And the golden rats, corresponding to all the Philistine cities under the five lords, from the fortified cities to country villages, even to the large stone of Abel where they set the ark. (Fortified cities: heavily protected cities; Abel: stone marker) **18.** The stone remains in the field of Joshua in Beth Shemesh to this day. **19.** God struck 50,070 men of Beth Shemesh for looking into the ark. The people mourned because of this great slaughter. (Mourned: felt sadness) **20.** The men of Beth Shemesh said, "Who can stand before this holy God? Where should the ark go?" **21.** They sent messengers to the people of Kirjath Jearim, saying, "The Philistines have returned the ark. Come and take it up with you." (Kirjath Jearim: a city)

Chapter 7

1. The men of Kirjath Jearim came and took the ark of the Lord, bringing it to the house of Abinadab on the hill. They appointed his son Eleazar to guard the ark. (Kirjath Jearim: town in ancient Israel) **2.** The ark stayed in Kirjath Jearim for 20 years, and the people of Israel mourned for the Lord during that time. **3.** Samuel addressed the Israelites, saying, "If you turn back to the Lord with all your hearts, remove the foreign gods and idols of Ashtoreth from among you, prepare yourselves to serve Him alone, and He will rescue you from the Philistines." **4.** The Israelites removed the Baals and Ashtoreths, committing to serve only the Lord. **5.** Samuel instructed, "Assemble all Israel at Mizpah, and I will pray to the Lord on your behalf." (Mizpah: place of gathering) **6.** The people gathered at Mizpah, drew water, and poured it out before the Lord. They fasted and confessed, "We have sinned against the Lord." Samuel judged Israel there. **7.** When the Philistines heard that Israel had gathered at Mizpah, their leaders moved against them. The Israelites became afraid. (Philistines: enemy people) **8.** The Israelites said to Samuel, "Please don't stop crying out to the Lord for us, that He may save us from the Philistines." **9.** Samuel took a young lamb and offered it as a whole burnt offering to the Lord, then cried out to Him for Israel. The Lord answered him. **10.** As Samuel offered the sacrifice, the Philistines advanced to fight. But the Lord sent a mighty thunderstorm, causing confusion among the Philistines, and Israel defeated them. **11.** The Israelites chased the Philistines, driving them back as far as below Beth Car. **12.** Samuel took a stone, placed it between Mizpah and Shen, and called it Ebenezer, saying, "Thus far the Lord has helped us." (Shen: place name) **13.** The Philistines were defeated and did not return to attack Israel. The Lord's hand was against them all the days of Samuel's leadership. **14.** The towns that the Philistines had captured from Israel were returned, from Ekron to Gath, and Israel regained its territory. There was peace between Israel and the Amorites. (Ekron, Gath: Philistine cities) **15.** Samuel served as Israel's judge throughout his life. **16.** Every year, he made a circuit to Bethel, Gilgal, and Mizpah, judging Israel in these places. (Bethel, Gilgal: towns in ancient Israel) **17.** He always returned to Ramah, where he lived, judged Israel, and built an altar to the Lord. (Ramah: Samuel's home)

Chapter 8

1. As Samuel became old, he appointed his sons to serve as judges over Israel (Israel: nation of God's people). **2.** His firstborn son was Joel, and the second was Abijah; they acted as judges in Beersheba (Beersheba: southern town). **3.** However, his sons did not follow his example. They sought dishonest profit, accepted bribes, and distorted justice (dishonest profit: unfair earnings; bribes: unlawful gifts; distorted justice: unfair rulings). **4.** The elders of Israel gathered and approached Samuel in Ramah (Ramah: Samuel's city). **5.** They said, "You are old, and your sons do not walk in your ways. Appoint a king to lead us, like the nations around us (nations: other people groups)." **6.** Samuel was upset by their demand for a king, so he prayed to the Lord (upset: troubled). **7.** The Lord replied, "Listen to the people. They are not rejecting you but Me as their ruler (rejecting: refusing to follow). **8.** They have done this ever since I brought them out of Egypt—abandoning Me to worship other gods (abandoning: leaving behind; other gods: false idols). Now they are treating you the same way." **9.** "Listen to their request, but make sure to warn them about the rights the king will claim over them (rights: demands)." **10.** Samuel conveyed all of the Lord's words to the people. **11.** He said, "This is what a king who rules over you will do: He will take your sons for his chariots, horses, and to run ahead of them (chariots: war vehicles)." **12.** "He will assign some of them as commanders, others as farmers, and still others to make weapons and equipment (commanders: leaders; weapons: tools for war)." **13.** "He will also take your daughters to be perfumers, cooks, and bakers (perfumers: makers of fragrances; bakers: bread makers)." **14.** "The best of your fields, vineyards, and olive groves will be taken and given to his servants (fields: land for farming; servants: workers)." **15.** "He will take a tenth of your grain and wine for his officials and attendants. **16.** "He will take your male and female servants, your finest young men, and your donkeys to work for him (donkeys: animals used for labor)." **17.** "He will demand a tenth of your flocks, and you will become his servants (servants: slaves)." **18.** "At that time, you will cry out because of the king you chose, but the Lord will not answer you (cry out: call for help; answer: respond)." **19.** Despite Samuel's warning, the people refused to listen. They insisted, "No! We want a king to rule over us (refused: rejected; king: ruler)." **20.** "We want to be like the other nations, with a king to lead us and fight our battles (battles: wars)." **21.** Samuel heard everything the people said and told it to the Lord (told: reported). **22.** The Lord answered, "Give them a king." Then Samuel said to the people, "Each of you, return to your cities (cities: towns)."

Chapter 9

1. There was a man from Benjamin named Kish, son of Abiel, son of Zeror, son of Bechorath, son of Aphiah, a mighty man. (strong: powerful) **2.** Kish had a handsome son named Saul, the most handsome among the Israelites. He was taller than anyone. (attractive: good-looking) **3.** The donkeys of Kish were lost. He told Saul, "Take a servant, go, and search for them." (lost: missing) **4.** They searched through Ephraim, Shalisha, and Shaalim, but didn't find them. They passed through Benjamin, but still found nothing. (traveled: went) **5.** When they reached Zuph, Saul said, "Let's return, or my father will worry more about us than the donkeys." (care: concern) **6.** The servant said, "There's a man of God in this city, an honorable man. Maybe he can show us the way." (wise: intelligent) **7.** Saul replied, "But what do we bring him? We have no bread, and no gift for the man of God." (gift: offering) **8.** The servant said, "I have a small coin of silver. I'll give it to him to show us the way." **9.** (Note: In Israel, when seeking guidance, people used to say, "Let's go to the seer"; a prophet was once called a seer.) **10.** Saul agreed, "That's a good idea. Let's go." **11.** As they climbed the hill, they met some young women drawing water, and asked, "Is the seer here?" **12.** They answered, "Yes, just ahead. He's here today because of a sacrifice on the high place." (Celebration: feast) **13.** "When you enter, you'll find him before he eats. The people won't eat until he blesses the sacrifice. Go now; you'll find him soon." (Blessing: prayer) **14.** They went up to the city, and found Samuel coming out to meet them. (Meeting: encounter) **15.** The Lord had told Samuel the day before that a man from Benjamin would come, and he was to anoint him as Israel's leader. (Future: plan) **16.** "I will send a man from Benjamin tomorrow. Anoint him as commander to save Israel from the Philistines. I've heard their cry." (rescue: deliver) **17.** When Samuel saw Saul, the Lord said, "This is the man I spoke of. He will reign over My people." (king: rule) **18.** Saul asked Samuel, "Where is the seer's house?" **19.** Samuel replied, "I am the seer. Come, eat with me today. Tomorrow I'll tell you what's on your mind." (prophet: seer) **20.** "Don't worry about the donkeys; they've been found. But all of Israel's hope is on you and your family." (concern: care) **21.** Saul said, "I'm from Benjamin, the smallest tribe, and my family is the least. Why are you speaking to me like this?" (humble: modest) **22.** Samuel took Saul and his servant to the banquet hall and seated them in the place of honor among about thirty guests. (gathering: assembly) **23.** Samuel told the cook, "Bring the portion I set aside." (meal: dish) **24.** The cook brought the thigh and set it before Saul. Samuel said, "This was saved for you. Eat, because it was kept for you." (Special: reserved) **25.** After the meal, they went down from the high place to the city. Samuel spoke with Saul on the roof. (conversation: talk) **26.** They got up early, and Samuel called Saul to send him on his way. (Departure: leave) **27.** As they reached the city's edge, Samuel told the servant to go on ahead. "But you stay here while I announce God's word." (Message: revelation)

Chapter 10

1. Then Samuel took a flask of oil, poured it on Saul's head, kissed him, and said, "The Lord has anointed you as ruler over His people." (anointed: bless; ruler : leader) (Saul: First King of Israel) **2.** When you leave me today, you'll meet two men at Rachel's tomb near Benjamin's territory at Zelzah. They will say, "The donkeys you were searching for have been found, and your father is worried about you, asking, 'What should I do about my son?'" (Rachel's tomb : a burial place; Benjamin : Saul's tribe) **3.** Then, continue to the terebinth tree of Tabor. Three men going to Bethel to worship will meet you, one carrying three goats, another with three loaves of bread, and the third with wine. (Tabor : mountain in Israel; Bethel : place of worship) **4.** They will greet you and give you two loaves of bread, which you should accept from them. **5.** Afterward, go to the hill of God where the Philistine outpost is. You will meet a group of prophets coming down from the high place, playing instruments and prophesying. (Hill of God : place where God's presence was; Philistine : enemy) (prophets : people who speak for God; high place : elevated worship site) **6.** The Spirit of the Lord will come upon you, and you'll prophesy with them, becoming a new person. **7.** When these signs happen, do what is needed, for God is with you. **8.** Go to Gilgal before me, and I will come to offer sacrifices. Wait there seven days until I arrive and show you what to do." (Gilgal : place where people gathered for worship) **9.** When Saul left Samuel, God changed his heart, and all the signs happened that day. **10.** When Saul arrived at the hill, a group of prophets met him. The Spirit of God came upon him, and he prophesied with them. **11.** When people who knew him saw him prophesying, they asked, "What has happened to Kish's son? Is Saul also among the prophets?" (Kish : Saul's father) **12.** A man answered, "Who is their father?" So, it became a saying: "Is Saul also among the prophets?" **13.** After he finished prophesying, Saul went to the high place. (high place : elevated worship site) **14.** Saul's uncle asked him,

"Where did you go?" Saul replied, "We were looking for the donkeys. When we couldn't find them, we went to Samuel." **15.** His uncle asked, "What did Samuel say to you?" **16.** Saul answered, "He told us the donkeys were found," but he didn't mention anything about the kingdom. (kingdom : state) **17.** Samuel gathered Israel at Mizpah, and said, "The Lord says: 'I brought Israel out of Egypt, delivered you from oppression, and saved you from your enemies.'" (Mizpah : place where Israel gathered for decisions; Egypt : land of slavery) (oppression : being treated badly) **19.** But today, you have rejected your God, who saved you, and asked for a king. Present yourselves by tribe and clan." (tribe : family group; clan : smaller family unit) **20.** When Samuel called the tribes, Benjamin was chosen. (Benjamin : Saul's tribe) **21.** When the families of Benjamin came forward, the family of Matri was selected. Saul, son of Kish, was chosen, but he was missing. (Matri : Saul's family) **22.** They asked the Lord, "Has he come?" The Lord replied, "He's hiding among the equipment." (equipment : things to carry) **23.** They brought him out, and when he stood among the people, he was taller than anyone. **24.** Samuel said, "Do you see whom the Lord has chosen? There is no one like him!" The people shouted, "Long live the king!" **25.** Samuel explained the duties of kingship, wrote them in a book, and placed it before the Lord. Then he sent the people home. (duties: responsibilities) **26.** Saul went home to Gibeah, and brave men whose hearts God had touched went with him. (Gibeah: city of Saul) **27.** But some rebels asked, "How can this man save us?" They despised him and gave him no gifts. Saul kept quiet. (Rebels: people who resisted authority; despised: treated with disrespect)

Chapter 11

1. Then Nahash, the Ammonite, came and set up camp against Jabesh Gilead. The men of Jabesh pleaded, "Make a treaty with us, and we will serve you." (Nahash: from the nation of Ammon; Jabesh Gilead: a town in Israel) **2.** Nahash responded, "I will agree to a treaty if you allow me to gouge out the right eye of every one of you and bring disgrace upon all of Israel." (gouge out: remove; disgrace: shame) **3.** The elders of Jabesh said, "Give us seven days to send messengers throughout Israel. If no one comes to our aid, we will surrender." (elders: leaders) **4.** The messengers went to Gibeah of Saul and told the people. Upon hearing this, the people wept loudly. (Gibeah: town of Saul, the future king) **5.** Saul, returning from the field, asked, "Why are the people crying?" They told him what the men of Jabesh had said. **6.** When Saul heard this, the Spirit of God came upon him, and his anger was greatly stirred. **7.** Saul took a pair of oxen, cut them into pieces, and sent them throughout Israel with the message: "Anyone who refuses to join Saul and Samuel in battle, this will happen to their oxen." The people feared the Lord, and they came together to fight. (yoke: coupling; Samuel: prophet of Israel) **8.** Saul numbered the people at Bezek, and there were 300,000 men of Israel and 30,000 men of Judah. (Bezek: place in Israel; Judah: tribe of Israel) **9.** They instructed the messengers, "Tell the men of Jabesh, 'By tomorrow, when the sun is hot, you will receive help.'" The messengers returned, and the men of Jabesh were filled with joy. **10.** The men of Jabesh responded, "Tomorrow, we will come out to you, and you can do whatever seems good to you." **11.** The next day, Saul divided the army into three groups and attacked the Ammonites in the early morning, defeating them until the heat of the day. Those who survived scattered and no two of them were left together. (Ammonites: people from Ammon) **12.** The people then asked Samuel, "Who opposed Saul's rule? Bring them to us, and we will put them to death." **13.** But Saul replied, "No one will be put to death today, for today the Lord has given Israel victory." (Salvation: rescue) **14.** Samuel said, "Let us go to Gilgal and renew the kingdom there." (Gilgal: place in Israel; renew: make new) **15.** All the people went to Gilgal, made Saul king before the Lord, offered peace offerings, and rejoiced with great joy. (Peace offerings: sacrifices of thanks)

Chapter 12

1. Now Samuel said to all Israel: "I have listened to your request and made a king over you." (King: Saul) **2.** "Here is the king, walking before you. I am old, and my sons are with you. I've led you from my youth until now." **3.** "Here I am. Testify against me before the Lord and His anointed: Whose ox or donkey have I taken? Whom have I wronged or accepted a bribe from?" (Ox : cow, Bribe : payment to do wrong) **4.** They answered, "You have not wronged us, oppressed us, or taken anything." (Wronged : hurt, Oppressed : treated unfairly) **5.** Samuel said, "The Lord and His anointed are witnesses that I have done nothing wrong." And they agreed, "He is a witness." (Anointed: chosen one) **6.** Samuel said, "It was the Lord who raised up Moses and Aaron and brought your ancestors out of Egypt." (Egypt: country, Ancestors: forefathers) **7.** "Now stand still, and I'll remind you of the righteous acts the Lord did for you and your ancestors." (Righteous: good, just) **8.** "When Jacob entered Egypt and your ancestors cried out, the Lord sent Moses and Aaron to bring them out and settle them here." (Jacob: Israel) **9.** "But when they forgot the Lord, He gave them over to their enemies—Sisera, the Philistines, and the king of Moab." (Sisera: enemy commander, Moab: enemy kingdom) **10.** "They cried to the Lord, confessing their sin, and He delivered them when they promised to serve Him." (Confessing: admitting, Delivered: rescued) **11.** "The Lord sent leaders like Jerubbaal, Bedan, Jephthah, and Samuel to save you from your enemies, and you lived in peace." **12.** "When you saw Nahash king of the Ammonites coming against you, you asked for a king, even though the Lord was your king." (Nahash : king of Ammonites) **13.** "Now, here is the king you asked for. The Lord has set him over you." **14.** "If you fear the Lord, serve Him, and obey His commands, you and the king will follow Him." (Fear: terror) **15.** "But if you disobey and rebel against the Lord, His hand will be against you, as it was against your ancestors." (Disobey : not obey, Rebel : fight against, Hand : power) **16.** "Now, stand and see this great thing the Lord will do before your eyes." **17.** "Isn't today the wheat harvest? I'll pray to the Lord, and He will send thunder and rain to show you how great your sin is in asking for a king." **18.** Samuel prayed, and the Lord sent thunder and rain. The people feared the Lord and Samuel. **19.** The people said to Samuel, "Pray for us, or we will die, for we have added sin to sin by asking for a king." **20.** Samuel replied, "Don't be afraid. You've done wrong, but don't turn away from following the Lord. Serve Him with all your heart." **21.** "Don't follow worthless things that can't help you; they are nothing." (Worthless: useless). **22.** "The Lord won't abandon His people for His great name's sake. He's pleased to make you His people." (Abandon: leave) **23.** "As for me, I won't sin by stopping my prayers for you. I'll teach you the right way." **24.** "Only fear the Lord and serve Him with all your heart. Consider all the great things He has done for you." **25.** "But if you continue in sin, you and your king will be swept away." (Swept away: destroyed)

Chapter 13

1. Saul had been king for one year and after two years of his reign over Israel, **2.** He selected three thousand men from Israel. Two thousand stayed with Saul in Michmash and the area of Bethel, while one thousand were with Jonathan in Gibeah of Benjamin. The rest were sent back to their tents. (Michmash: town in Israel, Bethel: mountain region, Gibeah of Benjamin: town) **3.** Jonathan attacked the Philistine outpost in Geba, and the Philistines were informed. Saul then sounded the trumpet across the land, saying, "Let the Hebrews hear!" (Outpost: a small military camp) **4.** When Israel learned that Saul had struck a Philistine garrison and that the Philistines now despised them, the people were called to join Saul at Gilgal. (Detestable: hated, Gilgal: town) **5.** The Philistines gathered their forces to fight Israel, bringing thirty thousand chariots, six thousand horsemen, and troops as numerous as the sand on the seashore. They camped in Michmash, east of Beth Aven. (Beth Aven: place) **6.** Seeing their dire situation, the Israelites, filled with anxiety, hid in caves, bushes, rocks, holes, and pits. (Distressed: anxious, thickets: bushes) **7.** Some Hebrews crossed the Jordan River into the regions of Gad and Gilead. Meanwhile, Saul remained in Gilgal, and his followers trembled with fear. (Jordan: river, trembling: fearful) **8.** Saul waited seven days, as Samuel had instructed, but Samuel did not come to Gilgal, and Saul's men began to scatter. **9.** So Saul said, "Bring the burnt offering and peace offerings to me," and he offered the burnt offering himself. (Burnt offering: sacrifice) **10.** Just as Saul finished the offering, Samuel arrived. Saul went out to greet him. **11.** Samuel asked, "What have you done?" Saul replied, "When I saw the people scattering, that you hadn't arrived on time, and that the Philistines were gathering at Michmash, **12.** I thought, 'The Philistines will attack me at Gilgal before I seek the Lord's favor.' So I felt compelled to offer the burnt offering." (Supplication: prayer, compelled: forced) **13.** Samuel said, "You have acted foolishly. You didn't obey the Lord's command. If you had, the Lord would have established your kingdom over Israel forever. **14.** But now your kingdom will not endure. The Lord has sought a man after His own heart and appointed him as leader of His people, because you did not follow His command." (Commandment: order, commander: leader) **15.** Samuel left Gilgal and went to Gibeah of Benjamin. Saul counted his troops, about six hundred men. **16.** Saul, Jonathan, and their men stayed in Gibeah of Benjamin, while the Philistines camped at Michmash. (Michmash: town) **17.** Raiders came out of the Philistine camp in three divisions. One headed toward Ophrah in the land of Shual, **18.** another toward Beth Horon, and the third to the border road overlooking the Valley of Zeboim toward the desert. (Ophrah: town, Shual: place, Beth Horon: town, Zeboim: valley, wilderness: desert) **19.** No blacksmiths were found in Israel because the Philistines feared the Hebrews might make swords or spears. (Blacksmith: metalworker) **20.** The Israelites had to go to the Philistines to sharpen their plows, mattocks, axes, and sickles. (Plowshare: plow, mattock: digging tool, sickle: tool for cutting) **21.** The sharpening fee was a pim for plows, mattocks, forks, and axes, and to sharpen goad points. (Pim: coin, goads: sharp tools) **22.** On the day of battle, no swords or spears were found with any of Saul's or Jonathan's men, except for Saul and Jonathan themselves. **23.** Meanwhile, the Philistine garrison advanced to the pass at Michmash. (Garrison: military post, pass: narrow road)

Chapter 14
1. One day, Jonathan, son of Saul, said to his armor-bearer, "Let's go to the Philistine garrison across the way." He did not tell his father. **2.** Saul was staying on the outskirts of Gibeah, under a pomegranate tree in Migron, with about six hundred men. (Gibeah: Saul's hometown) **3.** Ahijah, the son of Ahitub and grandson of Eli, priest at Shiloh, was wearing the ephod. Meanwhile, the people did not realize that Jonathan had left. (Ephod: priestly garment) **4.** Between the passes where Jonathan planned to approach the Philistine garrison were two sharp rocks—one called Bozez and the other Seneh. (Bozez & Seneh: rock names) **5.** One rock faced north toward Michmash and the other south toward Gibeah. **6.** Jonathan said to his armor-bearer, "Let's approach these uncircumcised men. Perhaps the Lord will help us, for He can save by many or by few." **7.** His armor-bearer replied, "Do whatever you think best. I'm with you completely." **8.** Jonathan said, "We'll show ourselves to them. **9.** If they say, 'Wait, we'll come to you,' we'll stay put. **10.** But if they say, 'Come up to us,' that will be the sign that the Lord has delivered them into our hands." **11.** So they revealed themselves to the Philistine garrison. The Philistines mocked, "Look, the Hebrew are crawling out of their hiding places!" **12.** They called out, "Come up, and we'll teach you a lesson!" Jonathan told his armor-bearer, "Follow me, for the Lord has handed them over to Israel." **13.** Jonathan climbed up on hands and knees, with his armor-bearer following. The Philistines fell before Jonathan, and his armor-bearer killed those who remained. **14.** In this initial attack, about twenty men were struck down in an area of half an acre. **15.** Panic spread through the Philistine camp, from the garrison to the raiders. The earth quaked, and fear gripped everyone. **16.** Saul's watchmen in Gibeah saw the Philistine army scattering. **17.** Saul ordered, "Count the troops to see who is missing." They found that Jonathan and his armor-bearer were absent. **18.** Saul then said to Ahijah, "Bring the ark of God here." (Ark: sacred chest, symbol of God's presence) **19.** But as Saul spoke to the priest, the noise in the Philistine camp grew louder, and Saul told him, "Withdraw your hand." **20.** Then Saul and his men joined the battle, finding the Philistines in chaos, fighting each other. **21.** Even Hebrews who had previously joined the Philistines turned back to fight with Saul and Jonathan. **22.** Israelites hiding in the region of Ephraim joined the pursuit when they heard the Philistines were fleeing. (Ephraim: region in Israel) **23.** That day, the Lord saved Israel, and the battle moved to Beth Aven. (Beth Aven: location near Michmash) **24.** However, the Israelites were weakened because Saul had made them swear not to eat until evening, before he avenged himself on his enemies. **25.** When they reached a forest, they found honey dripping from trees. **26.** Although the honey was abundant, no one ate because of Saul's oath. **27.** But Jonathan, unaware of the oath, dipped his rod into the honeycomb and ate. His strength was renewed. **28.** One soldier told him, "Your father commanded us not to eat, saying, 'Cursed is anyone who eats today.' The people are exhausted." **29.** Jonathan said, "My father has troubled the nation. Look how much better I feel after eating this honey. **30.** If the people had eaten freely from the spoils of their enemies, the victory would have been even greater." **31.** That day, the Israelites chased the Philistines from Michmash to Aijalon, but they were weak from hunger. (Aijalon: city in Judah) **32.** In desperation, the people slaughtered sheep, oxen, and calves on the ground and ate the meat with the blood. **33.** Someone informed Saul, "The people are sinning by eating meat with blood." Saul said, "You have sinned. Roll a large stone to me." **34.** He then instructed, "Bring your oxen and sheep here. Slaughter them properly and eat, so you don't sin against the Lord by eating with blood." Everyone complied that night. **35.** Saul built an altar to the Lord; it was his first altar. **36.** Saul suggested pursuing the Philistines all night and leaving no survivors. The people agreed, but the priest said, "Let us consult the Lord." **37.** Saul inquired of God, "Shall I pursue the Philistines? Will You deliver them into Israel's hands?" But there was no answer. **38.** Saul said, "Bring all the leaders here. We must find out who sinned today. **39.** Even if it's my son Jonathan, he will die." But no one spoke. **40.** Saul divided the people, placing himself and Jonathan on one side and the rest on the other. The people agreed. **41.** Saul prayed, and the lot fell on him and Jonathan. **42.** When lots were cast again, Jonathan was chosen. **43.** Saul asked, "What have you done?" Jonathan admitted, "I tasted a little honey with my rod. Must I die?" **44.** Saul declared, "May God punish me if you don't die, Jonathan." **45.** But the people intervened, saying, "Jonathan brought victory to Israel with God's help. He must not die!" So Jonathan was spared. **46.** Saul ended his pursuit of the Philistines, who returned to their land. **47.** Saul's reign included battles against Moab, Ammon, Edom, Zobah, and the Philistines. (Moab, Ammon: enemy nations; Edom: region southeast of Israel; Zobah: Syrian kingdom) **48.** He defeated the Amalekites and saved Israel from their plunderers. (Amalekites: enemy tribe) **49.** Saul's sons were Jonathan, Jishui, and Malchishua, and his daughters were Merab and Michal. **50.** Saul's wife was Ahinoam, and his army commander was Abner, his uncle's son. **51.** Saul's father was Kish, and Abner's father was Ner, son of Abiel. **52.** Throughout Saul's reign, there was constant war with the Philistines. He recruited every strong and brave man he saw into his army.

Chapter 15
1. Samuel said to Saul, "The Lord selected me to anoint you as the ruler over His people, Israel. Therefore, pay attention to the instructions from the Lord." (Israel: God's chosen people) **2.** The Lord Almighty has declared, "I will bring justice to Amalek for their actions against Israel, specifically for attacking them as they journeyed from Egypt." (Amalek: enemy of Israel) **3.** "Now, go and strike Amalek,

completely eliminating everything they have. Show no mercy—kill men, women, children, livestock, sheep, camels, and donkeys." (Eliminating: destroying fully) **4.** Saul assembled his troops at Telaim, counting 200,000 infantry and an additional 10,000 men from Judah. (Telaim: gathering place) **5.** He advanced to the city of Amalek and stationed his forces in the valley, ready for battle. (Stationed: positioned) **6.** Saul said to the Kenites, "Withdraw from the Amalekites to avoid being destroyed with them, for you were kind to the Israelites during their exodus from Egypt." The Kenites obeyed and departed from the Amalekites. (Withdraw: move away) **7.** Saul launched an attack on the Amalekites, striking them from Havilah to Shur, near Egypt. (Havilah: eastern region, Shur: desert near Egypt) **8.** He captured Agag, the Amalekite king, but utterly destroyed the rest of the people with his forces. (Utterly: completely) **9.** However, Saul and his men spared Agag and kept the finest sheep, oxen, and livestock, along with other valuable items. They destroyed only what was deemed useless. (spared: saved, deemed: considered) **10.** Then the Lord spoke to Samuel, saying, **11.** "I regret making Saul king because he has turned away from Me and ignored My commands." Samuel was deeply troubled and prayed to the Lord throughout the night. (regret: feel sorrow, troubled: distressed) **12.** Early the next morning, Samuel went to meet Saul but learned that Saul had gone to Carmel to set up a memorial for himself before proceeding to Gilgal. (Carmel: mountain in Israel, memorial: monument) **13.** When Samuel arrived, Saul greeted him, saying, "Blessed are you in the Lord's name! I have carried out the Lord's orders." (carried out: fulfilled) **14.** But Samuel asked, "Then why do I hear the sounds of sheep and cattle?" **15.** Saul replied, "The people brought them from the Amalekites. They spared the best of the sheep and oxen to offer as sacrifices to the Lord, but we destroyed the rest." (Offer: dedicate) **16.** Samuel interrupted, "Stop! Let me tell you what the Lord said to me last night." Saul responded, "Speak." (Interrupted: cut short) **17.** Samuel said, "Though you once saw yourself as insignificant, were you not made the leader of Israel's tribes? The Lord anointed you as king. (Insignificant: unimportant, anointed: chosen by God) **18.** He sent you on a mission, commanding you to destroy the Amalekites completely. **19.** Why did you disobey the Lord? Why did you seize the plunder and commit this wrong in His sight?" (Seize: take, plunder: loot) **20.** Saul defended himself, "I did obey the Lord! I completed the mission and brought back Agag, the king of Amalek, while destroying the Amalekites. **21.** But the people took the best of the livestock to offer as sacrifices to the Lord at Gilgal." (Gilgal: city near Jericho) **22.** Samuel replied, "Does the Lord value sacrifices as much as obedience? To obey is far better than offering sacrifices; to follow His commands is better than presenting the fat of rams. **23.** Rebellion is as sinful as witchcraft, and arrogance is like idolatry. Because you have rejected the Lord's command, He has rejected you as king." (Rebellion: defiance, arrogance: pride, idolatry: worship of idols) **24.** Saul admitted, "I have sinned. I violated the Lord's instructions and your words because I feared the people and listened to them." (violated: broke) **25.** "Now, please forgive my sin and return with me so I can worship the Lord." (Forgive: pardon) **26.** Samuel refused, saying, "I will not go with you. You rejected the Lord's command, and He has rejected you as king over Israel." **27.** As Samuel turned to leave, Saul grabbed his robe, tearing a piece of it. (Grabbed: seized) **28.** Samuel declared, "Today, the Lord has torn the kingdom of Israel from you and given it to a neighbor who is better than you. **29.** The Eternal One of Israel does not lie or change His mind, for He is not human." (Change His mind: reconsider) **30.** Saul pleaded, "I have sinned, but please honor me before my people and the elders of Israel. Come back with me so I may worship the Lord." (honor: respect) **31.** Samuel returned with Saul, and Saul worshiped the Lord. (Worshiped: praised) **32.** Then Samuel said, "Bring me Agag, the Amalekite king." Agag came forward, thinking, "Surely the pain of death has passed." (Agag: Amalekite king) **33.** But Samuel declared, "As your sword has left many women childless, so your mother will now be childless among women." Samuel then executed Agag at Gilgal. (childless: without children) **34.** Samuel went to Ramah, while Saul returned to his home in Gibeah. (Ramah: Samuel's city) **35.** Samuel never saw Saul again during his lifetime, but he mourned for him, and the Lord regretted making Saul king over Israel. (Mourned: grieved, regretted: felt sorrow)

Chapter 16

1. The Lord spoke to Samuel, saying, "How long will you grieve over Saul, since I have rejected him as king over Israel? Fill your horn with oil and go. I am sending you to Jesse from Bethlehem. I have chosen one of his sons to be king." (Rejected: dismissed, Bethlehemite: from Bethlehem) **2.** Samuel asked, "How can I go? Saul might kill me." The Lord responded, "Take a heifer with you and tell them you have come to offer a sacrifice to the Lord." (Heifer: young cow) **3.** "Invite Jesse to the sacrifice, and I will show you what to do. I will guide you to the one I have chosen." (Anoint: select) **4.** Samuel followed the Lord's command and went to Bethlehem. When the elders saw him, they were afraid and asked, "Have you come in peace?" (Trembled: shook with fear) **5.** Samuel replied, "Yes, I come to offer a sacrifice to the Lord. Purify yourselves and join me in the sacrifice." He consecrated Jesse and his sons for the event. (Consecrated: made holy) **6.** When they arrived, Samuel thought, "Surely this must be the one the Lord has chosen." (Anointed: selected one) **7.** But the Lord said to Samuel, "Do not look at his appearance or his height, for I have rejected him. The Lord sees the heart, not just the outward appearance." (Rejected: dismissed) **8.** Jesse brought forth Abinadab, but the Lord did not choose him. **9.** Then Shammah came before Samuel, but the Lord did not choose him either. **10.** Jesse presented seven of his sons before Samuel, but the Lord did not select any of them. **11.** Samuel asked, "Are these all your sons?" Jesse replied, "There is still the youngest, who is tending the sheep." Samuel told him, "We will not sit down until he arrives." (Youngest: smallest) **12.** When David arrived, he was fair in appearance, with bright eyes, and good-looking. The Lord said, "Anoint him; this is the one!" (Ruddy: red, healthy) **13.** Samuel anointed David in front of his brothers, and the Spirit of the Lord came upon him from that day forward. Samuel then returned to Ramah. (Anointed: selected) **14.** The Spirit of the Lord left Saul, and an evil spirit sent by God began to trouble him. (Distressing: disturbing). **15.** Saul's servants said to him, "A troubling spirit from God is tormenting you." **16.** "Let's find someone skilled at playing the harp to soothe you when the spirit troubles you." **17.** Saul agreed, "Find me someone who plays well." **18.** One of the servants said, "I know a son of Jesse who is a talented harpist, a warrior, wise, and handsome, and the Lord is with him." **19.** Saul sent messengers to Jesse, saying, "Send your son David to me." **20.** Jesse sent David to Saul, bringing with him bread, wine, and a goat. **21.** David stood before Saul, and Saul took a liking to him, making him his armor-bearer. (armor-bearer: soldier) **22.** Saul asked Jesse to let David stay because he had found favor with him. **23.** Whenever the evil spirit troubled Saul, David would play the harp, and Saul would feel at peace. The troubling spirit would leave him.

Chapter 17

1. Now the Philistines gathered their armies for battle, and camped at Sochoh, in Judah, between Sochoh and Azekah, in Ephes Dammim. (Sochoh: A town in Judah, Azekah: A town near Sochoh, Ephes Dammim: Location between Sochoh and Azekah) **2.** Saul and the men of Israel gathered and camped in the Valley of Elah, preparing for battle against the Philistines. (Saul: Israel's king, Elah: A valley) **3.** The Philistines stood on a mountain on one side, and Israel on the other, with a valley between them. (Mountain: A high area of land) **4.** A champion named Goliath, from Gath, went out from the Philistines, and he was over nine feet tall. (Goliath: A giant from Gath, Philistines: Enemies of Israel) **5.** He wore a bronze helmet, a coat of mail weighing 5,000 shekels of bronze. (Helmet: Head armor, Mail: Armor made of small metal rings) **6.** He had bronze armor on his legs and a bronze javelin on his back. (Javelin: A type of spear) **7.**

The shaft of his spear was like a weaver's beam, and its iron tip weighed 600 shekels; a shield-bearer went before him. (Shaft: Long part of the spear, Shield-bearer: One who carried Goliath's shield) **8.** Goliath called out to the Israelite army, "Why have you come to line up for battle? I am a Philistine, and you are Saul's servants. Choose a man and let him come fight me. **9.** If he kills me, we will serve you, but if I kill him, you will serve us." (Defy: To challenge or insult) **10.** Goliath said, "I defy Israel today! Give me a man to fight me." (Defy: Challenge) **11.** When Saul and Israel heard these words, they were afraid. (Dismayed: Feeling hopeless or scared) **12.** David was the son of Jesse, an old man from Bethlehem in Judah. He had eight sons. (Bethlehem : Town in Judah, Jesse : David's father) **13.** Jesse's three oldest sons went to battle with Saul: Eliab, Abinadab, and Shammah. (Eliab: Oldest son of Jesse, Abinadab: Second son of Jesse, Shammah : Third son of Jesse) **14.** David was the youngest, and the three oldest followed Saul. **15.** David occasionally returned to Bethlehem to tend his father's sheep. (Tend: To care for, Bethlehem: David's hometown) **16.** For forty days, Goliath came forward morning and evening. (Defy: To challenge) **17.** Jesse sent David with food for his brothers and to learn news of them. (Ephah : A measure of grain) **18.** He also sent ten cheeses to the captain and asked how his brothers were doing. (Cheese: Dairy food, Captain : Leader) **19.** Saul and the Israelites were in the Valley of Elah, fighting the Philistines. (Valley: A low area of land) **20.** David rose early, left the sheep with a keeper, and obeyed his father. He came to the camp as the army was going out to battle. (Keeper: One who watches or takes care of) **21.** Israel and the Philistines were lined up for battle. (Array: Arrangement for battle) **22.** David left his supplies with the keeper, ran to the army, and greeted his brothers. (Supplies: Necessary items) **23.** As David talked with them, Goliath came out, repeating his challenge, and David heard him. **24.** When the Israelites saw Goliath, they fled in fear. (Fled: Ran away in fear) **25.** The men of Israel said, "Have you seen this man? Whoever kills him will be richly rewarded, given the king's daughter, and freed from taxes." (Rewarded: Given gifts for bravery, Taxes: Money paid to the government) **26.** David asked, "What will be done for the man who defeats this Philistine and removes Israel's disgrace? Who is this uncircumcised Philistine who defies God's army?" (Disgrace: Shame, Uncircumcised: Not following Israel's tradition) **27.** The people replied, "So it will be done for the man who kills him." **28.** Eliab, David's older brother, became angry and said, "Why are you here? Who is watching the few sheep? I know your pride; you just came to watch the battle." (Pride: Self-importance, Battle: Fight) **29.** David replied, "What have I done now? Is there not a cause?" (Cause: A reason) **30.** David turned to others and asked the same, and they answered the same. **31.** When David's words were heard, they were reported to Saul, who sent for him. **32.** David said to Saul, "Don't let anyone be afraid. I will fight this Philistine." **33.** Saul replied, "You can't fight him. You are just a youth, and he's been a warrior since youth." (Warrior: Soldier) **34.** David said, "I have kept my father's sheep. When a lion or bear came and took a lamb, **35.** I went after it, struck it, and saved the lamb. When it turned on me, I grabbed it by the beard and killed it. (Beard: Hair on the chin) **36.** I've killed lions and bears, and this uncircumcised Philistine will be like them, for he has defied God's army." **37.** David said, "The Lord who saved me from the lion and bear will save me from this Philistine." Saul replied, "Go, and may the Lord be with you." **38.** Saul clothed David in armor, and put a bronze helmet on his head. (Armor: Protective clothing) **39.** David fastened the armor and tried to walk, but said, "I cannot walk in these, I have not tested them." So he took them off. (Tested: Tried to see if they work) **40.** David took his staff, chose five smooth stones, and put them in his shepherd's bag. He approached Goliath with his sling. (Staff: Walking stick, Sling: Weapon for throwing stones) **41.** Goliath, with his shield-bearer, came toward David. **42.** Goliath looked at David and mocked him, for he was young and handsome. (Mocked: Made fun of) **43.** He said, "Am I a dog, that you come at me with sticks?" and cursed David. **44.** Goliath said, "Come to me, and I'll give your flesh to the birds and beasts!" **45.** David said, "You come with a sword, spear, and javelin, but I come in the name of the Lord, the God of Israel, whom you have defied. **46.** Today, the Lord will deliver you into my hands. I will strike you down, and give the Philistine army's bodies to the birds and beasts, so all the earth will know there is a God in Israel." **47.** "The battle is the Lord's, and He will give you into our hands." **48.** As Goliath advanced, David ran toward him. **49.** David took a stone, slung it, and struck Goliath in the forehead. The stone sank into his head, and he fell face-first to the ground. **50.** David defeated Goliath with a sling and stone, and killed him. He had no sword. **51.** David ran, stood over Goliath, took his sword, and killed him. He cut off Goliath's head. When the Philistines saw their champion was dead, they fled. **52.** Israel and Judah shouted and chased the Philistines to Ekron, and the dead Philistines lay along the road. (Ekron: A city of the ancient Philistines) **53.** The Israelites returned from pursuing the Philistines and plundered their camps. (Plundered: Took valuables) **54.** David took Goliath's head to Jerusalem, but put his armor in his tent. (Jerusalem: City in Judah, Tent: A portable shelter) **55.** When Saul saw David, he asked Abner, "Whose son is this youth?" Abner replied, "I don't know." **56.** Saul said, "Find out whose son he is." **57.** After the battle, Abner brought David to Saul with Goliath's head. **58.** Saul asked, "Whose son are you, young man?" David replied, "I am the son of your servant Jesse from Bethlehem."

Chapter 18

1. Now, after speaking to Saul, Jonathan's soul was bound to David's, and he loved him like his own soul. (Bound: connected) **2.** Saul took David that day and would not let him return to his father's house. **3.** Jonathan and David made a covenant because of their deep love for each other. (Covenant: agreement) **4.** Jonathan gave David his robe, armor, sword, bow, and belt. (Armor: protective clothing) **5.** David went wherever Saul sent him and acted wisely. Saul made him commander over the army, and everyone, including Saul's servants, accepted him. (Wisely: carefully, commander: leader) **6.** As they were returning from defeating the Philistines, women from all cities came out to meet King Saul with joy, tambourines, and music. (Defeating: beating, tambourines: musical instruments) **7.** The women sang: "Saul has slain his thousands, and David his ten thousands." (Slain: killed) **8.** Saul was angry and said, "They've given David ten thousands, and only thousands to me. What more can he have but the kingdom?" (Kingdom: state) **9.** From that day on, Saul watched David closely. (Closely: carefully) **10.** The next day, a troubling spirit from God came upon Saul, and he prophesied in the house. David played music as usual, but Saul had a spear. (Troubling: bothering, prophesied: spoke from God, spear: sharp weapon) **11.** Saul threw the spear, saying, "I'll pin David to the wall!" But David escaped twice. (Pin: stick) **12.** Saul feared David because the Lord was with him, but had left Saul. **13.** So Saul removed David from his presence and made him captain of a thousand. David went out and came in before the people. (Captain: leader). **14.** David continued to act wisely, and the Lord was with him. **15.** When Saul saw that David acted so wisely, he became afraid of him. **16.** All of Israel and Judah loved David because of his actions. **17.** Saul said to David, "I will give you my older daughter Merab as a wife. Only fight the Lord's battles." He thought, "Let the Philistines defeat him, not me." (Merab: Saul's older daughter). **18.** David replied, "Who am I, and what is my family, that I should be son-in-law to the king?" **19.** When it was time for Merab to marry David, she was given to Adriel the Meholathite instead. (Meholathite: man from Meholah) **20.** Saul's daughter Michal loved David, and when Saul heard this, he was pleased. **21.** Saul said, "I will give her to David as a snare, so the Philistines will harm him." He told David again, "You shall be my son-in-law today." (Snare: trap) **22.** Saul ordered his servants to secretly tell David, "The king delights in you, and all his servants love you. Become the king's son-in-law." **23.** David responded, "Do you think being the king's son-in-law is a small thing? I'm poor and of little reputation." (Reputation: importance) 24. Saul's servants reported David's words to him. 25. Saul said, "Tell David the king wants no dowry but one hundred foreskins of the Philistines to take vengeance on his enemies." He hoped the Philistines would kill David. (Dowry: marriage settlement, vengeance: revenge) 26. When Saul's servants delivered this message, David was pleased to become the king's son-in-law. 27. David and his men killed two hundred Philistines and brought their foreskins to Saul, so David became the king's son-in-law. Saul gave him Michal as a wife. 28. Saul saw that the Lord was with David, and that Michal loved him. 29. Saul became even more afraid of David and made him his enemy forever. 30. When the Philistine princes went to war, David behaved more wisely than all Saul's servants, and his name became highly honored. (princes: leaders)

Chapter 19

1. Saul spoke to his son Jonathan and his servants, instructing them to kill David; but Jonathan, Saul's son, loved David deeply (greatly). (Saul : king of Israel) 2. Jonathan warned David, saying, "My father Saul wants to kill you. Be cautious (on your guard) and hide until the morning." (Cautious : careful) 3. "I will go out and speak to my father about you. I'll let you know what I find out." 4. Jonathan spoke favorably (well) about David to Saul, saying, "Don't sin against David, for he hasn't wronged you, and his actions toward you have been good." (Favorably : in a positive manner) 5. "He risked his life to defeat the Philistine, and the Lord brought great victory to Israel. You rejoiced then. Why should you kill an innocent man without reason?" (Risked: put his life in danger) 6. Saul listened to Jonathan and vowed, "As the Lord lives, he will not be killed." 7. Jonathan called David and shared everything with him. He brought David back to Saul, and David was in his presence again, as before. (Presence : in front of him) 8. A battle broke out again, and David fought the Philistines, defeating them with great force, and they fled. (Philistines : enemies of Israel) 9. A troubling spirit from the Lord took hold of Saul while he sat in his house with a spear in his hand, and David was playing music. (Distressing: troubling, Spear: a weapon) 10. Saul tried to pin David to the wall with the spear, but David escaped, and the spear struck the wall. David fled that night. (Pin: to stab or fix in place) 11. Saul sent messengers to watch David's house and kill him in the morning. Michal, David's wife, warned him, saying, "If you don't escape tonight, you'll be killed tomorrow." 12. Michal let David down through a window, and he fled to safety. (Fled: ran away) 13. Michal placed an idol (image) in the bed and covered it with goat's hair for its head and clothes. (Idol: a statue of a god) 14. When Saul's messengers came to take David, she said, "He's sick." 15. Saul sent the messengers back, saying, "Bring him to me in the bed so I can kill him." (Messengers: people sent to deliver a message) 16. When the messengers arrived, they found the idol in the bed with the goat's hair cover. 17. Saul asked Michal, "Why have you deceived me, sending my enemy away?" Michal answered, "He told me, 'let me go, why I should kill you?'" (Deceived: tricked or lied to) 18. David fled to Samuel at Ramah and told him everything Saul had done. They went and stayed in Naioth. (Ramah: a city in ancient Israel) (Naioth : a place near Ramah) 19. Saul was informed, "David is at Naioth in Ramah!" 20. Saul sent messengers to capture David. When they saw a group of prophets prophesying, with Samuel leading them, the Spirit of God came upon Saul's messengers, and they also prophesied. (Prophesied: spoke messages from God) 21. Saul sent more messengers, and they prophesied as well. Then he sent a third group, and they also prophesied. 22. Saul went to Ramah and came to the great well at Sechu. He asked, "Where are Samuel and David?" They answered, "They are at Naioth in Ramah." (Ramah : a town in Israel) (Sechu : a place near Ramah) 23. Saul went to Naioth in Ramah. The Spirit of God came upon him, and he prophesied until he arrived. 24. Saul took off his clothes and prophesied before Samuel, lying naked all day and night. So it was said, "Is Saul also among the prophets?" (Prophesied: Acted under divine inspiration)

Chapter 20

1. David fled from Naioth in Ramah and went to Jonathan, asking, "What have I done? What is my wrongdoing and what is my sin before your father that he wants to kill me?" (Naioth in Ramah: a town in ancient Israel) (Wrongdoing: immoral or illegal behavior) 2. Jonathan replied, "That's not true! You won't die! My father does not do anything without informing me. Why would he keep this from me? It's not like that." 3. David swore again, saying, "Your father knows that I've found favor with you, and he has said, 'Don't let Jonathan know, or he'll be upset.' But as the Lord lives and your soul lives, I'm only one step away from death." (Swore: made a serious promise; favor: approval or kindness) 4. Jonathan said, "I'll do whatever you ask." 5. David explained, "Tomorrow is the New Moon, and I am expected to sit with the king for the meal. But instead, I will hide in the field until the evening of the third day." (New Moon: a Jewish festival; evening: the time when it gets dark) 6. "If your father notices my absence, tell him, 'David asked permission to go to Bethlehem for the annual family sacrifice.'" (Bethlehem: a town in Israel) (Sacrifice: a religious offering) 7. "If he says, 'That's fine,' then I will be safe. But if he reacts angrily, you will know he has bad intentions toward me." (Intention: plan or goal) 8. "Please show me kindness, as we made a covenant (covenant: formal agreement) before the Lord. If I've wronged you, then let me be killed by you, but don't bring me before your father." 9. Jonathan responded, "No! If I knew my father intended to harm you, I would definitely warn you." (Harm: hurt or injure) 10. David asked, "Who will let me know if your father answers harshly?" (Harshly: in a rude or severe manner) 11. Jonathan said, "Let's go out to the field." So they both went. (Field: open area of land) 12. Jonathan swore by the Lord, saying, "I will speak with my father tomorrow or the third day. If he is favorable toward you, I will tell you." (Swore: made a serious promise; favorable: approving) 13. "But if he plans evil, I will send word to you and send you away safely. May the Lord be with you, as He has been with my father?" (Evil: wicked or harmful actions). 14. "And show kindness to me while I live, so I won't die; 15. And when the Lord has defeated all of David's enemies, continue showing kindness to my family forever." (Enemies: people who oppose or harm you; forever: for all time) 16. Jonathan made a covenant with David's family, saying, "Let the Lord deal with those who oppose David." (Oppose: resist or go against) 17. Jonathan made David swear again because of his deep love for him, as he loved him like his own soul. (swear: make a serious promise; soul: the essence of a person) 18. Jonathan said, "Tomorrow is the New Moon, and you will surely be missed because your seat will be empty." (Missed: noticed that someone is absent) 19. "After three days, go quickly to the place where you hid before, near the stone Ezel." (Stone Ezel: a landmark in the field) (Hid: concealed yourself) 20. "I will shoot three arrows beside it as though I'm aiming at a target." (Shoot: launch an arrow; target: a point aimed at) 21. "Then I'll send a boy to say, 'Go, find the arrows.' If I tell him, 'The arrows are this side of you, pick them up,' then you will know I am safe. But if I say, 'The arrows are beyond you,' then go, for the Lord has sent you away." (Beyond: farther than). 22. "As for the matter we've discussed, may the Lord watch over us forever." (matter: topic or issue; watch over: protect) 23. So David hid, and when the New Moon arrived, the king (Saul) sat down to eat the feast. (feast: large meal) 24. Saul sat in his usual spot by the wall. Jonathan stood, and Abner (Abner: military leader) sat beside him. David's seat was empty. (seat: place to sit) 25. Saul said nothing, thinking, "Something must have happened to him; he must be unclean." (unclean: ritually impure) 26. On the second day, when David's seat was still empty, Saul asked Jonathan, "Why hasn't the son of Jesse (Son of Jesse: David) come to eat, either yesterday or today?" 27. Jonathan replied, "David asked to go to Bethlehem." 28. "He said, 'Please let me go, for my family is having a sacrifice, and my

brother has asked me to attend. If I have found favor with you, please let me go.'" (favor: kindness or approval) **29.** Saul became furious with Jonathan, shouting, "You son of a rebellious woman! Don't you know you've chosen the son of Jesse to your own disgrace and that of your mother?" (furious: very angry; rebellious: refusing to obey) **30.** "As long as the son of Jesse is alive, you will not be king. Go and bring him to me; he must die." **31.** Jonathan asked, "Why should he be killed? What has he done?" **32.** Saul threw a spear at Jonathan, trying to kill him. Jonathan realized that his father was determined to kill David. (spear: a weapon with a long shaft) **33.** In great anger, Jonathan stood up from the table and didn't eat on the second day, grieving over David because his father had shamed him. (grieving: feeling deep sadness) **34.** The next morning, Jonathan went out to the field with a young boy. (boy: a young male) **35.** He told the boy, "Run and find the arrows I shoot." As the boy ran, Jonathan shot an arrow beyond him. **36.** When the boy reached the spot where the arrow had fallen, Jonathan called out, "Isn't the arrow beyond you?" **37.** Jonathan shouted to the boy, "Hurry, don't stop!" The boy gathered the arrows and returned to Jonathan. (gathered: collected) **38.** The boy didn't understand anything; only Jonathan and David knew the plan. (Understand: comprehend) **39.** Jonathan gave his weapons to the boy and told him, "Take them back to the city." (Weapons: tools used for defense) **40.** When the boy left, David came from hiding, bowed before Jonathan three times, and they kissed each other, weeping, with David weeping the most. **41.** Jonathan said, "Go in peace. We have sworn in the name of the Lord, saying, 'The Lord be between you and me, and between your descendants and mine, forever.'" (Descendants: future generations). **42.** David left, and Jonathan returned to the city. (returned: came back)

Chapter 21
1. Now David came to Nob, to Ahimelech the priest. Ahimelech was scared (afraid) when he met David and asked, "Why are you alone, and no one is with you?" (Nob: a city of priests) **2.** David replied, "The king sent me on a mission and told me, 'Do not tell anyone about the mission or what I have commanded.' I have sent my men to such and such a place." (King: Saul, Israel's king) **3.** "What do you have here? Give me five loaves of bread, or whatever you have." (Loaves: types of bread) **4.** The priest said, "We have no common bread, only holy bread, if your men have stayed away from women." (Holy: sacred or dedicated) **5.** David answered, "We've been away from women for three days. The men are holy, and the bread is ordinary (not holy), even though it was sanctified today." (Sanctified: made sacred or pure) **6.** So the priest gave him the holy bread, as there was no other bread but the showbread, which had been taken from before the Lord to be replaced with fresh bread. (Showbread: bread set apart for religious purposes) **7.** A man named Doeg, an Edomite, Saul's chief herdsman, was there that day, detained before the Lord. (Edomite: a person from Edom, a nation southeast of Israel) **8.** David asked Ahimelech, "Do you have a spear or sword? I didn't bring my weapons because I was in a hurry." (Spear: long weapon with a pointed tip, Sword: bladed weapon) **9.** The priest said, "The sword of Goliath (Philistine giant whom you killed) is here, wrapped behind the ephod (priest's garment). Take it, there's no other sword." (Goliath: giant defeated by David, Ephod: priest's sacred vestment) **10.** David took the sword and fled from Saul, going to Achish, the king of Gath. (Gath: Philistine city) **11.** The servants of Achish said, "Isn't this David, the king of the land? Didn't they sing of him: 'Saul killed thousands, and David tens of thousands'?" (David: future king of Israel) **12.** David became afraid of Achish and took these words seriously. (Afraid: feeling fear) **13.** So he pretended to be mad (insane), scratched at the gate doors, and let his saliva drip down his beard. (Mad: insane) **14.** Achish said, "Why have you brought me this madman? (Madman: insane person) **15.** I have no need of madmen. Why bring him here to act crazy in front of me? Should this man come into my house?" (Madmen: people pretending or acting insane)

Chapter 22
1. David left and escaped to the cave of Adullam. When his brothers and family heard, they joined him there. (Adullam: a place in Judah) **2.** Everyone in distress, in debt, or discontented gathered to him, and he became their leader. About 400 men were with him. (Distress: feeling troubled, discontented: unhappy) **3.** David went to Mizpah of Moab and asked the king, "Please let my parents stay here until I know what God will do for me." (Mizpah: a place, Moab: an area east of Israel) **4.** The king allowed them to stay, and they lived with him while David was in the stronghold. (Stronghold: a protected place) **5.** The prophet Gad told David, "Leave the stronghold and go to Judah." David then went to the forest of Hereth. (Gad: prophet, Judah: an area of Israel) **6.** Saul heard that David and his men were found. Saul was in Gibeah (town in Benjamin) under a tamarisk tree, holding a spear with his servants nearby. (Gibeah: a town, Benjamin: a tribe of Israel) **7.** Saul asked his servants, "Will the son of Jesse give each of you land and make you captains? (captains: leaders of men) **8.** You've all conspired against me! No one tells me my son has made a pact with Jesse's son. No one feels sorry for me or informs me about my son's betrayal." (Conspired: secretly planned, pact: agreement, betrayal: unfaithfulness) **9.** Doeg the Edomite (man from Edom), Saul's servant, said, "I saw Jesse's son at Nob with Ahimelech, son of Ahitub. (Edomite: person from Edom, Nob: a town with priests) **10.** Ahimelech asked God for him, gave him food, and the sword of Goliath." (Goliath: the giant warrior from the Philistines) **11.** Saul called for Ahimelech and all the priests of Nob. They came to him. **12.** Saul said, "Listen, son of Ahitub!" Ahimelech replied, "Here I am, my lord." **13.** Saul accused him, "Why did you help David, giving him food and a sword and asking God for him to rebel?" (rebel: fight against authority) **14.** Ahimelech answered, "Who among your servants is as loyal as David? He's the king's son-in-law, does your bidding, and is honored in your house. (loyal: faithful, bidding: command) **15.** I didn't ask God for him before. I knew nothing about this." **16.** Saul replied, "You will surely die, Ahimelech, and your family too!" **17.** He told his guards, "Kill the priests!" But they wouldn't harm the Lord's priests. (harm: hurt) **18.** Saul ordered Doeg to kill them. Doeg killed 85 priests wearing linen ephods. (ephods: special priest garments) **19.** Doeg also killed everyone in Nob, including men, women, children, infants, and animals. (infants: babies) **20.** Only Abiathar, son of Ahimelech, escaped and fled to David. **21.** Abiathar told David that Saul had killed the priests. **22.** David said, "I knew that day, when Doeg was there, that he would tell Saul. I've caused the death of your family. **23.** Stay with me, don't be afraid. Those who seek my life also seek yours, but you will be safe with me." (seek: look for, want)

Chapter 23
1. Then they told David, "The Philistines are attacking Keilah and stealing the grain." (Keilah: a city in Israel) **2.** David asked the Lord, "Should I go and fight them?" The Lord replied, "Go and save Keilah." (Save: protect or rescue) **3.** But David's men said, "We're afraid here in Judah. How much more if we go to Keilah against the Philistines?" (Judah: a kingdom of northern Israel) **4.** David asked the Lord again, and the Lord said, "Go to Keilah. I will hand the Philistines over to you." (Hand over: give or deliver) **5.** So David and his men fought the Philistines, defeated them, and took their animals. David saved Keilah's people. (Defeated: won against, Animals: livestock or farm animals) **6.** When Abiathar, son of Ahimelech, fled to David at Keilah, he brought the ephod (priest's garment) with him. (Ephod: a special garment worn by priests) **7.** Saul heard that David had gone to Keilah. He said, "God has given him to me, for he's trapped in a town with gates and bars." (Saul: King of Israel, Trapped: caught or surrounded) **8.** Saul gathered his army to attack Keilah and capture David. (Army: group of soldiers) **9.** David, knowing Saul's evil plan, said to Abiathar, "Bring the ephod." (Evil: bad or harmful) **10.** David prayed, "Lord, I've

heard Saul plans to destroy Keilah for my sake. (Destroy: ruin or damage) **11.** Will the people of Keilah hand me over to Saul? Will Saul come here as I've heard? Please tell me." The Lord answered, "He will come." (Hand over: betray or give up) **12.** David asked, "Will the people of Keilah hand me and my men to Saul?" The Lord answered, "They will hand you over." **13.** So David and his 600 men left Keilah and went wherever they could. When Saul learned they escaped, he stopped his pursuit. (Pursuit: chasing or following) **14.** David stayed in strongholds in the wilderness, in the Ziph mountains. Saul sought him daily, but God didn't give David to Saul. (Strongholds: fortified places, Wilderness: barren or empty land, Ziph: a place in Israel) **15.** David knew Saul was after his life and was in the Wilderness of Ziph, in a forest. (Forest: large area of trees) **16.** Jonathan, Saul's son, went to David in the woods and encouraged him in God. (Encouraged: gave hope or strength) **17.** He said, "Don't fear, Saul won't find you. You will be king of Israel, and I'll be next to you. Even Saul knows this." (Fear: be afraid of) **18.** They made a covenant before the Lord. David stayed in the woods, and Jonathan went home. (Covenant: formal agreement) **19.** The Ziphites told Saul, "David is hiding with us, in the strongholds of the Hachilah hill, south of Jeshimon." (Ziphites: people from Ziph, Hachilah: a hill, Jeshimon: a desert region) **20.** "Come down, king, as you desire, and we'll hand him over." (Desire: wish or want) **21.** Saul said, "Bless you, for showing kindness to me." (Kindness: being nice or helpful) **22.** "Go and find out where he is hiding and who's seen him. I've heard he's crafty." (Crafty: sneaky or tricky) **23.** "Search for all his hiding places, then come back with certainty, and I'll search for him throughout Judah." (Certainty: surety or clear knowledge) **24.** They went to Ziph before Saul, but David was in the Wilderness of Maon, south of Jeshimon. (Maon: a place in ancient Israel) **25.** When Saul pursued him, David moved to the rock in the Wilderness of Maon. Saul heard and pursued him. **26.** Saul went one side of the mountain, and David the other. David hurried to escape, for Saul's men surrounded him. (Mountain: large hill or raised land, Surrounded: trapped or encircled) **27.** A messenger told Saul, "Hurry, the Philistines are attacking!" (Messenger: one who delivers a message) **28.** Saul stopped chasing David and went to fight the Philistines. They named the place the Rock of Escape. (Rock of Escape: place where David narrowly escaped). **29.** David went from there and lived in the strongholds at En Gedi. (En Gedi: a place with fresh water, near the Dead Sea)

Chapter 24

1. When Saul returned from pursuing the Philistines, he was told, "David is in the Wilderness of En Gedi." (Philistines: enemy group, En Gedi: desert area near the Dead Sea) **2.** Saul chose three thousand men from all of Israel to search for David and his men in the Rocks of the Wild Goats. (Chosen men: selected soldiers, Rocks of the Wild Goats: rocky hills near En Gedi) **3.** As he reached the sheepfolds along the road, Saul entered a cave to take care of his needs. (David and his men were hidden in the cave's recesses.) (Sheepfolds: place where sheep are kept, relieve himself: attend to his needs, recesses: hidden areas) **4.** David's men said, "This is the day the Lord spoke of, when He promised to deliver your enemy into your hands. You may do whatever you choose with him." David secretly cut off a corner of Saul's robe. **5.** Afterward, David felt guilty for cutting off the corner of Saul's robe. (Troubled him: felt guilty) **6.** He said to his men, "The Lord forbid that I harm my master, the Lord's anointed, by laying a hand on him, since he is God's chosen one." (Anointed: chosen by God) **7.** David restrained his men with these words and did not allow them to rise against Saul. Saul left the cave and went on his way. **8.** David then got up, went out of the cave, and called, "My lord the king!" When Saul turned around, David bowed down to the ground. (Arose: stood up, bowed low: knelt down) **9.** David asked Saul, "Why do you listen to those who say, 'David is trying to harm you'?" **10.** "Today, you saw that the Lord gave you into my hands in the cave, and someone advised me to kill you. But I spared you, saying, 'I will not harm my lord, for he is the Lord's anointed.'" **11.** "Look, my father, see the corner of your robe in my hand! I cut off a piece, but did not kill you. Know that I have done no wrong or disobedience against you, yet you seek my life." (Evil: bad action, rebellion: disobedience, sinned: done wrong) **12.** "Let the Lord decide between us. Let Him punish me, but I won't harm you." (Avenge: punish) **13.** "As the saying goes, 'Wickedness comes from the wicked,' but I won't harm you." (Wickedness: evil) **14.** "Whom are you chasing, the king of Israel? A dead dog? A flea?" (Dead dog: worthless, flea: tiny insect) **15.** "Let the Lord be the judge and determine our case, and rescue me from your hand." (Deliver: rescue). **16.** After hearing David's words, Saul said, "Is that you, my son David?" And Saul wept aloud. **17.** He told David, "You are more righteous than I, for you have shown me kindness, while I have repaid you with harm." (Righteous: good) **18.** "Today you have shown kindness to me, for when the Lord gave me into your hands, you did not kill me." (Kindness: goodness) **19.** "If a man finds his enemy, will he let him go free? May the Lord reward you for what you have done for me today?" **20.** "Now I know for sure that you will be king, and the kingdom of Israel will be yours." (Kingdom: nation). **21.** "Please swear to me by the Lord that you will not destroy my descendants or my family name." (descendants: children). **22.** David swore to Saul, and Saul returned home, but David and his men went to the stronghold. (Stronghold: fortified place)

Chapter 25

1. When Samuel passed away, the Israelites gathered together to mourn his death and buried him in his hometown of Ramah. Afterward, David set out for the Wilderness of Paran. (Ramah: a town in Israel; Paran: a desert region in Israel) **2.** There was a wealthy man in Maon, whose business operations were in Carmel. He had 3,000 sheep and 1,000 goats and was shearing his sheep in Carmel. (Maon: a town in Israel; Carmel: a region in Israel) **3.** The man's name was Nabal, and his wife was Abigail. She was a woman of great wisdom and beauty, but Nabal was cruel and wicked in his actions. He was a descendant of Caleb. (Wisdom: discernment and prudence; Actions: deeds or conduct; Caleb: a figure from the Bible, known for his faithfulness) **4.** When David learned that Nabal was shearing his sheep in the wilderness, **5.** He sent ten of his young men to deliver a message to Nabal, saying, "Go to Carmel and greet Nabal in my name, **6.** And tell him, 'Peace be with you, peace be upon your household, and peace to all that you own!' (Wealth: abundance or property) **7.** I've heard that you are shearing your sheep. While your shepherds were with us, we did them no harm, and they didn't lose anything during their time with us in Carmel. **8.** Ask your servants, and they will confirm this. Please show kindness to my men, as we've come on a feast day. Whatever you can provide for us will be greatly appreciated, for we are your servants and your son David's men.'" **9.** When David's servants delivered the message, they waited for Nabal's reply. **10.** Nabal answered David's men, saying, "Who is David, and who the son of Jesse is? There are many slaves these days that break away from their masters. **11.** Should I take my food, my water, and my meat, which I've prepared for my shearers, and give them to strangers whom I don't know?" **12.** David's men turned and left, returning to David with this message. (Walked away: turned and departed) **13.** David then said to his men, "Let each of you put on his sword." So they did, and David also strapped on his sword. Around four hundred men went with David, while two hundred stayed behind to guard their supplies. (Put on his sword: prepare for battle) **14.** One of Nabal's servants informed Abigail, his wife, saying, "David sent messengers to greet our master, but he insulted them. (Insulted: offended or disrespected) **15.** The men treated us kindly; we weren't harmed, and we didn't miss anything as long as we were with them in the fields. **16.** They were like a wall of protection to us, both day and night, as we watched over the sheep. (Protection: safety or security) **17.** Now consider what you should do, because our master is an evil man, and no one can reason with him. (Think about: reflect on; Wicked man: morally corrupt) **18.** Abigail quickly gathered two hundred loaves of bread, two skins of wine, five prepared sheep, five measures of roasted grain, one hundred clusters of raisins, and two hundred cakes of figs, and loaded them onto donkeys. (Hurried: acted with urgency; Prepared: ready for use; Measure of grain: an amount of grain) **19.** She instructed her servants, "Go on ahead of me; I'll follow behind." But she didn't tell Nabal. **20.** As she rode her donkey and descended through the valley, she met David and his men, who were coming toward her. (Shelter: a place of refuge or protection) **21.** David had said, "I've guarded all that this man has in the wilderness, without any harm, yet he has returned evil for good. (Man: person; Harm: injury or loss) **22.** May God punish me severely if I leave even one man alive from Nabal's household by morning?" **23.** When Abigail saw David, she hurriedly dismounted from her donkey, fell at his feet, and bowed down to the ground. (Quickly: with speed; Get off: dismounted) **24.** She knelt before him and said, "Let the blame fall on me, my lord. Please let your servant speak and hear what I have to say. (Sin: wrongdoing or moral failure) **25.** Don't let my lord pay any attention to this worthless man, Nabal. His name means fool, and foolishness is his way. I didn't see the men you sent. (Think of: consider; Foolishness: lack of wisdom) **26.** As surely as the Lord lives and as you live, the Lord has prevented you from avenging yourself. Let your enemies be like Nabal. (Punishing: inflicting retribution) **27.** This gift I've brought to you, please give it to your men who follow you. (Gift: offering or present). **28.** Please forgive the wrong I've done, for the Lord will certainly establish an enduring house for you, as you fight the Lord's battles and live a life of integrity. (Wrongdoing: moral misdeed; Lasting: permanent or enduring). **29.** While others may try to harm you and take your life, the Lord will protect you. He will cast your enemies aside like stones from a sling. (Chase: pursue or hunt; Protection: safety or shielding) **30.** When the Lord has fulfilled all His promises to you and made you king over Israel, **31.** this will not be a regret or burden to you, for you will have shed no blood in vain, and you won't have taken vengeance yourself. When the Lord has dealt favorably with you, please remember me." (Sorrow: grief or sadness; Wrong: an immoral action) **32.** David replied, "Blessed be the Lord, who sent you to me today! **33.** Blessed is your advice, and blessed are you, for you've kept me from bloodshed and taking vengeance on my own. (Punishing: inflicting punishment) **34.** As sure as the Lord lives, if you had not hurried to meet me, not one man would have survived by morning." (Hurried: acted with urgency) **35.** David accepted the gifts she brought and said to her, "Go back to your house in peace. I have listened to you and respected your judgment." (Listened to: heeded or paid attention to) **36.** When Abigail returned to Nabal, he was hosting a feast in his house, as if it were a royal banquet. He was very drunk, so she didn't tell him anything until the next morning. (Happy: celebrating or in a good mood) **37.** The next morning, when the wine had worn off, Abigail told Nabal what had happened. His heart failed him, and he became as stiff as a stone. **38.** About ten days later, the Lord struck Nabal, and he died. **39.** When David heard that Nabal had died, he praised the Lord, saying, "Praise the Lord, who has avenged my shame by bringing justice upon Nabal. The Lord has kept me from doing evil." David then sent word to Abigail, asking her to become his wife. (Defended: protected; Shame: dishonor or humiliation; Asked: requested) **40.** When David's servants came to Abigail in Carmel, they said, "David has sent us to ask you to be his wife." (Carmel: a region in Israel) **41.** She bowed low to the ground and said, "I am your servant, ready to wash the feet of your lord's servants." **42.** She quickly mounted her donkey, accompanied by five of her maidservants, and followed David's messengers to become his wife. (Quickly: with speed) **43.** David also took Ahinoam from Jezreel as his wife, and both women became his wives. (Jezreel: a town in Israel) **44.** Meanwhile, Saul gave his daughter Michal to Palti, the son of Laish. (Michal: David's first wife; Laish: a man from Gallim, a town in Israel)

Chapter 26

1. Now the Ziphites came to Saul at Gibeah, saying, "Is David not hiding on Hachilah Hill, opposite Jeshimon?" (Gibeah: a town, Hachilah Hill: a mountain, Jeshimon: a desert place) **2.** Saul went down to the Wilderness of Ziph with 3,000 chosen men to find David. (Wilderness of Ziph: a desert area) **3.** Saul camped on Hachilah Hill, opposite Jeshimon, near the road, while David stayed in the wilderness and saw Saul was after him. **4.** David sent spies and learned Saul had indeed come. (Spies: secret watchers) **5.** David went to where Saul camped and saw Saul lying there with Abner, his army commander, surrounded by his men. (Abner: army leader) **6.** David asked Ahimelech the Hittite and Abishai, "Who will go with me to Saul's camp?" Abishai agreed. (Ahimelech: a Hittite, Abishai: son of Zeruiah, brother of Joab) **7.** They reached Saul's camp at night, where Saul lay sleeping with his spear by his head, surrounded by Abner and his men. (Spear: weapon) **8.** Abishai said, "God has given your enemy to you today. Let me strike him with the spear, and I won't need to do it twice." **9.** David replied, "Don't harm him; who can harm the Lord's anointed and be guiltless?" (Anointed: chosen one, Guiltless: not guilty) **10.** David added, "As the Lord lives, He will deal with him, or his time will come, or he will die in battle." **11.** "I won't harm the Lord's anointed, but take his spear and water jug, and let's go." (Water jug: container) **12.** David took the spear and jug, and they escaped. No one saw or woke because God caused them to fall into a deep sleep. **13.** David went to the other side, standing on a hill far off. **14.** He called out to Abner, "Don't you answer, Abner?" Abner replied, "Who are you calling to the king?" **15.** David said, "Aren't you a man? Why didn't you guard the king? Someone came to kill him." **16.** "You've done wrong. As the Lord lives, you deserve to die for not guarding your master. Look, the spear and jug are here." **17.** Saul recognized David's voice, saying, "Is that you, my son David?" David answered, "Yes, my lord, O king." **18.** David asked, "Why are you pursuing me? What have I done wrong?" **19.** "If the Lord stirred you against me, let Him accept my offering. But if men did this, may they be cursed, for they've driven me away from the Lord's inheritance." **20.** "Don't let my blood fall to the ground, for the king of Israel is chasing a flea, like hunting a partridge in the mountains." (Flea: small thing, Partridge: small bird) **21.** Saul said, "I have sinned. Return, my son David, I won't harm you anymore. I see now I've acted foolishly and made a great mistake." (Foolishly: silly, Err: made a mistake) **22.** David replied, "Here is the king's spear. Let someone come and take it. **23.** "May the Lord reward each man for his righteousness and faithfulness. He gave you into my hand today, but I didn't harm you." (Righteousness: good actions, Faithfulness: loyalty) **24.** "Just as your life was precious in my eyes, may my life be precious in the Lord's eyes, and may He deliver me from all trouble." **25.** Saul said, "Blessed are you, my son David. You will do great things and succeed." (Blessed: happy) So David went on his way, and Saul returned home.

Chapter 27

1. And David said to himself, "I will eventually be killed by Saul. There's nothing better than to quickly escape to the Philistines; Saul will stop searching for me in Israel. Then I'll be safe from him." (Philistines: people from a neighboring region) **2.** So David and his 600 men went to Achish, son of Maoch, king of Gath. (Achish: king of a Philistine city, Gath: a Philistine city, Maoch: a person's name) **3.** David lived with Achish in Gath, along with his men and their families, including his two wives, Ahinoam and Abigail, Nabal's widow. (Ahinoam: a woman from Jezreel, Abigail: from Carmel, Jezreel and Carmel: places in Israel) **4.** Saul learned that David had fled to Gath, so he no longer pursued him. **5.** David said to Achish, "If I have found favor with you, please give me a place in one of the towns in the countryside. Why should I live in your royal city?" (Countryside: rural areas) **6.** Achish gave him Ziklag that day, and it has belonged to the kings of Judah ever since. (Ziklag: a town, Judah: a kingdom of northern Israel) **7.** David stayed in Philistine territory for one year and four months. (Philistine: a neighboring region) **8.** David and his men raided the Geshurites, Girzites, and Amalekites, nations living from ancient times, from Shur to Egypt. (Shur: an Arabian desert region) **9.** When David attacked, he killed everyone and took their animals and goods, returning to Achish. **10.** Achish would ask, "Where did you raid today?" David would reply, "Against the southern areas of Judah, the Jerahmeelites, or the Kenites." (Judah: tribe of Israel, Jerahmeelites and Kenites: people groups) **11.** David killed everyone to prevent anyone from reporting his actions in Gath, saying, "So they won't tell on us." This was his constant behavior in Philistine territory. (Philistine: a neighboring region) **12.** Achish believed David, thinking, "He has made himself hated by his own people, so he will be my servant forever."

Chapter 28

1. Now, in those days, the Philistines gathered for battle against Israel. Achish said to David, "You know you and your men will fight with me." (Philistines: enemy people of Israel) 2. David replied, "You know what your servant can do." Achish answered, "I will make you my chief guard forever." (Servant: someone who serves another) 3. Samuel had died, and all Israel mourned and buried him in Ramah. Saul had expelled mediums and spiritists from the land. (Mediums: people who contact spirits) 4. The Philistines camped at Shunem, and Saul gathered Israel at Gilboa. (Shunem: place of the Philistine camp; Gilboa: mountain in Israel where Saul gathered his army) 5. When Saul saw the Philistine army, he was afraid, and his heart trembled. (Trembled: shook from fear) 6. Saul asked the Lord, but the Lord did not answer him through dreams, Urim, or prophets. (Urim: method of receiving answers from God) 7. Saul told his servants, "Find me a medium so I can ask her what to do." They replied, "There is one in En Dor." (En Dor: village with a medium) 8. Saul disguised himself, took two men, and went to the woman at night. He said, "Please conduct a seance and bring up the one I name." (Seance: ceremony to call spirits) 9. The woman said, "You know what Saul has done, how he banned mediums. Why put my life in danger?" (Banned: made illegal) 10. Saul swore by the Lord, "As the Lord lives, no harm will come to you." (Swore: promised strongly) 11. The woman asked, "Whom shall I bring up?" Saul answered, "Bring up Samuel." (Samuel: prophet, former leader of Israel) 12. When she saw Samuel, she cried out loudly, "Why have you deceived me? You are Saul!" (Deceived: tricked) 13. Saul said, "Don't be afraid. What did you see?" She replied, "I saw a spirit rising from the earth." (Spirit: ghost or soul of a dead person) 14. Saul asked, "What does he look like?" She answered, "An old man, covered in a cloak." Saul recognized it was Samuel, bowed to the ground. (Cloak: large piece of cloth worn over the body) 15. Samuel asked, "Why have you disturbed me?" Saul answered, "I am in deep distress. The Philistines are waging war, and God has abandoned me. I need your guidance." (Distress: trouble or worry) 16. Samuel replied, "Why ask me? The Lord has left you and is now your enemy." (Enemy: one who opposes you) 17. "The Lord has done as He said through me: He has torn the kingdom from you and given it to David." (Torn: taken away forcefully) 18. "Because you disobeyed the Lord and didn't punish Amalek, this is happening today." (Disobeyed: did not follow) 19. "The Lord will also give Israel to the Philistines. Tomorrow, you and your sons will be with me. Israel's army will fall to the Philistines." (Sons: male children) 20. Saul collapsed, terrified by Samuel's words. He had no strength, as he hadn't eaten all day or night. (Collapsed: fell down suddenly) 21. The woman saw Saul's distress and said, "I obeyed you and risked my life. Please, listen to me now." (Risked: put in danger) 22. "Let me give you some food to strengthen you for your journey." (Strengthen: give energy or power) 23. Saul refused, but his servants and the woman persuaded him. He got up and sat on the bed. (Persuaded: convinced) 24. The woman killed a fatted calf, made unleavened bread, and served it. (Fatted: fattened for eating) 25. They ate, then left that night. (Ate: consumed food

Chapter 29

1. Then the Philistines gathered all their armies at Aphek, and the Israelites camped by a spring in Jezreel. (Fountain: source of water, a valley in Israel) **2.** The Philistine lords reviewed their troops by hundreds and thousands, but David and his men were at the rear with Achish. (Philistine king: leader of the Philistines) **3.** The Philistine princes asked, "What are these Hebrews doing here?" Achish answered, "This is David, Saul's servant, who has been with me for years. I've found no fault in him." (Hebrews: Israelites, Saul's servant: David serving King Saul) **4.** The princes were angry and said, "Send him back to the place you assigned him, so he doesn't fight with us. What better way for him to gain favor with his master than by defeating us?" (Princes: leaders of the Philistines) **5.** "Is this not the David they sang about, saying, 'Saul has slain his thousands, and David his ten thousands'?" **6.** Achish called David and said, "As the Lord lives, you have been good to me, and I've found no fault in you since you came to me. But the lords do not approve." (Lord: God, lords: Philistine leaders) **7.** "So, return in peace, so you don't upset the Philistine lords." (lords: leaders of the Philistines) **8.** David replied, "What have I done? What have you found in me since I've been with you that would prevent me from fighting your enemies?" **9.** Achish answered, "I know you are like an angel to me, but the princes said, 'He cannot join us in battle.'" (Princes: leaders of the Philistines) **10.** "So, rise early with your men and leave as soon as it's light." **11.** David and his men rose early to leave for the Philistine land, while the Philistines went up to Jezreel. (a valley in Israel)

Chapter 30

1. Now it happened, when David and his men came to Ziklag on the third day, the Amalekites had attacked the South and Ziklag, burning it with fire, (Amalekites: a group of people; Ziklag: a city in Judah) **2.** and taking captive the women and all who were there, from small to great; they did not kill anyone, but carried them off. (captive: taken as prisoners) **3.** David and his men arrived to find the city burned and their wives, sons, and daughters taken captive. **4.** They wept loudly until they had no strength left. **5.** David's two wives, Ahinoam and Abigail, were among those taken. **6.** David was deeply distressed, as the people spoke of stoning him, but he strengthened himself in the Lord his God. (distressed: very upset; stoning: throwing stones to kill someone) **7.** David asked Abiathar the priest, "Bring me the ephod." (Abiathar: a priest; ephod: a special garment used for prayer) **8.** David inquired of the Lord, "Should I pursue this troop? Shall I overtake them?" The Lord answered, "Pursue, for you will surely overtake them and recover all." (inquired: asked; troop: group of soldiers) **9.** David and his 600 men reached the Brook Besor; some stayed behind. (Besor: a stream or small river) **10.** David and 400 men pursued; 200 stayed behind, too weary to cross. (weary: very tired) **11.** They found an Egyptian in the field, gave him bread and water, **12.** and offered him figs and raisins. After eating, his strength returned, as he hadn't eaten or drunk for three days. **13.** David asked, "Who are you, and where are you from?" He replied, "I'm an Egyptian, servant of an Amalekite; my master left me behind when I fell sick. **14.** We attacked the southern region of the Cherethites, Judah's territory, and burned Ziklag." (Cherethites: a people group; Judah: a region in Israel) **15.** David asked, "Can you lead me to this troop?" He replied, "Swear to me you won't kill me or hand me over to my master, and I'll lead you to them." **16.** He led David to where the Amalekites were spread out, eating, drinking, and celebrating their spoils. (Spoils: things taken from others) **17.** David attacked them from twilight until the next evening. Only 400 young men escaped on camels. (Twilight: the time between sunset and night) **18.** David recovered everything the Amalekites took, including his two wives. **19.** Nothing was missing, not even the smallest thing; David recovered it all. **20.** David took all the flocks and herds, calling it "David's spoil." (Flocks and herds: groups of sheep and cattle) **21.** David came to the 200 men who had stayed behind at the Brook Besor. They went out to meet him, and he greeted them. **22.** Some men from the group argued, "Since they didn't come with us, we won't share the spoil, except for their wives and children." **23.** But David said, "You won't do that with what the Lord has given us. He has protected us and delivered the enemy into our hands." **24.** "Everyone shares equally—those who fight and those who stay behind with the supplies." **25.** From that day on, it became a rule for Israel. **26.** When David returned to Ziklag, he sent some of the spoil to the elders of Judah, his friends, saying, "This is a gift from the enemies of the Lord." **27.** He sent it to those in Bethel, Ramoth, Jattir, (Bethel: a town in Israel; Ramoth: a place in the southern region of Israel; Jattir: a town in Judah) **28.** Aroer, Siphmoth, Eshtemoa, (Aroer: a city in southern Judah; Siphmoth: a place in Judah; Eshtemoa: a town in Judah) **29.** Rachal, the cities of the Jerahmeelites, the Kenites, (Rachal: a town; Jerahmeelites: a group of people; Kenites: a people group) **30.** Hormah, Chorashan, Athach, (Hormah: a town in Judah; Chorashan: a place in the southern region; Athach: a place in the region of Judah) **31.** Hebron, and all the places where David and his men had roamed. (Hebron: a city in Judah, where David was anointed as king)

Chapter 31
1. The Philistines battled Israel, causing the Israelites to flee, and many were killed on Mount Gilboa. (Mount Gilboa: a mountain in Israel) **2.** The Philistines pursued Saul and his sons, killing Jonathan, Abinadab, and Malchishua, Saul's sons. **3.** The fighting intensified around Saul, and the archers wounded him severely. (Archers: bowmen) **4.** Saul instructed his armorbearer, "Take your sword and kill me, so these uncircumcised men don't come and mistreat me." But the armorbearer was too afraid, so Saul took his own sword and fell on it. (Armorbearer: the one who carries his armor, Mistreat: abuse) **5.** When the armorbearer saw Saul was dead, he also fell on his sword and died. **6.** Thus, Saul, his three sons, his armorbearer, and all his men died that day. **7.** When the Israelites across the valley and the Jordan saw that their soldiers had fled and that Saul and his sons had died, they abandoned their cities, and the Philistines took over. (Valley: a low area between hills, Jordan: a river) **8.** The following day, the Philistines came to take the belongings from the dead and found Saul and his sons on Mount Gilboa. **9.** They severed his head, removed his armor, and sent word throughout the Philistine territories to announce it in their idol temples and to the people. (Idol: false god). **10.** They placed his armor in the temple of Ashtoreth and hung his body on the wall of Beth Shan. (Ashtoreth: a goddess of the Philistines, Beth Shan: a city in Israel, Hung: fastened) **11.** When the people of Jabesh Gilead heard what the Philistines had done to Saul, (Jabesh Gilead: a region in Israel) **12.** The courageous men traveled through the night, took Saul and his sons' bodies from the wall of Beth Shan, and brought them to Jabesh where they cremated them. (Courageous: brave, Cremated: burned) **13.** They buried their bones under a tamarisk tree in Jabesh and fasted for seven days. (Tamarisk tree: a type of tree, Fasted: refrained from eating)

10 – 2 Samuel
Chapter 1
1. After Saul's death, when David returned from defeating the Amalekites and stayed in Ziklag for two days (Amalekites: enemies of Israel; Ziklag: David's city). **2.** On the third day, a man came from Saul's camp, with torn clothes and earth on his head (signs of mourning and grief). He bowed to David. **3.** David asked, "Where are you from?" The man replied, "I escaped from Israel's camp." **4.** David inquired about the battle. The man said, "Israel fled, many died, including Saul and Jonathan" (Jonathan: Saul's son). **5.** David asked, "How do you know Saul and Jonathan are dead?" **6.** The man said, "On Mount Gilboa, I saw Saul leaning on his spear, with chariots and horsemen chasing him" (Gilboa: battlefield). **7.** Saul saw me, called me, and I answered, 'Here I am.' **8.** He asked, 'Who are you?' I replied, 'An Amalekite' (enemy group member). **9.** Saul told me, 'Kill me, for I am in anguish but still alive'" (anguish: severe pain). **10.** "So, I killed him, as he couldn't survive. I took his crown and bracelet and brought them to you" (crown and bracelet: royal insignia). **11.** David tore his clothes, and so did his men (tearing clothes: symbol of grief). **12.** They mourned, wept, and fasted for Saul, Jonathan, the Lord's people, and Israel's fallen (mourning: deep sorrow). **13.** David asked the man, "Who are you?" He replied, "An Amalekite foreigner's son" (foreigner: non-Israelite). **14.** David said, "Weren't you afraid to kill the Lord's anointed?" (anointed: chosen one). **15.** David ordered a young man, "Kill him." The Amalekite was struck dead. **16.** David declared, "Your blood is on your head. Your own words condemned you, saying you killed the Lord's anointed" (blood on your head: responsibility). **17.** David sang this lament for Saul and Jonathan (lament: mournful song). **18.** He commanded the teaching of "The Bow" to Judah, recorded in the Book of Jasher (The Bow: battle song; Book of Jasher: ancient text). **19.** "Israel's beauty lies slain on your heights. How the mighty have fallen!" (heights: high places). **20.** "Don't announce this in Gath or Askelon, lest their daughters rejoice" (Gath and Askelon: Philistine cities). **21.** "O Mount Gilboa, let no dew or rain fall on you, nor fields of offerings. Saul's shield lies disgraced, as though not anointed" (shield: warrior's defense). **22.** "Jonathan's bow never failed, and Saul's sword always succeeded" (bow and sword: weapons of war). **23.** "Saul and Jonathan, loved and delightful, united in life and death, swifter than eagles, stronger than lions" (eagles and lions: symbols of speed and strength). **24.** "Daughters of Israel, mourn for Saul, who adorned you with scarlet and gold" (scarlet: fine clothing). **25.** "How the mighty have fallen in battle! Jonathan, slain on your heights." **26.** "I grieve for you, Jonathan, my brother. Your love was more wonderful than a woman's love" (grieve: feel sorrow). **27.** "How the mighty have fallen, and the weapons of war perished!" (weapons of war: instruments of battle).

Chapter 2
1. After this, David asked the LORD, "Should I go to a city of Judah?" The LORD replied, "Go." David asked, "Which one?" The LORD said, "Hebron" (Hebron: Judah's city). **2.** David went with his two wives, Ahinoam of Jezreel and Abigail, the widow of Nabal of Carmel. **3.** David brought his men and their households, and they lived in Hebron's towns. **4.** The men of Judah anointed David king over Judah's house and told him that the men of Jabesh-gilead buried Saul (Jabesh-gilead: Saul's supporters). **5.** David sent messengers to Jabesh-gilead, saying, "May the LORD bless you for showing kindness by burying Saul." **6.** "May the LORD reward your kindness and truth, and I will also repay you." **7.** "Be strong and brave, for Saul is dead, and Judah's house has anointed me as king." **8.** Meanwhile, Abner, Saul's army commander, took Ish-bosheth, Saul's son, to Mahanaim (Mahanaim: eastern town). **9.** He made him king over Gilead, the Ashurites, Jezreel, Ephraim, Benjamin, and all Israel. **10.** Ish-bosheth was forty when he began his two-year reign over Israel, but Judah followed David. **11.** David ruled Judah in Hebron for seven years and six months. **12.** Abner and Ish-bosheth's men went to Gibeon (Gibeon: battle location). **13.** Joab, David's commander, and his men met them by the pool of Gibeon. They sat on opposite sides. **14.** Abner said, "Let the young men fight before us." Joab agreed. **15.** Twelve men from Benjamin for Ish-bosheth and twelve of David's servants fought. **16.** Each man seized his opponent and killed him, so the place was called Helkath-hazzurim in Gibeon (Helkath-hazzurim: "Field of Swords"). **17.** A fierce battle occurred, and David's men defeated Abner and Israel. **18.** Joab's brothers, Abishai and Asahel, were there. Asahel was swift like a wild deer. **19.** Asahel pursued Abner, not turning aside. **20.** Abner looked back and asked, "Are you Asahel?" He replied, "Yes." **21.** Abner said, "Turn aside and take another's armor." Asahel refused. **22.** Abner warned, "Stop pursuing me, or I will kill you and face Joab with shame." **23.** Asahel refused, so Abner struck him with the back of his spear under the fifth rib, killing him. All who passed by stood still where Asahel died. **24.** Joab and Abishai pursued Abner until sunset, reaching the hill of Ammah near Giah (Ammah: battlefield hill). **25.** The Benjamites gathered

around Abner on a hill. **26.** Abner called to Joab, "Shall the sword devour forever? Call off your men!" **27.** Joab replied, "If you hadn't spoken, the men would have stopped by morning." **28.** Joab blew a trumpet, stopping the battle. **29.** Abner and his men marched through the plain, crossed the Jordan, and reached Mahanaim. **30.** Joab gathered his men; they had lost 19 men and Asahel. **31.** David's men killed 360 of Abner's men, mostly Benjamites. **32.** They buried Asahel in his father's tomb in Bethlehem. Joab and his men marched all night, arriving in Hebron at dawn.

Chapter 3

1. The war between Saul's house and David's house was long, but David grew stronger while Saul's house weakened (conflict). **2.** Sons were born to David in Hebron: Amnon by Ahinoam the Jezreelitess (Hebron: city of Judah). **3.** Chileab by Abigail (Nabal's widow); Absalom by Maacah, daughter of Talmai, king of Geshur (Geshur: Aramean kingdom). **4.** Adonijah by Haggith; Shephatiah by Abital (Abital: David's wife). **5.** Ithream by Eglah. All these sons were born in Hebron (city of Judah). **6.** During the war, Abner became powerful in Saul's house (Abner: Saul's army commander). **7.** Saul's son, Ish-bosheth, accused Abner of taking Saul's concubine Rizpah (concubine: secondary wife). **8.** Abner was furious, defending his loyalty to Saul's house and accusing Ish-bosheth of ingratitude (ingratitude: lack of thanks). **9.** Abner swore to help David fulfill the LORD's promise of kingship (kingship: royal authority). **10.** He vowed to establish David as king over Israel and Judah, from Dan to Beer-sheba (Dan: northern city, Beer-sheba: southern city). **11.** Ish-bosheth couldn't oppose Abner due to fear (fear: dread). **12.** Abner sent messengers to David offering to unite Israel under his rule (unite: bring together). **13.** David agreed but demanded the return of his wife Michal before meeting Abner (Michal: Saul's daughter). **14.** David reminded Ish-bosheth that he had earned Michal with Philistine foreskins (Philistines: enemies of Israel). **15.** Ish-bosheth took Michal from her husband, Phaltiel (Phaltiel: Michal's second husband). **16.** Phaltiel followed, weeping, until Abner ordered him to return (weeping: crying). **17.** Abner persuaded Israel's elders to make David king, as the LORD promised (elders: community leaders). **18.** He reminded them of God's promise to save Israel through David (save: deliver). **19.** Abner spoke to the Benjamites and then to David in Hebron, gaining their agreement (Benjamites: Saul's tribe). **20.** Abner, with 20 men, met David, who hosted them (hosted: entertained). **21.** Abner pledged to unite Israel under David, and David sent him away in peace (peace: goodwill). **22.** Joab, returning from a raid, learned of Abner's visit (raid: military attack). **23.** Joab accused David of trusting Abner, who he claimed was spying (spying: gathering secrets). **24.** Joab secretly summoned Abner back without David's knowledge (secretly: without notice). **25.** Joab met Abner at the gate and killed him to avenge Asahel, his brother (avenge: seek revenge). **26.** David declared himself guiltless of Abner's blood, cursing Joab's family with suffering (cursing: calling harm). **27.** Joab and Abishai killed Abner for Asahel's death (Abishai: Joab's brother). **28.** David ordered public mourning for Abner, showing his sorrow (mourning: grief). **29.** He lamented Abner's death as unjust and caused by wicked men (lamented: mourned). **30.** David fasted, pleasing the people who saw his actions as sincere (fasted: refrained from eating). **31.** The people realized David was innocent of Abner's death (innocent: blameless). **32.** David declared Abner a great man who fell to evil (evil: wrongdoing). **33.** He admitted his own weakness despite being king and entrusted judgment to the LORD (weakness: lack of strength).

Chapter 4

1. When Saul's son heard of Abner's death in Hebron, he became weak (feeble: lacking strength), and Israel was troubled (Hebron: city of Judah). **2.** Saul's son had two captains, Baanah and Rechab, sons of Rimmon the Beerothite from Benjamin (Beeroth: city in Benjamin). **3.** The Beerothites had fled to Gittaim and lived there as strangers (sojourners: temporary residents). **4.** Jonathan, Saul's son, had a lame son named Mephibosheth. At five years old, when news of Saul and Jonathan's death at Jezreel came, his nurse dropped him while fleeing, making him lame (Jezreel: battlefield). **5.** Rechab and Baanah entered Ish-bosheth's house at noon as he rested (Ish-bosheth: Saul's son). **6.** Pretending to fetch wheat, they struck Ish-bosheth under the fifth rib and escaped (struck: attacked). **7.** They killed him in his bedroom, beheaded him, and carried his head through the night across the plain (plain: flat land). **8.** They brought the head to David in Hebron, claiming the LORD had avenged David of Saul and his descendants (avenged: sought justice). **9.** David responded, affirming the LORD as his deliverer from adversity (adversity: hardship). **10.** He recounted how he executed the man who brought news of Saul's death, expecting a reward (Ziklag: city of Judah). **11.** David condemned them for killing a righteous man in his house, declaring their guilt (righteous: innocent). **12.** David ordered their execution, cutting off their hands and feet, and hanging them by the pool in Hebron. Ish-bosheth's head was buried in Abner's tomb in Hebron (pool: water source).

Chapter 5

1. All the tribes of Israel came to David at Hebron, saying, "We are your bone and flesh" (Hebron: city of Judah). **2.** They reminded David that even when Saul was king, he led Israel, and the LORD said, "You shall shepherd my people and be their ruler" (shepherd: guide). **3.** The elders of Israel made a covenant with David at Hebron before the LORD, anointing him king over Israel. **4.** David was thirty years old when he began to reign, and he ruled for forty years. **5.** In Hebron, he reigned over Judah for seven years and six months, and in Jerusalem, he reigned over Israel and Judah for thirty-three years. **6.** David and his men went to Jerusalem, where the Jebusites (inhabitants) said, "You cannot enter here unless you remove the blind and the lame." **7.** Yet David captured the stronghold of Zion, now called the City of David (Zion: stronghold in Jerusalem). **8.** David declared, "Whoever climbs the water shaft and strikes the Jebusites, the blind and lame despised by my soul, will be chief and captain" (water shaft: underground channel). **9.** David lived in the stronghold, named it the City of David, and built it from Millo inward (Millo: fortification). **10.** David became increasingly great because the LORD God of hosts was with him. **11.** Hiram, king of Tyre, sent cedar, carpenters, and masons to build David a house (Tyre: coastal city). **12.** David realized the LORD had established him as king for Israel's sake, exalting the kingdom. **13.** After moving from Hebron to Jerusalem, David took more concubines and wives, and more sons and daughters were born. **14.** His children in Jerusalem were Shammua, Shobab, Nathan, Solomon, **15.** Ibhar, Elishua, Nepheg, Japhia, **16.** Elishama, Eliada, and Eliphalet. **17.** When the Philistines learned David was anointed king over Israel, they sought him, so David retreated to a stronghold (Philistines: enemies of Israel). **18.** The Philistines spread out in the valley of Rephaim (Rephaim: valley near Jerusalem). **19.** David asked the LORD if he should attack the Philistines, and the LORD assured him of victory. **20.** At Baal-perazim, David defeated them, saying, "The LORD has broken through my enemies like water breaks through," naming the place Baal-perazim (Baal-perazim: place of breakthrough). **21.** The Philistines abandoned their idols, which David and his men burned (idols: false gods). **22.** The Philistines regrouped in the valley of Rephaim. **23.** David sought the LORD again, who told him to circle behind them and attack near the mulberry trees. **24.** The LORD instructed David to act when he heard the sound of marching in the tops of the trees, signifying the LORD's advance. **25.** David obeyed and defeated the Philistines from Geba to Gazer (Geba and Gazer: cities in Israel).

Chapter 6

1. Again, David gathered all the chosen men of Israel, thirty thousand. (chosen men: selected leaders) **2.** David went with all the people from Baale of Judah to bring up the ark of God, whose name is called by the LORD of hosts who dwells between the cherubims. (Baale of Judah: city in Judah, cherubims: angelic beings) **3.** They set the ark on a new cart and brought it from the house of Abinadab in Gibeah; Uzzah and Ahio, Abinadab's sons, drove the cart. (cart: vehicle) **4.** They brought it from the house of Abinadab in Gibeah, and Ahio went before the ark. **5.** David and all Israel played before the LORD on various instruments, such as harps, psalteries, timbrels, cornets, and cymbals. (Instruments: musical tools) **6.** When they came to Nachon's threshing floor, Uzzah reached out and touched the ark because the oxen stumbled. (threshing floor: area for separating grain) **7.** The LORD's anger was kindled against Uzzah, and He struck him down for his mistake; Uzzah died by the ark. (Anger: wrath, mistake: error) **8.** David was upset because the LORD had punished Uzzah, so he named the place Perez-uzzah. (Upset: displeased) **9.** David was afraid of the LORD that day and asked, "How can the ark come to me?" (Afraid: fearful) **10.** David did not move the ark to the city of David but placed it in the house of Obed-edom the Gittite. (Gittites: man from Gath) **11.** The ark stayed in Obed-edom's house for three months, and the LORD blessed Obed-edom and his household. (Blessed: favored) **12.** David heard that the LORD had blessed Obed-edom's house, so he went to bring the ark back to the city of David with joy. **13.** When they carried the ark, they stopped every six steps to offer sacrifices. (Sacrifices: animal offerings) **14.** David danced before the LORD with all his strength, wearing a linen ephod. (Danced: leaped, ephod: priestly garment) **15.** David and all Israel brought the ark with shouting and trumpet sounds. (Shouting: rejoicing, trumpet: musical instrument) **16.** As the ark entered the city of David, Michal, Saul's daughter, saw David dancing and despised him in her heart. (Despised: hated) **17.** They set the ark in its place within the tabernacle David had made for it; he offered burnt and peace offerings. (Burnt offerings: sacrifices, peace offerings: thanksgiving) **18.** After the offerings, David blessed the people in the name of the LORD of hosts. (Blessed: prayed for) **19.** David gave everyone in Israel a cake of bread, a piece of meat, and wine before they went home. (Cake: bread, meat: food) **20.** David returned to bless his household, but Michal came out and criticized him for his actions. (Criticized: scolded) **21.** David replied it was before the LORD who chose him over her father to be ruler over Israel, so he would dance before the LORD. (Ruler: leader) **22.** David said he would humble himself even more and be honored by the maidservants, as she spoke of them. (Humble: lower oneself, maidservants: female servants) **23.** Michal had no children until the day of her death. (No children: barren)

Chapter 7
1. When the king sat in his house and the LORD had given him peace from all his enemies. (Peace: rest) **2.** The king said to Nathan the prophet, "I live in a house of cedar, but the ark of God is in a tent." (cedar: wood) **3.** Nathan said to the king, "Do what is in your heart, for the LORD is with you." **4.** That night, the word of the LORD came to Nathan, saying, **5.** "Go and tell my servant David, 'Are you the one to build me a house to dwell in?'" **6.** "I have not dwelt in a house since bringing Israel out of Egypt; I have lived in a tent and tabernacle." (Tabernacle: tent structure) **7.** "In all the places I have walked with Israel, I never asked any tribe to build me a house of cedar." (tribe: family group) **8.** "Say to David, 'I took you from following the sheep to be ruler over Israel.'" (sheep: flock) **9.** "I was with you wherever you went, defeated your enemies, and made your name great, like the greatest men on earth." **10.** "I will appoint a place for my people Israel, plant them so they can dwell safely, and not be afflicted anymore." (appointed: chosen, afflicted: harmed) **11.** "Since I gave Israel judges, I've given you rest from your enemies. The LORD will make you a house." **12.** "When your days are over and you rest with your ancestors, I will raise up your descendant to establish his kingdom." **13.** "He will build a house for my name, and I will establish his throne forever." **14.** "I will be his father, and he will be my son. If he sins, I will correct him, but my mercy will not depart from him as it did with Saul." (correct: punish) **15.** "My mercy will remain with him, unlike with Saul whom I removed." **16.** "Your house and kingdom will endure forever; your throne will be established forever." **17.** Nathan told David all these words and visions. (visions: divine revelations) **18.** David went in, sat before the LORD, and said, "Who am I, O Lord God, and what is my family that you have brought me this far?" (family: house) **19.** "This is a small thing to you, O Lord God; but you've also spoken of my family for the future. Is this the way of men, O Lord God?" (small thing: insignificant) **20.** "What can I say to you? You, Lord God, know your servant." **21.** "For your word's sake, and according to your heart, you've done all these great things to make your servant understand them." **22.** "You are great, O Lord God, for there is none like you, nor any God besides you, according to what we've heard." **23.** "What nation is like your people Israel, whom God redeemed to make a name for himself, doing great and terrible things for them in the land?" (terrible: awesome) **24.** "You have confirmed Israel as your people forever, and you, LORD, have become their God." **25.** "Now, O Lord God, fulfill the promise you made to your servant and his house forever." **26.** "Let your name be praised forever, saying, 'The LORD of hosts is the God of Israel,' and let David's house be established before you." **27.** "You, O LORD of hosts, God of Israel, have revealed to your servant that you will build him a house, so I've prayed this prayer." **28.** "Now, O Lord God, you are God, your words are true, and you've promised this good thing to your servant." **29.** "Please bless the house of your servant, that it may continue forever before you, for you, O Lord God, have spoken it. Bless the house of your servant forever." (good thing: blessing)

Chapter 8
1. After this, David defeated the Philistines and subdued them, taking Metheg-ammah from them. (subdued: brought under control) **2.** He smote Moab, measuring them to determine who would die and who would live, making them his servants who brought gifts. **3.** David also defeated Hadadezer, king of Zobah, as he tried to recover his border at the Euphrates River. (Euphrates: river in the Middle East) **4.** David took a thousand chariots, seven hundred horsemen, and twenty thousand foot soldiers, and he crippled all the chariot horses, except for enough to keep a hundred chariots. (crippled: hamstrung) **5.** When the Syrians of Damascus came to help Hadadezer, David killed twenty-two thousand Syrians. **6.** David placed garrisons in Damascus, and the Syrians became his servants, bringing gifts. The LORD kept David safe wherever he went. **7.** David took the gold shields from Hadadezer's servants and brought them to Jerusalem. **8.** From Betah and Berothai, cities of Hadadezer, David took much bronze. (bronze: a type of metal) **9.** When Toi, king of Hamath, heard that David had defeated Hadadezer's army, **10.** Toi sent his son Joram to bless David for defeating Hadadezer, who had fought with Toi. Joram brought silver, gold, and bronze vessels. (bless: honor) **11.** David dedicated these to the LORD, along with the silver and gold from the nations he had defeated. **12.** This included Syria, Moab, Ammon, the Philistines, Amalek, and the spoil from Hadadezer. (spoil: plundered goods) **13.** David gained a great reputation after defeating the Syrians in the Valley of Salt, killing eighteen thousand men. **14.** David set up garrisons in Edom, and all the people of Edom became his servants. The LORD kept David safe wherever he went. **15.** David reigned over all Israel, ensuring justice and fairness for his people. **16.** Joab, son of Zeruiah, was the commander of the army, and Jehoshaphat, son of Ahilud, was the recorder. (recorder: official historian) **17.** Zadok, son of Ahitub, and Ahimelech, son of Abiathar, were the priests, and Seraiah was the scribe. **18.** Benaiah, son of Jehoiada, led the Cherethites and Pelethites, and David's sons were chief rulers. (Cherethites: an elite group, Pelethites: another elite group)

Chapter 9
1. David inquired, "Is there anyone still alive from Saul's family to whom I can show kindness for Jonathan's sake?" **2.** A servant from Saul's household named Ziba was summoned. The king asked him, "Are you Ziba?" He answered, "Yes, I am your servant." **3.** The king then asked, "Is there anyone remaining from Saul's family to whom

I can show God's kindness?" Ziba replied, "Jonathan has a son who is crippled (unable to walk) in both feet." **4.** The king asked, "Where is he?" Ziba said, "He is staying in the house of Machir, son of Ammiel, in Lo-debar." (Lo-debar: a town in Gilead) **5.** David sent for him and brought him from the house of Machir, son of Ammiel, in Lo-debar. **6.** When Mephibosheth, Jonathan's son and Saul's grandson, appeared before David, he bowed low in respect. David said, "Mephibosheth." He responded, "I am your servant." **7.** David assured him, "Do not be afraid. For your father Jonathan's sake, I will show you kindness, return (restore) all the land that belonged to Saul, and you will always eat at my table." **8.** Mephibosheth bowed again and said, "What is your servant that you would regard a person as insignificant as a dead dog like me?" (dead dog: someone unworthy) **9.** The king summoned Ziba and declared, "I have given your master's grandson all that belonged to Saul and his family." **10.** He instructed Ziba, "You, your sons, and your servants will farm the land and harvest it for Mephibosheth, so he has food. But Mephibosheth himself will always dine at my table." Ziba had fifteen sons and twenty servants. **11.** Ziba said, "I will carry out everything my lord the king commands." From that time, Mephibosheth dined at David's table like one of the king's own sons. **12.** Mephibosheth had a young son named Micha, and everyone in Ziba's household became servants to Mephibosheth. **13.** Mephibosheth lived in Jerusalem and ate continually at the king's table, even though he was disabled (lame) in both feet. (Jerusalem: the capital of Israel)

Chapter 10
1. After this, the king of the Ammonites died, and his son Hanun became king in his place. (Ammonites: descendants of Ammon) **2.** David said, "I will show kindness to Hanun, son of Nahash, just as his father showed kindness to me." So David sent his servants to console him concerning his father. When David's servants entered the land of the Ammonites, (console: comfort) **3.** the Ammonite leaders said to Hanun, "Do you think David is honoring your father by sending comforters? Hasn't he sent them to spy out the city and overthrow it?" (spy out: secretly examine) **4.** So Hanun seized David's servants, shaved off half their beards, cut their garments at the hips, and sent them away humiliated. (humiliated: deeply shamed) **5.** When David was informed, he sent messengers to meet them because they were greatly ashamed. The king said, "Stay in Jericho until your beards grow back, then return." (Jericho: city near Jordan) **6.** When the Ammonites realized they had angered David, they hired 20,000 Syrian footmen from Beth-rehob and Zoba, 1,000 men from King Maacah, and 12,000 from Ish-tob. **7.** On hearing this, David sent Joab and his entire army of warriors. (Joab: David's general) **8.** The Ammonites formed their battle lines at the city gate while the Syrians of Zoba, Rehob, and others assembled in the field. **9.** When Joab saw the enemy positioned in front and behind, he selected Israel's best troops to face the Syrians. **10.** He placed the rest of the forces under his brother Abishai to confront the Ammonites. **11.** Joab said, "If the Syrians overpower me, you must help; if the Ammonites overpower you, I will help you." (overpower: defeat) **12.** "Be courageous! Let's fight bravely for our people and the cities of our God. May the LORD do what seems good to Him." **13.** Joab and his troops advanced against the Syrians, who fled before them. **14.** When the Ammonites saw the Syrians retreat, they also fled from Abishai into their city. Joab then returned to Jerusalem. **15.** After being defeated, the Syrians regrouped. **16.** Hadarezer brought additional Syrian forces from beyond the river, led by Shobach, his army commander, who assembled them at Helam. (Hadarezer: a Syrian king; Helam: battle site) **17.** When David heard, he gathered all Israel, crossed the Jordan, and confronted the Syrians at Helam. **18.** The Syrians fled, and David killed 700 chariot soldiers, 40,000 horsemen, and struck down Shobach, their commander, who died there. **19.** Seeing their defeat, the kings allied with Hadarezer made peace with Israel and became their servants. From then on, the Syrians feared aiding the Ammonites.

Chapter 11
1. At the start of spring, when kings go to battle, David sent Joab, his servants, and all Israel to destroy the Ammonites and besiege Rabbah. But David stayed in Jerusalem. (besiege: surround; Rabbah: Ammonite city) **2.** One evening, David rose from his bed and walked on the palace roof. From there, he saw a very beautiful woman bathing. **3.** David inquired about her, and someone said, "She is Bathsheba, daughter of Eliam and wife of Uriah the Hittite." (Hittite: an ancient group) **4.** David sent for her, and after she came, he lay with her. She then returned home. (lay: had relations) **5.** The woman conceived and informed David, saying, "I am pregnant." (conceived: became pregnant) **6.** David sent word to Joab, asking for Uriah the Hittite, who then came to David. **7.** David asked about Joab, the people, and the war's progress. **8.** He told Uriah, "Go home and wash your feet." Uriah left, and David sent food to his house. (wash your feet: rest) **9.** But Uriah slept at the palace door with the servants and did not go to his house. **10.** When David heard, he asked Uriah, "Why didn't you go home after your journey?" **11.** Uriah replied, "The ark, Israel, Judah, Joab, and the soldiers are in tents. Should I go home to eat, drink, and lie with my wife? I will not do this." (ark: sacred chest) **12.** David told Uriah to stay another day, and he remained in Jerusalem. **13.** David invited Uriah to eat and drink, making him drunk. But Uriah still slept with the servants and did not go home. **14.** In the morning, David wrote a letter to Joab and sent it with Uriah. **15.** The letter instructed Joab to place Uriah in the fiercest battle and then retreat, leaving him to die. (retreat: withdraw) **16.** Joab placed Uriah where the strongest enemy soldiers were. **17.** The city's men fought Joab's forces, killing some of David's servants, including Uriah. **18.** Joab sent a full report of the battle to David. **19.** He told the messenger, "If the king gets angry about our proximity to the city walls, **20.** remind him of Abimelech's death by a millstone in Thebez. Then tell him, 'Uriah the Hittite is dead too.'" (Thebez: a city; millstone: heavy grinding stone) **21.** The messenger delivered Joab's report to David. **22.** He said, "The men came out against us; we pushed them back to the gate. **23.** But archers shot from the walls, killing some of the king's servants, including Uriah." (archers: bowmen) **24.** David told the messenger, "Tell Joab not to be upset. The sword kills randomly. Strengthen your attack and overthrow the city. Encourage him." (overthrow: capture) **25.** When Uriah's wife heard of his death, she mourned for him. **26.** After her mourning, David brought her to his house. She became his wife and bore him a son, but David's actions displeased the LORD. (mourned: grieved)

Chapter 12
1. The LORD sent Nathan to David, saying, "There were two men in one city, one rich and one poor." (city: town) **2.** The rich man had many flocks and herds. (flocks: sheep; herds: livestock) **3.** The poor man had only one ewe lamb, which he nourished as a daughter. (ewe: female sheep; nourished: cared for) **4.** A traveler came to the rich man, who took the poor man's lamb to prepare it for his guest. (traveler: visitor; prepare: cook) **5.** David, angry, said, "As the LORD lives, the man who did this deserves to die!" (deserves: is worthy of) **6.** He must restore the lamb fourfold, for having no pity. (restore: repay; fourfold: four times) **7.** Nathan said, "You are the man! The LORD says: I made you king over Israel and saved you from Saul. (Saul: former king) **8.** I gave you your master's house, wives, and all Israel and Judah. I would have given even more. (Judah: southern kingdom) **9.** Why did you despise the LORD's word by killing Uriah and taking his wife? (despise: disregard; Uriah: Hittite soldier) **10.** The sword will never leave your house because you took Uriah's wife. (sword: violence) **11.** The LORD declares: I will raise trouble from your own family, and others will take your wives publicly. **12.** What you did in secret, I will expose before all Israel and under the sun. (expose: make known) **13.** David admitted, "I have sinned against the LORD." Nathan replied, "The LORD forgives your sin, but consequences remain." (forgives: pardons) **14.** The child born to you will die because you gave the LORD's enemies a reason to mock Him.

(mock: disrespect) **15.** Nathan left, and the LORD struck the child born to Uriah's wife, making him very sick. (struck: afflicted) **16.** David prayed, fasted, and lay on the ground all night for the child. (fasted: refrained from eating) **17.** The elders of his household tried to help him rise and eat, but he refused. (elders: household leaders) **18.** On the seventh day, the child died. The servants feared telling David, thinking he would grieve excessively. (grieve: mourn deeply) **19.** David noticed their whispers and asked, "Is the child dead?" They replied, "Yes, he is dead." **20.** David rose, washed, anointed himself, changed clothes, worshiped the LORD, and then ate. (anointed: applied oil; worshiped: honored God) **21.** The servants asked, "Why fast when the child lived, but eat now after his death?" **22.** David explained, "I fasted, hoping the LORD might show mercy and spare the child. (mercy: compassion; spare: save) **23.** But now he is dead. I cannot bring him back. I will go to him, but he will not return to me." **24.** David comforted Bathsheba, and she bore Solomon, whom the LORD loved. (Solomon: future king of Israel) **25.** Nathan named him Jedidiah because of the LORD's love. (Jedidiah: "Beloved of the LORD") **26.** Meanwhile, Joab fought against Rabbah, the royal city of the Ammonites. (Rabbah: Ammonite capital) **27.** Joab sent word to David: "I have taken the city's water supply. (water supply: vital part) **28.** Gather the people and capture the city, or it will be named after me." **29.** David gathered the army, captured Rabbah, and defeated the Ammonites. (Ammonites: neighboring enemies) **30.** He took the king's crown, weighing a talent of gold with jewels, and wore it. He brought back abundant spoils. (talent: heavy gold unit; spoils: treasures) **31.** He put the people under labor with saws, iron tools, and brickkilns. Thus, he treated all Ammonite cities. David returned to Jerusalem. (brickkilns: brick ovens; Jerusalem: Israel's capital)

Chapter 13
1. After this, Absalom, David's son, had a beautiful sister named Tamar, and Amnon, another of David's sons, loved her. (beautiful: attractive) **2.** Amnon was so distressed that he became sick because of Tamar, who was a virgin. He thought it would be hard to do anything to her. (distressed: upset; virgin: unmarried woman) **3.** Amnon had a crafty friend named Jonadab, the son of Shimeah, David's brother. (crafty: deceitful) **4.** Jonadab asked, "Why are you, the king's son, so lean every day? Tell me." Amnon replied, "I love Tamar, my brother Absalom's sister." (lean: thin) **5.** Jonadab suggested, "Pretend to be sick, and when your father comes to visit, ask him to send Tamar to make food for you." **6.** Amnon followed Jonadab's advice, and when the king came to visit, Amnon requested, "Please let Tamar make some cakes for me." **7.** David sent Tamar to Amnon to prepare food for him. **8.** Tamar went to Amnon's house, found him lying down, and made cakes in his sight. **9.** She poured them out before him, but Amnon refused to eat and ordered everyone to leave. **10.** Amnon then told Tamar, "Bring the food to my chamber so I can eat from your hand." **11.** As she brought the food, Amnon grabbed her and said, "Come, lie with me, my sister." **12.** Tamar pleaded, "Do not force me, for this should not happen in Israel. Do not commit this shameful act." (shameful: disgraceful) **13.** "Where would I go with my disgrace? And you would be seen as a fool in Israel. Ask the king, and he will not keep me from you." (disgrace: dishonor; fool: foolish person) **14.** But Amnon refused to listen, overpowering her, and raped her. **15.** Afterward, Amnon hated her with a greater hatred than he had loved her. He told her to leave. **16.** Tamar protested, "Sending me away is worse than what you just did," but Amnon would not listen. **17.** Amnon then called his servant and told him to throw her out and lock the door behind her. **18.** Tamar wore a multicolored robe, the usual attire for king's daughters who were virgins. The servant locked her out. (multicolored robe: special garment) **19.** Tamar put ashes on her head, tore her multicolored robe, and cried aloud. **20.** Absalom asked, "Has Amnon harmed you? Be silent, for he is your brother. Do not take it to heart." Tamar remained desolate in Absalom's house. (desolate: in sorrow) **21.** When King David heard of it, he was very angry. **22.** Absalom said nothing to Amnon, for he hated him because he had raped his sister. **23.** Two years later, Absalom held a sheep-shearing feast at Baal-hazor near Ephraim and invited all the king's sons. (Baal-hazor: a place; Ephraim: a region) **24.** Absalom asked the king to come, but David refused, saying it would be too much trouble. **25.** Absalom persisted, and David blessed him, though he did not go. **26.** Then Absalom asked for Amnon to come, and David hesitated but agreed. **27.** Absalom insisted, and David let Amnon and all the king's sons go with him. **28.** Absalom told his servants, "When Amnon is drunk, I will tell you to kill him. Do not be afraid; I have commanded you to do this. Be brave." **29.** The servants followed Absalom's orders and killed Amnon. The king's sons fled on mules. (mules: animals) **30.** News reached David that all his sons were dead, and he mourned deeply. **31.** The king tore his clothes and lay on the ground, and his servants stood by, also mourning. **32.** Jonadab, David's brother's son, explained, "Do not think all the king's sons are dead—only Amnon is dead, as Absalom planned because of what Amnon did to Tamar." **33.** He reassured the king, saying only Amnon was dead. **34.** Absalom fled. A lookout saw many people coming from the hillside. **35.** Jonadab said, "The king's sons are returning, just as I said." **36.** As soon as Jonadab finished speaking, the king's sons arrived, crying loudly. David and his servants wept with them. **37.** Absalom fled to Talmai, the king of Geshur, and David mourned for his son every day. (Talmai: king of Geshur) **38.** Absalom stayed in Geshur for three years. **39.** King David longed to go to Absalom, for he had been comforted over Amnon's death.

Chapter 14
1. Joab, son of Zeruiah, realized that King David's heart was set on Absalom. (set: focused) **2.** Joab sent for a wise woman from Tekoah and asked her to pretend to be a mourner. She should wear mourning clothes and not use oil, acting like a woman who had mourned for a long time. (mourning: grieving) **3.** Joab gave her the words to say to the king. **4.** The woman of Tekoah came to the king, bowed down, and asked for help. **5.** The king asked her, "What is troubling you?" She replied, "I am a widow, and my husband is dead." **6.** "I had two sons, and they fought in the field. No one was there to stop them, and one killed the other." **7.** "Now my family demands that the one who killed his brother be killed, and they want to destroy my remaining son, leaving no heir to my husband's name." (heir: successor) **8.** The king told her, "Go home, and I will take care of this matter." **9.** The woman replied, "My lord, the guilt is mine and my family's, but let the king and his throne be innocent." **10.** The king said, "Anyone who speaks against you, bring them to me, and they will not harm you." **11.** The woman said, "Please, remember the LORD your God, and do not let the avengers of blood kill my son. As the LORD lives, not a hair of your son will fall to the ground." (avengers of blood: relatives who seek vengeance) **12.** She asked the king to hear one more word. He replied, "Speak." **13.** She said, "Why do you, the king, treat the people of God this way? You speak as if you are guilty, because you have not brought back your banished son, Absalom." **14.** "We all must die, like water spilled on the ground, which cannot be gathered. Yet God provides a way for the banished not to remain separated from him." **15.** "I came to speak to the king because the people made me afraid. I hope the king will grant my request." **16.** "The king will listen and save me and my son from those who would destroy us and our inheritance." **17.** She said, "Your words are comforting. You, like an angel of God, can distinguish good from evil, and the LORD will be with you." **18.** The king asked, "Do not hide from me what I am about to ask. Is Joab behind this?" **19.** She replied, "As the king lives, nothing can turn you away from what you have spoken. Joab instructed me and gave me all these words to say." **20.** "Joab planned this, and you, my lord, are as wise as an angel of God in knowing everything." **21.** The king told Joab, "I have done this. Go, bring Absalom back to Jerusalem." **22.** Joab bowed down, thanked the king, and said, "Today I know I have found favor in your sight, for you have granted my request." **23.** Joab

went to Geshur and brought Absalom to Jerusalem. **24.** The king said, "Let him return to his house and not see my face." So Absalom went to his own house and did not see the king. **25.** There was no one in all Israel more admired for his beauty than Absalom; he had no blemish from head to toe. **26.** Once a year, Absalom cut his hair, which was heavy. He weighed it at 200 shekels (about 5 pounds). **27.** Absalom had three sons and a daughter named Tamar, who was very beautiful. **28.** Absalom lived in Jerusalem for two years without seeing the king. **29.** Absalom sent for Joab to ask him to speak to the king, but Joab refused to come. When Absalom sent again, Joab still would not come. **30.** So Absalom told his servants, "Joab's field is near mine, and he has barley there. Go set it on fire." They set the field on fire. **31.** Joab came to Absalom's house and asked, "Why have your servants burned my field?" **32.** Absalom replied, "I asked you to come, so I could send you to the king. Why did I leave Geshur? It would have been better for me to stay there. Let me now see the king's face; if I have done wrong, let him kill me." **33.** Joab went to the king, told him, and brought Absalom to him. When Absalom came, he bowed before the king, and the king kissed him.

Chapter 15
1. And after this, Absalom got chariots, horses, and fifty men to run before him. (chariots: horse-drawn vehicles) **2.** Absalom rose early and stood by the gate, and when anyone came to the king for judgment, he asked, "What city are you from?" The man replied, "I'm from one of Israel's tribes." **3.** Absalom told him, "Your case is good, but there's no one appointed by the king to hear you." (appointed: chosen) **4.** Absalom added, "I wish I were made judge, so everyone with a case could come to me, and I would give them justice." **5.** Whenever someone came to him, Absalom reached out, took their hand, and kissed them. (obeisance: act of respect) **6.** Absalom did this to all the people who came to the king, stealing the hearts of Israel. (stealing: winning) **7.** After forty years, Absalom asked the king to allow him to go to Hebron to fulfill a vow he made to God. (vow: promise) **8.** He explained, "I vowed to God while I was in Geshur, saying, 'If God brings me back to Jerusalem, I will serve Him.'" **9.** The king said, "Go in peace," so Absalom went to Hebron. (Hebron: city) **10.** But Absalom sent spies throughout Israel, instructing them to announce, "Absalom is king in Hebron!" when they heard the trumpet. (spies: secret agents) **11.** Two hundred men from Jerusalem went with him, unaware of the conspiracy. (conspiracy: secret plan) **12.** Absalom also called for Ahithophel, David's counselor, who joined him, and the conspiracy grew stronger as more people joined Absalom. (counselor: advisor) **13.** A messenger came to David, saying, "The hearts of Israel are with Absalom." **14.** David told his servants, "We must flee; Absalom will attack us and destroy the city with the sword." **15.** The king's servants replied, "We are ready to do whatever you command." **16.** David and his household left, leaving ten concubines to keep the house. (concubines: secondary wives) **17.** The king and all his people went on, stopping in a distant place. **18.** The king's servants passed with him, along with the Cherethites, Pelethites, and 600 Gittites from Gath. (Gath: Philistine city) **19.** David asked Ittai the Gittite, "Why are you coming with us? Return to your place, as you're a foreigner and exile." **20.** "You came only yesterday; should I make you travel with us today? Go back, and may God be with you." **21.** Ittai answered, "As God lives, and as you live, wherever you go, whether in life or death, I will be with you." **22.** David said, "Go ahead and cross over." Ittai and his men, with their children, passed on. **23.** The people cried out loudly as they crossed over, and the king went across the Kidron brook, heading toward the wilderness. (Kidron: brook near Jerusalem) **24.** Zadok and the Levites brought the Ark of the Covenant of God, but David told them to take it back to Jerusalem. **25.** The king said, "If God is pleased with me, He will bring me back and allow me to see the Ark again." **26.** "But if God does not want me, let Him do as He wills." **27.** David told Zadok, "You're a seer, so return to the city with your two sons, Ahimaaz and Jonathan. (seer: prophet) **28.** "I'll wait here until you send word to update me." **29.** Zadok and Abiathar took the Ark back to Jerusalem and stayed there. (Abiathar: priest) **30.** David went up Mount Olivet, weeping, with his head covered and barefoot. All the people with him did the same. (Mount Olivet: hill near Jerusalem) **31.** Someone informed David, "Ahithophel is with Absalom." David prayed, "Lord, turn Ahithophel's counsel into foolishness." **32.** As David reached the top of the mount where he worshiped God, Hushai the Archite met him, with his coat torn and dust on his head. (Hushai: David's friend) **33.** David said, "If you come with me, you'll be a burden." **34.** "But if you return to the city and say to Absalom, 'I will serve you as I served your father,' you can help me by defeating Ahithophel's advice." **35.** "You have Zadok and Abiathar there; tell them whatever you hear in the king's house." **36.** "Their sons, Ahimaaz and Jonathan, will carry the messages for me." **37.** So Hushai went to the city, and Absalom entered Jerusalem.

Chapter 16
1. As David passed the hill's top, Ziba, Mephibosheth's servant, met him with donkeys, 200 loaves of bread, 100 bunches of raisins, 100 summer fruits, and wine. (Mephibosheth: son of Saul) **2.** The king asked, "What is this for?" Ziba replied, "The donkeys are for the king's household, the bread and fruit for the young men, and the wine for the faint in the wilderness." (faint: weak) **3.** The king asked, "Where is your master's son?" Ziba answered, "He is staying in Jerusalem, thinking the people will restore his father's kingdom to him." **4.** David said, "Everything that belonged to Mephibosheth is now yours." Ziba humbly requested favor from the king. **5.** When David reached Bahurim, a man from Saul's family, named Shimei, cursed him. (Bahurim: town near Jerusalem) **6.** Shimei threw stones at David and his servants, with David's mighty men on both sides. **7.** Shimei cursed, "Get out, bloody man! You took Saul's place; now God has given the kingdom to Absalom!" **8.** "God is punishing you for the blood of Saul's family; Absalom will be king now." **9.** Abishai, son of Zeruiah, said, "Why should this man curse my king? Let me kill him." **10.** David replied, "Why do you interfere? Let him curse, for God has told him to. Who can stop him?" **11.** David said to Abishai and his servants, "My son is seeking my life; how much more should this Benjamite curse me? Let him be." **12.** "Maybe God will see my suffering and repay me with good for this cursing." **13.** As David and his men continued, Shimei cursed, threw stones, and threw dust. **14.** The king and his people were weary but rested there. **15.** Absalom and the men of Israel entered Jerusalem, with Ahithophel. (Ahithophel: David's counselor) **16.** When Hushai, David's friend, met Absalom, he said, "Long live the king!" **17.** Absalom asked, "Is this how you repay your friend? Why didn't you go with him?" **18.** Hushai replied, "No, I will serve the one God and Israel choose, and I will stay with him." **19.** "Should I serve Absalom? As I served your father, I will now serve you." **20.** Absalom asked Ahithophel for advice on what to do next. **21.** Ahithophel advised, "Sleep with your father's concubines in public, and all Israel will know you've broken with him. This will strengthen your position." (concubines: secondary wives) **22.** So a tent was set up on the roof, and Absalom slept with his father's concubines in full view of Israel. (roof: top of the house) **23.** Ahithophel's advice was highly respected, as if it were from God's oracle, both with David and Absalom.

Chapter 17
1. Ahithophel advised Absalom, "Let me choose 12,000 men and pursue David tonight." (pursue: chase) **2.** "I will surprise him when he's tired and afraid, and all his people will flee; then I will kill only the king." **3.** "I will bring all the people back to you, and those you seek will be as if they all returned, and there will be peace." **4.** Absalom and the elders of Israel approved the plan. **5.** Then Absalom said, "Call Hushai the Archite to hear his opinion." **6.** When Hushai arrived, Absalom asked, "Ahithophel's advice—should we follow it? If not, what do you suggest?" **7.** Hushai replied, "Ahithophel's advice is not good this time." **8.** "You know your father and his men; they are fierce and like a bear robbed of her cubs. Your father is a warrior

and won't stay with the people." (fierce: angry) **9.** "He's hiding now, and if any are defeated, it will look like a slaughter of those who follow you." **10.** "Even the bravest men will panic because everyone knows your father is strong and his men are warriors." **11.** "I suggest gathering all Israel from Dan to Beer-sheba, as many as the sand by the sea, and that you lead them yourself." **12.** "We will surprise him wherever he is, and not one of his men will survive." **13.** "If he hides in a city, we will pull it down with ropes and throw it into the river until not even a stone is left." (pull down: destroy) **14.** Absalom and the Israelites agreed, saying, "Hushai's advice is better than Ahithophel's," for God had decided to defeat Ahithophel's good advice to bring disaster to Absalom. **15.** Hushai then told Zadok and Abiathar, the priests, "This is what Ahithophel advised and what I suggested." **16.** "Send word to David to not spend the night in the wilderness but to cross over quickly, or the king and his people will be caught." **17.** Jonathan and Ahimaaz hid near En-rogel, and a servant girl informed them, and they told David. (En-rogel: place near Jerusalem) **18.** A boy saw them and informed Absalom. They quickly escaped and hid in a man's house in Bahurim, where there was a well. **19.** The woman covered the well's mouth with a cloth and spread grain on top, hiding them. **20.** When Absalom's men asked the woman about Jonathan and Ahimaaz, she said they had crossed the water. When they could not find them, they returned to Jerusalem. **21.** After they left, Jonathan and Ahimaaz emerged, went to David, and warned him to cross the water quickly, as Ahithophel had advised against him. **22.** David and his men immediately crossed the Jordan River, and by morning, all had crossed safely. (Jordan: river) **23.** When Ahithophel saw his advice was not followed, he returned home, set his affairs in order, and hanged himself. **24.** David reached Mahanaim, and Absalom crossed the Jordan with all his people. (Mahanaim: place near Jordan) **25.** Absalom made Amasa, the son of Ithra, his army commander instead of Joab. **26.** They camped in Gilead. **27.** When David arrived at Mahanaim, Shobi, Machir, and Barzillai brought supplies for him and his people. (Mahanaim: place near Jordan) **28.** They provided beds, food, and drink, including wheat, barley, beans, lentils, and honey, saying, "The people are hungry, tired, and thirsty in the wilderness."

Chapter 18

1. And David counted the people with him, and set commanders over thousands and hundreds. (counted : numbered) **2.** He divided the army into three parts: one under Joab, one under Abishai, and one under Ittai the Gittite. David said, "I will go with you." (divided : sent forth) **3.** But the people said, "You should stay behind. If we flee, they won't care about us. You are more valuable than ten thousand of us. It's better if you stay and help us from the city." **4.** David agreed and stood by the gate as the people went out in groups of hundreds and thousands. (gate : entrance) **5.** David commanded Joab, Abishai, and Ittai, "Be gentle with Absalom for my sake." The people heard this command. **6.** The army fought in the forest of Ephraim. (forest : wood) **7.** The Israelites were defeated by David's men, and 20,000 were killed that day. **8.** The battle spread out across the land, and more were killed by the forest than by the sword. (spread out : scattered) **9.** Absalom met David's men, riding a mule. His head got caught in an oak tree, and he was left hanging as the mule ran away. **10.** A man saw this and reported it to Joab, saying, "I saw Absalom hanging in an oak." **11.** Joab asked, "Why didn't you kill him right there? I would have given you ten shekels of silver and a belt." (belt : girdle) **12.** The man replied, "Even if you gave me a thousand shekels, I wouldn't touch the king's son. We heard the king command you, Abishai, and Ittai not to harm Absalom." **13.** "If I had killed him, I would be betraying my own life, for the king would know, and you would turn against me." **14.** Joab said, "I can't wait here with you." He took three javelins and thrust them through Absalom's heart while he was still alive in the tree. **15.** Ten young men who carried Joab's armor surrounded Absalom and struck him dead. **16.** Joab blew the trumpet, and the soldiers stopped chasing the Israelites. Joab had called them back. **17.** They threw Absalom into a pit in the forest and covered him with a large pile of stones. Then the Israelites scattered, each to their home. **18.** Absalom had built a monument for himself in the king's valley because he had no son to carry on his name. It is still called "Absalom's Place." (king's valley : Absalom's place) **19.** Ahimaaz, son of Zadok, wanted to run and tell the king the news, that God had avenged him on his enemies. **20.** Joab said, "You won't carry the news today. You will another time, but not today, because the king's son is dead." **21.** Joab told Cushi to go and report to the king. Cushi bowed and ran. **22.** Ahimaaz begged Joab to let him run too. Joab said, "Why run if you don't have any news?" **23.** Ahimaaz insisted, so Joab said, "Run." Ahimaaz outran Cushi. **24.** David was sitting between the gates, and the watchman went up to the roof and saw a man running alone. **25.** The watchman told the king, who said, "If he's alone, he has news." The man ran closer. **26.** Then the watchman saw another man running alone and told the king. The king said, "He also brings news." **27.** The watchman said, "The first man looks like Ahimaaz." The king replied, "He is a good man and brings good news." **28.** Ahimaaz called to the king, "All is well," and fell on his face before the king, saying, "Praise God who has delivered your enemies into your hand." **29.** The king asked, "Is Absalom safe?" Ahimaaz replied, "I saw a great commotion, but I don't know what happened." **30.** The king said, "Step aside and stand there." Ahimaaz stepped aside. **31.** Then Cushi came and said, "My lord, the king, God has avenged you today over those who rose up against you." **32.** The king asked, "Is Absalom safe?" Cushi replied, "May your enemies be like him." **33.** The king was deeply moved and went to the chamber over the gate, crying, "O my son Absalom! My son, my son Absalom! I wish I had died instead of you!"

Chapter 19

1. Joab received word that the king was weeping and mourning for Absalom. (mourning: showing sorrow) **2.** The victory of the day turned into mourning for the people because they heard how the king was grieving for his son. (grieving: deeply saddened) **3.** The people quietly entered the city, ashamed, as if they were fleeing a lost battle. (ashamed: embarrassed) **4.** The king covered his face and cried out loudly, "O Absalom, my son, my son!" (covered: hid, cried: shouted) **5.** Joab went to the king's house and rebuked him, saying, "You have shamed your servants today, the very ones who saved your life, as well as the lives of your family and your concubines." (shamed: humiliated, concubines: secondary wives) **6.** "You love your enemies but hate your friends. You have shown that you care more for Absalom than for us, and it seems that if Absalom were alive and we were all dead, you would have been pleased." (care: show concern) **7.** "So rise up, speak kindly to your servants, or none of us will stay with you tonight, and that will be worse than all the hardships you have faced from your youth." (kindly: gently) **8.** The king stood up and sat at the gate, and the people heard that the king was at the gate, so they came to him. All the people of Israel had gone home. (gate: a public place) **9.** The people of Israel argued among themselves, saying, "The king saved us from our enemies and the Philistines, but now he fled for Absalom." (argued: disputed, fled: ran) **10.** "Absalom, whom we made king over us, is dead in battle. Why then do we not bring back the king?" (made: appointed) **11.** David sent word to the priests Zadok and Abiathar, saying, "Tell the elders of Judah, 'Why are you the last to bring the king back to his house when all of Israel has already done so?'" (priests: religious leaders) **12.** "You are my relatives, my own flesh and blood. Why are you the last to bring back the king?" (relatives: family) **13.** "And tell Amasa, 'Are you not of my flesh and blood? May God do so to me and more, if you are not made the commander of my army instead of Joab.'" (commander: leader, army: military) **14.** The words of the king softened the hearts of the men of Judah, and they sent word to David, saying, "Return, and bring back all your servants." (softened: calmed) **15.** So the king returned and crossed the Jordan River. Judah went to Gilgal to meet him and lead him across. (Jordan: river, Gilgal:

meeting place) **16.** Shimei, son of Gera from Benjamin, hurried with his 1,000 men to meet the king. (Benjamin: tribe of Israel, hurried: rushed) **17.** Ziba, the servant of Saul's house, came with his 15 sons and 20 servants, and they crossed the Jordan before the king. (Ziba: servant, Saul: former king) **18.** A ferry was used to carry the king's household across, and Shimei fell before the king as he crossed the river. (ferry: small boat) **19.** Shimei said to the king, "Please don't hold my wrongs against me, and don't remember the evil I did when you left Jerusalem. Please don't take it to heart." (wrong: sin, evil: misdeed) **20.** "I know I've sinned, and I'm here today first from all the tribe of Joseph to meet the king." (sinned: wronged) **21.** But Abishai, son of Zeruiah, said, "Should Shimei not die for cursing the Lord's anointed king?" (anointed: chosen) **22.** David replied, "What do I have to do with you, sons of Zeruiah? Should anyone be put to death today in Israel? I am king over Israel today!" (Zeruiah: David's sister) **23.** The king told Shimei, "You will not die." And he swore an oath to him. (oath: promise) **24.** Mephibosheth, son of Saul, came to meet the king, looking unkempt and dirty since the day David fled. (Mephibosheth: son of Saul) **25.** When Mephibosheth met the king, David asked, "Why didn't you come with me, Mephibosheth?" (come: follow) **26.** Mephibosheth answered, "My servant deceived me. He said, 'I'll saddle a donkey for you so you can ride to the king,' but I am lame." (deceived: tricked, lame: unable to walk) **27.** "He has lied about me, but you, my king, are like an angel of God. Do what seems best to you." (lied: misrepresented, angel: messenger) **28.** "When my family was doomed, you invited me to eat at your table. What reason do I have to cry to the king?" (doomed: destined for death) **29.** The king said, "Why talk more about this? I've decided you and Ziba will share the land." (share: divide) **30.** Mephibosheth said, "Let him take it all, since my lord the king has returned in peace." (peace: safely) **31.** Barzillai, the Gileadite, came from Rogelim to cross the Jordan with the king. (Barzillai: wealthy supporter, Rogelim: place) **32.** Barzillai was 80 years old and had cared for the king during his time at Mahanaim. (80: old, cared: provided) **33.** The king invited Barzillai to come with him to Jerusalem and promised to provide for him. (invited: asked, provide: supply) **34.** Barzillai replied, "I am too old to enjoy such a journey. I can no longer tell the difference between good and bad, nor enjoy food or drink. Why should I be a burden to the king?" (burden: trouble) **35.** "I'll go a little way with you, but I don't deserve such a reward." (reward: repayment) **36.** "Let me return to my city to die and be buried by my parents. But let Chimham, my servant, go with you instead, and do for him as you wish." (return: go back) **37.** The king agreed, saying, "Chimham will go with me, and I'll do whatever you ask for him." (agree: consent) **38.** The people crossed the Jordan, and when the king was safely across, he kissed Barzillai and blessed him before Barzillai returned to his own home. (kissed: greeted, blessed: thanked) **39.** The king continued to Gilgal, with Chimham accompanying him. Judah led the king, along with half the people of Israel. (Gilgal: meeting place, Judah: tribe) **40.** The people of Israel confronted the king, saying, "Why did the men of Judah take the king and his household across the Jordan?" (confronted: challenged) **41.** The men of Judah answered, "The king is our relative, why should you be angry? We haven't taken anything from the king." (relative: family member) **42.** The men of Israel responded, "We have ten parts in the king and more right to David than you. Why then have you despised us?" (despised: ignored) **43.** The men of Judah spoke even more harshly than the men of Israel. (harshly: angrily)

Chapter 20
1. A man named Sheba, son of Bichri, a Benjamite, appeared and blew a trumpet, saying, "We have no part in David nor in Jesse's son. Every man to his tents, O Israel!" (Benjamite: tribe of Israel, tents: homes) **2.** So, all the men of Israel followed Sheba, but the men of Judah stayed loyal to their king, from Jordan to Jerusalem. (loyal: faithful) **3.** When David arrived at Jerusalem, he took his ten concubines, whom he left to take care of his house, and placed them under guard. He provided for them but did not sleep with them, so they lived as widows. (concubines: secondary wives, widows: without a husband) **4.** David told Amasa, "Gather the men of Judah in three days and be here." (gather: assemble) **5.** Amasa went to gather the men of Judah, but he delayed beyond the time David set. (delayed: took longer) **6.** David said to Abishai, "Sheba will do more harm than Absalom. Take the king's servants and chase him, or he may escape to a fortified city." (harm: damage, fortified: protected) **7.** Joab's men, along with the Cherethites, Pelethites, and mighty men, left Jerusalem to pursue Sheba. (Cherethites: warriors, Pelethites: mercenaries) **8.** When they reached the large stone at Gibeon, Amasa met them. Joab was dressed for battle, and his sword fell out as he moved. (Gibeon: place) **9.** Joab asked Amasa, "Are you well, my brother?" He grabbed Amasa's beard with his right hand to kiss him. (well: healthy, brother: relative) **10.** But Amasa didn't notice the sword in Joab's hand. Joab struck him in the side, killing him, and they continued after Sheba. (struck: hit) **11.** One of Joab's men shouted, "Who is for Joab and David? Follow Joab!" (follow: go after) **12.** Amasa lay in a pool of blood on the road, and when people stopped to look, the man moved him off the path and covered him with a cloth. (covered: hid) **13.** After Amasa was moved, the people continued following Joab to pursue Sheba. (continued: moved forward) **14.** Joab went through all the tribes of Israel to Abel and Beth-maachah, and the Berites joined him. (Abel: city, Beth-maachah: place) **15.** They besieged Sheba in Abel of Beth-maachah, building a siege ramp against the city's wall. (besieged: surrounded) **16.** A wise woman from the city called out, "Listen to me! Speak to Joab and come near so I can talk to him." (wise: intelligent) **17.** Joab approached, and the woman said, "Are you Joab?" He replied, "Yes." Then she said, "Listen to your servant." (servant: woman) **18.** She said, "In the old days, people would ask counsel at Abel, and matters were settled there." (counsel: advice) **19.** "I am one of the peaceful and loyal ones in Israel. Why are you trying to destroy a city that belongs to God?" (loyal: faithful) **20.** Joab answered, "I don't want to destroy the city. It's Sheba the son of Bichri who rebelled against David." (rebelled: went against) **21.** "Hand him over, and I will leave the city." The woman said, "We will throw his head over the wall to you." (hand: give) **22.** The woman went to the people, and they cut off Sheba's head and threw it to Joab. He blew a trumpet, and they returned to their tents. Joab went back to Jerusalem to the king. (cut off: removed, tents: homes) **23.** Joab was over all Israel's army, and Benaiah, son of Jehoiada, led the Cherethites and Pelethites. (army: soldiers) **24.** Adoram was in charge of taxes, and Jehoshaphat, son of Ahilud, was recorder. (taxes: tribute, recorder: official) **25.** Sheva was scribe, and Zadok and Abiathar were priests. (scribe: secretary) **26.** Ira the Jairite was a chief ruler over David. (ruler: leader)

Chapter 21
1. There was a famine for three years in David's time. David prayed to the LORD, and the LORD said it was because of Saul and his bloody house, who killed the Gibeonites. (famine: lack of food, bloody: violent) **2.** David called the Gibeonites and asked them, for they were not Israelites but the remnant of the Amorites. Israel had promised not to harm them, but Saul had tried to kill them. (remnant: survivors) **3.** David asked the Gibeonites what he could do to atone (make up) for Saul's actions so they could bless Israel. (atonement: forgiveness) **4.** The Gibeonites said they didn't want silver, gold, or anyone killed from Israel, but they wanted something else. (silver: money, atonement: compensation) **5.** They replied, "The man who destroyed us and planned our annihilation in Israel's land, **6.** let seven of his sons be handed over to us to be hanged before the LORD in Gibeah, Saul's chosen city." David agreed. (annihilation: destruction) **7.** But David spared Mephibosheth, Saul's grandson, because of the oath between David and Jonathan. (Oath: promise) **8.** David took the two sons of Rizpah, Saul's concubine, Armoni and Mephibosheth, and the five sons of Michal, Saul's daughter, who had been raised by Adriel. (concubine: secondary wife, raised: cared for)

9. He gave them to the Gibeonites, who hanged them on the hill before the LORD. They died during the beginning of the barley harvest. (barley: crop) **10.** Rizpah, the daughter of Aiah, spread sackcloth on a rock and stayed there from the start of harvest until rain fell, preventing birds and animals from disturbing the bodies. (sackcloth: rough cloth, rain: water) **11.** David was told what Rizpah did for her sons. (sons: children) **12.** David took Saul and Jonathan's bones from Jabesh-gilead, where the Philistines had hung them, after they killed Saul at Gilboa. (Jabesh-gilead: town, Gilboa: mountain) **13.** David brought the bones to Zelah in Benjamin and buried them in Kish's tomb, fulfilling the king's command. Afterward, God ended the famine. (Zelah: place, Kish: father) **14.** The Philistines fought Israel again, and David and his men went to battle. David grew weak. (battle: fight, weak: tired) **15.** Ishbi-benob, a giant, tried to kill David with his heavy spear, but Abishai, David's nephew, saved him and killed the Philistine. (giant: large man, spear: weapon) **16.** The men of David swore not to let David fight again to protect Israel's light. (Light: strength) **17.** There was another battle at Gob, where Sibbechai killed Saph, another giant's son. (Gob: place) **18.** In a battle at Gob, Elhanan, from Bethlehem, killed Goliath's brother, whose spear was huge. (Bethlehem: place) **19.** Another battle in Gath saw a giant with six fingers on each hand and six toes on each foot, born of giants. (Gath: city, giant: large man) **20.** This giant challenged Israel, but Jonathan, David's nephew, killed him. (Nephew: son of brother) **21.** These four giants, born in Gath, were slain by David and his men. (slain: killed) **22.** These four were born to the giant in Gath and fell by the hand of David and his servants. (giant: large man)

Chapter 22

1. And David spoke this song to the LORD the day the LORD delivered him from all his enemies and Saul's hand. (Delivered: saved) **2.** He said, "The LORD is my rock, fortress, and deliverer; (rock: strong support) (fortress: safe place) **3.** The God of my rock, in Him I trust; He is my shield, the horn of my salvation, my high tower, refuge, and savior; You save me from violence. (Shield: protector) (Horn: strength) (High tower: strong place) (Refuge: safe place) **4.** I will call on the LORD, who is worthy to be praised; I will be saved from my enemies. (Call: pray) **5.** When death's waves surrounded me, and wicked men made me afraid. (Waves: troubles) **6.** The sorrows of hell surrounded me; the snares of death trapped me. (Sorrows: deep troubles) (Snares: traps) **7.** In my distress I called to the LORD; He heard me from His temple, and my cry reached His ears. (Distress: trouble) **8.** Then the earth shook, and the heavens moved because He was angry. (Earth: ground) **9.** Smoke came from His nostrils, and fire from His mouth, burning coals. (Nostrils: nose) **10.** He bent the heavens and came down, with darkness beneath His feet. (bent: curved) **11.** He rode on a cherub and flew; He was seen on the wings of the wind. (cherub: angel) **12.** He made darkness His covering, with dark waters and thick clouds. (covering: protection) **13.** Before Him, fire blazed. (Blazed: burned brightly) **14.** The LORD thundered from heaven, and the Most High spoke. (Thundered: made loud noise) **15.** He sent arrows and scattered them; lightning struck and confused them. (arrows : weapons) (scattered: spread out) **16.** The sea's channels appeared, and the world's foundations were seen when the LORD rebuked and the blast of His breath came. (channels : pathways) (rebuked : scolded) **17.** He reached down from above and took me out of many waters. (took : saved) **18.** He delivered me from my strong enemy and those who hated me, for they were too strong for me. (delivered : saved) **19.** They attacked me in my calamity, but the LORD was my support. (calamity : disaster) (support : help) **20.** He brought me into a large place and saved me because He delighted in me. (large place : safe area) **21.** The LORD rewarded me for my righteousness and the purity of my hands. (rewarded : gave) (righteousness : right living) **22.** I have followed the LORD's ways and have not departed from Him. (departed : turned away) **23.** All His judgments were before me; I did not depart from His statutes. (statutes : rules) **24.** I was upright before Him and kept myself from sin. (upright : honest) (sin : wrong) **25.** Therefore, the LORD rewarded me for my righteousness and the purity of my actions. (rewarded : gave) **26.** With the merciful, You show mercy; with the upright, You show Yourself upright. (merciful : kind) (upright : righteous) **27.** With the pure, You show Yourself pure; but with the crooked, You show Yourself hostile. (crooked : dishonest) (hostile : unfriendly) **28.** You save the humble but bring down the proud. (humble : lowly) (proud : haughty) **29.** You are my lamp, O LORD; the LORD will light my darkness. (lamp : guide) **30.** By You, I can run through a troop, and by my God, I can leap over a wall. (troop : army) **31.** As for God, His way is perfect; the word of the LORD is tested; He is a shield for all who trust in Him. (tested : proven) (shield : protector) **32.** For who is God besides the LORD? Who is a rock except our God? (rock : strong support) **33.** God is my strength and power; He makes my way perfect. (strength : power) **34.** He makes my feet like the feet of a deer and sets me on high places. (deer : fast runner) (high places : strong ground) **35.** He teaches my hands to fight so that my arms can bend a bow of bronze. (Teaches: trains) (Bronze: strong metal) **36.** You have given me the shield of Your salvation, and Your gentleness has made me great. (Gentleness: kindness) **37.** You have enlarged my steps under me so that my feet did not slip. (Enlarged: made wider) **38.** I pursued my enemies and destroyed them, and did not stop until they were consumed. (pursued : chased) **39.** I wounded them, and they could not rise; they fell under my feet. (wounded : hurt) **40.** For You have girded me with strength for battle; You have subdued those who rose against me. (girded : equipped) (subdued : defeated) **41.** You gave me the necks of my enemies to destroy those who hate me. (necks : vulnerability) **42.** They looked, but there was no one to save them, even to the LORD, but He didn't answer. (save : rescue) **43.** I crushed them as fine dust, as the mire of the street, and scattered them. (crushed : beat down) (mire : mud) **44.** You delivered me from the struggles of my people and made me head of the nations; a people I did not know will serve me. (struggles: fights) (head : leader) **45.** Foreigners will submit to me; as soon as they hear, they will obey me. (foreigners : strangers) (submit : obey) **46.** Foreigners will fade away, and they will be afraid in their strongholds. (fade : disappear) (strongholds : secure places) **47.** The LORD lives; blessed be my rock; exalted be the God of my salvation. (exalted : lifted up) **48.** It is God who avenges me and brings down the nations under me, (avenges : punishes) **49.** Who brings me out from my enemies; You lift me up above those who rise against me and deliver me from the violent man. (delivers : saves) (violent : harsh) **50.** Therefore, I will praise You, O LORD, among the nations, and sing praises to Your name. (praise : thank) (sing : worship) **51.** He is the tower of salvation for His king and shows mercy to His anointed, to David and his descendants forever. (tower : strong place) (anointed : chosen) (descendants : children)

Chapter 23

1. These are the last words of David. David, son of Jesse, the man raised on high, the anointed of the God of Jacob, and the sweet psalmist of Israel, said, (psalmist : singer) **2.** The Spirit of the LORD spoke through me, and His word was on my tongue. (spoke : said) **3.** The God of Israel said, the Rock of Israel spoke to me: He who rules over men must be just, ruling in the fear of God. (Rock : strong support) (just : fair) **4.** He shall be as the morning light when the sun rises, a morning without clouds, like fresh grass growing after rain. (fresh : new) **5.** Though my house is not so with God, yet He has made with me an everlasting covenant, ordered in all things and sure; this is my salvation and desire, even if He doesn't cause it to grow. (everlasting : lasting forever) (covenant : agreement) **6.** But the sons of Belial will be like thorns, thrown away, and cannot be taken with hands. (sons of Belial : wicked people) (thorns : dangerous plants) **7.** The man who touches them must be armed with iron and a spear; they will be burned with fire in the same place. (armed : protected) **8.** These are the names of David's mighty men: The Tachmonite who sat in the seat, chief among the captains, Adino the Eznite, who killed eight hundred with his spear at one time. (captains : leaders) **9.** After him was Eleazar, son of Dodo, the Ahohite, one of the three mighty men with David when they defied the Philistines, and the men of Israel fled. (defied : challenged) **10.** He rose and struck the Philistines until his hand grew tired, and his hand stuck to the sword. The LORD gave a great victory that day, and the people only returned to take the spoil. (struck : hit) (spoil : goods) **11.** After him was Shammah, son of Agee the Hararite. The Philistines gathered into a troop in a field full of lentils, and the people fled. (lentils : type of plant) **12.** But he stood and defended the field, striking the Philistines, and the LORD gave a great victory. (defended : protected) **13.** Three of the thirty chief went down to David during harvest time to the cave of Adullam, and the Philistines camped in the valley of Rephaim. (Adullam : cave) (Rephaim : valley) **14.** David was in a stronghold, and the Philistine garrison was in Bethlehem. (stronghold : safe place) **15.** David longed and said, "Oh, that someone would give me water from the well of Bethlehem by the gate!" (longed : desired) **16.** The three mighty men broke through the Philistine camp, drew water from the well of Bethlehem by the gate, and brought it to David. But he wouldn't drink it, and poured it out to the LORD. (broke through : fought through) **17.** He said, "Far be it from me, O LORD, to drink this; is it not the blood of the men who risked their lives?" So, he wouldn't drink it. The three mighty men did this. (risked : endangered) **18.** Abishai, the brother of Joab, son of Zeruiah, was chief of three. He lifted his spear and killed three hundred men, gaining a name among the three. (spear: weapon) **19.** Was he not most honorable of the three? Therefore, he was their captain, though he didn't reach the first three. (captain : leader) **20.** Benaiah, son of Jehoiada, a valiant man of Kabzeel, who did many deeds, killed two lion-like men of Moab, and also went down and killed a lion in a pit during snow. (valiant: brave) (Kabzeel : place) **21.** He killed an Egyptian, a tall man with a spear, but went down with a staff, took the spear from the Egyptian, and killed him with his own spear. (tall: strong) **22.** These things Benaiah son of Jehoiada did, and he had a name among the three mighty men. **23.** He was more honorable than the thirty, but did not reach the first three, and David set him over his guard. (guard : soldiers) **24.** Asahel, brother of Joab, was one of the thirty; Elhanan, son of Dodo of Bethlehem, **25.** Shammah the Harodite, Elika the Harodite, **26.** Helez the Paltite, Ira son of Ikkesh of Tekoa, **27.** Abiezer the Anethothite, Mebunnai the Hushathite, **28.** Zalmon the Ahohite, Maharai the Netophathite, **29.** Heleb son of Baanah, a Netophathite, Ittai son of Ribai from Gibeah in Benjamin, **30.** Benaiah the Pirathonite, Hiddai of the brooks of Gaash, **31.** Abi-albon the Arbathite, Azmaveth the Barhumite, **32.** Eliahba the Shaalbonite, of the sons of Jashen, Jonathan, **33.** Shammah the Hararite, Ahiam son of Sharar the Hararite, **34.** Eliphelet son of Ahasbai, the Maachathite, Eliam son of Ahithophel the Gilonite, **35.** Hezrai the Carmelite, Paarai the Arbite, **36.** Igal son of Nathan of Zobah, Bani the Gadite, **37.** Zelek the Ammonite, Naharai the Beerothite, armor-bearer to Joab son of Zeruiah, **38.** Ira the Ithrite, Gareb the Ithrite, **39.** Uriah the Hittite: thirty-seven in all. (Ithrite : from Ithra) (Gibeah : town)

Chapter 24
1. Again, the LORD's anger burned against Israel, and He stirred David to say, "Go, number Israel and Judah." (anger: strong displeasure, stirred: moved) **2.** The king said to Joab, the commander, "Go through Israel and Judah, from Dan to Beer-sheba, and count the people so I can know their number." (commander: leader) **3.** Joab replied, "May the LORD your God increase the people a hundredfold, and may you see it, but why does my lord delight in this?" (delight: take pleasure) **4.** But the king's command prevailed, and Joab and the commanders went out to number Israel. (prevailed: was followed) **5.** They crossed the Jordan and camped in Aroer, near the city in the river of Gad, and near Jazer. (Aroer: city in Israel, Jazer: region of Israel) **6.** They went to Gilead, Tahtim-hodshi, Dan-jaan, and Zidon. (Gilead: region, Zidon: ancient Phoenician city)

7. They reached the stronghold of Tyre and all the cities of the Hivites and Canaanites, and went to the south of Judah, to Beer-sheba. (Tyre: city, Hivites: group of people) **8.** After going through the whole land, they returned to Jerusalem after nine months and twenty days. (Jerusalem: capital of Israel) **9.** Joab reported the count to the king: 800,000 warriors in Israel and 500,000 in Judah. (Warriors: soldiers) **10.** David regretted counting the people and said to the LORD, "I have sinned greatly; please take away my sin." (Regretted: felt bad, sinned: done wrong) **11.** The word of the LORD came to the prophet Gad the next morning. (Gad: prophet) **12.** The LORD offered David three choices: famine for seven years, fleeing from enemies for three months, or three days of pestilence in the land. (Pestilence: deadly disease) **13.** Gad asked David to choose one. (Choose: select) **14.** David, in distress, chose to fall into the LORD's hand, trusting in His mercy, not into human hands. (Distress: stress, mercy: kindness) **15.** The LORD sent a plague, killing 70,000 from Dan to Beer-sheba. (Plague: disease) **16.** When the angel stretched out his hand to destroy Jerusalem, the LORD stopped him, saying, "It is enough." The angel was by the threshingfloor of Araunah the Jebusite. (threshingfloor: place for separating grain, Araunah: a man) **17.** David saw the angel and said, "I have sinned, but these people have done nothing wrong. Let your hand fall on me and my family." (Sinned: done wrong) **18.** Gad told David to build an altar to the LORD at Araunah's threshingfloor. (Altar: place of sacrifice) **19.** David went up as the LORD commanded. (went up: climbed) **20.** Araunah saw David coming and bowed before him, asking why he was there. (bowed: showed respect) **21.** David replied, "I have come to buy your threshingfloor to build an altar so the plague will stop." (Buy: purchase) **22.** Araunah offered everything: oxen for sacrifice and tools for wood. (Oxen: cattle) **23.** Araunah gave everything, saying, "May the LORD accept you." (Accept: be pleased with) **24.** David refused, saying he would buy it for a price and not offer something that costs him nothing. He bought the threshingfloor and oxen for fifty shekels of silver. (Refused: did not accept) **25.** David built an altar, offered sacrifices, and the LORD stopped the plague. (Sacrifices: offerings)

11 – 1 king
Chapter 1
1. Whilst King David became very vintage, he could not hold heat even if they located covers over him. **2.** So his attendants stated to him, "Let us look for a younger virgin to serve the king and take care of him. She will be able to lie beside him so that our lord the king might also preserve warm." (Attendants: helpers) **3.** Then they searched in the course of Israel for a lovely younger female and discovered Abishag, a Shunammite, and brought her to the king. (Shunammite: from Shunem, a city in Israel) **4.** The female became very beautiful; she took care of the king and waited on him, but the king had no sexual relations together with her. **5.** Now Adonijah, whose mom became Haggith, set himself up as king, pronouncing, "I might be king." So he were given chariots and horses equipped, with fifty guys to run ahead of him. (Chariots: horse-drawn carts) **6.** (His father had in no way rebuked him by way of asking, "Why do you behave as you do?") He became also very good-looking and turned into born next after Absalom.) (Rebuked: criticized) **7.** Adonijah conferred with Joab son of Zeruiah and with Abiathar the priest, and that they gave him their support. (Conferred: talked) **8.** but Zadok the priest, Benaiah son of Jehoiada, Nathan the prophet, Shimei and Rei, and David's special protect did now not join Adonijah. **9.** Adonijah then sacrificed sheep, cattle, and fattened calves at the Stone of Zoheleth close to En Rogel. He invited all his brothers, the king's sons, and all the royal officials of Judah, (Fattened calves: well-fed animals) (En Rogel: a spring or well close to Jerusalem) **10.** but he did not invite Nathan the prophet or Benaiah or the unique shield or his brother Solomon. **11.** Then Nathan requested Bathsheba, Solomon's mother, "Have you no longer heard that Adonijah, the son of Haggith, has become king, and our lord David knows not anything

approximately it? **12.** Now then, let me advocate you how you may keep your personal life and the life of your son Solomon." **13.** "Go in to King David and say to him, 'My lord the king, did you no longer swear to me your servant, 'Clearly Solomon your son shall be king after me, and he'll take a seat on my throne'? Why then has Adonijah come to be king?' **14.** even as you are nonetheless there talking to the king, i'm able to are available in and upload my phrase to what you have got said." **15.** So Bathsheba went to peer the elderly king in his room, where Abishag the Shunammite was attending him. **16.** Bathsheba bowed down, prostrating herself earlier than the king. "What is it you want?" the king asked. (Prostrating: bowing down fully) **17.** She said to him, "My lord, you yourself swore to me your servant through the LORD your God: 'Solomon your son can be king after me, and he will take a seat on my throne.' **18.** but now Adonijah has end up king, and also you, my lord the king, do now not recognize about it. **19.** He has sacrificed big numbers of farm animals, fattened calves, and sheep, and has invited all the king's sons, Abiathar the priest, and Joab the commander of the navy, but he has now not invited Solomon your servant. **20.** My lord the king, the eyes of all Israel are on you, to learn from you who will sit down on the throne of my lord the king after him. **21.** in any other case, as soon as my lord the king is laid to relaxation together with his ancestors, I and my son Solomon can be handled as criminals." (Laid to rest: died) **22.** at the same time as she was nevertheless speak me with the king, Nathan the prophet arrived. **23.** And the king changed into informed, "Nathan the prophet is right here." So he went before the king and bowed along with his face to the floor. **24.** Nathan stated, "Have you ever, my lord the king, declared that Adonijah will be king when you, and that he's going to sit to your throne? **25.** Today he has long past down and sacrificed big numbers of cattle, fattened calves, and sheep. He has invited all of the king's sons, the commanders of the army, and Abiathar the priest. Right now they're consuming and drinking with him and saying, 'Long live King Adonijah!' **26.** However me, your servant, and Zadok the priest, and Benaiah son of Jehoiada, and your servant Solomon he did now not invite. **27.** is that this something my lord the king has accomplished without letting his servants recognize who ought to sit at the throne of my lord the king after him?" **28.** Then King David said, "Call in Bathsheba." So she came into the king's presence and stood earlier than him. **29.** The king then took an oath: "As clearly because the LORD lives, who has added me out of each problem, **30.** i'm able to truly perform this very day what I swore to you by the LORD, the God of Israel: Solomon your son will be king after me, and he will take a seat on my throne in my region." **31.** Then Bathsheba bowed down along with her face to the ground, prostrating herself before the king, and said, "May my lord King David stay forever!" **32.** King David said, "Call in Zadok the priest, Nathan the prophet, and Benaiah son of Jehoiada." once they got here earlier than the king, **33.** he stated to them, "Take your lord's servants with you and feature Solomon my son mount my own mule and take him right down to Gihon. (Mount: experience) (Gihon: a spring or water supply close to Jerusalem) **34.** There have Zadok the priest and Nathan the prophet anoints him king over Israel. Blow the trumpet and shout, 'Long live King Solomon!' **35.** Then you are to go up with him, and he is to come back and sit down on my throne and reign in my location. i've appointed him ruler over Israel and Judah." **36.** Benaiah son of Jehoiada spoke back the king, "Amen! may additionally the LORD, the God of my lord the king, so claim it. **37.** Because the LORD became with my lord the king, so may also he be with Solomon to make his throne even more than the throne of my lord King David!" **38.** So Zadok the priest, Nathan the prophet, Benaiah son of Jehoiada, the Kerethites and the Pelethites went down and had Solomon mount King David's mule, and they escorted him to Gihon. (Kerethites: elite soldiers) (Pelethites: elite infantrymen) **39.** Zadok the priest took the horn of oil from the sacred tent and anointed Solomon. Then they sounded the trumpet, and all of the humans shouted, "Lengthy live King Solomon!" (Anointed - consecrated; Trumpet - horn) **40.** And all the humans went up after him, playing pipes and rejoicing substantially, so that the ground shook with the sound. (Rejoicing - celebrating; Substantially : greatly) **41.** Adonijah and all the guests who had been with him heard it as they had been completing their banquet. On hearing the sound of the trumpet, Joab requested, "What's the means of all of the noise inside the metropolis?" (Banquet: feast; Means : reason) **42.** When he became talking, Jonathan son of Abiathar the priest arrived. Adonijah stated, "Come in. A worthy guy such as you must be bringing excellent information." (Worthy: deserving) **43.** "On no account!" Jonathan replied. "Our lord King David has made Solomon king. (On no account: never) **44.** The king has dispatched with him Zadok the priest, Nathan the prophet, Benaiah son of Jehoiada, the Kerethites, and the Pelethites, and they have placed him at the king's mule (Dispatched : sent; Kerethites : mercenaries; Pelethites - guards) **45.** and Zadok the priest and Nathan the prophet have anointed him king at Gihon. From there they have got long gone up cheering, and the city resounds with it. That's the noise you listen. (Resounds - echoes) **46.** furthermore, Solomon has taken his seat at the royal throne. (Furthermore: additionally; Throne : seat) **47.** also, the royal officials have come to congratulate our lord King David, saying, 'May your God make Solomon's name greater than yours, and his throne greater than yours!' And the king bowed in worship on his bed. (Congratulate: praise; Bow: kneel) **48.** And stated, 'Praise be to the LORD, the God of Israel, who has allowed my eyes to see a successor on my throne today.' (Successor : heir) **49.** At this, all Adonijah's visitors rose in alarm and dispersed. (Dispersed : scattered; Alarm : fear) **50.** But Adonijah, in fear of Solomon, went and took hold of the horns of the altar. (Horns : projections) **51.** Then Solomon changed into informed, "Adonijah is frightened of King Solomon and is clinging to the horns of the altar. He says, 'Let King Solomon swear to me nowadays that he's going to not placed his servant to demise with the sword.'" (Horns of the altar: the corners of the altar, symbolizing shelter) **52.** Solomon replied, "If he shows himself to be worthy, not a hair of his head will fall to the floor; but if evil is found in him, he will die." **53.** Then King Solomon despatched guys, and they introduced him down from the altar. And Adonijah got here and bowed all the way down to King Solomon, and Solomon stated, "Go to your home."

Chapter 2

1. When the time drew near for David to die, he gave a charge to Solomon his son. (Drew near: approached, charge: command) **2.** "I am about to go the way of all the earth," he said. "So be strong, act like a man, (way: path, act: behave) **3.** And observe what the LORD your God requires: Walk in obedience to him, and keep his decrees and commands, his laws and regulations, as written in the Law of Moses. Do this so that you may prosper in all you do and wherever you go. (Observe: follow, decrees: rules, regulations: guidelines, prosper: succeed) **4.** And that the LORD may keep his promise to me: 'If your descendants watch how they live, and if they walk faithfully before me with all their heart and soul, you will never fail to have a successor on the throne of Israel.' (Descendants: children, faithfully: loyally, successor: heir) **5.** "Now you yourself know what Joab son of Zeruiah did to me—what he did to the two commanders of Israel's armies, Abner son of Ner and Amasa son of Jether. He killed them, shedding their blood in peacetime as if in battle, and with that blood he stained the belt around his waist and the sandals on his feet. (Shed: spilled, peacetime: during peace, stained: marked) **6.** Deal with him according to your wisdom, but do not let his gray head go down to the grave in peace. (Wisdom: understanding, gray head: old age, grave: tomb) **7.** "But show kindness to the sons of Barzillai of Gilead and let them be among those who eat at your table. They stood by me when I fled from your brother Absalom. (Kindness: favor, fled: ran) **8.** "And remember, you have with you Shimei son of Gera, the Benjamite from Bahurim, who called down bitter curses on me the day I went to Mahanaim. When he came down to meet me at the Jordan, I swore to him by the LORD: 'I will not put you to death by the sword.' (Remember: recall, bitter: harsh, curses: insults) 9. But now, do not consider him innocent. You are a man of wisdom; you will know what to do to him. Bring his gray head down to the grave in blood." (Consider: think, innocent: blameless, wisdom: understanding) 10. Then David rested with his ancestors and was buried in the City of David. (Rested: passed away, ancestors: forefathers, buried: laid down) 11. He had reigned forty years over Israel—seven years in Hebron and thirty-three in Jerusalem. (Reigned: ruled, years: period, Hebron: city, Jerusalem: capital) 12. So Solomon sat on the throne of his father David, and his rule was firmly established. (Sat: took seat, rule: reign, firmly: securely) 13. Now Adonijah, the son of Haggith, went to Bathsheba, Solomon's mother. Bathsheba asked him, "Do you come peacefully?" He answered, "Yes, peacefully." (Peacefully: without conflict) 14. Then he added, "I have something to say to you." "You may say it," she replied. (Added: said, replied: answered) 15. "As you know," he said, "the kingdom was mine. All Israel looked to me as their king. But things changed, and the kingdom has gone to my brother; for it has come to him from the LORD. (Looked: viewed, kingdom: rule) 16. Now I have one request to make of you. Do not refuse me." "You may make it," she said. (Refuse: deny, request: plea) 17. So he continued, "Please ask King Solomon—he will not refuse you—to give me Abishag the Shunammite as my wife." (Continued: went on, wife: spouse) 18. "Very well," Bathsheba replied, "I will speak to the king for you." (Replied: answered, speak: talk) 19. When Bathsheba went to King Solomon to speak to him for Adonijah, the king stood up to meet her, bowed down to her and sat down on his throne. He had a throne brought for the king's mother, and she sat down at his right hand. (Stood: rose, bowed: leaned, throne: seat) 20. "I have one small request to make of you," she said. "Do not refuse me." The king replied, "Make it, my mother; I will not refuse you." (Small: minor, refused: declined) 21. So she said, "Let Abishag the Shunammite be given in marriage to your brother Adonijah." (Given: granted, marriage: union) 22. King Solomon answered his mother, "Why do you request Abishag the Shunammite for Adonijah? You might as well request the kingdom for him—after all, he is my older brother—yes, for him and for Abiathar the priest and Joab son of Zeruiah!" (answered: replied, request: ask) 23. Then King Solomon swore by the LORD: "May God deal with me, be it ever so severely, if Adonijah does not pay with his life for this request! (swore: vowed, severely: harshly, pay: suffer) 24. And now, as surely as the LORD lives—he who has established me securely on the throne of my father David and has founded a dynasty for me as he promised—Adonijah shall be put to death today!" (established: set up, securely: firmly, dynasty: line) 25. So King Solomon gave orders to Benaiah son of Jehoiada, and he struck down Adonijah and he died. (Orders: commands, struck down: killed) 26. To Abiathar the priest the king said, "Go back to your fields in Anathoth. You deserve to die, but I will not put you to death now, because you carried the ark of the Sovereign LORD before my father David and shared all my father's hardships." (Deserve: merit, death: end, carried: bore, hardships: difficulties) 27. So Solomon removed Abiathar from the priesthood of the LORD, fulfilling the word the LORD had spoken at Shiloh about the house of Eli. (Removed: took away, fulfilling: completing, priesthood: office) 28. When the news reached Joab, who had conspired with Adonijah though not with Absalom, he fled to the tent of the LORD and took hold of the horns of the altar. (Conspired: plotted, fled: ran, horns: projections) 29. King Solomon was told that Joab had fled to the tent of the LORD and was beside the altar. Then Solomon ordered Benaiah son of Jehoiada, "Go, strike him down!" (Ordered: commanded, strike: kill) 30. So Benaiah entered the tent of the LORD and said to Joab, "The king says, 'come out!' " But he answered, "No, I will die here." Benaiah reported to the king, "This is how Joab answered me." (Reported: told, answered: replied) 31. Then the king commanded Benaiah, "Do as he says. Strike him down and bury him, and so clear me and my whole family of the guilt of the innocent blood that Joab shed. (Commanded: ordered, guilt: blame, shed: spilled) 32. The LORD will repay him for the blood he shed, because without my father David knowing it he attacked two men and killed them with the sword. Both of them—Abner son of Ner, commander of Israel's army, and Amasa son of Jether, commander of Judah's army—were better men and more upright than he. (Repay: punish, attacked: assaulted, upright: honest) 33. May the guilt of their blood rest on the head of Joab and his descendants forever. But on David and his descendants, his house and his throne, may there be the LORD's peace forever." (guilt: blame, rest: remain, descendants: heirs, throne: seat, peace: harmony) 34. So Benaiah son of Jehoiada went up and struck down Joab and killed him, and he was buried at his home out in the country. (Struck down: killed) 35. The king put Benaiah son of Jehoiada over the army in Joab's position and replaced Abiathar with Zadok the priest. (Put: appointed, replaced: substituted) 36. Then the king sent for Shimei and said to him, "Build yourself a house in Jerusalem and live there, but do not go anywhere else. (Sent: called, live: reside) 37. The day you leave and cross the Kidron Valley, you can be sure you will die; your blood will be on your own head." (Cross: pass, valley: low area) 38. Shimei answered the king, "What you say is good. Your servant will do as my lord the king has said." And Shimei stayed in Jerusalem for a long time. (Answered: replied, servant: follower) 39. But three years later, two of Shimei's slaves ran off to Achish son of Maakah, king of Gath, and Shimei was told, "Your slaves are in Gath." (Slaves: servants, ran off: escaped) 40. At this, he saddled his donkey and went to Achish at Gath in search of his slaves. So Shimei went away and brought the slaves back from Gath. (Saddled: prepared, search: seek) 41. When Solomon was told that Shimei had gone from Jerusalem to Gath and had returned, (told: informed, returned: came back) 42. the king summoned Shimei and said to him, "Did I not make you swear by the LORD and warn you, 'On the day you leave to go anywhere else, you can be sure you will die'? At that time you said to me, 'What you say is good. I will obey.' (Summoned: called, swear: vow, warn: caution, obey: follow) 43. Why then did you not keep your oath to the LORD and obey the command I gave you?" (keep: honor, command: order) 44. The king also said to Shimei, "You know in your heart all the wrong you did to my father David. Now the LORD will repay you for your wrongdoing. (wrong: harm, repay: punish, wrongdoing: offense) 45. But King Solomon will be blessed, and David's throne will remain secure before the LORD forever." (blessed: favored, secure: safe) 46. Then the king gave the order to Benaiah son of Jehoiada, and he went out and struck Shimei down and he died. The kingdom was now established in Solomon's hands. (Order: command, struck down: killed, established: secured)

Chapter 3

1. Solomon made an alliance with Pharaoh King of Egypt and married his daughter. He introduced her to the city of David until he finished constructing his palace, the LORD's temple, and the town partitions. (Alliance: a formal agreement among two events) 2. The humans nevertheless sacrificed at excessive places, due to the fact a temple had not been constructed for the LORD's call. (High places: extended sites used for worship) 3. Solomon confirmed his love for the LORD with the aid of following his father David's instructions, but he nevertheless presented sacrifices and burned incense on the excessive places. 4. The king went to Gibeon to provide sacrifices, the most critical high place, and provided a thousand burnt offerings. 5. At Gibeon, the LORD regarded to Solomon in a dream and stated, "Ask for something you need me to offer you." (Dream: a series of mind or snap shots experienced at some stage during sleep) 6. Solomon spoke back, "you have got shown exquisite kindness in your servant, my father David, due to the fact he became trustworthy and upright. You've persevered your kindness by means of giving him a

son to sit down on the throne nowadays." **7.** "Now, LORD, you have got made me king rather than my father. I'm like a child and do now not recognize how to rule." (Infant: metaphor for being inexperienced) **8.** Your servant is amongst your selected people, too severe to be counted. **9.** Deliver me a discerning coronary heart to govern your human beings and distinguish proper from wrong. Who can govern this kind of extremely good people? (Discerning: having properly judgment) **10.** The Lord became pleased with Solomon's request. **11.** God said, "due to the fact you requested for expertise and no longer lengthy existence or wealth, nor the loss of life of your enemies, **12.** I will come up with a smart and discerning heart, unrivaled by way of all of us earlier than or when you. **13.** I can additionally come up with what you did now not ask for—wealth and honor—making you the best among kings. **14.** in case you stroll in obedience to me as David did, I will come up with a protracted life." (Obedience: compliance with commands) **15.** Solomon woke and found out it had been a dream. He lower back to Jerusalem, stood before the ark of the LORD's covenant, sacrificed services, and held a dinner party. (Ark: a sacred chest containing the 10 Commandments) **16.** Two prostitutes got here to the king and stood earlier than him. **17.** One stated, "This woman and that i live collectively, and I had a child while she was with me. **18.** The 0.33 day after my infant become born, she also had an infant. We had been alone inside the house. **19.** One night, her son died because she lay on him. **20.** She got up, took my son even as I used to be asleep, and located her useless son by my side. **21.** The subsequent morning, I saw my son become dead, but when I appeared closely, I saw it wasn't my son." **22.** The other woman stated, "No! The dwelling one is my son; the lifeless one is yours." They argued before the king. **23.** The king said, "One says, 'My son is alive and your son is dead,' at the same time as the alternative says, 'No, your son is lifeless and mine is alive.'" **24.** The king ordered, "carry me a sword." **25.** He commanded, "cut the dwelling infant in two and supply half of to each of them." **26.** The woman whose son turned into alive, moved by using love for her son, said, "Please, my lord, give her the residing infant! Don't kill him!" The alternative female stated, "Neither I nor you shall have him. Cut him in two!" **27.** The king dominated, "Give the residing toddler to the primary lady. She is his mom." **28.** When Israel heard the king's verdict, they held him in awe, due to the fact that he had awareness from God to manage justice. (Administer: to control or perform)

Chapter 4
1. So King Solomon ruled over all Israel. **2.** And those have been his chief officials: Azariah son of Zadok—the priest; **3.** Elihoreph and Ahijah, sons of Shisha—secretaries; Jehoshaphat son of Ahilud—recorder; **4.** Benaiah son of Jehoiada—commander in leader; Zadok and Abiathar—clergymen; **5.** Azariah son of Nathan—in charge of the district governors; Zabud son of Nathan—a clergyman and adviser to the king; **6.** Ahishar—palace administrator; Adoniram son of Abda—in fee of pressured hard work. (Administrator: individual in rate, compelled exertions: required work, often without pay) **7.** Solomon had twelve district governors over all Israel, who furnished provisions for the king and the royal family. Everyone had to offer substances for one month inside the year. **8.** These are their names: Ben-Hur—in the hill country of Ephraim; (Ephraim: one of the tribes of Israel) **9.** Ben-Deker—in Makaz, Shaalbim, Beth Shemesh, and Elon Bethhanan; (Makaz, Shaalbim, Beth Shemesh: cities in Israel) **10.** Ben-Hesed—in Arubboth (Sokoh and all the land of Hepher were his); (Arubboth: location or region in Israel, Sokoh: city in Judah) **11.** Ben-Abinadab—in Naphoth Dor (he was married to Taphath, daughter of Solomon); (Naphoth Dor: a place in Israel) **12.** Baana son of Ahilud—in Taanach and Megiddo, and in all of Beth Shan next to Zarethan below Jezreel, from Beth Shan to Abel Meholah across to Jokmeam; (Taanach, Megiddo, Beth Shan, Zarethan: towns in Israel, Abel Meholah: a place near Jordan River) **13.** Ben-Geber—in Ramoth Gilead (the settlements of Jair son of Manasseh in Gilead were his, as well as the region of Argob in Bashan and its sixty large walled cities with bronze gate bars); (Ramoth Gilead: city in Gilead, Argob: region, Bashan: ancient land, Walled cities: cities with strong defenses) **14.** Ahinadab son of Iddo—in Mahanaim; (Mahanaim: location on east side of Jordan River) **15.** Ahimaaz—in Naphtali (he had married Basemath, daughter of Solomon); (Naphtali: northern Israelite tribe) **16.** Baana son of Hushai—in Asher and in Aloth; (Asher: tribe in northern Israel, Aloth: area or region) **17.** Jehoshaphat son of Paruah—in Issachar; (Issachar: one of the tribes of Israel) **18.** Shimei son of Ela—in Benjamin; (Benjamin: one of the tribes of Israel) **19.** Geber son of Uri—in Gilead (the country of Sihon king of the Amorites and the country of Og king of Bashan). He was the only governor over the district. (Gilead: region east of Jordan, Sihon: Amorite king, Og: king of Bashan) **20.** The people of Judah and Israel were as numerous as the sand on the seashore; they ate, they drank and they were happy. (Seashore: edge of the sea) **21.** And Solomon ruled over all the kingdoms from the Euphrates River to the land of the Philistines, as far as the border of Egypt. These countries brought tribute and were Solomon's subjects all his life. (Euphrates: river in Mesopotamia, Philistines: coastal enemies of Israel, Tribute: payment made for protection, Subjects: people under rule) **22.** Solomon's daily provisions were thirty cors of the finest flour and sixty cors of meal, (Cors: unit of measurement for grain) **23.** ten head of stall-fed cattle, twenty of pasture-fed cattle and a hundred sheep and goats, as well as deer, gazelles, roebucks and choice fowl. (Stall-fed: fed in pens, Pasture-fed: fed on grass) **24.** For he ruled over all the kingdoms west of the Euphrates River, from Tiphsah to Gaza, and had peace on all sides. (Tiphsah: city on the Euphrates, Gaza: Philistine city) **25.** During Solomon's lifetime, Judah and Israel, from Dan to Beersheba, lived in safety, everyone under their own vine and under their own fig tree. (Dan: northern border of Israel, Beersheba: southern border, Vine: symbol of peace, Fig tree: symbol of prosperity) **26.** Solomon had four thousand stalls for chariot horses, and twelve thousand horses. (Stalls: enclosed areas for horses) **27.** The district governors, each in his month, supplied provisions for King Solomon and all who came to the king's table. They saw to it that nothing was lacking. **28.** They also brought to the proper place their quotas of barley and straw for the chariot horses and the other horses. (Quotas: assigned amounts) **29.** God gave Solomon wisdom and very great insight, and a breadth of understanding as measureless as the sand on the seashore. (Insight: deep understanding, Measureless: impossible to measure) **30.** Solomon's wisdom was greater than the wisdom of all the people of the East, and greater than all the wisdom of Egypt. (East: nations east of Israel, Egypt: powerful kingdom to the southwest) **31.** He was wiser than anyone else, including Ethan the Ezrahite—wiser than Heman, Kalkol, and Darda, the sons of Mahol. And his fame spread to all the surrounding nations. (Ethan, Heman, Kalkol, Darda: wise men of Israel, Mahol: family of wisdom) **32.** He spoke three thousand proverbs and his songs numbered a thousand and five. (Proverbs: short sayings with wisdom) **33.** He spoke about plant life, from the cedar of Lebanon to the hyssop that grows out of walls. He also spoke about animals and birds, reptiles, and fish. (Cedar of Lebanon: strong tree, Hyssop: small plant, Reptiles: animals with scaly skin, Fish: aquatic animals) **34.** From all nations people came to listen to Solomon's wisdom, sent by all the kings of the world, who had heard of his wisdom. (Nations: groups of people, Kings: rulers of nations)

Chapter 5
1. When Hiram, king of Tyre, heard that Solomon was now king after David, he sent messengers to Solomon, having been friends with David. (Messengers: people who deliver messages, friendly: good relationship) **2.** Solomon replied to Hiram: **3.** "You know that my father, David, could not build a temple for the LORD because of the wars he faced, until the LORD gave him victory over his enemies. (Victory: success in battle) **4.** But now the LORD has granted me peace, with no enemies or calamities. (Calamities: disasters) **5.** I plan

to build the temple for the LORD, as He promised my father David, saying, 'Your son will build the temple.' (Plan: intend) **6.** Order the cedars of Lebanon to be cut for me. My men will work with yours, and I will pay your workers whatever wages you set. You know the Sidonians are skilled at cutting timber." (Cedars: trees, Sidonians: people from Sidon) **7.** Hiram was pleased and said, "Praise the LORD for giving David such a wise son to rule." (Praise: express admiration) **8.** Hiram replied: "I will send the cedar and juniper logs as you requested. (Juniper: type of tree) **9.** My men will bring them down from Lebanon to the sea and float them to the place you specify. Then you can take them. In return, provide food for my household." **10.** In this way, Hiram supplied Solomon with the logs, **11.** And Solomon gave Hiram twenty thousand cors of wheat and twenty thousand baths of olive oil for his household, doing this year after year. (Cors: units of grain, Baths: units of liquid) **12.** The LORD gave Solomon wisdom, as promised. Solomon and Hiram made a treaty. (Treaty: formal agreement) **13.** Solomon drafted thirty thousand men from Israel to work. (Drafted: selected for service) **14.** They worked in shifts of ten thousand per month, one month in Lebanon and two months at home. Adoniram was in charge of the labor. (Shifts: work periods) **15.** Solomon had seventy thousand carriers and eighty thousand stonecutters, (Carriers: people who carry materials) **16.** plus three thousand three hundred supervisors managing the project. (Supervisors: managers) **17.** They removed large stone blocks from the quarry to form the temple's foundation. (Quarry: stone source) **18.** Solomon, Hiram, and workers from Byblos prepared the wood and stone for the temple. (Byblos: city known for trade)

Chapter 6

1. In the 480th year after the Israelites came out of Egypt, during the fourth year of Solomon's reign, in the second month (Ziv), he started the construction of the temple for the LORD. (Ziv: a month in the Hebrew calendar) **2.** The temple Solomon built was 60 cubits long, 20 cubits wide and 30 cubits high. (Cubit: a unit of measurement; approximately 18 inches or 45 cm) **3.** A porch at the front of the temple extended 20 cubits in width and projected 10 cubits from the main building. (Porch: a structure attached to a building, usually with a roof) **4.** He designed narrow windows high in the temple walls. (Narrow: limited in width) **5.** Around the main hall and inner sanctuary, Solomon built a surrounding structure with side rooms. (Sanctuary: a holy or sacred space) **6.** The first floor was 5 cubits wide, the second floor 6 cubits, and the third 7 cubits. There were ledges on the outside to prevent the insertion of anything into the walls. (Ledges: a flat horizontal surface) **7.** Only stones cut and prepared at the quarry were used, and no iron tools were heard at the construction site. (Quarry: a place where stone is extracted from the earth) **8.** The entrance to the lowest floor was on the south side, with stairs leading up to the second and third floors. (Stairs: steps for going from one level to another) **9.** Solomon completed the temple, roofing it with beams and cedar planks. (Beams: large, heavy pieces of wood or metal) **10.** He constructed side rooms around the temple, each 5 cubits high, supported by cedar beams. (Side rooms: additional spaces or chambers next to the main building) **11.** The LORD spoke to Solomon, saying: (Spoke: communicated) **12.** "If you follow my commands and observe my laws, I will keep the promise I made to your father David, and I will live among the Israelites, never forsaking them." (Forsaking: abandoning, leaving behind) **13.** Solomon finished the construction of the temple. (Construction: the act of building or creating something) **14.** He covered the inner walls with cedar, paneling from floor to ceiling, and laid juniper planks on the floor. (Paneling: wooden or other material applied to the walls as a covering) **15.** At the back of the temple, he partitioned off 20 cubits to form the Most Holy Place, also made from cedar wood. (Partitioned off: divided into sections) **16.** The main hall in front of the inner sanctuary was 40 cubits long. (Main hall: the primary room or space in a building) **17.** The interior was entirely cedar, intricately carved with designs of gourds and open flowers. No stone was visible. (Intricately: detailed and complicated) **18.** Solomon prepared the inner sanctuary to house the ark of the covenant. (Ark: a large, sacred container or chest) **19.** The inner sanctuary was 20 cubits in all dimensions and was overlaid with pure gold, as was the cedar altar. (Overlay: to cover with a layer of something) **20.** The interior of the temple was fully covered in gold, and gold chains were placed across the front of the Most Holy Place. (Chains: a series of connected metal links) **21.** Solomon overlaid every part of the inner sanctuary with gold, including the altar. (Overlay: to cover with a layer of something) **22.** For the inner sanctuary, he crafted two cherubim from olive wood, each 10 cubits tall. (Cherubim: angelic beings in religious art or texts) **23.** Each cherub had a wingspan of 10 cubits, with one wing 5 cubits long and the other similarly sized. (Wingspan: the distance from the tip of one wing to the tip of the other) **24.** The cherubim were positioned inside the innermost room, with their wings spread, touching opposite walls and meeting in the center. (Innermost: the very center or deepest part) **25.** The cherubim were covered in gold. (Covered: coated with a material) **26.** The temple's walls, both inside and outside, were adorned with carvings of cherubim, palm trees, and open flowers. (Adorned: decorated) **27.** Both the inner and outer rooms had gold-covered floors. (Outer: the exterior or outside part) **28.** He made doors of olive wood for the entrance to the inner sanctuary, one-fifth the width of the sanctuary. (Olive wood: wood from the olive tree, valued for its quality) **29.** He carved cherubim, palm trees, and flowers on the doors, and overlaid them with hammered gold. (Hammered: shaped or molded by striking with a hammer) **30.** For the entrance to the main hall, he made doorframes from olive wood, one-fourth the width of the hall, and crafted two doors of juniper wood, which were covered with gold. (Doorframes: the structure that surrounds a door) **31.** He carved cherubim, palm trees, and flowers on the doors, and then applied gold over the carvings. (Applied: placed or spread onto) **32.** Solomon built the inner courtyard with three layers of dressed stone and one layer of trimmed cedar beams. (Dressed stone: stone shaped and smoothed for construction purposes) **33.** The foundation for the temple was laid in the fourth year, in the month of Ziv. (Foundation: the solid base or support for a building) **34.** In the eleventh year, in the month of Bul (the eighth month), the temple was completed to its exact specifications after seven years of construction.

Chapter 7

1. Solomon took thirteen years to build his palace. (Palace: royal home) **2.** He built the Palace of the Forest of Lebanon, 100 cubits long, 50 wide, and 30 high, supported by four rows of cedar columns and cedar beams. (Cedar: type of durable wood; Columns: vertical support structures) **3.** The roof was made of cedar beams resting on the columns—45 beams in total, arranged in three rows of 15 each. (Beams: long pieces of wood for support) **4.** The windows were placed high, in sets of three facing each other. (Windows: openings for light and air) **5.** The doorways had rectangular frames and were grouped in sets of three, facing each other. (Doorways: openings for entry) **6.** He made a colonnade 50 cubits long and 30 cubits wide, with a portico in front, followed by pillars and an overhanging roof. (Colonnade: row of columns; Portico: covered entrance supported by columns) **7.** He built the Hall of Justice, where he would judge, and covered it with cedar from floor to ceiling. (Hall of Justice: place for judgment) **8.** The palace where Solomon would live was set farther back and was similar in design. He also made a palace for Pharaoh's daughter, whom he married. (Pharaoh's daughter: wife of Solomon, daughter of Egyptian king) **9.** All these structures, from the outside to the courtyard and from the foundation to the roof, were made of high-quality stone, carefully cut and smoothed on both sides. (Courtyard: open space surrounded by buildings) **10.** The foundations were made of large stones, some 10 cubits long and others 8 cubits. (Foundations: base of a building) **11.** Above the foundation were stones cut to size and cedar beams. (Beams: long horizontal supports) **12.** The great courtyard was surrounded by a wall made of three rows of dressed stone and one row of trimmed cedar beams, just like the inner courtyard of the Lord's temple. (Dressed: shaped or cut for use) **13.** Solomon sent to Tyre and brought Huram, (Tyre: ancient city known for skilled craftsmen) **14.** Huram's mother was from the tribe of Naphtali, and his father was a skilled craftsman in bronze from Tyre. He had great wisdom and understanding to work with bronze and came to Solomon to do the work. (Bronze: a metal alloy; Craftsman: skilled worker) **15.** He cast two bronze pillars, each 18 cubits tall and 12 cubits around. (Cubits: an ancient unit of length) **16.** He made two bronze capitals to place on top of the pillars, each 5 cubits high. (Capitals: decorative tops of columns) **17.** He decorated the capitals with interwoven chains, seven chains for each. (Chains: linked metal rings) **18.** He placed pomegranates in two rows around each capital to decorate them. He did the same for both capitals. (Pomegranates: decorative fruit symbol) **19.** The capitals were shaped like lilies and were 4 cubits high. (Lilies: flower shape used for design) **20.** On top of the capitals were 200 pomegranates, arranged in rows around the decorative chains. (Pomegranates: fruit-shaped decorations) **21.** He set the pillars at the temple's portico. He named the southern pillar "Jakin" and the northern pillar "Boaz." (Portico: covered entrance; Jakin: means "he will establish"; Boaz: means "in him is strength") **22.** The capitals were shaped like lilies, and the work on the pillars was finished. (Capitals: decorative tops of columns) **23.** He made the Sea of bronze, circular, measuring 10 cubits across and 5 cubits high, with a 30-cubit circumference. (Sea: large basin or container). **24.** Around its rim, there were ten gourds for each cubit, cast in two rows with the Sea. (Gourds: round, decorative shapes). **25.** The Sea stood on twelve bronze bulls, three facing each direction—north, west, south, and east. The bulls' backs faced inward. (Bulls: large male cattle). **26.** The Sea was one handbreadth thick, with a rim like a lily blossom and could hold 2,000 baths. (Handbreadth: width of a hand; Baths: ancient unit of liquid measurement) **27.** Huram made ten movable bronze stands, each 4 cubits long, 4 cubits wide and 3 cubits high. **28.** The stands had side panels attached to vertical supports. (Panels: flat surfaces) **29.** Between the supports, the panels had carvings of lions, bulls, and cherubim, with wreaths around them. (Cherubim: angelic beings) **30.** Each stand had four bronze wheels with bronze axles, and a basin resting on four supports, also decorated with wreaths. (Wheels: circular objects for movement) **31.** Inside each stand was a circular opening one cubit deep, with an engraving around its base. The panels were square. (Opening: a hole or space) **32.** The four wheels were placed under the panels, with axles connecting them to the stand. Each wheel was 1.5 cubits in diameter. (Diameter: length across a circle) **33.** The wheels were designed like chariot wheels, with metal axles, rims, spokes, and hubs. (Rims: the circular edges of the wheels) **34.** Each stand had four handles, one at each corner, sticking out. (Handles: parts for lifting or holding) **35.** The top of each stand had a circular band, half a cubit deep, where the supports and panels were attached. (Band: circular strip) **36.** He engraved cherubim, lions, and palm trees on the stands and panels, with wreaths around the decorations. (Engraved: carved or etched designs) **37.** These ten stands were all made in the same molds and were identical in size and shape. (Molds: forms used to shape metal) **38.** Huram made ten bronze basins, each holding 40 baths and measuring 4 cubits across, one for each stand. (Basins: large bowls or containers) **39.** Five stands were placed on the south side of the temple and five on the north. The Sea was placed at the southeast corner. (Southeast: direction between south and east) **40.** Huram also made pots, shovels, and sprinkling bowls. He completed all the work Solomon had given him for the temple of the Lord. (Pots: containers for use) **41.** This included the two pillars, the two capitals with bowl-shaped designs on top of the pillars, the networks decorating them, (Bowl-shaped: like a cup) **42.** the 400 pomegranates for the two sets of networks (two rows of pomegranates for each network decorating the capitals on the pillars), (Rows: lines of objects) **43.** the ten stands with their ten basins, (Basins: large bowls) **44.** the Sea and the twelve bulls beneath it, (Bulls: large male cattle) **45.** the pots, shovels, and sprinkling bowls. All these items were made from burnished bronze. (Burnished: polished to a shine) **46.** These items were cast in molds in the plain of the Jordan, between Sukkoth and Zarethan. (Molds: forms for shaping; Sukkoth: a place in Israel; Zarethan: an ancient city) **47.** Solomon did not weigh the bronze because there were so many items, and their total weight was not determined. (Weighed: measured by weight) **48.** Solomon also made all the furnishings for the Lord's temple: the golden altar, the table with the bread of the Presence, (Furnishings: items for use in the temple) **49.** the gold lampstands (five on the right and five on the left in front of the inner sanctuary), the gold floral designs, lamps, and tongs, (Lampstands: holders for lamps) **50.** the pure gold basins, wick trimmers, sprinkling bowls, dishes, and censers, and the gold sockets for the doors of the innermost room, the Most Holy Place, and also for the doors of the main hall of the temple. (Wick trimmers: tools for trimming lamp wicks; Censers: containers for burning incense) **51.** When all the work Solomon had done for the temple was finished, he brought in the things his father David had dedicated—the silver, gold, and furnishings—and placed them in the treasuries of the Lord's temple. (Treasure: storage of valuable items)

Chapter 8

1. King Solomon called together the elders of Israel, the leaders of the tribes, and the heads of the families to bring the ark of the Lord's covenant from Zion, the City of David, to Jerusalem. (Ark: chest; Covenant: agreement; Zion: hill; City of David: Jerusalem's part) **2.** All of Israel gathered at the time of the festival in the seventh month, Ethanim, to meet King Solomon. (Ethanim: seventh month) **3.** When the elders had gathered, the priests took the ark. (Priests: religious leaders) **4.** They brought the ark of the Lord, the tent of meeting, and all its sacred furnishings. The priests and Levites carried them up. (Levites: tribe members; Sacred: holy) **5.** Solomon and the entire assembly of Israel stood before the ark, offering so many sacrifices of sheep and cattle that they could not be counted. (Assembly: gathering; Sacrifices: offerings) **6.** The priests placed the ark in its rightful place in the inner sanctuary of the temple, the Most Holy Place, under the wings of the cherubim. (Sanctuary: holy place; Cherubim: angels) **7.** The cherubim spread their wings over the ark and its poles. (Poles: rods) **8.** The poles were so long that their ends could be seen from the Holy Place but not from outside it; and they remain there to this day. (Ends: tips) **9.** Inside the ark were only the two stone tablets that Moses had placed there at Horeb, where the Lord made a covenant with the Israelites after their exodus from Egypt. (Tablets: stones; Exodus: departure) **10.** When the priests left the Holy Place, a cloud filled the temple. (Cloud: mist) **11.** The priests could not perform their duties because the cloud represented the Lord's glory. (Glory: majesty) **12.** Solomon said, "The Lord said he would dwell in a dark cloud. (Dwell: live) **13.** I have built a magnificent temple for you, a place for you to live forever." (Magnificent: impressive) **14.** While all Israel stood, the king turned and blessed them. (Blessed: praised) **15.** He said: "Praise be to the Lord, the God of Israel, who has kept his promise to my father David. He said, (Praise: honor) **16.** 'Since I brought Israel out of Egypt, I have never chosen a city for my Name to be there, nor a man to rule my people Israel. But I chose David to rule them.' (Chosen: selected) **17.** My father David wanted to build a temple for the Lord, the God of Israel. (Wanted: desired) **18.** But the Lord said to him, 'You did well to desire this, (Desire: want) **19.** but you are not to build the temple; your son will build it for my Name.' (Son: child) **20.** The Lord has kept his promise: I have succeeded my father David and now sit on Israel's throne, as the Lord promised. I have built the temple for the Lord, the God of Israel. (Succeeded: followed; Throne: seat of power) **21.** I have prepared a place for the ark, in which the covenant is the Lord made with our ancestors when he brought them out of Egypt. (Prepared: arranged) **22.** Solomon stood before the altar of the Lord, in front of the entire assembly of Israel, and spread out his hands toward heaven. (Altar: platform; Assembly: gathering) **23.** He said: "Lord, God of Israel, there is no God like you in heaven or on earth—who keeps his covenant of love with those who walk faithfully in his way. (Covenant: agreement) **24.** You have kept your promise to my father David. You spoke, and with your hand you fulfilled it, as we see today. (Fulfilled: completed) **25.** Now, Lord, God of Israel, fulfill your promise to your servant David, when you said, 'You will never fail to have a descendant on the throne of Israel, if your sons are careful to walk in my ways as you have done.' (Descendant: offspring) **26.** And now, Lord, God of Israel, let your word to your servant David come true. (Word: promise) **27.** "But can God really dwell on earth? The heavens, even the highest heaven, cannot contain you. How much less this temple I have built! (Dwell: live; Contain: hold) **28.** Yet, pay attention to your servant's prayer and plea, Lord my God. Hear the cry and the prayer your servant is making in your presence today. (Plea: request) **29.** May your eyes be open toward this temple, night and day, the place you said, 'My Name shall be there,' so that you will hear the prayer your servant prays toward this place? (Open: attentive) **30.** Hear the supplication of your servant and of your people Israel when they pray toward this place. Hear from heaven, your dwelling place, and forgive. (Supplication: request) **31.** When anyone wrongs their neighbor and takes an oath before your altar in this temple, (Wrongs: harms) **32.** hear from heaven and act. Judge between your servants, condemning the guilty and acquitting the innocent. (Condemning: punishing; Acquitting: absolving) **33.** When Israel is defeated by an enemy because of sin, and when they turn back to you, praying and asking forgiveness in this temple, (Defeated: beaten) **34.** hear from heaven and forgive the sin of your people, and bring them back to the land you gave to their ancestors. (Forgive: pardon) **35.** When the heavens are shut up and there is no rain because your people have sinned, and they pray toward this place and repent, (Repent: regret) **36.** hear from heaven and forgive their sin. Teach them the right way to live, and send rain on the land you gave to your people. (Teach: instruct) **37.** When famine or plague comes, or blight, mildew, locusts, or grasshoppers, or when an enemy besieges them in their cities—whatever disaster or disease— (Famine: hunger; Plague: disease; Besieges: surrounds) **38.** and when a prayer is made by anyone among your people, being aware of their own afflictions, and spreading their hands toward this temple, (Afflictions: sufferings) **39.** hear from heaven, your dwelling place. Forgive and act, dealing with everyone according to their deeds, for you alone know every human heart. (Deeds: actions) **40.** May they fear you all the days they live in the land you gave to our ancestors. (Fear: respect) **41.** As for the foreigner who is not of your people Israel but has come from a distant land because of your name— (Foreigner: outsider) **42.** they will hear of your great name and mighty deeds—when they come and pray toward this temple, (Mighty: powerful) **43.** hear from heaven and do whatever the foreigner asks, so that all peoples on earth may know your name and fear you, as your own people Israel do. (Peoples: nations) **44.** When your people go to war against their enemies and pray to the Lord toward the city you have chosen and the temple I have built for your Name, (War: battle) **45.** hear from heaven and uphold their cause. (Uphold: support) **46.** When they sin against you—for no one is without sin—and you become angry and give them over to their enemies, and they are taken captive, (Sin: wrongdoing) **47.** if they change their hearts in the land of their captors and repent, saying, 'We have sinned,' (Captors: captors) **48.** and turn back to you with all their heart and soul and pray toward the land you gave their ancestors, (Turn: return) **49.** then from heaven, hear their prayer and forgive them. (Forgive: pardon) **50.** Forgive your people's sins, and show mercy to their captors. (Mercy: compassion) **51.** They are your people, whom you brought out of Egypt, out of the furnace of iron. (Furnace: smelting oven) **52.** May your eyes be open to the pleas of your servant and of your people, and listen to them whenever they call to you. (Pleas: requests) **53.** For you chose them from all the nations to be your inheritance, as you declared through Moses when you brought our ancestors out of Egypt. (Inheritance: possession) **54.** After finishing these prayers, Solomon rose from before the altar of the Lord, where he had been kneeling with his hands spread out toward heaven. (Kneeling: bowing) **55.** He stood and blessed the whole assembly of Israel with a loud voice, saying: (Blessed: praised) **56.** "Praise be to the Lord, who has given rest to his people Israel, as he promised. Not one word of all his good promises has failed. (Rest: peace) **57.** May the Lord our God be with us as he was with our ancestors; may he never leave us nor forsake us. (Forsake: abandon) **58.** May he turn our hearts to him, to walk in obedience to him, keeping his commands, decrees, and laws. (Obedience: compliance) **59.** May my prayers be near to the Lord, that he may uphold the cause of his servant and of Israel each day. (Uphold: support) **60.** So that all the peoples of the earth may know that the Lord is God and that there is no other. (Peoples: nations) **61.** May our hearts be fully committed to the Lord our God, living by his decrees and obeying his commands, as we do today." (Committed: devoted) **62.** Then Solomon and all Israel offered sacrifices before the Lord. (Sacrifices: offerings) **63.** Solomon offered 22,000 cattle and 120,000 sheep and goats as fellowship offerings. Thus, the king and all Israel dedicated the temple of the Lord. (Fellowship: communion) **64.** On that day, Solomon consecrated the middle part of the courtyard, offering burnt offerings, grain offerings, and fellowship offerings, because the bronze altar could not hold all the offerings. (Consecrated: sanctified) **65.** Solomon and all Israel celebrated the festival for 14 days—seven days, then seven more, before the Lord their God. (Festival: celebration) **66.** On the last day, Solomon sent the people home, and they blessed the king. They went home joyful, knowing all the good the Lord had done for David and his people Israel. (Blessed: praised)

Chapter 9

1. When Solomon had finished building the temple and the royal palace, and completed all his plans, **2.** The LORD appeared to him a second time, as he had at Gibeon. (Gibeon: city where Solomon made an offering to God) **3.** The LORD said to him, "I have heard your prayer and consecrated this temple you built by placing my Name there forever. My eyes and heart will always be there." (Consecrated: made holy or set apart) **4.** "If you walk before me with integrity and uprightness, as your father David did, and obeys my commands and decrees, **5.** I will establish your throne over Israel forever, as I promised David, saying, 'You will always have a successor on the throne of Israel.'" **6.** "But if you or your descendants turn away from me, do not keep my commands, and worship other gods, **7.** I will cut off Israel from the land I gave them and reject this temple. Israel will become a byword and a subject of ridicule among the nations." (Byword: a proverb or saying of mockery) **8.** "This temple will become a heap of ruins. People passing by will be appalled and ask, 'Why has the LORD done this to this land and temple?'" **9.** "They will answer, 'Because they abandoned the LORD their God, who brought their ancestors out of Egypt, and worshiped other gods.'" (Ancestors: forebears) **10.** After twenty years, during which Solomon built the temple and the royal palace, **11.** Solomon gave twenty towns in Galilee to Hiram, king of Tyre, because Hiram supplied him with cedar, juniper, and gold. (Tyre: ancient Phoenician city) **12.** When Hiram visited the towns Solomon had given him, he was not pleased. **13.** "What kind of towns are these, my brother?" he asked, and called them the Land of Kabul, a name that remains today. (Kabul: a name meaning "good for nothing") **14.** Hiram had sent 120 talents of gold to Solomon. (Talents: units of weight, usually used for gold or silver) **15.** Here is the record of the forced labor Solomon used to build the LORD's temple, his palace, and other projects. **16.** (Pharaoh, king of Egypt, had attacked and burned Gezer, killed its Canaanite inhabitants, and gave it as a wedding gift to his daughter, Solomon's wife.) **17.** Solomon rebuilt Gezer and also built Lower Beth Horon, **18.** Baalath and Tadmor in the desert within his land. (Tadmor: city in the desert). **19.** He also built store cities, and towns for his chariots and horses—whatever he desired, including in Jerusalem, Lebanon, and throughout his kingdom. **20.** There were still people left from the Amorites, Hittites, Perizzites, Hivites, and Jebusites (all non-Israelite nations). **21.** Solomon conscripted these remaining peoples to serve as slave labor for his building projects. (Conscripted: forced to work) **22.** But Solomon did not make slaves of any Israelites. They were his fighting men, officers, and commanders of his chariots. **23.** They also served as chief officials over Solomon's projects—550 overseers supervising the workers. **24.** After Pharaoh's daughter moved into the palace Solomon built for her, he constructed the terraces. **25.** Three times a year, Solomon offered burnt and fellowship offerings on the altar he built for the LORD, fulfilling his temple duties. **26.** Solomon also built ships at Ezion Geber, near Elath in Edom, on the Red Sea. (Ezion Geber: port city on the Red Sea; Elath: ancient city in Edom) **27.** Hiram sent his sailors to join Solomon's men in the fleet. **28.** They sailed to Ophir and brought back 420 talents of gold, which they delivered to Solomon. (Ophir: a distant region known for its wealth)

Chapter 10
1. When the queen of Sheba heard of Solomon's fame and his deep connection to the LORD, she traveled to test him with challenging questions. (Sheba: Arabia) **2.** She arrived in Jerusalem with an impressive caravan—camels loaded with spices, abundant gold, and precious stones. She came to Solomon and discussed everything that was on her mind. (Caravan: group) **3.** Solomon answered all her questions, leaving nothing too difficult for him to explain. **4.** When the queen observed the wisdom of Solomon and the grandeur of the palace he had built, **5.** the lavish food on his table, the arrangement of his officials, the servants in fine robes, his cupbearers, and the burnt offerings made at the LORD's temple, she was amazed. (Attendants: helpers) **6.** She said to the king, "What I heard in my homeland about your achievements and wisdom is true." **7.** "But I didn't believe it until I came and saw it with my own eyes. I've been told only half the truth; your wisdom and wealth far surpass what I heard." **8.** "How blessed are your people! How fortunate your officials, who stand before you continually and hear your wisdom!" **9.** "Praise be to the LORD your God, who has taken such pleasure in you and placed you on Israel's throne. Because of the LORD's eternal love for Israel, He has made you king to establish justice and righteousness." (Eternal: everlasting) **10.** The queen gave the king 120 talents of gold, a great quantity of spices, and precious stones. There was no record of spices as valuable as those she brought to Solomon. (talents: weight) **11.** (Hiram's ships brought gold from Ophir, along with large shipments of almugwood and precious stones. (Ophir: wealthy region, almugwood: rare wood) **12.** Solomon used the almugwood to make supports for the temple and the royal palace, as well as musical instruments like harps and lyres. Such an import of almugwood had never been seen before or after.) **13.** Solomon gave the queen of Sheba everything she asked for, plus what he had given her from his royal treasures. Then she returned to her land with her entourage. (Retinue: attendants) **14.** The weight of gold Solomon received every year was 666 talents, **15.** Not including the wealth from merchants, traders, and all the Arabian kings and governors. (Talents: weight) **16.** Solomon made two hundred large shields from hammered gold, with each shield containing six hundred shekels of gold. (Shekels: currency). **17.** He also made three hundred smaller shields from hammered gold, each containing three minas of gold. The king placed them in the Palace of the Forest of Lebanon. (Minas: weight) **18.** He then crafted a magnificent throne covered in ivory and plated with pure gold. (Ivory: elephant tusks) **19.** The throne had six steps, and its back was curved. On either side were armrests, with a lion standing next to each armrest. **20.** Twelve lions stood at the base of the six steps, one lion on each step. No other kingdom had ever made anything like it. **21.** All of King Solomon's goblets were made of gold, and every household item in the Palace of the Forest of Lebanon was made of pure gold. Silver was considered too insignificant to be used. (Goblets: cups) **22.** Solomon's fleet of trading ships, in partnership with Hiram's ships, returned once every three years, bringing gold, silver, ivory, and even exotic animals like apes and baboons. (Hiram: ally, apes: monkeys) **23.** Solomon surpassed all other kings of the earth in wealth and wisdom. (surpassed : exceed) **24.** The entire world sought his counsel to hear the wisdom God had placed in his heart. (sought: search for) **25.** Year after year, visitors brought gifts—gold, silver, robes, weapons, spices, and even horses and mules. **26.** Solomon accumulated 1,400 chariots and 12,000 horses, which were kept in chariot cities and in Jerusalem. (chariots: war vehicles) **27.** He made silver as common as stones in Jerusalem, and cedar as abundant as sycamore-fig trees in the foothills. (sycamore: tree) **28.** Solomon imported horses from Egypt and Kue, with royal merchants buying them at the going price. (Kue: Cilicia) **29.** A chariot from Egypt cost six hundred shekels of silver, and a horse one hundred and fifty. These were then exported to the kings of the Hittites and Arameans. (Hittites: Anatolia, Arameans: Syria)

Chapter 11
1. King Solomon, however, loved many foreign women in addition to Pharaoh's daughter, including Moabites, Ammonites, Edomites, Sidonians, and Hittites. (Edomites: people from Edom; Sidonians: people from Sidon; Hittites: people from the Hittite empire) **2.** These women came from nations that the LORD had warned the Israelites about, saying, "Do not intermarry with them, or they will turn your hearts toward their gods." But Solomon was deeply attached to them. (Intermarry: marry outside one's group) **3.** He had seven hundred wives from royal families and three hundred concubines, and they led him astray. (Concubines: secondary wives) **4.** As Solomon grew older, his wives turned his heart toward other gods, and his heart was no longer completely loyal to the LORD, his God, as David, his father, had been. (Loyal: faithful) **5.** He followed Ashtoreth, the goddess of the Sidonians, and Molech, the detestable god of the Ammonites. (Detestable: abhorrent) **6.** Solomon did evil in the eyes of the LORD and did not follow Him fully, as his father David had done. (Evil: sin) **7.** Solomon built high places on a hill east of Jerusalem for Chemosh, the detestable god of Moab, and for Molech, the detestable god of the Ammonites. (High places: altars) **8.** He built similar places for all his foreign wives, who burned incense and offered sacrifices to their gods. (Incense: fragrance) **9.** The LORD became angry with Solomon because his heart had turned away from Him, the God of Israel, who had appeared to him twice. (Turned away: departed) **10.** Despite God's warnings, Solomon did not obey His command to avoid other gods. (Obey: follow) **11.** The LORD said to Solomon, "Since you have acted this way and not kept My covenant and laws, I will certainly tear the kingdom from you and give it to one of your subordinates. (Covenant: agreement) **12.** However, for the sake of David your father, I will not do it during your lifetime. I will take it from your son's rule. (Subordinate: assistant) **13.** Yet I will not take the entire kingdom from him; I will give him one tribe for the sake of David My servant and for the sake of Jerusalem, the city I have chosen." (Tribe: clan) **14.** Then the LORD raised up an adversary against Solomon: Hadad the Edomite, from the royal family of Edom. (Adversary: enemy) **15.** Earlier, when David fought the Edomites, Joab, the commander of the army, had struck down all the men in Edom. (Commander: leader) **16.** Joab and the Israelites remained in Edom for six months, destroying every male. (Destroyed: wiped out) **17.** Hadad, still a boy, fled to Egypt with some officials who had served his father. (Fled: escaped) **18.** They traveled through Midian to Paran and then to Egypt, where Pharaoh gave Hadad a house, land, and food. (Provisions: supplies) **19.** Pharaoh

was pleased with Hadad and gave him his wife's sister, Queen Tahpenes, to marry. (Queen: ruler's wife) **20.** Tahpenes bore him a son named Genubath, whom she raised in the royal palace alongside Pharaoh's children. (Raised: nurtured) **21.** While in Egypt, Hadad heard that David and Joab had died. He then asked Pharaoh for permission to return to his own country. (Permission: consent) **22.** Pharaoh asked him, "What do you lack here that you want to go back?" (Lack: need) **23.** Hadad answered, "Nothing, but please let me go!" (Answer: reply) **24.** At the same time, the LORD raised up another adversary against Solomon: Rezon, the son of Eliada, who had fled from his master, King Hadadezer of Zobah. (Raised up: caused) **25.** When David defeated Zobah's army, Rezon gathered men to himself, and they took control of Damascus, where he ruled and became an enemy to Israel. (Took control: dominated) **26.** Jeroboam, the son of Nebat, also rebelled against the king. He was an Ephraimite from Zeredah, and his mother was a widow named Zeruah. (Rebelled: defied) **27.** Solomon had built the terraces and filled in the gap in the city of David. (Terraces: raised platforms) **28.** Jeroboam was an industrious man, and when Solomon saw how well he worked, he made him overseer of the labor force of the tribes of Joseph. (Industrious: hardworking) **29.** One day, as Jeroboam was leaving Jerusalem, the prophet Ahijah met him on the road, wearing a new cloak. (Prophet: seer) **30.** Ahijah tore his new cloak into twelve pieces. (Tore: ripped) **31.** He said to Jeroboam, "Take ten pieces for yourself. This is what the LORD, the God of Israel, says: 'I am going to tear the kingdom from Solomon's hand and give you ten tribes. (Kingdom: realm) **32.** But for the sake of My servant David and the city of Jerusalem, which I have chosen from all the tribes, Solomon will keep one tribe. (Sake: purpose) **33.** This will happen because they have forsaken Me, worshipped other gods, and have not obeyed My laws as David did. (Forsaken: abandoned) **34.** However, I will not take the whole kingdom from Solomon. I will allow him to rule his whole life for the sake of David My servant, who obeyed Me. (Obeyed: followed) **35.** After Solomon's death, I will take the kingdom from his son's hands and give you ten tribes. (Son: heir) **36.** I will leave one tribe for his son, so that David My servant may always have a lamp before Me in Jerusalem, the city where I have chosen to place My Name. (Lamp: symbol of life) **37.** But you will rule over all that your heart desires, and you will be king over Israel. (Rule: govern) **38.** If you obey My commands and walk in righteousness, just as David did, I will be with you. I will establish a dynasty for you as enduring as David's. (Righteousness: justice) **39.** I will humble David's descendants because of this, but not forever." (Humble: lower in status) **40.** Solomon tried to kill Jeroboam, but Jeroboam fled to Egypt, where he stayed with King Shishak until Solomon's death. (Tried: attempted) **41.** The other events of Solomon's reign, including all he did and the wisdom he displayed, are written in the annals of Solomon. (Annals: records) **42.** Solomon reigned in Jerusalem over all Israel for forty years. (Reigned: ruled) **43.** Solomon died and was buried in the city of David. His son Rehoboam succeeded him as king. (Succeeded: followed)

Chapter 12

1. Rehoboam went to Shechem, where all of Israel had collected to make him king: (Shechem: a town in Israel) **2.** when Jeroboam, son of Nebat, heard about this (he changed into still in Egypt, having fled from King Solomon), he back from exile: (Jeroboam: former servant of Solomon, fled to Egypt) **3.** The humans sent for Jeroboam, and he, in conjunction with the entire meeting of Israel, went to satisfy Rehoboam. They spoke to him, pronouncing: **4.** "Your father made our burdens unbearable, but if you lighten the harsh exertions and the heavy yoke he positioned on us, we can serve you:" (yoke: heavy burden or work) **5.** Rehoboam replied, "Supply me three days to suppose it over, and then go back to me." So the humans left. **6.** Rehoboam consulted the older advisors who had served his father Solomon. He asked, "What is your recommend on how I ought to reply to these humans?" (Counsel: recommendation) **7.** The elders spoke back, "If you will be kind to the humans these days, and communicate favorably to them, they'll be unswerving and serve you for all time:" (elders: sensible old guys) **8.** but Rehoboam disregarded the advice of the elders and consulted with the young men who had grown up with him and had been now his counselors: (counselors: advisors) **9.** He requested them, "What do you recommend I say to those individuals who are asking me to lighten the yoke my father located on them?" **10.** The young men, who were raised with Rehoboam, spoke back, "inform them this: 'My little finger is thicker than my father's waist:" (waist: the a part of the body among chest and hips) **11.** If my father made your yoke heavy, i'm able to make it even heavier. If he flogged you with whips, i will scourge you with scorpions.'" (Scourge: punish severely with a whip or something sharp) **12.** three days later, Jeroboam and the human beings lower back as Rehoboam had informed. **13.** Rehoboam spoke back them harshly, rejecting the advice of the elders: (harshly: in a merciless or unkind manner) **14.** He instructed them, "My father made your yoke heavy, however i can make it even heavier. My father flogged you with whips, but i will scourge you with scorpions." **15.** The king did now not pay attention to the human beings, for this turn of occasions changed into directed with the aid of the LORD to meet the prophecy given to Jeroboam, son of Nebat, via the prophet Ahijah: (prophecy: a message from God) **16.** when the Israelites saw that Rehoboam refused to listen to them, they spoke back, "What will we ought to do with David? We don't have any element in the son of Jesse! on your tents, O Israel! Appearance after your very own residence, David!" So the human beings of Israel lower back to their houses: (David: the second one king of Israel) **17.** Most effective the human beings of Judah remained unswerving to Rehoboam: (Judah: a tribe of Israel, additionally a state) **18.** Rehoboam despatched Adoniram, who was in price of forced hard work, however the Israelites stoned him to demise. Rehoboam managed to get away to Jerusalem in his chariot: (Adoniram: reputable in charge of forced exertions) **19.** Thus, Israel rebelled against the residence of David, and this division has endured to the present day: (rebel: the act of refusing to obey authority) **20.** When all the Israelites heard that Jeroboam had again, they known as him to a meeting and made him their king. Simplest the tribe of Judah remained trustworthy to Rehoboam. **21.** When Rehoboam came to Jerusalem, he assembled all the house of Judah and the tribe of Benjamin, 180,000 chosen warriors, to fight against the house of Israel to restore the kingdom to Rehoboam, the son of Solomon. (Assembled: gathered; House: people; Chosen: selected; Warriors: soldiers; Restore: reclaim) **22.** but the word of God got here to the prophet Shemaiah, **23.** Who informed Rehoboam, King of Judah, and all of the human beings of Judah and Benjamin: **24.** "this is what the LORD says: Do no longer go to war towards your brothers, the Israelites. pass back home, for i've ordained this department:" (ordained: determined or organized by God) **25.** The human beings obeyed God's word and lower back to their homes. **26.** Jeroboam fortified Shechem within the hill country of Ephraim and lived there. He additionally constructed up Peniel: (fortified: made more potent or safer) (Ephraim: a region of Israel) (Peniel: an area in Israel) **27.** Jeroboam concept to himself, "If these humans preserve to go to Jerusalem to offer sacrifices on the temple of the LORD, they will eventually go back their allegiance to Rehoboam, king of Judah. If that takes place, they will kill me and restore Rehoboam to the throne:" (allegiance: loyalty or faithfulness) **28.** After seeking counsel, Jeroboam made two golden calves. He informed the humans, "it's far too a long way so as to visit Jerusalem. Here are your gods, O Israel, who introduced you out of Egypt:" (calves: younger cows, used as idols here) **29.** He placed one calf in Bethel and the opposite in Dan: (Bethel: an area in Israel) (Dan: a city in Israel) **30.** This became a sinful exercise, as the human beings worshiped the calf in Bethel or even traveled as a ways as Dan to worship the other calf: (sinful: morally incorrect) **31.** Jeroboam constructed excessive places for worship and appointed priests from all varieties of human beings, even those who were now not Levites: (excessive locations: regions on hills used for worship) (Levites: participants of the tribe of Levi, who had been selected to serve in religious duties) **32.** He additionally instituted a competition on the fifteenth day of the eighth month, much like the one held in Judah, and offered sacrifices on the altar. This he did in Bethel, providing sacrifices to the golden calves he had made. He additionally appointed clergymen for the high places he had built. **33.** on the 15th day of the 8th month, a month he had chosen for the competition, Jeroboam went as much as the altar in Bethel and supplied sacrifices, for this reason organizing this new competition for Israel: (competition: a time for religious birthday celebration)

Chapter 13

1. With the aid of the word of the LORD, a prophet from Judah came to Bethel at the same time as King Jeroboam became standing by the altar to make an offering. (Bethel: a city in Israel; Jeroboam: king of Israel) **2.** He cried out against the altar: "Altar, altar! This is what the LORD says: A son named Josiah will be born into the family of David. He will sacrifice the priests who serve at these high places on you, and human bones will be burned on you." **3.** The prophet gave a sign that same day: "This is the sign the LORD has promised: The altar will be torn apart, and its ashes will be poured out." **4.** When King Jeroboam heard what the prophet said, he stretched out his hand from the altar and shouted, "Capture him!" But as he did, his hand became shriveled and could not be pulled back. (Shriveled: withered or dried up) **5.** The altar was also torn apart, and its ashes were poured out, exactly as the prophet had said in the word of the LORD. **6.** The king said to the prophet, "Pray to the LORD your God and ask Him to heal my hand." The prophet prayed, and the king's hand was healed and became as it was before. **7.** The king invited the prophet, saying, "Come home with me, and I will reward you with a gift." **8.** But the prophet answered, "Even if you gave me half of your wealth, I would not go with you. I cannot eat or drink in this place." (Wealth: possessions) **9.** "The LORD told me, 'You must not eat or drink here, nor return by the same way you came.'" (Return: come back) **10.** So the prophet took another road and did not return the same way he had come to Bethel. (Road: path) **11.** Meanwhile, an old prophet lived in Bethel. His sons came and told him what the man of God had done that day and what he had said to the king. (Prophet: messenger; Sons: children) **12.** The old prophet asked them, "Which way did he go?" His sons showed him the road the prophet from Judah had taken. (Showed: pointed out) **13.** So he said to his sons, "Saddle my donkey." They did so, and he rode off. (Saddle: prepare; Donkey: animal) **14.** The old prophet found the man of God sitting under an oak tree and asked him, "Are you the prophet who came from Judah?" "Yes," he answered. (Oak: tree) **15.** The old prophet said, "Come home with me and eat." (Eat: consume) **16.** But the man of God said, "I cannot go back with you, nor can I eat bread or drink water with you here." (Bread: food) **17.** "I have been told by the LORD not to eat or drink in this place or return by the way I came." (Told: instructed) **18.** The old prophet replied, "I too am a prophet, as you are. An angel spoke to me by the word of the LORD and told me to bring you back to my house so that you can eat and drink." (But he was lying to him.) (Replied: responded; Lying: deceiving) **19.** So the man of God returned with him and ate and drank in his house. (Returned: came back) **20.** While they were sitting at the table, the word of the LORD came to the old prophet. (Table: surface for eating) **21.** He cried out to the man of God from Judah, "This is what the LORD says: You have disobeyed the LORD's command. You did not keep the word that the LORD your God gave you. (Disobeyed: ignored; Command: order) **22.** You came back and ate bread and drank water in the place where the LORD told you not to. Therefore, your body will not be buried in the tomb of your ancestors." (Tomb: grave) **23.** After they ate and drank, the old prophet saddled the donkey for the man of God to continue his journey. (Saddled: prepared; Journey: trip) **24.** As the man of God traveled, a lion met him on the road and killed him. His body was left on the road, and the donkey and the lion stood beside it. (Traveled: journeyed; Met: encountered) **25.** Some people passed by and saw the body and the lion standing beside it. They went and reported it in the city where the old prophet lived. (Passed by: went by; Reported: told) **26.** When the old prophet heard what had happened, he said, "It is the man of God who disobeyed the LORD's command. The LORD has given him over to the lion, which has killed him as the LORD said it would." (Given over: handed over; Command: order) **27.** The old prophet said to his sons, "Saddle the donkey for me." They did so, (Saddle: prepare) **28.** and he went out and found the body lying on the road, with the donkey and lion standing beside it. The lion had not eaten the body nor harmed the donkey. (Lying: resting; Harmed: hurt) **29.** The old prophet lifted the man of God's body, placed it on the donkey, and brought it back to his city to mourn and bury him. (Lifted: picked up; Mourn: grieve) **30.** He laid the man of God's body in his own tomb and mourned over him, saying, "Alas, my brother!" (Tomb: grave; Alas: expression of sorrow) **31.** After burying him, the old prophet said to his sons, "When I die, bury me in the tomb where the man of God is buried. Lay my bones next to his. (Bury: inter) **32.** For the message he declared by the word of the LORD against the altar in Bethel and the high places in Samaria will certainly come true." (Message: prophecy; Declared: proclaimed) **33.** Even after these events, King Jeroboam did not change his wicked ways. He continued to appoint priests for the high places from among all kinds of people, consecrating anyone who wanted to serve. (Consecrating: making sacred) **34.** This was the sin of Jeroboam that led to the downfall of his dynasty and caused its destruction from the face of the earth. (Dynasty: a family or institution that holds power for several generations)

Chapter 14

1. During this time, Abijah, the son of Jeroboam, became seriously ill. Jeroboam told his wife, "Disguise yourself so no one will know you're my wife. Then go to Shiloh, where the prophet Ahijah lives—the one who told me I would become king over Israel." (Shiloh: a city in ancient Israel) **2.** "Take ten loaves of bread, some cakes, and a jar of honey with you. Go to him, and he will tell you what will happen to our son." **3.** Jeroboam's wife followed his instructions and went to the prophet Ahijah's house in Shiloh. Ahijah was unable to see because of his old age. (Ahijah: a prophet) **4.** However, the LORD had spoken to Ahijah, saying, "Jeroboam's wife is coming to ask you about her sick son. She will pretend to be someone else, but you will give her the answer I have given you." **5.** When Ahijah heard the sound of her footsteps at the door, he said, "Come in, wife of Jeroboam. Why are you pretending? I have a message from the LORD for you." (Pretending: acting as though something is not true) **6.** "Go back and tell Jeroboam, 'this is what the LORD, the God of Israel, says: "I raised you from among the people and made you ruler over Israel. **7.** I tore the kingdom from the house of David and gave it to you, but you have not followed my servant David, who obeyed my commands and followed me wholeheartedly, doing what was right in my eyes. (wholeheartedly : deeply) **8.** You have done more evil than any before you. You have made idols of metal, aroused my anger, and turned away from me." (Idols of metal: idols made from materials like gold or silver) **9.** "'Because of your actions, I will bring disaster upon your family. I will destroy every male descendant of yours in Israel—whether they are free or slaves. I will completely destroy your house, like dung being burned up.' (Dung: refuse or waste that is burned) **10.** 'Dogs will eat the bodies of those from your family who die in the city, and scavenger birds will feed on those who die in the open fields. The LORD has spoken!' **11.** "'As for you, go back to your home. The moment you step into your city, your son will die. **12.** The people of Israel will mourn for him and bury him. He is the only member of your family who will be buried, because he is the only one in your house whom the LORD has found to be good.'" **13.** "'The LORD will rise up a king for Israel who will cut off your family. This is already starting to take place.'" **14.** "'The LORD will strike Israel, making them like a reed that sways in the water. He will uproot them from this land, which he gave their ancestors, and scatter them beyond the Euphrates River, because they angered the LORD by making idols of Asherah.' (Asherah: a goddess in idol worship; Euphrates River: a major river in the ancient Near East) **15.** "'He will turn Israel over because of the sins you have committed, and because you led Israel into sin.'" **16.** Jeroboam's wife got up, left, and headed back to Tirzah. As soon as she entered her home, her son died. (Tirzah: a city in Israel) **17.** They buried the boy, and all Israel mourned for him, just as the LORD had said through His servant, the prophet Ahijah. **18.** The rest of the events in Jeroboam's reign—his wars and how he ruled—are written in the book of the annals of the kings of Israel. (Annals: official records or history) **19.** He ruled for twenty-two years, and then joined his ancestors in death. His son Nadab succeeded him as king. (Nadab: Jeroboam's son) **20.** Rehoboam King of Judah **21.** Rehoboam, the son of Solomon, became king in Judah. He was forty-one years old when he began his reign, and he ruled for seventeen years in Jerusalem, the city that the LORD had chosen from all the tribes of Israel to place His Name. His mother's name was Naamah, and she was an Ammonite. (Rehoboam: king of Judah; Jerusalem: the capital city of Judah) **22.** Judah sinned greatly in the eyes of the LORD. Their sins provoked the LORD's anger more than the sins of those who came before them. **23.** They built high places, set up sacred stones, and made Asherah poles on every high hill and under every tree. (High places: places of idol worship; Asherah poles: wooden objects used in worship) **24.** Even male prostitutes served at these shrines, and the people practiced all the detestable acts of the nations that the LORD had driven out before the Israelites. (Male prostitutes: men who performed ritual sexual acts for idols) **25.** In the fifth year of Rehoboam's reign, Shishak, the king of Egypt, attacked Jerusalem. (Shishak: Pharaoh of Egypt) **26.** He took the treasures from the LORD's temple and from the royal palace, including all the gold shields Solomon had made. **27.** King Rehoboam replaced them with bronze shields and gave them to the commanders of his guard, who were stationed at the palace entrance. **28.** Whenever the king went to the LORD's temple, the guards would carry the bronze shields, and afterward, they would return them to the guardroom. **29.** The rest of the events of Rehoboam's reign and all that he did are written in the annals of the kings of Judah. (Annals: official records or history) **30.** There was constant warfare between Rehoboam and Jeroboam. (War: ongoing conflict between the two kingdoms) **31.** Rehoboam rested with his ancestors and was buried in the City of David. His mother's name was Naamah, an Ammonite, and his son Abijah succeeded him as king. (City of David: Jerusalem)

Chapter 15
1. In the 18th year of Jeroboam's reign, Abijah, the son of Jeroboam, became king over Judah. (Jeroboam: King of Israel, Judah: the southern kingdom) **2.** Abijah ruled in Jerusalem for three years. His mother's name was Maakah, the daughter of Abishalom. (Maakah: his mother, Abishalom: her father) **3.** Abijah followed the sinful practices of his father and did not have a heart fully committed to the LORD his God, like his ancestor David. (Committed: devoted) **4.** Yet, for the sake of David, the LORD kept a lamp burning in Jerusalem, raising up a successor for Abijah and strengthening the city. (Lamp: symbol of enduring kingship) **5.** David had done what was right in the eyes of the LORD and had obeyed His commands throughout his life, except in the matter of Uriah the Hittite. (Uriah: a soldier wronged by King David) **6.** There was constant conflict between Abijah and Jeroboam during his reign. (Conflict: ongoing warfare) **7.** The details of Abijah's reign, his actions, and his wars are recorded in the annals of the kings of Judah. (Annals: official records) **8.** Abijah passed away and was buried in the City of David. His son, Asa, succeeded him as king. (City of David: Jerusalem) **9.** In the 20th year of Jeroboam's reign, Asa became king of Judah. (Jeroboam: King of Israel) **10.** Asa ruled in Jerusalem for 41 years. His grandmother's name was Maakah, the daughter of Abishalom. (Maakah: his grandmother, Abishalom: her father) **11.** Asa did what was right in the eyes of the LORD, following the example of his ancestor David. (Example: a model of righteousness) **12.** Asa removed all the male shrine prostitutes from the land and destroyed the idols his ancestors had made. (Male shrine prostitutes: men who served in pagan worship, Idols: false gods) **13.** He also deposed his grandmother Maakah from her position as queen mother, because she had made a vile image to worship Asherah. Asa burned it in the Kidron Valley. (Asherah: a pagan goddess, Kidron Valley: a valley near Jerusalem) **14.** Although Asa did not remove all the high places where idols were worshipped, he remained wholeheartedly devoted to the LORD throughout his life. (High places: locations for idol worship) **15.** Asa brought into the LORD's temple the silver, gold, and sacred articles that he and his father had dedicated. (Dedicated: consecrated for divine use) **16.** There was constant conflict between Asa and Baasha, the king of Israel, throughout their reigns. (Baasha: King of Israel) **17.** Baasha, king of Israel, attacked Judah and built up Ramah to prevent anyone from leaving or entering Asa's territory. (Ramah: a city near the border of Israel and Judah) **18.** Asa then took all the remaining silver and gold from the treasures of the LORD's temple and his own palace. He sent them to Ben-Hadad, king of Aram, who was ruling in Damascus. (Aram: a region to the northeast of Israel, Damascus: the capital of Aram) **19.** Asa sent this message to Ben-Hadad: "Let us make a treaty, just like the one between my father and yours. I am sending silver and gold as a gift. Break your treaty with Baasha, the king of Israel, so that he will withdraw from me." (Treaty: an agreement of peace) **20.** Ben-Hadad agreed with King Asa and sent his army commanders to attack the cities of Israel. They conquered Ijon, Dan, Abel Beth Maakah, and all of Kinnereth, as well as Naphtali. (Ijon, Dan, Abel Beth Maakah, Kinnereth: cities of Israel, Naphtali: a northern tribe) **21.** When Baasha heard about this, he stopped fortifying Ramah and withdrew to Tirzah. (Tirzah: a city in Israel) **22.** Asa commanded all Judah to carry away the materials from Ramah that Baasha had used for his fortifications. With these, Asa fortified Geba in Benjamin and Mizpah. (Geba: a city in Benjamin, Mizpah: a city of Judah) **23.** The rest of Asa's deeds, his victories, and the cities he built are recorded in the annals of the kings of Judah. However, in his later years, Asa suffered from a disease in his feet. (Annals: official historical records) **24.** Asa passed away and was buried with his ancestors in the city of David. His son Jehoshaphat succeeded him as king. (Jehoshaphat: Asa's son) **25.** In the second year of Asa's reign over Judah, Nadab, son of Jeroboam, became king of Israel. He ruled for two years. (Jeroboam: King of Israel) **26.** Nadab did evil in the sight of the LORD, following in his father's sinful ways and continuing the sins that had led Israel astray. (Led astray: caused Israel to sin) **27.** Baasha, son of Ahijah from the tribe of Issachar, conspired against Nadab and killed him at Gibbethon, a Philistine city, while Nadab and his forces were besieging it. (Gibbethon: a Philistine city, Besieging: surrounding a city to capture it) **28.** Baasha killed Nadab in the third year of Asa, king of Judah, and became king of Israel. **29.** As soon as Baasha began his reign, he killed the entire family of Jeroboam, fulfilling the prophecy of the LORD spoken through the prophet Ahijah. (Ahijah: a prophet of the LORD) **30.** This occurred because of Jeroboam's sins, which had led Israel to sin and provoked the LORD's anger. (Provoked: made God angry) **31.** The other events of Nadab's reign, and all his deeds, are written in the annals of the kings of Israel. (Annals: official records) **32.** There was constant conflict between Asa and Baasha throughout their reigns. **33.** In the third year of Asa's reign, Baasha, son of Ahijah, became king of Israel, ruling from Tirzah for 24 years. (Tirzah: a city in Israel) **34.** Baasha did evil in the eyes of the LORD, continuing the sins of Jeroboam and causing Israel to sin. (Causing Israel to sin: leading the nation into idolatry)

Chapter 16

1. The Lord spoke to Jehu, son of Hanani, about Baasha: 2. "I raised you from the dust and made you king over Israel, but you followed the wicked ways of Jeroboam, causing the people of Israel to sin and provoke my anger with their evil actions. 3. So I will destroy Baasha and his descendants, just as I did to the house of Jeroboam. 4. The bodies of Baasha's family who die in the city will be eaten by dogs, and those who die in the open fields will be eaten by birds." 5. The rest of Baasha's actions and his achievements—aren't they written in the Book of the Chronicles of the Kings of Israel? (Israel: country in the Southern Levant region) 6. Baasha died and was buried in Tirzah. His son Elah became king after him. (Tirzah: city in Israel) 7. The word of the Lord came to Baasha's family through the prophet Jehu, son of Hanani, because of the wickedness they had done in the Lord's sight, making Israel sin and angering God by their idolatry. (Idolatry: worshiping idols instead of God) 8. In the 26th year of Asa, king of Judah, Elah, son of Baasha, became king of Israel and reigned for two years from Tirzah. (Asa: king of Judah, Tirzah: city in Israel) 9. Zimri, one of Elah's officers who led half of the king's chariots, plotted against him. Elah was drinking in the house of Arza, the palace administrator, in Tirzah at the time. (Arza: palace administrator) 10. Zimri entered, struck Elah, and killed him in the 27th year of Asa's reign. Zimri then became king. 11. As soon as Zimri became king, he killed all of Baasha's relatives, sparing no males. 12. Zimri destroyed the whole family of Baasha, fulfilling the word of the Lord spoken through Jehu, 13. because of all the sins that Baasha and Elah had committed, leading Israel into sin and angering the Lord by their worthless idols. 14. The rest of Elah's reign and his deeds are written in the Book of the Chronicles of the Kings of Israel. 15. In the 27th year of Asa, king of Judah, Zimri became king of Israel and reigned for seven days. The Israelite army was camped near Gibbethon, a Philistine town. (Gibbethon: Philistine town, Philistine: enemies of Israel) 16. When the army heard that Zimri had killed Elah, they proclaimed Omri, the commander of the army, as king. (Omri: commander of the army) 17. Omri and his followers withdrew from Gibbethon and attacked Tirzah. 18. When Zimri saw the city was taken, he went to the royal palace's citadel and set it on fire, dying in the flames. (Citadel: stronghold) 19. Zimri's death came because of the evil he did, following in the footsteps of Jeroboam and leading Israel into sin. 20. The events of Zimri's short reign and the rebellion he led are written in the Book of the Chronicles of the Kings of Israel. 21. After Zimri's death, Israel was divided into two groups: one supported Tibni, son of Ginath, and the other supported Omri. (Tibni: rival claimant to the throne) 22. Omri's supporters were stronger, and Tibni died, leaving Omri as king. 23. In the 31st year of Asa's reign in Judah, Omri became king of Israel and ruled for 12 years, six of which were spent in Tirzah. (Asa: king of Judah, Tirzah: city in Israel) 24. Omri bought the hill of Samaria from Shemer for two talents of silver and built a city on it, naming it Samaria. (Samaria: city in Israel, later the capital) 25. Omri did evil in the eyes of the Lord, sinning more than any king before him. 26. He followed the ways of Jeroboam, leading Israel further into sin and provoking the Lord's anger with idols. 27. The rest of Omri's reign, his deeds, and achievements are written in the Book of the Chronicles of the Kings of Israel. 28. Omri died and was buried in Samaria. His son Ahab succeeded him as king. (Ahab: Omri's son) 29. In the 38th year of Asa's reign in Judah, Ahab, son of Omri, became king of Israel and ruled for 22 years in Samaria. (Asa: king of Judah, Samaria: city in Israel, capital of Israel later) 30. Ahab did more evil in the sight of the Lord than all the kings before him. 31. Not only did he continue the sins of Jeroboam, but he also married Jezebel, daughter of Ethbaal, king of the Sidonians. Ahab began to serve and worship Baal. (Jezebel: daughter of Ethbaal, Baal: a false god) 32. He built an altar to Baal in the temple of Baal in Samaria. (Samaria: city in Israel) 33. Ahab also made an Asherah pole, and he did more to provoke the Lord's anger than any king before him. (Asherah: a pagan goddess) 34. During Ahab's reign, Hiel of Bethel rebuilt the city of Jericho. He laid the foundations of the city at the cost of his firstborn son, Abiram, and set up its gates at the cost of his youngest son, Segub, fulfilling the word of the Lord spoken through Joshua, son of Nun. (Jericho: ancient city of Israel, Joshua: leader who brought Israel into the Promised Land)

Chapter 17

1. Elijah, the prophet from Tishbe in Gilead, spoke to King Ahab, saying, "As surely as the LORD, the God of Israel, lives and whom I serve, there will be no dew or rain for the coming years until I give the word." (Ahab: King of Israel, Tishbe: a town in Gilead, Gilead: area east of the Jordan River) 2. Then the word of the LORD came to Elijah: 3. "Go east, hide by the Kerith Brook, near the Jordan River." (Kerith Ravine: a stream east of the Jordan River) 4. "Drink from the brook, and I have commanded the ravens to bring you food there." (Ravens: large black birds) 5. Elijah obeyed the LORD's command and went to the Kerith Brook, where he stayed. 6. The ravens brought him bread and meat in the morning and evening, and he drank from the brook. (Meat: cooked flesh of animals, bread: food made from flour) 7. After some time, the brook dried up because there was no rain in the land. 8. The word of the LORD came to Elijah again: 9. "Go to Zarephath in the region of Sidon and stay there. I have commanded a widow in that town to provide you with food." (Zarephath: a city in Sidon, Sidon: ancient city in Phoenicia, now Lebanon, widow: a woman whose husband has died) 10. Elijah obeyed and went to Zarephath. Upon arriving at the city gate, he saw a widow gathering sticks. He called to her and said, "Please, bring me a little water in a jar so I can drink." (Sticks: small branches for a fire) 11. As she went to get it, he called after her, "Please bring me a small piece of bread as well." (Bread: food made from flour) 12. She answered, "As surely as the LORD your God lives, I have no bread—only a handful of flour in a jar and a little olive oil in a jug. I'm gathering sticks to make a final meal for myself and my son, that we may eat it and die." (jug: a container) 13. Elijah said to her, "Don't be afraid. Go ahead and do what you said, but first make a small loaf for me from what you have and bring it to me, and then prepare something for yourself and your son. (Loaf: a shaped piece of bread) 14. For this is what the LORD, the God of Israel, says: 'The flour in your jar will not run out, and the oil in your jug will not run dry until the day the LORD sends rain upon the land.'" 15. She went away and did as Elijah had told her. For many days, she, Elijah, and her son had enough food to eat. 16. The jar of flour was never empty, and the jug of oil never ran dry, because the LORD had promised through Elijah. 17. After some time, the widow's son became ill, and his condition worsened until he stopped breathing. 18. She said to Elijah, "What have you against me, O man of God? Did you come here to remind me of my sin and take my son's life?" (Sin: wrongdoing) 19. Elijah responded, "Give me your son." He took the boy from her arms, carried him to the upper room where he was staying, and laid him on his bed. (Upper room: a room on a higher floor) 20. Elijah cried out to the LORD, "LORD my God, have you brought tragedy upon this widow by causing her son to die?" (tragedy: great sorrow) 21. He stretched himself out on the boy three times and prayed, "LORD my God, let this boy's life return to him." 22. The LORD heard Elijah's prayer, and the boy's life returned to him, and he revived. (Revived: came back to life) 23. Elijah took the child, carried him down from the room into the house, and gave him back to his mother. He said, "Look, your son is alive!" 24. The woman replied to Elijah, "Now I know that you are a man of God, and that the word of the LORD from your mouth is truth."

Chapter 18

1. After a long period, in the third year of the drought, the LORD spoke to Elijah: "Go and present yourself to Ahab, and I will bring rain upon the land." (Ahab: King of Israel) 2. Elijah went to meet Ahab. By this time, the famine in Samaria had become very severe. (Samaria: capital of the northern kingdom of Israel) 3. Ahab had called Obadiah, who was in charge of his palace. (Obadiah: a faithful

servant of the LORD) **4.** While Jezebel was killing the LORD's prophets, Obadiah had hidden a hundred of them in caves, fifty in each, and provided them with food and water. (Jezebel: Queen of Israel, known for her evil acts) **5.** Ahab said to Obadiah, "Go through the land to all the springs and valleys. Perhaps we can find some grass to keep the horses and mules alive so we won't have to kill any of them." (Springs: natural water sources, valleys: low land areas between hills) **6.** They split the land between them, with Ahab heading one way and Obadiah the other. **7.** As Obadiah was walking, he encountered Elijah. When Obadiah recognized him, he bowed to the ground and asked, "Is it really you, my lord Elijah?" (Elijah: prophet of God) **8.** "Yes," Elijah answered. "Go tell your master, 'Elijah is here.'" **9.** Obadiah replied, "What have I done wrong, that you would put your servant in danger by sending me to Ahab, who may kill me?" (Servant: someone who serves another person) **10.** "I swear to you, as surely as the LORD your God lives, there is no kingdom or nation where my master has not sent someone to search for you. And whenever they couldn't find you, he made them swear they hadn't seen you." (Swear: to make a serious promise) **11.** "Now you want me to go and tell Ahab that Elijah is here? What will happen to me if you disappear on me again?" **12.** "I don't know where the Spirit of the LORD might take you after I leave. If I tell Ahab and he doesn't find you, he will kill me. Yet I have served the LORD from my youth." (Spirit: God's presence) **13.** "Haven't you heard, my lord, how I hid a hundred of the LORD's prophets when Jezebel was killing them? I kept them in two caves, fifty in each, and gave them food and water." (Prophets: people chosen by God to speak His word) **14.** "Now you tell me to go and tell Ahab, 'Elijah is here.' He will kill me!" **15.** Elijah responded, "As surely as the LORD Almighty lives, whom I serve, I will present myself to Ahab today." (LORD Almighty: God, who is all-powerful) **16.** Obadiah went to meet Ahab and informed him, and Ahab went to find Elijah. **17.** When Ahab saw Elijah, he said, "Is that you, you who have brought trouble to Israel?" (Trouble: caused problems) **18.** Elijah replied, "I haven't troubled Israel, but you and your father's house have. You have forsaken the LORD's commands and followed the Baals." (Baal: a false god) **19.** "Now, summon all the people of Israel to meet me on Mount Carmel. And bring the four hundred and fifty prophets of Baal, along with the four hundred prophets of Asherah, who eat at Jezebel's table." (Mount Carmel: a mountain in Israel, Asherah: a goddess worshipped with Baal) **20.** Ahab sent word throughout Israel and gathered the prophets on Mount Carmel. **21.** Elijah went before the people and said, "How long will you hesitate between two opinions? If the LORD is God, follow Him; but if Baal is God, follow him." But the people remained silent. (Hesitate: waver, be unsure) **22.** Then Elijah said, "I am the only prophet of the LORD left, but Baal has four hundred and fifty prophets." **23.** "Bring two bulls. Let the prophets of Baal choose one, cut it into pieces, and put it on the wood without setting fire to it. I will prepare the other bull and place it on the wood without setting fire to it." **24.** "Then you call on the name of your god, and I will call on the name of the LORD. The god who answers by fire—He is God." All the people agreed, saying, "What you say is good." **25.** Elijah said to the prophets of Baal, "Choose your bull and prepare it first, since there are so many of you. Call on the name of your god, but do not light the fire." **26.** They took the bull given to them and prepared it. Then they called on the name of Baal from morning until noon, shouting, "Baal, answer us!" But there was no response; no one answered. They danced around the altar they had made. (Altar: a structure for sacrifices). **27.** At noon, Elijah began to mock them. "Shout louder!" he said. "Surely he is a god! Perhaps he is deep in thought, or busy, or traveling. Maybe he is sleeping and needs to be awakened." (Mock: make fun of) **28.** So they shouted louder and cut themselves with swords and spears, as was their custom, until their blood flowed. (Cut: wound themselves, custom: a traditional practice) **29.** They continued their frantic prophesying until the time of the evening sacrifice, but there was no response, no one answered, and no one paid attention. (Frantic: wild or excited). **30.** Elijah then said to the people, "Come closer to me." They approached, and he repaired the altar of the LORD, which had been broken down. (Repaired: fixed or rebuilt) **31.** Elijah took twelve stones, one for each of the tribes of Israel, to whom the word of the LORD had come, saying, "Your name shall be Israel." (Tribes: the twelve groups descended from the sons of Jacob) **32.** With the stones, he built an altar in the name of the LORD. He dug a trench around it large enough to hold two seahs of seed. (Seah: a unit of measurement). **33.** He arranged the wood, cut the bull into pieces, and laid it on the wood. Then he said, "Fill four large jars with water and pour it on the offering and on the wood." **34.** "Do it again," he said, and they did it. "Do it a third time," he ordered, and they did it again. **35.** The water ran down around the altar and even filled the trench. **36.** At the time of the evening sacrifice, Elijah stepped forward and prayed, "LORD, the God of Abraham, Isaac, and Israel, let it be known today that you are God in Israel, and I am your servant. I have done all these things according to your command." (Abraham, Isaac, Israel: the patriarchs of Israel) **37.** "Answer me, LORD, answer me, so these people will know that you, LORD, are God, and that you are turning their hearts back again." (Hearts: thoughts and feelings). **38.** Then the fire of the LORD fell and consumed the sacrifice, the wood, the stones, and the soil. It also burned up the water in the trench. (Consumed: destroyed completely) **39.** When the people saw this, they fell on their faces and cried, "The LORD—He is God! The LORD—He is God!" (Faces: in worship or awe). **40.** Elijah commanded, "Seize the prophets of Baal. Don't let anyone escape!" They seized them, and Elijah had them taken to the Kishon Valley and executed there. (Kishon Valley: a valley near Mount Carmel) **41.** Elijah told Ahab, "Go, eat, and drink, for there is the sound of heavy rain." **42.** Ahab went to eat and drink, but Elijah climbed to the top of Mount Carmel, bent down to the ground, and placed his face between his knees. (Carmel: mountain in Israel) **43.** "Go and look toward the sea," Elijah told his servant. The servant went, but came back saying, "There is nothing there." Elijah told him seven times, "Go back." **44.** On the seventh time, the servant reported, "I see a small cloud rising from the sea, the size of a man's hand." Elijah said, "Go and tell Ahab, 'prepare your chariot and go down before the rain stops you.'" (Chariot: a vehicle drawn by horses) **45.** Meanwhile, the sky grew dark with clouds, the wind picked up, and a heavy rain began to fall. Ahab rode off to Jezreel. (Jezreel: a town in Israel). **46.** The power of the LORD came upon Elijah. He tucked his cloak into his belt and outran Ahab's chariot all the way to Jezreel. (Cloak: a long, flowing outer garment).

Chapter 19

1. Ahab told Jezebel everything that Elijah had done, including how he had killed all the prophets with a sword. **2.** Jezebel sent a messenger to Elijah with a warning: "May the gods deal with me, severely if I do not make your life like that of one of those prophets by this time tomorrow." (Prophets: religious leaders) **3.** Elijah was afraid and ran for his life. When he arrived at Beersheba in Judah, he left his servant there. (Beersheba: a city in Judah) **4.** Elijah then traveled alone for a day's journey into the wilderness. He found a broom tree, sat under it, and prayed, "I have had enough, LORD. Take my life; I am no better than my ancestors." (Broom tree: a type of shrub) **5.** He lay down under the tree and fell asleep. Suddenly, an angel touched him and said, "Get up and eat." **6.** Elijah looked around and saw that beside him was some bread baked on hot coals and a jar of water. He ate and drank, then lay down again. **7.** The angel of the LORD came back a second time and touched him, saying, "Get up and eat, for the journey is too much for you." **8.** Elijah ate and drank, and with new strength, he traveled for forty days and forty nights until he reached Horeb, the mountain of God. (Horeb: another name for Mount Sinai, where God spoke to Moses) **9.** There, he went into a cave and spent the night. The word of the LORD came to him: "Why are you here, Elijah?" **10.** Elijah answered, "I have been very zealous for the LORD God Almighty. The Israelites have rejected Your covenant, torn down Your altars, and killed Your prophets. I am the only one left, and now they are trying to kill me too." **11.** The LORD said, "Go out and stand on the mountain in My presence, for I am about to pass by." A great wind tore through the mountains, breaking the rocks into pieces before the LORD, but the LORD was not in the wind. **12.** After the wind, there was an earthquake, but the LORD was not in the earthquake. **13.** After the earthquake, there was a fire, but the LORD was not in the fire. And after the fire, there came a gentle whisper. **14.** When Elijah heard it, he pulled his cloak (a large piece of cloth worn over the body) over his face and went out to the mouth of the cave. Then, a voice asked, "What are you doing here, Elijah?" **15.** Elijah answered, "I have been very zealous for the LORD God Almighty. The Israelites have rejected Your covenant, torn down Your altars, and killed Your prophets. I am the only one left, and now they are trying to kill me too." **16.** The LORD said to him, "Go back the way you came, and go to the Desert of Damascus. (Damascus: a city in Syria) When you get there, anoint Hazael king over Aram. (Aram: ancient region, now part of Syria) **17.** Also, anoint Jehu son of Nimshi as king over Israel, and anoint Elisha son of Shaphat from Abel Meholah (Abel Meholah: a town in Israel) to succeed you as prophet. **18.** Jehu will put to death those who escape the sword of Hazael, and Elisha will put to death those who escape the sword of Jehu. **19.** Yet I have reserved seven thousand in Israel, all whose knees have not bowed down to Baal (Baal: a false god) or kissed him." **20.** Elijah went from there and found Elisha son of Shaphat. Elisha was plowing with twelve pairs of oxen, and he was driving the twelfth pair. Elijah went up to him and threw his cloak over him. **21.** Elisha immediately left his oxen and ran after Elijah, saying, "Let me kiss my father and mother goodbye, and then I will follow you." Elijah replied, "Go back. What have I done to you?" **22.** Elisha returned, took his oxen, slaughtered them, used the plowing equipment to cook the meat, and gave it to the people, and they ate. Then he set out to follow Elijah and became his servant.

Chapter 20

1. Now Ben-Hadad king of Aram mustered his entire army. Accompanied by thirty-two kings with their horses and chariots, he went up and besieged Samaria and attacked it. (Aram: region, now Syria; Samaria: capital of Israel) **2.** He sent messengers into the city to Ahab king of Israel, saying, "This is what Ben-Hadad says: **3.** 'Your silver and gold are mine, and the best of your wives and children are mine.'" **4.** The king of Israel answered, "Just as you say, my lord the king. I and all I have are yours." **5.** The messengers came again and said, "This is what Ben-Hadad says: 'I sent to demand your silver and gold, your wives and your children. **6.** But about this time tomorrow I am going to send my officials to search your palace and the houses of your officials. They will seize everything you value and carry it away.'" **7.** The king of Israel summoned all the elders of the land and said to them, "See how this man is looking for trouble! When he sent for my wives and my children, my silver and my gold, I did not refuse him." **8.** The elders and the people all answered, "Don't listen to him or agree to his demands." **9.** So he replied to Ben-Hadad's messengers, "Tell my lord the king, 'Your servant will do all you demanded the first time, but this demand I cannot meet.'" They left and took the answer back to Ben-Hadad. **10.** Then Ben-Hadad sent another message to Ahab: "May the gods deal with me, be it ever so severely, if enough dust remains in Samaria to give each of my men a handful." (Samaria: capital of Israel) **11.** The king of Israel answered, "Tell him: 'One who puts on his armor should not boast like one who takes it off.'" **12.** Ben-Hadad heard this message while he and the kings were drinking in their tents, and he ordered his men: "Prepare to attack." So they prepared to attack the city. **13.** Meanwhile, a prophet came to Ahab king of Israel and announced, "This is what the LORD says: 'Do you see this vast army? I will give it into your hand today, and then you will know that I am the LORD.'" **14.** "But who will do this?" asked Ahab. The prophet replied, "This is what the LORD says: 'The junior officers under the provincial commanders will do it.'" "And who will start the battle?" he asked. The prophet answered, "You will." **15.** So Ahab summoned the 232 junior officers under the provincial commanders. Then he assembled the rest of the Israelites, 7,000 in all. **16.** They set out at noon while Ben-Hadad and the 32 kings allied with him were in their tents getting drunk. **17.** The junior officers under the provincial commanders went out first. Now Ben-Hadad had dispatched scouts, who reported, "Men are advancing from Samaria." (Samaria: capital of Israel) **18.** He said, "If they have come out for peace, take them alive; if they have come out for war, take them alive." **19.** The junior officers under the provincial commanders marched out of the city with the army behind them **20.** and each one struck down his opponent. At that, the Arameans fled, with the Israelites in pursuit. But Ben-Hadad king of Aram escaped on horseback with some of his horsemen. (Aram: region, now Syria) **21.** The king of Israel advanced and overpowered the horses and chariots and inflicted heavy losses on the Arameans. **22.** Afterward, the prophet came to the king of Israel and said, "Strengthen your position and see what must be done, because next spring the king of Aram will attack you again." **23.** Meanwhile, the officials of the king of Aram advised him, "Their gods are gods of the hills. That is why they were too strong for us. But if we fight them on the plains, surely we will be stronger than they. **24.** Do this: Remove all the kings from their commands and replace them with other officers. **25.** You must also raise an army like the one you lost—horse for horse and chariot for chariot—so we can fight Israel on the plains. Then surely we will be stronger than they." He agreed with them and acted accordingly. **26.** The next spring Ben-Hadad mustered the Arameans and went up to Aphek to fight against Israel. (Aphek: city of battle) **27.** When the Israelites were also mustered and given provisions, they marched out to meet them. The Israelites camped opposite them like two small flocks of goats, while the Arameans covered the countryside. **28.** The man of God came up and told the king of Israel, "This is what the LORD says: 'Because the Arameans think the LORD is a god of the hills and not a god of the valleys, I will deliver this vast army into your hands, and you will know that I am the LORD.'" **29.** For seven days they camped opposite each other, and on the seventh day the battle was joined. The Israelites inflicted a hundred thousand casualties on the Aramean foot soldiers in one day. **30.** The rest of them escaped to the city of Aphek, where the wall collapsed on twenty-seven thousands of them. And Ben-Hadad fled to the city and hid in an inner room. **31.** His officials said to him, "Look, we have heard that the kings of Israel are merciful. Let us go to the king of Israel with sackcloth around our waists and ropes around our heads. Perhaps he will spare your life." **32.** Wearing sackcloth around their waists and ropes around their heads, they went to the king of Israel and said, "Your servant Ben-Hadad says: 'Please let me live.'" The king answered, "Is he still alive? He is my brother." **33.** The men took this as a good sign and were quick to pick up his word. "Yes, your brother Ben-Hadad!" they said. "Go and get him," the king said. When Ben-Hadad came out, Ahab had him come up into his chariot. **34.** "I will return the cities my father took from your father," Ben-Hadad offered. "You may set up your own market areas in Damascus, as my father did in Samaria." (Damascus: capital of Aram) Ahab said, "On the basis of a treaty I will set you free." So he made a treaty with him, and let him go. **35.** By the word of the LORD one of the company of the prophets said to his companion, "Strike me with your weapon," but he refused. **36.** So the prophet said, "Because you have not obeyed the LORD, as soon as you leave me a lion will kill you." And after the man went away, a lion found him and killed him. **37.** The prophet found another man and said, "Strike me, please." So the man struck him and wounded him. **38.** Then the prophet went and stood by the road waiting for the king. He disguised himself with his headband down over his eyes. (disguised : personate) **39.** As the king passed by, the prophet called out to him, "Your servant went into the thick of the battle, and someone came to me with a captive and said, 'Guard this man. If he is missing, it will be your life for his life, or you must pay a talent of silver.' **40.** While your servant was busy here and there, the man disappeared." "That is your sentence," the king of Israel said. "You have pronounced it yourself." **41.** Then the prophet quickly removed the headband from his eyes, and the king of Israel recognized him as one of the prophets. **42.** He said to the king, "This is what the LORD says: 'You have set free a man I had determined should die. Therefore it is your life for his life, your people for his people.'" **43.** Sullen and angry, the king of Israel went to his palace in Samaria. (Samaria: capital of Israel)

Chapter 21

1. Sometime later there was an incident involving a vineyard belonging to Naboth the Jezreelite. The vineyard was in Jezreel, close to the palace of Ahab king of Samaria. (Jezreel: a city in Israel; Ahab: king of Israel; Samaria: capital of Israel) **2.** Ahab said to Naboth, "Let me have your vineyard to use for a vegetable garden, since it is close to my palace. In exchange I will give you a better vineyard or, if you prefer, I will pay you whatever it is worth." **3.** But Naboth replied, "The LORD forbids that I should give you the inheritance of my ancestors." (Inheritance: something passed down through generations) **4.** So Ahab went home, sullen and angry because Naboth the Jezreelite had said, "I will not give you the inheritance of my ancestors." He lay on his bed sulking and refused to eat. (Sullen: gloomy) **5.** His wife Jezebel came in and asked him, "Why are you so sullen? Why won't you eat?" **6.** He answered her, "Because I said to Naboth the Jezreelite, 'Sell me your vineyard; or if you prefer, I will give you another vineyard in its place.' But he said, 'I will not give you my vineyard.'" **7.** Jezebel his wife said, "Is this how you act as king over Israel? Get up and eat! Cheer up. I'll get you the vineyard of Naboth the Jezreelite." (Israel: the northern kingdom; king over Israel: Ahab's role) **8.** So she wrote letters in Ahab's name, placed his seal on them, and sent them to the elders and nobles who lived in Naboth's city with him. (Seal: official mark or signature) **9.** In those letters she wrote: "Proclaim a day of fasting and seat Naboth in a prominent place among the people. **10.** But seat two scoundrels opposite him and have them bring charges that he has cursed both God and the king. Then take him out and stone him to death." (Scoundrels: dishonest people). **11.** So the elders and nobles who lived in Naboth's city did as Jezebel directed in the letters she had written to them. **12.** They proclaimed a fast and seated Naboth in a prominent place among the people. **13.** Then two scoundrels came and sat opposite him and brought charges against Naboth before the people, saying, "Naboth has cursed both God and the king." So they took him outside the city and stoned him to death. (Stoned: executed by throwing stones) **14.** Then they sent word to Jezebel: "Naboth has been stoned to death." **15.** As soon as Jezebel heard that Naboth had been stoned to death, she said to Ahab, "Get up and take possession of the vineyard of Naboth the Jezreelite that he refused to sell you. He is no longer alive, but dead." **16.** When Ahab heard that Naboth was dead, he got up and went down to take possession of Naboth's vineyard. **17.** Then the word of the LORD came to Elijah the Tishbite: (Elijah: prophet of God; Tishbite: from Tishbe, a town) **18.** "Go down to meet Ahab king of Israel, who rules in Samaria. He is now in Naboth's vineyard, where he has gone to take possession of it. (Samaria: capital of Israel) **19.** Say to him, 'this is what the LORD says: Have you not murdered a man and seized his property?' Then say to him, 'This is what the LORD says: In the place where dogs licked up Naboth's blood, dogs will lick up your blood—yes, yours!'" (Dogs: scavengers; symbolic of disgrace). **20.** Ahab said to Elijah, "So you have found me, my enemy!" "I have found you," he answered, "because you have sold yourself to do evil in the eyes of the LORD. (sold yourself: committed to evil actions) **21.** He says, 'I am going to bring disaster on you. I will wipe out your descendants and cut off from Ahab every last male in Israel—slave or free. (disaster: ruin; descendants: children and their offspring) **22.** I will make your house like that of Jeroboam son of Nebat and that of Baasha son of Ahijah, because you have aroused my anger and have caused Israel to sin.' (Jeroboam: former king of Israel, known for leading Israel into sin; Baasha: king of Israel, also associated with sin) **23.** "And also concerning Jezebel the LORD says: 'Dogs will devour Jezebel by the wall of Jezreel.' (Jezreel: city in Israel). **24.** "Dogs will eat those belonging to Ahab who die in the city, and the birds will feed on those who die in the country." (birds: symbolic of scavengers) **25.** (There was never anyone like Ahab, who sold himself to do evil in the eyes of the LORD, urged on by Jezebel his wife. (sold himself: committed fully to evil) **26.** He behaved in the vilest manner by going after idols, like the Amorites the LORD drove out before Israel.) (Amorites: ancient people whom God ordered Israel to drive out). **27.** When Ahab heard these words, he tore his clothes, put on sackcloth and fasted. He lay in sackcloth and went around meekly. (Sackcloth: rough cloth worn as a sign of mourning; meekly: humbly) **28.** Then the word of the LORD came to Elijah the Tishbite: **29.** "Have you noticed how Ahab has humbled himself before me? Because he has humbled himself, I will not bring this disaster in his day, but I will bring it on his house in the days of his son." (humbled himself: showed remorse)

Chapter 22

1. For three years, there was peace between the kingdoms of Aram and Israel. **2.** In the third year, Jehoshaphat, the king of Judah, went to visit Ahab, the king of Israel. (Jehoshaphat: King of Judah; Ahab: King of Israel) **3.** Ahab said to his officials, "Don't you know that Ramoth Gilead belongs to us, but we're doing nothing to take it back from Aram?" (Ramoth Gilead: A city east of Israel, contested by Israel and Aram) **4.** Ahab asked Jehoshaphat, "Will you go with me to fight for Ramoth Gilead?" Jehoshaphat replied, "I am as you are, my people are your people, and my horses are your horses." **5.** But Jehoshaphat also said, "First, let's ask the LORD what He thinks." **6.** So Ahab gathered about four hundred prophets and asked them, "Should we go to war against Ramoth Gilead, or should we hold back?" They all answered, "Go ahead, for the LORD will give you victory." **7.** Jehoshaphat wasn't convinced, and asked, "Is there no prophet of the LORD here whom we can ask?" **8.** Ahab answered, "There is one more, Micaiah son of Imlah, but I hate him because he never says anything good about me, only bad." Jehoshaphat replied, "The king should not speak like that." (Micaiah: A prophet who speaks the truth, even when it's unpleasant) **9.** So Ahab called one of his officials and said, "Bring Micaiah son of Imlah at once." **10.** Both Ahab and Jehoshaphat were sitting on their thrones in royal robes at the entrance to the gate of Samaria, with all the prophets prophesying before them. (Samaria: Capital city of ancient Israel) **11.** One of the prophets, Zedekiah son of Kenaanah, made iron horns and declared, "This is what the LORD says: 'With these you will gore the Arameans until they are destroyed.'" **12.** All the other prophets said the same thing, "Attack Ramoth Gilead and be victorious, for the LORD will give it into your hands." **13.** The messenger who had gone to summon Micaiah told him, "Look, all the other prophets are predicting success for the king. Please let your words agree with theirs and speak favorably." **14.** But Micaiah said, "As surely as the LORD lives, I can only speak what the LORD tells me." **15.** When Micaiah arrived, the king asked him, "Micaiah, should we go to war against Ramoth Gilead or not?" Micaiah answered, "Attack and be victorious, for the LORD will give it into the king's hands." **16.** The king said to him, "How many times must I make you swear to tell me nothing but the truth in the name of the LORD?" **17.** Then Micaiah replied, "I saw all Israel scattered on the hills like sheep without a shepherd, and the LORD said, 'These people have no leader; let each one return home in peace.'" (no shepherd: A metaphor for a leaderless nation) **18.** Ahab said to Jehoshaphat, "Didn't I tell you that he never prophesies anything good about me, only disaster?" **19.** Micaiah continued, "Therefore hear the word of the LORD: I saw the LORD sitting on His throne with all the heavenly hosts around

Him, on His right and left. (Hosts: armies) **20.** And the LORD said, 'Who will entice Ahab into attacking Ramoth Gilead and meeting his death there?' Some spirits suggested one thing, others another. (Entice: tempt; Spirits: beings) **21.** Finally, one spirit came forward and said, 'I will entice him.' (Came forward: approached) **22.** The LORD asked, 'How will you do that?' The spirit answered, 'I will go and put a lying spirit in the mouths of all his prophets.' The LORD replied, 'You will succeed in enticing him, go and do it.' (Lying: false; Prophets: messengers) **23.** So now the LORD has put a lying spirit in the mouths of all these prophets of yours. The LORD has decreed disaster for you." (Decreed: declared; Disaster: calamity) **24.** Then Zedekiah son of Kenaanah went up to Micaiah and slapped him in the face. "Which way did the spirit from the LORD go when he left me to speak to you?" he asked. (Slapped: struck; Face: cheek) **25.** Micaiah replied, "You will find out on the day you go to hide in an inner room." (Hide: shelter; Inner: private) **26.** The king of Israel then ordered, "Take Micaiah and send him back to Amon, the ruler of the city, and to Joash, the king's son, (Ordered: commanded; Ruler: governor) **27.** and say, 'This is what the king says: Put this man in prison and feed him only bread and water until I return safely.'" (Prison: jail) **28.** Micaiah declared, "If you ever return safely, the LORD has not spoken through me. Listen to this, all you people!" (Declared: proclaimed; Safely: unharmed) **29.** So the king of Israel and Jehoshaphat, king of Judah, went up to Ramoth Gilead. (Went up: traveled; Ramoth Gilead: location) **30.** The king of Israel told Jehoshaphat, "I will disguise myself in the battle, but you wear your royal robes." So the king of Israel disguised himself, and they entered the battle. (Disguise: conceal; Royal: regal) **31.** The king of Aram had ordered his thirty-two chariot commanders, "Don't fight anyone, small or great, except the king of Israel." (Aram: A neighboring kingdom of Israel) **32.** When the chariot commanders saw Jehoshaphat, they thought he was the king of Israel and turned to attack him. But when Jehoshaphat cried out, **33.** the chariot commanders realized he was not Ahab, and they stopped pursuing him. **34.** A man randomly shot an arrow and struck Ahab between the joints of his armor. Ahab told his chariot driver, "Turn the chariot around and get me out of the battle, I've been wounded." **35.** The battle continued all day, and Ahab was propped up in his chariot, facing the Arameans. His wound bled onto the floor of the chariot, and by evening he died. **36.** As the sun was setting, a cry went through the army: "Every man to his town, every man to his land!" **37.** So the king died and was brought back to Samaria, where he was buried. (Samaria: central region of the Land of Israel) **38.** They washed the chariot at the pool in Samaria (a place where prostitutes bathed), and the dogs licked up his blood, just as the word of the LORD had foretold. **39.** The other events of Ahab's reign, including all he did, the palace he built and decorated with ivory, and the cities he fortified, are they not written in the book of the annals of the kings of Israel? (ivory: a luxury material; annals: royal records) **40.** Ahab rested with his ancestors, and his son Ahaziah succeeded him as king. (Ahaziah: Ahab's son and successor) **41.** Jehoshaphat, son of Asa, became king of Judah in the fourth year of Ahab's reign. (Asa: Jehoshaphat's father) **42.** Jehoshaphat was thirty-five when he began his reign and ruled for twenty-five years in Jerusalem. His mother's name was Azubah, daughter of Shilhi. (Jerusalem: city in the Southern Levant) **43.** Jehoshaphat followed the ways of his father Asa, doing what was right in the eyes of the LORD. However, the high places were not removed, and people continued to offer sacrifices there. (High places: areas for idol worship) **44.** Jehoshaphat was at peace with the king of Israel. (Peace: friendly relationship). **45.** The other events of Jehoshaphat's reign, including his military victories, are recorded in the annals of the kings of Judah. (Annals: royal records). **46.** He removed the male shrine prostitutes who remained even after his father's reign. (shrine prostitutes: men who engaged in cultic sexual practices) **47.** At that time, there was no king in Edom; a provincial governor ruled. (Edom: A kingdom to the south of Judah) **48.** Jehoshaphat built ships to sail to Ophir for gold, but they were wrecked at Ezion Geber. (Ophir: A distant, rich land; Ezion Geber: A port on the Red Sea) **49.** Ahaziah, son of Ahab, suggested that his men sail with Jehoshaphat's, but Jehoshaphat refused. **50.** Then Jehoshaphat died and was buried with his ancestors in the city of David. His son Jehoram succeeded him as king. **51.** Ahaziah, son of Ahab, became king of Israel in Samaria in the seventeenth year of Jehoshaphat's reign. He reigned over Israel for two years. **52.** Ahaziah did evil in the sight of the LORD, following the ways of his father, mother, and Jeroboam, who caused Israel to sin. (Jeroboam: the first king of the divided northern kingdom of Israel) **53.** Ahaziah served and worshiped Baal, provoking the LORD's anger, just as his father had done. (Baal: a false god worshiped by the Canaanites)

12 – 2 Kings
Chapter 1

1. After Ahab's death, Moab mutinied against Israel. (Mutinied : defied authority; Moab : an ancient area east of Israel) **2.** Ahaziah, king of Israel, fell through the latticework of his upper room in Samaria and was poorly injured. He transferred couriers, saying, "Go ask Baal:Zebub, the god of Ekron, if I'll recover." (Latticework : bisecting strips; Ekron : an ancient Philistine megacity) **3.** the angel of the Lord spoke to Elijah the Tishbite, saying, "Go meet the couriers of the king of Samaria and say to them, 'Is there no God in Israel that you interrogate of Baal:Zebub, the god of Ekron?'" (Angel –Divine creatures; Tishbite : from Tishbe in Gilead) **4.** "Thus, the Lord says, 'You won't rise from your bed; you'll surely die.'" Elijah departed. (Rise : get up; Bed : place of rest) **5.** When the couriers returned, the king asked, "Why have you come back?" (Couriers : those who deliver dispatches) **6.** they replied, "A man met us and said, 'Return to the king and tell him, "Therefore says the Lord: Is it because there's no God in Israel that you interrogate of Baal:Zebub, the god of Ekron? You'll die."' (Inquire : ask for information) **7.** The king asked, "What kind of man was it who met you?" (Kind : type, sort) **8.** They answered, "A man with a rough appearance, wearing a leather belt." The king said, "It was Elijah the Tishbite." (Rough : harsh or wild in appearance; Leather : made from beast hide) **9.** The king transferred a captain with fifty dogfaces to find Elijah. They set up him sitting on a hill. The captain called, "Man of God, the king says, 'Come down!'" (Captain : leader; Hill : raised land) **10.** Elijah answered, "If I'm a man of God, let fire come down from heaven and consume you and your fifty men." Fire came down and consumed them. (Consume : destroy fully; incontinently : without detention) **11.** The king transferred another captain with fifty men. He called to Elijah, "Man of God, the king says, 'Come down snappily!'" (Snappily : without detention; Called : spoke audibly) **12.** Elijah answered, "If I'm a man of God, let fire come down from heaven and consume you and your fifty men." Again, fire came down and consumed them. (Fire : a hot, burning substance) **13.** the king transferred a third captain with fifty men. The captain approached, fell on his knees, and contended, "Man of God, please spare my life and the lives of these fifty men." (Approached : came near to; Plead : request earnestly) **14.** "Look, fire has consumed the first two captains and their men. But let my life be precious." (Destroyed : caused to cease to live; Precious : of great value) **15.** The angel of the Lord told Elijah, "Go down with him; don't be hysterical." Elijah arose and went down with him to the king. (Arose : got up; Hysterical : feeling fear) **16.** Elijah told the king, "The Lord says, 'Because you transferred couriers to interrogate of Baal:Zebub, the god of Ekron, is it because there's no God in Israel to seek His counsel? You'll die.'" (Inquire : seek information; Counsel : advice) **17** Ahaziah failed as the Lord had spoken. Since Ahaziah had no son, Jehoram, son of Jehoshaphat, came king in his place during the alternate time of Jehoram, king of Judah. (Jehoram : a king of Israel; Jehoshaphat : a king of Judah) **18** The rest of Ahaziah's deeds are written in the book of the chronicles of the lords of Israel. (Deeds : conduct or acts)

Chapter 2

1. When the Lord was ready to take Elijah up to heaven in a whirlwind, Elijah and Elisha traveled from Gilgal together. (Whirlwind : rotating wind) 2. Elijah said to Elisha, "Please stay also, for the Lord has transferred me to Bethel." Elisha replied, "As the Lord lives and as you live, I will not leave you!" So, they went to Bethel. 3. The prophets from Bethel approached Elisha and asked, "Do you know the Lord will take your master moment?" He replied, "Yes, I know. Be quiet!" 4. Elijah said, "Stay also, for the Lord has transferred me to Jericho." Elisha answered, "As the Lord lives and as you live, I will not leave you!" So, they went to Jericho. 5. The prophets from Jericho asked Elisha, "Do you know the Lord will take your master moment?" He responded, "Yes, I know. Be silent!" 6. Elijah said, "Stay also, for the Lord has transferred me to the Jordan River." Elisha replied, "As the Lord lives and as you live, I will not leave you!" So, they went on. (Jordan : swash) 7. Fifty prophets stood at a distance while Elijah and Elisha stood by the Jordan River. 8. Elijah took his cloak, rolled it up, and struck the water. It parted, and they crossed on dry land. (Cloak : garment) 9. After crossing, Elijah asked, "What can I do for you before I am taken?" Elisha answered, "Please let a double portion of your spirit be upon me." (Spirit : power). 10. Elijah replied, "You've asked for something difficult. However, it will be granted; if not, it won't, if you see me taken." 11. As they walked, suddenly a chariot and horses of fire appeared, separating them. Elijah was taken up by a whirlwind. (Whirlwind : rotating wind) 12. Elisha cried, "My father, my father, the chariot of Israel and its horsemen!" He no longer saw Elijah and tore his clothes in grief. (Tore : ripped) 13 Elisha picked up Elijah's departed cloak and went back to the Jordan River. 14 He struck the water with the cloak and asked, "Where is the Lord God of Elijah?" The water parted, and Elisha crossed. 15 The prophets from Jericho saw this and said, "The spirit of Elijah rests on Elisha." They bowed to him in respect. (Spirit : power) 16 they said, "There are fifty strong men with your retainers. Let them search for your master, in case the Lord's spirit took him down." Elisha replied, "Don't shoot anyone." 17 When they claimed, Elisha reluctantly agreed. They searched for three days but didn't find him. 18 When they returned, Elisha asked, "Didn't I say not to go?" 19 The men of the municipality came and said, "The municipality is good, but the water is defiled and the land unproductive." (Defiled : weakened) 20 Elisha said "Bring me a new bowl with tar." They brought it. (Bowl : vessel) 21 Elisha went to the water's source, threw in the tar, and declared, "The Lord says 'I have healed this water. It will no longer beget death or emptiness.'" (Healed : restored) 22 The water remains healed to this day, according to Elisha's word. 23 Elisha went to Bethel. On the road, some immature people mocked him, saying, "Get out, baldhead!" (Mocked : derided) 24 Elisha turned, cursed them in the Lord's name, and two womanish bears came out, mishandling forty:two youths. (Cursed : condemned) 25 Elisha went to Mount Carmel and also returned to Samaria. (Mount Carmel : a mountain range now in northern Israel)

Chapter 3

1. Now Jehoram, the son of Ahab, came king over Israel in Samaria during the eighteenth time of Jehoshaphat, king of Judah, and reigned twelve times. (Samaria : capital megacity of ancient Israel) 2. He did evil in the sight of the Lord, but not as his parents; he removed the Baal pillar his father made. (Baal : false god) 3. He continued the sins of Jeroboam, son of Nebat, who led Israel to stray. He didn't turn down from them. (Jeroboam : first king of Israel; Nebat : Jeroboam's father) 4. Mesha, king of Moab, a cowgirl, regularly paid the king of Israel one hundred thousand innocents and hair from one hundred thousand rams. (Mesha : king of Moab; homage : payment) 5. When Ahab failed, the king of Moab mutinied against Israel's king. (Mutinied : defied authority) 6. King Jehoram left Samaria and gathered Israel's forces. (Samaria : capital megacity of Israel) 7. He transferred a communication to Jehoshaphat, king of Judah: "The king of Moab has mutinied. Will you fight with me against him?" Jehoshaphat replied, "I'll go; my people are your people, my nags are yours." (Jehoshaphat : king of Judah) 8. Jehoram asked, "Which way shall we go?" Jehoshaphat said, "Through the Nature of Edom." (Edom : region southeast of Israel) 9. The king of Israel, Judah, and Edom marched on a circular route for seven days, but there was no water for the army or creatures. (Circular : circular) 10. The king of Israel said, "Alas! The Lord has brought these three lords together to deliver them to Moab." (Alas : expression of remorse) 11. Jehoshaphat asked, "Is there no prophet of the Lord we can consult?" One menial of Israel's king replied, "Elisha, son of Shaphat, is then; he served Elijah by pouring water on his hands." (Elisha : prophet of Israel) 12. Jehoshaphat said, "The word of the Lord is with him." So the three lords went to Elisha. (Word of the Lord : God's communication) 13. Elisha said to the king of Israel, "What do I have to do with you? Go to your father's and mama's prophets." The king replied, "No, the Lord has called these three lords together to deliver us to Moab." (Prophets : Messenger chosen by God) 14. Elisha answered, "As the Lord of hosts lives, if it weren't for Jehoshaphat, king of Judah, I wouldn't even look at you." (Lord of hosts : God, sovereign of heavenly armies) 15. "But bring me a musician." As the musician played, the hand of the Lord came upon Elisha. (Hand of the Lord : God's power) 16. Elisha said, "The Lord says, 'Dig fosses in this vale.'" (Fosses : dikes) 17. The Lord says, 'You won't see wind or rain, but this vale will be filled with water for you, your cattle, and creatures.' (Cattle –Domesticated animals) 18. This is easy for the Lord; He'll also deliver Moab into your hands. (Moab : bordering area of Israel) 19. You'll attack every fortified megacity and choice megacity, cut down every good tree, stop up every spring of water, and ruin the land with monuments. (Fortified : defended) 20. the coming morning, when the grain immolation was made, water suddenly came from Edom and filled the land. (Grain offering : food immolation to God) 21. When the Moabites heard the lords were coming, all who could bear arms gathered and stood at the border. (Moabites : people of Moab; Bear arms : carry weapons) 22. They rose beforehand, and the sun shone on the water, which appeared as red as blood. (Red as blood : pictorial color) 23. They said, "This is blood; the lords must have fought and killed each other. Now, Moab, to the loot!" (Spoil : plunder) 24. When they reached Israel's camp, Israel rose up and attacked the Moabites, causing them to flee. They pursued them, killing Moabites. (Pursued : chased) 25. They destroyed metropolises, threw monuments on every good piece of land, stopped all the springs of water, and cut down every good tree, except at Kir Haraseth, where slingers attacked it. (Slingers : Special troops who use slings) 26. When the king of Moab saw the battle was too fierce, he took seven hundred men with brands to break through to the king of Edom, but they failed. (Fierce : violent) 27. He also took his eldest son, who was to succeed him, and offered him as a burnt immolation on the wall. This caused great outrage against Israel, and they withdrew to their land. (Burnt immolation : immolation by fire; outrage : wrathfulness)

Chapter 4

1. A woman, whose husband was one of the prophets' disciples, cried out to Elisha, saying, "My husband, your servant, has passed away, and you know he honored the Lord. Now, the creditor is coming to take my two sons as his slaves." (Creditor: lender, Slaves: servants) 2. Elisha asked her, "What can I do for you? Tell me, what do you have in your house?" She replied, "I have nothing in my house except a small jar of oil." (Jar: container) 3. Elisha instructed her, "Go, ask your neighbors for empty containers—borrow as many as you can." 4. "Once you have gathered them, go inside your home, shut the door behind you and your sons, and start pouring oil into the containers. Set aside each one as it becomes full." 5. She followed his instructions, closing the door and pouring oil as her sons brought the containers to her. She filled them all. 6. When all the containers were full, she said to her son, "Bring me another container." He replied, "There are no more." Then the oil stopped flowing. (Ceased:

stopped) **7.** She went back to Elisha and told him what had happened. He said, "Go, sell the oil to pay your debt, and you and your sons can live on what is left." **8.** One day, Elisha traveled to Shunem, where a wealthy woman invited him to eat. From that time on, whenever he passed by, he would stop there for a meal. (Shunem: town) **9.** She said to her husband, "I know this man who passes by is a holy man of God." **10.** "Let's build a small room on the roof with a bed, table, chair, and lamp for him. Whenever he comes, he can rest there." **11.** One day, Elisha came to that room, entered, and rested there. **12.** He said to his servant Gehazi, "Call the woman from Shunem." When she came, she stood before him. **13.** Elisha asked her, "You have shown great kindness to us. What can I do for you? Would you like me to speak on your behalf to the king or the commander of the army?" She replied, "I live among my own people." (Commander: leader) **14.** Elisha asked, "What can be done for her then?" Gehazi answered, "She has no son, and her husband is old." **15.** Elisha told Gehazi, "Call her." When she came to the doorway, (Gehazi: servant) **16.** Elisha said, "This time next year, you will hold a son in your arms." She replied, "No, my lord. Man of God, please do not deceive me!" (Deceive: mislead) **17.** But, just as Elisha had promised, the woman became pregnant and gave birth to a son when the time came, exactly as Elisha had foretold. (Foretold: predicted) **18.** The boy grew, and one day he went out to his father, who was working with the reapers. (Reapers: harvesters) **19.** He complained to his father, "My head! My head!" His father told a servant, "Take him to his mother." **20.** The servant brought the boy to his mother, and he sat on her lap until noon, when he died. **21.** She carried him up to Elisha's room, laid him on the prophet's bed, shut the door, and left. (Lay: placed) **22.** She called her husband and said, "Send me one of the servants and a donkey so I can go quickly to the man of God and return." **23.** He asked, "Why go to him today? It's neither the New Moon nor the Sabbath." She answered, "It is fine." (Sabbath: day of rest) **24.** She saddled a donkey, told the servant, "Lead on, don't slow down unless I tell you." **25.** She set out and traveled to Mount Carmel. When Elisha saw her coming from a distance, he said to Gehazi, "Look, there is the Shunammite woman!" **26.** "Run to meet her and ask her, 'Are you well? Is your husband well? Is your son well?'" She answered, "Yes, everything is fine." (Carmel: mountain in present day northern Israel) **27.** When she reached Elisha, she took hold of his feet. Gehazi tried to push her away, but Elisha said, "Leave her alone. She is in great distress, and the Lord has not revealed to me what is wrong." (Distress: suffering) **28.** She said, "Did I ask for a son, my lord? Didn't I tell you not to deceive me?" (Deceive: trick) **29.** Also Elisha instructed Gehazi, "Prepare yourself, take my staff, and go. However, do n't stop to hail them; and if anyone greets you, do n't respond, If you come across anyone. Lay my staff on the child's face." (Staff: rod; hail : admit; respond : reply) **30.** But the child's ma replied, "As surely as the Lord lives and as you live, I will not leave you." So Elisha stood up and followed her. (Surely : easily; live : exist) **31.** Gehazi rushed ahead and placed the staff on the child's face, but there was no response — no sound or sign of life. He returned to meet Elisha and reported, "The child has not revived." (Revived : restored) **32.** when Elisha entered the house, he saw the child lying dead on the bed. **33.** He went in, shut the door behind him and the child, and appealed to the Lord. (appealed : solicited) **34.** Also Elisha lay on top of the child, pressing his mouth to the child's mouth, his eyes to the child's eyes, and his hands to the child's hands. He stretched out over the child, and the child's body came warm. (Pressed : applied pressure; stretched out : extended) **35.** Elisha walked back and forth in the room, also returned to stretch himself over the child again. The child sneezed seven times and opened his eyes. (Sneezed : exhaled explosively) **36.** Elisha called to Gehazi and said, "Summon the Shunammite woman." Gehazi called her, and when she arrived, Elisha said, "Take your son." (Summon : call) **37** She entered, fell at his bases, and bowed in appreciativeness. Also, she picked up her son and left the room. (Bowed : Incline the head) **38.** Elisha went back to Gilgal. There was a deficit in the land, and the prophets' sons sat before him. He said to his slavish, "Prepare a large pot and cook a stew for the sons of the prophets." (deficit : failure; stew : haze) **39.** One went to gather gravies, set up a wild vine, picked a basketful of wild gourds, sliced them, and put them in the stew, though they didn't know what they were. (vine : plant; gourds –a type of Vegetable) **40.** As they served the stew, one cried, "Man of God, there's bane in the pot!" They couldn't eat it **41.** Elisha said, "Bring me some flour." He threw it in the pot and said, "Now serve it to the people, and they can eat." There was no detriment in the stew. (Flour : ground grain) **42.** A man came from Baal Shalisha, bringing Elisha twenty loaves of barley chuck and some fresh grain in his sack. He said, "Give it to the people to eat." (Baal Shalisha : a place; barley : grain) **43.** Elisha's slavish asked, "How can I serve this to one hundred men?" Elisha replied, "Give it to the people, for the Lord says, 'They will eat and have leavings.'" (Leavings : remnants) **44.** The slavish served the loaves, and they ate until satisfied, with leavings, as the Lord had promised. (Satisfied : full)

Chapter 5

1. Now Naaman, commander of the Syrian army, was a great and honorable man in his master's eyes, as the Lord had given palm to Syria through him. He was a potent man of valor, but a pariah. (pariah : person with a skin complaint) **2.** The Syrians had raided Israel and brought back a youthful girl, who came a menial to Naaman's woman. (Raids : surprise attacks) **3.** She told her doxy, "If only my master were with the prophet in Samaria, he'd heal him of his leprosy." (Doxy : womanish head of ménage) **4.** Naaman told his master, "The girl from Israel said this." (Master : sovereign or king) **5.** The king of Syria said, "Go, and I'll shoot a letter to the king of Israel." He took ten bents of tableware, six thousand shekels of gold, and ten changes of apparel. (Bents : a unit of weight; Shekels : plutocrat **6.** He delivered the letter to the king of Israel, saying, "I've transferred Naaman to you to be healed of his leprosy." **7.** When the king read the letter, he tore his clothes and said, "Am I God, to heal him? This is a trap to quarrel with me." (Quarrel : argument) **8.** When Elisha heard the king had torn his clothes, he transferred a communication, "Why tear your clothes? Let him come to me, and he'll know there's a prophet in Israel." (Prophet : runner of God) **9.** Naaman went with his nags and chariot and stood at Elisha's door. (Chariot : a vehicle drawn by Horses.) **10.** Elisha transferred a runner, saying, "Wash in the Jordan seven times, and your meat will be restored and you'll be clean." (Messenger : person delivering a communication) **11.** Naaman came furious and said, "I allowed he'd come out, call on the Lord, surge his hand over me, and heal me." (Furious: very angry) **12.** "Are not the gutters of Damascus better than all of Israel's waters? Could I not wash in them and be clean?" He turned down in a rage. (Rage: extreme wrathfulness) **13.** His retainers said, "If the prophet had asked you to do commodity great, would you not have done it? How much further to wash and be clean?" (Father : regardful address) **14.** So he dipped seven times in the Jordan, and his meat was restored like a little child's, and he was clean. (Dipped : immersed; Restored : healed) **15.** He returned to Elisha, saying, "Now I know there's no God but in Israel. Please take a gift from me." (helpers: sidekicks) **16.** Elisha refused, saying, "As the Lord lives, I'll take nothing." Naaman prompted him, but he refused. (prompted: explosively asked) **17.** Naaman said, "If not, let me take two mule:loads of earth, for I'll no longer offer offerings to other gods, but only to the Lord." (Mule:loads : cargo carried by mules) **18.** "But may the Lord pardon me when I bow in the tabernacle of Rimmon with my master." (Temple: place of deification; Rimmon: a idolater god) **19.** Elisha replied, "Go in peace." Naaman left a short distance. (Go in peace: be at peace) **20.** Gehazi, Elisha's menial, said, "My master has spared Naaman but not taken his gifts. As the Lord lives, I'll run after him and take commodity." (Gehazi: Elisha's menial; Extra chorus from taking) **21.** Gehazi pursued Naaman, who asked, "Is each well?" (Pursued: chased) 22. Gehazi prevaricated, saying, "My master has transferred me to ask for two bents of tableware and two changes of garments for two youthful men of the prophets." 23. Naaman gave him two bents of tableware, two changes of garments, and transferred them ahead with his retainers. (Set : wrapped up) 24. At the stronghold, Gehazi took the gifts, stored them, and transferred the retainers down. (Citadel : fort) 25. Elisha asked Gehazi, "Where did you go?" Gehazi prevaricated, saying, "I didn't go anywhere." (Master : superior) 26. Elisha said, "Did my heart not go with you when Naaman turned to meet you? Is this the time for gifts? Why seek wealth and retainers?" (Olive groves : areas where olive trees are grown; Stations : grape granges) 27. "Naaman's leprosy will cleave to you and your descendants ever." Gehazi left, leprous, as white as snow. (Cleave: stick to)

Chapter 6
1. The votaries of the prophets spoke to Elisha, saying, "The place where we live with you is too confined for us." (Disciple: a follower or pupil of a schoolteacher; confined : lacking space, too small) 2. "Let us go to the Jordan River," they said, "and each of us will cut a ray to make a new place for us to stay." Elisha replied, "Go ahead." (Jordan River: a swash in Israel; beam: a long piece of wood used in construction) 3. One of them said, "Please, allow us to have you go with us." Elisha answered, "I'll go." 4. Elisha went with them. When they arrived at the Jordan, they began cutting trees. 5. As one was mincing a tree, the iron dismissal head fell into the water. He cried, "Oh, master! It was espoused!" (Axe head: the sharp essence part of the dismissal; espoused: taken temporarily) 6. the man of God asked, "Where did it fall?" The menial showed the spot. Elisha threw a stick in, causing the iron to float. (Man of God: a title for a prophet; stick: a small piece of wood) 7. "Pick it up," Elisha told him. The man reached out and took it. 8. Meanwhile, the king of Syria was preparing to wage war against Israel. He consulted his officers, saying, "I'll set up my camp then." (Consulted: asked for advice) 9. The man of God advised the king of Israel, "Be conservative and avoid this place, for the Syrians are hiding there." (Conservative: careful) 10. The king of Israel transferred men to check the place Elisha advised about. He was careful, and this happened constantly. 11. The king of Syria was worried and asked his officers, "Who among us is informing the king of Israel?" (Summoned: called or ordered; informing: telling) 12. One of his retainers replied, "None, my lord, but Elisha, the prophet in Israel, tells the king of Israel what you speak in your bedroom." (retainers : attendants or aides; prophet : a person who speaks for God) 13. The king said, "Go find where he is, so I can shoot men to capture him." They told him, "He's in Dothan." 14. The king transferred nags, chariots, and a large army to compass Dothan by night. (Chariots: large vehicles drawn by horses used in battle; compass : to encircle) 15. When Elisha's menial woke up and went outdoors, he saw the megacity girdled by an army. He shocked and said, "Oh, my master, what shall we do?" (Panicked : came anxious or spooked) 16. Elisha replied, "Don't sweat. Further are with us than with them." 17. Elisha supplicated, "Lord, open his eyes." The Lord opened his eyes, and he saw the hills full of nags and chariots of fire girding Elisha. (Nags and chariots of fire: a heavenly army of angels or important beings; girding : girding fully) 18. When the Syrians approached, Elisha supplicated, "Lord, strike them with blindness." The Lord struck them with blindness. (Strike: to hit or affect; dazed: made unfit to see) 19. Elisha said, "This isn't the way, nor is this the megacity. Follow me, and I'll lead you to the man you seek." He led them to Samaria. (Lead: companion; Samaria: a megacity in ancient Israel) 20. When they entered Samaria, Elisha supplicated, "Lord, open their eyes." The Lord opened their eyes, and they set up themselves in Samaria. 21. The king of Israel saw them and asked Elisha, "Should I kill them, my father? Should I kill them?" 22. Elisha answered "Don't kill them. Would you kill those you've captured? Set food and water before them, so they can eat and return to their master." (Sword: An armament for slice; bow: An armament for shooting arrows) 23. The king prepared a feast for them. After they ate and drank, he transferred them back to their master. The Syrian aggressors stopped coming into Israel. (Feast: a large, elaborate mess; aggressors : bushwhackers) 24. Lately, Ben:Hadad, king of Syria, gathered his army and besieged Samaria. (Besieged: girdled and attacked) 25. There was a great shortage in Samaria, and they besieged it until a jackass's head was vended for eighty shekels of tableware, and dove feces for five shekels of tableware. (Dove feces: waste produced by doves; shekels: ancient currency) 26. As the king of Israel walked along the wall, a woman cried, "Help, my lord, O king!" 27. He answered, "If the Lord doesn't help you, where can I find help? From the threshing bottom or the winepress?" (Threshing bottom: a place where grain is separated from chaff; winepress: a place where grapes are pressed to make wine) 28. The king asked, "What troubles you?" She said, "This woman told me, 'Give me your son so we may eat him moment, and we will eat my son hereafter.' 29. So we boiled my son and ate him. When I asked her for her son the coming day, she hid him." 30. When the king heard this, he tore his clothes in despair. As he walked, the people saw he was wearing sackcloth underneath. (Sackcloth: a rough, uncomfortable material worn as a symbol of mourning) 31. He said, "May God do to me and further if Elisha remains alive moment!" 32. Elisha was sitting with the elders when the king transferred a runner ahead of him. Before the runner arrived, Elisha said, "Do you see how this killer's son is transferring someone to take my life? Lock the door when the runner arrives." (Messenger : a person who carries a communication; steps : the sound of someone walking) 33. While Elisha was still speaking, the runner arrived, and the king said, "This disaster is from the Lord; why should I stay any longer for the Lord's help?" (Disaster: a great mischance or disaster)

Chapter 7
1. Also Elisha said, "Hear the word of the Lord. This is what the Lord says: 'By this time hereafter, a seah of fine flour will be vended for a shekel, and two seahs of barley will also be vended for a shekel, at the gate of Samaria.'" (Seah: a dimension of volume; Shekel: a gray coin) 2. An officer, who was the king's close counsel, replied to the man of God, "If the Lord were to open windows in heaven, could such a thing be?" Elisha answered, "You'll indeed see it with your own eyes, but you won't get to eat any of it." 3. Four men suffering from leprosy sat at the entrance of the megacity gate. They said to each other, "Why should we sit here staying to die?" (Leprosy: a habitual skin complaint) 4. "If we enter the megacity, we will die from the shortage there. However, we will die too, if we stay here. So, let's go and surrender to the Syrian army. However, we will live; if they kill us, at least we will die quickly, if they spare us." (Shortage: extreme deficit of food) 5. At twilight, they got up and headed for the Syrian camp. To their amazement, when they reached the edge of the camp, no one was there. 6. The Lord had caused the Syrian army to hear the sound of chariots and nags, like the noise of a large army. They thought, "The king of Israel has hired the lords of the Hittites and the Egyptians to attack us!" (Hittites: an ancient people) 7. So, the Syrians got up and fled in the twilight, leaving behind their canopies, nags, and burros. They ran for their lives. 8. When the lepers arrived at the edge of the camp, they entered one of the canopies, ate and drank, and took tableware, gold, and apparel. They went and hid their treasures. Subsequently, they returned to another tent, took more items, and hid them again. 9. Then they said to each other, "We aren't doing the right thing. Today is a day of good news, and we're keeping silent. If we stay until morning, some punishment will come upon us. Let's go tell the king's household what has happened." 10. So, they went and called out to the city doorkeepers, saying, "We went to the Syrian camp, and to our surprise, no one was there. There was no sound of people, only nags and burros tied up, and the tents were still standing." 11. The doorkeepers cried this out, and the news reached the king's

household. **12.** That night, the king got up and said to his retainers, "I'll tell you what the Syrians have done. They know we're starving, so they've left their camp and hidden in the fields, thinking, 'When the Israelites come out of the city, we will capture them alive and get back into the city.'" **13.** One of the retainers suggested, "Let several men take five of the remaining nags left in the city. They may either die like all the Israelites who have already perished, or they may survive. Let's send them to see what's happened." **14.** So, the king sent two chariots with nags, instructing them, "Go and check." **15.** They followed the path to the Jordan River, and saw that the road was scattered with garments and munitions that the Syrians had abandoned in their fear. The couriers returned and reported this to the king. **16.** Then the people of Samaria went out and pillaged the tents of the Syrians. As the Lord had said, a seah of fine flour was vended for a shekel, and two seahs of barley for a shekel. **17.** The king had assigned the officer who was his close counsel to be in charge of the city gate. But when the people rushed out, they trampled him at the gate, and he died just as Elisha had said when the king came to him. **18.** This happened just as the man of God had prophesied, saying, "By this time hereafter, a seah of fine flour will be vended for a shekel, and two seahs of barley for a shekel, at the gate of Samaria." **19.** The officer had responded to Elisha, "Indeed, if the Lord opened the windows of heaven, could such a thing be?" Elisha had replied, "You'll see it with your own eyes, but you won't eat any of it." **20.** And so it happened: the officer was trampled at the gate and died, just as the man of God had said.

Chapter 8
1. Also Elisha spoke to the woman whose son he'd revived, saying, "Get up and go with your family. Stay wherever you can, for the Lord has called for a shortage that will last seven years." (Shortage: deficit of food) **2.** So the woman followed the man of God's advice, going with her family to live in the land of the Philistines for seven years. (Philistines: people near Israel) **3.** After seven years, the woman returned from the Philistines and went to the king to reclaim her house and land. (Land of the Philistines: region controlled by the Philistines) **4.** The king was speaking with Gehazi, Elisha's servant, and said, "Tell me all the great things Elisha has done." (Gehazi: Elisha's servant) **5.** As Gehazi spoke of Elisha raising the dead, the woman whose son had been revived appeared, seeking her house and land. Gehazi said, "This is the woman, and her son whom Elisha brought back to life." (Restored to life: revived) **6.** When the king asked the woman, she verified it. So the king appointed an officer to help her, saying, "Give her back everything she owns, including all the crops from the fields since the day she left." (Officer: functionary in charge) **7.** Elisha went to Damascus, and Ben-Hadad, king of Syria, was ill. It was reported to him, "The man of God is here." (Damascus: capital of Syria) **8.** The king said to Hazael, "Take a gift and go ask the Lord through him, 'Will I recover from this illness?'" (Hazael: king's servant) **9.** So Hazael went to Elisha with forty camel-loads of the finest goods from Damascus. He stood before him and said, "Your servant, Ben-Hadad, king of Syria, has sent me to ask, 'Will I recover from this illness?'" (Camel-loads: large volume of goods) **10.** Elisha replied, "Go and tell him, 'You'll recover.' But the Lord has revealed to me that he'll die." (Revealed: shown) **11.** Elisha stared at Hazael until he felt ashamed. The man of God wept. (Stared: looked intensively) **12.** Hazael asked, "Why is my lord crying?" Elisha said, "I know the harm you will do to Israel. You'll burn their fortresses, kill their young men with the sword, dash their babies to the ground, and rip open their pregnant women." (Fortresses: defenses; Sword: weapon) **13.** Hazael asked, "What is your servant—a dog—that I should do such a thing?" Elisha answered, "The Lord has shown me that you will be king of Syria." (Servant: one who serves; Dog: lowly personality) **14.** Hazael went to his master. The king asked, "What did Elisha say to you?" He replied, "He said you'll recover." (Master: the king) **15.** The next day, Hazael took a cloth, dipped it in water, and spread it over the king's face, causing his death. Then Hazael became king. (Cloth: fabric) **16.** In the fifth year of Joram, son of Ahab, king of Israel, Jehoshaphat was still king of Judah. Also, Jehoram, son of Jehoshaphat, became king of Judah. (Joram: king of Israel; Jehoshaphat: king of Judah) **17.** Jehoram was thirty-two years old when he became king and reigned for eight years in Jerusalem. (Reign: to rule) **18.** He followed the ways of Israel's kings, as Ahab's house did, because he married Ahab's daughter. He did evil in the Lord's sight. (Ways: practices; Sight: view) **19.** But the Lord did not destroy Judah for the sake of His servant David, as He had promised to give David and his descendants a lasting lamp. (Lamp: symbol of leadership) **20.** During Jehoram's reign, Edom revolted and set up their own king. (Edom: area southeast of Israel) **21.** Jehoram went to Zair with all his chariots, rose by night, and attacked the Edomites who had surrounded him. But the Edomites fled. (Zair: city in Edom; Chariots: vehicles) **22.** As a result, Edom remains in rebellion against Judah. Libnah also revolted. (Rebellion: resistance) **23.** The other events of Jehoram's reign are recorded in the Book of the Chronicles of the Kings of Judah. (Chronicles: records) **24.** Jehoram died and was buried with his ancestors in the City of David. His son Ahaziah succeeded him. (City of David: Jerusalem) **25.** In the twelfth year of Joram, son of Ahab, king of Israel, Ahaziah, son of Jehoram, became king of Judah. (Ahaziah: king of Judah) **26.** Ahaziah was twenty-two years old when he began to reign, and he ruled for one year in Jerusalem. His mother's name was Athaliah, granddaughter of Omri, king of Israel. (Athaliah: queen of Judah; Omri: king of Israel) **27.** Ahaziah followed the ways of Ahab's house and did evil in the sight of the Lord, as Ahab's house did, since he was son-in-law to Ahab. (Son-in-law: husband of daughter) **28.** Ahaziah went with Joram, son of Ahab, to war against Hazael, king of Syria, at Ramoth Gilead. The Syrians wounded Joram. (Ramoth Gilead: city east of Jordan) **29.** King Joram went back to Jezreel to recover from his injuries, and Ahaziah, king of Judah, went to visit him there, since he was sick. (Jezreel: city in ancient Israel)

Chapter 9
1. Elisha, the prophet, summoned one of the young prophets and instructed him, "Prepare yourself, take this flask of oil, and go to Ramoth Gilead." (Flask: small vessel; Ramoth Gilead: city in Israel) **2.** "When you arrive, look for Jehu, son of Jehoshaphat, grandson of Nimshi. Go in, take him from among his companions, and bring him into a private room." (Companions: associates; Private room: isolated space) **3.** "Then, pour the oil on his head and declare, 'The Lord says, I have chosen you as king over Israel.'" (Declare: announce) **4.** So, the young prophet did as instructed and went to Ramoth Gilead. **5.** Upon arrival, he found the army commanders sitting. He approached one and said, "I have a message for you, Commander." Jehu replied, "Which one of us?" The young man answered, "For you, Commander." (Commanders: officers) **6.** Jehu stood up and went inside. The prophet poured the oil on his head and said, "This is the word of the Lord: 'I have made you king over Israel.'" **7.** "You will destroy the house of Ahab, your master, to avenge the death of My prophets and servants slain by Jezebel." (Avenge: seek justice for; Slain: killed) **8.** "The entire house of Ahab will be wiped out, and I will cut off every male descendant of Ahab, slave or free." (Wiped out: destroyed; Descendant: seed) **9.** "I will make your family like that of Jeroboam and Baasha." (Jeroboam: first king of Israel; Baasha: king of Israel) **10.** "The dogs will devour Jezebel in the field of Jezreel, and no one will bury her." (Devour: eat greedily) Then, the prophet opened the door and fled. **11.** Jehu came out to his officers. One asked, "Is everything all right? Why did that madman visit you?" Jehu replied, "You know the man and his talk." (Talk: speech) **12.** They responded, "Tell us what happened." Jehu said, "He said, 'The Lord has anointed you as king over Israel.'" (Anointed: chosen) **13.** Each man quickly took off his cloak, spread it under him on the steps, and blew the trumpet, crying, "Jehu is king!" (Cloak: garment) **14.** Jehu, the son of Jehoshaphat, conspired against King Joram. (Plot: plan secretly) **15.** Joram had returned to Jezreel to

recover from injuries inflicted by Hazael, king of Syria. Jehu said, "If you support me, do not let anyone escape to Jezreel." (Inflicted: caused; Support: help) **16.** Jehu mounted his chariot and went to Jezreel, where Joram was staying. Ahaziah, king of Judah, had come to visit him. (Mounted: rode) **17.** A lookout saw Jehu's company approaching and reported, "I see a group coming." Joram asked, "Send a rider to ask, 'Is it peace?'" (Lookout: watcher; Rider: messenger) **18.** The rider went and asked, "The king says, 'Is it peace?'" Jehu replied, "What does peace have to do with you? Turn around and follow me." The lookout reported, "The rider went to meet them but did not return." (Peace: absence of conflict) **19.** A second rider was sent, asking the same question. Jehu answered again, "What does peace have to do with you? Turn around and follow me." **20.** The lookout reported, "The second rider did not return either. The way he drives is reckless, just like Jehu!" (Reckless: careless) **21.** Joram ordered his chariot to be prepared. He and Ahaziah mounted their chariots and went to meet Jehu, meeting him on Naboth's property. (Ordered: instructed; Property: land) **22.** When Joram saw Jehu, he asked, "Is it peace, Jehu?" Jehu replied, "What peace can there be as long as your mother Jezebel's idolatry and witchcraft continue?" (Idolatry: false worship; Witchcraft: magic) **23.** Joram turned and fled, crying, "Treason, Ahaziah!" (Treason: betrayal) **24.** Jehu drew his bow and shot Joram between the shoulders. The arrow pierced his heart, and he sank down in his chariot. (Pierced: entered; Bow: weapon used for shooting arrows) **25.** Jehu ordered Bidkar, "Pick him up and throw him into Naboth's field, for I remember when you and I rode behind Ahab, and the Lord spoke against him, saying, **26.** 'I have seen the blood of Naboth and his sons, and I will repay it in this field.'" (Repay: recompense) **27.** When Ahaziah saw this, he fled to Beth Haggan. Jehu pursued him, saying, "Shoot him in his chariot." They shot him at the ascent of Gur, near Ibleam. He fled to Megiddo and died there. (Pursued: followed) **28.** His attendants took his body to Jerusalem and buried him with his ancestors in the City of David. (Attendants: servants; Ancestors: forebears) **29.** In the eleventh year of Joram, Ahaziah became king of Judah. **30.** When Jehu arrived in Jezreel, Jezebel heard of it. She painted her eyes, arranged her hair, and looked out of the window. (Painted her eyes: applied makeup; Arranged: prepared) **31.** As Jehu entered the gate, she shouted, "Is it peace, Zimri, murderer of your master?" (Shouted: mocked) **32.** Jehu looked up and asked, "Who is on my side?" Two or three eunuchs looked out. (Eunuchs: castrated men) **33.** Jehu commanded, "Throw her down." They threw her down, and her blood splattered on the wall and on the horses. Jehu trampled her underfoot. (Trampled: crushed) **34.** Then, Jehu went inside, ate, and drank. He said, "Go, bury this cursed woman, for she was a king's daughter." (Cursed: condemned) **35.** When they went to bury her, they found only her skull, her feet, and the palms of her hands. (Skull: head bones) **36.** They returned and told Jehu. He said, "This is the fulfillment of the word of the Lord spoken through Elijah: 'In the field of Jezreel, the dogs will eat Jezebel's flesh.'" (Fulfillment: completion) **37.** "Jezebel's body will be like dung on the ground in the field of Jezreel, so that no one will say, 'This is Jezebel's grave.'" (Dung: waste)

Chapter 10

1. Ahab had seventy sons in Samaria. Jehu transferred a letter to the autocrats of Jezreel, the elders, and those minding for Ahab's sons, saying (Samaria: capital; Jezreel: megacity; elders: leaders). **2.** "When this letter reaches you, since your master's sons are with you, and you have chariots, nags, a fortified megacity, and munitions, (fortified defended). **3.** Choose the stylish of your master's sons, put him on his father's throne, and defend your master's house." (able: suitable). **4.** They were hysterical and said, "Two lords could not repel him; how can we stand against him?" (alarmed: hysterical; repel: oppose). **5.** The palace functionary, megacity functionary, elders, and those minding for the sons transferred a communication to Jehu saying, "We're your retainers and will observe, but we won't make anyone king. Do what seems right." (retainers: followers; king: sovereign). **6.** Jehu wrote again, "If you support me, take the heads of your master's sons and bring them to me at Jezreel by hereafter. Seventy sons are with the megacity's leaders." (observe: follow; raising: caring). **7.** When the letter arrived, they killed the seventy sons, put their heads in baskets, and transferred them to Jehu. (youthful men: youths). **8.** A runner told Jehu, "They have brought the heads." Jehu said, "Pile them in two stacks at the gate until morning." (runner: courier; piles: heaps). **9.** In the morning, Jehu went out, stood before the people, and said, "You're righteous. I killed my master, but who killed all these?" (conspired: colluded; righteous: just). **10.** "Know that God's words about Ahab's house won't fail. The Lord has done what He said through His menial Elijah." (fail: remain unfulfilled; menial: follower). **11.** Jehu killed all of Ahab's family in Jezreel, his officers, close musketeers, and preachers, leaving none. (officers: leaders; preachers: religious leaders). **12.** Jehu also set out for Samaria. On the way, at Beth scrounge of the Goatherds, (set out: started; Beth scrounge: place name). **13.** Jehu met the sisters of Ahaziah, king of Judah, and asked, "Who are you?" They answered, "We're the sisters of Ahaziah. We came to hail the sons of the king and queen mama." (hail: hello). **14.** Jehu said, "Take them alive!" They took them and killed forty-two men at Beth scrounge. None survived. (alive: living; survived: lived). **15.** Jehu met Jehonadab, son of Rechab, saluted him, and asked, "Is your heart pious to me as mine is to you?" Jehonadab replied, "It is." Jehu said, "If so, give me your hand." Jehonadab gave his hand, and Jehu took him into his chariot. (pious: faithful; chariot: vehicle). **16.** Also Jehu said, "Come see how devoted I'm to the Lord." Jehonadab rode in his chariot. (devoted: married). **17.** When they reached Samaria, Jehu killed everyone from Ahab's family, fulfilling God's word through Elijah. (fulfilled: completed). **18.** Jehu gathered the people and said, "Ahab served Baal a little; Jehu will serve him more." (served: worshiped). **19.** "Call all Baal's prophets, retainers, and preachers. Let no bone be missing, for I've a great immolation for Baal. Anyone absent will die." Jehu planned to destroy Baal's worshipers. (immolation: sacrifice; worshipers: followers). **20.** Jehu said, "Declare a holy assembly for Baal." So they did. (placarded: announced). **21.** Jehu transferred couriers throughout Israel, and all Baal's worshipers gathered, filling his tabernacle. (tabernacle: sanctuary). **22.** Jehu told the one in charge, "Bring out blankets for all the worshipers." He brought out the blankets. (wardrobe: apparel; blankets: garments). **23.** Jehu and Jehonadab entered Baal's tabernacle and said to the worshipers, "Make sure there are no retainers of the Lord then, only Baal's worshipers." (precisely: cautiously). **24.** The worshipers offered offerings. Meanwhile, Jehu set up eighty men outdoors and said, "If any man escapes, the one who lets him escape will die in his place." (burnt immolations: offerings). **25.** After offering the burnt immolation, Jehu told the guards, "Go in and kill them all; let no bone escape!" They killed the worshipers and threw their bodies out, entering Baal's inner room. (guards: defenders; captains: leaders). **26.** They took the sacred pillars from Baal's tabernacle and burned them. (pillars: columns; sacred: holy). **27.** They broke Baal's pillar, tore down his tabernacle, and made it a potty. (potty: restroom). **28.** Therefore Jehu destroyed Baal's deification in Israel. (destroyed: canceled). **29.** Still, Jehu didn't turn from the sins of Jeroboam, son of Nebat, which caused Israel to stray, especially the golden pins at Bethel and Dan. (golden pins: idols). **30.** The Lord said to Jehu, "Because you have done what's right in My eyes and fulfilled My plan for Ahab's house, your descendants will rule Israel for four generations." (descendants: children). **31.** But Jehu didn't completely follow God's law and didn't turn from the sins of Jeroboam. (careful: active; law: commandments). **32.** In those days, the Lord began to reduce Israel, and Hazael conquered Israel's home, (reduce: shrink; home: land). **33.** from the Jordan eastward Gilead, Gad, Reuben, Manasseh, Aroer by the Arnon River, Gilead, and Bashan. (eastward: toward the east; Gilead: region). **34.** The rest of Jehu's deeds and might are written in the chronicles of Israel's lords. (deeds: conduct; chronicles: records). **35.** Jehu rested with his ancestors and was buried in Samaria. His son Jehoahaz succeeded him. (rested: died; succeeded: followed). **36.** Jehu reigned in Samaria for twenty-eight times. (reigned: ruled).

Chapter 11
1. When Athaliah, the mama of Ahaziah, saw that her son was dead, she killed all the royal descendants (heirs at law those entitled to inherit the throne). **2.** But Jehosheba, the son of King Joram and family of Ahaziah, took Joash, the son of Ahaziah, and intimately saved him from being killed with the other royal children. She hid him and his nanny in a private room to cover him from Athaliah's wrath (wrath violent wrathfulness). **3.** Joash remained retired in the house of the Lord for six times, while Athaliah ruled the land (ruled held authority as a queen). **4.** In the seventh time, Jehoiada summoned the commanders of the guards — the captains of the hundreds and brought them to the house of the Lord. He made a covenant with them, swore them to a pledge, and revealed the king's son (covenant formal agreement, pledge solemn pledge). **5.** He instructed them, "One-third of you, on guard duty on the Sabbath, shall watch over the king's palace" (palace hearthstone of the king). **6.** "Another third will guard the gate of Sur, and the remaining third will guard the gate behind the escorts. You must cover the palace to insure it isn't traduced" (traduced forcefully entered). **7.** "The two groups finishing duty on the Sabbath shall stay on guard at the house of the Lord to cover the king" (duty assigned responsibility). **8.** "Form a defensive circle around the king, each man holding a armament. Anyone who comes near is to be killed. Stay with the king wherever he goes" (defensive circle girding line of guards). **9.** The commanders followed Jehoiada's instructions. They took their men who were on duty and those finishing their shifts and came to Jehoiada the clerk (clerk religious leader). **10.** Jehoiada gave the commanders the pikestaffs and securities of King David, kept in the tabernacle of the Lord (securities defensive bias for defense). **11.** The guards stood in place, girding the king from the right to the left wing of the tabernacle, by the balcony and the house (balcony structure used for deification). **12.** Jehoiada brought out the king's son, placed a crown on his head, and gave him the evidence. They placarded him king, besmeared him, and celebrated by clapping and shouting, "Long live the king!" (evidence sacred law, besmeared set piecemeal with holy oil painting). **13.** When Athaliah heard the noise of the guards and people celebrating, she came to the tabernacle (tabernacle sacred place of deification). **14.** She saw the king standing by a pillar, in the customary place for a king. The leaders and trumpet players were by him, and all the people were rejoicing and blowing trumpets. Athaliah tore her clothes in torture and cried, "disloyalty! disloyalty!" (customary traditional, torture great suffering). **15.** Jehoiada ordered the commanders to take Athaliah outdoors under guard and kill anyone who followed her, but commanded that she not be killed in the tabernacle (commanded gave an authoritative order). **16.** They seized her, and she was led out through the entrance of the nags into the palace, where she was put to death (seized captured). **17.** Jehoiada made a covenant between the Lord, the king, and the people, to remain pious to the Lord. He also made a covenant between the king and the people (pious faithful). **18.** The people went to the tabernacle of Baal, tore it down, smashed its stages and icons, and killed Mattan, the clerk of Baal, in front of the stages. Jehoiada appointed officers to oversee the house of the Lord (icons images of false gods, oversee supervise). **19.** Jehoiada took the captains, guards, escorts, and all the people. They brought the king from the house of the Lord, through the gate of the escorts, to the palace and placed him on the throne (escorts guards, throne seat of authority). **20.** The people rejoiced, and the megacity was peaceful, for Athaliah had been executed with the brand at the palace (executed put to death). **21.** Jehoash was seven times old when he came king (king sovereign of a area).

Chapter 12
1. In the seventh year of Jehu's reign, Jehoash became king of Judah and reigned for forty years in Jerusalem. His mother's name was Zibiah, from Beersheba. (Beersheba: a town in southern Judah) **2.** Jehoash did what pleased the Lord throughout the days when the priest Jehoiada guided him. (Jehoiada: a priest; guided: instructed) **3.** However, the high places were not removed, and the people continued to offer sacrifices and burn incense at those locations. (High places: elevated areas for worship) **4.** Jehoash instructed the priests, saying, "All the money brought as offerings to the Lord's house, including the census tax and voluntary gifts, (Census money: a tax based on population; assessment money: a required contribution) **5.** let the priests take it from each person in their care and use it to repair the temple wherever it is in disrepair." (Repair: restore; dilapidation: damage) **6.** But by the twenty-third year of King Jehoash's reign, the priests had not yet repaired the temple. (Reign: the time a king rules) **7.** So King Jehoash summoned Jehoiada the priest and the other priests, and asked, "Why haven't you repaired the temple? Don't collect any more money from the people, but use the funds already brought in for repairs." (Summoned: called together; collect: gather money) **8.** The priests agreed to no longer take money from the people and to use the collected funds for repairs. (Agree: consent) **9.** Jehoiada the priest then made a chest, drilled a hole in its lid, and placed it beside the altar on the right side as one enters the Lord's house. The priests who kept watch at the door put all the offerings into it. (Chest: a box for storing things; Lid: the cover) **10.** Whenever the chest was full, the king's scribe and the high priest would count it, putting it into bags for safekeeping. (Scribe: a person who records; High priest: the chief priest) **11.** The money was given to the supervisors of the temple work, who paid the carpenters, builders, masons, and stonecutters, as well as for timber and cut stones to repair the temple. (Supervisors: those in charge of the work; Masons: stoneworkers) **12.** They used the money for all other necessary repairs to the temple. (Repairs: fixing or restoring) **13.** However, no silver basins, trimming tools, bowls, trumpets, or articles made of gold or silver were made for the temple from this money. (Basins: large bowls; Trimmers: cutting tools) **14.** The money was entirely used for the workmen who repaired the temple. (Entirely: fully) **15.** They did not require an accounting from the men who handled the funds, because they trusted them to use the money honestly. (Accounting: a record of expenses; Trust: confidence) **16.** The money from the guilt offerings and sin offerings was not brought into the temple; it belonged to the priests. (Guilt offerings: offerings for wrongdoings; Sin offerings: offerings for sins committed) **17.** Hazael, king of Syria, attacked Gath and captured it. He then turned his attention to Jerusalem. (Captured: took by force) **18.** Jehoash, king of Judah, took all the sacred items that his ancestors—Jehoshaphat, Jehoram, and Ahaziah, kings of Judah—had dedicated, along with his own sacred offerings and all the gold from the treasuries of the Lord's house and his palace, and sent them to Hazael, king of Syria, to avoid a siege. (Sacred items: consecrated objects; Treasuries: collections of valuable items) **19.** The rest of Jehoash's deeds are recorded in the Book of the Chronicles of the Kings of Judah. (Chronicles: historical records) **20.** His officials conspired against him and assassinated him in the house of the Millo, on the way down to Silla. (Conspired: secretly planned harm; Assassinated: murdered for political reasons) **21.** Jozachar son of Shimeath and Jehozabad son of Shomer, two of his servants, struck him down, and he died. They buried him with his ancestors in the City of David. His son Amaziah became king after him. (Servants: attendants; Struck him down: killed him)

Chapter 13
1 In the twenty:third time of Joash, son of Ahaziah, king of Judah, Jehoahaz, son of Jehu, began to control over Israel in Samaria for seventeen times. (Samaria a region and megacity in ancient Israel) **2** Jehoahaz did evil in the Lord's eyes, following the sins of Jeroboam,

son of Nebat, and did n't turn from them. (depart leave or abandon) **3** The Lord's wrathfulness burned against Israel, handing them over to Hazael, king of Syria, and Ben:Hadad, his son. (aroused stirred up, made active) **4** Jehoahaz sought the Lord's favor, and the Lord heeded, seeing Israel's suffering due to the king of Syria. (oppression cruel treatment) **5** The Lord handed a deliverer, freeing Israel from Syrian control, and they lived in their homes as ahead. (deliverer one who rescues) **6** Yet, they did n't turn from Jeroboam's sins, and the rustic image remained in Samaria. (rustic image hero used for deification) **7** Jehoahaz's army was reduced to fifty horsewomen, ten chariots, and ten thousand bottom dogfaces, as the king of Syria devastated them like trampled dust. (threshing grain separation) **8** The rest of Jehoahaz's deeds are recorded in the chronicles of Israel's lords. (chronicles literal records) **9** Jehoahaz failed and was buried in Samaria, and his son Joash came king. (rested with his fathers failed and was buried) **10** In the thirty:seventh time of Joash, king of Judah, Jehoash, son of Jehoahaz, came king over Israel, ruling for sixteen times. **11** He did evil in the Lord's sight, not turning from Jeroboam's sins. **12** The rest of Joash's deeds, including his battles with Amaziah, king of Judah, are in the chronicles of Israel's lords. **13** Joash failed and was buried in Samaria with Israel's lords, and Jeroboam succeeded him. **14** Elisha had come sick with the illness that would lead to his death. Joash, king of Israel, wept over him, saying, "My father, my father, the chariots of Israel and their horsewomen!" (chariots of Israel symbol of protection) **15** Elisha said, "Get a arc and arrows," and Joash did so. **16** Elisha said, "Put your hand on the arc," and placed his hands over the king's. **17** He said, "Open the east window," and Joash opened it. Elisha commanded, "Shoot," declaring it the Lord's arrow of deliverance over Syria at Aphek. (deliverance deliverance) **18** Elisha said, "Strike the ground," and Joash struck three times, also stopped. **19** The man of God, angry, said, "You should have struck five or six times for complete palm over Syria. Now, you'll only master them three times." (angry derangement) **20** Elisha failed and was buried. Aggressors from Moab raided the land each spring. (aggressors raiders) **21** While burying a man, people saw aggressors and put the man in Elisha's grave. Touching Elisha's bones, the man revived and stood up. (revived came back to life) **22** Hazael, king of Syria, tyrannized Israel during Jehoahaz's reign. (tyrannized harsh treatment) **23** Yet the Lord showed compassion due to His covenant with Abraham, Isaac, and Jacob, not destroying them. (gracious kind; covenant solemn agreement) **24** Hazael failed, and his son Ben:Hadad came king. **25** Jehoash, son of Jehoahaz, reclaimed metropolises taken by Ben:Hadad through battle. Joash defeated him three times and restored Israel's metropolises. (reclaimed: recovered)

Chapter 14
1. In the second year of Joash, son of Jehoahaz, king of Israel, Amaziah, son of Joash, became king of Judah. (Judah: southern kingdom) **2.** Amaziah was 25 years old when he began his reign, and he ruled for 29 years in Jerusalem. His mother's name was Jehoaddan, from Jerusalem. (reign: rule) **3.** He did what was right in the sight of the Lord, though not with the complete devotion of David, his ancestor. He followed the example set by his father, Joash. (devotion: commitment; ancestor: forefather) **4.** However, the high places were not removed, and the people still sacrificed and burned incense there. (sacrifices: offerings; incense: aromatic substance) **5.** When his authority over the kingdom was secure, Amaziah executed the officials who had murdered his father, the king. (executed: put to death; assassinated: killed secretly) **6.** But he did not put to death the children of the murderers, following the command in the Book of the Law of Moses, which says, "Parents shall not be executed for their children's sins, nor children for their parents'; each will die for their own sin." (command: order; sin: wrongdoing) **7.** He struck down ten thousand Edomites in the Valley of Salt and captured Sela in battle, renaming it Joktheel, a name it holds to this day. (Edomites: descendants of Esau; captured: seized by force) **8.** Amaziah sent envoys to Jehoash, son of Jehoahaz, son of Jehu, king of Israel, saying, "Come, let us face one another in battle." (envoys: messengers) **9.** Jehoash, king of Israel, replied to Amaziah, king of Judah, saying, "The thistle in Lebanon sent a message to the cedar in Lebanon, saying, 'Give your daughter to my son as wife.' But a wild beast passed by and trampled the thistle." (thistle: prickly plant; cedar: tall tree) **10.** "You have defeated Edom, and your pride has lifted you up. Glory in that and stay home. Why should you meddle with trouble and fall—both you and Judah with you?" (pride: self-esteem; meddle: interfere) **11.** But Amaziah did not listen. Therefore, Jehoash, king of Israel, advanced, and he and Amaziah, king of Judah, met at Beth Shemesh, which belongs to Judah. (advanced: moved forward) **12.** Judah was defeated by Israel, and each man fled to his tent. (defeated: beaten) **13.** Jehoash, king of Israel, captured Amaziah, king of Judah, at Beth Shemesh. He went to Jerusalem and broke down the wall of Jerusalem from the Gate of Ephraim to the Corner Gate—400 cubits. (cubits: ancient unit of length) **14.** He took all the gold and silver, the articles found in the house of the Lord and in the treasuries of the king's house, and hostages, and returned to Samaria. (hostages: prisoners) **15.** The rest of Jehoash's deeds, his strength, and his war with Amaziah, king of Judah, are written in the book of the chronicles of the kings of Israel. (chronicles: historical records) **16.** Jehoash passed away and was buried in Samaria with the kings of Israel. His son, Jeroboam, succeeded him. (passed away: died; succeeded: took over) **17.** Amaziah, son of Joash, king of Judah, lived for 15 more years after the death of Jehoash, son of Jehoahaz, king of Israel. **18.** The remaining acts of Amaziah are written in the book of the chronicles of the kings of Judah. **19.** A conspiracy formed against him in Jerusalem, and he fled to Lachish. They pursued him there and killed him. (conspiracy: secret plan; pursued: chased) **20.** His body was brought back on horses and buried in Jerusalem with his ancestors in the City of David. (ancestors: forefathers) **21.** The people of Judah made Azariah, who was 16, king in place of his father, Amaziah. **22.** He rebuilt Elath and brought it back under Judah's control after the king's death. (rebuilt: restored; Elath: city near the Red Sea) **23.** In the 15th year of Amaziah, king of Judah, Jeroboam, son of Joash, became king of Israel in Samaria and ruled for 41 years. (Samaria: capital of Israel) **24.** He did evil in the Lord's sight and did not depart from the sins of Jeroboam, son of Nebat, who had caused Israel to sin. (sin: wrongdoing) **25.** He restored Israel's territory from the entrance of Hamath to the Sea of the Arabah, according to the Lord's word spoken through His servant Jonah, the prophet from Gath Hepher. (territory: land; prophet: messenger of God) **26.** The Lord saw Israel's bitter suffering, with no one to help, whether bond or free. (suffering: pain; bond: enslaved) **27.** The Lord did not declare He would erase Israel's name from under heaven but saved them through Jeroboam, son of Joash. (erase: remove) **28.** The rest of Jeroboam's deeds, his power, and how he recaptured territories from Damascus and Hamath, are written in the book of the chronicles of the kings of Israel. **29.** Jeroboam passed away and was buried with the kings of Israel. His son, Zechariah, succeeded him. (succeeded: followed)

Chapter 15
1. In the twenty-seventh year of Jeroboam's reign over Israel, Azariah, son of Amaziah, became king of Judah. (reign: the period during which a king rules) **2.** He was sixteen when he began to reign and ruled fifty-two years in Jerusalem. His mother was Jecholiah of Jerusalem. (reigned: ruled, Jerusalem: the capital city of Judah) **3.** He did what was right in the Lord's eyes, as his father Amaziah had done. (right: morally correct, eyes: perception) **4.** However, the high places were not removed, and the people continued offering sacrifices and incense there. (high places: elevated areas used for idol worship) **5.** The Lord struck Azariah with leprosy, and he remained a leper until his death, living in isolation. His son Jotham took charge of the palace and judged the people. (struck: inflicted with, leprosy: a skin disease,

separate house: isolated dwelling) **6.** The rest of Azariah's deeds are written in the Book of the Chronicles of the Kings of Judah. (recorded: written down) **7.** Azariah died and was buried with his ancestors in the City of David. His son Jotham succeeded him. (passed away: died, ancestors: forefathers) **8.** In the thirty-eighth year of Azariah, Zechariah, son of Jeroboam, ruled Israel in Samaria for six months. (reigned: governed, Samaria: the capital city of Israel) **9.** He did evil in the Lord's sight, following the sinful ways of Jeroboam, son of Nebat. (evil: wrongdoing, sinful: morally wrong, led into sin: caused to sin) **10.** Shallum, son of Jabesh, conspired against him, killed him in front of the people, and took the throne. (conspired: secretly planned, struck: attacked) **11.** The rest of Zechariah's acts are written in the Chronicles of the Kings of Israel. (remaining: other) **12.** This fulfilled the Lord's word to Jehu: "Your descendants will sit on Israel's throne for four generations." (descendants: offspring, spoken: communicated) **13.** Shallum, son of Jabesh, became king in the thirty-ninth year of Uzziah and ruled for one month. (reigned: ruled) **14.** Menahem, son of Gadi, came from Tirzah, killed Shallum, and took the throne. (attacked: launched an assault, Tirzah: a city in Israel) **15.** The rest of Shallum's acts and his conspiracy are written in the Chronicles of the Kings of Israel. (acts: actions, conspiracy: secret plan) **16.** Menahem then attacked Tiphsah and its surrounding areas because they refused to surrender, even killing pregnant women. (ruthlessly: without mercy, surrender: give up, pregnant: carrying a child) **17.** In the thirty-ninth year of Azariah, Menahem, son of Gadi, became king and reigned for ten years in Samaria. (reigned: ruled) **18.** He did evil in the Lord's sight and continued in the sins of Jeroboam, son of Nebat. (never turned away: did not stop, sins: wrong actions) **19.** Pul, king of Assyria, invaded Israel. Menahem gave him a thousand talents of silver to gain his support and secure his kingdom. (invaded: attacked, talents: a unit of weight/money, ensure: guarantee) **20.** Menahem taxed the wealthy in Israel, collecting fifty shekels from each to send to the Assyrian king, who then withdrew. (taxing: imposing a fee, withdrew: left) **21.** The rest of Menahem's acts are written in the Chronicles of the Kings of Israel. (remaining: other, deeds: actions) **22.** Menahem died and was buried with his ancestors. His son Pekahiah succeeded him. (died: passed away, ancestors: forefathers) **23.** In the fiftieth year of Azariah, Pekahiah, son of Menahem, became king and reigned two years in Samaria. (reigned: ruled) **24.** He did evil in the Lord's sight and followed Jeroboam's sinful ways. (continuing: following, sinful ways: wrong practices) **25.** Pekah, son of Remaliah, an officer, conspired against and killed Pekahiah in Samaria, taking the throne. (plotted: secretly planned, citadel: fortress, took the throne: became king) **26.** The rest of Pekahiah's acts are written in the Chronicles of the Kings of Israel. (other acts: remaining actions) **27.** In the fifty-second year of Azariah, Pekah, son of Remaliah, became king in Samaria and reigned for twenty years. (reigned: ruled) **28.** He did evil in the Lord's sight and continued the sins of Jeroboam, son of Nebat. (continued: persisted in) **29.** During Pekah's reign, Tiglath-Pileser, king of Assyria, captured many cities in Israel and carried the people into captivity. (captured: seized, captivity: taken as prisoners) **30.** Hoshea, son of Elah, conspired against Pekah, killed him, and took the throne in the twentieth year of Jotham, son of Uzziah. (conspiracy: secret plan, took his place: became his successor) **31.** The rest of Pekah's acts are written in the Chronicles of the Kings of Israel. (other acts: remaining actions) **32.** In the second year of Pekah's reign, Jotham, son of Uzziah, began his reign as king of Judah. (reign: rule) **33.** Jotham was twenty-five when he became king and reigned for sixteen years in Jerusalem. His mother was Jerusha, daughter of Zadok. (became: ascended, Jerusalem: capital of Judah) **34.** Jotham did right in the Lord's sight, following his father Uzziah's example. (footsteps: example, following: emulating) **35.** However, the high places remained, and the people continued offering sacrifices there. Jotham also built the Upper Gate of the House of the Lord. (Continued: kept on, incense: fragrant substances burned as an offering) **36.** The rest of Jotham's deeds are written in the Chronicles of the Kings of Judah. (Deeds: actions) **37.** During Jotham's reign, the Lord began sending Rezin, king of Syria, and Pekah, son of Remaliah, against Judah. (Send: direct) **38.** Jotham died and was buried with his ancestors in the City of David. His son Ahaz succeeded him. (Passed away: died, succeeded: became the next ruler)

Chapter 16

1. In the seventeenth year of Pekah son of Remaliah, Ahaz, the son of Jotham, king of Judah, began to reign. **2.** Ahaz was twenty years old when he began his reign and ruled sixteen years in Jerusalem, but he did not follow the Lord's ways, as his ancestor David had. **3.** Instead, he followed the practices of the kings of Israel, even making his son pass through fire, imitating the detestable practices of the nations the Lord had driven out before Israel. (Detestable: greatly disliked or condemned.) **4.** He also offered sacrifices and burned incense on the high places, hills, and under every green tree. **5.** At that time, King Rezin of Syria and King Pekah of Israel waged war against Jerusalem, besieging Ahaz, but could not defeat him. (Siege: a military operation where forces surround a town or building to force surrender.) **6.** King Rezin of Syria captured Elath for Syria, driving out the people of Judah. The Edomites took over Elath and still dwell there. **7.** Ahaz sent messengers to Tiglath-Pileser, king of Assyria, saying, "I am your servant and your son. Rescue me from the hands of the king of Syria and Israel, who are rising against me." **8.** Ahaz took silver and gold from the house of the Lord and the royal treasuries and sent it as tribute to the king of Assyria. (Tribute: a payment made by one ruler or nation to another, often as a sign of submission or protection.) **9.** The king of Assyria responded by marching against Damascus, capturing it, exiling its people to Kir, and killing King Rezin. **10.** When King Ahaz visited Damascus to meet King Tiglath-Pileser, he saw an altar there. He sent the design and specifications to Urijah the priest in Jerusalem to replicate it. (Specifications: detailed descriptions or instructions.) **11.** Urijah built the altar exactly as King Ahaz had instructed, completing it before the king's return. **12.** Upon returning, Ahaz saw the altar, approached it, and offered sacrifices. **13.** He burned burnt offerings, grain offerings, poured drink offerings, and sprinkled the blood of peace offerings on it. **14.** He also moved the bronze altar from in front of the Lord's temple and placed it between the new altar and the temple on the north side of the new altar. **15.** King Ahaz ordered Urijah to use the new altar for daily offerings: morning burnt offerings, evening grain offerings, the king's burnt sacrifice, grain offerings, and the people's offerings, sprinkling the blood on it. He reserved the bronze altar for personal inquiries. (Inquiries: questions or requests for information.) **16.** Urijah followed all the king's commands. **17.** King Ahaz dismantled the wheels of the carts, removed the basins, took down the large bronze basin ("The Sea") from the bronze oxen, and placed it on a stone pavement. (Dismantled: took apart.) **18.** He also removed the pavilion built for the Sabbath and the king's outer entrance to the temple, all because of the king of Assyria. (Pavilion: a small, open-sided structure.) **19.** The remaining actions of King Ahaz are recorded in the chronicles of the kings of Judah. (Chronicles: detailed historical records.) **20.** Ahaz passed away and was buried with his ancestors in the City of David. His son Hezekiah succeeded him as king.

Chapter 17

1. In the twelfth year of Ahaz, king of Judah, Hoshea, son of Elah, became king of Israel in Samaria and reigned nine years. (Samaria: capital city of Israel; reigned: ruled) **2.** He did evil in the Lord's sight, but not as the kings before him. (Wickedly: evilly) **3.** Shalmaneser, king of Assyria, came against him, and Hoshea became his servant, paying tribute. (Tribute: payment) **4.** The Assyrian king uncovered Hoshea's plot to Egypt, refusing to pay tribute, so he captured him and imprisoned him. (Plot: scheme) **5.** The Assyrian king besieged Samaria for three years. (Besieged: surrounded and attacked) **6.** In

Hoshea's ninth year, Samaria was taken, and Israel was deported to Assyria, settled in Halah, the Habor River, and the Medes' cities. (Conquered: defeated; Habor: river) **7.** This happened because Israel sinned against the Lord, who had brought them out of Egypt and had them worship other gods. (Sinned: wronged) **8.** They followed the ways of nations the Lord had cast out and the kings of Israel who had made these practices. (Adopted: accepted) **9.** They secretly did what was wrong in the Lord's eyes, building high places in cities from watchtowers to fortified ones. (High places: altars; Watchtower: observation tower; Fortified city: protected city) **10.** They set up sacred pillars and wooden idols on high hills and under trees. (Sacred pillars: stone monuments; Idols: false gods) **11.** They burned incense on these high places, like the nations before them, provoking the Lord to anger. (Incense: aromatic substance; Provoke: anger) **12.** They worshiped idols, though the Lord had forbidden it. (Idols: false gods) **13.** The Lord sent prophets to call Israel and Judah to repent, follow His laws, and the commandments given to their ancestors. (Repent: turn away from sin) **14.** But they refused, hardening their hearts like their ancestors who didn't trust the Lord. (Hardened their hearts: refused to listen) **15.** They rejected His laws and covenant, following idols, idol worship, and the ways of surrounding nations. (Statutes: commands; Covenant: agreement) **16.** They abandoned all the commands, made idols, worshiped stars, and served Baal. (Abandoned: forsook; Calves: idolized bulls; Baal: a pagan god) **17.** They sacrificed their children, practiced sorcery and divination, and did evil to provoke the Lord. (Pass through the fire: ritual sacrifice; Sorcery: magic; Divination: fortune telling) **18.** The Lord became angry with Israel and removed them from His presence, leaving only Judah. (Removed from His presence: cast out) **19.** Judah did not keep the Lord's commandments, following Israel's sinful ways. (Walked in: followed) **20.** Therefore, the Lord rejected Israel's descendants, afflicting them and handing them to plunderers, casting them out. (Afflicted: caused suffering; Plunderers: robbers) **21.** He tore Israel from David's house, and they made Jeroboam their king, leading them to sin. (Tore away: separated; Jeroboam: king of Israel) **22.** Israel continued in the sins of Jeroboam and did not turn from them, (Sins: wrongdoings) **23.** until the Lord removed Israel from His presence, as He had warned through His prophets. Israel was exiled to Assyria, where they remain. (Removed from His presence: cast out) **24.** The Assyrian king brought people from Babylon, Cuthah, Ava, Hamath, and Sepharvaim, settling them in Samaria in place of Israel. (Settled: placed; Possession: control) **25.** At first, they didn't fear the Lord, so lions were sent among them, killing some. (Fear the Lord: reverence for God) **26.** The Assyrians told the king, "The nations you relocated don't know the customs of the God of the land, so He has sent lions." (Customs: practices) **27.** The king ordered, "Send a priest from Samaria to teach them the customs of the God of the land." (Commanded: ordered) **28.** A priest came to Bethel and taught them how to fear the Lord. (Bethel: a city in ancient Israel) **29.** But each nation still made its own gods and placed them in the shrines the Samaritans built. (Shrines: places of worship) **30.** The people of Babylon made Succoth Benoth, the people of Cuth made Nergal, the people of Hamath made Ashima, (Succoth Benoth, Nergal, Ashima: names of gods) **31.** the Avites made Nibhaz and Tartak, and the Sepharvites burned their children to Adrammelech and Anammelech, the gods of Sepharvaim. (Nibhaz, Tartak, Adrammelech, Anammelech: names of gods) **32.** They feared the Lord, but appointed priests of the high places to offer sacrifices. (Appointed: selected) **33.** They feared the Lord, but also served their gods, following the rituals of the nations they had been exiled from. (Exiled: removed) **34.** To this day, they continue their old rituals, not truly fearing the Lord, nor following His laws, statutes, and commands given to Jacob's children, Israel. (Rituals: ceremonies, Statutes: laws). **35.** The Lord made a covenant, charging them: "You shall not fear other gods, bow down to, serve, or sacrifice to them. (Covenant: agreement) **36.** But you shall fear the Lord, who brought you out of Egypt with great power and a mighty arm. You shall worship Him and sacrifice to Him. (Mighty arm: power) **37.** The laws, statutes, and commandments He wrote, you must observe forever, not fearing other gods. (Observe: follow carefully) **38.** And the covenant I made with you, do not forget, nor fear other gods. (Forget: fail to remember) **39.** You shall fear the Lord your God, and He will deliver you from all your enemies." (Deliver: save) **40.** They did not obey but continued in their former rituals. (Obey: listen to) **41.** So, they feared the Lord but served their carved images, and their children followed their ancestors' ways to this day. (Carved images: idols)

Chapter 18:
1. In the third year of Hoshea, son of Elah, king of Israel, Hezekiah, son of Ahaz, began his reign over Judah. (Hoshea: a king of Israel, Ahaz: Hezekiah's father) **2.** Hezekiah was twenty-five when he became king and reigned for twenty-nine years in Jerusalem. His mother's name was Abi, daughter of Zechariah. (Abi: Hezekiah's mother, Zechariah: her father) **3.** He did what was right in the sight of the Lord, following his ancestor David's example. (David: a king of Israel known for his faithfulness to God) **4.** He removed the high places, broke the sacred pillars, cut down the wooden idol, and shattered the bronze serpent that Moses had made. Until then, Israel had burned incense to it, calling it Nehushtan. (High places: elevated sites for idol worship, Nehushtan: the bronze serpent, an idol made by Moses) **5.** He trusted in the Lord God of Israel, and no king of Judah was like him, either before or after. (Judah: the southern kingdom of Israel) **6.** He remained loyal to the Lord, following His commandments. (Loyal: devoted, obedient) **7.** The Lord was with him, and he prospered. He rebelled against Assyria and refused to serve the king. (Assyria: an empire that conquered Israel) **8.** He defeated the Philistines, from Gaza to its surrounding cities. (Philistines: a people living along the coast of Israel) **9.** In the fourth year of Hezekiah, seventh of Hoshea, king of Israel, Shalmaneser, king of Assyria, attacked Samaria and besieged it. (Shalmaneser: a king of Assyria, Samaria: the capital of Israel) **10.** After three years, Samaria fell in Hezekiah's sixth year, Hoshea's ninth. (Besieged: surrounded to force surrender) **11.** The Assyrian king took Israel captive, sending them to Halah, the Habor River, and the Medes' cities. (Halah, Habor: locations in Assyria, Medes: a people from modern-day Iran) **12.** They did not obey the Lord but broke His covenant and disregarded Moses' commandments. (Covenant: a solemn agreement between God and Israel) **13.** In the fourteenth year of Hezekiah, Sennacherib, king of Assyria, attacked Judah and took its fortified cities. (Sennacherib: a king of Assyria) **14.** Hezekiah sent to Sennacherib at Lachish, saying, "I have sinned. Please withdraw; I will pay whatever you demand." The Assyrian king required three hundred talents of silver and thirty of gold. (Lachish: a city in ancient Judah) **15.** Hezekiah gave him all the silver from the temple and royal treasuries. (Treasuries: storehouses for wealth) **16.** He stripped the gold from the temple doors and pillars and gave it to the Assyrian king. (Stripped: removed the gold) **17.** The Assyrian king sent his chief officer, the Rabshakeh, with a large army to Jerusalem. They reached the aqueduct near the upper pool on the road to the Fuller's Field. (Rabshakeh: a high-ranking officer, Aqueduct: a water supply system) **18.** Eliakim, Shebna, and Joah went out to meet them. (Eliakim, Shebna, Joah: officials in Hezekiah's court) **19.** The Rabshakeh asked, "What is this confidence you have? (Confidence: trust or reliance) **20.** You speak of power for war, but in whom do you trust to rebel against me? (Rebel: resist authority) **21.** You trust in Egypt, that broken reed. If anyone leans on it, it will pierce their hand. So is Pharaoh to those who trust him. (Reed: a weak support, Pharaoh: the king of Egypt) **22.** If you trust in the Lord, isn't He the one whose high places and altars Hezekiah has removed, saying to Judah, 'Worship before this altar in Jerusalem'? (High places: sites for idol worship, Altars: places of sacrifice) **23.** Now, make peace with my master, and I will give you two thousand horses, if you can

provide riders for them. (Master: the king of Assyria) **24.** How can you defeat even one officer of my master's army while trusting Egypt for chariots and horsemen? (Officers: soldiers in charge) **25.** Did I come here without the Lord's approval to destroy this place? The Lord told me, 'Go up against this land and destroy it.'" (Approval: permission, land: referring to Judah) **26.** Eliakim, Shebna, and Joah asked the Rabshakeh to speak in Aramaic, not Hebrew, so the people on the wall would not hear. (Aramaic: a language spoken in the region, Hebrew: the language of Israel) **27.** The Rabshakeh replied, "Did my master send me only to speak to you, not to those on the wall, who will eat and drink their waste with you?" (Waste: refuse, excrement) **28.** Then he called out in Hebrew, saying, "Hear the word of the great king of Assyria: (Called out: shouted) **29.** Do not let Hezekiah deceive you. He cannot deliver you. (Deceive: mislead) **30.** Don't listen to Hezekiah's words when he says, 'The Lord will deliver us; this city will not fall to Assyria.' (Deliver: rescue, fall: be conquered) **31.** Do not listen to Hezekiah. The king of Assyria says, 'Make peace with me, and come out. Each of you can have your own vine, fig tree, and cistern.' (Cistern: a water storage tank) **32.** I will take you to a land like your own, with grain, new wine, bread, and vineyards. Live and not die. But do not listen to Hezekiah, for he will deceive you saying, 'The Lord will deliver us.' (Grain: food, vineyards: places where grapes are grown) **33.** Has any god of any nation delivered their land from Assyria's hand? (Hand: power) **34.** Where are the gods of Hamath, Arpad, Sepharvaim, Hena, and Ivah? Have they delivered Samaria? (Gods: idols worshipped by various nations) **35.** Which gods have delivered their lands from my hand, that the Lord should deliver Jerusalem?" (Land: territory, delivered: rescued) **36.** But the people were silent, following the king's command not to answer him. (Silent: remained quiet) **37.** Eliakim, Shebna, and Joah tore their clothes and reported the Rabshakeh's words to Hezekiah. (Tore their clothes: an expression of mourning or distress)

Chapter 19
1. When King Hezekiah heard this, he tore his clothes, put on sackcloth, and went to the tabernacle of the Lord. (Sackcloth: coarse cloth for mourning) **2.** He transferred Eliakim, Shebna, and the preachers, all in sackcloth, to Isaiah the prophet. (Scribe: a person who writes) **3.** They told him, "Hezekiah says 'This is a day of trouble, disgrace, and sacrilege; the children are ready to be born, but there's no strength to deliver them.'" (Sacrilege: discourteous speech against God) **4.** Maybe the Lord will hear to the field commander, whom the king of Assyria transferred to mock God, and will rebuke him for what the Lord has heard. Thus, supplicate for the remnant left." (Remnant: the remaining part) **5.** King Hezekiah's retainers came to Isaiah. **6.** Isaiah said, "Tell your master 'This is what the Lord says: Don't sweat the words you have heard, with which the Assyrian retainers have mocked Me. **7.** I'll shoot a spirit on him, and he'll hear a scuttlebutt and return to his land, where I'll make him fall by the brand.'" (Spirit: influence) **8.** The field commander returned and set up the king of Assyria fighting against Libnah, having moved from Lachish. **9.** The king of Assyria also heard that Tirhakah, king of Cush, was coming out to fight him. So he transferred couriers to Hezekiah saying (Cush: an ancient area south of Egypt) **10.** "Say to Hezekiah 'Don't let your God deceive you, saying, "Jerusalem won't fall into the hands of the king of Assyria." **11.** You have heard what the lords of Assyria did to other lands, destroying them. Do you suppose you'll be saved? **12.** Have the gods of the nations delivered those my ancestors destroyed—Gozan, Haran, Rezeph, and Eden's people in Telassar? **13.** Where is the king of Hamath, Arpad, Sepharvaim, Hena, and Ivah?" **14.** Hezekiah entered the letter from the couriers, read it, and went to the tabernacle of the Lord, spreading it before the Lord. **15.** Hezekiah supplicated, "O Lord God of Israel, You who are ennobled between the cherubim, You alone are God over all fiefdoms. You made heaven and earth. (Cherubim: angelic beings) **16.** Incline Your observance, O Lord, and hear; open Your eyes and see; hear to the words of Sennacherib, who has mocked the living God. (Incline: bend) **17.** It's true, Lord, that the lords of Assyria have devastated nations, **18.** and thrown their gods into the fire, for they weren't gods but mortal-made — wood and gravestone. Thus, they destroyed them. **19.** Now, O Lord, save us from his hand, that all fiefdoms may know that You alone are God." **20.** Isaiah transferred to Hezekiah "This is what the Lord says: 'Because you have supplicated to Me concerning Sennacherib, I've heard. **21.** The Lord says: 'The virgin son of Zion mocks you; Jerusalem laughs at you as you flee. (Virgin: symbol of chastity or Jerusalem) **22.** Whom have you disrespected and mocked? You have raised your voice against the Holy One of Israel! (Disrespected: offended) **23.** By your couriers, you have disrespected the Lord, saying, "By my chariots, I'll climb the mountains, cut down its altitudinous cedars, and enter its rich timber. (Chariots: battle vehicles) **24.** I've dug and drunk strange water, and with my bases I've dried up Egypt's aqueducts." (Strange water: foreign water sources) **25.** Have you not heard? I ordained this long agone. Now I've brought it to pass, to crush fortified metropolises into remains. (Ordained: appointed) **26.** Their occupants had little power; they were like lawn in the field, scorched before it grows. (Frustrated: shocked) **27.** But I know your lodging, your rage against Me. **28.** Because your rage and tumult have reached My cognizance, I'll put My hook in your nose and turn you back by the way you came. (Tumult: noisy disturbance) **29.** This shall be a sign to you: You'll eat what grows by itself this time, and in the alternate time, what springs from that. But in the third time, sow, reap, plant stations, and eat their fruit. **30.** The remnant of Judah will take root and bear fruit. (Root: grow deep) **31.** Out of Jerusalem will come a remnant, and those who escape from Zion. The zeal of the Lord will do this. (Zeal: passionate commitment) **32.** The king of Assyria won't enter this megacity, nor shoot an arrow, nor make a siege ramp against it. (Siege ramp: structure used for attacking metropolises) **33.** By the way he came, he'll return, and won't enter the megacity, says the Lord. **34.** I'll defend this megacity for My sake and for David's sake." **35.** That night the Lord's angel struck down 185,000 Assyrians. When people got up, all the bodies were dead. (Struck down: killed) **36.** Sennacherib left, returned to Nineveh, and stayed there. **37.** While worshiping in the tabernacle of his god Nisroch, his sons Adrammelech and Sharezer killed him with the brand and escaped to Ararat. Esarhaddon, his son, succeeded him. (Nisroch: an Assyrian god; Ararat: an ancient region)

Chapter 20
1. In those days, King Hezekiah was seriously ill and near death. The prophet Isaiah, son of Amoz, went to him and said, "Prepare your house, for you're going to die, and won't recover." (Ill: sick, near death; prepare: arrange) **2.** Hezekiah turned his face toward the wall and supplicated, **3.** "Lord, flash back how I've walked before You in verity and with a pious heart, and have done what's good in Your sight." Hezekiah wept plaintively. (Faithfully: actually) **4.** Before Isaiah left the court, the Lord spoke to him, **5.** "Go back and tell Hezekiah, the sovereign of My people, 'I've heard your prayer and seen your gashes. I'll heal you. On the third day, you'll go up to the Lord's tabernacle." (Sovereign: leader; ancestor: father; tabernacle: house of deification) **6.** I'll add fifteen further times to your life. I'll deliver you and this megacity from the Assyrian king and cover it for My sake and for the sake of My menial David.'" (Deliverance: deliver) **7.** Also Isaiah told them, "Take a lump of figs." They applied it to the pustule, and Hezekiah recovered. (Boil: a painful, infected area on the skin) **8.** Hezekiah asked, "What's the sign that the Lord will heal me and I'll go to His tabernacle on the third day?" **9.** Isaiah replied, "This will be the sign: Should the shadow move forward or backward ten degrees?" (Shadow: the shadow of the sun) **10.** Hezekiah responded, "It's easy for the shadow to go forward, but let it go backward ten degrees." **11.** Also Isaiah cried out to the Lord, and the Lord made the shadow move backward ten degrees on the chronograph of Ahaz. (Chronograph: an ancient chronometer device that uses the sun's shadow) **12.** At that time, Berodach-Baladan, king

of Babylon, transferred letters and a gift to Hezekiah because he'd heard of his illness. (Gift: a present) **13.** Hezekiah showed them all his treasures — tableware, gold, spices, precious canvases, and all his magazine — everything in his area. (Wealth: riches, magazine: munitions and armor) **14.** Isaiah asked, "What did these men say, and where did they come from?" Hezekiah replied, "From a distant land, from Babylon." (Distant: away) **15.** Isaiah asked, "What did they see in your palace?" Hezekiah answered, "They saw everything in my palace, nothing among my treasures was hidden." **16.** Also Isaiah said, "Hear to the word of the Lord: **17.** 'The days are coming when everything in your palace and everything your ancestors have stored will be carried off to Babylon. Nothing will be left,' says the Lord. **18.** 'Some of your descendants will be taken down and come eunuchs in the palace of the king of Babylon.'" (Eunuchs: men made unfit to have children, frequently serving in royal courts) **19.** Hezekiah replied, "The word of the Lord is good!" For he allowed, "At least there will be peace and security in my continuance." (Peace: tranquility, calm; security: safety) **20.** The rest of Hezekiah's acts, his strength, and the pool and lair he erected to bring water into the megacity are written in the Book of the Chronicles of the lords of Judah. (Strength: power, pool: a force of water; lair: an underground passage) **21.** Hezekiah passed down and was buried with his ancestors. His son Manasseh succeeded him as king. (Passed down: failed)

Chapter 21

1. Manasseh was twelve times old when he came king and reigned fifty-five times in Jerusalem. His mama's name was Hephzibah. **2.** He did evil in the sight of the Lord, following the execrations of the nations whom the Lord had cast out before Israel. (Execrations: despicable acts) **3.** He rebuilt the high places Hezekiah his father had destroyed, raised stages for Baal, made a rustic image, and worshiped the host of heaven. (High places: elevated deification spots) **4.** He also erected stages in the house of the Lord, where the Lord had said, "In Jerusalem, I'll put My name." **5.** He erected stages for the host of heaven in the two courts of the house of the Lord. (Courts: out-of-door areas) **6.** He made his son pass through the fire, rehearsed auguring, necromancy, and consulted spiritists. He did important wrong to provoke the Lord. (Soothsaying: augury) **7.** He set a sculpted image of Asherah in the house of the Lord, where the Lord said to David and Solomon, "I'll put My name ever." (Sculpted image: hero) **8.** I'll not make Israel wander from the land I gave their fathers, only if they observe all I commanded. (Bases: people) **9.** They paid no attention, and Manasseh enticed them to do more evil than the nations before them. (Enticed: led amiss) **10.** The Lord spoke through His prophets, saying, **11.** "Because Manasseh has done these execrations, acted more spitefully than the Amorites, and made Judah sin, (Execrations: despicable acts) **12.** I'll bring disaster upon Jerusalem and Judah, that whoever hears it, his cognizance will chink. **13.** I'll stretch the measuring line of Samaria and the dip of Ahab's house; I'll wipe Jerusalem like a dish. (Measuring line: a tool for marking distances) **14.** I'll leave My heritage, deliver them to their adversaries, and they will be despoiled. (Leave: abandon) **15.** They've done wrong in My sight and provoked Me since the day their fathers came out of Egypt. **16.** Manasseh exfoliated important innocent blood, filling Jerusalem with it, and led Judah into sin. (Exfoliated: revealed) **17.** The rest of Manasseh's acts and sins are written in the book of the chronicles of the lords of Judah. (Chronicles: sanctioned records) **18.** Manasseh rested with his fathers and was buried in his theater, in the theater of Uzza. His son Amon reigned in his place. **19.** Amon was twenty-two when he came king and reigned two times in Jerusalem. His mama's name was Meshullemeth, son of Haruz of Jotbah. **20.** He did evil in the sight of the Lord, as his father Manasseh had done. **21.** He walked in his father's ways, served his icons, and worshiped them. **22.** He quit the Lord God of his fathers and didn't walk in His ways. (Forsook: abandoned) **23.** The retainers of Amon conspired against him, killing him in his own house. (Conspired: colluded) **24.** The people executed those who had conspired against Amon and made his son Josiah king. (Executed: carried out the death judgment) **25.** The rest of Amon's acts are written in the book of the chronicles of the lords of Judah. (Acts: deeds) **26.** He was buried in the theater of Uzza, and Josiah, his son, reigned in his place.

Chapter 22

1. Josiah was eight times old when he came king, and he reigned thirty-one times in Jerusalem. His ma's name was Jedidah, the son of Adaiah from Bozkath. (Bozkath: a megacity in Judah kingdom) **2.** He did what was right in the sight of the Lord and followed the ways of his ancestor David, not turning to the right or left. (Erred: swerved) **3.** In the eighteenth time of King Josiah's reign, he transferred Shaphan the scribe, the son of Azaliah, the son of Meshullam, to the house of the Lord with the following command (Scribe: a pen or clerk) **4.** "Go to Hilkiah the high clerk, and have him count the capitalist brought into the house of the Lord by the doorkeepers from the people. (Doorkeepers: guards of the temple doors) **5.** Give the capitalist to those in charge of the work in the house of the Lord, to pay for repairs to the structure — **6.** Including carpenters, builders, and masons and to buy timber and cut monument to fix the house. (Hewn: cut or shaped) **7.** No account will be demanded from them, for they are secure. (Secure: reliable) **8.** Hilkiah the high clerk said to Shaphan, "I have set up the Book of the Law in the house of the Lord." He gave the book to Shaphan, and Shaphan read it. (Book of the Law: sacred Book, presumably the Torah) **9.** Shaphan the scribe went to the king and reported, "Your retainers have gathered the capitalist set up in the house, and have given it to those who are overseeing the repairs of the Lord's house." **10.** He also said, "Hilkiah the clerk has given me a book." And Shaphan read it to the king. **11.** When the king heard the words of the Book of the Law, he tore his clothes. (Tore: ripped as a sign of mourning or torture) **12.** Also the king instructed Hilkiah the clerk, Ahikam the son of Shaphan, Achbor the son of Michaiah, Shaphan the scribe, and Asaiah, a domestic of the king, saying, **13.** "Go and interrogate of the Lord for me, for the people, and for all Judah concerning the words of this book that has been set up. For the Lord's outrage is great against us because our ancestors didn't observe the words of this book, failing to do everything written in it." **14.** So Hilkiah, Ahikam, Achbor, Shaphan, and Asaiah went to Huldah the prophetess, the woman of Shallum the son of Tikvah, the son of Harhas, the keeper of the wardrobe. (She lived in Jerusalem in the Alternate Quarter.) They spoke with her. (Palmist: a womanish prophet) **15.** She said to them, "This is what the Lord God of Israel says: 'Tell the man who transferred you to Me, **16.** 'This is what the Lord says: "I will bring disaster upon this place and its inhabitants, fulfilling everything written in the book the king of Judah has read — **17.** because they have abandoned Me and burned incense to other gods, provoking Me to incense with everything they have done. Therefore, My outrage will be poured out on this place and won't be quenched."'" (Quenched: stopped or extinguished) **18.** But concerning the king of Judah, who transferred you to interrogate of the Lord, this is what you will tell him: "This is what the Lord, the God of Israel, says: **19.** 'Because your heart was tender, and you lowered yourself before the Lord when you heard what I spoke against this place and its people — that they would come to desolation and a curse — and you tore your clothes and wept before Me, I have heard you,' says the Lord. **20.** 'Therefore, I will gather you to your ancestors, and you will be buried in peace. You won't see the disaster I am going to bring upon this place.'" So they returned and reported this to the king.

Chapter 23

1. The king called for all the elders of Judah and Jerusalem to come before him. (Elders: aged leaders) **2.** The king went up to the house of the Lord with all the men of Judah, the preachers, the prophets, and all the people, from the topmost to the least. He read aloud all the words of the Book of the Covenant that had been set up in the house of the Lord. (Prophets: messenger of God) **3.** The king stood by a pillar and made a covenant before the Lord, to follow the Lord, keep His commandments, laws, and testimonies with all his heart and soul, and perform the words of the covenant written in the book. All the people agreed to this covenant. (Covenant: agreement) **4.** The king ordered Hilkiah the high clerk, the preachers of the alternate order, and the doorkeepers to bring out of the tabernacle of the Lord all the items made for Baal, Asherah, and the host of heaven. He burned them outside Jerusalem in the Kidron Valley and carried their ashes to Bethel. (Papers: sacred objects; Host of heaven: stars, moon, etc.) **5.** He removed the idolatrous preachers whom the lords of Judah had appointed to burn incense at the high places in Judah and Jerusalem, and those who burned incense to Baal, the sun, the moon, the constellations, and the host of heaven. (Idolatrous: idol-worshiping; High places: locales for idol deification) **6.** He brought out the rustic image from the house of the Lord, burned it at the Brook Kidron outside Jerusalem, bashed it to ashes, and threw its ashes on the graves of the common people. (Rustic image: idol; Common people: ordinary people) **7.** He tore down the ritual cells of the demoralized persons that were in the house of the Lord, where the women wove garments for the rustic image. (Demoralized persons: those involved in immoral acts) **8.** He brought all the preachers from the cities of Judah and defiled the high places where the preachers had burned incense, from Geba to Beersheba. He also broke down the high places at the gates of the city near the Gate of Joshua, the governor of the city. (Defiled: made sick) **9.** The preachers of the high places didn't come to the balcony of the Lord in Jerusalem, but ate unleavened bread among their fellow preachers. (Unleavened bread: without yeast) **10.** He defiled Topheth in the Valley of the Son of Hinnom, so that no one could make their children pass through the fire to Molech. (Defiled: made sick; Molech: a god associated with child immolation) **11.** He removed the horses that the lords of Judah had devoted to the sun at the entrance to the house of the Lord. He burned the chariots of the sun with fire. (Devoted: set aside for deification; Chariots: battle vehicles) **12.** He broke down the stages on the roof of the upper chamber of Ahaz, and the stages made by Manasseh in the two courts of the house of the Lord. He pulverized them and threw their dust into the Brook Kidron. (Stages: places of idol worship; Pulverized: crushed into powder) **13.** He defiled the high places east of Jerusalem, south of the Mount of Corruption, which Solomon had erected for Ashtoreth, Chemosh, and Milcom. (Defiled: made sick; High places: places for idol worship) **14.** He broke the sacred pillars, cut down the rustic images, and filled their places with human bones. (Sacred pillars: idol statues) **15.** He broke down the balcony at Bethel, and the high place erected by Jeroboam. He burned the high place, crushed it to powder, and burned the rustic image. (Bethel: a city; Jeroboam: the first king of Israel) **16.** As Josiah turned, he saw sepulchers on the mountain. He went over and took the bones out of the sepulchers, burned them on the balcony, and defiled it as the prophet had read. (Sepulchers: burial spots) **17.** He asked, "What monument is this I see?" The men replied, "It's the grave of the man of God who came from Judah and proclaimed these things against the altar at Bethel." (Monument: grave marker) **18.** The king said, "Let him be; don't move his bones." They left his bones undisturbed with the bones of the prophet from Samaria. (Undisturbed: not touched) **19.** Josiah removed all the sanctuaries at the high places in Samaria, which the lords of Israel had made to provoke the Lord. He dealt with them as he had in Bethel. (Sanctuaries: places of idol worship) **20.** He executed all the preachers of the high places, burning human bones on their altars. Also, he returned to Jerusalem. (Executed: put to death) **21.** The king commanded the people to keep the Passover to the Lord, as it is written in the Book of the Covenant. (Passover: a Jewish festival) **22.** Such a Passover had not been celebrated since the days of the judges or the kings of Israel and Judah. (Judges: leaders before the monarchy) **23.** In the eighteenth year of King Josiah's reign, this Passover was held before the Lord in Jerusalem. (Reign: rule as king) **24.** Josiah removed those who consulted mediums, spiritists, household gods, and idols. He did this to fulfill the law written in the book that Hilkiah the clerk had set up in the house of the Lord. (Mediums: spirit agents; Spiritists: those who seek supernatural knowledge) **25.** There was no king like Josiah before or after him, who turned to the Lord with all his heart, soul, and strength, following the entire Law of Moses. (Heart, soul, strength: all of one's being) **26.** Yet the Lord did not turn from His fierce wrath, because of the provocations of Manasseh. (Fierce: strong; Provocations: conduct that provokes wrath) **27.** The Lord said, "I will remove Judah from My sight, just as I have removed Israel. I will cast off Jerusalem and the temple where My name is placed." (Cast off: reject) **28.** The acts of Josiah, all he did, are written in the Book of the Chronicles of the kings of Judah. (Acts: deeds or conduct) **29.** During his reign, Pharaoh Necho of Egypt went to help the king of Assyria at the Euphrates River. Josiah confronted him at Megiddo, where Pharaoh Necho killed him. (Brazened: confronted in battle; Megiddo: a city) **30.** Josiah's attendants moved his body from Megiddo, brought him to Jerusalem, and buried him in his own grave. The people of the land made Jehoahaz, Josiah's son, king in his place. (Retainers: attendants) **31.** Jehoahaz was 23 years old when he became king, and he reigned three months. His mother's name was Hamutal. (Reigned: ruled) **32.** He did evil in the sight of the Lord, following the ways of his ancestors. (Sight: presence or view) **33.** Pharaoh Necho imprisoned him at Riblah in the land of Hamath, preventing him from reigning in Jerusalem. Necho also imposed a tribute on the land. (Locked: imprisoned; Homage: tribute) **34.** Pharaoh Necho made Eliakim king instead of Jehoahaz and changed his name to Jehoiakim. Pharaoh took Jehoahaz to Egypt, where he died. (Changed: altered; Took: brought) **35.** Jehoiakim gave Pharaoh the tribute and gold, but he taxed the people of the land to pay Pharaoh. (Tested: took money) **36.** Jehoiakim was 25 years old when he became king, and he reigned for 11 years. His mother's name was Zebudah. (Reigned: ruled) **37.** He did evil in the sight of the Lord, just as his ancestors had. (Sight: view)

Chapter 24

1. During his reign, Nebuchadnezzar, king of Babylon, came up against Judah. Jehoiakim, king of Judah, became his vassal for three years, and then rebelled. (Vassal: a subordinate or servant) **2.** The Lord sent bands of Chaldeans, Syrians, Moabites, and Ammonites to destroy Judah, fulfilling the prophecy by the Lord's prophets. (Chaldeans: Babylonian people) **3.** This occurred at the Lord's command to remove Judah because of Manasseh's sins and his many wicked deeds. (Manasseh: a former king of Judah) **4.** It was also due to the innocent blood he shed, filling Jerusalem with blood that the Lord would not forgive. (Innocent: not guilty of wrongdoing) **5.** Aren't the rest of Jehoiakim's acts written in the Book of the Chronicles of the Kings of Judah? (Chronicles: detailed historical records) **6.** Jehoiakim died and was buried with his ancestors. His son, Jehoiachin, succeeded him. (Reigned: ruled as king) **7.** The king of Egypt no longer came out of his land because the king of Babylon had taken all his territory from the Brook of Egypt to the River Euphrates. (Euphrates: a river in the Middle East) **8.** Jehoiachin was eighteen when he became king and reigned in Jerusalem for three months. His mother's name was Nehushta, daughter of Elnathan of Jerusalem. (Reigned: ruled as king) **9.** Jehoiachin did evil in the sight of the Lord, as his father had. (Evil: morally wrong) **10.** At that time, Nebuchadnezzar's servants came against Jerusalem, and the city was besieged. (Besieged: surrounded) **11.** Nebuchadnezzar came while his servants besieged the city. (Besieging: surrounding or attacking) **12.** Jehoiachin, his mother, servants, princes, and officers went out to Nebuchadnezzar, who took him prisoner in the eighth year of his reign. (Princes: noble or royal leaders) **13.** He carried away all the treasures of the Lord's house and the king's house, cutting up all the gold articles Solomon made for the temple, as the Lord had said.

(Treasures: valuable items) **14.** He took all Jerusalem into captivity, including captains, mighty men, ten thousand captives, and all the craftsmen. Only the poor were left. (Captivity: being taken as prisoners) **15.** He took Jehoiachin captive to Babylon, with the king's mother, wives, officers, and the mighty men of the land. (Captive: prisoner) **16.** All the valiant men, seven thousand, and craftsmen, one thousand, fit for war, Nebuchadnezzar brought captive to Babylon. (Valiant: brave) **17.** The king of Babylon made Mattaniah, Jehoiachin's uncle, king, changing his name to Zedekiah. (Uncle: a brother of one's parent) **18.** Zedekiah was twenty-one when he became king and reigned eleven years in Jerusalem. His mother was Hamutal, daughter of Jeremiah of Libnah. (Reigned: ruled as king) **19.** He did evil in the sight of the Lord, as Jehoiakim had. (Evil: morally wrong) **20.** Because of the Lord's anger, this happened in Jerusalem and Judah, and He cast them out. Then Zedekiah rebelled against Babylon. (Rebelled: resisted or defied)

Chapter 25

1. In the ninth year of King Zedekiah's reign, during the tenth month and on the tenth day, King Nebuchadnezzar of Babylon, along with his entire army, came against Jerusalem. They set up camp around the city and built a siege wall to cut off all access. (siege wall: a wall built to block access and starve the people inside) **2.** The city remained under siege until the eleventh year of King Zedekiah's reign. (siege: military action of surrounding and isolating a city) **3.** By the ninth day of the fourth month, the famine in the city had grown so intense that the people were left without any food. (famine: severe food shortage) **4.** Eventually, the city's wall was breached, and all the soldiers fled during the night through a gate between two walls near the king's garden. Though the Chaldeans (Babylonians) were still surrounding the city, the king managed to escape toward the plains. (breached: broken through; Chaldeans: Babylonians) **5.** The Chaldean army pursued the king and caught up with him in the plains near Jericho. His army scattered, leaving him alone. (pursued: chased) **6.** They captured the king and took him to Riblah, where they presented him before the king of Babylon, who passed judgment on him. (Riblah: a place where judgments were made) **7.** They killed King Zedekiah's sons in his presence, then blinded him, binding him with bronze chains and taking him to Babylon. (blinded: caused to lose sight) **8.** In the fifth month, on the seventh day of the month, during the nineteenth year of King Nebuchadnezzar, Nebuzaradan, the captain of the Babylonian guard, arrived in Jerusalem. (Nebuzaradan: Babylonian officer in charge of the army) **9.** He set fire to the temple of the Lord, the king's palace, and all the significant buildings of the city, destroying them in flames. (set fire to: burned down) **10.** The Chaldean army with Nebuzaradan broke down the entire wall of Jerusalem. (broke down: demolished) **11.** Nebuzaradan then carried away the remaining people who were still in the city, including those who had defected to the Babylonians. (defected: abandoned to join the enemy) **12.** However, he left some of the poor people of the land to tend vineyards and farms. (tend: take care of) **13.** The Chaldeans took the bronze pillars from the temple of the Lord, along with the carts and the bronze Sea, and smashed them to pieces, carrying the bronze to Babylon. (bronze Sea: a large basin used in the temple) **·14.** They also took the pots, shovels, trimmers, spoons, and all the bronze tools used by the priests for worship. (shovels: tools for digging; trimmers: tools for cutting) **15.** The firepans, basins, and the solid gold and silver items were also taken away by the Babylonian captain. (firepans: containers for fire in offerings; basins: large bowls) **16.** The two large bronze pillars, the Sea, and the carts, which King Solomon had made for the temple, were so large and valuable that their bronze was immeasurable. (Immeasurable: too great to measure) **17.** The height of each pillar was 18 cubits, with a bronze capital on top that was 3 cubits high, and a network of bronze with pomegranates surrounding it. The second pillar was identical. (Capital: top part of the pillar; cubit: a unit of measurement, about 18 inches) **18.** Nebuzaradan took Seraiah, the chief priest, Zephaniah, the second priest, and the three doorkeepers. (doorkeepers: temple guards) **19.** He also took a military officer, five of the king's close associates, the chief recruiting officer, and sixty men from the people, all of whom were found in the city. (Recruiting officer: the one in charge of gathering soldiers) **20.** Nebuzaradan brought them to the king of Babylon at Riblah. (Riblah: place for military judgment) **21.** The king of Babylon had them executed at Riblah, in the land of Hamath, thus completing the captivity of Judah. (Executed: put to death) **22.** Nebuchadnezzar appointed Gedaliah, the son of Ahikam, as governor over the people who remained in Judah after the conquest. (Governor: leader or ruler) **23.** When all the army leaders and their men heard that Gedaliah had been appointed, they came to him at Mizpah, including Ishmael, Johanan, Seraiah, and Jaazaniah, with their followers. (Mizpah: a town in Judah) **24.** Gedaliah took an oath before them and assured them not to fear the Chaldeans. He told them to live in the land, serve the king of Babylon, and all would go well. (Oath: a solemn promise) **25.** But in the seventh month, Ishmael, the son of Nethaniah, of the royal family, came with ten men, killed Gedaliah and the Jews with him, along with the Chaldeans. (Royal family: the king's family) **26.** Fearful of the Chaldeans, all the people, both great and small, fled to Egypt for safety. (Fled: ran away) **27.** In the thirty-seventh year of Jehoiachin's exile, on the twenty-seventh day of the twelfth month, King Evil-Merodach of Babylon, in his first year of reign, released Jehoiachin from prison. (Evil-Merodach: the king of Babylon) **28.** He spoke kindly to Jehoiachin and gave him a higher position than the other kings held in Babylon. (Position: rank) **29.** Jehoiachin was given new clothes, and he ate at the king's table for the rest of his life. (New clothes: replacement for prison clothes) **30.** The king also provided him with a regular food supply for every day of his life. (Food supply: daily meals)

13 – 1 Chronicles

Chapter 1

1. Adam, Seth, Enosh, **2.** Cainan, Mahalalel, Jared, **3.** Enoch, Methuselah, Lamech, **4.** Noah, Shem, Ham, and Japheth. **5.** The sons of Japheth have been Gomer, Magog, Madai, Javan, Tubal, Meshech, and Tiras. **6.** The sons of Gomer had been Ashkenaz, Diphath, and Togarmah. **7.** The sons of Javan had been Elishah, Tarshishah, Kittim, and Rodanim. **8.** The sons of Ham had been Cush, Mizraim, placed, and Canaan. **9.** The sons of Cush have been Seba, Havilah, Sabta, Raama, and Sabtecha. The sons of Raama were Sheba and Dedan. **10.** Cush fathered Nimrod; he became a powerful warrior in the world. (Nimrod: a potent hunter and king within the Bible) **11.** Mizraim fathered Ludim, Anamim, Lehabim, Naphtuhim, **12.** Pathrusim, Casluhim (from whom came the Philistines and the Caphtorim). **13.** Canaan fathered Sidon, his firstborn, and Heth; **14.** the Jebusite, the Amorite, and the Girgashite; **15.** the Hivite, the Arkite, and the Sinite; **16.** the Arvadite, the Zemarite, and the Hamathite. **17.** The sons of Shem have been Elam, Asshur, Arphaxad, Lud, Aram, Uz, Hul, Gether, and Meshech. **18.** Arphaxad fathered Shelah, and Shelah fathered Eber. **19.** Eber had two sons: one was named Peleg, due to the fact in his time the earth turned into divided; his brother's name become Joktan. (Peleg: relating to a division of the earth's population or geography) **20.** Joktan fathered Almodad, Sheleph, Hazarmaveth, Jerah, **21.** Hadoram, Uzal, Diklah, **22.** Ebal, Abimael, Sheba, **23.** Ophir, Havilah, and Jobab. some of these were the sons of Joktan. **24.** Shem, Arphaxad, Shelah, **25.** Eber, Peleg, Reu, **26.** Serug, Nahor, Terah, **27.** and Abram, who's Abraham. **28.** The sons of Abraham were Isaac and Ishmael. **29.** those are their genealogies: The firstborn of Ishmael changed into Nebajoth; then Kedar, Adbeel, Mibsam, **30.** Mishma, Dumah, Massa, Hadad, Tema, **31.** Jetur, Naphish, and Kedemah. these had been the sons of Ishmael. **32.** Now the sons born to Keturah, Abraham's concubine, have been Zimran, Jokshan, Medan, Midian, Ishbak, and Shuah. The sons of Jokshan were Sheba and Dedan. (Keturah: Abraham's second spouse after Sarah's demise) **33.** The sons of Midian had been Ephah,

Epher, Hanoch, Abida, and Eldaah. a lot of these have been the children of Keturah. **34.** Abraham fathered Isaac. The sons of Isaac have been Esau and Israel. **35.** The sons of Esau have been Eliphaz, Reuel, Jeush, Jaalam, and Korah. **36.** The sons of Eliphaz had been Teman, Omar, Zephi, Gatam, and Kenaz; and by Timna, Amalek. (Teman: a descendant of Esau; Amalek: a tribe often in warfare with Israel) **37.** The sons of Reuel have been Nahath, Zerah, Shammah, and Mizzah. **38.** The sons of Seir were Lotan, Shobal, Zibeon, Anah, Dishon, Ezer, and Dishan. **39.** The sons of Lotan had been Hori and Homam; Lotan's sister turned into Timna. **40.** The sons of Shobal were Alian, Manahath, Ebal, Shephi, and Onam. The sons of Zibeon were Ajah and Anah. **41.** The son of Anah became Dishon. The sons of Dishon have been Hamran, Eshban, Ithran, and Cheran. **42.** The sons of Ezer were Bilhan, Zaavan, and Jaakan. The sons of Dishan had been Uz and Aran. **43.** Now those were the kings who reigned in the land of Edom before a king reigned over the youngsters of Israel: Bela the son of Beor, and the name of his metropolis turned into Dinhabah. **44.** And when Bela died, Jobab the son of Zerah of Bozrah reigned in his vicinity. **45.** when Jobab died, Husham of the land of the Temanites reigned in his place. **46.** And when Husham died, Hadad the son of Bedad, who attacked Midian in the field of Moab, reigned in his vicinity. The call of his metropolis became Avith. **47.** when Hadad died, Samlah of Masrekah reigned in his location. **48.** And when Samlah died, Saul of Rehoboth-via-the-River reigned in his place. **49.** when Saul died, Baal-Hanan the son of Achbor reigned in his place. **50.** And when Baal-Hanan died, Hadad reigned in his location; and the name of his town became Pai. His wife's name turned into Mehetabel the daughter of Matred, the daughter of Mezahab. **51.** Hadad additionally died. And the chiefs of Edom were chief Timnah, leader Aliah, chief Jetheth, **52.** leader Aholibamah, chief Elah, leader Pinon, **53.** leader Kenaz, chief Teman, leader Mibzar, **54.** leader Magdiel, and chief Iram. those had been the chiefs of Edom. (Edom: a territory and those descended from Esau).

Chapter 2

1. These are the sons of Israel: Reuben, Simeon, Levi, Judah, Issachar, Zebulun, **2.** Dan, Joseph, Benjamin, Naphtali, Gad, and Asher. (Israel's sons: leaders of the twelve tribes) **3.** The sons of Judah were Er, Onan, and Shelah. They were born to him by the Canaanite woman, Shua. Er was wicked, so the Lord killed him. (Judah's sons and God's judgment on Er) **4.** Tamar, Judah's daughter-in-law, bore him Perez and Zerah. Judah had five sons in total. (Tamar bore twins, Perez and Zerah) **5.** Perez had two sons: Hezron and Hamul. (Perez's descendants) **6.** Zerah's sons were Zimri, Ethan, Heman, Calcol, and Dara: five in all. (Zerah's sons, notable figures in Judah's line) **7.** The son of Carmi was Achan, who caused Israel's trouble by sinning. (Achan, the troublemaker who took forbidden items) **8.** Ethan's son was Azariah. (Genealogy of Ethan's descendants) **9.** Hezron had three sons by his wife: Jerahmeel, Ram, and Chelubai. (Hezron's children and their line) **10.** Ram fathered Amminadab, and Amminadab fathered Nahshon, a leader of Judah. (Key leader in Judah's genealogy) **11.** Nahshon fathered Salma, and Salma fathered Boaz. (The line leading to Boaz, a prominent figure) **12.** Boaz fathered Obed, and Obed fathered Jesse. (The lineage leading to King David) **13.** Jesse had seven sons: Eliab (firstborn), Abinadab (second), Shimea (third), **14.** Nethanel (fourth), Raddai (fifth), Ozem (sixth), and David (seventh). (David, the youngest son, chosen as king) **16.** Their sisters were Zeruiah and Abigail. Zeruiah's sons were Abishai, Joab, and Asahel: three mighty men. (Zeruiah's sons: military leaders) **17.** Abigail bore Amasa; his father was Jether, an Ishmaelite. (Amasa, another leader, is mentioned) **18.** Caleb, Hezron's son, had children by Azubah and Jerioth. Their sons were Jesher, Shobab, and Ardon. (Caleb's family and offspring) **19.** After Azubah's death, Caleb married Ephrath, who bore him Hur. (Caleb's second wife and child) **20.** Hur fathered Uri, and Uri fathered Bezalel, the craftsman of the tabernacle. (Line leading to Bezalel, skilled in crafting holy artifacts) **21.** Later, Hezron married the daughter of Machir. She bore him Segub. (Hezron's second wife and child) **22.** Segub fathered Jair, who controlled twenty-three cities in Gilead. (Jair's cities in Gilead) **23.** Geshur and Syria took these cities, including Kenath and its towns. (The conflict over Jair's cities) **24.** After Hezron's death, Caleb's wife Abijah bore him Ashhur, the father of Tekoa. (Caleb's legacy and descendants) **25.** Jerahmeel, Hezron's firstborn, had sons: Ram, Bunah, Oren, Ozem, and Ahijah. (Jerahmeel's children) **26.** Jerahmeel married Atarah, who bore Onam. (Jerahmeel's second wife and child) **27.** Ram, Jerahmeel's firstborn, had sons: Maaz, Jamin, and Eker. (Ram's descendants) **28.** Onam had sons: Shammai and Jada. (Onam's children) **29.** Shammai's sons were Nadab and Abishur. (Shammai's descendants) **30.** Abishur's wife was Abihail, and they had two sons: Ahban and Molid. (Abishur's family line) **31.** Nadab's sons were Seled and Appaim. Seled died childless. (Nadab's sons, Seled's death) **32.** Appaim's son was Ishi, and Ishi's son was Sheshan. (Appaim's descendants) **33.** Sheshan had no sons, only daughters, and gave his daughter to his Egyptian servant, Jarha, as a wife. (Sheshan's daughter and servant marriage) **34.** Jarha and Sheshan's daughter had a son named Attai. (Attai, descendant through the servant's line) **35.** Attai's son was Nathan, and Nathan's son was Zabad. (The descendants of Attai) **36.** Zabad's son was Ephlal, and Ephlal's son was Obed. (Line from Zabad to Obed) **37.** Obed's son was Jehu, and Jehu's son was Azariah. (Descendants of Obed) **38.** Azariah's son was Helez, and Helez's son was Eleasah. (Genealogy through Azariah and Helez) **39.** Eleasah's son was Sismai, and Sismai's son was Shallum. (Eleasah's descendants) **40.** Shallum's son was Jekamiah, and Jekamiah's son was Elishama. (The final step in this lineage) **42.** Caleb's brother, Jerahmeel, had descendants: Mesha, his firstborn, the father of Ziph, and the sons of Mareshah, the father of Hebron. (Caleb's brother's descendants and their territories) **43.** Hebron's sons were Korah, Tappuah, Rekem, and Shema. (Hebron's family line) **44.** Shema's son was Raham, the father of Jorkoam; Rekem's son was Shammai. (Shema and Rekem's descendants) **45.** Shammai's son was Maon, who fathered Beth Zur. (Shammai's descendants and their territory) **46.** Ephah, Caleb's concubine, bore Haran, Moza, and Gazez. Haran fathered Gazez. (Caleb's concubine's children) **47.** Jahdai, another of Caleb's concubines, bore Regem, Jotham, Geshan, Pelet, Ephah, and Shaaph. (Another line of Caleb's family) **48.** Maachah, Caleb's concubine, bore Sheber and Tirhanah. (Caleb's concubine Maachah's children) **49.** Maachah also bore Shaaph, the father of Madmannah, Sheva, the father of Machbenah, and the father of Gibea. (Caleb's concubine's children and their territories) **50.** The daughter of Caleb was Achsah. **51.** The sons of Hur, Caleb's firstborn, were Shobal, the father of Kirjath Jearim, Salma, the father of Bethlehem, and Hareph, the father of Beth Gader. (Hur's descendants and cities they fathered) **52.** Shobal had descendants in Kirjath Jearim: Haroeh, and half the families of Manuhoth. (Shobal's descendants) **53.** The families of Kirjath Jearim were the Ithrites, Puthites, Shumathites, and Mishraites, from whom the Zorathites and Eshtaolites came. (The clans of Kirjath Jearim) **54.** Salma's descendants were Bethlehem, the Netophathites, Atroth Beth Joab, half of the Manahethites, and the Zorites. (Salma's territories) **55.** The scribes living in Jabez were from the families of the Tirathites, Shimeathites, and Suchathites, the Kenites from Hammath, the father of the house of Rechab. (The scribes of Jabez and their families.)

Chapter 3

1. These were the sons of David born to him in Hebron: Amnon, his firstborn, by Ahinoam from Jezreel; Daniel, by Abigail from Carmel; **2.** Absalom, the third, son of Maacah, daughter of Talmai, king of Geshur; Adonijah, the fourth, by Haggith; **3.** Shephatiah, the fifth, by Abital; Ithream, the sixth, by Eglah. (Hebron: City in Judah where David ruled for 7 years and 6 months) **4.** These six sons were born to him in Hebron, where he reigned for 7.5 years. In Jerusalem, he reigned 33 years. **5.** Born in Jerusalem were Shimea, Shobab, Nathan, and Solomon: four by Bathshua, daughter of Ammiel. **6.** Also

173

Ibhar, Elishama, Eliphelet, **7.** Nogah, Nepheg, Japhia, **8.** Elishama, Eliada, and Eliphelet: nine in total. **9.** These were all David's sons, besides those from his concubines, and Tamar, their sister. (Concubines: Secondary wives of lower status; Tamar: Daughter of David and sister of Absalom) **10.** Solomon's son was Rehoboam, who fathered Abijah, Asa, Jehoshaphat, **11.** Joram, Ahaziah, Joash, **12.** Amaziah, Azariah, Jotham, **13.** Ahaz, Hezekiah, Manasseh, **14.** Amon, and Josiah. **15.** The sons of Josiah: Johanan (firstborn), Jehoiakim (second), Zedekiah (third), and Shallum (fourth). **16.** The sons of Jehoiakim: Jeconiah and Zedekiah. **17.** The sons of Jeconiah were Assir, Shealtiel, **18.** Malchiram, Pedaiah, Shenazzar, Jecamiah, Hoshama, and Nedabiah. (Jeconiah: King of Judah, exiled to Babylon) **19.** The sons of Pedaiah were Zerubbabel and Shimei. **20.** The sons of Zerubbabel: Meshullam, Hananiah, Shelomith their sister, **21.** Hashubah, Ohel, Berechiah, Hasadiah, and Jushab-Hesed: five in total. (Zerubbabel: Leader of the return from exile, descendant of David) **22.** The sons of Hananiah: Pelatiah and Jeshaiah, and the sons of Rephaiah, Arnan, Obadiah, and Shechaniah. **23.** The son of Shechaniah: Shemaiah. The sons of Shemaiah were Hattush, Igal, Bariah, Neariah, and Shaphat: six in total. **24.** The sons of Neariah: Elioenai, Hezekiah, and Azrikam: three in total. **25.** The sons of Elioenai: Hodaviah, Eliashib, Pelaiah, Akkub, Johanan, Delaiah, and Anani: seven in total. (Elioenai: Likely a post-exilic priestly family)

Chapter 4

1. The sons of Judah were Perez, Hezron, Carmi, Hur, and Shobal. (Judah's kids, key ancestors) **2.** Reaiah, Shobal's son, fathered Jahath, who fathered Ahumai and Lahad, the families of the Zorathites. (Descendants of Shobal and their households) **3.** The sons of the father of Etam were Jezreel, Ishma, Idbash, and their sister Hazelelponi. (Family of Etam, including their sister) **4.** Penuel was the father of Gedor, and Ezer fathered Hushah. These were the sons of Hur, firstborn of Ephrathah, father of Bethlehem. **5.** Ashhur, father of Tekoa, had two wives: Helah and Naarah. (Ashhur's family and wives) **6.** Naarah bore Ahuzzam, Hepher, Temeni, and Haahashtari. These were her sons. (Naarah's kids) **7.** Helah bore Zereth, Zohar, and Ethnan. **8.** Koz fathered Anub, Zobebah, and the families of Aharhel, son of Harum. (Koz's descendants and their families) **9.** Jabez was more honorable than his brothers, and his mother named him Jabez, meaning "born in pain." **10.** Jabez prayed to the God of Israel: "Bless me, enlarge my territory, be with me, keep me from evil, and prevent me from causing pain." God granted his request. (Jabez's prayer for blessing and protection) **11.** Chelub, Shuhah's brother, fathered Mehir, who fathered Eshton. (Chelub's descendants) **12.** Eshton fathered Beth-Rapha, Paseah, and Tehinnah, father of Ir-Nahash. These were the men of Rechah. (Eshton's sons and their cities) **13.** The sons of Kenaz were Othniel and Seraiah. Othniel's sons were Hathath and Meonothai, who fathered Ophrah. (Kenaz's descendants, including Othniel, a future judge of Israel) **14.** Seraiah fathered Joab, the father of Ge Harashim, for they were craftsmen. **15.** The sons of Caleb, son of Jephunneh, were Iru, Elah, and Naam. Elah's son was Kenaz. (Caleb's sons, including Kenaz) **16.** The sons of Jehallelel were Ziph, Ziphah, Tiria, and Asarel. (Jehallelel's descendants) **17.** The sons of Ezrah were Jether, Mered, Epher, and Jalon. Mered's wife bore Miriam, Shammai, and Ishbah, father of Eshtemoa. **18.** Mered's wife Jehudijah bore Jered, father of Gedor, Heber, father of Sochoh, and Jekuthiel, father of Zanoah. (Mered's wife and her children) **19.** The sons of Hodiah's wife, the sister of Naham, were the fathers of Keilah (the Garmite) and Eshtemoa (the Maachathite). (Hodiah's descendants) **20.** The sons of Shimon were Amnon, Rinnah, Ben-Hanan, and Tilon. Ishi's sons were Zoheth and Ben-Zoheth. (Shimon's children) **21.** The sons of Shelah, son of Judah, were Er (father of Lecah), Laadah (father of Mareshah), and the families of the linen workers of Ashbea. **22.** Jokim, the men of Chozeba, Joash, Saraph (who ruled in Moab), and Jashubi-Lehem. These facts are historical. (Shelah's further descendants and key figures) **23.** These were the potters who lived at Netaim and Gederah, working for the king. (Craftsmen living in cities and working for the king) **24.** The sons of Simeon were Nemuel, Jamin, Jarib, Zerah, and Shaul. (Simeon's children) **25.** Shallum fathered Mibsam, and Mibsam fathered Mishma. (Simeon's descendants) **26.** Mishma's sons were Hamuel, Zacchur, and Shimei. (Mishma's descendants) **27.** Shimei had 16 sons and 6 daughters, but his brothers had fewer children. (Shimei's many children compared to his brothers) **28.** They lived in Beersheba, Moladah, Hazar Shual, Bilhah, Ezem, Tolad, Bethuel, Hormah, Ziklag, Beth Marcaboth, Hazar Susim, Beth Biri, and Shaaraim until David's reign. (Simeon's cities until the time of David) **29.** Their villages were Etam, Ain, Rimmon, Tochen, and Ashan: five towns with surrounding villages as far as Baal. (Simeon's villages) **30.** These were their dwelling places, and they maintained their genealogy. (The families' record of descent) **31.** Meshobab, Jamlech, Joshah (son of Amaziah), Joel, Jehu (son of Joshibiah), and others were leaders of their households. (Notable leaders among Simeon's descendants) **39.** They went to the entrance of Gedor, seeking pasture for their flocks, and found rich, peaceful land. (Simeonites finding good pasture in Gedor) **40.** The land was large, quiet, and peaceful, once inhabited by Hamites. (The fertile land they found) **41.** During Hezekiah's reign, they attacked the Meunites in their tents and destroyed them, and settled in their place due to the rich pasture. (Simeonites' victory over the Meunites and settlement) **42.** Five hundred men of Simeon went to Mount Seir, led by Pelatiah, Neariah, Rephaiah, and Uzziel, sons of Ishi. (Simeon's men lead a raid on Mount Seir) **43.** They defeated the last Amalekites who had escaped, and have dwelt there to this day. (Defeating the Amalekites and settling there).

Chapter 5

1. The sons of Reuben, Israel's firstborn: though he was the firstborn, his birthright was given to the sons of Joseph because he defiled his father's bed. Therefore, the genealogy is not listed according to the birthright. **2.** Judah prevailed over his brothers, and from him came a ruler, though the birthright was Joseph's. (Judah: Tribe from which King David and Jesus Christ descended) **3.** The sons of Reuben, Israel's firstborn, were Hanoch, Pallu, Hezron, and Carmi. **4.** The sons of Joel were Shemaiah, Gog, Shimei, **5.** Micah, Reaiah, Baal, **6.** and Beerah, whom Tiglath-Pileser, king of Assyria, took into captivity. He was the leader of the Reubenites. (Tiglath-Pileser: Assyrian king known for his military campaigns) **7.** And his brethren by their families were registered: Jeiel, Zechariah, **8.** and Bela son of Azaz, son of Shema, son of Joel, who lived in Aroer, as far as Nebo and Baal Meon. (Aroer: City east of the Jordan River; Nebo: Mountain near the land of Moab) **9.** They settled eastward as far as the entrance of the wilderness on this side of the Euphrates River, because their cattle had increased in Gilead. (Euphrates: Major river in Mesopotamia, often a border in biblical narratives) **10.** In the days of Saul, they fought against the Hagrites, who were defeated, and they settled in their tents across the entire area east of Gilead. (Hagrites: Nomadic group defeated by the Reubenites) **11.** The children of Gad lived next to them in Bashan as far as Salcah. **12.** Joel was the chief, followed by Shapham, Jaanai, and Shaphat in Bashan. **13.** Their brethren, by their father's house, were Michael, Meshullam, Sheba, Jorai, Jachan, Zia, and Eber: seven in all. **14.** These were the children of Abihail, son of Huri, son of Jaroah, son of Gilead, son of Michael, son of Jeshishai, son of Jahdo, son of Buz. **15.** Ahi, son of Abdiel, son of Guni, was the chief of their father's house. **16.** The Gadites lived in Gilead, in Bashan and its villages, and in all the common lands of Sharon within their borders. **17.** These were registered by genealogies during the reigns of Jotham, king of Judah, and Jeroboam, king of Israel. **18.** The sons of Reuben, Gad, and half the tribe of Manasseh had 44,760 men of valor, skilled in war, able to bear shield and sword, and to shoot with the bow. **19.** They made war against the Hagrites, Jetur, Naphish, and Nodab. **20.** They were helped against them, and the Hagrites and their allies were handed over to them. They cried out to God during the battle, and He heard them because they trusted in Him. **21.** They took 50,000 camels, 250,000 sheep, 2,000 donkeys, and 100,000 men in spoils. **22.** Many died in the battle, because it was God's war. The Reubenites, Gadites, and half-tribe of Manasseh lived in their place until the exile. **23.** The half-tribe of Manasseh dwelt in the land, from Bashan to Baal Hermon, that is, to Senir or Mount Hermon. **24.** These were the heads of their father's houses: Epher, Ishi, Eliel, Azriel, Jeremiah, Hodaviah, and Jahdiel: mighty men of valor, famous men, and heads of their houses. **25.** But they were unfaithful to the God of their ancestors and worshiped the gods of the people of the land, whom God had destroyed before them. **26.** So the God of Israel stirred up the spirit of Pul, king of Assyria (that is, Tiglath-Pileser), who took the Reubenites, Gadites, and half-tribe of Manasseh into captivity. He brought them to Halah, Habor, Hara, and the river of Gozan, where they remain to this day.

Chapter 6

1. The sons of Levi were Gershon, Kohath, and Merari. (Levites' roles) **2.** The sons of Kohath were Amram, Izhar, Hebron, and Uzziel. (Kohath's descendants) **3.** The children of Amram were Aaron, Moses, and Miriam. The sons of Aaron were Nadab, Abihu, Eleazar, and Ithamar. (Aaron's priesthood) **4.** Eleazar fathered Phinehas, and Phinehas fathered Abishua; **5.** Abishua fathered Bukki, and Bukki fathered Uzzi; **6.** Uzzi fathered Zerahiah, and Zerahiah fathered Meraioth; **7.** Meraioth fathered Amariah, and Amariah fathered Ahitub; **8.** Ahitub fathered Zadok, and Zadok fathered Ahimaaz; **9.** Ahimaaz fathered Azariah, and Azariah fathered Johanan; **10.** Johanan fathered Azariah, who served as priest in the temple that Solomon built in Jerusalem; (Priestly lineage) **11.** Azariah fathered Amariah, and Amariah fathered Ahitub; **12.** Ahitub fathered Zadok, and Zadok fathered Shallum; **13.** Shallum fathered Hilkiah, and Hilkiah fathered Azariah; **14.** Azariah fathered Seraiah, and Seraiah fathered Jehozadak. **15.** Jehozadak went into captivity when the Lord carried Judah and Jerusalem into exile by the hand of Nebuchadnezzar. (Exile of priests) **16.** The sons of Levi were Gershon, Kohath, and Merari. **17.** These are the names of the sons of Gershon: Libni and Shimei. **18.** The sons of Kohath were Amram, Izhar, Hebron, and Uzziel. **19.** The sons of Merari were Mahli and Mushi. These are the families of the Levites according to their fathers: (Levite families) **20.** Of Gershon: Libni his son, Jahath his son, Zimmah his son, **21.** Joah his son, Iddo his son, Zerah his son, and Jeatherai his son. **22.** The sons of Kohath were Amminadab his son, Korah his son, Assir his son, **23.** Elkanah his son, Ebiasaph his son, Assir his son, **24.** Tahath his son, Uriel his son, Uzziah his son, and Shaul his son. **25.** The sons of Elkanah were Amasai and Ahimoth. **26.** The sons of Elkanah were Zophai his son, Nahath his son, **27.** Eliab his son, Jeroham his son, and Elkanah his son. **28.** The sons of Samuel were Joel, the firstborn, and Abijah, the second. (Genealogy of Levites) **29.** The sons of Merari were Mahli, Libni his son, Shimei his son, Uzzah his son, **30.** Shimea his son, Haggiah his son, and Asaiah his son. (Merari's descendants) **31.** These are the men whom David appointed over the service of song in the house of the Lord, after the ark came to rest. **32.** They ministered with music before the dwelling place of the tabernacle of meeting, until Solomon built the temple of the Lord in Jerusalem. They served in their office according to their order. (David's music ministry) **33.** These are the ones who ministered with their sons: Of the sons of the Kohathites, Heman the singer, the son of Joel, the son of Samuel, **34.** the son of Elkanah, the son of Jeroham, the son of Eliel, the son of Toah, **35.** the son of Zuph, the son of Elkanah, the son of Mahath, the son of Amasai, **36.** the son of Elkanah, the son of Joel, the son of Azariah, the son of Zephaniah, **37.** the son of Tahath, the son of Assir, the son of Ebiasaph, the son of Korah, **38.** the son of Izhar, the son of Kohath, the son of Levi, the son of Israel. **39.** His brother Asaph, who stood at his right hand, was Asaph the son of Berachiah, the son of Shimea, **40.** the son of Michael, the son of Baaseiah, the son of Malchijah, **41.** the son of Ethni, the son of Zerah, the son of Adaiah, **42.** the son of Ethan, the son of Zimmah, the son of Shimei, **43.** the son of Jahath, the son of Gershon, the son of Levi. **44.** Their brethren, the sons of Merari, on the left hand, were Ethan the son of Kishi, the son of Abdi, the son of Malluch, **45.** the son of Hashabiah, the son of Amaziah, the son of Hilkiah, **46.** the son of Amzi, the son of Bani, the son of Shamer, **47.** the son of Mahli, the son of Mushi, the son of Merari, the son of Levi. (Levitical singers) **48.** Their brethren, the Levites, were appointed to every kind of service in the tabernacle of the house of God. (Levites' duties) **49.** But Aaron and his sons offered sacrifices on the altar of burnt offering and on the altar of incense, for all the work of the Most Holy Place, and to make atonement for Israel, according to all that Moses the servant of God had commanded. (Priestly sacrifices) **50.** The sons of Aaron were Eleazar his son, Phinehas his son, Abishua his son, **51.** Bukki his son, Uzzi his son, Zerahiah his son, **52.** Meraioth his son, Amariah his son, Ahitub his son, **53.** Zadok his son, and Ahimaaz his son. (Aaron's priestly line) **54.** These were their dwelling places in their settlements, for they were allotted by lot to the sons of Aaron, of the family of the Kohathites: **55.** They gave them Hebron in the land of Judah, with its surrounding common-lands. (Aaron's cities) **56.** But the fields of the city and its villages were given to Caleb, son of Jephunneh. **57.** To the sons of Aaron, they gave one of the cities of refuge, Hebron; also Libnah with its common-lands, Jattir, Eshtemoa with its common-lands, **58.** Hilen with its common-lands, Debir with its common-lands, **59.** Ashan with its common-lands, and Beth Shemesh with its common-lands. **60.** And from the tribe of Benjamin: Geba with its common-lands, Alemeth with its common-lands, and Anathoth with its common-lands. All their cities among their families were thirteen. (Cities of refuge) **61.** To the rest of the Kohathite families, they gave ten cities from half the tribe of Manasseh. **62.** To the sons of Gershon, throughout their families, they gave thirteen cities from the tribe of Issachar, the tribe of Asher, the tribe of Naphtali, and the tribe of Manasseh in Bashan. **63.** To the sons of Merari, across their families, they gave twelve cities from the tribe of Reuben, the tribe of Gad, and the tribe of Zebulun. **64.** So the children of Israel gave these cities with their common-lands to the Levites. (Levites' city allotment) **65.** And by lot, they gave from the tribe of Judah, the tribe of Simeon, and the tribe of Benjamin these cities, which are called by their names. (Lot allocation) **66.** Some of the families of the Kohathites were given cities from the tribe of Ephraim. **67.** They gave them one of the cities of refuge, Shechem with its common-lands, in the mountains of Ephraim, also Gezer with its common-lands, **68.** Jokmeam with its common-lands, Beth Horon with its common-lands, **69.** Aijalon with its common-lands, and Gath Rimmon with its common-lands. **70.** From the half-tribe of Manasseh: Aner with its common-lands and Bileam with its common-lands, for the rest of the Kohathites. (Cities in Ephraim and Manasseh) **71.** From the half-tribe of Manasseh the sons of Gershon were given Golan in Bashan with its common-lands and Ashtaroth with its common-lands. **72.** From the tribe of Issachar: Kedesh with its common-lands, Daberath with its common-lands, **73.** Ramoth with its common-lands, and Anem with its common-lands. **74.** From the tribe of Asher: Mashal with its common-lands, Abdon with its common-lands, **75.** Hukok with its common-lands, and Rehob with its common-lands. **76.** From the tribe of Naphtali: Kedesh in Galilee with its common-lands, Hammon with its common-lands, and Kirjathaim with its common-lands. (Cities in northern tribes) **77.** From the tribe of Zebulun, the remaining sons of Merari were given Rimmon with its common-lands and Tabor with its common-lands. (Zebulun's cities) **78.** On the other side of the Jordan, across from Jericho, they were given from the tribe of Reuben: Bezer in the wilderness with its common-lands, Jahzah with its common-lands, **79.** Kedemoth with its common-lands, and Mephaath with its common-lands. **80.** From the tribe of Gad: Ramoth in Gilead with its common-lands, Mahanaim with its common-lands, **81.** Heshbon with its common-lands, and Jazer with its common-lands. (East of Jordan cities)

Chapter 7

1. The sons of Issachar were Tola, Puah, Jashub, and Shimron: 4 in all. (Issachar; Jacob's ninth son") 2. The sons of Tola were Uzzi, Rephaiah, Jeriel, Jahmai, Jibsam, and Shemuel, heads of their father's house. The sons of Tola were mighty men of valor in their generations; their number in the days of David was twenty-six thousand. 3. The son of Uzzi was Izrahiah, and the sons of Izrahiah were Michael, Obadiah, Joel, and Ishiah. All 5 of them were chief men. 4. And with them, by their generations, according to their fathers' houses, were thirty-six thousand troops prepared for war; for they had many wives and sons." 5. Now their brethren (fellow Christians or members) among all the families of Issachar were strong men of valor, listed by their genealogies, 87,000 in all. 6. The sons of Benjamin were Bela, Becher, and Jediael: 3 in all. 7. The sons of Bela were Ezbon, Uzzi, Uzziel, Jerimoth, and Iri: five in all. They were heads of their fathers' houses, and they were listed by their genealogies, twenty-two thousand and thirty-four mighty men of valor. 8. The sons of Becher were Zemirah, Joash, Eliezer, Elioenai, Omri, Jerimoth, Abijah, Anathoth, and Alemeth. Some of these are the sons of Becher. 9. And they were recorded by genealogy according to their generations, heads of their fathers' houses, twenty thousand two hundred strong men of valor. 10. The son of Jediael was Bilhan, and the sons of Bilhan were Jeush, Benjamin, Ehud, Chenaanah, Zethan, Tharshish, and Ahishahar. 11. These were the sons of Jediael, heads of their fathers' houses; there were seventeen thousand hundred mighty men of valor fit to go out for war and battle. 12. Shuppim and Huppim were the sons of Ir, and Hushim was the son of Aher. 13. The sons of Naphtali were Jahziel, Guni, Jezer, and Shallum, the sons of Bilhah. 14. The descendants (sons) of Manasseh: his Syrian concubine bore him Machir the father of Gilead, the father of Asriel. 15. Machir took as his wife the sister of Huppim and Shuppim, whose name was Maachah. The name of Gilead's grandson was Zelophehad, but Zelophehad begot only daughters. 16. Maachah, the wife of Machir, bore a son, and she called his name Peresh. The name of his brother was Sheresh, and his sons were Ulam and Rakem. 17. The son of Ulam was Bedan. These were the descendants of Gilead the son of Machir, the son of Manasseh. 18. His sister Hammoleketh bore Ishhod, Abiezer, and Mahlah. 19. The sons of Shemida were Ahian, Shechem, Likhi, and Aniam. 20. The sons of Ephraim were Shuthelah, Bered his son, Tahath his son, Eladah his son, Tahath his son. 21. Zabad his son, Shuthelah his son, and Ezer and Elead. The men of Gath who were born in that land killed them because they came down to get their livestock. 22. Then Ephraim their father mourned (feel or show sorrow) many days, and his brethren came to comfort him. 23. And when he went in to his wife, she conceived and bore a son; and he called his name Beriah, because tragedy had come upon his house. 24. Now his daughter was Sheerah, who built Lower and Upper Beth Horon and Uzzen Sheerah; 25. And Rephah was his son, and Resheph, and Telah his son, Tahan his son, ("Sons of Ephraim") 26. Laadan his son, Ammihud his son, Elishama his son, 27. Nun his son, and Joshua his son. 28. Now their possessions and dwelling places were Bethel and its towns: to the east Naaran, to the west Gezer and its cities, and Shechem and its cities, as far as Ayyah and its towns; 29. and by the borders of the children of Manasseh were Beth Shean and its cities, Taanach and its towns, Megiddo and its cities, Dor and its towns. In these dwelt the children of Joseph, the son of Israel. 30. The sons of Asher were Imnah, Ishvah, Ishvi, Beriah, and their sister Serah. 31. The sons of Beriah were Heber and Malchiel, who was the father of Birzaith. 32. And Heber begot Japhlet, Shomer, Hotham, and their sister Shua. 33. The sons of Japhlet were Pasach, Bimhal, and Ashvath. These were the children of Japhlet. 34. The sons of Shemer were Ahi, Rohgah, Jehubbah, and Aram. 35. And the sons of his brother Helem were Zophah, Imna, Shelesh, and Amal. 36. The sons of Zophah were Suah, Harnepher, Shual, Beri, Imrah, 37. Bezer, Hod, Shamma, Shilshah, Jithran, and Beera. 38. The sons of Jether were Jephunneh, Pispah, and Ara. 39. The sons of Ulla were Arah, Haniel, and Rizia. 40. All these were the children of Asher, heads of their fathers' houses, choice men, mighty men of valor, chief leaders. And they were recorded by genealogies among the army, fit for war; their number was twenty-six thousand.

Chapter 8

1. Benjamin had five sons: Bela, his eldest; Ashbel, his 2nd; Aharah, his third; 2. Nohah, the fourth; and Rapha, the fifth. 3. Bela's descendants protected Addar, Gera, Abihud, (Addar: A private call, a leader of the tribe of Benjamin) 4. Abishua, Naaman, and Ahoah. 5 .Gera, Shephuphan, and Huram. 6. The own family of Ehud, who had been leaders of a few of the population of Geba, had their houses relocated to Manahath. 7 Naaman, Ahijah, and Gera have been instrumental in the move, with Gera fathering Uzza and Ahihud. 8 Shaharaim, after sending away his wives Hushim and Baara, had children in the area of Moab. 9. From his wife Hodesh, he had Jobab, Zibia, Mesha, Malcam, 10. Jeuz, Sachiah, and Mirmah. These were the heads of their families. 11. With Hushim, he had sons Abitub and Elpaal. 12. Elpaal's children included Eber, Misham, and Shemed, who were responsible for building Ono and Lod and their surrounding villages. (Ono and Lod: towns in Benjamin's territory later noted in the Bible) 13. Beriah and Shema led the families of Aijalon and drove out the people of Gath. 14. Ahio, Shashak, Jeremoth, 15. Zebadiah, Arad, and Eder, 16. Michael, Ispah, and Joha were Beriah's sons. 17 Zebadiah, Meshullam, Hizki, Heber, 18. Ishmerai, Jizliah, and Jobab were Elpaal's sons. 19. Jakim, Zichri, Zabdi, 20 Elienai, Zillethai, and Eliel, 21 Adaiah, Beraiah, and Shimrath were Shimei's sons. 22 Ishpan, Eber, Eliel, 23 Abdon, Zichri, Hanan, 24. Hananiah, Elam, Antothijah, 25. Iphdeiah, and Penuel were Shashak's children. 26. Shamsherai, Shehariah, Athaliah, 27. Jaareshiah, Elijah, and Zichri were the sons of Jeroham. 28 These were the prominent leaders in their families, dwelling in Jerusalem. 29. The father of Gibeon, Maacah, resided in Gibeon, 30. And his firstborn was Abdon, followed by Zur, Kish, Baal, Nadab, 31. Gedor, Ahio, Zecher, 32. and Mikloth, who fathered Shimeah. They lived alongside their relatives in Jerusalem. 33. Ner fathered Kish, and Kish fathered Saul, who had four sons: Jonathan, Malchishua, Abinadab, and Esh-Baal. (Esh-Baal: another name for Ishbosheth, son of Saul and later king of Israel) 34. Jonathan's son was Merib-Baal, who fathered Micah. 35. Micah's children were Pithon, Melech, Tarea, and Ahaz. 36. Ahaz fathered Jehoaddah, and Jehoaddah had Alemeth, Azmaveth, and Zimri; Zimri fathered Moza. 37. Moza fathered Binea, Raphah, Eleasah, and Azel. 38. Azel had six sons: Azrikam, Bocheru, Ishmael, Sheariah, Obadiah, and Hanan. These were his sons. 39. Eshek's children, his brother, included Ulam, his firstborn; Jeush, his second; and Eliphelet, his third. 40. The sons of Ulam were powerful warriors, professional archers. They had one hundred and fifty descendants in total, including sons and grandsons. All of these were from the tribe of Benjamin.

Chapter 9

1. All of Israel was recorded by genealogies, and their names were written in the book of the kings of Israel. However, Judah was exiled to Babylon because of their unfaithfulness. 2. The first inhabitants to settle in their allotted land in their cities were the Israelites, priests, Levites, and the Nethinim (temple servants). 3. In Jerusalem, the descendants of Judah lived, along with some from Benjamin, Ephraim, and Manasseh: 4. Uthai, the son of Ammihud, the son of Omri, the son of Imri, the son of Bani, from the family of Perez, the son of Judah. (Perez: one of the sons of Judah, whose descendants are significant in the genealogical line of Israel) 5. From the Shilonites: Asaiah, the firstborn, and his sons. 6. From the descendants of Zerah: Jeuel, and his brothers: six hundred and ninety in total. (Zerah: a descendant of Judah, known for his large family) 7 From the descendants of Benjamin: Sallu, son of Meshullam, son of Hodaviah, son of Hassenuah; 8. Ibneiah, son of Jeroham; Elah, son of Uzzi, son of Michri; Meshullam, son of

Shephatiah, son of Reuel, son of Ibnijah; **9.** and their brothers, listed according to their generations: nine hundred and fifty-six in total. These were the heads of their father's houses. **10.** The priests were: Jedaiah, Jehoiarib, and Jachin; (Jachin: one of the priests in charge of the house of the Lord) **11.** Azariah, son of Hilkiah, son of Meshullam, son of Zadok, son of Meraioth, son of Ahitub, who served as the officer over the house of God; **12.** Adaiah, son of Jeroham, son of Pashur, son of Malchijah; Maasai, son of Adiel, son of Jahzerah, son of Meshullam, son of Meshillemith, son of Immer; **13.** and their brothers, heads of their father's houses: 1,760 in total. These men were skilled and dedicated for the work in the service of God's house. **14.** The Levites were: Shemaiah, son of Hasshub, son of Azrikam, son of Hashabiah, of the family of Merari; (Merari: one of the Levitical families responsible for certain tasks in the temple) **15.** Bakbakkar, Heresh, Galal, and Mattaniah, son of Micah, son of Zichri, son of Asaph; (Asaph: a prominent Levite musician and one of David's chief musicians) **16.** Obadiah, son of Shemaiah, son of Galal, son of Jeduthun; and Berechiah, son of Asa, son of Elkanah, who lived in the villages of the Netophathites. (Netophathites: a Levitical group who lived in villages near Jerusalem) **17.** The gatekeepers were: Shallum, Akkub, Talmon, Ahiman, and their brothers. Shallum was their chief. **18.** These gatekeepers were responsible for guarding the camps of the Levites at the King's Gate on the east. **19.** Shallum, son of Kore, son of Ebiasaph, son of Korah, and his brothers, the Korahites, had charge of the service at the gates. Their ancestors had been in charge of guarding the entrance to the Lord's camp. (Korahites: descendants of Korah, assigned the responsibility of guarding the temple gates) **20.** Phinehas, son of Eleazar, had previously been the officer over them, and the Lord was with him. **21.** Zechariah, son of Meshelemiah, was responsible for keeping the door of the tabernacle of meeting. **22.** In total, two hundred and twelve gatekeepers were chosen, recorded by their genealogies in their villages. David and Samuel the seer had appointed them to this position of trust. (Gatekeepers: Levites assigned to guard the entrance of the temple or tabernacle) **23.** These gatekeepers, along with their children, were in charge of the gates of the Lord's house, the tabernacle, as assigned to them. **24.** The gatekeepers were appointed to four directions: east, west, north, and south. (Tabernacle: the portable temple used by the Israelites during their wanderings) **25.** Their brothers from other villages came to assist them for a week at a time. **26.** Four chief gatekeepers, all Levites, were in charge of the chambers and treasuries of God's house. **27.** They camped around the house of God, as they had the responsibility to open it each morning. **28.** Some were entrusted with the care of the serving vessels, ensuring they were brought in and taken out by count. (Serving vessels: the utensils used in the temple for worship) **29.** Others were responsible for the furnishings and all the sacred instruments, including the fine flour, wine, oil, incense, and spices. **30.** Some of the priests' sons prepared the sacred ointment for the spices. **31.** Mattithiah, a Levite and the firstborn of Shallum the Korahite, was assigned to oversee the baking of the offerings made in pans. (Korahite: descendant of Korah, assigned to temple duties) **32.** Some of the Kohathites were responsible for preparing the showbread for the Sabbath. (Kohathites: a Levitical family entrusted with the care of sacred items) **33.** These were the singers, heads of their father's houses, who lived in the chambers and were exempt from other duties; they were dedicated to the work of worship day and night. (Singers: Levites responsible for leading worship through music in the temple) **34.** These heads of the Levite families were leaders throughout their generations and resided in Jerusalem. **35.** Jeiel, the father of Gibeon, whose wife's name was Maacah, lived at Gibeon. **36.** His firstborn son was Abdon, followed by Zur, Kish, Baal, Ner, Nadab, **37.** Gedor, Ahio, Zechariah, and Mikloth. **38.** Mikloth fathered Shimeam, and they lived alongside their relatives in Jerusalem. **39.** Ner fathered Kish, Kish fathered Saul, and Saul fathered Jonathan, Malchishua, Abinadab, and Esh-Baal. **40.** Jonathan's son was Merib-Baal, who fathered Micah. **41.** The sons of Micah were Pithon, Melech, Tahrea, and Ahaz. **42** Ahaz fathered Jarah, and Jarah fathered Alemeth, Azmaveth, and Zimri; Zimri fathered Moza. **43** Moza fathered Binea, who fathered Rephaiah, Eleasah, and Azel. **44.** Azel had six sons: Azrikam, Bocheru, Ishmael, Sheariah, Obadiah, and Hanan. These were the sons of Azel.

Chapter 10

1. The Philistines engaged in battle with Israel, and the men of Israel fled from them, many falling dead on Mount Gilboa (Mount Gilboa; a mountain in northern Israel). **2.** The Philistines relentlessly pursued Saul and his sons, killing Jonathan, Abinadab, and Malchishua: Saul's sons. **3.** The battle raged fiercely against Saul, and he was struck and injured by enemy archers. **4.** Saul then said to his armor-bearer, "Draw your sword and kill me, so these uncircumcised enemies won't capture and torture me." But his armor-bearer, too afraid, refused. So Saul took his own sword and fell on it. **5.** When his armor-bearer saw Saul was dead, he also fell on his own sword and died alongside him. **6.** Thus, Saul, his three sons, and his household perished together (die, especially in a violent or sudden way). **7.** When the Israelites in the valley realized their army had fled and Saul and his sons were dead, they abandoned their cities. The Philistines then occupied them. **8.** The following day, as the Philistines came to loot the dead, they discovered Saul and his sons' bodies on Mount Gilboa. **9.** They stripped Saul of his belongings, took his head and armor, and sent word across their land to announce the victory in their temples and among their people. **10.** Saul's armor was placed in the temple of their gods, and his head was fastened in the temple of Dagon (Dagon ;a Philistine deity). **11.** When the residents of Jabesh Gilead heard of what the Philistines had done to Saul, (Jabesh Gilead; a city east of the Jordan River) **12.** all their brave men retrieved the bodies of Saul and his sons. They brought them to Jabesh, buried their bones under a tamarisk tree (a desert tree), and fasted for seven days. **13.** Saul died because he was unfaithful to the Lord, disobeyed His word, and sought guidance from a medium (unfaithful ;do not trust) .**14.** He did not seek help from the Lord, so God allowed him to die and gave his kingdom to David, the son of Jesse (David's father from Bethlehem).

Chapter 11

1. The people of Israel gathered at Hebron and said to David, "We are your own kin, your bone and flesh." **2.** They reminded him, "Even when Saul was king, you led Israel in battles. The Lord said, 'You will shepherd My people Israel and rule over them.'" (shepherd: a leader and guide) **3.** The elders of Israel met with David at Hebron, where he made a covenant with them before the Lord. They anointed him king over Israel, fulfilling the word of the Lord through Samuel. (Hebron: a significant city in Judah; Samuel: a prophet who anointed David) **4.** David and all Israel went to Jerusalem, then called Jebus, where the Jebusites lived. (Jebus: ancient name of Jerusalem; Jebusites: original inhabitants of Jerusalem) **5.** The Jebusites said, "You cannot enter here!" But David captured Zion, which became the City of David. (Zion: a fortress in Jerusalem; City of David: the area named after King David) **6.** David declared, "The first to attack the Jebusites will become chief and captain." Joab, son of Zeruiah, responded first and earned the title. (Joab: a commander in David's army) **7.** David lived in the stronghold, which was then called the City of David in his honor. **8.** He rebuilt the city, starting from the Millo and extending outward. Joab repaired the rest of the city. (Millo: a defensive structure in Jerusalem) **9.** David grew more powerful because the Lord of hosts was with him. (Lord of hosts: God as the commander of heavenly armies) **10.** These were the leaders among David's mighty warriors who supported him in establishing his kingdom, fulfilling the Lord's promise to Israel. (mighty warriors: elite fighters loyal to David) **11.** Jashobeam, a Hachmonite, was chief of the captains. Using his spear, he killed 300 men in one battle. (Jashobeam: a valiant warrior; Hachmonite: his lineage) **12.** Eleazar, son of Dodo the Ahohite, was also among the top three warriors. (Dodo: Eleazar's father; Ahohite: his clan) **13.** Eleazar stood with David at Pasdammim when the Philistines gathered for battle near a barley field. (Pasdammim: a battlefield location; Philistines: enemies of Israel) **14.** Despite others fleeing, they defended the field, killed the Philistines, and the Lord granted victory. (victory: triumph by God's intervention) **15.** Three of David's thirty warriors went to the cave of Adullam, where David was hiding, while the Philistines camped in the Valley of Rephaim. (Adullam: a cave of refuge; Valley of Rephaim: a valley near Jerusalem) **16.** At that time, David was in a stronghold, while Bethlehem was under Philistine control. (Bethlehem: David's birthplace) **17.** David expressed a longing, saying, "If only I could have water from the well near Bethlehem's gate!" (well: a source of water in Bethlehem) **18.** The three warriors broke through the Philistine camp, drew water from the well, and brought it to David. Yet, David refused to drink and poured it out as an offering to the Lord. **19.** He said, "I cannot drink this water, as it represents the lives of those who risked themselves for me!" Such deeds were done by these three warriors. **20.** Abishai, Joab's brother, led another group of three warriors. He used his spear to kill 300 men, earning a great reputation. (Abishai: a leader and Joab's sibling) **21.** Though honored above the other two, he did not attain the rank of the first three but was made their captain. **22.** Benaiah, son of Jehoiada from Kabzeel, performed notable feats, such as killing two champions of Moab and a lion on a snowy day. (Jehoiada: Benaiah's father; Moab: an enemy nation of Israel) **23.** He also killed a giant Egyptian, five cubits tall, by taking his spear and killing him with it. (cubit: an ancient measurement, about 18 inches) **24.** Benaiah's achievements earned him fame among David's mighty men. **25.** Although more respected than the thirty, he did not rank with the first three. David appointed him over his royal guard. **26.** Other notable warriors included Asahel (Joab's brother), Elhanan (son of Dodo from Bethlehem), **27.** Shammoth the Harorite, Helez the Pelonite, **28.** Ira (son of Ikkesh from Tekoa), Abiezer the Anathothite, **29.** Sibbechai the Hushathite, Ilai the Ahohite, **30.** Maharai the Netophathite, Heled (son of Baanah of Netophath), **31.** Ithai (son of Ribai from Gibeah in Benjamin), Benaiah the Pirathonite, **32.** Hurai from the brooks of Gaash, Abiel the Arbathite, **33.** Azmaveth the Baharumite, Eliahba the Shaalbonite, **34.** sons of Hashem the Gizonite, Jonathan (son of Shageh the Hararite), **35.** Ahiam (son of Sacar the Hararite), Eliphal (son of Ur), **36.** Hepher the Mecherathite, Ahijah the Pelonite, **37.** Hezro the Carmelite, Naarai (son of Ezbai), **38.** Joel (Nathan's brother), Mibhar (son of Hagri), **39.** Zelek the Ammonite, Naharai the Berothite (Joab's armor-bearer), **40.** Ira the Ithrite, Gareb the Ithrite, **41.** Uriah the Hittite, Zabad (son of Ahlai), **42.** Adina (son of Shiza, leader of the Reubenites) with thirty warriors, **43.** Hanan (son of Maachah), Joshaphat the Mithnite, **44.** Uzzia the Ashterathite, Shama and Jeiel (sons of Hotham the Aroerite), **45.** Jediael (son of Shimri) and Joha the Tizite, **46.** Eliel the Mahavite, Jeribai and Joshaviah (sons of Elnaam), Ithmah the Moabite, **47.** Eliel, Obed, and Jaasiel the Mezobaite.

Chapter 12

1. A group of men joined David at Ziklag while he was fleeing from Saul, son of Kish. These were mighty warriors who assisted him in battle. (Ziklag: a city given to David by the Philistines) **2.** They were skilled with bows and could use both hands equally well to hurl stones and shoot arrows. They were from the tribe of Benjamin, Saul's relatives. (Benjamin: one of the tribes of Israel) **3.** The leaders included Ahiezer and Joash, sons of Shemaah the Gibeathite; Jeziel and Pelet, sons of Azmaveth; Berachah; and Jehu the Anathothite. (Gibeathite: a native of Gibeah; Anathothite: a native of Anathoth) **4.** Other notable men were Ishmaiah the Gibeonite, a leader among the thirty, as well as Jeremiah, Jahaziel, Johanan, and Jozabad the Gederathite. **5.** Eluzai, Jerimoth, Bealiah, Shemariah, and Shephatiah the Haruphite also joined. **6.** Additionally, Elkanah, Jisshiah, Azarel, Joezer, and Jashobeam, who were Korahites, came to support David. (Korahites: descendants of Korah, often warriors or Levites) **7.** Joelah and Zebadiah, sons of Jeroham from Gedor, were among them. **8.** Some men from the tribe of Gad joined David at his stronghold in the wilderness. They were skilled warriors, adept with shield and spear, with faces fierce like lions and swift as gazelles. (Gad: one of the tribes of Israel; stronghold: a fortified hiding place) **9.** These included Ezer the first, Obadiah the second, and Eliab the third. **10.** Others were Mishmannah the fourth, Jeremiah the fifth, Attai the sixth, **11.** Eliel the seventh, Johanan the eighth, Elzabad the ninth, **12.** Jeremiah the tenth, and Machbanai the eleventh. **13.** These sons of Gad were leaders of the army, with the least commanding 100 men and the greatest over 1,000. **14.** They crossed the Jordan during the first month when it overflowed its banks, defeating enemies on both the eastern and western sides. (Jordan: a significant river in Israel) **15.** Some men from Benjamin and Judah also came to David at the stronghold. **16.** David approached them, saying, "If you come peacefully to help me, I will welcome you. But if you intend to betray me, may the God of our ancestors judge between us." (God of our ancestors: a reference to the God of Abraham, Isaac, and Jacob) **17.** Amasai, leader of the captains, responded under the Spirit's influence: "We are with you, David, son of Jesse! Peace to you and your allies, for your God supports you." David accepted them and made them leaders of his troops. **18.** Men from Manasseh joined David when he was aligning with the Philistines against Saul. However, they were sent back by the Philistine rulers, who feared David might switch allegiance. (Manasseh: one of the tribes of Israel; Philistines: adversaries of Israel) **19.** The Manassites who joined David at Ziklag included Adnah, Jozabad, Jediael, Michael, Jozabad, Elihu, and Zillethai, all commanders of thousands. **20.** These warriors aided David against raiders, as they were valiant and experienced leaders. **21.** Daily, more men joined David until his army became as powerful as the army of God. (army of God: a metaphor for divine strength) **22.** At Hebron, armed divisions gathered to transfer Saul's kingdom to David, as foretold by the Lord. (Hebron: David's first capital as king) **23.** Judah contributed 6,800 men equipped with shields and spears. **24.** From Simeon, 7,100 brave and skilled warriors came. **25.** Levi sent 4,600 men, **26.** including Jehoiada, leader of Aaron's descendants, with 3,700 men. (Aaronites: descendants of Aaron, the first high priest) **27.** Young and valiant Zadok came with 22 captains from his family. **28.** Benjamin, Saul's own tribe, sent 3,000 men, though many had remained loyal to Saul's house. **29.** Ephraim contributed 20,800 renowned warriors, famous in their clans. (Ephraim: a tribe known for its strength) **30.** The half-tribe of Manasseh sent 18,000 men, chosen by name to support David's kingship. **31.** From Issachar came 200 chiefs with wisdom to understand the times and advise Israel on what to do. (Issachar: a tribe known for discernment) **32.** Zebulun sent 50,000 expert warriors who could keep rank. **33.** Naphtali provided 1,000 captains and 37,000 men with shields and spears. **34.** Dan sent 28,600 skilled soldiers. **35.** Asher contributed 40,000 capable warriors. **36.** From the Reubenites, Gadites, and the half-tribe of Manasseh east of the Jordan, 120,000 armed men joined with every kind of weapon. **37.** All these warriors, loyal in heart and united in purpose, came to Hebron to crown David king of Israel. **38.** They stayed with David for three days, feasting on the provisions their fellow Israelites had prepared. **39.** People from Issachar, Zebulun, Naphtali, and other regions brought supplies: flour, fig cakes, raisins, wine, oil, cattle, and sheep: celebrating the joy of Israel. **40.** Additionally, those from nearby regions, as well as distant places like Issachar, Zebulun, and Naphtali, brought abundant provisions. They transported flour, cakes of figs, raisins, wine, oil, oxen, and sheep on donkeys, camels, mules, and oxen. There was great joy throughout Israel. (Issachar, Zebulun, Naphtali: tribes of Israel known for their unity and support of David).

Chapter 13

1. David consulted with the commanders of the army and all the leaders. **2.** David addressed the assembly of Israel, saying, "If this plan seems good to you and aligns with the will of the Lord our God, let us send word to our fellow Israelites who remain across the land of Israel, along with the priests and Levites in their towns and surrounding areas, to gather together for us." **3.** "Let us bring back the ark of our God, for we have not sought it since the time of Saul." (Saul was the first king of Israel.) **4.** The entire assembly agreed to this, for it seemed right to them. **5.** David gathered all of Israel, from Shihor in Egypt to the entrance of Hamath, to bring the ark of God from Kirjath Jearim. (Kirjath Jearim was a town where the ark had been kept.) **6.** David and all of Israel traveled to Baalah, which is also called Kirjath Jearim, a city belonging to Judah, to bring the ark of God, the Lord who is enthroned between the cherubim, where His name is proclaimed. **7.** They placed the ark on a new cart, brought from the house of Abinadab, and Uzza and Ahio, the sons of Abinadab, drove the cart. **8.** David and all of Israel played music before God with all their strength, singing and playing on harps, stringed instruments, tambourines, cymbals, and trumpets. **9.** When they arrived at Chidon's threshing floor, Uzza reached out to steady the ark because the oxen stumbled. **10.** The Lord's anger was aroused against Uzza, and He struck him for touching the ark; Uzza died there before God. **11.** David was angry because of the Lord's outburst against Uzza, and that place was named Perez Uzza (which means "the outbreak against Uzza") to this day. **12.** David was afraid of God on that day and said, "How can I bring the ark of God to me?" **13.** So David did not bring the ark into the City of David, but instead took it to the house of Obed-Edom the Gittite. (Obed-Edom was a man from Gath, a Philistine city.) **14.** The ark of God remained in the house of Obed-Edom for three months, and the Lord blessed Obed-Edom and all his household.

Chapter 14

1. King Hiram of Tyre sent messengers to David, bringing cedar trees, masons, and carpenters to build him a house. (Hiram: Phoenician king) **2.** David recognized that the Lord had established him as king over Israel, and his kingdom was exalted for the sake of God's people. (David's kingdom: divinely appointed) **3.** David took more wives in Jerusalem and had additional sons and daughters. **4.** These are the names of his children born in Jerusalem: Shammua, Shobab, Nathan, Solomon, **5.** Ibhar, Elishua, Elpelet, **6.** Nogah, Nepheg, Japhia, **7.** Elishama, Beeliada, and Eliphelet. (David's children: royal line) **8.** When the Philistines heard that David was king over all Israel, they went to search for him. David went out to meet them. (Philistines: Israel's enemies) **9.** The Philistines raided the Valley of Rephaim. (Valley: battleground) **10.** David asked God, "Should I go up against the Philistines? Will You deliver them into my hands?" The Lord said, "Go, I will give them to you." (David seeks God's guidance) **11.** They went to Baal Perazim, where David defeated them. He said, "God has broken through my enemies like a flood!" So, the place was called Baal Perazim. (Baal Perazim: "Lord of the breakthrough") **12.** When the Philistines left their gods, David commanded them to be burned with fire. **13.** The Philistines raided the valley again. (Philistines persist) **14.** David again inquired of God, and He told him, "Do not pursue them; wait near the mulberry trees." (Mulberry trees: strategic position) **15.** "When you hear marching in the tops of the trees, go out to battle, for I have gone ahead to strike the Philistines." (God's presence: victory) **16.** David obeyed and defeated the Philistines from Gibeon to Gezer. (Gibeon to Gezer: distance of victory) **17.** David's fame spread, and the nations feared him as God brought terror upon them. (David's fame: widespread)

Chapter 15

1. David built houses for himself in the City of David and set up a place for the ark of God, pitching a tent for it. (City of David: Jerusalem's ancient center) **2.** David declared, "Only the Levites may carry the ark of God, for the Lord has chosen them to bear it and serve Him forever." (Levites: priestly tribe) **3.** David gathered all Israel in Jerusalem to bring the ark of the Lord to the place he had prepared for it. (Ark of the Lord: sacred chest containing the tablets of the law) **4.** David assembled the descendants of Aaron and the Levites: **5.** Uriel, the chief of the Kohathites, with 120 of his relatives; **6.** Asaiah, the chief of the Merarites, with 220 of his relatives; **7.** Joel, the chief of the Gershonites, with 130 of his relatives; **8.** Shemaiah, the chief of the Elizaphanites, with 200 of his relatives; **9.** Eliel, the chief of the Hebronites, with 80 of his relatives; **10.** Amminadab, the chief of the Uzzielites, with 112 of his relatives. (Levite divisions: families with specific roles) **11.** David called for the priests Zadok and Abiathar, and for the Levites: Uriel, Asaiah, Joel, Shemaiah, Eliel, and Amminadab. (Zadok and Abiathar: high priests) **12.** He told them, "You are the heads of the Levite families; consecrate yourselves and your brothers, so you can bring the ark of the Lord to the place I have prepared for it." (Consecrate: make holy) **13.** "Because you did not do it the first time, the Lord's anger broke out against us, for we did not seek Him about the proper order." (First time: referring to earlier improper handling of the ark) **14.** So the priests and Levites consecrated themselves to bring the ark of the Lord God of Israel to its place. (Consecrated: purified for service) **15.** The Levites carried the ark of God on their shoulders, using its poles, as Moses had commanded, following the word of the Lord. (Moses' command: carrying by poles, not by hand) **16.** David instructed the Levite leaders to appoint their brothers as singers, with instruments such as stringed instruments, harps, and cymbals, to raise their voices with joy. (Musical instruments: part of worship) **17.** The Levites appointed Heman son of Joel, Asaph son of Berechiah, and Ethan son of Kushaiah. (Heman, Asaph, Ethan: prominent musicians) **18.** With them, the second group: Zechariah, Ben, Jaaziel, Shemiramoth, Jehiel, Unni, Eliab, Benaiah, Maaseiah, Mattithiah, Elipheleh, Mikneiah, Obed-Edom, and Jeiel, the gatekeepers. (Gatekeepers: responsible for the ark's security) **19.** The singers, Heman, Asaph, and Ethan, were to play the bronze cymbals. (Cymbals: percussion instruments in worship) **20.** Zechariah, Aziel, Shemiramoth, Jehiel, Unni, Eliab, Maaseiah, and Benaiah played stringed instruments according to Alamoth. (Alamoth: musical style) **21.** Mattithiah, Elipheleh, Mikneiah, Obed-Edom, Jeiel, and Azaziah led with harps on the Sheminith. (Sheminith: a musical scale or style) **22.** Chenaniah, leader of the Levites, was in charge of the music because he was skillful. (Chenaniah: music leader) **23.** Berechiah and Elkanah were doorkeepers for the ark. (Doorkeepers: guardians of the sacred space) **24.** Shebaniah, Joshaphat, Nethanel, Amasai, Zechariah, Benaiah, and Eliezer, the priests, were to blow trumpets before the ark of God, and Obed-Edom and Jehiah were doorkeepers. (Priests and trumpets: signaling God's presence) **25.** So David, the elders of Israel, and the captains of thousands went to bring the ark of the covenant from the house of Obed-Edom with joy. (Obed-Edom: a man who had been blessed by the ark's presence) **26.** When God helped the Levites who carried the ark, they offered seven bulls and seven rams as sacrifices. (Sacrifices: offerings of thanksgiving) **27.** David was clothed in fine linen, as were all the Levites who carried the ark, the singers, and Chenaniah, the music leader. David also wore a linen ephod. (Linen ephod: sacred garment) **28.** All Israel brought up the ark of the Lord with shouting, trumpets, cymbals, stringed instruments, and harps. (Celebration: worship with music) **29.** When the ark arrived at the City of David, Michal, Saul's daughter, looked out the window and saw King David dancing and playing music; and she despised him in her heart. (Michal's reaction: disapproval of David's public display of worship)

Chapter 16

1. They brought the ark of God and placed it in the tent David had prepared, offering burnt and peace offerings to God. (Ark: sacred box of God's covenant) **2.** After the offerings, David blessed the people in the name of the Lord. (Blessed: invoked God's favor) **3.** David gave each person in Israel a loaf of bread, a piece of meat, and a raisin cake. (Gifts: symbolic offerings) **4.** David appointed Levites to minister before the ark, to thank, praise, and commemorate God. (Levites: chosen servants) **5.** Asaph was chief, followed by Zechariah, Jeiel, Shemiramoth, Jehiel, Mattithiah, Eliab, Benaiah, and Obed-Edom. Jeiel played stringed instruments, while Asaph played cymbals. (Asaph: leader of music) **6.** Benaiah and Jahaziel, the priests, blew trumpets before the ark regularly. (Priests: responsible for trumpet sound) **7.** On that day, David gave this psalm to Asaph and his brethren to thank the Lord: (Psalm: sacred song or hymn) **8.** "Give thanks to the Lord! Proclaim His deeds among the peoples!" (Proclaim: declare God's wonders) **9.** "Sing to Him, recount His marvelous works!" (Marvelous works: miraculous deeds) **10.** "Glory in His name; let those who seek the Lord rejoice!" (Glory: honor and praise) **11.** "Seek the Lord and His strength; seek His presence always!" (Strength: God's power) **12.** "Remember His wonders and judgments." (Wonders: miraculous actions) **13.** "O Israel, His servant, children of Jacob, His chosen ones!" (Jacob: patriarch of Israel) **14.** "He is the Lord, and His judgments are throughout the earth." (Judgments: God's laws) **15.** "Remember His covenant forever, the word He gave for a thousand generations." (Covenant: binding promise) **16.** "The covenant He made with Abraham, His oath to Isaac," (Abraham, Isaac: patriarchs of Israel) **17.** "And confirmed to Jacob as a statute, to Israel as an everlasting covenant." (Statute: law or decree) **18.** "To you I will give Canaan as your inheritance." (Canaan: promised land) **19.** "When you were few in number, strangers in the land," (Strangers: foreigners in Canaan) **20.** "When they moved from nation to nation, from one kingdom to another," (Nations: different peoples) **21.** "He did not allow others to harm them and rebuked kings for their sake." (Rebuked: corrected kings) **22.** "Saying, 'Do not touch My anointed ones, and do My prophets no harm.'" (Anointed: God's chosen ones) **23.** "Sing to the Lord, all the earth; proclaim His salvation daily." (Salvation: deliverance by God) **24.** "Declare His glory among the nations, His wonders among all peoples." (Declare: announce God's greatness) **25.** "The Lord is great, to be feared above all gods." (Feared: reverenced) **26.** "The gods of the peoples are idols, but the Lord made the heavens." (Idols: false gods) **27.** "Honor and majesty are before Him; strength and joy fill His place." (Strength and joy: attributes of God) **28.** "Give to the Lord, O families of the earth, give to the Lord glory and strength." (Glory: honor due to God) **29.** "Give to the Lord the glory due His name; bring offerings and worship Him in holiness." (Holiness: purity of worship) **30.** "Tremble before Him, the earth is fixed and unmovable." (Tremble: show reverence) **31.** "Let the heavens rejoice and the earth be glad, saying, 'The Lord reigns!'" (Reigns: God rules) **32.** "Let the sea roar and the fields rejoice in all their fullness." (Fullness: everything in nature) **33.** "The trees will sing for joy before the Lord, for He will judge the earth." (Judge: execute justice) **34.** "Give thanks to the Lord for His goodness! His mercy endures forever." (Endures: lasts forever) **35.** "Say, 'Save us, God of our salvation; gather us from the nations to give thanks and praise.'" (Triumph: victory in praise) **36.** "Blessed be the Lord God of Israel, from everlasting to everlasting!" And all the people said, "Amen!" and praised the Lord. (Amen: affirmation) **37.** David left Asaph and his brethren before the ark to serve regularly, as required daily. (Regular service: daily worship) **38.** Obed-Edom and his sixty-eight relatives, including Obed-Edom the son of Jeduthun, and Hosah, were appointed gatekeepers. (Gatekeepers: guards of sacred space) **39.** Zadok the priest and his fellow priests served before the tabernacle at Gibeon. (Tabernacle: worship structure) **40.** They offered burnt offerings morning and evening, following the Law of the Lord for Israel. (Burnt offerings: sacrifices for atonement) **41.** Heman, Jeduthun, and others were chosen to give thanks to the Lord, for His mercy endures forever. (Chosen: set apart for service) **42.** Heman and Jeduthun played trumpets, cymbals, and other instruments, with Jeduthun's sons as gatekeepers. (Instruments: used in worship) **43.** The people returned home, and David went to bless his household. (Blessed: invoked God's favor)

Chapter 17

1. As David was living in his house, he said to Nathan the prophet, "Look, I live in a house made of cedar, but the ark of God is under a tent." (Cedar: luxury material; Tent: a symbol of God's temporary dwelling.) **2.** Nathan replied, "Do whatever you have in mind, for the Lord is with you." (Mind: referring to David's sincere desires.) **3.** That night, God's word came to Nathan: (God's word: divine revelation or instruction.) **4.** "Go and tell David: 'The Lord says you will not build Me a house to live in.'" (Servant: God's chosen leader, David.) **5.** "I have never dwelt in a house since bringing Israel up, but I have moved in a tent and tabernacle." (Dwelling: God's presence wasn't confined to a building.) **6.** "Did I ever ask any of the judges of Israel why they didn't build Me a house of cedar?" (Judges: leaders appointed by God to guide Israel.) **7.** "I took you from shepherding the flock and made you ruler over My people Israel. I have been with you wherever you went and defeated your enemies." (Shepherding: David's humble origins) **8.** "I will appoint a place for Israel to dwell safely, free from oppression, and I will subdue all your enemies. The Lord will build you a house." (Appoint: to set aside; Subdue: to defeat; House: a lasting dynasty.) **9.** "When your days are fulfilled, I will raise up your son to succeed you and establish his kingdom." (Fulfilled: completion of David's reign; Establish: setting up a lasting reign.) **10.** "He will build a house for Me, and I will establish his throne forever." (Throne: symbol of kingship; Forever: enduring reign.) **11.** "I will be his Father, and he will be My son. I will not take My mercy away from him." (Mercy: God's unwavering faithfulness.) **12.** "I will make his kingdom last forever, and his throne will be established eternally." (Last: enduring; Established: firmly set up.) **13.** Nathan conveyed all these words to David. (Conveyed: shared God's message to David.) **14.** David went into the presence of the Lord and said, "Who am I, O Lord, that You've brought me so far?" (Presence: God's divine presence; Humility: acknowledging David's smallness.) **15.** "This is but a small thing in Your eyes, O God, and You have spoken of my house for the long term, elevating me like a man of high rank." (Small thing: David's humble recognition of God's favor.) **16.** "What can I say to You, Lord, about the honor You've given Your servant? You know Your servant well." (Servant: David's role of obedience.) **17.** "For Your servant's sake, and according to Your heart, You have accomplished these great deeds." (Heart: God's desire to bless David.) **18.** "There is no one like You, O Lord, nor any other god, as we have heard with our own ears." (God: unique, sovereign.) **19.** "Who is like Israel, Your people, whom You redeemed to be Your own people, performing great and awesome deeds by driving out nations before them?" (Redeemed: God's act of rescuing Israel.) **20.** "You made Israel Your people forever, and You became their God." (Forever: eternal relationship; God: the true and eternal God.) **21.** "Now, O Lord, let Your word to Your servant and his house be established forever, and do as You have promised." (Established: firmly confirmed; Promise: God's commitment.) **22.** "Let Your name be exalted forever, and let the house of Your servant remain established before You." (Exalted: honored; Established: made permanent.) **23.** "For You have revealed that You will build me a house. Therefore, I pray before You." (Revealed: God's disclosure of His plan.) **24.** "Lord, You are God, and You've promised this great blessing to Your servant." (Promise: God's assurance of favor.) **25.** "You have blessed my house so that it may remain before You forever, as You have blessed it, O Lord." (Blessed: God's favor ensuring prosperity.) **26.** "Let the word You spoke about Your servant and his house be established forever." (Established: made permanent; Word: God's promise to David.) **27.** "For You, O Lord, have blessed it, and it will remain blessed forever." (Blessed: ongoing favor and divine support.)

Chapter 18

1. Afterward, David attacked the Philistines, defeated them, and took control of Gath and its surrounding towns. (Gath: one of the Philistine cities.) **2.** He then conquered Moab, making the Moabites his servants, who paid tribute to him. (Servants: subjects who owed allegiance and tribute.) **3.** David also defeated Hadadezer, the king of Zobah, extending his control to Hamath as he sought to strengthen his rule along the Euphrates River. (Hamath: a region near the Euphrates; Euphrates: major river in the ancient Near East.) **4.** David captured one thousand chariots, seven thousand horsemen, and twenty thousand foot soldiers from Hadadezer. He hamstrung all the chariot horses, keeping only enough for one hundred chariots. (Hamstrung: disabled the horses by cutting their tendons to prevent them from being used in battle.) **5.** When the Syrians of Damascus came to aid Hadadezer, David killed twenty-two thousand of them. (Damascus: a major city-state; Syrians: people from Damascus.) **6.** David established garrisons in Damascus, making the Syrians his servants, and they brought tribute to him. The Lord protected David wherever he went. (Garrisons: military posts; Tribute: payment made by subjects to their ruler.) **7.** David took the golden shields carried by Hadadezer's servants and brought them to Jerusalem. (Shields of gold: symbolic of victory and wealth.) **8.** From Tibhath and Chun, cities of Hadadezer, David collected a large amount of bronze, which Solomon later used to make the bronze Sea, the pillars, and other bronze items. (Bronze Sea: a large basin in Solomon's temple; Pillars: significant elements of temple construction.) **9.** When Tou, king of Hamath, learned of David's victory over Hadadezer, **10.** he sent his son Hadoram to greet and bless David, for Hadadezer had been at war with Tou. Hadoram brought gold, silver, and bronze as gifts. (Hadoram: son of Tou; Tribute: gifts offered as a sign of peace or alliance.) **11.** David dedicated all these gifts to the Lord, along with the silver and gold he had taken from other nations, including Edom, Moab, Ammon, the Philistines, and Amalek. (Dedicated: set apart for God's service.) **12.** Abishai, son of Zeruiah, killed eighteen thousand Edomites in the Valley of Salt. (Valley of Salt: a place of military conflict.) **13.** David placed garrisons in Edom, making all the Edomites his servants. The Lord preserved David wherever he went. (Edomites: people from Edom; Servants: subjects under David's rule.) **14.** David ruled over all Israel, administering justice and righteousness to his people. (Justice and righteousness: fair rule and godly leadership.) **15.** Joab, son of Zeruiah, commanded the army; Jehoshaphat, son of Ahilud, served as the recorder; **16.** Zadok, son of Ahitub, and Abimelech, son of Abiathar, were the priests; Shavsha was the scribe; **17.** Benaiah, son of Jehoiada, led the Cherethites and Pelethites, and David's sons were chief ministers at his side. (Cherethites and Pelethites: elite military forces; Scribe: one who recorded official matters.)

Chapter 19
1. After Nahash, the king of the Ammonites, died, his son Hanun took the throne. **2.** David decided to show kindness to Hanun, as Nahash had shown kindness to him. He sent messengers to comfort Hanun regarding his father's death. **3.** The princes of Ammon, however, wondered Hanun's belief in David, suggesting that David's messengers had been spies sent to overthrow the land. (spies: sellers for espionage) **4.** In reaction, Hanun humiliated David's servants by way of shaving their beards, cutting their clothes, and sending them away. (humiliated: brought about shame) **5.** While David discovered of this, he dispatched messengers to meet the men, who were deeply ashamed, teaching them to wait in Jericho until their beards grew back. (deeply ashamed: felt super embarrassment) **6.** Knowing they'd angered David, Hanun and the Ammonites sent 1000 talents of silver to hire chariots and horsemen from Mesopotamia, Maachah, and Zobah. (talents: devices of weight or currency) **7.** They employed thirty-two thousand chariots and allied with the king of Maachah, putting in camp near Medeba. The Ammonites gathered their forces for war. (allied: formed an alliance) **8.** Upon hearing this, David sent Joab and all of his strong men to confront the Ammonites. (amazing men: elite infantrymen) **9.** The Ammonites placed their army at the city gates, while the allied kings gathered their forces in the field. (placed: organized in battle formation) **10.** Since he was surrounded, Joab selected Israel's best men to fight the Syrians. (surrounded: encircled) **11.** The rest of the army was placed under the command of Joab's brother, Abishai, who was to face the Ammonites. (command: leadership role) **12.** Joab told Abishai, "If the Syrians are too strong for me, you help me; if the Ammonites are too strong for you, I will help you. Let's be strong for our people and for the cities of our God, and may the Lord do what is good in His sight." (strong: resilient or courageous) **13.** Joab and his forces attacked the Syrians, causing them to flee. (attacked: launched an offensive) **14.** When the Ammonites saw that the Syrians had fled, they also retreated into the city. Joab then returned to Jerusalem. (retreated: pulled back in defeat) **15.** The Syrians, knowing they were defeated, sent messengers to acquire reinforcements from across the river, led by Shophach, the commander of Hadadezer's army. (reinforcements: additional troops) **16.** When David learned of this, he assembled all of Israel, crossed the Jordan, and arranged for battle. (arranged: prepared for war) **17.** The battle began, and the Syrians fled before Israel. David's forces killed seven thousand chariot riders, forty thousand foot soldiers, and Shophach, the commander. (chariot riders: drivers of chariots) **18.** When Hadadezer's servants saw their defeat, they made peace with David and became his subjects. From that point, the Syrians no longer supported the Ammonites. (subjects: under David's rule) **19.** When the servants of Hadadezer saw that they had been defeated by Israel, they made peace with David and became his servants. From that point on, the Syrians no longer helped the Ammonites. (made peace: entered into a truce or alliance)

Chapter 20
1. In the spring, when kings typically go to war, Joab led the army to attack the Ammonites and besieged their city, Rabbah. But David stayed in Jerusalem. Joab captured and destroyed the city. **2.** David took the crown from the Ammonite king's head. It weighed a talent of gold and had precious stones. David placed it on his own head and took the city's spoils in great abundance. **3.** David took the people of the city and forced them to work with saws, iron picks, and axes. He did this to all the Ammonite towns. David and his army then returned to Jerusalem. **4.** Later on, a war broke out at Gezer with the Philistines. Sibbechai the Hushathite killed Sippai, one of the descendants of the giants, and they were subdued. (giants: refers to the Nephilim, a race of giants mentioned in the Bible) **5.** Another war with the Philistines occurred, in which Elhanan, son of Jair, killed Lahmi, the brother of Goliath the Gittite. Lahmi's spear shaft was like a weaver's beam. **6.** Yet another battle took place at Gath, where a giant man with twenty-four hands and feet: six on each hand and foot: was born to the giants. **7.** When this giant defied Israel, Jonathan, son of Shimea (David's brother), killed him. **8.** These giants were born in Gath, and all were defeated by David and his servants. (Gath: an ancient Philistine city, known as the home of Goliath)

Chapter 21
1. Now Satan rose up against Israel, and incited David to take a census of Israel. **2.** David instructed Joab and the leaders of the people, saying, "Go, count Israel from Beersheba to Dan, and report back to me the total count." **3.** Joab responded, "May the Lord increase His people a hundred times, but why does my lord the king require this? Why should this bring guilt upon Israel?" (Joab questioned David's motive and the possible consequences.) **4.** Nevertheless, David's command prevailed, and Joab went throughout Israel and returned to Jerusalem. **5.** Joab reported to David that there were 1,100,000 men who could draw the sword in Israel, and 470,000 in Judah. **6.** However, Joab did not include Levi and Benjamin in the count, for David's order was detestable to him. **7.** God was displeased with the census, and He struck Israel with a plague. (The census was seen as an act of pride, showing reliance on

numbers rather than on God's power.) **8.** David acknowledged his sin, saying, "I have sinned greatly in this matter. Please forgive me and remove this iniquity, for I have acted foolishly." **9.** The Lord spoke to Gad, David's prophet, saying, **10.** "Go, tell David, 'The Lord offers you three options. Choose one, and I will carry out your punishment.'" **11.** Gad presented David with three choices: **12.** "You can choose either three years of famine, three months of defeat by your enemies, or three days of plague from the Lord, with the angel of the Lord bringing judgment upon Israel. Choose one and tell me what to relay to God." **13.** David said to Gad, "I am in great distress. Let me fall into the Lord's hands, for His mercy is very great, but do not let me fall into the hands of men." (David chose God's mercy over human enemies.) **14.** The Lord sent a plague upon Israel, and 70,000 men of Israel died. **15.** God sent an angel to Jerusalem to destroy it, but as the angel was about to destroy the city, the Lord relented and said to the angel, "Enough! Restrain your hand." The angel stood by the threshing floor of Ornan the Jebusite. (God's mercy intervened before complete destruction.) **16.** David looked up and saw the angel of the Lord standing with a drawn sword stretched over Jerusalem. David and the elders, clothed in sackcloth, fell on their faces. **17.** David said to God, "It was I who ordered the census. I am the one who has sinned and done wrong, but these people are innocent. Let Your hand be against me and my family, but not against Your people." (David took responsibility for his sin, asking God to show mercy to Israel.) **18.** The angel commanded Gad to tell David to go to the threshing floor of Ornan the Jebusite and build an altar to the Lord. **19.** David obeyed the command of God through Gad, and went up to the threshing floor of Ornan. **20.** Ornan saw the angel, and his four sons hid, but Ornan continued threshing wheat. **21.** When David approached, Ornan bowed down to him, and David asked for the threshing floor to build an altar to God. **22.** David said to Ornan, "Sell me this place for the full price, so I can build an altar to the Lord, and the plague may be stopped." (David wanted to pay for the land, not take it for free, showing his sincerity.) **23.** Ornan offered to give David the threshing floor, the oxen for burnt offerings, the threshing tools for wood, and wheat for a grain offering. "Take it all," he said. **24.** But David refused, saying, "I will buy it at full price. I cannot offer to God something that costs me nothing." (David emphasized the importance of personal sacrifice in worship.) **25.** David paid Ornan 600 shekels of gold for the site. **26.** David built an altar to the Lord there, and offered burnt offerings and peace offerings. He called upon the Lord, and the Lord answered him by sending fire from heaven to consume the offerings. **27.** The Lord commanded the angel to put his sword back in its sheath, ending the destruction. **28.** When David saw that the Lord had answered him on the threshing floor of Ornan, he sacrificed there. **29.** At that time, the tabernacle of the Lord and the altar of burnt offerings, made by Moses in the wilderness, were at the high place in Gibeon. **30.** But David could not go there to inquire of God, because he was afraid of the sword of the angel of the Lord. (David was still fearful of God's wrath and the angel's presence.)

Chapter 22

1. Then David stated, "This is the residence of our Lord God, and this is the altar of burnt offering for Israel." **2.** So David commanded the foreigners in Israel to be gathered, and he appointed masons to cut stones for the construction of the house of God. **3.** David also prepared an abundance of iron for the nails of the gates and doors, and for the joints, as well as a great amount of bronze, **4.** and cedar wood in extraordinary quantities, for the Sidonians and Tyrians brought much cedar to David. (David made large preparations for the temple.) **5.** David said, "My son Solomon is younger and inexperienced, and the house to be built for the Lord must be extraordinarily magnificent, renowned, and wonderful throughout all nations. I will now make preparations for it." So David made plentiful preparations before his death. (David realized his son Solomon would take on the responsibility of building the temple.) **6.** Then David called for Solomon and told him to build a house for the Lord God of Israel. **7.** David said to Solomon: "My son, I had intended to build a house for the name of the Lord my God, **8.** but the word of the Lord came to me, saying, 'You have shed much blood and fought many wars; you will not build a house for My name, because you have shed so much blood on the earth in My sight. **9.** Behold, a son shall be born to you, who will be a man of peace; I will give him rest from all his enemies on every side. His name will be Solomon, for I will give peace and quietness to Israel during his reign. **10.** He will build a house for My name, and he will be My son, and I will be his Father. I will establish his kingdom over Israel forever.'" **11.** Now, my son, may the Lord be with you, and may you prosper as you build the house of the Lord your God, as He has promised you. **12.** Only may the Lord give you wisdom and understanding, and put you in charge of Israel, that you may obey the law of the Lord your God. **13.** Then you will prosper if you carefully follow the statutes and judgments with which the Lord commanded Moses regarding Israel. Be strong and courageous; do not fear or be discouraged. **14.** I have taken great pains to prepare for the house of the Lord: one hundred thousand talents of gold and one million talents of silver, along with bronze and iron in abundance. The wood and stones are also prepared, and you can add to them. **15.** Furthermore, there are craftsmen with you in abundance: woodworkers, stonecutters, and other skilled workers for every type of project. **16.** Of gold, silver, bronze, and iron, there is no limit. Get up and begin the work, and may the Lord be with you." **17.** David also commanded all the leaders of Israel to assist Solomon, saying, **18.** "Is not the Lord your God with you? Has He not given you peace on every side? He has given the land into my hand, and it is subdued before the Lord and His people. **19.** Now set your heart and soul to seek the Lord your God. Therefore, rise up and build the sanctuary of the Lord, to bring the ark of the covenant of the Lord and the holy vessels of God into the house to be built for the name of the Lord." (David encouraged the leaders to support Solomon in building the temple as an act of devotion to God.)

Chapter 23

1. When David grew old and his days were complete, he appointed his son Solomon as the king of Israel. **2.** David gathered all the leaders of Israel, including the priests and Levites. **3.** The Levites were counted from the age of thirty and older, and the total number of men reached thirty-eight thousand. **4.** Among these, twenty-four thousand were assigned to oversee the work in the house of the Lord, six thousand were appointed as officers and judges, **5.** four thousand served as gatekeepers, and four thousand were chosen to lead the praise of God using musical instruments, which David had personally created for this purpose. (Gatekeepers: Those who guarded the entrances; Musical instruments: Instruments used for worship and praise in the temple) **6.** David divided the Levites into groups based on the sons of Levi: Gershon, Kohath, and Merari. **7.** The Gershonites were Laadan and Shimei. **8.** The descendants of Laadan included Jehiel (the first), Zetham, and Joel: three in total. **9.** The sons of Shimei were Shelomith, Haziel, and Haran: three in total. These were the heads of the families of Laadan. **10.** Shimei's sons were Jahath, Zina, Jeush, and Beriah. These four were the sons of Shimei. **11.** Jahath was the eldest, and Zizah was the second. However, Jeush and Beriah had fewer sons, so they were counted as one family. **12.** The sons of Kohath were Amram, Izhar, Hebron, and Uzziel: four in total. **13.** The children of Amram were Aaron and Moses. Aaron, along with his descendants, was consecrated forever to perform sacred duties, such as burning incense before the Lord, ministering to Him, and blessing His name forever. (Consecrated: Set apart as holy for specific religious duties) **14.** The descendants of Moses, the servant of God, were counted within the tribe of Levi. **15.** Moses' sons were Gershon and Eliezer. **16.** Gershon's firstborn was Shebuel. **17.** Eliezer's firstborn was Rehabiah. Eliezer had no other sons, but Rehabiah's descendants were numerous. **18.** Izhar's firstborn was Shelomith. **19.** The sons of Hebron were Jeriah (the first), Amariah (the second), Jahaziel (the third), and Jekameam (the fourth). **20.** The sons of Uzziel were Michah (the first) and Jesshiah (the second). **21.** The sons of Merari were Mahli and Mushi. Mahli's children were Eleazar and Kish. **22.** Eleazar passed away without sons, only daughters, and his brothers, the sons of Kish, took them as wives. **23.** Mushi's sons were Mahli, Eder, and Jeremoth: three in total. **24.** These were the Levites, sorted by their family heads. They were counted according to their names, and they were responsible for the work in the house of the Lord from the age of twenty and above. **25.** David said, "The Lord, the God of Israel, has provided peace for His people, allowing them to settle in Jerusalem for good." **26.** David also told the Levites, "You will no longer carry the tabernacle or its furnishings as you did before." (Tabernacle: The portable sanctuary used by the Israelites before the Temple was built in Jerusalem) **27.** By David's final instructions, the Levites were registered from the age of twenty and above. **28.** Their primary responsibility was to assist the descendants of Aaron in the service of the Lord's house, whether in the courtyards, chambers, or in the purification of sacred items. **29.** They were also in charge of maintaining the showbread, preparing the grain offerings, the unleavened cakes, and everything that was cooked, mixed, or measured. (Showbread: The consecrated loaves of bread offered to God in the temple) **30.** They were to stand each morning and evening to give thanks and praise to the Lord. **31.** They were responsible for presenting burnt offerings to the Lord on Sabbaths, New Moons, and appointed feasts, following the prescribed order for each occasion. **32.** The Levites were also tasked with attending to the needs of the tabernacle, the holy place, and assisting the sons of Aaron with the work in the Lord's house. (New Moons: The celebration of the beginning of each month in the Hebrew calendar, often marked by sacrifices and special observances)

Chapter 24

1. These are the descendants of Aaron: Nadab, Abihu, Eleazar, and Ithamar. (Aaron: The brother of Moses, and the first high priest of Israel.) **2.** Nadab and Abihu died before their father and had no children, so Eleazar and Ithamar became priests. (Priests: Religious leaders responsible for performing sacred rituals.) **3.** David, with Zadok from Eleazar's line and Ahimelech from Ithamar's, assigned the priests to their service according to a set schedule. (Zadok: A high priest during King David's reign.) **4.** There were more leaders from Eleazar's descendants than from Ithamar's. Eleazar had sixteen, while Ithamar had eight. (Leaders: Individuals chosen to lead or represent their families or groups.) **5.** The priests and Levites were divided by lot into two groups, with both Eleazar and Ithamar's families serving in the sanctuary and house of God. (Levites: Members of the tribe of Levi, who assisted in temple duties.) **6.** Shemaiah, the Levite scribe, recorded the names before King David, Zadok, Ahimelech, and the heads of the priestly and Levitical families, selecting one family from Eleazar and one from Ithamar. (Scribe: A person responsible for writing or recording official documents.) **7.** The first lot fell to Jehoiarib, the second to Jedaiah, **8.** the third to Harim, the fourth to Seorim, **9.** the fifth to Malchijah, the sixth to Mijamin, **10.** the seventh to Hakkoz, the eighth to Abijah, **11.** the ninth to Jeshua, the tenth to Shecaniah, **12.** the eleventh to Eliashib, the twelfth to Jakim, **13.** the thirteenth to Huppah, the fourteenth to Jeshebeab, **14.** the fifteenth to Bilgah, the sixteenth to Immer, **15.** the seventeenth to Hezir, the eighteenth to Happizzez, **16.** the nineteenth to Pethahiah, the twentieth to Jehezekel, **17.** the twenty-first to Jachin, the twenty-second to Gamul, **18.** the twenty-third to Delaiah, the twenty-fourth to Maaziah. (Lot: A method of selection, often used to determine outcomes or assignments.) **19.** This was their schedule of service in the house of the Lord, as commanded by Aaron their father, according to the will of God. (Schedule: A fixed plan or timetable for activities.) **20.** The other Levites were: Shubael, son of Amram; Jehdeiah, son of Shubael. (Amram: The father of Moses, Aaron, and Miriam.) **21.** From Rehabiah, his first son was Isshiah. (Rehabiah: A Levite leader, one of the descendants of Levi.) **22.** Shelomoth, from the line of Izhar, had a son named Jahath. (Izhar: A son of Kohath, a tribe of Levi.) **23.** Jeriah, from the family of Hebron, was the first, Amariah the second, Jahaziel the third, and Jekameam the fourth. (Hebron: A city and also a descendant of Kohath, of the tribe of Levi.) **24.** From Uzziel, his son Michah had a son named Shamir. (Uzziel: A Levite from the tribe of Kohath.) **25.** Michah's brother Isshiah had a son named Zechariah. (Zechariah: A name meaning "God remembers.") **26.** The sons of Merari were Mahli and Mushi, and the son of Jaaziah was Beno. (Merari: A descendant of Levi, responsible for certain duties in the temple.) **27.** The sons of Jaaziah were Beno, Shoham, Zaccur, and Ibri. (Jaaziah: A Levite, the son of Merari.) **28.** Eleazar, from Mahli's line, had no sons. (Eleazar: The son of Aaron and high priest in Israel.) **29.** Jerahmeel, from the descendants of Kish, was a leader. (Kish: A name, referring to a family or lineage within the Levites.) **30.** The sons of Mushi were Mahli, Eder, and Jerimoth. These were the Levitical families according to their ancestral lines. (Mushi: A descendant of Merari, one of Levi's sons.) **31.** Just as the sons of Aaron, the Levites also cast lots for their duties before King David, Zadok, Ahimelech, and the heads of their families. The leaders and younger members followed the same procedure. (Casting lots: A method of decision-making, similar to drawing lots or casting dice.)

Chapter 25

1. David and the army commanders selected some of the sons of Asaph, Heman, and Jeduthun to prophesy with harps, stringed instruments, and cymbals. The number of skilled musicians was: (Prophesy: To speak or sing under divine inspiration.) **2.** The sons of Asaph were Zaccur, Joseph, Nethaniah, and Asharelah, under the direction of Asaph, who prophesied as directed by the king. (Asaph: A prominent Levite musician and prophet during David's reign.) **3.** The sons of Jeduthun were Gedaliah, Zeri, Jeshaiah, Shimei, Hashabiah, and Mattithiah, six in total, who prophesied with harps to praise the Lord under their father's leadership. (Jeduthun: A Levite musician and prophet, responsible for worship through music.) **4.** The sons of Heman included Bukkiah, Mattaniah, Uzziel, Shebuel, Jerimoth, Hananiah, Hanani, Eliathah, Giddalti, Romamti-Ezer, Joshbekashah, Mallothi, Hothir, and Mahazioth. (Heman: A Levite, seer, and musician, known for his wisdom and musical skill.) **5.** These were the sons of Heman, the king's seer, who prophesied to exalt his name. God gave Heman fourteen sons and three daughters. (Seer: A prophet, one who receives divine revelation.) **6.** These musicians were under their father's direction for the service in the Lord's house, using cymbals, stringed instruments, and harps. Asaph, Jeduthun, and Heman served under the king's authority. (Cymbals: Percussion instruments used in religious rituals; Stringed instruments: Instruments like harps used in worship.) **7.** The total number of skilled musicians, including those trained in the songs of the Lord, was two hundred and eighty-eight. (Skilled: Having the necessary expertise or ability.) **8.** They cast lots for their duties, both the small and great, teacher and student alike. (Casting lots: A method of decision-making through random selection.) **9.** The first lot for Asaph was Joseph; the second for Gedaliah and his sons, twelve in total; **10.** the third for Zaccur, his sons and brethren, twelve; **11.** the fourth for Jizri, his sons and brethren, twelve; **12.** the fifth for Nethaniah, his sons and brethren, twelve; **13.** the sixth for Bukkiah, his sons and brethren, twelve; **14.** the seventh for Jesharelah, his sons and brethren, twelve; **15.** the eighth for Jeshaiah, his sons and brethren, twelve; **16.** the ninth for Mattaniah, his sons and brethren, twelve; **17.** the tenth for Shimei, his sons and brethren, twelve; **18.** the eleventh for Azarel, his sons and brethren, twelve; **19.** the twelfth for Hashabiah, his sons and brethren, twelve; **20.** the thirteenth for Shubael, his sons and brethren, twelve; **21.** the fourteenth for Mattithiah, his sons and brethren, twelve; **22.** the fifteenth for Jeremoth, his sons and brethren, twelve; **23.** the sixteenth for Hananiah, his sons and brethren, twelve; **24.** the seventeenth for Joshbekashah, his sons and brethren, twelve; **25.** the eighteenth for Hanani, his sons and brethren, twelve; **26.** the nineteenth for Mallothi, his sons and brethren, twelve; **27.** the twentieth for Eliathah, his sons and brethren, twelve; **28.** the twenty-first for Hothir, his sons and brethren, twelve; **29.** the twenty-second for Giddalti, his sons and brethren, twelve; **30.** the twenty-third for Mahazioth, his sons and brethren, twelve; **31.** the twenty-fourth for Romamti-Ezer, his sons and brethren, twelve. (Lot: A method of selecting or assigning duties by chance or random selection.)

Chapter 26

1. Concerning the gatekeepers' divisions: of the Korahites, Meshelemiah, son of Kore, from the sons of Asaph. (Korahites: Descendants of Korah, a family of Levites responsible for guarding the temple.) **2.** The sons of Meshelemiah were Zechariah the firstborn, Jediael the second, Zebadiah the third, Jathniel the fourth, **3.** Elam the fifth, Jehohanan the sixth, Eliehoenai the seventh. (Meshelemiah: A Levite gatekeeper, a descendant of Korah.) **4.** The sons of Obed-Edom were Shemaiah the firstborn, Jehozabad the second, Joah the third, Sacar the fourth, Nethanel the fifth, **5.** Ammiel the sixth, Issachar the seventh, Peulthai the eighth; for God blessed him. (Obed-Edom: A Levite who was entrusted with guarding the ark of the covenant.) **6.** To Shemaiah his son were born men who governed their fathers' homes because they were men of exceptional ability. (Ruled: Managed or had authority over the households.) **7.** The sons of Shemaiah were Othni, Rephael, Obed, and Elzabad, whose brothers Elihu and Semachiah were also capable men. **8.** These were of the sons of Obed-Edom, with their sons and brethren, strong men for the work: sixty of Obed-Edom. **9.** Meshelemiah had sons and brothers, eighteen capable men. (Capable: Professional, equipped for the responsibilities to hand.) **10.** Hosah, of the children of Merari, had sons: Shimri the first (although he was not the firstborn, his father made him first), **11.** Hilkiah the second, Tebaliah the third, Zechariah the fourth; all the sons and brothers of Hosah numbered thirteen. (Merari: A family of Levites responsible for the physical duties of the tabernacle and later the temple.) **12.** These were the divisions of the gatekeepers among the chief men, serving like their brothers in the house of the Lord. **13.** They cast lots for each gate, from the smallest to the greatest, according to their father's house. (Casting lots: A method of decision-making through random choice.) **14.** The lot for the East Gate fell to Shelemiah, and for his son Zechariah, a wise counselor, the lot was for the North Gate. **15.** Obed-Edom received the South Gate, and to his sons, the storehouse. **16.** To Shuppim and Hosah the lot fell for the West Gate, with the Shallecheth Gate on the ascending highway: watchman opposite watchman. (Shallecheth Gate: Likely a gate with a ramp.) **17.** At the east were six Levites, at the north four every day, at the south four every day, and two by two for the storehouse. **18.** For the Parbar on the west, there were four on the highway and at the Parbar. (Parbar: A location, probably a part of the temple or an area near the gate.) **19.** These were the divisions of the gatekeepers of the sons of Korah and Merari. **20.** Ahijah, of the Levites, was over the treasuries of God's house and the treasuries of the dedicated things. (Treasuries: Storage areas for tithes, offerings, and sacred items.) **21.** The sons of Laadan, descendants of the Gershonites: Jehieli, the head of their father's house. **22.** The sons of Jehieli were Zetham and Joel, who were over the treasuries of the house of the Lord. **23.** Of the Amramites, the Izharites, the Hebronites, and the Uzzielites: **24.** Shebuel, the son of Gershom, the son of Moses, was the overseer of the treasuries. **25.** His brethren by Eliezer were Rehabiah his son, Jeshaiah his son, Joram his son, Zichri his son, and Shelomith his son. (Amramites: Descendants of Amram, Uzzielites: Levite clans with duties in the temple.) **26.** Shelomith and his brethren were over all the treasuries of the dedicated matters, which King David and the heads of the families had dedicated, including the spoils of battle. **27.** Some spoils from battles were also dedicated to maintain the house of the Lord. (Dedicated matters: Objects consecrated or set apart for the Lord's service.) **28.** Everything dedicated by Samuel the seer, Saul son of Kish, Abner son of Ner, and Joab son of Zeruiah was under the care of Shelomith and his brethren. **29.** Chenaniah and his sons, of the Izharites, were responsible as officers and judges over Israel outside Jerusalem. (Seer: A prophet, someone chosen to receive divine revelation.) **30.** Hashabiah and his brethren, from the Hebronites, a thousand seven hundred capable men, had oversight of Israel west of the Jordan, overseeing all matters related to the Lord and the king. **31.** Many of the Hebronites, Jerijah was head of the family. In the fortieth year of David's reign, capable men were found in Jazer of Gilead. **32.** His brethren were two thousand seven hundred capable men, heads of families, whom David appointed as officials over the Reubenites, Gadites, and half-tribe of Manasseh. (Jazer of Gilead: A region in Gilead known for capable men chosen by King David.)

Chapter 27

1. The Israelites, by their families and leaders, along with the commanders of thousands and hundreds, served the king in all military matters. Each division, consisting of 24,000 men, rotated monthly throughout the year. (Military divisions: groups in the army based on rank) **2.** Jashobeam, son of Zabdiel, led the first division in the first month, with 24,000 men in his unit. (Zabdiel: a Hebrew name) **3.** He was from the tribe of Perez and was the chief commander for the first month. (Perez: a son of Judah) **4.** In the second month, Dodai the Ahohite led the division, and Mikloth assisted him. His division also had 24,000. (Ahohite: a member of a family from the tribe of Benjamin) **5.** Benaiah, son of Jehoiada the priest, led the third division for the third month, with 24,000 men. (Jehoiada: a high-ranking priest) **6.** Benaiah was a mighty warrior, leading the 30, and his son Ammizabad joined him in the division. (30: a group of elite warriors in David's army) **7.** Asahel, brother of Joab, led the fourth division in the fourth month, followed by his son Zebadiah. The division numbered 24,000. **8.** Shamhuth the Izrahite commanded the fifth division for the fifth month, with 24,000 in his unit. (Izrahite: a member of the family of Izrah) **9.** Ira, son of Ikkesh the Tekoite, led the sixth division for the sixth month, with 24,000 men. (Tekoite: a town in Judah) **10.** Helez the Pelonite from Ephraim led the seventh division in the seventh month, with 24,000 men. **11.** Sibbechai the Hushathite from the Zarhites led the eighth division in the eighth month, with 24,000 men. (Hushathite: a descendant of Hushah, a place in Judah) **12.** Abiezer the Anathothite from Benjamin led the ninth division in the ninth month, with 24,000. (Anathoth: a town in Benjamin) **13.** Maharai the Netophathite from the Zarhites led the tenth division in the tenth month, with 24,000 men. (Netophathite: a person from Netophah, a town in Judah) **14.** Benaiah the Pirathonite from Ephraim led the eleventh division in the eleventh month, with 24,000 men. **15.** Heldai the Netophathite from Othniel led the twelfth division in the twelfth month, with 24,000 men. (Othniel: a judge of Israel, from the tribe of Judah) **16.** Over the tribes, Eliezer the son of Zichri governed the Reubenites, and Shephatiah the son of Maachah governed the Simeonites. (Zichri: a Levite leader) **17.** Hashabiah, son of Kemuel, led the Levites; Zadok was in charge of the Aaronites. (Kemuel: a leader in the Levite tribe) **18.** Elihu, David's brother, led Judah; Omri, son of Michael, led Issachar. (Elihu: a name meaning "my God is He") **19.** Ishmaiah, son of Obadiah, governed Zebulun, and Jerimoth, son of Azriel, governed Naphtali. (Obadiah: a prophet in the Old Testament) **20.** Hoshea, son of Azaziah, led Ephraim; Joel, son of Pedaiah, led the half-tribe of Manasseh. (Pedaiah: a name meaning "Jehovah has redeemed") **21.** Iddo, son of Zechariah, governed the half-tribe of Manasseh in Gilead; Jaasiel, son of Abner, led Benjamin. **22.** Azarel, son of Jeroham, governed Dan. These were the leaders of Israel's tribes. (Jeroham: a common Hebrew name) **23.** David did not count those under 20 years old, as God had promised to multiply Israel as the stars of the heavens. (Multiply: God's promise to bless Israel) **24.**

Joab, son of Zeruiah, began the census but did not finish, for God's anger was upon Israel because of it. The numbers were not recorded in the chronicles. (Zeruiah: David's sister, mother of Joab) 25. Azmaveth, son of Adiel, was in charge of the king's treasuries; Jehonathan, son of Uzziah, managed the storehouses. (Uzziah: a king of Judah) 26. Ezri, son of Chelub, was in charge of the field workers who tilled the ground. (Chelub: a descendant of Caleb) 27. Shimei the Ramathite oversaw the vineyards, and Zabdi the Shiphmite managed the wine production. (Ramathite: someone from Ramah) 28. Baal-Hanan the Gederite managed the olive and sycamore trees in the lowlands, and Joash handled the oil storage. (Gederite: someone from Geder, a place in Judah) 29. Shitrai the Sharonite oversaw the herds in Sharon, and Shaphat, son of Adlai, managed the herds in the valleys. (Sharon: a fertile plain along the Mediterranean) 30. Obil the Ishmaelite oversaw the camels; Jehdeiah the Meronothite managed the donkeys. (Ishmaelite: descendant of Ishmael) 31. Jaziz the Hagrite managed the flocks. These were the officials over King David's property. 32. Jehonathan, David's uncle, was a counselor, wise man, and scribe; Jehiel, son of Hachmoni, assisted the king's sons. (Hachmoni: a family of wise men) 33. Ahithophel was the king's chief counselor, and Hushai the Archite was his companion. (Archite: a person from the city of Archi) 34. After Ahithophel, Jehoiada, son of Benaiah, served as counselor, followed by Abiathar. Joab was the commander of the army. (Abiathar: a high priest in the Bible)

Chapter 28

1. David gathered all the leaders of Israel in Jerusalem: the officials of the tribes, the captains of lots and masses, the stewards of the king's possessions, and the valiant guys and powerful warriors. (Valiant men: brave and heroic warriors.) 2. King David stood and stated, "Pay attention, my people: I meant to construct a resting place for the ark of the covenant and the footstool of our God, and that I made arrangements to accomplish that." (Ark of the covenant: sacred chest containing the 10 Commandments.) 3. However, God said to me, 'You may not construct a residence for My name because you have been a warrior and shed blood.' (Warrior: a person skilled in combat.) 4. But the Lord selected me peculiarly from my father's house to be king of Israel forever. He selected Judah to be the ruler, and from the house of Judah, He selected me to be king over all Israel. (Judah: a tribe of Israel, from which King David descended.) 5. Of all my sons, the Lord has chosen my son Solomon to take a seat on the throne of the kingdom of the Lord over Israel. (Solomon: David's son, recognized for wisdom and building the temple.) 6. The Lord said to me, 'Your son Solomon will build My house and courts; he is My son, and I will be his Father.' (Father: a term denoting God's unique relationship with Solomon.) 7. I am able to establish his kingdom forever, if he stays faithful to observe My commandments as he does today. (Devoted: dependable and obedient to God's instructions.) 8. Now, in the presence of all Israel, the assembly of the Lord, and before our God, be careful to observe all of God's commandments so you can possess this good land and leave it as an inheritance for your children. (Inheritance: something passed down to future generations.) 9. "As for you, my son Solomon, know the God of your father and serve Him with a loyal heart and willing mind. For the Lord searches all hearts and understands the mind of all men. If you seek Him, He will be found; but if you forsake Him, He will reject you forever." (Forsake: to abandon or shrink back from.) 10. "Remember this, for the Lord has chosen you to build a house for His sanctuary. Be strong and do it." (Sanctuary: a holy or sacred area.) 11. David gave Solomon the plans for the vestibule, the houses, treasuries, upper chambers, inner chambers, and the place for the mercy seat; (Vestibule: a small entryway or hall.) 12. And all the plans by the Spirit for the courts of the Lord's house, the chambers around it, the treasuries of the house of God, and the treasuries for the dedicated things. (Dedicated things: services or items set apart for spiritual purposes.) 13. He also provided plans for the division of the priests and Levites, for all the work in the service of the Lord's house, and for all the articles used inside the house of the Lord. (Levites: members of the tribe of Levi, dedicated to spiritual duties.) 14. He gave weights of gold for all gold articles, and silver for all silver items, for every service. (Weights: specific amounts used to measure gold and silver.) 15. He provided weights for the golden lampstands and their lamps, and for the silver lampstands, each according to its use. (Lampstands: stands that held lamps, used for lighting the temple.) 16. He gave gold by weight for the tables of showbread and silver for the silver tables; (Showbread: bread placed in the temple as an offering.) 17. He gave 24-karat gold for the forks, basins, pitchers, and bowls, each by weight. (Pure gold: gold refined to remove impurities.) 18. He also gave refined gold for the altar of incense and for the chariot of gold cherubim that spread their wings over the ark of the covenant. (Chariot: a vehicle or structure, in this case, symbolic of divine glory.) 19. David said, "All of this the Lord made me understand in writing, through His hand upon me, the knowledge of these plans." (Plans: the specific design for the temple.) 20. David said to Solomon, "Be strong and courageous, and do the work. Do not be afraid or discouraged, for the Lord my God will be with you. He will not forsake you until the work of the Lord's house is completed." (Discouraged: feeling disheartened or losing confidence.) 21. "Here are the divisions of the priests and Levites for the service of God's house. Every willing craftsman will be with you for all kinds of work, and all the leaders and people will support you in your work." (Craftsman: skilled worker in temple construction.)

Chapter 29

1. King David addressed the assembly: "My son Solomon, whom God alone has chosen, is young and inexperienced, and the task is great, for the temple is not for man but for the Lord God." (Assembly: a meeting of people) 2. "I have prepared with all my might for the house of my God: gold for gold, silver for silver, bronze for bronze, iron for iron, wood for wood, onyx stones, stones to be set, glistening stones in various colors, all kinds of precious stones, and abundant marble slabs." (Precious stones: valuable gemstones used for decoration) 3. "Because of my love for the house of my God, I have given above and beyond what I have already prepared for the holy house: my personal treasure of gold and silver." (Holy house: a term for the temple of God) 4. "I gave 3,000 talents of gold from Ophir, and 7,000 talents of refined silver to overlay the temple walls." (Ophir: a region known for its wealth, especially gold) 5. "The gold for gold, the silver for silver, and for all the work of the craftsmen. Who will consecrate themselves today to the Lord?" (Consecrate: to dedicate or set aside for sacred use) 6. Then the leaders of Israel: the heads of the tribes, captains of hundreds and thousands, and the officials over the king's work: gave willingly. (Leaders of the tribes: leaders of Israel's twelve tribes) 7. They gave 5,000 talents and 10,000 darics of gold, 10,000 talents of silver, 18,000 talents of bronze, and 100,000 talents of iron. (Darics: ancient Persian gold coins) 8. All who had precious stones gave them to the treasury of the house of the Lord, under the care of Jehiel the Gershonite. (Gershonite: a member of the Levite family descended from Gershon) 9. The people rejoiced because they had given willingly with loyal hearts, and King David rejoiced greatly. (Loyal hearts: hearts dedicated to God with sincerity) 10. David blessed the Lord before the assembly: "Blessed are You, Lord God of Israel, our Father, forever and ever." (Assembly: gathering of people) 11. "Yours, O Lord, is greatness, power, glory, victory, and majesty. All in heaven and earth is Yours. Yours is the kingdom, and You are exalted above all." (Exalted: raised up in honor or position) 12. "Riches and honor come from You. You rule over all. In Your hand is power and might; it is in Your hand to make great and to give strength to all." (Might: great power or strength) 13. "Now, our God, we thank You and praise Your glorious name." (Glorious: full of beauty or grandeur) 14. "But who am I, and who are my people, that we should be able to offer so willingly? All things come from You, and out of

Your hand we have given to You." (Willingly: with a free and open heart) **15.** "For we are foreigners and strangers before You, as were all our ancestors; our days on earth are like a shadow, and there is no lasting hope." (Foreigners: people who do not belong to the land) **16.** "O Lord, all this abundance we have prepared to build You a house for Your holy name is from Your hand; it is all Yours." (Abundance: a large quantity of resources) **17.** "I know, O God, that You test the heart and take pleasure in uprightness. With a pure heart, I have willingly offered all these things; and I have seen Your people offering willingly." (Uprightness: honesty and integrity) **18.** "O Lord God of Abraham, Isaac, and Israel, our ancestors, keep this forever in the hearts of Your people, and direct their hearts toward You." (Direct: to guide or lead) **19.** "Give my son Solomon a loyal heart to keep Your commandments and to build the temple for which I have made provision." (Loyal heart: a heart fully committed to God) **20.** David said to the assembly, "Now bless the Lord your God." So the assembly blessed the Lord, the God of their ancestors, and bowed their heads, worshiping the Lord and the king. (Worshiping: showing reverence or honor) **21.** The next day, they made sacrifices to the Lord: 1,000 bulls, 1,000 rams, 1,000 lambs, with their drink offerings and sacrifices in abundance for all Israel. (Drink offerings: offerings of liquid poured out as a sacrifice) **22.** They ate and drank with great joy before the Lord, and made Solomon king again, anointing him before the Lord to be chief, and Zadok as priest. (Anointing: the act of pouring oil on a person to consecrate them) **23.** Solomon sat on the throne of the Lord as king, replacing his father David, and prospered; all Israel obeyed him. (Prospered: succeeded and grew in power) **24.** All the leaders, mighty men, and the sons of David submitted themselves to Solomon as king. (Mighty men: strong and brave warriors) **25.** The Lord greatly exalted Solomon in the sight of all Israel and bestowed royal majesty on him, beyond any king of Israel before him. (Exalted: honored or raised to a high position) **26.** Thus, David the son of Jesse reigned over all Israel. (Jesse: David's father, a man from Bethlehem) **27.** David reigned over Israel for forty years: seven years in Hebron and thirty-three years in Jerusalem. (Hebron: a city where David ruled for a time before Jerusalem) **28.** David died at a good old age, full of days, riches, and honor, and his son Solomon succeeded him as king. (Full of days: having lived a complete and fulfilling life) **29.** The acts of King David, from the beginning to the end, are written in the records of Samuel the seer, Nathan the prophet, and Gad the seer. (Seer: a prophet or visionary) **30.** They include his entire reign, his power, and the events that happened to him, to Israel, and to the surrounding kingdoms. (Reign: the period during which a king rules).

14 – 2 Chronicles

Chapter 1

1. Solomon, the son of David, became firmly established as king, with the LORD his God by his side, greatly enhancing his power and influence. (Established: stable, influence: power) **2.** Solomon then addressed all of Israel—commanders of thousands and hundreds, judges, and the leaders of every tribe and family. (Commanders: leaders, tribes: groups, judges: adjudicators) **3.** He, along with the entire assembly, traveled to Gibeon, where the tabernacle of the LORD, built by Moses in the wilderness, was located. (Assembly: gathering, tabernacle: sanctuary) **4.** However, David had moved the Ark of God from Kirjath-Jearim to Jerusalem, where he had set up a special tent for it. (Ark: chest, special tent: tabernacle) **5.** In front of the tabernacle, Solomon placed the bronze altar, crafted by Bezaleel, the son of Uri, son of Hur, and it became the focus of the congregation's offerings. (Bronze: metal, crafted: made, congregation: group) **6.** Solomon approached the bronze altar before the LORD, at the tabernacle, and offered a thousand burnt offerings in worship. (Burnt offerings: sacrifices) **7.** That night, God appeared to Solomon and said, "Ask for whatever you want, and I will give it to you." (Appeared: showed) **8.** Solomon responded, "You have shown great kindness to my father, David, and have made me king in his place." (Kindness: mercy) **9.** "Now, O LORD, let Your promise to my father be fulfilled. You have made me king over a people as numerous as the dust of the earth." (Fulfilled: completed, numerous: countless) **10.** "Give me wisdom and knowledge so that I can lead these people well. Who is able to govern such a great nation?" (Wisdom: insight, govern: rule, nation: people) **11.** God replied, "Because you have asked for wisdom and knowledge, and not for riches, honor, or the life of your enemies, I will grant your request. You will have wisdom and knowledge, and in addition, I will give you wealth, honor, and power—greater than any king before or after you." (Riches: wealth, honor: respect, power: authority) **12.** God's promise was fulfilled: Solomon received the wisdom and knowledge he asked for, along with an abundance of wealth, honor, and glory. (Abundance: plenty) **13.** Solomon then returned from Gibeon to Jerusalem, from the tabernacle, and took his place as the ruler of Israel. (Ruler: leader) **14.** Solomon gathered chariots and horsemen—1,400 chariots and 12,000 horsemen—and stationed them in various cities, as well as in Jerusalem itself. (Chariots: vehicles, horsemen: cavalry, stationed: placed) **15.** In Jerusalem, Solomon accumulated silver and gold so abundantly that it became as common as stones, and he cultivated cedar trees to rival the sycamore trees found in the valley. (accumulated: collected, abundantly: plentifully, rival: compete) **16.** He also imported horses from Egypt, along with fine linen, which his merchants sold at a profit. (Imported: brought, linen: fabric, merchants: traders, profit: earnings) **17.** The merchants brought chariots from Egypt, each costing 600 shekels of silver, and horses for 150 shekels each. These horses were sold to the kings of the Hittites and the kings of Syria through his trade network. (shekels: currency, Hittites: ancient people, Syria: nation, network: system)

Chapter 2

1. Solomon decided to construct a temple for the name of the LORD and a palace for his reign. (decided: chose, construct: build) **2.** He assigned 70,000 men to carry heavy loads, 80,000 to cut stones in the mountains, and 3,600 to oversee their work. (assigned: designated, heavy loads: burdens) **3.** Solomon sent a message to Huram, the king of Tyre, saying, "Just as you provided cedars for my father David to build a dwelling, do the same for me." (message: letter, cedars: trees) **4.** "I am building a house for the LORD my God to dedicate to Him, where incense will be burned, where the showbread will be maintained, and where daily sacrifices will be made — in accordance with the ordinances of the LORD, including offerings on the sabbaths, new moons, and festivals. This is a law for Israel forever." (dedicate: consecrate, ordinances: laws) **5.** The house I am building is magnificent because our God is greater than all gods. (magnificent: grand) **6.** But who can truly build a house for God, since even the heavens cannot contain Him? Who am I to build a house for Him, except to offer sacrifices before Him? (contain: hold) **7.** Send me a skilled craftsman, able to work with gold, silver, bronze, iron, and fabric of purple, crimson, and blue, who can also engrave, to work with the skilled artisans already here in Judah and Jerusalem, whom my father David provided. (craftsman: artisan, fabric: cloth, engrave: carve) **8.** Also send me cedar, fir, and algum wood from Lebanon, as I know your men are skilled in cutting timber in Lebanon. My workers will assist yours. (timber: wood) **9.** I need plenty of timber, as the house I am building will be extraordinary. (extraordinary: immense) **10.** In return, I will provide your workers, who cut the timber, with twenty thousand measures of wheat, twenty thousand measures of barley, twenty thousand baths of wine, and twenty thousand baths of oil. (measures: amounts, baths: containers) **11.** King Huram of Tyre responded in writing to Solomon, "Because the LORD has loved His people, He has made you king over them." (responded: replied) **12.** Huram continued, "Praise the LORD God of Israel, who created heaven and earth, and who has given David a wise son, filled with understanding, to build a temple for the LORD and a palace for his kingdom." (praise: bless, filled: endowed)

13. "I have sent you a skilled man, filled with wisdom, from my father Huram, (skilled: expert) **14.** The son of a woman from the tribe of Dan, whose father was a craftsman from Tyre, experienced in working with gold, silver, bronze, iron, stone, wood, purple, blue, fine linen, and crimson. He is also skilled in engraving and can create any design you need, working alongside your craftsmen and those of my father David." (craftsman: artisan, fine linen: high-quality cloth) **15.** As for the wheat, barley, oil, and wine that you mentioned, please send them to us, and we will fulfill your request. (mentioned: referred to) **16.** We will cut timber from Lebanon as much as you need, and transport it to you by rafts to Joppa, and you can bring it up to Jerusalem. (rafts: floating platforms) **17.** Solomon took a census of all the foreign workers in Israel, following the same counting that his father David had done, and they were found to number 153,600. (census: count) **18.** He assigned 70,000 of them to carry loads, 80,000 to cut stones in the mountains, and 3,600 to oversee the workers. (assigned: designated, oversee: supervise)

Chapter 3

1. Solomon began to build the temple of the LORD on Mount Moriah in Jerusalem, the site where the LORD appeared to David, his father, at the threshing floor of Ornan the Jebusite. (Threshing floor: granary) **2.** He started the construction on the second day of the second month in the fourth year of his reign. (reign: rule) **3.** The temple's dimensions were sixty cubits in length and twenty cubits in width, according to the standard measurement. (Dimensions: size) **4.** The porch in front of the temple was the same width as the temple, measuring twenty cubits, with a height of one hundred and twenty cubits. It was overlaid with pure gold. (Porch: entrance, overlaid: coated) **5.** The main hall was built with fir wood and covered with fine gold, decorated with palm tree carvings and chains. (Main hall: central area) **6.** Precious stones adorned the temple for beauty, and the gold used came from Parvaim. (Parvaim: gold source) **7.** The beams, pillars, walls, and doors were all coated with gold, and cherubim were engraved on the walls. (Beams: supports, cherubim: angels) **8.** The Most Holy Place measured twenty cubits by twenty cubits and was overlaid with six hundred talents of fine gold. (Most Holy Place: sanctuary) **9.** The nails weighed fifty shekels of gold, and the upper chambers were also covered in gold. (Nails: fasteners) **10.** In the Most Holy Place, Solomon made two cherubim from hammered gold, completely overlaid with gold. (Hammered: shaped) **11.** The cherubim's wings were twenty cubits long, with one wing of each cherub reaching five cubits to the temple wall, and the other five cubits reaching the other cherub. (reaching: extending) **12.** The opposite cherub's wings also extended five cubits to the wall and five cubits to the first cherub's wing. **13.** The span of their wings was twenty cubits, and their faces were turned inward. (span: width) **14.** Solomon made the veil separating the Holy of Holies from the rest of the temple from blue, purple, crimson, and fine linen, with cherubim woven into it. (woven: interlaced) **15.** He set up two massive pillars in front of the temple, each thirty-five cubits tall, with capitals five cubits high. (capitals: tops of pillars) **16.** Solomon made chains for the pillars and decorated them with one hundred pomegranates. (decorated: adorned, pomegranates: ornaments) **17.** The two pillars were placed on the right and left sides of the temple. The one on the right was named Jachin, and the one on the left was named Boaz. (positioned: placed, Jachin: establishment, Boaz: strength)

Chapter 4

1. Solomon constructed a large bronze altar, measuring twenty cubits in length, twenty cubits in width, and ten cubits in height. (bronze: brass) **2.** He also made a molten sea, ten cubits across its diameter, five cubits high, with a thirty-cubit circumference. (molten sea: large basin, circumference: perimeter) **3.** Beneath the sea were sculpted oxen, ten in a cubit, arranged in two rows around the entire basin. (sculpted: shaped) **4.** The sea rested on twelve oxen, with three facing each direction—north, west, south, and east—and their backs facing inward. (rested: placed, inward: toward the center) **5.** The sea was a handbreadth thick, and its rim was designed like a cup with lily-like flowers; it could hold three thousand baths. (handbreadth: width of a hand, rim: edge) **6.** Solomon also made ten lavers, placing five on each side, for washing the offerings; the sea was reserved for the priests to wash in. (lavers: washing basins, offerings: sacrificial gifts) **7.** He created ten golden lampstands in the temple, five on the right and five on the left, according to their design. (lampstands: holders for lamps) **8.** Solomon also made ten tables and placed five on each side, along with one hundred gold basins. (basins: bowls) **9.** He constructed the priestly court, the great court, and its doors, which were overlaid with brass. (priestly: related to priests, overlaid: coated) **10.** He positioned the molten sea on the right side at the east end, opposite the south. (positioned: placed) **11.** Huram crafted the pots, shovels, and basins, completing the work assigned to him by King Solomon for the temple. (crafted: made) **12.** He made the two pillars, their capitals, and the wreaths that adorned the tops of the pillars. (capitals: tops of pillars, wreaths: circular decorations) **13.** On the two wreaths, Huram added four hundred pomegranates, two rows on each wreath, covering the capitals. (pomegranates: fruit-like ornaments) **14.** He also made bases and lavers to place upon the bases. (bases: stands) **15.** One large sea, supported by twelve oxen, was made as well. (supported: held up) **16.** Huram also made the pots, shovels, fleshhooks, and other instruments for the temple, all from bright brass. (fleshhooks: hooks for meat, instruments: tools) **17.** The vessels were cast in the plain of Jordan, between Succoth and Zeredathah, using clay. (cast: molded) **18.** Solomon made these items in great quantity, so much so that the weight of the brass was unmeasurable. (quantity: amount) **19.** He also made the golden altar and tables for the showbread. (showbread: sacred bread) **20.** The golden lampstands with their lamps were made to burn continually before the Most Holy Place. (continually: without interruption) **21.** Solomon created gold flowers, lamps, and tongs, all from pure gold. (tongs: tools for handling) **22.** Additionally, he made snuffers, basins, spoons, and censers, all of pure gold. The inner doors of the temple and the most holy place were also gold-plated. (snuffers: tools for trimming lamps, censers: incense holders)

Chapter 5

1. When Solomon completed all the work for the house of the LORD, he brought in all the dedicated items his father David had set apart—silver, gold, and other instruments—and placed them in the treasures of God's house. (dedicated: consecrated) **2.** Solomon gathered the elders of Israel, the heads of the tribes, and the leaders of the families to Jerusalem to bring up the ark of the covenant from the City of David, Zion. (gathered: assembled, leaders: heads) **3.** All the men of Israel gathered for the feast in the seventh month. (feast: celebration) **4.** The elders of Israel came, and the Levites took up the ark. (Levites: priestly tribe) **5.** The priests and Levites brought the ark, the tabernacle, and all the holy vessels to the temple. (vessels: sacred items) **6.** Solomon and the congregation sacrificed sheep and oxen in such great numbers that they couldn't be counted. (congregation: assembly) **7.** The priests placed the ark in its designated place, inside the most holy place under the wings of the cherubim. (designated: appointed) **8.** The cherubim spread their wings over the ark, covering it and the staves above. (spread: extended, staves: carrying poles) **9.** The staves were drawn out, and their ends were visible before the oracle, but not outside. The ark remained in this position. (oracle: inner sanctum) **10.** The ark contained only the two tablets Moses had placed in it at Horeb, when the LORD made the covenant with Israel after their exodus from Egypt. (tablets: stone slabs, exodus: departure) **11.** When the priests came out of the holy place—having sanctified themselves and not following their usual rotation— (sanctified: consecrated, rotation: order) **12.** The Levite singers, all from Asaph, Heman, and Jeduthun, along with their sons and brothers, dressed in white linen and playing cymbals, psalteries, and harps, stood at the east end of the altar. With them were 120 priests sounding trumpets. (singers: musicians) **13.** When the trumpeters and singers united in praise and thanksgiving, lifting their voices with trumpets, cymbals, and other instruments, they praised the LORD, saying, "For He is good, and His mercy endures forever." The house was filled with a cloud, the glory of the LORD. (united: joined, praise: worship) **14.** The priests could not continue their duties because the cloud filled the temple with the glory of the LORD. (duties: ministry, glory: divine presence)

Chapter 6

1. Solomon declared, "The LORD has promised that He would dwell in the thick darkness." (Thick darkness: mystery) **2.** "Yet I have built a house for You, a place for Your eternal dwelling." (Eternal: everlasting) **3.** The king then turned to bless the whole congregation of Israel, and all the people stood up. (Congregation: assembly) **4.** He said, "Praise be to the LORD, the God of Israel, who with His hands has fulfilled the promise He made to my father David, saying, (Fulfilled: accomplished) **5.** 'From the day I brought My people out of Egypt, I did not choose a city from all the tribes of Israel to build a temple for My name, nor did I choose anyone to lead My people Israel.' (Tribes: groups) **6.** "But I have chosen Jerusalem for My name to be there, and I have chosen David to lead My people Israel." (Jerusalem: city) **7.** "It was in my father David's heart to build a house for the name of the LORD, the God of Israel. (Heart: intention) **8.** "But the LORD said to David, 'It was good that it was in your heart to build a temple for My name, (Good: pleasing) **9.** "'However, you shall not build the house; your son, who will come from your own body, will build it for My name.'" (Body: lineage) **10.** "The LORD has kept His word to David, for I have succeeded him as king and have built this house for the name of the LORD, the God of Israel." (Succeeded: replaced) **11.** "In it, I have placed the ark, the covenant which the LORD made with the Israelites." (Ark: chest) **12.** Solomon stood before the altar of the LORD, in front of the entire congregation, and spread his hands out toward heaven. (Altar: platform) **13.** He had made a bronze platform, five cubits long, five cubits wide, and three cubits high, and placed it in the center of the courtyard. He stood on it, knelt down, and spread his hands toward heaven. (Bronze: metal) (Cubits: measure) **14.** And he said, "O LORD God of Israel, there is no God like You in heaven or on earth, You who keep Your covenant and show mercy to Your servants who walk before You with all their hearts." (Mercy: compassion) **15.** "You who have kept Your promise to Your servant David, my father, speaking with Your mouth and fulfilling it with Your hand, as it is today." (Promise: assurance) **16.** "Now, O LORD God of Israel, let Your promise to Your servant David be confirmed, saying, 'There will always be a man on the throne of Israel if his descendants walk before Me as you have done.'" (Confirmed: verified) **17.** "Now, O LORD God of Israel, let Your word be true, as You spoke to Your servant David." (True: accurate) **18.** "But will God really live on earth with men? The heavens, even the highest heavens, cannot contain You, how much less this temple I have built!" (Contain: hold) (Heavens: sky) **19.** "Yet, O LORD my God, regard the prayer and plea of Your servant, listen to the cry and prayer Your servant is making before You." (Plea: request) **20.** "May Your eyes be open to this house day and night, the place where You have said You would put Your name. Hear the prayer Your servant prays toward this place." (Eyes: attention) **21.** "Hear the supplications of Your servant and of Your people Israel when they pray toward this place. Hear from heaven, Your dwelling place, and when You hear, forgive." (Supplications: petitions) **22.** "If a man wrongs his neighbor and is forced to take an oath, and comes to take an oath before Your altar in this temple," (Wrongs: harms) **23.** "Then hear from heaven and act. Judge Your servants by repaying the wicked, and rewarding the righteous, according to what they have done." (Repaying: compensating) (Wicked: evil) **24.** "If Your people Israel are defeated by an enemy because they have sinned against You, and they turn back to You, confess Your name, and pray and plead with You in this temple," (Plead: beg) **25.** "Then hear from heaven and forgive the sin of Your people Israel, and bring them back to the land You gave to their ancestors." (Sin: wrongdoing) **26.** "When the heavens are shut up and there is no rain because they have sinned against You, if they pray toward this place, and confess Your name, and turn from their sin because You have afflicted them," (Afflicted: harmed) **27.** "Then hear from heaven and forgive the sin of Your servants and of Your people Israel, teach them the good way to walk in, and send rain on the land You gave them as an inheritance." (Inheritance: possession) **28.** "If there is famine in the land, or pestilence, or blight, or mildew, locusts or caterpillars; if their enemies besiege them in the cities of their land, whatever disaster or sickness may come," (Famine: hunger) (Besiege: surround) **29.** "Then whatever prayer or supplication is made by any man, or by all Your people Israel, when each knows his own affliction and his own pain, and spreads out his hands toward this temple," (Supplication: prayer) (Affliction: suffering) **30.** "Then hear from heaven, Your dwelling place, and forgive, and deal with each person according to all they do, whose heart You know, for You alone know the hearts of all men." (Dwelling place: home) **31.** "So that they may fear You and walk in Your ways as long as they live in the land You gave to our ancestors." (Fear: reverence) **32.** "As for the foreigner who does not belong to Your people Israel but has come from a distant land because of Your great name and Your mighty hand, and Your outstretched arm—if they come and pray toward this temple," (Foreigner: stranger) (Outstretched: extended) **33.** "Then hear from heaven, Your dwelling place, and do whatever the foreigner asks of You, so that all peoples of the earth may know Your name, and fear You, as do Your own people Israel, and that they may know this house I have built is called by Your name." (Dwelling place: residence) **34.** "If Your people go to war against their enemies wherever You send them, and they pray to You toward this city You have chosen and the temple I have built for Your name," (War: battle) **35.** "Then hear from heaven their prayer and plea, and uphold their cause." (Uphold: support) **36.** "If they sin against You—there is no one who does not sin—and You become angry with them, and give them over to their enemies who take them captive to a land far or near," (Sin: offense) (Give them over: surrender) **37.** "And if they repent in the land where they were taken captive, and turn and pray to You in the land of their captivity, saying, 'We have sinned, we have done wrong, and we have acted wickedly,'" (Repent: regret) (Wickedly: evilly) **38.** "And if they return to You with all their heart and soul in the land of their captivity, and pray toward their land, which You gave their ancestors, toward the city You have chosen, and toward the temple I have built for Your name," (Return: come back) (Toward: facing) **39.** "Then hear from heaven, Your dwelling place, their prayer and their supplications, and uphold their cause, and forgive Your people who have sinned against You." (Uphold: maintain) **40.** "Now, O my God, may Your eyes be open and Your ears attentive to the prayers offered in this place." (Attentive: focused) **41.** "Now arise, O LORD God, and come to Your resting place, You and the ark of Your strength. May Your priests be clothed with salvation, and may Your faithful people rejoice in goodness." (Resting place: home) (Salvation: deliverance) **42.** "O LORD God, do not reject Your anointed one; remember the great love promised to Your servant David." (Anointed: chosen) (Reject: dismiss)

Chapter 7

1. When Solomon finished praying, fire came down from heaven, consuming the burnt offering and sacrifices, and the glory of the LORD filled the temple. (Consumed: devoured) (Glory: presence) (Temple: house) **2.** The priests could not enter the LORD's temple because the glory of the LORD had filled it. (Enter: go in) (Filled: occupied) **3.** When all the Israelites saw the fire and the glory of the LORD on the temple, they bowed down with their faces to the ground, worshipped, and praised the LORD, saying, "He is good, His mercy endures forever." (Worshipped: adored) (Praise: honor) (Mercy: compassion) **4.** Then, the king and all the people offered sacrifices before the LORD. (Sacrifices: offerings) **5.** King Solomon offered 22,000 oxen and 120,000 sheep. So, the king and all the people dedicated the temple of God. (Dedicated: consecrated) **6.** The priests carried out their duties, and the Levites played musical instruments that King David had made to praise the LORD because His mercy endures forever. The priests blew trumpets, and all Israel stood. (Levites: tribe of priests) (Instruments: tools) (Blowed: played) **7.** Solomon also consecrated the middle of the courtyard in front of the LORD's house, offering burnt offerings and the fat portions of peace offerings, because the bronze altar he had made couldn't hold all the offerings. (Consecrated: made holy) (Courtyard: open area) (Fat portions: best parts) **8.** At the same time, Solomon kept the feast for seven days, and all Israel with him, a large congregation, from the entrance of Hamath to the river of Egypt. (Feast: celebration) (Congregation: assembly) (Entrance: beginning) **9.** On the eighth day, they held a solemn assembly. They celebrated the dedication of the altar for seven days and the feast for seven days. (Solemn: serious) (Assembly: gathering) **10.** On the twenty-third day of the seventh month, Solomon sent the people home to their tents, happy and joyful for all the good things the LORD had done for David, Solomon, and His people Israel. (Joyful: pleased) (Goodness: kindness) **11.** Solomon finished building the temple of the LORD and the royal palace, and everything he had planned for the temple and his own palace was successfully completed. (Successfully: effectively) **12.** The LORD appeared to Solomon at night and said, "I have heard your prayer and have chosen this place to be a house of sacrifice for Myself." (Appeared: showed) (Sacrifice: offering) **13.** "If I shut up the heavens and there is no rain, or if I command locusts to devour the land, or if I send pestilence among My people;" (Shut up: stop) (Locusts: insects) (Pestilence: disease) **14.** "If My people, who are called by My name, humble themselves, pray, seek My face, and turn from their wicked ways, then I will hear from heaven, forgive their sin, and heal their land." (Humble: lower) (Sin: wrongdoing) (Heal: cure) **15.** "Now My eyes will be open, and My ears attentive to the prayer offered in this place." (Attentive: focused) **16.** "I have chosen and consecrated this house so that My name may be there forever. My eyes and My heart will be there always." (Consecrated: made holy) (Heart: focus) **17.** "As for you, if you walk before Me as your father David did, and do everything I command, and observe My decrees and laws," (Walk: live) (Decrees: commands) (Observe: follow) **18.** "Then I will establish your royal throne, as I covenanted with your father David, saying, 'You shall never lack a man to rule Israel.'" (Establish: secure) (Covenanted: promised) (Lack: be without) **19.** "But if you turn away and forsake My laws and commandments, and go and serve other gods and worship them," (Forsake: abandon) (Serve: worship) **20.** "Then I will uproot them from My land, which I have given them, and I will reject this temple that I have consecrated for My name. I will make it a byword and an object of ridicule among all nations." (Uproot: remove) (Reject: abandon) (Byword: saying) (Ridicule: mockery) **21.** "This temple, which is exalted, will become an astonishment to everyone who passes by. They will ask, 'Why has the LORD done this to this land and to this temple?'" (Exalted: high) (Astonishment: amazement) **22.** "And the answer will be, 'Because they forsook the LORD, the God of their ancestors, who brought them out of Egypt, and they embraced other gods, worshipped them, and served them. That is why He brought all this disaster upon them.'" (Embraced: accepted) (Disaster: calamity)

Chapter 8
1. After twenty years, during which Solomon built the temple of the LORD and his own palace, (During: throughout) (Built: constructed) **2.** Solomon also built the cities that Huram had restored to him, and he settled the Israelites there. (Restored: returned) (Settled: established) **3.** Solomon went to Hamath-zobah and defeated it. (Defeated: conquered) **4.** He also built Tadmor in the wilderness, along with all the storage cities he built in Hamath. (Storage: supply) (Wilderness: desert) **5.** Solomon built both Upper Beth-horon and Lower Beth-horon, fortified cities with walls, gates, and bars. (Fortified: strengthened) (Bars: locks) **6.** He also built Baalath and all the storage cities, chariot cities, and cities for horsemen that Solomon desired, in Jerusalem, Lebanon, and throughout his kingdom. (Chariot: carriage) (Kingdom: realm) **7.** As for the remaining people from the Hittites, Amorites, Perizzites, Hivites, and Jebusites, who were not Israelites, (Remaining: leftover) (Israelites: descendants of Jacob) **8.** These people's children, left in the land after their ancestors were defeated, Solomon made them pay tribute to him, and they still do so to this day. (Tribute: tax) (Defeated: conquered) **9.** However, Solomon did not make the Israelites work as servants. They were his soldiers, commanders, and captains of his chariots and cavalry. (Soldiers: warriors) (Cavalry: mounted troops) **10.** These were the chief officers of King Solomon, numbering 250, who ruled over the people. (Officers: leaders) **11.** Solomon brought Pharaoh's daughter from the City of David to the palace he had built for her, saying, "My wife shall not live in the palace of David, king of Israel, because the places are holy where the ark of the LORD has come." (Palace: residence) (Holy: sacred) **12.** Solomon then offered burnt offerings to the LORD on the altar he had built before the porch. (Burnt offerings: sacrifices) (Porch: entrance) **13.** He offered sacrifices regularly, according to the instructions given by Moses: on the Sabbaths, new moons, and during the three annual feasts—the Feast of Unleavened Bread, the Feast of Weeks, and the Feast of Tabernacles. (Sabbaths: weekly rest days) (Feasts: celebrations) (Unleavened: without yeast) **14.** Solomon arranged the duties of the priests and Levites, according to the order established by his father David, to praise and serve before the priests as required each day. He also assigned porters to each gate, as David the man of God had commanded. (Porters: gatekeepers) (Assigned: designated) **15.** They did not depart from the commands of the king regarding the priests, Levites, or the treasures. (Depart: stray) **16.** All the work of Solomon was completed from the day the foundation of the temple was laid until it was finished. Thus, the temple of the LORD was completed. (Foundation: base) (Completed: finished) **17.** Solomon then went to Ezion-geber and Eloth, on the coast of Edom. (Coast: shore) (Edom: region south of Israel) **18.** Huram sent ships and sailors who were skilled in the sea to Solomon, and together they sailed to Ophir, bringing back 450 talents of gold. They delivered it to King Solomon. (Skilled: experienced) (Talents: units of weight) (Delivered: brought)

Chapter 9
1. When the queen of Sheba heard of Solomon's renown, she traveled to Jerusalem to test his wisdom with challenging questions. She came with a great retinue—many camels carrying spices, gold in great quantity, and precious gems. Upon meeting Solomon, she spoke with him about everything on her mind. (Retinue: entourage; Gems: stones) **2.** Solomon answered all of her questions, leaving nothing unanswered; he revealed everything she inquired about. (Inquired: asked) **3.** When the queen of Sheba saw Solomon's wisdom, the palace he had built, (Wisdom: insight) **4.** the food at his table, the seating of his attendants, the way his ministers were dressed, and the grandeur of his ascent to the temple of the LORD, she was left in awe. (Attendants: servants; Ascent: rise) **5.** She said to the king, "The reports I heard in my own land about your deeds and wisdom were true." (Deeds: acts) **6.** However, I did not believe it until I arrived and saw it with my own eyes. In truth, I was only told half of the greatness of your wisdom. What I witnessed surpassed what I had heard. (Surpassed: exceeded) **7.** How fortunate are your men and your servants who always stand before you and listen to your wisdom. (Fortunate: lucky) **8.** Blessed be the LORD your God, who was pleased to set you on the throne as king for the LORD your God. Because the LORD loved Israel and wanted to establish them

forever, He made you their king to uphold justice and righteousness. (Righteousness: virtue) **9.** She gave King Solomon 120 talents of gold, a vast quantity of spices, and precious stones. Never before had the queen of Sheba given such a gift. (Talents: units; Spices: seasonings) **10.** Huram's servants, along with Solomon's own servants, brought gold from Ophir, along with algum wood and precious stones. (Ophir: region; Algum: wood) **11.** The king used the algum wood to make terraces for the temple and the royal palace, as well as harps and lyres for the singers. There had never been anything like them in the land of Judah. (Terraces: platforms; Lyres: instruments) **12.** King Solomon gave the queen of Sheba everything she desired, besides what she had already brought him. Then she returned to her own country with her servants. (Desired: wanted) **13.** The total amount of gold that came to Solomon each year was 666 talents. (Talents: units) **14.** This was apart from what the merchants and traders brought, and from the tribute that kings of Arabia and regional governors paid to him. (Tribute: payment) **15.** King Solomon made 200 golden shields, each crafted from beaten gold. Each shield weighed 600 shekels of gold. (Shekels: units) **16.** He also made 300 golden shields, with each shield requiring 300 shekels of gold. He placed them in the House of the Forest of Lebanon. (Shields: armor) **17.** The king also created a magnificent throne made of ivory, overlaid with pure gold. (Magnificent: grand) **18.** The throne had six steps, with a golden footstool, attached firmly to the throne. There were also stays on either side of the throne, with two lions standing beside them. (Stays: supports) **19.** There were twelve lions, six on each side of the steps. Such a throne had never been made in any other kingdom. (Kingdom: realm) **20.** All of Solomon's drinking vessels were made of gold, and the vessels in the House of the Forest of Lebanon were also pure gold. Silver was not valued in Solomon's day. (Valued: regarded) **21.** The king's ships sailed to Tarshish every three years, bringing back gold, silver, ivory, monkeys, and peacocks. (Tarshish: city; Ivory: tusk) **22.** Solomon surpassed all the kings of the earth in wealth and wisdom. (Surpassed: exceeded) **23.** All the kings of the earth sought to visit Solomon to hear the wisdom that God had given him. (Sought: desired) **24.** Each one brought a gift—silver and gold vessels, clothing, armor, spices, horses, and mules. These gifts were given year after year. (Mules: hybrids) **25.** Solomon had 4,000 stalls for horses and chariots, and 12,000 horsemen, whom he stationed in the chariot cities and in Jerusalem. (Horsemen: riders) **26.** He ruled over all the kings from the Euphrates River to the land of the Philistines and to the border of Egypt. (Euphrates: river) **27.** In Jerusalem, Solomon made silver as common as stones, and he made cedar wood as plentiful as sycamore trees in the lowlands. (Sycamore: tree) **28.** Horses were brought to Solomon from Egypt and from all other nations. (Nations: countries) **29.** The rest of Solomon's actions, both early and late in his reign, are written in the records of the prophet Nathan, the prophecy of Ahijah the Shilonite, and the visions of Iddo the seer regarding Jeroboam son of Nebat. (Seer: prophet) **30.** Solomon ruled in Jerusalem for forty years over all of Israel. (Ruled: governed) **31.** Solomon passed away and was buried in the city of David, his father. His son Rehoboam succeeded him as king. (Succeeded: followed)

Chapter 10
1. Rehoboam went to Shechem, for all of Israel had gathered there to make him king. (Shechem: a city in ancient Israel) **2.** When Jeroboam, son of Nebat, who had fled to Egypt to escape King Solomon, heard of this, he returned from Egypt. (Fled: ran away) **3.** They sent for him, and Jeroboam and all Israel spoke to Rehoboam, saying, (Sent: called) **4.** "Your father made our yoke unbearable. Now, if you lighten the heavy burden your father put on us, we will serve you." (Yoke: a burden or oppression) **5.** He replied, "Come back to me in three days." And the people went away. (Replied: answered) **6.** King Rehoboam consulted the elders who had served Solomon his father during his lifetime, asking, "What do you advise me to say to this people?" (Consulted: asked for advice) **7.** They responded, "If you are kind to this people, please them, and speak good words to them, they will serve you forever." (Kind: benevolent; Please: make happy) **8.** But Rehoboam rejected the advice of the elders and instead consulted the young men who had grown up with him and were now serving him. (Rejected: dismissed; Consulted: asked) **9.** He asked the young men, "What do you advise that we should answer the people, who have asked me to lighten the yoke my father placed on them?" (Advise: recommend) **10.** The young men answered, "This is what you should tell the people: 'My little finger is thicker than my father's waist. (Waist: the part of the body between the ribs and hips) **11.** If my father put a heavy yoke on you, I will make it heavier; if he beat you with whips, I will beat you with scorpions.'" (Scorpions: a whip with sharp metal tips; Beat: struck) **12.** So Jeroboam and all the people came to Rehoboam on the third day, as the king had instructed, saying, "Return to me in three days." (Instructed: commanded) **13.** The king answered them harshly and rejected the advice of the elders. (Harshly: severely) **14.** He told them what the young men had advised, "My father made your yoke heavy, but I will make it heavier. My father beat you with whips, but I will beat you with scorpions." (Beat: struck) **15.** The king did not listen to the people, for the turn of events was from God, so that the LORD might fulfill the word He spoke through Ahijah the Shilonite to Jeroboam son of Nebat. (Fulfill: complete; Events: occurrences; Shilonite: from Shiloh) **16.** When all Israel saw that the king refused to listen to them, they answered, "What share do we have in David? We have no inheritance in the son of Jesse. Every man to his tent, O Israel! Look after your own house, David." So all Israel went to their tents. (Inheritance: right to property) **17.** But the people of Judah remained loyal to Rehoboam, and he ruled over them. (Loyal: faithful) **18.** King Rehoboam sent Hadoram, who was in charge of the forced labor, but the Israelites stoned him to death. Rehoboam quickly got into his chariot and fled to Jerusalem. (Hadoram: officer; Stoned: killed with rocks) **19.** So Israel has been in rebellion against the house of David to this day. (Rebellion: defiance)

Chapter 11
1. When Rehoboam arrived in Jerusalem, he gathered 180,000 elite warriors from the tribes of Judah and Benjamin to fight against Israel, aiming to restore the kingdom under his rule. (elite: select; special, restore: bring back, warriors: soldiers) **2.** But the word of the LORD came to Shemaiah, a prophet, saying, (prophet: a person who is believed to be chosen to speak for God) **3.** "Say to Rehoboam, son of Solomon, king of Judah, and to all the people of Judah and Benjamin, (say: to speak or tell, Judah: a tribe of Israel, Benjamin: a tribe of Israel) **4.** 'This is what the LORD says: Do not march up to fight your brothers. Every man should return home, for this matter is part of My will.' And they obeyed the LORD's command, returning from their pursuit of Jeroboam. (pursuit: the act of chasing or following) **5.** Rehoboam stayed in Jerusalem and began building fortified cities in Judah. (fortified: strengthened or made secure, cities: towns or urban areas) **6.** He constructed the cities of Bethlehem, Etam, and Tekoa, (constructed: built or formed) **7.** and also built Beth-zur, Shoco, and Adullam, (built: created, Beth-zur: a city name, Shoco: a city name, Adullam: a city name) **8.** as well as Gath, Mareshah, and Ziph, (Gath: a city, Mareshah: a city, Ziph: a city) **9.** and Adoraim, Lachish, and Azekah, (Adoraim: a city, Lachish: a city, Azekah: a city) **10.** including Zorah, Aijalon, and Hebron—cities located in the territories of Judah and Benjamin. (territories: regions, Zorah: a city, Aijalon: a city, Hebron: a city) **11.** He fortified these strongholds, placed commanders in charge, and stocked them with food, oil, and wine. (fortified: strengthened, strongholds: fortified places, commanders: leaders, stocked: filled or provided, wine: an alcoholic beverage) **12.** In every city, he placed shields and spears, making them very secure, as Judah and Benjamin were aligned with him. (aligned: in agreement or partnership, shields: protective devices, spears: weapons) **13.** The priests and Levites from all across Israel came to him in Judah. (priests: religious leaders, Levites: members

of the Hebrew tribe of Levi, Israel: the nation or the people) 14. The Levites left their towns and property and moved to Judah and Jerusalem because Jeroboam and his sons had excluded them from serving as priests to the LORD. (excluded: kept out, property: land or possessions, priests: religious leaders) 15. Jeroboam had appointed his own priests for the high places, idols, and the golden calves he had made. (appointed: chosen, idols: false gods or images, calves: a young cow, golden: made of gold) 16. But many from the tribes of Israel, who truly sought the LORD, came to Jerusalem to worship and offer sacrifices to the God of their ancestors. (ancestors: forebears, worship: to honor or revere) 17. As a result, the kingdom of Judah was strengthened, and Rehoboam, son of Solomon, became strong for three years, as they followed the ways of David and Solomon. (strengthened: made stronger, followed: adhered to) 18. Rehoboam married Mahalath, the daughter of Jerimoth (son of David), and Abihail, the daughter of Eliab (son of Jesse); (married: took as a wife, daughter: female offspring) 19. She bore him children: Jeush, Shamariah, and Zaham. (bore: gave birth to, children: sons or daughters) 20. After her, he married Maachah, daughter of Absalom, who gave birth to Abijah, Attai, Ziza, and Shelomith. (married: took as a wife, gave birth to: had children) 21. Rehoboam loved Maachah, daughter of Absalom, more than all his other wives and concubines, for he had taken eighteen wives and sixty concubines, and fathered twenty-eight sons and sixty daughters. (loved: had affection for, concubines: women in a lower status than wives, fathered: became the father of) 22. Rehoboam made Abijah, son of Maachah, his chief and appointed him to be ruler among his brothers, planning to make him king. (appointed: selected or designated, chief: leader) 23. He also wisely distributed his children throughout the cities of Judah and Benjamin, providing them with plenty of food, and he sought many wives. (wisely: in a smart and thoughtful manner, distributed: spread out, plenty: more than enough)

Chapter 12

1. After Rehoboam had solidified his position as king and grown strong, he turned away from following the LORD's commands, and all of Israel followed his example. (Rehoboam: King of Judah; solidified: made firm; forsook: abandoned) 2. In the fifth year of Rehoboam's reign, Shishak, the king of Egypt, attacked Jerusalem because Israel had sinned against the LORD. (Shishak: Pharaoh of Egypt; sinned: committed wrong or transgressed God's law) 3. Shishak brought twelve hundred chariots, sixty thousand horsemen, and an innumerable army from Egypt, including the Lubims, the Sukkiims, and the Ethiopians. (chariots: war vehicles with wheels; Lubims, Sukkiims, Ethiopians: various ethnic groups or peoples) 4. Shishak captured the fortified cities of Judah and then advanced to Jerusalem itself. (fortified: protected with strong defenses) 5. The prophet Shemaiah came to Rehoboam and the leaders of Judah who had gathered in Jerusalem, warning them, "The LORD says: 'You have abandoned Me, and now I have handed you over to Shishak.'" (Shemaiah: a prophet; princes: leaders, nobles) 6. When the leaders and Rehoboam heard this, they humbled themselves and acknowledged, "The LORD is righteous." (humbled: showed repentance or submission; righteous: just, morally right) 7. When the LORD saw that they had humbled themselves, He spoke to Shemaiah, saying, "Because they have humbled themselves, I will not destroy them completely. I will grant them some relief, and My anger will not be poured out on Jerusalem through Shishak." (relief: rescue or deliverance; poured out: released or unleashed) 8. However, they will become Shishak's servants, so they may learn the difference between serving Me and serving the kingdoms of the world. (service: being subservient or in the service of; kingdoms: nations or realms) 9. Shishak, the king of Egypt, came up against Jerusalem and took away all the treasures from the house of the LORD and from the king's palace. He even carried off the golden shields that Solomon had made. (treasures: valuable items or wealth; shields: protective armament; Solomon: King of Israel, son of David) 10. In place of the golden shields, Rehoboam made shields of brass and gave them to the officers of the guard who kept watch at the entrance of the king's palace. (brass: a type of metal made from copper and zinc; officers of the guard: senior security or military officials) 11. Whenever the king entered the house of the LORD, the guards would retrieve the brass shields and return them to the guardroom. (house of the LORD: the temple in Jerusalem) 12. When Rehoboam humbled himself, the LORD turned away His anger and chose not to destroy him entirely. Conditions in Judah began to improve. (withdrew: took away; wrath: intense anger or fury) 13. Rehoboam regained strength in Jerusalem and continued to rule. He was forty-one years old when he became king and reigned for seventeen years in Jerusalem, the city the LORD had chosen out of all the tribes of Israel to set His name. His mother was Naamah, an Ammonite. (regained: regained strength or power; reigned: ruled as king; Naamah: Rehoboam's mother, an Ammonite woman) 14. But Rehoboam did wrong because he did not prepare his heart to seek the LORD. (did wrong: acted wickedly; prepare his heart: did not commit or devote himself to seeking God) 15. The acts of Rehoboam, from beginning to end, are written in the book of Shemaiah the prophet and Iddo the seer, who also recorded the genealogies. There were continuous wars between Rehoboam and Jeroboam throughout his reign. (acts: deeds or actions; genealogies: records of family lineage; Iddo: a prophet who documented events) 16. Rehoboam passed away and was buried in the city of David. His son Abijah succeeded him as king. (slept with his fathers: died; buried in the city of David: buried in Jerusalem, where King David was buried; Abijah: Rehoboam's son)

Chapter 13

1. In the eighteenth year of King Jeroboam's reign, Abijah ascended the throne over Judah. (Jeroboam: the first king of Israel's northern kingdom; reign: rule or governance) 2. Abijah ruled for three years from Jerusalem. His mother was Michaiah, daughter of Uriel from Gibeah. During his reign, conflict broke out between Abijah and King Jeroboam. (reigned: ruled; Michaiah: Abijah's mother; Gibeah: a town within the tribe of Benjamin) 3. Abijah mustered an army of four hundred thousand brave warriors, while Jeroboam gathered eight hundred thousand seasoned soldiers to face him in battle. (mustered: assembled; brave warriors: men of valor or courage) 4. Standing on Mount Zemaraim in the hill country of Ephraim, Abijah called out to Jeroboam and all of Israel, saying, "Hear me, Jeroboam, and all you people of Israel!" (Zemaraim: a location in Ephraim's territory) 5. "Do you not know that the LORD, the God of Israel, gave the kingdom of Israel to David and his descendants by a covenant of salt, which is everlasting?" (covenant of salt: a deep, unbreakable agreement) 6. Yet, Jeroboam, son of Nebat, a servant of Solomon, rose up and rebelled against his king. (Nebat: Jeroboam's father; servant: one who served King Solomon) 7. He gathered corrupt and worthless men, the sons of Belial, who opposed Rehoboam, the son of Solomon, when Rehoboam was young and inexperienced, unable to resist them. (sons of Belial: corrupt, wicked men; inexperienced: unfit or unprepared) 8. And now, you think you can rise against the kingdom of the LORD, which belongs to the descendants of David? You have a great army, and with you are golden calves that Jeroboam made to be worshiped as gods. (golden calves: idols created by Jeroboam) 9. You have cast out the priests of the LORD, the descendants of Aaron, and the Levites, and have appointed your own priests, like the other nations. Anyone who dedicates himself with a young bull and seven rams can become a priest to these false gods. (cast out: expelled or removed; dedicates: sanctifies or consecrates) 10. But we, on the other hand, have not abandoned the LORD. The priests who serve the LORD are the descendants of Aaron, and the Levites perform their sacred duties. (abandoned: forsaken or left behind) 11. Every morning and evening, they offer burnt offerings and incense to the LORD. The showbread is arranged on the holy table, and the golden lampstand burns with its lamps each evening.

We are faithful in keeping the charge of the LORD our God, but you have turned away from Him. (showbread: consecrated bread; charge: sacred responsibility) **12.** And look, God Himself is leading us, with His priests and the trumpets sounding the alarm against you. Do not fight against the LORD, the God of your ancestors, for you will not succeed. (trumpets sounding: trumpets blown as a signal or warning) **13.** But Jeroboam had secretly placed an ambush behind them, so Judah was trapped, with enemies before and behind. (ambush: a surprise attack; trapped: surrounded) **14.** When the men of Judah saw they were surrounded, they cried out to the LORD, and the priests blew the trumpets to signal the call to arms. (cried out: called in distress) **15.** Then the men of Judah raised their voices in battle cry, and as they did, God struck down Jeroboam and all of Israel before Abijah and Judah. (struck down: defeated; raised their voices: shouted in battle) **16.** The Israelites turned and fled before Judah, and the LORD delivered them into the hands of Judah's army. (delivered: handed over or granted victory) **17.** Abijah and his forces inflicted a great slaughter, killing five hundred thousand of Israel's finest soldiers. (slaughter: massacre; finest: chosen or elite soldiers) **18.** At that time, the people of Israel were humbled, while the people of Judah triumphed because they trusted in the LORD, the God of their ancestors. (humbled: defeated or subdued; trusted in: relied on) **19.** Abijah pursued Jeroboam, capturing several cities from him, including Bethel with its surrounding villages, Jeshnah with its towns, and Ephraim with its settlements. (pursued: chased; towns: smaller communities) **20.** Jeroboam never regained his strength during Abijah's reign, for the LORD struck him down, and he died. (regained strength: recovered power; struck: defeated) **21.** However, Abijah grew stronger, took fourteen wives, and fathered twenty-two sons and sixteen daughters. (grew stronger: became prosperous or powerful) **22.** The rest of Abijah's reign, his actions, and his words are recorded in the chronicles written by the prophet Iddo. (actions: deeds or acts; chronicles: historical records)

Chapter 14

1. When Abijah died and was buried in the city of David, his son Asa became king. During his reign, the land enjoyed peace for ten years. (Passed away: died; Reigned: ruled; Experienced peace: tranquility) **2.** Asa did what was righteous and just in the sight of the LORD, his God. (Good: righteous; Right: just) **3.** He removed the foreign altars, destroyed the idol worship sites, and cut down the Asherah poles. (Altars: shrines; High places: worship sites; Idols: statues; Asherah poles: pagan symbols) **4.** Asa commanded Judah to seek the LORD and follow His laws and commandments. (Commanded: ordered; Seek: pursue; Laws: instructions) **5.** He removed the idols from all Judah's cities, and the kingdom enjoyed peace during his reign. (Removed: eliminated; Enjoyed peace: was at rest) **6.** Asa strengthened the cities of Judah, as there was no war during those years, for the LORD had given them peace. (Fortified: strengthened; Rest: peace) **7.** Asa urged Judah to rebuild and fortify the cities while the land was peaceful, saying, "Since we sought the LORD and He granted us peace, let us build and prosper." (Fortify: strengthen; Prosper: succeed) **8.** Asa had a mighty army: 300,000 men from Judah with shields and spears, and 280,000 from Benjamin with shields and bows. (Mighty warriors: strong fighters) **9.** Zerah the Ethiopian came against them with a million men and 300 chariots, marching to Mareshah. (Ethiopian: African; Chariots: war vehicles) **10.** Asa met him in battle at the valley of Zephathah in Mareshah. (Arranged: organized) **11.** Asa prayed, "LORD, nothing is impossible for You. Help us, for we rely on You, and we go into battle in Your name. Do not let man prevail over You." (Rely: depend) **12.** The LORD struck down the Ethiopians, and they fled before Asa and Judah. (Struck down: defeated) **13.** Asa and his men pursued them to Gerar, where the Ethiopians were utterly defeated, and they took much spoil. (Pursued: chased; Spoil: loot) **14.** They destroyed the cities around Gerar, looted them, and gathered an abundance of spoil, for the fear of the LORD had fallen on the people. (Struck down: destroyed; Looted: plundered; Abundance: plenty) **15.** They raided the livestock camps, took many sheep and camels, and returned to Jerusalem. (Attacked: raided; Cattle: livestock)

Chapter 15

1. The Spirit of God came upon Azariah, the son of Oded. (Spirit: divine presence; Azariah: "Yahweh has helped") **2.** Azariah met Asa and said, "Listen, Asa, and all Judah and Benjamin: The LORD is with you as long as you are with Him. Seek Him, and He will be found; forsake Him, and He will forsake you." (Forsake: abandon) **3.** For a long time, Israel lacked the true God, a teaching priest, and the law. (Teaching priest: one who instructs in God's ways) **4.** But when they turned to the LORD in their distress and sought Him, He was found by them. (Trouble: distress, difficulty) **5.** At that time, there was no peace, and great turmoil spread across the nations. (Turmoil: confusion, unrest) **6.** Nation crushed nation, and city crushed city, for God brought them into great distress. (Crushed: defeated; Distress: suffering) **7.** Be strong, do not lose heart, for your work will be rewarded. (Hands be weak: lose strength or resolve) **8.** When Asa heard the prophecy of Azariah, he gained courage, removed the idols from Judah and Benjamin, and repaired the LORD's altar. (Detestable idols: abominable images; Took courage: gained strength) **9.** He gathered all Judah, Benjamin, and those from Ephraim, Manasseh, and Simeon who had joined him, because they saw that the LORD was with him. (Defected: left their previous allegiance) **10.** They assembled in Jerusalem in the third month, in the fifteenth year of Asa's reign. (Gathered: assembled) **11.** They offered 700 oxen and 7,000 sheep to the LORD from the spoil they had taken. (Spoil: goods taken after a battle) **12.** They made a covenant to seek the LORD with all their heart and soul. (Covenant: agreement, promise; Heart and soul: with full devotion) **13.** They swore an oath that anyone who would not seek the LORD should be put to death, whether small or great, man or woman. (Oath: vow, promise) **14.** They swore their oath with a loud voice, shouting, trumpets, and cornets. (Cornets: brass instruments) **15.** All Judah rejoiced at the oath, for they sought the LORD with all their heart, and He gave them rest on every side. (Rejoiced: celebrated, was happy; Rest: peace) **16.** Asa removed Maachah, his mother, from being queen mother because she made an idol in a grove. He destroyed the idol and burned it in the Kidron Valley. (Removed: took away; Queen mother: the king's mother; Grove: wooded area, often associated with pagan worship; Stamped: crushed, destroyed) **17.** However, the high places were not removed from Israel, but Asa remained faithful throughout his reign. (High places: pagan worship sites) **18.** Asa brought into God's house the dedicated items his father had consecrated, and those he had dedicated—silver, gold, and various vessels. (Dedicated: set apart for sacred use) **19.** There was no war until the thirty-fifth year of Asa's reign. (Reign: rule, period of leadership)

Chapter 16

1. In the 36th year of Asa's reign, King Baasha of Israel attacked Judah and built Ramah to prevent anyone from entering or leaving Judah. (Ramah: a city in Israel) **2.** Asa took silver and gold from the treasures of the Lord's house and his own palace, and sent it to Ben-hadad, king of Syria in Damascus, saying, (Damascus: capital of Syria, Ben-hadad: king of Syria) **3.** "We have a treaty, like our fathers had. I've sent you silver and gold—break your alliance with Baasha of Israel so he will leave us alone." (Treaty: a formal agreement) **4.** Ben-hadad agreed and sent his commanders to attack Israel's cities: Ijon, Dan, Abel-maim, and the store cities of Naphtali. (Commanders: military leaders, Ijon, Dan, Abel-maim, Naphtali: places in Israel) **5.** When Baasha heard this, he stopped building Ramah and abandoned his work. (Abandoned: left behind) **6.** Asa took the stones and timber from Ramah and used them to build Geba and Mizpah. (Timber: wood, Geba and Mizpah: cities in Judah) **7.** At that time, Hanani the seer (prophet) came to Asa and said, "You relied on Syria, not on God, so Syria escaped your control." (Seer: prophet, Syria: a neighboring kingdom) **8.** "Didn't God deliver you from the huge

Ethiopian army when you trusted Him? Now you've acted foolishly, so from now on, you'll face wars." (Ethiopian: from Ethiopia, foolishly: without wisdom) 9. "The Lord looks throughout the earth to strengthen those whose hearts are fully committed to Him. You've been foolish, and now you will have constant conflict." (Conflict: wars or struggles) 10. Asa was angry with the prophet and threw him in prison, also oppressing some of the people. (Oppressing: mistreating or burdening) 11. Asa's deeds, from beginning to end, are recorded in the book of the kings of Judah and Israel. (Recorded: written down) 12. In the 39th year of his reign, Asa became severely ill in his feet, but he sought help from physicians, not from God. (Physicians: doctors) 13. Asa died in the 41st year of his reign. (Reign: period of rule) 14. He was buried in his own tomb in the city of David, with a fragrant bed of spices and a large funeral pyre. (Tomb: burial place, Pyre: a pile for burning, spices: fragrant plants)

Chapter 17

1. Jehoshaphat, the son of Asa, became king and strengthened Judah against Israel. (Strengthened: made stronger) 2. He placed troops in all Judah's fortified cities and in the cities of Ephraim that his father Asa had captured. (Fortified: protected, Ephraim: a region in Israel) 3. The LORD was with Jehoshaphat because he followed the ways of his ancestor David and did not worship false gods. (False gods: idols, Baalim: false gods worshiped in ancient times) 4. Instead, he sought the Lord God of his father and followed His commandments, not the practices of Israel. (Practices: customs or actions) 5. Because of this, the LORD established his kingdom, and Judah brought him gifts. Jehoshaphat became rich and honored. (Established: made stable, Gifts: offerings or presents) 6. His heart was devoted to the ways of the LORD, and he removed idol worship from Judah. (Devoted: fully committed, Idol worship: worshiping false gods) 7. In the third year of his reign, Jehoshaphat sent his officials—Ben-hail, Obadiah, Zechariah, Nethaneel, and Michaiah—to teach in the cities of Judah. (Reign: period of ruling, Officials: leaders or representatives) 8. With them, he sent Levites—Shemaiah, Nethaniah, Zebadiah, Asahel, Shemiramoth, Jehonathan, Adonijah, Tobijah, and Tob-adonijah—and priests Elishama and Jehoram. (Levites: members of the Hebrew tribe of Levi, Priests: religious leaders) 9. They taught the people, carrying the Book of the Law of the LORD, and visited all the cities of Judah. (Law: divine rules or commandments) 10. The fear of the LORD came upon the surrounding kingdoms, so they did not fight against Jehoshaphat. (Fear: reverence or awe) 11. Some Philistines brought Jehoshaphat gifts and tribute silver, and the Arabians brought him 7,700 rams and 7,700 male goats. (Philistines: a neighboring people, Tribute: a payment made for protection, Arabians: people from the Arabian Peninsula) 12. Jehoshaphat grew very powerful and built strongholds and store cities throughout Judah. (Strongholds: fortified places, Store cities: places for storing goods) 13. He had many business dealings in Judah, and his military was strong, with valiant warriors in Jerusalem. (Valiant: brave, Military: army) 14. The leaders of Judah's armies were: Adnah, the chief, with 300,000 mighty warriors. (Mighty: strong, Warriors: fighters) 15. Jehohanan, the next captain, with 280,000. (Captain: leader of a group) 16. Amasiah, the son of Zichri, who willingly offered himself to the LORD, with 200,000 mighty warriors. (Willingly: voluntarily, Offered: gave himself) 17. Eliada of Benjamin, a mighty man with 200,000 armed with bows and shields. (Armed: equipped with weapons, Bows and shields: weapons for defense) 18. Jehozabad, with 180,000 fully prepared for battle. (Prepared: ready for action) 19. These warriors served the king, alongside those stationed in fortified cities throughout Judah. (Stationed: assigned to stay)

Chapter 18

1. Jehoshaphat, rich and honored, allied with Ahab. (allied: joined in partnership) 2. After some years, he visited Ahab in Samaria, where Ahab prepared a feast of sheep and oxen, urging him to join the battle at Ramoth-gilead. (feast: large meal) 3. Ahab asked, "Will you go with me to battle?" Jehoshaphat replied, "I am one with you and your people; we'll fight together." (replied: answered) 4. Jehoshaphat added, "Let us seek the Lord's guidance today." (added: also said) 5. Ahab gathered 400 prophets, asking if they should go to Ramoth-gilead. They all said, "Go, for God will give you victory." (gathered: assembled) 6. But Jehoshaphat asked, "Is there no prophet of the Lord left to consult?" (consult: ask for advice) 7. Ahab replied, "There's one—Micaiah, but I hate him. He always speaks against me." Jehoshaphat said, "Don't say that." (replied: answered) 8. Ahab ordered his officers to bring Micaiah. (ordered: commanded) 9. The kings sat on their thrones, and the prophets prophesied before them. (prophesied: foretold events) 10. Zedekiah, one of the prophets, made iron horns, declaring, "With these, you will defeat Syria." (declaring: stating) 11. All the prophets agreed, saying, "Go up and prosper, for the Lord will deliver it to you." (prosper: succeed) 12. A messenger urged Micaiah to speak favorably, as the others did. (urged: encouraged) 13. Micaiah responded, "I will only speak what the Lord tells me." (responded: replied) 14. When Micaiah came, Ahab asked, "Shall we go to Ramoth-gilead?" Micaiah answered, "Go, and you will succeed." (answered: replied) 15. Ahab demanded, "How many times must I warn you to speak the truth?" (warn: instruct) 16. Micaiah said, "I saw Israel scattered, like sheep without a shepherd. The Lord said, 'Let them return home in peace.'" (scattered: spread out) 17. Ahab complained, "I told you he only speaks evil about me!" (complained: expressed dissatisfaction) 18. Micaiah continued, "I saw the Lord on His throne, with the heavenly host around Him." (host: army) 19. The Lord asked, "Who will entice Ahab to go to Ramoth-gilead?" Various spirits offered suggestions. (entice: persuade) 20. A spirit stood before the Lord and said, "I will entice him." (stood: took a position) 21. The spirit said, "I will become a lying spirit in the mouths of his prophets." The Lord allowed it. (lying: false) 22. "The Lord has put a lying spirit in these prophets," Micaiah declared, "and spoken against you." (declared: stated) 23. Zedekiah slapped Micaiah and mocked him, "Which way did the Lord's spirit leave me?" (mocked: ridiculed) 24. Micaiah replied, "You will see on the day you hide in a room." (replied: answered) 25. Ahab ordered Micaiah to be imprisoned, saying, "Feed him only bread and water until I return safely." (ordered: commanded) 26. Micaiah boldly responded, "If you return safely, then the Lord didn't speak through me." (boldly: confidently) 27. Micaiah's declaration was heard by all. (declaration: statement) 28. Jehoshaphat and Ahab went to battle at Ramoth-gilead. (went: traveled) 29. Ahab disguised himself for the battle, but Jehoshaphat wore his royal robes. (disguised: changed appearance) 30. The Syrian king ordered his chariot commanders to focus only on killing Ahab. (ordered: instructed) 31. The chariot captains mistook Jehoshaphat for Ahab and surrounded him, but when he cried out, the Lord saved him. (mistook: confused) 32. When they realized it was not Ahab, they stopped chasing Jehoshaphat. (realized: understood) 33. A random archer shot an arrow, hitting Ahab between his armor's joints. (random: by chance) 34. Ahab told his charioteer to turn away, as he was wounded. He stayed in his chariot until evening, when he died. (wounded: injured)

Chapter 19

1. Jehoshaphat, the king of Judah, returned peacefully to his house in Jerusalem. 2. Jehu, son of Hanani the prophet, met him and said, "Should you help the wicked and love those who hate the LORD? Because of this, God's anger is upon you." (Wrath: intense anger) 3. However, there is good in you, for you removed idol worship from the land and set your heart to seek God. (Groves: places of idol worship) 4. Jehoshaphat stayed in Jerusalem but traveled through Judah, from Beer-sheba to Mount Ephraim, bringing the people back to the LORD, the God of their ancestors. (Beer-sheba: a town in southern Judah; Ephraim: a region in Israel) 5. He appointed judges in all the fortified cities of Judah, one in each city. 6. He instructed them, "Be careful in your judgments, for you do not judge for men

but for the LORD, who is with you in judgment." **7.** Therefore, let the fear of the LORD be upon you. Be careful to follow His commands, for He has no injustice, favoritism, or bribery." (Iniquity: wickedness; Respect of persons: showing favoritism; Taking of gifts: accepting bribes) **8.** Jehoshaphat also appointed Levites, priests, and family leaders in Jerusalem to settle disputes according to the LORD's laws. **9.** He commanded them, "Do this in the fear of the LORD, faithfully, and with a sincere heart." (Sincere: genuine, without pretense) **10.** Any case between your people—whether involving bloodshed, law, or commandments—warn them not to sin against the LORD, or His wrath will fall on you and them." (Trespass: sin or wrongdoing) **11.** Amariah, the chief priest, is in charge of all matters of the LORD, and Zebadiah, the ruler of Judah's house, oversees the king's matters. The Levites will assist you. Be courageous, and the LORD will be with the good." (Courageously: with bravery; Officers: officials or assistants)

Chapter 20

1. Afterward, the Moabites, Ammonites, and others joined them to fight against Jehoshaphat. (Ammonites: people) **2.** Messengers told Jehoshaphat, "A great army is coming from beyond the sea, from Syria, and they are at Hazazon-tamar, which is En-gedi." (Hazazon-tamar: town; En-gedi: location) **3.** Jehoshaphat was afraid, so he sought the LORD and proclaimed a fast throughout Judah. (Fast: abstention) **4.** All Judah gathered to ask for help from the LORD, coming from all their cities to seek Him. (Seek: search) **5.** Jehoshaphat stood in the temple of the LORD before the new court, (Court: area) **6.** and prayed, "O LORD God of our ancestors, are You not in heaven? Do You not rule over all kingdoms? Is there not power in Your hand to defeat any enemy?" (Ancestors: forebears) **7.** "Are You not our God who drove out the inhabitants of this land before Your people, Israel, and gave it to the descendants of Abraham forever?" (Inhabitants: residents; Descendants: offspring) **8.** They lived here and built a sanctuary for Your name, saying, (Sanctuary: temple) **9.** "If disaster strikes—such as war, judgment, pestilence, or famine—and we stand before this house, calling on Your name, You will hear and help us." (Pestilence: plague; Famine: hunger) **10.** "Now the Ammonites, Moabites, and people of Mount Seir, whom You did not allow Israel to invade when they came from Egypt, are attacking us." (Seir: region) **11.** "See how they repay us by trying to drive us out of the land You gave us to inherit?" (Repay: recompense; Inherit: receive) **12.** "O our God, will You not judge them? We have no strength against this vast army; we do not know what to do, but our eyes are on You." (Vast: immense; Judge: decide) **13.** All Judah stood before the LORD, including their children, wives, and little ones. (Little ones: children) **14.** The Spirit of the LORD came upon Jahaziel, a Levite, in the midst of the congregation. (Levite: priest; Congregation: assembly) **15.** Jahaziel said, "Listen, all Judah and Jerusalem, and King Jehoshaphat: The LORD says to you, 'Do not be afraid or discouraged by this great army; the battle is not yours, but God's.'" (Discouraged: disheartened; Battle: conflict) **16.** "Tomorrow, go down against them. They will come up by the Ziz pass, and you will find them at the end of the valley, before the wilderness of Jeruel." (Ziz: pass; Jeruel: desert) **17.** "You will not need to fight. Stand still, and watch the LORD's deliverance. Do not be afraid, for the LORD will be with you." (Deliverance: rescue) **18.** Jehoshaphat bowed down, and all Judah and Jerusalem fell before the LORD, worshipping Him. (Bow down: kneel; Worshipping: adoring) **19.** The Levites from the Kohathites and Korahites stood up to praise the LORD with loud voices. (Kohathites: family; Korahites: descendants) **20.** Early the next morning, they went out to the wilderness of Tekoa. Jehoshaphat stood and said, "Listen, Judah and Jerusalem: Believe in the LORD your God, and you will be established; believe His prophets, and you will prosper." (Tekoa: town; Prosper: succeed) **21.** After consulting the people, Jehoshaphat appointed singers to praise the beauty of holiness, to march ahead of the army, and say, 'Give thanks to the LORD, for His mercy endures forever.'" (Consulting: advising; Beauty: splendor) **22.** As they began to sing, the LORD set ambushes against the Ammonites, Moabites, and Mount Seir, and they were defeated. (Ambushes: traps) **23.** The Ammonites and Moabites turned against the people of Mount Seir and destroyed them. Then, when they finished, they turned on each other. (Turned against: attacked) **24.** When Judah reached the lookout point in the wilderness, they saw only dead bodies, and no one had escaped. (Lookout: vantage; Wilderness: desert) **25.** They gathered the spoils, finding riches and jewels among the dead, more than they could carry. It took them three days to collect the plunder. (Spoils: loot; Plunder: treasure) **26.** On the fourth day, they gathered in the valley of Berachah, where they blessed the LORD. This place was named the Valley of Berachah, meaning "blessing," and still carries that name today. (Berachah: blessing) **27.** Then, all the men of Judah and Jerusalem, with Jehoshaphat leading them, returned to Jerusalem with joy, for the LORD had given them victory over their enemies. (Victory: triumph) **28.** They came to Jerusalem with harps, lyres, and trumpets to the house of the LORD. (Harps: instruments; Lyres: stringed instruments; Trumpets: horns) **29.** The fear of God fell on all the surrounding kingdoms when they heard how the LORD fought for Israel. (Fear: awe) **30.** Jehoshaphat's kingdom was at peace, for his God gave him rest on every side. (Rest: peace) **31.** Jehoshaphat reigned in Judah for 25 years, beginning at age 35. His mother was Azubah, daughter of Shilhi. (Reigned: ruled) **32.** He followed the ways of his father Asa and did what was right in the eyes of the LORD. (Followed: obeyed) **33.** However, the high places were not removed, for the people had not yet set their hearts on the God of their ancestors. (High places: altars) **34.** The acts of Jehoshaphat, from beginning to end, are recorded in the book of Jehu, son of Hanani, as mentioned in the book of the kings of Israel. (Acts: deeds) **35.** Later, Jehoshaphat allied with Ahaziah, king of Israel, who did wickedly. (Allied: partnered) **36.** They made ships to go to Tarshish and built them in Ezion-geber. (Ships: vessels; Ezion-geber: port) **37.** But the prophet Eliezer son of Dodavah prophesied against Jehoshaphat, saying, "Because you joined with Ahaziah, the LORD has destroyed your works, and the ships were broken, unable to sail to Tarshish." (Prophesied: foretold; Destroyed: ruined)

Chapter 21

1. Jehoshaphat died and was buried with his ancestors in the City of David. His son Jehoram became king in his place. (Died: passed away; Ancestors: forefathers) **2.** Jehoshaphat had other sons: Azariah, Jehiel, Zechariah, Azariah, Michael, and Shephatiah. These were his sons, the king of Judah. (Sons: children; Ancestors: forebears) **3.** Their father gave them great gifts of silver, gold, and precious items, along with fortified cities in Judah, but he gave the kingdom to Jehoram, as he was the firstborn. (Fortified: strong; Firstborn: eldest) **4.** When Jehoram became king, he secured his rule by killing all his brothers and many of the princes of Israel. (Secured: strengthened; Princes: leaders) **5.** Jehoram was 32 when he began to reign, and he ruled for 8 years in Jerusalem. (Reign: rule) **6.** He followed the ways of the kings of Israel, like the house of Ahab, because he married Ahab's daughter, and did evil in the eyes of the LORD. (Evil: wickedness) **7.** However, the LORD did not destroy the house of David due to the covenant He made with David, and as He promised to give a legacy to David's descendants forever. (Covenant: agreement; Legacy: inheritance) **8.** During his reign, the Edomites rebelled from Judah's control and made their own king. (Rebelled: revolted; Dominion: control) **9.** Jehoram went out with his commanders and all his chariots, rising by night to attack the Edomites and their leaders. (Commanders: leaders; Chariots: carts) **10.** The Edomites revolted from Judah's control, and at the same time, Libnah also rebelled, because Jehoram had forsaken the LORD. (Forsaken: abandoned; Revolted: rebelled) **11.** Jehoram built high places in Judah, causing the people of Jerusalem to sin, and he compelled Judah to follow. (Sin: transgress; Compelled: forced) **12.**

A message came from Elijah the prophet saying, "Thus says the LORD God of David your father: You did not follow the ways of your father Jehoshaphat or King Asa of Judah," (Message: writing; Prophet: seer) **13.** "But you followed the kings of Israel, making Judah and Jerusalem sin, like the house of Ahab, and even killed your brothers, who were better than you." (Sin: transgressed; Whoredoms: idolatry) **14.** "The LORD will strike your people, your children, wives, and all your wealth with a great plague." (Plague: affliction) **15.** "You will suffer a great illness in your intestines, until your bowels fall out day by day." (Intestines: bowels; Illness: disease) **16.** The LORD stirred up against Jehoram the Philistines and the Arabians, near the Ethiopians. (Stirred: provoked; Philistines: enemies) **17.** They invaded Judah, broke into it, and took all the treasures from the king's house, including his sons and wives, leaving only Jehoahaz, his youngest son. (Invaded: attacked; Treasures: wealth) **18.** After all this, the LORD struck him with an incurable disease in his intestines. (Incurable: untreatable; Struck: afflicted) **19.** After two years, his intestines fell out due to his sickness, and he died from the disease. His people did not burn his body as they did for his ancestors. (Sickness: illness; Died: passed away; Burn: cremate) **20.** He was 32 when he began to reign and ruled for 8 years. He died unlamented and was buried in the City of David, but not in the royal tombs. (Unlamented: unloved; Tombs: graves)

Chapter 22
1. The people of Jerusalem made Ahaziah, the youngest son of Jehoram, king after his death, for the band of Arabian men had killed all his older brothers. (Band: group; Slain: killed) **2.** Ahaziah was 42 years old when he became king, and he reigned for one year in Jerusalem. His mother was Athaliah, the daughter of Omri. (Reigned: ruled) **3.** Ahaziah followed the ways of the house of Ahab, for his mother counseled him to do evil. (Counseled: advised; Evil: wickedness) **4.** He did evil in the sight of the LORD, like the house of Ahab, because his counselors led him to destruction after his father's death. (Destruction: ruin) **5.** Ahaziah followed their advice and went with Jehoram, son of Ahab, to war against Hazael, king of Syria at Ramoth-gilead. The Syrians wounded Jehoram. (Wounded: injured; War: battle) **6.** He returned to Jezreel to recover from his wounds, and Azariah, son of Jehoram, went to visit him because he was ill. (Recover: heal; Visit: go to see) **7.** The LORD's plan led to Ahaziah's destruction when he visited Jehoram, as he joined him in going to confront Jehu, whom the LORD had chosen to destroy Ahab's house. (Plan: purpose; Confront: face) **8.** When Jehu was executing judgment on Ahab's house, he found the princes of Judah and the sons of Ahaziah who served him, and he killed them. (Executing: carrying out; Judgment: punishment) **9.** Jehu sought out Ahaziah, who was hiding in Samaria, and brought him to Jehu. They killed him and buried him because he was the son of Jehoshaphat, who had sought the LORD wholeheartedly. The house of Ahaziah could not hold onto the kingdom. (Hiding: concealing; Sought: worshipped) **10.** When Athaliah, Ahaziah's mother, saw her son was dead, she rose up and destroyed all the royal family of Judah. (Rose up: acted; Destroyed: killed) **11.** Jehosheba, the daughter of King Jehoram and sister of Ahaziah, took Joash, Ahaziah's son, and hid him and his nurse in a bedroom, so that Athaliah did not kill him. Jehosheba was the wife of Jehoiada the priest. (Took: rescued; Hid: concealed; Priest: religious leader) **12.** Joash was hidden in the house of God for six years, while Athaliah reigned over the land. (Reigned: ruled; Land: country)

Chapter 23
1. In the seventh year, Jehoiada strengthened himself and made a covenant with the captains of hundreds: Azariah the son of Jeroham, Ishmael the son of Jehohanan, Azariah the son of Obed, Maaseiah the son of Adaiah, and Elishaphat the son of Zichri. (Strengthened: made strong; Covenant: agreement; Captains: leaders) **2.** They went throughout Judah, gathering the Levites from all the cities and the chief of the fathers of Israel, and they came to Jerusalem. (Gathering: collecting; Levites: members of the tribe of Levi; Chief: leaders) **3.** All the congregation made a covenant with the king in the house of God, and Jehoiada said to them, "Behold, the king's son shall reign, as the LORD has promised the sons of David." (Congregation: assembly; Reign: rule; Promised: pledged) **4.** Jehoiada instructed them on their duties: a third of you, of the priests and Levites, shall be porters of the doors on the Sabbath. (Porters: gatekeepers) **5.** A third shall be at the king's house, and a third shall be at the gate of the foundation; and all the people shall be in the courts of the house of the LORD. (Foundation: main entrance or support structure) **6.** But let no one enter the house of the LORD except the priests and those who serve the Levites, for they are holy; but all the people shall keep watch over the LORD. (Watch: guard) **7.** The Levites shall surround the king with weapons in their hands; and anyone else who enters the house shall be put to death. Be with the king when he enters and leaves. (Surround: encircle; Weapons: arms) **8.** The Levites and all Judah did as Jehoiada the priest commanded, and each man took his turn on the Sabbath, both those coming in and those going out. Jehoiada did not dismiss the courses. (Courses: groups or rotations of priests and Levites) **9.** Jehoiada gave the captains of the hundreds the spears, shields, and bucklers that had been King David's, which were in the house of God. (Bucklers: small shields) **10.** He set the people in position, each with his weapon in hand, from the right side of the temple to the left side, along the altar and the temple, surrounding the king. (Position: placement; Surrounding: encircling) **11.** They brought out the king's son, put the crown on him, gave him the testimony, made him king, and anointed him. Jehoiada and his sons said, "Long live the king!" (Testimony: royal decree or law; Anointed: consecrated) **12.** When Athaliah heard the noise of people running and praising the king, she came to the people in the house of the LORD. (Noise: loud sound; Praising: celebrating) **13.** She looked, and saw the king standing by the pillar at the entrance, with the princes and the trumpets by the king. All the people of the land rejoiced, and sounded trumpets, with singers and musicians leading the praise. Then Athaliah tore her clothes and cried, "Treason, treason!" (Pillar: column; Rejoiced: celebrated; Treason: betrayal; Tore: ripped) **14.** Jehoiada the priest brought out the captains of the hundreds, who were over the army, and said to them, "Take her away from the ranks, and whoever follows her, kill with the sword. Do not kill her in the house of the LORD." (Ranks: groups or divisions; Sword: weapon) **15.** So they took hold of her, and when they reached the entrance of the horse gate by the king's house, they killed her there. (Took hold of: seized; Entrance: doorway) **16.** Jehoiada made a covenant between himself, the people, and the king, that they should be the LORD's people. (Covenant: agreement) **17.** Then all the people went to the house of Baal, broke it down, destroyed its altars and images, and killed Mattan, the priest of Baal, before the altars. (Broke down: destroyed; Altars: places of worship; Images: idols) **18.** Jehoiada appointed the officers of the house of the LORD by the hands of the priests, the Levites, whom David had distributed in the house of the LORD, to offer burnt offerings to the LORD, as it is written in the law of Moses, with rejoicing and singing, as was commanded by David. (Appointed: assigned; Officers: leaders; Burnt offerings: sacrifices) **19.** He set the porters at the gates of the house of the LORD, so that no one unclean in any way should enter. (Porters: gatekeepers; Unclean: impure) **20.** Jehoiada took the captains of the hundreds, the nobles, the governors of the people, and all the people of the land, and brought the king down from the house of the LORD. They came through the high gate into the king's house and set the king on the throne. (Nobles: high-ranking people; Governors: rulers; Throne: seat of power) **21.** All the people rejoiced, and the city was quiet, after they had slain Athaliah with the sword. (Rejoiced: celebrated; Quiet: peaceful; Slain: killed)

Chapter 24
1. Joash became king at seven years old and reigned for forty years in Jerusalem. His mother was Zibiah from Beer-sheba. (Beer-sheba:

A city in the southern part of ancient Judah) **2.** Joash did what was right in the LORD's eyes as long as Jehoiada the priest was alive to guide him. (Jehoiada: A priest who guided King Joash) **3.** Jehoiada arranged for Joash to marry two wives, and Joash had sons and daughters. (Arranged: Made plans for) **4.** Joash decided to repair the temple of the LORD. (Repair: Restore, fix) **5.** He gathered the priests and Levites and instructed them to collect money from all Israel to fund the repairs, but they did not act quickly. (Levites: Members of the priestly tribe of Israel) **6.** The king called Jehoiada, the chief priest, asking why the Levites had not collected the money as commanded by Moses for the tabernacle. (Tabernacle: Portable sanctuary used by the Israelites in the wilderness) **7.** The sons of Athaliah had defiled the temple, giving its sacred items to Baal. (Defiled: Made impure or unholy) **8.** A chest was made and placed outside the temple gate to collect donations for the repairs. (Chest: A large box for storage) **9.** A proclamation was made throughout Judah and Jerusalem, asking for the donations Moses had commanded for the temple. (Proclamation: Official announcement) **10.** The people rejoiced and brought their contributions, filling the chest. (Contributions: Donations, offerings) **11.** When the chest was brought to the king's officials, they saw the large amount of money and emptied it daily, gathering more funds. (Emptied: Removed the contents from) **12.** The king and Jehoiada used the money to pay for the temple repairs, hiring workers to restore it. (Restored: Brought back to its former state) **13.** The work was completed, and the temple was strengthened and returned to its original state. (Strengthened: Made stronger, fortified) **14.** The remaining funds were used to make sacred vessels for the temple, and burnt offerings were made continuously. (Vessels: Sacred containers) **15.** Jehoiada lived to be 130 and was buried among the kings for his good deeds in Israel. (Deeds: Actions, works) **16.** After Jehoiada's death, the leaders of Judah approached Joash, and he listened to their advice. (Approached: Came to, went to) **17.** They abandoned the LORD and began worshipping idols, bringing God's wrath upon Judah and Jerusalem. (Wrath: Anger, intense fury) **18.** Despite sending prophets to call them back, the people ignored them. (Ignored: Paid no attention to) **19.** The Spirit of God came upon Zechariah, the son of Jehoiada, and he rebuked them for forsaking the LORD. (Rebuked: Scolded, reprimanded) **20.** The people conspired and stoned Zechariah to death in the temple courtyard, ignoring his warning. (Conspired: Planned together secretly) **21.** Joash, who had forgotten Jehoiada's kindness, had Zechariah killed. Zechariah's last words were, "May the LORD see this and take vengeance." (Vengeance: Revenge, punishment for wrongdoing) **22.** At the end of the year, a Syrian army came, defeated Judah, and plundered the city. (Plundered: Took goods by force) **23.** Although the Syrian army was small, the LORD delivered them into the Syrians' hands because Judah had abandoned God. (Delivered: Gave into their hands, allowed to defeat) **24.** Afterwards, Joash was left in great suffering. His own servants conspired against him and killed him in his bed. (Suffering: Pain or distress) **25.** Joash was buried in the City of David, but not in the royal tombs. (Royal tombs: The burial place for kings) **26.** The conspirators who killed him were Zabad, the son of Shimeath, an Ammonite woman, and Jehozabad, the son of Shimrith, a Moabite woman. (Ammonite/Moabite: People from neighboring nations) **27.** Joash's sons and the story of the temple's restoration are written in the book of the kings. His son Amaziah succeeded him. (Amaziah: Joash's son who became king after him)

Chapter 25

1. Amaziah was 25 years old when he became king, and he ruled for 29 years in Jerusalem. His mother was Jehoaddan from Jerusalem. (Reign: Period of ruling as a king) **2.** He did what was right in the LORD's sight, but his heart was not fully devoted to Him. (Devoted: Committed, dedicated) **3.** When his reign was firmly established, he had the servants who had killed his father, the king, put to death. (Firmly established: Made stable and secure) **4.** However, he did not execute their children, following the law of Moses, which says that each person is responsible for their own sin. (Execute: To carry out a death sentence) **5.** Amaziah gathered the men of Judah and Benjamin, divided them into groups by families, and counted 300,000 men capable of going to war, armed with spears and shields. (Divided: Separated into groups) **6.** He hired 100,000 brave men from Israel, paying them 100 talents of silver. (Brave: Showing courage or valor in battle) **7.** A man of God warned him not to take Israel's army with him, for the LORD was not with Israel, especially the children of Ephraim. (Warned: Told in advance of danger) **8.** The prophet said, "If you go, you will be defeated, for God has the power to help or to bring you down." (Defeated: Overcome or beaten) **9.** Amaziah asked what he should do about the 100 talents he had already paid the Israelite army. The prophet assured him that God could provide much more than this. (Assured: Made certain or confident) **10.** Amaziah sent the Israelite soldiers home, and they were very angry, returning to their land in rage. (Rage: Intense anger) **11.** Amaziah gathered his forces, went to the Valley of Salt, and defeated 10,000 men from Seir. (Defeated: Overcame in battle) **12.** Another 10,000 captives from Seir were taken by the men of Judah, brought to a high rock, and thrown down, killing them all. (Captives: Prisoners of war) **13.** The Israelite soldiers, sent home by Amaziah, attacked cities in Judah from Samaria to Beth-horon, killing 3,000 people and taking much loot. (Loot: Stolen goods or treasure) **14.** After the victory over the Edomites, Amaziah took the gods of Seir, set them up as his own gods, and worshipped them, burning incense to them. (Incense: A substance burned to produce a fragrant smoke in worship) **15.** This angered the LORD, and He sent a prophet to confront Amaziah, asking why he would worship gods that couldn't even save their own people. (Confront: To face or challenge directly) **16.** Amaziah dismissed the prophet, saying, "Are you part of the king's counsel? Why should I be punished?" The prophet replied, "I know that God has decided to destroy you because you have rejected His advice." (Dismissed: To reject or send away) **17.** Amaziah, seeking advice, sent a challenge to Joash, the king of Israel, asking him to meet face-to-face. (Challenge: To invite for a contest or confrontation) **18.** Joash responded with a parable, saying, "The thistle in Lebanon asked the cedar to give his daughter to his son, but a wild beast trampled the thistle." (Parable: A simple story used to teach a moral lesson) **19.** Joash warned Amaziah not to be proud of his victory over Edom, and advised him to stay at home, as meddling would bring disaster upon Judah. (Meddling: Interfering in something that doesn't concern you) **20.** But Amaziah refused to listen, for God had determined to deliver Judah into the hands of their enemies because they had sought after the gods of Edom. (Determined: Decided firmly) **21.** Joash and Amaziah met face-to-face at Beth-shemesh, where Judah was defeated, and its men fled. (Defeated: Beaten or overcome in battle) **22.** Judah was defeated before Israel, and every man fled to his own tent. (Tent: A portable shelter used by armies or travelers) **23.** Joash captured Amaziah, took him to Jerusalem, and broke down a section of the city wall, from the gate of Ephraim to the corner gate, 400 cubits long. (Captured: Took control of by force) **24.** Joash took all the gold, silver, and sacred vessels from the house of God, along with treasures from the royal palace, and returned to Samaria with hostages. (Hostages: People held as security for compliance) **25.** Amaziah, son of Joash, king of Judah, lived 15 years after the death of Joash, king of Israel. (Lived: Survived and continued to live) **26.** The acts of Amaziah, from beginning to end, are written in the book of the kings of Judah and Israel. (Acts: Deeds or actions) **27.** After Amaziah turned away from following the LORD, a conspiracy was formed against him in Jerusalem, and he fled to Lachish, where he was killed. (Conspiracy: A secret plan to harm someone) **28.** His body was brought back to Jerusalem and buried with his ancestors in the city of Judah. (Ancestors: Past generations of one's family)

Chapter 26

1. The people of Judah chose Uzziah, just 16 years old, to succeed his father Amaziah as king. (Chosen: selected) 2. He rebuilt Eloth and returned it to Judah after his father died. (Rebuilt: restored) 3. Uzziah was 16 when he began his reign, which lasted 52 years in Jerusalem. His mother was Jecoliah. (Reign: rule, lasted: continued, Jerusalem: city in Israel) 4. He did what was right in God's eyes, following his father's example. (Right: righteous, example: model) 5. Uzziah sought God's guidance through Zechariah, who understood divine visions. As long as he sought God, he prospered. (Guidance: direction, prospered: succeeded) 6. He fought the Philistines, destroying their city walls and building new cities around Ashdod. (Fought: battled, destroying: breaking down) 7. God helped Uzziah defeat the Philistines, Arabs, and Mehunims. (Defeat: conquer, Arabs: people from Arabian regions) 8. The Ammonites gave gifts to Uzziah, and his fame spread to Egypt, as he grew stronger. (Fame: reputation, grew: became) 9. Uzziah built towers around Jerusalem and fortified them for protection. (Fortified: strengthened) 10. He also built towers in the desert and dug wells, as he had many animals and workers. (Desert: dry land, wells: water sources) 11. Uzziah had an army of mighty men, organized by Jeiel, Maaseiah, and Hananiah. (Mighty: powerful, organized: arranged) 12. There were 2,600 leaders of warriors. (Leaders: commanders, warriors: soldiers) 13. Under their command was a force of 307,500 soldiers, all ready to fight for the king. (Force: army, soldiers: fighters) 14. Uzziah equipped them with shields, spears, helmets, bows, and slings for battle. (Equipped: provided, slings: devices for throwing stones) 15. He also built war machines in Jerusalem to launch arrows and large stones from towers. His name spread widely, as he was greatly helped by God. (War machines: siege engines, launched: fired) 16. But his success led to pride. He entered the temple to burn incense, which was reserved for priests. (Pride: arrogance, reserved: meant for) 17. Azariah the priest and 80 others confronted him, saying only priests could burn incense. (Confronted: challenged, priests: religious leaders) 18. They told Uzziah he had sinned, and his actions would not bring honor from God. (Sinned: wronged, honor: respect) 19. Uzziah became angry, but as he stood with the incense burner, leprosy broke out on his forehead. (Angry: enraged, leprosy: a skin disease) 20. The priests saw his condition and quickly forced him out. Uzziah fled, knowing God had punished him. (Forced: pushed, fled: ran away, punished: afflicted) 21. Uzziah remained a leper until his death, living in isolation. His son Jotham governed in his place. (Isolation: separation, governed: ruled) 22. The prophet Isaiah recorded Uzziah's deeds. (Recorded: wrote down) 23. Uzziah died and was buried in a royal tomb, but because of his leprosy, they did not bury him with other kings. His son Jotham became king. (Royal tomb: burial place of kings)

Chapter 27

1. Jotham became king at 25 and ruled 16 years in Jerusalem. His mother was Jerushah, daughter of Zadok. (Became: took office, ruled: reigned) 2. He did what was right in God's sight, just like his father Uzziah, but he did not enter the LORD's temple. The people, however, remained corrupt. (Corrupt: morally wrong) 3. Jotham built the high gate of the LORD's temple and made significant additions to the wall of Ophel. (Significant: considerable, additions: improvements) 4. He also built cities in the mountains of Judah and castles and towers in the forests. (Castles: fortified structures, towers: tall buildings) 5. He fought the Ammonite king, defeated him, and received tribute: 100 talents of silver, 10,000 measures of wheat, and 10,000 of barley. The Ammonites paid him the same tribute for two more years. (Tribute: payment, defeated: overcame) 6. Jotham grew strong because he followed the ways of the LORD his God. (Grew: became, followed: adhered to) 7. The rest of Jotham's deeds, wars, and actions are written in the book of the kings of Israel and Judah. (Deeds: actions, wars: battles) 8. Jotham was 25 when he began his reign and ruled 16 years in Jerusalem. (Reign: rule) 9. Jotham died and was buried in the City of David; his son Ahaz succeeded him as king. (Succeeded: took over, succeeded him: became king after him)

Chapter 28

1. Ahaz was 20 years old when he began his reign, and he ruled for 16 years in Jerusalem. However, he did not follow the ways of righteousness like his ancestor, David. (Righteousness: The quality of being morally right or justifiable) 2. He followed the sinful practices of the kings of Israel and made idols for Baal, the false god. (Idols: Statues or images representing gods, used for worship) 3. He even burned incense in the valley of Hinnom and sacrificed his own children by fire, following the wicked customs of the nations whom the Lord had driven out before Israel. (Incense: A substance that produces a pleasant fragrance when burned, used in rituals) 4. He made offerings at high places, on hills, and under every green tree. (High places: Elevated areas used for worship, often associated with idolatry) 5. Because of this, the Lord allowed the king of Syria to defeat him and take many of his people captive to Damascus. Ahaz was also struck by the king of Israel, who dealt him a great blow. (Defeat: To overcome or win a victory over someone) 6. Pekah, son of Remaliah, killed 120,000 valiant soldiers of Judah in one day because they had forsaken the Lord, the God of their ancestors. (Valiant: Brave and courageous) 7. Zichri, a mighty warrior from Ephraim, killed Maaseiah, the king's son, along with Azrikam, the governor of the royal palace, and Elkanah, the king's next in line. (Mighty: Powerful or strong) 8. The Israelites carried away 200,000 of their brothers—women, children, and spoils—and brought them to Samaria. (Spoils: Goods or valuables taken during a battle or war) 9. But a prophet of the Lord named Oded went out to meet the army returning to Samaria. He said, "Because the Lord was angry with Judah, He gave them into your hands, but your anger has been so great it has reached to heaven." (Wrath: Intense anger) 10. "Now you intend to enslave the people of Judah and Jerusalem. But don't you realize that you also have sinned against the Lord your God?" (Enslave: To make someone a slave or captive) 11. "Listen to me, and return the captives you have taken, for the fierce anger of the Lord is upon you." (Fierce: Intense, violent) 12. Then some of the leaders of Ephraim—Azariah, son of Johanan; Berechiah, son of Meshillemoth; Jehizkiah, son of Shallum; and Amasa, son of Hadlai—rose up against those coming from battle. (Leaders: People in positions of authority or leadership) 13. They said, "You must not bring the captives here, for we have already sinned against the Lord, and adding more to our sin will only bring more wrath upon us." (Trespass: A sin or wrongdoing) 14. So the soldiers agreed, and they left the captives and the spoil in front of the leaders and the entire congregation. (Congregation: A group of people assembled for worship) 15. The leaders named above took the captives, clothed those who were naked, gave them food and drink, anointed them with oil, and helped the weak ones by placing them on donkeys. They then brought them to Jericho, the city of palm trees, and returned to Samaria. (Anointed: To rub or smear with oil, often as part of a religious or ceremonial act) 16. At that time, King Ahaz sent a message to the kings of Assyria, asking for their help. (Sent: Dispatched or communicated) 17. For the Edomites had attacked Judah again and taken captives. (Edomites: People from the land of Edom, located southeast of Israel) 18. The Philistines also invaded the cities in the lowlands and south of Judah, capturing several towns including Beth-shemesh, Ajalon, Gederoth, Shocho, Timnah, and Gimzo, and settled there. (Invaded: Entered forcefully with the intent to conquer) 19. The Lord humbled Judah because of Ahaz, king of Israel, who had caused Judah to sin greatly against the Lord. (Humbled: Brought down in power or status) 20. King Tiglath-pileser of Assyria came to him, but instead of strengthening him, he brought even more distress. (Distressed: Caused great trouble or hardship) 21. Ahaz took treasures from the house of the Lord, the royal palace, and the officials, and gave them to the king of Assyria, hoping for help. But the Assyrian king did not assist him. (Treasures: Valuable

goods or possessions) 22. In his time of distress, Ahaz became even more rebellious, sinning against the Lord. (Rebellious: Disobedient or resisting authority) 23. He sacrificed to the gods of Damascus, believing that they had helped the kings of Syria, and said, "Since the gods of the Syrians helped them, I will sacrifice to them so that they may help me." But these gods were the downfall of him and all Israel. (Downfall: A sudden loss of power, prosperity, or status) 24. Ahaz took the sacred vessels from the house of God, cut them into pieces, locked the doors of the temple, and built altars in every corner of Jerusalem. (Vessels: Sacred items used in worship) 25. In every city of Judah, he set up high places to burn incense to other gods, provoking the Lord God of his ancestors to anger. (Provoking: Causing anger or irritation) 26. The rest of his acts, both the early and later ones, are written in the book of the kings of Judah and Israel. (Acts: Deeds or actions) 27. Ahaz died and was buried in Jerusalem, but not in the tombs of the kings of Israel. His son Hezekiah became king in his place. (Tombs: Burial places)

Chapter 29

1. Hezekiah became king at 25 and reigned 29 years in Jerusalem. His mother was Abijah, daughter of Zechariah. (Zechariah: A biblical name meaning "God remembers") 2. He did what was right in God's sight, following the example of his ancestor David. (Ancestor: A family member from past generations) 3. In the first year of his reign, Hezekiah opened and repaired the doors of the Lord's temple. (Repaired: Fixed or restored) 4. He called the priests and Levites to gather in the eastern courtyard. (Levites: Members of the Hebrew tribe assigned religious duties) 5. He told them to purify themselves and the temple, removing all defilement. (Defilement: Pollution or impurity) 6. Our ancestors sinned against God, forsaking Him and turning their backs on His temple. (Forsaking: Abandoning or leaving behind) 7. They closed the temple doors, extinguished the lamps, and stopped offering incense or sacrifices to God. (Extinguished: Put out or extinguished) 8. Therefore, God's anger has struck Judah, and we have suffered disgrace and trouble. (Disgrace: Shame or dishonor) 9. Our ancestors died in battle, and our families are in captivity because of this. (Captivity: Being held as prisoners) 10. I am determined to make a covenant with the Lord to turn away His anger. (Covenant: A solemn agreement) 11. Do not be careless, for God has chosen you to serve in His temple and offer incense. (Careless: Negligent or inattentive) 12. The Levites, including Mahath, Joel, Kish, and others, rose up to purify the temple. (Purify: Cleanse or make holy) 13. They gathered their fellow Levites and began the cleansing process, following the king's command. (Fellow: A companion or associate) 14. The Levites took the impurities from the temple and carried them to the Kidron Valley. (Impurities: Defilements or contaminants) 15. The priests entered to cleanse the inner temple and removed all uncleanness. (Uncleanness: Defilement or impurity) 16. The Levites carried the impurities out to the Kidron Brook. (Brook: A small stream of water) 17. They began the purification on the first day of the first month, finishing on the sixteenth. (Purification: The act of making pure) 18. They reported to King Hezekiah, saying the temple, altar, and vessels had been cleansed. (Vessels: Sacred instruments or utensils) 19. They also sanctified the vessels that King Ahaz had desecrated. (Sanctified: Made holy or consecrated) 20. King Hezekiah gathered the city leaders and went to the temple. (Leaders: Rulers or heads of communities) 21. They brought seven bulls, seven rams, seven lambs, and seven goats for sin offerings for the kingdom. (Sin offering: A sacrifice to atone for sins) 22. The priests slaughtered the animals and sprinkled their blood on the altar. (Sprinkled: Scattered in small drops) 23. They presented goats for a sin offering and laid their hands on them. (Laid their hands: Symbolic act of transfer of guilt) 24. The priests sacrificed them to atone for Israel, as the king had commanded. (Atone: To make amends for sin) 25. Hezekiah organized the Levites with instruments for praise, following David's command. (Instruments: Musical tools like cymbals, harps, and psalteries) 26. The Levites stood with their instruments and the priests with trumpets. (Trumpets: A brass wind instrument) 27. Hezekiah ordered the burnt offering to begin, and worship with music followed. (Burnt offering: A sacrifice wholly consumed by fire) 28. The congregation worshipped with songs and trumpet blasts until the offerings were completed. (Congregation: A group of people assembled for religious worship) 29. After the offerings, the king and all present bowed and worshipped God. (Worshipped: Showed reverence and adoration) 30. Hezekiah and the leaders encouraged the Levites to praise God with David's psalms. (Psalms: Sacred songs or hymns) 31. Hezekiah invited the people to bring sacrifices and thank offerings to the temple. (Thank offerings: Offerings of gratitude to God) 32. The congregation brought 70 bulls, 100 rams, and 200 lambs as burnt offerings. (Burnt offerings: Sacrificial animals consumed by fire) 33. The people also brought 600 oxen and 3,000 sheep as consecrated offerings. (Consecrated: Made sacred or dedicated to God) 34. The priests were too few, so the Levites assisted until the work was done. (Assisted: Helped or supported) 35. There was an abundance of offerings, and the service in the temple was organized. (Abundance: A large quantity or supply) 36. Hezekiah and the people rejoiced because God had prepared their hearts, and the work was done swiftly. (Rejoiced: Felt great happiness)

Chapter 30

1. Hezekiah sent letters to all Israel and Judah, including Ephraim and Manasseh, inviting them to Jerusalem to celebrate the Passover to the Lord God of Israel. (Passover: A Jewish feast commemorating the Israelites' escape from Egypt) 2. The king, his officials, and all Jerusalem had agreed to hold the Passover in the second month. (Officials: Leaders or government representatives) 3. They couldn't celebrate at the appointed time because the priests hadn't purified themselves, and the people hadn't gathered in Jerusalem. (Purified: Made clean or holy) 4. The plan pleased the king and all the people. (Pleased: Made happy or satisfied) 5. A decree was sent throughout Israel, from Beer-sheba to Dan, urging everyone to come to Jerusalem for the Passover, as it hadn't been done properly for many years. (Decree: An official order or decision) 6. The messengers went to all Israel and Judah, proclaiming, "Return to the Lord God of your ancestors, and He will show mercy to those who survived the Assyrian invasion." (Proclaiming: Announcing publicly) 7. Don't be like your ancestors who sinned against God and were punished with desolation. (Desolation: Destruction or ruin) 8. Don't be stubborn as they were, but submit to God, enter His holy temple, and serve Him so His anger may turn away. (Stubborn: Unwilling to change or yield) 9. If you return to God, your children and brethren will be shown mercy and brought back from captivity, for God is gracious and merciful. (Gracious: Kind and forgiving) 10. The messengers traveled through Ephraim, Manasseh, and Zebulun, but many mocked and scorned them. (Scorned: Showed contempt or ridicule) 11. However, some from Asher, Manasseh, and Zebulun humbled themselves and came to Jerusalem. (Humbled: Lowered themselves in submission) 12. In Judah, God moved the people to unite in obeying the king's command, as the Lord had spoken. (Moved: Inspired or influenced) 13. A large crowd gathered in Jerusalem to keep the Feast of Unleavened Bread in the second month. (Feast of Unleavened Bread: A seven-day Jewish festival after Passover) 14. They removed all altars in Jerusalem, including those used for incense, and threw them into the Kidron Valley. (Altars: Places of sacrifice or worship) 15. They slaughtered the Passover lambs on the fourteenth day of the second month. The priests and Levites purified themselves and offered burnt offerings. (Slaughtered: Killed for sacrifice) 16. The priests performed their duties as prescribed by the law of Moses, sprinkling the blood from the sacrifices. (Prescribed: Set out as a rule or guideline) 17. Since many people were not purified, the Levites took charge of the Passover sacrifices for those who weren't clean. (Purified: Made ritually clean) 18. Many from Ephraim, Manasseh,

Issachar, and Zebulun hadn't purified themselves properly but ate the Passover anyway. Hezekiah prayed for them, asking God to forgive them. (Ritually: According to religious customs or rules) **19.** Hezekiah prayed, "Lord, forgive those who sincerely seek You, even if they haven't followed the purification rituals." (Sincerely: With genuine intent) **20.** The Lord heard Hezekiah's prayer and healed the people. (Healed: Restored to health or purity) **21.** The Israelites who were in Jerusalem celebrated the Feast of Unleavened Bread with joy for seven days, while the priests and Levites praised God daily with loud instruments. (Instruments: Musical tools) **22.** Hezekiah spoke kindly to the Levites who taught the people, and they ate offerings during the feast, giving thanks to God. (Kindly: In a compassionate or gentle manner) **23.** The people decided to extend the feast for another seven days, and they celebrated with joy. (Extend: Lengthen or prolong) **24.** Hezekiah provided a thousand bulls and seven thousand sheep for the feast, and the princes added another thousand bulls and ten thousand sheep. A large number of priests purified themselves. (Provided: Supplied or gave) **25.** The entire congregation, including those from Israel and Judah, rejoiced together with the priests and Levites. (Congregation: A gathering of people for worship) **26.** There was great joy in Jerusalem, for nothing like it had been seen since Solomon, son of David, ruled Israel. (Great joy: Extreme happiness) **27.** The priests and Levites blessed the people, and their prayers were heard by God in His holy dwelling. (Blessed: Pronounced favor or well-being upon)

Chapter 31
1. When all was completed, the people of Israel who were present went to the cities of Judah. They destroyed the idols, cut down the Asherah poles (sacred groves), and demolished the high places and altars in Judah, Benjamin, Ephraim, and Manasseh, until everything was destroyed. Then they returned to their own cities. (Asherah poles: Sacred trees or wooden symbols associated with the goddess Asherah) **2.** Hezekiah organized the priests and Levites by their divisions, assigning each person to their duties: priests for burnt offerings, peace offerings, ministry, giving thanks, and praising God at the gates of the Lord's temple. (Divisions: Groups or sections) **3.** He also set aside a portion of his own wealth for the burnt offerings, including those for the mornings and evenings, the Sabbaths, new moons, and festivals, as prescribed in the Law of the Lord. (Prescribed: Ordered or set down as a rule) **4.** He commanded the people of Jerusalem to give their portion to the priests and Levites so they could be encouraged in following the Law of the Lord. (Encouraged: Motivated or strengthened) **5.** When the command was announced, the Israelites brought generous offerings of firstfruits—grain, wine, oil, honey, and the increase of their fields—and tithed abundantly. (Firstfruits: The first and best part of the harvest, offered to God) **6.** Those in the cities of Judah also brought tithes of their cattle, sheep, and sacred offerings, which were consecrated to the Lord, and they piled them up in heaps. (Consecrated: Set apart as holy or sacred) **7.** In the third month, they began to stack the offerings, and by the seventh month, the work was completed. (Stack: To arrange in piles) **8.** When Hezekiah and the princes saw the piles, they praised the Lord and blessed His people Israel. (Princes: Leaders or rulers) **9.** Hezekiah asked the priests and Levites about the heaps of offerings. (Heaps: Large piles or mounds) **10.** Azariah, the chief priest, responded, "Since the people began bringing their offerings to the Lord's house, we've had more than enough. God has blessed His people, and the leftovers are this great abundance." (Abundance: A large quantity) **11.** Hezekiah ordered storage rooms to be prepared in the temple for the offerings. (Storage rooms: Chambers or areas for keeping things) **12.** The offerings, tithes, and dedicated items were faithfully brought in, overseen by Conaniah the Levite, with his brother Shimei next in charge. (Faithfully: In a trustworthy and consistent manner) **13.** Other Levites, including Jehiel, Azaziah, and others, assisted under the leadership of Conaniah and Shimei, according to the command of King Hezekiah and Azariah, the ruler of the house of God. (Assisted: Helped or supported) **14.** Kore, a Levite from the east, was in charge of the freewill offerings, distributing them to the priests for the most sacred items. (Freewill offerings: Voluntary offerings given out of generosity) **15.** Alongside him were Eden, Miniamin, Jeshua, and others, who served in the priests' cities, distributing portions to their fellow priests and Levites, large and small. (Distributing: Giving out or handing over) **16.** They gave portions to all males from three years old and up who entered the temple to serve, according to their duties. (Portions: Allocated shares or amounts) **17.** The priests and Levites, starting at age 20, also received their portions for service in the temple, according to their duties. (Duties: Responsibilities or tasks) **18.** They also distributed portions to their families—wives, sons, and daughters—based on their positions and service. (Distributed: Shared out or allotted) **19.** Some priests, living in the fields outside their cities, were given portions in the same way, ensuring that all priests and Levites received their due. (Portions: Shares or allotments) **20.** Hezekiah did what was right, good, and true before the Lord, throughout all Judah. (Right: Morally correct; True: Faithful to God) **21.** In every work he began in the service of God's temple, in following the Law and commandments, he did it wholeheartedly, and God prospered him. (Wholeheartedly: With full devotion and commitment; Prospered: Succeeded or thrived)

Chapter 32
1. After these events, and once everything was established, Sennacherib, the king of Assyria, came to Judah and attacked the fortified cities, planning to capture them. (Fortified: Protected by strong walls or defenses) **2.** When Hezekiah saw that Sennacherib had come and intended to attack Jerusalem, **3.** he consulted with his officials and mighty men, deciding to stop the water from the springs outside the city to prevent the Assyrians from using it. They helped him with this plan. **4.** So, they gathered a large group of people to block all the springs and the river running through the land, asking, "Why should the Assyrian king find plenty of water here?" **5.** Hezekiah also strengthened the city by repairing broken walls, adding towers, building another wall outside, and improving the Millo (a fortification in Jerusalem). He made many spears and shields. (Millo: A fortification or structure in ancient Jerusalem) **6.** He appointed military commanders, gathered the people at the city gate, and encouraged them, saying, **7.** "Be strong and courageous; don't be afraid of the Assyrian king or his army. We have more on our side than he does. **8.** He only has human strength, but we have the Lord our God to help us and fight our battles." The people were comforted by these words of Hezekiah. (Comforted: Given peace or reassurance) **9.** After this, Sennacherib sent his officials to Jerusalem (he was laying siege to Lachish with all his forces) to speak to Hezekiah and the people there, saying, **10.** "What are you trusting in, staying in Jerusalem while I lay siege to it? **11.** Didn't Hezekiah deceive you, telling you that God will deliver you from my hand, while you are dying from hunger and thirst?" **12.** "Hasn't Hezekiah removed the high places and altars, saying that you must worship at one altar in Jerusalem?" **13.** "Don't you know what I and my ancestors have done to other nations? Were their gods able to save them from me? **14.** Which god of those nations my fathers destroyed could deliver his people from my hand? How much less will your God save you?" **15.** "So don't let Hezekiah deceive you; no god of any nation has been able to save their people from my hand, and your God will not be able to save you either." **16.** His servants spoke even more against the Lord God and against Hezekiah. **17.** Sennacherib also wrote letters mocking the God of Israel, saying, "Just as the gods of other nations didn't save them, neither will the God of Hezekiah save Jerusalem." **18.** They shouted loudly in the Jewish language to frighten and confuse the people on the city walls, hoping to take the city. (Frighten: Scare or intimidate) **19.** They spoke against the God of Jerusalem, comparing Him to the gods of other nations, who were mere idols made by human hands. **20.** In response, Hezekiah and the

prophet Isaiah prayed to God. **21.** The Lord sent an angel who struck down the mighty men, leaders, and commanders of the Assyrian army. Sennacherib returned home in disgrace. When he entered the temple of his god, his own sons killed him with a sword. **22.** Thus, the Lord saved Hezekiah and the people of Jerusalem from Sennacherib and all other enemies, guiding them on every side. **23.** Many people brought gifts to the Lord in Jerusalem and presents to Hezekiah, making him famous among the nations. **24.** During this time, Hezekiah became deathly ill and prayed to the Lord. God answered him and gave him a sign. (Sign: A miraculous indication of God's power) **25.** However, Hezekiah did not fully repay God for His kindness, and his pride grew. This angered God, bringing wrath upon Hezekiah, Judah, and Jerusalem. **26.** Despite this, Hezekiah humbled himself, and so God's anger did not come upon them during his reign. **27.** Hezekiah had great wealth and honor. He built storehouses for silver, gold, precious stones, spices, shields, and other valuable items. **28.** He also made storehouses for grain, wine, and oil, and stables for livestock. **29.** He built cities and accumulated large flocks and herds, for God had blessed him with great wealth. **30.** Hezekiah stopped the upper water source of Gihon and redirected it to the west side of the city of David. He prospered in all his works. **31.** However, when ambassadors from the princes of Babylon came to inquire about the miracle God performed, God withdrew from Hezekiah to test him, to see what was in his heart. (Tested: To examine or try to see one's true character) **32.** The rest of Hezekiah's deeds and his goodness are written in the visions of the prophet Isaiah and the books of the kings of Judah and Israel. **33.** Hezekiah died and was buried in the royal tombs of the descendants of David. The people of Judah and Jerusalem honored him, and his son Manasseh became king in his place.

Chapter 33

1. Manasseh was twelve years old when he began to reign, and he reigned fifty and five years in Jerusalem. (Reigned: ruled) **2.** But did that which was evil in the sight of the LORD, like unto the abominations of the heathen, whom the LORD had cast out before the children of Israel. (Evil: immoral; Abominations: detestable; Heathen: pagans) **3.** For he built again the high places which Hezekiah his father had broken down, and he reared up altars for Baalim, and made groves, and worshipped all the host of heaven, and served them. (High places: shrines; Reared up: built; Baalim: idols; Groves: sacred trees; Host: stars) **4.** Also he built altars in the house of the LORD, whereof the LORD had said, In Jerusalem shall my name be forever. (Altars: shrines) **5.** And he built altars for all the host of heaven in the two courts of the house of the LORD. (Courts: enclosures) **6.** And he caused his children to pass through the fire in the valley of the son of Hinnom: also he observed times, and used enchantments, and used witchcraft, and dealt with a familiar spirit, and with wizards: he wrought much evil in the sight of the LORD, to provoke him to anger. (Pass through the fire: sacrifice; Observed: practiced; Enchantments: spells; Witchcraft: sorcery; Familiar spirit: medium; Wizards: sorcerers) **7.** And he set a carved image, the idol which he had made, in the house of God, of which God had said to David and to Solomon his son, In this house, and in Jerusalem, which I have chosen before all the tribes of Israel, will I put my name for ever. (Carved image: idol) **8.** Neither will I any more remove the foot of Israel from out of the land which I have appointed for your fathers; so that they will take heed to do all that I have commanded them, according to the whole law and the statutes and the ordinances by the hand of Moses. (Take heed: obey) **9.** So Manasseh made Judah and the inhabitants of Jerusalem to err, and to do worse than the heathen, whom the LORD had destroyed before the children of Israel. (Err: sin) **10.** And the LORD spake to Manasseh, and to his people: but they would not hearken. (Hearken: listen) **11.** Wherefore the LORD brought upon them the captains of the host of the king of Assyria, which took Manasseh among the thorns, and bound him with fetters, and carried him to Babylon. (Captains: leaders; Host: army; Fetters: chains) **12.** And when he was in affliction, he besought the LORD his God, and humbled himself greatly before the God of his fathers, (Affliction: suffering; Besought: begged; Humbled: lowered) **13.** And prayed unto him: and he was intreated of him, and heard his supplication, and brought him again to Jerusalem into his kingdom. Then Manasseh knew that the LORD he was God. (Intreated: responded; Supplication: prayer) **14.** Now after this he built a wall without the city of David, on the west side of Gihon, in the valley, even to the entering in at the fish gate, and compassed about Ophel, and raised it up a very great height, and put captains of war in all the fenced cities of Judah. (Without: outside; Compassed: surrounded; Fenced: fortified) **15.** And he took away the strange gods, and the idol out of the house of the LORD, and all the altars that he had built in the mount of the house of the LORD, and in Jerusalem, and cast them out of the city. (Strange gods: idols; Cast out: expelled) **16.** And he repaired the altar of the LORD, and sacrificed thereon peace offerings and thanks offerings, and commanded Judah to serve the LORD God of Israel. (Repaired: restored; Sacrificed: offered; Peace offerings: gratitude; Thank offerings: thanksgiving) **17.** Nevertheless the people did sacrifice still in the high places, yet unto the LORD their God only. (High places: shrines) **18.** Now the rest of the acts of Manasseh, and his prayer unto his God, and the words of the seers that spake to him in the name of the LORD God of Israel, behold, they are written in the book of the kings of Israel. (Seers: prophets) **19.** His prayer also, and how God was intreated of him, and all his sin, and his trespass, and the places wherein he built high places, and set up groves and graven images, before he was humbled: behold, they are written among the sayings of the seers. (Trespass: sin; Graven images: idols) **20.** So Manasseh slept with his fathers, and they buried him in his own house: and Amon his son reigned in his stead. (Slept: died) **21.** Amon was two and twenty years old when he began to reign, and reigned two years in Jerusalem. (Two and twenty: twenty-two) **22.** But he did that which was evil in the sight of the LORD, as did Manasseh his father: for Amon sacrificed unto all the carved images which Manasseh his father had made, and served them; (Sacrificed: offered) **23.** And humbled not himself before the LORD, as Manasseh his father had humbled himself; but Amon trespassed more and more. (Trespassed: sinned) **24.** And his servants conspired against him, and slew him in his own house. (Conspired: plotted; Slew: killed) **25.** But the people of the land slew all them that had conspired against king Amon; and the people of the land made Josiah his son king in his stead. (Stead: place)

Chapter 34

1. Josiah was eight years old when he began to reign, and he reigned in Jerusalem for thirty-one years. (Reigned: ruled) **2.** He did what was right in the sight of the LORD, following the ways of his ancestor David, without turning aside. (Declined: turned away) **3.** In the eighth year of his reign, while still young, Josiah sought after the God of David, his father. In the twelfth year, he began to remove idol worship from Judah and Jerusalem, destroying high places, groves, carved images, and molten images. (Purged: cleansed; Groves: places of idol worship; Carved images: statues) **4.** He broke down the altars of Baal in his presence, cut down the images above them, and smashed the groves and molten images, scattering the dust on the graves of those who had sacrificed to them. (Baalim: idols of Baal) **5.** He burned the bones of the priests on their altars and cleansed Judah and Jerusalem. (Burned: set fire to) **6.** He did the same in the cities of Manasseh, Ephraim, Simeon, and Naphtali, destroying idols and altars everywhere. (Mattocks: digging tools) **7.** After breaking down the altars and idols across the land of Israel, he returned to Jerusalem. (Beaten: crushed) **8.** In the eighteenth year of his reign, after purging the land and the temple, he sent officials—Shaphan, Maaseiah, and Joah—to repair the temple of the LORD his God. (Purge: cleanse) **9.** They brought the collected money to Hilkiah, the high priest, from the Levites who had gathered it from the people of Manasseh, Ephraim, and all of Judah and Benjamin. (Levites: temple assistants) **10.** The money was given to the workers overseeing the repairs of the temple. (Oversight: supervision) **11.** The workers bought hewn stone, timber for couplings, and materials to repair the damage caused by the former kings of Judah. (Hewn: shaped; Couplings: joints or connections) **12.** The workers did their tasks faithfully, overseen by Levites from the Merari and Kohath families, and musicians were involved as well. (Artificers: craftsmen) **13.** The Levites also supervised the bearers of burdens and all other workers in the temple. (Porters: doorkeepers) **14.** While sorting the temple's money, Hilkiah found the Book of the Law given by Moses. (Scribe: a writer) **15.** Hilkiah gave the book to Shaphan the scribe. (Scribe: a person who writes) **16.** Shaphan brought the book to the king and reported that everything had been done according to the king's commands. (Committed: entrusted) **17.** They had gathered the money and handed it to the overseers and workmen. (Delivered: handed over) **18.** Shaphan then read the Book of the Law to the king. (Read: recited) **19.** Upon hearing the words of the law, the king tore his clothes in sorrow. (Rent: tore) **20.** The king ordered Hilkiah, Ahikam, Abdon, Shaphan, and Asaiah to go and inquire of the LORD about what to do, because God's anger was upon them for not following His word. (Inquire: seek information) **21.** The king feared God's wrath because their ancestors had disobeyed the law. (Wrath: anger) **22.** The group went to Huldah the prophetess, who lived in Jerusalem, to ask God's will. (Prophetess: female prophet) **23.** Huldah spoke to them on behalf of God, telling them that disaster was coming upon the land because of their idolatry. (Provoke: stir up) **24.** The curses written in the law would fall upon the people for forsaking God and worshipping other gods. (Forsaken: abandoned) **25.** God's anger would burn against this place and not be quenched until the judgment came. (Quenched: extinguished) **26.** God told them to convey to the king that, because his heart was tender and he humbled himself, he would not witness the coming destruction. (Tender: soft, compassionate) **27.** Because Josiah humbled himself, tore his clothes, and wept before God, God promised to hear his prayer. (Humbled: made low, repentant) **28.** God promised Josiah would be gathered to his ancestors in peace and would not see the destruction of the land. (Gathered: collected to) **29.** Josiah gathered all the elders of Judah and Jerusalem. (Elders: leaders) **30.** The king went to the temple and read aloud to the people the words of the Book of the Covenant that had been found. (Covenant: agreement) **31.** Josiah made a covenant before the LORD to obey His commandments with all his heart and soul. The people agreed. (Testimonies: written records; Statutes: laws) **32.** He made all the people of Judah and Benjamin stand by the covenant. (Inhabitants: residents) **33.** Josiah removed all the detestable idols from Israel and led the people to serve only the LORD. They remained faithful to God throughout his reign. (Abominations: detestable things)

Chapter 35
1. Josiah celebrated the Passover to the LORD in Jerusalem, slaughtering the Passover lambs on the fourteenth day of the first month. (Passover: a Jewish festival commemorating the Exodus from Egypt) **2.** He assigned the priests to their duties and encouraged them in their service at the temple. (Charges: responsibilities) **3.** Josiah told the Levites who taught Israel and were consecrated to God to place the holy ark in the temple built by Solomon, and not carry it anymore. (Consecrated: made holy) **4.** He instructed them to prepare by their family divisions, following the instructions in the writings of David and Solomon. (Courses: divisions or orders) **5.** The priests were to stand in the holy place according to the divisions of the families of Israel and the Levites. (Divisions: groupings) **6.** They were to kill the Passover lamb, sanctify themselves, and prepare the people to obey the LORD's commands through Moses. (Sanctify: make holy) **7.** Josiah provided 30,000 lambs and kids, and 3,000 oxen for the Passover offerings from his own possessions. (Kids: young goats) **8.** The princes gave willingly to the priests and Levites for the Passover offerings, including 2,600 small cattle and 300 oxen. (Willingly: voluntarily) **9.** Conaniah and his fellow Levite leaders gave 5,000 small cattle and 500 oxen for the Passover. (Levite: member of the tribe of Levi, responsible for temple duties) **10.** The service was arranged, and the priests and Levites took their places according to the king's orders. (Service: duties) **11.** The priests killed the Passover lambs, sprinkled the blood, and the Levites prepared the animals. (Flayed: skinned) **12.** They removed the burnt offerings and divided them as required by Moses' law, doing the same with the oxen. (Burnt offerings: sacrifices completely burned on the altar) **13.** They roasted the Passover lambs with fire as prescribed; other holy offerings were cooked in pots and divided quickly among the people. (Ordinance: regulation) **14.** Afterward, the priests were busy offering burnt offerings until night, so the Levites prepared food for the priests. (Burnt offerings: offerings burned completely as a sign of dedication) **15.** The singers, descendants of Asaph, and the temple porters did their duties as commanded by David and other leaders, not leaving their posts. (Porters: doorkeepers) **16.** All the temple service was prepared that day to celebrate the Passover and offer burnt offerings as commanded by Josiah. (Prepared: made ready) **17.** The people of Israel who were present kept the Passover and the Feast of Unleavened Bread for seven days. (Feast of Unleavened Bread: a festival commemorating the Exodus, where bread without yeast was eaten) **18.** No Passover had been kept like this since the days of the prophet Samuel. Josiah's Passover was unmatched by any king of Israel. (Unmatched: unequaled) **19.** This Passover occurred in the eighteenth year of Josiah's reign. (Reign: period of ruling) **20.** After the Passover, when Josiah had prepared the temple, King Necho of Egypt came to fight at Carchemish by the Euphrates River. Josiah went out to meet him. (Carchemish: an ancient city, important in battles; Euphrates: a river in the ancient Near East) **21.** Necho sent messengers to Josiah, saying, "I am not coming to fight you, but to fight another nation. God has commanded me to hurry—don't interfere, or God will destroy you." (Ambassadors: messengers) **22.** Josiah, ignoring God's warning, disguised himself and went to fight in the Valley of Megiddo. (Hearkened: listened) **23.** The archers shot at Josiah, and he was wounded. He told his servants to take him away. (Archers: bowmen) **24.** His servants took him out of the chariot, put him in another one, and brought him back to Jerusalem where he died and was buried. All Judah and Jerusalem mourned for him. (Sepulchres: tombs) **25.** The prophet Jeremiah lamented for Josiah, and the people of Israel made a tradition of singing songs of mourning in his honor. These are written in the Lamentations. (Lamented: expressed sorrow) **26.** The rest of Josiah's deeds and his righteous actions, as written in the law of the LORD, are recorded. (Goodness: acts of kindness and righteousness) **27.** Josiah's deeds, both first and last, are written in the books of the kings of Israel and Judah. (Deeds: actions)

Chapter 36
1. The people made Jehoahaz, son of Josiah, king in his father's place in Jerusalem. (Jehoahaz: a king of Judah) **2.** Jehoahaz was 23 when he began to reign and ruled for three months. (Reign: to rule) **3.** The king of Egypt removed him, demanding 100 talents of silver and one talent of gold from the land. (Talents: large units of weight or money) **4.** The Egyptian king made Jehoahaz's brother Eliakim king, renaming him Jehoiakim. He took Jehoahaz to Egypt. (Renamed: gave a new name) **5.** Jehoiakim began his reign at 25, ruling for 11 years in Jerusalem. He did evil in God's sight. (Evil: morally wrong or wicked) **6.** Nebuchadnezzar, king of Babylon, captured him and bound him to take him to Babylon. (Captured: seized) **7.** Nebuchadnezzar took sacred vessels from the Lord's temple and placed them in his own temple in Babylon. (Vessels: sacred items or containers) **8.** The acts of Jehoiakim, his evil deeds, and his reign are recorded in the book of the kings. His son Jehoiachin succeeded him. (Acts: deeds or actions) **9.** Jehoiachin, only 8 years old, reigned for three months and ten days, doing evil in God's sight. (Succeeded: followed) **10.** After a year, Nebuchadnezzar brought Jehoiachin to Babylon and made

Zedekiah king of Judah. (Proclamation: a formal announcement) **11.** Zedekiah was 21 when he became king, reigning for 11 years in Jerusalem. (Reigned: ruled) **12.** He did evil, refusing to humble himself before Jeremiah, the prophet of the Lord. (Humble: to lower oneself in submission) **13.** Zedekiah rebelled against Nebuchadnezzar, breaking his oath to God, and stubbornly refused to repent. (Rebelled: resisted authority) **14.** The leaders and people followed the wicked practices of foreign nations, defiling God's temple in Jerusalem. (Defiling: polluting or desecrating) **15.** The Lord sent messengers, warning His people out of compassion for them, but they mocked and rejected the prophets. (Messengers: those sent with a message) **16.** They despised God's word and His messengers, leading to His anger and irreversible punishment. (Despised: hated or scorned) **17.** God allowed the Chaldeans to kill the young men, showing no mercy to anyone, and took them into captivity. (Chaldeans: Babylonians) **18.** The Babylonians took all the temple vessels, treasures, and royal items to Babylon. (Vessels: items used in worship) **19.** They destroyed the temple, tore down Jerusalem's walls, and burned the palaces, taking everything of value. (Destroyed: ruined or demolished) **20.** Those who survived were carried to Babylon as servants until the Persian kingdom came to power. (Servants: those in bondage or slavery) **21.** This fulfilled God's word through Jeremiah, as the land rested, keeping its Sabbaths for 70 years. (Sabbaths: days of rest) **22.** In the first year of Cyrus, king of Persia, to fulfill God's word through Jeremiah, Cyrus proclaimed that God had appointed him to rebuild the temple in Jerusalem. (Proclaimed: officially announced) **23.** Cyrus declared that anyone from Israel should return to rebuild God's house in Jerusalem. (Proclaim: announce)

15 – Ezra
Chapter 1

1. In the first year of Cyrus, king of Persia, the LORD fulfilled His word through Jeremiah by stirring Cyrus's spirit to proclaim and write this decree: (fulfilled : completed; Cyrus : Persian king who conquered Babylon; Persia : ancient empire, present-day Iran) **2.** "Thus says Cyrus, king of Persia: The LORD, the God of heaven, has given me all the kingdoms of the earth and instructed me to build Him a house in Jerusalem, in Judah." (Charged: commanded; Jerusalem: capital of Judah, sacred city) **3.** "Whoever among you belongs to His people, may God be with you! Let him go to Jerusalem in Judah and build the house of the LORD, the God of Israel. He is the God in Jerusalem." (Judah: southern kingdom of Israel) **4.** "Let those who remain in any place they dwell support them with silver, gold, goods, livestock, and freewill offerings for the house of God in Jerusalem." (Sojourn: reside; freewill offerings: voluntary gifts) **5.** The leaders of Judah and Benjamin, along with priests, Levites, and everyone whose spirit God had moved, rose up to rebuild the LORD's house in Jerusalem. (Judah and Benjamin: tribes of Israel; Levites: tribe of Israel set apart for religious duties) **6.** Their neighbors gave them silver, gold, goods, livestock, and valuable items, along with freewill offerings. (strengthened: supported) **7.** King Cyrus returned the vessels of the LORD's house, which Nebuchadnezzar had taken from Jerusalem and placed in his gods' temple. (vessels: containers; Nebuchadnezzar : king of Babylon who destroyed Jerusalem and took sacred items) **8.** Cyrus handed these items over through Mithredath, the treasurer, who counted them out to Sheshbazzar, prince of Judah. (Mithredath : Persian official; Sheshbazzar : leader of the exiles returning to Jerusalem) **9.** The inventory included 30 gold dishes, 1,000 silver dishes, 29 knives, **10.** 30 gold bowls, 410 silver bowls of another kind, and 1,000 other vessels. **11.** In total, 5,400 gold and silver vessels were brought back by Sheshbazzar along with the exiles returning from Babylon to Jerusalem. (Exiles: people who were taken captive and later returned)

Chapter 2

1. These are the descendants of those who returned from captivity, whom King Nebuchadnezzar of Babylon had taken to Babylon. They came back to Jerusalem and Judah, each to their own city. (Nebuchadnezzar: King of Babylon; Jerusalem: Capital of Judah.) **2.** Those who returned with Zerubbabel included: Jeshua, Nehemiah, Seraiah, Reelaiah, Mordecai, Bilshan, Mispar, Bigvai, Rehum, and Baanah. The total number of the Israelites: (Zerubbabel: Leader of the returning exiles.) **3.** The children of Parosh numbered 2,172. **4.** The children of Shephatiah numbered 372. **5.** The children of Arah numbered 775. **6.** The children of Pahath-moab, from the descendants of Jeshua and Joab, numbered 2,812. **7.** The children of Elam numbered 1,254. **8.** The children of Zattu numbered 945. **9.** The children of Zaccai numbered 760. **10.** The children of Bani numbered 642. **11.** The children of Bebai numbered 623. **12.** The children of Azgad numbered 1,222. **13.** The children of Adonikam numbered 666. **14.** The children of Bigvai numbered 2,056. **15.** The children of Adin numbered 454. **16.** The children of Ater from Hezekiah numbered 98. **17.** The children of Bezai numbered 323. **18.** The children of Jorah numbered 112. **19.** The children of Hashum numbered 223. **20.** The children of Gibbar numbered 95. **21.** The children of Bethlehem numbered 123. **22.** The men of Netophah numbered 56. **23.** The men of Anathoth numbered 128. **24.** The children of Azmaveth numbered 42. **25.** The children of Kirjath-arim, Chephirah, and Beeroth numbered 743. **26.** The children of Ramah and Geba numbered 621. **27.** The men of Michmas numbered 122. **28.** The men of Bethel and Ai numbered 223. **29.** The children of Nebo numbered 52. **30.** The children of Magbish numbered 156. **31.** The children of the other Elam numbered 1,254. **32.** The children of Harim numbered 320. **33.** The children of Lod, Hadid, and Ono numbered 725. **34.** The children of Jericho numbered 345. **35.** The children of Senaah numbered 3,630. **36.** The priests: the children of Jedaiah, from the house of Jeshua, numbered 973. **37.** The children of Immer numbered 1,052. **38.** The children of Pashur numbered 1,247. **39.** The children of Harim numbered 1,017. **40.** The Levites: the children of Jeshua and Kadmiel, from the children of Hodaviah, numbered 74. **41.** The singers: the children of Asaph numbered 128. **42.** The children of the porters: the children of Shallum, Ater, Talmon, Akkub, Hatita, and Shobai, totaled 139. **43.** The Nethinims: the children of Ziha, Hasupha, Tabbaoth, (Nethinims: Temple servants.) **44.** The children of Keros, Siaha, Padon. **45.** The children of Lebanah, Hagabah, Akkub. **46.** The children of Hagab, Shalmai, Hanan. **47.** The children of Giddel, Gahar, Reaiah. **48.** The children of Rezin, Nekoda, Gazzam. **49.** The children of Uzza, Paseah, Besai. **50.** The children of Asnah, Mehunim, Nephusim. **51.** The children of Bakbuk, Hakupha, Harhur. **52.** The children of Bazluth, Mehida, Harsha. **53.** The children of Barkos, Sisera, Thamah. **54.** The children of Neziah, Hatipha. **55.** The children of Solomon's servants: the children of Sotai, Sophereth, Peruda. **56.** The children of Jaalah, Darkon, Giddel. **57.** The children of Shephatiah, Hattil, Pochereth of Zebaim, and Ami. **58.** All the Nethinims and the children of Solomon's servants totaled 392. **59.** These people came from Tel-melah, Tel-harsa, Cherub, Addan, and Immer, but could not prove their lineage to Israel. (Tel-melah: A place; Addan: A place.) **60.** The children of Delaiah, Tobiah, and Nekoda numbered 652. **61.** Of the priests: children of Habaiah, Koz, and Barzillai, who married daughters of Barzillai the Gileadite and took their name. (Barzillai: A Gileadite; Gilead: A region.) **62.** These men searched for their names in the genealogy records but were not found, so they were excluded from the priesthood. **63.** The governor told them they could not eat of the holy offerings until a priest with Urim and Thummim arose. (Urim and Thummim: Sacred objects used by priests.) **64.** The total congregation was 42,360. **65.** Apart from their servants and maids, who numbered 7,337, there were 200 singers, both men and women. **66.** Their horses numbered 736; their mules, 245. **67.** Their camels numbered 435; their donkeys, 6,720. **68.** Some of the leaders, when they arrived at the house of the LORD in Jerusalem, offered freely for the rebuilding of God's house. **69.** They gave according to their ability, totaling 61,000 gold drachmas, 5,000 pounds of silver, and 100 priestly garments. **70.** The priests, Levites, people, singers, porters, and Nethinims all lived in their cities, and all of Israel resided in their cities.

Chapter 3

1. When the seventh month arrived and the Israelites had settled in their cities, the people gathered together as one to Jerusalem. (Jerusalem: capital city of Judah) **2.** Jeshua, son of Jozadak, and his fellow priests, along with Zerubbabel, son of Shealtiel, and his relatives, rose up to build the altar of the God of Israel. They did this to offer burnt offerings on it, as commanded in the law of Moses, the servant of God. (Jozadak: a priest, Zerubbabel: leader of exiles) **3.** They placed the altar on its base, although they were afraid of the neighboring nations. In spite of their fear, they offered burnt offerings to the LORD, both in the morning and evening. (Burnt offering: animal sacrifice) **4.** They also celebrated the Feast of Tabernacles as instructed, offering the required daily burnt offerings according to the prescribed rituals. (Feast of Tabernacles: Jewish festival) **5.** Afterwards, they continued offering the regular burnt offerings for the new moons, the appointed feasts of the LORD, and those who freely gave voluntary offerings to the LORD. (Freewill offering: voluntary gift) **6.** From the first day of the seventh month, they began offering burnt offerings to the LORD, though the foundation of the temple had not yet been laid. (Temple: place of worship) **7.** They gave money to the masons and carpenters, and sent food, drink, and oil to the people of Sidon and Tyre, to bring cedar trees from Lebanon to the port of Joppa, in accordance with the permission granted by King Cyrus of Persia. (Sidon, Tyre: cities in ancient Phoenicia, Joppa: ancient port city, Cyrus: king of Persia) **8.** In the second year of their arrival at the house of God in Jerusalem, in the second month, Zerubbabel, son of Shealtiel, and Jeshua, son of Jozadak, along with the priests, Levites, and all those who returned from exile, began the work. They appointed Levites, aged twenty and older, to supervise the construction of the LORD's house. (Levites: members of the priestly tribe) **9.** Jeshua, with his sons and relatives, Kadmiel and his sons, from the tribe of Judah, stood together to supervise the workers in the house of God. In addition, the sons of Henadad, with their sons and relatives, the Levites, helped in the work. (Kadmiel: a leader, Judah: one of the 12 tribes of Israel) **10.** When the builders laid the foundation of the temple, the priests in their robes, with trumpets, and the Levites, descendants of Asaph, with cymbals, praised the LORD as instructed by King David of Israel. (Asaph: a musician, David: king of Israel) **11.** They sang together, giving praise and thanks to the LORD, saying: "For He is good, and His mercy endures forever toward Israel." The people shouted joyfully as they praised the LORD because the foundation of the house of the LORD had been laid. (Mercy: kindness) **12.** However, many of the priests, Levites, and older leaders who had seen the first temple wept aloud when they saw the foundation of this temple being laid, while many others rejoiced. (First temple: Solomon's temple) **13.** The sound was so mixed that the people could not tell the difference between the joyful shouting and the weeping. The noise was heard from afar.

Chapter 4

1. When the enemies of Judah and Benjamin heard that the exiled Israelites were building a temple to the Lord, the God of Israel, **2.** They approached Zerubbabel and the leaders of the families, saying, "Let us join you in building, as we also worship your God. We have been offering sacrifices to Him since the time of Esarhaddon, king of Assyria, who brought us here." (Esarhaddon: King of Assyria) **3.** But Zerubbabel, Jeshua, and the leaders of Israel's families replied, "You have no part with us in building a house for our God. We alone will build it for the Lord God of Israel, as King Cyrus of Persia commanded us." (Cyrus: King of Persia) **4.** The people of the land then discouraged the Judahites and made their work difficult, **5.** Hiring advisors to frustrate their efforts throughout the reign of King Cyrus of Persia, even until the time of King Darius of Persia. (Darius: King of Persia) **6.** During the reign of King Ahasuerus, at the beginning of his reign, they wrote an accusation against the people of Judah and Jerusalem. (Ahasuerus: King of Persia) **7.** Later, during the reign of King Artaxerxes, Bishlam, Mithredath, Tabeel, and their companions wrote to King Artaxerxes of Persia. The letter was written in the Aramaic language and translated. (Artaxerxes: King of Persia) **8.** Rehum the commander and Shimshai the scribe wrote a letter accusing Jerusalem to King Artaxerxes, saying, **9.** "Rehum the commander, Shimshai the scribe, and the others—Dinaites, Apharsathchites, Tarpelites, Apharsites, Archevites, Babylonians, Susanchites, Dehavites, and Elamites— **10.** And the people brought by the great and noble Asnappar, who settled in the cities of Samaria, and others across the river, have written this letter." (Asnappar: Leader who settled people in Samaria) **11.** This is a copy of the letter they sent to King Artaxerxes: "Your servants, the people from beyond the river, send greetings." (Beyond the river: Referring to the area across the Euphrates River) **12.** "We inform the king that the Jews who came from you are in Jerusalem, rebuilding the rebellious city and fortifying its walls and foundations." **13.** "Now, if this city is rebuilt and its walls are restored, they will not pay tribute, customs, or taxes, and this will harm the royal revenue." **14.** "Since we are supported by the king's palace, we do not want to see the king dishonored, so we have sent this report." **15.** "Let a search be made in the records of your ancestors, and you will find that this city has always been a rebellious city, harmful to kings and provinces, and that it has a history of sedition; this is why it was destroyed." **16.** "We inform the king that if this city is rebuilt and its walls restored, you will have no control over this region." **17.** King Artaxerxes sent a reply to Rehum the commander, Shimshai the scribe, and the other officials in Samaria and beyond the river: "Peace, and greetings." **18.** "The letter you sent has been read before me." **19.** "I ordered a search, and it was found that this city has long been a center of rebellion and sedition against kings." **20.** "There were powerful kings who ruled over Jerusalem and its surrounding lands, and tribute, taxes, and customs were paid to them." (Jerusalem: Capital city of Israel) **21.** "Now give the order to stop these men, and ensure that the city is not rebuilt until I give further instructions." **22.** "Be sure to follow this command carefully so that the king's interests are not harmed." **23.** When the copy of King Artaxerxes' letter was read to Rehum, Shimshai, and their companions, they quickly went to Jerusalem and forced the Jews to stop building. **24.** As a result, the work on the house of God in Jerusalem was halted, and it remained unfinished until the second year of the reign of King Darius of Persia. (Darius: King of Persia)

Chapter 5

1. The prophets Haggai and Zechariah, son of Iddo, delivered their messages to the people of Judah and Jerusalem in the name of the God of Israel, who was watching over them. (Haggai and Zechariah: Prophets urging the rebuilding of the temple; Iddo: Zechariah's father) **2.** Zerubbabel, the son of Shealtiel, and Jeshua, the son of Jozadak, took the initiative and began the reconstruction of the temple in Jerusalem, with the support and encouragement of the prophets of God. (Zerubbabel: Leader of the returning exiles; Jeshua: High priest; Temple: The house of God) **3.** At that time, Tatnai, the governor of the region beyond the River, along with Shethar-boznai and their associates, approached them and demanded, "Who authorized you to build this temple and complete its construction?" (Tatnai: Persian governor; Region beyond the River: Area east of the Euphrates, including Samaria) **4.** They also asked for the names of those who were overseeing the building of the temple. **5.** However, the protection of God was upon the elders of the Jews, and the work continued without interruption until a report could be sent to King Darius and a response received regarding the matter. (The eye of God: A sign of God's favor and protection) **6.** Here is the content of the letter sent to King Darius by Tatnai, the governor of the region beyond the River, Shethar-boznai, and their colleagues, the officials of the region: **7.** They sent a report saying, "To King Darius, greetings and peace." **8.** "Let it be known to the king that we went to the province of Judah, to the temple of the great God. It is being rebuilt with large stones, and timber is being laid in the walls. The work is progressing well and is being done with great care." (Temple of the great God: The house of God in Jerusalem) **9.** "We questioned the elders and asked, 'Who authorized you to build this temple and complete its construction?'" **10.** "We also asked for their names so we could inform the king of the leaders overseeing the work." **11.** "They replied, 'We are servants of the God of heaven and earth, and we are rebuilding the temple that was built many years ago by a great king of Israel.'" (God of heaven and earth: A title of God emphasizing His supreme authority) **12.** "However, because our ancestors angered the God of heaven, He handed them over to Nebuchadnezzar, king of Babylon, the Chaldean, who destroyed the temple and exiled the people to Babylon." (Nebuchadnezzar: King of Babylon who destroyed the first temple and exiled the Israelites) **13.** "But in the first year of King Cyrus of Babylon, he issued a decree to rebuild the house of God." (Cyrus: The Persian king who conquered Babylon and allowed the exiles to return) **14.** "He also returned the gold and silver vessels from the house of God that Nebuchadnezzar had taken from the temple in Jerusalem and placed in the temple of Babylon. These items were entrusted to a man named Sheshbazzar, whom Cyrus appointed as governor." (Gold and silver vessels: Sacred items taken from the temple; Sheshbazzar: Leader of the exiles) **15.** "Cyrus instructed him, 'Take these vessels, go, and place them in the temple in Jerusalem. Let the house of God be rebuilt at its original site.'" **16.** "So, Sheshbazzar came and laid the foundation of the house of God in Jerusalem. From that time until now, construction has continued, but the work is not yet finished." **17.** "Therefore, if it pleases the king, let a search be made in the royal archives in Babylon to confirm whether King Cyrus issued a decree to rebuild the house of God in Jerusalem. Then let the king send his decision on this matter." (Royal archives: Official records kept by the king)

Chapter 6

1. King Darius issued an official order, and a search was conducted in the archives where treasures were stored in Babylon. (Babylon: ancient city, capital of the Babylonian Empire) **2.** A scroll was found in the fortress of Achmetha in Media, which read: (Achmetha: fortress in Media, Media: ancient region in the Persian Empire) **3.** "In the first year of King Cyrus, he decreed that the temple in Jerusalem be rebuilt, with its foundations firmly laid, standing 60 cubits high and wide. (Cyrus: king of Persia who allowed the Jews to return and rebuild the temple, cubit: ancient unit of length, about 18 inches) **4.** The construction should use three layers of large stones and one layer of timber. The costs will be paid from the royal treasury. (timber: wood, treasury: funds or resources of the kingdom) **5.** Additionally, the gold and silver vessels that Nebuchadnezzar took from the temple in Jerusalem must be returned to the house of God. (vessels: sacred items used in worship, Nebuchadnezzar: king of Babylon who captured Jerusalem and took the sacred items) **6.** "Tatnai, governor beyond the River, and all your officials, stay away from the temple. (Tatnai: Persian governor, the River: Euphrates River, beyond the River: areas east of it) **7.** Let the Jews rebuild the temple on its site. (site: the exact location) **8.** The costs for rebuilding must be paid from royal revenues without delay. (revenues: income from taxes or other sources) **9.** Provide whatever is needed for offerings and sacrifices to the God of heaven, including animals and supplies. (animals: bulls, rams, lambs; supplies: wheat, salt, wine, and oil, God of heaven: a title for the God of Israel) **10.** These offerings will help ensure pleasing sacrifices and prayers for the king and his family. **11.** Any interference with this order will result in severe punishment: the person will be impaled on a beam and his house destroyed. (impaled: executed in a cruel way by being pierced, beam: a large piece of wood) **12.** "May God, who has chosen this place for His name, punish anyone who tries to destroy or change this temple. (place: the temple in Jerusalem) I, Darius, have issued this order, and it must be followed carefully." **13.** Tatnai, Shethar-boznai, and their associates followed King Darius' orders carefully. (Shethar-boznai: Persian official, associates: helpers or companions) **14.** The Jewish elders continued to rebuild, encouraged by the prophets Haggai and Zechariah. They completed the temple as commanded by the God of Israel and the Persian kings. (Haggai and Zechariah: prophets who encouraged the people to rebuild) **15.** The temple was completed on the third day of Adar, in the sixth year of King Darius' reign. (Adar: the twelfth month of the Hebrew calendar) **16.** The people of Israel, including priests, Levites, and exiles, celebrated the dedication of the temple with joy. **17.** For the dedication, they offered 100 bulls, 200 rams, 400 lambs, and 12 male goats as a sin offering for Israel. (sin offering: sacrifice made for atonement) **18.** The priests and Levites were arranged in their groups for service in the temple, as written in the Book of Moses. (Levites: tribe of Israel, responsible for temple service) **19.** On the 14th day of the first month, the returned exiles celebrated the Passover. (Passover: Jewish festival commemorating the Israelites' escape from Egypt) **20.** The priests and Levites purified themselves, and they slaughtered the Passover lamb for all the exiles, priests, and themselves. **21.** The Israelites who returned from exile and those who had separated from foreign nations to worship the Lord ate the Passover meal. **22.** They celebrated the Festival of Unleavened Bread for seven days with joy, for the Lord had made them happy by changing the attitude of the king of Assyria, who supported their efforts to rebuild the temple. (king of Assyria: Persian king, possibly Darius or Artaxerxes)

Chapter 7

1. After these events, during the reign of King Artaxerxes of Persia, Ezra, son of Seraiah, son of Azariah, son of Hilkiah, (Persian king) **2.** Son of Shallum, son of Zadok, son of Ahitub, **3.** son of Amariah, son of Azariah, son of Meraioth, **4.** Son of Zerahiah, son of Uzzi, son of Bukki, **5.** Son of Abishua, son of Phinehas, son of Eleazar, son of Aaron, the first high priest, (Aaron: First high priest of Israel) — **6.** Ezra arrived from Babylon, a skilled scribe in the Law of Moses, which the LORD, the God of Israel, had given him. The king granted him everything he requested because the hand of the LORD, his God, was upon him. (Babylon: Capital of Babylonia; scribe: writer; hand: support) **7.** A group of Israelites, including priests, Levites, singers, gatekeepers, and temple servants, also made the journey to Jerusalem in the seventh year of King Artaxerxes. (Jerusalem: City of Israel) **8.** Ezra reached Jerusalem in the fifth month of the seventh year of the king's reign. **9.** He began his journey from Babylon on the first day of the first month and arrived in Jerusalem on the first day of the fifth month, as the gracious hand of his God was upon him. (Gracious: kind, generous) **10.** Ezra had committed to studying the Law of the LORD, practicing it, and teaching its rules and decisions to the people of Israel. (Heart: determined; statutes: rules; judgments: decisions) **11.** This is the text of the letter King Artaxerxes sent to Ezra the priest, a scribe knowledgeable in the Law of the God of heaven: **12.** "Artaxerxes, king of kings, to Ezra the priest, a scribe of the Law of the God of heaven: Peace, (king of kings: Title for Persian kings) **13.** I issue an order that any Israelites in my kingdom, including priests and Levites, who wish to go to Jerusalem, may accompany you. (Decree: official order; volunteer: choose freely) **14.** You are appointed by the king and his seven advisors to investigate Judah and Jerusalem in accordance with the Law of your God, which is in your possession. (Counselors: advisors; inquire: ask about) **15.** Also, take the silver and gold offered by the king and his advisors for the God of Israel, whose dwelling is in Jerusalem, **16.** Along with any additional silver and gold you can gather from the province of Babylon, as well as the freewill offerings of the people and priests for the house of their God in Jerusalem. (Province: region; freewill offerings: voluntary gifts) **17.** With this money, you are to purchase bulls, rams, and lambs, along with their grain and drink offerings, to offer them on the altar of the house of your God in Jerusalem. (Grain offerings: cereal offerings; drink offerings: liquid offerings; altar: sacrifice place) **18.** You and your associates may use the remainder of the silver and gold as it seems best to you, in accordance with the will of your God. (Will: desire) **19.** Deliver all the items entrusted to you for the service of the house of your God in Jerusalem. (Articles: items; entrusted: given in trust; service: work) **20.** If anything else is needed for the house of your God that you are responsible for providing, you may take from the royal treasury. (Royal treasury: king's treasury) **21.** I, King Artaxerxes, issue a decree to all the treasurers beyond the River: Whatever Ezra, the priest and scribe of the Law of the God of heaven, requests, must be provided without delay, (treasurers: officials handling money; region beyond the River: area beyond the Euphrates River) **22.** up to 100 talents of silver, 100 cors of wheat, 100 baths of wine, 100 baths of oil, and unlimited salt. (talents: large units of weight; cors: measure of grain; baths: measure of liquid) **23.** Whatever is commanded by the God of heaven must be done diligently for the house of the God of heaven, so His anger will not fall upon the kingdom of the king and his sons. (carefully: diligently; wrath: anger; realm: kingdom) **24.** Additionally, it is decreed that no tribute, duty, or toll shall be imposed on any priests, Levites, singers, gatekeepers, temple servants, or any other workers in the house of God. (tribute: tax; duty: fees; toll: tax) **25.** You, Ezra, according to the wisdom of your God, are to appoint magistrates and judges to judge all the people in the region beyond the River—those who know the laws of your God. You are also to teach those who do not know them. (magistrates: judges) **26.** Anyone who does not obey the law of your God and the law of the king must be punished without delay, whether by death, exile, confiscation of property, or imprisonment. (Banishment: exile; confiscation: taking away; imprisonment: jail) **27.** Blessed be the LORD, the God of our ancestors, who has put it into the king's heart to honor the house of the LORD in Jerusalem, (blessed: praised; honor: respect) **28.** and who has shown mercy to me before the king, his counselors, and all his powerful officials. Because the hand of the LORD my God was upon me, I took courage and gathered leading men from Israel to go with me. (mercy: kindness; courage: strength)

Chapter 8

1. These are the leaders of their families, and the genealogy of those who came with me from Babylon during the reign of King Artaxerxes (Persian king). **2.** From Phinehas' descendants: Gershom; from Ithamar: Daniel; from David's line: Hattush. **3.** From Shechaniah, of Pharosh's line: Zechariah, with 150 males (men counted by family). **4.** From Pahath-moab: Elihoenai, son of Zerahiah, with 200 males. **5.** From Shechaniah, son of Jahaziel, with 300 males. **6.** From Adin: Ebed, son of Jonathan, with 50 males. **7.** From Elam: Jeshaiah, son of Athaliah, with 70 males. **8.** From Shephatiah: Zebadiah, son of Michael, with 80 males. **9.** From Joab: Obadiah, son of Jehiel, with 218 males. **10.** From Shelomith: Josiphiah's son, with 160 males. **11.** From Bebai: Zechariah, son of Bebai, with 28 males. **12.** From Azgad: Johanan, son of Hakkatan, with 110 males. **13.** The last of Adonikam's sons: Eliphelet, Jeiel, and Shemaiah, with 60 males. **14.** From Bigvai: Uthai, Zabbud, with 70 males. **15.** I gathered them by the river Ahava (river: a waterway near Babylon), where we camped for three days. I reviewed the people and priests but found no Levites (Levites: priests from the tribe of Levi). **16.** I sent for Eliezer, Ariel, Shemaiah, Elnathan, Jarib, Nathan, Zechariah, Meshullam, and other leaders and wise men (wise men: those who understood). **17.** I sent them to Iddo, the chief at Casiphia (place: a location in Babylon), instructing them to ask Iddo and his fellow Nethinims (Nethinims: temple servants) to send ministers for the house of our God. **18.** By God's help, they brought a wise man, Sherebiah, son of Mahli, a Levite, with 18 relatives. **19.** Hashabiah and Jeshaiah, sons of Merari (Merari: a branch of the Levites), with 20 relatives. **20.** From the Nethinims, 220 were appointed for service, all named. **21.** I proclaimed a fast (fast: a period of prayer and self-denial) at the river Ahava to humble ourselves before God, seeking His guidance for us, our children, and our possessions. **22.** I was ashamed to ask the king for soldiers to protect us, since we had told him, "God's hand is with those who seek Him, but against those who forsake Him." **23.** So we fasted and prayed, and God heard us. **24.** I appointed twelve priests: Sherebiah, Hashabiah, and ten others with them. **25.** I gave them the silver, gold, and vessels for the house of our God, which the king, his advisors, lords, and Israel had offered. **26.** I weighed out 650 talents of silver (talents: units of weight), 100 talents of silver vessels, and 100 talents of gold; **27.** 20 gold basins (basins: bowls) (worth a thousand drams) and two fine copper vessels as valuable as gold. **28.** I told them, "You are holy to the LORD; the vessels are holy, and the silver and gold are a freewill offering to the LORD." **29.** "Guard them carefully, and deliver them to the chief priests, Levites, and leaders in Jerusalem." **30.** The priests and Levites took the silver, gold, and vessels to bring to the house of God in Jerusalem. **31.** We left the river Ahava on the 12th day of the first month, heading for Jerusalem. God protected us from enemies and ambushes. **32.** We arrived in Jerusalem and stayed for three days. **33.** On the fourth day, the silver, gold, and vessels were weighed in the house of God by Meremoth, son of Uriah the priest, with Eleazar, son of Phinehas, and Jozabad, son of Jeshua, and Noadiah, son of Binnui, Levites. **34.** Each item was counted and weighed, and all was recorded. **35.** The exiles offered burnt offerings: twelve bulls for all Israel, 96 rams, 77 lambs, and 12 goats for sin offerings. **36.** They delivered the king's orders to the king's officers and governors on this side of the river, and they supported the people and the house of God.

Chapter 9

1. After these things were finished, the leaders came to me and said, "The people of Israel, including the priests and Levites, have not separated themselves from the people of the surrounding nations. They are doing the same abominations as the Canaanites, Hittites, Perizzites, Jebusites, Ammonites, Moabites, Egyptians, and Amorites." (Abominations: evil acts; Canaanites, Hittites, etc.: various nations that lived in and around ancient Israel) **2.** They have taken wives from these people for their sons and given their daughters to these people's sons. As a result, the holy descendants have mixed with the nations, and the leaders and rulers have been the most responsible for this sin. (Holy descendants: children; Leaders and rulers: chief authorities) **3.** When I heard this, I tore my clothes and mantle, pulled out the hair from my head and beard, and sat down in shock. (Mantle: cloak; Shock: astonishment, surprise) **4.** All those who trembled at the words of the God of Israel gathered around me because of the sin of those exiled. I sat there in shock until the evening sacrifice. (Trembled: feared; exiled: taken away; Evening sacrifice: offering made at sunset) **5.** At the evening sacrifice, I rose from my state of mourning. After tearing my clothes and mantle, I knelt and spread my hands out to the LORD my God. (Mourning: grief) **6.** I said, "O my God, I am ashamed and embarrassed to lift my face to you, my God. Our wrongdoings have piled up over our heads, and our guilt has reached the heavens." (Wrongdoings: sins) **7.** Since the days of our ancestors, we have greatly sinned, and because of our sins, we, our kings, and priests have been handed over to foreign kings, to the sword, to captivity, to plunder, and to disgrace, as we still experience today. (Ancestors: forefathers; Sword: killed; Captivity: forced imprisonment; Plunder: steal) **8.** But now, for a brief moment, the LORD our God has shown us mercy, leaving us a surviving remnant, providing a foothold in His holy place, giving light to our eyes, and offering a little relief in our bondage. (Mercy: kindness; Surviving remnant: small group; Foothold: small support; Holy place: temple; Bondage: slavery) **9.** Although we were slaves, our God did not abandon us in our slavery. He showed us mercy before the kings of Persia, giving us a fresh start, allowing us to rebuild the house of our God, repair its ruins, and fortify Judah and Jerusalem. (Mercy: kindness; Kings of Persia:

empire in the East; Ruins: destroyed parts; Judah and Jerusalem: the southern kingdom and capital city) **10.** Now, O our God, what can we say after all this? We have forsaken Your commands. (Forsaken: abandoned) **11.** You commanded through Your prophets, saying, "The land you are going to possess is defiled because of the wickedness of its people, whose sins have made it unclean from one end to the other." (Prophets: messengers; Wickedness: evil deeds) **12.** Therefore, do not give your daughters in marriage to their sons, nor take their daughters for your sons. Do not seek their peace or prosperity forever, so that you may grow strong, eat the good of the land, and leave it as an inheritance for your children forever. (Peace: well-being; Prosperity: success) **13.** After all that has happened to us because of our evil deeds and great sins, seeing that You, our God, have punished us less than we deserve, and have given us such a deliverance as this. (Evil deeds: wrong actions; Deliverance: rescue) **14.** Should we again break Your commands by intermarrying with the people who practice these abominations? Would You not be angry with us to the point of destroying us, leaving no survivors? (Intermarrying: marrying between groups; Abominations: evil acts) **15.** O LORD God of Israel, You are righteous. Although we are a remnant, we are still here today. We are before You in our guilt, for we cannot stand in Your presence because of this. (Righteous: just; Remnant: small group; Guilt: sin)

Chapter 10

1. When Ezra prayed and confessed, weeping and falling down before God's house, a large assembly of men, women, and children gathered to him from Israel, for the people wept bitterly. (Ezra: Jewish priest and scribe, God's house: temple) **2.** Shechaniah, son of Jehiel, a member of Elam's descendants, answered Ezra, saying, "We have sinned against our God by marrying foreign women from the people of the land, but now there is hope for Israel in this matter." (Shechaniah: man from priestly family, Elam: ancient region) **3.** Let us now make a covenant with our God to send away all the foreign wives and their children, in accordance with the counsel of my lord and those who fear God's commandments. Let it be done according to the law. (Covenant: formal agreement) **4.** Arise, for this matter belongs to you; we will support you. Be strong and do it. (Be strong: a call for courage) **5.** Ezra arose and made the chief priests, Levites, and all Israel swear to do as instructed. And they swore to it. (Levites: tribe of priests) **6.** Ezra then stood up from before God's house and went to the chamber of Johanan, son of Eliashib. He did not eat bread or drink water, for he mourned because of the transgression of the exiles. (Johanan: a priestly figure, Eliashib: high priest) **7.** A proclamation was made throughout Judah and Jerusalem to all the children of the exile, to gather together in Jerusalem. (Judah and Jerusalem: regions in Israel) **8.** Whoever did not come within three days, as instructed by the leaders and elders, would lose his property and be separated from the assembly of the exiles. (Exiles: those who were taken captive) **9.** All the men of Judah and Benjamin gathered in Jerusalem within three days, on the twentieth day of the ninth month. They sat in the street of God's house, trembling because of the matter and the heavy rain. (Judah and Benjamin: tribes of Israel) **10.** Ezra the priest stood up and said, "You have sinned by marrying foreign women, thus increasing the guilt of Israel." (Guilt: responsibility for wrongdoing) **11.** Now confess to the LORD God of your ancestors, do His will, and separate yourselves from the people of the land and from the foreign wives. (Confess: admit sins) **12.** The whole congregation answered with a loud voice, "As you have said, so we will do." **13.** But the people are many, and it is a time of much rain. We cannot stand outside, and this work is not for one or two days, for many have sinned in this matter. (Heavy rain: a practical difficulty) **14.** Let our leaders stand, and let those who have taken foreign wives from our cities come at appointed times, along with the elders and judges of each city, until the fierce wrath of our God for this matter is turned away from us. (Leaders: those in charge) **15.** Only Jonathan, son of Asahel, and Jahaziah, son of Tikvah, were employed in this matter, and Meshullam and Shabbethai the Levite helped them. (Jonathan: leader, Asahel: his father) **16.** The exiles did so. Ezra the priest, along with certain heads of the families, and all of them by their names, sat down on the first day of the tenth month to examine the matter. (Tenth month: when the action started) **17.** By the first day of the first month, they had finished dealing with all the men who had taken foreign wives. (First month: the beginning of the year) **18.** Among the priests, those who had taken foreign wives were Maaseiah, Eliezer, Jarib, and Gedaliah, descendants of Jeshua, son of Jozadak. (Jozadak: high priest) **19.** They promised to put away their wives, and for their guilt, they offered a ram from the flock as a trespass offering. (Guilt offering: for atonement) **20.** Of the sons of Immer, Hanani and Zebadiah were found. (Immer: priestly family) **21.** Of the sons of Harim, Maaseiah, Elijah, Shemaiah, Jehiel, and Uzziah were found. (Harim: priestly family) **22.** Of the sons of Pashur, Elioenai, Maaseiah, Ishmael, Nethaneel, Jozabad, and Elasah were found. (Pashur: priestly family) **23.** Of the Levites, Jozabad, Shimei, Keliah (also called Kelita), Pethahiah, Judah, and Eliezer were found. (Levites: tribe of priests) **24.** Of the singers, Eliashib was found; and of the gatekeepers, Shallum, Telem, and Uri were found. (Singers: worship leaders, Gatekeepers: temple guards) **25.** Of the sons of Parosh, Ramiah, Jeziah, Malchiah, Miamin, Eleazar, Malchijah, and Benaiah were found. (Parosh: a family name) **26.** Of the sons of Elam, Mattaniah, Zechariah, Jehiel, Abdi, Jeremoth, and Eliah were found. (Elam: ancient Persian region) **27.** Of the sons of Zattu, Elioenai, Eliashib, Mattaniah, Jeremoth, Zabad, and Aziza were found. (Zattu: a family name) **28.** Of the sons of Bebai, Jehohanan, Hananiah, Zabbai, and Athlai were found. (Bebai: a family name) **29.** Of the sons of Bani, Meshullam, Malluch, Adaiah, Jashub, Sheal, and Ramoth were found. (Bani: a family name) **30.** Of the sons of Pahath-moab, Adna, Chelal, Benaiah, Maaseiah, Mattaniah, Bezaleel, Binnui, and Manasseh were found. (Pahath-moab: a family name) **31.** Of the sons of Harim, Eliezer, Ishijah, Malchiah, Shemaiah, and Shimeon were found. (Harim: a family name) **32.** Of the sons of Benjamin, Malluch and Shemariah were found. (Benjamin: a tribe) **33.** Of the sons of Hashum, Mattenai, Mattathah, Zabad, Eliphelet, Jeremai, Manasseh, and Shimei were found. (Hashum: a family name) **34.** Of the sons of Bani, Maadai, Amram, and Uel were found. **35.** Benaiah, Bedeiah, Chelluh, **36.** Vaniah, Meremoth, Eliashib, **37.** Mattaniah, Mattenai, and Jaasau were found. (Benaiah: a family name) **38.** Bani, Binnui, Shimei, **39.** Shelemiah, Nathan, Adaiah, **40.** Machnadebai, Shashai, Sharai, **41.** Azareel, Shelemiah, Shemariah, **42.** Shallum, Amariah, and Joseph **43.** Of the sons of Nebo, Jeiel, Mattithiah, Zabad, Zebina, Jadau, Joel, and Benaiah were found. (Nebo: a place) **44.** All these had taken foreign wives, and some of them had children by them. (Foreign wives: women from outside Israel)

16 – Nehemiah

Chapter 1

1. These are the words of Nehemiah, the son of Hachaliah. During the month of Chisleu, in the twentieth year of the king's reign, I was staying in the palace of Shushan. (Chisleu: November-December; Shushan: city in Persia) **2.** Hanani, one of my relatives, came with some men from Judah. I asked them about the Jews who had survived the exile and about the condition of Jerusalem. (Exile: banishment) **3.** They told me, "The people who remain in the province after the captivity are in great suffering and shame. The walls of Jerusalem are in ruins, and its gates have been burned down." (Captivity: imprisonment) **4.** When I heard this news, I sat down and cried. I mourned for many days, fasting and praying to the God of heaven. (Fasting: abstaining from food) **5.** I said, "O LORD, God of heaven, the great and awe-inspiring God who keeps His promises and shows mercy to those who love Him and obey His commandments. (Mercy: compassion) **6.** Please be attentive to my prayer and open Your eyes to hear the prayers of Your servant, which I offer day and night for the Israelites, Your people. I confess the sins of the Israelites, including my own and those of my father's family, which we have committed against You. (Confess: admit) **7.** We have behaved corruptly toward You and have not kept Your commandments, statutes, or judgments that You gave to Your servant Moses. (Corruptly: dishonestly) **8.** Remember the words You gave to Moses, saying, 'If you disobey My commands, I will scatter you among the nations. (Scatter: disperse) **9.** But if you return to Me and obey My commands, I will gather you from even the farthest corners and bring you back to the place I have chosen for My name to dwell.' (Dwell: reside) **10.** These are Your people and servants, whom You have redeemed by Your great power and strong hand. (Redeemed: saved) **11.** Lord, I humbly ask You to listen to my prayer and to the prayers of those who fear Your name. Let Your servant succeed today and grant me mercy in the sight of this man." At that time, I was the king's cupbearer. (Cupbearer: wine steward)

Chapter 2

1. In the month of Nisan in the twentieth year of King Artaxerxes, when wine was brought for him, I took the wine and gave it to the king. I had not been sad in his presence before, (Nisan: first month of Jewish calendar; Artaxerxes: Persian king of the Achaemenid Empire) **2.** so the king asked me, "Why does your face look so sad when you are not ill? This can be nothing but sadness of heart." I was very much afraid, (sadness of heart: deep sorrow) **3.** but I said to the king, "May the king live forever! Why should my face not look sad when the city where my ancestors are buried lies in ruins, and its gates have been destroyed by fire?" (ruins: state of destruction) **4.** The king said to me, "What is it you want?" Then I prayed to the God of heaven, (prayed: offered a supplication) **5.** and I answered the king, "If it pleases the king and if your servant has found favor in his sight, let him send me to the city in Judah where my ancestors are buried so that I can rebuild it." (Judah: region of southern Israel) **6.** Then the king, with the queen sitting beside him, asked me, "How long will your journey take, and when will you get back?" It pleased the king to send me; so I set a time. (pleased: satisfied or contented) **7.** I also said to him, "If it pleases the king, may I have letters to the governors of Trans-Euphrates, so that they will provide me safe-conduct until I arrive in Judah? (Trans-Euphrates: area west of the Euphrates River; safe-conduct: assurance of safety) **8.** And may I have a letter to Asaph, keeper of the royal park, so he will give me timber to make beams for the gates of the citadel by the temple and for the city wall and for the residence I will occupy?" And because the gracious hand of my God was on me, the king granted my requests. (citadel: fortress; beams: supportive structures) **9.** So I went to the governors of Trans-Euphrates and gave them the king's letters. The king had also sent army officers and cavalry with me. (cavalry: soldiers on horseback) **10.** When Sanballat the Horonite and Tobiah the Ammonite official heard about this, they were very much disturbed that someone had come to promote the welfare of the Israelites. (Sanballat: governor of Samaria; welfare: well-being) **11.** I went to Jerusalem, and after staying there three days, (Jerusalem: ancient city and capital of Judah) **12.** I set out during the night with a few others. I had not told anyone what my God had put in my heart to do for Jerusalem. There were no mounts with me except the one I was riding on. (mounts: horses or donkeys) **13.** By night I went out through the Valley Gate toward the Jackal Well and the Dung Gate, examining the walls of Jerusalem, which had been broken down, and its gates, which had been destroyed by fire. (Valley Gate: western gate of Jerusalem; Dung Gate: southern gate of the city) **14.** Then I moved on toward the Fountain Gate and the King's Pool, but there was not enough room for my mount to get through; (Fountain Gate: eastern gate near the Gihon spring; King's Pool: possibly part of an ancient reservoir) **15.** so I went up the valley by night, examining the wall. Finally, I turned back and reentered through the Valley Gate. (examining: inspecting carefully) **16.** The officials did not know where I had gone or what I was doing, because as yet I had said nothing to the Jews or the priests or nobles or officials or any others who would be doing the work. (officials: leaders or administrators) **17.** Then I said to them, "You see the trouble we are in: Jerusalem lies in ruins, and its gates have been burned with fire. Come, let us rebuild the wall of Jerusalem, and we will no longer be in disgrace." (disgrace: shame or dishonor) **18.** I also told them about the gracious hand of my God on me and what the king had said to me. They replied, "Let us start rebuilding." So they began this good work. (gracious: kind or merciful) **19.** But when Sanballat the Horonite, Tobiah the Ammonite official, and Geshem the Arab heard about it, they mocked and ridiculed us. "What is this you are doing?" they asked. "Are you rebelling against the king?" (mocked: made fun of; rebelling: defying authority) **20.** I answered them by saying, "The God of heaven will give us success. We his servants will start rebuilding, but as for you, you have no share in Jerusalem or any claim or historic right to it." (claim: entitlement; historic right: ancestral ownership)

Chapter 3

1. Then Eliashib, the high priest, along with his fellow priests, rose up to rebuild the Sheep Gate. They consecrated it and installed its doors. They also sanctified it all the way to the Tower of Meah and the Tower of Hananeel. (Consecrated: set apart as holy) **2.** Next, the men of Jericho built alongside him, and Zaccur, the son of Imri, worked right after them. **3.** The sons of Hassenaah rebuilt the Fish Gate. They put in the beams, set the doors, and installed the locks and bars. (Beams: support structures; Locks: fastening devices; Bars: rods for securing) **4.** Meremoth, the son of Urijah, son of Koz, repaired the next section. Then, Meshullam, the son of Berechiah, son of Meshezabeel, followed by Zadok, the son of Baana, repaired the section after him. **5.** The Tekoites also worked on the repairs, but their nobles did not put their shoulders to the work of the Lord. (Nobles: high-ranking people) **6.** Jehoiada, the son of Paseah, and Meshullam, the son of Besodeiah, repaired the Old Gate. They put in the beams, the doors, the locks, and the bars. **7.** Melatiah, the Gibeonite, and Jadon, the Meronothite, along with the men of Gibeon and Mizpah, worked on the section up to the governor's palace near the river. (Governor: ruler) **8.** Uzziel, the son of Harhaiah, a goldsmith, repaired the next section, and after him, Hananiah, the son of one of the apothecaries, worked on the next. They strengthened the walls up to the Broad Wall. (Goldsmith: worker of gold; Apothecaries: medicine makers) **9.** Rephaiah, the son of Hur, the ruler of half of Jerusalem, repaired the section next. (Ruler: one who governs) **10.** Jedaiah, the son of Harumaph, repaired the section opposite his house, and Hattush, the son of Hashabniah, worked next to him. **11.** Malchijah, the son of Harim, and Hashub, the son of Pahath-moab, repaired the next section, including the Tower of the Furnaces. (Furnaces: heating or smelting structures) **12.** Shallum, the son of Halohesh, the ruler of half of Jerusalem, repaired the next section along with his daughters. (Daughters: female children) **13.** Hanun and the residents of Zanoah repaired the Valley Gate. They built it, set the doors, locks, and bars, and extended the wall a thousand cubits up to the Dung Gate. (Cubit: unit of length; Dung: waste matter) **14.** Malchiah, the son of Rechab, the ruler of Beth-haccerem, repaired the Dung Gate. He built it, set up its doors, locks, and bars. **15.** Shallun, the son of Col-hozeh, the ruler of part of Mizpah, repaired the Gate of the Fountain. He covered it, set up its doors, locks, and bars, and repaired the wall of the Pool of Siloah by the king's garden, extending to the stairs that go down to the City of David. (Fountain: water source; Covered: provided a surface) **16.** Nehemiah, the son of Azbuk, the ruler of half of Beth-zur, repaired the section near the tombs of David, the pool made for water, and the House of the Mighty. (Mighty: powerful people) **17.** Rehum, the son of Bani, a Levite, repaired the next section. Then, Hashabiah, the ruler of half of Keilah, repaired the section in his district. (Levite: member of the tribe of Levi) **18.** Bavai, the son of Henadad, the ruler of half of Keilah, repaired the next section. **19.** Ezer, the son of Jeshua, the ruler of Mizpah, repaired the section opposite the ascent to the armory, near the turning of the wall. (Ascent: upward path;

Armory: weapons storage) **20.** Baruch, the son of Zabbai, zealously repaired the next section from the turning of the wall to the door of the house of Eliashib, the high priest. (Zealously: with enthusiasm) **21.** Meremoth, the son of Urijah, the son of Koz, repaired another section, from the door of Eliashib's house to the end of the house of Eliashib. **22.** The priests, the men from the surrounding area, repaired the next section. **23.** Benjamin and Hashub repaired the section opposite their house, and Azariah, the son of Maaseiah, the son of Ananiah, repaired the section near his house. **24.** Binnui, the son of Henadad, repaired another section from Azariah's house to the corner of the wall. (Corner: point where walls meet) **25.** Palal, the son of Uzai, repaired the section at the turning of the wall, near the tower by the king's high house, beside the prison courtyard. After him, Pedaiah, the son of Parosh, worked on the next section. (Turning: shift in direction) **26.** The Nethinims lived in Ophel, repairing the section near the Water Gate, toward the east, and the tower that projects out. (Nethinims: temple servants; Projects: extends outward) **27.** The Tekoites repaired another section, opposite the Great Tower that projects out, as far as the wall of Ophel. (Great Tower: large tower) **28.** The priests, each one opposite his house, repaired the section above the Horse Gate. **29.** Zadok, the son of Immer, repaired the section opposite his house, and Shemaiah, the son of Shechaniah, the keeper of the East Gate, worked next to him. (Keeper: guardian) **30.** Hananiah, the son of Shelemiah, and Hanun, the sixth son of Zalaph, repaired the next section. Then, Meshullam, the son of Berechiah, repaired the section opposite his chamber. (Chamber: room) **31.** Malchiah, the goldsmith's son, repaired the section near the Nethinims and merchants, opposite the Gate Miphkad, and the rise to the corner. (Goldsmith: gold worker; Merchants: traders) **32.** The goldsmiths and merchants repaired the final section, from the corner to the Sheep Gate. (Sheep Gate: gate near where sheep were brought for sacrifice)

Chapter 4

1. When Sanballat heard we started rebuilding the wall, he became furious and mocked the Jews. (Wroth: very angry, Indignation: strong displeasure**2.** He said to his companions and the Samarian army, "What are these weak Jews doing? Do they think they can protect themselves? Will they offer sacrifices? Can they finish in one day? Will they bring stones from the burned rubble?" (Feeble: weak, Sacrifice: offering, Rubbish: waste) **3.** Tobiah the Ammonite said, "Even if a fox climbs on their wall, it will collapse!" **4.** Hear us, O God, for we are mocked! Turn their insults back on them and deliver them as captives in a foreign land. (Reproach: disgrace, Prey: victim, Captivity: imprisonment) **5.** Do not forgive their wrongdoings, nor erase their sins, for they have provoked You in front of the builders. (Iniquity: wickedness, Blotted out: erased) **6.** We continued rebuilding the wall, and it was halfway finished, for the people were determined to work. (Mind: determination) **7.** When Sanballat, Tobiah, the Arabs, Ammonites, and Ashdodites heard the wall was being repaired, they became very angry. (Ashdodites: people from Ashdod) **8.** They conspired together to fight Jerusalem and stop the work. (Conspired: secretly planned) **9.** We prayed to our God and stationed a guard day and night because of them. (Stationed: positioned) **10.** The people of Judah said, "The strength of those carrying loads is weakening, and there is too much rubble to rebuild the wall." (Bearers of burdens: load carriers, Decayed: exhausted) **11.** Our enemies said, "They won't know what hit them; we'll invade, kill, and stop the work." (Adversaries: enemies, Slay: kill) **12.** Jews near them warned us ten times, "Our enemies will attack from every direction." **13.** I stationed people in the lower sections and on higher ground, armed with swords, spears, and bows. (Lower places: lower sections, Higher places: elevated positions) **14.** I said to the nobles, rulers, and people, "Do not be afraid. Remember the Lord, who is powerful. Fight for your families and homes!" (Nobles: important people, Terrible: powerful) **15.** When our enemies heard we knew their plans and God frustrated them, we returned to the wall, each to his task. (Counsel: plan, Nought: nothing, Frustrated: stopped) **16.** Half of my servants worked on the wall, the other half stood guard with spears, shields, bows, and armor. Leaders stayed behind all of Judah. (Wrought: worked, Habergeons: light armor) **17.** Those working on the wall and carrying heavy loads worked with one hand and held a weapon in the other. (Laded: loaded) **18.** Every builder had a sword strapped to his side, and the man with the trumpet stood by me. (Girded: fastened, Trumpet: signaling instrument) **19.** I told the nobles, rulers, and people, "The work is large and spread out, and we're far apart." (Nobles: important people, Separated: spread out, Large: vast**20.** "When you hear the trumpet, gather with us. Our God will fight for us!" (Resort: gather) **21.** We continued our work: half of us stood guard with spears from dawn till nightfall. (Labored: worked hard) **22.** I told the people, "Let everyone stay in Jerusalem with their servants overnight to guard us and work during the day." (Lodge: stay) **23.** Neither I, my brothers, my servants, nor the guards took off their clothes, except to wash. (Put off: remove, Habergeons: light armor)

Chapter 5

1. And there was a loud roar from the people and their women against their fellow Jews. (roar loud complaint) **2.** For some said, "We, our sons, and our daughters are numerous. We need to gather grain so that we can eat and survive." (grain food) **3.** Others said, "We've pledged our fields, stations, and homes to buy grain because of the shortage." (pledged pledged as security for a loan; shortage food deficit) **4.** Some also said, "We've espoused plutocrat to pay the king's duty, and we've put our fields and stations as collateral." (contributory security for a loan) **5.** "Now, our bodies are no different from our sisters', and our children are the same as theirs. Yet, we're forced to bring our sons and daughters into yoke. Some of our daughters are formerly in yoke, and we've no power to free them. Others have taken our fields and stations." (yoke slavery) **6.** When I heard their complaints and these words, I came veritably angry. **7.** After I considered the matter, I rebuked the patricians and the officers, and I said to them, "You're charging your fellow Jews interest!" also I gathered a large assembly to deal with them. (rebuked blamed) **8.** I said to them, "We've redeemed our Jewish sisters who were vended to the nations, but now you're dealing your own sisters, and they will be vended back to us!" They remained silent and had nothing to say. (redeemed bought back) **9.** also I said, "What you're doing is n't good. Should not you walk in the fear of our God to avoid the reproach of the nations, our adversaries?" (reproach shame) **10.** "I, along with my sisters and my retainers, have n't taken plutocrat or grain from them. Let us stop this charging of interest." **11.** "I ask you to return to them, indeed moment, their fields, stations, olive groves, and homes, and the interest on the plutocrat, grain, wine, and oil painting that you have been taking from them." (olive groves vineyards) **12.** They replied, "We'll give it back and wo n't bear anything further from them. We'll do as you say." So I summoned the preachers and made them swear an pledge to do as they had said. (swear an pledge make a solemn pledge) **13.** I also shook out the crowds of my mask and said, "May God shake out every man from his house and his work who does n't keep this pledge. May he be shaken out and voided!" And the whole assembly said, "Amen," and praised the Lord. The people did as they had promised. **14.** likewise, from the time I was appointed governor of Judah, in the twentieth time until the thirty-alternate time of King Artaxerxes, I and my sisters did n't eat the food distributed to the governor. (appointed chosen) **15.** The before governors had burdened the people by taking food and wine from them, in addition to forty shekels of tableware. Indeed their retainers ruled over the people. But I did n't do so because of the fear of God. (burdened worried) **16.** also, I continued to work on the wall, and we did n't buy any land. My retainers and I worked on the construction of the wall. **17.** There were also at my table 150 Jews and officers, besides those who came from the girding nations. (officers leaders) **18.** Each day, a bull, six fine lamb, and some catcalls were prepared for me. Every ten days, an cornucopia of all kinds of wine was handed for me. But I did n't ask for the governor's food allowance because the people were suffering so much. (cornucopia large force) **19.** Think about me, my God, for good, for all that I've done for this people.

Chapter 6
1. When Sanballat, Tobiah, Geshem the Arab, and our other adversaries heard I had finished the wall and there were no gaps though the doors weren't yet in place —(Geshem Arabian leader; breach gap). **2.** Sanballat and Geshem transferred a communication, saying, "Let's match in one of the townlets in Ono. " But they were conniving to harm me.(Ono position; mischief detriment). **3.** I transferred couriers, saying, "I'm doing an important task and cannot come down. Why should the work stop while I meet with you?"(great work important task). **4.** They transferred this communication four times, and I responded the same each time.(after this kind in the same manner). **5.** Sanballat transferred his menial the fifth time with an open letter.(open letter closed letter). **6.** The letter said, "It's reported among the nations, and Gashmu says, that you and the Jews plan to mutiny, which is why you're erecting the wall to come their king."(rebellion insurrection). **7.** "You've appointed prophets to say, 'There's a king in Judah!' And now these reports will reach the king. Let's match to bandy this."(prophets spokespersons for God; king in Judah royal claim). **8.** I replied, "Nothing you say is true. You're making it up."(dissemble pretend). **9.** They were trying to scarify us, saying, "The work will stop if we weaken their hands." But, O God, strengthen my hands.(weakened made weak). **10.** I went to Shemaiah, son of Delaiah, who was confined to his house. He said, "Let's match in the tabernacle and shut the doors, for they're coming to kill you at night."(Shut up confined; tabernacle holy place). **11.** I replied, "Should I flee? Who would go into the tabernacle to save his life? I'll not go."(flee run). **12.** I realized that God hadn't transferred him. He was hired by Tobiah and Sanballat to blackjack me.(perceived realized; hired paid). **13.** He was hired to make me hysterical, so I would stray, giving them a reason to charge and disgrace me.(reproach disgrace). **14.** My God, flash back Tobiah, Sanballat, and Noadiah, and the other prophets who tried to make me hysterical.(palmist womanish prophet). **15.** The wall was finished on the twenty-fifth day of Elul, in fifty-two days.(Elul Hebrew month). **16.** When our adversaries heard this, and the girding nations saw it, they were discouraged, realizing the work was done with God's help.(wrought accomplished). **17.** During those days, the officers of Judah transferred numerous letters to Tobiah, and he replied.(patricians leaders). **18.** Numerous in Judah were pious to him, because he was the son-in-law of Shechaniah, and his son had married Meshullam's son.(sworn unto him pledged constancy). **19.** They spoke of his good deeds in my presence and told him everything I said. Tobiah transferred letters to blackjack me.(blackjack scarify).

Chapter 7
1. When the wall was finished and the doors set up, I appointed the gatekeepers, singers, and Levites to serve. (Gatekeepers – those in charge of guarding the city's gates, Levites – members of the tribe of Levi, designated for religious duties) **2.** I entrusted the responsibility of Jerusalem to my brother Hanani and Hananiah, the governor of the citadel. Hananiah was a trustworthy man who feared God more than many. (Citadel – a fortified area of a city) **3.** I instructed them, "Do not open the gates of Jerusalem until the sun is fully up. While the guards are posted, keep the doors shut and securely fastened. Assign guards from the people of Jerusalem, each near their home." (Guards – those who watch over the city, fastened – locked or secured) **4.** The city was large and impressive, but the population was small and the houses had not yet been built. (Population – the number of people living in the city) **5.** God put it in my heart to gather the leaders, rulers, and people to count them by family lines. I found a record of those who first returned from exile and discovered it was written. (Exile – the state of being sent away from one's homeland, Family lines – genealogies, Record – written documentation) **6.** These are the people who returned from captivity, exiled by King Nebuchadnezzar of Babylon, and came back to Jerusalem and Judah, each to their own city. (Captivity – the state of being held in another land as prisoners, Exiled – sent away from their homeland) **7.** They came with Zerubbabel, Jeshua, Nehemiah, Azariah, Raamiah, Nahamani, Mordecai, Bilshan, Mispereth, Bigvai, Nehum, and Baanah. The number of men from Israel was: (Zerubbabel, Jeshua, Nehemiah – leaders of the returning exiles, Mordecai – a prominent figure in the book of Esther) **8.** The descendants of Parosh numbered two thousand one hundred seventy-two. (Descendants – children or family members) **9.** The descendants of Shephatiah numbered three hundred seventy-two. **10.** The descendants of Arah numbered six hundred fifty-two. **11.** The descendants of Pahath-moab, including Jeshua and Joab, numbered two thousand eight hundred eighteen. (Pahath-moab – a family line, Jeshua – a name, also a priest) **12.** The descendants of Elam numbered one thousand two hundred fifty-four. **13.** The descendants of Zattu numbered eight hundred forty-five. **14.** The descendants of Zaccai numbered seven hundred sixty. (Zaccai – another family line) **15.** The descendants of Binnui numbered six hundred forty-eight. **16.** The descendants of Bebai numbered six hundred twenty-eight. **17.** The descendants of Azgad numbered two thousand three hundred twenty-two. **18.** The descendants of Adonikam numbered six hundred sixty-seven. **19.** The descendants of Bigvai numbered two thousand sixty-seven. **20.** The descendants of Adin numbered six hundred fifty-five. **21.** The descendants of Ater, from Hezekiah's family, numbered ninety-eight. (Hezekiah – a king of Judah) **22.** The descendants of Hashum numbered three hundred twenty-eight. **23.** The descendants of Bezai numbered three hundred twenty-four. **24.** The descendants of Hariph numbered one hundred twelve. **25.** The descendants of Gibeon numbered ninety-five. (Gibeon – a city in ancient Israel) **26.** The people from Bethlehem and Netophah numbered one hundred eighty-eight. (Netophah – a place or city) **27.** The people from Anathoth numbered one hundred twenty-eight. **28.** The people from Beth-azmaveth numbered forty-two. **29.** The people from Kirjath-jearim, Chephirah, and Beeroth numbered seven hundred forty-three. (Kirjath-jearim – a city, Chephirah – a village) **30.** The people from Ramah and Geba numbered six hundred twenty-one. **31.** The people from Michmas numbered one hundred twenty-two. **32.** The people from Bethel and Ai numbered one hundred twenty-three. (Ai – a city mentioned in the Bible) **33.** The people from the other Nebo numbered fifty-two. (Nebo – a city or region) **34.** The descendants of the other Elam numbered one thousand two hundred fifty-four. **35.** The descendants of Harim numbered three hundred twenty. **36.** The descendants of Jericho numbered three hundred forty-five. **37.** The descendants of Lod, Hadid, and Ono numbered seven hundred twenty-one. **38.** The descendants of Senaah numbered three thousand nine hundred thirty. **39.** The priests: the descendants of Jedaiah, from Jeshua's family, numbered nine hundred seventy-three. (Priests – religious leaders or officiants) **40.** The descendants of Immer numbered one thousand fifty-two. **41.** The descendants of Pashur numbered one thousand two hundred forty-seven. **42.** The descendants of Harim numbered one thousand seventeen. **43.** The Levites: the descendants of Jeshua, Kadmiel, and Hodevah numbered seventy-four. (Levites – priests and their helpers) **44.** The singers: the descendants of Asaph numbered one hundred forty-eight. (Singers – those who led in worship) **45.** The gatekeepers: descendants of Shallum, Ater, Talmon, Akkub, Hatita, and Shobai numbered one hundred thirty-eight. **46.** The Nethinims: the descendants of Ziha, Hashupha, and Tabbaoth, (Nethinims – temple servants who helped with tasks related to the temple) **47.** The descendants of Keros, Sia, and Padon, **48.** The descendants of

Lebana, Hagaba, and Shalmai, **49.** The descendants of Hanan, Giddel, and Gahar, **50.** The descendants of Reaiah, Rezin, and Nekoda, **51.** The descendants of Gazzam, Uzza, and Phaseah, **52.** The descendants of Besai, Meunim, and Nephishesim, **53.** The descendants of Bakbuk, Hakupha, and Harhur, **54.** The descendants of Bazlith, Mehida, and Harsha, **55.** The descendants of Barkos, Sisera, and Tamah, **56.** The descendants of Neziah and Hatipha. **57.** The descendants of Solomon's servants: the descendants of Sotai, Sophereth, and Perida, **58.** The descendants of Jaala, Darkon, and Giddel, **59.** The descendants of Shephatiah, Hattil, Pochereth of Zebaim, and Amon. **60.** The total number of Nethinims and descendants of Solomon's servants was three hundred ninety-two. (Nethinims – temple servants who helped with tasks related to the temple) **61.** These are the people from Telmelah, Telharesha, Cherub, Addon, and Immer. They couldn't prove their lineage to confirm they were of Israel. (lineage - ancestry; descendants - offspring) **62.** The descendants of Delaiah, Tobiah, and Nekoda numbered six hundred and forty-two. (descendants - offspring; Nekoda - a family name) **63.** Among the priests were the descendants of Habaiah, Koz, and Barzillai, who married a daughter of Barzillai the Gileadite, and their descendants were named after him. (descendants - offspring; Gileadite - from Gilead) **64.** They searched genealogical records but weren't found, so they were considered unclean and excluded from the priesthood. (genealogical - family history; polluted - unclean) **65.** The Tirshatha (governor) told them not to eat sacred offerings until a priest stood with the Urim and Thummim (divine tools). (Tirshatha - governor; Urim and Thummim - decision-making tools) **66.** The total assembly numbered forty-two thousand three hundred and sixty. (assembly - group of people; numbered - counted) **67.** There were seven thousand three hundred and thirty-seven servants, with two hundred and forty-five singers. (servants - workers; singers - worship leaders) **68.** They had seven hundred and thirty-six horses, two hundred and forty-five mules, (mules - hybrid animals; horses - travel animals) **69.** Four hundred and thirty-five camels, and six thousand seven hundred and twenty donkeys. (camels - travel animals; donkeys - transport animals) **70.** Some leaders contributed: The Tirshatha gave one thousand drachmas of gold, fifty basins, and five hundred and thirty priestly garments. (drachmas - currency; basins - containers) **71.** Some leaders gave twenty thousand drachmas of gold and two thousand two hundred pounds of silver. (drachmas - currency; pounds - weight) **72.** The rest gave twenty thousand drachmas of gold, two thousand pounds of silver, and sixty-seven priestly garments. (priestly garments - clothing; drachmas - currency) **73.** The priests, Levites, gatekeepers, singers, and some of the people, including the Nethinims (temple servants), lived in their cities. When the seventh month arrived, the children of Israel settled. (Levites - tribe of Levi; Nethinims - temple servants)

Chapter 8
1. All the people gathered in the road near the Water Gate, asking Ezra the scribe to bring the Book of the Law of Moses, which the LORD had commanded for Israel. (Water Gate: A gate in Jerusalem; Scribe: A person who clones or writes documents.) **2.** Ezra the clerk brought the Law before the assembly of men, women, and those who could understand, on the first day of the seventh month. (Priest: A religious leader; Assembly: A group gathered together.) **3.** He read from the book at the Water Gate, from morning until noon, and everyone heeded attentively to the Law. (Attentively: Paying close attention.) **4.** Ezra stood on a rustic platform they had made for the occasion, with Mattithiah, Shema, Anaiah, Urijah, Hilkiah, and Maaseiah on his right, and Pedaiah, Mishael, Malchiah, Hashum, Hashbadana, Zechariah, and Meshullam on his left wing. (Platform: A raised structure; Occasion: A specific event or purpose.) **5.** Ezra opened the book in front of all the people (for he was standing above them), and as he opened it, the people stood up. (Opened: Began reading from the scroll of the Law.) **6.** Ezra praised the LORD, and all the people answered, "Amen, Amen," raising their hands. They bowed and worshiped the LORD, facing the ground. (Amen: "So be it"; Worshiped: Showed reverence.) **7.** The Levites — Jeshua, Bani, Sherebiah, Jamin, Akkub, Shabbethai, Hodijah, Maaseiah, Kelita, Azariah, Jozabad, Hanan, Pelaiah — and the Levites helped the people understand the Law, and the people stayed in their places. (Levites: Members of the clerkly lineage; Helped: Guided.) **8.** They read from the Law easily, explained it, and helped the people understand it. (Easily: In an accessible way.) **9.** Nehemiah (the governor), Ezra the clerk, and the Levites who tutored the people said, "This day is holy to the LORD; don't mourn or weep." For all the people were weeping when they heard the Law. (Governor: Overseer; Mourn: To suffer.) **10.** They told the people, "Go and celebrate! Eat rich food, drink sweet drinks, and shoot portions to those with nothing. This day is holy to the LORD. Don't be sad, for the joy of the LORD is your strength." (Celebrate: Rejoice; Portions: Shares of food.) **11.** The Levites quieted the people, saying, "Be still, for the day is holy; don't suffer." (Quieted: Made quiet; Still: Calm.) **12.** All the people went down to eat, drink, shoot portions, and rejoice, because they understood the words explained to them. (Rejoice: Celebrate.) **13.** On the alternate day, the heads of the families, preachers, and Levites gathered to understand the Law. (Heads of families: Household leaders.) **14.** They set up written that the LORD commanded through Moses that the Israelites should live in cells during the jubilee of the seventh month. (Cells: Temporary harbors.) **15.** And they should advertise in all their municipalities and in Jerusalem, saying, "Go to the mountain and gather branches to make cells, as it's written." (Advertise: Make known.) **16.** The people went out, gathered branches, and made cells, each on the roof of his house, in their yards, in the house of God, and in the road near the Water Gate and the Ephraim Gate. (Cells: Temporary harbors.) **17.** All who had returned from exile made cells and sat under them. Since the days of Joshua son of Nun, the Israelites had not done this. And there was great joy. (Exile: Being away from one's homeland; Joshua son of Nun: Israel's leader after Moses.) **18.** Ezra read from the Law daily, and they celebrated the jubilee for seven days. On the eighth day, there was a solemn assembly, according to the constitution. (Solemn: Serious; Constitution: A rule.)

Chapter 9
1. On the twenty-fourth day of the month, the Israelites gathered, fasting, dressed in sackcloth, and sprinkled with dust (Sackcloth: a rough material worn as a sign of mourning; Dust: symbol of humility or mourning). **2.** They separated from foreigners, stood to confess their sins and those of their ancestors (Confess: to admit or acknowledge; Iniquities: immoral actions or sins). **3.** They read from the book of the law for one-fourth of the day, and for another one-fourth, they confessed and worshiped the LORD (Worshiped: to show reverence and adoration). **4.** The Levites—Jeshua, Bani, Kadmiel, Shebaniah, Bunni, Sherebiah, Bani, and Chenani—cried out loudly to the LORD (Levites: members of the tribe of Levi who served in religious duties). **5.** They called, "Stand and bless the LORD your God forever! Blessed be Your glorious name, exalted above all praise" (Bless: to speak well of; Exalted: raised in status or dignity). **6.** You alone are the LORD; You made the heavens, the earth, and all in them, and You preserve them. The heavenly hosts worship You (Hosts: armies or beings; Preserve: to maintain or protect). **7.** You are the LORD who chose Abram, brought him from Ur of the Chaldeans, and gave him the name Abraham (Chaldeans: an ancient people of Mesopotamia). **8.** You found his heart faithful, made a covenant to give his descendants the land of the Canaanites, Hittites, Amorites, Perizzites, Jebusites, and Girgashites. You fulfilled Your word because You are righteous (Covenant: a formal agreement or promise; Descendants: offspring; Righteous: morally right). **9.** You saw our ancestors' suffering in Egypt, and heard their cry by the Red Sea (Suffering: pain or distress). **10.** You performed signs and wonders against Pharaoh and his people, knowing their arrogance

against Your people, making a name for Yourself (Signs: miraculous events; Wonders: extraordinary events that inspire awe; Arrogantly: in a proud and superior way). **11.** You divided the sea, allowing them to pass on dry land, while their enemies were drowned (Mighty: powerful). **12.** You led them by a pillar of cloud by day and by a pillar of fire at night, lighting their path (Pillar: a vertical structure used for support or guidance). **13.** You came down on Mount Sinai, gave them right judgments, true laws, and good commandments (Judgments: decisions or verdicts; Statutes: laws or regulations). **14.** You revealed the holy Sabbath and gave them precepts, statutes, and laws through Moses (Precepts: principles or rules). **15.** You gave them bread from heaven when hungry and water from the rock when thirsty, promising to bring them into the land You swore to give them (Swore: made a solemn promise). **16.** But they and their ancestors became proud, stubborn, and refused to obey (Stubborn: unwilling to change or yield). **17.** They rejected Your law, forgot Your wonders, and appointed a leader to return them to slavery in Egypt. Yet You are a forgiving God, gracious, merciful, slow to anger, abounding in love, and did not abandon them (Rebellion: opposition or defiance; Forgives: pardons; Merciful: showing compassion; Abandon: to leave behind). **18.** Even when they made a golden calf and called it their god, they provoked You (Provoked: angered or stirred up). **19.** But in Your mercy, You did not abandon them in the wilderness; the cloud and fire never left them (Mercy: compassion or forgiveness). **20.** You gave Your Spirit to instruct them, provided manna and water for their needs (Withhold: to keep back). **21.** For forty years, You sustained them in the wilderness, so that they lacked nothing, their clothes did not wear out, and their feet did not swell (Sustained: supported; Swell: to enlarge or expand). **22.** You gave them kingdoms and nations, and they took possession of the lands of Sihon and Og (Possession: ownership or control; Sihon and Og: kings of lands conquered by Israel). **23.** You made their children as numerous as the stars, bringing them into the land You promised (Numerous: many; Ancestors: forefathers). **24.** The children entered, took possession of the land, and subdued the Canaanites and their kings (Subdued: brought under control). **25.** They captured fortified cities and rich land, taking possession of houses filled with goods, wells, vineyards, olive groves, and fruit trees in abundance. They ate, were satisfied, and delighted in Your goodness (Fortified: strengthened; Abundance: a large quantity). **26.** Yet, they became disobedient, rebelled against You, rejected Your law, and killed Your prophets (Disobedient: not following orders; Provocations: actions that cause anger). **27.** So You handed them to their enemies, who oppressed them. But when they cried out, You heard them and sent deliverers (Oppressed: treated harshly; Deliverers: those who save or rescue). **28.** After peace, they again did evil, and You allowed them to be ruled by their enemies. When they returned to You, You rescued them according to Your mercy (Dominated: had control over). **29.** You warned them, but they acted arrogantly and sinned against Your laws (Arrogantly: in a proud way; Stubborn: unwilling to change). **30.** For many years, You were patient with them, sending prophets, but they would not listen, so You handed them over to the people of the land (Patience: the ability to endure delay; Spirit: God's guiding presence). **31.** Yet, in Your mercy, You did not destroy them or abandon them, for You are gracious and merciful (Gracious: kind and giving). **32.** Our God, the great, mighty, and awesome God, who keeps covenant and shows mercy, let not the hardships upon us seem insignificant. These troubles have affected our kings, princes, priests, prophets, ancestors, and all Your people, from the kings of Assyria to today (Hardships: difficulties). **33.** You are just in everything that has come upon us. You have been faithful, but we have acted wickedly (Just: fair and righteous; Wickedly: in a morally wrong way). **34.** Our kings, princes, priests, and ancestors did not follow Your law or listen to Your commandments and testimonies (Testimonies: statements or teachings). **35.** They did not serve You in their kingdom or appreciate Your goodness, but turned to evil (Fertile: rich in resources). **36.** We are today servants in the land You gave our ancestors, yet we are still servants (Servants: those who serve others). **37.** The land produces for the kings You set over us because of our sins. These kings control our bodies and cattle, and we are in great distress (Distress: great pain or suffering). **38.** Therefore, we make a solemn covenant, writing it down. Our leaders, Levites, and priests affix their seals to it (Solemn: serious and formal; Affixing: attaching).

Chapter 10

1. Now, the names of those who sealed the agreement were Nehemiah, the governor(Tirshatha), the son of Hachaliah, and Zidkijah, **2.** Seraiah, Azariah, Jeremiah, **3.** Pashur, Amariah, Malchijah, **4.** Hattush, Shebaniah, Malluch, **5.** Harim, Meremoth, Obadiah, **6.** Daniel, Ginnethon, Baruch, **7.** Meshullam, Abijah, Mijamin, **8.** Maaziah, Bilgai, Shemaiah these were the preachers, **9.** And the Levites Jeshua, son of Azaniah, Binnui, of the sons of Henadad, Kadmiel;(Levites lineage responsible for religious duties) **10.** And their fellow Levites Shebaniah, Hodijah, Kelita, Pelaiah, Hanan, **11.** Micha, Rehob, Hashabiah, **12.** Zaccur, Sherebiah, Shebaniah, **13.** Hodijah, Bani, Beninu, **14.** The leaders of the people Parosh, Pahath- moab, Elam, Zatthu, Bani, **15.** Bunni, Azgad, Bebai, **16.** Adonijah, Bigvai, Adin, **17.** Ater, Hizkijah, Azzur, **18.** Hodijah, Hashum, Bezai, **19.** Hariph, Anathoth, Nebai, **20.** Magpiash, Meshullam, Hezir, **21.** Meshezabeel, Zadok, Jaddua, **22.** Pelatiah, Hanan, Anaiah, **23.** Hoshea, Hananiah, Hashub, **24.** Hallohesh, Pileha, Shobek, **25.** Rehum, Hashabnah, Maaseiah, **26.** Ahijah, Hanan, Anan, **27.** Malluch, Harim, Baanah, **28.** The rest of the people, including the preachers, Levites, doorkeepers(janitors), vocalizers, the Nethinim(tabernacle retainers), and all who had separated themselves from the foreign nations to follow the law of God, their women, sons, and daughters, each with understanding and knowledge, **29.** joined with their fellow Israelites and leaders in taking an pledge, pledging to follow the law of God, as it was given through Moses, the menial of God. They promised to observe all the commandments, rules, and bills of the LORD our God, **30.** They agreed not to give their daughters in marriage to the people of the land, nor take their daughters for their sons, **31.** And if the people of the land brought goods or food to vend on the Sabbath, they pledged not to buy it on the Sabbath or on the holy day, and to release every debt in the seventh time(time of release), **32.** Also, we established rules for ourselves, agreeing to pay a third of a shekel(small unit of currency) each time for the service of the house of our God, **33.** for the showbread(chuck placed on the balcony), the continual grain immolation, the diurnal burnt immolations, the immolations for the Sabbaths, the new moons, the appointed feasts, and the holy offerings. These immolations were to make atonement(cover sins) for Israel and support the work of the house of our God, **34.** We also cast lots to determine who would bring wood immolations to the house of our God, at the appointed times, time by time, as commanded in the law, to burn on the balcony of the LORD our God, **35.** We agreed to bring the firstfruits of our crop and the first fruits of all the fruit from our trees, time by time, to the house of the LORD, **36.** We also promised to bring the firstborn of our sons and cattle, as well as the firstborn of our herds and flocks, to the house of our God, to the preachers who serve there, **37.** We'll also bring the firstfruits of our dough, our immolations, and the fruit of all kinds of trees, wine, and oil painting to the preachers in the tabernacle chambers, and the tithes(a tenth part) of our crops to the Levites. The Levites will admit their tithes from the tithes in all the metropolises where we work the land, **38.** A clerk, a assignee of Aaron, will be with the Levites when they collect the tithes, and the Levites will bring a tenth of the tithes to the house of our God, to the lockers of the tabernacle, **39.** The Israelites and the Levites will bring the immolations of grain, new wine, and oil painting to the tabernacle lockers, where the sacred vessels and the preachers, doorkeepers, and vocalizers serve. We'll not neglect the house of our God.

Chapter 11

1. The leaders lived in Jerusalem, and the rest drew lots to decide that one in ten would live in the holy megacity, the rest in other metropolises. (Holy megacity: Jerusalem, set piecemeal for God) **2.** The people praised those who donated to live in Jerusalem. (Donated: offered willingly) **3.** These are the leaders in Jerusalem, while others—Israelites, preachers, Levites, Nethinim (tabernacle retainers), and Solomon's descendants—lived in their metropolises in Judah. (Nethinim: tabernacle workers) **4.** Some of Judah and Benjamin's descendants lived in Jerusalem. From Judah: Athaiah, the son of Uzziah, the son of Zechariah, the son of Amariah, the son of Shephatiah, the son of Mahalaleel, a assignee of Perez. (Perez: a son of Judah) **5.** Maaseiah, the son of Baruch, the son of gap-hozeh, the son of Hazaiah, the son of Adaiah, the son of Joiarib, the son of Zechariah, the son of Shiloni, was another occupant of Jerusalem. (Resident: living in a place) **6.** The descendants of Perez who lived in Jerusalem numbered 468 potent men. (Potent men: strong, able men) **7.** The descendants of Benjamin: Sallu, the son of Meshullam, the son of Joed, the son of Pedaiah, the son of Kolaiah, the son of Maaseiah, the son of Ithiel, the son of Jesaiah. (Benjamin: one of the 12 lines) **8.** After him, Gabbai and Sallai, with 928 men. (Men: male individualities) **9.** Joel, the son of Zichri, was in charge, and Judah, the son of Senuah, supported in overseeing the megacity. (Overseeing: managing) **10.** Among the preachers were Jedaiah, the son of Joiarib, and Jachin. (Preachers: religious leaders) **11.** Seraiah, the son of Hilkiah, the son of Meshullam, the son of Zadok, the son of Meraioth, the son of Ahitub, was the head of the tabernacle. (Head: leader) **12.** Their fellow preachers numbered 822, including Adaiah, the son of Jeroham, the son of Pelaliah, the son of Amzi, the son of Zechariah, the son of Pashur, the son of Malchiah. (Fellow: people belonging to the same group) **13.** Their leaders were Amashai, the son of Azareel, the son of Ahasai, the son of Meshillemoth, the son of Immer. (Leaders: those in charge) **14.** The gallant men serving with them numbered 128, and their administrator was Zabdiel, the son of a prominent family. (Valiant: stalwart, strong) **15.** The Levites included Shemaiah, the son of Hashub, the son of Azrikam, the son of Hashabiah, the son of Bunni. (Levites: lineage of Levi) **16.** Shabbethai and Jozabad, leaders of the Levites, oversaw work outside the tabernacle. (Overseeing: managing) **17.** Mattaniah, the son of Micha, the son of Zabdi, the son of Asaph, led thanksgiving and prayer. Bakbukiah, his alternate-in-command, and Abda, the son of Shammua, the son of Galal, the son of Jeduthun, supported him. (Alternate-in-command: deputy) **18.** 284 Levites lived in Jerusalem. (Holy megacity: set piecemeal for God) **19.** The doorkeepers were Akkub, Talmon, and their fellow keepers, numbering 172. (Doorkeepers: those guarding the gates) **20.** The remaining Israelites, preachers, and Levites lived in Judah, each in their heritage. (Heritage: land or property passed down) **21.** The Nethinim lived in Ophel, and Ziha and Gispa were in charge of them. (Nethinim: tabernacle retainers) **22.** Uzzi, the son of Bani, the son of Hashabiah, the son of Mattaniah, the son of Micha, supervised the Levites. The vocalizers, descendants of Asaph, were responsible for the tabernacle music. (Vocalizers: those leading deification with music) **23.** The king ordered a portion be given to the vocalizers daily. (Portion: a share or allowance) **24.** Pethahiah, the son of Meshezabeel, from the lineage of Zerah, the son of Judah, represented the king in matters concerning the people. (Representative: acting on behalf) **25.** The descendants of Judah lived in townlets: Kirjath-arba, Dibon, and Jekabzeel, with girding townlets. (Townlets: small municipalities) **26.** Some lived in Jeshua, Moladah, and Beth-phelet. (Metropolises: inhabited places) **27.** Others lived in Hazar-shual, Beer-sheba, and their girding townlets. (Townlets: small municipalities) **28.** And in Ziklag, Mekonah, and near townlets. (Hard: close) **29.** Some lived in En-rimmon, Zareah, and Jarmuth. (Municipalities: inhabited areas) **30.** Zanoah, Adullam, and girding townlets, Lachish, the fields hard, and Azekah and its townlets, were also inhabited by Judah's descendants. They lived from Beer-sheba to the vale of Hinnom. (Fields: areas of land) **31.** The descendants of Benjamin lived in Geba, Michmash, Aija, Bethel, and their townlets. (Townlets: small agreements) **32.** They lived in Anathoth, Nob, and Ananiah. (Municipalities: inhabited areas) **33.** Others lived in Hazor, Ramah, Gittaim. (Municipalities: inhabited areas) **34.** Hadid, Zeboim, and Neballat were also inhabited by Benjamin's descendants. (Inhabited: enthralled by people) **35.** Lod, Ono, and the vale of tradesmen were places where Benjamin's people lived. (Valley: low area of land, tradesmen: professed workers) **36.** The Levites were spread across Judah and Benjamin, serving in their divisions. (Divisions: separate sections)

Chapter 12

1. These are the priests and Levites who went with Zerubbabel, son of Shealtiel, and Jeshua: Seraiah, Jeremiah, Ezra, (Priests: religious leaders; Levites: members of the tribe of Levi, responsible for temple duties; Accompanied: went with) **2.** Amariah, Malluch, Hattush, **3.** Shechaniah, Rehum, Meremoth, **4.** Iddo, Ginnetho, Abijah, **5.** Miamin, Maadiah, Bilgah, **6.** Shemaiah, Joiarib, Jediah, **7.** Sallu, Amok, Hilkiah, Jedaiah. These were the chief priests in Jeshua's time. (Chief: leaders; Fellow: associates) **8.** The Levites were: Jeshua, Binnui, Kadmiel, Sherebiah, Judah, and Mattaniah, responsible for thanksgiving with their brethren. (In charge: responsible for; Thanksgiving: gratitude) **9.** Bakbukiah and Unni, with their brethren, took turns on duty. (Took turns: alternated; Duty: responsibility) **10.** Jeshua fathered Joiakim, who fathered Eliashib, who fathered Joiada, (Fathered: became the parent of) **11.** and Joiada fathered Jonathan, who fathered Jaddua. (Fathered: became the parent of) **12.** In Joiakim's time, the priests leading their families were: Seraiah, Meraiah; Jeremiah, Hananiah; (Leading: guiding; Families: groups of related people) **13.** Ezra, Meshullam; Amariah, Jehohanan; **14.** Melicu, Jonathan; Shebaniah, Joseph; **15.** Harim, Adna; Meraioth, Helkai; **16.** Iddo, Zechariah; Ginnethon, Meshullam; **17.** Abijah, Zichri; Miniamin, Moadiah, Piltai; **18.** Bilgah, Shammua; Shemaiah, Jehonathan; **19.** Joiarib, Mattenai; Jedaiah, Uzzi; **20.** Sallai, Kallai; Amok, Eber; **21.** Hilkiah, Hashabiah; Jedaiah, Nethaneel. **22.** During Eliashib, Joiada, Johanan, and Jaddua's time, the priests were recorded, continuing through Darius' reign. (Recorded: written down; Reign: rule) **23.** The Levites and leaders were listed in the record until Johanan, son of Eliashib. (Listed: named; Record: documentation) **24.** The Levites, including Hashabiah, Sherebiah, and Jeshua, son of Kadmiel, and their brethren, led praise and thanksgiving as commanded by David. (Praise: gratitude) **25.** Mattaniah, Bakbukiah, Obadiah, Meshullam, Talmon, and Akkub were the gatekeepers. (Gatekeepers: protectors of the gates) **26.** These events occurred during the time of Joiakim, son of Jeshua, and Nehemiah, the governor, and Ezra, the priest and scribe. (Governor: ruler; Scribe: writer) **27.** At the dedication of the wall, the Levites were summoned from all locations to Jerusalem, to celebrate with joy, thanksgiving, and music. (Summoned: called; Dedication: consecration) **28.** The singers gathered from the surrounding areas, including Netophathi, (Gathered: assembled) **29.** Gilgal, Geba, and Azmaveth, where they had built villages near Jerusalem. (Built: constructed) **30.** The priests and Levites purified themselves, the people, the gates, and the wall. (Purified: cleansed) **31.** I led the leaders of Judah onto the wall and arranged two groups of thanksgivers. One group went toward the Dung Gate. (Arranged: organized) **32.** Hoshaiah and half the leaders of Judah followed. (Followed: came after) **33.** Azariah, Ezra, Meshullam, **34.** Judah, Benjamin, Shemaiah, and Jeremiah, **35.** and some priests' sons with trumpets, including Zechariah, son of Jonathan, son of Shemaiah, son of Mattaniah, and Asaph's descendants. (Trumpets: musical instruments) **36.** Their brethren, Shemaiah, Azarael, Milalai, Gilalai, Maai, Nethaneel, Judah, and Hanani, followed with musical instruments, led by Ezra. (Brethren: brothers) **37.** They went up from the Fountain Gate to the City of David, past the House of David, to the Water Gate. (Fountain Gate: water access point) **38.** The other group of thanksgivers went the opposite way, and I followed, with half the people, from the Tower of Furnaces to the Broad Wall. (Opposite: reverse direction) **39.** They passed above the Gate of Ephraim, Old Gate, Fish Gate, Tower of Hananeel, Tower of Meah, and the Sheep Gate, stopping at the Prison Gate. (Passed: went by; Stopped: paused) **40.** The two groups stood in the house of God, and I, with half the leaders, stood with them: (House of God: temple) **41.** The priests—Eliakim, Maaseiah, Miniamin, Michaiah, Elioenai, Zechariah, and Hananiah—had trumpets. (Trumpets: instruments) **42.** Maaseiah, Shemaiah, Eleazar, Uzzi, Jehohanan, Malchijah, Elam, and Ezer were present, and the singers sang loudly, led by Jezrahiah, their overseer. (Loudly: with great volume) **43.** Great sacrifices were offered, and the people rejoiced greatly, for God had given them great joy, with their wives and children celebrating, and their joy was heard far away. (Rejoiced: celebrated) **44.** Certain people managed the storerooms for treasures, offerings, firstfruits, and tithes, gathered to support the priests and Levites as commanded by the law. (Managed: oversaw; Storerooms: storage places) **45.** The singers and gatekeepers maintained their duties as commanded by David and Solomon. (Maintained: kept up) **46.** In David and Asaph's time, there were leaders of singers who led praise and thanksgiving to God. (Leaders: heads) **47.** During Zerubbabel and Nehemiah's time, all of Israel gave portions for the singers and gatekeepers each day, sanctifying what was holy for the Levites, who sanctified it for Aaron's descendants. (Sanctifying: making holy)

Chapter 13
1. On that day, the book of Moses was read aloud to the people, and it was found written that the Ammonites and Moabites were forbidden to join God's congregation forever. (Ammonites: people from Ammon; Moabites: people from Moab; congregation: assembly) **2.** This was because they did not offer food and water to the Israelites but hired Balaam to curse them. However, God turned the curse into a blessing. (Balaam: a prophet hired to curse Israel; curse: prayer for harm) **3.** When they heard the law, the people separated from Israel all those who were not part of it. (Law: God's commandments; mixed multitude: people of different backgrounds) **4.** Eliashib the priest, who was in charge of the rooms in God's house, was allied with Tobiah. (Priest: religious leader; allied: united) **5.** He prepared a large room for Tobiah, where they stored food offerings, incense, vessels, and the tithes for the Levites, singers, and gatekeepers. (Tithes: offerings of a tenth; Levites: temple workers; singers: those leading worship) **6.** But I was not in Jerusalem. In the thirty-second year of King Artaxerxes of Babylon, I went to see the king and was allowed to return. (Artaxerxes: Persian king) **7.** When I arrived in Jerusalem, I learned of the wrong Eliashib had done by preparing a room for Tobiah in God's house. (Courts: outer areas of the temple) **8.** This upset me, so I threw out Tobiah's belongings. (Grieved me sore: deeply upset) **9.** I gave orders to cleanse the rooms and returned the vessels of God's house with the offerings of food and incense. (Cleanse: purify) **10.** I realized that the Levites had not received their portions, and the Levites and singers had gone to their fields. (Portions: shares of offerings) **11.** I confronted the leaders, asking, "Why is the house of God neglected?" I gathered them and restored them to their duties. (Contended: argued; forsaken: abandoned) **12.** Then all of Judah brought the tithes of grain, wine, and oil to the storerooms. (Tithes: offerings) **13.** I appointed Shelemiah the priest, Zadok the scribe, and Pedaiah from the Levites as treasurers, along with Hanan the son of Zaccur, as they were trustworthy. (Treasurers: those managing resources) **14.** Remember me, O my God, for this, and do not erase my good deeds for the house of God. (Erase: forget) **15.** I saw some people in Judah treading wine presses and bringing in grain, donkeys, wine, grapes, figs, and other goods on the Sabbath. I rebuked them for selling on the Sabbath. (Treading wine presses: crushing grapes; Sabbath: day of rest) **16.** Men from Tyre also lived in the city, bringing fish and goods to sell to the people of Judah on the Sabbath. (Tyre: a city-state) **17.** I confronted the nobles of Judah and asked, "What is this evil you are doing by profaning the Sabbath?" (Profane: disrespect) **18.** Did not your ancestors do this, and did not God bring judgment upon us and this city? Yet you are making it worse by profaning the Sabbath. (Profaning: treating with disrespect) **19.** When the gates of Jerusalem began to darken before the Sabbath, I ordered the gates to be shut until after the Sabbath. Some servants were stationed to prevent burdens from being brought in. (Servants: workers) **20.** So the merchants camped outside Jerusalem once or twice. (Merchants: sellers of goods) **21.** I warned them, saying, "Why are you camping by the wall? If you do this again, I will lay hands on you." From then on, they no longer came on the Sabbath. (Lay hands: physically stop) **22.** I commanded the Levites to purify themselves, guard the gates, and keep the Sabbath holy. Remember me, O my God, and show mercy according to your great love. (Purify: cleanse) **23.** I also saw Jews who had married women from Ashdod, Ammon, and Moab. (Ashdod: a Philistine city; Ammon: a neighboring nation; Moab: a neighboring nation) **24.** Their children spoke the language of Ashdod and not Judah's language, but the languages of their people. (Ashdod: a city of the Philistines) **25.** I rebuked them, cursed them, beat some of them, and pulled out their hair, making them swear by God to not give their daughters to foreign sons or take their daughters for their sons. (Rebuked: scolded; cursed: called for harm) **26.** Did not Solomon of Israel sin in this way? Yet, no king like him was beloved by God, and God made him king over all Israel. Nevertheless, foreign women caused him to sin. (Foreign women: women from other nations) **27.** Shall we listen to you and sin against our God by marrying foreign women? (Heed: listen to) **28.** Even one of the sons of Joiada, the son of Eliashib the high priest, was married to Sanballat the Horonite's daughter, so I drove him away. (Sanballat: an enemy of Israel) **29.** Remember them, O my God, for defiling the priesthood and the covenant of the priesthood and Levites. (Defiled: made unclean; covenant: agreement) **30.** I purified them from everything foreign and assigned duties to the priests and Levites. (Purified: cleansed) **31.** I also arranged for the wood offerings at the appointed times and the firstfruits. Remember me, O my God, for good. (Wood offerings: offerings of wood for the altar; firstfruits: first harvest offered to God).

17 – Esther

Chapter 1
1. Now it happened in the days of Ahasuerus, who reigned from India to Ethiopia, over 127 provinces. (Ahasuerus: Persian king, provinces: regions) **2.** In those days, when Ahasuerus sat on the throne in Shushan, the royal city, (Shushan: royal city, throne: seat of power) **3.** In the third year of his reign, he held a feast for all his princes and servants, the leaders of Persia and Media, and the nobles of the provinces. (feast: banquet, princes: high-ranking officials) **4.** He showed the riches of his kingdom and the glory of his greatness for 180 days. (glory: splendor, greatness: magnificence) **5.** After these days, he held another feast for everyone in Shushan, great and small, for seven days in the palace garden. (garden: outdoor space) **6.** The decorations were luxurious, with white, green, and blue curtains, fastened with fine linen and purple cords to silver rings and marble pillars. The beds were gold and silver, on a floor of marble. **7.** They drank from gold vessels, each different, and the king's wine flowed freely. (vessels: containers, flowed freely: abundant) **8.** The drinking was without compulsion; each person could drink as they wished, as the king had commanded his servants. (compulsion: force) **9.** Queen Vashti also held a feast for the women in the royal palace. (royal palace: king's residence) **10.** On the seventh day, when the king was happy from wine, he commanded seven chamberlains to bring Queen Vashti with her royal crown to show off her beauty to the people and princes. (chamberlains: servants, royal crown: crown of royalty) **11.** But Vashti refused to come at the king's command, and the king became furious. (refused: rejected, furious: very angry) **12.**

The king was very angry, and his wrath burned within him. (wrath: fury, burned: grew stronger) **13.** The king consulted the wise men who understood the law, (consulted: asked for advice, wise men: legal experts) **14.** and his closest advisers—Carshena, Shethar, Admatha, Tarshish, Meres, Marsena, and Memucan—who were princes of Persia and Media, and had access to the king. **15.** The king asked, "What should we do to Queen Vashti for disobeying my command?" (disobeying: refusing to follow) **16.** Memucan answered, "Vashti has wronged not only the king but all the princes and people in all the provinces of the king." (wronged: harmed, provinces: regions) **17.** "Her refusal will make all women despise their husbands when they hear of it, saying, 'King Ahasuerus commanded Vashti to come, but she didn't.'" (despise: hate, refusal: rejection) **18.** The women of Persia and Media will follow her example, causing contempt and anger. (contempt: disrespect, anger: fury) **19.** If it pleases the king, let a royal decree be issued that Vashti can never appear before the king again, and let her royal position be given to someone better. (decree: official order, position: role) **20.** When this decree is made known, all women will honor their husbands, from the greatest to the smallest. (honor: respect) **21.** This proposal pleased the king and his princes, and he followed Memucan's advice. (proposal: suggestion) **22.** He sent letters to all his provinces, in their own language, ordering that every man should rule his household, and that this command be proclaimed in every language. (proclaimed: announced, household: family)

Chapter 2
1. After King Ahasuerus' anger subsided, he remembered Vashti, her actions, and the decree against her. (Ahasuerus: Persian king; decree: official order) **2.** The king's servants suggested, "Let young virgins be chosen for the king." **3.** Officers should be sent to gather beautiful young virgins to Shushan, to the women's house, under Hege, for purification. (Shushan: capital city of Persia; Hege: king's chamberlain) **4.** The maiden who pleases the king should replace Vashti as queen. The king liked the idea and agreed. **5.** In Shushan, there was a Jew named Mordecai, a Benjamite. (Mordecai: Esther's cousin and guardian; Benjamite: descendant of the tribe of Benjamin) **6.** Mordecai had been taken from Jerusalem with the exile of King Jeconiah by King Nebuchadnezzar. (Jerusalem: city in Judah; Jeconiah: king of Judah; Nebuchadnezzar: king of Babylon) **7.** Mordecai raised Esther, his uncle's daughter, after her parents died. She was very beautiful. **8.** When the king's decree went out, Esther was also brought to Hege's care at the king's palace. **9.** Esther pleased Hege, who gave her special treatment, including her purification and seven maidens to attend her. **10.** Esther did not reveal her heritage, as Mordecai had instructed her. **11.** Mordecai checked daily on Esther's well-being at the women's house. **12.** After twelve months of purification (six months with myrrh oil, six with perfumes), each maiden's turn came to visit the king. **13.** Each maiden was given whatever she desired to take with her to the king's house. **14.** She spent the night with the king and then returned to the second house of the women, unless the king called for her by name. **15.** When it was Esther's turn, she took only what Hege advised, and won favor from all who saw her. **16.** Esther was brought to King Ahasuerus in the tenth month, the month of Tebeth, in his seventh year. (Ahasuerus: Persian king; Tebeth: the tenth month in the Jewish calendar) **17.** The king loved Esther more than all the others, made her queen, and replaced Vashti. **18.** The king held a great feast in Esther's honor, gave gifts, and granted a release to the provinces. (provinces: districts or regions under the king's rule) **19.** When the virgins were gathered a second time, Mordecai sat at the king's gate. (king's gate: royal entrance or court) **20.** Esther still kept her heritage secret, following Mordecai's command. **21.** Two of the king's chamberlains, Bigthan and Teresh, plotted against the king. (chamberlains: high-ranking officials or servants) **22.** Mordecai learned of the plot and told Esther, who reported it to the king in Mordecai's name. **23.** The plot was investigated, the conspirators hanged, and the event was recorded in the king's chronicles. (chronicles: official records or history books)

Chapter 3
1. After these events, King Ahasuerus promoted Haman, son of Hammedatha the Agagite, raising him above all his officials. (Ahasuerus: Persian king) **2.** All the king's servants at the gate bowed and honored Haman, as the king had commanded, but Mordecai did not bow or honor him. (Gate: entrance to the palace) **3.** The king's servants at the gate asked Mordecai, "Why do you disobey the king's command?" **4.** When they spoke to him daily and he ignored them, they told Haman to see if Mordecai's actions would stand, since he had told them he was a Jew. (Ignored: did not listen) **5.** When Haman saw that Mordecai did not bow or honor him, he was filled with rage. (Rage: extreme anger) **6.** He felt it was beneath him to only punish Mordecai, so he planned to destroy all the Jews in the kingdom of Ahasuerus, the people of Mordecai. (Beneath: too low or unworthy for him) **7.** In the first month, Nisan, of King Ahasuerus' twelfth year, they cast Pur before Haman daily, deciding on the month to act, which was the twelfth month, Adar. (Nisan: Jewish month; Pur: casting lots—random choice) **8.** Haman said to King Ahasuerus, "There is a certain people scattered across your kingdom, with laws different from everyone else, who don't obey the king's laws. It's not in your best interest to let them live." **9.** "If it pleases the king, let a decree be made to destroy them, and I will give 10,000 talents of silver to the king's officials to deposit in the treasury." (Decree: official order) **10.** The king took off his ring and gave it to Haman, the enemy of the Jews. (Ring: symbol of royal authority) **11.** The king told Haman, "The silver is yours, and the people are too. Do as you see fit." **12.** On the 13th day of the first month, the king's scribes wrote everything Haman had commanded to the king's governors, officials, and rulers in every province, in their own languages, in the name of King Ahasuerus, sealed with the king's ring. (Scribes: writers, Governors: officials ruling provinces) **13.** The letters were sent to all provinces, ordering the destruction of all Jews—young and old, men and women—on the 13th day of Adar, and their belongings would be plundered. (Plundered: stolen or taken as loot) **14.** Copies of the decree were made public in each province, telling the people to be ready for that day. **15.** The couriers rushed out with the king's command, and the decree was proclaimed in the citadel of Susa. The king and Haman sat down to drink, but the city of Susa was bewildered. (Citadel: fortress, Susa: capital city of Persia, Bewildered: confused)

Chapter 4
1. When Mordecai saw all that had happened, he tore his clothes, put on sackcloth and ashes, and went into the city, crying loudly and bitterly. (sorrowfully) **2.** He went as far as the king's gate, but no one in sackcloth could enter the king's gate. (King's gate: entrance to the palace) **3.** Throughout every province where the king's order was sent, Jews mourned, fasted, wept, and cried out loud; many lay in sackcloth and ashes. (mourning: sadness, fasting: going without food, weeping: crying) **4.** Esther's servants told her, and she was deeply distressed. She sent clothes to Mordecai to remove his sackcloth, but he refused. (distressed: upset, troubled) **5.** Esther then called Hatach, one of the king's attendants, and ordered him to find out why Mordecai was acting this way. (attendants: servants) **6.** Hatach went to Mordecai at the city square near the king's gate. (City square: open area near the palace) **7.** Mordecai explained what had happened to him and the money Haman promised to give the king to destroy the Jews. (Haman: king's official) **8.** He also gave Hatach a copy of the king's decree to show Esther, urging her to plead with the king for her people. (decree: official order, plead: request) **9.** Hatach told Esther what Mordecai had said. **10.** Esther replied to Hatach with instructions for Mordecai: **11.** "Everyone knows that anyone who enters the king's inner court without being called is sentenced to death unless the king holds out his golden scepter. I haven't been called in thirty days." (scepter: staff) **12.** Hatach

relayed Esther's message to Mordecai. (relayed: delivered) **13.** Mordecai responded, "Don't think you'll escape in the king's palace more than the other Jews. (escape: avoid danger) **14.** If you keep quiet now, deliverance will come from another place, but you and your family will perish. Perhaps you've become queen for this very moment." (deliverance: rescue, perish: die) **15.** Esther sent this answer back to Mordecai. **16.** "Gather all the Jews in Shushan to fast for me for three days and nights, without eating or drinking. I, along with my attendants, will do the same. Then I will approach the king, even though it's against the law. If I perish, I perish." **17.** Mordecai went and did as Esther had commanded. (commanded: instructed)

Chapter 5

1. On the third day, Esther dressed in her royal garments and stood in the inner court of the king's palace, across from the king's hall, where the king was seated on his throne near the gate. (King's house: royal palace) **2.** When the king saw Queen Esther standing in the court, he was pleased and extended his golden scepter toward her. Esther approached and touched its tip. (Scepter: royal staff) **3.** The king asked, "What is your request, Queen Esther? What do you want? I will grant it, even if it's up to half of my kingdom." **4.** Esther replied, "If it pleases the king, let him and Haman come today to the banquet I have prepared for them." (Banquet: feast, large meal) **5.** The king ordered, "Hurry, bring Haman quickly, so he can do as Esther has requested." They both went to the banquet Esther had set. **6.** At the banquet, the king asked Esther again, "What is your request, Queen Esther? It will be granted, even up to half the kingdom." **7.** Esther responded, "Here is my request: **8.** If I have found favor with the king and if it pleases him, let the king and Haman come to another banquet I will prepare tomorrow, and then I will make my request known." (Favor: kindness, approval) **9.** That day, Haman left the banquet feeling pleased and content. But when he saw Mordecai at the king's gate, who did not rise or show him respect, he became furious. (Gate: entrance) **10.** Haman controlled his anger and went home, where he called for his friends and his wife, Zeresh. **11.** He bragged about his wealth, the large number of his children, and how the king had promoted him above all the other officials. (Promoted: raised in rank) **12.** Haman continued, "I am the only one invited to the queen's banquet with the king, and tomorrow I will be invited again." **13.** "But none of this matters to me as long as I see Mordecai the Jew sitting at the gate." **14.** Zeresh and his friends suggested, "Build a gallows 75 feet high, and ask the king to have Mordecai hanged on it. Then go to the banquet in a joyful mood." Haman approved of this plan and ordered the gallows to be built. (Gallows: structure for hanging)

Chapter 6

1. That evening, the king was unable to sleep and ordered the book of records to be brought to him and read aloud. (King Ahasuerus: Persian king) **2.** It was found written that Mordecai had reported Bigthana and Teresh, two of the king's guards, who had plotted to assassinate King Ahasuerus. (Bigthana & Teresh: royal servants, assassinate: kill) **3.** The king asked, "What reward has been given to Mordecai for this?" The servants replied, "Nothing has been done for him." (reward: respect or recognition) **4.** The king asked, "Who is in the court?" Haman had come to speak to the king about hanging Mordecai on the gallows he had made. (court: area in the palace, gallows: structure for hanging) **5.** The servants answered, "Haman is in the court." The king said, "Let him come in." (court: area in the palace) **6.** Haman entered, and the king asked, "What should be done for the person the king wants to honor?" Haman thought, "Who else would the king want to honor more than me?" (honor: respect or recognition) **7.** Haman answered, "For the person the king wants to honor, **8.** Let royal clothes be brought, along with the king's horse and crown; **9.** Let one of the king's top officials dress him, lead him on the horse through the city, and announce, 'This is what is done for the person the king honors.'" (royal: belonging to the king or queen, officials: important servants) **10.** The king said, "Quickly, do all you have suggested for Mordecai the Jew, who sits at the king's gate. Do not leave out a single detail." (Mordecai the Jew: a man of Jewish faith) **11.** Haman took the royal clothes and the horse, dressed Mordecai, and led him through the city, announcing, "This is what is done for the person the king honors." (announcing: proclaiming) **12.** Mordecai returned to the king's gate, but Haman hurried home, grieving with his head covered. (grieving: feeling sad or regret) **13.** Haman told his wife Zeresh and his friends everything that had happened. They replied, "If Mordecai is of Jewish descent, you will not defeat him, but will certainly fall before him." (descent: family origin) **14.** While they were talking, the king's servants arrived to hurry Haman to the banquet Esther had prepared. (banquet: large meal or party)

Chapter 7

1. So the king and Haman came to the banquet with Queen Esther. (King Ahasuerus: Persian king) **2.** The king asked again on the second day of the wine banquet, "What is your request, Queen Esther? It will be granted, even up to half of my kingdom." (banquet: formal feast, wine: alcoholic drink) **3.** Esther replied, "If I have found favor in your sight, O king, and if it pleases you, grant my life at my request, and the lives of my people." (favor: approval, request: plea) **4.** "We are sold to be destroyed, killed, and wiped out. If we were only sold as slaves, I would have stayed silent, for the king would not suffer loss." (suffer loss: lose money or power) **5.** The king asked, "Who is responsible for this, and where is he?" (responsible: to blame) **6.** Esther answered, "The enemy is this wicked Haman." Haman was terrified. (wicked: evil) **7.** The king, enraged, left the banquet and went into the palace garden. Haman stayed to beg Esther for his life, realizing the king intended harm. (enraged: very angry, palace garden: royal outdoor area) **8.** When the king returned from the garden, he saw Haman on Esther's couch and asked, "Will he also assault the queen in my presence?" As the words left his mouth, Haman's face was covered. (assault: attack) **9.** Harbonah, one of the attendants, said, "Look, the gallows Haman built for Mordecai stand in his house, fifty cubits high." The king said, "Hang him on it." (gallows: structure for hanging, cubits: ancient unit of measurement) **10.** So Haman was hanged on the gallows he had prepared for Mordecai, and the king's anger was appeased. (appeased: calmed down)

Chapter 8

1. On that day, King Ahasuerus gave Haman's estate to Queen Esther. Mordecai came before the king, as Esther had revealed his relationship to her. (estate : house, revealed : told) **2.** The king took off his ring, which had been Haman's, and gave it to Mordecai. Esther put Mordecai in charge of Haman's estate. (put in charge : set over) **3.** Esther spoke to the king again, falling at his feet, pleading with tears to undo the evil Haman had planned against the Jews. (pleading : besought, undo : put away) **4.** The king extended the golden scepter to Esther. She rose and stood before him. (extended : held out) **5.** Esther said, "If it pleases the king, and if I have found favor with him, let it be written to reverse the letters Haman wrote to destroy the Jews." (favor : grace, reverse : change) **6.** "How can I bear to see the evil that will come upon my people, or the destruction of my family?" (bear : endure) **7.** King Ahasuerus said to Esther and Mordecai, "I have given Haman's estate to Esther, and Haman was hanged because he attacked the Jews." (estate : house, attacked : laid his hand upon) **8.** "Write a new decree for the Jews, as you wish, in the king's name, sealed with the king's ring. No one can reverse it." (decree : writing, reverse : undo) **9.** The king's scribes wrote the decree in the third month (Sivan), on the 23rd day, according to Mordecai's instructions, for the Jews and officials across the 127 provinces. (wrote : commanded, officials : lieutenants) **10.** The letters were written in the king's name, sealed with his ring, and sent by messengers on horseback, mules, camels, and young dromedaries. (messengers : posts) **11.** The king granted the Jews in every city the right to gather, defend themselves, and destroy those who attacked them, even taking the spoil. (granted : gave, spoil : plunder) **12.** This was set for one day in all provinces—on the 13th of Adar, the 12th month. (set : appointed) **13.** A copy of the decree was published in every province, and the Jews were prepared to defend themselves. (published : made known, prepared : ready) **14.** The messengers rode out, hurrying under the king's command, and the decree was issued at the palace in Shushan. (hurried : hastened, issued : given) **15.** Mordecai left the king's presence in royal clothes, with a gold crown and fine linen, and the city of Shushan rejoiced. (royal : kingly, rejoiced : was glad) **16.** The Jews had light, joy, gladness, and honor. (light : hope) **17.** In every province, wherever the king's decree was known, the Jews celebrated with joy, feasting, and a good day. Many people became Jews, fearing them.

Chapter 9

1. In the twelfth month, which is the month of Adar, on the thirteenth day of that month, when the king's order and decree were about to be executed, the enemies of the Jews had hoped to overpower them. But the situation turned around, and instead, the Jews gained authority over those who hated them. (decree: official order; executed: carried out) **2.** The Jews gathered in their cities across all the provinces of King Ahasuerus to defend themselves against those who sought to harm them. No one could stand against them, for fear of the Jews spread over all people. (gathered: assembled; oppose: resist) **3.** The rulers, lieutenants, deputies, and officials in the king's provinces supported the Jews because the fear of Mordecai had gripped them. (lieutenants: assistants) **4.** Mordecai was well-respected in the king's palace, and his fame spread throughout the provinces. His influence continued to grow stronger. (powerful: influential; court: royal household) **5.** The Jews struck down all their enemies with swords, killing and destroying them, and did whatever they pleased to those who hated them. (struck down: defeated) **6.** In the city of Shushan, the Jews killed five hundred men. **7.** The names of those slain include Parshandatha, Dalphon, Aspatha, **8.** Poratha, Adalia, Aridatha, **9.** Parmashta, Arisai, Aridai, and Vajezatha, **10.** as well as the ten sons of Haman, the enemy of the Jews. However, they did not take any of the spoils from the dead. (plunder: loot) **11.** On that day, the king was informed of how many had been killed in Shushan. **12.** The king asked Queen Esther, "The Jews have killed five hundred men in Shushan and the ten sons of Haman. What have they done in the rest of the provinces? What is your request? It will be granted." (petition: request) **13.** Esther replied, "If it pleases the king, let the Jews in Shushan be allowed to act again tomorrow according to today's decree, and let Haman's ten sons be hanged on the gallows." (hanged: executed) **14.** The king commanded it to be done, and a decree was issued in Shushan. The ten sons of Haman were hanged. **15.** On the fourteenth day of Adar, the Jews in Shushan gathered again and killed three hundred more men, but they did not take any of the loot. **16.** Meanwhile, Jews in other provinces of the king gathered together, defended themselves, and had peace from their enemies. They killed seventy-five thousand of their foes, but again, did not take any of the plunder. **17.** On the thirteenth day of Adar, and then again on the fourteenth day, they rested, celebrating with feasting and joy. **18.** Jews in Shushan gathered on the thirteenth and fourteenth days, and rested on the fifteenth, making it a day of feasting and gladness. **19.** Jews in rural areas, living in unwalled towns, observed the fourteenth day of Adar with joy, feasting, and giving gifts to one another. (unwalled: without walls) **20.** Mordecai recorded these events and sent letters to all Jews in every province of King Ahasuerus, both near and far, **21.** instructing them to observe the fourteenth and fifteenth days of Adar each year. **22.** These days were to commemorate the Jews' rest from their enemies, as the month had been changed from sorrow to joy, and from mourning to a day of celebration. They were to be days of feasting, joy, and giving gifts, including charity to the poor. (feast: celebration) **23.** The Jews agreed to continue observing this practice as Mordecai had written to them. **24.** This was because Haman, the son of Hammedatha, the Agagite, had planned to destroy the Jews, casting lots (Pur) to determine their fate, but his evil plan was reversed. (lots: chance) **25.** When Esther came before the king, he issued a decree in writing that Haman's wicked plot would be returned upon his own head, and that Haman and his sons would be hanged on the gallows. **26.** These days were called Purim, named after the casting of the lot. They were established as a remembrance for all the events described in this letter. **27.** The Jews made an oath, along with their descendants and all who joined them, to continue observing these two days every year, according to the instructions written in the letter. **28.** These days were to be kept and remembered in every generation, by every family, province, and city. The observance of Purim was to remain unbroken, and its memory was not to perish from among the Jews. **29.** Queen Esther, daughter of Abihail, and Mordecai the Jew, wrote with full authority to confirm the second letter regarding Purim. **30.** These letters were sent to all the Jews in the one hundred twenty-seven provinces of Ahasuerus's kingdom, with words of peace and truth, **31.** to confirm the observance of Purim in their proper time, as Mordecai and Esther had instructed them, and according to the fasts and cries they had established. **32.** The decree of Esther confirmed these matters regarding Purim, and it was recorded in the official records.

Chapter 10

1. And King Ahasuerus imposed a tax on the land and the coastal islands. **2.** Are not all his mighty acts and the promotion of Mordecai, whom the king honored, written in the chronicles of Media and Persia? (acts: deeds, promotion: advancement) **3.** Mordecai the Jew was second to King Ahasuerus, highly respected by the Jews, and beloved by his people, seeking their welfare and speaking peace to all his descendants. (respected: honored, welfare: well-being, descendants: children)

18 – Job

Chapter 1

1. In the land of Uz, there was a man named Job. He was a righteous and upright man who feared God and avoided evil. (righteous: virtuous, upright: honorable, feared: respected, avoided: shunned) **2.** Job had seven sons and three daughters. **3.** His wealth was immense: 7,000 sheep, 3,000 camels, 500 yoke of oxen, 500 donkeys, and a large household. He was the wealthiest man in the East. (wealth: riches, immense: vast, yoke of oxen: pairs of oxen, household: family, wealthiest: richest) **4.** His sons took turns holding feasts at their homes, inviting their sisters to join them for meals and celebrations. (feasts: banquets, inviting: asking, join: participate, celebrations: festivities) **5.** After these feasts, Job would send for them to purify them. He would rise early in the morning and offer burnt sacrifices, thinking, "Perhaps my children have sinned and cursed God in their hearts." This was Job's usual practice. (Purify: cleanse, burnt sacrifices: offerings, thinking: considering, usual: regular) **6.** One day, the sons of God gathered before the LORD, and Satan came with them. (Gathered: assembled, came: appeared) **7.** The LORD asked Satan, "Where have you come from?" Satan replied, "I have been roaming throughout the earth, going back and forth on it." (Roaming: wandering, throughout: across, going back and forth: moving to and fro) **8.** The LORD said to Satan, "Have you considered my servant Job? There is no one like him; he is blameless and upright, a man who fears God and shuns evil." (Considered: thought about, servant: follower, blameless: innocent, upright: righteous, fears: respects, shuns: avoids) **9.** Satan replied, "Does Job fear God for no reason? (no reason: without cause) **10.** You have put a protective hedge around him and his household, and everything he owns. You have blessed the work of his hands, and his possessions have grown. (Protective hedge: shield, owns: possesses, blessed: favored, work: labor, possessions: belongings, grown: increased) **11.** But take away everything he has, and he will surely curse you to your face." (Take away: remove, surely: certainly, curse: speak against) **12.** The LORD said to Satan, "Very well, everything he has is in your hands, but on the man himself, do not lay a finger." Then Satan left the LORD's presence. (Very well: okay, hands: control, lay a finger: harm) **13.** One day, while Job's children were eating and drinking wine in their eldest brother's house, (eating: feasting, drinking wine: having a drink, eldest: firstborn) **14.** a messenger came to Job and said, "The oxen were plowing and the donkeys were grazing nearby, (messenger: bearer of news, plowing: tilling, grazing: eating) **15.** When the Sabeans attacked, took them, and killed the servants with the sword. I alone have escaped to bring you the news." (Attacked: assaulted, took: stole, killed: murdered, servants: workers, escaped: fled) **16.** Before the messenger finished, another came and said, "Fire from heaven fell and burned up the sheep and the servants, and I alone have escaped to tell you." (Finished: completed, burned up: consumed, heaven: sky) **17.** While that messenger was still speaking, another came and said, "The Chaldeans formed three raiding parties, attacked your camels, and carried them off. They killed the servants with the sword, and I alone have escaped to tell you." (Chaldeans: Babylonians, raiding parties: groups of invaders, attacked: ambushed, carried off: stole) **18.** As he was speaking, another messenger arrived and said, "Your sons and daughters were feasting in the oldest brother's house, (sons and daughters: children, feasting: eating, oldest: firstborn) **19.** When a great wind swept in from the desert and struck the four corners of the house. It collapsed on them, and they are dead. I alone have escaped to tell you." (great: mighty, swept in: blew in, struck: hit, collapsed: fell down) **20.** At this, Job stood up, tore his robe, shaved his head, and fell to the ground in worship. (Stood up: rose, tore: ripped, shaved: cut off, worship: reverence) **21.** He said, "Naked I came from my mother's womb, and naked I will depart. The LORD gave, and the LORD has taken away; may the name of the LORD be praised." (naked: bare, depart: leave, taken away: removed, praised: honored) **22.** In all of this, Job did not sin or blame God for the calamities that befell him. (sin: do wrong, blame: accuse, calamities: misfortunes, befell: happened to)

Chapter 2
1. Again, the sons of God came to present themselves before the LORD, and Satan came with them. (Present: appear) **2.** The LORD asked, "Where have you come from?" Satan replied, "I have been roaming the earth." (Roaming: wandering) **3.** The LORD said, "Have you considered my servant Job? He is blameless, upright, and fears God. He still maintains his integrity despite your efforts to harm him without reason." (considered: thought about, blameless: innocent, upright: righteous, maintains: keeps, integrity: honesty, efforts: attempts, harm: hurt) **4.** Satan answered, "A man will give all he has for his life." (Life: survival) **5.** But if you strike his flesh and bones, he will curse you." (strike: afflict, flesh and bones: body, curse: speak against) **6.** The LORD said, "Very well, he is in your hands, but spare his life." (very well: okay, spare: save, life: survival) **7.** So Satan afflicted Job with painful sores from head to toe. (afflicted: struck, painful: agonizing, sores: boils) **8.** Job took a piece of broken pottery to scrape himself and sat in ashes. (scrape: rub, broken: shattered, pottery: clay, ashes: dust) **9.** His wife said, "Are you still holding on to your integrity? Curse God and die." (holding on: clinging, integrity: honor, curse: speak against) **10.** He replied, "You speak like a foolish woman. Should we accept good from God and not trouble?" In all this, Job did not sin. (foolish: senseless, accept: receive, trouble: hardship, sin: wrong) **11.** When Job's three friends—Eliphaz, Bildad, and Zophar—heard of his troubles, they agreed to visit him to comfort him. (heard: learned, troubles: misfortunes, agreed: decided, comfort: console) **12.** When they saw him from afar, they wept, tore their clothes, and sprinkled dust on their heads. (afar: a distance, wept: cried, tore: ripped, sprinkled: scattered, dust: ashes) **13.** They sat with him for seven days and nights in silence, seeing his great suffering. (sat: remained, silence: quiet, great: intense, suffering: pain).

Chapter 3
1. After this, Job opened his mouth and cursed the day of his birth. (opened: spoke, cursed: condemned) **2.** Job said: **3.** "Let the day I was born perish, and the night I was conceived. (perish: die, conceived: formed) **4.** Let that day be filled with darkness; may God not notice it, and may light never shine on it. (filled: covered, notice: see, shine: appear) **5.** Let darkness and death cover it; may a cloud rest over it, and may the day be filled with terror. (cover: envelop, rest: settle, terror: fear) **6.** Let that night be lonely; may it not be counted among the days of the year or included in the months. (lonely: desolate, counted: listed, included: part of) **7.** Let no joy come from that night. (joy: happiness) **8.** Let those who curse the day curse it, those who are ready to bring mourning. (curse: condemn, bring: cause, mourning: grief) **9.** Let the stars of that night be dark; let it long for light, but never see dawn. (dark: hidden, long for: desire, dawn: daybreak) **10.** Because it did not shut the doors of my mother's womb, nor hide my sorrow from my eyes. (shut: close, hide: conceal, sorrow: pain) **11.** Why did I not die at birth? Why did I not perish when I came from the womb? (die: pass away, perish: vanish) **12.** Why did my mother keep me? Why did she nurse me? (keep: bear, nurse: care for) **13.** For then I would have been at rest, sleeping peacefully. (rest: at peace, sleeping: resting, peacefully: calmly) **14.** I would be with kings and rulers who built ruins for themselves, (kings: monarchs, rulers: leaders, ruins: monuments) **15.** Or with princes who had gold and filled their homes with silver. (gold: riches, filled: stocked, silver: wealth) **16.** Or like a miscarriage that is never seen, like infants who never saw the light. (Never saw the light: never lived) **17.** There the wicked cease from troubling, and the weary are at rest. (Wicked: evil, cease: stop, troubling: tormenting, weary: tired, at rest: peaceful) **18.** There the prisoners are at peace, free from the voice of their oppressors. (Prisoners: captives, free: liberated, voice: commands, oppressors: tormentors) **19.** Both the small and great are there, and the servant is free from his master. (small: lowly, great: powerful, servant: worker, master: employer) **20.** Why is light given to those in misery, and life to those with bitter souls, (misery: suffering, bitter: sorrowful, souls: spirits) **21.** Who long for death but it does not come, who dig for it more than treasure? (long for: desire, dig for: seek, treasure: riches) **22.** Who rejoice when they find the grave? (rejoice: celebrate, grave: tomb) **23.** Why is light given to someone whose way is hidden, whom God has surrounded with obstacles? (way: path, hidden: obscured, surrounded: encircled, obstacles: hindrances) **24.** My sighs come before I eat, and my groans pour out like water. (sighs: breaths, groans: moans, pour out: flow, like water: abundantly) **25.** What I feared has come upon me; what I dreaded has happened to me. (feared: dreaded, come upon: overtaken, happened: occurred) **26.** I have no peace, no rest, and no quiet; trouble keeps coming. (peace: calm, rest: relaxation, quiet: stillness, keeps coming: persists).

Chapter 4
1. Then Eliphaz the Temanite replied: (replied: answered) **2.** "If we speak to you, will you be offended? But who can remain silent? (speak: talk, offended: hurt, remain silent: stay quiet) **3.** You have taught many, and supported the weak. (taught: instructed, supported: helped) **4.** Your words have helped those who were falling, and strengthened the weak. (helped: encouraged, falling: stumbling, strengthened: empowered) **5.** But now, when it has come upon you, you faint; it troubles you. (faint: collapse, troubles: disturbs) **6.** Is this not the confidence and hope you've placed in your righteousness? (confidence: trust, hope: assurance, righteousness: goodness) **7.** Remember, who ever perished being innocent? Where have the righteous been destroyed? (perished: died, innocent: blameless, destroyed: punished) **8.** As I have seen, those who sow iniquity reap wickedness. (sow: plant, iniquity: sin, reap: harvest, wickedness: evil) **9.** They perish by God's judgment; His breath consumes them. (perish: die, judgment: punishment, breath: spirit, consumes: destroys) **10.** The roar of the lion and the strength of the young lions are broken. (roar: growl, strength: power, broken:

crushed) **11.** The old lion dies for lack of prey, and the cubs scatter. (old: elderly, prey: food, scatter: flee) **12.** A secret thought came to me, and my ear caught a whisper. (secret thought: hidden idea, caught: heard, whisper: murmur) **13.** In the visions of the night, when deep sleep falls on people, (visions: dreams, deep sleep: deep slumber) **14.** fear and trembling overwhelmed me, and my bones shook. (fear: dread, trembling: shaking, overwhelmed: consumed) **15.** A spirit passed by my face, and my hair stood on end. (spirit: apparition, passed by: brushed past, stood on end: rose) **16.** It stood still, but I couldn't make out its form. In the silence, I heard a voice saying, (stood still: halted, make out: discern, form: shape) **17.** "Can a mortal be more righteous than God? Can a man be purer than his Maker? (mortal: human, purer: more innocent) **18.** God does not trust His servants; He charges His angels with error. (trust: rely on, charges: accuses, error: mistake) **19.** How much less those who live in fragile bodies, built from dust, who are easily destroyed! (fragile: weak, bodies: flesh, built from dust: made of earth, destroyed: ruined) **20.** They die without notice, and their greatness fades. (die: pass away, notice: awareness, fades: diminishes) **21.** They die without wisdom, and no one even notices." (wisdom: understanding, notices: cares)

Chapter 5
1. "Call now, is there anyone who will answer you? Which of the holy ones will you turn to? (call: shout, holy ones: saints) **2.** For wrath kills the foolish, and envy destroys the simple. (wrath: anger, foolish: ignorant, envy: jealousy, simple: naive) **3.** I've seen the foolish take root, but suddenly I cursed their home. (foolish: unwise, take root: establish themselves, cursed: condemned) **4.** Their children are in danger, crushed at the gate with no one to save them. (children: offspring, danger: peril, crushed: beaten, gate: entrance) **5.** The hungry eat their harvest, taking it from the thorns, and the thief devours their wealth. (hungry: starving, harvest: crops, thorns: brambles, thief: robber, devours: consumes) **6.** Trouble does not come from the dust, nor does distress spring from the ground; (trouble: hardship, dust: earth, distress: suffering, spring: arise) **7.** Yet, man is born to trouble, as sparks fly upward. (born: destined, trouble: affliction, sparks: embers) **8.** I would turn to God and commit my cause to Him, (turn: seek, commit: entrust, cause: case) **9.** Who does great and unsearchable things, marvelous things beyond number: (great: mighty, unsearchable: beyond understanding, marvelous: wonderful, beyond number: countless) **10.** He sends rain upon the earth and waters the fields; (rain: showers, waters: nourishes, fields: lands) **11.** He lifts up the lowly and exalts those who mourn to safety. (lifts up: raises, lowly: humble, exalts: honors, mourn: grieve, safety: security) **12.** He frustrates the plans of the crafty, so their hands cannot succeed. (frustrates: thwarts, plans: schemes, crafty: cunning, succeed: prosper) **13.** He traps the wise in their own cleverness, and the plans of the devious are overturned. (traps: ensnares, wise: prudent, cleverness: wisdom, devious: deceitful, overturned: reversed) **14.** They stumble in the dark, groping in the midday as if it were night. (stumble: fall, dark: darkness, groping: feeling around, midday: noon) **15.** But He saves the poor from the sword, from their mouths, and from the hand of the mighty. (saves: rescues, poor: needy, sword: blade, mouths: speech, hand: power, mighty: strong) **16.** So the poor have hope, and iniquity is silenced. (hope: expectation, iniquity: sin, silenced: quieted) **17.** Blessed is the man whom God corrects; do not despise the discipline of the Almighty. (blessed: happy, corrects: chastens, despise: scorn, discipline: instruction) **18.** For He wounds but He heals, He strikes but His hands make whole. (wounds: hurts, heals: restores, strikes: smites, whole: complete) **19.** He will deliver you from six troubles; in seven, no harm will touch you. (deliver: rescue, troubles: difficulties, harm: damage, touch: affect) **20.** In famine, He will redeem you from death, and in war, from the power of the sword. (famine: hunger, redeem: save, death: demise, war: conflict, power: strength) **21.** You will be hidden from the scourge of the tongue, and will not fear destruction when it comes. (hidden: protected, scourge: punishment, tongue: speech, destruction: ruin) **22.** You will laugh at destruction and famine, and will not fear wild beasts. (laugh: mock, famine: hunger, wild beasts: predators) **23.** For you will be in harmony with the stones of the field, and the beasts will be at peace with you. (harmony: peace, stones: rocks, field: land, beasts: animals, peace: tranquility) **24.** You will know that your tent is secure; you will visit your home and find nothing wrong. (tent: dwelling, secure: safe, visit: go to, wrong: amiss) **25.** You will know your descendants will be many, and your children will flourish like grass. (descendants: offspring, flourish: thrive, grass: plants) **26.** You will come to your grave in a ripe old age, like a sheaf of grain gathered in season. (grave: tomb, ripe old age: long life, sheaf: bundle, season: harvest) **27.** "We have carefully examined all this, and it is true. Hear it and apply it to your life." (examined: studied, true: certain, apply: follow)

Chapter 6
1. Job replied, (replied: answered) **2.** "If only my suffering could be weighed, and my troubles measured on a scale! (suffering: pain, troubles: afflictions, measured: quantified) **3.** They would be heavier than the sand of the sea, so my words are overwhelmed. (heavier: more burdensome, overwhelmed: consumed) **4.** The arrows of God have pierced me; the poison of His judgment drains my spirit. His terrors surround me. (arrows: darts, pierced: wounded, poison: venom, judgment: wrath, drains: depletes, terrors: fears) **5.** Does a wild donkey bray when it has grass? Does an ox low over its food? (wild donkey: donkey of the wilderness, bray: cry, ox: bull, low: moo) **6.** Can anything tasteless be eaten without salt? Or is there any flavor in egg whites? (tasteless: bland, eaten: consumed, flavor: taste) **7.** The things I refuse to touch are like my sorrowful food. (refuse: reject, touch: handle, sorrowful: painful) **8.** If only God would grant my wish, (grant: fulfill) **9.** that He would destroy me and end my life, (destroy: annihilate, end: terminate) **10.** then I could find some comfort, even in my pain, for I would not hide the words of God. (comfort: solace, pain: suffering, hide: conceal) **11.** What is my strength that I should hope? What is my future that I should continue? (strength: power, hope: expect, future: destiny, continue: persevere) **12.** Is my strength like stone, or my body made of bronze? (body: flesh, bronze: metal) **13.** Have I no help in myself? Has wisdom left me? (wisdom: understanding, left: departed) **14.** A friend should show compassion to the suffering, but you forsake the fear of God. (compassion: empathy, forsake: abandon, fear of God: reverence) **15.** My brothers have been deceitful like a dry creek, (deceitful: dishonest, dry creek: empty riverbed) **16.** darkened by ice, hidden in snow. (darkened: obscured, ice: frost, hidden: concealed) **17.** When they warm up, they vanish; in heat, they are gone. (warm up: melt, vanish: disappear, heat: warmth) **18.** Their paths turn aside, and they disappear. (paths: ways, turn aside: divert, disappear: fade) **19.** The people of Tema and Sheba waited for them, (Tema: a tribe, Sheba: a region) **20.** but they were ashamed when they were disappointed. (ashamed: embarrassed, disappointed: let down) **21.** Now you are all nothing; you see my misery and are afraid. (nothing: insignificant, misery: distress, afraid: fearful) **22.** Did I ask for anything from you? Did I ask for your wealth or help against my enemies? (ask: request, wealth: riches, help: assistance) **23.** Did I plead for you to rescue me or redeem me from the mighty? (plead: beg, rescue: save, redeem: deliver, mighty: powerful) **24.** Teach me, and I will be silent; help me understand where I've gone wrong. (teach: instruct, silent: quiet, understand: grasp, gone wrong: erred) **25.** How powerful are right words! But what does your arguing prove? (powerful: effective, right: correct, arguing: disputing, prove: demonstrate) **26.** Do you think you can correct my words or the speech of a man in despair, like wind? (correct: fix, speech: words, despair: hopelessness, wind: breath) **27.** You overwhelm the fatherless and dig a pit for your friend. (overwhelm: oppress, fatherless: orphaned, dig a pit: set a trap) **28.** Look at me and see the truth; you know I'm not lying. (look:

behold, truth: reality, lying: deceiving) **29.** Return to me, for my cause is righteous, (return: come back, cause: case, righteous: just) **30.** and there is no wrong in my speech. Can't my taste recognize what is false? (wrong: error, taste: discernment, false: untrue)

Chapter 7

1. "Is there not a time for man on earth? Are his days not like those of a hired worker? (Time: season, hired worker: laborer) **2.** As a servant longs for shade and a laborer for his pay, (servant: worker, longs: desires, pay: wages) **3.** So I am given months of misery and nights of pain. (Misery: suffering, pain: anguish) **4.** When I lie down, I wonder when I will rise, and the night drags on, full of restless tossing. (Lie down: recline, drag on: lingers, restless: uneasy, tossing: turning) **5.** My body is covered with worms and dust; my skin is broken and disgusting. (Covered: infested, worms: maggots, broken: shattered, disgusting: repulsive) **6.** My days pass faster than a weaver's shuttle, and they end in despair. (Pass: fly by, weaver's shuttle: loom tool, despair: hopelessness) **7.** Remember, my life is fleeting; my eyes will never see happiness again. (Fleeting: short-lived, happiness: joy) **8.** Those who see me now will never see me again; they look at me, but I'll be gone. (Look: gaze, gone: departed) **9.** Like a cloud that fades, I will go to the grave and never return. (Cloud: vapor, fades: dissipates, grave: tomb) **10.** I will not return to my house, and my place will forget me. **11.** I will speak out in my pain and complain in my soul's bitterness. (Speak out: cry out, pain: suffering, complain: lament, bitterness: sorrow) **12.** Am I like the sea or a sea monster that You keep watch over me? (sea monster: Leviathan, keep watch: guard) **13.** When I think my bed will bring relief and my couch will ease my pain, (relief: comfort, ease: soothe) **14.** You disturb me with dreams and frighten me with visions. (disturb: unsettle, frighten: scare, visions: nightmares) **15.** My soul would rather choose death than this constant torment. (choose: prefer, torment: suffering) **16.** I despise my life and do not want to live forever. Leave me alone, for my days are meaningless. (despise: loathe, meaningless: futile) **17.** Why do You care so much about man? Why do You focus on him? (care: concern, focus: pay attention) **18.** Why do You visit him every morning and test him continually? (visit: approach, test: try) **19.** How long will You not leave me alone, even until I swallow my saliva? (leave me alone: depart, swallow: gulp) **20.** I have sinned—what can I do to You, O God? Why have You made me Your target and a burden to myself? (sinned: wronged, target: focus, burden: weight) **21.** Why don't You forgive my sin and take away my wrongs? For I will soon lie in the dust, and when You seek me in the morning, I will be gone." (Forgive: pardon, wrongs: sins, seek: look for)

Chapter 8

1. Bildad the Shuhite responded: (responded: answered) **2.** "How long will you speak like this? How long will your words be like a strong wind? (speak: talk, words: speeches, strong wind: violent gust) **3.** Does God pervert justice? Does the Almighty twist what is right? (pervert: distort, Almighty: all-powerful, twist: corrupt) **4.** If your children sinned against God, He allowed their punishment. (sinned: wronged, allowed: permitted, punishment: retribution) **5.** If you seek God early and make your plea to the Almighty, (seek: search for, early: earnestly, plea: request) **6.** and if you are pure and upright, then God will restore you and bless your righteousness. (pure: clean, upright: righteous, restore: renew, bless: favor) **7.** Though your beginnings were humble, your end will prosper greatly. (Beginnings: start, humble: modest, end: outcome, prosper: succeed) **8.** Ask the generations before you, and learn from their fathers, (ask: inquire, generations: ancestors, learn: understand) **9.** for we are but a shadow on earth, knowing little. (Shadow: fleeting presence, knowing little: ignorant) **10.** Let them teach you and speak wisdom from the heart. (speak: impart, wisdom: understanding, heart: inner being) **11.** Can reeds grow without water? Can they thrive without mire? (reeds: plants, thrive: flourish, mire: mud) **12.** While still young and uncut, they wither before other plants. (young: tender, uncut: unharvested, wither: die, plants: crops) **13.** So it is with those who forget God; the hope of the hypocrite will perish. (forget: neglect, hypocrite: deceitful person, perish: vanish) **14.** His hope will be cut off, like a spider's web. (cut off: destroyed, spider's web: fragile structure) **15.** He will lean on his house, but it will not stand; he will grasp it, but it won't endure. (Lean: rely, house: home, stand: remain, endure: last) **16.** He flourishes in the sunlight, and his branches grow in his garden. (Flourishes: thrives, branches: offshoots, garden: field) **17.** His roots are tangled in the stones and around the pile of earth. (roots: foundation, tangled: entangled, stones: rocks, pile of earth: heap) **18.** If God removes him, his place will deny him, saying, "I never knew you." (removes: removes from, deny: refuse, place: position) **19.** This is the joy of his life, but others will rise from the earth in his place. (joy: happiness, rise: take his place) **20.** God will not reject a blameless man, nor help the wicked. (reject: cast aside, blameless: innocent, help: assist) **21.** He will fill your mouth with laughter and your lips with joy. **22.** Those who hate you will be clothed with shame, and the wicked's dwelling will be destroyed." (dwelling: house)

Chapter 9

1. Job answered: **2.** "I know this is true, but how can a man be just before God? **3.** If he contends with Him, he can't answer even one of a thousand questions. (Contends: argues,) **4.** God is wise and mighty; who can stand against Him and succeed? (Wise: knowledgeable, mighty: powerful, stand against: oppose, succeed: prevail) **5.** He moves mountains without their knowing, overturns them in anger. (Moves: shifts, overturns: topples, anger: fury) **6.** He shakes the earth from its place, and its pillars tremble. (Shakes: quakes, pillars: foundations) **7.** He commands the sun, and it doesn't rise; He seals the stars. (Commands: orders, rises: ascends, seals: holds in place) **8.** He alone spreads out the heavens and walks on the sea. (Spreads out: extends, heavens: sky) **9.** He made the constellations: Arcturus, Orion, and Pleiades, and the chambers of the south. (Constellations: star formations, chambers of the south: southern regions) **10.** He does great things beyond comprehension, wonders without number. (great things: marvelous acts, beyond comprehension: beyond understanding, wonders: miracles) **11.** He passes by me, and I don't see Him; He moves on, and I don't perceive Him. (Passes by: moves past, perceive: recognize) **12.** If He takes away, who can stop Him? Who can question His actions? (takes away: removes, question: challenge) **13.** If He doesn't withdraw His anger, even the proud helpers fall before Him. (Withdraw: turn away, helpers: assistants) **14.** How can I answer Him or choose my words to reason with Him? **15.** Even if I were righteous, I wouldn't answer but would plead for mercy with my Judge. (Righteous: innocent, plead for mercy: beg for forgiveness) **16.** If I called and He answered, I wouldn't believe He had listened to me. (Called: cried out, listened: heard) **17.** He breaks me with a storm and multiplies my wounds without cause. (Breaks: crushes, multiplies: increases, wounds: afflictions) **18.** He doesn't let me breathe, but fills me with bitterness. (Breathe: rest, bitterness: sorrow) **19.** If I speak of strength, He is stronger; if I speak of judgment, who can set a time to plead? (strength: power, judgment: justice, set a time: designate a moment) **20.** If I justify myself, my own words condemn me; if I claim perfection, it proves me corrupt. (Justify: defend, condemn: accuse, claim: assert, proves: shows) **21.** Even if I were perfect, I wouldn't know my soul; I would despise my life. (Perfect: blameless, despise: loathe) **22.** God destroys both the perfect and the wicked. (Destroys: annihilates, wicked: evil) **23.** If a sudden calamity strikes, He laughs at the trial of the innocent. (Calamity: disaster, strikes: hits, trial: suffering) **24.** The earth is in the hands of the wicked; He hides the faces of the judges—if not, where is He? (in the hands of: controlled by, hides: conceals, faces of the judges: authority of the rulers) **25.** My days are faster than a runner; they vanish without hope. (Faster: quicker, vanish: disappear, without hope: hopeless) **26.** They pass like ships or like an eagle rushing to its prey. (pass: move, rushing: flying swiftly) **27.** If I try to forget my complaint and comfort myself, (forget: dismiss, complaint: grievance) **28.** I fear my suffering will prove I'm guilty, and You won't hold me innocent. (fear: worry, suffering: pain, prove: show, hold me innocent: declare me innocent) **29.** If I'm wicked, why am I trying so hard in vain? (wicked: sinful, in vain: without result) **30.** If I wash myself with snow and make my hands clean, (wash: cleanse, snow: snowflakes) **31.** You will plunge me into a pit, and even my clothes will reject me. (plunge: throw, pit: grave, reject: disown) **32.** He is not a man like me that I should answer Him or come together in judgment. (man: human, answer: respond, come together: meet) **33.** There is no mediator between us to bring us together. (mediator: intermediary, bring us together: reconcile) **34.** Let God remove His rod from me, and let His terror not frighten me. (rod: discipline, terror: fear) **35.** Then I could speak without fear, but it is not so with me." (speak: respond, fear: dread).

Chapter 10
1. My soul is exhausted with life; I'll leave my complaint to myself and speak from the bitterness of my heart. (Bitterness: anger) **2.** I'll ask God, "Don't condemn me; show me why You argue with me. (Condemn: judge) **3.** Is it right for You to oppress me, to despise the work of Your hands, and favor the plans of the wicked? (Oppose: harm, despise: hate) **4.** Do You have human eyes? Do You see as we see? **5.** Are Your days like ours, and Your years like human years? **6.** Why do You search for my sin and look into my wrongs? (sin: wrongdoing, wrongs: faults) **7.** You know I'm not wicked, and no one can rescue me from Your power. (wicked: evil, rescue: save) **8.** You created me and shaped me, yet You destroy me. (destroy: ruin) **9.** Remember, You made me from clay; will You return me to dust? (clay: earth, return: bring back) **10.** You poured me out like milk and made me into a solid form, like cheese. (poured out: spilled, solid: firm) **11.** You clothed me with flesh and skin, and You built my bones and sinews. (sinews: tendons) **12.** You gave me life, favor, and protection; Your care has preserved my spirit. (preserved: kept safe) **13.** These things are hidden in Your heart, and I know they're with You. (hidden: concealed) **14.** If I sin, You mark it and won't forgive me. (mark: note, forgive: pardon) **15.** If I'm wicked, woe to me; if I'm righteous, I still can't lift my head in pride, for I am confused by my suffering. (woe: trouble, righteous: good) **16.** My suffering increases; You pursue me like a lion, showing Your power against me. (pursue: chase, power: strength) **17.** You renew Your accusations against me, and Your anger grows. I face changes and constant battle. (accusations: charges, anger: wrath) **18.** Why did You bring me into life if it's like this? I wish I had died at birth, unseen by anyone. (unseen: unnoticed) **19.** I should have never existed, but been taken straight from the womb to the grave. (womb: mother's body, grave: tomb) **20.** Aren't my days few? Leave me alone so I can find some comfort, (comfort: rest) **21.** before I go to the land of darkness, the shadow of death, (darkness: gloom, shadow of death: deep darkness) **22.** a land where darkness is the only thing, and where even light is as dark as night. (Darkness: gloom, light: brightness)

Chapter 11
1. Then Zophar the Naamathite answered and said: (Naamathite: a person from the town of Naamah) **2.** Shouldn't you be answered for all your words? Can a man full of talk be justified? (Answered: held accountable, talk: words, justified: declared righteous) **3.** Should your lies silence others? When you mock, should no one be ashamed? (Lies: falsehoods, silence: shut down, mock: ridicule, ashamed: embarrassed) **4.** You claim your doctrine is pure and that you are clean in God's sight. (doctrine: teaching, clean: innocent) **5.** But I wish God would speak and open His lips to correct you. (speak: respond, open His lips: speak out, correct: rebuke) **6.** He would show you the deep secrets of wisdom, which are far beyond what you know. Know this: God is giving you less punishment than your sins deserve. (deep secrets: hidden depths, far beyond: far greater, punishment: retribution, deserve: warrant) **7.** Can you search out God? Can you find out the Almighty completely? (search out: understand, find out: grasp, completely: fully) **8.** His wisdom is higher than the heavens—what can you do? It's deeper than the grave—what can you know? (higher: exalted, deeper: profound, grave: realm of the dead) **9.** His reach is longer than the earth and wider than the sea. (reach: extent, longer: greater, wider: broader) **10.** If He decides to close something off, or gather something, who can stop Him? (decides: determines, close something off: shut it down, gather: collect) **11.** He knows people's thoughts and sees wickedness—won't He take that into account? (Knows: understands, sees: observes, wickedness: evil) **12.** A man born of a woman is foolish and ignorant, like a wild donkey's colt. (Foolish: foolish, ignorant: unwise) **13.** If you prepare your heart and stretch your hands to Him, (prepare: ready, stretch: reach out) **14.** if you remove wickedness from your life, and don't let it dwell in your home, (remove: eliminate, wickedness: evil, dwell: live) **15.** then you will lift your face without shame, and you will stand firm without fear. (lift your face: raise your head, stand firm: remain steadfast) **16.** You will forget your suffering, remembering it like water that has passed. (Suffering: pain, remembering: recalling, passed: gone by) **17.** Your life will be brighter than noon, and you will shine like the morning sun. (Brighter: more radiant, noon: midday, shine: glow) **18.** You will be secure, because there is hope. You will rest safely. (Secure: safe, hope: confidence, rest safely: lie down in peace) **19.** You will lie down, and no one will make you afraid. Many will seek your favor. (Lie down: sleep, make you afraid: disturb you, seek your favor: desire your approval) **20.** But the wicked will lose hope, their eyes will fail, and they will have no escape. Their hope will be like the breath leaving their body. (Lose hope: despair, fail: fade, no escape: perish, hope: expectation).

Chapter 12
1. Job replied: **2.** You think you are the wise ones, but wisdom will die with you. (wise ones: sages, die with you: depart with you) **3.** I also have understanding, and I'm not inferior to you. Who doesn't know what you say? (Understanding: knowledge, inferior: lesser) **4.** I am like someone mocked by his friends, one who calls to God and is answered, while the righteous man is scorned. (Mocked: ridiculed, scorned: despised) **5.** The one who is about to fall is seen as a light to be extinguished by those who are comfortable. (About to fall: on the verge of ruin, extinguished: snuffed out, comfortable: secure) **6.** The tents of robbers prosper, and those who provoke God are secure. God brings them great wealth. (Tents: dwellings, robbers: thieves, provoke: challenge, wealth: riches) **7.** But ask the animals, and they will teach you; ask the birds, and they will tell you **8.** Speak to the earth, and it will teach you; or ask the fish of the sea, and they will declare it. (Declare: reveal) **9.** Everyone knows that the Lord created all this. **10.** In His hand is the life of every living thing and the breath of all mankind. **11.** Doesn't the ear test words as the mouth tastes food? **12.** Wisdom is found with the elderly, and understanding comes with length of life. (length of life: experience) **13.** With God is wisdom and strength; He has counsel and understanding. (counsel: guidance) **14.** If He breaks something down, it can't be rebuilt. If He locks someone up, no one can set them free. (breaks down: destroys, locks up: imprisons, set them free: release) **15.** He can withhold the waters and cause them to dry up; He can send them and flood the earth. (Withhold: restrain, cause to dry up: make evaporate, flood: overwhelm) **16.** God has strength and wisdom; He controls both the deceived and the deceiver. (strength: power, deceived: misled, deceiver: liar) **17.** He leads counselors away spoiled and makes judges look foolish. (counselors: advisors, spoiled: ruined, judges: rulers) **18.** He loosens the bonds of kings and wraps them in a belt. (loosens: loosens, bonds: chains, wraps in a belt: binds) **19.** He leads princes away as captives and overthrows the mighty. (princes: nobles, captives: prisoners, overthrows: topples) **20.** He removes speech from trusted advisors and takes understanding from the aged. (speech: eloquence, takes understanding: removes wisdom) **21.** He pours contempt on rulers

and weakens the strength of the mighty. (Pours contempt: scorns, weakens: diminishes, strength: power) **22.** He uncovers deep secrets and brings darkness into the light. (Uncovers: reveals, deep secrets: hidden things, darkness into the light: exposes the unknown) **23.** He increases and destroys nations; He enlarges and shrinks them. (Increases: enlarges, destroys: ruins, nations: countries) **24.** He removes the understanding of the leaders of the earth and makes them wander in uncharted wilderness. (Removes: takes away, understanding: wisdom, wander: roam, uncharted: unknown) **25.** They grope in the darkness without light, and He causes them to stumble like drunken men. (Grope: feel around, stumble: fall, drunken: intoxicated)

Chapter 13
1. I have seen and heard all this; I understand it just as you do. I'm not inferior to you. (Understand: comprehend, inferior: lesser) **2.** What you know, I know as well. **3.** I want to speak to the Almighty and reason with God. (Almighty: God) **4.** But you are all deceivers, pretending to be healers but offering no real help. (Deceivers: liars, healers: helpers, offering: providing) **5.** I wish you would just be silent—it would be wiser. (Silent: quiet, wiser: more prudent) **6.** Listen to my reasoning and the words I speak. (Reasoning: argument, words: speech) **7.** Are you speaking wrongly on behalf of God? Are you deceiving people for Him? (Speaking wrongly: misrepresenting, deceiving: misleading) **8.** Will you show favoritism to God? Will you argue on His behalf? (Favoritism: bias, argue: defend) **9.** Is it good for God to search you out? Are you mocking Him like you mock one another? (Search you out: examine, mocking: ridiculing) **10.** He will surely rebuke you if you show partiality. (rebuke: correct, partiality: favoritism) **11.** Shouldn't His majesty make you afraid? Shouldn't His terror fall on you? (Majesty: greatness, terror: fear) **12.** Your memories are like ashes, and your bodies like clay. (Memories: recollections, ashes: dust) **13.** Be quiet and let me speak, no matter what happens. (happens: occurs) **14.** Why should I risk my life and hold my soul in my hands? (Risk: jeopardize, soul: life) **15.** Even if He kills me, I will still trust Him; I will argue my case before Him. (Kills: takes my life, trust: have faith in, argue: plead) **16.** He will be my salvation; no hypocrite can stand before Him. (Salvation: deliverance, hypocrite: deceiver) **17.** Listen carefully to my words and the way I argue. (Carefully: attentively, argue: present my case) **18.** I know my case is just, and I'm confident that I will be justified. (case: cause, just: right, justified: proven innocent) **19.** Who will argue with me? If I remain silent, I will die. (argue: contend, remain silent: stay quiet) **20.** Just two things I ask: (things: requests) **21.** Take Your hand away from me, and stop frightening me. (hand: judgment, frightening: terrifying) **22.** Then call to me, and I'll answer, or let me speak, and You answer me. (call to me: summon me, answer: respond) **23.** How many wrongs and sins have I committed? Show me my sin. (Wrongs: offenses, sins: transgressions) **24.** Why do You hide Your face from me? Why do You treat me as Your enemy? (Hide your face: withdraw Your presence, treat: regard, enemy: adversary) **25.** Will You torment me like a leaf tossed by the wind, or pursue me like dry straw? (torment: afflict, tossed: blown, pursue: chase) **26.** You've written harsh things about me and made me carry the consequences of my youth. (Harsh: severe, consequences: repercussions) **27.** You put my feet in the stocks and watch every step I take. You leave a mark on the heels of my feet. (stocks: restraints, watch: observe, mark: trace) **28.** My body decays like something rotten, like a garment eaten by moths. (decays: deteriorates, rotten: spoiled, eaten by moths: consumed by insects).

Chapter 14
1. People are born with a short life, full of trouble. (Born: come into existence, short life: brief existence, trouble: hardship) **2.** They are like flowers that bloom and are quickly cut down, or like shadows that disappear and don't last. (Bloom: flourish, quickly: rapidly, disappear: vanish, last: endure) **3.** Why do You focus on someone like me, bringing me to judgment? (Focus: pay attention to, bringing: leading, judgment: trial) **4.** Who can make something pure from something unclean? No one. (Pure: clean, unclean: impure) **5.** Our days are numbered by You; You decide how long we live and set boundaries we cannot cross. (Numbered: counted, decide: determine, boundaries: limits, cross: surpass) **6.** Leave me alone, so I can rest, like a worker finishing their day. (Leave me alone: stop troubling me, rest: find peace) **7.** There's hope for a tree—it may be cut down, but it can sprout again, and its branches will grow back. (Hope: possibility, sprout: grow, grow back: regenerate) **8.** Even if its roots are old and the stump dies, (roots: base, stump: remainder) **9.** With water, it can bloom and produce new branches. (Bloom: flower, produce: grow) **10.** But when a person dies, they waste away—when they breathe their last, where do they go? **11.** Just like water that dries up, people lie down and don't rise again until the heavens are no more. (Dries up: evaporates, lie down: fall asleep, rise again: awaken) **12.** They will not wake up or be raised from their sleep. (Wake up: rouse, raised: revived) **13.** Oh, if only You would hide me in the grave, keep me secret until Your anger passes, and then remember me! (Hide: conceal, grave: tomb, secret: hidden, anger: wrath, remember: restore) **14.** If a person dies, can they live again? I'll wait for my change to come. (Live again: return to life, change: transformation) **15.** You will call, and I will answer; You will desire the work of Your hands. (Call: summon, answer: respond, desire: take pleasure in, work: creation) **16.** You count my steps and keep track of my sin. (Count: measure, keep track: record, sin: wrongdoing) **17.** My sins are sealed in a bag, and You have tied them up. (sealed: enclosed, bag: pouch, tied up: secured) **18.** Just like a mountain collapsing and a rock being moved from its place, (collapsing: crumbling, moved: shifted, place: position) **19.** You wear away what's strong, and destroy the hope of man. (wear away: erode, destroy: undo, hope: expectation) **20.** You overpower him forever, and he passes away. You change his appearance and send him away. (Overpower: dominate, passes away: dies, change: alter, send away: remove) **21.** His children may prosper, but he doesn't know it; if they are brought low, he doesn't perceive it. (Prosper: succeed, brought low: humbled, perceive: recognize) **22.** His body suffers, and his soul mourns within him. (Suffers: endures pain, mourns: grieves, soul: spirit).

Chapter 15
1. Then Eliphaz the Temanite answered and said: **2.** should a wise man speak empty words and fill his belly with useless ideas? (Empty: meaningless, useless: futile, ideas: notions) **3.** Should he reason with useless talk or with words that don't help? **4.** You reject fear and stop praying to God. (reject: dismiss, fear: reverence, stop: cease) **5.** Your words reveal your wickedness, and you speak deceitfully. (reveal: expose, wickedness: evil, deceitfully: falsely) **6.** Your own mouth condemns you, not I; your words testify against you. (condemns: accuses, testify: bear witness) **7.** Are you the first man ever born? Were you made before the hills? **8.** Have you heard the secret of God? Do you keep all wisdom to yourself? (Secret: counsel, keep: hoard) **9.** What do you know that we don't? What do you understand that we haven't heard? (Know: comprehend, understand: grasp, heard: learned) **10.** We have wise, older men here, many who are older than your father. (Wise: knowledgeable, older men: elders, father: ancestor) **11.** Do you think God's comfort is too small for you? Do you have special knowledge? (Comfort: solace, special: exclusive) **12.** Why does your heart deceive you? Why do you look away and speak against God? (Deceive: mislead, look away: turn away, speak against: accuse) **13.** What is a person that they can be pure? What is a human born of woman that they can be righteous? (Righteous: just) **14.** God doesn't trust His angels; even the heavens are not pure in His sight. (Trust: rely on, pure: spotless, sight: eyes) **15.** How much more unclean and sinful is a man who drinks iniquity like water? (Unclean: impure, sinful: wicked, drinks: absorbs, iniquity: sin) **16.** Listen to me, I'll show you what I've seen, (seen: witnessed) **17.** What wise men have passed down from their fathers and didn't hide it.

(Passed down: handed down, fathers: ancestors didn't hide: openly shared) **18.** They were the ones to whom the earth was given, and no strangers passed among them. **19.** The wicked live in pain all their days, and their years are hidden from the oppressor. (Wicked: evildoers, pain: suffering, hidden: concealed, oppressor: tyrant) **20.** A terrifying sound fills their ears; in times of prosperity, destruction comes upon them. (Terrifying: dreadful, fills: overwhelms, prosperity: success, destruction: ruin) **21.** They don't believe they will return from darkness; they wait for the sword to strike. (Darkness: trouble, sword: judgment). **22.** They wander for food, asking, "Where is it?" They know the day of darkness is near. (Wander: search, food: sustenance, day of darkness: time of calamity) **23.** Trouble and fear overwhelm them, as a king facing a battle. (Trouble: distress, fear: dread, overwhelm: engulf, facing: confronting) **24.** They strike out against God, strengthening themselves against the Almighty. (Strike out: rebel, strengthening: emboldening, Almighty: God) **25.** They charge at Him, with their necks stiff, their shields strong. (Charge: attack, necks stiff: defiant, shields: defenses). **26.** They cover themselves with their fatness and fatten their sides with excess. (Cover: surround, fatness: abundance, fatten: enrich) **27.** They live in ruins, in desolate cities and houses that are ready to collapse. (Ruins: decay, desolate: forsaken, collapse: fall) **28.** They won't be wealthy; their wealth won't last, and their prosperity won't last on earth. (Wealthy: rich, last: endure, prosperity: success) **29.** They will not escape darkness; fire will consume their branches, and they will wither away. (escape: avoid, consume: destroy, branches: offshoots, wither away: perish) **30.** Let no one deceived trust in false hopes—they will be rewarded with emptiness. (Deceived: misled, false: empty, hopes: expectations) **31.** Their punishment will come quickly, and their branch will not thrive. (Punishment: retribution, thrive: prosper) **32.** They will shake off their unripe fruit like a vine, and cast off their flowers like an olive tree. (Shake off: drop, unripe: immature, cast off: discard, flowers: blossoms) **33.** The homes of the wicked will be destroyed by fire, and the corrupt will be consumed. (Destroyed: devastated, consumed: destroyed) **34.** They conceive evil and give birth to lies, their lives are filled with deceit. (Conceive: conceive, evil: wickedness, give birth to: produce, deceit: falsehood) **35.** Their hearts prepare mischief and their bellies are filled with deceit. (Prepare: devise, mischief: wickedness, bellies: hearts).

Chapter 16
1. Then Job answered and said: **2.** I have heard many such things; you're all miserable comforters. (Miserable: wretched, comforters: consolers) **3.** Do empty words ever end? What makes you so bold to answer me? (Bold: arrogant) **4.** I could speak like you, if your positions were reversed. I could heap up words against you and shake my head at you. (Positions: places, reversed: switched, heap up: pile up, shake my head: mock) **5.** But instead, I would comfort you with my words and ease your grief with my lips. (Comfort: console, ease: alleviate, grief: sorrow) **6.** Even if I speak, my grief is not relieved; and if I stay silent, what do I gain? (Grief: sorrow, relieved: eased, stay silent: remain quiet, gain: benefit) **7.** But now, God has made me weary, and you've made me desolate. (Weary: exhausted, desolate: forsaken) **8.** My suffering is a witness against me; my thinness testifies to my pain. (Suffering: agony, witness: testimony, thinness: emaciation, testifies: bears witness) **9.** He tears me apart in His wrath; He gnashes His teeth at me. My enemy looks at me with hatred. (Tears apart: rends, wrath: anger, gnashes: grinds, looks: glares) **10.** They gape at me with their mouths, strike me on the cheek with contempt, and gather against me. (Strike: slap, contempt: disdain) **11.** God has delivered me to the wicked and handed me over to the ungodly. (Delivered: given, wicked: evil, handed over: surrendered) **12.** I was at ease, but He has shattered me. He grabbed me by the neck and shook me to pieces, setting me up as His target. (ease: comfort, shattered: crushed, grabbed: seized, target: mark) **13.** His archers surround me and tear at me without mercy, pouring out my insides on the ground. (Archers: bowmen, surround: encircle, tear at: rip, mercy: compassion, pouring out: spilling) **14.** He breaks me with repeated blows, attacking me like a warrior. (breaks: crushes, repeated: successive, blows: strikes, warrior: soldier) **15.** I have clothed myself in sackcloth and covered my head in the dust. (Clothed: donned, sackcloth: mourning clothes, covered: veiled) **16.** My face is swollen with weeping, and my eyelids are shadowed by death. (Swollen: puffed, weeping: crying, eyelids: lashes, shadowed: darkened) **17.** I have not wronged anyone, and my prayer is pure. (Wronged: harmed, prayer: plea) **18.** O earth, do not cover my blood, and let my cry not be hidden. (Cover: conceal, cry: plea) **19.** Even now, my witness is in heaven, and my record is on high. (Witness: testimony, record: account) **20.** My friends mock me, but my tears are poured out to God. (Mock: ridicule, poured out: spilled) **21.** Oh, that someone would plead with God for me, as a man pleads for his friend! (plead: intercede, friend: companion) **22.** For when my few years are finished, I will go the way from which I will never return.

Chapter 17
1. My breath is corrupt, my days are numbered, and the grave is ready for me. (Breath: life, corrupt: foul, numbered: limited, grave: tomb, ready: prepared) **2.** Are there not mockers around me? Does my eye not continue to see their insults? (Mockers: scorners, insults: taunts) **3.** Lay down a pledge for me with yourself; who will stand as my guarantor? (Pledge: security, guarantor: surety) **4.** You have hidden their hearts from understanding, so You will not exalt them. (Hidden: concealed, hearts: minds, exalt: raise) **5.** He who speaks flattery to his friends, even his children will be brought to shame. (Flattery: praise, children: offspring, brought to shame: disgraced) **6.** He has made me a byword for the people, and once I was like a drum, a symbol of joy. (Byword: proverb, drum: tambourine, symbol: sign, joy: celebration) **7.** My eyes are dim with sorrow, and my whole body is a shadow. (Dim: clouded, sorrow: grief, shadow: faint image) **8.** Upright people are appalled at this, and the innocent will rise up against the hypocrite. (Upright: righteous, appalled: horrified, hypocrite: pretender) **9.** But the righteous will keep going on his way, and the one with clean hands will grow stronger. (Righteous: just, keep going: persevere) **10.** But as for you all, come back and try again, for I cannot find a wise man among you. (come back: return, try again: attempt again, wise man: sage) **11.** My days are past, my plans are shattered, even the thoughts of my heart. (Past: over, shattered: ruined, thoughts: intentions, heart: mind) **12.** They turn night into day, and the light is short because of the darkness. (Turn: make, darkness: gloom) **13.** If I wait for death, the grave will be my home; I have made my bed in darkness. (wait: expect, home: resting place, darkness: despair) **14.** I say to the grave, "You are my father," and to the worm, "You are my mother and sister." **15.** Where is my hope now? Who can see any hope for me? (Hope: expectation, see: perceive) **16.** They will go down to the grave's gates, when we all rest together in the dust. (Grave's gates: entrance to the grave, rest together: lie together, dust: earth)

Chapter 18
1. Then Bildad the Shuhite replied, **2.** How long will you speak like this? Let us listen, and then we will respond. **3.** Why are we treated like animals, regarded as vile in your eyes? (Treated: seen, regarded: considered, vile: despicable) **4.** You tear yourself in your anger. Will the earth be abandoned for you? Will the rock be moved from its place? (Tear yourself: harm yourself, abandoned: forsaken, rock: foundation) **5.** The light of the wicked will be extinguished, and the spark of his fire will go out. (Light: hope, extinguished: quenched, spark: flame, fire: passion) **6.** His dwelling will be dark, and his lamp will go out. (Dwelling: home, dark: gloomy, lamp: light) **7.** His power will be weakened, and his own plans will bring him down. (Weakened: diminished, plans: schemes bring him down: destroy him) **8.** He is caught in a net by his own feet and walks into a trap. (Caught: ensnared, net: snare, trap: pitfall) **9.** The snare will take him

by the heel, and the robber will overpower him. (Snares: traps, heel: foot, overpower: defeat) **10.** A trap is set for him on the ground, and there's a snare in his path. (Trap: snare, set: placed, path: way) **11.** Terrors will surround him, driving him to his feet. (Terrors: fears, surround: encircle, driving: forcing) **12.** His strength will be hungry, and destruction is at his side. (Strength: power, hungry: lacking, destruction: ruin) **13.** His skin will be devoured by disease; the firstborn of death will consume his strength. (Devoured: consumed, disease: sickness, firstborn of death: death's harbinger, consume: drain) **14.** His confidence will be uprooted from his tent, and he will be brought to the king of terrors. (Confidence: security, uprooted: removed, tent: dwelling, king of terrors: death) **15.** Brimstone will be scattered on his dwelling. (Brimstone: sulfur, scattered: scattered, dwelling: home). **16.** His roots will dry up beneath him, and his branches will be cut off above. (Roots: foundation, dry up: wither, branches: limbs) **17.** His memory will vanish from the earth, and he will have no name in the streets. (Memory: remembrance, vanish: disappear) **18.** He will be driven from light into darkness, chased out of the world. (Light: hope, chased out: exiled, world: existence). **19.** He will have no descendants among his people, nor any left in his home. (Descendants: offspring, people: family, home: household). **20.** Those who come after him will be astonished at his fate, as those before were terrified. (Astonished: amazed, fate: end, terrified: horrified) **21.** This is the fate of the wicked, the place of those who do not know God. (Fate: end, wicked: ungodly, place: destiny, do not know God: reject God).

Chapter 19
1. Job replied, **2.** "How long will you torment me and crush me with words? (Torment: afflict, crush: oppress) **3.** You've insulted me ten times without shame, treating me like a stranger. (Insulted: mocked, without shame: relentlessly, stranger: outsider) **4.** Even if I've sinned, that's my concern alone. (Sinned: wronged, concern: responsibility) **5.** If you exalt yourselves over me and blame me for my suffering, (exalt: lift yourselves up, blame: accuse, suffering: affliction) **6.** Know that God has brought me low and trapped me in His net. (Brought me low: humbled me trapped: ensnared) **7.** I cry for help, but no one listens; I call for justice, but it doesn't come. (Cry for help: plead, justice: fairness) **8.** He has blocked my way and plunged me into darkness. (Blocked: obstructed, plunged: cast, darkness: despair) **9.** He has stripped me of honor and taken my crown. (Stripped: removed, honor: dignity, crown: glory) **10.** He's destroyed me completely, uprooting my hope like a tree. (Destroyed: shattered, uprooting: severing, hope: expectation) **11.** His anger burns against me; He counts me as an enemy. (Anger: wrath, burns: rages, counts: regards, enemy: foe) **12.** His forces surround me, attacking and laying siege to my tent. (Forces: troops, surround: encircle, attacking: assaulting, laying siege: besieging) **13.** My relatives have abandoned me; my friends have turned away. (Abandoned: forsaken, turned away: deserted) **14.** My family fails me, and my closest friends have forgotten me. (Fails: rejects, forgotten: neglected) **15.** My household sees me as a stranger; to them, I'm like a foreigner. (Household: family, stranger: outsider, foreigner: alien) **16.** I call my servant, but he doesn't answer—even when I beg. (Servant: attendant, doesn't answer: ignores, beg: plead) **17.** My own wife finds me repulsive, though I pleaded for her compassion. (Repulsive: revolting, pleaded: begged, compassion: mercy) **18.** Even children mock me, speaking against me when I rise. (mock: ridicule, speaking against: slandering) **19.** My closest friends despise me; those I love have turned on me. (despise: scorn, turned on: betrayed) **20.** My body is wasting away; I barely survive. (Wasting away: deteriorating, barely survive: barely endure) **21.** Have mercy, my friends, for God's hand has struck me. (Mercy: compassion, struck: afflicted) **22.** Why do you persecute me as God does? Isn't my suffering enough? (persecute: oppress, suffering: affliction) **23.** Oh, that my words were written and engraved forever in stone! (engraved: inscribed, forever: eternally) **24.** That they were carved with an iron tool and lead into rock! (carved: etched, iron tool: chisel, rock: stone) **25.** But I know my Redeemer lives, and in the end, He will stand on the earth. (Redeemer: Savior, lives: is alive, end: last days, stand: appear) **26.** Even after my body is destroyed, in my flesh, I will see God. (destroyed: decayed, flesh: body) **27.** I will see Him with my own eyes—I, and not another. My heart yearns for this! (see: behold, eyes: sight, yearns: longs) **28.** So why do you say, 'Let's pursue him,' when the truth is within me? (pursue: chase, truth: righteousness, within me: in my heart) **29.** Fear the sword yourselves, for God's wrath brings judgment!" (sword: judgment, wrath: anger, brings: delivers).

Chapter 20
1. Then Zophar the Naamathite replied, **2.** "My thoughts compel me to respond, and I can't hold back. (compel: urge, respond: reply, hold back: restrain) **3.** I've heard your rebuke, and my understanding prompts my answer. (rebuke: criticism, understanding: wisdom, prompts: urges) **4.** Don't you know that since the beginning of mankind, (beginning: foundation, mankind: humanity) **5.** The triumph of the wicked is brief, and the joy of the hypocrite lasts only a moment? (triumph: victory, wicked: ungodly, hypocrite: deceiver, lasts: endures) **6.** Even if he rises to the heavens and his head touches the clouds, (rises: ascends, heavens: sky, touches: reaches) **7.** He will perish forever like waste; those who saw him will ask, 'Where is he?' (perish: vanish, waste: refuse, saw: witnessed, ask: wonder) **8.** He will vanish like a dream, chased away like a night vision. (vanish: disappear, chased away: driven off, night vision: dream) **9.** The eye that saw him will see him no more, and his place will remember him no longer. (eye: sight, remember: recall) **10.** His children will seek favor from the poor, and his wealth will be restored to others. (seek favor: beg, wealth: riches, restored: returned) **11.** The sins of his youth fill his bones and go with him to the grave. (sins: transgressions, fill: consume, grave: death) **12.** Though wickedness tastes sweet and he hides it under his tongue, (wickedness: wrongdoing, tastes: feels, hides: conceals, under his tongue: secretly) **13.** Refusing to let it go, (refusing: clinging, let it go: release it) **14.** It will turn sour in his stomach and become poison within him. (turn sour: sour, poison: toxin) **15.** He swallows riches but will vomit them out; God will force them from him. (swallow: consume, vomit: reject, force: take away) **16.** He will taste the poison of serpents; the viper's tongue will kill him. (taste: experience, poison: venom, serpents: snakes, viper's tongue: snakebite) **17.** He will not see streams of honey and butter. (streams: rivers, honey and butter: abundance) **18.** What he gained, he must give back without enjoying it. (gained: acquired, give back: return, enjoying: savoring) **19.** For he oppressed the poor and stole what was not his to build his house. (Oppressed: exploited, stole: took, not his: unjustly, build: construct) **20.** His greed will leave him restless; his desires will not be fulfilled. (Greed: avarice, restless: unsettled, desires: cravings, fulfilled: satisfied) **21.** Nothing will remain of his wealth; no one will want what's left. (Remain: be left, want: desire) **22.** In his abundance, he will be in distress; the wicked will attack him. (Abundance: plenty, distress: trouble, attack: assail) **23.** When he fills his belly, God's wrath will rain down upon him. (Fill: satisfy, wrath: anger, rain down: pour) **24.** He will flee from an iron weapon, but a bronze arrow will strike him down. (Flee: escape, bronze arrow: weapon, strike down) **25.** The arrow is pulled from his body, glittering as it exits; terror surrounds him. (Pulled: extracted, glittering: shining, exits: leaves, terror: fear) **26.** Darkness will consume him; fire will destroy what remains of his tent. (Consume: engulf, destroy: burn, remains: belongings) **27.** Heaven will expose his guilt, and earth will rise against him. (Expose: reveal, guilt: shame, rise against: rebel) **28.** His wealth will vanish in the day of God's wrath. (Vanish: disappear, wrath: fury) **29.** This is the fate of the wicked, the portion God has decreed for them." (Fate: destiny, portion: lot, decreed: determined).

Chapter 21

1. But Job replied, 2. "Listen carefully to my words; let this be your comfort to me. (Listen carefully: pay attention, comfort: consolation) 3. Allow me to speak, and after I'm done, you may mock if you wish. (Allow: permit, mock: ridicule) 4. Is my complaint directed to man? If it were, why wouldn't my spirit be troubled? (Complaint: grievance, directed: aimed at, troubled: distressed) 5. Look at me and be shocked; cover your mouths in silence. (Shocked: astounded, cover your mouths: stop speaking, silence: quietness) 6. When I remember, fear grips me, and my body trembles. (Remembers: recall, grips: seizes, trembles: shakes) 7. Why do the wicked live long, grow old, and grow strong? (Wicked: ungodly, grow old: age, grow strong: become powerful) 8. Their children flourish before them, and their descendants thrive. (Flourish: prosper, thrive: succeed) 9. Their homes are safe from fear; God's rod does not strike them. (Rod: punishment, strike: hit) 10. Their bulls breed without fail, and their cows calve without miscarrying. (Bulls: cattle, breed: reproduce, calve: give birth, miscarrying: losing offspring) 11. They send their children out like a flock; their little ones dance with joy. (Flock: group, little ones: children). 12. They sing to the tambourine and harp, and rejoice to the sound of the pipe. (Rejoice: celebrate, pipe: flute) 13. They spend their days in prosperity and go to the grave in peace. (Prosperity: abundance, peace: tranquility) 14. Yet they say to God, 'Leave us alone! We want nothing to do with Your ways. (Leave us alone: depart from us, nothing to do with: no concern for) 15. Who is the Almighty, that we should serve Him? What benefit is there in prayer to Him?' (Benefit: gain, prayer: supplication) 16. But their prosperity is not in their own power; I reject the advice of the wicked. (Prosperity: success, reject: dismiss, advice: counsel) 17. How often is the lamp of the wicked snuffed out? How often does calamity overtake them? (Snuffed out: extinguished, calamity: disaster, overtake: engulf) 18. They are like straw blown by the wind, like chaff carried away by a storm. (Straw: hay, chaff: husks, carried away: swept away) 19. God stores up their punishment for their children, but He repays the wicked directly so they will know it. (Stores up: reserves, punishment: judgment, repays: recompenses) 20. They will see their destruction and drink the wrath of the Almighty. (Destruction: ruin, drink: experience, wrath: anger) 21. What do they care about their family after death, when their time is cut short? (care: concern, cut short: shortened) 22. Can anyone teach God knowledge, since He judges even the highest? (Teach: instruct, knowledge: wisdom, judges: evaluates, highest: exalted) 23. One man dies in strength, at ease and secure, (strength: vigor, ease: comfort, secure: safe) 24. With a healthy body and strong bones. (Healthy: robust, strong: powerful, bones: frame) 25. Another dies in bitterness, never tasting joy. (bitterness: sorrow, tasting: experiencing, joy: happiness) 26. Both lie down in the dust, covered by worms. (lie down: rest, covered: enveloped) 27. I know what you're thinking and the wrong conclusions you're drawing about me. (wrong conclusions: misguided judgments, drawing: making) 28. You ask, 'Where is the house of the prince? Where is the tent of the wicked?' (House: dwelling, prince: ruler, tent: residence). 29. Have you not asked those who travel? Do you not recognize their testimony: (testimony: witness) 30. The wicked are spared from the day of disaster and rescued from wrath. (Spared: delivered, disaster: calamity, rescued: saved) 31. Who confronts them with their deeds? Who repays them for their actions? (Confronts: challenges, deeds: actions, repays: rewards, actions: behavior) 32. Yet they are carried to their graves, and their tombs are guarded. (Carried: taken, guarded: protected) 33. The soil of the valley feels soft to them, and many follow after them, as countless others have gone before. (Soil: earth, feels: seems, follow after: pursue, countless: innumerable) 34. So how can you comfort me with empty words, when your answers are full of lies?" (Empty words: meaningless talk, answers: responses, full of lies: deceitful).

Chapter 22

1. Then Eliphaz the Temanite replied, 2. "Can a man benefit God? Even the wise benefit only themselves. (Benefit: add value, wise: knowledgeable, themselves: personally) 3. Does the Almighty gain anything from your righteousness or perfection? (Righteousness: moral uprightness, perfection: faultlessness) 4. Will He rebuke you or take you to court because of fear? (Rebuke: reprimand, court: legal action, fear: reverence) 5. Isn't your wickedness great and your sins endless? (Wickedness: evil, great: immense, sins: transgressions, endless: without end) 6. You took pledges from your brothers without cause and stripped the poor of their clothing. (Pledges: promises, without cause: unjustly, stripped: deprived, poor: needy) 7. You denied water to the thirsty and withheld bread from the hungry. (denied: refused, thirsty: those in need of water, withheld: kept back, hungry: those in need of food) 8. The powerful owned the land, and the honored dwelled in it. (owned: possessed, honored: esteemed, dwelled: lived) 9. You sent widows away empty-handed and crushed the orphans. (Sent away: dismissed, empty-handed: without aid, crushed: oppressed) 10. That's why traps surround you, sudden fear troubles you, (traps: snares, surround: enclose, sudden fear: unexpected dread, troubles: disturbs) 11. Darkness blinds you, and floods overwhelm you. (Darkness: obscurity, blinds: incapacitates, floods: torrents, overwhelm: inundate) 12. Isn't God in heaven above? Look how high the stars are! (Heaven: sky, high: lofty, stars: celestial bodies) 13. Yet you ask, 'What does God know? Can He judge through thick clouds?' (judge: evaluate, thick clouds: dense clouds) 14. You say clouds hide Him, and He walks the vault of heaven. (hide: conceal, walks: moves, vault: expanse, heaven: sky) 15. Have you considered the ancient path of the wicked, (ancient: old, path: way, wicked: unrighteous) 16. Who were swept away before their time, their foundation washed away by the flood? (swept away: destroyed, before their time: prematurely, foundation: base, washed away: destroyed by water) 17. They said to God, 'Leave us alone! What can the Almighty do to us?' (leave us alone: depart from us, Almighty: all-powerful, do: accomplish) 18. Yet He filled their homes with good things. But the wicked's advice is far from me. (filled: filled up, homes: households, good things: blessings, advice: counsel) 19. The righteous see their end and rejoice; the innocent mock them. (righteous: just, end: downfall, rejoice: celebrate, innocent: blameless, mock: ridicule) 20. 'Our wealth is intact,' they say, 'while fire consumes the wicked's remnant.' (wealth: riches, intact: untouched, fire: destruction, remnant: leftovers) 21. Get to know God and be at peace; this will bring you good. (know: understand, peace: tranquility, bring you good: bring you prosperity) 22. Listen to His words and store them in your heart. (listen: heed, store: treasure, heart: innermost being) 23. If you return to the Almighty and put sin far from your home, (return: turn back, Almighty: God, put sin far: remove iniquity) 24. You will treat gold like dust and gold from Ophir like river stones. (gold: riches, dust: dirt, Ophir: a place known for wealth, river stones: common stones) 25. The Almighty will be your treasure, and you'll have plenty of silver. (treasure: wealth, plenty: abundance, silver: riches) 26. You will delight in God and lift up your face to Him. (delight: take joy, lift up your face: approach with favor) 27. You will pray to Him, and He will hear you; you'll fulfill your vows. (pray: petition, hear: answer, fulfill: keep, vows: promises) 28. What you decide will succeed, and light will shine on your path. (succeed: prosper, light: guidance) 29. When others are humbled, you'll say, 'Lift them up!' and God will save the lowly. (humbled: brought low, lift them up: exalt, lowly: meek) 30. He will deliver even the guilty through the purity of your hands." (deliver: rescue, guilty: condemned, purity: innocence).

Chapter 23

1. Then Job replied, 2. "Even today my complaint is bitter; my suffering outweighs my groaning. (complaint: grievance, bitter: harsh, suffering: pain, outweighs: exceeds, groaning: lamenting) 3. If only I knew where to find Him, that I might go to His throne! (find: locate, throne: seat of authority) 4. I would present my case before

Him and argue my cause. (present: bring forward, case: complaint, argue: plead, cause: reason) **5.** I would learn His response and understand His words to me. (response: answer, understand: comprehend, words: message) **6.** Would He use His great power against me? No, He would give me strength. (power: might, against me: oppose me, give: provide, strength: courage) **7.** The upright could argue their case with Him, and I would be delivered forever from my judge. (upright: righteous, argue: plead, delivered: saved, judge: accuser) **8.** But if I go forward, He is not there; backward, I cannot find Him. (forward: ahead, backward: behind) **9.** On the left, where He works, I cannot see Him; He hides on the right, and I cannot perceive Him. (left: to the left, works: acts, hides: conceals, perceive: sense) **10.** Yet He knows the path I take; when He tests me, I will come out as gold. (path: way, tests: refines, come out: emerge, gold: pure) **11.** My feet have followed His steps; I have stayed on His way without turning aside. (feet: steps, followed: walked in, stayed: remained, without turning aside: not deviating) **12.** I have not departed from His commands; I treasure His words more than daily food. (departed: strayed, commands: laws, treasure: cherish, daily food: necessary sustenance) **13.** But He is unchanging; who can turn Him back? He does whatever He desires. (unchanging: constant, turn back: alter, desires: wills) **14.** He carries out His plans for me, and many such purposes are with Him. (carries out: fulfills, plans: intentions, purposes: decrees) **15.** That is why I am terrified in His presence; when I think of Him, I am afraid. (terrified: fearful, presence: presence, think of: contemplate, afraid: filled with dread) **16.** God has made my heart faint; the Almighty has terrified me. (heart: spirit, faint: weak, Almighty: all-powerful, terrified: struck with fear) **17.** Yet I am not destroyed by the darkness, nor has He hidden it from me." (destroyed: consumed, darkness: obscurity, hidden: concealed).

Chapter 24

1. "Why does the Almighty not set times for judgment? Why do those who know Him not see His justice? (justice: fairness) **2.** Some move boundary stones, steal flocks, and pasture them. (boundary stones: markers, pasture: graze) **3.** They drive away the fatherless's donkey and take a widow's ox as security. (fatherless: orphaned, security: collateral) **4.** They force the needy off the path, and the poor must hide together. (need: impoverished, hide: shelter) **5.** Like wild donkeys in the desert, they go out to work, searching for food; the wilderness provides for their children. (wilderness: desert) **6.** They harvest fields they do not own and gather grapes from the wicked. (own: possess, wicked: immoral) **7.** They leave the poor without clothing, making them shiver in the cold. (clothing: garments, shiver: tremble) **8.** Without shelter, they are drenched by mountain rains and cling to rocks for refuge. (shelter: protection, drenched: soaked, refuge: safety) **9.** They snatch the fatherless from their mothers and take pledges from the poor. (snatch: seize, pledges: promises) **10.** They leave the poor naked without clothing and take away food from the hungry. (naked: bare, take away: steal) **11.** They press olives and tread grapes but remain thirsty. (press: squeeze, tread: stomp) **12.** The dying groan in the city, and the wounded cry out, but God does not charge them with wrong. (dying: near death, groan: moan, charge: accuse) **13.** These people rebel against the light; they don't understand its ways or stay in its paths. (rebel: resist, understand: comprehend, ways: methods, paths: directions) **14.** The murderer rises early to kill the poor and needy; at night, he becomes a thief. (murderer: killer, rises: wakes, thief: robber) **15.** The adulterer waits for twilight, thinking, 'No one will see me,' and disguises his face. (adulterer: cheater, twilight: dusk, disguises: conceals) **16.** In the dark, they break into houses they marked in the day, avoiding the light. (break into: burglarize, marked: targeted) **17.** To them, morning is like the shadow of death; they fear being recognized. (shadow of death: grave, recognized: identified) **18.** They are swift as water, their land cursed; they avoid the vineyards. (swift: fast, cursed: doomed) **19.** Just as drought and heat consume snow, the grave devours those who sin. (drought: dry spell, consume: melt, devours: swallows) **20.** The womb forgets them, worms feast on them, and they are no longer remembered; wickedness is broken like a tree. (womb: mother's belly, feast: devour, wickedness: evil) **21.** They mistreat the childless woman and do no good for the widow. (mistreat: harm, childless: barren) **22.** By His power, God drags away the strong; they may rise, but no one feels safe. (drags: pulls, strong: mighty, rise: stand) **23.** God may allow them security for a time, but He watches their every move. (security: protection, watches: observes) **24.** They are exalted briefly, then gone; cut down like heads of grain. (exalted: raised, cut down: harvested) **25.** If this isn't true, who can prove me wrong and make my words meaningless?" (prove: disprove).

Chapter 25

1. Then Bildad the Shuhite said: **2.** "God is supreme and inspires awe; He brings peace in the heavens above. (supreme: highest, inspires: evokes, awe: reverence, brings: establishes) **3.** Who can count His armies? Who is not touched by His light? (Armies: hosts, counted: numbered, touched: affected, light: radiance) **4.** How can anyone be right before God? How can one born of a woman be pure? (Right: just, pure: clean) **5.** Even the moon does not shine brightly, and the stars are not flawless in His eyes. **6.** How much more so is man, who is frail like a worm, and humanity, weak as maggots? (frail: delicate, humanity: mankind, weak: fragile)"

Chapter 26

1. Then Job answered: **2.** "How have you helped the powerless? How have you saved those with no strength? (Powerless: weak, strength: power) **3.** How have you advised the one lacking wisdom? How have you explained things so clearly? (Advised: guided, lacking: without, explained: clarified, clearly: plainly) **4.** To whom have you spoken, and whose spirit was behind your words? (Spirit: influence) **5.** The dead are formed beneath the waters, and their inhabitants. (inhabitants: dwellers) **6.** Hell lies bare before Him, and destruction has no covering. (Hell: underworld, bare: exposed, destruction: ruin, covering: concealment) **7.** He stretches the north over empty space and hangs the earth upon nothing. (Stretches: extends, empty space: void) **8.** He holds the waters in His clouds, yet they do not burst under their weight. (Holds: contains, burst: break) **9.** He conceals His throne and spreads His cloud over it. (Conceals: hides, spreads: covers) **10.** He set boundaries for the waters, until day and night come to an end. (Boundaries: limits, end: close) **11.** The pillars of heaven tremble at His rebuke. (pillars: supports, tremble: shake, rebuke: correction) **12.** He divides the sea by His power; by His understanding, He strikes down the proud. (Divides: parts, power: might, understanding: wisdom, strikes down: brings low) **13.** By His Spirit, He adorned the heavens; His hand formed the twisted serpent. (Spirit: breath, adorned: decorated, formed: created, twisted: coiled) **14.** These are only a small part of His ways. How little we hear of Him! Who can truly understand the thunder of His power? (Small part: fraction, hear: learn, thunder: roar)"

Chapter 27

1. Job continued: **2.** "As surely as God lives, who has taken away my judgment, and the Almighty, who has troubled my soul, (lives: exists, judgment: justice, troubled: distressed, soul: spirit) **3.** As long as my breath is in me and the spirit of God in my nostrils, (breath: life, spirit: presence, nostrils: nose) **4.** My lips will not speak wickedness, nor will my tongue utter deceit. (Wickedness: evil, deceit: falsehood) **5.** God forbid that I should justify you! I will not abandon my integrity until I die. (Forbid: prevent, justify: defend, integrity: honesty) **6.** I hold fast to my righteousness and will not let it go; my conscience will not condemn me as long as I live. (Hold fast: cling, righteousness: virtue, conscience: moral sense, condemn: accuse) **7.** Let my enemy be like the wicked, and let those who rise against me be like the unrighteous. (Enemy: foe, wicked: immoral, rise against: oppose, unrighteous: unjust) **8.** What hope does the hypocrite have, even if he prospers, when God takes his soul? (Hope: expectation, hypocrite: deceiver, prospers: succeeds, soul: life) **9.** Will God hear his cry when distress comes upon him? (Hear: listen, cry: plea, distress: trouble) **10.** Will he find joy in the Almighty? Will he keep calling on God?) **11.** I will teach you what the hand of God has revealed to me; I will not hide what the Almighty has shown me. (Teach: instruct, revealed: disclosed, hide: conceal, shown: revealed) **12.** You have all seen it yourselves, so why are you being so vain? **13.** This is the portion of the wicked from God, the inheritance of the oppressors they will receive from the Almighty. (Portion: share, wicked: immoral, inheritance: legacy, oppressors: tyrants) **14.** If his children increase, it is for the sword; his descendants will not have enough to eat. (Increase: multiply, sword: destruction, descendants: offspring). **15.** Those who survive him will die by the sword; his widows will not mourn. (Survive: outlive, sword: violence, widows: bereaved) **16.** Though he piles up silver like dust and clothes like clay, (piles up: amasses, silver: money, dust: dirt, clothes: garments) **17.** He may store it, but the righteous will wear it, and the innocent will divide the wealth. (Store: save, righteous: virtuous, wear: use, divide: share) **18.** He builds his house like a moth's nest, like a shelter made by a watchman. (Builds: constructs, moth's nest: fragile home, shelter: refuge, watchman: guardian) **19.** The rich man may lie down, but he will not be gathered to his people; he opens his eyes, and he is no more. (Lie down: rest, gathered: reunited, no more: gone) **20.** Terrifying forces take hold of him like floodwaters; a storm sweeps him away in the night. (Terrifying: frightening, forces: powers, floodwaters: torrents, sweeps: carries) **21.** The east wind carries him away, and he vanishes; a storm hurls him out of his place. (East wind: destructive wind, carries away: blows away, vanishes: disappears, hurls: throws) **22.** God will throw His wrath upon him without mercy, and he will try to escape but will not. (Wrath: anger, mercy: compassion, escape: flee) **23.** People will clap their hands at him and hiss him out of his place. (Clap: applaud, hiss: mock).

Chapter 28

1. Surely there is a place where silver is mined, and a place where gold is refined. (Mined: extracted, refined: purified) **2.** Iron is extracted from the earth, and brass is smelted from stone. (smelted: melted) **3.** He ends the darkness and searches out all perfection, even the hidden stones of darkness and the shadow of death. (searches out: seeks, perfection: completeness, hidden: concealed, shadow of death: realm of death) **4.** The flood breaks out from the ground, from waters that no foot remembers; they dry up and vanish from men. (breaks out: bursts forth, remembers: recalls, dry up: evaporate, vanish: disappear) **5.** The earth produces food, and underneath it is as though fire has been kindled. (Produces: yields, kindled: ignited) **6.** The earth's stones are the source of sapphires, and it has dust that is pure gold. (stones: rocks, source: origin, sapphires: gemstones, pure: unrefined) **7.** There is a path that no bird knows, and the vulture's eye has never seen. (Path: trail, knows: discovers, vulture's eye: bird's vision) **8.** The young lions have not walked on it, nor has the fierce lion passed over it. (Walked: trod, fierce: mighty) **9.** He stretches his hand to the rock and moves mountains from their roots. (Stretches: extends, moves: shifts, roots: foundations) **10.** He cuts out rivers among the rocks and sees every precious thing. (Cuts out: carves, rivers: streams, precious: valuable) **11.** He stops the floods from overflowing, and brings hidden things to light. (Stops: halts, overflowing: spilling over, brings: reveals) **12.** But where can wisdom be found? Where is the place of understanding? (Found: discovered, understanding: insight) **13.** Man does not know its value, and it is not found among the living. (Value: worth, living: mortals) **14.** The deep says, "It is not in me," and the sea says, "It is not with me." **15.** It cannot be bought with gold, and silver cannot be weighed for its price. (Bought: purchased, weighed: measured, price: cost) **16.** It cannot be compared to the gold of Ophir, nor to precious onyx or sapphires. (Compared: matched, Ophir: a place known for wealth, precious: rare) **17.** Gold and crystal cannot match it; the exchange of it will not be for fine jewels. (fine jewels: precious gems) **18.** No mention will be made of coral or pearls; wisdom is more valuable than rubies. (Mention: reference, coral: red marine growth, pearls: ocean gems, valuable: priceless) **19.** The topaz of Ethiopia cannot compare to it; it cannot be valued with pure gold. (Topaz: gemstone, Ethiopia: ancient land, valued: appraised) **20.** So where does wisdom come from, and where is the place of understanding? (Come from: originate, place: source) **21.** It is hidden from the eyes of all living, and kept from the birds of the air. (Hidden: concealed, kept: guarded, eyes: sight) **22.** Death and destruction say, "We have heard of it with our ears." (heard: learned) **23.** God understands the way to it, and He knows its place. **24.** For He looks to the ends of the earth and sees everything under the heavens. **25.** He established the weight for the winds and measures the waters by His standards. (Established: set, weight: measure, winds: air currents, standards: guidelines) **26.** When He made a law for the rain and a path for the thunder's lightning, (law: rule, path: course, thunder's lightning: storm's fury) **27.** He saw it, declared it, prepared it, and searched it out. (saw: observed, declared: announced, prepared: arranged, searched it out: investigated) **28.** And He said to man, "The fear of the Lord is wisdom, and turning from evil understands." (Turning from: forsaking, evil: wickedness).

Chapter 29

1. Job continued his speech and said, **2.** Oh, if only I were like I was in the past, when God watched over me, (watched over: protected) **3.** When His light guided me, and by His light, I walked through darkness, (light: guidance, walked: journeyed, darkness: uncertainty) **4.** Like I was in the days of my youth, when God's secret presence was with my home, (secret presence: hidden protection, home: household) **5.** When the Almighty was with me, and my children were around me, (Almighty: powerful one, around me: beside me) **6.** When I enjoyed abundance, and the rocks provided me with streams of oil, (abundance: plenty, rocks: foundations, provided: gave) **7.** When I went to the city gate and prepared my seat in the street, (city gate: entrance) **8.** The young men saw me and stepped aside, and the elders rose up and stood in respect, **9.** The leaders stopped talking and placed their hands over their mouths, **10.** The nobles remained silent, their tongues stuck to the roof of their mouths, (nobles: aristocrats, remained: stayed, silent: quiet, stuck: clung) **11.** When the ear heard me, it blessed me, and when the eye saw me, it gave witness to my character, (ear: listener, blessed: praised, eye: observer, witness: testified, character: integrity) **12.** Because I helped the poor who cried for help, the fatherless, and those with no one to support them, (helped: assisted, poor: needy, cried for help: pleaded, fatherless: orphaned, support: care) **13.** The blessing of those near death came upon me, and I made the widow's heart rejoice, (blessing: favor, near death: dying, widow's heart: widow's sorrow, rejoice: glad) **14.** I wore righteousness like a garment, and judgment was my crown and robe, (wore: donned, righteousness: justice, garment: clothing, judgment: fairness, crown: symbol of authority) **15.** I was a guide to the blind and a support to the lame, (support: helper, lame: crippled) **16.** I became a father to the poor and investigated cases I did not know about, (father: protector, investigated: examined, cases: matters) **17.** I broke the jaws of the wicked and rescued the victim from their grasp, (broke: shattered, jaws: mouths, wicked: evildoers, rescued: saved, victim: helpless one, grasp: control) **18.** I thought to myself, "I will die in my nest, and my days will be as many as the grains of sand." (nest: home, grains of sand: endless) **19.** My roots grew by the water, and the dew rested on my branches all night, (roots: foundation, grew: spread, dew: moisture, branches: limbs) **20.** My glory was renewed in me, and my strength was restored, (renewed: refreshed, strength: vitality, restored: revived) **21.** People listened to me, waiting for my advice, (listened: heard, waiting: anticipating, advice: counsel) **22.** After I spoke, they didn't interrupt, and my words settled in their hearts, (interrupt: cut in, settled: found a place, hearts: minds) **23.** They waited for me as they wait for rain, and opened their mouths wide as for the late rain, (waited: hoped, rain: downpour, opened their mouths wide: eagerly anticipated) **24.** If I smiled at them, they did not doubt me, and the light of my face never discouraged them, (smiled: beamed, doubted: questioned, light: radiance, discouraged: disheartened) **25.** I led their way, sat as a leader, and comforted those in sorrow, like a king among his people. (Comforted: consoled, sorrow: grief).

Chapter 30

1. But now, those younger than I mock me, whose fathers I would have considered unworthy to sit with the dogs of my flock. (unworthy: undeserving, flock: herd) **2.** What good would their strength have been to me, when their old age is gone? **3.** They were lonely and poor, fleeing to the wilderness in times past, desolate and barren. (lonely: isolated, poor: destitute, fleeing: running, wilderness: desert, desolate: forsaken, barren: infertile) **4.** They would gather mallows and juniper roots for food. (Gather: collect, mallows: wild plants, juniper: shrub, roots: tubers) **5.** They were driven away by others, as if they were thieves, (driven away: cast out, thieves: criminals) **6.** Forced to live in the cliffs, caves, and rocky places of the earth. (Forced: compelled, cliffs: steep rocks, caves: caverns, rocky: stony) **7.** They would bray among the bushes, and gather under the nettles. (Bray: cry, nettles: stinging plants) **8.** They were children of fools, born of lowly people; they were worse than the earth itself. (lowly: humble, worse: more vile) **9.** And now I have become their song, their mocking proverb. (song: chant, mocking: derisive, proverb: saying) **10.** They despise me, keep their distance, and don't hesitate to spit in my face. (despise: hate, keep their distance: avoid, hesitate: pause, spit: insult) **11.** Because God has untied my ropes and afflicted me, they have no restraint and act with cruelty. (afflicted: tormented, restraint: self-control, cruelty: harshness) **12.** On my right side, young men rise up against me; they push me away, and make my path full of destruction. (Right side: beside me, rise up: oppose, push away: shove, destruction: ruin) **13.** They make my journey harder, adding to my misery, with no one to help. (Journey: path, harder: more difficult, misery: suffering) **14.** They overwhelm me like a flood, rolling over me in their devastation. (Overwhelm: overpower, flood: torrent, rolling over: crashing down, devastation: destruction) **15.** Terrifying forces press upon me, chasing my soul like the wind, and my hope vanishes like a cloud. (Terrifying: frightening, press: bear down, chasing: pursuing, vanishes: disappears) **16.** My soul is poured out, and the days of suffering have gripped me. (Poured out: emptied, gripped: seized) **17.** My bones are in agony through the night, and my muscles refuse to rest. (Agony: pain, muscles: limbs, refuse: resist, rest: relax) **18.** The weight of my illness changes the way my clothes fit; they tighten around me like a collar. (Weight: burden, illness: sickness, tighten: constrict, collar: neckband) **19.** God has thrown me into the dirt, and I have become like dust and ashes. (Throw: cast, dirt: earth, dust: powder, ashes: soot). **20.** I cry out to You, but You do not hear me; I stand, but You do not regard me. (cry out: call, hear: listen, regard: notice) **21.** You have become cruel toward me; with Your powerful hand, You oppose me. (Cruel: harsh, powerful: mighty, oppose: resist) **22.** You lift me up and carry me away like the wind, and destroy everything I have. (Lift: raise, carry away: take, destroy: ruin) **23.** I know You will bring me to death and to the place reserved for all the living. (Bring: lead, death: demise, reserved: set aside) **24.** But You will not stretch out Your hand to help me, even when they cry out for help. (Stretch out: extend, help: assist, cry out: call) **25.** Didn't I weep for those in trouble? Didn't my soul grieve for the poor? (Weep: mourn, trouble: distress, grieve: sorrow, poor: needy) **26.** When I expected good, evil came instead; when I waited for light, darkness overtook me. (Expected: hoped for, good: favor, evil: misfortune, light: brightness, darkness: gloom) **27.** My insides churned, and I couldn't find rest; the days of suffering overwhelmed me. (Churned: twisted, couldn't: was unable to, rest: peace, overwhelmed: overtaken) **28.** I went about in mourning without the sun, standing up and crying out in the assembly. (Mourning: grieving, without the sun: in darkness, crying out: shouting, assembly: gathering) **29.** I have become like a brother to dragons and a companion to owls. (Dragons: mythical beasts, companion: associate) **30.** My skin is darkened, and my bones burn with fever. (Darkened: discolored, burn: ache, fever: heat) **31.** My harp has become a song of mourning, and my flute a voice of sorrow. (Harp: instrument, song of mourning: lament, flute: pipe, voice: sound).

Chapter 31

1. I made a promise to my eyes: why then should I think about a young woman? **2.** What portion of God comes from above? What inheritance does the Almighty give from on high? (Portion: share, inheritance: legacy) **3.** Isn't destruction the fate of the wicked? And isn't a strange punishment the consequence for those who do evil? (destruction: ruin, fate: destiny, wicked: immoral, strange: unusual, consequence: result) **4.** Doesn't He see my ways and count all my steps? (count: number, steps: actions) **5.** If I have walked in vanity, or if my foot has rushed into deceit, (walked: lived, vanity: pride, rushed: hastened, deceit: dishonesty) **6.** Let me be weighed in an even balance, so God can know my integrity. (Weighed: measured, balance: scale, integrity: righteousness) **7.** If my path has gone off course, and my heart has followed my eyes, and if any sin has stuck to my hands, (path: way, off course: strayed, followed: pursued, stuck: clung, sin: wrongdoing) **8.** Then let me sow, and let someone else eat; let my descendants be uprooted. (Sow: plant, descendants: offspring, uprooted: destroyed) **9.** If my heart has been deceived by a woman, or if I have waited secretly at my neighbor's door, (deceived: led astray, secretly: stealthily, neighbor's: fellow's) **10.** Then let my wife grind grain for another man, and let others bow down to her. (Grind: mill, bow down: honor) **11.** This is a great sin, an evil to be punished by the judges. (Great: serious, evil: wickedness, punished: judged) **12.** It's like a fire that destroys everything, burning up all I have worked for. (Fire: blaze, destroys: consumes, burning up: destroying, worked for: labored for) **13.** If I have mistreated my servants when they argued with me, (mistreated: wronged, argued: disagreed) **14.** What will I do when God rises up? When He visits, what will I say? (Rises up: stands up, visits: examines) **15.** Didn't He who made me in the womb make my servant as well? Didn't the same God form both of us? (Womb: belly). **16.** If I have withheld what the poor desired, or caused the widow's eyes to grow dim, (withheld: denied, desired: longed for, grow dim: fade, widow's: bereaved woman's) **17.** Or eaten my food alone without sharing it with the fatherless, (eaten: consumed, alone: selfishly, fatherless: orphaned) **18.** (For from my youth, I have cared for them, like a father, and guided them from my mother's womb,) (Cared for: looked after, guided: led) **19.** If I have seen someone perish without clothing, or the poor lacking cover, (perish: die, lacking: without, cover: shelter) **20.** If they didn't bless me with their loins, or if they weren't warmed by the wool from my sheep, (bless: thank, loins: bodies, warmed: clothed, wool: fleece) **21.** If I raised my hand against the fatherless when I saw help in the gate, (raised: lifted, hand: fist, fatherless: orphaned, help: aid, gate: city entrance) **22.** Then let my arm fall from my shoulder blade, and let my arm be broken. (Arm: limb, fall: drop, shoulder blade: scapula, broken: shattered) **23.** For the terror of God was upon me, and I could not bear His greatness. (Terror: fear, upon: over, bear: endure) **24.** If I have put my hope in gold, or said to fine gold, "You are my security," (hope: trust, gold: wealth, security: safety) **25.** If I have rejoiced because my wealth was great, and because my hand had gotten much, (rejoiced: delighted, wealth: riches, gotten: gained) **26.** If I looked at the sun when it shone, or the moon walking in brightness, (looked at: gazed upon, sun: sunlight, walking in brightness: shining, moon: lunar light) **27.** And my heart was secretly enticed, or my mouth kissed my hand, (enticed: seduced, secretly: covertly, kissed: honored, hand: palm) **28.** This would be a sin to be judged, for I would have denied God above. (sin: wrongdoing, judged: punished, denied: rejected, above: heaven) **29.** If I rejoiced at the downfall of someone who hated me, or lifted myself up when evil came upon them, (rejoiced: celebrated, downfall: misfortune, hated: despised, lifted up: exalted, evil: misfortune) **30.** I never allowed my mouth to sin by cursing them. (allowed: permitted, sin: wrong, cursing: condemning) **31.** If the people of my household said, "Oh, if only we had some of his flesh to eat," (people: members, household: family, flesh: meat) **32.** The stranger did not stay outside; I opened my doors to the traveler. (Stranger: foreigner, traveler: guest) **33.** If I covered my sins like Adam, hiding my guilt in my heart, (covered: concealed, sins: wrongdoings, hiding: concealing, guilt: shame) **34.** If I feared a great multitude or the contempt of families and kept silent, not going out of my door, (feared: dreaded, multitude: crowd, contempt: disdain, kept silent: remained quiet, going out: stepping out) **35.** Oh, that someone would hear me! My desire is that the Almighty would answer me, and that my accuser would write a book. (desire: wish, Almighty: God, answer: respond, accuser: adversary, write: record) **36.** I would take it on my shoulder, and wear it like a crown. (Take: carry, shoulder: back, wear: adorn, crown: diadem) **37.** I would tell Him exactly how I have lived, and I would approach Him like a prince. **38.** If my land cries out against me, or its furrows complain, (cries out: pleads, furrows: fields) **39.** If I have eaten its fruits without paying, or caused its owners to lose their lives, (fruits: crops, paying: compensating, owners: landholders, lose their lives: suffer) **40.** Let thistles grow instead of wheat, and weeds instead of barley. The words of Job are finished. (Thistles: prickly plants grow: sprout, instead of: in place of, wheat: grain, weeds: unwanted plants).

Chapter 32
1. So, these three men stopped answering Job because they believed he was righteous in his own eyes. (Stopped: ceased, answering: responding, believed: thought, righteous: just, eyes: sight) **2.** Then Elihu, the son of Barachel the Buzite from the family of Ram, became angry. His anger burned against Job because Job justified himself rather than God. (burned: flared, justified: defended) **3.** He was also angry with Job's three friends because they had not found an answer to Job's arguments, but still condemned him. (Found: discovered, condemned: accused) **4.** Elihu had waited for the others to speak because they were older than him. (Waited: delayed, older: senior) **5.** But when Elihu saw that no one had an answer, his anger was stirred up. (Stirred up: provoked, answer: response) **6.** Elihu, the son of Barachel the Buzite, spoke up and said: "I am young, and you are very old, so I was afraid to express my opinion. (spoke up: addressed, young: inexperienced, old: elderly, afraid: hesitant, express: share, opinion: view) **7.** I thought that wisdom comes with age and that the elderly should teach wisdom. (Wisdom: knowledge, comes: accompanies, teach: impart) **8.** But there is a spirit in man, and the inspiration of the Almighty gives understanding. (inspiration: guidance, gives: imparts, understanding: insight) **9.** Not all wise men are great, and not all older people understand what is right. (Wise: knowledgeable, great: eminent, older: senior, understand: comprehend, right: just) **10.** So I say: Listen to me; I will share my opinion. (Listen: hear, share: express, opinion: view) **11.** I waited for your words; I listened as you searched for what to say. (Waited: bided time, listened: heard, searched: sought) **12.** But none of you proved Job wrong or answered his words. (Proved: demonstrated, wrong: erroneous, answered: responded) **13.** You might say, "We've found wisdom," but it is God who brings him down, not man. (Wisdom: insight, brings down: humbles) **14.** Job didn't speak against me, and I will not answer him in your way. **15.** They were all amazed and had no more answers; they stopped speaking. (amazed: astonished, answers: responses) **16.** When I saw they were silent and had no response, (silent: mute, response: reply) **17.** I decided to speak up, for I am also eager to share my thoughts. (speak up: address, eager: ready, thoughts: opinions) **18.** I am full of words; the spirit within me compels me to speak. (full: brimming, compels: urges) **19.** My belly is like wine without a vent, ready to burst like new wineskins. (belly: heart, vent: release, burst: rupture, wineskins: vessels) **20.** I must speak, so I can be refreshed. I will open my lips and respond. (refreshed: relieved, respond: reply) **21.** I pray, don't expect me to show favoritism or flatter anyone. (flatter: praise) **22.** For I don't know how to flatter; if I did, my Creator would quickly take me away. (Don't know: am not familiar with, flatter: praise, Creator: Maker).

Chapter 33
1. Job, listen to my words and pay attention to what I say. (listen: heed) **2.** I have opened my mouth, and my tongue speaks. **3.** My words come from the sincerity of my heart, and my lips speak clearly. (Sincerity: honesty) **4.** God made me, and the breath of the Almighty gave me life. (Breath: spirit) **5.** If you can answer me, present your case and stand up. (Present: present) **6.** I am speaking in God's place, as I too am made from clay. **7.** My presence will not make you afraid, nor will my hand weigh heavily on you. (Weigh: burden) **8.** You've spoken before me, saying, (before: previously) **9.** "I am pure, innocent, and free from sin." (Innocent: blameless) **10.** Yet you accuse me, treating me as an enemy, (accuse: blame) **11.** Putting my feet in stocks, watching my every move. (Stocks: restraints) **12.** But in this, you are wrong. God is greater than man. (Wrong: mistaken) **13.** Why do you argue with God? He doesn't have to explain Himself. (Argue: dispute) **14.** God speaks once, even twice, but man doesn't understand. (Understand: comprehend) **15.** He speaks through dreams and visions at night, when sleep falls upon men. **16.** He opens their ears and gives them instruction, (instruction: teaching) **17.** To turn man from his ways and keep him from pride. **18.** He saves them from death, keeping them from the sword. (saves: rescues) **19.** He chastens with pain on the bed and strong suffering in the bones. (chastens: disciplines) **20.** Their appetite fades, and they refuse food. (fades: diminishes) **21.** Their flesh wastes away until they are unrecognizable, and their bones become visible. (wastes: deteriorates) **22.** Their soul approaches the grave, and death draws near. (approaches: nears) **23.** If a messenger appears, an interpreter, to show them their righteousness, (interpreter: mediator) **24.** God is gracious, saying, "Rescue him from the pit; I've found a ransom." (ransom: payment) **25.** His body will be restored, like a young person's, and he will return to health. (restored: renewed) **26.** He will pray to God, and God will favor him, restoring his joy and righteousness. (favor: bless) **27.** If any man admits his sin, saying, "I've done wrong, but it hasn't helped me," (admits: confesses) **28.** God will save him from death and give him light. (light: guidance) **29.** God does these things repeatedly with people, (repeatedly: often) **30.** To bring them from death to life, guiding them to the light. (bring: lead) **31.** Listen carefully, Job, and be quiet while I speak. (quiet: silent) **32.** If you have anything to say, speak up, for I want to justify you. (justify: defend) **33.** If not, listen to me and I will teach you wisdom. (wisdom: knowledge)

Chapter 34
1. Then Elihu answered and said, **2.** "Listen to me, wise men, and give ear to me, you who have knowledge. **3.** The ear tests words, as the mouth tastes food. (Tests: examines, tastes: experiences) **4.** Let us choose judgment and agree on what is good. (Choose: select, judgment: fairness) **5.** Job has said, 'I am righteous, but God has taken away my right.' (Righteous: just, taken away: removed) **6.** Should I lie about my rights? My wound is incurable without sin. (Lie: deceive, incurable: unhealable) **7.** Who is like Job, who drinks in mockery like water? (Mockery: ridicule) **8.** He joins with the workers of evil and walks with the wicked. (Workers of evil: wrongdoers, wicked: immoral) **9.** For he says, 'It does not benefit a man to delight in God.' (Benefit: help, delight: take pleasure) **10.** Listen to me, you who understand: it is far from God to do wrong; the Almighty does not commit iniquity. (Understand: comprehend, wrong: evil, commit: do, iniquity: injustice) **11.** God rewards a man's work and gives him what he deserves. **12.** Surely, God does not do evil, nor

does the Almighty pervert justice. (Pervert: distort) **13.** Who has appointed Him over the earth? Who has set the whole world in place? (Appointed: made, set; placed) **14.** If He took His mind off man, gathering back His spirit and breath, (mind off: withdrew, gathering back: returning) **15.** all flesh would perish together, and mankind would return to dust. (Perish: die, mankind: humans) **16.** If you have understanding, listen to this; hear the words I speak. (Understanding: wisdom, hear: listen) **17.** Can someone who hates justice govern? Will you condemn the just? (Hate: dislike, govern: rule, condemn: judge) **18.** Is it right to say to a king, 'You are wicked,' and to princes, 'You are ungodly?' (right: fair, wicked: evil, ungodly: immoral) **19.** How much less to Him who does not show partiality to rulers or regard the rich more than the poor; all are His work. (partiality: favoritism, regard: favor) **20.** They die in an instant; people are troubled at midnight and pass away. The mighty are taken away without a hand. (instant: moment, troubled: distressed, mighty: powerful) **21.** His eyes are on the ways of man, and He sees all his actions. (eyes: gaze, actions: deeds) **22.** There is no darkness or shadow where the workers of iniquity can hide. (darkness: obscurity, shadow: gloom, hide: conceal) **23.** He will not punish more than what is just; no man can argue with God. (punish: judge, just: fair, argue: dispute) **24.** He breaks mighty men into pieces and replaces them with others. (breaks: shatters, replaces: substitutes) **25.** He knows their works and overturns them in the night, destroying them. (knows: understands, overturns: changes, destroying: ruining) **26.** He strikes them as wicked men in plain sight, (strikes: hits, plain sight: open view) **27.** because they turned back from Him and did not consider His ways. (turned back: abandoned, consider: follow) **28.** They cause the cry of the poor to reach Him, and He hears the cry of the afflicted. (cause: make, afflicted: suffering) **29.** When He gives peace, no one can cause trouble; when He hides His face, no one can see Him, whether against a nation or an individual. (gives: grants, cause: create, hides: conceals) **30.** He does this to prevent a hypocrite from ruling, lest the people become ensnared. (prevent: stop, hypocrite: pretender, ensnared: trapped) **31.** Surely it is right to say to God, 'I have borne chastisement; I will not sin anymore. (borne: endured, chastisement: punishment) **32.** Teach me what I do not see; if I have done wrong, I will not do it again.' (wrong: sin) **33.** Should He repay you according to your thoughts? He will repay you, whether you refuse or choose; speak what you know. **34.** Let wise men tell me; let a man of understanding listen. **35.** Job speaks without knowledge, and his words lack wisdom. (Knowledge: insight, lack: are without) **36.** My desire is that Job be tested to the end for his answers to wicked men. (Desire: wish, tested: tried) **37.** For he adds rebellion to his sin; he claps his hands among us and multiplies his words against God." (Rebellion: defiance, multiplies: increases)

Chapter 35
1. Elihu continued and said, **2.** "Do you think it is right to say, 'My righteousness is greater than God's'? **3.** For you ask, 'What benefit is it to me? What do I gain if I am free from sin?' **4.** I will answer you and your friends who are with you. **5.** Look up to the heavens and see; observe the clouds, which are higher than you. **6.** If you sin, what harm do you bring to God? If your sins are many, how do they affect Him? **7.** If you are righteous, what do you give to Him? What does He receive from your hand? **8.** Your wickedness affects only people like yourself, and your righteousness benefits other humans. (wickedness: evil, benefits: helps) **9.** People cry out because of oppression and plead for help against the powerful. (Oppression: injustice, plead: ask) **10.** But no one asks, 'Where is God my Maker, who gives songs in the night, **11.** who teaches us more than the animals of the earth and makes us wiser than the birds of the sky?' (Wiser: more knowledgeable) **12.** They cry out, but He does not answer because of the arrogance of evil men. **13.** Surely God does not listen to empty cries, and the Almighty pays no attention to them. (Empty: meaningless, pays attention: listens) **14.** Even if you say you cannot see Him, judgment is still before Him; so trust in Him. (Judgment: justice, trust: rely) **15.** But now, because His anger is not immediate, He does not punish as severely as He could. (Immediate: instant, severely: harshly) **16.** So Job speaks in vain; he multiplies words without knowledge." (Vain: useless, multiplies: increases).

Chapter 36
1. Elihu continued and said, **2.** "Give me a moment, and I will show you that I still have more to say on God's behalf. (Behalf: interest) **3.** I will bring my knowledge from a distant source and give glory to my Maker for His righteousness. (Glory: praise, righteousness: goodness) **4.** My words are true, and one who is perfect in knowledge is with you. (Perfect: complete, knowledge: understanding) **5.** Look, God is mighty and does not despise anyone; He is strong in wisdom and power. (Despise: hate, mighty: powerful) **6.** He does not let the wicked prosper but gives justice to the poor. (Prosper: succeed, wicked: evil) **7.** He watches over the righteous, exalting them with kings on thrones, establishing them forever in honor. (Exalting: lifting up, establishing: securing) **8.** But if they are bound in chains and caught in trouble, (bound: trapped, caught: ensnared) **9.** He shows them their deeds and their sins, how they have exceeded. (Deeds: actions, exceeded: gone beyond) **10.** He opens their ears to instruction and commands them to turn from wrongdoing. **11.** If they obey and serve Him, they will spend their days in prosperity and their years in happiness. (prosperity: success, happiness: joy) **12.** But if they do not obey, they will perish by the sword and die without understanding. **13.** The proud store up anger; they cry out for help only when it is too late. (Proud: arrogant, store up: gather) **14.** They die young, living among the corrupt. (corrupt: wicked) **15.** But He rescues the poor in their suffering and opens their ears during oppression. (Rescues: saves, oppression: hardship) **16.** He would have led you to a wide place of freedom, where you would enjoy abundant blessings. (Wide: spacious, freedom: liberty, abundant: plentiful) **17.** But you have followed the path of the wicked, and justice has caught up with you. (wicked: evil, justice: fairness) **18.** Beware of His wrath, lest it sweep you away with a blow that no ransom can redeem. (wrath: anger, sweep away: carry off, ransom: payment, redeem: save) **19.** Will your wealth save you? Not gold, nor the mightiest forces, can deliver you. (deliver: rescue) **20.** Do not long for the night when people vanish in judgment. (long: desire, vanish: disappear) **21.** Be careful not to choose wrongdoing over enduring suffering. (wrongdoing: evil, enduring: enduring) **22.** See, God is exalted by His power; who is a teacher like Him? (exalted: honored, teacher: instructor) **23.** Who can tell Him what to do, or accuse Him of wrongdoing? (accuse: blame) **24.** Remember to praise His works, which all people admire. (praise: celebrate, admire: respect) **25.** Everyone can see them, even from a distance. (see: witness, distance: afar) **26.** Behold, God is great, beyond our understanding; His years cannot be counted. (behold: look, beyond: surpassing) **27.** He draws up drops of water, which distill as rain from His vapor. (draws up: pulls, distill: condense) **28.** The clouds pour it down abundantly on humanity. (pour: release, abundantly: plentifully) **29.** Can anyone understand the spreading of the clouds or the thunder from His dwelling? **30.** He spreads His lightning across the skies and covers the depths of the sea. (spreads: extends, depths: bottom) **31.** Through these, He judges nations and provides food in abundance. (judges: decides, provides: gives) **32.** He controls the clouds, hiding the light or releasing it as He wills. (controls: directs, releasing: letting go, wills: desires) **33.** The thunder announces His presence, and even animals sense the coming storm.

Chapter 37
1. "At this, my heart trembles and leaps from its place. (trembles: shakes, leaps: jumps) **2.** Listen carefully to the rumble of His voice and the sound that comes from His mouth. (Rumble: roar, carefully: attentively) **3.** He sends it across the whole sky, and His lightning flashes to the ends of the earth. (flashes: strikes, ends: farthest parts) **4.** After it comes a roaring sound—God's majestic voice thunders,

and He does not hold it back when His voice is heard. (majestic: grand, thunders: booms, hold it back: restrain) **5.** God's voice is wondrous; He does great things beyond our understanding. (wondrous: amazing, understanding: comprehension) **6.** He commands the snow to fall on the earth and sends the gentle and heavy rains. (commands: orders, gentle: light, heavy: strong) **7.** He halts the work of every person so all may recognize His deeds. (halts: stops, recognize: see) **8.** Animals retreat to their dens and remain in their shelters. (retreat: withdraw, remain: stay) **9.** The whirlwind comes from the south, and cold winds blow from the north. (whirlwind: storm, blow: gust) **10.** By God's breath, ice is formed, and the broad waters freeze solid. (breath: wind, broad: wide, freeze: harden) **11.** He loads the clouds with moisture and scatters His lightning-filled clouds. (loads: fills, moisture: water, scatters: spreads) **12.** They swirl under His direction, accomplishing whatever He commands over the earth. (swirl: spin, direction: guidance, accomplishing: completing) **13.** He sends the weather for correction, for His land, or as an act of mercy. (correction: discipline, mercy: compassion) **14.** Listen to this, Job! Stand still and consider the amazing works of God. (consider: think about, amazing: remarkable) **15.** Do you know how God controls them or how He makes His lightning shine? (controls: directs, shine: flash) **16.** Do you understand the clouds' balance—the wondrous works of Him who is perfect in knowledge? (balance: arrangement, wondrous: marvelous, perfect: complete) **17.** Why are your clothes warm when He stills the earth with the south wind? (stills: calms, warm: hot) **18.** Can you help Him spread out the skies, hard as a polished mirror? (spread out: stretch, hard: firm, polished: smooth) **19.** Teach us what to say to Him, for we cannot speak because of our ignorance. (ignorance: lack of knowledge) **20.** Should someone tell Him I want to speak? If anyone does, they would surely be overwhelmed. (Overwhelmed: overpowered) **21.** Now we cannot see the bright light in the clouds, but the wind clears them. (Bright: shining, clears: removes) **22.** Golden splendor comes from the north, and God is clothed in awesome majesty. (splendor: brilliance, awesome: awe-inspiring) **23.** The Almighty is beyond our reach; He is great in power, justice, and abundant righteousness. He does not oppress. (beyond: outside of, abundant: overflowing, oppress: mistreat) **24.** Therefore, people revere Him. He shows no favor to those who think they are wise. (Revere: respect, favor: partiality).

Chapter 38

1. Then the LORD spoke to Job out of the storm and said: **2.** "Who is this questioning my wisdom with words that lack understanding? (understanding: insight) **3.** Brace yourself like a man; I will ask you questions, and you will answer me. **4.** Where were you when I laid the earth's foundation? Tell me, if you have knowledge. (foundation: base, knowledge: understanding) **5.** Who decided its dimensions? Surely you know! Who stretched the measuring line across it? (dimensions: size, stretched: extended, measuring line: ruler) **6.** On what is its foundation set? Or who placed its cornerstone, (placed: set, cornerstone: key element) **7.** While the morning stars sang together, and all the angels shouted with joy? (morning stars: bright stars, shouted: proclaimed) **8.** Who set limits for the sea when it burst from the womb, (limits: boundaries, burst: broke out) **9.** When I made clouds its covering and thick darkness its blanket, (covering: garment, blanket: covering) **10.** When I established its boundaries and set gates and doors, (established: set, boundaries: limits, gates: barriers) **11.** Saying, 'This far you may come, no farther; here your proud waves must stop'? (proud: rebellious, must stop: cease) **12.** Have you ever commanded the morning or shown the dawn its place, (commanded: ordered, shown: directed) **13.** So it would light up the edges of the earth and shake the wicked from it? (light up: brighten, edges: corners) **14.** The earth takes shape like clay pressed with a seal, and its features stand out. (features: details) **15.** But light is withheld from the wicked, and their strength is broken. (Withheld: kept back, strength: power) **16.** Have you explored the springs of the sea or walked in its depths? (Explored: searched, depths: bottom) **17.** Have the gates of death been revealed to you? Have you seen the entrance to the deepest darkness? (Gates: doors, revealed: shown) **18.** Do you understand the vastness of the earth? Tell me, if you know all this. (Vastness: immensity, understand: comprehend) **19.** Where does light live, and where does darkness reside? (Live: dwell, reside: remain) **20.** Can you take them to their proper places or understand the paths to their homes? (Proper: correct, paths: routes) **21.** Surely you know, for you were already born! You have lived so many years! (Lived: existed, many years: long time) **22.** Have you visited the storehouses of the snow or seen the reserves of hail, (visited: explored, reserves: stockpiles) **23.** Which I have saved for times of trouble, for days of war and battle? (Saved: reserved, trouble: difficulty) **24.** Do you know the way light is scattered or where the east wind is unleashed over the earth? (Scattered: spread, unleashed: sent) **25.** Who carves channels for the rain and paths for the thunder, (carves: shapes, channels: paths) **26.** To water lands where no one lives, desolate, empty deserts, (water: irrigate, desolate: barren, empty: uninhabited) **27.** To satisfy the dry wasteland and make it sprout with grass? (Satisfy: nourish, wasteland: barren land, sprout: grow) **28.** Does the rain have a father? Who gives birth to the drops of dew? **29.** Who gives birth to ice and frost from the heavens, (ice: frozen water, frost: cold) **30.** When the waters become as hard as stone, and the surface of the deep freezes solid? **31.** Can you fasten the chains of the Pleiades or loosen Orion's belt? (fasten: bind, chains: clusters, loosen: untie) **32.** Can you bring out the constellations at the right times or lead the Bear with its cubs? (bring out: cause to appear, constellations: star groups, lead: guide) **33.** Do you know the laws of the universe? Can you set them in control over the earth? (laws: principles, universe: heavens, set in control: establish dominion) **34.** Can you call to the clouds and command a flood to cover you? **35.** Can you send lightning bolts, and will they respond to you, saying, 'Here we are'? (Send: dispatch, respond: reply) **36.** Who gave wisdom to the inner being? Who gave understanding to the mind? (Inner being: heart, understanding: insight) **37.** Who can count the clouds in wisdom, or tip over the water jars of the sky, (count: number, tip over: overturn, jars: vessels) **38.** When the dust hardens into clumps and the soil clings together? (Clumps: lumps, soil: earth, clings: sticks) **39.** Can you hunt prey for the lion or feed its young, (prey: food, feed: provide for) **40.** When they crouch in their dens or wait in hiding? (Crouch: kneel, dens: shelters) **41.** Who provides food for the raven when its chicks cry out to God and wander in search of food?" (Provides: supplies, chicks: young birds, wander: roam).

Chapter 39

1. Do you know when mountain goats give birth or when deer deliver their calves? (Mountain goats: ibex, calves: young) **2.** Can you count the months they are pregnant or know the time they give birth? (Count: number) **3.** They crouch, give birth to their young, and are relieved of their pain. (Crouch: kneel, relieved: freed) **4.** Their young grow strong, thrive in the wild, and leave without returning. (Grow: develop, thrive: prosper) **5.** Who set the wild donkey free or untied its bonds? (Set free: released, untied: loosened, bonds: restraints) **6.** I made the wilderness· its home, the barren land its dwelling. (Wilderness: desert) **7.** It mocks the noise of the city and pays no attention to the shouts of the driver. (mocks: ridicules, pays no attention: ignores) **8.** Its pasture is in the mountains, and it searches for any green plant. (Pasture: grazing land, searches for: looks for) **9.** Will the unicorn serve you or stay by your crib? (unicorn: wild ox, crib: stable) **10.** Can you bind the unicorn to plow your fields or make it work in the valleys? (work: labor) **11.** Will you trust it because of its great strength, or leave your work to it? (trust: rely on, strength: power) **12.** Will you believe it will bring in your harvest and gather it into your barn? (believe: expect, harvest: crop) **13.** Did you give wings to the peacock or feathers to the ostrich? (feathers: plumage) **14.** The ostrich leaves her eggs in the earth and warms them in the dust. **15.** She forgets that the foot may crush them or the wild beast may break them. (Forgets: overlooks, crush: smash) **16.** She is indifferent to her young, as though they aren't hers. She labors in vain without fear. (Indifferent: unconcerned, labors in vain: works uselessly) **17.** Because God has denied her wisdom and understanding. (Denied: withheld, wisdom: knowledge) **18.** When she lifts herself high, she scorns the horse and its rider. (Scorns: mocks) **19.** Did you give the horse its strength or clothe its neck with thunder? (Strength: power, clothe: adorn) **20.** Can you make it afraid like a grasshopper? Its nostrils are terrifying. (Afraid: scared, nostrils: nose, terrifying: frightening) **21.** It paws in the valley, rejoicing in its strength and charging at armed men. (Pauses: strikes, charging: charging) **22.** It mocks fear and isn't frightened; it doesn't turn back from the sword. (Mock: ridicules, frightened: afraid, sword: weapon) **23.** The quiver rattles against it, and the glittering spear and shield. (Quiver: bow case, rattles: shakes, glittering: shining) **24.** It swallows the ground with fierceness and rage, ignoring the sound of the trumpet. (Swallows: devours, fierceness: fierceness, ignoring: dismisses) **25.** It shouts among the trumpets, "Ha! Ha!" and smells battle afar off—the thunder of commanders and the shouting. (Shouts: yells, thunder: roar) **26.** Does the hawk fly by your wisdom, stretching its wings toward the south? (Hawk: bird of prey) **27.** Does the eagle soar at your command and build its nest on high? (soar: fly, command: order) **28.** It dwells on the rock, in the crag of the rock, and the stronghold. (Dwells: lives, crag: cliff) **29.** From there it seeks its prey, and its eyes observe from afar. (seeks: hunts, observe: watch) **30.** Its young drink blood, and where the slain are, there it is. (Drink: consume, slain: dead).

Chapter 40
1. Then the LORD spoke to Job, saying, **2.** Can anyone who argues with the Almighty teach Him? If someone challenges God, let them answer. (argues: debates, teaches: instructs, challenges: questions) **3.** Job replied to the LORD and said, **4.** I am worthless; what can I say to You? I will keep silent and cover my mouth. (Worthless: insignificant, silent: quiet) **5.** I've spoken once, but I won't respond again; I've spoken twice, but I will not say more. (Respond: reply, say more: speak further) **6.** Then the LORD spoke to Job out of the storm and said, **7.** Prepare yourself like a man; I will ask you questions, and you will answer. (Prepare: brace, questions: inquiries) **8.** Will you cancel my judgment? Will you declare me wrong so you can be right? (cancel: undo, declare: proclaim, wrong: in the wrong) **9.** Do you have a mighty arm like God's? Can you thunder with a voice like His? (mighty: powerful, thunder: roar) **10.** Put on glory and splendor, dress yourself in honor and majesty. (Glory: brilliance, splendor: magnificence, honor: dignity, majesty: grandeur) **11.** Unleash your anger; look at the proud and bring them down. (Unleash: release, proud: arrogant, bring them down: humble them) **12.** Look at the arrogant and humble them; crush the wicked where they stand. (Arrogant: prideful, humble: abase, crush: defeat) **13.** Bury them in the dust, and hide their faces in the darkness. (Bury: cover, hide: conceal) **14.** Then I will acknowledge that your own right hand can save you. (Acknowledge: admit, right hand: power) **15.** Look at behemoth, which I created with you. It eats grass like an ox. (Behemoth: giant beast, ox: cow) **16.** Its strength is in its back and its power in the muscles of its belly. (Strength: might) **17.** Its tail swings like a cedar tree; the sinews of its thighs are tightly bound. (tail: rear, swings: sways, sinews: tendons, tightly: firmly) **18.** Its bones are like bronze beams; its limbs are like iron rods. (Bones: skeleton, limbs: legs, rods: bars) **19.** It is the most powerful of God's creations; only its Creator can approach it with a sword. (Powerful: strong, Creator: Maker) **20.** The mountains provide it with food, where all the wild animals roam. (provide: supply, roam: wander) **21.** It rests under the lotus trees, in the secret places of the reeds and marshes. (reeds: grasses) **22.** The trees cover it with shade, and the willows by the river encircle it. (willows: trees, encircle: surround) **23.** It drinks from the river and is not in a hurry; it believes it can draw the Jordan into its mouth. (Drinks: gulps, hurry: rush, draw: pull) **24.** It watches the river with its eyes, and its nose pushes through the traps. (Watches: observes, pushes: breaks, traps: snares).

Chapter 41
1. Can you catch Leviathan with a hook or his tongue with a rope? (Catch: capture) **2.** Can you pierce his nose or bore his jaw with a thorn? (Pierce: stab, bore: pierce) **3.** Will he beg you for mercy or speak gentle words to you? (Mercy: forgiveness, gentle: kind) **4.** Will he make a covenant with you, or will you make him your servant forever? (Covenant: agreement, servant: slave) **5.** Will you play with him like a bird or keep him for your maids? (play: amuse, maids: servants) **6.** Will his companions feast on him or divide him among traders? (feast: eat, divide: share) **7.** Can you fill his skin with iron or his head with fish spears? (fill: stuff, skin: hide, spears: javelins) **8.** Lay your hand on him, remember the battle, and don't try again. (lay: place, battle: fight) **9.** Behold, hope of conquering him is in vain; just seeing him strikes fear. (Hope: expectation, conquering: defeating, vain: useless, strikes: causes) **10.** No one dares provoke him; who can stand before me? (Dares: challenges, provoke: annoy, stand: confront) **11.** Who has claimed anything from me that I must repay? Everything under heaven is mine. (Claimed: demanded, repay: give back) **12.** I will not hide his form, power, or majestic appearance. (Hide: conceal, form: shape, majestic: glorious) **13.** Who can uncover his garment or approach him with a bridle? (Uncover: reveal, garment: covering, bridle: rein) **14.** Who can open his face, with his terrifying teeth all around? (open: unfasten, terrifying: fearsome) **15.** His scales are his pride, tightly sealed together. (scales: plates, pride: boast, tightly: firmly) **16.** They are so close that no air can pass between them. (Close: tight, pass: go) **17.** They are joined together and cannot be separated. **18.** When he sneezes, light shines, and his eyes are like the dawn. **19.** From his mouth come burning lamps, and sparks of fire leap out. (Burning: blazing,) **20.** Smoke pours from his nostrils like a boiling pot. **21.** His breath ignites coals, and a flame comes from his mouth. (ignites: lights, coals: embers, flame: fire) **22.** Strength rests in his neck, and joy turns to fear before him. (Rests: lies, joy: gladness, turns: changes) **23.** His flesh is tightly bound, firm and immovable. (flesh: body, bound: held, firm: solid, immovable: unshakeable) **24.** His heart is as hard as a stone, as unyielding as a millstone. (Heart: core, unyielding: rigid) **25.** When he rises, the mighty are afraid and purify themselves from fear. (mighty: powerful, purify: cleanse) **26.** Weapons cannot harm him: neither sword, spear, nor armor. (Weapons: arms, spear: javelin, armor: protection) **27.** He treats iron like straw and brass like rotten wood. (treats: handles, straw: hay, brass: copper, rotten: decayed) **28.** Arrows cannot make him flee; stones are like stubble to him. (flee: escape, stones: rocks, stubble: chaff) **29.** Darts are like straw; he laughs at the shaking of a spear. (laughs: mocks, shaking: trembling) **30.** Sharp stones are beneath him; he spreads sharp objects on the mud. (sharp: pointed, beneath: below, spreads: scatters) **31.** He makes the sea boil like a pot, like a pot of ointment. (Ointment: fragrance oil) **32.** He leaves a shining trail in the water, making the deep seem gray. (shining: glowing). **33.** On earth, there is no one like him, made without fear. (earth: world, made: created, without: free of) **34.** He watches all high things; he is the king of all the proud. (watches: observes, high: lofty, king: ruler, proud: arrogant).

Chapter 42
1. Job answered the LORD and said, **2.** I know You can do anything, and nothing is hidden from You. (hidden: concealed) **3.** Who is the one who speaks without understanding? I spoke of things I didn't know, things too marvelous for me. (understanding: comprehension, marvelous: amazing) **4.** Please listen, and I will speak; I will ask, and You will answer. (listen: hear, ask: inquire, answer: respond) **5.** I had heard of You by word, but now I see You with my own eyes. (heard: known, word: report) **6.** Therefore, I repent in dust and ashes. (repent: regret) **7.** After speaking to Job, the LORD said to Eliphaz the Temanite, "My anger is against you and your two friends because

you did not speak rightly about Me as Job did." (anger: wrath, rightly: truthfully) **8.** Take seven bulls and seven rams, go to Job, and offer a burnt offering for yourselves. Job will pray for you, and I will accept him, or I will punish you for not speaking rightly about Me. (bulls: cattle, rams: sheep, punish: chastise) **9.** Eliphaz, Bildad, and Zophar did as the LORD commanded, and the LORD accepted Job. (commanded: instructed) **10.** The LORD restored Job when he prayed for his friends and gave him twice as much as he had before. (restored: returned, prayed: interceded) **11.** His brothers, sisters, and former friends came, ate with him, comforted him for all the evil the LORD had brought upon him, and each gave him money and a gold earring. (comforted: consoled, evil: hardship, gave: presented) **12.** The LORD blessed Job's latter days more than his beginning. He had 14,000 sheep, 6,000 camels, 1,000 oxen, and 1,000 donkeys. (blessed: favored, latter: final) **13.** Job also had seven sons and three daughters. (sons: boys, daughters: girls) **14.** He named his first daughter Jemima, the second Kezia, and the third Keren-happuch. (named: called) **15.** No women were as beautiful as Job's daughters, and he gave them an inheritance along with their brothers. (beautiful: lovely, inheritance: fortune) **16.** Job lived 140 years, saw his children and grandchildren, four generations. (lived: existed, generations: descendants) **17.** Job died old and full of days. (old: elderly).

19 – Psalms
Chapter 1
1. Blessed is the person who doesn't follow the advice of the wicked, who doesn't stand in the path of wrongdoers, nor sit with those who mock others. (Wicked: morally wrong; Mock: to make fun of or ridicule.) **2.** But rather, their joy is in the training of the LORD, and they meditate on it day and night. (Meditate: to think deeply about something.) **3.** They're like a tree planted near aqueducts of water, which produces fruit at the right time, and whose leaves remain healthy; everything they do will succeed. (Stream: a small river; Prosper: to succeed or thrive.) **4.** The wicked, still, aren't like this; they're like chaff that the wind blows down. (Chaff: the outer husk of grain, which is useless and blown away.) **5.** Thus, the wicked won't stand establishment in the judgment, nor will wrongdoers be set up among the righteous. (Judgment: the final decision or verdict at the end of life.) **6.** For the LORD knows the way of the righteous, but the path of the wicked will be destroyed. (Righteous: morally right or just.)

Chapter 2
1. Why do the nations rage, and why do people imagine useless plans? (Rage: to be angry or violent; Imagine: to think of or devise.) **2.** The lords of the earth stand united, and autocrats compass together against the LORD and His chosen one, saying, (Plot: to plan secretly.) **3.** "Let us break their chains and throw off their ropes!" (Chains: something that binds; Ropes: figurative of control.) **4.** The One who sits in the welkin laughs at them; the LORD mocks them. (Mocks: makes fun of.) **5.** Also, He'll speak to them in His wrathfulness, and scarify them with His wrath. (Wrath: intense anger.) **6.** But I've installed my King on Zion, my holy mountain. (Installed: placed in position.) **7.** I'll declare the decree: The LORD has said to me, "You're my Son; today I've become your Father." (Decree: an official order or decision.) **8.** Ask me, and I'll make the nations your heritage, the ends of the earth your possession. (Heritage: something passed down; Possession: something owned.) **9.** You'll rule them with an iron scepter; you'll shatter them like crockery. (Scepter: a staff symbolizing power; Shatter: to break into pieces.) **10.** Thus, be wise, you lords; be instructed, you autocrats of the earth. (Instructed: taught or advised.) **11.** Serve the LORD with reverence and rejoice with pulsing. (Reverence: deep respect.) **12.** Kiss the Son, lest He be angry and you be destroyed in your way, when His wrath is snappily burned. Blessed are all who take retreat in Him. (Kiss the Son: a gesture of loyalty or submission; Burned: aroused or started.)

Chapter 3
1. LORD, how numerous are my adversaries! How numerous rise up against me! (Adversaries: those who oppose or are hostile to someone. **2.** Numerous say of me, "God won't deliver him." Selah. (Deliver: to rescue or save; Selah: a pause for reflection or musical interlude.) **3.** But You, LORD, are a guard around me; You're my glory and the One who lifts my head. (Shield: a protector; Glory: honor and praise.) **4.** I cried out to the LORD, and He answered me from His holy mountain. Selah. (Cried out: called urgently.) **5.** I lay down and slept; I woke up, for the LORD sustained me. (Sustained: kept alive or supported.) **6.** I'll not sweat the knockouts of thousands who have set themselves against me on every side. (Fear: to be afraid; Knockouts of thousands: many people.) **7.** Arise, LORD, save me, my God. You have struck all my adversaries on the jaw; You have broken the teeth of the wicked. (Teeth: metaphor for power.) **8.** Salvation belongs to the LORD; Your blessing is upon Your people. Selah. (Salvation: deliverance or saving; Blessing: favor or approval.)

Chapter 4
1. Answer me when I call, O God of my righteousness; You have relieved me in my torture; have mercy on me and hear my prayer. (Relieved: made less anxious or troubled.) **2.** How long will you people turn my glory into shame? How long will you love visions and seek false gods? Selah. (Visions: false beliefs or ideas.) **3.** Know that the LORD has set apart the godly for Himself; the LORD will hear when I call to Him. (Set apart: separated or chosen for a special purpose; Godly: righteous or devout.) **4.** Fluctuate and don't stray; when you're on your beds, search your hearts and be silent. Selah. (Fluctuate: shake with fear or emotion.) **5.** Offer offerings that are right, and trust in the LORD. (Offerings: offerings made to God.) **6.** Numerous are asking, "Who'll show us any good?" LORD, let the light of Your face shine upon us. (Light of Your face: metaphor for God's favor.) **7.** You have filled my heart with lesser joy than when their grain and new wine pullulate. (Abound: to exist in large quantities.) **8.** I'll lie down and sleep in peace, for You alone, LORD, make me dwell in safety. (Safety: being free from harm or danger.)

Chapter 5
1. Hear to my words, O LORD, and consider my studies. (Contemplation: deep thinking) **2.** Pay attention to my cry, my King and my God; I'll supplicate to You. (Cry: loud call for help) **3.** In the morning, O LORD, You'll hear my voice; I'll direct my prayers to You and look up. (Direct: companion) **4.** For You don't delight in wickedness; wrong cannot dwell with You. (Wickedness: immoral gesture) **5.** The foolish won't stand before You; You detest all who do wrong. (Foolish: lacking wisdom) **6.** You'll destroy those who lie; the LORD detests the violent and deceitful. (Deceitful: dishonest) **7.** But I'll enter Your house because of Your mercy; in admiration of You, I'll worship. (Mercy: compassion) **8.** Lead me, O LORD, in Your righteousness because of my adversaries; make Your way clear before me. (Righteousness: moral correctness) **9.** There's no verity in their speech; their hearts are filled with wrong; their throats are open graves; they flatter with their speeches. (Flatter: insincere praise) **10.** Destroy them, O God; let them fall by their own plans; cast them out for their numerous sins, for they've mutinied against You. (Mutinied: defied authority) **11.** Let all who take retreat in You rejoice; let them always be glad and sing for joy, for You cover them. (Refuge: protection) **12.** For You, O LORD, bless the righteous; You compass them with Your favor as with a guard. (Favor: support)

Chapter 6
1. O LORD, don't rebuke me in Your wrathfulness, nor correct me in Your displeasure. (Reproach: condemn; Displeasure: wrathfulness) **2.** Have mercy on me, O LORD, for I'm weak; O LORD, heal me, for my bones are in agony. (Agony: extreme pain) **3.** My soul is deeply worried; how long, O LORD, will You allow this suffering? (Distressed: worried) **4.** Return, O LORD, and deliver my soul; save me because of

Your loving: kindness. (Loving: kindness: compassion) **5.** For in death, there's no remembrance of You; who'll praise You from the grave? (Remembrance: memory) **6.** I'm worn out from my groaning; all night long I submerge my bed with gashes. (Moaning: expressing pain) **7.** My eyes grow weak with anguish; they fail because of all my adversaries. (Anguish: grief) **8.** Depart from me, all you who do wrong, for the LORD has heard my weeping. (Depart: leave) **9.** The LORD has heard my plea; the LORD will accept my prayer. (Plea: critical request) **10.** Let all my adversaries be shamed and greatly worried; let them turn back in shame. (Worried: distressed)

Chapter 7
1. O LORD my God, in You I take retreat; save me from all who pursue me, and deliver me. (Refuge: protection; Pursue: chase) **2.** Else, they will tear my soul piecemeal like a captain, dragging it down with no bone to deliver. (Tear: rip piecemeal; Deliverance: save) **3.** O LORD my God, if I've done this, if there's injustice in my hands. (Injustice: unfairness) **4.** Still, (Repay: return) **5.** If I've repaid evil to one who was at peace with me. Let my adversary pursue and catch my soul; let him champ my life and lay my honor in the dust. Selah. (Trample: crush) **6.** Arise, O LORD, in Your wrathfulness; rise up against my adversaries; awake for the judgment You have commanded. (Fury: rage) **7.** Let the people gather around You; return to Your throne on high. (Throne: seat of authority) **8.** The LORD will judge the people; judge me, O LORD, according to my righteousness and integrity. (Integrity: moral honesty) **9.** End the wickedness of the wicked, and establish the righteous, for You test hearts and minds. (Establish: set; Test: examine) **10.** My guard is with God, who saves the upright in heart. (Shield: protection) **11.** God is a righteous judge, and He's angry with the wicked every day. (Righteous: innocently just) **12.** Still, He'll edge His brand; He has bent His arc and made it ready, if the wicked don't rue. (Rue: feel guilt) **13.** He has prepared deadly munitions for them; He makes His arrows deadly. (Deadly: fatal) **14.** The wicked conceive wrong and give birth to falsehoods. (Conceive: form) **15.** They dig a hole and fall into the hole they made. (Hole: pit) **16.** The trouble they beget will return on their own heads; their violence will fall on their own heads. (Violence: detriment) **17.** I'll give thanks to the LORD because of His righteousness; I'll sing praises to His name. (Righteousness: moral correctness)

Chapter 8
1. O LORD, our Lord, how majestic is Your name in all the earth! You have set Your glory above the welkin. (Majestic: grand) **2.** Out of the mouths of babes, You have ordained strength to silence the foe and the chastiser. (Ordained: established) **3.** When I consider Your welkin, the work of Your fritters, the moon and the stars You set in place. (Consider: suppose about) **4.** What's humanity that You're aware of him, the son of man that You watch for him? (Aware: apprehensive) **5.** You made him a little lower than the angels and culminated him with glory and honor. (Angels: heavenly beings) **6.** You made him sovereign over the workshop of Your hands; You put everything under his bases. (Sovereign: leader) **7.** All the flocks and herds, and the creatures of the wild, **8.** The catcalls of the air, and the fish of the ocean, all that swim the paths of the swell. (Swim: move through water) **9.** O LORD, our Lord, how majestic is Your name in all the earth! (Majestic: grand)

Chapter 9
1. I will praise You, O LORD, with all my heart; I will proclaim Your deeds. (deeds: acts) **2.** I will rejoice in You and sing praises to Your name, O Most High. (rejoice: show joy) **3.** When my enemies turn back, they will stumble and perish before You. (stumble: trip, perish: be destroyed) **4.** You have defended my rights and sit on the throne, judging justly. (defended: protected) **5.** You have rebuked nations, destroyed the wicked, and wiped their name out. (rebuked: scolded, wicked: evil) **6.** O enemy, ruin is ended for you; You destroyed cities, and their memory is gone. (ruin: destruction) **7.** But the LORD will endure forever; His throne is for judgment. (endure: last, judgment: decision) **8.** He will judge the world in righteousness and render just decisions to all. (righteousness: moral justice, render: make) **9.** The LORD will be a refuge for the oppressed, a safe haven in trouble. (refuge: safe place, oppressed: treated harshly) **10.** Those who know Your name will trust You, for You have not abandoned those who seek You. (abandoned: forsaken, seek: search for) **11.** Sing praises to the LORD who dwells in Zion; declare His deeds among nations. (dwells: resides, deeds: actions) **12.** When He demands justice for bloodshed, He remembers them; He does not forget the cry of the afflicted. (afflicted: sufferers) **13.** Have mercy on me, O LORD; consider my distress from my enemies. Lift me from death's gates. (mercy: compassion, distress: suffering, gates of death: place of death) **14.** That I may declare Your praises in Zion; I will rejoice in Your salvation. (declare: proclaim, zion: Jerusalem, salvation: deliverance) **15.** The nations have fallen into their own pit; their feet are caught in their own net. (pit: trap) (net: trapping device) **16.** The LORD is known by His judgment; the wicked are trapped by their hands. (judgment: decision) (wicked: evil) (trapped: ensnared) **17.** The wicked go to the grave, and all nations that forget God. (grave: burial place) **18.** The needy will not be forgotten, and the hope of the poor will not perish. (needy: those in need) (hope: desire for a good outcome) **19.** Arise, O LORD; do not let mortals triumph. Let the nations be judged before You. (mortals: human beings) **20.** Strike fear into them, so they know they are merely human. (strike fear: cause terror)

Chapter 10
1. Why do You stand far away, O LORD? Why do You hide in times of trouble? (hide: conceal) (trouble: hardship) **2.** The wicked, in their pride, persecute the poor; let them be caught in their schemes. (pride: superiority) (persecute: treat cruelly) (schemes: deceitful plans) **3.** The wicked boast of their desires, and bless the greedy, whom the LORD despises. (boast: brag) (greedy: desiring more than needed) (despises: hates) **4.** The wicked, through pride, do not seek God; God is not in their thoughts. (countenance: appearance) **5.** Their ways are oppressive; Your judgments are beyond their sight. They sneer at enemies. (oppressive: burdensome) (judgments: decisions) (sneer: contemptuous smile) **6.** They say, "I will not be moved; I will never face adversity." (adversity: difficulty) **7.** Their mouths are full of cursing, lies, and deceit; under their tongues are mischief and wickedness. (mischief: harm) (wickedness: evil) **8.** They lurk in secret places; in hidden places, they murder the innocent. (lurk: hide) (murder: unlawfully kill) **9.** They crouch like a lion in its den; they trap the poor in their nets. (crouch: lower oneself) (den: lair) (nets: traps) **10.** They humble themselves, that the weak may fall by their hands. (humble: lower oneself) **11.** They say, "God has forgotten; He hides His face and will never see it." (forgotten: ignored) (hides: conceals) **12.** Arise, O LORD; lift up Your hand; do not forget the humble. (humble: modest) **13.** Why does the wicked disdain God? They say, "You will not hold us accountable." (disdain: contempt) (accountable: responsible) **14.** But You have seen it; You behold mischief and spite, and You will repay. The poor commit to You; You are the helper of the fatherless. (behold: observe) (mischief: harm) (spite: desire to hurt) (fatherless: without a father) **15.** Break the arm of the wicked; search out their wickedness until none remains. (wickedness: evil) **16.** The LORD is King forever; nations are perishing from His land. (perishing: being destroyed) **17.** LORD, You have heard the desire of the humble; You will strengthen their heart. (humble: modest) **18.** To defend the fatherless and oppressed, so mortals may no longer oppress them. (defend: protect) (oppressed: treated harshly)

Chapter 11
1. In the LORD I take refuge; why do you say, "Flee like a bird to your mountain"? (refuge: safe place) **2.** For behold, the wicked bend their bows, prepare arrows to shoot at the upright. (behold: observe) (bows: archery equipment, upright: just) **3.** If the foundations are destroyed, what can the righteous do? (foundations: basic principles, righteous: just) **4.** The LORD is in His holy temple; His

throne is in heaven. His eyes behold, His eyelids test men. (holy: sacred, throne: authority seat, test: examine) **5.** The LORD tests the righteous, but the wicked and those who love violence, His soul hates. (tests: examines. violence: harm through force) **6.** Upon the wicked, He will rain snares, fire, brimstone, and burning wind. This will be their cup. (snares: traps, brimstone: sulfur, portion: part, cup: fate) **7.** For the righteous LORD loves righteousness; His face beholds the upright. (righteousness: moral justice, upright: just)

Chapter 12
1. Help me, O Lord, for the godly and faithful are disappearing. (godly: righteous; faithful: loyal) **2.** Everyone speaks deceitfully and with double motives. (deceitfully: dishonestly; double motives: hypocritically) **3.** The Lord will cut off the proud and boastful tongues. (boastful: those who speak arrogantly) **4.** They say, "With our words we will triumph; who can control us?" (triumph: victory) **5.** I will arise to protect the poor and needy from their mockers. (mockers: those who scorn) **6.** The Lord's words are pure, refined like silver. (refined: purified) **7.** You will protect them from this generation forever. (generation: people of this age) **8.** The wicked flourish when the vilest are exalted. (vilest: most wicked)

Chapter 13
1. How long, O Lord, will you forget me? (forget: neglect) **2.** How long will I have sorrow in my heart? (sorrow: grief) **3.** Answer me, Lord, and grant me help. (answer: hear me) **4.** My enemies will rejoice if I am shaken. (shaken: unsettled) **5.** I trust in your love; my heart rejoices in your salvation. (salvation: deliverance) **6.** I will sing to the Lord, for he has been good to me. (good: kind)

Chapter 14
1. The fool says, "There is no God." They are corrupt. (fool: those who reject wisdom) **2.** The Lord looks for those who seek him. (seek: search for) **3.** They have turned away and become corrupt. (corrupt: immoral) **4.** The wicked devour my people and don't call on the Lord. (devour: consume greedily) **5.** The righteous are protected by God. (righteous: just) **6.** The Lord is the refuge of the poor. (refuge: safe place) **7.** Oh, that Israel's salvation would come from Zion! (salvation: rescue)

Chapter 15
1. Lord, who may live in your presence? (presence: dwelling) **2.** Those who walk uprightly and speak truth. (uprightly: honestly) **3.** Those who do no wrong to others. (wrong: unjust actions) **4.** They despise the wicked and honor the God: fearing. (despise: reject; honor: respect) **5.** They do not take bribes or lend at interest. (bribes: gifts for influence; interest: money charged for lending unfairly)

Chapter 16
1. Protect me, O God, for I trust in you. (protect: guard) **2.** You are my Lord, and apart from you, I have nothing good. (apart: separate) **3.** The saints are my delight. (saints: holy people) **4.** I will not follow other gods or honor their rituals. (rituals: religious practices) **5.** The Lord is my inheritance and my portion. (inheritance: legacy; portion: share) **6.** My life is secure in pleasant places. (secure: safe) **7.** I will bless the Lord, who gives me counsel. (counsel: advice) **8.** With the Lord at my right hand, I will not be moved. (right hand: symbolizing support and favour) **9.** My heart is glad, and my body rests in peace. (rest: be at ease) **10.** You will not leave me in the grave. (grave: death) **11.** You will show me the path of life and eternal joy in your presence. (path of life: righteous way; eternal joy: lasting happiness)

Chapter 17
1. O LORD, hear my plea for justice, my cry, and my prayer, which is sincere. (deceitful: false or pretended) **2.** Let my case be judged fairly in Your presence. **3.** You have tested my heart and found no wrong; I am determined not to speak inappropriately. **4.** I have kept from destructive paths by Your guidance. **5.** Guide my steps, that I do not stumble. **6.** I call to You, for You will hear me. **7.** Show me Your mercy and save those who trust in You. **8.** Protect me like the pupil of Your eye. (pupil: the center of the eye) **9.** Save me from the wicked who oppress me. **10.** They are full of pride, speaking arrogantly. (arrogantly: excessively proud) **11.** They surround us with their plans, watching us closely. **12.** Like a lion waiting to ambush its prey. **13.** Arise, LORD, defeat them and rescue my soul. **14.** Save me from men whose riches and inheritance are in this life. (portion: inheritance) **15.** I will see Your face in righteousness and be satisfied with Your likeness. (likeness: in Your image)

Chapter 18
1. I will love You, O LORD, my strength. **2.** The LORD is my rock, my fortress, my deliverer; my God, my strength, the one I trust; my shield, the source of my salvation, and my stronghold. (stronghold: a place of safety) **3.** I will call upon the LORD, worthy of praise, and I will be saved from my enemies. **4.** The terrors of death surrounded me, and wicked forces made me fearful. (wicked: evil) **5.** The terror of the grave engulfed me; the snares of death closed in. (snares: entanglement) **6.** In my distress, I called to the LORD, and He heard me from His temple. **7.** The earth shook; the foundations of the mountains trembled because He was angry. (foundations: bases) **8.** Smoke rose from His nostrils, and fire devoured from His mouth; burning coals blazed. (blazed: caught fire) **9.** He bent down the heavens and came down; darkness was under His feet. **10.** He rode on a cherub, flying swiftly; He soared on the wind. (cherub: angel) **11.** Darkness was His hiding place; His canopy surrounded by dark waters and thick clouds. (canopy: covering) **12.** At His brightness, dark clouds scattered with hailstones and burning coals. (hailstones: frozen ice balls) **13.** The LORD thundered from the heavens; hailstones and burning coals. **14.** He sent arrows and scattered them; lightning bolts dismayed them. (dismayed: frightened) **15.** The channels of the sea were exposed; the earth's foundations were laid bare at Your rebuke, O LORD. (channels: paths) **16.** He reached down from on high, took hold of me, and pulled me from deep waters. **17.** He rescued me from my powerful enemies, for they were too strong. **18.** They confronted me in my time of trouble, but the LORD was my support. (trouble: distress) **19.** He brought me out into a spacious place and rescued me because He delighted in me. (spacious: wide space) **20.** The LORD rewarded me for my righteousness; He repaid me according to my hands' purity. **21.** For I have followed the ways of the LORD, and have not turned from my God. **22.** His laws were before me, and I have not disregarded His commands. (laws: commands) **23.** I have lived with integrity before Him, and kept myself from sin. (integrity: honesty) **24.** Therefore, the LORD has rewarded me according to my righteousness, according to my hands' purity in His sight. **25.** With the merciful You show Yourself merciful; with the upright You show Yourself upright. (merciful: compassionate, upright: just) **26.** With the pure You show Yourself pure; with the crooked You show Yourself difficult to deal with. (pure: clean, crooked: dishonest) **27.** You save the humble, but bring down the proud. (humble: modest, proud: arrogant) **28.** You light my lamp; the LORD my God lights up my darkness. **29.** With Your help, I can run through a troop of enemies and leap over a wall. (troop: group) **30.** As for God, His way is perfect; His word is tested; He is a shield to all who take refuge in Him. (refuge: protection) **31.** For who is God except the LORD? Who is a rock except our God? (rock: safety) **32.** It is God who arms me with strength and makes my way perfect. **33.** He makes my feet like those of a deer and sets me on high places. **34.** He trains my hands for battle so that my arms can bend a bow of bronze. (bronze: metal) **35.** You have given me the shield of salvation; Your right hand has supported me; Your gentleness has made me great. (gentleness: kindness) **36.** You enlarged my steps so that my feet do not slip. **37.** I pursued my enemies and overtook them; I did not turn back until they were destroyed. **38.** I wounded them, and they could not rise; they fell beneath my feet. **39.** For You armed me with strength for the battle; You subdued my enemies. **40.** You made my enemies turn their backs to me; I destroyed those who hated me. **41.** They cried out, but there was no one to save them; they cried to the LORD, but He

did not answer. **42.** I beat them like dust before the wind; I cast them out like dirt in the streets. **43.** You rescued me from disputes of the people and made me head of the nations; people I did not know serve me. (disputes: conflicts) **44.** As soon as they hear of me, they obey me; foreigners submit to me. (foreigners: strangers) **45.** Foreigners lose heart and tremble from their strongholds. (strongholds: secure places) **46.** The LORD lives! Praise be to my Rock! Exalted be the God of my salvation! **47.** It is God who avenges me and subdues nations under me. (avenges: seeks justice) **48.** He rescues me from my enemies; You lift me above those who rise up against me; You deliver me from violent men. (violent: aggressive) **49.** Therefore, I will praise You, O LORD, among the nations and sing praises to Your name. **50.** Great deliverance He gives to His king, and shows mercy to His anointed, to David, and his descendants forever. (deliverance: rescue, anointed: chosen one)

Chapter 19
1. The heavens declare the glory of God, and the sky shows His work. **2.** Day and night speak, revealing knowledge. **3.** There is no speech or language where their message is not understood. **4.** Their message stretches across the earth, and their words reach the world. He has set a home for the sun in them (tabernacle: a sacred dwelling). **5.** The sun is like a bridegroom rejoicing to run a race (bridegroom: a man about to marry). **6.** Its path reaches the ends of the sky, and nothing escapes its heat. **7.** The law of the LORD is perfect, restoring the soul. The testimony of the LORD is dependable, making the simple wise (simple: inexperienced). **8.** The statutes of the LORD bring joy; His commandment gives light to the eyes. **9.** The fear of the LORD is clean, lasting forever. The judgments are righteous. **10.** They are more precious than gold and sweeter than honey. **11.** By them your servant is warned, and in keeping them, there is great reward. **12.** Cleanse me from hidden faults. **13.** Keep me from willful sins; let them not rule over me (willful: presumptuous, arrogant). **14.** May the words of my mouth and the meditation of my heart be pleasing to you, O LORD, my strength and my redeemer.

Chapter 20
1. May the LORD answer you in trouble; may the God of Jacob protect you. **2.** May He send help from His sanctuary (holy place) and strengthen you from Zion. **3.** May He accept your offerings and burnt sacrifices. Selah. **4.** May He give you the desires of your heart and fulfill your plans. **5.** We will rejoice in your salvation and raise our banners. May the LORD fulfill all your requests. **6.** I know the LORD saves His anointed (chosen one); He will answer with strength. **7.** Some trust in chariots, but we trust in the name of the LORD. **8.** They have fallen, but we have risen and stand firm. **9.** Save us, LORD; let the king hear us when we call.

Chapter 21
1. The king rejoices in your strength, O LORD; he greatly rejoices in your salvation. **2.** You have granted him the desires of his heart. Selah. **3.** You meet him with blessings and crown him with pure gold. **4.** He asked for life, and you gave it to him forever. **5.** His glory is great because of your salvation; you have bestowed honor and majesty on him (majesty: greatness). **6.** You have made him blessed forever and exceedingly glad in your presence (exceedingly: in overwhelming joy). **7.** The king trusts in the LORD, and through His mercy, he will not be shaken. **8.** Your hand will find all your enemies; your right hand will find those who hate you. **9.** You will make them like a blazing oven in your anger; the LORD will destroy them with fire. **10.** You will destroy their descendants and offspring. **11.** They planned evil but cannot carry it out. **12.** You will make them turn their back when you aim your bow at them. **13.** Be exalted (raised in honor), O LORD, in your strength; we will praise your power.

Chapter 22
1. My God, my God, why have you abandoned me? Why are you so far away from offering your help, and from hearing the words of my cries? (abandoned: forsaken; help: assistance; cries: loud cries of pain) **2.** My God, I call to you during the day, but you do not respond; I cry out at night, but remain silent. (respond: answer) **3.** Yet you are holy, O God, who is praised by the people of Israel. (holy: pure, set apart; praised: honored) **4.** Our ancestors trusted in you; they trusted, and you saved them. (ancestors: forefathers; trusted: believed in) **5.** They cried to you, and you delivered them; they trusted in you, and were never disappointed. (delivered: rescued; disappointed: let down) **6.** But I am like a worm, not even a man; a disgrace to humanity, despised by the people. (disgrace: shame; despised: hated, looked down upon) **7.** All those who see me mock me; they curl their lips and shake their heads, saying, (mock: make fun of) **8.** "He trusted in the Lord, let the Lord rescue him; if the Lord delights in him, let him save him." (delights: takes pleasure in) **9.** But you are the one who brought me out of my mother's womb; you made me trust you even when I was nursing at my mother's breast. (brought: delivered; trust: rely on) **10.** I was cast upon you from my birth; you have been my God from the moment I was born. (cast: placed, entrusted) **11.** Do not be far from me, for trouble is near, and there is no one to help me. (trouble: difficulty, distress) **12.** Many strong bulls surround me; mighty bulls from Bashan encircle me. (mighty: powerful; encircle: surround) **13.** They open their mouths wide at me, like roaring and hungry lions. (roaring: growling, making loud noises; hungry: eager for food) **14.** I feel like water spilling out; my bones are dislocated, my heart is like melted wax within me. (dislocated: out of joint; melted: turned to liquid) **15.** My strength is gone, like a broken piece of pottery; my tongue sticks to the roof of my mouth, and you have laid me in the dust of death. (strength: energy; broken: shattered; laid: placed) **16.** For wild dogs surround me; a gang of evildoers has closed in on me; they pierce my hands and feet. (wild dogs: ferocious enemies; gang: group; pierce: wound with a sharp object) **17.** I can count all my bones; they stare and gloat over me. (gloat: look with malicious satisfaction) **18.** They divide my clothes among them and cast lots for my garments. (cast lots: gamble) **19.** But do not be far from me, O Lord; my strength, hurry to help me. (strength: sustaining power) **20.** Save my soul from the sword; my precious life from the power of the dogs. (precious: valuable; sword: weapon; dogs: enemies) **21.** Rescue me from the lion's mouth; answer me from the horns of wild oxen. (horns: symbolic of power and aggression, hard projections) **22.** I will praise your name to my brothers; I will praise you in the congregation. (congregation: gathering of people) **23.** All you who revere the Lord, praise him; all you descendants of Jacob, honor him; stand in awe of him, all you descendants of Israel. (revere: respect deeply; descendants: children, offspring; awe: wonder) **24.** For he has not despised or ignored the suffering of the afflicted; he has not hidden his face from them, but when they cried to him, he listened. (afflicted: suffering; despised: hated; hidden: concealed) **25.** I will praise you in the great assembly; I will fulfill my vows before those who fear you. (assembly: gathering; fulfill: keep; vows: promises) **26.** The humble will eat and be satisfied; those who seek the Lord will praise him; may your hearts live forever. (humble: lowly, meek; satisfied: content; seek: look for) **27.** All the ends of the earth will remember and turn to the Lord, and all the families of the nations will bow down before you. (ends: farthest parts; nations: groups of people; bow down: show respect by lowering oneself) **28.** For the kingdom belongs to the Lord, and he rules over the nations. (kingdom: reign, domain; rules: governs) **29.** All those who are fat on earth will eat and worship; all those who go down to the dust will bow before him; no one can keep their soul alive. (fat: wealthy; worship: show reverence; dust: death) **30.** A future generation will serve him; they will proclaim the Lord to the next generation. (proclaim: announce, declare) **31.** They will declare his righteousness to a people yet to be born, for he has done it. (righteousness: goodness; declare: announce)

Chapter 23
1. The Lord is my shepherd; I shall not lack anything. (shepherd:

guide, protector; lack: be without) **2.** He lets me lie down in lush green pastures; he leads me beside peaceful waters. (lush: rich, fertile; pastures: grassy fields; peaceful: calm) **3.** He refreshes my soul; he guides me along right paths for the sake of his name. (refreshes: renews; guides: leads; paths: ways) **4.** Even though I walk through the darkest valley, I will not fear any evil, for you are with me; your rod and your staff comfort me. (darkest: most dangerous; valley: low area between mountains; rod: a symbol of authority and protection; staff: a tool for comfort and guidance) **5.** You prepare a feast for me in the presence of my enemies; you anoint my head with oil, my cup overflows. (feast: meal; anoint: bless) **6.** Surely your goodness and love will follow me all the days of my life, and I will dwell in the house of the Lord forever. (goodness: kindness; dwell: live)

Chapter 24
1. The earth is the Lord's, and everything in it, the world, and all who live in it. (earth: planet; live: exist and thrive under God's authority.) **2.** For he founded it upon the seas and established it upon the waters. (founded: created; established: set up) **3.** Who may ascend the mountain of the Lord? Who may stand in his holy place? (ascend: climb; stand: remain; holy: pure) **4.** The one who has clean hands and a pure heart, who does not trust in idols or swear by false gods. (clean: innocent; pure: free from sin; idols: false gods) **5.** They will receive blessing from the Lord and righteousness from the God of their salvation. (blessing: favor; righteousness: goodness; salvation: rescue) **6.** Such is the generation of those who seek him, who seek your face, O God of Jacob. Selah. (generation: group of people; seek: earnestly desire; face: presence) **7.** Lift up your heads, O gates; be lifted up, you ancient doors, that the King of glory may come in. (ancient: old; gates: entrances) **8.** Who is this King of glory? The Lord strong and mighty, the Lord mighty in battle. (mighty: powerful) **9.** Lift up your heads, O gates; lift them up, you ancient doors, that the King of glory may come in. (gates: entrances) **10.** Who is he, this King of glory? The Lord Almighty—he is the King of glory. Selah. (Almighty: all-powerful)

Chapter 25
1. To You, O LORD, I lift my soul. (soul: inner being, mind, and emotions) **2.** My God, I trust in You; do not let me be disgraced or let my enemies win. (triumph: succeed or celebrate victory) **3.** None who hope in You will be ashamed, but shame will come to those who act without cause. (shame: dishonor or embarrassment) **4.** Show me Your ways, O LORD, and teach me Your paths. (paths: ways of living) **5.** Guide me in truth and teach me, for You are my Savior; my hope is in You. **6.** Remember, O LORD, Your compassion and love from of old. (tender mercies: deep compassion) **7.** Forget the sins of my youth; in mercy, remember me for Your goodness. **8.** The LORD is good and just; He shows sinners the right way. **9.** He teaches the humble His way. **10.** The LORD's paths are love and truth for those who follow His covenant. (covenant: sacred agreement) **11.** For Your name's sake, LORD, forgive my great sin. (iniquity: moral corruption) **12.** The reverent will learn the right way. (feareth: shows reverence) **13.** They will live in peace, and their children will inherit the land. (inherit: to receive possession) **14.** The LORD reveals His covenant to those who fear Him. **15.** My eyes are on the LORD, for He rescues me from traps. **16.** Turn to me and show mercy, for I am troubled. **17.** Free me from my growing distress. **18.** Look on my suffering and forgive my sins. **19.** See how many enemies hate me fiercely. (cruel hatred: intense hostility) **20.** Protect my soul and save me; I trust in You. (trust: confidence) **21.** Let integrity preserve me, for I wait on You. (integrity: moral uprightness) **22.** Redeem Israel, O God, from all troubles. (redeem: rescue from hardship)

Chapter 26
1. Judge me, LORD, for I walk in integrity and trust You. (slide: fall away) **2.** Test my heart, O LORD. (reins: emotions) **3.** Your love is before me; I walk in Your truth. **4.** I avoid deceitful and hypocritical people. (dissemblers: deceivers) **5.** I hate evildoers and the wicked. (congregation: assembly) **6.** I wash my hands in innocence and approach Your altar. (innocency: blamelessness) **7.** I proclaim thanks and Your wonders. (wondrous: miraculous) **8.** LORD, I love Your house, where Your glory dwells. (habitation: dwelling) **9.** Do not group me with sinners or the violent. (bloody men: violent people) **10.** Their hands are evil, and they take bribes. (mischief: wrongdoing) **11.** I walk in integrity; redeem me with mercy. (mercy: kindness) **12.** I stand on solid ground and bless the LORD in the assembly. (even place: stable ground)

Chapter 27
1. The LORD is my light and salvation—whom should I fear? (salvation: rescue) **2.** When the wicked attacked, they stumbled and fell. **3.** Even if war rises, I will be confident. **4.** I desire to dwell in the LORD's presence and see His beauty. **5.** In trouble, He shelters me and sets me high on a rock. (pavilion: shelter) **6.** I will offer joyful sacrifices and sing praises to Him. (sacrifices of joy: gratitude offerings) **7.** Hear my cry, LORD; have mercy and answer me. (mercy: compassion) **8.** You said, "Seek My face," and I said, "I will seek You." (face: presence) **9.** Do not turn from me, O God of my salvation. **10.** If my parents forsake me, the LORD will care for me. (care for me: protect, forsake: leave) **11.** Teach me Your way and guide me on a clear path. (plain path: upright direction) **12.** Do not hand me to false accusers. **13.** I believed I would see the LORD's goodness in the living. **14.** Wait on the LORD; be brave, and He will strengthen you.

Chapter 28
1. To You, O LORD, I call; You are my rock. Do not stay silent, or I will become like those who fall into the grave. (grave: pit, destruction) **2.** Listen to my pleas when I call, lifting my hands toward Your holy place. (holy place: sacred place) **3.** Do not drag me with the wicked, who speak peace to neighbors but harbor evil. (wickedness: evil) **4.** Give them the punishment they deserve for their deeds and evil plans. **5.** Since they ignore the LORD's works, He will destroy them and not build them up. **6.** Blessed be the LORD, who has heard my pleas. **7.** The LORD is my strength and protector; my heart trusts, and He helps me. I will praise Him with joy. **8.** The LORD is the strength of His people and the saving strength of His anointed. (anointed: chosen, set apart) **9.** Save Your people, bless Your inheritance, and lift them forever. (inheritance: God's people)

Chapter 29
1. Give glory and strength to the LORD, O mighty ones. (mighty: those with great power) **2.** Give the glory due His name. Worship Him in holiness. (holiness: sacredness, purity) **3.** The LORD's voice thunders over the waters; He is over many waters. (thundereth: thunders) **4.** The voice of the LORD is powerful and majestic. (majesty: grandeur) **5.** The LORD's voice breaks the cedars of Lebanon. (cedars of Lebanon: tall, strong trees) **6.** He makes them leap like calves, Lebanon and Sirion like wild oxen. (Sirion: Mount Hermon; unicorn: wild ox) **7.** The voice of the LORD divides the flames of fire. (divide: separates) **8.** The LORD's voice shakes the wilderness, the wilderness of Kadesh. (shakes: causes to tremble) **9.** The LORD's voice causes deer to give birth and reveals forests. In His temple, all speak of His glory. (female deer: hinds) **10.** The LORD sits above the flood, reigning as King forever. (flood: overwhelming waters) **11.** The LORD gives strength to His people and blesses them with peace. (Peace: Amity)

Chapter 30
1. I will exalt You, O LORD, for You have lifted me up and not let my enemies rejoice. (extol: praise greatly) **2.** O LORD, I cried, and You healed me. (healed: restored to health) **3.** O LORD, You saved my soul from the grave and kept me alive. (grave: place of death) **4.** Sing praises to the LORD, all His faithful ones, and give thanks for His holiness. (faithful ones: holy ones) **5.** His anger lasts a moment, but His favor brings life. Weeping lasts for the night, but joy comes in the morning. (favor: kindness, grace) **6.** When I prospered, I thought I would never be shaken. (prosperity: success) **7.** By Your favor, You made my mountain stand strong. When You hid Your face, I was

troubled. (mountain: symbol of stability) **8.** I cried to You, O LORD, and pleaded for mercy. (pleaded: request for help) **9.** What good is there in my death? Will the dust praise You or declare Your truth? **10.** Hear me, O LORD, and show mercy. Be my helper. (mercy: compassion) **11.** You turned my mourning into dancing and put off my sackcloth, and girded me with gladness. (mourning: sadness; sackcloth: garment worn during mourning) **12.** That my soul may praise You and not be silent. O LORD, my God, I will give thanks forever. (praise: glory)

Chapter 31
1. In You, O Lord, I trust; let me never be ashamed. Rescue me for Your righteousness. (righteousness: God's justice) **2.** Answer quickly, O Lord. Be my rock of protection and safe refuge. (rock: strength; refuge: shelter) **3.** You are my fortress; lead and guide me for Your name's sake. (fortress: strong protection) **4.** Rescue me from the trap of my enemies, for You are my strength. (trap: danger) **5.** Into Your hands I commit my spirit. You have redeemed me, O Lord, God of truth. (redeemed: saved; truth: faithfulness) **6.** I despise those who worship false idols, but trust in You, Lord. **7.** I will rejoice in Your mercy, for You have seen my troubles. **8.** You have set my feet in a spacious place, not letting me fall to my enemies. (spacious: safe place) **9.** Have mercy, O Lord, for I am in distress. My soul and body are in anguish. (anguish: suffering) **10.** My life is filled with grief, and my strength is gone from my sins. (iniquity: sin) **11.** I am a disgrace to my enemies and a fear to my neighbors. **12.** I am forgotten, like a dead person; like a broken vessel. (broken vessel: discarded, useless) **13.** I have heard gossip and fear, for they plot to harm me. (gossip: unconstrained conversation about other people; plot: secret plans) **14.** But I trust in You, O Lord, and declare, "You are my God." **15.** My life is in Your hands; rescue me from my enemies. **16.** Let Your face shine on me, and save me for Your mercy's sake. **17.** Do not let me be ashamed, but let the wicked be silenced. (wicked: evil) **18.** Silence the liars who speak against the righteous. **19.** How great is Your goodness, stored up for those who fear You. (fear: reverence) **20.** You hide them in Your presence from man's pride and protect them from strife. (pride: arrogance; strife: conflict) **21.** Blessed be the Lord for His marvelous love. **22.** I said, "I am cut off," but You heard my cry. (cut off: abandoned) **23.** Love the Lord, all His saints, for He preserves the faithful and rewards the proud doer. **24.** Be strong, all who hope in the Lord; He will strengthen your heart. (courageous: brave)

Chapter 32
1. Blessed is the one whose sin is forgiven. (sin: wrongdoing) **2.** Blessed is the person to whom the Lord does not charge sin, and in whose spirit there is no deceit. (deceit: dishonesty) **3.** When I kept silent, my bones grew old from my groaning. (groaning: mournful sounds) **4.** Your hand was heavy on me, and my strength drained like summer heat. (drained: exhausted) **5.** I confessed my sin, and You forgave my guilt. (guilt: responsibility for wrong) **6.** Let the godly pray to You when You may be found; they won't be overwhelmed. (overwhelm: overpower) **7.** You are my hiding place, protecting me from trouble with songs of deliverance. (deliverance: rescue) **8.** I will guide you in the way you should go. **9.** Do not be like the mule, without understanding, controlled by bit and bridle. (bit and bridle: control tools) **10.** The wicked will have many sorrows, but those who trust in the Lord are surrounded by mercy. **11.** Rejoice in the Lord, you righteous; shout for joy, all you upright in heart. (upright: morally right)

Chapter 33
1. Rejoice in the LORD, all who are righteous; praise is fitting for the upright.(befitting: suitable) **2.** Praise the LORD with the harp and stringed instruments. **3.** Sing a new song to Him, play adroitly and loudly. **4.** The word of the LORD is right; His workshop are done in verity.(right: morally pure) **5.** He loves righteousness and justice; the earth is full of His virtuousness.(justice: fairness) **6.** By His word, the welkin were made; by His breath, their host.(host: heavenly beings or bodies) **7.** He gathers the ocean's waters and stores the depths.(stores: collect and preserve) **8.** Let all the earth sweat the LORD and stand in admiration of Him.(admiration: awe or reverence in response to God's majesty) **9.** He spoke, and it was done; He commanded, and it stood establishment.(stood establishment: remained stable) **10.** The LORD frustrates the plans of the nations.(frustrates: remains) **11.** His counsel stands ever, His studies to all generations.(counsel: advice) **12.** Blessed is the nation whose God is the LORD.(blessed: favored) **13.** The LORD looks from heaven and sees all men. **14.** From His lodging, He watches all who live on earth.(lodging: home) **15.** He made their hearts and considers their workshop.(considers observes) **16.** No king is saved by his army, nor a legionnaire by strength.(legionnaire: dogface) **17.** A steed can not save by its strength. **18.** The LORD's eye is on those who sweat Him and hope in His mercy.(mercy: kindness) **19.** To deliver them from death and keep them alive in shortage.(deliver: deliverance) **20.** Our soul delays for the LORD; He's our help and guard. **21.** Our hearts rejoice in Him, for we trust in His holy name. **22.** Let Your mercy, LORD, be upon us as we hope in You.

Chapter 34
1. I'll bless the LORD at all times; His praise will always be on my lips. **2.** My soul will boast in the LORD; let the humble hear and be glad.(boast: speak with pride) **3.** Magnify the LORD with me; let us exalt His name.(magnify: praise greatly; exalt: raise in honor) **4.** I sought the LORD, and He answered me, delivering me from my fears. **5.** They looked to Him and were radiant; their faces weren't shamed.(radiant: glowing with joy) **6.** This poor man cried, and the LORD heard him and saved him.(poor: humble) **7.** The angel of the LORD surrounds and delivers those who sweat Him. **8.** Taste and see that the LORD is good blessed is the one who trusts in Him. **9.** sweat the LORD, you His saints; there's no lack for those who sweat Him.(saints: holy bones, faithful) **10.** The youthful Napoleons may suffer hunger, but those who seek the LORD warrant no good thing. **11.** I'll educate you the fear of the LORD. **12.** Who desires life and good days? **13.** Keep your lingo from evil and lips from dishonesty.(dishonesty: falsehoods) **14.** Turn from wrong, do good, seek peace, and pursue it. **15.** The LORD's eyes are on the righteous, and His cognizance are open to their cry. **16.** The face of the LORD is against those who do wrong. **17.** The righteous cry, and the LORD hears them, delivering them from troubles. **18.** The LORD is near to the brokenhearted and saves the crushed in spirit. **19.** numerous are the afflictions of the righteous, but the LORD delivers them. **20.** He protects all their bones; none will be broken. **21.** Evil will slay the wicked; adversaries of the righteous will be condemned. **22.** The LORD redeems the life of His retainers; no bone who takes retreat in Him will be condemned.(redeems rescues; retreat: safe place)

Chapter 35
1. Defend me, O LORD, against those who oppose me. (Defend protect; Oppose: go against) **2.** Take up Your shield and armor to help me. (Shield: protective armor) **3.** Draw Your spear and stop those who pursue me. (Spear: weapon; Pursue: chase after) **4.** Let my enemies be ashamed and defeated. (Enemies: opponents; Ashamed: embarrassed; Defeated: overcome) **5.** Let them be like chaff, blown away by the wind. (Chaff: husks of grain, discarded; Blown away: scattered) **6.** Make their path dark and slippery. (Slippery: hard to walk on, dangerous) **7.** They have laid traps for me without cause. (Traps: snares or devices to catch; Cause: reason) **8.** Let their own trap catch them. (Trap: snare or pitfall) **9.** I will rejoice in Your salvation. (Rejoice: be glad; Salvation: deliverance) **10.** Who is like You, who saves the weak from the strong? (Weak: vulnerable; Strong: powerful) **11.** False witnesses accuse me with lies. (False: untrue; Witnesses: people giving testimony) **12.** They repay me with evil for good. (Repay: return; Evil: bad actions) **13.** I prayed for them when they were ill. (Prayed: asked for help from God; Ill: sick) **14.** I treated them as friends, but they rejoiced in my troubles. (Troubles: difficulties) **15.** They mocked me cruelly. (Mocked: made fun of;

Cruelly: in a harmful way) **16.** LORD, save my soul from destruction. (Save: rescue; Soul: inner being; Destruction: ruin) **17.** I will thank You in the great assembly. (Assembly: gathering of people) **18.** Do not let my enemies rejoice over me. (Rejoice: be glad; Enemies: opposers) **19.** They plot evil against the peaceful. (Plot: plan secretly; Peaceful: calm, not causing trouble) **20.** They open their mouths against me. (Open their mouths: speak against) **21.** You have seen this, LORD; do not be silent. (Silent: quiet, inactive) **22.** Awake and stand up for my cause. (Awake: rouse to action; Cause: reason or matter) **23.** Judge me according to Your righteousness. (Judge: decide fairly; Righteousness: justice) **24.** Do not let them say they have defeated me. (Defeated: beaten, overcome) **25.** Let them be ashamed who rejoice over my downfall. (Ashamed: embarrassed; Downfall: defeat) **26.** Let those who support me rejoice in Your righteousness. (Support: help or stand with; Rejoice: be glad) **27.** Let them praise You all day long. (Praise: speak highly of) **28.** I will speak of Your righteousness and praise You forever. (Speak: talk about; Forever: eternally)

Chapter 36
1. The wicked have no fear of God. (Wicked: evil; Fear: reverence or respect) **2.** They deceive themselves, believing their ways are good. (Deceive: trick; Believing: thinking to be true) **3.** Their words are full of lies and evil. (Lies: untruths; Evil: wrongdoing) **4.** They plot evil and do not hate it. (Plot: plan secretly; Hate: strongly dislike) **5.** Your mercy is vast, and Your faithfulness is unending. (Mercy: compassion; Vast: very large; Faithfulness: loyalty) **6.** Your righteousness is like great mountains, and Your judgments are deep. (Righteousness: justice; Judgments: decisions; Deep: profound) **7.** How precious is Your love! People take refuge under Your wings. (Precious: valuable; Refuge: shelter; Wings: protection) **8.** They will be satisfied with the abundance of Your house. (Satisfied: fulfilled; Abundance: plenty) **9.** With You is the fountain of life, and in Your light, we see light. (Fountain: source; Life: existence; Light: knowledge) **10.** Continue Your love and righteousness toward those who know You. (Continue: keep going; Love: care; Righteousness: justice) **11.** Do not let the proud defeat me. (Proud: arrogant; Defeat: overcome) **12.** The workers of evil have fallen and will not rise again. (Workers: doers; Evil: bad actions; Fallen: collapsed)

Chapter 37
1. Do not fret over the wicked or envy those who do evil (Fret: to worry; envy: to feel jealous). **2.** They will soon fade away like grass (Fade: to gradually disappear). **3.** Trust in the LORD and do good; He will provide for you (Trust: to rely on; provide: to supply). **4.** Delight in the LORD, and He will grant your heart's desires (Delight: to find joy and fulfillment in God's presence and will) **5.** Commit your way to the LORD, and He will make it happen (Commit: to dedicate or entrust). **6.** He will reveal your righteousness like the light (Reveal: to make known; righteousness: moral correctness). **7.** Rest in the LORD and wait patiently for Him (Rest: to be still or calm; patiently: without haste or frustration). **8.** Cease from wrath and do not do evil (Cease: to stop; wrath: intense anger). **9.** The wicked will be cut off, but those who wait on the LORD will inherit the earth (Cut off: removed or destroyed; inherit: to receive as a legacy). **10.** In a short time, the wicked will be no more (No more: no longer exist). **11.** The meek will inherit the land and enjoy peace (Meek: humble and gentle). **12.** The wicked plot against the righteous (Plot: to plan secretly). **13.** The LORD laughs at the wicked because their day is coming (Laugh: to mock or scorn). **14.** The wicked aim to harm the poor and needy, but their weapons will turn against them (Aim: to intend or direct; weapons: tools used for harm). **15.** Their swords will pierce their own hearts (Pierce: to go through). **16.** A little that the righteous have is better than much from the wicked (Righteous: morally right). **17.** The LORD upholds the righteous (Upholds: to support or sustain). **18.** The LORD knows the days of the righteous, and their inheritance is forever (Inheritance: what is passed down or given). **19.** In times of trouble, they will be satisfied (Satisfy: to fulfill needs). **20.** The wicked will perish, but the righteous will endure (Perish: to die or be destroyed; endure: to last or continue). **21.** The wicked borrow and do not repay, but the righteous give generously (Repay: to pay back; generously: freely and abundantly). **22.** Those blessed by the LORD will inherit the earth (Blessed: favored by God). **23.** The LORD directs the steps of the righteous (Directs: guides or leads). **24.** Though they stumble, the LORD will lift them up (Stumble: to trip or lose balance). **25.** I have never seen the righteous forsaken (Forsaken: abandoned or left behind). **26.** The righteous are merciful and lend (Merciful: showing compassion). **27.** Turn from evil and do good (Evil: morally wrong or bad). **28.** The LORD loves justice and preserves the faithful (Justice: fairness; faithful: loyal or devoted). **29.** The righteous will dwell in the land forever (Dwell: to live or stay in a place). **30.** The righteous speak wisdom and justice (Wisdom: knowledge and good judgment). **31.** The law of their God is in their hearts (Law: a system of rules). **32.** The wicked watch for opportunities to harm the righteous (Watch: to observe carefully). **33.** The LORD will not abandon the righteous (Abandon: to leave behind). **34.** Wait on the LORD, and He will exalt you (Exalt: to raise up). **35.** I have seen the wicked in power, but they will soon vanish (Vanish: to disappear). **36.** The wicked will be gone, though they once flourished (Flourished: grew or thrived). **37.** The blameless will have peace (Blameless: without fault). **38.** The wicked will be destroyed (Destroyed: wiped out or ruined). **39.** The LORD is the strength of the righteous in times of trouble (Strength: power or support). **40.** The LORD will deliver them because they trust in Him (Deliver: to rescue or save).

Chapter 38
1. LORD, do not rebuke me in Your anger (Rebuke: to reprimand or criticize). **2.** Your arrows pierce me, and Your hand presses me (Arrows: pointed weapons; Presses: to apply pressure). **3.** My body is in pain because of Your anger, and there is no peace due to my sin (Pain: physical suffering; Sin: immoral act). **4.** My sins weigh heavily on me (Weigh: to be a burden). **5.** My wounds stink because of my foolishness (Stink: to have a foul odor; Foolishness: lack of wisdom). **6.** I am deeply troubled and mourn all day (Mourn: to express sorrow). **7.** My body is filled with pain and there is no health in me (Health: well: being). **8.** I am weak and cry out in distress (Distress: extreme anxiety or pain). **9.** LORD, You know my desires and my groaning is not hidden (Groaning: making low sounds due to pain or sorrow). **10.** My strength fails, and I cannot see (Fail: to become weak or unable to function). **11.** My loved ones avoid me due to my illness (Loved ones: family and friends). **12.** My enemies seek to harm me with deceit (Deceit: dishonesty). **13.** I act as though I do not hear or speak (Mute: unable to speak). **14.** I remain silent before my enemies (Remain: to stay in one place). **15.** I trust in You, O LORD, and You will answer (Trust: reliance or confidence). **16.** Do not let my enemies rejoice over me (Rejoice: to be happy). **17.** I am close to falling, and my pain is constant (Fall: to stumble or collapse). **18.** I confess my sin and am sorry for it (Confess: to admit wrongdoing). **19.** My enemies are strong and hateful (Hateful: full of hatred). **20.** Those who repay good with evil oppose me (Repay: to return something). **21.** Do not forsake me, O LORD (Forsake: to abandon). **22.** Hurry to help me, O LORD, my Savior (Hurry: to move quickly; Savior: one who rescues).

Chapter 39
1. I said, I will take heed to my ways, that I sin not with my tongue: I will keep my mouth with a bridle, while the wicked is before me. (Bridle: a restraint or control) **2.** I was dumb with silence, I held my peace, even from good; and my sorrow was stirred. (Dumb: silent) **3.** My heart was hot within me, while I was musing the fire burned: then spake I with my tongue. (Musing: thinking deeply; Fire burned: intense emotion) **4.** LORD, make me to know mine end, and the measure of my days, what it is; that I may know how frail I am. (Frail: weak or delicate) **5.** Behold, thou hast made my days as an

handbreadth; and mine age is as nothing before thee: verily every man at his best state is altogether vanity. Selah. (Handbreadth: a short measure, symbolizing brevity; Vanity: emptiness or futility) **6.** Surely every man walketh in a vain shew: surely they are disquieted in vain: he heapeth up riches, and knoweth not who shall gather them. (Vain shew: an illusion or empty display; Disquieted: troubled) **7.** And now, Lord, what wait I for? my hope is in thee. (Hope: expectation or trust) **8.** Deliver me from all my transgressions: make me not the reproach of the foolish. (Transgressions: sins; Reproach: shame or disgrace) **9.** I was dumb, I opened not my mouth; because thou didst it. (Dumb: silent) **10.** Remove thy stroke away from me: I am consumed by the blow of thine hand. (Stroke: a blow or affliction) **11.** When thou with rebukes dost correct man for iniquity, thou makest his beauty to consume away like a moth: surely every man is vanity. Selah. (Rebukes: scolding or reprimands; Iniquity: sin; Beauty: strength or vitality) **12.** Hear my prayer, O LORD, and give ear unto my cry; hold not thy peace at my tears: for I am a stranger with thee, and a sojourner, as all my fathers were. (Stranger: foreigner; Sojourner: temporary resident) **13.** O spare me, that I may recover strength, before I go hence, and be no more. (Spare: have mercy; Recover strength: regain vitality)

Chapter 40
1. I waited patiently for the LORD; and he inclined unto me, and heard my cry. (Inclined: bent down or listened closely) **2.** He brought me up also out of an horrible pit, out of the miry clay, and set my feet upon a rock, and established my goings. (Miry: muddy or slippery) **3.** And he hath put a new song in my mouth, even praise unto our God: many shall see it, and fear, and shall trust in the LORD. (Fear: reverence or awe) **4.** Blessed is that man that maketh the LORD his trust, and respecteth not the proud, nor such as turn aside to lies. (Respecteth: does not follow or honor) **5.** Many, O LORD my God, are thy wonderful works which thou hast done, and thy thoughts which are to us: ward: they cannot be reckoned up in order unto thee: if I would declare and speak of them, they are more than can be numbered. (Reckoned: counted or listed; Us: ward: toward us) **6.** Sacrifice and offering thou didst not desire; mine ears hast thou opened: burnt offering and sin offering hast thou not required. (Sacrifice: offerings made to God; Burnt offering: a whole offering burned on the altar) **7.** Then said I, Lo, I come: in the volume of the book it is written of me, **8.** I delight to do thy will, O my God: yea, thy law is within my heart. (Delight: take joy; Law: God's commandments) **9.** I have preached righteousness in the great congregation: lo, I have not refrained my lips, O LORD, thou knowest. (Preached: proclaimed; Refrained: held back) **10.** I have not hid thy righteousness within my heart; I have declared thy faithfulness and thy salvation: I have not concealed thy lovingkindness and thy truth from the great congregation. (Righteousness: goodness and justice; Faithfulness: loyalty; Salvation: deliverance) **11.** Withhold not thou thy tender mercies from me, O LORD: let thy lovingkindness and thy truth continually preserve me. (Tender mercies: compassionate love) **12.** For innumerable evils have compassed me about: mine iniquities have taken hold upon me, so that I am not able to look up; they are more than the hairs of mine head: therefore my heart faileth me. (Innumerable: countless; Iniquities: sins; Compassed: surrounded) **13.** Be pleased, O LORD, to deliver me: O LORD, make haste to help me. (Make haste: hurry) **14.** Let them be ashamed and confounded together that seek after my soul to destroy it; let them be driven backward and put to shame that wish me evil. (Confounded: bewildered; Driven backward: forced to retreat) **15.** Let them be desolate for a reward of their shame that say unto me, Aha, aha. (Desolate: empty or abandoned) **16.** Let all those that seek thee rejoice and be glad in thee: let such as love thy salvation say continually, The LORD be magnified. (Magnified: made great or honored) **17.** But I am poor and needy; yet the Lord thinketh upon me: thou art my help and my deliverer; make no tarrying, O my God. (Tarrying: delay)

Chapter 41
1. Blessed is he that considereth the poor; the LORD will deliver him in time of trouble. (Considereth: cares for) **2.** The LORD will save him, and keep him alive; and he shall be blessed upon the earth, and thou wilt not deliver him unto the will of his adversaries. (Save: cover) **3.** The LORD will strengthen him upon the bed of sagging; thou wilt make all his bed in his sickness. (Sagging: suffering from illness) **4.** I said, LORD, be merciful unto me; heal my soul, for I've trespassed against thee. (Heal: restore) **5.** Mine adversaries speak wrong of me, When shall he die, and his name corrupt? (Perish: be destroyed) **6.** And if he come to see me, he speaketh vanity; his heart gathereth iniquity to itself; when he goeth abroad, he telleth it. (Vanity: falsehood; Iniquity: sin) **7.** All that detest me bruit together against me; against me do they concoct my hurt. (Concoct: plan) **8.** An evil complaint, say they, cleaveth fast unto him; and now that he lieth he shall rise up no further. (Cleaveth: clings) **9.** Yea, mine own familiar friend, in whom I trusted, which did eat of my chuck, hath lifted up his heel against me. (Heel: a symbol of treason) **10.** But thou, O LORD, be merciful unto me, and raise me up, that I may requite them. (Requite: repay) **11.** By this I know that thou favourest me, because mine adversary doth not triumph over me. (Favourest: favor or bless) **12.** And as for me, thou upholdest me in mine integrity, and settest me before thy face for ever. (Integrity: moral uprightness) **13.** Blessed be the LORD God of Israel from everlasting, and to everlasting. Amen, and Amen. (Everlasting: eternal)

Chapter 42
1. As the hart panteth after the water becks, so panteth my soul after thee, O God. (Hart: deer) **2.** My soul thirsteth for God, for the living God; when shall I come and appear before God? (Thirsteth: longs or solicitations) **3.** My gashes have been my meat day and night, while they continually say unto me, Where is thy God? (Meat: food; Continually: constantly) **4.** When I flash back these effects, I pour out my soul in me; for I had gone with the multitude, I went with them to the house of God, with the voice of joy and praise, with a multitude that kept holiday. (Pour out: express deeply; Multitude: large group; Holyday: jubilee) **5.** Why art thou cast down, O my soul? and why art thou disquieted in me? hope thou in God; for I shall yet praise him for the help of his countenance. (Cast down: sad or dejected; Disquieted: worried or restless) **6.** O my God, my soul is cast down within me; thus will I flash back thee from the land of Jordan, and of the Hermonites, from the hill Mizar. (Hermonites: those from Mount Hermon) **7.** Deep calleth unto deep at the noise of thy spouts; all thy swells and thy waves are gone over me. (Spouts: vortices; Billows: large swells) **8.** Yet the LORD will command his lovingkindness in the day, and in the night his song shall be with me, and my prayer unto the God of my life. (Lovingkindness: loyal love) **9.** I'll say unto God my rock, Why hast thou forgotten me? why go I mourning because of the oppression of the adversary? (Rock: strong support; Oppression: atrocity or burden) **10.** As with a brand in my bones, mine adversaries reproach me; while they say diurnal unto me, Where is thy God? (Reproach: shame or disgrace) **11.** Why art thou cast down, O my soul? and why art thou disquieted within me? hope thou in God; for I shall yet praise him, who's the health of my countenance, and my God. (Health: deliverance or well: being)

Chapter 43
1. Judge me, O God, and defend my cause against a nation that has turned away from You; rescue me from those who are deceitful and unjust. (Deceitful: dishonest; Unjust: unfair) **2.** You are my strength, O God. Why have You rejected me? Why must I walk in sorrow because of my enemy's oppression? (Oppression: cruel domination) **3.** Send Your light and truth to guide me, and bring me to Your holy mountain and sacred dwelling place. (Dwelling place: worship place) **4.** Then I will go to the altar of God, my source of joy, and praise You with the harp, O God. (Harp: stringed instrument) **5.** Why are you

discouraged, my soul? Why are you restless? Hope in God, for I will praise Him—my Savior and my God. (Discouraged: disheartened; Savior: deliverer)

Chapter 44

1. O God, we have heard from our ancestors about the great deeds You performed. (Ancestors: forefathers) **2.** You drove out nations with Your power, crushed our enemies, and established our people. (established: planted) **3.** They did not win by their own strength, but by Your hand, power, and favor. (Favor: grace) **4.** You are my King, O God; command victories for Israel. (Jacob: Israel) **5.** Through You, we will defeat our enemies and trample those who rise against us. (Defeat: overpower) **6.** I do not trust in my bow, nor can my sword save me. (Bow: weapon for arrows) **7.** You saved us from our enemies and shamed those who hated us. (Shamed: humiliated) **8.** We boast in God all day and will praise Your name forever. Selah. (Boast: take pride; Selah: pause) **9.** But now, You have rejected us and brought disgrace. Our armies no longer have Your support. (Disgrace: dishonor) **10.** You made us retreat, and our enemies plundered us. (Plundered: robbed) **11.** You made us like sheep for slaughter, scattered among the nations. (Scattered: dispersed) **12.** You sold Your people for nothing, gaining no wealth in exchange. (Wealth: riches) **13.** You made us a reproach to our neighbors, mocked by those around us. (Reproach: shame; Ridiculed: mocked) **14.** We are a proverb among the nations, a source of scorn. (Proverb byword; Scorn: disrespect) **15.** My disgrace is ever before me, and my face is covered with shame. (Disgrace: shame; Humiliation: embarrassment) **16.** This is due to the insults and mocking from those seeking revenge. (Insult: disrespect; Revenge: retaliation) **17.** Despite this, we have not forgotten You or been unfaithful to Your covenant. (Covenant: agreement) **18.** Our hearts have not turned away or strayed from Your path. (Strayed: wandered) **19.** Yet You have crushed us and overwhelmed us with suffering. (Desolate: deserted; Shadow of death: deep suffering) **20.** If we had forgotten Your name or worshiped another god, (Foreign: strange) **21.** would not God know it? He understands every heart. (Secrets: hidden thoughts) **22.** For Your sake, we face death all day and are like sheep to be slaughtered. (Slaughtered: killed) **23.** Wake up, Lord! Why do You sleep? Do not reject us forever. (Reject: abandon) **24.** Why do You hide Your face and forget our misery and oppression? (Misery: suffering; Oppression: harsh treatment) **25.** Our souls are bowed to the dust; our bodies cling to the ground. (Cling: stick closely) **26.** Rise up and help us! Redeem us because of Your steadfast love. (Redeem: rescue; Steadfast: unwavering)

Chapter 45

1. My heart overflows with a noble theme as I write about the king; my tongue is like a skilled writer's pen. (Noble: worthy) **2.** You are more beautiful than any man; grace flows from Your lips, and God has blessed You forever. (Grace: kindness) **3.** Strap Your sword at Your side, O mighty warrior, in all Your glory and majesty. (Majesty: royal splendor) **4.** Ride triumphantly in Your majesty, with truth, humility, and justice; Your right hand will perform awe: inspiring deeds. (Humility: modesty; Justice: righteousness) **5.** Your arrows are sharp, piercing the hearts of Your enemies; nations fall before You. (Piercing: deeply striking) **6.** Your throne, O God, lasts forever; the scepter of Your kingdom is righteous. (Scepter: royal authority) **7.** You love righteousness and hate wickedness; therefore, God has anointed You with joy above Your companions. (Righteousness: moral goodness; Wickedness: evil) **8.** All Your robes are fragrant with myrrh, aloes, and cassia, from palaces that bring You joy. (Fragrant: sweet: smelling; Myrrh, Aloes, Cassia: aromatic spices) **9.** Daughters of kings honor You; the queen stands at Your right hand, adorned in gold. (Adorned: decorated) **10.** Listen, daughter, and forget your people and father's house. (Forget: leave behind) **11.** The king will desire your beauty; worship Him. (Desire: cherish) **12.** The wealthy from Tyre will come with gifts, seeking Your favor. (Wealthy: rich; Favor: approval) **13.** The royal daughter is glorious within; her clothing is woven with gold. (Glorious: magnificent) **14.** She will be led to the king in embroidered garments, followed by young women. (Embroidered: decorated with needlework) **15.** They are led into the king's palace with joy and celebration. (Celebration: festivity) **16.** Your sons will succeed Your ancestors and be made princes. (Ancestors: forefathers; Princes: rulers) **17.** I will make Your name remembered through all generations, and nations will praise You forever. (Generations: descendants)

Chapter 46

1. God is our retreat and strength, a present help in trouble. (retreat: sanctum, protection) **2.** We'll not sweat, though the earth shakes and mountains fall into the ocean. (shakes: trembles) **3.** Though the waters roar and mountains fluctuate. Selah. (roar: roar; fluctuate: shake) **4.** A swash makes the megacity of God rejoice, the holy place of the Most High. (swash: sluice) **5.** God is in her; she'll not be moved. He'll help her at dawn. (dawn: morning) **6.** The nations raged, fiefdoms shaken; He spoke, and the earth melted. (raged: were angry; melted: dissolved) **7.** The LORD of hosts is with us; the God of Jacob is our retreat. Selah. (hosts: armies) **8.** Come, see the workshop of the LORD, the desolations He has made. (desolations: remains) **9.** He causes wars to cease; He breaks the arc, cuts the shaft, and burns the chariot. (check: stop; becks: consumes) **10.** Be still, and know I'm God; I'll be exalted among the nations and on earth. (exalted: honored) **11.** The LORD of hosts is with us; the God of Jacob is our retreat. Selah.

Chapter 47

1. Clap your hands, all you people roar to God with a voice of triumph. (triumph: palm) **2.** For the LORD most high is stupendous; He's a great King over all the earth. (stupendous: admiration: inspiring) **3.** He'll subdue the people under us, and the nations under our bases. (subdue: defeat) **4.** He'll choose our heritage, the excellence of Jacob whom He loved. Selah. (heritage: effects) **5.** God has mounted with a cry, the LORD with the sound of a trumpet. (mounted: risen) **6.** Sing praises to God, sing praises to our King. (praises: deification songs) **7.** For God is King of all the earth; sing praises with understanding. (understanding: wisdom) **8.** God reigns over the nations; He sits on His holy throne. (reigns: rules) **9.** The autocrats have gathered, the people of the God of Abraham; the securities of the earth belong to God; He's greatly exalted. (securities: defenders; exalted: honored)

Chapter 48

1. Great is the LORD, greatly to be praised in the megacity of our God, in the mountain of His godliness. (godliness: chastity) **2.** Beautiful in elevation, the joy of the earth, is Mount Zion, the megacity of the great King. (elevation: height) **3.** God is known in her palaces as a retreat. (palaces: royal structures) **4.** Behold, the lords assembled; they passed by together. (behold: see) **5.** They saw it, marveled, and hastened down. (marveled: amazed) **6.** Fear gripped them, and pain, like a woman in labor. (gripped: seized; labor: parturition) **7.** You broke the vessels of Tarshish with an east wind. (Tarshish: distant vessels) **8.** As we've heard, so we've seen in the megacity of the LORD; God will establish it ever. Selah. (establish: secure) **9.** We've allowed of Your loving: kindness, O God, in the midst of Your tabernacle. (loving: kindness: loyal love) **10.** According to Your name, O God, so is Your praise to the ends of the earth; Your right hand is full of righteousness. (right hand: power) **11.** Let Mount Zion rejoice, let Judah's daughters be glad because of Your judgments. (judgments: opinions) **12.** Walk about Zion, count her halls. (count: observe) **13.** Consider her bulwarks and palaces, that you may tell it to the ensuing generation. (bulwarks: protective walls) **14.** For this God is our God ever; He'll be our companion indeed to death. (companion: protection)

Chapter 49

1. Hear this, all you people hear, all you occupants of the world. (occupants: residers) **2.** Both low and high, rich and poor, together. (low: humble; high: elevated) **3.** My mouth will speak wisdom, and the contemplation of my heart will be of understanding. (contemplation: reflection) **4.** I'll incline my observance to a fable; I'll open my dark saying on the harp. (incline: give attention; fable: story with an assignment) **5.** Why should I sweat in times of trouble, when the iniquity of my adversaries surrounds me? (iniquity: sin) **6.** Those who trust in their wealth, and pride of their riches; (pride: pridefully speak) **7.** None can redeem his family, nor give a rescue for him. (redeem: save) **8.** (For the redemption of their soul is precious, and ceases ever.) (precious: expensive; ceases: ends) **9.** That he should live ever, and not see corruption. (corruption: decay) **10.** For he sees that the wise bones, likewise the foolish corrupt, and leave their wealth to others. (corrupt: bones) **11.** Their inward allowed is that their houses will last ever; they call their lands by their names. (inward study: plan) **12.** Nonetheless, man in honor doesn't remain; he's like the beasts that corrupt. (honor: respect) **13.** This way is their idiocy yet their offspring authorize their aphorisms. Selah. (idiocy: foolishness; offspring: descendants) **14.** Like lambs, they're laid in the grave; death shall feed on them, and the upright will have dominion over them in the morning. (laid: placed; dominion: control) **15.** But God will redeem my soul from the grave; for He shall admit me. Selah. (redeem: save; soul: life) **16.** Don't be hysterical when a man becomes rich, when the glory of his house increases; (glory: wealth) **17.** For when he dies, he'll carry nothing down; his glory won't follow him. (glory: wealth) **18.** Though while he lived, he blessed himself: men will praise you when you do well for yourself. (blessed: prospered) **19.** He shall go to the generation of his fathers; they shall never see light. (generation: descendants) **20.** A man in honor, yet lacking understanding, is like the beasts that perish. (understanding: wisdom)

Chapter 50
1. The Almighty God, the LORD, has spoken and called the earth from where the sun rises to where it sets. (Almighty: powerful and supreme; LORD: God's title) **2.** Out of Zion, the place of perfect beauty, God has shone forth. (Zion: Jerusalem, symbolizing God's presence) **3.** Our God is coming, with a consuming fire before Him and a great storm surrounding Him. (Consuming fire: a fire that destroys; tempestuous: stormy) **4.** He will call the heavens and the earth to witness as He judges His people. (Witness: to observe) **5.** Gather My faithful ones who have made a covenant with Me through sacrifice. (Covenant: a formal agreement) **6.** The heavens will proclaim His righteousness, for God is the Judge. Selah. (Righteousness: moral correctness; Selah: a pause to reflect) **7.** Listen, My people, I will testify against you. I am your God. **8.** I will not rebuke you for your sacrifices or burnt offerings. (Rebuke: to express disapproval) **9.** I will not accept bulls or goats from your house. (Pens: enclosures for animals) **10.** Every beast and cattle on a thousand hills are Mine. (Beast: wild animal) **11.** I know the birds of the mountains and the wild animals of the field. (Birds: fowl) **12.** If I were hungry, I would not tell you; the world belongs to Me. **13.** Do I eat the flesh of bulls or drink the blood of goats? (Blood: symbolic of life in sacrifice) **14.** Offer thanksgiving and fulfill your vows to the Most High. (Vows: promises made to God) **15.** Call on Me in trouble, and I will deliver you. **16.** But to the wicked, God says, Why speak of My laws and take My covenant in your mouth? (Wicked: those who do wrong; Covenant: sacred agreement) **17.** You hate discipline and ignore My words. **18.** When you see a thief, you join in, and you associate with adulterers. (Adulterers: those who betray in marriage) **19.** You speak evil, and your tongue deceives. (Deceit: dishonesty) **20.** You slander your brother, speaking against your mother's son. (Slandering: spreading false information) **21.** I kept silent, but I will rebuke you and expose your actions. **22.** Consider this, lest I tear you apart, and no one can save you. **23.** Whoever offers praise glorifies Me, and to those who live rightly, I will show My salvation. (Praise: gratitude; Salvation: deliverance)

Chapter 51
1. Have mercy on me, O God, according to Your loving kindness; wipe out my offenses. (Mercy: compassion; Loving kindness: God's faithful love) **2.** Wash me thoroughly from my guilt and cleanse me from sin. **3.** I acknowledge my wrongdoing; my sin is before me. **4.** I have sinned against You alone and done evil in Your sight. You are justified when You speak. (Justified: proven to be right) **5.** I was born in sin; my mother conceived me in sin. **6.** You desire truth in the inner parts; You teach me wisdom in secret. (Wisdom: understanding) **7.** Purge me with hyssop, and I will be clean; wash me, and I will be whiter than snow. (Purge: cleanse thoroughly; Hyssop: a plant used for purification) **8.** Let me hear joy and gladness; let the bones You crushed rejoice. (Crushed: broken) **9.** Hide Your face from my sins and blot out my transgressions. (Blot out: erase completely) **10.** Create in me a clean heart, O God, and renew a right spirit within me. (Renew: restore) **11.** Do not cast me from Your presence or take Your Holy Spirit from me. **12.** Restore to me the joy of Your salvation, and uphold me with a willing spirit. (Restore: bring back; Salvation: rescue) **13.** Then I will teach transgressors Your ways, and sinners will return to You. (Transgressors: those who break moral laws) **14.** Deliver me from bloodshed, O God, and my tongue will sing of Your righteousness. (Bloodshed: murder) **15.** O Lord, open my lips, and my mouth will declare Your praise. **16.** You do not delight in sacrifice; You do not take pleasure in burnt offerings. (Delight: find joy in) **17.** The sacrifices God desires are a broken spirit; You will not despise a contrite heart. (Contrite: feeling regret) **18.** Do good to Zion; build the walls of Jerusalem. (Zion: Jerusalem, God's kingdom) **19.** Then You will be pleased with the sacrifices of righteousness, with burnt offerings and whole offerings.

Chapter 52
1. Why boast of evil, O mighty man? The goodness of God endures forever. (Boast: to brag) **2.** Your tongue plots destruction; it is like a sharp razor, working deceitfully. (Deceitfully: dishonestly) **3.** You love evil more than good, and lies more than truth. Selah. (Selah: pause) **4.** You love devouring words, O deceitful tongue! (Devour: consume) **5.** God will destroy you forever; He will tear you from your tent and uproot you from the land of the living. Selah. (Tent: dwelling) **6.** The righteous will see and fear, and they will laugh at you: **7.** "Look at the man who did not make God his refuge, but trusted in his wealth and wickedness." (Refuge: safe place) **8.** But I trust in God's unfailing love forever. **9.** I will praise You forever because You have done it; I will wait for Your name, for it is good before Your saints.

Chapter 53
1. The fool says," There's no God." They're loose, committing wrongs; no bone does good. (Fool: lacking wisdom; loose: innocently rotten) **2.** God looked from heaven to see if anyone understood or sought God. (Sought: after pursued) **3.** All have turned away; they have all become corrupt; there is no one who does good, not even one." (Turned away: strayed from the right path; Corrupt: morally degraded, immoral) **4.** Do the workers of wrong not understand? They devour my people as chuck; they don't call on God. (Evil: wrongdoing; Devour: destroy) **5.** They're overwhelmed with terror; God has scattered the bones of those who chamber against you. (Overwhelmed: filled with; Scattered: broken) **6.** Oh, that deliverance would come from Zion! When God restores His people from prison, Jacob will rejoice. (Zion: God's presence; Captivity: thrall)

Chapter 54
1. Save me, O God, by Your name, and judge me with Your strength. **2.** Hear my prayer, O God; hear to my words. **3.** Nonnatives rise against me, and violent men seek my life; they don't set God before them. (Nonnatives: foreigners; Violent: cruel) **4.** God is my coadjutor; the Lord supports my soul. (Support: uphold) **5.** He'll repay my adversaries with wrong; cut them off in Your verity. (Repay: give what's justified; Cut them off: destroy) **6.** I'll offer a immolation to You; I'll praise Your name, for it's good. **7.** He has delivered me

from troubles, and I've seen the downfall of my adversaries. (Downfall: defeat)

Chapter 55

1. Hear to my prayer, O God, and don't hide from my plea. 2. Pay attention to me; I'm worried and moan in my complaint. (Worried: distressed; Moan: suffer) 3. Because of my adversary's voice, the oppression of the wicked; they cast iniquity upon me. (Oppression: cruel treatment; Iniquity: sin) 4. My heart is in anguish, and the demons of death have fallen upon me. (Anguish: pain; demons: sweat) 5. Fear and pulsing have come over me, and horror has overwhelmed me. (Pulsing: shaking; Overwhelmed: overcome) 6. I wish I had bodies like a dove! I would fly down and rest. 7. I would escape and dwell in the nature. (Dwell: live) 8. I would flee from the stormy wind and tempest. (Tempest: violent storm) 9. Destroy, O Lord, and confuse their speech; I've seen violence in the megacity. (Confuse: smatter) 10. Day and night, they go around the megacity; trouble and wickedness are in it. (Wickedness: wrong) 11. Destruction is in its midst; dishonesty and fraud don't depart. (Dishonesty: deceitfulness; Fraud: deception) 12. It wasn't an adversary who reproached me; I could have borne it. 13. But it was you, my companion and friend. (Companion: supporter) 14. We took sweet counsel and walked to the house of God. (Counsel: guidance) 15. Let death take them by surprise; let them go to the grave, for wrong is in their homes. 16. As for me, I'll call upon God, and the Lord will save me. 17. I'll supplicate morning, noon, and night, and He'll hear my voice. (Cry: audibly roar in torture) 18. He has redeemed my soul from the battle; numerous were against me. (Redeemed: saved) 19. God will hear and torment them, for they don't sweat God. (Ennobled: seated as king; Afflict: cause suffering) 20. He has broken His covenant. (Covenant: pledge) 21. His words were smooth as adulation, but war was in his heart. (Brands: munitions of attack) 22. Cast your burden on the Lord, and He'll sustain you; He'll noway let the righteous be shaken. (Sustain: uphold) 23. But You, O God, will bring them down to destruction; men of blood and dishonesty won't live half their days, but I'll trust in You. (Hole of destruction: grave or ruin)

Chapter 56

1. Be merciful to me, O God, for man would swallow me up; he fights me diurnal and oppresses me. 2. My adversaries seek to swallow me daily; numerous fight against me. 3. Whenever I'm hysterical, I'll trust in You. 4. In God, whose word I praise, I trust; I'll not sweat what man can do to me. 5. All day long they twist my words; their studies are against me for wrong. (Twist: distort meaning) 6. They gather and watch my way as they stay to take my life. 7. Shall they escape by iniquity? In Your wrathfulness, O God, cast down the peoples. (Iniquity: sin) 8. You keep track of my wanderings; put my gashes in Your bottle. Are they not in Your book? (Wanderings: struggles) 9. When I cry out to You, my adversaries will turn back; this I know, for God is for me. 10. In God, whose word I praise, in the Lord, whose word I praise, 11. In God I trust; I'll not sweat. What can man do to me? 12. Your promises are upon me, O God; I'll praise You. (Promises: pledges) 13. You have delivered my soul from death. Will You not deliver my bases from stumbling, that I may walk before God in the light of life? (Stumbling: tripping; Light of life: godly blessing)

Chapter 57

1. Show me your kindness, O God; be gracious to me, for my soul depends on you. I find shelter under your wings until these hardships pass. (hardships: severe difficulties or misfortunes) 2. I cry out to the God Most High, to the One who fulfills His purpose for me. (fulfills: brings to completion) 3. He will send help from heaven to save me from those who want to destroy me. Pause and reflect. (reflect: think deeply; Selah: a pause to think) 4. My soul is surrounded by enemies, fierce like lions. Their tongues are like sharp swords. (fierce: intense or aggressive) 5. Be lifted high, O God, above the heavens; may your majesty shine over all the earth. (majesty: greatness or splendor) 6. They laid a trap for me; but they fell into it themselves. Pause and reflect. (trap: a device to catch or harm; Selah: a pause to think) 7. My heart is steadfast, O God; I will sing and praise you with joy. (steadfast: firmly fixed and unwavering) 8. Awake, my soul! Awake, instruments of music! I will wake early to praise you. (instruments: tools used for music) 9. I will thank you, Lord, among the nations. 10. Your love reaches beyond the skies, and your faithfulness stretches to the clouds. (faithfulness: loyalty or reliability) 11. Be lifted high, O God, above the heavens; may your glory cover the earth. (glory: honor and greatness)

Chapter 58

1. Do you truly speak with righteousness, you who gather as a people? (righteousness: moral rightness or justice) 2. No, you devise wickedness; your hands deal out violence. (devise: plan or invent; violence: physical harm or force) 3. The wicked are corrupt from birth, speaking lies as soon as they learn to talk. (wicked: evil or immoral; corrupt: morally wrong) 4. Their actions are as deadly as snake venom. (venom: poisonous substance) 5. They ignore the voices of charmers. (charmers: those who use magic or skill to control) 6. O God, shatter their teeth so they cannot harm others. (shatter: break into pieces) 7. Let them vanish like water running away. (vanish: disappear) 8. May they waste away like a snail that melts. (waste away: weaken or disappear) 9. Sweep them away in your anger like a fierce storm. (fierce: powerful or intense) 10. The righteous will rejoice when they see justice done. (righteous: morally upright; rejoice: feel joy) 11. Then everyone will say, "Surely there is a reward for the godly; truly God judges the earth." (reward: something given in return for good deeds)

Chapter 59

1. Rescue me from my enemies, O God. (rescue: save from danger; enemies: those who oppose or harm) 2. Deliver me from evildoers, and save me from those who thirst for blood. (evildoers: people who commit wrongs; thirst: desire strongly) 3. Powerful people conspire against me, but not for any wrong I have done, Lord. (conspire: plan secretly against someone) 4. They rush to attack me without cause. (attack: aggressive action; cause: reason) 5. O Lord Almighty, rise to judge the nations. Pause and reflect. (judge: decide fairly; Selah: a pause to think) 6. Each evening, they prowl like growling dogs. (prowl: move around stealthily; growling: making a low threatening sound) 7. Their mouths spout vile words, and they arrogantly ask, "Who will hear us?" (vile: offensive or disgusting; arrogantly: pridefully) 8. But you, Lord, will laugh at them. (laugh: show scorn by laughing) 9. I will wait on you, my strength, for you are my defense. (defense: protection from harm) 10. God, my protector, will show me kindness and allow me to see justice. (protector: one who shields from harm; justice: fairness) 11. Do not kill them outright. Scatter them and bring them down, O Lord. (scatter: spread out or disperse) 12. Their prideful speech and lies will be their downfall. (prideful: overly self-important; downfall: failure) 13. Consume them in your anger until they are no more, so all will know that God reigns over the earth. Pause and reflect. (consume: destroy completely; reigns: rules; Selah: a pause to think) 14. Each evening, they return, growling like dogs. 15. Let them wander in search of food, unsatisfied. (wander: move without a set direction; unsatisfied: not fulfilled) 16. But I will sing of your strength and love every morning. (strength: power or ability) 17. To you, my fortress and protector, I will sing praises. (fortress: a strong and secure place)

Chapter 60

1. O God, you have rejected and scattered us in anger. Turn back to us and restore us. (restore: bring back to the original state) 2. You caused the earth to quake. Repair its cracks because it is shaking. (quake: tremble or shake violently) 3. You have made your people endure hardships. (endure: withstand or suffer through) 4. But you have given a banner to those who revere you. Pause and reflect. (banner: a flag representing unity; revere: deeply respect; Selah: a pause to think) 5. Rescue your beloved ones with your strong hand. (beloved: dearly loved) 6. God has declared, "I will rejoice! I will

divide Shechem." (rejoice: express great joy; Shechem: a historic location in Israel) **7.** Gilead and Manasseh belong to me; Ephraim is my helmet, and Judah is my staff. (helmet: protective headgear; staff: symbol of leadership) **8.** Moab will serve me like a washing bowl; Philistia will hear my shout of triumph. (triumph: victory or success) **9.** Who will guide me to Edom? (guide: lead or direct) **10.** Will you not, O God, who has rejected us? **11.** Give us help in troubles, for human help is useless. (useless: without value or effect) **12.** With God, we will be victorious and defeat our enemies. (victorious: having achieved success; enemies: opponents or adversaries)

Chapter 61
1. Hear to my cry, O God; pay attention to my prayer. **2.** From the furthest corners of the earth, I'll cry when my heart is overwhelmed. Lead me to the gemstone that's advanced than I. (overwhelmed: filled with strong feelings) **3.** You have been my sanctum and strong defense against my adversaries. (sanctum: a place of protection; defense: protection) **4.** I'll stay in Your sacred place ever, trusting in the safety of Your bodies. Selah. (sacred place: a holy or blessed area) **5.** For You, O God, have heard my pledges; You have given me the heritage of those who recognize Your name. (recognize: respect or reverence) **6.** You'll extend the king's life, making his times last through generations. **7.** He'll stand before You ever; prepare mercy and verity to keep him safe. (mercy: compassion or remission; verity: fastness) **8.** I'll sing praises to Your name ever, so I may fulfill my pledges daily.

Chapter 62
1. Truly, my soul delays for God alone; from Him comes my deliverance. (deliverance: the action of being rescued or set free) **2.** He alone is my gemstone, deliverance, and defense; I'll not be moved. **3.** How long will you try to harm a man? You'll be destroyed; like a collapsing wall, you'll fall. (collapsing: falling down or breaking piecemeal) **4.** They seek to bring him down from his position, enjoying falsehoods and dishonesty. They bless with their mouths, but curse inwardly. Selah. (dishonesty: misleading others) **5.** My soul, stay patiently for God alone, for my stopgap comes from Him. **6.** He alone is my gemstone and deliverance; He's my defense; I'll not be shaken. **7.** In God is my deliverance and glory; the gemstone of my strength and retreat is in God. (retreat: a safe place) **8.** Trust in Him at all times; pour out your hearts to Him. God is our retreat. Selah. **9.** People of low status are empty; those of high rank are deceitful. They're lighter than vanity when counted. (vanity: emptiness or worthlessness) **10.** Don't trust in oppression or robbery; if wealth increases, don't set your heart on it. (oppression: unjust treatment; stealing: taking without authorization) **11.** God has spoken formerly; doubly I've heard power belongs to God. **12.** And to You, O Lord, belongs mercy; You award everyone according to their deeds.

Chapter 63
1. O God, You're my God; beforehand I'll seek You. My soul thirsts for You, my body longs for You in a dry land where there's no water. (longs: deeply solicitations) **2.** To see Your power and glory, as I've seen You in the sanctuary. (sanctuary: a holy place of deification) **3.** Because Your lovingkindness is better than life, my lips will praise You. (lovingkindness: a deep, pious love and compassion) **4.** I'll bless You as long as I live; I'll lift my hands in Your name. **5.** My soul will be satisfied as with the richest foods; my mouth will praise You with joyous lips. **6.** When I flash back You on my bed, I meditate on You during the night. (meditate: reflect deeply) **7.** Because You have been my help, I'll rejoice in the shadow of Your bodies. (shadow: a defensive covering) **8.** My soul follows hard after You; Your right hand upholds me. (upholds: supports or sustains) **9.** But those who seek to destroy me will be cast down. **10.** They will fall by the brand and come food for foxes. (food for foxes: come vulnerable prey) **11.** The king will rejoice in God; all who swear by Him will glory, but the mouths of prevaricators will be silenced.

Chapter 64
1. Hear my voice, O God, as I supplicate; cover my life from the fear of my adversaries. (cover: keep safe) **2.** Hide me from the secret plots of the wicked, from the rebellion of evil workers. (wicked: evil people; rebellion: defiance against authority) **3.** They edge their speeches like brands and shoot bitter words like arrows. **4.** They attack the innocent from caching, suddenly without fear. **5.** They encourage evil and intimately plan traps, asking, "Who'll see us?" **6.** They search for evil deeds; their hearts are deeply wicked. **7.** But God will shoot them with His arrows; they will suddenly be wounded. **8.** Their own speeches will beget their downfall; all who see them will flee in fear. **9.** People will sweat and declare the work of God, wisely considering what He has done. **10.** The righteous will be glad in the LORD and trust in Him; all the upright will glory.

Chapter 65
1. Praise delays for You, O God, in Zion; to You, the oath will be fulfilled. (Zion: the megacity of Jerusalem; covenant: a solemn pledge) **2.** O You who hear prayer, to You all people will come. **3.** immoralities overwhelm me; You'll forgive our transgressions. (transgressions: violations of law or moral law) **4.** Blessed is the one You choose to bring near to You, to live in Your courts. We'll be satisfied with the virtuousness of Your house, the godliness of Your tabernacle. **5.** By stupendous deeds in righteousness, You answer us, O God of our deliverance, the stopgap of all the earth and those far on the swell. (righteousness: moral correctness) **6.** You establish the mountains with Your strength, clothed with power. **7.** You calm the roaring of the swell, the raging swells, and the uproar of the people. **8.** Those who live at the ends of the earth stand in admiration of Your signs; You make the daylight and evening joyous. **9.** You visit the earth and water it, perfecting it with the swash of God. You give grain when You prepare it. **10.** You water-soak the crests abundantly, settling its furrows, softening it with showers, and blessing its growth. **11.** You cap the time with Your virtuousness; Your paths drop with cornucopia. **12.** The wilderness pastures overflow, and the little hills rejoice. **13.** The meadows are clothed with flocks; the valleys are covered with grain; they shout for joy and sing.

Chapter 66
1. Let all the earth shout joyfully to God! (Joyful shout: loud praise) **2.** Sing praises to His name, glorifying His greatness. (Glorifying: honoring) **3.** Tell God, "How awe-inspiring are Your deeds! Your power makes enemies bow to You." (bow: submit) **4.** All will worship You and sing praises to Your name. Selah. (Worship: honor) **5.** Come and see God's amazing deeds toward humanity. (Amazing: wondrous) **6.** He turned the sea to dry land; His people walked through. We rejoiced in Him. (Rejoiced: celebrated) **7.** He rules with power forever; His eyes watch the nations. Let the proud not rise against Him. Selah. (Proud: arrogant) **8.** Bless our God, all people, and let His praise be heard! (Bless: praise) **9.** He preserves our lives, keeping us steady. (Steady: firm) **10.** You, O God, have tested us like silver. (Tested: purified) **11.** You brought us into danger and laid heavy burdens on us. (Burden: difficulty) **12.** You allowed others to oppress us, but You brought us to abundance. (Abundance: prosperity) **13.** I will bring burnt offerings and fulfill my vows. (Fulfill: carry out) **14.** which I made when I was in trouble. (Trouble: distress) **15.** I will offer the best sacrifices. Selah. (Best: finest) **16.** Come and hear, all who respect God, and I will tell what He's done for me. (Respect: fear) **17.** I cried to Him, and He was praised. (Praised: admired) **18.** If I cherished sin, the Lord would not have listened. (Cherished: held dear) **19.** But God heard my prayer. (Heard: paid attention) **20.** Blessed be God, who hasn't rejected my prayer or His mercy from me. (Mercy: compassion)

Chapter 67
1. May God bless us and shine His face upon us. Selah. (Bless: show favor) **2.** That Your way may be known across the earth and Your salvation among all nations. (Salvation: deliverance) **3.** Let all people praise You, O God. (Praise: honor) **4.** Let the nations rejoice, for You

will judge fairly. Selah. (Rejoice: be glad; judge: rule) **5.** Let all the people praise You, O God. (Praise: honor) **6.** Then the earth will yield its harvest, and God will bless us. (Yield: give forth) **7.** God will bless us, and all the earth will fear Him. (Fear: respect)

Chapter 68

1. Let God arise and let His enemies scatter; let those who hate Him flee. (Arise: stand up; scatter: disperse) **2.** As smoke is driven away, so drive them away; as wax melts before the fire, let the wicked perish before God. (Perish: be destroyed) **3.** Let the righteous be glad and rejoice before God. (Righteous: virtuous) **4.** Sing to God, sing praises to His name, and rejoice before Him. (Rejoice: celebrate) **5.** God is a father to the fatherless and a judge for widows. (Fatherless: without a father) **6.** God sets the lonely in families, releases prisoners, but the rebellious live in desolation. (Lonely: without companionship; desolation: emptiness) **7.** When You went before Your people, the earth trembled. Selah. (Trembled: shook) **8.** The earth shook, and the heavens poured at Your presence. (Poured: dropped) **9.** You sent abundant rain to refresh Your people. (Abundant: plentiful) **10.** Your people settled there; You provided for the poor. (Poor: needy) **11.** The Lord gave the word; great was the company who proclaimed it. (Proclaimed: announced) **12.** Kings fled quickly, and those at home divided the spoils. (Spoils: rewards) **13.** Even if you lie among pots, you will shine like a dove's wings covered with silver and gold. (Shine: stand out) **14.** When the Almighty scattered kings, it was like snow on Mount Salmon. (Almighty: all-powerful) **15.** God's hill is like the hill of Bashan. (Bashan: fertile region) **16.** Why do you leap, O hills? This is the hill God desires to dwell in. (Leap: jump) **17.** The chariots of God are thousands of angels; the Lord is among them. (Chariots: vehicles) **18.** You ascended on high and led captives in Your train; You received gifts for men. (Ascended: rose) **19.** Blessed be the Lord, who daily loads us with blessings, the God of our salvation. Selah. (Blessings: gifts) **20.** Our God is the God of salvation, and to Him belong the issues of death. (Salvation: deliverance) **21.** But God will strike the head of His enemies. (Strike: wound) **22.** The Lord will bring them back from the depths of the sea. (Back: return) **23.** So that your feet may be dipped in the blood of your enemies. (Dipped: immersed) **24.** They have seen Your procession, O God, in the sanctuary. (Procession: march) **25.** The singers went before, the musicians followed; the young women played timbrels. (Timbrels: tambourines) **26.** Bless God in the congregations, even the Lord, from the fountain of Israel. (Congregations: worshippers) **27.** There is little Benjamin with their ruler, the princes of Judah with their council, the princes of Zebulun, and the princes of Naphtali. (Princes: leaders) **28.** Your God has commanded your strength; strengthen what You have done for us. (Strength: might) **29.** Because of Your temple in Jerusalem, kings will bring gifts to You. (Temple: worship place) **30.** Rebuke the beast of the reeds, the herd of bulls with the calves of the nations, till everyone submits with silver pieces. Scatter the people who delight in war. (Rebuke: correct; beast: wild animal; submits: surrenders) **31.** Princes will come from Egypt; Ethiopia will stretch out her hands to God. (Stretch out: extend) **32.** Sing to God, you kingdoms of the earth; sing praises to the Lord, Selah. (Kingdoms: nations) **33.** To Him who rides the ancient heavens, behold, He sends forth His mighty voice. (Behold: observe) **34.** Ascribe strength to God; His greatness is over Israel, and His power is in the clouds. (Ascribe: attribute; greatness: superiority) **35.** O God, You are awesome from Your sanctuary; the God of Israel gives strength and power to His people. Blessed be God. (Sanctuary: sacred place; awesome: causing awe)

Chapter 69

1. Save me, O God, the waters have reached my soul. (Floodwaters: overwhelming waters) **2.** I sink in deep mire with no firm ground, and the floods overflow me. (Mire: swampy ground) **3.** I am weary from crying, my throat is dry, and my eyes fail as I wait for God. (Fail: become weak) **4.** My enemies are many and powerful, and I'm punished for things I didn't take. (Mighty: powerful) **5.** O God, you know my foolishness; my sins are not hidden. (Foolishness: lack of judgment) **6.** Do not let those who wait for you be ashamed because of me, O God. (Armies: God's powerful forces) **7.** I've borne disgrace for your sake; shame covers my face. (Reproach: disgrace) **8.** I'm a stranger to my brothers and an outsider to my mother's children. (Stranger: not accepted) **9.** Zeal for your house has consumed me, and the insults fall on me. (Zeal: passion) **10.** My fasting brought me more disgrace. (Chastened: humbled) **11.** I wore sackcloth and became a proverb among them. (Sackcloth: mourning garment) **12.** They mock me, and I'm a joke to drunkards. (Gate: public place) **13.** My prayer is to you, O Lord, hear me in your mercy and truth. (Salvation: deliverance) **14.** Rescue me from the mud and the deep waters. (Floods: overwhelming water) **15.** Don't let the floods drown me or the pit close over me. (Pit: deep hole) **16.** Answer me, for your love is good, and your mercy is abundant. (Tender mercies: deep compassion) **17.** Don't hide your face from me; answer me quickly. (Trouble: distress) **18.** Redeem my soul and rescue me from my enemies. (Redeem: rescue) **19.** You know my disgrace and shame; my enemies are before you. (Adversaries: enemies) **20.** My heart is broken from insults, and I found no comfort. (Reproach: insult) **21.** They gave me gall for food and vinegar to drink. (Gall: bitterness) **22.** Let their table become a trap to them. (Table: provision) **23.** Blind their eyes and make them tremble. (Loins: lower back) **24.** Pour out your anger on them. (Indignation: righteous fury) **25.** Let their homes be desolate. (Habitation: dwelling) **26.** They persecute the one you've struck and mock the wounded. (Persecute: oppress) **27.** Add guilt to their iniquity; don't let them enter your righteousness. (Iniquity: sin) **28.** Erase them from the book of the living, and not with the righteous. (Book of the living: list of the blessed) **29.** I am poor and in pain; lift me up through your salvation. (Sorrowful: full of grief) **30.** I will praise God with a song and thanksgiving. (Magnify: praise) **31.** This pleases the Lord more than sacrifices. (Bullock: castrated bull) **32.** The humble will be glad, and those who seek God will live. (Humble: modest) **33.** The Lord hears the poor and does not despise his prisoners. (Prisoners: oppressed) **34.** Let all creation praise him. (Seas: creation) **35.** God will save Zion and rebuild Judah's cities. (Zion: God's people) **36.** His servants' descendants will inherit it, and those who love his name will dwell there. (descendants: offspring)

Chapter 70

1. O God, hurry to save me; help me, O Lord. (Hasten: hurry) **2.** Let those who seek to harm me be ashamed and confounded. (Confounded: embarrassed) **3.** Let them be turned back who mock me, saying, "Aha!" (Shame: disgrace) **4.** Let those who seek you rejoice and say, "Let God be exalted!" (Exalted: praised) **5.** I am poor and needy; help me, O God; you are my deliverer. (Deliverer: savior)

Chapter 71

1. In You, O LORD, I place my trust; let me never be shamed. **2.** Rescue me by Your righteousness and save me. (Righteousness: The quality of being morally right.) **3.** Be my habitation; You are my rock and fortress. (Habitation: A place to live; Fortress: A stronghold.) **4.** Save me from the wicked and cruel. (Unrighteous: Not morally right.) **5.** You are my hope and trust from youth. (Trust: Firm belief in someone's ability.) **6.** I've relied on You since birth; my praise will always be to You. **7.** I am a wonder to many, but You are my refuge. (Wonder: A cause of admiration.) **8.** Let my mouth praise and honor You all day. (Honor: High respect.) **9.** Do not forsake me when I grow old or weak. (Forsake: Abandon or leave.) **10.** My enemies speak against me and conspire. (Conspire: Make secret plans to harm.) **11.** They say, "God has abandoned him; no one will help him." (Forsaken: Abandoned.) **12.** O God, hurry to help me! (Hurry: Move with speed.) **13.** Let those who oppose me be ashamed and disgraced. **14.** I will hope in You and praise You continually. (Hope: Expectation for something good.) **15.** My mouth will declare Your righteousness and salvation all day long. (Righteousness: The state of being morally right.) **16.** I will walk in the strength of the LORD and speak of Your righteousness. (Dominion: Control or sovereignty.) **17.** You have taught me from youth, and I proclaim Your mighty works. (Marvelous: Causing wonder.) **18.** Even in old age, do not forsake me until I declare Your power to the next generation. (Grayheaded: Having gray hair.) **19.** Your righteousness is very high; who is like You? (Righteousness: Right actions.) **20.** You have allowed me great trials, but You will revive me again. (Revive: To restore life.) **21.** You will increase my greatness and comfort me. (Comfort: Strengthen or encourage.) **22.** I will praise You with the lyre and harp, O Holy One of Israel. (Lyre: A stringed instrument.) **23.** My lips will rejoice as I sing to You, and my redeemed soul will rejoice. (Redeemed: Saved from evil.) **24.** My tongue will speak of Your righteousness all day, while those who seek to harm me will be ashamed.

Chapter 72
1. Give the king Your judgments, O God, and righteousness to the king's son. (Judgments: Legal decisions.) **2.** He will judge Your people with righteousness and the poor with justice. (Judge: To make decisions.) **3.** The mountains will bring peace, and the hills righteousness. (Righteousness: Morally just actions.) **4.** He will protect the poor and oppressors will be broken. (Oppressor: A cruel ruler.) **5.** People will fear You as long as the sun and moon endure. (Endure: To last or persist.) **6.** He will come down like rain upon the mown grass. (Mown: Cut grass.) **7.** In his days, the righteous will flourish, and peace will abound. (Flourish: To grow vigorously.) **8.** He will rule from sea to sea and to the ends of the earth. (Dominion: Sovereignty over a territory.) **9.** Those in the wilderness will bow before him, and his enemies will lick the dust. (Lick: To touch with the tongue, indicating submission.) **10.** Kings of Tarshish and the islands will bring gifts. (Presents: Special gifts.) **11.** All kings will bow before him; all nations will serve him. (Bow: To bend forward as a sign of respect.) **12.** He will deliver the needy when they cry; the poor and helpless. (Deliver: Rescue or save.) **13.** He will have compassion on the poor and needy. (Compassion: Sympathy for others' suffering.) **14.** He will redeem their lives from deceit and violence. (Redeem: To restore or save something.) **15.** He will live, and gold from Sheba will be given to Him; prayers will be made continually for Him. (Continually: Without interruption.) **16.** There will be an abundance of grain, and the fruit will wave like Lebanon. (Flourish: To grow well.) **17.** His name will endure forever; all nations will be blessed through Him. (Endure: To last or persist.) **18.** Blessed be the LORD God, the God of Israel, who alone does marvelous things. (Marvelous: Causing admiration.) **19.** Blessed be His glorious name forever; may the earth be filled with His glory. (Glorious: Having great beauty or splendor.) **20.** The prayers of David, son of Jesse, are finished. (Finished: Completed.)

Chapter 73
1. Truly, God is good to Israel, to those with a pure heart. (Pure heart: sincere) **2.** But I almost stumbled; my steps nearly slipped. (Slipped: faltered) **3.** I envied the wicked when I saw their prosperity. (Prosperity: success) **4.** They have no struggles in death; their strength is firm. (Struggles: troubles) **5.** They don't face troubles like others. (Troubles: difficulties) **6.** Pride surrounds them; violence is their clothing. (Pride: arrogance) **7.** They are fat and satisfied; they have more than they desire. (Fat: prosperous) **8.** They speak evil about oppression and speak proudly. (Evil: wickedly) **9.** They mock God, spreading their words across the earth. (Mock: disrespect) **10.** People follow them, drinking from their excess. (Excess: overabundance) **11.** They ask, "Does God know?" (Know: understand) **12.** The wicked prosper and grow rich. (Prosper: succeed) **13.** I've kept my heart pure for nothing. (Pure: innocent) **14.** I'm troubled daily, disciplined every morning. (Troubled: burdened) **15.** If I spoke this way, I'd hurt your people. (Hurt: mislead) **16.** It was too painful to understand until I entered your sanctuary. (Sanctuary: presence) **17.** Then I understood their end. (End: destiny) **18.** You set them on slippery ground, leading to destruction. (Slippery ground: risk) **19.** In an instant, they are ruined by terror. (Ruined: destroyed) **20.** They are like a dream when one wakes up; you will despise their illusion. (Illusion: false appearance) **21.** My heart was grieved, and I was troubled. (Grieved: distressed) **22.** I was foolish and ignorant, like an animal before you. (Animal: irrational) **23.** Yet, I am with you; you support me. (Support: guide) **24.** You guide me with counsel, then take me to glory. (Counsel: advice) **25.** Who do I have in heaven but you? I desire nothing on earth but you. (Desire: long for) **26.** My heart and flesh fail, but God is my strength and portion forever. (Portion: inheritance) **27.** Those far from you will perish; you destroy all who are unfaithful. (Unfaithful: disloyal) **28.** It is good for me to be near God, my refuge, to declare your works. (Refuge: shelter)

Chapter 74
1. O God, why have you rejected us forever? Why does your anger burn against your people? (Reject: abandon) **2.** Remember your people, whom you redeemed; remember Mount Zion. (Redeemed: rescued) **3.** Lift your feet to the ruins, the enemy has ravaged your sanctuary. (Ruins: destruction) **4.** Your enemies roar in your place of worship, setting up banners. (Roar: shout) **5.** They are known for chopping trees with axes. (Known: famous) **6.** Now they tear down the carvings with axes and hammers. (Carvings: designs) **7.** They've burned your sanctuary, defiling your dwelling. (Defiling: making impure) **8.** They say, "Let's destroy everything, we've burned all your places of worship." (Destroy: ruin) **9.** We don't see signs, no prophet to tell us how long this will last. (Signs: evidence) **10.** How long will the enemy mock you? Will they revile your name forever? (Revile: speak abusively) **11.** Why do you hold back your hand? Take it and destroy them. (Hold back: withhold) **12.** God is my King, working salvation in the earth. (Salvation: deliverance) **13.** You divided the sea by your strength, crushing the heads of dragons. (Dragons: sea creatures) **14.** You crushed Leviathan and gave him to the people of the wilderness. (Leviathan: sea monster) **15.** You opened springs and dried up rivers. (Springs: water sources) **16.** The day and night are yours; you created the sun and moon. (Created: made) **17.** You set the earth's boundaries, making summer and winter. (Boundaries: limits) **18.** Remember how the enemy mocked you, O LORD, and how the foolish reviled your name. (Mocked: ridiculed) **19.** Don't give the soul of your dove to the wicked; don't forget the poor. (Dove: symbol of peace) **20.** Remember your covenant; the earth is full of cruelty. (Covenant: sacred agreement) **21.** Don't let the oppressed return in shame, let the poor praise your name. (Oppressed: unjustly treated) **22.** Arise, God, defend your cause, remember how the foolish mock you. (Cause: reason for defending) **23.** Don't forget the noise of your enemies; their uproar grows. (Uproar: commotion)

Chapter 75
1. We give thanks to You, O God, for Your name is near, and Your mighty deeds are proclaimed. (mighty deeds: powerful acts) **2.** When I gather the assembly, I will judge with fairness. (assembly: group of people) **3.** The earth will shake, but I hold its foundations. (foundations: base) (Selah: pause for reflection) **4.** I warned the foolish, "Do not act foolishly," and the wicked, "Do not raise your power." (wicked: morally wrong) **5.** Do not act arrogantly, nor speak with pride. (arrogantly: self-importance) **6.** Promotion does not come from east, west, or south. **7.** God is the judge; He brings down one and raises another. **8.** In God's hand is a cup of judgment for the wicked. **9.** I will sing praises to the God of Jacob. **10.** I will cut off the strength of the wicked, but the righteous will be raised high. (righteous: morally right)

Chapter 76
1. God is known in Judah; His name is exalted in Israel. (exalted: praised) **2.** His dwelling place is in Salem, His home in Zion. (dwelling place: home) **3.** There, He broke weapons and stopped the battle. (weapons: fighting tools, stopped: halted) (Selah: pause for reflection) **4.** You are more glorious than the mountains filled with prey. (glorious: full of splendor, prey: hunted animals) **5.** The

warriors are defeated, unable to move. **6.** At Your rebuke, chariots and horses fall asleep. (rebuke: correction) **7.** Who can stand before You when You are angry? **8.** You declared judgment, and the earth stood still. **9.** When God arose to save the meek. (meek: humble) (Selah: pause for reflection) **10.** Human wrath will praise You, and You will restrain the rest. (wrath: anger, restrain: hold back) **11.** Make vows to the LORD and fulfill them. **12.** He will cut off the spirit of rulers; He is feared by kings. (spirit: will)

Chapter 77

1. I cried out to God, and He listened. (cried out: called for help) **2.** In my trouble, I sought the Lord, but my soul refused comfort. (comfort: peace) **3.** I remembered God, and was troubled. (troubled: disturbed, Selah: pause for reflection) **4.** You kept my eyes awake, and I could not speak. **5.** I considered the days of old. **6.** I remembered my song in the night, and my spirit searched for understanding. **7.** Will the Lord reject me forever? **8.** Has His mercy vanished? (mercy: compassion) **9.** Has God forgotten to be gracious? (gracious: kind, Selah: pause for reflection) **10.** I will remember Your strength, O Most High. **11.** I will remember Your works and wonders. **12.** I will meditate on Your deeds. (meditate: think deeply) **13.** Your way is in the sanctuary; who is greater than our God? (sanctuary: holy place) **14.** You are the God who works wonders. **15.** With Your arm, You redeemed Your people. (redeemed: rescued) **16.** The waters saw You and were afraid. **17.** The clouds poured down water, Your arrows flashed. **18.** The thunder was heard, and the earth trembled. **19.** Your way was in the sea; Your footsteps were unseen. **20.** You led Your people like a flock by Moses and Aaron. (flock: a group of sheep)

Chapter 78

1. Listen, my people, to my teachings; hear the words of my mouth. **2.** I will speak in parables, sharing ancient mysteries. (parable: story) **3.** These are things passed down by our ancestors. (known: understood, fathers: ancestors) **4.** We will tell future generations about the Lord's praise, strength, and wonders. (shewing: showing, generation to come: future) **5.** He set a law in Israel for our forefathers to teach their children. (testimony: witness, appointed: set) **6.** So future generations might know them, even those unborn, to share with their children. (arise: rise up, declare: announce) **7.** They could trust in God, remember His deeds, and obey His commands. (set their hope: trust, works: deeds) **8.** They should not be like their ancestors, whose hearts were not loyal. (stubborn: unwilling, steadfast: firm) **9.** The children of Ephraim, armed with bows, retreated in battle. (armed: equipped, turned back: retreated) **10.** They did not keep God's covenant or follow His law. (covenant: agreement, refused: declined) **11.** They forgot His works and wonders. (wonders: signs) **12.** He did amazing things in front of their ancestors in Egypt and Zoan. (marvellous: amazing, Zoan: Egypt) **13.** He parted the sea and led them through; He made the waters stand like a wall. (divided: separated, heap: pile) **14.** By day, He led them with a cloud, by night, with light from fire. (led: guided, cloud: vapor) **15.** He split rocks and gave them water from deep seas. (clave: split, wilderness: barren land) **16.** He brought streams from the rock and made waters flow like rivers. (streams: small rivers, rivers: flowing water) **17.** Yet they sinned more by provoking the Most High in the desert. (sinned: acted wrong, provoking: angering) **18.** They tested God by asking for food to satisfy their cravings. (tempted: tested, lust: craving) **19.** They spoke against God, asking, "Can God spread a table in the wilderness?" (furnish: provide, wilderness: barren land) **20.** He struck the rock and water poured out; can He provide bread and meat? (smote: struck, gushed out: flowed forcefully) **21.** The Lord heard and became angry, fire burned against Jacob. (wroth: angry, kindled: sparked) **22.** They did not believe in God or trust His salvation. (believed not: did not trust, salvation: deliverance) **23.** Though He had commanded the skies to open. (commanded: ordered, clouds from above: skies) **24.** He sent manna to eat, food from heaven. (manna: food, angels' food: heavenly food) **25.** Men ate the food of angels; He gave them all they needed. (angels' food: heavenly food, full: satisfied) **26.** He caused the east wind to blow and brought the south wind by His power. (east wind: wind from the east, south wind: wind from the south) **27.** He rained meat on them like dust, and birds like sand on the seashore. (rained: sent down, feathered fowls: birds) **28.** It fell in their camp, around their tents. (fell: dropped, habitations: dwellings) **29.** They ate and were filled, for He gave them what they desired. (filled: satisfied, desire: want) **30.** They were not tired of their cravings, but while the food was still in their mouths, (estranged: tired, lust: craving) **31.** The anger of God rose against them, and He killed the strongest of them. (wrath: anger, slew: killed) **32.** Despite this, they continued to sin and did not trust in His wonders. (sinned still: continued to sin, wondrous works: miraculous deeds) **33.** So He consumed their days in futility and their years in trouble. (consumed: ended, futility: uselessness) **34.** When He killed them, they sought Him and quickly turned to God. **35.** They remembered that God was their Rock, and the High God their Redeemer. (Rock: foundation, Redeemer: rescuer) **36.** But they flattered Him with their words, lying to Him with their tongues. (flattered: praised insincerely, lied: deceived) **37.** Their hearts were not loyal, and they were not faithful to His covenant. (right: loyal, steadfast: faithful) **38.** Yet, He was full of compassion, forgave their sins, and did not destroy them. (compassion: mercy, iniquity: sin) **39.** He remembered they were only flesh, a passing breeze. (flesh: human beings, wind: breeze) **40.** How often they provoked Him in the wilderness and grieved Him in the desert! (grieved: saddened, wilderness: desert) **41.** They tested God, limiting the Holy One of Israel. (limited: restricted, Holy One: God) **42.** They did not remember His mighty hand, nor the day He rescued them. (hand: power, delivered: rescued) **43.** How He performed miracles in Egypt and wonders in Zoan. (wrought: performed, Zoan: Egypt) **44.** He turned their rivers into blood, and they could not drink from their streams. (rivers into blood: a plague in Egypt, streams: small rivers) **45.** He sent flies to devour them, and frogs that destroyed them. (divers: various, devoured: consumed) **46.** He gave their crops to locusts and their labor to grasshoppers. (increase: crops, caterpillar: locust) **47.** He destroyed their vines with hail and their sycamore trees with frost. (destroyed: ruined, hail: ice pellets) **48.** He gave their cattle to the hail, and their flocks to thunderbolts. (flocks: animals, thunderbolts: lightning strikes) **49.** He unleashed His anger on them, sending destructive angels. (fierceness: anger, evil angels: destructive forces) **50.** He made a way for His anger, handing them over to pestilence. (path: way, pestilence: disease) **51.** He struck down the firstborn of Egypt, the strongest in Ham's tents. (firstborn: oldest children, tents: dwellings) **52.** But He led His own people like sheep and guided them through the wilderness. (flock: group of sheep, wilderness: barren land) **53.** He led them safely, and the sea overwhelmed their enemies. (overwhelmed: consumed, enemies: adversaries) **54.** He brought them to His holy land, to the mountain He took by His power. (sanctuary: holy place, right hand: power) **55.** He drove out nations before them and gave them land, settling Israel in their tents. (heathen: foreign nations, inheritance: land) **56.** Yet they tested and disobeyed the Most High and did not keep His commands. (provoked: angered, testimonies: commandments) **57.** They turned back and were unfaithful like a deceitful bow. (deceitful: dishonest, turned aside: strayed) **58.** They angered God with their high places and made Him jealous with idols. (high places: idol worship, graven images: idols) **59.** When God heard this, He became angry and despised Israel. (abhorred: hated, forsook: abandoned) **60.** He abandoned the tabernacle at Shiloh, the tent where He dwelt among men. (forsook: abandoned, tabernacle: portable temple) **61.** He gave His strength into captivity and His glory to the enemy. (strength: power, captivity: imprisonment) **62.** He handed His people over to the sword and was angry with His inheritance. (sword: weapon, inheritance: people) **63.** The fire consumed their young men, and their women did not marry. (consumed: destroyed, maidens: young women) **64.** Their priests were slain by the sword, and their widows did not mourn. (priests: leaders, slain: killed) **65.** Then the Lord woke like a warrior asleep, shouting as if drunk. (awaked: woke up, mighty man: warrior) **66.** He struck His enemies from behind and put them to shame forever. (smote: struck, perpetual: eternal) **67.** He rejected Joseph's tribe and chose Judah. (refused: rejected, Ephraim: tribe) **68.** He chose Judah, the mountain of Zion which He loves. (Zion: Jerusalem, loves: favors) **69.** He built His sanctuary like grand palaces, like the earth He established forever. (palaces: grand buildings, established: set up) **70.** He chose David, His servant, from the sheepfolds. (servant: chosen leader, sheepfolds: sheep pens) **71.** From following the ewes, He brought him to shepherd Israel. (ewes: female sheep, feed: guide) **72.** He led them with integrity of heart and skillful hands. (integrity: honesty, skilfulness: expertise)

Chapter 79
1. O God, the nations have defiled Your temple, leaving Jerusalem in ruins. (Ruins: heaps of destruction) **2.** They have thrown Your servants' bodies to the birds and wild animals. **3.** They have shed the blood of Your people around Jerusalem, with no one to bury them. **4.** We have become a disgrace and mockery to our neighbors. (Disgrace: reproach; Mockery: derision) **5** How long will Your righteous anger burn like fire? **6.** Pour out Your wrath on nations that do not know You or call on Your name. (Wrath: intense anger) **7.** They have devoured Israel and laid waste its home. (devoured: consumed; Laid waste: devastated) **8.** Do not remember our wrongs; let Your mercies come quickly, for we are brought very low. (Mercies: compassions; Humbled: brought very low) **9.** Help us, O God of salvation, for Your name's glory; deliver us, and forgive our sins. (Forgive: purge away) **10.** Why should the nations ask, "Where is their God?" Let it be known that You avenge the blood of Your servants. (Avenging: revenging) **11.** Hear the cries of the prisoners and save those appointed to die. (Prisoners: sighing of the prisoner; Condemned: appointed) **12.** Give back seven times the disgrace they have brought upon us, for they have mocked You. (Disgrace: reproach; Mock: reproached) **13.**We, Your people, will give You thanks forever and declare Your praise throughout generations. (Declare: show forth)

Chapter 80
1. Listen, O Shepherd of Israel, lead Joseph like a flock; shine forth from above the cherubim. (Shepherd: leader; Cherubim: angelic beings) **2.** Awaken Your power before Ephraim, Benjamin, and Manasseh to save us. (Ephraim, Benjamin, and Manasseh: tribes of Israel) **3.** Restore us, O God, and show favor upon us so we may be saved. (Restore: turn us again; Cause Your face to shine: show favor) **4.** O Lord God of heavenly armies, how long will You be angry with Your people's prayers? (heavenly armies: Hosts) **5.** You have fed them the bread of suffering and tears in great measure. (Bread of tears: suffering; Abundance: great measure) **6.** You have made us a quarrel for our neighbors, and our enemies mock us. (Quarrel: strife; Mock: laugh among themselves) **7.** Restore us, O God of heavenly armies, and let Your face shine upon us, so we may be saved. (Restore: turn us again; Face shine: favor) **8.** You brought Israel out of Egypt, drove out nations, and planted it. (Drove out: cast out) **9.** You cleared the land for it, and it became established, filling the land. (Took root: established; Filled: spread) **10.** The hills were covered with its shade, and its branches were like tall cedars. (Shade: shadow; Cedars: large, strong trees) **11.** It spread toward the sea and the river. (Sea: Mediterranean Sea; River: Euphrates River) **12.** Why have You destroyed its walls, letting everyone pick its fruit? (Broken down: destroyed; Pluck: pick) **13.** The wild boar ravages it, and wild animals devour it. (Boar: wild pig; Ravages: wastes) **14.** Return, O God of heavenly armies, care for this vine. (Visit: care for) **15.** The vineyard Your right hand planted, the branch You made strong. (Right hand: power; Vineyard: Israel) **16.** It is burned and cut down; they perish at Your rebuke. (Burned: destroyed; Rebuke: correction) **17** Let Your hand be on the man of Your right hand, the son of man You have made strong. (Man of Your right hand: leader chosen by God; Son of man: human representative) **18.** Then we will not turn away; revive us, and we will call on Your name. (Revive: quicken) **19.** Restore us, O Lord God of heavenly armies, and cause Your face to shine upon us, so we may be saved. (Face shine: favor)

Chapter 80
1. Listen, O Shepherd of Israel, who leads Joseph like a flock; you who are enthroned above the cherubim, reveal your glory. (Cherubim: heavenly beings) **2.** Stir your power before Ephraim, Benjamin, and Manasseh; come and deliver us. (Ephraim, Benjamin, Manasseh: the northern Tribes of Israel) **3.** Restore us, O God, and let your face shine upon us, that we may be rescued. (Restore: bring back) **4.** How long, O LORD God of armies, will you remain angry with the prayers of your people? (God of armies: God who commands forces) **5.** You give them tears to eat, and a full cup of sorrow to drink. (Sorrow: grief) **6.** You have made us a cause of strife to our neighbors; our enemies mock us. (Mock: ridicule) **7.** Restore us once more, O God of armies, and let your face shine upon us, that we may be saved. (Restore: bring back) **8.** You brought a vine out of Egypt and cast out the nations to plant it. (Egypt: land where Pharaoh ruled) **9.** You made space for it to grow; it took root deeply and spread across the land. (Root: foundation) **10.** Its shade covered the hills, and its branches were as grand as the cedars. (Cedars: tall trees) **11.** It reached out its branches to the sea, its shoots to the river. (Shoots: new growth) **12.** Why then have you broken down its protective walls, so that passersby can pick its fruit? (Pluck: gather) **13.** The wild boar from the forest destroys it, and the beasts of the field consume it. (Boar: wild pig) **14.** Return, we ask, O God of armies, look down from heaven and tend to this vine. (Tend: care for) **15.** The vineyard that your mighty hand has planted, the branch you have strengthened for yourself. (Vineyard: plant of vines) **16.** It is burned with fire and cut down; they perish at the rebuke of your face. (Rebuke: God's judgment, often leading to destruction) **17.** Let your hand rest on the man you have chosen, the son of man whom you have made strong. (Son of man: chosen leader) **18.** Then we will never turn away from you; revive us, and we will call on your name. (Revive: restore life) **19.** Restore us again, O LORD God of armies, let your face shine upon us, that we may be saved. (Restore: bring back)

Chapter 81
1. Sing loudly to God our strength; shout joyfully to the God of Jacob. (Shout: make a loud sound) **2.** Play a song, and bring the tambourine, the sweet harp with the lyre. (Tambourine: hand drum, Lyre: small harp) **3.** Blow the trumpet at the new moon, at the appointed time, on our feast day. (Feast day: special celebration) **4.** This was a rule for Israel, a law from the God of Jacob. (Rule: Commandments of God) **5.** He set this in place for Joseph as a testimony when he left Egypt, where I heard a language I didn't understand. (Testimony: evidence or reminder, Egypt: land of Pharaoh) **6.** I removed his burden from his shoulder; his hands were freed from the heavy pots. (Burden: load, Pots: cooking vessels) **7.** You called out in trouble, and I saved you; I answered you from the thunder and tested you at Meribah's waters. Selah. (Thunder: loud noise of storms, Meribah: place of quarrel) **8.** Listen, O my people, and I will testify to you: O Israel, if you will listen to me; **9.** There will be no foreign god among you; you will not worship any strange god. (Foreign god: god of another nation) **10.** I am the LORD your God, who brought you out of Egypt; open your mouth wide, and I will fill it. (Open wide: ask boldly) **11.** But my people would not listen to me, and Israel refused to follow me. (Listen: heed or obey.) **12.** So I let them follow their own desires and walk in their own plans. (Desires: wishes, Plans: ideas) **13.** Oh, if my people had listened to me, and Israel had walked in my ways! **14.** I would have quickly defeated their enemies and turned my hand against their foes. (Foes: enemies) **15.** Those who hated the LORD would have bowed to him, and their time would

have lasted forever. (Bowed: submitted) **16.** I would have given them the best of wheat and satisfied them with honey from the rock. (Honey from the rock: a symbol of great abundance)

Chapter 82

1. God stands in the assembly of the powerful; He judges among the gods. (Assembly: gathering, Powerful: mighty beings) **2.** How long will you judge unfairly and show favor to the wicked? Selah. (Unfairly: unjustly, Favor: partiality) **3.** Defend the poor and orphans; give justice to the suffering and those in need. (Orphans: fatherless children, Suffering: in pain) **4.** Rescue the poor and needy; save them from the hands of the wicked. (Rescue: deliver, Wicked: evil) **5.** They don't know or understand; they continue walking in darkness. The foundations of the earth are shaken. (Darkness: ignorance, Foundations: basic principles) **6.** I said, "You are gods, and all of you are children of the Most High." (Most High: God) **7.** But you will die like ordinary people and fall like any other ruler. (Ordinary: human, Ruler: leader) **8.** Rise up, O God, judge the earth, for You will inherit all the nations. (Inherit: take possession)

Chapter 83

1. Do not remain silent, O God; do not keep still or be quiet, O God. (Remain silent: stay quiet) **2.** See, your enemies are making a loud noise, and those who hate you have risen up. (Loud noise: commotion) **3.** They have plotted against your people and conspired against your hidden ones. (Plotted: planned secretly) **4.** They said, "Let's cut them off from being a nation so that Israel's name is forgotten." (Cut off: destroy, Forgotten: no longer remembered) **5.** They have joined together with one mind and are united against you. (Joined: united, United: in agreement) **6.** The tents of Edom, the Ishmaelites, Moab, and the Hagarenes; (Ishmaelites: descendants of Ishmael, Moab: an ancient nation) **7.** Gebal, Ammon, Amalek, the Philistines, and the people of Tyre; (Gebal: a city, Amalek: an enemy nation) **8.** Assyria has also joined them and helped the children of Lot. Selah. (Assyria: ancient empire, Lot: nephew of Abraham) **9.** Do to them as you did to the Midianites, to Sisera and Jabin by the river Kishon. (Midianites: enemies of Israel in the time of Gideon, Sisera/Jabin: leaders defeated by Deborah and Barak) **10.** They were destroyed at Endor and became like dung on the earth. (Dung: waste) **11.** Make their leaders like Oreb and Zeeb, all their rulers like Zebah and Zalmunna, (Leaders: important figures) **12.** Who said, "Let us take the houses of God as our own." (Houses of God: places of worship) **13.** O my God, make them like chaff, like the stubble before the wind. (Chaff: he worthless husk) **14.** Like fire that burns wood, and like flames that set mountains ablaze; (Flames: intense heat) **15.** So chase them with your storm, and terrify them with your tempest. (Tempest: violent storm) **16.** Fill their faces with shame so they will seek your name, O LORD. (Shame: dishonor) **17.** Let them be embarrassed and troubled forever; let them be put to shame and vanish. (Embarrassed: humiliated) **18.** Let people know that you, whose name alone is JEHOVAH, are the Most High over all the earth. (Jehovah: the LORD, Most High: supreme ruler)

Chapter 84

1. How delightful are your dwelling places, O LORD of hosts! (Delightful: pleasing) **2.** My soul yearns, even faints, to be in your courts; my heart and flesh cry out for the living God. (Yearns: longs, Courts: sacred spaces) **3.** The sparrow has found a home and the swallow a place to rest, near your altars, O LORD of hosts, my King and my God. (Rest: place to lay eggs) **4.** Blessed are those who live in your house; they are continually praising you. Selah. (Blessed: truly happy) **5.** Blessed is the person who draws strength from you, whose heart is set on walking your paths. (Strength: source of power, Paths: righteous ways) **6.** Those who travel through the valley of Baca turn it into a place of springs; the rain fills the pools. (Baca: valley of weeping, Pools: places of refreshment,) **7.** They go from strength to strength, each one appearing before God in Zion. (Strength: power) **8.** O LORD God of hosts, listen to my prayer; hear me, O God of Jacob. Selah. (Hear: respond) **9.** Look, O God, our protector, and consider the face of your anointed one. (Protector: shield, Anointed one: chosen leader) **10.** One day in your courts is better than a thousand elsewhere. I would rather stand at the door of the house of my God than live in the tents of the wicked. (Stand at the door: be a doorkeeper) **11.** For the LORD God is a sun and a shield; the LORD grants grace and glory; He withholds no good thing from those who walk uprightly. (Sun: source of light, Shield: protector) **12.** O LORD of hosts, happy is the person who places their trust in you. (Trust: confidence)

Chapter 85

1. LORD, you have shown kindness to your land; you have restored the fortunes of Jacob. (Kindness: favor, Fortunes: captivity) **2.** You have pardoned the guilt of your people; you have covered all their wrongs. Selah. (Pardoned: forgiven, Guilt: sins) **3.** You have taken away all your anger; you have turned from the burning heat of your wrath. (Burning heat: fierce anger) **4.** Bring us back, O God of our salvation, and let your anger towards us end. (Bring back: restore) **5.** Will you remain angry with us forever? Will your anger continue through all generations? (Remain: stay, Continue: endure) **6.** Will you not revive us again, so that your people may rejoice in you? (Revive: restore life) **7.** Show us your unfailing love, O LORD, and give us your salvation. (Unfailing love: mercy) **8.** I will listen to what the LORD God will say; He will promise peace to His people and to His faithful followers. But may they not return to foolishness. (Promise: speak, Faithful followers: saints) **9.** Surely His deliverance is near those who revere Him, that His glory may be seen in our land. (Deliverance: salvation, Revere: honor) **10.** Love and truth have met; justice and peace have embraced each other. (Love: mercy, Justice: righteousness, Embraced: joined) **11.** Truth will spring up from the ground, and righteousness will look down from the sky. (Spring up: grow, Righteousness: right living) **12.** The LORD will bless us with what is good, and our land will bear its fruit. (Bless: give, Bear its fruit: yield its increase) **13.** Righteousness will lead the way before Him and guide us along His paths. (Lead the way: go before, Guide: direct)

Chapter 86

1. O LORD, bend your ear and listen to me; for I am in desperate need and poverty. (Bend your ear: pay attention) **2.** Guard my life, for I am devoted to you; O my God, rescue your servant who places trust in you. (Guard: preserve, Devoted: holy, Rescue: save) **3.** Be compassionate toward me, O Lord, for I cry out to you daily. (Compassionate: merciful, Cry out: call) **4.** Fill your servant's heart with joy, for I lift my soul up to you, O Lord. (Fill: rejoice, Lift up: offer) **5.** You, Lord, are good and quick to forgive; you abound in mercy to all who call on you. (Abound: are plentiful, Mercy: love) **6.** Listen to my prayer, O LORD; hear my pleading for help. (Pleading: supplications) **7.** In my time of trouble, I will call on you, for you will surely answer me. (Time of trouble: distress) **8.** There is no god like you, O LORD; none can compare to your works. (Compare: match) **9.** All the nations you've created will come and bow down before you, O LORD, and give glory to your name. (Bow down: worship, Glory: honor) **10.** You are great and perform wonders; you alone are God. (Perform: do, Wonders: marvelous deeds) **11.** Teach me your ways, O LORD, that I may walk in your truth; unite my heart to honor your name. (Unite: bring together) **12.** I will give you thanks, O Lord my God, with all my heart; I will glorify your name forever. (Thanks: praise, Glorify: honor) **13.** Your mercy toward me is vast, and you have delivered my soul from the depths of death. (Vast: great, Delivered: saved) **14.** O God, the proud rise against me, and ruthless men seek my life, with no regard for you. (Rise against: oppose, Ruthless: violent) **15.** But you, O LORD, are full of compassion and grace, slow to anger, and rich in mercy and truth. (Rich: abundant) **16.** Turn toward me and show mercy; give your strength to your servant, and save the son of your maidservant. (Turn toward: look at, Maidservant: handmaid) **17.** Show me a clear sign of your favor, that those who hate me may see it and be ashamed, for you, LORD, have helped and comforted me. (Sign of your favor: token for good, Helped: assisted, Comforted: encouraged)

Chapter 87

1. His foundation is set upon the sacred mountains. (Set upon: established on) 2. The LORD holds the gates of Zion more precious than all the dwellings of Jacob. 3. Glorious things are proclaimed about you, O city of God. Selah. (Proclaimed: spoken) 4. I will mention Rahab and Babylon to those who are acquainted with me; look at Philistia, Tyre, and Ethiopia—this person was born there. (Acquainted: know, Look at: behold) 5. Of Zion, it will be said, "This one and that one were born in her," and the Most High Himself will establish her. (Will be said: shall declare, Establish: set up) 6. The LORD will count, when He writes down the people, that this one was born there. Selah. (Writes down: registers) 7. Both singers and instrumentalists will be there; all my sources of joy are in you. (Sources of joy: springs)

Chapter 88

1. O LORD God, my Deliverer, I have cried out to you day and night. (Cried out: called, Deliverer: salvation) 2. Let my prayer reach your ears; incline your ear to my desperate plea. (Incline: turn your ear, desperate plea: cry) 3. My soul is overwhelmed with troubles, and I feel my life is slipping into the grave. (Overwhelmed: filled, Slipping: drawing near) 4. I am counted among those who descend into the pit; I am like one with no strength. (Descend: go down, Pit: the depths, No strength: helpless) 5. I am like the dead who are left in the grave, forgotten and cut off from your hand. (Left: lying, forgotten: no more remembered) 6. You have placed me in the deepest pit, in the dark depths. (Deepest: lowest, Dark depths: darkness) 7. Your fierce anger weighs heavily on me, and your waves have overwhelmed me. Selah. (Weighs heavily: lies hard upon, Overwhelmed: filled with trouble) 8. You have made my friends far from me; you have made me an object of horror to them. I am trapped and cannot escape. (Trapped: shut up) 9. My eyes are weary from grief; I call to you, LORD, every day, reaching out my hands to you. (Weary: mourn, Reaching out: stretching) 10. Will you perform wonders for the dead? Can the dead rise up and give you praise? Selah. (Perform wonders: show wonders) 11. Will your lovingkindness be declared in the grave, or your faithfulness in the place of destruction? (Declared: known) 12. Can your miracles be seen in the dark, and your justice in the land of forgetfulness? (Miracles: wonders, Justice: righteousness) 13. But I cry to you, O LORD, and my prayer will come to you at dawn. (Dawn: morning) 14. LORD, why have you rejected me? Why do you hide your face from me? (Rejected: cast off, Hide your face: turn away) 15. I have been suffering since my youth, and I am near the end of my strength; I am overwhelmed by your terrors. (Near the end: ready to die, Overwhelmed: distracted) 16. Your wrath sweeps over me like a storm; your terrors have shut me out. (Sweeps over: goes over) 17. They surround me like a flood, coming around me from every side. (Coming around: compassing) 18. You have distanced my loved ones and friends from me; my companions are now in darkness. (Distanced: put far, Companions: acquaintances)

Chapter 89

1. I will continually sing of the LORD's great mercy: I will proclaim His loyalty to every generation. (mercy: steadfast love, loyalty: faithfulness) 2. I declared that His mercy will endure forever, and His faithfulness will be established in the heavens. 3. I made a solemn promise to My chosen one, to David, My servant. (solemn promise: covenant) 4. I will secure your descendants forever, and establish your throne for generations to come. (descendants: offspring) 5. The heavens will praise Your wonders, O LORD, and Your faithfulness will be declared by the saints. (saints: holy ones) 6. Who in the heavens can match the LORD? Who among the divine beings is like Him? (divine beings: mighty) 7. God is deeply revered among His people; He is held in awe by all who surround Him. (revered: feared, surround: are near) 8. O LORD God of hosts, who is as strong as You? Your faithfulness surrounds You like a shield. 9. You control the waves of the sea; when they rise, You calm them. 10. You crushed Rahab, and scattered Your enemies with Your mighty power. (Rahab: symbolic enemy of God) 11. The heavens belong to You, and the earth is Yours too; You created the world and everything in it. 12. You made the north and south, and even the mountains of Tabor and Hermon rejoice in Your name. (Tabor, Hermon: mountains) 13. Your arm is powerful, Your right hand is exalted and strong. 14. Righteousness and justice are the foundation of Your throne; mercy and truth go before You. (righteousness: right judgment) 15. Blessed are those who know the joyful sound; they walk in the light of Your presence. 16. They will rejoice in Your name all day long, and be exalted because of Your righteousness. 17. You are the glory of their strength, and in Your favor, their power is lifted up. 18. For the LORD is our protector; the Holy One of Israel is our king. 19. You spoke to Your holy one in a vision, saying, "I have provided help for the mighty, and I have chosen one from the people." (holy one: prophet) 20. I found David, My servant, and anointed him with My sacred oil. (anointed: chosen) 21. With him, My hand will remain, and My power will strengthen him. 22. No enemy will overpower him, nor will the wicked afflict him. (wicked: evil ones) 23. I will crush his enemies before him and strike down those who oppose him. 24. My faithfulness and mercy will be with him, and his strength will be exalted in My name. 25. I will place his power over the sea, and his right hand over the rivers. (power: hand) 26. He will call to Me, "You are my Father, my God, the rock of my salvation." 27. I will make him My firstborn, and he will be higher than the kings of the earth. 28. My mercy will remain with him forever, and My covenant will stay firm with him. 29. His descendants will last forever, and his throne will endure like the heavens. 30. If his sons turn away from My law and fail to follow My decrees, (decrees: commands) 31. If they disregard My commands and do not obey My statutes, 32. I will correct their wrongdoing with discipline and their sins with punishment. (discipline: correction) 33. Yet My mercy will not be taken from him, nor will My faithfulness be shaken. 34. I will never break My covenant, nor alter what has come from My mouth. (alter: change) 35. Once I swore by My holiness that I will never lie to David. 36. His descendants will remain forever, and his throne will be as enduring as the sun. 37. It will be as constant as the moon, a faithful witness in the sky. (moon: symbol of constancy) 38. But You have rejected and despised him, O LORD; You have been angry with Your anointed one. 39. You have broken the covenant with Your servant and cast his crown down. 40. You have torn down all his defenses and brought his strongholds to ruin. (strongholds: fortresses) 41. All who pass by mock him; he has become a disgrace to his neighbors. 42. You have made his enemies victorious, and his adversaries rejoice. 43. You have turned his sword away, and he has been unable to stand against his foes. 44. You have humbled his glory and cast his throne to the ground. 45. You have shortened his life and covered him with shame. Selah. (shortened: limited his time) 46. How long, LORD? Will You hide Yourself forever? Will Your anger burn like fire? 47. Remember how short my life is; why have You created man for nothing? (nothing: vanity) 48. Who can live and not face death? Who can rescue his soul from the grave? Selah. (rescue: save) 49. LORD, where are Your former mercies, which You promised to David in Your truth? 50. Remember, LORD, how Your enemies have reproached, how I bear their insults. 51. They have mocked You, O LORD, and ridiculed the footsteps of Your anointed. (mocked: laughed at) 52. Blessed be the LORD forevermore. Amen and Amen.

Chapter 90

1. LORD, You have been our safe refuge throughout all generations. (refuge: safe heaven) 2. Before the mountains were even created, or before You formed the earth and the world, You have always been God, from eternity to eternity. 3. You return man to dust, and say, "Return, O sons of men." 4. A thousand years to You are like a single day that quickly passes, or like a watch in the night. (watch: time

period) **5.** You carry them away like a flood; they are like a dream: in the morning they are like grass that springs up. **6.** In the morning it flourishes and grows; by evening it is cut down and withers. **7.** We are consumed by Your anger, and Your wrath overwhelms us. (overwhelms: causes distress) **8.** You place our iniquities (sins) before You; even our hidden faults are revealed in the light of Your presence. **9.** All our days pass away under Your anger; we live our years like a story that is told. **10.** Our lives last for seventy years, or eighty if we are strong, but their strength is filled with trouble and sorrow; soon our lives end, and we are gone. **11.** Who can truly understand the power of Your anger? Your fury matches the reverence You deserve. (reverence: deep respect) **12.** Teach us to wisely count our days, that we may gain a heart of wisdom. **13.** O LORD, how long will You hide Yourself? Have compassion on Your servants. **14.** Satisfy us early with Your love, so we can rejoice and be glad all our days. **15.** Make us glad as many days as You have caused us trouble, and the years we have seen adversity. (adversity: hardship) **16.** Let Your works be known to Your servants, and let Your glory shine on their children. **17.** Let the favor of the LORD our God be upon us; establish the work of our hands, yes, establish the work of our hands.

Chapter 91

1. Whoever finds refuge in the protection of the Most High will rest under the shadow of the Almighty. (refuge: safe place) **2.** I will declare to the LORD, "You are my safe haven and my fortress, my God, in whom I place my trust." **3.** He will certainly rescue you from the traps set by the enemy and from harmful diseases. (rescue: save) **4.** He will shield you with His wings, and you can trust in His protection. His faithfulness will surround you like armor. **5.** You will not fear the terror that comes at night, nor the arrows that strike during the day. **6.** You need not fear the sickness that creeps in the dark, or the destruction that strikes at midday. **7.** Although thousands may fall around you, and ten thousand may fall at your right side, it will not affect you. **8.** You will only see the punishment of the wicked with your eyes. **9.** Since you have made the LORD your refuge, the Most High your place of residence, **10.** No harm will touch you, and no plague will approach your home. **11.** He will command His angels to guard and protect you wherever you go. **12.** They will lift you up in their hands to prevent you from stumbling. **13.** You will walk upon the lion and the snake; you will trample on dangerous beasts and serpents. **14.** Because he holds fast to me in love, I will deliver him; I will protect him, for he acknowledges my name. **15.** When he calls upon me, I will answer him. I will be with him in trouble, and I will rescue and honor him. **16.** I will grant him long life and reveal to him my salvation. (salvation: deliverance, rescue)

Chapter 92

1. It is good to thank the LORD and sing praises to Your name, O Most High. (praises: expressions of gratitude) **2.** To proclaim Your love every morning and Your faithfulness each night, **3.** Using instruments with ten strings, the harp, and a solemn tune. **4.** For, LORD, You have made me glad through what You've done; I will rejoice in the works of Your hands. (rejoice: celebrate joyfully) **5.** O LORD, how great are Your actions! Your thoughts are deep and beyond understanding. (deep: profound) **6.** A senseless man cannot understand this, nor can a foolish person grasp it. (foolish: lacking wisdom) **7.** When the wicked grow like grass and those who do evil prosper, it is because they are doomed to be destroyed. **8.** But You, LORD, are exalted forever. (exalted: lifted high, honored) **9.** Look, LORD, Your enemies will perish; all those who do wrong will be scattered. **10.** But You will lift me up, like the horn of a wild ox, and anoint me with fresh oil. (wild ox: symbol of strength and power) **11.** My eyes will see the downfall of my enemies, and my ears will hear the defeat of those who rise up against me. **12.** The righteous will grow strong like a palm tree, and will thrive like a mighty cedar tree in Lebanon. (righteous: those who follow God's ways) **13.** Those who are planted in the house of the LORD will flourish in His presence. **14.** Even in old age, they will continue to bear fruit, remaining strong and healthy. (flourish: grow and thrive) **15.** This will show that the LORD is fair; He is my rock, and there is no wrong in Him. (rock: symbol of stability and safety)

Chapter 93

1. The LORD reigns, dressed in majesty; He is wrapped in strength, which He has used to gird Himself. The earth is firmly established, and it cannot be shaken. (reigns: rules, majesty: greatness, girded: prepared) **2.** Your throne was set up long ago; You have existed from eternity. (eternity: without beginning or end) **3.** The floods have risen, O LORD; the waters roar loudly, and the waves are lifted high. **4.** The LORD is greater than the roar of many waters, even greater than the mighty waves of the sea. (roar: loud noise) **5.** Your laws are completely trustworthy; holiness is the foundation of Your temple, O LORD, and it will last forever. (holiness: purity, trustworthy: reliable)

Chapter 94

1. O LORD God, to whom vengeance belongs, reveal Yourself. (vengeance: Gods righteous anger) **2.** Lift Yourself up, O Judge of the earth; give the proud what they deserve. (judge: ruler, render: give) **3.** How long, LORD, will the wicked triumph? How long will they prosper? (triumph: succeed) **4.** How long will they speak arrogantly and boast about their wrongdoings? (arrogantly: with pride) **5.** They hurt Your people, O LORD, and oppress Your inheritance. (inheritance: people or possessions God cares for) **6.** They kill the widow, the foreigner, and the orphan. (foreigners: strangers, orphan: fatherless child) **7.** They say, "The LORD will not see, nor will the God of Jacob pay attention." **8.** Understand, you fools among the people: when will you learn wisdom? (fools: unwise ones) **9.** The One who made the ear, can He not hear? The One who formed the eye, can He not see? (formed: shaped) **10.** The One who disciplines nations, will He not correct? The One who teaches man knowledge, will He not know? **11.** The LORD knows the thoughts of man, and they are empty. (empty: worthless) **12.** Blessed is the man whom You discipline, O LORD, and teach out of Your law; (discipline: correct, teach: guide) **13.** So that You may give him rest from days of trouble, until the wicked are punished. (rest: peace, punished: judged) **14.** For the LORD will not abandon His people, nor forsake His inheritance. (forsake: leave behind) **15.** But justice will return to the righteous, and the upright will follow it. (upright: those who are just) **16.** Who will stand up for me against the wicked? Who will rise against those who do evil? (stand up: defend, rise: act) **17.** If the LORD had not been my help, my soul would have been silent in death. (silent: lost) **18.** When I said, "I am slipping," Your mercy, O LORD, upheld me. (slipping: about to fall) **19.** In the midst of my worries, Your comfort brings joy to my soul. (worries: concerns) **20.** Can the throne of injustice partner with You, one who makes evil a law? (injustice: unrighteousness, partner: associate) **21.** They gather against the righteous and condemn the innocent. (gather: assemble, condemn: accuse) **22.** But the LORD is my defense; my God is my rock of refuge. (defense: protector, refuge: safe place) **23.** He will repay them for their evil deeds and destroy them in their own wickedness; the LORD our God will cut them off. (repay: punish, destroy: destroy completely)

Chapter 95

1. Come, let's sing for joy to the LORD; let's shout aloud to the rock that brings us salvation. (sing for joy: praise joyfully, brings us salvation: saves us) **2.** Let us approach Him with grateful hearts, and celebrate Him with music and song. (approach: come to, grateful hearts: thankfulness) **3.** The LORD is a mighty God, the greatest King over all other gods. (mighty: powerful, greatest: supreme) **4.** His hands hold the foundations of the earth, and the strength of the mountains is His alone. (foundations: deep places, strength: power) **5.** The sea belongs to Him, for He made it; and He also formed the dry land with His hands. (belongs: is His, formed: created) **6.** Come, let us bow down and worship; let's kneel before the LORD who made us. (bow down: humble ourselves, kneel: bow in reverence) **7.** He is our God, and we are His people, the sheep under His care. Today, if you hear His voice, (under His care: protected by Him) **8.** Do not harden your hearts, as they did when they rebelled, as they did when they tested Me in the desert. (rebelled: provoked, tested: tempted) **9.** When your ancestors challenged Me and saw what I did. (ancestors: forefathers) **10.** For forty years I was upset with that generation, and I said, "They are a people who go astray in their hearts, and they have not followed My ways." (upset: grieved, go astray: err) **11.** So I declared in My anger, "They will never enter My place of rest." (declared: swore, place of rest: promised peace)

Chapter 96
1. Sing to the LORD a fresh song: let the entire earth join in praise. (fresh song: a new song of praise) **2.** Praise His name and share His salvation, declaring His wonders from day to day. (wonders: miraculous deeds or marvelous acts) **3.** Announce His glory to the nations, and His miraculous deeds to all people. (glory: greatness or magnificence; nations: peoples or countries) **4.** The LORD is great and worthy of tremendous praise: He is to be revered above all gods. (revered: deeply respected) **5.** The gods of other nations are mere idols: but the LORD is the Creator of the heavens. (idols: false gods or statues; Creator: the one who made everything) **6.** Majesty and honor are before Him: strength and beauty fill His sacred place. (majesty: greatness, dignity; sacred place: holy or set-apart place) **7.** Give the LORD the glory due His name, O you peoples: give Him the power and honor He deserves. (due: owed or deserved; peoples: nations or groups) **8.** Bring offerings to the LORD and enter His courts, acknowledging His glorious name. (offerings: gifts or sacrifices; courts: areas of a temple or sacred place) **9.** Worship the LORD in the splendor of holiness: let the entire earth stand in awe of Him. (splendor: brilliance or beauty; holiness: sacredness or purity; awe: reverence or respect) **10.** Declare to the nations that the LORD reigns: He has firmly established the world and it will not be shaken. He will judge the nations with fairness. (reigns: rules or governs; established: made firm or set; shaken: moved or destroyed; fairness: justice or equity) **11.** Let the heavens rejoice and the earth be glad: let the sea roar and all that fills it. (rejoice: be happy or celebrate; roar: make a loud sound) **12.** Let the fields and all their produce rejoice: let all the trees of the forest shout for joy. (produce: crops or fruits; shout for joy: express happiness or praise loudly) **13.** Before the LORD, for He is coming to judge the earth: He will judge the world justly and the nations in His truth. (justly: fairly or with righteousness; truth: reality or faithfulness)

Chapter 97
1. The LORD is King; let the earth be glad, and let the far-off lands rejoice. (King: ruler or sovereign; far-off lands: distant regions or countries) **2.** Clouds and darkness surround Him; His throne is established on righteousness and justice. (surround: encircle or encompass; established: built or grounded; throne: seat of authority) **3.** A fire precedes Him, consuming all who oppose Him. (precedes: comes before; consuming: burning up or destroying) **4.** His lightning lights up the world; the earth witnesses it and trembles. (witnesses: observes or sees; trembles: shakes or quivers) **5.** The mountains melt like wax before the LORD's presence, before the Lord of all the earth. (melt: dissolve or soften; presence: nearness or appearance) **6.** The heavens announce His righteousness, and all the peoples witness His splendor. (announce: declare or proclaim; splendor: brilliance or magnificence) **7.** Let those who worship idols and boast of false gods be ashamed; let all the gods bow before Him. (idols: statues or false gods; boast: take pride in or brag) **8.** Zion hears this and rejoices; the daughters of Judah are glad because of Your righteous judgments, O LORD. (Zion: a hill in Jerusalem; daughters of Judah: people of Judah; righteous: just or fair; judgments: decisions or actions of justice) **9.** For You, LORD, are exalted above the earth; You are lifted high above all other gods. (exalted: raised up in honor, lifted high: elevated or placed above) **10.** You who love the LORD, hate evil; He protects the lives of His loyal servants and delivers them from the wicked. (protects: guards or defends; loyal servants: faithful followers; delivers: saves or rescues) **11.** Light is given to the righteous, and joy to the upright in heart. (given: provided or granted; upright: morally right or just) **12.** Rejoice in the LORD, you righteous; give thanks to His holy name. (rejoice: be glad or celebrate; holy: sacred or divine)

Chapter 98
1. Sing a fresh melody to the LORD, for He has performed amazing acts; His mighty hand and holy arm have secured victory for Him. (Victory: success in defeating an enemy) **2.** The LORD has made His salvation known; He has revealed His righteousness openly for all the nations to see. (Salvation: the act of being saved or delivered, Righteousness: being morally right or just) **3.** He has remembered His mercy and truth to Israel, and the entire earth has witnessed the saving power of our God. (Mercy: compassion or forgiveness shown to someone, Truth: honesty or reality) **4.** Shout joyfully to the LORD, all the earth! Let your voices rise in a loud celebration and song. (Rejoice: feel or show great joy) **5.** Sing to the LORD with the harp, with the harp and the melody of a song of praise. (Melody: a sequence of musical notes that is pleasing to the ear) **6.** Let trumpets and horns sound a joyful tune before the LORD, the King. (Trumpets: brass musical instruments, Horns: instruments that produce a loud sound) **7.** Let the seas roar, and everything in it; let the earth and all its people rejoice. (Roar: a loud, deep sound) **8.** Let the rivers clap their hands, let the mountains shout with joy together. (Clap: make a sound by striking the palms of hands together, Shout: to make a loud vocal sound of joy or excitement) **9.** Before the LORD, for He is coming to judge the earth; He will judge the world with fairness and the people with righteousness. (Judge: to make decisions about the actions of others, Fairness: treating everyone equally and justly, Righteousness: being morally right or just)

Chapter 99
1. The LORD reigns; let the people tremble in awe. He sits enthroned on the cherubim; let the earth quake. (Reigns: rules, Cherubim: divine beings, Tremble: shake with fear, Quake: shake) **2.** The LORD is great in Zion; He is exalted above all nations. (Exalted: raised high in honor, Zion: city of God) **3.** Let them praise Your mighty and revered name, for it is holy. (Revered: highly respected, Holy: sacred or pure) **4.** The strength of the King loves fairness; You establish justice and carry out righteousness in Israel. (Fairness: impartiality, Justice: right judgment, Righteousness: moral correctness, Israel: God's people) **5.** Lift up the LORD our God, and bow down at His feet, for He is holy. (Bow down: humble yourself in worship, Feet: symbolic of authority) **6.** Moses and Aaron were His priests, and Samuel was among those who called on His name; they called to the LORD, and He answered them. (Priests: religious leaders, Called on: prayed to, Answered: responded) **7.** He spoke to them from the cloud; they obeyed His commands and kept the teachings He gave them. (Obeyed: followed, Commands: orders, Teachings: instructions) **8.** You answered them, O LORD our God; You were a God who forgave them, though You punished their wrongs. (Forgave: pardoned, Punished: avenged, Wrongs: sins) **9.** Lift up the LORD our God, and worship at His holy mountain; for the LORD our God is holy. (Holy: sacred, Mountain: symbol of God's presence and power)

Chapter 100
1. Shout joyfully to the LORD, all you nations. (Shout joyfully: raise your voice in happiness, Nations: all people) **2.** Serve the LORD with delight; come into His presence with joyful singing. (Serve: worship or work for, Delight: happiness, Presence: being near, Joyful singing: singing with joy) **3.** Understand that the LORD is God: He is the one who made us, and we did not create ourselves; we are His people, and He cares for us like a shepherd cares for his sheep. (Understand: realize, Made: created, Shepherd: someone who takes care of sheep,

Cares: watches over) **4.** Enter His gates with thanksgiving, and His courts with praise; thank Him and honor His name. (Gates: entrances to a city, Courts: areas around a temple, Thank: express gratitude, Honor: respect and admire) **5.** For the LORD is kind; His love is forever; and His truth lasts for all generations. (Kind: good and generous, Forever: without end, Truth: faithfulness, Generations: all future people)

Chapter 101

1. I will sing of Your love and justice: to You, O LORD, I offer my song. (Love: mercy, Justice: fairness) **2.** I will live with wisdom in a perfect manner. When will You come to me? I will walk through my house with a sincere heart. (Sincere: genuine, Perfect: complete, Blameless) **3.** I will not let any wicked thing appear before my eyes; I despise the actions of those who stray from the right path; they will have no hold on me. (Despise: strongly dislike, Stray: go off course, Hold: influence) **4.** A dishonest heart will leave me; I will not tolerate a person who does wrong. (Dishonest: untruthful, Tolerate: endure or accept) **5.** Whoever secretly speaks ill of their neighbor, I will remove from my presence; I will not allow those with pride or arrogance to stay. (Secretly: in private, Ill: harmfully, Arrogance: excessive pride) **6.** My attention will be on the trustworthy people of the land, so that they may dwell with me; those who live uprightly shall serve me. (Trustworthy: reliable, Uprightly: morally correct) **7.** Anyone who practices deceit will not stay in my home; those who speak lies will not remain in my sight. (Deceit: trickery, Remain: stay) **8.** I will quickly remove all the wicked from the land, to rid the LORD's city of all evil-doers. (Quickly: promptly, Rid: remove, Evil-doers: wrongdoers)

Chapter 102

1. Listen to my prayer, O LORD, and let my plea reach Your presence. (Plea: earnest request) **2.** Do not hide Your face from me in my distress; listen to me when I cry out: answer me without delay. (Distress: trouble, Cry out: call for help, Delay: wait) **3.** My life is wasting away like smoke, and my bones are scorched as if by fire. (Wasting away: disappearing, Scorched: burned) **4.** My heart is broken, it withers like dry grass, and I forget to eat my food. (Broken: emotionally crushed, Withers: dries up) **5.** Because of my groaning, my bones stick to my flesh. (Groaning: deep sighs, Stick: adhere) **6.** I am like a pelican in the desert; I am like an owl in a desolate place. (Pelican: bird, Desolate: barren) **7.** I keep watch like a solitary sparrow perched alone on the roof. (Solitary: single, Perched: sitting) **8.** My enemies insult me all day long, and those who hate me have sworn to destroy me. (Insult: mock, Destroy: ruin) **9.** I have eaten ashes instead of food, and mixed my drink with tears. (Ashes: burnt remnants, Drink: liquid) **10.** This is because of Your anger and fury; You lifted me up, only to cast me down. (Fury: intense anger, Cast down: threw down) **11.** My days are like a fading shadow, and I am withered like dried grass. (Fading: disappearing, Withered: shriveled) **12.** But You, O LORD, will endure forever; Your name will last through every generation. (Endure: last, Generation: descendants) **13.** You will rise and have compassion on Zion, for the appointed time to show favor to her has come. (Compassion: pity, Appointed: set) **14.** Your servants love her very stones and have compassion for her dust. (Servants: faithful followers, Compassion: affection) **15.** The nations will be filled with awe at the name of the LORD, and all the kings of the earth will honor Your glory. (Filled with awe: amazed, Honor: respect) **16.** When the LORD rebuilds Zion, He will appear in His splendor. (Rebuilds: restores, Splendor: brilliance) **17.** He will pay attention to the prayer of the needy and not ignore their cry. (Pay attention: listen, Needy: poor, Cry: appeal) **18.** This will be recorded for the future generations, and those who are yet to be born will praise the LORD. (Recorded: written down, Generations: future people) **19.** For He has looked down from His holy heights; from heaven, the LORD observed the earth. (Heights: elevated places, Observed: looked at) **20.** To hear the groaning of those in captivity, to free those sentenced to death. (Groaning: lamenting, Sentenced: condemned) **21.** To declare the name of the LORD in Zion, and to praise Him in Jerusalem. (Declare: proclaim, Praise: worship) **22.** When people gather together and kingdoms unite to serve the LORD. (Gather: assemble, Unite: join) **23.** He weakened my strength along the way; He shortened my life. (Weakened: diminished, Shortened: made shorter) **24.** I said, "O my God, do not take me in the middle of my years; Your years last forever." (Take me: end my life, Years: lifetime) **25.** In the past, You laid the foundation of the earth; and the heavens are the work of Your hands. (Foundation: base, Work: creation) **26.** They will perish, but You will endure; everything will grow old like a garment; You will change them, and they will be made new. (Perish: decay, Endure: last, Grow old: wear out) **27.** But You are unchanging, and Your years will have no end. (Unchanging: constant, Years: time span) **28.** The children of Your servants will continue, and their descendants will be established in Your presence. (Descendants: offspring, Established: settled)

Chapter 103

1. Bless the LORD, my soul, and let every part of me honor His sacred name. (Bless: praise, Sacred: holy) **2.** Bless the LORD, my soul, and remember all the wonderful things He has done for you. (Remember: recall, Wonderful: amazing) **3.** He forgives all your wrongdoings and heals all your afflictions. (Forgives: pardons, Afflictions: troubles) **4.** He saves you from destruction and surrounds you with love and compassion. (Saves: rescues, Surrounds: envelops, Compassion: mercy) **5.** He fills your life with good things, renewing your strength like the eagle's. (Fills: satisfies, Renewing: refreshing) **6.** The LORD executes justice and fairness for all those who are treated unfairly. (Executes: carries out, Fairness: equity, Unfairly: unjustly) **7.** He made His ways known to Moses and revealed His deeds to the people of Israel. (Made known: revealed, Deeds: actions) **8.** The LORD is merciful and full of grace, slow to anger, and abounding in love. (Merciful: kind, Abounding: overflowing) **9.** He will not remain angry with us forever, nor will He always accuse us. (Remain: stay, Accuse: blame) **10.** He doesn't repay us according to our sins, nor does He punish us based on our wrongdoings. (Repay: reward, Wrongdoings: transgressions) **11.** As high as the sky is above the earth, so great is His love for those who honor Him. (Honor: reverence) **12.** As far as the east is from the west, that's how far He has removed our sins from us. (Removed: taken away, Sins: transgressions) **13.** Just as a father feels deep compassion for his children, the LORD feels that same compassion for those who revere Him. (Revere: respect, Compassion: pity) **14.** For He understands our limitations and remembers that we are made from dust. (Limitations: frailties, Dust: earth) **15.** People's lives are like grass: they bloom for a while, then fade away like flowers. (Bloom: flourish, Fade: wilt) **16.** The wind blows over them, and they are gone; their place is no longer remembered. (Blows: passes, Gone: disappeared) **17.** But the LORD's love is everlasting toward those who fear Him, and His righteousness extends to their descendants. (Everlasting: eternal, Righteousness: justice, Descendants: children) **18.** For those who keep His covenant and follow His commandments. (Covenant: agreement, Follow: obey) **19.** The LORD has set His throne high in the heavens, and His reign is over all things. (Set: established, Reign: rule) **20.** Praise the LORD, you powerful angels, who carry out His commands, listening to His word with attention. (Powerful: mighty, Attention: focus) **21.** Praise the LORD, all His heavenly hosts, you who serve Him and fulfill His will. (Heavenly hosts: angelic armies, Fulfill: complete) **22.** Praise the LORD, all His creations, everywhere in His dominion; bless the LORD, my soul. (Creations: works, Dominion: realm, Bless: praise)

Chapter 104

1. Bless the LORD, O my soul! O LORD, my Creator, You are magnificent, adorned with splendor and majesty. (splendor: grandeur) **2.** You cover Yourself with light like a garment, spreading the sky like a tent. (garment: covering, tent: shelter) **3.** You have placed the beams of Your home in the deep waters, and You ride upon the clouds, moving swiftly on the wind. (beams: supports, clouds: vapor, wind: air currents) **4.** You make Your angels winds, and Your servants like fiery flames. (servants: ministers, fiery: burning) **5.** You founded the earth upon its unshakable base, secure for all time. **6.** You draped it with the sea as a cloak, and the waters stood over the mountains. (sea: ocean) **7.** At Your rebuke, the waters scatter; at the sound of Your thunder, they flee in haste. (rebuke: command, thunder: loud noise) **8.** They ascend to the mountains, and descend to the valleys, to the place You've prepared for them. **9.** You set boundaries that they cannot cross, preventing them from flooding the earth again. **10.** You send streams into the valleys, where they flow freely among the hills. **11.** These waters provide drink for every wild animal, and the donkeys of the desert satisfy their thirst. (donkeys: asses) **12.** The birds of the sky nest by them, singing joyfully among the trees. **13.** You water the hills from Your chambers, and the earth is nourished by the fruits of Your labor. **14.** You cause the grass to grow for the cattle, and plants for mankind, bringing forth food from the earth. **15.** You provide wine that cheers the heart, oil to brighten the face, and bread that strengthens the soul. **16.** The trees of the LORD are full of sap, including the cedars of Lebanon that You planted. (sap: juice) **17.** The birds make their nests in them, and the storks have their homes in the fir trees. **18.** The high mountains are a refuge for the wild goats, and the rocks serve as a hiding place for the conies. (refuge: shelter, conies: rabbits) **19.** You made the moon to mark the changing seasons, and the sun knows when to set. **20.** You bring the night by darkening the sky, when the wild animals of the forest move about. **21.** The young lions roar for their prey, and seek their food from You. **22.** When the sun rises, they gather, and lie down in their dens. **23.** Man goes out to work and to labor until evening. **24.** O LORD, how vast are Your works! In wisdom, You have made everything; the earth is filled with Your abundance. **25.** The vast sea belongs to You, teeming with creatures, both great and small. **26.** There go the ships, and the leviathan, which You made to frolic in the sea. **27.** All of them look to You to provide their food at the proper time. **28.** When You give, they gather; You open Your hand, and they are satisfied with good things. **29.** When You hide Your face, they are troubled; when You take away their breath, they die and return to the dust. **30.** You send Your Spirit, and they are created; You renew the face of the earth. **31.** The glory of the LORD will endure forever; the LORD rejoices in His works. **32.** He looks at the earth, and it shakes; He touches the mountains, and they smoke. **33.** I will sing to the LORD as long as I live; I will praise my God while I have life. **34.** My meditation of Him will be pleasant; I will rejoice in the LORD. **35.** Let the sinners be wiped from the earth, and let the wicked be no more. Bless the LORD, O my soul. Praise the LORD.

Chapter 105

1. Give thanks to the LORD; call upon His name and declare His mighty acts to all nations. (declare: announce, mighty acts: powerful deeds) **2.** Sing praises to Him, and recount all His marvelous works. (recount: tell, marvelous: amazing) **3.** Boast in His holy name; let those who seek the LORD be filled with joy. (boast: glory, filled: made, joy: happiness) **4.** Seek the LORD and His strength; always search for His presence. (strength: power, presence: nearness) **5.** Remember the great things He has done, His wonders, and the commands He has spoken. (wonders: miracles, commands: words) **6.** O descendants of Abraham, His servant, O children of Jacob, whom He chose. (descendants: offspring, chosen: selected) **7.** He is the LORD our God; His laws are seen throughout the world. (laws: judgments, world: earth) **8.** He remembers His covenant forever, the promise He made for a thousand generations. (covenant: agreement, promise: pledge, generations: family lines) **9.** The covenant He made with Abraham, and His vow to Isaac; (vow: oath) **10.** And He confirmed it to Jacob as a decree, and to Israel as an eternal promise. (confirmed: established, decree: law, eternal: lasting forever) **11.** He said, "I will give you the land of Canaan as your inheritance." (inheritance: possession) **12.** When they were few in number, just a handful, and strangers in the land. (strangers: foreigners) **13.** When they wandered from one nation to another, from one kingdom to another people, (wandered: moved, kingdom: realm) **14.** He allowed no one to harm them; He rebuked kings for their sake. (rebuked: scolded, sake: benefit) **15.** Saying, "Do not touch My anointed ones, and do not harm My prophets." (anointed: chosen, prophets: messengers) **16.** He called for a famine upon the land, breaking the supply of food. (famine: scarcity, supply: provision) **17.** He sent ahead of them a man, Joseph, who was sold as a slave. (slave: servant) **18.** They bound his feet with shackles; his soul was placed in irons, (shackles: chains, irons: metal restraints) **19.** Until the time came for his word to be fulfilled, the word of the LORD tested him. (fulfilled: accomplished, tested: tried) **20.** The king sent for him and freed him; the ruler of the people let him go. (freed: released, ruler: leader) **21.** He made him master of his house and ruler over all his possessions, (master: overseer, possessions: property) **22.** To control his princes and teach wisdom to his counselors. (control: bind, princes: leaders, counselors: advisors) **23.** Israel came into Egypt, and Jacob lived in the land of Ham. (Ham: a region in Egypt) **24.** He caused His people to grow greatly, and made them stronger than their enemies. (grow: increase, enemies: foes) **25.** He turned the hearts of the Egyptians to hate His people, and to deal deceitfully with His servants. (hearts: minds, deceitfully: dishonestly, servants: followers) **26.** He sent Moses, His servant, and Aaron, whom He had chosen. (chosen: selected) **27.** They performed His signs among them, and wonders in the land of Ham. (performed: carried out, signs: miracles, wonders: extraordinary acts) **28.** He sent darkness and made it thick; they did not defy His command. (thick: dense, defy: resist) **29.** He turned their waters into blood, and destroyed their fish. (destroyed: killed) **30.** Their land swarmed with frogs, even in the royal palaces. (swarmed: filled, palaces: chambers of kings) **31.** He commanded flies and lice to appear everywhere. (flies: insects, lice: parasitic insects) **32.** He gave them hail instead of rain, and fiery lightning in their land. (hail: frozen rain, lightning: flashes of fire) **33.** He struck their vines and fig trees, and shattered the trees of their land. (struck: hit, shattered: broke) **34.** He spoke, and locusts and countless caterpillars came, (locusts: grasshoppers, caterpillars: larvae) **35.** Which devoured all the plants in their land and destroyed the fruit of their crops. (devoured: consumed, crops: harvest) **36.** He struck down the firstborn in their land, the first fruits of their strength. (firstborn: eldest, strength: power) **37.** He led them out with silver and gold, and there was no weak person among their tribes. (led: brought, weak: feeble) **38.** Egypt rejoiced when they departed, for the fear of them had fallen upon the Egyptians. (rejoiced: was glad, departed: left, fear: dread) **39.** He spread a cloud for their covering, and fire to light their way at night. (covering: shelter, light: guide) **40.** The people asked, and He provided quails, and fed them with the bread of heaven. (provided: gave, quails: birds) **41.** He opened a rock, and water flowed out; it ran like a river in the dry land. (rock: stone, flowed: poured, dry land: desert) **42.** For He remembered His sacred promise, and Abraham, His servant. (sacred: holy, promise: covenant) **43.** He brought His people out with joy, and His chosen ones with gladness. (brought out: led, chosen ones: select people) **44.** He gave them the lands of the nations, and they inherited the labor of the peoples, (inherited: received, labor: work) **45.** So that they might observe His statutes and obey His laws. Praise the LORD! (observe: follow, statutes: rules, obey: heed)

Chapter 106

1. Praise the LORD! Give thanks to Him, for He is good; His mercy lasts forever. (mercy: compassion) **2.** Who can speak of the mighty deeds of the LORD? Who can declare all His praise? (declare: proclaim) **3.** Blessed are those who uphold justice and do what is right at all times. (uphold: maintain, right: righteousness) **4.** Remember me, O LORD, with the favor You show to Your people; visit me with Your salvation. (favor: kindness, salvation: deliverance)

5. That I may see the prosperity of Your chosen ones, rejoice in the gladness of Your nation, and glory with Your inheritance. (prosperity: good fortune, inheritance: possession) **6.** We have sinned, just like our ancestors; we have done wrong and acted wickedly. (wrong: evil) **7.** Our ancestors did not understand Your miracles in Egypt; they forgot the abundance of Your mercies, but rebelled at the Red Sea. (miracles: wonders, rebelled: provoked) **8.** Yet He saved them for the sake of His name, that He might make His mighty power known. (might: power) **9.** He rebuked the Red Sea, and it dried up; He led them through the deep, as through a wilderness. (rebuked: commanded, dried up: became dry) **10.** He saved them from the enemy's hand, and redeemed them from the grasp of the foe. (redeemed: rescued, foe: enemy) **11.** The waters covered their enemies, not one was left. (covered: drowned) **12.** Then they believed His promises and sang His praise. (believed: trusted, promises: words) **13.** But they soon forgot His deeds, and did not wait for His counsel. (deeds: actions, counsel: advice) **14.** Instead, they craved excessively in the desert and tested God in the wilderness. (craved: desired, tested: provoked) **15.** He gave them what they wanted, but sent leanness into their souls. (leaning: emptiness) **16.** They became envious of Moses in the camp, and Aaron, the holy one of the LORD. (envious: jealous, holy: set apart) **17.** The earth opened and swallowed up Dathan, covering the group of Abiram. (swallowed: engulfed, covering: consumed) **18.** A fire broke out and consumed the wicked. (broke out: ignited, consumed: burned) **19.** They made a golden calf at Horeb and worshiped the idol they had made. (idol: false god, Horeb: a mountain) **20.** They exchanged their glory for the likeness of an ox that eats grass. (glory: greatness) **21.** They forgot God, their Savior, who had done great things in Egypt. (forgot: ignored, Savior: deliverer) **22.** Wonders in the land of Ham, and awesome deeds by the Red Sea. (wonders: marvelous acts, Ham: Egypt) **23.** Therefore, He said He would destroy them, had not Moses, His chosen servant, stood in the gap to turn away His wrath. (gap: breach, stood in the gap: interceded) **24.** They despised the pleasant land and did not believe His promise. (despised: rejected, pleasant: good) **25.** Instead, they grumbled in their tents and did not listen to the voice of the LORD. (grumbled: complained, listen: obey) **26.** So He raised His hand against them and made them fall in the wilderness. (raised: lifted, fall: perish) **27.** He scattered their descendants among the nations and dispersed them throughout the lands. (scattered: spread, dispersed: scattered) **28.** They joined in worshiping Baal of Peor and ate the sacrifices of the dead. (joined: became involved, Baal: a Canaanite god, Peor: a location) **29.** They angered God with their actions, and a plague broke out among them. (angered: provoked, actions: deeds, plague: disease) **30.** Then Phinehas stood up and executed judgment, and the plague was stopped. (executed: carried out, judgment: justice) **31.** This act was counted as righteousness for him, to be remembered for all generations. (righteousness: justice, remembered: honored) **32.** They provoked Him at the waters of Meribah, and things went badly for Moses because of them. (provoked: angered, Meribah: place of strife) **33.** They rebelled against his spirit and he spoke rashly with his lips. (rebelled: provoked, rashly: impulsively) **34.** They did not destroy the nations the LORD had commanded them to. (destroy: eliminate) **35.** Instead, they mingled with the nations and learned their practices. (mingled: mixed, practices: ways) **36.** They worshiped idols, which became a trap for them. (worshiped: adored, trap: snare) **37.** They even sacrificed their children to demons, shedding innocent blood. (sacrificed: offered, demons: evil spirits) **38.** They polluted the land with the blood of their sons and daughters, whom they sacrificed to the idols of Canaan. (polluted: defiled, sacrificed: offered, idols: false gods) **39.** They defiled themselves with their actions and followed their own sinful desires. (defiled: corrupted, desires: lusts) **40.** Therefore, the LORD's anger was aroused against His people, and He loathed His inheritance. (aroused: stirred up, loathed: hated) **41.** He handed them over to the hands of their enemies, and those who hated them ruled over them. (handed over: gave, ruled over: dominated) **42.** Their enemies oppressed them, and they were subject to their authority. (oppressed: afflicted, subject: subjugated) **43.** Many times He delivered them, but they continued to rebel with their advice and were brought low by their sin. (delivered: saved, rebel: provoked, brought low: humbled) **44.** Yet He looked upon their distress when He heard their cry. (distress: trouble) **45.** He remembered His covenant with them and showed mercy because of His great compassion. (showed mercy: had compassion, compassion: kindness) **46.** He made them objects of pity among those who carried them captive. (objects of pity: recipients of mercy) **47.** Save us, O LORD our God, and gather us from among the nations, that we may give thanks to Your holy name and glory in Your praise. (gather: collect, glory: boast) **48.** Blessed be the LORD, the God of Israel, from everlasting to everlasting. Let all the people say, "Amen." Praise the LORD! (everlasting: eternal)

Chapter 107

1. Give thanks to the LORD, for He is good; His love endures forever. (love: mercy, enduring: lasting) **2.** Let those who have been rescued by the LORD speak out, those He has saved from the hand of their enemies. (rescued: delivered, speak out: declare) **3.** He gathered them from various lands, from the east, west, north, and south. (gathered: brought together) **4.** They roamed in the wilderness, lost and without a place to settle. (roamed: wandered, settle: dwell) **5.** Hungry and thirsty, their spirits grew weak within them. (spirits: souls, weak: faint) **6.** They called to the LORD in their time of trouble, and He rescued them from their difficulties. (difficulties: distress) **7.** He guided them along the right path, leading them to a place to call home. (guided: led, call home: settle) **8.** Oh, that people would praise the LORD for His kindness and amazing works toward all mankind! (kindness: goodness, amazing: wondrous) **9.** He fills the soul that thirsts, and nourishes the hungry soul with good things. (fills: satisfies, nourishes: feeds) **10.** Those who sit in darkness and the shadow of death, imprisoned in suffering and chains. (suffering: affliction, chains: bondage) **11.** Because they defied God's word and rejected the guidance of the Most High. (defied: rebelled, rejected: despised, guidance: counsel) **12.** So He humbled their hearts with hardship; they stumbled and had no one to help them. (humbled: brought down, hardship: labor) **13.** Then they called out to the LORD in their distress, and He rescued them from their troubles. (rescued: delivered, troubles: hardships) **14.** He brought them out of darkness and the shadow of death, shattering their chains. (shattering: breaking) **15.** Oh, that people would praise the LORD for His kindness and amazing works toward all mankind! (kindness: goodness, amazing: wondrous) **16.** He has broken the gates of bronze and torn apart the bars of iron. (bronze: brass, torn apart: shattered) **17.** Foolish people, because of their rebellion and sins, face affliction. (foolish: sinful, rebellion: disobedience) **18.** They loathe all food and come close to death's door. (loathe: detest, come close: near) **19.** Then they cried to the LORD in their misery, and He saved them from their troubles. (misery: distress, troubles: suffering) **20.** He sent His word to heal them and rescued them from their ruin. (ruin: destruction) **21.** Oh, that people would praise the LORD for His kindness and amazing works toward all mankind! (kindness: goodness, amazing: wondrous) **22.** Let them offer sacrifices of thanks and declare His works with joy. (sacrifices of thanks: gratitude offerings, declare: proclaim) **23.** Those who go down to the sea in ships, engaging in trade on the mighty waters. (engaging: working, trade: commerce) **24.** They witness the works of the LORD and His wonders in the deep. (wonders: miracles) **25.** For He commands and raises a stormy wind, lifting the waves high. (raises: summons, lifting: raising) **26.** The waves soar to the heavens, then plunge to the depths; their hearts melt in fear. (plunge: descend, soar: rise) **27.** They stagger and reel, like drunken men, and lose all sense of direction. (stagger: sway, lose: have no) **28.** Then they cried to the

LORD in their distress, and He rescued them from their troubles. (rescued: delivered, troubles: danger) **29.** He calms the storm, making the waves quiet. (calms: soothes, waves: waters) **30.** Then they are glad because the sea is calm, and He guides them to their desired haven. (glad: relieved, guides: leads, haven: safe place) **31.** Oh, that people would praise the LORD for His kindness and amazing works toward all mankind! (kindness: goodness, amazing: wondrous) **32.** Let them honor Him in the gathering of the people and praise Him in the assembly of the elders. (honor: exalt, gathering: congregation) **33.** He turns rivers into dry land and springs of water into parched ground. (turns: changes, springs: sources, parched: dry) **34.** He transforms fruitful land into a barren wasteland because of the wickedness of those who live there. (fruitful: fertile, barren: empty, wasteland: desolate) **35.** He transforms deserts into pools of water and dry land into flowing springs. (transforms: changes, flowing: running) **36.** There He settles the hungry, allowing them to build a city for living. (settles: makes home, build: prepare) **37.** They sow fields and plant vineyards, yielding crops that multiply. (sow: plant, crops: produce) **38.** He blesses them so they are greatly increased, and their herds do not diminish. (blesses: favors, herds: livestock) **39.** But again, they are brought low through oppression, suffering, and sorrow. (brought low: humbled, oppression: hardship) **40.** He pours contempt on rulers, making them wander in the wilderness, where there is no path. (contempt: scorn, rulers: princes, wander: roam) **41.** Yet He lifts the poor from their affliction and makes them prosperous like a flock of sheep. (lifts: raises, flock: group) **42.** The upright see it and rejoice, and all wickedness is silenced. (upright: righteous, silenced: stopped) **43.** Whoever is wise and takes heed to this will understand the LORD's unfailing love. (heed: listens, unfailing: steadfast)

Chapter 108

1. O God, my heart is unwavering; I will sing and offer You praise, even with all my glory. (unwavering: fixed) **2.** Awake, my stringed instruments! I will rise early to offer You praise. (stringed instruments: harp, lyre) **3.** I will praise You, O LORD, among the nations, and sing Your praises among all people. (nations: peoples, sing praises: offer songs) **4.** For Your mercy is greater than the heavens, and Your faithfulness extends far beyond the clouds. (mercy: love, faithfulness: truth) **5.** Be lifted up, O God, above the heavens, and let Your majesty fill the entire earth. (majesty: glory) **6.** Save Your chosen ones with Your powerful right hand, and answer my call for help. (chosen ones: beloved, powerful: mighty) **7.** God has spoken from His holy sanctuary; I will rejoice and divide the land of Shechem and the valley of Succoth. (spoken: declared, sanctuary: holy place) **8.** Gilead is Mine; Manasseh is Mine; Ephraim is the strength of My head; Judah is the ruler of My people. (strength: might, ruler: lawgiver) **9.** Moab is like my washing basin; I will cast my sandal over Edom; I will shout in victory over the Philistines. (washing basin: washpot, victory: triumph) **10.** Who will bring me into the fortified city? Who will lead me into Edom? (fortified: strong, Edom: kingdom southeast of Israel) **11.** Will You not help us, O God, You who have rejected us? Will You not go out with our armies? (rejected: cast us off, go out: march out) **12.** Help us in our time of distress, for human strength is of no use. (distress: trouble, human strength: vain help) **13.** Through God we will achieve great things; He will help us defeat our enemies. (achieve: do valiantly, defeat: tread down)

Chapter 109

1. O God, who is the source of my praise, do not remain silent. (Silent: not speaking) **2.** The mouths of the wicked and deceitful are open against me; they speak lies and slander me. (Deceitful: dishonest, misleading; Slander: making false statements) **3.** They surround me with hateful words and unjustly fight against me. (Hateful: full of hatred; Unjustly: without fair reason) **4.** For the love I showed them, they have become my enemies, but I turn to You in prayer. (Enemies: those who oppose or harm) **5.** They repay my goodness with evil and return my love with hatred. (Repay: give in return; Goodness: kindness or virtue) **6.** Appoint a wicked man over him, and let Satan stand by his right hand. (Wicked: evil, morally wrong) **7.** When he is judged, let him be found guilty, and let his prayers turn into sin. (Judged: assessed or evaluated; Guilty: responsible for wrongdoing) **8.** Let his life be brief, and let another take his place. (Brief: short, of short duration) **9.** Let his children be left without a father, and his wife without a husband. (Orphaned: without parents; Widow: a woman whose husband has died) **10.** Let his children be homeless beggars, seeking sustenance from desolate places. (Beggars: those who ask for money or food; Desolate: empty, barren) **11.** Let the extortioner seize all that he owns, and let strangers plunder the fruits of his labor. (Extortioner: one who takes something by force or threat; Plunder: to steal or rob) **12.** Let no one show him mercy, nor favor his orphaned children. (Mercy: compassion, forgiveness; Favor: to support or assist) **13.** Let his descendants be cut off, and his name be erased from the earth. (Descendants: children or future generations; Erased: wiped out, removed) **14.** Let the iniquity of his ancestors be remembered, and his mother's sin be not forgotten. (Iniquity: wickedness, sin) **15.** Let them remain before the LORD continually, that He may blot out their memory from the earth. (Continually: without interruption; Blot out: erase, remove) **16.** Because he did not show mercy but persecuted the poor and needy, seeking to destroy those who were brokenhearted. (Persecuted: mistreated, oppressed; Brokenhearted: deeply sorrowful) **17.** As he delighted in curses, let curses be upon him; as he refused blessings, let them stay far from him. (Delighted: took pleasure in; Curses: spoken harm or misfortune) **18.** As he wrapped himself in curses like a garment, let them sink into him like water, and like oil into his bones. (Wrapped: covered, surrounded; Garment: clothing; Sink: to be absorbed deeply) **19.** Let it be to him as a garment that covers him, and as a belt he wears continuously. (Belt: a band worn around the waist) **20.** Let this be the reward of my enemies and those who speak evil against me. (Reward: compensation, return for actions) **21.** But You, O LORD, do it for the sake of Your name, for Your mercy is great; deliver me. (Sake: for the benefit or reason of; Deliver: save or rescue) **22.** For I am poor and needy, and my heart is deeply wounded within me. (Needy: lacking in basic needs; Wounded: hurt, emotionally affected) **23.** I fade away like a shadow in the evening, I am tossed about like a locust. (Fade: diminish, disappear; Tossed: thrown about, unsettled) **24.** My knees are weak from fasting, and my body is frail from lack of nourishment. (Fasting: going without food for spiritual reasons; Frail: weak, delicate) **25.** I have become a reproach to them; they shake their heads as they see me. (Reproach: disgrace, shame; Shake their heads: gesture indicating disapproval) **26.** Help me, O LORD my God, and save me because of Your great mercy. (Mercy: compassion, kindness) **27.** Let them know that it is Your hand, O LORD, that has done it. (Hand: power or action) **28.** Let them curse me, but You bless me; let my accusers be ashamed, but let Your servant rejoice. (Accusers: those who accuse or blame) **29.** Let my adversaries be clothed in shame, and let them cover themselves with disgrace as a garment. (Adversaries: enemies, opponents; Disgrace: dishonor, shame) **30.** I will greatly praise the LORD with my mouth; I will glorify Him among the multitudes. (Multitudes: large crowds, people) **31.** For He stands at the right hand of the poor, to save them from those who condemn their souls. (Condemn: judge negatively, accuse)

Chapter 110

1. The LORD spoke to my Master, saying, "Sit at My right hand until I make Your enemies a place to rest Your feet." (Right hand: position of honor; Footstool: a symbol of domination over enemies) **2.** The LORD will send out Your strength from Zion: You will reign among Your foes. (Zion: the city of Jerusalem, representing God's authority; Reign: rule or govern) **3.** Your people will willingly serve You on the day of Your power, in the beauty of holiness, like the freshness of the morning dew. (Willingly: eagerly; Beauty of holiness: the attractive purity of divine nature; Dew of youth: the vitality and energy of youth) **4.** The LORD has made an unchangeable oath, "You are a priest forever, just like Melchizedek." (Oath: a solemn promise; Priest: a religious leader; Melchizedek: a mysterious priest-king in the Bible) **5.** The Lord at Your right hand will defeat kings when He shows His anger. (Right hand: position of strength and honor; Wrath: powerful anger) **6.** He will judge the nations, filling the land with the slain; He will strike down the rulers of many lands. (Judge: make final decisions or punishment; Slain: those who have been killed; Strike down: defeat or attack) **7.** He will drink from the stream on His way, and because of this, He will lift His head in victory. (Stream: small flowing water; Lift His head: a sign of triumph or success)

Chapter 111

1. Praise the LORD! I will give Him thanks with all my heart, in the assembly of the righteous, and among the gathered people. (Assembly: gathering of people; Upright: those who live justly) **2.** The works of the LORD are magnificent, sought after by all who take pleasure in them. (Magnificent: impressive and worthy of admiration; Sought after: looked for, desired) **3.** His deeds are honorable and full of glory; His righteousness lasts forever. (Deeds: actions or works; Righteousness: moral rightness or justice) **4.** He has made His amazing works known, and the LORD is gracious and full of compassion. (Amazing works: extraordinary actions; Gracious: showing kindness; Compassion: deep sympathy and concern for others) **5.** He provides food for those who fear Him; He will always remember His covenant with them. (Fear: reverence and respect; Covenant: a sacred promise or agreement) **6.** He has shown His people the power of His works, and has given them the inheritance of other nations. (Power of His works: the strength and impact of His actions; Inheritance: a possession passed down to someone) **7.** The works of His hands are truth and justice; all His commandments are reliable. (Truth: accuracy and honesty; Justice: fairness and righteousness) **8.** They stand firm forever, completed in truth and righteousness. (Stand firm: remain strong and unshaken; Completed: carried out fully) **9.** He sent redemption to His people; He has established His covenant forever. Holy and awe-inspiring is His name. (Redemption: rescue or salvation; Established: firmly set; Awe-inspiring: causing reverence or respect) **10.** The fear of the LORD is the beginning of wisdom; those who follow His commandments gain understanding. His praise endures forever. (Wisdom: the ability to make good judgments; Understanding: comprehension and insight)

Chapter 112

1. Praise the LORD! Happy is the person who reveres the LORD and takes great pleasure in following His commandments. (Reveres: shows deep respect; Pleasures: enjoys deeply) **2.** His descendants will be powerful on earth; the children of the righteous will be blessed. (Descendants: children and grandchildren; Righteous: morally just) **3.** His house will be full of wealth and prosperity; and his righteousness will last forever. (Prosperity: financial success and abundance) **4.** For those who are upright, light will shine in the darkness; he is kind, full of mercy, and just. (Upright: morally right; Kind: compassionate; Mercy: showing kindness to others) **5.** A good person shows generosity and lends without hesitation; he manages his affairs with wisdom. (Generosity: willingness to give; Wisdom: careful decision-making) **6.** He will never be shaken; the righteous will be remembered forever. (Shaken: disturbed or moved; Righteous: people who live justly) **7.** He will not fear bad news; his heart is steady because he trusts in the LORD. (Steady: unwavering or firm) **8.** His heart is secure, and he will not fear, until he sees the downfall of his enemies. (Secure: firmly established; Downfall: defeat or destruction) **9.** He is generous, giving to the poor; his righteousness will endure forever, and he will be honored. (Generous: willing to give; Honored: held in high esteem) **10.** The wicked will see this and be upset; they will grind their teeth in anger and eventually fade away; the wicked's desires will vanish. (Grind their teeth: expression of anger or frustration; Fade away: disappear or weaken)

Chapter 113

1. Praise the LORD! All of you who serve the LORD, give praise to His holy name. (Serve: work for or honor; Holy: sacred or divine) **2.** May the name of the LORD be praised both now and forever. (Praised: celebrated, honored) **3.** From the time the sun rises to when it sets, the name of the LORD should be praised. (Rises: appears above the horizon; Sets: sinks below the horizon) **4.** The LORD is exalted above all nations, and His glory stretches beyond the heavens. (Exalted: raised in honor; Glory: magnificence, splendor) **5.** Who can compare to the LORD our God, who sits high in the heavens? (Compare: be similar or equal to; Sits high: is in a position of great authority) **6.** He humbles Himself to look down upon the heavens and the earth. (Humbles: lowers Himself in honor; Behold: look at, observe) **7.** He lifts the poor from the dust, and raises the needy from the ashes. (Lifts: raises, elevates; Ashes: dirt or refuse, often symbolic of low status) **8.** He places them with princes, even with the leaders of His people. (Places: positions; Princes: high-ranking leaders) **9.** He makes the childless woman the head of a family, and a joyful mother of children. Praise the LORD! (Head of a family: central figure in a household; Joyful: full of happiness)

Chapter 114

1. When Israel left Egypt, and the descendants of Jacob left a people speaking a foreign language; (Descendants: offspring; Foreign language: non-native language) **2.** Judah became God's sacred place, and Israel His kingdom. (Sacred: holy, Kingdom: dominion) **3.** The sea saw them and fled; the Jordan River turned back. (Fled: ran away quickly; Jordan: a river that flows through Israel) **4.** The mountains trembled like rams, and the hills skipped like young lambs. (Trembled: shook; Rams: male sheep; Lambs: young sheep) **5.** Why, O sea, did you flee? Why, O Jordan, did you turn back? (Flee: run away in fear, Turn back: reverse direction) **6.** Why did the mountains tremble like rams, and the hills skip like lambs? (Tremble: shake in fear; Skip: jump lightly) **7.** Earth, tremble at the presence of the LORD, at the presence of the God of Jacob; (Tremble: shake with fear or awe; Presence: nearness, being in the company of) **8.** He turned the rock into a pool of water, the hard stone into a spring of waters. (Turned: transformed, Pool of water: a body of water; Flint: a hard stone used for striking fire)

Chapter 115

1. Not to us, O LORD, not to us, but let Your name receive all the glory, for Your steadfast love and truth. (Steadfast: firm, unwavering; Truth: reliability, faithfulness) **2.** Why should the nations ask, "Where is their God?" (Nations: other peoples; Ask: question, wonder) **3.** Our God is enthroned in the heavens; He accomplishes all that He pleases. (Enthroned: seated as ruler, reigning; Pleases: desires, chooses) **4.** Their idols are made of precious metals, the product of human craftsmanship. (Precious metals: valuable materials; Craftsmanship: skill in making things) **5.** They have mouths, yet they cannot speak; they have eyes, but they cannot see. (Cannot: are unable to) **6.** They have ears, but they cannot hear; they have noses, but they cannot smell. (Unaware: lacking sensory functions) **7.** They have hands, yet they cannot feel; they have feet, but they cannot walk; they cannot make a sound. (Feel: touch, sense; Make a sound: speak) **8.** Those who fashion them become like them, as do all who trust in them. (Fashion: create, make; Trust: rely on, depend on) **9.** O Israel, place your trust in the LORD; He is your help and your protector. (Protector: defender, shield) **10.** O descendants of Aaron, trust in the LORD; He is your help and your protector. (Descendants: children, offspring) **11.** All who fear the LORD, place your trust in Him; He is your help and your protector. (Fear: reverence, deep respect) **12.** The LORD has not forgotten us; He will bless us; He will bless the house of Israel, and the house of Aaron. (Forget: overlook, neglect) **13.** He will bless those who honor Him, both the humble and the exalted. (Honor: respect, revere; Humble: lowly, meek; Exalted: elevated, honored) **14.** The LORD will increase your prosperity, both you and your descendants. (Prosperity: success, well-being) **15.** You are blessed by the LORD, the Creator of heaven and earth. (Creator: Maker, Originator) **16.** The heavens belong to the LORD, but He has entrusted the earth to humanity. (Entrusted: given responsibility for) **17.** The dead cannot praise the LORD, nor can those who descend into the grave. (Descend: go down, enter) **18.** But we will bless the LORD now and forever. Hallelujah! (Hallelujah: Praise the LORD)

Chapter 116
1. I deeply love the LORD because He has listened to my voice and heard my cries for help. (Cries: urgent pleas for assistance) **2.** He has bent down His ear to me, so I will call on Him for as long as I live. (Bent down: listened attentively) **3.** The pains of death surrounded me, and the terrors of the grave gripped me; I faced distress and grief. (Surrounded: encircled; Gripped: seized) **4.** Then I called on the name of the LORD: "O LORD, I beg You, save my life!" (Beg: earnestly request) **5.** The LORD is compassionate and just; yes, our God is full of mercy. (Compassionate: full of care and kindness; Just: fair) **6.** The LORD protects the humble: I was in deep trouble, and He rescued me. (Humble: simple, lowly; Rescued: saved, helped) **7.** Return to your rest, O my soul, for the LORD has been so good to you. (Return: find peace again; Rest: quietness, peace) **8.** You have saved my life from death, my eyes from tears, and my feet from stumbling. (Stumbling: falling, tripping) **9.** I will continue to walk in the presence of the LORD, here in the land of the living. (Presence: before God; Land of the living: earth, among the living) **10.** I believed in the LORD, and that is why I spoke; I was in great distress. (Distress: intense suffering, trouble) **11.** In my panic, I said, "Everyone is deceitful." (Panic: sudden fear; Deceitful: dishonest, lying) **12.** What can I give back to the LORD for all the good things He has done for me? (Give back: repay, offer) **13.** I will take the cup of salvation and call upon the name of the LORD. (Cup of salvation: symbol of God's deliverance) **14.** I will fulfill my promises to the LORD in the presence of all His people. (Fulfill: keep, carry out; Promises: vows, commitments) **15.** The death of His faithful ones is precious in the sight of the LORD. (Faithful ones: His saints, His people) **16.** O LORD, I am truly Your servant; I am Your servant, and the son of Your servant. You have freed me from my chains. (Freed: released, set free; Chains: bonds, fetters) **17.** I will bring You a sacrifice of thanksgiving and call on Your name. (Sacrifice of thanksgiving: offering of gratitude) **18.** I will fulfill my vows to the LORD in the presence of His people. (Fulfill: perform, carry out) **19.** In the courts of the LORD's house, in the midst of Jerusalem, praise the LORD! (Courts: areas of the temple; Midst: center)

Chapter 117
1. O praise the LORD, all you nations; exalt Him, all you peoples of the earth. (Exalt: lift up, honor) **2.** For His unfailing love toward us is vast, and His faithfulness endures forever. Praise the LORD! (Unfailing love: merciful kindness; Vast: great, immeasurable; Faithfulness: truth, reliability)

Chapter 118
1. Give thanks to the LORD, for He is truly good; His love is everlasting. (Love: steadfast, unchanging affection) **2.** Let Israel declare: "His love is forever faithful." (Declare: proclaim openly) **3.** Let the house of Aaron announce: "His mercy lasts forever." (House of Aaron: the priestly lineage) **4.** Let all who honor the LORD say: "His mercy endures through all time." (Honor: respect and reverence) **5.** In my time of distress, I called on the LORD; He answered me and gave me freedom in a spacious place. (Distress: time of difficulty or trouble; Spacious: open, wide) **6.** The LORD is on my side, I have no reason to fear; what harm can anyone do to me? (Harm: injury, damage) **7.** The LORD takes my side against my enemies, and I will see the downfall of those who oppose me. (Oppose: resist, fight against) **8.** It is better to trust in the LORD than to rely on human strength. (Rely: depend on) **9.** It is better to trust in the LORD than to put confidence in rulers or princes. (Princes: powerful leaders) **10.** Though all nations surrounded me, in the name of the LORD, I will defeat them. (Defeat: overcome, win over) **11.** Yes, they surrounded me on every side, but in the name of the LORD, I will prevail against them. (Prevail: succeed, triumph) **12.** They surrounded me like swarming bees, but they vanished like a fire burning thorns; in the name of the LORD, I will crush them. (Crush: defeat, destroy) **13.** You pushed me hard to make me fall, but the LORD came to my aid. (Pushed hard: exerted pressure) **14.** The LORD is my strength and my song, He has become my salvation. (Salvation: deliverance, rescue) **15.** In the tents of the righteous, the sound of joy and victory is heard; the powerful right hand of the LORD brings great deeds. (Righteous: morally upright) **16.** The LORD's right hand is raised in triumph; the right hand of the LORD accomplishes mighty works. (Triumph: victory) **17.** I will not die, but I will live to tell of the LORD's mighty works. (Tell of: proclaim, declare) **18.** Though the LORD has disciplined me severely, He has not handed me over to death. (Disciplined: corrected, chastised) **19.** Open the gates of righteousness for me, I will enter and give thanks to the LORD. (Gates of righteousness: the entrance to a place of moral integrity) **20.** This is the gate that belongs to the LORD, through which the righteous shall pass. (Righteous: morally upright) **21.** I will praise You, for You have answered me and have become my deliverance. (Deliverance: rescue, salvation) **22.** The stone that was rejected by the builders has now become the cornerstone. (Cornerstone: the most important part of a structure) **23.** This is the LORD's doing, and it is marvelous in our eyes. (Marvelous: extraordinary, wonderful) **24.** This is the day the LORD has made; we will rejoice and be glad in it. (Rejoice: express joy) **25.** Save us now, LORD, we ask You; O LORD, grant us success. (Grant: give, bestow) **26.** Blessed is he who comes in the name of the LORD; we bless you from the house of the LORD. (Comes in the name of: comes with the authority of) **27.** The LORD is God, and He has shown us light; bind the sacrifice with cords and offer it at the altar. (Shown us light: revealed truth and guidance) **28.** You are my God, and I will praise You; You are my God, I will exalt You. (Exalt: lift up in honor) **29.** Give thanks to the LORD, for He is good; His love endures forever. (Endures: lasts, persists)

Chapter 119
1. Blessed are the pure in heart, who walk in God's law. (undefiled : pure, way : path) **2.** Blessed are those who keep His rules and seek Him wholeheartedly. (testimonies : rules, seek : look for) **3.** They do no wrong, but walk in His ways. (iniquity : wrong, walk : follow) **4.** You have commanded us to follow Your precepts carefully. (precepts : rules) **5.** Oh, that my path would be directed to follow Your laws! (statutes : laws) **6.** Then I will not be ashamed when I obey all Your commands. (respect : obey) **7.** I will praise You with a sincere heart when I learn Your righteous decisions. (righteous : good, judgments : decisions) **8.** I will keep Your laws; do not completely forsake me. (forsake : abandon) **9.** How can a young person stay pure? By following Your word. (cleanse : stay pure) **10.** I have sought You with all my heart; do not let me stray from Your commands. (wander : stray) **11.** I have hidden Your word in my heart so I might not sin against You. (sin : do wrong) **12.** Blessed are You, O Lord; teach me Your laws. (statutes : laws) **13.** I have declared Your judgments with my mouth. (judgments : decisions) **14.** I rejoice in Your testimonies more than in all riches. (testimonies : rules) **15.** I will think about Your rules and follow Your ways. (precepts : rules, ways : paths) **16.** I will find delight in Your laws and never forget Your word. (statutes : laws) **17.** Deal generously with Your servant so I can live and keep Your word. (bountifully : generously) **18.** Open my eyes to see wonders in Your law. (wondrous : amazing) **19.** I am a stranger on earth; don't hide Your commands from me. (stranger : foreigner) **20.** My soul is broken with longing for Your judgments at all times. (longing : yearning) **21.** You have rebuked the proud, who are cursed and wander from Your commands. (rebuked : scolded, cursed : punished) **22.** Take away disgrace from me, for I have obeyed Your laws.

(reproach : disgrace) **23.** Princes speak against me, but I meditate on Your rules. (princes : leaders, meditate : think deeply) **24.** Your rules are my delight and my counselors. (testimonies : rules, counselors : advisors) **25.** My soul clings to the dust; revive me with Your word. (cleaveth : clings, quicken : revive) **26.** I declared my ways, and You answered me; teach me Your laws. (ways : actions) **27.** Help me understand the way of Your rules so I can talk about Your great works. (precepts : rules, wondrous : amazing) **28.** My soul melts with sorrow; strengthen me through Your word. (melteth : weakens, quicken : strengthen) **29.** Take away falsehood from me and graciously give me Your law. (lying : falsehood) **30.** I have chosen the way of truth; Your decisions are before me. (truth : honesty, judgments : decisions) **31.** I cling to Your testimonies; do not let me be put to shame. (testimonies : rules) **32.** I will run the path of Your commandments when You expand my heart. (run : follow, enlarge : expand) **33.** Teach me Your laws, and I will obey them to the end. (statutes : laws) **34.** Give me understanding, and I will follow Your law with all my heart. (understanding : wisdom) **35.** Make me walk in the path of Your commands, for I delight in them. (path : way) **36.** Turn my heart toward Your rules, not toward selfish gain. (incline : turn, covetousness : selfish gain) **37.** Turn my eyes from looking at worthless things; revive me in Your way. (vanity : worthless things, quicken : revive) **38.** Confirm Your word to Your servant, who fears You. (stablish : confirm, fear : respect) **39.** Take away my disgrace, which I dread, for Your judgments are good. (reproach : disgrace) **40.** Behold, I long for Your precepts; revive me in Your righteousness. (precepts : rules, quicken : revive) **41.** Let Your mercies come to me, O Lord, even Your salvation, according to Your word. (mercies : kindness) **42.** Then I can answer those who mock me, for I trust in Your word. (reproacheth : mocks) **43.** Never take Your truth away from my mouth, for I have hoped in Your judgments. (truth : word, judgments : decisions) **44.** I will keep Your law forever and ever. (law : command) **45.** I will walk in freedom, for I seek Your rules. (liberty : freedom) **46.** I will speak about Your testimonies before kings and will not be ashamed. (testimonies : rules) **47.** I will delight in Your commandments, which I love. (commandments : rules) **48.** I will lift up my hands to Your commandments, which I love, and meditate on Your statutes. (statutes : laws) **49.** Remember the word to Your servant, upon which You have caused me to hope. (hope : trust) **50.** This is my comfort in my suffering: Your word has revived me. (comfort : relief) **51.** The proud have mocked me, but I have not turned away from Your law. (derision : mockery) **52.** I remember Your ancient judgments, O Lord, and find comfort. (judgments : decisions) **53.** I am terrified by the wicked who forsake Your law. (horror : terrified) **54.** Your statutes are my songs in my pilgrimage. (songs : comfort, pilgrimage : journey) **55.** I remember Your name, O Lord, at night, and I keep Your law. (name : reputation) **56.** This has been my practice because I have kept Your precepts. (precepts : rules) **57.** You are my portion, O Lord; I have promised to keep Your words. (portion : inheritance) **58.** I have sought Your favor with all my heart; be merciful to me according to Your word. (favor : kindness) **59.** I thought about my ways and turned my feet to Your testimonies. (testimonies : rules) **60.** I hurried and did not delay to keep Your commandments. (delayed : postponed) **61.** Though the wicked have robbed me, I have not forgotten Your law. (robbed : stolen from) **62.** At midnight, I will rise to thank You for Your righteous judgments. (judgments : decisions) **63.** I am a companion of all who fear You and keep Your precepts. (companions : friends) **64.** The earth is full of Your mercy; teach me Your statutes. (statutes : laws) **65.** You have done good to Your servant, O Lord, according to Your word. (good : kindly) **66.** Teach me good judgment and knowledge, for I believe Your commandments. (judgment : wisdom) **67.** Before I was afflicted, I went astray, but now I keep Your word. (afflicted : troubled) **68.** You are good and do good; teach me Your statutes. (good : kind) **69.** The proud have spread lies about me, but I will keep Your precepts with all my heart. (lies : falsehood) **70.** Their hearts are fat and indifferent, but I delight in Your law. (fat : hard, grease : fat) **71.** It was good for me that I was afflicted, so that I might learn Your statutes. (afflicted : troubled) **72.** Your word is more precious to me than thousands of gold and silver pieces. (better : more precious) **73.** Your hands made and formed me; give me understanding to learn Your commandments. (formed : shaped) **74.** Those who fear You will be glad when they see me, because I have hoped in Your word. (fear : respect) **75.** I know, O Lord, that Your judgments are right, and that in faithfulness You have afflicted me. (judgments : decisions) **76.** Let Your merciful kindness be for my comfort, according to Your word to Your servant. (merciful kindness : compassion) **77.** Let Your tender mercies come to me so I can live, for Your law is my delight. (mercies : kindness) **78.** Let the proud be ashamed, for they dealt falsely with me without cause, but I will meditate on Your precepts. (proud : arrogant) **79.** Let those who fear You turn to me, and those who know Your testimonies. (turn : come) **80.** Let my heart be perfect in Your statutes, that I may not be ashamed. (perfect : whole, statutes : laws) **81.** My soul longs for Your salvation; I hope in Your word. (fainteth : longs) **82.** My eyes fail from longing for Your word, saying, "When will You comfort me?" (fail : weaken) **83.** I am like a wineskin in the smoke, yet I do not forget Your statutes. (bottle : wineskin) **84.** How long will Your servant suffer? When will You bring judgment on those who persecute me? (persecute : harass) **85.** The proud have dug pits for me, but they are not in line with Your law. (pits : traps) **86.** All Your commandments are trustworthy; they persecute me wrongfully; help me. (faithful : trustworthy) **87.** They have almost destroyed me on earth, but I have not forsaken Your precepts. (forsook : abandoned) **88.** Revive me according to Your lovingkindness, so I can keep the testimony of Your mouth. (quicken : revive, testimony : message) **89.** Forever, O Lord, Your word is settled in heaven. (settled : established) **90.** Your faithfulness extends to all generations; You established the earth, and it stands firm. (faithfulness : loyalty) **91.** Your laws continue to this day, for all things serve You. (ordinances : laws) **92.** If Your law had not been my delight, I would have perished in my affliction. (delights : joy) **93.** I will never forget Your precepts, for by them You have given me life. **94.** I am Yours; save me, for I have sought Your precepts. **95.** The wicked wait to destroy me, but I will meditate on Your testimonies. (testimonies : rules) **96.** I have seen the end of all perfection, but Your commandment is exceedingly broad. (perfection : completeness) **97.** Oh, how I love Your law! It is my meditation all day. (meditation : reflection) **98.** Through Your commandments, I am wiser than my enemies, for they are always with me. (enemies : foes) **99.** I have more understanding than all my teachers, for Your testimonies are my meditation. (teachers : instructors) **100.** I understand more than the ancients, because I keep Your precepts. (ancients : old ones) **101.** I have kept my feet from every evil way to follow Your word. (refrained : kept, evil : wrong) **102.** I have not turned away from Your decisions, for You have taught me. (departed : turned away, judgments : decisions) **103.** How sweet are Your words to my taste! Yes, sweeter than honey. (sweet : pleasing) **104.** Your rules give me understanding; that's why I hate every false way. (precepts : rules) **105.** Your word is a lamp to my feet and a light to my path. (path : way) **106.** I have sworn to keep Your righteous decisions. (sworn : promised, righteous : right) **107.** I am greatly afflicted; revive me, Lord, according to Your word. (afflicted : troubled, quicken : revive) **108.** Accept my freewill offerings, Lord, and teach me Your decisions. (freewill offerings : voluntary gifts) **109.** My soul is always in danger, but I don't forget Your law. (soul : life, law : command) **110.** The wicked have set traps for me, but I have not strayed from Your rules. (laid a snare : set traps) **111.** Your testimonies are my eternal heritage; they are my joy. (testimonies : rules, heritage : inheritance) **112.** I have set my heart to follow Your statutes always, to the end. (statutes : laws) **113.** I hate worthless thoughts, but I love Your law. (vain : worthless) **114.** You are my hiding place and shield; I hope in

Your word. (shield : protector) **115.** Depart from me, you evildoers, for I will keep God's commandments. (evildoers : wrongdoers) **116.** Uphold me according to Your word, so I can live; don't let me be ashamed of my hope. (uphold : support) **117.** Hold me up, and I will be safe; I will honor Your statutes continually. (safe : secure) **118.** You have destroyed all who stray from Your statutes; their deceit is false. (err : stray, deceit : lies) **119.** You remove all the wicked from the earth like dross; that's why I love Your rules. (dross : waste) **120.** My flesh trembles with fear of You; I am afraid of Your judgments. (flesh : body) **121.** I have done what is right and just; do not leave me to my oppressors. (judgment : fairness, oppressors : enemies) **122.** Be surety for Your servant for good; don't let the proud oppress me. (surety : guarantee, proud : arrogant) **123.** My eyes fail from longing for Your salvation and Your righteous word. (fail : weaken, salvation : rescue) **124.** Deal with Your servant according to Your mercy, and teach me Your statutes. (mercy : kindness) **125.** I am Your servant; give me understanding to know Your testimonies. (testimonies : rules) **126.** It is time for You, Lord, to act, for they have made Your law void. (made void : ignored) **127.** I love Your commandments more than gold, yes, more than fine gold. (commandments : laws) **128.** Therefore, I consider all Your precepts right and hate every false way. (precepts : rules) **129.** Your testimonies are wonderful; that's why my soul keeps them. (testimonies : teachings, soul : inner self) **130.** The entrance of Your words gives light; it gives understanding to the simple. (entrance : beginning, simple : humble) **131.** I opened my mouth and panted, for I longed for Your commandments. (panted : sighed, commandments : laws) **132.** Look upon me and be merciful, as You have done to those who love Your name. (merciful : kind) **133.** Guide my steps according to Your word; don't let sin have power over me. (steps : actions, iniquity : sin) **134.** Deliver me from man's oppression, so I can keep Your precepts. (deliver : rescue) **135.** Shine Your face upon Your servant and teach me Your statutes. (shine : show) **136.** Streams of tears flow from my eyes because people don't keep Your law. (streams : rivers) **137.** You are righteous, Lord, and Your judgments are upright. (righteous : just) **138.** Your testimonies, which You have commanded, are righteous and very faithful. (testimonies : commands, faithful : true) **139.** My zeal has consumed me because my enemies have forgotten Your words. (zeal : passion) **140.** Your word is pure; that's why Your servant loves it. (pure : clean) **141.** I am small and despised, yet I don't forget Your precepts. (despised : rejected) **142.** Your righteousness is everlasting, and Your law is truth. (righteousness : goodness) **143.** Trouble and anguish have overtaken me, but Your commandments are my delight. (trouble : distress, anguish : sorrow) **144.** The righteousness of Your testimonies is eternal; give me understanding, and I will live. (testimonies : teachings) **145.** I cried with my whole heart; hear me, Lord, I will keep Your statutes. (cried : prayed) **146.** I cried to You; save me, and I will keep Your testimonies. (save : rescue) **147.** I rise early and cry out; I hope in Your word. (rise early : wake up early) **148.** My eyes stay open through the night watches, so I can meditate on Your word. (meditate : think deeply) **149.** Hear my voice according to Your lovingkindness; revive me according to Your judgment. (lovingkindness : compassion, revive : restore) **150.** The wicked draw near to harm me, but they are far from Your law. (mischief : harm) **151.** You are near, Lord, and all Your commandments are truth. (near : close) **152.** I have known from long ago that You have founded Your testimonies forever. (testimonies : laws) **153.** Consider my suffering and deliver me, for I do not forget Your law. (suffering : trouble) **154.** Defend my cause and deliver me; revive me according to Your word. (defend : plead for) **155.** Salvation is far from the wicked, for they don't seek Your statutes. (wicked : evil) **156.** Great are Your tender mercies, Lord; revive me according to Your judgments. (mercies : kindness) **157.** Many are my persecutors and enemies, but I don't turn away from Your testimonies. (persecutors : harassers, enemies : foes) **158.** I have seen the transgressors and was grieved, because they don't keep Your word. (transgressors : wrongdoers) **159.** Consider how I love Your precepts; revive me, Lord, according to Your lovingkindness. (precepts : rules, lovingkindness : mercy) **160.** Your word is true from the beginning, and every one of Your righteous decisions endures forever. (righteous : just, decisions : judgments) **161.** Princes have persecuted me without cause, but my heart stands in awe of Your word. (princes : leaders) **162.** I rejoice at Your word, as one who finds great treasure. (rejoice : celebrate, spoil : treasure) **163.** I hate and abhor lying, but I love Your law. (abhor : dislike) **164.** Seven times a day I praise You for Your righteous judgments. (praise : worship) **165.** Great peace have those who love Your law; nothing shall make them stumble. (peace : calm) **166.** Lord, I have hoped for Your salvation, and I have done Your commandments. (salvation : rescue) **167.** My soul has kept Your testimonies, and I love them exceedingly. (testimonies : teachings) **168.** I have kept Your precepts and testimonies; all my ways are before You. (precepts : rules) **169.** Let my cry come near to You, Lord; give me understanding according to Your word. (cry : plea) **170.** Let my supplication come before You; deliver me according to Your word. (supplication : request) **171.** My lips shall praise You when You teach me Your statutes. (statutes : laws) **172.** My tongue will speak of Your word, for all Your commandments are righteous. (tongue : speech) **173.** Let Your hand help me, for I have chosen Your precepts. (precepts : commands) **174.** I have longed for Your salvation, Lord, and Your law is my delight. (longed : waited) **175.** Let my soul live, and it shall praise You; let Your judgments help me. (soul : life) **176.** I have gone astray like a lost sheep; seek Your servant, for I do not forget Your commandments. (gone astray : wandered, lost sheep : lost person)

Chapter 120

1. In my trouble, I called out to the Lord, and He answered me. (trouble : distress, called out : cried) **2.** Rescue my soul, O Lord, from deceitful lips and false words. (rescue : deliver, deceitful : lying) **3.** What will be done to you, O deceitful tongue, and what will be your reward? (deceitful : false, reward : punishment) **4.** You will face sharp arrows from the strong, and burning coals of juniper. (sharp : piercing, burning coals : hot embers) **5.** How miserable I am, living in Mesech, and staying among the tents of Kedar! (miserable : woe, Mesech : distant place, Kedar : nomadic tribe) **6.** My soul has long been among those who despise peace. (despise : hate) **7.** I long for peace, but whenever I speak, they are bent on war. (long for : desire, bent on : eager for)

Chapter 121

1. I will look to the mountains; from where will my help come? (look : gaze, mountains : hills) **2.** My help comes from the Lord, who created the heavens and the earth. (created : made) **3.** He will not allow your feet to stumble; the One who watches over you will never rest. (stumble : slip, watches over : keeps guard, rest : sleep) **4.** The One who guards Israel will never fall asleep or grow weary. (guards : keeps, weary : tired) **5.** The Lord is your protector; He will shield you with His presence at your side. (protector : keeper, shield : cover) **6.** The sun won't strike you during the day, nor the moon at night. (strike : harm) **7.** The Lord will guard you from all evil; He will protect your life. (guard : preserve, protect : keep safe) **8.** The Lord will protect you wherever you go, both now and forever. (protect : watch over, wherever : in all places)

Chapter 122

1. I was filled with joy when they invited me to go to the Lord's house. (filled with joy : glad, invited : said) **2.** Our feet will stand within your gates, O Jerusalem. (stand : rest, gates : city entrances) **3.** Jerusalem is built like a city that is closely united. (closely united : compact) **4.** There the tribes ascend, the tribes of the Lord, to give thanks and honor His name. (ascend : go up, honor : give thanks) **5.** In that city, thrones of judgment are placed, the thrones of David's house. (thrones : seats of authority, placed : set) **6.** Pray for the peace of Jerusalem: those who love you will prosper. (pray : ask, prosper : thrive) **7.** May peace dwell within your walls, and prosperity within your palaces. (dwell : be, palaces : royal buildings) **8.** For the sake of my family and friends, I now say, May peace be with you. (family : brethren, say : declare) **9.** Because of the house of the Lord our God, I will seek your well-being. (well-being : good)

Chapter 123

1. I raise my eyes to You, O You who reside in the heavens. (raise : lift, reside : dwell) **2.** Just as a servant watches closely for his master's signal, and a maid looks to her mistress, so we look to You, our Lord, eagerly waiting for Your mercy. (watches closely : looks, signal : hand, eagerly : expectantly) **3.** Show us mercy, O Lord, show us mercy, for we are overwhelmed by disdain. (show us : have, mercy : kindness, disdain : contempt) **4.** Our souls are burdened by the mockery of those at ease, and the disdain of the proud. (burdened : filled, mockery : scorn, disdain : contempt)

Chapter 124

1. If the Lord had not been on our side, Israel would now declare: (declare : say) **2.** If the Lord had not been with us when people rose up against us, (with us : on our side, rose up : attacked) **3.** They would have quickly swallowed us alive, when their anger was stirred up against us. (quickly : instantly, swallowed us : devoured us, anger : wrath) **4.** The waters would have engulfed us, the torrent would have swept over our very soul. (engulfed : overwhelmed, torrent : flood) **5.** The raging waters would have swept over us. (raging : proud) **6.** Praise be to the Lord, who has not let us be torn apart by their jaws. (torn apart : given as prey, jaws : teeth) **7.** Our soul has escaped like a bird from the trap of the hunters; the trap is broken, and we are free. (escaped : delivered, trap : snare, free : escaped) **8.** Our help comes from the name of the Lord, the Creator of heaven and earth. (help : support, Creator : maker)

Chapter 125

1. Those who trust in the Lord are like Mount Zion, which cannot be shaken but endures forever. (endures : abides, shaken : moved) **2.** Just as the mountains surround Jerusalem, the Lord surrounds His people both now and forevermore. (surround : encircle) **3.** The wicked's power will not rest on the righteous' inheritance, or the righteous might be tempted to do wrong. (power : rod, inheritance : lot, tempted : put forth their hands) **4.** Do good, O Lord, to those who are good, and to those who are upright in their hearts. (upright : honest) **5.** But those who turn to crooked paths, the Lord will lead along with the evildoers; yet peace will be upon Israel. (crooked : dishonest, evildoers : workers of iniquity)

Chapter 126

1. When the Lord brought back the captives of Zion, we felt as though we were dreaming. (brought back : turned again, captives : captivity) **2.** Our mouths were filled with joy, and our tongues with songs of praise. Then even the nations said, "The Lord has done wonderful things for them." (filled : made, joy : laughter, songs of praise : singing) **3.** The Lord has done marvelous things for us, and we are full of joy. (marvelous : great, full : glad) **4.** Restore us again, O Lord, like the refreshing streams in the dry south. (refreshing : streams, dry : south, restore : turn again) **5.** Those who sow in sorrow will eventually harvest with joy. (sow : plant, sorrow : tears, harvest : joy) **6.** Those who go out weeping, carrying their seeds for planting, will return rejoicing, bringing in their sheaves. (weeping : mourning, seeds for planting : precious seed, rejoicing : with joy)

Chapter 127

1. If the Lord does not build the house, the builders are wasting their effort; if the Lord does not guard the city, the watchman is on guard for nothing. (wasting : in vain, on guard : waketh, nothing : in vain) **2.** It's pointless for you to get up early and stay up late, to work hard and worry: for the Lord gives restful sleep to those He loves. (pointless : vain, work hard : rise up early, worry : bread of sorrows, restful sleep : sleep) **3.** Behold, children are a gift from the Lord; the offspring of the womb are His reward. (gift : heritage, offspring : fruit) **4.** Like arrows in the hands of a strong man, so are children born in the prime of life. (strong : mighty, prime of life : youth) **5.** Blessed is the man whose quiver is filled with them; they will not be shamed, but will confidently face their adversaries at the city gates. (blessed : happy, filled : full, confidently face : speak with, adversaries : enemies)

Chapter 128

1. Happy is the person who fears the Lord and follows His ways. (fears : reveres, follows : walketh) **2.** You will enjoy the fruits of your labor, and you will be content and well off. (enjoy : eat, fruits : labour, content : happy) **3.** Your wife will be like a productive vine within your home, and your children will be like young olive trees around your table. (productive : fruitful, young olive trees : olive plants) **4.** See, this is how the man who fears the Lord will be blessed. (blessed : favored) **5.** The Lord will bless you from Zion, and you will experience the prosperity of Jerusalem all your days. (prosperity : good, from : out of) **6.** You will live to see your grandchildren, and peace will reign over Israel. (grandchildren : children's children)

Chapter 129

1. From the days of my youth, I have been oppressed, let Israel testify: (oppressed : afflicted) **2.** They have oppressed me since I was young, yet they have not triumphed over me. (triumph : prevailed) **3.** They plowed deep furrows across my back, lengthening their wounds. (plowed : plowed, furrows : long) **4.** The Lord is just; He has severed the ropes of the wicked. (just : righteous, severed : cut asunder) **5.** Let all who despise Zion be humiliated and driven away. (despise : hate, humiliated : confounded) **6.** Let them be like grass on rooftops that withers before it even has a chance to grow. (withers : withereth, chance to grow : groweth) **7.** The reaper does not gather it in his hand, nor does the one bundling it gather it into his arms. (reaper : mower, bundling : bindeth) **8.** And those who pass by do not speak words of blessing: "May the Lord's favor be upon you; we bless you in the name of the Lord." (pass by : go by, favor : blessing)

Chapter 130

1. From the depths of despair, I call out to You, O LORD. (despair : depths) **2.** Lord, hear my voice; let Your ears be open to my cries for help. (cries for help : supplications) **3.** If You, LORD, held our sins against us, who could stand before You? (held : marked, stand : endure) **4.** But with You, there is forgiveness, so that You may be honored. (forgiveness : pardon, honored : feared) **5.** I wait for the LORD, my soul is patient, and I place my hope in His promise. (patient : doth wait, promise : word) **6.** My soul waits for the LORD more eagerly than watchmen wait for the dawn; yes, more than those who watch for the morning. (eagerly : longs, watchmen : those that watch) **7.** Let Israel trust in the LORD, for with Him is unfailing love, and plentiful redemption. (unfailing love : mercy, plentiful : plenteous) **8.** He will redeem Israel from all their sins. (redeem : deliver)

Chapter 131

1. O LORD, my heart is not proud, nor are my eyes raised in arrogance; I do not concern myself with things too great or too difficult for me. (proud : haughty, raised in arrogance : lofty, concern : exercise) **2.** Instead, I have calmed and quieted my soul, like a child who is weaned from his mother; my soul is like a weaned child within me. (calmed : behaved, weaned : grown, within me : in me) **3.** Let Israel place their hope in the LORD, now and forevermore. (place their hope : hope, now and forevermore : henceforth and for ever)

Chapter 132

1. O LORD, remember Your servant David, and all the hardships he faced. (hardships : afflictions) **2.** How he swore an oath to the LORD, and made a vow to the Almighty God of Jacob: (Almighty : mighty) **3.** I will not enter my house or lie down to rest, (enter : come into, lie down : go up) **4.** Nor will I allow sleep to my eyes or slumber to my eyelids, (slumber : rest) **5.** Until I find a dwelling place for the LORD, a place for the mighty God of Jacob. (dwelling place : habitation) **6.** We heard of it in Ephrathah, and found it in the fields of the wood. (found : discovered) **7.** Let us go into His sanctuary, let us bow before His footstool. (sanctuary : tabernacle) **8.** Arise, O LORD, come to Your resting place, You and the ark of Your power. (resting place : rest, ark : strength) **9.** Let Your priests be clothed in righteousness, and let Your faithful people rejoice. (faithful people : saints, rejoice : shout for joy) **10.** For the sake of Your servant David, do not reject Your anointed one. (rejected : turn away) **11.** The LORD swore to David in truth, He will not break His promise. "I will set one of your descendants on your throne." (break : turn from) **12.** If your children keep My covenant and follow My laws, their descendants will sit on your throne forever. (follow : keep, laws : testimony) **13.** For the LORD has chosen Zion, He has desired it as His home. (desired : chosen, home : habitation) **14.** This is My resting place forever; here I will stay, for I have longed for it. (resting place : rest, stay : dwell) **15.** I will bless her provisions abundantly, and satisfy her poor with bread. (bless : abundantly bless, provisions : provision, bread : food) **16.** I will clothe her priests with salvation, and her faithful people will rejoice in joy. (faithful people : saints, salvation : righteousness) **17.** There I will cause the horn of David to grow, I have prepared a light for My anointed one. (horn : strength, light : lamp) **18.** His enemies will be covered with shame, but his crown will shine brightly. (shine brightly : flourish)

Chapter 133
1. Look, how wonderful and delightful it is when brothers live together in harmony! (harmony : unity) **2.** It is like the sacred oil poured on the head, which flowed down onto the beard, even Aaron's beard, and extended to the hem of his robes. (sacred : precious, flowed down : ran down, hem : skirts) **3.** It is like the dew of Mount Hermon, falling upon the mountains of Zion; for there the LORD ordained His blessing, even life that endures forever. (dew : dewfall, ordained : commanded, endures : forevermore)

Chapter 134
1. Look, praise the LORD, all you who serve Him, who stand in the house of the LORD by night (praise: bless, serve: servants). **2.** Raise your hands in the holy place, and offer your blessings to the LORD (raise: lift up, holy place: sanctuary). **3.** The LORD who created the heavens and the earth bless you from Zion (created: made, bless: bless thee).

Chapter 135
1. Praise the LORD! Exalt His name, all you who serve Him, lift Him up in honor (Exalt: Praise, lift up: honor). **2.** You who stand in the temple of the LORD, within the courts of our God's sanctuary (stand: are positioned, sanctuary: holy place). **3.** Give praise to the LORD, for He is good; sing joyful songs to His name, for it is pleasing (pleasing: delightful). **4.** The LORD has chosen Jacob for Himself and made Israel His treasured possession (treasured possession: special inheritance). **5.** For I know the LORD is great, and our God is greater than all other gods (greater than: above). **6.** Whatever the LORD desires, He does in the heavens, on the earth, in the seas, and in all the depths (desires: pleases, depths: deep waters). **7.** He makes the clouds rise from the ends of the earth, He sends lightning with the rain, and brings forth the wind from His storehouses (storehouses: treasuries). **8.** He struck down the firstborn of Egypt, both of humans and animals (struck down: smote). **9.** He sent signs and wonders into Egypt, against Pharaoh and all his servants (signs and wonders: miraculous signs). **10.** He defeated powerful kings and destroyed mighty rulers (defeated: struck, destroyed: overthrew). **11.** Sihon, the king of the Amorites, and Og, the king of Bashan, along with all the kings of Canaan (kings: rulers). **12.** He gave their land as a possession to Israel, His people, as an inheritance (possession: heritage, inheritance: inheritance). **13.** Your name, O LORD, is eternal, and Your renown is remembered throughout all generations (renown: fame, remembered: remembered throughout). **14.** The LORD will judge His people and show mercy to His servants (judge: defend, show mercy: have compassion). **15.** The idols of the nations are made of silver and gold, crafted by human hands (crafted: made, human hands: the work of men). **16.** They have mouths, but cannot speak; they have eyes, but cannot see (cannot speak: speak not, cannot see: see note). **17.** They have ears, but cannot hear; there is no breath in their mouths (cannot hear: hear not). **18.** Those who make them become like them, and so does everyone who trusts in them). **19.** Bless the LORD, O house of Israel; bless the LORD, O house of Aaron (house of: descendants of). **20.** Bless the LORD, O house of Levi; you who fear the LORD, bless the LORD (fear: reverence). **21.** Blessed be the LORD from Zion, who dwells in Jerusalem. Praise the LORD! (dwells: resides).

Chapter 136
1. Give thanks to the LORD, for His goodness is everlasting; His steadfast love endures forever (goodness: kindness, steadfast love: mercy). **2.** Give thanks to the God who reigns supreme, for His steadfast love endures forever (reigns supreme: above all gods). **3.** Give thanks to the Master of all lords, for His steadfast love endures forever (Master of all lords: the Lord of lords). **4.** To the One who alone performs great wonders, for His steadfast love endures forever (great wonders: marvelous deeds). **5.** To the One who established the heavens with wisdom, for His steadfast love endures forever (established: created, wisdom: understanding). **6.** To the One who spread the earth above the waters, for His steadfast love endures forever (spread: stretched, above the waters: over the seas). **7.** To the One who created the great lights, for His steadfast love endures forever (great lights: the sun, moon, and stars). **8.** The sun to rule the day, for His steadfast love endures forever (rule: govern, day: daylight). **9.** The moon and the stars to guide the night, for His steadfast love endures forever (guide: govern, night: darkness). **10.** To the One who struck down Egypt's firstborn, for His steadfast love endures forever (struck down: smote, firstborn: sons). **11.** And led Israel out from their midst, for His steadfast love endures forever (led out: delivered, midst: among them). **12.** With a powerful hand and an outstretched arm, for His steadfast love endures forever (powerful hand: strong hand, outstretched arm: raised arm). **13.** To the One who parted the Red Sea, for His steadfast love endures forever (parted: divided, Red Sea: sea of reeds). **14.** And made Israel walk through the midst of it, for His steadfast love endures forever (walk through: pass through, midst: middle). **15.** But cast Pharaoh and his army into the sea, for His steadfast love endures forever (cast: overthrew, army: host). **16.** To the One who guided His people through the wilderness, for His steadfast love endures forever (guided: led, wilderness: desert). **17.** To the One who struck down great kings, for His steadfast love endures forever (struck down: defeated, great: mighty). **18.** And killed renowned rulers, for His steadfast love endures forever (killed: overthrew, renowned rulers: famous kings). **19.** Sihon, king of the Amorites, for His steadfast love endures forever (king of the Amorites: ruler of the Amorites). **20.** And Og, king of Bashan, for His steadfast love endures forever (king of Bashan: ruler of Bashan). **21.** And gave their land as an inheritance, for His steadfast love endures forever (gave: provided, inheritance: heritage). **22.** A heritage for His servant Israel, for His steadfast love endures forever (servant: people). **23.** Who took notice of our lowly condition, for His steadfast love endures forever (took notice: remembered, lowly condition: humble estate). **24.** And rescued us from our enemies, for His steadfast love endures forever (rescued: redeemed, enemies: foes). **25.** Who provides food for all living creatures, for His steadfast love endures forever (provides: gives, creatures: all flesh). **26.** Give thanks to the God of heaven, for His steadfast love endures forever (God of heaven: Sovereign of the heavens).

Chapter 137
1. By the waters of Babylon, we sat and wept, remembering the lost city of Zion (sat and wept: we sat there in sorrow, remembering: recalling). **2.** We hung our harps on the branches of the willow trees (hung: placed, branches of the willow trees: upon the willow's boughs). **3.** For those who had taken us captive demanded songs from us, and those who had crushed us urged us to be joyful, saying, "Sing us one of your joyful songs of Zion!" (demanded: insisted on,

those who had crushed us: our oppressors, urged: called for, joyful songs: songs of happiness). **4.** How can we sing the songs of the LORD while we are in a foreign land? (foreign land: a land that is not our own). **5.** If I forget you, O Jerusalem, may my right hand lose its skill (right hand: the hand that plays, lose its skill: forget how to play). **6.** If I fail to remember you, may my tongue cling to the roof of my mouth; may I never find joy if I do not prioritize Jerusalem (fail to remember: fail to keep in mind, cling: cleave, never find joy: may my joy be lost). **7.** Remember, LORD, the deeds of the Edomites on the day Jerusalem fell, when they shouted, "Tear it down, tear it down to its foundations!" (deeds: actions, shouted: they cried out, foundations: base of the city). **8.** O Babylon, you who are destined for destruction, blessed is the one who repays you for the harm you've done to us (destined for destruction: about to be destroyed, blessed: happy, repays: gives back). **9.** Blessed is the one who takes your children and shatters them against the stones (takes: seizes, shatters: dashes).

Chapter 138
1. I will praise You, Lord, with all my heart, and I will sing Your praises before all other powers (with all my heart: wholeheartedly, before all other powers: before any other authority or idols). **2.** I will bow toward Your holy sanctuary and give thanks for Your constant love and faithfulness, for You have exalted Your word even above Your name (bow toward: turn in reverence to, Your constant love: Your unfailing love, exalted: lifted up, Your word: Your promises). **3.** On the day I called out to You, You answered me and gave me strength, filling my soul with Your power (called out to You: cried out to You, filled my soul with Your power: empowered me deeply). **4.** All the kings of the earth will praise You, O Lord, when they hear the truth of Your words (the truth of Your words: the message You speak). **5.** They will sing of Your ways, for Your greatness and glory are beyond measure (Your greatness and glory: the magnitude of Your greatness). **6.** Although the Lord is high above all, He cares for the humble, but the proud are far from His sight (cares for: looks after, far from His sight: distant from His favor). **7.** Even in the midst of troubles, You will revive me. You will stretch out Your hand against my enemies' wrath, and Your right hand will bring me salvation (revive me: restore me, bring me salvation: rescue me from danger). **8.** The Lord will fulfill His purpose for me. Your lovingkindness, O Lord, is eternal; do not abandon the work You have begun in me (fulfill His purpose: complete His plans for me, eternal: forever enduring, do not abandon: forsake not).

Chapter 139
1. O Lord, You have searched and fully examined me; You understand all of my being (searched: investigated, fully examined: known thoroughly, all of my being: every part of me). **2.** You know when I sit down and when I stand up; You discern my thoughts from a distance (sit down: rest, stand up: rise, discern: understand). **3.** You surround all my actions and resting places, and You are familiar with every step I take (surround: compass, actions and resting places: paths and lying down, familiar with: acquainted with). **4.** There is no word on my tongue that You do not already know fully, O Lord (already know fully: know it altogether). **5.** You have enclosed me both behind and before, and placed Your hand on me (enclosed: beset, placed Your hand on me: laid Your hand upon me). **6.** This knowledge is too wonderful for me; it's beyond my reach (too wonderful: too marvelous, beyond my reach: too high for me to attain). **7.** Where can I go to escape Your presence, or where can I hide from You? (escape: flee, hide: run from). **8.** If I ascend to the heavens, You are there; if I descend to the depths, You are there as well (ascend: rise, descend to the depths: make my bed in Sheol). **9.** If I fly on the wings of the dawn or settle at the farthest part of the sea (fly on the wings of the dawn: take the wings of the morning, settle: dwell, farthest part: uttermost parts). **10.** Even there Your hand will guide me, Your right hand will hold me tightly (guide me: lead me, hold me tightly: uphold me firmly). **11.** If I say, "Surely the darkness will cover me," the night will shine as bright as the day (cover me: hide me, shine as bright as the day: will be as light). **12.** Darkness cannot hide from You; the night is as bright as the day, for darkness and light are the same to You (cannot hide: hides not, as bright as the day: as light as the day). **13.** You created my innermost being; You knitted me together in my mother's womb (created: formed, innermost being: reins, knitted together: wove together). **14.** I will praise You, for I am fearfully and wonderfully made; Your works are marvelous, and my soul fully knows this (fearfully: with reverence, wonderfully made: made in a wondrous way, soul fully knows this: my soul is fully aware). **15.** My frame was not hidden from You when I was made in secret, when I was woven in the depths of the earth (frame: substance, made in secret: formed in a hidden place, woven: intricately crafted). **16.** Your eyes saw me before I was even fully formed; all my days were written in Your book before any came to be (before I was even fully formed: while yet unformed, all my days: all the days of my life). **17.** How precious are Your thoughts toward me, O God! How vast the sum of them! (precious: valuable, thoughts: plans, sum of them: number of them). **18.** If I tried to count them, they would outnumber the grains of sand; when I awake, I am still with You (outnumber: surpass, grains of sand: sands of the sea, when I awake: when I wake up). **19.** Surely You will punish the wicked, O God; depart from me, you violent men (punish: slay, depart from me: avoid me, you violent men: you bloodthirsty people). **20.** They speak against You with evil intent; they misuse Your name (misuse Your name: take Your name in vain). **21.** Do I not hate those who hate You, O Lord? And do I not loathe those who oppose You? (loathe: despise, oppose You: rise up against You). **22.** I have a perfect hatred for them; I count them as my enemies (perfect hatred: total hatred, count them: consider them). **23.** Search me, O God, and know my heart; test me and know my thoughts (test me: try me, thoughts: anxieties, worries). **24.** See if there is any wicked way in me, and lead me in the path of everlasting life (wicked way: sinful path, lead me: guide me, everlasting life: the way of eternal life).

Chapter 140
1. O Lord, rescue me from those who are evil; keep me safe from the violent ones (rescue me: deliver me, keep me safe: preserve me). **2.** They plan wicked schemes in their hearts, always gathering for conflict (wicked schemes: mischiefs, gathering: assembling for war, conflict: battle). **3.** Their speech is like venom from serpents; their words are filled with poison like that of vipers. Selah (venom from serpents: sharpened tongues like a serpent, filled with poison: adders' poison). **4.** Protect me, Lord, from the wicked, from those who seek to harm me and trap my every step (protect me: keep me, seek to harm me: purposed to overthrow, trap my every step: snare my ways). **5.** The proud have laid snares for me, they've set traps and hidden nets along my path. Selah (laid snares: hid a snare, set traps: spread a net, hidden nets: set gins). **6.** I cry out to You, O Lord, my God: hear my plea and listen to my voice (cry out: said, listen to my voice: hear the voice of my supplications). **7.** O Lord God, the strength of my salvation, You have protected me in the day of battle (strength of my salvation: God the Lord, protected me: covered my head, day of battle: day of war). **8.** Do not grant the desires of the wicked, Lord; do not let their evil plans succeed, or they will be lifted up in pride. Selah (evil plans: wicked device, lifted up: exalt themselves). **9.** Let the harm they intend for me fall back upon their own heads (harm: mischief, fall back: cover them). **10.** Let burning coals fall upon them, let them be cast into the fire, into deep pits from which they will never rise (burning coals: let burning coals fall upon them, cast into the fire: cast into the fire, deep pits: deep pits, never rise: rise not up again). **11.** Let no liar be established on the earth; let the wicked be hunted down and brought to ruin (liar: evil speaker, established: be grounded, hunted down: pursued, brought to ruin: overthrown). **12.** I know the Lord will defend the cause of the oppressed and uphold the rights of the poor (defend the cause:

maintain the cause, oppressed: afflicted, uphold: right of the poor). **13.** Surely the righteous will praise Your name; those who are upright will dwell in Your presence forever (praise: give thanks, dwell: live, upright: just).

Chapter 141
1. O Lord, I cry out to You; hurry to answer me. Let my voice reach You swiftly when I call. (cry out to You: cry unto thee, answer me: make haste unto me, swiftly: quickly) **2.** Let my prayer rise before You like fragrant incense, and may the lifting of my hands be as the evening offering of praise. (prayer rise: set forth before thee, incense: as incense, offering of praise: evening sacrifice) **3.** Set a guard, O Lord, over my lips, and watch closely over the doorway of my mouth. (guard: watch, doorway: door, watch closely: keep) **4.** Do not let my heart be inclined to evil, or allow me to engage in wickedness with those who commit evil deeds. Do not let me partake in their indulgences. (inclined: incline, engage in: practise, evil deeds: wicked works, partake: eat) **5.** Let the righteous rebuke me, and may their correction be a blessing to me. Let their rebuke be like healing oil on my head, which brings no harm. I will still pray for them in their time of trouble. (rebuke me: smite me, blessing: kindness, correction: reproof, healing oil: excellent oil, no harm: not break my head, pray for them: my prayer also shall be) **6.** When their leaders fall, they will hear my words, for they will be sweet to their ears. (leaders: judges, fall: overthrown, hear my words: hear my words, sweet: sweet) **7.** Our bones lie scattered near the grave's mouth, like logs chopped and split for firewood. (bones: bones, scattered: scattered, near the grave: at the grave's mouth, chopped: cutteth and cleaveth wood, for firewood: upon the earth) **8.** But my eyes are fixed on You, O Lord God, in You I place my trust; do not leave me alone in my distress. (fixed on: unto, trust: hope, distress: destitute) **9.** Guard me from the traps they have set for me, and from the snares laid by those who do evil. (guard me: keep me from, traps: snares, laid: laid for me, those who do evil: workers of iniquity) **10.** Let the wicked fall into the very traps they've set, while I am able to escape safely. (fall into: fall, traps: nets, safely: withal escape)

Chapter 142
1. I cried out to the Lord with my voice; to Him I made my plea. (cried out: cried, made my plea: made my supplication) **2.** I poured out my grief before Him, showing Him all my distress. (poured out my grief: poured out my complaint, distress: trouble) **3.** When my spirit was overwhelmed within me, You knew my way. They secretly set snares along my path. (overwhelmed within me: overwhelmed, secretly set snares: privily laid a snare) **4.** I looked to my right, but no one took notice of me; there was no refuge, and no one cared for my well-being. (no one took notice: no man that would know me, no refuge: refuge failed me, cared for my well-being: no man cared for my soul) **5.** I called out to You, O Lord: You are my shelter and my portion in the land of the living. (shelter: refuge, portion: inheritance, land of the living: land of the living) **6.** Listen to my cry, for I am in deep need. Rescue me from those who are stronger than I. (deep need: brought very low, rescue me: deliver me, stronger than I: they are stronger than I) **7.** Bring my soul out of this prison that I may give You praise; the righteous will surround me, for You will deal generously with me. (bring my soul out of prison: bring my soul out of prison, deal generously: bountifully)

Chapter 143
1. O Lord, I call out to You; hurry to my aid. Listen to my cry and respond to my plea. (I call out to You: Hear my prayer, O Lord; listen to my cry) **2.** Do not bring me to trial, for no one alive can stand justified before You. (No one alive: no man living can be justified before You) **3.** My enemy has chased me down, crushed my life to the earth, and made me feel as if I were among the dead. (My enemy: the enemy has pursued me, crushed my life: beaten my life down to the earth, made me feel as if I were among the dead: made me dwell in darkness like the dead) **4.** My spirit is exhausted, and my heart is weighed down with despair. (My heart is weighed down: my spirit is overwhelmed within me, my heart: my heart within me is desolate) **5.** I reflect on the days gone by; I recall Your mighty works and think about the things You have done. (Recall Your mighty works: I meditate on all your works, think about the things You have done: muse on the work of your hands) **6.** I lift my hands to You in prayer; my soul thirsts for You like a dry and barren land. Selah. (My soul thirsts for You: my soul thirsts after Thee, like a dry land) **7.** Hurry, O Lord, to answer me, for my spirit is weak. Do not hide Your face from me, or I will be like those who descend into the grave. (Answer me quickly: Hear me speedily, O Lord; I am weak: my spirit faileth) **8.** Let me hear Your loving kindness each morning, for I place my trust in You. Show me the path I should walk, for I surrender my soul to You. (Show me the path: cause me to know the way, I surrender my soul: for I lift up my soul unto thee) **9.** Rescue me from my enemies, O Lord, for I have taken refuge in You. (Rescue me: Deliver me from mine enemies, I have taken refuge in You: I flee to thee for refuge) **10.** Teach me to follow Your will, for You are my God. Your good Spirit will guide me on the straight path. (Your good Spirit: Thy spirit is good, Guide me on the straight path: lead me into the land of uprightness) **11.** Give me new life, O Lord, for Your name's sake. In Your righteousness, bring me out of this distress. (Give me new life: Quicken me, O Lord, in Your righteousness: for thy righteousness' sake bring my soul out of trouble) **12.** In Your mercy, destroy my enemies and put an end to those who oppress my soul, for I belong to You. (Destroy my enemies: cut off mine enemies, put an end to those who oppress me: destroy all them that afflict my soul)

Chapter 144
1. Praised be the Lord, my strength, who trains my hands for battle and my fingers for combat. (battle: warfare, struggle) **2.** He is my goodness, my fortress, my high tower, my deliverer, my shield, and in Him I place my trust; He subdues my enemies under me. (subdues: conquers, brings under control) **3.** Lord, what is mankind that You take notice of him? Or the son of man that You regard him so highly? (regard: consider, respect) **4.** Human life is fleeting, like a breath; their days pass like a shadow that vanishes. (fleeting: short-lived; shadow: image, fleeting presence) **5.** Stretch out Your heavens, O Lord, and come down; touch the mountains and cause them to smoke. (smoke: emit fire and vapor) **6.** Let Your lightning flash and scatter them; send Your arrows and destroy them. (scatter: disperse, spread; destroy: annihilate, wipe out) **7.** Reach down from on high and rescue me, deliver me from the deep waters, and from the grasp of foreign nations. (foreign: unfamiliar, strange) **8.** Their words are empty and false, and their right hand is deceitful. (deceitful: dishonest, fraudulent) **9.** I will sing a new song to You, O God, and I will play music on a ten-stringed instrument to praise You. (ten-stringed: referring to a type of stringed instrument) **10.** It is You who grants deliverance to kings, who rescues David, Your servant, from the harmful sword. (harmful: dangerous, injurious) **11.** Free me and deliver me from the hands of foreign nations, whose words are deceitful and whose hands are full of falsehood. (falsehood: lies, deception) **12.** May our sons grow strong, like plants nurtured in their youth; may our daughters be like polished cornerstones in a palace. (cornerstones: foundational stones, pillars) **13.** May our barns be full, providing every kind of good; may our flocks multiply in the fields, and may our streets be filled with abundance. (barns: storage, granaries; abundance: plenty) **14.** May our oxen be strong for labor; may there be no breach in our walls or complaints in our streets. (breach: break, hole; complaints: grievances, murmurs) **15.** Blessed is the people who are so situated; blessed is the people whose God is the Lord. (situated: placed, in such a condition)

Chapter 145
1. I will exalt You, my God, O King, and I will bless Your name eternally. (exalt: lift up, praise; eternally: forever) **2.** Each day I will bless You, and Your name I will praise forevermore. (praise: express admiration, worship; forevermore: for all time) **3.** The LORD is

magnificent, and His praise is beyond measure; His greatness cannot be fully understood. (magnificent: grand, impressive; beyond measure: immeasurable) **4.** One generation will recount Your deeds to the next, and will speak of Your mighty works. (recount: tell, narrate; mighty works: powerful acts) **5.** I will proclaim the honor of Your splendor, and speak of Your marvelous works. (splendor: brilliance, grandeur; marvelous: extraordinary) **6.** People will speak of the awesome power of Your acts, and I will declare Your greatness. (awesome: inspiring awe or fear) **7.** They will overflow with the remembrance of Your abundant goodness, and will sing of Your just ways. (overflow: be filled, brimming; abundant: plentiful) **8.** The LORD is compassionate and full of grace; He is slow to anger and great in mercy. (compassionate: sympathetic, caring; grace: kindness, unmerited favor) **9.** The LORD is kind to all, and His tender mercies extend to all He has made. (kind: gentle, considerate; tender mercies: deep compassion) **10.** All Your works will praise You, O LORD, and Your devoted followers will bless You. (devoted: dedicated, loyal) **11.** They will speak of the glorious majesty of Your reign, and talk about the might of Your power. (reign: rule, authority) **12.** To make known to mankind Your mighty deeds and the splendor of Your kingdom. (mankind: humanity, all people; splendor: brilliance, grandeur) **13.** Your kingdom is everlasting, and Your dominion lasts throughout all generations. (everlasting: without end; dominion: rule, authority) **14.** The LORD supports those who fall and raises up those who are bowed low. (supports: strengthens, upholds; bowed low: humbled, bent) **15.** The eyes of all creatures look to You, and You provide for them in due time. (creatures: living beings, animals; due time: the right moment) **16.** You open Your hand and satisfy the desires of every living being. (satisfy: meet, fulfill; desires: longings, needs) **17.** The LORD is righteous in all His ways, and holy in all His deeds. (righteous: just, morally right; holy: pure, sacred) **18.** The LORD is near to all who call on Him, to all who call on Him in truth. (near: close, accessible) **19.** He will grant the desires of those who revere Him; He will hear their cry and deliver them. (revere: honor, respect; deliver: rescue) **20.** The LORD protects all who love Him, but He will destroy all the wicked. (protects: keeps safe, guards) **21.** My mouth will declare the praises of the LORD, and all living beings will bless His holy name forevermore. (declare: announce, proclaim; forevermore: for all time)

Chapter 146

1. Praise the LORD, all that I am, praise His holy name (praise: express gratitude or admiration). **2.** While I still have breath, I will praise the LORD; I will sing songs of praise to my God as long as I live (breath: life force, vitality). **3.** Do not rely on rulers or on mortal men who cannot save you (rely: depend, trust; rulers: those in power; mortal: subject to death). **4.** Their life is fleeting; they return to dust, and their thoughts vanish the moment they die (fleeting: short-lived, temporary; vanish: disappear, fade away). **5.** Blessed is the one who has the God of Jacob as their help, whose hope is firmly placed in the LORD (blessed: fortunate, happy; hope: expectation, trust). **6.** He is the Creator of heaven and earth, the sea, and everything in it; He is faithful to keep His promises forever (Creator: maker, originator; faithful: loyal, true; promises: commitments). **7.** He upholds justice for the oppressed, provides food for the hungry, and releases those in chains (upholds: supports, defends; justice: fairness, righteousness; oppressed: mistreated, suffering). **8.** The LORD gives sight to the blind, raises up the humble, and loves those who are righteous (gives sight: restores vision; humble: lowly, meek; righteous: morally right, just). **9.** He watches over foreigners, cares for the orphan and widow, but He overturns the plans of the wicked (watches over: protects, guards; foreigners: strangers, outsiders; overturns: reverses, destroys). **10.** The LORD will reign forever, O Zion, your God will reign throughout all generations. Praise the LORD! (reign: rule, govern; generations: groups of people born in the same period).

Chapter 147

1. Praise the LORD! How good it is to sing songs of gratitude to our God; it is a delightful and fitting thing to do (delightful: pleasing, enjoyable; fitting: appropriate, suitable). **2.** The LORD strengthens Jerusalem; He gathers the exiled people of Israel (strengthens: fortifies, supports; exiled: cast out, displaced). **3.** He mends the hearts of the brokenhearted and bandages their wounds (mends: heals, repairs; wounds: injuries, hurts). **4.** He knows the number of the stars, calling each one by its name (knows: counts, recognizes; calling: naming, summoning). **5.** Our LORD is great and mighty in strength; His wisdom has no end (wisdom: understanding, insight). **6.** The LORD exalts the humble, but He brings the proud down low (exalts: lifts up, elevates; proud: arrogant, haughty). **7.** Sing to the LORD with grateful hearts; praise Him with music and songs on the harp (grateful: thankful, appreciative). **8.** He blankets the heavens with clouds, sends rain upon the earth, and causes the grass to grow on the hills (blankets: covers, spreads; causes: makes, brings about). **9.** He feeds the creatures of the field and provides for the young ravens when they cry for food (feeds: nourishes, sustains; ravens: large, black birds). **10.** The LORD takes no delight in the strength of horses or in the swift legs of men (delight: joy, pleasure; swift: fast, quick). **11.** The LORD delights in those who fear Him, in those who place their hope in His steadfast love (delights: takes pleasure, enjoys; steadfast: unwavering, constant). **12.** Praise the LORD, O Jerusalem; praise your God, O Zion (praise: honor, glorify). **13.** He has made your gates secure; He has blessed your children within you (secure: strong, protected; blessed: favored, enriched). **14.** He brings peace to your borders and fills you with the finest wheat (borders: boundaries, edges; fills: provides, supplies). **15.** He sends His command across the earth, and His word moves swiftly (moves: travels, spreads; swiftly: quickly, rapidly). **16.** He gives snow like wool and scatters frost like ashes (scatters: spreads, distributes). **17.** He casts ice like small pieces of food; who can withstand the power of His cold? (casts: throws, sends out; withstand: endure, resist). **18.** He sends out His word and the ice melts; He causes the wind to blow, and the waters flow (melts: dissolves, thaws; flows: moves, runs). **19.** He has made known His word to Jacob, His laws and commands to Israel (made known: revealed, disclosed; laws: rules, commands). **20.** He has not done this for any other nation; as for His judgments, they do not know them. Praise the LORD (done: given, bestowed; judgments: decrees, rulings).

Chapter 148

1. Praise the LORD! Praise Him from the heavens, praise Him from the highest places (heavens: sky, celestial realms; highest: uppermost). **2.** Praise Him, all you angels, praise Him, all you heavenly armies (angels: messengers, celestial beings; armies: hosts, heavenly battalions). **3.** Praise Him, sun and moon; praise Him, all you stars that shine (shine: gleam, sparkle). **4.** Praise Him, you who are in the heavens above, and you waters above the sky (heavens: skies, expanse; waters: clouds, mist). **5.** Let them praise the name of the LORD, for He spoke and they came into being (spoke: commanded, decreed; came into being: were created). **6.** He made them firm forever; His decree remains unshaken (firm: stable, secure; decree: command, law; unshaken: unalterable). **7.** Praise the LORD from the earth, you creatures of the sea and all depths (creatures: beings, animals; depths: abyss, ocean). **8.** Lightning, hail, snow, and mist, stormy winds that obey His word (lightning: electric discharge; hail: ice pellets; mist: vapor; obey: follow, carry out). **9.** You mountains and all hills, you trees that bear fruit and all cedars (bear fruit: produce fruit, yield crops; cedars: tall trees, evergreens). **10.** Beasts of the field and all livestock, creatures that crawl and birds that fly (beasts: wild animals, creatures; livestock: domesticated animals). **11.** Kings of the earth and all people, rulers and judges of the world (rulers: monarchs, leaders; judges: magistrates, authorities). **12.** Young men and women, the elderly and children (women: maidens, virgins; elderly: older adults, seniors). **13.** Let them all praise the name of the LORD, for His name alone is supreme;

His glory exceeds the earth and the sky (supreme: highest, greatest; glory: majesty, grandeur; exceeds: surpasses, transcends). **14.** He has raised up the strength of His people, the praise of all His faithful ones, the children of Israel, a people near to Him. Praise the LORD! (raised up: elevated, strengthened; faithful: devoted, loyal; near: close, intimate).

Chapter 149
1. Praise the LORD! Sing to Him a new song, and let His praises fill the assembly of His faithful followers (followers: people who support or believe in something). **2.** Let Israel rejoice in the Creator who made them, and let the children of Zion celebrate in their King (Zion: a biblical name for Jerusalem or God's people). **3.** Let them praise His name with joyful dancing, and sing praises to Him with tambourines and harps (tambourines: a musical instrument). **4.** For the LORD delights in His people; He will crown the humble with salvation (delights: takes great pleasure, humble: modest, not proud; crown: to give honor). **5.** Let the saints rejoice in their glory; let them sing aloud on their beds (saints: holy or good people; glory: great honor or praise). **6.** Let the praises of God be on their lips, and a sharp sword in their hands (sword: a weapon). **7.** To bring judgment upon the nations, and punish the people (nations: large groups of people or countries). **8.** To bind their kings with chains, and their rulers with iron shackles (bind: tie up; rulers: leaders; shackles: chains or restraints). **9.** To carry out the written judgment: this honor is given to all His faithful servants (servants: those who serve or follow someone). Praise the LORD!

Chapter 150
1. Praise the LORD! Give praise to God in His holy place; praise Him for His power in the heavens (holy place: a sacred area; power: great strength or ability). **2.** Praise Him for His great works; praise Him according to His magnificent greatness (works: deeds or actions; magnificent: impressive in appearance or size). **3.** Praise Him with the blast of the trumpet; praise Him with stringed instruments and the harp (blast: a loud sound; stringed: having strings like a violin or guitar). **4.** Praise Him with tambourines and dancing; praise Him with stringed instruments and pipes (tambourines: small hand-held percussion instruments; pipes: wind instruments like flutes). **5.** Praise Him with loud cymbals; praise Him with clashing cymbals (cymbals: flat, round metal plates used in music; clashing: striking together). **6.** Let all things that breathe praise the LORD. Praise the LORD!

20 – Proverbs
Chapter 1
1. These are the proverbs of Solomon, the son of David, king of Israel. (Solomon: King of Israel; David: King of Israel) **2.** To gain wisdom and guidance, and to understand the words of insight. (Wisdom: the ability to make good decisions; Insight: understanding) **3.** To accept wisdom's teaching, justice, and fairness, along with equity. (Justice: fairness; Equity: impartiality) **4.** To offer prudence to the inexperienced and knowledge and discretion to young men. (Prudence: caution; Discretion: good judgment) **5.** A wise person will listen and grow in learning; a discerning individual will seek wise advice. (Discerning: insightful) **6.** To comprehend proverbs and their meaning, and the words of the wise, including their riddles. (Proverbs: short wise sayings; Riddles: complex statements) **7.** The fear of the LORD is the foundation of knowledge, but fools reject wisdom and instruction. (Fear: respect; LORD: God; Foundation: basis) **8.** My child, listen to your father's teaching, and do not forsake your mother's guidance. (Forsake: abandon) **9.** They will be like a crown of grace on your head, and a necklace around your neck. (Grace: favor) **10.** My child, if sinners try to entice you, do not agree. (Sinners: wrongdoers; Entice: tempt) **11.** If they say, "Join us, let's ambush the innocent for no reason," (Ambush: attack unexpectedly) **12.** "Let's swallow them alive like the grave, whole, like those who go down into the pit," (Grave: a place where people are buried; Pit: a deep hole) **13.** "We'll find all kinds of valuable things; we'll fill our houses with stolen goods," (Valuable things: precious possessions) **14.** "Throw in your lot with us, and let's all share the same purse." (Lot: share; Purse: money) **15.** My child, do not walk along their path; avoid their way. **16.** For their feet rush to evil, and they are quick to shed blood. (Evil: wrong actions; Shed blood: kill) **17.** It is futile to spread a net in full view of a bird. (Futile: useless; Net: trap) **18.** They are setting a trap for their own lives; they are lying in wait for their own destruction. (Trap: a device to catch someone; Destruction: downfall) **19.** The paths of greed lead to death, as it robs its victims of life. (Greed: desire for more than one needs) **20.** Wisdom calls out in the streets, raising her voice in the public squares. **21.** She speaks at the city gates, proclaiming her message. (City gates: where people gather) **22.** "How long will you simple ones love simplicity? How long will mockers delight in mocking, and fools hate knowledge?" (Simple ones: naive people; Mockers: those who make fun of others; Fools: unwise people) **23.** Turn to me when I correct you; I will pour out my spirit to you and share my words with you. (Spirit: influence) **24.** Because I have called out, and you refused; I stretched out my hand, but no one paid attention. **25.** You rejected all my advice and did not accept my rebuke. (Rebuke: correction) **26.** I will laugh at your disaster and mock when fear strikes you. (Disaster: trouble; Fear: terror) **27.** When your fear comes like a storm, and your destruction like a whirlwind, when distress and anguish overwhelm you, (Storm: strong wind; Whirlwind: a powerful rotating wind; Distress: anxiety; Anguish: sorrow) **28.** Then you will call to me, but I will not answer; you will seek me, but will not find me. **29.** Because you hated knowledge and did not choose the fear of the LORD, (Knowledge: wisdom; Fear: respect; LORD: God) **30.** You ignored my counsel and despised my correction. (Counsel: advice; Correction: guidance) **31.** Therefore, you will eat the fruit of your ways and be filled with the consequences of your actions. (Fruit: results; Consequences: outcome) **32.** The turning away of the naive will kill them, and the complacency of fools will destroy them. (Naive: easily deceived people; Complacency: self-satisfaction) **33.** But whoever listens to me will live in safety, free from the fear of harm. (Safety: security)

Chapter 2
1. My son, if you accept my teachings and treasure my commands; (commands: instructions) **2.** Listening to wisdom and focusing your heart on understanding; (wisdom: knowledge, understanding: clarity) **3.** If you cry out for knowledge and seek understanding; **4.** If you search for it like silver, and look for it like hidden treasure; (hidden: concealed) **5.** Then you will understand the fear of the LORD and find the knowledge of God. **6.** The LORD gives wisdom, and from His mouth come knowledge and understanding. **7.** He stores wisdom for the righteous, and protects those who live honestly. (righteous: just, uprightly: honestly) **8.** He watches over the paths of justice and preserves the way of His faithful. (faithful: holy ones) **9.** Then you will understand what is right, just, and fair; every good path. (fair: equitable) **10.** When wisdom fills your heart, and knowledge delights your soul; **11.** Discretion (judgment) will protect you, and understanding will guard you; **12.** To save you from the evil man, from those who speak perversely; (crooked: dishonest) **13.** Who leave the paths of uprightness and walk in darkness; **14.** Who delight in doing evil and rejoice in wickedness; **15.** Whose ways are twisted and crooked; (twisted: distorted) **16.** To rescue you from the immoral woman, from the one who flatters with her words; (flatters: praises falsely) **17.** Who abandons her youth's guidance and forgets her God's covenant. (guide: mentor) **18.** For her house leads to death, and her paths to the grave. (grave: pointing toward destruction) **19.** None who follow her return or find the paths of life. **20.** So you can walk with the righteous and keep their ways. (good: virtuous) **21.** The upright will live in the land, and the blameless will remain there. (blameless: innocent) **22.** But the wicked will be cut off from the earth, and sinners will be removed from it. (wicked: evil)

Chapter 3

1. My son, don't forget my law; keep my commandments in your heart (law: God's instructions or divine principles). **2.** They will add years to your life and bring you peace (peace: calmness). **3.** Don't let mercy and truth leave you; wear them around your neck and write them in your heart (mercy: kindness, truth: honesty). **4.** Then you will find favor and understanding with God and people (favor: approval, understanding: insight). **5.** Trust the LORD with all your heart; don't rely on your own understanding (understanding: judgment). **6.** Acknowledge Him in all your ways, and He will guide your path (acknowledge: submit, guide: lead). **7.** Don't think you're wise; fear the LORD and avoid evil (fear: reverence). **8.** It will bring health to your body and strength to your bones (health: well-being, body: physical self). **9.** Honor the LORD with your wealth and the first fruits of all your increase (honor: respect, wealth: money, first fruits: first harvested crops). **10.** Then your barns will overflow, and your vats will be full of wine (barns: storage for crops, vats: containers for liquids). **11.** My son, don't despise the LORD's discipline, and don't grow weary of His correction (discipline: training, weary: tired). **12.** The LORD corrects those He loves, just like a father corrects the son he delights in (corrects: teaches, delights: takes pleasure in). **13.** Blessed is the man who finds wisdom, and the man who gains understanding (blessed: happy, wisdom: good judgment). **14.** Wisdom is more valuable than silver, and her profit is better than fine gold (profit: spiritual gain, fine gold: precious gold). **15.** She is more precious than rubies, and nothing you desire can compare to her (precious: valuable, rubies: red gems). **16.** Long life is in her right hand, and wealth and honor are in her left (right hand: power, left hand: resources). **17.** Her paths are pleasant, and all her ways lead to peace (paths: directions, pleasant: enjoyable, ways: methods). **18.** She is a tree of life to those who take hold of her; those who hold her fast are happy (tree of life: source of life, hold fast: keep). **19.** The LORD used wisdom to create the earth and understanding to establish the heavens (earth: world, heavens: sky). **20.** By His knowledge, the depths were opened, and the clouds give rain (depths: oceans, clouds: vapor). **21.** My son, don't let wisdom and discretion leave you; keep them close (discretion: carefulness). **22.** They will give life to your soul and grace to your neck (soul: inner self, grace: favor). **23.** You will walk safely, and your feet won't stumble (stumble: trip). **24.** You won't be afraid when you lie down; your sleep will be peaceful (lie down: rest, peaceful: calm). **25.** Don't fear sudden danger or the destruction of the wicked when it comes (destruction: ruin, wicked: evil). **26.** The LORD will be your confidence and keep you from falling (confidence: trust, falling: failing). **27.** Don't withhold good from those who deserve it when you have the power to help (withhold: hold back). **28.** Don't tell your neighbor, "Come back tomorrow," when you can help today (neighbor: nearby person). **29.** Don't plan harm against your neighbor who lives peacefully with you (harm: injury, peacefully: without conflict). **30.** Don't quarrel with someone who hasn't harmed you (quarrel: argue). **31.** Don't envy the violent or choose any of their ways (envy: be jealous, violent: aggressive). **32.** The LORD hates the perverse, but His secret is with the righteous (perverse: crooked, righteous: morally right). **33.** The LORD's curse is on the house of the wicked, but He blesses the home of the righteous (curse: bad luck, blesses: gives favor). **34.** He mocks the mockers, but gives grace to the humble (mockers: those who make fun, humble: modest). **35.** The wise will be honored, but fools will experience shame (honored: respected, fools: unwise).

Chapter 4

1. Listen, children, to a father's teaching, and pay attention to gain wisdom (wisdom: knowledge and good judgment) **2.** I give you good guidance; do not abandon my law (guidance: direction, law: rules) **3.** I was my father's son, cherished and loved by my mother. (cherished: dearly loved) **4.** He taught me and said, "Keep my words in your heart; follow my commands, and live." (commands: instructions) **5.** Get wisdom and understanding; don't forget them, nor stray from my words. (understanding: the ability to grasp ideas, stray: move away) **6.** Don't abandon wisdom, and she will protect you; love her, and she will guard you. (abandon: give up, guard: protect) **7.** Wisdom is the most important thing; so, get wisdom and understanding with all you have. (most important: top priority) **8.** Honor her, and she will lift you up; she will bring you honor when you embrace her. (honor: respect, lift up: raise status or dignity) **9.** She will place a crown of grace on your head and give you glory. (grace: kindness, glory: honor or fame) **10.** Listen, my son, and accept my teachings; your life will be long. (teachings: instructions, long: extended) **11.** I have taught you the way of wisdom; I have guided you in the right path. (path: direction) **12.** Your steps will not be hindered, and you will not stumble when you run. (hindered: blocked, stumble: trip) **13.** Hold tightly to instruction; don't let it go, for she is your life. (instruction: guidance) **14.** Do not walk the path of the wicked, nor follow evil people. (wicked: bad, evil: harmful) **15.** Avoid it, don't go near, turn away, and leave. (avoid: stay away from) **16.** They can't sleep unless they do wrong; their rest is lost unless they cause harm. (wrong: bad actions, harm: damage) **17.** They feast on wickedness and drink the wine of violence. (feast: enjoy greatly, wickedness: evil actions, violence: use of force) **18.** But the righteous path is like light, shining brighter until the full day. (righteous: good, full day: perfect time) **19.** The way of the wicked is dark, and they don't know what causes them to stumble. (dark: unclear, stumble: trip or fall) **20.** My son, pay attention to my words and listen carefully. (pay attention: focus, carefully: with thought) **21.** Keep them in front of you, and let them stay in your heart. (front: ahead, stay: remain) **22.** They are life to those who find them and health to their body. (health: well-being) **23.** Guard your heart diligently, for it determines your life. (guard: protect, diligently: with careful attention, determines: decides) **24.** Remove corrupt speech, and keep deceitful lips far away from you. (corrupt: dishonest, deceitful: misleading) **25.** Let your eyes focus ahead, and keep your gaze straight. (gaze: look steadily) **26.** Think carefully about your path, and make sure all your ways are firm. (firm: stable) **27.** Don't turn aside to the right or left; keep away from evil. (turn aside: change direction, keep away from: avoid)

Chapter 5

1. My son, listen to my wisdom and understand. (Insight: understanding) **2.** So you value discretion and speak with knowledge. (Judgment: wise decision-making) **3.** The lips of an immoral woman are sweet like honey, and her mouth is smooth as oil. **4.** But her end is bitter like wormwood, sharp as a sword. (Wormwood: a bitter, poisonous plant) **5.** Her feet lead to death, her steps to the grave. (Grave: hell) **6.** Her ways are unpredictable, you can't understand them. (Unpredictable: not fixed) **7.** Listen, children, and don't turn from my words. **8.** Stay far from her and don't come near her house. **9.** Otherwise, you'll give your honor to others and your years to the cruel. **10.** Strangers will take your wealth, and your work will benefit others. **11.** You'll regret it when your body wastes away. **12.** You'll say, "I hated instruction and despised correction." (Instruction: teaching, correction: rebuke) **13.** I didn't obey my teachers or listen to those who taught me. **14.** I almost fell into evil in the assembly. (Assembly: group) **15.** Drink from your own well and cistern. (Cistern: reservoir) **16.** Let your streams flow freely, and rivers in the streets. **17.** Let them be only yours, not for others. **18.** Be blessed and find joy in your wife's love. **19.** Let her satisfy you, and be captivated by her love. **20.** Why be captivated by another woman and embrace someone else's body? **21.** The LORD sees all man's ways and examines his actions. **22.** The wicked will be trapped by their own sins, bound by their wrongdoings. (Wrongdoings: sins) **23.** He will die without correction, and in foolishness, he will go astray. (Foolishness: lack of wisdom, correction: teaching)

Chapter 6

1. My son, if you guarantee for a friend or make an agreement with a stranger, (Guarantee: promise) **2.** You're trapped by your words, caught by what you say. (Trapped: caught) **3.** Free yourself, son, when you're in your friend's power; humble yourself and fix it. (Control: authority) **4.** Don't let sleep overtake you or close your eyes. (Sleep: rest) **5.** Escape like a deer from the hunter, like a bird from the trapper. (trap: snare) **6.** Go to the ant, you lazy one; learn from her ways. (Lazy: idle) **7.** She has no guide or ruler, (supervisor: overseer) **8.** Yet she gathers food in summer and harvests what she needs. (Collects: gathers) **9.** How long will you sleep, O lazy one? When will you wake up? (Rest: slothful inactivity) **10.** A little more sleep, a little more rest— **11.** And poverty will come like a traveler, and need like an armed man. **12.** A wicked person speaks deceitfully. (Evil: wicked, lying: deceitful) **13.** He signals with his eyes, feet, and fingers; (signals: gestures) **14.** He plans evil and stirs up conflict. (Plans: devises, conflict: disagreement) **15.** His disaster will come suddenly, and he will be broken without remedy. (Disaster: calamity, fix: solution) **16.** The LORD hates six things; seven are an abomination to Him. (Disgusting: abomination) **17.** A proud look, a lying tongue, and hands that shed innocent blood, **18.** A heart that plans evil, feet that run to evil, (Plans: devises) **19.** A false witness who speaks lies, and one who stirs up division among brothers. (Division: discord) **20.** My son, keep your father's command and don't forsake your mother's teaching. (Abandon: forsake) **21.** Keep them close to your heart, tie them around your neck. (Always: constantly) **22.** They will guide you, protect you, and speak to you. **23.** The command is a lamp, the law is light, and correction is the way of life. (Discipline: correction) **24.** To keep you from the evil woman and her flattering words. (Sweet-talking: deceptive) **25.** Don't desire her beauty or let her captivate you. (Seduce: allure) **26.** A man is brought to poverty by an immoral woman; the adulteress hunts for his life. (Bad: immoral, cheating: adulteress) **27.** Can a man hold fire in his chest and not be burned? **28.** Can one walk on hot coals and not burn his feet? **29.** So, he who sleeps with his neighbor's wife will not go unpunished. (Unpunished: guilt-free) **30.** A thief is not despised if he steals to satisfy his hunger, (dislike: despise) **31.** But if caught, he must repay sevenfold, giving all he has. (Seven times: sevenfold, wealth: possessions) **32.** He who commits adultery lacks understanding and destroys his soul. (Understanding: wisdom) **33.** He will be wounded and dishonored, and his shame will not be erased. (Disgrace: humiliation) **34.** Jealousy is a man's fury; he will not spare in revenge. (Anger: rage, revenge: retribution) **35.** He will not accept any ransom, even if many gifts are offered. (Payment: ransom, relentless: unyielding)

Chapter 7
1. My son, keep my words, and store my commands in your heart. (heart: mind) **2.** Obey my commands and live; value my law deeply. (deeply: strongly) **3.** Tie them to your fingers; write them on your heart. **4.** Call wisdom your sister, and understanding your close friend. (friend: companion) **5.** They will protect you from the unfaithful woman, whose words deceive. (deceive: lie) **6.** I looked through my window. (window: opening for light or air) **7.** and saw among the foolish, a young man lacking wisdom. (foolish: unwise, wisdom: understanding) **8.** walking by her street, heading toward her house. **9.** It was evening, and the night was dark. (dark: black) **10.** A woman met him, dressed like a prostitute, and clever in her heart. (clever: sly, heart: mind) **11.** She is loud and rebellious, never at home. (loud: noisy, rebellious: stubborn) **12.** Now outside, now in the streets, waiting at every corner. **13.** She caught him, kissed him, and boldly said. (boldly: without shame) **14.** I have peace offerings; today I fulfilled my vows. (peace offerings: sacrifices, vows: promises) **15.** I came to find you, and here you are. **16.** I have made my bed with fine decorations. (decorations: fancy designs) **17.** and perfumed it with myrrh, aloes, and cinnamon. (perfumed: fragranced, myrrh: a sweet-smelling resin, aloes: fragrant wood, cinnamon: a spice) **18.** Come, let us enjoy love until morning, and comfort ourselves. (love: passion, comfort: make happy) **19.** For my husband is away on a long trip. **20.** and will return at the set time. (set time: appointed hour) **21.** Her flattering words persuaded him; with her lips, she led him. (flattering: sweet-talking) **22.** He followed her quickly, like an ox to slaughter, or a fool to punishment. (ox: cow, slaughter: killing, fool: someone unwise, punishment: discipline) **23.** Until an arrow strikes his heart; like a bird rushing to a trap, unaware it's deadly. (arrow: sharp weapon, heart: inner self, trap: danger) **24.** Listen to me, children, and pay attention to my words. (children: young ones) **25.** Don't let your heart turn to her ways; don't stray down her paths. (stray: wander) **26.** She has caused many to fall; even strong men have been defeated by her. (fall: fail, defeated: overcome) **27.** Her house leads to death, to the chambers of hell. (death: destruction, chambers: rooms, hell: place of punishment after death)

Chapter 8
1. Does wisdom not cry out? And understanding raises her voice? (Wisdom: deep knowledge; Understanding: ability to comprehend) **2.** She stands at the highest points, by the wayside, at the crossroads. (Crossroads: where roads meet) **3.** She calls at the gates, at the city entrance, and at the doors. (Gates: city entrances) **4.** To you, O men, I call; my voice is to all mankind. **5.** O simple ones, understand wisdom; and you fools, have a discerning heart (judging rightly). (Simple: lacking knowledge; Fool: someone who acts without wisdom) **6.** Listen; I will speak of excellent things, and my words will be truthful. (Excellent: very good, worthy) **7.** My mouth speaks truth; wickedness is an abomination (disgust) to my lips. (Abomination: something greatly hated) **8.** All my words are righteous; nothing deceitful or crooked is in them. (Righteous: morally right; Deceitful: dishonest; Crooked: dishonest) **9.** They are clear to those who understand, and right to those who seek knowledge. (Clear: easy to understand) **10.** Receive my teaching, not silver; and knowledge, rather than fine gold. (Teaching: instructions) **11.** For wisdom is better than rubies; nothing desired compares to it. (Rubies: precious red stones) **12.** I, wisdom, dwell with prudence, and discover knowledge of clever ideas. (Prudence: carefulness; Clever: intelligent) **13.** The fear of the LORD is to hate evil: pride, arrogance, and the wicked way, I hate. (Fear: deep respect; Arrogance: overconfidence) **14.** Counsel is mine, and sound wisdom; I am understanding; I have strength. (Counsel: advice; Sound: solid, reliable) **15.** By me kings reign, and rulers make just laws. (Reign: rule) **16.** By me princes govern, and all judges of the earth. (Govern: lead, rule) **17.** I love those who love me; and those who seek me early will find me. (Early: with eagerness, first) **18.** Riches and honor are with me; yes, lasting wealth and righteousness. (Lasting: continuing over time) **19.** My fruit is better than gold, even fine gold; and my profit more than silver. (Fruit: results, benefits) **20.** I lead in the way of righteousness, in the paths of justice. (Righteousness: goodness, moral right) **21.** I give those who love me an inheritance; I fill their treasuries. (Inheritance: gifts passed down) **22.** The LORD made me at the beginning of His creation, before His ancient works. (Ancient: very old, from the past) **23.** I was established from eternity, before the earth began. (Eternity: forever) **24.** When there were no deep waters, I was brought forth; when there were no springs of water. (Brought forth: created) **25.** Before the mountains were set in place, before the hills, I was born. (Mountains: large landforms) **26.** Before He made the earth, fields, or the dust of the world. (Fields: large areas of land) **27.** When He set the heavens, I was there; when He marked out the depths. (Heavens: sky, outer space) **28.** When He made the clouds above, and strengthened the fountains of the deep. (Clouds: vaporized water in the sky; Fountains: water sources) **29.** When He set the sea's boundaries, that its waters should not pass His command, when He laid the earth's foundations. (Boundaries: limits; Foundations: bases) **30.** Then I was with Him, as a master workman; I was daily His delight, rejoicing always before Him. (Master workman: expert creator) **31.** Rejoicing in the inhabited part of the earth, and my delight was with the sons of men. (Inhabited: lived in) **32.** Now listen to me, O children: blessed are those who

keep my ways. (Blessed: happy, favored) **33.** Listen to instruction, be wise, and do not reject it. (Instruction: guidance, teaching) **34.** Blessed is the man who hears me, watching daily at my gates, waiting at my doors. (Watching: observing, waiting) **35.** For whoever finds me finds life, and will receive favor from the LORD. (Favor: approval, blessing) **36.** But those who sin against me harm their own soul; all who hate me love death. (Sin: wrongdoings; Harm: cause injury)

Chapter 9

1. Wisdom has built her house, with seven strong pillars. (Seven pillars: firm foundation) **2.** She has prepared her animals, mixed her wine, and set the table. (Animals: beasts; Wine: drink) **3.** She calls out from the city's highest places, sending her maidens. **4.** "Let the naive come here; those lacking wisdom, listen." (Naive: simple, lacking wisdom) **5.** "Come, eat my bread, drink the wine I have mixed." (Bread: food, Wine: drink) **6.** "Leave foolishness and live; follow the path of understanding." (Foolishness: folly) **7.** Correcting a mocker brings shame; rebuking the wicked stains you. (Mocker: one who mocks, Stains: marks badly) **8.** Don't correct a mocker, or they will hate you; rebuke a wise man, and he will love you. (Rebuke: correct) **9.** Teach a wise man, and he will grow wiser; instruct a righteous man, and he will learn more. (Wise: smart, Instruct: teach, Righteous: just) **10.** The fear of the Lord is the beginning of wisdom; knowing the holy is understanding. (Fear of the Lord: reverence, Holy: sacred) **11.** Through me, your days will be long, and your life will increase. (Increase: grow) **12.** If you are wise, it benefits you alone; if you mock, you suffer alone. (Mock: make fun of) **13.** A foolish woman is loud, naive, and ignorant. (Naive: unaware, Ignorant: unknowing) **14.** She sits at the door of her house, in the city's high places, (House: home, City: high place) **15.** Calling to those passing by on their way. (Passing by: walking past) **16.** "Let the naive come here; those lacking wisdom, listen." (Naive: simple, Lacking wisdom: without understanding) **17.** "Stolen water is sweet; secret bread is pleasant." (Stolen: taken without permission, Secret: hidden) **18.** But they don't know the dead are there, and her guests are in the depths of the grave. (Dead: the deceased, Grave: death, Depths of the grave: place of death)

Chapter 10

1. The proverbs of Solomon: A wise son makes his father happy, but a foolish one brings grief to his mother. **2.** Wicked treasures are useless, but righteousness saves from death. (useless: not helpful) **3.** The LORD won't let the righteous go hungry, but He rejects the wealth of the wicked. (rejects: turns away) **4.** The lazy become poor, but the diligent grow rich. (diligent: hard-working) **5.** A son who gathers in summer is wise, but one who sleeps during harvest brings shame. **6.** Blessings are on the just, but the wicked face violence. **7.** The memory of the just is a blessing, but the name of the wicked fades. (fades: disappears) **8.** The wise accept guidance, but fools who talk too much will fall. (guidance: advice) **9.** Those who walk uprightly are secure, but those who twist their ways will be exposed. (uprightly: honestly, exposed: revealed) **10.** Winking causes sorrow, but fools who talk too much will fall. **11.** The mouth of the righteous is a source of life, but the wicked spread violence. **12.** Hatred stirs conflict, but love covers all wrongs. **13.** Wisdom is found in the lips of the understanding, but a fool faces punishment. (understanding: wise) **14.** Wise people store up knowledge, but the fool's speech leads to destruction. (Destruction: ruin) **15.** The rich see wealth as their protection, but the poor are destroyed by poverty. (protection: safety) **16.** The righteous work for life, but the wicked lead to sin. (sin: wrongdoing) **17.** Those who follow instruction are on the path of life, but rejecting correction leads astray. (instruction: teachings, leads astray: off course) **18.** He who hides hatred with lies, or speaks slander, is a fool. (Slander: false accusations) **19.** Many words lead to sin, but those who control their speech are wise. (speech: words) **20.** The tongue of the just is valuable, but the heart of the wicked is worthless. (valuable: precious) **21.** The righteous help many, but fools die for lack of wisdom. **22.** The LORD's blessing makes rich without adding sorrow. (sorrow: pain) **23.** Fools enjoy mischief, but the wise have true understanding. (mischief: trouble) **24.** The wicked's fear will come upon them, but the righteous' desires will be granted. (granted: given) **25.** The wicked are like a passing storm, but the righteous stand firm forever. **26.** Like vinegar to teeth and smoke to eyes, so is the lazy to those who send him. (lazy: inactive) **27.** The fear of the LORD adds years to life, but the wicked's time is shortened. (fear: respect) **28.** The righteous have hope and gladness, but the wicked's hope will vanish. (hope: joy) **29.** The LORD strengthens the upright, but the wicked face destruction. (destruction: ruin, upright: righteous) **30.** The righteous will never be shaken, but the wicked will be removed. (shaken: moved) **31.** The righteous speak wisdom, but the perverse tongue will be silenced. (perverse: twisted) **32.** The lips of the righteous know what is right, but the wicked speak perversely. (perversely: dishonestly)

Chapter 11

1. A false balance is detestable to the LORD, but a just weight pleases Him. (detestable: hated) **2.** Pride brings shame, but humility brings wisdom. (humility: modesty) **3.** The upright's integrity leads them, but the wicked's deceit destroys them. (deceit: dishonesty) **4.** Riches don't help in wrath's day, but righteousness saves from death. (wrath: anger) **5.** The perfect one's righteousness guides him, but the wicked fall by their own evil. (perfect: complete) **6.** The upright are saved by their righteousness, but the wicked are trapped by their own sin. **7.** When the wicked die, their hope vanishes. (vanishes: disappears) **8.** The righteous are rescued from trouble, and the wicked replace them. **9.** A hypocrite destroys with his words, but the just are saved through knowledge. (hypocrite: fake person) **10.** When the righteous prosper, the city rejoices; when the wicked perish, there's celebration. **11.** The city is lifted by the upright's blessing, but ruined by the wicked's words. **12.** A foolish person despises his neighbor, but the wise remain silent. (foolish: lacking wisdom) **13.** A gossip exposes secrets, but the faithful keep things hidden. (gossip: talebearer) **14.** Without counsel, people fall; in many advisors, there's safety. (counsel: advice) **15.** A surety for a stranger will suffer, but avoiding it ensures safety. (surety: guarantee) **16.** A gracious woman keeps honor; strong men keep wealth. **17.** A merciful man benefits his soul, but cruelty harms him. (merciful: kind) **18.** The wicked deceive, but those who sow righteousness receive a reward. (deceive: lie) **19.** Righteousness leads to life; pursuing evil leads to death. **20.** The perverse are detestable to the LORD, but the upright delight Him. (perverse: crooked) **21.** The wicked won't escape punishment, but the righteous will be saved. **22.** A beautiful woman without discretion is like gold in a pig's snout. (discretion: wisdom) **23.** The righteous desire only good; the wicked seek wrath. (wrath: anger) **24.** Some give freely and gain more, while others hoard and end in poverty. (hoard: keep more than needed) **25.** A generous soul prospers, and those who bless others will be blessed. (generous: giving) **26.** He who withholds grain will be cursed, but those who sell it will be blessed. **27.** Seeking good brings favor, but seeking mischief brings harm. (mischief: trouble) **28.** Trusting in riches leads to failure, but the righteous thrive like branches. **29.** A person who causes trouble at home will lose it all; the wise will rule over fools. **30.** The righteous' fruit is a tree of life; winning souls is wise. (fruit: result) **31.** The righteous will be rewarded on earth, much more the wicked and sinner.

Chapter 12

1. Whoever loves instruction loves knowledge, but he who hates correction is foolish. (correction: reproof, foolish: senseless) **2.** A good man finds favor with the LORD, but the wicked will be condemned. (wicked: evil) **3.** Wickedness does not secure a man, but the righteous will stand firm. (firm: established) **4.** A virtuous wife is a crown to her husband, but one who brings shame is like decay in his bones. (decay: rottenness) **5.** The righteous think rightly, but the wicked give deceitful advice. (deceitful: lies) **6.** The words of the wicked lie in wait for harm, but the upright speak deliverance. (deliverance: salvation) **7.** The wicked are destroyed, but the house of the righteous stands. (destroyed: overthrown) **8.** A man is praised for his wisdom, but a crooked heart is despised. (crooked: perverse) **9.** Better to be despised with a servant than to honor oneself and lack food. (lack: hunger) **10.** The righteous care for their animals, but the wicked are cruel even in kindness. (kindness: mercies) **11.** He who works the land will be satisfied with food, but the foolish lack understanding. (foolish: vain) **12.** The wicked crave evil, but the righteous bear good fruit. (crave: desire, fruit: yield) **13.** The wicked are trapped by their words, but the righteous are delivered from trouble. (trapped: snared) **14.** A man is satisfied by the fruit of his words, and his actions will repay him. (repay: recompence) **15.** A fool thinks his way is right, but the wise listen to advice. (advice: counsel) **16.** A fool's anger is quick, but a wise man covers his shame. (anger: wrath) **17.** A truthful speaker shows righteousness, but a false witness spreads lies. (false: deceit) **18.** Some speak like sword blows, but the wise bring healing with their words. (healing: restoration) **19.** Truthful lips endure forever, but lies are short-lived. (short-lived: momentary) **20.** Deceit is in the hearts of those who plan evil, but those who counsel peace find joy. (deceit: dishonesty, counsel: advice) **21.** No harm comes to the righteous, but the wicked are filled with trouble. (harm: evil) **22.** Lying lips are detestable to the LORD, but those who speak truth are His delight. (detestable: repulsive) **23.** A wise man hides knowledge, but a fool openly proclaims his foolishness. (proclaims: reveals) **24.** The diligent will rule, but the lazy will serve. (lazy: slothful) **25.** A heavy heart weighs a man down, but a kind word brings joy. (weighs down: stoops) **26.** The righteous are better than their neighbors, but the wicked lead others astray. (lead astray: mislead) **27.** The lazy do not enjoy what they hunt, but the diligent make their possessions valuable. (diligent: hardworking, possessions: substance) **28.** In the way of righteousness is life; there is no death in its path. (path: journey)

Chapter 13
1. A wise son listens to his father's guidance, but a mocker ignores correction. (mocker: someone who ridicules; correction: guidance) **2.** A man enjoys good from his words, but the wicked bring violence to themselves. (wicked: evil or immoral) **3.** He who controls his tongue protects his life, but a talkative man invites destruction. (talkative: talk too much; destruction: ruin) **4.** The lazy long for more but get nothing, while the diligent prosper. (lazy: unwilling to work; diligent: hardworking) **5.** The righteous hate lies, but the wicked are detestable and end in shame. (detestable: hated by others; shame: disgrace) **6.** Righteousness guards the upright, but wickedness ruins sinners. (upright: morally right; ruins: destroys) **7.** Some grow rich but have nothing, while others become poor yet have great wealth. (wealth: abundance of money or property) **8.** A man's wealth can save his life, but the poor ignore rebuke. (rebuke: criticism or correction) **9.** The righteous shine with joy, but the wicked's light is extinguished. (extinguished: put out) **10.** Pride causes conflict, but the wise avoid it. (pride: arrogance; conflict: disagreement) **11.** Wealth gained by vanity fades, but hard-earned wealth grows. (vanity: excessive pride; fades: diminishes) **12.** Hope delayed makes the heart sick, but fulfilled desire brings joy. (fulfilled: completed or satisfied) **13.** Those who reject the word face ruin, but those who respect commands will be rewarded. (reject: refuse; commands: orders) **14.** The wise's teachings are a life source, keeping them from death's traps. (teachings: lessons; traps: dangers) **15.** Good understanding earns favor, but the way of sinners is hard. (understanding: wisdom) **16.** The prudent act wisely, while fools expose their ignorance. (prudent: careful; ignorance: folly) **17.** A wicked messenger causes trouble, but a faithful one brings health. (wicked: evil; messenger: person delivering a message) **18.** Rejecting instruction leads to poverty and shame, but accepting reproof brings honor. (Instruction: teaching; reproof: correction) **19.** A desire fulfilled is sweet, but fools hate turning from evil. (fulfilled: satisfied; fools: foolish people) **20.** Walking with the wise makes you wise, but fools lead to destruction. (destruction: ruin or collapse) **21.** Sinners are pursued by evil, but the righteous are rewarded with good. (pursued: chased) **22.** A good man leaves an inheritance to his grandchildren, while the sinner's wealth is for the righteous. (inheritance: assets passed down) **23.** The poor's fields yield much food, but some lose it due to poor judgment. (yield: produce; judgment: decision-making) **24.** He who withholds discipline hates his son, but one who loves him corrects him. (withholds: holds back; discipline: training or correction) **25.** The righteous are satisfied, but the wicked go hungry. (satisfied: contented; hungry: lacking food)

Chapter 14
1. Every wise woman builds her home, but the foolish destroy it with their hands. (destroys: ruins) **2.** The one who walks uprightly fears the LORD; the perverse despises Him. (evil: immoral, perverse: corrupt) **3.** The foolish speak proudly, but the wise will protect themselves. (boast: act arrogantly) **4.** Without oxen, the stable is clean, but much gain comes from their strength. (barn: a place for farm animals) **5.** A truthful witness will not lie, but a false witness speaks lies. (untruths: false statements) **6.** The scoffer seeks wisdom but finds none, but knowledge is easy for the understanding. (mock: scorn, scoffer: one who mocks) **7.** Leave the foolish when they lack knowledge. (understanding: insight, wisdom) **8.** The wise understand their path, but fools deceive. (foolishness: lack of wisdom, deceive: mislead) **9.** Fools mock sin, but the righteous find favor. (mockery: disrespect, sin: wrongdoing) **10.** A heart knows its own pain; a stranger does not share in its joy. (sorrow: sadness, bitterness) **11.** The wicked's house will fall, but the upright will prosper. (destroyed: ruined, wicked: evil) **12.** There's a way that seems right, but it leads to death. (end: outcome) **13.** Even in laughter, the heart may be sorrowful; the end of joy is heaviness. (sadness: sorrow, heaviness: sorrowful state) **14.** A backslider is filled with his own ways, but a good man is satisfied with himself. (turns away: returns to wrong, backslider: one who falls back into sin) **15.** The simple believe everything, but the wise consider their steps. (foolish: easily deceived, simple: naive) **16.** The wise fear the LORD and avoid evil, but the fool is reckless. (dangerous: careless, reckless: without care) **17.** Quick anger leads to foolishness, and wicked people are hated. (rage: strong anger, foolishness: lack of sense) **18.** The simple inherit foolishness, but the wise are crowned with knowledge. (silliness: foolish behavior, inheritance) **19.** The evil bow before the good, and the wicked at the gates of the righteous. (humble: show respect, bow: show honor) **20.** The poor are hated even by their neighbors, but the rich have many friends. (despised: disliked, poor: in need) **21.** Whoever despises their neighbor sins, but showing mercy to the poor brings happiness. (rejects: treats with contempt, despises: hates) **22.** Those who plan evil go astray, but mercy and truth belong to those who plan good. (wrongdoing: evil deeds, err: go astray) **23.** Hard work brings profit, but empty words lead to poverty. (speech: talking, words: empty talk) **24.** The Wise's wealth is their crown, but the fool's folly is their disgrace. (shame: dishonor, crown: reward) **25.** A truthful witness saves lives, but a false witness speaks lies. (deceit: falsehoods, false: untrue) **26.** The fear of the LORD is a strong defense, and His children find refuge. (protection: safety, refuge: a safe place) **27.** The fear of the LORD is a source of life, keeping us from death's traps. (danger: harmful situations, snares: traps) **28.** The king's honor is in a large people, but in a lack of people, a prince's ruin. (loss: downfall, ruin: destruction) **29.** A patient person has great understanding, but a quick temper exalts folly. (rage: strong anger, temper: emotional outburst) **30.** A calm heart gives life to the body, but envy rots the bones. (jealousy: bitterness, envy: covetousness) **31.** Oppressing the poor dishonors the Creator, but showing mercy honors Him. (oppresses: treats unfairly, dishonors: disrespects) **32.** The wicked are driven away in their wickedness, but the righteous have hope in death. (sin: evil actions, wicked: morally wrong) **33.** Wisdom rests in the heart of

those who understand, but in fools, it is revealed. (known: made obvious, fools: ignorant people) **34.** Righteousness lifts up a nation, but sin brings disgrace to any people. (shame: dishonor, disgrace: shameful outcome) **35.** The king favors a wise servant, but his wrath is against those who bring shame. (anger: fury, wrath: intense anger)

Chapter 15

1. A gentle answer calms anger, but harsh words stir it up. (Anger: Wrath) **2.** The wise use knowledge well, but fools speak foolishness. (Foolishness: silly talk) **3.** The LORD observes both good and evil everywhere. (LORD: God) **4.** A wholesome tongue gives life, but perverse speech breaks the spirit. (Wholesome: healthy, Perverseness: bad, harmful) **5.** A fool rejects his father's teaching, but a wise person listens to correction. (Teaching: Instruction, Wise: Prudent) **6.** The righteous have much treasure; the wicked's wealth causes trouble. (Treasure: wealth) **7.** The wise spread knowledge, but fools keep it to themselves. **8.** The LORD hates the wicked's sacrifices, but delights in the prayers of the righteous. (Sacrifice: offering) **9.** The LORD hates the ways of the wicked, but loves those who seek righteousness. (Righteousness: right living) **10.** Correction is grievous for those who turn from the right way; those who hate rebuke will perish. (Grievous: painful, rebuke: correction) **11.** Hell and destruction are before the LORD; how much more the hearts of men? (Hell: eternal punishment, Destruction: ruin) **12.** A scorner rejects correction and avoids the wise. (Scorner: mocker) **13.** A cheerful heart makes the face bright, but sorrow breaks the spirit. (Sorrow : grief) **14.** A wise heart seeks knowledge; the fool feeds on foolishness. **15.** The afflicted have evil days, but the cheerful heart enjoys constant joy. (Afflicted : troubled) **16.** Better little with the fear of the LORD than great wealth with trouble. (Fear : reverence, reverence) **17.** Better a simple meal with love than a feast filled with hatred. **18.** A wrathful person causes strife, but a patient person calms it. (Wrathful : angry, Strife : conflict) **19.** The lazy are blocked by obstacles, but the righteous have a clear path. (lazy : Slothful , obstacles: hurdles) **20.** A wise son brings joy to his father, but a foolish one despises his mother. **21.** Folly is fun for the fool, but the wise walk rightly. (Folly : foolishness) **22.** Without counsel, strategies fail, but with many advisors, they succeed. (Counsel : advice, strategies: plans) **23.** A joyful word brings joy, and a timely word is very good. **24.** The way of life leads the wise away from destruction. (Destruction : ruin) **25.** The LORD will destroy the proud but protect the widow. (Widow : woman whose husband has died) **26.** The wicked's thoughts are vile, but pure words are pleasing to the LORD. (Vile : wicked) **27.** Greed ruins a household, but avoiding bribes brings life. (Greedy : wanting too much, Bribes : gifts for favors) **28.** The righteous think before speaking; the wicked speak evil things. **29.** The LORD is far from the wicked but hears the prayers of the righteous. **30.** The light in the eyes brings joy, and a good report strengthens the heart. (Light : joy) **31.** The ear that listens to life's reproof dwells among the wise. (Reproof : correction) **32.** Rejecting instruction harms the soul, but those who accept correction gain understanding. **33.** The fear of the LORD is the beginning of wisdom, and humility comes before honor. (Humility : being humble)

Chapter 16

1. The heart's plans and the tongue's response come from the LORD. **2.** A man's ways seem pure to him, but the LORD weighs the spirit. (judges: evaluates; inner nature: true self) **3.** Commit your actions to the LORD, and your thoughts will be steady. (firm: stable) **4.** The LORD made everything for Himself, even the wicked for the day of trouble. **5.** Pride in the heart is detestable to the LORD; no matter how united they are, the proud will be punished. (disliked: hated) **6.** Mercy and truth cleanse sin; the fear of the LORD turns people from evil. (purify: remove sin) **7.** When a man's ways please the LORD, even his enemies are at peace with him. **8.** Better a little with righteousness than great wealth gained unjustly. (wrongly: unfairly) **9.** A man plans his way, but the LORD directs his steps. (guides: shows the way) **10.** The king's lips speak divine judgment; he does not err in his decisions. (make mistakes: fail) **11.** Just weights and measures belong to the LORD; all the scales are His work. **12.** Kings find wickedness detestable because a throne is built on righteousness. (right behavior: just actions) **13.** Kings delight in righteous speech; they love those who speak truth. **14.** A king's anger is like a messenger of death, but a wise man can calm it. **15.** The king's favor is life; his smile is like the latter rain. (a good season of rain for crops: life-giving) **16.** Wisdom is better than gold, and understanding is more valuable than silver. **17.** The upright avoid evil; those who keep their way protect their soul. (righteous: morally good) **18.** Pride leads to destruction, and arrogance to a fall. (excessive pride: overbearing self-importance) **19.** It's better to be humble with the poor than to share spoil with the proud. (treasure: wealth) **20.** Wise decisions bring good, and trusting in the LORD makes one happy. **21.** The wise are called prudent, and kind words increase learning. (careful: cautious) **22.** Understanding is a fountain of life for the wise, but foolish guidance is folly. (source: spring; foolishness: lack of sense) **23.** The wise heart guides the tongue and adds knowledge to the lips. **24.** Pleasant words are sweet like honey, bringing joy and health to the bones. **25.** There is a way that seems right to a man, but it leads to death. **26.** A man works for himself, for his own needs urge him on. **27.** The wicked dig up evil, and their words are like a raging fire. (strong destructive force: uncontrollable) **28.** A perverse man causes conflict, and a whisperer separates close friends. (contrary: opposing; gossiper: one who spreads rumors) **29.** A violent man lures his neighbor into evil. **30.** He closes his eyes to plot evil and speaks to bring it to pass. (plan: secretly arrange; to make happen: fulfill) **31.** A gray head is a crown of honor when found in the way of righteousness. **32.** A patient man is stronger than the mighty; self-control is better than conquering a city. (calm: slow to anger) **33.** The lot is cast into the lap, but the LORD determines the outcome. (chance, drawing: random choice)

Chapter 17

1. A dry morsel with peace is better than a house full of sacrifices and strife. (strife: conflict) **2.** A wise servant will rule over a son who brings shame, and will share in the inheritance with the brothers. (inheritance: property passed down) **3.** The refining pot is for silver, and the furnace for gold, but the LORD tests hearts. (LORD: God) **4.** A wicked person listens to lies, and a liar listens to evil speech. (wicked: evil) **5.** Mocking the poor insults their Maker; those who rejoice in calamity will not go unpunished. (calamity: disaster) **6.** Grandchildren are the crown of the elderly; the glory of children is their father. (elderly: old people) **7.** Fools do not deserve excellent speech, nor do lying lips belong to a prince. (prince: ruler) **8.** A gift is like a precious stone to its possessor; wherever it goes, it prospers. (prosper: succeed) **9.** He who covers a sin seeks love, but repeating matters separates close friends. (sin: wrong act) **10.** A wise man learns more from rebuke than a fool from a hundred stripes. (rebuke: criticism; stripes: punishment) **11.** The wicked only seek rebellion; a cruel messenger will be sent against them. (rebellion: defiance) **12.** Better to meet a bear robbed of her cubs than a fool in his folly. (folly: foolishness) **13.** Anyone who repays good with evil will face evil in their own house. (repay: give back) **14.** The start of strife is like water breaking out; avoid contention before it escalates. (escalates: increases) **15.** The LORD abhors both justifying the wicked and condemning the righteous. (abhors: hates; justifying: declaring right) **16.** Why should a fool try to buy wisdom when he lacks the heart for it? (lacks: doesn't have) **17.** A friend loves at all times, and a brother is born for adversity. (adversity: hardship) **18.** A man lacking understanding strikes hands and becomes surety for his friend. (lacking: not having; strikes hands: agrees; surety: guarantee) **19.** He who loves strife loves transgression; he who exalts his gate seeks destruction. (transgression: wrongdoing; exalts: raises) **20.** A crooked heart finds no good, and a perverse tongue leads to mischief. (crooked: dishonest; perverse: twisted) **21.** A father of a fool will grieve, and the mother of a fool will experience bitterness.

(grieve: feel sorrow) **22.** A merry heart is good like medicine, but a broken spirit dries up the bones. (broken spirit: sadness) **23.** A wicked person takes a bribe to pervert justice. (bribe: illegal payment; pervert: distort) **24.** Wisdom is ahead of the understanding person, but the fool's eyes wander far. (wander: move aimlessly) **25.** A foolish son brings grief to his father and bitterness to his mother. (grief: sorrow; bitterness: anger) **26.** It's wrong to punish the just or strike princes for righteousness. (just: fair; strike: hit) **27.** A wise person spares their words; a person of understanding has a noble spirit. (noble: honorable) **28.** Even a fool, if he keeps quiet, is considered wise; he who holds his tongue is esteemed. (esteemed: respected)

Chapter 18
1. Through desire, a man, separating himself, seeks and meddles with all wisdom. (desire: pursuit of knowledge in isolation) **2.** A fool takes no pleasure in understanding, only in revealing his own heart. (fool: focused on self-expression, not learning) **3.** When the wicked come, so does contempt and disgrace. (wicked: evil people, contempt: disdain, disgrace: shame) **4.** A man's words are deep waters, and wisdom's wellspring is like a flowing stream. (words: thoughtful, wisdom: deep understanding, wellspring: source) **5.** It's wrong to favor the wicked and wrong the righteous in judgment. (wrong: unjust, judgment: decision-making) **6.** A fool's words lead to strife, and his mouth invites punishment. (fool: foolish person, strife: conflict, mouth: speech, punishment: consequences) **7.** A fool's mouth brings his ruin, and his lips trap his soul. (ruin: destruction, lips: speech, trap: ensnare) **8.** Gossip is like wounds, sinking deep into the heart. (gossip: harmful talk, wounds: emotional harm, sinking: deeply affecting) **9.** A lazy worker is like a great wasteful. (lazy: idle, wasteful: prodigal, worker: one who works) **10.** The LORD's name is a strong tower; the righteous run to it and are safe. (LORD: God, tower: refuge, righteous: virtuous people, safe: protected) **11.** The rich man's wealth is his strong city, and he believes it's an unbreakable wall. (wealth: riches, strong: secure, unbreakable: immovable) **12.** Before destruction, a man's heart is proud; before honor, there's humility. (destruction: downfall, heart: inner attitude, proud: arrogant, humility: modesty) **13.** Answering a matter before hearing it is foolish and shameful. (matter: issue, foolish: unwise, shameful: embarrassing) **14.** A man's spirit can bear his weakness, but who can bear a wounded spirit? (spirit: inner strength, weakness: physical ailment, wounded: emotionally hurt) **15.** The wise heart seeks knowledge, and the wise ear listens for it. (wise: prudent, heart: inner understanding, ear: receptive attitude, seeks: desires) **16.** A man's gift makes room for him, and brings him before the great. (gift: offering, makes room: creates opportunity, brings: leads, great: influential people) **17.** The first in his own cause seems right, but his neighbor examines him. (first: initial, cause: case, seems: appears, examines: scrutinizes) **18.** The lot ends disputes and divides the mighty. (lot: random choice, disputes: arguments, divides: separates, mighty: powerful) **19.** An offended brother is harder to win than a strong city, and their quarrels are like fortified bars. (offended: hurt, brother: close relative, win: reconcile, quarrels: disagreements, fortified: strong, bars: barriers) **20.** A man's stomach is filled by the fruit of his words; his lips bring him satisfaction. (stomach: desires, fruit: result, lips: speech, satisfaction: fulfillment) **21.** Death and life are in the power of the tongue, and those who love it will eat its fruit. (death: destruction, life: prosperity, tongue: speech, power: influence, fruit: results) **22.** He who finds a wife finds a good thing and receives favor from the LORD. (wife: spouse, good thing: blessing, favor: grace) **23.** The poor plead for help, but the rich answer roughly. (poor: needy, plead: beg, answer: respond, roughly: harshly) **24.** A man with friends must show himself friendly; and there is a friend closer than a brother. (friends: companions, show: demonstrate, friendly: kind, closer: more loyal)

Chapter 19
1. Better is a poor man who lives with integrity than a deceitful fool. (deceitful: dishonest) **2.** A soul without knowledge is not good; rushing leads to sin. (rushing: hastiness) **3.** A man's foolishness distorts his path, and his heart resents the LORD. (distorts: misleads) **4.** Wealth attracts many friends, but the poor is separated from others. **5.** A false witness will be punished; liars will not escape. **6.** Many seek the favor of the ruler, and everyone befriends those who give gifts. **7.** The poor's brothers hate him; his friends stay far away, even when he begs. **8.** Whoever gains wisdom loves their own soul; understanding brings good. **9.** A false witness will face punishment; liars will perish. (perish: die) **10.** Foolishness is not fit for delight; a servant ruling over princes is worse. **11.** A man's wisdom delays his anger; it's his glory to forgive offenses. **12.** A king's wrath is like a lion's roar; his favor is like dew on grass. **13.** A foolish son brings disaster to his father; a wife's quarrels are constant. **14.** A house and wealth are an inheritance from fathers, but a wise wife is a gift from the LORD. **15.** Laziness brings deep sleep; an idle soul suffers hunger. (idle: lazy) **16.** Keeping the commandment preserves life; despising it leads to death. **17.** He who helps the poor lends to the LORD, and God will repay. **18.** Discipline your son while there is hope; don't pity his tears. **19.** A man of great anger will be punished; if you save him, he'll need saving again. **20.** Listen to advice and learn; it will make you wise in the end. **21.** Many plans are in a man's heart, but the LORD's purpose will stand. **22.** A man's kindness shows his true desire; a poor man is better than a liar. **23.** The fear of the LORD leads to life; it keeps you content and free from harm. **24.** A lazy man hides his hand in his pocket and won't bring it to his mouth. **25.** Strike a mocker, and the simple will learn; correct the wise, and they'll grow in knowledge. (mocker: scoffer) **26.** A son who wastes his father's wealth and drives away his mother brings shame. **27.** Stop listening to instruction that leads you away from knowledge. **28.** An ungodly witness mocks justice; the mouth of the wicked devours evil. (devours: consumes) **29.** Scorners face judgment, and fools are punished with stripes.

Chapter 20
1. Wine mocks, strong drink stirs up anger: whoever is deceived by them is unwise. (deceived: misled) **2.** The fear of a king is like a lion's roar: those who provoke him sin against themselves. **3.** It's honorable for a man to avoid conflict, but fools love to meddle. (meddle: interfere) **4.** The lazy won't work in the cold; so, they'll beg at harvest and have nothing. (lazy: sluggard) **5.** Counsel in a man's heart is deep water; but a wise man will draw it out. (counsel: advice) **6.** Most men boast of their goodness, but a faithful man is rare. (boast: proclaim) **7.** The just walk with integrity; their children are blessed after them. (integrity: honesty) **8.** A king on the throne of judgment drives away all evil with his eyes. (drives away: scatters) **9.** Who can say, "I have made my heart clean, I am pure from sin"? (pure: free) **10.** False weights and measures are both an abomination to the LORD. (abomination: detestable) **11.** Even a child is known by his actions, whether they are pure and right. (actions: doings) **12.** The hearing ear and seeing eye are both made by the LORD. (hearing: ear) **13.** Don't love sleep, or you'll become poor; open your eyes, and you'll have enough. (love: desire) **14.** The buyer says, "It's worthless," but then boasts when he leaves. (worthless: naught) **15.** Gold and rubies are abundant, but the lips of knowledge are a precious gem. (lips: words) **16.** Take the coat of the one who guarantees for a stranger, and take a pledge for a stranger woman. (guarantees: surety) **17.** Deceptive bread tastes sweet, but in the end, the mouth is filled with gravel. (deceptive: deceitful) **18.** Every plan is established by advice, and good advice is needed for war. (advice: counsel) **19.** A talebearer reveals secrets, so don't meddle with a flatterer. (flatterer: deceiver) **20.** Anyone who curses father or mother will have their light put out in darkness. (light: lamp) **21.** An inheritance may be gained quickly, but its end won't be blessed. (quickly: hastily) **22.** Don't say, "I'll repay evil," but wait for the LORD, and He will save you. (repay: recompense) **23.** False weights are

detestable to the LORD; a false balance is not good. **24.** A man's steps are directed by the LORD; how can he understand his own way? (steps: goings) **25.** It's a trap for someone to eat something holy and then inquire about their vows. (trap: snare) **26.** A wise king scatters the wicked and crushes them with his wheel. (crushes: brings) **27.** The spirit of man is the candle of the LORD, searching the inward parts. (candle: lamp) **28.** Mercy and truth protect the king, and his throne is supported by mercy. (protect: safeguarding) **29.** The glory of young men is their strength, and the beauty of old men is their gray hair. (glory: beauty) **30.** The blueness of a wound cleanses away evil; so do stripes to the inner parts. (blueness: bruising)

Chapter 21

1. The king's heart is in the LORD's hand, like rivers of water; He guides it wherever He wants. (guides: directs) **2.** Every man thinks his way is right, but the LORD weighs the heart. (weighs: examines) **3.** Doing justice is more pleasing to the LORD than sacrifice. (pleasing: acceptable) **4.** Pride, arrogance, and the wickedness of the sinner are sin. (arrogance: haughty, wickedness: evil) **5.** The diligent's thoughts lead to abundance, but the hasty will lack. (diligent: hardworking, lack: be in need) **6.** Gaining wealth through lying is empty and leads to death. (empty: worthless) **7.** The wicked's robbery destroys them because they refuse justice. (robbery: theft, refuse: reject) **8.** A man's way is crooked, but the pure's work is right. (crooked: deceitful, pure: righteous) **9.** It's better to live in a corner of a roof than with a quarrelsome wife in a big house. (quarrelsome: argumentative) **10.** The wicked crave evil; their neighbor finds no favor. (crave: desire, favor: kindness) **11.** When a scoffer is punished, the simple become wise; when the wise are taught, they gain knowledge. (scoffer: mocker, simple: naive) **12.** The righteous understand the wicked's house, but God overthrows them for their evil. (overthrows: destroys) **13.** Whoever ignores the cry of the poor will also cry but not be heard. (ignores: shuts out) **14.** A secret gift calms anger, and a hidden reward soothes strong wrath. (soothes: pacifies) **15.** Justice brings joy to the righteous, but destruction comes to evildoers. (evildoers: wrongdoers) **16.** The man who strays from understanding will remain among the dead. (strays: wanders, understanding: wisdom) **17.** He who loves pleasure will be poor; he who loves wine and oil will not be rich. (pleasure: indulgence) **18.** The wicked will be a ransom for the righteous, and the treacherous for the upright. (treacherous: dishonest) **19.** It's better to live in the desert than with a quarrelsome, angry wife. (quarrelsome: argumentative) **20.** The wise have treasures and oil in their homes, but the fool wastes it. (wastes: spends recklessly) **21.** Whoever pursues righteousness and mercy finds life, righteousness, and honor. (pursues: seeks) **22.** A wise man can break through the stronghold of the mighty and bring down their power. (stronghold: fortress, power: strength) **23.** Whoever controls their tongue keeps their soul from trouble. (controls: restrains) **24.** The proud, haughty scoffer is known for his angry wrath. (scoffer: mocker, haughty: arrogant) **25.** The lazy man's desire kills him because he refuses to work. (lazy: slothful, refuses: avoids) **26.** The greedy man covets all day long, but the righteous give freely. (covets: desires, freely: generously) **27.** The wicked's sacrifice is detestable, especially if offered with evil intent. (detestable: loathsome, intent: purpose) **28.** A false witness will perish, but a truthful speaker will endure. (false: lying, endure: last) **29.** The wicked harden their face, but the upright direct their path. (harden: set, direct: guide) **30.** There is no wisdom or counsel against the LORD. (counsel: advice) **31.** The horse is prepared for battle, but safety comes from the LORD. (prepared: readied)

Chapter 22

1. A good name is better than great wealth, and favor is worth more than silver or gold. **2.** The rich and poor meet; the LORD made them both. **3.** The wise foresee danger and hide, but the simple go on and suffer. **4.** Humility and the fear of the LORD bring wealth, honor, and life. **5.** The froward face thorns and traps; he who guards his soul stays far from them. (Froward: stubborn, difficult) **6.** Train a child in the right way, and they won't depart from it when they grow. **7.** The rich rule over the poor, and the borrower is servant to the lender. (Borrower: someone who owes money) **8.** He who sows iniquity will reap vanity, and the rod of his anger will fail. (Iniquity: wickedness, Vanity: emptiness) **9.** The generous eye will be blessed, for he gives to the poor. (Generous: willing to give) **10.** Expel the mocker, and strife and reproach will cease. (Mocker: someone who mocks, Strife: conflict) **11.** He who loves purity of heart and has gracious speech will be the king's friend. (Gracious: kind, polite) **12.** The LORD preserves knowledge and overthrows the words of the wicked. (Wicked: evil people) **13.** The slothful man says, "There's a lion outside; I'll be killed in the streets." (Slothful: lazy) **14.** The mouth of a seductive woman is a deep pit; those abhorred by the LORD will fall in. (Seductive: tempting, Abhorred: hated) **15.** Foolishness is bound in a child's heart, but correction drives it far from him. (Bound: trapped) **16.** He who oppresses the poor to increase wealth, or gives to the rich, will surely come to need. **17.** Listen to the wise and apply your heart to knowledge. (Knowledge: understanding) **18.** It's a pleasant thing to keep wisdom within you; it will guide your speech. **19.** I've made known to you today that you should trust in the LORD. **20.** Have I not written excellent counsel and knowledge for you? (Counsel: advice) **21.** To make you sure of the truth, so you can answer with truth when others ask. **22.** Do not rob the poor because they are poor, or oppress the afflicted at the gate. (Afflicted: those who suffer, Gate: a public place in the city) **23.** For the LORD will defend their cause and punish those who wrong them. (Cause: reason for action) **24.** Don't make friends with an angry person or a furious man, or **25.** you'll learn their ways. (Furious: irate) **26.** Do not join those who cosign loans, or risk losing everything. (Cosign: agree to take responsibility for a loan) **27.** If you have nothing to pay, why should he take your bed? (Bed: something to sleep on) **28.** Don't remove ancient landmarks set by your ancestors. (Ancient landmarks: boundaries set long ago) **29.** Do you see a diligent man? He will stand before kings, not ordinary men. (Diligent: hardworking, Kings: rulers)

Chapter 23

1. When you sit to eat with a ruler, pay close attention to what's before you. **2.** Don't indulge, control yourself. (Indulge: overeat; control yourself: be cautious) **3.** Don't desire his rich food; it's deceptive. (deceptive: misleading) **4.** Don't work to get rich; stop relying on your own wisdom. **5.** Do you want to focus on what's fleeting? Riches fly away like an eagle. (fleeting: temporary) **6.** Don't eat with someone who is greedy, nor crave his fine foods. **7.** His heart isn't with you, even if he invites you. **8.** You'll regret it and lose your good words. **9.** Don't speak to a fool; he'll disregard your wisdom. (fool: stupid person; disregard: ignore) **10.** Don't move the old boundary stones or trespass the fatherless' land. (trespass: invade) **11.** Their protector is strong; He'll defend them. (defend: God) **12.** Focus on learning and open your ears to knowledge. **13.** Don't withhold discipline from a child; if you discipline them, they won't die. (withhold: hold back; discipline: correction) **14.** Discipline them, and you'll save their soul from destruction. (soul: life) **15.** My son, if your heart is wise, I will rejoice. (rejoice: be glad) **16.** My inner being will rejoice when you speak the truth. **17.** Don't envy sinners; always respect the LORD. (envy: desire) **18.** There's a reward; your hope won't be lost. (lost: disappointed) **19.** Listen, my son, be wise, and guide your heart in the right way. **20.** Don't hang around drunkards or gluttons. (drunkards: drunk people; gluttons: people who overeat) **21.** Drunkards and gluttons will end up poor, and laziness will make them beggars. **22.** Listen to your father and don't neglect your aging mother. (neglect: ignore) **23.** Buy truth and don't sell it; also wisdom, instruction, and understanding. **24.** A righteous father will be happy, and a wise child brings joy. **25.** Your parents will rejoice and be proud of you. (rejoice: be glad) **26.** My son, give me your heart and pay attention to my ways. **27.** A prostitute is like a deep pit, and an immoral woman is a trap. (prostitute: sex worker; immoral: unfaithful) **28.** She lies in wait to trap men and increase their sins. (lies in wait: hides) **29.** Who suffers? Who has sorrow, strife, complaints, wounds, and red eyes? (suffers: has pain; strife: arguments) **30.** Those who linger at wine and seek out mixed drinks. (linger: stay) **31.** Don't stare at wine when it's red, when it sparkles and moves in the cup. **32.** In the end, it bites like a serpent and stings like a viper. (serpent: snake; viper: poisonous snake) **33.** You'll see strange women, and your heart will speak twisted things. (strange: immoral; twisted: evil) **34.** You'll feel like you're lying in the sea or on top of a mast. (mast: top of a ship) **35.** You'll say, "They struck me, but I wasn't hurt; they beat me, but I didn't feel it. When will I wake up? I'll look for more."

Chapter 24

1. Do not envy evil men, nor desire to be with them. **2.** Their heart plans destruction, and their words speak evil. (evil: wickedness) **3.** A house is built through wisdom, and established by understanding. (understanding: clear thought) **4.** Knowledge fills rooms with valuable and delightful riches. (valuable: precious) **5.** A wise man is strong; a man of knowledge grows stronger. **6.** Wise counsel wins battles; in many advisors, there is safety. (safety: protection) **7.** Wisdom is too high for a fool; he does not speak in public. (public: gate: a place of public gathering) **8.** The one who plans evil will be called wicked. (wicked: evil person) **9.** Foolish thoughts are sin; mocking people are detestable. (mocking: scornful, detestable: hated) **10.** If you faint in times of trouble, your strength is weak. (weak: small) **11.** If you fail to save those facing death, **12.** and claim ignorance, does not God know your heart and judge your actions? **13.** My son, eat honey, for it is good, and honeycomb is sweet. **14.** So wisdom will be sweet to your soul; find it and be rewarded. **15.** Do not lie in wait against the righteous; do not harm his home. (righteous: good) **16.** A just man may fall seven times, but he rises again; the wicked will fall into trouble. (just: fair) **17.** Do not rejoice when your enemy falls, nor be glad when he stumbles. **18.** Lest the LORD be displeased, and His anger turn away from him. **19.** Do not fret over evil men or envy the wicked, **20.** for they will have no reward, and their light will fade. (light: success, fade: end) **21.** My son, fear the LORD and the king; avoid those who stir up change. (king: ruler, change: revolution) **22.** Sudden disaster will strike them; who knows their ruin? (disaster: trouble, ruin: fall) **23.** Wise people know it's wrong to show favoritism in judgment. (favoritism: bias) **24.** Whoever calls the wicked righteous will be cursed by the people. (wicked: evil person, cursed: hated) **25.** But those who rebuke him will be honored, and blessings will come to them. (rebuke: correct) **26.** People will praise those who give a truthful answer. (truthful: right) **27.** Prepare your work outside, and make it ready in the field; then build your house. **28.** Do not accuse your neighbor without cause, nor deceive with your words. (accuse: blame, deceive: lie) **29.** Do not say, "I will repay him as he has done to me." **30.** I passed by the field of the lazy man and the vineyard of the fool; **31.** it was overgrown with thorns, weeds had covered it, and the wall was broken. (lazy: slothful, fool: ignorant, broken: damaged) **32.** I saw this and considered it; I learned from it. (considered: thought about) **33.** A little sleep, a little rest, folding hands to sleep, **34.** and poverty will come like a traveler, and need like an armed man. (poverty: lack of money; need: lack, armed: strong)

Chapter 25

1. These are also Solomon's proverbs, copied by Hezekiah's men, king of Judah. (Judah: southern kingdom of Israel) **2.** It is God's glory to hide things, but kings' honour is to seek them out. (honour: respect) **3.** The heaven is high, the earth deep, and kings' hearts are beyond understanding. (beyond: hard to) **4.** Remove impurities from silver, and a refined vessel will result. (impurities: dross, refined: pure) **5.** Remove the wicked from the king's presence, and his throne will be firm in justice. (wicked: evil people) **6.** Don't put yourself forward before the king, nor in the place of great men. **7.** It's better to be told, "Come up here," than to be humbled before the prince you have seen. (humbled: made lower) **8.** Don't rush into arguments; you may not know how to finish, and be shamed. (rush: hastily, arguments: strive) **9.** Settle things with your neighbour, and don't reveal secrets to others. (settle: solve) **10.** Lest hearing it, they shame you, and your disgrace won't be removed. (disgrace: dishonour) **11.** A well-chosen word is like gold apples in silver settings. (well-chosen: rightly selected) **12.** Like gold earrings, a wise rebuke on a listening ear. (rebuke: reproof, listening: willing to hear) **13.** As snow in harvest, a faithful messenger refreshes his masters. (faithful: loyal, refreshes: gives comfort) **14.** One who boasts of a false gift is like clouds without rain. (boasts: brags, false: untrue) **15.** A prince is won by patience, and a gentle word can break a bone. (won: persuaded) **16.** Have you found honey? Eat only what's enough, lest you be sick. (enough: just right) **17.** Don't overstay at your neighbour's house, or he will tire of you and hate you. (overstay: stay too long, tire: become weary) **18.** A false witness is like a hammer, sword, and sharp arrow. (false witness: lying testimony) **19.** Trusting an unfaithful man in trouble is like a broken tooth or a dislocated foot. (unfaithful: unreliable) **20.** Like taking a coat in cold weather, or vinegar on soda, so is singing to a heavy heart. (heavy: sorrowful) **21.** If your enemy is hungry, feed him; if thirsty, give him water. **22.** You will heap burning coals on his head, and the LORD will reward you. (heap: place, coals: hot embers) **23.** The north wind drives away rain; an angry face stops gossip. (gossip: backbiting) **24.** Better to live in a corner of the roof than in a house with a quarrelsome wife. (quarrelsome: argumentative) **25.** Good news from a distant land is like cold water to a thirsty soul. (distant: far) **26.** A righteous man bowing before the wicked is like a disturbed fountain, a corrupt spring. (righteous: just, bowing: lowering oneself) **27.** It's not good to eat too much honey, nor to seek one's own glory. (glory: praise) **28.** A person without self-control is like a city with broken walls. (self-control: mastery over desires)

Chapter 26

1. Honour is out of place for a fool, like snow in summer or rain at harvest. (out of place: unsuitable) **2.** A curse without cause will not come, like a bird that wanders or a swallow that flies. **3.** A whip for the horse, a bridle for the donkey, and a rod for the fool's back. **4.** Don't answer a fool according to his foolishness, or you'll be like him. (foolishness: silliness) **5.** Answer a fool according to his foolishness, or he'll think he's wise. **6.** Sending a message by a fool is like cutting off your feet and inviting harm. **7.** The legs of the lame are uneven, so is a parable in the mouth of fools. (lame: crippled) **8.** Giving honour to a fool is like putting a stone in a sling. **9.** A thorn in the hand of a drunk is like a parable in a fool's mouth. **10.** God rewards both fools and wrongdoers. **11.** A fool returns to his folly, like a dog to its vomit. **12.** A man wise in his own eyes has less hope than a fool. (wise in his own eyes: self-conceited) **13.** The lazy man says there's a lion in the road, or lions in the streets. **14.** The lazy man turns on his bed like a door on its hinges. **15.** The slothful hides his hand and finds it hard to feed himself. (slothful: lazy) **16.** The lazy man thinks he's wiser than seven men who can reason. (reason: think clearly) **17.** A man who meddles in another's strife is like one who grabs a dog by the ears. (meddles: interferes, strife = conflict) **18.** A madman throwing fire and arrows is like a man who deceives his neighbour, then claims he's joking. (deceives: tricks) **19.** A man who deceives and says, "I was just kidding," is dangerous. **20.** Where there's no wood, the fire goes out; where there's no gossip, strife ends. (gossip: rumours) **21.** Like coals to burning coals, a contentious man stirs up conflict. (contentious: argumentative) **22.** Gossip wounds like a knife and sinks deep into the heart. **23.** Flattering lips and a wicked heart are like a broken pot covered with silver. (flattering: complimenting, wicked: evil) **24.** A man who hates pretends to be friendly, but stores deceit in his heart. **25.** Don't trust a man who speaks kindly, for he hides seven evils in his heart. **26.** A man who covers hatred with deceit will be exposed in front of everyone. (deceit: lies) **27.** He who digs a pit will fall into it; rolling a stone will bring it back on him. **28.** A lying tongue hates those it hurts, and a flattering mouth brings ruin.

Chapter 27

1. Don't brag about tomorrow; you can't predict what it will bring. **2.** Let others praise you, not your own mouth; a stranger, not your own lips. **3.** A stone is heavy, and sand weighs a lot, but a fool's anger is even heavier. **4.** Anger is harsh, and wrath is fierce; but who can endure jealousy? (wrath: intense anger) **5.** Open criticism is better than hidden affection. (Criticism: judgment or reproach) **6.** The wounds of a faithful friend are trustworthy, but enemy kisses are deceitful. (deceitful: misleading) **7.** A full person rejects honeycomb, but to the hungry, even bitterness tastes sweet. **8.** A bird that leaves its nest is like a man who abandons his place. **9.** Fragrance and perfume cheer the heart; so does the advice of a true friend. **10.** Don't abandon your close friend or your father's friend; a neighbor nearby is better than a distant brother in times of trouble. **11.** Be wise, my son, and make me proud, so I can respond to my accusers. **12.** A wise man sees danger ahead and hides, but the naive keep going and suffer. (naive: innocent or inexperienced) **13.** Take the coat of one who stands as a guarantee for a stranger, and secure a pledge for a foreign woman. (Pledge: assurance) **14.** A loud blessing early in the morning will seem like a curse. (curse: bad result) **15.** A constant drip on a rainy day and a quarrelsome woman are the same. (quarrelsome: combative) **16.** Whoever tries to hide her hides the wind, and the ointment on his right hand exposes him. **17.** Iron sharpens iron, and one man sharpens another. (sharpens: improves or strengthens) **18.** He who cares for the fig tree will enjoy its fruit; so the servant who serves his master will be honored. **19.** As a face reflects in water, so a man's heart reflects his thoughts. **20.** Hell and destruction are never full, and human desire is never satisfied. **21.** As the refiner's pot for silver and the furnace for gold, so is a man's praise tested. (refiner's pot: a container for melting silver) **22.** You can crush a fool in a mortar with wheat, but his foolishness won't leave him. (mortar: a bowl for crushing, foolishness: lack of wisdom) **23.** Be careful to know the state of your flocks and pay attention to your herds. (careful: diligent, flocks: groups of animals) **24.** Riches don't last forever, and a crown doesn't endure for every generation. (crown: symbol of kingship, generation: family line) **25.** The hay appears, fresh grass grows, and mountain herbs are gathered. (hay: dried grass) **26.** Lambs are used for clothing, and goats are the price of the field. **27.** You'll have plenty of goats' milk for your food, your household, and your maidens' care.

Chapter 28

1. The wicked flee without cause, but the righteous are bold like lions. (Wicked: evil people, flee: run away) **2.** A land in turmoil has many rulers, but a wise and understanding man brings stability. (Turmoil: confusion, stability: peace) **3.** A poor man who oppresses the poor is like a storm that leaves nothing. (Oppresses: treats unfairly) **4.** Those who abandon the law praise the wicked; those who follow it challenge them. (Abandon: leave, praise: support, challenge: oppose) **5.** Evil men don't understand justice, but those who seek the Lord understand all. (Justice: fairness, seek: look for) **6.** Better is the poor who lives uprightly than the rich who is crooked. (Uprightly: honestly, crooked: dishonest) **7.** A wise son keeps the law, but a companion of rebels shames his father. (Rebels: troublemakers, shames: dishonors) **8.** One who gains wealth through usury will leave it for those who pity the poor. (Usury: charging unfair interest) **9.** Anyone who turns away from the law will find their prayers detestable. (Detestable: hated) **10.** Those who mislead the righteous will fall into their own trap; the upright will prosper. (Mislead: lead astray) **11.** The rich think themselves wise, but the poor with understanding exposes their folly. (Folly: foolishness) **12.** When the righteous rejoice, glory abounds, but when the wicked rise, men hide. (Rejoice: celebrate, glory: honor, wicked: evil people) **13.** Those who hide their sins will not prosper, but those who confess and forsake them will find mercy. (Confess: admit, forsake: give up) **14.** Blessed is the man who fears the Lord always, but those who harden their hearts will fall into mischief. (Fears: respects, harden: refuse to listen, mischief: trouble) **15.** A wicked ruler is like a roaring lion or a bear over the poor. (Ruler: leader, roaring: loud, lion/bear) **16.** A ruler lacking understanding is an oppressor, but one who hates greed will have a long reign. (Lacking: without, oppressor: someone who treats people unfairly, reign: rule) **17.** A man guilty of violence will flee to the pit; no one should stop him. (Guilty: responsible for wrongdoing) **18.** Those who walk uprightly will be saved; those who are perverse will fall suddenly. (Uprightly: honestly, perverse: twisted) **19.** He who tills his land will have plenty, but he who follows empty pursuits will suffer poverty. (Tills: works, empty pursuits: worthless goals,) **20.** A faithful man will be blessed, but those who rush to get rich will not go unpunished. (Faithful: loyal, blessed: rewarded, rush: hurry) **21.** Showing partiality is wrong; even for a loaf of bread, a person will sin. (Partiality: favoritism, loaf: piece of bread) **22.** The one who hastes to get rich is blind to the fact that poverty will catch up with him. (Hastes: rushes) **23.** One who rebukes a man later will find favor over the one who flatters. (Rebukes: reprove, flatters: praises falsely, favor: approval) **24.** A thief who robs his parents and says it's not wrong is a companion of destroyers. (Robs: steals) **25.** A proud heart stirs up strife, but those who trust in the Lord will prosper. (Proud: arrogant, strife: conflict, trust: rely) **26.** Trusting in your own heart is foolish, but walking wisely brings deliverance. (Foolish: silly, deliverance: rescue) **27.** Those who give to the poor will never lack, but those who ignore them will face curses. (Lack: have none, ignore: disregard, curses: bad luck) **28.** When the wicked rise, people hide; when they perish, the righteous increase. (Perish: die, righteous: good people)

Chapter 29

1. He who is often reproved and hardens his heart will be destroyed without remedy (Reproved: corrected). **2.** When the righteous rule, people rejoice; when the wicked rule, they mourn. **3.** A lover of wisdom brings joy to his father; a companion of prostitutes wastes his wealth. **4.** A king who judges justly secures the land, but a gift-taker destroys it **5.** A flatterer traps his neighbor in a snare (Flatterer: someone who praises insincerely). **6.** The evil man's sin is a snare, but the righteous rejoice (Sin: wrongdoing). **7.** The righteous care for the poor; the wicked ignore them. **8.** Scornful men trap a city; wise men avert anger (Scornful: mocking). **9.** A wise man has no rest when contending with a fool, whether in rage or laughter (Contending: arguing). **10.** The bloodthirsty hate the upright; the just seek their soul (Bloodthirsty: violent). **11.** A fool speaks without restraint; a wise man holds his thoughts until later (Restraint: self-control). **12.** A ruler who listens to lies makes all his servants wicked (Servants: those who work for someone). **13.** The poor and deceitful meet, but the LORD gives them both light (Deceitful: dishonest). **14.** A king who judges the poor justly will have an enduring throne. **15.** The rod and reproof bring wisdom, but an undisciplined child brings shame to his mother. **16.** When the wicked multiply, sin increases, but the righteous will witness their downfall (Multiply: increase). **17.** Correct your son, and he will bring you peace and joy. **18.** Where there is no vision, people perish; those who obey the law are happy (Vision: guiding purpose). **19.** A servant will not be corrected by words; he understands but will not answer (Servant: worker). **20.** A hasty speaker has less hope than a fool (Hasty: quick). **21.** A servant raised carefully will become like a son (Carefully: with attention). **22.** An angry man stirs up conflict; a furious man multiplies transgressions (Furious: extremely angry). **23.** Pride brings a man low; humility preserves his honor (Pride: excessive self-importance). **24.** A thief's partner hates his own soul; he hears cursing but says nothing (Partner: accomplice). **25.** The fear of man is a snare, but trusting in the LORD brings safety. **26.** Many seek the ruler's favor, but judgment comes from the LORD (Favor: approval). **27.** The unjust are an abomination to the just, and the upright are an abomination to the wicked (Abomination: something hated).

Chapter 30
1. These are the words of Agur, son of Jakeh, the prophecy: he spoke to Ithiel, to Ithiel and Ucal. 2. I am more ignorant than any man, and I lack understanding. (Ignorant: lacking knowledge) 3. I have not gained wisdom, nor do I have knowledge of the sacred. 4. Who has ascended to heaven or descended? Who has gathered the wind in His hands? Who has wrapped up the waters in a cloak? Who has set the boundaries of the earth? What is His name, and what is the name of His Son, if you know? 5. Every word of God is flawless; He is a shield to those who trust in Him. 6. Do not add to His words, or He will correct you and prove you to be a liar. 7. I ask two things from You; please do not refuse me before I die: 8. Keep lies and deceit far from me; give me neither poverty nor riches, but provide for my needs. (Deceit: dishonesty) 9. Otherwise, I may become full and deny You, saying, "Who is the Lord?" or become poor, steal, and dishonor Your name. 10. Do not accuse a servant to his master, or he will curse you, and you will be found guilty. 11. There is a generation that curses their father and does not bless their mother. 12. There is a generation that appears pure in their own eyes but is still filthy. (Filthy: unclean) 13. There is a generation that is proud, with their eyes lifted high and their eyelids raised. (Proud: haughty) 14. There is a generation whose teeth are like swords and their jaws like knives, devouring the poor and the needy. (Devouring: destroying) 15. The leech has two daughters, always crying, "Give, give." There are three things that are never satisfied, and four that never say, "Enough": 16. The grave, the barren womb, the earth that is never filled with water, and the fire that says, "Enough." 17. The eye that mocks his father and scorns his mother, ravens from the valley will pluck it out, and young eagles will eat it. (Mocks: disrespects; Scorns: despises; Ravens: large black birds) 18. There are three things that are too wonderful for me, and four that I do not understand: 19. The way of an eagle in the sky, the way of a snake on a rock, the way of a ship on the sea, and the way of a man with a young woman. (Ship: vessel) 20. Such is the way of an adulterous woman; she eats, wipes her mouth, and says, "I've done nothing wrong." (Adulterous: unfaithful) 21. The earth is troubled by three things, and cannot bear four: 22. A servant who becomes a king, a fool who is full of food, 23. A woman who is hateful when married, and a maidservant who inherits her mistress's position. (Hateful: detestable; Maidservant: female servant) 24. Four things on earth are small, but they are exceedingly wise: 25. The ants, though they are not strong, store up food in the summer; 26. The conies, though weak, make their homes in the rocks; (Conies: small, rock-dwelling animals) 27. The locusts, with no king, go forward in swarms; (Locusts: grasshoppers) 28. The spider, who takes hold with her hands and lives in kings' palaces. (Spider: small arachnid) 29. There are three things that are graceful in their movement, and four that are lovely to behold: (Graceful: elegant) 30. A lion, the strongest of beasts, who does not turn away from anyone; 31. A greyhound, a male goat, and a king against whom no one can stand. (Greyhound: breed of dog; Male goat: he-goat) 32. If you have acted foolishly by raising yourself up, or if you have planned evil, put your hand on your mouth. 33. Just as churning milk makes butter, and pressing the nose makes blood, so stirring up anger causes strife. (Strife: conflict, disagreement)

Chapter 31
1. The words of King Lemuel, the prophecy his mother taught him. (Lemuel: a king's name) 2. What, my son, the son of my womb and vows? (Vows: promises made to God) 3. Do not give your strength to women or to things that ruin kings. 4. It is not for kings, Lemuel, to drink wine or princes strong drink. (Princes: royal leaders) 5. Lest they forget the law and pervert judgment for the afflicted. (Afflicted: those who suffer) 6. Give strong drink to those near death and wine to the heavy-hearted. (Strong drink: alcohol) 7. Let them drink and forget their poverty and misery. 8. Speak for the mute and those destined for destruction. (Mute: unable to speak) 9. Judge righteously and defend the poor and needy. (Righteously: with fairness) 10. Who can find a virtuous woman? Her worth is far above rubies. (Virtuous: good, moral) 11. Her husband trusts her fully, lacking no need of spoil. (Spoil: goods taken in war) 12. She does him good, not evil, all her life. (Evil: harm or wrongdoing) 13. She seeks wool and flax, working willingly with her hands. (Willingly: eagerly, without hesitation) 14. She is like a merchant's ship, bringing food from afar. (Afar: from distant places) 15. She rises early, feeding her household and maidens. (Maidens: young women who serve her) 16. She buys a field and plants a vineyard with her earnings. 17. She strengthens her arms and prepares for work. (Strengthens: makes stronger) 18. She knows her merchandise is good; her candle burns at night. (Merchandise: goods for sale) 19. She spins and weaves with her hands. (Spins: twists thread into yarn) 20. She reaches out to the poor and needy. 21. She is not afraid of the snow; her household is clothed in scarlet. (Scarlet: rich red cloth) 22. She makes herself coverings of tapestry, wearing silk and purple. (Tapestry: woven cloth for decoration) 23. Her husband is respected at the gates, sitting with the elders. (Gates: city gates, place of leadership) 24. She makes fine linen, sells it, and delivers girdles to merchants. (Girdles: belts or sashes) 25. Strength and honor are her clothing; she will rejoice in the future. (Rejoice: feel great joy) 26. She speaks with wisdom, and her tongue holds kindness. 27. She manages her household well, not idly eating bread. (Idly: without doing work) 28. Her children rise up and call her blessed, and her husband praises her. (Blessed: happy and honored) 29. Many daughters have done well, but you surpass them all. (Surpass: exceed or be better than) 30. Charm is deceitful, beauty is vain, but a woman who fears the LORD will be praised. (Deceitful: misleading, vain: empty) 31. Give her the fruit of her hands; let her works praise her in the gates.

21 – Ecclestiates

Chapter 1
1. These are the words of the teacher, son of David, king in Jerusalem. 2. "The whole lot is incomprehensible," says the teacher. "All is futile." (Futile: needless) 3. What do people gain from their hard work underneath the sun? (Hard work: effort) 4. Generations come and go, but the earth remains all the time. 5. The sun rises, sets, and returns to its vicinity. 6. The wind blows south, then turns north, constantly transferring in its cycle. 7. Rivers circulate the sea, but the ocean is in no way full. The rivers return to their source. (Rivers: flowing bodies of water) 8. Everything is tiresome, extra than words can express. The attention is in no way glad with seeing, nor the ear with hearing. 9. What has came about will show up once more; there is nothing new underneath the sun. 10. Can absolutely everyone say, "That is new"? It changed into here earlier than us. 11. Nobody remembers past generations, and future ones could be forgotten too. 12. I, the teacher, turned out to be king over Israel in Jerusalem. 13. I set my heart to apprehend all that takes place under the heavens. What a heavy burden God has given humanity! (Burden: weight) 14. I've seen everything underneath the sun, and it's all meaningless, like chasing the wind. (Chasing the wind: futile pursuit) 15. What is crooked can't be straightened, and what is lacking cannot rely. 16. I notion, "I've turn out to be wiser than all who ruled earlier than me. I've received a good deal understanding." 17. Then I tried to understand information, insanity, and folly, but I discovered it all to be like chasing after the wind. 18. With understanding comes sorrow; the greater understanding, the greater grief. (Grief:unhappiness).

Chapter 2
1. I stated to myself, "I will check myself with pleasure to see what is ideal." But that too proved meaningless. 2. "Laughter," I thought, "is madness. And what does delight gain?" (Madness: foolishness) 3. I tried cheering myself with wine and indulging in foolishness, while still guiding myself with knowledge. I wanted to see what is truly good for people to do during their brief lives. 4. I took on big projects:

I built homes and planted vineyards. **5.** I made gardens and parks, planting all kinds of fruit trees. **6.** I built reservoirs to water groves of thriving trees. **7.** I bought servants, both male and female, and had others born in my family. I owned more herds and flocks than anyone before me in Jerusalem. **8.** I accumulated silver and gold, the treasures of kings and provinces. I obtained singers and a harem—the pleasures of a man's heart. **9.** I became greater than anyone in Jerusalem before me, and my wisdom remained with me. **10.** I denied myself nothing my eyes desired; I refused my heart no pleasure. My heart determined pleasure in all my work, and that was the reward of my labor. **11.** But when I looked at all my achievements and the work I had done, everything was meaningless—a chasing after the wind; nothing was gained under the sun. **12.** Then I turned to consider wisdom, madness, and folly. What more can a king's successor do than what has already been done? **13.** I realized that wisdom is better than folly, just as light is better than darkness. **14.** The wise can see, while the fool walks in darkness; but I saw that the same fate awaits them both. **15.** I said to myself, "The fool's fate will even come to me. What do I gain by being wise?" I concluded, "This too is incomprehensible." **16.** The wise, like the fool, are not long remembered; both will be forgotten. Just like the fool, the wise must die. **17.** So I hated life, because the work done under the sun was grievous to me. All of it is meaningless, like chasing after the wind. **18.** I hated all the things I had worked for under the sun, because I must leave them to the one who comes after me. **19.** And who knows if that person will be wise or foolish? Yet they will take control of all the fruit of my labor, which I toiled for under the sun. This too is meaningless. **20.** So my heart despaired over all my work under the sun. **21.** Someone may go with wisdom, knowledge, and skill, only to leave everything they have to someone who hasn't worked for it. This too is meaningless and a great misfortune. **22.** What do people gain from all their toil and stressful striving under the sun? **23.** All their days are filled with grief and pain; even at night, their minds do not rest. This too is incomprehensible. **24.** Someone can do nothing better than to eat, drink, and find delight in their labor. This too I see as a gift from God. (Pleasure: success) **25.** For without God, who can eat or enjoy life? **26.** To those who please Him, God gives wisdom, knowledge, and pleasure, but to the sinner, He gives the task of accumulating wealth to hand over to those who please Him. This too is meaningless, like chasing after the wind.

Chapter 3

1. There is a time for everything, and a season for every activity under the heavens. **2.** A time to be born and a time to die, a time to plant and a time to uproot. **3.** A time to kill and a time to heal, a time to tear down and a time to build. **4.** A time to weep and a time to laugh, a time to mourn and a time to dance. **5.** A time to scatter stones and a time to gather them, a time to embrace and a time to refrain from embracing. **6.** A time to look and a time to give up, a time to keep and a time to throw away. **7.** A time to tear and a time to mend, a time to be silent and a time to speak. **8.** A time to love and a time to hate, a time for war and a time for peace. **9.** What do people gain from their toil? (Toil: continuous work) **10.** I've seen the burden God has placed on humanity. **11.** He has made everything beautiful in its time. He has set eternity in the human heart, yet no one can fully understand what God has done from beginning to end. (Eternity: endless time) **12.** I know that there's nothing better for people than to be happy and to do right while they live. **13.** That each may eat, drink, and find satisfaction in all their work—this is a gift from God. **14.** I know that whatever God does will last forever; nothing can be added to it or taken from it. God does it so that people will fear Him. (Fear: respect) **15.** Whatever exists has already been; what will be has already occurred. God will bring the past to account. **16.** I saw wickedness in the place of judgment, and wickedness in the place of justice. **17.** God will bring both the righteous and the wicked into judgment, for there is a time for every activity. **18.** I said to myself, "God tests people so they'll see that they are like animals." **19.** The fate of humans is like that of animals; the same fate awaits them both: as one dies, so dies the other. All of them share the same breath; humans have no advantage over animals. Everything is incomprehensible. **20.** All go to the same place; all come from dust, and to dust all return. **21.** Who knows if the human spirit rises upward and if the animal spirit goes down into the earth? **22.** So I saw that there is nothing better for a person than to enjoy their work, for that is their lot. Who can tell what will happen after them?

Chapter 4

1. I saw all the oppression under the sun: the tears of the oppressed (subject to harsh), with no one to comfort them; power was on the side of their oppressors, with no one to comfort them. **2.** I declared that the dead, who have already died, are happier than the living. **3.** But better than both is the one who has never been born, who has not seen the evil done under the sun. **4.** All toil and achievement spring from one's envy of another. This too is meaningless, a chasing after the wind. (Envy: desire for what others have) **5.** Fools fold their hands and destroy themselves. **6.** Better one handful with peace than two handfuls with toil and chasing after the wind. **7.** Again I saw something meaningless: **8.** A man was all alone; he had neither son nor brother. There was no end to his toil, yet he was not content with his wealth. "For whom am I working?" he asked, "and why am I depriving myself of enjoyment?" This too is meaningless. **9.** Two are better than one, because they have a good return for their labor. **10.** If one falls, the other can help them up. But pity anyone who falls and has no one to help them. **11.** If two lie down together, they will keep warm. But how can one keep warm alone? **12.** Though one may be overpowered, two can defend themselves. A cord of three strands is not easily broken. **13.** Better a poor but wise youth than an old but foolish king who no longer knows how to heed a warning. **14.** The youth may have come from prison to the kingship, or been born in poverty. **15.** I saw that all who live under the sun followed the youth, the king's successor. **16.** There was no end to those before them, but those who came later were not pleased with the successor. This too is meaningless, a chasing after the wind.

Chapter 5

1. Shield your steps when you go to the house of God. Go near to listen, instead of offering the sacrifice of fools who do not know they're wrong. (Sacrifice of fools: offering that is insincere or unwise) **2.** Do not be quick with your mouth, or hasty in your heart to utter anything before God. God is in heaven, and you are on earth, so let your words be few. **3.** A dream comes with many cares, and many words mark the speech of a fool. **4.** When you make a vow to God, do not delay in fulfilling it. He takes no pleasure in fools; satisfy your vow. **5.** It's better not to make a vow than to make one and not fulfill it. **6.** Do not let your mouth lead you into sin. Do not protest to the temple messenger, "My vow was a mistake." Why should God be angry at your words and destroy the work of your hands? **7.** Much dreaming and many words are meaningless. Therefore, fear God. **8.** If you see the poor oppressed in a district, and justice and rights denied, do not be surprised, for one official is watched by a higher one, and over them both are others better still. **9.** The increase from the land is taken by all; even the king profits from the fields. **10.** Whoever loves money never has enough; whoever loves wealth is never satisfied with their income. This too is incomprehensible. **11.** As goods increase, so do those who consume them. What benefit are they to the owners except to feast their eyes on them? **12.** The sleep of a laborer is good, whether they eat little or much, but the abundance of the rich prevents them from sleeping. **13.** I have seen a grievous evil under the sun: wealth hoarded to the harm of its owners, (Grievous: deeply troubling or serious) **14.** Or wealth lost through misfortune, so that when they have children, there is nothing left to inherit. **15.** Everyone comes naked from their mother's womb, and as they come, so they depart. They take nothing from their toil that they can carry in their hands. **16.** This too is a grievous evil: As everyone comes, so they depart, and what do they gain, since they toil for the wind? **17.** All their days they eat in darkness, with great frustration, agony, and anger. **18.** This is what I have seen to be good: It's fitting for someone to eat, drink, and find pleasure in their labor under the sun during the brief life God has given them. **19.** When God gives someone wealth and possessions, and the ability to enjoy them, to accept their lot and be happy in their toil—this is a gift from God. **20.** They seldom reflect on the days of their life, because God keeps them occupied with gladness of heart. (Gladness: pleasure)

Chapter 6

1. I have seen another evil under the sun, and it weighs heavily on mankind. **2.** God gives some people wealth, possessions, and honor, so they lack nothing, yet He does not grant them the ability to enjoy them. Strangers enjoy them instead. That is meaningless, a grievous evil. (Grievous: deeply troubling or severe) **3.** A man may have 100 children and live many years, but if he cannot enjoy his prosperity or receive a proper burial, I say that a stillborn infant is better off than he. (Stillborn: a child born dead) **4.** It comes without meaning, it departs in darkness, and its name is forgotten. **5.** Even though it never saw the sun or knew anything, it has more rest than that man. **6.** Even if he lives a thousand years twice over but cannot enjoy his prosperity. Do not all go to the same place? **7.** Everyone's toil is for their mouth, yet their appetite is never satisfied. (Toil: hard work) **8.** What advantage does the wise have over fools? What do the poor gain by knowing how to behave? (Benefit: advantage or gain) **9.** Better what the eye sees than the wandering of the appetite. This too is meaningless, a chasing after the wind. (Chasing after the wind: a futile pursuit) **10.** Whatever exists has already been named, and humanity's nature is known. No one can argue with someone stronger than themselves. (Stronger: someone more powerful) **11.** The more words, the less meaning. What gain is there in them? (Advantage: benefit or gain) **12.** For who knows what is good for someone during the few and meaningless days they pass through like a shadow? (Shadow: a fleeting or short existence) Who can tell what will happen after they're gone?

Chapter 7

1. An excellent name is better than fine fragrance, and the day of dying is better than the day of birth. (Perfume: a aromatic heady scent) **2.** It is better to go to a house of mourning than to a house of feasting, for death is the destiny of every person; the living should take this to heart. (Mourning: a time of sorrow after death) **3.** Frustration is better than laughter, because a sad face is good for the heart. **4.** The heart of the wise is in the house of mourning, but the heart of fools is in the house of pleasure. **5.** It is better to heed the rebuke of the wise than the song of fools. (Heed: pay attention to) **6.** Like the crackling of thorns beneath a pot, so is the laughter of fools. This too is incomprehensible. (Crackling: a sharp snapping noise) **7.** Extortion turns a wise person into a fool, and a bribe corrupts the heart. (Extortion: the act of obtaining something through force or threats) **8.** The end of a matter is better than its beginning, and patience is better than pride. **9.** Do not be quick to provoke your spirit, for anger rests in the lap of fools. (Lap: symbolizing the nature of foolishness) **10.** Do not say, "Why were the old days better than these?" For it is not wise to ask such questions. **11.** Wisdom, like an inheritance, is a good thing and benefits those who see the sun. (Inheritance: something passed down from ancestors) **12.** Knowledge is a shelter, as money is a refuge, but the advantage of knowledge is this: It preserves those who have it. (Preserves: maintains safe or protects) **13.** Consider what God has done: Who can straighten what He has made crooked? (Crooked: morally bent or wrong) **14.** When times are good, be happy; but when times are bad, consider: God made the one as well as the other. No one can discover anything about their future. **15.** In this meaningless life of mine, I have seen each of these: the righteous perishing in their righteousness and the wicked living long in their wickedness. (Or coming to an end) **16.** Do not be overly righteous, nor overly wise—why destroy yourself? **17.** Do not be overly wicked, nor be a fool—why die before your time? **18.** It is good to grasp one, and not let go of the other. Whoever fears God will avoid extremes. **19.** Wisdom makes one wise person more powerful than ten rulers in a city. (Rulers: leaders). **20.** Indeed, there is no one on earth who is righteous, no one who does what is right and never sins. (Righteous: morally right) **21.** Do not pay attention to every word people say, or you may hear your servant cursing you— (Servant: an employee or person under your authority) **22.** For you know in your heart that many times you have cursed others. **23.** All this I tested by wisdom, and I said, "I am determined to be wise"— but this was beyond me. **24.** What exists is far off and most profound— who can discover it? (Profound: deep or complex) **25.** So I turned my mind to understand, to investigate and to search out wisdom and the scheme of things, to understand the stupidity of wickedness and the madness of folly. (Scheme: plan) **26.** I find bitterer than death the woman who is a snare, whose heart is a trap and whose hands are chains. The man who pleases God will escape her, but the sinner she will ensnare. (Snare: a trap) **27.** "Look," says the teacher, "this is what I have found: **28.** Adding one thing to another to discover the scheme of things—while I was still searching but not finding— I found one upright man among a thousand, but not one upright woman among them all. (Upright: morally right or virtuous) **29.** This only have I found: God created mankind upright, but they have gone in search of many schemes."

Chapter 8

1. Who is like the wise? Who knows the explanation of things? Someone's knowledge brightens their face and changes its hard look. (Hard look: a stern or harsh expression) **2.** Obey the king's command, because you took an oath before God. (Oath: a solemn promise) **3.** Do not be in a hurry to leave the king's presence. Do not stand up for a bad reason, for he will do whatever he pleases. **4.** Since a king's word is supreme, who can say to him, "What are you doing?" (Supreme: of the highest authority) **5.** Whoever obeys his command will come to no harm, and the wise heart will know the right time and procedure. **6.** There is a right time and procedure for every matter, although a person may be weighed down by distress. (Weighed down: pressured or overwhelmed) **7.** Since no one knows the future, who can tell someone else what is to come? **8.** Just as no one has power over the wind to contain it, no one has power over the time of their death. As no one is discharged in wartime, so wickedness will not release those who practice it. (Discharged: released or freed) **9.** All this I saw as I applied my mind to all that is done under the sun. There is a time when a man lords it over others to his own hurt. **10.** Then too, I saw the wicked buried—those who used to come and go from the holy place and receive praise in the city where they did this. This too is meaningless. **11.** When the sentence for a crime is not quickly carried out, people's hearts are filled with schemes to do wrong. (Sentence: a penalty) **12.** Even though a wicked person who commits a hundred crimes may live a long time, I know that it will go better with those who fear God, who are reverent before Him. (Reverent: showing deep respect) **13.** Yet because the wicked do not fear God, it will not go well with them, and their days will not extend like a shadow. **14.** There is something else meaningless that happens on the earth: the righteous who get what the wicked deserve, and the wicked who get what the righteous deserve. This too is incomprehensible. **15.** So I commend the enjoyment of life, because there is nothing better for a person under the sun than to eat, drink, and be glad. Pleasure will accompany them in their toil all the days of the life God has given them under the sun. (Commend: encourage) **16.** After I applied my mind to understand wisdom and to observe the work that is done on earth—people getting no sleep day or night— **17.** Then I saw all that God has done. No one can comprehend what goes on under the sun. Despite all their efforts to search it out, no one can discover its meaning. Although the wise claim they know, they cannot truly understand it.

Chapter 9

1. I reflected and concluded that the righteous, the wise, and their actions are in God's hands, but no one knows if love or hate awaits them. **2.** All share the same fate—the good and the wicked, the clean and unclean, those who sacrifice and those who don't. As it is with the good, so with the sinful; as it is with those who take oaths, so with those who avoid them. (Fate: inevitable outcome) **3.** This is the evil under the sun: the same fate comes to all. People's hearts are full of evil, and insanity rules them while they live. Later, they join the dead. (Insanity: irrational behavior) **4.** The living have hope—even a living dog is better than a dead lion! (Dog: common pet; lion: symbol of power) **5.** The living know they will die, but the dead know nothing; they receive no reward, and even their memory is forgotten. (Reward: gain or compensation; memory: recollection) **6.** Their love, hate, and jealousy have long passed; they'll never again participate in what happens under the sun. (Jealousy: envy) **7.** Eat with joy and drink with a satisfied heart, for God has already approved of your actions. (Satisfied: pleased; approved: accepted) **8.** Always wear white, and anoint your head with oil. (White: purity; anoint: apply oil) **9.** Enjoy life with your spouse, whom you love, all the days of this fleeting life that God has given you under the sun—these are your days of toil. (Fleeting: trouble) **10.** Whatever you do, do it with all your might, for in the grave, where you are going, there is no work, planning, knowledge, or wisdom. (Might: strength; grave: tomb) **11.** I've seen that the race is not for the swift, nor the battle for the strong; food does not come to the wise, wealth to the talented, or favor to the learned; time and chance affect them all. (Talented: very gifted; learned: educated) **12.** No one knows when their time will come: as fish are caught in a cruel net or birds in a snare, people are trapped by evil times that come unexpectedly. (Snare: trap;) **13.** I also saw under the sun this wise example that deeply moved me: (Moved: deeply impressed) **14.** There was a small city with few people. A mighty king surrounded it with siege works. (Siege works: military equipment for attack) **15.** A poor but wise man lived there and saved the city with his wisdom, but no one remembered him. **16.** I said, "Wisdom is better than strength." But the wisdom of the poor is despised, and their words are ignored. (Despised: looked down on; ignored: not paid attention to) **17.** The quiet words of the wise are more valuable than the loud shouts of a fool in charge. (Valuable: more important) **18.** Wisdom is better than weapons of war, but a single sinner can destroy much good. (Sinner: wrongdoer)

Chapter 10

1. Just as dead flies make perfume stink, a little folly can outweigh wisdom and honor. (Folly: foolishness) **2.** The wise lean toward the right, but fools lean to the left. (Right: symbol of correctness; left: symbol of foolishness) **3.** Even fools, as they walk along the road, show their lack of sense, exposing their stupidity to everyone. (Exposing: revealing) **4.** If a ruler's anger rises against you, stay calm; serenity can calm great offenses. (Serenity: peacefulness) **5.** I have seen an evil under the sun: an error that comes from a ruler. (Error: mistake) **6.** Fools are placed in high positions, while the rich occupy low ones. **7.** I've seen slaves riding horses, and princes walking like slaves. (Slaves: those in servitude; princes: royalty) **8.** Whoever digs a pit may fall into it; whoever breaks a wall may be bitten by a snake. (bitten: harmed) **9.** Whoever quarries stones may be hurt by them; whoever splits logs may be endangered. (Quarries: stone pits; logs: large pieces of wood) **10.** If the ax is dull and its edge not sharpened, more strength is needed, but skill brings success. (Dull: blunt) **11.** If a snake bites before it is charmed, the charmer gets no fee. (Charmed: controlled) **12.** Words from the wise are gracious, but fools are consumed by their own words. (Consumed: overwhelmed) **13.** At first, their words are folly, but in the end, they become wicked madness. (Wicked: evil) **14.** Fools multiply words. No one knows what's ahead, so who can tell what comes next? (Multiply: increase) **15.** The toil of fools wearies them, for they don't even know the way to town. (Toil: hard work; wearies: exhausts) **16.** Woe to a land whose king is a servant, and whose princes feast in the morning. (Feast: eat lavishly) **17.** Blessed is the land whose king is noble, and whose princes eat at the right time—for strength, not drunkenness. (drunkenness: excessive drinking) **18.** Through laziness, beams sag; because of idle hands, the house leaks. (Beams: structural supports; idle: inactive) **19.** A feast is for laughter, wine brings joy, and money answers everything. (Answers: resolves) **20.** Do not speak ill of the king, even in your thoughts, or curse the rich in your bedroom, for a bird may carry your words, and a bird on the wing may repeat them. (Ill: negatively)

Chapter 11

1. Ship your grain across the sea; after many days, you may receive a return. (Ship: send by boat; return: profit) **2.** Invest in seven ventures, yes, in eight; you don't know what disaster may strike. (Ventures: business projects; disaster: misfortune) **3.** When clouds are full, they pour rain. A tree falls either north or south, where it falls, it stays. (Full: containing enough; stays: remains) **4.** Whoever watches the wind will never plant; whoever looks at the clouds will never reap. (Reap: harvest) **5.** Just as you don't know the path of the wind, or how life forms in the womb, you can't understand God's work, the Maker of all. (Path: direction; womb: place where babies grow) **6.** Sow your seed in the morning, and don't let your hands rest in the evening, for you don't know what will succeed. (Sow: plant; succeed: prosper) **7.** Light is sweet, and it's a joy to see the sun. (Sweet: pleasant) **8.** However many years you live, enjoy them all, but remember the days of darkness, for they will be many. Everything to come is meaningless. (Darkness: hardships; meaningless: futile) **9.** You who are young, be happy in your youth, and let your heart lead you. But know that God will bring everything to judgment. **10.** Banish anxiety from your heart and remove the troubles of your body, for youth and vigor are meaningless. (Anxiety: worry; vigor: energy)

Chapter 12

1. Remember your Creator while you are young, before trouble comes and you say, "I find no joy in life." **2.** Before the sun, moon, and stars grow dark, and the clouds return after the rain. (Grow dark: become unclear) **3.** When the keepers of the house tremble, and strong men stoop, when grinders cease because they are few, and those who look through windows grow dim. **4.** When the doors are closed and the sound of grinding fades; when people rise at the sound of birds, but all their songs are faint. (Grinding: mill work; faint: weak) **5.** When people are afraid of heights and dangers in the streets; when the almond tree blossoms and the grasshopper drags itself, and desire is no longer stirred. Then people go to their eternal home. (Almond tree: tree with white flowers; eternal home: afterlife) **6.** Remember him before the silver cord is severed, and the golden bowl is broken; before the pitcher is shattered at the spring, and the wheel broken at the well. (Silver cord: life's thread; golden bowl: life's vessel) **7.** The dust returns to the ground, and the spirit returns to God who gave it. (Spirit: soul) **8.** "Meaningless! Meaningless!" says the Teacher. "Everything is meaningless!" (Teacher: the preacher) **9.** Not only was the Teacher wise, but he imparted knowledge to the people, pondering and setting in order many proverbs. (Imparted: shared) **10.** The Teacher sought the right words, and what he wrote was upright and true. **11.** The words of the wise are like goads, their sayings like nails—given by one Shepherd. (Goads: sticks used to drive animals; Shepherd: God) **12.** Be warned, my son, about anything beyond these. Making many books has no end, and much study wearies the body. (Warned: cautioned) **13.** Now all has been heard; here's the conclusion: Fear God and keep His commandments—this is the duty of all. (Conclusion: final thought) **14.** For God will bring every deed into judgment, including hidden things, whether good or evil. (Deeds: actions)

22 – Song of Solomon
Chapter 1
1. The Song of Songs, written by Solomon. (Solomon: Wisdom) **2.** Let him kiss me with his lips; your love is sweeter than wine. (Wine: Fermentation) **3.** Your name is like a fragrant perfume, and because of it, young women adore you. (Perfume: Fragrance) **4.** Draw me in, we will chase after you; the king has brought me to his chambers. We'll rejoice in your love, which is better than wine; the righteous cherish you. (Righteous: Virtuous) **5.** Though I am dark-skinned, I am beautiful, daughters of Jerusalem, like the tents of Kedar, like the curtains of Solomon. (Kedar: Nomads) **6.** Don't look down on me because I'm dark; the sun has tanned me. My brothers were angry with me, so they made me care for the vineyards, but I didn't tend my own. (Vineyards: Grapes) **7.** Tell me, whom my soul loves, where you graze your flock, where they rest at noon. Why should I wander among the flocks of your companions? (Flock: Herd) **8.** If you don't know, O fairest of women, follow the path of the flock and feed your goats near the shepherds' tents. (Fairest: Beautiful) **9.** I compare you, my love, to a chariot of horses, like Pharaoh's finest. (Chariot: Vehicle) **10.** Your cheeks are lovely, adorned with jewels, and your neck with chains of gold. (Jewels: Gems) **11.** We will make you gold-bordered garments, studded with silver. (Studded: Adorned) **12.** As the king sits at his table, my spikenard releases its fragrance. (Spikenard: Scent) **13.** A bundle of myrrh is my beloved to me; he rests between my breasts all night. (Myrrh: Resin) **14.** My beloved is like a cluster of henna flowers in the vineyards of En-gedi. (En-gedi: Oasis) **15.** You are beautiful, my love; your eyes are like doves. (Doves: Peace) **16.** You are fair and lovely, my beloved; our bed is green. (Fair: Light) **17.** The beams of our house are made of cedar, and our rafters of fir. (Cedar: Wood)

Chapter 2
1. I am the rose of Sharon, and the lily of the valleys. (Sharon: plain; Lily: beauty) **2.** As the lily among thorns, so is my love among the daughters. (Thorns: hardships) **3.** As the apple tree among the trees of the forest, so is my beloved among the sons. I sat under his shadow with delight, and his fruit was sweet to my taste. (Shadow: protection; Fruit: sweetness) **4.** He brought me to the banqueting house, and his banner over me was love. (Banqueting: feast) **5.** Support me with flagons, comfort me with apples, for I am lovesick. (Flagons: vessels; Lovesick: heart-stricken) **6.** His left hand is under my head, and his right hand embraces me. (Embraces: holds) **7.** I charge you, daughters of Jerusalem, by the roes and hinds of the field, stir not up nor awake my love until he pleases. (Charge: command; Roes: deer) **8.** The voice of my beloved! Behold, he comes leaping over mountains, skipping upon hills. (Leaping: jumping) **9.** My beloved is like a roe or young hart: he stands behind our wall, looking through the windows, showing himself through the lattice. (Roe: deer; Lattice: framework) **10.** My beloved spoke and said, "Rise up, my love, my fair one, and come away." (Spoke: said) **11.** The winter is past, the rain is over and gone. (Past: finished) **2:12.** The flowers appear on the earth; the time of singing birds is come, and the voice of the turtle is heard in our land. (Turtle: dove) **13.** The fig tree puts forth green figs, and the vines with tender grapes give a good scent. Arise, my love, my fair one, and come away. (Tender: young) **14.** O my dove, in the clefts of the rock, in the secret places of the stairs, let me see your face, let me hear your voice; for sweet is your voice, and your face is beautiful. (Clefts: cracks; Sweet: pleasant) **15.** Take us the little foxes that spoil the vines, for our vines have tender grapes. (Foxes: harmful animal; Spoil: damage) **16.** My beloved is mine, and I am his: he feeds among the lilies. (Feeds: rests) **17.** Until the day breaks and the shadows flee away, turn, my beloved, be like a roe or young hart on the mountains of Bether. (Bether: division; Flee: escape)

Chapter 3
1. During the night, I searched for the one my soul desires. I looked for him, but couldn't find him. (Soul: inner being or heart) **2.** I decided to rise and wander through the city—through its streets and open squares—seeking the one my heart longs for. But still, I couldn't find him. (Squares: open public spaces) **3.** The city watchmen came across me, and I asked, "Have you seen the one my soul loves?" (Watchmen: city guards) **4.** I had barely moved past them when I finally found him, the one I so deeply love. I held him tightly and refused to let go, taking him to my mother's house, to the room where I was born. (Barely: just; Room: a private space) **5.** I urge you, daughters of Jerusalem, by the graceful gazelles and deer of the field do not stir my love or awaken him until he desires. (Graceful: elegant or beautiful; stir: disturb) **6.** Who is this emerging from the desert, rising like pillars of smoke, with fragrance of myrrh and frankincense, carrying the sweet perfumes of the merchant? (Emerging: coming out; Frankincense: aromatic resin) **7.** Look at Solomon's bed, surrounded by sixty brave men, the warriors of Israel. (Brave: courageous or valiant; Warriors: soldiers) **8.** All of them are armed with swords, skilled in battle, each keeping his sword at his side, ready for danger in the night. (Skilled: experienced in combat) **9.** King Solomon crafted for himself a chariot from Lebanon's finest wood. (Crafted: made with skill) **10.** Its pillars are silver, its base is golden, its covering is purple, and its interior is adorned with love, made for the daughters of Jerusalem. (Adorned: decorated or embellished; Covering: top layer) **11.** Go, daughters of Zion, and behold King Solomon wearing the crown his mother gave him on his wedding day, when his heart was filled with joy. (Zion: symbolic name for Jerusalem)

Chapter 4
1. Behold, you are beautiful, my love; your eyes are like doves nestled in your hair, as goats descending from Mount Gilead. (Nestled: settled; Gilead: region) **2.** Your teeth are like shorn sheep, freshly washed, each with twins, none barren. (Shorn: trimmed; barren: unfruitful) **3.** Your lips are like scarlet thread, your speech graceful; your temples like pomegranates within your hair. (Scarlet: red; Graceful: elegant) **4.** Your neck is like the Tower of David, a fortress adorned with shields of mighty men. (Fortress: stronghold) **5.** Your breasts are like two young deer, twins, feeding among the lilies. (Deer: graceful; Lilies: flowers) **6.** Until the day breaks and shadows vanish, I will go to the mountain of myrrh and hill of frankincense. (Myrrh: resin; Frankincense: gum) **7.** You are all beautiful, my love, with no flaw in you. (Flaw: imperfection) **8.** Come with me from Lebanon, my bride; from the heights of Amana, Shenir, and Hermon, from the dens of lions and leopards. (Lebanon: mountains; Dens: lairs) **9.** You have stolen my heart, my sister, my bride, with a glance and a jewel from your necklace. (Stolen: captivated) **10.** How beautiful is your love, my sister, my bride! Your love is better than wine, and your ointment's fragrance more exquisite than all spices. (Exquisite: delicate) **11.** Your lips drop honeycomb; honey and milk are under your tongue, and your garments smell like Lebanon. (Drop: flow) **12.** You are a closed garden, my sister, my bride; a sealed fountain. (Sealed: tightly closed) **13.** Your plants are an orchard of pomegranates, camphire, and spikenard. (Orchard: grove) **14.** Spikenard, saffron, calamus, cinnamon, frankincense, myrrh, and aloes, with all finest spices. (Aloes: resin) **15.** You are a fountain of gardens, a well of living waters, flowing with streams from Lebanon. (Living waters: fresh

water) **16.** Awake, O north wind; come, south wind, and blow upon my garden, that its spices may flow out. Let my beloved enter his garden and enjoy its fruits. (Spices: aromas)

Chapter 5

1. I've entered my garden, my bride; I've gathered my spices and my myrrh, savored honey and honeycomb, and enjoyed wine and milk. Come, friends, and feast with me; drink deeply, O beloved. (Garden: intimate place) **2.** Though I sleep, my heart is awake, for I hear my beloved's voice, "Open to me, my sister, my dove, my perfect one. My head is wet with dew, and my hair with night's rain." (Awake: attentive) **3.** I've taken off my coat—how can I put it back on? I've washed my feet—how could I soil them again? (Soil: dirty) **4.** My beloved reached through the door, and my heart was stirred by his touch. (Stirred: deeply moved) **5.** I rose to open to my beloved, and my hands were covered in fragrant myrrh, the scent lingering on the door handles. (Fragrant: sweet) **6.** When I opened, he was gone. My heart sank at his words. I searched for him but couldn't find him; I called, but he didn't respond. (Sank: heavy) **7.** The watchmen found me, beat me, and took away my veil. (Veil: modest covering) **8.** I implore you, daughters of Jerusalem, if you find my beloved, tell him I am faint with love. (Faint: overwhelmed) **9.** What makes your beloved so special, O fairest among women? Why do you charge us to search for him? (Fairest: most beautiful) **10.** My beloved is radiant, like the finest ruby, the most splendid of ten thousand. (Radiant: glowing) **11.** His head is pure gold, his hair thick and black, like a raven's feathers. (Thick: voluminous) **12.** His eyes are like doves by the waters, washed in milk, perfectly placed. (Symmetry: balanced) **13.** His cheeks are like a bed of spices, his lips like lilies, dripping with sweet myrrh. (Spices: aromatic) **14.** His hands are like gold rings set with beryl, and his torso like ivory, gleaming with sapphires. (Beryl: gemstone) **15.** His legs are like marble pillars, set on golden pedestals; his appearance is majestic, like the cedars of Lebanon. (Majestic: grand) **16.** His speech is sweet; he is the epitome of beauty. This is my beloved, my companion, O daughters of Jerusalem. (Epitome: perfect example)

Chapter 6

1. Where has your beloved gone, O fairest of women? Where has he turned, that we might seek him alongside you? (Fairest: most beautiful) **2.** My beloved has gone down into his garden, to the spice beds, to enjoy the gardens and gather lilies. (Spice: fragrant plants) **3.** I am my beloved's, and my beloved is mine; he dwells among the lilies. (Dwells: resides) **4.** You are beautiful, my love, as stunning as Tirzah, as lovely as Jerusalem, and as awe-inspiring as an army with banners. (Stunning: striking) **5.** Turn your eyes away from me, for they have captivated me; your hair is like a flock of goats descending from Gilead. (Captivated: enchanted) **6.** Your teeth are like a flock of sheep freshly washed, each bearing twins, and none are barren. (Barren: fruitless) **7.** Your temples are like a pomegranate within your hair. (Temples: sides of the head) **8.** There are sixty queens, eighty concubines, and countless virgins. (Concubines: secondary wives) **9.** But my dove, my pure one, is only one; she is the only one of her mother, the most beloved of her who bore her. The daughters saw her and called her blessed; even the queens and concubines praised her. (Pure: undefiled) **10.** Who is she who shines like the morning, as beautiful as the moon, as radiant as the sun, and awe-inspiring as an army with banners? (Radiant: glowing) **11.** I went down into the garden of nuts to view the fruits of the valley, to see if the vine had flourished and if the pomegranates had budded. (Flourished: thrived) **12.** Before I knew it, my soul was carried away like the chariots of Amminadib. (Carried away: swept off) **13.** Return, return, O Shulamite, return, that we may gaze upon you. What do you see in the Shulamite? It is as though we see the beauty of two armies. (Gaze: look intently)

Chapter 7

1. How beautiful are your feet in shoes, O princess! Your thighs like jewels, crafted by a skilled artisan. (Artisan: craftsman) **2.** Your navel is like a goblet, never empty; your belly likes a heap of wheat surrounded by lilies. (Goblet: cup) **3.** Your breasts are like two young deer, twins. (Deer: graceful) **4.** Your neck is an ivory tower; your eyes like the fishpools of Heshbon by Bath-rabbim; your nose like Lebanon's tower facing Damascus. (Ivory: white; Heshbon: city) **5.** Your head is like Carmel, and your hair like purple; the king is captivated. (Carmel: mountain; Captivated: enthralled) **6.** How fair and delightful you are, my love! (Fair: beautiful) **7.** Your figure is like a palm tree, and your breasts like grape clusters. (Figure: shape) **8.** I will climb the palm tree, grasp its branches; your breasts will be like grape clusters, and your breath like apples. (Breath: scent) **9.** Your mouth is like the finest wine; sweetly flowing, making the lips of sleepers speak. (Finest: best) **10.** I belong to my beloved, and his desire is for me. (Desire: longing) **11.** Come, my beloved, let's go into the field; let's stay in the villages. (Stay: lodge) **12.** Let's rise early to the vineyards, to see if the vines flourish and the pomegranates bloom; there I will give you my love. (Flourish: grow) **13.** The mandrakes smell sweet, and at our gates are all kinds of pleasant fruits, new and old, stored for you, my beloved. (Mandrakes: fragrant; stored: kept)

Chapter 8

1. If only you were like my brother, nursed by my mother! Then I could meet you openly and kiss you without being scorned. (Scorned: mocked or despised) **2.** I would take you to my mother's house, where she would teach me; I would give you spiced wine and pomegranate juice to drink. (Spiced wine: wine mixed with fragrant spices; pomegranate: a fruit symbolizing abundance or love) **3.** His left hand would support my head, and his right hand would hold me close. (Embrace: to hold lovingly) **4.** I urge you, daughters of Jerusalem, not to awaken love until it desires. **5.** Who is this coming from the wilderness, leaning on her beloved? I awakened you under the apple tree, where your mother gave you birth. (Wilderness: a deserted or uncultivated area) **6.** Place me like a seal on your heart and arm, for love is as strong as death, and jealousy as fierce as the grave. Its flames are like blazing fire, an intense flame. (Seal: a mark of ownership or protection; vehement: strong or passionate) **7.** Love cannot be extinguished by waters or floods; if one offered all their wealth for love, it would be utterly rejected. (Quench: to extinguish or put out; contemned: treated with contempt) **8.** We have a young sister without maturity; what should we do for her when she is sought in marriage? (Spoken for: considered for marriage or a proposal) **9.** If she is like a wall, we will build on her a silver palace; if she is like a door, we will secure her with cedar panels. **10.** I am a wall, and my breasts like towers; because of this, I found favor in his eyes. (Favor: approval or delight) **11.** Solomon had a vineyard at Baal-hamon, leased to keepers who each paid a thousand pieces of silver for its fruit. (vineyard: a plantation of grapevines; Baal-hamon: possibly a place of wealth or abundance) **12.** My vineyard is mine to tend. Solomon may keep his thousand pieces of silver, and those who care for it may have two hundred. (Keepers: those who manage or guard something) **13.** You who dwell in the gardens, let your companions listen to your voice, but let me also hear it. (Hearken to listen attentively) **14.** Hurry, my beloved, and be like a gazelle or young deer leaping on the mountains of spices. (Roe: a small deer; spices: fragrant plants or areas of delight)

23 – Isahia

Chapter 1

1. This is the prophetic vision of Isaiah, son of Amoz, concerning Judah and Jerusalem at some point of the reigns of Uzziah, Jotham, Ahaz, and Hezekiah, kings of Judah. (Amoz: Isaiah's father) **2.** Pay attention, O heavens, and pay interest, O earth! The Lord has spoken: "I raised and cared for kids, but they have got became against Me." **3.** The ox is aware of its proprietor, and the donkey its grasp's manger; however Israel does not know, My humans do now not recognize. (Manger: a feeding trough for animals) **4.** Woe to the sinful country, full with iniquity, a brood of wrongdoers, youngsters who are corrupt! They forsake the Lord, angered the Holy one in all Israel, and grew to become far from Him. (Iniquity: sinful conduct) **5.** Why continue to be punished? you are best growing extra rebellious. The complete head is unwell, and the coronary heart is faint. **6.** From head to toe, there's no fitness; handiest wounds, bruises, and open sores that have not been handled or bandaged. **7.** Your land is desolate, your towns are burned with fireplace. Strangers consume your land in full view, leaving it desolate. **8.** The daughter of Zion is left like a shelter in a winery, like a hut in a cucumber field, like a metropolis under siege. **9.** If the Lord of hosts had no longer left us a small remnant, we might have end up like Sodom and Gomorrah. **10.** Pay attention the phrase of the Lord, you rulers of Sodom; listen to the law of our God, you people of Gomorrah. (Gomorrah: an historic city destroyed for its wickedness) **11.** "Why do you deliver so many sacrifices to Me?" says the Lord. "i've had enough of your burnt services. I do not pride within the blood of bulls, lambs, or goats." **12.** When you come to appear before Me, who has asked you to trample My courts? **13.** Forestall bringing nugatory offerings; incense is detestable to Me. Your festivals, New Moons, and assemblies are a burden I cannot endure. **14.** Your New Moons and feasts I hate; they have turn out to be a burden to Me, and I am weary of bearing them. **15.** When you unfold out your fingers to wish, I will conceal My eyes from you. Even in case you pray many prayers, i will not pay attention, to your hands are complete of blood. **16.** "Wash yourselves, make yourselves easy; take your evil deeds out of My sight. Forestall doing evil. **17.** Learn to do right, are looking for justice, correct the oppressor, guard the fatherless, plead for the widow." **18.** "Come now, allow us to cause collectively," says the Lord. "Even though your sins are like scarlet, they will be as white as snow; though they're red as red, they'll be like wool." **19.** If you are willing and obedient, you may consume the coolest of the land; **20.** But if you refuse and rebellion, you may be devoured through the sword." For the mouth of the Lord has spoken. **21.** How the trustworthy town has turn out to be a prostitute! It became full of justice and righteousness, but now murderers. **22.** Your silver has grow to be dross, your wine is watered down. (Dross: impurities in metals) **23.** Your rulers are rebellious, partners of thieves. They love bribes and chase after rewards. They do not shield the fatherless, nor do they plead for the widow. **24.** Therefore, the Lord, the Lord of hosts, the effective certainly one of Israel, says: "I can take vengeance on My enemies and deal with folks that oppose Me." **25.** "I'm able to turn My hand in opposition to you, and purify your dross, eliminating all your impurities." **26.** I'm able to restore your judges to their former country, and your counselors to their unique position. Then you will be referred to as the town of righteousness, the faithful town. **27.** Zion may be redeemed with justice, and her repentant ones with righteousness. **28.** But rebels and sinners might be destroyed together, and those who forsake the Lord will perish. **29.** You may be ashamed of the idols you desired, and embarrassed via the gardens you chose. **30.** You will be like a terebinth tree whose leaves wither, or like a garden without water. (Terebinth: a form of tree often symbolizing electricity and staying power) **31.** The sturdy could be like tinder, and their works like sparks. Both will burn together, and nobody will quench them. (Tinder: dry cloth that catches hearth easily).

Chapter 2
1. The phrase that Isaiah, son of Amoz, saw concerning Judah and Jerusalem. **2.** In the closing days, the mountain of the Lord's house can be hooked up as the best of mountains, and exalted particularly hills. All international locations will flow to it. **3.** Many human beings will say, "Come, allow us to pass up to the mountain of the Lord, to the residence of the God of Jacob. He'll train us His approaches, and we can walk in His paths." For the law will go out from Zion, and the phrase of the Lord from Jerusalem. **4.** He'll choose between the countries and rebuke many human beings. They may beat their swords into plowshares and their spears into pruning hooks. Nations will no longer combat towards each different, and they will never examine conflict once more. **5.** O house of Jacob, come, allow us to walk in the light of the Lord. **6.** For you've got forsaken Your human beings, the residence of Jacob, because they may be packed with jap customs. They're soothsayers like the Philistines, and they satisfaction inside the kids of foreigners. (Soothsayers: those who exercise divination) **7.** Their land is complete of silver and gold, and their treasures are limitless. Their land is complete of horses, and their chariots cannot be counted. **8.** Their land is complete of idols; they worship the paintings of their personal palms, the matters their fingers have made. (Idols: Statues of God) **9.** Humans bow down and humble themselves, but do not forgive them. **10.** Enter the rocks, and disguise within the dirt, from the fear of the Lord and the splendor of His majesty. **11.** The pleasure of man could be humbled, and the vanity of guys might be brought low. The Lord on my own may be exalted in that day. **12.** The day of the Lord of hosts will encounter all that is proud and lofty, upon the whole thing lifted up—and it will be delivered low. **13.** Upon the cedars of Lebanon which are excessive and exalted, and upon the oak of Bashan; (Lebanon: a region acknowledged for its tall timber; Bashan: a fertile land east of Israel) **14.** Upon the high mountains, and the hills which can be lifted up; **15.** Upon each high tower, and each fortified wall; **16.** Upon all the ships of Tarshish, and all the beautiful sloops. (Tarshish: an ancient port metropolis known for its wealth) **17.** The delight of guy could be humbled, and the vanity of fellows may be added low. The Lord alone will be exalted in that day, **18.** And He's going to completely abolish the idols. **19.** They may conceal within the rocks and caves, from the terror of the Lord and the beauty of His majesty, whilst He rises to shake the earth. **20.** On that day, a person will throw away his idols of silver and gold, which he made to worship, to the moles and bats. (Moles: small burrowing animals; bats: flying mammals) **21.** They may conceal inside the crevices of the rocks and within the crags of the rugged mountains, from fear of the Lord and the splendor of His majesty, when He rises to shake the earth. **22.** Stop trusting in mortal guy, whose breath is in his nostrils. For why need to he be esteemed? (Mortal guy: a person whose lifestyles is fragile)

Chapter 3
1. Look, the Lord, the Lord of hosts, will remove from Jerusalem and Judah the food and water supply, the whole stock of bread and water. **2.** He will take away the mighty man, the soldier, the judge, the prophet, the diviner, and the elder. (Diviner: one who predicts the future through supernatural means) **3.** He will remove the captain of fifty, the respected man, the counselor, the skilled artisan, and the expert enchanter. (Enchanter: one who uses magic or spells) **4.** "I will appoint children to be their rulers, and babes shall govern them." **5.** The people will be oppressed, everyone by their neighbor; children will be disrespectful to the elderly, and the lowly to the honorable. **6.** When a man holds his brother in his father's house, saying, "You have clothes; be our ruler and take charge of this ruin," **7.** That day, he will refuse, saying, "I cannot help you; I have no food or clothes. Don't make me a ruler." **8.** Jerusalem has stumbled, and Judah has fallen, because their words and actions are against the Lord, provoking His glory. **9.** Their faces show their guilt, and they openly declare their sin like Sodom; they do not hide it. Woe to them! They have brought harm upon themselves. **10.** "Say to the righteous that it will go well with them, for they will enjoy the fruit of their deeds." **11.** Woe to the wicked! It will be disastrous for him, for he will receive the reward of his actions. **12.** My people are oppressed by children, and women rule over them. O My people, those who lead you mislead you and destroy your path. **13.** The Lord rises to plead His case and stands to judge the people. **14.** The Lord will bring judgment against the elders and rulers: "You have destroyed the vineyard; the plunder of the poor is in your homes." **15.** "What do you mean by oppressing My people and grinding the faces of the poor?" says the Lord, the God of hosts. **16.** The Lord says:

"Because the daughters of Zion are proud, walking with necks stretched out and lustful eyes, walking with measured steps and jingling with their feet, **17.** Therefore, the Lord will strike them with a scab on their heads, and He will uncover their secret parts." **18.** In that day, the Lord will remove their finery: the jingling anklets, scarves, and crescent-shaped ornaments; **19.** the pendants, bracelets, veils; **20.** The headdresses, leg ornaments, headbands; the perfume boxes, charms, **21.** rings, and nose jewels; **22.** Their festive clothes, mantles, outer garments, purses, **23.** Mirrors, fine linen, turbans, and robes. **24.** Instead of sweet perfume, there will be a foul odor; instead of a sash, a rope; instead of well-groomed hair, baldness; instead of a rich robe, sackcloth; and branding instead of beauty. **25.** Your men will fall by the sword, and your mighty warriors will be killed in battle. **26.** Her gates will mourn and lament (lament; a passionate expression of grief), and she will sit in the dust, desolate.

Chapter 4
1. in that day, seven women will cling to one man, saying, "We will provide our own food and clothes; only let us be called by your name to take away our disgrace." **2.** In that day, the Branch of the Lord will be beautiful and glorious, and the fruit of the earth will be excellent for those in Israel who have survived. (Branch of the Lord: messianic title) **3.** Those who remain in Zion and Jerusalem will be called holy—everyone whose name is recorded among the living in Jerusalem. **4.** When the Lord has cleansed the filth of Zion's daughters and purged the blood of Jerusalem by the spirit of judgment and burning, **5.** He will create a cloud and smoke by day and a shining fire by night above every dwelling on Mount Zion. Over all the glory, there will be a covering. (Mount Zion: Jerusalem, Glory: divine presence) **6.** There will be a shelter from the heat in the daytime, a refuge, and a place of protection from storm and rain. (Refuge: place of safety)

Chapter 5
1. Let me sing a song to my Beloved about His vineyard. My Beloved has a vineyard on a fertile hill. (Beloved: term of endearment) **2.** He dug it up, cleared its stones, and planted it with the best vine. He built a tower in the middle and made a winepress, hoping for good grapes, but it produced wild ones. (Wild grapes: bad results) **3.** "Now, inhabitants of Jerusalem and men of Judah, judge between Me and My vineyard. (Inhabitants: residents) **4.** What more could I have done for My vineyard that I did not? Why, when I expected good grapes, did it produce wild ones? (Vineyard: metaphor for Israel) **5.** Now I will remove its hedge, and it will be burned. I will break down its wall, and it will be trampled. (Hedge: protective boundary) **6.** I will let it lie waste; it will not be pruned or dug, and thorns and briers will grow. I will command the clouds not to rain on it." (Pruned: trimmed, Briers: weeds) **7.** The vineyard of the Lord of hosts is the house of Israel, and the men of Judah are His pleasant plant. He sought justice, but found oppression; righteousness, but a cry for help. (House of Israel: the people) **8.** Woe to those who join house to house, adding field to field, until there is no room for others to live in the land! (Woe: warning, sorrow) **9.** The Lord of hosts said, "Many houses will be desolate, great and beautiful ones without inhabitant. (Desolate: abandoned) **10.** Ten acres of vineyard will yield only a bath, and a homer of seed will produce only an ephah." (Bath: liquid measure) **11.** Woe to those who rise early to pursue strong drink and continue late into the night until wine inflames them! (Inflames: excites) **12.** Harp, strings, tambourine, flute, and wine are in their feasts, but they do not consider the work of the Lord or His actions. (Feasts: celebratory meals) **13.** Therefore, My people are exiled because they lack knowledge. Their leaders are hungry, and their people are thirsty. (Exiled: forced out) **14.** Therefore, Sheol has enlarged its mouth and opened it wide; their glory, crowds, and celebrations will descend into it. (Sheol: realm of the dead) **15.** People will be humbled, and the proud will be brought low, but the Lord of hosts will be exalted in judgment, and God who is holy will be glorified in righteousness. (Exalted: honored) **16.** Then lambs will graze where the rich once fed, and strangers will eat in their desolate fields. (Lambs: young sheep) **17.** Woe to those who draw iniquity with cords of vanity and sin as if with a cart rope, (Iniquity: wickedness, Cords: means) **18.** who say, "Let Him hurry and do His work, so we may see it! Let the Holy One of Israel come near, so we may know it." (Holy One of Israel: God) **19.** Woe to those who call evil good and good evil, who substitute darkness for light, and light for darkness, who replace bitter with sweet and sweet with bitter! (Substitute: replace, Bitter: sour) **20.** Woe to those wise in their own eyes and prudent in their own sight! (Prudent: wise) **21.** Woe to men mighty at drinking wine, and men valiant in mixing strong drinks, (Mighty: powerful) **22.** who justify the wicked for a bribe and take justice from the righteous! (Bribe: money for influence) **23.** Therefore, like fire that consumes stubble and flame that devours chaff, their roots will rot, and their blossoms will turn to dust, for they have rejected the law of the Lord and despised His word. (Stubble: dry stalks, Chaff: husks) **24.** The anger of the Lord is stirred against His people; He has raised His hand against them and struck them. The hills trembled, and their bodies lay like refuse in the streets. For all this, His anger is not turned away, His hand is still stretched out. (Refuse: waste) **25.** He will lift up a banner to the nations from afar and whistle to them from the ends of the earth. They will come quickly and swiftly. (Banner: signal, Whistle: call) **26.** None will be weary or stumble; none will sleep or slumber; their belts and sandals will not loosen or break. (Slumber: sleep) **27.** Their arrows will be sharp, their bows bent, their horses' hooves like flint, and their wheels like a whirlwind. (Flint: hard stone, Whirlwind: fast-moving wind) **28.** They will roar like lions, and like young lions, they will seize their prey, carry it away, and no one will rescue it. (Prey: hunted animals) **29.** In that day, they will roar like the sea. If one looks at the land, there will be darkness and distress, and the light will be obscured by the clouds. (Obscured: hidden)

Chapter 6
1. Inside the year when King Uzziah passed away, I saw the Lord seated on a throne, towering and exalted, and the train of His robe filled the temple. (Train of His gown: hem of His garment, Temple: God's living) **2.** Above the throne stood seraphim, each with six wings—wings covering their faces, two covering their feet, and with two, they flew. (Seraphim: angelic beings, Wings: symbols of strength and reverence) **3.** And they called to one another, saying, "Holy, holy, holy is the Lord of hosts; the whole earth is filled with His glory!" (God's sovereignty, Majesty: grandeur) **4.** The doorposts trembled at the sound of their voices, and the temple was filled with smoke. (Doorposts: door frames, Trembled: shook) **5.** Then I cried out, "Woe is me! I am ruined, for I am a man of unclean lips, and I live among a people of unclean lips; for my eyes have seen the King, the Lord of hosts." (Woe: sorrow, lost: ruined, Impure speech: sinful words) **6.** One of the seraphim flew to me, holding a burning coal that he had taken with tongs from the altar. (Seraphim: angelic beings, Coal: cleansing fire, Altar: place of sacrifice) **7.** He touched my lips with it and said, "This has touched your lips; your guilt is removed, and your sin is atoned for." (Guilt: moral stain, Atoned for: cleansed) **8.** Then I heard the voice of the Lord saying, "Whom shall I send, and who will go for Us?" And I said, "Here am I, send me." (Us: the plural of God, representing the Trinity) **9.** He said, "Go and tell this people, 'You will keep listening, but you will not understand; you will keep looking, but you will not perceive.'" (See: understand deeply) **10.** "Make the hearts of this people calloused, their ears dull, and their eyes closed—otherwise they might see with their eyes, hear with their ears, understand with their hearts, and turn and be healed." (Calloused: unresponsive, Blind: spiritually unaware) **11.** I asked, "How long, Lord?" And He answered, "Until the cities lie ruined and without inhabitant, and the houses are left deserted, and the fields are ruined and ravaged." (Ruined: destroyed, Desolate: abandoned) **12.** The Lord will remove people far away, and the land will be utterly forsaken. (Remove: exile, Desolate: abandoned) **13.**

And though a tenth remains in the land, it will again be laid waste. But as the terebinth and oak leave stumps when they are cut down, so the holy seed will be its stump." (Remnant: survivors, Stump: remaining portion of a tree)

Chapter 7

1. In the time of Ahaz, son of Jotham, son of Uzziah, king of Judah, Rezin king of Syria and Pekah son of Remaliah, king of Israel, came up to Jerusalem to wage war against it but could not defeat it. (Defeat: conquer) 2. The news reached the royal house, saying, "Syria has allied with Ephraim," and the hearts of Ahaz and his people were shaken as trees are shaken by the wind. 3. Then the Lord spoke to Isaiah, saying, "Go meet Ahaz, you and your son Shear-Jashub, at the end of the aqueduct from the upper pool, on the road to the laundries. (Aqueduct: water channel, Shear-Jashub: "a remnant shall return") 4. Tell him, 'Stay calm, do not be afraid, do not let your heart faint because of these two smoldering firebrands, because of the fierce anger of Rezin and Syria, and the son of Remaliah. (Faint: become fearful, Firebrands: burning sticks) 5. Syria, Ephraim, and the son of Remaliah have plotted to do evil against you, saying, (Plot: plan, Evil: harm) 6. 'Let us attack Judah, let us tear down its defenses, and appoint a king from the son of Tabel.'" (Tear down: breach, Appoint: make) 7. But the Lord says, "It will not happen; it will not come to pass." 8. The head of Syria is Damascus, and the head of Damascus is Rezin. Within sixty-five years Ephraim will be shattered and cease to be a people. (Ephraim: northern kingdom) 9. The head of Ephraim is Samaria, and the head of Samaria is the son of Remaliah. If you do not stand firm in your faith, you will not stand at all." (Faith: trust in God) 10. Again the Lord spoke to Ahaz, saying, 11. "Ask for a sign from the Lord your God, ask for it to be as deep as the grave or as high as the heavens." (Sign: proof, Deep: below, High: above) 12. But Ahaz replied, "I will not ask, nor will I test the Lord!" (Test: challenge God) 13. Then Isaiah said, "Hear now, O house of David! Is it not enough to weary men, but will you weary my God also? (Weary: trouble) 14. Therefore, the Lord Himself will give you a sign: the virgin will conceive and give birth to a Son, and will call Him Immanuel. (Virgin: young woman, Immanuel: "God with us") 15. He will eat curds and honey, and learn to reject evil and choose good. 16. Before the child learns to reject evil and choose good, the land you fear will be deserted by both kings. (Reject: turn away from) 17. The Lord will bring the king of Assyria against you and your people, and against your father's house—days like none since the time Ephraim broke away from Judah. (Assyria: empire) 18. On that day, the Lord will whistle for the fly from the farthest part of the Nile, and for the bee from the land of Assyria. (Whistle: call, Fly: symbol of invasion) 19. They will come, and they will settle in the desolate valleys, in the clefts of the rocks, and on all the thorny ground. (Desolate: abandoned, Thorny: difficult land) 20. On that day, the Lord will use the king of Assyria to shave you with a razor from beyond the Euphrates—your head, your legs, and even your beard will be shaved off. (Shave: humiliation) 21. On that day, a man will keep alive a young cow and two sheep. (Young cow: scarcity) 22. From the milk of these, he will eat curds, and everyone who is left in the land will eat curds and honey. (Curds: dairy) 23. In that day, even if a thousand vines worth a thousand shekels are planted, they will only be thorns and briars. (Shekels: silver coins, Briars: thorns) 24. People will use bows and arrows to gather the thorns, for the land will be overrun with them. (Thorns: difficult terrain) 25. Even the hills that can be plowed will be overrun with thorns and briars, and they will become pastureland for oxen and sheep to graze. (Pastureland: grazing area).

Chapter 8

1. The Lord told me, "Take a large scroll and write on it with a man's handwriting, concerning Maher-Shalal-Hash-Baz." 2. I will choose trustworthy witnesses to record this: Uriah the priest and Zechariah, the son of Jeberechiah. 3. I went to the prophetess, and she conceived a son. The Lord then told me, "Name him Maher-Shalal-Hash-Baz; 4. before the child can say 'Father' or 'Mother,' the riches of Damascus and the spoil of Samaria will be taken by the king of Assyria." 5. The Lord spoke to me again, saying: 6. "Since these people rejected the quiet waters of Shiloah, and rejoice in Rezin and in the son of Remaliah; (Shiloah: a stream or pool near Jerusalem; Rezin: king of Aram; Remaliah: the father of Pekah, king of Israel) 7. now, the Lord will bring upon them the waters of the River, powerful and mighty—the king of Assyria and all his glory. He will rise above all his channels and overflow all his banks. 8. He will pass through Judah, flooding and reaching to the neck; his wings will stretch across your land, O Immanuel. (Immanuel: meaning "God with us") 9. "Be shattered, O nations, and be broken! Listen, all you distant lands. Prepare yourselves, but be shattered; prepare yourselves, but be broken! 10. Plan together, but it will come to nothing. Speak a word, but it will not stand, for God is with us." 11. The Lord spoke to me firmly and told me not to follow the ways of this people, saying: 12. "Do not call a conspiracy everything this people calls a conspiracy, and do not fear what they fear or be troubled. 13. The Lord Almighty, Him you shall honor. Let Him be your fear, and let Him be your dread. (Lord of hosts: title for God as a military leader) 14. He will be a sanctuary, but also a stone of stumbling and a rock of offense to both houses of Israel, a trap and a snare to the people of Jerusalem. (The two houses of Israel: the northern kingdom of Israel and the southern kingdom of Judah) 15. Many will stumble and fall; they will be broken, trapped, and captured." 16. Bind up the testimony, and seal the law among my followers. 17. I will wait for the Lord, who has hidden His face from the house of Jacob; I will put my trust in Him. 18. Here am I, and the children the Lord has given me! We are signs and wonders in Israel from the Lord of hosts, who dwells in Mount Zion. 19. And when they say to you, "Seek those who consult spirits and whisper secrets," should not a people seek their God? Should they consult the dead on behalf of the living? 20. To the law and to the testimony! If they do not speak according to this word, it is because there is no light in them. 21. They will pass through troubled and hungry; and when they are hungry, they will become angry, curse their king and their God, and look up. 22. They will look to the earth, and see only distress, darkness, and the gloom of anguish; they will be thrust into deep darkness.

Chapter 9

1. However, the gloom will not last for those in misery, as it was when the land of Zebulun and Naphtali were lightly oppressed, and later more severely, by the way of the sea, beyond the Jordan, in Galilee of the Gentiles. (Zebulun and Naphtali: two tribes of Israel; Galilee: northern region of Israel, home to many Gentiles) 2. The people who walked in darkness have seen a great light; those who lived in the shadow of death, light has shined upon them. 3. You have multiplied the nation and increased its joy; they rejoice before You as people do when they harvest or divide the spoils of victory. 4. You have broken the yoke of their burden and the rod of their oppressors, as You did in the day of Midian. (Midian: the land of the Midianites, defeated by Gideon) 5. Every warrior's sandal and blood-soaked garment will be burned as fuel for fire. 6. For unto us a child is born, to us a Son is given, and the government will be on His shoulders. His name will be called Wonderful, Counselor, Mighty God, Everlasting Father, Prince of Peace. 7. Of the increase of His government and peace there will be no end, on the throne of David and His kingdom, to establish it with judgment and justice from that time forward, even forever. The zeal of the Lord of hosts will accomplish this. (David: the great king of Israel; Lord of hosts: name for God as a divine warrior) 8. The Lord sent a message against Jacob, and it has fallen upon Israel. 9. All the people will know, including Ephraim and the inhabitants of Samaria, who boast with pride and arrogance: (Ephraim: a tribe of Israel; Samaria: capital of the northern kingdom) 10. "The bricks have fallen, but we will rebuild with hewn stones; the sycamores are cut down, but we will replace them with cedars." 11. Therefore, the Lord will bring adversaries

against them, and stir up their enemies, **12.** the Syrians in the front and the Philistines at the back; they will devour Israel with open mouths. Yet, His anger is not turned away, His hand is still stretched out. (Syrians: people from Syria; Philistines: ancient enemies of Israel) **13.** The people do not turn to the one who strikes them, nor do they seek the Lord of hosts. **14.** Therefore, the Lord will cut off both head and tail from Israel, in one day. **15.** The elder and honorable are the head, but the prophet who leads in lies is the tail. **16.** The leaders of this people deceive them, and those they lead are destroyed. **17.** Therefore, the Lord will have no joy in their young men, nor mercy on their orphans and widows; for all are hypocrites and evildoers, and every mouth speaks foolishness. Yet, His anger is not turned away, His hand is still stretched out. **18.** Wickedness burns like fire, devouring briers and thorns, and kindling in the forest thickets, growing like smoke. **19.** By the wrath of the Lord of hosts, the land will be scorched, and the people will become fuel for the fire; no one will spare his neighbor. **20.** They will seize food on the right, but still be hungry; eat on the left, yet not be satisfied; each will eat the flesh of his own arm. **21.** Manasseh will devour Ephraim, and Ephraim Manasseh; together they will attack Judah. But His anger is not turned away, His hand is still stretched out. (Manasseh and Ephraim: two tribes of Israel; Judah: the southern kingdom of Israel)

Chapter 10

1. Woe (great sorrow or distress) to those who make unjust laws, who write oppression into regulation, **2.** To rob the needy of justice and take what's right from the terrible, making widows their prey and stripping the fatherless. **3.** What will you do when punishment comes, and destruction from afar? Where will you flee for help, and where will you leave your glory? **4.** Without Me, they will bow down the many captives and fall among the slain. For all this, His anger is not turned away, but His hand remains outstretched. **5.** Woe to Assyria, the rod of My anger, the staff in whose hand is My fury. **6.** I will send him against a godless state, against the people of My wrath. He will capture the wreck, take the plunder, and trample them like dust in the streets. **7.** But he does not intend this, nor does his heart think so; but he plans to break and cut off many nations. **8.** He boasts (encourages), "Are not my princes all kings? Isn't Calno like Carchemish? Isn't Hamath like Arpad? Isn't Samaria like Damascus?" (Calno, Carchemish, Hamath, Arpad: ancient cities known for their military power) **9.** As my hand has located the kingdoms of idols, whose images were more glorious than those of Jerusalem and Samaria, **10.** as I have done to Samaria and her idols, shall I not do the same to Jerusalem and her idols? **11.** When the Lord has done His work on Mount Zion and Jerusalem, He will punish the proud heart of the king of Assyria and his haughty eyes. **12.** For he says: "By my own power, I have done it; by my understanding, for I am wise. I have removed the boundaries of nations, and plundered their treasures, like a mighty man. **13.** My hand has found the riches of the nations, as one gathers eggs, I have amassed all the earth; no one flapped a wing or opened a mouth to protest." **14.** Shall the ax boast against the one who swings it? Or the saw against the one who uses it? As though a rod should wield itself, or a staff lift itself up—when it is only wood! **15.** Therefore, the Lord, the Lord of hosts, will send weakness upon his strong warriors; under his glory, a fire will burn, like a flame. **16.** The light of Israel will be a fire, and His Holy One a flame; it will burn and consume his thorns and briers in one day. **17.** It will eat the glory of his forest and fruitful field, both soul and body; and it will be as when a sick man wastes away. **18.** The rest of the trees in his forest will be so few that a child could count them. **19.** In that day, the remnant of Israel, and those who have escaped from the house of Jacob, will not depend upon the one who struck them, but will trust in the Lord, the Holy One of Israel, in truth. **20.** The remnant of Jacob will return to the Mighty God. **21.** Though your people, O Israel, be as numerous as the sand of the sea, only a remnant will return; the destruction decreed will overflow with righteousness. **22.** For the Lord God of hosts will make a decisive end in the midst of all the land. **23.** Therefore, thus says the Lord God of hosts: "O My people who live in Zion, do not be afraid of the Assyrian. He will strike you with a rod and lift his staff against you, as Egypt once did. **24.** But in a little while, My indignation (anger or annoyance) will cease, and My anger will be directed at their destruction." **25.** The Lord of hosts will raise up a plague for him, like the slaughter of Midian at the rock of Oreb; as He did with the sea, so He will lift it up in the way of Egypt. (Midian: a place defeated by Gideon) **26.** In that day, his burden will be lifted from your shoulder, and his yoke from your neck, and the yoke will be destroyed because of the anointing oil. **27.** He has come to Aiath, passed Migron, and at Michmash he has made arrangements. **28.** They have gone along the ridge, and lodged at Geba. Ramah is afraid, Gibeah of Saul has fled. **29.** Cry aloud, O daughter of Gallim! Let it be heard as far as Laish—O poor Anathoth! **30.** Madmenah has fled, and the inhabitants of Gebim seeking refuge. **31.** Still, he will remain at Nob that day, and shake his fist at the mount of the daughter of Zion, the hill of Jerusalem. **32.** Behold, the Lord of hosts will lop off the bough with terror; those of high stature will be cut down, and the proud will be humbled. **33.** He will cut down the thickets of the forest with iron, and Lebanon will fall before the mighty One. (Lebanon: famous for its tall cedar trees) **34.** He will cut down the thickets of the forest with iron, and Lebanon's towering trees will fall before the mighty One.

Chapter 11

1. A shoot will emerge from the lineage of Jesse, and a branch will grow from his roots. (Jesse: David's father) **2.** The Spirit of the Lord will rest upon Him, the Spirit of wisdom and understanding, the Spirit of counsel and might, the Spirit of knowledge and the reverence for the Lord. **3.** He will take delight in revering the Lord; He will not judge by mere appearances, nor make decisions based on what He hears. (Revering: respecting God) **4.** But with equity He will judge the poor and uphold justice for the meek of the earth; He will strike down the wicked with the word of His mouth and kill them with the breath of His lips. **5.** Righteousness will be the belt around His waist, and faithfulness will be the belt around His hips. (Righteousness: justice, Faithfulness: loyalty) **6.** The wolf will live with the lamb, the leopard will lie down with the young goat, and the calf, lion, and fattened calf will be together; and a child will lead them. **7.** The cow and the bear will graze together, their young will lie down side by side, and the lion will eat straw like the ox. **8.** A nursing infant will play near the den of a cobra, and a weaned child will put his hand into the hole of a viper. (Cobra: deadly snake) **9.** They will not harm or destroy on My holy mountain, for the earth will be filled with the knowledge of the Lord as the waters cover the sea. **10.** On that day, the root of Jesse will stand as a banner to the peoples; the nations will seek Him, and His resting place will be glorious. (Root of Jesse: Messiah) **11.** On that day, the Lord will again raise His hand to reclaim the remnant of His people, who remain, from Assyria, Egypt, Pathros, Cush, Elam, Shinar, Hamath, and the islands of the sea. (Remnant: God's people) **12.** He will raise a banner for the nations and gather the exiles of Israel, He will assemble the scattered people of Judah from the four corners of the earth. (Outcasts: scattered Israelites) **13.** The envy of Ephraim will depart, and the enemies of Judah will be cut off; Ephraim will not envy Judah, and Judah will not harass Ephraim. **14.** They will swoop down on the Philistines to the west, plundering the people of the East; they will take control of Edom and Moab, and the Ammonites will obey them. (Philistines: ancient enemies) **15.** The Lord will dry up the tongue of the Egyptian Sea, and with His mighty wind, He will wave His hand over the Euphrates River, splitting it into seven streams, so that people can walk across on dry ground. (Egyptian Sea: Red Sea) **16.** There will be a highway for the remnant of His people, who remain from Assyria, as there was for Israel when they came up from the land of Egypt. (Highway: return route)

Chapter 12

1. On that day, you will proclaim: "Lord, I give You thanks! Though You were angry with me, Your anger has been turned away, and You have comforted me." **2.** Look, God is my Savior; I will place my trust in Him and have no fear. For the Lord, Yah, is my strength and my song; He has become my salvation. (Yah: a shortened form of Yahweh) **3.** With joy, you will draw water from the fountains of salvation. **4.** On that day, you will declare: "Praise the Lord! Call on His name; tell the nations of His mighty works, and make known that His name is to be honored." **5.** Sing praises to the Lord, for He has done marvelous things; His deeds are known throughout the earth. **6.** Shout aloud, O people of Zion, for great is the Holy One of Israel, who dwells among you!)

Chapter 13

1. This is the prophecy concerning Babylon, which Isaiah son of Amoz received through vision. **2.** "Lift up a banner on the mountain heights, call out to them, wave your hand to signal that they may enter the gates of the rulers." (Banner: signal for battle, Gates of nobles: city gates of the elite) **3.** I have commanded My consecrated ones and summoned My mighty warriors to execute My anger, those who delight in My triumph. **4.** The sound of a multitude rises from the mountains, like a vast assembly! It is the tumult of kingdoms gathered together. The Lord of hosts is assembling an army for battle. (Tumult: loud commotion, Host: heavenly armies) **5.** They come from a distant land, from the farthest reaches of heaven, the Lord and His weapons of wrath, to destroy the entire earth. (Weapons of wrath: divine judgment) **6.** Mourn, for the day of the Lord is near! It will come with devastation from the Almighty. (Day of the Lord: time of divine judgment) **7.** Therefore, every hand will grow weak, and every heart will melt in fear. **8.** People will be filled with terror; pangs and pain will grip them, like a woman in labor. They will look at each other in astonishment, their faces burning with fear. **9.** See, the day of the Lord approaches, cruel with both wrath and fierce anger, to lay waste the land and remove its sinners. (Wrath: divine anger, Sinners: the wicked) **10.** The stars and constellations will not give their light; the sun will be darkened in its rising, and the moon will not shine. **11.** "I will punish the world for its evil, and the wicked for their sin; I will humble the pride of the arrogant and lay low the haughtiness of the ruthless." **12.** I will make a man more scarce than pure gold, a human being rarer than the gold of Ophir. **13.** Therefore, I will shake the heavens, and the earth will be removed from its place in the wrath of the Lord of hosts and the day of His fierce anger. (Fierce anger: intense divine fury) **14.** It will be like a hunted gazelle, like a sheep with no one to gather it; each will flee to their own people, and everyone will go back to their own land. (Gazelle: fleeing prey) **15.** Whoever is found will be struck down, and whoever is captured will fall by the sword. **16.** Their children will be dashed to pieces before their eyes; their homes will be plundered, and their wives will be raped. (Dashed to pieces: violent destruction) **17.** "Look, I will stir up the Medes against them, who will not value silver or delight in gold. **18.** Their bows will kill the young men, and they will show no mercy to the fruit of the womb; their eyes will not spare children." (Fruit of the womb: unborn children) **19.** Babylon, the glory of kingdoms and the splendor of the Chaldeans, will be overthrown as God overthrew Sodom and Gomorrah. (Babylon: empire, Chaldeans: Babylonians) **20.** It will never be inhabited again, nor will it be settled from generation to generation; the Arab will not pitch his tent there, nor will shepherds make their flocks lie down there. **21.** But wild animals will rest there, and their houses will be full of owls; ostriches will live there, and wild goats will leap about. **22.** Hyenas will howl in their fortresses, and jackals in their luxurious palaces. The time of Babylon's downfall is near, and its days will not be prolonged." (Hyenas: scavengers)

Chapter 14

1. The Lord will have mercy on Jacob, and will again choose Israel, settling them in their own land. Strangers will join them, and they will cling to the house of Jacob. **2.** Nations will bring them to their place, and the house of Israel will possess them as servants and maidens in the land of the Lord; they will take captive those who once held them captive, and rule over their oppressors. (Servants and maidens: captives, Oppressors: enemies) **3.** When the Lord gives you rest from your sorrow and the hardships which you endured, **4.** you will take up this taunt against the king of Babylon and say, "How the oppressor has ceased, the golden city is no more!" (Taunt: mocking song) **5.** The Lord has broken the rod of the wicked, the scepter of the rulers, (Rod: symbol of power) **6.** He who struck the nations in anger with unceasing blows, who ruled the kingdoms in fury, is now being persecuted with no one to stop him. **7.** The whole earth is at rest and quiet; they break into singing. **8.** Even the cypress trees rejoice over you, and the cedars of Lebanon say, 'Now that you have fallen, no woodcutter will come against us.' (Cypress: trees, Woodcutter: oppressor) **9.** "The grave below is stirred up to meet you when you arrive; it rouses the spirits of the dead, all the kings of the nations. They rise from their thrones to greet you." (Grave: Sheol, Kings of nations: rulers of the earth) **10.** All will speak and say to you, 'You too have become as weak as we? Have you become like us?' (Weakness: shared fate) **11.** Your pomp is brought down to the grave, and the sound of your harps is silenced; maggots are spread beneath you, and worms cover you." (Maggots: decay, Worms: dying) **12.** "How you have fallen from heaven, O Lucifer, son of the morning! How you are cut down to the ground, you who weakened the nations!" (Lucifer: fallen angel) **13.** For you said to your heart, 'I will ascend to heaven; I will raise my throne above the stars of God; I will sit on the mount of assembly, on the utmost heights of the sacred mountain; **14.** I will ascend above the clouds, I will make myself like the Most High.' **15.** Yet you are brought down to the grave, to the depths of the pit. **16.** "Those who see you will stare at you and ponder: 'Is this the man who shook the earth and made kingdoms tremble, (Shook the earth: caused great upheaval) **17.** who made the world a wilderness and destroyed its cities, who did not let his prisoners go home?'" (Prisoners: captives) **18.** All the kings of the nations, all of them, sleep in glory, each in his own tomb. (Sleep in glory: resting peacefully) **19.** But you are cast out of your grave like a rejected branch, like a slain man who is thrown aside, pierced by the sword, descending to the stones of the pit, trampled underfoot. (Rejected branch: dishonor) **20.** You will not be united with them in burial, for you have destroyed your land and killed your people. The offspring of the wicked will never be remembered. (Offspring: descendants) **21.** Prepare for the slaughter of his children, because of the sins of their fathers, so that they will not rise up and take possession of the land or fill the world with cities. (Slaughter: judgment on descendants) **22.** "I will rise up against them," says the Lord of hosts, "and cut off from Babylon its name and survivors, its offspring and descendants." (Call: legacy) **23.** "I will make it a place for owls and a marsh of stagnant water; I will sweep it with the broom of destruction," says the Lord of hosts. (Place for owls: desolation)

Chapter 15

1. This is the burden concerning Moab. In the night, Ar of Moab is devastated and destroyed; in the night, Kir of Moab is likewise overthrown. (Moab: a kingdom east of Israel, Ar and Kir: cities in Moab) **2.** Moab ascends to the temple and to Dibon, to the high places to mourn. They will lament over Nebo and Medeba; all their heads will be shaved, and every beard will be cut off. (Skinned: signs of mourning, Nebo and Medeba: cities of Moab) **3.** In the streets, they will wear sackcloth; on their rooftops and in the streets, everyone will cry out in bitter mourning. (Sackcloth: a sign of grief) **4.** Heshbon and Elealeh will cry out, their voices heard as far as Jahaz. Moab's armed forces will shout in distress; their lives will be burdensome to them. (Heshbon and Elealeh: cities in Moab, Jahaz: a city in Moab) **5.** "My heart will cry out for Moab; its fugitives will flee to Zoar, like a young heifer. They will ascend the Ascent of Luhith, weeping; they will raise a cry of destruction from the way of

Horonaim." (Zoar: a city of refuge, Ascent of Luhith: a mountain path, Horonaim: a city in Moab) **6.** The waters of Nimrim will dry up; the green grass will wither away, and nothing green will remain. (Nimrim: a stream, symbolizing desolation) **7.** Therefore, the wealth they accumulated and what they laid up will be carried away to the Brook of the Willows. (Brook of the Willows: a place of desolation) **8.** A cry has echoed around Moab's borders, its wailing reaching Eglaim and Beer Elim. (Eglaim and Beer Elim: places in Moab) **9.** The waters of Dimon will be full of blood, for I will bring even more upon Dimon—lions to consume those who escape, and the remnant of Moab will be destroyed. (Dimon: a city in Moab, Lions: symbolizing judgment)

Chapter 16

1. Send the lamb to the ruler of the land, from Sela to the wilderness, to the mountain of the daughter of Zion. (Lamb: a symbol of tribute, Sela: a city of Moab) **2.** It will be like a bird driven from its nest; so will Moab's daughters be at the fords of the Arnon. (Arnon: a river marking the boundary of Moab) **3.** "Take counsel, execute judgment; make your shadow like the night at midday; hide the refugees, do not betray the one who has escaped." (Shadow like night: offering protection) **4.** Let My exiled people stay with you, Moab; be a refuge from the destroyer. The oppressors will be gone, devastation will cease, and the plunderers will be gone from the land. (Exiled people: refugees, Destroyer: enemy forces) **5.** A throne will be established with mercy, and One will sit upon it in truth, from the house of David, seeking justice and swift righteousness. (Throne of mercy: Messianic promise) **6.** We have heard of Moab's pride, of its arrogance, and its rage; but its boasting will come to nothing. (Pride: arrogance, Rage: fury) **7.** Therefore, Moab will wail for Moab; everyone will mourn. The foundations of Kir Hareseth will mourn; they will be utterly stricken. (Kir Hareseth: a city in Moab) **8.** The fields of Heshbon and the vine of Sibmah will mourn. The rulers of the nations have broken its choice plants, which reached to Jazer and wandered into the wilderness. (Sibmah: a town known for vineyards, Jazer: a place near Moab) **9.** I will weep for the vine of Sibmah, and for the weeping of Jazer; I will flood Heshbon and Elealeh with tears, for battle cries have fallen over your summer fruits and harvests. (Summer fruits: symbolizing prosperity, Battle cries: destruction) **10.** Gladness and joy are taken away from the plentiful fields; there will be no singing or shouting in the vineyards. No one will tread out wine in the presses; I have caused their joy to cease. (Presses: winepresses) **11.** Therefore, my heart will sound like a harp for Moab, and my innermost being for Kir Heres. (Harp: a symbol of mourning) **12.** When Moab grows weary on the high places, he will go to his sanctuary to pray, but he will not prevail. (High places: places of idol worship) **13.** This is the message the Lord has spoken concerning Moab since that time. (Since that time: since the prophecy began) **14.** But now the Lord says, "Within three years, like the years of a hired worker, Moab's glory will be humbled, and its great multitude will diminish. Only a few will remain." (Three years: a set period of judgment)

Chapter 17

1. This is the burden concerning Damascus: "Behold, Damascus will cease to be a city and will become a heap of ruins." (Damascus: capital of Syria) **2.** The cities of Aroer will be abandoned; they will become places for flocks, where no one will disturb them. (Aroer: a city in Syria) **3.** The fortress of Ephraim will vanish, and the kingdom of Damascus will come to an end. The remnant of Syria will be like the glory of Israel," says the Lord of hosts. (Ephraim: the northern kingdom of Israel, Syria: the neighboring enemy) **4.** "In that day, the glory of Jacob will fade, and the fatness of his flesh will grow lean." (Glory of Jacob: the pride of Israel) **5.** It will be like when a harvester gathers the grain and reaps the heads with his arm; it will be like one gathering heads of grain in the Valley of Rephaim. (Rephaim: a valley near Jerusalem) **6.** Yet a few gleanings will remain, like the shaking of an olive tree, two or three olives at the top of the boughs, or four or five on the most fruitful branches," says the Lord God of Israel. (Gleanings: the leftovers after harvest) **7.** In that day, a man will look to his Maker and respect the Holy One of Israel. (Look to Maker: turn to God for salvation) **8.** He will not look to the altars, the work of his hands, nor will he respect what his fingers have made, neither the wooden images nor the incense altars. (Altars: places of idol worship) **9.** In that day, his fortified cities will be like abandoned branches, left because of the children of Israel; and desolation will come. (Fortified cities: cities of strength) **10.** Because you have forgotten the God of your salvation and have not remembered the Rock of your refuge, therefore you will plant beautiful plants and sow foreign seedlings. (God of salvation: God as the Savior) **11.** On the day you plant, you will make it grow, and in the morning, you will make your seed flourish, but the harvest will be a heap of ruins in the day of grief and despair. (Harvest: a symbol of judgment) **12.** Woe to the multitude of many nations that make a noise like the roar of the seas, and to the rushing of nations that make a rushing like the rushing of mighty waters! (Multitude: large, aggressive nations) **13.** The nations will rush like the rushing of many waters, but God will rebuke them, and they will flee far away, like chaff on the mountains before the wind, like a rolling thing before the whirlwind. (Chaff: symbol of destruction) **14.** At evening, trouble will come, and before morning, he will be gone. This is the fate of those who plunder us and the lot of those who rob us. (Fate of plunderers: sudden destruction)

Chapter 18

1. Woe to the land of buzzing wings, beyond the rivers of Cush, (Buzzing wings: a symbol of the Ethiopians) **2.** Which sends ambassadors by sea in vessels made of reeds, saying, "Go, swift messengers, to a nation tall and smooth of skin, to a people feared from their beginning, a nation strong and conquering, whose land the rivers divide." (Ethiopia: an ancient kingdom) **3.** All inhabitants of the world and dwellers on the earth, when he lifts up a banner on the mountains, you will see it; and when he blows a trumpet, you will hear it. (Trumpet: call to attention) **4.** For so the Lord has said to me, "I will rest and look from My dwelling place, like the heat of the sun at midday, like the dew in the heat of harvest." (God's rest: a time of judgment) **5.** Before the harvest, when the bud is perfect and the sour grape is ripening, He will cut off the branches with pruning hooks and take away the branches. (Pruning: judgment) **6.** They will be left for the birds of prey and the wild beasts of the earth; the birds of prey will summer on them, and the wild beasts will winter on them. (Desolation: abandonment) **7.** At that time, a gift will be brought to the Lord of hosts from a people tall and smooth of skin, a powerful nation whose land is divided by rivers, to the place of the name of the Lord of hosts, to Mount Zion. (Gift: tribute to God, Mount Zion: God's holy place)

Chapter 19

1. A burden in opposition to Egypt: See, the Lord comes riding on a rapid cloud, and Egypt's idols will tremble before Him. Their hearts will soften inside them. (Idols: fake gods) **2.** "I will stir Egyptians to combat amongst themselves—brother against brother, neighbor towards neighbor, metropolis towards town, state against kingdom." (Social unrest: inner warfare) **3.** Egypt's spirit will fail within them; their advisors will turn to idols, mediums, and sorcerers for assistance. **4.** "I will give Egypt into the hands of a harsh ruler, and a merciless king will govern them," says the Lord Almighty. **5.** The waters of the sea will dry up, and the river will be parched. **6.** The canals will become foul; the streams will dry up; the reeds and rushes will wither. (Canals: man-made water channels) **7.** All the papyrus plants along the river will wither and be scattered; nothing will remain. **8.** Fishermen will mourn, and those who cast nets into the waters will languish. (Fishermen: people who catch fish) **9.** Those who work with fine flax and weave fine fabric will be ashamed. (Flax: linen-producing plant) **10.** Egypt's foundations will disintegrate, and all who work for a living will be afflicted. (Foundations: economies)

11. The princes of Zoan are silly; Pharaoh's wise counselors give worthless advice. "How will you say, 'I am the son of wise men, the descendant of ancient kings'?" (Zoan: an ancient Egyptian city) **12.** "Where are your wise men now? Let them tell you what the Lord has planned for Egypt." **13.** The princes of Zoan are fools, the rulers of Noph are deceived; they've led Egypt off course. (Noph: ancient Egyptian city of Memphis) **14.** The Lord has mixed a perverse spirit in Egypt, and they will stumble in their ways, like a drunken man stumbling in his own vomit. **15.** Egypt will have no work left, from the highest to the bottom. **16.** In that day, Egypt will be like women—afraid and trembling at the wave of the Lord's hand against them. (Lord's hand: God's judgment) **17.** The land of Judah will terrify Egypt; everyone who mentions it will fear because of the Lord's purpose against Egypt. (Judah: southern kingdom of Israel) **18.** In that day, five cities in Egypt will speak the language of Canaan and swear allegiance to the Lord; one will be called the city of Destruction. **19.** In that day, an altar to the Lord will be in Egypt, and a monument to Him will stand at its border. **20.** It will serve as a sign and witness to the Lord in Egypt. When they cry out to Him because of their oppressors, He will send them a Savior, and He will deliver them. **21.** The Lord will make Himself known to Egypt, and they will know the Lord. They will offer sacrifices and vows to Him. **22.** The Lord will strike Egypt and then heal them; they will return to Him, and He will respond and heal them. (Strike and heal: judgment and healing) **23.** In that day, there will be a highway from Egypt to Assyria; the Egyptians will go to Assyria, and the Assyrians will go to Egypt, and Egypt will serve Assyria. **24.** In that day, Israel will be a blessing along with Egypt and Assyria, a blessing in the midst of the land. (Blessing: divine favor) **25.** The Lord of hosts will bless them, saying, "Blessed is Egypt, My people, and Assyria, the work of My hands, and Israel, My inheritance."

Chapter 20

1. In the year when Tartan came to Ashdod, sent by King Sargon of Assyria, and captured it, (Tartan: Assyrian general, Ashdod: Philistine city) **2.** the Lord spoke through Isaiah, son of Amoz, saying, "Take off your sackcloth and sandals." So Isaiah obeyed and walked naked and barefoot.
(Sackcloth: mourning garment, Naked: sign of humiliation) **3.** Then the Lord said, "Just as My servant Isaiah has walked naked and barefoot for three years as a sign to Egypt and Cush, (Cush: Ethiopia) **4.** so the king of Assyria will take away the Egyptians as captives, and the Cushites will be led away, young and old, naked and exposed, bringing shame to Egypt. **5.** They will be dismayed and ashamed of their hope in Cush and their pride in Egypt. (Cush: Ethiopia) **6.** The people in this region will say, 'This is what happens when we trust in Assyria—how can we escape?'

Chapter 21

1. The prophecy against the Wilderness of the Sea: like whirlwinds from the South, it comes from a dreadful land. (Wilderness of the Sea: likely referring to the desert regions near the sea) **2.** A troubling vision has been revealed to me. The betrayer betrays, and the plunderer plunders. "Go up, Elam! Attack, Media! All their groaning I will end." **3.** My body is in anguish; pain grips me like a woman in labor. I am distressed by what I hear, and terrified by what I see. **4.** My heart wavers; fear overwhelms me. The night I longed for has become a nightmare. **5.** "Prepare the table, set the watchman, eat and drink. Arise, princes, anoint the shield!" (Shield: symbolizing defense) **6.** The Lord says to me, "Set a watchman, and let him report what he sees." (Watchman: a sentinel or lookout) **7.** He sees chariots with horsemen, donkeys, and camels. He listens intently. (Chariots: symbolizing military forces) **8.** "A lion!" he cries. "I stand on the watchtower day and night." **9.** "Look! Here come men with chariots!" He replies, "Babylon has fallen! All the idols of her gods have been shattered." **10.** "My work and my harvest are in vain," says the Lord, "I declare this to you." **11.** The prophecy against Dumah: "Watchman, what of the night?" (Dumah: an ancient city, possibly in Edom) **12.** The watchman answers, "Morning is coming, but also night. If you wish to inquire, inquire; return and come back." **13.** The prophecy against Arabia: In the forests of Arabia, you will lodge, O Dedanites. **14.** "O inhabitants of Tema, bring water to the thirsty; meet those fleeing with bread." (Tema: another Arabian region) **15.** For they fled from swords, bows, and the distress of war. **16.** The Lord says, "Within a year, the glory of Kedar will vanish." (Kedar: a tribe in the Arabian desert) **17.** The remaining archers of Kedar will be few, for the Lord has spoken. (Archers: warriors skilled in using bows)

Chapter 22

1. The prophecy against the Valley of Vision: What's wrong with you, who have gone up to the rooftops? (Valley of Vision: possibly Jerusalem, known for prophecies) **2.** You are filled with noise and joy, yet your slain are not from battle, but from slaughter. **3.** Your rulers flee together, captured by archers; those who remain are bound. (Archers: warriors with bows) **4.** I said, "Look away from me; I will weep bitterly. Do not comfort me for the destruction of my people." (Bitterly: intense sorrow) **5.** It's a day of trouble, confusion, and destruction in the Valley of Vision—walls are being broken down and cries are heard. (Valley of Vision: likely Jerusalem) **6.** Elam carries the quiver with chariots and horsemen; Kir uncovers the shield. (Elam: an ancient kingdom, quiver: carrying weapons) **7.** Your best valleys will be filled with chariots, and horsemen will be at the gates. **8.** You removed Judah's protection, and looked to the armor of the House of the Forest. **9.** You saw the damage to the city of David and fortified the wall by gathering water. **10.** You counted the houses of Jerusalem and tore down some to strengthen the wall. **11.** You made a reservoir between the walls for water but did not look to God who made it. (Reservoir: water storage, Maker: God) **12.** In that day, the Lord called for mourning, baldness, and sackcloth, but you chose joy instead. (Sackcloth: mourning garment) **13.** You rejoiced, killing oxen and sheep, eating and drinking, saying, "Let us eat and drink, for tomorrow we die." **14.** Then the Lord revealed, "Because of this sin, there will be no atonement for you even to your death." (Atonement: reconciliation with God) **15.** The Lord commands, "Go to Shebna, the steward of the house, and ask him, (Shebna: a royal official) **16.** 'Why have you carved yourself a tomb in a high place, a tomb for yourself in the rock?'" **17.** "The Lord will cast you down, O mighty man, and will toss you like a ball into a distant land, and there you will die." **18.** "I will remove you from your office, and another will take your place." (Office: position of authority) **19.** "I will appoint Eliakim son of Hilkiah to replace you. **20.** I will clothe him with your robe and belt, and place him in charge of Jerusalem and Judah." **21.** "He will have the key to the house of David; he will open, and no one will shut, and shut, and no one will open." (Key: authority to control access) **22.** "I will make him like a peg in a secure place, a glorious throne for his family." (Peg: symbol of security) **23.** "They will hang all the glory of his family on him, and he will become a place of honor." (Honor: respect and authority) **24.** "But in that day, the peg will be removed, and all the weight it holds will fall, for the Lord has spoken."

Chapter 23

1. Wail, ships of Tarshish, for Tyre has been destroyed. There are no homes or harbors left. The news comes from Cyprus. (Tarshish: a Phoenician city, Cyprus: an island in the Mediterranean) **2.** Be still, people of the coast and merchants of Sidon, who filled the seas with their trade. (Sidon: another Phoenician city) **3.** The grain from Shihor and the harvest of the river formed Tyre's wealth, making it a marketplace for the nations. (Shihor: a river, often identified with the Nile) **4.** Be ashamed, Sidon, for the sea speaks and says, "I do not labor or give birth. I do not raise young men or virgins." **5.** When Egypt hears of Tyre's fall, they too will be filled with terror. **6.** Cry out, you people of Tarshish! Your strength is gone. (Tarshish: a trading city) **7.** Is this the city of joy, whose origins stretch back to ancient times? It once traveled far and settled in distant lands. **8.**

Who has devised this plan against Tyre, the great city, whose merchants were princes and whose traders were the elite of the earth? (Princes: wealthy merchants) **9.** The Lord of hosts has decided to humble the pride of all glory, to disgrace the esteemed of the earth. (Pride of glory: Tyre's arrogance) **10.** Overflow, daughter of Tarshish, for your strength has been destroyed. **11.** The Lord has stretched His hand over the sea, shaking kingdoms. He has commanded the destruction of Canaan's strongholds. **12.** You will rejoice no more, Sidon. Cross over to Cyprus, but even there you will find no rest. (Sidon: Tyre's sister city) **13.** Look at the land of the Chaldeans. This people, once unknown, was established by Assyria. It became a desolate place, with its towers and palaces in ruins. (Chaldeans: Babylonians) **14.** Wail, ships of Tarshish, for your power has been destroyed. **15.** Tyre will be forgotten for seventy years, like the lifespan of a king. After seventy years, Tyre will return, as in the song of a harlot: **16.** "Take a harp, wander through the city, forgotten harlot; sing many songs to be remembered." (Harlot: symbol of Tyre's decadence and unfaithfulness) **17.** After seventy years, the Lord will visit Tyre. She will return to her trade and once again engage with the kingdoms of the earth. **18.** However, her profits will be dedicated to the Lord; they will not be stored up but used for His people, to provide food and fine clothing.

Chapter 24

1. Behold, the Lord empties the earth and makes it desolate; He distorts its surface and scatters its inhabitants. (Desolate: empty) **2.** It will be the same for all: the people and priests, servants and masters, maids and mistresses, buyers and sellers, creditors and debtors. (Servants: people) **3.** The land will be utterly emptied and plundered, for the Lord has decreed it. **4.** The earth mourns and fades away, the world weakens and fades; the proud people of the earth wither. (Mourns: grieves, Weaken: grows feeble) **5.** The earth is defiled by its people because they have broken God's laws, altered His statutes, and violated the everlasting covenant. (Defiled: made unclean, Statutes: laws, Covenant: sacred agreement) **6.** Therefore, a curse consumes the earth, and its inhabitants are left in ruins. The earth's people are burned, and only a few remain. (Curse: punishment) **7.** The new wine fails, the vine withers, and all the happy-hearted groan. **8.** The music of tambourines stops, the sound of celebration ends, and the joy of the harp is silenced. (Tambourines: musical instruments) **9.** People will not drink wine with song; strong drinks will be bitter to those who drink them. (Strong drinks: alcoholic beverages) **10.** The city of chaos is broken down; every house is locked, and no one can enter. (Chaos: disorder) **11.** There is a cry for wine in the streets; all joy is gone, and the happiness of the land has vanished. **12.** The city is in ruins, and its gates have been destroyed. **13.** When this happens in the land among the people, it will be like the shaking of an olive tree, like the leftovers after harvest. (Leftovers: remaining vegetation) **14.** They will raise their voices, singing for the majesty of the Lord, and they will shout from the sea. (Majesty: greatness) **15.** Therefore, glorify the Lord in the light of dawn, and praise the name of our Lord God of Israel from the coastlands. (Coastlands: remote shores) **16.** From the ends of the earth, we hear songs: "Glory to the righteous!" but I say, "I am ruined, I am ruined! Woe to me! The traitors have betrayed me." (Traitors: deceitful people) **17.** Terror, pit, and snare await you, O inhabitants of the earth. (Pit: a deep hollow, Snare: trap) **18.** Whoever flees from the terror will fall into a pit, and whoever escapes from the pit will be caught in a snare. The windows from on high are open, and the foundations of the earth tremble. (Tremble: shake, Windows: heavens) **19.** The earth is violently broken, it is split open, and it shakes uncontrollably. (Violently: forcefully) **20.** The earth will stagger like a drunkard and totter like a hut; its transgression will weigh it down, and it will fall, never to rise again. (Totter: wobble) **21.** On that day, the Lord will punish the host of the high ones in the heavens and the kings of the earth. **22.** They will be gathered together as prisoners are gathered in a pit and shut up in a prison; after many days, they will be punished. **23.** Then the moon will be ashamed, and the sun disgraced, for the Lord of hosts will reign on Mount Zion and in Jerusalem, and before His elders, gloriously.

Chapter 25

1. O Lord, my God, I will exalt and praise Your name, for You have performed magnificent deeds; Your historical plans are devoted and real. (Superb: splendid, Plans: counsels) **2.** You have turned a thriving city into a destroy, a fortified metropolis into desolation, and a foreigner's palace will not exist; it'll never be rebuilt. **3.** As a result, mighty nations will honor You, and the city of fearsome peoples will keep You in awe. (Fearsome: terrifying, Awe: wonderful admire) **4.** You have been a shelter for the poor and a stronghold for the needy in their misery. You are a refuge from the storm and a shade from the heat; the fierce wind of the wicked is like a storm battering a wall. **5.** You will silence the chaos of foreign nations, like heat in a dry land, and the song of the wicked will fade, like the shadow of a cloud. (Chaos: uproar, Wicked: evil people) **6.** On this mountain, the Lord of Hosts will prepare a lavish dinner for all peoples, a banquet of rich foods, aged wine, and the finest cuts of meat, with well-refined wines. (Lavish: generous, Cuts of meat: portions of meat) **7.** He will destroy the veil that covers all nations and remove the blanket that shrouds all peoples. **8.** He will swallow up death forever, and the Lord God will wipe away all tears from their faces. He will remove the disgrace of His people from the whole earth, for the Lord has spoken. (Swallow up: spoil absolutely, Disgrace: shame) **9.** On that day, it will be declared, "This is our God; we have waited for Him, and He has delivered us. This is the Lord; we have waited for Him; let us rejoice and be glad in His salvation." **10.** For on this mountain, the Lord's hand will rest, and Moab will be trampled underfoot, like straw in a refuse heap. (Trampled: beaten, Refuse: waste) **11.** He will stretch out His hands as a swimmer stretches out to swim, and He will humble their pride, along with the deceitfulness of their hands. (Pride: arrogance, Deceitfulness: trickery) **12.** The fortress of your proud cities will be torn down and taken low, and their strong walls will be reduced to dirt. (Fortress: stronghold, Proud: boastful).

Chapter 26

1. On that day, this song will be sung in Judah: "We have a strong city; salvation will be its walls and ramparts." (Ramparts: defensive walls) **2.** Open the gates, that the righteous nation may enter, the people who keep the truth. **3.** You will keep in perfect peace the one whose mind is fixed on You, because he trusts in You. **4.** Trust in the Lord forever, for in Yah, the Lord, is eternal strength. **5.** For He brings down those who live in high places, the proud city; He will level it, and it will lie in the dust. (Level: bring down) **6.** The poor and needy will trample it down with their feet. (Trample: walk on) **7.** The path of the righteous is straight; O Most Upright, You make the way of the just level. **8.** Yes, we have waited for You in Your ways, O Lord; our souls long for Your name and Your remembrance. **9.** With my soul, I have desired You in the night; and with my spirit within me, I will seek You early; for when Your judgments are in the earth, the people will learn righteousness. (Judgments: decisions) **10.** Though the wicked are shown grace, they will not learn righteousness; in the land of uprightness, they will act unjustly and refuse to see the glory of the Lord. (Uprightness: honesty) **11.** Lord, when Your hand is lifted up, they will not see it. But they will be ashamed, seeing the fire of Your enemies consume them. **12.** Lord, You will establish peace for us, for You have done all our works in us. **13.** O Lord our God, other masters have ruled us, but by You alone do we mention Your name. **14.** They are dead and will not live again; they are deceased and will not rise. You have punished and destroyed them, and their memory has perished. (Deceased: dead) **15.** You have increased the nation, O Lord, and You are glorified; You have expanded the borders of the land. (Expanded: widened) **16.** In trouble, they have sought You; when Your discipline was upon them, they poured out a prayer. **17.** As a woman in labor cries out in her pain near her time of delivery, so have we been in Your sight, O Lord. (Labor: childbirth) **18.** We have been in labor, but we have brought forth nothing but wind; we have not brought salvation to the earth, nor have the inhabitants of the world fallen. (Salvation: deliverance) **19.** Your dead shall live; together with my dead body, they will rise. Awake and sing, you who dwell in dust; for your dew is like the dew of herbs, and the earth will give up the dead. (Dew: moisture, Herbs: plants) **20.** Come, my people, enter your rooms and shut the doors behind you; hide yourselves for a little while, until the indignation has passed. (Indignation: anger) **21.** For behold, the Lord is coming out of His place to punish the inhabitants of the earth for their iniquity; the earth will disclose her bloodshed and will no longer cover her slain. (Iniquity: wickedness)

Chapter 27
1. In that day, the Lord will use His mighty sword to punish Leviathan, the fleeing serpent, Leviathan, the twisted serpent, and He will slay the dragon in the sea. (Leviathan: a mythical sea monster) **2.** On that day, sing to the vineyard of red wine: (Vineyard: grape plantation) **3.** I, the Lord, keep it; I will water it continually; I will guard it day and night, lest anyone harm it. **4.** I have no fury; who would attack Me with thorns and briers? I would burn them all together. (Fury: anger) **5.** Or let them take hold of My strength, that they may make peace with Me, and they will make peace with Me. **6.** Those who come to Me will take root in Jacob; Israel will blossom and bud, and fill the face of the earth with fruit. **7.** Has Israel been struck like those who struck it? Or has it been slain like those who killed it? (Slain: killed) **8.** In measure, when You send it away, You contend with it; You remove it with Your fierce wind on the day of the east wind. (Contend: struggle, Fierce: strong) **9.** By this, the iniquity of Jacob will be atoned for; and this will be the result of removing his sin: when he makes all the altar stones like chalkstones, beaten to dust. The wooden images and incense altars will not stand. (Atoned for: forgiven, Chalkstones: soft stones) **10.** Yet the fortified city will be deserted; the habitation abandoned, left like a wilderness; there the calf will feed, and there it will lie down, consuming its branches. (Fortified: protected) **11.** When its boughs are withered, they will be broken off; women will come and set them on fire. For it is a people of no understanding; therefore, He who made them will have no mercy on them, and He who formed them will show them no favor. (Boughs: branches) **12.** And it will come to pass that the Lord will thresh from the Euphrates to the Brook of Egypt; and you will be gathered one by one, O children of Israel. (Thresh: separate, Euphrates: river in the Middle East) **13.** On that day, the great trumpet will be blown; those who are perishing in Assyria and those outcast in Egypt will come and worship the Lord on the holy mountain in Jerusalem. (Outcast: exiled, Perishing: dying)

Chapter 28
1. Woe to the proud crown of Ephraim, to the drunkards of that town, whose superb splendor fades like a withering flower at the pinnacle of the fertile valley. The ones triumph over with the aid of wine are in problem. (Withering: fading, Fertile: wealthy in resources) **2.** Behold, the Lord has a powerful and powerful one, like a typhoon of hail, a negative typhoon, like a flood of mighty waters in order to overflow. He will convey them down to the earth together with His hand. (Overflow: flood over) **3.** The crown of Ephraim's pride, the drunkards, can be trampled underfoot. **4.** Their superb beauty will fade like a flower at the pinnacle of the valley, like an early fruit that a passerby sees and eats earlier than it ripens. **5.** In that day, the Lord of hosts will be a crown of glory and a diadem of beauty for the remnant of His human beings. (Remnant: final, Diadem: crown) **6.** He will be a spirit of justice to folks that take a seat in judgment, and energy to individuals who flip again the war at the gate. (Judgment: honest selection-making) **7.** But they too are in mistakes thru wine, and by intoxicating drink they have misplaced their manner. The clergymen and prophets have erred via drink; they're swallowed up by wine, they stagger in imaginative and prescient and stumble in judgment. (Stagger: lose balance, Erred: made errors) **8.** All their tables are filled with vomit and dust, and no location is smooth. (Vomit: thrown-up meals) **9.** "Whom will He educate understanding? And to whom will He give an explanation for the message? To people who are like babes, simply weaned from milk?" (Weaned: now not nursing) **10.** For guidance need to be line upon line, principle upon principle, a bit right here, and a bit there. (Precept: command or rule) **11.** For with stammering lips and any other tongue, He'll talk to this humans, (Stammering: talking with pauses or errors) **12.** To those to whom He said, "This is the relaxation to offer the weary relaxation, and this is the refreshing"; yet they might not concentrate. (Refreshing: revival) **13.** But the word of the Lord to them can be "precept upon principle, line upon line, here a little, there a bit," in order that they will go, fall returned, and be damaged, snared, and caught. (Snared: trapped) **14.** Therefore, pay attention the phrase of the Lord, you scornful guys who rule this human beings in Jerusalem. (Scornful: Disrespectful) **15.** You have got said, "We have made a covenant with death, and with Sheol we are in settlement. When the overflowing scourge passes thru, it'll not come to us; for we've got made lies our shelter, and beneath falsehood we've hidden ourselves." (Covenant: settlement, Sheol: the grave) **16.** Therefore, thus says our Lord God: "Behold, I lay in Zion a stone, a tested stone, a valuable cornerstone, a sure basis; whoever believes will no longer act hastily." (Cornerstone: the foundational stone, Hastily: hurriedly) **17.** I will make justice the measuring line and righteousness the plumb line; the hail will sweep away the refuge of lies, and the waters will overflow the hiding location. (Measuring line: preferred for size, Plumb line: device for measuring uprightness) **18.** Your covenant with loss of life will be annulled, and your settlement with Sheol will no longer stand; when the overflowing scourge passes through, you'll be trampled down with the aid of it. (Annulled: canceled) **19.** Every time it goes out, it will take you; by day and by means of night time, it will likely be a fear just to apprehend the record. (Terror: extreme worry) **20.** For the mattress is simply too quick to stretch out on, and the blanket too narrow to wrap round you. (Stretch out: lie fully) **21.** For the Lord will upward thrust up, as He did at Mount Perazim; He may be indignant as He changed into in the Valley of Gibeon, to do His strange paintings, and to deliver to skip His uncommon act. (Odd: unusual, Perazim and Gibeon: locations of struggle) **22.** Now therefore, do now not be mockers, lest your bonds be made stronger; for I've heard from our Lord God of hosts, a destruction decided even upon the whole earth. (Mockers: folks who mock) **23.** Concentrate and listen my voice, pay attention and listen my speech. (Pay attention: concentrate attentively) **24.** Does the plowman plow all day to sow? Does he keep turning the soil and breaking apart the clods? (Clods: lumps of earth) **25.** When he has leveled the surface, does he no longer sow the black cumin, scatter the cumin, plant the wheat in rows, the barley in its place, and the spelt in its region? (Cumin: spice, Spelt: a kind of wheat) **26.** For He instructs him in the proper judgment, His God teaches him. (Judgment: choice-making) **27.** The black cumin isn't always threshed with a threshing sledge, nor is a cartwheel rolled over the cumin; the black cumin is overwhelmed out with a stick, and the cumin with a rod. (Thresh: separate grains from flowers, Rod: a tool for beating) **28.** Bread flour should be ground; therefore, he does not thresh it for all time, break it together with his cartwheel, or weigh down it together with his horsemen. (Flour: ground wheat) **29.** This also comes from the Lord of hosts, who's awesome in recommend and splendid in steerage. (steerage: route)

Chapter 29
1. Woe to you, Ariel, Ariel, the city where David lived! Add year to year, and let your festivals continue as usual. (Festivals: celebrations) **2.** Yet I will lay siege to Ariel, and it will mourn and lament. It will become to me like an altar hearth, a place of sacrifice. (Altar hearth: the base or foundation of an altar) **3.** I will surround you on every

side, and I will set up my siege works against you. (Siege works: military structures used in besieging a city) **4.** You will be brought down low, and you will speak from the ground. Your speech will come from the dust, as if ghostly, whispering from the earth. **5.** But your many enemies will be like fine dust, and the ruthless armies like chaff blown away. In a moment, suddenly, (Chaff: husks of grain that are separated and discarded) **6.** The LORD Almighty will come with thunder, an earthquake, and loud noise, with a whirlwind and tempest, and flames of a consuming fire. **7.** The nations that attack Ariel, her fortress, and besiege her will be like a dream, like a vision in the night— **8.** As when a hungry man dreams of eating but wakes still hungry, or when a thirsty man dreams of drinking but wakes still parched—so will it be with the armies that fight against Mount Zion. (Parched: dry) **9.** Be astonished and amazed! Blind yourselves and be sightless. Stagger, but not from wine; reel, but not from strong drink. **10.** The LORD has caused you to fall into a deep sleep. He has closed the eyes of the prophets and covered the heads of the seers. (Seers: those who receive visions or prophecies) **11.** For you, this entire vision is like words sealed in a scroll. If you give it to someone who can read and ask them to read it, they will say, "I cannot, for it is sealed." **12.** Or if you give the scroll to someone who cannot read and ask them to read it, they will answer, "I don't know how to read." (Scroll: a roll of parchment or paper) **13.** The LORD says: "These people come near to me with their words and honor me with their lips, but their hearts are far from me. Their worship is based on human traditions they have been taught." **14.** Therefore, I will again astonish these people with wonder upon wonder. The wisdom of the wise will perish, and the understanding of the discerning will vanish. **15.** Woe to those who go to great depths to hide their plans from the LORD, who do their deeds in darkness and think, "Who sees us? Who will know?" **16.** You turn things upside down, as though the potter were like the clay! Shall the thing formed say to the one who formed it, "You did not make me"? Can the pot say to the potter, "You know nothing"? (Potter: one who molds clay, Formed: created) **17.** In a very short time, Lebanon will be turned into a fertile field, and the fertile field will seem like a forest. **18.** In that day, the deaf will hear the words of the scroll, and the eyes of the blind will see out of the gloom and darkness. (Gloom: partial or complete darkness) **19.** Once again, the humble will rejoice in the LORD, and the needy will rejoice in the Holy One of Israel. (Humble: those who are modest or lowly) **20.** The ruthless will vanish, and the mockers will disappear. All who plot evil will be cut off— (Mockers: those who scorn or ridicule) **21.** Those who, with a word, make someone guilty, who trap the defender in court and deprive the innocent of justice through false testimony. **22.** Therefore, this is what the LORD, who redeemed Abraham, says to the descendants of Jacob: "No longer will Jacob be ashamed; no longer will their faces grow pale." **23.** When they see among them their children, the work of my hands, they will honor my name. They will acknowledge the holiness of the Holy One of Jacob, and stand in awe of the God of Israel. **24.** Those who were confused in spirit will gain understanding, and those who complained will accept instruction. (Confused in spirit: uncertain or lost)

Chapter 30

1. Woe to the rebellious children, declares the LORD, to those who plan without consulting Me, who make alliances not directed by My Spirit, and add sin to sin. (Rebellious: defiant) **2.** They go down to Egypt without seeking My counsel, looking to Pharaoh for protection and Egypt for shelter. (Pharaoh: the king of Egypt) **3.** But Pharaoh's protection will bring you nothing but shame, and Egypt's refuge will disgrace you. (Shame: dishonor) **4.** Though they have officials in Zoan and messengers who travel to Hanes, (Zoan: a city in Egypt) **5.** All will be put to shame because they rely on a nation that offers them no help. Egypt brings them no advantage, only dishonor and disgrace. (Advantage: benefit) **6.** This is a prophecy concerning the animals of the Negev: In a land of hardship and distress, where lions, lionesses, and venomous snakes dwell, the envoys carry their treasures on the backs of donkeys and camels, traveling to that unprofitable nation, (Negev: a desert region) **7.** To Egypt, whose help is utterly useless. I will call her Rahab the Do-Nothing. (Rahab: a poetic name for Egypt) **8.** Now, go and write this down for them; inscribe it on a scroll so that in the future it may serve as a lasting witness. (Scroll: a rolled-up document) **9.** These are a rebellious people, deceitful children, unwilling to listen to the LORD's instruction. (Deceitful: dishonest) **10.** They say to the seers, "Do not see visions!" and to the prophets, "Do not prophesy what is right! Tell us pleasant things, prophesy illusions. **11.** Get out of our way, stop confronting us with the Holy One of Israel! (Holy One of Israel: a title for God) **12.** Therefore, this is what the Holy One of Israel says: "Because you have rejected My message, relied on oppression, and depended on deceit, (Oppression: unjust treatment) **13.** This sin will become like a high wall, cracked and bulging, which suddenly collapses, in an instant. (Bulging: swelling outward) **14.** It will break into pieces like fragile pottery, shattered so mercilessly that not a single fragment will remain that could be used to take coals from a fire or scoop water from a cistern." (Cistern: a water storage container) **15.** This is what the Sovereign LORD, the Holy One of Israel, says: "In repentance and rest is your salvation; in quietness and trust is your strength, but you would not have it. (Repentance: turning away from sin) **16.** You said, 'No, we will flee on horses.' Therefore, you will flee! You said, 'We will ride on swift horses.' Therefore, your pursuers will be swift! (Swift: fast) **17.** A thousand will flee at the threat of one, and at the threat of five, you will all flee away, until you are left like a banner on a mountaintop, like a flag on a hill." (Banner: a flag) **18.** Yet the LORD longs to be gracious to you; He will rise up to show you compassion. For the LORD is a God of justice. Blessed are all who wait for Him! (Gracious: merciful) **19.** O people of Zion, who live in Jerusalem, you will weep no more. How gracious He will be when you cry for help! As soon as He hears, He will answer you. (Zion: a poetic name for Jerusalem) **20.** Although the Lord gives you the bread of adversity and the water of affliction, your teachers will no longer be hidden; with your own eyes, you will see them. (Affliction: suffering) **21.** Whether you turn to the right or the left, your ears will hear a voice behind you, saying, "This is the way; walk in it." (Walk: follow) **22.** Then you will desecrate your idols overlaid with silver and your images covered with gold; you will throw them away like a used menstrual cloth, and say to them, "Away with you!" (Desecrate: treat with disrespect) **23.** He will also send you rain for the seed you sow in the ground, and the food from the land will be rich and plentiful. In that day, your cattle will graze in wide meadows. **24.** The oxen and donkeys that work the land will eat well, with plenty of fodder and mash, spread out with fork and shovel. (Fodder: animal feed) **25.** In the day of great slaughter, when the towers fall, streams of water will flow on every high mountain and every lofty hill. (Slaughter: sacrifice) **26.** The moon will shine as bright as the sun, and the sunlight will be seven times brighter, like the light of seven full days, when the LORD binds up the bruises of His people and heals the wounds He inflicted. (Bruises: injuries) **27.** See, the Name of the LORD comes from afar, with burning anger and thick clouds of smoke; His lips are filled with wrath, and His tongue is like a consuming fire. (Wrath: intense anger) **28.** His breath is like a rushing torrent, rising up to the neck. He shakes the nations in the sieve of destruction; He places a bit in the jaws of the people, leading them astray. (Torrent: strong current) **29.** And you will sing, as on the night of a holy festival; your hearts will rejoice as when people playing pipes ascend to the mountain of the LORD, to the Rock of Israel. (Holy festival: sacred celebration) **30.** The LORD will make His majestic voice heard, and He will cause people to see His powerful arm coming down with raging anger, consuming fire, cloudbursts, thunderstorm, and hail. (Majestic: grand) **31.** The voice of the LORD will shatter Assyria; with His rod, He will strike them down. **32.** Every blow the LORD delivers to them with His punishing club will be accompanied by music, the sound of tambourines and harps, as He fights them in battle with His powerful arm. **33.** Topheth has been prepared long ago; it is made ready for the king. Its fire pit is deep and wide, with abundant fuel and wood; the breath of the LORD, like a stream of burning sulfur, sets it ablaze.

Chapter 31

1. Woe to those who go to Egypt for help, relying on horses, trusting in the power of chariots and horsemen, but fail to seek guidance from the Holy One of Israel. (Woe: warning of judgment) **2.** Yet God is wise and can bring calamity; He will act against the wicked and those who support evil. (Calamity: great disaster) **3.** Egypt is only human, not God; their horses are mere flesh, not spirit. When the LORD extends His hand, those who rely on Egypt will fall together. (Flesh: human strength; Spirit: divine power) **4.** The LORD says, "Like a lion growling over its prey, undisturbed by the noise of many shepherds, so will the LORD come to battle on Mount Zion." (Clamor: loud disturbance) **5.** Like birds flying, the LORD will protect Jerusalem, shield it, and pass over to rescue it. (Pass over: protect and deliver) **6.** Return to the LORD, O Israelites, whom you have greatly rebelled against. (Rebelled: turned away) **7.** In that day, you will renounce the idols of silver and gold made by your hands. (Idols: false gods) **8.** Assyria will fall by a divine sword; their young men will be enslaved. (Divine sword: judgment from God; Enslaved: made to work against their will) **9.** Their strongholds will crumble in terror, their leaders will panic at the sight of the battle flag," says the LORD, whose fire is in Zion and whose furnace is in Jerusalem. (Strongholds: fortified defenses; Furnace: place of judgment)

Chapter 32

1. A righteous king will reign, and rulers will govern justly. **2.** Each ruler will be like a shelter from the wind, a refuge from the storm, like streams in the desert and the shadow of a rock in a dry land. (Refuge: safe place; Shelter: protection) **3.** The eyes of the blind will be opened, and the ears of the deaf will hear. (Opened: become aware; Deaf: unable to hear) **4.** The fearful heart will understand, and those who stutter will speak clearly. (Fearful: anxious or worried) **5.** The fool will no longer be called noble, nor the scoundrel be respected. (Fool: person who lacks wisdom) **6.** Fools speak foolishness, their hearts are bent on evil; they practice ungodliness and spread lies about the LORD; they leave the hungry starving and withhold water from the thirsty. (Bent on: determined by) **7.** Scoundrels use evil methods, devising wicked plans to destroy the poor with lies, even when the needy are in the right. (Scoundrels: dishonest people) **8.** But the noble make noble plans and stand by their noble deeds. (Noble: honorable) **9.** Women who are complacent, rise and listen; you daughters who feel safe, hear my words! (Complacent: self-satisfied) **10.** Within a year, you will tremble; the grape harvest will fail, and the fruit harvest will not come. (Tremble: be filled with fear) **11.** Tremble, you complacent women, and shudder, you daughters of security! Strip off your fine clothes and wrap yourselves in rags. (Shudder: shake with fear) **12.** Mourn for the fields and vineyards, for the land of my people, which is overgrown with thorns and briars. Mourn for the houses of joy and the city of revelry. (Revelry: celebration) **13.** The fortress will be abandoned, the noisy city deserted; citadels and watchtowers will become wastelands, a place for donkeys and flocks. (Citadels: strongholds) **14.** Until the Spirit is poured upon us from on high, and the desert turns into a fertile field, and the fertile field becomes like a forest. (Poured: bestowed) **15.** The LORD's justice will be in the desert, His righteousness will dwell in the fertile fields. **16.** The result of righteousness will be peace; its effect will be quietness and confidence forever. (Righteousness: moral correctness) **17.** My people will live in peaceful homes, in secure dwellings, in undisturbed places of rest. (Undisturbed: free from trouble) **18.** Though hail flattens the forest and the city is completely destroyed, (Flattened: crushed) **19.** You will be blessed, sowing your seed by streams and letting your cattle and donkeys roam freely.

Chapter 33

1. Woe to you, O destroyer, who has never been destroyed! Woe to you, O betrayer, who has never been betrayed! When you cease your destruction, destruction will fall upon you. When you stop your betrayal, you will be betrayed. **2.** LORD, show us mercy; we eagerly await You. Be our strength every morning and our deliverance in times of trouble. **3.** When Your army makes a sound, nations flee; when You rise, the peoples scatter. **4.** Like locusts swarming for their plunder, the nations will hasten to take it. (Plunder: stolen treasures) **5.** The LORD is exalted and reigns on high; He will fill Zion with justice and righteousness. (Exalted: raised up in honor) **6.** He will be the solid foundation for your future, a treasure chest of salvation, wisdom, and knowledge. The fear of the LORD is the key to these riches. (Foundation: firm support) **7.** Look, the brave men are crying in the streets, and the messengers of peace weep bitterly. (Messengers: envoys) **8.** The highways are desolate, and no one travels on them. The treaty has been broken, witnesses are scorned, and no one is honored. (Treaty: agreement) **9.** The land is parched and withers; Lebanon is ashamed and fades away. Sharon becomes barren like a desert, and Bashan and Carmel lose their lushness. (Parched: dried out) **10.** "Now I will rise," declares the LORD. "Now I will be exalted; now I will be lifted up." (Rise: stand to act) **11.** You bring forth only useless chaff, and your breath is like fire that consumes you. (Chaff: worthless waste; Breath: actions or words) **12.** The nations will be reduced to ashes; like dry thorns, they will be set aflame. (Set aflame: ignited by fire) **13.** Those far off will hear what I have done; those nearby will acknowledge My power! (Acknowledge: recognize the authority of) **14.** The sinners in Zion are struck with terror; the wicked tremble in fear: "Who can endure this consuming fire? Who can withstand the eternal flames?" (Terror: fear of judgment) **15.** Those who live righteously, speak the truth, reject dishonest gain, and refuse to accept bribes will dwell safely on the heights. Their refuge will be in a secure fortress, and their basic needs will be met. (Righteously: justly) **16.** You will behold the King in His glory, and see a land that stretches out before you. (Behold: see with wonder) **17.** You will reflect on past terror and wonder, "Where is the tax collector? Where is the officer in charge of the towers?" (Terror: fear of former oppression) **18.** You will no longer see the proud, or hear their language that is foreign and hard to understand. (Proud: arrogant) **19.** Look at Zion, the city of our festivals. You will see Jerusalem, a peaceful home, a tent that will never be moved, whose stakes will never be pulled up. (Festivals: sacred celebrations) **20.** There, the LORD will be our Mighty One, like broad rivers and streams that no ship can navigate, no mighty vessel can cross. (Mighty One: powerful protector) **21.** The LORD is our judge, our lawgiver, and our King; He alone will save us. (Judge: one who renders justice) **22.** The rigging of your ships will be slack; the mast will be unsteady, and the sail will not be spread. Yet, even the crippled will take their share of the spoil. (Rigging: ship's equipment) **23.** In Zion, no one will say, "I am ill." The sins of its people will be forgiven.

Chapter 34

1. Come close, you nations, and listen; pay attention, all you peoples! Let the earth hear, and everything in it, the world and all that comes from it! **2.** The LORD is furious with all nations; His anger burns against their armies. He will utterly destroy them and hand them over to slaughter. (Furious: extremely angry) **3.** Their dead bodies will be scattered; they will stink, and their blood will soak the mountains. (Soak: saturate) **4.** All the stars in the sky will vanish; the heavens will roll up like a scroll. The stars will fall like withered leaves from vines or shriveled figs from fig trees. (Vanishing: disappearing) **5.** My sword is drenched in the heavens; behold, it descends in judgment upon Edom, the people I have utterly destroyed. **6.** The LORD's sword is filled with blood, covered in fat— the blood of lambs and goats, fat from rams' kidneys. The LORD has prepared a sacrifice in Bozrah and a great slaughter in Edom's land. (Sacrifice: ritual offering) **7.** Wild oxen will fall with them, along with bull calves and great bulls. Their land will be soaked in blood, and the dust will be thick with fat. (Thick: heavy and dense) **8.** For the LORD has a day of vengeance, a year of retribution to defend Zion's cause. **9.** Edom's streams will become pitch, her dust will turn to burning sulfur; her land will be a blazing pit of fire. **10.** It will burn forever, night and day; its smoke will rise without end. From generation to generation, it will lie waste, and no one will ever pass through it again. (Waste: desolate and uninhabited) **11.** The desert owl and screech owl will inherit it; the great owl and raven will make their nests there. The LORD will measure out Edom with chaos and plumb it with desolation. (Chaos: disorder) **12.** Her rulers will have no kingdom left, and all her leaders will vanish. (Rulers: those in power) **13.** Thorns will overrun her cities, nettles and thistles will grow in her strongholds. She will be a place for jackals, a home for owls. (Thistles: prickly plants; Jackals: wild dogs) **14.** Desert creatures will meet hyenas, and wild goats will bleat to each other. Night creatures will rest and find places to rest. (Hyenas: scavenging animals) **15.** The owl will build her nest and lay eggs, then hatch and care for her young under her wings. Falcons will gather there with their mates. **16.** Look at the scroll of the LORD and read: None of these creatures will be missing; not one will lack its mate. It is His mouth that has decreed it, and His Spirit will gather them. (Decreed: ordered) **17.** He has assigned them their portion and measured out their land. They will possess it forever and live there from generation to generation.

Chapter 35
1. The desert and dry land will rejoice; the wilderness will be glad and bloom like a flower. **2.** It will burst into full bloom and celebrate with joy. The glory of Lebanon, the beauty of Carmel and Sharon will be given to it. They will witness the splendor of the LORD, the magnificence of our God. (Splendor: great beauty or grandeur) **3.** Strengthen the weak hands and steady the trembling knees. **4.** Say to those with fearful hearts, "Be strong, don't be afraid! Your God is coming to save you. He will come with vengeance and divine retribution to rescue you." (Vengeance: punishment for wrongdoing) **5.** Then the eyes of the blind will be opened, and the ears of the deaf will hear. **6.** The lame will leap like a deer, and the mute will shout for joy. In the wilderness, water will flow, and streams will appear in the desert. **7.** The dry land will turn into a pool, and the parched ground into bubbling springs. In places where jackals once roamed, lush grass, reeds, and papyrus will grow. (Jackals: wild animals; Papyrus: aquatic plants) **8.** A highway will be there, called the Way of Holiness. It will be for those who walk on this path. The unclean will not travel on it, and wicked fools will not walk on it. (Unclean: impure; Wicked fools: those who are morally corrupt) **9.** There will be no lions or dangerous beasts on it—none will be there. Only the redeemed will walk on it. **10.** Those whom the LORD has rescued will return and come to Zion with singing. Everlasting joy will crown their heads. They will be filled with gladness and joy, and sorrow and sighing will vanish. (Redeemed: saved, rescued).

Chapter 36
1. In the fourteenth year of King Hezekiah's reign, Sennacherib, the king of Assyria, attacked and captured all of Judah's fortified cities. (Fortified cities: cities with strong defenses) **2.** Then, the Assyrian king sent his field commander with a large army from Lachish to Jerusalem. They stopped at the aqueduct near the Upper Pool, along the road leading to the Launderer's Field. (Aqueduct: a structure for carrying water) **3.** Eliakim, the palace administrator, Shebna the secretary, and Joah the recorder went out to meet him. **4.** The field commander spoke to them: "Tell Hezekiah, 'This is what the mighty king of Assyria says: What makes you so confident? **5.** You claim to have strength and advice for battle, but your words are hollow. Who are you relying on that causes you to defy me? (Defy: resist or challenge) **6.** I know you are relying on Egypt, but Egypt is like a broken reed. It pierces the hand of anyone who leans on it. That's how Pharaoh, king of Egypt, is to all who trust him. (Broken reed: weak and unreliable) **7.** But if you claim to be depending on the LORD our God, isn't He the same God whose altars and high places Hezekiah destroyed, saying to Judah and Jerusalem, 'You must worship only before this altar'? **8.** Come now, make a deal with my king. I'll give you 2,000 horses—if you can find enough men to ride them! (A challenge meant to highlight their weakness) **9.** How could you possibly withstand even one officer of my king's lowest officials, especially since you are relying on Egypt for horses and chariots? (Low-ranking: of a lower status) **10.** Did I come to attack and destroy this land without the LORD's command? The LORD Himself told me to come here and destroy it.'" (Destruction authorized: the commander claims divine backing for his mission) **11.** Eliakim, Shebna, and Joah replied, "Please speak to us in Aramaic, since we understand it. Do not speak in Hebrew, so that the people on the wall can hear." (Aramaic: a common language of diplomacy at the time, Hebrew: the native language of the people on the wall) **12.** The commander retorted, "Has my master only sent me to speak to your king and you? Am I not speaking to those sitting on the wall, who will have to eat their own excrement and drink their own urine, just like you?" (A cruel threat meant to frighten and demoralize) **13.** The commander then stood and shouted out loudly in Hebrew: "Listen to the words of the great king, the king of Assyria! **14.** This is what he says: Do not let Hezekiah deceive you. He cannot save you! **15.** Do not let Hezekiah try to convince you that the LORD will rescue you. He says, 'This city will not fall to the king of Assyria,' but don't believe him! **16.** Do not listen to Hezekiah's words. This is what the king of Assyria says: Make peace with me and surrender. Then each of you can enjoy the fruits of your own vine and fig tree and drink from your own cistern. (Cistern: a tank or container for holding water) **17.** I will take you to a land just like your own— a land full of grain, new wine, bread, and vineyards. **18.** Don't listen to Hezekiah when he says, 'The LORD will rescue us.' Have any of the gods of other nations ever saved their lands from my hand? (Mislead: to lead someone into deception or false beliefs) **19.** Where are the gods of Hamath and Arpad? Where are the gods of Sepharvaim? Have they saved Samaria from my power? (Sepharvaim: a city of ancient Syria) **20.** Which of all the gods of these nations has been able to deliver their lands from me? How can the LORD rescue Jerusalem from my power?" **21.** But the people remained silent and did not respond, because King Hezekiah had commanded, "Do not answer him." **22.** Then Eliakim, Shebna, and Joah, with their clothes torn in grief, went to Hezekiah and reported what the field commander had said. (Torn clothes: a sign of distress or mourning)

Chapter 37
1. When King Hezekiah heard this message, he tore his clothes in distress, put on sackcloth (a sign of mourning and repentance), and went to the temple of the LORD to pray. **2.** He sent Eliakim, the palace administrator, Shebna the secretary, and the leading priests—dressed in sackcloth—to the prophet Isaiah, son of Amoz. **3.** They told him, "This is what Hezekiah says: Today is a day of trouble, disgrace, and rebuke, like the time when a woman is about to give birth but has no strength to deliver the child." (Distress: a moment of overwhelming difficulty) **4.** Perhaps the LORD, your God, will listen to the words of the Assyrian field commander, whom his master, the king of Assyria, has sent to defy the living God. May He rebuke the commander for his blasphemies. Therefore, pray for the remnant of people that remains in Judah." **5.** When King Hezekiah's officials came to the prophet Isaiah, **6.** Isaiah replied, "Tell your king: 'This is what the LORD says: Do not be afraid of what you have heard—the words the Assyrian king's servants have used to mock me. **7.** I will soon make the king of Assyria hear a report that will cause him to return to his own country, and there I will have him struck down with the sword.'" (Mock: to make fun of or show contempt) **8.** When the field commander heard that King Sennacherib of Assyria had left Lachish, he withdrew from his siege

and found the king of Assyria fighting against Libnah. **9.** Sennacherib then received a report that Tirhakah, the king of Cush was marching to oppose him. When he heard this, he sent messengers to King Hezekiah with the following message: **10.** "Say to Hezekiah, king of Judah: Do not let your God deceive you by saying, 'Jerusalem will not be handed over to the king of Assyria.' **11.** You must have heard how the kings of Assyria have destroyed all the nations and their lands— how could you possibly escape? **12.** Did the gods of the nations I've conquered protect them—such as the gods of Gozan, Harran, Rezeph, and the people of Eden who were in Tel Assar? (Gozan, Harran, Rezeph: ancient cities conquered by Assyria) **13.** Where are the kings of Hamath or Arpad? Where are the kings of Lair, Sepharvaim, Hena, and Ivvah? **14.** Hezekiah received the letter from the messengers and read it. Then he went up to the temple of the LORD, spread the letter out before the LORD, **15.** and prayed: **16.** "LORD Almighty, God of Israel, enthroned between the cherubim, You alone are God over all the kingdoms of the earth. You created the heavens and the earth. **17.** Hear me, LORD, and listen. Open Your eyes, LORD, and see; hear the insults that Sennacherib has sent to mock the living God. **18.** It is true, LORD, that the Assyrian kings have laid waste to all the nations and their lands. **19.** They have burned the gods of those nations because they were not gods at all, but merely idols made of wood and stone, crafted by human hands. (Idols: false gods made by people) **20.** Now, LORD our God, deliver us from his hand, so that all the kingdoms of the earth may know that You alone, LORD, are God." **21.** Then Isaiah, son of Amoz, sent a message to Hezekiah: "This is what the LORD, the God of Israel, says: Because you prayed to me about Sennacherib, king of Assyria, **22.** here is the word the LORD has spoken against him: 'Virgin Daughter Zion despises you and mocks you. Daughter Jerusalem shakes her head at you as you flee. **23.** Who have you mocked and blasphemed? Against whom have you raised your voice and looked with such pride? Against the Holy One of Israel! (Blasphemed: spoken disrespectfully of God) **24.** By your messengers, you have mocked the Lord. You have said, 'With my many chariots, I have climbed the heights of the mountains, the highest peaks of Lebanon. I have cut down its tallest cedars, the best of its junipers. I have reached its most distant heights, the finest of its forests. (Arrogance: boastfully claiming power over everything) **25.** I have dug wells in foreign lands and drunk water there. With the soles of my feet, I have dried up all the streams of Egypt.' **26.** "Have you not heard? Long ago I planned this. In days of old, I ordained it. Now I have brought it to pass, that you have turned fortified cities into piles of rubble. **27.** Their people, drained of strength, are dismayed and put to shame. They are like plants in the field, like tender shoots, like grass on the roof, scorched before it can grow." (Scorched: burned and ruined before reaching maturity) **28.** "But I know where you are, when you come and go, and how you rage against me. **29.** Because you rage against me and your insolence has reached my ears, I will put my hook in your nose and my bit in your mouth, and I will make you return by the same way you came." (Insolence: rude or disrespectful behavior; Hook and bit: metaphors for control or subjugation) **30.** "This will be the sign for you, Hezekiah: This year you will eat what grows by itself, and the next year what springs from that. But in the third year, you will sow and reap, plant vineyards and eat their fruit. **31.** A remnant of the kingdom of Judah will take root below and bear fruit above. **32.** For out of Jerusalem will come a remnant, and out of Mount Zion a band of survivors. The zeal of the LORD Almighty will accomplish this." **33.** "Therefore, this is what the LORD says about the king of Assyria: He will not enter this city or shoot an arrow here. He will not come before it with a shield or build a siege ramp against it. **34.** By the way he came, he will return, and he will not enter this city," declares the LORD. **35.** "I will defend this city and save it, for my sake and for the sake of David my servant!" **36.** Then the angel of the LORD went out and struck down 185,000 men in the Assyrian camp. When the people got up the next morning, all the dead bodies were there! **37.** So Sennacherib, king of Assyria, broke camp and withdrew. He returned to Nineveh and stayed there. **38.** One day, while he was worshiping in the temple of his god Nisrok, his sons Adrammelek and Sharezer killed him with the sword. They then escaped to the land of Ararat. Esarhaddon, his son, succeeded him as king.

Chapter 38

1. During this time, King Hezekiah fell seriously ill and was near death. The prophet Isaiah, son of Amoz, visited him and said, "The LORD says: Set your house in order, for you are going to die and will not recover." **2.** Hezekiah turned to the wall and prayed: "LORD, remember how I have walked before you in faithfulness and done what is good in your eyes." And Hezekiah wept bitterly. **3.** "LORD, remember how I have walked before you in faithfulness and done what is good in your eyes." And Hezekiah wept bitterly. (faithfulness: loyalty) **4.** Then the word of the LORD came to Isaiah: **5.** "Go back and tell Hezekiah, 'The LORD, the God of your ancestor David, says: I have heard your prayer and seen your tears. I will add fifteen years to your life. (ancestor: forefather) **6.** I will also save you and this city from the king of Assyria." (Assyria: a powerful empire) **7.** "This will be the LORD's sign to you that he will fulfill his promise: **8.** I will make the shadow on the stairway of Ahaz move back ten steps." So, the sun's shadow went back ten steps. (Ahaz: King of Judah) **9.** Hezekiah's poem after recovery: **10.** I thought, "In my prime, must I die and lose all my future years?" **11.** "I will never see the LORD in the land of the living again, nor any man alive." **12.** My home has been dismantled like a shepherd's tent; my life was rolled up like a weaver's cloth, and the LORD cut it off. Day and night, you brought my life to an end. **13.** I waited for dawn, but like a lion, he crushed my bones; day and night, you ended my life. **14.** I cried like a swallow, moaned like a mourning dove. My eyes grew weak from looking to the heavens. I was in distress; Lord, help me!" **15.** But what can I say? He has spoken, and done this. I will walk humbly all my years because of this sorrow. **16.** LORD, these things give life, and my spirit finds hope in them. You healed me and gave me life. **17.** Surely it was for my benefit that I suffered. In your love, you kept me from the pit of destruction and forgave my sins. **18.** The grave cannot praise you; those in the pit cannot trust in your faithfulness. **19.** The living praise you, as I do today. Parents will teach their children about your faithfulness. (faithfulness: loyalty, truth) **20.** The LORD will save me, and we will sing with stringed instruments all our days in his temple. (stringed instruments: musical instruments like lyres) **21.** Isaiah said, "Prepare a poultice of figs and place it on the boil, and he will recover." (poultice: medicinal compress) **22.** Hezekiah asked, "What will be the sign that I will go up to the temple of the LORD?"

Chapter 39

1. At that time, Marduk-Baladan, son of Baladan, the king of Babylon, sent letters and gifts to Hezekiah because he had heard of his illness and recovery. (Marduk-Baladan: king of Babylon) **2.** Hezekiah welcomed the envoys and showed them everything in his storehouses—his silver, gold, spices, fine olive oil, his entire armory, and all his treasures. Nothing in his palace or kingdom was left hidden from them. **3.** Then the prophet Isaiah went to King Hezekiah and asked, "What did those men say, and where did they come from?" Hezekiah replied, "They came from a distant land, from Babylon." **4.** The prophet asked, "What did they see in your palace?" Hezekiah answered, "They saw everything in my palace. I showed them all my treasures." **5.** Isaiah then said to Hezekiah, "Hear the word of the LORD Almighty: **6.** The day will come when everything in your palace, and all that your ancestors have stored up until now, will be carried off to Babylon. Nothing will be left, says the LORD. **7.** Some of your descendants, your own children who will be born, will be taken away and made eunuchs in the palace of the king of Babylon." (eunuchs: castrated men who served in royal courts) **8.** "The word of the LORD you have spoken is good," Hezekiah replied. He thought, "There will be peace and security during my lifetime."

Chapter 40

1. "Comfort, comfort my people," says your God. 2. "Speak kindly to Jerusalem, and announce that her punishment is complete, that her sin has been forgiven, and that she has received from the LORD double for all her wrongs." 3. A voice calls out: "Prepare a way for the LORD in the wilderness (desert); make a straight path in the desert for our God." 4. Every valley will be lifted up, every mountain and hill made low; the rough ground will become level, the rugged places a plain. 5. Then the glory of the LORD will be revealed, and all people will see it together. For the mouth of the LORD has spoken." 6. A voice says, "Cry out." And I said, "What shall I cry?" "All people are like grass, and all their faithfulness like the flowers of the field." 7. The grass withers, the flowers fall, because the breath of the LORD blows on them. Surely, the people are like grass. 8. The grass withers, the flowers fall, but the word of our God endures forever." 9. You who bring good news to Zion, go up on a high mountain. You who bring good news to Jerusalem, lift up your voice with a shout, do not be afraid; say to the towns of Judah, "Here is your God!" 10. See, the Sovereign LORD comes with power, and he rules with a mighty arm. His reward is with him, and his recompense accompanies him. 11. He cares for his flock like a shepherd: He gathers the lambs in his arms and carries them close to his heart; he gently leads those that have young. 12. Who has measured the waters in the hollow of his hand, or with the breadth of his hand marked off the heavens? Who has held the dust of the earth in a basket, or weighed the mountains on scales and the hills in a balance? 13. Who can fathom the Spirit of the LORD, or instruct the LORD as his counselor? 14. Who did the LORD consult to enlighten him, and who taught him the right way? Who showed him knowledge or taught him understanding? 15. Surely the nations are like a drop in a bucket; they are regarded as dust on the scales; he weighs the islands as though they were fine dust. 16. Lebanon's trees are not enough for altar fires, nor its animals enough for burnt offerings. (Lebanon: known for its cedar trees) 17. Before him, all the nations are as nothing; they are regarded by him as worthless and less than nothing. 18. With whom will you compare God? To what image will you liken him? 19. An idol is made by a craftsman, who casts it in metal; a goldsmith covers it with gold and makes silver chains for it. 20. A poor person selects wood that will not rot and seeks a skilled worker to create an idol that will not topple. 21. Do you not know? Have you not heard? Has it not been told you from the beginning? Have you not understood since the earth was founded? 22. He sits enthroned above the circle of the earth, and its people are like grasshoppers. He stretches out the heavens like a canopy and spreads them out like a tent to live in. 23. He brings princes to nothing and reduces the rulers of this world to nothing. 24. No sooner are they planted, no sooner sown, no sooner take root in the ground, than he blows on them and they wither, and a whirlwind sweeps them away like chaff. (chaff: the husks separated from grain) 25. "To whom will you compare me? Or who is my equal?" says the Holy One. 26. Lift your eyes and look to the heavens: Who created all these? He who brings out the starry host one by one and calls each by name. Because of his great power and mighty strength, not one of them is missing. 27. Why do you complain, Jacob? Why do you say, Israel, "My way is hidden from the LORD; my cause is disregarded by my God"? 28. Do you not know? Have you not heard? The LORD is the everlasting God, the Creator of the ends of the earth. He will not grow tired or weary, and his understanding no one can fathom. 29. He gives strength to the weary and increases the power of the weak. 30. Even youths grow tired and weary, and young men stumble and fall; 31. But those who hope in the LORD will renew their strength. They will soar on wings like eagles; they will run and not grow weary, they will walk and not faint.

Chapter 41

1. "Be nonetheless in my presence, you islands! allow the international locations accumulate their power! let them come forward and present their case; let us meet together for judgment." 2. "Who has raised up one from the east, calling him in righteousness to fulfill his purpose? He palms countries over to him and subdues kings earlier than him. He makes them like dust along with his sword, like chaff blown by the wind along with his bow." (East: a direction associated with the rising solar, regularly linked with the origin of effective conquerors) 3. He pursues them relentlessly and actions forward unhurt, following a direction that has never been traveled earlier than. 4. "Who has performed this, bringing forth generations from the very beginning? it's miles I, the LORD, who is with the first and the final— i'm he." 5. The islands see this and are full of worry; the ends of the earth tremble. they arrive ahead collectively, collecting near. (Islands: frequently symbolic of distant lands or countries) 6. They inspire one another, saying, "Be sturdy!" 7. The metalworker supports the goldsmith, and the only who smooths with the hammer urges the only hanging the anvil. One approves of the work, announcing, "it is nicely." the opposite secures the idol to prevent it from falling. (Metalworker: someone who works with metallic; Goldsmith: one who crafts gold into items) 8. "but you, Israel, my servant, Jacob, whom i have chosen, you descendants of Abraham, my buddy, 9. I referred to as you from the ends of the earth, from the farthest corners I summoned you. I declared, 'you're my servant.' i have selected you and could no longer reject you. 10. Do now not be afraid, for i'm with you; do now not be dismayed, for i'm your God. i can beef up you, help you, and uphold you with my righteous proper hand." 11. "All those who oppose you will be humiliated and disgraced; people who face up to you will be as nothing and will vanish." 12. you'll search for folks that fought towards you, but you will no longer discover them. those who made struggle in opposition to you will be as if they in no way existed. 13. "For i'm the LORD, your God, who holds your proper hand and tells you, 'Do now not be afraid, i will help you.'" 14. "Do no longer worry, O Jacob, you little Israel, for i can assist you," publicizes the LORD, your Redeemer, the Holy certainly one of Israel. 15. "Behold, i'm able to make you a new threshing sledge, sharp and with many teeth. you will thresh mountains and crush them, and make the hills like chaff." (Threshing sledge: a heavy tool used for separating grain from the stalks) 16. "you'll winnow them, and the wind will deliver them away. but you may have fun inside the LORD and exult inside the Holy considered one of Israel." 17. "The bad and needy look for water, however discover none; their tongues are dry with thirst. however I, the LORD, will solution them; the God of Israel will not abandon them." 18. "i'm able to make rivers glide at the barren heights and springs inside the valleys. i'm able to flip the barren region into swimming pools of water, and the parched ground into springs." 19. "i'm able to plant cedars, acacias, myrtles, and olives inside the wasteland. i can location junipers inside the wastelands, in conjunction with firs and cypress trees." 20. "So that each one may also see and understand, may don't forget and know, that the hand of the LORD has carried out this, and that the Holy one among Israel has created it." 21. "gift your case," says the LORD. "deliver your arguments forward," says the King of Jacob. (King of Jacob: name relating to God's rule over Israel, the descendants of Jacob) 22. "tell us, you idols, what will manifest subsequent. inform us about the past, so we can also mirror and realize its very last final results. Or announce what's to return, 23. inform us what the destiny holds, so we may additionally recognize in case you are gods. Do something, whether or not accurate or bad, so we can be surprised and packed with awe." 24. "however you are nothing and your deeds are nugatory; whoever chooses you is detestable." 25. "i've raised up one from the north, and he is coming— one from the rising solar who calls on my name. He tramples on rulers as though they were mortar, as a potter treads on clay." (North: regularly associated with powerful empires like Babylon or Assyria) 26. "Who foretold this from the beginning, so we should understand, or earlier, so lets say, 'He became proper'? no one proclaimed it, nobody declared it, no person heard your phrases." 27. "i was the first to tell Zion,

'appearance, right here they may be!' I gave Jerusalem a messenger with desirable information." **28.** "I seemed, but there has been nobody— no person a number of the gods to provide suggest, nobody to respond once I requested." **29.** "See, they're all false! Their works are futile; their pix are however wind and emptiness." (Wind and emptiness: signifying their idols' lack of electricity or substance).

Chapter 42
1. "Here is my servant whom I guide, my chosen one, in whom I take pleasure. I will place my Spirit upon him, and he will bring justice to the nations." **2.** "He will not shout or raise his voice, nor cause a commotion in the streets." **3.** "He will not break a bruised reed, nor extinguish a smoldering wick. In faithfulness, he will bring justice." **4.** "He will not falter until justice is established on the earth. The islands will place their hope in his teachings." (Islands: distant lands or countries) **5.** "Thus says the LORD, the Creator of the heavens, who stretches them out and gives breath to the people on this earth." **6.** "I, the LORD, have called you in righteousness; I will hold your hand and make you a covenant for the people, a light to the Gentiles." **7.** "You will open the eyes of the blind, free captives from prison, and release those in darkness." (Captives: those in bondage, physically or spiritually) **8.** "I am the LORD; this is my name! I will not give my glory to another, nor share my praise with idols." **9.** "See, the former things have passed, and I announce new things before they spring into being." **10.** "Sing to the LORD a new song, his praise from the ends of the earth, you who go down to the sea, and all that is in it, you islands, and all who live in them." (New song: a fresh expression of praise for God's actions) **11.** "Let the desert and its towns raise their voices; let the settlements of Kedar rejoice. Let the people of Sela sing for joy, shouting from the mountaintops." (Kedar: a tribe living in the wilderness) **12.** "Let them give glory to the LORD and proclaim his praise in the islands." **13.** "The LORD will go out like a warrior, stirring his zeal like a champion. With a shout, he will raise the battle cry and overcome his enemies." **14.** "For a long time I have been silent, but now, like a woman in labor, I cry out in agony." **15.** "I will lay waste to the mountains, dry up rivers, and turn pools into dry land." **16.** "I will guide the blind along strange paths, turning darkness into light and making rough places smooth. I will not forsake them." **17.** "Those who trust in idols will be ashamed and turn back in disgrace." **18.** "Listen, you deaf; look, you blind, and see!" **19.** "Who is blind but my servant, and deaf like the messenger I send? Who is blind like the one in covenant with me, like the servant of the LORD?" **20.** "You have seen many things, but you do not understand; your ears are open, but you do not listen." (Covenant: formal agreement with God) **21.** "It pleased the LORD, for the sake of his righteousness, to make his law great and glorious." (Righteousness: moral rightness) **22.** "This is a people plundered and looted, trapped in pits or prisons, with no one to rescue them." (Plunder: stolen goods, often in conflict) **23.** "Who will listen and pay attention to this in time to come?" **24.** "Who gave Jacob to the looters and Israel to the plunderers? Was it not the LORD, because of their sin, for they did not follow his ways or obey his law?" **25.** "So he poured out his burning anger, and the violence of war consumed them, but they did not understand." (Burning anger: God's intense wrath)

Chapter 43
1. "Now, this is the word of the LORD— the one who created you, Jacob, and formed you, Israel: 'Do not be afraid, for I have redeemed you. I have called you by name; you are mine.' **2.** "When you pass through deep waters, I will be with you; the rivers will not overwhelm you. Even if you walk through fire, you will not be burned; the flames will not scorch you." (Redeemed: rescued or bought back from danger) **3.** "I am the LORD your God, the Holy One of Israel, your Savior. I gave Egypt as your ransom, and Cush and Seba as substitutes for you." **4.** "Because you are precious and honored in my sight, and I love you, I will exchange nations for your life, and peoples in exchange for you." **5.** "Do not fear, for I am with you. I will bring your descendants from the east and gather you from the west." **6.** "I will command the north to give them up, and tell the south, 'Do not keep them back.' Bring my sons from afar and my daughters from the ends of the earth." **7.** "All those who are called by my name, whom I created for my glory, whom I formed and made." (Glory: the honor and praise due to God alone) **8.** "Lead out the blind who have eyes, and those who are deaf but still have ears." (Blind and deaf: those who are spiritually unresponsive) **9.** "All the nations are gathering together, the peoples assembling. Which of their gods proclaimed this, or foretold the past? Let them bring their witnesses to prove they were right, so others may say, 'It is true.'" **10.** "You are my witnesses," declares the LORD, "and my chosen servant, so that you may know and trust me, and understand that I am the only true God. No god existed before me, and there will be none after me." **11.** "I, even I, am the LORD, and there is no savior besides me." **12.** "I have revealed, saved, and proclaimed my name— I alone, and not any foreign god among you. You are my witnesses," says the LORD, "that I am the one true God." **13.** "Yes, from ancient times, I am he. No one can deliver from my hand. When I act, who can undo it?" (Ancient times: God's eternal existence) **14.** "This is what the LORD says— your Redeemer, the Holy One of Israel: 'For your sake, I will send to Babylon and bring down all the Babylonians, those who boast of their ships.'" **15.** "I am the LORD, your Holy One, the Creator of Israel, your King." **16.** "This is what the LORD says— the one who made a way through the sea, a path through mighty waters," **17.** "who brought out the chariots and the army, and they all fell, never to rise again, extinguished like a wick." **18.** "Do not dwell on the past; forget what happened before." **19.** "Behold, I am doing a new thing! Now it springs up; do you not see it? I am making a way in the wilderness and streams in the desert." (Wilderness: barren land, Desert: dry and uninhabitable) **20.** "Even the wild animals honor me, the jackals and the owls, because I provide water in the wilderness and streams in the desert, to refresh my people, my chosen ones." **21.** "The people I formed for myself, that they may proclaim my praise." (Chosen: selected by God for a special purpose) **22.** "But you have not called on me, Jacob, and you have not wearied yourself seeking me, Israel." **23.** "You have not offered me sheep for burnt offerings, nor honored me with your sacrifices. I have not burdened you with grain offerings or demands for incense." **24.** "You have not bought any fragrant calamus for me, nor offered the fat of your sacrifices. Instead, you have burdened me with your sins and wearied me with your offenses." (Calamus: a fragrant plant used in worship) **25.** "I, even I, am the one who blots out your transgressions for my own sake and will remember your sins no more." (Blots out: completely forgives, wipes away) **26.** "Review the past for me; let us argue the case together; state your case and prove your innocence." **27.** "Your first ancestor sinned, and those I sent to teach you rebelled against me." **28.** "Therefore, I disgraced the leaders of your temple; I gave Jacob to destruction and Israel to scorn." (Dignitaries: influential leaders, temple: the place of worship)

Chapter 44
1. "However now concentrate, Jacob, my helper, Israel, whom I have selected. **2.** "This is what the LORD says— he created you, formed you in the womb, and could help you: Do no longer be afraid, Jacob, my servant, Jeshurun, whom I have chosen. **3.** "I will pour water at the thirsty land, streams at the dry floor; my Spirit for your offspring, and my blessing for your descendants." **4.** "They may grow like grass in a meadow, like poplars by means of streams." (Streams: life-giving blessing) **5.** "Some will say, 'I belong to the LORD'; others will call themselves by Jacob's name; others will write, 'The LORD's,' on their hand and take the name Israel." **6.** "This is what the LORD says— Israel's King and Redeemer, the LORD Almighty: I am the first and the last; there's no God beside me." **7.** "Who is like me? Let him claim it. Let him foretell the future, from the beginning to what's to come." **8.** "Do not tremble or be afraid. Did I not declare this long ago? You

are my witnesses. Is there any God except me? There's no other Rock; I know not one." **9.** "All who make idols are nothing, and what they treasure is nugatory. Folks that talk for them are blind and ignorant." **10.** "Who shapes a god or casts an idol that benefits nothing?" **11.** "Individuals who do will be shamed. The craftsmen are human. Let them stand collectively and be terrified." **12.** "The blacksmith works the iron within the hearth, shaping an idol with hammers, dropping power within the technique." **13.** "The carpenter measures and shapes a human form to place in a shrine." **14.** "He cuts down cedars or takes a pine tree, the use of rain to make it grow." **15.** "He uses part for firewood, warming himself and baking bread. But he also makes an idol and bows to it." (Idol: crafted god) **16.** "He burns half to cook, and with the other half, makes a god to worship." **17.** "He prays to his idol, 'Save me, you're my god!'" **18.** "They're blind, unable to understand, their eyes are covered, and their minds closed." **19.** "No one thinks, 'I used part for firewood; shall I now make an idol from the rest?'" **20.** "Such people feed on ashes; a deluded heart leads them off track. They cannot keep themselves, nor see their mistakes." **21.** "Remember these things, Jacob, for you, Israel, are my servant. I created you, and you're my servant; I cannot forget you." **22.** "I have wiped out your sins like a cloud, your offenses like mist. Return to me, for I've redeemed you." **23.** "Sing for joy, heavens, for the LORD has done this. Shout aloud, earth, burst into song, you mountains and forests, for the LORD has redeemed Jacob." **24.** "This is what the LORD says— your Redeemer, who formed you: I am the LORD, Maker of all things, who stretches out the heavens, and spreads out the earth." **25.** "I frustrate false prophets and turn their knowledge into foolishness." **26.** "I fulfill my servants' words, and satisfy their prophecies. Jerusalem will be inhabited, Judah's cities rebuilt, and their ruins restored." **27.** "I can dry up the seas and their streams." **28.** "I say of Cyrus, 'He's my shepherd; he will accomplish my purpose. He'll say of Jerusalem, 'Let it be rebuilt,' and of the temple, 'Let its foundations be laid.'"

Chapter 45
1. "This is what the LORD says to His chosen one, Cyrus (Cyrus: Persian king), whom I empower to defeat nations and strip kings of their power, opening gates that will never be closed. **2.** I will go ahead of you, level mountains, break bronze gates, and cut through iron bars. **3.** I will give you hidden treasures and riches in secret places so you will know I am the LORD, the God of Israel (Israel: the nation), who calls you by name. **4.** For the sake of Jacob (Jacob: the patriarch of Israel), my servant, and Israel, my chosen, I call you by name and honor you, though you do not recognize me. **5.** I am the LORD, and there is no other; apart from me, there is no God. I will strengthen you, even if you do not acknowledge me, **6.** so that everyone from east to west will know that I am the LORD, and there is no other. **7.** I create light and darkness, prosperity and disaster; I, the LORD, do all these things. **8.** "Heavens above, rain down righteousness; let the earth open and salvation grow. I, the LORD, have created it." **9.** "Woe to those who argue with their Maker, like clay questioning the potter. Does clay say to the potter, 'What are you making?' (Potter: one who shapes clay into objects) **10.** Woe to those who question parents, 'What have you given birth to?' **11.** "This is what the LORD says: Do you question me about my children or give orders about my work? **12.** I made the earth and created mankind; My hands stretched out the heavens, and I brought forth their stars (Stars: celestial bodies). **13.** I will raise up Cyrus in righteousness, make his paths straight, and he will rebuild my city and free my people without payment, says the LORD Almighty (LORD Almighty: title for God showing His sovereignty and power). **14.** The products of Egypt (Egypt: neighboring nation) and the wealth of Cush (Cush: kingdom south of Egypt) will come to you in chains, acknowledging that God is with you, and there is no other. **15.** Truly, you are a God who has hidden Himself, the Savior of Israel (Israel: the nation). **16.** All idol makers will be ashamed and disgraced; they will be humiliated together (Idols: man-made representations of gods). **17.** But Israel will be saved by the LORD with everlasting salvation; they will never be ashamed. **18.** For the LORD, who created the heavens and the earth, says: "I did not create the earth to be empty, but to be inhabited. I am the LORD, and there is no other. **19.** I have not spoken in secret or told Jacob's descendants to seek me in vain. I, the LORD, speak truth and declare what is right. **20.** "Gather together, you survivors from the nations. Foolish are those who carry idols and pray to gods that cannot save (Idols: man-made objects worshiped as gods). **21.** Announce what will happen. Who foretold it long ago? Was it not I, the LORD? There is no God besides me, a righteous God and Savior (Savior: one who rescues or delivers). **22.** "Turn to me and be saved, all you ends of the earth; for I am God, and there is no other. **23.** I have sworn by myself, my word will not be changed: Before me, every knee will bow, and every tongue will swear allegiance (Knee: symbolizing submission and honor). **24.** They will say, 'In the LORD alone is salvation and strength.' All who opposed Him will come and be ashamed. **25.** But all of Israel will be saved by the LORD and will take pride in Him."

Chapter 46
1. Bel bows down, Nebo stoops low; their idols are borne by beasts of burden. The images that are carried about are burdensome, a burden for the weary. (Bel: a Babylonian god; Nebo: a Babylonian god) **2.** They stoop and bow down together; unable to rescue the burden, they themselves go off into captivity. **3.** "Listen to me, you descendants of Jacob, all the remnant of the people of Israel, you whom I have upheld since your birth, and have carried since you were born. **4.** Even to your old age and gray hairs I am he, I am he who will sustain you. I have made you and I will carry you; I will sustain you and I will rescue you. **5.** "With whom will you compare me or count me equal? To whom will you liken me that we may be compared? **6.** Some pour out gold from their bags and weigh out silver on the scales; they hire a goldsmith to make it into a god, and they bow down and worship it. **7.** They lift it to their shoulders and carry it; they set it up in its place, and there it stands. From that spot it cannot move. Even though someone cries out to it, it cannot answer; it cannot save them from their troubles. **8.** "Remember this, keep it in mind, take it to heart, you rebels. (Rebels: those who oppose authority) **9.** Remember the former things, those of long ago; I am God, and there is no other; I am God, and there is none like me. **10.** I make known the end from the beginning, from ancient times, what is still to come. I say, 'My purpose will stand, and I will do all that I please.' **11.** From the east I summon a bird of prey; from a far-off land, a man to fulfill my purpose. What I have said, that I will bring about; what I have planned, that I will do. (Bird of prey: a metaphor for a strong conqueror) **12.** Listen to me, you stubborn-hearted, you who are now far from my righteousness. (Stubborn-hearted: those who refuse to change) **13.** I am bringing my righteousness near, it is not far away; and my salvation will not be delayed. I will grant salvation to Zion, my splendor to Israel. (Zion: a symbol for Jerusalem)

Chapter 47
1. "Go down, sit in the dust, Virgin Daughter Babylon; sit on the ground without a throne, queen city of the Babylonians. No more will you be called tender or delicate. (Virgin Daughter Babylon: untainted city) **2.** Take millstones and grind flour; take off your veil. Lift up your skirts, bare your legs, and wade through the streams. **3.** Your nakedness will be exposed and your shame uncovered. I will take vengeance; I will spare no one." **4.** Our Redeemer—the LORD Almighty is His name—is the Holy One of Israel. (Redeemer: Savior) **5.** "Sit in silence, go into darkness, queen city of the Babylonians; no more will you be called queen of kingdoms. **6.** I was angry with my people and desecrated my inheritance; I gave them into your hand, and you showed them no mercy. Even on the aged you laid a very heavy yoke. (Yoke: burden) **7.** You said, 'I am forever—the eternal queen!' But you did not consider these things or reflect on what might happen. **8.** "Now then, listen, you lover of pleasure, lounging

in your security and saying to yourself, 'I am, and there is none besides me. I will never be a widow or suffer the loss of children.' (Lover of pleasure: indulgent person) **9.** Both of these will overtake you in a moment, on a single day: loss of children and widowhood. They will come upon you in full measure, in spite of your many sorceries and all your potent spells. (Sorceries: magic; Spells: incantations) **10.** You have trusted in your wickedness and have said, 'No one sees me.' Your wisdom and knowledge mislead you when you say to yourself, 'I am, and there is none besides me.' **11.** Disaster will come upon you, and you will not know how to conjure it away. A calamity will fall upon you that you cannot ransom; a catastrophe you cannot foresee will suddenly come upon you. (Calamity: disaster) **12.** "Keep on, then, with your magic spells and your many sorceries, which you have labored at since childhood. Perhaps you will succeed, perhaps you will cause terror. **13.** All the counsel you have received has only worn you out! Let your astrologers come forward, those stargazers who make predictions month by month, let them save you from what is coming upon you. **14.** Surely they are like stubble; the fire will burn them up. They cannot even save themselves from the power of the flame. These are not coals for warmth; this is not a fire to sit by. **15.** That is all they are to you— these you have dealt with and labored with since childhood. All of them go on in their error; there is not one that can save you.

Chapter 48

1. "Hear this, you descendants of Jacob, called by the name of Israel, from the line of Judah, who swear by the name of the LORD but not in truth or righteousness— **2.** You claim to live in the holy city and trust in the God of Israel— the LORD Almighty is His name. **3.** Long ago, I foretold these things, I declared them with my mouth, and they came to pass when I acted suddenly. **4.** I knew how stubborn you were; your neck was as hard as iron, and your forehead as tough as bronze. (Stubborn: unyielding; Iron and bronze: symbols of hardness) **5.** That's why I revealed these things to you long before they happened, so you wouldn't claim, 'My idols did this, my gods made it happen.' (Idols: false gods) **6.** You've heard these things, now look at them. Will you not admit it? "From now on, I will tell you of things not known to you. **7.** They have been created recently, not from long ago; you've never heard of them before. So you cannot say, 'I knew of them.' **8.** You haven't heard nor understood, for your ears have been closed. You've been rebellious since birth. (Rebellious: disobedient) **9.** For the sake of my name, I have delayed my anger; for the sake of my praise, I have held it back from you, so I wouldn't destroy you completely. **10.** See, I've refined you, but not as silver; I have tested you in the furnace of affliction. (Refined: purified; Furnace of affliction: hardship) **11.** For my own sake, I do this. How could I let my name be dishonored? I won't give my glory to anyone else. **12.** "Listen, Jacob, and Israel whom I've called: I am the first and the last. (Jacob: another name for Israel; First and last: eternal nature of God) **13.** It was my hand that laid the earth's foundations, and my right hand that stretched out the heavens. When I call them, they stand together. (Right hand: symbol of power) **14.** "Gather, and listen: Which of your idols has predicted these things? The LORD's chosen ally will accomplish His purpose against Babylon; His strength will be used against the Babylonians. (Idols: false gods; Chosen ally: God's servant) **15.** It is I who have spoken; I've called him and will bring him to succeed in what I've planned. **16.** "Come close and listen: I've never spoken in secret; when it happens, I'm there." And now the Sovereign LORD has sent me, with His Spirit. (Sovereign LORD: God as ruler; Spirit: God's empowering presence) **17.** This is what the LORD says—your Redeemer, the Holy One of Israel: "I am the LORD your God, who teaches you what is best and leads you in the way you should go. (Redeemer: Savior; Holy One: sacred God) **18.** If you had only listened to my commands, your peace would be like a flowing river, your prosperity like the endless waves of the sea. (Peace: tranquility; Prosperity: well-being) **19.** Your descendants would have been as numerous as the sand, your children as countless as its grains; their name would never be erased or destroyed before me. (Descendants: children; Sand: numerous) **20.** Leave Babylon, flee from the Babylonians! Shout for joy and proclaim it to the ends of the earth: "The LORD has redeemed His servant Jacob." (Babylon: the city; Redeemed: rescued) **21.** When He led them through deserts, they didn't thirst; He made water flow from the rock and split it open, causing water to gush out. **22.** "There is no peace," says the LORD, "for the wicked."

Chapter 49

1. "Listen to my words, you islands, remote countries: before I was born, the LORD called me; from the womb of my mother He called my name." **2.** He made my words like a sharp sword, concealed me in His hand; He made me a refined arrow and hid me in His quiver. **3.** He said, "You are my servant, Israel, in whom I will display my glory." **4.** But I said, "I've labored in vain; yet my reward is in the LORD's hands." (Worked in vain: no visible result) **5.** And now the LORD says, "It is too small a thing to restore Jacob and bring back Israel; I will also make you a light for the Gentiles, so that my salvation may reach the ends of the earth." (Light: revelation; Gentiles: non-Israelites) **6.** The LORD, the Redeemer and Holy One of Israel, says: "Kings will see and arise, princes will bow down because of the LORD, who has chosen you." **7.** The LORD says, "In the time of favor, I will answer you; in the day of salvation, I will help you. I will make you a covenant to restore the land and deliver the captives." (Covenant: binding promise; Deliver: set free) **8.** "Say to the captives, 'Come out,' and to those in darkness, 'Be free!' They will find pasture and be led beside springs of water." (Captives: those in exile; Darkness: oppression) **9.** "I will turn mountains into roads and raise up highways **10.** "They will come from afar—north, west, and Aswan." (Aswan: a location in Egypt) **11.** "Shout, heavens; rejoice, earth; burst into song, mountains! For the LORD comforts His people and shows compassion to the troubled." (Comforts: brings relief; Troubled: struggling) **12.** But Zion said, "The LORD has forsaken me." (Zion: Jerusalem; Forsaken: abandoned) **13.** "Can a mother forget her baby? Even though she may forget, I will not forget you!" (Forget: neglect; Compassion: mercy) **14.** "I have engraved you on the palms of my hands; your walls are ever before me." (Engraved: marked permanently; Walls: Jerusalem's safety) **15.** "Your children will return, and those who destroyed you will leave." (Destroyed: ruined; Return: restoration) **16.** "Lift up your eyes and look; your children gather to you like adornments on a bride." (Adornments: decoration; Bride: metaphor for Israel's beauty) **17.** "Though you have been desolate, now your people will grow, and those who devoured you will be far away." (Desolate: abandoned; Devoured: oppressors) **18.** "Your children, born during your bereavement, will ask for more space." (Bereavement: loss; Space: room to grow) **19.** You will wonder, "Who bore these children? I was left alone; who raised them?" (Bereavement: loss; Left alone: deserted) **20.** The LORD says, "I will call the nations and bring your sons in their arms; they will carry your daughters on their hips." (Nations: foreign nations; Children: Israel's restoration) **21.** "Kings will be your foster fathers, and queens your nursing mothers. They will bow to you, and you will know I am the LORD." (Foster fathers: rulers who care for Israel; Nursing mothers: queens offering care) **22.** "Can plunder be taken from warriors, or captives rescued from the fierce?" (Plunder: treasure; Warriors: strong enemies) **23.** "Yes, captives will be freed, and I will save your children. I will make your oppressors eat their own flesh and drink their own blood." (Oppressors: enemies; Plunder: treasure) **24.** "Then all mankind will know that I, the LORD, am your Savior and Redeemer, the Mighty One of Jacob." (Redeemer: Savior; Mighty One: powerful protector) **25.** "Can plunder be taken from warriors, or captives rescued from the fierce?" (Plunder: treasures taken from defeated enemies; Fierce: powerful adversaries) **26.** "Yes, captives will be freed, and I will save your children. I will make your oppressors eat their own flesh and drink their own blood." (Oppressors: enemies; Freed: liberated; Plunder: treasures)

Chapter 50

1. "This is what the LORD says: Where is the certificate of divorce for your mother whom I sent away? To which creditor did I sell you? You were sold because of your sins, and your mother was sent away because of your transgressions." **2.** "When I came, why was there no one? When I called, why did no one answer? Is my arm too short to save you? I can dry up seas with a word, turn rivers into deserts, causing fish to die from thirst." **3.** "I cover the heavens in darkness and make it like a sackcloth." (Sackcloth: a coarse fabric often worn in mourning) **4.** "The Sovereign LORD has given me a well-trained tongue, to speak words that sustain the weary. He wakes me each morning, opening my ears to listen like a student." (Well-trained tongue: skillful speech) **5.** "The Sovereign LORD has opened my ears; I have not been rebellious, nor have I turned away." (Opened my ears: received instruction humbly) **6.** "I offered my back to those who beat me, my cheeks to those who pulled out my beard. I did not hide my face from mockery and spitting." (Mockery: ridicule) **7.** "Because the Sovereign LORD helps me, I will not be disgraced. I have set my face like flint, knowing I will not be put to shame." (Face like flint: firm resolve) **8.** "He who justifies me is near. Who will accuse me? Let us face each other! Who is my accuser? Let him confront me!" (Justifies: declares righteous; Accuser: someone who makes accusations) **9.** "The Sovereign LORD helps me. Who will condemn me? They will wear out like a garment; moths will eat them." (Condemn: pass judgment; Garment: clothing) **10.** "Who among you fears the LORD and obeys His servant? Let the one walking in darkness and having no light trust in the name of the LORD and rely on their God." (Fears: reveres; Trust: place confidence) **11.** "But you who light your own fires and walk in the light of your torches, you will lie down in torment, receiving what comes from my hand." (Torches: self-made guidance)

Chapter 51

1. "Hear me, you who seek righteousness and pursue the LORD: Reflect on the rock you were carved from, and the quarry from which you were hewn." (Rock: foundation of faith) **2.** "Look at Abraham, your father, and Sarah, the one who bore you. When I called Abraham, he was just one man, but I blessed him and made him many." **3.** "The LORD will comfort Zion, turning her desolation into Eden, her wastelands into the garden of the LORD. Joy, gratitude, and song will fill her." (Eden: paradise) **4.** "Listen, my people, and hear me, my nation: I will bring forth instruction, and my justice will shine as a guiding light for the nations." **5.** "My righteousness is near, salvation is on the way, and my power will bring justice to the nations. Distant lands will look to me with hope." **6.** "Lift your gaze to the heavens, look at the earth below; the heavens will vanish like smoke, the earth will wear out like a garment, and its people will die. But my salvation will endure forever, and my righteousness will never fail." **7.** "Listen, you who know what is right, and those who follow my instruction: Do not fear the mockery of mortals or be disturbed by their insults." (Mockery: criticism) **8.** "Like a moth consuming fabric, or a worm devouring wool, they will fade. But my righteousness endures forever, my salvation across all generations." (Moth and worm: destructive forces) **9.** "Awake, O arm of the LORD, clothe yourself with power! As in ancient times, when you defeated Rahab and pierced the dragon." (Arm of the LORD: God's strength; Rahab: chaos or Egypt) **10.** "Did you not dry up the sea, part the great deep, and make a path for the redeemed to cross?" (Redeemed: saved people) **11.** "Those rescued by the LORD will return to Zion with songs of joy, crowned with everlasting joy. Gladness will overtake them, and sorrow will flee." (Rescued: saved people; Zion: Jerusalem) **12.** "I, the LORD, am the one who comforts you. Why then fear mere mortals, who are like grass?" (Mere mortals: human beings) **13.** "Why forget your Maker, who stretches out the heavens and lays the earth's foundations, living in constant terror from the wrath of the oppressor?" (Oppressor: enemy) **14.** "Soon, the captives will be freed, they will not die in prison nor lack bread." (Captives: exiled people) **15.** "I am the LORD, your God, who stirs up the sea, and its waves roar—my name is the LORD Almighty." (God's power: control over nature) **16.** "I have placed my words in your mouth, shielding you with the shadow of my hand— I who established the heavens and the earth, saying to Zion, 'You are my people.'" **17.** "Awake, Jerusalem, who has drunk the cup of the LORD's wrath, drained the goblet that makes people stagger." (Cup of wrath: punishment) **18.** "Among your children, none are left to guide you; none who raised you can take you by the hand." (Guidance: leadership) **19.** "Double calamities have struck—ruin, destruction, famine, and sword—who can comfort you?" (Calamities: disasters) **20.** "Your children have fallen, lying helpless at every street corner, trapped like antelope in a net, filled with the wrath of the LORD." (Children: people; Antelope: trapped) **21.** "Listen, you afflicted ones, drunk not on wine but on your sorrow." (Afflicted: suffering; Drunk: overwhelmed) **22.** "The Sovereign LORD declares: I have removed from you the cup that made you stagger; from this cup of wrath, you will never drink again." (Cup of wrath: punishment) **23.** "I will give it into the hands of your tormentors, who made you lie down so they could walk over you." (Tormentors: oppressors)

Chapter 52

1. "Awake, Zion! Strengthen yourself, Jerusalem, the holy city! No uncircumcised or defiled will enter you again." (Strengthen: rise up) **2.** "Shake off the dust, rise, and sit in glory, Jerusalem. Free yourself from the chains of captivity, Daughter Zion." (Chains: captivity) **3.** "The LORD declares: You were sold for nothing, and you will be redeemed without cost." (Redeemed: rescued) **4.** "The Sovereign LORD says: My people went to Egypt at first, but now Assyria oppresses them." **5.** "What do I have here?" says the LORD. "My people have been taken for nothing, and their rulers mock them. My name is constantly blasphemed." (Blasphemed: dishonored) **6.** "Therefore, my people will know my name. On that day, they will know that I foretold it— I, the LORD." (Foretold: promised) **7.** "How beautiful are the feet of those who bring good news, proclaim peace, salvation, and say to Zion, 'Your God reigns!'" **8.** "Listen! Your watchmen raise their voices in joy. When the LORD returns to Zion, they will witness it." (Watchmen: messengers) **9.** "Burst into song, ruins of Jerusalem, for the LORD has comforted and redeemed his people." (Ruins: desolation) **10.** "The LORD will reveal his holy arm before all nations, and all the earth will see our God's salvation." **11.** "Depart, depart, come out from there! Do not touch anything unclean! Purify yourselves, you who carry the LORD's articles." (Purify: sanctify) **12.** "You will not leave in haste, for the LORD will lead you, and the God of Israel will protect you from behind." **13.** "See, my servant will act wisely, be raised, exalted, and lifted up." (Exalted: glorified) **14.** "Many were appalled by his appearance, disfigured beyond human recognition." (Disfigured: marred) **15.** "He will sprinkle many nations. Kings will be silent before him; they will understand what they never heard or were told." (Kings: rulers; Sprinkle: cleanse)

Chapter 53

1. "Who has believed our message, and to whom has the arm of the LORD been revealed?" (Revealed: shown) **2.** "He grew up like a tender shoot, a root in dry ground. He had no beauty or majesty to draw us to him, nothing in his appearance that would make us desire him." (Draw: attract) **3.** "He was despised and rejected by men, a man of suffering and acquainted with pain. People hid their faces from him, and we held him in low esteem." (Acquainted with pain: familiar with suffering) **4.** "Yet he bore our pain and carried our suffering, but we thought he was being punished by God, stricken and afflicted." (Punished: judged) **5.** "He was pierced for our transgressions, crushed for our iniquities; the punishment that brought us peace was on him, and by his wounds, we are healed." (Healed: restored) **6.** "We all, like sheep, have gone astray; each of us has turned to our own way, and the LORD has laid on him the iniquity of us all." (Iniquity: sin) **7.** "He was oppressed and afflicted, yet he remained silent; like a lamb to the slaughter, and as a sheep before its shearers, he did not speak." (Silent: mute) **8.** "He was taken away by oppression and judgment. Who protested? He was cut off from the land of the living, punished for the transgression of my people." (Protested: objected) **9.** "He was assigned a grave with the wicked, but with the rich in his death, though he had done no violence, nor was deceit in his mouth." (Deceit: falsehood) **10.** "Yet it was the LORD's will to crush him and cause him to suffer; though he makes his life an offering for sin, he will see his descendants and prolong his days. The LORD's will will prosper through him." (Prolong: extend) **11.** "After his suffering, he will see the light of life and be satisfied; by his knowledge, my righteous servant will justify many, and he will bear their iniquities." (Justify: make right) **12.** "Therefore, I will give him a portion among the great, and he will divide the spoils with the strong, because he poured out his life unto death, and was numbered with the transgressors. He bore the sin of many and interceded for the transgressors." (Interceded: pleaded)

Chapter 54

1. "Sing, O barren lady, you who've never borne a child; burst into music, shout with joy, you who've by no means been in labor. For greater are the youngsters of the desolate than the ones of the woman with a husband," publicizes the LORD. (Desolate: forsaken) **2.** "Extend the area of your tent, stretch your tent curtains huge, do no longer keep again; extend your ropes and beef up your stakes." **3.** "For you may spread out to the proper and to the left; your descendants will dispossess countries and inhabit their desolate towns." **4.** "Do now not fear, for you will no longer be ashamed. Do now not be dismayed; you'll no longer be disgraced. you may overlook the shame of your young people and will not recall the reproach of your widowhood." (Dismayed: humiliated) **5.** "To your Maker is your husband— the LORD Almighty is his name— the Holy One among Israel is your Redeemer; he's referred to as the God of all the earth." **6.** "The LORD will call you again, as if you had been a spouse abandoned and grieved in spirit— a wife who turned into married young but rejected," says your God. (Grieved: distressed) **7.** "For a moment, I deserted you, but with terrific compassion, I will convey you again." (Deserted: abandoned) **8.** "In a burst of anger, I concealed my face from you for a quick time, but with everlasting kindness, I will have compassion on you," says the LORD, your Redeemer. (Burst: surge) **9.** "That is just like the days of Noah to me, after I swore that the waters of Noah would in no way once more flood the earth. Now, I have sworn no longer to be irritated with you and by no means to rebuke you once more." (Sworn: vowed) **10.** "Even though the mountains be shaken and the hills be removed, my love for you will in no way be shaken, nor will my covenant of peace be taken away," says the LORD, who has compassion on you. (Shaken: disturbed) **11.** "O troubled metropolis, lashed by storms and not comforted, I can rebuild you with turquoise stones, and your foundations may be made from lapis lazuli." (Afflicted: distressed) **12.** "I can make your partitions of treasured stones, your battlements of rubies, and your gates of glowing jewels." (Battlements: defenses) **13.** "All of your youngsters could be taught by means of the LORD, and first rate could be their peace." (Peace: prosperity) **14.** "You will be firmly hooked up in righteousness; tyranny can be a long way from you, and you may have nothing to worry. Terror can be some distance removed; it'll now not method you." (Firmly hooked up: securely founded) **15.** "If anyone attacks you, it's going to no longer be by my doing; whoever assails you may be defeated." (Assails: attacks) **16.** "See, I've created the blacksmith who stirs up the coals and forges weapons suit for their cause, and I have additionally created the destroyer to convey wreck." (Stirs up: fans) **17.** "No weapon cast against you may prevail, and you'll refute every tongue that accuses you. This is the inheritance of the servants of the LORD, and their vindication comes from me," broadcasts the LORD. (Vindication: justification)

Chapter 55

1. "Come, all who are thirsty, come to the waters! And you who have no money, come, buy and eat! Come, buy wine and milk without cost, without spending anything." (Thirsty: longing) **2.** "Why waste your money on food that doesn't satisfy? Why labor for what doesn't nourish? Listen, listen to me, and enjoy what is good; you will delight in the finest of foods." (Waste: spend) **3.** "Pay attention and come to me; listen, and you will live. I will establish an everlasting covenant with you, a promise of my unfailing love to David." (Establish: make) **4.** "See, I have made him a witness to the nations, a ruler and commander of peoples." (Witness: sign) **5.** "You will call upon nations you do not know, and nations unknown to you will come running to you, because of the LORD your God, the Holy One of Israel, who has adorned you with splendor." (Adorned: gifted) **6.** "Seek the LORD while He may be found; call upon Him while He is near." (Seek: search) **7.** "Let the wicked forsake their ways, and the unrighteous their thoughts. Let them turn to the LORD, and He will have mercy on them, and to our God, for He will freely pardon." (Forsake: abandon) **8.** "For my thoughts are not your thoughts, nor are your ways my ways," declares the LORD. (Declare: says) **9.** "As the heavens are higher than the earth, so are my ways higher than your ways, and my thoughts higher than your thoughts." (Higher: greater) **10.** "Just as the rain and snow fall from the sky and do not return without watering the earth, making it bud and flourish, producing seed for the sower and bread for the eater," (Flourish: grow) **11.** "So is my word that goes out from my mouth: it will not return to me empty, but will achieve the purpose I intended, and fulfill what I sent it to accomplish." (Fulfill: complete) **12.** "You will go out with joy and be led forth in peace; the mountains and hills will break into singing before you, and all the trees of the field will clap their hands." (Break: burst) **13.** "Instead of the thornbush, the juniper will grow, and instead of briers, the myrtle will appear. This will be for the LORD's renown, a sign that will last forever." (Appear: spring up)

Chapter 56

1. The LORD says: "Uphold justice and do what's right, for my salvation is close to, and my righteousness will soon be discovered." (Uphold: hold) **2.** "Blessed is the one who does this, the one who holds fast to it, who maintains the Sabbath holy and refrains from doing evil." (Holds fast: clings) **3.** "Let no foreigner who has joined the LORD say, 'The LORD will certainly exclude me from His people.' And let no eunuch say, 'I am only a dried-up tree.'" (Joined: bound) **4.** "For that is what the LORD says: 'To the eunuchs who keep my Sabbaths, who choose what pleases me, and hold fast to my covenant—'" (Choose: take pleasure in) **5.** "I will give them within my temple and its walls a name and a memorial better than sons and daughters. I will give them an everlasting name that will never fade away.'" (Memorial: renown) **6.** "And to the foreigners who bind themselves to the LORD, to serve Him, who love His name, and become His servants— those who keep the Sabbath holy and hold firmly to my covenant—" (Bind: commit) **7.** "These I will bring to my holy mountain and give them joy in my house of prayer. Their offerings and sacrifices will be accepted on my altar, for my house will be called a house of prayer for all nations." **8.** The Sovereign LORD says: "He who gathers the exiles of Israel: 'I will gather others to them, in addition to those already gathered.'" **9.** "Come, all you wild animals, come and eat! All you beasts of the forest, come and banquet!" (Wild animals: beasts) **10.** "Israel's watchmen are blind; they lack understanding. They are like mute dogs who cannot bark. They lie around dreaming and love to sleep." **11.** "They are dogs with insatiable appetites, never satisfied. They are shepherds without understanding. They follow their own way and look for their own advantage." (Insatiable: infinite) **12.** "Everyone calls out, 'Come, let us get wine! Let us drink our fill of beer! And the next day will be even better than today.'" (Fill: indulge)

Chapter 57

1. The righteous are taken from us, but no one can pay attention. The devout are removed, and no one knows that they are taken away to be spared from evil. 2. Those who live with integrity find peace and rest in dying. (Integrity: uprightness) 3. "But you—come here, you children of a sorceress, offspring of adulterers and prostitutes! 4. Who are you mocking? At whom do you sneer and stick out your tongues? Are you not a brood of rebels, the offspring of liars? (Sneer: scorn) 5. You burn with lust under every spreading tree; you sacrifice your children in the ravines and beneath the crags. (Burn with lust: take pleasure in sinful desires) 6. The idols of some of the smooth stones of the ravines are your portion; you have poured drink offerings and grain offerings to them. Must I be lenient with you in light of this? 7. You made your bed on high hills, offering sacrifices there. 8. Behind your doors and doorposts, you have placed pagan symbols. You have abandoned me, uncovered your bed, climbed into it, and made agreements with those you desire. (Exposed: discovered) 9. You went to Molek with olive oil, extended your perfumes, sent your ambassadors far, and even descended to the world of the dead! (Molek: a Canaanite god) 10. You wearied yourself with all your travels, yet you would not admit, "It is hopeless." You found strength in your actions, so you did not give up. (Weary: fatigued) 11. "Whom have you feared so much that you have not remained faithful to me? You have forgotten me and did not take it to heart. Is it not because I've been silent for so long that you do not fear me?" (Remain faithful: stay true) 12. "I will disclose your righteousness and works, and they will be of no use to you." (Disclose: reveal) 13. "When you call for help, let your idols save you! But the wind will scatter them; they are like an insignificant breath, easily blown away. Whoever takes shelter in me, however, will inherit the land and own my holy mountain." (Safe haven: refuge) 14. It will be said: "Prepare the way! Clear the obstacles from the course of my people." (Prepare: clear) 15. The high and exalted One, who lives forever and whose name is holy, says: "I live in a high and holy place, but I am also with those who are humble and contrite in spirit, to revive their spirits and heal their hearts." (Humble: lowly) 16. "I will not accuse forever, nor will I always be angry, for that would cause them to faint from the weight of my wrath—the very people I created." (Accuse: blame) 17. "I was enraged by their greed and punished them, hiding my face in anger, but they continued in their rebellious ways." (Enraged: angered) 18. "I have seen their ways, but I will heal them. I will guide them and restore comfort to Israel's mourners." (Mourners: those who grieve) 19. "I will create praise on their lips: 'Peace, peace, to those far and near,' says the LORD, 'and I will heal them.'" (Reward: songs of gratitude) 20. But the wicked are like the restless sea, constantly tossing up dirt and mud. (Restless: unsettled) 21. "There is no peace," says my God, "for the wicked."

Chapter 58

1. "Shout aloud, do not hold back! Raise your voice like a trumpet and proclaim to my people their rebellion, to the descendants of Jacob their sins. 2. They are seeking me day by day, as though eager to know my ways. They act as though they are a nation that does right, one that has not forsaken the commands of its God. They ask me for just judgments and seem eager for God to draw near. 3. 'Why have we fasted,' they complain, 'and you did not notice? Why have we humbled ourselves, and you did not acknowledge it?' "But on the day of your fast, you do as you please and exploit your people. (Mistreat: exploit) 4. Your fasting leads to quarrels and disputes; you strike each other with wicked fists. You cannot fast in this way and expect your voice to be heard on high. (Quarrels: arguments) 5. Is this the fast I have chosen? A mere day for people to humble themselves? Is it only for bowing down like a reed, for wearing sackcloth and ashes? Is that really what you call a fast, a day acceptable to the LORD? 6. "Is this not the fast I desire: to loose the chains of injustice, to untie the cords of the yoke, to loose the oppressed and break every burden? (Chains of injustice: bonds of oppression) 7. Is it not to share your food with the hungry, to provide shelter for the poor and homeless, to clothe the naked, and not to turn away from your own flesh and blood? 8. Then your light will shine like the dawn, and your healing will appear quickly. Your righteousness will go before you, and the glory of the LORD will be your rear guard. (Righteousness: right living) 9. Then you will call, and the LORD will answer. You will cry for help, and He will say, "Here I am." If you remove the yoke of oppression, the pointing of fingers, and malicious talk, (Malicious talk: harmful speech) 10. And if you devote yourself to feeding the hungry and meeting the needs of the oppressed, your light will rise in the darkness, and your night will become as bright as the noonday. 11. The LORD will guide you always; He will satisfy your needs in a sun-scorched land and will strengthen your frame. You will be like a well-watered garden, like a spring whose waters never fail. 12. Your people will rebuild the ancient ruins and restore the foundations that have long been desolate. You will be called the Repairer of Broken Walls, the Restorer of Streets with Dwellings. (Rebuild: repair) 13. "If you keep your feet from breaking the Sabbath, from doing as you please on my holy day, if you call the Sabbath a delight and honor the LORD's holy day, and if you refrain from doing your own thing, from speaking idle words, (Refrain: avoid) 14. Then you will find your joy in the LORD. I will make you ride on the heights of the land and feast on the inheritance of your father Jacob." The mouth of the LORD has spoken. (Triumph: victory)

Chapter 59

1. "The LORD's power is not restricted in saving, neither is His hearing too dull to respond. 2. But your sins have created a divide between you and your God; they have hidden His face, so He will not listen. 3. Your hands are covered in blood, your fingers guilty. You speak lies, and your tongue spreads evil. 4. No one seeks justice, nor defends the truth with integrity. They rely on false arguments, spreading deceit and planning evil. 5. They lay viper's eggs and weave spider webs. Everyone who eats their eggs will die, and if one breaks, a venomous snake is born. (Viper: toxic snake) 6. Their webs provide no protection; they cannot cover themselves with what they create. Their deeds are evil, and violence fills their hands. 7. They rush to sin, shedding innocent blood. Their plans are evil, and violence follows their steps. 8. They don't understand peace, and their paths lack justice. They have twisted their roads; those who walk them find no peace. 9. Justice is far from us, and righteousness is out of reach. We look for light, but darkness surrounds us; we long for brightness, but we walk in shadows. 10. Like the blind, we feel our way along the walls, stumbling as though it were night at noon. Among the strong, we seem like the dead. (Twilight: the period of dim light after sundown) 11. We growl like bears and moan like doves, seeking justice but finding none; we long for deliverance, but it remains far away. 12. Our sins are many before You, and our wrongs testify against us. We acknowledge our guilt: 13. Rebellion against the LORD, turning our backs on our God, stirring up rebellion, and speaking lies from our hearts. (Rebellion: insurrection; Oppression: unjust treatment) 14. Justice is disregarded, and righteousness is distant. Truth stumbles in the streets; honesty cannot enter. 15. Truth is nowhere to be found, and everyone who avoids evil is targeted. The LORD looked and was displeased that no justice existed. 16. He saw no one to intervene and was appalled. So His own arm brought salvation, and His righteousness supported Him. (Intervene: step in; Salvation: deliverance) 17. He wore righteousness as armor, and salvation as a helmet. He wrapped Himself in vengeance and zeal, like a cloak. (Zeal: passion) 18. He will repay His enemies for their deeds, giving retribution to those who oppose Him; He will give the islands their due. (Retribution: payback or punishment for wrongdoing) 19. From the west, people will fear

the name of the LORD, and from the east, they will honor His glory. For He will come like a mighty flood, driven by the breath of the LORD. **20.** "The Redeemer will come to Zion, to those in Jacob who turn from their sins," says the LORD. (Zion: Jerusalem or God's holy city; Jacob: another name for Israel) **21.** "That is My covenant with them," says the LORD. "My Spirit will remain on you, and My words will be on your lips, on your children's lips, and on their descendants forever." (Covenant: an agreement or promise; Spirit: God's power or presence)

Chapter 60

1. "Rise up, shine, for your light has come, and the LORD's glory shines upon you. **2.** See, darkness covers the earth, and deep darkness envelops the people, but the LORD rises over you, and His glory appears upon you. **3.** Nations will be drawn to your light, and kings to the radiance of your rising. **4.** Lift up your eyes and look around: All will gather to you; your sons will come from afar, and your daughters will be carried on their arms. **5.** Then you will gaze in awe, your heart will rejoice, and your joy will overflow. The wealth of the seas will be brought to you, and the riches of nations will come. **6.** Camels from Midian and Ephah will cover your land; people from Sheba will come, bringing gold, incense, and proclaiming the praises of the LORD. (Midian: a region in the Arabian Peninsula; Ephah: a region in the Arabian desert; Sheba: an ancient kingdom, probably in southern Arabia) **7.** The flocks of Kedar will be gathered to you, and the rams of Nebaioth will serve you. They will be offered on My altar, and I will glorify My temple. (Kedar: a desert tribe, descendants of Ishmael; Nebaioth: another tribe from Ishmael's descendants) **8.** "Who are these who fly like clouds, like doves to their nests?" **9.** Surely, the islands look to Me; Tarshish's ships will lead the way, bringing your children from afar, with silver and gold, to honor the LORD your God, the Holy One of Israel, who has endowed you with beauty. (Tarshish: an ancient Phoenician city, probably in Spain) **10.** "Foreigners will rebuild your walls, and their kings will serve you. Although I struck you in anger, I will show you compassion in My favor." **11.** Your gates will stay open day and night, so that the wealth of the nations may be brought to you, and their kings will come in triumph. **12.** Any nation or kingdom that refuses to serve you will perish; it will be utterly destroyed. **13.** "The honor of Lebanon will come to you, the juniper, fir, and cypress, to beautify My sanctuary; and I will glorify the place of My feet." (Lebanon: known for its forests of cedar trees, used in building temples) **14.** The children of your oppressors will come bowing before you; all who once despised you will bow at your feet and call you the city of the LORD, Zion of the Holy One of Israel. **15.** "Although you were forsaken and despised, with no one passing through, I will make you the eternal joy and delight of every generation." **16.** You will drink the milk of nations and be nourished at royal breasts. Then you will know that I, the LORD, am your Savior, your Redeemer, the Mighty One of Jacob. **17.** Instead of bronze, I will bring you gold; instead of iron, I will bring you silver. Instead of wood, I will bring you bronze, and instead of stones, iron. I will make peace your ruler, and well-being your governor. **18.** Never again will violence be heard in your land, nor destruction within your borders; you will call your walls Salvation and your gates Praise. **19.** The sun will no longer be your light by day, nor will the moon give you its light. The LORD will be your everlasting light, and your God will be your glory. **20.** Your sun will never set again, and your moon will never wane. The LORD will be your everlasting light, and the days of your sorrow will cease. **21.** All your people will be righteous, and they will inherit the land forever. They are the offspring I have planted, the work of My hands, to display My splendor. **22.** The least of you will become a thousand, and the smallest a mighty nation. I, the LORD, will do this in My time, and I will do it swiftly."

Chapter 61

1. The God's spirit is on me because He has anointed me to carry good news to the poor people. He sent me to heal the brokenhearted, declare freedom for captives, and release prisoners from darkness. **2.** I am to proclaim the year of the LORD's favor and the day of vengeance of our God, to comfort all who mourn. (Vengeance: divine justice) **3.** To provide for those who grieve in Zion, to give them a crown of beauty instead of ashes, the oil of joy instead of mourning, and a garment of praise instead of despair. They will be called oaks of righteousness, a planting of the LORD, to display His splendor. **4.** They will rebuild ancient ruins, restore devastated places, and renew cities ruined for generations.(Ruins: destroyed buildings) **5.** Foreigners will shepherd your flocks, and strangers will work your fields and vineyards. **6.** You will be called priests of the LORD, ministers of our God. You will enjoy the wealth of nations, and in their riches, you will boast. (Priests: spiritual leaders) **7.** Instead of shame, you will receive a double portion; instead of disgrace, you will rejoice in your inheritance. You will inherit double in your land, and everlasting joy will be yours. **8.** "For I, the LORD, love justice; I hate robbery and wrongdoing. In My faithfulness, I will reward My people and make an everlasting covenant with them." (Covenant: divine promise) **9.** Their descendants will be known among the nations, and their offspring will be recognized by the peoples. All who see them will acknowledge they are a people the LORD has blessed. **10.** I greatly rejoice in the LORD; my soul exults in my God. He has clothed me with garments of salvation and wrapped me in a robe of righteousness, like a bridegroom adorned with a crown, and a bride with her jewels. (Garments: symbolic of salvation) **11.** Just as soil makes plants grow and gardens cause seeds to sprout, so the LORD will make righteousness and praise spring up before all nations. (Righteousness: right living; Praise: worship)

Chapter 62

1. For the sake of Zion, I will not stay silent, and for Jerusalem's sake, I will not rest, until her righteousness shines like the dawn and her salvation burns brightly like a torch. **2.** The nations will witness your righteousness, and all kings will see your glory; a new name, given by the LORD, will be yours. **3.** You will be a crown of splendor in the LORD's hand, a royal diadem in the palm of your God. (Diadem: royal crown) **4.** They will no longer call you abandoned, nor will your land be called Desolate. You will be named Hephzibah, and your land Beulah; for the LORD will delight in you, and your land will be married. (Hephzibah: "My delight is in her") **5.** As a young man rejoices over his bride, so your Builder will rejoice over you. Like a bridegroom with his bride, your God will find joy in you. **6.** I have stationed watchmen on your walls, Jerusalem; they will never be quiet, day or night. You who call on the LORD, give yourselves no rest, (Watchmen: spiritual guardians) **7.** and give Him no rest until He establishes Jerusalem and makes her the praise of the earth. **8.** The LORD swears by His right hand and mighty arm: "Never again will I give your grain to your enemies, nor will foreigners drink the new wine you worked for; (Right hand: strength; mighty arm: power) **9.** but those who harvest it will eat it and praise the LORD, and those who gather the grapes will drink it in My sanctuary's courts." **10.** Go through the gates! Prepare the way for the people. Build up the highway! Remove the obstacles. Raise a banner for the nations. **11.** The LORD has made a proclamation to the ends of the earth: "Say to Daughter Zion, 'Look, your Savior comes! His reward is with Him, and His recompense follows Him.'" **12.** They will be called the Holy people, the Redeemed of the LORD; you will be called sought after, the city no longer deserted.

Chapter 63

1. Who is this coming from Edom, from Bozrah, with red-stained garments? Who is this, clothed in glory, advancing in the power of His might? "It is I, proclaiming victory, mighty to save." **2.** Why are your garments crimson, like a man treading the winepress? **3.** "I alone have trodden the winepress; no one from the nations was with me. I trampled them in My anger and beaten them in My wrath; their blood stained My garments, and I defiled all My clothing." (Wrath:

excessive anger) **4.** The day of vengeance was for Me, and the year of My redemption had come. (Vengeance: divine justice) **5.** I looked around, but there was no one to help. I was astonished that no one offered support. So, My own arm brought salvation, and My own wrath upheld Me. **6.** I trampled the nations in My anger; in My wrath, I made them drunk and spilled their blood on the ground. (Wrath: anger; Drunk: crushed) **7.** I will recount the LORD's lovingkindnesses, the deeds for which He deserves praise, all He has done for us—the many good things He did for Israel, according to His great compassion and kindness. (Lovingkindnesses: acts of grace) **8.** He said, "Surely they are My people, children who are true to Me"; and so He became their Savior. (True to Me: faithful) **9.** In all their affliction, He was afflicted. The angel of His presence saved them. In His love and mercy, He redeemed them; He lifted them up and carried them all the days of old. **10.** Yet they rebelled and grieved His Holy Spirit. So, He turned against them and became their enemy, fighting against them Himself. **11.** Then His people remembered the days of old, the time of Moses and his followers— "Where is the one who brought them through the sea, with the shepherd of His flock? Where is the one who placed His Holy Spirit among them, **12.** who sent His glorious arm of power to be at Moses' side, who divided the waters before them to make for Himself an everlasting name, (Glorious arm: God's power in action) **13.** who led them through the depths, like a horse in the wilderness, they did not stumble; (Depths: deep waters; Stumble: falter) **14.** Like cattle that go down to the plains, the Spirit of the LORD gave them rest. This is how You led Your people, to make for Yourself a glorious name. **15.** Look down from heaven and see, from Your lofty and holy throne. Where is Your zeal and Your strength? Your tenderness and compassion seem to be withheld from us. (Zeal: passionate devotion; Compassion: sympathy) **16.** Yet You are our Father. Though Abraham does not know us and Israel does not acknowledge us, You, LORD, are our Father. You have been our Redeemer from ancient times. (Redeemer: one who saves) **17.** Why, LORD, do You let us stray from Your ways and harden our hearts so we do not fear You? Return, for the sake of Your servants, the tribes that are Your inheritance. (Hardened hearts: become stubborn) **18.** For a little while, Your people possessed Your holy place, but now our enemies have trampled down Your sanctuary. (Holy place: sacred land; Sanctuary: holy temple) **19.** We were Yours from the beginning, but You have not ruled over them; they are not called by Your name.

Chapter 64
1. Oh, that You would tear open the heavens and come down, that the mountains might quake at Your presence! (Tear open: rend, break open) **2.** As fire sets dry wood ablaze and makes water boil, come down to make Your name known to Your enemies and let the nations tremble before You! (Tremble: shake with fear) **3.** For when You did amazing things we did not expect, You came down, and the mountains quaked at Your presence. **4.** From ancient times no one has heard, no ear has perceived, nor eye seen any god besides You, who works on behalf of those who wait for You. **5.** You help those who rejoice in doing right, who remember Your ways. But when we sinned against You, You became angry. How then can we be saved? (Rejoice: delight in) **6.** We have all become like someone unclean, and all our righteous deeds are like filthy rags; we wither like leaves, and our sins blow us away like the wind. (; Filthy rags: worthless deeds) **7.** No one calls on Your name or seeks to hold on to You; You have hidden Your face from us and given us over to our sins. **8.** Yet You, LORD, are our Father; we are the clay, and You are the potter; we are all the work of Your hands. (Clay: moldable, like people; Pottery: shaping us as He wills) **9.** Do not be angry beyond measure, LORD; do not remember our sins forever. Look at us, we pray, for we are all Your people. (Beyond measure: excessively; Remember: hold against us) **10.** Your holy cities have become a wilderness; even Zion is a desolation, and Jerusalem a ruin. (Zion: Jerusalem; Desolation: destruction) **11.** Our sacred and glorious temple, where our ancestors praised You, has been burned with fire, and all that we treasured lies in ruins. (Sacred temple: holy place of worship) **12.** After all this, LORD, will You restrain Yourself? Will You remain silent and punish us without measure.

Chapter 65
1. "I revealed Myself to a people who never sought Me, and I was found by those who never called on My name. To a nation that did not ask, I said, 'Here I am, here I am.'" **2.** I have stretched out My hands all day long to a rebellious people who walk in ways that aren't good, following their own plans. (Rebellious: stubborn) **3.** A people who provoke Me to My face, offering sacrifices in gardens and burning incense on brick altars. (Provoke: insult; Incense: services to idols) **4.** They sit among graves and practice secret rituals; they eat the flesh of pigs and prepare broth from unclean meat. (Graves: tombs of the dead; Unclean: forbidden food in Jewish law) **5.** They say, 'Stay away from me, I am too holy for you!' These people are like smoke in My nostrils, a fire that burns forever. (Smoke in nostrils: repugnant to God) **6.** "Look, it is written before Me: I will not remain silent but will repay them fully; I will bring their deeds back to them." (Repay: vengeance) **7.** "Both their sins and the sins of their ancestors," says the LORD. "Because they offered sacrifices on the mountains and provoked Me on the hills, I will repay them fully for their actions." **8.** The LORD says, "Just as there is still juice in a bunch of grapes, and people say, 'Do not destroy it, for there is a blessing in it,' so I will not destroy all of My servants." (Blessing: grace; Servants: faithful people) **9.** I will bring descendants from Jacob, and from Judah, people who will inherit My mountains. My chosen people will live there, and their descendants will possess the land. **10.** Sharon will become a pasture for flocks, and the Valley of Achor a resting place for herds, for those who seek Me. (Sharon: fertile plain; Achor: valley, traditionally associated with rebellion) **11.** "But those of you who forsake the LORD and forget My holy mountain, who set tables for Fortune and pour mixed wine for Destiny, (Forsake: abandon; Destiny: fate) **12.** I will assign you to the sword, and all of you will fall by the sword; you forsook My name, you did evil in My sight, and chose what I hate." **13.** Therefore, this is what the Sovereign LORD says: "My servants will eat, but you will go hungry; My servants will drink, but you will thirst. My servants will rejoice, but you will be ashamed." (Sovereign: all-powerful; Rejoice: be happy) **14.** My servants will sing with joy, but you will cry out in distress and mourn with broken hearts. (Distress: suffering; Broken hearts: depression) **15.** You will leave your name to My chosen ones, and they will use it in curses. The Sovereign LORD will bring about your end, but He will give a new name to His servants. (Curses: negative speech; New name: blessing) **16.** Whoever blesses in the land will do so by the true God, and whoever makes an oath will swear by the true God. The former troubles will be forgotten and hidden from My eyes." (Blesses: invokes favor; Oath: pledge) **17.** "Look, I will create a new heaven and a new earth. The former things will not be remembered, nor will they come to mind." (New heaven: new creation; Former things: old suffering) **18.** Be glad and rejoice forever in what I am creating. I will make Jerusalem a joy, and its people a delight. (Delight: pride) **19.** I will take delight in Jerusalem, and My people. There will be no more weeping or crying heard in it. (Weeping: mourning) **20.** Never again will there be an infant who dies early or an old man who does not live out his years. The one who dies at a hundred will be considered young, and the one who does not reach a hundred will be cursed. (Cursed: doomed) **21.** They will build houses and live in them, plant vineyards and eat their fruit. (Vineyards: fields) **22.** They will not build for others to live in, or plant for others to eat. Like trees, they will live long and enjoy the fruit of their labor. (Trees: durability) **23.** They will not labor in vain, and their children will not suffer misfortune. They will be blessed by the LORD, along with their descendants. (Blessed: favored; Misfortune: disaster) **24.** Before they call, I will answer; while they are still speaking, I will hear. (Answer: respond to prayers) **25.** The wolf and

the lamb will graze together, the lion will eat straw like the ox, and dust will be the serpent's food. They will not harm or destroy anyone on My holy mountain," says the LORD.

Chapter 66

1. The LORD says, "Heaven is My throne, and the earth is My footstool. What kind of house will you build for Me? Where will My resting place be?" **2.** "Did not My hand make all things, and thus they came into being?" says the LORD. "I look favorably on those who are humble, contrite in spirit, and who tremble at My word." (Contrite: remorseful) **3.** "But those who sacrifice a bull are as guilty as murderers, and those who offer a lamb are like those who break a dog's neck. Those who bring grain offerings are like offering pig's blood, and those who burn incense are like worshiping idols. They follow their own ways and pride in abominations." (Abominations: detestable acts) **4.** "So I will choose to punish them and bring upon them what they dread. When I called, no one answered; when I spoke, no one listened. They did evil in My sight and chose what displeases Me." **5.** Hear the word of the LORD, you who fear His word: "Your own people who hate and exclude you because of My name say, 'Let the LORD be glorified, that we may witness your joy!' But they will be put to shame." (Exclude: reject) **6.** Hear the uproar from the city and the noise from the temple! It is the sound of the LORD repaying His enemies for all they deserve. (Uproar: chaos) **7.** "Before she goes into labor, she gives birth. Before the pain comes, she delivers a son." **8.** "Who has ever heard of such things? Who has seen such things? Can a country be born in a day? Can a nation be born in an instant? Yet, no sooner does Zion go into labor than she gives birth to her children." **9.** "Shall I bring to the point of birth and not cause delivery?" says the LORD. "Shall I, who cause labor, shut the womb?" says your God. **10.** "Rejoice with Jerusalem and be glad for her, all you who love her. Rejoice greatly with her, all who mourn over her." **11.** "You will be nourished and satisfied at her comforting breasts. You will drink deeply and delight in her abundance." (Nourished: cared for) **12.** "I will extend peace to her like a river, and the wealth of nations like a flooding stream. You will be nourished and carried on her arm, dandled on her knees." (Dandled: cradled) **13.** "As a mother comforts her child, so will I comfort you; and you will be comforted over Jerusalem." **14.** "When you see this, your heart will rejoice and you will flourish like grass. The hand of the LORD will be made known to His servants, but His fury will be shown to His enemies." (Flourish: thrive) **15.** "See, the LORD is coming with fire, and His chariots are like a whirlwind. He will bring His anger with fury and His rebuke with flames of fire." (Whirlwind: destructive force) **16.** "With fire and with His sword, the LORD will execute judgment on all people. Many will be slain by the LORD." **17.** "Those who consecrate and purify themselves to enter gardens and follow one who eats the flesh of pigs, rats, and other unclean things— they will meet their end together with those they follow," says the LORD. (Consecrate: dedicate) **18.** "Because of what they have planned and done, I am about to gather the people of all nations and languages, and they will see My glory." **19.** "I will set a sign among them, and I will send some of those who survive to the nations— to Tarshish, to the Libyans and Lydians, to Tubal and Greece, and to the distant islands who have not heard of My fame or seen My glory. They will declare My glory among the nations." (Tarshish: far-off lands) **20.** "They will bring all your people, from all nations, to My holy mountain in Jerusalem as an offering to the LORD— on horses, in chariots, on mules and camels. They will bring them, just as the Israelites bring their grain offerings, to the temple of the LORD in clean vessels." **21.** "And I will select some of them to be priests and Levites," says the LORD. (Priests: religious leaders) **22.** "As the new heavens and the new earth that I create will endure before Me," says the LORD, "so will your name and descendants endure." (Endure: last forever) **23.** "From one New Moon to another and from one Sabbath to another, all mankind will come and bow down before Me," says the LORD. **24.** "And they will go out and look on the dead bodies of those who rebelled against Me; the worms that eat them will not die, the fire that burns them will not be quenched, and they will be loathsome to all mankind." (Rebelled: opposed; Unquenched: eternal judgment)

24 – Jeremiah

Chapter 1

1. The words of Jeremiah, son of Hilkiah, a priest from Anathoth in the land of Benjamin. (Anathoth: A town in the region of Benjamin, ancient Israel) **2.** The LORD's message came to him during the reign of King Josiah of Judah, in the 13th year of his rule. (Reign: The period during which a king rules) **3.** It continued through the reign of King Jehoiakim, Josiah's son, until the 11th year of King Zedekiah, ending with the exile of Jerusalem. (Exile: Forced removal from one's country or home) **4.** Then the LORD spoke to me, saying, **5.** "Before I formed you in the womb, I knew you; before you were born, I set you apart and chose you as a prophet to the nations." (Set apart: To make holy or designate for a special purpose) **6.** I responded, "Ah, Sovereign LORD! I cannot speak because I am too young." (Sovereign: Supreme ruler or authority) **7.** But the LORD answered, "Do not say, 'I am too young.' You will go wherever I send you, and speak whatever I command." (Command: An order or instruction) **8.** "Do not be afraid of them, for I am with you to protect you," says the LORD. (Protect: To keep safe from harm) **9.** The LORD then touched my mouth and said, "I have placed My words in your mouth." (Placed: Put or set in a specific location) **10.** "Today, I have appointed you to oversee nations and kingdoms, to uproot, destroy, and tear down, as well as to build and plant." (Uproot: To remove completely by pulling up) **11.** The LORD asked, "Jeremiah, what do you see?" I replied, "I see a branch of an almond tree." (Almond tree: A tree symbolizing watchfulness in the Bible) **12.** The LORD said, "You have seen correctly, for I am ready to fulfill My word." (Ready: Prepared or willing to act) **13.** Then the LORD asked me again, "What do you see?" I said, "I see a boiling pot, tilted toward the north." (Boiling: Heating to the point of bubbling) **14.** The LORD replied, "Disaster will come from the north and will strike all the people of the land." **15.** "I will summon the kingdoms of the north," declares the LORD, "and they will come and set their thrones at the gates of Jerusalem, surrounding its walls and the cities of Judah." (Summon: To call or gather) **16.** "I will judge them for their wickedness: they have forsaken Me, burned incense to other gods, and worshiped idols they made." (Forsaken: Abandoned or turned away from) **17.** "Prepare yourself; stand up and speak everything I command you. Do not be afraid of them, or I will shame you in front of them." (Shame: To dishonor or disgrace) **18.** "Today I have made you like a fortified city, an iron pillar, and bronze walls against the kings of Judah, their leaders, priests, and people." (Fortified: Made strong or secure) **19.** "They will fight against you but will not defeat you, for I am with you to deliver you," says the LORD. (Defeat: To overcome or conquer)

Chapter 2

1. The word of the Lord came to me: (Came: arrived) **2.** "Go and proclaim in Jerusalem: 'I remember your devotion in youth, when you followed me through the wilderness, in a land barren and unplanted.'" (Devotion: loyalty; Unplanted: uncultivated) **3.** "Israel was consecrated to the Lord, the firstfruits of His harvest; those who devour her will be punished," says the Lord. (Consecrated: sacred; Devours: consumes) **4.** "Hear the word of the Lord, O house of Jacob, all the families of Israel." (Families: descendants) **5.** "What wrong did your ancestors find in me that they turned from me, following idols and becoming worthless?" (Wrong: injustice; Worthless: futile) **6.** "They didn't ask, 'Where is the Lord who brought us out of Egypt and led us through the desert, a land of pits and drought, where no one lived?'" (Drought: dry spell; Pits: danger) **7.** "I brought you into a fertile land, but when you entered, you defiled it and turned my inheritance into something detestable." (Fertile: rich; Defiled: corrupted) **8.** "The priests didn't ask, 'Where is the Lord?' The leaders rebelled, and the prophets followed Baal, pursuing what's useless." (Rebelled: opposed; Useless: unprofitable) **9.** "Therefore, I will plead with you, and your descendants, I will continue to argue." (Plead: argue) **10.** "Go to distant places like Chittim and Kedar and see if you find anything like this." (Distant: far off) **11.** "Has any nation exchanged its gods, though they're no gods? But my people have exchanged their glory for something that has no value." (Exchanged: swapped; Glory: honor) **12.** "Be amazed, O heavens, and shudder at this," says the Lord. (Amazed: astonished) **13.** "My people have committed two evils: they've forsaken me, the fountain of living water, and dug broken cisterns that can hold no water." (Forsaken: abandoned; Broken: cracked) **14.** "Is Israel a servant, born into slavery? Why has she become plundered?" (Plundered: spoiled) **15.** "The lions have roared against her, and her land is desolate. Her cities are burned down and deserted." (Desolate: abandoned; Roared: attacked) **16.** "The children of Noph and Tahapanes have broken your crown." (Broken: shattered) **17.** "Have you not brought this upon yourself by forsaking the Lord your God, who led you on the right path?" (Forsaking: abandoning) **18.** "Why go to Egypt to drink from the Nile, or to Assyria for the Euphrates?" (Euphrates: river) **19.** "Your own wickedness will correct you, and your backsliding will rebuke you. See how bitter and evil it is to forsake me," says the Lord. (Wickedness: evil; Backsliding: relapse) **20.** "I broke your chains long ago, but you said, 'I will not serve.' You gave yourself to idol worship on every hill and under every tree." (Chains: bondage) **21.** "I planted you as a good vine, but you have turned into a wild and corrupt vine." (Wild: degenerate) **22.** "Even if you wash with lye and use soap, your guilt remains before me," says the Lord. (Lye: cleansing agent) **23.** "How can you say, 'I am not defiled; I've not followed Baal'? Look at your ways; you're like a swift camel running freely." (Defiled: polluted; Swift: fast) **24.** "You're like a wild donkey in the desert, sniffing for pleasure. No one can turn her back." (Sniffing: searching) **25.** "You refuse to be controlled, saying there is no hope. You love other gods and pursue them." (Controlled: restrained) **26.** "Like a thief caught in the act, Israel is ashamed—her kings, princes, priests, and prophets." (Caught: trapped) **27.** "They say to wood, 'You are my father,' and to stone, 'You gave birth to me.' They turn their backs to me, but in trouble, they cry out, 'Arise and save us!'" (Arise: stand up) **28.** "Where are the gods you made? Let them rise and save you in your time of trouble. For as many cities as you have, you have as many gods, O Judah." (Rise: stand up) **29.** "Why argue with me? You have all rebelled against me," says the Lord. (Rebelled: defied) **30.** "I struck your children in vain; they did not learn. Your own sword has destroyed your prophets, like a lion devours its prey." (Struck: smitten; Devours: consumes) **31.** "O generation, consider the word of the Lord. Have I been a wilderness to Israel, a land of darkness? Why do my people say, 'We will not return to you anymore?'" (Masters: lords) **32.** "Can a young woman forget her jewelry? Yet my people have forgotten me for countless days." (Countless: many) **33.** "Why go to such lengths to find love? You've even taught the wicked your ways." (Great lengths: much effort) **34.** "In your skirts is found the blood of the innocent. I did not find it by secret search, but openly on all your actions." (Skirts: garments; Innocent: poor souls) **35.** "And yet you say, 'I am innocent. His anger will turn away from me.' I will bring my case against you, because you say, 'I have not sinned.'" (Claim: assert) **36.** "Why change your ways so much? You will be ashamed of Egypt as you were of Assyria." (Ashamed: embarrassed) **37.** "You will leave Egypt, hands on your head, for the Lord has rejected your trust, and you will not succeed in them." (Rejected: dismissed; Trust: reliance)

Chapter 3

1. They ask: If a man divorces his wife and she marries another, can she ever return to him? Wouldn't that make the land unclean? Yet you've played the harlot with many lovers, but still, I call you back to Me, says the LORD. (Unclean: ceremonially impure; Harlot: unfaithful) **2.** Look around and see how far you've gone—how many places you've defiled with your adulteries. Like a wandering traveler in the desert, you waited for lovers everywhere, polluting the land with your sin. (Defiled: morally or spiritually tainted) **3.** Because of this, the rains have been withheld, and the skies remain dry. You've worn the shame of a prostitute, yet refused to be embarrassed. (Withheld: held back) **4.** Will you not, even now, call to Me, saying, "You are my Father, the guide of my youth?" (Guide: leader) **5.** Will I remain angry forever, or will My anger end? Look at how you've spoken and done evil, without hesitation. (Hesitation: pause or delay) **6.** The LORD spoke to me in the days of King Josiah: "Have you seen what Israel, the rebellious nation, has done? She has gone to every high hill and every shady tree, and there, she's been unfaithful to Me." (Rebellious: resisting authority) **7.** I called Israel to return, but she did not. Her treacherous sister Judah watched and did the same. (Treacherous: deceitful) **8.** Though I gave Israel a certificate of divorce for her adultery, Judah did not fear but followed in the same footsteps. (Certificate of divorce: legal separation) **9.** Her sin was so light and reckless that it defiled the land, and she committed idolatry, worshipping stones and wood. (Reckless: careless) **10.** Still, Judah has not turned back to Me with all her heart, but only pretends, says the LORD. (Pretends: feigns sincerity) **11.** The LORD said, "Israel, who has fallen away, has been more honest than Judah, who is deceitful." (Fallen away: turned from faith) **12.** Proclaim to the north: "Return, wayward Israel, says the LORD. I will not stay angry forever because I am merciful." (Wayward: straying from the right path) **13.** Acknowledge your sin, that you have rebelled against the LORD, scattered your ways to false gods, and failed to listen to My voice. (Acknowledge: confess; Rebelled: turned away) **14.** "Return, you disobedient children," says the LORD. "I am married to you, and I will bring you back, one from a city, two from a family, and I will restore you to Zion." (Disobedient: refusing to follow God's commands) **15.** I will give you leaders after My own heart, who will guide you with knowledge and wisdom. (Leaders: shepherds or teachers) **16.** In those days, when you grow in number and prosper, you will no longer talk about the Ark of the Covenant. It will be forgotten, no longer needed. (Prosper: grow in wealth or success) **17.** At that time, Jerusalem will be called the throne of the LORD, and all nations will come to worship there, turning away from their wicked hearts. (Wicked: immoral or sinful) **18.** In those days, the houses of Judah and Israel will unite, and they will come together from the north to the land I promised to your ancestors. (Unite: come together) **19.** I asked, "How can I give you a beautiful land, an inheritance among the nations, and you call Me Father and never turn away from Me?" (Inheritance: birthright or land passed down) **20.** Just as a wife betrays her husband, so have you betrayed Me, O house of Israel, says the LORD. (Betrays: is unfaithful) **21.** I hear the cries of Israel on the high hills, weeping for the path they've perverted and the God they've forgotten. (Perverted: twisted or corrupted) **22.** "Return, you rebellious children, and I will heal your waywardness. We come to You, for You alone are our God." (Waywardness: straying from the right path) **23.** It is useless to hope for salvation from the hills or mountains. Only in the LORD, our God, is the salvation of Israel. (Useless: of no value) **24.** Shame has consumed the work of our ancestors: their livestock, their children, and all they labored for. (Consumed: completely devoured) **25.** We lie in shame, our confusion covering us, because we have sinned against the LORD, from our youth until now, and have not obeyed His voice. (Confusion: mental or emotional disorder)

Chapter 4

1. "Return to Me, O Israel," says the LORD. "Turn away from your idols and sin, and I will not reject you." (idols: false gods or images worshipped instead of the true God) **2.** "Swear by the living LORD in truth, fairness, and righteousness. Then all nations will bless themselves through Him and honor His name." (fairness: justice, equality ; honor: respect, reverence) **3.** "Break up your unplowed ground, and do not plant among thorns." (unplowed: land not prepared for planting ; thorns: sharp, prickly plants) **4.** "Purify your hearts, O people of Judah and Jerusalem, or my anger will consume you like an unquenchable fire because of your sinful actions." (purify: cleanse, ; consume: destroy completely ; unquenchable: impossible to stop) **5.** "Announce it in Judah, sound the trumpet in Jerusalem, and gather the people to the fortified cities." (announce: declare, make known ; fortified: strengthened and protected) **6.** "Raise a signal toward Zion, do not hesitate, for I will bring disaster from the north and great destruction." (signal: sign, indicator) **7.** "The lion from the thicket has come, the enemy is on the move, and your cities will be left desolate, without inhabitants." (thicket: tangled growth of plants ; desolate: empty, abandoned) **8.** "Wrap yourselves in mourning clothes, weep and cry aloud, for the LORD's fierce anger has not turned away from us." (mourning clothes: sackcloth, worn in sorrow) **9.** "On that day, the hearts of the king, rulers, priests, and prophets will be filled with shock and disbelief." (disbelief: denial or rejection of divine truth) **10.** "I said, 'Lord, you have greatly misled this people and Jerusalem by promising peace, when war is at hand.'" (misled: deceived, led astray) **11.** "A scorching wind will blow from the wilderness, not to refresh, but to destroy." (scorching: extremely hot ; refresh: cool or renew) **12.** "I will judge them, for the winds from the wilderness will soon arrive." (judge: bring decision or punishment) **13.** "He will come like a storm, his chariots will be like a whirlwind, his horses faster than eagles. Woe to us, for we are doomed!" (whirlwind: a strong, rotating wind ; woe: deep sorrow or distress) **14.** "Jerusalem, cleanse your heart from wickedness so that you may be saved. How long will your evil thoughts remain within you?" (cleanse: purify, remove impurity ; wickedness: sinful actions) **15.** "A voice from Dan declares distress, and from Mount Ephraim comes the sound of suffering." (distress: great pain, sorrow) **16.** "Tell the nations and announce it against Jerusalem: Watchmen from a distant land are raising their voices against Judah's cities." (watchmen: guards or observers watching for danger) **17.** "Like farmers surrounding their fields, the enemy will encircle her because she has rebelled against Me," says the LORD. (rebelled: resisted authority, disobeyed) **18.** "Your actions have brought this disaster upon you; it is bitter, and it reaches to your very heart." (bitter: painful, difficult) (disaster: great damage or destruction) **19.** "My heart aches deeply, I cannot be silent. I hear the trumpet's call and the sound of war approaching." (aches: feels pain or sorrow) **20.** "Disaster upon disaster is declared, the land is ruined, my tents and dwellings are destroyed in a moment." (disaster: great misfortune, calamity) **21.** "How long must I watch the battle standard and hear the trumpet sound?" (battle standard: flag or symbol of war) **22.** "My people are foolish; they don't know Me. They are stubborn and have no understanding. They are clever at doing evil but lack the knowledge to do good." (stubborn:determined, unwilling to change) **23.** "I looked at the earth, and it was empty and void; the skies had no light." (void: completely empty, lacking) **24.** "The mountains trembled, and all the hills shook." (trembled: shook, quivered) **25.** "I looked again, and there was no one, and all the birds had flown away." (flown away: escaped, fled) **26.** "The fertile land became a desert, and all the cities were destroyed because of the LORD's fierce anger." (fertile: rich in nutrients, capable of supporting life ; desert: barren, dry land) **27.** "The LORD has said, 'The whole land will be desolate, but I will not destroy it entirely.'" (desolate: empty, abandoned) **28.** "The earth will mourn, and the heavens will be dark because I have decreed it, and I will not change My mind." (decreed: ordered, decided) **29.** "The entire city will flee at the sound of the horsemen and archers; they will hide in thickets and climb the rocks. Every city will be deserted and uninhabited." (archers: those who shoot arrows ; thickets: dense bushes or trees) **30.** "When you are devastated, what will you do? Even if you dress in fine clothes and adorn yourself with gold, it will be in vain. Your lovers will despise you and seek your life." (devastated: severely damaged, destroyed ; adorn: decorate, embellish) **31.** "I hear the voice of a woman in labor, in pain like the daughter of Zion, crying out in anguish, 'Woe is me! My soul is exhausted by the violence.'" (anguish: extreme pain or suffering ; exhausted: very tired, worn out)

Chapter 5

1. Go through the streets of Jerusalem and look closely—if you can find even one man who acts justly and seeks the truth, I will forgive the city. (Justly: in a fair and righteous manner) **2.** Though they claim, "The LORD lives," they speak falsely. (Falsely: untruthfully) **3.** O LORD, aren't your eyes focused on the truth? You struck them, but they did not repent; you consumed them, but they refused to be corrected. Their hearts are hard as stone, and they won't return to you. (Repent: feel regret or remorse) **4.** I thought, surely these people are poor and foolish, for they do not know the ways of the LORD or understand His justice. (Justice: fair treatment or judgment) **5.** I will speak to the great leaders, who should know the way of the LORD, but they too have broken the laws and freed themselves from His authority. (Authority: control or power to enforce rules) **6.** So, a lion from the forest will destroy them, a wolf will plunder them, and a leopard will watch over their cities—everyone who goes outside will be torn apart. Their sin and rebellion are countless. (Plunder: to steal goods ; Rebellion: resistance or defiance of authority) **7.** How can I forgive this? Your children have turned away from me and worship false gods. After I fed them abundantly, they committed adultery and gathered in the brothels. (Adultery: unfaithfulness in marriage) **8.** They were like well-fed horses in the morning, each one lusting after his neighbor's wife. (Lusting: having strong desire, especially sexual desire) **9.** Shall I not punish these deeds? says the LORD. Shall I not avenge such a nation? (Avenge: to seek revenge or justice) **10.** Go up to her walls and destroy, but don't completely wipe her out—remove her defenses, for they do not belong to the LORD. (Defenses: protection or security) **11.** Both Israel and Judah have betrayed me, says the LORD. (Betrayed: treated someone unfairly) **12.** They have lied about the LORD, saying, "He will not punish us; no harm will come to us." (Lied: told falsehoods) **13.** The prophets will be as empty as wind, for their words hold no truth. This will happen to them. (Empty: lacking substance or truth) **14.** Therefore, says the LORD, because you speak these lies, I will make my words in your mouth like fire, and this people will be the wood—it will consume them. (Consume: to destroy completely) **15.** Look, I will bring a nation from afar, a mighty and ancient people whose language you do not understand. (Mighty: powerful, strong) **16.** Their warriors are like a grave full of death, and they are all mighty men. (Grave: a place of burial, symbolizing death) **17.** They will devour your crops, your bread, your flocks and herds, and they will destroy your fortified cities with the sword. (Devour: to eat up completely) **18.** But in those days, says the LORD, I will not destroy you completely. (Completely: entirely, fully) **19.** When you ask, "Why is the LORD doing this to us?" the answer will be, "As you have forsaken Me and served foreign gods, now you will serve strangers in a foreign land." (Forsaken: abandoned) **20.** Declare this to the people of Jacob and Judah. (Declare: to make known publicly) **21.** Listen, O foolish people without understanding! You have eyes but do not see, ears but do not hear. (Foolish: lacking wisdom or sense) **22.** Do you not fear Me, says the LORD? Do you not tremble before My presence? I who set the sand as a boundary for the sea, a decree that it cannot cross. (Tremble: to shake or be afraid) **23.** But this people has a rebellious and stubborn heart; they have turned away from Me. (Rebellious: defying authority) **24.** They do not even think, "Let us fear the LORD who gives us rain and ensures our harvest." (Ensure: to make sure of) **25.** Your sins have turned away these blessings, and your wrongdoings have withheld good things from you. (Withheld: kept back or refused) **26.** Among my people are wicked men who set traps to catch others. (Wicked: morally wrong or evil) **27.** Their homes are full of deceit, like a cage full of birds, and they are becoming rich and powerful. (Deceit: dishonesty or trickery) **28.** They are growing fat and prosperous, yet they ignore justice for the needy and the fatherless. (Prosperous: successful or flourishing) **29.** Shall I not punish these deeds, says the LORD? Shall I not avenge such a nation? (Avenge: to seek justice or revenge) **30.** A dreadful and horrible thing has been committed in this land. (Dreadful: causing fear or terror) **31.** The prophets lie, the priests rule unjustly, and my people love it this way. What will you do in the end? (Unjustly: not in a fair or righteous way)

Chapter 6

1. Children of Benjamin, flee from Jerusalem, sound the trumpet in Tekoa, and set a fire signal in Beth-haccerem, for great destruction comes from the north. (Destruction: Ruin) **2.** I have compared Zion's daughter to a beautiful, fragile woman. (Zion: Jerusalem) **3.** The shepherds with their flocks will surround her, setting camp and feeding in their place. (Shepherds: Leaders; Flocks: People) **4.** Prepare for war; let's attack at noon! Woe to us, for the day is fading and evening shadows grow long. (Woe: Sorrow; Shadows: Dusk) **5.** Let's go by night and destroy her palaces. **6.** The LORD says, cut down trees and build ramps against Jerusalem, for this city is full of oppression. (Ramps: Mounds; Oppression: Injustice) **7.** Like a fountain pouring out water, she pours out wickedness; violence and destruction are heard within her, and I see continual grief and wounds. (Wickedness: Sin; Grief: Sorrow) **8.** Jerusalem, take warning, lest I abandon you and make you desolate, a land without inhabitants. (Desolate: Empty) **9.** The LORD says, they will gather the last few of Israel like grapes, turning back to gather the harvest. (Glean: Collect; Grapegatherer: Picker) **10.** Who will listen? Their ears are closed and they will not hear; God's word is a reproach to them, and they have no delight in it. (Reproach: contempt or disdain; Delight: Joy) **11.** I am filled with the LORD's fury, and I can no longer hold it back. I will pour it out on the children and young men. Even husband and wife, the elderly and young, will be taken. (Fury: Anger) **12.** Their homes, fields, and wives will be taken, for I will stretch out my hand against the land's inhabitants, says the LORD. (Inhabitants: People) **13.** From the least to the greatest, all are greedy; even the prophets and priests act deceitfully. (Deceitfully: Dishonestly) **14.** They heal the hurt of my people lightly, saying, "Peace, peace," when there is no peace. (Heal: Soothe; Lightly: Casually) **15.** Were they ashamed of their abominations? No, they were not ashamed at all, so they will fall with the others. (Abominations: Sins) **16.** The LORD says, stand in the ways, look for the old paths, and walk in the good way, and you will find rest for your souls. But they refused. (Old paths: Traditions; Rest: Peace) **17.** I set watchmen over you to warn you, but you would not listen. (Watchmen: Guardians) **18.** Hear, nations, and know what is happening among them. **19.** Hear, O earth: I will bring disaster upon this people, the result of their thoughts, because they have ignored my words and law. (Disaster: Calamity; Ignored: Neglected) **20.** What use are your incense from Sheba and sweet cane from a distant land? Your offerings are not acceptable to me. (Incense: Perfume; Sweet cane: Fragrance) **21.** The LORD says, I will place stumbling blocks before this people, and both fathers and sons will fall. (Stumbling blocks: Obstacles) **22.** A great nation from the north will rise up, and they will come against you. **23.** They will be armed with bow and spear, cruel with no mercy, their voice like the roaring sea, riding on horses, ready for war against you, O daughter of Zion. (Cruel: Harsh; Roaring: Loud; Array: Formation) **24.** We've heard of them, our hands grow weak, and pain grips us, like a woman in labor. (Grips: Seizes; Labor: Childbirth) **25.** Don't go into the field or walk along the road, for the enemy's sword and fear are everywhere. (Sword: Weapon; Fear: Dread) **26.** Daughter of my people, dress in sackcloth and mourn like for an only son, for the destroyer will suddenly come upon us. (Sackcloth: Cloth; Mourn: Grieve) **27.** I have made you a fortress among my people, so you may test their ways. (Fortress: Stronghold; Test: Examine) **28.** They are rebellious, full of slander, and corrupt like iron and brass. (Rebellious: Disobedient; Slander: Lies; Corrupt: Wicked) **29.** The bellows are burned, and the lead melts in vain; the wicked are not removed. (Bellows: Tools; Lead: Metal) **30.** Men will call them worthless silver because the LORD has rejected them. (Worthless: Useless; Rejected: Cast aside)

Chapter 7

1. The word of the LORD came to Jeremiah, saying: **2.** "Stand at the entrance of the LORD's house and proclaim this message: Hear the word of the LORD, all you people of Judah, who enter through these gates to worship Him." **3.** The LORD Almighty, the God of Israel, says, "Change your ways and actions, and I will allow you to remain in this place." (Change: to transform; Remain: to stay) **4.** "Do not place your trust in empty, deceptive words, saying, 'The temple of the LORD, the temple of the LORD,' as if it alone will protect you." (Empty: vain; Deceptive: misleading) **5.** "If you truly reform your ways and actions, and deal fairly with each other, **6.** If you do not oppress the foreigner, the orphan, or the widow, and do not shed innocent blood, nor follow after other gods to your own harm, **7.** Then I will allow you to live in this land, the land I gave to your ancestors, forever." (Reform: to improve; Oppress: to wrongfully treat) **8.** "Look, you place your trust in lies that will not benefit you." **9.** "Will you steal, murder, commit adultery, lie, offer incense to Baal, and follow gods you do not even know? **10.** And then, you come and stand in this house, called by My name, and say, 'We are saved to commit all these abominations!'" (Abominations: detestable acts; Saved: delivered) **11.** "Has this house, which is called by My name, become a den of thieves in your sight? I have seen it too, says the LORD." (Den: a hideout; Thieves: robbers) **12.** "Go to My place at Shiloh, where I first established My name, and see what I did there because of the wickedness of My people Israel." (Established: set up; Wickedness: evil acts) **13.** "Now, because you have done all these things, I spoke to you again and again, but you would not listen; I called you, but you refused to answer." **14.** "Therefore, I will treat this house, called by My name, and this place you trust in, just as I treated Shiloh." (Therefore: for this reason; Trust: reliance) **15.** "I will drive you out of My sight, as I have driven out all your relatives, even the entire nation of Ephraim." (Drive out: expel; Sight: presence) **16.** "Do not pray for these people, nor raise cries or prayers for them, nor intercede with Me, for I will not listen to you." (Intercede: to plead on behalf of others; Cries: calls for help) **17.** "Do you not see what they are doing in the towns of Judah and the streets of Jerusalem?" **18.** "The children gather wood, the fathers light the fire, and the women make dough to bake cakes for the queen of heaven and pour drink offerings to other gods, thus provoking Me to anger." (Provoke: to anger; Offerings: gifts) **19.** "Do they provoke Me to anger? says the LORD. Do they not bring destruction upon themselves?" **20.** "Therefore, the LORD God says: My anger and fury will be poured out upon this place—on humans, animals, crops, and trees—and it will burn without being extinguished." (Fury: intense anger; Extinguished: put out) **21.** "The LORD of hosts, the God of Israel, says: 'Add your burnt offerings to your other sacrifices, and eat the meat.'" **22.** "For when I brought your ancestors out of Egypt, I did not command them concerning burnt offerings or sacrifices." **23.** "But I gave them this command: 'Obey My voice, and I will be your God, and you will be My people; walk in all the ways I have commanded you, so that it may go well with you.'" (Obey: to listen and follow; Well: good) **24.** "But they did not listen or pay attention, but followed the stubbornness of their evil hearts, and turned away from Me, instead of moving forward." (Stubbornness: hard-heartedness; Pay attention: heed) **25.** "From the day your ancestors left Egypt until now, I have sent My servants the prophets, rising early and sending them daily." **26.** "Yet they did not listen to Me, nor did they pay attention, but they became more stubborn than their ancestors." (Stubborn: refusing to change; Neck: figuratively hard-heartedness) **27.** "Therefore, you will speak all these words to them, but they will not listen; you will call to them, but they will not answer." **28.** "But tell them, 'This is a nation that does not listen to the voice of the LORD their God, nor accept correction. Truth has perished, and is cut off from their lips.'" (Correction: guidance; Perished: destroyed) 29. "Cut off your hair, Jerusalem, and throw it away, and take up a lament on the high hills, for the LORD has rejected and abandoned the generation of His anger." (Lament: a mourning cry; Abandoned: forsaken) 30. "For the people of Judah have done evil in My sight, says the LORD; they have set their detestable idols in My house, defiling it." (Detestable: repulsive; Defiling: making unclean) 31. "They have built high places for Baal, in the valley of the son of Hinnom, to burn their children in the fire—something I never commanded, nor did it ever come to My mind." (High places: elevated worship sites; Valley: low area) 32. "The days are coming, says the LORD, when it will no longer be called Tophet or the valley of Hinnom, but the valley of slaughter, where they will bury the dead, until there is no more room." (Slaughter: mass killing; Valley: a low area) 33. "The bodies of these people will be food for the birds of the sky and the animals of the earth, and no one will scare them away." (Carcasses: dead bodies; Fray: to scare away) 34. "Then I will cause the sounds of joy and gladness to cease in the cities of Judah and the streets of Jerusalem. The voice of the bridegroom and the bride will be silenced, for the land will become desolate." (Mirth: joy; Desolate: uninhabited)

Chapter 8

1. The LORD declares: At that time, they will dig up the bones of the kings, princes, priests, prophets, and all the people of Jerusalem from their graves. (Declare: announce; Dig up: remove from the ground) 2. They will lay them out before the sun, moon, and stars they worshiped, and those they served, loved, and followed. They will not be buried but left to decay on the earth. (Decay: rot or decompose) 3. The survivors of this wicked family will choose death over life, wherever I have scattered them, says the LORD. (Wicked: evil or immoral) 4. Say to them: "Will they fall and never rise? Will they turn away and not return?" (Turn away: abandon) 5. Why does Jerusalem continually backslide, holding on to deceit and refusing to return to the LORD? (Backslide: fall back into sin; Deceit: dishonesty) 6. I listened, but they did not speak rightly. No one repented, saying, "What have I done?" They all continued in their evil ways, like horses rushing into battle. (Repented: felt remorse; Evil: morally wrong) 7. Even the stork knows its appointed seasons, and the birds know when to migrate. But my people don't know the judgment of the LORD. (Appointed: designated; Migrating: moving seasonally) 8. How can you claim wisdom when you have rejected the law of the LORD? Your scholars' writings are useless. (Claim: assert; Scholars: learned individuals) 9. The wise are ashamed, dismayed, and captured. They rejected the word of the LORD; what wisdom is left in them? (Dismayed: filled with fear or concern) 10. I will give their wives to others, and their lands to those who will inherit them. Everyone, from the least to the greatest, is greedy, even the prophets and priests. (Greedy: wanting more than needed) 11. They have tried to heal my people's wounds lightly, saying, "Peace, peace," when there is no peace. (Lightly: insufficiently) 12. Were they ashamed of their abominations? No, they were not ashamed, nor could they even blush. They will fall when the time comes for judgment. (Abominations: detestable acts; Blush: show embarrassment) 13. I will surely destroy them. There will be no fruit on the vine or fig tree, and what I gave them will be taken away. (Destroy: ruin; Vine: grape plant) 14. Why do we sit idly? Let's go into fortified cities and stay there, for the LORD has silenced us and given us bitter water to drink because we have sinned against Him. (Fortified: protected; Bitter: unpleasant) 15. We hoped for peace, but there was none. We waited for healing, but instead, trouble came. (Healing: recovery; Trouble: distress) 16. We hear the snorting of horses from Dan, and the land trembles at the sound of their neighing. The invaders have come and devastated the land, including the cities and people. (Snorting: exhaling loudly; Neighing: horse sound; Invaders: attackers) 17. Look, I will send venomous snakes among you, which cannot be charmed, and they will bite you, says the LORD. (Venomous: poisonous; Charms: magic to control) 18. When I try to comfort myself over my sorrow, my heart grows faint. (Faint: weak or weary) 19. I hear the cries of my people from a distant land: "Is the LORD not in Zion? Is her King not there? Why have they angered me with their idols and foolishness?" (Angered: provoked to anger; Idols: false gods) 20. The harvest is over, summer is gone, and we are not saved. (Harvest: gathering of crops; Saved: rescued) 21. I am in pain for my people. I am deeply troubled and overwhelmed. (Troubled: disturbed; Overwhelmed: overcome with emotion) 22. Is there no balm in Gilead? Is there no healer there? Why has the health of my people not been restored? (Balm: soothing medicine; Healer: one who cures)

Chapter 9

1. Oh, if my head were waters, and my eyes a fountain of tears, so I could weep day and night for the slain of my people! (Slain: killed; fountain: source) 2. If only I had a resting place in the wilderness, where travelers stay, so I could leave my people, for they are all adulterers, a treacherous group. (Adulterers: betrayers; treacherous: deceitful) 3. They bend their tongues like bows to lie; they are not brave for the truth. They go from evil to evil, and they do not know Me, says the LORD. (Bend: curve; valiant: brave; proceed: continue) 4. Be careful, and trust no one—every brother will deceive, and every neighbor will slander. (Slander: defamation) 5. They deceive their neighbors and speak lies; they weary themselves committing wickedness. (Wickedness: immorality) 6. You live in the midst of deceit, and through it they refuse to know Me, says the LORD. (Deceit: dishonesty) 7. Therefore, says the LORD of Hosts, I will refine and test them; how else can I help My people? (Refine: purify; hosts: armies) 8. Their words are like arrows, speaking deceit. They speak peace with their mouths, but in their hearts, they plot harm. (Plot: scheme) 9. Shall I not punish them for these things? Will I not avenge My soul on such a nation? (Avenge: retaliate) 10. I will weep for the mountains and the wilderness because they are burned and desolate, with no living creatures left. (Desolate: barren) 11. I will make Jerusalem a heap of ruins, a den for wild animals, and the cities of Judah empty, with no inhabitants. (Heap: pile; den: lair) 12. Who is wise enough to understand this? Who can explain why the land perishes, burned like a wilderness with no one passing through? (Perishes: decays) 13. The LORD says, because they have forsaken My law and disobeyed My voice, following their own hearts and the false gods their ancestors taught them. (Forsaken: abandoned; disobeyed: ignored) 14. They have followed the desires of their own hearts and the idols their fathers worshiped. (Desires: cravings; idols: false gods) 15. Therefore, says the LORD of Hosts, I will feed them bitter poison and give them gall to drink. (Gall: bitterness) 16. I will scatter them among nations they do not know, and a sword will chase them until they are destroyed. (Scatter: disperse; sword: weapon) 17. The LORD says, call for the mourning women and skilled wailers to come quickly and mourn for us, so our eyes may overflow with tears. (Wailers: mourners) 18. Let them hurry and wail for us, so our eyes may run down with tears, and our eyelids gush out with waters. (Gush: pour) 19. A voice of wailing is heard from Zion—how devastated we are! We are ashamed because we have forsaken the land, and our homes have cast us out. (Devastated: destroyed; ashamed: guilty) 20. Listen to the word of the LORD, O women, and teach your daughters to mourn, and each neighbor to lament. (Lament: grieve) 21. For death has entered our homes, cutting off children and young men from the streets. (Entered: arrived) 22. Say, the LORD declares, the bodies of men will fall like dung in the field, and no one will gather them. (Dung: waste) 23. The LORD says, let not the wise man boast of his wisdom, nor the mighty man of his strength, nor the rich man of his wealth. (Boast: brag) 24. Let the one who boasts, boast in understanding Me, for I am the LORD who delights in lovingkindness, justice, and righteousness on the earth. (Delights: rejoices) 25. The days are coming, says the LORD, when I will punish those who are

circumcised as well as the uncircumcised— (Circumcised: ritual) **26.** Egypt, Judah, Edom, Ammon, Moab, and all who dwell in the wilderness—because all these nations are uncircumcised, and the house of Israel is uncircumcised in heart. (Uncircumcised: unclean)

Chapter 10

1. Listen to the message that the LORD speaks to you, O people of Israel: (People of Israel: Israelites) **2.** This is what the LORD says: Do not follow the practices of the nations, nor be afraid of the signs in the sky, for the nations are frightened by them. (Frightened: Scared) **3.** The customs of the people are pointless; one cuts a tree from the forest, a craftsman shapes it with an axe. (Pointless: Useless; Craftsman: Worker) **4.** They cover it with silver and gold, fastening it with nails and hammers to keep it from falling. (Fastening: Securing) **5.** They stand straight like a palm tree but cannot speak. They must be carried, as they cannot walk. Do not fear them; they can neither harm nor help you. (Straight: Upright; Must be carried: Need to be moved)**6.** There is no one like You, O LORD; You are great, and Your power is unmatched. (Unmatched: Unequaled) **7.** Who would not revere You, King of the nations? For it is right for You to be honored, as there is no one like You among all the wise men of the nations or their kingdoms. (Revere: Respect; Wise men: Scholars) **8.** But they are altogether foolish and senseless; their teachings are mere illusions. (Foolish: Unwise; Senseless: Absurd) **9.** Silver is brought from Tarshish and gold from Uphaz, the work of artisans and metalworkers; their garments are made of blue and purple, crafted by skilled men. (Artisans: Skilled workers; Metalworkers: Founders) **10.** But the LORD is the true God, the living God, and an eternal King. At His wrath, the earth will tremble, and the nations will not withstand His fury. (Wrath: Anger; Tremble: Shake; Fury: Rage) **11.** Say to them: The gods who did not create the heavens and the earth will vanish from the earth and from beneath the heavens. (Vanish: Disappear) **12.** It is He who made the earth by His power, who established the world by His wisdom, and stretched out the heavens by His understanding. (Established: Founded; Stretched out: Expanded) **13.** When He speaks, the heavens are filled with water, and He causes vapor to rise from the ends of the earth. He brings the rain with lightning and brings forth wind from His storehouses. (Vapor: Moisture; Storehouses: Reserves) **14.** Every man is senseless in his knowledge; the craftsmen are confused by their idols, for their molten images are falsehoods, and there is no breath in them. (Senseless: Foolish; Molten: Melted; Falsehoods: Lies) **15.** They are empty, and the work of errors; when the time comes for them to be judged, they will perish. (Empty: Worthless; Errors: Mistakes) **16.** Jacob's inheritance is not like theirs; He is the Creator of all things, and Israel is His chosen people. The LORD Almighty is His name. (Inheritance: Possession; Creator: Maker) **17.** Gather your belongings, O people of the stronghold. (Stronghold: Fortress) **18.** The LORD says: I will cast out the people of the land at this time and bring distress upon them so they will know the truth. (Distress: Hardship) **19.** Woe is me! My wound is severe; this is a deep sorrow, and I must endure it. (Woe: Grief; Severe: Intense; Endure: Bear) **20.** My tent is destroyed, my ropes are broken, my children have gone, and I have no one to rebuild my home. (Destroyed: Ruined; Rebuild: Restore) **21.** The leaders have become foolish and have not sought the LORD; therefore, they will fail, and their people will scatter. (Leaders: Pastors; Scatter: Disperse) **22.** Listen! A great noise is coming, a commotion from the north, to make the cities of Judah desolate, a place for wild animals. (Commotion: Chaos; Desolate: Empty; Wild animals: Beasts) **23.** O LORD, I know that man cannot guide his own steps; it is not within man to direct his path. (Guide: Lead; Direct: Control) **24.** Correct me, LORD, but do so with fairness; do not correct me in Your anger, or I will be destroyed. (Correct: Discipline; Fairness: Justice) **25.** Pour out Your wrath on the nations that do not know You, and on the families that do not call on Your name; for they have consumed Israel and made its land desolate. (Wrath: Fury; Consume: Devour; Desolate: Ruin)

Chapter 11

1. The word of the LORD came to Jeremiah, saying: **2.** Declare the terms of this covenant to the people of Judah and to those living in Jerusalem. (Covenant: Agreement) **3.** Tell them, "This is what the LORD, the God of Israel, says: Cursed is anyone who does not obey the terms of this covenant." (Cursed: Damned) **4.** It is the same covenant I made with your ancestors when I brought them out of Egypt, out of the iron furnace. I said, "Obey my voice and follow all my commands, and you will be my people, and I will be your God." **5.** Then I will fulfill the promise I made to your ancestors, to give them a land flowing with milk and honey, as it is today. And I said, "Amen, LORD." (Promise: Oath ; Milk and honey: Prosperity) **6.** The LORD said to me, "Preach these words in the cities of Judah and the streets of Jerusalem, telling them to listen to and obey this covenant." (Proclaim: Announce) **7.** For I have warned your ancestors from the day I brought them out of Egypt, rising early and speaking to them: "Obey my voice." **8.** But they did not listen or pay attention. Instead, each followed the stubbornness of their evil hearts. Therefore, I will bring upon them all the consequences of this covenant, which I commanded them to obey, but they refused. (Incline: Listen ; Imagination: Thoughts) **9.** The LORD revealed to me that there is a conspiracy among the people of Judah and the inhabitants of Jerusalem. (Conspiracy: Plot) **10.** They have turned back to the sins of their forefathers who refused to listen to my words. They followed other gods and served them. Both Israel and Judah have broken the covenant I made with their ancestors. (Iniquities: Sins) **11.** Therefore, the LORD says, "I will bring disaster upon them that they cannot escape. Even if they cry out to me, I will not listen." (Evil: Harm) **12.** Then the cities of Judah and the people of Jerusalem will cry out to their gods, the ones to whom they offer incense, but they will not save them in their time of trouble. (Incense: Smoke) **13.** Judah's cities and Jerusalem's streets are filled with altars to these false gods, like Baal, to which they burn incense. (Baal: Idol) **14.** Do not pray for these people, and do not plead on their behalf, for I will not listen when they call to me in their distress. **15.** What does my beloved have to do in my house, when she has committed such evil, turning away from me? You rejoice in doing wrong. **16.** The LORD once called you a green olive tree, beautiful and full of good fruit, but now with the great uproar he has set it on fire, and its branches are broken. (Uproar : Tumult) **17.** The LORD of hosts, who planted you, has spoken disaster against you because of the evil done by Israel and Judah, which provoked him to anger by offering incense to Baal. (Hosts: Armies) **18.** The LORD has shown me their deeds, and I know them. **19.** But I was like a lamb or an ox led to slaughter; I did not realize they were plotting against me, saying, "Let us destroy the tree with its fruit; let us cut him off from the land of the living, so his name is forgotten." (Slaughter: Killing) **20.** But, O LORD of hosts, who judges justly and tests the heart and mind, let me see your vengeance on them, for I have revealed my cause to you. (Vengeance: Revenge) **21.** Therefore, the LORD says concerning the men of Anathoth, who seek your life, saying, "Do not prophesy in the name of the LORD, lest you die by our hand." (Anathoth: Town) **22.** Therefore, the LORD of hosts says, "I will punish them. The young men will die by the sword, and their children will die by famine." (Sword: Weapon ; Famine: Hunger) **23.** There will be no survivors, for I will bring judgment upon the men of Anathoth in the year of their visitation. (Visitation: Judgment)

Chapter 12

1. You are righteous, O LORD, when I argue with you. Yet, let me question your judgments: Why do the wicked thrive? Why are those who act deceitfully so happy? (Righteous: Just; Argue: Plead; Thrive: Succeed) **2.** You have planted them, they have taken root and grown; they bear fruit. They speak of you, but their hearts are far from you. (Planted: Settled; Reins: Heart) **3.** But you know me, LORD. You have seen my heart. Tear them down like sheep for slaughter, and prepare them for their end. (Slaughter: Kill) **4.** How long will the land mourn and the fields wither because of the wickedness of those who live there? The animals and birds suffer because they say, "God won't see our end." (Mourn: Grieve; Wither: Fade; Suffer: Endure) **5.** If you've been weary from running with the footmen, how will you compete with the horses? If you've been troubled in peaceful lands, what will you do when danger rises? (Footmen: Soldiers; Compete: Contend; Swelling: Rising) **6.** Even your own family has betrayed you. They speak kindly, but don't trust them. (Betrayed: Deceived; Trust: Rely) **7.** I've abandoned my house and given my beloved into the hands of enemies. (Beloved: Loved) **8.** My inheritance feels like a lion in the forest, roaring against me—so I have come to despise it. (Inheritance: Legacy; Despise: Hate) **9.** My inheritance is like a speckled bird, with enemies circling it. Gather the beasts of the field to devour it. (Speckled: Spotted; Devour: Eat) **10.** Many leaders have ruined my vineyard, trampling my land and turning it into a wasteland. (Vineyard: Cropland; Wasteland: Desert) **11.** They have made it desolate, and it mourns. The whole land is in ruin, because no one cares. (Desolate: Barren; Mourns: Grieves) **12.** The destroyers are coming across all high places in the wilderness. The sword of the LORD will consume the land from one end to the other. No one will have peace. (Destroyers: Ruiners; Consume: Devour) **13.** They planted wheat but will harvest thorns; they labored in vain and will face shame because of God's anger. (Thorns: Brambles; Labor: Work; Vain: Fruitless) **14.** The LORD will deal with all my evil neighbors who harm the land I gave Israel. He will uproot them and remove Judah from among them. (Evil: Wicked; Uproot: Eradicate) **15.** After uprooting them, I will return and show mercy, restoring each person to their land and heritage. (Mercy: Compassion; Heritage: Inheritance) **16.** If they learn my people's ways and swear by my name, as they once taught my people to swear by idols, they will be rebuilt among my people. (Idols: False-gods; Rebuilt: Restored) **17.** But if they refuse, I will destroy them completely, says the LORD. (Refuse: Reject; Destroy: Annihilate)

Chapter 13

1. The LORD instructed me, "Go and take a linen belt, tie it around your waist, but don't dip it in water." (Linen: Fabric) **2.** I obeyed the LORD's command, taking the belt and wearing it around my waist. **3.** Then the word of the LORD came to me again, saying, **4.** "Take the belt you are wearing, go to the Euphrates River, and hide it there in a crack of the rocks." (Euphrates: River) **5.** I went to the Euphrates and hid the belt, as the LORD had told me. **6.** After many days, the LORD spoke to me again: "Go to the Euphrates and take the belt from where you hid it." **7.** I went, dug up the belt, and found that it was ruined—it was completely useless. (ruined: Damaged) **8.** Then the word of the LORD came to me, saying, **9.** "This is how I will destroy the pride of Judah, and the great pride of Jerusalem." (Pride: Arrogance) **10.** "This wicked people, who refuse to listen to my words, follow the stubbornness of their hearts, and worship false gods, will become like this belt, useless." (Wicked: Evil ; Stubbornness: Obstinacy ; Imagination: Thoughts) **11.** "Just as a belt clings to a man's waist, so I wanted the entire house of Israel and Judah to cling to me. They were meant to be my people, my name, and my glory. But they refused to listen." (Clings: Sticks ; Glory: Honor) **12.** "Say to them, 'This is what the LORD God of Israel says: Every bottle will be filled with wine.' And they will say, 'Of course, we know that every bottle will be filled with wine!'" (Bottles: vessels) **13.** "Then tell them, 'The LORD says: I will fill the people of this land—including the kings, the priests, the prophets, and all the inhabitants of Jerusalem—with drunkenness.'" (Drunkenness: Intoxication) **14.** "I will cause them to clash with one another—fathers and sons together. I will show no pity, no mercy, but will bring about their destruction." (Pity: sympathy) **15.** "Listen carefully and pay attention: Don't be proud, for the LORD has spoken." (Proud: Arrogant) **16.** "Give glory to the LORD your God before darkness comes, before you stumble on dark mountains. And while you look for light, he will turn it into deep shadow." (Glory: Honor) **17.** "But if you refuse to listen, my soul will weep in secret because of your pride. My eyes will overflow with tears, for the LORD's people will be taken away as captives." **18.** "Tell the king and the queen, 'Humble yourselves and sit down, for your crowns of glory will be removed.'" (Humble: Lower) **19.** "The southern cities will be shut up, and no one will open them. Judah will be completely taken into captivity." **20.** "Lift up your eyes and look to the north. Where is the flock you were given, the beautiful flock?" **21.** "What will you say when punishment comes? You taught them to be leaders over you. Will not sorrow grip you like a woman in labor?" (Punishment: Discipline) **22.** "And if you ask, 'Why are these things happening to me?' It's because your sins have been exposed, and your shame is visible for all to see." **23.** "Can the Ethiopian change his skin or the leopard his spots? Then you who are used to doing evil, can you do good?" (Ethiopian: an ancient kingdom located south of Egypt) **24.** "Therefore, I will scatter them like stubble blown away by the wind in the wilderness." (Stubble: Remnants) **25.** "This is your lot, the portion I have set aside for you, because you have forgotten me and trusted in lies." (Portion: Share) **26.** "So I will uncover your shame and make it visible for all to see." (Uncover : Discover) **27.** "I have seen your adulteries, your lustful acts, your immoral actions, and your detestable practices in the hills and fields. Woe to you, Jerusalem! Will you never be cleansed? When will it end?" (Adulteries: Infidelity in marriage)

Chapter 14

1. This is the word of the LORD to Jeremiah about the drought. (Drought: dry spell) **2.** Judah mourns, and its gates are in despair; the city of Jerusalem cries out. (Mourns: grieves; Despair: hopelessness) **3.** The nobles sent their children to gather water, but the wells were dry; they returned empty and ashamed, covering their heads. (Nobles: aristocrats; Ashamed: embarrassed) **4.** The ground is cracked because there has been no rain; the farmers are ashamed, covering their heads. (Cracked: split; Plowmen: farmers) **5.** Even the deer abandoned their young in the fields because there was no grass.(Hind: female deer) **6.** The wild donkeys stand on the high ground, sniffing the wind like dragons; their eyes grow weak from lack of grass. (Snuffed up: sniffed; Dragons: A mythical creature) **7.** LORD, though our sins accuse us, act for the sake of Your name, for we have greatly sinned. (Accuse: blame) **8.** O hope of Israel, our Savior in times of trouble, why are You like a traveler passing through, stopping only for the night? (Savior: rescuer) **9.** Why are You like someone stunned, unable to save? Yet You are with us, and we bear Your name—do not leave us. (stunned : Astonied) **10.** The LORD says to the people: They love to wander; they do not turn from their ways. Because of this, the LORD will not accept them and will remember their sins. **11.** The LORD said to me, "Do not pray for their well-being." (Well-being: health) **12.** When they fast, I will not listen to their cries; when they offer sacrifices, I will not accept them. I will destroy them with the sword, famine, and plague. (Fast: abstain) **13.** I replied, "Ah, Lord GOD! The prophets tell them, 'You will not see war, and there will be no famine. I will give you peace.'" **14.** But the LORD replied, "The prophets lie in My name. I did not send them, nor did I speak to them. They are deceiving you with false visions, empty predictions, and lies from their own hearts." (False vision: misleading dream) **15.** Therefore, the LORD says, "These false prophets who say there will be no sword or famine will themselves die by sword and famine." (Famine: starvation) **16.** The people they prophesy to will be left in the streets of Jerusalem, dying from hunger and the sword, with no one to bury them—neither their wives, nor children. I will pour out their wickedness on them. (Prophesy: predict; Pour out: release) **17.** Tell them: "Let my eyes weep night and day without ceasing, for the virgin daughter of my people is suffering a grievous wound."(Grievous: severe) **18.** If I go into the field, I see those slain by the sword. If I enter the city, I see those dying from famine. Both the prophet and the priest wander in a land they do not know. (Slain: killed; Priest: clergyman) **19.** "Have You utterly rejected Judah? Why has Your soul loathed Zion? Why have You struck us, and there is no cure? We hoped for peace, but there is no peace; we sought healing, but only trouble remains!" (Loathed: hated; Struck: afflicted) **20.** We confess, O LORD, our wickedness and the sins of our ancestors; we have sinned against You. (Confess: admit; Wickedness: evil) **21.** Do not reject us for the sake of Your name, do not disgrace the throne of Your glory. Remember Your covenant with us and do not break it. (Disgrace: dishonor; Covenant: agreement) **22.** Are there any false gods among the nations who can send rain? Can the heavens give showers? Are You not the LORD, our God? We will wait for You, for You made all things. (False gods: idols)

Chapter 15
1. The LORD told me, "Even if Moses and Samuel stood before Me, I would not show mercy to this people. Cast them away from My sight and let them go." (Mercy: compassion; cast away: reject) **2.** If they ask, "Where should we go?" tell them: "Those meant for death will die; those for the sword will be killed; those for famine will starve; those for captivity will be taken." (Famine: hunger; captivity: imprisonment) **3.** I will bring four punishments upon them: the sword to kill, dogs to tear apart, birds to devour, and beasts to destroy. (Tear apart: rip; devour: consume) **4.** I will scatter them among all nations because of what Manasseh, son of Hezekiah, did in Jerusalem. (Scatter: spread; nations: countries) **5.** Who will pity you, Jerusalem? Who will mourn for you or ask how you are? (Mourn: grieve) **6.** You have abandoned Me, says the LORD; you have turned away. So I will stretch out My hand to destroy you. I am tired of holding back My anger. (Abandoned: forsaken; stretch out: extend) **7.** I will sweep them away at the gates of the city, taking their children and destroying My people because they refuse to change. (Sweep away: remove; refuse: decline) **8.** Their widows outnumber the sands of the sea. I will bring a destroyer at noon to strike suddenly, bringing terror to the city. (Widows: bereaved; destroyer: annihilator) **9.** The woman who had seven children now suffers and has lost them all; her sun has set while it was still day. She is ashamed, and the rest will die by the sword. (Languish: suffer; residue: remainder) **10.** Alas, my mother, that you bore me a man of conflict and strife! I have never borrowed or lent money, yet they all curse me. (Alas: woe; strife: conflict) **11.** The LORD said, "It will be well with your remnant; I will make the enemy treat you kindly in times of trouble." (Remnant: remainder) **12.** Can iron break northern iron and steel? (Break: fracture) **13.** I will give your wealth and treasures to your enemies because of your sins, in all your lands. (Substance: wealth; spoil: loot) **14.** I will send you and your enemies to a foreign land, for My anger is like a fire that will burn against you. (Foreign: unfamiliar; burn: scorch) **15.** O LORD, remember me, visit me, and take vengeance on my persecutors. Do not take me away in Your patience, for I have suffered for Your sake. (Vengeance: retribution; persecutors: oppressors) **16.** Your words were found, and I ate them. They became the joy and delight of my heart, for I am called by Your name, O LORD of hosts. (Delight: pleasure; hosts: armies) **17.** I did not sit with the mockers or rejoice, but I sat alone because of Your hand, filled with anger. (Mockers: ridiculers; hand: power) **18.** Why is my pain unending and my wound incurable? Will You be like a liar to me, or like water that fails? (Incurable: unhealable; liar: deceiver) **19.** The LORD said, "If you return to Me, I will bring you back and make you stand before Me. If you separate the precious from the worthless, you will be My messenger. Let them return to you, but do not return to them." (Separate: distinguish; messenger: herald) **20.** I will make you like a strong wall to this people. They will fight against you, but they will not overcome you. I am with you to save and protect you." (Overcome: defeat; protect: shield) **21.** I will rescue you from the wicked and redeem you from the ruthless. (Redeem: rescue)

Chapter 16
1. The LORD spoke to me, saying, **2.** "Do not take a wife or have sons or daughters in this place." **3.** "For this is what the LORD says about the children born here, their mothers who gave birth to them, and their fathers who fathered them in this land:" **4.** "They will die from severe afflictions; they will not be mourned or buried, but will lie like refuse on the ground. They will be killed by the sword and famine, and their bodies will be devoured by birds and beasts." (Afflictions: hardships; refuse: waste; devoured: eaten) **5.** "Do not enter the house of mourning or join in lamenting for them, because I have removed My peace from this people, as well as My love and mercy," says the LORD. (Lamenting: mourning) **6.** "Both the great and the lowly will die in this land. No one will bury them or mourn for them; neither will they cut themselves or shave their heads in grief." (Grief: sorrow; cut themselves: self-inflict wounds) **7.** "No one will offer them comfort or give them the cup of consolation for their parents." (Consolation: comfort) **8.** "Do not enter the house of feasts, nor sit down to eat and drink with them." **9.** "For this is what the LORD of hosts, the God of Israel, says: I will cause the sounds of celebration, joy, and happiness to cease from this place, including the voices of the bridegroom and the bride, while you are still here to see it." (Cease: stop; bridegroom: man marrying) **10.** "When you share these words with the people, they will ask you, 'Why has the LORD brought such great disaster upon us? What have we done wrong, and what is our sin against the LORD our God?'" **11.** "Then say to them, 'It is because your ancestors abandoned Me, followed other gods, served and worshiped them, and refused to keep My laws.'" (Abandoned: forsaken; followed: pursued) **12.** "You have acted even worse than your ancestors, each of you following the wickedness of your own heart, refusing to listen to Me." (Wickedness: evil; refuse: decline) **13.** "So I will cast you out of this land into a land that neither you nor your ancestors know. There you will serve other gods, day and night, and I will show you no mercy." **14.** "The time is coming," says the LORD, "when it will no longer be said, 'The LORD lives, who brought Israel up from Egypt.'" **15.** "Instead, it will be said, 'The LORD lives, who brought Israel up from the land of the north and from all the lands where He had scattered them. I will bring them back to the land I gave to their forefathers.'" (Scattered: dispersed; forefathers: ancestors) **16.** "I will send many fishermen to gather them, and later many hunters to track them down from every mountain, hill, and the caves of the earth." (hunters: pursuers) **17.** "For My eyes are on all their ways; nothing escapes My notice, and their sin is not hidden from Me." **18.** "I will repay them double for their sin and iniquity, for they have polluted My land with the remains of their detestable idols." (Polluted: defiled; detestable: loathsome) **19.** "O LORD, my strength, my fortress, and my refuge in times of trouble, the nations will come from the ends of the earth and say, 'Surely our ancestors have inherited lies, emptiness, and worthless things.'" (Nations: Gentiles; emptiness: vanity) **20.** "Can a man make gods for himself, when they are not gods?" **21.** "Therefore, I will make them know My power and might, and they will recognize that My name is the LORD." (Might: strength; recognize: acknowledge)

Chapter 17
1. The sin of Judah is deeply etched, like iron on stone, engraved on their hearts and altars.(etched: carved, engraved: carved deeply) **2.** Their children remember the altars and sacred groves, where green trees grow on high hills. (groves: small woods or thickets) **3.** O my mountain, I will give your riches and treasures to be plundered, and your high places will be destroyed. (plundered: stolen or taken by force) **4.** You will lose the inheritance I gave you and serve enemies in a land you do not know, for you have angered me with your sin, and my wrath will last forever. (inheritance: something passed down, wrath: divine anger) **5.** The LORD says: Cursed is the man who trusts in others and turns his heart away from God. (cursed: condemned, turns: moves away) **6.** He will be like a desert bush, blind to the good around him, and will live in barren, uninhabited places. (barren: dry and infertile, inhabited: lived in) **7.** Blessed is the man who trusts in the LORD, and whose hope is in God. (blessed: fortunate, favored) **8.** He will be like a tree planted by water, with roots spreading, unshaken by heat, and always bearing fruit.

(unshaken: not disturbed or moved) **9.** The heart is deceitful and wicked; who can truly understand it? (deceitful: misleading, wicked: morally wrong) **10.** I, the LORD, search hearts and minds, rewarding everyone based on their actions and the fruits of their deeds. (rewarding: giving as a result, fruits: outcomes or results) **11.** Like a bird that sits on eggs it cannot hatch, so will the one who gains riches unjustly lose them, and be a fool at the end. (unjustly: unfairly) **12.** From the beginning, a glorious throne is the place of our sanctuary. (sanctuary: holy or sacred place) **13.** LORD, the hope of Israel, all who abandon You will be ashamed, for they have forsaken You, the source of life. (forsaken: abandoned, source: origin) **14.** Heal me, LORD, and I will be healed; save me, and I will be saved, for You are my praise. (praise: worship or adoration directed to God.) **15.** They mock me, saying, "Where is the word of the LORD? Let it come now." (mock: openly ridicule or reject) **16.** I have not rushed to follow my own desires or longed for disaster; what I say is true before You. (rushed: hurried, disaster: ruin or destruction) **17.** Do not be a terror to me; You are my hope in times of trouble. (terror: fear, hope: trust) **18.** Let those who persecute me be ashamed, but not me. Let them be dismayed, but not me; bring evil upon them and destroy them double. (persecute: harass or oppress, dismayed: distressed) **19.** The LORD said to me: Stand in the gate where the kings of Judah enter and leave, and speak to all the people. (gate: entrance, speak: proclaim) **20.** Say to them: Hear the word of the LORD, you kings and people of Judah, all who enter through these gates. (proclaim: announce) **21.** The LORD says: Be careful not to carry burdens or do work on the Sabbath day, and do not bring anything through Jerusalem's gates. (burdens: heavy loads, Sabbath: day of rest) **22.** Do not carry any burden from your homes on the Sabbath; keep the day holy as I commanded your ancestors. (holy: sacred, ancestors: forebears) **23.** But they refused, stubbornly ignoring my commands, and turned their backs on me. (stubbornly: determinedly, ignoring: disregarding) **24.** If you obey Me and keep the Sabbath holy, then kings and princes will enter through these gates, and the city will remain forever. (obey: follow commands, remain: stay) **25.** Kings, princes, and the people will come, bringing offerings and praises to the house of the LORD. (offerings: gifts or sacrifices) **26.** They will come from all over Judah, bringing sacrifices of thanksgiving to the LORD. (thanksgiving: gratitude, sacrifices: offerings) **27.** But if you refuse to obey and keep the Sabbath holy, I will set fire to the gates of Jerusalem, and it will consume the palaces, never to be quenched. (quench: extinguish or put out)

Chapter 18

1. The word of the LORD came to Jeremiah, saying, (word: message or command) **2.** "Go down to the potter's house, and there I will make you hear my words." (potter: a person who makes pottery, hear: understand) **3.** So I went to the potter's house, and saw him working with clay on the wheel. (wheel: a spinning device for shaping clay) **4.** The vessel he made was flawed, so he reshaped it into a new one, as he saw fit. (flawed: damaged, reshaped: made again) **5.** Then the LORD spoke to me, saying, (spoke: said) **6.** "O house of Israel, can't I do with you as this potter does? As clay is in the potter's hand, so are you in My hand, O Israel." (clay: a malleable substance that can be shaped, potter's hand: the control of the maker) **7.** If I decide to destroy a nation or kingdom, (destroy: completely ruin) **8.** but that nation repents of its evil ways, I will change my mind and not bring disaster upon it. (repents: turns away from sin, disaster: calamity) **9.** And if I decide to build and plant a nation, (build: create, plant: to establish) **10.** but it does evil and disobeys My voice, I will change my mind and no longer bless it. (bless: show favor) **11.** Now go and speak to the people of Judah and Jerusalem: "The LORD says, I am planning evil against you; turn from your wicked ways and do what is right." (wicked: sinful, right: good) **12.** But they replied, "There is no hope. We will follow our own plans and do what our evil hearts desire." (hope: expectation of good, evil: wrong) **13.** Therefore, the LORD says, "Ask the nations: has anyone seen such things? The virgin of Israel has done a horrible thing." (horrible: terrible, virgin: a metaphor for purity or faithfulness) **14.** Will anyone leave the snow from Lebanon, or the cold flowing waters that come from another place? (Lebanon: a mountain range known for its snow and waters) **15.** Because My people have forgotten Me, they worship false gods and have gone off the right path, walking in unfamiliar ways. (worship: give reverence, false gods: idols, unfamiliar: not known) **16.** This will make their land desolate, and everyone who passes by will be astonished and shake their head. (desolate: empty and ruined, astonished: shocked) **17.** I will scatter them like a storm before their enemies; I will turn my back on them in their time of trouble. (scatter: spread out, storm: strong wind, turn my back: withdraw my support) **18.** They said, "Let us plot against Jeremiah; the law will not fail the priest, nor the wisdom of the wise, nor the prophet's word. Let us silence him with our words and ignore what he says." (plot: plan secretly, silence: make quiet) **19.** "Hear me, O LORD, and listen to those who oppose me." (oppose: fight against) **20.** "Should evil be repaid with good? They dug a pit for me. Remember that I spoke well for them, trying to turn Your anger away." (repaid: returned, dug a pit: set a trap) **21.** "So deliver their children to famine, and let them be killed by the sword. Let their wives become widows, and their men be slain in battle." (famine: hunger or starvation, slain: killed) **22.** "Let a cry be heard from their homes when You bring a sudden attack on them. They have set traps for me." (traps: snares, attack: assault) **23.** "But You, LORD, know all their plans to kill me. Do not forgive their sin, but let them be overthrown in Your anger." (forgive: pardon, overthrown: destroyed)

Chapter 19

1. The LORD commands: "Go and take a clay pot, along with the elders of the people and priests. (Elders: Older, respected leaders in the community) **2.** Head to the valley of Hinnom, by the east gate, and declare the message I give you there. (Valley of Hinnom: A place associated with idolatry and child sacrifice) **3.** Say, 'Listen, O kings of Judah and people of Jerusalem! The LORD of Hosts, the God of Israel, says: I will bring disaster on this place, and everyone who hears it will be shocked.' (Disaster: Great harm or misfortune; Shocked: Stunned or horrified) **4.** They have abandoned me and defiled this place, burning incense to foreign gods unknown to them, their ancestors, or the kings of Judah, filling the place with innocent blood. (Defiled: Made unclean or impure; Incense: Fragrant smoke offered to gods) **5.** They have even built altars to Baal, burning their sons as sacrifices to him, a practice I never commanded, nor did it ever enter my mind. (Baal: A pagan god of fertility and storm; Altars: Structures for sacrifices) **6.** Therefore, the days are coming when this place will no longer be called Tophet or the valley of Hinnom, but the valley of slaughter. (Tophet: A place of child sacrifice; Slaughter: Mass killing) **7.** I will destroy the plans of Judah and Jerusalem here; they will fall by the sword before their enemies, their bodies left for scavengers to consume. (Scavengers: Animals that feed on dead bodies) **8.** This city will be ruined, and those who pass by will be shocked and mock it because of its suffering. (Ruined: Destroyed or severely damaged; Mock: To ridicule or show disrespect) **9.** In the siege, they will be so desperate that they will eat the flesh of their sons, daughters, and neighbors. (Siege: Military blockade or attack of a city) **10.** You will break the clay pot in front of the people with you, (Clay pot: Symbolizing the fragility of the people) **11.** and tell them, 'The LORD says: I will shatter this people and city, just like this pot that can never be repaired. They will be buried here, until there is no more room.' (Shatter: To break into pieces; Repaired: Fixed or restored) **12.** This is what will happen to this place, and to its people—it will become like Tophet. **13.** Even the homes of Jerusalem and the kings of Judah will be defiled, because they worshipped the stars and poured out drink offerings to other gods. (Defiled: Made unclean or profaned; Drink offerings: Liquids poured out as a ritual offering) **14.** After prophesying at Tophet, Jeremiah returned to the temple court and said to the people: (Prophesying: Speaking messages inspired by God) **15.** 'The LORD of Hosts, the God of Israel, says: I will bring all the disasters I've declared on this city and its towns, because they have stubbornly refused to listen to my words.' (Hosts: Armies or forces; Stubbornly: With persistence in refusing to change)

Chapter 20

1. Pashur, the son of Immer, a priest and the chief official in the LORD's temple, heard that Jeremiah was delivering these prophecies. (Immer: priest; chief official: leader) **2.** In response, Pashur struck Jeremiah and placed him in the stocks at the Benjamin Gate, near the temple of the LORD. (stocks: restraints) **3.** The next morning, Pashur brought Jeremiah out of the stocks. Jeremiah told him, "The LORD has changed your name from Pashur to Magor-missabib." (Magor-missabib: terror) **4.** "For the LORD says: I will make you a terror to yourself and your friends. Your enemies will slay them with the sword, and you will witness it with your own eyes. All of Judah will be handed over to the king of Babylon, who will take them captive and execute them with the sword." (terror: fear; captivity: imprisonment) **5.** The treasures, strength, and labor of this city, as well as all the wealth of the kings of Judah, will be taken by their enemies, who will plunder everything and carry it to Babylon. (plunder: loot) **6.** You, Pashur, and your entire household will be taken into exile. You will die in Babylon and be buried there, along with your friends who have spoken lies." (exile: banishment) **7.** "O LORD, You have deceived me, and I have been deceived. You are stronger than I, and You have triumphed. I am ridiculed every day, and everyone mocks me." (deceived: tricked; triumphed: prevailed) **8.** "Whenever I speak, I cry out, 'Violence and destruction!' because the word of the LORD has become a source of reproach to me every day." (reproach: shame) **9.** "I said to myself, 'I will not mention Him or speak in His name anymore.' But Your word was like a fire burning within me, shut up in my bones. I grew weary of holding it in, and I could not do it." (shut up: confined; weary: exhausted) **10.** "I heard many people whispering, 'Terror on every side! Report him! Let's report him!' All my friends are watching for me to slip, saying, 'Perhaps he will be deceived, and we will overcome him and get our revenge.'" (whispering: gossiping; overcome: defeat) **11.** "But the LORD is with me like a mighty warrior. Therefore, my persecutors will stumble and not prevail. They will be greatly ashamed, for they will not succeed. Their shame will never be forgotten." (persecutors: oppressors; shame: disgrace) **12.** "O LORD of Hosts, You who test the righteous and know the heart and mind, let me see Your vengeance on them. I have committed my case to You." (hosts: armies; vengeance: punishment) **13.** "Sing to the LORD, praise the LORD, for He has delivered the soul of the poor from the hands of the wicked." (delivered: saved; wicked: evil) **14.** "Cursed be the day I was born! Let the day my mother bore me not be blessed." (cursed: condemned) **15.** "Cursed be the man who brought the news to my father, saying, 'A son has been born to you,' and made him glad." (cursed: condemned) **16.** "Let that man be like the cities that the LORD overthrew and did not relent. Let him hear cries of anguish in the morning and screams of distress at noon." (anguish: pain; relent: spare) **17.** "Why did I not die at birth, or why didn't my mother's womb become my tomb, so that I would never have seen the light of day?" (tomb: grave) **18.** "Why was I born to endure toil and sorrow, that my days should be filled with shame?" (toil: labor; sorrow: grief)

Chapter 21

1. The word of the LORD came to Jeremiah when King Zedekiah sent Pashur, son of Melchiah, and Zephaniah, son of Maaseiah, to ask for a prophecy. (Inquire: ask) **2.** They said, "Please ask the LORD for us, because King Nebuchadrezzar of Babylon is at war with us. Perhaps the LORD will act as He has before and make him leave." (Wondrous works: miraculous deeds) **3.** Jeremiah replied, "Tell Zedekiah this:" **4.** "The LORD of Israel says, 'I will take back the weapons you use to fight the Babylonians and Chaldeans who are besieging your city. I will bring them into the city instead.'" (Besiege: surround in an attempt to capture) **5.** "I will fight against you with an outstretched hand, in anger, fury, and great wrath." (Outstretched: extended; Wrath: intense anger) **6.** "I will strike down the people of this city, both human and animal, with a deadly plague." (Pestilence: deadly disease) **7.** "Afterward, I will deliver King Zedekiah, his officials, and the remaining people into the hands of Nebuchadrezzar, their enemies, and those who seek their lives. He will kill them with the sword, showing no mercy." (Mercy: compassion) **8.** "To the people, say this: 'The LORD sets before you two paths—life and death.'" **9.** "Those who stay in the city will die by sword, famine, or plague. But those who surrender to the Babylonians will live, and their lives will be spared." **10.** "I have turned against this city for destruction, not for good. It will be handed over to the king of Babylon, who will burn it down." **11.** "Concerning the house of Judah's king, hear the word of the LORD:" **12.** "O house of David, the LORD says: 'Administer justice in the morning, and rescue the oppressed from their oppressors, or My fury will burn like fire, unstoppable because of your evil deeds.'" (Execute: carry out; Spoiled: plundered; Oppressor: those who exploit others) **13.** "I am against you, O inhabitants of the valley and rock of the plain, who say, 'Who can attack us? Who can enter our homes?'" (Inhabitant: dweller) **14.** "I will punish you for what you have done. I will set your forests on fire, and it will burn everything around it." (Devour: consume; Forest: wooded area)

Chapter 22

1. The LORD commands: Go to the house of Judah's king and speak this word: (Judah: Kingdom) **2.** "Hear the word of the LORD, O king on David's throne, you and your servants and people who enter through these gates: (David's throne: Dynasty) **3.** Execute justice and righteousness; rescue the oppressed. Do not harm foreigners, orphans, or widows, and do not shed innocent blood here. (Righteousness: Justice; Oppressed: Victims; Foreigners: Outsiders; Orphans: Parentless; Widows: Bereaved) **4.** If you do this, kings of David's line will enter through these gates, riding in chariots and on horses with their people. (Chariots: Vehicles) **5.** But if you refuse to listen, I swear by Myself, this house will become desolate. (Desolate: Abandoned) **6.** You are like Gilead and Lebanon to Me, but I will turn you into a desolate wilderness, cities without inhabitants. (Gilead: Region; Lebanon: Mountains) **7.** I will send destroyers to cut down your choice cedars and burn them. (Destroyers: Ravagers; Cedars: Trees) **8.** Many nations will pass by and ask, "Why has the LORD done this to such a great city?" (Nations: Peoples) **9.** They will answer, "Because they abandoned the LORD's covenant, worshipped other gods, and served them." (Covenant: Agreement) **10.** Do not mourn for the dead, but for the one who will never return to his homeland. (Mourn: Grieve; Homeland: Birthplace) **11.** This is the fate of Shallum, son of Josiah, king of Judah, who reigned after his father and left this place—he will never return. (Fate: Destiny) **12.** He will die in the land to which he was exiled and never see Judah again. (Exiled: Banished) **13.** Woe to the one who builds his house with injustice and his chambers with wrong, who exploits his neighbor without paying him. (Injustice: Unfairness; Exploits: takes advantage of) **14.** He says, "I will build a large house with wide rooms, paneled with cedar and painted with vermilion." (Vermilion: Red) **15.** Will you rule because you dress in cedar? Didn't your father live well by practicing justice and caring for the poor? (Rule: Govern; Cedar: Wood) **16.** He judged fairly, and it was well with him—this is what it means to know Me, says the LORD. (Judged fairly: Decided justly; Know Me: Understand) **17.** But your heart is set on greed, shedding innocent blood, and oppression. (Greed: Avarice; Shedding: Spilling; Oppression: Cruelty) **18.** Therefore, concerning Jehoiakim, son of Josiah, king of Judah: People will not mourn for him, saying, "Ah, my brother!" or "Ah, his glory!" (Glory: Honor) **19.** He will be buried like a donkey, dragged and thrown beyond Jerusalem's gates. (Dragged: Pulled) **20.** Cry out from Lebanon and Bashan; your lovers are destroyed. (Cry out: Shout; Bashan: Region) 21. I spoke to you when you prospered, but you refused to listen. This has been your way since youth—you did not obey My voice. (Prospered: Thrived; Refused: Rejected; Obey: Follow) 22. Your shepherds will be swept away by the wind, and your lovers will go into captivity. You will be ashamed of your wickedness. (Shepherds: Leaders; Swept away: Taken; Wickedness: Evil) 23. O inhabitant of Lebanon, who nests in the cedars, how will you fare when pain comes, like the labor of a woman? (Inhabitant: Resident; Nests: Dwells; Labor: Pain) 24. As I live, says the LORD, even if Coniah, son of Jehoiakim, were My signet ring, I would remove you. (Signet: Seal) 25. I will give you into the hands of those who seek your life, to Nebuchadnezzar, king of Babylon, and the Chaldeans. (Seek: Pursue; Chaldeans: Babylonians) 26. I will cast you and your mother into a land where you were not born, and you will die there. (Cast: Throw; Exile: Banishment) 27. You will not return to the land you long for. (Long for: Desire) 28. Is Coniah like a despised broken vessel? Why are he and his descendants cast into a land they do not know? (Despised: Hated; Vessel: Container) 29. O earth, earth, earth, hear the word of the LORD! (Earth: World) 30. Thus says the LORD: Write this man childless—none of his descendants will succeed him on the throne of David in Judah. (Childless: Without heirs; Descendants: Offspring)

Chapter 23

1. Woe to the shepherds who destroy and scatter my flock, declares the LORD. (Shepherds: Leaders; Scatter: Disperse) 2. This is what the LORD, the God of Israel, says to the shepherds who are supposed to care for my people: You have scattered my sheep, driven them away, and failed to tend to them. I will bring the consequences of your actions upon you, declares the LORD. (Tend: Care; Consequences: Punishment) 3. But I will gather the remnants of my people from all the nations where I have scattered them, and I will bring them back to their own pasture, where they will thrive and multiply. (Remnants: Survivors; Thrive: Flourish) 4. I will appoint new shepherds who will care for them, and they will no longer be afraid or disheartened. None will go hungry, declares the LORD. (Appoint: Place; Disheartened: Discouraged) 5. The days are coming, says the LORD, when I will raise up a righteous descendant of David. A king will reign wisely, bringing justice and righteousness to the land. (Descendant: Offspring; Reign: Rule) 6. In his reign, Judah will be saved, and Israel will live in peace. His name will be called, "The LORD Our Righteousness." (Saved: Delivered; Peace: Safety) 7. The time will come, says the LORD, when they will no longer speak of the LORD who brought Israel out of Egypt. (Speak: Declare) 8. Instead, they will say, "The LORD lives, who brought up the descendants of Israel from the north and from all the nations where He had driven them. They will live in their own land." (Descendants: Offspring; Driven: Exiled) 9. My heart is broken because of the prophets; my bones tremble. I am like a drunkard, overcome with grief because of the LORD and His holy words. (Overcome: Weakened; Grief: Sorrow) 10. The land is full of adulterers, and the curse of swearing has made it mourn. The fruitful fields are withered, and their paths are corrupt, their actions evil.(Adulterers: Cheaters; Withered: Dried up; Corrupt: Wicked) 11. Both prophets and priests are corrupt, and even in my house, I find their wickedness, says the LORD. (Corrupt: Unholy; Wickedness: Evil) 12. Because of this, their paths will be slippery, and they will stumble in the darkness. I will bring disaster upon them—the year of their punishment, says the LORD. (Slippery: Perilous; Punishment: Judgment) 13. I have seen the folly of the prophets of Samaria; they prophesied in the name of Baal, leading Israel astray. (Folly: Foolishness; Baal: Idol) 14. I have also seen the wickedness of the prophets in Jerusalem: they commit adultery, live in lies, and support evildoers, causing no one to turn away from their wickedness. They are like Sodom and its people like Gomorrah, says the LORD. (Wickedness: Sin; Adultery: Unfaithfulness; Evildoers: Wrongdoers) 15. Therefore, the LORD of Hosts says, I will feed them with bitterness and make them drink the poison of their own actions. The profaneness of the prophets of Jerusalem has spread throughout the land. (Bitterness: Wormwood; Poison: Gall) 16. The LORD says, Do not listen to the words of these prophets, for they speak delusion. They follow their own imagination, not the words of the LORD. (Delusion: Deception; Imagination: Desire) 17. They say to those who despise me, "The LORD says you will have peace," and to those who follow their own evil desires, "No harm will come to you." (Despise: Reject; Harm: Evil) 18. Who has truly stood in the counsel of the LORD and heard His word? Who has paid attention to it and listened? (Counsel: Guidance; Attention: Heeded) 19. Look, a great storm from the LORD has gone out in wrath, a violent storm that will fall on the wicked. (Wrath: Anger; Violent: Fierce) 20. The LORD's anger will not be turned back until He has fully executed His judgment. In the latter days, you will understand this perfectly. (Executed: Fulfilled; Latter days: Future) 21. I have not sent these prophets, yet they run with their messages. I have not spoken to them, yet they prophesy. (Run: Act hastily; Prophesy: Predict) 22. If they had stood in My counsel, they would have turned my people from their evil ways and deeds. (Counsel: Guidance; Turned: Repented) 23. Am I only a God near at hand, says the LORD, and not a God far away? (Near: Close; Far away: Distant) 24. Can anyone hide from Me in secret places? Do I not fill heaven and earth? says the LORD. (Hide: Escape; Fill: Occupy) 25. I have heard what the prophets are saying, those who prophesy lies in My name, claiming, "I had a dream! I had a dream!" (Prophesy: Predict; Lies: Falsehoods) 26. How long will these deceitful prophets continue to deceive? They are prophets of their own deceitful hearts. (Deceitful: Dishonest) 27. They want to make My people forget My name through their false dreams. They tell these lies as their ancestors turned to Baal. (Forget: Neglect; Lies: Falsehoods) 28. If a prophet has a dream, let him tell it. But if he has My word, let him speak it faithfully. What is the chaff to the wheat? says the LORD. (Chaff: Worthless; Wheat: Valuable) 29. Is not My word like a fire, declares the LORD, and like a hammer that breaks the rock to pieces? (Fire: Powerful; Hammer: Forceful) 30. Therefore, I am against the prophets who steal My words from one another. (Steal: Take unlawfully; Words: Messages) 31. I am against the prophets who use their tongues to declare, "The LORD says." (Declare: Proclaim; Tongues: Words) 32. I am against those who prophesy false dreams, leading My people astray with their lies and trivialities. I did not send them, and they will not benefit the people at all, says the LORD. (False: Untrue; Trivialities: Lightness; Benefit: Help) 33. When the people, prophet, or priest ask you, "What is the burden of the LORD?" you will answer, "What burden? I will forsake you," says the LORD. (Forsake: Abandon) 34. If anyone, prophet, priest, or people, says, "The burden of the LORD," I will punish that person and his household. (Punish: Discipline) 35. Each person should ask his neighbor or brother, "What has the LORD answered?" or "What has the LORD spoken?" (Answered: Responded; Spoken: Said) 36. You will no longer mention the burden of the LORD. Each person's word will be his own burden, for you have perverted the words of the living God, the LORD of Hosts. (Perverted: Distorted;) 37. Ask the prophet, "What has the LORD answered you? What has the LORD spoken?" (Answered: Responded; Spoken: Said) 38. But because you say, "The burden of the LORD," this is what the LORD says: Since you use this phrase, "The burden of the LORD," I will tell you, you shall no longer say it. (Use: Say) 39. Therefore, I will utterly forget you, forsake you, and the city I gave you and your ancestors. I will cast you out of My presence. (Forget: Abandon; Cast: Throw) 40. I will bring an everlasting disgrace upon you, a perpetual shame that will never be forgotten. (Everlasting: Unending; Perpetual: Constant)

Chapter 24

1. The LORD showed me a vision: Two baskets of figs were placed in front of the LORD's temple, following the time when King Nebuchadnezzar of Babylon had carried away Jeconiah, the son of Jehoiakim, king of Judah, along with the leaders, craftsmen, and

blacksmiths from Jerusalem to Babylon. (Vision: Revelation; Carried away: Taken captive) **2.** One basket contained excellent figs, similar to the first fruits of the harvest, while the other had figs that were so spoiled they were inedible. (Excellent: Good; Inedible: Rotten) **3.** Then the LORD asked me, "Jeremiah, what do you see?" I replied, "I see figs: the good ones are very good, but the bad ones are so bad they cannot be eaten." (Replied: Answered; Bad: Spoiled) **4.** The word of the LORD came to me again, saying: **5.** "This is what the LORD, the God of Israel, says: Just as these good figs represent the exiles of Judah whom I have sent to the land of Babylon, so I will take care of them for their own good." (Exiles: Captives; Take care: Bless) **6.** "I will look after them for their benefit and will eventually return them to this land. I will rebuild them and not destroy them. I will plant them, and they will not be uprooted." (Benefit: Welfare; Rebuild: Restore) **7.** "I will give them a heart to know that I am the LORD. They will truly become my people, and I will be their God. They will return to me with all their hearts." (Return: Repent) **8.** "But the spoiled figs, which are too bad to be eaten, represent King Zedekiah of Judah, his officials, and the people of Jerusalem who remain in the land, as well as those who have gone to Egypt." (Spoiled: Rotten; Remain: Stay) **9.** "I will scatter them among the nations, where they will bring disgrace. They will be ridiculed, mocked, and cursed wherever I send them." (Scatter: Disperse; Ridiculed: Shamed; Cursed: Disgraced) **10.** "I will bring destruction upon them through sword, famine, and plague, and they will be completely wiped out from the land I gave to them and their ancestors." (Wiped out: Destroyed; Destruction: Judgment)

Chapter 25

1. The word of the Lord came to Jeremiah in the fourth year of King Jehoiakim, son of Josiah, and in the first year of King Nebuchadnezzar of Babylon. (Jehoiakim: a king of Judah; Nebuchadnezzar: a Babylonian king) **2.** Jeremiah spoke to all the people of Judah and Jerusalem, declaring: (declaring: proclaiming) **3.** From the thirteenth year of King Josiah until today, the word of the Lord has come to me, but you have not listened, despite my persistent warnings. (persistent: ongoing) **4.** The Lord sent His prophets, rising early to speak to you, but you refused to listen. (refused: declined, rejected) **5.** They urged you to turn from your evil ways and stay in the land God gave you, but you ignored them. (urged: strongly advised) **6.** Do not follow other gods, for I will not harm you if you do not provoke me. (provoke: stir up anger) **7.** Yet you have not listened to me, and you have made me angry with your actions. (actions: deeds, behaviors) **8.** Therefore, because you refused my words, **9.** I will bring all the families of the north, led by Nebuchadnezzar, my servant, to destroy this land and its people. (servant: one who serves, often with authority) **10.** The sound of joy and celebration will be gone; this land will become desolate. (desolate: abandoned, empty) **11.** The land will be a wasteland for seventy years, and these nations will serve Babylon. (Wasteland: barren, empty place) **12.** After seventy years, I will punish Babylon and its king for their sins, making their land desolate forever. (Punish: inflict a penalty) **13.** I will bring to pass all the prophecies written in this book, including the judgment on all the nations. (prophecies: predictions, divine messages) **14.** Many nations and kings will be punished for what they have done, as I repay them for their actions. (repay: give back in kind) **15.** The Lord told me to give all the nations a cup of His wrath to drink. (wrath: fury) **16.** They will be shaken and mad because of the sword I will send among them. (shaken: disturbed, troubled) **17.** I made the nations drink the cup, as the Lord commanded. **18.** Jerusalem and Judah, their kings, and leaders, will become a desolation, as they are today. (desolation: complete destruction) **19.** Egypt, its rulers, and its people will also drink the cup of judgment. **20.** And the other nations—Uz, Philistia, and many others—will suffer too. (Philistia: a region along the Mediterranean coast) **21.** Edom, Moab, and Ammon will face judgment. **22.** So will the kings of Tyre, Sidon, and the distant lands across the seas. (Tyre: an ancient Phoenician city; Sidon: another Phoenician city) **23.** The kings of Arabia and the remote desert peoples will also drink it. **24.** The kings of Elam, Media, and the northern lands will drink too. (Elam: an ancient kingdom in the east; Media: an ancient empire in the north) **25.** All the kings of the world will be judged, including the king of Sheshach. (Sheshach: a cryptic name for Babylon, used to symbolize its downfall) **26.** Tell them, "Drink the cup, and suffer; you will not escape, for the sword will follow you." (escape: flee, avoid) **27.** If they refuse, tell them they will certainly drink it. **28.** For I will bring disaster on the city called by my name—should you go unpunished? No, you will be punished too. (disaster: calamity) **29.** I will send a sword upon all the inhabitants of the earth. **30.** The Lord will roar from heaven, shaking the earth, and calling for judgment on all nations. (roar: shout loudly, as a lion does) **31.** The cry of judgment will reach the ends of the earth as the Lord contends with the wicked. (contends: argues, disputes) **32.** A great whirlwind of destruction will spread from nation to nation. (whirlwind: a violent, rotating wind; a metaphor for upheaval) **33.** The slain of the Lord will be from one end of the earth to the other, left unburied, and treated like dung. (slain: killed) **34.** Shepherds, lament your fate, for the time of your destruction has come. (lament: mourn, express grief) **35.** The leaders of the flock will have no escape. (leaders: heads, rulers) **36.** A cry of distress will rise from the leaders, for the Lord has destroyed their pasture. (pasture: place of feeding or care) **37.** The peaceful homes are gone, destroyed by the Lord's fierce anger. (fierce: intense, violent) **38.** Like a lion leaving its den, the Lord has abandoned His land to its enemies. (den: lair, home of a lion)

Chapter 26

1. At the beginning of King Jehoiakim's reign, the Lord gave Jeremiah this message: (Jehoiakim: king of Judah) **2.** "Stand in the court of the Lord's house and speak to all the people of Judah who come to worship, delivering all the words I command you. Do not leave out a single word." (court: area outside the temple; command: order) **3.** "Perhaps they will listen, turn from their evil ways, and I will forgive the evil I planned to bring upon them because of their actions." (forgive: pardon, stop punishment) **4.** "But if you refuse to listen and obey my law, **5.** and ignore the words of my prophets, whom I sent early to warn you, **6.** then I will make this house like Shiloh and this city a curse to all the nations." (Shiloh: a former religious center, now destroyed; curse: divine punishment) **7.** The priests, prophets, and all the people heard Jeremiah speak these words in the Lord's house. **8.** When Jeremiah finished speaking, they took him and said, "You must die!" (finished: completed) **9.** "Why have you prophesied in the Lord's name, saying this house will be destroyed like Shiloh, and the city will become desolate?" The people gathered against Jeremiah. (desolate: empty, destroyed) **10.** When the princes of Judah heard this, they came from the king's palace and sat at the new gate of the Lord's house. (princes: leaders, rulers) **11.** The priests and prophets told the princes and people, "This man deserves to die because he has prophesied against this city." **12.** Jeremiah responded, "The Lord sent me to speak these words to you. **13.** Now, change your ways and obey the Lord, and He will relent from the judgment He has pronounced against you." (relent: withdraw, change His mind) **14.** "As for me, I am in your hands. Do as you see fit." **15.** "But know this: if you kill me, you will bring innocent blood upon yourselves and this city, for the Lord has truly sent me to speak these words." (innocent: not guilty) **16.** The princes and people said to the priests and prophets, "This man is not worthy to die, for he has spoken to us in the name of the Lord." **17.** Then some elders of the land spoke up, saying: (elders: senior leaders) **18.** "Micah of Moresheth prophesied in the days of King Hezekiah, saying that Zion would be plowed like a field and Jerusalem would become a heap of ruins. **19.** Did King Hezekiah put him to death? No, he feared the Lord, prayed for mercy, and the Lord spared Judah from destruction. If we kill this man, we may bring great harm upon ourselves." (plowed: made into farmland, destroyed) **20.** There was also a prophet named Urijah, who spoke against this city and land like Jeremiah. 21. When King Jehoiakim and his men heard his prophecy, they sought to kill him. Urijah fled to Egypt, 22. but Jehoiakim sent men to bring him back, 23. and they killed him with a sword, burying his body in a common grave. (common: belonging to the general public) 24. However, the hand of Ahikam, son of Shaphan, was with Jeremiah, so they did not give him over to the people to be killed. (hand: influence, support)

Chapter 27

1. In the early days of King Jehoiakim's reign, the Lord spoke to Jeremiah, saying, (Reign: rule) 2. "Make bonds and yokes, and place them on your neck," (Bonds: restraints; Yokes: burden) 3. "Send them to the kings of Edom, Moab, Ammon, Tyre, and Sidon by the messengers who come to King Zedekiah of Judah," (Messengers: couriers) 4. "And tell them to say, 'This is what the Lord of hosts, the God of Israel, says:'" (Hosts: armies) 5. "I created the earth, mankind, and animals by my great power, and I gave them to whom I chose." (Mankind: humans) 6. "Now, I have given all these lands into the hands of Nebuchadnezzar, king of Babylon, my servant, and I gave him the beasts of the field to serve him." (Beasts: animals) 7. "All nations will serve him, his son, and his grandson, until his time ends. Then many nations and mighty kings will rise up against him." (Mighty: powerful; Rise up: rebel) 8. "But any nation that refuses to serve Nebuchadnezzar and refuses to submit to his yoke will be punished by the sword, famine, and disease, until I destroy them." (Submit: yield; Yoke: control) 9. "Do not listen to your prophets, diviners, dreamers, enchanters, or sorcerers who tell you not to serve Babylon's king." (Diviners: fortune-tellers; Enchanters: magicians; Sorcerers: witches) 10. "They are lying to you, trying to lead you away from your land and bring about your destruction." (Lying: deceiving; Destruction: ruin) 11. "But nations that submit to the yoke of Babylon and serve him will remain in their own land, till it, and live there." (Submit: obey; Yoke: burden) 12. "I spoke to Zedekiah, king of Judah, saying, 'Submit to the king of Babylon, serve him, and live.'" (Submit: obey) 13. "Why should you die, you and your people, by sword, famine, and disease, as the Lord has declared against nations who refuse Babylon's rule?" (Famine: hunger; Disease: illness) 14. "Do not listen to the false prophets who say, 'You will not serve the king of Babylon.' They are lying." (False: untrue; Lying: deceiving) 15. "I did not send them, says the Lord. They lie in my name to drive you out and bring about your destruction." (Send: commission; Lie: deceive) 16. "I also spoke to the priests and the people: 'Do not listen to the false prophets who say the sacred vessels will soon be returned from Babylon. They are lying.'" (Priests: clergy; Vessels: sacred items) 17. "Do not listen to them. Serve the king of Babylon, and live. Why should this city be destroyed?" (Destroyed: ruined) 18. "But if they are true prophets, let them pray to the Lord of hosts for the vessels in the Lord's house, the king's house, and in Jerusalem, that they not go to Babylon." (True: genuine; Intercession: prayer) 19. "Concerning the pillars, the sea, the bases, and the remaining vessels in this city," (Pillars: columns; Sea: basin; Bases: foundations) 20. "Which Nebuchadnezzar did not take when he took Jeconiah, son of Jehoiakim, and the nobles of Judah into captivity," (Nobles: aristocrats; Captivity: imprisonment) 21. "The Lord says concerning these vessels: they will be taken to Babylon."
(Taken: carried) 22. "They will remain there until the day I visit them, says the Lord, and then I will bring them back and restore them to this place." (Visit: come; Restore: return)

Chapter 28

1. In the fourth year of Zedekiah's reign, in the fifth month, Hananiah the prophet from Gibeon spoke to me in the LORD's house, in front of the priests and people, saying: (Reign: Period of rule or government; Gibeon: A place in ancient Israel.) 2. "The LORD of hosts, the God of Israel, declares: I have broken the yoke of the king of Babylon. (Hosts: Armies or heavenly beings; Yoke: A device used to harness animals, here symbolizing oppression or control.) 3. In two years, I will bring back all the sacred objects that King Nebuchadnezzar took to Babylon. (Sacred: Holy or religious; Nebuchadnezzar: The king of Babylon.) 4. I will also return King Jeconiah and all Judah's exiles from Babylon." (Exiles: People who have been forced to leave their homeland.) 5. Then I, the prophet Jeremiah, responded to Hananiah before the priests and the people, saying: (Response: A reply or answer.) 6. "Amen! May the LORD fulfill your prophecy and restore the sacred vessels and captives." (Fulfill: To complete or carry out; Prophecy: A prediction or message from God; Vessels: Sacred items or containers used in worship.) 7. "But listen to what I say to you and the people. (Listen: Pay attention to.) 8. Prophets before us prophesied wars, disasters, and plagues. (Plagues: Widespread diseases or calamities.) 9. A prophet who speaks of peace will be known when his words come true—then we will know the LORD truly sent him." (Peace: A state of calm or harmony; Known: Recognized or acknowledged.) 10. Hananiah then took the yoke from my neck and broke it. (Took: Seized or removed.) 11. He said, "Thus says the LORD: I will break the yoke of Babylon from the neck of all nations in two years." Then I went on my way. (Thus: In this way; Neck: The part of the body connecting the head and torso.) 12. After Hananiah broke the yoke, the LORD spoke to me again: (Again: Once more.) 13. "Tell Hananiah: You have broken wooden yokes, but you will now make iron yokes for them. (Wooden: Made of wood; Iron: A strong, metallic element.) 14. I have placed an iron yoke on these nations to serve Nebuchadnezzar, and they will serve him." (Serve: To work for or obey.) 15. "Hananiah, you are lying. The LORD has not sent you. You are misleading the people." (Lying: Saying something false; Misleading: Causing someone to believe something wrong.) 16. "Because of this, you will die this year for leading people to rebel against the LORD." (Rebel: To resist or oppose authority.) 17. Hananiah died in the seventh month of the same year. (Seventh: The number after sixth.)

Chapter 29

1. These are the words of the letter that the prophet Jeremiah sent from Jerusalem to the surviving elders, priests, prophets, and all the people whom King Nebuchadnezzar had taken from Jerusalem to Babylon. (Surviving: Remaining) 2. This was after King Jeconiah, the queen, the eunuchs, the leaders of Judah and Jerusalem, and the craftsmen had left Jerusalem. (Eunuchs: Castrates; Craftsmen: Artisans) 3. The letter was sent by Elasah, the son of Shaphan, and Gemariah, the son of Hilkiah, whom King Zedekiah of Judah had sent to Nebuchadnezzar in Babylon. (Sent: Delivered) 4. The LORD of armies, the God of Israel, says to all the exiles whom I caused to be carried away from Jerusalem to Babylon: (Exiles: Deportees) 5. "Build homes and live in them. Plant gardens and enjoy the fruit of your labor." (Labor: Work) 6. "Take wives, have children, and let your sons marry and your daughters be married, so your families may grow, not decrease." (Decrease: Shrink) 7. "Seek the well-being of the city where I have sent you into exile, and pray for its prosperity, for when it prospers, you will prosper."(Well-being: Welfare; Prosperity: Success) 8. "Do not let the false prophets or dreamers in your midst deceive you. Do not listen to their dreams." (Deceive: Mislead) 9. "They are prophesying lies in my name; I have not sent them, says the LORD." (Prophesy: Predict) 10. "After seventy years have passed in Babylon, I will visit you and keep my promise to bring you back to your land." (Visit: Aid) 11. "For I know the plans I have for you, declares the LORD, plans for your peace and well-being, not for harm, to give you a future full of hope." (Plans: Intentions; Well-being: Health) 12. "Then you will call upon me, and I will listen to you." (Call: Pray) 13. "You will search for me and find me when you seek me with all your heart." (Seek: Search) 14. "I will be found by you, declares the LORD, and I will end your exile. I will gather you from all the places where I have scattered you and bring you back to the land from which I exiled you." (Exile: Banishment; Scattered: Dispersed) 15. "Because you have said, 'The LORD has raised up prophets for us in Babylon,'" (Raised: Appointed) 16. "Know that the

LORD of the king on David's throne, and of all the people living in this city, says:" (Throne: Seat) **17.** "I will send the sword, famine, and plague upon them, and they will become like bad figs, too spoiled to eat." (Sword: Weapon; Famine: Starvation; Plague: Disease) **18.** "I will pursue them with the sword, famine, and plague, and scatter them among all the kingdoms of the earth, where they will be a disgrace, a horror, and a ridicule among the nations." (Pursue: Chase; Ridicule: Mockery) **19.** "Because they did not listen to my words, which I sent to them by my servants the prophets, whom I sent early and often, but they refused to listen." (Servants: Messengers) **20.** "Therefore, hear the word of the LORD, all you exiles whom I have sent from Jerusalem to Babylon:" (Hear: Listen) **21.** "Thus says the LORD of armies, the God of Israel, concerning Ahab son of Kolaiah and Zedekiah son of Maaseiah, who prophesy lies to you in my name: I will give them into the hand of King Nebuchadnezzar of Babylon, and he will kill them before your eyes." (Give: Deliver; Slay: Kill) **22.** "They will become a curse for all the exiles in Babylon, saying, 'May the LORD treat you like Ahab and Zedekiah, whom the king of Babylon roasted in the fire.'" (Curse: Malediction; Roasted: Burned) **23.** "Because they have done vile deeds in Israel, committed adultery with their neighbors' wives, and spoken lies in my name, which I did not command them to say." (Vile: Wicked; Adultery: Infidelity) **24.** "Now speak to Shemaiah the Nehelamite, saying:" (Nehelamite: Distant group) **25.** "This is what the LORD of armies, the God of Israel says: Because you have sent letters in your name to all the people in Jerusalem, and to Zephaniah the priest, saying:" (Zephaniah: Priest) **26.** "The LORD has made you priest in place of Jehoiada, and you are to arrest anyone who falsely claims to be a prophet." (Arrest: Detain) **27.** "Why have you not rebuked Jeremiah of Anathoth, who claims to be a prophet to you?" (Rebuked: Scolded) **28.** "He has sent us a letter saying, 'This exile will be long, so build houses and plant gardens.'" (Exile: Banishment; Gardens: Cultivated plots) **29.** "And Zephaniah the priest read this letter to Jeremiah the prophet." (Read: Recite) **30.** "Then the word of the LORD came to Jeremiah:" (Word: Message) **31.** "Send to all the exiles, saying, 'Thus says the LORD concerning Shemaiah the Nehelamite: Because he prophesied to you and I did not send him, and has caused you to trust in lies:" (Prophesied: Predicted; Lies: Falsehoods) **32.** "I will punish Shemaiah and his descendants. He will have no one left among the people, nor will he see the good that I will bring to my people, for he has led them into rebellion against the LORD.'" (Descendants: Offspring; Rebellion: Defiance)

Chapter 30

1. This is the word that came to Jeremiah from the LORD: (Word: Message) **2.** "The LORD, the God of Israel, commands you: Write down everything I have told you in a book." (Told: Spoke; Command: Instruct) **3.** "A time is coming, says the LORD, when I will restore my people Israel and Judah. I will bring them back to the land I gave to their forefathers, and they will inherit it once again." (Restore: Bring back; Inherit: Possess) **4.** These are the words the LORD spoke concerning the fate of Israel and Judah.(Fate: Destiny; Concerning: Regarding) **5.** "The LORD declares: We hear a sound of fear, a cry of distress, not peace." (Distress: Suffering; Peace: Calm) **6.** "Ask yourselves: Can a man give birth? Why do I see men holding their waists as though in labor, with their faces pale?" (Labor: Childbirth; Pale: Colorless) **7.** "Alas! That day is so dreadful, unlike any other. It is a time of Jacob's distress, but he will be saved from it." (Dreadful: Terrifying; Distress: Trouble) **8.** "In that day, says the LORD, I will break the yoke off your neck and shatter the chains that bind you. No foreign nations will oppress you any longer." (Yoke: Burden; Chains: Bonds) **9.** "Instead, you will serve the LORD your God and David, the king I will raise up for you." (Serve: Worship) **10.** "Do not fear, O Jacob, says the LORD. Do not be discouraged, Israel. I will bring you back from the lands where you have been scattered. Jacob will return in peace, and no one will cause him to fear." (Fear: Be afraid; Discouraged: Dismayed; Cause: Make) **11.** "I am with you to save you, declares the LORD. Though I will bring an end to all the nations where I have scattered you, I will not bring an end to you. I will correct you in measure, but I will not leave you completely unpunished." (Correct: Discipline; Measure: Limit) **12.** "For the LORD says: Your wound is incurable, and your injury is deep." (Incurable: Untreatable; Deep: Severe) **13.** "No one is here to defend you, to bind up your wounds. There is no one to heal you." (Defend: Plead; Bind up: Heal) **14.** "All your former allies have forsaken you. They do not seek you anymore. I have struck you with the wound of an enemy, as punishment for the multitude of your sins." (Forsaken: Forgotten; Punishment: Judgment) **15.** "Why do you cry over your pain? Your sorrow cannot be healed because your sins have multiplied. I have done this because of your wickedness." (Cry: Weep; Healed: Cured; Wickedness: Sinfulness) **16.** "All who devour you will themselves be devoured. All your enemies will go into captivity. Those who take what belongs to you will be plundered, and those who attack you will be attacked." (Devour: Consume; Plundered: Looted; Attack: Prey) **17.** "I will restore your health and heal your wounds, says the LORD, because they called you an outcast, saying, 'This is Zion, whom no one seeks.'" (Restore: Bring back; Outcast: Exile) **18.** "The LORD says: I will bring back the tents of Jacob and have mercy on his dwelling places. The city will be rebuilt on its ruins, and the palace will remain as it was." (Mercy: Compassion; Ruins: Wreckage) **19.** "Songs of thanksgiving and joy will come from them. I will multiply them, and they will not be few. I will also honor them, and they will not be small." (Multiply: Increase; Honor: Glorify) **20.** "Their children will be as they were in the past, and their community will be established before me. I will punish those who oppress them." (Community: Congregation; Oppress: Afflict) **21.** "Their leaders will come from among them, and their ruler will arise from their own people. I will bring him near, and he will approach me. For who is this who has devoted himself to approach me?" says the LORD. (Leaders: Rulers; Devoted: Committed) **22.** "You will be my people, and I will be your God." **23.** "The whirlwind of the LORD will go forth with fury, a continuing storm. It will strike the wicked with pain." (Whirlwind: Storm; Fury: Anger) **24.** "The fierce anger of the LORD will not be turned back until he has accomplished his purpose. In the last days, you will understand it."(Accomplished: Fulfilled; Last: Final)

Chapter 31

1. "At that time," declares the LORD, "I will be the God of all Israel's families, and they will be My people." (families: descendants or households) **2.** This is what the LORD says: "Those who survived the sword found favor in the wilderness; I gave rest to Israel." (favor: grace or blessing) **3.** The LORD appeared long ago, saying, "I have loved you with an everlasting love; I have drawn you with kindness." (everlasting: eternal; drawn: brought close) **4.** "I will rebuild you, Israel, and you will be restored. You will once again dance joyfully with tambourines." (tambourines: small drums) **5.** "You will plant vineyards on Samaria's mountains, and those who plant will enjoy the fruit freely." (vineyards: grape gardens) **6.** The day will come when watchmen on Ephraim's hills will call, "Let us go to Zion to worship the LORD." (Zion: symbolic name for Jerusalem or God's holy place) **7.** The LORD says, "Sing with joy for Jacob, shout for Israel, and declare: 'Save Your people, O LORD, the remnant of Israel.'" (remnant: a small remaining group) **8.** "I will bring them from the north and gather them from distant lands—among them the blind, the lame, pregnant women, and those in labor—a great assembly will return." (assembly: group or gathering) **9.** "They will come with tears and prayers. I will lead them beside streams of water on a smooth path. I am Israel's Father, and Ephraim is My firstborn." (firstborn: one with special status or privilege) **10.** "Hear the LORD's word, nations, and proclaim it afar: The One who scattered Israel will gather them and care for them as a shepherd does his flock." (shepherd: caretaker of sheep) **11.** The LORD has redeemed Jacob and freed him from one stronger than he. (redeemed: saved or delivered) **12.** They will sing joyfully in Zion and rejoice in the LORD's blessings: grain, wine, oil, flocks, and herds. Their souls will flourish like a watered garden, and they will grieve no more. (flourish: thrive) **13.** "The young women will dance with joy, and the young and old will celebrate together. I will turn their sorrow into joy and comfort them." (sorrow: sadness) **14.** "I will satisfy the priests with abundance, and My people will be filled with My goodness," declares the LORD. (abundance: plenty) **15.** The LORD says, "A voice is heard in Ramah—Rachel weeping for her children, refusing comfort because they are gone." (weeping: crying) **16.** The LORD says, "Hold back your tears, for your work will be rewarded, and your children will return from the enemy's land." (rewarded: repaid or compensated) **17.** "There is hope for your future," declares the LORD. "Your children will return to their homeland." (hope: expectation or assurance) **18.** "I have heard Ephraim lamenting, 'You disciplined me, and I was corrected, like an untrained ox. Restore me, LORD, for You are my God.'" (lamenting: expressing sorrow) **19.** "After I turned back, I repented and felt shame for the sins of my youth." (repented: showed regret for wrongdoing) **20.** The LORD says, "Is Ephraim My dear son? Though I spoke against him, I still remember him and have compassion on him." (compassion: deep sympathy) **21.** "Mark the road signs and set your heart on the path to return, O Israel." (path: direction or way) **22.** "How long will you wander, O rebellious daughter? The LORD has created something new: a woman will protect a man." (rebellious: disobedient) **23.** This is what the LORD Almighty, the God of Israel, says: "Once again in Judah and its cities, people will say, 'The LORD bless you, O righteous home, O holy mountain.'" (righteous: morally right) **24.** Farmers and shepherds will live in Judah's cities. (shepherds: caretakers of sheep) **25.** "I will refresh the weary soul and fill the sorrowful soul," declares the LORD. (refresh: revive or renew) **26.** After this, I awoke and found my sleep to be peaceful. (peaceful: calm or restful) **27.** The days are coming," says the LORD, "when I will establish people and animals in Israel and Judah." **28.** "Just as I oversaw their destruction, I will now watch over their rebuilding and growth," declares the LORD. (oversaw: supervised) **29.** In those days, people will no longer say, "The fathers ate sour grapes, and the children's teeth were set on edge." (sour grapes: bitter or unpleasant outcomes) **30.** "Each person will die for their own sin; those who eat sour grapes will face the consequences themselves." (sin: wrongdoing) **31.** "The days are coming," declares the LORD, "when I will establish a new covenant with Israel and Judah." (covenant: agreement or promise) **32.** "It will not be like the covenant I made with their ancestors when I led them out of Egypt, which they broke," declares the LORD. (ancestors: forefathers) **33.** "This is the covenant I will make: I will write My law in their hearts and be their God, and they will be My people." (hearts: innermost thoughts) **34.** "They will no longer need to teach each other about Me, for all will know Me. I will forgive their sins and forget their wrongdoing." (forgive: pardon) **35.** The LORD, who sets the sun, moon, and stars in their courses and controls the sea's waves, is His name. (courses: paths or movements) **36.** "If these laws of nature vanish, only then will Israel cease to be My nation," declares the LORD. (vanish: disappear) **37.** The LORD says, "If the heavens can be measured or the earth's foundations fully explored, only then will I reject Israel for all they've done." (foundations: base or core) **38.** "The days are coming," declares the LORD, "when the city will be rebuilt for the LORD from Hananeel's Tower to the Corner Gate." (rebuilt: constructed again) **39.** The boundary line will extend from Gareb Hill to Goath. (boundary: dividing line) **40.** "The entire valley of ashes and all the fields to Kidron Brook will be holy to the LORD and never uprooted or destroyed again." (holy: sacred)

Chapter 32

1. The message from the LORD came to Jeremiah during the tenth year of King Zedekiah of Judah, which was also the eighteenth year of King Nebuchadnezzar of Babylon. (Zedekiah: last king of Judah, Nebuchadnezzar: king of Babylon) **2.** At that time, the Babylonian army had surrounded Jerusalem, and Jeremiah the prophet was imprisoned in the court of the king's palace. (Jerusalem: capital of Judah, Babylon: empire) **3.** King Zedekiah had imprisoned Jeremiah, asking, "Why are you prophesying that the LORD will hand this city over to the king of Babylon, and it will fall?" (Zedekiah: last king of Judah) **4.** Zedekiah would not escape the Babylonians but would be captured and face Nebuchadnezzar, meeting him eye to eye. **5.** Zedekiah would be taken to Babylon, where he would remain until God would visit him, though the people would not prevail against the Babylonians in battle. (Babylon: empire) **6.** Then the LORD spoke to me, saying, **7.** "Hanameel, the son of your uncle Shallum, will come to you, asking you to buy his field in Anathoth. You have the right to redeem it." (Hanameel: Jeremiah's cousin, Anathoth: town in Benjamin) **8.** Just as the LORD said, Hanameel came to me in the prison courtyard and offered to sell me his field in Anathoth. He said, "The right of redemption belongs to you, so buy it for yourself." Then I knew this was the word of the LORD. **9.** I bought the field from Hanameel in Anathoth and paid him seventeen shekels of silver. (Shekels: currency) **10.** I signed the deed, sealed it, and had witnesses present as I weighed out the silver for him. (Deed: legal contract) **11.** I took both the sealed and open copies of the purchase deed. (Sealed deed: formal agreement) **12.** I gave the purchase documents to Baruch, the son of Neriah, in front of the witnesses, and all the people who were in the court of the prison. (Baruch: Jeremiah's scribe) **13.** I instructed Baruch before them all, saying, (Baruch: Jeremiah's scribe) **14.** "Thus says the LORD of hosts, the God of Israel: 'Take these deeds, both sealed and open, and place them in an earthen jar, so they may remain for many years.'" (LORD of hosts: title for God) **15.** "For the LORD says: 'Houses, fields, and vineyards will again be bought in this land.'" (LORD of hosts: title for God) **16.** After I gave Baruch the deeds, I prayed to the LORD, saying, (Deeds: legal papers) **17.** "Ah, Sovereign LORD, you made the heavens and earth by your great power; nothing is impossible for you." (Sovereign LORD: title for God) **18.** "You show love to thousands and repay the sins of the fathers to their children. The great and mighty God, the LORD of hosts, is his name." (LORD of hosts: title for God) **19.** "You are great in wisdom and mighty in deeds; your eyes are open to all the ways of men, rewarding each person according to their actions." (Great in counsel: wise in decisions) **20.** "You performed wonders in Egypt, Israel, and other nations, and made a name for yourself that endures to this day." (Egypt: ancient kingdom) **21.** "You brought Israel out of Egypt with mighty signs and wonders, with an outstretched arm and great terror." **22.** "You gave them this land, a land flowing with milk and honey, as you promised their forefathers." (Land flowing with milk and honey: abundant land) **23.** "They entered and possessed it, but they did not listen to your voice or follow your laws. As a result, you brought all this disaster upon them." (Law: God's commands) **24.** "Now, the siege mounts have come to the city, and it has been handed over to the Babylonians, because of sword, famine, and pestilence. What you foretold has come true, and you see it happening." (Chaldeans: Babylonians, Siege mounts: large earthen ramps) **25.** "And you instructed me, 'Buy the field for money and get witnesses,' for the city has already fallen to the Chaldeans." (Chaldeans: Babylonians) **26.** Then the LORD spoke to me again, saying, (Word of the LORD: divine message) **27.** "I am the LORD, the God of all flesh. Is anything too difficult for me?" (LORD of all flesh: Creator of all people) **28.** "I will hand this city over to the Babylonians and their king, Nebuchadnezzar, and they will capture it." (Nebuchadnezzar: king of Babylon) **29.** "The Chaldeans will set fire to the city and burn it, including the houses where they have burned incense to Baal and made offerings to other gods, provoking me to anger." (Chaldeans: Babylonians, Baal: false god) **30.** "The Israelites and Judahites have been wicked from their youth, and their actions have provoked me to anger, says the LORD." (Provoked: angered) **31.** "This city has been a source of my anger and fury since it was built, and I will remove it from my sight." **32.** "Because of the evil done by the Israelites and Judahites, including their kings, priests, prophets, and people, all of them have provoked me to anger." (Evil: sin) **33.** "They have turned their backs to me, not their faces, though I taught them early and persistently, yet they would not listen." (Back to me: rejection) **34.** "They have defiled my temple by setting up idols in it." (Idols: false gods) **35.** "They built altars to Baal in the valley of Hinnom and caused their children to pass through fire to Molech, which I never commanded." (Molech: pagan god) **36.** "Now, concerning this city, you say it will be destroyed by the sword, famine, and pestilence at the hands of Babylon **37.** "But I will gather my people from all the nations where I have driven them in my anger, and I will bring them back to this place to live in safety." **38.** "They will be my people, and I will be their God." (God: their protector) **39.** "I will give them one heart and one way, so they will fear me forever, for their good and the good of their children." (Heart: inner will) **40.** "I will make an everlasting covenant with them that I will never break. I will put my fear in their hearts so that they will never turn away from me." (Everlasting covenant: unbreakable promise) **41.** "I will rejoice over them and do them good, and I will plant them securely in this land with all my heart and soul." (Plant them securely: establish firmly) **42.** "Just as I brought great disaster upon them, I will also bring all the good I have promised them." (Disaster: punishment) **43.** "Fields will again be bought in this land, even though it is desolate and given over to the Chaldeans." (Desolate: abandoned) **44.** "Men will buy fields for money, make formal agreements, and take witnesses in the land of Benjamin, the surrounding areas of Jerusalem, and throughout Judah. I will restore their fortunes, says the LORD." (Chaldeans: Babylonians)

Chapter 33
1. The word of the LORD came to Jeremiah a second time while he was still imprisoned in the court of the palace, saying, (Jeremiah: prophet of God, imprisoned for his prophecies) **2.** "Thus says the LORD, the Creator and establisher of all things; the LORD is His name." **3.** "Call to Me, and I will answer you, revealing great and mighty things that you do not know." (Call to Me: God's invitation to prayer) **4.** "For this is what the LORD, the God of Israel, says about the houses in this city, and the houses of the kings of Judah, which are being destroyed by the siege ramps and the sword." (Chaldeans: Babylonians) **5.** "The enemy comes to fight the Babylonians, but their streets will be filled with the dead, whom I have struck down in My anger and fury, because of the wickedness of the people who have caused Me to turn My face away from this city." (Dead bodies: result of judgment) **6.** "But look, I will restore health and healing to it. I will heal them and show them the abundance of peace and truth." (Restore health: promise of restoration) **7.** "I will bring back the captives of Judah and Israel and rebuild them as they were before." (Captivity: Israel and Judah's exile) **8.** "I will cleanse them from all their sin against Me, and I will forgive all their iniquities by which they have sinned and rebelled against Me." (Cleansing: purification from sin) **9.** "It will be a name of joy, praise, and honor before all the nations of the earth, which will hear of all the good things I do for them. They will fear and tremble at the goodness and prosperity I bring upon them." (Prosperity: blessing for the people) **10.** "Again, in this place, which you say is desolate, without man or beast, and in the cities of Judah and the streets of Jerusalem, that are now empty—" (Desolate: destroyed city) **11.** "The sound of joy and gladness will be heard again—the voice of the bridegroom and the bride, the voices of those who will say, 'Give thanks to the LORD of hosts, for the LORD is good; His love endures forever.' And they will bring offerings of praise into the house of the LORD. For I will restore the fortunes of the land as they were in the past." (Praise: worship and gratitude) **12.** "Once more, in this place, which is desolate, without man or beast, and in all its cities, there will be the dwelling of shepherds and their flocks." (Shepherds: caretakers of the land) **13.** "In the cities of the mountains, the valleys, the south, and in the land of Benjamin, around Jerusalem, and in the cities of Judah, the flocks will again pass under the care of their shepherds." (Flocks: symbolizing restoration) **14.** "The days are coming," says the LORD, "when I will fulfill the good promise I made to the house of Israel and the house of Judah." (Promise: God's faithfulness to His people) **15.** "At that time, I will cause the Righteous Branch to grow from David's line. He will do what is just and right in the land." (Righteous Branch: a reference to the Messiah, Jesus) **16.** "In those days, Judah will be saved, and Jerusalem will live in safety. And this is the name by which it will be called: 'The LORD is our righteousness.'" (Judah: the southern kingdom, Jerusalem: the capital) **17.** "For this is what the LORD says: 'David will never fail to have a man sit on the throne of Israel.'" (David: the royal line) **18.** "Nor will the Levitical priests lack a man to offer burnt offerings, grain offerings, and sacrifices before Me." (Levitical priests: the priestly lineage) **19.** The word of the LORD came again to Jeremiah, saying, (Word of the LORD: divine revelation) **20.** "Thus says the LORD: If you can break My covenant of day and night, so that there is no day or night in their appointed seasons," (Covenant: agreement between God and His people) **21.** "Then My covenant with David My servant can also be broken, so that he will not have a son to sit on his throne, and My covenant with the Levites, My ministers, can be broken." (David: the kingly line, Levites: the priestly line) **22.** "As the stars of heaven cannot be numbered, nor the sand of the sea measured, so I will multiply the descendants of David My servant, and the Levites who minister to Me." (Descendants: promise of multiplication) **23.** The word of the LORD came to Jeremiah, saying, (Divine message: God's ongoing communication) **24.** " Have you not noticed what these people have spoken, saying, 'The two families the LORD chose—He has rejected them'? They have despised My people, and they no longer consider them a nation." (Rejection: the people's despair) **25.** "Thus says the LORD: If My covenant with day and night is not fixed, and I have not established the laws of heaven and earth," (Covenant: God's unbreakable promises) **26.** "Then I will reject the descendants of Jacob and David My servant, so that I will not take any of his descendants to be rulers over the descendants of Abraham, Isaac, and Jacob. For I will restore their fortunes and have mercy on them." (Reject: God's judgment would be reversed)

Chapter 34
1. The word of the LORD came to Jeremiah when King Nebuchadnezzar of Babylon, his army, and all the kingdoms under his rule attacked Jerusalem and its cities, saying: **2.** The LORD, the God of Israel, said to Jeremiah: "Go speak to Zedekiah, king of Judah, and tell him, 'I am giving this city into the hands of the king of Babylon, and he will destroy it with fire.'" **3.** "You will not escape; you will be captured and taken to Babylon. You will see the king of Babylon face to face and speak with him directly before going to Babylon." (Escape: run away, avoid capture) **4.** "But listen to the LORD's word, Zedekiah: you will not die in battle." **5.** "You will die in peace, and like your ancestors, the kings before you, people will mourn for you with burning incense." (Incense: a substance burned for its fragrance) **6.** Jeremiah spoke all these words to King Zedekiah in Jerusalem, **7.** while the Babylonian army fought against Jerusalem and the remaining cities of Judah: Lachish and Azekah, which were the last fortified cities left. (Fortified: strengthened, protected) **8.** This message came to Jeremiah after Zedekiah had made a covenant with the people of Jerusalem to proclaim liberty. (Covenant: a formal agreement) **9.** Every person was to release their Hebrew servants and maidservants, allowing them to go free. No one was to keep another Hebrew as a servant. (Servant: someone who works for another) **10.** When the people and leaders heard this, they obeyed and let their servants go free. **11.** But afterward, they reversed their decision and forced the freed servants and maidservants to return and serve them again. (Reversed: changed, turned back) **12.** Therefore, the word of the LORD came to Jeremiah, saying: **13.** "I made a covenant with your ancestors when I brought them out of

Egypt, out of slavery, saying: (Slavery: the condition of being owned by another) **14.** 'After seven years, every Hebrew slave must be freed if they've served for six years.' But your ancestors did not listen to me." **15.** "Now, you have done what is right by proclaiming liberty, and you made a covenant in my temple." **16.** "But you broke that covenant by forcing the freed servants back into servitude." (Servitude: the condition of being a servant) **17.** "Therefore, I declare liberty to you," says the LORD, "but it will be a liberty to the sword, famine, and plague. I will scatter you across all the kingdoms of the earth." (Plague: a deadly disease) **18.** "I will punish those who broke my covenant, those who did not keep their promises when they cut the calf in two and passed between its parts." (covenant: violated, broke) **19.** "The leaders of Judah, Jerusalem, the eunuchs, priests, and people who passed between the pieces of the calf will face judgment." (Eunuchs: men who were castrated, often held high office) **20.** "I will hand them over to their enemies, and their bodies will become food for birds and wild animals." **21.** "King Zedekiah and his officials will be delivered into the hands of their enemies, the Babylonian army, and they will be destroyed." **22.** "I will order the Babylonian army to return, fight against the city, capture it, and burn it. The cities of Judah will be left desolate, with no one living in them." (Desolate: empty, abandoned

Chapter 35

1. The word of the LORD came to Jeremiah during the reign of Jehoiakim, son of Josiah, king of Judah, saying: (Reign: the period during which a king rules) **2.** "Go to the Rechabites' house, speak to them, bring them to the LORD's house, and offer them wine to drink." (Rechabites: a nomadic family who followed strict traditions) **3.** So, I brought Jaazaniah, the son of Jeremiah, with his family, and all the Rechabites, (Jaazaniah: a leader among the Rechabites) **4.** Into a room in the LORD's house, near the chamber of the princes, above the room of the doorkeeper, Maaseiah. (Princes: noble or royal figures; Chamber: a room) **5.** I placed wine before them and said, "Drink the wine." (Placed: set) **6.** But they replied, "We won't drink wine, for our ancestor Jonadab, son of Rechab, commanded us not to drink wine, nor should our sons, forever." (Ancestor: forefather) **7.** "We shall not build houses, plant vineyards, or own land. We will live in tents all our days, that we may live long in the land as strangers." (Strangers: foreigners in the land) **8.** "We have obeyed our father Jonadab's command not to drink wine, nor to build homes, or own land, and to live in tents." (Obeyed: followed) **9.** "We have stayed true to his instructions all our lives, we and our children." (True: faithful) **10.** "We live in tents and follow all that Jonadab our father commanded." (Tents: portable homes) **11.** "But when Nebuchadnezzar, king of Babylon, came to attack, we fled to Jerusalem for safety from the armies of the Chaldeans and Syrians."(Fled: ran away) **12.** Then the LORD spoke to Jeremiah, saying: (Spoke: communicated) **13.** "Tell the people of Judah and Jerusalem: 'Will you not learn from the Rechabites and listen to my words?'" (Learn: receive guidance) **14.** "Jonadab's descendants obey his command not to drink wine; they still obey it today. But I have spoken to you persistently, and you have not listened." (Persistently: repeatedly) **15.** "I have sent my prophets, urging you to turn from evil and follow me, but you have refused to listen." (Urging: encouraging strongly) **16.** "The Rechabites have obeyed their father, but you have not obeyed me." (Obeyed: followed) **17.** "So I will bring disaster on Judah and Jerusalem, for they have not listened or answered my call." (Disaster: great harm) **18.** "But because you have obeyed Jonadab's commands, the LORD says, your descendants will always stand before me." (Descendants: future generations) **19.** "Jonadab the son of Rechab will have descendants who serve me forever." (Descendants: future generations)

Chapter 36

1. In the fourth year of Jehoiakim, the son of Josiah, king of Judah, the Lord spoke to Jeremiah, saying, (Jehoiakim: King of Judah; Josiah: Former king of Judah) **2.** "Take a scroll and record all the words I've given you to speak against Israel, Judah, and all the surrounding nations—from the time I first spoke to you during King Josiah's reign until now." (Josiah: A former righteous king of Judah) **3.** "Perhaps the people of Judah will listen to the disaster I plan to bring upon them, so that they may turn from their wickedness and I will forgive their sin." (House of Judah: Refers to the people of Judah) **4.** Jeremiah then summoned Baruch, the son of Neriah, and Baruch wrote down all the words of the Lord that Jeremiah spoke to him on a scroll. (Baruch: Jeremiah's faithful scribe) **5.** Jeremiah instructed Baruch, "I am confined and cannot go to the temple of the Lord, but you must go." (Temple of the Lord: The sacred place of worship in Jerusalem) **6.** "Take the scroll you've written and read it aloud to the people in the temple during the day of fasting. Also read it to everyone from Judah who has come to Jerusalem." (Fasting day: A day set aside for prayer and repentance) **7.** "Maybe they will plead for mercy before the Lord and turn away from their evil ways, for the Lord's anger is great against this nation." (Great anger: God's righteous judgment on sin) **8.** Baruch did exactly as Jeremiah had instructed, reading the scroll with the Lord's words to the people in the temple. (Baruch's obedience: He faithfully delivered God's message) **9.** In the fifth year of Jehoiakim, in the ninth month, a fast was proclaimed for all the people in Jerusalem and from the towns of Judah who gathered there. (Jehoiakim: The current king of Judah) **10.** Baruch read aloud the words of Jeremiah in the temple, in the chamber of Gemariah, son of Shaphan the scribe, in the upper courtyard at the entrance of the new gate, while all the people listened. (Gemariah: A scribe and royal servant; Shaphan: A well-known official) **11.** When Michaiah, the son of Gemariah, heard Baruch read the scroll aloud, (Michaiah: A listener to God's word) **12.** he went to the king's palace, to the scribe's room, where the princes were sitting—Elishama the scribe, Delaiah son of Shemaiah, Elnathan son of Achbor, Gemariah son of Shaphan, Zedekiah son of Hananiah, and other officials. (Elishama: A scribe; Zedekiah: A prince and royal official) **13.** Michaiah reported to them everything he had heard when Baruch read the scroll to the people. (Princes: High-ranking officials of the king) **14.** The princes sent Jehudi, son of Nethaniah, to Baruch with the message, "Take the scroll you read and come." Baruch brought the scroll with him. (Jehudi: A servant of the king) **15.** "Sit down and read it to us," they said. Baruch read the scroll aloud to them. (Reading aloud: The public proclamation of God's message) **16.** After hearing the words, they were greatly disturbed and said to Baruch, "We must report all these words to the king." (Report: The princes' concern for the king's response) **17.** They asked Baruch, "How did you come to write all these words?" (Writing: The process of recording God's message) **18.** Baruch explained, "Jeremiah spoke them to me, and I wrote them down with ink on the scroll." (Baruch's explanation: The method of recording) **19.** The princes then told Baruch, "Go and hide, you and Jeremiah, and do not let anyone know where you are." (Hiding: The need to protect the messengers of God) **20.** The princes took the scroll to the king's court but placed it in the chamber of Elishama, the scribe, and informed the king of all that was written. (Elishama: The royal scribe who kept the scroll safe) **21.** The king sent Jehudi to get the scroll from Elishama's chamber. Jehudi read it to the king and the princes standing beside him. (Jehudi: The king's messenger) **22.** The king was sitting in his winter apartment, with a fire burning before him. (Winter apartment: The king's seasonal residence) **23.** As Jehudi read, the king cut off the portions he read with a knife and threw them into the fire until the entire scroll was consumed. (The scroll burned: The king's rejection of God's message) **24.** Despite this, neither the king nor his officials showed any sign of fear or repentance. (No repentance: The king's defiance) **25.** Elnathan, Delaiah, and Gemariah pleaded with the king not to destroy the scroll, but he refused to listen. (Intercession: The princes' attempt to stop the burning) **26.** The king ordered that Baruch and Jeremiah be captured, but the Lord hid them. (God's protection: The Lord protected His messengers) **27.** After the king burned the scroll, the word of the Lord came to Jeremiah, saying, (God's message: A new command) **28.** "Take another scroll and write again the same words that were in the first scroll, which Jehoiakim, king of Judah, burned." (Second scroll: A new opportunity to deliver God's message) **29.** "Tell Jehoiakim, king of Judah, that the Lord says: 'You burned the scroll and questioned why it contained the prophecy that the king of Babylon would come and destroy this land, wiping out both man and beast.'" (Jehoiakim's question: The king's refusal to accept God's warning) **30.** "Therefore, the Lord says regarding Jehoiakim: He will not have a descendant to sit on David's throne, and his body will be exposed to the heat during the day and to the cold at night." (David's throne: The royal line of David) **31.** "I will punish him, his descendants, and his officials for their wickedness, and I will bring upon them all the disaster I have declared, because they have not heeded my words." (God's punishment: A divine judgment) **32.** So, Jeremiah took another scroll, and gave it to Baruch, who again wrote down all the words of the Lord from Jeremiah, and many similar words were added to it. (Baruch's faithful recording: The message continued)

Chapter 37

1. King Zedekiah, son of Josiah, succeeded Coniah, son of Jehoiakim, whom King Nebuchadnezzar of Babylon had appointed over Judah. (Zedekiah: Last king of Judah; Josiah: A righteous king of Judah; Nebuchadnezzar: King of Babylon) **2.** Neither Zedekiah, his officials, nor the people of Judah listened to the words of the LORD through the prophet Jeremiah. (Jeremiah: A prophet of God) **3.** Zedekiah sent Jehucal, son of Shelemiah, and Zephaniah, son of Maaseiah the priest, to ask Jeremiah to pray to the LORD for them. (Jehucal: A royal official; Zephaniah: A priest) **4.** Jeremiah was free to move among the people, as he was not imprisoned. (Jeremiah: A prophet who had freedom) **5.** When Pharaoh's army came from Egypt, the Chaldeans besieging Jerusalem withdrew. (Pharaoh: The ruler of Egypt; Chaldeans: Babylonians) **6.** The word of the LORD came to Jeremiah, saying: **7.** "Tell the king of Judah who sent you to inquire of me: Pharaoh's army, which came to help you, will return to Egypt. (Pharaoh: The ruler of Egypt) **8.** The Chaldeans will return, conquer this city, and burn it with fire." **9.** "Do not deceive yourselves, thinking the Chaldeans will leave; they will not." **10.** "Even if you defeated the Chaldeans, they would rise up and burn this city." **11.** When the Chaldeans withdrew from Jerusalem because of Pharaoh's army, (Chaldeans: Babylonians) **12.** Jeremiah left Jerusalem for the land of Benjamin to separate himself among the people. (Benjamin: A region in Israel) **13.** At the Benjamin Gate, Irijah, captain of the guard, arrested Jeremiah, accusing him of defecting to the Chaldeans. (Irijah: A captain of the guard) **14.** Jeremiah denied this, saying he was not defecting, but Irijah did not believe him and brought him to the officials. (Defecting: Joining the enemy) **15.** The officials were angry, beat Jeremiah, and imprisoned him in the house of Jonathan the scribe, which had been turned into a prison. (Jonathan the scribe: A person whose house was used as a prison) **16.** Jeremiah remained in the dungeon for many days. (Dungeon: A dark, confined prison) **17.** King Zedekiah secretly called for Jeremiah and asked, "Is there a word from the LORD?" Jeremiah answered, "Yes, you will be handed over to the king of Babylon." (Zedekiah: King of Judah; Babylon: The empire that would conquer Judah) **18.** Jeremiah asked, "What have I done to be imprisoned? What wrong have I done to you or your people?" (Officials: Those in positions of power) **19.** "Where are the prophets who said the king of Babylon would not attack?" (Prophets: Those who speak for God) **20.** "I beg you, my lord the king, let my request be granted. Do not send me back to the house of Jonathan the scribe, or I will die there." (Plea: A humble request) **21.** Zedekiah ordered that Jeremiah be moved to the court of the prison, where he would receive daily bread from the baker's street until the city's bread was gone. So Jeremiah stayed in the court of the prison. (Court of the prison: A less harsh prison area; Baker's street: A place where bread was made)

Chapter 38

1. Shephatiah, son of Mattan, Gedaliah, son of Pashur, Jucal, son of Shelemiah, and Pashur, son of Malchiah, all heard the message that Jeremiah had delivered to the people, saying, **2.** "The LORD declares, those who stay in this city will die by sword, famine, or disease. But anyone who surrenders to the Babylonians will live, for their life will be spared." (Babylonians: The people of Babylon, an ancient empire) **3.** "The LORD has spoken: This city will certainly fall to the forces of the Babylonian king's army, and they will take it over." (Babylonian king: The ruler of Babylon) **4.** The princes told the king, "Please, let us execute this man. His words are discouraging the soldiers and the people, and he is not speaking for their good but for their harm." (Princes: Royal officials or high-ranking leaders) **5.** King Zedekiah responded, "He is in your hands; the king cannot oppose your actions." (Zedekiah: The final king of Judah) **6.** They seized Jeremiah and threw him into the dungeon of Malchiah, son of Hammelech, in the courtyard of the prison. They lowered him with ropes. The dungeon had no water, only mud, and Jeremiah sank into the mire. (Dungeon: A dark, underground prison cell; Malchiah: A name; Hammelech: A name) **7.** When Ebed-melech, an Ethiopian eunuch in the king's house, heard that Jeremiah was thrown into the dungeon, the king was sitting at the Benjamin Gate. (Ebed-melech: An Ethiopian servant; Benjamin Gate: A gate in Jerusalem) **8.** Ebed-melech went out from the king's house and spoke to the king, saying, **9.** "My lord, these men have acted wrongly in throwing Jeremiah into the dungeon. He is at risk of dying from hunger, for there is no more bread in the city." (Dungeon: A dark, underground prison cell) **10.** The king ordered Ebed-melech, "Take thirty men with you and pull Jeremiah out of the dungeon before he dies." (Ebed-melech: A name) **11.** So Ebed-melech gathered the men, went to the royal treasury, and took old rags and torn cloths. He lowered them by ropes into the dungeon to Jeremiah. (Treasury: A room where the king's valuables are stored) **12.** Ebed-melech instructed Jeremiah, "Place these old rags under your armpits and tie the ropes around you." Jeremiah did as he was told. (Rags: Old or worn-out pieces of cloth) **13.** They pulled Jeremiah up using the ropes and brought him to the prison courtyard, where he stayed. (Ropes: Strong cords used to pull or bind) **14.** King Zedekiah sent for Jeremiah and brought him to the third entrance of the temple. The king said to him, "I have a question for you; do not hide anything from me." (Temple: A place of worship) **15.** Jeremiah answered, "If I tell you, will you not surely kill me? And if I advise you, will you not listen?" (Advise: To give guidance or counsel) **16.** King Zedekiah swore to Jeremiah in secret, saying, "As the LORD lives, who created us, I will not kill you or hand you over to those who seek your life." (Swore: Made a solemn promise) **17.** Then Jeremiah said to him, "The LORD of Hosts, the God of Israel, says: If you surrender to the Babylonian officers, your life will be spared, and the city will not be destroyed by fire. You and your household will survive." (LORD of Hosts: A title for God, meaning Lord of the heavenly armies; Surrender: To give up or yield) **18.** "But if you refuse to surrender, the city will fall to the Babylonians, they will burn it, and you will not escape." (Refuse: To decline or reject) **19.** Zedekiah replied, "I am afraid of the Jews who have already defected to the Babylonians. They may hand me over to them, and I will be mocked." (Defected: Left for another group or cause) **20.** Jeremiah assured him, "They will not hand you over. Listen to the voice of the LORD, and it will go well with you, and your life will be spared." (Assured: To make certain or promise) **21.** "But if you refuse, this is the word the LORD has shown me:" (Refuse: To decline or reject) **22.** "The women left in the king's palace will be brought to the Babylonian officials, and they will mock you, saying: 'Your allies have deceived you; your feet are stuck in the mud, and they have turned against you.'" (Deceived: Misled or tricked) **23.** "Your wives and children will be taken by the Babylonians. You will not escape but will be captured by the king of Babylon, and this city will be burned." (Captured: Taken by force) **24.** Zedekiah said to

Jeremiah, "Do not let anyone know about our conversation, or you will die." (Conversation: A discussion between two or more people) 25. "But if the princes find out that I have spoken with you and ask you what we talked about, tell them that you were begging the king not to send you back to Jonathan's house to die." (Princes: Ruling leaders) 26. So Jeremiah did as the king had instructed when the princes came to ask him. (Instructed: Given directions or orders) 27. The princes asked, and Jeremiah told them everything the king had commanded. They stopped questioning him, for they did not understand the seriousness of the matter. (Seriousness: The importance or gravity of the situation) 28. Jeremiah remained in the court of the prison until the fall of Jerusalem, and he was there when the city was captured. (Jerusalem: The capital city of Judah)

Chapter 39

1. In the ninth year of King Zedekiah of Judah, during the tenth month, King Nebuchadnezzar of Babylon and his army laid siege to Jerusalem. (Zedekiah: The last king of Judah; Nebuchadnezzar: The king of Babylon; Siege: A military blockade) 2. In Zedekiah's eleventh year, on the fourth month, ninth day, the city's walls were breached. (Breached: Broken through) 3. Babylonian officials entered and sat at the main gate, including Nergal-sharezer, Samgar-nebo, Sarsechim, Rab-saris, Nergal-sharezer again, and Rabmag, with other officials. (Rab-saris: Chief officer; Rabmag: High official) 4. When King Zedekiah and his soldiers saw them, they fled the city at night through the king's garden, between two walls, heading toward the plain. (Fled: Ran away; Garden: A royal park or garden; Plain: A flat, open area) 5. The Chaldeans pursued and captured him near Jericho. They brought him to Nebuchadnezzar at Riblah, in Hamath, where he was judged. (Chaldean: Babylonian; Jericho: A city near the Jordan River; Riblah: A place of judgment; Hamath: A region in Syria) 6. At Riblah, Nebuchadnezzar had Zedekiah's sons killed in front of him, and also executed Judah's leaders. (Leaders: High-ranking men) 7. The king then gouged out Zedekiah's eyes, bound him in chains, and took him to Babylon. (Gouged out: Removed; Chained: Bound with chains) 8. The Chaldeans burned the king's palace and the people's homes, and destroyed Jerusalem's walls. (Set fire: Burned; Destroyed: Tore down completely) 9. Nebuzar-adan, the captain of the guard, took the remaining people, including those who surrendered, to Babylon. (Nebuzar-adan: Babylonian officer; Captain of the guard: Military leader) 10. Nebuzar-adan left the poor behind in Judah, giving them vineyards and fields. (Vineyards: Grape-growing land; Fields: Areas for farming) 11. Nebuchadnezzar gave instructions to Nebuzar-adan about Jeremiah, saying, (Instructions: Orders) 12. "Take Jeremiah, treat him well, and follow his instructions." 13. Nebuzar-adan sent for Jeremiah, along with other Babylonian officials, to bring him out of the prison courtyard. (Sent for: Ordered to bring) 14. They gave Jeremiah to Gedaliah, son of Ahikam and Shaphan, to bring him home. He lived among the people. 15. While in prison, the LORD spoke to Jeremiah, saying, (Confined: Kept in prison) 16. "Go to Ebed-melech the Ethiopian and tell him, 'The LORD of Hosts, the God of Israel, says: I will bring disaster on this city, and you will see it happen.'" (Ebed-melech: A name; Ethiopian: Person from Cush; Hosts: Armies or heavenly beings) 17. "But I will rescue you on that day; you will not be handed over to those you fear." (Rescue: Save from harm; Handed over: Given to the enemy) 18. "I will deliver you, and your life will be spared because you trusted in me," declares the LORD. (Delivered: Saved from danger)

Chapter 40

1. After Jeremiah was released by Nebuzar-adan, the captain of the guard, at Ramah, where he had been taken, bound in chains with those exiled from Jerusalem and Judah to Babylon, the word of the LORD came to him. (Ramah: A town in the territory of Benjamin; Exiled: Forced to leave their homeland) 2. The captain of the guard spoke to Jeremiah, saying, "The LORD your God has declared this disaster upon this city." (Declared: Announced) 3. "The LORD has done exactly what He said He would, because you have sinned against Him and failed to listen to His voice. That is why this destruction has come upon you." (Destruction: Ruin or downfall; Failed to listen: Did not obey) 4. "Today, I am releasing you from your chains. If it seems right to you to come with me to Babylon, then come, and I will care for you. But if you prefer not to come, all the land is before you. Go where you choose, to any place that seems good to you." (Releasing: Setting free; Care for: Take care of) 5. Before Jeremiah could leave, the captain of the guard added, "Go back to Gedaliah, son of Ahikam, whom the king of Babylon has appointed as governor over Judah's cities. Stay with him among the people, or go anywhere else you prefer." The captain provided him with food and a reward, then let him go. (Governor: Ruler or administrator; Reward: Payment or gift) 6. Jeremiah went to Gedaliah, son of Ahikam, at Mizpah, where he settled with the people who remained in the land. (Mizpah: A town in Judah) 7. When the military leaders in the fields, and their men, heard that King Nebuchadnezzar had made Gedaliah the governor and had put in his care the remaining men, women, children, and the poor who had not been taken to Babylon, (Military leaders: Captains or commanders) 8. They came to Gedaliah at Mizpah: Ishmael, son of Nethaniah, Johanan and Jonathan, sons of Kareah, Seraiah, son of Tanhumeth, and the sons of Ephai the Netopathite, and Jezaniah, son of a Maachathite, with their followers. (Ishmael, Johanan, Ephai, etc.: Names of leaders or groups) 9. Gedaliah swore an oath to them and their men, saying, "Do not be afraid of the Chaldeans. Stay in the land, serve the king of Babylon, and it will go well for you." (Chaldeans: Babylonians; Oath: A solemn promise) 10. "As for me, I will remain in Mizpah, serving the Chaldeans who come to us. But you, gather wine, summer fruits, and oil, store them in your vessels, and settle in the cities you have taken." (Gather: Collect; Vessels: Containers) 11. When Jews living in Moab, Ammon, Edom, and other lands heard that the king of Babylon had left a remnant in Judah and made Gedaliah governor, (Moab, Ammon, Edom: Regions surrounding Judah) 12. They returned from the places they had fled and came to Judah, to Gedaliah at Mizpah, bringing with them much wine and summer fruits. (Returned: Came back; Fled: Escaped) 13. Johanan, son of Kareah, and the other military leaders from the fields also came to Gedaliah at Mizpah, (Military leaders: Captains or commanders) 14. and warned him, "Do you know that Baalis, king of the Ammonites, has sent Ishmael, son of Nethaniah, to kill you?" But Gedaliah did not believe them. (Baalis: A name; Ammonites: People from the region of Ammon) 15. Johanan secretly told Gedaliah, "Let me go and kill Ishmael. No one will know about it. Why should he kill you and scatter all the people who have gathered to you, causing the remnant of Judah to be lost?" (Secretly: Privately; Remnant: Those left behind) 16. But Gedaliah, son of Ahikam, replied to Johanan, son of Kareah, "Do not do this. You are accusing Ishmael falsely." (Accusing: Blaming)

Chapter 41

1. In the seventh month, Ishmael, son of Nethaniah and of royal lineage, came to Gedaliah at Mizpah with ten men, and they ate together. (Royal lineage: descendants of the king's family) 2. Ishmael and his men killed Gedaliah, whom the king of Babylon had appointed as governor. (Governor: an official in charge of governing a region) 3. Ishmael also killed the Jews and Chaldean soldiers who were with Gedaliah at Mizpah. (Chaldeans: Babylonians; soldiers: armed warriors) 4. Two days after Gedaliah's murder, no one knew about it yet. (Murder: unlawful killing of someone) 5. Eighty men from Shechem, Shiloh, and Samaria arrived, mourning with shaved beards, torn clothes, and offerings for the LORD's temple. (Mourning: expressing grief; temple: place of worship) 6. Ishmael met them, pretending to weep, and invited them to see Gedaliah. (Pretending: acting falsely) 7. When they entered the city, Ishmael and his men killed them and threw their bodies into a pit. (Pit: a deep hole in the ground) 8. Ten men pleaded for their lives, offering

hidden supplies of wheat, barley, oil, and honey, so Ishmael spared them. (Spared: refrained from killing or harming) 9. Ishmael filled the pit King Asa had made long ago with the bodies of those he killed for Gedaliah's sake. (King Asa: a former king of Judah) 10. He took the rest of Mizpah's people, including the king's daughters, captive and headed toward the Ammonites. (Captive: held against one's will; Ammonites: a neighboring nation east of Israel) 11. Johanan, son of Kareah, and the army captains heard of Ishmael's actions. (Captains: leaders of military groups) 12. They gathered their forces, pursued Ishmael, and found him near the great waters of Gibeon. (Pursued: followed to capture or attack) 13. When Ishmael's captives saw Johanan and his forces, they rejoiced. (Rejoiced: celebrated or felt great joy) 14. The captives turned back and joined Johanan's group. (Turned back: changed direction or allegiance) 15. Ishmael escaped with eight men to the Ammonites. (Escaped: fled or got away from capture) 16. Johanan and his captains rescued the remaining people—soldiers, women, children, and eunuchs—that Ishmael had taken from Mizpah. (Eunuchs: royal servants or officials, often celibate) 17. They settled at Chimham, near Bethlehem, planning to flee to Egypt. (Settled: made a temporary home; Bethlehem: a town in Judah) 18. They feared the Babylonians because Ishmael had killed Gedaliah, the governor appointed by Babylon's king. (Feared: felt afraid; Babylonians: people of Babylon)

Chapter 42

1. Johanan, Jezaniah, all the captains, and the people, from the least to the greatest, approached Jeremiah. (Captains: military leaders; least to greatest: people of all social statuses) 2. They said, "Please accept our plea and pray to the LORD your God for this remnant, for we are few, as you see." (Remnant: the small group remaining; plea: earnest request) 3. "Pray that the LORD shows us the path we should take and what we must do." (Path: direction or course of action) 4. Jeremiah replied, "I will pray to the LORD for you and share everything He answers without holding anything back." (Answers: divine responses) 5. They promised, "May the LORD be a true witness if we fail to do what He instructs through you." (Witness: someone who confirms a statement or event) 6. "Whether pleasant or hard, we will obey the LORD's voice to ensure our well-being." (Obey: follow instructions; well-being: state of being safe and prosperous) 7. Ten days later, the LORD's word came to Jeremiah. (Word: divine message or command) 8. Jeremiah called Johanan, the captains, and all the people, from the least to the greatest. (Called: summoned or gathered) 9. He said, "This is what the LORD, the God of Israel, says: You sent me to present your plea before Him." (Plea: request or petition) 10. "If you remain in this land, I will establish and not destroy you, plant and not uproot you, for I regret the harm I brought upon you." (Establish: make secure; uproot: remove completely) 11. "Do not fear the Babylonian king, for I am with you to save and rescue you from his hand," declares the LORD. (Rescue: deliver from harm) 12. "I will grant you mercy so that the king may show you kindness and allow you to return to your land." (Mercy: compassion or forgiveness; kindness: consideration) 13. "But if you refuse to stay in this land and disobey the LORD," (Disobey: refuse to follow instructions) 14. "And say, 'We will go to Egypt to avoid war, trumpet sounds, and hunger, and live there,'" (Trumpet sounds: signals of war) 15. "Then hear this from the LORD: If you set your hearts on entering Egypt to live there," (Set your hearts: firmly decide) 16. "The sword you fear will find you there, and the famine you dread will pursue you; there you will die." (Sword: war or violence; pursue: follow closely) 17. "All who go to Egypt will perish by sword, famine, and plague, leaving none to escape the disaster I will send." (Plague: widespread calamity or disease) 18. "As My anger poured out on Jerusalem, it will pour out on you in Egypt. You will become a curse, scorn, and disgrace, never returning here." (Scorn: contempt; disgrace: loss of respect) 19. "The LORD commands you, O remnant of Judah: Do not go to Egypt! Be sure I have warned you today." (Warned: alerted to danger) 20. "You were deceitful when you asked me to pray to the LORD for you, saying you would obey whatever He commands." (Deceitful: dishonest or insincere) 21. "Today, I told you His will, but you have not obeyed the LORD or His commands." (Commands: authoritative orders) 22. "Now, be certain that you will die by sword, famine, and plague in the place you desire to go." (Certain: without doubt; desire: wish or intend)

Chapter 43

1. After Jeremiah finished delivering all the words that the LORD their God had sent him to speak, the people heard everything (Jeremiah: a prophet chosen by God; LORD: the God of Israel). 2. Azariah, the son of Hoshaiah, Johanan, the son of Kareah, and all the proud men said to Jeremiah, "You are lying! The LORD our God has not sent you to warn us against going to Egypt and staying there." (Azariah: a leader of the people; Johanan: a military officer). 3. They claimed, "Baruch, the son of Neriah, is the one who has influenced you to speak against us, leading us into the hands of the Chaldeans, so they can kill us and take us captive to Babylon." (Baruch: scribe and companion of Jeremiah; Neriah: Baruch's father). 4. Johanan, the son of Kareah, the military leaders, and all the people refused to follow the LORD's command to remain in Judah. (Kareah: Johanan's father). 5. Instead, Johanan and the leaders took all the remaining people of Judah who had returned from the nations where they had been scattered, and they brought them back to live in Judah. 6. This included men, women, children, the king's daughters, and everyone whom Nebuzar-adan, the captain of the guard, had left with Gedaliah, son of Ahikam, and Jeremiah the prophet, as well as Baruch, son of Neriah. (Gedaliah: governor appointed by Babylon; Nebuzar-adan: Babylonian military commander). 7. They traveled to Egypt because they refused to listen to the LORD, and they reached the city of Tahpanhes. (Tahpanhes: a city in Egypt where they took refuge). 8. While they were in Tahpanhes, the word of the LORD came to Jeremiah, saying: 9. "Take large stones in your hands and bury them in the clay of the brick kiln at the entrance to Pharaoh's palace in Tahpanhes, in full view of the people of Judah." (Pharaoh: the ruler of Egypt). 10. "Then tell them, 'This is what the LORD of Hosts, the God of Israel, says: I will summon Nebuchadnezzar, the king of Babylon, my servant, and I will set his throne on these stones that I have buried. He will spread his royal tent over them.'" (Nebuchadnezzar: king of Babylon; Babylon: the empire that conquered Judah). 11. "When he comes, he will strike the land of Egypt, and those meant for death will die, those meant for captivity will be taken captive, and those meant for the sword will be struck down by the sword." 12. "I will set fire to the temples of Egypt's gods, and he will burn them down and carry their idols away. He will dress in Egypt like a shepherd wearing his cloak, and he will leave in peace." 13. "He will destroy the idols in Beth-shemesh, located in Egypt, and burn down the temples of Egypt's gods." (Beth-shemesh: a city in Egypt where some Israelites had worshipped false gods).

Chapter 44

1. The word came to Jeremiah concerning the Jews living in Egypt, including those in Migdol, Tahpanhes, Noph, and Pathros, saying, 2. "The LORD of hosts, the God of Israel, says: You have seen the destruction I brought upon Jerusalem and Judah, where cities are now desolate and uninhabited.(Desolate: barren, empty, or uninhabited.) 3. This happened because of their wickedness in angering me by offering incense and serving gods they did not know—gods neither you nor your ancestors knew.(Incense: a substance burned to create a fragrant smoke, often used in worship; Wickedness: immoral or sinful behavior.) 4. I sent my prophets early to warn you, saying, 'Do not do what I hate!' 5. But you refused to listen and ignored the warnings, continuing to burn incense to other gods. 6. Therefore, my anger was poured out on Judah, and its cities were destroyed. They remain desolate, as they are today.(Desolate: barren, empty, or uninhabited.) 7. Now, why commit such a great evil against your own souls by cutting off man, woman, child, and

infant from Judah, leaving none to remain? (Evil: morally wrong or sinful; Souls: the spiritual or immaterial part of a person.) **8.** You provoke me by burning incense to other gods in Egypt, where you have gone to live. This will make you a curse and a disgrace among all nations.(Provoke: to incite or anger; Curse: a prayer or invocation for harm to come upon someone; Disgrace: a loss of reputation or respect.) **9.** Have you forgotten the wickedness of your ancestors, the kings of Judah, their wives, and your own wickedness? (Wickedness: immoral or sinful behavior.) **10.** They have not humbled themselves or obeyed my law, even to this day. (Humbled: to lower oneself in humility; Obeyed: to follow or comply with a command or law.) **11.** Therefore, I will set my face against you for destruction and will cut off all Judah. (Set my face against: to turn against or oppose; Destruction: the action or process of ruining something.) **12.** Those who fled to Egypt will die there by sword or famine, from the least to the greatest. They will be a disgrace, a curse, and an astonishment. (Fled: ran away; Sword: a weapon used for cutting or thrusting; Famine: extreme scarcity of food; Astonishment: great shock or amazement.) **13.** I will punish those in Egypt as I punished Jerusalem, with sword, famine, and pestilence. (Pestilence: a deadly disease or plague.) **14.** None of the remnant of Judah who went to Egypt will escape to return to Judah, except those who are spared. (Remnant: a small remaining quantity of something; Spared: saved from harm or destruction.) **15.** All those who knew their wives were burning incense to other gods in Egypt responded to Jeremiah, saying, **16.** "We will not listen to you, but we will do whatever we want, offering incense to the queen of heaven and pouring out drink offerings to her, as we did in Judah and Jerusalem. Then we had plenty and no harm. (Listen: to pay attention to sound or words; Incense: a substance burned to create a fragrant smoke, often used in worship; Drink offerings: a ritual pouring of liquid in honor of a deity.) **17.** But since we stopped offering incense to her, we have lacked everything and suffered by sword and famine.(Lacked: to be without or have insufficient; Suffered: to experience pain or hardship.) **18.** When we burned incense to the queen of heaven, did we do so without our men?" **19.** Jeremiah answered all the people, saying, **20.** "Did the LORD not remember the incense you burned in Judah and Jerusalem? It entered His mind, (Incense: a substance burned to create a fragrant smoke, often used in worship.) **21.** and the LORD could no longer bear your evil and abominations. That's why your land is desolate, without inhabitants. (Bear: to endure or tolerate; Abominations: things that cause disgust or hatred.) **22.** Because you sinned against the LORD, this evil has happened to you. (Sinned: acted in a way that violates divine law or moral principles; Evil: morally wrong or sinful.) **23.** You burned incense, sinned against the LORD, and disobeyed His law. Therefore, this destruction is upon you. (Disobeyed: failed to follow or comply with a command or law.) **24.** Then Jeremiah spoke to all the people, especially the women, saying, **25.** "You and your wives made vows to burn incense to the queen of heaven and pour drink offerings to her. You will surely fulfill these vows. (Vows: solemn promises or commitments; Fulfill: to carry out or complete.) **26.** But the LORD says, I have sworn by my great name that no man of Judah in Egypt will ever again speak my name, saying, 'The LORD lives!' (Sworn: taken an oath or made a solemn promise.) **27.** I will watch over them for evil, not for good. Those in Egypt will be consumed by sword and famine until none remain. (Consumed: destroyed or devoured; Famine: extreme scarcity of food.) **28.** Yet a small number will escape the sword and return to Judah, and the rest will know whose words will stand—mine or theirs. (Escape: to get away from something dangerous; Sword: a weapon used for cutting or thrusting.) **29.** This will be a sign to you that I will punish you here, so you will know my words will stand against you for evil. (Punish: to inflict a penalty for wrongdoing; Sign: a symbol or mark that communicates something.) **30.** I will give Pharaoh-hophra, king of Egypt, into the hands of his enemies, as I gave King Zedekiah into Nebuchadnezzar's hands.

Chapter 45
1. The message that Jeremiah the prophet delivered to Baruch, the son of Neriah, after Baruch had written down these words at Jeremiah's command, during the fourth year of King Jehoiakim, son of Josiah of Judah, saying: **2.** "This is what the LORD, the God of Israel, says to you, Baruch;**3.** You have said, 'Alas for me! The LORD has added sorrow to my pain. I am exhausted from my groaning and can find no relief.' (Alas: an expression of sorrow or regret; Groaning: a low sound made due to pain or distress; Relief: the alleviation of pain or discomfort.) **4.** Tell him this: 'The LORD declares: I will tear down what I have built, and uproot what I have planted—this entire land.' (Tear down: to destroy or demolish; Uproot: to remove by pulling out from the roots; Entire: complete or whole.) **5.** 'And are you seeking great things for yourself? Do not seek them! For I am bringing disaster upon all people, says the LORD, but I will protect your life wherever you go as if it were a spoil of war.' (Disaster: a sudden event causing great damage or loss; Spoil: goods taken from the defeated in war; Protect: to keep safe from harm or danger.)

Chapter 46
1. The word of the LORD came to Jeremiah, concerning the nations: (Nations: Gentiles, foreign peoples) **2.** Against Egypt, and the army of Pharaoh-necho, which Nebuchadrezzar, king of Babylon, defeated by the Euphrates in Carchemish in the fourth year of Jehoiakim. (Carchemish: an ancient city on the Euphrates) **3.** Prepare your shields and bucklers; get ready for battle. (Buckler: small shield) **4.** Harness the horses, and rise, horsemen, with your helmets on; sharpen the spears and put on your armor. (Harness: to prepare for use) **5.** Why do I see them dismayed and retreating? The mighty are beaten and fleeing in panic, afraid on every side, says the LORD. (Dismayed: discouraged, afraid) **6.** Let not the swift escape, nor the strong man flee; they will stumble and fall by the Euphrates River. (Stumble: to fall or lose balance) **7.** Who is this coming like a flood, whose waters are restless like rivers? (Flood: a large, overwhelming surge) **8.** Egypt rises like a flood, with waters that rage like rivers, saying, "I will cover the earth and destroy cities and people." (Rage: to be violent and uncontrolled) **9.** Come, horses, rage, chariots! Let the mighty men come forth—Ethiopians, Libyans, and Lydians with shields and bows. (Ethiopians, Libyans, Lydians: ancient peoples in Africa and Asia Minor) **10.** This is the day of the LORD's vengeance, a day to punish His enemies. The sword will devour and be drunk with their blood. The LORD has a sacrifice prepared by the Euphrates River. (Vengeance: revenge, punishment) **11.** Go to Gilead, and take balm, O virgin daughter of Egypt. But it will be in vain, for you will not be healed. (Balm: a healing ointment) **12.** The nations have heard of your shame, and your cry fills the land. The mighty have stumbled, and they both fell together. (Shame: dishonor, disgrace) **13.** The LORD told Jeremiah that Nebuchadrezzar, king of Babylon, would strike Egypt. (Strike: to attack or defeat) **14.** Declare this in Egypt, in Migdol, Noph, and Tahpanhes: Stand firm and prepare, for the sword will devour you. (Declare: to announce, to proclaim) **15.** Why are your warriors swept away? They stood not, for the LORD drove them away. (Warriors: soldiers) **16.** Many have fallen, one upon another, saying, "Let us return to our own land from the oppressing sword." (Oppressing: harsh or cruel) **17.** They cry, "Pharaoh, king of Egypt, is nothing but noise; his time has passed." (Noise: meaningless talk) **18.** As surely as Tabor is among the mountains, and Carmel by the sea, so shall he come. (Tabor, Carmel: well-known mountains in Israel) **19.** O daughter of Egypt, prepare to go into captivity. Noph will be wasted and empty of inhabitants. (Captivity: being taken as a prisoner) **20.** Egypt is a beautiful heifer, but destruction is coming from the north. (Heifer: young cow, symbolizing strength) **21.** Her hired soldiers are like fatted calves, but they are turning back and fleeing together. They could not stand because the day of their disaster has come. (Fatted calves: animals being fattened for sacrifice or slaughter) **22.** The enemy's voice will be like a serpent, as they march with axes to cut down her trees, like lumberjacks.

(Lumberjacks: woodcutters) **23.** They will cut down her forest, says the LORD, though it cannot be counted, for their numbers are like locusts. (Locusts: swarming insects, symbolizing destruction) **24.** Egypt's daughter will be humiliated and given into the hands of the northern nations. (Humiliated: made to feel ashamed) **25.** The LORD of Hosts says: I will punish the multitudes of No, Pharaoh, Egypt, and their gods, and kings; I will hand them over to those who seek their lives. (No: ancient city of Egypt) **26.** I will deliver them into the hands of Nebuchadrezzar, king of Babylon, and afterward Egypt will be inhabited again, as in ancient times. (Deliver: to hand over) **27.** But do not fear, O my servant Jacob. I will save you from afar and bring your descendants back to their land. Jacob will return in peace, and none will make him afraid. (Descendants: offspring, children) **28.** Do not fear, O Jacob, for I am with you. I will end all the nations where I have scattered you, but I will not end you. I will discipline you, but not leave you unpunished. (Discipline: to correct or punish for wrong behavior)

Chapter 47

1. The word of the LORD came to the prophet Jeremiah concerning the Philistines, before Pharaoh attacked Gaza. (Gaza: a major city in ancient Philistia; Pharaoh: the king of Egypt at that time) **2.** The LORD says: Look, waters rise from the north, flooding the land and everything in it, including the cities and their inhabitants. People will cry out, and all the land's residents will wail. (Philistines: people from the ancient coastal region of Philistia) **3.** At the sound of the pounding hooves of his powerful horses, the rushing of his chariots, and the noise of their wheels, fathers will not turn back to their children, weakened by fear. (Chariots: two-wheeled vehicles used in battle) **4.** The day is coming to destroy all the Philistines and cut off the last helpers from Tyre and Sidon. The LORD will bring ruin to the Philistines, the survivors from the land of Caphtor. (Tyre and Sidon: ancient cities in Phoenicia, present-day Lebanon; Caphtor: a region, possibly Crete) **5.** Baldness has come to Gaza; Ashkelon is devastated, and their valley is left desolate. How long will you continue to mourn? (Ashkelon: one of the five Philistine cities) **6.** O sword of the LORD, how long will you be still? Return to your sheath, rest, and be quiet. (Sword of the LORD: a symbol of God's judgment) **7.** How can it be still, when the LORD has given it a task against Ashkelon and the coastal regions? He has assigned it there. (Ashkelon: a major city of the Philistines; sea shore: the coastal region of the Philistines)

Chapter 48

1. This is the message against Moab from the LORD of hosts, the God of Israel: Woe to Nebo! It has been laid waste. Kiriathaim is ashamed and captured. Misgab is in disarray and fear. (Nebo: a Moabite city, Kiriathaim: another city of Moab, Misgab: a fortress, laid waste: destroyed) **2.** No longer will Moab be praised; in Heshbon, they have plotted evil against her, saying, "Let us cut Moab off from being a nation." Madmen, you too will fall, and the sword will chase you down. (Heshbon: an ancient city of Moab, plotted evil: planned harm, Madmen: a city of Moab, sword: symbol of war) **3.** A voice of mourning rises from Horonaim, a cry of devastation and great ruin. (Horonaim: a city of Moab, devastation: destruction, ruin: total collapse) **4.** Moab is destroyed, and her little ones raise a bitter lament. (Lament: mourning or grieving) **5.** On the ascent of Luhith, there will be endless weeping, and as the descent from Horonaim, enemies will hear the cries of destruction. (Descent: downward path) **6.** Flee, save yourselves, and become like a lone heath in the wilderness. (wilderness: uninhabited area) **7.** Because you have relied on your strength and wealth, you too will be taken. Chemosh, along with his priests and princes, will be exiled. (Chemosh: the chief god of Moab, priests) **8.** The destroyer will strike every city, and no place will remain safe. The valley will be desolate, and the plains will be wiped out, as the LORD has decreed. (Destroyer: invader, desolate: empty, wiped out: completely destroyed, decreed: ordered by God) **9.** Give wings to Moab so it can flee and escape, for its cities will be empty, with no one left to dwell in them. (Wings: symbolizing the ability to flee, dwell: live) **10.** Cursed is the one who performs the work of the LORD deceitfully, and cursed is the one who withholds their sword from shedding blood. (Deceitfully: dishonestly, withholds: holds back, shedding blood: causing death) **11.** Moab has been complacent since its youth, like wine settled on its dregs, unshaken and not taken into captivity. Therefore, its pride remains unbroken, and its scent unchanged. (Complacent: self-satisfied, dregs: the sediment of wine, unshaken: not disturbed, scent: character or nature) **12.** But the days are coming, says the LORD, when I will send wanderers to Moab, who will drain its vessels and shatter its bottles. (Wanderers: those who cause wandering, vessels: containers, shatter: break into pieces) **13.** Moab will be ashamed of Chemosh, just as Israel was ashamed of Bethel, the place of their trust. (Ashamed: feeling dishonored, Bethel: an important place of worship in Israel) **14.** How can you say, "We are mighty and brave for battle?" (Mighty: strong, brave: courageous) **15.** Moab is ruined, its cities abandoned, and its chosen young men are slain, declares the King, whose name is the LORD of hosts. (Ruined: destroyed, slain: killed) **16.** The disaster of Moab is swiftly approaching, and its suffering is drawing near. (Disaster: great misfortune, suffering: pain or hardship) **17.** All who are around Moab, mourn for it; those who know its name, lament, saying, "How is the strong staff broken, and the glorious rod?" (Lament: mourn, strong staff: symbol of strength, glorious rod: symbol of authority) **18.** Daughter of Dibon, descend from your glory and sit in the dust, for the invader of Moab will soon overtake you and destroy your fortresses. (Dibon: a city of Moab, invader: attacker, fortresses: strong defenses) **19.** Inhabitants of Aroer, stand by the way and watch. Ask those who flee and those who escape, "What has happened?" (Aroer: a city of Moab, flee: run away, escape: get away) **20.** Moab is shattered; it is broken. Cry out in sorrow, and proclaim in Arnon that Moab has been spoiled. (Shattered: broken into pieces, spoiled: ruined) **21.** Judgment has come to the cities of the plains— Holon, Jahazah, Mephaath. (Judgment: punishment, plains: flat land, Holon, Jahazah, Mephaath: cities of Moab) **22.** Dibon, Nebo, and Beth-diblathaim, (Dibon, Nebo, Beth-diblathaim: cities of Moab) **23.** Kiriathaim, Beth-gamul, and Beth-meon, (Kiriathaim, Beth-gamul, Beth-meon: cities of Moab) **24.** Kerioth, Bozrah, and all the cities of Moab, whether far or near, (Kerioth, Bozrah: cities of Moab) **25.** The strength of Moab is cut off, and its arm is broken, says the LORD. (Strength: power, arm: symbol of strength) **26.** Make Moab drunk, for it has exalted itself against the LORD. Moab will wallow in its own vomit and become an object of mockery. (Exalted: lifted up in pride, wallow: lie in, vomit: rejected waste, mockery: derision) **27.** Was Israel not a mockery to you? Did you find them among thieves? Whenever you spoke of them, you rejoiced. (Mockery: derision, thieves: criminals) **28.** Inhabitants of Moab, leave your cities and dwell in the rocks. Be like a dove nesting in the side of a ravine. (Dwell: live, ravine: deep narrow valley) **29.** We have heard of Moab's pride, its arrogance, its haughtiness, and its boastful heart. (Pride: excessive self-importance, arrogance: overbearing, haughtiness: arrogance) **30.** I know Moab's fury, says the LORD, but it will not prevail. Its lies will not stand. (Fury: intense anger, prevail: succeed, lies: falsehoods) **31.** Therefore, I will weep for Moab and cry for all Moab. My heart will grieve for the men of Kir-heres. (Grieve: feel sorrow for) **32.** O vine of Sibmah, I will mourn for you with the mourning of Jazer. Your vines have spread beyond the sea, reaching as far as Jazer. The destroyer has fallen upon your summer fruits and your harvest. (Vine: grapevine, Sibmah: a city of Moab, Jazer: a city of Moab, summer fruits: harvest crops, destroyer: invader) **33.** Joy and gladness are gone from the fertile fields and from the land of Moab. I have made the wine fail from the winepresses; there will be no more rejoicing. (Fertile fields: productive land, winepresses: place where grapes are crushed, rejoicing: celebration) **34.** From the cry of Heshbon to Elealeh, and from Jahaz to Zoar, a lament is heard, like a young heifer in distress. Even the waters of Nimrim will be desolate. (Cry: mourning, lament: sorrowful song, heifer: young cow, distress: suffering, desolate: abandoned) **35.** Furthermore, says the LORD, I will put an end to the offerings made on the high places and the burning of incense to foreign gods in Moab. (Offerings: gifts to gods, high places: sites for worship, incense: fragrant smoke offered in worship) **36.** Therefore, my heart will sound like pipes for Moab, and for the men of Kir-heres. All that they had gathered is now gone. (Pipes: musical instruments, gathered: accumulated wealth) **37.** Every head will be shaved, every beard cut off. There will be marks on every hand, and sackcloth on every waist. (Shaved: hair cut off, sackcloth: coarse cloth worn as a sign of mourning) **38.** There will be mourning in all the rooftops and streets of Moab, for I have shattered Moab like an unpleasing vessel, says the LORD. (Shattered: broken, unpleasing: unwanted, vessel: container) **39.** Moab will cry out, "How is it destroyed? How is Moab turned away in shame? Moab will become a laughingstock and a source of terror to all those around it." (Destroyed: ruined, turned away: forsaken, laughingstock: object of mockery, terror: fear) **40.** For the LORD says, "Moab will fly like an eagle and spread its wings over Moab." (Fly: soar, wings: power or protection) **41.** Kerioth will be captured, and the strongholds will be taken. On that day, the hearts of Moab's mighty men will be like the hearts of a woman in labor. (Captured: seized, strongholds: fortified places, mighty men: warriors, labor: childbirth) **42.** Moab will cease to be a nation, for it has exalted itself against the LORD. (Cease: stop, exalted: lifted in pride) **43.** Fear, pit, and snare will come upon you, O Moab, says the LORD. (Pit: trap, snare: snaring device) **44.** The one who flees from the terror will fall into the pit, and the one who climbs out of the pit will be caught in the snare. I will bring upon Moab the year of its punishment, says the LORD. (Terror: extreme fear, punishment: retribution) **45.** Those who fled have taken refuge under the shadow of Heshbon because of the threat, but a fire will come out from Heshbon and a flame from the heart of Sihon, devouring the corner of Moab and the crown of the head of its tumultuous people. (Refuge: safety, threat: danger, tumultuous: disorderly) **46.** Woe to you, Moab! The people of Chemosh are destroyed. Your sons and daughters have been taken captive. (Woe: great sorrow, Chemosh: the god of Moab, captive: taken as prisoners) **47.** Yet I will restore the fortunes of Moab in the days to come, says the LORD. This concludes the judgment of Moab. (Restore: bring back, fortunes: prosperity)

Chapter 49
1. Concerning the Ammonites, the LORD says: Does Israel have no sons or descendants? Why does their king take possession of Gad, and why do his people settle in its cities? (Ammonites: descendants of Lot, an ancient people; Gad: a tribe of Israel) **2.** The days are coming, declares the LORD, when I will send a war cry to Rabbah of the Ammonites; it will become a ruin, and its towns will burn. Then Israel will take possession of what was once theirs. (Rabbah: capital city of the Ammonites) **3.** Howl, O Heshbon, for Ai is devastated! Cry, O daughters of Rabbah, put on sackcloth, mourn, and run to and fro by the gates, for their king and his leaders will be captured. (Heshbon: ancient city of the Amorites; Ai: a Canaanite city destroyed by Joshua) **4.** Why do you boast in the valleys, your fertile valley, O unfaithful daughter? You trust in your riches, saying, "Who will come against me?" (Backsliding daughter: a term used for unfaithful Israel) **5.** I will bring fear upon you, says the Lord of Hosts, from all around you. You will be driven out, and no one will gather those who stray. (Host: God's title as the leader of heavenly armies) **6.** Afterward, I will restore the captives of Ammon, says the LORD. (Ammon: an ancient Semitic kingdom) **7.** Concerning Edom, the LORD of Hosts asks: Has wisdom disappeared from Teman? Has counsel vanished from the wise? Is their wisdom gone? (Teman: a city in Edom known for its wisdom) **8.** Flee, turn back, dwell deep, O inhabitants of Dedan; for I will bring destruction upon Esau, at the time I visit him. (Dedan: a region and people south of Edom) **9.** If grape harvesters come to you, wouldn't they leave some grapes behind? If thieves come at night, they only take what they need. (Gleaning: leaving behind remnants of harvest for the poor) **10.** But I have exposed Esau, uncovering his hidden places. He cannot hide; his descendants, brothers, and neighbors are all gone. (Esau: ancestor of the Edomites) **11.** Leave your orphans; I will protect them. Let your widows trust in me. (Orphans and widows: symbols of vulnerability and God's care) **12.** The LORD declares: Those who were not supposed to drink from the cup of judgment will surely drink. And you, will you go unpunished? No, you will drink from it too. (Judgment cup: a metaphor for God's judgment) **13.** I have sworn by myself, says the LORD, that Bozrah will be a desolation, a disgrace, a wasteland, and a curse. All its cities will become eternal ruins. (Bozrah: capital of Edom) **14.** I have heard a report from the LORD: An envoy is sent to the nations, saying, "Gather, and come against her for battle." (Envoy: a messenger, often of war) **15.** I will make you insignificant among the nations and despised by men. (Despicable: regarded with contempt) **16.** Your arrogance deceives you, O you who live in the rock clefts, who dwell high on the hill. Though you make your nest like an eagle, I will bring you down, says the LORD. (Rock clefts: Edom was known for its mountain strongholds) **17.** Edom will be a desolation, and all who pass by will be horrified and hiss at its plagues. (Desolation: complete destruction) **18.** As with the destruction of Sodom and Gomorrah, no one will remain, and no one will live there. (Sodom and Gomorrah: ancient cities destroyed for their sin) **19.** A lion will rise from the Jordan against the stronghold, but I will make him flee suddenly. Who can challenge me? Who can appoint the time of judgment? (Jordan: a river in Israel, symbolizing strength and security) **20.** Listen to the LORD's plans against Edom, His purpose against Teman: Even the least of the flock will draw them out, and their homes will be left desolate. (Teman: a region in Edom) **21.** The earth shakes at the sound of their fall, and the cry is heard all the way to the Red Sea. (Red Sea: the body of water between Egypt and the Arabian Peninsula) **22.** He will come up like an eagle, spreading his wings over Bozrah, and that day the hearts of Edom's mighty men will be filled with fear, like a woman in labor. (Bozrah: an important city in Edom) **23.** Concerning Damascus: Hamath and Arpad are dismayed; they have heard bad news. They are distressed, unable to find peace. (Damascus: capital of Syria; Hamath and Arpad: ancient cities in Syria) **24.** Damascus grows weak and turns to flee; terror grips her; anguish has taken hold, like a woman in labor. (Damascus: ancient city, now the capital of Syria) **25.** How is the city of praise, the city of my joy, not left desolate? (City of praise: a title for Damascus) **26.** Therefore, her young men will fall in the streets, and all her warriors will be cut off, says the LORD of Hosts. (Young men: often symbolizing strength and future generations) **27.** I will set fire to the walls of Damascus, and it will consume the palaces of Ben-Hadad. (Ben-Hadad: a name of kings of Aram, associated with Damascus) **28.** Concerning Kedar and the kingdoms of Hazor, which Nebuchadnezzar, king of Babylon, will strike: Arise, attack Kedar and spoil the men of the East. (Kedar: a region of nomadic Arab tribes; Hazor: an ancient city) **29.** Their tents and flocks will be taken, their belongings and camels will be seized. They will cry out in fear on every side. (Tents: temporary dwellings of nomads; flocks: sheep or cattle) **30.** Flee far away, O inhabitants of Hazor, says the LORD, for Nebuchadnezzar, king of Babylon, has planned disaster against you. (Nebuchadnezzar: king of Babylon who conquered many nations) **31.** Rise up against the nation that is carefree, says the LORD, the nation without gates or walls, dwelling alone. (Wealthy nation: refers to an isolated, prosperous land) **32.** Their camels and cattle will be plundered, and I will scatter those in the corners of the earth. Their calamity will come from all directions, says the LORD. (Plundered: taken by force or theft) **33.** Hazor will be a home for wild animals, a place of desolation forever. No one will live there, and no man will

dwell in it. (Wild animals: symbolizing desolation) **34**. The word of the LORD came to Jeremiah concerning Elam at the beginning of the reign of Zedekiah, king of Judah, saying: (Zedekiah: last king of Judah) **35**. The LORD of Hosts says: I will break the power of Elam, the source of their strength. (Elam: an ancient kingdom located in modern-day Iran) **36**. I will send the four winds to scatter the people of Elam to all corners of the earth; no nation will escape their exile. (Four winds: symbolic of global scattering) **37**. I will bring fear upon Elam's enemies and those who seek their life. I will bring disaster and my fierce anger, says the LORD, and I will pursue them with the sword until I destroy them. (Fierce anger: God's intense judgment) **38**. I will set my throne in Elam and destroy its king and rulers, says the LORD. (Throne: symbol of God's sovereignty) **39**. But in the later days, I will bring the captives of Elam back, says the LORD. (Captives: those taken as prisoners of war)

Chapter 50

1. This is the prophecy that the LORD spoke against Babylon and the land of the Chaldeans, delivered by the prophet Jeremiah. (Chaldeans: ancient people from the southern part of Babylon) **2**. Announce it to the nations, broadcast the message, raise a banner, and leave no room for secrecy: declare that Babylon is fallen! Bel is shamed, and Merodach is shattered; her idols are defeated, and her images are smashed to pieces. (Bel: a chief god of the Babylonians; Merodach: another Babylonian god) **3**. From the north, a nation rises against her, a people that will make her land desolate, with no one left to dwell there. All will flee: man and beast alike will depart. (Desolate: barren, empty, abandoned) **4**. At that time, says the LORD, the children of Israel and Judah will return, united in their journey. With tears in their eyes, they will seek the LORD their God. (United: joined together, in harmony) **5**. They will ask the way to Zion, their faces set toward it, saying, "Let us go, and make an everlasting covenant with the LORD, one that will never be forgotten." (Covenant: an agreement or promise) **6**. My people have become like lost sheep; their shepherds led them astray, guiding them away from the true path. They wandered from hill to hill, forgetting where they once rested. (Shepherds: leaders or guides; Astray: away from the correct path) **7**. Those who found them devoured them, and their enemies said, "We have done no wrong; they have sinned against the LORD, the true God, the hope of their ancestors." (Devoured: consumed, destroyed; Sinned: done wrong, disobeyed God) **8**. Leave Babylon, flee from the land of the Chaldeans, and be like goats leading the flock to safety. (Flee: run away, escape) **9**. I will raise up a mighty coalition of nations from the north against Babylon. They will form ranks and surround her; she will be captured. Their arrows will strike with precision, and none will miss. (Coalition: a group formed for a common purpose; Precision: accuracy, exactness) **10**. The land of the Chaldeans will become a spoil. All who plunder her will be satisfied, says the LORD. (Spoil: goods or treasure taken in war; Plunder: to rob or steal) **11**. You rejoiced when you destroyed my people. You grew fat and strong like heifers in the grass, roaring like bulls. (Heifers: young cows, often used for breeding) **12**. But now your mother will be shamed, the one who gave you birth will be disgraced. Babylon will become the least of the nations, a desolate wasteland, dry and barren. (Disgraced: shamed, dishonored) **13**. Because of the fierce anger of the LORD, it will remain uninhabited, a place so desolate that those who pass by will be horrified and will hiss at its ruin. (Horrified: filled with fear or shock; Hiss: a sound expressing disdain or disgust) **14**. Surround Babylon on all sides! All who are armed, shoot your arrows at her—spare none. For she has sinned greatly against the LORD. (Spare: to save from harm, avoid destroying) **15**. Shout aloud against her! Her defenses have crumbled; her walls are shattered. This is the LORD's vengeance. Let justice be carried out as she has done to others. (Crumbled: fallen apart; Vengeance: punishment in return for wrongs) **16**. Cut off the workers from Babylon—those who harvest crops and sow seeds. They will flee in fear, seeking refuge in their own lands, leaving Babylon to fall. (Refuge: safety, protection) **17**. Israel, like a scattered sheep, was driven away by fierce lions. First, the king of Assyria devoured them; then, King Nebuchadrezzar of Babylon broke their bones. (Scattered: dispersed, separated; Devoured: consumed or destroyed) **18**. Therefore, the LORD of hosts, the God of Israel, declares: I will punish the king of Babylon and his land, just as I have punished the king of Assyria. (Hosts: armies or heavenly beings) **19**. I will bring Israel back to its rightful place, where they will find peace. They will be nourished in Carmel and Bashan, and their souls will be satisfied in Ephraim and Gilead. (Nourished: fed, taken care of; Bashan: a fertile region east of Israel; Ephraim and Gilead: regions in ancient Israel) **20**. In those days, says the LORD, the sins of Israel and Judah will be forgiven, and no trace of their guilt will remain. I will pardon those whom I have preserved. (Pardon: to forgive, to release from guilt) **21**. Go against the land of Merathaim and the people of Pekod. Completely destroy them, says the LORD, and carry out all my commands. (Merathaim: a place or region; Pekod: another region or people associated with Babylon) **22**. A sound of destruction fills the land, a mighty roar of battle. (Destruction: ruin, devastation) **23**. How has the hammer of the earth been broken and shattered! Babylon, once the dominant power, has now become a desolation among the nations. (Hammer: symbol of great strength; Desolation: complete emptiness, ruin) **24**. I have laid a trap for you, O Babylon. You are caught, though you did not realize it. You are found and ensnared because you opposed the LORD. (Ensnared: trapped, caught) **25**. The LORD has opened his armory and brought out his weapons of judgment. This is the work of the Lord GOD of hosts in the land of the Chaldeans. (Armory: a place where weapons are stored) **26**. Come against her from every direction. Open her storehouses, lay her bare, and destroy everything. Leave nothing behind. (Storehouses: places where goods are kept) **27**. Slay all her cattle; send them to the slaughter. Woe to them, for their time of reckoning has come. (Slay: kill; Woe: a declaration of grief or distress; Reckoning: a time of judgment) **28**. Listen to the voices of those who escape Babylon, declaring the vengeance of the LORD and the vengeance of His temple in Zion. (Vengeance: punishment for wrongs) **29**. Gather together the archers against Babylon. Surround her, and let none escape. Give her what she deserves—what she has done to others, do to her. For she has been arrogant against the LORD, the Holy One of Israel. (Archers: those who use bows and arrows; Arrogant: proud, showing a lack of respect) **30**. Therefore, her young men will fall in the streets, and her warriors will be cut off in that day, says the LORD. (Cut off: destroyed, removed) **31**. I am against you, O most proud Babylon, says the Lord GOD of hosts. Your day has come, the time when I will bring judgment upon you. (Proud: haughty, thinking oneself superior) **32**. The proud will stumble and fall, and none will rise to help them. I will set fire to their cities, and it will consume everything around them. (Stumble: to fall or trip; Consume: to destroy completely) **33**. The LORD of hosts says: Israel and Judah were oppressed together. Those who captured them held them fast and refused to let them go. (Oppressed: mistreated, harmed; Held fast: kept tightly, captured) **34**. But their Redeemer is strong. The LORD of hosts is His name. He will defend their cause, bring rest to the land, and trouble those who dwell in Babylon. (Redeemer: one who rescues or saves; Cause: reason, argument; Dwell: to live or reside) **35**. A sword is coming against the Chaldeans, the inhabitants of Babylon, her princes, and her wise men. (Princes: leaders, rulers) **36**. A sword will strike the liars, and they will go mad. A sword will strike her mighty warriors, and they will be dismayed. (Dismayed: frightened, alarmed) **37**. A sword will strike her horses and chariots, and the mixed peoples within her will become like women. A sword will strike her treasures, and they will be plundered. (Mixed peoples: diverse or foreign populations; Plundered: looted, robbed) **38**. A drought is coming upon her waters, and they will be dried up. Babylon is a land of idols, and her people are mad with their worship. (Drought: a long period without rain; Idols: false gods, images of worship) **39**. Therefore, wild beasts of the desert and islands will make their home in her, and owls will dwell in her ruins. Babylon will be uninhabited forever, a desolate wasteland. (Wild beasts: untamed animals; Owls: birds that often symbolize desolation) **40**. Just as God overthrew Sodom and Gomorrah and their neighboring cities, says the LORD, so no man will live there, and no human will dwell there. (Overthrew: destroyed, turned upside down) **41**. Look! A people comes from the north, a great nation, with many kings from the farthest reaches of the earth. (Farthest: most distant) **42**. They will wield bows and lances, fierce and merciless. Their roar will be like the sea as they ride upon horses, ready for battle against you, O daughter of Babylon. (Wield: to carry and use; Lances: long spears) **43**. The king of Babylon has heard their report, and his hands grow weak. Anguish overtakes him, like the pain of a woman in labor. (Anguish: extreme pain, distress) **44**. Like a lion coming from the banks of the Jordan, he will come to her stronghold. But I will cause them to flee from her, and no one will stand against me. Who can compare to me? Who can challenge my appointed time? Who can stand before me? (Stronghold: a fortified place) **45**. Therefore, hear the counsel of the LORD, His plan against Babylon. His purpose concerning the Chaldeans will be carried out. Even the smallest among them will lead them to ruin, and He will desolate their land. (Counsel: advice, plan) **46**. At the news of Babylon's fall, the earth will tremble, and a cry of distress will be heard among the nations. (Distress: great suffering or pain)

Chapter 51

1. Thus speaks the LORD: "I will rise up against Babylon and those who dwell in its midst, those who oppose Me, with a destructive wind. (destructive: harmful) **2**. I will send men with fans to sweep through Babylon, emptying its lands, for in the time of judgment, they will be surrounded by foes. (fans: blowers ; foes: enemies) **3**. Let the archer take aim at the one who bends, and the one clothed in armor; let no mercy be shown to her young men, but utterly destroy her entire army. (archer: bowman ; armor: protection) **4**. The slain shall fall within the land of the Chaldeans, and those pierced will lie in her streets. (slain: killed ; pierced: stabbed) **5**. Israel has not been abandoned, nor Judah by its God, the LORD of hosts, despite the land being filled with sin against the Holy One of Israel. (hosts: armies) **6**. Escape from the midst of Babylon, let each man save his life; do not be consumed by her iniquity, for the time of the LORD's vengeance has come—He will repay her. (iniquity: wickedness ; vengeance: retribution) **7**. Babylon was a golden cup in the hand of the LORD, causing the earth to stagger; the nations have drunk her wine, and now the nations rage. (stagger: wobble ; rage: anger) **8**. Babylon is suddenly fallen and destroyed; mourn for her, try to heal her wounds, if it is possible. (mourn: grieve) **9**. We sought to heal Babylon, but she could not be healed. Leave her, and let each one return to his own land, for her judgment reaches to the heavens, and her fate is sealed. (healed: restored ; judgment: punishment) **10**. The LORD has made our righteousness known. Come, let us declare the work of the LORD in Zion. (righteousness: virtue) **11**. Sharpen the arrows, gather the shields: the LORD has stirred the spirit of the kings of the Medes, for His purpose is against Babylon, to destroy it, as vengeance for the LORD's temple. (stirred: provoked ; vengeance: retaliation) **12**. Raise the standard upon the walls of Babylon, strengthen the watch, station the guards, and prepare ambushes, for the LORD has planned and will execute what He spoke against Babylon. (standard: banner ; ambushes: attacks) **13**. O you who dwell by many waters, rich in treasures, your end has come, and the measure of your greed is full. (dwell: live ; treasures: wealth ; measure: amount) **14**. The LORD of hosts has sworn by Himself, "I will fill you with men like locusts, and they will shout against you." (locusts: pests) **15**. He has made the earth by His power, established the world by His wisdom, and spread out the heavens by His understanding. (established: set ; understanding: insight) **16**. When He speaks, waters rise in the heavens, vapor ascends from the ends of the earth, lightning strikes with the rain, and the wind blows from His storehouses. (vapor: mist ; ascends: rises) **17**. Every man is foolish in his knowledge; the craftsman is ashamed of his idols, for the molten image is a lie and holds no breath. (foolish: ignorant ; craftsman: creator ; molten: melted ; idol: statue) **18**. They are vanity, the product of errors; in the time of reckoning, they will perish. (vanity: emptiness ; errors: mistakes ; reckoning: judgment) **19**. But the portion of Jacob is not like them; He is the Creator of all things, and Israel is His inheritance. The LORD of hosts is His name. (portion: share ; inheritance: legacy) **20**. You are My battle axe and weapon of war: with you, I will shatter nations and destroy kingdoms. (battle axe: weapon) **21**. With you, I will crush both horse and rider, chariot and driver. (crush: smash) **22**. With you, I will break both man and woman, old and young, and the young man with the maiden. (maiden: girl) **23**. With you, I will shatter the shepherd and his flock, the farmer and his oxen, the captains and rulers. (flock: herd ; captains: leaders) **24**. I will repay Babylon and all the Chaldeans for the evil they have done to Zion, declares the LORD. (repay: avenge ; Chaldeans: Babylonians) **25**. Look, I am against you, O destroying mountain, says the LORD, who devastates the whole earth. I will stretch out My hand against you, and bring you down from the rocks, making you a burnt mountain. (devastates: destroys) **26**. No stone from you will be taken for a cornerstone or foundation; you will be desolate forever, says the LORD. (cornerstone: base ; desolate: abandoned) **27**. Raise a banner in the land, sound the trumpet among the nations, summon the kingdoms of Ararat, Minni, and Ashchenaz against her; appoint a commander and bring the horses like swarming locusts. (summon: call ; swarming: gathering) **28**. Gather the nations, the kings of the Medes, their leaders, and the rulers of their lands. (Medes: ancient people) **29**. The earth will tremble and sorrow, for the LORD's plan against Babylon will be carried out, making it an empty desolation. (tremble: shake) **30**. The mighty men of Babylon have given up the fight, retreating to their strongholds. Their strength has failed, and they have become like women. Their houses are burned, their gates broken. (strongholds: fortresses) **31**. One messenger will meet another to announce to the king of Babylon that his city is captured from one side. (captured: seized) **32**. The passages are blocked, and the reeds are set afire. The warriors are terrified. (passages: routes ; reeds: plants) **33**. Thus says the LORD of hosts, the God of Israel: "The daughter of Babylon is like a threshing floor; it is time to thresh her, for the harvest is coming." (threshing floor: grain area ; harvest: gathering) **34**. Nebuchadnezzar, king of Babylon, has devoured me, crushed me, made me an empty vessel, and swallowed me up like a serpent. He filled his belly with my delicacies and cast me out. (devoured: consumed ; vessel: container ; delicacies: treats) **35**. The violence done to me and to my flesh will be upon Babylon, and my blood will be upon the inhabitants of Chaldea, says Jerusalem. (violence: harm ; inhabitants: residents) **36**. Therefore, says the LORD: "I will plead your case and avenge you. I will dry up her sea and make her springs dry." (plead: argue ; avenge: punish) **37**. Babylon will become heaps of ruins, a dwelling place for dragons, an astonishment, and a hissing, uninhabited forever. (heaps: piles ; dragons: monsters) **38**. They will roar like lions, and like lion's cubs, they will shout. (roar: yell) **39**. In their heat, I will prepare their feasts and make them drunk, so they may rejoice and fall into a perpetual sleep, never to wake again, says the LORD. (feasts: banquets ; perpetual: eternal) **40**. I will bring them down like lambs to the slaughter, like rams and goats. (lambs: sheep) **41**. How is Sheshach captured! How is the praise of the whole earth surprised! How has Babylon become an astonishment among the nations! (Sheshach: Babylon) (astonishment: shock) **42**. The sea has risen against Babylon; she is covered with the multitude of her waves. (waves: swells) **43**. Her cities are desolate, a dry land, and a wilderness; no one lives there, and no one passes through. (desolate: ruined ; wilderness: barren) **44**. I will punish Bel in Babylon and will take back what he has consumed; the nations will no longer gather to him. The wall of Babylon will fall. (punish: discipline ; consume: devour) **45**. My people, come out of her, and save yourselves from the fierce anger of the LORD. (save: rescue) **46**. Do not fear the rumors that will spread; one year after another, rumors of violence and conflict will come. (rumors: gossip ; conflict: battle) **47**. The days are coming when I will judge the idols of Babylon, and her entire land will be confused; all her slain will fall within her borders. (idols: statues ; confused: chaotic) **48**. Then heaven and earth, and everything in them, will rejoice over Babylon, for the destroyers will come from the north, says the LORD. (destroyers: wreckers) **49**. Just as Babylon caused the slain of Israel to fall, so Babylon will fall with the slain of all the earth. (slain: dead) **50**. You who have escaped the sword, go, do not stand still; remember the LORD from afar and let Jerusalem come to mind. (escape: flee) **51**. We are ashamed because we have heard reproach; shame has covered our faces, for foreigners have entered the sanctuaries of the LORD's house. (reproach: disgrace ; sanctuaries: temples) **52**. Therefore, the days are coming, says the LORD, when I will judge the idols of Babylon, and the wounded will groan throughout the land. (groan: moan) **53**. Even if Babylon rises to heaven and strengthens her defenses, the spoilers will still come upon her, says the LORD. (defenses: barriers) **54**. A cry is heard from Babylon, a great destruction from the land of the Chaldeans. (destruction: ruin) **55**. The LORD has spoiled Babylon and destroyed her great voice; her waves roar like mighty waters, a noise that shakes the earth. (spoiled: ruined ; waves: surges) **56**. The destroyer has come upon Babylon, and her mighty men are captured; every bow is broken. The LORD God of recompenses will surely repay. (destroyer: wrecking force ; recompenses: rewards) **57**. I will make her princes, wise men, captains, rulers, and mighty men drunk; they will fall into a perpetual sleep, never to wake again, says the King, whose name is the LORD of hosts. (princes: lords) **58**. The broad walls of Babylon will be completely destroyed, and her high gates will be burned with fire; the people will work in vain, and their efforts will wear them out. (broad: wide ; vain: pointless) **59**. The word that Jeremiah the prophet commanded Seraiah, the son of Neriah, to take with him when he went to Babylon with King Zedekiah in the fourth year of his reign. Seraiah was a quiet prince. (commanded: directed ; quiet: reserved) **60**. Jeremiah wrote in a book all the disasters that would come upon Babylon, all the words spoken against it. (disasters: tragedies) **61**. When you reach Babylon and read this book, (reach: arrive) **62**. say, "LORD, You have spoken against this place to destroy it, so that nothing and no one will remain in it, neither man nor beast, but it will be desolate forever." (desolate: barren) **63**. When you finish reading this book, tie a stone to it and throw it into the Euphrates River, (tie: bind) **64**. and say, "Thus Babylon will sink, and never rise again from the disaster I will bring upon her." So ends the words of Jeremiah. (sink: submerge ; disaster: catastrophe)

Chapter 52

1. Zedekiah was twenty-one years old when he began his reign, and he ruled in Jerusalem for eleven years. His mother's name was Hamutal, daughter of Jeremiah from Libnah. (Libnah: A town in ancient Judah) **2**. He acted wickedly in the sight of the LORD, just as Jehoiakim had done. (Wickedly: In a morally wrong manner) **3**. Because of the LORD's anger, it came to pass that in Jerusalem and Judah, the people were cast out of His presence. During this time, Zedekiah rebelled against the king of Babylon. (Rebelled: To rise up against authority) **4**. In the ninth year of his reign, on the tenth day of the tenth month, Nebuchadrezzar, king of Babylon, came against Jerusalem with his entire army. They camped around the city and built siege works to surround it. (Siege: A military operation where forces surround a city to capture it) **5**. The city remained under siege until the eleventh year of King Zedekiah's reign. (Siege: The act of surrounding and blockading a city or fortress) **6**. In the fourth month, on the ninth day, the famine became severe within the city, leaving the people with no bread to eat. (Famine: A severe shortage of food) **7**. Eventually, the city walls were breached, and all the soldiers fled under the cover of night, escaping through a gate between two walls near the king's garden. The Chaldeans had surrounded the city, and the soldiers fled toward the plains. (Breached: Broken through ; Pursued: Followed with the intent to capture or attack) **8**. The Chaldean army pursued the king and caught up with Zedekiah in the plains of Jericho, where his soldiers scattered and fled. **9**. They captured the king and took him to Riblah, in the land of Hamath, where the king of Babylon passed judgment on him. (Riblah: A place in northern Syria where the king of Babylon passed judgment) **10**. The Babylonian king killed Zedekiah's sons before his eyes and also executed all the officials of Judah in Riblah. (Executed: Killed as a punishment or sentence) **11**. Afterward, the king of Babylon gouged out Zedekiah's eyes, bound him in chains, and took him to Babylon, where he remained imprisoned until his death. (Gouged out: Removed by force, especially referring to the eyes) **12**. In the fifth month, on the tenth day of the month, during the nineteenth year of Nebuchadrezzar, the captain of the guard, Nebuzar-adan, who served the king of Babylon, came to Jerusalem. (Captain of the guard: A high-ranking military officer responsible for the army's protection and security) **13**. He set fire to the house of the LORD, the king's palace, all the houses of Jerusalem, and the homes of the leading men of the city. (Set fire to: Burned) **14**. The entire army of the Chaldeans, under the command of the captain of the guard, tore down the city walls surrounding Jerusalem. (Tore down: Destroyed or demolished) **15**. Nebuzar-adan then took some of the poor people of the land, along with the rest of those who were left behind in the city, including those who had defected to the Babylonian king, and carried them away as captives. (Defected: Abandoned one's allegiance to join the enemy) **16**. However, the captain of the guard left behind some of the poor people of the land to work as vine growers and farmers. (Vine growers: People who cultivate grapevines) **17**. He also took the bronze pillars, the bases, and the large bronze basin (the "brasen sea") from the temple of the LORD, as well as all the bronze items, and took them to Babylon. (Brasen sea: A large bronze basin used in the temple for ceremonial washing) **18**. The caldrons, shovels, snuffers, bowls, spoons, and other bronze vessels used in temple service were also taken by the Chaldeans. (Snuffers: Tools used to trim or extinguish the wicks of lamps) **19**. The golden and silver items, such as basins, firepans, bowls, candlesticks, spoons, and cups, were all taken by the captain of the guard, who carried them away. (Firepans: Shallow pans used for carrying fire) **20**. The two bronze pillars, the large basin, and the twelve bronze bulls under the bases, all made by King Solomon for the temple, were also removed. The weight of all these bronze vessels was beyond measure. (Bulls: Bronze animal figures placed beneath the bases of the pillars) **21**. The height of one pillar was eighteen cubits, with a twelve-cubit circumference, and it was four fingers thick. It was hollow. (Cubit: A unit of length based on the forearm, approximately 18 inches) **22**. A brass chapiter was placed on it, and the chapiter itself was five cubits tall, decorated with a network and pomegranates, all made of brass. The second pillar and its pomegranates were similar. (Chapiter: The ornamental top of a pillar ; Pomegranates: Decorative fruit-shaped designs used in the temple's architecture) **23**. There were ninety-six pomegranates on the sides of the pillars, and a total of one hundred pomegranates around the network. **24**. The captain of the guard took Seraiah, the chief priest, Zephaniah, the second priest, and three keepers of the temple gate. **25**. He also took an eunuch in charge of the soldiers, seven of the king's close attendants, the principal scribe of the army, who had counted the people, and sixty others from the land who were found in the city. (Scribe: A person who writes or keeps records) **26**. Nebuzar-adan took all these people and brought them to the king of Babylon in Riblah. **27**. The king of Babylon struck them down and executed them in Riblah, in the land of Hamath. This marked the end of Judah's captivity. (Struck down: Killed or struck with force) **28.** In the seventh year of Nebuchadrezzar's reign, three thousand and twenty-three Jews were taken captive. (Taken captive: Captured and brought into captivity) **29.** In the eighteenth year of Nebuchadrezzar, eight hundred thirty-two people were carried off from Jerusalem. (Carried off: Taken away by force or capture) **30.** In the twenty-third year of Nebuchadrezzar, Nebuzar-adan, the captain of the guard, took seven hundred forty-five Jews as captives, making the total number of exiled persons four thousand six hundred. (Exiled: Forced to live away from one's homeland, usually due to political or military reasons) **31.** In the thirty-seventh year of the exile of King Jehoiachin of Judah, in the twelfth month on the twenty-fifth day, Evil-merodach, king of Babylon, in his first year, released Jehoiachin from prison. **32.** The king spoke kindly to him, raised his position above the other kings in Babylon, **33.** changed his prison clothes, and gave him a place at his table for the rest of his life. (Prison clothes: The attire worn by prisoners) **34.** The king of Babylon provided Jehoiachin with daily provisions until his death, ensuring that he would always have food to eat.(Provisions: Supplies, especially food and necessities)

25 – Lamentations
Chapter 1

1. How does the city sit solitary, once full of people? She has become like a widow, once great among the nations, now a tribute-bearer. **2.** She weeps bitterly at night; no one comforts her. Her lovers have betrayed her, and her friends have become enemies. **3.** Judah is in captivity, suffering greatly and finding no rest among the nations. Her persecutors have overtaken her. (persecutors : those who harm her) **4.** Zion mourns as no one comes to its feasts. Its gates are desolate; the priests sigh, the virgins suffer, and bitterness overwhelms it. (Zion : two hills of ancient Jerusalem, desolate : empty) **5.** Her enemies are prosperous, for the LORD has afflicted her due to her many transgressions. Her children are in captivity. (enemies : those who oppose her, transgressions : sins) **6.** The beauty of Zion has departed. Its princes, like deer with no pasture, have no strength before their pursuers. (princes: leaders, pursuers : those chasing her) **7.** Jerusalem remembers its former glory and the days when it fell into enemy hands, with no one to help. Her adversaries mock her. (adversaries: enemies) **8.** Jerusalem has grievously sinned and been cast down. Those who once honored her now despise her, seeing her shame. (grievously: seriously, cast down : thrown down, shame : nakedness) **9.** Her filthiness is evident, and she has forgotten her end. She is brought low, with no comforter. O LORD, behold my affliction. (filthiness: impurity, brought low : humbled, affliction : suffering) **10.** The enemy has taken all her precious things, and even desecrated the sanctuary, which was forbidden to foreigners. (sanctuary: holy place, desecrated : defiled) **11.** Her people sigh, seeking food; they have sold their treasures to survive. LORD, look upon me, for I have become vile. (treasures: valuable items, vile : disgusting) **12.** Is it nothing to you, all who pass by? See the sorrow done to me by the LORD in His fierce anger. (sorrow : grief, fierce anger : strong wrath) **13.** From above, He has sent fire into my bones, prevailing against me. He has trapped me and made me desolate. (fire: suffering, desolate : empty) **14.** The burden of my transgressions is heavy; they have weakened me, and the LORD has handed me over to my enemies. (burden: weight, transgressions : sins) **15.** The LORD has crushed my mighty men and called an assembly to destroy my young men, as if pressing grapes in a winepress. (Mighty men : warriors, assembly : group) **16.** I weep because no comforter is near, and my children are desolate, overcome by the enemy. (comforter: someone to help, desolate : abandoned) **17.** Zion stretches out her hands, but there is no one to comfort her. The LORD has surrounded Jacob with enemies, and Jerusalem is defiled. (Zion: Jerusalem, Jacob : Israel, defiled : made unclean) **18.** The LORD is righteous; I have rebelled against His commands. Hear my sorrow, for my young men and virgins are in captivity. (righteous: just, rebellion : disobedience, young men : warriors, virgins : unmarried women) **19.** I called for help, but my lovers deceived me. My priests and elders have died, seeking food for their souls. (deceived: tricked, priests : religious leaders) **20.** O LORD, I am in distress; my heart is overwhelmed, for I have rebelled greatly. The sword kills outside, and death is within. (distress: suffering, sword : war, overwhelmed : burdened) **21.** My enemies rejoice at my trouble. They know the day you've appointed will come, and they will suffer as I have. (enemies: those who oppose me, appointed : planned) **22.** Let their wickedness be before you. Do to them as you've done to me for my sins, for my sighs are many and my heart is faint. (wickedness: evil deeds, sighs : groans, faint : weak)

Chapter 2

1. How has the Lord covered the daughter of Zion with a cloud in His anger, and thrown down from heaven to earth Israel's beauty, forgetting His footstool on the day of His wrath? (Footstool: symbolic reference to the Temple or Jerusalem) **2.** The Lord has consumed all of Jacob's dwellings, showing no mercy. He has thrown down the strongholds of Judah in His wrath, defiling its kingdom and princes. (Strongholds: places of defense) **3.** In fierce anger, He has cut off Israel's horn, withdrawn His protection from before the enemy, and burned against Jacob like a fire that devours everything. (Horn: strength or power) **4.** He has bent His bow like an enemy, standing as an adversary, and destroyed everything pleasant in Zion's tabernacle, pouring out His fury like fire. (Tabernacle: place of worship) **5.** The Lord has become like an enemy, swallowing up Israel and all her palaces, destroying her strongholds, and bringing mourning to Judah. (**Palaces: royal residences**) **6.** He violently took away His tabernacle, destroyed His places of assembly, and caused Zion to forget her feasts and Sabbaths, despising king and priest in His anger. (Assembly: gathering place) **7.** The Lord has rejected His altar and abhorred His sanctuary, giving control of her walls to the enemy, making noise in the house of the Lord as if it were a feast day. (Altar: place of sacrifice; sanctuary: holy place) **8.** The Lord has planned the destruction of Zion's walls, and He has continued His destruction until both the ramparts and walls lament and wither. (**Ramparts: defensive walls**) **9.** Her gates have fallen into the ground; He has destroyed and broken her bars. Her king and princes are among the Gentiles. The law is no more, and her prophets find no vision from the Lord. (Bars: gates' metal parts; Gentiles: foreign nations) **10.** The elders of the daughter of Zion sit on the ground in silence; they have thrown dust on their heads and put on sackcloth. The virgins of Jerusalem hang down their heads. (Elders: wise men; sackcloth: mourning clothes) **11.** My eyes fail with tears; my heart is troubled for the destruction of my people. Children and infants faint in the streets. (fail: become weak) **12.** They ask their mothers for food, but faint as if they were wounded in the streets, their souls poured out into their mothers' arms. (Faint: fade) **13.** What can I compare to you, O daughter of Jerusalem? What can heal your great wound, like the sea, which cannot be healed? **14.** Your prophets have seen false visions and have not revealed your sin, causing your exile. They have given you false hopes and causes for banishment. (Prophets: spiritual leaders) **15.** All who pass by clap their hands at you, mocking Jerusalem, saying, "Is this the city called 'The perfection of beauty, the joy of the whole earth'?" (pass by: travelers; clap hands: mock) **16.** All your enemies open their mouths against you; they hiss and gnash their teeth, saying, "We have swallowed her up; this is the day we waited for." (gnash: grind teeth in anger) **17.** The Lord has done what He planned, fulfilling His word that He commanded long ago. He has thrown down without mercy and caused your enemies to rejoice over you, exalting their power. (Fulfilling: completing; word: promise) **18.** Let your tears flow like a river, day and night, O daughter of Zion; give yourself no rest, nor stop grieving. (grieving: mourning) **19.** Arise, cry out in the night; at the beginning of the watches pour out your heart like water before the Lord. Lift up your hands to Him for the lives of your young children who faint for hunger in every street. (watches: night periods) **20.** O Lord, look and see to whom You have done this. Shall the women eat their fruit, and the priests and prophets be slain in the sanctuary? (fruit: children; slain: killed) **21.** The young and the old lie dead in the streets; my virgins and young men are fallen by the sword; You have slain them in the day of Your anger, with no pity. (virgins: young women) **22.** You called my terrors to surround me on the day of Your anger; none escaped, and those I raised were consumed by the enemy. (terrors: fears; consumed: destroyed)

Chapter 3

1. I am the man who has seen suffering under God's anger. (suffering: affliction, anger: wrath) **2.** He has led me into darkness, not light. (darkness : despair) **3.** He is against me; His hand is upon me all day. (against : opposed) **4.** He has worn out my flesh and skin; He has broken my bones. (flesh : body, broken : shattered) **5.** He has built walls against me, surrounding me with bitterness and hardship. (bitterness: gall, hardship: travail) **6.** He has placed me in darkness, like the dead of old. (dead of old : ancient graves) **7.** He has surrounded me so I cannot escape; my chains are heavy. (surrounded: hedged) **8.** Even when I cry out, He shuts out my prayer. (shut : refuses) **9.** He has blocked my way with hewn stone and made my paths crooked. (Hewn stone : cut stone, crooked : twisted) **10.** He waits for me like a bear or a lion in hiding. (hiding: in secret places) **11.** He has turned my way and torn me apart; He has made me desolate. (desolate : abandoned) **12.** He has bent His bow and set me as a target for His arrows. (bow : weapon, target : aim) **13.** His arrows pierce my innermost being. (innermost: inmost) **14.** I am a mockery to my people, their song all day. (mockery: derision) **15.** He has filled me with bitterness; He has made me drunk with wormwood. (drunken : overwhelmed, wormwood : bitter herb) **16.** He has broken my teeth with gravel and covered me with ashes. (gravel: sharp stones, ashes : dust) **17.** You have removed my peace; I have forgotten prosperity. (prosperity : well-being) **18.** I said, "My strength and hope are gone from the LORD." (hope : trust) **19.** I remember my suffering, my bitterness, and the gall. (gall : bitterness) **20.** My soul remembers them and is humbled within me. (humbled : made low) **21.** Yet this I recall, and therefore I have hope: **22.** It is because of the LORD's mercies that we are not consumed, for His compassion never fails. (mercies : kindness, compassion : deep care) **23.** They are new every morning; great is Your faithfulness. (faithfulness : loyalty) **24.** The LORD is my portion, says my soul; therefore, I will hope in Him. (portion : share, soul : inner being) **25.** The LORD is good to those who wait for Him, to the soul that seeks Him. (wait : trust, seeks : searches for) **26.** It is good to hope and quietly wait for the salvation of the LORD. (salvation : rescue) **27.** It is good for a man to bear the yoke in his youth. (yoke : burden, youth : young age) **28.** He sits alone and keeps silent because He has borne it. (keeps silent : remains quiet) **29.** He puts his mouth in the dust, hoping there may be hope. (dust : ground, hope : mercy) **30.** He gives his cheek to the one who strikes him; He is full of reproach. (cheek : face, reproach : shame) **31.** For the Lord will not cast off forever. (cast off : reject) **32.** Though He causes grief, He will show compassion because of His great mercies. (grief : sorrow, compassion : care) **33.** He does not afflict willingly nor grieve the children of men. (afflict : cause pain) **34.** To crush underfoot all the prisoners of the earth, (crush underfoot : tread down) **35.** To deprive a man of his rights before the Most High, (deprive : take away, Most High : God) **36.** To subvert a man in his cause, the Lord does not approve. (subvert : twist, cause : case) **37.** Who is he who speaks and it happens when the Lord has not commanded it? (commandeth : ordered) **38.** Does not both evil and good come from the mouth of the Most High? (evil : harm, good : blessing) **39.** Why should a living man complain, a man for the punishment of his sins? (complain : complain, punishment : consequence) **40.** Let us examine our ways and return to the LORD. (examine : check) **41.** Let us lift up our hearts with our hands to God in heaven. (heavens : sky, God) **42.** We have transgressed and rebelled; You have not pardoned. (transgressed : sinned, pardoned : forgiven) **43.** You have covered us with anger and pursued us; You have slain, You have not pitied. (slain : killed, pitied : shown mercy) **44.** You have covered Yourself with a cloud so that our prayers cannot pass through. (cloud : veil, prayers : requests) **45.** You have made us scum and refuse among the nations. (scum : worthless, refuse : trash) **46.** All our enemies have opened their mouths against us. (enemies : foes) **47.** Fear and a snare have come upon us, desolation and destruction. (fear : terror, snare : trap) **48.** My eyes pour down rivers of water for the destruction of the daughter of my people. (rivers : streams, destruction : ruin) **49.** My eyes flow without ceasing, with no intermission, (intermission : break) **50.** Until the LORD looks down and sees from heaven. (heaven : sky, LORD : God) **51.** My eyes bring grief to my soul because of all the daughters of my city. (grief : sorrow, daughters : people) **52.** My enemies have chased me like a bird, without cause. (chased : pursued) **53.** They have cut off my life in the dungeon and thrown stones at me. (dungeon : prison) **54.** The waters rose above my head; I thought I was cut off. (cut off : finished) **55.** I called on Your name, O LORD, from the low dungeon. (low dungeon : deep prison) **56.** You have heard my voice; do not hide Your ear from my cry. (cry : plea) **57.** You drew near on the day I called to You, saying, "Do not fear." (drew near : came closer) **58.** O Lord, You have pleaded the cause of my soul; You have redeemed my life. (redeemed : saved) **59.** O LORD, You have seen my wrong; judge my cause. (judge : make judgment) **60.** You have seen all their vengeance and their schemes against me. (vengeance : revenge, schemes : plans) **61.** You have heard their reproach, O LORD, and all their schemes against me. (reproach : insult) **62.** The lips of those who rose up against me, and their plans against me all day long. (lips : words) **63.** Behold their sitting down and their rising up; I am their subject of mockery. (mockery : ridicule) **64.** Reward them, O LORD, according to their deeds, O LORD, according to the work of their hands. (reward : repay) **65.** Give them sorrow of heart; Your curse be upon them. (sorrow : grief) **66.** Pursue and destroy them in Your anger from under the heavens of the LORD. (anger : wrath)

Chapter 4

1. How has the gold lost its shine! How has the purest gold changed! The stones of the sanctuary are scattered in the streets. (Sanctuary: sacred place) **2.** The precious sons of Zion, once like fine gold, are now regarded as clay pots, the work of a potter's hands. (Zion: holy city) **3.** Even sea creatures nurse their young; but the daughter of my people has become cruel, like desert ostriches. (Ostriches: large birds) **4.** The infant's tongue sticks to the roof of his mouth from thirst; young children beg for bread, but no one gives it to them. **5.** Those who once ate well now lie in the streets; those raised in luxury now embrace piles of dung. (Dung: animal waste) **6.** The punishment for my people's sin is worse than Sodom's, which was destroyed in an instant, with no one to help. (Sodom: destroyed city) **7.** Her Nazarites were purer than snow, whiter than milk, more ruddy than rubies, their appearance like sapphire. (Nazarites: those set apart for God) **8.** Their faces are darker than coal; they are unrecognizable in the streets. Their skin clings to their bones, withered and dry, like sticks. **9.** Those slain by the sword are better off than those who die of hunger, for hunger causes them to waste away. **10.** The compassionate women have boiled their own children; they became their food during the destruction of my people. (Compassionate: caring) **11.** The LORD has finished pouring out His anger; He has set Zion on fire, and it has consumed its foundations. **12.** The kings of the earth and all its inhabitants never imagined that the enemy would breach Jerusalem's gates. (Breach: break through) **13.** It is for the sins of her prophets and priests, who shed the blood of the innocent in her midst. (Prophets: messengers of God, Priests: religious leaders) **14.** They wandered blind in the streets, polluted by blood, so no one could touch their garments. (Polluted: made unclean) **15.** They cried, "Stay away, it's unclean; don't touch us." When they fled, they said among the nations, "They can no longer stay here." (Fled: ran away) **16.** The LORD's anger has scattered them; He will no longer regard them. The priests and elders are ignored. (Elders: senior leaders) **17.** We hoped in vain for help; we watched for a nation that could not save us. **18.** Our enemies hunt us so we can't walk the streets; our end is near, our days are done. (Enemies: those who oppose us) **19.** Our pursuers are swifter than eagles; they chased us over mountains and ambushed us in the wilderness. (Eagles: fast birds, Wilderness: uninhabited area) **20.** The LORD's anointed, our breath of life, was captured in their traps. We thought, "Under his shadow, we would live among the nations." (Anointed: chosen leader) **21.** Rejoice, O daughter of Edom, who lives in Uz; the cup of punishment will reach you too. You will be drunk and exposed. (Edom: nation to the southeast of Israel, Uz: region where Job lived) **22.** The punishment for your sins, O daughter of Zion, is complete. You will no longer be taken into exile, but the LORD will punish Edom for their sins. (Zion: Jerusalem)

Chapter 5

1. Remember, O LORD, what has come upon us; look, and see our disgrace. (disgrace: shame) **2.** Our land is given to foreigners, our homes to strangers. **3.** We are orphans, with no fathers; our mothers are like widows. **4.** We pay for water; our wood is sold to us. **5.** Our necks are under oppression; we work, but find no rest. (oppression: suffering) **6.** We have turned to Egypt and Assyria, hoping for food. (Egypt: ancient kingdom in Africa; Assyria: ancient empire in the Middle East) **7.** Our ancestors sinned and are gone, and we bear their guilt. (guilt: wrongdoings) **8.** Servants rule over us; no one rescues us from their control. **9.** We risk our lives for food, due to the sword in the wilderness. (sword: danger) **10.** Our skin became dark, like an oven, from the famine's heat. (famine: extreme hunger) **11.** They violated the women of Zion and the girls in Judah's cities. (Zion: Jerusalem, the holy city) **12.** Princes are hung by their hands; elders are dishonored. (Princes: royalty; elders: older leaders; dishonored: disrespected) **13.** Young men are forced to grind grain, and children fall under the wood. (wood: heavy burdens) **14.** Elders no longer sit at the gate, and young men have stopped singing. (gate: place of public decision) **15.** The joy of our hearts is gone; our dancing is turned to sorrow. **16.** The crown has fallen from our head; woe to us, for we have sinned! (woe: misery) **17.** Our hearts are faint, and our eyes grow dim because of this. (faint: weak; dim: tired) **18.** The mountain of Zion is desolate, and foxes roam on it. (Zion: city of holiness) **19.** But you, O LORD, remain forever; your throne endures through all generations. **20.** Why do you forget us forever and forsake us for so long? **21.** Restore us to yourself, O LORD, and we will return; renew our days as in the past. **22.** Yet you have utterly rejected us; you are very angry with us.

26 – Ezekiel

Chapter 1

1. In the thirtieth year, on the fifth day of the fourth month, as I was among the captives by the river Chebar, the heavens opened, and I saw visions of God. (captives: prisoners, visions: revelations) **2.** On the fifth day of the month, the fifth year of King Jehoiachin's captivity, **3.** The word of the LORD came to Ezekiel the priest, son of Buzi, by the river Chebar in the land of the Chaldeans; the hand of the LORD was upon him. (priest: clergyman, hand: power) **4.** I looked, and a whirlwind came from the north, a great cloud with fire and brightness around it, and amber-colored fire within. (whirlwind: storm, brightness: light) **5.** From the midst of it came four living creatures, with the likeness of a man. (midst: center, likeness: appearance) **6.** Each had four faces and four wings. (faces: features) **7.** Their feet were straight, with the soles like a calf's foot, shining like burnished brass. (straight: upright, soles: bottoms, calf's foot: hooves, burnished: polished) **8.** They had hands under their wings on all four sides, with faces and wings. (hands: arms) **9.** Their wings were joined; they did not turn when they moved, but went straight forward. (joined: connected) **10.** Their faces were like a man's, a lion's on the right, an ox's on the left, and an eagle's face. (faces: features) **11.** Their wings were stretched upward, with two wings joined and two covering their bodies. (stretched: extended, covering: shielding) **12.** They went straight forward, following the direction of the spirit, without turning. (direction: path) **13.** Their appearance was like burning coals of fire, and like lamps with fire and lightning. (appearance: form, coals: embers) **14.** The living creatures moved like flashes of lightning. (flashes: streaks) **15.** I saw one wheel on the earth beside the creatures, with four faces. (wheel: disc) **16.** The wheels appeared like beryl, with a wheel inside another wheel. (beryl: precious stone) **17.** They moved in any direction without turning. (direction: way) **18.** Their rings were high and full of eyes all around. (rings: rims, full of: covered with) **19.** When the living creatures moved, the wheels moved with them, and when the creatures rose, the wheels rose too. (rose: lifted) **20.** Wherever the spirit went, the creatures and the wheels followed, for the spirit of the living creatures was in the wheels. (spirit: force) **21.** When they moved, the wheels moved; when they stood, the wheels stood; when they rose, the wheels rose. (stood: stopped) **22.** Above the creatures was the likeness of a firmament, as clear as crystal, stretched over their heads. (firmament: sky, stretched: extended) **23.** Under the firmament, their wings were spread out, each having two wings covering their bodies. (spread: unfolded, covering: shielding) **24.** I heard the sound of their wings like great waters, the voice of the Almighty, like a host's noise. When they stood, they let down their wings. (sound: noise, great waters: rushing waters, Almighty: God, host: army) **25.** A voice came from the firmament above when they stood and let down their wings. (voice: sound, firmament: sky) **26.** Above the firmament was the likeness of a throne, like sapphire stone, and on the throne was the appearance of a man. (throne: seat, sapphire: blue gem) **27.** I saw amber-like fire within, from the waist up and down, with brightness all around. (amber-like: golden, brightness: light) **28.** The brightness around was like a rainbow in the cloud on a rainy day. This was the likeness of the glory of the LORD. When I saw it, I fell on my face and heard a voice speaking. (rainbow: arc, glory: majesty).

Chapter 2

1. He said, "Son of man, stand up, and I will speak to you." **2.** As He spoke, the Spirit entered me, raised me to my feet, and I listened. (Spirit: force, raised: lifted) **3.** He said, "I am sending you to Israel, a rebellious nation that has sinned against Me to this day. (sending: sending forth, rebellious: disobedient, sinned: wronged) **4.** They are stubborn and hardhearted. Tell them, 'This is what the Lord GOD says.' (stubborn: obstinate, hardhearted: unyielding) **5.** Whether they listen or not, they will know a prophet was among them. (listen: hear, prophet: messenger) **6.** Do not fear them, their words, or their looks, though you dwell among thorns and scorpions. (fear: be afraid, words: speech, dwell: live, thorns: prickles, scorpions: dangerous creatures) **7.** Speak My words, whether they listen or not, for they are rebellious. (speak: proclaim, listen: hear) **8.** Listen to Me, son of man. Do not rebel like them. Open your mouth and eat what I give you." (rebel: disobey, eat: consume) **9.** I saw a hand holding a scroll. (hand: palm, scroll: parchment) **10.** It was unrolled, covered with words of lamentation, mourning, and woe. (unrolled: unfolded, lamentation: sorrow, mourning: grief, woe: distress).

Chapter 3

1. God said to me, "Son of man, take and consume this scroll, then go and deliver My message to the people of Israel." **2.** I opened my mouth, and He gave me the scroll to eat. (opened: parted, gave: handed) **3.** He said, "Fill yourself with this scroll I am giving you." I ate it, and it tasted sweet like honey. (fill: consume, sweet: pleasant) **4.** He said, "Now go to the Israelites and speak My words to them." (speak: deliver, words: message) **5.** "You are not being sent to people with a foreign language you cannot understand but to the house of Israel." (sent: dispatched, foreign: unfamiliar) **6.** "Not to nations with unfamiliar speech. If I had sent you to them, they would have listened to you." (nations: peoples, listened: heeded) **7.** "But the

Israelites will not listen to you because they refuse to listen to Me. They are stubborn and hard-hearted." (refuse: reject, stubborn: obstinate, hard-hearted: unyielding) **8.** "I have made you just as resolute as they are, with a forehead as tough as theirs." (resolute: determined, tough: unyielding) **9.** "Like the hardest stone, I have made you resilient. Do not fear them or their defiance, even though they are a rebellious people." (resilient: strong, defiance: resistance, rebellious: disobedient) **10.** He said, "Take all My words into your heart and listen carefully." (take into heart: internalize, carefully: attentively) **11.** "Go to your people in exile and tell them, 'This is what the Lord God says,' whether they choose to listen or ignore." (exile: captivity, ignore: disregard) **12.** Then the Spirit lifted me, and I heard a loud voice behind me saying, "Praise the glory of the Lord in His place!" (loud: powerful, praise: honor) **13.** I also heard the sound of the living creatures' wings touching each other, the wheels beside them, and a loud roaring noise. (roaring: thunderous, noise: sound) **14.** The Spirit carried me away, and I went, feeling bitterness and anger, but the Lord's power was strong upon me. (bitterness: sorrow, anger: frustration, power: strength) **15.** I went to the exiles living at Tel Abib near the Chebar River. For seven days, I sat there with them, overwhelmed. (overwhelmed: stunned) **16.** After seven days, the Lord spoke to me, saying, (spoke: communicated) **17.** "Son of man, I have appointed you as a watchman for Israel. Listen to My words and warn them on My behalf." (appointed: designated, watchman: guardian, warn: alert) **18.** "If I warn the wicked they will die, and you do not warn them, they will die in their sins, but I will hold you accountable for their blood." (wicked: evil, accountable: responsible) **19.** "However, if you warn them and they do not repent, they will die in their sin, but you will have saved yourself." (repent: turn, saved: spared) **20.** "If a righteous person turns from doing right and sins, and I cause them to stumble, they will die because you did not warn them. Their previous good deeds will not be remembered, and I will hold you responsible." (stumble: fall, righteous: virtuous, remembered: recalled) **21.** "But if you warn the righteous not to sin and they heed the warning, they will live, and you will have saved yourself." (heed: obey) **22.** The Lord's power came upon me, and He said, "Go out to the plain, and I will speak to you there." (plain: field) **23.** I went to the plain and saw the glory of the Lord, just as I had seen it by the Chebar River. I fell on my face. (glory: majesty, fell: collapsed) **24.** The Spirit entered me, lifted me to my feet, and said, "Go and shut yourself in your house." (shut: lock, entered: filled) **25.** "You will be bound with ropes and unable to go out among the people." (bound: tied, unable: restricted) **26.** "I will make you mute so you cannot rebuke them, for they are a rebellious people." (mute: silent, rebuke: criticize) **27.** "But when I give you a message, I will enable you to speak, and you will say, 'This is what the Lord God says.' Whoever listens will listen, and whoever refuses will refuse, for they are rebellious." (enable: empower, refuses: rejects).

Chapter 4

1. "Son of man, take a clay tablet, place it in front of you, and draw the city of Jerusalem on it." (clay: ceramic, tablet: slab) **2.** "Depict a siege against it: build a fort, set up a ramp, pitch camps around it, and position battering rams against it." (depict: show, siege: attack, battering rams: assault devices) **3.** "Take an iron pan and place it as a wall between you and the city. Face it as though you are laying siege. This will be a sign to Israel." (iron pan: metal plate, wall: barrier, laying siege: attacking) **4.** "Lie on your left side and take on the guilt of Israel's sins. You will bear it for as many days as I assign you." (guilt: responsibility, bear: carry) **5.** "I have assigned you 390 days to represent the years of their sin. During this time, you will carry Israel's guilt." (assigned: given, represent: symbolize) **6.** "When you finish, lie on your right side and carry Judah's guilt for 40 days—one day for each year." (finish: complete, carry: bear) **7.** "Turn your face toward Jerusalem under siege, with your arm bared, and prophesy against it." (bared: uncovered, prophesy: speak, siege: attack) **8.** "I will tie you up so you cannot turn from side to side until you have completed the days of the siege." (tie up: bind, completed: finished) **9.** "Take wheat, barley, beans, lentils, millet, and spelt, mix them in a container, and use them to make bread. Eat it during the 390 days you lie on your side." (wheat: grain, barley: cereal, beans: legumes, lentils: pulses) **10.** "Your food will be rationed: twenty shekels of bread per day. Eat it at set times." (rationed: limited, set times: scheduled) **11.** "You will drink water by measure—about one-sixth of a hin—at set times." (measure: amount, hin: ancient volume unit) **12.** "You will eat the bread as barley cakes baked over human dung in the sight of the people." (barley cakes: flatbreads, baked: cooked, dung: excrement) **13.** The LORD said, "This is how Israel will eat unclean food in the nations where I scatter them." (unclean: impure, scatter: disperse) **14.** I protested, "Ah, Lord GOD! I have never defiled myself. From my youth, I have never eaten anything that died naturally, was torn by beasts, or was impure." (defiled: contaminated, torn: ripped, impure: unclean) **15.** He replied, "Very well, I allow you to use cow dung instead of human dung to bake your bread." (allow: permit, cow dung: manure) **16.** He said, "Son of man, I am about to cut off the food supply in Jerusalem. They will eat bread by weight and drink water by measure, anxiously rationing both." (cut off: stop, rationing: distributing) **17.** "They will lack food and water, grow desperate, and waste away because of their sins." (lack: be without, desperate: hopeless, waste away: perish).

Chapter 5

1. "Son of man, take a sharp sword, use it as a barber's razor to shave your head and beard, and then divide the hair using scales." (sharp: keen, razor: blade, divide: separate) **2.** "Burn one-third of the hair in the center of the city after the siege days are completed. Take another third, strike it with the sword around the city, and scatter the last third to the wind. I will send a sword to chase them." (burn: set on fire, strike: hit, scatter: disperse) **3.** "Take a few strands of the hair, and tuck them into the folds of your garment." (strands: locks, tuck: place, folds: layers) **4.** "From these, take some again, throw them into the fire, and burn them. From this fire, judgment will spread to the entire house of Israel." (throw: cast, judgment: punishment, spread: extend) **5.** "This is what the Lord GOD says: This is Jerusalem. I placed her at the center of the nations, surrounded by other lands." (placed: positioned, center: heart, surrounded: encircled) **6.** "But she rebelled against my commands and laws more than the nations around her. She rejected my rules and did not follow them." (rebelled: defied, rejected: refused, rules: commands) **7.** "Therefore, this is what the Lord GOD says: Because you have been more rebellious than the nations around you, failing to obey my laws or even follow the practices of other nations—" (rebellious: disobedient, failing: neglecting, practices: customs) **8.** "I, the Lord GOD, declare that I am against you. I will bring judgment upon you in front of all the nations." (declare: proclaim, against: opposed, judgment: punishment) **9.** "I will do to you what I have never done before and will never do again because of your detestable sins." (detestable: abhorrent, sins: wrongdoings) **10.** "As a result, fathers will eat their children, and children will eat their fathers. I will carry out my judgment, and the survivors will be scattered to the winds." (result: consequence, carry out: execute, scattered: dispersed) **11.** "As surely as I live, says the Lord GOD, because you defiled my temple with your vile idols and detestable practices, I will show you no pity or mercy." (defiled: desecrated, vile: disgusting, mercy: compassion) **12.** "One-third of you will die from plague or famine inside the city. Another third will fall by the sword outside it. The final third will be scattered to the winds, and I will pursue them with the sword." (plague: disease, famine: starvation, pursue: chase) **13.** "My anger will be spent, and my wrath will subside. When I have unleashed my fury, they will know that I, the LORD, acted in my zeal." (anger: rage, wrath: fury, subside: lessen, fury: violence, zeal: passion) **14.** "I will make you a ruin and an object of scorn among the nations around you. Everyone who passes by will be appalled." (ruin: destruction, scorn: contempt, appalled: horrified) **15.** "You will become a warning, a taunt, and an object of shock to the nations around you when I bring judgment with anger, fury, and fierce rebuke. I, the LORD, have spoken." (warning: alert, taunt: mockery, shock: astonishment, rebuke: reprimand) **16.** "When I send famine, like deadly arrows of destruction, I will weaken your food supply and increase the famine among you." (send: deliver, deadly: lethal, arrows: projectiles, weaken: diminish, increase: intensify) **17.** "I will send famine, wild beasts, disease, and bloodshed. The sword will come against you. I, the LORD, have spoken." (wild beasts: animals, disease: illness, bloodshed: killing, sword: weapon).

Chapter 6

1. The LORD spoke to me and said: **2.** "Son of man, face the mountains of Israel and deliver a message against them. **3.** Say this: 'Mountains of Israel, listen to the words of the Lord GOD! The Lord GOD says to the mountains, hills, streams, and valleys: I will bring a sword against you and destroy your worship sites. (worship sites: shrines) **4.** Your altars will be demolished, your idols shattered, and the bodies of your people will fall in front of these idols. (demolished: destroyed, shattered: broken) **5.** I will scatter the bones of your people around your altars. (scatter: spread, altars: shrines) **6.** Wherever you live, your towns will be ruined, and your high places destroyed. Your altars will be broken, idols smashed, and all the works you have made wiped out. (ruined: devastated, destroyed: demolished, smashed: crushed, wiped out: erased) **7.** The dead will lie among you, and then you will know that I am the LORD. **8.** However, I will allow some of you to survive and escape the sword as you are scattered among other nations. (survive: live, escape: flee) **9.** Those who survive will remember me in the lands where they are held captive. They will realize how deeply I was hurt by their unfaithfulness and idolatry. They will despise themselves for the wickedness and abominations they committed. (unfaithfulness: betrayal, idolatry: idol worship, despise: hate, wickedness: evil, abominations: detestable acts) **10.** Then they will understand that I am the LORD and that my warnings of disaster were not empty threats. (disaster: calamity, empty: meaningless) **11.** The Lord GOD says this: Clap your hands and stomp your feet as you cry, 'How terrible!' for the evil actions of Israel. The people will fall by sword, famine, and disease. (famine: starvation, disease: plague) **12.** Those far away will die from disease, those nearby will be killed by the sword, and those under siege will perish from hunger. This is how I will unleash my wrath. (siege: blockade, perish: die, wrath: anger) **13.** You will know that I am the LORD when you see the dead lying around their idols and altars, on hilltops, mountaintops, under green trees, and beneath large oaks—everywhere they offered sacrifices to their false gods. (lying: resting, offered: made, false gods: idols) **14.** I will stretch out my hand against them and turn the land into a desolation, more barren than the wilderness near Diblath. Wherever they live, they will know that I am the LORD." (desolation: ruin, barren: empty).

Chapter 7

1. The word of the LORD came to me, saying: **2.** "Son of man, this is what the Lord GOD says to the land of Israel: The end has come upon the whole land. **3.** The time has come; I will pour out My anger, judge you by your deeds, and repay you for all your sins. (pour out: unleash, repay: reward) **4.** I will not show mercy or pity. I will repay you for your actions, and your sins will be evident. Then you will know that I am the LORD. (mercy: compassion, pity: sympathy, evident: clear) **5.** This is what the Lord GOD says: Disaster—an unprecedented disaster—is coming. (unprecedented: unparalleled) **6.** The end is here! It has arrived and is watching you. **7.** The morning has come, the day of trouble is near, not a joyful sound from the mountains. (trouble: distress) **8.** Soon, I will unleash My fury and fulfill My wrath against you. I will judge you for your deeds and repay you for your sins. (unleash: release, fury: anger, fulfill: complete) **9.** I will not spare or pity you but will repay you according to your ways. You will know that I, the LORD, strike you. (spare: forgive, strike: punish) **10.** Look, the day has come! Pride has blossomed, and arrogance has grown. (blossomed: flourished, arrogance: conceit) **11.** Violence has become a rod of wickedness. None will survive—not their wealth, nor their numbers, nor their mourning. (violence: brutality, rod: symbol, wickedness: evil) **12.** The time has come, the day is near. Buyers and sellers alike will face wrath. (wrath: anger) **13.** Sellers will not regain what they sold, even if they live, because the entire crowd is under judgment, and no one will escape. (regain: recover, crowd: people, judgment: punishment) **14.** They sound the trumpet and prepare for battle, but no one goes because My wrath is upon them all. (wrath: anger, prepare: get ready) **15.** Outside, the sword will strike; inside, famine and disease will consume. Those in the field will die by the sword, and those in the city by famine and plague. (strike: hit, consume: destroy, plague: disease) **16.** The survivors will flee to the mountains, mourning like doves over their sins. (mourning: grieving) **17.** All hands will be weak, and knees will tremble. (weak: feeble, tremble: shake) **18.** They will wear sackcloth, and horror will cover them. Shame will be on their faces, and they will shave their heads in despair. (sackcloth: rough cloth, horror: fear, despair: hopelessness) **19.** They will throw their silver into the streets, and their gold will be worthless. These will not save them on the day of the LORD's wrath. Their greed has led to their downfall. (worthless: useless, greed: selfishness, downfall: ruin) **20.** They took pride in their treasures but used them to make detestable idols, so I will reject them. (treasures: riches, detestable: repulsive) **21.** I will hand their wealth over to foreigners and their treasures to the wicked, who will defile them. (wealth: riches, defile: pollute) **22.** I will turn away from them, and robbers will invade and defile My sanctuary. (turn away: abandon, invade: attack, sanctuary: holy place) **23.** Forge chains, for the land is full of bloodshed and the city full of violence. (forge: create, chains: bonds, bloodshed: murder) **24.** I will bring the most ruthless nations against them to occupy their homes and desecrate their holy places. (ruthless: merciless, desecrate: profane) **25.** Destruction is coming. Though they seek peace, there will be none. (destruction: ruin, seek: search) **26.** Calamity will follow calamity, and rumors will spread. People will seek prophetic visions, but the law will be lost to priests, and guidance will fail from elders. (calamity: disaster, prophetic: divinely inspired, fail: be absent) **27.** The king will mourn, the prince will despair, and the people will be paralyzed with fear. I will treat them according to their actions and judge them by their deeds. Then they will know I am the LORD." (mourn: grieve, despair: lose hope, paralyzed: immobilized, judge: evaluate).

Chapter 8

1. In the sixth year, on the fifth day of the sixth month, as I sat in my house with the elders of Judah before me, the hand of the Lord GOD came upon me. **2.** I saw a figure that looked like fire—from the waist down it was fire, and from the waist up it was bright, like glowing amber. (bright: shining, glowing: radiant) **3.** He stretched out what seemed like a hand and grabbed me by my hair. The Spirit lifted me between heaven and earth and took me in a vision of God to Jerusalem, to the north gate of the inner courtyard, where a statue that provokes jealousy stood. (grabbed: seized, provokes: stirs up) **4.** There I saw the glory of the God of Israel, just as I had seen in the vision in the plain. (glory: majesty) **5.** He said, "Son of man, look north." When I looked, I saw the idol of jealousy near the altar gate. (idol: image, jealousy: envy) **6.** He said, "Do you see the great sins Israel is committing here, driving Me away from My sanctuary? But you will see even greater abominations." (sins: wrongdoings, sanctuary: holy place, abominations: detestable acts) **7.** Then He brought me to the entrance of the courtyard. I saw a hole in the wall. (courtyard: yard, hole: opening) **8.** He said, "Son of man, dig through the wall." So I dug and found a door. (dig: excavate, door: entrance) **9.** He said, "Go in and see the wicked acts they are committing here." (wicked: evil) **10.** Inside, I saw walls covered with images of crawling creatures, unclean animals, and all the idols of Israel. (crawling creatures: insects, unclean: impure, idols: false gods) **11.** Seventy elders of Israel stood before them, with Jaazaniah son of Shaphan among them. Each held a censer, and a thick cloud of incense rose. (elders: leaders, censer: container, incense: fragrance) **12.** He said, "Son of man, do you see what Israel's elders are doing in secret, thinking, 'The LORD doesn't see us; He has abandoned the land'?" (secret: privately, abandoned: forsaken) **13.** He added, "You will see even worse abominations." (worse: more severe) **14.** He brought me to the entrance of the LORD's temple, where women were sitting and weeping for Tammuz (a Babylonian fertility god). (weeping: crying, fertility: reproduction) **15.** He said, "Do you see this, son of man? You will see even greater abominations." (greater: more detestable) **16.** He brought me to the inner courtyard of the LORD's temple. There, at the entrance between the porch and the altar, were twenty-five men worshiping the sun, with their backs to the temple of the LORD. (inner courtyard: inner yard, porch: entranceway) **17.** He said, "Is it not enough that Judah commits these abominations, filling the land with violence and provoking My anger? They even put a branch to their noses as an insult to Me! (violence: bloodshed, provoking: arousing, insult: offense) **18.** Therefore, I will act in fury. I will show no pity or mercy. Even if they cry out loudly, I will not listen to them." (fury: rage, pity: compassion, mercy: grace, cry out: shout).

Chapter 9

1. Then He cried out loudly in my ears, "Summon those who have charge over the city, each with a weapon of destruction in hand." (summon: call, destruction: ruin) **2.** I saw six men coming from the north gate, each carrying a deadly weapon. Among them was a man dressed in linen with a writing kit at his side. They stood beside the bronze altar. (bronze: metal, altar: sacred table) **3.** The glory of the God of Israel rose from above the cherubim and moved to the threshold of the temple. The LORD called to the man clothed in linen with the writing kit. (glory: majesty, cherubim: angelic beings, threshold: entrance) **4.** He said, "Go through Jerusalem and put a mark on the foreheads of those who mourn and grieve over all the sins committed there." (mourn: weep, grieve: sorrow, sins: wrongdoings) **5.** To the others, He said, "Follow him through the city and strike down everyone. Show no pity or mercy." (strike down: kill, pity: compassion, mercy: forgiveness) **6.** Kill the old, the young, women, children, and maidens, but do not touch anyone with the mark. Begin at My sanctuary." So they started with the elders in front of the temple. (maidens: young women, sanctuary: holy place, elders: leaders) **7.** He commanded, "Defile the temple by filling its courts with the dead. Go out and kill." And they went through the city, striking people down. (defile: desecrate, courts: open areas, striking down: killing) **8.** While they were carrying out the slaughter, I was left alone. I fell facedown and cried, "Ah, Lord GOD! Will You destroy the entire remnant of Israel in Your fury against Jerusalem?" (slaughter: massacre, remnant: remaining people, fury: anger) **9.** He answered, "The sin of Israel and Judah is exceedingly great. The land is filled with bloodshed, and the city is full of corruption. They claim, 'The LORD has abandoned the land; He does not see us.' (exceedingly: extremely, bloodshed: violence, corruption: wickedness, abandoned: left) **10.** But I will not spare or show pity. I will repay them for their deeds." (spare: forgive, pity: compassion, deeds: actions) **11.** Then the man clothed in linen with the writing kit returned and reported, "I have done as You commanded." (commanded: instructed).

Chapter 10

1. I looked up and saw above the cherubim, something that seemed like a sapphire stone, appearing as a throne. (seemed: appeared, sapphire: precious stone, appearing: looking) **2.** He spoke to the man dressed in linen and instructed him, "Go between the wheels, beneath the cherubim, and take coals of fire from between them, then spread them over the city." The man went in while I was watching. (dressed: clothed, instructed: told, spread: scatter) **3.** The cherubim stood to the right of the temple as the man entered, and a cloud filled the inner court. (right: east, filled: covered, court: yard) **4.** The glory of the LORD lifted from the cherub and stood at the threshold of the temple, the entire house was filled with the cloud, and the court glowed with the LORD's glory. (glory: majesty, lifted: rose, threshold: entrance, glowing: shining) **5.** The sound of the cherubim's wings could be heard even outside the court, like the voice of the Almighty when He speaks. (sound: noise, heard: listened, Almighty: powerful one) **6.** When the man in linen was instructed to take fire from between the wheels and the cherubim, he entered and stood beside the wheels. (instructed: told, entered: went, beside: next to) **7.** One of the cherubim reached out from between them, took fire from the middle, and handed it to the man in linen, who then went out with it. (reached out: extended, middle: center, handed: gave) **8.** Under the wings of the cherubim, I saw the form of a man's hand. (wings: appendages, form: shape, hand: palm) **9.** I saw four wheels beside the cherubim, one beside each. The wheels were like beryl stones in appearance. (wheels: circles, beryl: greenish stone, appearance: look) **10.** All four wheels had the same appearance, like a wheel within a wheel. (same: identical, within: inside) **11.** As they moved, they moved on all four sides; they did not turn as they moved, but went wherever the face of the cherubim directed them. (sides: directions, turn: rotate, directed: guided) **12.** Their entire bodies, backs, hands, wings, and the wheels were full of eyes all around, even the wheels themselves. (entire: whole, backs: rear, full: covered, around: everywhere) **13.** I heard a voice call to the wheels, "O wheel." (call: shout) **14.** Each of the cherubim had four faces: one of a cherub, one of a man, one of a lion, and one of an eagle. (faces: heads, cherub: angel) **15.** The cherubim were lifted up; this was the living creature I had seen by the river Chebar. (lifted: raised, living creature: being) **16.** When the cherubim moved, the wheels moved with them; when they raised their wings to lift from the ground, the wheels remained beside them. (moved: shifted, raised: lifted, remained: stayed) **17.** When they stood, the wheels stood; when they lifted up, the wheels lifted up with them, for the spirit of the living creatures was in them. (stood: stayed, lifted up: rose, spirit: essence) **18.** Then the glory of the LORD left the threshold of the temple and moved over the cherubim. (left: departed, threshold: entrance) **19.** The cherubim lifted their wings and rose from the earth in my sight, and as they went out, the wheels were beside them, standing at the east gate of the LORD's house, with the glory of the God of Israel above them. (rose: ascended, went out: left, standing: positioned) **20.** This was the living creature I had seen near the river Chebar, and I realized they were the cherubim. (realized: understood) **21.** Each had four faces and four wings, and under their wings was the likeness of a man's hands. (likeness: appearance, hands: palms) **22.** The faces of the cherubim were the same as those I had seen by the river Chebar; they moved straight forward without turning. (same: identical, straight: direct).

Chapter 11

1. The Spirit lifted me and brought me to the east gate of the LORD's house, where I saw 25 men, including Jaazaniah son of Azur and Pelatiah son of Benaiah, the leaders of the people. (lifted: raised, brought: took, leaders: rulers) **2.** The LORD said to me, "Son of man, these are the men who plan evil and give wicked advice in this city. (plan: devise, evil: wrongdoing, wicked: sinful, advice: counsel) **3.** They say, 'The end is not near; let us build houses. This city is a cauldron, and we are the meat.' (end: destruction, cauldron: pot, meat: flesh) **4.** Therefore, prophesy against them, son of man." (prophesy: speak, against: in opposition to) **5.** The Spirit of the LORD came upon me, saying, "Speak to them, 'This is what the LORD says: I know what you are thinking, every thought.' (thinking: planning, thought: intention) **6.** You have increased the slain in this city and filled its streets with death. (slain: killed, filled: crowded, death: violence) **7.** Therefore, this is what the LORD says: The dead you have left are the meat, and this city is the cauldron, but I will bring you out of it. (dead: corpses, left: abandoned, bring you out: remove) **8.** You fear the sword, but I will bring a sword against you," says the LORD. (sword: weapon) **9.** "I will remove you from the city and hand you over to strangers, executing judgment among you. (remove: take out, strangers: foreigners, executing: carrying out, judgment: punishment) **10.** You will fall by the sword, and I will judge you at the border of Israel, and you will know that I am the LORD. (fall: die, judge: punish, border: edge) **11.** This city will no longer be your cauldron, nor will you be the meat; I will judge you at Israel's border. (cauldron: pot) **12.** You will know that I am the LORD, for you have not followed my laws or kept my commandments, but have behaved like the surrounding nations." (behaved: acted, surrounding: neighboring) **13.** When I prophesied, Pelatiah son of Benaiah died. I fell on my face and cried out, "Ah, LORD GOD, will you completely destroy the remnant of Israel?" (prophesied: spoke, cried out: pleaded, remnant: remainder) **14.** The LORD answered me, saying, **15.** "Son of man, your relatives, your fellow exiles, and all the house of Israel have said, 'Get away from the LORD; this land is ours.' (relatives: kin, fellow exiles: companions in exile, house: people) **16.** Therefore, say this: 'Although I have scattered them among the nations, I will be a small sanctuary for them wherever they go.' (scattered: dispersed, sanctuary: refuge) **17.** I will gather you from the nations, bring you back to the land of Israel, (gather: collect, bring back: return) **18.** and they will remove all the detestable things and abominations from it. (remove: eliminate, detestable: disgusting, abominations: sinful acts) **19.** I will give them one heart and a new spirit, removing their heart of stone and giving them a heart of flesh, (spirit: attitude, heart: inner being, removing: replacing) **20.** so they can follow my statutes, keep my laws, and obey them. They will be my people, and I will be their God. (statutes: laws, keep: observe, obey: follow) **21.** But those whose hearts follow their detestable things will be punished according to their deeds," says the LORD. (follow: pursue, detestable: sinful, deeds: actions) **22.** The cherubim lifted their wings, and the wheels beside them, with the glory of the God of Israel above them. (lifted: raised, beside: next to) **23.** The glory of the LORD moved from the city and stood on the mountain east of it. (moved: departed, stood: stopped) **24.** The Spirit took me in a vision to the exiles in Chaldea. The vision I had seen left me. (took: carried, vision: revelation, left: departed) **25.** I spoke to the exiles all that the LORD had shown me. (spoken: told, shown: revealed).

Chapter 12

1. The word of the LORD came to me, saying, (word: message) **2.** "Son of man, you live among a rebellious people who have eyes but do not see, ears but do not hear. (rebellious: disobedient, see: understand, hear: listen) **3.** Therefore, prepare for exile. Carry your belongings during the day in their sight and move from one place to another. Perhaps they will realize their rebellion. (prepare: get ready, exile: captivity, belongings: possessions, realize: understand) **4.** Bring your belongings in their sight as if you are going into exile, and at evening, leave as if being taken captive. (taken captive: captured) **5.** Dig through the wall in their sight and carry your belongings through it. (dig: break, carry: move) **6.** Carry them on your shoulders, cover your face, and do not look at the ground. You are a sign to the house of Israel." (sign: symbol) **7.** I obeyed the LORD's command: I carried my belongings in daylight as if for exile, dug through the wall in the evening, and carried them on my shoulder. (obeyed: followed, command: order) **8.** The word of the LORD came to me in the morning, saying, (morning: dawn) **9.** "Son of man, hasn't the rebellious house of Israel asked, 'What are you doing?' (asked: questioned) **10.** Tell them, 'This message is for the prince of Jerusalem and all the people of Israel among them.' (message: word) **11.** Say, 'I am a sign for you. Just as I have done, so will it happen to them; they will go into exile.' (happen: occur) **12.** The prince will leave at twilight, carrying his belongings on his shoulders, digging through the wall, covering his face so he cannot see the ground. (twilight: dusk) **13.** I will catch him in a trap, and he will be taken to Babylon, but he will not see it, though he will die there. (trap: snare, taken: captured, see: witness) **14.** I will scatter those who support him to the winds, and draw my sword against them. (scatter: disperse, support: back, sword: weapon) **15.** They will know I am the LORD when I scatter them among the nations. (nations: countries) **16.** But I will spare a few from the sword, famine, and plague so they can declare their abominations among the nations, and they will know I am the LORD." (spare: save, plague: disease, declare: proclaim, abominations: sinful acts) **17.** The word of the LORD came to me again, saying, (again: once more) **18.** "Son of man, eat your bread with trembling and drink your water with fear, (eat: consume, trembling: fear, drink: consume) **19.** and tell the people of the land, 'Thus says the Lord GOD: They will eat and drink in fear, for the land will be desolate because of the violence of its inhabitants.' (land: country, desolate: empty, violence: wrongdoing, inhabitants: people) **20.** The cities will be laid waste, and the land will be desolate. Then they will know I am the LORD." (laid waste: destroyed) **21.** The word of the LORD came to me, saying, (again: once more) **22.** "Son of man, what is this proverb you have in Israel, 'The days go on, and every vision fails'? (proverb: saying, vision: prophecy) **23.** Tell them, 'This is what the Lord GOD says: I will end this proverb, and they will no longer say it in Israel. The days are near, and the fulfillment of every vision is at hand. (fulfillment: completion, at hand: near) **24.** There will be no more false visions or flattering prophecies in Israel. (false: untrue, flattering: pleasing) **25.** For I, the LORD, will speak, and what I say will happen; it will no longer be delayed. In your days, O rebellious house, I will fulfill my words.'" (delayed: postponed, fulfill: complete) **26.** The word of the LORD came to me again, saying, (again: once more) **27.** "The house of Israel says, 'The vision he sees is for many years from now, and he prophesies about distant times.' (distant: far off) **28.** Therefore, say to them, 'The LORD GOD says: None of my words will be delayed anymore. The words I have spoken will be fulfilled.'" (delayed: postponed, fulfilled: completed).

Chapter 13

1. The word of the LORD came to me, saying, (word: message) **2.** "Son of man, prophesy against the prophets of Israel who speak from their own hearts, saying, 'Hear the word of the LORD.' (prophesy: speak, prophets: messengers, speak: speak out, hearts: desires) **3.** This is what the Lord GOD says: Woe to the foolish prophets who follow their own spirit and see nothing! (woe: disaster, foolish: senseless, follow: follow after, spirit: emotions, see: perceive) **4.** O Israel, your prophets are like foxes in the desert. (foxes: cunning animals) **5.** You have not stood in the gaps or built a defense for the house of Israel to stand in battle on the day of the LORD. (stood: defended, gaps: openings, defense: protection, stand: remain firm, battle: conflict) **6.** They have seen false visions and deceptive prophecies, claiming, 'The LORD says,' when the LORD has not sent them. They give false hope by confirming what isn't true. (false: misleading, deceptive: dishonest, confirming: supporting, true: real) **7.** Have you not seen false visions and spoken lying prophecies, saying, 'The LORD says,' when I have not spoken? (lying: untruthful) **8.** Therefore, this is what the Lord GOD says: Because you speak lies and see vanity, I am against you. (lies: untruths, vanity: empty thoughts) **9.** My hand will be against the prophets who see false visions and tell lies. They will not be in the assembly of my people, nor written in Israel's record, nor enter the land of Israel. Then you will know that I am the LORD GOD. (hand: power, assembly: congregation, record: book, enter: come into) **10.** They have misled my people, saying, 'Peace,' when there is no peace. One builds a wall, and others cover it with untempered mortar. (misled: deceived, peace: safety, builds: constructs, cover: conceal, untempered: untested) **11.** Say to those who cover it with untempered mortar, 'It will fall. There will be an overflowing shower, and great hailstones will fall, and a stormy wind will tear it down.' (overflowing: abundant, shower: rain, hailstones: ice pellets, tear: destroy) **12.**

When the wall falls, will you not be asked, 'Where is the mortar you used to cover it?' (asked: questioned) **13.** Therefore, this is what the Lord GOD says: I will tear it down with a storm in my fury, and there will be an overflowing shower and great hailstones in my anger. (tear: destroy, storm: tempest, fury: wrath) **14.** I will break down the wall you covered with untempered mortar and bring it to the ground. The foundation will be revealed, and it will fall, and you will be consumed in the midst of it. You will know that I am the LORD. (break down: demolish, foundation: base, consumed: destroyed) **15.** I will complete my wrath on the wall and those who covered it with untempered mortar. The wall will be no more, and neither will those who covered it. (complete: finish, wrath: anger) **16.** These are the prophets of Israel who prophesy about Jerusalem, claiming to see visions of peace, but there is no peace, says the Lord GOD. (prophesy: speak, claiming: saying, visions: revelations) **17.** Likewise, son of man, set your face against the women of your people who prophesy from their own hearts, and prophesy against them, (set: direct, women: females) **18.** and say, 'This is what the Lord GOD says: Woe to the women who sew pillows for all armholes and make kerchiefs on every head to hunt souls. Will you hunt the souls of my people and let others live? (sew: stitch, armholes: sleeves, kerchiefs: head coverings, hunt: capture, souls: lives) **19.** Will you pollute me among my people for handfuls of barley and pieces of bread, killing those who should not die and sparing those who should not live, by lying to my people who listen to your lies? (pollute: defile, handfuls: small portions, sparing: saving, listen: heed) **20.** Therefore, this is what the Lord GOD says: I am against your pillows with which you hunt souls. I will tear them from your arms and let the souls go free. (against: opposed to, tear: rip) **21.** I will tear your kerchiefs and deliver my people from your hands, and they will no longer be your prey. You will know that I am the LORD. (deliver: rescue, prey: victims) **22.** Because you have made the righteous sad with your lies, whom I have not made sad, and have encouraged the wicked not to turn from their wickedness by promising them life, (righteous: innocent, sad: grieve, encouraged: urged, wicked: sinful, turn: change) **23.** therefore, you will see no more false visions or divinations. I will deliver my people from your hand, and you will know that I am the LORD." (divinations: predictions)

Chapter 14

1. Some of Israel's elders came to me and sat in front of me. (elders: leaders, sat: settled) **2.** The word of the LORD came to me, saying, (word: message) **3.** "Son of man, these men have placed idols in their hearts and put obstacles of sin before them. Should I listen to them when they come to inquire of me? (placed: set, idols: false gods, obstacles: hindrances, inquire: ask) **4.** Therefore, speak to them and tell them: 'This is what the Lord GOD says: Any man of Israel who places idols in his heart and faces the obstacle of his sin, then comes to ask me for guidance, I will answer them based on the number of their idols. (guidance: direction, number: amount) **5.** I will allow them to follow their own hearts because they have turned away from me through their idols.' (allow: permit, follow: pursue, turned away: separated) **6.** Therefore, tell the people of Israel: 'This is what the Lord GOD says: Repent, turn from your idols, and stop all your abominations. (repent: change your ways, turn from: reject, abominations: detestable acts) **7.** Any man of Israel, or foreigner living in Israel, who separates himself from me, sets up idols in his heart, and faces sin as a stumbling block before him, then comes to seek a prophet for advice, I the LORD will answer them directly. (foreigner: stranger, separates: distances, advice: counsel, directly: personally) **8.** I will turn my face against that person, make them a symbol of disgrace, and cut them off from my people. You will know that I am the LORD. (turn my face: direct my attention, symbol: sign, disgrace: shame, cut off: remove) **9.** If the prophet speaks falsely, I will allow the deception. I will act against that prophet and remove them from my people Israel. (speaks falsely: gives false prophecy, allow: permit, deception: lies) **10.** Both the one who seeks counsel and the prophet will bear the consequences of their sin. (counsel: advice, bear: endure, consequences: punishments) **11.** This will stop Israel from going astray and defiling themselves with their sins, so they will be my people, and I will be their God, says the Lord GOD.' (astray: off course, defiling: polluting, sins: wrongdoings) **12.** The word of the LORD came again to me, saying, (word: message) **13.** "Son of man, if a land sins against me by committing great wickedness, I will stretch out my hand against it. I will destroy its food supply, send famine, and wipe out both people and animals. (sins: wrongs, committing: doing, wickedness: evil, stretch out: extend, wipe out: destroy) **14.** Even if Noah, Daniel, and Job were in that land, they would only save their own lives by their righteousness, says the Lord GOD. (righteousness: goodness, save: rescue) **15.** If I send wild animals to ravage the land, making it desolate and impassable, (ravage: destroy, desolate: empty, impassable: unreachable) **16.** even if Noah, Daniel, and Job were there, they would not save their sons or daughters; only they would be spared, and the land would be desolate. (spared: saved, sons: children, daughters: female children) **17.** Or if I bring war upon the land and say, 'Let the sword pass through,' cutting off both man and beast, (war: conflict, sword: weapon, pass through: sweep through) **18.** even if these three men were in it, they would not save their sons or daughters; only they would be saved. (saved: rescued) **19.** Or if I send a deadly disease upon the land, pouring out my wrath in blood to destroy man and beast, (deadly disease: plague, wrath: anger) **20.** even if Noah, Daniel, and Job were present, they would only save themselves by their righteousness, not their sons or daughters. (righteousness: moral integrity, present: here) **21.** How much more will this be true when I send my four severe judgments—war, famine, wild animals, and disease—to Jerusalem, cutting off all life? (severe: intense, judgments: punishments) **22.** However, a remnant will survive, both sons and daughters, who will be brought out. When you see them and understand their actions, you will be comforted about the destruction I brought upon Jerusalem. (remnant: remainder, survive: remain, comforted: consoled, destruction: ruin) **23.** You will be comforted when you see their deeds and understand that I did all this with purpose, says the Lord GOD." (comforted: consoled, deeds: actions, purpose: reason).

Chapter 15

1. The word of the LORD came to me, saying, (word: message) **2.** "Son of man, what is the vine tree more than any other tree, or a branch among the forest trees?" (vine tree: grapevine, branch: limb) **3.** "Can wood from it be used for any work? Can a pin be made to hang anything?" (wood: timber, work: purpose, pin: peg) **4.** "It is cast into the fire for fuel, burning at both ends, with the middle consumed. Is it fit for any work?" (cast: thrown, fuel: heat, consumed: destroyed, fit: suitable) **5.** "When it was whole, it was not fit for work, how much less after the fire has burned it?" (whole: intact, fit: suitable, work: use) **6.** "Therefore, I will give the people of Jerusalem over to destruction like the vine in the fire." (give over: hand over, destruction: ruin) **7.** "I will set my face against them. They will escape one fire, only to face another, and you will know I am the LORD." (set: turn, escape: avoid, face: meet, know: understand) **8.** "I will make the land desolate because of their sin," says the Lord GOD. (desolate: empty, sin: wrongdoing)

Chapter 16

1. The word of the LORD came to me, saying, (word: message) **2.** "Son of man, make Jerusalem aware of her abominations," (aware: know, abominations: wickedness) **3.** "Say to her: 'Your birth and origins are from Canaan; your father was an Amorite and your mother a Hittite.'" (origins: beginnings, father: parent, mother: parent) **4.** "When you were born, no one cared for you; your navel was not cut, you were not washed, and no one took pity on you." (navel: belly button, washed: cleansed, pity: sympathy) **5.** "You were abandoned in the open field, loathed in the day you were born." (abandoned: left, loathed: hated) **6.** "When I passed by, I saw you polluted in your own blood and said, 'Live!' and I made you thrive." (polluted: tainted, thrive: flourish) **7.** "I caused you to grow like a plant, and you became beautiful, your breasts were formed, and your hair grew." (grew: developed, formed: shaped) **8.** "When I passed by, you were ready for love, and I covered you with my garment, entered into a covenant with you, and you became mine." (garment: clothing, covenant: agreement) **9.** "I washed you with water, cleaned away your blood, and anointed you with oil." (cleaned: removed, anointed: smeared) **10.** "I clothed you in embroidered cloth, and put shoes of leather on you. I girded you with fine linen and covered you with silk." (embroidered: decorated, girded: strapped, covered: draped) **11.** "I adorned you with jewelry: bracelets, a chain for your neck," (adorned: decorated, chain: necklace) **12.** "a jewel for your forehead, earrings in your ears, and a beautiful crown on your head." (jewel: gem, earrings: studs) **13.** "You were decked with gold and silver, your clothing was fine linen and silk, and you ate the best food, becoming very beautiful and prosperous." (decked: decorated, prosperous: wealthy) **14.** "Your fame spread among the nations because of your beauty, which was perfected through my splendor." (fame: reputation, splendor: glory) **15.** "But you trusted in your beauty and became a prostitute, offering yourself to everyone, pouring out your fornications." (trusted: relied, fornications: immoral acts) **16.** "You took your garments and made high places with various colors, playing the harlot on them." (garments: clothes, high places: altars, harlot: prostitute) **17.** "You took my gold and silver, which I gave you, and made images of men, committing adultery with them." (images: statues, adultery: unfaithfulness) **18.** "You took your embroidered garments and covered them, and set my oil and incense before them." (covered: draped, incense: fragrance) **19.** "You offered my food — fine flour, oil, and honey — to your idols for a sweet fragrance." (offered: gave, fragrance: scent) **20.** "You sacrificed your sons and daughters to these idols. Is this not enough wickedness?" (sacrificed: offered, wickedness: evil) **21.** "You killed my children and passed them through the fire for your idols." (killed: murdered, passed through: burned) **22.** "In all your abominations, you forgot the days of your youth when you were naked, polluted in your blood." (abominations: sins, polluted: tainted) **23.** "Woe, woe to you! After all your wickedness," (woe: disaster, wickedness: sin) **24.** "You built an eminent place for yourself in every street." (eminent: prominent, place: site) **25.** "You built your high places at the head of every street and defiled your beauty by exposing yourself to everyone who passed by." (high places: altars, defiled: polluted, exposed: revealed) **26.** "You committed fornication with the Egyptians, your neighbors, and with Assyrians, provoking me to anger." (fornication: immorality, neighbors: companions) **27.** "I have stretched out my hand over you and reduced your food, delivering you to the will of those who hate you." (stretched out: extended, reduced: cut, will: desires) **28.** "You played the harlot with the Assyrians and could never be satisfied." (harlot: prostitute, satisfied: content) **29.** "You multiplied your fornications in Canaan and Chaldea, but still were not satisfied." (multiplied: increased, fornications: immoral acts) **30.** "How weak is your heart, says the LORD, seeing you do all these things like a stubborn prostitute." (weak: foolish, stubborn: obstinate) **31.** "You built your high places at the head of every street, showing contempt for hire, like a wife who commits adultery." (showing: displaying, contempt: disrespect, hire: payment) **32.** "You took strangers instead of your husband!" (strangers: outsiders, husband: spouse) **33.** "Others give gifts to prostitutes, but you gave gifts to all your lovers, hiring them to come to you from every direction." (lovers: partners, hiring: paying) **34.** "You are different from other prostitutes, for none followed you to commit prostitution; you paid your lovers, and they didn't pay you." (different: unique, followed: pursued, commit: engage) **35.** "Therefore, hear the word of the LORD." (hear: listen, word: message) **36.** "Because your filthiness was poured out and your nakedness exposed, you gave your children to idols." (filthiness: uncleanness, exposed: revealed) **37.** "I will gather all your lovers, whom you took pleasure in, and I will expose your nakedness to them." (gather: collect, pleasure: enjoyment, expose: reveal) **38.** "I will judge you as adulterous women are judged, and I will make you drink blood in fury and jealousy." (adulterous: unfaithful, fury: rage, jealousy: envy) **39.** "I will give you into their hands, and they will destroy your high places, strip you of your clothes, and take your jewels, leaving you naked." (destroy: demolish, strip: remove, jewels: ornaments) **40.** "They will bring a company against you, stone you, and pierce you with swords." (company: group, stone: throw stones, pierce: stab) **41.** "They will burn down your houses and execute judgments on you in front of many women. I will make you stop being a prostitute." (burn down: destroy, execute: carry out, judgments: punishments) **42.** "I will calm my fury and stop being angry with you." (calm: soothe, fury: rage) **43.** "Because you didn't remember your youth but provoked me, I will repay you for your actions." (repay: punish, actions: deeds) **44.** "Everyone will use this proverb against you: 'Like mother, like daughter.'" (proverb: saying, daughter: child) **45.** "You are your mother's daughter, who loathed her husband and children. You are the sister of your sisters who also loathed their husbands and children." (loathed: hated, sisters: siblings) **46.** "Your older sister is Samaria, and your younger sister is Sodom." (older: elder, younger: junior) **47.** "Yet you have not followed their ways but have surpassed them in your corruption." (surpassed: exceeded, corruption: depravity) **48.** "As I live, says the LORD, Sodom didn't sin as you have." (sin: transgress, live: exist) **49.** "Sodom's sin was pride, excess, and neglecting the poor and needy." (excess: overindulgence, neglecting: ignoring) **50.** "They committed abomination, and I destroyed them when I saw fit." (abomination: wickedness, destroyed: wiped out) **51.** "Samaria didn't commit half your sins, but you have multiplied your abominations more than they did." (multiplied: increased, sins: wrongs) **52.** "You judged your sisters, but you are more abominable than they. You should be ashamed of your actions." (judged: condemned, abominable: detestable, ashamed: embarrassed) **53.** "When I restore the captives of Sodom and Samaria, I will also restore yours among them." (restore: return, captives: prisoners) **54.** "You will bear your shame, as you comfort them." (bear: carry, comfort: console) **55.** "When Sodom and Samaria are restored, you will also return to your former state." (former: previous, state: condition) **56.** "You didn't mention Sodom when you were proud." (mention: refer, proud: arrogant) **57.** "Before your wickedness was revealed, you mocked the daughters of Syria and the Philistines, who despised you." (mocked: ridiculed, despised: hated) **58.** "You bore your lewdness and abominations," says the LORD. (lewdness: immorality, abominations: sins) **59.** "I will deal with you as you have dealt with others, despising the oath and breaking the covenant." (deal: treat, oath: promise, breaking: violating) **60.** "But I will remember my covenant with you and establish an everlasting one." (establish: set, everlasting: eternal) **61.** "You will remember your ways and be ashamed when you receive your sisters, but not by your covenant." (ways: actions, ashamed: embarrassed) **62.** "I will establish my covenant with you, and you will know that I am the LORD." (establish: set, know: understand) **63.** "Then you will remember and be ashamed and never speak again because of your shame when I am pacified toward you." (pacified: calmed, ashamed: embarrassed)

Chapter 17

1. The word of the LORD came to me, saying, (word: message) **2.** "Son of man, tell the house of Israel a parable and a riddle." (parable: story, riddle: puzzle) **3.** "Say, 'This is what the Lord GOD says: A mighty eagle with expansive wings, long feathers, and many colors came to Lebanon and took the highest branch of the cedar tree. (mighty: strong, expansive: wide, highest: top) **4.** He cut off the top of its young shoots and took it to a bustling trade city, placing it in a merchant's center. (young shoots: small branches, bustling: busy, merchant's center: market) **5.** He then took a seed from the land and planted it in fertile soil near abundant waters, growing it like a willow tree. (seed: sprout, fertile: rich, abundant: plentiful) **6.** It grew into a small vine, spreading out its branches toward the eagle, with its roots placed beneath him. It became a vine that grew branches and sprouted new shoots. (small: little, spreading out: extending, sprouted: grew) **7.** But then another great eagle, with many feathers, appeared. The vine bent its roots and stretched its branches to him, hoping he would water it in the fields where it had been planted. (appeared: showed up, stretched: extended) **8.** It was planted in good soil by plenty of water to bear fruit and be a strong vine. (soil: ground, bear fruit: produce, strong: sturdy) **9.** Say to them, 'The Lord GOD says: Will it thrive? If the eagle pulls up its roots and cuts off its fruit, the vine will wither. It will lose its leaves in the spring, and no great power or people can save it.' (thrive: grow, wither: dry up, lose: shed) **10.** Yes, when it was planted, will it thrive? Will it not wither when the east wind touches it? It will wither in the furrows where it grew." (touches: strikes, furrows: grooves) **11.** Then the word of the LORD came to me, saying, (word: message) **12.** "Say to the rebellious people of Israel, 'Do you not understand the meaning of this? Look, the king of Babylon has come to Jerusalem, taken its king and leaders, and brought them to Babylon. (rebellious: disobedient, meaning: significance, leaders: rulers) **13.** He took the king's descendants and made a covenant with him, requiring him to take an oath. He also took the strongest men of the land, (descendants: children, covenant: agreement, oath: vow, strongest: mightiest) **14.** so the kingdom would be humbled and would not rise again. If he kept his covenant, the kingdom could stand. (humbled: lowered, rise again: be restored, stand: endure) **15.** But the king broke his covenant by sending messengers to Egypt, asking for horses and soldiers. Will he succeed in this? Will he escape after breaking the covenant? (broke: violated, messengers: envoys, succeed: prosper, escape: flee) **16.** As I live, says the Lord GOD, in the place where the king made himself king, whose oath he despised and whose covenant he broke, he will die in Babylon. (despised: scorned, place: location) **17.** Pharaoh with his large army and many soldiers will not help him when war comes, when they build siege walls and ramparts to try to stop many people. (large: vast, ramparts: defensive walls, stop: halt) **18.** Since he despised the oath and broke the covenant after making it, he will not escape. (despised: scorned, escape: flee) **19.** Therefore, the Lord GOD says: As I live, I will repay him for breaking my covenant and despising my oath. (repay: punish, despising: scorn) **20.** I will catch him in my trap and bring him to Babylon, where I will judge him for his sin against me. (trap: snare, judge: punish, sin: wrong) **21.** All his allies and their bands will fall by the sword, and the survivors will be scattered to the winds. Then you will know that I, the LORD, have spoken." (allies: supporters, bands: groups, scattered: dispersed) **22.** The Lord GOD says: "I will take a branch from the top of the high cedar and plant it. I will cut off a young, tender shoot from its highest branches and plant it on a high, exalted mountain. (branch: limb, tender: soft, exalted: elevated) **23.** On the mountain in the heights of Israel, I will plant it, and it will grow, bearing fruit and becoming a beautiful cedar. All kinds of birds will nest under it, and in the shade of its branches, they will find shelter. (beautiful: splendid, nest: settle, shelter: refuge) **24.** Then all the trees of the field will know that I, the LORD, have humbled the proud tree and lifted up the low tree. I have dried up the green tree and made the dry tree thrive. I, the LORD, have spoken and will do it." (humble: lower, proud: arrogant, thrive: grow).

Chapter 18

1. The word of the LORD came to me, saying, (word: message) **2.** Why do you use this proverb in Israel: "The fathers have eaten sour grapes, and the children's teeth are set on edge?" (proverb: saying, sour grapes: bitter fruit) **3.** As I live, says the Lord GOD, you will no longer use this proverb in Israel. (longer: anymore) **4.** All souls are mine; the soul of the father and the soul of the son are mine. The soul that sins shall die. (souls: lives, sins: wrongs) **5.** If a man is righteous and does what is lawful and right, (righteous: just, lawful: legal) **6.** He does not worship idols, commit adultery, or defile himself. (worship: adore, adultery: unfaithfulness, defile: corrupt) **7.** He does not oppress anyone, restores pledges, does not rob, feeds the hungry, and clothes the naked. (oppress: mistreat, restores: returns, rob: steal) **8.** He does not charge usury or take interest, avoids evil, and judges justly. (usury: excessive interest, interest: charge, avoids: shuns) **9.** He follows my laws and does what is right; he is righteous and will surely live, says the Lord GOD. (follows: obeys, surely: certainly) **10.** If he has a son who is a robber, a murderer, or does any of these wicked things, (robber: thief, murderer: killer, wicked: evil) **11.** And does not follow his father's example but defiles others, (defiles: corrupts) **12.** Oppresses the poor, robs, and worships idols, (poor: needy) **13.** Takes interest, and commits abominations, he will not live; he will surely die for his sins. (takes: charges, abominations: vile acts, sins: wrongdoings) **14.** But if this son sees his father's wickedness and chooses to live righteously, (chooses: decides, wickedness: evil) **15.** He does not commit idol worship, does not defile others, (idol worship: idolatry, defile: corrupt) **16.** Does not oppress anyone, and provides for the needy, (oppress: mistreat, provides: helps) **17.** He does not take interest, but follows God's laws. This son will live, not die. (interest: charge) **18.** His father, who oppressed others and did evil, will die for his sins. (oppressed: mistreated, evil: wicked) **19.** You ask, "Why should the son not bear the father's iniquity?" If the son does what is right, he will live. (iniquity: sin, right: righteous) **20.** The soul that sins will die. The son will not bear the father's guilt, and the father will not bear the son's guilt. The righteous will live by their righteousness, and the wicked will die by their wickedness. (guilt: blame, righteousness: justice, wickedness: evil) **21.** If the wicked person turns from their sins, follows God's laws, and does what is right, they will live. (turns: repents, right: just) **22.** All the wickedness they committed will be forgiven, and they will live in their righteousness. (wickedness: wrongs, forgiven: pardoned) **23.** I do not delight in the death of the wicked, says the Lord GOD. I desire that they turn from their ways and live. (delight: take pleasure, desire: want) **24.** If the righteous person turns away from their righteousness and does evil, their past righteousness will not be remembered. They will die for their sins. (turns away: forsakes, past: previous, remembered: recalled) **25.** You say, "The way of the Lord is not fair." Hear me, O house of Israel, is not my way fair? Are not your ways unfair? (fair: just, unfair: unjust) **26.** When a righteous person turns from their righteousness and commits iniquity, they will die for it. (commits: does, iniquity: sin) **27.** When the wicked person turns from their wickedness and does what is right, they will live. (turns: repents, wickedness: wrongs) **28.** If they turn from all their transgressions, they will surely live and not die. (transgressions: sins, surely: certainly) **29.** Yet you say, "The way of the Lord is not fair." O house of Israel, are not my ways fair? Are not your ways unfair? (unfair: unjust) **30.** Therefore, I will judge you, O house of Israel, each according to their ways, says the Lord GOD. Repent and turn from all your sins, so your iniquity does not bring ruin upon you. (judge: punish, repent: change, ruin: destruction) **31.** Cast away your transgressions and make for yourselves a new heart and a new spirit. Why should you die, O house of Israel? (cast away: throw away, transgressions: sins, spirit: attitude) **32.** I do not take pleasure in the death of anyone, says the Lord GOD. Turn from your ways and live. (take pleasure: delight, ways: actions).

Chapter 19

1. Take up a lament for the princes of Israel, (lament: mourn) **2.** And say, "What is your mother? A lioness: she lay among lions and raised her cubs among young lions." (lioness: female lion, cubs: young) **3.** She raised one of her cubs, and it became a lion; it learned to hunt and devoured men. (hunted: chased, devoured: consumed) **4.** The nations heard of him; he was caught in their trap and brought in chains to Egypt. (nations: peoples, caught: trapped, chains: shackles) **5.** When she saw her hope was lost, she took another of her cubs and made him a lion. (hope: expectation, lost: gone) **6.** He roamed among the lions, became a lion, learned to hunt, and devoured men. (roamed: wandered, hunt: chase) **7.** He attacked their cities, laid waste to their palaces, and the land was desolate by his roar. (attacked: assaulted, laid waste: destroyed, desolate: barren) **8.** Nations surrounded him from all sides, trapped him in their pit. (surrounded: encircled, trapped: caught) **9.** They put him in chains and brought him to the king of Babylon, where his voice would no longer be heard in Israel. (chains: shackles, voice: cry) **10.** Your mother was like a vine by the waters, fruitful and full of branches. (vine: plant, fruitful: productive, branches: limbs) **11.** She had strong branches like the scepters of rulers, her stature was exalted among the thick branches. (strong: sturdy, scepters: staffs, stature: height, exalted: elevated) **12.** But she was uprooted in fury, thrown down, and the east wind dried up her fruit. Her strong branches were broken and consumed by fire. (uprooted: torn out, fury: anger, dried up: withered, consumed: destroyed) **13.** Now she is planted in the wilderness, in a dry and thirsty land. (planted: set, wilderness: desert, thirsty: parched) **14.** A fire has come from her branches, devouring her fruit. She has no strong branch to rule with. This is a lamentation, and it shall remain a lamentation. (fire: blaze, devouring: consuming, lamentation: mournful song, remain: endure).

Chapter 20

1. In the seventh year, on the tenth day of the fifth month, the elders of Israel came to inquire of the LORD and sat before me. (inquire: ask) **2.** The word of the LORD came to me, saying, (saying: spoke) **3.** "Son of man, speak to the elders of Israel and say, 'This is what the Lord GOD says: Are you here to inquire of me? As I live, I will not be inquired of by you.'" (inquire: ask, live: exist) **4.** "Will you judge them, son of man? Make them understand the abominations of their ancestors." (judge: decide, abominations: evils) **5.** "Say: When I chose Israel, I revealed myself to them in Egypt and declared, 'I am the LORD your God.'" (revealed: showed, declared: proclaimed) **6.** "I lifted my hand to bring them out of Egypt, to a land flowing with milk and honey, the most glorious of lands." (lifted: raised, glorious: splendid) **7.** "I told them to throw away their idols and not defile themselves with the idols of Egypt, for I am the LORD your God." (throw away: discard, defile: pollute) **8.** "But they rebelled, did not listen, and kept their idols. So I decided to pour out my fury on them in Egypt." (rebelled: resisted, fury: anger) **9.** "But for my name's sake, I acted, so it would not be profaned among the nations where they were."

(profaned: dishonored, acted: did) **10.** "So I brought them out of Egypt into the wilderness." (wilderness: desert) **11.** "I gave them my statutes and judgments, which if followed, would give them life." (statutes: laws, judgments: rules) **12.** "I also gave them my Sabbaths, a sign that I sanctify them." (sanctify: make holy) **13.** "But Israel rebelled in the wilderness, despising my statutes, polluting my Sabbaths, and following idols. I decided to pour out my fury on them there." (rebelled: resisted, despising: hating, polluting: defiling) **14.** "But I acted for my name's sake, so it wouldn't be profaned among the nations." (profaned: dishonored) **15.** "I swore not to bring them into the promised land because they despised my judgments and followed idols." (promised: given, despised: hated) **16.** "Yet I spared them from being destroyed in the wilderness." (spared: saved, destroyed: wiped out) **17.** "I told their children not to follow their ancestors' sins but to walk in my statutes and keep my Sabbaths." (ancestors: forefathers, walk: follow) **18.** "But they too rebelled, polluting my Sabbaths. I decided to pour out my fury on them in the wilderness." (rebelled: resisted, fury: anger) **19.** "I am the LORD your God. Walk in my statutes and keep my judgments." (statutes: laws, judgments: rules) **20.** "Keep my Sabbaths holy, a sign between us, so you know I am the LORD who sanctifies you." (holy: sacred, sanctifies: makes holy) **21.** "But their children also rebelled, not following my statutes, despising my Sabbaths. I said I would pour out my fury on them in the wilderness." (rebelled: resisted, fury: anger) **22.** "But I withdrew my hand, acting for my name's sake, so it would not be profaned." (withdrew: pulled back, acted: did) **23.** "I lifted my hand to scatter them among the nations and disperse them." (scatter: spread, disperse: separate) **24.** "They had not kept my judgments, polluted my Sabbaths, and followed idols." (polluted: defiled, followed: worshipped) **25.** "So I gave them statutes that were not good and judgments they couldn't live by." (statutes: laws, couldn't live by: were not helpful) **26.** "I polluted them through their own sacrifices, making them desolate so they would know I am the LORD." (polluted: defiled, desolate: barren) **27.** "Speak to Israel: Your fathers blasphemed me by trespassing against me." (blasphemed: insulted, trespassing: sinning) **28.** "When I brought them into the land, they sacrificed on high hills, provoking me with their offerings." (sacrificed: offered, provoking: angering) **29.** "I asked them, 'What is this high place you go to?' It is called Bamah to this day." (high place: altar) **30.** "Say to Israel: Are you polluted like your fathers, committing idolatry?" (polluted: defiled, idolatry: idol worship) **31.** "When you offer gifts, making your children pass through fire, you pollute yourselves with idols. Shall I be inquired of by you? As I live, I will not be inquired of by you." (pollute: defile, inquired: asked) **32.** "What you think will not happen. You say, 'We will be like the nations, serving idols of wood and stone.'" (nations: peoples, idols: false gods) **33.** "As I live, I will rule over you with a mighty hand, outstretched arm, and fury poured out." (fury: anger, outstretched: extended) **34.** "I will gather you from the nations where you are scattered, with a mighty hand and fury." (gather: collect, scattered: dispersed) **35.** "I will bring you into the wilderness of the nations and plead with you face to face." (plead: argue, face to face: directly) **36.** "Like I pleaded with your ancestors in Egypt, so I will plead with you." (pleaded: argued) **37.** "I will cause you to pass under the rod and bring you into the bond of the covenant." (cause: make, rod: staff) **38.** "I will purge the rebels from among you. They will not enter Israel, and you will know I am the LORD." (purge: cleanse, rebels: wrongdoers) **39.** "As for you, house of Israel, go serve your idols, but pollute my holy name no more with your gifts and idols." (pollute: defile, holy: sacred) **40.** "On my holy mountain in Israel, all of Israel will serve me. I will accept your offerings and firstfruits." (mountain: hill, offerings: gifts) **41.** "I will accept your sweet savor when I bring you out from the nations, and I will be sanctified in you before the nations." (savor: fragrance, sanctified: made holy) **42.** "You will know I am the LORD when I bring you into the land I promised to your ancestors." (promised: gave) **43.** "There you will remember your sinful ways and loathe yourselves for your evils." (loathe: hate, evils: sins) **44.** "You will know I am the LORD when I act for my name's sake, not according to your wicked ways." (wicked: evil) **45.** The word of the LORD came to me, saying, (saying: spoke) **46.** "Son of man, set your face toward the south, and prophesy against the forest of the south." (prophesy: speak) **47.** "Say to the forest: Hear the word of the LORD. I will kindle a fire in you, burning every green and dry tree. The flame will not be quenched, and all faces from south to north will be burned." (kindle: start, quenched: put out, faces: people) **48.** "All flesh will see that I, the LORD, have kindled it. It will not be quenched." (flesh: people, kindled: started) **49.** I said, "Ah Lord GOD! They say I speak in parables." (parables: riddles).

Chapter 21
1. The word of the LORD came to me. (word: message) **2.** "Son of man, face Jerusalem, speak against the holy places, and prophesy against the land of Israel." (prophesy: foretell) **3.** "Say to Israel: 'I am against you. I will draw my sword from its sheath to cut off both the righteous and the wicked.'" (draw: pull out, sheath: scabbard) **4.** "Since I will cut off both the righteous and the wicked, my sword will strike from south to north." (strike: hit) **5.** "All will know that I, the LORD, have drawn my sword, and it will not return." (return: withdraw) **6.** "Sigh, son of man, with sorrow, and let them see your bitterness." (bitterness: grief) **7.** "When they ask, 'Why do you sigh?' answer, 'The news is coming: terror will strike. Hearts will melt, hands will be weak, spirits will faint, and knees will tremble. It is coming, says the Lord GOD.'" (terror: fear, strike: hit, faint: collapse) **8.** The word of the LORD came to me again. (again: once more) **9.** "Son of man, prophesy, and say, 'The sword, the sword is sharpened and polished.'" (sharpened: honed, polished: smoothed) **10.** "It is sharpened for slaughter, polished to shine. Should we rejoice? It despises the rod of my son and is ready to strike." (slaughter: killing, despises: rejects) **11.** "It has been polished to be handled, sharpened and ready for the slayer." (handled: used, slayer: killer) **12.** "Cry and mourn, son of man, for it will strike my people, even the princes of Israel. The sword will bring terror to my people. Strike your thigh in grief." (mourn: grieve, terror: fear) **13.** "This is a trial, and what if even the rod is despised? It will be no more, says the Lord GOD." (trial: test, despised: rejected) **14.** "Prophesy again, strike your hands together, and let the sword be doubled. It is the sword of the slain, striking the great ones in their private chambers." (doubled: increased, slain: killed) **15.** "I have set the sword against all their gates to cause their hearts to faint and multiply their ruin. It is bright and wrapped for slaughter." (ruin: destruction, wrapped: prepared) **16.** "Go whichever way your face is set, to the right or to the left." (face: direction) **17.** "I will strike my hands together, and my fury will rest. I, the LORD, have said it." (fury: anger, rest: cease) **18.** The word of the LORD came again to me. (again: once more) **19.** "Son of man, appoint two ways for the sword of the king of Babylon to come. Both will come from the same land. Choose a place at the crossroads to the city." (appoint: set, crossroads: junction) **20.** "Appoint a way for the sword to reach Rabbath of the Ammonites and Judah in Jerusalem." (reach: come to) **21.** "The king of Babylon will stand at the crossroads, using divination. He will make his arrows bright, consult images, and examine the liver." (divination: fortune-telling, images: idols) **22.** "The divination for Jerusalem will lead him to appoint captains, open the mouth for slaughter, lift the voice with shouting, and prepare battering rams and fortifications." (divination: prophecy, slaughter: killing, captains: leaders) **23.** "It will be like a false divination in their eyes, but he will remember their iniquity, and they will be captured." (false: fake, iniquity: sin) **24.** "Because your iniquity is remembered, your sins revealed, and your actions exposed, you will be taken." (iniquity: sin, exposed: uncovered) **25.** "You, profane and wicked prince of Israel, your day has come when iniquity will end." (profane: unholy, wicked: evil) **26.** "Remove the crown and the diadem. It will not be the same. Exalt the low and abase the high." (remove: take off, diadem: crown, abase: lower) **27.** "I will overturn, overturn, overturn it, and it will be no more until he comes whose right it is. I will give it to him." (overturn: flip, right: entitlement) **28.** "Son of man, prophesy against the Ammonites and their reproach, saying, 'The sword is drawn for slaughter.'" (reproach: disgrace, slaughter: killing) **29.** "They will see vanity and false divination in you. It will bring them upon the necks of the slain, for their iniquity will end." (vanity: emptiness, false: fake, iniquity: sin) **30.** "Shall I cause the sword to return to its sheath? I will judge you in the land of your nativity." (cause: make, nativity: birth) **31.** "I will pour out my wrath on you, blow against you with the fire of my anger, and deliver you to men skilled in destruction." (wrath: fury, skilled: expert) **32.** "You will be fuel for the fire, your blood will fill the land, and you will no longer be remembered. I, the LORD, have spoken." (fuel: material, fill: cover, remembered: recalled).

Chapter 22
1. The word of the LORD came to me, saying, (word: message) **2.** "Son of man, will you judge the bloody city? Show her all her abominations." (judge: condemn, abominations: wickedness) **3.** "Say, 'Thus says the Lord GOD: The city sheds blood and makes idols to defile herself.'" (defile: pollute) **4.** "You are guilty of shedding blood and defiling yourself with idols. Your days are numbered, and you are a reproach to the nations." (guilty: at fault, reproach: disgrace) **5.** "Those near and far will mock you, for you are infamous and greatly troubled." (mock: ridicule, infamous: notorious) **6.** "The princes of Israel are in you, using their power to shed blood." (princes: leaders, shed: spill) **7.** "They show no respect for father and mother, oppress strangers, vex the fatherless and the widow." (vex: distress) **8.** "You despise my holy things and profane my Sabbaths." (despise: scorn, profane: disrespect) **9.** "There are those who spread lies to shed blood, eat on the mountains, and commit lewd acts in your midst." (spread: tell, lewd: immoral) **10.** "They reveal their father's nakedness, humiliate the one set apart for impurity." (reveal: expose, humiliate: shame) **11.** "One has committed adultery, another defiled his

daughter-in-law, and another humiliated his sister, his father's daughter." (adultery: infidelity, defiled: polluted) **12.** "They take bribes to shed blood, practice usury and extortion, and forget me, says the Lord GOD." (bribes: payments, usury: lending at high interest) **13.** "Therefore, I strike my hand at your dishonest gain and the blood in your midst." (strike: slap, dishonest: unfair) **14.** "Can your heart endure and your hands be strong when I deal with you? I, the LORD, have spoken it, and I will do it." (endure: withstand, deal: act) **15.** "I will scatter you among the nations, disperse you across the countries, and remove your filth from you." (scatter: disperse, filth: impurity) **16.** "You will take your inheritance in the sight of the nations, and you will know that I am the LORD." (inheritance: possession) **17.** The word of the LORD came to me, saying, (word: message) **18.** "Son of man, Israel has become dross to me: brass, tin, iron, and lead in the furnace, the dross of silver." (dross: waste, furnace: smelter) **19.** "Because you have become dross, I will gather you into the midst of Jerusalem." (gather: assemble) **20.** "Just as silver, brass, iron, lead, and tin are gathered in the furnace to be melted, so will I gather you in my anger and fury, and melt you there." (melted: liquefied, fury: rage) **21.** "I will gather you, blow on you with the fire of my wrath, and you will be melted in the furnace." (wrath: anger) **22.** "As silver is melted, so you will be melted in the midst of it, and you will know that I, the LORD, have poured out my fury on you." (melted: liquefied, poured out: released) **23.** The word of the LORD came to me, saying, (word: message) **24.** "Son of man, say to her: You are the land that is not cleansed, nor rained on in the day of indignation." (cleansed: purified, indignation: anger) **25.** "There is a conspiracy of her prophets, like a roaring lion ravaging the prey. They devour souls, take treasures, and make many widows." (conspiracy: plot, devour: consume, ravaging: destroying) **26.** "Her priests have violated my law and profaned my holy things. They have not distinguished between the holy and the profane, nor between the clean and unclean. They have disregarded my Sabbaths, and I am profaned among them." (violated: broken, disregarded: ignored) **27.** "Her princes are like wolves, shedding blood and destroying lives for dishonest gain." (princes: leaders, dishonest: unfair) **28.** "Her prophets have covered their lies with untempered mortar, seeing vanity and divining lies. They say, 'Thus says the Lord GOD,' when the LORD has not spoken." (covered: concealed, divining: predicting, untempered: weak) **29.** "The people use oppression, practice robbery, and mistreat the poor and needy. They wrongfully oppress the stranger." (oppression: cruelty, wrongfully: unjustly) **30.** "I searched for a man among them who would build the wall and stand in the gap before me to prevent destruction, but I found none." (searched: looked for, gap: breach) **31.** "Therefore, I have poured out my wrath upon them. I have consumed them with the fire of my anger, and repaid them for their actions, says the Lord GOD." (consumed: destroyed, repaid: rewarded).

Chapter 23
1. The word of the LORD came to me again. **2.** Son of man, there were two women, daughters of one mother. (daughters: offspring) **3.** They prostituted themselves in Egypt in their youth, losing their virginity and being defiled. (prostituted: engaged in immorality, defiled: corrupted) **4.** Their names were Aholah (the elder) and Aholibah (her sister). They were mine and bore sons and daughters. Aholah represents Samaria, and Aholibah represents Jerusalem. (bore: gave birth to, represents: symbolizes) **5.** Aholah became a prostitute when she was mine, lusting after her lovers, the Assyrians. (prostitute: immoral woman, lusting: desiring) **6.** The Assyrians were well-dressed, captains, rulers, and handsome young men on horseback. (well-dressed: fashionable, captains: leaders, rulers: officials) **7.** She prostituted herself with the Assyrians, defiling herself with their idols. (prostituted: engaged in immorality, defiling: corrupting) **8.** She did not give up her prostitution from Egypt, where she lost her virginity. (prostitution: immorality, lost her virginity: became unchaste) **9.** Therefore, I handed her over to her lovers, the Assyrians. (handed over: gave) **10.** They exposed her nakedness, took her children, and killed her with the sword. She became infamous for this punishment. (exposed: revealed, nakedness: vulnerability, infamous: notorious) **11.** When her sister Aholibah saw this, she became even more corrupt in her lust and prostitution. (corrupt: wicked, lust: desire) **12.** She lusted after the Assyrians, captains and rulers, all handsome young men on horseback. (lusted: desired) **13.** I saw that she was defiled and followed the same path. (defiled: corrupted) **14.** She increased her prostitution when she saw images of the Chaldeans on the wall. (increased: intensified, images: pictures) **15.** The Chaldeans were dressed in fine attire, with princes resembling Babylonian royalty. (fine attire: elegant clothing, princes: leaders) **16.** When Aholibah saw them, she lusted after them and sent messengers to Chaldea. (lusted: desired) **17.** The Babylonians came to her and defiled her, causing her to become polluted. (defiled: corrupted, polluted: contaminated) **18.** She exposed her prostitution, and my mind was alienated from her, just as it was from her sister. (alienated: distanced) **19.** She multiplied her prostitution, recalling the days of her youth in Egypt. (multiplied: increased, recalling: remembering) **20.** She lusted after their lovers, whose flesh was like that of donkeys, and whose semen was like that of horses. (lusted: desired, semen: seed) **21.** You remembered the sexual sins of your youth in Egypt. (sexual sins: immoral acts) **22.** Therefore, I will bring your enemies, whom you hate, against you. (enemies: adversaries) **23.** The Babylonians, Chaldeans, and all the Assyrians will come, young men, captains, and rulers on horseback. (captains: leaders, rulers: officials) **24.** They will attack with chariots and troops, surrounding you with shields, helmets, and judgment. (chariots: vehicles, troops: soldiers, judgment: punishment) **25.** I will bring my jealousy upon you, and they will treat you with fury, cutting off your nose and ears, and your survivors will be killed by the sword. (jealousy: anger, fury: rage) **26.** They will strip you of your clothes and take away your beautiful jewels. (strip: remove) **27.** I will put an end to your prostitution and idolatry from Egypt, so you will no longer look to them. (end: stop, idolatry: idol worship) **28.** I will hand you over to those whom you hate and alienate you from them. (alienate: separate) **29.** They will treat you hatefully, taking all your work and leaving you naked, exposing your prostitution. (hatefully: maliciously) **30.** I will do this because you prostituted yourself with idols. (prostituted: engaged in immorality, idols: false gods) **31.** You followed your sister's path, so I will give you the same punishment. (path: way) **32.** You will drink from your sister's cup, deep and full. You will be mocked and ridiculed, as it contains much. (mocked: ridiculed, ridiculed: scorned) **33.** You will be filled with drunkenness and sorrow, the cup of astonishment and desolation from Samaria. (astonishment: amazement, desolation: ruin) **34.** You will drink it, break the shards, and pull off your breasts. I have spoken it. (shards: pieces) **35.** Because you have forgotten me and cast me behind you, you will bear the consequences of your actions. (forgotten: ignored, cast behind: rejected, consequences: results) **36.** Will you judge Aholah and Aholibah? Declare their abominations to them. (abominations: wickedness) **37.** They committed adultery, blood is on their hands, and they sacrificed their children to idols. (adultery: infidelity, sacrificed: offered) **38.** They defiled my sanctuary and profaned my Sabbaths. (defiled: corrupted, profaned: desecrated) **39.** After killing their children, they profaned my sanctuary on the same day. (killing: murdering) **40.** You sent for men from afar, and when they came, you washed yourself, painted your eyes, and adorned yourself. (adorned: decorated) **41.** You sat on a fine bed with a prepared table, offering my incense and oil. (prepared: set) **42.** A crowd of people came, and you were joined by men from the wilderness, who gave you bracelets and crowns. (wilderness: desert, bracelets: adornments, crowns: headwear) **43.** I asked, will they commit adultery with her? Yet they did, just as they do with a prostitute. (adultery: infidelity) **44.** They went into Aholah and Aholibah, the lewd women. (lewd: immoral) **45.** The righteous men will judge them as adulteresses and murderers, because blood is on their hands. (adulteresses: unfaithful women, murderers: killers) **46.** I will bring a company to punish them, and they will be spoiled. (company: group, spoiled: plundered) **47.** They will stone them with stones, kill their children, and burn their houses. (stone: execute, kill: slay, burn: set aflame) **48.** I will end lewdness in the land, teaching all women not to follow your ways. (lewdness: immorality, teaching: instructing) **49.** You will bear the consequences of your lewdness and idolatry, and know that I am the Lord GOD. (lewdness: immorality, idolatry: idol worship).

Chapter 24
1. On the tenth day of the tenth month in the ninth year, the word of the LORD came to me. (word: message) **2.** Son of man, write the date, for on this day the king of Babylon besieged Jerusalem. (besieged: surrounded) **3.** Tell the rebellious house a parable: "Set a pot on the fire, and pour water into it. (rebellious: disobedient, parable: story) **4.** Put the choice pieces of meat in it—thighs, shoulders, and choice bones. (choice: select) **5.** Take the best of the flock, and burn the bones beneath to make it boil well, so the bones cook in it." (flock: group, boil: cook) **6.** Woe to the bloody city, the pot whose scum is still in it! Remove it piece by piece, leaving nothing behind. (woe: sorrow, scum: residue) **7.** Her blood is in her midst; she poured it on a rock, not covering it with dust. (midst: center, covering: hiding) **8.** to provoke fury and vengeance. I have set her blood on the rock for all to see, uncovered. (provoke: stir up, fury: anger, vengeance: revenge) **9.** Woe to the bloody city! I will make the fire great. (woe: sorrow, bloody: violent) **10.** Heap wood, kindle the fire, consume the flesh, and spice it well. Let the bones burn. (heap: pile, kindle: start, consume: burn) **11.** When it's empty, put it on the coals to heat, melting its impurities and consuming its scum. (impurities: dirt, coals: embers) **12.** She has exhausted herself with lies; her scum remains. It will be burned. (exhausted: drained, lies: falsehoods) **13.** Her filthiness is lewdness. Though I tried to cleanse her, she was not purified. She will not be cleansed

until my fury is complete. (filthiness: wickedness, lewdness: immorality, cleansed: purified) **14.** I, the LORD, have spoken. It will happen as I say. I will not change, spare, or repent. Your actions will determine your judgment. (spoken: declared, repent: regret) **15.** The word of the LORD came to me again. (word: message) **16.** Son of man, I will take away the desire of your eyes with a stroke, but you shall not mourn or weep. (desire: longing, stroke: blow) **17.** Do not cry; do not mourn for the dead. Wear your turban and shoes, cover not your lips, and do not eat the bread of others. (turban: headpiece, cover: hide, bread: food) **18.** I spoke to the people in the morning, and in the evening, my wife died. I did as commanded the next morning. (commanded: instructed) **19.** The people asked me, "Why are you acting this way? What does it mean?" (acting: behaving, mean: signify) **20.** I replied, "The word of the LORD came to me, saying, (word: message) **21.** 'I will defile my sanctuary, the strength of your glory, the desire of your eyes, and the objects of your pity. Your sons and daughters will die by the sword. (defile: desecrate, sanctuary: holy place, strength: power, pity: compassion) **22.** You will act as I have: you will not cover your lips or eat others' bread. (cover: hide) **23.** You will wear turbans and shoes, and will not mourn or weep, but you will pine away for your iniquities and mourn for one another.' (pine away: waste away, iniquities: sins) **24.** Ezekiel is a sign to you; you will do as he has done, and when it happens, you will know that I am the LORD. (sign: symbol) **25.** When I take away their strength, the joy of their glory, the desire of their eyes, and their children, (strength: power, glory: honor) **26.** The one who escapes will come to you to tell you what has happened. (escapes: survives) **27.** On that day, your mouth will be opened to the survivor. You will speak again and be a sign to them, and they will know that I am the LORD." (survivor: refugee, sign: symbol)

Chapter 25

1. The word of the LORD came to me again, saying, (word: message) **2.** Son of man, direct your face toward the Ammonites and prophesy against them. (direct: turn, prophesy: foretell) **3.** Say to them, "Hear the word of the Lord GOD: Because you said, 'Aha!' when my sanctuary was profaned, when the land of Israel was desolate, and when Judah went into captivity, (profaned: desecrated, desolate: ruined, captivity: exile) **4.** I will give you to the men of the east as a possession. They will set up their palaces and live in you, eating your fruit and drinking your milk. (possession: property, palaces: homes) **5.** I will make Rabbah a place for camels, and the Ammonites a place for flocks. You will know that I am the LORD. (Rabbah: capital city, flocks: herds) **6.** Because you clapped your hands and stamped your feet, rejoicing in heart over Israel's destruction, (rejoicing: celebrating, destruction: ruin) **7.** I will stretch out my hand against you, delivering you to the nations as plunder. I will cut you off from the people and destroy you, and you will know that I am the LORD. (plunder: loot, cut off: remove) **8.** Because Moab and Seir said, 'The house of Judah is like all the other nations,' (house: people) **9.** I will open the side of Moab, from the cities on its borders, including Beth-jeshimoth, Baal-meon, and Kiriathaim, (open: expose, borders: edges) **10.** and give them to the men of the east and the Ammonites as possession, so Moab will be forgotten among the nations. (possession: property, forgotten: erased) **11.** I will execute judgments on Moab, and they will know that I am the LORD. (execute: carry out, judgments: decisions) **12.** Because Edom has taken vengeance against Judah, (vengeance: revenge) **13.** I will stretch out my hand against Edom, cutting off man and beast from it, making it desolate from Teman. Those of Dedan will fall by the sword. (desolate: empty, fall: perish) **14.** I will pour out my vengeance on Edom through my people Israel, and they will carry out my anger and fury, making Edom know my vengeance. (pour out: unleash, fury: rage) **15.** Because the Philistines have acted in vengeance, with a spiteful heart, seeking to destroy Judah out of old hatred, (spiteful: hateful, hatred: animosity) **16.** I will stretch out my hand against the Philistines, cutting off the Cherethites and destroying the remnants of the coastal regions. (remnants: remains, coastal: shore) **17.** I will bring great vengeance upon them with furious rebukes, and they will know that I am the LORD when I pour out my vengeance on them." (bring: deliver, rebukes: reprimands).

Chapter 26

1. On the first day of the eleventh year, the LORD spoke to me, saying, (spoke: said) **2.** Son of man, because Tyre has rejoiced over Jerusalem's downfall, saying, "She is ruined; the gates of the people have been broken. Now, she will turn to me, and I will prosper," (ruined: destroyed, broken: shattered, prosper: succeed) **3.** Therefore, the Lord GOD declares: I am against you, Tyre, and I will bring many nations against you, just as waves crash upon the shore. (bring: send, waves: surges) **4.** They will demolish your walls and destroy your towers. I will strip you bare and turn you into a flat rock. (demolish: destroy, strip: remove) **5.** You will become a place for fishermen to spread their nets. I have declared it, says the Lord GOD, and you will be plundered by the nations. (spread: lay, plunder: loot) **6.** Your cities in the countryside will be destroyed by the sword, and everyone will know that I am the LORD. (destroyed: ruined) **7.** The Lord GOD says: I will bring Nebuchadnezzar, the king of Babylon, from the north against you, with his cavalry, chariots, and a vast army. (bring: send, cavalry: horsemen, vast: large) **8.** He will slay your cities in the countryside, set up a siege against you, and attack with his weapons. (slay: kill, siege: blockade) **9.** He will use siege engines against your walls, and with his axes, he will tear down your towers. (siege engines: war machines, axes: tools) **10.** The dust from his horses will cover you; the noise of his chariots and soldiers will shake your city when he enters through your gates, like a city whose walls have been breached. (dust: debris, shake: tremble, breached: broken) **11.** He will trample your streets with his horses' hooves. Your people will be slaughtered, and your strongholds will fall. (trample: crush, slaughtered: killed, strongholds: fortresses) **12.** They will plunder your wealth, seize your goods, destroy your walls, and break down your beautiful homes. They will throw your stones, timber, and rubble into the sea. (plunder: loot, seize: take, beautiful: fine, timber: wood, rubble: debris) **13.** The music of your songs will cease, and the sound of your harps will no longer be heard. (cease: stop, harps: stringed instruments) **14.** I will make you like a bare rock, a place where fishermen spread their nets. You will never be rebuilt, for I, the LORD, have spoken. (bare: exposed, spread: lay) **15.** The Lord GOD says to Tyre: When you fall, will not the islands be shaken at the sound of your destruction? When your wounded cry out, and the slaughter is great within you, (shaken: tremble, slaughter: killing) **16.** The rulers of the coastlands will come down from their thrones, remove their robes, and clothe themselves in trembling. They will sit down in shock, horrified by your fate. (rulers: leaders, trembling: fear, horrified: terrified) **17.** They will lament over you, saying, "How has the mighty city fallen, once so powerful in the sea, and a terror to all who sailed upon it?" (lament: mourn, mighty: strong, terror: fear) **18.** The islands will tremble on the day of your fall, and the coastal lands will be disturbed at your departure. (tremble: shake, disturbed: shaken) **19.** The Lord GOD declares: When I make you desolate, like cities that are uninhabited, and when the waters of the sea cover you, (desolate: empty, uninhabited: abandoned) **20.** When I bring you down to the pit with the ancient dead, and place you in the desolate parts of the earth, you will never be inhabited again. (pit: grave, desolate: empty) **21.** You will become a horror to others, and though people seek you, you will never be found again, says the Lord GOD. (horror: terror, seek: look for).

Chapter 27

1. The word of the LORD came to me again, saying, (word: message) **2.** Son of man, take up a lament for Tyre, (lament: mourning) **3.** And say to Tyre, you who are situated at the gateway to the sea, a trader among many islands, the Lord GOD says: Tyre, you have said, "I am perfect in beauty." (gateway: entrance, perfect: flawless) **4.** Your borders are in the heart of the seas, and your builders have perfected your beauty. (borders: boundaries, perfected: completed) **5.** They made your shipboards from fir trees of Senir, and used cedars from Lebanon to make your masts. (shipboards: planks, masts: posts) **6.** Your oars were made from the oaks of Bashan, and the artisans from Ashur crafted your benches of ivory, brought from the islands of Chittim. (oars: paddles, crafted: made, benches: seats) **7.** Fine linen from Egypt, embroidered with designs, was your sail, and blue and purple cloth from the islands of Elishah covered you. (embroidered: decorated, cloth: fabric) **8.** The people of Zidon and Arvad were your sailors, and your wise men, O Tyre, served as your pilots. (sailors: seamen, pilots: navigators) **9.** The elders of Gebal and their skilled workers were your caulkers; the ships of the sea and their sailors traded in your markets. (elders: leaders, skilled: expert, caulkers: sealers) **10.** The men of Persia, Lud, and Phut were your soldiers, your warriors, who displayed their shields and helmets to enhance your beauty. (soldiers: fighters, enhance: improve) **11.** The men of Arvad were stationed around your walls, and the Gammadims were stationed in your towers; they hung their shields on your walls to perfect your beauty. (stationed: placed, towers: fortresses, perfect: complete) **12.** Tarshish was your merchant, trading in many kinds of goods, including silver, iron, tin, and lead. (merchant: trader, goods: products) **13.** Javan, Tubal, and Meshech were your merchants, trading people and brass vessels in your markets. (brass: metal) **14.** The house of Togarmah brought horses, horsemen, and mules to your markets. (horsemen: cavalry) **15.** The men of Dedan were your merchants, and many islands were your trading partners, bringing you ivory and ebony as tribute. (tribute: offering) **16.** Syria traded with you, bringing emeralds, purple fabrics, embroidered cloth, fine linen, coral, and agate. (emeralds: jewels, coral: sea plants) **17.** Judah and Israel were your merchants, trading wheat, honey, oil, and balm. (wheat: grain, balm: ointment) **18.** Damascus traded with you, bringing wine from Helbon and white wool. (wool: fleece)

19. Dan and Javan traveled back and forth in your markets, trading bright iron, cassia, and calamus. (cassia: spice, calamus: reed) **20.** Dedan brought precious clothes for chariots to your markets. (precious: valuable, chariots: carts) **21.** Arabia and the princes of Kedar traded with you, bringing lambs, rams, and goats as goods. (lambs: sheep, rams: male sheep) **22.** The merchants of Sheba and Raamah traded with you, bringing spices, precious stones, and gold. (spices: seasonings, stones: gems) **23.** Haran, Canneh, Eden, Sheba, Assur, and Chilmad were your merchants. (merchants: traders) **24.** These merchants traded all sorts of goods, including blue garments, embroidered work, chests of rich apparel bound with cords, and cedar wood. (garments: clothes, apparel: clothing) **25.** The ships of Tarshish sang your praises in your markets; you were filled with wealth and made glorious in the heart of the seas. (praises: compliments, filled: loaded) **26.** Your rowers brought you into deep waters, but the east wind will break you in the heart of the seas. (rowers: oarsmen, break: destroy) **27.** Your riches, merchandise, sailors, pilots, caulkers, and all your warriors, along with your entire company, will be cast into the sea when your ruin comes. (merchandise: goods, warriors: fighters, company: group) **28.** The surrounding areas will shake at the cry of your sailors. (surrounding: nearby, shake: tremble) **29.** All who handle the oar, the sailors, and the pilots will come down from their ships, stand on the shore, (handle: steer, shore: coastline) **30.** And they will raise their voices in sorrow, crying bitterly and throwing dust on their heads, while they roll in ashes. (raise: lift, sorrow: grief) **31.** They will shave their heads in mourning for you, wear sackcloth, and weep for you with deep sorrow. (mourning: grieving, sackcloth: rough fabric) **32.** They will lament for you, saying, "What city is like Tyre, destroyed in the midst of the sea?" (lament: mourn, midst: center) **33.** When your goods went out to sea, you enriched many nations; you made the kings of the earth wealthy through the abundance of your goods. (enriched: made rich, abundance: plenty) **34.** But when you are broken by the seas and your merchandise and all your people fall into the depths, (broken: shattered, depths: abyss) **35.** The inhabitants of the islands will be stunned by your destruction, and their kings will be filled with fear, their faces troubled. (inhabitants: residents, stunned: shocked, troubled: worried) **36.** The merchants among the nations will hiss at you, and you will be a terror, never to be found again. (hiss: mock, terror: fear)

Chapter 28

1. The word of the LORD came to me again, saying, (word: message) **2.** Son of man, speak to the ruler of Tyre and say, "This is what the Sovereign LORD says: Because your heart is proud and you claim to be a god, sitting on the throne of a god in the heart of the sea, but you are just a mortal, not a god, even though you consider yourself as wise as a god." (proud: arrogant, claim: declare, mortal: human) **3.** You are wiser than anyone, with no secrets hidden from you. (wiser: smarter, secrets: mysteries) **4.** With your wisdom and understanding, you have acquired wealth, amassing gold and silver in your treasuries. (acquired: gained, amassing: collecting, treasuries: vaults) **5.** Through your extensive trade and clever dealings, you have grown even richer, and your heart has become proud because of your wealth. (extensive: large, clever: shrewd, richer: wealthier) **6.** Therefore, this is what the Sovereign LORD says: Because you have set your heart like that of a god, (set: placed) **7.** I will bring against you foreigners, ruthless nations, who will draw their swords against your great wisdom and defile your splendor. (foreigners: outsiders, ruthless: harsh, defile: dishonor) **8.** They will bring you down to the pit, and you will die the death of the slain in the heart of the sea. (pit: abyss, slain: killed) **9.** Will you still claim to be a god when the one who slays you comes? You will be a mere man, not a god, in the hands of your destroyer. (slays: kills, mere: simple) **10.** You will die the deaths of the uncircumcised by the hands of foreigners. I have spoken it," says the Sovereign LORD. (uncircumcised: outsiders) **11.** Then the word of the LORD came to me again, saying, (again: once more) **12.** Son of man, lament for the king of Tyre and tell him, "This is what the Sovereign LORD says: 'You were the seal of perfection, full of wisdom and perfect in beauty. (lament: mourn, seal: mark, perfection: flawlessness) **13.** You were in Eden, the garden of God; every precious stone adorned you: sardius, topaz, and diamond, beryl, onyx, jasper, sapphire, emerald, carbuncle, and gold. Your tambourines and pipes were prepared for you on the day you were created. (adorned: decorated, tambourines: drums) **14.** You were the anointed cherub who was set apart, and I appointed you. You were on the holy mountain of God and walked among fiery stones. (anointed: chosen, cherub: angel, set apart: designated) **15.** You were flawless in your ways from the day you were created until wickedness was found in you. (flawless: perfect, wickedness: sin) **16.** Through the abundance of your trade, you became filled with violence and sinned. So, I will cast you out as a defiled thing from the mountain of God, and I will destroy you, O covering cherub, from the midst of the fiery stones. (abundance: plenty, defiled: unclean, cast out: expel) **17.** Your heart was lifted up because of your beauty, and you corrupted your wisdom because of your splendor. I will throw you to the ground and expose you to the gaze of kings. (lifted up: exalted, corrupted: spoiled, splendor: magnificence) **18.** You defiled your sanctuaries by your many sins, and by the unrighteousness of your trade. Therefore, I will bring fire from within you that will consume you, and I will bring you to ashes on the earth in the sight of all who see you. (sanctuaries: temples, unrighteousness: wickedness, consume: burn) **19.** All who know you among the nations will be horrified at you; you will become a terror, and you will never exist again.'" (horrified: shocked, terror: fear, exist: remain) **20.** The word of the LORD also came to me, saying, (also: once again) **21.** Son of man, turn your face toward Sidon and prophesy against it. (turn: direct, prophesy: foretell) **22.** Say, "This is what the Sovereign LORD says: I am against you, O Sidon, and I will show my glory within you. They will know that I am the LORD when I bring judgment upon her and sanctify myself in her. (glory: honor, sanctify: make holy) **23.** I will send a plague into her, and blood will flow in her streets. The slain will fall on every side by the sword, and they will know that I am the LORD. (plague: disease, flow: spill, slain: killed) **24.** There will no longer be any pricking thorn or painful brier for the house of Israel, from all those who despised them. They will know that I am the Sovereign LORD." (pricking: sharp, brier: thornbush, despised: hated) **25.** This is what the Sovereign LORD says: "When I gather the people of Israel from the nations where they have been scattered, and show my holiness in them in the sight of the nations, they will return to the land I gave to my servant Jacob. (gather: collect, scattered: dispersed, holiness: sanctity) **26.** They will live there in safety, build houses, and plant vineyards. They will live in peace when I execute judgment on all those who despise them around them. Then they will know that I am the LORD their God." (safety: security, execute: carry out, peace: tranquility).

Chapter 29

1. In the tenth year, on the tenth month, the word of the LORD came to me, saying: (word: message) **2.** "Son of man, prophesy against Pharaoh, king of Egypt, and against all Egypt. (prophesy: foretell) **3.** Say, 'I am against you, Pharaoh, the great dragon in the river, who claims, "My river is mine, and I made it." (claims: says, dragon: serpent) **4.** I will put hooks in your jaws, pull you out of the river, and make the fish stick to you. (hooks: snares) **5.** I will throw you into the wilderness, where you and the fish will fall on the open fields, uncollected, and become food for wild animals and birds. (wilderness: desert, uncollected: scattered) **6.** Egypt will know that I am the LORD, because they were like a broken reed to Israel. (reed: stick) **7.** When Israel leaned on you, you broke and caused them to stumble. (leaned: relied, stumble: fall) **8.** Therefore, I will bring a sword upon you and cut off both man and beast. (sword: weapon) **9.** Egypt will become desolate, and they will know that I am the LORD, as they claimed the river was theirs. (desolate: empty) **10.** I will make Egypt desolate from Syene to Ethiopia. (desolate: ruined) **11.** No one will pass through it for forty years. (pass: travel) **12.** I will make Egypt a desolation, and its cities will remain waste for forty years. I will scatter the Egyptians among the nations. (desolation: ruin, waste: destroyed, scatter: disperse) **13.** After forty years, I will gather Egypt back from where it was scattered. (gather: collect) **14.** Egypt will return to Pathros and become a lowly kingdom. (lowly: humble) **15.** It will be the lowest of kingdoms, and it will no longer rule over the nations. (lowest: least, rule: govern) **16.** Egypt will no longer be a source of confidence for Israel, who will remember their sins. (source: place, confidence: trust, remember: recall) **17.** In the twenty-seventh year, on the first day of the first month, the word of the LORD came to me, saying: (month: period) **18.** "Nebuchadnezzar, king of Babylon, served a great hardship against Tyre, but did not receive payment for his army. (hardship: difficulty, payment: reward) **19.** Therefore, I will give Egypt to Nebuchadnezzar, and he will take its people and spoil as payment for his army. (spoil: loot) **20.** I have given Egypt to him for his service, because he worked for me." (service: labor) **21.** "On that day, I will make Israel's strength grow, and they will know that I am the LORD." (strength: power, grow: increase).

Chapter 30

1. The word of the LORD came to me, saying: (word: message) **2.** "Son of man, prophesy and say, 'Woe to the day!' (woe: sorrow) **3.** For the day of the LORD is near, a cloudy day, a time for the nations. (cloudy: dark, nations: peoples) **4.** The sword will come upon Egypt, and Ethiopia will be in great pain as Egypt's people are slain, and her foundations are destroyed. (slain: killed, foundations: bases) **5.** Ethiopia, Libya, Lydia, and all her allies will fall by the sword. (allies: supporters) **6.** Those who support Egypt will fall, and her power will be humbled; from Syene to the border, they will fall by the sword. (support: help, humbled: weakened) **7.** Egypt will be desolate among desolate nations, and her cities among ruined cities. (desolate: empty, ruined: destroyed) **8.** Egypt will know that I am the LORD when I set fire to her and destroy all her helpers. (helpers: allies) **9.** In that day, messengers will go to the careless Ethiopians, bringing fear and pain, like the day of Egypt. (careless: unconcerned, pain: suffering) **10.** I will cause the multitude of Egypt to cease by the hand of Nebuchadnezzar, king of Babylon. (multitude: mass) **11.** He and his terrible army will come to destroy Egypt, filling the land with the slain. (terrible: mighty, slain: dead) **12.** I will dry up the rivers, give the land to the wicked, and make it waste by the hand of strangers. (dry up: drain, wicked: evil) **13.** I will destroy Egypt's idols, cease their images in Noph, and there will be no more rulers in Egypt, but fear will spread throughout the land. (idols: statues, cease: stop, rulers: leaders) **14.** Pathros will be desolate, Zoan will burn, and I will execute judgments in No. (execute: carry out) **15.** I will pour my fury on Sin, Egypt's strength, and cut off the multitude in No. (fury: anger, strength: power, multitude: many) **16.** I will set fire in Egypt: Sin will suffer, No will be shattered, and Noph will be in daily distress. (suffer: endure, shattered: broken, distress: trouble) **17.** The young men of Aven and Pi-beseth will fall by the sword, and these cities will go into captivity. (fall: die, captivity: exile) **18.** At Tehaphnehes, the day will darken, and I will break Egypt's yoke, ending her strength. A cloud will cover her, and her daughters will go into captivity. (darken: grow dim, yoke: oppression, strength: power) **19.** I will execute judgments in Egypt, and they will know that I am the LORD. (execute: carry out, judgments: punishments) **20.** In the eleventh year, first month, on the seventh day, the word of the LORD came to me, saying: (year: period) **21.** "Son of man, I have broken Pharaoh's arm, and it will not be healed or strengthened to hold the sword. (broken: shattered, healed: fixed, strengthened: made strong) **22.** I am against Pharaoh and will break both his strong and broken arms, causing the sword to fall from his hand. (strong: mighty, fall: drop) **23.** I will scatter the Egyptians among the nations and disperse them through the countries. (scatter: spread, disperse: distribute) **24.** I will strengthen the arms of the king of Babylon and put my sword in his hand, but Pharaoh's arms will weaken, and he will groan like a wounded man. (strengthen: empower, groan: moan, wounded: hurt) **25.** I will strengthen the arms of the king of Babylon, and Pharaoh's arms will fail. Then they will know that I am the LORD, when I put my sword in the hand of Babylon's king to strike Egypt. (fail: weaken, strike: hit) **26.** I will scatter the Egyptians among the nations and disperse them among the countries, and they will know that I am the LORD." (disperse: spread).

Chapter 31
1. In the eleventh year, the third month, on the first day, the word of the LORD came to me, saying: (year: period, word: message) **2.** "Son of man, speak to Pharaoh king of Egypt and his multitude: Who are you like in greatness? (multitude: people) **3.** The Assyrian was like a cedar in Lebanon, tall, with beautiful branches and a shadowing canopy. (canopy: covering) **4.** The waters made him great, setting him high with rivers flowing around his roots, sending out streams to all the trees of the field. (roots: base, streams: channels) **5.** His height exceeded all the trees, and his branches grew long, nurtured by the abundance of water. (height: size, nurtured: nourished) **6.** Birds nested in his branches, and animals gave birth under his shade, and great nations lived under his shadow. (nested: made homes, shade: protection) **7.** His beauty was in his size, with roots by great waters. (size: mass) **8.** No trees in God's garden were like him; the cedars, fir trees, and chestnut trees could not compare to his beauty. (garden: paradise, compare: match) **9.** I made him beautiful with his many branches, so all the trees of Eden envied him. (branches: limbs, envied: desired) **10.** Therefore, the Lord says: Because of your pride and exaltation, (pride: arrogance, exaltation: high position) **11.** I will deliver you into the hands of a mighty enemy, who will deal with you for your wickedness. (deliver: give, mighty: powerful, wickedness: evil) **12.** Foreigners, the cruelest of nations, will cut you down. Your branches will fall, and your boughs will break. The nations will leave your shadow. (cruelest: harshest, cut down: destroy, boughs: limbs) **13.** Birds will remain on your ruin, and beasts will rest on your branches. (ruin: destruction, beasts: animals) **14.** No tree by the waters will be exalted for its height, nor will any tree rise above others, for all will be delivered to death, to the depths of the earth. (exalted: lifted up, depths: lowest parts) **15.** When you went to the grave, I caused mourning. The deep waters were held back, and Lebanon mourned for you; the trees of the field fainted. (grave: tomb, mourning: grieving, fainted: withered) **16.** The nations trembled at your fall when I cast you down to the pit with those who descend to the grave. The trees of Eden, the best of Lebanon, will be comforted in the underworld. (trembled: shook, fall: destruction, cast down: thrown down, pit: abyss, underworld: grave) **17.** They went down with you, those who were your allies, living under your shadow. (allies: supporters) **18.** Who are you like in glory among the trees of Eden? Yet, you will be brought down to the depths of the earth, to lie with the uncircumcised, among those slain by the sword. This is Pharaoh and all his multitude," says the Lord GOD. (glory: honor, uncircumcised: unclean, slain: killed).

Chapter 32
1. In the twelfth year, twelfth month, on the first day, the word of the LORD came to me. (year: period, word: message) **2.** "Son of man, lament for Pharaoh, king of Egypt, and say: 'You are like a young lion among nations, a sea monster stirring rivers and muddying the waters.' (lament: mourn, sea monster: beast) **3.** The Lord GOD says: 'I will spread my net over you with many people, and they will haul you up in my net.' (net: trap, haul: catch) **4.** I will leave you on the land, cast onto the open field, where birds will feed on you and beasts will be filled with your flesh. (cast: throw, filled: satisfied) **5.** I will scatter your flesh on the mountains and fill the valleys with your remains. (scatter: spread, remains: corpses) **6.** Your blood will soak the land to the mountains, and the rivers will overflow with it. (soak: saturate, overflow: spill) **7.** When I put you out, I will darken the heavens, cover the sun with clouds, and dim the moon. (darken: dim, dim: obscure) **8.** I will darken all the bright lights of the heavens and bring darkness over your land, declares the Lord GOD. (bright: shining, bring: cast) **9.** I will trouble many nations when I bring your destruction to lands you do not know. (trouble: disturb, bring: cause) **10.** Many people will be shocked by you, and their kings will tremble when I wield my sword against you. (shocked: astounded, tremble: shake, wield: raise) **11.** The Lord GOD says: 'The sword of the king of Babylon will come against you. (sword: weapon) **12.** I will let the swords of mighty warriors destroy your multitudes and end Egypt's pride, leaving its people in ruins. (ruins: devastation) **13.** I will wipe out all the animals near Egypt's rivers; neither human nor beast will stir the waters. (wipe out: erase, stir: move) **14.** I will calm the waters, making the rivers flow smoothly, says the Lord GOD. (calm: settle, smoothly: steadily) **15.** When I make Egypt desolate and strike down its inhabitants, they will know that I am the LORD. (desolate: empty, strike down: smite) **16.** This is the lamentation that the daughters of the nations will sing for Egypt and its multitudes, says the Lord GOD. (lamentation: dirge, daughters: nations) **17.** On the fifteenth day of the twelfth month, the word of the LORD came to me. (word: message) **18.** "Son of man, wail for Egypt's multitudes and send them down to the grave with the nations that have fallen. (wail: weep, grave: pit) **19.** Say, 'Are you better than others? Go down and lie with the uncircumcised.' (better: superior, lie: rest) **20.** They will fall among the slain by the sword, delivered to death with all their multitudes. (fall: die, slain: dead, delivered: sent) **21.** Mighty leaders in the grave will taunt Pharaoh and his armies as they lie uncircumcised, killed by the sword. (taunt: mock) **22.** Assyria is there with her people, their graves surrounding her, all slain by the sword. (slain: killed) **23.** Their graves are deep in the pit, with her multitudes lying around, all killed in battle. (pit: abyss) **24.** Elam is there with her multitudes, uncircumcised, slain by the sword, and disgraced in death, lying with others who went to the pit. (disgraced: humiliated) **25.** Her grave is surrounded by her people, all uncircumcised and slain, bearing their shame in the grave. (grave: tomb, bearing: carrying) **26.** Meshech and Tubal are there with their multitudes, all uncircumcised, slain by the sword. (multitudes: masses) **27.** They do not lie with the fallen warriors buried with their weapons, for their iniquity remains on them in death. (iniquity: sin) **28.** Pharaoh will lie with the uncircumcised, slain by the sword. (slain: killed) **29.** Edom is there with her kings and princes, who lie with the uncircumcised, slain by the sword. (princes: rulers) **30.** The princes of the north and the Zidonians are there, disgraced in death, lying uncircumcised with the slain. (disgraced: shamed) **31.** Pharaoh will see them and be comforted over his armies, though all are slain by the sword, says the Lord GOD. (comforted: consoled) **32.** I caused terror in the land of the living, and Pharaoh and his multitudes will lie uncircumcised with the slain by the sword, says the Lord GOD. (terror: fear, multitudes: dead).

Chapter 33
1. The word of the LORD came to me again, saying, (word: message) **2.** "Son of man, speak to your people and say: 'When I bring a sword against a land, the people appoint a watchman from among them. (sword: weapon, watchman: guard) **3.** If the watchman sees the sword coming and blows the trumpet to warn the people, (blows: sounds, trumpet: horn) **4.** then anyone who hears the trumpet but ignores the warning and is killed, their death is their own responsibility. (ignores: disregards, responsibility: fault) **5.** They heard the warning but did not act; their death is their fault. But if they heed the warning, they save their lives. (heed: listen to, save: protect) **6.** If the watchman sees the sword coming but does not blow the trumpet, and someone dies, that person will die in their sin, but I will hold the watchman accountable for their blood. (accountable: responsible, blood: death) **7.** Son of man, I have made you a watchman for Israel. Hear my words and give them my warning. (warning: message) **8.** If I say to the wicked, 'You will surely die,' and you do not warn them to turn from their ways, they will die in their sin,

and I will hold you accountable. (warn: advise, ways: actions) **9.** But if you warn the wicked and they do not turn, they will die in their sin, but you will have saved yourself. (warn: advise, saved: protected) **10.** Son of man, speak to Israel: 'You say, "Our sins weigh us down; how can we live?" (weigh: burden, live: survive) **11.** Say to them: As surely as I live, declares the Lord GOD, I take no pleasure in the death of the wicked. Turn back from your evil ways! Why should you die, O house of Israel?' (pleasure: delight, evil: wrong) **12.** Tell your people: The righteous will not be saved by their righteousness if they sin, and the wicked will not die for their wickedness if they turn from it. (saved: delivered, sin: wrongs, turn: repent) **13.** If I tell the righteous they will live, but they trust in their righteousness and sin, none of their righteous acts will be remembered, and they will die for their sin. (trust: rely, acts: deeds) **14.** If I say to the wicked, 'You will surely die,' but they turn from their sin and do what is right, (turn: repent, right: just) **15.** returning what they took in pledge, restoring what they stole, and following my decrees, they will live and not die. (returning: giving back, restoring: returning, decrees: commands) **16.** None of their past sins will be remembered; they have done what is right and will live. (remembered: recalled) **17.** Yet your people say, 'The way of the Lord is not fair.' But it is their way that is not fair. (way: path) **18.** If the righteous turn from righteousness and sin, they will die for it. (turn: abandon, die: perish) **19.** If the wicked turn from their wickedness and do right, they will live. (wickedness: sin) **20.** Yet you say, 'The way of the Lord is not fair.' But I will judge each of you according to your ways, O house of Israel." (judge: evaluate, ways: actions) **21.** In the twelfth year of our exile, on the fifth day of the tenth month, a survivor from Jerusalem came to me and said, "The city has fallen!" (survivor: remnant, fallen: collapsed) **22.** The hand of the LORD was on me the evening before the survivor arrived, and my mouth was opened; I could speak again. (hand: power) **23.** Then the word of the LORD came to me: (word: message) **24.** "Son of man, the people living in the ruins of Israel say, 'Abraham was one man and inherited the land; we are many, so the land belongs to us.' (ruins: desolation, inherited: received) **25.** Tell them: 'This is what the Lord GOD says: You eat meat with the blood, worship idols, and commit murder—should you possess the land? (possess: own) **26.** You rely on violence, commit abominations, and defile your neighbor's wife— should you possess the land?' (rely: depend, abominations: sins, defile: desecrate) **27.** Tell them: 'This is what the Lord GOD says: Those in the ruins will die by the sword, those in the fields will be eaten by wild animals, and those in forts and caves will die of disease. (ruins: desolate places, eaten: consumed, disease: plague) **28.** I will make the land desolate, destroy its pride, and leave its mountains empty. (desolate: barren, destroy: ruin) **29.** When I make the land desolate because of their sins, they will know that I am the LORD.' (desolate: ruined, sins: wrongdoings) **30.** "Son of man, your people talk about you by the walls and doors, saying, 'Come and hear what the LORD says.' (talk: gossip) **31.** They come to you, sit before you as my people, and hear your words but do not act on them. They speak love with their mouths, but their hearts pursue selfish gain. (pursue: seek, selfish: self-centered) **32.** To them, you are like a singer with a lovely voice, playing an instrument beautifully—they hear your words but do not obey them. (lovely: beautiful, obey: follow) **33.** But when all this happens, as it surely will, they will know that a prophet has been among them." (happens: occurs).

Chapter 34
1. The word of the LORD came to me, saying, (word: message) **2.** "Son of man, prophesy against the shepherds of Israel. Say to them: 'This is what the Lord GOD says: Woe to the shepherds of Israel who only care for themselves! Shouldn't shepherds take care of the flock? (prophesy: speak, woe: disaster, flock: herd) **3.** You take the best parts—the fat and the wool—and slaughter the best sheep, but you do not care for the flock. (slaughter: kill) **4.** You have not strengthened the weak, healed the sick, bandaged the injured, brought back the strays, or searched for the lost. Instead, you rule harshly and with cruelty. (strengthened: supported, healed: cured, bandaged: treated, strays: wanderers, rule: govern) **5.** So the sheep were scattered because there was no shepherd, and they became food for wild animals. (scattered: dispersed, food: prey) **6.** My sheep wandered over mountains and hills, scattered over the earth, with no one searching for them or looking after them. (searched: seeking, looking after: caring for) **7.** Therefore, shepherds, hear the word of the LORD: (hear: listen to) **8.** As surely as I live, declares the Lord GOD, because my flock has become prey and food for wild animals, and because the shepherds did not care for the flock but only fed themselves, (prey: victims) **9.** hear the word of the LORD: (hear: listen to) **10.** This is what the Lord GOD says: I am against the shepherds and will hold them accountable for my flock. I will stop them from feeding the flock and from feeding themselves. I will rescue my sheep from their mouths, so they will no longer be food for them. (accountable: responsible, feeding: caring for) **11.** For this is what the Lord GOD says: I myself will search for my sheep and take care of them. (search: seek, take care: provide for) **12.** Just as a shepherd looks for his scattered sheep, so I will seek out my flock. I will rescue them from all the places where they were scattered on a day of clouds and darkness. (scattered: dispersed, rescue: save, clouds and darkness: uncertainty) **13.** I will bring them back from the nations and gather them from the lands. I will lead them to their own land and feed them on the mountains of Israel, by the streams, and in the fertile areas of the land. (bring back: return, feed: nourish, fertile: productive) **14.** I will give them good pasture, and their grazing place will be on Israel's high mountains. There they will rest in a good place and feed on rich pasture. (pasture: land, grazing: feeding, rich: plentiful) **15.** I myself will take care of my sheep and give them rest, declares the Lord GOD. (take care: provide for, rest: peace) **16.** I will search for the lost, bring back the strays, bandage the injured, and strengthen the weak. But the fat and strong I will destroy—I will shepherd them with justice. (strays: wanderers, bandage: treat, destroy: remove, justice: fairness) **17.** As for you, my flock, this is what the Lord GOD says: I will judge between one sheep and another, between rams and goats. (judge: separate, rams: male sheep, goats: animals) **18.** Is it not enough that you eat good pasture, but you trample the rest with your feet? That you drink clean water, but muddy the rest with your feet? (trample: stomp, muddy: pollute) **19.** Must my flock eat what you have trampled and drink what you have muddied? (trampled: stomped on, muddied: polluted) **20.** Therefore, this is what the Lord GOD says: I will judge between the fat sheep and the lean sheep. (judge: separate, lean: weak) **21.** Because you push with your sides and shoulders and butt the weak with your horns until they are scattered, (push: shove, weak: vulnerable) **22.** I will save my flock, and they will no longer be prey. I will judge between sheep and sheep. (save: rescue, prey: victims) **23.** I will set one shepherd over them— my servant David. He will tend them and be their shepherd. (set: appoint, tend: care for) **24.** I, the LORD, will be their God, and my servant David will be a prince among them. I, the LORD, have spoken. (prince: leader) **25.** I will make a covenant of peace with them and remove the dangerous animals from the land so they can live safely in the wilderness and sleep in the forests. (covenant: agreement, remove: take away, dangerous: harmful) **26.** I will make them and the area around my hill a blessing. I will send rain at the right time—showers of blessing. (blessing: favor, right time: proper season) **27.** The trees will bear fruit, and the land will produce crops. They will live safely on their land, and when I break their chains and rescue them from those who enslaved them, they will know I am the LORD. (bear fruit: produce, chains: bondage, enslaved: oppressed) **28.** They will no longer be prey to other nations, nor will wild animals devour them. They will live in safety, and no one will make them afraid. (prey: victims, devour: consume, safety: security) **29.** I will provide a place of renown for them; they will no longer suffer hunger or the shame brought by other nations. (renown: honor, shame: disgrace) **30.** They will know that I, the LORD their God, am with them and that they, the house of Israel, are my people, declares the Lord GOD. (know: recognize, house of Israel: people of Israel) **31.** You are my flock, the sheep of my pasture. I am your God, declares the Lord GOD." (flock: herd).

Chapter 35
1. The word of the LORD came to me, saying, (word: message) **2.** "Son of man, turn your face toward Mount Seir and prophesy against it. (prophesy: speak, Seir: region) **3.** Say to it, 'This is what the Lord GOD says: I am against you, Mount Seir. I will stretch out my hand against you and make you a desolate wasteland. (desolate: barren, wasteland: deserted place) **4.** I will destroy your cities, and you will become desolate. Then you will know that I am the LORD. (destroy: demolish, cities: towns) **5.** Because you have harbored eternal hatred and shed the blood of the Israelites with the sword during their time of trouble, when their punishment had ended, (harbored: held, eternal: lasting, shed: spilled, Israelites: people of Israel) **6.** as surely as I live,' declares the Lord GOD, 'I will prepare you for bloodshed, and blood will pursue you. Since you have not hated bloodshed, it will pursue you. (prepare: ready, pursue: follow) **7.** I will make Mount Seir a desolate waste and cut off everyone who comes and goes. (cut off: remove, desolate: barren) **8.** I will fill your mountains with the dead. Those killed by the sword will fall on your hills, in your valleys, and in your ravines. (fill: cover, dead: corpses, ravines: deep valleys) **9.** I will make you a permanent wasteland, and your cities will never be rebuilt. Then you will know that I am the LORD. (permanent: lasting, wasteland: desert, rebuilt: restored) **10.** Because you have said, 'These two nations and these two lands will be ours, and we will take possession of them,' even though the LORD was there, (nations: peoples, lands: territories, possession: ownership) **11.** as surely as I live,' declares the Lord GOD, 'I will deal with you according to the anger and envy you showed in your hatred toward them. And I will make myself known to them when I judge you. (deal with: act toward, anger: wrath, envy: jealousy, hatred: hostility, judge: punish) **12.** Then you will know that I am the LORD. I have heard all the

blasphemies you spoke against the mountains of Israel, saying, 'They are desolate; we will devour them.' (blasphemies: insults, devour: consume) **13.** You boasted against me with your words and multiplied your insults against me. I heard it all. (boasted: bragged, multiplied: increased, insults: offenses) **14.** This is what the Lord GOD says: 'While the whole earth rejoices, I will make you desolate. (rejoices: celebrates) **15.** Just as you rejoiced when Israel's inheritance became desolate, so I will make you desolate. You, Mount Seir, and all of Edom will become a wasteland. Then they will know that I am the LORD.'" (inheritance: possession, desolate: barren, wasteland: deserted place)

Chapter 36
1. The word of the LORD came to me, saying, (word: message) **2.** "Son of man, prophesy to the mountains of Israel and say, 'Mountains of Israel, hear the word of the LORD. (prophesy: speak) **3.** This is what the Lord GOD says: Because your enemies mocked you, saying, "Aha! The ancient high places are now ours," (mocked: ridiculed, high places: elevated areas) **4.** therefore, prophesy and say, 'This is what the Lord GOD says to the mountains, hills, rivers, valleys, desolate ruins, and abandoned cities that have become plunder and ridicule to the surrounding nations: (prophesy: speak, plunder: loot, ridicule: contempt) **5.** In my burning jealousy, I have spoken against the remaining nations and all Edom, who eagerly took my land as their possession, rejoicing with spite and hatred to plunder it. (jealousy: zealous anger, eagerly: eagerly, possession: ownership, spite: malice, plunder: steal) **6.** Therefore, prophesy about the land of Israel and say to the mountains, hills, rivers, and valleys, "This is what the Lord GOD says: I have spoken in jealousy and anger because you have suffered the shame of the nations. (prophesy: speak, jealousy: intense anger, anger: wrath, suffered: endured, shame: disgrace) **7.** Therefore, this is what the Lord GOD says: I have sworn that the surrounding nations will bear their shame. (sworn: promised, bear: endure, shame: disgrace) **8.** But you, mountains of Israel, will grow branches and bear fruit for my people Israel, for they will soon return. (branches: offshoots, bear: produce, return: come back) **9.** See, I care for you and will turn to you so that you may be cultivated and sown. (care: tend, turn: look after, cultivated: prepared, sown: planted) **10.** I will multiply people upon you—the entire house of Israel. The ruined cities will be rebuilt, and the desolate lands will be inhabited. (multiply: increase, ruined: destroyed, cities: towns, desolate: barren) **11.** I will increase the population of people and animals. They will thrive and multiply. I will restore you to your former prosperity and make you better than before. Then you will know that I am the LORD. (increase: grow, thrive: flourish, restore: return, prosperity: wealth) **12.** I will have my people, Israel, walk upon you again. They will possess you, and you will no longer rob them of their children. (walk: tread, possess: own, rob: steal) **13.** This is what the Lord GOD says: Because people say you devour your children and deprive your nation, (devour: consume, deprive: take away) **14.** you will no longer consume people or cause your nation to stumble, declares the Lord GOD. (consume: devour, stumble: fall) **15.** I will no longer let you hear the insults of the nations, and you will no longer bear the shame or cause your nation to fall again, declares the Lord GOD. (insults: mockery, bear: endure, shame: disgrace, fall: fail) **16.** The word of the LORD came to me again: (word: message) **17.** "Son of man, when the people of Israel lived in their land, they defiled it with their behavior and actions. Their ways were unclean, like a woman's impurity. (defiled: polluted, behavior: actions, unclean: impure, impurity: filthiness) **18.** So I poured out my wrath on them for the blood they shed in the land and for the idols they worshiped, which defiled it. (wrath: anger, shed: spilled, idols: false gods, defiled: corrupted) **19.** I scattered them among the nations, and they were dispersed into other countries. I judged them according to their actions. (scattered: dispersed, judged: punished, actions: deeds) **20.** But wherever they went, they dishonored my holy name. People said about them, 'These are the LORD's people, yet they had to leave his land.' (dishonored: profaned, holy: sacred) **21.** But I had concern for my holy name, which the people of Israel had profaned among the nations. (concern: care, profaned: defiled, holy: sacred) **22.** Therefore, say to the people of Israel, 'This is what the Lord GOD says: I am not acting for your sake, Israel, but for my holy name, which you profaned among the nations. (acting: doing, sake: benefit, profaned: desecrated) **23.** I will show the holiness of my great name, which has been profaned among the nations—the name you dishonored. Then the nations will know that I am the LORD when I am shown holy through you before their eyes. (holiness: sacredness, dishonored: defiled, shown holy: revealed as holy) **24.** For I will gather you from the nations, bring you back from all the countries, and return you to your own land. (gather: collect, bring back: return, own: ancestral) **25.** I will sprinkle clean water on you, and you will be clean. I will cleanse you from all your impurities and idols. (sprinkle: pour, cleanse: purify, impurities: defilements) **26.** I will give you a new heart and put a new spirit within you. I will remove your heart of stone and give you a heart of flesh. (heart: will, spirit: soul, remove: take away, flesh: soft) **27.** I will place my Spirit within you and move you to follow my laws and carefully obey my commands. (Spirit: Holy Spirit, move: guide) **28.** You will live in the land I gave your ancestors. You will be my people, and I will be your God. (ancestors: forefathers) **29.** I will save you from your uncleanness. I will summon grain and make it plentiful, so you will not experience famine. (summon: call, plentiful: abundant, famine: scarcity) **30.** I will increase the fruit of your trees and the crops of your fields so you will no longer endure famine among the nations. (increase: grow, endure: suffer, crops: harvests) **31.** Then you will remember your evil ways and wicked deeds, and you will hate yourselves for your sins and detestable actions. (evil: immoral, wicked: sinful, detestable: abhorrent) **32.** Know that I am not doing this for your sake, declares the Lord GOD. Be ashamed and humbled by your actions, Israel. (ashamed: embarrassed, humbled: humbled) **33.** This is what the Lord GOD says: On the day I cleanse you from all your sins, I will resettle your cities, and the ruins will be rebuilt. (cleanse: purify, resettle: restore, ruins: destruction) **34.** The desolate land will be cultivated instead of lying waste in the sight of everyone who passes by. (cultivated: farmed, waste: barren) **35.** They will say, 'This land that was desolate is now like the garden of Eden, and the ruined cities are fortified and inhabited.' (desolate: barren, garden of Eden: paradise, fortified: strengthened, inhabited: populated) **36.** Then the surrounding nations will know that I, the LORD, have rebuilt the ruins and replanted the desolate areas. I, the LORD, have spoken, and I will do it. (replanted: restored, desolate: barren, spoken: declared) **37.** This is what the Lord GOD says: I will allow the people of Israel to ask me to increase their numbers like a flock. (increase: grow, flock: herd) **38.** Like the numerous flocks brought to Jerusalem for festivals, so the ruined cities will be filled with people. Then they will know that I am the LORD." (numerous: many, ruined: destroyed, filled: populated)

Chapter 37
1. The hand of the LORD came upon me, and by the Spirit of the LORD, I was taken to a valley full of bones. (hand: power, Spirit: Holy Spirit, valley: plain, bones: skeletal remains) **2.** He led me around the valley, and I saw a vast number of very dry bones. (led: guided, vast: immense, dry: withered, bones: skeletal remains) **3.** He asked me, "Son of man, can these bones live?" I replied, "O Lord GOD, only you know." (asked: inquired, live: come to life, replied: answered) **4.** Then He said, "Prophesy to these bones and tell them, 'Dry bones, hear the word of the LORD! (prophesy: speak, dry: withered, hear: listen) **5.** This is what the Lord GOD says to these bones: I will put breath in you, and you will live. (breath: life force) **6.** I will attach tendons to you, bring flesh upon you, cover you with skin, and breathe life into you. Then you will know that I am the LORD.'" (tendons: ligaments, flesh: muscle, skin: covering, breathe life: give breath) **7.** So I prophesied as He commanded. While I was speaking, I heard a rattling sound. The bones came together, bone to bone. (prophesied: spoke, rattling sound: noise, came together: assembled) **8.** As I watched, tendons and flesh appeared, and skin covered them, but there was no breath in them. (appeared: formed, covered: enveloped) **9.** Then He said, "Prophesy to the breath, son of man. Say, 'This is what the Lord GOD says: Come, breath, from the four winds, and breathe into these slain that they may live.'" (breath: spirit, slain: dead) **10.** I prophesied as He commanded, and breath entered them. They came to life and stood up on their feet—a vast army. (prophesied: spoke, breath: spirit, came to life: revived, stood up: rose) **11.** Then He said, "Son of man, these bones represent the people of Israel. They say, 'Our bones are dried up, and our hope is lost; we are cut off.'" (represent: symbolize, dried up: withered, hope: expectation, cut off: separated) **12.** Therefore, prophesy and say, 'This is what the Lord GOD says: I will open your graves and bring you out of them, my people, and I will bring you back to the land of Israel. (prophesy: speak, open: unseal, graves: tombs, bring back: return) **13.** You will know that I am the LORD when I open your graves and bring you out of them, my people. (graves: tombs, bring out: raise) **14.** I will put my Spirit in you, and you will live. I will settle you in your land, and you will know that I, the LORD, have spoken and will do it.'" (Spirit: breath, settle: establish) **15.** The word of the LORD came to me again, saying, (word: message) **16.** "Son of man, take two sticks. Write on one, 'For Judah and the Israelites associated with him.' On the other, write, 'For Joseph—the stick of Ephraim—and the Israelites associated with him.' (take: hold, sticks: pieces of wood, associated: allied) **17.** Join them together into one stick so that they become one in your hand. (join: unite, become one: merge) **18.** When your people ask you, 'What does this mean?' (ask: inquire) **19.** Tell them, 'This is what the Lord GOD says: I am taking the stick of Joseph, which is in Ephraim's hand, along with the tribes of Israel, and I will join it to Judah's stick. They will become one stick in my hand.' (taking: gathering, tribes: clans, join: unite) **20.** Hold the sticks in your hand

so the people can see them. (hold: carry, see: observe) **21.** Say to them, 'This is what the Lord GOD says: I will gather the Israelites from among the nations where they have been scattered. I will bring them back to their land. (gather: collect, scattered: dispersed) **22.** I will make them one nation in the land, on the mountains of Israel. They will have one king, and they will no longer be two nations or divided into two kingdoms. (one: united, divided: split) **23.** They will no longer defile themselves with idols, detestable practices, or sins. I will save them from their sinful ways, cleanse them, and they will be my people, and I will be their God. (defile: pollute, detestable: abominable, sinful: wicked, cleanse: purify) **24.** My servant David will be their king, and they will have one shepherd. They will follow my laws and keep my commands. (servant: chosen one, shepherd: leader, laws: decrees, keep: observe) **25.** They will live in the land I gave to my servant Jacob, where their ancestors lived. They and their descendants will live there forever, and my servant David will be their prince forever. (ancestors: forefathers, prince: ruler) **26.** I will make a covenant of peace with them—it will be everlasting. I will establish them, increase their numbers, and place my sanctuary among them forever. (covenant: agreement, peace: harmony, everlasting: eternal, establish: secure, sanctuary: dwelling place) **27.** My dwelling place will be with them. I will be their God, and they will be my people. (dwelling place: residence, people: nation) **28.** Then the nations will know that I, the LORD, make Israel holy when my sanctuary is among them forever.'" (make holy: consecrate, sanctuary: holy place)

Chapter 38
1. The word of the LORD came to me, saying, (word: message) **2.** "Son of man, set your face against Gog, of the land of Magog, the chief prince of Meshech and Tubal. Prophesy against him (set your face: direct your attention, Gog: leader, prince: ruler, prophesy: speak) **3.** and say, 'This is what the Lord GOD says: I am against you, Gog, chief prince of Meshech and Tubal. (chief prince: ruler, against: opposed) **4.** I will turn you around, put hooks in your jaws, and lead you out with your entire army—horses and horsemen, all splendidly dressed, a great force with shields, bucklers, and swords. (turn around: redirect, hooks: hooks in your jaws: compel, splendidly dressed: well-equipped, great force: large army, shields: protection, bucklers: small shields) **5.** Persia, Ethiopia, and Libya will be with them, all equipped with shields and helmets. (Persia: Iran, Ethiopia: Cush, Libya: Phut, equipped: armed, shields: protection, helmets: headgear) **6.** Gomer and its troops, and the house of Togarmah from the far north with all its troops—many nations will accompany you. (Gomer: a people, Togarmah: region of Turkey, far north: distant northern lands, accompany: join) **7.** Be prepared! Prepare yourself and all your allies, and be ready to lead them. (prepared: ready, allies: supporters, lead: guide) **8.** After many days, you will be called upon. In the latter years, you will invade a land restored from war, whose people were gathered from many nations to the mountains of Israel, long desolate. These people now live in safety. (called upon: summoned, latter years: final years, invade: attack, restored: rebuilt, desolate: deserted) **9.** You will advance like a storm, covering the land like a cloud, you and all your troops and many nations with you. (advance: move forward, storm: tempest, covering: overshadowing, troops: soldiers) **10.** This is what the Lord GOD says: On that day, thoughts will arise in your mind, and you will plan evil. (thoughts: ideas, arise: come, evil: wickedness) **11.** You will say, 'I will invade a land of unwalled villages, a peaceful people who live in safety without walls, bars, or gates.' (invade: attack, unwalled: undefended, peaceful: tranquil, safety: security) **12.** You will seek to plunder and loot, attacking the resettled ruins and the people gathered from the nations, who have acquired livestock and wealth and live at the center of the land. (plunder: pillage, loot: steal, resettled ruins: rebuilt settlements, acquired: gained, livestock: animals, wealth: riches, center: heart) **13.** Sheba, Dedan, the merchants of Tarshish, and all their leaders will ask, 'Have you come to take plunder? Have you assembled your forces to loot, to carry off silver and gold, livestock, and goods, and to seize great wealth?' (merchants: traders, forces: armies, carry off: steal, seize: take) **14.** Therefore, prophesy, son of man, and say to Gog: 'This is what the Lord GOD says: On that day when my people Israel are living in safety, will you not notice? (prophesy: speak, notice: take note) **15.** You will come from your place in the far north, leading many nations with you, a mighty army on horseback. (far north: distant northern region, mighty: powerful, horseback: cavalry) **16.** You will advance against my people Israel like a cloud covering the land. In the latter days, I will bring you against my land so that the nations may know me when I demonstrate my holiness through you before their eyes, O Gog. (advance: move toward, cloud: fog, latter days: end times, demonstrate: show, holiness: sanctity) **17.** This is what the Lord GOD says: Are you the one I spoke of long ago through my servants, the prophets of Israel, who prophesied for years that I would bring you against them? (spoke of: foretold, servants: prophets, prophesied: spoke) **18.** On that day, when Gog invades the land of Israel, my anger will be aroused, declares the Lord GOD. (anger: wrath, aroused: stirred, declares: says) **19.** In my zeal and fiery wrath, I declare that there will be a great earthquake in the land of Israel. (zeal: passion, fiery wrath: intense anger, declare: announce, earthquake: tremor) **20.** The fish in the sea, the birds in the sky, the beasts of the field, every creeping thing, and all people on the earth will tremble at my presence. The mountains will be overturned, cliffs will collapse, and every wall will fall to the ground. (tremble: shake, presence: coming, overturned: shaken, collapse: fall, walls: barriers) **21.** I will summon a sword against Gog on all my mountains, declares the Lord GOD. Every man's sword will be against his brother. (summon: call, sword: weapon, against: directed toward) **22.** I will execute judgment on him with plague and bloodshed. I will pour down torrents of rain, hailstones, fire, and burning sulfur on him, his troops, and the many nations with him. (execute: carry out, plague: disease, bloodshed: slaughter, torrents: floods, hailstones: ice, burning sulfur: brimstone) **23.** In this way, I will show my greatness and holiness, making myself known to many nations. Then they will know that I am the LORD.'" (greatness: power, holiness: sanctity, making known: revealing).

Chapter 39
1. "Son of man, prophesy against Gog and say, 'This is what the Lord GOD says: I am against you, Gog, chief prince of Meshech and Tubal. (prophesy: declare, chief: ruler) **2.** I will turn you around, lead you from the far north, and bring you against the mountains of Israel. (turn: redirect, lead: guide) **3.** I will strike your bow from your left hand and your arrows will fall from your right hand. (strike: break, fall: drop) **4.** You and your armies will fall on the mountains of Israel. I will give you as food to the birds of prey and the wild animals. (fall: collapse, food: prey) **5.** You will fall in the open field, for I, the LORD, have spoken. (fall: perish, spoken: declared) **6.** I will send fire on Magog and on those who live securely on the coastlands, and they will know that I am the LORD. (send: unleash, securely: safely) **7.** I will make my holy name known among my people Israel and will no longer let it be dishonored. Then the nations will know that I am the LORD, the Holy One in Israel. (make known: reveal, dishonored: profaned) **8.** It is coming, and it will surely happen, declares the Lord GOD. This is the day I have spoken of. (surely: certainly, spoken: declared) **9.** Those who live in the cities of Israel will go out and burn the weapons—shields, bows, arrows, clubs, and spears. They will use them as fuel for seven years. (burn: consume, fuel: fire) **10.** They will not need to gather firewood from the fields or cut it from the forests because they will use the weapons for fuel. They will plunder those who plundered them and loot those who looted them, declares the Lord GOD. (plunder: rob, loot: steal) **11.** On that day, I will give Gog a burial place in Israel, in the Valley of the Travelers, east of the sea. It will block the way of travelers. There, Gog and all his army will be buried, and it will be called the Valley of Hamon-Gog (the horde of Gog). (block: obstruct) **12.** For seven months, the house of Israel will bury them to cleanse the land. (cleanse: purify) **13.** All the people will help bury them, and it will bring honor to them on the day I am glorified, declares the Lord GOD. (honor: glory) **14.** Men will be assigned to continually search the land and bury the remains to cleanse it. After seven months, they will continue searching. (assigned: appointed, cleanse: purify) **15.** When they find a human bone, they will mark it for the buriers to take to the Valley of Hamon-Gog. (find: discover, mark: identify) **16.** A nearby city will be named Hamonah (multitude). In this way, the land will be cleansed. (cleansed: purified) **17.** "Son of man, this is what the Lord GOD says: Call to every bird and wild animal: 'Gather and come to my sacrifice on the mountains of Israel. Eat flesh and drink blood! (gather: assemble, sacrifice: offering) **18.** Feast on the flesh of mighty men and drink the blood of the princes of the earth, as if they were rams, lambs, goats, and bulls, fattened animals of Bashan. (feast: gorge, mighty men: heroes) **19.** Eat fat until you are full and drink blood until you are drunk at the feast I have prepared for you. (full: satisfied, drunk: intoxicated) **20.** At my table, you will feast on horses, charioteers, warriors, and all kinds of soldiers, declares the Lord GOD. (feast: dine, charioteers: drivers) **21.** I will display my glory among the nations. All nations will see the judgment I have executed and the power of my hand laid upon them. (display: reveal, executed: carried out) **22.** From that day forward, the house of Israel will know that I am the LORD their God. (forward: onward, know: recognize) **23.** The nations will understand that the house of Israel went into exile because of their sin. They were unfaithful to me, so I hid my face from them and gave them into the hands of their enemies, and they all fell by the sword. (understand: realize, unfaithful: disloyal) **24.** I dealt with them according to their uncleanness and transgressions and hid my face from them. (dealt: acted, transgressions: sins) **25.** "Therefore, this is what the Lord GOD says: I will now restore the fortunes of Jacob and have mercy on the entire house of Israel. I will be zealous for my holy name. (restore: bring back, zealous: passionate) **26.** After they have borne their shame and

unfaithfulness, when they lived securely in their land without fear, (borne: carried, securely: safely) **27.** I will bring them back from the nations and gather them from the lands of their enemies. Through this, I will show my holiness in the sight of many nations. (bring back: return, gather: assemble) **28.** Then they will know that I am the LORD their God, who sent them into exile and has now gathered them back to their own land, leaving none behind. (sent: exiled, gathered: returned) **29.** I will no longer hide my face from them, for I have poured out my Spirit on the house of Israel, declares the Lord GOD.'" (hide: conceal, poured out: bestowed).

Chapter 40

1. In the twenty-fifth year of our exile, at the beginning of the year, on the tenth day of the month—14 years after Jerusalem had been destroyed—the hand of the LORD was upon me, and He brought me to a place. (exile: captivity, place: location) **2.** In visions from God, He brought me to the land of Israel and set me on a very high mountain. On its south side, I saw what looked like the framework of a city. (visions: revelations, framework: structure) **3.** He brought me closer, and I saw a man who looked like bronze, holding a linen cord and a measuring rod. He stood at the gate. (closer: nearer, rod: staff) **4.** The man said to me, "Son of man, look with your eyes, hear with your ears, and pay close attention to everything I show you. You were brought here so that I could show you these things. Report everything you see to the house of Israel." (attention: focus, report: tell) **5.** I saw a wall surrounding the temple area. The man had a measuring rod six cubits long (each cubit being a standard length plus a handbreadth). He measured the wall: it was one rod thick and one rod high. (surrounding: encircling, thick: wide) **6.** Then he went to the east gate, climbed its steps, and measured its threshold. It was one rod wide. (threshold: entrance) **7.** Each guardroom was one rod square, with a five-cubit space between them. The threshold of the gate next to the portico was also one rod deep. (guardroom: chamber, deep: length) **8.** Then he measured the portico of the gate, which was one rod deep. (portico: porch) **9.** He measured the portico, eight cubits deep, and its supporting posts, two cubits thick. The portico faced inward. (supporting: holding, inward: inside) **10.** There were three guardrooms on each side of the east gate, all the same size, and the posts on either side were also the same size. (guardrooms: chambers, size: dimensions) **11.** He measured the entrance to the gate: it was 10 cubits wide, and the gate itself was 13 cubits long. (entrance: opening, long: deep) **12.** The walls around each guardroom were one cubit thick, and the rooms themselves were six cubits square. (walls: barriers, thick: wide) **13.** He measured the width of the gate from roof to roof of opposing guardrooms: it was 25 cubits. Doorways faced each other. (width: span, opposing: opposite) **14.** He measured the posts of the gate: they were 60 cubits high, and the gateway extended all around to the courtyard. (posts: pillars, extended: reached) **15.** The total length of the gate passage from the outer entrance to the inner portico was 50 cubits. (total: overall, passage: corridor) **16.** The guardrooms and their posts had windows all around facing inward, and the porticos had palm trees carved on their posts. (windows: openings, carved: etched) **17.** Then he brought me into the outer court, where I saw chambers and a paved area around the court. There were 30 chambers along the pavement. (outer: external, paved: tiled) **18.** This pavement ran alongside the gates and corresponded to the length of the gates; it was the lower pavement. (ran: stretched, corresponded: matched) **19.** He measured the distance from the front of the lower gate to the outer front of the inner court: it was 100 cubits on the east and north sides. (distance: span, front: exterior) **20.** Next, he measured the north gate of the outer court, its dimensions matching those of the first gate. (dimensions: measurements, matching: identical) **21.** Its guardrooms, posts, and portico were the same size as the first gate, and it was 50 cubits long and 25 cubits wide. (guardrooms: chambers, wide: broad) **22.** Its windows, portico, and carvings of palm trees were identical to those of the east gate. Seven steps led up to it, and its portico faced inward. (identical: same, carvings: engravings) **23.** Across from it was the north gate of the inner court, 100 cubits away. (across: opposite, away: distant) **24.** He led me to the south gate, which also matched the measurements of the others. (led: guided, measurements: dimensions) **25.** It had windows all around like the others, and it was 50 cubits long and 25 cubits wide. (windows: openings, wide: broad) **26.** Seven steps led up to it, and its portico faced inward. Palm trees were carved on the posts of the gate, one on each side. (steps: stairs, carved: etched) **27.** The inner court also had a gate facing south, and the distance between the inner and outer gates on the south side was 100 cubits. (distance: span) **28.** Then he brought me to the south gate of the inner court. It had the same measurements as the others. (measurements: dimensions) **29.** Its guardrooms, posts, and portico were the same size as the other gates, with windows all around. It was 50 cubits long and 25 cubits wide. (guardrooms: chambers, windows: openings) **30.** The portico extended 25 cubits inward and was five cubits wide. (extended: reached, inward: inside) **31.** Its portico faced the outer court, and it had carvings of palm trees on its posts. Eight steps led up to it. (carvings: engravings, steps: stairs) **32.** Next, he brought me to the east gate of the inner court and measured it. It had the same dimensions as the others. (measured: gauged, dimensions: measurements) **33.** Its guardrooms, posts, and portico also matched the other gates, with windows all around. It was 50 cubits long and 25 cubits wide. (matched: were identical, windows: openings) **34.** Its portico faced the outer court, with palm trees carved on its posts, one on each side. Eight steps led up to it. (faced: oriented, carved: etched) **35.** Then he brought me to the north gate and measured it. It had the same dimensions as the others. (measured: gauged, dimensions: measurements) **36.** including its guardrooms, posts, portico, and windows all around. It was 50 cubits long and 25 cubits wide. (guardrooms: chambers, portico: porch) **37.** Its portico faced the outer court, with palm trees carved on its posts. Eight steps led up to it. (carved: etched, steps: stairs) **38.** There was a chamber by the gates where the burnt offerings were washed. (chamber: room, washed: cleansed) **39.** Inside the portico of the gate, there were two tables on each side for slaughtering the burnt offerings, sin offerings, and guilt offerings. (slaughtering: preparing, offerings: sacrifices) **40.** Outside, near the north gate entrance, there were two tables, and two more tables were at the other end of the portico. (entrance: doorway, end: opposite side) **41.** So there were eight tables in all for preparing sacrifices. (preparing: making, sacrifices: offerings) **42.** Four additional tables of hewn stone were for the burnt offerings, each 1.5 cubits long, 1.5 cubits wide, and one cubit high. The tools for slaughtering the offerings were kept there. (hewn: carved, tools: implements) **43.** Hooks, a handbreadth wide, were attached all around the room, and the offerings were placed on the tables. (attached: fixed, placed: arranged) **44.** Outside the inner gate were two rooms for the singers in the inner court, one near the north gate facing south, and the other near the east gate facing north. (rooms: chambers, facing: oriented) **45.** The man said, "The room facing south is for the priests who guard the temple, (guard: protect, priests: ministers) **46.** and the room facing north is for the priests who guard the altar. These are the descendants of Zadok, the Levites who are allowed to approach the LORD to serve Him." (descendants: offspring, serve: minister) **47.** He measured the inner court: it was 100 cubits square, with the altar in front of the temple. (measured: gauged, square: even) **48.** Then he brought me to the temple porch and measured the posts: five cubits on each side. The entrance was three cubits wide on each side. (posts: pillars, entrance: doorway) **49.** The porch was 20 cubits long and 11 cubits wide. Steps led up to it, and there were pillars on each side of the entrance. (long: deep, wide: broad, pillars: columns).

Chapter 41

1. He brought me to the temple and measured the posts, each six cubits wide on both sides, the same width as the tabernacle. (posts: pillars, width: breadth) **2.** The door was ten cubits wide, with five cubits on each side. The length was forty cubits, and the width was twenty cubits. (door: entrance, length: depth, width: breadth) **3.** He measured the doorposts, which were two cubits thick, and the door itself, six cubits wide. (doorposts: doorframes, thick: wide) **4.** The length in front of the temple was twenty cubits, and the width was twenty cubits. He said, "This is the most holy place." (length: depth, width: breadth) **5.** He measured the wall, six cubits thick, and the side chambers were four cubits wide around the house. (measured: gauged, chambers: rooms) **6.** The side chambers were three stories high, with thirty chambers, built into the walls of the temple. (stories: levels, chambers: rooms) **7.** The side chambers spiraled upward, increasing in width from the lowest to the highest. (spiraled: twisted, increasing: widening) **8.** The foundations of the side chambers were six cubits high. (foundations: bases, high: tall) **9.** The outer wall for the side chambers was five cubits thick, with space for the inner side chambers. (outer: external, space: gap) **10.** There was a twenty-cubit wide space between the chambers on all sides of the house. (space: gap) **11.** The doors of the side chambers faced the open space: one door to the north and another to the south. The open space was five cubits wide. (faced: oriented, space: area) **12.** The building in front of the separate place was seventy cubits wide and ninety cubits long, with five cubits thick walls. (building: structure, separate place: inner sanctum) **13.** The entire house, including the separate place and building, was one hundred cubits long. (entire: total, including: comprising) **14.** The width of the house and separate place toward the east was one hundred cubits. (toward: facing) **15.** The length of the building opposite the separate place, including the galleries on both sides, was one hundred cubits. (opposite: across, galleries: corridors) **16.** The doorposts, narrow windows, and galleries had three stories, with wood covering from the ground to the windows. (narrow: slim, covering: cladding) **17.** The carvings on the walls, inside and outside, extended from above the door to the inner house. (carvings: engravings, extended: stretched) **18.** The walls were decorated with cherubim and palm trees, with a palm tree between each pair of cherubim. (decorated: adorned, between: between each set) **19.** Each cherub had two faces: one of a man and one of a lion, displayed around the house. (faces: visages, displayed: shown) **20.** Cherubim and palm trees were carved from the ground up to above the door and along the temple walls. (carved: etched, along: upon) **21.** The temple posts were squared, and the appearance of the sanctuary was the same as the posts. (squared: shaped, appearance: form) **22.** The altar of wood was three cubits high, two cubits long, and made of wood. He said, "This is the table before the LORD." (altar: table, made of: crafted from) **23.** Both the temple and sanctuary had two doors. (sanctuary: holy place) **24.** Each door had two leaves, two turning leaves per door. (leaves: panels, turning: hinged) **25.** The doors were decorated with cherubim and palm trees, like the walls, with thick planks covering the porch. (decorated: adorned, planks: boards) **26.** The porch had narrow windows and palm trees on both sides, with thick planks covering the walls. (porch: portico, covering: cladding).

Chapter 42
1. He led me to the outer court, toward the north, and into a chamber opposite the separate place, in front of the northern building. (led: guided, chamber: room, opposite: across from) **2.** The north door was fifty cubits wide, and the length was one hundred cubits. (door: entrance, length: depth) **3.** Gallery over gallery, three stories high, faced the twenty cubits of the inner court and the pavement of the outer court. (gallery: corridor, stories: levels, faced: overlooked) **4.** In front of the chambers, there was a walk ten cubits wide and a path one cubit wide, with their doors facing north. (walk: path, facing: oriented) **5.** The upper chambers were shorter because their galleries were higher than the lower and middle sections of the building. (shorter: smaller, sections: levels) **6.** The upper chambers had no pillars like those in the courts, so they were narrower than the lower and middle stories. (pillars: columns, narrower: more narrow) **7.** The outer wall facing the chambers was fifty cubits long. (outer: external, facing: overlooking) **8.** The chambers in the outer court were fifty cubits long, while the space in front of the temple was one hundred cubits long. (space: area) **9.** The entrance to these chambers was on the east side, accessible from the outer court. (entrance: doorway, accessible: reachable) **10.** The chambers were built into the wall of the outer court, facing the separate place and the building. (built: constructed, wall: barrier) **11.** The walk before them was similar in size and design to the chambers facing the north, with doors aligned in the same manner. (similar: comparable, aligned: positioned) **12.** The doors of the chambers facing south had an entrance at the head of the walk, leading to the wall on the east. (head: top, leading: directing) **13.** He told me that the north and south chambers before the separate place were holy chambers where priests would eat the most holy offerings: meat, sin, and trespass offerings. (told: informed, holy: sacred, offerings: sacrifices) **14.** When priests enter these holy chambers, they must not exit into the outer court in their ministry garments. They must change into other garments before handling offerings for the people. (enter: enter into, garments: robes, handling: preparing) **15.** After measuring the inner house, he led me to the east gate and measured it all around. (measuring: gauging, led: guided) **16.** He measured the east side with the reed, five hundred reeds in total. (reed: rod, total: in all) **17.** He measured the north side, five hundred reeds. (north: northern) **18.** He measured the south side, five hundred reeds. (south: southern) **19.** He turned to the west side and measured five hundred reeds. (turned: faced, west: western) **20.** The whole area, with walls on all sides, measured five hundred reeds long and five hundred reeds wide, separating the sanctuary from the common area. (area: space, separating: dividing, common: secular).

Chapter 43
1. He brought me to the east gate. (brought: led, gate: entrance) **2.** Then the glory of the God of Israel came from the east, and His voice was like many waters, and the earth shone with His glory. (glory: presence, waters: rivers, shone: radiated) **3.** It was like the vision I saw when I came to destroy the city, similar to the vision by the river Chebar, and I fell on my face. (vision: revelation, destroy: devastate, similar: akin) **4.** The glory of the LORD entered the house through the east gate. (entered: came into, house: temple) **5.** The spirit lifted me and brought me to the inner court, where the glory of the LORD filled the house. (lifted: raised, filled: saturated) **6.** I heard God speak to me from the house, and the man stood beside me. (speak: speak out, beside: next to) **7.** He said, "Son of man, this is the place of My throne, the place of My feet, where I will dwell with Israel forever. My holy name will no longer be defiled by the sins of Israel and their kings." (place: location, throne: seat, defiled: desecrated) **8.** "They have defiled My name by placing their thresholds next to Mine and their posts by My posts, and by the abominations they committed, so I consumed them in My anger." (defiled: polluted, abominations: detestable acts, consumed: destroyed) **9.** "Let them remove their sins, and I will dwell among them forever." (remove: take away, dwell: live, among: with) **10.** "Show the house to Israel, that they may be ashamed of their iniquities and measure the pattern." (show: reveal, ashamed: humiliated, iniquities: sins, pattern: blueprint) **11.** "If they are ashamed, show them the form of the house, its exits and entrances, its laws, and its ordinances, and write it before them so they can follow all of them." (form: structure, exits: doors, laws: rules, ordinances: decrees) **12.** "This is the law of the house: the entire area atop the mountain will be most holy." (law: rule, area: space, atop: on top, holy: sacred) **13.** "These are the measurements of the altar: a cubit and a handbreadth; its base will be a cubit, and its border around the edge will be a span. This is the high place of the altar." (measurements: dimensions, base: foundation, border: perimeter, edge: rim) **14.** "From the ground to the lower settle will be two cubits high and one cubit wide; the upper settle will be four cubits high and one cubit wide." (settle: platform, wide: broad) **15.** "The altar will be four cubits high, with four horns on it." (horns: projections) **16.** "The altar will be twelve cubits long and twelve cubits wide, square on all sides." (long: length, square: rectangular) **17.** "The settle will be fourteen cubits long and fourteen cubits wide, with a half-cubit border and a cubit-wide base. Its stairs will face the east." (settle: platform, stairs: steps, face: point) **18.** "These are the ordinances for the altar when it is made, for burnt offerings and the sprinkling of blood." (ordinances: regulations, sprinkling: sprinkling of) **19.** "Give a young bull for a sin offering to the priests of Zadok's line, who serve Me." (sin offering: atonement sacrifice, serve: minister) **20.** "Take the blood of the bull and apply it to the four horns, the four corners of the settle, and the border to cleanse and purify it." (apply: put, corners: edges, cleanse: purify, purify: sanctify) **21.** "The bull for the sin offering will be burned outside the sanctuary." (burned: consumed by fire, sanctuary: holy place) **22.** "On the second day, offer a flawless goat for a sin offering and cleanse the altar as done with the bull." (flawless: perfect, cleanse: purify) **23.** "After cleansing, offer a young bull and a ram, both without blemish." (offer: present, blemish: defect) **24.** "Offer them before the LORD, and the priests shall sprinkle salt on them before burning them as an offering." (sprinkle: scatter, offering: sacrifice) **25.** "For seven days, prepare a goat for a sin offering daily, along with a young bull and a ram, without blemish." (prepare: offer, daily: every day) **26.** "For seven days, purge and purify the altar, and consecrate yourselves." (purge: cleanse, consecrate: sanctify) **27.** "After these days, on the eighth day and beyond, the priests shall offer your burnt and peace offerings, and I will accept you," says the Lord GOD. (beyond: after, offer: present, burnt: burnt offerings, peace: fellowship).

Chapter 44
1. He brought me back to the east gate of the outer sanctuary, and it was shut. (brought: led, sanctuary: temple, shut: closed) **2.** The LORD said, "This gate shall remain shut because the LORD, the God of Israel, has entered through it. No one will enter by it." (remain: stay, entered: came through) **3.** "It is for the prince. The prince will sit in it to eat bread before the LORD. He will enter through the porch of the gate and leave the same way." (prince: ruler, sit: stay, bread: food, porch: entrance) **4.** He took me to the north gate, and I saw the glory of the LORD fill the house. I fell on my face. (north: northern, glory: presence, fill: occupy, house: temple, fell: collapsed) **5.** The LORD told me, "Pay close attention, hear and see all I say about the house of the LORD, its laws, and all its ordinances. Watch carefully how the sanctuary enters and exits." (pay attention: observe, hear: listen, laws: rules, ordinances: decrees, sanctuary: holy place, enters: comes in, exits: goes out) **6.** "Tell the rebellious people of Israel, 'Enough of your abominations!'" (rebellious: disobedient, abominations: detestable acts) **7.** "You have brought uncircumcised people into My sanctuary, polluting it by offering My bread and breaking My covenant with your abominations." (uncircumcised: impure, sanctuary: temple, polluting: defiling, bread: offerings, breaking: violating, covenant: agreement) **8.** "You have not kept the charge of My holy things but set your own keepers in My sanctuary." (kept: maintained, charge: responsibility, holy things: sacred items, keepers: caretakers, sanctuary: temple) **9.** "No stranger, uncircumcised in heart or flesh, shall enter My sanctuary, not even those among Israel." (stranger: foreigner, uncircumcised: impure, enter: come into) **10.** "The Levites who went astray after idols will bear their sin." (went astray: strayed, bear: carry, sin: guilt) **11.** "They will still serve in My sanctuary but will not perform priestly duties. They will manage the gates and offer sacrifices for the people." (serve: minister, perform: carry out, duties: tasks, manage: oversee, offer: present) **12.** "Because they led Israel into sin by serving idols, they will bear their shame." (led: guided, into sin: to sin, bear: carry, shame: disgrace) **13.** "They will not come near to Me to serve as priests but will bear their disgrace and the abominations they committed." (near: approach, disgrace: dishonor, committed: performed) **14.**

"But I will make them keepers of the house, managing its service." (keepers: caretakers, house: temple, managing: overseeing) 15. "The priests of Zadok, who stayed faithful when Israel went astray, will come near to serve Me, offering sacrifices and ministering to Me." (faithful: loyal, stayed: remained, astray: deviated, ministering: serving) 16. "They will enter My sanctuary, minister at My table, and keep My charge." (enter: come into, table: altar, charge: responsibility) 17. "When they enter the inner court, they will wear linen garments, no wool, to avoid sweating while ministering." (inner court: holy place, wear: dress in, linen garments: priestly clothes, sweating: perspiring) 18. "They will wear linen bonnets and breeches. No other garments will be worn during their service." (wear: don, bonnets: head coverings, breeches: pants, garments: clothes) 19. "When they go into the outer court, they will change their garments, leaving their ministry clothes in the holy chambers." (outer court: courtyard, change: remove, garments: clothes, ministry clothes: service attire, holy chambers: sacred rooms) 20. "They will not shave their heads or grow their hair long but will trim their hair." (shave: cut, grow: allow, trim: shorten) 21. "They will not drink wine when entering the inner court." (drink: consume, wine: alcohol, entering: entering into) 22. "They will only marry virgins from Israel or a widow of a priest." (marry: wed, virgins: unmarried women, widow: bereaved wife) 23. "They will teach My people to distinguish between the holy and the profane, and between the clean and the unclean." (distinguish: differentiate, holy: sacred, profane: secular, clean: pure, unclean: impure) 24. "They will judge disputes according to My laws and keep My Sabbaths holy." (judge: settle, disputes: disagreements, laws: regulations, Sabbaths: holy days) 25. "They will not defile themselves by touching the dead, except for close family members like a father, mother, son, daughter, brother, or unmarried sister." (defile: pollute, touching: coming in contact with, dead: deceased, close family members: immediate relatives) 26. "After touching a dead body, they will be cleansed after seven days." (cleansed: purified, body: corpse) 27. "Before entering the sanctuary to minister, they must offer a sin offering." (offer: present, minister: serve) 28. "I will be their inheritance. They will have no land in Israel; I am their possession." (inheritance: heritage, land: territory, possession: possession) 29. "They will eat the meat, sin, and trespass offerings, and everything dedicated to the LORD will belong to them." (eat: consume, meat: flesh, offerings: sacrifices, dedicated: consecrated) 30. "The firstfruits and offerings of all things will go to the priests, including the first dough, so that the blessing may rest in your home." (firstfruits: first produce, offerings: gifts, blessing: favor) 31. "The priests will not eat anything that is dead of itself or torn, whether from birds or animals." (eat: consume, torn: mangled)

Chapter 45
1. When you divide the land for inheritance, you will set aside a holy portion for the LORD. This portion will be 25,000 reeds long and 10,000 reeds wide. It will be holy, with boundaries all around. (divide: distribute, inheritance: possession, set aside: allocate, portion: section, holy: sacred, boundaries: borders) 2. Within this portion, there will be a 500-reed square for the sanctuary, with 50 reeds around it for the suburbs. (square: area, sanctuary: temple, suburbs: outskirts) 3. The entire portion, 25,000 by 10,000 reeds, will include the sanctuary and the most holy place. (entire: complete, include: encompass) 4. The holy portion will be for the priests who minister in the sanctuary, providing space for their homes and for the sanctuary itself. (minister: serve, providing: offering, homes: dwellings, sanctuary: temple) 5. The remaining land within this 25,000 by 10,000 reed area will be for the Levites to use, giving them 20 chambers for their possession. (remaining: leftover, use: occupy, chambers: rooms, possession: ownership) 6. You will also set aside a 5,000 reed wide, 25,000 reed long portion for the city, next to the holy portion. This will be for all the people of Israel. (set aside: allocate, portion: area, next to: adjacent, city: town) 7. The prince will have land on both sides of the holy portion and the city portion, from the west to the east border. (prince: ruler, sides: edges, border: boundary) 8. This land will be for the prince in Israel. The princes will no longer oppress the people. The remaining land will be given to the tribes of Israel. (land: territory, oppress: mistreat, remaining: leftover, tribes: clans) 9. The LORD says, "Princes of Israel, stop using violence and taking what isn't yours. Act with justice and fairness." (violence: cruelty, taking: stealing, act: behave, justice: righteousness, fairness: equity) 10. "You will use just balances, and honest measurements like the ephah (grain measurement) and bath (liquid measurement)." (use: apply, just: fair, balances: scales, measurements: units, honest: truthful) 11. "Both the ephah and bath will hold the tenth part of a homer (a larger measure of grain), and their measurement will be according to the homer." (hold: contain, tenth part: tenth, measurement: size, according to: based on) 12. "The shekel will be twenty gerahs. Your manneh (a larger currency unit) will be twenty shekels or 25 or 15 shekels." (shekel: coin, gerahs: small currency units, manneh: monetary unit) 13. "You will offer a sixth part of an ephah of wheat and barley from every homer of grain." (offer: present, sixth part: one-sixth, barley: a type of grain) 14. "For oil, you will offer the tenth part of a bath from the cor, which holds 10 baths." (oil: fat, cor: vessel) 15. "One lamb will be offered for every 200 from the best pastures of Israel. This will be for burnt, meat, and peace offerings, to make reconciliation with the LORD." (lamb: sheep, pastures: grazing land, reconciliation: atonement) 16. "The people of Israel will give this offering for the prince." (give: present, offering: gift) 17. "The prince will provide burnt offerings, meat offerings, and drink offerings during feasts, new moons, and Sabbaths. He will offer sin offerings, meat offerings, burnt offerings, and peace offerings to make reconciliation for the people." (provide: supply, feasts: festivals, new moons: monthly festivals, reconciliation: atonement) 18. "On the first day of the first month, the prince will offer a bull without blemish to cleanse the sanctuary." (bull: ox, without blemish: perfect, cleanse: purify) 19. "The priest will take the blood of the sin offering and apply it to the posts of the house, the corners of the altar, and the posts of the inner court gate." (apply: put, posts: pillars, house: temple, altar: sacrificial table, gate: entrance) 20. "On the seventh day of the month, the same will be done for those who have sinned unknowingly, to cleanse the house." (same: identical, sinned unknowingly: sinned unintentionally) 21. "On the fourteenth day of the first month, you will celebrate Passover for seven days, eating unleavened bread." (celebrate: observe, unleavened: without yeast) 22. "On this day, the prince will prepare a bull for a sin offering for himself and all the people." (prepare: make, sin offering: atonement offering) 23. "For seven days, the prince will offer seven bullocks and seven rams daily as burnt offerings, with a goat each day for a sin offering." (bullocks: bulls, rams: male sheep, daily: every day) 24. "He will offer one ephah of grain with each bullock and ram, and one hin (about 1 gallon) of oil for every ephah of grain." (grain: flour, oil: fat) 25. "On the fifteenth day of the seventh month, during the feast, the prince will offer similar offerings as during Passover, including sin offerings, burnt offerings, meat offerings, and oil." (feast: celebration, similar: identical, offerings: sacrifices).

Chapter 46
1. The east gate of the inner court will be closed on regular days but opened on the Sabbath and the new moon. (regular: normal, opened: unlocked) 2. The prince will enter through the outer porch of the gate, stand by the post, and offer his burnt and peace offerings. He will worship at the gate's threshold and leave; the gate will stay open until evening. (porch: vestibule, stand: stop, post: pillar, threshold: entrance, evening: night) 3. The people will worship at this gate on the Sabbath and new moon. (worship: honor, new moon: monthly festival) 4. The prince will offer six unblemished lambs and one unblemished ram for a burnt offering on the Sabbath. (unblemished: perfect, offering: sacrifice, ram: male sheep) 5. The meat offering for the ram will be an ephah, and for the lambs, it will be according to his ability, with an hin of oil for every ephah. (meat offering: grain offering, ability: means, ephah: measure, oil: fat) 6. On the new moon, he will offer one unblemished bullock, six lambs, and a ram, all without blemish. (new moon: monthly festival, bullock: young bull, lambs: young sheep) 7. He will prepare a meat offering: one ephah for the bullock, one ephah for the ram, and for the lambs, as much as he can give, with an hin of oil for every ephah. (prepare: make, offering: sacrifice, as much as: whatever, give: provide) 8. When the prince enters, he will enter through the porch of the gate and leave the same way. (porch: vestibule, leave: exit) 9. During the feasts, if people enter through the north gate, they must leave through the south gate, and vice versa; they should not return through the gate they entered. (feasts: celebrations, enter: go in, leave: go out, vice versa: the other way around) 10. The prince will enter and exit with the people during their worship. (enter: go in, exit: go out, worship: reverence) 11. During the feasts, the meat offering will be one ephah for a bullock, one ephah for a ram, and as much as he can offer for the lambs, with an hin of oil for every ephah. (feasts: festivals, meat offering: grain offering, lambs: young sheep) 12. If the prince offers a voluntary burnt or peace offering, the east gate will be opened for him, and he will offer as he does on the Sabbath; the gate will be shut after he leaves. (voluntary: freewill, burnt: holocaust, peace offering: fellowship offering, shut: closed) 13. A daily burnt offering of an unblemished lamb will be prepared every morning. (daily: every day, offering: sacrifice) 14. A meat offering for the lamb will be prepared daily: one-sixth ephah of flour and one-third hin of oil, mixed together. (meat offering: grain offering, flour: meal, mixed: combined) 15. The lamb, meat offering, and oil will be prepared daily for a continual burnt offering. (continual: perpetual, burnt offering: holocaust) 16. If the prince gives a gift to one of his sons, it will be their inheritance forever. (gift: present, inheritance: possession, forever: eternally) 17. If the prince gives a gift from his inheritance to a servant, it will belong to the servant only until the year of

liberty, then it will return to the prince's family. (servant: worker, belong: be owned, liberty: freedom) **18.** The prince must not take land from the people by force; he must provide inheritance for his sons from his own possessions to prevent the people from being scattered. (take: seize, force: coercion, possessions: property, scattered: dispersed) **19.** The angel brought me through the entry beside the gate to the priests' chambers, which faced north, and there was a place on both sides to the west. (angel: messenger, entry: entrance, chambers: rooms) **20.** This is where the priests will boil the trespass and sin offerings, and bake the meat offering, so they do not bring them into the outer court. (boil: cook, trespass offering: guilt offering, bake: cook, outer court: exterior area) **21.** He led me through the outer court, where there were four corners, and in each corner, there was a court. (led: guided, corners: angles, court: area) **22.** Each of the four corner courts measured 40 cubits long and 30 cubits wide, all of the same size. (measured: was, cubits: unit of length, size: dimension) **23.** There were buildings around the courts, with boiling places under the buildings on all four sides. (buildings: structures, boiling places: cooking areas, sides: edges) **24.** These are the places where the ministers of the house will boil the people's sacrifices. (places: areas, ministers: servants, sacrifices: offerings)

Chapter 47
1. He brought me to the door of the house, where waters flowed out from under the threshold, eastward, as the house faced east. The waters came from the right side of the house, at the south of the altar. (door: entrance, flowed: streamed, threshold: entrance, right: east, altar: sacrificial table) **2.** He led me northward, then around to the outer gate that faced east, and waters ran out on the right side. (led: guided, northward: north, around: toward, outer gate: exterior gate) **3.** The man with the measuring line went eastward, measuring a thousand cubits. He led me through the waters, which were ankle-deep. (measuring line: measuring cord, went: traveled, ankle-deep: shallow, led: guided) **4.** He measured another thousand cubits, and the waters were knee-deep. He measured another thousand, and the waters were waist-deep. (knee-deep: deeper, waist-deep: higher) **5.** He measured another thousand, and it became a river I could not cross, for the waters were too deep, a river to swim in, impassable. (cross: traverse, swim in: wade through, impassable: unreachable) **6.** He asked, "Son of man, have you seen this?" Then he brought me back to the river's edge. (asked: inquired, brought: returned, edge: bank) **7.** When I returned, I saw many trees on both sides of the river. (returned: came back, saw: observed, trees: plants) **8.** He said, "These waters flow eastward, into the desert, and to the sea. When they reach the sea, the waters will be healed." (flow: stream, eastward: toward the east, healed: restored) **9.** Every living creature wherever the river flows will live. A great multitude of fish will be there, for the waters will be healed, and everything will live where the river goes. (living creature: being, multitude: large number, fish: aquatic life) **10.** Fishermen will stand along the river from En-gedi to En-eglaim, spreading their nets. The fish will be of many kinds, like the fish of the great sea. (fishermen: anglers, nets: traps, kinds: types) **11.** But the marshy areas and the salt pits will not be healed; they will remain salt. (marshy areas: wetlands, salt pits: saline pools) **12.** On both sides of the river, all kinds of fruit trees will grow. Their leaves will not wither, and their fruit will not fail. They will produce fresh fruit each month, and their leaves will be for medicine. (fruit trees: bearing trees, wither: fade, fail: fall short, produce: bear, medicine: healing) **13.** The Lord GOD says: "This will be the boundary for the land, which you will inherit, divided among the twelve tribes of Israel. Joseph will receive two portions." (boundary: border, inherit: possess, divided: apportioned, portions: shares) **14.** You will inherit it equally, as I swore to give it to your ancestors. This land will be your inheritance. (inherit: receive, equally: equally divided, swore: promised, ancestors: forefathers) **15.** The northern border will extend from the Great Sea, by the way of Hethlon, toward Zedad. (northern: upper, border: boundary, extend: stretch, Great Sea: Mediterranean, way of: route of) **16.** The border will continue through Hamath, Berothah, Sibraim, between Damascus and Hamath, and Hazar-hatticon, by the border of Hauran. (continue: proceed, through: passing, between: among, border: boundary) **17.** From the sea, the border will go to Hazar-enan, the border of Damascus, and extend northward, to the border of Hamath. This is the northern side. (sea: ocean, go to: reach, extend: stretch, northward: upwards) **18.** The eastern border will be measured from Hauran, Damascus, Gilead, and the land of Israel by the Jordan River, all the way to the east sea. (measured: calculated, from: starting at, all the way to: until, east sea: Dead Sea) **19.** The southern border will extend from Tamar to the waters of strife in Kadesh, and to the Great Sea. This is the southern side. (southern: lower, extend: stretch, waters of strife: disputed waters) **20.** The western border will be the Great Sea, from the border to a point opposite Hamath. This is the western side. (western: left, opposite: across from, point: location) **21.** You will divide this land among yourselves, according to the tribes of Israel. (divide: apportion, land: territory, yourselves: yourselves, tribes: clans) **22.** You will divide it by lot for an inheritance to you and to the strangers who live among you, who have children among you. They will be like native-born Israelites, and will inherit among the tribes of Israel. (by lot: randomly, inheritance: possession, strangers: foreigners, native-born: born in the land) **23.** Wherever a foreigner resides, you will assign him an inheritance in the tribe where he dwells, says the Lord GOD. (foreigner: outsider, resides: lives, assign: allocate, tribe: clan, dwells: stays)

Chapter 48
1. These are the names of the tribes. Starting from the north, along the coast of Hethlon, as one travels toward Hamath, Hazar-enan, and the border of Damascus to the north, this is the eastern and western boundary for Dan. (names: titles, coast: shore, travels: journeys, border: edge, boundary: perimeter) **2.** To the south of Dan, from east to west, will be Asher's portion. (south: beneath, portion: share, east to west: horizontally) **3.** To the south of Asher, from east to west, will be Naphtali's portion. (portion: allotment) **4.** To the south of Naphtali, from east to west, will be Manasseh's portion. (portion: share) **5.** To the south of Manasseh, from east to west, will be Ephraim's portion. (portion: lot) **6.** To the south of Ephraim, from east to west, will be Reuben's portion. (portion: area) **7.** To the south of Reuben, from east to west, will be Judah's portion. (portion: territory) **8.** The portion for Judah, from east to west, will include an offering of 25,000 reeds in width, and as long as the other portions, from east to west. The sanctuary will be in the center. (offering: gift, width: breadth, length: extent, sanctuary: temple) **9.** The oblation offered to the LORD will be 25,000 in length and 10,000 in breadth. (offering: sacrifice) **10.** This holy offering for the priests will be 25,000 in length to the north, 10,000 in breadth to the west, 10,000 in breadth to the east, and 25,000 in length to the south, with the LORD's sanctuary in the middle. (holy: sacred, offering: sacrifice, priests: clergy) **11.** This will be for the priests, the sons of Zadok, who have kept my charge and not gone astray when Israel went astray, unlike the Levites. (kept: followed, charge: command, gone astray: strayed, unlike: different from) **12.** The land offered will be most holy, located by the border of the Levites. (land: territory, offered: provided, most holy: consecrated) **13.** To the south of the priests' border, the Levites will have 25,000 in length and 10,000 in breadth. (border: boundary, Levites: priestly tribe) **14.** They will not sell or exchange it, nor alienate the firstfruits of the land, for it is holy to the LORD. (sell: trade, exchange: barter, alienate: transfer, firstfruits: initial produce) **15.** The remaining 5,000 in breadth, opposite the 25,000 for the priests, will be a profane area for the city, for dwelling and suburbs. The city will be in the center. (remaining: leftover, profane: secular, dwelling: residential, suburbs: outskirts) **16.** The city will measure 4,500 on each side—north, south, east, and west. (measure: span) **17.** The city's suburbs will measure 250 units on each side—north, south, east, and west. (suburbs: outskirts, units: measurements) **18.** The remaining land, 10,000 eastward and 10,000 westward, will be adjacent to the holy portion. It will be used for food for those who serve the city. (remaining: excess, adjacent: next to, serve: assist) **19.** Those who serve the city will be from all the tribes of Israel. (serve: minister) **20.** The entire oblation will measure 25,000 by 25,000, a square with the city's possession in the middle. (oblation: offering, square: rectangle, possession: territory) **21.** The remaining land will be for the prince, located on either side of the holy oblation and the city's possession, eastward and westward, in line with the prince's portion. The sanctuary will be in the center. (prince: ruler, line with: aligned with) **22.** The land between the Levites' possession and the city, in the areas between the borders of Judah and Benjamin, will be for the prince. (between: amid, areas: regions) **23.** To the east, from the border to the west, Benjamin will have a portion. (portion: allotment) **24.** To the south of Benjamin, from east to west, Simeon will have a portion. (portion: share) **25.** To the south of Simeon, from east to west, Issachar will have a portion. (portion: section) **26.** To the south of Issachar, from east to west, Zebulun will have a portion. (portion: allotment) **27.** To the south of Zebulun, from east to west, Gad will have a portion. (portion: share) **28.** To the south of Gad, the border will extend from Tamar to the waters of strife at Kadesh and to the river toward the Great Sea. (extend: stretch, waters of strife: disputed waters, river: stream, Great Sea: Mediterranean) **29.** This is the land you will divide by lot for the tribes of Israel as their inheritance, says the Lord GOD. (divide: distribute, inheritance: possession) **30.** These are the exits of the city to the north: 4,500 units. (exits: gateways) **31.** The city gates will be named after the tribes of Israel: three gates to the north—Reuben, Judah, and Levi. (gates: entrances, named after: titled) **32.** To the east: 4,500 units and three gates—Joseph, Benjamin, and Dan. (units: measurements, gates: entrances) **33.** To the south: 4,500 units and three gates—Simeon, Issachar, and Zebulun. (gates: entries) **34.** To the west: 4,500

units and three gates—Gad, Asher, and Naphtali. (units: measurements) **35.** The total area will be 18,000 units, and from that day on, the city will be called "The LORD is there." (total: complete, area: space, called: named).

27 – Daniel
Chapter 1

1. In the third year of King Jehoiakim's reign in Judah, King Nebuchadnezzar of Babylon laid siege to Jerusalem. (Judah: southern kingdom of ancient Israel; Babylon: ancient empire) **2.** The Lord gave King Jehoiakim of Judah into Nebuchadnezzar's hands, along with some of the sacred objects from the temple. Nebuchadnezzar took them to the land of Shinar and placed them in the temple of his god, storing them in the treasury of his god. (Shinar: entire Babylon; house of his God: temple) **3.** Nebuchadnezzar instructed Ashpenaz, the chief of his eunuchs, to select some young men from Israel, from the royal family and nobility. (eunuchs: castrated men) **4.** young men who were without blemish, handsome, wise, knowledgeable, and skilled in learning, capable of standing in the king's palace, and ready to learn the language and ways of the Chaldeans. (blemish: flaw; knowledgeable: intelligent; Chaldeans: Babylonians) **5.** The king ordered a daily provision of his own food and wine for them, intending to train them for three years, so they could serve him later. **6.** Among them were Daniel, Hananiah, Mishael, and Azariah from Judah. **7.** The chief eunuch gave them new names: Daniel became Belteshazzar, Hananiah became Shadrach, Mishael became Meshach, and Azariah became Abednego. **8.** But Daniel decided not to defile himself with the king's food or wine, and he asked the chief eunuch for permission to avoid defiling himself. (defile: pollute) **9.** God granted Daniel favor and kindness from the chief eunuch. (favor: like) **10.** The eunuch replied, "I am afraid of my lord the king, who has ordered your food and drink. Why should he see you looking worse than the other young men? Then I might be punished." (punished: executed) **11.** Daniel then spoke to Melzar, the steward appointed over them, **12.** "Please test us for ten days. Let us have only vegetables to eat and water to drink. (vegetables: plant foods) **13.** Then compare our appearance with the other young men who eat the king's food, and deal with us according to what you see." **14.** Melzar agreed to their request and tested them for ten days. **15.** After ten days, they appeared healthier and more robust than all the young men who ate the king's food. (healthier: stronger) **16.** So, Melzar removed their portion of food and wine, giving them vegetables instead. **17.** God gave these four young men wisdom and understanding in every area of learning and knowledge, and Daniel had the ability to interpret visions and dreams. (learning: education) **18.** When the training period was completed, the eunuch brought them before King Nebuchadnezzar. **19.** The king spoke with them, and among all of them, none was found to be as impressive as Daniel, Hananiah, Mishael, and Azariah, so they entered the king's service. **20.** In all matters of wisdom and understanding the king asked them about, he found them ten times better than all the magicians and astrologers in his entire kingdom. (magicians: sorcerers; astrologers: fortune tellers) **21.** Daniel remained in the king's service until the first year of King Cyrus. (Cyrus: Persian ruler)

Chapter 2

1. In the second year of Nebuchadnezzar's reign, he had troubling dreams that disturbed his sleep. (Nebuchadnezzar: King of Babylon) **2.** The king called for magicians, astrologers, sorcerers, and Chaldeans to explain his dreams. They stood before him. (Magicians: sorcerers, astrologers: stargazers, Chaldeans: wise men of Babylon) **3.** The king told them, "I had a dream, and my spirit is troubled to understand it." (spirit: soul) **4.** The Chaldeans spoke in Aramaic, "Live forever, O king! Tell us the dream, and we will explain it." (Aramaic: a language) **5.** The king replied, "The dream has left me. If you cannot tell me both the dream and its meaning, you will be cut to pieces, and your houses destroyed." (destroyed: ruined) **6.** "But if you tell me the dream and its interpretation, you will be rewarded with gifts, honor, and riches. Tell me the dream and its meaning." (gifts: prizes) **7.** They replied, "Tell your servants the dream, and we will explain it." **8.** The king said, "I know you're trying to buy time, since the dream is gone from me." **9.** "If you cannot tell me the dream, you will face one fate: you've prepared lies to delay until the time changes. Tell me the dream, and I'll know you can explain its meaning." **10.** The Chaldeans said, "No one on earth can reveal such a mystery! No king has ever asked this of any magician, astrologer, or Chaldean." **11.** "This is a rare request, and only the gods could reveal it, but they don't dwell among humans." **12.** The king was furious and ordered the wise men of Babylon to be killed. (wise men of Babylon: Babylonian scholars) **13.** The order to kill the wise men went out, and they sought Daniel and his companions to execute them. (Daniel: a young Hebrew man) **14.** Daniel spoke wisely to Arioch, the king's captain, who was sent to kill the wise men. (captain: leader) **15.** Daniel asked, "Why is the king's order so urgent?" Arioch explained the situation to Daniel. **16.** Daniel asked the king for time to reveal the dream's meaning. **17.** Daniel returned to his house and told his companions—Hananiah, Mishael, and Azariah—about the matter. **18.** They prayed to the God of heaven for mercy, that they might not perish with the other wise men of Babylon. (God of heaven: the true God) **19.** The secret was revealed to Daniel in a night vision. He praised the God of heaven. (night vision: a dream) **20.** Daniel said, "Blessed be God forever, for wisdom and power are His." **21.** "He changes times and seasons, removes kings, and raises others. He gives wisdom to the wise and knowledge to the discerning." (kings: rulers, discerning: understanding) **22.** "He reveals deep and hidden things. He knows what is in darkness, and light dwells with Him." **23.** "I thank and praise You, God of my ancestors, for giving me wisdom and power and revealing the king's mystery." (ancestors: descendants) **24.** Daniel went to Arioch, who was sent to kill the wise men, and said, "Don't destroy them. Take me to the king, and I will explain the dream." **25.** Arioch quickly brought Daniel before the king, saying, "I found a man from Judah who can explain your dream." (Judah: land of ancient Israel) **26.** The king asked Daniel, whose name was Belteshazzar, "Can you tell me the dream and its meaning?" (Belteshazzar: Daniel's Babylonian name) **27.** Daniel replied, "The mystery the king asks cannot be explained by wise men, astrologers, or magicians." **28.** "But there is a God in heaven who reveals secrets. He has made known to King Nebuchadnezzar what will happen in the future. Your dream and the visions on your bed are as follows:" (Nebuchadnezzar: King of Babylon) **29.** "While you lay on your bed, thoughts about what will happen in the future came to you. He who reveals secrets showed you what will happen." **30.** "This mystery wasn't revealed to me because I am wiser than others, but so that you, the king, may know the thoughts of your heart." **31.** "You saw a great image, whose brightness was stunning, standing before you, and it was terrifying." (terrifying: fearful) **32.** "Its head was of fine gold, its chest and arms were of silver, its belly and thighs were bronze," (bronze: brass) **33.** "Its legs were iron, and its feet were a mix of iron and clay." **34.** "You saw a stone, cut without hands, strike the feet of iron and clay, crushing them." **35.** "Then the iron, clay, bronze, silver, and gold were broken to pieces, like chaff from a threshing floor, and the wind blew them away. But the stone became a great mountain and filled the whole earth." (chaff: light pieces) **36.** "This is the dream, and now I will tell you its meaning. **37.** "You, O king, are the king of kings. The God of heaven has given you a kingdom, power, strength, and glory." **38.** "Wherever people live, He has given you dominion over them. You are the head of gold." (dominion: control) **39.** "After you, another kingdom will arise, inferior to yours, followed by a third kingdom of bronze that will rule over all the earth." (inferior: weaker) **40.** "The fourth kingdom will be strong as iron, because iron breaks and crushes everything. It will break all things and crush them." **41.** "As you saw the feet and toes mixed with clay and iron, this kingdom will be divided, but it will have the strength of iron, as you saw the iron mixed with clay." **42.** "The toes, part iron and part clay, mean that the kingdom will be partly strong and partly fragile." **43.** "Just as iron and clay don't mix, so the people will not unite, even as iron doesn't mix with clay." **44.** "In the time of those kings, the God of heaven will set up a kingdom that will never be destroyed. It will crush all other kingdoms and last forever." **45.** "As you saw the stone cut without hands, crushing the iron, bronze, clay, silver, and gold, the great God has shown you what will happen. The dream is certain, and its meaning is trustworthy." **46.** The king bowed before Daniel, worshipped him, and ordered offerings to be made in his honor. **47.** The king said, "Truly, your God is the God of gods, the Lord of kings, and a revealer of secrets, since you could reveal this mystery." (kings: rulers) **48.** The king made Daniel a powerful man, gave him many gifts, and made him ruler over all Babylon and chief of its wise men. (Babylon: capital city of Babylon) **49.** Daniel requested that the king appoint Shadrach, Meshach, and Abed-nego over Babylon's affairs, while Daniel remained at the king's gate. (Shadrach, Meshach, and Abed-nego: Daniel's three companions)

Chapter 3

1. King Nebuchadnezzar made a gold statue, 60 cubits high and 6 cubits wide, and set it up in the plain of Dura, in Babylon's province (Nebuchadnezzar: King of Babylon, plain of Dura: open land in Babylon's territory). **2.** He sent for all the leaders—princes, governors, captains, judges, treasurers, counselors, sheriffs, and rulers—to attend the image's dedication (dedication: unveiling, counselors: advisors, sheriffs: officials). **3.** The leaders gathered to the dedication and stood before the image (gathered: assembled). **4.** A herald shouted, "O peoples, nations, and languages, listen!" (herald: messenger). **5.** "When you hear the music—cornet, flute, harp, sackbut, psaltery, dulcimer, and all kinds of music—you must worship the golden image" (worship: bow down, music: instruments). **6.** "Anyone who does not worship will be thrown into a fiery furnace immediately" (furnace: fiery pit). **7.** When the music played, all people bowed and worshipped the golden image (bowed: fell down). **8.** Some Chaldeans approached and accused the Jews (Chaldeans: Babylonians, accused: reported). **9.** They said to King Nebuchadnezzar, "O king, live forever!" (live forever: reign forever). **10.** "You commanded that anyone who hears the music must worship the golden image" (commanded: ordered). **11.** "Anyone who refuses will be thrown into the fiery furnace" (refuses: does not obey). **12.** "There are certain Jews, Shadrach, Meshach, and Abed-nego, who do not serve your gods or worship the golden image" (serve: honor, worship: bow down). **13.** In fury, Nebuchadnezzar ordered Shadrach, Meshach, and Abed-nego to be brought before him (fury: rage, ordered: commanded). **14.** He asked, "Is it true you refuse to worship my gods or the image?" (Refuse: reject). **15.** "If you are ready to worship, well; if not, you will be thrown into the furnace—who can save you?" (ready: prepared). **16.** Shadrach, Meshach, and Abed-nego replied, "We don't need to answer you" (replied: answered, need: have to). **17.** "Our God can save us from the furnace and from your hand, O king" (save: deliver). **18.** "But even if He doesn't, we will not worship your gods or the image" (even if: even though). **19.** Nebuchadnezzar was furious, and his face changed; he ordered the furnace to be heated seven times hotter (furious: enraged, face: expression). **20.** He commanded his strongest soldiers to bind Shadrach, Meshach, and Abed-nego and throw them into the furnace (strongest: mightiest, bind: tie). **21.** The men were bound and thrown into the furnace (thrown: cast). **22.** The furnace was so hot that the soldiers who threw them in were burned (burned: killed by the flames). **23.** Shadrach, Meshach, and Abed-nego fell into the furnace, still bound (fell: dropped). **24.** Nebuchadnezzar jumped up, astonished, and asked his counselors, "Did we throw three men into the fire?" (astonished: amazed). **25.** "I see four men walking in the fire, unhurt, and the fourth looks like the Son of God" (unhurt: unharmed). **26.** Nebuchadnezzar approached the furnace and called, "Shadrach, Meshach, and Abed-nego, servants of the Most High God, come out!" (approached: came near, Most High God: Supreme Deity). **27.** When they came out, the leaders saw that the fire had not harmed them; their clothes were untouched, and they didn't even smell like smoke (untouched: unaffected). **28.** Nebuchadnezzar praised the God of Shadrach, Meshach, and Abed-nego, who sent an angel to save His servants, who trusted in Him and defied the king's command (praised: blessed, defied: rejected). **29.** "I decree that anyone who speaks against their God will be cut to pieces, and their houses made a heap of rubble, for no god can save like this" (decree: order, rubble: debris). **30.** Then Nebuchadnezzar promoted Shadrach, Meshach, and Abed-nego in Babylon (promoted: advanced).

Chapter 4
1. Nebuchadnezzar, king, to all people, nations, and languages on earth: Peace be multiplied to you. (Nebuchadnezzar: Babylonian king) **2.** I wish to show the signs and wonders the Most High God has done for me. (Signs: miracles; Wonders: amazing acts) **3.** How great are His signs! How mighty are His wonders! His kingdom is eternal, and His rule lasts from generation to generation. (Eternal: forever) **4.** I, Nebuchadnezzar, was at peace in my house, prospering in my palace. (Palace: royal residence) **5.** I had a dream that made me afraid; thoughts and visions troubled me. (Afraid: scared; Troubled: disturbed) **6.** So, I issued a decree to bring all the wise men of Babylon to interpret the dream for me. (Decree: command) **7.** The magicians, astrologers, Chaldeans, and soothsayers came, and I told them the dream, but they could not interpret it. (Magicians: sorcerers; Soothsayers: fortune tellers) **8.** Finally, Daniel came in, called Belteshazzar after my god, and in whom the spirit of the holy gods dwells. I told him the dream, saying, (Daniel: Jewish prophet, Belteshazzar: Babylonian name) **9.** "Belteshazzar, master of the magicians, because I know the spirit of the holy gods is in you, and no secret is too difficult for you, tell me the meaning of my dream." (Master: leader) **10.** The visions I saw in my bed: a tree stood in the middle of the earth, its height was great. (Visions: dreams; Earth: world) **11.** The tree grew strong, its height reached the heavens, and its sight extended to the ends of the earth. (Sight: view) **12.** Its leaves were beautiful, its fruit abundant, and it provided food for all. Beasts found shelter under it, and birds lived in its branches, and all flesh was nourished. (Abundant: plenty; Beasts: animals; Flesh: living creatures) **13.** I saw in the visions a holy watcher coming down from heaven. (Watcher: angel) **14.** He cried aloud, saying, "Cut down the tree, strip off its branches, shake off its leaves, scatter its fruit. Let the beasts flee from under it, and the birds from its branches." (Cried aloud: shouted) **15.** "But leave the stump with its roots in the earth, bound with iron and brass in the grass of the field. Let it be drenched with the dew of heaven and live among the beasts for seven years." (Stump: base; Drenched: soaked) **16.** "Let his heart be changed from a man's to a beast's, and let seven periods pass over him." (Periods: seasons, years) **17.** "This decision is made by the watchers, and the command of the holy ones, to show that the Most High rules the kingdom of men, gives it to whomever He pleases, and sets the lowest over it." (Decision: decree; Holy ones: angels) **18.** "I, King Nebuchadnezzar, have seen this dream. Now, Belteshazzar, interpret it, for none of my wise men can. You can, because the spirit of the holy gods is in you." **19.** Daniel, whose name was Belteshazzar, was stunned for an hour, and his thoughts troubled him. The king said, "Belteshazzar, do not be troubled by the dream or its meaning." Daniel answered, **20.** "My lord, this dream is for those who hate you, and its interpretation is for your enemies." (Enemies: those who oppose you) **21.** "The tree you saw, which grew and became strong, its height reached to heaven, and its sight to all the earth, **22.** whose leaves were beautiful, its fruit plentiful, and which fed all: it represents you, O king. Your greatness has grown, reaching to heaven, and your rule extends to the ends of the earth." (Represents: symbolizes) **23.** "The holy watcher you saw coming down from heaven saying, 'Cut down the tree, destroy it, but leave the stump with the roots in the field' means your kingdom will be taken from you. You will live among the beasts until you learn that the Most High rules." **24.** "This is the interpretation, O king, and the decree of the Most High: **25.** You will be driven away from men, and your dwelling will be with the beasts. You will eat grass like oxen, and seven years will pass over you until you acknowledge the Most High rules the kingdom of men." (Driven away: forced out; Dwelling: living place) **26.** "As for the stump left with the roots, your kingdom will return after you know that the heavens rule." (Stump: base; Heavens: God's rule) **27.** "Therefore, O king, accept my advice: Renounce your sins by doing what is right, and your wickedness by showing mercy to the poor. Perhaps your prosperity will be prolonged." (Renounce: reject; Wickedness: evil deeds; Prosperity: success) **28.** All this came upon King Nebuchadnezzar. **29.** Twelve months later, as he was walking on the roof of the royal palace of Babylon, (Royal palace: king's home in Babylon) **30.** he said, "Is this not the great Babylon I have built as the royal residence by my mighty power, and for the honor of my majesty?" (Majesty: greatness) **31.** While the words were still on his lips, a voice came from heaven, saying, "King Nebuchadnezzar, your kingdom has been taken from you." **32.** "You will be driven away from men, and live with the beasts. You will eat grass like oxen, and seven years will pass until you acknowledge the Most High rules over the kingdoms of men." **33.** The judgment was fulfilled immediately on Nebuchadnezzar. He was driven from men and ate grass like oxen. His body was wet with dew, and his hair grew like eagle feathers, and his nails like bird claws. (Dew: moisture) **34.** After the set time passed, I, Nebuchadnezzar, lifted my eyes to heaven, and my understanding returned to me. I praised the Most High, honored Him who lives forever, whose kingdom is everlasting and whose rule lasts for all generations. **35.** "All the inhabitants of the earth are considered as nothing. He does as He wills in heaven and on earth, and no one can stop Him or ask, 'What are You doing?'" **36.** "At the same time, my sanity returned to me. My honor and glory were restored, and my advisers and nobles sought me out. I was reestablished in my kingdom, and even greater majesty was added to me." **37.** "Now, I, Nebuchadnezzar, praise, exalt, and honor the King of heaven, whose works are true, and whose ways are just. He is able to humble those who walk in pride." (Pride: arrogance)

Chapter 5
1. King Belshazzar hosted a grand banquet for a thousand of his nobles and drank wine in their presence. (Belshazzar: King of Babylon) **2.** As he was enjoying the wine, he ordered that the gold and silver vessels taken by his father Nebuchadnezzar from the temple in Jerusalem be brought so that he, his nobles, wives, and concubines could drink from them. (Nebuchadnezzar: King of Babylon, Jerusalem: City in Israel) **3.** The vessels from God's temple in Jerusalem were brought, and everyone drank from them. (God's temple: Holy place in Jerusalem) **4.** They drank wine and praised the gods of gold, silver, bronze, iron, wood, and stone. (Bronze: A metal, Iron: Metal) **5.** At that very moment, a hand appeared and began writing on the wall near the lampstand in the palace. The king saw the hand that was writing. (Lampstand: Light source) **6.** The king's expression changed, and he became greatly disturbed; his joints weakened, and his knees trembled. (Disturbed: Troubled, Joints: Body parts that bend) **7.** He called for the magicians, Chaldeans, and sorcerers, saying, "Whoever can read and explain this writing will be honored with scarlet robes, a gold chain, and made third in command of the kingdom." (Magicians: Wise men, Chaldeans: Astrologers, Sorcerers: Magicians) **8.** The wise men came, but none could read or interpret the writing. **9.** Belshazzar was deeply troubled, his expression changed, and his nobles were confused. (Nobles: High-ranking officials) **10.** The queen entered due to the king's distress and said, "O king, live forever! Don't let your thoughts trouble you or change your expression." **11.** "There is a man in your kingdom who has the spirit of the holy gods. In your father's reign, he had great wisdom, understanding, and insight, like that of the gods. Nebuchadnezzar made him chief over all the magicians, astrologers, Chaldeans, and sorcerers." **12.** "This man, Daniel—whom the king named Belteshazzar—possesses an excellent

spirit, knowledge, and understanding, and can interpret dreams, explain riddles, and solve difficult problems. Let him be called, and he will give you the interpretation." (Daniel: Hebrew prophet, Belteshazzar: Daniel's Babylonian name) **13.** Daniel was brought before the king, who asked him, "Are you that Daniel from Judah, whom my father brought from Jerusalem?" (Judah: Region of ancient Israel) **14.** "I've heard that the spirit of the gods is in you, and that you have insight, wisdom, and understanding." **15.** "The wise men and astrologers were summoned to read the writing and interpret it, but they couldn't." **16.** "I've heard that you can explain riddles and solve mysteries. If you can read this writing and tell me its meaning, you will be clothed in scarlet, wear a gold chain, and be the third ruler in the kingdom." **17.** Daniel replied, "You may keep your rewards, and give your gifts to someone else. However, I will read the writing and interpret it for you." **18.** "O king, the Most High God gave your father Nebuchadnezzar a vast kingdom, glory, and honor." (Most High God: The supreme deity) **19.** "People, nations, and languages trembled before him; he could kill or spare anyone, and he could elevate or demote anyone he wished." **20.** "But when his heart became arrogant and his mind hardened in pride, he was deposed from his throne, and his glory was taken from him." **21.** "He was driven away from people; his heart became like that of an animal, and he lived with wild beasts. He ate grass like cattle, and his body was soaked with dew, until he acknowledged that the Most High God rules over the kingdom of men and appoints rulers as He chooses." **22.** "But you, Belshazzar, have not humbled yourself, even though you knew all of this." **23.** "Instead, you have defied the Lord of heaven. You brought the sacred vessels from His temple, drank wine from them, and praised gods of silver, gold, bronze, iron, wood, and stone—gods that cannot see, hear, or understand. Yet you have not honored the God who holds your life in His hands." (Defied: Disrespected, Vessels: Containers, Sacred: Holy) **24.** "That is why this hand was sent from Him, and this is what was written." **25.** "The writing says: MENE, MENE, TEKEL, UPHARSIN." (MENE: Numbered, TEKEL: Weighed, PERES: Divided) **26.** "This is what it means: MENE—God has numbered the days of your reign and brought it to an end." (Numbered: Counted and completed) **27.** "TEKEL—You have been weighed on the scales and found lacking." (Weighed: Judged, Lacking: Insufficient) **28.** "PERES—Your kingdom is divided and given to the Medes and Persians." (Medes and Persians: Ancient empires, Persia: Iran) **29.** Belshazzar commanded that Daniel be dressed in scarlet, given a gold chain, and made the third ruler in the kingdom. (Scarlet: Red, Chain: Necklace) **30.** That very night, Belshazzar, king of the Chaldeans, was slain. (Slain: Killed) **31.** Darius the Mede took control of the kingdom at the age of about sixty-two. (Darius: King of the Medes, Mede: Ancient people from Iran)

Chapter 6

1. It pleased Darius to appoint 120 governors over his kingdom; (Darius: king of Persia) **2.** And three presidents, with Daniel as the first, to oversee them, ensuring the king suffered no loss. **3.** Daniel was favored above the others because he had an excellent spirit; (excellent spirit: good character) the king considered making him ruler over the entire kingdom. **4.** The presidents and princes tried to find fault with Daniel regarding the kingdom, but they couldn't find any; he was trustworthy, with no error or fault. (princes: officials) **5.** They decided they could only trap Daniel through his faith in God. **6.** So they approached King Darius, saying, "Long live the king!" (Darius: king of Persia) **7.** "All the officials have agreed to establish a law that anyone who asks a petition of any god or man, except you, O king, within thirty days, shall be thrown into the lion's den." (petition: request) **8.** "O king, sign this decree, making it unchangeable, as per the laws of the Medes and Persians." (Medes and Persians: nations under Darius' rule) **9.** King Darius signed the decree. **10.** When Daniel learned the decree was signed, he went home and prayed three times a day, with his windows open toward Jerusalem, just as he had always done. (Jerusalem: city in Israel) **11.** The officials gathered and found Daniel praying to God. **12.** They approached the king, saying, "Did you not sign a decree that anyone who prays to anyone but you would be thrown into the lion's den?" The king confirmed it. **13.** They reported, "Daniel, a captive from Judah, ignores your decree and prays three times a day." (Judah: region in ancient Israel, captive: prisoner) **14.** The king was upset and tried all day to find a way to save Daniel. **15.** They reminded the king that no decree in the Medes and Persians could be changed. **16.** Reluctantly, the king ordered Daniel to be thrown into the lion's den, saying, "Your God, whom you serve, will rescue you." **17.** A stone was placed over the den's mouth, sealed with the king's signet to ensure the decision was final. (signet: stamp) **18.** The king went to his palace, fasting and unable to sleep. (palace: residence) **19.** Early the next morning, the king hurried to the lion's den. **20.** He cried out in a sorrowful voice, "Daniel, servant of the living God, has your God, whom you serve continually, saved you from the lions?" **21.** Daniel replied, "O king, live forever!" **22.** "My God sent an angel to shut the lions' mouths; they haven't harmed me, for I was innocent before him, and I've done no wrong to you, O king." **23.** The king was overjoyed and ordered Daniel to be lifted out of the den. He was unharmed because he trusted in his God. **24.** The king then ordered those who accused Daniel to be thrown into the den, along with their families. The lions overpowered them before they even reached the bottom. **25.** King Darius sent a decree to all peoples and nations: (Darius: king of Persia) **26.** "I decree that everyone in my kingdom must fear and tremble before the God of Daniel; for he is the living God, enduring forever. His kingdom cannot be destroyed, and his rule will last to the end." **27.** "He rescues, performs miracles, and delivered Daniel from the lions." **28.** So Daniel prospered during the reign of Darius and Cyrus the Persian. (Darius: king of Persia, Cyrus: king of Persia)

Chapter 7

1. In the first year of Belshazzar, king of Babylon, Daniel had a dream and visions on his bed. He wrote it down and shared the summary. (Babylon: ancient city) **2.** Daniel said, "In my night vision, I saw the four winds of heaven stirring the great sea." (heaven: sky, sea: large body of water) **3.** Four great beasts rose from the sea, each different from the others. (beasts: creatures) **4.** The first was like a lion, with eagle's wings. I watched until its wings were torn off, and it was lifted from the ground, standing like a man with a human heart. **5.** Then a second beast, like a bear, rose. It leaned on one side and had three ribs in its mouth. They told it, "Arise and eat much flesh." (ribs: bones) **6.** Next, I saw a leopard with four bird wings and four heads. Dominion was given to it. (dominion: power) **7.** Then I saw a fourth beast, terrifying and powerful, with iron teeth. It devoured, crushed, and trampled what remained. It was unlike the others, with ten horns. **8.** I watched the horns, and a little horn grew among them. Three of the first horns were uprooted. The little horn had human eyes and a mouth boasting great things. **9.** I watched until thrones were set up, and the Ancient of Days took His seat. His clothes were white as snow, and His hair like pure wool. His throne was a fiery flame, and its wheels like burning fire. (Ancient of Days: God) **10.** A fiery stream came from Him. Thousands served Him, and millions stood before Him. The judgment was set, and the books were opened. (stream: flowing water, judgment: decision, books: records) **11.** I watched because of the great words the little horn spoke. I saw the beast slain, its body destroyed, and burned in the fire. (slain: killed) **12.** The other beasts had their authority taken, but their lives were prolonged for a time. (authority: control) **13.** In my vision, I saw someone like the Son of Man coming with the clouds of heaven. He approached the Ancient of Days and was brought near to Him. (Son of Man: a title for Jesus, clouds: masses of vapor) **14.** Dominion, glory, and a kingdom were given to Him. All peoples, nations, and languages would serve Him. His dominion is everlasting and cannot be destroyed. (kingdom: ruled area) **15.** I, Daniel, was troubled in spirit and disturbed by the visions in my mind. (spirit: inner self) **16.** I asked one of those standing by to explain the meaning. He told me the interpretation. (standing by: nearby, interpretation: explanation) **17.** The four beasts are four kings who will arise from the earth. (kings: rulers) **18.** But the saints of the Most High will receive the kingdom and possess it forever. (saints: holy people, Most High: God) **19.** I wanted to understand the fourth beast, which was more terrifying than the others, with iron teeth and brass claws. It devoured, crushed, and trampled the rest. (claws: sharp nails) **20.** I also wanted to know about the ten horns on its head, and the other horn that grew up, removing three of them. This horn had eyes and a mouth boasting great things, appearing stronger than the others. (eyes: seeing organs) **21.** I saw that this horn made war with the saints and defeated them. (war: battle) **22.** Until the Ancient of Days came and judgment was given to the saints. Then the saints took possession of the kingdom. (Ancient of Days: God) **23.** He said, "The fourth beast will be a fourth kingdom on earth, unlike all others. It will devour and crush the whole earth." (kingdom: ruled area) **24.** The ten horns are ten kings who will arise. Another will come after them, different from the first, and will overthrow three kings. **25.** He will speak against the Most High, wear out the saints, and try to change laws and times. They will be given into his hand for a time, times, and half a time. (times: periods of time) **26.** But judgment will sit, and his dominion will be taken away and destroyed. (judgment: decision, dominion: control) **27.** The kingdom, dominion, and greatness under heaven will be given to the saints of the Most High. His kingdom will be everlasting, and all dominions will serve Him. (heaven: sky) **28.** This is the end of the matter. I, Daniel, was greatly troubled, and my face changed, but I kept the matter in my heart.

Chapter 8

1. In the third year of King Belshazzar's reign, I, Daniel, saw a vision, similar to the one I had before. (Belshazzar: King of Babylon). **2.** I saw in a vision while in Shushan, the palace of Elam, by the river Ulai. (Shushan: City of the Persian Empire, Ulai: River in Elam). **3.** I lifted my eyes and saw a ram with two horns by the river. One horn was higher, and the higher one came up last. (Ram:

Male sheep) **4.** The ram pushed westward, northward, and southward, defeating all beasts, and became very strong. (Beasts: Animals, defeating: Beating) **5.** I then saw a goat from the west, moving across the earth without touching the ground. It had a large horn between its eyes. **6.** The goat attacked the ram with fury, and struck it down, breaking both its horns. (Fury: Anger, struck: Hit) **7.** The ram had no power to resist; it was cast down, trampled, and none could save it. (Trampled: Stomped on, resist: Fight back) **8.** The goat grew very powerful, but when strong, its great horn broke, and four smaller horns grew in its place. (Powerful: Strong, smaller horns: New leaders) **9.** From one of these horns, a little horn emerged, growing toward the south, east, and the "pleasant land" (Israel). (Little horn: New ruler, pleasant land: Israel) **10.** The little horn grew to challenge the host of heaven, casting down stars and trampling them. (Challenge: Fight, host of heaven: Angels) **11.** It even exalted itself against the prince of the host, removing the daily sacrifice and defiling the sanctuary. (Exalted: Raised up, prince of the host: God, defiling: Polluting) **12.** A host was given to it against the daily sacrifice because of sin, and it cast truth to the ground, prospering in its actions. (Host: Army, sin: Wrongdoing, prospering: Succeeding) **13.** I heard one saint ask another how long this vision would last—concerning the sacrifices, the desolation, and the trampling of the sanctuary and host. (Saint: Holy one, desolation: Destruction) **14.** He answered, "For 2,300 days; then the sanctuary will be cleansed." (Cleansed: Made pure) **15.** After seeing the vision, I, Daniel, sought its meaning. Then, I saw a man-like figure. (Meaning: Explanation, figure: Shape) **16.** A voice called from between the banks of the Ulai, saying, "Gabriel, explain the vision to this man." (Gabriel: Angel, Ulai: River) **17.** Gabriel approached, and I was afraid, falling on my face. He said, "Understand, son of man, the vision concerns the end times." (End times: Future judgment) **18.** While speaking, I fell into a deep sleep, but he touched me and set me upright. (Upright: Standing) **19.** He said, "I will explain the end of the indignation. The appointed time for the end is near." (Indignation: Anger, appointed: Set) **20.** The ram with two horns represents the kings of Media and Persia. (Media: Ancient empire, Persia: Ancient empire) **21.** The goat is the king of Greece, and the large horn is the first king. (Greece: Ancient kingdom, large horn: First ruler) **22.** When the large horn breaks, four kingdoms will rise from it, but without its power. (Kingdoms: Territories, power: Strength) **23.** In the latter part of their reign, when wickedness is at its peak, a fierce king will arise with dark understanding. (Wickedness: Evil, fierce: Cruel) **24.** His power will be great, but not by his own strength. He will destroy many and prosper in his actions, even against the holy people. (Prosper: Succeed, holy people: Israelites) **25.** Through his cunning, he will make deceit thrive. He will exalt himself and, through peace, destroy many, even opposing the Prince of princes, but he will be broken without human hands. (Cunning: Trickery, deceit: Lies, Prince of princes: God) **26.** The vision of the evening and the morning is true. Seal up the vision, for it concerns many days ahead. (Seal up: Keep secret, many days ahead: Far future) **27.** I, Daniel, fainted and was sick for days. Afterward, I resumed my duties for the king, astonished by the vision, though no one understood it. (Fainted: Lost strength, astonished: Surprised)

Chapter 9
1. In the first year of Darius, son of Ahasuerus, who became king over the Chaldeans; (Darius: king of the Medes, Ahasuerus: Persian king, Chaldeans: Babylonians) **2.** In the first year of his reign, I, Daniel, understood from the writings the number of years, according to the word of the LORD to Jeremiah the prophet, that He would complete seventy years of Jerusalem's desolation. (writings: books, desolation: destruction) **3.** So I turned to the Lord God, seeking Him in prayer and supplication, with fasting, sackcloth, and ashes. (supplication: humble request, sackcloth: rough cloth) **4.** I prayed to the LORD my God, confessing, "O Lord, great and awesome God, who keeps the covenant and shows mercy to those who love Him and obey His commands." (covenant: promise, mercy: compassion) **5.** We have sinned, acted wickedly, rebelled, and turned away from Your laws and judgments. (wickedly: immorally, rebelled: defied, judgments: decisions) **6.** We did not listen to Your prophets who spoke in Your name to our kings, princes, fathers, and all the people of the land. (prophets: messengers of God, princes: leaders) **7.** O Lord, righteousness belongs to You, but shame belongs to us, to the men of Judah, the people of Jerusalem, and to all Israel, near and far, in all the countries where You've scattered them, because of their sins against You. (righteousness: right action, shame: disgrace, Judah: southern kingdom of Israel, Jerusalem: capital city of Judah, Israel: nation of Israel) **8.** O Lord, shame belongs to us, to our kings, princes, and fathers, because we have sinned against You. (shame: disgrace, princes: leaders) **9.** To the Lord our God belong mercy and forgiveness, though we have rebelled against Him. (mercy: compassion, forgiveness: pardon) **10.** We have not obeyed the voice of the LORD our God to walk in His laws, which He gave through His prophets. (voice: command, laws: teachings) **11.** All Israel has broken Your law, turning away from obeying You; therefore, the curse is upon us, and the oath in the law of Moses has come true, because we have sinned against Him. (curse: punishment, oath: promise) **12.** He has fulfilled His words against us, and against our leaders, bringing great disaster upon us—nothing like this has happened to Jerusalem. (disaster: calamity) **13.** As written in the law of Moses, all this evil has come upon us, but we did not pray to the LORD our God to turn from our sins and understand Your truth. (evil: suffering, truth: wisdom) **14.** Therefore, the LORD has watched over the evil and brought it upon us, for the LORD our God is righteous in all He does, but we have not obeyed His voice. (evil: suffering, righteous: just) **15.** Now, O Lord our God, who brought Your people out of Egypt with a mighty hand, and earned renown, as today; we have sinned and done wickedly. (renown: fame, Egypt: land of slavery) **16.** O Lord, according to Your righteousness, turn away Your anger and fury from Jerusalem, Your holy mountain, because of our sins and our fathers' iniquities; Jerusalem and Your people have become a reproach to those around us. (righteousness: right action, fury: anger, iniquities: wrongdoings, Jerusalem: capital city of Judah, reproach: disgrace, mountain: Zion, sacred hill) **17.** Now, O our God, hear the prayer and supplications of Your servant, and let Your face shine on Your desolate sanctuary, for Your sake. (supplications: humble requests, sanctuary: temple, desolate: ruined) **18.** O my God, incline Your ear and hear; open Your eyes and see our desolations, and the city called by Your name. We do not present our supplications because of our righteousness, but because of Your great mercy. (desolations: ruin, supplications: requests) **19.** O Lord, hear; O Lord, forgive; O Lord, listen and act; delay not, for Your own sake, O my God, for Your city and Your people are called by Your name. (delay: wait) **20.** While I was praying, confessing my sin and the sin of my people Israel, and presenting my supplication for the holy mountain of my God; (supplication: humble request, Israel: nation of Israel) **21.** Gabriel, whom I had seen in the vision at the beginning, came swiftly and touched me about the time of the evening sacrifice. (Gabriel: angel) **22.** He informed me, speaking, "O Daniel, I have now come to give you insight and understanding. (insight: wisdom, understanding: knowledge) **23.** At the start of your supplications, the command went out, and I have come to tell you, for you are greatly loved; therefore, consider the matter and understand the vision." (supplications: humble requests) **24.** Seventy weeks are determined for your people and your holy city, to finish transgression, put an end to sin, make atonement for iniquity, bring in everlasting righteousness, seal up the vision and prophecy, and anoint the Most Holy. (weeks: periods of seven years, atonement: reconciliation, iniquity: sin, righteousness: right action, Most Holy: sacred person/place) **25.** Know that from the issuing of the decree to restore and build Jerusalem to the Messiah the Prince, there will be seven weeks and sixty-two weeks. The street and wall will be rebuilt, even in troubled times. (decree: order, Messiah: anointed one, Prince: leader, Jerusalem: city, troubled: difficult) **26.** After sixty-two weeks, the Messiah will be cut off, but not for Himself. The people of the prince to come will destroy the city and the sanctuary, and its end will come in a flood. War and desolations are determined. (cut off: killed, prince: leader, desolations: ruin) **27.** He will confirm a covenant with many for one week, and in the middle of the week, He will put an end to sacrifice and offering. Because of abominations, He will make the sanctuary desolate, until the end, when judgment will be poured out on the desolate. (covenant: promise, sanctuary: temple, desolate: ruined, judgment: punishment)

Chapter 10
1. In the third year of King Cyrus of Persia, a revelation was given to Daniel (called Belteshazzar). The message was true, but it concerned a distant time; he understood it and the vision. (Cyrus : Persian king) **2.** At that time, I, Daniel, mourned for three weeks. **3.** I ate no tasty food, drank no wine, and didn't anoint myself until the three weeks were over. (rub oil on) **4.** On the 24th day of the first month, I was by the Tigris River. (Hiddekel: a river in Mesopotamia) **5.** I looked up and saw a man in linen, with a belt of fine gold from Uphaz. (Uphaz: a region known for fine gold) **6.** His body shone like beryl, his face like lightning, his eyes like flaming torches, and his arms and legs like polished bronze. His voice sounded like a crowd. (beryl: a precious stone) **7.** I, Daniel, alone saw the vision; the men with me didn't see it, but they trembled and fled. **8.** I was left alone, weak from the vision, my strength drained, and I fell into a weakened state. **9.** I heard his words and, overwhelmed, I fell into a deep sleep with my face on the ground. **10.** A hand touched me, lifting me to my hands and knees. **11.** He said, "Daniel, greatly loved, understand the words I speak. Stand up, for I've been sent to you." I stood, trembling. **12.** He reassured me, "Don't fear, Daniel. From the first day you sought understanding and humbled yourself before God, your words were heard, and I've come because of them." (humbled yourself: showed sorrow) **13.** "But

the prince of Persia opposed me for 21 days, until Michael, one of the chief princes, came to help. Now I've stayed with the Persian kings." (prince of Persia: a spiritual ruler of Persia) **14.** "I've come to explain what will happen to your people in the future, for the vision concerns a long time ahead." (your people: the Jews) **15.** After he said this, I bowed with my face to the ground and became speechless. **16.** Then someone like a man touched my lips, and I spoke, saying, "My lord, the vision has overwhelmed me, and I have no strength left." **17.** "How can I, your servant, speak to you? I have no strength or breath left in me." **18.** Again, one who looked like a man touched me and gave me strength. **19.** He said, "Don't fear, Daniel. Peace be to you. Be strong!" As he spoke, I felt strength return and said, "Let my lord speak, for you have strengthened me." **20.** He asked, "Do you know why I've come to you? Now I must return to fight against the prince of Persia. When I leave, the prince of Greece will come." (prince of Greece: a spiritual ruler of Greece) **21.** "But I will tell you what is written in the book of truth. No one supports me except Michael, your prince." (Michael: a spiritual ruler of Israel)

Chapter 11

1. In the first year of Darius the Mede, I stood to confirm and strengthen him. (Darius the Mede: a Persian king) **2.** Now I will reveal the truth: Three kings will rise in Persia, and the fourth will be wealthier than them all; through his riches, he will provoke all against Greece. (Persia: ancient empire, Greece: ancient civilization) **3.** A mighty king will rise, ruling with great power, doing as he pleases. (Mighty king: a very powerful ruler) **4.** His kingdom will be broken and divided to the four winds; not to his heirs or as he ruled, but to others. (Four winds: all directions, heirs: his children or descendants) **5.** The southern king will be strong, as will one of his princes, who will surpass him in power. (Southern king: ruler of Egypt) **6.** In time, they will unite; the southern king's daughter will marry the northern king for peace, but she will fail him. (Northern king: ruler of the Seleucid Empire) **7.** A branch from her roots will rise and defeat the northern king's fortress. (Branch: a descendant or offshoot) **8.** He will take captives and treasures to Egypt, and outlive the northern king. (Egypt: ancient kingdom in the south) **9.** The southern king will return to his land. (Land: territory of Egypt) **10.** His sons will gather great forces, but one will break through and return to his fortress. (Forces: military troops) **11.** The southern king will angrily fight the northern king; the northern king's forces will be defeated. (Angrily: with great anger) **12.** After his victory, the southern king will be prideful, but his strength will fade. (Prideful: arrogant or self-important) **13.** The northern king will return with an even greater army and more riches. (Army: soldiers) **14.** Many will oppose the southern king, including thieves among your people, but they will fail. (Thieves: robbers) **15.** The northern king will attack, taking the fortified cities, and the southern defense will crumble. (Fortified cities: cities with strong defenses) **16.** The northern king will conquer at will, even the glorious land, consuming it. (Glorious land: possibly referring to Israel or Judea) **17.** He will use his full strength to conquer, offering the daughter of women in marriage, but she will betray him. (Daughter of women: a princess, likely referring to a royal marriage) **18.** He will turn to the islands, winning many, but a prince will stop his reproach. (Islands: distant lands or territories, Prince: a ruler or leader) **19.** He will turn back to his land, but he will stumble and fall. (Stumble: to trip or fall) **20.** A tax raiser will rise in his place, but will quickly be destroyed, not in anger or battle. (Tax raiser: a person who imposes taxes) **21.** A vile man will take his place, gaining the kingdom by deception. (Vile: wicked or immoral) **22.** His forces will overflow, breaking the covenant with the prince. (Overflow: overpower, Covenant: agreement, Prince: a ruler) **23.** After a pact, he will betray, growing strong with a small group. (Pact: agreement) **24.** He will peacefully take the richest provinces, spoiling them and planning against strongholds for a time. (Richest provinces: wealthiest areas, Spoiling: looting or taking) **25.** He will fight the southern king with a great army, but the southern king's forces will be defeated by trickery. (Trickery: deception) **26.** His own forces will betray him, and many will fall. (Betray: to deceive or turn against) **27.** Both kings will plot evil and lie, but the end will come at the appointed time. (Plot: plan, Appointed time: the preordained moment) **28.** He will return with great wealth, but his heart will turn against the holy covenant. (Holy covenant: sacred agreement, possibly referring to God's covenant with Israel) **29.** He will return at the appointed time, but it will not be as before. (Appointed time: predestined moment) **30.** The ships of Chittim will oppose him, causing him grief, and he will turn to those who forsake the covenant. (Chittim: ancient lands, possibly referring to Cyprus) **31.** His forces will desecrate the sanctuary and abolish the daily sacrifice, placing the abomination that causes desolation. (Sanctuary: holy place, Abomination: a great evil) **32.** He will corrupt those who break the covenant with flatteries, but those who know their God will stand firm. (Flatteries: insincere praise) **33.** The wise will teach many, but they will suffer, even by sword and fire. (Wise: knowledgeable, Sword and fire: forms of execution or persecution) **34.** Some will receive little help, but many will join them in deception. (Deception: trickery) **35.** Some of the wise will fall to purify and refine them until the end, for the time is appointed. (Purify: cleanse, Refine: improve or purify) **36.** The king will act according to his will, exalting himself above all gods, speaking against the God of gods, prospering until the determined end. (Exalting: elevating, God of gods: supreme deity) **37.** He will disregard the God of his fathers, desiring no women, and magnify himself above all gods. (Desiring no women: possibly celibate or rejecting women) **38.** He will honor the god of forces with wealth, and increase his glory with treasures. (God of forces: a powerful or military god, Wealth: riches) **39.** He will strengthen his control with this strange god and divide the land for gain. (Strange god: an unfamiliar or foreign deity) **40.** At the end, the southern king will oppose him, and the northern king will come like a whirlwind, overwhelming many lands. (Whirlwind: a violent storm or attack) **41.** He will enter the glorious land, overthrowing many nations, but Edom, Moab, and Ammon will escape. (Edom, Moab, Ammon: regions in ancient Israel, now part of modern-day Jordan) **42.** He will stretch his hand over many countries, and Egypt will not escape. (Stretch his hand: extend his control) **43.** He will control Egypt's treasures, and Libya and Ethiopia will follow him. (Libya, Ethiopia: regions in Africa) **44.** News from the east and north will trouble him, and he will retaliate with fury, destroying many. (Retaliate: to get revenge) **45.** He will set his palace between the seas, but will meet his end, with no one to help him. (Palace between the seas: likely refers to the Holy Land or Jerusalem, situated between the Mediterranean and Dead Seas)

Chapter 12

1. At that time, Michael the great prince will rise up, protecting your people. There will be a time of trouble like never before, but your people will be saved, all whose names are in the book. (Michael: an archangel, prince: leader, saved: delivered, trouble: distress) **2.** Many who sleep in the dust will awake: some to eternal life, others to shame and eternal contempt. (awake: rise, eternal: forever, contempt: disgrace) **3.** The wise will shine like the sky, and those who lead many to righteousness will shine like stars forever. (righteousness: justice, shine: glow, wise: discerning) **4.** But you, Daniel, close the book until the end. Many will wander, and knowledge will grow. (Daniel: a prophet, wander: roam, grow: increase) **5.** Then I saw two others, one on each side of the riverbank. (riverbank: edge of the river) **6.** One asked the man in linen on the river, "How long until the end of these wonders?" (linen: cloth, wonders: marvels, end: conclusion) **7.** The man in linen raised both hands to heaven and swore it would be for a time, times, and half a time. When the scattering of the holy people is complete, everything will end. (swore: vowed, scattering: dispersing, complete: finished) **8.** I heard, but did not understand. I asked, "What will be the end of these things?" (understand: comprehend) **9.** He answered, "Go on, Daniel. The words are sealed until the end." (sealed: closed, end: conclusion) **10.** Many will be purified, made clean, and tested; but the wicked will continue their ways, and they won't understand. The wise will understand. (purified: cleansed, wicked: evil, tested: tried) **11.** From the time the daily sacrifice is removed and the abomination that causes desolation is set up, there will be 1,290 days. (Sacrifice: offering, abomination: defilement, desolation: destruction) **12.** Blessed is he who waits and reaches 1,335 days. (waits: endures, blessed: happy) **13.** But go on till the end. You will rest and rise at the end of days. (rest: sleep, rise: stand, end of days: final period)

28 – Hosea

Chapter 1

1. The message from the LORD that came to Chapter, the son of Beeri, during the reigns of Uzziah, Jotham, Ahaz, and Hezekiah, kings of Judah, and Jeroboam, the son of Joash, king of Israel. (Uzziah, Jotham, Ahaz, Hezekiah: kings of Judah; Jeroboam: a king of Israel) **2.** The beginning of the word of the LORD through Chapter. The LORD instructed Chapter to marry a woman who had been unfaithful, and to have children from such a woman, for the land of Israel has been unfaithful to God, turning away from Him. (unfaithful: disloyal) **3.** So Chapter obeyed and married Gomer, the daughter of Diblaim. She became pregnant and gave him a son. **4.** The LORD told him, "Name him Jezreel, for in a little while I will punish the house of Jehu for the bloodshed at Jezreel, and I will bring an end to the kingdom of Israel." (Jezreel: a place associated with the bloodshed caused by Jehu) **5.** On that day, I will break Israel's military strength in the valley of Jezreel. (military strength: the power or ability to fight, usually referring to an army) **6.** Gomer became pregnant again and had a daughter. The LORD instructed Chapter to name her Lo-ruhamah, which means "not loved," because He would no longer show mercy to the house of Israel but would completely remove them. (Lo-ruhamah: meaning "not loved," showing a lack of mercy) **7.** However, I will have compassion on the house of Judah. I will save them, not by military power, but by the LORD their God, and they will not be saved by bow, sword, or battle, nor by horses or horsemen. (compassion: deep sympathy and concern for others; bow: a weapon used to shoot arrows) **8.** After she had weaned Lo-ruhamah, Gomer became pregnant once more and had a son. (weaned: no longer nursing from the mother) **9.** God told him to name the child Lo-ammi, which means "not my people," because Israel was no longer God's people, and He would not be their God. (Lo-ammi: meaning "not my people") **10.** Yet, the number of the people of Israel will be as countless as the grains of sand by the sea, which cannot be measured. In the place where it was said to them, "You are not my people," it will be said, "You are the children of the living God." (countless: too many to be counted) **11.** Then the people of Judah and the people of Israel will be united, appointing one leader, and they will return from the land. The day of Jezreel will be great. (united: brought together; appointing: choosing; Jezreel: a place of significance)

Chapter 2

1. Say to your brothers, "Ammi" (meaning "my people"), and to your sisters, "Ru-hamah" (meaning "she has received mercy"). (Ammi: my people; Ru-hamah: she has received mercy) **2.** Plead with your mother; plead with her! She is not my wife, and I am not her husband. Let her remove her unfaithfulness from her sight and stop committing adultery. (Adultery: infidelity in marriage) **3.** Otherwise, I will strip her bare, leaving her as she was on the day she was born, and make her desolate like a desert, and cause her to die of thirst. (strip her bare: expose her completely; desolate: abandoned, empty) **4.** I will not show mercy to her children, because they are the children of unfaithfulness. (unfaithfulness: disloyalty, betrayal) **5.** Their mother has been unfaithful. She who conceived them has done shamefully, for she said, "I will go after my lovers, who give me my food and water, my wool and linen, my oil and drink." (conceived: became pregnant; shamefully: in a dishonorable way; lovers: those who she pursued instead of being faithful) **6.** Therefore, I will block her way with thorns, and I will build a wall around her so that she cannot find her paths. (block her way: prevent her from continuing; thorns: sharp, prickly plants; paths: ways or directions) **7.** She will chase after her lovers but will not catch them. She will search for them but will not find them. Then she will say, "I will return to my first husband, for it was better for me then than it is now." (chase after: pursue; lovers: false gods or people) **8.** She does not realize that it was I who gave her the grain, wine, and oil, and that I multiplied her silver and gold, which she used to make offerings to Baal. (Baal: a false god worshiped in Canaan) **9.** Therefore, I will return and take back my grain in its season, and my wine in its time. I will take away my wool and linen, which were meant to cover her nakedness. (grain: harvested crops; wool and linen: materials used for clothing) **10.** I will expose her shame before her lovers, and no one will rescue her from my hand. (expose: make visible; shame: dishonor) **11.** I will put an end to her celebrations, her feasts, new moon festivals, sabbaths, and all her appointed festivals. (end: stop; celebrations: special events, feasts; sabbaths: days of rest and worship) **12.** I will destroy her vines and fig trees, which she thought were the rewards given to her by her lovers. I will turn them into a forest, and wild animals will eat them. (destroy: completely ruin; vines and fig trees: symbols of prosperity; rewards: things given in exchange for loyalty) **13.** I will punish her for the days when she worshiped the Baals, when she burned incense to them, adorned herself with jewelry, and went after her lovers, forgetting me, declares the LORD. (worshiped: gave religious devotion; Baals: false gods; incense: a substance burned for fragrance) **14.** Therefore, I will woo her by bringing her into the wilderness, and speak tenderly to her. (woo: attract, entice; wilderness: a barren or desolate place) **15.** There I will give her back her vineyards, and the valley of Achor (meaning "trouble") will become a door of hope. There she will respond as in the days of her youth, as in the day when she came up from Egypt. (Achor: "trouble"; vineyards: land where grapes grow) **16.** In that day, declares the LORD, you will call me "Ishi" (meaning "my husband") and no longer call me "Baali" (meaning "my master"). (Ishi: my husband; Baali: my master) **17.** I will remove the names of the Baals from her lips, and she will no longer remember them by name. (remove: take away; Baals: false gods) **18.** In that day I will make a covenant for them with the animals of the field, the birds in the sky, and the creatures that crawl on the ground. I will break the bow, sword, and battle from the earth, and make them lie down safely. (covenant: a formal agreement; break: destroy; bow, sword, and battle: instruments of war) **19.** I will betroth you to me forever; I will betroth you to me in righteousness, justice, love, and compassion. (betroth: engage in a promise of marriage; righteousness: moral correctness; justice: fairness) **20.** I will betroth you to me in faithfulness, and you will know the LORD. (faithfulness: loyalty) **21.** In that day, I will answer, declares the LORD. I will answer the heavens, and they will answer the earth. (answer: respond) **22.** The earth will respond to the grain, the wine, and the oil, and they will respond to Jezreel. (grain: crops; wine: fermented juice; oil: olive oil) **23.** I will sow her for myself in the land. I will have compassion on the one who was not loved. I will say to those who were not my people, "You are my people," and they will respond, "You are our God." (sow: plant seeds; compassion: pity; not loved: rejected)

Chapter 3

1. The LORD said to me, "Go love a woman cherished by her lover, yet unfaithful, as I love the children of Israel, who worship other gods and delight in wine." (Unfaithful : adulteress; worship other gods : idol worship) **2.** I bought her for fifteen silver coins, a bushel of barley, and half a bushel of barley. (Bushel : unit of grain measurement) **3.** I told her, "You will stay with me for many days, not acting as a prostitute or being with any other man. I will also be faithful to you." (Prostitute : harlot) **4.** Israel will live for many days without a king, leader, sacrifices, idols, ephods (garments for guidance), and teraphim (household idols). (Ephod : sacred garment; Teraphim : small idols) **5.** Then, Israel will return, seek the LORD and David their king, and experience His goodness in the future.

Chapter 4

1. Listen to the LORD, O Israel, for He has a dispute with those in the land. There is no truth, mercy, or knowledge of God. (Dispute : controversy) **2.** Through swearing, lying, murder, stealing, and adultery, they break all bounds, and bloodshed follows. **3.** The land will mourn, and all will suffer, including animals and birds; even fish will disappear. (Mourn : grieve; Suffer : languish) **4.** Let no one argue, for your people are like those who contend with the priest. **5.** You will fall by day, and the prophet at night. I will destroy your mother. **6.** My people are destroyed for lack of knowledge. Since you reject knowledge, I will reject you as priests and forget your children. **7.** The more they increased, the more they sinned, and I will turn their glory into shame. **8.** They feed on the sin of my people and set their hearts on wickedness. (Wickedness : iniquity) **9.** Like people, like priests—so I will punish them for their deeds. **10.** They will eat but not be satisfied. They will commit spiritual adultery but will not increase, for they have abandoned the LORD. (Spiritual adultery : unfaithfulness to God) **11.** Prostitution, wine, and new wine take away their understanding. **12.** They consult idols (stocks) and seek guidance from their staff (symbols of false hope). The spirit of prostitution has led them astray. (Stocks : idols; Staff : divining idols) **13.** They sacrifice on mountaintops, burn incense under trees, and their daughters commit prostitution. **14.** I will not punish your daughters for prostitution, nor your brides for adultery. For the men go aside with harlots and offer sacrifices with prostitutes. Therefore, those without understanding will fall. **15.** Though Israel acts as a prostitute, let Judah not sin and avoid Gilgal or Beth-aven (House of Vanity). (Beth-aven : place of idol worship) **16.** Israel is stubborn like a heifer. The LORD will feed them like a lamb in an open field. (Heifer : young cow; Stubborn : rebellious) **17.** Ephraim is joined to idols; let him alone. **18.** Their wine has soured; they continually commit spiritual adultery. Their rulers love shameful things. **19.** The wind has wrapped her in its wings, and they will be ashamed of their sacrifices. (Sacrifices : acts of idolatry)

Chapter 5

1. Hear, O priests and people of Israel, for judgment is upon you. You have been a snare at Mizpah and a net at Tabor. (Snare: trap) **2.** The rebels deepen their corruption, despite my corrections. (Rebels: revolvers) **3.** I know Ephraim, and Israel is not hidden from me. Ephraim commits prostitution, and Israel is defiled. **4.** They will not turn to God, for the spirit of prostitution is within them, and they do not know the LORD. **5.** Israel's pride testifies against them. Therefore, Israel and Ephraim will fall in their sin; Judah will fall too. (Testifies: bears witness) **6.** They will seek the LORD with their flocks, but will not find Him, for He has withdrawn from them. **7.** They have dealt treacherously with the LORD and given birth to illegitimate children. Now a month will consume them. (Illegitimate: unlawful children) **8.** Blow the trumpet in Gibeah, and the horn in Ramah; cry aloud at Beth-aven. After you, O Benjamin! **9.** Ephraim will be desolate in the day of rebuke. I have declared what will surely happen to the tribes of Israel. **10.** The rulers of Judah remove the boundaries. Therefore, I will pour my wrath upon them. **11.** Ephraim is oppressed and broken by judgment, as he followed human commands. **12.** I will be like a moth to Ephraim, and rot to Judah. **13.** When Ephraim saw his sickness, he sought help from Assyria, but could not be healed. **14.** I will be like a lion to Ephraim, like a young lion to Judah. I will tear and leave; none shall rescue them. **15.** I will return to my place until they acknowledge their guilt and seek my face. In their distress, they will seek me early.

Chapter 6

1. Let us return to the LORD. He has wounded us, but He will heal us; He has struck us, but He will bind our wounds. (Bind: wrap up) **2.** After two days, He will revive us; on the third day, He will raise us up, and we will live in His presence. (Revive: bring back to life) **3.** Then we will truly know the LORD; He will come to us like rain, like the spring and autumn rains. (Autumn rains: second rainy season) **4.** Ephraim and Judah, what shall I do with you? Your goodness fades like the morning mist. (Mist: fine spray of water vapor) **5.** I have sent prophets and spoken through My words, and My judgments are clear. (Judgments: decisions from God) **6.** I desire mercy, not sacrifices, and knowledge of God more than burnt offerings. (Mercy: compassion; burnt offerings: sacrifices) **7.** But they have broken the covenant and betrayed Me. (Betrayed: violated loyalty) **8.** Gilead is a city of evil deeds, stained with blood. (Stained: made unclean) **9.** Like robbers ambushing a man, priests murder in the way; they commit vile acts. (Vile: wicked) **10.** I have seen terrible sin in Israel; Ephraim is defiled. (Defiled: impure) **11.** Judah, a harvest is set for you when I restore my people. (Harvest: judgment or reward)

Chapter 7
1. When I would heal Israel, Ephraim's sin was revealed, and the wickedness of Samaria: they lie, steal, and rob. (Wicked: morally wrong) **2.** They do not consider their actions; I remember their sins, and they are before me. (Actions: deeds) **3.** They make the king glad with their wickedness, and the princes with their lies. (Glad: pleased) **4.** They are all adulterers, like a furnace heated by the baker. (Adulterers: those who break vows) **5.** The princes have made the king ill with wine; he mocks. (Mock: ridicules) **6.** Their hearts are like an oven, waiting to burn; their baker sleeps through the night. (Baker: one who makes bread?) **7.** They devour their judges, and all their kings fall; none call on me. (Devour: destroy) **8.** Ephraim is like a half-baked cake. (Half-baked: not fully formed) **9.** Strangers consume his strength, and he doesn't realize it. (Strangers: foreign nations) **10.** Israel's pride testifies against them, yet they do not return to the LORD. (Testifies: proves) **11.** Ephraim is like a senseless dove, calling Egypt and Assyria for help. (Senseless: foolish) **12.** I will spread My net over them and punish them. (Punish: impose penalty) **13.** Woe to them for fleeing from Me; though I redeemed them, they lied against Me. (Redeemed: saved) **14.** They do not cry out to Me with all their heart, but rebel when they gather for food. (Rebel: resist authority) **15.** I strengthened them, but they imagine evil against Me. (Strengthened: made strong) **16.** They return, but not to the Most High; their rulers will fall by the sword. (Return: come back)

Chapter 8
1. Blow the trumpet! He will come like an eagle against the house of the LORD because they have broken My covenant and disobeyed My law. (Disobeyed: violated) **2.** Israel will cry to Me, "We know You, our God!" (Cry: call out in distress) **3.** Israel has rejected what is good, and the enemy will pursue him. (Rejected: cast off) **4.** They set up kings and princes not by Me; they made idols with their silver and gold. (Idols: false gods) **5.** Your calf, Samaria, will be destroyed; My anger burns against them. (Calf: false god statue) **6.** It was made by a craftsman, not by God; it will be broken. (Craftsman: skilled worker) **7.** They sow the wind and reap the whirlwind; their crops will fail and be consumed. (Sown: planted; whirlwind: violent storm) **8.** Israel is consumed and will be among the nations like a worthless vessel. (Consumed: destroyed) **9.** Ephraim has gone up to Assyria, like a wild donkey alone; he has hired lovers. (Wild donkey: undomesticated animal) **10.** Though they hire nations, I will gather them, and they will sorrow for the king's burden. (Sorrow: feel sadness) **11.** Ephraim has many altars to sin; altars will become places for sin. (Altars: places of worship) **12.** I wrote to them the great things of My law, but they considered it foreign. (Foreign: strange or unfamiliar) **13.** They offer sacrifices but eat the meat themselves; the LORD will not accept them. (Offer: present; sacrifices: offerings) **14.** Israel has forgotten his Maker and built temples; Judah has built fortified cities, but I will send fire upon their cities. (Forgotten: failed to remember; fortified: protected)

Chapter 9
1. Do not rejoice, Israel, as other nations do; you have strayed from God, chasing after rewards like grain. (Rewards: benefits or gains) **2.** The grain and winepress will not satisfy them, and the wine will fail. (Winepress: a place where grapes are crushed to make wine) **3.** They will not stay in the land of the LORD; Ephraim will return to Egypt and eat unclean things in Assyria. (Unclean: impure) **4.** Their sacrifices will be like mourners' bread; anyone who eats will be defiled. (Defiled: made impure) **5.** What will you do on the day of the LORD's feast? (Feast: a religious celebration) **6.** Egypt will gather them; their pleasant places will be overtaken by thorns. (Thorns: sharp-pointed plants) **7.** Judgment has come; Israel will know it. The prophet is seen as a fool because of their great sin. (Judgment: God's decision or punishment; Fool: lacking wisdom) **8.** The watchman of Ephraim is trapped by idols in God's house. (Watchman: a person who watches over others; Idols: false gods or images of worship) **9.** They are deeply corrupt like the days of Gibeah, and God will punish their sin. (Corrupt: morally wrong; Gibeah: a place in Israel known for sin) **10.** I found Israel like ripe grapes in the wilderness, but they turned to Baal-peor and their evil deeds followed. (Baal-peor: a false god worshiped by the Israelites) **11.** Ephraim's glory will vanish like a bird, from birth to conception. (Glory: honor, dignity) **12.** Even though they raise children, I will cause them to lose them. (Raise: bring up or nurture) **13.** Ephraim, like Tyre, is planted in a fertile place, but will lead their children to death. (Tyre: a wealthy city; Fertile: rich in nutrients) **14.** Give them a barren womb and dry breasts. (Barren: unable to bear children) **15.** Their wickedness in Gilgal makes God reject them. (Wickedness: evil deeds; Gilgal: a place associated with sin) **16.** Ephraim is struck down, their roots dried up, and they will bear no fruit. (Roots: the origin or source of something) **17.** My God will reject them because they did not listen, and they will wander among the nations. (Wander: move aimlessly)

Chapter 10
1. Israel is like a vine that grows for its own gain; the more they increase, the more idols they make. (Idols: false gods or images of worship) **2.** Their hearts are divided; they will be found guilty. (Divided: torn between conflicting choices) **3.** They will say, "We have no king because we did not fear the LORD." (Fear: reverence or respect) **4.** They made false oaths, and judgment will grow like poison. (Oaths: promises or vows; Judgment: God's decision or punishment) **5.** The people of Samaria will fear the calves of Beth-aven, mourning over it because its glory has departed. (Calves: idols shaped like young cows; Glory: honor, dignity) **6.** It will be taken to Assyria as a gift to King Jareb. (Assyria: an empire that conquered Israel) **7.** Samaria's king will be like foam on the water. (Foam: bubbles or froth on the surface of water) **8.** The high places of Aven will be destroyed, and thorns will grow on their altars. (High places: locations used for idol worship) **9.** Israel, you have sinned since Gibeah. (Sinned: committed wrongdoings) **10.** I will punish them, and the people will gather against them. (Punish: inflict a penalty) **11.** Ephraim is like a trained heifer, but I will put a yoke on her neck. (Heifer: a young cow; Yoke: a wooden frame placed on animals) **12.** Sow righteousness and seek the LORD until He comes and rains righteousness upon you. (Sow: plant seeds; Righteousness: moral correctness) **13.** You have reaped iniquity because you trusted in your way and your warriors. (Reaped: gathered the result; Iniquity: immoral actions) **14.** A great uproar will arise among your people, and your fortresses will be destroyed. (Uproar: noise or chaos; Fortresses: strongholds or defenses) **15.** Bethel will do the same to you because of your wickedness, and the king of Israel will be cut off in the morning. (Wickedness: evil deeds)

Chapter 11
1. When Israel was young, I loved him and called him out of Egypt, like a father calling his son. (Egypt: a land of captivity or oppression) **2.** But the more they were called, the more they turned away from me. They sacrificed to Baal and burned incense to idols. (Baal: a false god worshiped by the Canaanites; incense: fragrant smoke burned in worship)**3.** I taught Ephraim to walk, holding their hands, but they did not realize it was I who healed them. (Ephraim: a tribe of Israel, often representing the northern kingdom) **4.** I led them with kindness, like a loving person taking off the yoke from their necks, feeding them and caring for them. (Yoke: a wooden bar used to control animals)**5.** They will not return to Egypt, but Assyria will be their king, because they refused to return to me. (Assyria: the empire that would eventually conquer Israel)**6.** The sword will strike their cities, consuming their leaders and destroying them because of their own plans. (Sword: a symbol of destruction or judgment) **7.** My people are bent on turning away from me. Though they call to the Most High, no one exalts Him. (Most High: a title for God, emphasizing His supremacy) **8.** How can I give you up, Ephraim? How can I hand you over, Israel? How can I treat you like Admah or Zeboim? My heart is torn within me; my compassion for you burns. (Admah and Zeboim: cities destroyed with Sodom and Gomorrah)**9.** I will not unleash the full fury of my anger; I will not destroy Ephraim again. For I am God, not a mere man. The Holy One is among you, and I will not come in wrath. (Wrath: intense anger) **10.** They will follow the LORD; He will roar like a lion. When He roars, even the children will tremble, especially those from the west.(Tremble: to shake or fear) **11.** They will shake like birds coming from Egypt, like doves from Assyria. I will settle them in their homes, says the LORD. (Shake: to be afraid; Egypt and Assyria symbolize places of exile) **12.** Ephraim surrounds me with lies, and Israel with deceit. But Judah still walks with God, and is faithful to the saints.(Saints: holy ones or faithful followers of God)

Chapter 12
1. Ephraim feeds on wind, following the east wind. He constantly multiplies lies and destruction. He has made alliances with Assyria and brought oil to Egypt.(Feeds on wind: engaging in empty pursuits; alliances: agreements or partnerships)**2.** The LORD has a controversy with Judah, and He will punish Jacob for his deeds. He will repay him according to his actions.(Controversy: a dispute or judgment)**3.** In the womb, he grasped his brother's heel; by his strength, he wrestled with God.(Jacob: the ancestor of Israel, who fought with God and his brother Esau)**4.** He struggled with the angel and won. He cried and begged for mercy, and he found God at Bethel, where God spoke

with us.(Angel: a messenger from God; Bethel: a sacred place where Jacob had an encounter with God) **5.** Even the LORD God of hosts, the LORD, is his memorial. (God of hosts: the Almighty, ruler of all armies) **6.** So you must return to your God, practice mercy and justice, and always wait on your God.(Mercy: compassion and kindness; justice: fairness and right action) **7.** He is a merchant with false balances in his hands. He loves to cheat people. (Merchant: a trader; false balances: dishonest scales used to cheat in trade) **8.** Ephraim says, "I've become wealthy; I have found prosperity." In all my work, no sin can be found. (Prosperity: success or abundance; sin: moral wrongdoing) **9.** I am the LORD your God, who brought you out of Egypt. I will make you live in tents again, as in the days of the festival. (Festival: a time of religious celebration) **10.** I spoke through the prophets, gave many visions, and used parables to teach through them. (Parables: short stories used to teach lessons) **11.** Is there guilt in Gilead? Yes, they are worthless. They sacrifice bulls in Gilgal; their altars are like piles of stones in the fields. (Gilead and Gilgal: places of idol worship and false sacrifice) **12.** Jacob fled to Syria, and there Israel served for a wife, and kept sheep for her. (Syria: a region to the north, where Jacob fled; served for a wife: reference to Jacob working for Rachel) **13.** By a prophet the LORD brought Israel out of Egypt, and by a prophet he was protected. (Prophet: one who speaks for God) **14.** Ephraim has provoked God to great anger, so his blood will remain on him, and his disgrace will return upon him. (Provoked: angered; blood: a symbol of guilt)

Chaper13
1. When Ephraim spoke, people trembled, but when he sinned by worshiping Baal, he died. (Baal: a false god)**2.** Now they sin more and more, making silver idols according to their own ideas. They say to those who sacrifice, "Kiss the calves." (Idols: false gods made of silver; calves: a symbol of idol worship) **3.** Therefore, they will be like the morning mist, or the early dew that vanishes, like chaff blown by the wind, or smoke from a chimney.(Chaff: husks separated from grain, symbolizing worthlessness) **4.** I am the LORD your God, who brought you out of Egypt. You will have no god but me, for there is no savior besides me. (Savior: a deliverer or rescuer) **5.** I knew you in the wilderness, in a land of severe drought. (Drought: a prolonged period without rain) **6.** As they fed, they became satisfied; their hearts became proud, and they forgot me. (Proud: self-exalted; satisfied: content, with needs met) **7.** Therefore, I will be like a lion to them, and like a leopard along the way I will watch. (Leopard: a swift and dangerous animal) **8.** I will confront them like a bear who has lost her cubs, tearing open their hearts. I will devour them like a lion; wild animals will destroy them. (Heart: symbol of emotions and soul; devour: to destroy) **9.** Israel, you have destroyed yourself, but your help is found in me. (Help: rescue or deliverance) **10.** I will be your king. Where is any other that can save you in all your cities? Where are your kings and princes whom you once asked for?(Princes: rulers or leaders) **11.** I gave you a king in my anger and took him away in my wrath. (Wrath: intense anger)**12.** The guilt of Ephraim is bound up, his sin is hidden. (Bound up: stored up, kept; hidden: covered or concealed) **13.** The pain of a woman in labor will come upon him. He is an unwise son who does not know when to leave the place of childbirth. (Unwise: lacking wisdom or understanding) **14.** I will ransom them from the power of the grave; I will redeem them from death. Death, I will be your plagues; Grave, I will be your destruction. Compassion will be hidden from my eyes. (Ransom: to buy back; Redeem: to rescue or save; Plagues: disasters) **15.** Though he is fruitful among his brothers, an east wind will come, the wind of the LORD from the wilderness. His spring will become dry, and his well will dry up. He will spoil the treasures of every good vessel.(Fruitful: productive; east wind: a destructive wind from the desert) **16.** Samaria will be destroyed because she rebelled against her God. They will fall by the sword, their infants dashed to pieces, and their pregnant women ripped open. (Samaria: the capital city of Israel; ripped open: a horrific punishment)

Chapter 14
1. Return to the LORD your God, for you have stumbled because of your sin. (Stumbled: fallen or failed) **2.** Take words with you and return to the LORD. Say to Him, "Forgive all our sins and accept us graciously, that we may offer the fruit of our lips."(Fruit of lips: prayers or vows)**3.** Assyria will not save us; we will not rely on horses. We will no longer say, "Our gods" to the work of our hands, for in you the fatherless find mercy. (Assyria: a foreign empire; fatherless: orphans, symbolizing those in need) **4.** I will heal their waywardness and love them freely, for my anger has turned away from them. (Waywardness: rebelliousness or wandering; freely: without reservation) **5.** I will be like the dew to Israel. He will blossom like a lily and take root like the cedars of Lebanon. (Dew: refreshing moisture; cedars of Lebanon: strong, resilient trees) **6.** His branches will spread and his beauty will be like the olive tree, and his fragrance like the cedars of Lebanon. (Fragrance: pleasant smell) **7.** Those who live in his shadow will return. They will be revived like the grain and grow like the vine; his scent will be like the wine of Lebanon. (Revived: restored or made alive) **8.** Ephraim will say, "What have I to do with idols anymore? I have answered and observed Him; I am like a flourishing cypress tree. From me comes your fruit." (Idols: false gods; flourishing: thriving)**9.** Who is wise? Let them understand these things. Who is prudent? Let them know them. For the ways of the LORD are right, and the righteous walk in them, but the rebellious stumble in them.(Prudent: wise and careful; stumble: fall or falter)

29 – Joel
Chapter 1
1. The word of the LORD came to Joel, son of Pethuel. **2.** Listen, elders and all people of the land: Has this happened in your time or your ancestors' days? (Elders: older people, ancestors: family members from the past) **3.** Tell your children, and let them pass it on to the next generation. **4.** What the palmerworm (small caterpillar) left, the locust ate; what the locust left, the cankerworm (another type of insect) ate; and what the cankerworm left, the caterpillar ate. **5.** Wake up, you drunkards, and weep; mourn, you wine drinkers, for the new wine is gone. (Drunkards: people who drink too much, mourn: feel sorrow) **6.** A mighty, countless nations have invaded my land, with the teeth of lions and the jaws of great lions. (Teeth of lions: very strong) **7.** It has destroyed my vine (grapevine) and stripped my fig tree, leaving them bare, with only white branches. (Vine: grape plant, fig tree: tree that bears figs) **8.** Mourn like a young woman mourning the loss of her husband. (Mourning: grieving, loss: when something or someone is gone) **9.** The grain and drink offerings are cut off from the house of the LORD, and the priests, His ministers, mourn. (Offering: gift given in worship, priests: religious leaders, ministers: servants of God) **10.** The land is wasted; the grain is ruined, the new wine is dried up, and the oil is failing. (wasted: destroyed, failing: not working) **11.** Be ashamed, you farmers and vine growers, for the harvest has perished. (Farmers: people who grow crops, vine growers: people who grow vines) **12.** The vine, fig tree, pomegranate (fruit tree), palm, and apple trees have all withered; joy has vanished from the people. (Withered: dried up, pomegranate: a fruit-bearing tree vanished: disappeared) **13.** Gird yourselves in sackcloth, you priests; mourn, ministers of the altar; the offerings are withheld from the house of God. (Gird: prepare, sackcloth: rough clothing worn in mourning, altar: place of sacrifice) **14.** Declare a fast, call a solemn assembly, gather the elders and all the people to the house of the LORD, and cry out to Him. (Fast: no eating, solemn: serious, assembly: gathering) **15.** Woe to the day! The day of the LORD is near, a day of destruction from the Almighty. (Woe: great sorrow, destruction: complete ruin) **16.** The offerings have ceased, and joy has disappeared from the house of our God. (Ceased: stopped, disappeared: gone) **17.** The seeds have rotted in the soil, the barns are empty, and the corn withered. (Rotted: decayed, soil: ground, barns: storage buildings) **18.** The animals groan, the herds (groups of animals) are confused, and the flocks (groups of sheep) of sheep are devastated. (Groan: make a low sound of pain, confused: lost or unsure) **19.** O LORD, I cry to You, for fire has consumed the pastures (grassy areas), and flames have burned the trees. (Consumed: destroyed completely, pastures: grassy lands, flames: fire) **20.** The animals cry out to you, for the rivers have dried up and the fire has ravaged the wilderness (desert area). (Ravaged: destroyed completely, wilderness: wild, untamed area)

Chapter 2
1. Blow the trumpet in Zion, sound the alarm on My holy mountain. Let all the inhabitants tremble, for the day of the LORD is near. (Zion: a hill in Jerusalem, symbolic of God's kingdom) **2.** A day of darkness and gloom, clouds and thick darkness, like the morning spread on the mountains. A great and strong people, unmatched before or after, for generations. (gloom: sadness or darkness; thick darkness: very dense darkness) **3.** A fire devours before them, and behind them a flame burns. The land is like Eden before them, but a desolate wilderness behind. Nothing escapes them. (Eden: a paradise garden in the Bible) **4.** Their appearance is like horses, and they run like horsemen. (appearance: look or form) **5.** They leap like chariots on mountaintops, like the noise of a consuming fire, a strong army in battle formation. (chariots: two-wheeled vehicles used in battle) **6.** People will be in pain before them, their faces turning black. (faces turning black: a sign of fear and distress) **7.** They will run like mighty men, climb walls like warriors, march in order, not breaking ranks. (mighty men: strong and brave warriors) **8.** They won't push one another; each will follow their path, and if they fall on a sword, they will not be wounded. (path: a way or course they take) **9.** They will run through the city, scale walls, climb houses, and enter windows like thieves. (thieves: people who steal) **10.** The earth will quake before them, the heavens will tremble. The sun and moon will grow dark, and the stars will cease to shine. (quake: shake; cease: stop) **11.** The LORD will utter His voice before His army, for His camp is vast. He is powerful in executing His word.

The day of the LORD is great and terrible—who can endure it? (utter: speak; execute: carry out) **12.** Therefore, says the LORD, return to Me with all your heart, with fasting, weeping, and mourning. (mourning: showing sorrow) **13.** Rend your hearts, not your garments, and return to the LORD your God. He is gracious, merciful, slow to anger, kind, and relents from judgment. (rend: tear; relents: changes His mind from punishment) **14.** Who knows if He will return, relent, and leave behind a blessing—grain and drink offerings for the LORD your God? (blessing: a gift of favor) **15.** Blow the trumpet in Zion, sanctify a fast, call a solemn assembly. (sanctify: make holy or set apart) **16.** Gather the people, sanctify the congregation, assemble the elders, gather children, and those nursing. Let the bridegroom leave his room and the bride her chamber. (bridegroom: husband-to-be; chamber: room) **17.** Let the priests, ministers of the LORD, weep between the porch and the altar. Let them say, "Spare Your people, O LORD, and don't let Your heritage be a reproach. Why should the heathen ask, 'Where is their God?'" (reproach: shame or dishonor; heathen: people who do not believe in God) **18.** Then the LORD will be jealous for His land and have pity on His people. (jealous: protective and zealous; pity: feel compassion) **19.** The LORD will answer and say to His people, "I will send you grain, wine, and oil, and you will be satisfied. I will no longer make you a reproach among the nations." (grain: food crops; wine and oil: agricultural products) **20.** I will remove the northern army far from you, driving them into a barren, desolate land. Their stench will rise because of the great harm they caused. (stench: bad smell; barren: empty) **21.** Do not fear, O land; rejoice and be glad, for the LORD will do great things. (rejoice: be happy) **22.** Do not be afraid, you beasts of the field, for the wilderness pastures will spring up. The trees will bear fruit; the fig tree and vine will yield strength. (beasts of the field: animals in the wild) **23.** Be glad, O children of Zion, and rejoice in the LORD your God. He has given you the early rain in moderation, and He will send both the early and latter rains in the first month. (early rain: rain at the start of the growing season) **24.** The threshing floors will be full of grain, and the vats will overflow with wine and oil. (threshing floors: places where grain is separated from stalks; vats: containers for liquids) **25.** I will restore to you the years that the locust, the cankerworm, the caterpillar, and the palmerworm have eaten—My great army that I sent among you. (locust: a destructive insect; caterpillar and palmerworm: similar destructive pests) **26.** You will eat in plenty, be satisfied, and praise the name of the LORD your God, who has dealt wondrously with you. My people will never be ashamed. (wondrously: in a marvelous way) **27.** You will know that I am in the midst of Israel, and that I am the LORD your God, and there is no other. My people will never be ashamed. (midst: center; Israel: the nation of God's chosen people) **28.** Afterward, I will pour out My Spirit on all flesh. Your sons and daughters will prophesy, your old men will dream dreams, your young men will see visions. (prophesy: speak messages from God; visions: supernatural insights) **29.** I will pour out My Spirit on the servants and handmaids in those days. (servants and handmaids: workers, especially those in lower status) **30.** I will show wonders in the heavens and on the earth: blood, fire, and pillars of smoke. (wonders: miraculous signs) **31.** The sun will be turned to darkness, and the moon to blood, before the great and terrible day of the LORD comes. (terrible: awe-inspiring and fearful) **32.** Everyone who calls on the name of the LORD will be delivered. On Mount Zion and in Jerusalem, there will be deliverance, as the LORD has said, and among the remnant whom the LORD calls. (delivered: saved or rescued; Mount Zion: a hill in Jerusalem; remnant: those who remain)

Chapter 3

1. When I restore the fortunes of Judah and Jerusalem, (Judah: city in Israel, Jerusalem: city in Israel) **2.** I will gather all nations to the valley of Jehoshaphat to judge them for scattering My people and dividing My land. (Jehoshaphat: valley in Israel) **3.** They have sold My people, a boy for a prostitute and a girl for wine. (cast lots: deciding by chance) **4.** What do you want with Me, Tyre, Sidon, and Palestine? Will you repay Me? If so, I'll return your actions upon you. (Tyre: city in Lebanon, Sidon: city in Lebanon, Palestine: region near Israel) **5.** You took My silver and gold and carried My treasures into your temples. (temples: places of worship) **6.** You sold the children of Judah and Jerusalem to the Greeks, taking them far from their homeland. (Greeks: people of Greece) **7.** I will bring them back from the places you sold them and punish you for what you've done. (repay: punish) **8.** I will sell your sons and daughters to the people of Judah, who will sell them to the Sabeans, a far-off nation. (Sabeans: distant people) **9.** Declare to the nations: Prepare for battle. Let mighty warriors assemble. (mighty men: strong warriors) **10.** Turn your plowshares into swords and pruning hooks into spears; let the weak say, "I am strong." (plowshares: farming tools, pruning hooks: cutting tools) **11.** Gather, O nations, and bring down your strong ones, O LORD. **12.** Let the nations come to the valley of Jehoshaphat, where I will judge them. (Jehoshaphat: valley in Israel) **13.** The harvest is ripe, and their wickedness is great. (harvest ripe: ready for reaping, wickedness: evil actions) **14.** There are multitudes in the valley of decision, for the day of the LORD is near. (multitudes: many people) **15.** The sun and moon will darken, and the stars will stop shining. **16.** The LORD will roar from Zion, and the earth will tremble, but He will be the refuge and strength of His people, Israel. (Zion: Jerusalem) **17.** Then you will know I am the LORD, dwelling in Zion, My holy mountain. Jerusalem will be sacred, and no foreigners will enter it. (dwelling: living, foreigners: non-Israelites) **18.** On that day, the mountains will overflow with wine, the hills with milk, and Judah's rivers will fill with water. A spring will flow from the house of the LORD to water the valley of Shittim. (fountain: spring, Shittim: place in Israel) **19.** Egypt will be devastated, and Edom will be a wasteland because of the violence done to Judah. (desolate: empty, Edom: region near Israel, violence: harm) **20.** But Judah will last forever, and Jerusalem will endure through the generations. (dwell: live) **21.** I will purify the blood that has not been cleansed, for the LORD dwells in Zion. (cleanse: purify)

30 – Amos

Chapter 1

1. The words of Amos, a shepherd from Tekoa, which he saw concerning Israel during the reigns of Uzziah, king of Judah, and Jeroboam, son of Joash, king of Israel, two years before the earthquake. (Tekoa: a town in Judah; Uzziah: king of Judah; Jeroboam: king of Israel) **2.** He said, "The LORD will roar from Zion and speak from Jerusalem; the shepherds will mourn, and Mount Carmel will wither." (Zion: a hill in Jerusalem; Carmel: a mountain range in Israel) **3.** The LORD says: "For three sins of Damascus, and for four, I will not forgive them, because they threshed Gilead with iron sledges." (Damascus: capital of Syria; Gilead: region east of the Jordan River) **4.** "I will send fire on Hazael's house, consuming Ben-hadad's palaces." (Hazael: king of Aram; Ben-hadad: a title for kings of Aram) **5.** "I will break Damascus' gates, destroy Aven's people, and exile the Syrians to Kir," says the LORD. (Aven: a place in Syria; Kir: a place of exile) **6.** The LORD says, "For three sins of Gaza, and for four, I will not forgive them, because they took captives to Edom." (Gaza: a city of the Philistines; Edom: a neighboring nation) **7.** "I will send fire on Gaza's walls, consuming her palaces." **8.** "I will destroy Ashdod, Ashkelon, and Ekron, and the Philistines will perish," says the Lord GOD. (Ashdod, Ashkelon, Ekron: cities of the Philistines) **9.** The LORD says, "For three sins of Tyre, and for four, I will not forgive them, because they handed captives to Edom, breaking the brotherly covenant." (Tyre: an ancient Phoenician city; Edom: a nation southeast of Israel) **10.** "I will send fire on Tyre's walls, consuming her palaces." (Palaces: royal residences) **11.** The LORD says, "For three sins of Edom, and for four, I will not forgive them, because they pursued their brother with the sword and showed no mercy." (Edom: a nation southeast of Israel) **12.** "I will send fire on Teman, consuming Bozrah's palaces." (Teman: a region in Edom; Bozrah: a city in Edom) **13.** The LORD says, "For three sins of the Ammonites, and for four, I will not forgive them, because they attacked pregnant women in Gilead to expand their borders." (Ammonites: people of Ammon; Gilead: region east of the Jordan River) **14.** "I will set fire to Rabbah's walls, consuming her palaces with a battle cry and a whirlwind." (Rabbah: capital of the Ammonites) **15.** "Their king and princes will go into exile," says the LORD. (Princes: leaders or rulers)

Chapter 2

1. The LORD says: For three sins of Moab, and for four, I will not forgive them, because they burned the bones of the king of Edom to lime. (Edom: an ancient kingdom south of Israel; lime: act of destruction) **2.** I will send fire on Moab, consuming the palaces of Kerioth, and Moab will perish in chaos, with cries and trumpet blasts. (Kerioth: a city in Moab) **3.** I will remove their judges and destroy their princes, says the LORD. (judges: rulers or leaders; princes: rulers) **4.** The LORD says: For three sins of Judah, and for four, I will not forgive them, because they rejected the LORD's law and walked in their ancestors' lies. (lies: false statements) **5.** I will send fire on Judah, and it will burn the palaces of Jerusalem. (Jerusalem: capital of Judah) **6.** The LORD says: For three sins of Israel, and for four, I will not forgive them, because they sold the righteous for silver and the poor for sandals. (righteous: those who do what is right; sandals: footwear) **7.** They trample the poor and ignore the meek; a man and his father defile My holy name. (trample: step heavily on; meek: humble or gentle) **8.** They lie on clothes taken as pledges and drink wine bought with bribes in the house of their god. (pledges: promises; bribes: gifts for favor; god: false deity) **9.** I destroyed the powerful Amorite, whose height was like cedars and strength like oaks, cutting off their fruit and roots. (Amorites: ancient Canaanites; cedars: large trees; oaks: strong trees) **10.** I brought you up from Egypt, led you through the wilderness for forty years, to take the land of the Amorites. (Egypt: African kingdom; wilderness: barren desert) **11.** I raised prophets from your sons and Nazarites from your young men. Is this not true, O Israel? says the LORD. (prophets: messengers of God;

Nazarites: set-apart vow followers) **12.** But you gave the Nazarites wine to drink and told the prophets to stop prophesying. **13.** Look, I am crushed under you like a cart full of grain. (sheaves: bundles of grain) **14.** The swift will not escape, the strong will not find strength, and the mighty cannot save themselves. (swift: fast runners; strong: powerful; mighty: great power) **15.** The bowman will not stand firm, the runner will not escape, and the horseman cannot save himself. (bowman: archers; horseman: on horseback) **16.** Even the bravest warriors will flee naked in that day, says the LORD. (warriors: fighters; naked: without clothes)

Chapter 3

1. Listen to the word the Lord has spoken against you, O Israel, the family I brought up from Egypt: **2.** I have only known you among all the nations, so I will punish you for your sins. (Sins: wrongdoings) **3.** Can two walk together without agreeing? **4.** Does a lion roar without a reason? Does a young lion cry out if it hasn't caught anything? **5.** Can a bird be trapped without bait? Can a snare be set without catching something? **6.** Can a trumpet be blown in a city and the people not fear? Can disaster strike a city unless the Lord allows it? (Disaster: misfortune) **7.** The Lord does nothing without revealing His plans to His prophets. (Prophets: messengers of God) **8.** When the lion roars, who will not be afraid? When God speaks, who can remain silent? **9.** Announce in Ashdod and Egypt, saying, "Gather on the mountains of Samaria and see the chaos and oppression." (Ashdod: a Philistine city, Samaria: capital of Israel) **10.** They don't know how to do what is right, says the Lord, storing up violence and theft in their palaces. (Violence: harm, Theft: stealing) **11.** Therefore, the Lord says: "An enemy will surround the land, take away your strength, and plunder your palaces." (Plundered: looted) **12.** Like a shepherd rescuing parts of a lion's prey, Israel will be rescued—those in Samaria and Damascus will be spared. (Samaria: a city in Israel, Damascus: a city in Syria) **13.** Hear this and testify in the house of Jacob, says the Lord, the God of armies. (Jacob: the father of Israel, God of hosts: a title for God) **14.** When I visit Israel's sin, I will also punish the altars of Bethel; the horns of the altar will be cut off and fall. (Bethel: an Israelite city, Sin: wrongdoing) **15.** I will strike both the winter and summer houses; the houses of ivory will be destroyed, and the great houses will end. (Ivory: a precious material)

Chapter 4

1. Listen, you cows of Bashan, who live on the mountain of Samaria, oppress the poor, crush the needy, and tell your masters, "Bring us more to drink." (Cows of Bashan: metaphor for wealth; Samaria: capital of Israel) **2.** The Lord God has sworn by His holiness that the days are coming when He will drag you away with hooks, and your descendants with fishhooks. **3.** You will be led out through the gaps, each cow following the other, and thrown into the exile, says the Lord. (Breaches: gaps) **4.** Go to Bethel and sin, go to Gilgal and increase your rebellion. Bring your morning sacrifices and your tithes every third year. (Bethel: sacred city in Israel; Gilgal: important city in Israel; Tithes: one-tenth of income) **5.** Offer thank offerings with leaven and announce your freewill offerings; this pleases you, O Israel, says the Lord God. (Leaven: it indicate Israel disobedience as it was prohibited for offerings) **6.** I gave you hunger in all your cities and lack of food in every place, yet you did not return to Me, says the Lord. **7.** I withheld rain from you when there were three months left before harvest, sending rain on one city but not another. One field received rain, while another dried up. **8.** Two or three cities wandered to one city for water, but were still unsatisfied. Yet, you did not return to Me, says the Lord. **9.** I struck you with blight and mildew, and when your crops grew, the locust devoured them. Yet, you did not return to Me, says the Lord. (Blight: plant disease; Mildew: fungus) **10.** I sent a plague similar to that in Egypt among you, killed your young men with the sword, and took your horses. I made the stench of your camps rise to your nostrils. Yet, you did not return to Me, says the Lord. **11.** I overthrew some of you like God overthrew Sodom and Gomorrah. You were like a stick pulled from the fire, yet you did not return to Me, says the Lord. (Sodom: a city destroyed for sinfulness; Gomorrah: a city destroyed for sinfulness) **12.** Therefore, Israel, prepare to meet your God. **13.** For, He who forms the mountains, creates the wind, reveals His thoughts to man, turns the morning into night, and walks on the heights of the earth, the Lord, the God of hosts, is His name.

Chapter 5

1. Listen to this sorrowful message I bring against you, O house of Israel. (Sorrowful message: a mournful declaration) **2.** Israel has fallen and will not rise again. She is left desolate in her own land with no one to help her. (Desolate: abandoned or in ruin) **3.** The Lord GOD declares: The city that once had a thousand will be reduced to a hundred, and the city that had a hundred will be left with only ten, for Israel. (Israel: refers to the northern kingdom of Israel) **4.** The LORD says, "Search for me, and you will find life." (Search: to seek or pursue) **5.** But do not seek out Bethel, Gilgal, or Beer-sheba; for Gilgal will be taken into exile, and Bethel will come to nothing. (Bethel: a sacred site; Gilgal: an early settlement; Beer-sheba: a city in southern Israel) **6.** Seek the LORD and you will live, or He will erupt like fire in the house of Joseph and consume it, leaving no one to stop the flames. (Joseph: refers to the northern kingdom of Israel) **7.** You who twist justice into bitterness and ignore righteousness. (Bitterness: a harsh, corrupted condition) **8.** Seek the one who created the Pleiades and Orion, who turns night into dawn and calls forth the rains from the sea, pouring them over the earth—His name is the LORD. (Pleiades and Orion: constellations; the LORD: the Almighty Creator) **9.** He strengthens the weak against the powerful, so that the oppressed can break through the strongest fortifications. (Weak: the downtrodden; Powerful: the oppressors) **10.** You detest those who speak out against injustice and disdain those who speak truthfully. (Gate: a place of judgment) **11.** You trample the poor and take their grain; you build fine homes of hewn stone, but you will not live in them; you plant vineyards, but will not drink their wine. (Hewn stone: cut stones for construction) **12.** I know your many sins and wrongdoings. You oppress the innocent, accept bribes, and prevent the poor from receiving justice. (Oppress: to wrong or burden; Innocent: the righteous) **13.** The wise will be silent in such evil times. (Wise: those who understand the gravity of the moment) **14.** Seek good, not evil, so you may survive, and the LORD, the God of hosts, will be with you. (God of hosts: a title for the Almighty) **15.** Hate evil, love good, and restore justice at the gate. Perhaps the LORD of hosts will be merciful to the remnant of Joseph. (Gate: a place of judgment; Remnant: the remaining faithful ones) **16.** Therefore, the LORD, the God of hosts, declares: There will be mourning in every street, and people will cry out, "Alas!" Skilled mourners will be called to lament. (Lament: to grieve deeply) **17.** In all vineyards, there will be mourning, for I will pass through you, says the LORD. (Vineyards: symbolic of the land of Israel) **18.** Woe to those who long for the day of the LORD! What is the day of the LORD to you? It will be a time of darkness, not light. (Woe: a declaration of impending disaster) **19.** It will be like someone escaping from a lion, only to be met by a bear; or entering a house and leaning against the wall, only to be bitten by a snake. (Lions and bears: symbols of inevitable danger) **20.** The day of the LORD will be complete darkness, with no light at all. (Day of the LORD: a time of divine judgment) **21.** I despise your festivals and take no pleasure in your gatherings. (Festivals: religious holidays or feasts) **22.** Even if you bring me burnt offerings and grain offerings, I will not accept them. I will not look at your peace offerings. (Burnt offerings: sacrifices burned in worship; Peace offerings: sacrifices of reconciliation) **23.** Remove the noise of your songs; I will not listen to the sound of your harps. (Noise: distractions from true worship) **24.** Let justice flow like water, and righteousness like an ever-flowing stream. (Justice: fairness and equity) **25.** Did you bring me sacrifices for forty years in the wilderness, O house of Israel? (Wilderness: a barren desert region where Israel wandered) **26.** You carried the shrine of your king, Moloch (the god of the Ammonites), and Chiun (another idol), the star of your god, which you made for yourselves. (Moloch and Chiun: idols worshipped by Israel in disobedience) **27.** Therefore, I will send you into exile beyond Damascus, says the LORD, whose name is the God of hosts. (Damascus: capital of Syria; Exile: a forced removal from one's land)

Chapter 6

1. Woe to those who feel secure in Zion and trust in the strength of Samaria's mountain, the leading city to which Israel came! (Zion: Jerusalem; Samaria: Capital of the Northern Kingdom of Israel) **2.** Visit Calneh, then go to Hamath, and then to Gath of the Philistines. Are their kingdoms greater than yours or their land more expansive? (Calneh: ancient Mesopotamian city; Hamath: Syrian city; Gath: Philistine city) **3.** You who push away the day of disaster and bring nearer the reign of violence, (Violence: oppression) **4.** Who lie on luxurious ivory beds, stretch out on couches, and feast on lambs and calves, (Ivory: luxury material; Lambs: young sheep; Calves: young cattle) **5.** Who play harps and invent new instruments, like David did, (David: King of Israel, musician) **6.** Who drink wine from bowls and use the finest oils, yet are indifferent to Joseph's suffering. (Joseph: Israelite son symbolizing the tribes) **7.** Because of this, they will be the first taken into captivity, and their extravagant feasts will be taken away. (Captives: prisoners) **8.** The Lord has sworn by Himself, says the God of hosts, that He despises Israel's pride and palaces, and will give up the city and all within it. (Jacob: Israel; Palaces: royal homes) **9.** When ten men remain in one house, they will all die. (Ten men: a small number symbolizing destruction) **10.** A relative will burn the corpse and ask those near, "Is anyone still there?" They will reply, "No," and he will say, "Do not mention the name of the LORD." (Relative: family member; LORD: Yahweh) **11.** The LORD commands, and He will strike both large and small houses with ruin. (Strike: punish) **12.** Can horses run on rocky ground? Can one plow with oxen there? You have turned justice into bitterness and righteousness into poison. (Oxen: farm animals; Justice: fairness) **13.** You who take pride in your empty achievements, saying, "We have gained strength by

360

our own power!" (Rejoice: celebrate; pride in your empty achievements: pride in human strength) **14.** But I will raise up a nation against you, Israel, says the LORD, and they will oppress you from the northern boundary (Hamath) to the southern boundary (the wilderness river). (Oppress: harshly control; Hamath: Syrian city)

Chapter 7

1. The Sovereign Lord showed me a vision: He formed locusts at the start of the final growth, after the king's harvests. (Locusts: a type of grasshopper) **2.** When the locusts finished devouring the land's grass, I cried, "Lord God, forgive! How can Jacob survive? He is so small." (Jacob: the nation of Israel) **3.** The Lord relented, saying, "It will not happen." **4.** Then the Lord showed me another vision: He called to judge by fire, which consumed the deep waters and scorched part of the land. (The great deep: the oceans) **5.** Again, I pleaded, "Lord, stop! How can Jacob survive? He is too small." (Jacob: the nation of Israel) **6.** The Lord relented again, saying, "This also will not happen." **7.** Then I saw the Lord standing on a wall with a plumb line in His hand. (Plumb line: a tool used to measure vertical alignment) **8.** The Lord asked, "Amos, what do you see?" I said, "A plumb line." The Lord replied, "I am setting a plumb line among My people Israel. I will no longer overlook their sins." (Plumb line: a tool used to measure vertical alignment) **9.** The high places of Isaac will be destroyed, and Israel's sanctuaries will be laid waste. I will rise against Jeroboam's house with the sword. (Isaac: the patriarch of Israel, Jeroboam: the king of Israel) **10.** Amaziah, the priest of Bethel, sent a message to King Jeroboam, saying, "Amos is conspiring against you. The land cannot bear his words." (Bethel: a city in Israel, Jeroboam: the king of Israel) **11.** Amos says, "Jeroboam will die by the sword, and Israel will be taken into captivity." (Jeroboam: the king of Israel) **12.** Amaziah told Amos, "Go to Judah, eat your bread there, and prophesy there." (Judah: the southern kingdom) **13.** "But do not prophesy at Bethel, for it is the king's sanctuary and royal court." (Bethel: a city in Israel) **14.** Amos replied, "I am not a prophet, nor the son of one. I was a shepherd and a sycamore fruit gatherer. (Herder: a person who cares for livestock, Sycamore: a type of tree) **15.** But the Lord took me from following the flock and said, 'Go, prophesy to Israel.' (Israel: the northern kingdom) **16.** Listen to the word of the Lord: You say, 'Do not prophesy against Israel or the house of Isaac.' (Isaac: the patriarch of Israel, Israel: the northern kingdom) **17.** Therefore, the Lord says: 'Your wife will become a prostitute, your children will die by the sword, your land will be divided, and you will die in a polluted land. Israel will be taken into exile.' (Israel: the northern kingdom)

Chapter 8

1. The Lord showed me a vision of a basket filled with ripe summer fruit. (Summer fruit: fruit harvested in summer) **2.** He asked, "What do you see, Amos?" I replied, "A basket of summer fruit." The Lord said, "The end has come for Israel; I will no longer show mercy." (Israel: northern kingdom of Israel) **3.** The temple's joyful songs will turn to mourning, and many will die, their bodies discarded quietly. (Temple: place of worship; bodies: the dead) **4.** Listen, you who exploit the poor and make the needy suffer. (Exploit: take advantage of; Suffer: endure hardship) **5.** You ask, "When will the religious festival end so we can sell grain? When will the Sabbath be over so we can market wheat, reducing the measure, inflating the price, and using false scales?" (Sabbath: day of rest; False scales: dishonest weights) **6.** You buy the poor for silver and sell the needy for a pair of shoes, even selling the leftover grain. (Leftover: refuse or discarded grain) **7.** The Lord swears by the greatness of Jacob: "I will not forget their actions." (Jacob: Israel's ancestor, the patriarch) **8.** Will not the land tremble? Everyone will mourn, and it will rise like a flood, swept away as in Egypt. (Tremble: shake; Egypt: historical flood event) **9.** On that day, says the Lord, I will make the sun set at noon, and darkness will cover the earth in the middle of the day. (Noon: midday; Darken: bring darkness) **10.** I will turn your feasts into mourning and your songs into weeping. Sackcloth will be worn, and heads shaved, like mourning for an only son. (Sackcloth: rough garment worn during mourning; Baldness: sign of grief) **11.** The days are coming, says the Lord, when I will send a famine—not for food, but for hearing God's word. (Famine: shortage) **12.** People will wander from coast to coast, looking for the Lord's word, but will not find it. (Coast to coast: from one side of the land to another) **13.** On that day, young men and women will faint from thirst. (Faint: become weak) **14.** Those who swear by the sin of Samaria, and by gods like Dan and Beer-sheba, will fall and never rise again. (Samaria: worship of false gods; Dan: northern city; Beer-sheba: southern town)

Chapter 9

1. I saw the LORD by the altar, saying, "Strike the top of the doorframe, making the posts tremble and break. I will slay the last with the sword; no one will escape or survive." (Altar: place of sacrifice; Doorframe: the top of a door) **2.** If they descend to the grave, I will pull them up; if they ascend to the heavens, I will bring them down. (Hell: the grave or underworld; Heaven: sky or God's dwelling place) **3.** If they hide on Mount Carmel, I will search for them; if they flee to the sea, I will command the serpent to strike them there. (Carmel: a mountain in Israel; Sea: Mediterranean Sea) **4.** If they are taken captive, I will command the sword to strike them, and I will judge them harshly, not with favor. (Sword: a weapon; Captivity: being captured) **5.** The LORD God touches the land, making it melt, and those who dwell there will mourn. It will rise like a flood, and recede like Egypt's destruction. (Egypt: land along the Nile River) **6.** He builds His chambers in the heavens, calls the sea, and pours it over the earth; the LORD is His name. (Chambers: rooms in heaven; Sea: Mediterranean Sea) **7.** Are you not like the people of Cush to me, O Israel? Did I not bring Israel from Egypt, the Philistines from Caphtor, and the Syrians from Kir? (Cush: ancient kingdom in Africa; Caphtor: homeland of the Philistines; Kir: ancient city) **8.** The LORD's eyes are on the sinful kingdom, and I will destroy it, but I will not completely wipe out the house of Jacob. (Jacob: the ancestor of Israel) **9.** I will sift Israel among the nations like grain in a sieve; none will be lost. (Sifted: refined or separated) **10.** All sinners who claim evil will not harm them will die by the sword. (Sword: weapon of battle) **11.** On that day, I will rebuild the fallen house of David and restore it to its former glory. (House of David: King David's royal line) **12.** They will possess the remnant of Edom and all nations called by My name. (Edom: region southeast of Israel; Nations: other peoples) **13.** The days are coming when the plowman will overtake the reaper, and the hills will drip with sweet wine. (Plowman: one who plows; Reaper: one who harvests) **14.** I will restore Israel's captivity; they will rebuild cities, plant vineyards, and enjoy the fruit. (Captivity: exile or imprisonment) **15.** I will plant them in their land, and they will never be uprooted again. (Uprooted: removed from their land)

31 – Obadiah

Chapter 1

1. The vision of Obadiah: This is what the Sovereign Lord says concerning Edom: I have received a report from the Lord, and a messenger has been sent to the nations, calling, "Rise up, let us go to war against her." **2.** I have made you insignificant among the nations; you are deeply despised. **3.** The pride of your heart has misled you, you who live in the high places, in the clefts of the rocks, saying, "Who can bring me down?" (pride: inflated self-importance, clefts: cracks of the rocks) **4.** Even if you soar like the eagle and set your nest among the stars, I will bring you down, declares the Lord. **5.** If thieves or robbers came at night, would they not take only what they need and leave some behind? **6.** How thoroughly have Esau's hidden treasures been uncovered!("Esau's hidden treasures: the valuable possessions of Edom) **7.** All your allies have driven you to the edge, those who once shared peace with you have deceived you. They have set a trap for you. (allies: Allied nations) **8.** On the day of the Lord, I will eliminate the wise men from Edom and understanding from Esau's hills. (understanding: wisdom) **9.** Your warriors, O Teman, will be filled with fear, and all of Esau's mountains will be cut off by the sword. **10.** Because you acted violently against your brother Jacob, shame will cover you, and you will be utterly destroyed. (violence: unjust aggression) **11.** On the day you watched from the sidelines when strangers took his wealth and enemies entered his gates, you were like one of them. **12.** You should not have rejoiced over the downfall of your brother or celebrated Judah's destruction. (rejoiced: took malicious pleasure) **13.** You should not have entered my people's gates in their time of distress, nor have taken what belonged to them. (distress: calamity) **14.** You should not have cut off those who were fleeing or handed over those who remained. **15.** The day of the Lord is near for all nations. As you have done, so it will be done to you; your actions will be returned to you. **16.** Just as you drank on my holy mountain, so the nations will drink continually. They will be consumed as if they had never existed. (consumed: wiped out) **17.** But on Mount Zion, there will be deliverance, and it will be holy. The house of Jacob will reclaim their inheritance. (deliverance: rescue) **18.** The house of Jacob will become a fire, the house of Joseph a flame, but Esau will be like stubble. They will be consumed by the fire, and no survivors will remain from Esau. (stubble: useless remnants) **19.** Those in the south will possess the mountains of Esau, and those in the lowlands will inherit the Philistine territories. **20.** The exiles of Israel will reclaim the land of the Canaanites, as far as Zarephath, and the exiles from Jerusalem will possess the cities of the south. (Zarephath: a Phoenician town) **21.** Deliverers will ascend to Mount Zion to rule over Esau's mountains, and the kingdom will belong to the Lord.

32 – Jonah

Chapter 1

1. The word of the LORD came to the son of Amittai, saying, (Amittai: my faithfulness) **2.** "Go to Nineveh, that large city, and deliver a message against it, for its wickedness has reached me." (Nineveh: ancient city; wickedness: sinfulness) **3.** But he fled to Tarshish to escape the LORD, went to Joppa, found a ship, paid the fare, and boarded it. (Tarshish: distant city; Joppa: port city) **4.** The LORD sent a mighty storm, and the ship was in danger of breaking. (Mighty: violent storm) **5.** The sailors were afraid and cried to their gods. They threw cargo overboard, but he was asleep in the hold. (sailors: ship workers; hold: storage area) **6.** The captain said, "How can you sleep? Call on your God! Perhaps He will save us." (perish: die) **7.** The men said, "Let us cast lots to find who is responsible." The lot fell on him. (cast lots: decide by chance) **8.** They asked, "Who are you? Where are you from? What is your country and your people?" (trouble: problem) **9.** He answered, "I am a Hebrew, and I worship the LORD, the God of heaven, who made sea and land." (Hebrew: Israelite) **10.** The men were terrified and said, "What have you done?" They knew he was fleeing from the LORD. (fleeing: running away) **11.** They asked, "What should we do to calm the sea?" The storm grew worse. **12.** He said, "Throw me into the sea, and it will calm. This storm is my fault." (throw: cast) **13.** Instead, they rowed harder to reach land, but the storm grew stronger. **14.** They cried, "LORD, do not hold us guilty for killing him. You have done as You pleased." (accountable: responsible) **15.** They threw him into the sea, and it grew calm. (overboard: into water) **16.** The men greatly feared the LORD, offered a sacrifice, and made vows to Him. (vows: promises) **17.** The LORD prepared a great fish to swallow him, and he stayed in the belly of the fish three days and nights. (great fish: large sea creature)

Chapter 2

1. Inside the fish, he prayed to the LORD his God, **2.** saying, "In my trouble, I called to You, and You answered. From the grave, I cried for help, and You listened." (grave: the realm of the dead) **3.** "You cast me into the deep; the currents surrounded me, and Your waves swept over me." (currents: moving water) **4.** "I said, 'I am banished from Your sight,' yet I will look again toward Your temple." (banished: cast out) **5.** "The waters surrounded me; seaweed wrapped around my head." (engulfing: surrounding) **6.** "To the roots of the mountains I sank, but You, LORD, brought my life from the pit." (pit: depth) **7.** "When my life was ebbing away, I prayed, and it rose to Your temple." (ebb: decline) **8.** "Those clinging to idols forfeit Your grace." (forfeit: lose) **9.** "I will offer sacrifices with thanks and fulfill my vows. Salvation comes from the LORD." (sacrifice: offering) **10.** The LORD commanded the fish, and it vomited him onto land. (vomited: expelled)

Chapter 3

1. The word of the LORD came a second time: **2.** "Go to Nineveh and proclaim My message." (proclaim: announce) **3.** He obeyed and went to Nineveh, a very large city. It took three days to go through it. (large: vast) **4.** He proclaimed, "Forty days and Nineveh will be overturned." (overturned: destroyed) **5.** The Ninevites believed God, fasted, and put on sackcloth, from the greatest to the least. (fast: abstain from food) **6.** The king heard, rose from his throne, removed his robes, put on sackcloth, and sat in ashes. (robes: ceremonial clothes) **7.** He decreed, "Let no one, including animals, eat or drink." (decreed: ordered) **8.** "Let everyone call urgently on God and turn from evil and violence." (urgently: immediately) **9.** "Who knows? God may relent and turn from His anger so we will not perish." (relent: change His mind) **10.** God saw they turned from evil and did not bring the destruction He had threatened. (evil: wickedness)

Chapter 4

1. Jonah was very displeased and angry. (displeased: unhappy) **2.** He prayed, "LORD, I knew You are compassionate, slow to anger, and abounding in love, relenting from sending calamity." (calamity: disaster) **3.** "Take my life, for it is better to die than to live." (take my life: end my life) **4.** The LORD asked, "Is it right for you to be angry?" **5.** Jonah went east of the city, made a shelter, and sat in its shade to see what would happen. (shelter: hut) **6.** The LORD provided a plant to give shade and ease his discomfort, making him happy. (plant: gourd; discomfort: unease) **7.** At dawn, God sent a worm to chew the plant, and it withered. (withered: dried up) **8.** God sent a scorching wind, and the sun blazed on him. He grew faint and wished to die, saying, "It is better to die than to live." (scorching: very hot; faint: weak) **9.** God said, "Is it right to be angry about the plant?" He replied, "Yes, I'm so angry I could die." **10.** The LORD said, "You cared for a plant you didn't grow, which sprang up and died overnight." (cared: worried about) **11.** "Should I not care for Nineveh, with over 120,000 people who cannot tell their right hand from their left, and many animals?" (right hand: immature)

33 – Micah

Chapter 1

1. The LORD's message came to Micah during the reigns of Jotham, Ahaz, and Hezekiah, kings of Judah, about Samaria and Jerusalem. (Micah: a prophet; Jotham, Ahaz, and Hezekiah: kings of Judah) **2.** Listen, all peoples, and earth; let the Sovereign LORD testify against you from His holy temple. (Testify: bear witness; Sovereign: supreme ruler) **3.** The LORD is coming from His dwelling to trample the high places of the earth. (Dwelling: home; Trample: crush) **4.** Mountains will melt, and valleys will split like wax near fire or water on a steep slope. (Wax: soft substance; Steep slope: sharp incline) **5.** This is because of Jacob's rebellion and Israel's sins. Jacob's rebellion is Samaria, and Judah's high places are Jerusalem. (Rebellion: defiance; High places: worship sites) **6.** I will make Samaria a heap of rubble in the field, hurling its stones into the valley. (Heap: pile; Hurl: throw, Samaria: the capital of the Northern Kingdom, representing idolatry) **7.** Her idols will be shattered, her earnings burned, for they were gained immorally and will return to such use. (Idols: worship statues; immorally: against morals) **8.** I will weep, wail, and mourn like jackals and owls, going barefoot and naked. (Wail: lament loudly; Jackals: wild animals) **9.** Her wound is incurable and has reached the gates of Jerusalem. (Incurable: unhealable; Gates: entrances) **10.** Do not announce it in Gath; mourn in Beth Aphrah by rolling in the dust. (Gath: Philistine city; Dust: earth as mourning) **11.** In Shaphir, pass in shame; in Zaanan, they do not come out. Beth Ezel mourns, withdrawing its support. (Shaphir: pleasant town; Zaanan: city name; Support: help) **12.** Maroth hopes for good, but disaster from the LORD has reached Jerusalem's gates. (Maroth: bitter town; Disaster: calamity) **13.** Lachish, harness the chariot, for you began Judah's sins. (Harness: attach; Chariot: vehicle) **14.** Moresheth Gath will send gifts; Achzib will fail Israel's kings. (Achzib: false town; Fail: disappoint) **15.** A conqueror will come to Mareshah; Israel's glory will retreat to Adullam. (Conqueror: invader; Retreat: withdraw) **16.** Shave your heads in mourning for your children, who will be taken into exile. (Exile: forced removal; Mourning: grieving)

Chapter 2

1. Woe to those plotting evil, carrying it out at dawn because they have power. (Woe: sorrow; Plotting: planning) **2.** They covet fields and houses, seizing and oppressing owners and their inheritance. (Covet: desire with wrongful intent; Oppressing: mistreating) **3.** The LORD plans disaster; you cannot escape or walk proudly in this time of calamity. (Disaster: misfortune; Escape: avoid) **4.** People will lament, saying, "We are ruined! The LORD has divided our fields." (Lament: mourn; Ruined: destroyed) **5.** You will have no one in the LORD's assembly to divide land by lot. (Assembly: gathering; Lot: allocation) **6.** They say, "Do not prophesy," but prophets must not be silenced. (Prophesy: foretell; Silenced: stopped) **7.** Jacob's house, is the LORD's Spirit limited? His words bless the upright. (Limited: restricted; Upright: righteous) **8.** Recently, My people act as enemies, robbing peaceful passersby. (Enemies: adversaries; Peaceful: without harm) **9.** You evict women from their homes and rob their children of My glory forever. (Evict: expel; Rob: steal) **10.** Arise and leave; this defiled land will destroy you completely. (Defiled: polluted; Destroy: ruin) **11.** If a liar promises wine and beer, he would suit this people. (Liar: deceiver; Suit: fit) **12.** I will gather Jacob and Israel, assembling them like a noisy flock in a pen. (Assembling: gathering; Pen: enclosure) **13.** The breaker will lead them through the gate; their king and the LORD will be at their head. (Breaker: leader; Gate: entrance)

Chapter 3

1. And I said, "Listen, O leaders of Jacob, and rulers of Israel; isn't it your duty to understand what justice truly is?" (Leaders of Jacob : Rulers of Israel) **2.** "You despise what is good and embrace evil; you strip the skin from my people and tear their flesh from their bones." (Tear off : rip apart) **3.** "You consume the flesh of my people, remove their skin, and break their bones, chopping them like meat in a pot." (Devour : consume ruthlessly or violently.) **4.** "Then they will call on the LORD, but He will not answer; He will hide His face from them because of their wicked deeds." (Hide His face : withdraw His favor or protection) **5.** "This is what the LORD says about the false prophets who mislead my people, who cry 'Peace!' while preparing war against those who refuse to feed them." (Bite with teeth : attack or deceive for personal gain) **6.** "As a result, night will fall on you, and there will be no vision; darkness will cover their diviners, and you won't be able to predict the future." (Divine : Predict the future) **7.** "The seers will be ashamed, and the diviners will be humiliated; they will cover their lips because God will not respond.(Seers: individuals who receive visions or revelations from God) **8.** "But I am filled with the power of the LORD's Spirit, with justice and strength, to reveal to Jacob his wrongdoing and to Israel his sins." (Might :Divine power) **9.** "Listen, O leaders of Jacob, and rulers of Israel, who detest justice and twist what is right." (Despise: Hate) **10.** "You build Zion through violence and Jerusalem through corruption." (Zion : a symbolic or poetic reference to Jerusalem) **11.** "Her leaders judge for a bribe, her priests teach for money, and her prophets prophesy for a price; yet they still say, 'The LORD is among us, no harm will come.'" (Bribe : Payment for favor) **12.** "Therefore, Zion will be plowed like a field, and Jerusalem will become a heap of ruins, with the temple mount like a forested hill." (Plowed : Destroyed)

Chapter 4

1. "But in the last days, the mountain of the LORD's house will be the highest of all mountains, and it will rise above the hills, and peoples will come to it." (Exalted : elevated in honor by God) 2. "Many nations will say, 'Come, let us go up to the mountain of the LORD, to the house of the God of Jacob, so that He may teach us His ways, and we will follow His paths.'" (Nations : peoples or ethnic groups.) 3. "He will settle disputes among many nations, and they will turn their weapons into farming tools. Nations will no longer fight each other, and they will no longer train for war." (Swords : Weapons) 4. "Everyone will sit peacefully under their own vine and fig tree, and no one will make them afraid, for the LORD of hosts has spoken." (Vine : Grape plant) 5. "All people will walk in the name of their god, but we will walk in the name of the LORD our God forever." (Walk : Live according to) 6. "On that day, says the LORD, I will gather the crippled, bring together the scattered, and those I have afflicted." (Lame : Disabled) 7. "I will turn the crippled into a strong nation, and the scattered into a mighty people. The LORD will reign over them on Mount Zion forever." 8. "And you, O tower of the flock, the fortress of the daughter of Zion, to you it will come, the first dominion; the kingdom will be restored to the daughter of Jerusalem." (Tower of the flock : Place of protection) 9. "Why do you cry out? Is there no king in you? Has your advisor perished? You are in anguish like a woman in labor." (Advisor : Counselor) 10. "Be in pain and labor to give birth, O daughter of Zion. For now, you will go to Babylon. There you will be rescued, and the LORD will redeem you from your enemies." (Labor : Struggle to give birth) 11. "Many nations have gathered against you, saying, 'Let her be defiled, and let us look upon Zion.'" (Defiled : Made unclean) 12. "But they do not understand the plans of the LORD, for He will gather them like sheaves to the threshing floor." (Sheaves: Bundles of grain) 13. "Rise up and thresh, O daughter of Zion, for I will make your horn iron and your hooves bronze. You will crush many nations, and their plunder will be dedicated to the LORD

Chapter 5
1. Gather yourselves, O daughter of troops, for the enemy has laid siege against us, and they will strike Israel's judge on the cheek. (Siege: blockade; Judge: divinely appointed)2. But you, Bethlehem Ephrathah, though small, will give rise to one who will rule Israel, whose origins are from ancient times. (Bethlehem: town in Judah; Origins: preexistent existence)3. He will give them up until the one in labor gives birth, and then the remnant of his brothers will return to Israel. (Remnant: remainder)4. He will lead in the strength of the LORD and be great to the ends of the earth. (Strength: power; Great: mighty)5. This man will bring peace, and when the Assyrian comes into our land, we will raise seven shepherds and eight leaders against him. (Assyrian: empire)6. They will destroy Assyria and Nimrod's land with the sword, and He will deliver us from the Assyrian invader. (Nimrod: kingdom; Deliver: rescue)7. The remnant of Jacob will be like dew, not waiting for men. (Dew: moisture)8. The remnant will be like a lion among the nations, tearing apart, with no one able to stop them. (Lion: powerful; Tearing apart: defeating with unstoppable force.)9. Your hand will be lifted against your enemies, and they will all be destroyed. (Enemies: foes)10. In that day, I will destroy your horses and chariots. (Chariots: vehicles of war)11. I will demolish your cities and strongholds. (Strongholds: fortresses)12. I will remove sorcery and fortune-tellers from among you. (Sorcery: magic; Fortune-tellers: seers)13. I will cut off your idols and images, and you will no longer worship them. (Idols: statues; Images: likenesses)14. I will uproot your groves and destroy your cities. (Groves: sacred trees; Uproot: tear out)15. I will execute vengeance upon the nations in anger, like nothing they have ever heard. (Vengeance: revenge; anger: wrath)

Chapter 6
1. Hear what the LORD says; arise and plead before the mountains, and let the hills hear. (Plead: argue)2. Listen, mountains, to the LORD's case, for He has a dispute with His people, and He will argue with Israel. (Dispute: disagreement; Case: lawsuit)3. My people, what have I done to you? How have I burdened you? Testify against me. (Burdened: weighed down)4. I brought you out of Egypt and redeemed you from slavery, sending Moses, Aaron, and Miriam before you. (Redeemed: saved)5. Remember what Balak consulted, and Balaam answered, from Shittim to Gilgal, to know the righteousness of the LORD. (Balak: king; Balaam: prophet hired to curse Israel) 6. What shall I bring before the LORD—burnt offerings or year-old calves? (Burnt offerings: sacrifices)7. Will the LORD be pleased with thousands of rams or rivers of oil? Should I give my firstborn for my sin? (Rams: sheep; Firstborn: first child)8. The LORD has shown you what is good: to act justly, love mercy, and walk humbly with your God. (Justly: fairly; Mercy: kindness)9. The LORD calls to the city, and the wise person will hear. (Rod: symbol of authority)10. Are there still treasures of wickedness and deceitful measures in the house of the wicked? (Wickedness: evil; Deceitful: misleading)11. Should I count them pure with false balances and deceitful weights? (Balances: scales)12. The rich are full of violence, and their words are lies. (Violence: aggression)13. Therefore, I will bring sickness and desolation upon you because of your sins. (Desolation: ruin)14. You will eat but not be satisfied, sow but not reap, and whatever you harvest will be given to the sword. (Sow: plant; Reap: gather)15. You will sow but not reap, tread olives but not anoint yourselves, and press sweet wine but not drink it. (Tread: crush; Anoint: sprinkling of oil) 16. You have followed the statutes of Omri and Ahab so I will make you desolate and mock you. (Statutes: laws; Omri: king of Israel known for idolatry." "Ahab: king of Israel, infamous for leading Israel into idolatry.")

Chapter 7
1. Woe is me! I am like one who has sought the summer fruits or the last grapes, but there is nothing to eat; my soul longs for the first-ripe fruit. (summer fruits: fruits gathered at the end of the harvest)2. The good have vanished from the earth; there is no upright among them. They wait to shed blood; they trap their brothers in a net. (upright: honest or righteous)3. They are determined to do evil with both hands; the ruler asks for bribes, the judge seeks a reward, and the influential speak wickedly, covering it up. (bribes: money or rewards for favor)4. The best among them is like a thorn bush, and the most upright is sharper than a thorn hedge. The day of your watchmen and visitation is coming, and confusion will follow. (watchmen: guardians, those who warn of trouble)5. Do not trust a friend, rely on a companion; be cautious even with those closest to you. (bosom: the place near the chest, symbolizing closeness)6. A son dishonors his father, a daughter rises up against her mother, and a daughter-in-law against her mother-in-law. A man's enemies are those in his own household. (dishonors: shows disrespect)7. But I will look to the LORD; I will wait for the God of my salvation. My God will hear me.8. Do not rejoice over me, my enemy! When I fall, I will rise again; when I sit in darkness, the LORD will be my light.9. I will bear the Lord's anger because I have sinned against Him, until He pleads my case and brings justice for me. He will bring me into the light, and I will see His righteousness.10. Then my enemy will see this, and shame will cover her who asked, "Where is the LORD your God?" My eyes will see her destruction; she will be trampled like mud in the streets. (trampled: defeated)11. The day your walls are rebuilt will come, and on that day your borders will be far removed. (walls: protective barriers or fortifications)12. On that day, people will come from Assyria, from fortified cities, from the strongholds to the river, from sea to sea, and from mountain to mountain. (Assyria: an ancient empire; fortified cities: strong, protected cities)13. Yet the land will become desolate because of the people who live in it, due to the consequences of their deeds. (desolate: empty, ruined)14. Shepherd your people with your staff, the flock that belongs to you, who live in solitude in the forest of Carmel. Let them feed in Bashan and Gilead, as in the days of old. (Carmel: a mountain range in Israel; Bashan and Gilead: regions known for rich pasture)15. As in the days when you came out of Egypt, I will show them marvelous things. (Egypt: the land from which the Israelites were delivered, a reference to their Exodus)16. The nations will see and be ashamed of their strength. They will cover their mouths, and their ears will be deaf. (nations: foreign peoples; strength: military or political power)17. They will lick the dust like a snake, crawling from their holes like worms of the earth. They will fear the LORD our God, and be terrified of you. (lick the dust: humiliation and defeat; worms of the earth: creeping creatures symbolizing lowliness)18. Who is a God like you, who pardons iniquity and passes over the transgression of the remnant of His people? He does not remain angry forever, for He delights in showing mercy. (iniquity: wickedness or sin; remnant: remaining people after destruction)19. He will again have compassion on us; He will subdue our iniquities, and You will cast all their sins into the depths of the sea.20. You will be faithful to Jacob, and show mercy to Abraham, as You swore to our ancestors from days of old. (Jacob: the father of the twelve tribes of Israel; Abraham: the patriarch of Israel's people)

34 – Nahum
Chapter 1
1. The burden of Nineveh. The vision of Nahum the Elkoshite. 2. God is jealous, and the LORD avenges; the LORD avenges, and is furious; the LORD will take vengeance on His enemies, and reserves wrath for His adversaries. (vengeance: retribution, adversaries: opponents, wrath: anger) 3. The LORD is slow to anger, and great in power, and will not leave the wicked unpunished; the LORD has His way in the storm and in the whirlwind, and the clouds are the dust of His feet. (unpunished: without consequence, whirlwind: violent wind) 4. He rebukes the sea, dries it up, and dries up all the rivers; Bashan and Carmel and Lebanon wither. (rebukes: commands, Bashan: region of fertile land, Lebanon: mountain range, wither: dry up) 5. The mountains quake at Him, and the hills melt, and the earth is burned at His presence; the world, and all who live in it, tremble before Him. (quake:

shake, melt: disintegrate, burned: scorched, tremble: shake with fear) **6.** Who can stand before His indignation? Who can endure His fierce anger? His fury is like fire, and the rocks are thrown down by Him. (indignation: anger, endure: withstand, fierce: strong, fury: rage) **7.** The LORD is good, a stronghold in the day of trouble; He knows those who trust in Him. (stronghold: safe place) **8.** But with an overwhelming flood, He will make an end of the place, and darkness will pursue His enemies. (overwhelming: all-consuming, flood: overflowing water, darkness: complete darkness) **9.** What do you imagine against the LORD? He will make an end of it; trouble will not rise up a second time. (imagine: plan, end: finish, trouble: suffering) **10.** Though they are like tangled thorns and drunkards, they will be consumed as dry stubble. (tangled: twisted, drunkards: spiritually intoxicated, consumed: destroyed, stubble: dry plants) **11.** There is one from you who plots evil against the LORD, a wicked counselor. (plots: plans, wicked: evil, counselor: advisor) **12.** The LORD says: Though they are quiet and numerous, they will be cut down when He passes through. Though I have troubled you, I will trouble you no more. (quiet: inactive, numerous: many, cut down: destroyed, troubled: oppressed) **13.** Now I will break off their yoke from you, and burst your chains. (yoke: burden, burst: break) **14.** The LORD has commanded that no more of your name be remembered; He will destroy your idols, and you will have no descendants. You are vile. (remembered: known, destroy: annihilate, idols: false gods, descendants: family line of kings, vile: despicable) **15.** Look, on the mountains, the feet of him who brings good news, proclaiming peace! O Judah, celebrate your festivals, fulfill your vows, for the wicked will no longer pass through you; they are utterly cut off. (Judah: kingdom of Judah, utterly: utterly contemptible).

Chapter 2

1. The one who destroys is coming to confront you; secure your fortifications, watch the roads, strengthen your resolve, and powerfully fortify your defenses. (fortifications: defenses, resolve: determination) **2.** For the LORD has taken away the glory of Jacob, as He did with Israel; the plunderers have stripped them clean and ruined their vine branches. (plunderers: those who loot, stripped: emptied, ruined: destroyed) **3.** The shields of his warriors are stained red, the valiant men are clothed in scarlet; the chariots will be set ablaze with torches on the day of battle, and the fir trees will shake violently. (warriors: soldiers, stained: covered, set ablaze: kindled) **4.** The chariots will charge through the streets, crashing into one another in the wide roads; they will look like flaming torches, racing like lightning. (charge: rush, crashing: colliding) **5.** He will call out his best men; they will stumble as they march; they will hurry to the city wall, and the defense will be ready. (best men: elite soldiers, stumble: fall, hurry: rush) **6.** The gates of the rivers will be opened, and the palace will be destroyed. (gates: entrances, destroyed: ruined) **7.** Huzzab will be taken captive, led away, and her maids will lead her in mourning, making a sound like doves, beating their breasts. (Huzzab: a queen, captive: taken prisoner, mourning: grieving) **8.** But Nineveh, like an old pool of water, will see its people flee. They will cry out, "Stand, stand!" but no one will turn back. (Nineveh: the city, pool of water: stagnant, flee: run away) **9.** Take the spoils of silver, take the spoils of gold, for there is no end to the treasures and beautiful items. (spoils: loot, treasures: wealth) **10.** The city is empty, desolate, and ruined; the hearts of the people will melt, their knees will tremble, pain will grip them, and their faces will turn pale. (desolate: barren, ruined: destroyed, pale: turned white) **11.** Where is the home of the lions and the feeding ground for the young lions, where the lion, even the old lion, roamed, and none dared to disturb them? (home: lair, roamed: walked, disturbed: frightened) **12.** The lion tore apart enough prey for his cubs, killed for his lionesses, filled his dens with the spoils, and his lairs with the kill. (prey: hunt, cubs: young lions, spoils: loot) **13.** Look, I am against you, says the LORD of hosts; I will burn your chariots, and the sword will consume your young lions; I will cut off your prey from the earth, and the sound of your messengers will no longer be heard. (consume: destroy, prey: victims, messengers: envoys).

Chapter 3

1. Woe to the city of bloodshed! It is filled with lies and theft; the prey never stops. (bloodshed: violence, theft: robbery) **2.** The sound of whips, the rattling of wheels, the prancing of horses, and the thundering chariots. (prancing: galloping) **3.** The horsemen raise their bright swords and glittering spears; there is a great number of the slain, with many bodies; there is no end to their dead; they stumble over the corpses. (slain: killed, stumble: trip) **4.** Because of the countless immoral acts of the beautiful prostitute, the mistress of sorceries, who enslaves nations through her immorality and families through her witchcraft. (immoral: sinful, prostitute: idolatrous harlot, sorceries: magic) **5.** Look, I am against you, says the LORD of hosts; I will uncover your skirts and show the nations your nakedness, and the kingdoms your shame. (uncover: expose, skirts: clothing) **6.** I will throw filthy shame upon you, make you despicable, and set you as a spectacle for all to see. (filthy: disgraceful, despicable: vile, spectacle: public display) **7.** Then all who look at you will flee, saying, "Nineveh is destroyed! Who will mourn for her? Where will I find comforters for you?" (mourn: grieve) **8.** Are you better than the great city of No, that was situated by the rivers, with waters surrounding it, whose defenses were the sea, and whose wall was from the sea? (No: Thebes, located in Egypt, defenses: protection) **9.** Ethiopia and Egypt were her strength, and there was no limit to her power; Put and Lubim were her allies. (strength: power, allies: helpers) **10.** Yet she was taken captive, her children dashed to pieces at the city streets, and they cast lots for her leaders; her great men were bound in chains. (captured: taken, dashed: crushed) **11.** You too will be drunk and hide; you will seek strength because of your enemies. (drunk: overwhelmed, seek: search) **12.** All your strongholds will be like fig trees with ripe fruit; when shaken, they will fall into the mouth of the eater. (strongholds: defenses, ripe: mature, shaken: disturbed) **13.** Look, your people are women in the midst of you; the gates of your land will be wide open to your enemies; fire will devour your bars. (bars: gates) **14.** Draw water for the siege, strengthen your defenses; dig clay and tread the mortar, build strong the brick kilns. (siege: attack, mortar: binding material) **15.** There the fire will consume you; the sword will cut you off, devouring you like locusts; multiply like locusts, like the cankerworm. (consume: destroy, cankerworm: destructive worm) **16.** You have multiplied your merchants more than the stars of heaven; the locusts spoil and fly away. (merchants: traders, spoil: plunder) **17.** Your rulers are like locusts, and your officials like great grasshoppers, who camp in the hedges on cold days; but when the sun rises, they fly away, and no one knows where they have gone. (rulers: leaders, officials: captains) **18.** Your shepherds are asleep, O king of Assyria; your nobles lie in the dust; your people are scattered on the mountains, and no one gathers them. (shepherds: leaders, nobles: high-ranking people, scattered: dispersed) **19.** There is no healing for your wound; your injury is fatal; all who hear the news about you will clap their hands for joy; for who has not experienced your constant wickedness? (healing: recovery, fatal: deadly, injury: wound).

35 – Habakuk

Chapter 1

1. The vision that Habakkuk the prophet received. (vision: divine revelation) **2.** O LORD, how long will I cry out and you will not listen? I cry to you about violence, and you do not save! (cry out: call for help, violence: injustice) **3.** Why do you show me evil, and make me witness suffering? Destruction and violence are before me; there are people stirring up conflict and arguing. (evil: iniquity, suffering: grievance, destruction: devastation, conflict: strife) **4.** Therefore the law is paralyzed, and justice is never carried out; the wicked surround the righteous; therefore, wrong judgment prevails. (paralyzed: ineffective, justice: judgment, prevails: succeeds) **5.** Look among the nations and be amazed; I will do something in your time that you wouldn't believe even if it was told to you. (amazed: astounded) **6.** For I am raising up the Chaldeans, that ruthless and impetuous nation, who will sweep across the land to seize territories not their own. (ruthless: cruel, impetuous: hasty, sweep: march) **7.** They are terrifying and fearsome; their judgment and their dignity come from themselves. (fearsome: dreadful, dignity: authority) **8.** Their horses are swifter than leopards, and fiercer than evening wolves; their horsemen will spread out, and they will come from far away; they will fly like eagles hurrying to eat. (swifter: faster, fiercer: more intense, spread out: disperse) **9.** They come for violence; their faces are like the east wind, and they gather captives like sand. (violence: destruction, east wind: scorching wind, captives: prisoners) **10.** They mock kings, and princes are a joke to them; they laugh at every fortress, they pile up dirt and capture it. (mock: scoff, joke: scorn, fortress: stronghold, pile up: heap) **11.** Then they will change their mind, pass on, and blame their power on their god. (change: alter, blame: attribute) **12.** Are you not from everlasting, O LORD my God, my Holy One? We will not die. O LORD, you have appointed them for judgment; O mighty God, you have established them for correction. (appointed: ordained, everlasting: eternal, correction: discipline) **13.** You are too pure to look at evil and cannot tolerate wrongdoing. Why then do you look at those who act treacherously, and remain silent when the wicked devour those more righteous than themselves? (treacherously: deceitfully, tolerate: endure, devour: destroy) **14.** You make people like fish in the sea, like creeping things that have no ruler over them. (creeping things: animals, ruler: authority) **15.** They catch all of them with a hook, they gather them in their net, and haul them in their dragnet; so they rejoice and are glad. (catch: capture, net: fishing net, haul: drag) **16.** Therefore they sacrifice to their net and burn incense to their dragnet; because through them, their portion is fat and their food abundant. (sacrifice: worship, incense: offerings, abundant: plentiful) **17.** Will they keep emptying their nets and continually killing nations without mercy? (emptying: depleting, continually: constantly, mercy: compassion).

Chapter 2

1. I will stand at my post and watch on the lookout tower, waiting to see what the LORD will say to me, and how I will respond when I am corrected. (post: station, lookout: watch, corrected: rebuked). **2.** The LORD answered me, "Write down the vision clearly, making it easy to read so that those who read it may run." (vision: revelation, clearly: plainly). **3.** The vision has an appointed time, and though it may seem slow in coming, wait for it; it will certainly happen at the right time. (appointed: set, slow: tarry, certainly: surely). **4.** The proud man's soul is not right, but the righteous will live by faith. (proud: puffed up, righteous: just, live: be sustained). **5.** Because he is driven by his desires, he is arrogant and never stays at home, seeking to conquer more and more, but he will never be satisfied. (driven: consumed by desire, arrogant: proud, conquer: gather). **6.** Won't all the nations eventually mock him, saying, "Woe to him who takes what isn't his! How long will he continue to amass wealth?" (mock: taunt, wealth: riches, amass: accumulate). **7.** Enemies will rise up suddenly and strike you, and you will become their victim. (strike: attack, victim: prey). **8.** You've plundered many nations, but now the survivors will plunder you, because of the bloodshed and violence that you've caused in the land and the cities. (plundered: spoiled, survivors: remnant, caused: done). **9.** Woe to the man who desires evil gain for himself, setting up his home high to escape the consequences of his actions. (desires: covets, gain: profit, consequences: punishment). **10.** By killing many people, you have brought shame upon your house and harmed your own soul. (killing: murdering, harmed: sinned against). **11.** The stones will cry out from the walls, and the beams in the woodwork will speak. (cry out: witness, beams: timbers). **12.** Woe to the one who builds a city with bloodshed and establishes it with evil deeds. (bloodshed: violence, establishes: builds, evil: iniquity). **13.** Isn't it the will of the LORD that people labor for nothing and wear themselves out in vain? (will: purpose, labor: work, vain: emptiness). **14.** The earth will be filled with the knowledge of the glory of the LORD, just as the sea is covered with water. (knowledge: awareness, glory: majesty). **15.** Woe to him who gives his neighbor wine, making them drunk to look upon their shame. (drunk: intoxicated, shame: nakedness). **16.** You will be filled with shame instead of glory. Drink, and let your nakedness be exposed; the cup of the LORD's judgment is coming for you. (nakedness: exposed body, judgment: wrath). **17.** The violence you caused to Lebanon and the destruction of animals will come back upon you, because of the bloodshed and violence you have committed. (Lebanon: forests, violence: harm, destruction: spoil). **18.** What good is an idol, when its maker has carved it? It's nothing but a lie. The maker trusts in his own creation, making it a powerless idol. (good: profit, carved: shaped, powerless: dumb). **19.** Woe to the one who says to wood, "Wake up!" or to a stone, "Arise! Teach us!" It's covered in gold and silver, but it has no breath in it. (covered: overlaid, no breath: lifeless). **20.** But the LORD is in His holy temple; let the earth be silent before Him. (temple: sacred place, silent: still).

Chapter 3

1. A prayer from Habakkuk the prophet, in the style of Shigionoth. (Shigionoth: a musical term, possibly referring to a particular tune or type of lament). **2.** O LORD, I have heard Your words, and I was filled with fear. O LORD, revive Your work in the midst of the years; make Your power known in this time, and in Your wrath, remember mercy. (filled: overwhelmed, revive: restore, Your power: Your might). **3.** God came from Teman, and the Holy One from Mount Paran. Selah. His glory covered the sky, and the earth was full of His praise. (Teman: a region, Mount Paran: a mountain range, glory: divine radiance, sky: heavens). **4.** His radiance was like the light; His hands had rays of power coming from them, and His power was hidden. (radiance: brightness, rays: rays of light, hidden: concealed). **5.** Before Him went pestilence, and fiery coals spread at His feet. (pestilence: disease, fiery coals: burning wrath). **6.** He stood and measured the earth; He looked, and the nations scattered. The ancient mountains trembled, and the eternal hills bowed down. His ways are eternal. (measured: surveyed, scattered: trembled, eternal: perpetual). **7.** I saw the tents of Cushan in distress, and the tents of Midian shook in fear. (distress: affliction, shook: trembled). **8.** Was the LORD angry with the rivers? Was His wrath against the rivers, or His anger against the sea? Did He ride upon His horses and His chariots of salvation? (angry: displeased, chariots of salvation: divine deliverance). **9.** Your bow was laid bare, according to the promises made by the tribes, even Your word. Selah. You split the earth with rivers. (laid bare: revealed, promises: oaths, split: cleaved). **10.** The mountains saw You and shook in fear; the rushing waters passed by. The deep sea roared, and lifted its hands high. (roared: uttered, rushing waters: overflowing, lifted: raised). **11.** The sun and moon stood still in their places; at the brightness of Your arrows, they hurried along, at the light from Your shining spear. (hurry: went, brightness: light, shining: glittering). **12.** You marched through the land in anger; You threshed the nations in wrath. (marched: moved, threshed: crushed, wrath: fury). **13.** You came out to save Your people, to save Your anointed one; You struck the head of the house of the wicked, exposing their foundation to the neck. Selah. (anointed: chosen one, struck: wounded, exposed: uncovered). **14.** You pierced the head of the enemy's villages with their own weapons. They came out like a whirlwind to scatter me, rejoicing as if to devour the poor secretly. (pierced: struck through, villages: strongholds, devour: consume). **15.** You trampled through the sea with Your horses, through the mighty waters. (trampled: walked upon, mighty: heap). **16.** When I heard, my body trembled; my lips quivered at the sound. Decay entered my bones, and I shook in fear, waiting for the day of distress when He comes up against the people, and He will overwhelm them with His forces. (trembled: shook, distress: trouble). **17.** Though the fig tree does not blossom, and there is no fruit on the vines; the olive trees fail, and the fields produce no food; the flocks are gone from the fold, and there are no herds in the stalls. (fail: wither, no herds: no cattle). **18.** Yet I will rejoice in the LORD, I will take joy in the God of my salvation. (rejoice: exult, salvation: deliverance). **19.** The LORD God is my strength; He will make my feet like the feet of a deer, and He will enable me to walk on high places. For the director of music, on my stringed instruments. (strength: power, feet like the feet of a deer: swift, director: chief singer).

36 – Zaphaniah

Chapter 1

1. The word of the LORD came to Zephaniah, son of Cushi, grandson of Gedaliah, and descendant of Hezekiah, during Josiah's reign in Judah. (Judah: southern Israelite kingdom) **2.** The LORD says, "I will completely destroy everything on earth." (utterly: fully or completely) **3.** "I will eliminate people, animals, birds, fish, and idols of the wicked, erasing humanity from the earth," says the LORD. (idols: objects of worship) **4.** "I will act against Judah and Jerusalem, removing all traces of Baal and pagan priests." (Baal: Canaanite god) **5.** "I will also remove those worshiping heavenly bodies on rooftops or swearing by both the LORD and Molech." (Molech: pagan god) **6.** "And those who turn away from the LORD or fail to seek His guidance." (guidance: advice or direction) **7.** "Be silent before the Sovereign LORD, for His day is near. He has prepared a sacrifice and called His guests." (sacrifice: offering to God) **8.** "On that day, I will punish princes, the king's children, and those wearing foreign clothes." (foreign: not of their culture) **9.** "I will also punish those defiling their masters' houses with violence and deceit." (defiling: corrupting or staining) **10.** "On that day," says the LORD, "there will be cries from the Fish Gate, wailing from the second district, and crashing from the hills." (Fish Gate: city gate in Jerusalem) **11.** "Mourn, residents of Maktesh, for traders are ruined, and silver dealers are cut off." (Maktesh: merchant area in Jerusalem) **12.** "I will search Jerusalem with lamps and punish those who are complacent, thinking the LORD neither rewards nor punishes." (complacent: spiritual indifference) **13.** "Their riches will be taken, their homes ruined; they'll build houses they won't live in and plant vineyards but not enjoy the wine." (vineyard: grape plantation) **14.** The great day of the LORD is near and approaching quickly. Even the strongest will cry bitterly. (bitterly: with deep sorrow) **15.** That day is one of anger, distress, destruction, and thick darkness. (distress: severe trouble) **16.** It will bring trumpet alarms against fortified cities and high towers. (fortified: well-defended) **17.** "I will bring trouble so severe that people will stumble like the blind, for they've sinned against the LORD. Their blood will pour like dust, their bodies like waste." (waste: useless matter) **18.** "Neither silver nor gold can save them from the LORD's wrath. His fiery jealousy will consume the land and swiftly destroy all who live there." (jealousy: intense anger)

Chapter 2

1. Gather, O rejected nation, come together. (Rejected nation: God's rejection due to sin.) **2.** Do this before the decree takes effect, before the day fades like chaff, and before the LORD's fierce anger strikes. (Chaff: empty remains of grain) **3.** Seek the LORD, you humble ones who follow His ways. Pursue righteousness and humility; perhaps you will be sheltered from His anger. (Humble: those who recognize their dependence on God.) **4.** Gaza will be deserted, Ashkelon destroyed, Ashdod driven out, and Ekron uprooted. (Gaza, Ashkelon, Ashdod, Ekron: Philistine cities) **5.** Woe to the seacoast dwellers, the Cherethite nation! The LORD's judgment is against you, Canaan, land of the Philistines; I will leave you desolate. (Cherethites: a Philistine tribe) **6.** The seacoast will become pastures for shepherds and pens for flocks. (Flocks: herds of animals) **7.** This land will belong to Judah's remnant; they will rest in Ashkelon's homes, for the LORD will restore them. (Remnant: surviving group) **8.** I have heard Moab's insults and Ammon's taunts, mocking My people and boasting against their borders. (Moab, Ammon: nations east of Israel) **9.** As I live, declares the LORD, Moab will be like Sodom, and Ammon like Gomorrah—desolate and abandoned. My people will inherit their land. (Sodom, Gomorrah: cities destroyed for wickedness) **10.** This will be their fate for their pride and insults against the people of the LORD. (Pride: arrogance) **11.** The LORD will strike fear in them, destroy their idols, and everyone will worship Him, even from distant islands. (Idols: false gods) **12.** You Ethiopians too will fall by My sword. (Ethiopians: people from Cush) **13.** He will stretch His hand against the north, destroying Assyria and turning Nineveh into a wasteland. (Nineveh: Assyrian capital) **14.** Flocks will graze in her ruins, and animals will rest there; birds will roost on her columns, and desolation will cover her. (Cormorants, bitterns: birds) **15.** Once a proud city, now a desolate ruin, where animals rest. Those who pass will mock her. (Proud city: Nineveh)

Chapter 3

1. Woe to the unclean, corrupt city, full of oppression! (Woe: sorrow; Unclean: morally impure) **2.** She ignored the voice, refused correction, did not trust in the LORD, or come near to her God. (Correction: guidance to improve) **3.** Her leaders are like roaring lions, her judges are wolves at dusk, leaving nothing until morning. (Leaders: rulers; Judges: decision-makers) **4.** Her prophets are deceitful, her priests have profaned the sanctuary and broken the law. (Prophets: messengers; Priests: religious leaders) **5.** The just LORD is in her midst, bringing His judgments every morning. He never fails, but the wicked know no shame. (Just: righteous; Judgment: fair decision) **6.** I have destroyed the nations; their cities are desolate, their streets abandoned with no one left. (Desolate: abandoned; Abandoned: left empty) **7.** I hoped they would fear Me and change, but they persisted in corruption. (Corruption: moral decay) **8.** Wait for Me, says the LORD, until I rise to punish. I will gather nations to pour out My wrath on them. The earth will burn with My jealousy. (Wrath: strong anger; Jealousy: protective anger) **9.** At that time, I will give people a pure language to call upon the LORD's name and serve Him together. (Pure: free from idolatry and falsehood; Accord: harmony) **10.** From beyond the rivers of Cush (Ethiopia), My scattered people will bring offerings. (Cush: ancient region in Africa) **11.** On that day, you will no longer be ashamed for your sins, for I will remove those who are proud, and you will no longer boast. (Proud: arrogant) **12.** I will leave a humble and poor people, and they will trust in the LORD. (Humble: lowly; Poor: without wealth) **13.** The remnant of Israel will speak truth, not lies, and live in peace without fear. (Remnant: those left behind; Remain: stay) **14.** Sing, O Zion; rejoice, O Israel; be glad with all your heart, O Jerusalem. (Zion: symbolic for Jerusalem) **15.** The LORD has removed your punishment, He has defeated your enemy. The King of Israel, the LORD, is with you, and you will no longer see disaster. (King of Israel: God as ruler) **16.** On that day, it will be said to Jerusalem, "Do not fear," and to Zion, "Let your hands be strong." (Zion: Jerusalem or Israel) **17.** The LORD, mighty to save, is with you. He will rejoice over you with joy and quiet you with His love. (Mighty: powerful) **18.** I will gather those who mourn for the feasts, who found them burdensome. (Mourn: feel sorrow; Feasts: sacred celebrations) **19.** At that time, I will remove those who oppress you, save the lame, and gather the outcasts. They will be praised everywhere. (Oppress: mistreat; Outcasts: rejected people) **20.** I will bring you back, and make you a name and praise among all nations when I restore your fortunes, says the LORD. (Renowned: widely known; Restore: bring back)

37 – Haggai
Chapter 1

1 In the second year of King Darius, on the first day of the sixth month, the word of the Lord came through the prophet Haggai to Zerubbabel, son of Shealtiel, the governor of Judah, and to Joshua, son of Josedech, the high priest, saying, (Darius: King of Persia; Zerubbabel: Governor of Judah; Joshua: High priest) **2.** The Lord Almighty says, "The people are saying that now is not the time to rebuild the temple of the Lord." (Lord Almighty: God as the supreme ruler) **3.** Then the word of the Lord came through Haggai again, saying, **4.** "Is it right for you to live in well-built homes while my house remains in ruins?" (Well-built: Comfortable or luxurious) **5.** The Lord says, "Consider your ways." (Consider: Reflect or think about) **6.** You plant a lot but harvest little. You eat and drink, yet you are never satisfied. You clothe yourselves but stay cold. You earn money, but it seems to vanish, like money put into a purse with holes. **7.** The Lord says again, "Consider your ways." **8.** "Go up to the mountains, gather wood, and rebuild my house. I will take joy in it and be honored," says the Lord. (Mountains: High regions of land) **9.** You expected to have plenty, but when you brought it home, it was nothing. I blew it away. Why? Because my house lies in ruins while you focus on your own homes. **10.** That's why the heavens have withheld dew, and the earth has held back its crops. (Dew: moisture from the air; crops: Plants grown for food) **11.** I called for a drought on the fields, the mountains, the grain, the new wine, and everything the land produces, and on all your labor. (Drought: Lack of rain) **12.** Then Zerubbabel, Joshua, and the people obeyed the voice of the Lord their God and feared Him. **13.** Haggai, the Lord's messenger, gave the Lord's message to the people: "I am with you," declares the Lord. (Messenger: One who delivers God's message) **14.** The Lord stirred up the spirits of Zerubbabel, Joshua, and all the people, and they began working on the temple of the Lord their God. **15.** This happened on the twenty-fourth day of the sixth month, in the second year of King Darius.

Chapter 2

1. On the 21st day of the seventh month, the word of the Lord came through the prophet Haggai, saying, (Seventh month: Hebrew calendar month, 21st day: specific date) **2.** "Speak to Zerubbabel, governor of Judah, Joshua the high priest, and the remaining people, saying, (Zerubbabel: Governor of Judah, Joshua: High priest, Judah: Region in Israel) **3.** 'Who among you saw this temple in its former glory? How does it look now? Is it not like nothing in your sight, a shadow of its former greatness?' (Temple: Sacred building, glory: Greatness or splendor) **4.** But be strong, Zerubbabel, Joshua, and all the people, says the Lord. Work, for I am with you, says the Lord of hosts. (Strong: Courageous, Lord of hosts: God's heavenly army) **5.** My spirit remains with you, as I promised when you came out of Egypt. Do not fear. (Egypt: Ancient land where the Israelites were enslaved) **6.** In a little while, I will shake the heavens, earth, sea, and land; (Heavens: Sky or universe, shake: Cause to move violently) **7.** I will shake all nations, and the desire of all nations will come, and I will fill this house with glory, says the Lord of hosts. (Nations: Groups of people, house: Temple, glory: Greatness or honor) **8.** The silver and gold are mine, says the Lord of hosts. (Silver: Precious metal, gold: Valuable metal, Lord of hosts: God's heavenly army) **9.** The glory of this temple will be greater than the former one, and in this place, I will give peace, says the Lord. (Temple: Sacred building, glory: Greatness or splendor, peace: Harmony or tranquility) **10.** On the 24th day of the ninth month, the word of the Lord came through Haggai, saying, (Ninth month: Hebrew calendar month, 24th day: specific date) **11.** "Ask the priests about the law, (Priests: Religious leaders, law: Religious rules) **12.** 'If someone carries holy flesh on the edge of their garment and touches bread, stew, wine, oil, or any food, will it become holy?' The priests answered, 'No.' (Holy flesh: Sacred meat, garment: Clothing, holy: Sacred) **13.** Then Haggai asked, 'If someone unclean by a dead body touches these things, will they become unclean?' The priests replied, 'Yes, they will be unclean.' (Unclean: Ritually impure, dead body: Deceased person's body) **14.** Haggai said, 'So is this people, this nation, and everything they do. What they offer is unclean.' (Unclean: Ritually impure) **15.** Now consider this from today, from before the temple foundation was laid. (Temple foundation: The base or beginning of the temple) **16.** When you went to gather grain, you found only half of what you expected. (Grain: Seeds or cereal crops) **17.** I sent mildew, hail, and blight to all your work, yet you did not return to me, says the Lord. (Mildew: Fungus, hail: Icy rain, blight: Plant disease) **18.** Now, consider this from today, from the day the temple foundation was laid. (Temple foundation: The base or beginning of the temple) **19.** Is there yet any crop in the barn? The trees have not yet borne fruit, but from this day on, I will bless you. (Crop: Harvested produce, barn: Storage building for crops, bless: To bring favor or prosperity) **20.** Again, on the 24th day of the month, the word of the Lord came to Haggai, saying, (24th day: Specific date) **21.** "Tell Zerubbabel, governor of Judah, I will shake the heavens and the earth; (Zerubbabel: Governor of Judah, shake: Cause to move violently) **22.** I will overthrow the kingdoms and destroy their power, overthrow chariots and those who ride them, and the horses and riders will fall by the sword. (Overthrow: To defeat or destroy, chariots: Ancient war vehicles, sword: Weapon) **23.** On that day, I will take you, Zerubbabel, my servant, and make you like a signet ring, for I have chosen you, says the Lord of hosts." (Signet ring: A ring used as symbol of royal authority)

38 – Zechariah
Chapter 1

1. In the eighth month, second year of Darius, Zechariah received a message from the LORD. (LORD: The Almighty) **2.** The LORD was very angry with your ancestors. (ancestors: forefathers who turned away from God's commands) **3.** So, tell them, "Return to me, and I will return to you," says the LORD of hosts. (hosts: heavenly armies) **4.** Don't be like your ancestors, to whom the prophets said, "Turn from your evil ways," but they didn't listen. **5.** Where are your ancestors now? Do the prophets live forever? (forever: living eternally) **6.** Didn't my words and commands, delivered by the prophets, affect your ancestors? They realized that God dealt with them according to their actions. (ancestors: forefathers) **7.** On the 24th day of the 11th month, Zechariah received another message from the LORD. (LORD: God of Israel) **8.** In the night, Zechariah saw a man on a red horse, standing among myrtle trees, with other horses behind him, red, speckled, and white. (myrtle trees: a type of tree) **9.** Zechariah asked, "What are these?" **10.** The angel replied, 'I will show you.' **11.** The man answered, "These are the ones sent by the LORD to patrol the earth." (patrol: to survey or oversee) **12.** The horses said, "We've patrolled the earth, and everything is calm." (calm: peaceful, still) **13.** Then the angel asked, "LORD of hosts, how long until you show mercy on Jerusalem and Judah, after 70 years of anger?" (hosts: armies; Judah: southern kingdom of Israel) **14.** The LORD answered with good and comforting words. (comforting: words of hope and encouragement) **15.** The angel said, "Proclaim, 'The LORD is passionate about Jerusalem and Zion.'" (Zion: city and hill of Jerusalem) **16.** "I'm angry with the nations that are at peace. I was angry, but their actions intensified the suffering **17.** "So, I am returning to Jerusalem with mercy. My house will be rebuilt, and a measuring line will be stretched over it." (Mercy: kindness; measuring line: symbol of construction) **18.** "Proclaim, 'The cities will prosper, and the LORD will comfort Zion and choose Jerusalem again.'" (prosper: flourish) **19.** Zechariah then saw four horns. (horns: powers or oppressors) **20.** He asked the angel, "What are these?" **21.** The angel replied, "These are the horns that scattered Judah, Israel, and Jerusalem. But four carpenters will come to defeat them." (Judah: southern kingdom; Israel: northern kingdom; carpenters: agents of divine justice)

Chapter 2
1. I looked again and saw a man with a measuring line in his hand. (Measuring line: a tool used to measure distance.) **2.** I asked, "Where are you going?" He replied, "To measure Jerusalem, to find its width and length." (Jerusalem: the holy city; width: the extent from side to side; length: the extent from end to end.) **3.** Then the angel who spoke with me went out, and another angel met him. (Spoke: communicated; met: encountered.) **4.** The second angel said, "Run, tell the young man that Jerusalem will be populated like towns without walls, filled with people and animals." (Populated: inhabited; without walls: open, undefended.) **5.** The LORD says, "I will be a protective fire around her, and my glory will be in her midst." (Protective: guarding; glory: divine presence.) **6.** "Come out from the land of the north, for I have scattered you like the four winds," says the LORD. (Scattered: spread out; winds: the directions of the earth's air currents.) **7.** "Escape, Zion, who lives with Babylon." (Zion: Jerusalem or its people; Babylon: an enemy city.) **8.** The LORD says, "After glory, I was sent to the nations that harmed you. Anyone who harms you harms the apple of my eye." (Glory: divine honor; harmed: caused damage; apple of my eye: something cherished.) **9.** "I will shake my hand at them, and they will become spoils for their enemies. You will know the LORD sent me." (Shake my hand: a gesture of anger or judgment; spoils: rewards of conquest.) **10.** "Sing and rejoice, daughter of Zion, for I will come and dwell among you," says the LORD. (Dwell: live.) **11.** "Many nations will join with the LORD and become my people. I will be in the midst of you, and you will know that the LORD sent me." (Join: unite; midst: center.) **12.** "The LORD will inherit Judah as his portion and choose Jerusalem again." (Inherit: take possession of; portion: share.) **13.** "Be still, all people, before the LORD, for he has risen from his holy place." (Still: silent; risen: has stood up.)

Chapter 3
1. He showed me Joshua the high priest standing before the angel of the LORD, and Satan at his right to accuse him. (Accuse: To charge with wrongdoing) **2.** The LORD rebuked Satan, saying, "The LORD who chose Jerusalem rebukes you. Is this not a brand plucked from the fire?" (Rebuke: To express sharp disapproval) (Brand: a burning stick pulled from the fire) **3.** Joshua was wearing filthy clothes and stood before the angel. (Filthy: Extremely dirty) **4.** The angel told those standing by, "Take off his filthy clothes. I have forgiven your sins and will give you clean garments." (Iniquity: Wickedness or sin) **5.** I said, "Put a clean mitre on his head." So they did, and the angel stood by. (Mitre: A type of headdress worn by priests) **6.** The angel of the LORD spoke to Joshua, saying, (Protested: Expressed disapproval) **7.** "The LORD of hosts says: If you follow my ways and keep my commands, you will judge my house, guard my courts, and be given authority among these standing here." (Hosts: Armies or heavenly beings) **8.** "Listen, Joshua, and you priests: For you are a sign. I will send my servant, the BRANCH." (Branch: A symbolic title for a future leader or Messiah) **9.** "Look at the stone I have set before Joshua. It has seven eyes, and I will engrave it. I will remove the sins of the land in one day." (Engrave: To carve or etch into a surface) **10.** "On that day, you will invite your neighbors to sit under the vine and fig tree." (Invite: To request someone's presence)

Chapter 4
1. The angel who had spoken to me returned and woke me, just as someone awakens from a deep sleep. (Woke: roused) **2.** He asked, "What do you see?" I replied, "I see a golden lampstand, with a bowl on top, seven lamps on it, and seven tubes leading to them." (Lampstand: a holder for lamps, Tubes: narrow passages) **3.** There are two olive trees next to it, one on the right of the bowl and one on the left. (Olive trees: trees bearing olives) **4.** I questioned the angel, saying, "What do these things mean, my lord?" (Questioned: asked, Lord: a term of respect) **5.** The angel responded, "Don't you know what these are?" I answered, "No, my lord." (Responded: answered) **6.** Then he explained, "This is the message from the Lord to Zerubbabel: 'It will not be by human strength or power, but by My Spirit,' says the Lord Almighty." (Message: communication, Almighty: all-powerful) **7.** "Who are you, mighty mountain? Before Zerubbabel, you will become level ground, and he will bring out the final stone with a shout of 'Grace, grace to it!'" (Final stone: the last stone, Grace: divine favor) **8.** The word of the Lord came to me once more. **9.** "Zerubbabel's hands began the foundation of this temple, and his hands will complete it. You will know that the Lord Almighty has sent me to you." (Foundation: base, Temple: place of worship) **10.** "Who despises the small beginnings? They will rejoice when they see the measuring line in Zerubbabel's hand. These are the eyes of the Lord, moving throughout the whole earth." (Despises: looks down on, Measuring line: tool for measurement, Rejoice: celebrate) **11.** I asked again, "What are the two olive trees beside the lampstand, one on each side?" (Asked: inquired) **12.** I asked again, "What are these two olive branches that pour out golden oil through the golden tubes?" (Branches: tree limbs, Pour out: release) **13.** The angel replied, "Do you not know what these are?" I said, "No, my lord." (Replied: responded) **14.** He said, "These are the two chosen ones, who stand by the Lord of all the earth." (Chosen: selected for a special purpose)

Chapter 5
1. I turned, lifted my eyes, and saw a flying scroll. **2.** The angel asked, "What do you see?" I replied, "A flying scroll, 20 cubits long and 10 cubits wide." **3.** He said, "This is the curse over the earth: those who steal or swear falsely will be cut off." **4.** The Lord will send it, and it will enter the house of the thief or one who swears falsely by His name, consuming their house, timber and stones. (Timber: wood) **5.** The angel said, "Look again, see what comes next." **6.** I asked, "What is it?" He replied, "It's an ephah going forth; this is the appearance of evil in the whole earth." (Ephah: a unit of measure) **7.** I saw a talent of lead lifted, with a woman sitting inside the ephah. (Talent: a heavy weight) **8.** The angel said, "This is wickedness." He threw it back into the ephah and sealed it with the lead weight. **9.** Then I saw two women with wings like storks, lifting the ephah between earth and heaven. (Storks: large birds) **10.** I asked, "Where are they taking it?" **11.** The angel answered, "To build a house in Shinar, where it will be established on its own base." (Shinar: an ancient region)

Chapter 6
1. I looked up and saw four chariots emerging from between two mountains made of bronze. (Bronze: a strong, durable metal.) **2.** The first chariot had red horses, and the second had black horses. **3.** The third chariot carried white horses, and the fourth had spotted and strong horses. (Spotted: marked with patches of color.) **4.** I asked the angel speaking with me, "What do these represent, my lord?" **5.** The angel said, "These are the four spirits of heaven sent out from the presence of the Lord of all the earth." (Spirits: divine beings or forces.) **6.** The black horses went toward the north, the white ones followed them, and the spotted horses headed south. **7.** The strong horses sought permission to patrol the earth. The Lord said, "Go and patrol the earth," and they obeyed. (Patrol: to travel and watch over an area.) **8.** Then the angel called to me, saying, "Look! Those going toward the north have calmed My spirit there." (Calmed: brought peace or relief.) **9.** The word of the Lord came to me, saying: **10.** "Take silver and gold from Heldai, Tobijah, and Jedaiah, who have returned from Babylon, and go to the house of Josiah, son of Zephaniah." (Captivity: being taken prisoner.) **11.** Make crowns from the silver and gold and place one on the head of Joshua, the high priest. (High Priest: chief religious leader.) **12.** Say, 'This is what the Lord of Hosts says: Behold the man called The Branch! He will grow where He is and build the temple of the Lord.' (Branch: a metaphor for someone who brings life and renewal.) **13.** "Yes, He will build the temple of the Lord and rule in glory, sitting as both king and priest. He will bring harmony between both roles." (Harmony: peaceful agreement.) **14.** The crowns will be a memorial for Helem, Tobijah, Jedaiah, and Hen, son of Zephaniah, in the temple of the Lord. (Memorial: something kept to remember an event or person.) **15.** People from afar will come to build the temple of the Lord. Then you will know the Lord has sent me to you—if you diligently obey His voice. (Diligently: with careful and persistent effort.)

Chapter 7
1. In the fourth year of King Darius, on the fourth day of the ninth month (Chisleu), the word of the LORD came to Zechariah. (Chisleu: the ninth month in the Hebrew calendar) **2.** Sherezer, Regem-melech, and their men were sent to the house of God to pray to the LORD. **3.** They asked the priests and prophets in the temple, "Should we continue mourning and fasting in the fifth month, as we've done for many years?" **4.** The word of the LORD came to me, saying: **5.** "Tell the people and the priests: When you fasted and mourned in

the fifth and seventh months for seventy years, was it truly for Me? (Fasted: abstained from food or drink for religious purposes) **6.** And when you ate and drank, wasn't it only for yourselves?" **7.** "Why haven't you listened to the words I spoke through the prophets when Jerusalem was prosperous, and its surrounding cities were inhabited?" **8.** Then the word of the LORD came to Zechariah again: **9.** "This is what the LORD of hosts says: Be just, show kindness, and have compassion for one another. (Compassion: deep sympathy and concern for others) **10.** Do not oppress widows, orphans, foreigners, or the poor. Do not plot evil against others in your hearts. (Oppress: treat harshly or unfairly) **11.** But the people refused to listen. They turned away stubbornly and stopped their ears so they wouldn't hear. (Hearken: listen attentively) **12.** They hardened their hearts like stone to avoid hearing My law and the words I sent through the prophets. As a result, My great wrath came upon them. (Adamant: unyielding or stubborn) **13.** When I called out to them, they didn't listen. So, when they cried to Me, I didn't listen, says the LORD. **14.** I scattered them among foreign nations like a whirlwind, leaving the land empty and deserted. The once-beautiful land became a wasteland. (Desolate: abandoned and lifeless)

Chapter 8
1. The word of the LORD came to me again. **2.** The LORD says, "I am deeply passionate about Zion and fiercely protective of her." (Jealousy: deep passion or concern.) **3.** "I have returned to Zion and will live in Jerusalem, which will be called the City of Truth and the Holy Mountain. **4.** "Old men and women will once again live peacefully in Jerusalem, leaning on their staffs in their old age." (Staff: a walking stick.) **5.** "The streets will be filled with boys and girls playing joyfully." **6.** "If this seems impossible to the remnant of my people, should it be impossible for me?" (Remnant: the small remaining group.) **7.** "I will rescue my people from the east and west." **8.** "I will bring them back to live in Jerusalem. They will be my people, and I will be their God, in truth and righteousness." (Righteousness: moral correctness.) **9.** "Be strong, you who have heard these prophetic words since the foundation of the temple was laid." (Foundation: the base or starting point.) **10.** "Previously, there was no reward for work, and no peace, as people turned against each other." (Affliction: hardship or trouble.) **11.** "But now, I will not treat the remnant as I did before," says the LORD. **12.** "Seeds will flourish, vines will bear fruit, the land will yield abundance, and the heavens will send dew." (Dew: moisture from the atmosphere.) **13.** "You were once a curse among the nations, but I will save you and make you a blessing. Do not fear; be strong." (Heathen: people of other nations or beliefs.) **14.** "I once planned to punish your ancestors for their sins, and I did not relent." (Relent: become less strict.) **15.** "Now, I plan to bless Jerusalem and Judah. Do not be afraid." **16.** "Speak truth to one another, judge fairly, and promote peace." (Judgment: decision-making.) **17.** "Do not plot evil or make false promises, for I hate these things," says the LORD. (False oath: a dishonest promise.) **18.** The word of the LORD came again. **19.** "The fasts of the fourth, fifth, seventh, and tenth months will turn into joyful celebrations for Judah. Love truth and peace." **20.** "People from many cities will come together." **21.** "One city's people will call others to seek and pray to the LORD." **22.** "Strong nations and many peoples will come to Jerusalem to pray to the LORD." **23.** "In those days, people of all nations will seek the company of a Jew, saying, 'We want to go with you because we know God is with you.'"

Chapter 9
1. The burden of the LORD's word will fall on Hadrach, with Damascus as its resting place. All of Israel will turn their eyes toward the LORD. (Burden: a heavy responsibility) **2.** Hamath will border it, along with Tyre and Sidon, which are very wise. (Border: form the boundary; Sidon: an ancient Phoenician city) **3.** Tyre built a stronghold, gathering silver like dust and gold like street mud. (Stronghold: a fortified place) **4.** The Lord will cast her out, destroy her power in the sea, and she will be consumed by fire. (Cast out: expel; consume: destroy) **5.** Ashkelon will see it and fear; Gaza will mourn deeply, and Ekron's hope will be shattered. The king of Gaza will perish, and Ashkelon will be uninhabited. (Shattered: broken or ruined; Perish: die) **6.** A foreigner will live in Ashdod, and I will remove the pride of the Philistines. (Foreigner: a person from outside the area) **7.** I will cleanse their mouths and remove their abominations, but those who remain will belong to God. They will become rulers in Judah, and Ekron will be like the Jebusites. (Abominations: things hated by God; Jebusites: ancient people of Jerusalem) **8.** I will protect My house, ensuring no oppressor passes through, for I have seen with My own eyes. (Oppressor: one who oppresses or harms others) **9.** Rejoice greatly, daughter of Zion! Shout, daughter of Jerusalem! Your King comes, just and bringing salvation, humble and riding on a donkey, the foal of a donkey. (Zion: a hill in Jerusalem, symbolizing Israel) **10.** I will remove the chariot from Ephraim, the horse from Jerusalem, and cut off the battle bow. He will speak peace to the nations, and His rule will extend from sea to sea, from river to the ends of the earth. (Chariot: a wheeled war vehicle; Ephraim: a tribe of Israel) **11.** By the blood of the covenant, I will free your prisoners from the pit with no water. (Covenant: a sacred agreement; Pit: a deep hole or dungeon) **12.** Turn to the stronghold, prisoners of hope; today I declare that I will give you double. (Stronghold: a place of safety or defense) **13.** When I bend Judah for Myself and fill the bow with Ephraim, I will raise your sons, O Zion, against Greece, making you a mighty sword. (Bend: to make ready or prepare; Ephraim: a tribe of Israel) **14.** The LORD will be seen over them; His arrow will flash like lightning. He will blow the trumpet and come with southern whirlwinds. (Whirlwinds: powerful winds or storms) **15.** The LORD will defend them; they will conquer with slings and stones, rejoicing like wine-drunk men, filled like bowls and corners of the altar. (Sling stones: stones used in a slingshot) **16.** The LORD will save them as His flock, and they will be like jewels in a crown, raised as a banner in His land. (Flask: a container; Flock: a group of sheep) **17.** How great is His goodness and beauty! The young men will rejoice like corn, and the young women like new wine. (Goodness: kindness or generosity)

Chapter 10
1. Ask the LORD for rain in the season of latter rains; He will send bright clouds and showers to nourish the fields. (Latter rains – rains that come after the planting season, essential for crops) **2.** Idols speak emptiness, and diviners tell lies; their false dreams offer no comfort. Without a shepherd, they wander like a flock, troubled and lost. (Diviners – those who predict the future through supernatural means) **3.** I became angry with the shepherds and punished the goats. The LORD visited His people, Judah, making them like His powerful horse in battle. (Goats – leaders or rulers; the LORD of hosts – God, ruler of all) **4.** From Judah comes strength, leadership, and warriors who will defeat all oppressors. (Corner – a key leader or cornerstone; Nail – stability or support) **5.** They will be like mighty men, crushing their enemies in the streets, fighting with the LORD on their side. Even horse riders will be overwhelmed. (Mire – mud; Confounded – confused, defeated) **6.** I will strengthen Judah and save Joseph. I will restore them because of My mercy, and they will no longer feel abandoned. I am their God, and I will hear them. (Joseph – a tribe of Israel) **7.** Ephraim will be mighty, rejoicing like those who drink wine; their children will rejoice too, for their hearts will be glad in the LORD. (Ephraim – a tribe of Israel) **8.** I will gather them, having redeemed them, and they will grow in number. (Hiss – a call or signal) **9.** I will scatter them among nations; they will remember Me in distant lands, return to their children, and live in peace. (Scatter – spread out) **10.** I will bring them back from Egypt and Assyria, to the lands of Gilead and Lebanon, where there will be no room for them. (Gilead – a region; Lebanon – a region known for its mountains) **11.** They will cross the sea with difficulty, but I will dry up the rivers. The pride of Assyria will fall, and Egypt's power will be destroyed. (Sceptre – symbol of power or rule) **12.** I will strengthen them in the LORD, and they will walk in His name, says the LORD. (Sceptre – staff or authority of a ruler)

Chapter 11
1. Open your gates, O Lebanon, that fire may consume your cedars. (Lebanon: a country with famous cedar trees) **2.** Cry out, O fir tree, for the cedar has fallen; the mighty are ruined. Cry out, O oaks of Bashan, for the forest are destroyed. (Bashan: a region known for its oak trees) **3.** The shepherds' voices howl, for their glory is lost; the roar of young lions is heard, for the pride of Jordan is ruined. (Jordan: a river) **4.** Thus says the LORD: Feed the flock destined for slaughter. (Slaughter: sacrificial killing) **5.** The owners kill them without guilt, and those who sell them say, "Blessed be the LORD, for I am rich." But their shepherds show no compassion. (Shepherds: leaders or caretakers) **6.** I will no longer have pity on the people of the land, says the LORD. I will hand everyone over to his neighbor and his king, and they will strike the land; I will not rescue them. (King: ruler of a country) **7.** I will care for the flock of slaughter, the poor of the flock. I took two staffs: one called Beauty, the other Bands, and I fed the flock. (Staffs: wooden sticks used for support) **8.** I cut off three shepherds in one month, and my soul despised them, and theirs despised me. (Despised: hated) **9.** Then I said, "I will no longer feed you. Let the dying die, and the lost be lost. Let the rest feed on one another's flesh." **10.** I took my staff, Beauty, and broke it to break my covenant with the people. (Covenant: agreement or promise) **11.** It was broken that day, and the poor flock knew it was the word of the LORD. **12.** I said to them, "If you want, give me my wages; if not, then leave it." They weighed thirty pieces of silver for me. (Wages: payment for work) **13.** The LORD said, "Throw it to the potter!"—a worthless price they valued me at. So I threw the thirty pieces to the potter in the temple of the LORD. (Potter: a person who makes things from clay) **14.** Then I broke my other staff, Bands, to break the bond between Judah and Israel. (Judah and Israel: ancient kingdoms) **15.** The LORD said, "Take the tools of a foolish shepherd." (Foolish:

unwise) **16.** I will raise up a shepherd who will not care for the lost, seek the young, heal the broken, or feed the standing. He will devour the fat and tear the claws. (Devour: eat greedily) **17.** Woe to the idol shepherd who leaves the flock! The sword will strike his arm and his right eye. His arm will dry up, and his right eye will be darkened. (Idol: false, not real)

Chapter 12

1. The burden of the LORD's word for Israel, says the LORD, who created the heavens, set the earth's foundation, and placed the spirit in man. (Burden: a heavy message or responsibility) **2.** I will make Jerusalem a source of fear to all nearby nations, who will lay siege to both Judah and Jerusalem. (Siege: a military blockade) **3.** On that day, Jerusalem will become a stone too heavy for all to carry; those who try will be shattered, even if all the earth's nations gather against it. (Burden: weight, too difficult to handle) **4.** On that day, I will strike every horse with panic and its rider with madness. I will watch over Judah's people and blind the horses of the enemy. (Astonishment: shock or surprise; Madness: uncontrollable anger) **5.** The leaders of Judah will find strength in the LORD, the God of hosts, knowing that the people of Jerusalem will help them. (Hosts: armies or heavenly beings) **6.** On that day, I will make Judah's leaders like a blazing fire among dry wood, devouring all those around them, and Jerusalem will be secure in its place. (Hearth: a place of fire; Sheaf: a bundle of grain) **7.** The LORD will protect Judah's tents first, so the glory of David's house and Jerusalem's people will not be exalted over Judah. (Tents: dwellings or homes) **8.** On that day, the LORD will defend Jerusalem's people, making even the weakest among them strong like David, and the house of David will be like God, like the angel of the LORD. (Feeble: weak) **9.** I will destroy all nations that attack Jerusalem. (Seek: to attempt or plan) **10.** I will pour out a spirit of grace and prayer on the house of David and Jerusalem, and they will mourn for the one they pierced, as for a beloved son. (Grace: unmerited favor; Supplications: earnest requests) **11.** That day will bring great mourning in Jerusalem, like the mourning for Hadadrimmon in the valley of Megiddon. (Mourning: expressing sorrow or grief) **12.** Every family will mourn separately: the house of David apart, with their wives; the house of Nathan apart, with their wives; (Apart: separately or individually) **13.** The house of Levi apart, with their wives; the house of Shimei apart, with their wives; (Levi: a tribe of Israel; Shimei: a name of a family or individual) **14.** All remaining families will mourn apart, with their wives separately. (Remaining: left over or still existing)

Chapter 13

1. On that day, a fountain will be opened for the house of David and Jerusalem, to cleanse them from sin and impurity. (impurity: uncleanness) **2.** The Lord will remove idols from the land and they will be forgotten, and He will drive out false prophets and evil spirits. (false prophets: those who falsely claim to speak for God; evil spirits: unclean or harmful spirits) **3.** If someone prophesies lies in the Lord's name, his parents will say, "You shall die!" and will punish him for his false prophecy. (prophesies: foretells future events; false prophecy: a lie spoken as if from God) **4.** On that day, prophets will be ashamed of their visions and will stop pretending to deceive others by wearing rough garments. (deceive: mislead or trick) **5.** A prophet will admit, "I am no prophet; I am a farmer, raised to care for animals." (husbandman: farmer) **6.** When asked about the wounds on his hands, he will answer, "These are the wounds I received from my friends." (wounds: injuries) **7.** The Lord commands, "Awake, O sword, against my shepherd, and against the man who is my companion! Strike the shepherd, and the sheep will scatter; I will turn my hand against the little ones." (shepherd: leader; companion: fellow) **8.** Two-thirds of the people in the land will be cut off and die, but a third will remain. (cut off: removed or destroyed) **9.** The remaining third will be tested through trials, refined like silver and gold, and they will call on God's name. He will answer, "These are my people," and they will say, "The Lord is our God." (refined: purified through heat or pressure; trials: tests of endurance)

Chapter 14

1. The day of the LORD is coming, and your wealth will be divided among you. (Spoil: wealth, plunder) **2.** I will gather all nations to battle against Jerusalem; the city will be taken, homes looted, and women violated. Half of the city will go into captivity, but the rest will not be destroyed. (Rifled: looted, ravished: violated) **3.** Then the LORD will rise up and fight against these nations as He did in ancient battles. **4.** On that day, His feet will stand on the Mount of Olives, east of Jerusalem. The mountain will split, creating a vast valley with half moving north, the other south. (Cleave: split) **5.** You will flee to the valley of the mountains, just as you fled from the earthquake in Uzziah's time. The LORD will come with all His holy ones. (Azal: a place, tumult: confusion) **6.** On that day, the light will be neither clear nor dark. **7.** It will be a unique day, known only to the LORD, where it is neither day nor night, but light will shine at evening. **8.** Living waters will flow from Jerusalem, half to the eastern sea, half to the western sea, in summer and winter alike. **9.** The LORD will reign over the entire earth, and His name will be the only one. **10.** The land will be leveled, from Geba to Rimmon, south of Jerusalem, and it will be inhabited again, from Benjamin's gate to the first gate, and beyond. (Geba, Rimmon: locations, plain: flat land) **11.** People will live there in peace, and Jerusalem will no longer face destruction. **12.** The LORD will strike those who fought against Jerusalem with a plague: their flesh will decay while they stand, and their eyes and tongues will disintegrate. (Plague: a deadly disease or punishment) **13.** On that day, the LORD will stir up confusion among them; neighbors will fight against each other. **14.** Judah will also fight in Jerusalem, and the wealth of the surrounding nations—gold, silver, and clothes—will be gathered in great abundance. **15.** Even the animals—horses, mules, camels, and donkeys—will suffer from this plague. **16.** Those who remain from the nations that fought against Jerusalem will come each year to worship the King, the LORD of hosts, and to celebrate the Feast of Tabernacles. (host: army, tabernacles: a religious festival) **17.** If any nation refuses to come and worship the LORD, they will receive no rain. **18.** If Egypt refuses to come, they will also face the plague for not observing the Feast of Tabernacles. **19.** This will be the punishment for Egypt and any nation that refuses to keep the Feast. **20.** On that day, even the bells on the horses will say, "HOLINESS TO THE LORD," and the pots in the LORD's temple will be as sacred as the bowls before the altar. **21.** All pots in Jerusalem and Judah will be holy to the LORD, and those who offer sacrifices will use them. On that day, there will be no more Canaanites in the house of the LORD. (Canaanite: a member of the ancient people in Canaan, unclean)

39 – Malachi

Chapter 1

1. The word of the LORD to Israel, delivered through Malachi. **2.** "I have loved you," says the LORD. But you question, "How have You loved us?" Was not Esau Jacob's brother? Yet I chose Jacob, **3.** But rejected Esau, laying waste to his land, leaving it for desert creatures. (rejected: cast aside, not chosen) **4.** Edom says, "We've been ruined, but we will rebuild." But the LORD says, "They will rebuild, but I will destroy. They will be known as the land of wickedness, opposed by Me forever." (opposed: against, hostile) **5.** You will see this and say, "The LORD is exalted even beyond Israel's borders." **6.** A son honors his father, and a servant respects his master. If I am your Father, where is the honor due Me? If I am your Master, where is your reverence? O priests, you have shown contempt for My name. (contempt: disrespect, scorn) **7.** You present polluted offerings on My altar, and ask, "How have we defiled You?" By saying, "The LORD's table is worthless." (polluted: ritual impurity, defiled; worthless: of no value) **8.** When you offer blind, lame, or sick animals, is that not wrong? Would your governor accept such offerings? says the LORD. (governor: ruler, authority) **9.** Beg God to show favor and be merciful to us. Will He be pleased with your offerings? **10.** Who will even close the doors of My temple for nothing, or light My altar fire without purpose? I have no pleasure in you, says the LORD. (purpose: intention, reason) **11.** From the sunrise to sunset, My name will be honored among the nations with pure offerings. My name will be exalted among the Gentiles, says the LORD. (Gentiles: nations, non-Jews) **12.** But you have defiled it, calling My altar impure and its offerings contemptible. (defiled: made unclean, corrupt) **13.** You say, "What a burden!" and bring animals that are blind, lame, or sick. Should I accept such offerings from you? says the LORD. (burden: something tiresome, annoying) **14.** Cursed is the one who offers a flawed sacrifice, though he has a perfect animal in his flock. I am a great King, says the LORD, and My name is to be feared. (flawed: defective, imperfect; perfect: without defect)

Chapter 2

1. And now, O priests, this command is for you. **2.** If you will not listen and honor My name, says the LORD of Hosts, I will send a curse upon you, and I will curse your blessings. Indeed, I have already cursed them, because you have not taken this to heart. (blessings: good things, favor) **3.** I will defile your descendants and spread dung on your faces, the dung of your offerings, and you will be removed with it. (Defile: make unclean spiritually, dirty; descendants: children, offspring) **4.** You will know that I have sent this command, that My covenant may remain with Levi, says the LORD of Hosts. **5.** My covenant with him was one of life and peace, and I gave these to him because he revered Me and was in awe of My name. (revered: respected, honored; awe: deep respect, fear) **6.** He spoke truth, and there was no deceit in his mouth. He lived in peace and justice, turning many away from wickedness. (deceit: dishonesty; wickedness: evil, wrongdoing) **7.** The priest's lips should preserve knowledge, and people should seek the law from his mouth, for he is the messenger of the LORD of Hosts. (preserve: keep, maintain; messenger: one who delivers messages) **8.** But you have gone astray. You have caused many to stumble by misinterpreting the law, and you have corrupted the covenant of Levi, says the LORD of Hosts. **9.** Because of this, I have made you contemptible and low in the eyes of all the people, since you have not followed My ways and have been partial in administering the law. (partial: biased, unfair) **10.** Do we not all have one Father? Has not one God created us? Why do we break faith with one another, profaning the covenant of our ancestors? (break faith: act treacherously, betray; profaning: disrespecting, dishonoring) **11.** Judah has broken faith, and an abomination has been committed in Israel and Jerusalem. Judah has profaned the holiness of the LORD, and has married the daughter of a foreign god. (abomination: a detestable act; profaned: desecrated, violated) **12.** The LORD will cut off from Jacob's tents the man who does this, both the master and the scholar, and anyone who brings an offering to the LORD of Hosts. (cut off: remove, cast away) **13.** You do this again: you cover the LORD's altar with tears and weeping, but He no longer pays attention to your offering or receives it with favor. **14.** You ask, "Why?" It is because the LORD has been witness between you and the wife of your youth, with whom you have broken faith. Though she is your companion and the wife of your covenant. (companion: partner, friend) **15.** Did He not make you one? And why one? Because He sought godly offspring. So guard your heart, and let none break faith with the wife of his youth. (offspring: children, descendants) **16.** The LORD, the God of Israel, says He hates divorce. He who covers his wife with violence, says the LORD of Hosts, should take care not to break faith. (divorce: separation, putting away; violence: harm, mistreatment) **17.** You have wearied the LORD with your words. You ask, "How have we wearied Him?" By saying, "All who do evil are good in the LORD's sight, and He delights in them," or, "Where is the God of justice?" (wearied: tired, exhausted; evil: immoral, wrong; delights: takes pleasure in)

Chapter 3

1. Behold, I will send My messenger to prepare the way before Me. Then the Lord you seek will suddenly come to His temple—the messenger of the covenant you desire. He will come, says the LORD of Hosts. (Messenger: the one preparing the way for the Messiah) **2.** Who can endure His coming? Who will remain standing when He appears? He is like a refiner's fire and like fullers' soap. (Refiner's fire: purifying heat; Fullers' soap: cleansing agent) **3.** He will purify the sons of Levi, refining them like gold and silver, so that they can offer offerings to the LORD in righteousness. (Sons of Levi: the priestly class) **4.** Then the offerings of Judah and Jerusalem will be pleasing to the LORD, as in days gone by. (Judah: the southern kingdom) **5.** I will come to you in judgment, swiftly witnessing against sorcerers, adulterers, false swearers, oppressors, and those who disregard the rights of the foreigner, and do not fear Me, says the LORD of Hosts. (Foreigners: non-Israelites) **6.** For I am the LORD, and I do not change; that's why you, O descendants of Jacob, have not been destroyed. (Descendants of Jacob: the Israelites) **7.** You have turned away from My commands since the days of your ancestors. Return to Me, and I will return to you, says the LORD. But you ask, "How can we return?" (Commands: divine laws) **8.** Can a man rob God? Yet you have robbed Me. But you ask, "How have we robbed You?" In tithes and offerings. (Tithes: one-tenth of income) **9.** You are under a curse, for you have robbed Me—this whole nation. (Curse: divine judgment) **10.** Bring the full tithe into the storehouse, so there will be food in My house. Test Me in this, says the LORD, and see if I will open the heavens and bless you beyond measure. (Storehouse: the place to store tithes and offerings) **11.** I will rebuke the devourer for your sake, so it will not ruin your crops, and your vines will not drop fruit before its time, says the LORD of Hosts. (Devourer: pestilence or ruin) **12.** All nations will call you blessed, for you will be a delightful land, says the LORD. (Blessed: favored by God) **13.** You have spoken harshly against Me, says the LORD. Yet you ask, "What have we said against You?" (Harsh: accusatory and rebellious) **14.** You say, "It's pointless to serve God. What do we gain by keeping His commands and walking mournfully before the LORD of Hosts?" (Pointless: without benefit) **15.** Now we see that the arrogant are blessed, those who do evil are prosperous, and those who challenge God go unpunished. (Arrogant: prideful and defiant) **16.** Then those who feared the LORD spoke to one another, and the LORD listened. A book of remembrance was written for those who revere the LORD and honor His name. (Feared: held in deep respect) **17.** They will be Mine, says the LORD, on the day when I make them My special treasure. I will spare them as a man spares his son who serves him. (Special treasure: a prized possession) **18.** Then you will see the difference between the righteous and the wicked, between those who serve God and those who do not. (Righteous: those who follow God's will; Wicked: those who rebel)

Chapter 4

1. The day is coming that will burn like a furnace. All the proud and evil-doers will be like stubble, and the coming day will burn them up, leaving neither root nor branch, says the LORD of Hosts. (Stubble: dry, worthless remains) **2.** But for those who fear My name, the Sun of Righteousness will rise, bringing healing with His wings. You will grow strong like calves in the field. (Sun of Righteousness: a symbol of Christ bringing justice and healing) **3.** You will trample the wicked, for they will be like ashes under your feet on the day I act, says the LORD of Hosts. (Trample: symbolic of victory over the wicked) **4.** Remember the law of Moses, My servant, which I commanded him at Horeb for all Israel, with its statutes and ordinances. (Horeb: the mountain where God gave the law) **5.** I will send Elijah the prophet before the great and terrible day of the LORD comes. (Elijah: a prophet who will prepare the way for the coming of the Lord) **6.** He will turn the hearts of the fathers to the children, and the hearts of the children to their fathers, or else I will come and strike the land with a curse. (Turn: to restore relationships; Curse: the consequences of rebellion)

40 – Mathew

Chapter 1

1. This is the genealogy of Jesus Christ, who is descended from both David and Abraham. (genealogy: family history, David: King of Israel, Abraham: the Patriarch) **2.** Abraham was the father of Isaac, Isaac was the father of Jacob, and Jacob fathered Judah and his brothers. **3.** Judah fathered Perez and Zerah through Tamar; Perez fathered Hezron; Hezron fathered Ram. **4.** Ram fathered Amminadab; Amminadab fathered Nahshon; Nahshon fathered Salmon. **5.** Salmon fathered Boaz with Rahab; Boaz fathered Obed with Ruth; Obed fathered Jesse. **6.** Jesse fathered David, the king; and David, the king, fathered Solomon by the woman who had been married to Uriah. (King David, Solomon: King of Israel) **7.** Solomon fathered Rehoboam; Rehoboam fathered Abijah; Abijah fathered Asa. **8.** Asa fathered Jehoshaphat; Jehoshaphat fathered Joram; Joram fathered Uzziah. **9.** Uzziah fathered Jotham; Jotham fathered Ahaz; Ahaz fathered Hezekiah. **10.** Hezekiah fathered Manasseh; Manasseh fathered Amon; Amon fathered Josiah. **11.** Josiah fathered Jeconiah and his brothers at the time when they were taken into exile in Babylon. (Babylon: the ancient empire, exile: forced displacement) **12.** After the exile to Babylon, Jeconiah fathered Shealtiel; Shealtiel fathered Zerubbabel. **13.** Zerubbabel fathered Abiud; Abiud fathered Eliakim; Eliakim fathered Azor. **14.** Azor fathered Zadok; Zadok fathered Achim; Achim fathered Eliud. **15.** Eliud fathered Eleazar; Eleazar fathered Matthan; Matthan fathered Jacob. **16.** Jacob fathered Joseph, who was the husband of Mary, and from her came Jesus, known as the Christ. (Christ: The Messiah) **17.** In total, there are three sets of fourteen generations: from Abraham to David, from David to the exile in Babylon, and from the exile to Christ. (generation: line of descendants) **18.** Here is how the birth of Jesus Christ occurred: Mary, who was engaged to Joseph, was found to be pregnant before they came together, and the child was conceived by the Holy Spirit. (engaged: pledged to marry, conceived: became pregnant) **19.** Joseph, her husband, a man of integrity (moral uprightness), decided not to shame her publicly, but to break off the engagement quietly. (engagement: promise to marry, shame: disgrace) **20.** As Joseph pondered these things, an angel of the Lord appeared to him in a dream, saying, "Joseph, son of David, do not be afraid to take Mary as your wife, for the child she carries is from the Holy Spirit." (pondered: thought deeply, son of David: descendant of King David) **21.** She will bear a son, and you shall name him Jesus, because he will deliver his people from their sins. (deliver: save, sins: wrongdoings) **22.** This all happened to fulfill the prophecy spoken by the Lord through the prophet: (fulfill: bring to pass, prophecy: prediction made by a prophet) **23.** "The virgin will conceive and bear a son, and they will call him Immanuel," which means "God with us." (virgin: unmarried woman, conceive: become pregnant) **24.** When Joseph woke up, he did as the angel of the Lord had instructed him, and took Mary as his wife. (instructed: ordered) **25.** But he had no marital relations with her until after she gave birth to a son, and he named him Jesus. (marital relations: sexual union)

Chapter 2

1. After Jesus was born in the town of Bethlehem in Judea, during the reign of King Herod, a group of wise men from the East arrived in Jerusalem. (Bethlehem: a town in Judea, Herod: King of Judea) **2.** They asked, "Where is the one who has been born to be the King of the Jews? We saw his star in the East and have come to honor him." (honor: show respect) **3.** When King Herod heard about this, he became deeply disturbed, and so did all the people of Jerusalem. (disturbed: troubled) **4.** Herod gathered the leading priests and experts in the law and questioned them about where the Messiah (the anointed one) was to be born. (experts: scholars, Messiah: the Christ) **5.** They answered him, "In Bethlehem of Judea, for the prophet wrote:" **6.** "O Bethlehem, though you are small among the clans of Judah, out of you will come a ruler who will shepherd my people Israel." (ruler: leader, shepherd: guide) **7.** Herod secretly called the wise men and asked them to find out exactly when the star had appeared. (secretly: privately) **8.** He told them, "Go and search carefully for the child. When you find him, report back to me so that I can come and honor him too." (search: look for) **9.** After hearing the king, they left. The star they had seen in the East went ahead of them and stopped over the place where the child was. (stopped: rested) **10.** When they saw the star, they were filled with joy beyond measure. (joy beyond measure: overwhelming happiness) **11.** They entered the house and saw the child with Mary, his mother. They bowed down and worshipped him. Then they opened their treasures and gave him gifts: gold, frankincense, and myrrh. (bowed: knelt, worshipped: adored) **12.** After being warned in a dream not to return to Herod, they took a different route back to their own country. (warned: cautioned) **13.** Once the wise men had left, an angel of the Lord appeared to Joseph in a dream, saying, "Get up! Take the child and his mother and escape to Egypt. Stay there until I tell you, for Herod is planning to search for the child and kill him." (escape: flee) **14.** So Joseph got up, took the child and Mary, and left for Egypt during the night. (got up: woke up) **15.** They remained in Egypt until Herod died, fulfilling what the Lord had said through the prophet: "Out of Egypt I called my son." (fulfilled: completed) **16.** When Herod realized that he had been tricked by the wise men, he was furious and ordered the massacre of all boys in Bethlehem and the surrounding regions who were two years old and younger, based on the time he had learned from the wise men. (tricked: deceived, massacre: killing) **17.** Then the prophecy spoken by Jeremiah was fulfilled, which says: (prophecy: divine prediction) **18.** "A voice was heard in Ramah, weeping and mourning, Rachel weeping for her children and refusing to be comforted, because they were no more." (Ramah: a town, mourning: sorrow) **19.** After Herod's death, an angel of the Lord appeared to Joseph in a dream while he was in Egypt. (appeared: showed up) **20.** The angel said, "Get up! Take the child and his mother and go back to Israel, for those who wanted to take the child's life are dead." (go back: return) **21.** So Joseph got up, took the child and his mother, and returned to Israel. (got up: rose) **22.** But when Joseph learned that Archelaus was now ruling in Judea, in place of his father Herod, he was afraid to go there. After being warned again in a dream, he withdrew to the region of Galilee. (Archelaus: Herod's son, withdrew: moved away) **23.** He went and settled in a town called Nazareth, fulfilling what was spoken through the prophets: "He will be called a Nazarene." (Nazareth: a town in Galilee)

Chapter 3

1. During that time, John the Baptist began preaching in the wilderness of Judaea. **2.** He called out, "Repent, for the kingdom of heaven is near!" (repent: turn away from sin) **3.** This is the one the prophet Isaiah spoke about: "A voice calling out in the desert, 'Prepare the way for the Lord, make His paths straight.'" (Isaiah's prophecy) **4.** John wore clothes made of camel hair and a leather belt; his food was locusts and wild honey. (ascetic lifestyle: simple, self-denying way of life) **5.** People from Jerusalem, Judea, and the surrounding region of the Jordan River came to him. (Jordan River region: area where John preached and baptized) **6.** They were baptized by him in the Jordan River, confessing their wrongdoings. (baptized: immersed in water as a sign of repentance) **7.** When John saw many Pharisees and Sadducees coming to be baptized, he said, "You brood of vipers, who warned you to flee from the coming wrath?" (Pharisees: strict religious leaders, Sadducees: wealthy priests, brood of vipers: hypocrites, wrath: anger) **8.** "Produce fruit that shows you have truly repented." (fruit: results, repentance: turning away from sin) **9.** "Don't think you can say, 'We are descendants of Abraham.' God can raise up children of Abraham from these stones." (Abraham: ancestor of Israel, descendants: offspring) **10.** "The axe is already at the root of the trees; any tree that does not bear good fruit will be cut down and thrown into the fire." (axe: symbol of judgment, root: foundation, fire: destruction) **11.** "I baptize you with water for repentance, but the one coming after me is much greater than I. He will baptize you with the Holy Spirit and fire." (Holy Spirit: divine presence, fire: purification) **12.** "He has a winnowing fork in His hand to clear His threshing floor, gathering the wheat into the barn, but burning the chaff with unquenchable fire." (winnowing: separating good from bad, chaff: waste, fire: judgment) **13.** Then Jesus came from Galilee to the Jordan River to be baptized by John. (Galilee: northern region of Israel) **14.** John tried to prevent Him, saying, "I need to be baptized by You, and yet You come to me?" (humility: modesty, reluctance) **15.** Jesus replied, "Let it be so for now; it is proper to fulfill all that is right." Then John agreed. (righteousness: acting in accordance with God's will) **16.** As soon as Jesus was baptized, He came up from the water, and the heavens opened. He saw the Spirit of God descending like a dove and resting on Him. (Spirit of God: divine presence, dove: symbol of peace and the Holy Spirit) **17.** A voice from heaven said, "This is My beloved Son, in whom I am well pleased." (beloved: dearly loved, well pleased: fully satisfied)

Chapter 4

1. Then the Spirit led Jesus into the wilderness where He was tempted by the devil. (wilderness: a barren place) **2.** After fasting for forty days and nights, He became extremely hungry. (fasting: refraining from food) **3.** The devil came to Him and said, "If You are the Son of God, tell these stones to become bread." (devil: tempter, Son of God: divine title) **4.** Jesus replied, "It is written, 'Man does not live by bread alone, but by every word that proceeds from the mouth of God.'" (bread alone: physical sustenance, word: divine teaching) **5.** Then the devil took Him to the holy city and set Him on the highest point of the temple. (holy city: Jerusalem, pinnacle: highest point) **6.** He said, "If You are the Son of God, throw Yourself down. For it is written, 'He will command His angels to watch over You, and they will lift You up, so that You won't even strike Your foot against a stone.'" (angels: heavenly beings) **7.** Jesus answered, "It is also written, 'You shall not test the Lord your God.'" (test: challenge God's will) **8.** The devil then took Him to an exceedingly high mountain and showed Him all the kingdoms of the world and their splendor. (high mountain: elevated place, kingdoms: realms, splendor: glory) **9.** He said to Jesus, "All this I will give You, if You will bow down and worship me." (worship: show reverence) **10.** Jesus responded, "Get away from Me, Satan! For it is written, 'Worship the Lord your God, and serve Him alone.'" (Satan: adversary, serve: devote yourself to) **11.** Then the devil left Him, and angels came and took care of Him. (took care of: provided for His needs) **12.** When Jesus heard that John had been imprisoned, He moved to Galilee. (John: John the Baptist, imprisoned: arrested) **13.** He left Nazareth and settled in Capernaum, near the shore of the Sea of Galilee, in the areas of Zebulun and Naphtali. (Capernaum: a town by the sea, Zebulun and Naphtali: regions of Israel) **14.** This fulfilled what the prophet Isaiah had spoken: (fulfilled: brought about) **15.** "The land of Zebulun and the land of Naphtali, the road by the sea, beyond the Jordan, Galilee of the Gentiles." (Gentiles: non-Jews, road by the sea: coastal region) **16.** "The people who lived in darkness have seen a great light; on those who lived in the land of the shadow of death, light has dawned." (darkness: spiritual ignorance, light: divine revelation, shadow of death: grave danger) **17.** From that time, Jesus began to preach, saying, "Repent, for the kingdom of heaven has arrived." (repent: turn away from sin) **18.** As Jesus walked beside the Sea of Galilee, He saw two brothers, Simon (who is called Peter) and his brother Andrew, casting a net into the water because they were fishermen. (Galilee: northern region of Israel) **19.** "Come, follow Me," He said, "and I will make you fishers of men." (fishers of men: those who spread God's message) **20.** Immediately, they left their nets and followed Him. (immediately: without delay) **21.** Moving on from there, He saw two other brothers, James, the son of Zebedee, and John, his brother, in a boat with their father Zebedee, mending their nets. Jesus called them. (Zebedee: their father, mending: repairing) **22.** Without hesitation, they left the boat and their father, and followed Him. (hesitation: delay in action) **23.** Jesus traveled throughout Galilee, teaching in their synagogues, proclaiming the good news of the kingdom, and healing every kind of disease and sickness among the people. (synagogues: places of Jewish worship, proclaiming: preaching) **24.** News about Him spread across Syria, and people brought to Him all who were suffering from various illnesses, those in pain, the demon-possessed, the epileptic, and the paralyzed; and He healed them. (Syria: northern region, healed: restored to health) **25.** Large crowds followed Him from Galilee, the Decapolis, Jerusalem, Judea, and the regions beyond the Jordan. (Decapolis: ten cities, regions beyond the Jordan: areas east of the Jordan River)

Chapter 5

1. When Jesus saw the crowds, He climbed up a mountain, and His disciples gathered around Him. (mountain: elevated land) **2.** Then He began to speak and teach them, saying: **3.** "Blessed are those who recognize their spiritual poverty, for the kingdom of heaven belongs to them." (spiritual poverty: humility or lack of self-reliance, blessed: highly favored by God) **4.** "Blessed are those who mourn, for they will find comfort." (mourn: feel sorrow, comfort: be consoled) **5.** "Blessed are the humble, for they will inherit the earth." (humble: meek or gentle, inherit: receive as a gift) **6.** "Blessed are those who deeply long for righteousness, for they will be satisfied." (long: crave or desire intensely, righteousness: moral integrity, satisfied: fulfilled) **7.** "Blessed are those who show mercy, for they will be shown mercy in return." (mercy: compassion, return: reciprocate) **8.** "Blessed are those with a pure heart, for they will see God." (pure heart: sincere or free from impurity, see God: experience God's presence) **9.** "Blessed are the peacemakers, for they will be recognized as God's children." (peacemakers: those who bring peace, recognized: acknowledged) **10.** "Blessed are those persecuted for the sake of righteousness, for the kingdom of heaven is theirs." (persecuted: treated unfairly, righteousness: moral goodness) **11.** "Blessed are you when others insult and persecute you, falsely accusing you because of Me." (insult: verbally attack, falsely: untruthfully) **12.** "Rejoice and be glad, for your reward in heaven will be great. In the same way, they persecuted the prophets before you." (rejoice: be joyful, reward: recompense, prophets: messengers of God) **13.** "You are the salt of the earth. But if salt loses its flavor, it cannot be made salty again; it is good for nothing but to be thrown out and trampled underfoot." (salt: preservative, flavor: taste, trampled: crushed or stepped on) **14.** "You are the light of the world. A city on a hill cannot be hidden." (light: illumination or guide, city: large settlement) **15.** "People do not light a lamp and put it under a bowl. Instead, they place it on a stand so it gives light to everyone in the house." (lamp: light source, bowl: container, stand: platform) **16.** "Let your light shine before others, so they may see your good works and honor your Father in heaven." (shine: stand out, honor: praise or glorify) **17.** "Do not think that I have come to destroy the Law or the prophets. I have come not to abolish them, but to fulfill them." (abolish: cancel, fulfill: complete or make perfect) **18.** "For truly, I say to you, until heaven and earth pass away, not even the smallest part of the Law will be removed until everything is accomplished." (smallest part: tiniest detail, accomplished: fully completed) **19.** "Anyone who disregards even the smallest of these commands, and teaches others to do the same, will be called least in the kingdom of heaven. But whoever obeys and teaches them will be called great in the kingdom of heaven." (disregards: ignores, obeys: follows, teaches: instructs) **20.** "I tell you, unless your righteousness surpasses that of the Pharisees and the teachers of the law, you will not enter the kingdom of heaven." (surpasses: exceeds, righteousness: moral integrity) **21.** "You have heard it said, 'Do not commit murder,' and anyone who murders will be judged." (murder: unlawful killing) **22.** "But I say to you that anyone who is angry with their brother or sister without a cause is subject to judgment. And anyone who calls their brother 'Raca' is in danger of the council, and anyone who says, 'You fool!' is in danger of hell fire." (angry: furious, Raca: insulting term, council: Jewish court) **23.** "So, if you are offering your gift at the altar and remember that your brother or sister has something against you, **24.** leave your gift there and go be reconciled with them first, then return and offer your gift." (gift: offering, reconciled: restored to peace) **25.** "Settle matters quickly with your opponent while you are on your way, or they may hand you over to the judge, and the judge may send you to prison." (settle: resolve, opponent: adversary, prison: confinement) **26.** "Truly, I tell you, you will not leave until you have paid the last penny." **27.** "You have heard it said, 'Do not commit adultery.' **28.** But I tell you, anyone who looks at a woman lustfully has already committed adultery with her in his heart." (lustfully: with sinful desire, adultery: infidelity in marriage) **29.** "If your right eye causes you to sin, tear it out and throw it away. It is better to lose one part of your body than for your whole body to be cast into hell." (sin: wrongdoing, tear out: remove painfully, hell: eternal punishment) **30.** "And if your right hand causes you to sin, cut it off and throw it away. It is better for you to lose one part of your body than for your whole body to be thrown into hell." (cut off: amputate, sin: wrongdoing) **31.** "It has been said, 'Anyone who divorces his wife must give her a certificate of divorce.' **32.** But I tell you that anyone who divorces his wife, except for sexual immorality, causes her to commit adultery; and anyone who marries a divorced woman commits adultery." (certificate: written notice, immorality: sinful actions) **33.** "Again, you have heard it said, 'Do not break your oath, but fulfill your vows to the Lord.' **34.** But I tell you, do not swear at all: neither by heaven, for it is God's throne, **35.** nor by the earth, for it is His footstool, nor by Jerusalem, for it is the city of the great King." (footstool: resting place) **36.** "And do not swear by your head, for you cannot make even one hair white or black." (swear: make a promise, head: personal authority) **37.** "Simply let your 'Yes' be 'Yes,' and your 'No' be 'No.' Anything beyond this comes from evil." (evil: immoral or wrong) **38.** "You have heard it said, 'An eye for an eye, and a tooth for a tooth.' **39.** But I say to you, do not resist an evil person. If someone strikes you on the right cheek, turn the other cheek as well." (strike: hit, resist: fight back) **40.** "And if anyone wants to sue you and take your shirt, let them have your coat as well." (sue: take legal action, shirt: garment) **41.** "If anyone compels you to go one mile, go with them two." (compels: forces, mile: distance) **42.** "Give to those who ask, and do not turn away from those who want to borrow from you." (ask: request, borrow: take temporarily) **43.** "You have heard it said, 'Love your neighbor and hate your enemy.' **44.** But I say to you, love your enemies, bless those who curse you, do good to those who hate you, and pray for those who mistreat you and persecute you." (bless: wish good for, curse: speak evil of, mistreat: abuse) **45.** "That you may be children of your Father in heaven, for He makes His sun rise on the evil and the good, and sends rain on the righteous and the unrighteous." (sun: light, rain: water) **46.** "If you love those who love you, what reward will you get? Even tax collectors do the same." (reward: prize) **47.** "And if you only greet your own people, what are you doing more than others? Even pagans do that." (greet: salute, pagans: non-believers) **48.** "Be perfect, therefore, as your Father in heaven is perfect." (perfect: complete or mature)

Chapter 6

1. Be cautious not to perform your charitable acts in front of others to be noticed by them. If you do, your Father in heaven will not reward you. (charitable acts: deeds of kindness, reward: divine approval) **2.** When you give to the needy, don't announce it with fanfare like the hypocrites do in the synagogues or on the streets, seeking praise from others. Truly, they have already received their reward. (hypocrites: pretenders, fanfare: public display) **3.** But when you give to the poor, keep it private—don't even let your left hand know what your right hand is doing, **4.** so that your giving is done in secret. And your Father, who sees in secret, will reward you openly. (reward: recognition, secret: hidden from others) **5.** When you pray, don't be like the hypocrites who love to pray standing in the synagogues and on street corners just to be seen by others. Truly, they have already received their reward. (hypocrites: false believers, reward: recognition) **6.** But when you pray, go into your room, shut the door, and pray to your Father, who is unseen. Your Father, who sees what is done in secret, will reward you. (room: private place, unseen: invisible) **7.** And when you pray, don't use meaningless repetitions, as the pagans do, thinking they will be heard because of their many words. (repetitions: empty phrases, pagans: non-believers) **8.** Do not be like them, for your Father knows what you need even before you ask Him. (need: necessity, ask: request) **9.** This is how you should pray: Our Father in heaven, hallowed be Your name. (hallowed: revered, name: reputation) **10.** Your kingdom come. Your will be done on earth as it is in heaven. (kingdom: reign, will: desires) **11.** Give us today our daily bread. (daily bread: sustenance) **12.** And forgive us our sins, as we forgive those who sin against us. (sins: wrongdoings) **13.** And lead us not into temptation, but deliver us from evil. For Yours is the kingdom, the power, and the glory, forever. Amen. (temptation: trial, deliver: rescue, evil: harm) **14.** For if you forgive others their wrongs, your heavenly Father will forgive you. (forgive: pardon, wrongs: offenses) **15.** But if you do not forgive others, your Father will not forgive you. (forgive: pardon) **16.** When you fast, don't look gloomy like the hypocrites, who disfigure their faces to show others they are fasting. Truly, they have received their reward. (fast: abstain from food, gloomy: sad, disfigure: alter appearance) **17.** But when you fast, wash your face and anoint your head, **18.** so that it will not be obvious to others that you are fasting, but only to your Father, who is unseen. And your Father, who sees in secret, will reward you. (reward: recognition) **19.** Do not store up treasures on earth, where moth and rust destroy, and where thieves break in and steal. (treasures: wealth, moth: insects, rust: decay) **20.** Instead, store up treasures in heaven, where neither moth nor rust can destroy, and where thieves cannot break in or steal. (heaven: spiritual realm) **21.** For where your treasure is, there your heart will also be. (treasure: wealth or focus, heart: inner desires) **22.** The eye is the lamp of the body. If your eyes are healthy, your whole body will be full of light. (eye: vision, healthy: clear) **23.** But if your eyes are unhealthy, your body will be filled with darkness. If the light in you is darkness, how great is that darkness! (unhealthy: corrupted, light: understanding) **24.** No one can serve two masters. Either they will hate the one and love the other, or they will be loyal to the one and despise the other. You cannot serve both God and money. (masters: authorities, loyal: devoted) **25.** Therefore, I tell you, do not worry about your life, what you will eat or drink, or about your body, what you will wear. Is not life more than food, and the body more than clothing? (worry: be anxious, life: existence, body: physical self) **26.** Look at the birds in the sky: they do not sow or reap, no do they store away in barns, yet your heavenly Father feeds them. Are you not much more valuable than they? (sow: plant, reap: gather, barns: storage) **27.** Which of you can add a single moment to your life by worrying? (moment: time) **28.** And why worry about clothes? See how the lilies of the field grow. They do not labor or spin. (labor: work hard, spin: weave) **29.** Yet I tell you, not even Solomon in all his splendor was dressed like one of these. (splendor: glory or wealth) **30.** If that is how God clothes the grass of the field, which is here today and tomorrow is thrown into the fire, will He not much more clothe you, you of little faith? (clothes: dress, fire: destruction) **31.** So do not worry, saying, "What shall we eat?" or "What shall we drink?" or "What shall we wear?" (worry: be anxious, eat: consume, drink: imbibe) **32.** For the pagans run after these things, and your heavenly Father knows that you need them. (pagans: non-believers, run after: chase) **33.** But seek first His kingdom and His righteousness, and all these things will be given to you as well. (righteousness: moral integrity) **34.** Therefore, do not worry about tomorrow, for tomorrow will worry about itself. Each day has enough trouble of its own. (worry: be anxious, trouble: difficulty)

Chapter 7

1. Judge not, that ye be not judged. (judge: criticize, evaluate) **2.** For with what judgment ye judge, ye shall be judged: and with what measure ye mete, it shall be measured to you again. (mete: give, measure) **3.** And why beholdest thou the mote that is in thy brother's eye, but considerest not the beam that is in thine own eye? (beholdest: look at, mote: small particle, beam: large piece of wood) **4.** Or how wilt thou say to thy brother, Let me pull out the mote out of thine eye; and, behold, a beam is in thine own eye? (wilt: will, mote: small particle, beam: large piece of wood) **5.** Thou hypocrite, first cast out the beam out of thine own eye; and then shalt thou see clearly to cast out the mote out of thy brother's eye. (hypocrite: pretender, cast out: remove) **6.** Give not that which is holy unto the dogs, neither cast ye your pearls before swine, lest they trample them under their feet, and turn again and rend you. (holy: sacred, dogs: unworthy, pearls: valuable things, swine: pigs, trample: crush, rend: tear apart) **7.** Ask, and it shall be given you; seek, and ye shall find; knock, and it shall be opened unto you: (ask: request, seek: look for, knock: tap or strike) **8.** For every one that asketh receiveth; and he that seeketh findeth; and to him that knocketh it shall be opened. **9.** Or what man is there of you, whom if his son ask bread, will he give him a stone? (bread: food, stone: a hard rock) **10.** Or if he ask a fish, will he give him a serpent? (fish: food, serpent: snake) **11.** If ye then, being evil, know how to give good gifts unto your children, how much more shall your Father which is in heaven give good things to them that ask him? (evil: bad, gifts: presents, Father: God, heaven: God's realm) **12.** Therefore all things whatsoever ye would that men should do to you, do ye even so to them: for this is the law and the prophets. (whatsoever: whatever, law: God's commands, prophets: messengers of God) **13.** Enter ye in at the strait gate: for wide is the gate, and broad is the way, that leadeth to destruction, and many there be which go in thereat: (strait: narrow, gate: entrance, broad: wide, leadeth: leads, destruction: ruin) **14.** Because strait is the gate, and narrow is the way, which leadeth unto life, and few there be that find it. (strait: narrow, gate: entrance, narrow: tight, life: eternal life, few: not many) **15.** Beware of false prophets, which come to you in sheep's clothing, but inwardly they are ravening wolves. (beware: be careful, false: dishonest, prophets: messengers, sheep's clothing: looking harmless, ravening: greedy, wolves: predators) **16.** Ye shall know them by their fruits. Do men gather grapes of thorns, or figs of thistles? (fruits: actions, gather: collect, thorns: sharp points, thistles: prickly plants) **17.** Even so every good tree bringeth forth good fruit; but a corrupt tree bringeth forth evil fruit. (bringeth forth: produces, corrupt: bad, evil: harmful) **18.** A good tree cannot bring forth evil fruit, neither can a corrupt tree bring forth good fruit. (cannot: cannot do, good: beneficial, evil: harmful, corrupt: bad) **19.** Every tree that bringeth not forth good fruit is hewn down, and cast into the fire. (hewn down: cut down, cast: thrown, fire: destruction) **20.** Wherefore by their fruits ye shall know them. (fruits: actions) **21.** Not every one that saith unto me, Lord, Lord, shall enter into the kingdom of heaven; but he that doeth the will of my Father which is in heaven. (saith: says, Lord: master, kingdom: realm, heaven: God's domain, doeth: does, will: desire) **22.** Many will say to me in that day, Lord, Lord, have we not prophesied in thy name? and in thy name have cast out devils? and in thy name done many wonderful works? (prophesied: predicted, devils: evil spirits, wonderful works: miracles) **23.** And then will I profess unto them, I never knew you: depart from me, ye that work iniquity. (profess: declare, knew: recognized, depart: leave, iniquity: evil deeds) **24.** Therefore whosoever heareth these sayings of mine, and doeth them, I will liken him unto a wise man, which built his house upon a rock: (whosoever: whoever, heareth: hears, sayings: teachings, doeth: does, liken: compare, wise: smart, house: home, rock: solid foundation) **25.** And the rain descended, and the floods came, and the winds blew, and beat upon that house; and it fell not: for it was founded upon a rock. (descended: fell, floods: heavy water, winds: air currents, beat: struck, founded: built) **26.** And every one that heareth these sayings of mine, and doeth them not, shall be likened unto a foolish man, which built his house upon the sand: (foolish: unwise, house: home, sand: loose ground) **27.** And the rain descended, and the floods came, and the winds blew, and beat upon that house; and it fell: and great was the fall of it. (fell: collapsed, great: large, fall: collapse) **28.** And it came to pass, when Jesus had ended these sayings, the people were astonished at his doctrine: (doctrine: teachings) **29.** For he taught them as one having authority, and not as the scribes. (authority: power, scribes: religious teachers)

Chapter 8

1. When he was come down from the mountain, great multitudes followed him. **2.** And, behold, there came a leper and worshipped him, saying, Lord, if thou wilt, thou canst make me clean. (leper: person with skin disease, worshipped: showed reverence, wilt: want, canst: can) **3.** And Jesus put forth his hand, and touched him, saying, I will; be thou clean. And immediately his leprosy was cleansed. (put forth: extended, cleansed: healed, immediately: instantly) **4.** And Jesus saith unto him, See thou tell no man; but go thy way, shew thyself to the priest, and offer the gift that Moses commanded, for a testimony unto them. (saith: says, shew: show, priest: religious leader, testimony: proof) **5.** And when Jesus was entered into Capernaum, there came unto him a centurion, beseeching him, (Capernaum: a town, centurion: Roman officer, beseeching: urgently requesting) **6.** And saying, Lord, my servant lieth at home sick of the palsy, grievously tormented. (lieth: is lying, palsy: paralysis, grievously: severely, tormented: suffering) **7.** And Jesus saith unto him, I will come and heal him. (heal: cure) **8.** The centurion answered and said, Lord, I am not worthy that thou shouldest come under my roof: but speak the word only, and my servant shall be healed. (worthy: deserving, roof: house, speak: say) **9.** For I am a man under authority, having soldiers under me: and I say to this man, Go, and he goeth; and to another, Come, and he cometh; and to my servant, Do this, and he doeth it. (under authority: under command, soldiers: troops, doeth: does) **10.** When Jesus heard it, he marvelled, and said to them that followed, Verily I say unto you, I have not found so great faith, no, not in Israel. (marvelled: was amazed, verily: truly, faith: trust) **11.** And I say unto you, That many shall come from the east and west, and shall sit down with Abraham, and Isaac, and Jacob, in the kingdom of heaven. (sit down: dine, kingdom: realm, heaven: God's domain) **12.** But the children of the kingdom shall be cast out into outer darkness: there shall be weeping and gnashing of teeth. (cast out: thrown out, outer darkness: far from God, weeping: crying, gnashing: grinding) **13.** And Jesus said unto the centurion, Go thy way; and as thou hast believed, so be it done unto thee. And his servant was healed in the selfsame hour. (believed: trusted, selfsame: exact, hour: time) **14.** And when Jesus was come into Peter's house, he saw his wife's mother laid, and sick of a fever. (laid: lying down, fever: high temperature) **15.** And he touched her hand, and the fever left her: and she arose, and ministered unto them. (ministered: served) **16.** When the even was come, they brought unto him many that were possessed with devils: and he cast out the spirits with his word, and healed all that were sick: (even: evening, possessed with devils: controlled by evil spirits, cast out: expelled, spirits: demons, healed: cured) **17.** That it might be fulfilled which was spoken by Esaias the prophet, saying, Himself took our infirmities, and bare our sicknesses. (fulfilled: completed, infirmities: weaknesses, bare: carried) **18.** Now when Jesus saw great multitudes about him, he gave commandment to depart unto the other side. (depart: go, other side: the opposite shore) **19.** And a certain scribe came, and said unto him, Master, I will follow thee whithersoever thou goest. (scribe: religious teacher, whithersoever: wherever) **20.** And Jesus saith unto him, The foxes have holes, and the birds of the air have nests; but the Son of man hath not where to lay his head. (foxes: wild animals, holes: burrows, lay his head: rest) **21.** And another of his disciples said unto him, Lord, suffer me first to go and bury my father. (suffer: allow, bury: lay to rest) **22.** But Jesus said unto him, Follow me; and let the dead bury their dead. (Follow: come after, dead: spiritually dead) **23.** And when he was entered into a ship, his disciples followed him. (entered: got into, ship: boat) **24.** And, behold, there arose a great tempest in the sea, insomuch that the ship was covered with the waves: but he was asleep. (tempest: storm, insomuch: so much, covered: overwhelmed) **25.** And his disciples came to him, and awoke him, saying, Lord, save us: we perish. (awoke: woke him up, perish: die) **26.** And he saith unto them, Why are ye fearful, O ye of little faith? Then he arose, and rebuked the winds and the sea; and there was a great calm. (fearful: afraid, arose: stood up, rebuked: scolded, calm: peace) **27.** But the men marvelled, saying, What manner of man is this, that even the winds and the sea obey him! (manner: type, obey: follow orders) **28.** And when he was come to the other side into the country of the Gergesenes, there met him two possessed with devils, coming out of the tombs, exceeding fierce, so that no man might pass by that way. (other side: opposite shore, Gergesenes: region, tombs: burial places, exceeding fierce: extremely violent) **29.** And, behold, they cried out, saying, What have we to do with thee, Jesus, thou Son of God? art thou come hither to torment us before the time? (cried out: shouted, torment: torture) **30.** And there was a good way off from them an herd of many swine feeding. (herd: group of animals, swine: pigs, feeding: eating) **31.** So the devils besought him, saying, If thou cast us out, suffer us to go away into the herd of swine. (besought: begged, cast out: send away) **32.** And he said unto them, Go. And when they were come out, they went into the herd of swine: and, behold, the whole herd of swine ran violently down a steep place into the sea, and perished in the waters. (steep: sharp, perished: drowned) **33.** And they that kept them fled, and went their ways into the city, and told everything, and what was befallen to the possessed of the devils. (kept: watched, fled: ran away, befallen: happened) **34.** And, behold, the whole city came out to meet Jesus: and when they saw him, they besought him that he would depart out of their coasts. (coasts: region, depart: leave)

Chapter 9

1. And he entered into a ship, and passed over, and came into his own city. (passed over: crossed) **2.** And, behold, they brought to him a man sick of the palsy, lying on a bed: and Jesus seeing their faith said unto the sick of the palsy; Son, be of good cheer; thy sins be forgiven thee. (sick of the palsy: paralyzed, lying: reclining, faith: trust, cheer: joy) **3.** And, behold, certain of the scribes said within themselves, This man blasphemeth. (scribes: religious scholars, blasphemeth: speaks disrespectfully about God) **4.** And Jesus knowing their thoughts said, Wherefore think ye evil in your hearts? (knowing: understanding, thoughts: ideas, evil: wrong) **5.** For whether is easier, to say, Thy sins be forgiven thee; or to say, Arise, and walk? (easier: simpler, arise: get up) **6.** But that ye may know that the Son of man hath power on earth to forgive sins, (then saith he to the sick of the palsy,) Arise, take up thy bed, and go unto thine house. (power: authority, take up: pick up, bed: mat) **7.** And he arose, and departed to his house. (arose: got up, departed: went) **8.** But when the multitudes saw it, they marvelled, and glorified God, which had given such power unto men. (multitudes: large crowds, marvelled: were amazed, glorified: praised, power: authority) **9.** And as Jesus passed forth from thence, he saw a man, named Matthew, sitting at the receipt of custom: and he saith unto him, Follow me. And he arose, and followed him. (passed forth: went away, arose: got up) **10.** And it came to pass, as Jesus sat at meat in the house, behold, many publicans and sinners came and sat down with him and his disciples. (sat at meat: ate, publicans: tax collectors) **11.** And when the Pharisees saw it, they said unto his disciples, Why eateth your Master with publicans and sinners? (Pharisees: religious leaders, eateth: eats, Master: teacher) **12.** But when Jesus heard that, he said unto them, They that be whole need not a physician, but they that are sick. (whole: healthy, physician: doctor) **13.** But go ye and learn what that meaneth, I will have mercy, and not sacrifice: for I am not come to call the righteous, but sinners to repentance. (mercy: kindness, sacrifice: offerings, righteous: good people, repentance: turning from sin) **14.** Then came to him the disciples of John, saying, Why do we and the Pharisees fast oft, but thy disciples fast not? (fast: abstain from food) **15.** And Jesus said unto them, Can the children of the bridechamber mourn, as long as the bridegroom is with them? but the days will come, when the bridegroom shall be taken from them, and then shall they fast. (bridechamber: wedding hall, mourn: grieve, bridegroom: husband) **16.** No man putteth a piece of new cloth unto an old garment, for that which is put in to fill it up taketh from the garment, and the rent is made worse. (garment: clothing, rent: tear) **17.** Neither do men put new wine into old bottles: else the bottles break, and the wine runneth out, and the bottles perish: but they put new wine into new bottles, and both are preserved. (wine: grape juice, bottles: wine skins, perish: waste) **18.** While he spake these things unto them, behold, there came a certain ruler, and worshipped him, saying, My daughter is even now dead: but come and lay thy hand upon her, and she shall live. (ruler: leader, worshipped: showed reverence, lay: touch) **19.** And Jesus arose, and followed him, and so did his disciples. (arose: stood up) **20.** And, behold, a woman, which was diseased with an issue of blood twelve years, came behind him, and touched the hem of his garment: (diseased: suffering, issue of blood: bleeding, hem: edge) **21.** For she said within herself, If I may but touch his garment, I shall be whole. (whole: healed) **22.** But Jesus turned him about, and when he saw her, he said, Daughter, be of good comfort; thy faith hath made thee whole. And the woman was made whole from that hour. (turned about: turned around, comfort: encouragement, faith: trust) **23.** And when Jesus came into the ruler's house, and saw the minstrels and the people making a noise, (minstrels: musicians, making a noise: mourning loudly) **24.** He said unto them, Give place: for the maid is not dead, but sleepeth. And they laughed him to scorn. (Give place: move aside, maid: young girl, sleepeth: is sleeping, scorn: mock) **25.** But when the people were put forth, he went in, and took her by the hand, and the maid arose. (put forth: removed, arose: got up) **26.** And the fame hereof went abroad into all that land. (fame: news, abroad: spread) **27.** And when Jesus departed thence, two blind men followed him, crying, and saying, Thou Son of David, have mercy on us. (departed: left, blind: unable to see) **28.** And when he was come into the house, the blind men came to him: and Jesus saith unto them, Believe ye that I am able to do this? They said unto him, Yea, Lord. (believe: trust, able: capable) **29.** Then touched he their eyes, saying, According to your faith be it unto you. (touched: healed, according to: based on, faith: trust) **30.** And their eyes were opened; and Jesus straitly charged them, saying, See that no man know it. (straightly: strictly, charged: commanded) **31.** But they, when they were departed, spread abroad his fame in all that country. (departed: left, spread abroad: told everywhere) **32.** As they went out, behold, they brought to him a dumb man possessed with a devil. (dumb: unable to speak, possessed: controlled, devil: demon) **33.** And when the devil was cast out, the dumb spake: and the multitudes marvelled, saying, It was never so seen in Israel. (cast out: driven away, spake: spoke, marvelled: were amazed) **34.** But the Pharisees said, He casteth out devils through the prince of the devils. (casteth out: drives away, prince: leader) **35.** And Jesus went about all the cities and villages, teaching in their synagogues, and preaching the gospel of the kingdom, and healing every sickness and every disease among the people. (went about: traveled, synagogues: Jewish meeting places, preaching: telling) **36.** But when he saw the multitudes, he was moved with compassion on them, because they fainted, and were scattered abroad, as sheep having no shepherd. (moved with compassion: felt pity, fainted: exhausted, scattered abroad: lost) **37.** Then saith he unto his disciples, The harvest truly is plenteous, but the labourers are few; (harvest: work to be done, plenteous: abundant, labourers: workers) **38.** Pray ye therefore the Lord of the harvest, that he will send forth labourers into his harvest. (pray: ask, send forth: send out)

Chapter 10

1. And when he had called unto him his twelve disciples, he gave them power against unclean spirits, to cast them out, and to heal all manner of sickness and all manner of disease. (called unto him: summoned, power: authority, unclean spirits: evil spirits, cast them out: drive them away, manner: type) **2.** Now the names of the twelve apostles are these; The first, Simon, who is called Peter, and Andrew his brother; James the son of Zebedee, and John his brother; (apostles: messengers, called: named) **3.** Philip, and Bartholomew; Thomas, and Matthew the publican; James the son of Alphaeus, and Lebbaeus, whose surname was Thaddaeus; (publican: tax collector, surname: family name) **4.** Simon the Canaanite, and Judas Iscariot, who also betrayed him. (Canaanite: from Canaan, betrayed: betrayed, gave away) **5.** These twelve Jesus sent forth, and commanded them, saying, Go not into the way of the Gentiles, and into any city of the Samaritans enter ye not: (sent forth: sent out, Gentiles: non-Jews, Samaritans: a group of people from the region of Samaria) **6.** But go rather to the lost sheep of the house of Israel. (lost sheep: people who have strayed from God's ways, house of Israel: the people of Israel) **7.** And as ye go, preach, saying, The kingdom of heaven is at hand. (preach: proclaim, at hand: near) **8.** Heal the sick, cleanse the lepers, raise the dead, cast out devils: freely ye have received, freely give. (cleanse: purify, lepers: people with leprosy, cast out devils: drive out demons, freely: without charge) **9.** Provide neither gold, nor silver, nor brass in your purses, (provide: bring, purses: bags) **10.** Nor scrip for your journey, neither two coats, neither shoes, nor yet staves: for the workman is worthy of his meat. (scrip: bag or wallet, staves: walking sticks, workman: worker, meat: food) **11.** And into whatsoever city or town ye shall enter, inquire who in it is worthy; and there abide till ye go thence. (inquire: ask, worthy: deserving, abide: stay) **12.** And when ye come into an house, salute it. (salute: greet) **13.** And if the house be worthy, let your peace come upon it: but if it be not worthy, let your peace return to you. (worthy: deserving, peace: blessing) **14.** And whosoever shall not receive you, nor hear your words, when ye depart out of that house or city, shake off the dust of your feet. (receive: accept, shake off: symbolically reject) **15.** Verily I say unto you, It shall be more tolerable for the land of Sodom and Gomorrha in the day of judgment, than for that city. (verily: truly, tolerable: bearable, Sodom and Gomorrha: ancient cities known for sin, judgment: final decision by God) **16.** Behold, I send you forth as sheep in the midst of wolves: be ye therefore wise as serpents, and harmless as doves. (send you forth: send you out, midst: middle, wolves: danger, wise: smart, serpents: snakes, harmless: innocent) **17.** But beware of men: for they will deliver you up to the councils, and they will scourge you in their synagogues; (beware: be cautious, deliver you up: hand you over, councils: courts, scourge: beat) **18.** And ye shall be brought before governors and kings for my sake, for a testimony against them and the Gentiles. (governors: rulers, kings: monarchs, testimony: evidence) **19.** But when they deliver you up, take no thought how or what ye shall speak: for it shall be given you in that same hour what ye shall speak. (take no thought: do not worry, same hour: at that moment) **20.** For it is not ye that speak, but the Spirit of your Father which speaketh in you. (Spirit: Holy Spirit, speaketh: speaks) **21.** And the brother shall deliver up the brother to death, and the father the child: and children shall rise up against their parents, and cause them to be put to death. (deliver up: hand over, rise up: rebel, cause: make) **22.** And ye shall be hated of all men for my name's sake: but he that endureth to the end shall be saved. (endureth: perseveres, saved: rescued) **23.** But when they persecute you in this city, flee ye into another: for verily I say unto you, Ye shall not have gone over the cities of Israel, till the Son of man be come. (persecute: mistreat, flee: run away, gone over: visited, Son of man: Jesus) **24.** The disciple is not above his master, nor the servant above his lord. (disciple: student, master: teacher, servant: worker, lord: master) **25.** It is enough for the disciple that he be as his master, and the servant as his lord. If they have called the master of the house Beelzebub, how much more shall they call them of his household? (enough: sufficient, Beelzebub: a name for the devil, household: family) **26.** Fear them not therefore: for there is nothing covered, that shall not be revealed; and hid, that shall not be known. (covered: hidden, revealed: made known, hid: concealed) **27.** What I tell you in darkness, that speak ye in light: and what ye hear in the ear, that preach ye upon the housetops. (darkness: secrecy, speak ye: proclaim, light: openly, preach ye: declare, housetops: roofs) **28.** And fear not them which kill the body, but are not able to kill the soul: but rather fear him which is able to destroy both soul and body in hell. (kill: destroy, soul: spirit, destroy: ruin, hell: eternal punishment) **29.** Are not two sparrows sold for a farthing? and one of them shall not fall on the ground without your Father. (sparrows: small birds, farthing: small coin, fall: drop, ground: earth) **30.** But the very hairs of your head are all numbered. (hairs: strands of hair, numbered: counted) **31.** Fear ye not therefore, ye are of more value than many sparrows. (value: worth) **32.** Whosoever therefore shall confess me before men, him will I confess also before my Father which is in heaven. (confess: acknowledge, before: in front of) **33.** But whosoever shall deny me before men, him will I also deny before my Father which is in heaven. (deny: reject) **34.** Think not that I am come to send peace on earth: I came not to send peace, but a sword. (send: bring, sword: symbol of division or conflict) **35.** For I am come to set a man at variance against his father, and the daughter against her mother, and the daughter in law against her mother in law. (set at variance: cause division) **36.** And a man's foes shall be they of his own household. (foes: enemies, household: family) **37.** He that loveth father or mother more than me is not worthy of me: and he that loveth son or daughter more than me is not worthy of me. (loveth: loves, worthy: deserving) **38.** And he that taketh not his cross, and followeth after me, is not worthy of me. (taketh: carries, cross: burden, followeth after: follows) **39.** He that findeth his life shall lose it: and he that loseth his life for my sake shall find it. (findeth: gains, loseth: gives up, sake: purpose) **40.** He that receiveth you receiveth me, and he that receiveth me receiveth him that sent me. (receiveth: accepts, sent: sent out) **41.** He that receiveth a prophet in the name of a prophet shall receive a prophet's reward; and he that receiveth a righteous man in the name of a righteous man shall receive a righteous man's reward. (prophet: messenger, reward: compensation) **42.** And whosoever shall give to drink unto one of these little ones a cup of cold water only in the name of a disciple, verily I say unto you, he shall in no wise lose his reward. (little ones: children, cold water: refreshing drink, in no wise: in no way)

Chapter 11
1. After commanding His twelve disciples, Jesus went to teach and preach in their cities. **2.** When John heard of Jesus' works in prison, he sent two of his disciples, **3.** Asking, "Are you the one to come, or should we look for another?" **4.** Jesus replied, "Tell John what you hear and see: The blind see, the lame walk, lepers are cleansed, the deaf hear, the dead are raised, and the poor hear the gospel. **5.** Blessed is anyone not offended by me." (offended: caused to feel upset or angry) **6.** Jesus then spoke to the crowd about John: "What did you go into the wilderness to see? A reed shaken by the wind? (reed: a plant, metaphorically something unstable) **7.** A man dressed in fine clothes? Those who wear fine clothes live in kings' palaces. **8.** What did you go to see? A prophet? Yes, and more than a prophet. **9.** This is the one about whom it is written: 'I will send my messenger ahead of you, who will prepare your way before you.' **10.** Truly, among those born of women, none is greater than John the Baptist; yet whoever is least in the kingdom of heaven is greater than he." (least: the smallest or lowest in rank) **11.** From the time of John the Baptist, the kingdom of heaven has suffered violence, and the violent take it by force. (suffereth: endures; violence: aggressive actions) **12.** All the prophets and the law prophesied until John. (prophesied: foretold future events) **13.** And if you are willing to accept it, he is the Elijah who was to come. (Elijah: a prophet from the Old Testament, expected to return before the Messiah) **14.** Whoever has ears, let them hear. **15.** To what can I compare this generation? It's like children sitting in the markets, calling out to others, **16.** "We played the pipe for you, and you did not dance; we sang a dirge, and you did not mourn." (dirge: a song of sorrow, especially for the dead) **17.** John came neither eating nor drinking, and they said, "He has a demon." (demon: evil spirit) **18.** The Son of Man came eating and drinking, and they said, "Here is a glutton and a drunkard, a friend of tax collectors and sinners." (glutton: someone who eats too much, drunkard: someone who drinks too much alcohol) **19.** But wisdom is proven right by her deeds. (wisdom: knowledge applied rightly) **20.** Then Jesus began to denounce the cities where most of His miracles were performed, because they did not repent: (denounce: criticize publicly; repent: feel remorse or regret for sin) **21.** "Woe to you, Chorazin! Woe to you, Bethsaida! For if the miracles done in you had been done in Tyre and Sidon, they would have repented long ago in sackcloth and ashes. (sackcloth: rough fabric worn in mourning; ashes: symbol of mourning or repentance) **22.** But I tell you, it will be more bearable for Tyre and Sidon on the day of judgment than for you. (bearable: able to be endured; judgment: God's final evaluation of people's deeds) **23.** And you, Capernaum, will you be lifted to the heavens? No, you will go down to Hades. (Hades: the realm of the dead, often representing destruction) **24.** But I tell you, it will be more bearable for Sodom on the day of judgment than for you. (Sodom: an ancient city known for wickedness, destroyed by God) **25.** At that time, Jesus said, "I praise You, Father, Lord of heaven and earth, because You have hidden these things from the wise and learned, and revealed them to little children. (praise: express approval or gratitude) **26.** Yes, Father, for this is what You were pleased to do. (pleased: happy or satisfied with) **27.** All things have been committed to me by my Father. No one knows the Son except the Father, and no one knows the Father except the Son and those to whom the Son chooses to reveal Him. (committed: entrusted; reveal: make known) **28.** Come to me, all you who are weary and burdened, and I will give you rest. (weary: tired; burdened: weighed down by difficulties) **29.** Take my yoke upon you and learn from me, for I am gentle and humble in heart, and you will find rest for your souls. (yoke: a wooden frame used to harness animals, symbolizing submission or partnership) **30.** For my yoke is easy and my burden is light." (burden: something carried, often a responsibility or difficulty)

Chapter 12
1. Jesus and His disciples walked through cornfields on the sabbath; they were hungry and began eating the corn. (Sabbath: a day of rest; Cornfields: fields with crops of grain) **2.** The Pharisees criticized them for doing what was unlawful on the sabbath. (Pharisees: religious leaders) **3.** Jesus replied, "Have you not read what David did when he and his men were hungry? (David: King of Israel, known for his faith) **4.** He entered the house of God and ate the showbread, which only priests could eat." (Showbread: sacred bread offered to God) **5.** Or do you not know that priests break the sabbath in the temple and are innocent? **6.** I tell you, something greater than the temple is here. (Greater: more important or significant) **7.** If you understood, 'I desire mercy, not sacrifice,' you would not condemn the innocent. (Mercy: kindness, compassion; Sacrifice: offerings to God) **8.** The Son of Man is Lord even of the sabbath." (Son of Man: a title Jesus used for Himself; Lord: master, ruler) **9.** He went into their synagogue, **10.** And a man with a withered hand was there. They asked Him if it was lawful to heal on the sabbath to accuse Him. (Withered: dried up, deformed) **11.** He asked, "If one of you had a sheep fall into a pit on the sabbath, would you not lift it out?" (Pit: a deep hole) **12.** How much more valuable is a man than a sheep? It's lawful to do good on the sabbath." **13.** He told the man to stretch out his hand, and it was restored. (Restored: made whole again, healed) **14.** The Pharisees plotted to destroy Him. (Plotted: made secret plans) **15.** Jesus withdrew, and large crowds followed Him, and He healed them all, **16.** Telling them not to make Him known, **17.** To fulfill the prophecy, **18.** "Behold My servant, whom I have chosen, My beloved, in whom I am well pleased; I will put My Spirit upon Him, and He will bring justice to the Gentiles." (Servant: one who serves; Gentiles: non-Jews) **19.** He will not quarrel or shout, nor let anyone hear His voice in the streets. (Quarrel: argue; Streets: public places) **20.** He will not break a bruised reed or quench a smoldering wick until He brings justice to victory. (Bruised: broken or weakened; Quench: put out, extinguish; Wick: the part of a candle that burns) **21.** And in His name, the Gentiles will hope. **22.** A man possessed by a demon, blind and mute, was brought to Him, and He healed him. (Possessed: controlled by evil spirits; Mute: unable to speak) **23.** The people were amazed and asked, "Is this the Son of David?" (Son of David: a messianic title, referring to Jesus) **24.** The Pharisees said, "He casts out demons by Beelzebub, the prince of demons." (Beelzebub: another name for Satan, the prince of evil spirits) **25.** Jesus knew their thoughts and said, "A kingdom divided against itself will fall. (Thoughts: inner ideas; Kingdom: a realm ruled by a king) **26.** If Satan casts out Satan, his kingdom cannot stand." **27.** "If I cast out demons by Beelzebub, by whom do your sons cast them out? They will judge you." (Judge: criticize, convict) **28.** "But if I cast out demons by the Spirit of God, the kingdom of God has come upon you." (Spirit: the power of God) **29.** Or how can one enter a strong man's house and steal his goods unless he first binds the strong man? (Strong man: someone powerful, such as Satan; Binds: ties up, defeats) **30.** Whoever is not with Me is against Me; and whoever does not gather with Me scatters. (Scatter: spread apart, separate) **31.** Every sin and blasphemy will be forgiven, except the blasphemy against the Holy Spirit. (Blasphemy: disrespectful speech or action against God) **32.** Speaking against the Son of Man will be forgiven, but speaking against the Holy Spirit will not, in this world or the next. **33.** Make the tree good, and its fruit good, or make the tree bad, and its fruit bad; the tree is known by its fruit. (Fruit: the result or actions; Known: recognized by) **34.** You

brood of vipers, how can you speak good things, being evil? For out of the heart, the mouth speaks. (Brood: group; Vipers: poisonous snakes) **35.** A good man brings forth good from his heart, and an evil man brings forth evil from his heart. **36.** I tell you, every idle word will be accounted for on the Day of Judgment. (Idle: careless, unnecessary) **37.** By your words, you will be justified or condemned. **38.** Some scribes and Pharisees asked, "Teacher, show us a sign from You." (Scribes: religious scholars) **39.** Jesus answered, "An evil and adulterous generation seeks a sign, but the only sign will be that of Jonah, (Adulterous: spiritually unfaithful) **40.** For as Jonah was three days and nights in the belly of the great fish, the Son of Man will be three days and nights in the earth." (Belly: stomach) **41.** The people of Nineveh will rise up in judgment against this generation because they repented at Jonah's preaching. (Repented: changed their mind, turned from sin) **42.** The Queen of the South will rise in judgment against this generation because she came from afar to hear Solomon's wisdom; and one greater than Solomon is here. (Queen of the South: the Queen of Sheba; Afar: from a distance) **43.** When an unclean spirit leaves a man, it seeks rest but finds none. (Unclean: impure, evil) **44.** It returns to its former home, finding it empty, swept, and in order. (Empty: vacant; Swept: cleaned) **45.** It brings seven worse spirits, and the man's condition becomes worse. So it will be with this wicked generation." (Wicked: evil, immoral) **46.** While He was speaking, His mother and brothers stood outside wanting to speak with Him. **47.** Someone said, "Your mother and brothers are outside, wanting to speak with You." **48.** He replied, "Who is My mother, and who are My brothers?" **49.** He stretched out His hand toward His disciples and said, "Here are My mother and brothers! **50.** Whoever does the will of My Father in heaven is My brother, sister, and mother." (Will: desire, command)

Chapter 13

1. On that same day, Jesus left the house and sat by the sea. (sea: body of water) **2.** Large crowds gathered around Him, so He got into a boat and sat down while the people stood on the shore. (shore: land at the edge of the sea) **3.** He taught them many things in parables, saying, "A sower went out to plant seeds. (sower: farmer) **4.** As he sowed, some seeds fell along the path, and birds came and ate them up. (path: walking trail) **5.** Other seeds fell on rocky ground where there wasn't much soil. They sprouted quickly because the soil was shallow. (rocky ground: hard, stony area) **6.** But when the sun rose, they were scorched and withered because they had no roots. (scorched: dried up by heat) **7.** Some seeds fell among thorns, which grew and choked the plants. (thorns: prickly plants) **8.** But other seeds fell on good soil and produced a crop—some yielding a hundred, some sixty, and some thirty times what was sown. (yielding: producing) **9.** Let anyone with ears listen." **10.** The disciples asked Him, "Why do You speak to the people in parables?" (parables: stories with lessons) **11.** He replied, "Because you are allowed to know the mysteries of the kingdom of heaven, but others are not. (mysteries: hidden truths) **12.** To those who have, more will be given, and they will have an abundance. But to those who do not have, even what they have will be taken from them. (abundance: plenty) **13.** This is why I speak to them in parables: though they see, they do not perceive; though they hear, they do not understand. (perceive: recognize) **14.** In them, Isaiah's prophecy is fulfilled: 'You will listen but not understand; you will look but not see.' (Isaiah: a prophet) **15.** For these people's hearts have grown dull; their ears can barely hear, and their eyes are closed. Otherwise, they might see, hear, and understand, and I would heal them.' **16.** "But blessed are your eyes, for they see, and your ears, for they hear. (blessed: favored by God) **17.** Truly, many prophets and righteous people longed to see what you see but did not, and to hear what you hear but did not." (righteous: morally upright) **18.** "So listen to the parable of the sower: **19.** When anyone hears the message about the kingdom but doesn't understand it, the evil one comes and snatches away what was sown in their heart. This is the seed along the path. (evil one: devil) **20.** The seed on rocky ground is the one who hears the word and accepts it with joy at first. **21.** But they have no root and endure only a short time. When trouble or persecution comes because of the word, they quickly fall away. (persecution: mistreatment) **22.** The seed among thorns is like someone who hears the word, but worldly concerns and the deceitfulness of wealth choke it, making it unfruitful. (deceitfulness: dishonesty) **23.** But the seed on good soil represents someone who hears the word, understands it, and produces a harvest of a hundred, sixty, or thirty times what was planted. **24.** Jesus told them another parable: "The kingdom of heaven is like a man who sowed good seed in his field. **25.** But while he slept, his enemy came and planted weeds among the wheat and left. (weeds: unwanted plants) **26.** When the wheat sprouted and formed heads, the weeds also appeared. **27.** The landowner's servants asked him, 'Didn't you sow good seed in your field? Where did the weeds come from?' **28.** He replied, 'An enemy did this.' The servants asked, 'Should we pull them up?' **29.** He answered, 'No, because while pulling the weeds, you might uproot the wheat as well. (uproot: remove from roots) **30.** Let them both grow until harvest, and at harvest time, I will tell the reapers to collect the weeds to burn and gather the wheat into my barn.'" **31.** He gave them another parable: "The kingdom of heaven is like a mustard seed, the smallest of all seeds. (mustard seed: tiny seed) **32.** When it grows, it becomes the largest of garden plants and turns into a tree, where birds perch in its branches." **33.** He told another parable: "The kingdom of heaven is like yeast that a woman mixed into three measures of flour until it worked through the dough." (yeast: leavening agent) **34.** Jesus spoke all these things to the crowd in parables. He did not speak to them without using parables, **35.** to fulfill the prophet's words: "I will open my mouth in parables and reveal things hidden since creation." **36.** Then Jesus dismissed the crowd and went inside. His disciples asked Him to explain the parable of the weeds in the field. **37.** He replied, "The one who sows the good seed is the Son of Man, **38.** the field is the world, the good seed represents the children of the kingdom, and the weeds are the children of the evil one. **39.** The enemy who sowed them is the devil, the harvest is the end of the world, and the reapers are angels. **40.** Just as the weeds are gathered and burned, so it will be at the end of the world. **41.** The Son of Man will send His angels, and they will gather out of His kingdom all who cause sin and those who do evil. **42.** They will throw them into a fiery furnace, where there will be weeping and grinding of teeth. (fiery furnace: place of intense heat) **43.** Then the righteous will shine like the sun in their Father's kingdom. Let those with ears listen." **44.** "The kingdom of heaven is like treasure hidden in a field. When a man finds it, he hides it again, and in his joy, he sells everything he owns to buy that field." **45.** "The kingdom of heaven is like a merchant looking for fine pearls. **46.** When he finds one of great value, he sells everything he owns and buys it." **47.** "The kingdom of heaven is like a fishing net cast into the sea, gathering all kinds of fish. **48.** When it was full, the fishermen pulled it to shore, sorted the good fish into containers, and threw away the bad ones." **49.** "This is how it will be at the end of the world: angels will separate the wicked from the righteous. **50.** They will throw the wicked into the fiery furnace, where there will be weeping and grinding of teeth." **51.** Jesus asked, "Have you understood all this?" They answered, "Yes, Lord." **52.** Then He said, "Every scribe trained for the kingdom of heaven is like a homeowner who brings out treasures both new and old." **53.** After Jesus finished teaching these parables, He left that place. **54.** Returning to His hometown, He taught in their synagogue, and they were amazed. They asked, "Where did this man get this wisdom and these miracles?" (synagogue: Jewish place of worship) **55.** "Isn't this the carpenter's son? Isn't His mother named Mary, and His brothers James, Joseph, Simon, and Judas?" **56.** "And aren't His sisters here with us? Where did He get all this?" **57.** They were offended by Him. But Jesus said, "A prophet is honored everywhere except in his hometown and his own family." **58.** He did not do many miracles there because of their lack of faith.

Chapter 14

1. At that time, Herod the tetrarch heard about Jesus' fame, (Tetrarch: a ruler of one-quarter of a kingdom) and he told his servants, "This is John the Baptist; he has risen from the dead, and that's why such mighty works are being done through him." (Mighty works: powerful miracles or deeds) **2.** Herod had arrested John and imprisoned him because of Herodias, his brother Philip's wife, (Imprisoned: put in jail) since John had told him, "It is not lawful for you to have her." (Lawful: allowed by law) **3.** Although Herod wanted to kill John, he feared the people, who regarded him as a prophet. (Regarded: considered or thought of) **4.** On Herod's birthday, Herodias' daughter danced before him, pleasing him, (Pleasing: making happy or satisfied) and he promised with an oath to give her anything she asked. (Oath: a formal promise) **5.** Prompted by her mother, she asked, "Give me John the Baptist's head on a platter." (Prompted: urged or encouraged) **6.** The king was distressed but, because of his oath and the guests, he ordered it to be done. (Distressed: upset or troubled) **7.** So, he sent an executioner to behead John in prison. (Executioner: person who carries out the death sentence; Behead: to cut off someone's head) **8.** His head was brought on a platter and given to the girl, who took it to her mother. (Platter: a large, flat dish) **9.** John's disciples came, took his body, buried it, and reported the news to Jesus. (Disciples: followers or students) **10.** When Jesus heard this, He withdrew by boat to a remote place, but the people followed Him on foot from the towns. (Withdrew: moved away; Remote: far or distant) **11.** When He saw the crowd, He had compassion on them and healed their sick. (Compassion: deep sympathy and care) **12.** As evening came, His disciples said, "This is a remote place, and it's getting late; send the people away so they can buy food." (Evening: the time of day from late afternoon to night) **13.** Jesus replied, "They don't need to leave; give them something to eat." (Replied: answered) **14.** They said, "We have only five loaves and two fish." (Loaves: small loaves of bread) **15.** "Bring them to Me," Jesus said. (Bring: to carry or take something to someone) **16.** He made the people sit down on the grass, took the loaves and fish, gave thanks, broke them, and gave them to the disciples to distribute. (Distribute: to give out or hand out) **17.** All ate and were satisfied, and twelve baskets of leftovers were collected. (Leftovers: food remaining after a meal) **18.** About 5,000 men had eaten, not counting women and children. (Counting: including) **19.** Immediately, Jesus made His disciples get into the boat and go ahead of Him to the other side while He dismissed the crowd. (Dismissed: sent away) **20.** Afterward, He went up on a mountain alone to pray, and He remained there alone as evening came. (Afterward: later; Remained: stayed) **21.** Meanwhile, the boat was far from shore, buffeted by waves because the wind was against it. (Buffeted: struck or beaten; Against: in opposition to) **22.** During the fourth watch of the night, Jesus went to them, walking on the water. (Watch: a period of time during the night) **23.** When the disciples saw Him walking on the water, they were terrified, thinking He was a ghost, and cried out in fear. (Terrified: extremely scared; Ghost: a spirit of a dead person) **24.** But Jesus immediately said, "Take courage! It's I. Don't be afraid." (Immediately: right away; Courage: the ability to face fear) **25.** Peter replied, "Lord, if it's You, tell me to come to You on the water." (Replied: answered) **26.** "Come," Jesus said. So Peter stepped out of the boat and walked on the water toward Jesus. (Stepped out: went out of; Toward: in the direction of) **27.** But when he saw the strong wind, he became afraid and began to sink. "Lord, save me!" he cried. (Sink: to go down into water) **28.** Immediately, Jesus reached out His hand, caught him, and said, "You of little faith, why did you doubt?" (Doubt: to be unsure or uncertain) **29.** When they climbed into the boat, the wind died down. (Climbed: went up into; Died down: became calm) **30.** Those in the boat worshiped Him, saying, "Truly, You are the Son of God." (Worshiped: showed reverence; Truly: really, in fact) **31.** After crossing over, they landed at Gennesaret. (Crossing over: moving across from one side to another) **32.** When the people there recognized Jesus, they sent word throughout the surrounding region and brought all the sick to Him. (Recognized: identified; Region: an area) **33.** They begged Him to let them touch the edge of His cloak, and all who touched it were healed. (Begged: asked urgently or desperately; Cloak: a loose garment) **34.** Some Pharisees and teachers of the law came to Jesus from Jerusalem and asked, **35.** "Why do Your disciples break the tradition of the elders? They don't wash their hands before they eat!" **36.** Jesus replied, "And why do you break the command of God for the sake of your tradition?"

Chapter 15

1. Then some scribes and Pharisees from Jerusalem came to Jesus and asked, (Scribes: religious scholars; Pharisees: members of a Jewish religious group) **2.** "Why do Your disciples break the tradition of the elders? They don't wash their hands before eating." (Tradition: customs or practices passed down) **3.** Jesus answered, "Why do you break God's commandment because of your tradition?" (Commandment: an official rule or law) **4.** For God said, "Honor your father and mother," and, "Anyone who curses their father or mother is to be put to death." (Honor: respect; Curses: speak evil of) **5.** But you say, "If anyone declares what they might have given to their father or mother as a gift to God, they are not required to honor their parents." (Declare: announce or state) **6.** Thus, you nullify (make ineffective) the command of God for the sake of your tradition. (Nullify: make invalid or void) **7.** You hypocrites! Isaiah prophesied correctly about you when he said: (Hypocrites: people who pretend to be what they are not) **8.** "These people honor Me with their lips, but their hearts are far from Me." (Honor: respect or revere) **9.** "They worship Me in vain; their teachings are merely human rules." (Vain: without purpose or result) **10.** Jesus called the crowd and said, "Listen and understand: (Listen: pay attention) **11.** It's not what goes into the mouth that defiles a person, but what comes out of the mouth, this defiles a person." (Defiles: makes unclean or impure) **12.** Then the disciples came to Him and said, "Do you know that the Pharisees were offended when they heard this?" (Offended: upset or insulted) **13.** Jesus replied, "Every plant my Heavenly Father has not planted will be pulled up by the roots. (Planted: established or set in place) **14.** Leave them; they are blind guides. If the blind lead the blind, both will fall into a pit." (Guides: leaders; Pit: a large hole or danger) **15.** Peter said, "Explain this parable to us." (Parable: a short story with a moral lesson) **16.** Jesus said, "Are you still so dull?" (Dull: slow to understand) **17.** "Don't you see that whatever enters the mouth goes into the stomach and then out of the body?" (Enter: go in; Stomach: organ where food is processed) **18.** "But the things that come out of the mouth come from the heart, and these defile a person." (Heart: the center of emotions and intentions) **19.** "For out of the heart come evil thoughts, murder, adultery, sexual immorality, theft, false testimony, slander." (Slander: spreading false information to damage someone's reputation) **20.** "These are the things that defile a person; but eating with unwashed hands doesn't defile a person." (Unwashed: not cleaned) **21.** Jesus left that place and went to the region of Tyre and Sidon. (Region: an area or district) **22.** A Canaanite woman from that area came and cried out, "Lord, Son of David, have mercy on me! My daughter is severely demon-possessed." (Canaanite: from the ancient region of Canaan; Demon-possessed: under the control of evil spirits) **23.** Jesus did not answer her a word. His disciples came and urged Him, "Send her away, for she keeps crying after us." (Urged: strongly advised) **24.** He answered, "I was sent only to the lost sheep of Israel." (Lost sheep: people who have strayed from the right path) **25.** The woman came and knelt before Him, saying, "Lord, help me!" (Kneel: to bend the knees in respect) **26.** He replied, "It's not right to take the children's bread and toss it to the dogs." (Toss: throw casually) **27.** She said, "Yes, Lord, but even the dogs eat the crumbs that fall from their masters' table." (Crumbs: small pieces of food) **28.** Then Jesus answered, "Woman, you have great faith. Let it be done as you wish." And her daughter was healed at that moment. (Faith: belief and trust) **29.** Jesus moved on from there and went to the Sea of Galilee. He went up on a mountain and sat down. (Moved on: left the place) **30.** Great crowds came to Him, bringing the lame, blind, mute, maimed, and many others, and laid them at His feet, and He healed them. (Maimed: crippled or injured) **31.** The people were amazed when they saw the mute speaking, the maimed made whole, the lame walking, and the blind seeing; and they praised the God of Israel. (Amazed: surprised; Praised: gave thanks and honor) **32.** Jesus called His disciples to Him and said, "I have compassion for these people; they have been with Me for three days and have nothing to eat. I don't want to send them away hungry, or they may faint on the way." (Compassion: deep sympathy) **33.** His disciples asked, "Where could we get enough bread in this remote place to feed such a large crowd?" (Remote: distant or far away) **34.** "How many loaves do you have?" Jesus asked. "Seven, and a few small fish," they replied. (Loaves: bread) **35.** He told the crowd to sit down on the ground. (Sit down: to take a seat) **36.** Then He took the seven loaves and the fish, gave thanks, broke them, and gave them to His disciples to distribute to the people. (Distribute: to hand out) **37.** They all ate and were satisfied, and the leftovers were collected—seven baskets full. (Leftovers: remaining food) **38.** The number of men who ate was about four thousand, not counting women and children. (Counting: including) **39.** After sending the crowd away, He got into the boat and went to the region of Magdala. (Region: an area)

Chapter 16

1. The Pharisees and Sadducees came to Jesus, testing Him, asking for a sign from heaven. (Pharisees: Jewish religious leaders; Sadducees: another religious group; Testing: trying to challenge) **2.** He answered, "At evening, you say, 'It will be fair weather, for the sky is red.' (Fair: good or clear) **3.** And in the morning, 'It will be stormy today, for the sky is red and threatening.' You know how to interpret the appearance of the sky, but can you not interpret the signs of the times? (Stormy: bad weather; Threatening: looking dangerous or ominous) **4.** A wicked and adulterous generation seeks a sign, but no sign will be given to it except the sign of the prophet Jonah." And He left them and went away. (Adulterous: unfaithful; Jonah: an Old Testament prophet) **5.** When the disciples reached the other side, they had forgotten to bring bread. (Reached: arrived at) **6.** Jesus said to them, "Watch out and beware of the yeast of the Pharisees and Sadducees." (Yeast: a substance used to make bread rise, here symbolizing bad influence) **7.** They discussed among themselves, "It's because we didn't bring any bread." (Discussed: talked about) **8.** Jesus, knowing this, said, "You of little faith, why are you talking among yourselves about having no bread? (Little faith: lack of trust) **9.** Do you still not understand? Don't you remember the five loaves for the five thousand, and how many baskets you gathered? (Remember: recall or think back to) **10.** Or the seven loaves for the four thousand, and how many baskets you took up? (Loaves: pieces of bread) **11.** How is it you don't understand that I wasn't talking about bread? Be on guard against the yeast of the Pharisees and Sadducees." (Guard: protect or watch) **12.** Then they understood that He wasn't telling them to beware of bread, but of the teachings of the Pharisees and Sadducees. (Teachings: doctrines or lessons) **13.** When Jesus came to the region of Caesarea Philippi, He asked His disciples, "Who do people say the Son of Man is?" **14.** They replied, "Some say John the Baptist; others say Elijah; and still others say Jeremiah or one of the prophets." (Replied: answered) **15.** "But what about you?" He asked. "Who do you say I am?" (Asked: inquired) **16.** Simon Peter answered, "You are the Messiah, the Son of the living God." (Messiah: the promised savior) **17.** Jesus replied, "Blessed are you, Simon son of Jonah, for this was not revealed to you by flesh and blood, but by my Father in heaven." (Revealed: made known) **18.** "And I tell you that you are Peter, and on this rock I will build my church, and the gates of Hades will not overcome it." (Rock: a solid foundation; Hades: the realm of the dead) **19.** "I will give you the keys of the kingdom of heaven; whatever you bind on earth will be bound in heaven, and whatever you loose on earth will be loosed in heaven." (Keys: authority; Bind:

hold fast; Loose: release) **20.** Then He ordered His disciples not to tell anyone that He was the Messiah. (Ordered: instructed or commanded) **21.** From that time on, Jesus began to show His disciples that He must go to Jerusalem, suffer many things at the hands of the elders, the chief priests, and the teachers of the law, and that He must be killed and on the third day be raised to life. (Suffer: endure pain or hardship) **22.** Peter took Him aside and began to rebuke Him. "Never, Lord! This shall never happen to You!" (Rebuke: scold or correct) **23.** Jesus turned and said to Peter, "Get behind me, Satan! You are a stumbling block to me; you do not have in mind the concerns of God, but merely human concerns." (Satan: adversary or enemy; Stumbling block: an obstacle to progress) **24.** Then Jesus said to His disciples, "Whoever wants to be My disciple must deny themselves and take up their cross and follow Me." (Deny: refuse to acknowledge; Cross: a symbol of suffering and sacrifice) **25.** "For whoever wants to save their life will lose it, but whoever loses their life for My sake will find it." (Save: preserve; Lose: give up or sacrifice) **26.** "What good will it be for someone to gain the whole world, yet forfeit their soul? Or what can anyone give in exchange for their soul?" (Forfeit: lose or give up) **27.** "For the Son of Man is going to come in His Father's glory with His angels, and then He will reward each person according to what they have done." (Glory: honor or majesty) **28.** "Truly I tell you, some who are standing here will not taste death before they see the Son of Man coming in His kingdom." (Taste death: die)

Chapter 17
1. After six days, Jesus took Peter, James, and John his brother, and led them up a high mountain by themselves. (Took: led; High: elevated) **2.** He was transfigured before them. His face shone like the sun, and His clothes became as white as light. (Transfigured: changed in appearance) **3.** Suddenly, Moses and Elijah appeared and talked with Him. (Suddenly: unexpectedly) **4.** Peter said to Jesus, "Lord, it is good for us to be here. If You wish, I will make three shelters: one for You, one for Moses, and one for Elijah." (Shelters: temporary structures) **5.** While he was still speaking, a bright cloud overshadowed them, and a voice came from the cloud, saying, "This is My beloved Son, in whom I am well pleased; listen to Him." (Overshadowed: covered or concealed) **6.** When the disciples heard this, they fell facedown and were terrified. (Facedown: with their faces on the ground; Terrified: very scared) **7.** Jesus came and touched them, saying, "Get up, do not be afraid." (Touched: physically reached out to) **8.** When they looked up, they saw no one except Jesus. (Looked up: raised their eyes) **9.** As they came down the mountain, Jesus commanded them, "Do not tell anyone what you have seen until the Son of Man has been raised from the dead." (Commanded: instructed firmly) **10.** The disciples asked, "Why then do the scribes say that Elijah must come first?" (Scribes: religious teachers) **11.** Jesus replied, "Elijah indeed comes first and will restore all things. (Restore: return to proper state) **12.** But I tell you that Elijah has already come, and they did not recognize him, but have done to him whatever they wanted. Likewise, the Son of Man will suffer at their hands." (Recognize: identify) **13.** Then the disciples understood that He was talking about John the Baptist. (Understood: grasped the meaning) **14.** When they came to the crowd, a man approached Jesus, kneeling before Him and saying, (Kneeling: bowing down) **15.** "Lord, have mercy on my son. He has seizures and suffers terribly. He often falls into the fire or the water." (Seizures: uncontrollable shaking) **16.** "I brought him to Your disciples, but they could not heal him." (Heal: cure) **17.** Jesus replied, "You unbelieving and perverse generation, how long shall I stay with you? How long shall I put up with you? Bring the boy here to Me." (Unbelieving: lacking faith; Perverse: morally wrong) **18.** Jesus rebuked the demon, and it came out of the boy, and he was healed at that moment. (Rebuked: commanded forcefully) **19.** The disciples came to Jesus privately and asked, "Why couldn't we drive it out?" (Privately: away from others) **20.** He replied, "Because you have so little faith. Truly I tell you, if you have faith as small as a mustard seed, you can say to this mountain, 'Move from here to there,' and it will move. Nothing will be impossible for you." (Mustard seed: a very small seed) **21.** However, this kind does not go out except by prayer and fasting. (Fasting: abstaining from food for spiritual purposes) **22.** While they were staying in Galilee, Jesus said to them, "The Son of Man is going to be delivered into the hands of men, (Delivered: handed over) **23.** They will kill Him, and on the third day He will be raised to life." And the disciples were filled with grief. (Grief: sorrow) **24.** After they arrived in Capernaum, those who collected the temple tax came to Peter and asked, "Doesn't your teacher pay the temple tax?" (Temple tax: a religious tax paid to support the temple) **25.** "Yes, He does," he replied. When Peter went into the house, Jesus spoke to him first, saying, "What do you think, Simon? From whom do the kings of the earth collect duties and taxes— from their own children or from others?" (Duties: taxes or charges) **26.** "From others," Peter answered. "Then the children are exempt," Jesus said to him. (Exempt: free from obligation) **27.** "But so that we may not cause offense, go to the lake and throw out your line. Take the first fish you catch, open its mouth, and you will find a coin. Take it and give it to them for My tax and yours." (Cause offense: create a problem)

Chapter 18
1. At that time, the disciples came to Jesus and asked, "Who is the greatest in the kingdom of heaven?" (Greatest: most important) **2.** Jesus called a little child to Him and placed the child among them. (Placed: set; Among: in the middle of) **3.** He said, "Truly, I tell you, unless you change and become like little children, you will never enter the kingdom of heaven." (Change: be converted; Enter: be allowed into) **4.** Therefore, whoever humbles himself like this child is the greatest in the kingdom of heaven. (Humbles: lowers oneself; Greatest: most important) **5.** And whoever receives one such little child in My name receives Me. (Receives: welcomes) **6.** But whoever causes one of these little ones who believe in Me to stumble, it would be better for him to have a millstone hung around his neck and be drowned in the depths of the sea. (Causes to stumble: leads astray; Millstone: a large stone for grinding grain; Drowned: submerged in water) **7.** Woe to the world because of offenses! For it is inevitable that offenses come, but woe to the one through whom the offense comes! (Woe: great sorrow or trouble; Offenses: wrongdoings) **8.** If your hand or foot causes you to stumble, cut it off and throw it away. It is better to enter life maimed or crippled than to have two hands or two feet and be thrown into eternal fire. (Maimed: having a part of the body injured or missing; Crippled: unable to walk properly; Eternal fire: lasting punishment) **9.** If your eye causes you to stumble, gouge it out and throw it away. It is better to enter life with one eye than to have two eyes and be thrown into hellfire. (Gouge: force out) **10.** See that you do not look down on one of these little ones. For I tell you that their angels in heaven always see the face of My Father in heaven. (Look down: treat with disrespect; Angels: spiritual beings who serve God) **11.** For the Son of Man came to save what was lost. (Save: rescue; Lost: those who are spiritually lost) **12.** What do you think? If a man has 100 sheep and one of them goes astray, will he not leave the 99 on the hills and go to look for the one that wandered off? (Goes astray: strays away; Wandered off: got lost) **13.** And if he finds it, truly I tell you, he is happier about that one sheep than about the 99 that did not go astray. (Happier: more joyful) **14.** In the same way, your Father in heaven is not willing that any of these little ones should perish. (Perish: be lost or destroyed) **15.** If your brother sins against you, go and show him his fault just between the two of you. If he listens to you, you have won your brother over. (Sin: do wrong; Fault: wrongdoing) **16.** But if he will not listen, take one or two others along so that 'every matter may be established by the testimony of two or three witnesses.' (Testimony: statement of what happened) **17.** If he refuses to listen to them, tell it to the church; and if he refuses to listen even to the church, treat him as you would a pagan or a tax collector. (Treat: regard; Pagan: someone who does not believe in God; Tax collector: seen as a sinner by Jews) **18.** Truly I tell you, whatever you bind on earth will be bound in heaven, and whatever you loose on earth will be loosed in heaven. (Bind: forbid; Loose: permit) **19.** Again, I tell you that if two of you on earth agree about anything they ask for, it will be done for them by My Father in heaven. (Agree: are in agreement) **20.** For where two or three gather in My name, there am I with them. (Gather: come together) **21.** Then Peter came to Him and asked, "Lord, how many times shall I forgive my brother when he sins against me? Up to seven times?" (Forgive: pardon) **22.** Jesus answered, "I tell you, not seven times, but seventy-seven times." (Seventy-seven times: a way of saying an unlimited number) **23.** Therefore, the kingdom of heaven is like a king who wanted to settle accounts with his servants. (Settle accounts: resolve financial matters) **24.** As he began the settlement, a man who owed him ten thousand talents was brought to him. (Owed: was in debt to; Talents: a large unit of money) **25.** Since he was not able to pay, the master ordered that he and his wife and children and all that he had be sold to repay the debt. (Repay: pay back) **26.** The servant fell on his knees before him. "Be patient with me," he begged, "and I will pay back everything." (Knees: legs bent; Begged: asked desperately) **27.** The servant's master took pity on him, canceled the debt, and let him go. (Took pity: felt sorry; Canceled: forgave) **28.** But when that servant went out, he found one of his fellow servants who owed him a hundred denarii. He grabbed him and began to choke him. "Pay back what you owe me!" he demanded. (Fellow servants: other workers; Denarii: a small amount of money) **29.** His fellow servant fell to his knees and begged him, "Be patient with me, and I will pay you back." (Begged: pleaded) **30.** But he refused. Instead, he went and had the man thrown into prison until he could pay the debt. (Refused: did not agree) **31.** When the other servants saw what had happened, they were greatly distressed and went and told their master everything that had happened. (Distressed: upset) **32.** Then the master called the servant in. "You wicked servant," he said, "I canceled all that debt of yours because you

begged me to. (Wicked: evil; Canceled: forgave) **33.** Shouldn't you have had mercy on your fellow servant just as I had on you?" (Mercy: compassion) **34.** In anger, his master handed him over to the jailers to be tortured, until he should pay back all he owed. (Tortured: subjected to pain) **35.** This is how My heavenly Father will treat each of you unless you forgive your brother or sister from your heart. (Treat: deal with)

Chapter 19

1. When Jesus had finished teaching these things, He left Galilee and went to the region of Judea, beyond the Jordan River. (Region: area; Beyond: on the far side of) **2.** Large crowds followed Him, and He healed them there. (Crowds: large groups of people) **3.** The Pharisees came to test Him and asked, "Is it lawful for a man to divorce his wife for any reason?" (Test: challenge; Lawful: allowed by law) **4.** He answered, "Haven't you read that at the beginning, the Creator made them male and female, (Creator: God; Made: created) **5.** and said, 'For this reason a man will leave his father and mother and be united to his wife, and the two will become one flesh'? (United: joined; Flesh: body, togetherness) **6.** So they are no longer two, but one flesh. Therefore, what God has joined together, let no one separate." (Separate: divide) **7.** They asked Him, "Why then did Moses command that a man give his wife a certificate of divorce and send her away?" (Certificate of divorce: a legal document for separation) **8.** Jesus replied, "Moses allowed you to divorce your wives because your hearts were hard. But it was not this way from the beginning. (Allowed: permitted; Hard hearts: stubbornness) **9.** I tell you that anyone who divorces his wife, except for sexual immorality, and marries another woman commits adultery; and anyone who marries a divorced woman commits adultery." (Sexual immorality: fornication, sexual sin; Adultery: cheating in marriage) **10.** The disciples said to Him, "If this is the situation between a husband and wife, it is better not to marry." (Situation: condition) **11.** Jesus replied, "Not everyone can accept this teaching, but only those to whom it has been given. (Accept: agree with) **12.** For there are eunuchs who were born that way, and there are eunuchs who were made eunuchs by men, and there are those who choose to live like eunuchs for the sake of the kingdom of heaven. The one who can accept this should accept it." (Eunuchs: men who are unable to have children, often due to castration) **13.** Then people brought little children to Jesus for Him to place His hands on them and pray for them, but the disciples rebuked them. (Rebuked: scolded) **14.** Jesus said, "Let the little children come to Me and do not hinder them, for the kingdom of heaven belongs to such as these." (Hinder: prevent) **15.** And He placed His hands on them and went on from there. (Placed: laid; Went on: continued) **16.** A man came to Jesus and asked, "Teacher, what good thing must I do to get eternal life?" (Eternal life: life that never ends, in heaven) **17.** "Why do you ask Me about what is good?" Jesus replied. "There is only One who is good. If you want to enter life, keep the commandments." (Commandments: God's laws) **18.** "Which ones?" the man inquired. Jesus replied, "You shall not murder, you shall not commit adultery, you shall not steal, you shall not give false testimony, (Give false testimony: lie) **19.** honor your father and mother, and love your neighbor as yourself." (Honor: respect) **20.** "All these I have kept," the young man said. "What do I still lack?" (Lack: need, be missing) **21.** Jesus answered, "If you want to be perfect, go, sell your possessions and give to the poor, and you will have treasure in heaven. Then come, follow Me." (Perfect: complete; Possessions: things you own) **22.** When the young man heard this, he went away sad, because he had great wealth. (Sad: unhappy) **23.** Then Jesus said to His disciples, "Truly I tell you, it is hard for a rich man to enter the kingdom of heaven. (Rich: wealthy) **24.** Again I tell you, it is easier for a camel to go through the eye of a needle than for a rich man to enter the kingdom of God." (Camel: a large animal; Eye of a needle: a small hole; Imagery for something almost impossible) **25.** When the disciples heard this, they were greatly astonished and asked, "Who then can be saved?" (Astonished: surprised) **26.** Jesus looked at them and said, "With man this is impossible, but with God all things are possible." (Impossible: cannot be done; Possible: able to be done) **27.** Peter answered Him, "We have left everything to follow You. What then will there be for us?" (Left: abandoned) **28.** Jesus said to them, "Truly I tell you, at the renewal of all things, when the Son of Man sits on His glorious throne, you who have followed Me will also sit on twelve thrones, judging the twelve tribes of Israel. (Renewal: restoration; Glorious: magnificent) **29.** And everyone who has left houses, or brothers, or sisters, or father, or mother, or wife, or children, or fields for My sake will receive a hundred times as much and will inherit eternal life. (Fields: land) **30.** But many who are first will be last, and many who are last will be first." (First: important; Last: least important)

Chapter 20

1. For the kingdom of heaven is like a man who is a householder, who went out early in the morning to hire laborers for his vineyard. (Householder: owner of a house; Laborers: workers) **2.** He agreed with the laborers for a penny a day and sent them into his vineyard. (Agreed: made a deal; Penny: a coin, here meaning a day's wage) **3.** About the third hour, he went out and saw others standing idle in the marketplace, (Third hour: around 9:00 AM; Idle: not working) **4.** and said to them, "You also go into the vineyard, and whatever is right, I will give you." So they went. (Right: fair, what is just) **5.** He went out again at the sixth and ninth hours and did the same. (Sixth hour: around 12:00 PM; Ninth hour: around 3:00 PM) **6.** At about the eleventh hour, he went out and found others standing idle, and said to them, "Why have you been standing here all day doing nothing?" (Eleventh hour: around 5:00 PM) **7.** They said to him, "Because no one has hired us." He said to them, "You also go into the vineyard, and whatever is right, you will receive." (Hired: employed) **8.** When evening came, the lord of the vineyard said to his steward, "Call the laborers and give them their pay, beginning with the last hired and going to the first." (Steward: manager) **9.** The workers who were hired about the eleventh hour came, and each received a penny. (Came: arrived) **10.** When the first came, they expected to receive more, but each of them also received a penny. (Expected: thought they would get) **11.** When they received it, they grumbled against the householder, (Grumbled: complained) **12.** saying, "These last worked only one hour, and you have made them equal to us, who have borne the burden and heat of the day." (Burden: difficult work; Heat: the heat of the day, especially in the hot sun) **13.** But he answered one of them, "Friend, I am not being unfair to you. Didn't you agree with me for a penny? (Unfair: unjust) **14.** Take your pay and go. I want to give the one who was hired last the same as I gave you. (Pay: wages, money for work) **15.** Don't I have the right to do what I want with my own money? Or are you envious because I am generous?" (Right: authority; Envious: jealous) **16.** So the last will be first, and the first will be last. For many are called, but few are chosen. (Called: invited; Chosen: selected, picked) **17.** As Jesus was going up to Jerusalem, He took the twelve disciples aside and said to them, (Aside: separately) **18.** "We are going up to Jerusalem, and the Son of Man will be betrayed to the chief priests and the teachers of the law. They will condemn Him to death, (Betrayed: handed over; Condemn: judge guilty) **19.** and will turn Him over to the Gentiles to be mocked, flogged, and crucified. On the third day, He will be raised to life." (Gentiles: non-Jews; Mocked: ridiculed; Flogged: beaten with a whip) **20.** Then the mother of Zebedee's sons came to Jesus with her sons, kneeling down and asking a favor of Him. (Kneeling: bending down as a sign of respect) **21.** "What is it you want?" He asked. She said, "Grant that one of these two sons of mine may sit at Your right and the other at Your left in Your kingdom. (Grant: give; Right and left: places of honor) **22.** Jesus replied, "You do not know what you are asking. Can you drink the cup I am going to drink? Can you be baptized with the baptism I am going to be baptized with?" (Cup: a symbol of suffering; Baptism: immersion, often referring to suffering or trials) **23.** They answered, "We can." Jesus said to them, "You will indeed drink from My cup and be baptized with the baptism I am baptized with, but to sit at My right or left is not for Me to grant. These places belong to those for whom they have been prepared by My Father." (Indeed: truly; Grant: give permission) **24.** When the ten heard about this, they were indignant with the two brothers. (Indignant: angry) **25.** Jesus called them together and said, "You know that the rulers of the Gentiles lord it over them, and their high officials exercise authority over them. (Lords it over: rule harshly; Officials: leaders) **26.** Not so with you. Instead, whoever wants to become great among you must be your servant, (Servant: one who serves others) **27.** and whoever wants to be first must be your slave— (Slave: a person who serves without rights) **28.** just as the Son of Man did not come to be served, but to serve, and to give His life as a ransom for many." (Ransom: payment to free someone) **29.** As Jesus and His disciples were leaving Jericho, a large crowd followed Him. (Jericho: a city in ancient Israel) **30.** Two blind men were sitting by the roadside, and when they heard that Jesus was going by, they shouted, "Lord, Son of David, have mercy on us!" (Mercy: kindness, help) **31.** The crowd rebuked them and told them to be quiet, but they shouted all the louder, "Lord, Son of David, have mercy on us!" (Rebuked: scolded) **32.** Jesus stopped and called them, "What do you want Me to do for you?" (Stopped: paused, halted) **33.** "Lord," they answered, "we want our sight." (Sight: the ability to see) **34.** Jesus had compassion on them and touched their eyes. Immediately they received their sight and followed Him. (Compassion: sympathy, pity)

Chapter 21

1. And when they drew near to Jerusalem, and came to Bethphage, to the Mount of Olives, then Jesus sent two disciples, (Drew near: approached; Bethphage: a village near Jerusalem; Mount of Olives: a hill near Jerusalem) **2.** Saying to them, "Go into the village ahead of you, and immediately you will find a donkey tied, and a colt with her; untie them and bring them to Me. (Colt: a young donkey) **3.** If anyone says anything to you, say that the Lord needs them, and immediately he will send them." (Lord: a respectful title for

Jesus) **4.** This took place to fulfill what was spoken by the prophet, saying, (Fulfill: to complete or make happen) **5.** "Say to the daughter of Zion, 'See, your King comes to you, gentle and riding on a donkey, on a colt, the foal of a donkey.'" (Daughter of Zion: a symbolic reference to Jerusalem or Israel; Foal: a young animal, especially a young donkey) **6.** The disciples went and did as Jesus commanded them, (Commanded: ordered) **7.** They brought the donkey and the colt, placed their clothes on them, and Jesus sat on them. (Clothes: garments, outerwear) **8.** A very large crowd spread their cloaks on the road, while others cut branches from the trees and spread them on the road. (Cloaks: outer garments; Spread: laid down) **9.** The crowds that went ahead of Him and those that followed shouted, "Hosanna to the Son of David! Blessed is He who comes in the name of the Lord! Hosanna in the highest!" (Hosanna: an expression of praise and joy; Son of David: a title for the Messiah) **10.** When Jesus entered Jerusalem, the whole city was stirred and asked, "Who is this?" (Stirred: moved, excited) **11.** The crowds answered, "This is Jesus, the prophet from Nazareth in Galilee." (Prophet: someone who speaks for God) **12.** Jesus entered the temple and drove out all who were buying and selling there. He overturned the tables of the money changers and the seats of those who sold doves. (Drove out: forced out; Money changers: people who exchanged foreign money for temple currency) **13.** He said to them, "It is written, 'My house will be called a house of prayer,' but you are making it a den of thieves." (Written: referring to scripture; Den of thieves: a place of sinful activity) **14.** The blind and the lame came to Him at the temple, and He healed them. (Lame: unable to walk properly) **15.** When the chief priests and the teachers of the law saw the wonderful things He did and the children shouting in the temple, "Hosanna to the Son of David," they were indignant. (Indignant: angry or upset) **16.** "Do you hear what these children are saying?" they asked Him. "Yes," replied Jesus, "Have you never read, 'From the lips of children and infants You, Lord, have called forth Your praise'?" (Lips: part of the mouth; Called forth: created or brought out) **17.** And He left them and went out of the city to Bethany, where He spent the night. (Bethany: a village near Jerusalem) **18.** Early in the morning, as He was on His way back to the city, He was hungry. (On His way back: returning) **19.** Seeing a fig tree by the road, He went up to it but found nothing on it except leaves. Then He said to it, "May you never bear fruit again!" Immediately the tree withered. (Fig tree: a tree that produces figs; Withered: dried up, died) **20.** When the disciples saw this, they were amazed and asked, "How did the fig tree wither so quickly?" (Amazed: surprised) **21.** Jesus replied, "Truly I tell you, if you have faith and do not doubt, not only can you do what was done to the fig tree, but you can also say to this mountain, 'Go, throw yourself into the sea,' and it will be done. (Truly: certainly; Doubt: uncertainty) **22.** If you believe, you will receive whatever you ask for in prayer." (Believe: trust, have faith) **23.** Jesus entered the temple courts, and while He was teaching, the chief priests and the elders of the people came to Him. "By what authority are You doing these things?" they asked. "And who gave You this authority?" (Temple courts: outer areas of the temple; Authority: power to act) **24.** Jesus replied, "I will also ask you one question. If you answer Me, I will tell you by what authority I am doing these things. (Reply: answer) **25.** John's baptism—where did it come from? Was it from heaven, or of human origin?" They discussed it among themselves and said, "If we say, 'From heaven,' He will ask, 'Then why didn't you believe him?' (Baptism: a religious act of washing; Human origin: from people) **26.** But if we say, 'Of human origin,' we are afraid of the people, for they all hold that John was a prophet." (Afraid: scared) **27.** So they answered Jesus, "We don't know." Then He said, "Neither will I tell you by what authority I am doing these things." (Neither: not either) **28.** What do you think? There was a man who had two sons. He went to the first and said, 'Son, go and work today in the vineyard.' (Vineyard: a place where grapevines grow) **29.** "I will not," he answered, but later he changed his mind and went. (Changed his mind: decided differently) **30.** Then the father went to the other son and said the same thing. He answered, "I will, sir," but he did not go. (Sir: a respectful address) **31.** Which of the two did what his father wanted?" "The first," they answered. Jesus said to them, "Truly I tell you, the tax collectors and the prostitutes are entering the kingdom of God ahead of you. (Tax collectors: people who collected taxes; Prostitutes: people who sell sexual services) **32.** For John came to you to show you the way of righteousness, and you did not believe him, but the tax collectors and the prostitutes did. And even after you saw this, you did not repent and believe him." (Repent: feel sorry for, change one's mind) **33.** Listen to another parable: There was a landowner who planted a vineyard, put a wall around it, dug a winepress in it, and built a watchtower. Then he rented the vineyard to some farmers and went away on a journey. (Landowner: someone who owns land; Winepress: where grapes are crushed to make wine; Watchtower: a tall building for watching) **34.** When the harvest time approached, he sent his servants to the tenants to collect his fruit. (Harvest: gathering of crops) **35.** The tenants seized his servants; they beat one, killed another, and stoned a third. (Seized: took hold of; Stoned: threw stones at) **36.** Again, he sent other servants more than the first time, and the tenants treated them the same way. (Treated: acted toward) **37.** Last of all, he sent his son to them. "They will respect my son," he said. (Respect: show honor) **38.** But when the tenants saw the son, they said to each other, "This is the heir. Come, let's kill him and take his inheritance." (Heir: someone who inherits after someone dies) **39.** So they took him and threw him out of the vineyard and killed him. (Threw: cast out) **40.** Therefore, when the owner of the vineyard comes, what will he do to those tenants?" (Owner: the person who owns something) **41.** "He will bring those wicked men to a wretched end," they replied, "and he will rent the vineyard to other tenants, who will give him his share of the crop at harvest time." (Wicked: evil, sinful) **42.** Jesus said to them, "Have you never read in the Scriptures: 'The stone the builders rejected has become the cornerstone; the Lord has done this, and it is marvelous in our eyes'? (Cornerstone: the most important stone in a building, symbolic of Jesus) **43.** Therefore I tell you that the kingdom of God will be taken away from you and given to a people who will produce its fruit. (Taken away: removed) **44.** Anyone who falls on this stone will be broken to pieces; anyone on whom it falls will be crushed." (Crushed: destroyed, shattered) **45.** When the chief priests and the Pharisees heard Jesus' parables, they knew He was talking about them. (Pharisees: religious leaders) **46.** They looked for a way to arrest Him, but they were afraid of the crowd, because the people held that He was a prophet. (Arrest: capture)

Chapter 22

1. Jesus responded again by telling them a story, saying, (Story: A narrative or tale, often used to convey a moral lesson) **2.** "The kingdom of heaven can be compared to a king who arranged a marriage for his son, (Marriage: A formal union of two people, typically recognized by law and/or religion) **3.** And sent his servants to call those who were invited to the wedding, but they refused to come. (Servants: People employed to do domestic or administrative work) **4.** He sent more servants, saying, 'Tell those invited, "Look, I have prepared a feast: my oxen and fattened cattle (animals raised for food) are slaughtered, and everything is ready. Come to the wedding!"' (Fattened cattle: Animals that have been specially fed for the purpose of being slaughtered for meat; Slaughtered: Killed for food, usually in a ritual or systematic way) **5.** But they ignored the invitation and went their separate ways—one to his field, another to his business. (Ignored: Paid no attention to or disregarded; Field: An area of land used for agriculture or farming; Business: An occupation, profession, or trade) **6.** And the others mistreated the servants and even killed them. (Mistreated: Treated badly or cruelly; Killed: Took the life of) **7.** When the king heard this, he was furious, and he sent his army to destroy those murderers and burn their city. (Furious: Extremely angry; Army: A large group of soldiers organized for war; Murderers: People who kill another person unlawfully and with intent; City: A large and significant town or settlement) **8.** Then he said to his servants, 'The wedding banquet is prepared, but those who were invited were not worthy to attend. (Banquet: A large meal or feast, often in celebration; Worthy: Deserving or qualified) **9.** So go to the roads and invite everyone you find to the wedding.' (Roads: Paths or routes that people travel on) **10.** The servants went out into the streets and gathered all they could find, both good and bad, and the wedding hall was filled with guests. (Servants: People employed to perform duties for others; Gathered: Collected or brought together; Guests: People who are invited to an event or occasion) **11.** When the king came in to see the guests, he noticed a man who was not wearing the proper wedding clothes. (Notice: To observe or become aware of something; Proper: Correct or suitable for the purpose; Wedding clothes: Special attire worn for a wedding) **12.** He asked him, 'Friend, how did you get in here without the proper wedding garment?' The man was speechless. (Speechless: Unable to speak, usually due to shock, embarrassment, or being caught; Garment: A piece of clothing) **13.** Then the king told his servants, 'Tie him up hand and foot and throw him outside, into the darkness, where there will be weeping and gnashing of teeth.' (Servants: People employed to perform duties for others; Gnashing of teeth: A biblical expression of great pain, anguish, or despair; Weeping: Crying, usually in sorrow; Darkness: Complete absence of light, often symbolizing suffering or punishment) **14.** For many are called, but few are chosen." (Chosen: Selected or picked out from a group) **15.** Then the Pharisees (religious leaders) went out and plotted to trap Jesus in his words. (Pharisees: A religious group in ancient Judaism, known for strict adherence to the law; Plotted: Planned, often in a secretive or harmful way) **16.** They sent their followers, along with the Herodians (people who supported King Herod), to ask him, "Teacher, we know you are truthful and teach the way of God with sincerity. You do not show favoritism, for you treat all people equally. (Followers: People who follow or support a leader or teacher; Herodians: A political group that supported King Herod, a Roman-appointed ruler; Truthful: Honest, saying what is true; Sincerity: The quality of being genuine, without pretense or deceit; Favoritism: The unfair treatment of one person or group over others) **17.** Tell us, then, is it right to pay taxes to Caesar or not?" (Taxes: Money paid to the government by citizens for public services; Caesar: A title used by Roman emperors, particularly Augustus or his successors) **18.** But Jesus, knowing their evil intentions, replied, "Why do you try to trap me, you hypocrites (people who pretend to be something they are not)? (Evil intentions: Plans or desires to do something morally wrong; Hypocrites: People who act in contradiction to their stated beliefs or values) **19.** Show me the coin used for the tax." They brought him a denarius (a type of Roman coin). (Coin: A small, flat piece of metal used as money; Denarius: A Roman silver coin commonly used in the 1st century AD) **20.** Jesus asked them, "Whose image and inscription is this?" (Image: A representation or likeness of someone or something; Inscription: Words that are written or engraved on a surface) **21.** "Caesar's," they replied. (Caesar's: Belonging to Caesar, the Roman emperor) Then he said to them, "Give to Caesar what is Caesar's, and to God what is God's." (Emperor Caesar: The ruler of the Roman Empire; Render: To give or return something) **22.** When they heard this, they were amazed and left him, going away. (Amazed: Filled with wonder or surprise) **23.** That same day, some Sadducees (a group that denied the resurrection of the dead) came to Jesus and asked him, (Sadducees: A religious group in ancient Judaism, who denied the resurrection of the dead and the existence of angels) **24.** "Teacher, Moses told us that if a man dies without having children, his brother must marry the widow and raise up offspring for him. (Widow: A woman whose husband has died; Offspring: Children or descendants) **25.** Now, there were seven brothers with us: the first married and died, and since he had no children, his wife was left to his brother. (Brothers: Male siblings) **26.** The second brother did the same, and the third, and so on until all seven had married her. (Same: Identical, or similar in every way) **27.** Finally, the woman died. (Finally: In the end, after everything else) **28.** In the resurrection, whose wife will she be? For all seven were married to her." (Resurrection: The rising from the dead, especially in a religious context) **29.** Jesus replied, "You are in error because you do not understand the Scriptures or the power of God. (Error: A mistake or misunderstanding; Scriptures: Sacred writings or religious texts) **30.** In the resurrection, people will neither marry nor be given in marriage; they will be like the angels in heaven. (Angels: Spiritual beings believed to serve as messengers or servants of God) **31.** But about the resurrection of the dead, have you not read what God said to you, (Read: To look at and understand written or printed material) **32.** 'I am the God of Abraham, the God of Isaac, and the God of Jacob'? He is not the God of the dead, but of the living." (Abraham, Isaac, Jacob: Patriarchs in the Bible, ancestors of the Jewish people) **33.** When the crowd heard this, they were astonished at his teaching. (Astonished: Amazed, shocked, or surprised) **34.** When the Pharisees heard that Jesus had silenced the Sadducees, they gathered together. (Silenced: Made speechless or quiet, especially by an argument) **35.** One of them, an expert in the law, tested him with a question: (Expert: A person with specialized knowledge or skills in a particular area; Law: A set of rules or principles that govern a society) **36.** "Teacher, which is the greatest commandment in the Law?" (Commandment: A rule or directive given by a higher authority, especially in religious contexts) **37.** Jesus replied, "Love the Lord your God with all your heart, with all your soul, and with all your mind. (Heart: The emotional center of a person; also used metaphorically for feelings and desires; Soul: The immaterial essence of a person, often considered the seat of consciousness; Mind: The intellectual or thinking part of a person) **38.** This is the first and greatest commandment. (Greatest: The most important or significant) **39.** And the second is like it: 'Love your neighbor as yourself.' (Neighbor: A person who lives near or next to you; in a broader sense, any fellow human) **40.** All the Law and the Prophets hang on these two commandments." (Law: A body of rules or regulations; Prophets: People who are believed to be divinely inspired to deliver messages from God) **41.** While the Pharisees were gathered together, Jesus asked them, (Gathered: Came together in one place) **42.** "What do you think about the Messiah? Whose son is he?" (Messiah: A promised or expected deliverer or savior) They replied, "The Son of David." (David: A biblical king, considered the greatest of Israel's kings) **43.** Jesus said to them, "How is it then that David, speaking by the Spirit, calls him Lord? For he says, (Spirit: The spiritual or divine aspect of God or a person) **44.** 'The LORD said to my Lord, "Sit at my right hand until I put your enemies under your feet."' (Right hand: The place of honor or authority) **45.** If David calls him Lord, how can he be his son?" (David: A biblical king, considered the greatest of Israel's kings; Son: A male child or descendant) **46.** No one could answer him a word, and from that day on, no one dared to ask him any more questions. (Dared: Was bold or courageous enough)

Chapter 23

1. Then Jesus spoke to the crowd and his disciples, (Crowd: Large group) **2.** "The scribes and Pharisees sit in Moses' seat. (Scribes: Religious teachers) **3.** Follow what they say, but do not do as they do, for they do not practice what they preach. (Preach: Teach) **4.** They burden others with heavy loads but will not lift a finger to help. (Burden: Load) **5.** Everything they do is to be seen by others; they make their phylacteries large and love public recognition. (Phylacteries: Prayer boxes) **6.** They seek the best places at feasts and synagogues, (Feasts: Meals) **7.** and love being called 'Rabbi'. (Rabbi: Teacher) **8.** But you are all brothers, and Christ is your only Teacher. (Teacher: Instructor) **9.** Call no one your father on earth; you have one Father in heaven. (Father: Parent or authority) **10.** Do not be called 'masters'; Christ is your Master. (Masters: Authorities) **11.** The greatest among you will be your servant. (Servant: Helper) **12.** Those who exalt themselves will be humbled, but those who humble themselves will be exalted. (Exalt: Lift up) **13.** Woe to you, scribes and Pharisees, hypocrites! You shut the kingdom of heaven to others; you neither enter nor let others in. (Hypocrites: Pretenders) **14.** You devour widows' houses and make long prayers for show; you will receive greater condemnation. (Devour: Consume greedily) **15.** You travel to make one convert, but make them twice as much a child of hell as yourselves. (Convert: Follower) **16.** Woe to you, blind guides! You say swearing by the temple means nothing, but swearing by the gold of the temple binds a person. (Blind: Unaware) **17.** You blind fools! Which is greater: the gold, or the temple that makes the gold holy? (Fools: Unwise) **18.** You say swearing by the altar means nothing, but swearing by the gift on the altar makes someone guilty. (Altar: Sacred table) **19.** You blind men! Which is greater: the gift, or the altar that makes the gift holy? (Holy: Sacred) **20.** Anyone who swears by the altar swears by it and everything on it. (Swears: Promises) **21.** Anyone who swears by the temple swears by it and by God who dwells in it. (Dwells: Lives) **22.** Anyone who swears by heaven swears by God's throne and the One who sits on it. (Throne: Seat of power) **23.** Woe to you, scribes and Pharisees, hypocrites! You tithe small herbs but neglect justice, mercy, and faithfulness. (Tithe: Give a tenth of their income) **24.** You blind guides! You strain out a gnat but swallow a camel. (Strain: Filter) **25.** Woe to you, scribes and Pharisees, hypocrites! You clean the outside of the cup, but inside you are full of greed and self-indulgence. (Greed: Desire for more) **26.** Cleanse the inside first, so the outside will be clean. (Cleanse: Purify) **27.** Woe to you, scribes and Pharisees, hypocrites! You are like whitewashed tombs—beautiful outside but full of dead bones inside. (Whitewashed: Painted) **28.** In the same way, you appear righteous outwardly, but inside you are full of hypocrisy and wickedness. (Wickedness: Evil) **29.** Woe to you, scribes and Pharisees, hypocrites! You build tombs for the prophets and decorate the graves of the righteous, (Decorate: Adorn) **30.** saying, 'If we had lived in the past, we would not have killed the prophets.' (Killed: Murdered) **31.** You testify against yourselves that you are the descendants of those who murdered the prophets. (Testify: Witness) **32.** Fill up the measure of your ancestors' sin. (Measure: Amount) **33.** You serpents! You brood of vipers! How can you escape being condemned to hell? (Brood: Group) **34.** I am sending you prophets, wise men, and scribes. Some you will kill and crucify; others you will persecute. (Persecute: Oppress) **35.** All the righteous blood shed on earth will fall on you, from Abel to Zechariah, whom you murdered. (Righteous: Just) **36.** Truly, all these things will come upon this generation. (Generation: People born in the same time) **37.** O Jerusalem, Jerusalem, you who kill the prophets and stone those sent to you, how often I wanted to gather your children as a hen gathers her chicks, but you refused! (Stone: Throw rocks) **38.** Look, your house is left desolate. (Desolate: Empty) **39.** For I tell you, you will not see me again until you say, 'Blessed is he who comes in the name of the Lord.' (Blessed: Honored)

Chapter 24

1. Jesus left the temple, and his disciples came to show him its buildings. (Buildings: Structures for shelter.) **2.** Jesus replied, "Do you see all this? Truly, I tell you, not one stone here will be left on another; all will be thrown down." (Thrown: Propelled with force.) **3.** While sitting on the Mount of Olives, his disciples asked him privately, "When will these things happen, and what will be the sign of your coming and the end of the age?" (Privately: In secret.) **4.** Jesus answered, "Be careful that no one deceives you." (Deceives: Misleads or tricks.) **5.** "Many will come claiming to be the Christ and will deceive many." (Claiming: Asserting as true.) **6.** "You will hear of wars and rumors of wars. Do not be alarmed; these things must happen, but the end is not yet." (Rumors: Unverified stories.) **7.** "Nation will rise against nation, and kingdom against kingdom. There will be famines, plagues, and earthquakes in many places." (Famines: Severe food shortages.) **8.** "All these are the beginning of sorrows." (Sorrows: Deep sadness or grief.) **9.** "Then they will hand you over to be persecuted and killed. You will be hated by all nations because of me." (Persecuted: Oppressed or mistreated.) **10.** "Many will be offended, betray, and hate each other." (Betray: Be disloyal or expose secrets.) **11.** "False prophets will rise up and deceive many." (Prophets: Those claiming divine messages.) **12.** "Because of the increase in wickedness, the love of most will grow cold." (Wickedness: Immorality or evil.) **13.** "But the one who stands firm to the end will be saved." (Stands firm: Remains determined.) **14.** "And this gospel of the kingdom will be preached in all the world as a testimony to all nations, and then the end will come." (Gospel: The message of Christ.) **15.** "So when you see the abomination of desolation spoken of by the prophet Daniel standing in the holy place, let the reader understand," (Abomination: A disgusting offense.) **16.** "then those in Judea should flee to the mountains." (Flee: Escape from danger.) **17.** "Let no one on the roof come down to take anything from their house," (Roof: The top of a building.) **18.** "and let no one in the field return for their clothes." (Field: Open land used for farming.) **19.** "How dreadful it will be for pregnant women and nursing mothers in those days!" (Dreadful: Causing fear or discomfort.) **20.** "Pray that your flight will not happen in winter or on the Sabbath." (Flight: The act of fleeing.) **21.** "For there will be great distress, unequaled from the beginning of the world until now—and never to be equaled again." (Distress: Extreme sorrow or pain.) **22.** "If those days were not shortened, no one would survive, but for the sake of the elect, those days will be shortened." (Elect: Chosen ones.) **23.** "At that time, if anyone says to you, 'Look, here is the Christ!' or 'There he is!' do not believe it." (Christ: The Anointed One or Messiah.) **24.** "For false Christs and false prophets will appear and perform great signs and wonders to deceive, if possible, even the elect." (Wonders: Extraordinary signs.) **25.** "See, I have told you ahead of time." (Ahead: In advance.) **26.** "So if anyone tells you, 'He's in the desert,' do not go out; or 'He's in the inner rooms,' do not believe it." (Inner: Private or secluded.) **27.** "For as the lightning comes from the east and flashes to the west, so will be the coming of the Son of Man." (Flashes: Sudden bursts of light.) **28.** "Wherever the carcass is, there the vultures will gather." (Carcass: A dead body.) **29.** "Immediately after the tribulation of those days, the sun will be darkened, the moon will not give its light, the stars will fall from the sky, and the heavenly bodies will be shaken." (Tribulation: Great suffering.) **30.** "Then the sign of the Son of Man will appear in the sky, and all the nations of the earth will mourn. They will see the Son of Man coming on the clouds of heaven with power and great glory." (Mourn: Express sorrow.) **31.** "And he will send his angels with a loud trumpet call, and they will gather his elect from the four winds, from one end of the heavens to the other." (Angels: Divine messengers.) **32.** "Learn this lesson from the fig tree: As soon as its twigs get tender and its leaves come out, you know that summer is near." (Twigs: Small branches.) **33.** "Even so, when you see all these things, you know that it is near, right at the door." (Near: Close in time.) **34.** "Truly I tell you, this generation will not pass away until all these things have happened." (Generation: A group of people born at the same time.) **35.** "Heaven and earth will pass away, but my words will never pass away." (Pass away: Cease to exist.) **36.** "But about that day or hour no one knows, not even the angels in heaven, nor the Son, but only the Father." (Angels: Spiritual beings.) **37.** "As it was in the days of Noah, so it will be at the coming of the Son of Man." (Noah: A biblical figure who survived the flood.) **38.** "For in the days before the flood, people were eating, drinking, marrying, and giving in marriage, up to the day Noah entered the ark." (Flood: A large overflow of water.) **39.** "And they knew nothing about what would happen until the flood came and took them all away. That is how it will be at the coming of the Son of Man." (Took: Removed or captured.) **40.** "Two men will be in the field; one will be taken and the other left." (Taken: Removed or captured.) **41.** "Two women will be grinding with a hand mill; one will be taken and the other left." (Grinding: Breaking down into smaller parts.) **42.** "Therefore, keep watch, because you do not know on what day your Lord will come." (Watch: Stay alert.) **43.** "But understand this: If the owner of the house had known at what time of night the thief was coming, he would have kept watch and not let his house be broken into." (Thief: A person who steals.) **44.** "So you also must be ready, because the Son of Man will come at an hour you do not expect." (Ready: Prepared and able.) **45.** "Who then is the faithful and wise servant, whom the master has put in charge of the servants in his household to give them their food at the proper time?" (Servant: A person employed for tasks.) **46.** "It will be good for that servant whose master finds him doing so when he returns." (Good: Morally right.) **47.** "Truly I tell you, he will put him in charge of all his possessions." (Possessions: Things owned.) **48.** "But suppose that servant is wicked and says to himself, 'My master is staying away a long time,'" (Wicked: Morally wrong or evil.) **49.** "and he begins to beat his fellow servants and to eat and drink with drunkards." (Fellow: A companion or peer.) **50.** "The master of that servant will come on a day when he does not expect him, and at an hour he is not aware of." (Aware: Knowledgeable or conscious.) **51.** "He will cut him to pieces and assign him a place with the hypocrites, where there will be weeping and gnashing of teeth." (Hypocrites: Pretenders or deceivers.)

Chapter 25

1. The kingdom of heaven is like ten virgins who took their lamps and went out to meet the bridegroom. (Virgins: unmarried women, often symbolizing purity) **2.** Five were wise, and five were foolish. (Foolish: lacking wisdom or good judgment) **3.** The foolish took lamps but no oil, (Oil: a substance used to fuel lamps) **4.** while the wise took extra oil in vessels along with their lamps. (Vessels: containers or jars) **5.** As the bridegroom delayed, they all fell asleep. (Delayed: postponed or took longer than expected) **6.** At midnight, a shout was heard: "The bridegroom is coming, go meet him!" (Midnight: the middle of the night) **7.** All the virgins woke and trimmed their lamps. (Trimmed: adjusted or prepared, typically by cutting) **8.** The foolish asked the wise, "Give us some of your oil, our lamps have gone out." (Gone out: stopped burning) **9.** The wise replied, "There isn't enough; go buy some for yourselves." (Replied: answered) **10.** While they were gone, the bridegroom arrived, and those ready entered the wedding feast; the door was shut. (Feast: a large meal or celebration) **11.** Later, the other virgins came, saying, "Lord, open the door for us." (Virgins: unmarried women, often symbolizing purity) **12.** But he replied, "I don't know you." (Replied: answered) **13.** Be watchful, for you don't know the day or hour of the Son of Man's return. (Watchful: alert or vigilant) **14.** The kingdom of heaven is like a man traveling abroad, who entrusted his wealth to his servants. (Entrusted: gave responsibility for) **15.** He gave five talents to one, two to another, and one to the last, each according to their ability, and then departed. (Talents: units of money, or gifts and abilities) **16.** The one with five talents invested them and gained five more. (Invested: put money into something with the hope of gaining a return) **17.** Similarly, the one with two talents gained two more. (Gained: obtained or earned) **18.** But the servant with one talent buried it in the ground. (Buried: placed or hidden in the earth) **19.** After a long time, the master returned to settle accounts. (Settle: to resolve or clear up) **20.** The servant with five talents brought ten, saying, "You gave me five talents, and I've earned five more." (Earned: gained through effort) **21.** His master replied, "Well done, good and faithful servant. You were faithful with a few things; I'll put you in charge of many. Enter your master's joy." (Faithful: loyal and trustworthy) **22.** The servant with two talents did the same, saying, "You gave me two talents, and I've gained two more." (Same: in the same manner or way) **23.** The master replied, "Well done, good and faithful servant. You've been faithful in a little; I'll entrust you with much. Enter your master's joy." (Entrust: to give someone responsibility for something) **24.** The servant with one talent said, "Master, I knew you were hard, reaping where you didn't sow and gathering where you didn't scatter. (Reaping: gathering crops) **25.** I was afraid, so I hid your talent in the ground. Here's what belongs to you." (Hid: concealed or kept out of sight) **26.** The master answered, "You wicked, lazy servant! You knew I reap where I didn't sow and gather where I didn't scatter. (Wicked: morally wrong or evil) **27.** You should have at least put my money with the bankers so I could have earned interest." (Interest: extra money earned from investments) **28.** Take the talent from him and give it to the one who has ten talents. (Talent: a large sum of money, or an ability) **29.** To everyone who has, more will be given, and they will have abundance. But from those who have little, even what they have will be taken away. (Abundance: a large quantity or amount) **30.** And throw the worthless servant into outer darkness, where there will be weeping and gnashing of teeth. (Worthless: having no value or usefulness) **31.** When the Son of Man comes in His glory, and all His angels with Him, He will sit on His glorious throne. (Glory: great honor or magnificence) **32.** All nations will be gathered before Him, and He will separate them as a shepherd divides sheep from goats. (Separate: to divide into groups or categories) **33.** He will place the sheep on His right and the goats on His left. (Place: to position or put in a certain spot) **34.** Then the King will say to those on His right, "Come, you who are blessed by My Father, inherit the kingdom prepared for you since the world's foundation. (Inherit: to receive something passed down) **35.** For I was hungry, and you gave Me food; thirsty, and you gave Me drink; a stranger, and you took Me in; (Took in: welcomed or provided shelter) **36.** naked, and you clothed Me; sick, and you visited Me; in prison, and you came to Me." (Clothed: gave clothing to) **37.** Then the righteous will ask, "Lord, when did we see You hungry and feed You, thirsty and give You drink? (Righteous: morally right or just) **38.** When did we see You a stranger and take You in, or naked and clothe You? (Stranger: someone unknown or foreign) **39.** When did we see You sick or in prison and visit You?" (Visit: to go see someone, typically to provide help or support) **40.** The King will reply, "Truly, whatever you did for one of the least of these brothers and sisters of Mine, you did for Me." (Reply: to respond to a question or statement) **41.** Then He will say to those on His left, "Depart from Me, you cursed, into the eternal fire prepared for the devil and his angels. (Cursed: condemned or damned) **42.** For I was hungry, and you gave Me nothing to eat; thirsty, and you gave Me nothing to drink; (Nothing: not a single thing) **43.** a stranger, and you didn't take Me in; naked, and you didn't clothe Me; sick, and in prison, and you didn't visit Me." (Visit: to go see someone, typically to provide help or support) **44.** They will reply, "Lord, when did we see You hungry or thirsty or a stranger or naked or sick or in prison and did not help You?" (Help: to assist or provide aid) **45.** He will answer, "Truly, whatever you did not do for one of the least of these, you did not do for Me." (Answer: to respond to a question or statement) **46.** And these will go away into eternal punishment, but the righteous into eternal life. (Eternal: lasting forever)

Chapter 26

1. After Jesus finished speaking, he told his disciples, (Disciples: followers) **2.** "In two days is the Passover, and the Son of Man will be handed over to be crucified." (Passover: Jewish festival) **3.** The chief priests and elders gathered at Caiaphas's palace, (Elders: leaders) **4.** plotting to arrest Jesus secretly and kill him, (Plotting: planning harm) **5.** but decided to avoid the feast to prevent unrest. (Unrest: disturbance) **6.** While in Bethany at Simon the leper's house, (Leper: one with leprosy) **7.** a woman poured precious ointment on Jesus's head during the meal. (Ointment: scented oil) **8.** The disciples were upset, saying it was wasteful, (Wasteful: unnecessary use) **9.** claiming it could have been sold to help the poor. (Poor: needy people) **10.** Jesus replied, "Leave her alone; she has done a good deed for me. (Deed: act) **11.** The poor will always be with you, but I won't." (Always: continually) **12.** He explained, "She prepared my body for burial." (Burial: placing in a grave) **13.** He declared her act would be remembered wherever the gospel is preached. (Gospel: teachings of Christ) **14.** Judas Iscariot went to the chief priests, (Betray: disloyal act) **15.** asking what they'd pay him to betray Jesus. They agreed on thirty silver coins. (Coins: metal money) **16.** From then on, Judas sought an opportunity to betray Him. (Opportunity: chance) **17.** On the first day of the Feast of Unleavened Bread, the disciples asked where to prepare the Passover meal. (Unleavened: without yeast) **18.** Jesus directed them to a certain man's house, saying, "My time is near; we will celebrate here." (Celebrate: observe joyfully) **19.** The disciples obeyed and prepared the meal. (Obeyed: followed orders) **20.** That evening, Jesus sat with the twelve. (Evening: nightfall) **21.** He said, "One of you will betray me." (Betray: deceive) **22.** Sorrowful, they asked, "Is it I, Lord?" (Sorrowful: sad) **23.** He answered, "The one who shares my dish will betray me. (Dish: plate for food) **24.** Woe to that man—it would be better if he were never born." (Woe: distress) **25.** Judas asked, "Is it I?" Jesus replied, "You have said it." (Replied: answered) **26.** During the meal, Jesus blessed bread, broke it, and gave it to them, saying, "Take, eat; this is my body." (Blessed: made holy) **27.** He took a cup, gave thanks, and shared it, (Thanks: gratitude) **28.** saying, "This is my blood of the covenant, shed for many for the forgiveness of sins. (Covenant: sacred agreement) **29.** I won't drink wine again until I do so with you in my Father's kingdom." (Kingdom: God's realm) **30.** After singing a hymn, they went to the Mount of Olives. (Hymn: religious song) **31.** Jesus warned, "Tonight, you will all fall away because of me, as it is written: 'Strike the shepherd, and the sheep will scatter.' (Shepherd: guide) **32.** After I rise, I will go ahead of you to Galilee." (Galilee: region in Israel) **33.** Peter declared, "Even if all leave, I never will." (Declared: said firmly) **34.** Jesus said, "Before the rooster crows, you'll deny me three times." (Deny: refuse) **35.** Peter insisted, "I'd die before denying you," and the others agreed. (Insisted: asserted) **36.** Jesus went with them to Gethsemane and said, "Sit here while I pray." (Gethsemane: a garden for prayer) **37.** Taking Peter and Zebedee's sons, he became deeply troubled. (Troubled: distressed) **38.** He said, "My soul is overwhelmed with sorrow. Stay and watch with me." (Watch: stay alert) **39.** Going farther, he prayed, "Father, take this cup if possible, but your will be done." (Will: desire) **40.** Returning, he found them asleep and asked Peter, "Couldn't you stay awake for one hour?" (Awake: not sleeping) **41.** "Pray to avoid temptation. The spirit is willing, but the body is weak." (Temptation: lure to do wrong) **42.** He prayed again, "Father, if this cup must be taken, your will be done." (Cup: suffering) **43.** Returning, he found them sleeping again, their eyes heavy. (Heavy: weary) **44.** Leaving them, he prayed a third time with the same words. (Same: unchanged) **45.** He said, "The time has come. The Son of Man is betrayed into sinners' hands." (Betrayed: handed over) **46.** "Get up! My betrayer is here." (Betrayer: disloyal one) **47.** While speaking, Judas arrived with a crowd armed with swords and clubs. (Armed: carrying weapons) **48.** Judas signaled, "The one I kiss is him; arrest him." (Kiss: sign of affection) **49.** Approaching Jesus, Judas said, "Greetings, Rabbi," and kissed him. (Rabbi: teacher) **50.** Jesus replied, "Friend, do what you came for." They seized him. (Seized: captured) **51.** One disciple struck the high priest's servant, cutting off his ear. (Struck: hit) **52.** Jesus said, "Put away your sword. Those who use it will die by it." (Sword: weapon) **53.** "I could ask my Father for angels to protect me." (Angels: divine messengers) **54.** "But how would Scripture be fulfilled if this didn't happen?" (Scripture: holy text) **55.** Jesus told the crowd, "I taught openly in the temple; you didn't arrest me then." (Temple: place of worship) **56.** "This fulfills the prophets' words." The disciples fled. (Fled: ran away) **57.** Jesus was taken to Caiaphas, where the elders and scribes gathered. (Scribes: record keepers) **58.** Peter followed at a distance and sat with the guards to see what would happen. (Guards: protectors) **59.** The chief priests sought false witnesses against Jesus to have him killed. (False: untrue) **60.** Despite many witnesses, they found no evidence. Finally, two spoke up. (Evidence: proof) **61.** They said, "He claimed he could destroy God's temple and rebuild it in three days." (Destroy: ruin) **62.** The high priest asked, "Don't you respond to these accusations?" (Accusations: charges) **63.** Jesus stayed silent. The high priest demanded, "Are you the Christ, the Son of God?" (Silent: not speaking) **64.** Jesus replied, "You said it. You'll see the Son of Man at God's right hand, coming in the clouds." (Clouds: sky formations) **65.** The high priest tore his clothes, shouting, "Blasphemy! We don't need more witnesses." (Blasphemy: disrespect to God) **66.** The council declared, "He deserves death." (Death: end of life) **67.** They spat on him, struck him, and mocked him. (Mocked: ridiculed) **68.** They taunted, "Prophesy, Christ! Who hit you?" (Taunted: teased) **69.** Outside, a servant girl said to Peter, "You were with Jesus of Galilee." (Servant: helper) **70.** Peter denied it, saying, "I don't know what you mean." (Denied: refused) **71.** Another servant said, "This man was with Jesus of Nazareth!" (Nazareth: Jesus's hometown) **72.** Peter denied it again with an oath, "I don't know him." (Oath: solemn promise) **73.** Bystanders said, "You're one of them; your accent gives it away!" (Accent: speech style) **74.** Peter swore, "I don't know him!" The rooster crowed immediately. (Swore: vowed) **75.** Remembering Jesus's words, Peter wept bitterly after denying him three times. (Wept: cried)

Chapter 27

1. When morning came, all the chief priests and elders plotted against Jesus to have him killed. (Plotted: Planned secretly.) **2.** After binding him, they led him to the governor, Pontius Pilate. (Bound: Tied up securely.) **3.** Judas, who betrayed him, seeing that Jesus was condemned, regretted it and returned the thirty pieces of silver to the chief priests. (Regretted: Felt sorry or remorseful.) **4.** "I have sinned by betraying innocent blood," he said. They replied, "What's that to us? You take care of it." (Betraying: Being disloyal or deceptive.) **5.** Judas threw the silver into the temple, left, and hanged himself. (Hanged: Killed by suspension from a rope.) **6.** The chief priests took the silver but said, "It's unlawful to put it in the treasury because it's blood money." (Unlawful: Not permitted by law.) **7.** They decided to buy the potter's field to bury foreigners. (Foreigners: People from another country or place.) **8.** That field became known as the Field of Blood. (Field: An area of land.) **9.** Then what was spoken by the prophet Jeremiah was fulfilled, saying, "They took the thirty pieces of silver, the price set on him by the people of Israel." (Fulfilled: Completed or made true.) **10.** "And they gave them for the potter's field, as the Lord commanded me." (Commanded: Ordered or instructed.) **11.** Jesus stood before the governor, and Pilate asked him, "Are you the King of the Jews?" Jesus answered, "You have said so." (Governor: A person in charge of a province or region.) **12.** When accused by the chief priests, Jesus said nothing. (Accused: Charged with wrongdoing.) **13.** Pilate asked him, "Don't you hear how many things they are accusing you of?" (Accusing: Blaming for wrongdoing.) **14.** But Jesus gave no answer, which amazed Pilate. (Amazed: Surprised or astonished.) **15.** At the feast, the governor used to release a prisoner chosen by the crowd. (Feast: A special meal or celebration.) **16.** They had a notorious prisoner named Barabbas. (Notorious: Famous for bad reasons.) **17.** Pilate asked them, "Which one do you want me to release: Barabbas or Jesus called Christ?" (Release: To set free.) **18.** He knew it was out of envy that they had handed Jesus over to him. (Envy: Jealousy or resentment of others' success.) **19.** While sitting on the judgment seat, Pilate's wife sent him a message: "Don't have anything to do with that innocent man, for I have suffered in a dream because of him." (Judgment: The decision made in a legal case.) **20.** But the chief priests and elders persuaded the crowd to ask for Barabbas and to kill Jesus. (Persuaded: Convinced someone to do something.) **21.** Pilate asked again, "Which of the two do you want me to release?" They answered, "Barabbas!" (Release: Let go or free.) **22.** Pilate asked, "What shall I do with Jesus, who is called Christ?" They all answered, "Crucify him!" (Crucify: To kill by nailing to a cross.) **23.** Pilate asked, "Why, what wrong has he done?" But they shouted louder, "Crucify him!" (Wrong: Something harmful or unjust.) **24.** Pilate saw he was getting nowhere, and the crowd was getting unruly. So he washed his hands in front of them, saying, "I am innocent of this man's blood. It's your responsibility." (Unruly: Disorderly or uncontrollable.) **25.** The people

383

responded, "Let his blood be on us and on our children." (Response: A reply or reaction.) **26.** Pilate released Barabbas and, after having Jesus flogged, handed him over to be crucified. (Flogged: Whipped or beaten with a whip.) **27.** Then the soldiers took Jesus into the palace and gathered the whole company of soldiers around him. (Company: A group of people.) **28.** They stripped him and put a scarlet robe on him. (Scarlet: A bright red color.) **29.** They made a crown of thorns and placed it on his head, put a reed in his right hand, and mocked him, saying, "Hail, King of the Jews!" (Mocked: Ridiculed or made fun of.) **30.** They spat on him and struck him on the head with the reed. (Spat: Forcefully expelled saliva.) **31.** After mocking him, they took off the robe, put his own clothes back on, and led him away to be crucified. (Robes: Long, flowing garments.) **32.** As they left, they found a man from Cyrene, Simon, and forced him to carry Jesus' cross. (Forced: Made to do something unwillingly.) **33.** They came to a place called Golgotha, which means the place of a skull. (Golgotha: The place of crucifixion.) **34.** They offered him wine mixed with gall, but he refused to drink it. (Gall: Bitter substance, often associated with bitterness.) **35.** They crucified him, divided his clothes, and cast lots to fulfill the prophecy, "They divided my garments and cast lots for my clothing." (Divided: Separated into parts.) **36.** Sitting down, they watched him there. (Watched: Observed attentively.) **37.** They placed the accusation above his head: "THIS IS JESUS, THE KING OF THE JEWS." (Accusation: A charge or claim of wrongdoing.) **38.** Two criminals were crucified with him, one on his right and one on his left. (Criminals: People who break the law.) **39.** Those who passed by hurled insults at him, shaking their heads. (Hurled: Threw with force.) **40.** They said, "You who are going to destroy the temple and rebuild it in three days, save yourself! If you are the Son of God, come down from the cross." (Destroy: To break down or ruin completely.) **41.** Likewise, the chief priests, with the scribes and elders, mocked him, saying, (Scribes: Scholars who copied documents.) **42.** "He saved others, but he can't save himself. If he is the King of Israel, let him come down from the cross, and we will believe him." (Believe: Accept as true.) **43.** "He trusted in God; let God rescue him now if he wants him, for he said, 'I am the Son of God.'" (Rescue: Save or protect from harm.) **44.** Even the criminals who were crucified with him insulted him in the same way. (Insulted: Offended or treated with disrespect.) **45.** From noon until 3 p.m., darkness covered the land. (Noon: 12:00 PM.) **46.** At about 3 p.m., Jesus cried out, "Eli, Eli, lama sabachthani?" meaning, "My God, my God, why have you forsaken me?" (Forsaken: Abandoned or left behind.) **47.** Some of those standing there heard him and said, "He's calling Elijah." (Elijah: A prophet in the Old Testament.) **48.** Immediately, one of them ran and got a sponge, soaked it in vinegar, put it on a reed, and gave it to Jesus to drink. (Sponge: A soft, absorbent material.) **49.** The others said, "Leave him alone. Let's see if Elijah comes to save him." (Leave alone: Not interfere.) **50.** Jesus cried out again with a loud voice and gave up his spirit. (Spirit: The immaterial part of a person.) **51.** At that moment, the temple veil tore from top to bottom, the earth shook, and rocks split. (Veil: A piece of cloth that covers or hides.) **52.** The graves were opened, and many holy people who had died were raised to life. (Graves: Burial places.) **53.** After Jesus' resurrection, they came out of the graves and went into the city, appearing to many. (Resurrection: Rising from the dead.) **54.** When the centurion and those with him saw the earthquake and the events that had happened, they were terrified and said, "Truly, this was the Son of God." (Centurion: A Roman officer in charge of a hundred soldiers.) **55.** Many women were watching from a distance. They had followed Jesus from Galilee to care for him. (Galilee: A region in northern Israel.) **56.** Among them were Mary Magdalene, Mary the mother of James and Joseph, and the mother of Zebedee's sons. (Zebedee: A person mentioned in the Bible as the father of two disciples.) **57.** When evening came, a rich man from Arimathea, named Joseph, who had become a disciple of Jesus, (Arimathea: A town mentioned in the Bible.) **58.** Went to Pilate and asked for Jesus' body. Pilate ordered it to be given to him. (Ordered: Gave instructions for something to be done.) **59.** Joseph took the body, wrapped it in a clean linen cloth, (Linen: A type of cloth made from flax.) **60.** And placed it in his own new tomb, carved out of rock. He rolled a large stone in front of the tomb and left. (Tomb: A burial place for a body.) **61.** Mary Magdalene and the other Mary were sitting opposite the tomb. (Opposite: On the other side.) **62.** The next day, the chief priests and Pharisees went to Pilate, (Pharisees: A religious group in ancient Judaism.) **63.** Saying, "We remember that while he was alive, that deceiver said, 'After three days I will rise again.'" (Deceiver: A person who lies or misleads.) **64.** "So give the order to make the tomb secure until the third day. Otherwise, his disciples may come and steal the body and tell the people he has risen from the dead. This last deception will be worse than the first." (Secure: Make safe or prevent from being stolen.) **65.** Pilate answered, "Take a guard. Go, make the tomb as secure as you know how." (Guard: A person who watches over something.) **66.** So they went and made the tomb secure by sealing the stone and setting a guard. (Sealing: Closing or securing with a seal.)

Chapter 28

1. At the end of the Sabbath, as dawn approached on the first day of the week, Mary Magdalene and the other Mary came to see the tomb. (Sabbath: A day of rest, typically Saturday in Jewish tradition.) **2.** Suddenly, there was a great earthquake. The angel of the Lord came down from heaven, rolled back the stone from the tomb, and sat on it. (Earthquake: A sudden shaking of the ground.) **3.** His appearance was like lightning, and his clothes were as white as snow. (Countenance: Facial expression or appearance.) **4.** The guards trembled in fear of him and became like dead men. (Trembled: Shook with fear or cold.) **5.** The angel said to the women, "Do not be afraid. I know you are looking for Jesus, who was crucified." (Crucified: Killed by being nailed to a cross.) **6.** "He is not here; he has risen, just as he said. Come, see the place where he was laid." (Laid: Placed, especially in a tomb or grave.) **7.** "Go quickly and tell his disciples that he has risen from the dead. He is going ahead of you into Galilee. There you will see him. I have told you." (Disciples: Followers or students of a teacher, especially of Jesus.) **8.** They hurried away from the tomb, afraid yet filled with joy, and ran to tell his disciples. (Hurry: To move or act quickly.) **9.** As they went to tell his disciples, Jesus met them and said, "Greetings!" They came to him, took hold of his feet, and worshiped him. (Greetings: A friendly or respectful word of welcome.) **10.** Jesus said to them, "Do not be afraid. Go and tell my brothers to go to Galilee, where they will see me." (Brothers: Refers to Jesus' followers, often called his "disciples.") **11.** While they were on their way, some of the guards went into the city and reported to the chief priests everything that had happened. (Guards: Soldiers who are assigned to protect or watch over something.) **12.** The chief priests and elders gathered together, and after discussing, they gave a large sum of money to the soldiers. (Elders: Older or respected leaders in a community.) **13.** They said, "Tell people, 'His disciples came during the night and stole his body while we were asleep.'" (Sum: A total amount of money.) **14.** "If this gets to the governor, we will convince him and keep you out of trouble." (Convince: Persuade someone to believe or do something.) **15.** The soldiers took the money and did as they were instructed. This story has been widely spread among the Jews even to this day. (Widely: Over a large area or to many people.) **16.** The eleven disciples went to Galilee, to the mountain where Jesus had told them to go. (Eleven: The number of disciples remaining after Judas' betrayal.) **17.** When they saw him, they worshiped him, but some doubted. (Doubted: Were uncertain or lacked belief.) **18.** Jesus came to them and said, "All authority in heaven and on earth has been given to me." (Authority: Power or right to give orders or make decisions.) **19.** "Therefore, go and make disciples of all nations, baptizing them in the name of the Father, the Son, and the Holy Spirit." (Baptizing: Performing a religious ceremony of purification with water.) **20.** "Teach them to obey everything I have commanded you. And surely I am with you always, to the very end of the age." (Obey: To follow or comply with commands or instructions.) Amen

41 – Mark

Chapter 1

1. The beginning of the gospel of Jesus Christ, the Son of God. (Gospel: good news) **2.** As written in the prophets: "I send my messenger before you to prepare the way." (Messenger: one who carries a message) **3.** A voice in the wilderness says, "Prepare the way of the Lord, make His paths straight." (Wilderness: a deserted place; Lord: a title for God) **4.** John baptized in the wilderness, preaching a baptism of repentance for the forgiveness of sins. (Baptism: ritual washing; Repentance: feeling regret; Forgiveness: pardon) **5.** People from Judea and Jerusalem were baptized in the Jordan River, confessing their sins. (Judea: a region in ancient Israel; Jordan River: river in the region) **6.** John wore camel hair clothing and ate locusts and wild honey. (Locusts: insects) **7.** He said, "One mightier than I is coming, whose sandals I am unworthy to untie." (Mightier: greater) **8.** I baptize with water, but He will baptize with the Holy Spirit. (Holy Spirit: The third person of Trinity) **9.** Jesus came from Nazareth in Galilee and was baptized by John in the Jordan. (Nazareth: a town in Galilee) **10.** As He came out of the water, the Spirit, like a dove, descended on Him. (Dove: a bird symbolizing peace) **11.** A voice from heaven said, "You are my beloved Son, in whom I am well pleased." (Beloved: dearly loved) **12.** The Spirit immediately drove Him into the wilderness. (Drove: compelled) **13.** He was in the wilderness for forty days, tempted by Satan, and attended by angels. (Tempted: tested; Satan: the devil; Angels: divine beings) **14.** After John was imprisoned, Jesus went to Galilee, preaching the kingdom of God. (Imprisoned: put in prison; Galilee: a region; Kingdom: reign) **15.** He said, "The time has come; the kingdom of God is near. Repent and believe the good news." (Repent: turn from sin; Good news: the message of salvation) **16.** Walking by the Sea of Galilee, He saw Simon and Andrew casting a net. (Sea of Galilee: a large freshwater lake; Casting:

throwing) **17.** Jesus said, "Follow me, and I will make you fishers of men." (Fishers of men: those who bring others to faith) **18.** At once, they left their nets and followed Him. (Nets: fishing tools) **19.** Further, He saw James and John mending their nets in the boat. (Mending: repairing) **20.** Jesus called them, and they left their father, Zebedee, and followed Him. (Zebedee: their father) **21.** They went to Capernaum, and on the Sabbath, Jesus entered the synagogue and taught. (Capernaum: a town in Galilee; Sabbath: holy day of rest) **22.** The people were amazed, for He taught with authority, unlike the scribes. (Authority: power; Scribes: religious teachers) **23.** A man with an unclean spirit cried out in the synagogue. (Synagogue: place of worship; Unclean spirit: evil spirit) **24.** "What do you want with us, Jesus of Nazareth? I know you are the Holy One of God." (Nazareth: a town; Holy One: A title for Messiah) **25.** Jesus rebuked him, saying, "Be silent and come out." (Rebuked: scolded) **26.** The spirit left, and the man was healed. (Healed: made better) **27.** People were amazed, saying, "He commands even the unclean spirits, and they obey Him!" (Teaching: instruction) **28.** His fame spread throughout Galilee. (Fame: reputation) **29.** After leaving the synagogue, they went to Simon and Andrew's house. (House: residence) **30.** Simon's mother-in-law was sick with fever, and they told Jesus. (Mother-in-law: wife's mother; Fever: illness) **31.** He healed her, and she began to serve them. (Serve: help others) **32.** At sunset, they brought all who were sick or possessed by demons. (Sick: ill; Possessed: controlled by demons) **33.** The town gathered at the door. (Town: village) **34.** He healed many, casting out demons, and did not let them speak because they knew Him. (Drove out: forced to leave) **35.** Early the next morning, Jesus went to a solitary place to pray. (Solitary: alone) **36.** Simon and his companions searched for Him. (Companions: associates) **37.** When they found Him, they said, "Everyone is looking for You." (Exclaimed: cried out) **38.** He replied, "Let's go to other towns so I can preach there also. That's why I came." (Preach: deliver a message) **39.** He preached in Galilee and cast out demons. (Galilee: a region in southern Israel) **40.** A leper came to Him, saying, "If you are willing, you can make me clean." (Leprosy: skin disease) **41.** Jesus touched him and said, "I am willing. Be clean!" (Compassion: sympathy) **42.** The leprosy left him, and he was healed. (Cleansed: made pure) **43.** Jesus warned him sternly. (Stern: strict) **44.** "Don't tell anyone. Go to the priest and offer the sacrifices Moses commanded." (Priest: religious leader; Testimony: proof) **45.** The man went out and spread the news, so that Jesus could not enter the city openly, but stayed in lonely places. (Spreading: telling widely; Lonely places: isolated areas)

Chapter 2

1. Jesus returned to Capernaum, and after a few days, it was heard that he was at a house there. (Capernaum: a town in north Galilee)**2.** Immediately, many gathered, filling the house to the point that there was no room, not even at the door, and he preached the word to them.**3.** Four men brought a paralyzed man to him. (Paralyzed: unable to move)**4.** Unable to reach him because of the crowd, they uncovered the roof where he was. After breaking it open, they lowered the bed the paralyzed man was lying on. (Roof: top covering of the house)**5.** When Jesus saw their faith, he told the paralyzed man, "Son, your sins are forgiven." (Faith: belief in action) **6.** Some scribes were sitting there, questioning in their hearts, (Scribes: religious teachers) **7.** "Why does this man speak blasphemies? Who can forgive sins except God?" (Blasphemies: saying disrespectful things) **8.** Jesus, perceiving their thoughts, asked them, "Why are you reasoning like this in your hearts?" **9.** Which is easier to say to the paralyzed man: 'Your sins are forgiven,' or 'Get up, take your bed, and walk'? **10.** But to show you that the Son of Man has authority on earth to forgive sins," he said to the paralyzed man, **11.** "I tell you, get up, take your bed, and go home." **12.** Immediately, the man got up, took his bed, and walked out in front of everyone. They were all amazed, and praised God, saying, "We have never seen anything like this." **13.** Then Jesus went to the sea, and a large crowd came to him, and he taught them. (Sea: Sea of Galilee) **14.** As he passed by, he saw Levi, the son of Alphaeus, sitting at the tax collector's booth, and said to him, "Follow me." Levi got up and followed him. (Levi: a tax collector) **15.** Later, Jesus ate at Levi's house, and many tax collectors and sinners were dining with him and his disciples, for many had followed him. (Sinners: people considered morally wrong) **16.** When the Pharisees saw that he was eating with sinners and tax collectors, they asked his disciples, "Why does he eat with tax collectors and sinners?" (Pharisees: religious leaders) **17.** When Jesus heard this, he replied, "It is not the healthy who need a doctor, but the sick. I did not come to call the righteous, but sinners to repentance." (Repentance: turning away from sin) **18.** Now, the disciples of John and the Pharisees fasted. They came and asked, "Why do John's disciples and the Pharisees fast, but your disciples do not fast?" (Fasted: abstain from food as a religious practice) **19.** Jesus answered, "How can the guests of the bridegroom fast while he is with them? As long as they have the bridegroom with them, they cannot fast. (Bridegroom: the groom at a wedding) **20.** But the time will come when the bridegroom will be taken from them, and on that day they will fast." **21.** No one sews a patch of unshrunk cloth on an old garment. If they do, the new patch will pull away from the old, and the tear will be worse. (Unshrunk: not yet washed) **22.** No one pours new wine into old wineskins. If they do, the wine will burst the skins, and both the wine and the skins will be ruined. Instead, new wine must be poured into new wineskins. (Wineskins: containers made from animal skin) **23.** One Sabbath, Jesus and his disciples were walking through grain fields, and they began to pick some heads of grain as they went along. (Sabbath: a day of rest) **24.** The Pharisees said to him, "Look, why are they doing what is unlawful on the Sabbath?" (Pharisees: religious leaders) **25.** He answered, "Have you never read what David did when he and his companions were hungry and in need?" (David: the King of Israel) **26.** In the days of Abiathar, David entered the house of God and ate the consecrated bread, which is only lawful for priests to eat. He also gave some to his companions. (Abiathar: the high priest) (Consecrated: set apart for God) **27.** Then he said to them, "The Sabbath was made for man, not man for the Sabbath." **28.** So the Son of Man is Lord even of the Sabbath." (Son of Man: Jesus)

Chapter 3

1. Jesus returned to the synagogue, where a man with a withered hand was present. (Synagogue: Jewish place of worship) **2.** The people were watching to see if He would heal the man on the Sabbath, hoping to accuse Him. (Sabbath: a day of rest, typically Saturday) **3.** Jesus said to the man with the withered hand, "Step forward." **4.** He then asked the crowd, "Is it lawful to do good or harm on the Sabbath, to save life or to kill?" But they remained silent. **5.** Jesus, filled with anger and sorrow over their hard hearts, told the man, "Stretch out your hand." The hand was restored, as healthy as the other. (Hardness of heart: stubbornness or unwillingness to believe) **6.** Immediately, the Pharisees went out and conspired with the Herodians (supporters of King Herod) to destroy Jesus. (Pharisees: religious leaders; Herodians: political group loyal to King Herod) **7.** Jesus withdrew with His disciples to the sea, and a large crowd from Galilee followed Him, along with people from Judea, **8.** Jerusalem, Idumea and beyond the Jordan River, and from Tyre and Sidon because they had heard of His miracles. (Idumea: region south of Judea; Tyre and Sidon: cities on the Mediterranean) **9.** He instructed His disciples to have a small boat ready for Him, so the crowd wouldn't overwhelm Him. **10.** He had healed many, and those suffering from diseases pushed forward to touch Him. **11.** Evil spirits fell before Him, shouting, "You are the Son of God!" (Evil spirits: demons or unclean spirits) **12.** He strongly warned them not to make Him known. **13.** Jesus went up a mountain and called to Himself those He desired, and they came to Him. **14.** He appointed twelve men to be with Him and to send them out to preach, **15.** And to grant them the authority to heal sicknesses and cast out demons. **16.** He gave the name Simon to Peter; **17.** He also named James, son of Zebedee, and John, his brother, and called them Boanerges, meaning "Sons of Thunder"; (Boanerges: "Sons of Thunder," a reference to their strong personalities) **18.** Andrew, Philip, Bartholomew, Matthew, Thomas, James son of Alphaeus, Thaddaeus, Simon the Zealot, **19.** And Judas Iscariot, who later betrayed Him. Afterward, they went into a house. (Zealot: a group desiring to overthrow Roman rule; Iscariot: surname of Judas, the betrayer) **20.** The crowd gathered again, and there was no room for them to even eat. **21.** When His family heard about this, they went to take control of Him, thinking He was out of His mind. **22.** The scribes who came down from Jerusalem said, "He is possessed by Beelzebul (Satan), and by the prince of demons He casts out demons." (Beelzebul: another name for Satan) **23.** Jesus called them over and spoke to them in parables, "How can Satan drive out Satan? **24.** If a kingdom is divided against itself, it cannot stand. **25.** If a house is divided against itself, it cannot stand. **26.** If Satan rises against himself and is divided, he cannot stand but will come to an end. **27.** No one can enter a strong man's house and take his possessions unless they first bind him, then they can plunder his house. (Plunder: take goods by force) **28.** Truly, I tell you, all sins will be forgiven the children of men, and any blasphemy they utter, **29.** But whoever blasphemes against the Holy Spirit will never be forgiven, but is guilty of eternal sin." (Blaspheme: speak against God; Holy Spirit: God's presence) **30.** He said this because they were claiming, "He has an unclean spirit." **31.** Then His mother and brothers arrived, standing outside, and they sent someone to call Him. **32.** The crowd around Him said, "Your mother and brothers are outside looking for You." **33.** He replied, "Who are My mother and brothers?" **34.** Looking at those seated around Him, He said, "Here are My mother and brothers! **35.** Whoever does the will of God is My brother, sister, and mother." (God's will: what God desires or commands)

Chapter 4

1. Once again, Jesus began teaching beside the sea. A large crowd gathered, so he got into a boat and sat, while the people stayed on the shore. (shore:

edge of the sea) **2.** He shared many teachings with them using parables, saying, (parables: simple stories used to explain deeper truths) **3.** "Listen closely! A farmer went out to plant seeds." **4.** As he sowed, some of the seeds fell along the path, and birds came and ate them. (sowed: planted) **5.** Other seeds fell on rocky soil where there wasn't much earth. They grew quickly, but because the soil was shallow, **6.** when the sun came up, they were scorched, and because they had no roots, they withered. (scorched: burned) **7.** Some seeds fell among thorns. As they grew, the thorns choked them, preventing any fruit from forming. (choked: smothered) **8.** But some fell on good soil, where they grew and produced a crop—some thirty, some sixty, and some a hundred times more. (crop: harvest) **9.** He then said, "Anyone with ears to hear, let them listen carefully!" (ears: ability to understand) **10.** Later, when Jesus was alone, the disciples, along with others, asked him to explain the parable. (disciples: followers) **11.** He replied, "You have been given the secret knowledge of the kingdom of God, but to those outside, everything is told through parables." (secrets: hidden truths) **12.** "Though they look, they won't understand; though they hear, they won't grasp it. If they did, they might turn from their ways and be forgiven." (grasp: comprehend, turn: repent) **13.** He asked, "Do you not understand this parable? How then will you understand all parables?" **14.** The farmer sows the word. (word: message of God) **15.** Some people are like the seeds along the path where the word is sown. As soon as they hear it, Satan comes and takes the word away from them. (Satan: the Devil) **16.** Others are like the seeds on rocky soil. They hear the word and accept it with joy, **17.** but they don't have deep roots. They endure only for a short time. When trouble or persecution comes because of the word, they quickly fall away. (persecution: suffering for beliefs) **18.** Still others are like seeds that fall among thorns. They hear the word, **19.** but the worries of life, the deceitfulness of wealth, and the desire for other things come in and choke the word, making it unfruitful. (deceitfulness: dishonesty, choke: smother) **20.** But others are like seeds planted on good soil. They hear the word, accept it, and produce a harvest—some thirty, some sixty, and some a hundred times what was sown. (harvest: fruit) **21.** He asked, "Do you bring a lamp to hide it under a bowl or a bed? Don't you put it on a stand?" (lamp: light source) **22.** "For there is nothing hidden that will not be revealed, and nothing concealed that will not be brought to light." (concealed: hidden) **23.** "If anyone has ears to hear, let them listen!" **24.** "Consider carefully what you hear. The measure you use will be measured to you, and more will be given to those who listen." (measure: amount) **25.** "Whoever has will be given more, and whoever does not have, even what they have will be taken away." **26.** He also said, "This is what the kingdom of God is like: a man scatters seed on the ground, **27.** and though he sleeps and rises day and night, the seed grows without him knowing how." (scatters: spreads, grows: develops) **28.** "The soil produces crops on its own—first the stalk, then the ear, and finally the full grain in the ear." (stalk: stem of the plant) **29.** "As soon as the grain is ripe, he puts in the sickle, because the harvest has come." (sickle: harvesting tool) **30.** Then he asked, "What can we compare the kingdom of God to, or what parable can we use to describe it?" **31.** "It is like a mustard seed, which is the smallest of all seeds on earth." **32.** "Yet, when it is planted, it grows and becomes the largest of all garden plants, with such large branches that the birds can nest in its shade." (branches: parts of the plant) **33.** With many such parables, Jesus spoke the word to them, as much as they could understand. **34.** He explained everything privately to his disciples. **35.** That day, when evening came, he said to his disciples, "Let us go over to the other side." (other side: the opposite shore) **36.** They left the crowd behind and took him along in the boat, with other boats following them. **37.** A great storm arose, and the waves broke over the boat, so that it was nearly filled with water. (waves: large moving water) **38.** Jesus was in the back of the boat, sleeping on a cushion. They woke him and said, "Teacher, don't you care if we drown?" (cushion: soft pad). **39.** He stood up, rebuked the wind, and said to the sea, "Be quiet! Be still!" The wind stopped, and there was a great calm. (rebuked: commanded, still: calm)n **40.** He said to them, "Why are you afraid? Do you still have no faith?" **41.** They were terrified and asked each other, "Who is this? Even the wind and the sea obey him!" (Terrified: greatly afraid)

Chapter 5
1. They arrived on the other side of the sea, entering the region of the Gadarenes. (Gadarenes: region) **2.** As Jesus stepped out of the boat, a man with an impure spirit came from the tombs to meet him. (Impure: unclean, contaminated) **3.** This man lived among the tombs, and no one could restrain him, not even with chains. (Restrain: control, hold back) **4.** He had been bound with shackles and chains, but tore them apart. No one had the strength to subdue him. (Subdue: overpower, control) **5.** Day and night, he wandered in the mountains, crying out and hurting himself with stones. (Tombs: burial places, graves) **6.** When he saw Jesus from a distance, he ran to him and fell at his feet, worshiping him. **7.** He shouted, "What do you want with me, Jesus, Son of the Most High God? I beg you, do not torment me!" (Torment: torture, cause pain) **8.** For Jesus had already commanded the impure spirit to come out of the man. **9.** Then Jesus asked, "What is your name?" He replied, "Legion, for we are many." (Legion: multitude, large group) **10.** The spirits begged Jesus not to send them out of the area. (Begged: pleaded, asked urgently) **11.** Nearby, a large herd of pigs was feeding on the hillside. (Herd: group, flock) **12.** The spirits begged, "Send us into the pigs, let us enter them." **13.** At once, Jesus gave them permission. The spirits entered the pigs, and the herd, about two thousand, rushed into the lake and drowned. (Drowned: perished, died in water) (Steep: sharp, sudden incline) **14.** Those tending the pigs ran off and reported this in the town and countryside, and the people went out to see what had happened. (Tending: caring for, managing) (Countryside: rural areas, outskirts) **15.** When they came to Jesus, they saw the man who had been possessed, sitting, fully clothed, and in his right mind, and they were afraid. (Possessed: controlled, influenced) **16.** Those who had seen it told the people what happened to the demon-possessed man and the pigs. **17.** Then the people began to plead with Jesus to leave their region. (Plead: ask, beg) **18.** As Jesus was getting into the boat, the man who had been demon-possessed begged to go with him. (Demon-possessed: under evil influence, controlled) **19.** Jesus did not let him, but said, "Go home to your family and tell them how much the Lord has done for you, and how he has had mercy on you." (Mercy: compassion, kindness) **20.** So the man went away and began to tell in the Decapolis how much Jesus had done for him, and all were amazed. (Decapolis: ten cities, region of ten cities) **21.** When Jesus had crossed over by boat to the other side, a large crowd gathered, and he stayed by the lake. **22.** Then Jairus, a synagogue leader, came and fell at Jesus' feet. (Synagogue: place of worship, Jewish temple) **23.** He pleaded, "My little daughter is dying. Please come and heal her." (Earnestly: sincerely, seriously) (Healed: cured, restored) **24.** So Jesus went with him, and a large crowd followed and pressed around him. (Pressed: crowded, squeezed) **25.** And a woman who had been subject to bleeding for twelve years was there. (Subject: affected, influenced) **26.** She had suffered greatly under many doctors and spent all she had, yet grew worse. (Suffered: endured, experienced pain) **27.** When she heard about Jesus, she came up behind him in the crowd and touched his cloak. (Cloak: outer garment, robe) **28.** She thought, "If I just touch his clothes, I will be healed." **29.** Immediately, her bleeding stopped, and she felt freed from her suffering. (Freed: released, liberated) **30.** At once, Jesus realized that power had gone out from him. He turned and asked, "Who touched my clothes?" (Power: divine energy, strength) **31.** "You see the people crowding," his disciples answered, "and yet you ask, 'Who touched me?'" **32.** But Jesus kept looking to see who had done it. **33.** Then the woman, knowing what had happened, came, fell at his feet, trembling, and told him the truth. (Trembling: shaking, quivering) **34.** He said, "Daughter, your faith has healed you. Go in peace and be freed from your suffering." **35.** While Jesus was still speaking, some came from Jairus' house. "Your daughter is dead," they said. "Why bother the teacher anymore?" (Bother: trouble, disturb) **36.** Overhearing this, Jesus told him, "Don't be afraid; just believe." **37.** He did not let anyone follow except Peter, James, and John, the brother of James. **38.** When they came to Jairus' house, Jesus saw a commotion, with people crying and wailing loudly. (Commotion: disturbance, uproar) (Wailing: crying loudly, mourning) **39.** He went in and said, "Why all this commotion? The child is not dead but asleep." (Asleep: dead, in a state of unconsciousness) **40.** They laughed at him. After putting them all out, he took the child's parents and disciples in. **41.** He took her by the hand and said, "Talitha koum!" (Little girl, arise). (Talitha koum: Aramaic phrase for "Little girl, get up.") **42.** Immediately, the girl stood up and began to walk. They were astonished. (Astonished: amazed, shocked) **43.** He gave strict orders not to tell anyone and told them to give her something to eat.

Chapter 6
1. Jesus left that area and returned to His hometown, with His disciples following Him. **2.** When the Sabbath arrived, He began teaching in the synagogue. Many who heard Him were amazed and asked, "Where did this man get such knowledge? What kind of wisdom has been given to Him, and how can He perform such powerful works?" **3.** "Isn't He just the carpenter, the son of Mary, and the brother of James, Joses, Judas, and Simon? Aren't His sisters living here with us?" And they were offended by Him. (Offended: Feeling disrespected or shocked.) **4.** But Jesus said to them, "A prophet is not without honor, except in his own town, among his own family, and in his own home." **5.** He could not perform any significant miracles there, except for healing a few sick people by laying His hands on them. **6.** He was amazed by their lack of faith. Then He traveled to surrounding villages, continuing His teaching. **7.** Jesus called His twelve disciples to Him and began sending them out two by two, giving them power to cast out unclean spirits. (Unclean spirits: Evil or demonic forces.) **8.** He instructed them, "Take nothing for the

journey except a staff—no bag, no bread, and no money in your belts." **9.** "Wear sandals, but don't carry extra clothes." **10.** "Wherever you enter a house, stay there until you leave that place." **11.** "If any place does not welcome you or listen to you, leave and shake the dust off your feet as a testimony against them. Truly, I tell you, it will be more bearable for Sodom and Gomorrah on the day of judgment than for that city." (Sodom and Gomorrah: Two cities in the Bible that were destroyed because of their wickedness.) **12.** The disciples went out and proclaimed that people should repent. (Repent: To feel regret for one's wrongdoings and change.) **13.** They cast out many demons and anointed many sick people with oil, healing them. (Anointed: To apply oil, often as a symbol of healing or blessing.) **14.** King Herod heard about Jesus, for His name had become well-known. Some said, "John the Baptist has risen from the dead," and that's why such powerful works are being done by Him. **15.** Others said, "It's Elijah." Still others said, "It's a prophet, or one of the prophets." **16.** But when Herod heard this, he said, "It's John, the one I beheaded; he has come back to life." **17.** For Herod had arrested John, bound him, and put him in prison for the sake of Herodias, his brother Philip's wife, whom he had married. (Bound: Tied or restrained.) **18.** John had told Herod, "It is unlawful for you to have your brother's wife." (Unlawful: Not permitted by law.) **19.** So Herodias held a grudge against John and wanted to kill him, but she couldn't. (Grudge: A persistent resentment.) **20.** Herod feared John, knowing he was a righteous and holy man, and protected him. Whenever Herod heard him, he was greatly perplexed, yet enjoyed listening to him. **21.** An opportune moment came when Herod gave a banquet for his birthday, attended by his nobles, military commanders, and the leading men of Galilee. (Opportune: Favorable or well-timed.) **22.** When Herodias' daughter came in and danced, it greatly pleased Herod and his guests. The king said to the girl, "Ask me for anything you want, and I will give it to you." **23.** And he swore to her, "Whatever you ask, I will give you, up to half my kingdom." **24.** She went out and asked her mother, "What should I ask for?" Her mother replied, "The head of John the Baptist." **25.** So she hurried back to the king and made her request, "I want you to give me the head of John the Baptist on a platter right now." (Platter: A large flat dish or container.) **26.** The king was deeply distressed, but because of his oath and his guests, he could not refuse her. (Oath: A solemn promise or vow.) **27.** At once, the king sent an executioner to bring John's head. The executioner went, beheaded him in prison, **28.** and brought his head on a platter, giving it to the girl, who then gave it to her mother. **29.** When John's disciples heard of it, they came, took his body, and laid it in a tomb. **30.** The apostles gathered around Jesus and reported to Him everything they had done and taught. (Apostles: The twelve disciples chosen by Jesus to spread His message.) **31.** Jesus said to them, "Come with Me by yourselves to a quiet place and rest a while." For many people were coming and going, and they didn't even have time to eat. **32.** So they went away by themselves in a boat to a solitary place. (Solitary: Alone or remote, with no one else.) **33.** But many saw them leaving and recognized them. They ran on foot from all the towns and arrived ahead of them. **34.** When Jesus landed and saw the large crowd, He had compassion on them because they were like sheep without a shepherd. So He began teaching them many things. (Compassion: Deep sympathy for others' suffering.) **35.** By this time, it was late in the day, and His disciples came to Him, saying, "This is a remote place, and it's already very late." (Remote: Isolated or distant.) **36.** "Send the people away so they can go to the surrounding villages and buy themselves something to eat." **37.** But Jesus replied, "You give them something to eat." They asked Him, "Should we go and spend two hundred denarii on bread to give them something to eat?" **38.** He asked, "How many loaves do you have? Go and see." When they found out, they said, "Five loaves and two fish." **39.** Then Jesus instructed them to have the people sit down in groups on the green grass. **40.** So they sat down in groups of hundreds and fifties. **41.** Taking the five loaves and the two fish, Jesus looked up to heaven, blessed the food, and broke the loaves. He gave them to His disciples to distribute to the people. He also divided the two fish among them all. **42.** They all ate and were satisfied. **43.** The disciples picked up twelve basketfuls of leftover pieces of bread and fish. **44.** The number of men who had eaten was about five thousand. **45.** Immediately, Jesus made His disciples get into the boat and go ahead of Him to the other side, to Bethsaida, while He sent the people away. **46.** After dismissing the crowd, He went up on a mountain to pray. **47.** Later that night, the boat was in the middle of the lake, and Jesus was alone on the land. **48.** He saw them struggling at the oars, because the wind was against them. About the fourth watch of the night, He went out to them, walking on the water. He was about to pass by them, (Struggling: Making a great effort or difficulty.) **49.** but when they saw Him walking on the lake, they thought He was a ghost and cried out. **50.** They all saw Him and were terrified. But immediately, He spoke to them, "Take courage! It is I; don't be afraid." **51.** Then He climbed into the boat with them, and the wind calmed down. They were completely amazed, **52.** for they had not understood the significance of the loaves; their hearts were hardened. (Hardened: Resistant to understanding or belief.) **53.** When they had crossed over, they came to land at Gennesaret and anchored there. **54.** As soon as they got out of the boat, people recognized Jesus. **55.** They ran throughout the entire region and brought the sick on mats to wherever they heard He was. **56.** Wherever He went—into villages, towns, or the countryside—they placed the sick in the marketplaces. They begged Him to let them touch even the edge of His cloak, and all who touched it were healed.

Chapter 7

1. The Pharisees and some scribes from Jerusalem gathered around Him. (Pharisees :religious group, scribes :Jewish law experts) **2.** They noticed some of His disciples ate bread with unclean defiled hands and criticized them. (defiled :made unclean) **3.** The Pharisees and Jews follow the tradition of washing their hands before eating. (tradition of the elders :customs passed down) **4.** They also wash cups, pots, and brass vessels. (brass :copper and zinc alloy) **5.** The Pharisees asked why Jesus' disciples don't follow their tradition of washing hands. (scribes :law experts) **6.** He replied, "Isaiah prophesied about you hypocrites: 'You honor Me with your lips, but your hearts are far from Me.'" (hypocrites :pretenders) **7.** "You worship in vain, teaching human commands as doctrines." (vain :empty, doctrines :religious teachings) **8.** You reject God's command to hold human traditions like washing pots. (reject :refuse) **9.** You set aside God's command to keep your tradition. (commandments :God's laws) **10.** Moses said, "Honor your father and mother," and "Anyone who curses them must die." (Moses :Jewish lawgiver) **11.** But you say a man can dedicate his money to God (Corban) and not help his parents. (Corban :gift dedicated to God) **12.** You allow this and disregard care for parents. (disregard :ignore) **13.** Your tradition nullifies the word of God. (nullify :make ineffective) **14.** Jesus called the crowd and said, "Listen, understand: nothing outside a person can defile them." (understand :grasp meaning) **15.** "It is what comes out of a person that defiles them." (defile :make unclean) **16.** (If anyone has ears to hear, let them listen.) (ears to hear :ability to understand) **17.** His disciples asked about the parable. (parable :moral story) **18.** He asked, "Are you so lacking in understanding? What enters a person doesn't defile them." (dull :slow to understand) **19.** "It enters the stomach, then into the sewer, purging all foods." (purge :cleanse) **20.** "What comes out of a person defiles them." (defiles :makes impure) **21.** "Evil thoughts, adulteries, fornications, murders, (adulteries :sexual sin, fornications :sexual immorality) **22.** thefts, greed, wickedness, deceit, lewdness, blasphemy, pride, foolishness." (thefts :stealing, greed :material desire, wickedness :immorality) **23.** "All these evil things come from within and defile a person." (defile :make unclean) **24.** Jesus went to Tyre and Sidon, and tried to remain hidden, but could not. (Tyre and Sidon :ancient cities) **25.** A woman whose daughter had an unclean spirit came and begged Him. (unclean spirit :demon) **26.** She was Greek, a Syrophoenician by birth, and asked Jesus to cast out the demon. (Syrophoenician :from Syria and Phoenicia) **27.** Jesus said, "Let the children be filled first, for it's not right to take their bread and give it to dogs." (children's bread :God's promises, dogs :derogatory term for Gentiles) **28.** She replied, "Yes, Lord, but even dogs eat the crumbs from under the table." (crumbs :small bits of food) **29.** Jesus said, "Because of your answer, go; the demon has left your daughter." (answer :response) **30.** She found her daughter resting, free of the demon. (lying on the bed :resting peacefully) **31.** Jesus went to the Sea of Galilee, through the region of Decapolis. (Decapolis :ten cities) **32.** They brought Him a deaf man with a speech impediment and asked Him to heal him. (impediment :difficulty) **33.** Jesus took him aside, put His fingers in his ears, and touched his tongue. (spit :saliva used in healing) **34.** He sighed, looked up, and said, "Ephphatha," meaning, "Be opened." (Ephphatha :Aramaic for "be opened") **35.** Immediately his ears were opened, his tongue loosened, and he spoke clearly. (bond :restriction) **36.** Jesus told them not to tell anyone, but they spread the news more. (spread :share information) **37.** They were amazed, saying, "He does all things well; He makes the deaf hear and the mute speak." (mute :unable to speak)

Chapter 8

1. A large crowd had gathered, and they had nothing to eat. Jesus called His disciples. (Crowd: a large group of people.) **2.** "I have compassion on them because they have been with me three days and have no food." (Compassion: sympathy for others' suffering.) **3.** "If I send them away hungry, they might faint on the way, for many came from far." (Faint: lose strength.) **4.** His disciples asked, "Where can we find enough bread in this desert to feed them?" (Desert: a barren place.) **5.** Jesus asked, "How many loaves do you have?" They replied, "Seven." **6.** He told the crowd to sit. Then He took the loaves, gave thanks, broke them, and gave them to the disciples to distribute.

(Distribute: give out.) **7.** They had a few fish. Jesus blessed them and told His disciples to distribute them as well. **8.** They ate and were full, and the disciples collected seven baskets of leftovers. (Leftovers: remaining food.) **9.** About four thousand ate, and He sent them away. **10.** Immediately, He got into a boat with His disciples and went to Dalmanutha. (Dalmanutha: a location.) **11.** The Pharisees came, asking for a sign from heaven to test Him. (Pharisees: Jewish religious leaders.) **12.** He sighed deeply and said, "No sign will be given to this generation." (Sighed: exhaled with frustration.) **13.** He left them, entered the boat, and went to the other side. **14.** The disciples forgot to bring bread, only having one loaf. (Loaf: a single bread.) **15.** Jesus warned, "Beware of the yeast of the Pharisees and of Herod." (Yeast: influence.) **16.** They thought it was because they had no bread. **17.** Jesus said, "Why are you thinking about bread? Don't you understand yet?" (Understand: grasp the meaning.) **18.** "Having eyes, do you not see? And ears, do you not hear? Don't you remember?" **19.** "When I broke five loaves for five thousand, how many baskets of leftovers did you gather?" They said, "Twelve." **20.** "And when I broke seven loaves for four thousand, how many baskets of leftovers did you gather?" They answered, "Seven." **21.** He asked, "Why don't you understand?" **22.** They brought a blind man to Him, asking Him to touch him. **23.** Jesus took his hand, led him outside, spat on his eyes, and asked if he saw anything. (Spat: released saliva.) **24.** The man said, "I see people, but they look like trees walking." (Trees: metaphor for blurry vision.) **25.** Jesus touched his eyes again, and the man saw clearly. **26.** Jesus sent him home, telling him not to go into the village. (Village: small town.) **27.** Jesus asked His disciples, "Who do people say I am?" **28.** They replied, "John the Baptist, Elijah, or one of the prophets." **29.** "But what about you?" Jesus asked. Peter answered, "You are the Christ." (Christ: the anointed one.) **30.** Jesus warned them not to tell anyone about Him. **31.** He began to teach that the Son of Man must suffer, be rejected, die, and rise after three days. (Suffer: endure pain.) **32.** He spoke openly. Peter took Him aside and rebuked Him. **33.** Jesus rebuked Peter, saying, "Get behind me, Satan! You are focused on human things, not God's." (Rebuked: sternly corrected.) **34.** Jesus called the crowd and said, "Whoever wants to follow Me must deny themselves, take up their cross, and follow Me." **35.** "For whoever saves their life will lose it, but whoever loses their life for Me will save it." **36.** "What is it worth for a person to gain the whole world but lose their soul?" (Soul: inner being.) **37.** "Or what can someone give in exchange for their soul?" **38.** "If anyone is ashamed of Me in this sinful generation, I will be ashamed of them when I come in glory." (Ashamed: feeling embarrassed or guilty.)

Chapter 9

1. And he said, "Truly, some of you standing here will not die before seeing God's kingdom come in power." (Kingdom of God: God's rule or reign) **2.** After six days, Jesus took Peter, James, and John up a high mountain, where he was transfigured. (Transfigured: changed in appearance) **3.** His clothes became dazzling white, whiter than anyone on earth could bleach them. (Dazzling: very bright; Bleach: whiten) **4.** Elijah and Moses appeared, talking with Jesus. (Elijah: a prophet; Moses: leader of Israel) **5.** Peter said, "Rabbi, let us make three shelters, one for you, Moses, and Elijah." (Rabbi: teacher) **6.** He said this because he was afraid and didn't know what to say. (Afraid: feeling fear) **7.** A cloud overshadowed them, and a voice said, "This is my beloved Son; listen to him." (Beloved: dearly loved) **8.** When they looked, only Jesus remained with them. (Alone: without others) **9.** As they came down, Jesus told them not to share what they saw until he rose from the dead. (Rising from the dead: resurrection) **10.** They wondered what rising from the dead meant. (Rising from the dead: coming back to life) **11.** They asked, "Why do the scribes say Elijah must come first?" (Scribes: Jewish law experts) **12.** Jesus replied, "Elijah comes and restores all things, but the Son of Man must suffer." (Restore: fix or make right; Suffer: endure hardship) **13.** "Elijah has already come, and they did to him as written." (Elijah: John the Baptist) **14.** Jesus saw a crowd and scribes arguing with his disciples. (Arguing: disagreeing) **15.** When the crowd saw Jesus, they were amazed and ran to greet him. (Amazed: filled with wonder) **16.** Jesus asked, "What are you arguing about?" (Arguing: disagreeing) **17.** A man said, "I brought my son with a mute spirit, and your disciples couldn't cast it out." (Mute: unable to speak) **18.** "It throws him into convulsions, and they couldn't help." (Convulsions: violent movements) **19.** Jesus replied, "How long must I endure you? Bring him to me." (Endure: put up with) **20.** When they brought the boy, the spirit caused him to fall, foaming at the mouth. (Foaming: frothing at the mouth) **21.** Jesus asked, "How long has this been happening?" "Since childhood," the father replied. (Childhood: early years) **22.** "It often tries to harm him; help us if you can." (Help: assist) **23.** Jesus said, "Everything is possible for one who believes." (Believe: have faith) **24.** The father cried, "I believe; help my unbelief!" (Unbelief: doubt) **25.** Jesus rebuked the spirit, "Come out of him, and never enter him again." (Rebuked: corrected sharply) **26.** The spirit cried, threw the boy into convulsions, and came out. The boy appeared dead. (Convulsions: sudden violent movements) **27.** Jesus took the boy's hand, and he got up. (Hand: part of the body) **28.** His disciples privately asked, "Why couldn't we cast it out?" (Privately: in secret) **29.** Jesus replied, "This kind only comes out through prayer and fasting." (Fasting: abstaining from food for spiritual reasons) **30.** They passed through Galilee, not wanting anyone to know. (Galilee: a region in Israel) **31.** Jesus taught, "The Son of Man will be delivered, killed, and rise on the third day." (Delivered: handed over) **32.** They didn't understand and were afraid to ask him. (Afraid: filled with fear) **33.** At Capernaum, Jesus asked, "What were you arguing about?" (Capernaum: a town in Galilee) **34.** They remained silent because they had argued about who was the greatest. (Greatest: most important) **35.** Jesus said, "If you want to be first, be last and serve all." (Servant: one who serves) **36.** He placed a child among them, saying, "Whoever welcomes a child in my name, welcomes me." (Child: young person) **37.** John said, "We saw someone casting out demons in your name, and we stopped him." (Casting out demons: expelling evil spirits) **38.** Jesus replied, "Don't stop him; anyone who performs miracles in my name cannot speak against me." (Miracles: supernatural acts) **39.** "Whoever is not against us is for us." (For us: supporting us) **40.** "Anyone who gives you a cup of water in my name won't lose their reward." (Reward: gift for good deeds) **41.** "Anyone who causes a believer to stumble, it would be better for them to be thrown into the sea with a millstone around their neck." (Stumble: lead into sin) **42.** "If your hand causes you to stumble, cut it off; it's better to enter life maimed than to go to hell." (Maimed: injured) **43.** "Where the worm does not die, and the fire is not quenched." (Worm: decay; Unquenched: unextinguished) **44.** "If your foot causes you to stumble, cut it off." (Foot: part of the body) **45.** "Where the worm does not die, and the fire is not quenched." (Quenched: put out) **46.** "If your eye causes you to stumble, pluck it out." (Pluck: remove) **47.** "Where the worm does not die, and the fire is not quenched." (Worm: symbol of decay) **48.** "Everyone will be salted with fire, and every sacrifice will be salted with salt." (Salted: treated with salt) **49.** "Salt is good, but if it loses its saltiness, how can it be made salty again?" (Saltiness: quality of being salty) **50.** "Salt is good; have salt and peace with each other." (Peace: harmony)

Chapter 10

1. Jesus left that place and traveled to the region of Judea, across the Jordan. Again, people gathered, and as usual, he taught them. (Judea :region in Israel; Jordan :river; usual :customary practice) **2.** The Pharisees came to him, asking if a man can divorce his wife, trying to test him. (Pharisees :religious leaders; divorce :end a marriage) **3.** Jesus asked them, "What did Moses command you?" (Moses :Jewish lawgiver) **4.** They said, "Moses allowed a man to write a certificate of divorce and send her away." (certificate of divorce :legal document for divorce) **5.** Jesus answered, "Moses wrote this because your hearts were hard." (hard hearts :stubbornness) **6.** But from the beginning of creation, God made them male and female. (creation :God's act of making the world) **7.** For this reason, a man will leave his father and mother and be united with his wife. (united :joined together) **8.** The two will become one flesh, no longer two, but one. (one flesh :deep connection between husband and wife) **9.** What God has joined together, let no one separate. (joined together :united by God) **10.** Later, his disciples asked him again about this. (disciples :followers of Jesus) **11.** Jesus replied, "Anyone who divorces his wife and marries another commits adultery against her." (adultery :unfaithfulness in marriage) **12.** And if a woman divorces her husband and marries another, she commits adultery." (divorces :legally ends a marriage) **13.** People brought children for Jesus to touch, but the disciples rebuked them. (rebuked :scolded) **14.** Jesus was upset and said, "Let the little children come to me; do not hinder them, for the kingdom of God belongs to such as these." (hinder :stop or prevent) **15.** Truly, anyone who does not receive the kingdom of God like a child will not enter it." (receive :accept; kingdom of God :God's reign) **16.** He took the children in his arms, put his hands on them, and blessed them. (blessed :spoke favor) **17.** A man ran up, knelt before him, and asked, "Good Teacher, what must I do to inherit eternal life?" (knelt :showed respect) **18.** Jesus replied, "Why do you call me good? Only God is good." (good :morally perfect) **19.** You know the commandments: 'Do not murder, commit adultery, steal, give false testimony, defraud, honor your father and mother.'" (commandments :God's laws) **20.** The man said, "Teacher, I have followed all these since I was young." (followed :obeyed) **21.** Jesus looked at him and loved him. "One thing you lack: sell all you have, give to the poor, and follow me." (lack :missing something; treasure in heaven :eternal rewards) **22.** The man went away sad, for he had great wealth. (wealth :great possessions) **23.** Jesus said to his disciples, "How hard it is for the rich to enter God's kingdom!" (rich :wealthy) **24.** The disciples were amazed. Jesus said, "Children, how hard it is for those who trust in riches to enter God's kingdom!" (amazed :surprised) **25.** It is easier for a camel to go through the eye of a needle than for a rich man to enter God's kingdom." (eye of a needle :small opening) **26.** The disciples asked, "Who then can be saved?" (saved :rescued from sin) **27.** Jesus said, "With man it is impossible, but not with God. With God, all things are possible." (possible :able to happen) **28.** Peter said, "We have left everything to follow you!" (left everything :gave up possessions) **29.** Jesus replied, "No one who has left family or possessions for my sake and the gospel will fail to receive much more in this life, along with persecutions—and in the next, eternal life." (persecutions :suffering for beliefs) **30.** Many who are first will be last, and the last first." (first and last :positions of honor) **31.** As they went up to Jerusalem, Jesus led the way. The disciples were amazed, and others followed in fear. He took the Twelve aside and told them what would happen. (amazed :surprised; Twelve :disciples) **32.** "We are going to Jerusalem," he said, "where the Son of Man will be handed over to the chief priests and teachers of the law. They will condemn him to death and hand him over to the Gentiles, (Son of Man :Jesus; Gentiles :non-Jews) **33.** who will mock, beat, spit on, and kill him. After three days, he will rise again." (mock :ridicule; flog :whip) **34.** James and John, the sons of Zebedee, came to him. "Teacher, we want you to do for us whatever we ask." (sons of Zebedee :disciples) **35.** He asked, "What do you want me to do for you?" (asked :inquired) **36.** They said, "Grant that we sit, one on your right, the other on your left in your glory." (glory :honor and majesty) **37.** Jesus replied, "You don't know what you're asking. Can you drink the cup I drink or be baptized with the baptism I undergo?" (cup :suffering; baptism :identifying with Jesus' suffering) **38.** "We can," they answered. (answered :responded) **39.** Jesus said, "You will drink the cup I drink and be baptized as I am, (drink the cup :endure suffering) **40.** but to sit on my right and left is not for me to give. These places are for those for whom they have been prepared." (grant :give) **41.** The other disciples became angry with James and John. (angry :upset) **42.** Jesus called them together and said, "You know that rulers over the Gentiles lord it over them, and their high officials exercise authority over them. (lord it over :dominate; high officials :leaders) **43.** Not so with you. Instead, whoever wants to be great must be your servant, (servant :one who serves others) **44.** and whoever wants to be first must be the slave of all. (slave :one who serves without power) **45.** For even the Son of Man came not to be served, but to serve, and to give his life as a ransom for many." (ransom :payment to release) **46.** They came to Jericho. As Jesus and his disciples left the city, a blind man, Bartimaeus, sat by the roadside begging. (Jericho :city; Bartimaeus :blind man) **47.** When he heard it was Jesus, he shouted, "Jesus, Son of David, have mercy on me!" (Son of David :title for the Messiah) **48.** Many told him to be quiet, but he shouted louder, "Son of David, have mercy on me!" (rebuked :scolded) **49.** Jesus stopped and said, "Call him." So they called the blind man, "Cheer up! He is calling you." (cheer up :be encouraged) **50.** He threw off his cloak, jumped up, and came to Jesus. (cloak :outer garment) **51.** "What do you want me to do for you?" Jesus asked. "Rabbi, I want to see." (Rabbi :teacher) **52.** "Go," said Jesus, "your faith has healed you." Immediately, he could see and followed Jesus. (healed :made well)

Chapter 11

1. As they neared Jerusalem, near Bethphage and Bethany on the Mount of Olives, Jesus sent two disciples ahead. (Bethphage - a village near Jerusalem; Mount of Olives - a hill near Jerusalem) **2.** He told them, "Go to the village. You'll find a colt tied. Untie it and bring it here." (Colt - a young horse) **3.** "If anyone asks, say, 'The Lord needs it,' and they will let you take it." (Lord - a title for Jesus) **4.** The disciples found the colt and untied it. **5.** Some people asked, "Why are you untying the colt?" **6.** They replied as Jesus instructed, and the people let them take it. **7.** They brought the colt to Jesus, threw their cloaks on it, and Jesus sat on it. (Cloaks - outer garments) **8.** Many spread coats on the road, others cut palm branches and laid them down. (Palm branches - tree branches) **9.** The crowd shouted, "Hosanna! Blessed is he who comes in the name of the Lord!" (Hosanna - praise) **10.** "Blessed is the kingdom of David! Hosanna in the highest!" **11.** Jesus entered Jerusalem and went into the temple. Seeing everything, he left for Bethany with his disciples. (Temple - a place of worship) **12.** The next day, Jesus felt hungry as they left Bethany. (Bethany - a village near Jerusalem) **13.** He saw a fig tree with leaves, but no fruit because it wasn't the season for figs. (Fig tree - a tree that produces figs) **14.** Jesus said, "No one will ever eat fruit from you again." (Ever - at any time) **15.** Jesus entered the temple and drove out those buying and selling, overturning tables. (Money changers - people exchanging money) **16.** He didn't allow anyone to carry goods through the temple courts. (Merchandise - goods for sale) **17.** He taught, "My house shall be a house of prayer, but you've made it a den of thieves." (Den - a place of hiding) **18.** The chief priests and scribes feared him, as the crowd was amazed at his teaching. (Scribes - experts in religious law) **19.** At evening, they left the city. **20.** The next morning, they saw the fig tree withered from the roots. (Withered - dried up; Roots - plant foundation) **21.** Peter said, "The fig tree you cursed has withered." **22.** Jesus answered, "Have faith in God." (Faith - trust) **23.** "Truly, if you say to this mountain, 'Be thrown into the sea,' and believe, it will happen." (Doubt - uncertainty) **24.** "Whatever you ask for in prayer, believe that you have received it." (Prayer - communication with God) **25.** "When praying, forgive anyone you hold against, so your Father may forgive you." (Forgive - let go of wrongs) **26.** "If you don't forgive, neither will your Father forgive your sins." (Sins - wrongdoings) **27.** Jesus was approached by the chief priests, scribes, and elders. (Elders - respected leaders) **28.** They asked, "By what authority are you doing these things?" **29.** Jesus said, "I will ask you one question. Answer me, and I'll tell you." (Reply - answer) **30.** "Was John's baptism from heaven or men?" (Baptism - religious act) **31.** They debated, "If we say heaven, he'll ask why we didn't believe John." **32.** "If we say men, we fear the people who believe John was a prophet." **33.** They answered, "We don't know." Jesus said, "Neither will I tell you by what authority I do these things."

Chapter 12

1. Jesus began speaking to them in parables. A man planted a vineyard, built a fence, dug a winepress, and erected a tower. He leased it to farmers and went away. (Parables: stories with hidden meanings) **2.** At harvest time, he sent a servant to collect some of the fruit. (Harvest: time of gathering crops) **3.** They seized him, beat him, and sent him away empty. (Seized: caught, empty: without anything) **4.** He sent another servant, whom they struck on the head and treated shamefully. (Shamefully: in a way that brings dishonor) **5.** He sent others, some they beat, some they killed. (Beating: hitting, killing: causing death) **6.** Finally, he sent his beloved son, thinking, "They will respect my son." (Beloved: dearly loved) **7.** But the farmers plotted, "This is the heir. Let's kill him and take the inheritance." (Heir: person who inherits property) **8.** They killed him and threw him outside the vineyard. (Vineyard: a place where grapes are grown) **9.** What will the vineyard owner do? He will destroy those farmers and give the vineyard to others. (Vineyard: grape farm) **10.** Have you not read, "The stone the builders rejected has become the cornerstone"? (Cornerstone: the main stone in building) **11.** This is the Lord's doing, and it is marvelous. (Marvelous: wonderful) **12.** They wanted to arrest him but feared the crowd because they knew the parable was about them, so they left. (Arrest: take into custody) **13.** They sent Pharisees and Herodians to trap him with their words. (Pharisees: Jewish religious leaders, Herodians: supporters of King Herod) **14.** They asked, "Is it lawful to pay taxes to Caesar, or not?" (Lawful: allowed by law) **15.** Jesus, knowing their hypocrisy, asked them to bring a coin. (Hypocrisy: pretending to be something you're not) **16.** He asked, "Whose image is on this coin?" They replied, "Caesar's." (Image: likeness, Caesar: Roman emperor) **17.** "Give to Caesar what is Caesar's and to God what is God's," he said. They were amazed. (Amazed: surprised) **18.** Sadducees, who don't believe in the resurrection, asked him a question. (Sadducees: Jewish group that denied resurrection) **19.** "If a man dies without children, his brother must marry the widow to carry on the family line." (Widow: a woman whose husband has died) **20.** There were seven brothers; the first married but died without children. (Brothers: male siblings) **21.** The second and third brothers married her, but they also died without children. (Married: wed, died: passed away) **22.** All seven brothers married her and died, and then the woman died too. (Died: passed away) **23.** In the resurrection, whose wife will she be, since all seven had her? (Resurrection: rising from the dead) **24.** Jesus answered, "You err because you don't know the Scriptures or God's power." (Err: make a mistake, Scriptures: sacred writings) **25.** In the resurrection, people will not marry, but will be like angels. (Angels: spiritual beings) **26.** Have you not read about the burning bush, where God spoke to Moses, saying, "I am the God of Abraham, Isaac, and Jacob"? (Burning bush: a miraculous event in Moses' life) **27.** He is not the God of the dead, but of the living. You are mistaken. (Mistaken: wrong) **28.** A scribe, impressed by Jesus' answer, asked, "Which command is the most important?" (Scribe: scholar of the law) **29.** Jesus answered, "The most important command is: 'Hear, O Israel: The Lord our God is one Lord.'" (Hear: listen, Lord: a title for God) **30.** "Love the Lord with all your heart, soul, mind, and strength." (Heart: feelings, Soul: inner being, Mind: intellect, Strength: physical power) **31.** "The second is: Love your neighbor as yourself." These are the greatest commandments. (Neighbor: others around you) **32.** The scribe agreed, saying, "To love God and your neighbor is more important than all offerings." (Offerings: gifts to God) **33.** Jesus replied, "You are close to the kingdom of God." No one dared ask him more questions. (Kingdom: reign, authority) **34.** While teaching in the temple, Jesus asked, "Why do the scribes say the Messiah is David's son?" (Messiah: the anointed one) **35.** David, speaking by the Holy Spirit, said, 'The Lord said to my Lord, sit at my right hand.' (Holy Spirit: God's presence) **36.** If David calls him Lord, how can he be his son? (Lord: master) **37.** The crowd listened to him gladly. (Gladly: with joy) **38.** Jesus warned, "Beware of the scribes who love to wear robes and seek honors." (Beware: be cautious) **39.** They love the best seats and the places of honor at feasts. (Feasts: large meals or celebrations) **40.** They take advantage of widows and make long prayers. They will be punished severely. (Widows: women whose husbands have died) **41.** Jesus watched as people put money into the treasury. The rich gave much. (Treasury: place where money is stored) **42.** A poor widow came and gave two small coins. (Coins: money) **43.** Jesus said, "This widow gave more than all the rich, for she gave everything she had." (Everything: all) **44.** The rich gave from their abundance, but she gave from her poverty. (Abundance: plenty, Poverty: lack of money)

Chapter 13

1. As Jesus left the temple, one of His disciples remarked, "Teacher, look at these massive stones and splendid buildings!" (splendid: impressive, magnificent) **2.** Jesus replied, "Do you see these impressive buildings? Not one stone will remain upon another; all will be torn down." (torn down: destroyed) **3.** Later, sitting on the Mount of Olives facing the temple, Peter, James, John, and Andrew asked Him privately, **4.** "Tell us, when will these things happen, and what sign will show their fulfillment?" (fulfillment: completion) **5.** Jesus began, "Watch out that no one deceives you. (deceives: misleads) **6.** Many will claim to be me, saying, 'I am the Messiah,' and will mislead many. (Messiah: savior or chosen one; mislead: lead astray) **7.** When you hear of wars and rumors of wars, do not panic. These events must occur, but the end is not yet. (rumors: reports; panic: feel sudden fear) **8.** Nations and kingdoms will clash. Earthquakes and famines will happen in various places. These are just the start of distress. (clash: fight; famines: extreme scarcity of food; distress: suffering) **9.** Be cautious! They will hand you over to councils, beat you in synagogues, and you'll testify of me before rulers and kings. (synagogues: Jewish places of worship; testify: speak on behalf) **10.** But first, the gospel must be spread to all nations. (gospel: good news) **11.** When you are arrested, don't worry about what to say. The Holy Spirit will guide your words. (arrested: taken into custody) **12.** Family members will betray one another, leading to death, and children will rise against parents. (betray: act against) **13.** You will be hated by all for my name, but whoever endures until the end will be saved. (endures: perseveres, remains steadfast) **14.** When you see the 'abomination of desolation,' as spoken by Daniel, flee to the mountains. (abomination: disgraceful act; desolation: destruction; flee: escape quickly) **15.** Do not return home for belongings if you are on the rooftop. (belongings: possessions) **16.** If you are in the field, don't go back for your cloak. (cloak: outer garment) **17.** How dreadful for pregnant and nursing mothers in those days! (dreadful: terrible, distressing) **18.** Pray your escape won't be during winter. (escape: act of getting away) **19.** That time will bring unmatched suffering since creation began. (unmatched: never before seen) **20.** If God hadn't shortened those days, no one would survive, but He shortened them for His chosen people. (shortened: made brief) **21.** If anyone says, 'Here is the Messiah!' or 'There He is!' don't believe it. **22.** False messiahs and prophets will appear, performing signs to mislead even the elect. (prophets: people claiming divine authority; mislead: deceive; elect: chosen believers) **23.** So stay alert! I've warned you about this ahead of time. (alert: watchful) **24.** After that distress, the sun will go dark, the moon will stop shining. (distress: great suffering or trouble) **25.** Stars will fall, and heavenly powers will be shaken. (heavenly: related to the skies or heavens) **26.** Then the Son of Man will come in clouds with power and glory. (glory: magnificent beauty or greatness) **27.** He will send His angels to gather His chosen ones from all directions. (directions: all parts of the world) **28.** Learn from the fig tree: when its branches soften and sprout leaves, you know summer is near. (soften: become tender; sprout: begin to grow) **29.** Similarly, when these events happen, know the time is near—at the door. (similarly: in the same way) **30.** I assure you, this generation won't pass away before all these things happen. (generation: people of a specific time) **31.** Heaven and earth will vanish, but my words will remain forever. (vanish: disappear completely) **32.** No one knows the exact day or hour—neither angels nor the Son, only the Father. (exact: precise) **33.** Stay alert and pray, because you don't know when the time will come. (alert: watchful) **34.** It's like a man leaving on a trip who assigns tasks to his servants and tells the doorkeeper to stay watchful. (assigns: gives responsibility) **35.** So, keep watch! You don't know if the master will come at evening, midnight, dawn, or morning. (dawn: early morning) **36.** Don't let him return suddenly and find you sleeping. (suddenly: unexpectedly) **37.** What I say to you, I say to all: Watch! (watch: remain attentive)

Chapter 14

1. After two days was the Passover feast and Unleavened Bread. The chief priests and scribes plotted to arrest and kill Jesus by trickery. (Passover: Jewish festival; Unleavened Bread: the week-long festival following Passover) **2.** But they decided not during the feast, fearing an uproar from the people. **3.** While in Bethany at Simon the leper's house, a woman broke an alabaster jar of expensive spikenard ointment and poured it on Jesus' head. (Bethany: village near Jerusalem; Simon the leper: man healed by Jesus) **4.** Some were upset, saying, "Why waste the ointment?" **5.** "It could be sold for 300 denarii and given to the poor," they murmured. (Denarii: a Roman coin) **6.** Jesus said, "Leave her alone; she has done a good deed for me. **7.** The poor are always here, but I won't be. **8.** She has anointed my body for burial. **9.** Wherever the gospel is preached, what she has done will be told in memory of her." **10.** Judas Iscariot went to the chief priests to betray Jesus. (Judas Iscariot: disciple who betrayed Jesus) **11.** They were pleased and promised to give him money. He looked for an opportunity to betray him. **12.** On the first day of Unleavened Bread, when the Passover lamb was slaughtered, the disciples asked where to prepare the meal. **13.** Jesus sent two disciples into the city, saying, "Follow the man carrying water. **14.** Ask the owner, 'Where is the guest room for the Passover with my disciples?'" **15.** He will show you a large upper room, furnished. Prepare for us there." **16.** The disciples went, found as he said, and prepared the meal. **17.** In the evening, Jesus came with the twelve. **18.** As they ate, Jesus said, "One of you will betray me." **19.** They were distressed and asked, "Is it I?" **20.** Jesus replied, "It is one of the twelve who dips with me." **21.** "The Son of Man will go as written, but woe to the betrayer! It would be better if he had not been born." **22.** While eating, Jesus took bread, blessed, broke it, and gave it, saying, "This is my body." **23.** Then he took the cup, gave thanks, and they drank from it. **24.** "This is my blood of the new covenant, poured out for many. **25.** I won't drink again until I do so in God's kingdom." **26.** After singing a hymn, they went to the Mount of Olives. (Mount of Olives: a hill near Jerusalem) **27.** Jesus said, "You will all fall away. It is written, 'I will strike the shepherd, and the sheep will scatter.' **28.** But after I rise, I will go to Galilee." (Galilee: region where Jesus preached) **29.** Peter said, "Even if all fall away, I won't." **30.** Jesus replied, "Tonight, before the rooster crows twice, you will deny me three times." **31.** Peter protested, "Even if I die, I will not deny you!" The others said the same. **32.** They came to Gethsemane, and Jesus said, "Sit here while I pray." (Gethsemane: garden outside Jerusalem) **33.** He took Peter, James, and John, and was deeply distressed. **34.** "My soul is sorrowful to death. Stay here and watch." **35.** He went a little farther, fell to the ground, and prayed, "If possible, let this hour pass, but not my will, yours be done." **36.** "Abba, Father, all is possible for you. Take this cup away, but let your will be done." **37.** He found them sleeping and said to Peter, "Couldn't you stay awake for one hour? **38.** Watch and pray, so you don't fall into temptation. The spirit is willing, but the flesh is weak." **39.** He prayed again with the same words. **40.** Returning, he found them asleep again. They didn't know how to respond. **41.** He said, "Sleep on; it's enough. The time has come. The Son of Man is betrayed into sinners' hands. **42.** Rise, let's go. The betrayer is near." **43.** Judas, with a crowd of armed men, approached. (Judas: disciple who betrayed Jesus) **44.** He gave them a sign, "The one I kiss, arrest him." **45.** He went straight to Jesus, kissed him, and said, "Rabbi!" **46.** They seized Jesus. **47.** One of them drew a sword and cut off the ear of the high priest's servant. (High priest: religious leader in Jerusalem) **48.** Jesus said, "Have you come to arrest me with swords and clubs? **49.** I was in the temple teaching daily, but you didn't arrest me. The Scriptures must be fulfilled." **50.** All deserted him and fled. **51.** A young man wearing only a linen cloth followed. They tried to seize him, **52.** but he ran away, leaving the cloth. **53.** They took Jesus to the high priest, where all the chief priests, elders, and scribes were gathered. **54.** Peter followed at a distance, into the high priest's courtyard, and warmed himself by the fire. **55.** The chief priests and council sought false testimony to condemn Jesus to death but found none. **56.** Many testified falsely, but their stories didn't match. **57.** Then some falsely said, **58.** "We heard him say, 'I will destroy this temple and build another in three days.'" **59.** Their testimony still didn't agree. **60.** The high priest asked, "Why don't you answer? What are they accusing you of?" **61.** But Jesus remained silent. The high priest asked, "Are you the Christ, the Son of the Blessed One?" **62.** Jesus said, "I am. You will see the Son of Man at God's right hand, coming in the clouds." **63.** The high priest tore his clothes. "Why do we need more witnesses? **64.** You've heard the blasphemy. What do you think?" They condemned him to death. **65.** Some spat at him, covered his face, struck him, and said, "Prophesy!" **66.** While Peter was below, a servant girl of the high priest saw him. **67.** She looked at him and said, "You were with Jesus of Nazareth." **68.** Peter denied it, "I don't know what you're talking about," and went outside. **69.** The girl saw him again and told others, "This man is one of them." **70.** Peter denied it. A little later, others said, "You're a Galilean; your speech gives you away." **71.** Peter cursed, saying, "I don't know him." **72.** The rooster crowed a second time. Peter remembered Jesus' words and wept.

Chapter 15

1. Early in the morning, the chief priests, elders, scribes, and entire council convened, bound Jesus, and handed him over to Pilate. (convened: gathered)

2. Pilate asked, "Are you the King of the Jews?" Jesus replied, "You have said so." (replied: answered) **3.** The chief priests accused him of many things, but he said nothing. (accused: blamed) **4.** Pilate asked, "A aren't you going to answer? Look at all the charges against you." (charges: accusations) **5.** But Jesus remained silent, and Pilate was amazed. (remained: stayed) **6.** During the festival, Pilate released one prisoner to the crowd. (released: set free) **7.** Barabbas, a murderer involved in an insurrection, was in prison. (insurrection: rebellion) **8.** The crowd demanded Pilate do as usual. (demanded: insisted) **9.** Pilate asked, "Do you want me to release the King of the Jews?" (release: set free) **10.** He knew the priests handed him over out of envy. (envy: jealousy) **11.** The priests persuaded the crowd to ask for Barabbas instead. (persuaded: convinced) **12.** Pilate asked, "What should I do with the one you call the King of the Jews?" (should: ought to) **13.** They cried, "Crucify him!" (cried: shouted) **14.** Pilate asked, "Why? What has he done wrong?" But they shouted, "Crucify him!" (wrong: bad) **15.** Pilate, wishing to please the crowd, released Barabbas and had Jesus flogged before sending him to be crucified. (wishing: desiring; flogged: beaten) **16.** The soldiers took him to the Praetorium and gathered the whole battalion. (battalion: group of soldiers) **17.** They clothed him in purple, made a crown of thorns, and placed it on his head. (crowned: placed a crown) **18.** They mocked him, saying, "Hail, King of the Jews!" (mocked: ridiculed) **19.** They struck him with a reed, spat on him, and knelt in mock worship. (mock: pretend; spat: ejected saliva) **20.** After mocking him, they dressed him in his own clothes and led him out to crucify him. (dressed: clothed) **21.** They forced Simon of Cyrene to carry Jesus' cross. (forced: compelled) **22.** They brought him to Golgotha, the place of a skull. (Golgotha: place of the skull) **23.** They offered him wine mixed with myrrh, but he refused it. (myrrh: a fragrant resin) **24.** After crucifying him, they divided his clothes by casting lots. (casting: throwing) **25.** It was about the third hour when they crucified him. (crucified: nailed to the cross) **26.** The inscription on his charge read: "THE KING OF THE JEWS." (inscription: written statement) **27.** Two thieves were crucified with him, one on his right and one on his left. (thieves: criminals) **28.** The scripture was fulfilled that he was numbered with the transgressors. (fulfilled: completed; transgressors: wrongdoers) **29.** Those passing by mocked him, saying, "Destroy the temple and rebuild it in three days, save yourself and come down." (mocked: ridiculed) **30.** Likewise, the chief priests mocked him, saying, "He saved others; he cannot save himself." (likewise: similarly) **31.** "Let the King of Israel come down from the cross that we may believe." Even those crucified with him mocked him. (crucified: nailed to the cross) **32.** At noon, darkness covered the land until the ninth hour. (darkness: absence of light) **33.** At the ninth hour, Jesus cried out, "My God, why have you forsaken me?" (forsaken: abandoned) **34.** Some bystanders thought he was calling Elijah. (bystanders: people standing nearby) **35.** One ran, soaked a sponge with vinegar, and offered it to him, saying, "Let's see if Elijah will come to take him down." (soaked: saturated) **36.** Jesus cried out loudly and died. (died: passed away) **37.** The temple veil was torn from top to bottom. (veil: curtain) **38.** When the centurion saw how he died, he declared, "Surely this man was the Son of God!" (centurion: Roman officer) **39.** Some women watched from a distance, including Mary Magdalene, Mary the mother of James the younger and Joses, and Salome. (watched: observed) **40.** These women had followed him in Galilee and supported him. (supported: helped) **41.** As evening approached, because it was the day before the Sabbath, (Sabbath: day of rest) **42.** Joseph of Arimathea, a respected council member, went to Pilate and asked for Jesus' body. (respected: esteemed) **43.** Pilate, surprised, asked the centurion if Jesus had already died. (surprised: astonished) **44.** When the centurion confirmed it, Pilate gave the body to Joseph. (confirmed: verified) **45.** Joseph bought fine linen, took the body down, wrapped it, and placed it in a tomb. (bought: purchased) **46.** He rolled a stone to seal the tomb's entrance. (rolled: moved in a circular manner) **47.** Mary Magdalene and Mary the mother of Joses saw where he was laid. (laid: placed)

Chapter 16

1. After the Sabbath, Mary Magdalene, Mary the mother of James, and Salome bought spices to anoint Him. **2.** Early on the first day of the week, they went to the tomb at sunrise. **3.** They wondered who would roll the stone away from the tomb's entrance. **4.** When they arrived, the stone was already rolled away; it was very large. **5.** Inside, they saw a young man in white robes sitting on the right side, and they were amazed. (Amazed: filled with wonder) **6.** He told them, "Do not be afraid. Jesus has risen, He is not here; see where He was laid. **7.** "Go and tell His disciples and Peter that He will meet you in Galilee, as He said." **8.** They fled from the tomb, trembling and silent, afraid to speak to anyone. **9.** Jesus first appeared to Mary Magdalene, from whom He had cast out seven demons. **10.** She told the disciples, but they did not believe her. **11.** When they heard she had seen Him alive, they refused to believe. **12.** He appeared in another form to two disciples walking in the country. (Form: appearance) **13.** They reported it to the others, but they did not believe them either. **14.** Later, He rebuked the eleven disciples for their unbelief and stubbornness, since they had not believed the ones who saw Him after His resurrection. (Rebuked: criticized, Stubbornness: unyielding attitude) **15.** He told them, "Go into all the world and preach the gospel to every creature." **16.** "Those who believe and are baptized will be saved; those who do not will be condemned." **17.** "These signs will follow believers: in My name, they will cast out demons, speak new languages." (Signs: wonders or miracles) **18.** "They will handle snakes, and if they drink poison, it will not harm them; they will heal the sick." **19.** After speaking to them, Jesus ascended into heaven and sat at God's right hand. (Ascended: rose up) **20.** The disciples went out, preaching everywhere, and the Lord confirmed their message with signs.

42 – Luke

Chapter 1

1. Many have tried to write a clear account of the things we believe, **2.** Just as they were shared with us by those who were first witnesses and servants of the word. **3.** Since I have carefully understood all things, I also decided to write to you, most excellent Theophilus, (Theophilus: a person who loved God) **4.** So you can be sure of the teachings you received. **5.** In the time of King Herod of Judea, there was a priest named Zacharias, from the division of Abijah, and his wife Elizabeth, a descendant of Aaron. (Herod: King of Judea, Abijah: a division of priests) **6.** They were both righteous before God, following His commandments and laws blamelessly. **7.** They had no children because Elizabeth was barren, and both were advanced in age. **8.** While Zacharias was serving as priest, **9.** He was chosen by lot to burn incense in the temple. **10.** The people were praying outside during the incense offering. **11.** An angel appeared to him on the right side of the altar. **12.** Zacharias was startled and afraid. **13.** But the angel said, "Do not fear, Zacharias, your prayer has been heard. Elizabeth will bear you a son, and you will name him John." **14.** You will have joy, and many will rejoice at his birth. **15.** He will be great in God's sight, and filled with the Holy Spirit from birth, without drinking wine or strong drink. **16.** Many of Israel's people will turn to God. **17.** He will go before the Lord in the spirit of Elijah, preparing people for the Lord. (Elijah: a prophet of Israel) **18.** Zacharias asked, "How can this be? I am old, and my wife is also elderly." **19.** The angel replied, "I am Gabriel, who stands before God, and I was sent to bring you this good news." **20.** "Now you will be mute until these things happen, because you didn't believe my words, which will come true in due time." **21.** The people waited, wondering why Zacharias stayed so long in the temple. **22.** When he came out, he couldn't speak, and they realized he had seen a vision. **23.** After his service, he returned home. **24.** Soon, Elizabeth became pregnant and hid herself for five months, saying, **25.** "The Lord has taken away my shame among people." **26.** In the sixth month, the angel Gabriel was sent to Nazareth, a town in Galilee, . (Nazareth: a town in Galilee, Joseph: Mary's husband, a descendant of King David) **27.** To a virgin named Mary, betrothed to Joseph, a descendant of David **28.** The angel greeted her, saying, "You are favored, and the Lord is with you. Blessed are you among women." **29.** Mary was confused and wondered what this greeting meant. **30.** The angel said, "Do not be afraid, Mary; you have found favor with God." **31.** "You will conceive and bear a son, and you will name Him Jesus." **32.** "He will be great, called the Son of the Most High, and God will give Him the throne of His ancestor David." **33.** "He will reign over the house of Jacob forever, and His kingdom will have no end." (Jacob: another name for Israel) **34.** Mary asked, "How will this happen, since I am a virgin?" **35.** The angel replied, "The Holy Spirit will come upon you, and the power of God will overshadow you, so the child will be called the Son of God." **36.** "Also, your cousin Elizabeth is pregnant in her old age, though she was once barren, and is now in her sixth month." **37.** "For no word from God will fail." **38.** Mary responded, "I am the Lord's servant; let it be as you have said." And the angel left. **39.** Mary quickly went to the hill country of Judea, **40.** Entering Zacharias' house and greeting Elizabeth. **41.** When Elisabeth heard Mary's greeting, the baby leaped in her womb, and she was filled with the Holy Spirit. (Holy Spirit: God's divine presence) **42.** She exclaimed, "You are blessed among women, and so is the child you carry." **43.** "Why am I so honored that the mother of my Lord should visit me?" **44.** "When I heard your greeting, the baby leaped for joy." **45.** "Blessed is she who believed, for the Lord will fulfill His promises." **46.** Mary replied, "My soul magnifies the Lord," **47.** "and my spirit rejoices in God my Savior." **48.** "He has looked upon my humble state, and all generations will call me blessed." **49.** "The Mighty One has done great things for me, and holy is His name." **50.** "His mercy extends to those who fear Him, from generation to generation." **51.** "He has shown His power, scattering the proud and lifting the humble." **52.** "He has brought down rulers and exalted the lowly." **53.** "He has filled the hungry with good things and sent the rich away empty." **54.** "He has helped His servant Israel, remembering His mercy," **55.** "as He promised Abraham and his descendants forever." **56.** Mary stayed with Elisabeth for three months before returning home. **57.** Elisabeth gave birth to a son. **58.** Her neighbors rejoiced, hearing how God had shown her great mercy. **59.** On the eighth day, they came to circumcise the child, planning to name him Zacharias. **60.** But his mother said, "No, his name will be John." **61.** They said, "No one in your family has that name." **62.** They asked his father, who wrote, "His name is John," and they were amazed. **63.** Immediately, Zacharias' mouth was opened, and he praised God. **64.** Fear spread throughout the region, and people talked about these events. **65.** Everyone wondered, "What kind of child will this be?" and God's hand was with him. **66.** Filled with the Holy Spirit, Zacharias prophesied: **67.** "Praise the Lord, the God of Israel, who has redeemed His people." **68.** "He has raised up a mighty Savior for us from the house of His servant David." (David: King of Israel, ancestor of Jesus) **69.** "As foretold by the prophets long ago," **70.** "to save us from our enemies and those who hate us." **71.** "To show mercy to our ancestors and remember His holy covenant," **72.** "the oath He swore to Abraham," **73.** "to deliver us from our enemies, so we can serve Him without fear," **74.** "in holiness and righteousness all our days." **75.** "And you, my child, will be the prophet of the Most High, preparing the way for the Lord," **76.** "giving His people the knowledge of salvation through the forgiveness of their sins." **77.** "Through the mercy of our God, the rising sun will visit us," **78.** "to shine on those in darkness and guide our feet into peace." **79.** The child grew strong in spirit and lived in the wilderness until his public appearance to Israel. (Wilderness: a harsh, desert-like area often used for spiritual preparation)

Chapter 2

1. In those days, Caesar Augustus ordered a census for tax purposes across the Roman world. (Caesar Augustus: the Roman Emperor) **2.** The tax was first introduced when Cyrenius was governor of Syria. (Cyrenius: the Roman governor) **3.** Everyone went to their hometowns to be registered. **4.** Joseph traveled from Nazareth in Galilee to Bethlehem in Judea, the city of David, as he was from David's lineage. (Bethlehem: town in Judea) **5.** He went with his betrothed, Mary, who was pregnant. **6.** While they were there, Mary's time to give birth arrived. **7.** She gave birth to her firstborn son, wrapped him in cloth, and placed him in a manger, as there was no room in the inn. (Manger: animal feeding trough) **8.** Nearby, shepherds were in the fields watching over their flocks at night. **9.** An angel appeared, and the glory of the Lord surrounded them, causing great fear. **10.** The angel reassured them, saying, "Do not be afraid. I bring you great joy for all people." **11.** A Savior, the Messiah, has been born today in the city of David. **12.** You'll find the baby wrapped in cloth and lying in a manger. **13.** Suddenly, a heavenly host appeared with the angel, praising God. **14.** "Glory to God in the highest, and peace on earth to those he favors." **15.** After the angels left, the shepherds said, "Let's go to Bethlehem and see what's happened." **16.** They hurried and found Mary, Joseph, and the baby in the manger. **17.** After seeing him, they shared what had been told about this child. **18.** All who heard were amazed at the shepherds' words. **19.** Mary treasured all these events and reflected on them. **20.** The shepherds returned, praising God for what they had seen and heard. **21.** Eight days later, Jesus was circumcised and named as the angel had instructed. (Circumcision: a Jewish tradition) **22.** When Mary's purification was complete, they took Jesus to Jerusalem to present him to the Lord. (Purification: a post-birth ritual) **23.** As the law required, every firstborn male is consecrated to the Lord. **24.** They offered a pair of doves or two pigeons, as prescribed in the law. **25.** Simeon, a righteous and devout man, was waiting for Israel's redemption, and the Holy Spirit was upon him. **26.** The Spirit had revealed that he would not die before seeing the Messiah. **27.** Moved by the Spirit, Simeon went to the temple when Jesus was presented. **28.** He took Jesus in his arms, praised God, and said: **29.** "Lord, you can now let me depart in peace as you promised." **30.** "My eyes have seen your salvation," **31.** "Prepared for all people;" **32.** "A light for the Gentiles and the glory of Israel." **33.** Mary and Joseph marveled at what Simeon said about Jesus. **34.** Simeon blessed them and told Mary, "This child will cause many to rise and fall in Israel, and will be opposed." **35.** "A sword will pierce your soul too, revealing hearts' thoughts." (Sword: symbol of suffering) **36.** Anna, a prophetess from the tribe of Asher, was very old and had been widowed for many years. (Anna: an elderly prophetess) **37.** She lived in the temple, worshiping with fasting and prayer day and night. **38.** Coming up at that moment, she gave thanks to God and spoke about the child to those waiting for redemption. **39.** After fulfilling the law, they returned to Galilee, to Nazareth. **40.** Jesus grew strong, filled with wisdom, and God's grace was upon him. **41.** Every year, his parents went to Jerusalem for Passover. **42.** When Jesus was twelve, they went to the feast. **43.** After the festival, Jesus stayed behind in Jerusalem without his parents' knowledge. **44.** Thinking he was in their group, they traveled a day's journey before realizing he was missing. **45.** They returned to Jerusalem and searched for him. **46.** After three days, they found him in the temple, listening to teachers and asking questions. **47.** Everyone who heard him was amazed at his understanding. **48.** When his parents found him, they were astonished. Mary asked, "Why have you treated us like this? We've been searching anxiously." **49.** Jesus replied, "Didn't you know I must be in my Father's house?" **50.** They didn't understand his words. **51.** Jesus returned to Nazareth with them, and was obedient. Mary kept these things in her heart. **52.** Jesus grew in wisdom, stature, and favor with God and people.

Chapter 3

1 In the fifteenth year of Tiberius Caesar's reign, during the governorship of Pontius Pilate in Judea, and with Herod as tetrarch of Galilee, Philip as tetrarch of Ituraea and Trachonitis, and Lysanias as tetrarch of Abilene. (Tiberius Caesar: Roman Emperor, Pontius Pilate: Governor of Judea, Herod: Ruler of Galilee, Galilee: Region in northern Israel, Trachonitis: Region near the Golan Heights, Abilene: Region in ancient Syria) **2.** The word of God came to John, son of Zacharias, while Annas and Caiaphas were high priests in the wilderness. (Annas and Caiaphas: High Priests of the time, Zacharias: John's father, wilderness: desert area) **3.** John went throughout the region near the Jordan, calling for baptism as a sign of repentance for the forgiveness of sins. (Jordan: Major river in Israel, repentance: turning away from sin, forgiveness: pardon) **4.** As the prophet Isaiah wrote, "A voice calls in the wilderness, 'Prepare the way for the Lord, make His paths straight.'" (Isaiah: Old Testament prophet, wilderness: desert area) **5.** "Fill every valley, lower every mountain and hill, make the crooked paths straight, and smooth out the rough ways." **6.** "All people will witness God's salvation." **7.** John warned the crowds, "You brood of vipers, who warned you to flee from the coming judgment?" (wrath: anger of God) **8.** "Show fruits worthy of repentance. Don't rely on being children of Abraham. God can raise children from stones." (repentance: turning away from sin) **9.** "The axe is at the tree's root; every tree that does not bear good fruit will be chopped down and thrown into the fire." **10.** The crowd asked, "What should we do?" **11.** John replied, "If you have two coats, share with the one who has none, and if you have food, do the same." **12.** Tax collectors asked, "Teacher, what should we do?" (Tax collectors: officials who collected taxes) **13.** He said, "Don't collect more than required." **14.** Soldiers asked, "What should we do?" He answered, "Don't abuse anyone, accuse falsely, and be content with your pay." (extort: forcefully take money) **15.** The people were wondering if John was the Messiah. (Messiah: Savior) **16.** John said, "I baptize with water, but someone more powerful than I will come, whose sandals I am not worthy to untie. He will baptize you with the Holy Spirit and fire." **17.** "His winnowing fork is in His hand, to clear the threshing floor, gathering the wheat into the barn, and burning the chaff with unquenchable fire." (winnowing fork: tool used for separating grain from chaff, threshing floor: area where grain is separated) **18.** John spoke many other things, encouraging the people and proclaiming the good news. (exhorted: urged) **19.** When John rebuked Herod the tetrarch for his immoral relationship with his brother's wife and his other wrongdoings, **20.** Herod had John imprisoned. (Herod: Ruler of Galilee) **21.** When everyone was baptized, Jesus also was baptized. As He prayed, the heaven opened, **22.** and the Holy Spirit descended like a dove, with a voice from heaven saying, "You are My beloved Son; with You I am well pleased." **23.** Jesus was about thirty years old, believed to be the son of Joseph, **24.** the son of Heli, Matthat, Levi, Simeon, Symeon, Joseph, **25.** Mattathias, Amos, Nahum, Esli, Naggai, **26.** Maath, Mattathias, Semein, Joseph, Judah, **27.** Joanna, Rhesa, Zerubbabel, Shealtiel, Neri, (Zerubbabel: leader who helped rebuild the temple) **28.** Melchi, Addi, Cosam, Elmodam, Er, **29.** Josech, Eliezer, Jorim, Matthat, Levi, **30.** Simeon, Judah, Joseph, Jonan, Eliakim, **31.** Melea, Menan, Mattatha, Nathan, David, (David: King of Israel) **32.** Jesse, Obed, Boaz, Salmon, Nahshon, **33.** Amminadab, Aram, Esrom, Phares, Judah, **34.** Jacob, Isaac, Abraham, Terah, Nahor, (Abraham: Founder of Israel, Jacob: Son of Isaac) **35.** Saruch, Reu, Peleg, Eber, Shelah, **36.** Cainan, Arphaxad, Shem, Noah, Lamech, (Noah: Biblical flood survivor) **37.** Methuselah, Enoch, Jared, Mahalalel, Cainan, **38.** Enos, Seth, Adam, the son of God. (Adam: First human)

Chapter 4

1. Jesus, filled with the Holy Spirit, returned from the Jordan and was led into the wilderness. **2.** For 40 days, the devil tempted him while he fasted, and he grew hungry. **3.** The devil challenged, "If you are the Son of God, turn this stone into bread." **4.** Jesus responded, "It is written: 'Man does not live by bread alone, but by God's word.'" **5.** The devil then showed him all the world's kingdoms. **6.** "I will give you all this power and glory, for it's mine to give," said the devil. **7.** "Worship me, and it will be yours." **8.** Jesus replied, "Get behind me, Satan! It is written: 'Worship the Lord your God alone.'" **9.** The devil took him to Jerusalem and placed him on the temple's highest point. **10.** "If you are the Son of God, throw yourself down," he said. **11.** "For it is written: 'His angels will guard you.'" **12.** Jesus answered, "It is said: 'Do not test the Lord your God.'" **13.** After the temptations, the devil left him for a time. **14.** Jesus returned to Galilee, empowered by the Spirit, and his fame spread. (Fame: widespread recognition) **15.** He taught in synagogues, and people praised him. (Synagogues: Jewish places of worship) **16.** He went to Nazareth, his hometown, and attended the Sabbath service. (Sabbath: a day of religious observance and rest) **17.** The scroll of the prophet Isaiah was given to him. He read: **18.** "The Spirit of the Lord is on me, anointed (Anointed: chosen for a special purpose) to bring good news to the poor, heal the brokenhearted, free prisoners, restore sight to the blind, and release the oppressed." **19.** "To proclaim the Lord's favor." **20.** He returned the scroll, sat down, and all eyes were on him. **21.** "Today, this scripture is fulfilled (Fulfilled: completed or realized) in your hearing," he declared. **22.** They were amazed but questioned, "Isn't this Joseph's son?" **23.** Jesus replied, "You'll quote, 'Physician, heal yourself,' and ask me to do in Nazareth what I did in Capernaum." **24.** "No prophet is accepted in his hometown," he said. **25.** "In Elijah's time, many widows (Widows: women whose husbands have died) existed in Israel during a famine (Famine: severe shortage of food), yet Elijah was sent to a widow in Sidon." **26.** "In Elisha's time, many lepers (Lepers: people with a contagious skin disease) were in Israel, but only Naaman, the Syrian, was healed." **27.** The crowd grew angry at his words. **28.** They drove him out and tried to throw him off a cliff. (Cliff: a steep rock face) **29.** But Jesus walked through the crowd and continued on. **30.** He went to Capernaum, where he taught on the Sabbath. **31.** His teaching amazed them, as he spoke with authority (Authority: the power to command or control). **32.** A man possessed by an evil spirit cried out in the synagogue. **33.** "What do you want with us, Jesus of Nazareth? I know you are the Holy One of God." **34.** Jesus rebuked (Rebuked: scolded or criticized sharply) the spirit, "Be quiet and leave him!" The demon left without harming him. **35.** The people were astonished (Astonished: greatly surprised), saying, "He commands demons with authority, and they obey." **36.** News of him spread throughout the region. **37.** Jesus went to Simon's house, where Simon's mother-in-law lay sick. They asked Jesus to help. **38.** He rebuked the fever, and it left her. She immediately got up and served them. **39.** At sunset, people brought the sick to Jesus, and he healed them all. **40.** Demons cried, "You are the Son of God!" but he rebuked them and told them not to speak, for they knew he was the Messiah. (Messiah: the Anointed One or Savior) **41.** Early the next morning, Jesus went to a quiet place. The people searched for him and tried to stop him from leaving. **42.** He said, "I must preach the kingdom of God in other towns as well, for this is why I was sent." **43.** And he preached in the synagogues of Judea. (Judea: a region in Israel)

Chapter 5
1. Jesus stood by the Lake of Gennesaret as the crowd gathered to hear His message. **2.** He saw two boats by the lake; the fishermen were washing their nets. **3.** Jesus entered Simon's boat, asking him to push it out a little. He sat and taught the people from the boat. **4.** When He finished, Jesus told Simon to go into deeper water and let down the nets for a catch. **5.** Simon replied, "We worked all night and caught nothing, but because you say so, I'll let down the net." **6.** They caught so many fish that their nets began to break. **7.** They signaled their partners in the other boat, and both boats filled, nearly sinking. **8.** Simon Peter, amazed, fell at Jesus' feet and said, "Lord, leave me, for I am a sinful man." (Sinful: morally wrong or bad) **9.** He and his companions were astonished by the large catch.(Astonished: greatly surprised or amazed) **10.** James and John, the sons of Zebedee, were also amazed. Jesus told Simon, "Do not fear; from now on, you will catch people." **11.** They left everything and followed Him. **12.** A man with leprosy saw Jesus in a town, fell before Him, and begged, "Lord, if you are willing, you can make me clean." (Leprosy: a skin disease) **13.** Jesus reached out, touched him, and said, "I am willing. Be clean!" Immediately, the leprosy left him. **14.** Jesus told him to be quiet but go to the priest and offer sacrifices as a testimony. (Testimony: a statement or evidence that supports a truth) **15.** Despite this, news of Jesus spread, and many came to hear Him and be healed. **16.** Jesus withdrew to lonely places to pray. (Withdraw: to move away or retreat) **17.** One day, as He taught, Pharisees and teachers of the law from Galilee, Judea, and Jerusalem sat nearby. The power of the Lord was with Him to heal. (Pharisees: religious leaders; Galilee, Judea, Jerusalem: regions) **18.** Some men brought a paralyzed man on a mat, trying to reach Jesus. (Paralyzed: unable to move; Mat: a flat surface used for carrying) **19.** Unable to get through the crowd, they climbed onto the roof and lowered him down. **20.** Seeing their faith, Jesus said, "Friend, your sins are forgiven." (Faith: belief or trust in something or someone) **21.** The Pharisees and teachers questioned, "Who can forgive sins but God alone?" **22.** Knowing their thoughts, Jesus asked, "Why are you thinking this?" **23.** "Which is easier: to say your sins are forgiven, or to say, 'Get up and walk'?" **24.** "But to show you that the Son of Man has authority to forgive sins," He said to the paralyzed man, "Get up, take your mat, and go home." (Authority: the power to make decisions) **25.** Immediately, the man stood, took his mat, and went home, praising God. **26.** Everyone was amazed, glorifying God, saying, "We have seen remarkable things today." (Glorifying: praising or honoring) **27.** After this, Jesus saw Levi, a tax collector, sitting at his booth, and said, "Follow me." **28.** Levi got up, left everything, and followed Him. **29.** Levi hosted a great banquet for Jesus, with a crowd of tax collectors and others. (Banquet: a large meal or feast) **30.** The Pharisees complained to His disciples, "Why do you eat with tax collectors and sinners?" **31.** Jesus replied, "It is not the healthy who need a doctor, but the sick." **32.** "I did not come to call the righteous, but sinners to repentance." (Repentance: the act of feeling remorse and changing behavior) **33.** They asked, "Why do John's disciples fast, but yours eat and drink?" (Fast: to abstain from food or drink for religious reasons) **34.** Jesus answered, "Can you make the friends of the bridegroom fast while he is with them?" (Bridegroom: the man who is getting married) **35.** "The time will come when the bridegroom will be taken away, and then they will fast." **36.** He told them this parable: "No one sews a patch from a new garment onto an old one. It will tear both the new and the old." (Parable: a simple story used to illustrate a moral or spiritual lesson) **37.** "No one pours new wine into old wineskins, or the wine will spill and the skins will be ruined." (Wineskins: containers made of animal skin to hold liquids) **38.** "New wine must be put into new wineskins, and both are preserved." **39.** "No one, after drinking old wine, wants the new, because they say, 'The old is better.'"

Chapter 6
1. After the first Sabbath, on another one, Jesus walked through the grain fields with his disciples. They picked the ears of corn, rubbed them in their hands, and ate them. (Sabbath: a day of rest; disciples: followers of Jesus) **2.** Some Pharisees questioned, "Why are you doing something forbidden on the Sabbath?" (Pharisees: a religious group who followed strict laws) **3.** Jesus responded, "Haven't you read what David did when he and his men were hungry? (David: a king of Israel) **4.** He entered the house of God, ate the consecrated bread, and gave it to his followers—something only priests are allowed to do. (Consecrated: made holy or sacred; priests: religious leaders) **5.** "The Son of Man is the Lord of the Sabbath." (Son of Man: a title Jesus used for himself; Lord: master, ruler) **6.** On another Sabbath, Jesus went into a synagogue to teach, where a man with a withered hand was present. (Synagogue: a Jewish place of worship; withered: dried up or shriveled) **7.** The Pharisees watched closely to see if he would heal on the Sabbath, hoping to accuse him. (Accuse: to charge someone with wrongdoing) **8.** Jesus, knowing their thoughts, called the man with the withered hand forward. He stood up. (Thoughts: ideas or plans in one's mind) **9.** Jesus asked, "Is it lawful to do good or harm on the Sabbath? To save life or destroy it?" (Lawful: permitted by law) **10.** He then told the man, "Stretch out your hand." The man did so, and his hand was completely healed. (Healed: made well or cured) **11.** The Pharisees were furious and began plotting what to do with Jesus. (Furious: very angry; plotting: secretly planning) **12.** Jesus went to a mountain to pray, spending the entire night in communion with God. (Communion: close relationship or communication with God) **13.** When daybreak came, he called his disciples and chose twelve, naming them apostles. (Daybreak: the moment the day begins; apostles: specially chosen messengers of Jesus) **14.** They were Simon (also called Peter), his brother Andrew, James and John, Philip and Bartholomew, (Simon: a disciple of Jesus) **15.** Matthew and Thomas, James (son of Alphaeus), and Simon the Zealot, (Zealot: a member of a group that sought to overthrow Roman rule) **16.** Judas (son of James), and Judas Iscariot, who would betray him. (Betray: to be disloyal or turn against) **17.** After coming down the mountain, he stood in a flat area, surrounded by his disciples and a large crowd from Judea, Jerusalem, and the coastal regions of Tyre and Sidon. (Judea: a region in ancient Israel; Jerusalem: the capital city of Israel; Tyre and Sidon: ancient cities in present-day Lebanon) **18.** Many who were troubled by evil spirits were also healed. (Troubled: disturbed or afflicted; evil spirits: harmful supernatural beings) **19.** People tried to touch him, because power flowed from him and healed them all. (Flowed: moved continuously) **20.** Jesus looked at his disciples and said, "Blessed are you who are poor, for the kingdom of God is yours." (Blessed: favored or happy; kingdom of God: the reign or rule of God) **21.** "Blessed are you who hunger now, for you will be satisfied. Blessed are you who weep now, for you will laugh." (Hunger: to feel the need for food; weep: to cry) **22.** "Blessed are you when people hate you, exclude you, insult you, and reject your name as evil because of the Son of Man." (Exclude: to leave out or deny entry; reject: to refuse or dismiss) **23.** "Rejoice and leap for joy, for your reward is great in heaven. That's how their ancestors treated the prophets." (Rejoice: to feel or show great happiness; ancestors: forebears, earlier generations) **24.** "But woe to you who are rich, for you have already received

your comfort." (Woe: a word expressing sorrow or warning; comfort: consolation or ease) **25.** "Woe to you who are full now, for you will go hungry. Woe to you who laugh now, for you will mourn and weep." (Mourn: to express grief or sorrow) **26.** "Woe to you when everyone speaks well of you, for that's how they treated the false prophets." (False prophets: people who claim to speak for God but do not) **27.** "But I tell you who hear me, love your enemies, do good to those who hate you." (Enemies: people who oppose you) **28.** "Bless those who curse you, and pray for those who mistreat you." (Curse: to wish harm upon; mistreat: to treat badly) **29.** "If someone strikes you on one cheek, offer the other also. If someone takes your cloak, don't stop them from taking your tunic." (Strike: to hit; cloak: an outer garment; tunic: a type of clothing) **30.** "Give to anyone who asks, and if someone takes your possessions, don't ask for them back." (Possessions: belongings or property) **31.** "Treat others the way you want to be treated." **32.** "If you love only those who love you, what credit is that? Even sinners love those who love them." (Credit: recognition or reward; sinners: those who commit wrongdoing) **33.** "If you do good to those who do good to you, what credit is that? Sinners do the same." **34.** "If you lend to those expecting to be repaid, what credit is that? Sinners lend to sinners, expecting to receive back the same." (Lend: to give something temporarily with the expectation it will be returned) **35.** "But love your enemies, do good to them, and lend without expecting anything back. Then your reward will be great, and you will be children of the Most High, who is kind to the ungrateful and wicked." (Ungrateful: not showing gratitude; wicked: evil or immoral) **36.** "Be merciful, just as your Father is merciful." (Merciful: showing compassion or forgiveness) **37.** "Do not judge, and you will not be judged. Do not condemn, and you will not be condemned. Forgive, and you will be forgiven." (Condemn: to declare someone guilty or deserving of punishment) **38.** "Give, and it will be given to you—pressed down, shaken together, and overflowing. For with the measure you use, it will be measured back to you." (Pressed down: packed tightly; overflowing: spilling over the top) **39.** Jesus told them a parable: "Can a blind person lead another blind person? Won't both fall into a pit?" (Parable: a simple story used to illustrate a moral or spiritual lesson) **40.** "A disciple is not above his teacher, but everyone who is fully trained will be like their teacher." (Disciple: a student or follower of a teacher) **41.** "Why do you notice the speck in your brother's eye, but don't see the plank in your own?" (Speck: a tiny particle; plank: a large piece of wood) **42.** "How can you say, 'Let me remove the speck from your eye,' when you do not see the plank in your own? First, remove the plank, and then you will see clearly to help your brother." **43.** "A good tree does not bear bad fruit, nor does a bad tree bear good fruit." (Bear: produce) **44.** "Each tree is recognized by its fruit. People do not pick figs from thornbushes, nor grapes from brambles." (Brambles: prickly shrubs) **45.** "A good person brings good things out of the good stored in their heart, and an evil person brings evil from the evil stored in their heart. For the mouth speaks what the heart is full of." **46.** "Why do you call me 'Lord, Lord,' and not do what I say?" (Lord: a title for a ruler or master) **47.** "Anyone who comes to me, hears my words, and puts them into practice is like someone who builds a house on solid rock." (Practice: to do something regularly or repeatedly) **48.** "When a flood comes and the stream beats against that house, it will not be shaken, because it is well-built." (Flood: a large amount of water covering land) **49.** "But the one who hears my words and does not put them into practice is like someone who builds a house on the ground without a foundation. When the stream strikes it, it collapses, and its destruction is great." (Foundation: the base or support for something; collapse: to fall down or give way)

Chapter 7

1. After teaching the crowd, Jesus entered Capernaum. **2.** A centurion's servant, whom he deeply cared for, was seriously ill. (Centurion: a Roman officer in charge of 100 soldiers) **3.** Hearing about Jesus, the centurion sent Jewish elders to ask for his help. (Elders: respected leaders within the Jewish community) **4.** The elders urgently urged Jesus, saying the centurion deserved help. **5.** He loves our nation and even built a synagogue for us. (Synagogue: a Jewish place of worship) **6.** Jesus went with them, but near the house, the centurion sent friends to say, "Lord, I am not worthy to have you enter my house." **7.** "I am not worthy to approach you; just say the word, and my servant will be healed." **8.** "I have authority over soldiers, and they obey my commands. My servant does what I tell him." (Authority: power or control over others) **9.** Jesus marveled and said, "I haven't found such faith in Israel." (Marveled: was amazed) **10.** The messengers returned and found the servant healed. **11.** The next day, Jesus went to Nain with his disciples and a crowd. (Nain: a town in Galilee) **12.** As they reached the gate, they saw a widow's only son being carried out, with a large crowd following her. (Widow: a woman whose husband has died) **13.** Jesus, feeling compassion, said, "Do not weep." (Compassion: deep sympathy and concern for others) **14.** He touched the bier, and the procession halted. "Young man, rise," he said. (Bier: a structure for carrying a dead body) **15.** The dead man sat up, spoke, and Jesus gave him back to his mother. **16.** Fear spread, and people praised God, saying, "A great prophet has arisen among us, and God has visited his people." **17.** News of Jesus spread throughout Judea and beyond. (Judea: a region in ancient Israel) **18.** John's disciples reported these events to him. **19.** John sent two disciples to ask Jesus, "Are you the one, or should we look for another?" **20.** The disciples asked, "John the Baptist sent us to ask if you are the one or should we wait for someone else?" (John the Baptist: a prophet who baptized people in the Jordan River) **21.** Jesus healed many, gave sight to the blind, and cured the sick. **22.** He replied, "Tell John what you have seen and heard: the blind see, the lame walk, the lepers are cleansed, the deaf hear, the dead are raised, and the gospel is preached to the poor." (Lepers: people with a contagious skin disease) **23.** "Blessed is the one who is not offended by me." (Offended: feeling upset or angry about something) **24.** After John's messengers left, Jesus spoke to the crowd about John, asking, "What did you go out to see? A reed shaken by the wind?" (Reed: a tall, slender plant, used metaphorically here to mean someone easily swayed or uncertain) **25.** "Did you go to see someone in luxury? Those who wear fine clothes live in palaces." (Luxury: expensive and comfortable living) **26.** "Did you go to see a prophet? Yes, and more than a prophet." **27.** "This is the one about whom it is written: 'I will send my messenger ahead of you to prepare your way.'" **28.** "Among those born of women, no one is greater than John the Baptist, yet the least in the kingdom of God is greater than he." (Kingdom of God: the reign or rule of God) **29.** All who heard him, including tax collectors, justified God by being baptized by John. (Justified: declared righteous or in the right) **30.** But the Pharisees rejected God's purpose by refusing baptism. (Pharisees: a religious group in ancient Judaism who strictly followed the law) **31.** Jesus asked, "What can I compare this generation to?" **32.** "They are like children in the marketplace calling to others, 'We played the pipe for you, but you didn't dance; we sang a lament, but you didn't weep.'" (Lament: a song or expression of sorrow) **33.** "John came not eating or drinking, and you said, 'He has a demon.'" **34.** "The Son of Man came eating and drinking, and you call him a glutton and drunkard, a friend of tax collectors and sinners!" (Glutton: someone who eats excessively) **35.** "But wisdom is proved right by her children." (Wisdom: the ability to make good decisions) **36.** A Pharisee invited Jesus to dinner, and he entered and reclined at the table. (Reclined: lay back, in this case, during a meal) **37.** A sinful woman, hearing Jesus was there, brought an alabaster jar of perfume. (Alabaster: a smooth, white stone often used for fine carvings or containers) **38.** She wept behind Jesus, washed his feet with her tears, wiped them with her hair, kissed them, and anointed them with perfume. **39.** The Pharisee thought, "If Jesus were a prophet, he would know who this woman is, a sinner." **40.** Jesus responded, "Simon, I have something to tell you." "Tell me, teacher," Simon replied. **41.** "Two people owed a lender money, one 500 denarii, the other 50." (Denarii: Roman coins used as currency) **42.** "Neither could repay, so the lender forgave both. Which one will love him more?" **43.** Simon answered, "The one who owed more." Jesus said, "You have judged correctly." **44.** Turning to the woman, he said to Simon, "Do you see this woman? I came into your house, and you didn't offer me water for my feet, but she washed them with her tears." **45.** "You didn't greet me with a kiss, but she hasn't stopped kissing my feet." **46.** "You didn't anoint my head with oil, but she has anointed my feet with perfume." **47.** "Her many sins are forgiven because of her great love; but the one forgiven little, loves little." **48.** Jesus told her, "Your sins are forgiven." **49.** The others at the table wondered, "Who is this who forgives sins?" **50.** Jesus said, "Your faith has saved you; go in peace."

Chapter 8

1. Jesus traveled from town to town, sharing the message of God's kingdom with his twelve disciples. **2.** Several women, including Mary Magdalene, who had been freed from demons, followed him. **3.** Joanna, the wife of Herod's steward Chuza, Susanna, and others supported him financially. **4.** A large crowd gathered, and Jesus told them a parable. (Parable: a simple story used to illustrate a moral or spiritual lesson) **5.** A farmer sowed seeds, some of which were trampled on the path and eaten by birds. (Path: a hardened ground, symbolizing a hardened heart) **6.** Some seeds fell on rocky soil, grew quickly, but withered without enough moisture. (Rocky soil: land with a shallow layer of soil) **7.** Other seeds fell among thorns, which choked the plants as they grew. (Thorns: weeds or plants that hinder growth) **8.** Some seeds fell on good soil, yielding a bountiful crop. Jesus then called, "Let anyone who has ears, listen." (Good soil: a heart receptive to God's word) **9.** The disciples asked him to explain the parable. **10.** He said that the mysteries of God's kingdom are revealed to them, but to others, it's through parables, so they may not understand. (Mysteries: hidden truths) **11.** The seed represents God's word. (Seed: symbolizing the message of God) **12.** The seed on the path symbolizes those who hear the word, but the devil steals it from them. (Devil: a fallen angel who opposes God) **13.** The seed on rocky ground represents those who accept the word but fall away when faced with difficulties. (Rocky ground: symbolizes shallow faith) **14.** The seed among thorns represents those distracted by life's worries, riches, and pleasures, preventing them from maturing. (Riches: desires) (Pleasures: desires) **15.** The good soil represents those who accept God's word and bear fruit through perseverance. (Good soil: a heart receptive to God's word) (Perseverance: steadfastness) **16.** A lamp is not hidden but placed on a stand so others can see its light. (Lamp: symbolizing knowledge or truth) **17.** Everything hidden will eventually be revealed. (Revealed: made known to all) **18.** Pay attention to how you listen; those who have will receive more, while those who don't will lose what they have. **19.** Jesus' family came but couldn't reach him because of the crowd. **20.** Someone told him his family was outside wanting to see him. **21.** He replied, "My family are those who hear and follow God's word." **22.** Jesus and his disciples set sail to the other side of the lake. (Lake: a large body of water) **23.** As they sailed, a storm arose, and their boat began to fill with water. (Storm: a violent disturbance in the weather) **24.** They woke Jesus, and he calmed the storm, asking, "Where is your faith?" **25.** The disciples were amazed and questioned who Jesus was, as even nature obeyed him. **26.** They reached the region of the Gadarenes. (Region: an area) **27.** A demon-possessed man, living among tombs, met them. (Demon-possessed: under the control of evil spirits) (Tombs: burial places) **28.** The man cried out, asking why Jesus had come, begging him not to torment him. **29.** Jesus had already commanded the demon to leave the man, but the demon had often seized him. (Demon: an evil spirit possessing the man) **30.** Jesus asked his name, and the man replied, "Legion," because many demons inhabited him. (Legion: a large number, referencing many demons) **31.** The demons begged not to be sent to the abyss. (Abyss: a deep, bottomless pit) **32.** Seeing pigs nearby, the demons asked to enter them, and Jesus allowed it. (Pigs: animals considered unclean in Jewish law) **33.** The demons entered the pigs, and the herd rushed into the lake and drowned. (Steep bank: a sharp incline) **34.** The herders fled and told others what had happened. (Herders: people who tend livestock) **35.** The people were afraid when they saw the healed man, now sane and clothed. (Sane: in his right mind) **36.** The witnesses explained how the man was healed. (Healed: restored to health or sanity) **37.** The people asked Jesus to leave, so he got in the boat and left. **38.** The healed man wanted to go with Jesus, but he was sent to tell others what God had done for him. **39.** He went through the city sharing his story. **40.** When Jesus returned, the people welcomed him. (Welcomed: greeted with joy) **41.** Jairus, a synagogue leader, came to Jesus, begging for help for his dying daughter. (Synagogue: a place of Jewish worship) **42.** As they went, the crowds pressed in. (Crowded: pushing or pressing together in a dense group) **43.** A woman, who had been bleeding for twelve years without finding a cure, touched Jesus' cloak and was instantly healed. (Cloak: a garment worn over clothes) **44.** Jesus asked, "Who touched me?" **45.** Peter, seeing the crowd, asked why Jesus would ask such a question. **46.** Jesus felt power leave him and knew someone had been healed. (Power: divine strength or healing ability) **47.** The woman, trembling, confessed, explaining her healing. (Trembling: shaking due to fear or excitement) **48.** Jesus told her, "Your faith has healed you; go in peace." (Faith: trust in God's ability to heal) **49.** While Jesus was speaking, someone informed Jairus that his daughter had died. **50.** Jesus reassured him to have faith, and she would be healed. (Healed: restored to life or health) **51.** At the house, Jesus took only his closest disciples and the girl's parents inside. (Disciples: followers of Jesus) **52.** He told the mourners not to weep, saying the girl was merely asleep. (Weeping: crying in sorrow) **53.** They mocked him, knowing she was dead. (Mocked: laughed at or ridiculed) **54.** Jesus took her hand and told her to rise from death. (Get up: rise from death) **55.** She stood up immediately, and he instructed them to give her food. (Spirit: the life force within a person) **56.** Her parents were astonished, and Jesus told them not to tell anyone about the miracle. (Astonished: surprised or amazed)

Chapter 9

1. Jesus gave his twelve disciples authority over demons and power to heal. (demons: evil spirits) **2.** He sent them to preach the kingdom of God and heal the sick. **3.** He told them, "Take nothing for your journey—no staff, bag, bread, money, or extra coat." (staff: walking stick) **4.** "Stay in one house until you leave that town." **5.** "If a town rejects you, shake off the dust from your feet as a testimony against them." (testimony: witness) **6.** The disciples went, preaching and healing everywhere. **7.** Herod, the ruler, heard of Jesus and was confused, as some thought John had risen from the dead. (ruler: leader) **8.** Others thought Elijah had returned, or one of the ancient prophets was alive again. (Elijah: prophet from the Old Testament) **9.** Herod said, "I beheaded John, but who is this?" He wanted to meet Jesus. (beheaded: killed) **10.** When the apostles returned, they reported to Jesus. He took them to a quiet place near Bethsaida. (apostles: disciples, Bethsaida: a town near the Sea of Galilee) **11.** The crowds followed, and Jesus welcomed them, teaching about God's kingdom and healing the sick. **12.** As the day ended, the disciples suggested sending the people away to find food and shelter, since they were in a remote place. (shelter: place to stay, remote: far) **13.** Jesus said, "You feed them." They replied, "We have only five loaves and two fish, unless we buy food for everyone." (loaves: bread) **14.** There were about five thousand men. Jesus had them sit in groups of fifty. **15.** They sat down. **16.** Jesus blessed the loaves and fish, broke them, and gave them to the disciples to distribute. (distribute: share) **17.** Everyone ate and was satisfied, with twelve baskets of leftovers. (baskets: containers, satisfied: full) **18.** While Jesus prayed alone, his disciples were with him. He asked, "Who do the crowds say I am?" **19.** They answered, "Some say John the Baptist, others say Elijah, and some think a prophet has come back to life." **20.** "What about you?" Jesus asked. Peter answered, "You are the Christ of God." (Christ: Messiah) **21.** Jesus warned them not to tell anyone. **22.** He told them, "The Son of Man must suffer, be rejected by leaders, be killed, and rise on the third day." (rejected: not accepted) **23.** "If anyone wants to follow me, they must deny themselves, take up their cross daily, and follow me." (deny themselves: give up their own desires, cross: a symbol of suffering) **24.** "Those who try to save their lives will lose them; but those who lose their lives for me will save them." **25.** "What good is it to gain the whole world but lose yourself?" **26.** "Whoever is ashamed of me, the Son of Man will be ashamed of when he comes in glory with the Father and angels." (ashamed: embarrassed, glory: splendor) **27.** "I tell you, some here will not die before they see God's kingdom." **28.** Eight days later, Jesus took Peter, John, and James to a mountain to pray. **29.** As he prayed, his face changed, and his clothes became dazzling white. (dazzling: very bright) **30.** Moses and Elijah appeared, speaking of his coming death in Jerusalem. (Moses: leader, Elijah: prophet) **31.** They appeared in glory and spoke of his departure. (departure: death) **32.** Peter and his companions were sleepy but saw Jesus' glory when they woke. **33.** As the men were leaving, Peter suggested building three shelters for Jesus, Moses, and Elijah, not understanding what he was saying. (Shelters: temporary homes) **34.** While speaking, a cloud covered them, and they were afraid. **35.** A voice from the cloud said, "This is my Son, listen to him." **36.** When the voice stopped, Jesus was alone. The disciples kept this to themselves and told no one. **37.** The next day, a crowd met Jesus as they came down from the mountain. **38.** A man begged Jesus to look at his only son, who was possessed by a spirit. (possessed: controlled) **39.** The spirit would throw him into convulsions, making him foam at the mouth. (convulsions: shaking) **40.** The disciples could not drive the spirit out. **41.** Jesus replied, "You unbelieving generation, how long must I be with you? Bring your son here." (unbelieving: doubting) **42.** As the boy came, the spirit threw him to the ground, but Jesus rebuked it, healed the boy, and gave him back to his father. (rebuked: commanded) **43.** The crowd was amazed at God's power, and Jesus told his disciples, **44.** "Listen carefully: the Son of Man will be delivered into men's hands." (delivered: handed over) **45.** They did not understand, and were afraid to ask him. **46.** An argument broke out among the disciples about who would be the greatest. **47.** Jesus, knowing their thoughts, took a child and said, **48.** "Whoever welcomes this child in my name welcomes me, and the one who sent me. The least among you is the greatest." (least: smallest) **49.** John said, "We saw someone casting out demons in your name and tried to stop him because he is not one of us." (casting out demons: expelling evil spirits) **50.** Jesus replied, "Do not stop him. Whoever is not against us is for us." **51.** When the time came for him to be taken up to heaven, Jesus set his face toward Jerusalem. **52.** He sent messengers ahead to a Samaritan village to prepare for him. (Samaritan: from Samaria) **53.** But the people did not receive him because he was going to Jerusalem. (receive: accept) **54.** James and John asked, "Lord, should we call down fire from heaven to destroy them like Elijah did?" **55.** Jesus rebuked them, saying, "You do not know what spirit you are of." **56.** "The Son of Man did not come to destroy people's lives but to save them." They moved on to another village. **57.** A man said to Jesus, "I will follow you wherever you go." **58.** Jesus replied, "Foxes have dens, birds have nests, but the Son of Man has no place to rest." (dens: homes) **59.** He told another, "Follow me." The man said, "Let me first bury my father." **60.** Jesus said, "Let the dead bury their own dead, but go and preach the kingdom of God." **61.** Another said, "I will follow you, but first let me say goodbye to my family." **62.** Jesus replied, "Anyone who starts plowing and looks back is not fit for the kingdom of God." (plowing: working)

Chapter 10

1. The Lord appointed seventy others and sent them, two by two, to every place He was about to visit. **2.** He told them, "The harvest is plentiful, but the workers are few. Ask the Lord of the harvest to send more workers." (Harvest: gathering souls, Workers: those who help spread the message) **3.** "Go! I am sending you like lambs among wolves." (Lambs: harmless, Wolves: dangerous enemies) **4.** "Do not take a purse, bag, or sandals, and don't greet anyone on the road." (Purse: small bag for money, Sandals: footwear) **5.** "When you enter a house, greet it with 'Peace to this house.'" (Peace: a greeting of goodwill) **6.** "If the house is peaceful, your peace will remain, but if not, it will return to you." **7.** "Stay in one house, eating and drinking what they offer, for the worker deserves their wages. Don't move from house to house." (Worker: someone earning a living, Wages: payment for work) **8.** "When you enter a city and they welcome you, eat what is given." **9.** "Heal the sick and tell them, 'The kingdom of God has come near.'" (Kingdom of God: God's reign or rule) **10.** "If they reject you, leave and shake the dust off your feet as a witness against them." **11.** "Even the dust from your city we shake off, but know this: the kingdom of God has come near." **12.** "It will be more bearable for Sodom than for that city on the day of judgment." (Sodom: a city destroyed for sin, Judgment: divine decision on one's actions) **13.** "Woe to you, Chorazin and Bethsaida! If the miracles performed in you had been done in Tyre and Sidon, they would have repented long ago." (Chorazin: a town in Galilee, Bethsaida: a village near the Sea of Galilee, Tyre & Sidon: ancient cities known for sin) **14.** "But it will be more bearable for Tyre and Sidon than for you." **15.** "And you, Capernaum, will be brought down to hell." (Capernaum: a place of Jesus' ministry, Hell: a place of punishment in the afterlife) **16.** "Whoever listens to you listens to me; whoever rejects you rejects me, and whoever rejects me rejects the one who sent me." **17.** The seventy returned with joy, saying, "Lord, even demons obey us in Your name." (Demons: evil spirits) **18.** He said, "I saw Satan fall like lightning from heaven." (Satan: the adversary, Heaven: God's domain) **19.** "I have given you authority over serpents, scorpions, and all the enemy's power; nothing will harm you." (Serpents: snakes, Scorpions: venomous creatures, Authority: power or control) **20.** "However, don't rejoice that spirits submit to you, but that your names are written in heaven." (Names in heaven: symbolizing salvation, Submission: yielding to authority) **21.** Jesus rejoiced, saying, "I thank You, Father, Lord of heaven and earth, that You have hidden these things from the wise and revealed them to little children." (Wise: knowledgeable, revealed: made known) **22.** "All things have been entrusted to me by my Father. No one knows the Son except the Father, and no one knows the Father except the Son, and those to whom the Son chooses to reveal Him." (Entrusted: given responsibility, Son: Jesus, Revealed: shown or made known) **23.** He turned to His disciples and said privately, "Blessed are the eyes that see what you see." (Disciples: followers, Blessed: fortunate or favored) **24.** "Many prophets and kings wanted to see what you see, but didn't, and hear what you hear, but didn't." (Prophets: people who speak God's truth, Kings: rulers of nations) **25.** A lawyer asked, "Teacher, what must I do to inherit eternal life?" (Lawyer: an expert in religious law, Inherit: receive as a legacy) **26.** Jesus replied, "What is written in the law? How do you interpret it?" (Interpret: understand or explain) **27.** He said, "Love the Lord with all your heart, soul, strength, and mind; and love your neighbor as yourself." (Soul: the spiritual part of a person, Neighbor: someone nearby or another person) **28.** Jesus said, "You've answered correctly. Do this, and you will live." **29.** He asked, "Who is my neighbor?" **30.** Jesus told the story: "A man was traveling from Jerusalem to Jericho and was attacked by thieves. They beat him and left him half-dead." (Jerusalem: holy city, Jericho: ancient city) **31.** "A priest came by and saw him but passed by on the other side." (Priest: religious leader) **32.** "A Levite did the same, passing by on the other side." (Levite: a member of the priestly tribe) **33.** "But a Samaritan came and had compassion on him." (Samaritan: a person from Samaria, Compassion: sympathy and concern) **34.** "He treated his wounds, took him to an inn, and cared for him." (Wounds: injuries, Inn: a place to stay) **35.** "The next day, he gave two silver coins to the innkeeper, saying, 'Take care of him, and I'll repay any extra when I return.'" (Silver coins: money, Innkeeper: the person who manages the inn) **36.** "Which of these three do you think was a neighbor to the man?" **37.** The lawyer replied, "The one who showed mercy." Jesus said, "Go and do likewise." (Mercy: compassion or forgiveness) **38.** As they went, Jesus entered a village where a woman named Martha welcomed Him into her home. (Martha: a woman from Bethany) **39.** She had a sister named Mary, who sat at Jesus' feet and listened to His teaching. (Mary: Martha's sister) **40.** Martha, distracted by the preparations, asked, "Lord, don't You care that my sister left me to serve alone? Tell her to help me." (Distracted: not focused) **41.** "Martha, Martha, you are worried about many things," Jesus replied. (Worried: anxious or concerned) **42.** "Only one thing is needed. Mary has chosen the better part, and it won't be taken from her." (Chosen: selected, Better part: the more important choice)

Chapter 11

1. While praying in a certain place, one of his followers asked him, "Lord, teach us to pray, just as John taught his disciples." (Followers: disciples) **2.** Jesus replied, "When you pray, say: 'Our Father in heaven, may your name be honored. Let your kingdom come and your will be done on earth, just as it is in heaven.'" (Honor: to show respect) **3.** Provide us with our daily bread. (Bread: food or sustenance) **4.** Forgive us our sins, as we forgive those who have wronged us. Do not lead us into temptation, but deliver us from evil. (Temptation: the desire to do something wrong) **5.** He then asked, "Which of you has a friend, and at midnight goes to him asking for three loaves of bread, (Midnight: 12:00 AM) **6.** because a friend has arrived and you have nothing to offer him?" (Offer: to present or give something to someone) **7.** The friend will respond, 'Don't disturb me; the door is locked, and the children are in bed. I cannot get up and give you anything.' (Disturb: to interrupt or bother) **8.** I tell you, though he won't get up and give it to him because of their friendship, his persistence will make him get up and give him whatever he needs. (Persistence: the quality of continuing to do something despite difficulties) **9.** Ask, and you will receive; seek, and you will find; knock, and the door will be opened to you. (Seek: to look for or search) **10.** Everyone who asks receives, the one who seeks finds, and to the one who knocks, the door will open. **11.** If a son asks for bread, will his father give him a stone? Or if he asks for a fish, will he give him a snake? (Snake: a reptile, commonly a dangerous one) **12.** Or if he asks for an egg, will he offer him a scorpion? (Scorpion: a small, venomous insect with a stinger) **13.** If you, though imperfect, know how to give good gifts to your children, how much more will your heavenly Father give the Holy Spirit to those who ask him? (Imperfect: not flawless or complete) **14.** He cast out a demon, and when it left, the mute person spoke, and the crowd marveled. (Mute: unable to speak) **15.** But some of them said, "He casts out demons by Beelzebub, the prince of demons." (Beelzebub: a name for the devil or Satan) **16.** Others, trying to trap him, asked for a sign from heaven. (Trap: to deceive or trick someone) **17.** Knowing their thoughts, he said, "A kingdom divided against itself will be destroyed, and a house divided will fall." (Thoughts: ideas or plans in one's mind) **18.** If Satan is divided against himself, his kingdom will not survive. You claim I cast out demons by Beelzebub. (Survive: to continue to exist or live) **19.** If I cast out demons by Beelzebub, who do your sons cast them out by? They will be your judges. (Judge: a person who makes decisions in a court of law) **20.** But if I cast out demons by the power of God, then the kingdom of God has come upon you. (Power: the ability or capacity to do something) **21.** When a strong man guards his house, his possessions are secure. (Possessions: things owned) **22.** But when someone stronger comes and overpowers him, he takes away his armor and divides his spoils. (Overpowers: to defeat or overcome someone) **23.** Whoever is not with me is against me, and whoever does not gather with me scatters. (Scatters: to spread out or disperse) **24.** When an unclean spirit leaves a person, it wanders through dry places, seeking rest. If it finds none, it returns to its former home. (Unclean: impure or contaminated) **25.** When it returns, it finds the house swept clean and in order. (Swept: cleaned by brushing away dirt) **26.** Then it brings seven more wicked spirits, and they enter and dwell there, making the last state worse than the first." (Wicked: evil or immoral) **27.** As he spoke, a woman in the crowd said, "Blessed is the mother who gave you birth and nursed you." (Blessed: favored or fortunate) **28.** He replied, "Blessed are those who hear the word of God and obey it." (Obey: to follow commands or rules) **29.** When the crowd gathered, he said, "This generation seeks a sign, but no sign will be given except the sign of Jonah the prophet." (Generation: a group of people born around the same time) **30.** Just as Jonah was a sign to the people of Nineveh, so the Son of Man will be to this generation. (Son of Man: a title Jesus used for himself) **31.** The Queen of the South will rise at judgment and condemn this generation. She traveled from a distant land to hear the wisdom of Solomon, and now something greater than Solomon is here. (Judgment: a formal decision or ruling) **32.** The people of Nineveh will rise at judgment and condemn this generation. They repented at Jonah's message, and now something greater than Jonah is here. (Repented: felt remorse or regret for wrongdoing) **33.** No one lights a lamp and hides it. Instead, they place it on a stand so that those who enter can see the light. (Lamp: a source of light) **34.** Your eye is the lamp of your body. If your eye is healthy, your whole body will be filled with light; if it is unhealthy, your body will be full of darkness. (Healthy: in good condition) **35.** Be careful that the light within you is not darkness. (Careful: paying attention to avoid harm) **36.** If your entire body is full of light, with no part dark, it will be as bright as when a lamp gives you light." (Entire: whole, complete) **37.** While he was speaking, a Pharisee invited him to dinner, and he went and sat down to eat. (Pharisee: a member of an ancient Jewish sect) **38.** When the Pharisee noticed that he did not first wash before eating, he was surprised. (Notice: to become aware of something) **39.** The Lord said, "You Pharisees clean the outside of the cup, but inside you are full of greed and wickedness." (Greed: a desire for more than needed) **40.** Did not the one who made the outside also make the inside? (Made: created or formed) **41.** But give what you have to the poor, and everything will be clean for you. (Poor: people lacking basic necessities) **42.** Woe to you, Pharisees! You tithe small herbs but neglect justice and love for God. You should do both. (Neglect: to fail to care for) **43.** Woe to you, Pharisees! You love the best seats in the synagogues and greetings in the marketplaces. (Synagogues: Jewish places of worship) **44.** Woe to you, scribes and Pharisees, hypocrites! You are like unmarked graves that people walk over unknowingly. (Hypocrites: people who pretend to have qualities they don't possess) **45.** One of the law experts replied, "Teacher, you are insulting us too." (Insulting: disrespectful or offensive) **46.** Jesus responded, "Woe to you, experts in the law! You load people with burdens too heavy to bear and do nothing to help them." (Burden: a heavy load or responsibility) **47.** Woe to you! You build the tombs of the prophets, but your ancestors killed them. (Tombs: burial places) **48.** You testify that you approve of what your ancestors did—they killed the prophets, and you build their tombs. (Testify: to give evidence or statement) **49.** So, God says, 'I will send them prophets and apostles, whom they will kill and persecute.' (Apostles: early Christian leaders) **50.** This generation will be held accountable for the blood of all the prophets shed since the world began. (Accountable: responsible for actions) **51.** From the blood of Abel to Zechariah, who was killed between the altar and the temple. (Zechariah: a prophet) **52.** Woe to you, experts in the law! You have taken away the key of knowledge. You did not enter, and you hindered those who were entering." (Hindered: prevented or blocked) **53.** As he said this, the Pharisees and law experts began to oppose him fiercely and provoke him with many questions, (Provoke: to cause someone to react strongly) **54.** waiting to trap him in something he might say. (Trap: to deceive or catch in a mistake)

Chapter 12

1. A large crowd gathered, pressing against each other. Jesus warned His disciples, "Beware of the Pharisees' hypocrisy." (Pharisees: Jewish religious group, Hypocrisy: pretending to be something one is not) **2.** Nothing hidden will stay secret; everything will be revealed. (Revealed: made known) **3.** What you speak in secret will be heard openly; what you whisper will be shouted. (Whisper: speak softly) **4.** Don't fear those who can kill the body but have no power beyond that. (Body: the physical form) **5.** Fear God, who after death can cast you into hell. (Hell: place of punishment) **6.** Even five sparrows are sold for two pennies, yet God doesn't forget any of them. (Sparrows: small birds, Pennies: small coins) **7.** God has counted every hair on your head. You are worth more than sparrows. **8.** Whoever acknowledges me before others, I will acknowledge before God's angels. **9.** But whoever denies me before others will be denied before God's angels. **10.** Speaking against the Son of Man can be forgiven, but blasphemy against the Holy Spirit won't be. (Blasphemy: disrespectful speech) **11.** When you're taken before rulers, don't worry about your defense. **12.** The Holy Spirit will guide you on what to say. **13.** A man asked, "Teacher, tell my brother to share the inheritance." **14.** Jesus replied, "Who made me a judge between you two?" **15.** Be careful not to fall into greed; life isn't about abundance of possessions. (Greed: excessive desire for wealth) **16.** He told them a parable: "A rich man's land produced a large harvest." (Parable: a story teaching a lesson) **17.** He wondered, "What will I do with all this? I have no space for my crops." **18.** "I'll tear down my barns and build bigger ones to store everything." **19.** He said to himself, "I'll relax and enjoy life now, for I have plenty." **20.** But God said, "You fool! Tonight your life will be demanded. Who will get your wealth?" (Demanded: required) **21.** This is how it is for anyone who stores up riches but is not rich toward God. **22.** Don't worry about what you will eat or wear. **23.** Life is more than food, and the body is more than clothes. **24.** Look at the ravens; they don't store or reap, yet God feeds them. You're much more valuable. (Ravens: a type of bird) **25.** Who can add to their life by worrying? **26.** If you can't do even that, why worry about other things? **27.** Consider how lilies grow. They don't work, but Solomon wasn't dressed as beautifully as one. **28.** If God clothes the grass, which is here today and gone tomorrow, how much more will He clothe you, O little faith? (Lilies: types of flowers) **29.** Don't focus on what to eat or drink. **30.** The nations seek these things, and your Father knows you need them. **31.** Seek His kingdom, and everything else will be added to you. **32.** Don't fear, little flock; it's your Father's pleasure to give you the kingdom. **33.** Sell your possessions and give to the poor. Store treasures in heaven, where nothing can destroy them. **34.** Where your treasure is, your heart will be also. **35.** Be ready, with your lamps burning. **36.** Be like servants waiting for their master to return from a wedding banquet. **37.** Blessed are those servants who are found ready when the master returns. **38.** Even if he comes late, blessed are those servants. **39.** If the house owner knew when the thief was coming, he would have stayed awake. **40.** Be ready, for the Son of Man will come when you least expect it. **41.** Peter asked, "Lord, is this for us or for everyone?" **42.** Jesus replied, "Who is the faithful manager, whom the master puts in charge to give others their food at the proper time?" **43.** Blessed is the servant found doing so when the master returns. **44.** Truly, the master will put him in charge of everything. **45.** But if the servant thinks the master is delayed and misbehaves, **46.** the master will come unexpectedly and punish him, assigning him a place with the unbelievers. **47.** The servant who knows the master's will but doesn't follow it will be punished severely. **48.** But the one who doesn't know and does wrong will be punished less. To those given much, much will be required. **49.** I've come to bring fire on the earth; how I wish it were already burning! (Fire: metaphor for change or purification) **50.** I have a baptism to undergo, and I'm distressed until it's finished. (Baptism: a symbolic ritual of cleansing) **51.** Do you think I came to bring peace? No, I bring division. **52.** Families will be divided—three against two and two against three. **53.** Fathers against sons, mothers against daughters, mothers-in-law against daughters-in-law. **54.** Jesus said to the crowd, "When you see a cloud in the west, you say, 'Rain is coming,' and it does." **55.** And when the south wind blows, you say, 'It will be hot,' and it happens. **56.** You hypocrites! You can interpret the weather, but not the present time. (Hypocrites: those pretending to be what they are not) **57.** Why don't you judge for yourselves what is right? **58.** When you go with your adversary to court, settle on the way to avoid being thrown into prison. **59.** I tell you, you won't leave until you've paid every last penny. (Adversary: opponent in a legal case)

Chapter 13

1. Some told Jesus about the Galileans blood Pilate mixed with their sacrifices. (Pilate: Roman governor) **2.** Jesus asked, "Do you think these whose Galileans were worse sinners because they suffered like this?" **3.** No, unless you repent, you will all perish in the same way. (Repent: feel remorse for one's wrongdoings, Perish: die) **4.** Or those killed when the tower of Siloam fell on them, do you think they were worse sinners than others in Jerusalem? (Siloam: a pool in Jerusalem) **5.** No, but unless you repent, you will perish too. **6.** Jesus told them this parable: A man planted a fig tree in his vineyard, but it bore no fruit. (Parable: a story with a lesson) **7.** He said to the gardener, "For three years I've sought fruit from this tree but found none. Why waste the ground? Cut it down." (Gardener: someone who tends a garden) **8.** The gardener replied, "Let it stay another year. I will dig around it and fertilize it." (Fertilize: add nutrients to soil) **9.** "If it bears fruit, great! If not, cut it down." **10.** Jesus taught in a synagogue on the Sabbath. (Synagogues: places of Jewish worship, Sabbath: a day of rest) **11.** A woman crippled for eighteen years was there, bent over and unable to stand. (Crippled: physically disabled) **12.** Jesus called her forward and said, "Woman, you are set free from your infirmity." (Infirmity: sickness) **13.** He laid His hands on her, and she immediately stood straight and praised God. **14.** The synagogue leader was upset because Jesus healed on the Sabbath, telling the people, "Come to be healed on the other days, not the Sabbath." (Indignant: angered) **15.** Jesus replied, "You hypocrite! Don't you untie your animals to water them on the Sabbath? (Hypocrite: one who contradicts their beliefs) **16.** Shouldn't this woman, a daughter of Abraham, be set free from Satan's bondage on the Sabbath?" (Daughter of Abraham: a Jewish woman) **17.** His critics were embarrassed, but the people rejoiced at His miracles. (Embarrassed: shamed) **18.** Jesus asked, "What is the kingdom of God like?" **19.** It is like a mustard seed, which grows into a large tree where birds can rest in its branches. (Mustard seed: a tiny seed that grows large) **20.** He asked again, "What shall I compare the kingdom of God to?" **21.** It is like yeast that a woman mixes into flour until the dough rises. (Yeast: a substance used in baking) **22.** Jesus continued traveling and teaching toward Jerusalem. **23.** Someone asked, "Lord, will only a few be saved?" **24.** Jesus said, "Make every effort to enter through the narrow door, for many will try and not succeed." (Effort: exertion of energy) **25.** When the owner locks the door, you will stand outside, pleading, "Lord, open for us!" but He will reply, "I don't know you." **26.** You will say, "We ate and drank with You, and You taught in our streets." **27.** But He will say, "I don't know you. Depart from me, you evildoers!" (Evildoers: wrongdoers) **28.** There will be weeping and gnashing of teeth when you see Abraham, Isaac, Jacob, and the prophets in God's kingdom, but you are thrown out. (Weeping: crying, Gnashing: grinding teeth) **29.** People will come from all directions and sit down in God's kingdom. **30.** The last will be first, and the first will be last. **31.** Some Pharisees warned Jesus, "Herod wants to kill You. Leave here." (Pharisees: a Jewish religious group, Herod: ruler of Galilee) **32.** Jesus replied, "Go tell that fox, 'I cast out demons and heal today and tomorrow, and I will reach my goal by the third day.'" (Fox: a sly person) **33.** I must continue today, tomorrow, and the next day—no prophet dies outside Jerusalem. **34.** Jerusalem, you who kill the prophets and stone those sent to you, how I longed to gather your children, but you refused! (Jerusalem: the capital city of Israel) **35.** Your house is left desolate, and you won't see Me again until you say, 'Blessed is He who comes in the name of the Lord.'" (Desolate: abandoned)

Chapter 14

1. Jesus went to a leading Pharisee's house on the Sabbath for a meal, and they watched him closely. (Pharisee: a member of a Jewish religious group; Sabbath: day of rest) **2.** A man with dropsy (swelling due to fluid buildup) was there. (Dropsy: swelling from fluid retention) **3.** Jesus asked the Pharisees and lawyers, "Is it lawful to heal on the Sabbath?" (Lawyers: experts in Jewish law) **4.** They didn't answer, so Jesus healed the man and let him go. **5.** He then asked them, "If your donkey or ox falls into a pit on the Sabbath, wouldn't you pull it out immediately?" (Donkey: a small animal; ox: a work animal) **6.** They couldn't respond. **7.** He spoke a parable to those invited, noticing they chose the best seats, saying, (Parable: a simple story with a moral) **8.** "Don't sit in the highest seat at a wedding, in case someone more honored arrives." (Wedding: a ceremony where two are united) **9.** "The host might ask you to move, and you would be embarrassed." (Embarrassed: feeling self-conscious or ashamed) **10.** "Instead, sit in the lowest seat. Then the host may invite you to move up, and you'll be honored." (Host: the one who invites and hosts guests) **11.** "Whoever exalts himself will be humbled, but the humble will be exalted." (Exalts: raises in status; humbled: lowered in status) **12.** Jesus said to the host, "Don't invite your friends or rich neighbors to a feast, lest they repay you." (Feast: a large meal or celebration) **13.** "Invite the poor, the crippled, the blind, and the lame." (Crippled: unable to walk properly; lame: unable to walk due to injury) **14.** "You'll be blessed because they cannot repay you, but you'll be rewarded at the resurrection of the righteous." (Blessed: favored by God; resurrection: rising from the dead) **15.** One man at the table said, "Blessed is the one who will feast in God's kingdom." (Kingdom of God: God's rule on Earth) **16.** Jesus replied, "A man prepared a great feast and invited many." **17.** "When it was time, he sent his servant to tell them, 'Come, everything is ready.'" (Servant: one who serves) **18.** They all made excuses. One said, "I bought a field and must inspect it." (Field: land area) **19.** Another said, "I bought five yoke of oxen and need to test them." (Yoke: a wooden bar connecting oxen) **20.** Another said, "I married a wife and can't come." (Wife: a woman married to a man) **21.** The servant told the master, who became angry and said, "Go to the streets and bring in the poor, the crippled, the blind, and the lame." (Master: the one in charge) **22.** The servant said, "I've done as you asked, but there's still room." **23.** The master told him, "Go to the highways and compel people to come, so my house may be filled." (Highways: main roads; compel: strongly urge) **24.** "None of those invited will taste my feast." **25.** Large crowds followed Jesus, and he said, (Crowds: large groups of people) **26.** "If anyone comes to me and doesn't hate his family and even his own life, he can't be my disciple." (Disciple: a follower or student) **27.** "Anyone who doesn't carry his cross and follow me can't be my disciple." (Cross: the structure Jesus was crucified on; carry his cross: endure the challenges of following Jesus) **28.** "If you want to build a tower, don't you first calculate the cost to see if you can finish it?" (Tower: a tall building) **29.** "Otherwise, people will mock you when you can't finish." (Mock: make fun of) **30.** "They will say, 'He started building but couldn't finish.'" **31.** "What king, going to war, doesn't first assess if he can face a larger army?" (King: a ruler; war: armed conflict) **32.** "If not, he'll send a messenger to ask for peace." (Messenger: one who delivers messages) **33.** "Similarly, anyone who doesn't give up everything cannot be my disciple." (Give up: surrender) **34.** "Salt is good, but if it loses its flavor, how can it be restored?" (Salt: a mineral used to season food) **35.** "It's useless for soil or manure; it's thrown away. Whoever has ears, let them listen." (Manure: animal waste used for fertilizer)

Chapter 15

1. Tax collectors and sinners gathered around Jesus to hear Him. **2.** The Pharisees and experts in the law grumbled, "This man associates with sinners and eats with them." (Grumbled: complained or muttered) **3.** Jesus told them a story: **4.** "Suppose you have 100 sheep, and one gets lost. Wouldn't you leave the 99 to search for the lost one until you find it?" **5.** "And when you do, you joyfully carry it back." (Joyfully: with great happiness) **6.** "When you get home, you call your friends and neighbors, saying, 'Rejoice with me, for I've found my lost sheep.'" (Rejoice: celebrate joyfully) **7.** "In the same way, there's more joy in heaven over one sinner who repents than over 99 righteous people who need no repentance." (Repents: turns away from sin and seeks forgiveness, Righteous: morally right) **8.** "Or, if a woman has 10 silver coins and loses one, wouldn't she light a lamp, sweep the house, and search carefully until she finds it?" (Carefully: with attention and caution) **9.** "And when she does, she calls her friends and neighbors, saying, 'Rejoice with me, for I've found my lost coin.'" **10.** "Similarly, there is joy in heaven over one sinner who turns back to God." (Sinner: someone who commits immoral acts) **11.** Jesus continued, "A man had two sons." **12.** "The younger asked for his inheritance, and the father divided his wealth between them." (Inheritance: property or money passed down after a person's death, Wealth: possessions or money) **13.** "The younger son went to a far country and wasted his money on reckless living." (Reckless: careless or irresponsible) **14.** "When a famine hit, he became desperate." (Famine: a severe shortage of food, Desperate: feeling hopeless and in urgent need) **15.** "He hired himself to a man who sent him to feed pigs." (Hired: employed, Pigs: domesticated animals raised for food) **16.** "He was so hungry he longed to eat the pigs' food, but no one gave him anything." (Longed: desired deeply) **17.** "Then he realized his mistake and said, 'My father's servants have more than enough to eat, and I'm starving!'" (Realized: became aware of, Starving: dying from hunger) **18.** "I'll go back and tell my father, 'I've sinned against heaven and you.'" (Sinned: did something wrong or immoral) **19.** "I'm not worthy to be called your son. Treat me as one of your servants.'" (Worthy: deserving of, Servants: workers employed by someone) **20.** So he returned to his father. When the father saw him from afar, he ran to him, embraced him, and kissed him. (Embraced: held closely, Afar: from a distance) **21.** The son said, "I've sinned against heaven and you. I'm not worthy to be your son." **22.** But the father said to his servants, "Quick, bring the best robe, a ring for his finger, and sandals for his feet." (Robe: a long, loose garment, Sandals: footwear) **23.** "Prepare the fattened calf for a feast. Let's celebrate!" (Fattened calf: a young cow raised for eating, Feast: a large meal) **24.** "This son of mine was lost and is now found." So they began to celebrate. (Lost: spiritually separated from God) **25.** Meanwhile, the older son was in the field. When he came near the house, he heard music and dancing. **26.** He asked a servant what was happening. **27.** "Your brother has returned," the servant said, "and your father has killed the fattened calf because he's back safe and sound." (Safe and sound: unharmed and well) **28.** The older brother became angry and refused to join the celebration. (Refused: declined or rejected) **29.** His father came out and pleaded with him. (Pleaded: asked earnestly) **30.** He replied, "I've worked for you all these years and never disobeyed you. Yet you never gave me even a young goat to celebrate with my friends. But when this son of yours wasted your money, you killed the fattened calf for him!" (Disobeyed: did not follow instructions, Squandered: wasted carelessly) **31.** "Son," the father replied, "you are always with me, and everything I have is yours." **32.** "But we had to celebrate because this brother of yours was lost and is now found, was dead and is alive again." (Dead: spiritually separated from God, Alive again: restored to life)

Chapter 16

1. Jesus told his disciples a story about a rich man with a steward who was accused of mismanaging his wealth. (Steward: a manager of property) **2.** The rich man asked the steward to explain, saying, "Give an account of your management; you can no longer be my steward." (Stewardship: managing someone else's property) **3.** The steward thought, "What will I do? My job is being taken from me, and I can't work in the fields or beg." **4.** He decided to act so that after losing his job, people would take him in. **5.** He called his master's debtors and asked the first, "How much do you owe?" **6.** "A hundred measures of oil," he replied. The steward said, "Quickly write fifty." **7.** He asked another, "How much do you owe?" The man answered, "A hundred measures of wheat." "Write eighty," said the steward. **8.** The master praised the dishonest steward for his cleverness. People of this world often act wiser than the faithful. **9.** I tell you, use wealth to make friends, so when it is gone, they will welcome you into eternal homes. (Mammon: worldly wealth) **10.** If you are faithful in small things, you will be faithful in greater matters; if dishonest in little, you will be dishonest in much. **11.** If you can't be trusted with worldly wealth, who will trust you with true riches? **12.** If you're unfaithful with another's property, who will give you your own? **13.** A servant can't serve two masters—he will either hate one or love the other. You can't serve both God and money. (Masters: those in control, Mammon: wealth) **14.** The Pharisees, who loved money, sneered at Jesus. (Pharisees: a religious group) **15.** He said, "You justify yourselves before people, but God knows your hearts. What men value highly is detestable to God." **16.** The law and prophets lasted until John; since then, the good news of God's kingdom is preached, and everyone tries to enter it. **17.** It's easier for heaven and earth to pass away than for one small part of the law to fail. (Void: ineffective) **18.** Anyone who divorces his wife and marries another commits adultery, and the one who marries a divorced woman also commits adultery. **19.** A rich man lived in luxury every day, dressed in purple and fine linen. (Luxury: extravagant living) **20.** At his gate lay a beggar named Lazarus, covered with sores. (Sores: painful skin wounds) **21.** Lazarus longed for scraps from the rich man's table, and even dogs licked his sores. **22.** The beggar died and was carried to Abraham's side. The rich man also died and was buried. (Abraham's side: a place of comfort) **23.** In hell, the rich man saw Abraham far off with Lazarus beside him. **24.** He cried, "Father Abraham, have mercy! Send Lazarus to cool my tongue, for I am in torment in this fire." **25.** Abraham replied, "You enjoyed good things in life, while Lazarus suffered. Now he is comforted, and you are in torment." **26.** There is a great divide between us; no one can cross from here to there or vice versa. (Chasm: a large gap) **27.** The rich man begged, "Send Lazarus to warn my five brothers." **28.** "Let him warn them, so they don't end up here in torment." **29.** Abraham answered, "They have Moses and the prophets—let them listen to them." (Moses and the prophets: the Jewish scriptures) **30.** The rich man said, "If someone rises from the dead, they will repent." **31.** Abraham said, "If they don't listen to Moses and the prophets, they won't be convinced even if someone rises from the dead."

Chapter 17

1. Jesus told His disciples, "Offenses will come, but woe to the one through whom they come!" (Offenses: wrongdoings) **2.** "It's better for him if a millstone were tied around his neck and he were thrown into the sea than to cause one of these little ones to stumble." (Millstone: a heavy grinding stone) **3.** "Be careful. If your brother sins, rebuke him; and if he repents, forgive him." (Repents: regrets his actions) **4.** "Even if he sins against you seven times in a day, forgive him when he repents." (Repents: asks for forgiveness) **5.** The apostles said, "Increase our faith." (Increase: strengthen) **6.** Jesus replied, "If you had faith like a mustard seed, you could uproot a sycamore tree and plant it in the sea." (Mustard seed: a tiny seed; Sycamore tree: a tree type) **7.** "Which of you would tell a servant who's worked in the field to sit down to eat right away?" (Servant: a person working for another) **8.** "Instead, would you not say, 'Prepare my meal, serve me, and afterward you may eat and drink'?" (Prepare: get ready) **9.** "Does the master thank the servant for doing what was required? I think not." (Required: expected duties) **10.** "Similarly, when you have done all you were commanded, say, 'We are unworthy servants, only doing our duty.'" (Duty: responsibility) **11.** As He was on His way to Jerusalem, He passed through Samaria and Galilee. (Jerusalem: a city; Samaria: a region) **12.** In a village, ten men with leprosy met Him from a distance. (Leprosy: a skin disease) **13.** They cried, "Jesus, Master, have mercy on us." (Mercy: compassion) **14.** He told them, "Go to the priests." As they went, they were healed. (Priests: religious leaders) **15.** One of them, seeing he was healed, returned, praising God. **16.** He fell at Jesus' feet and thanked Him; he was a Samaritan. (Samaritan: from Samaria) **17.** Jesus asked, "Weren't all ten healed? Where are the other nine?" **18.** "Only this foreigner returned to give glory to God." (Foreigner: someone from outside Israel) **19.** He said, "Rise and go; your faith has healed you." (Healed: restored to health) **20.** The Pharisees asked when the kingdom of God would come. Jesus answered, "The kingdom of God doesn't come with visible signs." (Pharisees: Jewish leaders) **21.** "You won't be able to say, 'Here it is!' because the kingdom of God is within you." (Kingdom of God: God's reign) **22.** He told His disciples, "The time will come when you will long to see the days of the Son of Man but won't be able to." (Son of Man: Jesus' title) **23.** "They'll say, 'Look here!' or 'Look there!' but don't follow them." **24.** "For the Son of Man's coming will be like lightning flashing across the sky." (Lightning: a flash of light) **25.** "But first, He must suffer many things and be rejected by this generation." (Suffer: endure pain) **26.** "Just as in Noah's days, so will it be when the Son of Man comes." (Noah: a biblical figure) **27.** "They ate, drank, married, and gave in marriage until Noah entered the ark, and the flood destroyed them." (Ark: a large boat) **28.** "Similarly, in Lot's days, they ate, drank, bought, sold, and built." (Lot: another biblical figure) **29.** "But when Lot left Sodom, fire and sulfur rained down and destroyed them." (Sodom: a city destroyed by God) **30.** "It will be the same when the Son of Man is revealed." (Revealed: made known) **31.** "On that day, those on the roof or in the field should not go back for their things." (Roof: top of a house) **32.** "Remember Lot's wife." (Lot's wife: turned to salt when she looked back) **33.** "Whoever tries to save their life will lose it, but whoever loses their life for Me will save it." (Save: protect) **34.** "That night, two will be in one bed; one will be taken and the other left." **35.** "Two women will be grinding grain together; one will be taken and the other left." (Grinding: crushing grains) **36.** "Two men will be in the field; one will be taken and the other left." (Field: farming area) **37.** They asked, "Where, Lord?" He replied, "Where the body is, the eagles will gather." (Eagles: large birds of prey)

Chapter 18

1. Jesus shared a story to teach that people should always pray without giving up. (faint: lose courage) **2.** In a city, there was a judge who neither feared God nor respected people. **3.** A widow in that city repeatedly asked him, "Grant me justice against my enemy." (widow: a woman whose husband has died) **4.** For a time, the judge ignored her but later thought, "Even though I don't fear God or care for people, **5.** I'll help her because her persistence is wearing me out." (troubleth: bothers; weary: tire out) **6.** Jesus said, "Listen to the unjust judge. **7.** If such a man grants justice, won't God quickly help His chosen ones who cry to Him day and night? **8.** He will act promptly, but when the Son of Man comes, will He find faith on earth?" (Son of Man: Jesus) **9.** To those confident in their own righteousness and who despised others, Jesus told this: (righteousness: moral virtue) **10.** "Two men went to pray at the temple—one a Pharisee, the other a tax collector." (Pharisee: religious leader) **11.** The Pharisee prayed, 'God, thank You that I'm not like other sinners or even this tax collector. **12.** I fast twice weekly and give a tenth of my income.' (tithes: religious offerings) **13.** But the tax collector stood far off, wouldn't look up, and prayed, 'God, have mercy on me, a sinner.' (afar: far away) **14.** Jesus said, "This man was made right with God, unlike the other. Those who exalt themselves will be humbled, and the humble will be lifted." **15.** Parents brought children to Jesus for a blessing, but the disciples tried to stop them. (rebuked: corrected harshly) **16.** Jesus said, "Let the children come to me, for God's kingdom belongs to such as these. **17.** Anyone who doesn't receive it like a child will never enter." **18.** A ruler asked, "Good Teacher, what must I do to inherit eternal life?" (ruler: local leader) **19.** Jesus replied, "Why call me good? Only God is good. **20.** You know the commandments: don't commit adultery, murder, steal, lie, or dishonor your parents." **21.** The ruler said, "I've followed these since my youth." **22.** Jesus replied, "You still lack one thing: sell your possessions, give to the poor, and follow me." **23.** The man left sorrowful because he was very rich. **24.** Jesus said, "It's hard for the wealthy to enter God's kingdom. **25.** A camel passing through a needle's eye is easier than a rich person entering heaven." **26.** The listeners asked, "Who can be saved?" **27.** Jesus said, "What's impossible for humans is possible with God." **28.** Peter said, "We've left everything to follow You." **29.** Jesus replied, "Anyone who sacrifices for God's kingdom **30.** will receive much more now and eternal life later." **31.** He told the disciples, "We're heading to Jerusalem, where all prophecies about the Son of Man will be fulfilled." (Jerusalem: holy city of Israel) **32.** "He'll be handed to Gentiles, mocked, insulted, and spat on." (Gentiles: non-Jews) **33.** "They'll whip Him, kill Him, and on the third day, He'll rise again." **34.** The disciples didn't understand; the meaning was hidden from them. **35.** Near Jericho, a blind man was begging by the roadside. (Jericho: ancient city in Palestine) **36.** Hearing a crowd, he asked what was happening. **37.** They told him, "Jesus of Nazareth is passing by." (Nazareth: Jesus' hometown) **38.** He shouted, "Jesus, Son of David, have mercy on me!" (Son of David: descendant of King David) **39.** Though people tried to silence him, he cried louder, "Son of David, have mercy on me!" **40.** Jesus stopped and asked for the man to be brought to Him. **41.** He asked, "What do you want me to do?" The man replied, "Lord, I want to see." (sight: vision) **42.** Jesus said, "Receive your sight; your faith has healed you." **43.** Instantly, the man could see and followed Jesus, praising God. Everyone who witnessed it glorified God.

Chapter 19

1. Jesus entered and passed through Jericho. (Jericho: an ancient city in Israel) **2.** A man named Zacchaeus, the chief tax collector, was rich. **3.** He wanted to see Jesus but couldn't because of the crowd, as he was short. (Stature: height) **4.** He climbed a sycamore tree to see Him, for Jesus was passing that way. (Sycamore tree: a broad-leaved tree) **5.** When Jesus came to the place, He looked up and said, "Zacchaeus, hurry down; I must stay at your house today." **6.** Zacchaeus quickly came down and received Him joyfully. **7.** The people murmured, saying, "He's gone to stay with a sinner." **8.** Zacchaeus stood up and said, "Lord, I'll give half of my wealth to the poor, and repay four times any wrongs." **9.** Jesus said, "Salvation has come to this house, for he is a son of Abraham." (Abraham: a key biblical patriarch) **10.** The Son of Man came to seek and save the lost. (Son of Man: a title for Jesus) **11.** As they heard this, He told them a parable, because He was near Jerusalem and they thought the kingdom of God would appear immediately. (Parable: a moral story) **12.** He said, "A nobleman went to a far country to receive a kingdom and return." (Nobleman: a high-ranking person) **13.** He gave ten servants a mina each and told them to do business until He returned. **14.** His citizens hated him and sent a message saying, "We do not want him as king." **15.** Upon His return, He called the servants to see what they had gained. **16.** The first servant said, "Your mina has earned ten more." **17.** "Well done!" the master said. "Because you've been faithful in a little, you will rule over ten cities." (Cities: urban areas) **18.** The second servant said, "Your mina has earned five more." **19.** The master replied, "You will rule over five cities." **20.** Another servant said, "Here is your mina, which I kept hidden." **21.** "I was afraid of you, for you are a harsh man," he explained. (Harsh: severe) **22.** The master said, "I will judge you by your words. You knew I am strict, so why didn't you at least put my money in the bank?" **23.** He ordered, "Take the mina from him and give it to the one with ten." **24.** The others protested, "But he already has ten!" **25.** The master replied, "Everyone who has will be given more, but from those who have nothing, even what they have will be taken away." **26.** "As for my enemies who didn't want me to rule over them, bring them here and kill them." (Reign: rule) **27.** After saying this, He went up to

Jerusalem. (Jerusalem: a major city in Israel) **28.** Near Bethphage and Bethany, at the Mount of Olives, He sent two disciples ahead. (Mount of Olives: a hill near Jerusalem) **29.** "Go to the village ahead; you'll find a colt tied there. Untie it and bring it to me." **30.** "If anyone asks why you're untying it, tell them, 'The Lord needs it.'" **31.** The disciples found everything as Jesus had said. **32.** As they untied the colt, the owners asked, "Why are you untying it?" **33.** They replied, "The Lord needs it." **34.** They brought the colt to Jesus, placed their cloaks on it, and set Jesus on it. (Cloaks: outer garments) **35.** As Jesus rode along, people spread their cloaks on the road. **36.** When He neared the descent of the Mount of Olives, His disciples began praising God loudly for all the miracles they had seen. **37.** They shouted, "Blessed is the King who comes in the name of the Lord! Peace in heaven and glory in the highest!" (King: ruler of a kingdom) **38.** Some Pharisees in the crowd said, "Teacher, rebuke your disciples!" **39.** He replied, "If they were silent, the stones would cry out." (Stones: rocks) **40.** As He neared Jerusalem, He wept over the city, **41.** saying, "If only you had known what would bring you peace today, but now it's hidden from your eyes." (Peace: tranquility) **42.** "The days will come when your enemies will surround you, destroy you, and leave no stone on another." **43.** "Because you did not recognize the time of God's coming to you." **44.** He entered the temple and began driving out those who were selling. (Temple: a sacred place) **45.** He said, "It's written, 'My house will be a house of prayer,' but you've made it a den of thieves." (Thieves: robbers) **46.** He taught daily in the temple, but the chief priests and leaders tried to kill Him. (Chief priests: high-ranking religious leaders) **47.** They couldn't figure out how to do it, for all the people were eagerly listening to Him. (Eagerly: with great interest) **48.** Every day He taught in the temple, but at night He went out to stay at the mount called the Mount of Olives. (Mount of Olives: a hill near Jerusalem)

Chapter 20
1. One day, as Jesus taught in the temple and preached, the chief priests, scribes, and elders approached him. (Temple: a sacred place of worship) **2.** They asked, "By whose authority are you doing these things? Who gave you this authority?" **3.** Jesus replied, "I'll ask you one question; answer me first: **4.** Was John's baptism from heaven or from men?" (Baptism: a religious ritual) **5.** They reasoned, "If we say, 'From heaven,' he'll ask why we didn't believe him." **6.** "If we say, 'From men,' the people will stone us, for they believe John was a prophet." **7.** They replied, "We don't know." **8.** Jesus said, "Neither will I tell you by what authority I do these things." **9.** Then Jesus told a parable: "A man planted a vineyard, rented it to farmers, and went away for a long time." **10.** "At harvest time, he sent a servant to collect fruit, but they beat him and sent him away empty." **11.** "He sent another servant, but they treated him the same and sent him away empty." **12.** "He sent a third, but they wounded him and threw him out." **13.** "The owner said, 'I will send my beloved son; surely they will respect him.'" **14.** "But when they saw the son, they said, 'Let's kill him and take his inheritance.'" **15.** "So, they threw him out of the vineyard and killed him. What will the owner do to them?" **16.** "He will destroy those farmers and give the vineyard to others." The people said, "God forbid!" **17.** Jesus said, "What does this mean: 'The stone the builders rejected has become the cornerstone?'" (Cornerstone: a key stone in the foundation of a building) **18.** "Anyone who falls on this stone will be broken, and anyone on whom it falls will be crushed." **19.** The chief priests and scribes wanted to arrest him, but they feared the people who knew he spoke against them. **20.** They sent spies pretending to be honest men, to trap him in his words and hand him over to the governor. (Governor: a ruler of a province) **21.** They asked, "Teacher, we know you speak the truth and teach the way of God, without favoritism. Is it lawful to pay taxes to Caesar?" (Caesar: title of Roman emperors) **22.** Jesus saw through their trickery and replied, "Why do you test me?" **23.** "Show me a coin. Whose image and inscription are on it?" They said, "Caesar's." **24.** "Give to Caesar what is Caesar's, and to God what is God's." **25.** They were amazed and couldn't trap him in front of the people. **26.** Some Sadducees, who deny the resurrection, came to him with a question. (Sadducees: a Jewish sect denying the resurrection) **27.** They asked, "Moses wrote that if a man's brother dies childless, his brother should marry the widow and raise offspring for him." **28.** "There were seven brothers. The first married and died without children. The second did the same, and the third also, until all seven had married her and died." **29.** "Finally, the woman died. In the resurrection, whose wife will she be, since all seven had her?" **30.** Jesus answered, "People of this age marry, but those worthy of the resurrection neither marry nor are given in marriage." **31.** "They cannot die anymore, as they are like angels and children of God." **32.** "Moses showed that the dead are raised when he calls God the God of Abraham, Isaac, and Jacob." (Bush: the burning bush where Moses encountered God) **33.** "God is not the God of the dead, but of the living, for all live to him." **34.** Some scribes agreed, "Teacher, you've answered well." **35.** They dared not ask him any further questions. **36.** He then asked, "Why do they say the Christ is David's son?" (David: the second king of Israel) **37.** David himself says, 'The Lord said to my Lord, Sit at my right hand, **38.** until I make your enemies a footstool for your feet.'" (Psalms: a book in the Bible with songs and prayers) **39.** "If David calls him Lord, how can he be his son?" **40.** Then, in front of the crowd, Jesus warned his disciples, **41.** "Beware of the scribes, who like to walk in long robes, seek respect in the marketplaces, and want the best seats at feasts." **42.** "They devour widows' homes and make long prayers for show. They will receive a greater judgment." **43.** Jesus sat near the offering box and watched how people gave. Many rich people gave large amounts, **44.** but a poor widow came and put in two small coins. **45.** Jesus said, "This poor widow has put in more than all the others, **46.** for they gave out of their wealth, but she gave out of her poverty, all she had to live on." **47.** As some spoke about the temple, how it was adorned with beautiful stones and gifts, Jesus said, "The time will come when everything here will be destroyed, not one stone will be left on another."

Chapter 21
1. He looked up and saw rich people putting their gifts into the treasury. **2.** He also saw a poor widow putting in two small coins. (Mites: small coins) **3.** He said, "Truly, this poor widow has given more than all others." **4.** The rich gave from their excess, but she gave everything she had to live on. (Excess: abundance or surplus) **5.** As people admired the temple's beautiful stones and gifts, he said, **6.** "The days will come when not one stone will remain; all will be destroyed." (Temple: a holy building) **7.** They asked him, "When will this happen, and what sign will show it's near?" **8.** He warned, "Do not be deceived; many will claim to be the Christ, saying the end is near. Do not follow them." (Deceived: tricked or misled) **9.** "When you hear of wars and uprisings, don't panic; these things must happen first, but the end is not yet." (Uprisings: rebellions or revolts) **10.** "Nation will rise against nation, and kingdom against kingdom. **11.** There will be earthquakes, famines, and signs from heaven." (Famines: widespread hunger) **12.** "Before all this, you will be seized, persecuted, and brought before rulers and kings for my name's sake." (Persecuted: mistreated for belief) **13.** "This will serve as an opportunity for you to testify." (Testify: give evidence or show proof) **14.** "Do not worry about what to say; **15.** I will give you wisdom and words that no one can resist or contradict." (Adversaries: enemies) **16.** "You will be betrayed by family and friends, and some of you will be killed." (Betrayed: deceived by trusted ones) **17.** "You will be hated by all because of my name." **18.** "But not a single hair of your head will be harmed." (Perish: destroyed or harmed) **19.** "By your endurance, you will keep your lives." (Endurance: ability to bear hardship) **20.** "When you see Jerusalem surrounded by armies, know its destruction is near." (Jerusalem: the capital of Israel) **21.** "Those in Judea should flee to the mountains, and those in the city should leave." (Judea: a region of Israel) **22.** "These are the days of vengeance, to fulfill all that is written." (Vengeance: retribution) **23.** "Woe to those who are pregnant or nursing, for there will be great distress and wrath upon this people." (Distress: great trouble or suffering) **24.** "They will fall by the sword and be taken as captives, and Jerusalem will be trampled by the Gentiles until their time is fulfilled." (Sword: weapon for fighting; Gentiles: non-Jews) **25.** "There will be signs in the sun, moon, and stars, and on the earth, nations will be in turmoil, with the sea and waves roaring." (Anguish: suffering) **26.** "People will be terrified, seeing what's coming, as the powers of heaven will be shaken." (Apprehensive: fearful) **27.** "Then, they will see the Son of Man coming in a cloud with power and glory." (Son of Man: title for Jesus) **28.** "When these things begin to happen, stand tall and look up, for your redemption is near." (Redemption: being saved) **29.** He told them, "Look at the fig tree and all the trees." (Fig tree: a fruit-bearing tree) **30.** "When they begin to bud, you know summer is near." (Sprout: start growing) **31.** "In the same way, when you see these signs, know the kingdom of God is near." (Kingdom of God: God's rule) **32.** "Truly, this generation will not pass until all is fulfilled." (Generation: people born at the same time) **33.** "Heaven and earth will pass away, but my words will remain forever." **34.** "Be on guard, so your hearts aren't weighed down by excess, drunkenness, and life's worries, and that day doesn't surprise you." (Carousing: excessive partying) **35.** "It will come upon all who live on earth." **36.** "Be alert, praying that you can escape these events and stand before the Son of Man." **37.** During the day, he taught in the temple, and at night, he went to the Mount of Olives. (Mount of Olives: a hill near Jerusalem) **38.** The people came early in the morning to hear him teach in the temple.

Chapter 22
1. The Feast of Unleavened Bread, also called Passover, was near. (Passover: Jewish holiday marking Exodus) **2.** The chief priests and scribes sought a way to kill Jesus, fearing the people. (Scribes: Jewish law experts) **3.** Satan entered Judas Iscariot, one of the twelve disciples. (Iscariot: surname of Judas) **4.**

Judas went to the chief priests and temple officers to arrange betraying Jesus. (Temple officers: in charge of the temple security) **5.** They were glad and agreed to give him money. **6.** Judas agreed and waited for the right time to betray Jesus without the crowds. **7.** The day of Unleavened Bread arrived, and the Passover lamb had to be sacrificed. **8.** Jesus sent Peter and John, saying, "Go prepare the Passover meal for us." **9.** They asked, "Where should we prepare it?" **10.** He answered, "In the city, you will meet a man carrying water. Follow him to the house he enters." **11.** Tell the owner, 'Where is the room where I can eat the Passover with My disciples?' **12.** He will show you a large, furnished room; prepare there." **13.** They found everything as He had told them and prepared the meal. **14.** At the appointed time, Jesus sat with the twelve apostles. **15.** "I have eagerly desired to share this Passover with you before I suffer," He said. **16.** "I will not eat it again until it is fulfilled in the kingdom of God." **17.** He took the cup, gave thanks, and said, "Share this among yourselves." **18.** "I will not drink from the vine again until God's kingdom comes." **19.** He took the bread, broke it, and said, "This is My body, given for you. Do this in remembrance of Me." **20.** After supper, He took the cup again, saying, "This is the new covenant in My blood, shed for you." **21.** "But the one who betrays Me is at the table with Me." **22.** "The Son of Man will go as planned, but woe to the one who betrays Him!" **23.** They questioned who among them would do it. **24.** A dispute broke out over who was the greatest. **25.** Jesus told them, "Gentile kings lord it over their people, but you should serve one another." (Gentiles: non-Jews) **26.** "The greatest among you should be like the a prisoner known for sedition and murder.) **20.** Pilate, wanting to release Jesus, spoke to them again. **21.** But they cried, "Crucify him!" **22.** Pilate asked, "What has he done wrong? I find no reason for his death. I will punish him and release him." **23.** But they insisted with loud voices, demanding his crucifixion. **24.** Pilate gave in and sentenced Jesus as they wished. **25.** He released Barabbas but handed Jesus over to be crucified. **26.** As they led him away, they seized Simon, a Cyrenian, to carry the cross behind Jesus. (Cyrenian: from Cyrene in North Africa) **27.** A large crowd followed, including women who mourned for him. **28.** Jesus turned and said, "Daughters of Jerusalem, do not weep for me, but for yourselves and your children." **29.** "The days are coming when people will say, 'Blessed are the barren and those who never bore children.'" **30.** "Then they will say to the mountains, 'Fall on us,' and to the hills, 'Cover us.'" **31.** "If they do this to a green tree, what will happen to the dry?" **32.** Two other criminals were led with him to be executed. **33.** When they arrived at Calvary, they crucified him, with the criminals on his right and left. (Calvary: the hill where Jesus was crucified) **34.** Jesus said, "Father, forgive them, for they do not know what they do." They divided his clothes and cast lots. **35.** The people stood watching, and the rulers mocked him, saying, "He saved others; let him save himself if he is the Christ." **36.** The soldiers also mocked him, offering him vinegar, **37.** saying, "If you are the King of the Jews, save yourself." **38.** Above him was a sign written in Greek, Latin, and Hebrew: "THIS IS THE KING OF THE JEWS." **39.** One of the criminals insulted him, "If you are the Christ, save yourself and us." **40.** But the other criminal rebuked him, "Don't you fear God, since you are condemned to die?" **41.** "We deserve our punishment, but this man has done nothing wrong." **42.** Then he said to Jesus, "Remember me when you come into your kingdom." **43.** Jesus replied, "Today you will be with me in paradise." **44.** At noon, darkness covered the land until three in the afternoon. **45.** The sun was darkened, and the temple curtain was torn in two. **46.** Jesus cried out loudly, "Father, into your hands I commit my spirit," and breathed his last. **47.** The centurion, seeing what happened, praised God, saying, "This was a righteous man." **48.** The crowd, witnessing all this, struck their breasts and went away. **49.** All his acquaintances, including the women who had followed from Galilee, stood at a distance, watching. (Galilee: region in northern Israel) **50.** A man named Joseph, a good and just member of the council, **51.** (Joseph, from Arimathaea, had not agreed with the council's decision and awaited God's kingdom.) **52.** He went to Pilate and asked for Jesus' body. **53.** He took it down, wrapped it in linen, and placed it in a tomb, never used before. **54.** It was the day of preparation, and the Sabbath was approaching. **55.** The women who had followed Jesus from Galilee saw the tomb and how Jesus' body was laid. **56.** They went home to prepare spices and ointments and rested on the Sabbath according to the commandment.

Chapter 24

1. Early on the first day of the week, the women came to the tomb with spices they had prepared. (Tomb: burial place) **2.** They found the stone rolled away from the tomb. (Stone: large rock blocking the tomb) **3.** They entered and found no body of Jesus. **4.** They were puzzled, and two men in shining clothes appeared. (Puzzled: confused) **5.** As they were afraid and bowed, the men said, "Why seek the living among the dead?" (Living: alive) **6.** "He is not here, but has risen. Remember what He said in Galilee, **7.** 'The Son of Man must be handed over, crucified, and rise on the third day.'" **8.** Then they remembered His words. **9.** They returned from the tomb and told the eleven and others. (Eleven: the remaining disciples) **10.** It was Mary Magdalene, Joanna, Mary the mother of James, and other women who told the apostles. **11.** The apostles thought their words were nonsense and didn't believe them. (Nonsense: untrue or foolish) **12.** Peter ran to the tomb, saw the linen cloths, and left, amazed at what had happened. **13.** That same day, two disciples were going to Emmaus, about seven miles from Jerusalem. (Emmaus: a village near Jerusalem) **14.** They were discussing all that had happened. **15.** As they talked, Jesus Himself came and walked with them. **16.** But they were kept from recognizing Him. **17.** He asked, "What are you discussing as you walk, and why are you sad?" **18.** One of them, named Cleopas, asked, "Are you the only visitor in Jerusalem who doesn't know what happened?" (Cleopas: a disciple) **19.** Jesus replied, "What happened?" They said, "Concerning Jesus of Nazareth, a prophet powerful in word and deed, **20.** who was handed over to be condemned and crucified." (Nazareth: Jesus' hometown) **21.** "We had hoped He would redeem Israel. It's been three days since this happened." **22.** "Some women of our group amazed us. They went to the tomb early **23.** and found it empty, but also saw angels who said He was alive." **24.** "Some of our companions went to the tomb and found it as the women said, but they didn't see Him." **25.** Jesus said, "How foolish you are, and slow to believe what the prophets have said. **26.** Didn't Christ have to suffer and enter His glory?" (Glory: great honor or power) **27.** Beginning with Moses and the prophets, He explained the scriptures concerning Himself. (Moses: a prophet, the lawgiver) **28.** As they approached Emmaus, He acted as though He would go further. **29.** But they urged Him, "Stay with us; the day is nearly over." So He went in to stay. **30.** When He was at the table, He took bread, gave thanks, broke it, and gave it to them. (Broke: divided into pieces) **31.** Their eyes were opened, and they recognized Him, but He vanished from their sight. **32.** They said to each other, "Didn't our hearts burn within us as He spoke and explained the scriptures?" (Burn: felt strongly) **33.** They got up and returned to Jerusalem, where they found the eleven and others gathered. **34.** They said, "The Lord has risen and appeared to Simon!" **35.** Then they told how they recognized Him in the breaking of bread. **36.** While they were speaking, Jesus stood among them and said, "Peace be with you." (Peace: calm, absence of trouble) **37.** They were startled and frightened, thinking they saw a ghost. **38.** He said, "Why are you troubled? Why do doubts rise in your hearts?" (Doubts: uncertain thoughts) **39.** "Look at My hands and feet; it is I. Touch Me and see; a ghost doesn't have flesh and bones as I do." **40.** After saying this, He showed them His hands and feet. **41.** While they still did not believe because of joy and amazement, He asked, "Do you have any food?" **42.** They gave Him a piece of broiled fish and honeycomb, **43.** and He ate it in their presence. **44.** He said, "These are the words I spoke to you while I was with you, that everything written in the law of Moses, the prophets, and the Psalms must be fulfilled." (Psalms: a book of the Bible) **45.** Then He opened their minds so they could understand the scriptures. (Opened: made clear) **46.** He told them, "It is written that the Messiah will suffer and rise from the dead on the third day, **47.** and repentance and forgiveness of sins will be preached in His name to all nations, beginning in Jerusalem." (Repentance: turning away from sin) **48.** "You are witnesses of these things." **49.** "I am going to send you what My Father has promised, but stay in the city until you are clothed with power from on high." **50.** He led them out to Bethany, lifted His hands, and blessed them. (Bethany: a village near Jerusalem) **51.** While blessing them, He was taken up into heaven. (Heaven: the place where God lives) **52.** They worshiped Him and returned to Jerusalem with great joy. **53.** They stayed continually at the temple, praising God. Amen.

43 – John

Chapter 1

1. In the beginning, the Word existed, and the Word was with God, and the Word was God. **2.** He was with God in the beginning. **3.** Through Him all things were made; without Him nothing was made that has been made. **4.** In Him was life, and that life was the light of all mankind. **5.** The light shines in the darkness, and the darkness has not overcome it. **6.** There was a man sent from God, whose name was John. **7.** He came as a witness to testify concerning that light, so that through him all might believe. **8.** He himself was not the light; he came only as a witness to the light. **9.** The true light that gives light to everyone was coming into the world. **10.** He was in the world, and though the world was made through Him, the world did not recognize Him. **11.** He came to that which was His own, but His own did not receive Him. **12.** Yet to all who did receive Him, to those who believed in His name, He gave the right to become children of God— **13.** children born not of natural descent, nor of human decision or a husband's will, but born of God. **14.** The Word became flesh and made His dwelling among us. We have seen His glory, the glory of the One and Only Son, who came from the Father, full of grace and truth. **15.** John testified concerning Him. He cried out, saying, "This is the one I spoke about when I said, 'He who comes after me has surpassed me because He was before me.'" **16.** Out of His fullness we have all received grace in place of grace already given. **17.** For the law was given through Moses; grace and truth came through Jesus Christ. **18.** No one has ever seen God, but the One and Only Son, who is Himself God and is in closest relationship with the Father, has made Him known. **19.** Now this was John's testimony when the Jewish leaders in Jerusalem sent priests and Levites to ask him who he was. **20.** He did not fail to confess, but confessed freely, "I am not the Messiah." **21.** They asked him, "Then who are you? Are you Elijah?" He said, "I am not." "Are you the Prophet?" He answered, "No." **22.** Finally they said, "Who are you? Give us an answer to take back to those who sent us. What do you say about yourself?" **23.** John replied in the words of Isaiah the prophet, "I am the voice of one calling in the wilderness, 'Make straight the way for the Lord.'" (Isaiah: a major Old Testament prophet) **24.** Now the Pharisees who had been sent **25.** asked him, "Why then do you baptize if you are not the Messiah, nor Elijah, nor the Prophet?" **26.** "I baptize with water," John replied, "but among you stands one you do not know. **27.** He is the one who comes after me, the straps of whose sandals I am not worthy to untie." **28.** This all happened at Bethabara on the other side of the Jordan, where John was baptizing. (Bethabara: a place near the Jordan River) **29.** The next day John saw Jesus coming toward him and said, "Look, the Lamb of God, who takes away the sin of the world!" (Lamb of God: a title regarding Jesus as the ultimate sacrifice) **30.** This is the one I meant when I said, 'A man who comes after me has surpassed me because He was before me.' **31.** I myself did not know Him, but the reason I came baptizing with water was that He might be revealed to Israel." **32.** Then John gave this testimony: "I saw the Spirit come down from heaven as a dove and remain on Him. **33.** And I myself did not know Him, but the one who sent me to baptize with water told me, 'The man on whom you see the Spirit come down and remain is the one who will baptize with the Holy Spirit.' **34.** I have seen and I testify (justify) that this is God's Chosen One." **35.** The next day John was there again with two of his disciples. **36.** When he saw Jesus passing by, he said, "Look, the Lamb of God!" **37.** When the two disciples heard him say this, they followed Jesus. **38.** Turning around, Jesus saw them following and asked, "What do you want?" They said, "Rabbi" (which means "Teacher"), "where are You staying?" **39.** "Come," He replied, "and you will see." So they went and saw where He was staying, and they spent that day with Him. It was about the tenth hour. **40.** Andrew, Simon Peter's brother, was one of the two who heard what John had said and who had followed Jesus. (Andrew: one of Jesus' first disciples, brother of Peter) **41.** The first thing Andrew did was to find his brother Simon and tell him, "We have found the Messiah" (that is, the Christ). (Messiah: the Anointed One, or Christ) **42.** And he brought him to Jesus. Jesus looked at him and said, "You are Simon son of John. You will be called Cephas" (which, when translated, is Peter). (Cephas: the Aramaic name for Peter, meaning "rock") **43.** The next day Jesus decided to leave for Galilee. Finding Philip, He said to him, "Follow Me." **44.** Philip, like Andrew and Peter, was from the town of Bethsaida. (Bethsaida: a town on the Sea of Galilee) **45.** Philip found Nathanael and told him, "We have found the one Moses wrote about in the Law, and about whom the prophets also wrote—Jesus of Nazareth, the son of Joseph." (Nazareth: a town in Galilee) **46.** "Nazareth! Can anything good come from there?" Nathanael asked. "Come and see," said Philip. **47.** When Jesus saw Nathanael approaching, He said of him, "Here truly is an Israelite in whom there is no deceit!" (Israelite: a true descendant of Israel) **48.** "How do you know me?" Nathanael asked. Jesus replied, "I saw you while you were still under the fig tree before Philip called you." **49.** Then Nathanael declared, "Rabbi, You are the Son of God; You are the King of Israel!" **50.** Jesus replied, "You believe because I told you I saw you under the fig tree. You will see greater things than that." **51.** He then added, "Very truly I tell you, you will see 'heaven open, and the angels of God ascending and descending on' the Son of Man." (Son of Man: a title Jesus used for Himself)

Chapter 2

1. On the third day, a wedding took place in Cana, and Jesus' mother was there. (Cana: a town in Galilee) **2.** Both Jesus and His disciples were invited to the wedding. **3.** When the wine ran out, Jesus' mother told Him, "They have no wine." **4.** Jesus replied, "Woman, why is that my concern? My time has not yet come." **5.** His mother said to the servants, "Do whatever He tells you." **6.** Nearby were six stone jars used for Jewish purification rituals, each holding 20 to 30 gallons. (Purification: Jewish ritual cleansing) **7.** Jesus instructed them, "Fill the jars with water." They filled them to the top. **8.** He then said, "Draw some out and take it to the master of the feast." They did so. **9.** When the master tasted the water, now wine, he didn't know where it had come from (but the servants knew), so he called the bridegroom. **10.** He said, "Everyone serves the best wine first, and when the guests have drunk freely, the cheaper wine. But you have kept the best wine until now!" **11.** This was the first of the signs Jesus performed in Cana, revealing His glory, and His disciples believed in Him. (Signs: Miraculous acts showing divine power) **12.** After this, He went to Capernaum with His mother, brothers, and disciples, staying there only a few days. (Capernaum: a town on the Sea of Galilee) **13.** The Jewish Passover was near, and Jesus went up to Jerusalem. (Passover: Jewish festival commemorating the Exodus) **14.** In the temple, He found people selling oxen, sheep, and doves, and money changers sitting at their tables. **15.** He made a whip from cords, drove them all out of the temple, along with the animals, and poured out the money of the changers, overturning their tables. **16.** He told those selling doves, "Get these out of here! Do not make My Father's house a marketplace!" **17.** Then His disciples remembered that it is written, "Zeal for Your house will consume Me." (Zeal: intense devotion) **18.** The Jews asked Him, "What sign can You show us for doing these things?" **19.** Jesus answered, "Destroy this temple, and in three days I will raise it up." **20.** They replied, "It took forty-six years to build this temple, and will You raise it in three days?" **21.** But Jesus was speaking about the temple of His body. **22.** After He was raised from the dead, His disciples remembered that He had said this, and they believed both the Scripture and the word Jesus had spoken. **23.** While in Jerusalem during the Passover, many believed in His name when they saw the signs He performed. **24.** But Jesus did not trust them, because He knew all people, **25.** and did not need anyone to testify about mankind, for He knew what was in a person. (Testify: give witness or evidence)

Chapter 3

1. There was a Pharisee named Nicodemus, a leader of the Jewish people. (Pharisee: a religious group known for strict observance of the law) **2.** Nicodemus came to Jesus by night and said, "Rabbi, we know that You are a teacher who has come from God, for no one can perform the signs You do unless God is with Him." **3.** Jesus replied, "Very truly I tell you, no one can see the kingdom of God unless they are born again." **4.** Nicodemus asked, "How can someone be born when they are old? Can they re-enter their mother's womb and be born again?" **5.** Jesus answered, "Very truly I tell you, no one can enter the kingdom of God unless they are born of water and the Spirit. **6.** Flesh gives birth to flesh, but the Spirit gives birth to spirit. **7.** You should not be surprised at My saying, 'You must be born again.' **8.** The wind blows wherever it pleases. You hear its sound, but you cannot tell where it comes from or where it is going. So it is with everyone born of the Spirit." **9.** Nicodemus responded, "How can this be possible?" **10.** Jesus said, "You are Israel's teacher, and do you not understand these things? **11.** Very truly I tell you, we speak of what we know, and we testify to what we have seen, but you people do not accept our testimony. **12.** I have spoken to you of earthly things and you do not believe; how then will you believe if I speak of heavenly things? **13.** No one has ever gone into heaven except the one who came from heaven—the Son of Man, who is in heaven." (Son of Man: a title Jesus used for Himself) **14.** Just as Moses lifted up the serpent in the wilderness, so the Son of Man must be lifted up, **15.** that everyone who believes may have eternal life in Him. **16.** For God so loved the world that He gave His one and only Son, that whoever believes in Him shall not perish but have eternal life. **17.** For God did not send His Son into the world to condemn the world, but to save the world through Him. **18.** Whoever believes in Him is not condemned, but whoever does not believe stands condemned already because they have not believed in the name of God's one and only Son. **19.** This is the verdict: Light has come into the world, but people loved darkness instead of light because their deeds were evil. **20.** Everyone who does evil hates the light, and will not come into the light for fear that their deeds will be exposed. **21.** But whoever lives by the truth comes into the light, so that it may be seen plainly that what they have done has been done in the sight of God." **22.** After this, Jesus and His disciples went into the Judean countryside, where He spent some time with them and baptized people. (Judean countryside: the rural area surrounding Jerusalem) **23.** John was also baptizing at Aenon near Salim, because there was plenty of water, and people were coming and being baptized. (Aenon: a place near the Jordan River) **24.** John had not yet been imprisoned. **25.** An argument developed between some of John's disciples and a certain Jew over the matter of ceremonial washing. **26.** They came to John and said to him, "Rabbi, that man who was with you on the other side of the Jordan—the one you testified about—look, He is baptizing, and everyone is going to Him!" **27.** To this John replied, "A person can receive only what is given them from heaven. **28.** You yourselves can testify that I said, 'I am not the Messiah but am sent ahead of Him.' **29.** The bride belongs to the bridegroom. The friend who attends the bridegroom waits and listens for him, and is full of joy when he hears the bridegroom's voice. That joy is mine, and it is now complete. **30.** He must become greater; I must become less. **31.** The one who comes from above is above all; the one who is from the earth belongs to the earth and speaks as one from the earth. The one who comes from heaven is above all. **32.** He testifies to what He has seen and heard, but no one accepts His testimony. **33.** Whoever has accepted it has certified that God is truthful. **34.** For the one whom God has sent speaks the words of God, for God gives the Spirit without limit. **35.** The Father loves the Son and has placed everything in His hands. **36.** Whoever believes in the Son has eternal life, but whoever rejects the Son will not see life, for God's wrath remains on them."

Chapter 4
1. While Jesus learned that the Pharisees had heard He was making more disciples and baptizing more people than John, **2.** Though Jesus Himself was not baptizing, but His disciples were, **3.** He decided to leave Judea and return to Galilee. **4.** He had to pass through Samaria (an ancient region in central Palestine). **5.** So, He arrived at a Samaritan town called Sychar, near the land Jacob had given to his son Joseph. **6.** Jacob's well was there. Jesus, tired from His journey, sat down by the well. It was about noon. **7.** A Samaritan woman came to draw water, and Jesus asked her, "Please give Me a drink." **8.** His disciples had gone into the town to buy food. **9.** The woman was surprised. "You are a Jew, and I am a Samaritan woman. Why are You asking me for a drink?" (Jews did not associate with Samaritans.) **10.** Jesus answered, "If you knew the gift of God, and who it is that asks you for a drink, you would have asked Him, and He would have given you living water." (Living water: eternal life) **11.** "Sir," the woman said, "You have nothing to draw with, and the well is deep. How can You give me this living water? **12.** Are You greater than our father Jacob, who gave us this well and drank from it himself, as did his sons and his livestock?" **13.** Jesus answered, "Everyone who drinks this water will thirst again, **14.** but whoever drinks the water I give them will never thirst. Indeed, the water I give them will become in them a spring of water, welling up to eternal life." (Eternal life: everlasting joy) **15.** The woman said, "Sir, give me this water so that I won't get thirsty and have to keep coming here to draw water." **16.** Jesus told her, "Go, call your husband, and come back." **17.** She replied, "I have no husband." Jesus said to her, "You are right when you say you have no husband. **18.** In fact, you have had five husbands, and the man you now have is not your husband. What you have said is true." **19.** The woman said, "Sir, I can see that You are a prophet. **20.** Our ancestors worshiped on this mountain, but you Jews claim that the place where we must worship is in Jerusalem." (Prophet: God's messenger) **21.** Jesus replied, "Believe Me, woman, a time is coming when you will worship the Father neither on this mountain nor in Jerusalem. **22.** You Samaritans worship what you do not know; we worship what we do know, for salvation is from the Jews. **23.** Yet a time is coming and has now come when true worshipers will worship the Father in the Spirit and in truth, for they are the kind of worshipers the Father seeks. **24.** God is spirit, and His worshipers must worship in the Spirit and in truth." (Spirit and truth: sincere worship) **25.** The woman said, "I know that Messiah (called the Christ) is coming. When He comes, He will explain everything to us." **26.** Jesus declared, "I, the one speaking to you, am He." **27.** Just then, His disciples returned and were surprised to find Him talking with a woman. But no one asked, "What do You want?" or "Why are You talking with her?" **28.** Then, leaving her water jar, the woman went back to the town and said to the people, **29.** "Come, see a man who told me everything I ever did. Could this be the Messiah?" **30.** They came out of the town and made their way toward Him. **31.** Meanwhile, His disciples urged Him, "Rabbi, eat something." **32.** But He said to them, "I have food to eat that you know nothing about." **33.** Then His disciples said to each other, "Could someone have brought Him food?" **34.** Jesus said, "My food is to do the will of Him who sent Me and to finish His work. **35.** Don't you have a saying, 'It's still four months until the harvest'? I tell you, open your eyes and look at the fields! They are ripe for harvest. **36.** Even now the one who reaps draws a wage and harvests a crop for eternal life, so that the sower and the reaper may be glad together. **37.** Thus the saying 'One sows and another reaps' is true. **38.** I sent you to reap what you have not worked for. Others have done the hard work, and you have reaped the benefits of their labor." (Sowing and reaping: spreading the Gospel) **39.** Many of the Samaritans from that town believed in Him because of the woman's testimony, "He told me everything I ever did." **40.** So when the Samaritans came to Him, they urged Him to stay with them, and He stayed two days. **41.** And because of His words, many more became believers. **42.** They said to the woman, "We no longer believe just because of what you said; now we have heard for ourselves, and we know that this man really is the Savior of the world." (Savior: the Messiah) **43.** After the two days, He left for Galilee. **44.** (Now Jesus Himself had pointed out that a prophet has no honor in his own country.) **45.** When He arrived in Galilee, the Galileans welcomed Him. They had seen all that He had done in Jerusalem at the Passover festival, for they had also been there. **46.** Once more He visited Cana in Galilee, where He had turned the water into wine. And there was a certain royal official whose son was ill at Capernaum. **47.** When he heard that Jesus had arrived in Galilee from Judea, he went to Him and begged Him to come and heal his son, who was close to death. **48.** "Unless you people see signs and wonders," Jesus told him, "you will never believe." **49.** The royal official said, "Sir, come down before my child dies." **50.** "Go," Jesus replied, "your son will live." The man took Jesus at His word and departed. **51.** While he was still on his way, his servants met him with the news that his boy was living. **52.** When he inquired as to the time when his son got better, they said to him, "Yesterday at one in the afternoon the fever left him." **53.** Then the father realized that this was the exact time at which Jesus had said to him, "Your son will live." So he and his whole household believed. **54.** This was the second sign Jesus performed after coming from Judea to Galilee. (Sign: miracle or proof of divine power)

Chapter 5
1. Sometime later, there was a Jewish festival, and Jesus went up to Jerusalem to attend it. **2.** In Jerusalem, near the Sheep Gate, there is a pool, called Bethesda in Hebrew, which has five covered porches. **3.** A large number of disabled people—blind, lame, and paralyzed—lay there, waiting for the water to be stirred. **4.** For an angel would come down at a certain time to stir the water, and the first person to go in after it was stirred would be healed of whatever disease they had. **5.** One man had been there for thirty-eight years, suffering from a long-term illness. **6.** Jesus saw him lying there and knew that he had been in that condition for a long time. He asked him, "Do you want to be healed?" **7.** The man answered, "Sir, I have no one to help me get into the pool when the water is stirred. By the time I get there, someone else gets in before me." **8.** Jesus told him, "Get up, pick up your mat, and walk." **9.** Immediately, the man was healed. He picked up his mat and started walking. It was the Sabbath day when this happened. (Sabbath: day of rest) **10.** The Jewish leaders said to the man who had been healed, "It's the Sabbath. It is unlawful for you to carry your mat." **11.** The man replied, "The one who healed me told me, 'Pick up your mat and walk.'" **12.** "Who is this fellow who told you to do that?" they asked. **13.** But the healed man did not know who it was, for Jesus had slipped away into the crowd that was there. **14.** Later, Jesus found him at the temple and said to him, "See, you are well again. Stop sinning or something worse may happen to you." (Sin: disobedience to God) **15.** The man went away and told the Jewish leaders that it was Jesus who had healed him. **16.** Because of this, the Jewish leaders began to persecute Jesus, for He was doing these things on the Sabbath. (Persecute: mistreat for beliefs) **17.** In response, Jesus said, "My Father is always at His work to this very day, and I too am working." **18.** This made the Jews even more determined to kill Him, not only because He was breaking the Sabbath, but also because He was calling God His own Father, making Himself equal with God. (Equal with God: claiming divine authority) **19.** Jesus gave them this answer: "Very truly I tell you, the Son can do nothing by Himself; He can do only what He sees His Father doing. Because whatever the Father does, the Son also does. **20.** For the Father loves the Son and shows Him all He does. Yes, and He will show Him even greater works than these, so that you will be amazed. **21.** For just as the Father raises the dead and gives them life, even so the Son gives life to whom He is pleased to give it. **22.** Moreover, the Father judges no one, but has entrusted all judgment to the Son, **23.** that all may honor the Son just as they honor the Father. Whoever does not honor the Son does not honor the Father who sent Him. (Judgment: divine assessment) **24.** Very truly I tell you, whoever hears My word and believes Him who sent Me has eternal life and will not be judged, but has crossed over from death to life. (Eternal life: everlasting life) **25.** Very truly I tell you, a time is coming—and has now come—when the dead will hear the voice of the Son of God, and those who hear will live. **26.** For as the Father has life in Himself, so He has granted the Son also to have life in Himself. **27.** And He has given Him authority to judge because He is the Son of Man. (Son of Man: title Jesus used for Himself) **28.** Do not be amazed at this, for a time is coming when all who are in their graves will hear His voice **29.** and come out—those who have done what is good will rise to live, and those who have done what is evil will rise to be condemned. (Resurrection: rising from the dead) **30.** By Myself I can do nothing; I judge only as I hear, and My judgment is just, for I seek not to please Myself but Him who sent Me. (Judgment: fair decision) **31.** If I testify about Myself, My testimony is not true. **32.** There is another who testifies in My favor, and I know that His testimony about Me is true. **33.** You have sent to John, and he has testified to the truth. **34.** Not that I accept human testimony; but I mention it that you may be saved. **35.** John was a lamp that burned and gave light, and you chose to rejoice for a while in his light. (Lamp: source of truth) **36.** But I have a greater testimony than that of John; for the works that the Father has given Me to finish—the very works I am doing—testify that the Father has sent Me. **37.** And the Father who sent Me has Himself testified concerning Me. You have never heard His

voice nor seen His form. **38.** Nor do you have His word living in you, for you do not believe the one He sent. **39.** You study the Scriptures diligently because you think that in them you have eternal life. These are the very Scriptures that testify about Me, **40.** yet you refuse to come to Me to have life. **41.** I do not accept glory from human beings. **42.** But I know you; I know that you do not have the love of God in your hearts. **43.** I have come in My Father's name, and you do not accept Me. But if someone else comes in his own name, you will accept him. **44.** How can you believe since you accept glory from one another but do not seek the glory that comes from the only God? **45.** But do not think I will accuse you before the Father; your accuser is Moses, on whom your hopes are set. **46.** If you believed Moses, you would believe Me, for he wrote about Me. **47.** But since you do not believe what he wrote, how are you going to believe what I say?"

Chapter 6

1. After these events, Jesus crossed over to the Sea of Galilee, which is also known as the Sea of Tiberias. **2.** A large crowd followed Him because they witnessed the miraculous signs He performed on the sick. (Signs: miracles) **3.** Jesus went up a mountain and sat down with His disciples. **4.** The Jewish Passover festival was approaching. (Passover: Jewish festival) **5.** As Jesus looked up, He saw a great crowd coming toward Him, and He asked Philip, "Where can we buy enough bread for all these people to eat?" **6.** He asked this to test him, for Jesus already knew what He was going to do. (Test: trial of faith) **7.** Philip replied, "Even two hundred denarii worth of bread wouldn't be enough for each person to have a little." **8.** Andrew, Simon Peter's brother, spoke up, **9.** "There's a boy here with five barley loaves and two fish, but what good is that with such a large crowd?" (Barley loaves: basic food) **10.** Jesus said, "Tell the people to sit down." There was plenty of grass in that area, and about five thousand men sat down. **11.** Then Jesus took the loaves, gave thanks, and distributed them to those who were seated. He did the same with the fish, giving them as much as they wanted. **12.** When everyone was full, He told His disciples, "Gather the leftover pieces, so that nothing is wasted." (Leftovers: food collected) **13.** So they gathered the pieces, filling twelve baskets with the fragments from the five barley loaves that remained after everyone had eaten. **14.** When the people saw this miracle, they said, "This is truly the Prophet who is to come into the world." (Prophet: expected Messiah) **15.** Realizing that they intended to come and force Him to become their king, Jesus withdrew again to the mountain by Himself. (King: earthly ruler) **16.** When evening came, His disciples went down to the sea, **17.** got into a boat, and started across the sea toward Capernaum. By this time, it was already dark, and Jesus had not yet joined them. (Capernaum: town of Jesus) **18.** A strong wind began to blow, and the waters grew rough. **19.** After rowing about three or four miles, they saw Jesus walking on the sea and approaching the boat. They were terrified. (Walking on water: miracle) **20.** But He said to them, "It's Me; don't be afraid." **21.** Then they gladly took Him into the boat, and immediately the boat reached the shore where they were heading. (Arrival: miracle at sea) **22.** The next day, the crowd that had stayed on the other side of the sea realized that only one boat had been there, and that Jesus had not entered it with His disciples. They saw that His disciples had left alone. (Crowd: seeking Jesus) **23.** Other boats had arrived from Tiberias, near the place where they had eaten the bread after Jesus gave thanks. (Tiberias: location of boats) **24.** When the crowd saw that Jesus and His disciples were no longer there, they got into the boats and went to Capernaum in search of Jesus. **25.** When they found Him on the other side of the sea, they asked Him, "Rabbi, when did You get here?" **26.** Jesus answered, "Very truly I tell you, you are looking for Me, not because you saw the signs, but because you ate the loaves and had your fill. (Signs: divine miracles) **27.** Do not labor for food that spoils, but for food that endures to eternal life, which the Son of Man will give you. For on Him, God the Father has placed His seal of approval." (Eternal life: lasting reward) **28.** Then they asked Him, "What must we do to do the works God requires?" **29.** Jesus answered, "The work of God is this: to believe in the One He has sent." (Faith: belief in Jesus) **30.** So they asked Him, "What sign will You perform then, so that we may see it and believe You? What will You do? **31.** Our ancestors ate the manna in the wilderness, as it is written, 'He gave them bread from heaven to eat.'" (Manna: heavenly bread) **32.** Jesus replied, "Very truly I tell you, it was not Moses who gave you the bread from heaven, but My Father gives you the true bread from heaven. (True bread: Jesus Himself) **33.** For the bread of God is He who comes down from heaven and gives life to the world." **34.** "Sir," they said, "always give us this bread." **35.** Jesus declared, "I am the bread of life. Whoever comes to Me will never go hungry, and whoever believes in Me will never be thirsty." (Bread of life: spiritual sustenance) **36.** But I told you that you have seen Me and still do not believe. **37.** All those the Father gives Me will come to Me, and whoever comes to Me I will never drive away. **38.** For I have come down from heaven not to do My will but to do the will of Him who sent Me. (Will of God: divine mission) **39.** And this is the will of Him who sent Me: that I shall lose none of all those He has given Me, but raise them up at the last day. **40.** For My Father's will is that everyone who looks to the Son and believes in Him shall have eternal life, and I will raise them up at the last day." (Resurrection: raising from death) **41.** At this, the Jews began to grumble about Him because He said, "I am the bread that came down from heaven." (Grumbling: murmuring) **42.** They said, "Isn't this Jesus, the son of Joseph, whose father and mother we know? How can He now say, 'I came down from heaven'?" **43.** Jesus replied, "Stop grumbling among yourselves. **44.** No one can come to Me unless the Father who sent Me draws them, and I will raise them up at the last day. (Drawn to Jesus: divine calling) **45.** It is written in the prophets: 'They will all be taught by God.' Everyone who has heard the Father and learned from Him comes to Me. **46.** No one has seen the Father except the One who is from God; only He has seen the Father. **47.** Very truly I tell you, the one who believes has eternal life. **48.** I am the bread of life. **49.** Your ancestors ate the manna in the wilderness, yet they died. **50.** But here is the bread that comes down from heaven, which anyone may eat and not die. (Manna vs. Jesus: contrast) **51.** I am the living bread that came down from heaven. Whoever eats this bread will live forever. This bread is My flesh, which I will give for the life of the world." (Living bread: Christ's sacrifice) **52.** Then the Jews began to argue sharply among themselves, "How can this man give us His flesh to eat?" (Dispute: misunderstanding) **53.** Jesus said to them, "Very truly I tell you, unless you eat the flesh of the Son of Man and drink His blood, you have no life in you. (Flesh and blood: essential for eternal life) **54.** Whoever eats My flesh and drinks My blood has eternal life, and I will raise them up at the last day. **55.** For My flesh is real food, and My blood is real drink. **56.** Whoever eats My flesh and drinks My blood remains in Me, and I in them. **57.** Just as the living Father sent Me, and I live because of the Father, so the one who feeds on Me will live because of Me. **58.** This is the bread that came down from heaven. Your ancestors ate manna and died, but whoever eats this bread will live forever." **59.** He said this while teaching in the synagogue in Capernaum. (Synagogue: place of worship) **60.** On hearing it, many of His disciples said, "This is a hard teaching. Who can accept it?" **61.** Aware that His disciples were grumbling about this, Jesus asked them, "Does this offend you? **62.** Then what if you see the Son of Man ascend to where He was before? **63.** It is the Spirit who gives life; the flesh counts for nothing. The words I have spoken to you are spirit and life. (Spirit: life-giving force) **64.** But some of you do not believe." For Jesus knew from the start who would not believe and who would betray Him. **65.** He continued, "That's why I told you that no one can come to Me unless the Father has enabled them." **66.** From that point onward, many of His disciples turned back and no longer followed Him. **67.** So Jesus asked the Twelve, "Do you also want to leave?" **68.** Simon Peter answered Him, "Lord, where would we go? You have the words that give eternal life. **69.** We have come to believe and know that You are the Holy One of God." (Holy One: divine title) **70.** Jesus replied, "Did I not choose you, the Twelve? Yet one of you is a devil." **71.** He was referring to Judas Iscariot, the son of Simon, for he, though one of the Twelve, would eventually betray Him. (Betrayal: act of treason)

Chapter 7

1. After these activities, Jesus walked in Galilee, fending off Judea because the Jews sought to kill Him. (Galilee: region in northern Israel; Judea: region in southern Israel) **2.** The Festival of Tabernacles was approaching. (Festival of Tabernacles: Jewish celebration of harvest) **3.** His brothers said, "Go to Judea so Your disciples can see Your works." **4.** "No one wants to remain hidden when they want to be seen. If You do these things, show Yourself to the world." **5.** Even His brothers didn't believe in Him. **6.** Jesus answered, "My time has not yet come, but yours is always ready." **7.** The world does not hate you, but it hates Me because I reveal its evil deeds. **8.** "You go to the festival. I am not going yet, because My time has not fully come." **9.** After talking to them, He stayed in Galilee. **10.** After His brothers left for the festival, He went too, but secretly. **11.** At the feast, the Jews searched for Him, asking, "Where is He?" **12.** People were divided: some said, "He's a good man," others said, "He deceives the people." **13.** No one openly spoke about Him for fear of the Jews. **14.** Midway through the festival, Jesus went to the temple and taught. (Temple: sacred place of worship) **15.** The Jews were amazed, saying, "How does He know letters, having never studied?" **16.** Jesus answered, "My teaching is not Mine, but from Him who sent Me." **17.** "If anyone is willing to do His will, they will know whether My teachings are from God or from Myself." **18.** "He who speaks for personal glory seeks selfish gain, but He who seeks the honor of the one who sent Him is truthful, without unrighteousness." **19.** "Didn't Moses give you the law? Yet, none of you obey it. Why do you seek to kill Me?" **20.** The people responded, "You have a demon. Who wants to kill You?" **21.** Jesus responded, "I did one miracle, and you are all amazed." **22.** "Moses gave you circumcision (though it comes from the fathers, not him), and you circumcise on the Sabbath." 23. "If circumcision is allowed on the Sabbath to fulfill the law, why are you angry when I heal a man completely on the Sabbath?" 24. "Do not judge by appearances, but judge with righteous judgment." 25. Some in Jerusalem said, "Isn't this the one they want to kill? 26. But, He speaks boldly, and they do nothing. Do the rulers know that He is the Christ?" 27. "We know where He's from, but when the Christ comes, no one will know His origin." 28. Jesus cried out in the temple, "You know Me, and where I am from. I did not come on My own, but He who sent Me is true, and you do not know Him." 29. "But I know Him, because I am from Him, and He sent Me." 30. They tried to arrest Him, but no one laid a hand on Him, for His time had not yet come. 31. Many believed in Him, saying, "When the Christ comes, will He perform more signs than this man?" 32. The Pharisees heard the crowd murmuring and sent officers to arrest Him. 33. Jesus said, "I'll be with you a little longer, and then I will go to Him who sent Me." 34. "You will look for Me, but you won't find Me. Where I am going, you cannot come." 35. The Jews asked one another, "Where does He intend to go that we won't find Him? Will He go to some of the Greeks and teach them?" 36. "What does He mean by saying, 'You will look for Me, but will not find Me,' and 'Where I am going, you cannot come'?" 37. On the last day of the festival, Jesus stood and shouted, "If anyone is thirsty, let him come to Me and drink." 38. "Whoever believes in Me, as the Scripture says, rivers of living water will flow from within him." 39. He was referring to the Spirit, whom those who believed in Him would receive. The Spirit had not yet been given, because Jesus had not yet been glorified. (Glorified: honored or exalted) 40. Many in the crowd, hearing His words, said, "This is truly the Prophet." 41. Others said, "This is the Christ." But some argued, "Can the Christ come from Galilee?" 42. "Doesn't the Scripture say the Christ comes from the line of David and from Bethlehem, where David lived?" 43. A division arose among the people because of Him. 44. Some wanted to arrest Him, but no one laid hands on Him. 45. The officers returned to the chief priests and Pharisees, who asked, "Why didn't you bring Him?" 46. The officers responded, "No man ever spoke like this!" 47. The Pharisees responded, "Have you also been deceived?" 48. "Have any of the rulers or Pharisees believed in Him?" 49. "But this crowd, who doesn't know the law, is cursed." 50. Nicodemus (the Pharisee who came to Jesus by night) asked, 51. "Does our law condemn a man without first hearing from him and understanding his actions?" 52. They replied, "Are you from Galilee too? Search the Scriptures. No prophet comes from Galilee." 53. Then everyone went to their homes.

Chapter 8

1. Jesus went to the Mount of Olives. (Mount of Olives: a hill near Jerusalem) 2. Early the next morning, He returned to the temple, where the people gathered around Him, and He sat down to teach. 3. The scribes and Pharisees brought to Him a woman caught in adultery (voluntary sexual intercourse), placing her in front of Him. 4. They said, "Teacher, this woman was caught in the act of adultery. 5. According to Moses' law, we are commanded to stone such a person. What do you say?" (Stone: to kill by throwing stones) 6. They were testing Him, hoping to find a reason to accuse Him. But Jesus bent down and began writing on the ground with His finger, pretending not to listen to them. 7. When they kept asking Him, He stood up and said, "Let the one who is without sin throw the first stone at her." 8. Then He bent down again and continued writing on the ground. 9. Those who heard Him were convicted by their consciences, and one by one, they left, beginning with the oldest. Soon, only Jesus and the woman remained. 10. Jesus looked up and asked her, "Where are your accusers? Has no one condemned you?" 11. She replied, "No one, Lord." Jesus said, "Neither do I condemn you. Go and leave your life of sin." (Condemn: to express disapproval or punishment) 12. Jesus then declared, "I am the light of the world. Whoever follows Me will never walk in darkness but will have the light of life." (Light of life: guidance, truth, and salvation) 13. The Pharisees challenged Him, saying, "You testify about Yourself. Your testimony is not valid." 14. Jesus responded, "Even though I testify about Myself, My testimony is true, for I know where I came from and where I am going. You, however, do not know where I come from or where I am going." 15. "You judge by human standards, but I do not judge anyone." 16. "But if I do judge, My judgment is just because I am not alone in this. The Father who sent Me is with Me." 17. "Your law says that the testimony of two witnesses is true." 18. "I testify about Myself, and the Father who sent Me also testifies about Me." 19. They asked, "Where is Your Father?" Jesus answered, "You don't know Me or My Father. If you knew Me, you would know My Father also." 20. These words He spoke while teaching in the temple courts. No one arrested Him because His time had not yet come. 21. He said to them, "I am going away, and you will look for Me, but you will die in your sin. Where I am going, you cannot come." 22. The Jews questioned, "Will He kill Himself because He says, 'Where I am going, you cannot come'?" 23. Jesus answered, "You are from below, I am from above. You belong to this world; I do not." 24. "That's why I told you that you will die in your sins, for unless you believe that I am He, you will die in your sins." 25. They asked, "Who are You?" Jesus answered, "I am exactly what I have been telling you from the beginning." 26. "I have much to say in judgment of you, but the one who sent Me is true, and I speak to the world what I have heard from Him." 27. They did not understand that He was talking about the Father. 28. Jesus continued, "When you have lifted up the Son of Man, then you will know that I am He, and that I do nothing on My own but speak just what the Father has taught Me." 29. "The Father who sent Me is with Me. He has not left Me alone, for I always do what pleases Him." 30. As He spoke, many believed in Him. 31. To those who believed in Him, Jesus said, "If you hold to My teaching, you are really My disciples. 32. Then you will know the truth, and the truth will set you free." 33. They answered, "We are descendants of Abraham, and we have never been enslaved. How can You say, 'You will be set free'?" 34. Jesus replied, "Very truly I tell you, everyone who sins is a slave to sin." (Slave: someone under the power of sin) 35. "A slave does not remain in the house forever, but a son belongs to it forever." 36. "So if the Son sets you free, you will be free indeed." 37. "I know you are Abraham's descendants, but you are trying to kill Me because My word has no place in you." 38. "I speak what I have seen with My Father, and you do what you have heard from your father." 39. They answered, "Abraham is our father." Jesus replied, "If you were Abraham's children, you would do what Abraham did. 40. But now you are trying to kill Me, a man who has told you the truth that I heard from God. Abraham did not do such things." 41. "You are doing the works of your father." They answered, "We are not illegitimate children. We have one Father—God." 42. Jesus said, "If God were your Father, you would love Me, for I came from God and now am here. I did not come on My own, but He sent Me." 43. "Why is My language not clear to you? It is because you are unable to hear what I say." 44. "You belong to your father, the devil, and you want to carry out your father's desires. He was a murderer from the beginning, not holding to the truth, for there is no truth in him. When he lies, he speaks his native language, for he is a liar and the father of lies." 45. "Yet because I tell the truth, you do not believe Me." 46. "Can any of you prove Me guilty of sin? If I am telling the truth, why don't you believe Me?" 47. "Whoever belongs to God hears what God says. The reason you do not hear is that you do not belong to God." 48. The Jews replied, "Aren't we right in saying that You are a Samaritan and have a demon?" 49. Jesus answered, "I am not possessed by a demon. I honor My Father, and you dishonor Me." 50. "I am not seeking glory for Myself; but there is One who seeks it, and He is the judge." 51. "Very truly I tell you, whoever obeys My word will never see death." 52. The Jews responded, "Now we know You are demon-possessed! Abraham and the prophets died, and yet You say, 'Whoever obeys My word will never taste death.' 53. Are You greater than our father Abraham, who died? And the prophets died. Who do You think You are?" 54. Jesus replied, "If I honor Myself, My honor means nothing. It is My Father who honors Me, of whom you say, 'He is our God.'" 55. "But you do not know Him. I know Him, and if I said I did not, I would be a liar like you. But I do know Him and obey His word." 56. "Your father Abraham rejoiced at the thought of seeing My day; he saw it and was glad." 57. The Jews said, "You are not yet fifty years old, and You have seen Abraham?" 58. Jesus replied, "Very truly I tell you, before Abraham was born, I AM." 59. At this, they picked up stones to throw at Him, but Jesus hid Himself, slipping away from the temple through the crowd.

Chapter 9

1. As Jesus walked along, He noticed a man who had been blind since birth. 2. His disciples asked, "Rabbi, who sinned—this man or his parents—that he was born blind?" 3. Jesus answered, "Neither this man nor his parents sinned. Rather, this happened so that God's works might be revealed in him." 4. "I must do the work of Him who sent Me while it is still day; night is coming when no one can work." (Sent: send off to a destination or for a purpose) 5. "As long as I am in the world, I am the light of the world." (Light: metaphor for guidance and truth) 6. After saying this, Jesus spat on the ground, made mud with the saliva, and applied it to the man's eyes. 7. Then He told him, "Go, wash in the Pool of Siloam" (which means "sent"). So the man went, washed, and came home seeing. (Siloam: a pool in Jerusalem, symbolizing sending or mission) 8. His neighbors and those who had seen him begging asked, "Isn't this the same man who used to sit and beg?" 9. Some said, "Yes, he is." Others said, "No, he only looks like him." The man himself said, "I am the man." 10. They asked him, "How were your eyes opened?" 11. He answered, "A man called Jesus made mud, put it on my eyes, and told me to wash in the Pool of Siloam. I went, washed, and now I see." 12. They asked him, "Where is He?" He replied, "I don't know." 13. They took the man, who had been blind, to the Pharisees. 14. It was a Sabbath when Jesus made the

mud and opened his eyes. (Sabbath: a day of rest, Saturday in Jewish law) **15.** The Pharisees asked him how he had received his sight. He answered, "He put mud on my eyes, I washed, and now I see." **16.** Some of the Pharisees said, "This man is not from God, for He does not keep the Sabbath." Others asked, "How can a sinner perform such signs?" And a division arose among them. **17.** They asked the man again, "What do you say about Him, since He opened your eyes?" He replied, "He is a prophet." **18.** But the Jews refused to believe that he had been blind and received his sight until they called his parents. **19.** They asked them, "Is this your son, who you say was born blind? How is it that he now sees?" **20.** His parents answered, "We know that this is our son, and that he was born blind; **21.** but we don't know how he now sees, or who opened his eyes. He is of age; ask him. He will speak for himself." **22.** His parents said this because they were afraid of the Jews, for the Jews had already agreed that anyone who acknowledged Jesus as the Messiah would be put out of the synagogue. **23.** That's why his parents said, "He is of age; ask him." **24.** So they called the man who had been blind a second time and said, "Give glory to God. We know this man is a sinner." **25.** The man answered, "Whether He is a sinner or not, I don't know. One thing I do know: I was blind, but now I see." **26.** They asked him, "What did He do to you? How did He open your eyes?" **27.** He replied, "I have told you already, and you did not listen. Why do you want to hear it again? Do you want to become His disciples too?" **28.** Then they hurled insults at him and said, "You are this man's disciple! We are disciples of Moses. **29.** We know that God spoke to Moses, but as for this man, we don't even know where He comes from." **30.** The man answered, "Now that is remarkable! You don't know where He comes from, yet He opened my eyes! **31.** We know that God does not listen to sinners; He listens to the godly person who does His will. **32.** Nobody has ever heard of opening the eyes of a man born blind. **33.** If this man were not from God, He could do nothing." **34.** To this they replied, "You were steeped in sin at birth; how dare you lecture us?" And they threw him out. (Utter: complete or absolute) **35.** When Jesus heard that they had thrown him out, He found him and asked, "Do you believe in the Son of God?" **36.** The man asked, "Who is He, Lord, that I may believe in Him?" **37.** Jesus said, "You have now seen Him; in fact, He is the one speaking with you." **38.** Then the man said, "Lord, I believe," and he worshiped Him. **39.** Jesus said, "For judgment I have come into this world, so that the blind will see and those who see will become blind." **40.** Some of the Pharisees who were with Him heard Him say this and asked, "What? Are we blind too?" **41.** Jesus replied, "If you were blind, you would not be guilty of sin; but now that you claim you can see, your guilt remains."

Chapter 10

1. Very truly I tell you, anyone who does not enter the sheep pen through the door but climbs in some other way is a thief and a robber. **2.** But the one who enters through the door is the shepherd of the sheep. (shepherd; tend (sheep) as a shepherd)**3.** The doorkeeper opens the door for him, and the sheep listen to his voice. He calls his own sheep by name and leads them out. **4.** When he has brought out all his own, he goes on ahead of them, and his sheep follow him because they know his voice. (follow; obey) **5.** But they will never follow a stranger; in fact, they will run away from him because they do not recognize a stranger's voice. **6.** Jesus used this figure of speech, but the Pharisees did not understand what he was telling them. **7.** Therefore Jesus said again, "Very truly I tell you, I am the door for the sheep. **8.** All who have come before me are thieves and robbers, but the sheep have not listened to them. **9.** I am the door; whoever enters through me will be saved. They will come in and go out, and find pasture. **10.** The thief comes only to steal and kill and destroy; I have come that they may have life, and have it to the full." **11.** "I am the good shepherd. The good shepherd lays down his life for the sheep. **12.** The hired hand is not the shepherd and does not own the sheep. When he sees the wolf coming, he abandons the sheep and runs away. Then the wolf attacks the sheep and scatters them. **13.** The man runs away because he is a hired hand and cares nothing for the sheep. **14.** I am the good shepherd; I know my sheep and my sheep know me— **15.** just as the Father knows me and I know the Father—and I lay down my life for the sheep. **16.** I have other sheep that are not of this pen. I must bring them also. They too will listen to my voice, and there shall be one flock and one shepherd. **17.** The reason my Father loves me is that I lay down my life—only to take it up again. **18.** No one takes it from me, but I lay it down of my own accord. I have authority to lay it down and authority to take it up again. This command I received from my Father." **19.** The Jews who heard these words were again divided. **20.** Many of them said, "He is demon-possessed and raving mad. Why listen to him?" **21.** But others said, "These are not the sayings of a man possessed by a demon. Can a demon open the eyes of the blind?" **22.** Then came the Festival of Dedication (Hanukkah) at Jerusalem. It was winter, **23.** and Jesus was in the temple courts walking in Solomon's Colonnade. **24.** The Jews who were there gathered around him, saying, "How long will you keep us in suspense? If you are the Messiah, tell us plainly." **25.** Jesus answered, "I did tell you, but you do not believe. The works I do in my Father's name testify about me. **26.** But you do not believe because you are not my sheep. **27.** My sheep listen to my voice; I know them, and they follow me. **28.** I give them eternal life, and they shall never perish; no one will snatch them out of my hand. **29.** My Father, who has given them to me, is greater than all; no one can snatch them out of my Father's hand. **30.** I and the Father are one." **31.** Again, his Jewish opponents picked up stones to stone him. **32.** But Jesus said to them, "I have shown you many good works from the Father. For which of these do you stone me?" **33.** They replied, "We are not stoning you for any good work, but for blasphemy, because you, a mere man, claim to be God." **34.** Jesus answered, "Is it not written in your Law, 'I have said you are gods'? **35.** If he called them 'gods,' to whom the word of God came—and Scripture cannot be set aside— **36.** what about the one whom the Father set apart as his very own and sent into the world? Why then do you accuse me of blasphemy because I said, 'I am God's Son'? **37.** Do not believe me unless I do the works of my Father. **38.** But if I do them, even though you do not believe me, believe the works, that you may know and understand that the Father is in me, and I am in the Father." **39.** Again they tried to seize him, but he escaped their grasp. **40.** Then Jesus went back across the Jordan to the place where John had been baptizing in the early days. There he stayed, **41.** And many people came to him. They said, "Though John never performed a sign, all that John said about this man was true." **42.** And in that place many believed in Jesus.

Chapter 11

1. A man named Lazarus was sick. He was from Bethany, the village of Mary and her sister Martha. **2.** (This Mary, whose brother Lazarus now lay sick, was the same one who poured perfume on the Lord and wiped his feet with her hair.) **3.** So the sisters sent word to Jesus, saying, "Lord, the one you love is sick." (Sick: unwell, ill) **4.** When Jesus heard this, he said, "This sickness will not end in death. No, it is for God's glory so that God's Son may be glorified through it." **5.** Now Jesus loved Martha, her sister, and Lazarus. **6.** So when he heard that Lazarus was sick, he stayed where he was two more days. (Glorified: honored or made to appear important) **7.** Then he said to his disciples, "Let us go back to Judea." **8.** "But Rabbi," they said, "a short while ago the Jews tried to stone you, and you are going back?" **9.** Jesus answered, "Are there not twelve hours of daylight? Anyone who walks in the daytime will not stumble, for they see by this world's light." (Rabbi: teacher, often used for a Jewish scholar) **10.** "It is when a person walks at night that they stumble, for they have no light." **11.** After saying this, he went on to tell them, "Our friend Lazarus has fallen asleep; but I am going there to wake him up." **12.** His disciples replied, "Lord, if he sleeps, he will get better." (Stumble: trip or lose balance) **13.** Jesus had been speaking of his death, but his disciples thought he meant natural sleep. **14.** So he told them plainly, "Lazarus is dead, **15.** and for your sake I am glad I was not there, so that you may believe. But let us go to him." **16.** Then Thomas (also called Didymus) said to the rest of the disciples, "Let us also go, that we may die with him." (Plainly: clearly, without ambiguity) **17.** On his arrival, Jesus found that Lazarus had already been in the tomb for four days. **18.** Bethany was less than two miles from Jerusalem, **19.** and many Jews had come to comfort Martha and Mary in the loss of their brother. (Tomb: a grave or burial place) **20.** When Martha heard that Jesus was coming, she went out to meet him, but Mary stayed at home. **21.** "Lord," Martha said to Jesus, "if you had been here, my brother would not have died. **22.** But I know that even now God will give you whatever you ask." **23.** Jesus said to her, "Your brother will rise again." **24.** Martha answered, "I know he will rise again in the resurrection at the last day." **25.** Jesus said to her, "I am the resurrection and the life. The one who believes in me will live, even though they die; **26.** and whoever lives by believing in me will never die. Do you believe this?" (Resurrection: the act of rising from the dead) **27.** "Yes, Lord," she replied, "I believe that you are the Messiah, the Son of God, who is to come into the world." **28.** After she had said this, she went back and called her sister Mary aside. "The Teacher is here," she said, "and is asking for you." **29.** When Mary heard this, she got up quickly and went to him. (Messiah: the Savior or anointed one) **30.** Now Jesus had not yet entered the village, but was still at the place where Martha had met him. **31.** When the Jews who had been with Mary in the house, comforting her, noticed how quickly she got up and went out, they followed her, supposing she was going to the tomb to mourn there. **32.** When Mary reached the place where Jesus was and saw him, she fell at his feet and said, "Lord, if you had been here, my brother would not have died. (Mourn: to express sadness after a loss) **33.** When Jesus saw her weeping, and the Jews who had come along with her also weeping, he was deeply moved in spirit and troubled. **34.** "Where have you laid him?" he asked. "Come and see, Lord," they replied.

35. Jesus wept. (Wept: shed tears, cried) 36. Then the Jews said, "See how he loved him!" 37. But some of them said, "Could not he who opened the eyes of the blind man have kept this man from dying?" 38. Jesus, once more deeply moved, came to the tomb. It was a cave with a stone laid across the entrance. (Entrance: the opening or doorway) 39. "Take away the stone," he said. "But, Lord," said Martha, the sister of the dead man, "by this time there is a bad odor, for he has been there four days." 40. Then Jesus said, "Did I not tell you that if you believe, you will see the glory of God?" 41. So they took away the stone. Then Jesus looked up and said, "Father, I thank you that you have heard me. (Odor: a smell, especially a bad one) 42. I knew that you always hear me, but I said this for the benefit of the people standing here, that they may believe that you sent me." 43. When he had said this, Jesus called in a loud voice, "Lazarus, come out!" 44. The dead man came out, his hands and feet wrapped with strips of linen, and a cloth around his face. Jesus said to them, "Take off the grave clothes and let him go." (Linen: a type of fabric, often used for wrapping) 45. Therefore many of the Jews who had come to visit Mary, and had seen what Jesus did, believed in him. 46. But some of them went to the Pharisees and told them what Jesus had done. 47. Then the chief priests and the Pharisees called a meeting of the Sanhedrin. "What are we accomplishing?" they asked. "Here is this man performing many signs. (Pharisees: a religious group known for strict adherence to Jewish laws) 48. "If we let him go on like this, everyone will believe in him, and then the Romans will come and take away both our temple and our nation." 49. Then one of them, named Caiaphas, who was high priest that year, spoke up, "You know nothing at all! 50. You do not realize that it is better for you that one man die for the people than that the whole nation perish." (Sanhedrin: the Jewish council or governing body) 51. He did not say this on his own, but as high priest that year he prophesied that Jesus would die for the Jewish nation, 52. and not only for that nation but also for the scattered children of God, to bring them together and make them one. 53. So from that day on, they plotted to take his life. (Prophesied: foretold as a prophecy) 54. Therefore Jesus no longer moved about publicly among the people of Judea. Instead, he withdrew to a region near the wilderness, to a village called Ephraim, where he stayed with his disciples. 55. When it was almost time for the Jewish Passover, many went up from the country to Jerusalem for their ceremonial cleansing before the Passover. 56. They kept looking for Jesus, and as they stood in the temple courts they asked one another, "What do you think? Isn't he coming to the festival at all?" (Passover: a Jewish festival commemorating the Exodus from Egypt) 57. But the chief priests and the Pharisees had given orders that anyone who found out where Jesus was should report it so that they might arrest him.

Chapter 12

1. Six days before the Passover, Jesus came to Bethany, where Lazarus lived, whom Jesus had raised from the dead. 2. Here a dinner was given in Jesus' honor. Martha served, while Lazarus was among those reclining at the table with him. 3. Then Mary took about a pint of pure nard, an expensive perfume; she poured it on Jesus' feet and wiped his feet with her hair. And the house was filled with the fragrance of the perfume. (Nard: a type of fragrant oil used in ancient times, often very costly) 4. But one of his disciples, Judas Iscariot, who was later to betray him, objected, 5. "Why wasn't this perfume sold and the money given to the poor? It was worth a year's wages." 6. He did not say this because he cared about the poor but because he was a thief; as keeper of the money bag, he used to help himself to what was put into it. (Thief: a person who steals) 7. "Leave her alone," Jesus replied. "It was intended that she should save this perfume for the day of my burial. 8. You will always have the poor among you, but you will not always have me." 9. Meanwhile, a large crowd of Jews found out that Jesus was there and came, not only because of him but also to see Lazarus, whom he had raised from the dead. (Burial: the act of burying a dead body) 10. So the chief priests made plans to kill Lazarus as well, 11. for on account of him many of the Jews were going over to Jesus and believing in him. 12. The next day the great crowd that had come for the festival heard that Jesus was on his way to Jerusalem. (Chief priests: high-ranking religious leaders) 13. They took palm branches and went out to meet him, shouting, "Hosanna! Blessed is he who comes in the name of the Lord! Blessed is the king of Israel!" 14. Jesus found a young donkey and sat on it, as it is written: 15. "Do not be afraid, Daughter Zion; see, your king is coming, seated on a donkey's colt." (Hosanna: an expression of praise or joy) 16. At first, his disciples did not understand all this. Only after Jesus was glorified did they realize that these things had been written about him and that these things had been done to him. 17. Now the crowd that was with him when he called Lazarus from the tomb and raised him from the dead continued to spread the word. 18. Many people, because they had heard that he had performed this sign, went out to meet him. (Glorified: honored, made to appear important) 19. So the Pharisees said to one another, "See, this is getting us nowhere. Look how the whole world has gone after him!" 20. Now there were some Greeks among those who went up to worship at the festival. 21. They came to Philip, who was from Bethsaida in Galilee, with a request. "Sir," they said, "we would like to see Jesus." (Greeks: people from Greek-speaking regions, often gentiles in the context of Jewish customs) 22. Philip went to tell Andrew; Andrew and Philip in turn told Jesus. 23. Jesus replied, "The hour has come for the Son of Man to be glorified. 24. Very truly I tell you, unless a kernel of wheat falls to the ground and dies, it remains only a single seed. But if it dies, it produces many seeds." (Kernel: the central, edible part of a seed) 25. Anyone who loves their life will lose it, while anyone who hates their life in this world will keep it for eternal life. 26. Whoever serves me must follow me; and where I am, my servant also will be. My Father will honor the one who serves me. 27. "Now my soul is troubled, and what shall I say? 'Father, save me from this hour'? No, it was for this very reason I came to this hour. (Troubled: experiencing distress or anxiety) 28. Father, glorify your name!" Then a voice came from heaven, "I have glorified it, and will glorify it again." 29. The crowd that was there and heard it said it had thundered; others said an angel had spoken to him. 30. Jesus said, "This voice was for your benefit, not mine. (Thundered: made a loud, booming noise) 31. Now is the time for judgment on this world; now the prince of this world will be driven out. 32. And I, when I am lifted up from the earth, will draw all people to myself." 33. He said this to show the kind of death he was going to die. (Prince of this world: a reference to Satan or the power of evil) 34. The crowd spoke up, "We have heard from the Law that the Messiah will remain forever, so how can you say, 'The Son of Man must be lifted up'? Who is this 'Son of Man'?" 35. Then Jesus told them, "You are going to have the light just a little while longer. Walk while you have the light, before darkness overtakes you. Whoever walks in the dark does not know where they are going. 36. Believe in the light while you have the light, so that you may become children of light." When he had finished speaking, Jesus left and hid himself from them. (Light: a symbol of truth or guidance) 37. Even after Jesus had performed so many signs in their presence, they still would not believe in him. 38. This was to fulfill the word of Isaiah the prophet: "Lord, who has believed our message and to whom has the arm of the Lord been revealed?" 39. For this reason, they could not believe, because, as Isaiah says elsewhere: (Signs: miraculous acts that serve as proof or evidence) 40. "He has blinded their eyes and hardened their hearts, so they can neither see with their eyes, nor understand with their hearts, nor turn—and I would heal them." 41. Isaiah said this because he saw Jesus' glory and spoke about him. 42. Yet at the same time, many even among the leaders believed in him. But because of the Pharisees, they would not openly acknowledge their faith for fear they would be put out of the synagogue; (Synagogue: a Jewish house of worship) 43. for they loved human praise more than praise from God. 44. Then Jesus cried out, "Whoever believes in me does not believe in me only, but in the one who sent me. 45. The one who looks at me is seeing the one who sent me. (Praise: approval or admiration) 46. I have come into the world as a light, so that no one who believes in me should stay in darkness. 47. "If anyone hears my words but does not keep them, I do not judge that person. For I did not come to judge the world, but to save the world. 48. There is a judge for the one who rejects me and does not accept my words; the very words I have spoken will condemn them at the last day. (Condemn: to declare guilty or to punish) 49. For I did not speak on my own, but the Father who sent me commanded me to say all that I have spoken. 50. I know that his command leads to eternal life. So whatever I say is just what the Father has told me to say."

Chapter 13

1. Before the Passover Feast, Jesus knew that His time to leave the world and return to the Father had come. He loved His disciples and showed them the full extent of His love. 2. After the meal, Judas Iscariot, the son of Simon, had already been influenced by the devil to betray Jesus. (Judas Iscariot: one of Jesus' disciples who would later betray Him) 3. Jesus, aware that the Father had entrusted everything to Him and that He had come from God and would return to God, 4. rose from the table, removed His outer garments, and wrapped a towel around Himself. 5. He then poured water into a basin and began washing His disciples' feet, drying them with the towel He had tied around Him. 6. When Jesus reached Peter, Peter questioned, "Lord, are You going to wash my feet?" 7. Jesus replied, "You do not understand what I am doing now, but you will understand later." 8. Peter protested, "You will never wash my feet!" Jesus answered, "If I do not wash you, you have no part with Me." 9. Peter then said, "Lord, not just my feet, but my hands and head as well!" 10. Jesus explained, "Anyone who has had a bath only needs to wash their feet to be clean. You are clean, but not all of you." 11. He knew who would betray Him, so He said, "You are not all clean." 12. After washing their feet, Jesus put on His clothes and sat down again. "Do you understand what

I have done for you?" He asked. **13.** "You call Me Teacher and Lord, and you are right, because that is what I am," He said. **14.** "If I, your Lord and Teacher, have washed your feet, you also should wash each other's feet. **15.** "I have set an example for you, that you should do as I have done for you." **16.** "Very truly I tell you, no servant is greater than their master, nor is the messenger greater than the one who sent them." **17.** "Now that you know these things, you will be blessed if you practice them." **18.** "I am not talking about all of you. I know whom I have chosen, but this is to fulfill Scripture: 'He who ate My bread has turned against Me.'" (He who ate My bread has turned against Me: a reference to betrayal) **19.** "I am telling you now, before it happens, so that when it does, you will believe that I am the One." **20.** "Very truly I tell you, whoever accepts anyone I send accepts Me; and whoever accepts Me accepts the One who sent Me." **21.** After saying this, Jesus was deeply troubled in His spirit and declared, "Very truly I tell you, one of you will betray Me." **22.** The disciples looked at each other, confused about whom He was speaking of. **23.** One of them, the disciple whom Jesus loved, was reclining next to Him. **24.** Peter gestured to him to ask Jesus who He meant. **25.** The disciple leaned back against Jesus and asked, "Lord, who is it?" **26.** Jesus replied, "It is the one to whom I will give this piece of bread after I have dipped it." He dipped the bread and handed it to Judas Iscariot, son of Simon. **27.** After Judas took the bread, Satan entered him. Jesus said to him, "What you are about to do, do quickly." **28.** No one at the table understood why Jesus had said this to Judas. **29.** Some thought that Jesus was telling him to buy the things they needed for the feast or to give something to the poor. **30.** Judas took the bread and immediately went out. It was night. **31.** Once Judas had left, Jesus said, "Now the Son of Man is glorified, and God is glorified in Him." **32.** "If God is glorified in Him, God will also glorify Him in Himself and will do so without delay." **33.** "My children, I will be with you only a little longer. You will look for Me, and just as I told the Jews, 'Where I am going, you cannot come,' now I tell you the same." **34.** "I give you a new command: Love one another. As I have loved you, you must love one another." **35.** "By this, everyone will know that you are My disciples, if you love one another." **36.** Peter asked, "Lord, where are You going?" Jesus replied, "Where I am going, you cannot follow now, but you will follow later." **37.** Peter asked, "Lord, why can't I follow You now? I will lay down my life for You." **38.** Jesus answered, "Will you lay down your life for Me? Very truly I tell you, before the rooster crows, you will deny Me three times." (Rooster: a bird known for crowing in the early morning, marking the time)

Chapter 14

1. "Do not let your hearts be troubled. You believe in God; believe in Me also." **2.** "In My Father's house, there are many rooms. If it were not so, I would have told you. I am going to prepare a place for you." **3.** "And if I go to prepare a place for you, I will come back and take you to be with Me, so that where I am, you may also be." **4.** "You know the way to the place where I am going." **5.** Thomas replied, "Lord, we do not know where You are going, so how can we know the way?" **6.** Jesus answered, "I am the way, the truth, and the life. No one comes to the Father except through Me." **7.** "If you had known Me, you would have known My Father also. From now on, you know Him and have seen Him." **8.** Philip said, "Lord, show us the Father, and that will be enough for us." **9.** Jesus replied, "Have I been with you so long, Philip, and yet you do not know Me? Anyone who has seen Me has seen the Father. How can you say, 'Show us the Father'? **10.** "Do you not believe that I am in the Father, and the Father is in Me? The words I say to you are not My own; it is the Father, living in Me, who is doing His work." **11.** "Believe Me when I say that I am in the Father, and the Father is in Me; or at least believe on the evidence of the works themselves." **12.** "Very truly I tell you, whoever believes in Me will do the works I have been doing, and they will do even greater things than these, because I am going to the Father." **13.** "And I will do whatever you ask in My name, so that the Father may be glorified in the Son." **14.** "If you ask anything in My name, I will do it." **15.** "If you love Me, keep My commandments." **16.** "And I will ask the Father, and He will give you another Helper, to be with you forever—" (Helper: someone who helps, referring to the Holy Spirit) **17.** "the Spirit of truth. The world cannot accept Him, because it neither sees Him nor knows Him. But you know Him, for He lives with you and will be in you." **18.** "I will not leave you as orphans; I will come to you." (Orphans: children without parents) **19.** "Before long, the world will not see Me anymore, but you will see Me. Because I live, you also will live." **20.** "On that day you will realize that I am in My Father, and you are in Me, and I am in you." **21.** "Whoever has My commandments and keeps them is the one who loves Me. The one who loves Me will be loved by My Father, and I too will love them and show Myself to them." **22.** Judas (not Iscariot) said, "But, Lord, why do You intend to show Yourself to us and not to the world?" **23.** Jesus replied, "Anyone who loves Me will obey My teaching. My Father will love them, and We will come to them and make Our home with them." **24.** "Anyone who does not love Me will not obey My teaching. These words you hear are not My own; they belong to the Father who sent Me." **25.** "All this I have spoken while still with you." **26.** "But the Advocate, the Holy Spirit, whom the Father will send in My name, will teach you all things and will remind you of everything I have said to you." (Advocate: one who supports or defends) **27.** "Peace I leave with you; My peace I give you. I do not give to you as the world gives. Do not let your hearts be troubled and do not be afraid." **28.** "You heard Me say, 'I am going away and I am coming back to you.' If you loved Me, you would be glad that I am going to the Father, for the Father is greater than I." **29.** "I have told you now before it happens, so that when it does happen, you will believe." **30.** "I will not say much more to you, for the prince of this world is coming. He has no hold over Me." (Prince of this world: a reference to Satan) **31.** "But He comes so that the world may learn that I love the Father and do exactly what My Father has commanded Me. Come now, let us leave."

Chapter 15

1. "I am the real vine, and My Father is the only who tends the vine (real Vine: The authentic supply or beginning of spiritual existence; Jesus as the issuer of life and sustenance)." **2.** "Every branch in Me that doesn't produce fruit, He eliminates; and every branch that does bear fruit, He prunes to help it produce even greater (Prunes: To trim or reduce back branches to promote healthier growth or more fruit)." **3.** "You have already been made clean because of the message I have spoken to you." **4.** "Stay in Me, and I will remain in you. Just as a branch cannot bear fruit by itself unless it stays connected to the vine, neither can you, unless you stay in Me (stay: To remain, maintain, or persist in a relationship or state)." **5.** "I am the vine, and you are the branches. Those who stay in Me, and I in them, will bear much fruit, for without Me, you can accomplish nothing." **6.** "Anyone who does not remain in Me is like a branch that is discarded, dried up, and gathered to be burned in the fire." **7.** "If you remain in Me and My words remain in you, ask anything you want, and it will be done for you." **8.** "This is how My Father is glorified: by bearing much fruit, and this is how you will show to be My disciples." **9.** "As the Father has loved Me, so I have loved you. Stay in My love." **10.** "If you obey My commandments, you will remain in My love, just as I have obeyed My Father's commandments and remain in His love (Obey: To comply with the commands or commandments given)." **11.** "I have told you this so that My joy may be in you and your joy may be complete." **12.** "This is My commandment: Love each other as I have loved you." **13.** "There is no greater love than to lay down one's life for one's friends." **14.** "You are My friends if you do what I command you." **15.** "I no longer call you servants because a servant does not know what his master is doing. I have called you friends, because I have made known to you everything I heard from My Father." **16.** "You did not choose Me, but I chose you. I appointed you to go and bear lasting fruit, so that whatever you ask the Father in My name, He will give you." **17.** "This is My command: Love each other." **18.** "If the world dislikes you, know that it hated Me first." **19.** "If you were part of the world, it would love you as one of its own. But because you are not of the world, and I have chosen you out of it, the world will hate you." **20.** "Remember the saying I told you: 'A servant is not greater than his master.' If they persecuted Me, they will also persecute you. If they followed My teachings, they will also follow yours (Persecuted: To be harassed, mistreated, or oppressed due to one's beliefs or actions)." **21.** "They will treat you this way because of My name, because they do not know the One who sent Me." **22.** "If I had not come and spoken to them, they would not be guilty of sin. But now they have no excuse for their sin." **23.** "Everyone who hates Me also hates My Father." **24.** "If I had not performed among them the works that no one else did, they would not be guilty of sin. But now they have seen these miracles and still hate both Me and My Father." **25.** "But this is happening so that the words written in their scriptures may be fulfilled: 'They hated Me without a cause.'" **26.** "When the Helper comes, whom I will send to you from the Father, the Spirit of truth, who comes from the Father, He will testify about Me (Helper: The Holy Spirit, as the one who comes to help and guide the disciples)." **27.** "And you also must testify, because you have been with Me from the beginning (Testify: To bear witness or provide proof of the truth)."

Chapter 16

1. "I have told you these things so you will not fall away (Fall away: To stumble or be led into error)." **2.** "They will expel you from the synagogues; indeed, the time is coming when anyone who kills you will think that they are offering service to God." (synagogue; a place of worship for Jewish people) **3.** "They will do these things because they have not known the Father or Me." **4.** "But I have told you these things so that when their time comes, you may remember that I told you. I did not mention them to you at first because I was with you." **5.** "But now I am going to the One who sent Me, and none of you asks, 'Where are You going?'" **6.** "But because I have said these things, grief has filled your hearts (Grief: Deep sorrow or sadness)." **7.** "However, I tell you the truth: It is for your good that I go away. For if I do not go away, the Helper will not come to you; but if I go, I will send Him to you (Helper: The Holy Spirit, who comes to assist and guide)." **8.** "When He comes, He will convict the world of sin, of righteousness, and of judgment." **9.** "He will convict them of sin, because they do not believe in Me." **10.** "He will convict them of righteousness, because I am going to the Father, and you will no longer see Me." **11.** "He will convict them of judgment, because the ruler of this world has been judged." **12.** "I still have many things to say to you, but you cannot bear them now (bear: To endure or tolerate)." **13.** "But when the Spirit of truth comes, He will guide you into all truth. He will not speak on His own authority, but will speak only what He hears; and He will tell you what is yet to come." **14.** "He will glorify Me, because He will take from what is Mine and declare it to you (Glorify: To honor or praise highly)." **15.** "All that the Father has is Mine; that is why I said that He will take from what is Mine and declare it to you." **16.** "In a little while, you will no longer see Me, and again, in a little while, you will see Me, because I am going to the Father." **17.** "Then some of His disciples said to one another, 'What does He mean by saying, "In a little while, you will not see Me; and again, in a little while, you will see Me"; and, "because I am going to the Father"?' **18.** "They kept asking, 'What does He mean by "a little while"? We do not understand what He is saying.'" **19.** "Jesus knew they wanted to ask Him about this, so He said to them, 'Are you asking one another about what I meant when I said, "In a little while, you will not see Me; and again, in a little while, you will see Me"?' " **20.** "Very truly I tell you, you will weep and mourn, while the world rejoices. You will grieve, but your grief will turn to joy." **21.** "A woman giving birth has pain because her time has come; but when her baby is born, she forgets the anguish because of her joy that a child is born into the world." **22.** "So with you: Now is your time of grief, but I will see you again, and you will rejoice, and no one will take away your joy." **23.** "In that day, you will not ask Me anything. Very truly I tell you, My Father will give you whatever you ask in My name." **24.** "Until now, you have not asked for anything in My name. Ask and you will receive, and your joy will be complete." **25.** "I have spoken to you in figures of speech, but the time is coming when I will no longer use this kind of language but will tell you plainly about the Father." **26.** "In that day, you will ask in My name. I am not saying that I will ask the Father on your behalf." **27.** "No, the Father Himself loves you because you have loved Me and have believed that I came from God." **28.** "I came from the Father and entered the world; now I am leaving the world and going back to the Father." **29.** "Then His disciples said, 'Now You are speaking plainly and without figures of speech!'" **30.** "Now we can see that You know all things and that You do not need to have anyone ask You questions. This makes us believe that You came from God." **31.** "Do you now believe?" **32.** "A time is coming, and in fact has come, when you will be scattered, each to your own home. You will leave Me all alone. Yet I am not alone, for My Father is with Me." **33.** "I have told you these things so that in Me you may have peace. In this world you will have trouble. But take heart! I have overcome the world."

Chapter 17
1. "Jesus spoke these words, lifted up His eyes to heaven, and said: 'Father, the hour has come. Glorify Your Son, that Your Son also may glorify You.' **2.** "As You have given Him authority over all flesh, that He should give eternal life to as many as You have given Him. **3.** "And this is eternal life, that they may know You, the only true God, and Jesus Christ whom You have sent." (eternal life: life that is never-ending, gained through knowledge and relationship with God and Jesus.) **4.** "I have glorified You on the earth. I have finished the work which You have given Me to do." **5.** "And now, O Father, glorify Me together with Yourself, with the glory which I had with You before the world was." (Glorify: To honor or make something or someone illustrious.) **6.** "I have manifested Your name to the men whom You have given Me out of the world. They were Yours, You gave them to Me, and they have kept Your word." (Manifested: Made visible or clear; word: the message or teaching of God.) **7.** "Now they have known that all things which You have given Me are from You." **8.** "For I have given to them the words which You have given Me; and they have received them, and have known surely that I came forth from You; and they have believed that You sent Me." (words: Teachings or messages from God.) **9.** "I pray for them. I do not pray for the world but for those whom You have given Me, for they are Yours." (Pray: To make a petition or request to God.) **10.** "And all Mine are Yours, and Yours are Mine, and I am glorified in them." (Glorified: Made to be of great honor and praise.) **11.** "Now I am no longer in the world, but these are in the world, and I come to You. Holy Father, keep through Your name those whom You have given Me, that they may be one as We are." (Keep: To protect or watch over.) **12.** "While I was with them, I kept them in Your name. Those whom You gave Me I have kept; and none of them is lost except the son of perdition, that the Scripture might be fulfilled." (Son of perdition: A person destined for destruction; Perdition: complete loss or destruction.) **13.** "But now I come to You, and these things I speak in the world, that they may have My joy fulfilled in themselves." (joy: Deep, abiding happiness or fulfillment.) **14.** "I have given them Your word; and the world has hated them because they are not of the world, just as I am not of the world. **15.** "I do not pray that You should take them out of the world, but that You should keep them from the evil one." (Evil one: Devil, representing evil and temptation.) **16.** "They are not of the world, just as I am not of the world." **17.** "Sanctify them by Your truth. Your word is truth." (Sanctify: To make holy or set apart for God's purposes.) **18.** "As You sent Me into the world, I also have sent them into the world." **19.** "And for their sakes I sanctify Myself, that they also may be sanctified by the truth." **20.** "I do not pray for these alone, but also for those who will believe in Me through their word;" (word: Message or teachings about Jesus that lead others to belief.) **21.** "That they all may be one, as You, Father, are in Me, and I in You; that they also may be one in Us, that the world may believe that You sent Me." (One: Unified in purpose and spirit.) **22.** "And the glory which You gave Me I have given them, that they may be one just as We are one:" (Glory: Honor, beauty, or greatness that reflects God's nature.) **23.** "I in them, and You in Me; that they may be made perfect in one, and that the world may know that You have sent Me, and have loved them as You have loved Me." (Perfect: Complete, mature, and unified in purpose and spirit.) **24.** "Father, I desire that they also whom You gave Me may be with Me where I am, that they may behold My glory which You have given Me; for You loved Me before the foundation of the world." (Behold: To see or look upon; Glory: Honor or majesty.) **25.** "O righteous Father! The world has not known You, but I have known You; and these have known that You sent Me." (Righteous: Just, morally right, in accordance with God's standards.) **26.** "And I have declared to them Your name, and will declare it, that the love with which You loved Me may be in them, and I in them." (Declared: Made known or proclaimed.)

Chapter 18
1. "When Jesus had spoken those words, He went out along with His disciples over the Brook Kidron, where there was a garden, which He and His disciples entered." **2.** "And Judas, who betrayed Him, also knew the place; for Jesus frequently met there with His disciples." (Betrayed: delivered someone into harm, being disloyal.) **3.** "Then Judas, having received a detachment of troops, and officers from the chief priests and Pharisees, came there with lanterns, torches, and weapons." (Detachment: a group sent on a specific mission.) **4.** "Jesus therefore, knowing all things that would come upon Him, went forward and said to them, 'Whom are you seeking?'" **5.** "They answered Him, 'Jesus of Nazareth.' Jesus said to them, 'I am He.' And Judas, who betrayed Him, also stood with them." (I am He: A declaration of divine identity) **6.** "Now when He said to them, 'I am He,' they drew back and fell to the ground." (Drew back: Moved away, possibly in fear.) **7.** "Then He asked them again, 'Whom are you seeking?' And they said, 'Jesus of Nazareth.'" **8.** "Jesus answered, 'I have told you that I am He. Therefore, if you seek Me, let these go their way.'" (Seeking: look for or pursue.) **9.** "That the saying might be fulfilled which He spoke, 'Of those whom You gave Me I have lost none.'" (Saying: A statement or prophecy.) **10.** "Then Simon Peter, having a sword, drew it and struck the high priest's servant, and cut off his right ear. The servant's name was Malchus." (Drew: Took out; Struck: Hit forcefully.) **11.** "So Jesus said to Peter, 'Put your sword into the sheath. Shall I not drink the cup which My Father has given Me?'" (Sword: A weapon; Sheath: A cover for the sword; Cup: Metaphor for suffering.) **12.** "Then the detachment of troops and the captain and the officers of the Jews arrested Jesus and bound Him." (Arrested: Taken into custody; Bound: Tied up.) **13.** "And they led Him away to Annas first, for he was the father-in-law of Caiaphas who was high priest that year." (Led: Taken; High priest: spiritual leader with the highest authority.) **14.** "Now it was Caiaphas who advised the Jews that it was expedient that one man should die for the people." (Expedient: useful; Die for: To sacrifice one's life for others.) **15.** "And Simon Peter followed Jesus, and so did another disciple. Now that disciple was known to the high priest, and went with Jesus into the courtyard of the high priest." (Followed: Went after; Disciple: Follower of Jesus.) **16.** "But Peter stood at the door outside. Then the other disciple, who was known to the high priest, went out and spoke to her who kept the door, and brought Peter in." (Kept the door: Guarded the entrance.) **17.** "Then the servant girl who kept the door said to Peter, 'You are not also one of this man's disciples, are you?' He said, 'I am not.'" (Servant girl: female worker; Disciple: Follower of Jesus.) **18.** "Now the servants and officers who had made a fire of coals stood there, for it was cold, and they warmed themselves. And Peter stood with them and warmed himself." (Officers: Temple or law enforcement people.) **19.** "The high priest then asked Jesus about His disciples and His doctrine." (Doctrine: the

teachings of Jesus.) **20.** "Jesus answered him, 'I spoke openly to the world. I always taught in synagogues and in the temple, where the Jews always meet, and in secret I have said nothing.'" (Synagogues: Jewish places of worship.) **21.** "Why do you question Me? Ask those who have heard Me what I said to them. Indeed they know what I said." **22.** "And when He had said these things, one of the officers who stood by struck Jesus with the palm of his hand, saying, 'Do You answer the high priest like that?'" (Struck: Hit forcefully; Palm: a part of the hand.) **23.** "Jesus answered him, 'If I have spoken evil, bear witness of the evil; but if well, why do you strike Me?'" (Evil: wrong actions; bear witness: Testify or give proof.) **24.** "Then Annas sent Him bound to Caiaphas the high priest." (Sent: Directed; Bound: Tied up.) **25.** "Now Simon Peter stood and warmed himself. Therefore they said to him, 'You are not also one of His disciples, are you?' He denied it and said, 'I am not!'" (Denied: Rejected the accusation.) **26.** "One of the servants of the high priest, a relative of him whose ear Peter cut off, said, 'Did I not see you in the garden with Him?'" **27.** "Peter then denied again; and immediately a rooster crowed." (Denied: Rejected; Rooster: A male bird known for crowing.) **28.** "Then they led Jesus from Caiaphas to the Praetorium, and it was early morning. But they themselves did not go into the Praetorium, lest they should be defiled, but that they might eat the Passover." (Led: Taken; Praetorium: The Roman governor's residence.) **29.** "Pilate then went out to them and said, 'What accusation do you bring against this man?'" (Accusation: A charge or claim of wrongdoing.) **30.** "They answered and said to him, 'If He were not an evildoer, we would not have brought Him up to you.'" (Evildoer: someone who does wrong.) **31.** "Then Pilate said to them, 'You take Him and judge Him according to your law.' Therefore the Jews said to him, 'It is not lawful for us to put anyone to death,'" (Lawful: in accordance with the law.) **32.** "That the saying of Jesus might be fulfilled which He spoke, signifying by what death He would die." (Saying: A prophecy; Fulfilled: completed.) **33.** "Then Pilate entered the Praetorium again, called Jesus, and said to Him, 'Are You the King of the Jews?'" (King: A ruler.) **34.** "Jesus answered him, 'Are you speaking for yourself about this, or did others tell you this regarding Me?'" **35.** "Pilate answered, 'Am I a Jew? Your own nation and the chief priests have delivered You to me. What have You done?'" **36.** "Jesus answered, 'My kingdom is not of this world. If My kingdom were of this world, My servants would fight, so that I should not be delivered to the Jews; but now My kingdom is not from here.'" (Kingdom: A realm of authority.) **37.** "Pilate therefore said to Him, 'Are You a king then?' Jesus answered, 'You say rightly that I am a king. For this cause I was born, and for this cause I have come into the world, that I should bear witness to the truth. Everyone who is of the truth hears My voice.'" (Bear witness: Testify.) **38.** "Pilate said to Him, 'What is truth?' And when he had said this, he went out again to the Jews, and said to them, 'I find no fault in Him at all.'" **39.** "But you have a custom that I should release someone to you at the Passover. Do you therefore want me to release to you the King of the Jews?'" (Passover: A Jewish holiday commemorating the Exodus.) **40.** "Then they all cried again, saying, 'Not this Man, but Barabbas!' Now Barabbas was a robber."

Chapter 19

1. Pilate had Jesus flogged. (flogged: whipped with a whip or lash) **2.** The squaddies made a crown of thorns and positioned it on His head, then dressed Him in a crimson gown. **3.** They mocked Him, announcing, "Hail, King of the Jews!" and struck Him with their palms. **4.** Pilate went outdoor again and said, "I am bringing Him to you so that you may additionally see that I discover no fault in Him." **5.** Jesus came out, carrying the crown of thorns and the purple gown. Pilate said, "study the person!" **6.** when the chief monks and officials saw Him, they shouted, "Crucify Him!" Pilate answered, "you're taking Him and crucify Him. I see no fault in Him." (leader monks: leading religious officers) **7.** The Jews answered, "we've a regulation, and in line with it, He should die due to the fact He claimed to be the Son of God." **8.** Upon hearing this, Pilate grew even greater fearful, **9.** and went lower back into the palace, asking Jesus, "where are You from?" however Jesus remained silent. (palace: the respectable residence of a ruler) **10.** Pilate said, "You refuse to talk to me? Don't i have authority to crucify You or loose You?" **11.** Jesus replied, "you will haven't any electricity over Me until it turned into given to you from above. the one who handed Me over to you is guilty of a more sin." **12.** Pilate attempted to loose Him, however the Jews shouted, "in case you allow this man go, you aren't any buddy of Caesar. anybody who calls himself a king is opposing Caesar." **13.** listening to this, Pilate sat at the judgment seat at an area known as The Pavement, which in Hebrew is called Gabbatha. (judgment seat: the vicinity where a choose gives rulings) (Pavement: a stone surface, Gabbatha: Aramaic word which means "place of the cranium") **14.** It became the day of education for the Passover, about the 6th hour. Pilate stated to the Jews, "here is your King!" (Passover: a Jewish pageant commemorating the Exodus) **15.** They shouted returned, "Take Him away! Crucify Him!" Pilate asked, "Shall I crucify your King?" The chief clergymen answered, "We haven't any king however Caesar!" **16.** So Pilate exceeded Jesus over to be crucified, and the soldiers took Him away. **17.** Jesus carried His go to an area called the place of a skull, that is referred to as Golgotha in Hebrew. (location of a skull: a hill corresponding to a skull) (Golgotha: Aramaic term for "location of the skull") **18.** They crucified Him there, in conjunction with two others, one on each facet, with Jesus within the middle. **19.** Pilate had a signal located above Jesus that study: JESUS OF NAZARETH, THE KING OF THE JEWS. **20.** Many Jews study the sign since the region of the crucifixion changed into near the city. It turned into written in Hebrew, Greek, and Latin. (Hebrew, Greek, and Latin: 3 commonplace languages on the time) **21.** The leader clergymen of the Jews told Pilate, "Don't write, 'The King of the Jews,' however that He said, 'i'm the King of the Jews.'" **22.** Pilate answered, "What i've written, i have written." **23.** while the soldiers crucified Jesus, they divided His garments into 4 parts, giving each soldier a part, alongside along with his tunic. The tunic changed into seamless, woven in one piece from pinnacle to backside. (tunic: a easy garment worn by using humans in historic times) **24.** They decided no longer to rip it, but solid masses to look who might get it, pleasurable the Scripture that says, "They divided My clothes among them, and forged plenty for My garment." So the infantrymen did this. (cast lots: draw lots to determine who will get it) **25.** status near the pass have been Jesus' mom, His mom's sister, Mary the wife of Clopas, and Mary Magdalene. **26.** whilst Jesus saw His mother and the disciple whom He loved status nearby, He stated to her, "woman, right here is your son!" (the disciple whom He loved: normally understood as John, the writer of this Gospel) **27.** Then He stated to the disciple, "right here is your mother!" And from that moment, the disciple took her into his domestic. **28.** Later, knowing that everything turned into finished, Jesus stated, "i am thirsty," to satisfy the Scripture. **29.** A jar of bitter wine become there, so they soaked a sponge in it, placed it on a hyssop department, and lifted it to His mouth. (hyssop: a sort of plant used for cleansing rituals) **30.** After Jesus drank the sour wine, He stated, "it's far finished!" He then bowed His head and gave up His spirit. (gave up His spirit: died) **31.** because it changed into education Day and the bodies could not continue to be on the cross at some stage during the Sabbath (due to the fact that Sabbath was a unique one), the Jews requested Pilate to have the legs of the crucified men damaged and their our bodies removed. (Sabbath: the day of rest and worship in Judaism) **32.** The infantrymen got here and broke the legs of the primary guy and the other who was crucified with Jesus. **33.** when they came to Jesus and noticed that He was already dead, they did no longer wreck His legs. **34.** alternatively, one soldier pierced His facet with a spear, and blood and water immediately flowed out. (spear: an extended, pointed weapon) **35.** the only who witnessed this has testified, and his testimony is authentic. He knows he is telling the fact so that you may additionally trust. **36.** those activities passed off to fulfill the Scripture: "now not one among His bones could be broken." **37.** And any other Scripture says, "they will appearance on the only they have pierced." **38.** Later, Joseph of Arimathea, a secret disciple of Jesus (due to the fact he feared the Jews), requested Pilate for permission to take Jesus' body. Pilate allowed it, so Joseph took the body away. (Joseph of Arimathea: a wealthy member of the Jewish council and secret follower of Jesus) **39.** Nicodemus, who had visited Jesus at night, also came, bringing an aggregate of myrrh and aloes, approximately seventy-five kilos. (Nicodemus: a Pharisee and mystery follower of Jesus, myrrh and aloes: fragrant spices used in burial preparations) **40.** the two of them took Jesus' frame, wrapped it in linen cloths with the spices, as changed into the Jewish custom for burial. **41.** near the crucifixion web page become a garden, and within the lawn, a brand new tomb wherein no one had but been buried. **42.** as it was the Jewish day of guidance, and the tomb turned into nearby, they laid Jesus there.

Chapter 20

1. Early on the first day of the week, while it was still dark, Mary Magdalene went to the tomb and saw that the stone had been rolled away. **2.** She ran to Simon Peter and the other disciple, the one Jesus loved, and said, "They've taken the Lord out of the tomb, and we don't know where they've put him!" **3.** Peter and the other disciple raced to the tomb. (Raced: ran quickly) **4.** The other disciple outran Peter and reached the tomb first. **5.** He bent down and saw the linen strips lying there but didn't go in. **6.** Simon Peter arrived, went straight into the tomb, and saw the linen strips. **7.** He also noticed the cloth that had been wrapped around Jesus' head, still in its place, separate from the linen. **8.** Then the other disciple, who had reached the tomb first, also went inside. He saw and believed. **9.** (They still didn't understand from Scripture that Jesus had to rise from the dead.) **10.** The disciples then returned to their place. **11.** Mary stood outside the tomb, crying. As she wept, she looked inside. **12.** She saw two angels in white sitting where Jesus' body had been, one at the head and the other at the foot. **13.** They asked her,

"Woman, why are you crying?" She replied, "They've taken my Lord away, and I don't know where they've put him." **14.** She turned around and saw Jesus standing there, but didn't recognize him. **15.** He asked, "Woman, why are you crying? Who are you looking for?" Thinking he was the gardener, she said, "Sir, if you've taken him away, tell me where you've put him, and I'll get him." **16.** Jesus said, "Mary." She turned toward him and exclaimed, "Rabboni!" (Rabboni: Teacher in Aramaic) **17.** Jesus replied, "Do not hold on to me, for I have not yet ascended to the Father. Go to my brothers and tell them, 'I am ascending to my Father and your Father, to my God and your God.'" **18.** Mary Magdalene went to the disciples and told them, "I have seen the Lord!" and shared what he had said to her. **19.** That evening, the disciples were gathered with the doors locked because of fear of the Jewish leaders. Jesus appeared and said, "Peace be with you!" **20.** He showed them his hands and side, and they were overjoyed to see the Lord. **21.** Again, he said, "Peace be with you! As the Father has sent me, I am sending you." **22.** He breathed on them and said, "Receive the Holy Spirit. **23.** If you forgive anyone's sins, they are forgiven; if you do not forgive them, they are not forgiven." **24.** Thomas, also called Didymus, one of the Twelve, wasn't with the disciples when Jesus came. **25.** The others told him, "We have seen the Lord!" But he said, "Unless I see the nail marks in his hands and put my finger in them, and my hand into his side, I will not believe." **26.** A week later, the disciples were again in the house, and Thomas was with them. Despite the doors being locked, Jesus appeared and said, "Peace be with you!" **27.** Then he said to Thomas, "Put your finger here; see my hands. Reach out your hand and put it into my side. Stop doubting and believe." **28.** Thomas responded, "My Lord and my God!" (Responded; replied) **29.** Jesus said, "Because you have seen me, you have believed; blessed are those who have not seen and yet have believed." **30.** Jesus performed many other signs in the presence of his disciples that aren't recorded in this book. **31.** But these are written so that you may believe that Jesus is the Messiah, the Son of God, and that by believing you may have life in his name.

Chapter 21
1. Later, Jesus appeared once again to his disciples at the Sea of Galilee, and this is how it unfolded: **2.** Simon Peter, Thomas (also known as Didymus), Nathanael from Cana, the sons of Zebedee, and two other disciples were together.(Didymus ; a Greek name meaning "twin") **3.** Pete.r said to the group, "I'm going fishing." The others agreed, saying, "We'll join you." So, they went out and got into the boat, but all through the night, they didn't catch a single fish (Fishing (the activity of catching fish). **4.** Just as the sun began to rise, Jesus stood on the shore, though the disciples did not immediately recognize him.(recognize; know) **5.** He called out to them, "Friends, have you caught anything?" "No," they answered. **6.** Jesus told them, "Throw your net over the right side of the boat, and you will find some." When they did, they found themselves unable to pull in the net because of the large catch. **7.** At that moment, the disciple whom Jesus loved said to Peter, "It's the Lord!" As soon as Peter heard him, he quickly wrapped his tunic around him (since he had removed it earlier) and leapt into the water to reach Jesus. **8.** The others followed in the boat, towing the heavy net of fish, about a hundred yards from shore. **9.** When they reached the land, they found a fire burning with fish and bread already on it. **10.** Jesus said, "Bring some of the fish you just caught." **11.** Simon Peter climbed into the boat and dragged the net ashore. It was full of large fish—153, but despite the number, the net was not torn. (Dragged ; pulled with effort) **12** Jesus invited them, "Come, have breakfast with me." None of the disciples dared ask him, "Who are you?" because they knew it was the Lord. **13.** Jesus took the bread, gave it to them, and did the same with the fish. **14.** This was now the third time that Jesus had appeared to his disciples since his resurrection. **15.** After they had finished eating, Jesus turned to Simon Peter and asked, "Simon son of John, do you love me more than these?" Peter responded, "Yes, Lord, you know I love you." Jesus said, "Feed my lambs." **16.** A second time, Jesus asked, "Simon son of John, do you love me?" Peter replied, "Yes, Lord, you know that I love you." Jesus told him, "Take care of my sheep." **17.** A third time, Jesus asked, "Simon son of John, do you love me?" This time, Peter was grieved because Jesus asked him the same question three times. He said, "Lord, you know all things. You know that I love you." Jesus replied, "Feed my sheep. **18.** Truly, I tell you, when you were younger, you dressed yourself and went wherever you chose. But when you are old, you will stretch out your hands, and someone else will dress you and take you where you do not want to go." **19** Jesus said this to indicate the kind of death by which Peter would glorify God. Then he said, "Follow me!" **20.** As Peter turned around, he noticed the disciple whom Jesus loved following them. This was the same disciple who had leaned back against Jesus at the Last Supper and had asked, "Lord, who is going to betray you?" **21.** Seeing him, Peter asked, "Lord, what about this man?" **22.** Jesus replied, "If I want him to remain alive until I return, what is that to you? You follow me!" **23.** As a result, rumors began to spread among the believers that this disciple would not die. However, Jesus did not say that he would not die; he simply said, "If I want him to remain alive until I return, what is that to you?" (Rumors; unverified information or gossip) **24.** This disciple is the one who testifies to these things and who wrote them down. We know that his testimony is trustworthy and true. **25.** Jesus did many more things that are not written here. If every one of them were recorded, I believe the world itself could not contain the books that would be written. (Contain; hold within)

44 – Acts
Chapter 1
1. I wrote a prior account, O Theophilus, detailing all Jesus began to do and teach. (Theophilus: likely a believer addressed by Luke) **2.** This continued until the day He ascended, after instructing the apostles He had chosen through the Holy Spirit. (Ascended: went up to heaven) **3.** He proved Himself alive after His suffering through undeniable evidence, appearing to them over forty days and teaching about God's kingdom. (undeniable evidence: clear and unquestionable signs) **4.** While gathering with them, He commanded them to remain in Jerusalem and wait for the Father's promise, which He had spoken of earlier. **5.** "John baptized with water," He said, "but soon you will be baptized with the Holy Spirit." (baptized: immersed as part of a religious ritual) **6.** When they met, they asked, "Lord, will You now restore Israel's kingdom?" **7.** He replied, "It's not for you to know the timing the Father has set by His authority." **8.** "But you will receive power when the Holy Spirit comes upon you, and you will testify about Me in Jerusalem, all Judea, Samaria, and to the ends of the earth." (testify: bear witness) **9.** After saying this, He was taken up as they watched, and a cloud hid Him from view. **10.** While they stared into the sky, two men in white clothing stood beside them. **11.** They said, "Men of Galilee, why do you stand gazing at the sky? This same Jesus, who was taken to heaven, will return the same way." (gazing: looking steadily) **12.** They returned to Jerusalem from the Mount of Olives, a Sabbath day's journey away. (Sabbath day's journey: a limited distance permitted on the Sabbath) **13.** Upon arriving, they went to an upstairs room where Peter, James, John, Andrew, Philip, Thomas, Bartholomew, Matthew, James son of Alphaeus, Simon the Zealot, and Judas son of James were staying. **14.** They united in prayer with the women, Mary (Jesus' mother), and His brothers. **15.** During those days, Peter addressed about 120 disciples, saying: **16.** "Brothers, Scripture had to be fulfilled concerning Judas, who guided those who arrested Jesus, as foretold by the Holy Spirit through David." (fulfilled: brought to completion) **17.** "He was one of us and shared in this ministry." **18.** "With the money earned from his wrongdoing, Judas bought a field, where he fell and burst open, spilling his insides." (wrongdoing: sinful act) **19.** This became known to Jerusalem's residents, who called the field 'Aceldama,' meaning 'Field of Blood.' **20.** "As written in Psalms: 'Let his dwelling be abandoned; let another take his position.'" (dwelling: place of residence) **21.** "So, one of the men who accompanied us throughout Jesus' ministry must join us as a witness to His resurrection." **22.** "Starting from John's baptism to His ascension, they must testify to His resurrection." **23.** They nominated Joseph (Barsabas, also called Justus) and Matthias. **24.** They prayed, "Lord, You know every heart; show us whom You have chosen." **25.** "Let him take over Judas' role, who turned away to his own destiny." (destiny: outcome or fate) **26.** They cast lots, and Matthias was selected to join the eleven apostles. (cast lots: used a method to make decisions)

Chapter 2
1. When the day of Pentecost arrived, they were all gathered in one place with unity. (Pentecost: A Jewish festival celebrating the harvest and the giving of the law) **2.** Suddenly, a sound like a rushing wind came from heaven and filled the house where they sat. (Rushing: Moving with speed) **3.** Tongues of fire appeared and rested on each of them. (Tongues: Languages, Cloven: Divided) **4.** They were filled with the Holy Spirit and began speaking in different languages as the Spirit enabled them. (Utterance: Speech or expression) **5.** Jews from every nation were living in Jerusalem. (Devout: Very religious) **6.** When the crowd heard the sound, they gathered and were amazed, for each person heard them speaking in their own language. (Noised abroad: Spread or reported widely) **7.** They were astonished and asked, "Aren't all these speakers Galileans?" (Astonished: Filled with surprise) **8.** "How do we hear them speaking in our own native languages?" (Native: Originating from a particular place) **9.** Parthians, Medes, Elamites, residents of Mesopotamia, Judaea, Cappadocia, Pontus, Asia, (Mesopotamia: Ancient region between the Tigris and Euphrates rivers) **10.** Phrygia, Pamphylia, Egypt, parts of Libya near Cyrene, Romans, Jews, and converts, (Phrygia: Ancient region in central Anatolia, now part of Turkey, Pamphylia: Region in southern Asia Minor) **11.** Cretans and Arabs—yet we hear them declaring the wonders of God in our languages." (Cretans: People from the island of Crete)

12. Everyone was amazed and confused, asking, "What does this mean?" (Confused: Bewildered, unsure) **13.** Some mocked, saying, "They're drunk on new wine." (Mocked: Made fun of or ridiculed) **14.** But Peter, with the other eleven apostles, stood and spoke loudly: "Men of Judaea and all Jerusalem, listen to me. (Apostles: Original messengers or leaders of the early church) **15.** These men aren't drunk as you think; it's only the third hour of the day. (Hour: A time period, specifically 9 AM in this case) **16.** This is what the prophet Joel spoke about: (Prophet: A person who is believed to receive and deliver messages from God) **17.** 'In the last days, God says, I will pour out My Spirit on all people. Your sons and daughters will prophesy, your young men will see visions, and your old men will dream dreams. (Prophesy: Predict or declare by divine inspiration) **18.** Even on My servants, both men and women, I will pour out My Spirit, and they will prophesy. (Servants: Those who serve or obey) **19.** I will show wonders in the heavens above and signs on the earth below: blood, fire, and smoke. (Wonders: Miraculous events, Signs: Indications or symbols) **20.** The sun will turn to darkness, and the moon to blood before the great and glorious day of the Lord. (Glorious: Full of splendor or greatness) **21.** And everyone who calls on the name of the Lord will be saved.' (Saved: Rescued from sin or harm) **22.** Men of Israel, listen to these words: Jesus of Nazareth, a man proven by God to you with miracles, wonders, and signs, which God did through Him among you, as you yourselves know. (Miracles: Supernatural events, Wonders: Extraordinary signs) **23.** He was handed over by God's plan and foreknowledge, and you, with wicked hands, crucified and killed Him. (Foreknowledge: Knowledge of events before they happen, Wicked: Morally wrong) **24.** But God raised Him from the dead, freeing Him from the agony of death, because it was impossible for death to hold Him. (Agony: Intense pain, Impossible: Not able to happen) **25.** David said about Him: 'I saw the Lord always before me. Because He is at my right hand, I will not be shaken. (Shaken: Moved or disturbed) **26.** Therefore my heart is glad, and my tongue rejoices; my body will also rest in hope, (Rejoices: Feels great joy, Rest: To relax or stop from activity) **27.** because You will not abandon me to the grave, nor will You let Your Holy One see decay.' (Abandon: To leave behind, Grave: Tomb, Decay: Decompose) **28.** You have made known to me the paths of life; You will fill me with joy in Your presence.' (Paths: Ways or courses, Joy: A feeling of great happiness) **29.** Brothers, I can tell you with confidence that the patriarch David is both dead and buried, and his tomb is here to this day. (Patriarch: A founding father or leader) **30.** But since he was a prophet and knew that God had promised him on oath that He would place one of his descendants on his throne, (Descendants: Offspring, Oath: A solemn promise) **31.** he spoke of the resurrection of the Christ, that He was not abandoned to the grave, nor did His body see decay. (Resurrection: Rising from the dead, Abandoned: Left behind) **32.** God has raised this Jesus to life, and we are all witnesses of it. (Witnesses: Those who see or experience something) **33.** Exalted to the right hand of God, He has received the promised Holy Spirit from the Father and has poured out what you now see and hear. (Exalted: Raised to a high position, Poured out: Given freely) **34.** For David did not ascend to heaven, and yet he said, 'The Lord said to my Lord, "Sit at my right hand until I make your enemies a footstool for your feet."' (Ascend: To rise up, Footstool: A piece of furniture to rest feet on) **35.** until I make your enemies a footstool for your feet.' (Enemies: Those who oppose you) **36.** Let all Israel be assured of this: God has made this Jesus, whom you crucified, both Lord and Christ. (Assured: Made certain, Crucified: Killed by being nailed to a cross) **37.** When the people heard this, they were cut to the heart and asked Peter and the other apostles, "Brothers, what should we do?" (Cut to the heart: Felt deeply convicted) **38.** Peter replied, "Repent and be baptized, each of you, in the name of Jesus Christ for the forgiveness of your sins. And you will receive the gift of the Holy Spirit. (Repent: To regret and turn away from sin, Baptized: Immersed in water as a sign of faith) **39.** The promise is for you, your children, and all who are far off—for all whom the Lord our God will call." (Promise: Assurance, Call: Invitation or summons) **40.** With many other words, he warned them and pleaded with them, "Save yourselves from this corrupt generation." (Warned: Informed of danger, Corrupt: Morally wrong) **41.** Those who accepted his message were baptized, and about three thousand were added to their number that day. (Accepted: Took in or agreed with, Baptized: Immersed in water) **42.** They devoted themselves to the apostles' teaching, to fellowship, to the breaking of bread, and to prayer. (Devoted: Committed fully, Fellowship: Communion or sharing) **43.** Everyone was filled with awe, and many wonders and miraculous signs were done by the apostles. (Awe: Reverent wonder, Miraculous: Supernatural) **44.** All the believers were together and had everything in common. (Believers: Those who trust in Jesus, Common: Shared) **45.** Selling their possessions and goods, they gave to anyone as they had need. (Possessions: Things owned, Goods: Items or property) **46.** Every day they continued to meet together in the temple courts, breaking bread in their homes and eating together with glad and sincere hearts, (Sincere: Genuine or honest) **47.** praising God and enjoying the favor of all the people. And the Lord added to their number daily those who were being saved. (Favor: Approval or goodwill)

Chapter 3

1. Peter and John went to the temple together at the time of prayer, which was the ninth hour of the day. (9th hour: Around 3 PM) **2.** A man, who had been lame from birth, was carried and placed daily at the temple's Beautiful gate to beg for alms from those entering. (Lame: Unable to walk, Alms: Charitable gifts or money) **3.** When he saw Peter and John about to enter, he asked them for money. (Money: Currency or wealth) **4.** Peter, along with John, fixed his gaze on him and said, "Look at us." (Fixed: Focused or directed) **5.** The man paid close attention, hoping to receive something from them. (Close attention: Focused interest) **6.** Peter said, "I have no silver or gold, but I will give you what I do have: In the name of Jesus Christ of Nazareth, stand up and walk." (Silver: A precious metal, Gold: A valuable metal, Nazareth: The hometown of Jesus) **7.** Taking him by the right hand, Peter helped him up, and immediately his feet and ankles were strengthened. (Strengthened: Made stronger or firmer) **8.** The man jumped up, stood, and began walking, leaping, and praising God as he entered the temple with them. (Leaping: Jumping with joy or excitement) **9.** Everyone saw him walking and praising God. (Praising: Expressing admiration or gratitude) **10.** They recognized him as the man who had sat begging at the Beautiful gate and were astonished and filled with wonder at what had occurred. (Astonished: Amazed or shocked, Wonder: Admiration or surprise) **11.** As the healed man held on to Peter and John, the people gathered around them in Solomon's Porch, amazed by the miracle. (Healed: Restored to health, Porch: A covered entrance or area, Miracle: A supernatural event) **12.** When Peter saw this, he addressed the crowd, "Men of Israel, why are you surprised by this? Why are you staring at us as if it were by our own power or godliness that we made this man walk?" (Addressed: Spoke to, Staring: Looking fixedly, Godliness: Holiness or righteousness) **13.** The God of Abraham, Isaac, and Jacob, the God of our ancestors, has glorified His servant Jesus, whom you handed over to Pilate and rejected, even though Pilate was willing to release Him. (Glorified: Honored or praised, Pilate: The Roman governor who sentenced Jesus) **14.** You denied the Holy and Righteous One, choosing a murderer to be released instead. (Holy: Sacred or divine, Righteous: Morally just) **15.** You killed the source of life, but God raised Him from the dead, and we are witnesses to this fact. (Source: Origin or cause, Witnesses: Those who testify to something they have seen or experienced) **16.** Through faith in His name, this man whom you see and know has been made strong. It is the faith in Him that has healed him completely in front of you all. (Faith: Belief or trust, Healed: Restored to health) **17.** Now, brothers, I know that you acted in ignorance, as did your leaders. (Ignorance: Lack of knowledge or awareness) **18.** But what God foretold through the prophets—that the Messiah would suffer—He has fulfilled. (Foretold: Predicted, Messiah: The promised Savior or Anointed One) **19.** Repent, and turn back to God so that your sins may be wiped away, and times of refreshment may come from the Lord. (Repent: To feel regret and turn away from sin, Wiped away: Erased or forgiven, Refreshment: Renewal or restoration) **20.** He will send you Jesus, whom He had already appointed for you. (Appointed: Chosen or designated) **21.** Heaven must receive Him until the time comes for the restoration of all things, which God promised long ago through His holy prophets. (Restoration: The act of bringing something back to its original state) **22.** Moses said, 'The Lord your God will raise up for you a prophet like me from among your own people; you must listen to everything He tells you.' (Raise up: To bring forward or cause to appear) **23.** Anyone who does not listen to that prophet will be completely cut off from the people. (Cut off: Removed or excluded) **24.** All the prophets, from Samuel to those after him, have foretold these days. (Foretold: Predicted or prophesied) **25.** You are the descendants of the prophets and of the covenant God made with your ancestors, saying to Abraham, 'Through your offspring, all peoples on earth will be blessed.' (Descendants: Offspring or children, Covenant: A sacred agreement or promise) **26.** When God raised up His servant, He sent Him first to you to bless you by turning each of you from your wicked ways. (Wicked: Morally wrong or evil)

Chapter 4

1. While Peter and John were speaking, the priests, temple captain, and Sadducees confronted them. (Sadducees: A Jewish sect that denied resurrection) **2.** They were upset because the apostles taught about Jesus and the resurrection. (Resurrection: Rising from the dead) **3.** They arrested them until the next day since it was evening. (Arrested: Taken into custody) **4.** Many who heard believed, and the number of men grew to about five thousand. (Believed: Had faith in Jesus) **5.** The next day, rulers, elders, and scribes assembled. (Scribes: Jewish law experts) **6.** Annas the high priest,

Caiaphas, John, Alexander, and others related to the high priest gathered in Jerusalem. (High priest: Chief religious leader) **7.** They asked, "By what power or name did you do this?" (Power: Authority or ability) **8.** Filled with the Holy Spirit, Peter said, "Rulers and elders, (Holy Spirit: God's divine presence) **9.** If we're questioned about healing a disabled man, (Disabled: Unable to function normally) **10.** Know that he was healed by the name of Jesus Christ, whom you crucified, but God raised. (Healed: Restored, Crucified: Executed on a cross) **11.** Jesus is the rejected stone now the cornerstone. (Cornerstone: Foundation stone) **12.** Salvation is found in no other name under heaven. (Salvation: Deliverance from sin) **13.** Seeing Peter and John's courage, though unlearned, they recognized they had been with Jesus. (Courage: Bravery) **14.** Seeing the healed man, they couldn't object. (Healed: Cured) **15.** They sent them out and discussed. (Discussed: Deliberated) **16.** They said, "A notable miracle is evident to all in Jerusalem; we can't deny it." (Notable: Significant, Miracle: Supernatural act) **17.** "Let's warn them not to speak of this name further." (Warn: Caution) **18.** They ordered Peter and John not to speak or teach in Jesus' name. (Ordered: Commanded) **19.** Peter and John replied, "Judge if obeying you over God is right. (Obeying: Following commands) **20.** We cannot stop speaking about what we've seen and heard." **21.** After more threats, they released them, as the people glorified God. (Glorified: Honored) **22.** The healed man was over forty years old. (Healed: Restored) **23.** Released, they returned to their group and shared what was said. **24.** Together, they prayed, "Lord, You made heaven, earth, and the sea." (Prayed: Spoke to God) **25.** Through David, You said, 'Why do nations rage and people plot in vain?' (Plot: Plan, Vain: Futile) **26.** Earthly kings and rulers gathered against the Lord and His Messiah. (Messiah: Savior) **27.** Indeed, Herod, Pilate, Gentiles, and Israelites conspired against Jesus, whom You anointed. (Conspired: Planned, Anointed: Chosen) **28.** They carried out Your predetermined will. (Predetermined: Decided in advance) **29.** Lord, consider their threats and grant us boldness to speak Your word. (Boldness: Confidence) **30.** Stretch out Your hand to heal and perform signs and wonders through Jesus' name. (Signs: Miraculous acts) **31.** After praying, the place shook, and they were filled with the Holy Spirit, speaking boldly. (Shook: Trembled, Boldly: With courage) **32.** The believers were united, sharing all they had. (United: Together as one) **33.** The apostles testified powerfully of Jesus' resurrection, and great grace was upon them. (Testified: Declared) **34.** None were needy; those owning land or houses sold them and gave the proceeds. (Needy: Lacking essentials) **35.** They gave it to the apostles for distribution to anyone in need. (Distribution: Sharing) **36.** Joseph, called Barnabas (meaning "Son of Encouragement"), was a Levite from Cyprus. (Encouragement: Support) **37.** He sold a field and brought the money to the apostles.

Chapter 5

1. A man named Ananias, along with his wife Sapphira, sold a piece of property. (Sapphira: a woman's name) **2.** However, they secretly kept part of the money from the sale, and his wife was aware of this. They brought a portion and laid it at the feet of the apostles. (Secretly: in a hidden manner; Portion: a part of something) **3.** Peter said to Ananias, "Why has Satan filled your heart to deceive the Holy Spirit and withhold part of the money from the sale?" (Satan: the devil; Deceive: to mislead or trick; Withhold: to keep back) **4.** "When it was yours, didn't you have control over it? And after selling it, wasn't the money still yours to manage? Why have you planned this in your heart? You have not lied to people, but to God." (Control: power or authority over something; Manage: handle or direct; Lied: told an untruth) **5.** When Ananias heard these words, he fell down and died, and great fear spread among all who heard about it. (Fear: dread or terror) **6.** The young men rose, wrapped him up, carried him out, and buried him. (Wrapped: covered or bound; Buried: placed in the ground) **7.** About three hours later, his wife, unaware of what had happened, came in. (Unaware: not knowing) **8.** Peter asked her, "Did you sell the land for this amount?" She replied, "Yes, for that amount." (Amount: the quantity or sum) **9.** Peter responded, "How is it that you have agreed together to test the Spirit of the Lord? The feet of those who buried your husband are at the door, and they will carry you out too." (Agree: to decide together; Test: to challenge or deceive) **10.** Immediately, she fell at his feet and died. The young men entered, found her dead, and buried her beside her husband. (Immediately: without delay; Buried: placed in the ground) **11.** Great fear came upon the whole church and all who heard of these events. (Church: the body of believers) **12.** The apostles performed many signs and wonders among the people, and all were united in Solomon's Porch. (Signs: miraculous events; Wonders: amazing acts; United: joined together) **13.** No one else dared join them, but the people held them in high esteem. (Dared: had the courage; Esteem: respect or admiration) **14.** More and more people came to believe in the Lord, both men and women. (Believe: accept as true; Lord: a title for Jesus) **15.** So much so that they brought the sick into the streets, placing them on beds and mats, hoping that even Peter's shadow might fall on some of them as he passed by. (Sick: those who are ill; Shadow: a dark shape made by blocking light) **16.** People also came from surrounding cities, bringing their sick and those tormented by evil spirits, and all were healed. (Surrounding: nearby; Tormented: afflicted; Evil spirits: harmful supernatural beings) **17.** The high priest and those with him, belonging to the Sadducees, became filled with jealousy. (Sadducees: a Jewish religious group; Jealousy: envy or resentment) **18.** They arrested the apostles and put them in the common prison. (Arrested: took into custody; Common: public) **19.** But during the night, an angel of the Lord opened the prison doors, led them out, and said, (Angel: a divine messenger) **20.** "Go, stand in the temple courts and tell the people the full message of this new life." (Temple courts: the outer parts of the temple; Message: the proclamation or teaching) **21.** At daybreak, they entered the temple and began teaching. The high priest and those with him convened the council, including all the elders of Israel, and sent officers to bring the apostles from the prison. (Daybreak: the time when the sun rises; Council: a gathering of leaders; Elders: senior or respected members) **22.** When the officers arrived, they did not find them in the prison and returned to report. (Officers: guards or soldiers; Report: to give an account) **23.** "The prison was securely locked, and the guards were standing outside the doors, but when we opened them, we found no one inside." (Securely: safely or tightly; Guards: those who watch over something) **24.** When the high priest and the captain of the temple guards heard this, they were puzzled and wondered what would happen next. (Captain: the leader; Puzzled: confused; Wondered: were unsure) **25.** Then someone came and told them, "Look, the men you put in prison are standing in the temple courts, teaching the people." (Look: see or observe) **26.** The captain and the officers went and brought the apostles in without force, for they feared the people, lest they be stoned. (Force: strength or violence; Feared: were afraid of) **27.** They brought them before the council, and the high priest questioned them. (Council: a gathering of religious leaders; Questioned: asked them) **28.** "Didn't we strictly order you not to teach in this name? Yet you have filled Jerusalem with your teaching and are trying to bring this man's blood upon us." (Strictly: in a firm manner; Order: command; Blood: the responsibility for Jesus' death) **29.** Peter and the other apostles replied, "We must obey God rather than men." (Obey: follow commands; Men: people) **30.** "The God of our ancestors raised Jesus, whom you killed by hanging him on a cross." (Ancestors: forefathers; Killed: took his life; Cross: the instrument of Jesus' crucifixion) **31.** "God has exalted him to his right hand as Prince and Savior, to grant repentance to Israel and forgiveness of sins." (Exalted: lifted up; Prince: leader; Savior: rescuer) **32.** "We are witnesses of these things, and so is the Holy Spirit, whom God has given to those who obey him." (Witnesses: those who testify; Obey: follow instructions) **33.** When the council heard this, they were furious and debated whether to kill the apostles. (Furious: very angry; Debated: discussed) **34.** But a Pharisee named Gamaliel, a respected teacher of the law, stood up in the council and ordered that the apostles be taken outside for a brief discussion. (Pharisee: a member of a Jewish religious group; Respected: held in high regard) **35.** He said, "Men of Israel, consider carefully what you are about to do with these men." (Consider: think about) **36.** "Some time ago, a man named Theudas appeared, claiming to be someone important. He gathered about four hundred followers, but he was killed, and all his followers were scattered and brought to nothing." (Claiming: stating; Followers: people who follow someone; Scattered: dispersed) **37.** "After him, Judas of Galilee rose up during the census and led many people after him. He also perished, and all his followers were scattered." (Perished: died or was destroyed; Census: a population count) **38.** "Therefore, I advise you to leave these men alone, for if their plan is of human origin, it will fail." (Advise: recommend; Origin: source or beginning) **39.** "But if it is from God, you will not be able to stop them. You might even find yourselves fighting against God." (Stop: prevent; Fighting: opposing) **40.** The council agreed with him. They called the apostles in, beat them, and ordered them not to speak in the name of Jesus, and let them go. (Beat: physically punished; Ordered: commanded) **41.** The apostles left the council, rejoicing that they had been counted worthy to suffer disgrace for the name of Jesus. (Rejoicing: celebrating; Worthy: deserving) **42.** Every day, both in the temple and from house to house, they never stopped teaching and proclaiming the message of Jesus Christ. (Proclaiming: announcing publicly; Message: the gospel)

Chapter 6

1. During those days, as the number of disciples grew, complaints arose among the Greek-speaking Jews against the Hebrew-speaking ones, as their widows were being overlooked in the daily distribution of aid. (Complaints: grievances; Distribution: giving) **2.** The twelve apostles gathered all the disciples and said, "It is not right for us to neglect the word of God in order to serve tables." (Neglect: abandon; Serve: attend to) **3.** "Therefore, brothers, choose seven men from among you who are known to be full of the Holy Spirit and wisdom, so we can appoint them to manage this task." (Brothers: fellow believers; Appoint: assign) **4.** "We will dedicate ourselves to prayer and the ministry of the word." (Dedicate: devote; Ministry: service) **5.** This proposal pleased everyone, and they chose Stephen, a man full of faith and the Holy Spirit, along with Philip, Prochorus, Nicanor, Timon, Parmenas, and Nicolas, a convert from Antioch. (Convert: proselyte; Antioch: city) **6.** They presented these men to the apostles, and after praying, the apostles laid their hands on them. (Presented: brought; Laid: blessed) **7.** The word of God spread, and the number of disciples in Jerusalem increased rapidly. Many priests also became obedient to the faith. (Spread: expanded; Obedient: submissive) **8.** Stephen, filled with faith and power, performed great wonders and signs among the people. (Wonders: miracles; Signs: acts) **9.** But some men from the synagogue, called the Synagogue of the Freedmen, including Cyrenians, Alexandrians, and those from Cilicia and Asia, argued with Stephen. (Synagogue: meeting place; Freedmen: Libertines) **10.** They were unable to withstand the wisdom and the Spirit by which he spoke. (Withstand: resist; Spirit: power) **11.** They then secretly bribed some men to say, "We have heard him speak blasphemous words against Moses and against God." (Secretly: covertly; Bribed: persuaded) **12.** They stirred up the people, the elders, and the teachers of the law, seized Stephen, and brought him before the Sanhedrin. (Stirred: provoked; Sanhedrin: council) **13.** They produced false witnesses, who claimed, "This man never stops speaking against this holy place and the law." (False: lying; Holy place: temple) **14.** "We have heard him say that Jesus of Nazareth will destroy this place and change the customs handed down to us by Moses." (Customs: traditions; Handed down: delivered) **15.** All those who were sitting in the Sanhedrin stared at Stephen, and they saw that his face was like the face of an angel. (Stared: gazed; Sanhedrin: council)

Chapter 7
1. The high priest asked, "Is this true?" **2.** Stephen responded, "Listen, brothers and fathers. The God of glory appeared to Abraham in Mesopotamia before he lived in Haran." (Mesopotamia: region, Haran: city) **3.** He told him, 'Leave your land and family and go to the place I will show you.' **4.** Abraham left the Chaldeans and settled in Haran. After his father died, God brought him here. (Chaldeans: Babylonians) **5.** God gave him no land, not even a place to stand, but promised to give it to him and his descendants. (Descendants: offspring) **6.** God told him his descendants would live as strangers in a foreign land, be enslaved and mistreated for 400 years. (Enslaved: imprisoned, Mistreated: abused) **7.** But God promised to judge the nation that enslaved them, and afterward, they would leave and worship Him here. (Judge: punish) **8.** God made a covenant with Abraham, and Abraham had Isaac, circumcised him on the eighth day, and Isaac had Jacob, who fathered twelve sons. (Covenant: agreement, Circumcised: cut) **9.** Jealous of Joseph, his brothers sold him to Egypt, but God was with him. (Jealous: envious) **10.** God rescued him from all troubles and gave him favor and wisdom before Pharaoh, making him governor of Egypt and his household. (Rescued: saved, Pharaoh: king) **11.** A famine struck Egypt and Canaan, and our ancestors could not find food. (Famine: shortage) **12.** When Jacob heard there was grain in Egypt, he sent our ancestors there first. (Grain: crops) **13.** The second time, Joseph revealed his identity to his brothers, and his family was introduced to Pharaoh. (Revealed: showed) **14.** Joseph called for Jacob and all his family— seventy-five people. (Seventy-five: 75) **15.** Jacob went to Egypt and died, as did our ancestors. **16.** They were buried in Shechem, in the tomb Abraham bought from Hamor's sons. (Shechem: city, Tomb: grave) **17.** As the time for God's promise to Abraham neared, the people grew in Egypt. (Promise: vow) **18.** A new king, who did not know Joseph, took power. (Power: authority) **19.** This king dealt deceitfully with our people, mistreated our ancestors, and ordered the death of their newborns. (Deceitfully: dishonestly) **20.** During this time, Moses was born, a beautiful child, and was hidden in his father's house for three months. (Hidden: concealed) **21.** When he was abandoned, Pharaoh's daughter adopted him. (Adopted: accepted) **22.** Moses was educated in Egyptian wisdom and was powerful in speech and action. (Wisdom: knowledge) **23.** At forty, Moses chose to visit the Israelites. (Israelites: Hebrews) **24.** He saw one being mistreated and defended him, striking down the Egyptian. (Striking: hitting) **25.** He thought his people would understand that God would use him to deliver them, but they did not. (Deliver: save) **26.** The next day, he tried to reconcile two Israelites fighting, but one rejected him, asking, "Who made you ruler and judge?" (Reconcile: settle, Rejected: dismissed) **27.** He even said, "Are you going to kill me like the Egyptian?" **28.** Moses fled and became a foreigner in Midian, where he had two sons. (Foreigner: outsider) **29.** Forty years later, an angel appeared to him in a burning bush on Mount Sinai. (Angel: messenger, Sinai: mountain) **30.** Moses, amazed by the sight, approached, and God spoke. (Amazed: awed) **31.** "I am the God of your ancestors, the God of Abraham, Isaac, and Jacob." Moses trembled and did not dare to look. (Trembled: shook, Dare: challenge) **32.** God told him to remove his sandals because the ground was holy. (Holy: sacred) **33.** God said, "I have seen the suffering of my people in Egypt. I have heard their cries, and I have come to rescue them. Now, I am sending you back to Egypt." (Suffering: pain) **34.** Moses, whom they rejected, saying, "Who made you ruler?" was sent by God to be both ruler and deliverer. (Rejected: denied, Deliverer: savior) **35.** Moses led the people out after performing wonders and signs in Egypt, at the Red Sea, and during forty years in the wilderness. (Wonders: miracles, Wilderness: desert) **36.** Moses told Israel, "God will raise up a prophet like me from among you, whom you must listen to." (Raise up: bring) **37.** Moses was with the people in the wilderness, received living words from God, and passed them on to us. (Living: active) **38.** Our ancestors refused to obey him and turned back to Egypt in their hearts. (Refused: declined, Turned back: returned) **39.** They told Aaron, "Make us gods to lead us, for we don't know what happened to Moses." **40.** They made a golden calf and worshiped it, rejoicing in their own works. (Golden calf: idol, Worshiped: adored) **41.** God turned away from them and let them worship the stars, as the prophet said. (Heavenly bodies: stars) **42.** God asked, "Did you offer sacrifices and offerings in the wilderness for forty years, O house of Israel?" (Sacrifices: offerings) **43.** "You carried the tabernacle of Moloch and the star of your god Rephan, idols you made to worship. I will send you beyond Babylon." (Tabernacle: tent, Idols: false gods) **44.** Our ancestors had the tabernacle of testimony in the wilderness, as God commanded Moses to build it. (Testimony: witness) **45.** Later, Joshua brought it into the land of the Gentiles, and God drove out the nations before them, until the time of David. (Gentiles: non-Jews, Drove out: removed) **46.** David found favor with God and requested to build a house for the God of Jacob. (Favor: grace) **47.** But it was Solomon who built the temple. (Temple: house) **48.** However, the Most High does not dwell in temples made by human hands, as the prophet says. (Most High: God) **49.** "Heaven is my throne, and the earth is my footstool. What kind of house will you build for me?" **50.** "Did not my hand make all these things?" **51.** You stiff-necked and uncircumcised in heart and ears, you always resist the Holy Spirit, just as your ancestors did. (Stiff-necked: stubborn, Uncircumcised: unspiritual) **52.** Which of the prophets did your ancestors not persecute? They killed those who foretold the coming of the Righteous One, whom you betrayed and murdered. (Persecuted: oppressed, Foretold: predicted) **53.** You received the law given through angels, but you did not obey it. **54.** When they heard this, they were furious and gnashed their teeth. (Furious: enraged, Gnashed: ground) **55.** But Stephen, full of the Holy Spirit, looked up to heaven and saw God's glory, and Jesus standing at the right hand of God. (Glory: brilliance) **56.** He said, "Look, I see heaven open and the Son of Man standing at the right hand of God." **57.** They screamed, stopped their ears, and rushed at him. (Screamed: yelled) **58.** They threw him out of the city and stoned him. The witnesses laid their clothes at the feet of a young man named Saul. (Stoned: killed, Witnesses: observers) **59.** As they stoned Stephen, he prayed, "Lord Jesus, receive my spirit." **60.** He knelt down and cried, "Lord, do not hold this sin against them." When he said this, he died. (Kneeling: bowing, Sin: wrong)

Chapter 8
1. Saul approved of Stephen's death. Soon, a great persecution arose against the church in Jerusalem, and the believers were scattered across Judea and Samaria, except for the apostles. (Persecution: oppression for beliefs) **2.** Devout men buried Stephen and mourned deeply for him. (Devout: deeply religious) **3.** Saul ravaged the church, entering homes youngest, and the leader like the one who serves." **27.** "Who is greater: the one at the table or the one who serves? I am among you as one who serves." **28.** "You have stood by Me in My trials." **29.** "I confer a kingdom on you, just as My Father did for Me." **30.** "You will eat and drink at My table and sit on thrones, judging the twelve tribes of Israel." **31.** "Simon, Satan has asked to sift you as wheat." (Satan: the adversary) **32.** "But I have prayed for you, that your faith may remain strong. When you return, strengthen your brothers." **33.** Peter replied, "I'm ready to go with You to prison and even death." **34.** Jesus answered, "Before the rooster crows, you will deny Me three times." **35.** He asked them, "When I sent you without purse or sandals, did you lack anything?" They replied, "Nothing." **36.** "Now, if you have a purse, take it, and if you don't have a sword, buy one." **37.** "What's written about Me must be fulfilled: 'He was numbered with the transgressors.'" (Transgressors: sinners) **38.** They said, "Lord, here are two swords." He replied, "That's enough." **39.** Jesus went to the Mount of Olives, and His disciples followed Him. (Mount of Olives: a hill near Jerusalem) **40.** He told them, "Pray that you will not fall into

temptation." **41.** He withdrew a little and prayed, **42.** "Father, if You are willing, take this cup from Me, but let Your will be done." **43.** An angel appeared, strengthening Him. **44.** In agony, He prayed more earnestly, and His sweat became like drops of blood. **45.** When He returned, He found the disciples asleep, overwhelmed with sorrow. **46.** "Why are you sleeping?" He asked. "Pray so you don't fall into temptation." **47.** As He spoke, Judas appeared, leading a crowd to betray Him with a kiss. (Judas: one of the twelve apostles) **48.** Jesus asked, "Judas, are you betraying Me with a kiss?" **49.** His followers asked, "Shall we strike with our swords?" **50.** One struck the high priest's servant and cut off his ear. **51.** Jesus said, "No more of this!" He healed the man's ear. **52.** He asked the chief priests, temple officers, and elders, "Why come against Me with swords? I was with you daily in the temple." **53.** "This is your hour, when darkness reigns." **54.** They arrested Him and took Him to the high priest's house. Peter followed from a distance. (High priest: head of the Jewish temple) **55.** Peter sat with them around a fire. **56.** A servant girl saw him and said, "This man was with Jesus." **57.** Peter denied it, "I don't know Him." **58.** A little later, another said, "You're one of them." Peter denied it again. **59.** An hour later, another said, "This man was with Him. He is a Galilean." (Galilean: from the region of Galilee) **60.** Peter replied, "I don't know what you're talking about!" The rooster crowed immediately. **61.** Jesus turned and looked at Peter. Peter remembered Jesus' words, "Before the rooster crows, you will deny Me three times." **62.** He went out and wept bitterly. **63.** The men guarding Jesus mocked and beat Him. **64.** They blindfolded Him and struck Him, asking, "Prophesy, who hit You?" **65.** They said many other insulting things to Him. **66.** At dawn, the elders, chief priests, and teachers of the law gathered and led Jesus to their council. **67.** "Are You the Christ? Tell us," they demanded. Jesus replied, "If I tell you, you will not believe." **68.** "And if I ask you, you will not answer." **69.** "From now on, the Son of Man will sit at the right hand of the mighty God." (Right hand: a position of power) **70.** They asked, "Are You the Son of God?" He answered, "You say that I am." **71.** "We don't need further testimony. We've heard it from His own mouth."

Chapter 23
1. The crowd rose and took him to Pilate. (Pilate: Roman governor) **2.** They accused him, claiming, "He is misleading the nation, forbidding tribute to Caesar, and calling himself Christ, a King." **3.** Pilate asked, "Are you the King of the Jews?" Jesus replied, "You say so." **4.** Pilate told the priests and people, "I find no fault in him." **5.** But they insisted, "He is stirring up trouble, teaching across Judea, starting from Galilee." **6.** Upon hearing about Galilee, Pilate asked if he was from there. (Galilee: region in northern Israel) **7.** When Pilate learned Jesus was under Herod's authority, he sent him to Herod, who was in Jerusalem at that time. (Herod: ruler of Judea) **8.** Herod was glad to see Jesus, having long wished to meet him, hoping to witness a miracle. **9.** He asked many questions, but Jesus said nothing. **10.** The chief priests and scribes accused him fiercely. **11.** Herod and his soldiers mocked Jesus, dressed him in a fine robe, and sent him back to Pilate. **12.** That day, Pilate and Herod became friends; they had been enemies before. **13.** Pilate summoned the chief priests, rulers, and the people, **14.** and said, "You brought this man to me as one misleading the people. I find no fault in him." **15.** "Herod found no reason to condemn him either. I sent him to him, and nothing deserving of death was done." **16.** "I will punish him and release him." **17.** (It was customary for Pilate to release a prisoner at the feast.) **18.** The crowd shouted, "Release Barabbas!" **19.** (Barabbas: and arresting men and women for imprisonment. (Ravaged: severely damaged) **4.** Those scattered preached wherever they went. (Scattered: spread out) **5.** Philip went to Samaria and preached about Christ. (Preached: delivered a message) **6.** The people listened attentively to Philip's message, amazed by his miracles. (Attentively: with focus) **7.** Evil spirits shrieked and left many, and numerous sick were healed. (Evil spirits: demons; Sick: ill) **8.** There was great joy in the city. (Joy: happiness) **9.** Simon, who practiced sorcery, deceived the people of Samaria, claiming to be someone great. (Sorcery: magic) **10.** From the least to the greatest, all believed Simon, thinking he had the power of God. (Least: lowest rank) **11.** They admired him, amazed by his magic for a long time. (Admired: respected) **12.** When they believed Philip's message of God's kingdom and Jesus, both men and women were baptized. (Believed: accepted as true) **13.** Even Simon believed and was baptized. He stayed with Philip, astonished by the miracles. (Astonished: filled with wonder) **14.** When the apostles in Jerusalem heard that Samaria had accepted God's word, they sent Peter and John. (Accepted: received) **15.** Peter and John prayed for the Samaritans to receive the Holy Spirit. (Prayed: asked for God's help) **16.** At that time, the Holy Spirit had not yet come upon any of them; they had only been baptized in Jesus' name. (Yet: up to that time) **17.** The apostles laid hands on them, and they received the Holy Spirit. (Laid hands: gesture of blessing) **18.** When Simon saw that the Holy Spirit was given through the apostles' hands, he offered them money. (Offered: gave for exchange) **19.** He asked, "Give me this power so anyone I touch can receive the Holy Spirit." (Asked: requested) **20.** Peter responded, "May your money perish with you, for you think God's gift can be bought." (Perish: be destroyed) **21.** "You have no share in this, for your heart is not right with God." (Share: involvement) **22.** "Repent of your wickedness and pray to God for forgiveness." (Repent: feel regret) **23.** "I see you are full of bitterness and enslaved by sin." (Bitterness: deep anger; Enslaved: trapped) **24.** Simon requested they pray for him so none of the consequences would come upon him. (Requested: asked for) **25.** They preached in many Samaritan villages before returning to Jerusalem. (Preached: delivered religious teachings) **26.** An angel told Philip to go south to the desert road from Jerusalem to Gaza. (Desert: barren land) **27.** Philip obeyed and met an Ethiopian eunuch, a high-ranking official under Queen Candace, who oversaw her treasure. He had come to Jerusalem to worship. (Eunuch: castrated man in royal service; Official: person in authority) **28.** The eunuch was returning, reading the prophet Isaiah in his chariot. (Chariot: horse-drawn vehicle) **29.** The Spirit told Philip to go near and join the chariot. (Spirit: divine presence) **30.** Philip ran to the chariot, heard the eunuch reading, and asked, "Do you understand what you're reading?" (Understand: grasp the meaning) **31.** The eunuch replied, "How can I unless someone guides me?" He invited Philip to sit with him. (Guides: teaches) **32.** The scripture spoke of a lamb led to slaughter, silent before its shearer, without protest. (Shearer: one who cuts wool) **33.** It spoke of how his judgment was taken away, and his life was removed from the earth. (Judgment: legal decision) **34.** The eunuch asked, "Who is the prophet referring to? Himself or someone else?" (Prophet: one who speaks for God) **35.** Philip began with this scripture and preached to him about Jesus. (Began: started) **36.** As they traveled, they came to water, and the eunuch asked, "What's stopping me from being baptized?" (Baptized: immersed for purification) **37.** Philip replied, "If you believe with all your heart, you may." The eunuch answered, "I believe Jesus Christ is the Son of God." (Believe: have faith) **38.** The eunuch commanded the chariot to stop, and they both entered the water, where Philip baptized him. (Ordered: commanded) **39.** After coming out of the water, the Spirit took Philip away, and the eunuch rejoiced as he continued his journey. (Rejoiced: celebrated joyfully) **40.** Philip was found in Azotus and preached in many cities until reaching Caesarea. (Preached: delivered religious messages)

Chapter 9
1. Saul, still threatening and seeking to harm the disciples, went to the high priest. (threatening: expressing intention to harm) **2.** He asked for letters to Damascus to arrest any followers of Jesus, men or women, and bring them to Jerusalem. (followers of Jesus: disciples or believers) **3.** As Saul neared Damascus, a bright light suddenly surrounded him from heaven. (bright: shining strongly) **4.** He fell to the ground and heard a voice saying, "Saul, why are you persecuting me?" (persecuting: mistreating or harming) **5.** Saul asked, "Who are you, Lord?" The voice replied, "I am Jesus, whom you are persecuting. It is hard for you to resist my will." (resist: fight against) **6.** Trembling and amazed, Saul asked, "What should I do?" The Lord told him to go to the city where he would be told further. (trembling: shaking in fear) **7.** The men with Saul stood speechless, hearing the voice but seeing no one. (speechless: unable to speak) **8.** Saul got up, but when his eyes opened, he was blind. His companions led him to Damascus. (companions: friends or associates) **9.** For three days, Saul was blind, and he neither ate nor drank. (blind: unable to see) **10.** A disciple named Ananias in Damascus was told in a vision to find Saul. (disciple: a follower of Christ) **11.** The Lord directed Ananias to the house of Judas on Straight Street, where Saul was praying. (praying: communicating with God) **12.** Saul had seen in a vision Ananias coming to restore his sight. (restore: return to normal) **13.** Ananias was afraid, knowing Saul's evil actions against Christians in Jerusalem. (evil: wicked or harmful) **14.** Saul had authority to arrest anyone calling on Jesus' name. (authority: official permission) **15.** The Lord reassured Ananias, saying Saul was chosen to spread His name to Gentiles, kings, and Israel. (Gentiles: non-Jews) **16.** The Lord would show Saul the suffering he must endure for His name. (endure: suffer patiently) **17.** Ananias went to Saul, laid hands on him, and said, "Jesus has sent me so you can receive your sight and the Holy Spirit." (laid hands: touched in a blessing) **18.** Immediately, scales fell from Saul's eyes, and he could see again. He was baptized. (scales: a covering or film) **19.** After eating, Saul regained strength and stayed with the disciples in Damascus. (regained: got back) **20.** Saul quickly began preaching in the

synagogues that Jesus is the Son of God. (synagogues: Jewish places of worship) **21.** Everyone was amazed, asking if this was the man who had destroyed Jesus' followers. (destroyed: harmed severely) **22.** Saul grew stronger and confounded the Jews in Damascus, proving Jesus is the Christ. (confounded: confused or amazed) **23.** After many days, the Jews plotted to kill Saul. (plotted: planned secretly) **24.** Saul learned of their plot, and they watched the gates day and night. (gates: city entrances) **25.** The disciples helped Saul escape by lowering him in a basket through a wall. (escape: to get away safely) **26.** When Saul arrived in Jerusalem, the disciples were afraid, not believing he was a true follower. (disciples: believers) **27.** Barnabas vouched for Saul, telling them of his encounter with Jesus and his bold preaching in Damascus. (vouched: confirmed the truth) **28.** Saul stayed with the disciples in Jerusalem, coming and going with them. (coming and going: visiting frequently) **29.** He boldly preached about Jesus, but some Grecians tried to kill him. (Grecians: Greek-speaking Jews) **30.** The brethren sent Saul to Caesarea and then to Tarsus for safety. (brethren: fellow believers) **31.** The churches had peace and grew stronger, walking in the fear of the Lord and the comfort of the Holy Spirit. (comfort: support) **32.** Peter visited the saints in Lydda. (saints: holy believers) **33.** There, he healed Aeneas, a man paralyzed for eight years. (paralyzed: unable to move) **34.** Peter told Aeneas, "Jesus heals you; get up and make your bed." Aeneas immediately stood up. (heals: makes well) **35.** People in Lydda and Saron saw Aeneas and turned to the Lord. (turned: changed direction or beliefs) **36.** In Joppa, a disciple named Tabitha, also called Dorcas, was known for her good deeds. (deeds: actions) **37.** Tabitha died, and her body was laid in an upper room. (laid: placed) **38.** The disciples sent for Peter, asking him to come quickly. (disciples: followers of Christ) **39.** Peter went with them, and when he arrived, the widows showed him the garments Tabitha made. (widows: women whose husbands had died) **40.** Peter prayed, turned to the body, and said, "Tabitha, arise." She opened her eyes and sat up. (arise: get up) **41.** He helped her stand, then called the saints and widows to see her alive. (saints: holy believers) **42.** This miracle spread throughout Joppa, and many believed in the Lord. (miracle: a supernatural act) **43.** Peter stayed in Joppa for many days with Simon, a tanner. (tanner: one who works with leather)

Chapter 10
1. A man named Cornelius lived in Caesarea, a centurion in the Italian regiment. (Centurion: Roman officer, Regiment: military unit) **2.** He was a devout man who feared God, along with his household. He gave generously to the poor and prayed regularly. (Devout: religious, Alms: charity) **3.** At 3 PM, Cornelius saw a vision of God's angel calling his name: "Cornelius." (Vision: supernatural appearance) **4.** Terrified, he asked, "What is it, Lord?" The angel replied, "Your prayers and acts of charity have been remembered by God." (Acts of charity: giving to others) **5.** "Send men to Joppa and ask for Simon, also known as Peter." (Joppa: a port city) **6.** "He is staying with Simon the tanner by the sea. He will tell you what to do." (Tanner: someone who processes hides) **7.** After the angel left, Cornelius called two servants and a devout soldier who served him. (Devout: religious) **8.** He explained everything to them and sent them to Joppa. (Explained: made clear) **9.** The next day, as they neared the city, Peter went to the rooftop to pray around noon. (Rooftop: top of a house) **10.** Hungry, Peter was about to eat, but while waiting, he fell into a trance. (Trance: a vision or deep focus) **11.** He saw heaven open and a large sheet lowered, held by four corners. (Sheet: large cloth) **12.** In the sheet were all kinds of animals, wild beasts, creeping creatures, and birds. (Creeping creatures: insects and reptiles) **13.** A voice said, "Get up, Peter; kill and eat." (Voice: divine call) **14.** Peter replied, "No, Lord; I've never eaten anything unclean." (Unclean: defiled) **15.** The voice said again, "Do not call unclean what God has made clean." (Unclean: defiled, Clean: pure) **16.** This happened three times, and the sheet was taken back into heaven. (Taken: lifted) **17.** Peter was puzzled when Cornelius' men arrived and stood at the gate. (Puzzled: confused) **18.** They called out, asking for Simon, known as Peter. (Called out: shouted) **19.** While Peter was thinking about the vision, the Spirit told him, "Three men are looking for you." (Spirit: divine presence) **20.** "Go downstairs and go with them without hesitation, for I have sent them." (Hesitation: doubt) **21.** Peter went down and said, "I'm the one you're looking for. Why have you come?" (Looking for: searching for) **22.** They replied, "Cornelius, a righteous man who fears God, was told by an angel to summon you to hear from you." (Righteous: morally right) **23.** Peter invited them in and gave them lodging. The next day, he left with them, and some believers from Joppa accompanied him. (Lodging: accommodation) **24.** The next day they arrived in Caesarea, where Cornelius had gathered his family and friends. (Caesarea: city in ancient Judea) **25.** As Peter entered, Cornelius met him, fell at his feet, and worshiped him. (Worshiped: showed reverence) **26.** Peter said, "Stand up; I am a man, too." (Stand up: rise) **27.** Peter entered the house, finding many gathered. (Gathered: assembled) **28.** Peter said, "It's forbidden for Jews to associate with Gentiles, but God showed me not to call anyone unclean." (Gentiles: non-Jews) **29.** "So I came without objection. Why have you summoned me?" (Objection: refusal) **30.** Cornelius said, "Four days ago, I was fasting and praying at 3 PM when a man in bright clothing appeared." (Fasting: refraining from food) **31.** "He said, 'Your prayer is heard, and your acts of charity are remembered by God.'" (Acts of charity: giving to others) **32.** "Send to Joppa for Simon, also called Peter, who is staying at Simon the tanner's house. He will tell you what to do." (Tanner: one who works with hides) **33.** "I immediately sent for you, and you've done well to come. We are all here to hear what God has commanded you." (Commanded: instructed) **34.** Peter said, "I now realize that God does not show favoritism." (Favoritism: partiality) **35.** "In every nation, anyone who fears God and does what is right is accepted by Him." (Accepted: welcomed) **36.** "You know the message God sent to Israel, preaching peace through Jesus Christ, who is Lord of all." (Preaching: delivering a message) **37.** "You know what happened throughout Judea, starting in Galilee after John's baptism." (Judea: a region, Galilee: a region) **38.** "God anointed Jesus of Nazareth with the Holy Spirit and power. He went around doing good and healing those oppressed by the devil." (Anointed: chosen, Oppressed: afflicted) **39.** "We are witnesses of all He did in the land of the Jews and in Jerusalem, where they killed Him by hanging on a tree." (Witnesses: those who testify) **40.** "But God raised Him from the dead on the third day and showed Him to us." (Raised: revived) **41.** "He was not seen by everyone, but by those God chose, by us who ate and drank with Him after He rose from the dead." (Ate: consumed food) **42.** "He commanded us to preach to the people and testify that He is the appointed Judge of the living and the dead." (Preach: deliver a sermon, Judge: decision-maker) **43.** "All the prophets testify that anyone who believes in Him will receive forgiveness of sins through His name." (Forgiveness: pardon) **44.** As Peter spoke, the Holy Spirit came upon all who heard the message. (Holy Spirit: divine presence) **45.** The Jewish believers with Peter were amazed that the Holy Spirit was given to the Gentiles. (Amazed: astonished) **46.** They heard them speaking in tongues and praising God. Then Peter said, (Tongues: languages spoken supernaturally) **47.** "Can anyone stop these people from being baptized, since they've received the Holy Spirit like we did?" (Stop: prevent) **48.** Peter ordered them to be baptized in Jesus' name, and they asked him to stay with them for a few days. (Ordered: instructed)

Chapter 11
1. The apostles and believers in Judea heard that the Gentiles had received God's word. (Gentiles: non-Jews) **2.** When Peter arrived in Jerusalem, those who followed the law criticized him, (Circumcision: the Jewish ritual of removing the foreskin, symbolizing the covenant with God) **3.** Saying, "You ate with uncircumcised men!" (Uncircumcised: not having undergone the Jewish ritual of circumcision) **4.** Peter explained the events from the beginning, saying, (Expounded: explained in detail) **5.** "I was praying in Joppa and had a vision: a large sheet came down from heaven, held by four corners, and came to me. (Trance: a deep, altered state of consciousness, often associated with visions) **6.** As I looked, I saw animals, wild creatures, reptiles, and birds. (Reptiles: cold-blooded animals, such as lizards and snakes) **7.** A voice told me, 'Get up, Peter; kill and eat.' **8.** I replied, 'No, Lord! I have never eaten anything impure or unclean.' (Impure: not clean or defiled) **9.** The voice said again, 'Do not call anything impure that God has made clean.' (Common: something considered ordinary or unclean in Jewish law) **10.** This happened three times, and everything was drawn back up to heaven. **11.** At once, three men arrived at the house where I was staying, sent from Caesarea. (Caesarea: a city on the Mediterranean coast in ancient Judea) **12.** The Spirit told me to go with them without hesitation, and six brothers went with me. We entered the man's house, **13.** And he told us how he saw an angel in his house who said, 'Send for Simon Peter, (Angel: a spiritual being who serves as a messenger of God) **14.** Who will tell you words by which you and your household will be saved.' (Saved: delivered from sin and its consequences) **15.** As I began speaking, the Holy Spirit came upon them, just as it did on us at the beginning. (Holy Spirit: the third person of the Christian Trinity) **16.** Then I remembered the Lord's words: 'John baptized with water, but you will be baptized with the Holy Spirit.' (Baptized: immersed in water as a sign of spiritual cleansing or initiation) **17.** Since God gave them the same gift He gave us, who believed in Jesus Christ, who was I to oppose God? (Withstand: resist or oppose) **18.** When they heard this, they praised God, saying, 'God has granted repentance that leads to life, even to the Gentiles.' (Repentance: the act of feeling regret and changing one's behavior, especially in a religious context) **19.** Those scattered by the persecution after Stephen's death traveled to places like Phoenicia, Cyprus, and Antioch, preaching only to Jews. (Persecution: hostility or ill-treatment) **20.** Some men from Cyprus and Cyrene went to Antioch and preached to the Greeks, proclaiming the Lord Jesus. (Proclaiming: announcing) **21.** The Lord's hand was with them, and

many believed and turned to the Lord. **22.** News of this reached the church in Jerusalem, and they sent Barnabas to Antioch. (Church: the community of Christian believers) **23.** When he arrived and saw the grace of God, he rejoiced and encouraged them all to remain faithful to the Lord. (Grace: God's unearned favor and kindness) **24.** He was a good man, full of the Holy Spirit and faith, and many people were added to the Lord. (Holy Spirit: God's presence and power) **25.** Barnabas then went to Tarsus to find Saul. (Tarsus: a city in the region of Cilicia, where Saul (Paul) was from) **26.** After finding him, he brought him to Antioch, and they spent a year teaching a large number of people. The disciples were first called Christians in Antioch. (Disciples: followers of Jesus Christ) **27.** During those days, prophets came from Jerusalem to Antioch. (Prophets: people who claim to receive messages from God) **28.** One of them, named Agabus, stood up and, by the Spirit, predicted a great famine that would spread across the world, which happened during the reign of Emperor Claudius. (Famine: a severe shortage of food) (Reign: the period during which a king or emperor rules) **29.** The disciples decided, each according to their ability, to send relief to the brothers in Judea. (Relief: aid or help, especially in times of need) **30.** They did this and sent the gift to the elders by Barnabas and Saul. (Elders: leaders or overseers in the church)

Chapter 12

1. Around that time, King Herod persecuted some members of the church. (persecuted: oppressed, members: followers) **2.** He had James, the brother of John, killed with the sword. (killed: executed, sword: weapon) **3.** When Herod saw that this pleased the Jews, he decided to arrest Peter as well. (This was during the Days of Unleavened Bread.) (pleased: satisfied, arrest: capture) **4.** After arresting Peter, he put him in prison, guarded by four squads of soldiers, planning to bring him before the people after the Passover. (arresting: capturing, guarded: protected) **5.** While Peter was in prison, the church prayed earnestly to God for him. (earnestly: fervently, prayed: petitioned) **6.** The night before Herod planned to bring him out, Peter was asleep between two soldiers, chained, with guards at the door. (planned: intended, chained: bound) **7.** Suddenly, an angel of the Lord appeared, a light shone in the prison, and the angel struck Peter on the side, waking him. The chains fell off his hands. (suddenly: unexpectedly, struck: hit) **8.** The angel told Peter, "Get dressed and put on your sandals." Peter did as instructed. The angel then said, "Wrap your cloak around you and follow me." (dressed: clothed, instructed: commanded) **9.** Peter followed the angel, unsure if this was real or a vision. (unsure: uncertain, vision: dream) **10.** They passed the first and second guards and reached the iron gate leading to the city, which opened by itself. They walked down one street, and then the angel left him. (reached: arrived at, itself: automatically) **11.** When Peter realized what had happened, he said, "Now I know for sure that the Lord has sent His angel and rescued me from Herod and the people's expectations." (realized: understood, rescued: saved) **12.** He went to the house of Mary, the mother of John Mark, where many people were gathered, praying. (gathered: assembled, praying: petitioning) **13.** When Peter knocked on the door, a servant girl named Rhoda came to answer. (knocked: tapped, servant: maid) **14.** She recognized Peter's voice but, overjoyed, didn't open the door. Instead, she ran to tell the others that Peter was outside. (recognized: identified, overjoyed: ecstatic) **15.** They said she was out of her mind, but she insisted. They then suggested, "It must be his angel." (insisted: persisted, suggested: proposed) **16.** Meanwhile, Peter continued knocking. When they opened the door and saw him, they were amazed. (continued: kept, amazed: astonished) **17.** Peter motioned for them to be quiet and told them how the Lord had rescued him. He then instructed them to tell James and the other believers. Afterward, he left and went to another place. (motioned: signaled, instructed: directed) **18.** The next day, there was a commotion among the soldiers about what had happened to Peter. (commotion: disturbance, soldiers: guards) **19.** When Herod couldn't find him, he interrogated the guards and ordered their execution. He then went from Judea to Caesarea, where he stayed. (interrogated: questioned, execution: killing) **20.** Herod was angry with the people of Tyre and Sidon. They came to him in one accord, making peace through the king's chamberlain, Blastus, because their region depended on his country for food. (angry: enraged, accord: unity) **21.** On a set day, Herod, dressed in royal attire, sat on his throne and gave a speech. (dressed: clothed, attire: garments) **22.** The people shouted, "This is the voice of a god, not a man!" (shouted: exclaimed, god: deity) **23.** Immediately, the angel of the Lord struck him down because he did not give glory to God. He was eaten by worms and died. (immediately: instantly, struck: struck down) **24.** But the word of God continued to grow and spread. (continued: persisted, spread: expanded) **25.** After completing their mission in Jerusalem, Barnabas and Saul returned, taking John Mark with them. (completed: finished, mission: task)

Chapter 13

1. In the early church at Antioch, there were several prophets and teachers: Barnabas, Simeon (nicknamed Niger), Lucius from Cyrene, Manaen (who had grown up with Herod the tetrarch), and Saul. (Tetrarch: ruler) (Cyrene: North Africa) **2.** As they served the Lord and were fasting, the Holy Spirit spoke, saying, "Set apart Barnabas and Saul for the task I have called them to." (Fasting: abstinence) (Holy Spirit: Paraclete) **3.** After they had fasted, prayed, and laid hands on them, they sent Barnabas and Saul on their mission. (Laid hands: blessing) **4.** Led by the Holy Spirit, they journeyed to Seleucia and sailed from there to the island of Cyprus. (Seleucia: port) (Cyprus: island) **5.** When they arrived in Salamis, they preached the word of God in the Jewish synagogues, and John served as their assistant. (Synagogues: places of worship) (Word of God: gospel) **6.** Traveling across the island to Paphos, they encountered a sorcerer, a false prophet, a Jewish man named Bar-Jesus. (Sorcerer: magician) (False prophet: deceiver) **7.** This man was in the service of the proconsul, Sergius Paulus, a wise leader who requested to hear the word of God from Barnabas and Saul. (Proconsul: governor) (Requested: asked) **8.** Elymas the sorcerer (as he was also called) opposed them, trying to turn the proconsul away from the faith. (Opposed: resisted) **9.** Filled with the Holy Spirit, Saul, now known as Paul, fixed his gaze on him (Filled: empowered) **10.** and said, "You are full of deceit and evil, a child of the devil, an enemy of all that is good. Will you never stop twisting the ways of the Lord?" (Deceit: dishonesty) (Twisting: distorting) **11.** "Now, behold, the hand of the Lord is upon you, and you will be blind for a time, unable to see the sun." Immediately, a darkness fell over him, and he began searching for someone to lead him. (Behold: see) (Blind: sightless) (Searching: groping) **12.** When the proconsul saw what had happened, he believed, astonished by the teaching of the Lord. (Astonished: amazed) (Teaching: doctrine) **13.** Paul and his companions left Paphos and traveled to Perga in Pamphylia, where John left them and returned to Jerusalem. (Pamphylia: region) **14.** Continuing from Perga, they arrived in Antioch in Pisidia and went into the synagogue on the Sabbath to sit down. (Pisidia: region) (Sabbath: rest day) **15.** After the reading of the Law and the Prophets, the synagogue leaders invited Paul and Barnabas, saying, "Brothers, if you have any message of encouragement, please speak." (Law: Torah) (Prophets: seers) **16.** Paul stood up, motioned for silence, and said, "Men of Israel, and you Gentiles who worship God, listen to me." (Beckoned: gestured) (Gentiles: non-Jews) **17.** "The God of Israel chose our ancestors and made them great when they lived in Egypt. With a mighty arm, He brought them out of bondage." (Ancestors: forebears) (Bondage: slavery) **18.** "For forty years, He tolerated their rebellious ways in the desert." (Tolerated: endured) **19.** "After destroying seven nations in Canaan, He divided their land among His people." (Canaan: promised land) (Divided: distributed) **20.** "He gave them judges for about 450 years, until Samuel the prophet." (Judges: leaders) **21.** "Then they asked for a king, and God gave them Saul, the son of Kish, from the tribe of Benjamin, who ruled for forty years." (Kish: Saul's father) **22.** "When God removed him, He raised up David as their king, and testified about him, saying, 'I have found David, son of Jesse, a man after my own heart; he will do everything I want him to.'" (Testified: affirmed) (Heart: soul) **23.** "From David's descendants, God has brought to Israel the Savior, Jesus, as He promised." (Savior: rescuer) **24.** "Before His coming, John preached a baptism of repentance to all the people of Israel." (Repentance: remorse) (Baptism: immersion) **25.** "When John finished his course, he said, 'Who do you think I am? I am not the Messiah. But one is coming after me, whose sandals I am not worthy to untie.'" (Course: journey) (Untie: loosen) **26.** "Brothers, descendants of Abraham, and you Gentiles who fear God, to us has been sent the message of salvation." (Fear God: reverence) (Salvation: deliverance) **27.** "The people of Jerusalem and their leaders did not recognize Jesus, nor understand the prophecies read every Sabbath. They fulfilled them by condemning Him." (Condemning: sentencing) **28.** "Even though they found no reason to execute Him, they asked Pilate to have Him crucified." (Pilate: governor) (Executed: killed) **29.** "After fulfilling all that was written about Him, they took Him down from the cross and laid Him in a tomb." (Cross: execution device) (Tomb: grave) **30.** "But God raised Him from the dead." (Raised: revived) **31.** "He was seen for many days by those who had come up with Him from Galilee to Jerusalem. They are now His witnesses to the people." (Witnesses: observers) **32.** "We bring you the good news: what God promised our ancestors, He has fulfilled for us, their children, by raising up Jesus." (Good news: gospel) (Fulfilled: completed) **33.** "As it is written in the second Psalm: 'You are my Son; today I have become your Father.'" (Psalm: sacred song) **34.** "God raised Him from the dead, never to decay again. As He said: 'I will give you the holy and sure blessings promised to David.'" (Sure blessings: promises) **35.** "Therefore, He says in another Psalm, 'You will not let Your Holy One see decay.'" (Holy One: Messiah) (Decay: corruption) **36.** "For David, after serving God's purpose in his generation, died, was buried with his ancestors, and saw decay." (Generation: age) **37.** "But the one whom God raised from the dead did not see decay." (Decay: rot) **38.** "Therefore, brothers, know that through Jesus the forgiveness of sins is proclaimed to you." (Forgiveness: pardon) **39.** "Through Him, everyone who believes is declared righteous from everything you could not be justified from by the law of Moses." (Justified: declared innocent) **40.** "Be careful that what the prophets warned about does not happen to you." (Careful: cautious) **41.** "'Look, you scoffers, wonder and perish; for I am doing something in your days that you would never believe, even if someone told you.'" (Scoffers: mockers) **42.** As the Jews left the synagogue, the Gentiles asked Paul and Barnabas to speak more about these things the next Sabbath. (Gentiles: non-Jews) **43.** After the meeting, many Jews and devout converts followed Paul and Barnabas, and they urged them to remain in God's grace. (Devout: pious) (Proselytes: converts) **44.** The next Sabbath, nearly the whole city gathered to hear the word of God. (Gathered: assembled) **45.** When the Jews saw the crowds, they were filled with jealousy and began to argue against what Paul was saying, even blaspheming. (Jealousy: envy) (Blaspheming: disrespecting) **46.** Boldly, Paul and Barnabas declared, "It was necessary to first speak to you. But since you reject it and do not consider yourselves worthy of eternal life, we now turn to the Gentiles." (Reject: dismiss) **47.** "For this is what the Lord has commanded us: 'I have made you a light for the Gentiles, to bring salvation to the ends of the earth.'" (Light: guide) **48.** When the Gentiles heard this, they rejoiced and honored God's message, and all who were destined for eternal life believed. (Destined: chosen) **49.** The message of the Lord spread throughout the whole region. (Spread: expanded) **50.** The Jews incited prominent women and leading men of the city, stirring up persecution against Paul and Barnabas, and expelled them from the region. (Incited: provoked) **51.** Paul and Barnabas shook the dust from their feet as a sign of rejection and went to Iconium. (Shook: brushed) **52.** The disciples were filled with joy and the Holy Spirit. (Disciples: followers)

Chapter 14
1. In Iconium, Paul and Barnabas entered the Jewish synagogue, spoke boldly, and many Jews and Greeks believed. (Iconium: city; synagogue: temple; boldly: confidently) **2.** But the unbelieving Jews stirred up the Gentiles and turned them against the apostles. (Unbelieving: faithless; Gentiles: non-Jews) **3.** They continued speaking boldly for a long time, with the Lord confirming their message through signs and wonders. (Boldly: courageously; confirming: validating; signs: miracles) **4.** The city was divided; some sided with the Jews, others with the apostles. (Divided: split; sided: supported) **5.** The Gentiles and Jews, with their leaders, plotted to mistreat and stone them. (Mistreat: harm; stone: kill) **6.** Aware of the plot, they fled to Lystra and Derbe in Lycaonia and preached there. (Aware: conscious; fled: escaped) **7.** In Lystra, they preached the gospel. (Gospel: message) **8.** There was a man in Lystra, crippled from birth, who had never walked. (Crippled: disabled; birth: origin) **9.** When he heard Paul, Paul saw he had faith to be healed. (Faith: belief) **10.** Paul told him to stand up, and the man leaped to his feet. (Leaped: jumped) **11.** The crowd, amazed, declared that gods had come down in human form. (Amazed: astonished; declared: said) **12.** They called Barnabas "Zeus" and Paul "Hermes" because Paul was the main speaker. (Zeus/Hermes: gods; speaker: orator) **13.** The priest of Zeus brought oxen and offerings to sacrifice to them. (Priest: cleric; oxen: cattle) **14.** When the apostles saw this, they tore their clothes and rushed to stop them, shouting, (Tore: ripped; rushed: hurried) **15.** "Why are you doing this? We are just like you and preach about the living God who made everything." (Preach: proclaim; living God: active deity) **16.** In the past, God allowed nations to follow their own ways. (Allowed: permitted; nations: peoples) **17.** But He showed His goodness by sending rain and providing food, filling our hearts with joy. (Goodness: kindness; joy: happiness) **18.** With these words, they barely stopped the crowd from sacrificing to them. (Barely: hardly) **19.** Some Jews from Antioch and Iconium came and convinced the crowd to stone Paul, thinking he was dead. (Convinced: persuaded; stoned: killed) **20.** But when his disciples gathered around him, Paul stood up and went back into the city. The next day, he and Barnabas left for Derbe. (Disciples: followers; stood up: rose) **21.** After preaching in Derbe and teaching many, they returned to Lystra, Iconium, and Antioch. (Preaching: teaching) **22.** They strengthened the believers, urging them to stay faithful, explaining that suffering is part of entering God's kingdom. (Strengthened: encouraged; suffering: hardship) **23.** They appointed elders in each church, prayed, and entrusted them to the Lord. (Appointed: chose; entrusted: gave) **24.** After passing through Pisidia, they reached Pamphylia. (Pisidia/Pamphylia: regions) **25.** They preached in Perga, then sailed to Attalia. (Preached: proclaimed; sailed: traveled) **26.** From Attalia, they sailed back to Antioch, where they had been sent by God's grace for this mission. (Grace: favor; mission: task) **27.** Upon returning, they gathered the church and shared how God had opened the door of faith to the Gentiles. (Gathered: assembled; door: opportunity) **28.** They stayed there a long time, teaching and encouraging the disciples. (Encouraging: supporting)

Chapter 15
1. Certain men came from Judea and taught the brothers, saying, "Unless you are circumcised according to Moses' law, you cannot be saved." (Circumcised: cut; Judea: region) **2.** Paul and Barnabas strongly disagreed with them, so they decided to go to Jerusalem to consult the apostles and elders about this issue. (Disagreed: argued) **3.** On their journey, the church sent them through Phoenicia and Samaria, where they shared the conversion of the Gentiles, bringing joy to all the believers. (Gentiles: non-Jews; Phoenicia: region) **4.** In Jerusalem, they were welcomed by the church, apostles, and elders, and they reported all that God had done through them. (Apostles: followers; Elders: leaders) **5.** But some believers from the Pharisees argued that Gentiles must be circumcised and follow the Law of Moses. (Pharisees: religious group; Law: rules) **6.** The apostles and elders gathered to discuss the matter. (Gathered: assembled) **7.** After much debate, Peter stood up and reminded them that God chose him to bring the gospel to the Gentiles, who then believed. (Debate: discussion) **8.** God, who knows the heart, testified by giving them the Holy Spirit, just as He did to us. (Testified: proved; Holy Spirit: divine) **9.** He made no distinction between us and them, purifying their hearts through faith. (Distinction: difference; Purifying: cleansing) **10.** Why then would you test God by putting a yoke (burden) on the disciples that neither we nor our ancestors could bear? (Yoke: burden) **11.** We believe that we are saved through the grace of the Lord Jesus, just as they are. (Grace: favor) **12.** Everyone listened in silence as Barnabas and Paul shared how God worked wonders among the Gentiles. (Wonders: miracles) **13.** Afterward, James spoke, saying, "Listen to me." (James: leader) **14.** Simeon (Peter) explained how God visited the Gentiles to take from them a people for His name. (Simeon: Peter) **15.** This agrees with the words of the prophets, as written: (Agree: match; Prophets: speakers) **16.** "I will rebuild the fallen tabernacle of David, restoring its ruins and setting it up again." (Tabernacle: tent) **17.** So that the rest of mankind may seek the Lord, including all the Gentiles who are called by my name," says the Lord, who does these things. (Mankind: humans; Called: chosen) **18.** God knows all His works from the beginning of the world. (Works: deeds) **19.** Therefore, my judgment is that we should not trouble the Gentiles who are turning to God. (Judgment: decision) **20.** Instead, we should write to them to avoid idol worship, sexual immorality, consuming strangled animals, and blood. (Immorality: sin) **21.** Moses has long been preached in every city, read in synagogues every Sabbath. (Preached: taught; Sabbath: rest) **22.** The apostles and elders, together with the whole church, chose men to send with Paul and Barnabas to Antioch: Judas (called Barsabbas) and Silas, leading men among the believers. (Chosen: selected) **23.** They wrote letters to the Gentiles in Antioch, Syria, and Cilicia, greeting them: (Cilicia: region) **24.** "We heard that some people from us troubled you, teaching that you must be circumcised and obey the law, which we did not command. (Troubled: disturbed) **25.** So we decided, with one accord, to send these men to you, along with Barnabas and Paul, (One accord: united) **26.** who have risked their lives for the name of our Lord Jesus Christ. (Risked: endangered) **27.** We have sent Judas and Silas to speak the same things to you in person. (Speak: tell) **28.** It seemed good to the Holy Spirit and to us not to impose any greater burden than these necessary requirements: (Impose: force) **29.** Abstain from food offered to idols, from blood, from strangled animals, and from sexual immorality. If you do this, you will do well. Farewell." (Abstain: refrain; Farewell: goodbye) **30.** They were sent off and went to Antioch, where they gathered the believers and read the letter. (Gathered: assembled) **31.** When they heard it, they rejoiced at the encouragement. (Rejoiced: celebrated; Encouragement: support) **32.** Judas and Silas, both prophets, spoke many words to strengthen and confirm the brothers. (Strengthen: support; Confirm: affirm) **33.** After staying for a time, they were sent off in peace by the believers to the apostles. (Sent off: dismissed) **34.** However, Silas chose to remain in Antioch. (Remain: stay) **35.** Paul and Barnabas stayed in Antioch, teaching and preaching with many others. (Preaching: teaching) **36.** After some time, Paul suggested to Barnabas, "Let us return to visit the brothers in every city where we preached and see how they are doing." (Suggested: proposed) **37.** Barnabas wanted to take John Mark with them, (Wanted: desired) **38.** but Paul disagreed, since Mark had left them earlier in Pamphylia and not continued the work. (Disagreed: opposed; Pamphylia: region) **39.** The disagreement was so sharp that they parted ways: Barnabas took Mark and sailed to Cyprus, (Disagreement: argument) **40.** and Paul chose Silas and left, entrusted by the believers to the grace of God. (Entrusted: trusted) **41.** Paul and Silas traveled through Syria and Cilicia, strengthening the churches. (Strengthening: encouraging)

Chapter 16

1. Paul then traveled to Derbe and Lystra, where he found a disciple named Timothy. His mother was a Jewish believer, but his father was Greek. (Derbe and Lystra: towns in Asia Minor; Timothy: companion of Paul) 2. Timothy was well spoken of by the believers in Lystra and Iconium. (Iconium: an ancient city in Asia Minor) 3. Paul wanted Timothy to join him in his travels, so he had him circumcised, as many Jews in the area knew his father was Greek. (Circumcision: a rite practiced by Jews) 4. As they traveled from city to city, they shared the decrees set by the apostles and elders in Jerusalem for the believers to follow. (Apostles: Jesus' closest followers; Jerusalem: the central city for early Christianity) 5. The churches grew stronger in their faith, and the number of believers increased every day. (Faith: trust and belief in God) 6. They passed through Phrygia and Galatia, but the Holy Spirit stopped them from preaching the message in Asia. (Phrygia and Galatia: regions in ancient Asia Minor) 7. When they reached Mysia, they attempted to go into Bithynia, but the Spirit did not allow it. (Mysia: a region in Asia Minor; Bithynia: a region to the north) 8. Afterward, they bypassed Mysia and headed for Troas. (Troas: a city by the coast in Asia Minor) 9. That night, Paul had a vision of a man from Macedonia standing and asking, "Come to Macedonia and help us." (Macedonia: a region in northern Greece) 10. After seeing the vision, we immediately decided to go to Macedonia, convinced that God had called us to bring the gospel to them. (Gospel: the good news of Jesus) 11. So, leaving Troas, we sailed directly to Samothrace, and the following day we reached Neapolis. (Samothrace: an island in the northern Aegean; Neapolis: a port in Macedonia) 12. From Neapolis, we traveled to Philippi, the main city in that part of Macedonia, and a Roman colony. We stayed there for several days. (Philippi: a leading city in Macedonia) 13. On the Sabbath, we went outside the city to the river, where people often gathered to pray. We sat down and spoke to the women who had assembled. (Sabbath: the day of rest) 14. One of them was Lydia, a seller of purple goods from Thyatira, who worshiped God. She listened to us, and the Lord opened her heart to respond to Paul's message. (Lydia: a businesswoman from Thyatira; Thyatira: an ancient city in Asia Minor) 15. After being baptized, along with her household, she invited us to stay at her home, saying, "If you consider me a believer, please come and stay with us." And she convinced us. (Baptized: a Christian ritual of immersion in water) 16. As we went to pray, a slave girl with the ability to tell fortunes met us. She earned much money for her masters by predicting the future. (Fortunes: predicting events through supernatural means) 17. She followed Paul and us, shouting, "These men are servants of the Most High God, and they are showing you the way of salvation!" (Most High God: a title for the one true God) 18. She continued this for several days until Paul, troubled by her actions, turned and said to the spirit, "In the name of Jesus Christ, come out of her!" And it left her immediately. (Spirit: a supernatural force) 19. When her owners realized their hope of making money was gone, they seized Paul and Silas and dragged them to the marketplace to face the authorities. (Marketplace: a public square) 20. They brought them before the magistrates, accusing them of causing trouble in the city by promoting customs that were not allowed for Romans. (Magistrates: city officials) 21. "These men are teaching customs that are not lawful for Romans to accept or practice," they said. (Romans: citizens of the Roman Empire) 22. The crowd joined in attacking Paul and Silas, and the magistrates ordered that they be stripped and beaten. (Beaten: physically punished) 23. After being severely beaten, they were thrown into prison, and the jailer was ordered to keep them securely. (Jailer: person in charge of prison) 24. The jailer followed these instructions and put them into the innermost cell, fastening their feet in stocks. (Stocks: a device for locking prisoners' feet) 25. Around midnight, Paul and Silas prayed and sang hymns to God, and the other prisoners were listening to them. (Hymns: songs of praise) 26. Suddenly, there was a violent earthquake, causing the prison to shake. At once, all the doors opened, and everyone's chains came loose. (Earthquake: a shaking of the ground) 27. When the jailer awoke and saw the prison doors open, he drew his sword, intending to kill himself, assuming the prisoners had escaped. (Sword: a weapon for defense) 28. But Paul shouted, "Don't harm yourself! We are all here." (Harm: injury) 29. The jailer called for lights, rushed in, and trembling, fell at the feet of Paul and Silas. (Lights: sources of illumination) 30. He brought them outside and asked, "Sirs, what must I do to be saved?" (Saved: rescued from sin) 31. They replied, "Believe in the Lord Jesus, and you will be saved—you and your household." (Believe: to have faith in Jesus) 32. They spoke the word of the Lord to him and to everyone in his house. (Word of the Lord: God's message) 33. At that hour, the jailer took them and washed their wounds, and immediately he and his whole household were baptized. (Wounds: injuries) 34. He then brought them into his house, set food before them, and rejoiced, as he and his entire household had come to believe in God. (Food: a meal) 35. The next day, the magistrates sent officers with orders to release them. (Officers: assistants to magistrates) 36. The jailer told Paul, "The magistrates have ordered that you be set free. Now you may go in peace." (Peace: absence of conflict) 37. But Paul replied, "They beat us publicly without a trial, even though we are Romans, and threw us into prison. Now they want to send us away secretly? No, let them come and release us themselves." (Romans: citizens of the Roman Empire) 38. The officers reported this to the magistrates, and when they learned Paul and Silas were Romans, they were alarmed. (Alarmed: afraid or surprised) 39. The magistrates came and apologized, escorting them out of the prison, and requested that they leave the city. (Apologized: expressed regret) 40. After leaving the prison, Paul and Silas went to Lydia's house. They met with the believers, encouraged them, and then departed. (Encouraged: provided comfort and support)

Chapter 17

1. After passing through Amphipolis and Apollonia, they arrived in Thessalonica, where there was a Jewish synagogue. (Amphipolis: a city in Macedonia; Apollonia: another ancient city) 2. As usual, Paul went into the synagogue and, for three Sabbaths, reasoned with them from the Scriptures. (Sabbath: the day of Jewish rest and worship) 3. He explained that the Messiah had to suffer and rise from the dead, declaring that Jesus, whom he was preaching, is the Christ. (Messiah: the Anointed One) 4. Some of them believed and joined Paul and Silas, including many devout Greeks and prominent women. (Greeks: non-Jews who followed Jewish customs) 5. But the jealous Jews stirred up trouble by recruiting unruly men from the marketplace to incite a riot. They attacked Jason's house, searching for Paul and Silas. (Unruly: disruptive) 6. When they didn't find them, they dragged Jason and others before the city officials, accusing them of turning the world upside down and spreading trouble. (City officials: local authorities) 7. "Jason has welcomed these men," they said, "and they are preaching that another king, Jesus, is in opposition to Caesar." (Caesar: the Roman emperor) 8. This caused unrest among the people and city leaders when they heard these accusations. (Unrest: disturbance) 9. After securing a guarantee from Jason and the others, they let them go. (Guarantee: assurance for their behavior) 10. The believers immediately sent Paul and Silas away to Berea by night. When they arrived, they went into the synagogue. (Berea: a town in Macedonia) 11. The Bereans were more open-minded than those in Thessalonica, eagerly listening to Paul's teachings and examining the Scriptures daily. (Open-minded: willing to consider new ideas) 12. Many believed, including some prominent Greek women and a number of men. (Prominent: of high status) 13. When the Thessalonian Jews heard that Paul was preaching in Berea, they came to stir up trouble as they had in Thessalonica. (Trouble: conflict) 14. The believers immediately sent Paul to the coast, but Silas and Timothy stayed in Berea. (Timothy: Paul's close companion) 15. Those who escorted Paul brought him to Athens and told Silas and Timothy to join him soon. (Athens: the capital city of Greece) 16. While waiting for them in Athens, Paul was troubled to see the city full of idols. (Troubled: distressed) 17. Paul spoke with the Jews and the Gentiles in the synagogue and with anyone he met in the marketplace. (Gentiles: non-Jews) 18. Some philosophers from the Epicurean and Stoic schools began to debate him. Some said, "What is this speaker trying to say?" Others remarked, "He seems to be proclaiming foreign gods," because he preached Jesus and the resurrection. (Epicurean: followers of a pleasure-focused philosophy; Stoic: followers of a virtue-focused philosophy) 19. They took him to the Areopagus, asking, "Can you explain this new teaching?" (Areopagus: the high court of Athens) 20. "You bring strange ideas to our ears," they said. "We want to know what these things mean." (Strange: unfamiliar) 21. (All the Athenians and foreigners there spent their time discussing or hearing new ideas.) (Athenians: citizens of Athens) 22. Paul stood in the middle of the Areopagus and said, "Men of Athens, I see that you are very religious." (Religious: devoted to worship) 23. "As I walked around, I saw your objects of worship, including an altar with the inscription: 'To an Unknown God.' The God you worship unknowingly, I now proclaim to you." (Objects of worship: idols) 24. "The God who made the world and everything in it is Lord of heaven and earth, and does not live in temples made by human hands." (Temples: buildings of worship) 25. "Nor is he served by human hands, as if he needed anything. Rather, he gives life, breath, and everything to all people." (Served: worshipped) 26. "From one man, God made all nations to inhabit the earth. He set the times and boundaries of their lands." (Nations: peoples) 27. "He did this so that they would seek him, though he is not far from any of us." (Seek: search for) 28. "In him we live, move, and exist," as some of your poets have said, "For we are his children." (Poets: writers of songs or poems) 29. "Since we are God's offspring, we should not think the divine being is like gold, silver, or stone—an image made by human art." (Divine being: God) 30. "In the past, God overlooked such ignorance, but now commands everyone

everywhere to repent." (Repent: to turn away from sin) **31.** "For he has set a day to judge the world in righteousness by the man he has appointed. He has provided proof to everyone by raising him from the dead." (Judge: to make a fair decision) **32.** When they heard about the resurrection, some mocked, while others said, "We will hear you again about this matter." (Mocked: ridiculed) **33.** Paul left their meeting. (Meeting: gathering) **34.** However, some joined him and believed, including Dionysius, a member of the Areopagus, and a woman named Damaris, along with others. (Dionysius: a member of the Athenian council)

Chapter 18

1. After leaving Athens, Paul traveled to Corinth. (Corinth: City) **2.** There, he met Aquila, a Jewish man from Pontus, who had recently come from Italy with his wife, Priscilla, after Emperor Claudius had ordered all Jews to leave Rome. (Pontus: Region; Claudius: Emperor) **3.** Since they shared the same trade, Paul stayed with them and worked as a tentmaker. (Trade: Occupation) **4.** Every Sabbath, he preached in the synagogue, convincing both Jews and Greeks. (Sabbath: Rest; Synagogue: Temple) **5.** When Silas and Timothy arrived from Macedonia, Paul was filled with the Holy Spirit and preached to the Jews that Jesus is the Messiah. (Macedonia: Region; Messiah: Savior) **6.** When they opposed him and insulted him, Paul shook out his clothes and declared, "Your blood is on your heads; I am innocent. From now on, I will preach to the Gentiles." (Opposed: Resisted; Insulted: Offended; Gentiles: Non-Jews) **7.** Paul then left and stayed in the house of Justus, a man who worshipped God and lived next to the synagogue. (Worshipped: Revered; Synagogue: Temple) **8.** Crispus, the synagogue leader, and his entire household believed in the Lord. Many Corinthians also believed and were baptized. (Crispus: Leader; Baptized: Initiated) **9.** That night, the Lord spoke to Paul in a vision, telling him, "Do not be afraid, keep speaking, and don't be silent." (Vision: Revelation) **10.** "I am with you, and no one will harm you because I have many people in this city." (Harm: Injure) **11.** Paul stayed there for a year and a half, teaching God's word. (Teaching: Instruction) **12.** When Gallio was the proconsul of Achaia, the Jews united to bring Paul before the judgment seat. (Gallio: Official; Proconsul: Governor; Achaia: Region) **13.** They accused him of persuading people to worship God in ways contrary to the law. (Accused: Charged; Contrary: Opposite) **14.** Gallio responded, "If this were a matter of crime or immorality, I would judge you. (Immorality: Sin) **15.** But if it's about words or your law, handle it yourselves; I will not judge such matters." (Handle: Manage) **16.** Gallio dismissed the case. (Dismissed: Rejected) **17.** The Greeks then seized Sosthenes, the synagogue ruler, and beat him in front of the court. Gallio showed no concern. (Seized: Captured; Sosthenes: Person) **18.** After staying a while longer, Paul left, taking Priscilla and Aquila with him to Syria. He had his hair cut in Cenchrea due to a vow. (Syria: Region; Cenchrea: Port; Vow: Promise) **19.** They arrived in Ephesus, where Paul went to the synagogue to preach to the Jews. (Ephesus: City) **20.** Though they asked him to stay longer, Paul declined, (Declined: Refused) **21.** saying, "I must go to Jerusalem for a feast, but I will return if God wills." He then sailed from Ephesus. (Jerusalem: City; Feast: Celebration) **22.** After landing at Caesarea, Paul greeted the church and went down to Antioch. (Caesarea: City; Antioch: City) **23.** After spending some time there, he traveled through Galatia and Phrygia, strengthening the disciples. (Galatia: Region; Phrygia: Region; Disciples: Followers) **24.** Meanwhile, a Jewish man named Apollos from Alexandria, skilled in the Scriptures, arrived in Ephesus. (Alexandria: City; Scriptures: Writings) **25.** He was knowledgeable about the way of the Lord and taught passionately, but only knew of John's baptism. (Knowledgeable: Informed; Passionately: Emotionally) **26.** Aquila and Priscilla heard him and took him aside to explain God's way more fully. (Aquila: Person; Priscilla: Person) **27.** When Apollos planned to go to Achaia, the brethren wrote a letter of recommendation for him, and when he arrived, he helped many believers. (Brethren: Christians; Achaia: Region) **28.** He powerfully convinced the Jews, publicly proving from the Scriptures that Jesus is the Messiah. (Powerfully: Effectively; Convince: Persuade; Messiah: Savior)

Chapter 19

1. While Apollos was staying in Corinth, Paul traveled through the upper regions and arrived in Ephesus, where he found some disciples. (Disciples: Followers) **2.** He asked them, "Did you receive the Holy Spirit when you first believed?" They replied, "We have never even heard of the Holy Spirit." (Heard: Unaware) **3.** Paul then asked, "Then what baptism did you undergo?" They answered, "The baptism of John." (Baptism: Ritual washing for purification) **4.** Paul explained, "John baptized with a baptism of repentance, instructing people to believe in the one who would come after him—Jesus Christ." (Repentance: Regret or remorse for sin) **5.** After hearing this, they were baptized in the name of the Lord Jesus. (Baptized: Initiated through water) **6.** When Paul laid his hands on them, the Holy Spirit came upon them, and they began speaking in different languages and prophesying. (Prophesying: Predicting or speaking under divine inspiration) **7.** There were about twelve men in total. (Total: Full amount) **8.** Paul went to the synagogue and spoke boldly there for three months, engaging in discussions and persuading people about the Kingdom of God. (Boldly: Courageously) **9.** When some hardened their hearts and spoke out against the Way in public, Paul moved on and began teaching daily at the school of Tyrannus. (Hardened: Refused to believe; Way: Early Christian faith) **10.** This continued for two years, so that everyone in Asia, both Jews and Greeks, heard the message of the Lord Jesus. (Prevailed: Succeeded or spread widely) **11.** God performed extraordinary miracles through Paul, (Extraordinary: Remarkable or unusual) **12.** so that even cloths or aprons touched by him were taken to the sick, healing them, and evil spirits departed from them. (Evil spirits: Demons or malevolent beings) **13.** Some Jewish exorcists tried to invoke the name of Jesus over those with evil spirits, saying, "We command you by the Jesus whom Paul preaches." (Exorcists: Those who cast out demons) **14.** Seven sons of Sceva, a Jewish priest, were among them. (Sons: Male children) **15.** The evil spirit replied, "I know Jesus, and I know Paul, but who are you?" (Replied: Responded verbally) **16.** The man with the evil spirit jumped on them, overpowering them, and they fled the house naked and wounded. (Overpowered: Defeated or controlled completely) **17.** This became widely known in Ephesus, causing fear to fall on everyone, and the name of the Lord Jesus was greatly honored. (Honored: Respected or revered) **18.** Many who had believed came forward, confessing their sinful deeds, (Confessed: Admitted or acknowledged) **19.** and those who practiced sorcery brought their books together and burned them in front of everyone. The value of the books was calculated at fifty thousand silver coins. (Sorcery: Magical practices or witchcraft) **20.** As a result, the word of God spread widely and grew in power. (Prevailed: Flourished or succeeded) **21.** After these events, Paul decided to go to Jerusalem, then to Rome, after traveling through Macedonia and Achaia. (Events: Occurrences or happenings) **22.** He sent two of his helpers, Timothy and Erastus, into Macedonia, but he remained in Asia for a while. (Helpers: Assistants or supporters) **23.** Around that time, a major disturbance arose concerning the Way. (Disturbance: Uproar or public commotion) **24.** A silversmith named Demetrius, who made silver shrines of Diana, brought considerable profit to the craftsmen. (Silversmith: Metalworker who crafts objects from silver; Shrines: Small temples or altars) **25.** He gathered the workers and said, "You know that this trade brings us wealth. (Wealth: Accumulated riches or resources) **26.** And you see and hear that Paul has persuaded a large number of people in Ephesus and all across Asia that gods made by human hands are not gods. (Persuaded: Convinced or influenced to believe) **27.** This puts our business in jeopardy, as well as the honor of the temple of the great goddess Diana, whom all Asia and the world worship." (Jeopardy: Danger or risk) **28.** When the crowd heard this, they were enraged and cried out, "Great is Diana of the Ephesians!" (Enraged: Filled with intense anger) **29.** The whole city was thrown into chaos, and they seized Gaius and Aristarchus, Paul's traveling companions, and dragged them into the theater. (Chaos: Disorder or confusion) **30.** Paul wanted to enter the crowd, but his disciples prevented him. (Disciples: Followers or students of a teacher) **31.** Some leaders of Asia, who were friends of Paul, sent him a message urging him not to risk going into the theater. (Leaders: Authorities or influential figures) **32.** Some in the crowd shouted one thing, others another, and the assembly was in confusion, with most not even knowing why they had gathered. (Assembly: A group of people gathered together) **33.** They brought out Alexander, a Jew, to make a defense. (Defense: Justification or explanation) **34.** But when the crowd realized he was a Jew, they all shouted for about two hours, "Great is Diana of the Ephesians!" (Shouted: Cried out loudly) **35.** The town clerk finally quieted the crowd and said, "Men of Ephesus, does anyone not know that our city is the guardian of the great goddess Diana and the image that fell from the sky? (Guardian: Protector or custodian) **36.** Since these things cannot be denied, you should calm down and not act rashly. (Rashly: Without careful thought or consideration) **37.** You have brought these men here, who are neither temple robbers nor blasphemers of our goddess. (Blasphemers: Insulters or defamers of sacred things) **38.** If Demetrius and the craftsmen have a legitimate complaint, let the courts decide. (Legitimate: Valid or lawful) **39.** If it's about other matters, it should be settled in a lawful assembly. (Lawful: In accordance with the law) **40.** We are in danger of being charged with rioting today, for there is no reason for this disorder." (Rioting: Participating in a violent public disturbance) **41.** After saying this, he dismissed the assembly. (Dismissed: Sent away or disbanded)

Chapter 20

1. After the uproar ended, Paul gathered the disciples, embraced them, and set off for Macedonia. (Uproar: Disturbance) **2.** He traveled through those regions, encouraging them, then arrived in Greece. (Exhortation: Encouragement) **3.** He stayed there for three months, but when Jews plotted against him as he was about to sail to Syria, he decided to return through Macedonia. (Plot: Scheme) **4.** Sopater from Berea, Aristarchus and Secundus from Thessalonica, Gaius from Derbe, Timotheus, Tychicus, and Trophimus from Asia joined him. (Joined: Accompanied) **5.** They went ahead and waited for us in Troas. (Troas: City) **6.** After the Feast of Unleavened Bread, we sailed from Philippi and arrived at Troas after five days, staying there for seven days. (Feast of Unleavened Bread: Festival) **7.** On the first day of the week, as the disciples gathered to break bread, Paul preached to them, preparing to leave the next day, and continued until midnight. (Preached: Taught) **8.** The room was filled with many lamps. (Lamps: Lights) **9.** A young man named Eutychus, sitting in a window, fell asleep during Paul's long sermon, fell from the third floor, and was found dead. (Sermon: Speech) **10.** Paul went down, embraced him, and assured them, "Don't worry, his life is still in him." (Embraced: Hugged) **11.** After returning upstairs, breaking bread, and talking until dawn, Paul departed. (Dawn: Morning) **12.** The young man was revived, and they were greatly comforted. **13.** We sailed on to Assos to meet Paul, who had chosen to walk there. (Assos: Town) **14.** When he joined us in Assos, we sailed to Mitylene. **15.** The next day, we sailed past Chios, reached Samos, and stayed at Trogyllium, then arrived at Miletus the following day. (Chios: Island) (Samos: Island) (Trogyllium: Promontory) **16.** Paul decided not to visit Ephesus, as he was eager to reach Jerusalem for Pentecost. (Pentecost: Festival) **17.** From Miletus, he sent for the elders of the Ephesus church. (Elders: Leaders) **18.** When they arrived, he told them, "You know how I lived among you from the beginning, serving the Lord humbly with tears and trials caused by the Jews' plots." (Trials: Tests) **19.** "I withheld nothing helpful from you but taught you publicly and privately, urging both Jews and Greeks to repent and trust in Jesus Christ." (Withheld: Held back) (Repent: Regret) **20.** "Now, I'm compelled by the Spirit to go to Jerusalem, not knowing what will happen to me there." (Compelled: Forced) (Spirit: Ghost) **21.** "The Holy Spirit has warned me in every city that chains and suffering await me." (Chains: Shackles) (Await: Expect) **22.** "But none of this frightens me; I don't consider my life precious, only that I finish my course with joy, fulfilling the ministry the Lord gave me—to preach the gospel of God's grace." (Frightens: Scares) (Ministry: Service) **23.** "I know that you will not see my face again, because I've preached God's kingdom to you all." (Preached: Taught) (Kingdom: Rule) **24.** "Today, I declare that I am innocent of everyone's blood, for I've given you the full counsel of God." (Declare: State) (Innocent: Blameless) (Counsel: Advice) **25.** "Be careful, and watch over yourselves and the flock, which the Holy Spirit made you overseers of, to shepherd the church of God, which He purchased with His own blood." (Watch over: Guard) (Flock: Group) (Purchased: Bought) **26.** "I know that after I leave, fierce wolves will attack, not sparing the flock." (Fierce: Savage) (Sparing: Saving) **27.** "Even from among you, some will arise, distorting the truth to lead disciples astray." (Distorting: Twisting) (Disciples: Followers) (Astray: Off-course) **28.** "So stay alert and remember how I warned you for three years, night and day, with tears." (Alert: Watchful) (Warned: Cautioned) **29.** "Now, I entrust you to God and His grace, which can build you up and give you an inheritance among the sanctified." (Entrust: Entrust) (Inheritance: Legacy) (Sanctified: Holy) **30.** "I haven't coveted anyone's money, gold, or clothes." (Coveted: Desired) **31.** "You know I worked with my hands to support myself and those with me." (Support: Aid) **32.** "I showed you that we must work hard to help the weak and remember Jesus' words: 'It is more blessed to give than to receive.'" (Blessed: Fortunate) **33.** After speaking, he knelt and prayed with them all. (Kneeled: Bent) **34.** They wept and embraced him, sorrowful especially because they would never see his face again. They accompanied him to the ship. (Wept: Cried) (Accompanied: Followed)

Chapter 21

1. After leaving them behind and setting sail, we headed straight for Coos, then Rhodes, and finally reached Patara the next day. **2.** Finding a ship heading to Phoenicia, we boarded it and continued our journey. **3.** After spotting Cyprus, we sailed past it on the left and headed into Syria, landing in Tyre where the ship was unloading its cargo. (Unloading: taking off cargo or goods) **4.** There, we met disciples and stayed for seven days. They, through the Spirit, warned Paul not to go to Jerusalem. (Disciples: followers of Jesus) **5.** After our stay, we departed, and the disciples, along with their families, walked us out of the city. We knelt by the shore and prayed. (Departed: left) **6.** After saying our goodbyes, we boarded the ship, and they returned home. **7.** From Tyre, we traveled to Ptolemais, greeted the believers, and stayed with them for a day. (Believers: those who follow Christ) **8.** The next day, we continued to Caesarea and stayed at Philip the Evangelist's house, one of the seven deacons. (Evangelist: one who spreads the gospel) **9.** Philip had four daughters who were virgins and prophesied. (Prophesied: spoke by divine inspiration) **10.** After several days, a prophet named Agabus came down from Judea. **11.** He took Paul's belt, tied his own hands and feet, and declared, "The Holy Spirit says the Jews in Jerusalem will bind the owner of this belt and hand him over to the Gentiles." (Gentiles: non-Jews) **12.** Hearing this, both we and the local believers begged Paul not to go to Jerusalem. (Begged: urgently requested) **13.** Paul replied, "Why are you making me weep and break my heart? I'm ready to not only be bound, but to die in Jerusalem for the name of the Lord Jesus." (Weep: cry with sorrow, Bound: tied up or imprisoned) **14.** When he wouldn't be convinced, we stopped pleading, saying, "Let God's will be done." (Pleading: begging) **15.** After these days, we packed our belongings and went to Jerusalem. (Packed: gathered and carried) **16.** Some disciples from Caesarea went with us, including Mnason, an older disciple from Cyprus, who offered us lodging. (Lodging: a place to stay) **17.** When we arrived in Jerusalem, the believers welcomed us warmly. **18.** The next day, Paul went to James, and all the elders were present. (Elders: leaders of the church) **19.** After greeting them, Paul shared what God had done among the Gentiles through his ministry. (Ministry: service or work in spreading the gospel) **20.** They praised God and said, "Brother, you see how many thousands of Jews believe, and they are all zealous for the law." (Zealous: passionate or fervent) **21.** They've heard about you, that you teach Jews among the Gentiles to abandon Moses, saying they shouldn't circumcise their children or follow Jewish customs. (Customs: traditions or practices) **22.** What should we do? A crowd will gather, for they will hear you've arrived. **23.** So, we suggest you take these four men who have made a vow. (Vow: a solemn promise, often religious) **24.** Purify yourself with them and cover their expenses so they can shave their heads. This will show everyone that the rumors about you are false, and you also observe the law. (Purify: make clean ceremonially, Observe: follow) **25.** As for the Gentile believers, we've written that they should only avoid food sacrificed to idols, blood, meat from strangled animals, and sexual immorality. (Strangled: killed without draining the blood) **26.** Paul took the men, purified himself with them, and entered the temple to complete the days of purification until their offerings were made. (Purification: ceremonial cleaning) **27.** When the seven days were almost over, Jews from Asia saw Paul in the temple, caused a stir, and seized him. (Stir: commotion or disturbance) **28.** They shouted, "Men of Israel, help! This man teaches everyone everywhere against our people, the law, and this place. He even brought Greeks into the temple and defiled this holy place." (Defiled: made impure or unclean) **29.** (They had previously seen Paul with Trophimus, an Ephesian, and assumed he brought him into the temple.) **30.** The whole city was in an uproar. The crowd dragged Paul out of the temple and locked the doors. (Uproar: noisy commotion) **31.** As they were about to kill him, news reached the commander of the guard that Jerusalem was in chaos. (Chaos: complete disorder) **32.** He immediately took soldiers and officers and rushed to the crowd. When they saw the commander and his men, they stopped beating Paul. (Officers: high-ranking soldiers) **33.** The commander arrested Paul, ordered him to be bound with two chains, and asked who he was and what he had done. (Arrested: detained, Bound: tied up) **34.** Some in the crowd shouted one thing, some another, and the commander couldn't figure out the truth because of the uproar, so he ordered Paul to be taken to the barracks. (Uproar: loud noise, Barracks: a place where soldiers are housed) **35.** As they reached the steps, the soldiers had to carry Paul because the violence of the crowd was overwhelming. (Overwhelming: overpowering, hard to resist) **36.** The mob followed, shouting, "Away with him!" (Mob: a large, disorganized crowd) **37.** As Paul was about to be led into the barracks, he asked the commander, "May I speak to you?" (Barracks: building for soldiers) **38.** The commander replied, "Can you speak Greek? Aren't you the Egyptian who led a revolt and took four thousand murderers into the wilderness?" (Revolt: rebellion) **39.** Paul answered, "I'm a Jew from Tarsus in Cilicia, a citizen of a well-known city. Please allow me to speak to the people." (Cilicia: a region in modern-day Turkey) **40.** The commander granted him permission, and Paul stood on the stairs, motioned for silence, and spoke to the crowd in Hebrew, saying:

Chapter 22

1. Men, brothers, and fathers, listen to my defense now. (Defense: Justification) **2.** When they heard him speaking in Hebrew, they became quieter. He said, (Quieter: Silent) **3.** I am a Jew, born in Tarsus, Cilicia, but raised in this city under Gamaliel, taught in the strict tradition of our ancestors, and zealous for God, just as you are today. (Zealous: Devoted) **4.** I persecuted this faith, even to the point of death, imprisoning both men and women. (Persecuted: Harassed) **5.** The high priest and the council can testify to this; I received letters from them to arrest believers in Damascus and bring them to Jerusalem for punishment. (Testify: Confirm) (Council: Assembly) **6.** As I approached Damascus at noon, a great light from heaven suddenly shone around me. (Approached: Nearing) (Noon: Midday) **7.** I fell to the ground and heard a voice, "Saul, Saul, why are you persecuting me?" (Persecuting: Oppressing) **8.** I asked, "Who are you, Lord?" and the voice answered, "I am Jesus of Nazareth, whom you are persecuting." (Nazareth: Town) **9.** Those with me saw the light but did not hear the voice. (Heard: Listened) **10.** I asked, "What should I do, Lord?" and He replied, "Get up, go into Damascus, and you will be told what to do." (Replied: Answered) (Told: Informed) **11.** Blinded by the light, I was led by the hand to Damascus. (Blinded: Unseen) (Led: Guided) **12.** There, Ananias, a devout man respected by the Jews, came to me. (Devout: Pious) (Respected: Admired) **13.** He called me "Brother Saul," and I regained my sight at that very hour. (Regained: Recovered) (Sight: Vision) **14.** He said, "The God of our ancestors has chosen you to know His will, to see the Righteous One, and hear His voice." (Righteous: Just) (Will: Plan) **15.** "You will be His witness to all people of what you have seen and heard." (Witness: Testifier) **16.** "Now, why wait? Get baptized, wash away your sins, and call on the name of the Lord." (Baptized: Immersed) (Sins: Wrongdoings) **17.** Later, when I prayed in the temple in Jerusalem, I fell into a trance. (Prayed: Communed) (Temple: Shrine) (Trance: Reverie) **18.** I saw Jesus telling me, "Hurry, leave Jerusalem quickly, for they will not accept your testimony about me." (Testimony: Evidence) **19.** I replied, "Lord, they know how I persecuted and imprisoned believers, even consenting to the death of Stephen." (Consenting: Agreeing) **20.** "I stood by when Stephen was killed and guarded the clothes of those who murdered him." (Murdered: Killed) (Guarded: Watched) **21.** Jesus said, "Go, for I will send you far to the Gentiles." (Gentiles: Non-Jews) **22.** When they heard this, they shouted, "Away with him! He should not live!" (Shouted: Yelled) **23.** As they yelled, threw off their clothes, and tossed dust into the air, (Tossed: Threw) (Dust: Debris) **24.** The chief captain ordered Paul to be taken to the fortress and examined by scourging to find out why they were accusing him. (Captain: Leader) (Fortress: Stronghold) (Scourging: Flogging) **25.** As they bound him, Paul asked the centurion, "Is it lawful to scourge a Roman citizen who has not been condemned?" (Bound: Tied) (Centurion: Officer) **26.** The centurion reported this to the chief captain, saying, "Be careful! This man is a Roman." (Reported: Informed) **27.** The chief captain came and asked, "Are you a Roman?" Paul replied, "Yes." (Captain: Officer) **28.** The captain said, "I bought my citizenship at great cost." Paul answered, "I was born a Roman." (Citizenship: Status) (Cost: Price) **29.** Immediately, those who were about to interrogate Paul withdrew, and the captain was afraid because he had bound a Roman citizen. (Interrogate: Question) (Withdrew: Retreated) **30.** The next day, wanting to understand the charges against Paul, the chief captain released him, summoned the chief priests and council, and brought Paul before them. (Summoned: Called) (Charges: Accusations)

Chapter 23

1. Paul, looking intently at the council, said, "Brothers, I have always lived with a clear conscience before God until now." (Conscience: the inner sense of right and wrong) **2.** The high priest, Ananias, ordered those standing by Paul to strike him on the mouth. (Struck: hit) **3.** Paul replied, "God will strike you, you whitewashed wall! You sit to judge me by the law, yet you command I be struck unlawfully!" (Whitewashed: hypocritically clean or moral) **4.** Those present asked, "Do you insult God's high priest?" (Insult: disrespect) **5.** Paul said, "I didn't know, brothers, that he was the high priest; Scripture says, 'Do not speak evil of the ruler of your people.'" (Scripture: sacred writings) **6.** When Paul realized some were Sadducees and others Pharisees, he declared, "I am a Pharisee, the son of a Pharisee. I stand trial for the hope of the resurrection of the dead." (Pharisee: a member of a Jewish religious group; Sadducees: another Jewish group with different beliefs) **7.** This statement caused a division between the Pharisees and Sadducees, and the crowd was split. (Division: disagreement) **8.** The Sadducees deny the resurrection, angels, and spirits; but the Pharisees acknowledge both. (Resurrection: rising from the dead) **9.** The Pharisees' scribes shouted, "We find no fault in this man. If a spirit or angel spoke to him, we should not oppose God." (Scribes: experts in Jewish law) **10.** As the argument grew intense, the chief captain feared for Paul's safety and ordered soldiers to take him by force to the barracks. (Intense: very strong) **11.** That night, the Lord stood by Paul and said, "Take courage, Paul. You've testified about me in Jerusalem, and you must do the same in Rome." (Testified: gave witness) **12.** The next day, over forty Jews formed a conspiracy, vowing not to eat or drink until they killed Paul. (Conspiracy: secret plan) **13.** More than forty men joined the plot. (Plot: secret plan) **14.** They went to the chief priests and elders, saying, "We have sworn not to eat until we kill Paul." (Sworn: made a serious promise) **15.** They asked the council to request the chief captain bring Paul down, pretending they needed more information, but they planned to kill him on the way. (Pretending: making it seem false) **16.** Paul's today, might become what I am—except for these chains." (Chains: bonds) **30.** After Paul spoke, the king, governor, Bernice, and all present rose up. (Rose up: stood up) **31.** As they left, they discussed among themselves, saying, "This man has done nothing deserving of death or imprisonment." (Deserving: worthy) **32.** Agrippa told Festus, "This man could have been set free if he had not appealed to Caesar." (Appealed: requested)

Chapter 27

1. It was decided that we would sail to Italy, so Paul and several other prisoners were handed over to a centurion named Julius, who was part of Augustus' regiment. (Regiment: a military unit) **2.** We boarded a ship from Adramyttium, intending to travel along the coast of Asia. With us was Aristarchus, a Macedonian from Thessalonica. (Macedonian: from Macedonia, in Greece) (Intending: planning) **3.** The next day, we stopped at Sidon, where Julius treated Paul with kindness and allowed him to visit friends to rest and refresh. (Kindness: care or goodwill) (Refresh: regain energy) **4.** When we set sail again, we had to navigate under the island of Cyprus because the winds were against us. (Navigate: move along) (Against: contrary to) **5.** We continued our journey through the seas of Cilicia and Pamphylia and finally reached Myra, a city in Lycia. (Pamphylia: an ancient region in Asia Minor) **6.** At Myra, the centurion found a ship from Alexandria heading to Italy, and we transferred onto it. (Transferred: moved to) (Alexandria: a major port city in Egypt) **7.** The days passed slowly, and we struggled against the wind. After many days, we managed to sail under Crete, near a place called Salmone. (Struggled: had difficulty) (Managed: succeeded in doing) **8.** We finally reached a harbor called The Fair Havens, near the city of Lasea. (Harbor: a place for ships to dock) **9.** By this time, the season for sailing was dangerous, and since the Day of Atonement had passed, Paul warned everyone about the risks of continuing. (Day of Atonement: a Jewish holiday) (Warned: cautioned) **10.** Paul told them, "I fear this journey will end in disaster, not just for the cargo and ship, but for our lives as well." (Disaster: destruction) **11.** However, the centurion listened to the ship's captain and owner instead of Paul's advice. (Listened: paid attention to) (Advice: guidance) **12.** Since the harbor wasn't suitable for winter, most of the crew wanted to sail to Phenice, another harbor on Crete, to spend the winter there. (Suitable: appropriate for) (Winter: stay during the cold season) **13.** When the weather calmed and the south wind blew gently, they set out, thinking they had succeeded in their plan, sailing close to Crete. (Gently: softly) (Succeeded: achieved their goal) **14.** But soon, a violent wind called Euroclydon began to blow, throwing the ship off course. (Violent: strong and forceful) **15.** The ship was caught in the storm and could no longer face the wind, so we let it drift wherever the storm pushed it. (Drift: float aimlessly) **16.** As we passed a small island called Clauda, we had a difficult time securing the lifeboat. (Securing: fastening) (Lifeboat: emergency boat) **17.** Once the crew brought the lifeboat aboard, they reinforced the ship and, fearing it would crash on rocks, they took down the sails. (Reinforced: strengthened) (Crash: hit forcefully) **18.** As the storm continued, they threw cargo overboard to lighten the ship. (Cargo: goods being transported) (Lighten: reduce weight) **19.** On the third day, they threw the ship's equipment into the sea. (Equipment: tools and gear) **20.** With no sun or stars for many days, and the storm showing no sign of stopping, all hope of survival seemed lost. (Sign: indication) **21.** After not eating for a long time, Paul stood and said, "You should have listened to me and not sailed from Crete, sparing us from this trouble." (Sparing: avoiding) **22.** "But take heart—none of you will lose your life, though the ship will be destroyed." (Take heart: be encouraged) (Destroyed: ruined completely) **23.** "Last night, the angel of God, whom I serve, stood by me." (Angel: divine messenger) **24.** "He told me, 'Do not be afraid, Paul. You must stand before Caesar, and God has granted you the lives of all who sail with you.'" (Granted: given) **25.** "So take courage, I believe God, and everything will happen just as He told me." (Courage: bravery) **26.** "But we will be stranded on an island." (Stranded: left with no escape) **27.** On the fourteenth night, while drifting through the Adriatic Sea, the sailors thought they were near land. (Drifting: moving without control) (Adriatic Sea: between Italy and the Balkans) **28.** They took soundings and found the water was 20 fathoms deep. After sailing a bit further, they measured 15 fathoms. (Soundings: depth measurements) (Fathoms: depth units) **29.** Fearing they would crash on rocks, they dropped four anchors and waited for daylight. (Anchors: devices to hold the ship in place) **30.** As the sailors attempted to escape in the lifeboat, pretending to drop more anchors, Paul warned the centurion and soldiers, "Unless these men stay aboard, no one will be saved." (Pretending: faking) **31.** The soldiers cut the ropes to the lifeboat and let it drift away. (Cut: severed) **32.** As the sun was rising, Paul urged everyone to eat, saying, "It's been 14 days since you've eaten, and you need strength." (Urged: strongly suggested) **33.** "Eat for your health—none of you will lose even a hair from your head." (Health: well-being) **34.** After saying this, Paul took bread, thanked God, broke it, and began to eat. (Broke: divided) (Thanked: expressed gratitude) **35.** This encouraged everyone, and they also ate. (Encouraged: inspired) **36.** There were 276 people on board. (Board: the ship) **37.** After eating, they threw the rest of the wheat overboard to lighten the load. (Rest: remaining part) **38.** The next morning, they didn't recognize the land, but they saw a bay with a beach and decided to try to reach it. (Recognize: identify) **39.** They raised the sails and headed for the shore, preparing for landfall. (Headed: moved toward) (Landfall: reaching land) **40.** They ran the ship aground at a spot where two seas met, and while the front of the ship stuck fast, the back was smashed by the waves. (Ran aground: crashed on shore) (Smashed: broken) **41.** The soldiers planned to kill the prisoners to prevent them from escaping, but the centurion, wanting to save Paul, stopped them. (Prevent: stop) **42.** He ordered that those who could swim jump into the sea and swim to land, while the rest used pieces of the ship to float to safety. (Ordered: commanded) **43.** Everyone made it safely to shore, just as Paul had assured them. (Assured: promised)

Chapter 28

1. After they had safely escaped, they discovered the island was called Malta. (Malta: island) **2.** The locals showed us great kindness, starting a fire to warm us because of the rain and cold. (Kindness: hospitality) **3.** While Paul gathered sticks for the fire, a viper came out and bit him. (Viper: snake) **4.** The locals thought he was a murderer, as even though he survived the sea, justice wouldn't let him live. (Justice: retribution) **5.** Paul shook off the snake and suffered no harm. (Suffered: endured) **6.** They waited for him to swell up or die, but when nothing happened, they changed their minds and thought he was a god. (Swelling up: bloating) **7.** The estate of Publius, the island's chief official, was nearby. He welcomed us and showed us great hospitality for three days. (Estate: property) (Hospitality: kindness) **8.** Publius' father was sick with fever and dysentery. Paul prayed, laid hands on him, and healed him. (Dysentery: diarrhea) **9.** Others on the island who were sick came to Paul and were healed. (Sick: ill) **10.** The people honored us greatly and gave us everything we needed for the journey. (Honored: respected) **11.** After three months, we sailed on a ship from Alexandria that had wintered there. Its emblem was Castor and Pollux. (Emblem: symbol) **12.** We docked in Syracuse and stayed three days. (Docked: landed) **13.** From there, we sailed on to Rhegium, and the next day, the wind shifted, and we reached Puteoli. (Shifted: changed) **14.** In Puteoli, we found Christian brothers who invited us to stay with them for a week. After that, we continued toward Rome. (Brothers: Christians) **15.** When the brothers in Rome heard, they met us at Appii Forum and the Three Taverns. Paul thanked God and was encouraged. (Encouraged: uplifted) (Appii Forum: place) **16.** When we arrived in Rome, the centurion handed the prisoners over to the captain of the guard, but Paul was allowed to stay by himself with a soldier guarding him. (Centurion: officer) (Captain: leader) **17.** After three days, Paul called the Jewish leaders together. He said, "Though I've done nothing wrong, I was arrested in Jerusalem and handed to the Romans. (Leaders: chiefs) **18.** After they examined me, they wanted to release me, but the Jews opposed it. (Examined: investigated) **19.** I was compelled to appeal to Caesar—not because I have anything against my people. (Compelled: forced) (Appeal: request) **20.** I've called you here to explain that I am in chains for the hope of Israel." (Chains: shackles) (Hope: expectation) **21.** They replied, "We haven't received any letters about you, nor has anyone said anything bad." (Letters: messages) **22.** "But we'd like to hear your views, as we know this sect is spoken against everywhere." (Sect: movement) **23.** They set a day to meet, and many came to Paul's lodging. From morning until evening, he explained and testified about the kingdom of God, persuading them about Jesus from the Law and Prophets. (Lodging: accommodation) (Testified: declared) **24.** Some were convinced, but others didn't believe. (Convinced: persuaded) **25.** When they disagreed, Paul said, "Isaiah spoke truthfully about you, (Disagreed: argued) **26.** saying, 'You will hear but not understand, see but not perceive.' (Perceive: realize) **27.** The people's hearts have grown calloused, their ears dull, and their eyes closed. Otherwise, they might see, hear, understand, and turn, and I would heal them." (Calloused: hardened) (Turn: repent) **28.** Therefore, God's salvation has been sent to the Gentiles, and they will listen." (Gentiles: non-Jews) **29.** After this, the Jews argued among themselves. (Argued: debated) **30.** Paul spent two years in his rented house, welcoming all who came to him. (Rented: leased) **31.** He preached about the kingdom of God and taught about Jesus Christ boldly and without hindrance. (Boldly: confidently)

45 – Romans

Chapter 1

1. Paul, a servant of Jesus Christ, called to be an apostle, set apart for the gospel of God. (Servant : one who serves, set apart : chosen for a specific purpose) **2.** This gospel was promised by His prophets in the holy scriptures. (Prophets : messenger of God) **3.** Regarding His Son, Jesus Christ our Lord, descended from David according to the flesh. (Flesh : human nature) **4.** Declared to be the Son of God with power through His resurrection from the dead. (Declared : made known, resurrection : rising from the dead) **5.** Through Him, we have received grace and apostleship, to lead all nations to faith for His name. (Apostleship : t mission entrusted to apostles, grace : unearned favor) **6.** You also are called by Jesus Christ. (Called : invited or chosen) **7.** To all in Rome, beloved of God, called to be saints: Grace and peace from God our Father and the Lord Jesus Christ. (Saints : holy ones, grace : unearned favor, peace : inner calm) **8.** I thank God through Jesus Christ for you, as your faith is known worldwide. (Faith : trust or belief in God) **9.** God is my witness, whom I serve in the gospel of His Son, making mention of you in my prayers. (Gospel : good news) **10.** I pray that I may visit you, if it's God's will. (Prosperous: Blessed) **11.** I long to see you, to share some spiritual gift with you, so you may be strengthened. (Spiritual gift : abilities given by the Holy Spirit to strengthen believers) **12.** I wish to be encouraged by our shared faith. (Encouraged : strengthened) **13.** I have often wanted to visit you, but have been hindered, to have fruit among you. (Hindered : prevented, fruit : results of spreading the gospel) **14.** I am obligated to Greeks and barbarians, wise and foolish. (Obligated : indebted, barbarians : non-Greeks, wise : learned, foolish : unlearned) **15.** I am eager to preach the gospel to you in Rome. (Preach : proclaim or teach) **16.** I am not ashamed of the gospel of Christ, for it is the power of God for salvation to all who believe. (salvation : rescue from sin) **17.** In the gospel, the righteousness of God is revealed, from faith to faith: "The just shall live by faith." (Righteousness : God's perfect goodness, just : righteous people) **18.** God's wrath is revealed against all ungodliness and unrighteousness, who suppress the truth. (Wrath : anger, ungodliness : wickedness, suppress : hold down) **19.** What can be known about God is made clear to them, for God has shown it. (Manifest : made clear) **20.** His invisible attributes are clearly seen in creation, so they are without excuse. (Attributes : characteristics, creation : everything made by God) **21.** Although they knew God, they did not honor or thank Him, and became futile in their thinking. (Futile : useless) **22.** Professing to be wise, they became fools. (Professing : claiming) **23.** They exchanged the glory of God for images of man and animals. (Exchanged : traded) **24.** God gave them over to impurity to dishonor their bodies. (Impurity : uncleanness, dishonor : shame) **25.** They worshiped the creature more than the Creator, who is blessed forever. Amen. (Creature : creation, blessed : praised) **26.** God gave them over to degrading passions, as women exchanged natural relations. (Degrading : lowering, passions : strong desires) **27.** Likewise, men left natural relations with women and burned with lust for each other. (Lust : strong desire) **28.** Since they did not retain God in their knowledge, God gave them over to a depraved mind. (Depraved : morally corrupt) **29.** They were filled with all kinds of wickedness: envy, murder, deceit, and malice. (Malice : evil intentions) **30.** They were gossips, slanderers, God-haters, proud, and disobedient to parents. (Slanderers : people who speak false things about others) **31.** They were without understanding, unmerciful, and unloving. (Without understanding : foolish, unmerciful : without mercy) **32.** Though they know the righteous judgment of God, they not only do these things but approve of others who do them. (Righteous : just)

Chapter 2

1. You are without excuse, O man, who judges others, for by judging, you condemn yourself, doing the same things. (Excuse: a reason or explanation; Condemn: to declare guilty) **2.** God's judgment is based on truth, against those who commit such acts. (Acts: actions or deeds) **3.** Do you think you will escape God's judgment while doing the same things? (Escape: to avoid) **4.** Do you despise His kindness and patience, not realizing that it leads you to repentance? (Despise: to dislike intensely; Repentance: regret and change of heart) **5.** Your stubbornness and unrepentant heart store up wrath for the day of judgment. (Unrepentant: not feeling regret; Wrath: intense anger) **6.** God will repay each person according to their deeds. (Repay: to give back in return) **7.** To those who do good and seek glory, honor, and immortality, God gives eternal life. (Immortality: the ability to live forever) **8.** But to those who follow unrighteousness, there will be anger and wrath. (Unrighteousness: wickedness) **9.** There will be trouble for every soul that does evil, for the Jew first and also for the Gentile. (Soul: the immaterial part of a person; Gentile: a non-Jew) **10.** But glory, honor, and peace to everyone who does good, for the Jew first and also for the Gentile. (Glory: great honor or admiration) **11.** For God does not show favoritism. (Favoritism: unfair preference) **12.** All who sin apart from the law will perish without it, and all who sin under the law will be judged by it. (Perish: to die; Law: a set of rules or principles) **13.** It's not just those who hear the law, but those who obey it, who will be declared righteous. (Declared: officially stated) **14.** When Gentiles obey the law by nature, they are a law to themselves. (Obey: to follow; Law: rules or principles) **15.** They show the law written in their hearts, with their conscience bearing witness, accusing or excusing them. (Conscience: moral sense of right and wrong) **16.** God will judge people's secrets through Jesus Christ, as proclaimed by the gospel. (Proclaimed: declared publicly) **17.** You call yourself a Jew, boast in God, and rely on the law. (Rely: depend on) **18.** You know His will and approve of what is excellent, instructed by the law. (Approve: to accept as good; Instructed: taught) **19.** You think you are a guide for the blind, a light in darkness, (Guide: one who shows the way; Light: a source of illumination) **20.** an instructor of the foolish, a teacher of infants, with the truth in the law. (Teacher: one who imparts knowledge) **21.** You who teach others, do you not teach yourself? (Teach: to instruct) **22.** You say not to commit adultery, but do you commit it? (Adultery: voluntary sexual relations with someone other than one's spouse) **23.** By breaking the law, you dishonor God. (Dishonor: to treat with disrespect) **24.** As it is written, "God's name is blasphemed among the Gentiles because of you." (Blasphemed: spoken evil of) **25.** Circumcision is valuable if you obey the law, but if you break it, your circumcision is as if uncircumcision. (Circumcision: the removal of the foreskin, often a sign of religious identity) **26.** If the uncircumcised keep the law, their uncircumcision is as if circumcision. (Uncircumcised: not having undergone circumcision) **27.** The uncircumcised who obey the law will condemn you for breaking it. (Condemn: to judge negatively) **28.** A true Jew is one inwardly, and circumcision is of the heart, by the Spirit. (Inwardly: in the inner being; Spirit: divine influence) **29.** A true Jew's praise is from God, not from others. (Praise: approval or admiration)

Chapter 3
1. What's the benefit of being a Jew or circumcised? (circumcision: a religious ritual of cutting) **2.** There's much advantage, mainly because the oracles (divinely inspired messages or revelations) of God were entrusted to them. **3.** What if some didn't believe? Does their unbelief cancel out God's faithfulness? (unbelief: lack of faith) **4.** No! Let God be true and all men liars, as it's written, "So you can be justified in your words and win when judged." (justified: declared right) **5.** If our sin highlights God's righteousness, is God wrong to judge us? (sin: wrongdoing) **6.** No! How could God judge the world if that were true? **7.** If my lie brings more glory to God, why am I judged as a sinner? (lie: falsehood) **8.** Should we say, "Let's do evil so good comes"? Their condemnation is deserved. (condemnation: punishment) **9.** Are we better than others? No, for both Jews and Gentiles are under sin. (Gentiles: non-Jews) **10.** As it is written: "There is no one righteous, not even one." **11.** No one understands or seeks God. **12.** All have turned away and become worthless; no one does good. **13.** Their throats are like open graves, their tongues deceitful, and their lips poisonous. (deceitful: dishonest) **14.** Their mouths are full of cursing and bitterness. **15.** Their feet are quick to shed blood. (shed: spill) **16.** Their paths lead to ruin and misery. **17.** They do not know peace. **18.** There is no fear of God before their eyes. **19** We know that the law speaks to those under it, so everyone will be held accountable. (accountable: responsible) **20.** No one can be justified by the law; it shows us our sin. **21.** Now, God's righteousness has been revealed, witnessed by the law and prophets. **22.** This righteousness comes through faith in Jesus Christ to all who believe. (righteousness: right standing with God) **23.** All have sinned and fall short of God's glory. **24.** All are justified freely by his grace through Christ Jesus. (grace: unearned favor) **25.** God presented Jesus as a sacrifice through faith in his blood to show his righteousness in forgiving sins. (sacrifice: offering to God) **26.** He did this to show his righteousness, being both just and the one who justifies those with faith in Jesus. **27.** Where's the boasting? It's excluded. Not by works, but by faith. **28.** A person is justified by faith apart from the law. **29.** Is God only the God of the Jews? No, he's also the God of Gentiles. **30.** There is only one God, who justifies both Jews and Gentiles by faith. **31.** Do we nullify the law by faith? No! We uphold the law. (nullify: cancel)

Chapter 4
1. What can we say about Abraham, our forefather, in relation to the flesh? What did he discover? **2.** If Abraham was justified by actions, he could boast, but not before God. **3.** What does Scripture say? Abraham trusted God, and it was credited to him as righteousness. (Justified: declared righteous; Righteousness: the state of being morally right or justifiable) **4.** To someone who works, the reward is owed, not a gift of grace. **5.** But to someone who doesn't work, but believes in God who justifies the ungodly, their faith is credited as righteousness. **6.** David speaks of the blessedness of someone God grants righteousness apart from works, (Blessedness: happiness or state of being blessed) **7.** saying, "Blessed are those whose wrongdoings are forgiven, and whose sins are covered." **8.** Blessed is the one whom the Lord will not count as sinful. **9.** Does this blessing come to the circumcised only, or also to the uncircumcised? We say faith was credited to Abraham as righteousness. (Circumcised: the act of removing the foreskin of the male genitalia, a sign of the covenant in Judaism) **10.** How was it credited to him? Before or after circumcision? It was before circumcision. **11.** He received circumcision as a sign, a seal of the righteousness he had by faith while uncircumcised, to be the father of all who believe. **12.** He is the father of those who walk in the faith of Abraham, both circumcised and uncircumcised. **13.** The promise to inherit the world came not through the law, but through the righteousness of faith. **14.** If those of the law are heirs, faith is useless, and the promise is void. **15.** The law brings wrath, for where there is no law, there is no sin. (Transgression: the act of breaking a law or command) **16.** The promise depends on faith, so it may be by grace, guaranteed to all Abraham's descendants—both those of the law and those of faith. **17.** (As it is written, "I have made you a father of many nations") before God, who gives life to the dead and calls things that are not as though they were. **18.** Against hope, Abraham believed in hope and became the father of many nations, just as it was said, "So shall your offspring be." **19.** Without weakening in faith, he did not consider his body, nearly dead at a hundred, nor Sarah's womb. **20.** He did not doubt God's promise but was strengthened in faith, giving glory to God, **21.** fully persuaded that God could do what He promised. **22.** This is why "it was credited to him as righteousness." **23.** The words "it was credited to him" were not for Abraham alone, **24.** but also for us, to whom righteousness will be credited if we believe in God who raised Jesus our Lord from the dead. **25.** He was delivered over to death for our sins and raised to life for our justification.

Chapter 5
1. Since we are justified by faith, we have peace with God through Jesus Christ. (Justified: declared righteous by God) **2.** Through Him, we access grace by faith and rejoice in the hope of God's glory. (Rejoice: feel or show great joy) **3.** We even rejoice in sufferings, knowing that suffering produces patience. (Patience: the ability to endure without complaining) **4.** Patience leads to character, and character brings hope. (Experience: proven character that results from enduring trials or challenge) **5.** Hope does not disappoint, because God's love is poured into our hearts by the Holy Spirit. (Atonement: reconciliation with God) **6.** While we were powerless, Christ died for the ungodly. (Ungodly: those who do not follow God) **7.** Rarely will anyone die for a righteous person, but for a good person, someone might dare to die. (Righteous: morally right, just) **8.** But God shows His love by Christ dying for us while we were still sinners. (Sinners: those who commit wrongdoings against God) **9.** Now justified by His blood, we will be saved from wrath through Him. (Wrath: God's anger or judgment) **10.** If we were reconciled to God by the death of His Son, much more will we be saved by His life! (Reconciled: restored to a friendly relationship) **11.** We rejoice in God through Jesus Christ, through whom we've received reconciliation. (Reconciliation: restoration of relationship) **12.** Sin entered the world through one man, and death through sin, so death spread to all because all sinned. (Sin: wrongdoing or offense against God) **13.** (Before the law, sin was in the world, but sin isn't counted when there's no law.) (Imputed: credited or assigned) **14.** Death reigned from Adam to Moses, even over those who didn't sin like Adam, who represents the one to come. (Reigned: ruled) **15.** The gift is not like the trespass: if many died through one man's sin, God's grace through Jesus Christ has overflowed to many. (Trespass: sin or wrongdoing) **16.** The gift is not like the sin: one sin led to condemnation, but the gift brings justification. (Condemnation: punishment or judgment) **17.** If death reigned through one man's sin, how much more will grace and righteousness reign in life through Jesus Christ! (Righteousness: moral rightness or being just) **18.** Just as one trespass brought condemnation, one righteous act brought life for all people. (Righteous: morally right, just) **19.** Through one man's disobedience, many were made sinners, and through His obedience, many will be made righteous. (Disobedience: refusal to obey) **20.** The law entered to increase trespass, but where sin increased, grace increased more. (Grace: God's unearned favor or kindness) **21.** Just as sin reigned in death, grace reigns through righteousness to bring eternal life through Jesus Christ. (Eternal: lasting forever)

Chapter 6
1. What should we say? Should we continue sinning so grace may increase? (Grace: unearned favor or kindness from God) **2.** By no means! How can we, who have died to sin, live in it? (Sin: wrongdoing or immoral behavior) **3.** Don't you know that we were baptized into Jesus Christ's death? (Baptized: immersed in water as a sign of faith) **4.** We were buried with Him in baptism, so we can live a new life as He was raised from the dead. (Raised: brought back to life) **5.** If we've been united with Him in death, we will also share in His resurrection. (Resurrection: rising from the dead) **6.** Our old self was crucified with Him so sin's power over us is destroyed, and we no longer serve sin. (Crucified: put to death on a cross, Serve: work for or obey) **7.** Anyone who has died is free from sin. (Sin: wrongdoing or immoral behavior) **8.** If we've died with Christ, we will live with Him. (Christ: the anointed one, the Messiah) **9.** Since Christ was raised, death no longer has power over Him.

(Power: control or authority) **10.** He died to sin once; He lives for God. (Died: ceased to live) **11.** Consider yourselves dead to sin but alive to God in Christ. (Alive: living) **12.** Do not let sin control your body and lead you to evil desires. (Control: rule or dominate, Evil: morally wrong, Desires: strong feelings of wanting something) **13.** Do not offer any part of yourselves to sin, but offer yourselves to God as instruments of righteousness. (Offer: give or present, Instruments: tools or means) **14.** Sin shall not control you, for you are under grace, not the law. (Under grace: living with God's favor, not under judgment) **15** What then? Shall we sin because we are under grace? By no means! (Grace: unearned favor or kindness from God) **16.** Don't you know that whoever you obey becomes your master either sin leading to death or obedience leading to righteousness? (Master: controller, Obedience: following rules, Righteousness: moral rightness) **17.** Thanks to God, though you were once slaves to sin, you obeyed from your heart the teaching given to you. (Slaves: those controlled or forced to serve, Obeyed: followed, Heart: inner being) **18.** You are free from sin and now serve righteousness. (Free: no longer under control, Serve: work for or obey) **19.** I speak in human terms because of your weakness. Just as you gave yourselves to sin, now give yourselves to righteousness for holiness. (Human terms: everyday examples, Weakness: lack of strength, Holiness: being set apart for God) **20.** When you were slaves to sin, you were free from righteousness. (Slaves: those controlled or forced to serve, Righteousness: moral rightness) **21.** What benefit did you gain from the things you are now ashamed of? They lead to death. (Benefit: good result, Ashamed: feeling embarrassed, Death: separation from life) **22.** Now that you're free from sin and serve God, you gain holiness, leading to eternal life. (Holiness: being set apart for God, Eternal: lasting forever) **23.** The wages of sin is death, but the gift of God is eternal life in Christ Jesus our Lord. (Wages: payment for work, Sin: wrongdoing or immoral behavior, Gift: something given without payment, Eternal: lasting forever)

Chapter 7
1. Do you not know, brothers and sisters, that the law has authority over a person only as long as they live? **2.** A woman is bound to her husband as long as he lives, but if he dies, she is free from the law regarding her husband. **3.** If her husband is alive and she marries another, she is an adulteress, but if he dies, she is free from the law. **4.** Similarly, you have died to the law through Christ, so you may belong to Him, to bear fruit for God. **5.** When we were in the flesh, sinful passions stirred by the law led to death. (Flesh: human nature apart from God) **6.** But now we are free from the law and serve in the newness of the Spirit, not in the old way of the letter. (Letter: written law) **7.** Is the law sin? No! I would not have known sin without the law, especially coveting. (Coveting: desire for what belongs to another) **8.** Sin, using the commandment, stirred up all kinds of coveting. Without the law, sin was inactive. **9.** I once lived without the law, but when the commandment came, sin revived, and I died. **10.** The commandment, meant to bring life, brought death instead. **11.** Sin, using the commandment, deceived me and killed me. (Deceived: misled, tricked) **12.** So, the law is holy, and the commandment is good, just, and righteous. **13.** Did what is good cause my death? No! Sin used the good to bring death, making sin exceedingly sinful. (Exceedingly: to a great degree) **14.** We know the law is spiritual, but I am unspiritual, sold to sin. (Unspiritual: lacking spiritual strength) **15.** I don't understand my actions. What I want to do, I do not; what I hate, I do. **16** If I do what I do not want to do, I agree that the law is good. **17** It is no longer I who do it, but sin living in me. **18.** I know that nothing good dwells in me, that is, in my sinful nature. (Sinful nature: human tendency to sin) **19.** What I want to do, I do not do; what I don't want, I do. **20.** If I do what I do not want, it's no longer I but sin living in me. **21.** I find this law: when I want to do good, evil is present with me. **22.** I delight in God's law in my inner being. (Delight: take great pleasure in) **23.** But I see another law warring against my mind and making me a prisoner to sin. (Warring: fighting, attacking) **24.** What a wretched man I am! Who will deliver me from this body of death? (Wretched: miserable, distressed) **25.** Thanks be to God, who delivers me through Jesus Christ! So, with my mind, I serve God's law, but with my flesh, the law of sin. (Flesh: human nature)

Chapter 8
1. There is no condemnation for those in Christ Jesus who live by the Spirit, not the flesh. (Condemnation: the act of declaring someone guilty and deserving punishment) **2.** The law of the Spirit has freed me from the law of sin and death **3.** What the law couldn't do, God did by sending His Son in the likeness of sinful flesh to defeat sin. **4.** So, the law's righteous requirements are met in us who live by the Spirit, not the flesh. **5.** Those who live by the flesh focus on its desires; those who live by the Spirit focus on the things of the Spirit. **6.** The mind set on the flesh leads to death; the mind set on the Spirit leads to life and peace. **7.** The fleshly mind is hostile to God; it does not obey God's law and cannot do so. (Hostile: unfriendly, antagonistic) **8.** Those in the flesh cannot please God. **9.** You are in the Spirit, if God's Spirit lives in you; if not, you do not belong to Christ. **10.** If Christ is in you, your body is dead because of sin, but the Spirit gives life because of righteousness. **11.** The Spirit who raised Christ from the dead will give life to your bodies through His Spirit. **12.** We are not obligated to live according to the flesh. (Obligated: required or bound to do something) **13.** If you live by the flesh, you will die, but if through the Spirit you kill the deeds of the body, you will live. **14.** Those led by the Spirit are children of God. **15.** You received the Spirit of adoption, by which we cry, "Abba, Father." (Adoption: the act of accepting someone as a member of the family) **16.** The Spirit confirms with our spirit that we are God's children. **17.** If we are children, we are heirs of God and co-heirs with Christ, if we share in His suffering so we may also share in His glory. **18.** The sufferings of this time are not worth comparing with the glory to come. **19.** Creation eagerly waits for the revelation of the children of God. (Revelation: the act of revealing or disclosing something) **20.** Creation was subjected to frustration in hope, not by its own choice but by God's will. (Frustration: the feeling of being upset or discouraged) **21.** Creation will be freed from corruption into the glorious freedom of God's children. **22.** Creation groans and suffers together in pain. (Groans: deep, expressive sounds of pain or longing) **23.** We, who have the firstfruits of the Spirit, also groan as we wait for the redemption of our bodies. (Redemption: the act of being saved from sin or evil) **24.** We are saved by hope, but hope that is seen is not hope. **25.** But if we hope for what we do not see, we wait for it patiently. **26.** The Spirit helps us in our weakness; we do not know how to pray, but the Spirit intercedes for us with groans. (Intercedes: pleads on behalf of someone else) **27.** God, who knows the hearts, knows the mind of the Spirit, because the Spirit intercedes for God's people according to God's will. **28.** All things work for good for those who love God, who are called according to His purpose. (Purpose: the reason for which something is done) **29.** Those God foreknew, He predestined to be conformed to the image of His Son. (Predestined: determined beforehand) **30.** Those He predestined, He called; those He called, He justified; those He justified, He glorified. (Justified: declared righteous) **31.** If God is for us, who can be against us? **32.** He who did not spare His Son, but gave Him up for us, will also give us all things. **33.** Who can bring any charge against God's elect? It is God who justifies. (Elect: those chosen by God) **34.** Christ, who died and was raised, intercedes for us at God's right hand. (Intercedes: pleads on behalf of someone else) **35.** Who can separate us from the love of Christ? Trouble, hardship, persecution, famine, nakedness, danger, or sword? **36.** As it is written: "For Your sake, we are killed all day long; we are like sheep to be slaughtered." **37.** In all these things, we are more than conquerors through Him who loved us. (Conquerors: those who overcome or defeat) **38.** I am sure that neither death nor life, angels nor powers, present nor future, **39.** nor height nor depth, nor anything in creation, will be able to separate us from God's love in Christ Jesus our Lord.

Chapter 9
1. I speak the truth in Christ; my conscience, with the Holy Spirit, confirms this. (Conscience: a person's moral sense of right and wrong) **2.** I have deep sorrow and constant grief. (Sorrow: a feeling of sadness or grief) **3.** I would be willing to be separated from Christ for the sake of my fellow Israelites. **4.** They are Israelites, who have the adoption, glory, covenants, law, worship, and promises. **5.** The patriarchs are theirs, and Christ came from them, who is God over all, blessed forever. Amen. (Patriarchs: the male leaders or founders of a family or tribe) **6.** God's word has not failed, for not all of Israel are truly Israel. **7.** Not all Abraham's descendants are his children; only Isaac's descendants are the promised ones. **8.** It is not the children of the flesh but the children of the promise who are regarded as true descendants. **9** The promise was, "At the appointed time, Sarah will have a son." **10.** Rebekah also had children by Isaac, our father, **11.** though they had done nothing good or bad, so God's purpose in choosing might stand. **12.** It was said, "The older will serve the younger." **13.** As it is written, "Jacob I loved, but Esau I hated." **14.** Is there injustice with God? No! **15.** He says to Moses, "I will have mercy on whom I choose." **16.** It does not depend on human effort, but on God's mercy. **17.** God raised Pharaoh to show His power and declare His name throughout the earth. **18.** God shows mercy to whom He wills, and hardens whom He wills. (Harden: to make someone stubborn or resistant to change) **19.** Why then does God still find fault? Who can resist His will? **20.** Who are you, to question God? Can the clay say to the potter, "Why did you make me like this?" **21.** Does not the potter have the right to make different vessels from the same lump of clay? **22.** What if God endured with patience those destined for destruction, to make His glory known? **23.** What if He prepared vessels of mercy for glory? **24.** Even us, whom He has called, not only from the Jews but from the Gentiles. **25.** As Hosea said, "I will call them My people who were not My people." **26.** They will be called "children of the living God."

27. Isaiah said, "Though Israel's numbers are many, only a remnant will be saved." **28.** The Lord will quickly fulfill His purpose on the earth. **29.** Unless the Lord had left us descendants, we would have become like Sodom. **30.** The Gentiles, who didn't pursue righteousness, obtained it by faith. **31.** But Israel, who pursued righteousness by the law, did not attain it. **32.** Why? Because they sought it by works, not by faith. They stumbled over the stumbling stone. (Stumbling stone: an obstacle that causes people to fall or fail) **33.** As written: "I lay in Zion a stone that causes people to stumble; the one who believes in Him will not be ashamed."

Chapter 10
1. My heartfelt longing and prayer to God on behalf of Israel is for their salvation. (Salvation: deliverance from sin and its consequences, typically by God's grace) **2.** I testify that they are passionate about God, but their zeal is not based on true understanding. (Zeal: great energy or enthusiasm in pursuit of a cause or objective) **3.** They do not understand God's righteousness and are trying to establish their own righteousness, not submitting to the righteousness that comes from God. (Righteousness: the quality of being morally right or justifiable) **4.** Christ is the fulfillment of the law, bringing righteousness to everyone who believes. (Fulfillment: the completion or achievement of something) **5.** Moses described the righteousness that comes from the law, stating that anyone who follows its commands will live by them. (Described: explained or portrayed in detail) **6.** But the righteousness that comes through faith speaks differently: It does not ask, "Who will ascend to heaven?" (Ascend: go up or rise) **7.** or, "Who will go down into the depths?" (Depths: the profound or extreme part of something) **8.** But what does it say? The word is near you, in your mouth and in your heart; this is the message of faith we proclaim. (Proclaim: announce or declare something publicly) **9.** If you declare with your mouth that Jesus is Lord and believe in your heart that God raised Him from the dead, you will be saved. (Declare: state something formally or officially) **10.** For it is with the heart that one believes and is made righteous, and it is with the mouth that confession is made and salvation is declared. (Confession: the act of admitting or declaring something) **11.** The Scripture says, "Anyone who believes in Him will never be put to shame." (Scripture: sacred writings of Christianity, particularly the Bible) **12.** There is no distinction between Jew and Greek; the same Lord is Lord of all and richly blesses all who call on Him. (Distinction: a difference or contrast) **13.** Everyone who calls on the name of the Lord will be saved. (Calls: prays or appeals to for help or intervention) **14.** How, then, can they call on the one they have not believed in? And how can they believe in the one of whom they have not heard? And how can they hear without someone preaching to them? (Preaching: delivering a religious message, often in public) **15.** And how can anyone preach unless they are sent? As it is written, "How beautiful are the feet of those who bring good news!" (Sent: authorized or commissioned to act) **16.** But not all the Israelites accepted the good news. As Isaiah says, "Lord, who has believed our message?" (Accepted: received or embraced something willingly) **17.** Consequently, faith comes from hearing the message, and the message is heard through the word of Christ. (Consequently: as a result, therefore) **18.** But I ask, did they not hear? Of course they did: "Their voice has gone out into all the earth, their words to the ends of the world." (Voice: a declaration or message) **19.** Again I ask, did Israel not understand? First, Moses says, "I will make you envious by those who are not a nation; I will make you angry by a nation that has no understanding." (Envious: feeling of jealousy or desire for something that belongs to someone else) **20.** And Isaiah boldly says, "I was found by those who did not seek me; I revealed myself to those who did not ask for me." (Boldly: with courage and confidence) **21.** But concerning Israel, God says, "All day long I have held out my hands to a disobedient and obstinate people." (Obstinate: stubbornly refusing to change or be persuaded)

Chapter 11
1. I ask, has God rejected His people? No! I am an Israelite, from Abraham's lineage, from the tribe of Benjamin. (Rejected: cast off) **2.** God has not rejected His people whom He foreknew. Remember what Scripture says about Elijah, pleading with God against Israel: (Foreknew: knew beforehand) **3.** "Lord, they killed Your prophets and destroyed Your altars; I'm the only one left, and they seek to kill me." (Destroyed: tore down) **4.** But God answered: "I have kept seven thousand men who have not worshiped Baal." (Worshiped: bowed to) **5.** So, even now there is a remnant chosen by grace. (Remnant: remaining part) **6.** If by grace, it is not based on works; otherwise, grace is no longer grace. (Grace: unearned favor) **7.** Israel has not obtained what it sought, but the elect have obtained it, and the rest were hardened. (Hardened: made insensible) **8.** As it is written: "God gave them a spirit of stupor, eyes that can't see, ears that can't hear, to this day." (Stupor: confusion) **9.** David says, "Let their table become a snare and a trap, a stumbling block, and a recompense to them." (Recompense: reward) **10.** "Let their eyes be darkened so they cannot see, and their backs always bent." (Bent: stooped) **11.** I ask, have they stumbled so as to fall? No! Their fall brought salvation to the Gentiles, to provoke Israel to jealousy. (Provoke: arouse) **12.** If their fall means riches for the world, how much more their fullness? (Fullness: completeness) **13.** I speak to you Gentiles. I magnify my ministry, (Magnify: exalt) **14.** hoping to provoke some of my fellow Israelites to jealousy and save some. (Save: rescue) **15.** For if their rejection is the reconciliation of the world, what will their acceptance bring but life from the dead? (Reconciliation: restoration) **16.** If the firstfruit is holy, so is the whole batch; and if the root is holy, so are the branches. (Firstfruit: initial part) **17.** If some branches were broken off, and you, a wild olive shoot, were grafted in, sharing the nourishment of the olive tree, (Grafted: inserted) **18.** do not boast against the branches. If you do, remember the root supports you, not the other way around. (Boast: brag) **19.** You might say, "The branches were broken off so I could be grafted in." (Broken off: removed) **20.** True. They were broken off because of unbelief, and you stand by faith. Do not be proud, but fear. (Unbelief: lack of faith) **21.** If God did not spare the natural branches, He will not spare you either. (Spare: withhold) **22.** Consider the kindness and severity of God: severity to those who fell, but kindness to you, if you remain in His kindness. (Severity: harshness) **23.** If they do not persist in unbelief, they will be grafted in again, for God is able to do so. (Persist: continue) **24.** If you were cut from a wild olive tree and grafted into a cultivated tree, how much more will the natural branches be grafted into their own tree? (Cultivated: nurtured) **25.** I don't want you to be ignorant of this mystery, so you don't think too highly of yourselves. Israel has experienced a partial hardening until the full number of Gentiles comes in. (Mystery: hidden truth) **26.** And so all Israel will be saved. As it is written: "The Deliverer will come from Zion and turn godlessness from Jacob." (Deliverer: Savior) **27.** This is My covenant with them when I take away their sins." (Covenant: agreement) **28.** As far as the gospel is concerned, they are enemies for your sake, but as far as election is concerned, they are loved for the patriarchs' sake. (Election: chosen ones) **29.** For God's gifts and calling are irrevocable. (Irrevocable: unchangeable) **30.** Just as you Gentiles once were disobedient but now have received mercy, (Disobedient: rebellious) **31.** they too have now become disobedient, that through your mercy they also may receive mercy. (Mercy: compassion) **32.** For God has bound everyone over to disobedience, so He can have mercy on all. (Bound over: held accountable) **33.** Oh, the depth of the riches of God's wisdom and knowledge! How unsearchable His judgments, and His ways beyond finding out! (Unsearchable: impossible to understand) **34.** Who has known the mind of the Lord? Or who has been His counselor? (Counselor: advisor) **35.** Who has ever given to God, that God should repay them? (Repay: return) **36.** For from Him, through Him, and to Him are all things. To Him be the glory forever! Amen. (Glory: honor)

Chapter 12
1. I urge you, by God's mercy, to offer your bodies as living sacrifices—holy and pleasing to God, which is your reasonable act of worship. (mercy: compassion or forgiveness, reasonable: based on good sense) **2.** Do not conform to this world, but be transformed by renewing your mind, so you can discern God's will—what is good and perfect. (conform: behave according to, transformed: changed, discerning: recognizing clearly) **3.** By the grace God gave me, I say to everyone: Do not think too highly of yourself, but with sober judgment, as God has given each of you faith. (grace: unearned favor, sober: serious, judgment: ability to make decisions) **4.** Just as the body has many parts with different functions, **5.** so in Christ, we are one body, with each member belonging to the others. **6.** We have different gifts, according to God's grace. If your gift is prophecy, prophesy in proportion to your faith. (prophecy: inspired message) **7.** If your gift is serving, serve; if teaching, teach; **8.** If encouraging, encourage; if giving, give generously; if leading, lead diligently; if showing mercy, do so cheerfully. (generously: freely, diligently: with care, mercy: compassion) **9.** Love must be sincere. Hate evil; cling to good. (sincere: genuine, cling: hold tightly) **10.** Be devoted to one another in love. Honor others above yourselves. (devoted: loyal, honor: respect) **11.** Never lack zeal, but keep your spiritual fervor, serving the Lord. (zeal: enthusiasm, fervor: passion) **12.** Be joyful in hope, patient in trouble, faithful in prayer. (faithful: loyal) **13.** Share with those in need. Practice hospitality. (hospitality: kindness to guests) **14.** Bless those who persecute you; bless, don't curse. (persecute: treat cruelly, curse: speak evil) **15.** Rejoice with those who rejoice; mourn with those who mourn. (rejoice: be happy, mourn: grieve) **16.** Live in harmony with each other. Don't be proud, but associate with the humble. (harmony: agreement, associate: connect) **17.** Don't repay evil for evil. Do what is right in the eyes of everyone. (repay: give back) **18.** If possible, live at peace with everyone. (peace: calm) **19.** Do not take revenge, but leave room for God's wrath, for it is written, "I will repay," says the Lord. (revenge: payback, wrath: anger) **20.** If your enemy is hungry, feed him; if

thirsty, give him drink. In doing this, you will heap burning coals on his head. (heap: pile) **21.** Do not be overcome by evil, but overcome evil with good. (overcome: defeat)

Chapter 13

1. Let every person be in submission to the governing authorities. For there is no authority except that which is established by God; the authorities that exist are appointed by Him. (Submission: obedience) **2.** Therefore, anyone who resists the authority resists God's decree, and those who do so will face judgment. (Resists: opposes; Decree: command; Judgment: punishment) **3.** Rulers are not a threat to those who do right, but to those who do wrong. Do you want to avoid fear of authority? Then do what is right, and you will receive praise from them. (Threat: danger; Praise: approval) **4.** For the ruler is God's servant to promote your good. But if you do wrong, be afraid, for the ruler does not bear the sword in vain; they are God's servant, an avenger who carries out God's wrath on wrongdoers. (Servant: helper; Promote: encourage; Sword: a weapon used for punishment; Vain: without purpose; Avenger: punisher; Wrath: anger) **5.** Therefore, it is necessary to be subject, not only because of possible punishment, but also because of conscience. (Necessary: required; Subject: obedient; Conscience: moral sense of right and wrong) **6.** This is also why you pay taxes, for the authorities are God's servants who give their full time to governing. (Taxes: fees required by the government) **7.** Give everyone what you owe them: If you owe taxes, pay taxes; if revenue, then revenue; if respect, then respect; if honor, then honor. (Revenue: money or payment; Respect: regard or esteem; Honor: high regard) **8.** Let no debt remain outstanding except the continuing debt to love one another, for whoever loves others has fulfilled the law. (Debt: unpaid amount; Outstanding: remaining; Fulfilled: completed) **9.** The commandments, "You shall not commit adultery," "You shall not murder," "You shall not steal," "You shall not give false testimony," "You shall not covet," and any other commandment, are summed up in this one rule: "Love your neighbor as yourself." (Commandments: orders or rules; Adultery: cheating on one's spouse; False testimony: lie; Covet: desire wrongly; Summed up: condensed) **10.** Love does no harm to a neighbor. Therefore, love is the fulfillment of the law. (Harm: wrong; Fulfillment: completion) **11.** And do this, understanding the present time: the hour has already come for you to wake up from your slumber, because our salvation is nearer now than when we first believed. (Understanding: knowing; Slumber: sleep; Salvation: rescue from sin) **12.** The night is nearly over; the day is almost here. So let us put aside the deeds of darkness and put on the armor of light. (Deeds: actions; Armor: protection) **13.** Let us live decently, as in the daytime, not in carousing and drunkenness, not in sexual immorality and debauchery, not in dissension and jealousy. (Decently: properly; Carousing: partying; Drunkenness: intoxication; Sexual immorality: wrong sexual behavior; Debauchery: excessive indulgence; Dissension: disagreement; Jealousy: envy) **14.** Rather, clothe yourselves with the Lord Jesus Christ, and do not think about how to gratify the desires of the flesh. (Gratify: satisfy; Desires: wants; Flesh: the sinful nature)

Chapter 14

1. Welcome those weak in faith, but avoid arguments over differing beliefs. (Weak in faith: fragile or undeveloped belief) **2.** Some believe they can eat anything, but the weak eat only vegetables. (Vegetables: plant-based food, indicating restricted diet) **3.** Those who eat all foods shouldn't look down on those who abstain, nor should those who abstain judge others. God accepts both. (Abstain: refrain; Condemn: judge negatively) **4.** Who are you to judge another's servant? They answer to their master, who will uphold them. (Judge: form an opinion; Uphold: support) **5.** One person regards one day as sacred, another treats all days equally. Each should follow their convictions. (Sacred: holy; Convinced: certain) **6.** Observing or not observing special days, eating or abstaining—all should be done in gratitude to God. (Observe: celebrate; Abstain: refrain) **7.** None of us lives or dies solely for ourselves. (Alone: without others) **8.** In life and death, we belong to the Lord. (Belong: under authority or ownership) **9.** Christ died and rose to be Lord of the living and dead. (Returned to life: resurrected) **10.** Why judge or look down on others? We will all face God's judgment seat. (Look down: regard as inferior; Judgment seat: place of final decision) **11.** Scripture says every knee will bow and every tongue will acknowledge God. (Acknowledge: admit truth) **12.** Each will account for themselves to God. (Account: explanation of actions) **13.** Stop judging. Instead, avoid creating obstacles for others. (Stumbling block: hindrance; Obstacle: barrier) **14.** Nothing is unclean by nature, but if one considers it so, then for them, it is unclean. (Unclean: impure or forbidden) **15.** If your food distresses someone, you're not acting in love. Don't harm someone Christ died for. (Distressed: troubled; Acting in love: showing care) **16.** Do not let your good be spoken of as evil. (Spoken of: referred to) **17.** God's kingdom is about righteousness, peace, and joy in the Holy Spirit, not eating or drinking. (Righteousness: moral uprightness; Peace: harmony; Joy: great happiness) **18.** Those who serve Christ in this way please God and are approved by others. (Serves: works under; Approved: accepted) **19.** Strive for peace and mutual edification. (Edification: moral improvement) **20.** Don't ruin God's work over food. Though all food is clean, eating what causes others to stumble is wrong. (Work of God: God's plan; Stumble: falter spiritually) **21.** Avoid anything—like meat or wine—that may cause others to fall. (Fall: sin or stray) **22.** Keep personal beliefs between you and God. Blessed is one who doesn't condemn themselves by their choices. (Blessed: fortunate; Condemn: judge negatively) **23.** Doubts make actions sinful if not from faith, as everything not from faith is sin. (Doubts: uncertainty; Sin: moral wrongdoing)

Chapter 15

1. We who are strong must help the weak and not live for our own satisfaction. **2.** Each of us should aim to do good for our neighbor, helping them grow. **3.** Christ did not live to please Himself; as it says, "The insults of those who insulted You fell on Me." (insults: offenses or disrespectful words) **4.** Everything written earlier was to teach us, so we might find hope through patience and the Scriptures. **5.** May God, who gives patience and encouragement, make you united in Christ. (patience: the ability to endure difficulty) **6.** With unity, glorify God, the Father of Jesus Christ. **7.** Welcome one another, just as Christ welcomed you, for God's glory. **8.** Christ served the Jews to fulfill God's promises to the ancestors. (ancestors: forefathers or predecessors) **9.** Gentiles glorify God for His mercy; as written, "I will praise You among the Gentiles." **10.** Again, Scripture says, "Rejoice, Gentiles, with His people." (Gentiles: non-Jewish people) **11.** And, "Praise the Lord, all you Gentiles; praise Him, all peoples." **12.** Isaiah says, "The root of Jesse will rise to reign; Gentiles will hope in Him." (reign: rule as king) **13.** May God fill you with joy, peace, and overflowing hope through the Holy Spirit. **14.** I am confident, brothers and sisters, of your goodness, knowledge, and ability to guide one another. **15.** I've written boldly to remind you because of God's grace given to me. (grace: unearned favor or blessing) **16.** God appointed me as a minister of Christ to the Gentiles, so their offering would be acceptable, sanctified by the Spirit. (sanctified: made holy or pure) **17.** I glory in what Christ has accomplished through me for God. **18.** I only speak of what Christ has done through me to lead the Gentiles by word and deed. **19.** By God's power, I have fully preached Christ's gospel, from Jerusalem to Illyricum. (gospel: the message of Christ's salvation) **20.** My goal is to preach Christ where He is unknown, not building on others' work. **21.** As it says, "Those who never heard of Him will see and understand." **22.** This is why I've been delayed in visiting you. **23.** Now, with no place left to work here, I've longed to visit you for years. **24.** I hope to see you on my way to Spain and enjoy your company. **25.** But now, I go to Jerusalem to serve the saints. (saints: believers or holy ones) **26.** Macedonia and Achaia have given generously to help Jerusalem's poor believers. **27.** They are pleased to share material blessings, as they've received spiritual blessings from the Jews. (spiritual: related to the soul or faith) **28.** Once this task is done, I'll visit you on my way to Spain. **29.** I am sure I'll come to you with Christ's full blessing. **30.** I ask you, by Jesus and the Spirit's love, to pray with me. **31.** Pray I'll be rescued from unbelievers and that my service in Jerusalem will be accepted. **32.** Then I can come to you joyfully and be refreshed with you. **33.** May the God of peace be with you all. Amen. (peace: freedom from conflict or worry)

Chapter 16

1. I introduce Phebe, our sister and servant of the church in Cenchrea. (Cenchrea: a port city near Corinth) **2.** Welcome her in the Lord and support her in any matter where she needs help, as she has aided many, including me. **3.** Greetings to Priscilla and Aquila, my fellow workers in Christ Jesus. **4.** They risked their lives for me, and I, along with Gentile churches, am grateful. (Gentiles: non-Jews) **5.** Greet the church in their house and Epaenetus, the first to believe in Christ in Achaia. **6.** Send greetings to Mary, who worked hard for us. **7.** Salute Andronicus and Junia, my relatives and fellow prisoners, esteemed among the apostles. (Esteemed: highly regarded or honored) **8.** Send greetings to Amplias, whom I love in the Lord. **9.** Salute Urbanus, our coworker, and Stachys, my dear friend. **10.** Greet Apelles, proven faithful in Christ, and those in Aristobulus' household. **11.** Greetings to Herodion, my relative, and the household of Narcissus in the Lord. **12.** Salute Tryphena, Tryphosa, and Persis, who worked diligently in the Lord. (Diligently: with great effort) **13.** Greetings to Rufus, chosen by the Lord, and his mother, who has cared for me as well. **14.** Salute Asyncritus, Phlegon, Hermas, Patrobas, Hermes, and their companions. (Companions: people who are together in a shared activity or circumstance) **15.** Greet Philologus, Julia, Nereus, his sister, Olympas, and all the saints with them. (Saints: believers or followers of Christ) **16.** Greet one another with a holy kiss. Churches of Christ send their greetings. **17.** Watch out for those who create divisions and oppose the teaching you've received; stay away from them. (Divisions: disagreements or separations) **18.** They serve their own desires and use flattering words to deceive innocent people. (Deceive: to mislead) **19.** Your obedience is well-known, and I rejoice for you. Be wise in doing good and innocent about evil. (Innocent: free from wrongdoing or guilt) **20.** God will soon defeat Satan under your feet. May Christ's grace be with you. (Satan: the adversary, evil one) **21.** Timothy, Lucius, Jason, and Sosipater, my coworkers and relatives, send greetings. **22.** I, Tertius, who wrote this letter, send my greetings in the Lord. **23.** Gaius, my host and host of the church, greets you, as do Erastus, the city treasurer, and Quartus, our brother. (Treasurer: the person responsible for managing finances) **24.** May the grace of the Lord Jesus Christ be with you all. **25.** To the one able to strengthen you by the gospel and Jesus Christ's message, a mystery revealed after long ages— (Mystery: something hidden or unknown) **26.** now made known through the prophets' writings to inspire obedience among all nations— (Obedience: compliance with God's will) **27.** to God, the only wise one, be glory forever through Christ. Amen. (Glory: great honor or praise)

46 – 1 Corinthians
Chapter 1
1. Paul, called by God to be an apostle of Jesus Christ, and our brother Sosthenes. **2.** To the church of God in Corinth, to those sanctified in Christ Jesus, called to be saints, with all who call on Jesus Christ's name—both theirs and ours. **3.** Grace and peace to you from God our Father and the Lord Jesus Christ. **4.** I thank God for you, for the grace given to you through Jesus Christ. **5.** You have been enriched in every way, in speech and knowledge, **6.** As the testimony of Christ was confirmed in you. **7.** You lack no spiritual gift while waiting for the return of our Lord Jesus Christ. **8.** He will keep you firm to the end, so you will be blameless on the day of our Lord Jesus Christ. **9.** God is faithful, who called you into fellowship with His Son, Jesus Christ our Lord. (Fellowship: sharing in common or partnership) **10.** I urge you, brothers and sisters, in Jesus' name, to agree with each other, with no divisions, but to be united in thought and judgment. **11.** Some from Chloe's household have told me that there are divisions among you. **12.** Some say, "I follow Paul"; others say, "I follow Apollos"; or "Cephas"; or "Christ." **13.** Is Christ divided? Was Paul crucified for you? Were you baptized in Paul's name? **14.** I thank God I baptized none of you except Crispus and Gaius, **15.** So no one can say you were baptized in my name. **16.** I also baptized the household of Stephanas; I don't know if I baptized anyone else. **17.** Christ did not send me to baptize, but to preach the gospel, not with eloquence, so the cross would not lose its power. (Eloquence: fluent or persuasive speaking or writing) **18.** The message of the cross is foolishness to those perishing, but to us being saved, it's God's power. **19.** It is written: "I will destroy the wisdom of the wise, and frustrate the understanding of the intelligent." (Frustrate: to prevent from achieving a goal or making progress) **20.** Where is the wise person? Where is the teacher of the law? Has God not made foolish the wisdom of the world? **21.** For in God's wisdom, the world did not know Him, and it pleased God to save those who believe by preaching, which seems foolish. **22.** Jews want signs, and Greeks seek wisdom, **23.** But we preach Christ crucified, a stumbling block to Jews and foolishness to Greeks. (Stumbling block: something that hinders progress or causes failure) **24.** But to those called, both Jews and Greeks, Christ is God's power and wisdom. **25.** God's foolishness is wiser than human wisdom, and His weakness stronger than human strength. **26.** Think about your calling, brothers: not many were wise, influential, or of noble birth. **27.** But God chose the foolish things of the world to shame the wise and the weak things to shame the strong. **28.** God chose the lowly and despised things to nullify the things that are, (Nullify: to make something invalid or ineffective) **29.** So that no one may boast before Him. **30.** It is because of God that you are in Christ Jesus, who has become our wisdom, righteousness, holiness, and redemption. **31.** As it is written: "Let the one who boasts, boast in the Lord."

Chapter 2
1. When I came, I didn't use fancy speech or wisdom, but shared God's testimony. (Testimony: a statement or declaration of belief) **2.** I decided to know nothing except Jesus Christ, and Him crucified. **3.** I came to you in weakness, fear, and trembling. **4.** My message was not with persuasive words but with the Spirit's power. (Persuasive: able to convince) **5.** So your faith would rest on God's power, not human wisdom. **6.** We speak wisdom to the mature, but not the wisdom of this world or its rulers. (Mature: fully developed) **7.** We speak God's hidden wisdom, destined for our glory. (Destined: planned or intended) **8.** None of the rulers knew it; had they, they wouldn't have crucified Jesus. (Crucified: executed by nailing to the cross) **9.** As it is written: "No eye has seen or ear heard what God has prepared for those who love Him." **10.** God has revealed these things to us through His Spirit, who searches all things. (Revealed: made known) **11.** Who knows a person's thoughts except their own spirit? Likewise, no one knows God's thoughts except the Spirit of God. **12.** We have received God's Spirit, not the world's, so we can understand what He gives us. (Received: accepted) **13.** We speak not with human wisdom but with the Spirit's teachings, comparing spiritual things. **14.** The natural person cannot understand spiritual things; they are foolishness to him. (Natural: related to the physical world) **15.** The spiritual person judges all things but is not judged by anyone. **16.** "Who knows the mind of the Lord?" But we have the mind of Christ.

Chapter 3
1. Brothers, I couldn't speak to you as spiritual, but as worldly, mere infants in Christ. (Infants: immature or undeveloped believers) **2.** I gave you basic teachings, not solid food, because you weren't ready for more. (Solid food: deeper teachings of faith) **3.** You are still worldly with jealousy, conflict, and divisions—proving you're living like humans. (Jealousy: envy, Conflict: disputes, Divisions: separations) **4.** One says, "I follow Paul," another "I follow Apollos"—isn't this worldly? (Worldly: influenced by human ways instead of God's) **5.** Paul and Apollos are servants, working for your faith as God assigned. (Servants: those who serve or minister to others) **6.** I planted, Apollos watered, but only God makes it grow. (Grow: develop spiritually) **7.** The one who plants or waters is nothing—only God makes things grow. (Plant: begin a spiritual work, Water: nurture or help it grow) **8.** The planter and waterer are united, each will be rewarded for their labor. (Labor: work or effort) **9.** We are coworkers in God's service, and you are His field and building. (Coworkers: partners in work, Field: a place of growth, Building: a structure) **10.** By God's grace, I laid the foundation, and others are building on it. (Grace: unearned favor) **11.** No other foundation can be laid except Jesus Christ. (Foundation: the base or starting point of belief) **12.** Anyone can build with different materials: gold, silver, or wood, but fire will test them. (Materials: things used to build, Test: prove or examine by fire) **13.** Each person's work will be revealed by fire, testing its value. (Revealed: made known) **14.** If work survives, the builder will be rewarded. (Survives: remains intact) **15.** If burned up, the builder will suffer loss but still be saved. (Suffer loss: lose the reward) **16.** Don't you know that you are God's temple and His Spirit dwells in you? (Temple: a sacred place, Dwells: lives within) **17.** If anyone destroys God's temple, God will destroy them, for His temple is holy. (Destroys: harms or damages, Holy: sacred or set apart) **18.** Let no one deceive themselves; let the wise of this world become fools to be truly wise. (Deceive: mislead, Fools: lacking true wisdom) **19.** The wisdom of the world is foolishness to God. He catches the wise in their own tricks. (Tricks: clever but deceptive actions) **20.** The Lord knows that the thoughts of the wise are empty. (Empty: worthless or vain) **21.** So don't boast in human leaders—everything is yours, (Boast: show off or take pride) **22.** whether Paul, Apollos, Cephas, or the world, life, or death—everything is yours, (Cephas: another name for Peter) **23.** and you belong to Christ, and Christ belongs to God. (Belong: are owned by)

Chapter 4
1. Regard us as servants of Christ and stewards of God's mysteries. (Stewards: caretakers) **2.** Stewards must be faithful. (Faithful: trustworthy) **3.** I don't care if you or anyone judges me; I don't judge myself. **4.** I don't know anything against myself, but the Lord judges me. **5.** Don't judge before the right time; the Lord will reveal all secrets and motives. **6.** I use myself and Apollos as examples, so you don't think too highly of anyone. **7.** What do you have that you didn't receive? Why boast as if you didn't? **8.** You are already full and rich, like kings; I wish we could reign with you. **9.** God has placed us apostles last, like sentenced to death, a spectacle to all. (Spectacle: public display) **10.** We are fools for Christ, but you are wise; we are weak, but you are strong; we are despised. (Despised: hated or treated with disrespect) **11.** We hunger, thirst, are poorly clothed, beaten, and homeless. **12.** We work hard; when cursed, we bless; when persecuted, we endure; **13.** when slandered, we answer kindly. We are the scum of the earth. (Slander: false statements) (Scum: most despised) **14.** I warn you, not to shame you, but as my dear children. **15.** Though you have many teachers, you don't have many fathers. I became your father through the gospel. **16.** I urge you to imitate me. (Imitate: copy, follow as an example) **17.** I have sent Timothy, my faithful son, to remind you of my teachings. **18.** Some of you are arrogant, thinking I won't visit. (Arrogant: overbearing or prideful) **19.** I will come soon, and see not just what they say, but the power behind it. **20.** The kingdom of God is about power, not words. **21.** Should I come with a rod, or in love and gentleness? (Rod: discipline or correction)

Chapter 5
1. It is reported that there is sexual immorality among you, worse than even among the Gentiles, where one is with his father's wife. (sexual immorality: fornication:) **2.** You are proud instead of grieving, so the person who did this should be removed. (proud: puffed up) **3.** Though I am absent in body, I have already judged the one who committed this sin. (judged: made a decision) **4.** In the name of Jesus, when gathered, and with my spirit, with His power,

(gathered: assembled) **5.** Deliver him to Satan for the destruction of his flesh, so his spirit may be saved in the end. (deliver: hand over) **6.** Your boasting is wrong; don't you know that a little yeast affects the whole dough? (yeast: leaven) **7.** Remove the old yeast, so you may be a new batch, for Christ, our Passover, was sacrificed. (remove: purge ou) **8.** Let us celebrate with sincerity and truth, not with malice or wickedness. (malice: ill will, desire to hurt) **9.** I wrote to you not to associate with fornicators. **10.** Not with the immoral of the world, or with idolaters or greedy people, for you'd have to leave the world. (greedy: covetous) **11.** Now, I write not to eat with anyone claiming to be a brother but living in sin. **12.** What is my responsibility to judge those outside? Isn't it for you to judge those inside? (judge: pass judgment) **13.** God will judge those outside; expel the wicked person from your midst. (wicked: immoral, evil)

Chapter 6

1. Why go to court with another believer before unbelievers instead of the saints? (saints: God's holy people) **2.** Don't you know the saints will judge the world? If you judge the world, can't you judge small matters? **3.** Don't you know we will judge angels? How much more earthly matters? **4.** If you have disputes about earthly matters, appoint those with low status in the church to judge. (disputes: disagreements) **5.** I speak to your shame. Is there no wise person among you to settle matters between believers? **6.** But one brother sues another before unbelievers. **7.** There's a fault among you. Why not accept wrong? Why not be defrauded? **8.** Instead, you wrong and cheat one another, even fellow believers. (defrauded: cheated) **9.** Don't you know the unrighteous won't inherit God's kingdom? Don't be deceived: neither the immoral, idolaters, nor thieves, nor greedy, nor drunkards, nor slanderers, nor swindlers will inherit God's kingdom. (unrighteous: wrongdoers, deceived: misled, idolaters: those who worship idols, swindlers: cheats) **10.** These will not inherit God's kingdom. **11.** Some of you were like this, but you were washed, sanctified, and justified in Jesus' name and the Spirit. (washed: cleansed, sanctified: made holy, justified: declared righteous) **12.** "I can do anything," but not all things are beneficial. I will not be controlled by anything. **13.** Food is for the stomach, and the stomach for food, but God will destroy both. The body is for the Lord, and the Lord for the body. **14.** God raised the Lord and will raise us by His power. (power: strength) **15.** Don't you know your bodies are members of Christ? Should I unite them with a prostitute? Never! (members: parts, prostitute: person engaging in sexual immorality) **16.** Don't you know when you unite with a prostitute, you become one body with her? For, "The two will become one flesh." **17.** But whoever is united with the Lord is one spirit with Him. **18.** Flee sexual immorality. Every sin is outside the body, but sexual sin is against the body. (flee: run away from) **19.** Don't you know your body is a temple of the Holy Spirit, who is in you and from God? You are not your own. (temple: sacred place) **20.** You were bought at a price, so honor God with your body and spirit, which belong to God.

Chapter 7

1. Now concerning what you wrote to me: It is good for a man not to be with a woman. **2.** But to avoid immorality, each man should have his own wife, and each woman her own husband. **3.** The husband should fulfill his marital duty to his wife, and likewise, the wife to her husband. **4.** The wife does not have authority over her body, but the husband does; likewise, the husband's body belongs to the wife. **5.** Do not deprive each other, except by mutual consent for prayer, and come back together to avoid temptation. (deprive : withhold) **6.** I give this as a suggestion, not a command. **7.** I wish all were as I am, but each has a gift from God, one this way, another that. **8.** To the unmarried and widows, I say it is good to remain as I am. **9.** But if they cannot control themselves, let them marry, for it is better to marry than burn with passion. **10.** To the married, the Lord commands: A wife must not separate from her husband. **11.** But if she does, let her remain unmarried or be reconciled to her husband. A husband must not divorce his wife. **12.** If any brother has a wife who is not a believer, and she agrees to live with him, he must not divorce her. **13.** Likewise, if a woman has an unbelieving husband, and he is willing to stay, she must not divorce him. **14.** The unbelieving spouse is sanctified by the believing spouse; otherwise, your children would be unclean, but now they are holy. (sanctified : made holy or set apart) **15.** If the unbeliever leaves, let them leave. A believer is not bound in such cases, for God calls us to peace. (bound : obligated or restricted) **16.** How do you know, wife, whether you will save your husband? Or, husband, whether you will save your wife? **17.** Let each person live as God called them, and I instruct all the churches the same. **18.** Was anyone called while circumcised? Let him not become uncircumcised. If uncircumcised, let him not circumcise. **19.** Circumcision means nothing; what matters is keeping God's commandments. **20.** Each person should remain in the condition they were in when called. **21.** Were you a slave when called? Don't worry, but if you can be free, do so. (slave : someone who is owned by another person) **22.** A slave called to the Lord is the Lord's freed person, and a free person is Christ's servant. (freed : set free) **23.** You were bought at a price; do not become slaves to men. (slaves : someone who is owned by another person) **24.** Brothers and sisters, remain in the situation where God called you. **25.** Concerning virgins, I have no command, but I give my judgment as one trustworthy in the Lord. **26.** I think it is good for a man to remain as he is, given the present distress. (distress : a time of difficulty or trouble) **27.** Are you bound to a wife? Do not seek to be free. Are you free from a wife? Do not seek one. **28.** But if you marry, you have not sinned; yet you will face trouble, and I want to spare you. (spare : prevent from experiencing) **29.** The time is short, so those with wives should live as though they had none. **30.** Those who weep, as though they did not; those who rejoice, as though they did not; those who buy, as though they did not possess. **31.** Those who use the world's things should do so without being overly attached, for this world is passing away. (attached : overly invested or concerned) **32.** I want you to be free from concerns. An unmarried person cares for the Lord's things, how to please Him. **33.** A married person cares for worldly things, how to please their spouse. **34.** An unmarried woman cares for the Lord's things, to be holy in body and spirit. A married woman cares for worldly things. **35.** I say this for your benefit, not to restrict you, but to allow you to serve the Lord without distractions. **36.** If anyone feels he is acting wrongly toward his virgin, and it's necessary, let them marry; they do not sin. **37.** If a man is firm in his heart, has no need to marry, and has decided to keep his virgin, he does well. (firm : resolute or determined) **38.** So he who marries her does well, but he who does not marry her does better. **39.** A woman is bound to her husband as long as he lives. If he dies, she is free to marry anyone, but only in the Lord. (bound : obligated or restricted) **40.** She is happier if she remains as she is, and I think I have the Spirit of God.

Chapter 8

1 Concerning food offered to idols, we all have some knowledge, but knowledge puffs up, while love builds up. (Puffs up: makes proud, builds up: strengthens). **2** If anyone thinks they know something, they haven't yet fully understood. (Fully understood: grasped the full truth). **3** But if someone loves God, God knows them. (Knows: has a relationship with). **4** We know an idol is nothing, and there is only one true God. (Idol: false god). **5** There are many gods called so, but for us, there is one God, the Father. (Father: creator and source). **6** There is one Lord, Jesus Christ, through whom all things came, and through whom we live. (Lord: God, Christ: the anointed one). **7** Not everyone has this knowledge, and some still think food offered to idols is truly defiled. (Defiled: made impure). **8** Food doesn't affect our standing with God; we are not better or worse for eating or not eating. **9** Be careful that your freedom doesn't cause the weak to stumble. (Stumble: fall into sin). **10** If someone with a weak conscience sees you eating in an idol's temple, will they not be encouraged to do the same? (Conscience: inner sense of right and wrong). **11** Because of your knowledge, the weak person may be led astray, the one for whom Christ died. (Led astray: misled). **12** When you hurt others' consciences, you sin against Christ. **13** If eating meat causes my brother to fall, I'll never eat meat again. (Fall: stumble in faith).

Chapter 9

1. Am I not an apostle? Am I not free? Have I not seen Jesus Christ our Lord? Are you not my work in the Lord? **2.** Even if I am not an apostle to others, I am to you; you are the proof of my apostleship in the Lord. **3.** My answer to those who question me is this: **4.** Do we not have the right to eat and drink? **5.** Do we not have the right to bring a wife, like the other apostles and Cephas. **6.** Or is it just Barnabas and I who don't have the right to stop working? **7.** Who serves as a soldier at their own expense? Who plants a vineyard and doesn't eat its fruit? Or who tends a flock and doesn't drink its milk? (Tends: takes care of) **8.** Am I speaking from a human point of view, or does the law say the same? (Point of view: perspective) **9.** The law says, "You shall not muzzle an ox while it treads the grain." Does God care about oxen? (Muzzle: prevent from eating, Treads: walks on, Grain: seeds) **10.** Or is it for our benefit? Yes, it's written for us, because the plowman should plow in hope, and the thresher should share in the harvest. (Plowman: one who plows the field, Thresher: one who separates grain from husk) **11.** If we sow spiritual things, is it too much to reap material things from you? (Sow: plant, Reap: harvest) **12.** If others have the right to receive this, shouldn't we? Yet we haven't used it to avoid hindering the gospel. (Hindering: preventing) **13.** Don't you know those who serve in the temple get their food from the temple? (Serve: work, serve in the temple: perform sacred duties) **14.** In the same way, the Lord commanded those who preach the gospel should live by it. (Preach: deliver religious message) **15.** But I haven't used these rights. I would rather die than have anyone take away my reason to boast. (Boast: to take pride in) **16.** When I preach, I have no reason to boast, for I must preach. Woe to me if I don't! (Woe: great sorrow or distress, Preach: deliver religious message) **17.** If I do it willingly, I have a reward; if unwillingly, I am entrusted with a duty. (Entrusted: given responsibility) **18.** What's my reward? That when I preach, I offer the gospel free of charge, not abusing my rights. (Abusing: taking unfair advantage) **19.** Though I'm free, I've made myself a servant to all, to win as many as possible. (Servant: one who serves others, Win: gain) **20.** To the Jews, I became like a Jew, to win the Jews; to those under the law, I became like one under the law. (Under the law: following the Jewish law) **21.** To those without the law, I became like one without the law, to win those outside the law. (Outside the law: not following the Jewish law) **22.** To the weak, I became weak, to win the weak. I've become all things to all people, so that I might save some. (Weak: lacking strength, Save: rescue) **23.** I do this for the gospel's sake, to share in its blessings. (Sake: purpose) **24.** Do you not know that in a race, all run, but only one wins? Run in such a way to win. (Race: competition) **25.** Everyone in the games trains strictly to win a perishable crown, but we train for an imperishable one. (Games: athletic contests, Perishable: decaying, Imperishable: eternal) **26.** So I run with purpose, not aimlessly; I fight, not just shadow-boxing. (Aimlessly: without direction, Shadow-boxing: pretending to fight without an opponent) **27.** I discipline my body, making it my slave, so that after preaching to others, I will not be disqualified. (Discipline: train, Disqualified: not eligible)

Chapter 10
1. Brothers, I do not want you to be unaware that all our ancestors were under the cloud and passed through the sea. **2.** They were baptized into Moses in the cloud and the sea (baptized: immersed or identified with). **3.** They all ate the same spiritual food, **4.** and drank the same spiritual drink, for they drank from the spiritual rock that followed them, and that rock was Christ. **5.** But many of them displeased God and were overthrown in the wilderness. **6.** These things are examples for us, so we don't crave evil things as they did. **7.** Do not become idolaters, as some of them did; as it is written, "The people sat to eat and drink, and rose up to play" (idolaters: those who worship idols). **8.** Nor should we commit sexual immorality, as some of them did, and 23,000 fell in a day. **9.** Let us not test Christ, as some did and were destroyed by serpents (test: to challenge or provoke). **10.** Do not grumble, as some did and were destroyed by the destroyer (grumble: complain, destroyer: the agent of destruction, often a reference to God's judgment). **11.** These things happened as examples for us, written for our instruction, as the end of the ages has come. **12.** So if you think you stand, be careful not to fall. **13.** No temptation has overtaken you except what is common to man. God is faithful; He will not let you be tempted beyond what you can bear. But He will provide a way out. **14.** Therefore, my beloved, flee from idolatry. **15.** I speak as wise people; judge what I say. **16.** The cup of blessing we bless, is it not a sharing in the blood of Christ? The bread we break, is it not a sharing in the body of Christ? **17.** We, though many, are one body, for we all partake of the one loaf (partake: to share in or participate). **18.** Consider Israel: those who eat the sacrifices are participants in the altar. **19.** What do I mean? That an idol is anything, or that food sacrificed to idols is anything? **20.** No, but the Gentiles sacrifice to demons, not God, and I don't want you to share with demons. **21.** You cannot drink the cup of the Lord and the cup of demons. You cannot share the Lord's table and the table of demons. **22.** Do we provoke the Lord to jealousy? Are we stronger than He? (provoke: to cause or stir up) **23.** All things are lawful for me, but not all things are beneficial. All things are lawful for me, but not all things build up (edify: build up, improve morally or spiritually). **24.** Let no one seek their own good, but the good of others. **25.** Eat whatever is sold in the market without asking questions for the sake of conscience (conscience: awareness of right and wrong), **26.** for "the earth is the Lord's, and everything in it." **27.** If an unbeliever invites you and you want to go, eat whatever is put before you without asking questions. **28.** But if someone says, "This is offered to idols," don't eat it for their sake and for conscience' sake. The earth is the Lord's. **29.** I mean the conscience of the other person, not yours. For why should my freedom be judged by another's conscience? **30.** If I partake with thankfulness, why am I criticized for something I thank God for? (partake: to share in or participate) **31.** So, whether you eat, drink, or whatever you do, do it all for God's glory. **32.** Do not cause anyone to stumble, whether Jews, Greeks, or the church of God. **33.** Just as I try to please everyone in every way, not seeking my advantage, but the good of many, so that they may be saved (advantage: benefit, gain).

Chapter 11
1. Follow my example, as I follow Christ. **2.** I praise you for remembering me and keeping the teachings I passed on to you. **3.** The head of every man is Christ, the head of woman is man, and the head of Christ is God. **4.** A man who prays with his head covered dishonors his head. **5.** A woman who prays uncovered dishonors her head; it's like being shaved. (shaved: having hair cut very short or removed) **6.** If a woman does not cover her head, let her cut her hair, but if it's shameful, let her cover it. (shameful: something that brings disgrace) **7.** A man should not cover his head because he is the image and glory of God; the woman is the glory of man. **8.** The man is not from the woman; the woman is from the man. **9.** Man was not created for the woman; the woman was created for the man. **10.** That's why a woman should cover her head because of the angels. **11.** In the Lord, neither man nor woman is independent of the other. **12.** Woman came from man, but man is born of woman. All things come from God. **13.** Is it proper for a woman to pray to God uncovered? **14.** Does nature not teach you that long hair on a man is disgraceful? (disgraceful: shameful or dishonorable) **15.** But long hair on a woman is her glory; it's given to her as a covering. **16.** We have no such practice, nor do the churches of God. **17.** I do not praise you for coming together, because it causes harm, not good. **18.** I hear there are divisions among you when you meet, and I believe part of it. **19.** There must be divisions so that those approved by God may be evident. **20.** When you meet, it is not to eat the Lord's Supper. **21.** When you eat, some eat before others, leaving some hungry and others drunk. (drunk: intoxicated by alcohol) **22.** Don't you have homes to eat in? Or do you despise the church and shame those who have nothing? **23.** I received from the Lord what I passed on to you: Jesus took bread the night he was betrayed, **24.** gave thanks, broke it, and said, "This is my body, broken for you; do this to remember me." **25.** After supper, he took the cup and said, "This is the new covenant in my blood; do this to remember me." (covenant: agreement or promise) **26.** Whenever you eat and drink, you proclaim the Lord's death until he comes. **27.** Anyone who eats or drinks unworthily is guilty of sinning against the body and blood of the Lord. **28.** Let each person examine themselves before eating and drinking. **29.** Anyone who eats or drinks without recognizing Christ's body brings judgment on themselves. **30.** That's why many of you are weak, sick, and some have died. (died: fallen asleep refers to those who died in faith) **31.** If we judged ourselves, we would not be judged. **32.** When we are judged, we are disciplined by the Lord, so we won't be condemned with the world. **33.** So, when you come together to eat, wait for each other. **34.** If anyone is hungry, eat at home, so that your meetings do not bring judgment.

Chapter 12
1. Concerning spiritual gifts, brothers, I don't want you to be uninformed. (Uninformed: lacking knowledge.) **2.** You know that you were once led to worthless idols. (Worthless: without value.) **3.** No one speaking by the Spirit calls Jesus cursed, and no one can say Jesus is Lord except by the Holy Spirit. (Cursed: condemned; Lord: title of honor for Jesus.) **4.** There are different gifts, but the same Spirit. (Gifts: abilities from God.) **5.** There are different services, but the same Lord. (Services: acts of ministry.) **6.** There are different workings, but the same God works in all. (Workings: activities; God: the Father.) **7.** The Spirit is given to each for the common good. (Common good: benefit of all.) **8.** One receives wisdom, another knowledge, by the same Spirit. (Wisdom: good decision-making; Knowledge: understanding of truth.) **9.** To one, faith; to another, healing, by the same Spirit. (Faith: strong belief in God; Healing: divine restoration of health.) **10.** To another, miracles; to another, prophecy; to another, distinguishing spirits; to another, tongues; and to another, interpretation. (Miracles: supernatural acts; Prophecy: speaking God's messages; Distinguishing spirits: discerning God's will; Tongues: speaking unknown languages; Interpretation: explaining tongues.) **11.** All these are the work of the same Spirit, giving to each as He chooses. (Work: the result of effort; Chooses: selects.) **12.** The body is one, though made of many parts, and so is Christ. (Body: the church or believers.) **13.** We were all baptized into one body by the Spirit, whether Jew or Gentile, slave or free, and all were given one Spirit to drink. (Baptized: joined to; Spirit: the Holy Spirit; Jew/Gentile: Jewish or non-Jewish; Slave/free: different social statuses.) **14.** The body has many parts, not just one. (Parts: members of the church.) **15.** If the foot says, "I'm not the hand," is it still part of the body? (Foot/Hand: different members in the church.) **16.** If the ear says, "I'm not the eye," is it part of the body? (Ear/Eye: representing different roles.) **17.** If the body were only an eye, where would hearing be? (Body: the church; Eye/Hearing: different roles in the church.) **18.** God placed each part in the body as He chose. (Placed: positioned; Chose: selected.) **19.** If all were one part, where would the body be? (Body: the church, the collective group of believers.) **20.** There are many parts, but one body. (Parts: individuals; Body: the unified church.) **21.** The eye can't say to the hand, "I don't need you!" The head can't say to the feet, "I don't need you!" (Eye/Hand/Head/Feet: different members of the church.) **22.** The weaker parts are indispensable. (Weaker: less important in appearance; Indispensable: essential.) **23.** The less honorable parts we treat with honor. (Honorable: deserving respect.) **24.** God made the body with greater honor for the parts that lacked it. (Greater honor: more respect; Lacked: needed.) **25.** There should be no division, but the parts should care for one another. (Division: separation; Care: concern.) **26.** If one part suffers, all suffer. If one part is honored, all rejoice. (Suffers: experiences

pain; Honored: recognized; Rejoice: celebrate.) **27.** You are the body of Christ, and each of you is a part. (Body of Christ: the church, the believers.) **28.** God placed in the church apostles, prophets, teachers, miracles, healings, helps, guidance, and tongues. (Placed: assigned; Apostles: messengers; Prophets: speakers of God's truth; Teachers: instructors; Helps: assistance; Guidance: leadership.) **29.** Are all apostles? Are all prophets? Are all teachers? Do all do miracles? (Apostles: those who spread the gospel; Prophets: those who speak God's word; Teachers: those who instruct; Miracles: supernatural acts.) **30.** Do all heal? Do all speak in tongues? Do all interpret? (Heal: restore health; Tongues: speak in unknown languages; Interpret: explain tongues.) **31.** Desire the greater gifts, and I'll show you a better way. (Desire: strongly wish for; Greater gifts: more impactful spiritual gifts; Better way: a more excellent way of living, especially in love.)

Chapter 13

1. If I speak in all languages, but lack love, I am just noise. (Noise : meaningless sound) **2.** If I have prophecy and faith to move mountains, but no love, I am nothing. (Prophecy : foretelling future events) **3.** If I give all I have to the poor or die for others, but have no love, it's worthless. (Worthless : without value) **4.** Love is patient, kind, not jealous, boastful, or proud. (Jealous : envious) **5.** Love doesn't act shamefully, is not selfish, easily angered, or hold grudges. (Shamefully : dishonorably, Grudges : resentments) **6.** Love rejoices in truth, not wrongdoing. (Rejoices : takes pleasure, Wrongdoing : sin) **7.** Love bears, believes, hopes, and endures all things. (Bears : supports) **8.** Love never ends. Prophecies, tongues, and knowledge will fade. (Fade : disappear) **9.** We know and prophesy in part. (Prophesy : predict) **10.** But when completeness comes, partial things will end. (Completeness : perfection) **11.** When I was a child, I acted like one, but I matured. (Matured : became an adult) **12.** Now we see only a dim reflection; then we'll understand fully. (Dim : unclear) **13.** Now remain faith, hope, and love, but the greatest is love. (Remains : continues, Greatest : most important)

Chapter 14

1. Pursue love, and eagerly desire spiritual gifts, especially prophecy. **2.** The one who speaks in a tongue speaks to God, not men, and speaks mysteries in the Spirit. **3.** The one who prophesies speaks to others for their growth, encouragement, and comfort. **4.** Speaking in tongues builds up the self, but prophecy builds up the church. **5.** I wish you all spoke in tongues, but prophecy is better, for the prophet is greater unless they interpret. (Interpret: To explain or translate something) **6.** If I come speaking in tongues, how will you benefit unless I speak by revelation, knowledge, or teaching? (Revelation: A divine or supernatural disclosure) **7.** Even lifeless instruments, like a flute, must give a clear sound to be recognized. **8.** If a trumpet does not give a clear call, how will anyone prepare for battle? **9.** If you speak unintelligibly, how will others know what you mean? You will speak into the air. **10.** There are many kinds of voices in the world, each with meaning. **11.** If I don't understand the language, I will be like a foreigner to the speaker, and vice versa. (Foreigner: A person from a different country or culture) **12.** Seek spiritual gifts, especially those that build up the church. **13.** Let the one speaking in tongues pray for the ability to interpret. **14.** If I pray in a tongue, my spirit prays, but my mind does not benefit. **15.** I will pray and sing both with my spirit and understanding. **16.** If you bless in the spirit, how can the unlearned say "Amen" if they don't understand? (Unlearned: Lacking knowledge or education) **17.** You give thanks well, but others are not built up. **18.** I thank God I speak in tongues more than you all. **19.** But in church, I would rather speak five words with understanding than ten thousand in a tongue. **20.** Brothers, be mature in understanding, but innocent in evil. **21.** As it is written, "I will speak to this people in foreign tongues, but they will not listen," says the Lord. **22.** Tongues are a sign for unbelievers, while prophecy is for believers. **23.** If everyone speaks in tongues and unbelievers come in, they will think you are mad. **24.** But if all prophesy, an unbeliever will be convicted and worship God, saying, "God is truly among you." **25.** Their hearts will be revealed, and they will fall and worship God. **26.** When you come together, let everything be for building up—hymn, teaching, tongue, or interpretation. **27.** Let two or three speak in tongues, each in turn, with interpretation. **28.** If there is no interpreter, let them remain silent and speak to God. **29.** Let two or three prophets speak, and let others evaluate. **30.** If a revelation comes to another, the first should be silent. (Revelation: A divine or supernatural disclosure) **31.** You all can prophesy one by one so everyone may learn and be comforted. **32.** The spirits of prophets are subject to the prophets. **33.** God is not a God of confusion, but of peace. **34.** Women should remain silent in the church, as they must be in submission. **35.** If they want to learn, they should ask their husbands at home. **36.** Did the word of God come from you? Or are you the only ones it has reached? **37.** If anyone thinks themselves a prophet, let them acknowledge my words as God's command. **38.** If anyone ignores this, let them be ignored. **39.** Therefore, desire prophecy and do not forbid speaking in tongues. **40.** Let everything be done decently and in order.

Chapter 15

1. I remind you, brothers and sisters, of the gospel I preached, which you received and in which you stand. (gospel: good news) **2.** You are saved by this, if you hold fast to it, unless you believed in vain. (vain: without purpose) **3.** I passed on to you what I received: Christ died for our sins, as the Scriptures say. (passed on: delivered, received: accepted) **4.** He was buried, and rose on the third day, according to the Scriptures. (rose: came back to life) **5.** He appeared to Cephas, then to the twelve. (Cephas: Peter) **6.** Then He appeared to over 500 brothers, most of whom are still alive, but some have died. (brothers: fellow believers) **7.** He appeared to James, then to all the apostles. (apostles: those sent by Christ) **8.** Lastly, He appeared to me, as one born out of time. (born out of time: out of sequence) **9.** I am the least of the apostles, unworthy to be called an apostle, because I persecuted the church. (persecuted: attacked) **10.** But by God's grace, I am what I am, and His grace was not wasted; I worked harder than them all. (grace: unmerited favor) **11.** Whether it was I or they, we preach the same, and you believed. (preach: proclaim) **12.** If Christ is preached as risen, why do some of you say there is no resurrection? (resurrection: rising from the dead) **13.** If there's no resurrection, then Christ hasn't been raised. **14.** And if Christ hasn't risen, our preaching and your faith are in vain. (vain: without result) **15.** We are false witnesses of God, because we testified He raised Christ if the dead don't rise. (false witnesses: liars) **16.** If the dead don't rise, Christ hasn't risen. **17.** And if Christ hasn't risen, your faith is futile, and you're still in your sins. (futile: ineffective) **18.** Then those who died in Christ are lost. (lost: destroyed) **19.** If our hope in Christ is only for this life, we are most miserable. (miserable: wretched) **20.** But Christ is indeed risen and is the first to rise from the dead. (indeed: truly) **21.** Since death came through a man, the resurrection also comes through a man. (resurrection: rising again) **22.** As in Adam all die, in Christ all will be made alive. (alive: spiritually living) **23.** But each in their own order: Christ first, then those who belong to Him when He comes. (order: sequence) **24.** Then the end will come, when Christ gives the kingdom to God, after destroying all dominion and power. (dominion: control, power: authority) **25.** Christ must reign until all His enemies are under His feet. **26.** The last enemy to be destroyed is death. (enemy: foe) **27.** God has put everything under His feet, except Himself who put everything under Christ. (except: excluding) **28.** When everything is subject to Christ, He will submit to God, that God may be all in all. (subject: under control) **29.** If the dead don't rise, why are some baptized for the dead? (baptized: immersed in water) **30.** Why do we risk our lives every hour? (risk: endanger) **31.** I face death every day, and I boast in you in Christ Jesus our Lord. **32.** If I fought wild beasts at Ephesus, what did I gain if the dead don't rise? Let's eat and drink, for tomorrow we die. (wild beasts: dangerous opponents) **33.** Don't be deceived: bad company corrupts good character. (deceived: misled, corrupts: spoils) **34.** Wake up and stop sinning, for some don't know God. I say this to your shame. (sinning: doing wrong) **35.** Someone may ask, "How are the dead raised, and with what body do they come?" **36.** You fool! What you sow doesn't come to life unless it dies. (sow: plant) **37.** When you sow, you don't plant the body it will be, but just a seed, like wheat or another grain. (wheat: a type of grain) **38.** God gives it a body as He chooses, and each seed has its own body. (chooses: decides) **39.** Flesh is not all the same: there's human flesh, animal flesh, fish flesh, and bird flesh. (flesh: physical body) **40.** There are heavenly bodies and earthly bodies, with different glories. (heavenly: from the sky, glory: brilliance) **41.** The sun has one glory, the moon another, and stars differ in glory. (differ: are different) **42.** So is the resurrection: sown in corruption, raised in incorruption. (corruption: decay, incorruption: perfection) **43.** Sown in dishonor, raised in glory; sown in weakness, raised in power. (dishonor: shame, weakness: frailty, power: strength) **44.** Sown a natural body, raised a spiritual body. (spiritual: relating to the spirit) **45.** The first Adam was a living being, the last Adam a life-giving spirit. (life-giving: bringing life) **46.** The natural comes first, then the spiritual. (natural: physical) **47.** The first man is earthly, the second is from heaven. (earthly: from the ground) **48.** As the earthly man, so are those of the earth; as the heavenly man, so are those of heaven. (earthly: of the earth, heavenly: of heaven) **49.** We bore the image of the earthly, and we will bear the image of the heavenly. (image: likeness) **50.** Flesh and blood cannot inherit the kingdom of God, nor can corruption inherit incorruption. (inherit: receive) **51.** Listen, I tell you a mystery: not all will sleep, but all will be changed. (mystery: unknown truth) **52.** In the twinkling of an eye, at the last trumpet, the dead will be raised incorruptible, and we will be changed. (twinkling: quick moment, trumpet: loud sound) **53.** This corruptible body must put on incorruption, and this mortal body must put on immortality. (mortal: able to die, immortality: eternal life) **54.** When the corruptible puts on incorruption, death is swallowed up in victory. (swallowed up: defeated) **55.** "Where, O death, is your sting? Where, O grave, is your victory?" **56.** The sting of death is sin, and the power of sin is the law. (sting: pain) **57.** Thanks be to God, who gives us victory through our Lord Jesus Christ. **58.** Therefore, my dear brothers, stand firm, always giving yourselves fully to the work of the Lord, knowing your labor is not in vain. (labor: work)

Chapter 16

1. Now about the collection for the saints, as I instructed the Galatian churches, do the same. (Collection: a gathering of money or gifts for a cause) **2.** On the first day of each week, set aside money based on your earnings, so there's no need for collections when I arrive. (Earnings: money received from work) **3.** I'll send those you approve by letter to deliver your gift to Jerusalem. (Approve: agree or accept) **4.** If necessary, I'll also go with them. (Necessary: required) **5.** I'll visit you after passing through Macedonia. (Macedonia: region in Greece) **6.** I may stay and winter with you, and you can send me on my journey. (Winter: stay during the cold season) **7.** I hope to stay for a while, if the Lord allows. (Allows: permits) **8.** But I will stay in Ephesus until Pentecost. (Pentecost: Jewish feast, fifty days after Passover) **9.** A great opportunity for ministry is open to me, though there are many opponents. (Opportunity: a chance; Opponents: adversaries) **10.** If Timothy comes, make sure he is welcome and unafraid, for he works for the Lord like I do. (Unafraid: without fear) **11.** Don't despise him, but send him in peace, for I expect him with the brothers. (Despise: regard with disrespect) **12.** Apollos did not want to come now, but he will visit when the time is right. (Right: appropriate) **13.** Be alert, stand firm in the faith, be brave, and strong. (Alert: watchful) **14.** Do everything in love. (Love: charity, selfless concern for others) **15.** I urge you to follow the example of the household of Stephanas, who devoted themselves to serving the saints. (Urge: strongly encourage; Devoted: dedicated) **16.** Submit to such leaders and all who work with us. (Submit: yield or give in) **17.** I am happy for the arrival of Stephanas, Fortunatus, and Achaicus, as they made up for what you lacked. (Lacked: were missing) **18.** They refreshed both my spirit and yours, so honor such people. (Refresh: revitalize) **19.** The churches in Asia greet you. Aquila and Priscilla, with their church, send warm greetings. (Greet: send good wishes) **20.** All the brothers send greetings. Greet each other with a holy kiss. (Brothers: fellow believers) **21.** This greeting is from me, Paul, written with my own hand. (Greeting: message of well-wishing) **22.** If anyone does not love the Lord Jesus Christ, let him be accursed. Come, Lord Jesus! (Accursed: cursed, condemned) **23.** May the grace of the Lord Jesus Christ be with you all. (Grace: unearned favor) **24.** My love be with you all in Christ Jesus. Amen. (Love: deep affection)

47 – 2 Corinthians

Chapter 1

1. Paul, an apostle of Jesus Christ by God's will, and Timothy, our brother, to the church of God in Corinth, with all the saints in Achaia: (Apostle: Messenger with a mission.) **2.** Grace and peace to you from God our Father and the Lord Jesus Christ. (Grace: God's unearned favor.) **3.** Blessed be God, the Father of our Lord Jesus Christ, the Father of mercies, and the God of all comfort; (Mercies: Compassion and kindness.) **4.** Who comforts us in all our troubles, so that we can comfort others with the comfort we receive from God. (Comfort: Encouragement in distress.) **5.** For as the sufferings of Christ overflow in us, so also our comfort overflows through Christ. (Overflow: Abundance beyond limits.) **6.** Whether we are troubled, it is for your comfort and salvation, or whether we are comforted, it is for your comfort and salvation. (Effective: Produces desired results.) **7.** Our hope for you is steadfast, knowing that as you share in our sufferings, you will also share in our comfort. (Steadfast: Firm and unchanging.) **8.** We do not want you unaware, brothers, of the troubles we experienced in Asia, where we were under great pressure and even despaired of life. (Despaired: Felt hopeless.) **9.** Indeed, we felt we had received the sentence of death, so we would rely not on ourselves but on God, who raises the dead. (Sentence: Judgment or decree.) **10.** He has delivered us from deadly peril and will continue to deliver us; we have set our hope on him to keep delivering us. (Peril: Serious danger.) **11.** As you help us by your prayers, many will give thanks for the blessing given to us through the prayers of many. (Gift: Favor or blessing.) **12.** Our boast is this: the testimony of our conscience that we acted with simplicity and godly sincerity, not worldly wisdom but by God's grace. (Testimony: Declaration of truth.) **13.** We write nothing to you other than what you read or acknowledge, and I trust you will fully acknowledge it. (Acknowledge: Admit as true.) **14.** Just as you partially acknowledged us, we are your reason for rejoicing, as you are ours in the day of the Lord Jesus. (Rejoicing: Great joy.) **15.** With this confidence, I planned to visit you first so that you might have a second benefit, (Benefit: Advantage or blessing.) **16.** to pass through you into Macedonia, then return to you from Macedonia and be sent to Judea. (Macedonia: Northern Greek region.) **17.** When I planned this, did I act lightly? Or do I plan by the flesh, with yes and no? (Flesh: Human or worldly concerns.) **18.** But as God is faithful, our message to you has not been yes and no. (Faithful: Reliable and trustworthy.) **19.** For Jesus Christ, preached among you by me, Silvanus, and Timothy, was not yes and no but always yes in him. (Preached: Proclaimed or announced.) **20.** All God's promises in him are yes, and in him Amen, to God's glory through us. (Amen: Affirmation of agreement.) **21.** God establishes us with you in Christ and anointed us, (Establishes: Makes firm and secure.) **22.** sealed us and gave the Spirit as a guarantee in our hearts. (Sealed: Marked as authentic.) **23.** I call God as my witness that I refrained from coming to Corinth to spare you. (Refrained: Held back.) **24.** Not that we dominate your faith, but we are workers with you for your joy, for by faith you stand firm. (Lord it over: Exercise control.)

Chapter 2

1. I decided that I would not come to you again with sorrow. (Sorrow: Deep sadness or regret.) **2.** For if I make you sad, who will make me happy, except the one saddened by me? (Sad: Feeling unhappy.) **3.** I wrote to you so that when I come, I would not have sorrow from those who should make me rejoice; I trust that my joy is shared by all of you. (Rejoice: To feel great joy.) **4.** I wrote with much distress and anguish of heart, with many tears, not to make you sad, but to show how much I love you. (Distress: Severe pain or anxiety.) **5.** If anyone has caused grief, he has not grieved me, but partly, so I do not burden all of you. (Burden: A heavy responsibility.) **6.** The punishment imposed by the majority is sufficient. (Punishment: Penalty for wrongdoing.) **7.** Now you should forgive and comfort him, so he is not overwhelmed by excessive sorrow. (Overwhelmed: Overcome by emotion or circumstance.) **8.** I urge you to reaffirm your love for him. (Urge: Strongly encourage.) **9.** I wrote to test your obedience in all things. (Test: To evaluate or examine.) **10.** If you forgive anyone, I forgive them too. My forgiveness, in Christ's presence, is for your sake. (Forgive: To pardon wrongdoing.) **11.** This is so Satan does not take advantage of us, as we are not unaware of his schemes. (Schemes: Deceptive plans.) **12.** When I went to Troas to preach the gospel, the Lord opened a door for me. (Door: Opportunity.) **13.** I had no peace of mind because I didn't find Titus, my brother, so I left and went to Macedonia. (Peace of mind: Calm and freedom from worry.) **14.** Thanks be to God, who always leads us in Christ's triumph and spreads the fragrance of His knowledge everywhere. (Triumph: Great victory.) **15.** We are the aroma of Christ to God among the saved and the lost. (Aroma: A pleasing or symbolic influence.) **16.** To some, we are the aroma of death leading to death; to others, the aroma of life leading to life. Who is adequate for such a task? (Adequate: Sufficient or capable.) **17.** We are not like many who peddle God's word for profit; we speak sincerely, as from God, in Christ's presence. (Peddle: To promote for gain, often dishonestly.)

Chapter 3

1. Do we begin to commend ourselves again? Or do we need, like others, letters of recommendation to you or from you? (Commend: To praise or recommend.) **2.** You are our letter, written on our hearts, known and read by all people. (Letter: A communication or message.) **3.** You are clearly revealed as Christ's letter, delivered by us, written not with ink but by the Spirit of the living God, not on stone tablets but on hearts of flesh. (Revealed: Made clearly known.) **4.** Such confidence we have through Christ toward God. (Confidence: Trust or assurance.) **5.** Not that we are sufficient in ourselves to claim anything as from us, but our sufficiency is from God. (Sufficiency: Being adequate or enough.) **6.** He made us competent ministers of the new covenant—not of the letter but of the Spirit; for the letter kills, but the Spirit gives life. (Competent: Qualified or capable.) **7.** If the ministry of death, engraved on stones, came with glory so great that the Israelites could not gaze at Moses' face because of its fading glory, (Ministry: Service or work for God.) **8.** How much more glorious is the ministry of the Spirit? (Ministry of the Spirit: Work of the Holy Spirit in the gospel.) **9.** If the ministry that condemns was glorious, the ministry that brings righteousness exceeds it in glory. (Condemns: Declares guilty.) **10.** What was once glorious now seems without glory because of the surpassing glory. (Surpassing: Far exceeding.) **11.** If what was fading came with glory, how much greater is the glory of what remains! (Fading: Diminishing or passing away.) **12.** Since we have this hope, we speak with great boldness. (Boldness: Courage or confidence.) **13.** Not like Moses, who put a veil over his face so the Israelites could not see the end of what was fading. (Veil: A covering that obscures.) **14.** Their minds were blinded; to this day, the same veil remains when the old covenant is read—it is removed only in Christ. (Blinded: Unable to perceive clearly.) **15.** Even now, when Moses is read, a veil covers their hearts. (Heart: Inner understanding or emotions.) **16.** But when anyone turns to the Lord, the veil is removed. (Turns to the Lord: Seeks God for understanding.) **17.** Now the Lord is the Spirit, and where the Spirit of the Lord is, there is freedom. (Freedom: Liberty or release.) **18.** We all, with unveiled faces, reflecting the Lord's glory, are being transformed into His image, from glory to glory, by the Spirit of the Lord. (Transformed: Changed in form or character.)

Chapter 4

1. Therefore, since we have this ministry, as we have received mercy, we do not give up. (Ministry: Service in spreading the gospel.) **2.** We have renounced hidden dishonesty, not walking in craftiness or handling God's word deceitfully, but revealing the truth and commending ourselves to everyone's conscience before God. (Renounced: Rejected formally.) **3.** If our gospel is hidden, it is hidden to those who are lost. (Hidden: Not understood or revealed.) **4.** The god of this world has blinded the minds of unbelievers, so the light of Christ's glorious gospel, the image of God, will not shine on them. (Blinded: Prevented from understanding.) **5.** We do not preach ourselves, but Christ Jesus as Lord, and ourselves as your servants for Jesus' sake. (Preach: Proclaim or teach.) **6.** God, who commanded light to shine out of darkness, has shined in our hearts to reveal the knowledge of God's glory in Christ's face. (Shined: Illuminated or made known.) **7.** We hold this treasure in fragile earthen vessels, so the power is from God and not us. (Earthen vessels: Fragile human bodies.) **8.** We are troubled on every side but not distressed; perplexed but not despairing. (Perplexed: Confused or uncertain.) **9.** Persecuted but not forsaken; cast down but not destroyed. (Persecuted: Oppressed for beliefs.) **10.** We carry in our bodies the dying of Jesus, so His life is also made manifest in us. (Manifest: Made visible or clear.) **11.** We who live are continually delivered to death for Jesus' sake so that His life is revealed in our mortal flesh. (Mortal: Temporary or subject to death.) **12.** Death works in us, but life in you. (Works: Operates or produces effect.) **13.** With the same spirit of faith, as it is written, "I believed, and therefore I spoke," we also believe and speak. (Spirit of faith: Attitude of trust in God.) **14.** Knowing that the one who raised Jesus will also raise us and present us with you. (Raised: Brought to life.) **15.** Everything is for your sake, so abundant grace, through many thanks, overflows to God's glory. (Redound: Overflow or contribute.) **16.** Therefore, we do not give up. Though our outward self-perishes, our inward self is renewed daily. (Inward self: Inner spiritual being.) **17.** Our light affliction, momentary, works for us an eternal weight of glory far beyond measure. (Affliction: Pain or suffering.) **18.** We focus not on visible things, which are temporary, but on invisible things, which are eternal. (Temporal: Temporary and not lasting.)

Chapter 5

1. We know that if this earthly body is destroyed, God has prepared an eternal heavenly dwelling for us. (Dwelling: Home.) **2.** In this life, we long deeply to be clothed with our heavenly home. (Clothed: Covered.) **3.** If clothed, we won't be left exposed or unprepared. (Exposed: Vulnerable.) **4.** While in this body, we groan under its weight, desiring not to lose it but to be transformed into eternal life. (Transformed: Changed.) **5.** God Himself prepared us for this and gave His Spirit as a guarantee. (Guarantee: Assurance.) **6.** We remain confident, knowing that living in this body means being apart from the Lord. (Confident: Certain.) **7.** For we live by faith, not by sight. (Faith: Trust.) **8.** We are confident and prefer to leave the body and be with the Lord. (Prefer: Favor.) **9.** Therefore, we strive to please Him, whether in this life or the next. (Strive: Effort.) **10.** For everyone must appear before Christ's judgment to receive according to their deeds, good or bad. (Deeds: Actions.) **11.** Understanding the fear of the Lord, we seek to persuade others, being transparent before God and your consciences. (Persuade: Convince.) **12.** We do not praise ourselves but offer you a reason to be proud of us, not for outward show but genuine heart. (Genuine: Sincere.) **13.** If we seem out of our minds, it is for God; if rational, it is for your benefit. (Rational: Logical.) **14.** Christ's love compels us, as we believe that if He died for all, then all were spiritually dead. (Compels: Drives.) **15.** He died so those who live may no longer live for themselves but for Him who died and rose again. (Rose: Resurrected.) **16.** Thus, we no longer see anyone from a worldly perspective, not even Christ as He once was. (Perspective: Viewpoint.) **17.** Anyone in Christ is a new creation; the old life is gone, and everything is new. (Creation: Being.) **18.** All this comes from God, who reconciled us to Himself through Christ and gave us the ministry of reconciliation. (Reconciled: Restored.) **19.** God reconciled the world to Himself in Christ, not counting sins against them, entrusting us with His message of reconciliation. (Entrusting: Assigning.) **20.** As Christ's ambassadors, we plead on His behalf: Be reconciled to God. (Ambassadors: Representatives.) **21.** God made Christ, who knew no sin, to become sin for us so we might receive God's righteousness in Him. (Righteousness: Purity.)

Chapter 6

1. As co-workers with God, we urge you not to receive His grace in vain. (Vain: Without purpose.) **2.** (As God says, "In the right time, I heard you, and on the day of salvation, I helped you." Now is the time of salvation.) (Salvation: Deliverance.) **3.** We give no cause for offense so that our ministry is not discredited. (Offense: Wrongdoing.) **4.** In everything, we show ourselves as God's servants—with great patience in troubles, hardships, and difficulties. (Patience: Endurance.) **5.** Through beatings, imprisonments, riots, labor, sleepless nights, and fasting. (Fasting: Abstaining from food.) **6.** By purity, understanding, patience, kindness, the Holy Spirit, and sincere love. (Purity: Moral cleanliness.) **7.** By truthful speech, God's power, and the weapons of righteousness in both hands. (Weapons: Tools.) **8.** Through honor and dishonor, slander and praise; seen as deceivers, yet truthful. (Deceivers: Liars.) **9.** As unknown yet recognized; dying yet alive; disciplined yet not killed. (Disciplined: Corrected.) **10.** Sorrowful yet always rejoicing; poor yet enriching many; having nothing yet possessing everything. (Possessing: Holding.) **11.** Corinthians, we have spoken openly to you; our heart is wide open. (Wide: Generous.) **12.** You are not restricted by us, but by your own affections. (Restricted: Limited.) **13.** As a fair return (I speak as to children), open your hearts too. (Return: Response.) **14.** Do not team up with unbelievers; righteousness and wickedness have no fellowship, nor light with darkness. (Fellowship: Partnership.) **15.** Christ and Belial do not agree; believers and unbelievers share no common ground. (Belial: Evil.) **16.** The temple of God cannot align with idols; we are God's temple, as He said, "I will live and walk among them; I will be their God, and they will be my people." (Temple: Dwelling place.) **17.** Therefore, come out from among them, be separate, and avoid unclean things, says the Lord, and I will accept you. (Separate: Set apart.) **18.** I will be a Father to you, and you will be my sons and daughters, says the Lord Almighty. (Father: Protector.)

Chapter 7

1. Dearly beloved, having these promises, let us purify ourselves from all defilement of body and spirit, striving for holiness in reverence to God. (Defilement: Impurity.) **2.** Accept us; we have wronged, corrupted, or defrauded no one. (Defrauded: Cheated.) **3.** I do not say this to condemn you, for you are in our hearts to live and die with you. (Condemn: Criticize.) **4.** I am bold in speaking to you and proud of you. I am filled with comfort and overflowing with joy, even in all our troubles. (Bold: Confident.) **5.** When we came to Macedonia, we had no rest; we faced conflicts on the outside and fears within. (Conflicts: Struggles.) **6.** But God, who comforts the lowly, comforted us by Titus's arrival. (Lowly: Downcast.) **7.** Not only by his arrival, but also by the encouragement he received from you, as he told us about your longing, mourning, and zeal for me, making me rejoice even more. (Zeal: Passion.) **8.** Though I made you sorrowful with a letter, I do not regret it, though I did for a moment; I see that the letter caused sorrow, but only for a while. (Sorrowful: Upset.) **9.** I now rejoice, not because you were grieved, but because your grief led to repentance. It was a godly sorrow that left no harm. (Repentance: Turning back to God.) **10.** Godly sorrow leads to repentance and salvation without regret, but worldly sorrow leads to death. (Worldly: Earthly.) **11.** See what this godly sorrow has produced in you—earnestness, clearing yourselves, indignation, fear, longing, zeal, and a readiness for justice. You proved yourselves pure in this matter. (Indignation: Anger at wrongdoing.) **12.** I wrote not because of the wrongdoer or the victim, but so our care for you might be shown before God. (Victim: Sufferer.) **13.** We were comforted by your encouragement and even more joyful because Titus was refreshed by all of you. (Refreshed: Uplifted.) **14.** If I boasted to him about you, I was not embarrassed; just as our words to you were true, so was our boasting about you to Titus. (Boasting: Praising.) **15.** His affection for you grows as he remembers your obedience and how you welcomed him with respect and humility. (Humility: Modesty.) **16.** I rejoice because I trust you completely. (Trust: Confidence.)

Chapter 8

1. Brothers, we want you to know about the grace of God shown to the churches of Macedonia. (Grace: Favor.) **2.** Despite severe trials and deep poverty, their joy overflowed in rich generosity. (Generosity: Willingness to give.) **3.** I testify that they gave as much as they could, and even beyond their ability, willingly. (Ability: Capacity.) **4.** They pleaded with us earnestly to accept their gift and share in serving the saints. (Saints: Believers.) **5.** They went beyond our expectations, giving themselves first to the Lord and then to us by God's will. (Will: Purpose.) **6.** This prompted us to urge Titus to complete this act of grace among you as he had begun. (Prompted: Encouraged.) **7.** As you excel in faith, speech, knowledge, diligence, and love, also excel in this grace of giving. (Diligence: Careful effort.) **8.** I am not commanding you, but testing the sincerity of your love by comparing it with others' eagerness. (Sincerity: Genuine nature.) **9.** You know Christ's grace: though rich, he became poor for you, so you could become rich through his poverty. (Poverty: Humble state.) **10.** My advice benefits you, as you began this work a year ago with eagerness. (Eagerness: Enthusiasm.) **11.** Now complete it, so your willingness matches your actions, according to what you have. (Willingness: Readiness.) **12.** If the willingness is there, the gift is acceptable according to what one has, not what one lacks. (Acceptable: Pleasing.) **13.** I do not mean others should be eased while you are burdened. (Burdened: Weighed down.) **14.** Let your surplus meet their need now, and their surplus may meet yours later, so there is equality. (Surplus: Excess.) **15.** As written: "The one who gathered much did not have too much, and the one who gathered little had no lack." (Lack: Shortage.) **16.** Thanks to God, who put into Titus's heart the same concern for you. (Concern: Care.) **17.** Titus accepted our appeal and went to you eagerly on his own initiative. (Initiative: Willingness to act.) **18.** We sent with him the brother praised by all the churches for his work in spreading the gospel. (Gospel: Good news of Christ.) **19.** He was chosen by the churches to travel with us in handling this gift for God's glory and your readiness. (Readiness: Preparedness.) **20.** We aim to avoid any criticism about our handling of this generous gift. (Criticism: Judgment.) **21.** We ensure everything is honest, not just before God but also before people. (Honest: Upright.) **22.** We also sent another brother, proven diligent in many ways, and now even more so by our confidence in you. (Diligent: Hardworking.) **23.** Titus is my partner and coworker for your benefit, and our other brothers are messengers of the churches and Christ's glory. (Messengers: Representatives.) **24.** Therefore, show them proof of your love and of our pride in you before all the churches. (Proof: Evidence.)

Chapter 9
1. Regarding the service to the saints, I don't need to write to you. (Service: Helping.) **2.** I know your eagerness, which I boast about to the Macedonians, that Achaia was ready a year ago, and your zeal has inspired many. (Zeal: Passion.) **3.** I have sent the brothers to ensure our boasting of you is not in vain and that you are prepared as promised. (Boasting: Praising.) **4.** I don't want to be ashamed if Macedonians come with me and find you unprepared, which would dishonor our boasting. (Dishonor: Shame.) **5.** Therefore, I urged the brothers to go ahead and prepare your gift, so it's ready as a gift and not out of obligation. (Gift: Donation.) **6.** Remember, whoever sows sparingly will reap sparingly, and whoever sows generously will reap generously. (Sow: Give.) **7.** Let each person give as they decide in their heart, not reluctantly or under pressure, for God loves a cheerful giver. (Reluctantly: Unwillingly.) **8.** God is able to make all grace overflow to you, so you have enough for every good work. (Overflow: Abound.) **9.** As Scripture says, "He has freely given to the poor; his righteousness endures forever." (Righteousness: Moral quality.) **10.** The one who provides seed for sowing also provides bread for food and increases the fruits of your righteousness. (Sowing: Planting.) **11.** You will be enriched in everything, leading to thanksgiving to God through us. (Enriched: Blessed.) **12.** This service meets the needs of the saints and leads to abundant thanksgiving to God. (Service: Ministry.) **13.** Through this service, they glorify God for your obedience to the gospel of Christ and your generous giving to them and others. (Obedience: Compliance.) **14.** They pray for you, longing for God's grace in you. (Longing: Desire.) **15.** Thanks be to God for his indescribable gift. (Indescribable: Too great to express.)

Chapter 10
1. I, Paul, appeal to you by the meekness and gentleness of Christ. Though I am humble in person, I am bold when absent. (Appeal: Request.) **2.** I ask that I may not be bold when present, as I intend to be against some who think we live according to the flesh. (Intend: Plan.) **3.** Although we live in the flesh, we do not fight according to the flesh. (Fight: Struggle.) **4.** Our weapons are not physical, but powerful through God to demolish strongholds. (Strongholds: Obstacles.) **5.** We destroy arguments and anything that exalts itself against the knowledge of God, and make every thought obedient to Christ. (Destroy: Demolish.) **6.** We are ready to punish all disobedience once your obedience is complete. (Punish: Discipline.) **7.** Do you judge by outward appearance? If anyone believes they belong to Christ, remember we also belong to Christ. (Judge: Assess.) **8.** Though I could boast of the authority given to us by the Lord for building you up, I do not feel ashamed. (Boast: Praise.) **9.** I don't want to seem like I'm trying to frighten you with my letters. (Frighten: Intimidate.) **10.** Some say, "His letters are strong, but his presence is weak and speech contemptible." (Contemptible: Deserving of scorn.) **11.** Let such a person realize that, as we are in our letters, we will be in action when present. (Realize: Understand.) **12.** We do not compare ourselves with others who commend themselves. Those who measure by their own standard are not wise. (Commend: Praise.) **13.** We will not boast beyond our measure but according to the rule God has assigned to us, even reaching you. (Assigned: Given.) **14.** We do not stretch beyond our measure, as if we did not reach you, for we have come to you in preaching the gospel. (Stretch: Exaggerate.) **15.** We do not boast in others' work, but we hope that when your faith grows, we will be expanded abundantly through you. (Expanded: Increased.) **16.** Our aim is to preach the gospel in regions beyond you, not boasting in what others have already prepared. (Aim: Goal.) **17.** If anyone glories, let him glory in the Lord. (Glories: Boasts.) **18.** It is not he who commends himself that is approved, but the one whom the Lord commends. (Commends: Praises.)

Chapter 11
1. I wish you could bear with me a little in my foolishness, and indeed bear with me. (Wish: Desire.) **2.** I am jealous over you with godly jealousy, for I have promised you to one husband, to present you as a pure virgin to Christ. (Jealous: Zealous.) **3.** I fear, lest as the serpent deceived Eve, your minds should be corrupted from the simplicity that is in Christ. (Deceived: Misled.) **4.** If someone preaches another Jesus or spirit or gospel, which we have not preached, you might tolerate him. (Tolerate: Accept.) **5.** I believe I am not inferior to the chiefest apostles. (Inferior: Lesser.) **6.** Though I am unskilled in speech, I am not in knowledge; we have been clearly revealed among you. (Unskilled: Inexperienced.) **7.** Have I offended you by humbling myself so you could be exalted, preaching the gospel freely? (Offended: Hurt.) **8.** I took support from other churches to serve you. (Support: Assistance.) **9.** I didn't burden anyone while with you; what I lacked was supplied by the brethren from Macedonia. (Burden: Weigh down.) **10.** As the truth of Christ is in me, no one will stop me from boasting in Achaia. (Boasting: Praising.) **11.** Do I not love you? God knows. (Love: Care.) **12.** What I do, I do to avoid giving occasion to those who seek to boast like us. (Occasion: Opportunity.) **13.** False apostles, deceitful workers, transforming into apostles of Christ. (Deceitful: Dishonest.) **14.** No wonder; Satan transforms into an angel of light. (Transform: Change.) **15.** So it's no big deal if his ministers are transformed into ministers of righteousness; their end will be according to their works. (End: Outcome.) **16.** I say again, don't think me a fool; if you do, accept me as a fool so I can boast. (Boast: Brag.) **17.** I speak not from the Lord, but foolishly in this boasting. (Boasting: Bragging.) **18.** Many glory after the flesh, so I will also glory. (Glory: Boast.) **19.** You tolerate fools gladly, seeing yourselves as wise. (Tolerate: Endure.) **20.** You tolerate if someone brings you into bondage, devours you, takes from you, exalts himself, or smites you on the face. (Tolerate: Endure.) **21.** I speak reproachfully, as though we were weak. But if anyone dares to boast, I will boast too. (Reproachfully: Critically.) **22.** Are they Hebrews? So am I. Are they Israelites? So am I. Are they of Abraham's seed? So am I. (Hebrews: Jewish people.) **23.** Are they ministers of Christ? I am more: in labors abundant, stripes above measure, prisons frequent, deaths often. (Stripes: Beatings.) **24.** Five times I received thirty-nine stripes from the Jews. (Stripes: Beatings.) **25.** Three times I was beaten with rods, once stoned, thrice shipwrecked, a night and day in the deep. (Rod: Stick.) **26.** In journeys often, in perils of waters, robbers, my countrymen, heathens, cities, wilderness, sea, false brethren. (Perils: Dangers.) **27.** In weariness, pain, watchings, hunger, thirst, fastings, cold, and nakedness. (Watchings: Sleeplessness.) **28.** Besides all this, the daily care of all the churches. (Care: Concern.) **29.** Who is weak, and I am not weak? Who is offended, and I do not burn? (Burn: Be upset.) **30.** If I must boast, I will boast of my weaknesses. (Boast: Brag.) **31.** God the Father of Jesus Christ knows I am not lying. (Lying: Deceiving.) **32.** In Damascus, the governor kept the city under guard, wanting to capture me. (Guard: Watch.) **33.** I escaped through a window in a basket, lowered by the wall, and escaped his hands. (Escaped: Fled.)

Chapter 12
1. It is not profitable for me to boast, but I will speak of visions and revelations from the Lord. (Profitable: Useful.) **2.** I knew a man in Christ over fourteen years ago, (whether in the body or out, I cannot tell: God knows); he was caught up to the third heaven. (Caught up: Taken up.) **3.** I know this man, (whether in the body or out, I cannot tell: God knows); (Man: Refers to Paul himself.) **4.** He was caught up into paradise and heard unspeakable words, which it is not lawful for man to utter. (Paradise: Heaven.) **5.** I will boast of such a man, but not of myself, except in my weaknesses. (Weaknesses: Infirmities.) **6.** Though I want to boast, I won't be foolish; I will speak the truth, but I refrain, so no one thinks more of me than what they see or hear. (Refrain: Hold back.) **7.** To keep me humble because of the great revelations, I was given a thorn in the flesh, a messenger of Satan to torment me, so I wouldn't be too proud. (Thorn in the flesh: Ongoing struggle or difficulty.) **8.** I asked the Lord three times to remove it from me. (Asked: Begged.) **9.** He told me, "My grace is enough for you, for my strength is made perfect in weakness." So, I will gladly boast in my weaknesses, so Christ's power can rest upon me. (Boast: Brag.) **10.** I take pleasure in weaknesses, insults, hardships, persecutions, and troubles for Christ's sake: for when I am weak, I am strong. (Pleasure: Delight.) **11.** I have become a fool in boasting; you have forced me to it. I should have been commended by you, as I am no inferior to the greatest apostles, even though I am nothing. (Commended: Praised.) **12.** Truly, the signs of an apostle were displayed among you, in patience, signs, wonders, and mighty deeds. (Signs: Miracles.) **13.** What is it you lacked compared to other churches, except that I didn't burden you? Forgive me for

this wrong. (Burden: Weigh down.) **14.** I am coming to you for the third time, and I will not be a burden. I do not seek your wealth, but you. Parents should provide for their children, not the other way around. (Wealth: Possessions.) **15.** I will gladly spend and be spent for you; though the more I love you, the less you love me. (Spent: Exhausted.) **16.** I did not burden you, but being crafty, I took advantage of you. (Crafty: Cunning.) **17.** Did I gain anything from you by sending anyone to you? (Gain: Profit.) **18.** I sent Titus and another brother; did Titus gain anything from you? Did we not walk in the same spirit and steps? (Spirit: Attitude.) **19.** Do you think we are defending ourselves to you? We speak before God in Christ, but we do everything for your edification, dearly beloved. (Edification: Building up.) **20.** I fear that when I come, I will not find you as I hope, and you won't find me as you hope; there may be debates, envy, wrath, strife, gossip, arrogance, and disorder. (Disorder: Chaos.) **21.** I fear that when I come again, God will humble me among you, and I will mourn for those who have sinned and not repented of their impurity, fornication, and lustful practices. (Mourn: Grieve.)

Chapter 13

1. This is the third time I am coming to you. Every word will be established by two or three witnesses. (Witnesses: Those who testify.) **2.** I have warned you before, and now, as I am absent, I write to those who have sinned and to all others, that if I come again, I will not spare. (Warned: Informed.) **3.** Since you seek proof that Christ is speaking through me, know that He is not weak towards you, but mighty among you. (Mighty: Powerful.) **4.** Though He was crucified through weakness, He lives by the power of God. We too are weak in Him, but we will live with Him by God's power toward you. (Crucified: Killed on the cross.) **5.** Examine yourselves to see if you are in the faith; test yourselves. Do you not know yourselves, how Christ is in you, unless you are reprobates? (Reprobates: Unapproved.) **6.** But I trust that you will know that we are not reprobates. (Trust: Believe.) **7.** I pray to God that you do no evil; not to show we are approved, but that you do what is honest, even if we appear as reprobates. (Honest: Truthful.) **8.** For we can do nothing against the truth, but only for the truth. (Truth: God's will.) **9.** We are glad when we are weak and you are strong; our wish is for your perfection. (Perfection: Maturity in Christ.) **10.** Therefore, I write these things while absent, so I won't need to be harsh when present, using the authority given to me for edification, not destruction. (Edification: Building up.) **11.** Finally, brothers, farewell. Be perfect, be encouraged, be of one mind, live in peace; and the God of love and peace will be with you. (Farewell: Goodbye.) **12.** Greet one another with a holy kiss. (Holy kiss: A gesture of peace and love.) **13.** All the saints greet you. (Saints: Believers in Christ.) **14.** The grace of the Lord Jesus Christ, the love of God, and the communion of the Holy Spirit be with you all. Amen. (Grace: Favor; Communion: Fellowship.)

48 – Galatians

Chapter 1

1. Paul, an apostle (not by men or by man, but by Jesus Christ and God the Father who raised Him from the dead), **2.** and all the brethren with me, to the churches of Galatia: (Galatia: region in central Asia Minor) **3.** Grace and peace to you from God the Father and our Lord Jesus Christ, **4.** who gave Himself for our sins, to deliver us from this evil age, according to the will of our God and Father, **5.** to whom be glory forever. Amen. **6.** I am amazed that you are turning so quickly from Him who called you in Christ's grace to a different gospel, **7.** which is not another; but there are some who confuse you and want to distort the gospel of Christ. (Distort: alter the meaning) **8.** But if we, or an angel from heaven, should preach a gospel different from what we preached to you, let him be accursed. (Accursed: condemned) **9.** As I said before, I now repeat: if anyone preaches a gospel other than what you received, let him be accursed. **10.** Am I now trying to win the approval of men or of God? If I were still trying to please men, I would not be a servant of Christ. (Servant: bondservant) **11.** I want you to know, brothers, that the gospel I preached is not from man. **12.** I did not receive it from man, nor was I taught it, but it came through the revelation of Jesus Christ. (Revelation: divine disclosure) **13.** You have heard about my former way of life in Judaism, how I persecuted the church of God and tried to destroy it. (Persecuted: mistreated; Judaism: the Jewish religion) **14.** I advanced in Judaism beyond many of my contemporaries, being more zealous for the traditions of my ancestors. (Zealous: passionate) **15.** But when God, who set me apart from my mother's womb and called me by His grace, **16.** was pleased to reveal His Son in me, so that I might preach Him among the Gentiles, I did not immediately consult with anyone, **17.** nor did I go up to Jerusalem to those who were apostles before me; I went into Arabia, then returned to Damascus. (Arabia: region south of Israel) **18.** After three years, I went to Jerusalem to visit Peter and stayed with him for fifteen days. **19.** I saw no other apostles except James, the Lord's brother. (James: the brother of Jesus) **20.** (What I am writing to you, I assure you before God, I am not lying.) **21.** Then I went to the regions of Syria and Cilicia. (Cilicia: a region in southeastern Turkey) **22.** I was still unknown by sight to the churches of Judea in Christ. (Judea: region around Jerusalem) **23.** They only heard, "The man who formerly persecuted us now preaches the faith he once tried to destroy." **24.** And they praised God because of me. (Praise: glorified)

Chapter 2

1. Fourteen years later, I went to Jerusalem with Barnabas and took Titus. (Barnabas: companion of Paul; Titus: Greek Christian) **2.** I went by revelation and explained the gospel I preach among the Gentiles, privately to those of high reputation, lest I had run in vain. (Revelation: divine truth) **3.** Even Titus, a Greek, was not compelled to be circumcised. (Circumcised: Jewish ritual) **4.** This happened because of false brothers secretly brought in (to spy on our freedom in Christ, aiming to bring us into bondage). (False brothers: pretenders) **5.** We didn't yield to them, to preserve the truth of the gospel. (Yield: submit) **6.** Those who seemed important added nothing to my message. (Favoritism: partiality) **7.** When they saw I was entrusted with the gospel for the uncircumcised, as Peter was for the circumcised, (Uncircumcised: non-Jews) **8.** (He who worked in Peter also worked in me for the Gentiles). (Apostleship: role of an apostle) **9.** When James, Cephas, and John recognized the grace given to me, they gave me and Barnabas the right hand of fellowship, agreeing we would go to the Gentiles. (Pillars: key leaders) **10.** They only asked us to remember the poor, which I was eager to do. (Poor: needy) **11.** When Peter came to Antioch, I opposed him to his face because he was wrong. (Antioch: ancient city) **12.** Before certain men came from James, he ate with Gentiles, but withdrew when they came, fearing those of the circumcision group. (Circumcision group: Jews insisting on circumcision) **13.** The Jews joined his hypocrisy, and even Barnabas was led astray. (Hypocrisy: false appearance) **14.** I said to Peter, "You are a Jew, but you live like a Gentile—why force Gentiles to live as Jews?" (Gentile: non-Jew) **15.** We, Jews by birth, are not sinners like the Gentiles, (Sinners: outside the law) **16.** knowing that a person is justified by faith in Christ, not by works of the law, for no one will be justified by the law. (Justified: declared righteous) **17.** If, while seeking justification in Christ, we are found to be sinners, does that mean Christ is a servant of sin? Certainly not! (Servant of sin: one who encourages sin) **18.** If I rebuild what I destroyed, I prove myself a lawbreaker. (Lawbreaker: violator of the law) **19.** Through the law I died to the law, that I might live for God. (Died to the law: freed from condemnation) **20.** I have been crucified with Christ; I no longer live, but Christ lives in me. The life I live now, I live by faith in the Son of God, who loved me and gave Himself for me. (Crucified: executed on a cross) **21.** I do not set aside the grace of God, for if righteousness could come by the law, Christ died for nothing. (Grace: unearned favor)

Chapter 3

1. O foolish Galatians! Who has bewitched you, so that you no longer obey the truth, before whose eyes Jesus Christ was clearly shown as crucified? (Bewitched: deceived) **2.** I want to learn from you: Did you receive the Spirit by the law's works or by hearing with faith? (Spirit: Holy Spirit) **3.** Are you so foolish? Having started in the Spirit, are you now trying to be perfected by the flesh? (Flesh: human effort, works) **4.** Have you suffered so much for nothing—if indeed it was for nothing? (Suffered: endured hardships) **5.** Does He who gives you the Spirit and works miracles do so by the law or by hearing with faith? (Miracles: divine signs, wonders) **6.** Just as Abraham "believed God, and it was credited to him as righteousness." (Abraham: patriarch of Israel; Righteousness: right standing with God) **7.** Understand that those of faith are the true sons of Abraham. (Faith: trust in God) **8.** Scripture foresaw that God would justify the Gentiles by faith and preached the gospel to Abraham, saying, "In you all nations shall be blessed." (Gentiles: non-Jews; Justify: declare righteous) **9.** So, those of faith are blessed with believing Abraham. (Blessed: favored by God) **10.** All who rely on the law are under a curse, for it is written, "Cursed is everyone who does not continue to do everything in the law." (Law: the commandments in the Old Testament) **11.** It is clear that no one is justified by the law, for "the righteous will live by faith." (Justified: declared righteous) **12.** The law is not based on faith; "the person who does these things will live by them." (Live by them: obeying the law) **13.** Christ has redeemed us from the curse of the law, becoming a curse for us (for it is written, "Cursed is everyone who hangs on a tree"), (Redeemed: rescued, delivered; Tree: cross) **14.** so that the blessing of Abraham might come to the Gentiles through Christ, and we might receive the promise of the Spirit through faith. (Promise: the gift of the Holy Spirit) **15.** Brethren, I speak in human terms: Even a man's covenant, once confirmed, no one can annul or add to. (Covenant: formal agreement) **16.** The promises were made to Abraham and his Seed. Not "seeds" as many, but "Seed," which is Christ. (Seed: descendant) **17.** The law, which came 430 years later, does not annul the covenant confirmed by God in Christ. (Annul:

invalidate, cancel) **18.** If the inheritance is based on the law, it is no longer based on promise; but God gave it to Abraham by promise. (Inheritance: the blessings promised by God) **19.** What purpose then does the law serve? It was added because of transgressions, until the Seed should come to whom the promise was made. (Transgressions: sins) **20.** A mediator does not mediate for one only, but God is one. (Mediator: a person who intervenes between two parties) **21.** Is the law against God's promises? Certainly not! If a law had been given that could give life, righteousness would have come by the law. (Righteousness: right standing with God) **22.** But Scripture has confined everyone under sin, so that the promise by faith in Jesus Christ might be given to those who believe. (Confined: trapped, bound) **23.** Before faith came, we were held in custody under the law, until faith was revealed. (Custody: under control, protection) **24.** The law was our tutor to lead us to Christ, that we might be justified by faith. (Tutor: guardian, guide) **25.** But after faith has come, we are no longer under a tutor. (Tutor: guardian) **26.** For you are all sons of God through faith in Christ Jesus. (Sons of God: children of God) **27.** All who were baptized into Christ have clothed yourselves with Christ. (Baptized: immersed into Christ's identity) **28.** There is neither Jew nor Greek, neither slave nor free, neither male nor female; you are all one in Christ Jesus. (Jew: ethnic Israelite; Greek: non-Jew; One in Christ: united in Christ) **29.** And if you belong to Christ, then you are Abraham's seed, and heirs according to the promise. (Heirs: those who inherit the promise)

Chapter 4
1. As long as an heir is a child, he is no different from a servant, even though he owns everything, **2.** but he is under guardians until the set time by his father. **3.** In the same manner, when we were children, we were enslaved by worldly forces. (Worldly forces: basic principles of existence) **4.** But when the right time came, God sent His Son, born under the law, **5.** to redeem those under the law so we might receive adoption as sons. **6.** Because you are sons, God sent His Spirit into your hearts, calling, "Abba, Father!" (Abba: intimate term for father) **7.** You are no longer a servant, but a son, and if a son, then an heir through Christ. **8.** Before, you served idols, things that are not gods. (Idols: false gods) **9.** Now that you know God, why turn back to weak, powerless forces, wanting to be enslaved again? **10.** You observe rituals and special days. (Rituals: customs, special days: festivals) **11.** I fear I may have wasted my efforts on you. **12.** Brothers, become like me, for I became like you. You have not harmed me. **13.** You received me despite my illness when I first preached to you. **14.** You didn't reject me because of my condition, but welcomed me as though I were Christ. **15.** What was your blessing? You would have given me your eyes if you could. **16.** Have I become your enemy by telling you the truth? **17.** They seek to win you over, but for selfish reasons. **18.** It's good to be zealous for a good cause, not just when I am present. **19.** My children, for whom I labor until Christ is formed in you, **20.** I wish I could be with you now and change my tone, for I am unsure about you. **21.** You who want to be under the law, do you hear what it says? **22.** Abraham had two sons: one by a slave woman, the other by a free woman. **23.** The son of the slave woman was born according to the flesh, the son of the free woman by promise. (Promise: divine covenant) **24.** These are symbols of two covenants: one that brings bondage, and the other that brings freedom. **25.** Mount Sinai represents the present Jerusalem, enslaved with her children. **26.** But the Jerusalem above is free, and she is the mother of us all. **27.** Because the Scripture says: "Rejoice, you who were barren, for the desolate woman will have more children than the one with a husband." **28.** We, brothers, are children of promise, like Isaac. **29.** Just as the son born naturally persecuted the son born by the Spirit, so it is now. **30.** The Scripture says: "Cast out the slave woman and her son, for the son of the slave woman will not inherit with the son of the free woman." **31.** Therefore, we are not children of the slave woman, but of the free woman.

Chapter 5
1. Stand firm in the freedom Christ has given you, and do not return to a life of slavery. **2.** I, Paul, say that if you get circumcised, Christ will be of no benefit to you. **3.** Anyone who chooses circumcision is obligated to follow the entire law. **4.** You have been severed from Christ if you seek justification through the law; you have fallen from grace. **5.** We, through the Spirit, eagerly await the hope of righteousness by faith (faith; believe). **6.** In Christ, neither circumcision nor uncircumcision matters, but faith that works through love. **7.** You were doing well. Who stopped you from obeying the truth? **8.** This persuasion doesn't come from the One who called you. **9.** A little yeast leavens the whole batch of dough. (Yeast: small influence) **10.** I trust that you will remain firm in the Lord, and the one troubling you will face judgment. **11.** If I still preach circumcision, why am I persecuted? The offense of the cross would be removed. **12.** I wish those who cause you trouble would go further and cut themselves off! **13.** You are called to freedom, but don't use freedom to indulge the flesh; instead, serve one another in love. **14.** The entire law is summed up in one command: "Love your neighbor as yourself." **15.** But if you keep biting and devouring each other, beware, or you'll destroy one another! **16.** Walk in the Spirit, and you will not fulfill the desires of the flesh. **17.** The flesh desires what is opposed to the Spirit, and the Spirit what is opposed to the flesh; they are in conflict, so you don't do what you want. **18.** But if you are led by the Spirit, you are not under the law. **19.** The acts of the flesh are obvious: adultery, fornication, impurity, lust, (Lust; an intense desire for something) **20.** idolatry, witchcraft, hatred, discord, jealousy, fits of rage, selfishness, division, heresies, **21.** envy, murder, drunkenness, wild parties, and the like. I warn you, as I did before, that those who live like this will not inherit God's kingdom. **22.** The fruit of the Spirit is love, joy, peace, patience, kindness, goodness, faithfulness, **23.** Gentleness, and self-control. Against such things, there is no law. **24.** Those who belong to Christ have crucified the flesh with its passions and desires. **25.** If we live by the Spirit, let's also walk by the Spirit. **26.** Let us not be conceited, provoking or envying each other.

Chapter 6
1. Brothers, if someone is caught in sin, restore them gently, watching out for yourself so you're not tempted. (Restore: bring back to proper state) **2.** Bear each other's burdens to fulfill Christ's law. **3.** If anyone thinks they're something when they're not, they deceive themselves. (Deceive: mislead) **4.** Test your own actions, and take pride in your own work, not comparing yourself to others. (Test: evaluate) **5.** Everyone must carry their own load. **6.** Those taught the word should share all good things with their teacher. (Word: God's teachings) **7.** Don't be fooled: God can't be mocked. You reap what you sow. (Mocked: ridiculed) **8.** Those who sow to the flesh reap destruction, but those who sow to the Spirit reap eternal life. (Flesh: sinful nature; Spirit: Holy Spirit) **9.** Don't grow weary in doing good. In due time, we'll reap if we don't give up. (Weary: tired or discouraged) **10.** Let's do good to everyone, especially fellow believers. (Family of faith: fellow Christians) **11.** See the large letters I've written with my own hand! **12.** Some urge you to be circumcised to avoid persecution for Christ. (Circumcised: a Jewish rite) **13.** Even those circumcised don't keep the law; they want you to be circumcised to boast about it. **14.** I'll only boast in the cross of Christ, by which the world is dead to me and I to it. (Boast: take pride) **15.** In Christ, neither circumcision nor uncircumcision matters, only becoming a new creation. **16.** Peace and mercy to all who follow this rule, and to the true Israel of God. **17.** Let no one trouble me, for I bear the marks of Jesus. (Marks of Jesus: physical signs of suffering for Christ) **18.** May the grace of Jesus Christ be with your spirit. Amen.

49 – Ephasians

Chapter 1
1. Paul, an apostle of Jesus Christ by the will of God, to the saints who are in Ephesus, and to the faithful in Christ Jesus: **2.** Grace and peace to you from God our Father and the Lord Jesus Christ. **3.** Blessed be the God and Father of our Lord Jesus Christ, who has blessed us with every spiritual blessing in the heavenly realms in Christ. **4.** He chose us in Him before the foundation of the world, that we should be holy and blameless before Him in love. **5.** He predestined us to be adopted as His children through Jesus Christ, according to the good pleasure of His will. (Predestined: determined in advance) **6.** To the praise of His glorious grace, which He freely gave us in the Beloved. **7.** In Him, we have redemption through His blood, the forgiveness of sins, in accordance with the riches of His grace. (Redemption: freedom) **8.** Which He lavished on us with all wisdom and understanding. (Lavished: gave generously) **9.** He made known to us the mystery of His will, according to His good pleasure, which He purposed in Christ. (Mystery: hidden truth) **10.** To bring unity to all things in heaven and on earth under Christ, in the fullness of time. **11.** In Him, we have also received an inheritance, having been predestined according to His purpose, who works out everything in conformity with the purpose of His will. **12.** We were chosen to be for the praise of His glory, who first hoped in Christ. **13.** And you also, after hearing the word of truth, the gospel of your salvation, and having believed in Him, were sealed with the promised Holy Spirit. (Gospel: good news) **14.** The Spirit is a deposit guaranteeing our inheritance until the redemption of those who are God's possession, to the praise of His glory. (Deposit: guarantee) **15.** For this reason, ever since I heard about your faith in the Lord Jesus and your love for all the saints, **16.** I have not stopped giving thanks for you, remembering you in my prayers. **17.** I keep asking that the God of our Lord Jesus Christ, the Father of glory, may give you the Spirit of wisdom and revelation, so that you may know Him better. (Revelation: divine disclosure) **18.** I pray that the eyes of your heart may be enlightened, in order that you may know the hope to which He has called you, the riches of His glorious inheritance in the saints. (Enlightened: made aware) **19.** And His incomparable great power for us who believe, according to the working of His mighty strength. (Incomparable:

beyond comparison) **20.** That power He exerted in Christ when He raised Him from the dead and seated Him at His right hand in the heavenly realms. **21.** Far above all rule, authority, power, and dominion, and every name that is invoked, not only in the present age but also in the one to come. **22.** And God placed all things under His feet and appointed Him to be head over everything for the church, **23.** which is His body, the fullness of Him who fills everything in every way.

Chapter 2
1. You were once dead in your sins, but God made you alive. **2.** You used to follow the ways of this world and obey the ruler of the air, the spirit now at work in the disobedient. (Ruler: authority) **3.** We all lived in the desires of the flesh, by nature deserving of wrath, just like others. (Wrath: judgment) **4.** But God, rich in mercy, loved us with great love, **5.** Even when we were dead in sin, He made us alive with Christ—by grace you are saved. (Grace: unearned favor) **6.** He raised us up with Christ and seated us with Him in heavenly places. **7.** So that in the coming ages, He might show the immeasurable riches of His grace through Christ Jesus. **8.** For by grace you are saved through faith, not from yourselves, but as God's gift. **9.** Not by works, so no one can boast. (Boast: brag) **10.** We are God's creation, made in Christ Jesus to do good works, which He planned in advance. (Workmanship: creation) **11.** Remember, you were once Gentiles, called "Uncircumcision" by those who call themselves "Circumcision." (Gentiles: non-Jews) **12.** You were without Christ, excluded from Israel's promises, and without hope and God in the world. (Citizenship: belonging, Covenants: promises) **13.** But now, in Christ, you who were far away have been brought near by His blood. **14.** Christ is our peace, making both groups one and destroying the barrier of hostility. (Hostility: conflict) **15.** By abolishing the law's commands and creating one new humanity, He made peace. **16.** And through the cross, He reconciled both to God, putting to death their hostility. (Reconcile: bring together, hostility: conflict) **17.** He preached peace to those far and near. **18.** Through Him, we both have access to the Father by one Spirit. (Access: approach) **19.** You are no longer strangers, but fellow citizens with God's people, and members of His household. **20.** Built on the foundation of the apostles and prophets, with Christ as the cornerstone. (Cornerstone: foundation) **21.** In Him, the whole building is joined and grows into a holy temple. **22.** In Him, you are being built together to become a dwelling where God lives by His Spirit. (Dwelling: residence)

Chapter 3
1. For this reason, I, Paul, a prisoner of Jesus Christ for the sake of you Gentiles, **2.** If you have heard about the administration (dispensation) of God's grace given to me for you, **3.** How through revelation He made known to me the mystery, as I briefly wrote before. (Revelation: divine disclosure) **4.** By reading this, you can understand my insight into the mystery of Christ, **5.** Which was not made known in other generations, but is now revealed to His holy apostles and prophets by the Spirit. **6.** That the Gentiles are fellow heirs, members of the same body, and sharers of His promise in Christ through the gospel. **7.** I became a servant of this gospel, by the gift of God's grace given to me through the effective working of His power. (Servant: minister) **8.** Though I am the least of all God's people, this grace was given to me to preach the unsearchable riches of Christ to the Gentiles. (Unsearchable: beyond understanding) **9.** And to make everyone see the fellowship of this mystery, hidden in God, who created all things through Jesus Christ, **10.** So that the manifold wisdom of God might be made known to the rulers and authorities in heavenly places through the church. (Manifold: many-sided) **11.** This was in accordance with the eternal purpose He accomplished in Christ Jesus our Lord. **12.** In Him, we have boldness and access with confidence through faith in Him. **13.** Therefore, I ask that you not be discouraged by my suffering for you, which is for your glory. **14.** For this reason, I kneel before the Father of our Lord Jesus Christ, **15.** From whom the whole family in heaven and on earth derives its name. **16.** I pray that He may grant you, according to the riches of His glory, to be strengthened with power through His Spirit in your inner being. **17.** So that Christ may dwell in your hearts through faith, being rooted and established in love, **18.** That you may have the power to comprehend with all the saints what is the breadth, length, height, and depth, **19.** And to know the love of Christ that surpasses knowledge, that you may be filled with all the fullness of God. **20.** Now to Him who is able to do immeasurably more than all we ask or imagine, according to His power that is at work within us, (Immeasurably: beyond measure) **21.** To Him be glory in the church and in Christ Jesus throughout all generations, forever and ever. Amen.

Chapter 4
1. I, a prisoner of the Lord, urge you to live in a way that is worthy of your calling. **2.** With humility, gentleness, patience, bearing with one another in love, **3.** Making every effort to keep the unity of the Spirit through the bond of peace. **4.** There is one body and one Spirit, just as you were called to one hope, **5.** One Lord, one faith, one baptism, **6.** One God and Father of all, who is above all, through all, and in you all. **7.** But to each of us grace has been given according to Christ's gift. **8.** When He ascended on high, He took captivity captive and gave gifts to people. **9.** (What does "ascended" mean, except that He also descended to the lower parts of the earth? **10.** The One who descended is the same One who ascended far above all the heavens to fill all things.) **11.** He gave some to be apostles, some prophets, some evangelists, and some pastors and teachers, **12.** To equip the saints for the work of ministry, for building up the body of Christ, **13.** Until we all reach unity in the faith and in the knowledge of the Son of God, becoming mature, attaining to the fullness of Christ, **14.** So we will no longer be children, tossed back and forth by every wind of teaching, tricked by people's cunning and deceitful schemes. (Cunning craftiness: clever deceit) **15.** But speaking the truth in love, we will grow to become in every respect the mature body of Him who is the head, that is, Christ. **16.** From Him, the whole body, joined and held together by every supporting ligament, grows and builds itself up in love, as each part does its work. (Ligament: connective tissue, Effectual: effective, Measure: proportion) **17.** I say this and testify in the Lord: No longer live as the Gentiles do, in the futility of their thinking. (Futility: pointlessness) **18.** They are darkened in their understanding, separated from the life of God because of their ignorance, due to the hardness of their hearts. **19.** They have given themselves over to sensuality, indulging in every kind of impurity, with a desire for more. (Sensuality: indulgence of desires) **20.** But that is not the way you learned Christ. **21.** If you have heard about Him and were taught in Him, as the truth is in Jesus, **22.** You were taught to put off your former way of life, the old self, which is corrupted by deceitful desires, **23.** And be renewed in the spirit of your mind, **24.** And put on the new self, created to be like God in true righteousness and holiness. **25.** Therefore, put away falsehood, speak truthfully to your neighbor, for we are all members of one body. **26.** In your anger, do not sin; do not let the sun go down while you are still angry, **27.** And do not give the devil a foothold. **28.** Anyone who has been stealing must no longer steal, but must work, doing something useful with their own hands, that they may have something to share with those in need. (Needeth: needs) **29.** Do not let any unwholesome talk come out of your mouths, but only what is helpful for building others up, according to their needs, that it may benefit those who listen. (Unwholesome: harmful) **30.** And do not grieve the Holy Spirit of God, with whom you were sealed for the day of redemption. **31.** Get rid of all bitterness, rage, anger, brawling, slander, and every form of malice. (Malice: ill will) **32.** Be kind and compassionate to one another, forgiving each other, just as in Christ God forgave you.

Chapter 5
1. Be imitators of God, as dearly cherished youngsters, **2.** And stroll in love, just as Christ cherished us and gave Himself up for us, a fragrant offering and sacrifice to God. (fragrant: alluring) **3.** However sexual immorality, impurity, or greed should no longer also be named among you, as it is fallacious for saints. **4.** Nor have to there be obscenity, foolish communicate, or coarse joking, which might be out of region, but as an alternative thanksgiving. (Obscenity: offensive language) **5.** For that no immoral, impure, or greedy man or woman—such a person is an idolater—has any inheritance within the country of Christ and of God. **6.** Let no one deceive you with empty words, for because of such things, God's wrath comes upon the disobedient. (Empty: meaningless) **7.** Do not be companions with them. **8.** For you were once in darkness, but now you are light within the Lord. Stay as children of light, **9.** (For the fruit of the Spirit is found in all goodness, righteousness, and truth.) **10.** Find out what pleases the Lord. **11.** Don't have any fellowship with the unfruitful works of darkness, but instead expose them. **12.** It is shameful even to speak of what they do in secret. **13.** But everything uncovered by the light becomes visible, and everything that is illuminated becomes light. **14.** That is why it is said: "Wake up, sleeper, rise from the dead, and Christ will shine on you." **15.** Be careful, then, how you live—not as unwise, but as wise, **16.** Making the most of every opportunity, because the days are evil. **17.** Therefore, do not be foolish, but understand what the Lord's will is. **18.** Do not get drunk on wine, which leads to debauchery; instead, be filled with the Spirit. (Debauchery: excessive indulgence) **19.** Speak to each other with psalms, hymns, and spiritual songs, singing and making music from your heart to the Lord. **20.** Always give thanks to God the Father for everything, in the name of our Lord Jesus Christ. **21.** Submit to one another out of reverence for Christ. **22.** Wives, submit yourselves to your own husbands as to the Lord. **23.** For the husband is the head of the wife as Christ is the head of the church, and he is the Savior of the body. **24.** Because the church submits to Christ, so wives should submit to their husbands in everything. **25.** Husbands, love your wives, just as Christ loved the church and gave Himself up for her, **26.** To sanctify and cleanse her by the washing with water through the word, **27.**

And to present her to Himself as a radiant church, without spot or wrinkle or any other blemish, but holy and blameless. **28.** In the same way, husbands should love their wives as their own bodies. He who loves his wife loves himself. **29.** After all, no one ever hated their own body, but they feed and take care of it, just as Christ does the church— **30.** For we are members of His body. **31.** For this reason, a man will leave his father and mother and be united to his wife, and the two will become one flesh. (One flesh: united as one) **32.** This is a profound mystery, but I am talking about Christ and the church. **33.** However, each one of you must also love his wife as he loves himself, and the wife must respect her husband. (Respect: honor)

Chapter 6
1. Children, follow your parents' guidance in the Lord, as this is the right thing to do. **2.** Honor both your father and mother, for this is the first command with a promise attached. (Honor: respect) **3.** So that it may go well with you, and you may enjoy a long life on earth. (Prosper: succeed) **4.** Fathers, do not provoke your children to anger, but raise them with the Lord's discipline and instruction. (Provoke: annoy) **5.** Workers, be respectful and sincere toward your earthly masters, as if you were serving Christ. **6.** Do not work only when being watched, but sincerely as servants of Christ, doing God's will with your heart. **7.** Serve with a willing heart, as though you are serving the Lord and not people. (Willingly: freely) **8.** Remember that whatever good you do, the Lord will reward you, whether you are a slave or free. (Slave: servant) **9.** Masters, treat your workers kindly, without threatening them, because you both have a Master in heaven who shows no favoritism. (Masters: employers) **10.** Finally, be strong in the Lord and in His great power. (Strong: empowered) **11.** Put on all of God's armor so that you can stand firm against the devil's tricks. (Armor: protection) **12.** Our battle is not against people, but against spiritual rulers, powers, and forces of evil in the heavenly realms. (Struggle: fight) **13.** Therefore, take up God's full armor to remain strong when facing evil, and after everything, stand firm. (Stand firm: endure) **14.** Stand your ground, with truth as your belt, and righteousness as your chest armor. (Truth: honesty) **15.** Have your feet ready, equipped with the peace that comes from the gospel. (Readiness: preparation) **16.** Above all, take the shield of faith to block all the fiery arrows of the enemy. (Faith: trust) **17.** Put on the helmet of salvation, and take up the sword of the Spirit, which is God's Word. (Helmet: headgear) **18.** Pray at all times, in the Spirit, with every kind of prayer and request, and stay alert, praying for all God's people. (Pray: petition) **19.** Pray for me too, that I may speak boldly and reveal the mystery of the gospel. (Proclaim: declare) **20.** I am an ambassador in chains, so pray that I may speak boldly as I should. (Ambassador: representative) **21.** You will know how I am doing, for Tychicus, a dear brother and faithful servant, will tell you all. (Tychicus: companion) **22.** I sent him for this reason, to update you on our situation and bring you encouragement. **23.** May peace be upon the brothers and sisters, along with love and faith, from God the Father and the Lord Jesus Christ. **24.** Grace be given to all who love our Lord Jesus Christ with an undying love. Amen. (Grace: favor)

50 – Philipians
Chapter 1
1. Paul and Timothy, servants of Jesus Christ, to all the saints in Christ Jesus at Philippi, including the bishops and deacons. (Saints: holy ones) **2.** Grace and peace to you from God our Father and the Lord Jesus Christ. (Grace: favor, Peace: harmony) **3.** I thank God whenever I remember you. (Remember: recall) **4.** In every prayer, I always thank God with joy for you all. (Prayer: communication with God.) **5.** For your partnership in the gospel from the first day until now. (Partnership: fellowship) **6.** I am confident that God, who began a good work in you, will complete it until Christ's return. (Confident: sure) **7.** It's right for me to feel this way, because I have you in my heart; you share in God's grace with me, whether in my chains or defending the gospel. (Chains: imprisonment) **8.** God knows how deeply I long for you all with the love of Christ. (Long: deeply yearn for) **9.** I pray that your love will grow in knowledge and discernment. (Discernment: judgment) **10.** So you may approve what is best, be pure and blameless until Christ's return. (Pure: morally blameless) **11.** Filled with the fruits of righteousness that comes through Jesus Christ, to the glory of God. (Fruits: results) **12.** I want you to know that what happened to me has actually advanced the gospel. (Advanced: furthered) **13.** My imprisonment has become known to everyone in the palace and beyond. (Imprisonment: being in prison) **14.** Most of the believers, encouraged by my chains, are now more bold in speaking God's word. (Chains: imprisonment) **15.** Some preach Christ out of envy, others out of goodwill. (Envy: jealousy) **16.** The latter do it out of love, knowing I defend the gospel. (Love: affection) **17.** The former preach out of selfish ambition, not sincerely, to add pain to my imprisonment. (Selfish ambition: personal gain) **18.** But I rejoice, because Christ is preached, whether for good or bad motives. (Rejoice: be glad) **19.** I know this will turn out for my deliverance through your prayers and the Spirit of Jesus Christ. (Deliverance: salvation) **20.** I eagerly expect and hope that I will never be ashamed, but will always honor Christ, whether by life or death. (Eagerly: expectantly) **21.** For to live is Christ, and to die is gain. (Gain: advantage) **22.** If I live on, it means fruitful work for me, but I don't know what to choose. (Fruitful: spiritually productive) **23.** I am torn between the two: I want to be with Christ, which is far better. (Torn: conflicted) **24.** But staying in the flesh is more necessary for you. (Flesh: physical life) **25.** I am confident I will remain and continue with you for your growth and joy in faith. (Confident: assured) **26.** So you can rejoice more abundantly in Christ when I return to you. (Rejoice: celebrate) **27.** Live in a way worthy of the gospel, standing firm with one spirit, striving together for the faith. (Striving: working hard) **28.** Do not be intimidated by your enemies; this shows their defeat and your salvation. (Intimidated: frightened, Enemies: opponents) **29.** It has been granted to you, not only to believe in Christ, but also to suffer for Him. (Granted: given) **30.** You are facing the same struggle I had, and still have. (Struggle: conflict)

Chapter 2
1. If there is any comfort in Christ, any love, any fellowship in the Spirit, any compassion and mercy. (Comfort: encouragement, Fellowship: partnership) **2.** Make my joy complete by being like-minded, having the same love, being united in spirit and purpose. **3.** Do nothing out of selfish ambition or pride, but in humility consider others better than yourselves. (Ambition: desire) **4.** Do not only look out for your own interests, but also for the interests of others. **5.** Let the same attitude be in you that was in Christ Jesus: (Attitude: mindset) **6.** Who, being in the nature of God, did not consider equality with God something to cling to, (Cling: hold on tightly) **7.** But made Himself nothing, taking the form of a servant, and being made in human likeness. **8.** And being found as a man, He humbled Himself by becoming obedient to death—even death on a cross. (Humbled: self-abasement) **9.** Therefore, God exalted Him to the highest place and gave Him the name above all names, (Exalted: lifted up) **10.** That at the name of Jesus, every knee should bow, in heaven, on earth, and under the earth **11.** And every tongue confess that Jesus Christ is Lord, to the glory of God the Father. **12.** Therefore, my dear friends, as you have always obeyed, not just when I am present, but now much more in my absence, work out your salvation with fear and trembling. **13.** For it is God who works in you, both to desire and to act according to His good purpose. **14.** Do everything without complaining or arguing, (Complaining: grumbling) **15.** So that you may be blameless and pure, children of God without fault, in the midst of a crooked and perverse generation, shining like stars in the world. **16.** Hold firmly to the word of life, so that I can rejoice on the day of Christ that I did not run or labor in vain. (Firmly: with firm convocation) **17.** But even if I am poured out like a drink offering on the sacrifice and service of your faith, I rejoice and share my joy with you all. **18.** So you too should rejoice and share in my joy. (Rejoice: Deep joy) **19.** I hope in the Lord Jesus to send Timothy to you soon, so that I too may be encouraged when I hear about your condition. **20.** I have no one else like Timothy, who will genuinely care for your welfare. **21.** Everyone else looks out for their own interests, not those of Jesus Christ. **22.** But you know Timothy's proven worth, how as a son with his father, he has served with me in spreading the gospel. **23.** I hope to send him as soon as I see how things go with me. **24.** And I trust in the Lord that I myself will come soon. **25.** I considered it necessary to send Epaphroditus, my brother and fellow worker, and your messenger who ministered to my needs. **26.** He was longing to see you all and distressed because you heard he was sick. **27.** He was indeed sick and almost died, but God had mercy on him, and not only on him but also on me, to spare me sorrow upon sorrow. **28.** I am sending him back more eagerly, so that when you see him, you may rejoice and I may have less sorrow. **29.** Welcome him in the Lord with great joy, and honor people like him, **30.** Because he risked his life for the work of Christ, nearly dying to make up for your lack of service to me.

Chapter 3
1. Rejoice in the Lord. It is not a burden for me to remind you of this, but it is beneficial for you. (Rejoice: be glad) **2.** Watch out for those who do evil, for those who try to impose unnecessary rules on the flesh. (Impose: force upon) **3.** We are the true people of God, who worship Him in spirit, boast in Christ Jesus, and place no trust in human efforts. (Boast: glory in) **4.** Though I could have confidence in my own efforts, if anyone thinks they can rely on their own achievements, I have more reasons to do so: **5.** I was circumcised on the eighth day, a true Israelite, from the tribe of Benjamin, a Hebrew among Hebrews; as for the law, I was a Pharisee; **6.** I zealously persecuted the church and, in terms of the righteousness demanded by the law, I was blameless. (Zealously: passionately) **7.** But what I once considered gain, I now count as a loss for the sake of Christ. **8.** Yes, I consider everything a loss compared to the surpassing greatness of knowing Christ Jesus my Lord, for whose sake I have

lost everything and consider it worthless, in order to gain Christ. (Worthless: of no value) **9.** And be found in Him, not with my own righteousness that comes from obeying the law, but the righteousness that comes through faith in Christ—the righteousness that is given by God through faith. **10.** I want to know Christ and experience the power of His resurrection, and share in His sufferings, becoming like Him in His death, (Sufferings: hardships) **11.** And so, somehow, I hope to attain the resurrection of the dead. (Attain: reach) **12.** Not that I have already achieved this, or am already perfect, but I press on to take hold of that for which Christ Jesus took hold of me. (Press on: pursue with determination) **13.** Brothers, I do not consider myself to have already obtained it, but one thing I do: forgetting what is behind and striving toward what is ahead, **14.** I press on toward the goal to win the prize for which God has called me heavenward in Christ Jesus. **15.** All of us who are spiritually mature should think the same way; and if on some point you think differently, God will reveal this to you. (Spiritually mature: fully grown in faith) **16.** Only let us continue to live by the same standard to which we have attained. (Live by: follow the path) **17.** Join with others in following my example, brothers, and take note of those who live according to the pattern we gave you. **18.** For many, as I have often warned you, and now say even with tears, live as enemies of the cross of Christ. **19.** Their end is destruction, their god is their appetite, and their glory is in their shame. They set their minds on earthly things. (Glory: pride) **20.** But our citizenship is in heaven, and we eagerly await a Savior from there, the Lord Jesus Christ, (Eagerly: with anticipation) **21.** Who, by the power that enables Him to bring everything under His control, will transform our lowly bodies so that they will be like His glorious body. (Lowly: humble)

Chapter 4

1. Consequently, my dearly beloved brothers, whom I long for, my pleasure and crown, stand firm in the Lord, my cherished. **2.** I urge Euodia and I urge Syntyche to be of one mind in the Lord. (Urge: strongly encourage) **3.** Yes, and I ask you, my true companion, to help these women who have labored with me in the gospel, along with Clement and the other fellow workers, whose names are in the book of life. (Companion: partner) **4.** Rejoice in the Lord always. I will say it again: rejoice! (Rejoice: be glad) **5.** Let your gentleness be evident to all. The Lord is near. (Gentleness: kindness) **6.** Do not be anxious about anything, but in every situation, through prayer and petition, with thanksgiving, let your requests be made known to God. (Petition: request) **7.** And the peace of God, which surpasses all understanding, will guard your hearts and minds in Christ Jesus. (Surpasses: exceeds) **8.** Finally, brothers, whatever is true, whatever is noble, whatever is right, whatever is pure, whatever is lovely, whatever is admirable—if anything is excellent or praiseworthy—think about such things. (Admirable: worthy of respect) **9.** Whatever you have learned or received or heard from me, or seen in me—put it into practice. And the God of peace will be with you. **10.** I rejoiced greatly in the Lord that at last you have renewed your concern for me. Indeed, you were concerned, but you had no opportunity to show it. (Renewed: revived) **11.** I am not saying this because I am in need, for I have learned to be content whatever the circumstances. (Content: satisfied) **12.** I know what it is to be in need, and I know what it is to have plenty. I have learned the secret of being content in any and every situation, whether well-fed or hungry, whether living in plenty or in want. **13.** I can do all things through Christ who strengthens me. **14.** Yet it was good of you to share in my troubles. **15.** You Philippians know that in the early days of the gospel, when I left Macedonia, no church shared with me in the matter of giving and receiving, except you only; **16.** Even when I was in Thessalonica, you sent me aid more than once when I was in need. **17.** Not that I desire a gift, but I desire that you have credit to your account. (Spiritual benefit: rewards in heaven) **18.** I have received full payment and have more than enough. I am amply supplied, now that I have received from Epaphroditus the gifts you sent. They are a fragrant offering, an acceptable sacrifice, pleasing to God. (Aromatic offering: appealing gift) **19.** And my God will meet all your needs according to the riches of His glory in Christ Jesus. **20.** To our God and Father be glory forever and ever. Amen. **21.** Greet all God's people in Christ Jesus. The brothers and sisters who are with me send greetings. **22.** All God's people here send you greetings, especially those who belong to Caesar's household. **23.** The grace of the Lord Jesus Christ be with your spirit. Amen.

51 – Colossians

Chapter 1

1. Paul, an apostle of Jesus Christ by God's will, and Timothy, our brother. (apostle: messenger) **2.** To the faithful disciples of Christ in Colosse: May grace and peace be upon you from God our Father and the Lord Jesus Christ. (disciples: followers) **3.** We constantly praise God, the Father of our Lord Jesus Christ, in our prayers for you. (praise: give thanks) **4.** Because we have heard of your steadfast faith in Christ Jesus and your love for all of God's people. (steadfast: unwavering) **5.** This is the hope that is stored up for you in heaven, a hope you first heard through the authentic gospel message. (stored up: laid up) **6.** The gospel, which is spreading throughout the world and yielding fruit, has also been fruitful among you since the moment you understood and accepted God's grace in truth. (yielding fruit: bearing fruit) **7.** You learned it from Epaphras, our dear fellow servant, a faithful minister of Christ on your behalf. **8.** He also shared with us your love for one another, inspired by the Spirit. (shared: communicated) **9.** For this reason, since we first heard of you, we haven't stopped praying for you, asking God to fill you with knowledge of His will through all wisdom and spiritual understanding. (filled: equipped) **10.** We pray that you would live in a manner worthy of the Lord, producing good works and growing in your knowledge of God. (manner: way of life) **11.** May you be strengthened with all power, according to His glorious might, so that you may endure with patience and joy. (strengthened: empowered) **12.** Give thanks to the Father, who has made us worthy to share in the inheritance of His holy people in the kingdom of light. (worthy: qualified) **13.** He has saved us from the dominion of darkness and brought us into the kingdom of His beloved Son. (saved: rescued) **14.** In whom we have salvation and the forgiveness of sins. (salvation: redemption) **15.** He is the seen image of the invisible God, the firstborn over all creation. (seen: visible) **16.** Through Him, all things were made: things in the heavens, on earth, visible and invisible, whether thrones, powers, rulers, or authorities. Everything was made by Him and for Him. (made: created) **17.** He existed before all things, and in Him, everything remains united. (united: holds together) **18.** He is the head of the body, the church; the beginning and the first to rise from the dead, so that in everything He might be preeminent. (preeminent: supreme) **19.** God delighted to have all of His fullness dwell in Him. (delighted: was pleased) **20.** And through Him, to reconcile all things to Himself, whether on earth or in heaven, making peace through His blood shed on the cross. (reconcile: restore) **21.** At one time, you were separated from God and hostile in your thoughts and actions. (hostile: alienated) **22.** But now He has reconciled you through His physical body by His death, to present you holy, innocent, and free from accusation before Him. (innocent: blameless) **23.** If you remain firmly grounded in your faith, stable and unshaken, not departing from the hope of the gospel you received, which has been proclaimed to every creature under heaven. I, Paul, am a servant of this gospel. (firmly grounded: steadfast) **24.** Now, I celebrate in my suffering for you, and I am fulfilling what is lacking in Christ's afflictions for the sake of His body, the church. (celebrate: rejoice) **25.** I have become a servant of the church by God's commission, to complete the word of God. (commission: calling) **26.** This is the secret that was hidden for ages but has now been revealed to His saints. (secret: mystery) **27.** God wanted to make known to the Gentiles the magnificent riches of this secret: Christ in you, the hope of glory. (magnificent: glorious) **28.** We proclaim Christ, warning and teaching everyone with all wisdom, to present each person mature in Christ. (warning: admonishing) **29.** To this end, I strive, working with all His energy, which works powerfully within me. (strive: try hard)

Chapter 2

1. I want you to know the great concern I have for you, for those in Laodicea, and for all who haven't met me personally. (concern: care) **2.** My desire is that their hearts be encouraged, united in love, and led to the full assurance of understanding and the knowledge of God's mystery—Christ Himself. (encouraged: comforted) **3.** In Christ are hidden all the treasures of wisdom and knowledge. (treasures: riches) **4.** I say this to protect you from being deceived by persuasive arguments. (deceived: misled) **5.** Though I am physically absent, I am with you in spirit, rejoicing in your discipline and steadfast faith in Christ. (absent: away) **6.** Since you have received Christ Jesus as Lord, live your lives rooted in Him, (rooted: grounded) **7.** Firmly built up in Him, strengthened in faith as you were taught, and overflowing with thankfulness. (built up: established) **8.** Be cautious not to be misled by human traditions, worldly principles, or empty philosophies that are not based on Christ. (cautious: careful) **9.** In Christ, all the fullness of God lives in bodily form, (fullness: completeness) **10.** And in Him, you are made complete, for He is the head over every authority and power. (complete: whole) **11.** In Him, you were spiritually circumcised—removing sin's power—not by human hands, but by Christ. (circumcised: purified) **12.** You were buried with Him in baptism and raised to life through faith in God's power, who raised Him from the dead. (buried: submerged, raised: revived) **13.** When you were spiritually dead in sin, God made you alive with Christ, forgiving all your sins. (dead: lifeless, forgiving: pardoning) **14.** He erased the record of charges against us and nailed it to the cross. (erased: wiped out) **15.** Christ disarmed spiritual rulers and authorities, publicly exposing and triumphing over them through His cross. (disarmed: defeated) **16.** Therefore, don't let anyone judge you over food, drink, festivals, new moons, or Sabbaths, (judge: criticize) **17.**

Which are shadows of things to come; the reality is found in Christ. (shadows: symbols) **18.** Don't let anyone disqualify you with false humility, angel worship, or unspiritual visions—things rooted in pride. (disqualify: reject) **19.** Such people fail to hold onto Christ, the Head, who nourishes and unites the whole body, helping it grow as God intends. (nourishes: strengthens) **20.** Since you have died with Christ to worldly principles, why do you still follow human rules, (died: passed away, principles: teachings) **21.** Such as "Don't touch," "Don't taste," "Don't handle"? (touch: handle) **22.** These are based on human commands and teachings and will eventually perish. (commands: instructions) **23.** Though they appear wise with self-imposed worship, false humility, and harsh treatment of the body, they lack true value in restraining sin. (appear: seem).

Chapter 3
1. Since you have been raised with Christ, focus on things above, where Christ sits at God's right hand. (focus: concentrate) **2.** Set your minds on heavenly things, not earthly ones. (heavenly: spiritual) **3.** For you have died, and your life is now hidden with Christ in God. (hidden: concealed) **4.** When Christ, who is your life, appears, you will also appear with Him in glory. (glory: splendor) **5.** Put to death earthly desires like sexual immorality, impurity, lust, evil desires, and greed, which is idolatry. (idolatry: idol worship) **6.** These bring God's wrath on those who disobey. (wrath: anger) **7.** You once lived in these ways when you followed them. (lived: existed) **8.** But now rid yourselves of anger, rage, malice, slander, and filthy language. (slander: defamation) **9.** Don't lie to each other; you have taken off the old self with its practices. (practices: habits) **10.** And put on the new self, renewed in knowledge in the image of its Creator. (renewed: transformed) **11.** Here there is no Greek or Jew, circumcised or uncircumcised, barbarian, Scythian, slave, or free; Christ is all and in all. (circumcised: ritualistically purified) **12.** As God's chosen, holy, and loved, clothe yourselves with compassion, kindness, humility, gentleness, and patience. (clothe: dress) **13.** Bear with one another and forgive each other if you have grievances, just as Christ forgave you. (grievances: complaints) **14.** Above all, put on love, which binds everything together in perfect unity. (binds: unites) **15.** Let the peace of Christ rule in your hearts, since you were called to peace in one body. And be thankful. (peace: tranquility) **16.** Let Christ's word richly dwell in you. Teach and encourage one another with wisdom, singing psalms, hymns, and spiritual songs with gratitude to God. (encourage: motivate) **17.** Whatever you do, in word or action, do it in the name of the Lord Jesus, giving thanks to God the Father through Him. (action: deed) **18.** Wives, submit to your husbands, as is fitting in the Lord. **19.** Husbands, love your wives and do not be harsh with them. (harsh: severe) **20.** Children, obey your parents in everything, for this pleases the Lord. (obey: follow) **21.** Fathers, do not provoke your children, so they won't become discouraged. (provoke: irritate) **22.** Servants, obey your earthly masters sincerely, fearing the Lord, not just to please them when they're watching. (sincerely: genuinely) **23.** Whatever you do, work at it with all your heart, as working for the Lord, not for men. (work: labor) **24.** Know that you will receive the inheritance from the Lord as your reward; you are serving Christ. (inheritance: legacy) **25.** Anyone who does wrong will be repaid for their actions, without favoritism. (repaid: compensated)

Chapter 4
1. Masters, treat your servants fairly and justly, knowing you also have a Master in heaven. (justly: rightly) **2.** Continue in prayer, staying watchful and thankful. (watchful: alert) **3.** Pray also for us, that God may open a door for us to share the mystery of Christ, for which I am in chains. (chains: imprisonment) **4.** Pray that I may proclaim it clearly, as I should. (proclaim: announce) **5.** Walk in wisdom toward outsiders, making the most of every opportunity. (outsiders: nonbelievers) **6.** Let your speech always be gracious, seasoned with salt, so you know how to answer everyone. (gracious: kind) **7.** Tychicus, a beloved brother and faithful servant of the Lord, will inform you about my circumstances. (inform: update) **8.** I have sent him to encourage and comfort your hearts. (encourage: uplift) **9.** He is coming with Onesimus, a faithful and beloved brother, who is one of you. They will share all that is happening here. (faithful: loyal) **10.** Aristarchus, my fellow prisoner, sends his greetings, as does Mark, the cousin of Barnabas. If he visits, welcome him. (fellow: companion) **11.** Jesus, called Justus, also greets you. These are the only Jewish coworkers for God's kingdom here, and they have been a great comfort to me. (coworkers: partners) **12.** Epaphras, a servant of Christ and one of you, sends his greetings. He always prays fervently for you to stand firm in God's will. (fervently: earnestly) **13.** I testify to his deep concern for you and for those in Laodicea and Hierapolis. (testify: affirm) **14.** Luke, the beloved physician, and Demas greet you. (physician: doctor) **15.** Greet the believers in Laodicea, Nymphas, and the church in his house. (believers: followers) **16.** After this letter is read to you, ensure it is read to the church in Laodicea, and read the letter from Laodicea as well. (ensure: make sure) **17.** Tell Archippus to complete the ministry he received from the Lord. (complete: finish) **18.** I, Paul, write this greeting with my own hand. Remember my chains. Grace be with you. (greeting: salutation).

52 – 1 Thessalonians
Chapter 1
1. From Paul, Silvanus, and Timothy, to the church of the Thessalonians who belong to God the Father and the Lord Jesus Christ: Grace and peace to you from God our Father and the Lord Jesus Christ. (grace: favor, peace: harmony) **2.** We always express gratitude to God for all of you, remembering you in our prayers. (gratitude: thankfulness) **3.** We continually recall your faithful deeds, loving efforts, and steadfast hope in our Lord Jesus Christ before God our Father. (steadfast: unwavering) **4.** We are confident, dear brothers and sisters loved by God, that He has chosen you. (confident: assured) **5.** Our message to you was not just words but came with power, the Holy Spirit, and deep conviction. You know how we lived among you for your benefit. (conviction: certainty) **6.** You imitated us and the Lord, welcoming the message with joy from the Holy Spirit, even in the midst of great hardship. (hardship: difficulty) **7.** Because of this, you became examples to believers throughout Macedonia and Achaia. (examples: models) **8.** The word of the Lord has spread out from you—not just in Macedonia and Achaia, but everywhere your faith in God has been made known. We don't even need to say anything! (spread: extended) **9.** Others themselves tell about how we came to you and how you turned from idols to serve the living and true God. (idols: false gods) **10.** And you now wait for His Son from heaven, the one He raised from the dead—Jesus, who rescues us from the coming wrath. (wrath: anger)

Chapter 2
1. You yourselves know, brothers, that our visit to you was not without purpose. (purpose: intent) **2.** Despite previous suffering and mistreatment in Philippi, we boldly preached God's gospel to you amidst opposition. (opposition: resistance) **3.** Our appeal was not based on deceit, impurity, or trickery. (deceit: dishonesty) **4.** Instead, we speak as those approved by God to be entrusted with the gospel, aiming to please God, not people, for He tests our hearts. (approved: accepted) **5.** We never used flattery or masked greed, as you know, and God is our witness. (flattery: compliments) **6.** Nor did we seek glory from people, neither from you nor others, even though we could have been a burden as apostles of Christ. (glory: honor) **7.** Instead, we were gentle among you, like a nursing mother caring for her children. (gentle: kind) **8.** Because of our deep affection for you, we were delighted to share not only God's gospel but also our lives, for you had become dear to us. (affection: love) **9.** You remember, brothers, our hard work and toil; we labored night and day so as not to be a burden while preaching God's gospel to you. (toil: effort) **10.** You are witnesses, and so is God, of how holy, righteous, and blameless our conduct was among you who believe. (blameless: faultless) **11.** For you know that we treated each of you as a father treats his children. (treated: cared) **12.** Encouraging, comforting, and urging you to live worthy of God, who calls you into His kingdom and glory. (worthy: deserving) **13.** We also thank God continually because, when you received His word from us, you accepted it not as a human word but as it truly is—the word of God, which works in you who believe. (accepted: embraced) **14.** For you, brothers, became imitators of God's churches in Judea that are in Christ Jesus. You suffered from your own people just as they did from the Jews, (suffered: endured) **15.** Who killed the Lord Jesus and the prophets and persecuted us. They displease God and oppose all people, (displease: offend) **16.** Hindering us from speaking to the Gentiles so they may be saved. In doing so, they always heap up their sins, and God's wrath has overtaken them fully. (hindering: blocking) **17.** But brothers, though we were separated from you for a short time in person but not in heart, we longed intensely to see you again. (separated: apart) **18.** We wanted to come to you—certainly I, Paul, tried again and again—but Satan blocked our way. (blocked: prevented) **19.** For what is our hope, joy, or crown of boasting before our Lord Jesus at His coming? Isn't it you? (boasting: pride) **20.** Indeed, you are our glory and joy. (glory: splendor)

Chapter 3
1. When we could no longer wait, we decided to stay in Athens alone. (wait: delay) **2.** We sent Timothy, our brother and God's servant, to strengthen and encourage you in your faith. (encourage: uplift) **3.** We didn't want anyone to be unsettled by these trials, as you know we are destined for them. (trials: hardships) **4.** While we were with you, we warned that we would face suffering, and you have seen this happen. (suffering: pain) **5.** When I could wait no longer, I sent to learn about your faith, fearing the tempter might have led you astray, making our efforts fruitless. (fruitless: wasted) **6.** But Timothy has returned with good news about your faith and love, and your fond memories of us, longing to see us as we do you. **7.** This news has

comforted us in our affliction and troubles because of your faith. (affliction: distress) **8.** We are revived as you remain steadfast in the Lord. (revived: renewed) **9.** How can we thank God enough for the joy you bring us before Him? (joy: happiness) **10.** We pray earnestly night and day to see you again and help strengthen your faith. (earnestly: sincerely) **11.** May God our Father and Jesus our Lord guide our way to you. (guide: direct) **12.** May the Lord help you grow and overflow in love for one another and everyone, just as we love you. (overflow: abound) **13.** May He establish your hearts as blameless in holiness before God at the coming of our Lord Jesus with His saints. (establish: secure)

Chapter 4
1. We urge you, brothers, to follow what we taught you about living to please God and continue growing in it. (urge: encourage) **2.** You know the instructions we gave you through the Lord Jesus. (instructions: teachings) **3.** God's will is for your sanctification: abstain from sexual immorality. (sanctification: purity) **4.** Each of you should control your body in holiness and honor. (honor: respect) **5.** Do not act in passionate lust like those who don't know God. (lust: desire) **6.** Do not wrong or take advantage of a brother, for the Lord will avenge such actions, as we warned you. (avenge: repay) **7.** God has called us to holiness, not impurity. (holiness: righteousness) **8.** Anyone who rejects this teaching is rejecting God, who gave you His Holy Spirit. (rejecting: refusing) **9.** Regarding brotherly love, you've been taught by God to love one another. (love: care) **10.** You already love the believers in Macedonia, but we encourage you to love even more. (encourage: urge) **11.** Strive to lead a quiet life, handle your own affairs, and work with your hands as we instructed. (strive: aim) **12.** This way, you'll live honorably before outsiders and lack nothing. (honorably: respectably) **13.** We don't want you to be ignorant about those who have died, so you won't grieve like those without hope. (grieve: mourn) **14.** If we believe Jesus died and rose again, we also believe God will bring with Him those who have died in Christ. (rose: resurrected) **15.** According to the Lord's word, we who are alive at His return will not precede those who have died. (precede: go before) **16.** The Lord Himself will descend from heaven with a shout, the archangel's voice, and God's trumpet; the dead in Christ will rise first. (descend: come down) **17.** Then we who are alive will be caught up with them in the clouds to meet the Lord and be with Him forever. (caught up: gathered) **18.** Encourage each other with these words.

Chapter 5
1. Brothers, there's no need for me to write to you about the times and seasons. (seasons: periods) **2.** You are fully aware that the day of the Lord will arrive unexpectedly, like a thief in the night. (unexpectedly: suddenly) **3.** When people say, "Everything is calm and secure," sudden destruction will fall upon them, just like the pain of childbirth, and they will not escape. (destruction: ruin) **4.** But you, brothers, are not in darkness, so that day will not catch you off guard like a thief. (darkness: ignorance) **5.** You are all children of light and of the day; we do not belong to the night or the darkness. (light: truth) **6.** Therefore, let us not be asleep like others, but let us be alert and self-controlled. (alert: watchful) **7.** Those who sleep do so at night, and those who are drunk are drunk at night. (drunk: intoxicated) **8.** But we belong to the day, so let's stay sober, putting on faith and love as protection and the hope of salvation as a helmet. (sober: clear-minded) **9.** God has not chosen us for wrath, but for salvation through our Lord Jesus Christ, (wrath: punishment) **10.** Who died for us, so that whether we are awake or asleep, we may live together with Him. (awake: alive) **11.** So encourage each other and build one another up, just as you are doing now. (encourage: support) **12.** We ask you, brothers, to recognize those who labor among you, those who lead you in the Lord and instruct you, (instruct: teach) **13.** Show them the utmost respect and love for their work, and live in peace with each other. (respect: honor) **14.** We urge you, brothers, to warn those who are idle, encourage the fainthearted, support the weak, and be patient with everyone. (fainthearted: discouraged) **15.** Make sure no one repays wrong with wrong, but always strive to do what is good for one another and for all people. (strive: aim) **16.** Rejoice always. (rejoice: celebrate) **17.** Never stop praying. (praying: interceding) **18.** Give thanks in every situation, for this is God's will for you in Christ Jesus. (thanks: gratitude) **19.** Do not stifle the Spirit. (stifle: suppress) **20.** Do not dismiss prophecies. (dismiss: reject) **21.** Test everything and hold on to what is good. (test: examine) **22.** Stay away from every form of evil. (stay away: avoid) **23.** May the God of peace sanctify you completely, and may your spirit, soul, and body remain blameless until the coming of our Lord Jesus Christ. (sanctify: purify) **24.** The One who has called you is faithful, and He will bring it to pass. (faithful: trustworthy) **25.** Brothers, pray for us. (pray: intercede) **26.** Greet all the brothers with a holy kiss. (greet: welcome) **27.** I urge you before the Lord to have this letter read to all the holy brothers.

(urge: request) **28.** May the grace of our Lord Jesus Christ be with you. Amen. (grace: favor).

53 – 2 Thessolonians
Chapter 1
1. Paul, Silvanus, and Timothy to the church of the Thessalonians in God our Father and the Lord Jesus Christ. (Thessalonians: Believers of the Christ.) **2.** Grace and peace to you from God our Father and the Lord Jesus Christ. (Grace: Favor, Peace: Harmony.) **3.** We always thank God for you, brothers, as it is right, because your faith is growing abundantly, and your love for each other is increasing. (Faith: Trust in God, Charity: Love.) **4.** We boast of you in the churches of God because of your patience and faith during your persecutions and trials. (Patience: Endurance, Faith: Trust in God.) **5.** This is evidence of God's righteous judgment, that you may be counted worthy of God's kingdom, for which you suffer. (Worthy: Deserving.) **6.** It is right for God to repay trouble to those who trouble you. (Repay: Reward or punish.) **7.** And to you who are troubled, rest with us when the Lord Jesus is revealed from heaven with his mighty angels. (Rest: Peace, Revealed: Made known.) **8.** In flaming fire, taking vengeance on those who do not know God and do not obey the gospel of Jesus Christ. (Vengeance: Punishment.) **9.** They will be punished with eternal destruction, away from the presence of the Lord and the glory of His power. (Destruction: Loss, Glory: Majesty.) **10.** When He comes to be glorified in His saints and admired by all who believe, because our testimony among you was believed. (Glorified: Honored, Saints: Holy ones.) **11.** We always pray for you that God would make you worthy of His calling, fulfilling the good pleasure of His goodness, and empowering the work of your faith. (Worthy: Deserving, Calling: God's invitation.) **12.** That the name of our Lord Jesus Christ may be glorified in you, and you in Him, according to God's grace. (Glorified: Honored.)

Chapter 2
1. We ask you, brothers, by the coming of our Lord Jesus Christ and our gathering together to Him, (Coming: Jesus' return, Gathering: The believers' reunion with Christ.) **2.** Do not be quickly shaken in mind or troubled, whether by spirit, word, or letter supposedly from us, claiming that the day of Christ has already come. (Shaken: Disturbed, Troubled: Upset.) **3.** Let no one deceive you, for that day will not come unless the rebellion happens first, and the man of sin is revealed, the son of perdition (perdition: destruction, Rebellion: falling away.) **4.** He will oppose and exalt himself above everything that is called God or worshiped, even sitting in the temple of God, proclaiming himself to be God. (Exalted: Lifted up, Proclaiming: Claiming.) **5.** Do you not remember that I told you these things when I was still with you? (Remembrance: Paul's prior teaching.) **6.** And now you know what restrains him, so that he may be revealed in his time. (Restrains: Something holding back his revelation.) **7.** The mystery of iniquity (evil) is already at work, but the one who is currently holding it back will continue until he is removed. (Mystery of iniquity: Hidden evil plans.) **8.** Then the lawless one (the Antichrist) will be revealed, whom the Lord will destroy with the breath of His mouth and the brightness of His coming. (Lawless one: The Antichrist, Destroy: Overcome completely.) **9.** The Antichrist's coming will be in Satan's power, with all kinds of signs, wonders, and lies. (Satan's power: Evil and deceitful works.) **10.** He will deceive those who are perishing because they rejected the love of the truth and did not accept salvation. (Deceive: Lead into error.) **11.** Therefore, God will send them strong delusion, allowing them to believe what is false, (Delusion: Misleading belief.) **12.** So that they will be condemned for not believing the truth and taking pleasure in unrighteousness. (Condemned: Judged for their rejection of truth.) **13.** But we give thanks to God always for you, because He has chosen you for salvation, through sanctification by the Spirit and belief in the truth. (Sanctification: Being set apart for God's purpose.) **14.** God called you through our gospel, to obtain the glory of our Lord Jesus Christ. (Glory: Honor and praise.) **15.** Therefore, stand firm, and hold on to the traditions we taught you, whether by word or letter. (Traditions: Teachings we've passed on.) **16.** May our Lord Jesus Christ and God the Father, who loved us and gave us eternal comfort and good hope through grace, (Eternal comfort: Hope that lasts forever.) **17.** Comfort your hearts and strengthen you in every good word and work. (Strengthen: Encourage and support.)

Chapter 3
1. Finally, brothers, pray for us, that the gospel may spread and be honored as it is among you. **2.** Pray we're delivered from wicked, faithless men. (Wicked: Evil.) **3.** The Lord is faithful; He will strengthen and protect you. **4.** We trust you'll obey the things we command. **5.** May the Lord guide your hearts into God's love and patient waiting for Christ. **6.** We command you in Christ's name to avoid any brother living unruly and not following the traditions we've taught. (Unruly: Disorderly.) **7.** You know how to follow our example, for we lived properly among you. **8.** We didn't take anyone's bread

without paying; we worked hard to avoid being a burden. **9.** We had the right to ask for help, but we worked to set an example for you. **10.** We told you: if anyone won't work, they shouldn't eat. **11.** We hear some of you are idle, not working but meddling in others' business. (Idle: Lazy, Meddling: Interfering.) **12.** We command and encourage them to work quietly and provide for themselves. **13.** Don't grow weary in doing good. (Weary: Tired.) **14.** If anyone doesn't obey these instructions, avoid them, so they'll feel ashamed. **15.** Yet don't treat them as an enemy, but warn them as a brother. **16.** May the Lord of peace give you peace at all times and in every way. **17.** This is Paul's signature, which I write in every letter to prove it's from me. **18.** The grace of our Lord Jesus Christ be with you all. Amen.

54 – 1 Timmothy
Chapter 1
1. Paul, an apostle of Jesus Christ by God's command, our Savior, and the Lord Jesus Christ, our hope. (Apostle: Messenger.) **2.** To Timothy, my true son in the faith: grace, mercy, and peace from God our Father and Jesus Christ our Lord. (Grace: Unearned favor.) **3.** I urged you to remain in Ephesus when I left for Macedonia, to warn certain people not to teach false doctrines. (Doctrine: Belief system.) **4.** Avoid myths and endless genealogies, which cause more confusion than growth in faith. (Genealogy: Family history.) **5.** The goal of our command is love from a pure heart, a clear conscience, and genuine faith. (Conscience: Inner moral sense.) **6.** Some have strayed from these, turning to meaningless talk. (Strayed: Gone off course.) **7.** They desire to be teachers of the law, but they don't understand what they're saying or what they're affirming. (Affirming: Confirming as true.) **8.** We know the law is good if used properly. (Law: Set of rules.) **9.** It is not for the righteous but for the lawless and disobedient, the ungodly, and sinners, the unholy, and profane, for murderers, (Profane: Disrespectful.) **10.** the sexually immoral, slave traders, liars, perjurers, and anyone contrary to sound doctrine. (Perjurers: Liars under oath.) **11.** This is in line with the glorious gospel of the blessed God, entrusted to me. (Gospel: Good news of Christ.) **12.** I thank Christ Jesus our Lord, who gave me strength, considering me faithful, and appointed me to His service. (Appointed: Assigned a role.) **13.** I was once a blasphemer, persecutor, and violent man, but I received mercy because I acted in ignorance and unbelief. (Blasphemer: One who insults God.) **14.** The grace of our Lord overflowed with faith and love in Christ Jesus. (Overflowed: Poured out abundantly.) **15.** This is a trustworthy saying: Christ Jesus came into the world to save sinners, of whom I am the worst. (Trustworthy: Reliable.) **16.** But for this reason, I received mercy, so that in me Christ Jesus might display His immense patience as an example to those who would believe and receive eternal life. (Immense: Huge.) **17.** Now to the King eternal, immortal, invisible, the only wise God, be honor and glory forever and ever. Amen. (Immortal: Deathless.) **18.** I give you this charge, Timothy, based on the prophecies spoken over you, that you may fight the good fight, (Charge: Formal instruction.) **19.** holding on to faith and a good conscience, which some have rejected, leading to their shipwrecked faith. (Shipwrecked: Ruined.) **20.** Among them are Hymenaeus and Alexander, whom I've handed over to Satan to learn not to blaspheme. (Blaspheme: Insult God.)

Chapter 2
1. I urge, first of all, that supplications, prayers, intercessions, and thanksgiving be made for everyone. (Supplications: earnest requests) **2.** For kings and all those in authority, that we may lead peaceful, godly, and honest lives. (Authority: power over others) **3.** This is good and pleasing in the sight of God our Savior. (Pleasing: satisfactory) **4.** Who desires all people to be saved and to come to the knowledge of the truth. (Desires: strongly wants) **5.** There is one God, and one mediator between God and men, the man Christ Jesus. (Mediator: reconciler) **6.** Who gave Himself as a ransom for all, to be proclaimed in due time. (Ransom: payment for freedom) **7.** For this, I was appointed a preacher and an apostle (I speak the truth in Christ, and lie not), a teacher of the Gentiles in faith and truth. (Apostle: one sent) **8.** Therefore, I want men everywhere to pray, lifting holy hands, without anger or doubt. (Anger: strong displeasure) **9.** Similarly, women should dress modestly, with decency and self-control, not with braided hair, gold, pearls, or expensive clothes. (Modestly: humbly) **10.** But, with good works, as befits women who profess godliness. (Befits: is suitable for) **11.** Let a woman learn in quietness and full submission. (Submission: yielding to authority) **12.** I do not permit a woman to teach or have authority over a man, but to be in quietness. (Authority: power to control) **13.** For Adam was formed first, then Eve. (Formed: created) **14.** And Adam was not deceived, but the woman, being deceived, fell into transgression. (Transgression: violation) **15.** Yet, she will be saved through childbearing if they continue in faith, love, and holiness with self-control. (Self-control: restraint)

Chapter 3
1. This is a trustworthy saying: if anyone desires the office of a bishop, he desires a noble task. (Bishop: church overseer) **2.** A bishop must be blameless, the husband of one wife, vigilant, sober, respectable, hospitable, and able to teach. (Vigilant: watchful) **3.** Not given to wine, not violent, not greedy for dishonest gain, but gentle, not quarrelsome, not materialistic. (Quarrelsome: prone to arguing) **4.** He must manage his own household well, with children under control and dignified. (Dignified: respectful) **5.** (If a man doesn't know how to manage his own household, how can he take care of the church of God?) (Manage: control) **6.** He must not be a recent convert, or he may become proud and fall into the devil's condemnation. (Novice: inexperienced) **7.** He must also have a good reputation with outsiders, so he doesn't fall into disgrace and the devil's trap. (Reputation: how others see someone) **8.** Similarly, deacons must be worthy of respect, not deceitful, not given to much wine, and not greedy for dishonest gain. (Deceitful: dishonest) **9.** They must hold the deep truths of the faith with a clear conscience. (Conscience: inner sense of right and wrong) **10.** They must first be tested, and then, if found blameless, serve as deacons. (Tested: examined) **11.** Their wives must also be dignified, not slanderers, sober, and trustworthy in all things. (Slanderers: those who spread false information) **12.** Deacons must be the husband of one wife and manage their children and households well. (Manage: oversee) **13.** Those who serve well as deacons earn a good standing and great confidence in the faith in Christ Jesus. (Confidence: trust) **14.** I write these things to you, hoping to come to you soon. (Hope: desire) **15.** But if I am delayed, you will know how to behave in the house of God, which is the church of the living God, the pillar and foundation of the truth. (Foundation: core) **16.** Without question, great is the mystery of godliness: God was revealed in the flesh, justified in the Spirit, seen by angels, preached among the nations, believed on in the world, and taken up in glory. (Mystery: something hidden)

Chapter 4
1. The Spirit clearly says that in the later times, some will abandon the faith, following deceiving spirits and teachings of demons. (Deceiving: misleading) **2.** They will lie hypocritically, having their consciences seared as with a hot iron. (Hypocritically: pretending beliefs they do not truly hold) **3.** They will forbid marriage and demand abstinence from certain foods, which God created to be received with thanksgiving by those who believe and know the truth. (Abstinence: refraining) **4.** For everything God created is good, and nothing should be rejected if received with thanksgiving. (Rejected: dismissed) **5.** It is consecrated by God's word and prayer. (Consecrated: made sacred) **6.** If you remind the brethren of these things, you will be a good minister of Jesus Christ, nourished in the words of faith and sound doctrine. (Nourished: spiritually strengthened) **7.** Reject profane and old wives' tales, and instead train yourself in godliness. (Profane: disrespectful) **8.** Physical training has some value, but godliness is valuable for everything, promising benefits for this life and the next. (Godliness: living according to God's will) **9.** This is a trustworthy saying and deserves full acceptance. (Trustworthy: reliable) **10.** We work and suffer disgrace because we have put our hope in the living God, who is the Savior of all men, especially those who believe. (Disgrace: shame) **11.** Command and teach these things. (Command: instruct) **12.** Let no one look down on your youth, but set an example for believers in speech, conduct, love, faith, and purity. (Despise: treat with disrespect) **13.** Until I come, focus on reading, exhortation, and teaching. (Exhortation: urging strongly) **14.** Do not neglect the gift within you, which was given by prophecy when the elders laid hands on you. (Neglect: fail to care for) **15.** Reflect on these things, devote yourself to them, so that your progress may be evident to everyone. (Devote: give attention to) **16.** Watch your life and doctrine closely; persevere in them, for by doing so you will save both yourself and your hearers. (Persevere: continue firmly)

Chapter 5
1. Don't harshly rebuke an elder; treat him like a father, and younger men as brothers. (Rebuke: To criticize or reprimand sharply) **2.** Regard older women as mothers and younger ones as sisters, with complete purity. (Purity: Freedom from immorality or corruption) **3.** Show respect to widows who are truly in need. (Widows: Women whose husbands have died) **4.** If a widow has children or grandchildren, they should care for her, repaying their parents, as it pleases God. **5.** A true widow, left alone, relies on God and prays continually. **6.** But a widow living in pleasure is spiritually dead. (Pleasure: Self-indulgent enjoyment) **7.** Instruct them on these matters to keep them blameless. (Blameless: Free from guilt or wrongdoing) **8.** Anyone who doesn't care for their family has denied the faith and is worse than an infidel. (Infidel: A person who does not believe in religion or faith) **9.** A widow under Threescore and married to more than one man shouldn't be included in the list. (Threescore: Sixty) **10.** She should be known for good works, raising children, hosting strangers, serving the saints, and helping the needy. (Saints:

Devout or holy people) **11.** Don't enroll younger widows; their desires may lead them away from Christ into marriage. (Enroll: To officially register or admit) **12.** They face Damnation for abandoning their prior faith. (Damnation: Condemnation to eternal punishment) **13.** They become idle, gossiping and meddling in matters they shouldn't. (Idle: Avoiding work; lazy) **14.** Younger women should marry, raise children, manage homes, and avoid giving adversaries a reason to accuse. (Adversaries: Opponents or enemies) **15.** Some have already strayed to follow Satan. (Strayed: Wandered from the right path or direction) **16.** Believing men or women should care for their widows so the church can relieve those truly in need. (Relieve: To provide help or assistance) **17.** Elders who lead well deserve double honor, especially those teaching the word. (Elders: older individuals) **18.** As Scripture says, "Don't muzzle the ox while it treads grain," and, "A worker deserves their pay." (Muzzle: A device that prevents eating or speaking) **19.** Don't accept accusations against elders without two or three witnesses. (Accusations: Claims of wrongdoing or misconduct) **20.** Publicly correct those who sin so others may fear. (Sin: Acts against divine law or morality) **21.** In God's presence, keep these instructions without partiality or favoritism. (Partiality: Unfair bias or preference) **22.** Don't hastily appoint anyone or share in others' sins; remain pure. (Hastily: Done quickly without careful consideration) **23.** Stop drinking only water; use a little wine for your stomach and frequent infirmities. (Infirmities: Weaknesses or illnesses) **24.** Some sins are obvious and lead to judgment, while others are hidden. (Judgment: The act of forming decisions or conclusions) **25.** Likewise, good deeds are often evident, and even those that aren't can't remain hidden. (Evident: Clearly seen or understood)

Chapter 6
1. Servants must honor their masters to keep God's name and doctrine from being blasphemed. (Blasphemed: Spoken of disrespectfully) **2.** Those with believing masters shouldn't despise them but serve faithfully, as they are beloved. Teach these principles. (Despise: Look down on or scorn) **3.** Anyone who teaches contrary to wholesome, godly doctrine rejects the words of Christ. (Doctrine: A set of beliefs or teachings) **4.** Such a person is proud, ignorant, and focused on disputes, leading to envy, strife, and evil thoughts. (Strife: Conflict or fighting) **5.** These corrupt men, void of truth, argue perversely, thinking godliness is a means to gain—avoid them. (Perversely: In a stubborn or unreasonable way) **6.** True wealth lies in godliness combined with contentment. (Contentment: Satisfaction with what one has) **7.** We came into the world with nothing, and we'll leave with nothing. **8.** If we have food and raiment, we should be content. (Raiment: Clothing) **9.** Those who seek riches fall into temptation and harmful desires, leading to ruin. **10.** The love of money causes evil, making some stray from faith and suffer sorrows. **11.** Man of God, flee these desires and pursue righteousness, faith, love, patience, and meekness. (Meekness: Gentle, humble nature) **12.** Fight the good fight of faith, hold on to eternal life, and stay true to your profession of faith. (Profession: A declaration of belief or faith) **13.** In God's sight, quickeneth all things, and before Christ, who testified before Pilate, I command you. (Quickeneth: Brings to life or revives) **14.** Keep this command spotless and unrebukeable, until Christ appears. (Unrebukeable: Beyond criticism or fault) **15.** At the right time, Christ will reveal the blessed and potentate, King of kings and Lord of lords. (Potentate: A supreme ruler) **16.** He alone is immortal, living in unapproachable light, unseen by anyone. (Immortal: The state of living forever) **17.** Tell the rich not to be highminded or trust uncertain wealth but trust God, who gives abundantly. (Highminded: Arrogantly proud) **18.** Encourage them to do good, be rich in deeds, and share generously. **19.** By doing so, they secure a solid foundation for eternal life. (Foundation: A base or groundwork for something) **20.** Timothy, guard what's entrusted to you. Avoid godless chatter and contradictions of false knowledge. **21.** Some, professing this false knowledge, have strayed from faith. Grace be with you. Amen.

55 – 2 Timothy
Chapter 1
1. Paul, an apostle of Jesus Christ by God's will, called to the promise of life in Christ Jesus. (apostle: messenger) **2.** To Timothy, my dear son: Grace, mercy, and peace from God the Father and Christ Jesus our Lord. (mercy: compassion) **3.** I thank God, whom I serve with a clear conscience, as my ancestors did, remembering you in my prayers day and night. (conscience: sense of right and wrong) **4.** I long to see you, recalling your tears, so I may be filled with joy. (recalling: remembering) **5.** I am reminded of your sincere faith, which first lived in your grandmother Lois and mother Eunice, and now lives in you. (sincere: genuine) **6.** I encourage you to rekindle God's gift in you, given through the laying on of my hands. (rekindle: revive) **7.** For God gave us a spirit not of fear but of power, love, and sound judgment. (judgment: ability to make decisions) **8.** So don't be ashamed of the Lord's testimony or of me, His prisoner. Share in suffering for the gospel by God's power. (testimony: evidence or declaration) **9.** He saved us and called us to a holy life, not because of our works, but by His purpose and grace, given in Christ before time began. (grace: unearned favor) **10.** Now revealed through Jesus Christ, our Savior, who destroyed death and brought eternal life through the gospel. (eternal: everlasting) **11.** I was appointed a preacher, apostle, and teacher to the Gentiles. (Gentiles: non-Jewish people) **12.** For this reason, I suffer but am not ashamed, for I know whom I trust, and I'm sure He'll guard what I've entrusted to Him until that day. (entrusted: given responsibility for) **13.** Hold on to the sound teachings you've heard from me, grounded in faith and love in Christ Jesus. (grounded: based on) **14.** Guard the treasure entrusted to you through the Holy Spirit dwelling in us. (dwelling: living) **15.** You know that everyone in Asia has deserted me, including Phygellus and Hermogenes. (deserted: abandoned) **16.** May the Lord show mercy to Onesiphorus' household, for he often refreshed me and wasn't ashamed of my chains. (refreshed: encouraged or comforted) **17.** When in Rome, he searched hard for me and found me. (searched: looked thoroughly) **18.** May the Lord grant him mercy on that day. You know how much he helped me in Ephesus. (grant: give or allow)

Chapter 2
1. So, my son, be strong in the grace that is in Christ Jesus. (grace: unearned favor) **2.** What you've heard from me in the presence of many witnesses, entrust to reliable men who will be able to teach others. (entrust: give responsibility to) **3.** Endure hardship like a good soldier of Jesus Christ. (endure: withstand or bear) **4.** A soldier doesn't get involved in civilian affairs but focuses on pleasing the one who enlisted him. (civilian: non-military) **5.** An athlete isn't crowned unless he competes according to the rules. (crowned: awarded) **6.** The hard-working farmer should be the first to enjoy the crops. (hard-working: diligent) **7.** Reflect on what I say, and may the Lord give you understanding. (reflect: think deeply) **8.** Remember Jesus Christ, the descendant of David, raised from the dead according to my gospel. (descendant: offspring) **9.** I suffer for it, even to the point of imprisonment, but God's word is never chained. (chained: restricted) **10.** I endure all things for the sake of the elect, that they may receive the salvation in Christ Jesus with eternal glory. (elect: chosen ones) **11.** This is a trustworthy saying: If we die with Him, we will also live with Him. (trustworthy: reliable) **12.** If we endure, we will reign with Him; if we deny Him, He will deny us. (reign: rule) **13.** Even if we are faithless, He remains faithful; He cannot deny Himself. (faithless: lacking faith) **14.** Remind them of these things, urging them not to argue over words, which is useless and leads to the ruin of the hearers. (ruin: destruction) **15.** Do your best to present yourself to God as one approved, a worker who doesn't need to be ashamed, rightly handling the word of truth. (approved: accepted) **16.** Avoid godless chatter, for it will lead to more ungodliness. (godless: lacking reverence for God) **17.** Their talk will spread like cancer, among them are Hymenaeus and Philetus. (cancer: destructive growth) **18.** They have deviated from the truth, claiming that the resurrection has already happened, and they are destroying the faith of some. (deviated: strayed) **19.** But God's firm foundation stands with this seal: "The Lord knows those who are His," and, "Let everyone who calls on the name of the Lord turn away from sin." (seal: confirmation or mark) **20.** In a large house, there are not only vessels of gold and silver, but also of wood and clay, some for noble purposes, some for ignoble. (vessels: containers) **21.** If a person cleanses themselves from dishonorable things, they will be a vessel for honorable use, set apart, useful to the master, and ready for every good work. (cleanses: purifies) **22.** Flee youthful desires and pursue righteousness, faith, love, and peace, along with those who call on the Lord with a pure heart. (flee: run away from) **23.** Avoid foolish and ignorant disputes, as they only lead to quarrels. (disputes: arguments) **24.** And the Lord's servant must not quarrel, but be kind to everyone, able to teach, and patient. (quarrel: fight or argue) **25.** Gently instruct those who oppose themselves, in hope that God will grant them repentance leading to the knowledge of the truth. (repentance: regret for wrongdoings) **26.** And that they may escape the devil's trap, having been held captive by him to do his will. (captive: imprisoned)

Chapter 3
1. But know this: In the last days, difficult times will come. (difficult: challenging) **2.** People will be lovers of themselves, greedy, boastful, proud, blasphemers, disobedient to parents, ungrateful, and unholy. (blasphemers: those who speak disrespectfully about God) **3.** They will be without love, unforgiving, slanderers, without self-control, cruel, and haters of what is good. (slanderers: those who spread false information) **4.** They will be traitors, reckless, conceited, lovers of pleasure rather than lovers of God. (traitors: those who betray trust) **5.** They will have a form of godliness but deny its power. Stay away from such people. (form: outward appearance) **6.**

They are the ones who sneak into homes and capture weak women burdened with sins and led astray by various desires. (burdened: weighed down) **7.** Always learning but never able to come to the knowledge of the truth. (knowledge: understanding) **8.** Just as Jannes and Jambres opposed Moses, these men oppose the truth, their minds corrupt and their faith worthless. (corrupt: morally wrong) **9.** But they won't get far, for their folly will be evident to everyone, just as it was with them. (folly: foolishness) **10.** You, however, have fully known my teaching, conduct, purpose, faith, patience, love, and endurance, (conduct: behavior) **11.** including the persecutions and sufferings I faced in Antioch, Iconium, and Lystra. Yet, the Lord delivered me from them all. (persecutions: mistreatment for beliefs) **12.** Yes, everyone who desires to live godly in Christ Jesus will suffer persecution. (desires: wants) **13.** But evil men and impostors will go from bad to worse, deceiving and being deceived. (impostors: deceivers) **14.** Continue in the things you have learned and are convinced of, knowing those from whom you learned them. (convinced: fully persuaded) **15.** And from childhood, you have known the sacred Scriptures, which are able to make you wise for salvation through faith in Christ Jesus. (sacred: holy) **16.** All Scripture is God-breathed and useful for teaching, rebuking, correcting, and training in righteousness, (rebuking: criticizing or correcting) **17.** so that the servant of God may be thoroughly equipped for every good work. (equipped: prepared)

Chapter 4
1. I charge you before God and the Lord Jesus Christ, who will judge the living and the dead at His appearing and His kingdom. (charge: command) **2.** Preach the word; be ready in season and out of season; correct, rebuke, and encourage with patience and teaching. (rebuke: criticize or correct) **3.** The time will come when they will not tolerate sound doctrine, but will gather teachers who satisfy their own desires, having itching ears. (doctrine: teaching or beliefs) **4.** They will turn away from the truth and follow myths. (myths: false stories) **5.** Be watchful in all things, endure hardship, do the work of an evangelist, and fully carry out your ministry. (evangelist: preacher of the gospel) **6.** I am ready to be poured out, and my departure is near. (poured out: offered as a sacrifice) **7.** I have fought the good fight, finished the race, and kept the faith. (faith: trust or belief in God) **8.** Now there is a crown of righteousness laid up for me, which the Lord, the righteous judge, will give me on that day, and not only to me but to all who love His appearing. (righteousness: moral rightness) **9.** Do your best to come to me soon. (best: greatest effort) **10.** For Demas has deserted me, loving the present world, and has gone to Thessalonica. Crescens went to Galatia, and Titus to Dalmatia. (deserted: abandoned) **11.** Only Luke is with me. Bring Mark with you, for he is useful to me in ministry. (useful: helpful) **12.** I have sent Tychicus to Ephesus. (sent: dispatched) **13.** When you come, bring the cloak I left at Troas with Carpus, and the books, especially the parchments. (cloak: outer garment) **14.** Alexander the coppersmith did me much harm. May the Lord repay him for his actions. (repay: compensate or punish) **15.** Be on guard against him, as he strongly opposed our message. (guard: protect) **16.** At my first defense, no one stood with me; everyone deserted me. I pray that God does not hold it against them. (defense: legal argument) **17.** But the Lord stood by me and gave me strength, so that through me the message might be fully proclaimed, and all the Gentiles might hear. I was rescued from the lion's mouth. (proclaimed: announced publicly) **18.** The Lord will deliver me from every evil attack and bring me safely to His heavenly kingdom. To Him be glory forever and ever. Amen. (deliver: save or rescue) **19.** Greet Prisca and Aquila, and the household of Onesiphorus. (greet: send regards to) **20.** Erastus stayed in Corinth, and I left Trophimus sick at Miletus. (stayed: remained) **21.** Do your best to come before winter. Eubulus, Pudens, Linus, Claudia, and all the brethren send their greetings. (brethren: fellow believers) **22.** The Lord Jesus Christ be with your spirit. Grace be with you. Amen. (grace: unearned favor)

56 – 2 Titus
Chapter 1
1. Paul, a servant of God, and an apostle of Jesus Christ, according to the faith of God's elect, and the acknowledging of the truth which is after godliness; (Acknowledging: acceptance) **2.** In hope of eternal life, which God, that cannot lie, promised before the world began; (Eternal life: everlasting life) **3.** Hath manifested his word through preaching, committed unto me by the commandment of God our Saviour; (Manifested: revealed, committed: entrusted) **4.** To Titus, my son in the common faith: Grace, mercy, and peace, from God the Father and Jesus Christ our Saviour. (Common faith: shared faith) **5.** For this cause left I thee in Crete, to set in order the things that are lacking, and ordain elders in every city, as I appointed thee: (Lacking: missing) **6.** If any be blameless, the husband of one wife, having faithful children not accused of disorderly conduct. (Blameless: without fault, disorderly conduct: unruly behavior) **7.** For a bishop must be blameless, as God's steward; not self-willed, not soon angry, not given to wine, no striker, not greedy for money; (Steward: caretaker, self-willed: stubborn, striker: violent, greedy for money: dishonest) **8.** But a lover of hospitality, good men, sober, just, holy, temperate; (Hospitality: kindness to strangers, sober: clear-headed, temperate: self-controlled) **9.** Holding fast the faithful word as taught, able to exhort and convince the opposers. (Exhort: encourage, opposers: those who argue against) **10.** For many are unruly, vain talkers, and deceivers, especially those of the circumcision: (Unruly: disorderly, vain talkers: empty speakers, circumcision: Jews) **11.** Whose mouths must be stopped, who subvert whole households, teaching things they should not, for dishonest gain. (Subvert: undermine, dishonest gain: wrongful profit) **12.** One of their own prophets said, The Cretians are always liars, evil beasts, lazy gluttons. (Gluttons: overeaters) **13.** This is true. Rebuke them sharply, so they may be sound in the faith; (Rebuke: correct strongly, sound: healthy) **14.** Not giving heed to Jewish myths and commandments of men that turn from the truth. (Myths: fables) **15.** To the pure, all things are pure; but to the defiled and unbelieving, nothing is pure; even their minds and consciences are defiled. (Defiled: polluted, unbelieving: faithless) **16.** They profess to know God, but in works deny him, being abominable, disobedient, and unfit for every good work. (Profess: claim, abominable: detestable, unfit: unqualified)

Chapter 2
1. Speak things that align with sound doctrine. **2.** Teach older men to be sober, serious, self-controlled, faithful, loving, and patient. **3.** Teach older women to be holy, not slanderers, not addicted to wine, and to teach good things. (slanderers: false accusers) **4.** They should teach younger women to be sober, love their husbands and children, **5.** be sensible, pure, good homemakers, and obedient to their husbands, so God's word isn't dishonored. (sensible: wise) **6.** Encourage young men to be self-controlled. **7.** Be an example of good works, with purity, seriousness, and honesty in teaching. **8.** Speak with integrity so no one can criticize you, and your opponents will be ashamed. (integrity: honesty) **9.** Teach slaves to obey their masters, pleasing them in everything, not talking back, **10.** not stealing but showing full faithfulness, so they make God's teaching attractive. **11.** God's grace has appeared, bringing salvation to all people, **12.** teaching us to reject sin and live self-controlled, righteous, and godly lives. **13.** We await the blessed hope and the glorious return of Jesus Christ, (blessed hope: joyful expectation) **14.** who gave Himself to redeem us from sin and purify for Himself a special people, eager for good works. (redeem: rescue) **15.** Speak, encourage, and correct with authority—don't let anyone disregard you.

Chapter 3
1. Remind them to submit to rulers and authorities, to obey magistrates, and to be ready for good works. **2.** Speak no evil of anyone, be peaceful, gentle, and show humility to everyone. (peaceful: calm) **3.** We ourselves were once foolish, disobedient, deceived, living in lusts and pleasures, full of malice, envy, and hatred. **4.** But when the kindness and love of God appeared, **5.** not because of our righteous deeds, but because of His mercy, He saved us, through the washing of regeneration and renewal by the Holy Spirit; (regeneration: spiritual rebirth) **6.** whom He poured out on us richly through Jesus Christ, our Savior. **7.** Having been justified by His grace, we are heirs to the hope of eternal life. **8.** This is a trustworthy saying, and I want you to affirm these things, so believers will be careful to devote themselves to good works. These are profitable for people. **9.** Avoid foolish debates, genealogies, arguments, and disputes over the law, for they are unprofitable and useless. **10.** Reject a divisive person after one or two warnings. **11.** Knowing such a person is perverted and sinful, condemning themselves. (perverted: misguided) **12.** When I send Artemas or Tychicus, make every effort to come to me at Nicopolis, for I have decided to winter there. **13.** Help Zenas the lawyer and Apollos on their journey, providing everything they need. **14.** Let our people learn to devote themselves to good works for necessary tasks, so they are not unfruitful. **15.** All who are with me send greetings. Greet those who love us in the faith. Grace be with you all. Amen.

57 - 2 Philemon
Chapter 1
1. Paul, a prisoner of Jesus Christ, and Timothy, our brother, to Philemon, our beloved fellow laborer, **2.** and to Apphia, Archippus, and the church in your house: **3.** Grace and peace to you from God our Father and the Lord Jesus Christ. **4.** I thank God, mentioning you in my prayers, **5.** hearing of your love and faith toward Jesus and all saints, **6.** that your faith may become effective by acknowledging every good thing in you in Christ. **7.** We have great joy in your love, for the hearts of the saints are refreshed by you. (love for the hearts: affections) **8.** Though I could command you, **9.** I appeal to you for love's sake, I, Paul, an old man and prisoner of Christ. **10.** I appeal for my son Onesimus, whom I have fathered in my chains: (fathered: begotten) **11.** once unprofitable to you, now profitable to both of us. (unprofitable: useless,

profitable: useful) **12.** I send him back; receive him as you would me. **13.** I would have kept him to serve me in your place, **14.** but I didn't want to do anything without your consent, that it be voluntary, not forced. **15.** Perhaps he was separated from you for a while to receive him forever, (separated: parted) **16.** not as a servant, but a beloved brother. (beloved: dear) **17.** If you consider me a partner, receive him as you would me. (partner: companion) **18.** If he has wronged you or owes you anything, charge it to my account. (wronged: hurt) **19.** I, Paul, have written this with my own hand: I will repay it. **20.** Yes, brother, let me have joy from you in the Lord. Refresh my heart in Christ. (joy: delight) **21.** Confident you will obey, I wrote to you, knowing you will do even more. (obey: comply) **22.** Prepare a guest room for me, as I hope to be restored to you through your prayers. (Prepare: make ready, restored: returned) **23.** Epaphras, my fellow prisoner in Christ, greets you, **24.** as do Marcus, Aristarchus, Demas, and Luke, my fellow workers. **25.** The grace of the Lord Jesus Christ be with your spirit. Amen. (grace: favor)

58 – Hebrews
Chapter 1

1. God spoke in various ways through the prophets in the past. (Prophets: messengers of God) **2.** In these final days, He speaks through His Son, who is the heir of all things and the creator of the worlds. (Heir: someone who inherits; Creator: one who makes) **3.** The Son reflects God's glory, His exact likeness, and sustains all things with His powerful word. After cleansing our sins, He sat at the right hand of God. (Glory: God's divine presence; Right hand: position of honor) **4.** The Son is superior to angels, having inherited a more excellent name. (Superior: better, higher status) **5.** To which angel did God ever say, "You are my Son, today I have begotten you," or, "I will be a Father to him, and he will be my Son"? (Begotten: unique son ship of Christ; Father: Creator, protector) **6.** When He brings His firstborn into the world, He commands all the angels to worship Him. (Firstborn: the first child or creation) **7.** He makes His angels spirits and His ministers a flame of fire. (Ministers: servants or helpers) **8.** But to the Son, God says, "Your throne, O God, is eternal, and righteousness rules Your kingdom." (Throne: seat of authority or power; Righteousness: moral correctness) **9.** You love righteousness and hate wickedness, so God has anointed You with joy above all others. (Anointed: chosen and blessed by God) **10.** You, Lord, laid the earth's foundation in the beginning, and the heavens are the work of Your hands. (Foundation: base or starting point) **11.** They will perish, but You remain; they will age like a garment. (Perish: be destroyed or come to an end; Garment: clothing) **12.** Like clothing, You will fold them up, and they will change, but You remain the same, and Your years will never end. (Fold up: roll or gather up) **13.** To which angel did God ever say, "Sit at My right hand until I make Your enemies a footstool"? (Footstool: something to rest feet on, symbolizing submission) **14.** Aren't the angels ministering spirits sent to serve those who will inherit salvation? (Ministering: serving or helping; Salvation: deliverance from sin or danger)

Chapter 2

1. We must pay careful attention to what we've heard, so we don't drift away. (Drift away: to lose focus or fall into error) **2.** If the word delivered by angels was reliable and every disobedience was justly rewarded, (Angels: spiritual beings messengers of God) **3.** how can we escape if we neglect such great salvation, first spoken by the Lord and confirmed by those who heard Him? (Salvation: deliverance from sin and its consequences) **4.** God also testified through signs, wonders, miracles, and gifts of the Holy Spirit, as He willed. (Holy Spirit: God's presence and power in the world) **5.** The angels were not given dominion over the world to come, which we speak of. (Dominion: control or authority) **6.** But one has testified, "What is man that You are mindful of him? Or the son of man, that You care for him?" (Son of man: a title referring to humans or Jesus Christ) **7.** You made him a little lower than the angels, crowned him with glory and honor, and gave him authority over Your works. (Glory: great beauty or splendor) **8.** You put all things under his feet; nothing is left out, though we do not yet see all things subject to him. (Subject to: under the control or influence of) **9.** But we see Jesus, made lower than the angels for a time, crowned with glory and honor, that He, by God's grace, might taste death for everyone. (Grace: unearned favor or kindness from God) **10.** It was fitting for Him, through whom and for whom all things exist, to make the captain of our salvation perfect through suffering. (Captain: leader or guide; Salvation: deliverance from sin) **11.** Both the sanctifier and those sanctified are one, and so He is not ashamed to call them brothers, (Sanctifier: the one who makes holy) **12.** saying, "I will declare Your name to my brothers, and praise You among the congregation." (Congregation: a group of people gathered for religious worship) **13.** He also says, "I will trust in Him," and, "Here am I and the children God has given me." (Trust: reliance on someone or something) **14.** Since the children share in flesh and blood, He also shared in them, to destroy the devil, who holds the power of death, (Devil: the evil one, Satan) **15.** and to free those who, through fear of death, were in lifelong bondage. (Bondage: slavery or being trapped) **16.** He did not take the nature of angels, but the seed of Abraham. (Seed of Abraham: descendants of Abraham, a patriarch of Israel) **17.** In all things, He was made like His brothers, to be a merciful and faithful high priest, making reconciliation for the people's sins. (High priest: a religious leader who mediates between people and God) **18.** Because He Himself suffered and was tempted, He is able to help those who are tempted. (Tempted: tested or led into sin)

Chapter 3

1. Therefore, brothers and sisters, who share in the heavenly calling, consider Jesus, our Apostle and High Priest. (Apostle: a messenger of God; High Priest: a spiritual leader in ancient Israel) **2.** He was faithful to God, just as Moses was faithful in his role. (Moses: a key leader in Israel's history) **3.** Jesus deserves more honor than Moses, as the builder of a house has more glory than the house itself. (Glory: honor and praise) **4.** Every house has a builder, but God is the Creator of all things. (Creator: God as the origin of all life and existence) **5.** Moses was faithful as a servant in God's house, foreshadowing what was to come. (Servant: one who serves God; God's house: His people or temple) **6.** Christ, as the Son over His house, is the one we belong to if we remain confident and hopeful to the end. (Son: a position of authority, in contrast to a servant) **7.** As the Holy Spirit says, "Today, if you hear His voice, **8.** do not harden your hearts, as during the rebellion in the wilderness, (Wilderness: the desert area where the Israelites wandered after leaving Egypt) **9.** when your ancestors tested Me, despite seeing My works for forty years. (Ancestors: forebears, those who came before) **10.** I was displeased with that generation and said, 'They always go astray in their hearts and don't know My ways.' (Generation: the people living in the wilderness at the time) **11.** So, I swore, 'They will never enter My rest.'" (Rest: the promised land of peace, where God's people find reward) **12.** Be careful, brothers and sisters, that none of you has an unbelieving heart that turns away from the living God. (Unbelieving: lacking faith in God) **13.** Encourage each other daily to prevent being hardened by sin's deceit. (Deceit: the misleading nature of sin) **14.** We share in Christ if we hold firmly to our confidence until the end. (Share: to participate in; Confidence: trust in God's promises) **15.** As it's said, "Today, if you hear His voice, do not harden your hearts, as in the rebellion." (Harden: to refuse to listen or obey) **16.** Some provoked Him, but not all who left Egypt with Moses. (Egypt: the land where Israel was enslaved before the Exodus) **17.** With whom was He displeased for forty years? Was it not with those who sinned and whose bodies fell in the wilderness? (Wilderness: the desert area where Israel wandered) **18.** And to whom did He swear they wouldn't enter His rest, except those who did not believe? (Swear: to make an oath or promise) **19.** Therefore, they couldn't enter due to their unbelief. (Unbelief: lack of faith in God's promises)

Chapter 4

1. Let us fear, lest a promise remains for us to enter His rest, and we fall short of it. (Rest: spiritual peace or salvation) **2.** The gospel was preached to us as to them, but it did not benefit them because they did not mix it with faith. (Gospel: good news about Jesus Christ) **3.** We who believe enter His rest, as He swore in His anger, "They shall not enter My rest," even though the works were finished from the world's foundation. (Rest: spiritual peace or salvation) **4.** He spoke of the seventh day, saying, "God rested on the seventh day from all His works." (Seventh day: the Sabbath, day of rest in the Bible) **5.** And again, He says, "They shall not enter My rest." (Rest: spiritual peace or salvation) **6.** Some must still enter, but those who first heard did not, due to unbelief. (Unbelief: lack of faith) **7.** Again, He limits a day, saying through David, "Today, after so long, if you hear His voice, do not harden your hearts." (David: King of Israel, a prominent biblical figure) **8.** If Jesus had given them rest, He would not have spoken of another day. (Jesus: the central figure of Christianity) **9.** There remains a rest for the people of God. (Rest: spiritual peace or salvation) **10.** Whoever enters His rest ceases from their own works, just as God did from His. (Works: efforts or deeds) **11.** Let us strive to enter that rest, lest we fall into unbelief. (Rest: spiritual peace or salvation) **12.** The word of God is alive, powerful, sharper than any sword, dividing soul and spirit, joints and marrow, and discerning thoughts and intents. (Word of God: the teachings or message of the Bible) **13.** No creature is hidden from His sight; all are naked and open before Him. (Creatures: living beings; sight: perception or vision) **14.** Since we have a great high priest, Jesus the Son of God, let us hold firm to our faith. (High priest: spiritual leader in Judaism) **15.** Our high priest can sympathize with our weaknesses, having been tempted like us, yet without sin. (Tempted: tested or enticed to do wrong; sin: immoral act) **16.** Let us boldly approach the throne of grace to receive mercy and find grace in our time of need. (Throne of grace: the place where God's mercy is offered; mercy: compassion and forgiveness)

Chapter 5

1. Every high priest chosen from among men is appointed to serve in matters of God, offering gifts and sacrifices for sins. (High priest: a religious leader in Judaism) **2.** He can sympathize with the ignorant and straying, since he too is subject to weakness. (Ignorant: lacking knowledge, Straying: wandering off the right path) **3.** Therefore, he must offer sacrifices for both the people and himself. (Sacrifices: offerings made to God) **4.** No one takes this honor upon themselves, but only those called by God, as Aaron was. (Aaron: Moses' brother, first high priest of Israel) **5.** Likewise, Christ did not glorify Himself as high priest, but was called by God, who said, "You are my Son; today I have begotten You." (Christ: Jesus Christ, Son of God, Begotten: generated or created by God) **6.** He is also declared a priest forever, in the order of Melchizedek. (Melchizedek: a king and priest in the Bible, a mysterious figure) **7.** In His earthly life, He offered prayers and supplications, crying out to God who could save Him from death, and was heard because of His reverence. (Supplications: earnest requests or prayers, Reverence: deep respect or honor) **8.** Though He was the Son, He learned obedience through His suffering. (Obedience: following the will of God, Suffering: enduring pain or hardship) **9.** Having been perfected, He became the source of eternal salvation for those who obey Him. (Perfected: made complete or flawless, Eternal salvation: everlasting deliverance from sin) **10.** He was called by God as a high priest in the order of Melchizedek. (See verse 6 for Melchizedek) **11.** We have much to say about this, but it is hard to explain because you are slow to understand. (Slow to understand: lacking understanding or wisdom) **12.** By now, you should be teachers, but you need someone to teach you the basic principles of God's word. You are still like infants, needing milk, not solid food. (Basic principles: foundational teachings, Infants: young children, Milk: simple teachings) **13.** Those who drink milk are unskilled in the word of righteousness; they are still babies. (Unskilled: lacking experience or skill, Word of righteousness: teachings about what is right in God's eyes) **14.** But solid food is for the mature, those who, by practice, have trained their senses to distinguish good from evil. (Solid food: deeper or more advanced teachings, Mature: fully grown in faith, Distinguish: recognize the difference)

Chapter 6

1. Let us move beyond the basic teachings of Christ and strive for maturity, not repeatedly laying the foundation of repentance from dead works and faith in God. (Repentance: turning away from sin) **2.** This includes the teachings on baptism, laying on of hands, resurrection, and eternal judgment. (Baptism: Christian ritual of immersion in water; Resurrection: rising from the dead) **3.** We will do this if God allows. (God: the supreme being in Christianity) **4.** It is impossible to renew to repentance those who, having received the light, tasted the heavenly gift, and shared in the Holy Spirit, (Holy Spirit: God's presence in the world) **5.** Who have experienced God's word and the powers of the age to come, (The age to come: the future, especially in Christian theology) **6.** If they fall away, since they crucify the Son of God again and shame Him publicly. (Son of God: Jesus Christ) **7.** The earth that receives rain and produces useful crops is blessed by God, (Crops: plants grown for food) **8.** But that which bears thorns and thistles is rejected and near to being burned. (Thorns: sharp, pointed growths on plants; Thistles: prickly plants) **9.** We are confident of better things for you, things that accompany salvation. (Salvation: deliverance from sin and its consequences) **10.** God will not forget your labor of love, shown by your service to the saints. (Saints: holy people, especially those revered in Christianity) **11.** We desire each of you to show the same diligence, ensuring full assurance of hope to the end. (Diligence: careful and persistent work) **12.** Be not lazy, but follow those who, through faith and patience, inherit the promises. (Promises: God's commitments to His people) **13.** When God made a promise to Abraham, He swore by Himself, since there is no greater. (Abraham: the patriarch of the Jewish, Christian, and Islamic faiths) **14.** He promised, "I will bless you and multiply you." (Bless: to provide with divine favor) **15.** After enduring patiently, Abraham obtained the promise. (Enduring: lasting through difficulty) **16.** Men swear by the greater, and an oath ends all dispute. (Oath: a solemn vow) **17.** To show the unchangeability of His purpose, God confirmed His promise with an oath. (Unchangeability: unalterable, fixed) **18.** By two unchangeable things, in which it is impossible for God to lie, we have strong consolation, having fled to the hope set before us. (Consolation: comfort or encouragement) **19.** This hope is an anchor for the soul, sure and steadfast, entering the inner sanctuary. (Anchor: a device used to secure a ship; Inner sanctuary: the innermost part of the temple, a holy place) **20.** Jesus has entered ahead of us as the high priest forever, in the order of Melchizedek. (Jesus: the central figure of Christianity; Melchizedek: a king and priest mentioned in the Bible)

Chapter 7

1. Melchisedec, king of Salem and priest of the Most High God, met Abraham returning from the defeat of the kings and blessed him. (Melchisedec: a king and priest in the Bible; Salem: an ancient city, later known as Jerusalem) **2.** Abraham gave him a tenth of all; his name means King of Righteousness, and he is also King of Peace. (Tenth: a tenth part; Righteousness: the quality of being morally right or just) **3.** He had no father, mother, or genealogy, no beginning or end of life, made like the Son of God, and remains a priest forever. (Genealogy: family lineage; Son of God: a title for Jesus) **4.** Consider how great this man was, to whom even Abraham gave a tenth of the spoils. (Spoils: the goods or profits gained in battle) **5.** The sons of Levi, who receive the priesthood, are commanded to take tithes from their brethren, though they are descendants of Abraham. (Levi: one of the twelve tribes of Israel; Tithes: a tenth of earnings given to religious leaders) **6.** But Melchisedec, whose lineage is not counted from them, received tithes from Abraham and blessed him with the promises. (Lineage: ancestry or family descent; Promises: blessings made by God) **7.** Without doubt, the lesser is blessed by the greater. (Lesser: the one of lower rank) **8.** Here, men who die receive tithes, but there he receives them, being testified as living. (Testified: witnessed or proven) **9.** Levi, who receives tithes, paid tithes through Abraham. (Levi: the ancestor of the Levitical priests) **10.** For Levi was in Abraham's loins when Melchisedec met him. (Loins: the part of the body around the hips, used in reference to descendants) **11.** If the Levitical priesthood brought perfection, why was another priest needed, after Melchisedec's order, not Aaron's? (Levitical priesthood: the priesthood belonging to the tribe of Levi; Aaron: the brother of Moses, the first high priest) **12.** When the priesthood is changed, the law must change also. (Priesthood: the office or duties of a priest) **13.** The one spoken of belongs to another tribe, of which no one served at the altar. (Tribe: a group of people descended from a common ancestor) **14.** It is clear that Jesus came from Judah, of which Moses spoke nothing regarding priesthood. (Judah: one of the twelve tribes of Israel) **15.** It is more evident that another priest arises, like Melchisedec. (Arises: appears or comes into being) **16.** He is made not by the law of a fleshly commandment, but by the power of an endless life. (Fleshly: physical or earthly; Endless life: eternal life) **17.** God testified, "You are a priest forever after the order of Melchisedec." (Testified: declared or affirmed; Order: rank or system) **18.** The old commandment was set aside for its weakness and inefficiency. (Commandment: a divine rule or law; Inefficiency: lack of effectiveness) **19.** The law made nothing perfect, but a better hope brings us closer to God. (Hope: a belief in a better future; Closer: nearer in relationship) **20.** And He was made priest with an oath, unlike others. (Oath: a solemn promise) **21.** The priests were made without an oath, but this one, with an oath from God, "You are a priest forever." (Priests: religious leaders; Oath: a solemn promise) **22.** By this, Jesus became the guarantor of a better covenant. (Guarantor: someone who promises to fulfill something; Covenant: a sacred agreement or promise) **23.** There were many priests, because they were not able to continue due to death. (Priests: religious leaders; Continue: last or remain in office) **24.** But this priest, because He lives forever, has an unchangeable priesthood. (Unchangeable: not able to be altered) **25.** Therefore, He is able to save completely those who come to God through Him, since He lives forever to intercede for them. (Intercede: to act as a mediator or advocate) **26.** Such a high priest is fitting for us, holy, blameless, separate from sinners, and exalted above the heavens. (Blameless: without fault; Exalted: raised to a higher status) **27.** He does not need to offer sacrifices daily, as the other high priests do, for He offered Himself once for all. (Sacrifices: offerings made to God) **28.** The law appoints men with weaknesses as priests, but the oath made the Son, consecrated forever. (Consecrated: made holy or sacred; Oath: a solemn promise)

Chapter 8

1. The sum of what we've spoken is this: We have a high priest, seated at the right hand of the throne of the Majesty in heaven. (High priest: a religious leader in Judaism; Majesty in heaven: refers to God's royal presence) **2.** He is a minister of the sanctuary, the true tabernacle made by the Lord, not man. (Sanctuary: a sacred place; Tabernacle: a portable dwelling place for God used by the Israelites) **3.** Every high priest must offer gifts and sacrifices, so it's necessary for this priest to have something to offer. (Gifts and sacrifices: offerings made to God as acts of worship) **4.** If he were on earth, he wouldn't be a priest, since there are priests offering gifts according to the law. (Law: the religious laws of the Old Testament, especially the Mosaic Law) **5.** They serve as examples and shadows of heavenly things, as Moses was warned to make the tabernacle according to the pattern shown to him. (Moses: a prophet and leader of the Israelites; Tabernacle: the holy place built for God's presence) **6.** He now has a superior ministry, being the mediator of a better covenant, established on better promises. (Mediator: one who acts as an intermediary; Covenant: a formal agreement or promise, in this case, between God and His people) **7.** If the first covenant had been perfect, there would have been no need for a second. (Covenant: a sacred agreement or pact; First and second: referring to the Old and New Covenants) **8.** For he finds fault with them and says, "The days will come when I will make a new covenant with Israel and Judah." (Israel and Judah: two ancient kingdoms of the Israelites; New covenant: God's new promise with His people) **9.** This covenant won't be like the one made when I led them out of Egypt, as they didn't continue in it, and I disregarded them. (Egypt: the ancient kingdom where the Israelites were enslaved; Covenant: God's agreement with His people) **10.** I will put my laws in their minds and hearts; I will be their God, and they will be my people. (Laws: God's commandments; People: refers to the Israelites or believers) **11.** They won't need to teach each other to know the Lord, for all will know me, from the least to the greatest. (Lord: God; Least to greatest: all people, regardless of status) **12.** I will be merciful to their wrongdoings and remember their sins no more. (Merciful: showing compassion; Wrongdoings: sins or offenses) **13.** By declaring a new covenant, He has made the first obsolete, and what is fading away is ready to vanish. (Obsolete: no longer in use; Fading away: becoming outdated or no longer relevant)

Chapter 9

1. The first covenant had divine ordinances and a worldly sanctuary. (Covenant: a formal agreement) **2.** The first tabernacle had a candlestick, a table, and the shewbread, called the sanctuary. (Tabernacle: a portable sanctuary used by the Israelites) **3.** After the second veil, the tabernacle called the Holiest of all. (Veil: a curtain or divider in the temple) **4.** It had the golden censer, the ark of the covenant covered in gold, with manna, Aaron's rod, and the tablets of the covenant. (Censer: a container for burning incense; Ark of the Covenant: a sacred chest containing the tablets of the law) **5.** The cherubims overshadowed the mercy seat, which we cannot detail now. (Cherubims: angelic beings; Mercy seat: the lid of the Ark of the Covenant) **6.** The priests entered the first tabernacle regularly to perform the service of God. (Priests: religious leaders in the temple) **7.** The high priest entered the second tabernacle once a year, with blood for himself and the people's sins. (High priest: the chief religious leader) **8.** The Holy Spirit signified that the way to the holiest was not yet revealed, while the first tabernacle stood. (Holy Spirit: God's presence and power) **9.** The first tabernacle was a symbol, offering gifts and sacrifices that could not perfect the conscience. (Conscience: inner sense of right and wrong) **10.** It consisted of food, drinks, washings, and carnal ordinances, until the time of reformation. (Carnal ordinances: physical rituals or laws) **11.** Christ came as a high priest of good things, entering a greater, perfect tabernacle, not made with hands. (Christ: the anointed one, referring to Jesus) **12.** He entered with His own blood, obtaining eternal redemption for us. (Redemption: the act of being saved from sin) **13.** The blood of bulls and goats sanctified the flesh, purifying the unclean. (Sanctified: made holy or set apart) **14.** How much more will Christ's blood, offered through the eternal Spirit, purify our consciences from dead works to serve the living God? (Eternal Spirit: God's unchanging presence) **15.** Christ is the mediator of the new covenant, offering death for the redemption of transgressions, granting eternal inheritance. (Mediator: one who stands between two parties; Transgressions: sins or wrongdoings) **16.** A testament requires the death of the testator. (Testament: a will or covenant; Testator: the one who makes the will) **17.** A testament is valid only after the testator's death. (Valid: legally acceptable) **18.** The first covenant was dedicated with blood. (Dedicated: consecrated or sanctified) **19.** Moses spoke every precept to the people, then sprinkled the book, the people, and the tabernacle with the blood of calves and goats. (Precept: a command or instruction) **20.** He declared, "This is the blood of the covenant God enjoined to you." (Enjoined: instructed or commanded) **21.** He also sprinkled the tabernacle and all the ministry vessels with blood. (Ministry vessels: sacred objects used in religious ceremonies) **22.** Almost all things are purified with blood, and without it, there is no remission. (Remission: forgiveness or cancellation of sins) **23.** It was necessary for the heavenly things to be purified with better sacrifices. (Heavenly things: spiritual realities or divine things) **24.** Christ entered heaven itself to appear before God for us. (Heaven: the dwelling place of God) **25.** He does not offer Himself often, like the high priest, with the blood of others. (High priest: the chief priest in the temple) **26.** If He had to suffer repeatedly, He would have done so since the foundation of the world, but now He appeared to take away sin by His sacrifice. (Foundation of the world: the beginning of creation) **27.** It is appointed for men to die once, then judgment. (Appointed: destined or determined) **28.** Christ was offered once to bear the sins of many; He will appear a second time for salvation to those waiting for Him. (Salvation: deliverance from sin and its consequences)

Chapter 10

1. The law is a mere shadow of the good things to come, not the reality, and can never make those who offer sacrifices perfect. (Law: the Old Testament laws) **2.** If it could, sacrifices would have ceased, for those who are cleansed once would no longer have a consciousness of sin. (Sacrifices: ritual offerings) **3.** But with those sacrifices, sins are remembered every year. (Sins: wrongdoings) **4.** The blood of bulls and goats is incapable of removing sins. (Bulls and goats: animals used in sacrifices) **5.** When He entered the world, He said, "You did not desire sacrifices, but prepared a body for Me." (Christ: Jesus Christ) **6.** You took no delight in burnt offerings or sin offerings. (Burnt offerings: sacrifices completely burned) **7.** Then I said, "Here I am, to do Your will, O God, as it is written in the Scriptures about Me." (Will: God's plan for Jesus) **8.** He said, "You did not desire sacrifices, which are commanded by the law." (Law: the Mosaic law) **9.** He came to fulfill God's will, putting aside the old system to establish a new one. (First: the Old Covenant, Second: the New Covenant) **10.** Through that will, we are sanctified by the offering of Jesus Christ once and for all. (Sanctified: made holy) **11.** Every priest stands day after day, offering the same sacrifices, which can never take away sins. (Priest: religious leader) **12.** But this man, after offering Himself as a sacrifice for sin once and for all, sat down at God's right hand. (Right hand: a position of power) **13.** From that time, He waits for His enemies to be made His footstool. (Footstool: a symbol of victory over enemies) **14.** By His one sacrifice, He has made perfect forever those who are being sanctified. (Perfected: made complete) **15.** The Holy Spirit also testifies to us, saying, (Holy Spirit: the third person of the Trinity) **16.** "This is the covenant I will make with them, I will write My laws on their hearts and minds." (Covenant: an agreement with God) **17.** "And I will remember their sins no more." (Sins: moral wrongdoings) **18.** When there is forgiveness for sins, no more sacrifice is needed for sin. (Remission: forgiveness) **19.** Therefore, brothers, we have confidence to enter the Most Holy Place by the blood of Jesus, (Brothers: fellow believers, Most Holy Place: the Holy of Holies) **20.** by a new and living way He opened for us through His flesh, (Flesh: body, New and living way: a fresh approach to God) **21.** and having a high priest over God's house. (High priest: chief religious leader) **22.** Let us approach with a sincere heart, full of faith, having our hearts cleansed from a guilty conscience, and our bodies washed with pure water. (Guilty conscience: a feeling of guilt) **23.** Let us hold unswervingly to the hope we profess, for He who promised is faithful. (Profession: declaration of belief) **24.** Let us consider how we may spur one another on toward love and good deeds, (Spur: encourage, Good deeds: righteous actions) **25.** not neglecting to meet together, as some are in the habit of doing, but encouraging one another, and all the more as you see the day approaching. (Meet together: gather for worship, Day: the return of Christ) **26.** If we deliberately sin after receiving the knowledge of the truth, there is no longer any sacrifice for sin, (Deliberately: intentionally, Truth: the gospel) **27.** but only a fearful expectation of judgment and fiery wrath, which will consume God's enemies. (Wrath: divine anger) **28.** Anyone who rejected Moses' law died without mercy under two or three witnesses. (Moses: the leader and lawgiver) **29.** How much more severe do you think the punishment will be for those who reject the Son of God, treat His sacrifice as unholy, and insult the Spirit of grace? (Son of God: Jesus Christ, Spirit of grace: the Holy Spirit) **30.** For we know God has said, "Vengeance is Mine, I will repay," and "The Lord will judge His people." (Vengeance: divine retribution) **31.** It is a terrifying thing to fall into the hands of the living God. (Living God: the true and active God) **32.** But recall the former days, when after you were enlightened, you endured a great struggle with sufferings, (Enlightened: spiritually awakened) **33.** partly while you were publicly exposed to reproach and suffering, and partly while you shared in the suffering of others. (Reproach: public shame) **34.** You sympathized with me in my imprisonment and joyfully accepted the confiscation of your property, knowing you have a better and lasting possession in heaven. (Imprisonment: being in jail, Confiscation: taking away) **35.** So do not throw away your confidence, for it will be richly rewarded. (Confidence: trust in God's promises) **36.** You need to persevere so that when you have done the will of God, you will receive what He has promised. (Persevere: endure patiently) **37.** For in just a little while, He who is coming will come and will not delay. (Delay: take longer) **38.** But the righteous will live by faith, and if anyone shrinks back, I will not be pleased with them. (Righteous: just, Faith: trust in God) **39.** But we are not those who shrink back and are destroyed, but those who believe and are saved. (Destroyed: lost forever, Saved: redeemed)

Chapter 11

1. Faith is the assurance of things hoped for, the evidence of things unseen. (Faith: trust in God; Assurance: confidence in what is hoped for) **2.** By it, the elders gained a good reputation. (Elders: respected leaders or ancestors) **3.** Through faith, we understand that God created the worlds, and things visible were made from the invisible. (Worlds: universe; Invisible: unseen) **4.** By faith, Abel offered a better sacrifice than Cain, and through it, he was declared righteous, with God testifying of his gifts. Though dead, he still speaks. (Abel and Cain: sons of Adam and Eve; Righteous: morally right) **5.** By faith, Enoch was taken away to avoid death; he pleased God before his translation. (Enoch: a biblical figure; Translation: being taken to heaven without dying) **6.** Without faith, it's impossible to please God. To approach Him, one must believe He exists and rewards those who seek Him. (Faith: trust; Pleasing: making God happy) **7.** By faith, Noah, warned of things unseen, built an ark to save his family, condemning the world and inheriting righteousness by faith. (Noah: a biblical figure; Ark: a large boat) **8.** By faith, Abraham obeyed God's call to leave for a place he would later inherit, not knowing where he was going. (Abraham: a patriarch in the Bible; Inherit: to receive by inheritance) **9.** He lived in tents with Isaac and Jacob, heirs of the same promise. (Isaac and Jacob: Abraham's sons; Heirs: those who inherit) **10.** He sought a city with foundations, built by God. (City: a place of eternal home; Foundations: the base or origin) **11.** By faith, Sarah received strength to conceive, judging God faithful who had promised. (Sarah: Abraham's wife; Conceive: to become pregnant) **12.** From one man, nearly dead, came countless descendants, as numerous as the stars and sand. (Descendants: offspring; Stars and sand: representing many) **13.** All these died in faith, not having received the promises but seeing them afar off, embracing them as strangers on earth. (Strangers: foreign to this world; Promises: God's future blessings) **14.** Those who speak this way seek a homeland. (Homeland: their true, heavenly home) **15.** Had they remembered their former country, they might have returned. (Former country: the land they left) **16.** Now they desire a better, heavenly country, and God is proud to be called their God, having prepared a city for them. (Heavenly: eternal home with God; City: symbolic of the future divine home) **17.** By faith, Abraham offered Isaac, his only son, whom God promised to bless. (Isaac: Abraham's son; Only son: unique and precious) **18.** God promised that Isaac's descendants would be the chosen line. (Descendants: children and future generations) **19.** Abraham believed God could raise Isaac from the dead, and in a sense, he received him back. (Raise: bring back to life; Received back: figurative for restoring his son) **20.** By faith, Isaac blessed Jacob and Esau concerning future events. (Jacob and Esau: Isaac's sons; Blessed: gave blessings or prophecies) **21.** By faith, Jacob, near death, blessed Joseph's sons and worshiped leaning on his staff. (Jacob: Isaac's son; Joseph: Jacob's son, a key figure in Egypt) **22.** By faith, Joseph spoke of the Israelites' exodus and instructed them concerning his bones. (Exodus: departure of Israelites from Egypt) **23.** By faith, Moses' parents hid him for three months, not fearing the king's command. (Moses: a leader of the Israelites; King's command: the Pharaoh's order to kill Hebrew infants) **24.** By faith, Moses, when grown, refused to be called Pharaoh's daughter. (Pharaoh: the king of Egypt) **25.** He chose to suffer with God's people rather than enjoy the fleeting pleasures of sin. (Fleeting: temporary; Pleasures of sin: sinful enjoyments) **26.** He considered the reproach of Christ greater riches than the treasures of Egypt, focused on the eternal reward. (Reproach: shame or disgrace; Egypt: the ancient kingdom) **27.** By faith, he left Egypt, undeterred by the king's wrath, enduring because he saw the invisible God. (Wrath: anger; Endured: persisted through trials) **28.** By faith, he kept the Passover, protecting the firstborn from death. (Passover: Jewish festival celebrating God's protection in Egypt) **29.** By faith, Israel crossed the Red Sea as though on dry land, while the Egyptians drowned. (Red Sea: the sea separating Egypt and Israel; Israel: the descendants of Jacob) **30.** By faith, the walls of Jericho fell after being surrounded for seven days. (Jericho: an ancient city in Canaan) **31.** By faith, Rahab, the prostitute, spared the spies and was not destroyed with the unbelievers. (Rahab: a woman in Jericho who helped Israelite spies) **32.** And what more shall I say? Time fails to recount the deeds of Gideon, Barak, Samson, Jephthah, David, Samuel, and the prophets. (Gideon, Barak, Samson, Jephthah: judges in Israel's history; David: king of Israel) **33.** Through faith, they conquered kingdoms, brought justice, obtained promises, stopped lions' mouths, (Lions' mouths: defeating threats) **34.** quenched fires, escaped the sword, became strong in weakness, valiant in battle, and defeated foreign armies. (Sword: the weapon of war) **35.** Women received their dead back, while others endured torture for a better resurrection. (Resurrection: rising from the dead; Torture: suffering for their faith) **36.** Some faced mockings, scourgings, bonds, and imprisonment. (Scourgings: beatings; Bonds: chains) **37.** They were stoned, sawn in two, tempted, killed by the sword; they lived in poverty and torment, (Stoned: executed by throwing stones) **38.** of whom the world was not worthy, wandering in deserts, mountains, and caves. (Worthy: deserving of respect) **39.** These all, through faith, received a good testimony but did not receive the promise. (Testimony: approval or recognition; Promise: God's future blessings) **40.** God provided something better for us, so that they without us would not be made perfect. (Better: more complete blessing; Perfect: fulfilled purpose)

Chapter 12

1. Since we are surrounded by so many witnesses, let us cast aside every burden and sin, and run with perseverance the race before us. (Witnesses: those who set examples of faith) **2.** Focus on Jesus, the pioneer and perfecter of our faith, who endured the cross, disregarding its shame, and now sits at God's right hand. (Jesus: central figure of Christianity, right hand of God: position of honor) **3.** Reflect on Jesus, who endured opposition from sinners, so you don't grow weary or lose heart. (Opposition: resistance) **4.** You haven't yet struggled to the point of shedding blood against sin. (Struggled: fought, shedding blood: suffering to the point of death) **5.** Forgetting the encouragement: "My son, don't despise the Lord's discipline or lose heart when rebuked." (Discipline: correction, rebuked: reprimanded) **6.** The Lord disciplines those He loves and punishes every son He accepts. (Punishes: corrects, loves: showing care) **7.** If you endure discipline, God treats you as His children. What child is not disciplined? (Endure: accept, children of God: those accepted by God) **8.** If you're without discipline, you are illegitimate, not His children. (Illegitimate: not legitimate, lacking rightful status) **9.** We respected our earthly fathers who disciplined us; shouldn't we submit to the Father of spirits and live? (Father of spirits: God, who is the creator of life) **10.** They disciplined us briefly, but God does so for our benefit, to share in His holiness. (Holiness: moral purity, for our benefit: for our good) **11.** Discipline may seem painful now, but it later brings the peaceful fruit of righteousness to those trained by it. (Righteousness: moral rightness, trained by it: learning through correction) **12.** Strengthen your weak hands and knees; (Weak: feeble, knees: symbol of personal strength) **13.** Make straight paths so that the lame are not disabled but healed. (Lame: unable to walk properly, healed: restored to health) **14.** Pursue peace and holiness, without which no one will see the Lord. (Peace: harmony, holiness: purity) **15.** See that no one misses God's grace, and that no root of bitterness grows, causing trouble and defiling many. (Grace: God's unmerited favor, bitterness: resentment) **16.** Let there be no immoral person like Esau, who traded his birthright for a meal. (Esau: firstborn son of Isaac, birthright: inheritance rights) **17.** He later sought the blessing but was rejected, finding no place for repentance, despite his tears. (Repentance: regret or sorrow, blessing: divine favor) **18.** You haven't come to a mountain with fire, darkness, and a storm, (Mountain: symbol of God's presence, fire: representing God's holiness) **19.** Where a trumpet's blast and voice frightened those who heard it. (Trumpet: announcement of God's presence, voice: divine command) **20.** They couldn't bear the command, "If even an animal touches the mountain, it must be stoned." (Stoned: executed by throwing stones, mountain: a sacred place) **21.** The sight was terrifying; Moses trembled in fear. (Moses: leader of Israel, trembling: shaking with fear) **22.** But you've come to Mount Zion, the city of the living God, the heavenly Jerusalem, and to countless angels in joyful assembly. (Mount Zion: a sacred hill in Jerusalem, heavenly Jerusalem: the ultimate city of God) **23.** To the church of the firstborn, whose names are written in heaven, to God, the Judge of all, and to the spirits of the righteous. (Firstborn: those belonging to God, Judge of all: God) **24.** And to Jesus, the mediator of a new covenant, and to His blood, which speaks a better word than Abel's. (Jesus: the mediator of God's covenant, blood: symbol of Christ's sacrifice) **25.** Don't refuse Him who speaks. If they didn't escape when they rejected Him on earth, we surely won't escape if we turn from Him in heaven. (Refuse: reject, warned: cautioned) **26.** His voice once shook the earth, and now He promises to shake both earth and heaven. (Shook: caused to tremble, heaven: the celestial realm) **27.** "Once more" indicates the removal of what can be shaken, so that what remains is unshakable. (Shaken: altered or destroyed, unshakable: cannot be moved) **28.** Since we are receiving an unshakable kingdom, let us serve God with reverence and awe. (Kingdom: God's eternal reign, reverence: deep respect) **29.** For our God is a consuming fire. (Consuming fire: a metaphor for God's power and holiness)

Chapter 13

1. Let brotherly love continue. **2.** Don't forget to entertain strangers, as some have unknowingly entertained angels. (Angels: divine messengers) **3.** Remember those in bonds and suffering as if you were also in the body. (Bonds: imprisonment or chains) **4.** Marriage is honorable, but God will judge fornicators and adulterers. (Fornicators: those who engage in illicit sexual relations) **5.** Be content with what you have, for God said, "I will never leave you nor forsake you." (Forsake: abandon) **6.** We can boldly say, "The Lord is my helper; I will not fear what man does to me." **7.** Remember those who rule over you, who spoke the word of God. Follow their faith, considering their outcome. (Outcome: result or end) **8.** Jesus Christ is the same yesterday, today, and forever. **9.** Don't be led astray by strange doctrines. It is good for the heart to be established by grace, not foods that didn't benefit those who practiced them. (Doctrines: beliefs or teachings) **10.** We have an altar, and those who serve the tabernacle have no right to eat from it. (Tabernacle: a portable sanctuary in the Old Testament) **11.** The bodies of the beasts whose blood the high priest brings into the sanctuary for sin are burned outside the camp. (Beasts: animals; Sanctuary: holy place) **12.** Jesus, to sanctify the people with His own blood, suffered outside the gate. (Sanctify: to make holy or pure) **13.** Let us go to Him outside the camp, bearing His reproach. (Reproach: disgrace or shame) **14.** We seek a city to come, for we have no lasting city here. (City: a permanent place or home) **15.** Offer the sacrifice of praise to God continually, giving thanks to His name. **16.** Do good and share; these sacrifices please God. **17.** Obey those who rule over you, for they watch over your souls, and it's unprofitable for you if they do so with grief. (Grief: sorrow or distress) **18.** Pray for us; we trust we have a good conscience, willing to live honestly. (Conscience: moral sense of right and wrong) **19.** I ask that you do this so I can be restored to you sooner. (Restored: brought back or returned) **20.** Now, the God of peace, who brought again from the dead our Lord Jesus, the great shepherd, through the blood of the eternal covenant, (Eternal covenant: everlasting agreement) **21.** Make you perfect in every good work to do His will, pleasing in His sight through Jesus Christ, to whom be glory forever. Amen. (Glory: honor, praise, or worship) **22.** I urge you, brothers, to accept this word of exhortation; I have written briefly. (Exhortation: strong encouragement or urging) **23.** Know that our brother Timothy has been set free; if he comes soon, I will see you. (Timothy: a companion of Paul) **24.** Greet those who rule over you and all the saints. Those from Italy greet you. (Saints: holy or dedicated people) **25.** Grace be with you all. Amen. (Grace: unmerited favor or blessing)

59 – 1 Peter
Chapter 1

1. Peter, an apostle of Jesus Christ, to the scattered believers in Pontus, Galatia, Cappadocia, Asia, and Bithynia, (Pontus, Galatia, Cappadocia, Asia, Bithynia: regions in modern-day Turkey) **2.** Chosen by God's foreknowledge, sanctified by the Spirit for obedience to Christ, with grace and peace multiplied to you. (Sanctified: made holy or set apart for a special purpose) **3.** Praise be to God, who, by His mercy, has given us new birth into a living hope through the resurrection of Jesus Christ, (Mercy: compassion or forgiveness shown toward someone) **4.** To an imperishable inheritance, undefiled, and unfading, kept in heaven for you, (Imperishable: not subject to decay or destruction) **5.** Who are shielded by God's power through faith, ready to be revealed at the last time. (Shielded: protected or guarded) **6.** In this, you rejoice, though now, for a time, you may suffer various trials, (Trials: tests or challenges) **7.** That the trial of your faith, more precious than gold, may result in praise and glory at the appearing of Jesus Christ. (Faith: trust or belief in something or someone) **8.** Though you have not seen Him, you love Him; though you do not see Him now, you believe and rejoice with inexpressible joy, (Inexpressible: too great to be expressed in words) **9.** Receiving the outcome of your faith, the salvation of your souls. (Salvation: deliverance from sin and its consequences) **10.** The prophets inquired and searched carefully about this salvation, (Prophets: people chosen by God to deliver His messages) **11.** Wondering about the time and the Spirit of Christ within them, revealing the sufferings of Christ and the glory to follow. (Spirit of Christ: the Holy Spirit, God's presence within believers) **12.** It was revealed to them that they were serving not themselves but you, as those who preached the gospel, empowered by the Holy Spirit, with angels longing to understand it. (Gospel: the good news of Jesus Christ) **13.** Therefore, prepare your minds for action, be sober, and set your hope fully on the grace to be brought to you at the revelation of Jesus Christ. (Revelation: the revealing of something previously hidden) **14.** As obedient children, do not conform to your former ignorance, (Conform: to follow or adopt a standard) **15.** But be holy in all you do, just as He who called you is holy, (Holy: sacred, set apart for God's purposes) **16.** For it is written, "Be holy, for I am holy." (Quoted from the Old Testament) **17.** If you call on the Father, who judges impartially, live your lives in reverent fear during your time here, (Impartially: without favoritism) **18.** Knowing that you were not redeemed with perishable things like silver or gold, (Redeemed: bought back or saved from sin) **19.** But with the precious blood of Christ, a lamb without blemish or spot, (Blemish: a flaw or imperfection; Lamb: a symbol of Christ's sacrifice) **20.** Foreordained before the foundation of the world, but revealed in these last times for you, (Foreordained: predetermined, planned beforehand) **21.** Through Him, you believe in God, who raised Him from the dead and gave Him glory, so your faith and hope are in God. (Glory: honor, praise, and worship) **22.** Since you have purified your souls by obeying the truth, love one another deeply from a pure heart, (Purified: made clean, free from sin) **23.** Being born again, not of perishable seed, but of imperishable, through the living and enduring word of God. (Born again: spiritually reborn, a new life in Christ) **24.** For all flesh is like grass, and its glory is like the flower of the grass; the grass withers, and the flower falls, (Flesh: human beings or the physical world) **25.** But the word of the Lord endures forever. And this is the word preached to you through the gospel. (Endures: lasts or persists over time)

Chapter 2

1. Put away malice, deceit, hypocrisy, envy, and evil speaking. (Malice: desire to harm others; Deceit: dishonesty) **2.** Like newborn babies, desire pure spiritual milk to grow in your faith. (Spiritual milk: teachings of the faith) **3.** If you have tasted the Lord's goodness. (Tasted: experienced) **4.** Coming to Him, a living stone rejected by men but chosen and precious to God, (Living stone: symbol of Jesus Christ, who gives life) **5.** You too, as living stones, are being built into a spiritual house, a holy priesthood offering spiritual sacrifices acceptable to God through Jesus. (Spiritual house: the Church; Priesthood: group of people chosen to serve God) **6.** Scripture says, "I lay a precious cornerstone in Zion; whoever believes in Him will not be put to shame." (Zion: Jerusalem or God's chosen place) **7.** To believers, He is precious; to the disobedient, He is the stone rejected by builders, now the cornerstone, (Disobedient: those who refuse to follow) **8.** A stumbling stone and a rock of offense to those who are disobedient to the word. (Stumbling stone: something that causes people to fall, symbolizing Jesus as a point of division) **9.** But you are a chosen people, a royal priesthood, a holy nation, God's special possession, to proclaim His praises who called you out of darkness into His light. (Royal priesthood: a group of people serving God as kings and priests) **10.** Once not a people, now God's people; once without mercy, now have received mercy. (Mercy: compassion or forgiveness) **11.** Dear friends, I urge you to abstain from sinful desires that war against your soul. (Abstain: to refrain from; War: struggle or battle) **12.** Live honorably among Gentiles, so that even if they accuse you, they may glorify God by your good deeds. (Gentiles: non-Jews) **13.** Submit to every human authority for the Lord's sake, whether to the king or governors. (Governors: officials who govern regions) **14.** They are sent to punish wrongdoers and commend those who do right. (Commend: praise or approve) **15.** By doing good, silence the ignorance of foolish people. (Ignorance: lack of knowledge) **16.** Live as free people, but do not use your freedom to cover up evil; live as servants of God. (Servants of God: those who serve God) **17.** Honor everyone, love the brotherhood, fear God, honor the king. (Brotherhood: fellow believers) **18.** Servants, be subject to your masters, both good and harsh. (Masters: those who hold authority over servants or workers) **19.** It is commendable if, for the sake of your conscience, you endure suffering unjustly. (Conscience: inner sense of right and wrong) **20.** If you suffer for doing good and endure it, this pleases God. (Endure: to suffer patiently) **21.** To this you were called, because Christ suffered for you, leaving an example to follow His steps. (Called: chosen by God for a purpose) **22.** He committed no sin, and no deceit was found in His mouth. (Deceit: lying or trickery) **23.** When reviled, He did not revile back; when suffering, He did not threaten, but entrusted Himself to God, the righteous judge. (Reviled: insulted; Entrusted: gave control to) **24.** He bore our sins in His body on the cross, so that we might die to sin and live for righteousness; by His wounds, you were healed. (Bore: carried or took upon Himself; Righteousness: living in right relationship with God) **25.** You were like sheep going astray, but now you have returned to the Shepherd and Overseer of your souls. (Shepherd: leader or guide, referring to Jesus; Overseer: one who watches over)

Chapter 3

1. Wives, be submissive to your husbands, so that even if they don't obey the word, they may be won over by your conduct. (Submissive: yielding to the authority of another; won over: persuaded or converted) **2.** Let them observe your pure and respectful behavior. (Observe: to watch closely) **3.** Don't focus on outward adornment like braided hair, gold jewelry, or fine clothing. (Adorn: to decorate or embellish) **4.** But on the inner beauty of a gentle and quiet spirit, which is valuable to God. (Gentle: calm and kind; Quiet: peaceful) **5.** Holy women in the past, who trusted in God, adorned themselves this way by submitting to their husbands. (Adorned: decorated or enhanced their appearance) **6.** As Sarah obeyed Abraham, calling him lord, you are her daughters if you do good and are not afraid. (Sarah: wife of Abraham, considered a matriarch in Jewish and Christian faiths) **7.** Husbands, live with your wives with understanding, honoring them as the weaker vessel, and as co-heirs of grace, so your prayers are not hindered. (Weaker vessel: a metaphor suggesting physical or emotional frailty) **8.** Finally, be of one mind, compassionate, loving as brothers, humble, and courteous. (Compassionate: showing concern for others; Courteous: polite) **9.** Don't repay evil for evil or insult for insult, but bless others, knowing you are called to inherit a blessing. (Bless: to speak well of or wish good for) **10.** Whoever desires to love life and see good days must keep their tongue from evil and their lips from deceit. (Deceit: dishonesty or trickery) **11.** Let them turn from evil and do good, seek peace and pursue it. (Pursue: to chase or actively seek) **12.** The Lord watches over the righteous and listens to their prayers, but His face is against those who do evil. (Righteous: just, morally right; Evil: wicked or harmful actions) **13.** Who can harm you if you are devoted to doing good? (Devoted: dedicated or committed) **14.** If you suffer for righteousness' sake, you are blessed. Don't fear or be troubled by their threats. (Righteousness: acting in accordance with divine law; Blessed: favored by God) **15.** Sanctify the Lord in your hearts and always be ready to explain the hope within you, with gentleness and respect. (Sanctify: to make holy; Hope: confident expectation) **16.** Keep a good conscience, so that those who falsely accuse you will be ashamed. (Conscience: moral awareness) **17.** It's better, if it's God's will, to suffer for doing good than for doing evil. (Suffer: to endure pain or hardship) **18.** Christ also suffered for sins—the just for the unjust—to bring us to God, being put to death in the flesh but made alive by the Spirit. (Just: righteous; Unjust: wrong or sinful) **19.** Through the Spirit, He preached to the imprisoned spirits, (Spirit: the Holy Spirit) **20.** Who were disobedient during the time of Noah when God patiently waited while the ark was being built, saving only eight people by water. (Noah: a biblical figure who built the ark; Ark: a large boat built by Noah to survive the flood) **21.** Baptism now saves you, not by removing physical dirt, but by appealing to God for a clear conscience, through the resurrection of Jesus Christ. (Baptism: a Christian sacrament of initiation; Resurrection: rising from the dead) **22.** Who has gone into heaven and is at God's right hand, with angels, authorities, and powers subject to Him. (Heaven: the divine realm; Right hand: a position of honor and authority)

Chapter 4
1. Since Christ suffered for us, arm yourselves with the same mindset; those who suffer in the flesh have ceased from sin. (Arm: prepare, Mindset: attitude) **2.** They no longer live for human desires but to do God's will. (Desires: lusts) **3.** Our past life was enough to indulge in the sins of the Gentiles—lasciviousness, lusts, drunkenness, revelries, and idolatry. (Gentiles: non-Jews, Lasciviousness: immoral behavior, Revelries: wild parties) **4.** They are surprised when you don't join them in their excesses and speak evil of you. (Excesses: extreme behaviors) **5.** They will give an account to God, who will judge the living and the dead. (Account: explanation, Judge: decide fate) **6.** The gospel was also preached to the dead, so they may be judged like men in the flesh but live by God's Spirit. (Gospel: good news of Christ, Flesh: physical body) **7.** The end is near; be sober and watchful in prayer. (Sober: clear-minded, Watchful: alert) **8.** Above all, love each other deeply, for love covers a multitude of sins. (Multitude: many) **9.** Show hospitality without complaint. (Hospitality: generosity to guests) **10.** Use your gifts to serve one another as good stewards of God's grace. (Stewards: caretakers, Grace: unearned favor from God) **11.** If you speak, speak as God's words; if you serve, do it with God's strength, so God may be glorified through Jesus Christ. (Glorified: praised) **12.** Do not be surprised by the fiery trials you face. (Fiery: intense, Trials: tests) **13.** Rejoice, because you share in Christ's sufferings and will be glad when His glory is revealed. (Rejoice: be happy, Glory: divine splendor) **14.** If you are insulted for Christ's name, you are blessed, for God's Spirit rests upon you. (Insulted: criticized, Blessed: favored) **15.** Let none suffer as a murderer, thief, evildoer, or meddler. (Meddler: someone who interferes in others' affairs) **16.** If you suffer as a Christian, do not be ashamed, but glorify God in it. (Glorify: honor, Christian: follower of Christ) **17.** Judgment begins with God's house; what will be the outcome for those who do not obey the gospel? (Judgment: God's judgment, House: believers or Church) **18.** If the righteous are scarcely saved, where will the ungodly and sinners appear? (Righteous: those who live rightly, Ungodly: sinful) **19.** Let those who suffer according to God's will entrust their souls to Him in doing good, as to a faithful Creator. (Entrust: commit, Faithful: trustworthy)

Chapter 5
1. I urge the elders among you, who am also an elder and witness to Christ's sufferings, and a sharer in the coming glory: (Elders: leaders in the church; witness: someone who has seen or experienced something firsthand) **2.** Care for God's flock, overseeing them willingly, not for gain, but with a ready mind. (Flock: a group of people, especially a congregation; gain: personal profit) **3.** Don't act as rulers over God's heritage, but be examples to the flock. (Heritage: inheritance or possession of God; examples: role models or guides) **4.** When the Chief Shepherd appears, you will receive an unfading crown of glory. (Chief Shepherd: Jesus Christ, the main leader of the church; crown of glory: a reward of eternal life and honor) **5.** Likewise, submit to the elders, and be humble toward each other, for God resists the proud but gives grace to the humble. (Submit: to yield or surrender; grace: unmerited favor from God) **6.** Humble yourselves under God's mighty hand, so He may lift you up in due time. (Mighty hand: God's powerful control or authority; due time: the right or appointed time) **7.** Cast all your cares on Him, for He cares for you. (Cares: worries or concerns) **8.** Be sober and vigilant; your enemy, the devil, roams like a lion, seeking to devour. (Sober: clear-minded and self-controlled; vigilant: watchful and alert; devil: Satan, the enemy of God and mankind) **9.** Resist him firmly in the faith, knowing that your fellow believers face the same struggles. (Resist: to fight against; firm: steady, strong; faith: belief in God) **10.** The God of all grace, who called you to His eternal glory in Christ, will restore, strengthen, and establish you after you have suffered a while. (Restore: to bring back to a right state; strengthen: to make stronger; establish: to make firm or unshakable) **11.** To Him be glory and dominion forever. Amen. (Glory: praise and honor; dominion: supreme authority) **12.** Through Silvanus, a faithful brother, I have briefly written, urging you and testifying that this is the true grace of God in which you stand. (Silvanus: a Christian companion of Peter, also known as Silas; faithful: loyal and trustworthy) **13.** The church at Babylon, chosen with you, greets you, as does my son Marcus. (Babylon: a city, historically the capital of the Babylonian Empire, here used symbolically for Rome; Marcus: a companion of Peter, also known as Mark) **14.** Greet one another with a kiss of love. Peace to all in Christ. Amen. (Kiss of love: a traditional greeting signifying affection and unity among believers; Peace: a state of harmony, especially in Christ)

60 – 2 Peter
Chapter 1
1. Simon Peter, a servant and apostle of Jesus Christ, to those who share our faith through the righteousness of God and Jesus Christ. (Simon Peter: a disciple of Jesus) **2.** May grace and peace abound through knowing God and Jesus our Lord. **3.** His divine power grants us everything for life and godliness through knowing Him, who called us to glory and virtue. (Divine power: God's supreme authority) **4.** He has given us great promises, enabling us to share in His divine nature and escape worldly corruption caused by lust. **5.** Be diligent to add virtue to faith, knowledge to virtue, (Virtue: moral excellence) **6.** temperance to knowledge, patience to temperance, godliness to patience, (Temperance: self-control) **7.** brotherly kindness to godliness, and love to brotherly kindness. **8.** If these qualities abound in you, they will make you fruitful in the knowledge of Jesus Christ. (Fruitful: productive in spiritual growth) **9.** Lacking these traits shows blindness and forgetfulness of being cleansed from past sins. **10.** Be diligent to confirm your calling and election, and you will not stumble. (Election: God's choice of believers) **11.** In this way, you will receive a rich welcome into the eternal kingdom of our Lord and Savior Jesus Christ. (Eternal kingdom: God's everlasting reign) **12.** I will always remind you of these truths, even though you know them and are grounded in them. (Grounded: firmly established) **13.** As long as I live, I will stir you to remember them. (Stir: encourage or awaken) **14.** I know my earthly life will soon end, as Jesus Christ has revealed to me. (Earthly life: mortal existence) **15.** I will ensure you can recall these things after my departure. (Departure: death or leaving this life) **16.** We did not follow myths but were eyewitnesses of Jesus Christ's majesty. (Myths: false stories or fables) **17.** He received honor and glory from God when the voice declared, "This is My beloved Son, in whom I am well pleased." (Beloved Son: Jesus Christ) **18.** We heard this voice from heaven while with Him on the holy mountain. (Holy mountain: Mount of Transfiguration) **19.** We have the reliable prophetic word, a light in darkness, until the day dawns and Christ shines in your hearts. (Prophetic word: inspired message from God) **20.** Understand that no prophecy in Scripture is of private interpretation. (Private interpretation: one's personal understanding) **21.** Prophecy did not originate from human will but from men moved by the Holy Spirit. (Holy Spirit: God's spirit guiding believers)

Chapter 2
1. False prophets arose among the people, just as false teachers will secretly introduce destructive heresies, even denying the Lord, bringing swift destruction upon themselves. (Heresies: beliefs contrary to Christian doctrine) **2.** Many will follow their destructive ways, causing the truth to be maligned. (Maligned: spoken about in a harmful way) **3.** Through greed and deceptive words, they will exploit you; their judgment is certain, and their destruction does not delay. (Exploit: take advantage of) **4.** God did not spare sinful angels but cast them into hell, bound in darkness for judgment. (Hell: place of punishment) **5.** He did not spare the ancient world but saved Noah, a preacher of righteousness, when He brought the flood on the ungodly. (Noah: biblical figure who built the ark) **6.** He condemned Sodom and Gomorrah, reducing them to ashes as an example for the ungodly. (Sodom and Gomorrah: ancient cities destroyed for sin) **7.** Yet, He rescued righteous Lot, distressed by the wickedness around him. (Lot: nephew of Abraham in the Bible) **8.** Lot's righteous soul was tormented daily by the lawless deeds he witnessed and heard. (Tormented: deeply troubled) **9.** The Lord knows how to deliver the godly from trials and reserve the unrighteous for punishment on the Day of Judgment. (Judgment Day: time of divine reckoning) **10.** This especially applies to those who indulge in lust and despise authority; they are arrogant, self-willed, and unafraid to slander celestial beings. (Celestial

beings: angels or divine entities) **11.** Even angels, greater in might and power, do not bring slanderous accusations before the Lord. (Slanderous: falsely damaging one's reputation) **12.** These people, like unreasoning animals, speak against what they do not understand and will perish in their corruption. (Corruption: moral decay or sin) **13.** They will be repaid for their wickedness, reveling in their deception and shameless behavior. (Reveling: taking great pleasure in) **14.** Their eyes are full of adultery and sin; they deceive the unstable and are trained in greed, cursed children. (Adultery: sexual unfaithfulness) **15.** They have abandoned the right path, following Balaam, who loved unjust gain. (Balaam: Old Testament prophet led astray by greed) **16.** But Balaam was rebuked by a donkey that spoke with a human voice, restraining his madness. (Donkey: animal used in the Bible to carry burdens) **17.** These people are like waterless springs and storm-driven mists, destined for eternal darkness. (Waterless springs: metaphor for something unfruitful) **18.** They use boastful, empty words to entice those barely escaping error through fleshly desires. (Entice: attract or tempt) **19.** They promise freedom but are slaves of corruption, for one is enslaved by what overcomes them. (Slaves: people bound to something stronger than themselves) **20.** If they escape worldly corruption through Christ but are again entangled and overcome, their end is worse than their beginning. (Entangled: caught up and trapped) **21.** It would have been better for them not to know the way of righteousness than to turn away after knowing it. (Righteousness: living according to God's ways) **22.** They fulfill the proverb: "A dog returns to its vomit," and, "A washed pig returns to the mud." (Proverb: a short, wise saying)

Chapter 3
1. This second letter I write to stir your pure minds by way of remembrance. **2.** Be mindful of the words spoken by the holy prophets and the apostles of the Lord. (Apostles: Early followers of Jesus who spread His teachings) **3.** Know this: in the last days, scoffers will come, following their own desires. (Scoffers: Those who mock or ridicule) **4.** They will say, "Where is His coming?" since everything continues as it has since creation. (Creation: The act of God making the universe and everything in it) **5.** They ignore that, by God's word, the heavens existed, and the earth was formed out of water. (Heavens: The sky or the universe; Earth: The planet we live on) **6.** By these, the world of old perished, being flooded. (Flooded: Covered with water, as in the great flood during Noah's time) **7.** The present heavens and earth are reserved by the same word for fire on the day of judgment for the ungodly. (Judgment: The final evaluation by God of all people; Ungodly: Those who do not follow God's will) **8.** Do not forget: with the Lord, a day is like a thousand years, and a thousand years like a day. (Lord: Refers to God, the supreme ruler) **9.** The Lord is not slow in keeping His promise but is patient, wanting all to repent. (Repent: To feel remorse and turn away from sin) **10.** The day of the Lord will come like a thief; the heavens will pass away, and the earth will be burned up. (Thief: Someone who steals secretly, implying the unexpectedness of the Lord's return) **11.** Since these things will be dissolved, live in holiness and godliness. (Holiness: The state of being sacred or pure; Godliness: Living in a way that reflects God's will) **12.** Look for and hasten the day of God, when the heavens will burn and elements melt. (Hasten: To speed up or hurry) **13.** But according to His promise, we await new heavens and a new earth, where righteousness dwells. (Righteousness: The quality of being morally right or just) **14.** Be diligent to be found by Him in peace, spotless and blameless. (Diligent: Working hard and carefully) **15.** Consider the Lord's patience as salvation, as Paul has written with wisdom. (Salvation: The deliverance from sin and its consequences; Paul: An apostle who spread the Christian message) **16.** In Paul's letters are things hard to understand, which unstable people distort, leading to destruction. (Distort: To twist or misinterpret) **17.** Beloved, knowing this, guard against being led astray and falling from steadfastness. (Steadfastness: Firm and unwavering loyalty or faithfulness) **18.** Grow in grace and knowledge of our Lord Jesus Christ. To Him be glory forever. Amen. (Grace: God's favor and help; Jesus Christ: The central figure of Christianity)

61 – James
Chapter 1
1. James, a servant of God and the Lord Jesus Christ, to the scattered twelve tribes, greetings. **2.** Consider it joy when you face trials. (Trials: tests or challenges) **3.** Knowing that the testing of your faith produces perseverance. (Perseverance: persistence) **4.** Let perseverance complete its work, so you may be mature, lacking nothing. (Mature: fully developed) **5.** If you lack wisdom, ask God, who gives generously. (Wisdom: knowledge and good judgment) **6.** But ask in faith, without doubting, as doubt is like a tossed wave. (Doubt: uncertainty) **7.** Don't expect to receive anything from God if you doubt. **8.** A double-minded person is unstable in all their ways. (Double-minded: divided in thought or opinion) **9.** The lowly should rejoice in their exalted position. (Exalted: lifted up in honor) **10.** The rich should rejoice in their humble position. (Humble: lowly or modest) **11.** Like flowers, the rich will fade away when the sun scorches them. (Scorches: burns with intense heat) **12.** Blessed is the one who perseveres through trials, for they will receive the crown of life. (Perseveres: endures, Crown of life: eternal reward) **13.** God does not tempt anyone, for He cannot be tempted by evil. (Tempt: lure or entice into sin) **14.** Each person is tempted by their own desires. (Desires: strong feelings or cravings) **15.** Desire gives birth to sin, and sin brings death. (Birth: the beginning of, Sin: wrongdoing, Death: spiritual separation from God) **16.** Do not be deceived, brothers and sisters. (Deceived: misled or tricked) **17.** Every good gift comes from God, who does not change. (Gift: something given, Variableness: change) **18.** He gave us birth through the word of truth, making us His firstfruits. (Firstfruits: the first part of something, often given to God) **19.** Be quick to listen, slow to speak, and slow to anger. (Anger: strong feeling of displeasure) **20.** Human anger does not bring about the righteousness God desires. (Righteousness: moral correctness) **21.** Get rid of all evil and accept the word which can save you. (Evil: morally wrong) **22.** Do what the word says, not just listen to it. (Deceiving: misleading) **23.** A person who hears but doesn't act is like someone who forgets their reflection. (Reflection: image in a mirror) **24.** They forget what they look like after looking at themselves. **25.** But the person who acts on the law of freedom will be blessed. (Blessed: favored by God) **26.** If someone cannot control their tongue, their religion is worthless. (Tongue: speech) **27.** Pure religion is to care for orphans and widows and remain untainted by the world. (Tainted: polluted or corrupted)

Chapter 2
1. My brothers, do not show favoritism while holding the faith of our Lord Jesus Christ, the glorious one. (Favoritism: bias, Glorious: honorable) **2.** If a rich man in fine clothes and a poor man in shabby clothes enter your church, (Shabby: torn) **3.** and you give the rich man a good seat but tell the poor man to stand or sit on the floor, **4.** are you not being partial and judging with evil thoughts? (Partial: biased, Evil: wrong) **5.** Has not God chosen the poor to be rich in faith and heirs of His kingdom? (Heirs: inheritors) **6.** But you dishonor the poor. Aren't the rich the ones who oppress you and take you to court? (Dishonor: disrespect, Oppress: burden) **7.** Do they not slander the noble name by which you are called? (Slander: defamation, Noble: esteemed) **8.** If you love your neighbor as yourself, you do well. (Neighbor: others, Yourself: well-being) **9.** But if you show favoritism, you sin and break the law. (Sin: wrongdoing, Law: rule) **10.** Whoever keeps the whole law but stumbles in one part is guilty of breaking all of it. (Stumbles: errs, Guilty: liable) **11.** For the same God who said, "Do not commit adultery," also said, "Do not murder." If you do one but not the other, you still break the law. (Adultery: infidelity, Murder: killing) **12.** Speak and act as those who will be judged by the law of freedom. (Judged: evaluated, Freedom: liberty) **13.** Mercy triumphs over judgment for those who show mercy. (Triumphs: prevails, Mercy: compassion) **14.** What good is it if someone claims to have faith but has no actions? Can faith save them? (Faith: belief, Actions: deeds) **15.** If a brother or sister is hungry and lacks clothing, **16.** and you wish them well but do not give them what they need, what good is that? (Wish: desire, Good: benefit) **17.** Faith without works is dead. (Works: deeds) **18.** Someone might say, "You have faith, I have works." Show me your faith without works, and I'll show you mine by my actions. (Actions: deeds, Show: display) **19.** You believe in one God. Good! Even demons believe and shudder. (Shudder: tremble) **20.** Do you want evidence that faith without deeds is useless? (Evidence: proof, Deeds: works) **21.** Was Abraham not justified by what he did when he offered Isaac on the altar? (Justified: declared righteous, Offered: gave) **22.** His faith and actions worked together, and his faith was made complete by his deeds. (Deeds: actions, Complete: fulfilled) **23.** The Scripture was fulfilled that says, "Abraham believed God, and it was credited to him as righteousness," and he was called God's friend. (Credited: attributed, Righteousness: rightness) **24.** A person is justified by what they do, not by faith alone. (Justified: declared righteous, Alone: only) **25.** Likewise, Rahab the prostitute was justified by her works when she hid the spies. (Prostitute: sex worker, Works: deeds) **26.** As the body without the spirit is dead, so faith without deeds is dead. (Spirit: soul, Dead: lifeless)

Chapter 3
1. Don't aim to be many teachers, for we will face stricter judgment. (teachers: those who instruct others) **2.** We all make mistakes. If someone doesn't stumble in speech, they are perfect and can control their body. (stumble: fail or trip) **3.** We control horses with bits in their mouths, turning their entire body. (bits: small pieces of metal in the horse's mouth used for control) **4.** Ships are steered by a small rudder, despite strong winds. (rudder: a flat piece of wood or metal used to steer) **5.** The tongue, though small, boasts of great things. A small fire can start a huge blaze. (boasts: speaks

proudly) **6.** The tongue is a fire, full of evil, defiling the whole body and set on fire by hell. (defiling: corrupting or making unclean) **7.** Every kind of creature has been tamed by man. (tamed: domesticated or controlled) **8.** The tongue is untamable, a restless evil full of poison. (restless: unable to be still) **9.** With it, we praise God, and with it, we curse people made in God's image. (curse: speak badly of) **10.** Blessing and cursing come from the same mouth—this should not happen. (cursing: speaking harmfully) **11.** Can fresh and salty water flow from the same spring? (spring: a natural source of water) **12.** Can a fig tree bear olives, or a vine bear figs? No more can saltwater flow fresh. (bear: produce or give) **13.** The wise show it through good deeds done with humility. (humility: modesty or lack of pride) **14.** If you have bitter envy and selfish ambition, don't boast or lie. (envy: jealousy, selfish ambition: wanting success at others' expense) **15.** This wisdom is not from above but is earthly, unspiritual, and demonic. (demonic: relating to evil forces) **16.** Where envy and selfishness are, confusion and evil follow. (confusion: disorder or chaos) **17.** Heavenly wisdom is pure, peace-loving, gentle, full of mercy, impartial, and sincere. (impartial: fair and not biased, sincere: genuine) **18.** Peacemakers sow peace and reap righteousness. (sow: plant, reap: gather)

Chapter 4

1. Where do fights and quarrels come from? Do they not come from your desires that battle within you? (Desires: strong wants or cravings) **2.** You want things but don't get them; you kill, covet, and fight, but still lack, because you don't ask. (Covet: desire something someone else has) **3.** You ask, but don't receive, because you ask with wrong motives to satisfy your selfish desires. (Motives: reasons for doing something) **4.** You adulterers, don't you know friendship with the world is enmity with God? Anyone who is a friend of the world is God's enemy. (Adulterers: those unfaithful in a relationship; Enmity: hostility, opposition) **5.** Do you think the Scripture says without reason, "The Spirit in us longs for jealousy"? (Jealousy: desire to have what others have) **6.** But God gives more grace. Scripture says, "God resists the proud but gives grace to the humble." (Grace: unearned kindness; Humble: not proud) **7.** Submit to God. Resist the devil, and he will flee from you. (Submit: yield or surrender; Resist: oppose) **8.** Come near to God, and He will come near to you. Cleanse your hands, you sinners, and purify your hearts, you double-minded. (Double-minded: undecided, wavering) **9.** Be sorrowful, mourn, and weep; let your laughter turn to sorrow and joy to sadness. (Sorrowful: feeling sadness) **10.** Humble yourselves before the Lord, and He will lift you up. (Humble: be modest, not proud) **11.** Don't speak evil against each other. When you judge, you judge the law, not obey it. (Judge: criticize or condemn) **12.** There is only one Lawgiver and Judge, who can save and destroy. Who are you to judge another? (Lawgiver: the one who makes the law) **13.** You who say, "We'll go to such-and-such a city, trade, and make money," (Trade: exchange goods or services) **14.** You don't know what tomorrow will bring. Your life is a vapor that vanishes. (Vapor: mist, something fleeting) **15.** You should say, "If the Lord wills, we will live and do this or that." (Will: desire, plan) **16.** You boast in your arrogance; all such boasting is evil. (Arrogance: pride, overconfidence) **17.** If you know what is good and don't do it, it is sin for you. (Sin: wrongdoing, disobedience to God)

Chapter 5

1. Listen, wealthy ones, weep for the troubles coming upon you. (Wealthy: having great material possessions) **2.** Your riches have rotted, and your clothes are spoiled. (Rotted: decayed; Spoiled: damaged or ruined) **3.** Your gold and silver are rusted, and that rust will testify against you, burning your flesh like fire. You've hoarded treasures for the final days. (Hoarded: accumulated unnecessarily; Testify: serve as evidence) **4.** The workers you cheated cry out, and their cries have reached God's ears. (Cheated: wrongfully deprived of something owed) **5.** You have lived in luxury, indulging yourselves as though it were a day of slaughter. (Indulging: satisfying your desires excessively) **6.** You have condemned and killed the righteous, who does not resist you. (Condemned: judged or declared guilty) **7.** Be patient until the Lord comes, like a farmer waits for the crops. (Patient: enduring hardship without complaint) **8.** Be patient and strengthen your hearts, for the Lord is near. (Strengthen: make firm or strong) **9.** Don't grumble against each other, or you'll be judged. The Judge is at the door. (Grumble: complain in a low, murmuring way) **10.** Take the prophets as examples of suffering and patience. (Prophets: individuals chosen to speak for God) **11.** We consider those who endure blessed; you've seen how Job was patient and how the Lord showed mercy. (Endure: to withstand hardship; Mercy: compassion or forgiveness) **12.** Don't swear oaths, but let your yes be yes and no be no, to avoid condemnation. (Oaths: solemn promises; Condemnation: judgment or penalty) **13.** Is anyone in trouble? Let them pray. Is anyone happy? Let them sing praise. (Praise: express admiration or gratitude) **14.** Is anyone sick? Call the elders to pray and anoint with oil in the Lord's name. (Elders: mature or senior members of the church; Anoint: apply oil as a sign of blessing) **15.** The prayer of faith will heal the sick and forgive their sins. (Faith: trust in God's power; Heal: restore health) **16.** Confess your sins to each other and pray for healing. The prayer of a righteous person is powerful. (Confess: admit wrongdoing; Righteous: morally right) **17.** Elijah was human like us and prayed for no rain, and it didn't rain for three and a half years. (Human: mortal, with weaknesses) **18.** He prayed again, and rain came, and the earth yielded crops. (Yielded: produced or brought forth) **19.** If someone strays from the truth, bring them back. (Strays: moves away or deviates) **20.** Whoever turns a sinner from their error will save them from death and cover many sins. (Error: mistake or wrong action; Save: rescue from spiritual death)

62 – 1 John

Chapter 1

1. From the start, we heard, saw, and touched the Word of life. (Word of life: Gospel) **2.** This life was revealed to us, and we testify about it, sharing the eternal life that was with the Father and shown to us. (Testify: Witness, Revealed: Exposed) **3.** We declare to you what we've seen and heard, so you can share in our fellowship, which is with the Father and His Son, Jesus Christ. (Fellowship: Communion) **4.** We write these things so that your joy may be complete. (Complete: Full) **5.** The message we received and share is that God is light, and in Him, there is no darkness. (Light: Purity, Darkness: Evil) **6.** If we claim to have fellowship with Him but live in darkness, we are lying and not living by the truth. (Claim: Assert, Fellowship: Communion) **7.** But if we walk in the light, as He does, we have fellowship with each other, and Jesus' blood cleanses us from all sin. (Cleanse: Purify) **8.** If we deny our sin, we deceive ourselves, and the truth is not in us. (Deceive: Mislead) **9.** If we confess our sins, He is faithful and just to forgive and cleanse us from all unrighteousness. (Confess: Admit, Unrighteousness: Immorality) **10.** If we claim we haven't sinned, we make God a liar, and His word is not in us. (Claim: Assert, Liar: False)

Chapter 2

1. My dear children, I write these words to help you avoid sin. But if anyone does sin, we have Jesus Christ, the righteous One, who pleads our case before the Father. (Plead: Advocate) **2.** He is the atoning sacrifice for our sins—and not just ours, but for the sins of the world. (Atoning: Reconciling) **3.** We can be certain that we truly know Him if we obey His commandments. (Obey: Follow) **4.** Anyone who says, "I know Him," but does not keep His commandments, is deceiving themselves, and the truth is not in them. (Deceiving: Lying) **5.** But if we obey His word, God's love is perfected in us. This shows we are truly in Him. (Realized: Fulfilled) **6.** Whoever claims to live in Him must live as He did. (Live: Walk) **7.** I'm not writing a new commandment, but an old one you've known from the beginning. This is the message you've heard. (Commandment: Instruction) **8.** Yet, it's a new commandment I'm writing to you, true in Christ and in you, because darkness is passing away and the light is shining. (Darkness: Evil, Light: Truth) **9.** Whoever claims to be in the light but hates their brother is still in darkness. (Hates: Dislikes) **10.** But whoever loves their brother remains in the light, and there is no reason for them to stumble. (Stumble: Fall) **11.** Anyone who hates their brother lives in darkness, walks in darkness, and has no idea where they are going because the darkness has blinded them. (Blinded: Lost) **12.** I write to you, little children, because your sins are forgiven for Jesus' sake. (Forgiven: Pardoned) **13.** I write to you, fathers, because you know Him who is from the beginning. I write to you, young men, because you have overcome the evil one. (Overcome: Defeated) **14.** I've written to you, fathers, because you know Him from the beginning, and to young men because you are strong, the word of God remains in you, and you've overcome the evil one. (Strong: Powerful) **15.** Do not love the world or its desires. If anyone loves the world, the love of the Father is not in them. (Love: Desire) **16.** Everything in the world—the cravings of sinful desires, the lust of the eyes, and pride in our achievements—is not from the Father, but from the world. (Cravings: Desires, Pride: Arrogance) **17.** The world and its desires will pass away, but whoever does the will of God will live forever. (Will: Purpose) **18.** Dear children, this is the last hour. You have heard that the antichrist is coming, and now many antichrists have appeared. This shows it's the last hour. (Antichrist: Opponent of Christ) **19.** They left us because they were never truly part of us; if they had been, they would have stayed. Their leaving showed they didn't belong. (Departure: Leaving) **20.** But you have an anointing from the Holy One, and you know the truth. (Anointing: Empowerment) **21.** I'm writing to you not because you don't know the truth, but because you do, and no lie comes from the truth. (Lie: Falsehood) **22.** Who is a liar but the one who denies that Jesus is the Christ? That person is the antichrist, denying both the Father and the Son. (Denies: Rejects) **23.** Anyone who denies the Son does not have the Father. But whoever acknowledges the Son has both the Father and the Son. (Acknowledges: Accepts) **24.** Let what you have heard from the beginning remain in you. If it does, you will remain in the Son and the Father. (Remain:

Abide) **25.** And this is the promise He made to us: eternal life. (Promise: Assurance) **26.** I write these things to warn you about those who are trying to deceive you. (Deceive: Mislead) **27.** The anointing you received from Him remains in you, and you don't need anyone to teach you. The anointing teaches you about all things, and is true, not false. Continue to remain in Him. (Anointing: Teaching) **28.** Now, dear children, remain in Him so that when He appears, we will have confidence and not be ashamed at His coming. (Confidence: Assurance) **29.** If you know that He is righteous, you know that everyone who does what is right has been born of Him. (Righteous: Just)

Chapter 3

1. See what incredible love the Father has given us, that we should be called His children! The world does not recognize us because it did not know Him. (Incredible: amazing, Recognize: identify) **2.** Beloved, we are God's children now, and although we don't yet know what we will be, when He appears, we will be like Him, for we will see Him as He is. (Appears: shows, Beloved: dearly loved) **3.** Anyone who has this hope purifies themselves, just as He is pure. (Purifies: cleanses) **4.** Whoever sins breaks the law, for sin is lawlessness. (Lawlessness: disregard) **5.** You know that He appeared to take away our sins, and in Him, there is no sin. (Appeared: came, Sin: wrongdoing) **6.** Whoever remains in Him does not sin; whoever sins has not seen or known Him. (Remains: stays, Known: understood) **7.** Little children, do not be deceived: those who do what is right are righteous, just as He is righteous. (Deceived: tricked, Righteous: just) **8.** The one who sins belongs to the devil, who has sinned from the beginning. The Son of God appeared to destroy the devil's works. (Belongs: controlled, Destroy: end) **9.** No one born of God continues to sin, for His seed remains in them. They cannot sin because they are born of God. (Seed: inheritance, Continues: keeps) **10.** This is how we distinguish between God's children and the devil's: anyone who does not do right or love their brother is not of God. (Distinguish: differentiate, Brother: believer) **11.** This is the message you heard from the beginning: love one another. (Message: teaching) **12.** Not like Cain, who belonged to the evil one and killed his brother because his deeds were evil and his brother's righteous. (Belonged: controlled, Deeds: actions) **13.** Do not be surprised if the world hates you. (Hates: dislikes) **14.** We know we have passed from death to life because we love our brothers. Anyone who does not love remains in death. (Passed: moved, Remains: stays) **15.** Anyone who hates their brother is a murderer, and no murderer has eternal life in them. (Murderer: killer, Eternal: lasting) **16.** This is how we know love: Jesus laid down His life for us, and we should do the same for our brothers. (Laid down: gave up) **17.** If anyone has material possessions and sees their brother in need but ignores them, how can God's love be in them? (Material possessions: wealth, Ignores: overlooks) **18.** Let us not love with words or speech, but with actions and truth. (Actions: deeds, Truth: sincerity) **19.** This is how we know we belong to the truth and can set our hearts at rest before God. (Belong: are part of, Set at rest: reassure) **20.** If our hearts condemn us, God is greater than our hearts and knows everything. (Condemn: judge, Knows: understands) **21.** If our hearts do not condemn us, we have confidence before God. (Confidence: trust) **22.** And whatever we ask, we receive, because we keep His commands and do what pleases Him. (Pleases: satisfies) **23.** His command is to believe in the name of His Son, Jesus Christ, and love one another as He commanded. (Command: instruction) **24.** Those who obey His commands remain in Him, and He in them. We know He remains in us by the Spirit He has given us. (Obey: follow, Spirit: presence)

Chapter 4

1. Beloved, do not believe every spirit, but test the spirits to see if they are from God, because many false prophets have gone out into the world. (Test: examine, False prophets: deceivers) **2.** This is how you recognize the Spirit of God: Every spirit that confesses Jesus Christ has come in the flesh is from God. (Recognize: identify, Confesses: acknowledges) **3.** Every spirit that does not confess that Jesus Christ has come in the flesh is not from God. This is the spirit of the antichrist, which you have heard is coming, and is now already in the world. (Antichrist: deceiver, Confess: acknowledge) **4.** You are of God, little children, and have overcome them, because greater is He that is in you than he who is in the world. (Overcome: defeated, Greater: more powerful) **5.** They are of the world; therefore, they speak as the world does, and the world listens to them. (World: society, Listens: hears) **6.** We are of God; those who know God listen to us, but those who are not of God do not listen to us. By this, we know the spirit of truth and the spirit of error. (Know: understand, Error: mistake) **7.** Beloved, let us love one another, for love is from God. Everyone who loves is born of God and knows God. (Born: born again, Knows: understands) **8.** Anyone who does not love does not know God, because God is love. (Love: affection, Know: understand) **9.** In this, the love of God was revealed to us: God sent His only Son into the world, that we might live through Him. (Revealed: shown, Live: exist) **10.** Here is love: not that we loved God, but that He loved us and sent His Son to be the atoning sacrifice for our sins. (Atoning: reconciling, Sacrifice: offering) **11.** Beloved, if God so loved us, we also ought to love one another. (Ought: should) **12.** No one has ever seen God. If we love one another, God dwells in us, and His love is perfected in us. (Dwells: resides, Perfected: completed) **13.** By this we know that we dwell in Him and He in us, because He has given us His Spirit. (Dwell: live, Spirit: presence) **14.** And we have seen and testify that the Father sent the Son to be the Savior of the world. (Testify: declare, Savior: deliverer) **15.** Whoever confesses that Jesus is the Son of God, God dwells in him, and he in God. (Confesses: acknowledges, Dwells: lives) **16.** And we have known and believed the love that God has for us. God is love, and he who abides in love abides in God, and God in him. (Abides: remains, Known: understood) **17.** In this, love is made perfect, so that we may have boldness on the day of judgment; because as He is, so are we in this world. (Boldness: confidence, Judgment: evaluation) **18.** There is no fear in love, but perfect love drives out fear, because fear has to do with punishment. The one who fears has not been made perfect in love. (Drives out: expels, Punishment: penalty) **19.** We love Him because He first loved us. (Loved: cared for) **20.** If anyone says, "I love God," but hates his brother, he is a liar. For the one who does not love his brother whom he has seen, how can he love God whom he has not seen? (Liar: deceiver, Seen: perceived) **21.** And this commandment we have from Him: Whoever loves God must also love his brother. (Commandment: instruction, Must: has to)

Chapter 5

1. Anyone who believes Jesus is the Christ is born of God. And anyone who loves God loves His children too. (Christ: Anointed one) **2.** We know we love God's children when we love God and follow His commandments. (Commandments: Rules or laws) **3.** The love of God means keeping His commandments, and they are not burdensome. (Burdensome: Heavy or difficult to bear) **4.** Whatever is born of God overcomes the world. Our victory over the world is our faith. (Overcome: Defeat) **5.** Who can overcome the world accept those who believe Jesus is the Son of God? (accept: Only) **6.** Jesus Christ came through water and blood, not just water. The Spirit testifies to the truth. (Testifies: Gives evidence) **7.** In heaven, the Father, the Word, and the Holy Spirit testify together, and they are one. (Word: Refers to Jesus Christ; Spirit: Holy Spirit) **8.** On earth, the Spirit, water, and blood testify, and they agree as one. (Testify: Give witness or evidence) **9.** If we accept the witness of men, God's testimony is greater, for He has testified about His Son. (Testimony: Evidence or statement) **10.** Whoever believes in the Son of God has this testimony within themselves. Denying this makes them a liar, for they reject God's testimony. (Denying: Refusing to accept) **11.** God's testimony is this: He has given us eternal life, and this life is in His Son. (Testimony: Evidence or statement) **12.** Whoever has the Son has life; those without the Son do not have life. (Life: Eternal life through Jesus Christ) **13.** I write to you who believe in the Son of God, so that you may know you have eternal life and continue to believe in Him. (Eternal: Everlasting) **14.** We can be confident that if we ask anything according to God's will, He hears us. (Confident: Sure, certain) **15.** If we know He hears us, whatever we ask, we can be sure He will give us what we asked for. (Sure: Certain) **16.** If someone sees their brother sinning a non-death sin, they should pray, and God will give them life. There is a sin leading to death; I don't say you should pray for that. (Sin: Wrongdoing; Non-death sin: Not fatal to salvation) **17.** All wrongdoing is sin, but not all sin leads to death. (Wrongdoing: Unjust or immoral actions) **18.** We know that whoever is born of God does not sin; the one born of God keeps himself safe, and the evil one cannot touch him. (Evil one: Satan, or the devil) **19.** We know that we belong to God, while the whole world lies in evil. (Lie: Remain in a state) **20.** We know the Son of God has come and given us understanding, so we can know the true God and be in Him through His Son, Jesus Christ. He is the true God and eternal life. (Understanding: Insight) **21.** Dear children, keep yourselves from idols. Amen. (Idols: False gods or images of worship)

63 – 2 John

Chapter 1

1. To the dear lady and her family, whom I love deeply in the truth. And it's not just me, but all who share in the truth love you too. (dear: beloved; truth: the reality of God's word) **2.** Because the truth lives within us and will stay with us forever. (lives: remains; forever: eternally) **3.** May grace, mercy, and peace from God the Father and from Jesus Christ, the Son, be with you in truth and love. (grace: unearned favor; mercy: compassion; peace: calmness) **4.** I was overjoyed to find your children living according to the truth, just as the Father has commanded us. (overjoyed: filled with great joy) **5.** Now, I urge you, dear lady, not to receive a new commandment, but the one we've had from the start: to love one another. (urge: encourage strongly; commandment: instruction) **6.** And this is what love looks like: living by His commands. This is the command we've heard from the beginning: to live by it. (looks like: means; live by: follow) **7.** Many deceivers have entered the world, those who do not acknowledge that Jesus Christ came in the flesh. These are the ones who deceive and are against Christ. (deceivers: liars; against: opposed to) **8.** Be careful, so we don't lose what we've worked for, but instead receive the full reward. (be careful: watch out; worked for: earned) **9.** Anyone who does not remain in Christ's teachings does not have God. But anyone who stays true to His teachings has both the Father and the Son. (remain: stay; teachings: doctrine) **10.** If someone comes to you and does not bring these teachings, don't welcome them into your home or offer them any greeting. (offer: give) **11.** Whoever greets them shares in their evil work. (shares: participates in) **12.** I have many things to write to you, but I'd rather not do it with pen and paper. I hope to visit you and speak face to face so our joy can be complete. (complete: full) **13.** The children of your chosen sister send their greetings. Amen. (chosen: elect)

64 – 3 John
Chapter 1

1. To Gaius, my dearly beloved, whom I love in truth. **2.** I wish above all things for your prosperity and health, just as your soul prospers. (Prosperity: success or flourishing) **3.** I greatly rejoiced when the brothers testified about the truth in you, as you live by the truth. (Testified: gave evidence or proof) **4.** There is no greater joy for me than hearing that my children follow the truth. **5.** Beloved, you faithfully support the brothers and strangers alike. **6.** They've spoken of your charity to the church; if you help them on their journey in a godly way, you'll do well. (Charity: kindness or love for others; Godly: in a manner that reflects God's will) **7.** For they went out for God's name, taking nothing from the Gentiles. (Gentiles: people who are not Jewish) **8.** We should receive such people, so we can be fellow workers for the truth. (Fellow workers: those who collaborate or assist in a shared task) **9.** I wrote to the church, but Diotrephes, who loves being first, doesn't welcome us. (Preeminence: the state of being superior or more important) **10.** If I come, I will remind him of his actions—speaking against us with harmful words, refusing to welcome the brothers, and even stopping others from doing so, casting them out of the church. (Prating: talking foolishly or irresponsibly; Malicious: intending to cause harm or suffering) **11.** Beloved, don't follow evil, but good. Anyone who does good is from God, but anyone who does evil has not seen God. **12.** Demetrius is well spoken of by all and by the truth itself; we also testify, and you know our testimony is true. (Testify: give evidence or bear witness) **13.** I have many things to write, but I prefer to speak with you face to face. **14.** I hope to see you soon; peace be with you. Our friends send their greetings. Greet the friends by name.

65 – Jude
Chapter 1

1. Jude, a servant of Jesus Christ and the brother of James, to those who are set apart by God the Father, kept safe in Jesus Christ, and called to His purpose. (Set apart: made holy or distinguished for a special purpose) **2.** May mercy, peace, and love be greatly multiplied to you. **3.** Beloved, although I intended to write to you about our shared salvation, I found it necessary to urge you to contend strongly for the faith that was once for all entrusted to the saints. (Contend: strive or fight for) **4.** For certain individuals have secretly infiltrated your ranks—those destined for judgment—ungodly people who turn the grace of our God into a license for immorality, and deny the only Sovereign God and our Lord Jesus Christ. (License: permission; Immorality: wickedness) **5.** I want to remind you, even though you already know this, that the Lord, after rescuing the people from Egypt, later destroyed those who refused to believe. **6.** And the angels who did not keep their assigned positions but abandoned their rightful place, He has bound in everlasting chains under darkness, awaiting the judgment of the great day. (Assigned positions: designated places or duties) **7.** Similarly, Sodom and Gomorrah, along with their neighboring cities, gave themselves to immorality and pursued unnatural desires, serving as an example by suffering the eternal fire's judgment. (Immorality: sinful behavior; Unnatural desires: forbidden passions) **8.** In the same way, these defiled dreamers corrupt their own bodies, reject authority, and insult celestial beings. (Defiled: corrupted or tainted; Celestial: heavenly or spiritual beings) **9.** Yet Michael the archangel, when contending with the devil over the body of Moses, did not dare to bring a railing accusation, but said, "The Lord rebuke you." (Contending: struggling or disputing) **10.** But these people speak against things they don't understand, and like irrational animals, they follow their instincts and destroy themselves with what they naturally know. (Irrational: lacking reason; Instincts: natural, unlearned behaviors) **11.** Woe to them! For they have followed the way of Cain, rushed greedily into the error of Balaam for financial gain, and perished in the rebellion of Korah. (Woe: sorrow; Greedily: with selfish desire; Perished: died or came to ruin) **12.** These are blemishes at your love feasts, feasting with you without fear, clouds without water, carried about by winds; trees with no fruit, twice dead and uprooted. (Blemishes: flaws or stains; Love feasts: communal meals for fellowship; Upturned: removed from the roots) **13.** They are like wild waves of the sea, foaming up their shame; wandering stars, for whom darkness is reserved forever. (Wandering: unstable or aimless; Darkness: eternal punishment) **14.** Enoch, the seventh from Adam, prophesied about them, saying, "Look, the Lord is coming with thousands of His holy ones." (Prophesied: foretold; Holy ones: saints or angels) **15.** He will execute judgment on all, convicting the ungodly for all the wicked things they have done and for all the harsh words they have spoken against Him. (Convicting: proving guilty; Wicked: morally wrong) **16.** These people are grumblers and complainers, following their own selfish desires. Their mouths speak boastful words, showing favoritism for personal gain. (Grumblers: murmurers; Selfish desires: desires for personal pleasure) **17.** But, beloved, remember the words spoken by the apostles of our Lord Jesus Christ. **18.** They said to you that in the last days, there will be mockers who follow their own godless desires. (Mockers: those who mock or make fun of others) **19.** These are the ones who cause divisions, worldly-minded, and devoid of the Spirit. (Devoid: lacking or without) **20.** But you, beloved, build yourselves up in your most holy faith, praying in the Holy Spirit, (Build up: strengthen or encourage; Holy Spirit: God's presence living within believers) **21.** Keep yourselves in God's love, waiting for the mercy of our Lord Jesus Christ, which leads to eternal life. **22.** Show mercy to those who doubt. **23.** Save others by snatching them from the fire, showing even hatred toward the clothing stained by their sinful nature. **24.** Now, to Him who is able to keep you from stumbling and to present you faultless before His glorious presence with great joy, (Stumbling: falling into error; Faultless: without fault or sin) **25.** To the only wise God our Savior, be glory, majesty, dominion, and power, both now and forever. Amen.

66 – Revelation
Chapter 1

1. The revelation of Jesus Christ, which God gave Him to show His servants what will soon happen; He sent it through His angel to John. (Servants: those who serve God) **2.** John recorded the word of God, the testimony of Jesus, and everything he saw. (Testimony: evidence or witness) **3.** Blessed are those who read, hear, and obey this prophecy, for the time is near. (Obey: follow) **4.** To the seven churches in Asia: Grace and peace from God, who is, was, and is to come, and from the seven Spirits before His throne; (Grace: unearned favor; Spirits: symbolic of the Holy Spirit's presence) **5.** And from Jesus Christ, the faithful witness, the firstborn from the dead, and the ruler of the kings of the earth. To Him who loves us and freed us from our sins by His blood, (Ruler: one who governs) **6.** And has made us a kingdom and priests to God and His Father; to Him be glory and power forever. Amen. (Priests: those who serve in religious duties) **7.** He comes with clouds, and every eye will see Him, even those who pierced Him; all the earth will mourn because of Him. Amen. (Pierced: wounded with a sharp object) **8.** I am the Alpha and the Omega, the Beginning and the End, says the Lord, the Almighty. (Alpha & Omega: the first and last letters of the Greek alphabet, meaning "the beginning and the end") **9.** I, John, your brother in suffering and patience in Christ, was on Patmos for the word of God and Jesus' testimony. (Suffering: experiencing pain) **10.** I was in the Spirit on the Lord's Day, and heard a loud voice like a trumpet, (Spirit: under divine inspiration) **11.** Saying, "I am the Alpha and the Omega. Write what you see and send it to the seven churches." (Churches: local Christian communities) **12.** I turned to see the voice speaking to me and saw seven golden lampstands; (Lampstands: stands holding lamps, symbolizing churches) **13.** In the center, one like the Son of Man, clothed with a robe and a golden sash. (Sash: a band worn around the waist) **14.** His head and hair were white like wool, His eyes like a blazing fire; (Wool: soft, thick material) **15.** His feet like glowing bronze, and His voice like rushing waters. (Bronze: a metal alloy, often used for strength) **16.** He held seven stars in His right hand, and from His mouth came a sharp sword; His face was like the sun in its brilliance. (Sword: a weapon; Brilliance: shining intensity) **17.** When I saw Him, I fell as though dead, and He touched me, saying, "Do not fear. I am the First and the Last. (Fear: to be afraid) **18.** I am the Living One; I was dead, but I am alive forever and hold the keys of death and Hades. (Hades: the realm of the dead) **19.** Write what you have seen, what is now, and what will happen after this. (Happen: take place) **20.** The seven stars are the angels of the seven churches, and the seven lampstands are the churches. (Angels: spiritual messengers)

Chapter 2

1. To the angel of the church in Ephesus: These are the words of the One who holds the seven stars and walks among the seven golden lampstands (lampstands: symbolic holders of divine light). **2.** I know your deeds, hard work, and endurance. You cannot tolerate evil people and have tested false apostles. **3.** You've persevered for my name and not grown weary. **4.** Yet, you've abandoned your first love. **5.** Remember where you've fallen, repent, and do what you did at first. If not, I will remove your lampstand (lampstand: the church's spiritual influence). **6.** You hate the practices of the Nicolaitans which I also hate. (Nicolaitans: a sect promoting immorality), **7.** To the victor, I will give access to the tree of life in God's paradise (paradise: heaven). **8.** To the angel of the church in Smyrna: These are the words of the One who is the First and the Last, who was dead and is alive. **9.** I know your suffering, poverty (though you're spiritually rich), and the slander of false Jews, who are Satan's synagogue (synagogue: assembly). **10.** Fear not trials ahead; the devil will test some of you with imprisonment. Remain faithful even to death for a crown of life (crown: reward of eternal life). **11.** The one who overcomes will not be harmed by the second death (second death: eternal separation from God). **12.** To the angel of the church in Pergamum: These are the words of the One with the sharp, double-edged sword (sword: God's Word). **13.** I know you remain loyal in Satan's city, even during Antipas's martyrdom (martyr: one who dies for faith). **14.** Yet, you follow Balaam's teachings, leading to idolatry and immorality (idolatry: worship of idols). **15.** You also follow the Nicolaitans' ways. **16.** Repent, or I will come quickly with the sword of my mouth. **17.** To the victor, I will give hidden manna and a white stone with a secret name. (Manna: heavenly food) **18.** To the angel of the church in Thyatira: These are the words of the Son of God, whose eyes blaze like fire and feet shine like bronze. **19.** I know your love, faith, service, and growing deeds. **20.** Yet, you tolerate Jezebel, who misleads servants into immorality and idolatry. **21.** I gave her time to repent, but she refused. **22.** I will cast her and her followers into suffering unless they repent. **23.** All churches will know I examine hearts and minds and repay deeds (reins: innermost thoughts). **24.** To those in Thyatira who avoid Satan's so-called secrets, I place no burden. **25.** Hold firmly to what you have until I come. **26.** To the victor, I will give authority over nations, **27.** To rule them with an iron scepter and shatter them like pottery. **28.** I will also give them the morning star (morning star: Christ's light). **29.** Whoever has ears, let them hear what the Spirit says to the churches.

Chapter 3
1. To the angel of the church in Sardis, write: The one holding the seven Spirits of God and the seven stars says, I know your deeds; though you seem alive, you are dead. (angel: messenger) **2.** Stay alert and strengthen what remains, as it is close to dying. Your actions are not complete before God. (alert: watchful) **3.** Remember what you have received and heard; obey and repent. If you are not watchful, I will come like a thief at an unknown hour. (repent: turn back) **4.** Yet, a few in Sardis have not defiled their garments. They will walk with me in white, for they are worthy. (defiled: stained) **5.** The one who conquers will wear white garments, and I will never erase their name from the book of life but will acknowledge them before my Father and His angels. (conquers: overcomes) **6.** Let anyone who has an ear listen to what the Spirit says to the churches. **7.** To the angel of the church in Philadelphia, write: The holy and true one, holding the key of David, who opens and no one shuts, and shuts and no one opens, says: **8.** I know your deeds; I have placed an open door before you. You have little strength but have kept my word and not denied my name. **9.** I will make those of the synagogue of Satan, who lie about being Jews, come and bow before you, knowing I love you. (synagogue: place of worship) **10.** Since you obeyed my command to endure, I will protect you from the global trial that is coming. **11.** I am coming soon. Hold on tightly to what you have, so no one takes your crown. **12.** To the one who conquers, I will make them a pillar in God's temple, write on them God's name, the New Jerusalem, and my new name. (pillar: permanent part of a structure) **13.** Let anyone who has an ear listen to what the Spirit says to the churches. **14.** To the angel of the church in Laodicea, write: The Amen, the true and faithful witness, the beginning of God's creation, says: **15.** I know your deeds; you are neither cold nor hot. I wish you were one or the other. **16.** But because you are lukewarm, I will spit you out of my mouth. **17.** You claim to be rich and self-sufficient, but you are actually wretched, poor, blind, and naked. (self-sufficient: independent) **18.** Buy refined gold from me to become rich, white garments to cover your shame, and salve to heal your eyes. (salve: ointment) **19.** I correct those I love. Be eager to change and repent. **20.** I stand at the door and knock. If anyone hears and opens, I will enter and dine with them. **21.** To the one who conquers, I will give the right to sit with me on my throne, as I sat with my Father on His throne. **22.** Let anyone who has an ear listen to what the Spirit says to the churches.

Chapter 4
1. After this, I saw a door open in heaven, and a voice like a trumpet said, "Come up here, and I will show you what is to come." **2.** Immediately, I was in the Spirit, and saw a throne with someone sitting on it. **3.** The one who sat appeared like jasper and sardius, and a rainbow around the throne looked like emerald. (Jasper and Sardius: types of gemstones; Emerald: green gemstone) **4.** Around the throne were twenty-four thrones, with twenty-four elders wearing white robes and gold crowns. (Elders: senior figures; Robes: long garments) **5.** From the throne came lightning, thunder, and voices. Seven lamps burned before the throne, representing the seven Spirits of God. (Spirits of God: divine presence or power) **6.** Before the throne was a sea of glass, like crystal. Four creatures full of eyes were around it. (Crystal: clear, transparent material) **7.** The first creature was like a lion, the second like a calf, the third had a human face, and the fourth was like an eagle. **8.** Each creature had six wings and eyes all around. They never stop saying, "Holy, holy, holy, Lord God Almighty, who was, is, and is to come." (Wings: body parts used for flying; Holy: sacred or divine) **9.** When the creatures give glory, honor, and thanks to the one on the throne, **10.** The twenty-four elders fall down and worship the one who lives forever, casting their crowns before the throne, saying, **11.** "You are worthy, Lord, to receive glory, honor, and power, for you created all things, and by your will they exist." (Worthy: deserving; Glory: great honor; Honor: respect)

Chapter 5
1. I saw a scroll in the right hand of the one on the throne, sealed with seven seals. (scroll : a rolled-up document) **2.** A strong angel shouted, "Who is worthy to open the scroll and break its seals?" (worthy : deserving) **3.** No one in heaven, on earth, or under the earth could open or look at the scroll. **4.** I cried, for no one was worthy to open or look at the scroll. **5.** One elder said, "Do not weep; the Lion of Judah, the Root of David, has triumphed to open the scroll and break its seals." (Lion of Judah : a title for Jesus) **6.** I saw a Lamb standing as though slain, with seven horns and seven eyes, which are the seven Spirits of God sent to all the earth. (slain : killed) **7.** The Lamb took the scroll from the one on the throne. **8.** The four living creatures and twenty-four elders fell down, holding harps and bowls of incense, which are the prayers of the saints. (incense : symbol of prayer) **9.** They sang, "You are worthy to take the scroll and open its seals, for You were slain, and with Your blood, You redeemed people from every nation." **10.** You made them kings and priests to serve God, and they will reign on earth. **11.** I heard the voice of many angels, numbering countless thousands, around the throne and elders. **12.** They said, "Worthy is the Lamb to receive power, wealth, wisdom, strength, honor, glory, and praise!" **13.** I heard every creature in heaven, on earth, under the earth, and in the sea, saying, "To Him on the throne and the Lamb be blessing, honor, glory, and power forever!" **14.** The four living creatures said, "Amen!" and the elders worshiped the eternal One. (eternal : without end)

Chapter 6
1. I saw the Lamb open a seal, and heard a thunderous voice saying, "Come and see." (Thunderous: loud sound) **2.** I saw a white horse with a rider holding a bow and a crown, conquering and ready to conquer. (Conquering: gaining control) **3.** When the second seal opened, the second creature said, "Come and see." (Creature: living being) **4.** A red horse appeared, and the rider took peace from the earth, causing people to kill each other. He had a large sword. (Sword: weapon) **5.** When the third seal opened, the third creature said, "Come and see." I saw a black horse, and the rider had scales in his hand. (Scales: measurement tool) **6.** A voice said, "A day's wheat for a denarius, three measures of barley for a denarius, but don't harm the oil and wine." (Denarius: Roman coin) **7.** When the fourth seal opened, the fourth creature said, "Come and see." **8.** I saw a pale horse, and the rider's name was Death, with Hades following. They were given power to kill a quarter of the earth by sword, famine, death, and wild beasts. (Hades: the underworld) **9.** When the fifth seal opened, I saw souls of those slain for God's word under the altar. (Souls: spiritual essence) **10.** They cried, "How long, Lord, before you avenge us?" (Avenge: seek justice) **11.** White robes were given to each, and they were told to wait until their fellow servants were also martyred. (Martyred: killed for faith) **12.** When the sixth seal opened, there was a great earthquake, and the sun became black, the moon red. (Earthquake: ground shaking) **13.** The stars fell like figs shaken by wind. (Stars: celestial bodies) **14.** The sky disappeared, and mountains and islands were moved. (Mountains: large landforms) **15.** The kings, rich, powerful, and every person hid in caves and rocks. (Kings: rulers) **16.** They cried, "Fall on us, and hide us from God and the Lamb!" (Lamb: symbol of Christ) **17.** "For the great day of wrath has come, and who can stand?" (Wrath: intense anger)

Chapter 7
1. I saw four angels at earth's corners, holding back winds so they wouldn't blow on land, sea, or trees. (corners: edges) **2.** Another angel rose from the east with God's seal, calling to the four angels given power to harm the earth and sea. (seal: mark of authority) **3.** He said, "Do not harm the land, sea, or trees until we seal God's servants on their foreheads." (seal: mark for protection) **4.** I heard the sealed number: one hundred forty-four thousand

from Israel's tribes. **5.** Twelve thousand were sealed from Judah, Reuben, and Gad. **6.** Twelve thousand were sealed from Asher, Naphtali, and Manasseh. **7.** Twelve thousand were sealed from Simeon, Levi, and Issachar. **8.** Twelve thousand were sealed from Zebulun, Joseph, and Benjamin. **9.** I saw an uncountable multitude from all nations, standing before God's throne and the Lamb, dressed in white with palm branches. (multitude: large crowd) **10.** They shouted, "Salvation belongs to God on the throne and to the Lamb!" (salvation: deliverance from sin) **11.** Angels, elders, and creatures worshipped God at the throne. **12.** They said, "Amen! Blessing, glory, wisdom, and power to God forever!" (Amen: so be it) **13.** An elder asked, "Who are these in white robes, and where did they come from?" (elder: respected leader) **14.** I replied, "You know." He said, "These are from great suffering, made pure by the Lamb's blood." (tribulation: severe trouble) **15.** They serve God constantly, and He shelters them. **16.** They will never hunger, thirst, or suffer heat again. **17.** The Lamb will shepherd them, lead them to living waters, and God will wipe away their tears. (shepherd: guide or caretaker)

Chapter 8

1. When the seventh seal was opened, heaven became silent for about half an hour. (seal: a symbolic closure or judgment) **2.** Seven angels stood before God and were given trumpets. **3.** Another angel, with a golden censer, offered incense mixed with the prayers of saints on the golden altar. (censer: a container for burning incense) **4.** The smoke of the incense and prayers rose before God from the angel's hand. **5.** The angel filled the censer with fire from the altar and threw it to the earth, causing lightning, thunder, and an earthquake. **6.** The seven angels with trumpets prepared to blow them. **7.** The first trumpet brought hail and fire mixed with blood, burning a third of the trees and all green grass. **8.** The second trumpet cast a fiery mountain into the sea, turning a third of it to blood. **9.** A third of sea creatures died, and a third of ships were destroyed. **10.** The third trumpet caused a blazing star, Wormwood, to fall on a third of rivers and springs. (Wormwood: a bitter, poisonous plant) **11.** A third of the waters turned bitter, and many people died from drinking them. **12.** The fourth trumpet darkened a third of the sun, moon, and stars, dimming both day and night by a third. **13.** An angel flew through the heavens, crying, "Woe to the earth's people for the last three trumpet blasts!" (woe: great sorrow or distress)

Chapter 9

1. The fifth angel sounded his trumpet, and I saw a star fall from heaven to earth. To it was given the key to the abyss. (Abyss: a deep or bottomless pit) **2.** He opened the abyss, and smoke poured out, darkening the sun and sky. **3.** Locusts came from the smoke, given power like scorpions. (Locusts: large insects, Scorpions: venomous arachnids) **4.** They were told not to harm plants, only people without God's seal. (Seal: a mark of protection) **5.** They could not kill, only torment for five months, like a scorpion's sting. (Torment: severe pain) **6.** People will seek death but not find it, longing to die but death will escape them. (Escape: avoid, evade) **7.** The locusts looked like battle horses, with crowns and faces like men. (Crowns: ornamental headpieces) **8.** They had women's hair and lion's teeth. (Lion's: a large, powerful cat) **9.** They wore armor like iron and their wings sounded like many chariots. (Armor: protective covering, Chariots: ancient vehicles pulled by horses) **10.** Their tails were like scorpions, causing harm for five months. (Scorpions: venomous creatures) **11.** They had a king, the angel of the abyss, named Abaddon in Hebrew, Apollyon in Greek. (Abyss: bottomless pit, Abaddon: destruction, Apollyon: destroyer) **12.** The first woe is past, two more are coming. (Woe: great sorrow or trouble) **13.** The sixth angel blew his trumpet, and I heard a voice from the altar before God. (Altar: a structure for sacrifices) **14.** The voice said to release the four angels bound at the Euphrates River. (Bound: restrained, tied) **15.** These angels were prepared to kill a third of mankind. (Mankind: human beings) **16.** The army of horsemen numbered two hundred million. (Horsemen: riders on horses) **17.** The horses and riders had fiery armor, and fire, smoke, and sulfur came from their mouths. (Sulfur: a yellow mineral, often associated with fire) **18.** A third of humanity was killed by fire, smoke, and sulfur. (Humanity: human race) **19.** Their power was in their mouths and tails, which were like serpents' tails. (Serpents: snakes) **20.** Those not killed still did not repent of idol worship or evil deeds. (Repent: feel remorse, turn away from, Idol: a false god) **21.** They did not stop their murders, sorcery, sexual immorality, or thefts. (Sorcery: magical practices, Immorality: wrong or sinful behavior)

Chapter 10

1. I saw a mighty angel coming from heaven, clothed in a cloud, with a rainbow on his head, his face shining like the sun, and his feet like pillars of fire. (mighty: powerful, pillars: strong columns) **2.** He held an open book and placed his right foot on the sea and his left on the land. (sea: large body of water, land: solid ground) **3.** He shouted like a roaring lion, and seven thunders answered with their voices. (thunders: loud sounds from the sky) **4.** When the thunders spoke, I was about to write, but I heard a voice saying, "Do not write what they said." **5.** The angel raised his hand to heaven. (raised: lifted) **6.** He swore by the eternal One, who made the heavens, earth, and sea, that there would be no more delay. (swore: promised, eternal: forever lasting) **7.** When the seventh angel sounds his trumpet, the mystery of God will be complete, as He told the prophets. (mystery: hidden plan, trumpet: a loud instrument) **8.** The voice from heaven said, "Go and take the open book from the angel." **9.** I went and asked the angel for the book. He said, "Eat it. It will be sweet in your mouth but bitter in your stomach." (eat it: consume, bitter: unpleasant) **10.** I took the book, ate it, and it was sweet in my mouth but bitter in my stomach. (tasted: experienced, swallow: consume) **11.** He told me, "You must prophesy again to many peoples, nations, and kings." (prophesy: speak God's message, peoples: groups of people)

Chapter 11

1. I was given a reed like a rod, and the angel said, "Rise and measure the temple of God, the altar, and those who worship there." (reed: a measuring stick, rod: a staff or stick) **2.** Do not measure the outer court, for it is given to the Gentiles, and they will trample the holy city for forty-two months. (Gentiles: non-Jews) **3.** I will give power to my two witnesses, and they will prophesy for twelve hundred and sixty days, clothed in sackcloth. (sackcloth: rough fabric worn as a sign of mourning or repentance) **4.** These are the two olive trees and lampstands before the Lord of the earth. (lampstands: holders for lamps, symbolizing witnesses) **5.** If anyone harms them, fire will come from their mouths and destroy their enemies. (harm: injure or hurt) **6.** They have power to stop rain, turn water to blood, and bring plagues as often as they wish. (plagues: severe diseases or disasters) **7.** When their testimony ends, the beast from the abyss will kill them. (testimony: witness or message; beast: a destructive figure) **8.** Their bodies will lie in the streets of the city, spiritually called Sodom and Egypt, where our Lord was crucified. (crucified: nailed to the cross) **9.** People from all nations will see their bodies for three and a half days and refuse to bury them. (nations: countries, refuse: deny or not allow) **10.** People will rejoice and exchange gifts, because these two prophets tormented them. (tormented: caused great distress or pain) **11.** After three and a half days, they will come back to life, and great fear will fall on those who see them. (great: immense, fear: intense feeling of dread) **12.** They will hear a voice from heaven saying, "Come up here," and they will ascend in a cloud while their enemies watch. (ascend: rise upward) **13.** At that hour, a great earthquake will occur, killing seven thousand, and the rest will be terrified and give glory to God. (earthquake: a sudden shaking of the ground, terrified: filled with fear) **14.** The second woe is over; the third is coming quickly. (woe: a great sorrow or distress) **15.** The seventh angel sounded his trumpet, and voices in heaven proclaimed, "The kingdoms of this world belong to our Lord, and he will reign forever." (reign: rule or govern) **16.** The twenty-four elders fell on their faces and worshiped God, (elders: respected leaders) **17.** saying, "We thank you, Lord, for taking your power and beginning to reign." (thank: express gratitude) **18.** The nations were angry, and your wrath has come, the time to judge the dead and reward your servants. (wrath: intense anger, reward: give a prize or compensation) **19.** The temple of God was opened, and the ark of his covenant was seen with lightning, thunder, an earthquake, and hail. (ark: a sacred chest, covenant: a formal agreement)

Chapter 12

1. A great sight appeared in the sky: a woman clothed with the sun, the moon beneath her feet, and a crown of twelve stars on her head. (Clothed: covered, Beneath: under) **2.** She was pregnant and in pain, crying out as she was about to give birth. (Pregnant: carrying a child, Crying out: shouting in pain) **3.** Another sight appeared: a great red dragon with seven heads, ten horns, and seven crowns. (Heads: top parts of the body, Horns: pointed projections) **4.** His tail swept a third of the stars from the sky and threw them to the earth. The dragon stood before the woman to devour her child when it was born. (Devour: eat or destroy) **5.** She gave birth to a son, who would rule all nations, but her child was taken up to God. (Rule: govern, Taken up: lifted) **6.** The woman fled into the wilderness, where God had prepared a place for her, where she was nourished for 1,260 days. (Wilderness: deserted place, Nourished: fed) **7.** A war broke out in heaven: Michael and his angels fought the dragon and his angels. (Michael: an archangel, Fought: battled) **8.** The dragon did not win and lost his place in heaven. (Win: succeed, Lost: no longer had) **9.** The dragon, called the Devil and Satan, who deceives the world, was cast to the earth with his angels. (Deceives: misleads) **10.** A loud voice in heaven said, "Salvation, power, and the kingdom of God have come, for the accuser of our brothers has been cast down." (Salvation: rescue, Accuser: one who blames) **11.** They overcame him by the blood of the Lamb and their testimony; they did not love their lives even unto death. (Testimony: witness, Unto: until) **12.** Rejoice, heavens, but woe to the earth and sea, for the devil is furious, knowing his time is short. (Woe: great sorrow, Furious: very angry) **13.** When the dragon saw he was thrown to earth, he persecuted the woman who gave birth to the son. (Persecuted: harmed) **14.** The woman was given two eagle wings to fly to a place in the wilderness, where she was protected from the serpent. (Serpent: snake, Protected: kept safe) **15.** The serpent poured water like a river after the woman, to drown her. (Drown: submerge in water) **16.** The earth helped the woman, swallowing the flood the dragon sent. (Swallowing: taking in) **17.** The dragon was angry and made war on the rest of her offspring, those who keep God's commandments and hold to Jesus' testimony. (Offspring: descendants, Hold to: keep firmly)

Chapter 13

1. I stood by the sea and saw a beast rise with seven heads, ten horns, ten crowns, and blasphemous names on its heads. (Blasphemous: speaking evil or disrespectfully about God) **2.** The beast was like a leopard, with bear feet and a lion's mouth. The dragon gave it power, throne, and authority. (Throne: a seat of power, authority) **3.** One head appeared mortally wounded, but the wound healed, and the world marveled at the beast. (Mortally: fatally) **4.** They worshiped the dragon and the beast, asking, "Who can fight the beast?" (Worshiped: showed reverence or adoration) **5.** It spoke blasphemous things and was given authority to act for forty-two months. **6.** It blasphemed God, His name, His temple, and those in heaven. **7.** It was given power to wage war against and overcome the saints, ruling over all nations and tongues. (Saints: holy people, followers of God) **8.** All on earth will worship it, except those written in the Lamb's Book of Life. (Lamb: Jesus Christ, the Savior) **9.** Whoever has ears, let them listen. (Meaning: pay attention) **10.** Those who lead into captivity will be taken captive; those who kill with the sword will die by the sword. This is the patience of the saints. (Captivity: being held captive or imprisoned) **11.** Then another beast rose from the earth, with two horns like a lamb and speaking like a dragon. (Dragon: a symbol of evil or Satan) **12.** It caused people to worship the first beast, whose deadly wound was healed. (Deadly: fatal) **13.** It performed signs, making fire come down from heaven. (Signs: miraculous acts or wonders) **14.** It deceived people with miracles and told them to make an image of the beast. (Deceived: misled or tricked) **15.** It gave life to the image of the beast, so that it could speak and demand worship, killing those who refused. (Demand: required, insisted upon) **16.** It made everyone receive a mark on their hand or forehead. (Mark: a sign or symbol) **17.** No one could buy or sell without the mark, the beast's name, or its number. (Buy or sell: engage in commerce) **18.** Let those with understanding calculate the number of the beast: it is six hundred sixty-six. (Calculate: figure out, determine)

Chapter 14

1. I saw a Lamb on Mount Zion with 144,000, having His Father's name on their foreheads. (144,000: a symbolic number representing those faithful to God) **2.** I heard a voice from heaven like many waters and thunder, and harps playing. (harps: musical instruments) **3.** They sang a new song before the throne and elders, which only the 144,000 could learn. (elders: spiritual leaders) **4.** These are pure, following the Lamb wherever He goes, redeemed as the firstfruits to God. (firstfruits: the best or first of something, symbolizing purity) **5.** No deceit was found in them; they are blameless before God's throne. (blameless: without fault) **6.** I saw another angel with the everlasting gospel to preach to all nations. (everlasting gospel: the eternal message of salvation) **7.** He cried, "Fear God, give Him glory, for His judgment has come. Worship the Creator." (Creator: the one who made everything) **8.** Another angel said, "Babylon has fallen, she made nations drink of her sinful ways." (Babylon: a symbol of sinful, corrupt powers) **9.** A third angel warned, "If anyone worships the beast or takes its mark, **10.** they will suffer God's wrath, tormented forever in the presence of the Lamb." **11.** Their torment will last forever; no rest for those who worship the beast or its mark. (torment: great suffering) **12.** Here is the patience of the saints who keep God's commands and faith in Jesus. (saints: holy or faithful people) **13.** A voice from heaven said, "Blessed are those who die in the Lord; their works follow them." (blessed: honored and favored) **14.** I saw a cloud with one like the Son of Man, wearing a crown and holding a sickle. (sickle: a curvrd cutting tool) **15.** An angel told Him to reap the harvest, for the earth's harvest is ripe. (reap: to gather the harvest) **16.** The Lamb reaped the earth, gathering the harvest. (Lamb: a symbol of Jesus Christ) **17.** Another angel came with a sharp sickle. **18.** Another angel, with authority over fire, told him to gather the grapes. (fire: often a symbol of judgment) **19.** The angel gathered the grapes and cast them into God's winepress of wrath. (winepress: a place where grapes are crushed, symbolizing judgment) **20.** The winepress was trodden outside the city, and blood flowed as high as horses' bridles. (blood: a symbol of judgment and death)

Chapter 15

1. I saw a great sign in heaven: seven angels with the last seven plagues, completing God's wrath. (Plagues: destructive diseases or disasters) **2.** I saw a sea of glass mixed with fire, and those who conquered the beast and its mark standing on it, holding God's harps. (Conquered: defeated) **3.** They sang the song of Moses and the Lamb, praising God's great and true works, O King of saints. (Saints: holy or sacred people) **4.** "Who will not fear You, Lord, and glorify Your name? You alone are holy; all nations will worship You, for Your judgments are clear." (Judgments: decisions or decrees) **5.** Then, I saw the temple of the heavenly tabernacle open. (Tabernacle: a sacred place or tent) **6.** Seven angels came out of the temple in white linen with golden sashes. (Sashes: decorative bands) **7.** One of the living creatures gave the angels seven golden bowls full of God's eternal wrath. (Wrath: intense anger) **8.** The temple was filled with smoke from God's power, and no one could enter until the plagues were finished.

Chapter 16

1. A loud voice from the temple said to the seven angels, "Go and pour out God's wrath on the earth." **2.** The first angel poured out his bowl on the earth, causing painful sores on those who had the mark of the beast and worshiped its image. (Sores: painful skin ulcers) **3.** The second angel poured his bowl into the sea, turning it into blood, and every creature in it died. (Bowl: a container; Creature: living being) **4.** The third angel poured his bowl into the rivers and springs, turning them into blood. (Springs: natural sources of water) **5.** The angel of the waters said, "You are righteous, O Lord, for You have judged this way." (Righteous: morally right) **6.** "They shed the blood of saints, and You gave them blood to drink; they deserve it." (Shed: spilled, often violently) **7.** A voice from the altar said, "Yes, Lord Almighty, Your judgments are true and just." (Almighty: having complete power) **8.** The fourth angel poured his bowl on the sun, and it scorched people with fire. (Scorched: burned severely) **9.** People were burned and cursed God but did not repent and glorify Him. (Repent: feel remorse for one's actions) **10.** The fifth angel poured his bowl on the throne of the beast, plunging its kingdom into darkness; people gnawed their tongues in pain, (Plunging: causing to fall or move suddenly) **11.** and cursed God because of their pain, but did not repent. (Gnawed: bit or chewed repeatedly) **12.** The sixth angel poured his bowl on the Euphrates River, drying it up to prepare the way for the kings from the east. (Euphrates: a major river in the Middle East) **13.** I saw three unclean spirits like frogs come from the dragon, the beast, and the false prophet. (Unclean: impure, evil) **14.** They are spirits of demons, working signs to gather the kings for the great battle of God Almighty. (Demons: evil spirits) **15.** "I come like a thief! Blessed is the one who stays awake and keeps their clothes on." (Blessed: favored, happy) **16.** They gathered at a place called Armageddon. (Armageddon: the site of the final battle) **17.** The seventh angel poured his bowl into the air, and a voice from the throne said, "It is done." (Throne: the seat of authority) **18.** There were lightning, thunder, and a massive earthquake like no other in history. (Massive: large, powerful) **19.** The great city split into three parts, and Babylon was remembered before God to receive His fierce wrath. (Wrath: intense anger) **20.** Every island vanished, and the mountains were no longer found. (Vanished: disappeared) **21.** Hailstones, each weighing about a talent, fell from the sky, and people cursed God for the severe plague of hail. (Hailstones: small pieces of ice; Talent: a large unit of weight)

Chapter 17

1. One of the seven angels with the seven bowls came and said, "Come, I will show you the judgment of the great harlot on many waters." (Harlot = prostitute, waters = peoples) **2.** With her, the kings of the earth committed immorality, and the people were made drunk with her wickedness. (Immorality = sinful behavior, drunk = overwhelmed) **3.** He carried me in the spirit to the wilderness, where I saw a woman on a scarlet beast, full of blasphemous names, with seven heads and ten horns. (Blasphemous = disrespectful to God) **4.** The woman wore purple and scarlet, adorned with gold, jewels, and pearls, holding a golden cup full of her abominations. (Abominations = detestable things) **5.** On her forehead was written, "MYSTERY, BABYLON THE GREAT, THE MOTHER OF PROSTITUTES AND ABOMINATIONS OF THE EARTH." (Prostitutes = immoral women) **6.** I saw the woman drunk with the blood of saints and martyrs. I wondered greatly. (Drunk = overwhelmed, martyrs = those who die for their faith) **7.** The angel said, "Why are you amazed? I will explain the mystery of the woman and the beast with seven heads and ten horns." (Amazed = astonished, mystery = something difficult to understand) **8.** The beast was, is not, and will rise from the abyss to destruction. The earth's people will be astonished. (Abyss = bottomless pit, astonished = shocked) **9.** Here is wisdom: The seven heads are seven mountains where the woman sits. (Mountains = symbols of power) **10.** There are seven kings: five have fallen, one is, and one is yet to come. He will last only a little while. (Kings = rulers, yet = not yet) **11.** The beast that was, is not, is the eighth and goes to destruction. (Destruction = ruin) **12.** The ten horns are ten kings who have not yet received their kingdoms but will reign briefly with the beast. (Reign = rule) **13.** They will unite and give their power to the beast. (Unite = come together) **14.** They will fight the Lamb, but the Lamb will defeat them, for He is Lord of lords and King of kings, and those with Him are faithful. (Defeat = overcome) **15.** The waters are peoples, multitudes, nations, and languages. (Peoples = groups of people) **16.** The ten horns will hate the woman, strip her, eat her flesh, and burn her with fire. (Strip = remove her clothes, flesh = body) **17.** God has put it in their hearts to fulfill His will and give their power to the beast until His words are fulfilled. (Fulfill = complete) **18.** The woman you saw is the great city that rules over the kings of the earth. (Rules = has power over)

Chapter 18
1. I saw another angel with great power, and the earth was lit by his glory. (Glory: Great beauty or honor.) **2.** He cried loudly, "Babylon has fallen and become a home for demons and unclean spirits." (Demons: Evil spirits. Unclean: Not pure.) **3.** All nations shared in her immorality, and the kings and merchants grew rich from her luxury. (Immorality: Wrong behavior. Luxury: Great comfort or wealth.) **4.** A voice from heaven said, "Come out of her, my people, so you don't share in her sins or plagues." (Plagues: Disasters or punishments.) **5.** Her sins have reached heaven, and God has remembered her wrongs. (Wrongs: Actions that are morally wrong.) **6.** Pay her back as she has done, and double her punishment for her deeds. (Deeds: Actions or behaviors.) **7.** As she glorified herself and lived in luxury, give her that much sorrow. (Glorified: Praised. Luxury: Great comfort or wealth.) **8.** Her plagues will come in one day—death, mourning, and famine; she will be destroyed by fire, for God is strong. (Mourning: Grief. Famine: Lack of food.) **9.** The kings who sinned with her will mourn when they see her burning. (Sinned: Committed wrong acts.) **10.** They will stand far off, saying, "Alas, that great city, your judgment has come in one hour." (Alas: An expression of sorrow. Judgment: Final decision or punishment.) **11.** Merchants will weep, for no one buys their goods anymore. (Weep: Cry.) **12.** The goods of gold, silver, pearls, fine linen, purple, silk, and precious woods will be gone. (Goods: Products or merchandise.) **13.** Cinnamon, wine, oil, wheat, cattle, slaves, and even souls of men will no longer be bought or sold. (Souls: The immaterial essence of a person.) **14.** The luxury you desired is gone forever, and you will never find it again. (Luxury: Great comfort or wealth.) **15.** Merchants who grew rich from her will weep in fear of her torment. (Torment: Extreme pain or suffering.) **16.** They will cry, "Alas, that great city, which was adorned with wealth and luxury!" (Adorned: Decorated. Wealth: Abundance of resources.) **17.** In one hour, all her riches are destroyed. Sailors and shipmasters will stand far off, (Sailors: People who work on ships. Shipmasters: Captains of ships.) **18.** crying, "What city is like this great city?" (Crying: Expressing sorrow with tears.) **19.** They will mourn and say, "In one hour, she was made desolate." (Mourn: Express grief. Desolate: Empty or abandoned.) **20.** Rejoice, heaven and the saints, for God has avenged you on her. (Avenge: To punish in return for a wrong.) **21.** A mighty angel threw a huge stone into the sea, saying, "This is how Babylon will be destroyed, never to be found again." (Millstone: A large stone used for grinding grain.) **22.** The sounds of music, work, and celebration will be heard no more in you. (Celebration: The act of celebrating.) **23.** The light of a lamp will no longer shine, and the voices of the bride and bridegroom will never be heard again. (Bridegroom: A man on his wedding day.) **24.** In her was found the blood of prophets, saints, and all slain on earth. (Slain: Killed violently.)

Chapter 19
1. After this, I heard a great voice from many people in heaven saying, "Hallelujah! Salvation, glory, honor, and power belong to our God." (Halleluiah: an expression of praise, Salvation: deliverance from sin, Glory: great honor, Power: strength or control) **2.** For His judgments are true and righteous; He has judged the great harlot who corrupted the earth, and avenged His servants' blood. (Harlot: immoral woman, Avenge: to take revenge) **3.** They again said, "Hallelujah!" And her smoke rose forever. (Smoke: vapor or fumes from burning) **4.** The twenty-four elders and the four living creatures worshiped God, saying, "Amen; Hallelujah!" (Amen: so be it) **5.** A voice from the throne said, "Praise our God, all His servants, and those who fear Him, both small and great." (Fear: reverence or awe) **6.** I heard a great multitude, like many waters and mighty thunderings, saying, "Hallelujah! For the Lord God omnipotent reigns." (Omnipotent: all-powerful) **7.** Let us rejoice and honor Him, for the marriage of the Lamb has come, and His bride has prepared herself. (Lamb: a symbol for Jesus Christ) **8.** She was clothed in clean, white linen, which represents the righteous acts of the saints. (Saints: holy or devout people) **9.** He said, "Write: Blessed are those invited to the marriage supper of the Lamb." These are the true sayings of God. (Invited: called to join) **10.** I fell to worship him, but he said, "Do not do that! Worship God; the testimony of Jesus is the spirit of prophecy." (Testimony: evidence, Prophecy: a message from God) **11.** Then I saw heaven opened, and a white horse; the one on it was called Faithful and True, judging in righteousness. (Righteousness: moral correctness) **12.** His eyes were like fire, and He wore many crowns; He had a name no one knew but Himself. (Crowns: symbols of authority or victory) **13.** He was clothed in a robe dipped in blood, and His name is "The Word of God." (Robe: a long garment) **14.** The armies of heaven followed Him on white horses, dressed in fine, clean linen. (Armies: groups of soldiers, Linen: a type of cloth) **15.** A sharp sword came from His mouth, and He will strike the nations, ruling them with an iron rod. (Sword: a weapon, Rod: a staff or scepter) **16.** His robe and thigh bore the name "King of Kings and Lord of Lords." (Thigh: the upper leg) **17.** An angel stood in the sun and called to the birds, "Come to the great supper of God." (Supper: a meal) **18.** "So that you may eat the flesh of kings, captains, mighty men, horses, and all people, both free and slave." (Captains: military leaders, Flesh: the body) **19.** I saw the beast and the kings of the earth with their armies gathered to fight against Him and His army. (Beast: a symbol of evil, Army: a group of soldiers) **20.** The beast and the false prophet were captured and thrown alive into the lake of fire. (False prophet: one who deceives) **21.** The rest were killed with the sword from His mouth, and the birds ate their flesh. (Sword: a weapon, Flesh: the body)

Chapter 20
1. I saw an angel come down from heaven with the key to the abyss and a chain. (Abyss: a deep, bottomless pit) **2.** He grabbed the dragon, the Devil and Satan, and bound him for a thousand years. (Dragon: a symbol of Satan) **3.** He threw him into the abyss, locked him up, and sealed him so he couldn't deceive the nations until the thousand years ended. (Deceive: to mislead or trick) **4.** I saw thrones, and those sitting on them were given authority to judge. I saw the souls of martyrs who hadn't worshiped the beast or received his mark, and they ruled with Christ for a thousand years. (Martyrs: those who suffer or die for their faith) **5.** The rest of the dead didn't come back to life until after the thousand years. This is the first resurrection. **6.** Blessed are those who take part in the first resurrection; the second death has no power over them, and they will reign with Christ. (Resurrection: rising from the dead) **7.** When the thousand years are over, Satan will be set free from his prison. **8.** He will deceive the nations, Gog and Magog, to gather them for battle, as numerous as the sea's sand. (Gog and Magog: symbolic nations of evil) **9.** They will surround the saints' camp and the beloved city, but fire from heaven will destroy them. **10.** The devil who deceived them will be cast into the lake of fire, where the beast and false prophet are, tormented forever. (False prophet: a deceiver who claims to speak for God) **11.** I saw a great white throne, and the One sitting on it, whose presence made earth and heaven vanish. **12.** The dead, small and great, stood before God, and the books were opened; they were judged by what was written in them. **13.** The sea gave up the dead in it, and death and Hades gave up their dead, judged by their deeds. (Hades: the realm of the dead) **14.** Death and Hades were thrown into the lake of fire. This is the second death. **15.** Anyone not in the book of life was cast into the lake of fire. (Book of life: a register of those saved by God)

Chapter 21
1. I saw a new heaven and earth; the old ones had passed away, and there was no more sea. (Sea - symbol of chaos or separation) **2.** I, John, saw the holy city, new Jerusalem, coming down from God, like a bride for her husband. **3.** A loud voice from heaven said, "God's dwelling is with mankind; He will live with them, and they will be His people." **4.** God will wipe away every tear, and there will be no more death, sorrow, or pain, for the old things are gone. **5.** The One on the throne said, "I make all things new. Write, for these words are true." **6.** "It is finished. I am the Alpha and the Omega, the beginning and the end. I will give water to the thirsty freely." (Alpha and Omega - First and last letters of the Greek alphabet, meaning beginning and end) **7.** "The one who overcomes will inherit all things. I will be their God, and they will be My child." **8.** The fearful, unbelievers, murderers, sorcerers, and liars will be in the lake of fire, the second death. (Sorcerers - those who practice magic) **9.** One of the seven angels who had the final plagues spoke to me, saying, "Come, I will show you the Lamb's wife." **10.** He took me in the spirit to a high mountain and showed me the holy city, Jerusalem, descending from God. **11.** The city was filled with God's glory, shining like a precious jasper stone. **12.** It had a great wall with twelve gates, and twelve angels at the gates, with the names of Israel's twelve tribes. **13.** There were three gates on each side: east, north, south, and west. **14.** The city's wall had twelve foundations with the names of the twelve apostles of the Lamb. **15.** The angel used a golden reed to measure the city, its gates, and wall. **16.** The city was square, twelve thousand furlongs in length, width, and height. (Furlongs - a unit of distance, about 1/8 of a mile) **17.** The wall was 144 cubits thick, according to the angel's measure. (Cubit - an ancient measure, approximately

18 inches) **18.** The wall was made of jasper, and the city was pure gold, like glass. **19.** The city's foundations were adorned with precious stones: jasper, sapphire, chalcedony, and emerald. **20.** The other stones were sardonyx, sardius, chrysolite, beryl, topaz, chrysoprase, jacinth, and amethyst. **21.** The twelve gates were pearls, and the streets were pure gold, like transparent glass. **22.** I saw no temple, for God and the Lamb are its temple. **23.** The city had no need of sun or moon, for the glory of God and the Lamb gave it light. **24.** The saved nations will walk in its light, and kings will bring their glory into it. **25.** Its gates will never be shut, for there will be no night there. **26.** They will bring the glory and honor of the nations into it. **27.** Nothing impure will enter it, only those written in the Lamb's book of life.

Chapter 22

1. He showed me a clear river of life, flowing from the throne of God and the Lamb. (Lamb: Jesus Christ) **2.** On each side of the river stood the tree of life, bearing twelve fruits, one each month, with leaves for the healing of the nations. (Nations: different groups of people) **3.** There will be no curse; God and the Lamb will reign, and His servants will serve Him. (Curse: punishment) **4.** They will see His face, and His name will be on their foreheads. (Foreheads: the front part of the head) **5.** There will be no night, no need for light, for God will give them light, and they will reign forever. (Reign: rule) **6.** These words are true; God sent His angel to show His servants what will soon happen. (Angel: messenger) **7.** "I am coming quickly. Blessed are those who obey this prophecy." (Blessed: happy or fortunate) **8.** I, John, saw and heard these things and fell to worship the angel showing me. (Worship: show reverence) **9.** The angel said, "Do not worship me; I am a servant like you. Worship God." (Servant: one who serves) **10.** "Do not seal the words of this book, for the time is near." (Seal: close or hide) **11.** Let the unjust remain unjust, and the righteous remain righteous. (Unjust: unfair, unrighteous; Righteous: morally right) **12.** "I am coming quickly, and My reward is with Me, to repay each person for their actions." (Repay: reward or punish) **13.** I am the Alpha and Omega, the Beginning and End. (Alpha and Omega: the first and last letters of the Greek alphabet, symbolizing the beginning and end) **14.** Blessed are those who keep My commandments, for they will have the right to the tree of life and enter the city. (Commandments: instructions or laws) **15.** Outside are the evil—sorcerers, immoral people, murderers, idolaters, and liars. (Idolaters: those who worship false gods) **16.** I, Jesus, sent My angel to testify these things in the churches. I am the Root and Offspring of David, the bright morning star. (Testify: witness or tell; Offspring: descendants) **17.** The Spirit and the bride say, "Come! Let those who hear say, 'Come!'" (Bride: the Church or the faithful) **18.** If anyone adds to this book, God will add the plagues written in it. (Plagues: disasters or punishments) **19.** If anyone removes from this book, God will take away their part in the tree of life and the holy city. (Remove: take away; Part: share) **20.** The one who testifies says, "I am coming quickly. Amen. Come, Lord Jesus." (Testifies: witnesses or confirms)

67 – Tobit

Chapter 1

1. This is the record of the words of Tobit, son of Tobiel, descendant of Ananiel, Aduel, Gabael, Asael, from the tribe of Naphtali. (Tobiel: name, Naphtali: tribe) **2.** During the reign of Shalmaneser, king of the Assyrians, I was captured from the town of Thisbe, near the city of Naphtali in Galilee, above Aser. (Shalmaneser: king, Thisbe: town, Galilee: region) **3.** I, Tobit, have lived my life in truth and righteousness, performing many acts of charity for my people and relatives as we journeyed to Nineveh in Assyria. (Righteousness: virtue, Charity: generosity, Nineveh: city) **4.** When I was young, the tribe of Naphtali, including my family, abandoned Jerusalem, the city chosen for all Israel to offer sacrifices, where the temple of the Most High was established forever. (Abandoned: deserted, Jerusalem: city, Most High: God) **5.** While the others turned to idolatry, worshiping Baal, (Idolatry: idol worship, Baal: false god) **6.** I alone continued to visit Jerusalem for the festivals, as commanded by Israel's eternal law, bringing my tithes and offerings to the priests, the sons of Aaron. (Festivals: celebrations, Tithes: offerings, Aaron: priest) **7.** I gave one tenth of my earnings to the priests in Jerusalem, sold another tenth, and spent it there each year. (Earnings: income, Spent: used) **8.** The third portion I gave to those in need, as Deborah, my father's mother, had instructed me, since I was an orphan. (Portion: share, Deborah: name, Orphan: parentless) **9.** When I reached adulthood, I married Anna, a relative, and we had a son, Tobias. (Adulthood: maturity, Tobias: name) **10.** When we were exiled to Nineveh, my people ate the food of the Gentiles, (Exiled: banished, Gentiles: non-Jews) **11.** but I refrained, (Refrained: avoided) **12.** remembering God in my heart. (Heart: mind) **13.** The Most High granted me favor with King Enemessar, and I became his steward. (Steward: manager) **14.** I traveled to Media and entrusted ten talents of silver to Gabael, the brother of Gabrias, in Rages. (Media: region, Talents: currency, Rages: city) **15.** After Enemessar's death, his son Sennacherib took the throne, and I could not return to Media. (Throne: seat of power) **16.** During Enemessar's reign, I gave alms, sharing my bread with the hungry, (Reign: rule, Alms: charity) **17.** and provided clothes to the naked. If I saw any of my people dead or discarded in Nineveh, I buried them. (Naked: unclothed, Discarded: thrown away) **18.** If Sennacherib executed anyone, I secretly buried their bodies to keep them hidden from the king's wrath. (Executed: killed, Wrath: anger) **19.** When a Ninevite accused me of burying the dead, I fled to avoid execution. (Accused: blamed, Fled: escaped) **20.** All my possessions were taken, leaving me with nothing but my wife Anna and son Tobias. (Possessions: belongings) **21.** Within fifty-five days, two of Sennacherib's sons killed him and fled, and Sarchedonus succeeded him as king, appointing Achiacharus, my cousin, as overseer of his father's affairs. (Succeeded: replaced, Overseer: supervisor) **22.** Achiacharus interceded for me, and I returned to Nineveh. He was Sarchedonus's cupbearer and steward, and my brother's son. (Interceded: pleaded, Cupbearer: servant)

Chapter 2

1. When I returned home and my wife Anna and son Tobias were with me, during the feast of Shavuot, the feast of the seven weeks, a good meal was prepared. I sat down to eat. (Shavuot: festival) **2.** Seeing the abundance of food, I said to my son, "Go and find any poor man of our people who fears the Lord; wait for me." (Abundance: plenty) **3.** He returned and said, "Father, one of our people has been strangled and thrown into the marketplace." (Strangled: choked) **4.** Before eating, I stood up, took him into a room, and waited until sunset to bury him. **5.** Afterward, I washed and ate my meal in sorrow. (Sorrow: sadness) **6.** Remembering Amos' prophecy, "Your feasts will turn to mourning, and your joy to lamentation." (Prophecy: prediction; Lamentation: grief) **7.** I wept, and at sunset, I dug a grave and buried him. (Wept: cried; Grave: tomb) **8.** My neighbors mocked me, saying, "This man is not afraid to die for his actions. He fled, yet now he buries the dead again!" (Mocked: ridiculed; Fled: ran) **9.** That night, I slept by the wall of my courtyard, unclean, with my face uncovered. (Unclean: impure) **10.** I didn't know there were sparrows in the wall, and while I slept, their droppings got into my eyes, causing blindness. I went to the doctors, but they couldn't help. Achiacharus took care of me until I went to Elymais. (Droppings: waste; Elymais: city) **11.** Meanwhile, my wife Anna worked at women's tasks. (Tasks: chores) **12.** When she finished her work and gave it back to the owners, they paid her wages and also gave her a kid (a young goat). (Wages: payment; Kid: goat) **13.** When it cried in the house, I asked, "Where did this kid come from? Was it stolen? It's unlawful to eat stolen goods." (Stolen: taken; Unlawful: illegal) **14.** She replied, "It was a gift, more than my wages." I didn't believe her, and told her to return it. I was ashamed of her, but she responded, "Where are your alms and righteous deeds? All your works are known." (Alms: charity; Righteous: just; Deeds: actions)

Chapter 3

1. In my sorrow, I wept and prayed, saying: (Sorrow: sadness, Wept: cried) **2.** "Lord, You are righteous, and all Your actions are full of mercy and truth. You judge rightly and justly forever." (Righteous: just, Mercy: compassion, Truth: honesty) **3.** "Remember me and look upon me. Do not punish me for my sins or for the wrongs of my ancestors who sinned before You." (Punish: penalize, Sins: wrongdoings, Ancestors: forebears) **4.** "They disobeyed Your commandments, and because of this, You delivered us to be plundered, to face captivity and death, and to become a disgrace among the nations we were scattered to." (Plundered: robbed, Captivity: imprisonment, Disgrace: shame) **5.** "Now, Your judgments are true. Deal with me according to my sins and those of my ancestors, since we have not followed Your commandments or walked in truth before You." (Judgments: decisions, Commandments: laws, Truth: honesty) **6.** "Now, do what seems best to You, and take my soul from me, that I may return to the earth. It is better to die than to live with the false accusations and sorrow I face. Please command that I be released from this distress and enter into the everlasting realm. Do not turn Your face from me." (Soul: spirit, Distress: hardship, Everlasting realm: afterlife) **7.** On the same day, in Ecbatane, a city of Media, Sarah, daughter of Raguel, was also mocked by her maidservants, (Ecbatane: city, Mocked: ridiculed) **8.** because she had been married to seven husbands, all of whom Asmodeus, the evil spirit, had killed before they could consummate the marriage. "Don't you know," they said, "you've caused the deaths of your husbands? You've had seven, but none of their names are remembered by you." (Consummate: complete, Asmodeus: demon, Evil spirit: harmful being) **9.** "Why do you blame us for their deaths? If they're gone, go to them. We don't want to see you have any children." (Blame: accuse, Children: offspring) **10.** Hearing this, Sarah became deeply troubled and thought of taking her own life. She said, "I am my father's only child, and if I do this, it will bring shame upon him and sorrow to his old age." (Troubled: distressed, Shame: dishonor) **11.** She then prayed toward the window, saying, "Blessed are You, O Lord, my God, and Your holy name is worthy of praise forever. Let all Your works give You praise forever." (Blessed: honored, Worthy: deserving) **12.** "Now, O Lord, I direct my eyes and face toward You," (Eyes: vision, Face: presence) **13.** and say, "Take me from this earth, so I no longer hear reproach." (Reproach: shame) **14.** "You know, Lord, that I have been pure and free from sin with men," (Pure: clean, Sin: wrongdoing) **15.** "I have never defiled my name or my father's name while in this captivity. I am my father's only daughter, and he has no other heir. Why should I continue to live? But if it's not Your will for me to die, show mercy and put an end to this reproach." (Defiled: tarnished, Heir: successor, Reproach: shame) **16.** Both of their prayers were heard by God in His great majesty. (Majesty: greatness) **17.** Raphael was sent to heal them both: to restore Tobit's sight, to give Sarah, daughter of Raguel, to Tobias, and to bind Asmodeus, the evil spirit, because she was rightfully Tobias' wife by inheritance. At that time, Tobit returned to his house, and Sarah, the daughter of Raguel, came down from her room. (Heard: listened to, Heal: cure, Sight: vision, Bind: restrain, Inheritance: legal right)

Chapter 4

1. On that day, Tobit remembered the money he had entrusted to Gabael in Rages of Media. (Entrusted: gave) **2.** He thought to himself, "I have longed for death; why not call for my son Tobias and tell him about the money before I die?" (Longed: wished, Tell: inform) **3.** When he called Tobias, he said, "My son, when I die, bury me, and do not neglect your mother. Honor her all your life and do what pleases her, and do not cause her grief." (Neglect: disregard, Pleases: satisfies) **4.** "Remember, my son, how much danger she faced for you when you were in her womb. When she passes, bury her beside me in the same grave." (Danger: risk, Passes: dies) **5.** "My son, always remember the Lord our God and avoid sin. Keep His commandments and live uprightly. Do not follow paths of unrighteousness." (Avoid: shun, Uprightly: honorably) **6.** "If you live truthfully, your actions will succeed, and you will prosper along with those who live justly." (Prosper: thrive) **7.** "Give alms from your possessions; when you give, do not be grudging or envious. If you turn your face from the poor, God will turn His face from you." (Grudging: reluctant, Envious: jealous) **8.** "If you have plenty, give generously; if you have little, give what you can, without fear." (Generously: freely, Little: modest amount) **9.** "For you are storing up a treasure for yourself for times of need." (Storing up: saving) **10.** "Alms save from death and keep one from darkness." (Save: rescue, Darkness: misfortune) **11.** "Alms are a good offering to all who give them in the sight of the Most High." (Offering: gift) **12.** "Beware of immorality, my son, and marry a woman from your own people, not a foreigner. We are the descendants of the prophets—Noah, Abraham, Isaac, and Jacob. Remember, they married within their own kin and were blessed." (Immorality: unchastity, Descendants: children) **13.** "Love your brethren, and do not despise them in your heart. Pride leads to destruction, and lewdness brings poverty. Lewdness is the mother of famine." (Pride: arrogance, Lewdness: immorality, Famine: hunger) **14.** "Pay your workers promptly; if you serve God, He will repay you. Be wise and cautious in all your actions." (Promptly: without delay, Cautious: careful) **15.** "Do not do to others what you hate. Do not drink to drunkenness, nor let it accompany you on your journey." (Accompany: follow) **16.** "Give bread to the hungry, clothes to the naked, and alms according to your means. Do not be envious when giving." (Envious: jealous) **17.** "Donate bread for the burial of the righteous, but give nothing to the wicked." (Donate: contribute) **18.** "Seek advice from the wise and never disregard counsel that is helpful." (Disregard: ignore) **19.** "Bless the Lord your God always and pray that He guides your ways. He gives wisdom and humbles whom He chooses. Keep my commandments in mind always." (Guides: directs, Wisdom: knowledge) **20.** "I remind you of the ten talents I entrusted to Gabael, the son of Gabrias, in Rages of Media." (Remind: recall, Entrusted: gave) **21.** "Do not fear, my son, that we are poor. You are rich if you fear God, turn away from sin, and do what is pleasing in His sight." (Rich: wealthy)

Chapter 5

1. Tobias replied, "Father, I will do everything you have instructed me to do." (Replied: answered) **2.** "But how can I receive the money, since I don't know the man?" (Receive: take) **3.** Tobit gave him a written note and said, "Find someone who can travel with you while I am still alive, and I will pay him wages. Go, and collect the money." (Written note: document, Wages: payment) **4.** Tobias went to find a companion, and there he met Raphael, who was actually an angel, though Tobias didn't recognize him. (Companion: travel partner) **5.** Tobias asked him, "Can you accompany me to Rages? Do you know the way well?" (Accompany: go with) **6.** The angel replied, "I will go with you. I know the way well because I have stayed with our brother Gabael." (Stayed: lodged, Well: thoroughly) **7.** Tobias then said, "Wait here while I tell my father." (Wait: stay, Tell: inform) **8.** Raphael replied, "Go and don't delay." Tobias returned to his father and said, "I have found someone who will travel with me." (Delay: hesitate, Return: go back) **9.** Tobit said, "Call him in, so I can find out what tribe he is from and whether he is trustworthy to go with you." (Trustworthy: reliable) **10.** They greeted each other, and then Tobit asked, "Brother, tell me your family and tribe." (Greeted: saluted) **11.** The angel responded, "Are you looking for my tribe, my family, or just someone to accompany your son?" (Accompany: travel with) **12.** Tobit insisted, "I want to know your lineage and your name." (Insisted: urged) **13.** The angel replied, "I am Azarias, the son of Ananias, from your own family." (Lineage: ancestry) **14.** Tobit responded, "You are welcome, brother. I meant no offense in asking about your family. You come from a good and honorable line. I know Ananias and Jonathan, sons of the great Samaias. We traveled together to Jerusalem for worship and offered the firstborn and tithes. They did not fall into the errors of our people. You come from a noble family." (Offense: insult, Honorable: respected) **15.** Then Tobit asked, "What wages shall I pay you? Would one drachm a day and necessities like those for my own son be acceptable?" (Wages: payment) **16.** "Yes," the angel replied, "and if you return safely, I will add more to your wages." (Add: increase) **17.** Tobias was pleased, and the angel said to him, "Prepare for your journey, and may God bless your trip." When Tobias had gathered everything needed for the trip, his father said, "Go with this man. May God, who dwells in heaven, bless your journey, and may His angel accompany you." They set out together, with the young man's dog following them. (Bless: prosper, Accompany: travel with) **18.** Meanwhile, Anna, Tobias' mother, wept and said to Tobit, "Why did you send our son away? Isn't he the support of our lives, going in and out before us?" (Wept: cried, Support: help) **19.** "Don't be too eager to add more wealth. Let what the Lord has provided for us be enough for our child." (Eager: eager, Wealth: riches) **20.** Tobit reassured her, "Do not worry, my sister. He will return safe, and you will see him again." (Reassured: comforted) **21.** "The good angel will keep him safe, and his journey will be successful. He will return unharmed." (Unharmed: safe) **22.** After this, Anna stopped crying. (Crying: weeping)

Chapter 6

1. As they journeyed, they reached the Tigris River in the evening and camped there. (Continued: proceeded) **2.** Tobias went down to wash, and a fish jumped out, attempting to swallow him. (Attempting: trying) **3.** The angel said, "Catch the fish!" Tobias grabbed it and pulled it to shore. (Grabbed: seized) **4.** The angel instructed, "Open the fish and take out its heart, liver, and gall, and keep them safe." (Safe: preserve) **5.** Tobias followed the angel's instructions. After roasting and eating the fish, they continued toward Ecbatane. (Followed: obeyed) **6.** As they traveled, Tobias asked, "Brother Azarias, what are the heart, liver, and gall of the fish for?" (Asked: inquired) **7.** The angel replied, "The heart and liver create smoke to drive away evil spirits or devils." (Drive away: repel) **8.** "The gall is for anointing a person with eye problems, and it will heal them." (Anointing: applying, Heal: cure) **9.** As they neared Rages, (Nearing: approaching) **10.** The angel said, "Today we will stay with Raguel, your cousin. He has a daughter named Sara. I will speak to him so you may marry her." (Stay: lodge, Speak: talk) **11.** "You are the rightful one to marry her, as you are her closest relative." (Rightful: entitled) **12.** "She is beautiful and wise. I will speak to her father. After our visit, we will arrange the marriage. According to Moses' law, Raguel cannot marry her to anyone else, or he will be guilty of death, for the right of inheritance belongs to you." (Arrange: organize, Guilty: accountable) **13.** Tobias replied, "I've heard that Sara was married to seven men, and they all died in the marriage chamber." (Replied: responded) **14.** "I am my father's only son. If I marry her, I fear I will die like the others. A wicked spirit harms only those who marry her. I'm afraid my death will cause sorrow to my parents, as they have no other son to bury them." (Harm: injure) **15.** The angel reassured him, "Remember your father's advice to marry within your kin. She will be given to you as a wife. Do not fear the evil spirit. Tonight, she will become your wife." (Reassured: comforted) **16.** "When you enter the marriage chamber, burn some of the fish's heart and liver on perfume ashes. The smoke will drive the spirit away." (Burn: make smoke) **17.** "The demon will flee and never return. Pray to God for mercy when you come together, and He will save you. Do not fear, for she was meant to be your wife, and you will be blessed with children." (Flee: run away, Mercy: compassion) **18.** Upon hearing this, Tobias loved Sara, and his heart was joined to hers. (Joined: united)

Chapter 7

1. When they arrived at Ecbatane, they went to the house of Raguel, and Sara met them. After they greeted each other, she brought them inside. **2.** Raguel said to Edna, his wife, "How much this young man resembles Tobit, my cousin!" (Resemble: look like) **3.** Raguel asked, "Where are you from, brothers?" They answered, "We are from the sons of Naphtali, who are captives in Nineveh." (Captives: prisoners) **4.** Raguel asked, "Do you know

Tobit, our kinsman?" They replied, "We know him." He asked, "Is he in good health?" (Kinsman: relative) **5.** They replied, "He is alive and in good health." Tobias said, "He is my father." **6.** Raguel jumped up, kissed him, and wept. **7.** He blessed Tobias, saying, "You are the son of an honorable and good man." Upon hearing that Tobit was blind, he became sorrowful and wept. (Honorable: respected) **8.** Edna, Raguel's wife, and Sara, his daughter, also wept. They welcomed them warmly, and after killing a ram, they set food on the table. Tobias said to Raphael, "Brother Azarias, speak about what we discussed on the way, and let's settle this matter." (Warmly: kindly) **9.** Raphael explained the situation to Raguel, who said to Tobias, "Eat and drink, and be merry." **10.** "It is right for you to marry my daughter. But I will tell you the truth." **11.** "I've married my daughter to seven men, and each one died the night they married her. Still, for now, enjoy yourselves." Tobias said, "I will not eat until we agree and swear an oath to each other." (Oath: promise) **12.** Raguel said, "Take her as your wife according to tradition, for you are cousins, and she is yours. May the merciful God grant success to you both." **13.** He called his daughter Sara, took her hand, and gave her to Tobias, saying, "Take her as your wife according to Moses' law, and take her to your father. I bless you both." (Bless: wish good fortune) **14.** He called Edna, his wife, took a paper, wrote a marriage contract, and sealed it. (Contract: agreement) **15.** Then they began to eat. **16.** Raguel called his wife Edna and said, "Sister, prepare another room and bring her in." (Sister: term of affection) **17.** Edna obeyed and brought Sara to the room. Sara wept, and Edna comforted her, saying, **18.** "Be comforted, my daughter. May the Lord of heaven and earth give you joy in place of your sorrow. Be comforted, my daughter." (Comforted: consoled)

Chapter 8
1. After they had finished eating, they brought Tobias in to her. **2.** As he entered, he remembered Raphael's advice, took the ashes of the perfumes, placed the heart and liver of the fish on them, and made a smoke. (Ashes: residue) **3.** When the evil spirit smelled it, he fled to the farthest parts of Egypt, and the angel bound him. (Bound: captured) **4.** After they were alone, Tobias rose and said, "Sister, let us pray that God may have mercy on us." (Mercy: compassion) **5.** Tobias prayed, "Blessed art Thou, O God of our fathers, and blessed is Thy holy name forever. Let the heavens and all Thy creatures bless Thee." (Blessed: praised) **6.** "Thou made Adam and gave him Eve as a companion. From them came mankind. Thou said, 'It is not good for man to be alone.'" (Companion: partner) **7.** "Now, O Lord, I take this my sister uprightly, not for lust. Grant that we may grow old together." (Uprightly: honorably) **8.** She said, "Amen." (Amen: so be it) **9.** They both slept that night. Raguel arose and went to prepare a grave. (Grave: burial place) **10.** "I fear he may be dead." **11.** Raguel returned home, **12.** And said to Edna, "Send a maid to check if he is alive. If not, we'll quietly bury him." (Maid: servant) **13.** The maid entered and found them both asleep. **14.** She told them he was alive. **15.** Raguel praised God, saying, "Thou art worthy to be praised with holy praise; let Thy saints and angels praise Thee forever." (Praise: worship) **16.** "Thou art praised because Thou hast made me joyful. What I feared did not happen, and Thou hast shown great mercy." (Joyful: happy) **17.** "Thou art praised for having mercy on the two children of their fathers. Grant them mercy, and let their lives be completed in joy and health." (Mercy: compassion) **18.** Raguel told his servants to fill the grave. (Servants: workers) **19.** He kept the wedding feast for fourteen days. (Feast: celebration) **20.** Before the days ended, Raguel had sworn that Tobias should stay until the fourteen days were complete. (Sworn: promised) **21.** Afterward, Tobias would take half of his wealth and return to his father. The rest would be his after Raguel and Edna's death. (Wealth: possessions)

Chapter 9
1. Then Tobias called to Raphael and said, **2.** "Brother Azarias, take with thee a servant, and two camels, and go to Rages of Media to Gabael, and bring me the money, and bring him to the wedding." (Rages: city; camels: animals) **3.** For Raguel hath sworn that I shall not depart. (Sworn: pledged) **4.** But my father counteth the days; and if I tarry long, he will be very sorry. (Counteth: counts; tarry: delay) **5.** So Raphael went out, and lodged with Gabael, and gave him the handwriting: who brought forth bags which were sealed up, and gave them to him. (Lodged: stayed; handwriting: document; sealed: closed) **6.** And early in the morning they went forth both together, and came to the wedding: and Tobias blessed his wife. (Went forth: departed; blessed: prayed)

Chapter 10
1. As the days passed and the journey continued, Tobit anxiously counted the time. When the expected days had passed and his son had not returned, (anxiously: worried, expected: anticipated) **2.** he wondered, "Could they have been delayed? Or perhaps Gabael has died, and no one is left to deliver the money?" (delayed: postponed, died: passed away) **3.** Deeply distressed, Tobit sighed. (distressed: troubled) **4.** His wife, seeing his grief, lamented, "My son is lost, for he has been gone too long!" She began to weep. (lamented: mourned, grief: sorrow) **5.** "I care for nothing now, for the light of my eyes, my son, is gone." (light of my eyes: beloved, gone: lost) **6.** Tobit tried to comfort her, saying, "Do not grieve; he is safe." (comfort: console, grieve: mourn) **7.** But she refused to be comforted, insisting, "Do not lie to me; I know he is dead." She went out every day to the road where he had traveled, fasting and mourning. She did not cease her weeping until the fourteen days of the wedding had passed. (ceased: stopped, mourning: grieving, wedding: celebration) **8.** After the last day, Tobias said to Raguel, "Please, let me go. My father and mother no longer expect to see me." (expecting: waiting for) **9.** Raguel urged him, "Stay longer, and I will send word to your father about your welfare." (urged: encouraged, welfare: well-being) **10.** Tobias replied, "I must go now. Please let me return to my father." (replied: answered, return: go back) **11.** Raguel stood, gave Sara to Tobias as his wife, along with half his wealth, servants, livestock, and money. (stood: rose, wealth: riches, livestock: animals) **12.** He blessed them and sent them on their way, saying, "May the God of heaven grant you a prosperous journey, my children." (blessed: prayed for, prosperous: successful) **13.** Turning to his daughter, Raguel advised, "Honor your father and mother-in-law, so I may hear good reports of you." (advised: counseled, honor: respect) **14.** He kissed her goodbye, and Edna said to Tobias, "May the Lord of heaven bless you, my dear brother. I pray I may live to see children from you by my daughter, so I can rejoice in my old age. I entrust my daughter to you, with great faith. Treat her well." (entrust: confide, rejoice: be happy)

Chapter 11
1. After these events, Tobias continued his journey, praising God for a successful trip. He blessed Raguel and Edna, then traveled toward Nineve. (praising: honoring, successful: prosperous) **2.** Raphael said to Tobias, "You remember, brother, how you left your father behind: (remember: recall) **3.** "Let us hurry ahead of your wife and prepare the house." (hurry: rush, ahead: before) **4.** "Take with you the gall of the fish." So they traveled on, with the dog following them. (gall: bitter fluid) **5.** Meanwhile, Anna sat, anxiously looking for her son's return. (anxiously: eagerly) **6.** When she saw him approaching, she said to her husband, "Look, your son is coming, and the man who accompanied him." (approaching: nearing) **7.** Raphael then said, "I know, Tobias, that your father will soon regain his sight." (regain: recover) **8.** "Anoint his eyes with the gall, and after rubbing it in, the whiteness will fall away, and he will see you." (anoint: apply oil, whiteness: cataracts) **9.** Anna ran to her son, embraced him, and said, "Now that I have seen you, my son, I can die in peace." They both wept. (embraced: hugged, die in peace: content) **10.** Tobit, hearing them, came toward the door but stumbled. Tobias rushed to him, (rushed: hurried) **11.** took hold of him, and applied the gall to his father's eyes, saying, "Be of good courage, my father." (applied: put on, courage: hope) **12.** When his eyes began to sting, Tobit rubbed them. (sting: hurt) **13.** The whiteness from his eyes peeled off, and when he saw Tobias, he embraced him, (peeled off: came away) **14.** weeping and saying, "Blessed are you, O God, and blessed is your name forever. Blessed are all your holy angels." (blessed: praised) **15.** "You have chastised and shown mercy to me, for now I can see my son, Tobias." Tobias entered, rejoicing, and shared all that had happened in Media. (chastised: corrected, rejoicing: celebrating) **16.** Tobit went to meet his daughter-in-law at the gate of Nineve, joyfully praising God. Those who saw him were amazed, as he had regained his sight. (amazed: astonished) **17.** Tobit thanked God openly and, when he approached his wife, he blessed her, saying, "You are welcome, daughter; blessed be God, who has brought you to us, and blessed be your parents." There was great joy among all his relatives in Nineve. (blessed: praised, relatives: family) **18.** Achiacharus and Nasbas, his brother's son, arrived. (arrived: came) **19.** Tobias' wedding celebration lasted seven days, filled with great joy. (celebration: festivity)

Chapter 12
1. Then Tobit called Tobias and said, "My son, make sure to pay the man who traveled with you, and give him more." (pay: give money, traveled: journeyed) **2.** Tobias replied, "Father, it's no trouble to give him half of what I brought back." (trouble: difficulty) **3.** "For he brought me safely back to you, healed my wife, brought the money, and healed you too." (healed: cured) **4.** Tobit said, "He deserves it." (deserves: is entitled to) **5.** So he called the angel and said, "Take half of what we have brought and go in peace." (half: 50%) **6.** Then the angel took them aside and said, "Bless God, praise and magnify Him. Praise Him for all He has done in your sight. It's good to praise and honor God; don't be slow to do so." (magnify: glorify, slow: reluctant) **7.** "It is good to keep a king's secret, but it is honorable to reveal the works of God. Do what is good, and no evil will touch you." (honorable: respectable) **8.** "Prayer with fasting, almsgiving, and righteousness is good. A little with righteousness

is better than much with sin. It's better to give alms than to store up gold." (almsgiving: charity, righteousness: virtue) **9.** "Alms save from death and cleanse from sin. Those who practice righteousness and charity will live long." (cleanse: purify) **10.** "But those who sin harm their own life." (harm: hurt) **11.** "I will not keep anything from you. It's good to keep a king's secret, but revealing God's works is honorable." (revealing: disclosing) **12.** "When you prayed, and Sara your daughter-in-law, I presented your prayers before the Holy One; and when you buried the dead, I was with you." (presented: brought, buried: laid to rest) **13.** "Your act of kindness in burying the dead was not hidden from me. I was there with you." (kindness: compassion) **14.** "Now God has sent me to heal you and Sara." (heal: cure) **15.** "I am Raphael, one of the seven holy angels who present the prayers of the saints and serve before the glory of God." (saints: holy people) **16.** Both were astonished and fell to the ground in fear. (astonished: amazed, fear: dread) **17.** He said, "Do not fear. It will go well with you; praise God." (fear: be afraid) **18.** "I came not for any favor, but by God's will. Therefore, praise Him forever." (favor: kindness) **19.** "I have appeared to you these days, but I neither ate nor drank. You saw a vision." (appeared: showed up, vision: supernatural sight) **20.** "Now give thanks to God, for I am going back to Him who sent me. Write all that has happened in a book." (thanks: gratitude, book: record) **21.** When they got up, they no longer saw him. (got up: stood) **22.** They praised God for His great works and acknowledged how the angel of the Lord had appeared to them. (acknowledged: recognized)

Chapter 13
1. Tobit wrote a prayer of gratitude, saying, "Praise be to God, who lives eternally, and blessed is His kingdom." (eternally: forever lasting) **2.** "He corrects and shows mercy; He sends to the grave and raises up again. No one can escape His mighty hand." (corrects: punishes, grave: death) **3.** "Praise Him, all the children of Israel, among the nations, for He has scattered us among them." (praise: honor, nations: non-Israelites) **4.** "Proclaim His greatness and exalt Him before everyone; for He is our Lord and eternal Father." (exalt: lift up, everyone: all people) **5.** "Though He punishes us for our sins, He will show mercy again and gather us from the nations where He has scattered us." (punishes: disciplines, sins: wrongdoings) **6.** "If you return to Him with all your heart and soul, and live righteously before Him, He will turn to you and not hide His face. See what He will do for you, and give praise to the great and everlasting King. Even in my captivity, I praise Him and declare His greatness to this sinful nation. O sinners, turn and act justly, for who knows if He will accept you and show mercy?" (righteously: justly, sinful: wicked, accept: forgive, mercy: compassion) **7.** "I will honor my God, and my soul will rejoice in the King of heaven for His greatness." (rejoice: be joyful) **8.** "Let all speak and praise Him for His justice and righteousness." (justice: fairness, righteousness: goodness) **9.** "O Jerusalem, the holy city, He will punish you for your children's wrongdoings, but He will show mercy to the righteous." (wrongdoings: sinful actions, righteous: just) **10.** "Give thanks to the Lord, for He is good; praise the eternal King, that His sanctuary may be rebuilt in you with joy, and let those who are captive rejoice. May He love the afflicted forever." (sanctuary: place of worship, afflicted: suffering) **11.** "Many people from distant lands will come to honor the name of the Lord, bringing offerings to the King of heaven. All generations will praise you with great joy." (offerings: gifts, generations: future people) **12.** "Cursed are those who hate you, and blessed are those who love you forever." (cursed: condemned, blessed: favored) **13.** "Rejoice and be glad, O children of the just, for they will be gathered and praise the Lord of the righteous." (just: virtuous) **14.** "Blessed are those who love you, for they will rejoice in your peace; blessed are those who mourned your punishment, for they will rejoice when they see your glory and be glad forever." (mourning: grieving, glory: greatness) **15.** "Let my soul bless God, the great King." (bless: praise) **16.** "For Jerusalem will be rebuilt with precious stones, including sapphires and emeralds; her walls, towers and defenses will be made of pure gold." (defenses: battlements) **17.** "Her streets will be paved with gemstones from Ophir and other precious stones." (gemstones: precious jewels) **18.** "And all her streets will shout 'Hallelujah!' praising Him, saying, 'Blessed is God, who has made it glorious forever.'" (Hallelujah: praise God)

Chapter 14
1. Tobit finished praising God. **2.** At 58, he lost his sight, which was restored after 8 years. He gave alms, grew in reverence for God, and praised Him. (Alms: charity; Reverence: respect) **3.** As he grew old, he called his son and grandchildren, saying, "Take care of your children, for I am near the end of my life." **4.** "Go to Media, for I believe Jonah's prophecy about Nineveh's fall. Peace will be in Media, while our people will scatter. Jerusalem will be desolate, and God's house destroyed for a time." (Prophecy: prediction; Desolate: abandoned) **5.** "But God will have mercy, and they will return to rebuild the temple, though not as glorious as the first. Eventually, they'll rebuild Jerusalem and restore God's house forever, as foretold." (Glorious: splendid; Foretold: predicted) **6.** "All nations will turn to God, abandoning idols." (Idols: false gods) **7.** "Nations will praise the Lord, and His people will glorify Him. Those who love God in truth and justice will rejoice and show mercy." (Mercy: compassion) **8.** "Now, my son, leave Nineveh, for Jonah's prophecy will come true." **9.** "Keep the law, be merciful and just, so it will go well with you." (Merciful: compassionate) **10.** "Bury me and your mother decently, but don't stay in Nineveh. Remember how Aman mistreated Achiacharus, who raised him. Though Achiacharus was saved, Aman perished. Manasses gave alms and escaped death, but Aman died in darkness." (Perished: died) **11.** "So, my son, remember how almsgiving and righteousness bring salvation. After saying this, Tobit died at 158 and was buried honorably." (Righteousness: virtue; Honorably: respectably) **12.** "When Anna passed, Tobias buried her beside his father. He moved with his family to Ecbatane, to live with his father-in-law, Raguel." (Ecbatane: city) **13.** "There, Tobias lived honorably, buried his father- and mother-in-law, and inherited their wealth, along with his father's." (Inherited: received) **14.** "He lived 127 years in Ecbatane and died there." **15.** "Before his death, Tobias heard of Nineveh's destruction by Nabuchodonosor and Assuerus and rejoiced." (Destruction: ruin)

68 – Judith
Chapter 1
1. In the twelfth year of Nabuchodonosor's reign in Nineveh, during the rule of Arphaxad in Ecbatane over the Medes (reign: rule). **2.** Arphaxad fortified Ecbatane with massive stone walls, seventy cubits high and fifty cubits wide (fortified: strengthened; cubits: ancient unit of measurement). **3.** He built towers a hundred cubits high and gates seventy cubits tall for his armies (towers: tall structures). **4.** These gates, forty cubits wide, allowed the movement of troops and footmen (troops: soldiers; footmen: infantry). **5.** In those days, Nabuchodonosor waged war against Arphaxad in the plain near Ragau (waged: engaged in; plain: flat land). **6.** Many nations, including those near the Euphrates, Tigris, and Hydaspes, joined Nabuchodonosor for the battle (Euphrates, Tigris, Hydaspes: rivers). **7.** He called on people from Persia, Cilicia, Damascus, Libanus, Antilibanus, and coastal regions to join his cause (Persia: ancient empire; Cilicia: region; Damascus: city; Libanus, Antilibanus: mountain ranges). **8.** He extended his call to Carmel, Gilead, Galilee, and the plains of Esdrelom (Carmel, Gilead, Galilee: regions; Esdrelom: valley of Jezreel). **9.** He also summoned those in Samaria, Jerusalem, and beyond Jordan, including Egypt and Ethiopia (summoned: called upon). **10.** Despite this, the nations disregarded his command and sent his envoys away in disgrace (disregarded: rejected; envoys: messengers). **11.** Enraged, Nabuchodonosor vowed to punish Cilicia, Damascus, Syria, Moab, Ammon, Judea, and Egypt by the sword (vowed: promised; sword: weapon). **12.** In the seventeenth year of his reign, Nabuchodonosor fought Arphaxad and defeated his forces (defeated: overcame). **13.** He captured Ecbatane, destroying its towers, looting its streets, and leaving it in ruins (captured: took control of; looting: stealing; ruins: destruction). **14.** Arphaxad was killed in the mountains of Ragau, and his forces were utterly destroyed (killed: slain; utterly: completely). **15.** Nabuchodonosor returned to Nineveh with a vast army, victorious (vast: large; victorious: successful). **16.** He and his men celebrated their triumph with a grand feast for 120 days (triumph: victory; feast: banquet).

Chapter 2
1. In the eighteenth year, on the twenty-second day of the first month, Nabuchodonosor planned to avenge himself on the earth (avenge: take vengence). **2.** He gathered his officers and nobles, revealing his intent to afflict all nations (officers: military leaders; nobles: high-ranking individuals; afflict: cause harm). **3.** A decree was made to destroy all who disobeyed his commands (decree: official order; disobeyed: did not follow). **4.** Nabuchodonosor appointed Holofernes, his chief captain, to lead this campaign (appointed: chose; chief captain: top military leader; campaign: military operation). **5.** He instructed him to take 120,000 footmen and 12,000 horsemen to subdue the west (footmen: infantry; horsemen: cavalry; subdue: conquer). **6.** The mission was to punish those who defied his authority (defied: opposed). **7.** Holofernes was to demand submission by offering earth and water as tokens of surrender (submission: yielding; tokens: symbols). **8.** Nabuchodonosor threatened to devastate the land, filling valleys and rivers with the slain (devastate: destroy; slain: killed). **9.** He vowed to take captives from the farthest regions of the earth (vowed: promised; captives: prisoners). **10.** Holofernes was to reserve the compliant for judgment and destroy the rebellious (compliant: obedient; rebellious: resistant). **11.** Those who resisted were to be slaughtered and plundered without mercy (slaughtered: killed; plundered: looted; mercy: compassion). **12.** Nabuchodonosor declared that his word would be fulfilled by his power

(fulfilled: carried out). **13.** He ordered Holofernes to obey all commands and act swiftly (swiftly: quickly). **14.** Holofernes assembled the governors, captains, and officers of the Assyrian army (assembled: gathered). **15.** He organized 120,000 footmen and 12,000 archers on horseback (archers: soldiers with bows). **16.** The army was prepared with precision for war (precision: accuracy). **17.** Supplies included countless camels, asses, sheep, oxen, and goats for provisions (provisions: food and supplies). **18.** They carried abundant food and wealth from the king's treasury (abundant: plentiful; treasury: storage of wealth). **19.** Holofernes set out with his vast force to conquer the west (vast: large). **20.** Many joined him, forming an innumerable multitude like locusts or sand (innumerable: too many to count; multitude: large group). **21.** They traveled three days from Nineveh to the plain of Bectileth near the Cilician mountains (traveled: journeyed). **22.** From there, Holofernes led his army into the hill country (hill country: mountainous region). **23.** He destroyed Phud, Lud, and the children of Rasses, plundering their lands (plundering: stealing). **24.** Crossing the Euphrates, he ravaged Mesopotamia and cities along the Arbonai River (ravaged: destroyed; Mesopotamia: ancient region between the Euphrates and Tigris rivers). **25.** He reached the borders of Cilicia, killing all who resisted, and moved toward Japheth (borders: edges; Japheth: a region). **26.** He attacked the children of Midian, burning their tents and seizing their sheepfolds (seizing: taking by force; sheepfolds: pens for sheep). **27.** During the wheat harvest, he devastated Damascus, burning fields, destroying herds, and killing young men (devastated: destroyed; herds: groups of animals). **28.** Fear and dread of him spread to all coastal inhabitants, from Sidon to Tyre, and as far as Azotus and Ascalon (fear and dread: terror; coastal inhabitants: people living near the sea).

Chapter 3
1. Ambassadors were sent to Holofernes to negotiate peace (ambassadors: official representatives; negotiate: discuss terms). **2.** They declared themselves servants of Nabuchodonosor, submitting to his will (servants: subjects; submitting: yielding). **3.** They offered their homes, fields, flocks, herds, and tents for his use (flocks: groups of sheep; herds: groups of cattle). **4.** They pledged their cities and people to serve him as he saw fit (pledged: promised; saw fit: deemed appropriate). **5.** The men conveyed this message to Holofernes (conveyed: delivered). **6.** Holofernes advanced to the coast with his army, placing garrisons in fortified cities and selecting men for aid (advanced: moved forward; garrisons: military posts; fortified: strengthened). **7.** The people welcomed him with garlands, dances, and music (garlands: wreaths made of flowers or leaves). **8.** However, he destroyed their borders and sacred groves, intending to abolish all gods except Nabuchodonosor, whom he demanded all nations worship (borders: boundaries; sacred groves: holy wooded areas; abolish: eliminate). **9.** He reached Esdraelon near Judea and approached the great strait of Judea (strait: narrow passage of water). **10.** Holofernes camped between Geba and Scythopolis for a month to gather supplies for his army (camped: set up a military camp; supplies: provisions).

Chapter 4
1. The Israelites in Judea heard of Holofernes' actions against the nations and their temples (heard: became aware of). **2.** They feared greatly for Jerusalem and the temple of the Lord (feared greatly: were deeply afraid). **3.** Recently returned from captivity, they had sanctified the temple, altar, and vessels after their defilement (sanctified: purified; defilement: contamination). **4.** They sent messages to surrounding regions, including Samaria, Bethoron, Jericho, and the valley of Salem (surrounding: nearby). **5.** They fortified mountain tops, secured villages, and stored provisions since the harvest was complete (fortified: strengthened; secured: protected; provisions: supplies). **6.** Joacim, the high priest in Jerusalem, wrote to those in Bethulia and Betomestham near Dothaim (wrote: sent a letter). **7.** He commanded them to guard the hill passages, as they were narrow and easy to defend (guard: protect; passages: routes). **8.** The Israelites obeyed Joacim's orders, uniting under the leadership of Jerusalem's elders (obeyed: followed; uniting: coming together). **9.** With fervor, they cried out to God and humbled themselves (fervor: intense passion; humbled: showed humility). **10.** Men, women, children, strangers, and servants put on sackcloth, mourning deeply (sackcloth: coarse material worn as a sign of mourning; mourning: expressing grief). **11.** They covered themselves in ashes, spread sackcloth before the Lord, and draped the altar with it (covered: sprinkled; draped: covered). **12.** Together, they prayed earnestly that their families and cities would not fall to destruction and reproach (earnestly: sincerely; reproach: disgrace). **13.** God heard their prayers and saw their afflictions as they fasted throughout Judea and Jerusalem (afflictions: sufferings; fasted: refrained from food). **14.** Joacim and the priests, wearing sackcloth, continued offering daily sacrifices and freewill gifts (sacrifices: offerings to God; freewill gifts: voluntary offerings). **15.** They prayed with ashes on their mitres, pleading for God's mercy on the house of Israel (mitres: ceremonial headgear worn by priests; pleading: asking earnestly).

Chapter 5
1. Holofernes was informed that the Israelites had fortified the hill country and prepared for war, blocking access to the plains (fortified: strengthened; blocking: preventing). **2.** Angered, he summoned the princes of Moab, the captains of Ammon, and the governors of the coast (summoned: called for). **3.** He questioned them about the Israelites—who they were, their cities, their strength, and their leaders (questioned: asked; strength: military power). **4.** He also asked why they had not submitted to him like the other nations of the west (submitted: yielded or surrendered). **5.** Achior, captain of the Ammonites, replied, "Let me explain truthfully about this people living in the hill country" (truthfully: honestly). **6.** "They are descendants of the Chaldeans, **7.** who left Mesopotamia, refusing to worship their ancestral gods" (refusing: rejecting; ancestral: family-based). **8.** "Instead, they worship the God of heaven, who led them away from their land and into Canaan, where they prospered" (prospered: flourished). **9.** "When famine struck Canaan, they moved to Egypt, where they multiplied greatly" (multiplied: increased in number). **10.** "However, the Egyptian king enslaved them, forcing them to labor in brickmaking" (enslaved: made them slaves; brickmaking: producing bricks). **11.** "They cried out to their God, who struck Egypt with plagues, forcing the Egyptians to release them" (struck: afflicted; plagues: widespread disasters). **12.** "Their God parted the Red Sea for them, **13.** led them to Mount Sinai, and cleared their path through the wilderness" (cleared: made easy or accessible). **14.** "They conquered the Amorites, took Heshbon, and crossed the Jordan to occupy the hill country, **15.** driving out the Canaanites, Perizzites, Jebusites, Shechemites, and Girgashites" (drove out: expelled). **16.** "They thrived while obedient to their God, who hates iniquity" (thrive: prosper; iniquity: wickedness). **17.** "But when they sinned, they suffered defeats, captivity, and the destruction of their temple and cities" (suffered: experienced). **18.** "Now, they have returned to God, resettled Jerusalem, and rebuilt their sanctuary in the hill country" (sanctuary: holy place of worship; resettled: moved back to and established). **19.** "If they sin against their God, we will defeat them, for their sin will lead to their ruin" (ruin: destruction). **20.** "But if they are faithful, their God will defend them, and we will be shamed before the world" (faithful: loyal; shamed: dishonored). **21.** After Achior finished, those around the tent murmured, angered by his words (murmured: complained). **22.** The chiefs of Holofernes' army and those from Moab and the coast demanded Achior's death (demanded: requested firmly). **23.** They claimed the Israelites were weak and incapable of standing in battle (incapable: unable to withstand). **24.** They urged Holofernes to attack, declaring the Israelites as prey for his army to devour (prey: victim; devour: consume).

Chapter 6
1. After the uproar, Holofernes, the chief captain of Assyria, addressed Achior and the Moabites, saying before all the nations (uproar: commotion). **2.** "Who are you, Achior, and the hirelings of Ephraim, to prophesy against us, saying that Israel will not be defeated because their God will protect them? Who is God but Nabuchodonosor?" (hirelings: mercenaries, hired soldiers; prophesy: predict). **3.** "He will send his power to destroy them, and their God will not deliver them. We will destroy them easily, for they cannot withstand the strength of our horses" (withstand: resist). **4.** "We will trample them, their mountains will be soaked in blood, and their fields filled with the dead. None of my words will fail; they will perish, says Nabuchodonosor, lord of all the earth" (trample: crush underfoot; perish: die). **5.** "You, Achior, will not see my face again until I have taken vengeance on this nation that came out of Egypt" (vengeance: punishment for wrongs). **6.** "Then my army will strike you down, and you will fall among the slain" (strike down: kill). **7.** "My servants will take you back to the hill country, and you will be kept in one of the cities of the passages" (servants: attendants; passages: narrow paths). **8.** "You will not perish until you are destroyed with them" (perish: die). **9.** "If you think they will be defeated, do not let your face fall, for I have spoken, and none of my words will fail" (fall: show distress). **10.** Holofernes commanded his servants to take Achior to Bethulia and deliver him into the hands of the Israelites (deliver: hand over). **11.** They took him, led him to the plain, and from there to the hill country near Bethulia (plain: flat land). **12.** When the city's men saw them, they went out with weapons, keeping them from coming closer by casting stones (casting: throwing). **13.** However, they secretly captured Achior, bound him, and left him at the foot of the hill before returning to Holofernes (bound: tied up). **14.** The Israelites descended from the city, freed Achior, and brought him to Bethulia, presenting him to the city's leaders (descended: came down). **15.** The leaders were Ozias, son

of Micha of Simeon, Chabris, son of Gothoniel, and Charmis, son of Melchiel (leaders: heads of the people). **16.** They gathered all the elders, the youth, and the women, and placed Achior before the assembly. Ozias asked him to explain what had happened (assembly: group gathered together). **17.** Achior recounted Holofernes' council and all the proud words he had spoken against Israel (recounted: told; council: advice). **18.** The people fell down, worshipped God, and cried out, (fell down: bowed down). **19.** "O Lord God of heaven, see their pride, have mercy on our low estate, and look upon those sanctified to you today" (sanctified: set apart as holy). **20.** They comforted Achior and praised him greatly (comforted: consoled). **21.** Ozias took him to his house, held a feast for the elders, and they prayed to the God of Israel throughout the night for help (feast: large meal).

Chapter 7

1. Holofernes commanded his army to move against Bethulia, aiming to take the ascents of the hill country and wage war against Israel (ascents: upward slopes). **2.** The army, with 170,000 footmen and 12,000 horsemen, along with others, set out, a great multitude (multitude: large crowd). **3.** They camped near Bethulia by the fountain, spreading out from Dothaim to Belmaim, and from Bethulia to Cynamon, near Esdraelon (fountain: water source). **4.** The Israelites were greatly troubled and said, "These men will destroy us; the mountains and valleys cannot bear their weight" (bear: withstand). **5.** The men of Israel prepared for battle, lighting fires on their towers, and watched through the night (prepared: readied). **6.** On the second day, Holofernes brought his horsemen to view the city's entrances (horsemen: mounted soldiers). **7.** He seized the fountains of water and set garrisons over them, then returned to his camp (seized: took control of; garrisons: military posts). **8.** The leaders of Esau, Moab, and the sea coast advised Holofernes (advised: counseled). **9.** They warned him not to attack in battle, so his army wouldn't suffer defeat (warned: cautioned). **10.** They explained that the Israelites trust in the heights of their mountains, making it difficult to reach them (heights: elevated areas). **11.** They suggested Holofernes remain in camp, as their water source would lead to their downfall (downfall: destruction). **12.** The water from the mountain is essential for the people of Bethulia; taking it would cause them to surrender (essential: crucial). **13.** Once thirsty, they would be easy to defeat, and their families would be destroyed by fire or sword (defeat: overcome). **14.** This would punish them for rebelling against Holofernes (punish: inflict retribution). **15.** The council's plan pleased Holofernes, and he decided to act as advised (pleased: satisfied). **16.** Holofernes ordered the Ammonites to depart, and they took the waters of Israel (depart: leave). **17.** The Esauites joined the Ammonites, camping in the hills opposite Dothaim, while others spread across the plain (opposite: facing). **18.** The Assyrians' army covered the land, with their tents and equipment forming a vast camp (covered: spread across). **19.** The Israelites cried to God, as they were surrounded, and there was no escape (surrounded: encircled). **20.** For 34 days, the Assyrian army stayed, and the Israelites' water supply ran out (ran out: was exhausted). **21.** Their cisterns were emptied, and they were only given water in limited amounts (cisterns: storage tanks). **22.** The children, women, and young men grew weak from thirst, collapsing in the streets and at the gates (collapsed: fell down). **23.** The people gathered and cried out to their leaders, Ozias and the elders (gathered: assembled). **24.** They accused the leaders of failing to seek peace with the Assyrians, bringing them to the brink of destruction (brink: verge). **25.** They felt helpless and believed God had allowed them to suffer at the hands of the Assyrians (helpless: powerless). **26.** They proposed surrendering the city to Holofernes, rather than dying of thirst (proposed: suggested). **27.** They were willing to become servants to survive, to avoid seeing their families perish (perish: die). **28.** They called upon God as a witness, praying that He would not punish them for their words (witness: one who testifies). **29.** The assembly wept together, crying out to God for mercy (wept: cried). **30.** Ozias encouraged them to endure five more days, trusting that God would show mercy (endure: bear). **31.** If no help came after five days, he would act according to their wishes (wishes: desires). **32.** Ozias dismissed the people to their posts, sending women and children home as the city grew weaker (dismissed: sent away; posts: positions).

Chapter 8

1. At that time, Judith, daughter of Merari, of the tribe of Israel, heard of the people's plight (plight: serious difficulty). **2.** Her husband, Manasses, died during the barley harvest (barley: a type of grain). **3.** He fell ill from the heat while overseeing the harvest, died in Bethulia, and was buried near Dothaim and Balamo (overseeing: managing). **4.** Judith was a widow for three years and four months (widow: woman whose husband has died). **5.** She built a tent on her house's roof, wearing sackcloth and widow's attire (sackcloth: coarse cloth worn as a sign of mourning). **6.** She fasted during her widowhood, except on Sabbaths, new moons, and feast days (fasted: refrained from food). **7.** Judith was known for her beauty, and her late husband left her wealth, servants, cattle, and land (cattle: livestock). **8.** No one spoke ill of her, for she greatly feared God (feared: revered, held in awe). **9.** Upon hearing the people complain about the governor and their dire situation, Judith learned of Ozias' promise to surrender the city in five days (dire: urgent, severe). **10.** She sent her servant to summon Ozias, Chabris, and Charmis, the city's elders (summon: call for). **11.** When they came, she reproached them for their oath to deliver the city unless God helped them within five days (reproached: rebuked, criticized). **12.** She questioned their presumption in tempting God by setting such a limit (presumption: assuming without evidence). **13.** She warned them they would never understand God's will by testing Him (testing: challenging). **14.** She reminded them that humans cannot know the depth of God's heart or His plans (depth: extent). **15.** If God does not help them, He still has the power to defend or destroy them whenever He chooses (defend: protect). **16.** They should not bind God's counsel, for He is not like men who can be threatened or swayed (bind: limit; swayed: influenced). **17.** They should wait for God's salvation, calling upon Him in faith, and He will hear them if it pleases Him (salvation: deliverance). **18.** Our people have not worshipped man-made gods, unlike previous generations (man-made: created by humans). **19.** For that reason, our ancestors suffered defeat and ruin at the hands of enemies (defeat: loss; ruin: destruction). **20.** But we trust in the one true God, who will not abandon us (abandon: forsake). **21.** If we fall, all of Judah will be devastated, and the sanctuary desecrated, with God requiring justice for its profanation (desecrated: made unholy; profanation: disrespect). **22.** Our brethren will be slaughtered, the country exiled, and our inheritance lost, turning us into a reproach among the Gentiles (brethren: brothers; reproach: shame). **23.** Our servitude will bring dishonor, not favor, but the Lord will turn it into disgrace (servitude: slavery; disgrace: dishonor). **24.** Let us set an example for our brethren, as their faith and the sanctuary rest on us (example: model). **25.** Let us thank God, who tests us as He did our ancestors (tests: refines through trials). **26.** Remember how He tested Abraham, Isaac, and Jacob in their trials (trials: challenges). **27.** Unlike them, we have not been tested by fire, nor has God taken vengeance on us, but He disciplines those who approach Him (discipline: corrects). **28.** Ozias praised Judith's words, recognizing her wisdom and the goodness of her heart (praised: commended). **29.** The people knew her understanding and moral disposition from the beginning (disposition: character). **30.** Despite the people's thirst, which forced them to swear to deliver the city, they still sought her help (swear: vow). **31.** They asked her to pray for rain, believing that God would send it through her prayers (prayers: petitions to God). **32.** Judith promised to do something that would be remembered throughout future generations (promised: vowed). **33.** She told them to stay in the gate, while she and her servant would leave, trusting God to visit Israel through her actions (visit: intervene). **34.** She instructed them not to question her plans until they were completed (instructed: directed). **35.** Ozias and the princes blessed her and sent her on her way, trusting God to lead her in victory (blessed: honored). **36.** The elders returned to their posts, and Judith went to carry out her plan (posts: positions).

Chapter 9

1. Judith fell on her face, put ashes on her head, and removed her sackcloth. At the time of the evening incense in Jerusalem, she cried out loudly, saying (ashes: a sign of mourning). **2.** "O Lord God of my father Simeon, You gave him a sword to avenge the defilement of a maid by strangers. You declared it should not happen, yet they did (defilement: corruption, dishonor). **3.** Therefore, You gave their rulers to be slain in blood, deceived, and struck down, their servants with their lords, and their lords with their thrones (slain: killed). **4.** You gave their wives to be taken as prey, their daughters as captives, and their spoils to Your children who abhorred their blood's pollution, calling for Your help: O God, hear me, a widow (prey: victims; abhorred: hated). **5.** You have worked not only these deeds, but all things past and future. You have prepared Your ways, and Your judgments are in Your foreknowledge (foreknowledge: prior knowledge). **6.** What You determined was already prepared, and said, 'Lo, we are here,' for all Your ways are set, and Your judgments known (determined: decided). **7.** Behold, the Assyrians are strong, their horses and men exalted, trusting in their strength, yet they do not know that You are the Lord who breaks battles (exalted: raised in status; breaks: defeats). **8.** Cast down their strength, for they have purposed to defile Your sanctuary and pollute Your tabernacle, seeking to destroy Your altar (purposed: planned). **9.** Look at their pride and send Your wrath upon them; give me, a widow, the power I seek (wrath: anger). **10.** Strike by my words both the servant and the prince, breaking their pride through a woman's hand (prince: leader). **11.** For Your power is not in numbers or strength, but You are the God of the afflicted, the helper of the oppressed, the upholder of the weak, and the savior of the hopeless (afflicted: distressed; oppressed: burdened). **12.** I pray, O God of my father, God of Israel's inheritance, Creator of the waters, King of all creatures, hear my prayer (inheritance: possession). **13.** Make my speech and deceit a wound to those who have plotted evil against Your covenant, Your holy house, Sion, and Your children's inheritance (deceit: trickery). **14.** Let all nations and tribes acknowledge that You are the God of all power and might, and there is no other protector of Israel but You." (acknowledge: recognize).

Chapter 10
1. After Judith had finished praying to the God of Israel and saying these words, **2.** she rose from where she had fallen, called her maid, and went to the house she used during sabbaths and feasts (maid: servant). **3.** She removed her sackcloth, washed her body, anointed herself with ointment, braided her hair, put on a headpiece, and donned her clothes of gladness, which she wore during the life of her husband Manasses (headpiece: a decorative item for the head; gladness: happiness). **4.** She put sandals on her feet, wore her bracelets, chains, rings, earrings, and other ornaments to adorn herself and attract the gaze of all who would see her (adorn: decorate). **5.** Judith gave her maid a bottle of wine, oil, a bag of parched corn, figs, and fine bread, which she wrapped up and carried (parched corn: dried corn). **6.** They went to the gate of Bethulia, where they found Ozias and the city elders, Chabris and Charmis (elders: senior leaders). **7.** When they saw her beauty and changed appearance, they were greatly amazed and praised God, saying, **8.** "May the God of our fathers bless you and fulfill your plans for the glory of Israel and the exaltation of Jerusalem" (exaltation: raising in honor). **9.** She replied, "Command the gates to be opened, so I may go out to do as you have discussed." They ordered the young men to open the gates for her (discussed: talked about). **10.** Judith and her maid left, and the people watched her until she was out of sight, descending the mountain and crossing the valley (descending: going down). **11.** As they journeyed, the first watch of the Assyrians met them, **12.** and they asked her, "Who are you, where are you from, and where are you going?" She answered, **13.** "I am a Hebrew woman fleeing from my people. I am going to Holofernes, the chief captain of your army, to give him counsel on how to conquer the hill country without losing any men" (fleeing: escaping; counsel: advice). **14.** Hearing her words and seeing her beauty, the men marveled and said, **15.** "You have saved your life by coming before our lord. Now come to his tent, and some of us will escort you" (escort: guide). **16.** "Do not fear when you stand before him; speak as you have said, and he will treat you well," they told her. **17.** They chose 100 men to accompany her and her maid to Holofernes' tent. **18.** As Judith entered the camp, word spread throughout the tents, and people gathered around her, marveling at her beauty. **19.** They admired Israel for having such women and said, "Who would despise a people with such women? Surely, none should escape." **20.** Holofernes' attendants went out, bringing her to his tent. **21.** Holofernes rested on his bed under a canopy woven with purple, gold, emeralds, and precious stones (canopy: a covering). **22.** They informed him of Judith's arrival, and he came out before his tent with silver lamps lighting the way. **23.** When Judith arrived, the men marveled at her beauty. She fell at Holofernes' feet, showing him respect, and his servants helped her up (respect: honor).

Chapter 11
1. Holofernes said to her, "Do not fear; I never harm those who serve Nabuchodonosor, king of all the earth." **2.** "If your people in the mountains had not defied me, I would not have attacked them; they have brought this upon themselves." (defied: opposed) **3.** "But now, tell me why you fled from them and came to us; you came for protection, so be at ease. You will live through this night and beyond." **4.** "No harm will come to you, but you will be treated well, as all servants of King Nabuchodonosor are." **5.** Judith replied, "Let me speak honestly to my lord, I will not lie tonight." (honestly: truthfully) **6.** "If you follow my advice, God will bring success to your plans, and your goals will be achieved." **7.** "As Nabuchodonosor lives, so does his power, which governs all things, including men, beasts, cattle, and birds." (governs: controls) **8.** "We have heard of your wisdom, and all the earth praises you for your knowledge and military feats." (feats: achievements) **9.** "We know what Achior said in your council; the men of Bethulia saved him and heard his words." **10.** "Do not trust his words; they are true, but our nation will not be punished unless they sin against their God." **11.** "Now, death is upon them, and their sin will provoke God's anger when they act unlawfully." (provoke: stir up; unlawfully: against the law) **12.** "Their food is running out, and their water is scarce; they plan to eat what is forbidden by God." (scarce: in short supply) **13.** "They intend to consume the firstfruits and offerings reserved for the priests in Jerusalem, which is unlawful." (firstfruits: the first portion of the harvest offered to God) **14.** "They have sent messengers to Jerusalem for permission to break the law." **15.** "Once they receive approval, they will act immediately, and they will be destroyed that very day." **16.** "I, your servant, knowing this, have fled, and God has sent me to astonish the earth with His plans." (astonish: amaze) **17.** "I serve the God of heaven day and night. I will stay with you and pray, and He will reveal when they have sinned." **18.** "I will show you, and then you will lead your army, and none will resist you." **19.** "I will guide you through Judea to Jerusalem, where you will conquer them, as it was foretold to me." (foretold: predicted) **20.** Holofernes and his servants were pleased with her words and marveled at her wisdom. **21.** "There is no woman like her anywhere on earth, for her beauty and wisdom." **22.** Holofernes said, "God sent you to us so we could defeat those who despise my lord." **23.** "You are both beautiful and wise; if you do as you say, your God will be my God, and you will live in the house of King Nabuchodonosor, renowned across the earth." (renowned: famous)

Chapter 12
1. He commanded that she be brought to his banquet and prepared food and wine for her from his own supply. **2.** Judith replied, "I will not eat of it, lest it cause offense, but provide me with what I brought." (offense: displeasure) **3.** Holofernes asked, "If your provisions run out, how will we provide for you, since no one here is from your nation?" (provisions: supplies) **4.** Judith answered, "As the Lord lives, I will not use what I have until God works through me to accomplish His will." (accomplish: achieve) **5.** The servants brought her to her tent, where she slept until midnight, then woke toward the morning watch. (watch: a period of time in which guards are kept) **6.** She sent word to Holofernes, asking permission to go out and pray. **7.** Holofernes gave his guard orders to let her go, and she stayed in the camp for three days, going out at night to wash in a fountain near the camp. **8.** Afterward, she prayed to the God of Israel to guide her in helping her people. **9.** She returned, remained in her tent, and ate her meal in the evening. **10.** On the fourth day, Holofernes hosted a feast for his servants, excluding his officers. (excluding: leaving out) **11.** He instructed Bagoas, the eunuch, to persuade Judith to join the banquet and eat and drink with them. (persuade: convince) **12.** He feared that if she were not brought, it would shame them, and she might mock them. (shame: dishonor; mock: ridicule) **13.** Bagoas approached Judith, urging her not to fear, but to come, be honored, and enjoy the feast as one of Nabuchodonosor's servants. (urging: encouraging) **14.** Judith responded, "I will do as you say, and it will be my joy until my death." **15.** She dressed in her finest attire, and her maid laid soft skins for her to sit on near Holofernes. (attire: clothing; skins: animal pelts) **16.** When Judith entered, Holofernes was captivated by her beauty and eagerly awaited the opportunity to deceive her. (captivated: fascinated; deceive: mislead) **17.** Holofernes said to her, "Drink and enjoy yourself with us." **18.** Judith replied, "I will drink today, for my life is more precious to me today than ever before." **19.** She ate and drank what her maid had prepared before Holofernes. **20.** Holofernes delighted in her company and drank more wine than he ever had in a single day. (delighted: enjoyed)

Chapter 13
1. When evening came, Holofernes' servants quickly left, and Bagoas shut the tent and dismissed the waiters, as they were tired from the long feast. (dismissed: sent away) **2.** Judith was left alone in the tent, while Holofernes lay drunk on his bed. (drunk: intoxicated) **3.** Judith had instructed her maid to wait outside the bedchamber, as she would go out for prayer, and she informed Bagoas accordingly. (informed: notified) **4.** When everyone left, Judith stood by the bed, praying in her heart, "O Lord God of all power, look upon my actions for the exaltation of Jerusalem." (exaltation: glorification) **5.** "Now is the time to help Your people and destroy the enemies that have risen against us." **6.** Judith went to Holofernes' bed, took down his sword, **7.** and, holding his hair, prayed, "Strengthen me, O Lord God of Israel, this day." **8.** She struck his neck twice with all her strength and severed his head. (severed: cut off) **9.** She threw his body down from the bed, removed the canopy, and took the head to her maid. (canopy: covering) **10.** They went as usual to pray, passing through the camp, circling the valley, and climbing the mountain to Bethulia. **11.** At the gates, Judith called out to the watchmen, "Open the gate! God is with us, to show His power in Jerusalem, as He has done today." (watchmen: guards) **12.** The people of the city hurried to the gate and called for the elders. **13.** They ran to the gate, surprised by her return, opened it, and made a fire for light, gathering around her. **14.** Judith shouted, "Praise God, for He has not withdrawn His mercy from Israel, but has destroyed our enemies through my hands this night." (withdrawn: taken away) **15.** She revealed Holofernes' head, saying, "Behold the head of Holofernes, chief of the Assyrian army. The Lord struck him through the hands of a woman." (behold: look) **16.** "As the Lord lives, He guided my way and used my appearance to deceive him, though he never sinned with me to shame me." (deceive: mislead; shame: disgrace) **17.** The people were

amazed, bowed in worship, and praised God, saying, "Blessed be God, who has brought down our enemies today." (amazed: astonished) **18.** Ozias said, "Blessed are you, daughter, above all women, and blessed be God who directed you to cut off the head of our enemy's chief." **19.** "Your faith will remain in the hearts of men, remembering God's power forever." **20.** "God will reward you with eternal praise, for you have sacrificed yourself for our nation and avenged our ruin, walking faithfully before God." The people responded, "So be it, so be it." (avenged: punished for; ruin: destruction)

Chapter 14
1. Judith said, "Listen, my brethren, take this head and hang it on the highest part of your walls." (brethren: fellow members) **2.** "When morning comes and the sun rises, take up your weapons, and have every valiant man leave the city. Set a captain over them, as if going toward the Assyrian watch, but do not descend." (valiant: courageous) **3.** "Then, they will take their armor and enter the Assyrian camp, raising the captains, but they will find Holofernes gone. Fear will fall on them, and they will flee before you." (raising: summoning) **4.** "You and all Israel will pursue them, overthrowing them as they flee." (overthrowing: defeating) **5.** "Before doing this, call Achior the Ammonite, that he may witness the defeat of the one who despised Israel." (despised: scorned) **6.** They called Achior, who, upon seeing Holofernes' head, fell down, his spirit failing. (spirit: life force) **7.** After recovering him, he bowed at Judith's feet and said, "Blessed are you in all Judah and among all nations. Hearing your name, they will be astonished." (astonished: amazed) **8.** "Now tell me all you have done." Judith then explained all she had done since leaving until that moment. **9.** The people shouted joyfully, praising God for her actions. **10.** Achior, seeing God's work, believed greatly and was circumcised, joining Israel. (circumcised: underwent ritual removal of the foreskin) **11.** At dawn, they hung Holofernes' head on the wall, took their weapons, and moved out toward the mountain straits. (straits: narrow passages) **12.** The Assyrians saw them and sent word to their leaders. **13.** They went to Holofernes' tent, telling his servants to wake him, as they feared the Hebrews were preparing for battle. **14.** Bagoas, thinking Judith had slept with Holofernes, went into the tent, but no one answered. **15.** He opened the door, found Holofernes dead, and his head gone. **16.** Bagoas cried loudly, weeping and mourning, tearing his garments. (garments: clothes) **17.** He then searched for Judith, but when she was not found, he ran to the people, shouting, **18.** "The Hebrews have shamed King Nabuchodonosor's house. Holofernes lies dead, decapitated." (decapitated: beheaded) **19.** The Assyrian captains, hearing this, tore their clothes and were filled with dread. There was a great outcry throughout the camp. (dread: fear)

Chapter 15
1. When the people in the tents heard, they were astonished at what had happened. (astonished: amazed) **2.** Fear and trembling fell on them, and no one dared stay near his neighbor. They fled in all directions—into the plain and hill country. (trembling: anxiety) **3.** Those who camped in the mountains around Bethulia also fled. The Israelites, all the warriors among them, pursued them. (warriors: soldiers) **4.** Ozias sent messengers to Betomasthem, Bebai, Chobai, and Cola, and throughout Israel to spread the news and urge them to attack their enemies. (messengers: carriers of news) **5.** Upon hearing this, the Israelites united and slaughtered their enemies as far as Chobai. Men from Jerusalem and the surrounding hill country also joined in the pursuit, killing many until they reached Damascus and beyond. (slaughtered: killed in large numbers) **6.** The remaining people in Bethulia attacked the Assyrian camp, took their spoils, and became greatly enriched. (spoils: valuables taken in war) **7.** The Israelites who returned from the battle collected the remaining spoils, and the villages and cities of the mountains and plains were filled with riches. (riches: wealth) **8.** Joacim the high priest and the elders of Jerusalem came to see the blessings God had given Israel and to greet Judith. (blessings: divine favor) **9.** When they arrived, they blessed her, saying, "You are the exaltation of Jerusalem, the great glory of Israel, and the joy of our nation." (exaltation: lifting up, praise) **10.** "You have accomplished great things by your hand, and God is pleased. Blessed be you forever, from the Almighty Lord." All the people said, "So be it." **11.** The people plundered the enemy camp for thirty days. Judith was given Holofernes' tent, his valuables, and all his belongings. She took them and loaded them onto her mule and carts. (plundered: looted) **12.** All the women of Israel gathered to see Judith, blessing her and celebrating with a dance. She took branches and gave them to the other women. (branches: twigs or boughs) **13.** They crowned Judith and her maid with olive garlands and danced before all the people. The men followed in armor, wearing garlands and singing songs. (garlands: wreaths)

Chapter 16
1. Then Judith began to sing a thanksgiving, and all the people sang after her. (thanksgiving: expression of gratitude) **2.** Judith said, "Begin unto my God with timbrels, sing unto my Lord with cymbals; sing a new psalm to Him, exalt Him, and call upon His name." (timbrels: small hand drums, cymbals: percussion instruments) **3.** For God breaks battles; He delivered me from those who persecuted me. (delivered: rescued) **4.** Assur came from the north with tens of thousands, his army blocking the torrents and his horsemen covering the hills. (torrents: fast-moving streams) **5.** He boasted he would destroy my borders, kill my young men, dash infants to the ground, and make my virgins spoil. (spoil: plunder, damage) **6.** But the Almighty Lord defeated them through the hand of a woman. (Almighty: all-powerful) **7.** The mighty were not defeated by young men or Titans, but Judith, the daughter of Merari, overcame him with her beauty. (Titans: powerful figures, heroes) **8.** She put off her widow's garment, anointed her face, bound her hair, and wore a linen garment to deceive him. (anointed: applied oil to) **9.** Her sandals captivated his eyes, her beauty took his mind, and the sword passed through his neck. (captivated: enchanted) **10.** The Persians were terrified by her courage, and the Medes were daunted by her bravery. (daunted: intimidated) **11.** Then my afflicted shouted for joy, the weak cried aloud, and they were astonished; their voices were overthrown. (afflicted: suffering, overthrown: overwhelmed) **12.** The daughters of Israel pierced them through and wounded them as fugitives' children; they perished by the Lord's battle. (pierced: stabbed, fugitives: people fleeing) **13.** I will sing a new song to the Lord, for He is great, glorious, and invincible in strength. (invincible: unbeatable) **14.** Let all creatures serve Him: He spoke, and they were made; His voice created them, and none can resist it. (creatures: beings, resist: oppose) **15.** The mountains will move, the rocks will melt as wax, but God is merciful to those who fear Him. (merciful: compassionate, fear: revere) **16.** All sacrifice is too little for a sweet offering to Him; but he who fears the Lord is great always. (sacrifice: offerings made to God) **17.** Woe to the nations that rise against my people! The Lord will take vengeance on them with fire and worms, and they will weep forever. (vengeance: punishment) **18.** When they entered Jerusalem, they worshipped the Lord. After purification, they offered burnt offerings, free offerings, and gifts. (purification: cleansing rituals) **19.** Judith dedicated all the spoils of Holofernes to the Lord, including the canopy from his bedchamber. (dedicated: consecrated, spoils: war loot) **20.** The people feasted in Jerusalem before the sanctuary for three months, and Judith stayed with them. (feasted: celebrated with food) **21.** After this, everyone returned to their inheritance, and Judith went to Bethulia, where she remained honored in her land. (inheritance: family property) **22.** Many desired her, but none knew her after her husband Manasses died and was buried with his people. (desired: wanted, knew: had relations with) **23.** Judith grew in honor, lived to be 105, freed her maid, and died in Bethulia, where she was buried in the cave of her husband. (honor: respect, maid: servant) **24.** The house of Israel mourned her for seven days. Before her death, she distributed her goods to her husband's and her kin's nearest relatives. (mourning: grieving, distributed: shared) **25.** No one caused the children of Israel to fear during Judith's life or long after her death. (caused: made)

69 – Letter of Jeremiah
1. A letter from Jeremiah to individuals who could be taken captive to Babylon, to confirm what God had commanded him. **2.** Whilst you reach Babylon, you will stay there for decades—seven generations—and then I'm able to convey you back peacefully. **3.** In Babylon, you may see idols fabricated from silver, gold, and wood, carried by way of human beings and feared by using the nations. **4.** Do not be like foreigners, worshiping these idols, even when you see crowds bowing earlier than them. **5.** Instead, say on your hearts, "Lord, we worship You alone." (Worship: show reverence) **6.** My angel is with you, and I am looking after your souls. **7.** Their idols are crafted and gilded, but they're fake and can't talk. (Gilded: covered with gold) **8.** They use gold to crown their idols, as though making ready for a bride. (Crown: ceremonial headpiece) **9.** Clergy also take gold and silver from the idols for their own use. **10.** They even give a number of the idol's gold to prostitutes, dressing them in clothes as though they were gods. (Prostitutes: women conducting sexual offerings) **11.** These idols can't defend themselves from decay, although they're dressed in exceptional garments. **12.** The idols are wiped smooth of dust through their monks, who take care of them like fragile objects. **13.** The idols preserve scepters, as if judging the human beings, yet they can not punish offenders. **14.** They preserve daggers and axes, however can not guard themselves from war or thieves. **15.** This shows they are now not gods, so do not fear them. **16.** Like broken vessels, they're vain; their eyes are complete of dust, and that they cannot see. **17.** Priests lock up the temples to shield the idols from thieves. **18.** They light many candles for the idols, although the idols can not see. (Candles: mild sources) **19.** These idols are like beams within the temple; they claim their hearts are troubled, however they sense not anything. (Beams: long portions of timber) **20.** Their faces are blackened by means of smoke from the temple. **21.** Bats, birds, and cats sit down on them, proving they are now not gods. **22.** Those signs make

it clean they may be now not gods, so do now not fear them. **23.** Regardless of their gold, they may be not shining unless polished, and that they felt nothing after they had been melted down. (Melted: turned into liquid) **24.** These useless idols are offered at a high rate. (Useless: without breath) **25.** Carried by men on their shoulders, these idols don't have any feet, proving they are nugatory. (Nugatory: of no fee) **26.** Folks that serve them are ashamed; if the idols fall, they can not rise up or move without assist. **27.** Priests misuse offerings and provide nothing to the poor, while hoarding part of the sacrifices. (Priests: religious leaders, offerings: items made to gods) **28.** Women, consisting of those in menstruation or childbirth, eat the sacrifices, showing that those idols are not gods. **29.** How can they be gods when women prepare food for them? **30.** Priests sit down in their temples, carrying torn garments and having shaved heads, showing they are no longer gods. **31.** They cry and wail before their idols, as human beings do at a feast when someone dies. (Idols: statues or photographs worshipped as gods) **32.** The priests remove their robes and get dressed their wives and youngsters in them. **33.** Whether they receive good or evil, they can't pay off it; they can not establish or cast off a king. **34.** Further, they can't deliver wealth or money; if someone makes a promise to them but doesn't keep it, they'll now not ask for it. **35.** They can't save every person from death, nor give the weak from the strong. **36.** They can't restore sight to the blind, nor provide aid to anyone in trouble. (Blind: unable to see) **37.** They show no compassion to widows or orphans. **38.** Their idols, made of wood and covered with gold and silver, are like stones carved from the mountain; individuals who worship them will be disappointed. (Idols: representations of gods, Silver: a precious metallic, Gold: a precious yellow metal) **39.** How can anyone believe they're gods when even the Chaldeans (Babylonian people) dishonor them? (Chaldeans: an ancient people of Babylon, dishonor: show disrespect) **40.** If they see a mute person who can't speak, they bring him to Bel (a Babylonian god) hoping he'll speak, as though Bel could understand. (Mute: unable to speak, Bel: a Babylonian god) **41.** But they themselves can't understand this, and they leave the problem unresolved because they have no knowledge. (Knowledge: awareness or understanding) **42.** Women sitting by the roads, with cords around them, burn bran to make a fragrance; if one of them is taken by a passerby, she accuses her companion of not being as worthy, for her cord was not broken. (Bran: husks of grain, perfume: fragrance or sweet smell) **43.** Everything they do is false; so how can anyone think or say that they are gods? (False: not real or genuine) **44.** They are made by carpenters and goldsmiths, and they can only be what the craftsmen shape them to be. (Carpenters: woodworkers, Goldsmiths: metalworkers who work with gold) **45.** The creators of these idols will not last long; how, then, can the things made by them be gods? (Creators: makers or builders) **46.** They leave lies and shame for those who come after them. (Lies: falsehoods, shame: dishonor or disgrace) **47.** When war or disaster strikes, the priests consult among themselves to find a hiding place. **48.** How can people not see that these idols are not gods, when they cannot even protect themselves from war or calamity? (Calamity: great misfortune or disaster) **49.** Made of wood and covered with silver and gold, in time it will be evident that they are fake. (Silver: a precious metal, Gold: a precious yellow metal) **50.** It will be clear to all nations and rulers that these idols are not gods, but mere creations of human hands, without divine power in them. (Nations: groups of people united by common culture or government, Rulers: leaders or governors) **51.** Who then can fail to understand that they are not gods? **52.** They can't establish a king or send rain upon the earth. **53.** They can't even decide their own case or right a wrong, as they are powerless, like crows between heaven and earth. (Decide: judge or determine, Powerless: lacking power, Crows: large black birds) **54.** When fire falls on a wood idol, covered with gold or silver, the priests will flee, but the idol itself will burn like beams of wood. (Fire: flames or heat, Beams: long pieces of wood) **55.** They can't withstand any king or enemy; how can anyone believe they are gods? (Withstand: bear or endure, Enemy: opponent) **56.** These idols, made of wood and covered in silver and gold, can't protect themselves from thieves or robbers. (,Robbers: individuals who take things by force) **57.** The gold, silver, and clothes they're dressed in are taken by the strong, and they can't protect themselves. **58.** It is better to be a king who shows his strength, or a useful item in a house, than to be such false gods; or even to be a door that secures things inside, than to be such idols. (Door: a movable barrier, Secures: keeps safe) **59.** The sun, moon, and stars, bright and fulfilling their purposes, obey the instructions given to them. **60.** Further, lightning is easily seen when it strikes, and the wind blows through all nations. (Lightning: sudden electrical discharge, Wind: moving air) **61.** When God commands the clouds to move across the world, they do as instructed. (Clouds: masses of water vapor in the sky) **62.** Likewise, fire sent from above consumes hills and forests, obeying God's command; but these idols have neither the appearance nor the power to do the same. (Fire: flames or heat, Consumes: destroys) **63.** Therefore, it is not reasonable to say or believe that these idols are gods, as they cannot judge or do good for people. (Reasonable: logical or practical) **64.** Knowing they are not gods, do not be terrified of them. **65.** They cannot curse or bless kings. (Curse: invoke harm or misfortune, Bless: ask for divine favor) **66.** They can't show signs in the heavens, nor shine like the sun, nor give light like the moon. (Signs: indicators or wonders) **67.** The beasts are better than these idols, for they can take shelter and help themselves. (Beasts: animals, shelter: protection) **68.** It is clear that these idols are not gods, so do not fear them. **69.** Like a scarecrow in a cucumber field that serves no purpose, these idols of wood, covered with gold and silver, are useless. (Scarecrow: an object to frighten birds) **70.** Moreover, they are like a thorn bush in an orchard where every bird can sit, or like a dead body cast into darkness. (Thorn: a sharp point on a plant, Orchard: a place where fruit trees grow) **71.** You will know they are not gods because the bright red that decorates them will rot; they will eventually be consumed and become a disgrace in the land. (Red: a color often associated with royalty) **72.** Better is the righteous person who has no idols, for he will be free from reproach. (Righteous: morally right, Reproach: shame or complaint).

70 – The Prayer of Azariah

1. They walked in the flames, praising and blessing God. **2.** Azariah stood and prayed in the fire: **3.** Blessed are You, O Lord, God of our ancestors; Your name is worthy of eternal praise and glory. **4.** You are just in all Your deeds; Your works are true, Your ways righteous, and Your judgments just. **5.** You brought these things upon us and Jerusalem in justice, for we sinned. (execute; put a plan, order, or course of action into effect) **6.** We acted wickedly, turning away from You. (wickedly; immorally) **7.** We trespassed, disobeyed Your commandments, and failed to follow them. (trespassed; sinned) **8.** All You've done to us has been in righteous judgment. (judgment; decision) **9.** You delivered us to lawless enemies, the most wicked ruler. (wicked; evil or morally wrong) **10.** We are now a disgrace to Your servants and worshippers. (disgrace; shame) **11.** Do not abandon us, for Your name's sake; do not annul Your covenant. (covenant; agreement) **12.** For the sake of Abraham, Isaac, and Israel, do not withdraw Your mercy. (beloved; dearly loved) **13.** You promised to multiply their descendants like stars and sand. (descendants; offspring) **14.** We are now smaller than all nations, oppressed because of our sins. (oppressed; burdened) **15.** We have no leader, prophet, sacrifice, or incense to seek Your mercy. (oblation; offering) **16.** Let our humble, broken hearts be accepted as sacrifice. (humble; modest) **17.** Let this be like burnt offerings of rams and bulls, for those who trust You will not be shamed. (bullocks; young bulls) **18.** We now follow You wholeheartedly, seeking Your face. (seek; look for) **19.** Do not shame us but deal with us mercifully. (multitude; abundance) **20.** Deliver us by Your wonders and glorify Your name. Let our enemies be ashamed. (marvelous; wonderful) **21.** Confound their power and break their strength. (confounded; confused) **22.** Let them know You are the only God, glorious over all. (glorious; magnificent) **23.** The king's servants heated the furnace with resin, pitch, and wood. (resin; sticky substance) **24.** Flames leapt above the furnace, burning the nearby Chaldeans. (leapt; jumped) **25.** The angel of the Lord entered the furnace, extinguishing its flames. (struck; extinguished) **26.** The furnace felt like a moist, whistling wind, leaving them unharmed. (moist; damp) **27.** The three, in one voice, praised, glorified, and blessed God. (glorified; honored)

71 – Esdaras

Chapter 1

1. Josiah held the Passover in Jerusalem for the Lord on the fourteenth day of the first month. (Jerusalem: capital of Judah) **2.** He assigned the priests to their duties in the Lord's temple, wearing their garments. (Priests: religious leaders) **3.** He instructed the Levites, the temple servants, to consecrate themselves and place the Holy Ark in the temple built by King Solomon. (Levites: tribe of Levi; Ark: sacred chest) **4.** "No longer carry the ark. Serve the Lord and prepare for worship in your family groups," he said. (Israel: the Jewish kingdom) **5.** Follow King David's instructions, and stand in your positions according to your divisions." (Solomon: King of Israel) **6.** "Prepare the Passover, sacrifice for your relatives, and observe it as Moses commanded." (Passover: festival of the Exodus) **7.** Josiah gave thirty thousand lambs and kids, and three thousand calves, from his possessions for the people, priests, and Levites. (Lambs and kids: young sheep and goats) **8.** Temple leaders gave two thousand six hundred sheep and three hundred calves for the priests' Passover. (Temple officials: Helkiah, Zechariah, Jehiel) **9.** Military leaders gave five thousand sheep and seven hundred calves for the Levites. (Captains: military commanders) **10.** The priests and Levites, with unleavened bread, stood in their positions by families to offer sacrifices. (Unleavened bread: bread made without yeast) **11.** They performed the offerings as written in Moses' law, beginning in the morning. (Moses: leader of Israel) **12.** They roasted the Passover lamb and boiled the sacrifices in bronze vessels, filling the air with a pleasing aroma. (Bronze: a metal alloy) **13.** The priests, sons of Aaron, prepared the sacrifices for themselves and their families. (Aaron: brother of Moses, first high priest) **14.** The priests offered the fat until evening, while the Levites prepared for their families. (Fat: best parts of the animal) **15.** The singers, sons of Asaph, performed as David had instructed, with Asaph, Zechariah, and Ethan representing the king. (Asaph: musician and temple leader) **16.** The gatekeepers stood guard at every gate, and no one left their post as Levites prepared for others. (Gatekeepers: those who guarded the temple) **17.** All sacrifices for the Lord were completed that day, with the Passover celebration. (Lord: God) **18.** The offerings on the altar were made as commanded by King Josiah. (Altar: table for sacrifices) **19.** The Israelites celebrated the Passover and the Feast of Unleavened Bread for seven days. (Feast of Unleavened Bread: part of Passover) **20.** No Passover had been held in Israel like this since the time of Samuel. (Samuel: prophet and judge of Israel) **21.** No king of Israel had held such a Passover as Josiah, with priests, Levites, and all Israel in Jerusalem. (Jerusalem: capital city) **22.** This Passover occurred in the eighteenth year of Josiah's reign. (Reign: period of a king's rule) **23.** Josiah's actions were righteous before the Lord, full of devotion. (Righteous: morally right) **24.** The events of his reign are written, showing how the wickedness of others grieved the Lord, fulfilling His words against Israel. (Wickedness: morally wrong actions) **25.** Afterward, Pharaoh, king of Egypt, went to war at Carchemish by the Euphrates, and Josiah went out to meet him. (Pharaoh: king of Egypt; Carchemish: ancient city on the Euphrates) **26.** Pharaoh sent messengers, saying, "What do I have to do with you, king of Judah? (Judah: southern kingdom of Israel) **27.** I was not sent to fight you. My battle is with the Euphrates. The Lord is with me, urging me forward." (Euphrates: ancient river) **28.** Josiah did not heed the prophet Jeremiah's warning, but sought to fight, disregarding the Lord's message. (Jeremiah: prophet of Judah) **29.** They fought in Megiddo, and the commanders confronted Josiah. (Megiddo: battle site) **30.** The king said, "Take me from the battle, for I am weak!" His servants quickly carried him away. (Battlefield: location of the battle) **31.** He entered his second chariot, returned to Jerusalem, died, and was buried in his ancestors' tomb. (Chariot: a two-wheeled vehicle; Jerusalem: capital of Judah) **32.** All Judea mourned for Josiah. The prophet Jeremiah lamented, and the leaders and women mourned, a tradition still practiced in Israel. (Jeremiah: prophet of God; Josiah: king of Judah) **33.** The acts of Josiah, his glory, and his understanding of God's law are written in the book of the kings of Judea and Israel. (Judea: southern kingdom of Israel) **34.** The people made Joachaz, Josiah's son, king when he was twenty-three. (Joachaz: son of Josiah) **35.** He reigned for three months before the king of Egypt deposed him. (Jerusalem: capital of Judah) **36.** The Egyptian king imposed a tax of 100 talents of silver and one talent of gold. (Talent: a weight measure) **37.** The king of Egypt made Joakim, Joachaz's brother, king of Judah. (Joakim: brother of Joachaz) **38.** Joakim imprisoned the nobles and captured his brother Zarakes, bringing him from Egypt. (Zarakes: brother of Joakim) **39.** Joakim, twenty-five when he became king, did evil in God's sight. (Joakim: king of Judah) **40.** King Nebuchadnezzar of Babylon bound Joakim and took him to Babylon. (Nebuchadnezzar: king of Babylon) **41.** Nebuchadnezzar took the Lord's holy vessels to his temple in Babylon. (Vessels: sacred temple items) **42.** Joakim's deeds and his impurity are recorded in the royal chronicles. (Impurity: disrespect to God) **43.** Joakim's son, Jeconiah, became king at eighteen. (Jeconiah: son of Joakim) **44.** He reigned for three months and ten days in Jerusalem, doing evil in the Lord's eyes. (Jerusalem: capital of Judah) **45.** After a year, Nebuchadnezzar sent for him to be brought to Babylon with the holy vessels. (Nebuchadnezzar: king of Babylon) **46.** Nebuchadnezzar made Zedekiah, Jeconiah's uncle, king of Judah at twenty-one. He reigned eleven years. (Zedekiah: king of Judah) **47.** Zedekiah did evil, ignoring the Lord's commands through Jeremiah. (Jeremiah: prophet of God) **48.** Zedekiah swore allegiance to God but rebelled, becoming stubborn and disobeying God's laws. (Nebuchadnezzar: king of Babylon) **49.** The governors and priests did many wicked things, defiling the Lord's temple in Jerusalem. (Governors: leaders of the people) **50.** God sent messengers to call them back, but they mocked Him. (Messenger: one delivering God's message) **51.** They ridiculed His prophets until God sent the Chaldeans against them. (Prophets: speakers for God; Chaldeans: Babylonians) **52.** The Chaldeans killed young and old around the temple, sparing no one. (Sword: weapon of war) **53.** They took all the Lord's holy vessels and treasures to Babylon. (Holy vessels: sacred items) **54.** They burned the Lord's house, broke Jerusalem's walls, and set its towers on fire. (Jerusalem: capital of Judah) **55.** They destroyed everything glorious and carried the survivors to Babylon. (Glorious things: significant possessions) **56.** The survivors became servants to the Babylonian king until the Persian empire rose, fulfilling God's word through Jeremiah. (Persians: an empire replacing Babylonians) **57.** "The land will observe its Sabbaths, and her desolation will last seventy years." (Sabbaths: periods of rest or observance)

Chapter 2

1. In the first year of King Cyrus of Persia, the Lord's word through Jeremiah was fulfilled. (Cyrus: King of Persia; Jeremiah: a prophet) **2.** The Lord stirred King Cyrus of Persia, and he issued a proclamation throughout his kingdom, also in writing. (Persia: ancient empire covering modern-day Iran) **3.** Cyrus, king of Persia, declared: "The Lord God of Israel has made me ruler over the world, **4.** and commanded me to build a house for Him in Jerusalem, in Judea. (Judea: a region in ancient Israel) **5.** Anyone from His people, let the Lord be with them, and let them go up to Jerusalem in Judea to rebuild His house. He is the God who dwells in Jerusalem. **6.** Let those in their lands help with gold, silver, **7.** gifts, horses, cattle, and other offerings for the Lord's temple in Jerusalem." (Temple: a place of worship in Jerusalem) **8.** The leaders of Judah and Benjamin, along with the priests, Levites, and all whom the Lord stirred, set out to rebuild the Lord's house in Jerusalem. (Judah and Benjamin: two of the twelve tribes of Israel) **9.** People around them supported them with gold, silver, horses, cattle, and other gifts, as many had vowed. **10.** King Cyrus brought out the sacred vessels of the Lord, which King Nebuchadnezzar had taken from Jerusalem and stored in the temple of his gods. (Nebuchadnezzar: King of Babylon) **11.** Cyrus entrusted the vessels to Mithradates, his treasurer, **12.** who delivered them to Sanabassar, the governor of Judea. (Sanabassar: a governor of Judea) **13.** The total number of these items was: 1,000 gold cups, 1,000 silver cups, 29 silver censers, 30 gold bowls, 2,410 silver bowls, and 1,000 other vessels. **14.** In total, there were 5,479 vessels of gold and silver, **15.** carried back by Sanabassar with the exiles from Babylon to Jerusalem. (Babylon: an ancient city in Mesopotamia) **16.** During the reign of King Artaxerxes of Persia, Belemus, Mithradates, Tabellius, Rathumus, Beelethmus, and Samellius the scribe, with their associates, wrote to him about the situation in Judea and Jerusalem. (Artaxerxes: King of Persia; Samaria: region in ancient Israel) **17.** To King Artaxerxes from Rathumus, Samellius, and their council, including the judges of Coelesyria and Phoenicia: (Phoenicia: ancient coastal region) **18.** We inform you that the Jews who came from your land to Jerusalem are rebuilding that rebellious city. They are repairing its markets and walls and laying the foundation of a temple. **19.** If the city is rebuilt and its walls completed, they will refuse to pay tribute and even oppose kings. **20.** Since the temple work is in progress, we think it necessary to bring this matter to your attention, **21.** so, if it pleases you, a search can be made in the records of your ancestors. **22.** You will find that the city was rebellious, troubling kings and cities, **23.** and the Jews stirred up wars, which is why the city was destroyed. **24.** Therefore, we declare that if the city is rebuilt, you will lose access to Coelesyria and Phoenicia." **25.** King Artaxerxes replied to Rathumus, Beelethmus, Samellius, and their associates in Samaria, Syria, and Phoenicia. **26.** "I have read your letter. After investigation, it has been found that the city opposed kings, **27.** and its people rebelled, with powerful kings in Jerusalem who collected tribute from Coelesyria and Phoenicia. **28.** Therefore, I have ordered that the city's rebuilding stop, and no further work will proceed. **29.** Rebellious actions will be prevented to avoid disturbing kings." **30.** After receiving the decree, Rathumus, Samellius, and their associates hurried to Jerusalem with cavalry and a large force, disrupting the work. The rebuilding of the temple stopped until the second year of King Darius of Persia's reign. (Darius: King of Persia)

Chapter 3

1. King Darius hosted a grand feast for his officials, household, and rulers of Media and Persia. (Media: an ancient empire in the western part of modern Iran; Persia: an ancient empire in Iran) **2.** He invited governors, captains, and leaders from 127 provinces, from India to Ethiopia. (Ethiopia: India to Ethiopia, present-day Ethiopia) **3.** After eating and drinking, the guests returned home, and King Darius went to his room, fell asleep, and woke up. **4.** The three young guards discussed among themselves. **5.** "Each of us will state what is strongest. The wisest answer will earn great rewards." **6.** "The winner will receive purple clothes, drink from golden cups, sleep on a golden bed, and ride in a chariot with gold reins, wearing a linen turban and a gold chain." (Turban: a type of headwear) **7.** "This person will be honored and called a cousin of the king." **8.** They wrote their answers, sealed them, and placed them under Darius' pillow. **9.** "When the king wakes, the answers will be read, and the wisest will win." **10.** The first wrote, "Wine is the strongest." **11.** The second wrote, "The king is the strongest." **12.** The third wrote, "Women are strongest, but above all, Truth prevails." **13.** When Darius woke, he read the answers. **14.** He summoned the princes, governors, and officials to gather. **15.** The king sat in judgment and listened to the answers. **16.** "Call the young men to explain their answers," he commanded. They entered. **17.** "Explain what you wrote," the king asked. **18.** The first guard, who spoke of wine's strength, began: **19.** "Wine is powerful! It makes everyone lose their senses, from kings to commoners. **20.** It turns sorrow into joy and makes people forget their troubles. **21.** It makes them feel wealthy, disregarding rulers and officials. **22.** Drunken people forget loyalty and may even fight. **23.** When sober, they forget their actions. **24.** Isn't wine the strongest, since it makes people behave this way?" He finished.

Chapter 4

1. The second speaker, who had spoken of the king's power, said: **2.** "O sirs, aren't those who rule the sea and land mighty? **3.** But the king is stronger. He commands them, and they obey him. **4.** If he orders war, they fight. If he sends them against enemies, they conquer strongholds. **5.** They fight and die without disobeying the king's command. The spoils of victory are brought to the king. **6.** Even those who farm bring tribute to the king. **7.** He commands life and death, and they follow. **8.** If he orders destruction, they destroy. If he orders building, they build. **9.** If he tells them to cut down, they do. If he tells them to plant, they obey. **10.** His people and armies obey him. He rests while others watch over him. **11.** None may leave or disobey. **12.** How can the king not be the strongest, seeing he is obeyed like this?" **13.** The third speaker, Zerubbabel, who had spoken of women and truth, said: **14.** "O sirs, isn't the king mighty, and men many, but isn't wine powerful? Who rules them, but women? **15.** Women gave birth to the king and all rulers of the land. **16.** They nourished those who grew the vineyards that give wine. **17.** Women make garments for men, bringing them glory. Without women, men cannot exist. **18.** Men gather wealth, but when they see a beautiful woman, **19.** they forget their wealth and desire her more than gold or silver. **20.** A man leaves his father and country to be with his wife. **21.** He ends his days with her, forgetting his family and homeland. **22.** This proves women have dominion over you. Don't you work to provide for them? **23.** Men travel, rob, or sail, and after their deeds, they bring the rewards to the woman they love. **24.** A man loves his wife more than his parents. **25.** Many have become slaves or perished because of women. **26.** Women cause men to lose their minds and act foolishly. **27.** Many have perished, stumbled, and sinned because of women. **28.** Don't you see the king's power? Even he is ruled by women. **29.** I saw the king with Apame, his concubine, **30.** sitting at his side, taking the crown and placing it on her head, striking the king. **31.** The king gazed at her, and if she smiles, he laughs. If she is displeased, he flatters her. **32.** O sirs, how can it not be that women are strong, seeing they do this?" **33.** The king and nobles looked at each other. The king began to speak about truth: **34.** "Isn't the earth great, and the sky vast? The sun moves swiftly and returns each day. **35.** Isn't it the one who made these things who is great? Therefore, truth is greater than all things. **36.** The earth calls on truth, and the sky blesses it. **37.** All works tremble, but truth is unshaken. **38.** Wine, the king, and women may be unrighteous, but truth is eternal and strong. **39.** Truth does what is just, not wicked. All men approve truth's deeds. **40.** Truth's judgment is just. It is the strength, kingdom, and power of all ages. Blessed be the God of truth!" **41.** The people shouted, "Great is truth, and stronger than all!" **42.** The king said, "Ask for what you will, even more than written, and we will grant it, for you are wise. You shall sit next to me and be called my cousin." **43.** He asked the king to remember his vow to rebuild Jerusalem and return the vessels taken by Cyrus. **44.** He also reminded the king to rebuild the temple that was burned when Judea was desolate. **45.** "This is what I ask of you: fulfill your vow to the King of Heaven." **46.** King Darius stood, kissed him, and wrote letters to the treasurers and governors, **47.** directing them to help him and those with him rebuild Jerusalem. **48.** He also wrote to governors in Lebanon, ordering them to bring cedar wood for the city's construction. **49.** He decreed freedom for the Jews traveling to Judea, and the land they occupied was exempt from tribute. **50.** He ordered the Edomites to give up Jewish villages and set aside funds for the temple. **51.** He gave twenty talents for building the temple and ten talents for daily burnt offerings. **52.** He granted freedom to those coming from Babylon to build the city and support for the priests. **53.** He wrote to ensure the Levites were supported until the temple was completed. **54.** He commanded land and wages for those guarding the city. **55.** He also ordered the return of the vessels from Babylon, as commanded by Cyrus. **56.** When the young man left, he praised the King of Heaven, **57.** thanking Him for wisdom and success. **58.** He took the letters, went to Babylon, and shared the news with his family. **59.** They praised God for granting them freedom to build Jerusalem and the temple, celebrating with joy for seven days.

Chapter 5

1. The clan leaders, with their families—wives, children, servants, and livestock—were chosen to go up according to their tribes. (Clans: groups of families) **2.** Darius sent 1,000 horsemen to escort them safely to Jerusalem with musical instruments, drums, and flutes. (Darius: King of Persia; Jerusalem: capital of Israel) **3.** Their relatives rejoiced, and Darius commanded they travel together. **4.** These are the names of those who went, listed by family and tribe. (Divisions: groups or categories) **5.** The priests, descendants of Phinehas and Aaron: Jesus (Joshua) son of Josedek, son of Saraiah, Joakim, son of Zerubbabel, of the house of David, from Judah. (Zerubbabel: leader from exile) **6.** They spoke before King Darius in the second year of his reign, in the month of Nisan. (Darius: King of Persia; Nisan: first month of the Jewish year) **7.** These Judeans returned from captivity, taken by King Nebuchadnezzar to Babylon. (Nebuchadnezzar: King of Babylon) **8.** They returned to Jerusalem and Judea, each to their own city, led by Zerubbabel, Jesus, Nehemiah, and others. (Nehemiah: leader who rebuilt Jerusalem) **9.** The families and leaders: sons of Phoros, 2,172; sons of Saphat, 472. **10.** Sons of Ares, 756; **11.** Sons of Phaath Moab (Jesus and Joab's families), 2,812. (Joab: military leader) **12.** Sons of Elam, 1,254; Zathui, 945; Chorbe, 705; Bani, 648; **13.** Bebai, 623; Astad, 1,322; **14.** Adonikam, 667; Bagoi, 2,066; Adinu, 454; **15.** Ater (of Ezekias), 92; Kilan and Azetas, 67; Azaru 432; **16.** Annis, 101; Arom, Bassai, 323; Arsiphurith, 112; **17.** Baiteros, 3,005; Bethlomon, 123; **18.** Netophah, 55; Anathoth, 158; Bethasmoth, 42; (Anathoth: town in Judah) **19.** Kariathiarius, 25; Caphira and Beroth, 743; (Kariathiarius: town near Jerusalem) **20.** Chadiasai and Ammidioi, 422; Kirama and Gabbe, 621; **21.** Macalon, 122; Betolion, 52; Niphis, 156; **22.** Calamolalus and Onus, 725; Jerechu, 345; **23.** Sanaas, 3,330. **24.** The priests: Jeddu (a priestly family), son of Jesus, from Sanasib, 972; Emmeruth, 1,152; (Jeddu: priest from Jehoiarib's family) **25.** Phassurus, 1,247; Charme, 1,017. **26.** Levites: Jesus, Kadmiel, Banas, Sudias, 74. (Levites: helpers in the temple) **27.** Temple singers: Asaph's sons, 128. (Asaph: leader of temple music) **28.** Gatekeepers: Salum, Atar, Tolman, Dacubi, Ateta, Sabi, 139 total. (Gatekeepers: guards at the temple) **29.** Temple servants: Esau, Asipha, Tabaoth, Keras, Sua, Phaleas, Labana, Aggaba. **30.** Acud, Uta, Ketab, Accaba, Subai, Anan, Cathua, Geddur, **31.** Jairus, Daisan, Noeba, Chaseba, Gazera, Ozias, Phinoe, Asara, Basthai, Asana, Maani, Naphisi, Acub, Achipha, Asur, Pharakim, Basaloth, **32.** Meedda, Cutha, Charea, Barchus, Serar, Thomei, Nasi, Atipha. (Jairus: a biblical figure) **33.** The servants of Solomon: Assaphioth, Pharida, Jeeli, Lozon, Isdael, Saphuthi, **34.** Agia, Phacareth, Sabie, Sarothie, Masias, Gas, Addus, Subas, Apherra, Barodis, Saphat, Allon. (Solomon: King of Israel, builder of the Temple) **35.** All the temple servants and Solomon's descendants numbered 372. (Temple servants: workers in the temple) **36.** These people came from Thermeleth and Thelersas, led by Charaathalan and Allar. (Thermeleth: a place, Thelersas: a place, Charaathalan: a leader, Allar: a name) **37.** They couldn't trace their family lineage to Israel: the descendants of Dalan, son of Ban, and the sons of Nekodan numbered six hundred fifty-two. (Dalan: a name, Ban: a name, Nekodan: a name) **38.** Some priests, who claimed the office but lacked proper records, were the sons of Obdia, Akkos, and Jaddus, who married Augia, daughter of Zorzelleus. (Obdia: a name, Akkos: a name, Jaddus: a name, Augia: a name, Zorzelleus: a name) **39.** When their genealogies were searched and found lacking, they were excluded from the priesthood. (Genealogies: family records, Priesthood: sacred office) **40.** Nehemiah and Attharias told them they couldn't partake in holy offerings until a high priest wearing the Urim and Thummim arose. (Nehemiah: a leader, Attharias: a name, Urim and Thummim: sacred objects) **41.** All of Israel, twelve years old and older, excluding servants, numbered forty-two thousand three hundred sixty. (Israel: the people of God, Servants: male and female workers) **42.** Their male and female servants numbered seven thousand three hundred thirty-seven, and there were two hundred forty-five musicians and singers. (Musicians: those who played instruments, Singers: those who praised with songs) **43.** They had four hundred thirty-five camels, seven thousand thirty-six horses, two hundred forty-five mules, and five thousand five hundred twenty-five donkeys. (Camels: animals used for transport, Mules: crossbred animals for work) **44.** Some leaders, upon arriving in Jerusalem, vowed to restore the temple and contribute according to their ability. (Leaders: heads of families, Jerusalem: holy city) **45.** They donated one thousand minas of gold, five thousand minas of silver, and one hundred priestly garments to the temple treasury. (Minas: a unit of currency, Treasury: collection of funds for sacred work) **46.** The priests, Levites, singers, gatekeepers, and others lived in Jerusalem and nearby towns. (Levites: priests of the tribe of Levi, Gatekeepers: those guarding the temple gates) **47.** When the seventh month came, and everyone returned to their homes, they gathered in the open space before the eastern porch. (Seventh month: significant time for feasts, Eastern porch: part of the temple) **48.** Jesus, son of Josedek, and Zorobabel, son of Salathiel, prepared the altar to offer burnt offerings as prescribed by Moses. (Jesus: a name, Josedek: a name, Zorobabel: a leader, Salathiel: a name, Burnt offerings: sacrifices to God) **49.** Some from other nations joined them to rebuild the altar, as they were opposed by surrounding nations. They offered sacrifices morning and evening. (Other nations: non-Israelites, Sacrifices: offerings to God) **50.** They also celebrated the Feast of

Tabernacles, offering daily sacrifices. (Feast of Tabernacles: Jewish festival, Law: divine commandments) **51.** They made continual offerings for Sabbaths, new moons, and other holy feasts. (Sabbaths: holy days of rest, New moons: first day of the month in the Hebrew calendar) **52.** Those who had vowed to God began offering sacrifices from the first day of the seventh month, even though the temple was not yet built. (Vows: promises to God) **53.** They provided funds, food, and drink to the workers, and sent supplies to Sidon and Tyre to bring cedar from Lebanon to Joppa, following King Cyrus's orders. (Sidon: a Phoenician city, Tyre: a Phoenician city, Lebanon: a mountain region, Joppa: a port city, Cyrus: a Persian king) **54.** In the second year after arriving in Jerusalem, they began the work of rebuilding the temple. (Rebuilding: construction of the temple) **55.** They laid the foundation of the temple in the second month of the second year after their return to Judea and Jerusalem. (Foundation: the base of the temple, Judea: region in Israel) **56.** They appointed Levites over the work of the temple, and with one accord, the Levites, led by Jesus and his family, began the labor. (Levites: priests of the tribe of Levi) **57.** The priests, wearing their garments, with trumpets and cymbals, and the Levites, sons of Asaph, led the people in praise and thanksgiving according to David's instructions. (Asaph: a name, Cymbals: percussion instruments) **58.** They sang loud songs of thanksgiving to the Lord for His goodness and eternal glory. (Eternal: lasting forever) **59.** All the people sounded trumpets and shouted joyfully, praising the Lord for the temple's rebuilding. (Trumpets: brass instruments used for announcement) **60.** Some of the Levite priests and older men who had seen the first temple wept as they compared it with the new one. (Levite priests: religious workers from the tribe of Levi, Former temple: earlier temple of God) **61.** However, many others rejoiced and shouted joyfully with trumpets. (Joyfully: with great happiness) **62.** The noise was so loud that it could be heard far off. (Drowned out: covered by louder sounds) **63.** When the enemies of Judah and Benjamin heard it, they understood that the returnees were rebuilding the temple for the Lord. (Judah and Benjamin: tribes of Israel, Returnees: those who returned from exile) **64.** They approached Zorobabel, Jesus, and the leaders, offering to help build, saying they too had been worshipping the Lord since the days of King Asbasareth of the Assyrians. (Asbasareth: a name, Assyrians: an ancient empire) **65.** Zorobabel, Jesus, and the leaders refused, saying it was not for others to build the temple but only for the Israelites, as ordered by King Cyrus of Persia. (Cyrus: a Persian king) **66.** The neighboring nations opposed the building, cutting off supplies and hindering progress. (Opposed: acted against) **67.** Their opposition continued throughout Cyrus's reign, delaying the completion of the temple for two years until the reign of Darius. (Darius: a Persian king, Reign: period of rule) **68.** Now, when the enemies of Judah and Benjamin heard that the descendants of the captivity built the temple, (Judah and Benjamin: tribes of Israel, Enemies: those against the Israelites) **69.** They came to Zorobabel, Jesus, and the chief men, saying, "Let us build with you." (Chief men: leaders of the families, Zorobabel: a leader, Jesus: a name) **70.** "For we worship the same God and have sacrificed to Him since the reign of Asbasareth, king of Assyria." (Asbasareth: a name, Assyria: an ancient empire) **71.** But Zorobabel, Jesus, and the chief men responded, "You have no part in building the house of God; we will build it alone, as commanded by King Cyrus." (Cyrus: a Persian king) **72.** The surrounding nations pressed hard against the people of Judah, obstructing their efforts and halting supplies. (Judah: a tribe of Israel, Obstructing: hindering) **73.** Through secret plots and persuasion, they caused the work to cease during the reign of King Cyrus, continuing their interference until the reign of King Darius. (Darius: a Persian king, Reign: period of rule)

Chapter 6

1. In the second year of King Darius, the prophets Aggaeus and Zacharias, the son of Addo, prophesied to the Jews in Judea and Jerusalem in the name of the Lord, the God of Israel. **2.** Then Zorobabel, the son of Salathiel, and Jesus, the son of Josedek, began rebuilding the Lord's house in Jerusalem, with the prophets assisting them. **3.** At that time, Sisinnes, the governor of Syria and Phoenicia, came with Sathrabuzanes and others, asking them, **4.** "By whose authority are you rebuilding this house and performing these works?" **5.** The Jewish elders found favor because the Lord had visited the captives; **6.** They were not hindered from building until Darius was informed and responded. **7.** A copy of the letter from Sisinnes and Sathrabuzanes to King Darius: **8.** "To King Darius, greetings. We found the elders of the Jews in Jerusalem rebuilding the house of their God with costly stones and timber in the walls. **9.** The work is progressing quickly. **10.** We asked them by whose authority they were building, and they gave us their leaders' names. **11.** They answered, 'We are servants of the Lord who created heaven and earth. **12.** This house was built long ago by a powerful king of Israel and was completed. **13.** But when our ancestors sinned against God, He handed them over to King Nebuchadnezzar of Babylon. **14.** Nebuchadnezzar destroyed the house, burned it, and took the people to Babylon. **15.** But in the first year of King Cyrus, he ordered the rebuilding of the house of the Lord. **16.** The holy vessels of gold and silver that Nebuchadnezzar took from the house were returned by King Cyrus to Zorobabel and Sanabassarus, with orders to rebuild the temple. **17.** Sanabassarus laid the foundations of the Lord's house in Jerusalem, and we have been rebuilding it ever since.' **18.** If it pleases the king, let a search be made in the royal archives of Babylon. **19.** If it is found that King Cyrus authorized the rebuilding of the house in Jerusalem, let him send instructions on how to proceed." **20.** King Darius ordered a search in the archives, and a scroll was found in Ekbatana, which recorded: **21.** "In the first year of King Cyrus, he ordered the rebuilding of the house of the Lord in Jerusalem, where sacrifices are made. **22.** It is to be 60 cubits high and 60 cubits wide, built with three rows of hewn stones and one row of new timber from the land. Its costs are to be covered from the royal treasury. **23.** The holy vessels taken by Nebuchadnezzar should be restored to the house in Jerusalem." **24.** He also ordered that Sisinnes and Sathrabuzanes should not interfere, but allow Zorobabel and the elders of the Jews to rebuild the temple. **25.** "I command that it be fully rebuilt, and that those from the captivity of Judea be assisted until the work is finished. **26.** Funds from Coelesyria and Phoenicia should be given for the sacrifices and daily needs of the temple. **27.** Drink offerings should be made to the Most High God for the king and his family, so they may pray for their lives." **28.** Anyone who defies this command will be punished by having a beam taken from their house and being hanged on it. **29.** "May the Lord destroy any king or nation that attempts to hinder the work of the Lord's house in Jerusalem." **30.** King Darius has commanded these things be carried out diligently.

Chapter 7

1. Sisinnes, the governor of Coelesyria and Phoenicia, and Sathrabuzanes, along with their companions, carefully oversaw the sacred task, following King Darius's orders. (Sisinnes: a Persian governor; Coelesyria: an ancient region in the eastern Mediterranean; Phoenicia: an ancient civilization in the coastal region of the eastern Mediterranean; Darius: a king of Persia) **2.** They assisted the Jewish elders and temple leaders. **3.** The holy work thrived while the prophets Aggaeus and Zacharias spoke God's messages. (Aggaeus: a prophet; Zacharias: a prophet) **4.** The work was completed by the command of the Lord, with approval from Cyrus, Darius, and Artaxerxes, kings of Persia. (Cyrus: a king of Persia; Artaxerxes: a king of Persia) **5.** The temple was finished on the 23rd of Adar in the sixth year of King Darius's reign. (Adar: the twelfth month in the Hebrew calendar; Darius: a king of Persia) **6.** The Israelites, priests, Levites, and those returning from captivity followed the law of Moses. (Levites: members of the Hebrew tribe of Levi; captivity: state of being imprisoned or enslaved) **7.** For the temple's dedication, they offered one hundred bulls, two hundred rams, and four hundred lambs, **8.** along with twelve male goats for Israel's sin offering, corresponding to the twelve tribes. (Bulls: large male cattle; Rams: male sheep; Lambs: young sheep; Sin offering: sacrifice made for forgiveness of sin) **9.** The priests and Levites served in their prescribed garments, by family groups, as written in the book of Moses. The gatekeepers stood at the gates. (Gatekeepers: those who guarded the temple gates) **10.** The returning Israelites celebrated Passover on the 14th of the first month, after the priests and Levites were purified. (Passover: Jewish festival commemorating the Exodus from Egypt; Levites: members of the Hebrew tribe of Levi) **11.** All who returned from captivity, including the Levites, were purified and sanctified. (Sanctified: made holy) **12.** They offered the Passover sacrifice for themselves, their families, and the priests. **13.** They ate the Passover with all who had separated from idol worship and sought the Lord. (Idolatry: the worship of idols) **14.** They observed the Feast of Unleavened Bread for seven days, rejoicing before the Lord. **15.** They celebrated because the Lord had turned the king of Assyria's plans in their favor, strengthening their work for the Lord. (Assyria: an ancient empire located in Mesopotamia; Lord: a title for God)

Chapter 8

1. After these events, during the reign of Artaxerxes, the Persian king, Esdras, son of Azaraias, son of Zechrias, son of Helkias, son of Salem, (Artaxerxes: Persian king) **2.** son of Sadduk, son of Ahitob, son of Amarias, son of Ozias, son of Memeroth, son of Zaraias, son of Savias, son of Boccas, son of Abisne, son of Phinees, son of Eleazar, son of Aaron, the high priest, (Aaron: Brother of Moses, first high priest) **3.** Esdras, a skilled scribe in the law of Moses given by God, went up from Babylon. (Babylon: Ancient city, now Iraq) **4.** The king favored him and granted all his requests. **5.** Along with Esdras, some Israelites, priests, Levites, singers, gatekeepers, and temple servants went to Jerusalem. (Levites: Tribe responsible for religious duties; Jerusalem: Holy city) **6.** In the seventh year of Artaxerxes' reign, they left Babylon on the first day of the first month and reached Jerusalem, guided by the Lord on a successful journey. (Artaxerxes: Persian king) **7.** Esdras taught all Israel the laws and commandments of the Lord without omission. **8.** King Artaxerxes' letter to Esdras was as follows: **9.** "King Artaxerxes to Esdras the priest and teacher of the law, greetings. (Artaxerxes: Persian king) **10.** I have ordered that all Jews, priests, Levites, and others willing, may go with you to Jerusalem. (Jews: Descendants of Judah) **11.** Those who choose to go with you, as advised by my seven counselors, may depart with you, **12.** to manage the affairs of Judea and Jerusalem according to God's law, (Judea: Region in ancient Israel) **13.** and carry the offerings for the Lord of Israel in Jerusalem, which I and my counselors have pledged, along with all gold and silver found in Babylon for the Lord in Jerusalem, (Babylon: Ancient city) **14.** along with the people's offerings for the temple of the Lord their God in Jerusalem, including gold and silver for sacrifices, (Temple: Sacred worship building) **15.** to offer on the altar of the Lord in Jerusalem. (Altar: Structure for sacrifices) **16.** You may act according to the will of your God in handling the gold and silver. **17.** The holy vessels for the temple in Jerusalem, (Vessels: Sacred worship items) **18.** and any other necessary items, should be taken from the king's treasury. **19.** I have commanded the treasurers in Syria and Phoenicia to give whatever Esdras, the priest and teacher of God's law, requests with care, (Syria: Ancient region, Phoenicia: Coastal region) **20.** up to 100 talents of silver, 100 cors of wheat, 100 firkins of wine, and abundant salt. (Talent: Weight unit, Cors: Grain measure, Firkin: Liquid container) **21.** Everything must be done according to God's law, so His wrath does not fall upon the king and his sons. **22.** No taxes or impositions should be laid on the priests, Levites, singers, gatekeepers, temple servants, or anyone working in the temple. (Levites: Religious workers) **23.** Esdras, with God's wisdom, should appoint judges in Syria and Phoenicia to judge those who know the law of your God, and teach those who do not. (Judges: Legal authorities) **24.** Anyone who disobeys God's law or the king's law should be punished, whether by death, financial penalty, or imprisonment." **25.** Esdras the scribe said, "Blessed be the Lord, the God of my ancestors, who has moved the king's heart to honor His house in Jerusalem, (Ancestors: Forefathers, Jerusalem: Holy city) **26.** and granted me favor in the sight of the king, his counselors, and his nobles. (Nobles: High-ranking individuals) **27.** Therefore, encouraged by God's help, I gathered men from Israel to go with me. (Israel: God's chosen people) **28.** These are the leaders from their families who went with me from Babylon in the reign of King Artaxerxes: (Artaxerxes: Persian king) **29.** From Phinees' sons, Gerson; from Ithamar's sons, Gamael; from David's sons, Attus, son of Sechenias; (Phinees: Descendant of Aaron, David: King of Israel) **30.** From Phoros' sons, Zacharais, with 150 men; **31.** From Phaath Moab, Eliaonias, son of Zaraias, with 200 men; **32.** From Zathoes' sons, Sechenias, son of Jezelus, with 300 men; from Adin's sons, Obeth, son of Jonathan, with 250 men. (Phaath Moab: A family group, Zathoes: A family group, Adin: Another family group) **33.** From the sons of Elam: Jesias, son of Gotholias, with seventy men; **34.** From the sons of Saphatias: Zaraias, son of Michael, with seventy men; **35.** From the sons of Joab: Abadias, son of Jehiel, with 212 men; **36.** From the sons of Banias: Salimoth, son of Josaphias, with 160 men; **37.** From the sons of Babi: Zacharias, son of Bebai, with 28 men; **38.** From the sons of Azgad: Astath, Joannes, son of Hakkatan, with 110 men; **39.** From the sons of Adonikam: Eliphalat, Jeuel, and Sama- ias, with 70 men; **40.** From the sons of Bago: Uthi, son of Istalcurus, with 70 men. (Elam: an ancient region east of Mesopotamia; Joab: a military leader during King David's reign) **41.** I gathered them by the river Theras, where we camped for three days, and I inspected them. (Theras: A river in the region where the group camped) **42.** Finding no priests or Levites, **43.** I sent for Eleazar, Iduel, Maasmas; and Elnathan, Samaias, Joribus, Nathan, Ennatan, Zacharias, and Mosollamus—principal men of understanding. **45.** I instructed them to go to Loddeus, the captain of the treasury, **46.** and request him to send men who could serve in the priests' office. (Loddeus: a leader in charge of the temple treasury) **47.** By God's hand, they brought us understanding men from the sons of Mooli, the Levite, Asebebias and his 18 sons. (Mooli: a Levite family) **48.** Asebias, Annuus, and Osaias, from the sons of Chanuneus, with 20 men; **49.** From the temple servants appointed by David and the leaders, 220 temple servants. Their names were reported. (Chanuneus: a family of Levites; David: the king of Israel) **50.** I vowed a fast for the young men before the Lord, seeking a prosperous journey for us, our children, and livestock. **51.** I was ashamed to ask the king for an army, cavalry, or an escort, **52.** since we had claimed that our Lord would protect those who seek Him. (Cavalry: soldiers on horseback) **53.** We prayed to the Lord and found Him merciful. **54.** I appointed twelve men, including Eserebias, Assamias, and ten of their kin. **55.** I weighed out the silver, gold, and holy vessels given by the king, his counselors, and Israel. **56.** I gave them 650 talents of silver, 100 talents of silver vessels, 100 talents of gold, **57.** twenty golden vessels, and twelve fine brass vessels. (Talent: a unit of weight, used as currency) **58.** I told them, "You are holy to the Lord; the vessels, gold, and silver are a vow to Him. **59.** Guard them until you deliver them to the leaders of the priests, Levites, and Israel's families in Jerusalem, to the chambers of the Lord's house." (Jerusalem: the capital city of Israel, the site of the temple) **60.** The priests and Levites took the silver, gold, and vessels to the temple in Jerusalem. **61.** On the twelfth day of the first month, we left the river Theras and arrived in Jerusalem by God's mighty hand, **62.** protected from all enemies. Upon arrival, we spent three days, and on the fourth day, the silver and gold were weighed and delivered to Marmoth the priest, son of Urias. (Marmoth: a priest; Urias: his father, a priest) **63.** With him were Eleazar, son of Phinees, and Josabdus, son of Jesus, and Moeth, son of Sabannus, the Levites. They recorded everything by number and weight. (Phinees: a priest, son of Eleazar; Sabannus: a Levite) **64.** All was noted at the same hour. **65.** Those who had returned from captivity offered sacrifices to the Lord, including twelve bulls, ninety-six rams, **66.** Seventy-two lambs and twelve goats were offered as peace offerings, each dedicated to the Lord. (Peace offering: a sacrifice symbolizing reconciliation) **67.** The king's orders were delivered to his stewards and the governors of Coelesyria and Phoenicia, honoring the people and the temple of the Lord. (Coelesyria: a historical region in the Levant, Phoenicia: an ancient Mediterranean civilization) **68.** Afterward, the leaders came to me and said, **69.** "The people of Israel, including the princes, priests, and Levites, have not separated themselves from the foreign nations—the Canaanites, Hittites, Perizzites, Jebusites, Moabites, Egyptians, and Edomites. (Gentiles: non-Israelite nations) **70.** They and their children have intermarried with foreign nations, mixing holy descendants with others. The rulers and nobles have been involved in this from the beginning." **71.** Upon hearing this, I tore my clothes and holy garments, pulled the hair from my head and beard, and sat down grieving. **72.** Those who were troubled by the word of the Lord gathered around me as I mourned, and I remained sorrowful until the evening sacrifice. **73.** Then, rising from my fast with my clothes torn, I bowed my knees, stretched my hands to the Lord, and said, **74.** "O Lord, I am ashamed and humbled before You, **75.** for our sins have multiplied, and our wrongs have reached to the heavens. **76.** Since our ancestors, we have been in great sin, even to this day. **77.** For our sins, and those of our ancestors, we, along with our people, kings, and priests, have been given over to foreign kings, the sword, captivity, and shame, and still remain in shame. **78.** Yet, You, O Lord, have shown mercy, leaving us a remnant and a name in the place of Your sanctuary, **79.** bringing light to the house of our God and providing food during our servitude. **80.** Even in bondage, we were not forsaken, for You gave us favor with the kings of Persia to provide for us. (Persia: ancient empire located in modern Iran) **81.** They glorified the temple of the Lord, rebuilt Zion, and gave us a secure place to dwell in Judea and Jerusalem. (Zion: the hill of Jerusalem, Judea: a region in Israel, Jerusalem: capital city of Israel) **82.** "Now, O Lord, what can we say? We have broken Your commandments given by the prophets, who said, **83.** 'The land you will possess is polluted by foreign nations and their uncleanness. **84.** Therefore, do not intermarry with them or give your daughters to their sons. **85.** Do not seek peace with them, so that you may be strong and leave a lasting inheritance for your children.' **86.** All that has happened to us is due to our wickedness, yet You, O Lord, have made our sins lighter, **87.** and allowed us a remnant. But we have again turned back to mixing with the impurities of the land's heathen people. **88.** You were not angry enough to destroy us, leaving us with no root, seed, or name. **89.** O Lord of Israel, You are faithful, for we still have a root today. (Lord of Israel: title for God as protector of Israel) **90.** We stand before You in our iniquities, unable to stand because of these sins." **91.** As Esdras prayed and wept, lying on the ground before the temple, a large crowd gathered, for there was great mourning. (Esdras: another name for Ezra, a scribe and priest in the Hebrew Bible, Jerusalem: capital city of Israel) **92.** Then Jechonias, son of Jeelus, an Israelite, cried out, "O Esdras, we have sinned by marrying foreign women, but there is still hope for Israel. (Jechonias: a king of Judah) **93.** Let us vow to the Lord to put away all our foreign wives and their children, **94.** as seems good to you and to those who obey the Law of the Lord. **95.** Rise and take action, for this is your task, and we will support you in doing it bravely." **96.** So Esdras rose and took an oath from the chief priests and Levites to do this, and they swore to it. (Levites: members of the Hebrew tribe of Levi, responsible for temple duties)

Chapter 9

1. Esdras (a scribe and priest) left the temple court and went to Jonas' room, son of Eliasib (a priest), (Eliasib: high priest). **2.** He stayed there, fasting and mourning over the people's sins. **3.** A proclamation was sent across Judea and Jerusalem, calling all returnees from captivity to gather in Jerusalem. (Judea: region in Israel, Jerusalem: capital city). **4.** Anyone who failed to come within two or three days, as ordered by the elders, would lose their livestock to the temple and be excluded from the group of returnees. **5.** After three days, the people of Judah and Benjamin gathered in Jerusalem on the twentieth day of the ninth month. (Judah and Benjamin: tribes of Israel). **6.** The crowd sat outside shivering in the cold before the temple. (Temple: holy place in Jerusalem). **7.** Esdras stood and reproached them, saying, "You've broken the law by marrying foreign women, adding to Israel's sin." **8.** "Confess your sins and honor the Lord, the God of our ancestors," **9.** "and separate from the foreign women and their people." **10.** The assembly cried out, "We will obey as you've said." **11.** "But the crowd is large, and the weather harsh, so it cannot be settled quickly; our sin is widespread." **12.** "Let the leaders remain, and those with foreign wives must come at the set time," **13.** "along with their leaders and judges, so we can turn away God's anger." (Judges: local authorities in Israel). **14.** Jonathan, son of Azael, and Ezekias, son of Thocanus, took charge, assisted by Mosollamus, Levis, and Sabbateus as judges. **15.** The returnees followed these instructions. (Returnees: those who returned from exile). **16.** Esdras selected prominent men by name; they gathered on the first day of the tenth month to address the issue. (Tenth month: Hebrew month of Tevet). **17.** The cases of men with foreign wives were settled by the first day of the first month. (First month: Hebrew month of Nisan). **18.** Among the priests with foreign wives were found: **19.** the sons of Jesus (a variant of Joshua), son of Josedek (the high priest), and their relatives: Mathelas, Eleazar, Joribus, and Joadanus. (Josedek: high priest during exile). **20.** They agreed to divorce their wives and offer rams as a sin offering. (Rams: sacrificial animals). **21.** From the sons of Emmer: Ananias, Zabdeus, Manes, Sameus, Hiereel, and Azarias. **22.** From the sons of Phaisur: Elionas, Massias, Ishmael, Nathanael, Ocidelus, and Saloas. **23.** From the Levites: Jozabdus, Semeis, Colius (called Calitas), Patheus, Judas, and Jonas. (Levites: priestly tribe). **24.** From the singers: Eliasibus and Bacchurus. (Singers: temple musicians). **25.** From the gatekeepers: Sallumus and Tolbanes. (Gatekeepers: those who guarded the temple gates). **26.** From Israel, the sons of Phoros: Hiermas, Ieddias, Melchias, Maelus, Eleazar, Asibas, and Banneas. (Phoros: a family in Israel). **27.** From the sons of Ela: Matthanias, Zacharias, Jezrielus, Oabdius, Hieremoth, and Aedias. (Ela: a family group). **28.** From the sons of Zamoth: Eliadas, Eliasimus, Othonias, Jarimoth, Sabathus, and Zardeus. (Zamoth: family group). **29.** From the sons of Bebai: Joannes, Ananias, Jozabdus, and Ematheis. (Bebai: a family from Judah). **30.** The sons of Addi: Naathus, Moossias, Lac-cunus, Naidus, Matthanias, Sesthel, Balnuus, and Manasseas. (Addi: a priestly family) **31.** The sons of Annas: Elionas, Aseas, Melchias, Sabbeus, and Simon Chosameus. (Annas: high priest) **32.** The sons of Asom: Maltanneus, Mattathias, Sabanneus, Eliphalat, Manasses, and Semei. (Asom: a family group) **33.** The sons of Baani: Jeremias, Momdis, Ismaerus, Juel, Mamdai, Pedias, Anos, Carabasion, Enasibus, Mamnitemus, Eliasis, Bannus, Eliali, Someis, Selemias, and Nathanias. The sons of Ezora: Sesis, Ezril, Azaelus, Samatus, Zambri, and Josephus. (Baani: a family group, Ezora: a priestly family) **34.** The sons of Nooma: Mazitias, Zabadeas, Edos, Juel, and Banaias. (Nooma: a family group) **35.** They had foreign wives and sent them away with their children. (Foreign wives: marriages outside Israel) **36.** The priests, Levites, and Israelites lived in Jerusalem and surrounding areas during the seventh month, as well as in their settlements. (Levites: temple workers) **37.** The people gathered in unity in the wide area before the temple's east porch. (Temple: worship center in Jerusalem) **38.** They asked Esdras the priest, "Bring the law of Moses, given by the Lord, the God of Israel." (Esdras: a scribe and priest) **39.** Esdras brought the law to the congregation of men and women, including the priests, to be read on the new moon of the seventh month. (New moon: the start of the month) **40.** He read the law from morning until midday in the open space before the temple, and everyone paid attention. (Multitude: large crowd) **41.** Esdras stood on a wooden pulpit to read. (Pulpit: raised platform for reading) **42.** Mattathias, Sammus, Ananias, Azarias, Urias, Ezekias, and Baalsamus stood on his right, (Mattathias: a priestly name) **43.** and Phaldeus, Misael, Melchias, Lothasubus, Nabarias, and Zacharias stood on his left. (Zacharias: a prophet) **44.** Esdras took the law, sat in a prominent position, and opened it. (Book of the law: sacred scriptures) **45.** As he opened it, everyone stood. Esdras blessed the Lord, the Almighty. (Blessed: praised) **46.** The people answered "Amen" and worshiped, raising their hands and bowing down. (Amen: affirmation) **47.** Jesus, Annus, Sarabias, Iadinus, Jacubus, Sabateus, Auteas, Maiannas, Calitas, Azarias, Jozabdus, Ananias, and Phalias, the Levites, explained the law. (Levites: temple workers) **48.** They read and explained the law's meaning to the people. (Made clear: clarified) **49.** Attharates addressed Esdras and the Levites, saying, (Attharates: a leader) **50.** "This day is holy to the Lord—don't weep, for hearing the law caused sorrow." (Wept: expressed sorrow) **51.** "Eat rich food, drink sweet drinks, and share with those in need; (Fat: rich food, Sweet: sweet drinks) **52.** for this day is holy, and the Lord will honor you." (Holy: dedicated to God) **53.** The Levites instructed the people not to be sad, as this day was holy. (Levites: temple workers) **54.** The people went to enjoy the day, sharing food with those in need, and rejoicing greatly. (Rejoice: celebrate joyfully) **55.** They understood the law's message and were gathered for this purpose. (Understood: comprehended)

72 – Wisdom of Solomon
Chapter 1

1. Love righteousness, you who judge the earth; seek the Lord with a pure heart and sincerity. (Sincerity: honesty, without deceit) **2.** He is found by those who do not test Him, and reveals Himself to those who trust in Him. (Test: challenge; trust: confidence) **3.** Wrong thoughts separate us from God, and His power corrects the foolish when tested. (Foolish: lacking wisdom) **4.** Wisdom cannot enter a malicious soul, nor dwell in a sinful body. (Malicious: harmful, spiteful; sinful: morally wrong) **5.** The Holy Spirit of discipline avoids deceit and leaves when unrighteousness enters. (Discipline: training in right behavior; unrighteousness: injustice, immorality) **6.** Wisdom loves and does not excuse blasphemy; God knows the heart, intentions, and words. (Blasphemy: disrespectful speech against God) **7.** The Spirit of the Lord fills the world and knows all voices. (Spirit: divine influence; fills: permeates) **8.** Unrighteous words cannot be hidden; vengeance will find the wrongdoer. (Vengeance: punishment for wrongdoing) **9.** God will examine the plans of the wicked, and their words will reveal their deeds. (Examine: investigate; deeds: actions) **10.** The ear of jealousy hears all; complaints are never hidden. (Jealousy: protective desire; complaints: dissatisfaction) **11.** Avoid murmuring and backbiting; no secret word goes unnoticed. Lies destroy the soul. (Murmuring: complaining quietly; backbiting: speaking ill behind someone's back) **12.** Do not seek death through wrong choices, nor bring destruction upon yourself. (Destruction: ruin, downfall) **13.** God did not create death, nor delight in the ruin of the living. (Delight: take pleasure in) **14.** He created everything to thrive, with no poison or death in His creation. (Thrive: grow and develop well; poison: harmful substance) **15.** Righteousness is eternal. (Eternal: lasting forever) **16.** The wicked, through their actions, bring death upon themselves, thinking they can control it. (Wicked: morally wrong; bring upon: cause to happen)

Chapter 2

1. The ungodly reason to themselves, but wrongly: "Our life is short and full of suffering, and death has no remedy. No one returns from the grave." (Remedy: cure) **2.** We are born by chance and, after we're gone, it will be as though we never existed. Our breath is like smoke, and our hearts like fleeting sparks. (Chance: without purpose; fleeting: short-lived) **3.** When it goes out, our bodies turn to ash, and our spirits vanish like soft air. (Vanish: disappear) **4.** Our name will be forgotten, and no one will remember our deeds. Our life will fade like a cloud and disappear like mist driven by the sun. (Disperse: scatter) **5.** Our time is like a passing shadow; after death, there is no return. It is sealed, and no one comes back. (Sealed: fixed, final) **6.** Let us enjoy the present, indulging in life's pleasures like youth. (Indulge: enjoy freely) **7.** Let us drink fine wine and use luxurious oils; let us not miss the beauty of spring. (Luxurious: rich) **8.** Let us crown ourselves with roses before they wither. (Wither: die) **9.** Let none of us miss out on pleasure; let us leave signs of joy everywhere, for this is our portion. (Portion: share) **10.** Let us oppress the righteous poor, ignore the widow, and disrespect the elderly. (Oppress: mistreat; widow: woman whose husband has died) **11.** Let strength define justice, for the weak are worthless. (Strength: power) **12.** Let us ambush the righteous, for he is against our ways; he accuses us of breaking the law and exposing our sins. (Ambush: surprise; accuse: charge) **13.** He claims to know God and calls himself a child of the Lord. (claims: says) **14.** He was made to correct our thoughts. (Correct: rebuke) **15.** His life is so different from ours that we can't stand to look at him. (Stand to: tolerate) **16.** He sees us as counterfeit, avoiding our ways like filth, and boasts that the righteous will be blessed, claiming God is his father. (Counterfeit: fake; filth: corruption) **17.** Let's see if his words are true, and what will happen to him in the end. (End: outcome) **18.** If the righteous is truly God's son, He will rescue him from his enemies. (Rescue: save) **19.** Let us test his patience with cruelty and torture. (Cruelty: harshness) **20.** Let us condemn him to a shameful death, for he says he will be honored. (Condemn: judge) **21.** They imagined all this and were deceived by their own wickedness. (Deceived: misled) **22.** They did not understand God's mysteries or hope for the reward of the righteous. (mysteries: divine truths; reward: blessing) **23.** God created man to be immortal, in His own eternal image. (immortal: undying) **24.** But through envy of the devil, death entered the world, and those who follow him experience it. (envy: jealousy)

Chapter 3

1. The righteous are in God's care, and no harm can touch them. **2.** To the unwise, it seems they die in sorrow. (Unwise: foolish) **3.** Their departure is seen as destruction, but they are at peace. (Departure: passing; destruction: ruin; peace: rest) **4.** Though they suffer, their hope is in eternal life. (Suffer: endure; eternal life: immortality) **5.** After brief chastisement, they will be greatly rewarded, for God has tested and found them worthy. (Chastisement: punishment; tested: proved; worthy: deserving) **6.** Like gold in fire, He has refined them and accepted them as an offering. (Refined: purified; offering: sacrifice) **7.** When their time comes, they will shine like sparks among stubble. (Shine: glow; sparks: embers; stubble: remnants) **8.** They will judge nations and have dominion, and their Lord will reign forever. (judge: rule; dominion: authority; reign: rule) **9.** Those who trust in Him will gain wisdom, and the faithful will remain with Him, for grace and mercy are for His chosen. (Wisdom: understanding; faithful: loyal) **10.** The wicked will be punished for their evil thoughts, having neglected the righteous and forsaken the Lord. (wicked: ungodly; evil thoughts: sins; neglected: ignored; forsaken: abandoned) **11.** Those who scorn wisdom and discipline live in misery; their hopes are empty, and their deeds unfruitful. (scorn: despise; wisdom: knowledge) **12.** Their wives are foolish, and their children wicked. (Foolish: unwise; wicked: evil) **13.** Their descendants are cursed. Blessed is the barren woman who remains pure, for she will bear fruit in the spiritual harvest. (Descendants: offspring; cursed: damned) **14.** Blessed is the man who has done no wrong; he will receive the gift of faith and an inheritance in God's temple. (Wrong: sin; inheritance: legacy; gift: grace) **15.** The reward for good deeds is glorious, and the root of wisdom will never fail. (reward: benefit) **16.** Children of adulterers will not find fulfillment, and the seed of the unrighteous will be cut off. (Adulterers: cheaters; fulfillment: perfection) **17.** Though they live long, their lives are worthless, and their old age lacks honor. (Worthless: valueless) **18.** If they die young, they will have no hope or comfort in their trials. (Trials: suffering) **19.** The end of the wicked is dreadful. (Dreadful: horrible)

Chapter 4

1. It is better to have no children and possess virtue, for its memory is eternal, known by God and men. (virtue: moral excellence) **2.** When present, men take example from it; when absent, they long for it. It wears a crown, triumphs forever, having won victory, striving for pure rewards. (Striving: seeking) **3.** The ungodly's offspring will not prosper or take root from illegitimate origins. (Ungodly: immoral, without God) **4.** Though they may briefly flourish, they will be shaken by the wind and rooted out. (Flourish: grow healthily) **5.** Their branches will break their fruit unripe and useless. (Ripe: fully mature) **6.** Children born of unlawful unions are witnesses of wickedness against their parents in judgment. (Unlawful: not allowed) **7.** Though the righteous may die, they find rest. (Righteous: morally just) **8.** True honor is not measured by years. (Honor: respect) **9.** Wisdom is the gray hair of man, and an unblemished life is true old age. (Unblemished: flawless) **10.** He pleased God and was loved by Him, so he was taken from among sinners. (Sinners: those who break divine law) **11.** He was swiftly taken, lest wickedness alter his understanding or deceit deceive his soul. (Deceit: misleading) **12.** Wickedness obscures honesty, and lust undermines simplicity. (Undermines: weakens) **13.** He was perfected quickly, fulfilling a long life. (perfected: made flawless) **14.** His soul pleased the Lord, so He hastened to remove him from the wicked. (hastened: moved quickly) **15.** The people saw it but did not understand, nor did they reflect on God's grace and mercy with His saints, whom He respects. (grace: kindness; mercy: forgiveness; saints: holy people) **16.** The righteous dead condemn the living ungodly, and youthful perfection condemns the long years of the unrighteous. (Condemn: disapprove, punish) **17.** They will witness the wise's end but not understand God's purpose or the safety He grants him. (comprehend: fully understand) **18.** They will despise him, but God will mock them, and they will become a vile carcass and reproach among the dead forever. (vile: wicked; carcass: remains; reproach: disgrace) **19.** He will tear them down, casting them headlong, leaving them speechless, shaking them from their foundation, and they will be destroyed, with no memory. (headlong: recklessly) **20.** When they face their sins, they will come in fear, and their iniquities will confront them directly. (iniquities: immoral behavior)

Chapter 5

1. The righteous will stand boldly before those who wronged them, disregarding their efforts. (Righteous: morally right or justifiable) **2.** When the wrongdoers see this, they will be filled with fear and astonishment at how far beyond their expectations the righteous have been saved. (Astonishment: great surprise) **3.** In regret and anguish, they will admit to themselves, "This was the one we mocked and ridiculed." (Anguish: severe pain or distress) **4.** We foolishly thought his life was pointless and his end dishonorable. (Foolishly: in a manner showing lack of wisdom) **5.** How is he now counted among God's children, and his place among the saints? (Saints: holy or virtuous people) **6.** We strayed from the path of truth, and righteousness never shined on us. (Strayed: moved away from the correct path) **7.** We labored in wickedness and destruction, wandering through paths unknown, but we never knew God's way. (Wickedness: morally wrong or evil) **8.** What did pride gain us? What did our boasting bring us? (Boasting: excessive pride in oneself) **9.** All those things have passed like a shadow, or like a quick-moving post. (Passed: gone or disappeared) **10.** Like a ship sailing the water, leaving no trace behind once it's gone. (Trace: a mark or sign left by something) **11.** Like a bird flying through the air, leaving no sign of its path, only the air disturbed by its wings. (Disturbed: interrupted or moved) **12.** Or like an arrow shot at a target, splitting the air, but leaving no trace. (Split: divided or cut through) **13.** Just like that, we were born and quickly came to our end, with no sign of virtue, consumed by our own sin. (Virtue: moral excellence) **14.** The hope of the wicked is fleeting, like dust blown by the wind or smoke scattered by a storm. (Fleeting: lasting for a very short time) **15.** But the righteous live forever, their reward is with the Lord, and He cares for them. (Reward: a benefit or compensation for good actions) **16.** They will receive a glorious kingdom and a beautiful crown from the Lord, who will protect them. (Glorious: deserving great admiration) **17.** God will take His zeal as armor and use His creatures to avenge His enemies. (Zeal: great energy or enthusiasm) **18.** He will wear righteousness as a breastplate and true judgment as a helmet. (Breastplate: protective armor for the chest) **19.** He will take holiness as an invincible shield. (Invincible: too powerful to be defeated) **20.** His wrath will be sharpened as a sword, and the world will battle against the foolish. (Wrath: extreme anger) **21.** Then, thunderbolts will strike, and from the clouds, they will fly straight to their target. (Thunderbolts: bolts of lightning) **22.** Hailstones of wrath will be thrown like arrows, the sea will rage against them, and floods will drown them. (Hailstones: chunks of ice that fall from the sky) **23.** A mighty wind will blow them away, and iniquity will destroy the earth, overthrowing the powerful. (Iniquity: immoral or grossly unfair behavior)

Chapter 6

1. Listen, O kings, and understand; learn, you who judge the earth. (Judge: to make decisions or form opinions) **2.** Pay attention, you who rule nations and take pride in your people. (Pride: a feeling of deep satisfaction with one's achievements) **3.** Power is given to you by the Lord, and sovereignty from the Highest, who will examine your deeds and thoughts. (Sovereignty: supreme power or authority) **4.** As ministers of His kingdom, you have not judged correctly, nor followed His law or counsel. (Ministers: servants or officials) **5.** A sharp judgment will come upon those in high places. (Sharp: severe, intense) **6.** Mercy will soon pardon the humble, but the mighty will face torment. (Pardon: forgive, Torment: suffering) **7.** The Lord shows no favoritism nor is He awed by greatness, for He made both the small and great and cares for them equally. (Favoritism: unfair bias, Awe: wonder or admiration) **8.** A severe trial awaits the mighty. (Severe: intense, harsh) **9.** I speak to you, O kings, so you may gain wisdom and not stray. (Stray: to wander or turn away) **10.** Those who keep holiness will be judged holy, and those who learn wisdom will know how to answer. (Holiness: sacredness) **11.** Set your hearts on my words; desire them, and you will be taught. (Desire: wish or long for) **12.** Wisdom is glorious and never fades; she is seen by those who love her, and found by those who seek her. (Glorious: deserving admiration) **13.** She meets those who desire her and reveals herself to them. (Reveals: makes known) **14.** Those who seek her early will find her without trouble. (Trouble: difficulty) **15.** To think on her is the perfection of wisdom; those who watch for her will find peace. (Perfection: flawless state) **16.** She seeks those worthy of her, showing favor along their paths and in every thought. (Favor: approval) **17.** The true beginning of wisdom is the desire for discipline, and discipline's care is love. (Discipline: training) **18.** Love is keeping her laws, and paying attention to them ensures incorruption. (Incorruption: freedom from decay) **19.** Incorruption brings us closer to God. (Incorruption: purity) **20.** Desire for wisdom leads to a kingdom. (Desire: strong wanting) **21.** If you delight in thrones and scepters, honor wisdom to reign forever. (Delight: great pleasure, Scepters: staffs held by rulers) **22.** I will tell you what wisdom is, where she came from, and bring her knowledge into light. (Mysteries: things hard to understand) **23.** I will not speak with envy, for a man filled with envy cannot fellowship with wisdom. (Envy: resentment toward others' success) **24.** Wisdom of many is the welfare of the world, and a wise king supports the people. (Welfare: health and happiness) **25.** Receive instruction through my words, and it will benefit you. (Benefit: to gain good)

Chapter 7

1. I too am a mortal, like all others, descended from the first man formed from the earth. (Mortal: human; Descended: originated) **2.** In my mother's womb, I was shaped as flesh over ten months, crafted from blood, originating from human seed and the joy of union. (Womb: uterus; Crafted: formed) **3.** At birth, I inhaled life's air and fell upon the earth, which shares our essence. My first cry was like every other person's. (Inhaled: breathed; Essence: nature) **4.** I was wrapped in swaddling clothes and cared for tenderly. (Swaddling: wrapping; Tenderly: kindly) **5.** No king has ever had a different start to life. (Start: beginning) **6.** All humans enter life the same way and depart similarly. (Depart: leave) **7.** I prayed, and understanding was granted; I sought God, and wisdom came to me. (Granted: given; Sought: asked) **8.** I valued wisdom more than scepters and thrones, seeing riches as nothing in comparison to her. (Scepters: staffs; Comparison: contrast) **9.** Precious stones, gold, and silver seem insignificant compared to her. (Precious: valuable; Insignificant: unimportant) **10.** I loved her above health and beauty, choosing her over light, which fades, as her light is eternal. (Treasured: valued; Fades: dims) **11.** With her came all good things and countless riches in abundance. (Countless: endless; Abundance: plenty) **12.** I delighted in them, knowing wisdom precedes them all, though I didn't realize she was their source. (Delighted: enjoyed; Precedes: leads) **13.** I diligently learned and freely shared her insights, not hiding her wealth. (Diligently: carefully; Insights: wisdom) **14.** She is an unfailing treasure to those who embrace her, leading them to become friends of God and recipients of His gifts. (Unfailing: constant; Recipients: receivers) **15.** God allows me to speak and understand knowledge because He leads to wisdom and guides the wise. (Granted: allowed; Guides: directs) **16.** In His hands are we, our words, wisdom, and all skill in creation. (Creation: making) **17.** He gave me knowledge of the world's workings, its formation, and the elements' processes. (Elements: basics; Processes: methods) **18.** He revealed the beginning, end, and in-between of times, the sun's turning, and seasonal changes. (Revealed: shown; Turning: movement) **19.** I understood the cycles of years and the stars' arrangements. (Cycles: patterns; Arrangements: orders) **20.** I learned about creatures' natures, wild beasts' instincts, winds' power, human reasoning, plants, and roots. (Instincts: drives; Varieties: types) **21.** Both hidden and revealed things were made known to me. (Revealed: shown) **22.** Wisdom taught me; she holds a pure, vibrant, versatile, and unblemished spirit that loves good and is unstoppable. (Versatile: flexible; Vibrant: lively; Unblemished: perfect) **23.** She is kind, steadfast, powerful, and able to penetrate pure, subtle minds. (Steadfast: loyal; Subtle: fine) **24.** Wisdom moves faster than any force and fills all things with her purity. (Fills: permeates; Purity: clarity) **25.** She is God's breath, a pure emanation of His glory, free of impurity. (Emanation: flow; Impurity: imperfection) **26.** She is the radiance of eternal light, a spotless mirror of God's majesty, and an image of His goodness. (Radiance: glow; Majesty: greatness) **27.** Though one in essence, she renews all creation and enters holy souls, making them God's companions and prophets. (Essence: being; Companions: friends) **28.** God loves only those who dwell with wisdom. (Dwell: live) **29.** She surpasses the sun's beauty and all stars; compared to her, even light is secondary. (Surpasses: exceeds) **30.** Though light is followed by night, wisdom remains untouched by evil. (Untouched: pure)

Chapter 8
1. Wisdom stretches mightily from one end of the world to the other and gently orders all things. (Stretches: extends; Orders: organizes) **2.** I loved her and sought her from my youth, desiring her as my spouse and admiring her beauty. (Sought: pursued; Spouse: partner) **3.** Being close to God, she magnifies her nobility, and even the Lord Himself loves her. (Magnifies: elevates; Nobility: virtue) **4.** She knows God's mysteries and loves His works. (Mysteries: secrets; Works: creations) **5.** If wealth is to be desired, what is richer than wisdom, which accomplishes all? (Wealth: riches; Accomplishes: achieves) **6.** If prudence brings results, who is a more skillful creator than wisdom? (Prudence: wisdom; Skillful: capable) **7.** If one loves righteousness, her deeds are virtues: she teaches temperance, prudence, justice, and courage—qualities unmatched in life. (Deeds: actions; Courage: bravery) **8.** If experience is sought, she knows ancient truths, predicts the future, interprets speeches, explains riddles, and foresees signs and seasons. (Predicts: anticipates; Interprets: explains) **9.** I decided to live with her, knowing she would counsel me in good things and comfort me in grief. (Counsel: advise; Grief: sorrow) **10.** Because of her, I will gain respect among the people and honor from elders, even in my youth. (Respect: esteem; Honor: recognition) **11.** I will be quick-witted in judgment and admired by the great. (Quick-witted: perceptive; Judgment: decisions) **12.** When silent, they will wait for me; when I speak, they will listen intently; and if I talk long, they will be awed. (Intently: carefully; Awed: amazed) **13.** Through her, I will achieve immortality and leave behind an eternal legacy. (Immortality: eternal life; Legacy: remembrance) **14.** I will govern the people and subdue nations. (Govern: lead; Subdue: control) **15.** Tyrants will fear me at mere mention, and I will be praised among the people and courageous in war. (Tyrants: oppressors; Courageous: brave) **16.** When I return home, I will rest with her, as her companionship brings no bitterness, only joy and delight. (Companionship: presence; Delight: happiness) **17.** Reflecting on this, I realized that to be united with wisdom is immortality. (Reflecting: thinking; United: joined) **18.** Her friendship brings great joy, her works bring endless riches, and her conversations grant prudence and good reputation. (Endless: infinite; Reputation: honor) **19.** I sought her because, even as a child, I was insightful and had a good spirit. (Insightful: perceptive; Spirit: character) **20.** Being good, I was placed in a pure body. (Pure: undefiled) **21.** However, I understood I could only receive her if God granted her to me. Knowing this was also wisdom, I prayed and sought her with all my heart. (Granted: given; Sought: asked)

Chapter 9
1. O God of my ancestors and Lord of mercy, who created all things by your word. (Ancestors: forefathers; Mercy: compassion) **2.** You ordained man through wisdom to rule over the creatures you made. (Ordained: appointed; Rule: govern) **3.** To manage the world with fairness and justice, and to judge with integrity. (Fairness: equity; Integrity: honesty) **4.** Grant me wisdom, who sits by your throne, and do not reject me from among your children. (Grant: give; Reject: exclude) **5.** For I, your servant and child of your maidservant, am weak, short-lived, and too young to understand laws and judgment. (Maidservant: female servant; Short-lived: brief) **6.** Even the most perfect human is worthless without your wisdom. (Worthless: insignificant; Wisdom: insight) **7.** You have chosen me to rule your people and judge your sons and daughters. (Rule: lead; Judge: guide) **8.** You commanded me to build a temple on your holy mountain and an altar in the city where you dwell, resembling the holy tabernacle you prepared from the beginning. (Temple: sacred building; Tabernacle: sanctuary) **9.** Wisdom was with you, knowing your works and present when you created the world, understanding what pleases you and aligns with your commands. (Aligns: matches; Commands: instructions) **10.** Send her from your holy heavens and glorious throne to work with me so I may know what pleases you. (Glorious: majestic; Pleases: satisfies) **11.** She understands all things, will guide me wisely in my actions, and sustain me with her power. (Guide: lead; Sustain: uphold) **12.** My works will be acceptable, and I will judge your people justly, deserving to sit on my father's throne. (Justly: fairly; Deserving: worthy) **13.** Who can understand God's counsel or discern His will? (Counsel: advice; Discern: perceive) **14.** Human thoughts are fragile, and our plans are unreliable. (Fragile: weak; Unreliable: uncertain) **15.** Our mortal body burdens the soul, and the earthly tent weighs down the mind that reflects on many matters. (Burdens: oppresses; Reflects: ponders) **16.** We barely comprehend earthly things and only with effort find what is before us—how can heavenly things be known? (Comprehend: understand; Effort: struggle) **17.** Who can grasp your counsel unless you grant wisdom and send your Holy Spirit from above? (Grasp: comprehend; Spirit: divine essence) **18.** Through wisdom, humanity's ways were renewed, people learned what pleases you, and were saved. (Renewed: reformed; Saved: redeemed)

Chapter 10
1. She safeguarded the first man of the world, created alone, and lifted him from his fall. (Safeguarded: protected; Fall: failure) **2.** She granted him authority to rule over all things. (Granted: gave; Authority: power) **3.** But when the wicked abandoned her in anger, he perished in the rage that led him to kill his brother. (Abandoned: left; Perished: died) **4.** Because of this, the earth was flooded, but wisdom preserved it, guiding the righteous in a small, humble vessel. (Flooded: submerged; Vessel: boat) **5.** When nations plotted wickedly and were confused, she found and preserved the righteous, keeping him devoted despite his compassion for his son. (Plotted: conspired; Devoted: loyal) **6.** She delivered the righteous man who escaped the fire that fell on five cities. (Delivered: rescued; Escaped: fled) **7.** Their wickedness left a smoking wasteland, unripe fruit, and a pillar of salt—a reminder of disbelief. (Wasteland: barren area; Disbelief: unfaithfulness) **8.** By rejecting wisdom, they not only harmed themselves but left a legacy of foolishness, exposing their sins. (Rejecting: ignoring; Legacy: memory) **9.** Yet wisdom freed from pain those who followed her. (Freed: released; Pain: suffering) **10.** She guided the righteous fleeing his brother's anger, showed him God's kingdom, taught him holy truths, enriched his travels, and multiplied his work's rewards. (Enriched: blessed; Multiplied: increased) **11.** When greed overtook his oppressors, she supported and made him prosper. (Greed: selfishness; Prosper: succeed) **12.** She protected him from enemies, kept him safe, and granted victory in conflict to reveal that goodness triumphs over all. (Protected: defended; Triumphs: wins) **13.** When the righteous was sold, she stayed with him, freeing him from sin and descending with him into the pit. (Stayed: remained; Pit: prison) **14.** She freed him from bondage, raised him to rulership, and exposed his accusers as liars, granting him eternal honor. (Bondage: captivity; Eternal:

everlasting) **15.** She rescued the righteous and their innocent descendants from their oppressors. (Descendants: offspring; Oppressors: tyrants) **16.** She filled the servant of God with courage to oppose terrifying kings through wonders and signs. (Courage: bravery; Oppose: resist) **17.** She rewarded the righteous, guided them in miraculous ways, shading them by day and lighting their nights. (Rewarded: blessed; Miraculous: extraordinary) **18.** She led them through the Red Sea and across vast waters. (Led: guided; Vast: immense) **19.** She drowned their enemies and cast them from the ocean depths. (Drowned: submerged; Depths: bottom) **20.** The righteous plundered the wicked, praised your holy name, O Lord, and celebrated your powerful hand that fought for them. (Plundered: took from; Celebrated: honored) **21.** For wisdom gave speech to the mute and made eloquent those who could not speak. (Mute: silent; Eloquent: articulate)

Chapter 11

1. She prospered their works through the holy prophet. (Prospered: succeeded) **2.** They went through an uninhabited wilderness, pitching tents where no paths existed. (Uninhabited: empty, Pitched: set up) **3.** They stood against their enemies and were avenged on their adversaries. (Avenged: repaid) **4.** When they were thirsty, they called upon You, and You gave them water from the flinty rock, quenching their thirst. (Flinty: hard, Quenching: satisfying) **5.** By the same means their enemies were punished, they were helped in need. (Punished: judged, Helped: aided) **6.** Instead of a foul, flowing river, (Foul: dirty) **7.** Instead of the commandment that led to the slaying of infants, You gave them water by an unexpected means. (Slaying: killing, Abundance: plenty) **8.** Through their thirst, You showed how You had punished their enemies. (Thirst: dryness) **9.** When they were tested, mercifully chastised, they realized how the wicked were judged and tormented, thirsting differently than the just. (Tested: tried, Chastised: corrected, Wrath: anger) **10.** You admonished them as a father but condemned the wicked as a king. (Admonished: warned, Condemned: sentenced) **11.** Whether absent or present, they were troubled alike. (Troubled: disturbed) **12.** A double grief and groaning for past memories came upon them. (Grief: sorrow, Groaning: lamenting) **13.** When they saw others benefited by their own punishments, they felt some awareness of the Lord. (Benefited: helped, Awareness: recognition) **14.** They scorned whom they later admired after seeing the result. (Scorned: mocked, Admired: respected) **15.** For their foolishness in worshipping unreasonable beasts, You sent a multitude of irrational beasts for vengeance. (Foolishness: stupidity, Vile: disgusting, Vengeance: revenge) **16.** So they would know that the same way a man sins, he will be punished in the same manner. (Punished: judged) **17.** Your Almighty hand, which created the world from formless matter, had no shortage of ways to send wild beasts—bears, lions, (Almighty: all-powerful, Formless: shapeless) **18.** Or wild beasts, full of rage, newly created, breathing fire or emitting foul smoke. (Rage: anger, Emitting: releasing) **19.** These beasts could harm them immediately or destroy them with their terrifying sight. (Sight: vision, Destroy: ruin) **20.** Without these, they could have fallen with one blast from Your power, scattered by Your vengeance, but You ordered all things with measure. (Blast: force, Scattered: spread, Ordered: arranged) **21.** You can show Your strength anytime; who can resist Your arm? (Resist: withstand) **22.** The world before You is like a tiny grain on a scale, like a drop of morning dew on earth. (Grain: speck, Dew: moisture) **23.** You have mercy on all, for You can do all things and overlook men's sins, giving them a chance to repent. (Mercy: compassion, Overlook: forgive, Repent: change) **24.** You love everything You have made and abhor nothing. You would never have created anything if You hated it. (Abhor: detest, Created: made) **25.** How could anything endure if it were not Your will, or be preserved if not called by You? (Endure: last, Preserved: protected) **26.** But You spare all, for they are Yours, O Lord, Lover of souls. (Spare: save, Lover: protector)

Chapter 12

1. For Your incorruptible Spirit is in all things. (Incorruptible: unchanging) **2.** Therefore, You chasten them gradually, reminding them of their offenses, so they may turn from wickedness and believe in You, O Lord. (Chasten: correct, Offenses: wrongdoings) **3.** It was Your will to destroy the old inhabitants of Your holy land by our fathers' hands, (Inhabitants: residents) **4.** Whom You hated for their detestable witchcrafts and wicked sacrifices. (Detestable: loathsome) **5.** Also the merciless child murderers, flesh devourers, and blood feasts, (Merciless: cruel, Devourers: eaters) **6.** With their priests among their idolatrous crew, and parents killing helpless souls. (Idolatrous: idol-worshipping, Helpless: powerless) **7.** That the land You prized might receive a worthy colony of God's children. (Prized: valued) **8.** You spared men, sending wasps to destroy them gradually. (Spared: saved, Wasps: stinging insects) **9.** Not that You lacked power to defeat them with beasts or a single word, (Lacked: lacked, Defeat: conquer) **10.** But You gave them time to repent, knowing their malice and that they wouldn't change. (Repent: remorse, Malice: ill-will) **11.** For they were cursed from the start; You did not pardon them for anyone's sake. (Cursed: condemned) **12.** Who can challenge Your judgment, or accuse You for nations You created? (Challenge: question, Accuse: blame) **13.** For there is no God but You, who cares for all, showing that Your judgment is right. (Cares: loves, Right: just) **14.** Neither king nor tyrant can oppose Your judgment. (Oppose: resist, Tyrant: ruler) **15.** Since You are righteous, You order things righteously, never condemning the innocent. (Order: arrange, Condemning: judging) **16.** Your power is the foundation of righteousness, and You are gracious to all. (Foundation: basis, Gracious: kind) **17.** When men doubt Your full power, You show strength and make their boldness clear. (Doubt: question, Boldness: courage) **18.** But You, mastering Your power, judge with fairness, treating us with favor. (Mastering: controlling, Fairness: justice) **19.** By these actions, You've taught us to be merciful and gave us hope of repentance. (Actions: deeds, Hope: expectation) **20.** If You punished the enemies of Your children with care, giving them time to turn from malice, (Punished: judged, Care: consideration) **21.** How much more careful were You in judging Your sons, with whom You made covenants? (Careful: thoughtful, Covenants: agreements) **22.** As You chasten us, You scourge our enemies far more, teaching us to seek mercy when judged. (Chasten: correct, Scourge: punish) **23.** You torment the wicked with their own abominations. (Torment: afflict, Abominations: detestable acts) **24.** They went astray, worshipping false gods that even their enemies despised. (False: fake) **25.** You sent judgments to mock them, like children without reason. (Judgments: verdicts, Mock: ridicule) **26.** But those who would not be corrected will face a judgment worthy of God. (Corrected: reformed, Judgment: penalty) **27.** For they grudged when punished, thinking their gods superior, but acknowledged the true God, and received severe damnation. (Grudged: complained, Severe: extreme, nephew heard of their plot and went to the barracks to tell Paul. (Nephew: brother's or sister's son) **17.** Paul called a centurion and told him to take the young man to the chief captain, as he had urgent news. (Centurion: Roman officer) **18.** The centurion took the young man to the chief captain, saying, "Paul, the prisoner, called me and asked me to bring this young man to you, for he has something important to tell you." (Urgent: important and requiring immediate action) **19.** The chief captain took the boy aside and asked, "What is it you want to tell me?" (Aside: privately) **20.** The young man said, "The Jews are plotting to have you bring Paul down tomorrow, pretending to ask more about him, but they are waiting to kill him." (Plotting: making secret plans) **21.** "Do not give in to them. Over forty men have bound themselves with an oath not to eat or drink until they kill Paul. They are ready, waiting for your approval." (Bound: pledged) **22.** The chief captain sent the boy away, warning him not to tell anyone what he had revealed. (Revealed: disclosed) **23.** He ordered two centurions to prepare two hundred soldiers, seventy horsemen, and two hundred spearmen to guard Paul to Caesarea that night. (Spearmen: soldiers armed with spears) **24.** He also arranged for animals to carry Paul safely to Felix the governor. (Arranged: organized) **25.** He wrote a letter to Felix, saying: (Letter: written communication) **26.** "Claudius Lysias to the most excellent governor Felix, greetings." (Greetings: formal hello) **27.** "This man was seized by the Jews and nearly killed. I intervened with soldiers and saved him when I discovered he was a Roman." (Intervened: interfered to stop something) **28.** "When I tried to find out why they accused him, I brought him before their council." (Council: assembly of people for discussion) **29.** "I found that he was only accused over matters of their law, with no charges worthy of death or imprisonment." (Accused: charged with a crime) **30.** "When I learned of the plot against him, I immediately sent him to you with his accusers to state their case." (Immediately: without delay) **31.** The soldiers, following orders, took Paul by night to Antipatris. (Orders: instructions) **32.** The next day, the horsemen continued with Paul while the rest returned to the barracks. (Horsemen: soldiers on horseback) **33.** When they arrived in Caesarea, they delivered the letter to the governor and presented Paul to him. (Delivered: handed over) **34.** Felix read the letter and asked which province Paul was from. Learning he was from Cilicia, (Province: region) **35.** Felix said, "I will hear your case when your accusers arrive." He ordered Paul to be kept in Herod's palace. (Ordered: gave a command)

Chapter 24

1. Five days later, Ananias the high priest, with elders and the orator Tertullus, came to accuse Paul before the governor. (Orator: speaker) **2.** Tertullus began, "Since we enjoy peace thanks to you and your actions have benefited this nation, (Benefited: helped) **3.** We always thank you, most noble Felix, everywhere and at all times." (Noble: distinguished) **4.** "To avoid being lengthy, I ask you to hear a few words of mercy." (Mercy: compassion) **5.** "We've found this man to be a troublemaker, causing unrest among Jews worldwide, and leading the Nazarene sect." (Unrest: disturbance) (Sect:

group) **6.** "He tried to defile the temple, and we arrested him, planning to judge him by our laws." (Defile: desecrate) **7.** "But Lysias, the chief captain, intervened, taking him from us, (Intervened: interfered) (Forcefully: violently) **8.** Ordering his accusers to present their case to you, for you to examine the matter yourself." (Examine: inspect) **9.** The Jews agreed, affirming the accusations. (Affirming: confirming) **10.** Paul replied, "Since you've been a judge for many years, I gladly defend myself. (Gladly: willingly) **11.** It's only been twelve days since I went to Jerusalem to worship. (Worship: devotion) **12.** They didn't find me debating anyone in the temple, stirring up trouble, or causing disturbances in the city. (Debating: arguing) (Stirring up: provoking) (Disturbances: commotions) **13.** They can't prove the charges against me. (Charges: accusations) **14.** But I admit this: I follow the way they call heresy, worshiping the God of my fathers, believing the law and prophets. (Admit: confess) (Heresy: dissent) **15.** I hope in God, as they do, for the resurrection of the dead, both the righteous and the wicked. (Hope: expectation) (Resurrection: revival) (Righteous: just) (Wicked: evil) **16.** I strive to keep a clear conscience before God and men. (Strive: endeavor) (Conscience: morality) **17.** After many years, I came to bring gifts and offerings to my people. (Offerings: gifts) **18.** Some Asian Jews found me in the temple, purified and without a crowd or commotion. (Purified: cleansed) (Commotion: uproar) **19.** They should have been here to accuse me if they have charges. (Accuse: charge) **20.** Or let these men say if they found any wrongdoing when I stood before the council, (Wrongdoing: offense) **21.** Except for one issue: I declared, 'I am on trial today because of my belief in the resurrection of the dead.'" (Declared: stated) **22.** Felix, knowing more about the faith, postponed the case, saying, "I'll wait for Lysias to fully understand this matter." (Postponed: delayed) (Faith: belief) **23.** He ordered Paul to be guarded but allowed him some freedom and visitors. (Guarded: watched) **24.** After some days, Felix and his Jewish wife, Drusilla, summoned Paul to speak about faith in Christ. (Summoned: called) **25.** Paul discussed righteousness, self-control, and judgment to come. Felix, troubled, said, "Go away for now; when I have a convenient time, I'll call you." (Righteousness: justice) (Self-control: restraint) (Troubled: anxious) (Convenient: suitable) **26.** He hoped Paul would offer him a bribe to be released and called for him often. **27.** After two years, Festus replaced Felix, and to please the Jews, Felix left Paul in prison. (Replaced: succeeded) (Please: satisfy)

Chapter 25
1. When Festus arrived in the province, he went from Caesarea to Jerusalem three days later. (Province: territory) **2.** The high priest and Jewish leaders informed him against Paul and begged him to have Paul condemned. (Informed: accused) (Begged: pleaded) **3.** Asking for favor to have Paul sent to Jerusalem, planning to ambush and kill him. (Favor: favorability) (Ambush: surprise attack) **4.** But Festus replied that Paul should be kept at Caesarea, and he would go there shortly. (Replied: responded) **5.** "Let those among you who are able, go with me to accuse him if he has done anything wrong." (Able: capable) (Accuse: charge) **6.** After staying over ten days, he went to Caesarea; the next day, he ordered Paul to be brought before the court. (Ordered: commanded) **7.** When Paul arrived, the Jews from Jerusalem stood around him, bringing serious accusations that they couldn't prove. (Accusations: charges) (Serious: grave) **8.** Paul defended himself, saying, "I've done nothing wrong against Jewish law, the temple, or Caesar." (Defended: argued) **9.** Festus, wanting to please the Jews, asked, "Do you want to go to Jerusalem and be judged there?" (Pleased: satisfy) (Judged: tried) **10.** Paul replied, "I stand at Caesar's judgment seat where I should be judged; I have done no wrong to the Jews, as you know." (Judgment: trial) (Wrong: offense) **11.** "If I've committed any crime worthy of death, I won't refuse to die; but if not, no one can hand me over to them. I appeal to Caesar." (Committed: done) (Refuse: decline) (Hand over: surrender) **12.** Festus, after consulting with the council, said, "You've appealed to Caesar, and to Caesar you shall go." (Consulting: conferring) (Appealed: requested) **13.** After some days, King Agrippa and Bernice visited Festus in Caesarea to greet him. (Visited: came) (Greeted: welcomed) **14.** After staying several days, Festus told King Agrippa about Paul, (Told: informed) (Several: a few) **15.** Explaining that the chief priests and elders of the Jews wanted him judged. (Explaining: describing) (Judged: tried) **16.** "I told them it's not Roman practice to deliver a man for execution without facing his accusers and having a chance to defend himself." (Execution: death sentence) (Practice: custom) **17.** "So when they came here, I immediately sat on the judgment seat and had the man brought before me." (Immediately: promptly) **18.** "The accusers didn't bring any charges I expected, but had some issues about their own beliefs, especially concerning Jesus, who was dead, but Paul claimed was alive." (Issues: matters) (Beliefs: views) (Claimed: asserted) **19.** "I wasn't sure how to handle these questions, so I asked if he wanted to be judged in Jerusalem." (Handle: address) (Judged: tried) **20.** "But when Paul appealed to be kept for Caesar's hearing, I ordered him to be kept until I could send him to Caesar." (Kept: held) (Appealed: requested) **21.** Agrippa said to Festus, "I'd like to hear him myself. Tomorrow, you shall hear him." (Hear: listen) (Shall: will) **22.** The next day, Agrippa and Bernice entered with great pomp, and Festus ordered Paul to be brought. (Pomp: ceremony) (Ordered: commanded) **23.** Festus said, "King Agrippa, and all present, you see this man whom the Jews have accused, both in Jerusalem and here, crying that he should not live any longer." (Crying: shouting) (Accused: charged) **24.** "But I found no reason to condemn him to death, and since he appealed to Caesar, I've decided to send him there." (Condemn: judge guilty) (Reason: cause) (Appealed: requested) **25.** "I have nothing certain to write to my lord, so I brought him before you, especially before you, King Agrippa, to have something to write after his examination. (Certain: definite) (Examination: trial) **26.** "It seems unreasonable to send a prisoner without stating the charges against him." (Unreasonable: illogical) (Charges: accusations)

Chapter 26
1. Agrippa said to Paul, "You are permitted to speak for yourself." Paul stretched out his hand and answered: (Permitted: allowed) **2.** "I consider myself fortunate, King Agrippa, to answer for myself today regarding the accusations made by the Jews." (Fortunate: lucky) **3.** "Especially since I know you are well-versed in Jewish customs and disputes. Please listen patiently to me." (Well-versed: knowledgeable) **4.** "All the Jews know my life from my youth, which began in my homeland in Jerusalem." (Homeland: native land) **5.** "They know me from the beginning; if they testify, they will confirm that I lived as a Pharisee, the strictest sect of our religion." (Sect: group) (Pharisee: a member of an ancient Jewish sect) **6.** "Now I stand here, judged for the hope of the promise made by God to our ancestors." (Hope: expectation) (Ancestors: forebears) **7.** "Our twelve tribes, serving God day and night, hope to see the fulfillment of this promise. For this hope, I am accused by the Jews." (Fulfillment: completion) **8.** "Why is it considered unbelievable by you that God could raise the dead?" (Unbelievable: hard to believe) (Raise: resurrect) **9.** "I once thought I should do many things contrary to the name of Jesus of Nazareth." (Contrary: opposed) **10.** "I did this in Jerusalem, arresting many of the saints, having authority from the chief priests. When they were executed, I voted against them." (Saints: holy people) (Executed: killed) **11.** "I punished them often in synagogues and forced them to blaspheme. I was so furious that I persecuted them to foreign cities." (Blaspheme: speak irreverently about God) (Furious: enraged) (Persecuted: mistreated) **12.** "On my way to Damascus with authority from the chief priests," (Authority: official power) **13.** "At midday, O king, I saw a light from heaven, brighter than the sun, shining around me and those traveling with me." (Midday: noon) (Shining: glowing) **14.** "We all fell to the ground, and I heard a voice saying in Hebrew, 'Saul, Saul, why are you persecuting me? It is hard for you to kick against the goads.'" (Goads: sharp points) (Persecuting: attacking) **15.** "I said, 'Who are you, Lord?' And the voice replied, 'I am Jesus, whom you are persecuting.'" (Replied: answered) **16.** "But rise and stand on your feet; I have appeared to you to appoint you as a servant and witness of what you have seen and will see." (Appoint: designate) (Witness: observer) **17.** "I will rescue you from the people and from the Gentiles, to whom I am sending you." (Rescue: save) (Gentiles: non-Jews) **18.** "To open their eyes and turn them from darkness to light, and from Satan's power to God's, so they may receive forgiveness of sins and an inheritance among those sanctified by faith in me." (Inheritance: heritage) (Sanctified: made holy) **19.** "So, King Agrippa, I was not disobedient to the heavenly vision." (Disobedient: rebellious) **20.** "First, I preached to those in Damascus, then in Jerusalem, throughout Judea, and finally to the Gentiles, telling them to repent, turn to God, and do works worthy of repentance." (Repent: regret) (Worthy: deserving) **21.** "For this reason, the Jews seized me in the temple and tried to kill me." (Seized: captured) **22.** "But with God's help, I continue to this day, testifying to small and great, saying nothing other than what the prophets and Moses said would come." (Testifying: witnessing) (Small and great: all people) **23.** "That the Christ would suffer, rise from the dead, and bring light to both the people and the Gentiles." (Christ: Messiah) (Suffer: endure pain) **24.** As Paul spoke, Festus interrupted, shouting, "Paul, you're insane! Your learning is driving you mad!" (Interrupted: cut off) (Insane: crazy) (Learning: knowledge) **25.** Paul replied, "I am not mad, most excellent Festus, but I speak the words of truth and reason." (Reason: rationality) **26.** "The king knows about these matters, and I speak freely because I am sure none of this is hidden from him; it wasn't done in secret." (Freely: openly) (Hidden: concealed) **27.** "King Agrippa, do you believe the prophets? I know you do." (Believe: trust) **28.** Agrippa replied, "You almost persuade me to become a Christian." (Persuade: convince) **29.** Paul responded, "I would to God that not only you, but everyone listening Damnation: condemnation)

Chapter 13

1. Surely vain are all men by nature, who are ignorant of God, and could not know Him through the good things seen, nor acknowledge the workmaster by considering His works. (Vain: futile, Acknowledge: recognize) 2. They considered fire, wind, swift air, the stars, violent water, or the lights of heaven as gods governing the world. (Considered: thought, Governing: ruling) 3. If they were delighted by their beauty, let them know how much better the Lord of them is, for the first author of beauty created them. (Delighted: pleased, Author: creator) 4. If they admired their power, let them understand how much mightier is He who made them. (Admired: admired, Mightier: stronger) 5. By the greatness and beauty of the creatures, the maker of them is seen. (Creatures: beings) 6. They are less to be blamed, for perhaps they err in seeking God, desiring to find Him. (Err: mistake, Desiring: longing) 7. Being engaged in His works, they search diligently and trust their sight, as the things they see are beautiful. (Engaged: involved, Diligently: carefully) 8. However, they are not pardoned. (Pardoned: forgiven) 9. If they could understand so much, how did they not sooner find the Lord of the world? (Understand: comprehend, Sooner: earlier) 10. Miserable are they, whose hope is in dead things, calling them gods—works of men's hands, gold, silver, images of beasts, or useless stones. (Miserable: unfortunate, Useless: worthless) 11. A carpenter fells timber, skillfully removing the bark, then makes a vessel for man's service. (Fells: cuts, Vessel: container) 12. After using the refuse of his work to cook, he feeds himself. (Refuse: waste) 13. He carves a crooked, useless piece of wood into the image of a man or a vile beast, painting it red and covering spots. (Carves: shapes, Vile: despicable) 14. When finished, he places it on a wall, fastening it with iron, ensuring it won't fall, as it cannot help itself. (Fastening: securing, Ensuring: making sure) 15. He provides for it so it won't fall, knowing it needs help because it is just an image. (Provides: makes provision, Needs: requires) 16. Then he prays to it for his goods, wife, and children, ashamed to speak to that which has no life. (Goods: possessions) 17. He calls upon the weak for health, prays to the dead for life, and seeks aid from the powerless. (Calls upon: prays to, Seeks: asks for) 18. He asks for a safe journey from one who cannot walk, and for success from one who cannot act. (Safe: successful, Success: prosperity) 19. For gaining and success, he asks the most unable to help. (Gaining: acquiring)

Chapter 14

1. Once again, one preparing to sail, facing stormy seas, places his trust in a fragile piece of wood, weaker than the ship that carries him. (fragile: weak) 2. It is the desire for gain that led to its creation, and the craftsman built it with his skill. (craftsman: builder) 3. Yet Your providence, O Father, governs it all: You've made a path through the sea and a safe way through the waves. (providence: care) 4. Showing that You can deliver from all danger, even if a man sails without skill. (deliver: rescue) 5. But You didn't want Your wisdom to remain idle; so, men place their lives in fragile vessels and are saved through peril. (idle: inactive; peril: danger) 6. In ancient times, when giants perished, the world's hope was saved in a weak vessel, leaving a legacy for future generations. (perished: died; legacy: inheritance) 7. Blessed is the wood through which righteousness comes. (righteousness: justice) 8. But what is made by human hands is cursed, as is the maker: both are tainted— he for making it, and it for being corruptible yet called divine. (tainted: spoiled; corruptible: decaying) 9. The ungodly and their ungodliness are detestable to God. (ungodly: immoral; detestable: hateful) 10. What is made by hands will be punished with its maker. (punished: penalized) 11. Even the idols of the Gentiles will face judgment, for in God's creation, they have become abominations, leading souls astray. (Gentiles: non-Jews; abominations: horrors; astray: off course) 12. The making of idols was the start of spiritual immorality, and their creation brought corruption to life itself. (immorality: sinfulness; corruption: decay) 13. They were not there from the beginning, and they will not endure. (endure: last) 14. They entered the world due to men's empty pride and will soon end. (empty: vain; pride: arrogance) 15. A father mourning his child creates an image of the deceased and honors it as a god, though it was once a mortal, now passed away. (mourning: grieving; deceased: dead) 16. Over time, this ungodly practice became law, with images worshipped under royal command. (ungodly: sinful; royal: regal) 17. Those who couldn't honor their ruler in person made his image to honor in his stead, hoping to flatter him as though he were present. (stead: place; flatter: praise) 18. The craftsman's work fueled the superstition of the masses. (fuel: intensify) 19. Seeking favor, the artisan poured all his skill into creating the finest likeness. (artisan: maker; likeness: image) 20. The people, impressed by the craftsmanship, began to worship the image, which had previously been honored, not deified. (craftsmanship: skill; deified: worshipped) 21. This marked the start of the world's deception, as men, under hardship, ascribed the divine name to mere stone and wood. (deception: trickery; ascribed: attributed) 22. It wasn't enough that they were ignorant of God; they lived amidst a war of ignorance, calling their plagues "peace." (ignorant: unaware; plagues: disasters) 23. They sacrificed children, engaged in secret rites, or indulged in foreign feasts, (rites: rituals; indulged: indulged) 24. abandoning purity in lives and marriages—betrayals, adultery, and corruption. (purity: cleanness; adultery: infidelity) 25. Bloodshed, theft, lies, corruption, and unrest reigned among all people, with broken trust and perjury. (bloodshed: killing; perjury: lying) 26. Idol worship led to the defilement of souls, disordered marriages, adultery, and impurity. (defilement: corruption; impurity: contamination) 27. Idol worship is the root, cause, and end of all evil. (root: source; evil: immorality) 28. Idolaters are either mad with joy, speak false prophecies, live unjustly, or break their oaths. (idolaters: worshippers; prophecies: predictions) 29. Their trust in lifeless idols makes them swear falsely without fearing harm. (lifeless: dead) 30. They will face just punishment for their disregard of God and deceitful oaths, rejecting holiness. (disregard: neglect; deceitful: dishonest; holiness: purity) 31. It is not the power of those by whom they swear, but the righteous vengeance of sinners that punishes their wrongdoing. (vengeance: retribution)

Chapter 15

1. But You, O God, are kind, true, patient, and in Your mercy, You govern all things. (gracious: kind; longsuffering: patient) 2. When we sin, we belong to You, recognizing Your power; but we will not sin, for we know we are Yours. (sin: wrongdoing) 3. To know You is true righteousness; to understand Your power is the foundation of immortality. (righteousness: justice; immortality: eternal life) 4. The deceptive inventions of men and painted images do not deceive us; the artist's work is in vain. (inventions: creations; vain: pointless) 5. These images entice fools to desire them, longing for the form of a lifeless image that has no breath. (enticeth: attracts; lust: desire) 6. Those who make, desire, and worship these images are lovers of evil and are deserving of such false idols. (worship: adore; lovers: admirers) 7. The potter shapes clay with effort, creating vessels for our use, both clean and unclean, with the purpose judged by the potter. (potter: clay worker; vessels: containers) 8. But if he misuses his skill, he makes a false god from the same clay that will soon return to the earth when his life is required. (misuses: abuses; skill: ability) 9. His focus is not on labor or his short life, but on surpassing goldsmiths, silversmiths, and metalworkers, seeking glory in making false things. (surpassing: exceeding; glory: honor) 10. His heart is like ashes, his hope worse than earth, and his life is less valuable than clay. (ashes: dust; hope: expectation) 11. He does not know his Maker, nor the one who gave him life and spirit. (Maker: Creator; spirit: life force) 12. They view our lives as mere entertainment and our time as a market for gain, saying they must profit by any means, even evil. (pastime: entertainment; gain: profit) 13. The man who makes fragile vessels and carved images knows he offends more than others. (brittle: fragile; offend: insult) 14. All the enemies of Your people, who oppress them, are foolish and more miserable than babies. (oppress: dominate; miserable: wretched) 15. They consider all the idols of the nations as gods, yet these idols lack the ability to see, breathe, hear, or move. (idols: false gods; breathe: respire) 16. Man created them, borrowing his own spirit, yet no one can make a god like himself. (borrowed: took; spirit: soul) 17. Being mortal, he crafts a dead object with sinful hands; he is better than the idols he worships, for he once lived, but they never did. (mortal: subject to death; sinful: immoral) 18. They even worship the most hateful beasts, with some being worse than others. (hateful: detestable) 19. These idols are not even as desirable as real animals, yet they go without God's praise and blessing. (desirable: appealing; praise: admiration)

Chapter 16

1. Therefore, they were justly punished, tormented by the multitude of beasts. (justly: rightly) 2. Instead of such punishment, You dealt kindly with Your people, providing them with quails to stir their appetite. (kindly: graciously; appetite: hunger) 3. So they, desiring food, would loathe the beasts sent among them, and by experiencing hunger briefly, they would taste something new. (loathe: hate; penury: poverty) 4. It was necessary that those who exercised tyranny would face hunger, but for these, it was only to show them how their enemies were tormented. (tyranny: oppression; tormented: tortured) 5. When the fierce beasts came upon them, and they perished from the bites of serpents, Your anger was not everlasting. (fierce: intense; perished: died) 6. They were troubled for a short time to remind them, with a sign of salvation, to remember Your law's command. (troubled: distressed; admonished: warned) 7. Those who turned to it were not saved by the image they saw but by You, the Savior of all. (turned: directed; Savior: Redeemer) 8. And through this, You made Your enemies confess that You are the one who saves from all evil. (confess: admit) 9. The grasshoppers and flies killed them, and there was no cure for their lives, for they deserved such punishment. (cure: remedy) 10. But Your sons were not overcome even by the venomous dragon's bites, for Your

mercy was with them and healed them. (venomous: poisonous) 11. They were pricked to remember Your words and were quickly saved, so they wouldn't forget and might remain mindful of Your goodness. (pricked: stung) 12. It was not herbs or ointments that healed them, but Your word, O Lord, which heals all. (ointment: balm) 13. For You have power over life and death; You lead to the gates of death and bring back to life. (gates: doors) 14. A man kills through malice, and the spirit, once gone, doesn't return; neither does the soul come back after being received. (malice: hatred; received: taken) 15. Yet, it is impossible to escape Your hand. (impossible: unavoidable) 16. The ungodly, who refused to know You, were punished by Your mighty arm, with strange rains, hail, and showers, unable to escape, and they were consumed by fire. (refused: denied; mighty: strong) 17. What is most surprising is that the fire was more powerful in the water, which extinguishes all things, for the world fights for the righteous. (surprising: astonishing; extinguishes: puts out) 18. Sometimes, the flame was softened so that it did not consume the beasts sent against the wicked, but they could see and understand that they were being judged by God. (softened: reduced) 19. At other times, it burned even in the water, overcoming the power of fire to destroy the unjust land's fruits. (overcoming: defeating) 20. Instead, You fed Your people with food from angels, and sent them bread from heaven, ready-made without their effort, satisfying every desire and fitting every taste. (satisfying: fulfilling) 21. Your provision revealed Your sweetness to Your children, adapting to the eater's appetite and pleasing them all. (provision: supply; revealed: showed) 22. Snow and ice withstood the fire, not melting, so they could know that fire burning in hail and rain destroyed their enemies' crops. (withstood: endured; crops: produce) 23. Yet, the fire forgot its strength to nourish the righteous. (forgot: ignored) 24. The creatures that serve You, as their Maker, strengthen against the unrighteous for their punishment, but weaken for those who trust in You. (creatures: beings; unrighteous: wicked) 25. Thus, the elements were transformed in every way and obeyed Your grace, which nourishes all, fulfilling the needs of those who depend on You. (elements: forces; transformed: changed) 26. So, Your children, whom You love, may understand that it is not fruits that nourish man, but Your word, which preserves those who trust in You. (preserves: protects) 27. What wasn't destroyed by fire melted quickly with a little sun, (destroyed: ruined; melted: dissolved) 28. To show that we must honor You with thanks, and pray to You at dawn. (honor: praise) 29. The hope of the ungrateful will melt like frost and vanish like useless water. (ungrateful: thankless)

Chapter 17
1. For Your judgments are great and beyond expression; therefore, souls that lack understanding have gone astray. (judgments: decisions; unnurtured: unwise) 2. When unrighteous men sought to oppress the holy nation, they were trapped in their own homes, prisoners of darkness, bound by the chains of a long night, exiled from Your eternal providence. (oppose: wrongfully control; providence: divine care) 3. While they thought they could hide their sins in secret, they were engulfed in forgetfulness, overwhelmed by terrifying visions. (engulfed: surrounded; forgetfulness: oblivion) 4. The place that held them could not shield them from fear; sounds like falling waters surrounded them, and dreadful visions appeared with gloomy faces. (shield: protect; gloomy: sorrowful) 5. No power of fire could give them light; the bright stars' flames could not pierce the darkness of that terrible night. (pierce: penetrate) 6. Only a dreadful fire, kindled by itself, appeared to them, and terrified, they believed that what they saw was worse than what they could not see. (kindled: ignited; terrified: scared) 7. The illusions of magic were defeated, and their boastful wisdom was shown to be disgraceful. (illusions: deceptions; boastful: arrogant) 8. Those who promised to rid the soul of fear were themselves sick with terror, deserving to be mocked. (mocked: ridiculed) 9. Though no terrible thing truly frightened them, they were scared by the sight of passing beasts and hissing serpents, (frightened: terrified) 10. And died from fear, denying they even saw the air, which was unavoidable from every side. (denied: refused; unavoidable: inevitable) 11. Wickedness, condemned by its own conscience, is fearful, always anticipating further suffering. (wickedness: evil; condemned: judged) 12. Fear is nothing but a betrayal of the help reason offers. (betrayal: abandonment) 13. When inner expectations are low, ignorance seems worse than the actual cause of torment. (expectations: anticipations; ignorance: lack of knowledge) 14. That night, they slept a restless sleep, which came from the depths of inevitable hell. (restless: troubled; inevitable: certain) 15. They were tormented by monstrous apparitions and weakened, their hearts failing them, as sudden and unexpected fear struck them. (tormented: troubled; apparitions: visions) 16. Whoever fell down was tightly bound, trapped in a prison without iron bars. (tightly: firmly; trapped: confined) 17. Whether farmer, shepherd, or field worker, they were overtaken and could not escape their unavoidable fate, all bound by the same chain of darkness. (overtaken: caught; fate: destiny) 18. Whether it was a whistling wind, the sweet sound of birds among branches, or the forceful rush of water, (whistling: blowing; rush: flow) 19. Or the terrifying noise of stones falling, invisible beasts running, savage wild animals roaring, or the echoing sound from hollow mountains, these things made them faint with fear. (terrifying: frightening; echoing: reverberating) 20. The whole world was filled with clear light, and no one's work was hindered, (hindered: blocked) 21. But only over them was a heavy night, a shadow of the darkness that would later claim them, though they were more miserable than the darkness itself. (shadow: symbol; miserable: wretched)

Chapter 18
1. Nevertheless, Your saints were filled with great light. Hearing their voices but not seeing their form, they considered them happy, as they had not suffered as the saints had. (saints: holy people; form: appearance) 2. They did not harm those who had previously wronged them, thanking them and asking for pardon for having been enemies. (pardon: forgiveness) 3. Instead, You gave them a pillar of fire to guide them and a harmless sun to shelter them honorably. (harmless: non-threatening; shelter: protect) 4. Those who had imprisoned Your sons, who were to bring the pure light of the law to the world, deserved to be deprived of light and shut in darkness. (incorrupt: pure; deprived: denied) 5. When they decided to kill the saints' babies, one child was cast out and saved to rebuke them. You took away their children in a mighty flood. (rebuke: reprimand; mighty: powerful) 6. Our ancestors knew in advance of that night, so that, knowing the oaths they had trusted, they could be encouraged. (ancestors: forebears; encouraged: cheered) 7. For Your people, both the salvation of the righteous and the destruction of enemies were accepted. (salvation: deliverance) 8. By the means You punished our enemies, You glorified us, Your chosen people. (adversaries: enemies; glorified: honored) 9. The righteous secretly sacrificed, agreeing to a holy law that the saints should share both good and evil, with fathers now singing praise. (sacrificed: offered; share: partake) 10. On the other side, a wailing cry arose from the enemies, and a mournful sound spread for the children who were lamented. (wailing: crying; lamented: mourned) 11. The master and servant were punished the same way; as the king suffered, so did the common people. (common: ordinary) 12. All together, they had countless dead with the same kind of death; the living could not bury them, for in a single moment, their noblest children were destroyed. (countless: innumerable; noblest: best) 13. Though they had not believed due to their enchantments, after the death of the firstborn, they recognized this people as the sons of God. (enchantments: sorcery; recognized: acknowledged) 14. While all was quiet, and that night was swiftly passing, (swiftly: quickly) 15. Your Almighty word came down from heaven like a warrior into a land of destruction, (Almighty: all-powerful; warrior: fighter) 16. Your commandment, like a sharp sword, filled everything with death; it reached the heavens, but stood on the earth. (commandment: divine order) 17. Suddenly, visions of terrible dreams troubled them greatly, and unexpected terrors struck them. (visions: appearances; troubled: distressed) 18. Some were thrown here and there, half-dead, showing the cause of their demise. (demise: death) 19. The dreams that disturbed them foresaw this, so they might know the reason for their suffering. (foresaw: predicted) 20. Even the righteous experienced death's touch, and many perished in the wilderness, but Your wrath did not last long. (perished: died; wrath: anger) 21. Then the blameless man rushed to defend them, bringing the shield of his ministry, prayer, and incense, to end the calamity, declaring himself Your servant. (blameless: innocent; calamity: disaster) 22. He overcame the destroyer not with physical strength, but with the power of words, citing the oaths and covenants made with the ancestors. (overcame: defeated; citing: referring to) 23. When the dead were piled high, he stood between them, halting the wrath and creating a path for the living. (piled: stacked; halting: stopping) 24. In his long robe was the whole world, and on the stones were the fathers' glory engraved, with Your Majesty on his head. (robe: garment; engraved: carved) 25. The destroyer gave way, fearing them, for it was enough that they only tasted Your wrath. (tasted: experienced; wrath: anger)

Chapter 19
1. For the wicked, wrath came upon them without mercy, lasting to the end, for God had known their actions beforehand. (Wrath: intense anger; beforehand: in advance) 2. Though He had given them leave to depart and hastened their exit, they quickly regretted it and sought to overtake those they had urged to go. (Hastened: made faster) 3. While they wept by the graves of the dead, they devised another foolish plan, chasing those they had once dismissed. (Devised: thought up) 4. The fate they deserved led them to this end, making them forget what had already happened, so they might complete the punishment for their sins. (Fate: destiny; deserved:

earned) **5.** Thus, Your people traveled a wondrous path, encountering strange and fearsome fates. (Wondrous: wonderful; fates: outcomes) **6.** All creation was transformed, obeying its commands to keep Your children safe from harm. (Creation: all that exists; transformed: changed) **7.** A cloud covered the camp; where water had been, dry land appeared; through the Red Sea, a clear path emerged; and from the violent waters, a lush field grew. (Lush: rich, abundant) **8.** Through these marvels, Your people moved, protected by Your hand, seeing Your strange and marvelous wonders. (Marvels: extraordinary events; wonders: miraculous acts) **9.** They moved like horses, leapt like lambs, praising You, O Lord, their Deliverer. (Leapt: jumped; Deliverer: Savior) **10.** They remembered the plagues in the foreign land: how the earth brought forth flies instead of cattle, and the river turned up frogs instead of fish. (Plagues: disasters; foreign: land not their own) **11.** But soon after, they saw a new kind of bird, answering their hunger for delicacies. (Delicacies: special or luxurious foods) **12.** For quails rose from the sea to satisfy their desires. (Quails: small birds) **13.** Punishment came on the sinners, preceded by signs and thunder, justly inflicted for their wickedness, as they were cruel to strangers, more so than the Sodomites. (Inflicted: caused; wickedness: evil actions) **14.** The Sodomites did not welcome strangers, but these brought their benefactors into bondage. (Sodomites: people of Sodom, known for their sinfulness; benefactors: those who do good for others; bondage: captivity) **15.** Perhaps some will consider those who mistreated strangers. (Mistreated: treated cruelly or unfairly) **16.** These, who had feasted with them and shared in their laws, now cruelly oppressed those they had welcomed. (Feasted: ate and celebrated; oppressed: treated harshly) **17.** Like the blind stricken at the door of the righteous, they were surrounded by thick darkness, and each groped for his own door. (Stricken: struck, afflicted; groped: felt blindly for) **18.** The elements were transformed in harmony, like changing notes on a psaltery—though the sounds change, the essence remains, and these wonders could be seen in all that transpired. (Elements: natural forces; psaltery: a stringed instrument; essence: core nature; transpired: happened) **19.** Waters became earth, and creatures that once swam now walked on land. (Swam: moved through water) **20.** The fire overcame the water, defying its cooling power, and the water forgot its extinguishing nature. (Defying: resisting; extinguishing: putting out) **21.** Yet the flames did not consume the flesh of living creatures, nor did they melt the icy food from heaven, which naturally melts. (Consume: destroy; flesh: the body of a creature; icy: frozen) **22.** In all things, O Lord, You magnified and glorified Your people, never neglecting them, but supporting them at every time and place. (Magnified: made great; glorified: honored; neglecting: failing to care for)

73 – The First Book of Maccabees
Chapter 1

1. Alexander, son of Philip of Macedon, defeated Darius, king of Persia, and became the first ruler over Greece. (Philip: father of Alexander, Macedonia: ancient kingdom in Greece, Darius: Persian king, Persia: ancient empire) **2.** He waged many wars, captured strongholds, and defeated kings. (strongholds: fortified places) **3.** He conquered many lands and amassed great wealth, bringing peace to the earth, and his pride grew. (amassed: collected, pride: feeling of superiority) **4.** He built a large army, ruling over many nations, who paid him tribute. (tribute: payment made by one nation to another as a sign of submission) **5.** When he fell ill, he knew he was going to die. (ill: sick) **6.** He called his trusted servants, dividing his kingdom among them while still alive. (servants: attendants, trusted: loyal) **7.** Alexander ruled for twelve years before his death. (twelve: number of years) **8.** After his death, his servants ruled in his place. (servants: assistants, ruled: governed) **9.** They crowned themselves as kings, and evil increased on earth. (crowned: made kings, evil: wickedness) **10.** A wicked man named Antiochus Epiphanes arose, son of the former king, and began his reign in the 137th year of Greek rule. (wicked: evil, reign: rule, Epiphanes: title meaning "manifest," Greek: from Greece) **11.** Some Israelites persuaded others to make a pact with the surrounding nations, hoping to end their suffering. (pact: agreement, persuaded: convinced, suffering: hardship) **12.** This idea pleased them. (idea: thought, pleased: made happy) **13.** Some of them went to the king, who allowed them to follow the customs of the heathen. (heathen: non-Jewish nations) **14.** They built a gymnasium in Jerusalem, following foreign customs. (gymnasium: exercise place) **15.** They became uncircumcised, forsaking the holy covenant, and joined the heathen in evil actions. (uncircumcised: not undergoing a ritual, forsaking: abandoning, covenant: sacred agreement) **16.** Antiochus planned to conquer Egypt and rule over both realms. (realm: kingdom) **17.** He entered Egypt with a large army and fought against Ptolemy, the Egyptian king. (fought: battled) **18.** Ptolemy fled in fear, and many were killed. (fled: ran away) **19.** Antiochus took Egypt's strong cities and the spoils. (spoils: loot, goods taken after victory) **20.** After defeating Egypt, Antiochus returned and attacked Israel with a large army. (defeating: conquering) **21.** He entered the sanctuary, taking all the sacred items. (sanctuary: holy place) **22.** He took the golden altar, lampstand, utensils, and many other holy items. (altar: table for sacrifices, lampstand: holder for lamps) **23.** Antiochus seized the silver, gold, and precious vessels, including hidden treasures. (seized: took, precious: valuable) **24.** After plundering everything, he returned home, boasting arrogantly. (plundering: robbing) **25.** Israel mourned deeply everywhere. (mourned: expressed sorrow) **26.** Leaders, young men, and women grieved, and the land was in sorrow. (grieved: mourned) **27.** Every bridegroom lamented, and even those in marriage chambers were filled with sorrow. (lamented: expressed grief) **28.** The land trembled, and the house of Jacob was ashamed. (trembled: shook, ashamed: dishonored) **29.** After two years, the king sent his chief tax collector to the cities of Judah. (tax collector: one who gathers taxes) **30.** He deceived them with peace, then attacked, killing many Israelites. (deceived: tricked) **31.** After plundering the city, he set it on fire and destroyed it. (plundering: looting, destroyed: ruined) **32.** He took women and children as captives and took the cattle. (captives: prisoners) **33.** They rebuilt the city of David, fortifying it with a strong wall. (fortifying: strengthening) **34.** They placed a sinful nation in it and made it their stronghold. (sinful: wicked, stronghold: fortified place)**35.** They stored weapons and supplies, and after collecting the spoils of Jerusalem, placed them there, which became a trap. **36.** It became a place to ambush the sanctuary and a danger to Israel. **37.** They shed innocent blood around the sanctuary and defiled it. (Defiled: made unclean or impure) **38.** The people fled, and Jerusalem became a place for strangers, unrecognizable to its own people. **39.** The sanctuary was desolate, feasts turned to mourning, and sabbaths to disgrace. (Desolate: abandoned, in ruins) **40.** The city's glory was replaced by dishonor, and its honor became sorrow. **41.** King Antiochus ordered everyone to become one people. **42.** All nations agreed to follow the king's command. **43.** Many Israelites joined his religion, sacrificed to idols, and broke the sabbath. (Sabbaths: sacred days of rest) **44.** The king sent letters to Jerusalem and Judah to follow foreign laws. **45.** He forbade sacrifices and burnt offerings in the temple, profaned sabbaths and festivals. (Profaned: treated with disrespect) **46.** He ordered the sanctuary and people to be polluted. **47.** They built altars, sacrificed pigs, and unclean animals. (Polluted: made impure) **48.** They left children uncircumcised and polluted their souls with impurity. (Circumcised: removal of the foreskin, a religious practice; Polluted: made impure) **49.** The king wanted them to forget the law and change its ordinances. **50.** He decreed death for anyone who disobeyed. (Decreed: ordered or commanded) **51.** He wrote to his whole kingdom, appointing overseers to enforce sacrifices in Judah. (Overseers: supervisors or officials) **52.** Many joined those who abandoned the law, committing evil acts. **53.** They drove Israelites into hiding wherever they could. **54.** On the fifteenth day of Casleu, they set up the abomination on the altar and built idol altars in Judah. (Abomination: something that causes disgust or hatred) **55.** They burned incense at their homes and in the streets. **56.** They tore and burned the books of the law they found. **57.** Anyone with the covenant or practicing the law was to be put to death. **58.** They enforced this every month in the cities. **59.** On the 25th day, they sacrificed on the idol altar set up on God's altar. **60.** They killed women who circumcised their children, hanging infants and killing those who did the circumcising. **61.** Many in Israel refused to eat unclean food, preferring death rather than defilement. (Defilement: the act of making something impure) **62.** They chose death over profaning the holy covenant. (Profaning: treating with disrespect) **63.** They died in great numbers. **64.** Wrath greatly afflicted Israel.

Chapter 2

1. Mattathias, a priest from Modin, descended from Joarib, son of Simeon, and settled there. (Joarib: priestly lineage) **2.** He had five sons: Joannan (Caddis), **3.** Simon (Thassi), **4.** Judas (Maccabeus), **5.** Eleazar (Avaran), and Jonathan (Apphus). **6.** Seeing the blasphemy in Judah and Jerusalem, (Blasphemy: disrespectful speech or acts toward sacred things) **7.** Mattathias lamented, "Why was I born to see my people's misery, the city's ruin, and the sanctuary defiled?" (Lamented: expressed grief; Defiled: made unclean or impure) **8.** The temple lost its glory. (Glory: splendor or honor) **9.** Treasures were taken, infants killed, and young men slain. (Slain: killed violently) **10.** Every nation shared in her downfall. **11.** She's now a slave, once free. (Slave: a person without freedom or autonomy) **12.** The sanctuary, our pride, is ruined and profaned. (Profaned: treated disrespectfully) **13.** Why live any longer?" **14.** Mattathias and his sons mourned deeply. (Mourned: grieved or expressed sorrow) **15.** The king's officers came to Modin to enforce sacrifices. (Enforce: to compel obedience) **16.** Many Israelites came; Mattathias and his sons gathered. **17.** The officers said, "You're a respected leader, supported by family. (Respected: admired and held in high regard) **18.** So obey the king's command, and you'll be rewarded with wealth and honor." (Honor: high respect or privilege) **19.** Mattathias replied, "Though all nations obey the king, **20.** we will stay true to our covenant with God." (Covenant: a solemn agreement) **21.** "We will not forsake the Law," he declared. (Forsake: abandon or give up) **22.** "We will not follow the king's orders." **23.** As he spoke, a Jew went forward to sacrifice on the altar. (Sacrifice: an offering, often to a deity) **24.** Mattathias, filled with zeal, killed him and the king's officer, and tore down the altar. (Zeal: passionate devotion or enthusiasm) **25.** He acted with zeal for the Law, like Phinehas with Zimri. (Phinehas: a priest known for his zeal in protecting God's Law) **27.** Mattathias shouted, "Let those loyal to the Law follow me!" (Loyal: faithful to commitments) **28.** He and his sons fled, leaving everything behind. (Fled: ran away to escape danger) **29.** Many others seeking justice followed them to the wilderness. (Wilderness: a remote, uninhabited area) **30.** They went with their families, facing greater persecution. (Persecution: severe mistreatment due to beliefs) **31.** The king's officers pursued them and camped near. (Pursued: chased to capture) **32.** They attacked on the Sabbath. (Sabbath: a day of rest and worship) **33.** They demanded, "Come out and obey the king's command." **34.** They refused, saying, "We will not break the Sabbath." **35.** The battle quickly ensued. (Ensued: followed as a result) **36.** They did not respond or throw stones at them, nor did they block the places where they were hiding. **37.** They said, "Let us die innocent; heaven and earth will testify that you killed us wrongfully." **38.** They fought on the Sabbath, killing them, including their wives, children, and cattle—about a thousand people. **39.** When Mattathias and his companions heard, they mourned deeply. **40.** One said, "If we don't fight for our lives and laws, they will soon destroy us." **41.** They decided, "Whoever attacks us on the Sabbath, we will fight; we will not die as our brothers did." **42.** A group of devoted men (Assideans: Devout men of Israel who dedicated themselves to observing the law) joined them, those who followed the law. **43.** Persecuted people (Persecuted: Oppressed or harassed, especially for religious beliefs) joined and supported them. **44.** They fought sinful men (Sinful men: Those who lived in disobedience to God's laws) in anger; the rest fled to the Gentiles (Gentiles: Non-Jews, people from other nations) for help. **45.** Mattathias and his men destroyed the altars. **46.** They circumcised all uncircumcised children in Israel, showing great courage. **47.** They pursued proud men (Proud men: Those who were arrogant and opposed to God's law), and their work prospered. **48.** They restored the law from the Gentiles and kings, and did not let sinners succeed. **49.** As Mattathias neared death, he said, "Now pride and destruction have come; the time of wrath is near." **50.** "Be zealous (Zealous: Showing great energy or enthusiasm in support of a cause) for the law and give your lives for the covenant (Covenant: A formal agreement or promise, often referring to the sacred relationship between God and the Jewish people) of our ancestors." **51.** "Remember what our ancestors did; you will gain honor and a lasting name." **52.** "Abraham was faithful and his righteousness was counted." **53.** "Joseph kept the commandment in distress and became ruler of Egypt." **54.** "Phinehas, by zeal, gained the eternal priesthood." **55.** "Jesus fulfilled the word and became a judge in Israel." **56.** "Caleb bore witness and received the land." **57.** "David, for mercy, got the everlasting kingdom." **58.** "Elijah, zealous for the law, was taken to heaven." **59.** "Hananiah, Azariah, and Mishael were saved by faith from the fire." **60.** "Daniel, for his innocence, was saved from the lions." **61.** "Those who trust in Him will never be defeated." **62.** "Do not fear sinful men, for their glory is temporary and fades." **63.** "Today they may be powerful, but tomorrow they will be gone." **64.** "Be courageous for the law; through it, you will gain glory." **65.** "Listen to Simon, a man of wisdom; he will guide you." **66.** "Judas Maccabeus has been strong; let him lead you in battle." **67.** "Gather those who follow the law and avenge your people." **68.** "Repay the Gentiles and follow the law's commandments." **69.** He blessed them and was gathered to his ancestors. **70.** He died in the 146th year, and his sons buried him at Modin. Israel mourned greatly.

Chapter 3

1. Judas, called Maccabeus, took his father's place. (Maccabeus: "The Hammer" – a title for Judas, signifying strength) **2.** His brothers and all his allies joined him in the battle for Israel. (Allies: People or groups who support and help another) **3.** He gained great honor, wore armor like a giant, and led battles to protect his people. (Honor: High respect or esteem) **4.** He was fierce like a lion, roaring for his prey. (Prey: An animal hunted or killed for food) **5.** He hunted the wicked and destroyed those who troubled Israel. (Wicked: Evil or morally wrong) **6.** The wicked feared him, and evil workers were troubled as salvation thrived under his leadership. (Workers: Those who carry out an action; Salvation: Deliverance from harm or sin) **7.** He caused distress to kings and brought joy to Israel, and his memory is blessed. (Distress: Great pain, anxiety, or suffering) **8.** He destroyed the godless in the cities of Judah, turning away God's anger. (Godless: Lacking reverence for God; turning away: Preventing or stopping) **9.** His fame spread far, and those near death rallied to him. (Rallied: Gathered or came together for a common cause) **10.** Apollonius gathered an army from Samaria to fight Israel. (Gathered: Collected or assembled) **11.** Judas met him, defeated him, and many of his men were slain; the rest fled. (Slain: Killed violently) **12.** Judas took their spoils, including Apollonius' sword, which he used for life. (Spoils: Goods taken in battle or plundered) **13.** Seron, a Syrian commander, heard of Judas' growing force. (Commander: A person in charge of a military operation) **14.** He decided to gain glory by defeating Judas and his followers, who defied the king's orders. (Defied: Resisted or refused to obey) **15.** He marched out with a large army to avenge Israel. (Avenge: To take revenge for a wrong) **16.** Judas met him near Bethhoron with a small company. (Company: A group of people working together) **17.** Judas' men questioned how they could fight such a large force, being few and exhausted from fasting. (Exhausted: Extremely tired; Fasting: Going without food for a period of time) **18.** Judas answered, "It's not hard for the few to defeat the many with God's help." (Defeat: To win against; Help: Assistance or support) **19.** "Victory doesn't depend on the size of the army; strength comes from heaven." (Victory: Winning in a battle or contest) **20.** "They come in pride to destroy us and our families, but we fight for our lives and laws." (Pride: A feeling of superiority; Destroy: To ruin or put an end to) **21.** "The Lord will defeat them before us; don't fear them." (Fear: A feeling of anxiety caused by danger) **22.** After this, he charged, and Seron's army was defeated. (Charged: Attacked with force) **23.** They pursued them, killing 800 of Seron's men, while the rest fled to the Philistine territory. (Pursued: Followed in order to catch; Philistine: An ancient people who were enemies of Israel) **24.** Fear of Judas and his brothers spread to the surrounding nations. (Surrounding: Near or around) **25.** His fame reached the king, and all nations spoke of his victories. (Fame: The state of being known by many people; Victories: Successes in battles) **26.** King Antiochus, enraged, gathered his forces and a strong army. (Enraged: Filled with intense anger) **27.** He gave his soldiers pay for a year, preparing them for battle. (Pay: Compensation for work; Preparing: Getting ready for something) **28.** When his treasure ran low and taxes were weak, due to the plague and unrest from his policies, (Plague: A widespread disease; Unrest: A state of dissatisfaction and disorder) **29.** he feared he could no longer afford to maintain the army or give gifts as he had before. (Afford: To be able to pay for; Maintain: To keep in good condition) **30.** He had once been more prosperous than other kings but now faced financial strain. (Prosperous: Successful and wealthy; Strain: Pressure or stress, especially financial) **31.** The king, greatly troubled, resolved to go to Persia to collect tributes (payments or taxes). **32.** He left Lysias, a nobleman of royal blood, to oversee the kingdom's affairs (royal: relating to kings or queens). **33.** Lysias was also tasked with raising the king's son Antiochus. **34.** Half of the army, including elephants, was given to Lysias to manage Judaea and Jerusalem (elephants: large animals used in war). **35.** Lysias was ordered to send an army to destroy Israel's strength and remove their memorial (memorial: remembrance). **36.** He was commanded to settle strangers in their land and divide it by lot (lot: a method of random selection). **37.** The king left Antioch, crossed the Euphrates River, and traveled through high regions (Euphrates: a major river in the ancient world). **38.** Lysias appointed Ptolemee, Nicanor, and Gorgias, the king's strong allies (allies: supporters in war). **39.** He sent forty thousand foot soldiers and seven thousand horsemen to attack Judaea (foot soldiers: infantry; horsemen: cavalry). **40.** These forces encamped near Emmaus, preparing for war (encamped: set up camp). **41.** Merchants came with gold and silver to buy Israelites as slaves (merchants: traders). **42.** Judas and his brothers saw the growing miseries and prepared to resist. **43.** They said, "Let us restore our people and protect the sanctuary (sanctuary: a holy place)." **44.** The people gathered for battle and prayed for mercy and compassion (compassion: sympathy). **45.** Jerusalem was desolate, and the sanctuary was trampled, and strangers occupied the land (desolate: abandoned). **46.** The Israelites assembled at Mizpah, a place of ancient prayer (assembled: gathered). **47.** They fasted, wore sackcloth, scattered ashes on their heads, and tore their garments (sackcloth: rough fabric worn during mourning). **48.** They opened the law book defaced by heathen images (defaced: ruined; heathen: non-believers). **49.** They presented the priests' garments, firstfruits, and tithes and reinvigorated the Nazarites (Nazarites: people dedicated to God). **50.** They cried out, "What shall we do with these, and where can we take them?" **51.** "The sanctuary is desecrated, and the priests are grieving and humbled (desecrated: violated; humbled: brought low)." **52.** "The heathen are assembled against us; You know their plans (heathen: non-believers; assembled: gathered)." **53.** "We cannot survive unless You, O God, help us." **54.** They sounded trumpets and cried loudly to heaven (trumpets: instruments used in ceremonies or war). **55.** Judas organized the people into groups of thousands, hundreds, fifties, and tens (organized: arranged systematically). **56.** He allowed those building homes, newly betrothed, planting vineyards, or afraid to return (betrothed: engaged to be married). **57.** The camp moved south of Emmaus, readying for battle. **58.** Judas urged them, "Arm yourselves and prepare to fight to defend the sanctuary." **59.** "It is better to die in battle than witness the ruin of our people and sanctuary (ruin: destruction)." **60.** "But let the will of God, which is supreme, prevail (supreme: highest in authority)."

Chapter 4

1. Gorgias led five thousand infantry and a thousand elite cavalry, advancing under the cover of night. (Infantry: foot soldiers; Cavalry: soldiers on horseback) **2.** His goal was to surprise and attack the Jewish camp, with guidance from the fortress guards. (Fortress: a heavily fortified stronghold) **3.** Hearing this, Judas and his warriors prepared to confront the king's army at Emmaus. **4.** The enemy forces were scattered when Judas approached. **5.** Gorgias entered Judas' camp at night but, finding it empty, assumed they had fled into the mountains. **6.** At dawn, Judas revealed himself on the plain with three thousand men, though poorly armed. (Plain: flat and open land) **7.** They saw the enemy camp, fortified with experienced cavalry and war-ready soldiers. (Fortified: strengthened and protected) **8.** Judas encouraged his men, "Do not fear their numbers or their attack." **9.** He reminded them of their ancestors' deliverance at the Red Sea from Pharaoh's army. (Deliverance: rescue or liberation) **10.** Judas prayed for God's mercy and victory, asking Him to honor His covenant with their forefathers. (Covenant: a solemn agreement) **11.** He desired the nations to witness God's power to save Israel. **12.** The enemy noticed the Israelites approaching. **13.** They came out to fight, but Judas' men sounded their trumpets to rally their forces. (Rally: to unite or come together) **14.** The battle began, and the enemy, overwhelmed, fled into the plains. **15.** The Israelites pursued, killing three thousand enemies across the regions of Gazera and Idumea. (Pursued: chased or followed) **16.** Judas called his forces back, halting the pursuit. (Halted: stopped) **17.** He urged restraint, reminding them of an imminent battle. (Restraint: self-control; Imminent: about to happen) **18.** He warned of Gorgias' nearby army and encouraged them to focus on defeating the enemy. **19.** Even as he spoke, part of the enemy forces appeared from the mountains. **20.** Seeing the burning tents and defeated troops, the enemy was filled with fear. **21.** Terrified by Judas' readiness for battle, they fled into foreign lands. **22.** Judas and his men plundered the tents, finding great treasures. (Plundered: looted or robbed) **23.** They recovered gold, silver, fine silk, and other riches. **24.** Returning home, they sang praises to the Lord for His enduring mercy. (Enduring: lasting or eternal) **25.** That day, Israel experienced a remarkable victory. **26.** Survivors informed Lysias of the defeat, leaving him confused and discouraged. **27.** Lysias felt defeated, unable to achieve his goals or fulfill the king's commands. **28.** The following year, he gathered sixty thousand foot soldiers and five thousand cavalry to subdue Israel. (Subdue: bring under control) **29.** They camped at Bethsura, where Judas prepared to confront them with ten thousand men. **30.** Judas prayed, recalling God's past victories through David and Jonathan against stronger foes. (Foes: enemies)**31.** Deliver this army to Your people, Israel, and disgrace their power and cavalry. (cavalry: soldiers on horseback) **32.** Make them lose courage, weaken their strength, and let them tremble in fear. (tremble: shake with fear) **33.** Strike them down with the sword of Your faithful, and let those who know Your name praise You. (faithful: loyal followers) **34.** In battle, about five thousand of Lysias' men were slain. (slain: killed in combat) **35.** Seeing his defeat and the bravery of Judas' men, Lysias retreated to Antioch to gather a larger army. (retreated: withdrew from the battlefield) **36.** Judas and his brothers said, "Our enemies are defeated; let us cleanse and rededicate the sanctuary." (sanctuary: holy place) **37.** The assembly climbed Mount Zion to restore the temple. (assembly: gathering of people) **38.** They saw the temple desecrated, gates burned, and courts overgrown. (desecrated: treated with disrespect) **39.** They tore their garments, mourned deeply, and scattered ashes on their heads. (garments: clothing) **40.** Prostrating themselves, they sounded trumpets and cried out to heaven. (prostrating: lying flat in submission) **41.** Judas assigned men to fight until the sanctuary was purified. (purified: made clean or holy) **42.** He selected priests loyal to the Law to oversee the work. (oversee: supervise) **43.** They cleansed the temple and moved the defiled stones to an unclean place. (defiled: made impure) **44.** They debated what to do with the desecrated altar. (debated: discussed or considered) **45.** Deciding it was a disgrace, they dismantled the altar. (disgrace: shame or dishonor) **46.** The stones were stored on the temple mount until a prophet could advise. (prophet: one who speaks for God) **47.** Following the Law, they built a new altar from unhewn stones. (unhewn: not cut or shaped) **48.** The sanctuary and its courts were repaired and consecrated. (consecrated: made sacred) **49.** They replaced holy vessels and restored the lampstand, incense altar, and table. (vessels: containers used in rituals) **50.** The lamps were lit, filling the temple with light, and incense burned. (incense: aromatic substance burned for fragrance) **51.** Bread was set on the table, and veils were hung, completing the work. (veils: curtains) **52.** On the 25th of Casleu in 148, they rose early to offer sacrifices on the new altar. (sacrifices: offerings to God) **53.** They dedicated the altar with hymns, instruments, and great joy. (dedicated: set apart for a sacred purpose) **54.** Worshipers fell on their faces, praising God for His blessings. (worshipers: those who show reverence to God) **55.** The eight-day dedication was filled with offerings and thanksgiving. (thanksgiving: expression of gratitude) **56.** They adorned the temple with gold, rebuilt the gates, and installed new doors. (adorned: decorated) **57.** The people rejoiced, for the shame brought by the Gentiles was removed. (rejoiced: celebrated with joy) **58.** Judas and the assembly declared the altar dedication to be celebrated yearly with gladness. (declared: announced officially) **59.** They fortified Mount Zion with strong walls and towers to prevent future attacks. (fortified: strengthened against attack) **60.** Guards were stationed, and Bethsura was fortified to protect against Idumea. (stationed: assigned to a place) **61.** These actions secured the people's defense and ensured peace. (secured: made safe)

Chapter 5

1. The nations, upon hearing of the restored altar and sanctuary, were deeply displeased (sanctuary: a holy place). **2.** They conspired to destroy Jacob's descendants and began attacking them (conspired: planned secretly). **3.** Judas defeated the Edomites in Idumea at Arabattine, capturing their spoils (Edomites: descendants of Esau; spoils: loot taken from enemies). **4.** He punished the sons of Bean for ambushing the Israelites on the roads (ambushing: attacking suddenly by surprise). **5.** Judas besieged their towers, destroyed them, and burned all within (besieged: surrounded and attacked). **6.** Moving to Ammon, he faced Timotheus's strong army (Ammon: a region east of the Jordan River). **7.** After several battles, Judas defeated them and captured Jazer (Jazer: a city in Gilead). **8.** He returned to Judea after securing the towns (securing: making safe). **9.** The heathens of Galaad assembled to attack the Israelites, forcing them to flee to Dathema's fortress (fortress: a stronghold for protection). **10.** They sent pleas to Judas for rescue, saying enemies surrounded them (pleas: urgent requests). **11.** Timotheus prepared to capture the fortress (capture: take control by force). **12.** The letter urged Judas to help as many Israelites had been killed (urged: strongly encouraged). **13.** They reported widespread destruction in Tobie, with captives and loot taken (captives: prisoners of war; loot: stolen goods). **14.** Messengers from Galilee also brought news of enemies assembling there (assembling: gathering together). **15.** They spoke of hostile forces from Ptolemais, Tyre, Sidon, and Galilee (hostile: unfriendly or aggressive). **16.** Judas and the people convened to decide how to respond (convened: gathered). **17.** Judas sent Simon to rescue Galilee, while he and Jonathan went to Galaad (rescue: save from danger). **18.** Joseph and Azarias were left in Judea with orders not to engage the enemy (engage: involve in battle). **19.** Judas strictly commanded them to guard the people until his return (commanded: gave an authoritative order). **20.** Simon led three thousand men to Galilee; Judas took eight thousand to Galaad (led: guided or commanded). **21.** Simon defeated the heathens in Galilee, killing three thousand and taking spoils (defeated: overcame in battle). **22.** He brought the rescued Israelites to Judea with joy (rescued: saved from harm). **23.** Judas and Jonathan crossed the Jordan, traveling three days through wilderness (wilderness: uninhabited or wild area). **24.** They met Nabathites who peacefully informed them of their brethren's plight (Nabathites: Arabian nomads; plight: a difficult situation). **25.** They learned many Israelites were trapped in fortified cities like Bosora and Alema (fortified: strengthened for defense). **26.** The enemy planned a massive assault the next day (assault: an aggressive attack). **27.** Judas moved quickly to Bosora, captured it, killed the males, and burned the city (captured: took control by force). **28.** He advanced at night and reached a fortress under siege by a large army (siege: a military blockade). **29.** At dawn, Judas saw siege engines and ladders ready for attack (siege engines: tools used to breach fortifications). **30.** Encouraging his troops, he said, "Fight for your brethren today!" (troops: soldiers; brethren: fellow Israelites). **31.** Dividing his army into three groups, Judas prayed and sounded trumpets before attacking (trumpets: brass instruments used for signals). **32.** Recognizing Judas, the enemy fled; eight thousand were killed (fled: ran away). **33.** Judas then took Maspha, destroyed it, and claimed its spoils (claimed: took possession of). **34.** He continued to capture towns like Casphon and Maked in Galaad (capture: take by force). **35.** Timotheus regrouped and encamped near Raphon (regrouped: reorganized after defeat; encamped: set up a temporary camp). **36.** Scouts informed Judas of a massive enemy force, including hired Arabians (scouts: people sent ahead to gather information). **37.** The heathens were stationed beyond the brook, preparing for battle

481

(stationed: placed or positioned). **38.** Judas learned of their strategy and advanced to meet them (strategy: a planned approach to achieve a goal). **39.** Timotheus instructed his captains to act only if Judas crossed the brook first (instructed: gave directions or orders). **40.** He warned that Judas's strength would overwhelm them in a direct confrontation (overwhelm: defeat completely; confrontation: direct conflict). **41.** If he is afraid and camps beyond the river, we will cross over and defeat him. **42.** Judas reached the stream and instructed the scribes to stay behind, telling everyone to join the battle. **43.** He crossed first, followed by all the people. The enemy, discouraged, threw down their weapons and fled to the temple at Carnaim. **44.** They captured the city, burned the temple, and Carnaim was defeated. The enemy could no longer resist Judas (defeated: conquered). **45.** Judas gathered all the Israelites from Galaad, including men, women, children, and possessions, to march into Judea (possessions: belongings). **46.** They reached Ephron, a strong city, and had to pass through it. **47.** The people of Ephron shut the gates and blocked them (blocked: obstructed). **48.** Judas sent a message, asking to pass peacefully, but they refused (refused: denied). **49.** Judas ordered a proclamation for the camp to stay where they were (proclamation: announcement). **50.** The soldiers attacked the city until it was captured (taken: seized). **51.** They killed all the males, destroyed the city, took the spoils, and walked over the slain. **52.** They crossed the Jordan and camped near Bethsan. **53.** Judas gathered those behind and encouraged them until they reached Judea (encouraged: motivated) **54.** They arrived at Mount Sion joyfully and offered burnt offerings, thanking God for their safe return. **55.** While Judas and Jonathan were in Galaad, Simon his brother was in Galilee before Ptolemais. **56.** Joseph and Azarias, captains, heard of their victories (captains: leaders). **57.** They decided to fight the surrounding heathen to gain fame (heathen: non-Jews, Gentiles). **58.** After instructing their garrison, they marched to Jamnia (garrison: group of soldiers stationed in a fort). **59.** Gorgias and his men came to fight them. **60.** Joseph and Azarias were defeated, and about two thousand Israelites were slain (killed). **61.** This was a heavy defeat, as they acted without Judas' leadership (heavy defeat: loss). **62.** These men were not descendants of Israel's deliverers (descendants: offspring). **63.** Judas and his brothers were renowned throughout Israel and the surrounding nations (renowned: famous). **64.** People gathered to them, praising them joyfully (with great enthusiasm). **65.** Judas and his brothers fought against the Edomites in the south, striking Hebron, destroying its fortress, and burning its towers (striking: attacking). **66.** They moved toward the Philistines, passing through Samaria. **67.** Some priests, eager for battle, were slain for acting recklessly (without proper thought) (eager: eager to prove their bravery) (recklessly: without caution). **68.** Judas then attacked Azotus, destroying their altars, burning their idols, and plundering their cities before returning to Judea (idols: statues of gods) (plundering: looting).

Chapter 6
1. King Antiochus, traveling through the mountains, heard of Elymais in Persia, a city known for its wealth in silver and gold. (Elymais: a city in Persia; Antiochus: king of the Seleucid Empire) **2.** The city had a rich temple filled with gold-covered shields and breastplates, left by Alexander the Great. (Breastplates: armor for the chest) **3.** He tried to take the city, but the people fought back, and Antiochus fled. (Spoil: to plunder or take by force) **4.** He returned to Babylon, deeply upset. (Babylon: ancient city, capital of the Neo-Babylonian Empire) **5.** A messenger informed him that his armies in Judea had been defeated. (Judea: a region in ancient Israel) **6.** Lysias, who led the attack, had been driven off by the Jews, who had grown stronger from their spoils. (Spoils: goods taken in war) **7.** They had destroyed the idol he set up in Jerusalem and rebuilt the walls of the sanctuary. (Sanctuary: sacred or holy place) **8.** Antiochus was astonished and sickened, fearing he would die. (Astonished: greatly surprised) **9.** He lay in bed for many days, increasingly sorrowful. (Sorrowful: feeling sadness or grief) **10.** He called his friends and said, "Sleep is gone from my eyes, and my heart is troubled." (Troubled: worried or disturbed) **11.** He reflected on his fall from power, once beloved, now in misery. (Misery: great suffering) **12.** He regretted plundering Jerusalem and attacking the Jews unjustly. (Plundering: robbing or looting) **13.** He saw his troubles as punishment for his wrongs and feared death. (Punishment: penalty for wrongdoing) **14.** He called for Philip, a trusted companion, to prepare his son for the throne. (Philip: a loyal advisor) **15.** He gave Philip his crown, robe, and signet ring to guide his son, Antiochus, to rule. (Signet: a ring with a seal for authenticating documents) **16.** Antiochus died in the 149th year of his reign. (Reign: period of rule) **17.** Lysias made Antiochus' son, Eupator, king. (Eupator: name given to the new king) **18.** Meanwhile, the tower defenders continued to oppose the Jews and strengthened the Gentiles. (Gentiles: non-Jews) **19.** Judas called the people together to besiege the tower. (Besiege: to surround and attack) **20.** They laid siege in the 150th year, building ramps and siege engines. (Siege: military blockade) **21.** Some besieged men escaped and joined with traitors from Israel. (Traitors: those who betray their country) **22.** They went to the king, asking when he would avenge their suffering. (Avenge: to punish for a wrong) **23.** "We served your father and followed his commands," they said. (Commands: orders or instructions) **24.** "Now our own people besiege us, and they kill and rob us." (Rob: to steal by force) **25.** "They attack us and our borders." (Borders: boundaries of a region) **26.** "Today, they besiege Jerusalem, the sanctuary, and Bethsura." (Bethsura: a fortified city in Judea) **27.** "If you don't act, they will do worse, and you won't control them." (Control: to manage or govern) **28.** The king, enraged, gathered his advisors and army leaders. (Enraged: filled with anger) **29.** Mercenaries from other lands joined his army. (Mercenaries: soldiers for hire) **30.** His army grew to 100,000 infantry, 20,000 cavalry, and 32 war elephants. (Infantry: foot soldiers; Cavalry: soldiers on horseback; Elephants: large animals used in battle) **31.** The army moved through Idumea and besieged Bethsura, using war machines. The defenders burned the engines and fought valiantly. (Idumea: region south of Judea; besieged: surrounded to force surrender; valiant: courageous) **32.** Judas relocated to Bathzacharias, positioning his forces opposite the king's camp. (relocated: moved) **33.** At dawn, the king advanced with his troops, sounding their trumpets to prepare for battle. (dawn: early morning) **34.** They showed grape and mulberry juice to the elephants to provoke them into fighting. (provoke: stir into action) **35.** The elephants were accompanied by 1,000 armored men and 500 cavalry for protection. (cavalry: soldiers on horseback) **36.** These troops stayed close to the elephants, never straying from their sides. (straying: wandering away) **37.** Each elephant carried a wooden tower with 32 warriors and one handler. (handler: person controlling an animal) **38.** The remaining cavalry flanked the army, following signals while staying fully armored. (flanked: stationed on the sides; signals: gestures or actions used to communicate) **39.** The sunlight reflected off gold and brass shields, making the mountains shine like fire. (reflected: bounced back; shields: protective equipment) **40.** The king's army advanced in perfect order, some on mountains, others in valleys. (valleys: low-lying land between hills) **41.** The marching sounds of soldiers and clattering armor frightened all who heard them. (clattering: loud, continuous sound; frightened: scared) **42.** Judas attacked, killing 600 men from the king's forces. (forces: military troops) **43.** Eleazar noticed a royal elephant, taller than the rest, and thought the king was on it. (royal: associated with a king; taller: greater in height) **44.** To save his people, Eleazar took a great risk to make a lasting name for himself. (risk: danger; lasting: enduring) **45.** He charged, cutting down enemies, and reached the elephant. (charged: rushed forward; cutting down: killing) **46.** Crawling beneath it, he killed the elephant, but it fell and crushed him. (crushed: pressed down with force) **47.** Seeing the king's overpowering forces, the remaining Jews retreated. (overpowering: too strong to resist; retreated: withdrew) **48.** The king's army camped against Judea and Mount Sion. (camped: set up temporary living quarters) **49.** Those in Bethsura surrendered due to lack of supplies during the sabbatical year. (surrendered: gave up; sabbatical: rest year) **50.** The king captured Bethsura and stationed a garrison there. (stationed: assigned to stay; garrison: troops stationed in a fortress) **51.** The sanctuary was besieged for many days, with engines to throw fire, stones, and darts. (Engines: machines for warfare) **52.** They built their own counter-engines and fought for a long time. (Counter-engines: devices built to oppose the enemy's machines) **53.** Eventually, their supplies ran out, as it was the seventh year and food had been eaten up. (Seventh year: a year when land was to rest, and supplies were scarce) **54.** Only a few stayed in the sanctuary, as famine forced people to go home. (Famine: extreme scarcity of food) **55.** Lysias learned that Philip, appointed by King Antiochus to raise his son to be king, had returned. (Appointed: assigned) **56.** Philip had returned from Persia and Media and sought control of the kingdom's affairs. (Persia and Media: ancient regions in the east) **57.** Lysias told the king and commanders, "We lack food, the siege is strong, and the kingdom's matters are at risk." (Siege: military blockade) **58.** He proposed peace with the people and their nation. (Proposed: suggested) **59.** "Let them follow their laws, as they are angry because we changed them." (Angry: upset) **60.** The king and leaders agreed, and peace was made. (Leaders: high-ranking officials) **61.** The king and his nobles swore an oath, and the people left the stronghold. (Nobles: people of high rank) **62.** The king entered Mount Zion, but when he saw its strength, he broke his oath and ordered the wall to be torn down. (Torn down: demolished) **63.** He quickly returned to Antioch, where he found Philip in control and fought to take the city. (Antioch: ancient city in Syria)

Chapter 7
1. In the 150th year, Demetrius left Rome, came to a coastal city, and ruled there. **2.** He entered the palace and learned that his forces had captured Antiochus and Lysias. **3.** Upon hearing this, he declared, "I do not want to see

them." **4.** His army executed them, and Demetrius took the throne. **5.** Wicked men from Israel, led by Alcimus, came to him. (Alcimus: A man who wanted to be high priest) **6.** They accused Judas and his men of killing the king's supporters and driving them from their land. **7.** They urged the king to send a trusted man to punish Judas and his allies. **8.** The king sent Bacchides to handle the situation. (Bacchides: A loyal friend of the king) **9.** Bacchides, with Alcimus now appointed high priest, was told to punish the Israelites. **10.** They arrived in Judea with a large army, pretending to offer peace. **11.** Judas and his men saw their true intent and ignored the offer. **12.** Alcimus and Bacchides gathered scribes to seek justice. (Scribes: Scholars or teachers of the law) **13.** The Assideans were the first to seek peace, trusting Alcimus' priestly role. (Assideans: Pious Israelites) **14.** Alcimus assured them with peaceful words and a promise not to harm them. **15.** He swore to avoid any harm to them or their friends. **16.** They trusted him, but he took 60 men and killed them all in one day, as promised. **17.** "They have discarded the bodies of your saints and spilled their blood around Jerusalem, with no one to bury them." **18.** Fear and dread spread, and the people said, "There is no truth or righteousness in them; they broke the covenant and oath they swore." **19.** Bacchides left Jerusalem, camped in Bezeth, and took many of those who had turned against him, killing them and throwing them into a pit. **20.** Bacchides gave the region to Alcimus and left him with a force, then went to the king. (Alcimus: A man who wanted to be high priest) **21.** Alcimus fought for the high priesthood. **22.** Those who caused harm to Israel came to Alcimus, after taking Judea. **23.** Judas saw the harm done by Alcimus and his group, worse than that of the Gentiles. **24.** Judas took vengeance on those who had rebelled, ensuring they did not return to the countryside. **25.** Seeing that he couldn't withstand Judas, Alcimus went back to the king, accusing them falsely. **26.** The king sent Nicanor, who hated Israel, with orders to destroy them. (Nicanor: A prince sent by the king, who hated Israel) **27.** Nicanor arrived with a large force and sent a deceitful message to Judas, saying, **28.** "There will be no battle between us; I will come with a few men to meet you in peace." **29.** Nicanor met Judas, but his men were ready to attack. **30.** Judas, realizing their deceit, feared and refused to meet Nicanor. **31.** Nicanor, seeing his plan uncovered, went to fight Judas at Capharsalama. **32.** Nicanor's side lost about 5,000 men, and the rest fled to the city of David. **33.** Nicanor then went up to Mount Sion, where some priests and elders came out to greet him in peace. **34.** He mocked and insulted them, speaking arrogantly. **35.** He swore in his anger, "Unless Judas and his army are delivered to me, I will burn this house if I return safely!" **36.** The priests entered, stood before the altar and the temple, weeping, and prayed, **37.** "O Lord, You chose this house to be called by Your name, a house of prayer for Your people." **38.** "Avenge this man and his army, let them fall by the sword, and do not let them continue their evil." **39.** Nicanor camped in Bethhoron, where a Syrian army met him. **40.** Judas camped in Adasa with 3,000 men, and prayed, **41.** "O Lord, when Assyrians blasphemed, Your angel struck down 185,000 of them." (Blasphemed: To speak disrespectfully) **42.** "Destroy this army today, so they know they have insulted Your sanctuary, and judge them." **43.** On the 13th of Adar, the armies fought. Nicanor's army was defeated, and he was slain first in the battle. **44.** When Nicanor's army saw he was dead, they dropped their weapons and fled. **45.** They pursued them for a day's journey, from Adasa to Gazera, blowing their trumpets as they followed. **46.** The people from all the towns of Judea surrounded them, and the pursuers were killed with the sword. **47.** They took the spoils, cut off Nicanor's head and right hand, and hung them up toward Jerusalem. (Spoils: Loot or plunder) **48.** The people rejoiced greatly and made that day a day of great celebration. **49.** They decided to keep this day every year, the 13th of Adar. **50.** Thus, Judea had a brief time of peace.

Chapter 8

1. Judas had heard of the Romans, who were powerful and brave, and welcomed all who joined them, forming alliances with anyone who came to them. (Romans: people from the Roman Empire)**2.** He also learned of their great courage and many victories, including over the Galatians, whom they conquered and made pay tribute. (Galatians: people from a region in Asia Minor)**3.** He heard of their success in Spain, where they gained control of the silver and gold mines. (Spain: a country in Europe)**4.** Through wisdom and patience, they conquered distant lands and defeated kings from the farthest regions, forcing them to pay tribute each year. (Tribute: payment as a sign of submission)**5.** They also defeated Philip and Perseus, kings of the Citims, and others who opposed them. (Philip: King of Macedon; Perseus: last king of Macedon)**6.** Antiochus the Great, king of Asia, attacked them with 1.2.0 elephants and a large army, but was defeated. (Antiochus: Seleucid king; Asia: region in Western Asia)**7.** They captured him and made a treaty, requiring him and his successors to pay a large tribute and provide hostages. (Hostages: people pledged as security)**8.** They took the lands of India, Media, and Lydia from him and gave them to King Eumenes. (India, Media, Lydia: regions in Asia)**9.** The Greeks had also planned to destroy them. (Greeks: people from Greece)**10** The Romans sent a leader who defeated them, took captives, and claimed their land and forts, making them servants. (Leader: military commander)**11.** They also conquered kingdoms and islands that resisted them. (Islands: land masses surrounded by water)**12.** But they kept peaceful ties with their allies, and their name spread far, instilling fear in all who heard of them. (Allies: supporters)**13.** The Romans helped those they favored to become kings and removed those they didn't, growing in power.**14.** Despite their power, none of them wore crowns or purple robes to seek recognition. (Purple: royal color)**15.** They set up a senate with 3.2.0 men who met daily to govern for the people's welfare. (Senate: ruling body)**16.** They appointed one ruler each year, and all obeyed him without envy or rivalry. (Rivalry: competition)**1** After hearing of this, Judas sent Eupolemus and Jason to Rome to seek an alliance. (Eupolemus: a name; Jason: a name)**18.** They asked the Romans to free Israel from the oppression of the Greeks. (Greeks: people from Greece)**19.** They traveled to Rome and spoke to the senate, saying: **20.** "Judas Maccabeus and his people have sent us to form an alliance and be recognized as your friends." (Maccabeus: a leader of the Jewish revolt)**21.** The Romans were pleased with this request. (Romans: people from the Roman Empire)**22.** This is the copy of the letter the senate sent back on brass tablets to Jerusalem as a memorial of their peace and alliance. (Brass: a metal alloy of copper and zinc)**23.** "May the Romans and the Jewish people have success forever, by sea and land. May their enemies and sword stay far away." (Success: good fortune) **24.** "If war arises against the Romans or any of their allies in their territory,"**25.** "The Jewish people will support them fully when the time is set, with all their heart."**26.**"They will not provide supplies, weapons, money, or ships to those who fight against them, but will honor their agreement without expecting anything in return." (Supplies: food and necessities)**27.** "Similarly, if war comes to the Jewish people, the Romans will help them fully, as the time is appointed."**28.** "They will not provide supplies, weapons, money, or ships to those who fight against them, but will honor the covenant with honesty." (Covenant: agreement) **29.** The Romans made this agreement with the Jewish people according to these terms.**30.** If either party later wishes to add or change anything, they can do so freely, and any changes will be officially approved.**31.** As for the wrongs Demetrius has done to the Jews, we have written to him, asking why he has made their burden heavier. (Demetrius: a name).**32.** "If they continue to complain, we will bring justice and fight against you by sea and land." (Justice: fairness or righting wrongs)

Chapter 9

1. When Demetrius learned that Nicanor and his army had been defeated, he sent Bacchides and Alcimus to Judea a second time with the main force of his army. (Bacchides: a general; Alcimus: a high priest) **2.** They took the route to Galgala, camped near Masaloth in Arbela, and after capturing it, they killed many people. (Galgala: a location; Arbela: an ancient city) **3.** In the first month of the 152nd year, they camped outside Jerusalem. **4.** From there, they moved to Berea with 20,000 infantry and 2,000 cavalry. (Berea: a city) **5.** Judas set up camp at Eleasa, with 3,000 chosen men. (Eleasa: a location) **6.** Seeing the size of the enemy's army, they were greatly afraid, and many deserted, leaving only 800 men. (Deserted: left the army) **7.** Judas, seeing his army shrink and the battle approaching, was troubled and distressed, as he had no time to regroup. **8.** Yet he said to those who remained, "Let's rise and fight our enemies, perhaps we can prevail." **9.** But they discouraged him, saying, "We can't win; let's save ourselves now, and later we'll return with our brothers to fight. We are too few." **10.** Judas replied, "God forbid that I should flee! If it is our time to die, let us do so honorably, not staining our reputation." **11.** Bacchides' army then moved out and positioned themselves against them, with cavalry split into two groups, and slingers and archers leading the way. The frontline was filled with mighty men. **12.** Bacchides was on the right wing, while the army advanced on both sides, and their trumpets were sounded. **13.** Judas' men also blew their trumpets, and the earth shook with the noise of the armies. The battle raged from morning until night. **14.** When Judas saw that Bacchides and his main force were on the right, he led his bravest men. **15.** They defeated the right wing and chased them to Mount Azotus. (Azotus: a location) **16.** When the left wing saw their right side defeated, they pursued Judas and his men from behind. **17.** A fierce battle ensued, and many were slain on both sides. **18.** Judas was killed, and the remaining soldiers fled. **19.** Jonathan and Simon took their brother Judas' body and buried him in the tomb of their ancestors at Modin. (Modin: a town) **20.** They mourned for him, and all Israel grieved greatly for many days, saying, **21.** "How has the valiant man fallen, who delivered Israel?" **22.** The deeds and greatness of Judas, his wars, and noble acts are not written here, for they were many. **23.** After Judas' death, the wicked rose up across Israel, and those who practiced evil came to power. **24.** During this time, a great famine struck, causing the people to rebel and join the wicked. (Famine: extreme scarcity of food) **25.** Bacchides appointed the wicked as rulers over the land. (Bacchides: a general) **26.** Bacchides searched for Judas' friends, captured them, and took revenge on them with great cruelty. (Revenge: punishment; Cruelty: harsh treatment) **27.** This caused great suffering in Israel, unlike anything seen since the time when there were no prophets among them. **28.** Judas' friends then gathered and said to Jonathan: **29.** "Since your brother Judas died, we have no leader to fight our enemies, Bacchides, and those who oppose us from within our own nation." **30.** "Therefore, we have chosen you to be our leader and captain in his place, so that you may lead us in battle." **31.** Jonathan took the leadership and rose up to take his brother Judas' place. **32.** When Bacchides learned of this, he sought to kill Jonathan. **33.** Jonathan, his brother Simon, and their followers, realizing this, fled to the wilderness of Thecoe and set up camp by the pool of Asphar. (Thecoe: a place; Asphar: a location) **34.** Bacchides, hearing of their movements, advanced to the Jordan with his army on the Sabbath day. **35.** Jonathan sent his brother John, a commander, to ask the Nabathites to let them keep their provisions, as they had much. (Nabathites: a people or tribe) **36.** But the children of Jambri from Medaba seized John and his belongings. (Jambri: a group of people; Medaba: a city) **37.** Later, Jonathan and Simon learned that the children of Jambri were holding a grand wedding and bringing the bride from Nadabatha, the daughter of a prince of Chanaan. **38.** They remembered John and decided to ambush the wedding procession. **39.** When they looked out, they saw the wedding party with much celebration—drums, music, and many weapons. (Carriage: procession) **40.** Jonathan and his men attacked from their hiding place, slaughtering many, and the rest fled to the mountain. They took all the spoils. **41.** The wedding celebration turned to mourning, and the music became cries of lament. **42.** After avenging their brother's death, they returned to the Jordan marsh. **43.** Bacchides, hearing of this, came to the Jordan banks with a great army on the Sabbath. **44.** Jonathan said to his men, "Let us fight for our lives, for today is not like before. We are trapped on every side—with the battle before us, the Jordan on both sides, and no way to retreat." **45.** "Cry out to God for deliverance from our enemies!" **46.** They fought bravely, and Jonathan tried to strike Bacchides, but he retreated. **47.** Jonathan and his men leapt into the Jordan River and swam to the other side, but Bacchides' army did not follow. **48.** About a thousand of Bacchides' men were killed that day. **49.** Bacchides returned to Jerusalem, where he strengthened the fortresses of Judea: Jericho, Emmaus, Bethhoron, Bethel, Thamnatha, Pharathoni, and Taphon, fortifying them with high walls, gates, and bars. (Fortresses: strongholds) **50.** He placed garrisons in these cities to oppress Israel. **51.** Bacchides also fortified Bethsura, Gazera, and the tower, stationing forces there and providing them with food supplies. **52.** He took the sons of Israel's leaders as hostages and imprisoned them in the tower at Jerusalem. **53.** In the 153rd year, Alcimus ordered the inner wall of the sanctuary to be torn down, as well as the works of the prophets. **54.** But as he began this task, Alcimus was struck with a disease that paralyzed him, rendering him unable to speak or give orders. **55.** Alcimus died in great agony, unable to continue his work. **56.** Alcimus died in great torment. (torment: severe pain) **57.** Bacchides, seeing Alcimus was dead, returned to the king, and Judea had peace for two years. (peace: a state of rest or harmony) **58.** The ungodly men conspired to call Bacchides to capture Jonathan in one night. (ungodly: wicked; conspired: plotted secretly) **59.** They consulted with him. (consulted: discussed) **60.** Bacchides sent secret letters to seize Jonathan, but their plan was discovered. (seize: capture) **61.** Fifty conspirators were captured and killed. (conspirators: plotters against authority) **62.** Jonathan and Simon fortified Bethbasi in the wilderness. (fortified: strengthened) **63.** Bacchides attacked Bethbasi after gathering his army. (attacked: launched an assault) **64.** He laid siege to the city and used siege engines. (siege: surrounding of a place during battle; siege engines: war machines for attack) **65.** Jonathan left Simon in the city and went into the countryside with a group. (countryside: rural areas outside cities) **66.** He defeated Odonarkes and his brothers at their camp. (defeated: overcame in battle) **67.** Simon burned the siege engines while Jonathan attacked Bacchides. (burned: set on fire; attacked: fought against) **68.** Bacchides was defeated, and his efforts were in vain. (vain: useless, without success) **69.** Furious at his counselors, Bacchides killed many and returned to his land. (furious: very angry; counselors: advisors) **70.** Jonathan sent messengers to make peace and free the prisoners. (messengers: those who carry messages) **71.** Bacchides agreed, swearing never to harm Jonathan again. (swearing: making a solemn promise) **72.** Bacchides freed the prisoners and never returned to Judea. (freed: released from captivity) **73.** The fighting ceased, and Jonathan governed Israel, removing the ungodly. (ceased: ended; governed: ruled)

Chapter 10

1. In the 160th year, Alexander, son of Antiochus Epiphanes, took Ptolemais, where the people supported him and he became ruler. (Epiphanes: a title meaning "God manifest" or "God revealed") **2.** Hearing this, King Demetrius gathered a large army to fight him. (Demetrius: a Greek name, referring to the king in this context) **3.** Demetrius sent Jonathan a letter, praising him warmly. **4.** He said, "Let's make peace with him before he sides with Alexander." **5.** "Otherwise, he'll remember all the wrongs we did to him and his people." **6.** Demetrius gave Jonathan permission to raise an army, gather weapons, and receive the hostages in the tower. (Hostages: people held to ensure that an agreement or treaty is honored) **7.** Jonathan returned to Jerusalem, read the letter to the people and those in the tower. **8.** The people in the tower were afraid when they heard of Jonathan's new authority. **9.** They gave their hostages to Jonathan, who returned them to their families. **10.** Jonathan stayed in Jerusalem and began rebuilding the city. **11.** He ordered workers to strengthen the walls of Mount Zion with large stones for fortification. (Fortification: a defensive wall or structure meant to protect a place) **12.** The foreign soldiers in Bacchides' fortresses fled. (Fortresses: fortified military structures) **13.** Each man returned to his own country. **14.** In Bethsura, those who abandoned the law stayed, as it was their refuge. (Refuge: a place of safety or shelter) **15.** Hearing of Jonathan's deeds, King Alexander decided to make him an ally. **16.** He said, "Shall we find another like him? Let's make him our friend." **17.** He wrote a letter to Jonathan, saying: **18.** "King Alexander greets his brother Jonathan." **19.** "We know you are a powerful man and fit to be our friend." **20.** "We appoint you high priest and declare you the king's friend. We send a purple robe and a gold crown, asking for your support." (Purple robe: a symbol of royal authority) **21.** In the seventh month of the 160th year, during the Feast of Tabernacles, Jonathan wore the sacred robe, gathered his forces, and equipped them with armor. (Tabernacles: a Jewish feast, equipped: provided with necessary items) **22.** Hearing this, Demetrius was distressed and said, (distressed: upset) **23.** "What have we done wrong, that Alexander made peace with the Jews to strengthen himself?" (peace: amity) **24.** "I will write to them offering honors and gifts to gain their support." (honors: privileges, rewards) **25.** He sent this message: "King Demetrius greets the Jewish people: (greet: send regards) **26.** Since you have kept our covenant and stayed loyal, we are glad to hear of it. (covenant: agreement) **27.** "Continue loyal, and we will reward you." (reward: recompense) **28.** "We will grant you privileges and rewards." **29.** "I free all Jews from tribute, salt duties, and crown taxes." (tribute: payment to the ruler) **30.** "From today, I release all dues on land in Judea and surrounding regions, forever." (dues: owed payments) **31.** "Let Jerusalem and its borders be holy and free from taxes." (holy: sacred) **32.** "I give up control of the tower to the high priest to manage." **33.** "I free all Jews who were taken captive and instruct officials to cancel taxes on their cattle." **34.** "Jewish festivals and sabbaths will be days of freedom in my kingdom." **35.** "No one shall disturb or harm them." **36.** "I will enlist 30,000 Jews in the king's army, paid as soldiers." (enlist: listed, registered) **37.** "Some will serve in fortresses or royal tasks, and live by their own laws." **38.** "The three regions of Samaria will be joined to Judea, under the high priest's authority." **39.** "I give Ptolemais and its land as a gift to the sanctuary in Jerusalem." (sanctuary: holy place) **40.** "I will send 15,000 shekels annually for the sanctuary's expenses." (shekels: ancient currency) **41.** "The unpaid dues will now be used for the temple's work." **42.** "I will release the 5,000 shekels taken from the temple's funds, as they belong to the priests." **43.** "Those who seek refuge in the temple shall be free, and all their possessions in my realm." (refuge: protection) **44.** "Expenses for building the temple will come from the king's treasury." **45.** "Building Jerusalem's walls and fortifications will be funded by the king." **46.** Jonathan and the people did not trust Demetrius, recalling his harm to Israel. **47.** They trusted Alexander, who had offered real peace. **48.** Alexander gathered forces and camped near Demetrius. (gathered: assembled) **49.** After battle, Demetrius' army fled, and Alexander won **50.** The battle continued until sunset, and Demetrius was killed. **51.** Alexander sent ambassadors to King Ptolemy of Egypt, asking for peace. (Ambassadors: Representatives sent on a diplomatic mission) **52.** "Since I have returned to my kingdom, defeated Demetrius, and restored our land, **53.** we overcame him in battle, and now sit on his throne. **54.** Let us form an alliance, and give me your daughter as my wife; I will honor both you and her." **55.** Ptolemy replied, "Blessed is the day you returned to your father's land and took the throne. **56.** I will do as you ask. Meet me in Ptolemais, and I will give you my daughter in marriage." **57.** Ptolemy left Egypt with his daughter Cleopatra and arrived in Ptolemais in the 162nd year. **58.** King Alexander met him, gave Cleopatra to him, and they celebrated the marriage with great glory. **59.** Alexander also wrote to Jonathan, asking him to meet him. **60.** Jonathan traveled to Ptolemais, where he gave gifts and gained favor from the kings.

61. Some wicked men from Israel accused him, but the king ignored their charges. (Accusers: People who charge others with wrongdoing) 62. The king had Jonathan dressed in purple, symbolizing honor. (Purple: A color associated with royalty and honor) 63. He sent officials to announce that no one should accuse or disturb him. 64. Seeing Jonathan honored, his accusers fled. 65. The king made Jonathan one of his closest allies and gave him power. (Duke: A nobleman, often a ruler of land) 66. Jonathan returned to Jerusalem in peace and joy. 67. In the 165th year, Demetrius, son of Demetrius, came from Crete to claim his father's land. 68. Alexander, hearing this, was troubled and returned to Antioch. 69. Demetrius appointed Apollonius, governor of Coele-Syria, to lead an army and sent a message to Jonathan. (Celosyria: A region in the ancient Near East, part of modern Syria) 70. "You alone oppose us, and for you, I am mocked. Why boast of your power in the mountains?" (boast: to brag) 71. "If you rely on your own strength, come to the plain and let us settle this, for I control the cities." (Plain: flat land; Settle: resolve) 72. "Ask who I am and who stands with me, and they'll tell you your foot can't stand firm here." (Stand firm: remain stable) 73. "You won't withstand cavalry and a large force in the plain, where there's no place to escape." (Withstand: resist; Cavalry: soldiers on horseback) 74. Jonathan, moved by these words, chose ten thousand men and left Jerusalem, where Simon, his brother, met him to help. (Moved: emotionally affected) 75. They camped near Joppa, but the people denied them entry, as Apollonius had a garrison there. (Garrison: a group of soldiers stationed at a post) 76. Jonathan laid siege, and the people, fearing him, opened the gates. Jonathan took Joppa. (Siege: surrounding a city to force surrender) 77. Apollonius gathered three thousand cavalry and infantry and moved toward Azotus, hoping to draw Jonathan out. (Cavalry: soldiers on horseback; Infantry: soldiers on foot) 78. Jonathan pursued him to Azotus, where the two armies met in battle. (Pursued: chased) 79. Apollonius had left a thousand horsemen in ambush. (Ambush: a surprise attack) 80. Jonathan knew of the ambush, as the enemy surrounded and attacked them from dawn to dusk. (Dawn: morning; Dusk: evening) 81. Jonathan's soldiers stood firm, causing the enemy's cavalry to grow weary. (Firm: steady; Weary: tired) 82. Simon brought his forces forward, defeating the exhausted cavalry and making the enemy flee. (Forward: ahead) 83. The cavalry scattered, fleeing into Azotus and seeking refuge in the temple of Dagon. (Scattered: spread out; Refuge: safety) 84. Jonathan set fire to Azotus and surrounding cities, looted them, and burned Dagon's temple with those inside. (Looted: plundered) 85. Nearly eight thousand men were killed or burned. (Slain: killed) 86. Jonathan then camped at Ascalon, where the people greeted him with celebration. (Celebration: joyful event) 87. Jonathan and his men returned to Jerusalem with the spoils of victory. (Spoils: goods taken from the enemy) 88. King Alexander, hearing of these events, honored Jonathan even more. (Honored: recognized) 89. He sent Jonathan a golden buckle and granted him possession of Accaron and its borders. (Buckle: a metal clasp; Granted: gave; Possession: ownership)

Chapter 11

1. The king of Egypt gathered a large army and many ships, intending to deceitfully take Alexander's kingdom. (Deceitfully - dishonestly) 2. He traveled peacefully to Spain, and the cities welcomed him, as King Alexander had ordered. (Ordered - commanded) 3. Ptolemy stationed a garrison of soldiers in each city to maintain control. (Garrison - a group of soldiers stationed to defend a place) 4. When he came near Azotus, they showed him the ruined temple and bodies of the slain. (Ruined - destroyed; Slain - killed) 5. They told the king about Jonathan's actions, hoping to anger him, but he remained silent. (Anger - provoke to wrath) 6. Jonathan met the king at Joppa, where they greeted each other and stayed. (Greeted - saluted) 7. Jonathan returned to Jerusalem after accompanying the king to the river Eleutherus. (Accompanying - going with) 8. Ptolemy, having control over the coastal cities, plotted against Alexander. (Plot - secretly plan) 9. Ptolemy sent ambassadors to Demetrius to form an alliance, offering his daughter. (Ambassadors - representatives; Alliance - union) 10. He regretted giving his daughter to Alexander, as the king had tried to kill him. (Regretted - felt sorrow) 11. This was a false accusation due to Ptolemy's desire for the throne. (Accusation - a claim of wrongdoing) 12. Ptolemy took back his daughter and gave her to Demetrius, causing their hatred to show. (Hatred - intense dislike) 13. Ptolemy entered Antioch, wearing both crowns of Asia and Egypt. (Crowns - symbolic headpieces) 14. Meanwhile, Alexander was in Cilicia as the people there had revolted. (Revolted - rebelled) 15. Upon hearing this, Alexander gathered his forces to confront Ptolemy, but Ptolemy defeated him. (Confront - face in a hostile way) 16. Alexander fled to Arabia for refuge, while Ptolemy grew stronger. (Refuge - protection) 17. Zabdiel beheaded Alexander and sent his head to Ptolemy. (Beheaded - cut off his head) 18. Ptolemy died three days later, and those in the strongholds fought among themselves. (Strongholds - fortified places) 19. Thus, in the 167th year of the reign, Demetrius took the throne. (Reign - period of rule) 20. Jonathan gathered the people to capture the fortress in Jerusalem, preparing war engines. (Fortress - a fortified stronghold) 21. Wicked men reported that Jonathan was besieging the tower. (Besieging - surrounding to force surrender) 22. The king, enraged, wrote to Jonathan to stop the siege and come urgently. (Enraged - very angry) 23. Jonathan, despite the king's letter, continued the siege and risked himself. (Risked - exposed to danger) 24. He took gifts and went to Ptolemais to meet the king, who favored him. (Gifts - presents; Favored - showed approval) 25. Though some made complaints against him, Jonathan gained the king's favor. (Complaints - accusations) 26. The king treated him as his predecessors had, promoting him in the sight of his friends. (Predecessors :those who came before) 27. He confirmed Jonathan in the high priesthood and gave him special honor among his chief friends. (Priesthood :office of a priest) 28. Jonathan asked the king to free Judea and the three regions of Samaria, offering three hundred talents. (Talents :a unit of currency) 29. The king agreed and sent a letter to Jonathan confirming these details. 30. "King Demetrius greets Jonathan and the Jews." (Greets :sends regards) 31. "Here is a copy of the letter we wrote to our relative Lasthenes about you." (Relative :family member) 32. "King Demetrius sends greetings to his father Lasthenes." (Greetings :regards) 33. "We will show kindness to the Jews, our friends, due to their loyalty." (Loyalty :faithfulness) 34. "We confirm the borders of Judea, including the three regions, and the sacrifices in Jerusalem will be free from tribute." (Confirm :make official; Tribute :payment made to a ruler) 35. "We will no longer collect the tithes, taxes, or other dues from them." (Tithes :a tenth of income given as an offering) 36. "These terms will stand forever." (Terms :conditions) 37. "Make a copy of this agreement and deliver it to Jonathan to display on the holy mount." (Agreement :mutual understanding) 38. King Demetrius sent his forces home, keeping only mercenaries from distant islands, causing resentment. (Mercenaries :soldiers hired for pay; Resentment :anger due to unfair treatment) 39. Tryphon, noticing discontent, approached Simalcue to release Antiochus, the son of Alexander. (Discontent :dissatisfaction) 40. Tryphon urged Simalcue to give up Antiochus to reign in place of Demetrius, explaining the army's rebellion. (Urged :encouraged) 41. Jonathan sent a message asking the king to remove the men from the tower and fortresses in Jerusalem. (Fortresses :fortified buildings) 42. Demetrius agreed and promised to honor Jonathan further. (Honor :respect or recognition) 43. "Send me help, as my forces have been sent away." (Help :assistance) 44. Jonathan sent three thousand soldiers to Antioch, which pleased the king. (Pleased :made happy) 45. The citizens of Antioch gathered to kill the king. (Citizens :people living in a city) 46. The king fled, but the city's people blocked the gates and fought. (Blocked :obstructed) 47. The king called for the Jews' help, and they killed about one hundred thousand of the city's people. (Help :assistance) 48. They set fire to the city, looted it, and saved the king. (Looted :took goods by force) 49. The citizens, seeing the Jews' victory, begged for peace. (Begged :asked urgently) 50. "Grant us peace, and stop the Jews from attacking us." (Grant :give) 51. They laid down their weapons and made peace. The Jews were honored by the king and returned to Jerusalem with great spoils. (laid down : put down; spoils: plundered goods) 52. King Demetrius sat on his throne, and the land was peaceful under his rule. (throne : king's seat; rule : control) 53. However, he deceived Jonathan and did not reward him, troubling him greatly. (deceived : misled; troubling : causing distress) 54. Tryphon returned with young Antiochus, who was crowned king. (crowned : made king) 55. Demetrius' soldiers joined Tryphon and fought against him, forcing Demetrius to flee. (flee : escape) 56. Tryphon captured the elephants and took Antioch. (captured : seized) 57. Antiochus confirmed Jonathan as high priest and appointed him ruler of four regions. (confirmed : officially recognized; appointed : assigned) 58. He sent Jonathan golden vessels, allowed him to drink from gold, wear purple, and have a golden belt. (vessels : containers) 59. Simon was appointed commander from The Ladder of Tyre to Egypt's borders. (appointed : assigned; commander : leader) 60. Jonathan passed through cities across the water, with Syrian forces joining him. In Ascalon, the people honored him. (honored : showed respect) 61. He went to Gaza, but they shut him out, so he besieged and looted the city. (besieged : surrounded; looted : plundered) 62. The people of Gaza made peace, and Jonathan sent their leaders' sons as hostages to Jerusalem. (hostages : people held to ensure an agreement) 63. Jonathan heard Demetrius' generals were advancing toward Cades, planning to expel him. (advancing : moving forward; expel : force out) 64. He confronted them, leaving Simon in charge of the region. (confronted : faced) 65. Simon fought and besieged Bethsura, and the people asked for peace. (besieged : surrounded) 66. Simon granted peace, expelled the people, and set a garrison there. (granted : gave; garrison : military post) 67. Jonathan camped by the waters of Gennesar and moved toward the plain of Nasor. (camped : set up

a base) **68.** The enemy ambushed them in the plain and mountains. (ambushed : attacked by surprise) **69.** When the ambush began, Jonathan's men fled. (fled : ran away) **70.** Only two commanders, Mattathias and Judas, remained. (commanders : military leaders) **71.** Jonathan tore his clothes, sprinkled ashes on his head, and prayed. (tore : ripped; sprinkled : scattered) **72.** He rallied his forces, turned the battle, and drove the enemy to retreat. (rallied : gathered; retreat : withdraw) **73.** His men returned to him, chasing the enemy back to their camp. (chasing : following in pursuit) **74.** About three thousand enemies were slain, and Jonathan returned to Jerusalem. (slain : killed)

Chapter 12

1. When Jonathan saw the right time, he sent men to Rome to renew the alliance with them. (Alliance: a formal agreement) **2.** He also sent letters to the Lacedemonians and others for the same purpose. (Lacedemonians: people from Sparta) **3.** They went to Rome, entered the Senate, and said, "Jonathan the High Priest and the Jewish people sent us to renew the past friendship and alliance." (Senate: governing body) **4.** The Romans gave them letters to the governors, allowing peaceful entry into Judea. (Governors: regional leaders) **5.** Here is the copy of Jonathan's letter to the Lacedemonians: **6.** "Jonathan the High Priest, the elders, priests, and other Jews send greetings to the Lacedemonians, our brothers." (Elders: respected leaders) **7.** Letters from Darius to Onias confirmed that you are our brethren, as shown here. (Brethren: fellow members) **8.** Onias honored the ambassador, received the letters, and acknowledged the alliance. (Ambassador: official representative) **9.** Although we don't need this, we are sending to renew our bond of brotherhood. (Bond: connection) **10.** We don't want to be strangers to you, since it's been a long time since we heard from you. (Strangers: unfamiliar people) **11.** We remember you in our prayers and sacrifices during feasts, as is proper. (Sacrifices: offerings) **12.** We are glad for the honor you give us. (Honor: respect) **13.** We have faced great troubles, as surrounding kings fought against us. (Troubles: problems) **14.** But we don't wish to trouble you or our allies with these wars. (Allies: supporters) **15.** We have help from heaven, delivering us from enemies and putting them under our control. (Delivering: rescuing) **16.** For this reason, we sent Numenius and Antipater to renew the friendship and alliance with Rome. (Renew: restore) **17.** We also instructed them to visit you and deliver our letter about renewing brotherhood. (Instructed: directed) **18.** We hope you will respond to us. (Respond: reply) **19.** This is the copy of Onias' letter: **20.** "Areus, king of the Lacedemonians, to Onias the High Priest, greetings:" (Greetings: expressions of goodwill) **21.** It is written that the Lacedemonians and Jews are brethren, descendants of Abraham. (Descendants: offspring) **22.** Now that we know this, let us know of your well-being. (Well-being: health and happiness) **23.** We reply that your cattle and possessions are ours, and ours are yours. (Cattle: livestock; Possessions: belongings) **24.** When Jonathan heard that Demetrius' commanders came to fight with a larger army, (Commanders: military leaders) **25.** he met them in Amathis, preventing them from entering his land. (Land: territory) **26.** He sent scouts, and they reported an ambush planned for the night. (Scouts: people sent for observation, Ambush: a surprise attack) **27.** At sunset, Jonathan ordered his men to stay alert and armed throughout the night, with sentries around the camp. (Sentries: guards) **28.** The enemy, fearing Jonathan's readiness, lit fires in their camp to signal their unease. (Unease: discomfort or worry) **29.** Jonathan and his men were unaware of this until morning, seeing the fires still burning. (Unaware: not knowing) **30.** Jonathan pursued them but couldn't catch up as they crossed the Eleutherus River. (Pursued: followed) **31.** He then turned to the Zabadeans, attacked them, and took their goods. (Zabadeans: Arabian group, Goods: possessions) **32.** Jonathan moved on to Damascus, passing through the region. (Damascus: a city in Syria) **33.** Simon traveled to Ascalon and Joppa, taking them both. (Took: captured) **34.** He set a garrison in Joppa to control it, after hearing they would surrender it to Demetrius' followers. (Garrison: group of soldiers) **35.** Jonathan returned and consulted the elders about fortifying Judea. (Fortifying: strengthening) **36.** They planned to reinforce Jerusalem's walls and build a mound to isolate it. (Isolate: separate) **37.** The people rebuilt parts of the wall, especially near the east side, called Caphenatha. (Caphenatha: a specific place) **38.** Simon fortified Adida in Sephela with gates and bars. (Fortified: strengthened, Sephela: a region) **39.** Tryphon aimed to kill Antiochus and take the throne for himself. (Aimed: planned) **40.** He feared Jonathan would oppose him, so he plotted to capture and kill him. (Plotted: planned secretly) **41.** Jonathan, with 40,000 men, went to meet him in Bethsan. (Bethsan: an ancient city) **42.** Seeing Jonathan's large force, Tryphon did not attack. (Did not: refused) **43.** Tryphon greeted him with respect, gave him gifts, and ordered his men to obey Jonathan. (Obey: follow orders) **44.** Tryphon asked why Jonathan brought so many men, claiming there was no conflict. (Claiming: stating) **45.** He asked Jonathan to send his men home and come with him to Ptolemais, offering him control of it and other strongholds. (Strongholds: fortified places) **46.** Jonathan trusted him, sent his men back, and kept 3,000 soldiers. (Trusted: believed) **47.** He sent 2,000 to Galilee and took 1,000 with him. (Galilee: a region) **48.** But when they arrived at Ptolemais, they were captured and killed. (Captured: taken by force) **49.** Tryphon sent troops to destroy the rest of Jonathan's forces in Galilee. (Troops: soldiers) **50.** Upon hearing Jonathan's death, the survivors gathered and prepared to fight. (Gathered: assembled) **51.** Seeing their resolve, the attackers withdrew. (Withdraw: retreated) **52.** The survivors returned to Judea, mourning Jonathan and his men. (Mourning: grieving) **53.** Neighbors, seeing Israel without a leader, sought to destroy them, believing they were vulnerable. (Vulnerable: exposed to harm)

Chapter 13

1. Simon heard that Tryphon had gathered a great army to invade Judea and destroy it. (invade – attack, destroy – ruin) **2.** Seeing the people in fear, he went to Jerusalem and gathered them together, (fear – anxiety) **3.** He spoke, saying, "You know what I, my brothers, and my father's house have done for the laws, the sanctuary, and the battles we've fought." (sanctuary :holy place, battles :fights) **4.** "All my brothers have died for Israel, and I am left alone." (died :been killed) **5.** "It is unthinkable for me to save myself in troubled times, for I am no better than my brothers." (unthinkable :unimaginable) **6.** "I will avenge our nation, the sanctuary, our wives, and children, for the nations are gathered to destroy us." (avenge :seek justice, nations :foreign peoples) **7.** The people's spirits were lifted upon hearing these words. (spirits :morale) **8.** They said, "You will lead us in place of Judas and Jonathan, your brothers." (lead :guide) **9.** "Fight our battles, and we will obey your commands." (commands :orders) **10.** Simon gathered the army and quickly strengthened Jerusalem's walls. (strengthened :fortified) **11.** He sent Jonathan, son of Absolom, with a large force to Joppa, where they expelled the inhabitants. (expelled :drove out, inhabitants :residents) **12.** Tryphon left Ptolemais with a great army to invade Judea, and Jonathan was held captive. (captive :imprisoned) **13.** Simon camped at Adida, facing the plain. (camped :set up camp) **14.** Tryphon, learning Simon had replaced his brother Jonathan, sent messengers saying, (replaced :took the place of) **15.** "We hold Jonathan for a debt owed to the king; send one hundred talents and two sons as hostages." (debt :money owed, talents :units of money, hostages :people held as security) **16.** "Send the money and hostages, and we will release him." (release :set free) **17.** Simon sent the money and the children, fearing the people would blame him if Jonathan died. (blame :hold responsible) **18.** "If I hadn't sent the money, Jonathan would be dead," they might say. (might say :could claim) **19.** Simon sent them, but Tryphon did not release Jonathan. (release :free) **20.** Tryphon advanced to destroy the land, but Simon's army followed him everywhere. (advanced :moved forward) **21.** The people in the tower messaged Tryphon, asking him to hurry and bring supplies. (supplies :provisions) **22.** Tryphon prepared his cavalry, but a heavy snowstorm delayed him, and he withdrew to Gilead. (cavalry :soldiers on horseback, withdrew :retreated) **23.** Near Bascama, Tryphon had Jonathan killed and buried there. (killed :executed) **24.** Then, Tryphon returned to his own land. (returned :went back) **25.** Simon took Jonathan's bones and buried them in Modin, the city of their fathers. (bones :remains, buried :placed in a grave) **26.** All Israel mourned deeply and grieved for him for many days. **27.** Simon built a monument over his father and brothers' tomb, with stonework on both sides. **28.** He raised seven pyramids for his family. **29.** The pyramids had carvings, with armor displayed on large pillars and ships carved on them for sailors to see. **30.** This tomb still stands in Modin today. **31.** Tryphon deceived and killed King Antiochus. (Deceived: misled) **32.** Tryphon crowned himself king and caused great suffering. **33.** Simon fortified Judean strongholds, building high walls, gates, and storing food. (Fortified: strengthened and protected) **34.** Simon sent men to King Demetrius asking for land immunity. (Immunity: exemption from certain rules or taxes) **35.** Demetrius replied in writing: **36.** "King Demetrius to Simon, high priest, and the Jewish nation, greetings: **37.** We received the crown and robe you sent, and we agree to a lasting peace with you. **38.** All agreements stand, and the strongholds are yours. **39.** We forgive all past errors, including the crown tax, and no more tribute will be paid in Jerusalem. (Tribute: payments) **40.** If anyone is worthy to serve in our court, let them be enrolled, and let there be peace. (Enrolled: officially listed) **41.** Thus, in the 170th year, the yoke of the heathen was removed from Israel. (Yoke: burden; Heathen: non-Jews) **42.** From that time, Israel began writing: "In the first year of Simon the high priest and governor." **43.** Simon besieged Gaza, built a war engine, and took a tower. (Besieged: surrounded and blockaded; War engine: a military machine for attacking) **44.** Soldiers from the engine entered the city, causing chaos. **45.** The people tore their clothes and begged Simon for peace. **46.** They asked for mercy, not judgment. (Mercy: compassion) **47.** Simon spared them, purged the city of idols, and entered with songs. (Purged: cleansed) **48.** He purified the city, strengthened its defenses, and built himself a residence. (Purified: removed impurities from; Residence: place to live) **49.** The people in the Jerusalem tower were trapped and suffered famine. (Famine: severe shortage of food) **50.** They pleaded for peace, and Simon cleansed the tower. **51.** Simon entered the tower on the 23rd day of the second month with celebration, marking a victory. **52.** He made this day an annual celebration and strengthened the temple hill, where he settled. **53.** Simon appointed his son John as captain and stationed him in Gazera. (Captain: leader)

Chapter 14

1. In the year 172, King Demetrius gathered his army and marched into Media to seek support against Tryphone. (Media: ancient region in Iran; Tryphone: opponent of Demetrius) **2.** Arsaces, king of Persia and Media, hearing of Demetrius' invasion, sent an officer to capture him. (Arsaces: Persian king; dispatched: sent) **3.** The officer defeated Demetrius' army, captured him, and brought him to Arsaces, who imprisoned him. (struck: attacked; imprisoned: confined) **4.** Judea had peace under Simon, who worked for the people's well-being and earned their respect. (reign: period of rule; diligently: persistently; welfare: well-being) **5.** Simon took Joppa as a harbor and opened access to the islands. (honorable: worthy of respect; strategic: important; harbor: sheltered port) **6.** He expanded his territory, recovering lands and strengthening his rule. (expanded: made larger; territory: area; reclaiming: taking back) **7.** Simon gained captives and controlled Gazera, Bethsura, and the fortress, purging them of opposition. (captives: prisoners; dominion: control; purified: cleansed; opposition: enemies) **8.** The people worked the land in peace, and the earth produced plentiful crops. (tilled: worked the soil; yielded: produced; abundant: plentiful) **9.** Elders gathered to discuss wisdom, while young men wore glorious military attire. (elders: respected leaders; adorned: dressed; glorious: impressive; attire: clothing) **10.** Simon provided for the cities and equipped them with defenses, ensuring his name was honored worldwide. (provisions: supplies; equipped: prepared; defenses: protection; celebrated: praised) **11.** He brought peace to the land, and Israel rejoiced greatly. (established: set up; rejoiced: celebrated) **12.** People sat peacefully under their own vine and fig tree, free from fear. (intimidate: frighten) **13.** There was no one to oppose them, and even kings were defeated. (oppose: resist; defeated: overthrown) **14.** He strengthened the weak, examined the law, and removed the wicked. (strengthened: made stronger; thoroughly: completely; defied: resisted; wickedly: immorally) **15.** Simon beautified the sanctuary and added many new vessels to the temple. (beautified: decorated; sanctuary: holy place; vessels: religious containers) **16.** When news of Jonathan's death reached Rome and Sparta, they were saddened. (saddened: made sorrowful) **17.** Upon learning Simon became high priest and ruler, they sent a letter of congratulations. (succeeded: followed in position) **18.** They sent a letter to Simon engraved on brass to renew the alliance with his brothers. (engraved: carved; alliance: union) **19.** The letters were read aloud in the Jerusalem assembly. (assembly: gathering) **20.** A letter from Sparta's rulers to Simon and the Jewish people conveyed their greetings. (rulers: leaders; greetings: good wishes) **21.** The ambassadors reported Simon's glory, and Sparta welcomed them warmly. (ambassadors: representatives; esteemed: highly respected; glory: praise) **22.** We recorded their message in the council: Numenius and Antipater came to renew the bond of friendship. (contents: substance; council: decision-making body; bond: connection) **23.** The people honored them and recorded their mission in public records, ensuring Sparta's memory. (welcomed: greeted; lasting: enduring) **24.** Simon sent Numenius to Rome with a large golden shield to reaffirm the alliance. (subsequently: afterward; reaffirm: confirm; magnificent: grand) **25.** Upon hearing this, the people wondered, "What thanks shall we give to Simon and his sons?" (wondered: asked; thanks: gratitude) **26.** Simon, his brothers, and his family established Israel, defeated their enemies in battle, and secured their freedom. (Established: set up, founded.) **27.** They inscribed the events on brass tablets, which were placed on pillars on Mount Zion. The inscription reads: On the 18th day of Elul, in the 162nd year, third year of Simon's high priesthood, (Inscribed: wrote.) **28.** At Saramel, a large assembly of priests, leaders, and elders proclaimed these matters. (Assembly: gathering. Elders: respected leaders.) **29.** Simon, son of Mattathias, with his brothers, risked their lives to defend the sanctuary and the law, bringing great honor to Israel. (Sanctuary: holy place.) **30.** After Jonathan had gathered the nation and served as high priest, (Served: acted as.) **31.** Their enemies prepared to invade and destroy the land and seize the sanctuary. (Invade: enter forcefully. Seize: take by force.) **32.** At this time, Simon defended the nation, spending his wealth, arming the brave men, and paying them wages. (Arming: providing with weapons. Wages: payment.) **33.** He fortified Judea's cities, including Bethsura, where enemies had once camped, placing a Jewish garrison there. (Fortified: strengthened. Garrison: military post.) **34.** He also fortified Joppa and Gazera, where the enemies had previously lived, and stationed Jews there, equipping them for restoration. (Equipping: providing necessary supplies. Restoration: bringing back to good condition.) **35.** The people praised Simon, honoring him as their governor and high priest for his accomplishments and dedication to the nation. (Accomplishments: achievements.) **36.** Under his leadership, the nation prospered. The heathens were driven out, and the polluters of the holy place were removed. (Heathens: non-believers. Polluters: defilers.) **37.** Simon took charge of the tower, fortifying it for the safety of the city and strengthened Jerusalem's walls. (Fortifying: strengthening.) **38.** King Demetrius confirmed Simon as high priest, according to tradition, (Confirmed: officially supported.) **39.** And made him his ally, greatly honoring him. (Ally: partner.) **40.** Demetrius had heard that the Romans considered the Jews their allies and had honored Simon's ambassadors. (Ambassadors: representatives.) **41.** The Jews and priests were pleased that Simon should be their governor and high priest forever. (Forever: for all time.) **42.** Simon would lead the army, oversee the sanctuary, its works, the land, the army, and fortresses. (Oversee: supervise. Fortresses: strongholds.) **43.** All were required to obey him, and documents would be issued in his name, clothed in purple, adorned with gold. (Adorned: decorated.) **44.** No one could oppose his authority or break these rules. (Oppose: go against.) **45.** Anyone breaking these laws would face punishment. (Punishment: penalty.) **46.** The people agreed to these terms with joy. (Terms: conditions.) **47.** Simon accepted the role of high priest, leader, and protector of the people. (Protector: defender.) **48.** A decree was made to inscribe this agreement on brass tablets and display it in the sanctuary. (Decree: official order. Inscribe: write.) **49.** Copies were to be kept in the treasury for Simon and his descendants. (Descendants: offspring.)

Chapter 15

1. Antiochus, son of Demetrius, sent letters to Simon, the high priest, and the Jews, greeting them from across the seas. (Seas: regions across the sea from Judea, typically in the Mediterranean.) **2.** The letters stated: King Antiochus to Simon, high priest, and the Jewish people, greetings: (Letters: written messages.) **3.** Since wicked men now rule our ancestral kingdom, I plan to reclaim it with a large army and warships. (Reclaim: to take back possession of something. Warships: ships equipped for battle.) **4.** I will travel through the land, seeking vengeance against those who have devastated it, leaving cities ruined. (Vengeance: punishment for a wrong or injury. Devastated: severely damaged or destroyed.) **5.** I confirm all past offerings to you, as well as any additional gifts granted. (Confirm: to affirm or acknowledge something.) **6.** I also grant you the right to mint your own coins with your seal. (Mint: to make or produce money. Seal: a symbol or stamp used to authenticate documents.) **7.** Jerusalem and the sanctuary will remain free, and all your fortresses and armaments are yours. (Sanctuary: a sacred place or temple. Armaments: weapons and military equipment. Fortresses: large, strong buildings or defenses.) **8.** Any debt owed to the king will be forgiven, now and forever. (Forgiven: excused or pardoned.) **9.** When our kingdom is restored, we will honor you, your nation, and your temple, spreading your fame. (Restored: returned to a previous state. Fame: widespread reputation.) **10.** In 164, Antiochus entered his land, gathering his forces, leaving few with Tryphon. (Forces: military troops.) **11.** Faced with this, Tryphon fled to Dora, a coastal city. (Fled: ran away. Coastal: located on the coast.) **12.** Realizing his troubles and that his forces had deserted him, he sought refuge in Dora. (Troubles: difficulties or problems. Deserted: abandoned. Refuge: a place of safety.) **13.** Antiochus camped near Dora with 120,000 soldiers and 8,000 cavalry. (Cavalry: soldiers on horseback.) **14.** He surrounded the city, placing ships nearby, launching attacks by land and sea, blocking all entry and exit. (Launched: started or initiated. Attacks: aggressive actions against something.) **15.** Meanwhile, Numenius and his companions arrived from Rome with letters for kings and nations. (Companions: associates or friends.) **16.** Lucius, the Roman consul, to King Ptolemy, greetings: (Consul: a high-ranking official in ancient Rome.) **17.** The Jewish ambassadors, our allies, have come to renew the old treaty, sent by Simon, the high priest. (Ambassadors: official representatives. Renew: to make something valid again. Alliance: an agreement between parties for mutual benefit.) **18.** They presented a golden shield weighing 1,000 pounds. (Presented: gave as a gift. Shield: a defensive weapon.) **19.** We inform all kings and nations not to harm the Jews, their cities, or aid their enemies. (Inform: notify or tell. Harm: cause injury. Aid: assist.) **20.** We accept their shield as a token of friendship. (Token: a symbol or representation.) **21.** If troublesome individuals have fled to you, send them to Simon the high priest for punishment. (Troublesome: causing trouble or disturbance. Fled: ran away.) **22.** This message was sent to King Demetrius, Attalus, Ariarathes, and Arsaces, (Nations: countries or peoples.) **23.** and to other nations, including the Sampsames, Lacedemonians, Delus, Myndus, Sicyon, Caria, Samos, Pamphylia, Lycia, Halicarnassus, Rhodus, Aradus, Cos,

Side, Gortyna, Cnidus, Cyprus, and Cyrene. (Nations: countries or peoples.) **24.** A copy was also sent to Simon the high priest. (Copy: a duplicate of something written.) **25.** Antiochus continued his siege against Dora, attacking and constructing siege engines, trapping Tryphon inside. (Siege: a military blockade of a city. Engines: machines used in warfare, especially to break down walls.) **26.** Simon sent 2,000 men, silver, gold, and armor to assist him. (Assist: to help or support.) **27.** Antiochus refused their help, breaking his agreements with Simon, acting unfriendly. (Refused: declined. Agreements: formal arrangements.) **28.** He sent Athenobius to claim Simon was withholding Joppa, Gazera, and the Jerusalem tower. (Withholding: keeping back or not giving.) **29.** Antiochus accused Simon of ravaging borders and seizing lands outside Judea. (Ravaging: destroying. Seizing: taking control of.) **30.** He demanded the return of captured cities or 500 talents in silver for damages, threatening war if Simon refused. (Talents: large sums of money. Wage war: to engage in armed conflict.) **31.** Athenobius arrived in Jerusalem, astonished by Simon's grandeur, wealth, and retinue, then delivered the king's message. (Grandeur: magnificence. Retinue: a group of attendants.) **32.** Simon replied that they never took land unfairly, and what they held was their ancestral inheritance. (Inheritance: something passed down from ancestors.) **33.** Hence, Simon maintained his ancestors' land. (Maintained: kept or preserved.) **34.** For Joppa and Gazera, Simon offered 100 talents for their return. (Offered: proposed.) **35.** Athenobius remained silent. (Silent: not speaking.) **36.** He returned to the king, enraged by Simon's words and splendor. (Enraged: made very angry. Splendor: brilliance.) **37.** Meanwhile, Tryphon escaped to Orthosias. (Escaped: fled from danger.) **38.** The king appointed Cendebeus as captain of the coast, commanding him to gather troops and march toward Judea. (Appointed: designated. Cavalry: soldiers on horseback.) **39.** He instructed Cendebeus to fortify Cedron and wage war, while Antiochus continued pursuing Tryphon. (Fortify: strengthen. Wage war: to fight.) **40.** Cendebeus arrived in Jamnia, provoking and capturing the people. (Provoking: causing anger. Capturing: taking control of.) **41.** After fortifying Cedron, he stationed troops to raid the roads of Judea. (Stationed: placed. Raid: a sudden attack.)

Chapter 16
1. John came from Gazera and informed Simon of Cendebeus' actions. (Cendebeus: a military leader or enemy) **2.** Simon called his sons Judas and John, telling them that his family had always fought for Israel, succeeding in freeing the nation. (Succeeded: achieved success) **3.** Now, as he was old, Simon entrusted them to fight in his place with God's help. (Entrusted: gave responsibility or duty) **4.** He chose twenty thousand men, including cavalry, and camped at Modin. (Cavalry: soldiers mounted on horseback) **5.** The next morning, they faced a large army, separated by a water brook. (Brook: a small stream or creek) **6.** Simon crossed first, encouraging his men to follow. (Encouraging: giving support or confidence) **7.** He positioned the cavalry in the middle, anticipating the enemy's strength. (Anticipating: expecting or preparing for) **8.** The holy trumpets were sounded, and the enemy fled, many being killed. (Trumpets: musical instruments used for signaling) **9.** Judas was wounded, but John pursued the enemy to Cedron. (Pursued: followed in an attempt to catch) **10.** The enemy fled to Azotus, where John burned the towers and killed about two thousand men. (Fled: ran away, escaped) **11.** Ptolemaeus was made captain in Jericho, rich in gold and silver. (Captain: leader or commander) **12.** He was the high priest's son-in-law. (Son-in-law: the husband of one's daughter) **13.** Proud, he conspired to seize control and destroy Simon and his sons. (Conspired: planned secretly, usually to do something harmful) **14.** Simon visited Jericho with his sons to manage the cities, arriving in the 167th year in the month of Sabat. (Managed: oversaw or controlled) **15.** Ptolemaeus invited them to a banquet in a hidden fortress, where he had men waiting to ambush. (Banquet: a large formal meal, often with many guests) (Fortress: a strong, fortified building or military stronghold) (Ambush: a surprise attack) **16.** After drinking, Ptolemaeus' men attacked, killing Simon, his sons, and servants. (Servants: people who work for others, typically in a domestic or personal role) **17.** This was a treacherous act, repaying good with evil. (Treacherous: betraying trust, deceitful) **18.** Ptolemaeus sent word to the king, asking for reinforcements to help him control the land. (Reinforcements: additional support or troops) **19.** He also sent men to kill John in Gazera and promised rewards to the tribunes for their help. (Tribunes: official or military officers in ancient Rome) **20.** He also targeted Jerusalem and the Temple Mount. (Targeted: aimed at or focused on) **21.** A messenger told John of his family's death and the plot against him. (Messenger: someone who delivers messages) **22.** John killed those sent to destroy him, knowing their intentions. (Intentions: plans or aims) **23.** John's deeds, battles, fortifications, and actions are recorded in his priestly chronicles. (Deeds: actions or accomplishments) (Fortifications: structures built to defend an area) **24.** These are written from the time he became high priest after his father.

74 – The Second Book of Maccabees

Chapter 1
1. The Jews in Jerusalem and Judea send greetings and peace to the Jews in Egypt. (Judea: region in Israel) **2.** May God be kind and remember His covenant with Abraham, Isaac, and Jacob, His faithful servants. **3.** May He give you a heart to serve Him with courage and a willing spirit. **4.** May He open your hearts to His law and bring you peace. **5.** May He hear your prayers and never abandon you in times of trouble. **6.** We are praying for you. **7.** During the reign of Demetrius, in the 169th year, we wrote to you in the midst of our distress after Jason and his group turned from the holy land. (Demetrius: Greek king) **8.** They burned the porch and shed innocent blood. We prayed to God, offering sacrifices and lighting lamps, and He heard us. **9.** Now, observe the Feast of Tabernacles in the month of Casleu. (Casleu: Hebrew month) **10.** In the 188th year, people in Jerusalem, Judea, and the council sent greetings to Aristobulus, master of King Ptolemy, a descendant of the priests, and to the Jews in Egypt. (Aristobulus: Jewish leader) **11.** We thank God for saving us from great dangers, having fought against a king. **12.** God drove out those who fought within the holy city. **13.** The leader came to Persia with a powerful army, but they were defeated in the temple of Nanea through deception. (Nanea: temple in Persia) **14.** Antiochus, pretending to seek marriage, entered the temple with his men, seeking a dowry. **15.** The priests of Nanea locked the temple once Antiochus and his men entered. **16.** They opened a secret door and threw stones, killing the captain and scattering his men. **17.** Blessed be our God, who delivers the ungodly. **18.** We plan to observe the purification of the temple on the 25th of Casleu and invite you to join us. **19.** When our ancestors were in Persia, priests secretly hid the altar's fire in a dry pit, keeping it safe. **20.** Many years later, Nehemiah sent descendants of those priests to recover the fire but found only thick water. **21.** Nehemiah instructed the priests to use the water on the sacrifices. **22.** When the sun came out, a great fire ignited, surprising everyone. **23.** The priests prayed while the sacrifice burned, with Jonathan leading. **24.** Their prayer was: "O Lord, Creator of all, mighty, just, merciful, and King of all, **25.** You who deliver Israel, chose the fathers, and sanctified them, **26.** Accept this sacrifice for Israel, protect Your people, and sanctify them. **27.** Gather the scattered, save those in exile, and let the nations know You are our God. **28.** Punish those who oppress us. **29.** Restore Your people to the holy land, as Moses said." **30.** The priests sang psalms of thanksgiving. **31.** After the sacrifice was consumed, Nehemiah ordered the remaining water to be poured on the stones. **32.** The water caused a flame, but it was outshined by the light from the altar. **33.** The king of Persia was told that Nehemiah purified the sacrifices with the water, where fire had once been. **34.** The king closed the place and declared it holy after investigating. **35.** He gave many gifts to those he honored. **36.** Nehemiah called this event Naphthar, meaning "cleansing," though many call it Nephi.

Chapter 2
1. It is also written that the prophet Jeremiah instructed those carried away to take some of the fire, as indicated. (Jeremiah: prophet of Israel) **2.** He told them not to forget God's commandments, nor to be led astray by images of silver and gold with their ornaments. **3.** He urged them to keep the law in their hearts. **4.** The same writing mentions that God warned Jeremiah to take the tabernacle, ark, and altar of incense and go into the mountain where Moses saw God's inheritance. **5.** Jeremiah found a hidden cave, where he placed the tabernacle, ark, and altar, then sealed the entrance. **6.** Some followed him to mark the path, but they couldn't find it. **7.** Jeremiah told them the place would remain hidden until God gathers His people again and shows them mercy. **8.** Then God will reveal the place, and His glory and the cloud, as shown to Moses and when Solomon sanctified the place. (Solomon: King of Israel) **9.** The prophet, being wise, offered the dedication sacrifice and the completion of the temple. **10.** Just as Moses prayed and fire came down to consume the sacrifices, Solomon prayed, and fire came down from heaven to consume his offerings. **11.** Moses said the sin offering was consumed because it was not to be eaten. **12.** Solomon kept the feast for eight days. **13.** These events are also recorded in Nehemiah's writings, where he gathered records of the kings, prophets, and David, along with the epistles of the kings about the holy gifts. (Nehemiah: Jewish leader) **14.** Similarly, Judas Maccabeus gathered what had been lost in the war, and it remains with us. (Judas Maccabeus: Jewish warrior) **15.** If you need them, send someone to fetch them. **16.** We are about to celebrate the purification and encourage you to observe the same days. **17.** We hope that God, who delivered His people and gave them an inheritance, kingdom, priesthood, and sanctuary as promised, will soon have mercy on us. **18.** He will gather us from every land and bring us to the holy place, having delivered us from troubles and purified

it. **19.** Concerning Judas Maccabeus, his brothers, the purification of the great temple, and the dedication of the altar, **20.** the wars against Antiochus Epiphanes and his son Eupator, **21.** and the signs from heaven for those who bravely honored Judaism, so that a small group overcame the whole country, **22.** reclaimed the temple, freed the city, and upheld the laws, with God's favor: **23.** All these things are recorded by Jason of Cyrene in five books, which we will now condense into one volume. (Jason of Cyrene: historian) **24.** Given the vast amount of material, we aim to simplify the story for those who wish to read and remember it easily. **25.** Our goal is for those who read to enjoy it, those who wish to memorize to do so with ease, and all who read it to benefit. **26.** It was not an easy task for us to condense, but a labor of effort and focus. **27.** Just as preparing a banquet is hard work for the benefit of others, we willingly take on this challenge for the pleasure of many. **28.** We leave the detailed treatment of every point to the original author, focusing on presenting the main points clearly. **29.** As a builder plans the whole structure, but a decorator chooses what is best to adorn it, we aim for clarity and brevity in this abridgment. **30.** Detailed attention to every point belongs to the original author, **31.** but brevity and simplicity are granted to those making an abridgment. **32.** Therefore, we begin the story, avoiding a lengthy prologue, as it is foolish to do so when the main story is the focus.

Chapter 3

1. When the holy city was peaceful, and the laws well kept due to Onias the high priest's godliness, **2.** even kings honored the temple and enriched it with their gifts. **3.** Seleucus of Asia funded the sacrifices from his own revenue. **4.** Simon, a governor of the temple from Benjamin, quarreled with Onias over city matters. **5.** Failing to prevail, Simon went to Apollonius, governor of Celosyria and Phoenicia, **6.** and told him of the immense wealth in the Jerusalem treasury, which could be seized for the king. **7.** Apollonius informed the king, who sent his treasurer, Heliodorus, to take the money. **8.** Heliodorus journeyed under the guise of visiting the cities but had the king's true mission. (guise: a false appearance) **9.** Upon arrival in Jerusalem, he met the high priest, told him of the king's order, and asked if the rumors were true. **10.** The high priest explained that the money was meant for widows, orphans, and important individuals, not for the king. **11.** He clarified that the total was 400 talents of silver and 200 of gold, entrusted to the temple's care. (entrusted: given with responsibility) **12.** Heliodorus insisted on taking the funds, despite the high priest's objections. **13.** On the appointed day, Heliodorus entered the treasury, causing great distress throughout the city. (appointed: scheduled or chosen) **14.** The priests, in sacred garments, prayed for the preservation of the funds. (preservation: the act of keeping something safe) **15.** The high priest's face showed deep fear and sorrow. **16.** His agony was visible to all who saw him. (agony: intense pain or suffering) **17.** The people gathered, praying fervently for the safety of the temple. (fervently: with intense passion) **18.** Women in sackcloth and virgins from the temple also joined the prayers. **19.** Everyone raised their hands toward heaven, seeking God's mercy. **20.** The scene of their prayers and the high priest's distress was heart-wrenching. (heart-wrenching: causing deep emotional pain) **21.** They prayed for the security of the sacred treasures. **22.** Despite their prayers, Heliodorus continued his mission. **23.** While in the treasury, a divine vision appeared before them. (divine: related to God or gods) **24.** They saw a horse with a mighty rider, terrifying them all with its power. (mighty: powerful or strong) **25.** The rider was dressed in gold and struck at Heliodorus. **26.** Two young men appeared beside him, beating Heliodorus with whips. (whips: long, thin tools used for striking) **27.** Heliodorus fell, surrounded by darkness, and was carried away, unable to help himself. **28.** The once confident treasurer was now powerless, acknowledging God's power. (powerless: lacking strength or ability) **29.** He lay speechless, near death, but the people praised God for protecting the temple. (speechless: unable to speak, usually due to shock or awe) **30.** The temple, once filled with fear, was now filled with joy and thanksgiving. (thanksgiving: the act of giving thanks) **31.** Heliodorus' friends pleaded for the high priest to pray for his recovery. (pleaded: asked urgently or with emotion) **32.** Suspecting the king might think the Jews were involved in wrongdoing, Onias offered a sacrifice for Heliodorus' life. (wrongdoing: illegal or immoral behavior) **33.** As the sacrifice was offered, the same young men appeared again, telling Heliodorus to thank Onias for his life. **34.** They urged him to declare God's power. Then, they vanished. (urged: strongly advised or encouraged) **35.** Heliodorus made sacrifices, praised God, and returned to the king, telling everyone of God's mighty works. **36.** He testified to the king about the miraculous events he had witnessed. (testified: gave evidence or proof of something) **37.** The king, upon hearing this, warned that anyone sent to Jerusalem who was an enemy of God would suffer the same fate. (fate: a predetermined outcome or destiny) **38.** He advised that any traitor sent there would be severely punished, acknowledging God's power over the temple. (traitor: someone who betrays others) **39.** The king recognized that God watches over the temple and punishes those who harm it. **40.** Thus, the story of Heliodorus and the treasury concluded. (concluded: came to an end)

Chapter 4

1. Simon, who betrayed both the money and his country, slandered Onias, falsely accusing him of terrorizing Heliodorus and causing these troubles. (slandered: made false accusations against) **2.** He dared to call Onias a traitor, though Onias had served the city well, loved his nation, and was zealous for the law. (zealous: passionate or enthusiastic) **3.** The hatred grew so intense that murders were committed by Simon's followers. **4.** Seeing the danger, Onias recognized Apollonius, governor of Celosyria and Phoenicia, was fueling Simon's malice. (fueling: causing to grow or intensify) (malice: desire to harm others) **5.** Onias went to the king, not to accuse his people, but to seek the good of all. **6.** He saw that the peace of the state and Simon's folly could only be resolved if the king intervened. (folly: foolishness) (intervened: became involved to stop something) **7.** After Seleucus' death, Antiochus Epiphanes took the throne, and Jason, Onias' brother, schemed to become high priest. (schemed: secretly planned) **8.** Jason promised the king 360 talents of silver and an additional 80 talents from other revenues. **9.** He also offered 150 more talents to set up a place for Greek training and to rename the youth of Jerusalem as Antiochians. **10.** The king granted this, and Jason immediately led his people into Greek customs. **11.** Jason abolished royal privileges granted to Jews by John, father of Eupolemus, and introduced new customs against the law. (privileges: special rights or advantages) **12.** He built a gymnasium under the tower and forced young men to wear Greek hats. **13.** Greek fashions and heathen practices, fueled by Jason's impiety, led priests to abandon their duties and join in the forbidden activities at the gymnasium. (heathen: non-religious or not following the main religion) (impiety: lack of respect for religion) **14.** The priests, neglecting their sacred duties, joined in the unlawful activities, forgetting the glory of their forefathers. (neglecting: failing to care for) (sacred: holy or religiously important) (unlawful: illegal) (forefathers: ancestors) **15.** This led to great calamity, for they sought to imitate the very customs of their enemies. (calamity: disaster) (imitate: copy) **16.** Following such actions brings severe consequences, as those they sought to emulate would become their avengers. (emulate: try to match or surpass) (avengers: those who seek revenge) **17.** It is not a light matter to defy God's laws; the future will reveal the consequences. (defy: resist or refuse to obey) **18.** When the games were held at Tyre, the king was present. **19.** Jason sent Antiochian messengers with 300 drachms for a Hercules sacrifice, though even the bearers found it inappropriate for sacrifice. (drachms: a type of ancient Greek coin) **20.** Instead, the money intended for Hercules was used to build warships. **21.** Apollonius, sent to Egypt for Ptolemy Philometor's coronation, saw Antiochus was concerned for his safety and went to Joppa and Jerusalem. (coronation: the ceremony of crowning a king or queen) **22.** Jason and the city honored Apollonius, welcoming him with torches and shouts, and later he went to Phenice. **23.** Three years later, Jason sent Menelaus, Simon's brother, to deliver money to the king and discuss certain matters. **24.** Menelaus, praising the king's power, offered 300 talents more than Jason to secure the priesthood. (secure: obtain) **25.** He brought nothing worthy of the high priesthood but the cruelty of a tyrant. (tyrant: a cruel ruler) **26.** Jason, who had undermined his brother, was now overthrown by Menelaus and fled to the Ammonites. (undermined: weakened or sabotaged) (Ammonites: a group of ancient people) **27.** Menelaus took the priesthood but neglected the money owed to the king, though Sostratus, the castle ruler, demanded it. **28.** Both were summoned before the king regarding the money owed. **29.** Menelaus left his brother Lysimachus as high priest, and Sostratus appointed Crates to govern Cyprus. **30.** Meanwhile, Tarsus and Mallos revolted because of the king's concubine, Antiochus. (concubine: a woman who lives with a man without being married to him) **31.** The king rushed to quell the revolt, leaving Andronicus in charge. (quell: put an end to) **32.** Taking advantage of the situation, Menelaus stole golden vessels from the temple, giving some to Andronicus and selling the rest in Tyre. (vessels: containers) **33.** Onias, discovering this, reproved Menelaus and withdrew to the sanctuary at Daphne near Antioch. (reproved: criticized or scolded) (sanctuary: a holy or safe place) **34.** Menelaus, with Andronicus, tricked Onias into leaving the sanctuary, then imprisoned him unlawfully. (unlawfully: illegally) **35.** This unjust act caused outrage among Jews and other nations who mourned Onias' murder. (outrage: strong anger) **36.** When the king returned from Cilicia, the Jews and Greeks who abhorred the deed protested Onias' unjust killing. (Cilicia: an ancient region) (abhorred: hated) **37.** Antiochus, moved by Onias' modest behavior, wept in sorrow. (modest: humble or not boastful) **38.** Filled with anger, Antiochus stripped Andronicus of his purple, paraded him through the city, and executed him at the same place where he had wronged Onias. (purple: a royal color) **39.** Many sacrileges committed by Lysimachus and Menelaus became widely known, and the people gathered against Lysimachus as gold vessels were stolen. (sacrileges: violations of sacred things) **40.** The angry crowd, led by Auranus, a foolish old man, confronted Lysimachus, who armed 3,000 men to resist. (foolish: lacking sense) **41.** The crowd fought back with stones, clubs, and dust, wounding many, and forcing them to flee. Lysimachus was killed beside the treasury. **42.** The people accused Menelaus for these actions. **43.** When the king came to Tyre, three senators defended the cause. **44.** Menelaus, convicted, promised to pay Ptolemy, son of Dorymenes, to sway the king's favor. (sway: influence) **45.** Ptolemy, taking the king aside, changed his mind. **46.** He freed Menelaus from charges, despite his guilt, and condemned to death the innocent men who had pleaded their case. (condemned: declared to be wrong) **47.** The innocent men were punished while Menelaus, the cause of the turmoil, was spared. (turmoil: confusion or disorder) **48.** The righteous defenders of the city, its people, and the sacred vessels suffered unjust punishment. (righteous: morally right) (sacred: holy or religiously important) **49.** Even the people of Tyre, disgusted by Menelaus' actions, ensured the innocent men were honorably buried. (disgusted: filled with revulsion) **50.** Menelaus remained in power, growing more malicious, a great traitor to the people. (malicious: intending to harm) (traitor: someone who betrays)

Chapter 5

1. At the same time, Antiochus prepared for his second campaign in Egypt. **2.** For nearly forty days, horsemen in golden armor, armed with lances, appeared in the sky, resembling soldiers in battle. (lances: long spears) **3.** They fought in the air, clashing with shields, pikes, swords, and darts, with glittering armor and various weapons. (pikes: long, pointed weapons) (darts: small throwing weapons) **4.** People prayed that this vision would bring good. **5.** When a false rumor spread that Antiochus was dead, Jason took a thousand men and attacked the city, defeating those on the walls. Menelaus fled to the castle. (rumor: unverified information) **6.** Jason mercilessly killed his fellow citizens, thinking them enemies, not realizing the harm it would cause. (mercilessly: without pity or compassion) **7.** Despite his actions, Jason did not gain control but was shamed for his betrayal and fled to the Ammonites. (betrayal: the act of being disloyal or treacherous) **8.** Jason, pursued and hated, was accused before King Aretas of Arabia and cast out to Egypt. (pursued: chased) (cast out: thrown away or expelled) **9.** Having driven many from their land, Jason ended up in Sparta, seeking help from his kin. (kin: family or relatives) **10.** He who had denied the dead proper burials had no one to mourn him, nor a proper funeral. (denied: refused) (burials: the act of burying the dead) (mourn: show sorrow for a loss) **11.** When the king heard of these events, he thought Judea had rebelled, so he marched in fury from Egypt and took the city by force. (fury: extreme anger) **12.** Antiochus ordered his soldiers to kill anyone they encountered, including those on rooftops. (encountered: met) **13.** Men, women, children, virgins, and infants were all slaughtered. (virgins: young women who have not had sexual relations) **14.** Over three days, 80,000 were killed, and just as many were sold into slavery. (slavery: the condition of being owned and forced to work without pay) **15.** Antiochus, not content, entered the holy temple with Menelaus, desecrating it by taking sacred vessels and giving them away. (content: satisfied) (desecrating: treating something sacred with disrespect) (vessels: containers) **16.** He defiled the holy things dedicated by previous kings for the glory of the temple. (defiled: polluted or desecrated) (dedicated: set apart for a special purpose) **17.** Antiochus was arrogant, unaware that God was allowing the city's sins to bring about this judgment. (arrogant: showing a high opinion of oneself) (judgment: the act of judging or punishing) **18.** Had the people not been sinful, Antiochus would have been punished, as Heliodorus had been when he tried to rob the treasury. (sinful: guilty of sin or wrongdoings) (treasury: a place where money or valuables are stored) **19.** God did not choose the temple for the sake of the place, but for the people. (sake: purpose or reason) **20.** The temple shared in the nation's suffering but would later share in its restoration, once the people were reconciled to God. (restoration: the act of returning something to its original state) (reconciled: brought into agreement or peace) **21.** Antiochus took 1,800 talents from the temple and rushed to Antioch, planning to conquer more with his prideful ambition. (talents: units of weight or money in ancient times) (conquer: to gain control over by force) (prideful: having excessive self-importance) (ambition: a strong desire to achieve something) **22.** He left oppressive governors in charge: Philip in Jerusalem, Andronicus in Garizim, and Menelaus, who was cruel to the Jews. (oppressive: harsh and unjust) (governors: people who rule over a region) **23.** He sent Apollonius with 22,000 soldiers to kill all men of fighting age and enslave women and children. (enslave: make someone a slave) **24.** Apollonius came to Jerusalem, pretending peace, and waited for the Sabbath. (pretending: making something appear as if it were true) **25.** On the Sabbath, he commanded his soldiers to arm themselves and attacked, killing many who were observing the holy day. (Sabbath: a day of rest and worship in Judaism) (arm: equip with weapons) **26.** He slaughtered anyone he found celebrating the Sabbath, running through the city with weapons. (slaughtered: killed in a brutal manner) **27.** Judas Maccabeus and about nine others escaped into the wilderness, living like beasts and eating herbs to avoid defilement. (defilement: the act of making something unclean or impure) (wilderness: an uninhabited area of land) (herbs: plants used for food or medicine) (beasts: animals, especially wild ones)

Chapter 6

1. Shortly after, the king sent an old man from Athens to force the Jews to abandon their laws and not live by God's commandments. (commandments: rules or laws given by God) **2.** He also aimed to defile the temple in Jerusalem, renaming it the temple of Jupiter Olympius, and in Garizim, the temple of Jupiter the Defender of Strangers. (defile: to make unclean or impure) (Jupiter Olympius: a title for the Roman god Jupiter) (Garizim: a mountain in Samaria) **3.** This action brought great distress to the people. (distress: extreme worry or pain) **4.** The temple was filled with revelry, as Gentiles engaged in immoral acts and brought unlawful items into the holy places. (revelry: lively and noisy festivities) (Gentiles: non-Jews) (immoral: not conforming to accepted standards of morality) (unlawful: illegal) **5.** The altar was also defiled with forbidden offerings. (forbidden: not allowed) (offerings: gifts or sacrifices given to a god) **6.** It was illegal for anyone to observe the Sabbath, fasts, or to identify as a Jew. (observe: to follow or keep) (Sabbath: a day of rest and worship in Judaism) (fasts: periods of not eating for religious reasons) **7.** On the king's birthday, Jews were forced to partake in sacrifices, and during the Bacchus festival, they had to participate in idol processions. (Bacchus: the Roman god of wine and revelry) (idol: a false god or image worshipped) **8.** A decree was issued to neighboring cities, urging Jews to adopt Gentile customs and partake in their sacrifices. (decree: an official order) (urge: to strongly encourage) **9.** Anyone who refused to conform was sentenced to death, and the suffering was evident. (conform: to comply with rules or standards) **10.** Two women who circumcised their children were publicly executed by being thrown from the city wall. (circumcised: the act of removing the foreskin of the male genitals, a religious practice in Judaism) **11.** Others, who secretly kept the Sabbath in caves, were burned alive when discovered. (burned alive: killed by fire) **12.** Let those who read this not lose heart, for these punishments were not for destruction but to correct the nation. (heart: courage or spirit) (correct: to make right) **13.** It is a sign of God's goodness that wrongdoers are swiftly punished. (wrongdoers: people who commit wrong acts) **14.** Unlike other nations, God does not delay punishing us until our sin reaches its peak. (delay: to postpone) (sin: wrongdoing or moral failure) (peak: highest point) **15.** This is to prevent us from reaching the fullness of sin, after which punishment would be inevitable. (fullness: complete extent) (inevitable: certain to happen) **16.** God does not withdraw His mercy from us; even in adversity, He does not forsake His people. (withdraw: to take away) (mercy: compassion or forgiveness) (adversity: hardship or misfortune) (forsake: to abandon) **17.** Let this serve as a warning to us. Now, we will briefly explain the matter. (serve: to act as) (warning: a caution or advice) **18.** Eleazar, a respected elder and scribe, was forced to eat swine's flesh. (elder: an older, respected person) (scribe: a person who writes or copies documents) (swine: pigs) **19.** Choosing death over dishonor, he rejected the food and willingly faced torture. (dishonor: shame or disgrace) (rejected: refused or declined) (torture: the act of causing extreme pain to punish) **20.** Those who resist such unlawful demands should be prepared to suffer for righteousness. (resist: to oppose or fight against) (unlawful: illegal) (righteousness: morally right behavior) **21.** The authorities, recognizing Eleazar's age and friendship, tried to persuade him to pretend to eat lawful food, to save his life. (authorities: people in power) (persuade: to convince) (pretend: to act as if something is true) **22.** In doing so, they offered him a way out, believing he would find favor by pretending. (favor: approval or support) **23.** But Eleazar, valuing his honor, refused and chose to die rather than dishonor God. (valuing: considering as important or precious) **24.** At his age, he felt it would mislead others into thinking he had forsaken his faith. (mislead: to guide someone in the wrong direction) (forsaken: abandoned or given up) **25.** He feared that, for a moment's survival, young people might be deceived by his hypocrisy, tarnishing his legacy. (hypocrisy: pretending to have moral standards one does not have) (tarnishing: damaging or spoiling) (legacy: something handed down from the past) **26.** Though he could be spared from earthly punishment, he knew he could not escape God's judgment. (spared: saved from harm) (earthly: related to the physical world) (judgment: the act of judging or condemning) **27.** Therefore, he chose to face death bravely, as befitted his age and faith. (befitted: suited or appropriate for) **28.** He left an example for the youth to die courageously for God's laws. Eleazar went to his torment immediately after speaking these words. (example: a model for others to follow) (courageously: with bravery) (torment: severe physical or mental suffering) **29.** Those who led him, once filled with goodwill, now saw him as a desperate man because of his firm resolve. (goodwill: kindness or favor) (resolve: determination) **30.** As he endured beatings, Eleazar groaned, acknowledging that while he could have avoided death, his soul was at peace, knowing he suffered for God's sake. (endured: suffered through) (groaned: made a low sound of pain or discomfort) (acknowledging: admitting or recognizing) (sake: reason or purpose) **31.** Thus, Eleazar died, leaving a legacy of courage and virtue, inspiring not only the youth but all of Israel. (virtue: moral excellence or goodness)

Chapter 7
1. Seven brothers and their mother were captured, forced by the king to eat pork, and tortured. (pork: pig meat) **2.** The first said, "We are ready to die rather than break our fathers' laws." (fathers' laws: ancestral commandments) **3.** The king, angered, ordered the pans to be heated. (pans: cooking vessels) **4.** The first brother's tongue was cut out and his body dismembered while his family watched. (dismembered: torn apart) **5.** He was thrown into the fire, and his family encouraged each other to die courageously. (courageously: bravely) **6.** "The Lord sees us and comforts us," they said, "as Moses declared for His servants." (comforts: gives relief) **7.** After the first brother died, the second was mocked. They pulled off his scalp and asked if he would eat. (scalp: head skin) (mocked: ridiculed) **8.** He refused and endured the same fate. (endured: suffered) **9.** As he died, he said, "You take our lives, but God will raise us up to eternal life." (eternal: forever) **10.** The third brother was mocked, but he stuck out his tongue and held out his hands. (mocked: ridiculed) **11.** He said, "These hands are from heaven. I trust God will return them." (return: give back) **12.** The king marveled at his courage. (marveled: admired) **13.** After the third died, the fourth was tortured. (tortured: caused pain) **14.** He said, "It is good to die by human hands, for God will raise me again." (raise: bring back to life) **15.** The fifth brother was brought and tortured. **16.** He said to the king, "You have power over men, but you are mortal. God hasn't forsaken us." (mortal: subject to death) (forsaken: abandoned) **17.** "Wait and see His power. He will punish you and your descendants." (descendants: children and future generations) **18.** The sixth brother said, "We suffer for our sins, and marvelous things happen to us." (marvelous: extraordinary) **19.** "Do not think you will escape punishment for fighting against God." (escape: avoid) **20.** The mother showed great courage, enduring the deaths of her sons with hope in the Lord. (enduring: suffering through) **21.** She encouraged each of them with strong words, showing resolve. (resolve: determination) **22.** She said, "I did not give you life or form your bodies." (form: create) **23.** "But the Creator of the world will give you life again because you gave up yours for His laws." (Creator: maker) (life: existence) **24.** Antiochus, insulted, promised the youngest wealth and power if he turned from his fathers' laws. (insulted: offended) (wealth: riches) **25.** The king urged the mother to persuade her son to save his life. (persuade: convince) **26.** She agreed to speak with him. **27.** She mocked the king and said, "My son, I carried you for nine months and raised you with trouble." (mocked: ridiculed) (raised: cared for) **28.** "Look at the heavens and the earth, which God made from nothing, as He made mankind." (heavens: the sky or universe) (mankind: humanity) **29.** "Do not fear this tormentor. Die like your brothers, and I'll receive you again." (tormentor: one who causes suffering) **30.** The young man declared, "I will not obey the king. I will follow God's law." (declare: state firmly) **31.** "You will not escape God's judgment for what you've done to the Hebrews." (judgment: punishment) **32.** "We suffer for our sins." (sins: wrongs) **33.** "Though God is angry with us for a short time, He will reconcile with His servants." (reconcile: make peace) (servants: followers) **34.** "You, wicked man, will not escape the judgment of God, who sees all." (wicked: evil) **35.** "Our brothers are dead but under God's everlasting covenant. You will face punishment for your pride." (everlasting: eternal) (covenant: agreement) **36.** "I offer my life for our fathers' laws, hoping God will show mercy and end the wrath upon us." (wrath: anger) **37.** "May you acknowledge that only God is true, and may His wrath cease through us." (acknowledge: recognize) **38.** The king, enraged, tortured him more, offended by being mocked. (enraged: very angry) (offended: insulted) **39.** The man died pure, trusting fully in the Lord. (pure: sinless) **40.** Finally, after all her sons, the mother died. **41.** This concludes the account of the idolatrous feasts and extreme tortures. (idolatrous: idol-worshipping) **42.** Let this be enough to speak of the painful events.

Chapter 8
1. Judas Maccabeus and his followers gathered 6,000 men and prayed for God's mercy on the oppressed. (oppressed: suffering people) **2.** They asked God to restore the city and punish the wicked. (wicked: evil people) **3.** Maccabeus and his men, with God's help, struck down their enemies. (struck down: defeated) **4.** He burned towns, took key positions, and attacked by night. (key: important) **5.** Philip, seeing Maccabeus' success, asked Ptolemeus for reinforcements. (reinforcements: additional soldiers) **6.** Nicanor, with 20,000 men, was sent to destroy the Jews, assisted by Gorgias. **7.** Nicanor planned to sell Jews to raise money for the king's tribute. (tribute: payment to the king) **8.** He announced the sale of Jews at 90 for one talent. (talent: a unit of money) **9.** Hearing of Nicanor's arrival, some fled, while others prayed for deliverance. (deliverance: rescue) **10.** They prayed for God to save them for His name's sake. (name's sake: for His glory) **11.** Maccabeus gathered 6,000 men, urging them to trust God and fight. (urging: encouraging) **12.** He reminded them that their faith was in God, not in weapons. (faith: trust) **13.** Maccabeus recalled how God helped their ancestors, like defeating Sennacherib's army. **14.** He also shared the story of how 8,000 Jews defeated 120,000 Galatians. **15.** Encouraged, Maccabeus divided his army into four parts with his brothers. (encouraged: inspired) **16.** Each leader had 1,500 men, and Eleazar read the holy book. (Eleazar: a respected leader) **17.** With God's help, they killed 9,000 of Nicanor's men and scattered the rest. (scattered: dispersed) **18.** They took the enemy's money but stopped as the Sabbath approached. (Sabbath: holy day of rest) **19.** They gave thanks to God and observed the Sabbath. (observed: kept) **20.** Afterward, they shared the spoils with the needy. (spoils: loot) (needy: poor) **21.** They prayed for God's forgiveness and mercy. (forgiveness: pardon) **22.** They defeated 20,000 of Timotheus' men, taking strongholds and spoils. (strongholds: fortified positions) **23.** The poor and elderly shared in the spoils. **24.** They stored the armor and brought the spoils to Jerusalem. (stored: kept) **25.** They killed Philarches, who had harmed the Jews. (harmed: hurt) **26.** They burned Callisthenes, who had burned the holy gates. (burned: destroyed by fire) **27.** Nicanor, defeated, fled in disgrace to Antioch. (disgrace: shame) **28.** Nicanor admitted that God protected the Jews. (admitted: confessed) **29.** He acknowledged that the Jews could not be harmed because they followed God's laws. **30.** Nicanor's defeat showed God's protection over the Jews. **31.** Maccabeus and his men continued to succeed with God's help. (succeed: win) **32.** They celebrated their victory, thanking God for His protection. **33.** The enemy was defeated, and the Jews defended their land. (defended: protected) **34.** Maccabeus and his men showed courage, trusting in God. (courage: bravery) **35.** Their victory was seen as a sign of God's favor. (favor: approval) **36.** The story of their triumph spread, showing that God fought for them. (triumph: victory)

Chapter 9
1. Antiochus returned in shame from Persia. (shame: disgrace) **2.** He tried to seize Persepolis, but the people defended themselves, forcing him to flee. (seize: capture) **3.** Upon reaching Ecbatane, Antiochus learned of Nicanor and Timotheus' defeat. **4.** Angered, he swore to destroy Jerusalem and the Jews. **5.** But God struck him with a painful, incurable illness. (incurable: impossible to heal) **6.** This was just, as he had inflicted similar suffering on others. (just: deserved) **7.** Despite his pain, he continued boasting, but soon fell from his chariot in agony. (boasting: bragging) **8.** He, who once thought himself invincible, was now humiliated and carried in a litter. (invincible: unbeatable) (litter: a covered vehicle carried by men) **9.** Worms rose from his body, and his flesh rotted, causing unbearable stench. (rotted: decayed) (stench: horrible smell) **10.** His pride turned to shame as his body decayed. **11.** Finally, he admitted that no mortal should boast like a god. (mortal: human) **12.** He acknowledged God's judgment and repented, vowing to change his ways. (repented: regretted) **13.** Antiochus promised to free the Jews, restore the temple, and make amends. (amends: make things right) **14.** He pledged to treat the Jews equally with the Athenians. **15.** He offered to restore the temple with more gifts and funds for sacrifices. **16.** He even vowed to convert to Judaism and spread God's power. (convert: change beliefs) **17.** But his suffering continued, as God's judgment remained. **18.** Desperate, he wrote a letter to the Jews, apologizing and seeking forgiveness. (desperate: in great need) **19.** Antiochus wished the Jews prosperity and health. (prosperity: success) **20.** He thanked God for their welfare, hoping for his own recovery. **21.** He explained his illness and his concern for the safety of his kingdom. **22.** Despite his hopes, his sickness grew worse. **23.** He recalled how his father had prepared a successor in case of trouble. **24.** He named his son Antiochus as his successor, ensuring the kingdom's stability. **25.** He asked the Jews to remain loyal to him and his son. **26.** He believed his son would be kind to them. **27.** Antiochus urged the Jews to remember his past kindness. **28.** The wicked king died a painful death in a foreign land, far from his kingdom.

(wicked: evil) **29.** His body was taken by Philip, who fled to Egypt, fearing Antiochus' son.

Chapter 10

1. Maccabeus and his group, guided by God, reclaimed the temple and city. **2.** They tore down the heathen altars and chapels in the streets. (heathen: pagan) **3.** After cleansing the temple, they built a new altar and offered sacrifices, incense, lights, and shewbread. (shewbread: special bread offered in the temple) **4.** They prayed to God for mercy, asking not to face such troubles again. **5.** On the same day the temple had been defiled, it was cleansed, the 25th of Casleu. (defiled: polluted, made unclean) **6.** They celebrated eight days, like the Feast of Tabernacles, remembering their past suffering. **7.** They waved branches, palms, and sang psalms, thanking God for their success. **8.** A decree was made to celebrate these days annually. **9.** This marks the end of Antiochus Epiphanes. **10.** Now we recount the deeds of Antiochus Eupator, his son, briefly. **11.** Eupator appointed Lysias as governor of Syria and Phoenicia. **12.** Ptolemeus Macron, sympathetic to the Jews, sought peace with them. **13.** Accused of treason, Macron, discouraged, poisoned himself. (treason: betrayal) **14.** Gorgias, the governor, hired soldiers and waged war against the Jews. **15.** The Idumeans, holding strongholds, received exiled Jews and fostered conflict. (fostered: encouraged) **16.** Maccabeus and his men prayed for God's help and attacked the Idumean strongholds. **17.** They captured the strongholds, killing 20,000. **18.** Nine thousand Idumeans fled to two strong castles, well-stocked for a siege. (siege: military blockade) **19.** Maccabeus left Simon, Joseph, and Zaccheus to besiege the castles while he helped elsewhere. **20.** Simon's men, greedy for money, accepted a bribe, allowing some to escape. (bribe: illegal payment to influence actions) **21.** Maccabeus, learning of this, condemned the traitors and took the castles. (traitors: those who betray) **22.** He killed the traitors and captured both castles, killing over 20,000. **23.** Timotheus, who had been defeated before, gathered a great army to attack the Jews. **24.** Maccabeus and his men prayed and prepared for battle. **25.** They prayed for God's mercy, asking for victory over their enemies. **26.** After praying, they armed themselves and went to meet their foes. **27.** At dawn, the two forces clashed, with Maccabeus' army relying on God's help. **28.** In battle, five men on horses appeared from heaven, leading the Jews and protecting Maccabeus. **29.** The heavenly figures attacked the enemies with arrows and lightning, causing blindness and confusion. **30.** The enemy lost 20,500 foot soldiers and 600 horsemen. **31.** Timotheus fled to a stronghold called Gawra, where Chereas was governor. **32.** Maccabeus' men courageously laid siege to the fortress for four days. **33.** Inside, the enemies blasphemed, mocking the Jews. (blasphemed: insulted sacred things) **34.** On the fifth day, 20 young men from Maccabeus' army attacked the wall, killing many. **35.** Others set the towers on fire, burning the blasphemers alive, and broke open the gates. **36.** Maccabeus' army entered the fortress, killing Timotheus, Chereas, and Apollophanes. **37.** Afterward, they praised God for the great victory He had given them. **38.** They thanked God for delivering Israel and giving them triumph. (triumph: victory)

Chapter 11

1. Lysias, the king's protector and cousin, took great offense at what had been done. **2.** He gathered 80,000 men and horsemen, intending to turn the city into a Gentile settlement. (Gentile: non-Jewish person) **3.** He planned to profit from the temple, like other heathen temples, and sell the high priesthood every year. (heathen: pagan) **4.** He failed to consider God's power, relying on his vast army of foot soldiers, horsemen, and elephants. **5.** Lysias came to Judea, approached the strong town of Bethsura, about five furlongs from Jerusalem, and laid siege. (furlongs: a measure of distance) **6.** Upon hearing of the siege, Maccabeus and the people prayed for a good angel to deliver Israel. **7.** Maccabeus took up arms, urging others to join him in helping their brethren; they moved forward with determination. (brethren: brothers, fellow people) **8.** As they neared Jerusalem, they saw a figure on horseback in white, with golden armor. **9.** They praised God, gaining courage to fight not just men, but fierce beasts and even iron walls. **10.** With divine help, they marched in armor, for God was merciful to them. (divine: related to God) **11.** They charged their enemies like lions, defeating 11,000 foot soldiers, 1,600 horsemen, and scattering the rest. **12.** Many enemies, wounded, fled naked, and Lysias escaped in shame. **13.** Lysias, reflecting on his defeat, realized that the Hebrews, aided by God, could not be beaten, so he sent a message. **14.** He persuaded them to accept reasonable terms, promising to convince the king to be their friend. **15.** Maccabeus agreed to Lysias's terms, prioritizing the common good, and whatever Maccabeus wrote was accepted by the king. **16.** Lysias sent letters to the Jews saying: "Lysias sends greetings to the people of the Jews." **17.** "John and Absolom, whom you sent, delivered my petition and requested its fulfillment." **18.** "I have reported what was necessary to the king, and he has granted what was possible." **19.** "If you remain loyal, I will continue to support your interests." **20.** "I have also instructed those from me to discuss with you the specific matters." **21.** "Farewell. 148th year, 24th day of the month Dioscorinthius." (Dioscorinthius: a month in the ancient Greek calendar) **22.** The king's letter to Lysias read: "King Antiochus to his brother Lysias sends greetings." **23.** "Since our father has passed to the gods, we desire peace in our realm, allowing everyone to attend to their own affairs." **24.** "We know the Jews resisted our father's request to adopt Gentile customs and prefer to live by their own laws." **25.** "We have decided to grant them peace and restore their temple, so they may follow their forefathers' ways." **26.** "You should send them peace, assuring them of our intentions, so they can continue their affairs with confidence." **27.** The king's letter to the Jewish council and the people read: "King Antiochus sends greetings to the council and all Jews." **28.** "If you are well, we are pleased; we are also in good health." **29.** "Menelaus informed us of your wish to return home and follow your own business." (Menelaus: a high-ranking Jewish official) **30.** "Those who wish to leave may do so safely until the 30th day of Xanthicus." (Xanthicus: a month in the ancient Greek calendar) **31.** "The Jews may continue to follow their laws and customs, and none will be troubled for any unintentional mistakes." **32.** "I have sent Menelaus to comfort you." **33.** "Farewell. In the 148th year, 15th day of Xanthicus." **34.** The Romans sent a letter saying: "Quintus Memmius and Titus Manlius, Roman ambassadors, send greetings to the Jews." **35.** "We are pleased with all Lysias has granted." **36.** "For matters he referred to the king, send someone to advise us, and we will declare what is convenient." **37.** "Send someone quickly so we know your decision." **38.** "Farewell. 148th year, 15th day of Xanthicus."

Chapter 12

1. After these agreements, Lysias went to the king, and the Jews resumed their work. **2.** However, governors like Timotheus and Apollonius disturbed the Jews' peace. **3.** The people of Joppa deceived the Jews, inviting them onto boats, only to drown over two hundred. **4.** When Judas learned of this, he ordered his men to prepare for battle. **5.** He prayed to God for justice, then burned the boats and killed those who fled. **6.** After securing the town, Judas planned to attack Joppa. **7.** Hearing of a similar plot by the Jamnites, he attacked them at night. (Jamnites: people from Jamnia, an ancient city) **8.** The fire he set was seen from Jerusalem, two hundred and forty furlongs away. (furlongs: a unit of distance, about 220 yards or 201 meters) **9.** As Judas moved towards Timotheus, the Arabs attacked, but Judas' forces triumphed. **10.** The Arabs begged for peace, and Judas agreed, believing they would be useful. **11.** Judas then tried to build a bridge to Caspis, but the people resisted. **12.** They mocked Judas and trusted in their city's defenses. **13.** Judas prayed to God, then launched an assault and captured the city. (assault: a sudden attack) **14.** The slaughter was so great that a nearby lake was filled with blood. (slaughter: killing, especially in a brutal way) **15.** They traveled to Characa, where they found Timotheus had left. **16.** Dositheus and Sosipater killed over ten thousand of Timotheus' men. **17.** Judas divided his army and prepared to face Timotheus, who had a large force. **18.** Timotheus sent his baggage, women, and children to a fortress called Carnion. (baggage: personal belongings) **19.** Upon seeing Judas' forces, Timotheus' men fled, injuring each other in the chaos. (chaos: complete disorder) **20.** Judas pursued them, killing about thirty thousand of the enemy. **21.** Timotheus was captured by Dositheus and Sosipater but spared after promising peace. (spared: saved from harm) **22.** Judas then marched on Carnion and killed twenty-five thousand people. **23.** After the victory, he moved towards Ephron, a city with strong defenses. (defenses: structures or actions meant to protect) **24.** With God's help, they took the city and killed twenty-five thousand defenders. (defenders: people who protect a place) **25.** They then traveled to Scythopolis, six hundred furlongs from Jerusalem. (Scythopolis: an ancient city in the region of the Decapolis) **26.** The Jews there treated them kindly, and Judas thanked them. **27.** After the Feast of Weeks, they returned to Jerusalem. (Feast of Weeks: a Jewish festival, also called Shavuot, celebrating the giving of the Torah) **28.** They then confronted Gorgias, governor of Idumea, who came out with a large army. **29.** A few Jews were slain, but Judas' forces won the battle. (slain: killed) **30.** During the fight, Dositheus grabbed Gorgias, but a Thracian soldier injured him, forcing Gorgias to flee. (Thracian: a person from ancient Thrace, an area in modern-day Greece and Turkey) **31.** After a long struggle, Judas' army attacked and defeated Gorgias' men. (struggle: a fight or conflict) **32.** Judas sang psalms and led a surprise charge, putting the enemy to flight. (charge: a quick attack; psalms: sacred songs or hymns) **33.** They then camped in Odollam and rested on the Sabbath. (Sabbath: the Jewish day of rest, observed from Friday evening to Saturday evening) **34.** The next day, they gathered the bodies of their fallen comrades to bury them. (comrades: fellow soldiers or companions) **35.** Under the slain men's coats, they found idols, which violated Jewish law. (idols: images or statues worshiped as gods; violated: broke or disobeyed) **36.** The discovery revealed the cause of their deaths, and the Jews praised God. **37.** They prayed for forgiveness and urged others to avoid sin. (urged: strongly recommended) **38.** Judas gathered two thousand drachms for a sin offering, hoping for the resurrection of the dead. (drachms: ancient Greek coins; sin offering: a sacrifice to atone for sin) **39.** He believed praying for the dead was not in vain, as they would rise again. (vain: without success or result) **40.** Judas made a reconciliation for the dead, hoping to free them from sin. (reconciliation: the restoration of friendly relations) **41.** His actions showed his faith in the afterlife and God's justice. **42.** Judas exhorted the people to remain pure, mindful of the consequences of sin. (exhorted: strongly encouraged) **43.** He sent the offering to Jerusalem, hoping it would aid the dead in their resurrection. **44.** He believed in the power of prayer for the dead and the hope of resurrection. **45.** Judas' act of reconciliation showed his care for both the living and the dead.

Chapter 13

1. In the 149th year, Judas learned that Antiochus Eupator was coming with a great army into Judea. **2.** Antiochus had 110,000 foot soldiers, 5,300 horsemen, 22 elephants, and 300 chariots with hooks. **3.** Menelaus joined him, pretending to support Antiochus, hoping to become governor. **4.** However, God moved Antiochus against Menelaus, and Lysias informed the king of his wickedness, leading to his death. **5.** Menelaus was executed in a tower, as was the punishment for sacrilege. (sacrilege: violation or profanation of something sacred) **6.** He died a shameful death, without burial, because of his crimes against the altar. **7.** This death was just, as he had defiled the holy altar. (defiled: polluted or desecrated) **8.** Antiochus came with a cruel plan to harm the Jews even more than his father had. **9.** Judas, seeing this, called on the people to pray for God's help against the coming threat. **10.** He urged them to pray day and night, asking God to protect their law, land, and temple. **11.** They fasted and prayed for three days, seeking mercy and guidance. (fasted: abstained from food for religious reasons) **12.** After praying, Judas prepared his men for battle. **13.** Judas and the elders decided to fight before the king's army could take Judea. **14.** Trusting in God, Judas encouraged his soldiers to fight for their laws, temple, and land, camping at Modin. **15.** With the battle cry "Victory is of God," Judas led a night attack, killing 4,000 men and the chief elephant. **16.** The attack caused fear and chaos in the enemy camp, and Judas withdrew successfully. (chaos: complete disorder) **17.** The victory was granted by God and took place at dawn. **18.** The king, impressed by the Jews' courage, tried to capture their strongholds by strategy. **19.** He attacked Bethsura, a fortified Jewish city, but was defeated, losing many men. (fortified: strengthened or protected with defenses) **20.** Judas had sent supplies to Bethsura's defenders, strengthening their resistance. **21.** Rhodocus, a traitor in the Jewish camp, revealed the secrets to the enemy and was imprisoned. (traitor: a person who betrays trust) **22.** The king tried again to negotiate with the people of Bethsura, but was defeated by Judas. **23.** The king then learned that Philip, in Antioch, had been defeated, and he submitted to the Jews, offering peace. **24.** The king made Maccabeus the principal governor from Ptolemais to the Gerrhenians. (governor: a person in charge of a region or province) **25.** In Ptolemais, the people were upset about the agreements, wanting to break them. **26.** Lysias addressed the people, persuading them to accept the terms, then returned to Antioch.

Chapter 14

1. Seven brothers and their mother were captured, forced to eat pig's flesh, and tortured. (tortured: subjected to severe pain as punishment or to force a confession) **2.** The first brother said, "We are ready to die rather than break our fathers' laws." **3.** In his rage, the king heated pans and cauldrons. (cauldrons: large metal pots used for boiling) **4.** The first brother's tongue was cut, and his body mutilated while the others watched. (mutilated: severely damaged or disfigured) **5.** He was thrown into the fire, encouraging his family to die bravely. **6.** "The Lord sees and comforts us, as Moses said." **7.** The second brother was asked to eat, but he refused and endured the same torture. **8.** He said, "You take our lives, but God will raise us to life." **9.** The third brother courageously put out his tongue and hands, saying he despised them for God's laws. (despised: strongly disliked) **10.** The king marveled at his courage. **11.** The fourth brother said, "It's good to die for God's laws; you won't have resurrection." (resurrection: rising from the dead) **12.** The fifth brother, tortured, said the king should not think their nation is forsaken by God. (forsaken: abandoned or deserted) **13.** "Wait and see how God will punish you." **14.** The sixth brother said they suffered for their sins and warned the king not to fight God. **15.** "You will not escape punishment."

16. The mother endured her sons' deaths with courage, trusting in God's promise of life. **17.** She encouraged them to stay faithful, saying, "God will give you life again." **18.** Antiochus, angry, offered wealth to the youngest if he would abandon the laws. **19.** When the youngest refused, the king urged his mother to convince him to save his life. **20.** She promised, then mocked the king and said, "I gave you life; God will give it again." **21.** "Look at the heavens and earth—God made them and mankind." **22.** "Don't fear the torment; die bravely so I can be reunited with you." **23.** The youngest said, "I will obey God's law, not the king's." **24.** "You, who harmed the Hebrews, will not escape God's judgment." **25.** "We suffer for our sins, but God will reconcile with us." (reconcile: restore friendly relations) **26.** "You will not escape the judgment of God." **27.** "Our brothers died for God's covenant; you will be punished for your pride." (covenant: a solemn agreement) **28.** "I offer my life for our fathers' laws, praying for God's mercy on our nation." **29.** "May God's wrath cease through our deaths." (wrath: intense anger) **30.** The king, enraged, tortured the youngest more than the others. **31.** The youngest died, trusting fully in the Lord. **32.** After all the sons died, the mother also passed away. **33.** Let this suffice to describe the feasts and tortures they endured. (suffice: be enough) **34.** The mother's courage and faith stood as an example. **35.** The seven brothers' brave deaths were honored for their steadfastness. (steadfastness: loyalty or dedication) **36.** Their sacrifice was a testament to their faith in God. (testament: a statement of belief or principle) **37.** God's law and their willingness to die for it were the true victory. **38.** Their deaths showed the power of faith over tyranny. (tyranny: cruel and oppressive government rule) **39.** The mother's faith shone brightly in the face of grief. **40.** The family's courage was an inspiration for generations to come. **41.** Each brother's death brought them closer to eternal life. (eternal: lasting forever) **42.** Their story became a lasting legacy of faith and courage. (legacy: something handed down from the past)

Chapter 15

1. Nicanor, learning that Judas was in the strongholds near Samaria, planned to attack on the Sabbath. **2.** The Jews with him urged, "Honor the holy day God made above all others." **3.** Nicanor asked if there was a Mighty One in heaven who commanded the Sabbath. **4.** They answered, "The living Lord in heaven commanded the seventh day to be kept." **5.** Nicanor arrogantly said, "I command arms for the king's business," but his will was blocked. (arrogantly: with an attitude of superiority) **6.** Nicanor decided to build a monument to his victory over Judas and his group. (monument: a structure built to honor a person or event) **7.** Maccabeus trusted that the Lord would help him. **8.** He urged his people to remember past help from heaven and expect victory now. **9.** Comforting them with the law, the prophets, and past victories, he gave them courage. **10.** He armed them with words, reminding them of the heathens' falsehoods. (heathens: people who do not believe in God; falsehoods: lies) **11.** He shared a dream that greatly encouraged them. **12.** In his vision, Onias, the former high priest, prayed for the Jews. **13.** A glorious man appeared, and Onias said, "This is Jeremias, the prophet." **14.** Jeremias gave Judas a golden sword, saying, "Take this gift from God." **15.** Encouraged, they decided to fight to protect the temple. **16.** They feared for the holy temple more than their families. (holy: sacred or consecrated) **17.** Those in the city were anxious about the battle outside. (anxious: worried or fearful) **18.** As the battle neared, Maccabeus prayed for God's aid. **19.** "O Lord, you sent your angel to destroy 185,000 of Sennacherib's army." (angel: a messenger from God) **20.** "Send your angel now to strike fear into our enemies." **21.** "Let them be terrified as they come to blaspheme your people." (blaspheme: show disrespect or speak irreverently about God) **22.** His prayer ended. **23.** Nicanor and his army came with trumpets and songs. **24.** Judas and his men prayed, trusting in God. **25.** Fighting and praying, they killed 35,000 enemies, encouraged by God's presence. **26.** Afterward, they learned Nicanor had died in his armor. **27.** They rejoiced and praised God in their language. **28.** Judas ordered Nicanor's head and hand to be brought to Jerusalem. **29.** He showed them Nicanor's head and hand, which had been raised against the temple. **30.** He cut out Nicanor's tongue and had it given to the birds. (tongue: the organ in the mouth used for speaking) **31.** The people praised God, saying, "Blessed be the One who keeps His place undefiled." (undefiled: pure, not tainted) **32.** Nicanor's head was hung as a sign of God's help. **33.** They decreed the 30th of Adar should be celebrated every year. (decreed: officially ordered or commanded) **34.** From then on, the Hebrews had control of the city. **35.** If the story is well told, it's as I wished; if poorly, it's what I could manage. **36.** Just as wine with water delights the taste, well-crafted speech delights the reader. The end. (well-crafted: skillfully made or constructed) **37.** If I have told it well, it is as I desired; if poorly, it is what I could do. **38.** As wine mixed with water pleases the taste, so finely crafted speech delights the ear. The end. (finely crafted: made with great skill)

75 – The Third book of Maccabees

Chapter 1

1. When Philopater learned that Antiochus had taken control of his territories, he ordered his infantry and cavalry to assemble, taking his sister Arsinoe with him, and marched toward Raphia, where Antiochus had camped. (Raphia: a region near the Egyptian border) **2.** Theodotus, planning to execute his mission, took the bravest soldiers trusted by Ptolemy, and at night reached Ptolemy's tent to kill him and end the war. (Theodotus: a trusted military leader) **3.** Dositheus, a Jew who had renounced his faith, secretly helped Ptolemy escape, replacing him with an innocent man in the tent, who met Ptolemy's intended fate. (Dositheus: a Jewish renegade) **4.** A fierce battle ensued with Antiochus's forces initially gaining the upper hand. Arsinoe moved among the soldiers, pleading for them to fight for their families, offering two minas of gold to the victorious. (Minas: a unit of currency) **5.** The enemy was defeated in close combat, and many were taken prisoner. (Close combat: hand-to-hand fighting) **6.** After this victory, the king decided to visit neighboring cities to raise morale. (Morale: group confidence) **7.** His actions, including generous donations to temples, inspired his people. (Temples: places of worship) **8.** The Jewish elders sent representatives to greet him, and their warm welcome made him eager to visit Jerusalem. (Jewish elders: community leaders) **9.** Upon arriving in Jerusalem, he offered sacrifices and thank offerings to the Greatest God, following all the rituals of the sacred city, and entered the inner court. (Jerusalem: the capital city of ancient Israel) **10.** Impressed by the temple's beauty and order, he considered entering the sanctuary itself. (Sanctuary: the holiest part of the temple) **11.** When told only the high priest could enter once a year, he refused to accept this. (High priest: chief religious leader) **12.** Even after they read the law to him, he insisted on entering, arguing he should not be deprived of this honor. (The law: religious conduct rules) **13.** He questioned why no priests had stopped him from entering other temples. (Priests: religious leaders) **14.** Someone rebuked him for boasting about his actions. (Boasting: excessive pride) **15.** Undeterred, he asked, "Since I've come this far, should I not enter, with or without your consent?" (Consent: permission) **16.** The priests, in their sacred garments, knelt and prayed to the Greatest God for protection, crying out for help against the king's intrusion, **17.** while those in the city became fearful and rushed out, uncertain of what would happen. (Intrusion: unwelcome interference) **18.** Young women, secluded in their rooms, emerged with their mothers, throwing dust and ashes on their heads, filling the streets with cries of grief. (Lamentations: expressions of sorrow) **19.** Women, newly prepared for marriage, abandoned their bridal chambers and ran through the city in panic. (Bridal chambers: rooms for newlywed women) **20.** Mothers and nurses left newborns in homes and fields, but many gathered fervently at the Most High's temple. (Newborns: recently born babies) **21.** Prayers were offered by those assembled to oppose the king's sacrilegious actions. (Sacrilegious: disrespectful to the sacred) **22.** Some citizens, emboldened, refused to submit and rallied to defend their faith and traditions. (Emboldened: made brave) **23.** Calling for arms to defend the law, they caused an uproar, but the elders restrained them and returned them to prayer. (Arms: weapons) **24.** The prayers continued as the multitude gathered. (Multitude: large crowd) **25.** The king's advisers made many attempts to change his mind and stop his reckless actions. (Advisers: counselors) **26.** But he remained resolute, determined to carry out his plan. (Resolute: determined) **27.** Even his officers, seeing this, joined the Jews in praying to God for help against such arrogance. (Imploring: begging earnestly) **28.** The intensity of the cries from the crowd created a deafening uproar. (Uproar: loud commotion) **29.** The people, the walls, and the floor seemed to resound with the desire to protect the sanctity of the temple, preferring death over seeing it defiled. (Sanctity: holiness)

Chapter 2

1. At that moment, High Priest Simon knelt near the holy place, spread his hands in reverence, and prayed. (Holy place: sacred worship site) **2.** "O Lord, our King, Ruler of heaven and all creation, Holy among the holy, the only Sovereign, Almighty, hear us, your servants, oppressed by a wicked man who boasts in his power." **3.** "You, the Creator and Lord of the universe, are a just Governor who judges those who act with arrogance." **4.** "You destroyed the earlier wicked ones, including the giants, who relied on their strength, drowning them in a great flood. (Giants: powerful beings or Nephilim from ancient times)" **5.** "You made the Sodomites an example when You destroyed them with fire and brimstone. (Sodomites: people from Sodom, known for wickedness) (Brimstone: sulfur used in their destruction)" **6.** "You showed Your power when You caused Pharaoh, the enslaver of Your people, to suffer many afflictions. (Pharaoh: ruler of ancient Egypt)" **7.** "You drowned him in the sea when he pursued with chariots, but provided safe passage to those who trusted in You, Creator of all. (The Red Sea: the water parted for the Israelites' escape)" **8.** "They saw Your mighty works and praised You, the Almighty." **9.** "You, O King, when You created the earth, chose this city, making it holy for Your name, though You need nothing. You honored it with Your presence." **10.** "You promised, out of love for Israel, that if we sin, suffer, and pray here, You would hear us." **11.** "Truly, You are faithful and true." **12.** "You aided our ancestors in distress, rescuing them from great dangers." **13.** "Now, O Holy King, see how our sins have weakened us, leaving us vulnerable to our enemies." **14.** "In our suffering, this wicked man seeks to dishonor Your holy place, consecrated for Your name." **15.** "Your dwelling in the heavens is beyond human reach." **16.** "But You revealed Your glory among Israel by sanctifying this place." **17.** "Do not punish us for their impurity or profanity, lest the lawless boast, saying:" **18.** "'We have trampled the holy house as idolaters trample their temples. (Idolaters: those who worship false gods)'" **19.** "Forgive our sins, cleanse us of our iniquities, and show compassion now. (Iniquities: wicked actions)" **20.** "Let Your mercy guide us quickly, granting peace, so the broken-hearted may praise You." **21.** At that time, God, who sees all, heard this prayer and punished the proud and scornful man in justice. **22.** "Shaking him like a reed in the wind, He cast him down, powerless and speechless, by His righteous judgment. (Reed: symbolizing instability)" **23.** "His friends and guards, seeing his swift punishment, feared for his life and quickly removed him." **24.** "When he recovered, he showed no repentance and left, vowing revenge." **25.** "He went to Egypt, growing more wicked with his companions in sin. (Egypt: ancient powerful kingdom)" **26.** "His audacity grew as he spread evil rumors, drawing followers to his cause." **27.** "He aimed to dishonor our people, erecting a stone pillar with this inscription: (Pillar: monument or tall structure) **28.** "'No one may enter this temple unless they sacrifice. All Jews are to be enslaved. Those who resist will be killed.'" **29.** "Those registered will bear the ivy-leaf symbol of Dionysus, reduced to limited rights. (Dionysus: Greek god of wine and revelry)" **30.** "To avoid seeming to hate them all, it was written that those who join the initiated will have equal rights with Alexandrians. (Initiated: those who undergo a ritual to become part of a group) (Alexandrians: people of Alexandria in Egypt)" **31.** "Some leaders, eager to gain favor, submitted to the king, hoping for future honor." **32.** "Most, however, clung to their faith, paying money to avoid registration." **33.** "They looked forward to future help, rejecting the apostates and viewing them as enemies. (Apostates: those who abandon their faith)"

Chapter 3

1. Upon learning this, the king's rage grew, targeting not just the Jews in Alexandria but also those in the countryside. He ordered their gathering into one place for a brutal execution. (Alexandria: ancient Egyptian city) **2.** During this time, hostile rumors spread by conspirators accused the Jews of blocking adherence to legal decrees. (Ordinances: formal laws or decrees) **3.** The Jews had always been loyal to the ruling kings of Egypt, honoring their agreements with previous rulers. (Kings: rulers or monarchs) **4.** Their worship of God and adherence to His laws required avoiding certain practices, which made them disliked by some. (Distinctions: separations or differences) **5.** Despite this, their good deeds and upright behavior earned them respect. (Virtuous: morally excellent) **6.** This admiration was ignored by outsiders, **7.** who accused the Jews of being unsociable and disloyal to the king due to their exclusive worship and dietary laws, fueling hatred against them. (Animosity: strong hostility) **8.** The sudden oppression of an innocent people caught the attention of the Greek citizens, who sympathized but could not intervene. (Greeks: ancient people of Greece) **9.** "The all-knowing God will not overlook such a great people," they said. (Plight: difficult situation) **10.** Some Jewish neighbors, friends, and business associates secretly promised their support. (Associates: colleagues or partners) **11.** Meanwhile, the king, proud of his power and dismissive of God, wrote a letter against the Jews. (Steadfast: firm and unwavering) **12.** "From King Ptolemy Philopator: greetings to commanders and soldiers in Egypt and beyond! (Ptolemy Philopator: ruler of Egypt in the Ptolemaic dynasty) **13.** I am in good health, and so are my affairs. **14.** Since our successful Asian campaign, achieved with divine help and our strength, **15.** we resolved to treat the people of Coele-Syria and Phoenicia with kindness and generosity. (Coele-Syria: ancient Syrian region; Phoenicia: ancient maritime civilization) **16.** We even donated to their temples and visited Jerusalem to honor the temple of this foolish people. (Jerusalem: sacred city in Israel) **17.** Outwardly, they welcomed us, but their actions betrayed them. When we tried to enter their temple with gifts, **18.** their arrogance led them to deny us entry. Yet we refrained from using force. (Arrogance: pride or overconfidence) **19.** They alone defy kings and benefactors, refusing reason and showing hostility. (Rebellious: defying authority) **20.** On our victorious return, we treated all Egyptians kindly, **21.**

and sought to grant the Jews Alexandria citizenship and inclusion in our rituals. (Rituals: ceremonial acts) **22.** Instead, they rejected this kindness, showing their malice and spurning invaluable rights. (Malice: intent to harm) **23.** They even shunned their own people loyal to us, believing their corrupt ways would force us to abandon reform. (Defiance: bold resistance) **24.** Their hostility raises concerns of a sudden rebellion from these impious individuals. (Impious: lacking respect for God) **25.** Thus, all Jews, along with their families, must be sent in chains to face a harsh execution. (Chains: restraints made of metal links) **26.** We believe this punishment ensures the kingdom's stability. (Stability: firmness or steadiness) **27.** Anyone harboring a Jew will be tortured to death along with their household. **28.** Informers will receive the accused's property, 2,000 drachmas, freedom, and a crown. (Drachmas: ancient Greek coins) **29.** Any place sheltering Jews will be destroyed and rendered uninhabitable. **30.** The king's decree was issued in this form. (Decree: official order or command)

Chapter 4

1. Wherever this decree reached, people responded with loud joy and celebration, as if their long-hidden anger could now be openly expressed. (Decree: an official order) **2.** The Jews were overwhelmed with sorrow, weeping as their hearts burned with grief over the sudden destruction decreed against them. (Jews: Israelites, Decree: an official command) **3.** No home, city, or street was free from their cries of mourning. (Wailing: loud cries of grief) **4.** Expelled by generals with harshness, even some enemies wept, moved by human compassion and the uncertainty of life. (Generals: military leaders) **5.** Elderly people were driven forward, their weak, bent steps forced into swift movement by ruthless power. (Hoary-haired: having gray or white hair, Feeble: weak) **6.** Brides, recently married, exchanged joy for sorrow, their heads covered with dust instead of perfume, marching through insults and replacing wedding songs with mournful cries. (Myrrh: fragrant resin, Bridal chamber: room for newlyweds) **7.** Bound and exposed to shame, they were brutally forced onto ships. (Herded: forcefully gathered) **8.** Husbands, instead of crowns, wore ropes, spending their days in mourning with death looming ahead. (Prime: peak of youth) **9.** Some were shackled and forced to row, others had their feet bound in heavy chains. (Shackles: restraints for ankles) **10.** The deck above blocked out all light, leaving them in darkness, treated like traitors throughout the journey. (Traitors: betrayers) **11.** They were transported to Schedia, where the king had them confined in a large hippodrome, visible to everyone but denied help or humane treatment. (Schedia: a city in ancient Egypt, Hippodrome: an open-air arena) **12.** Upon learning their families mourned their plight, (Lament: express grief) **13.** the king became enraged, ordering them to endure the same harsh treatment, without mercy. (Leniency: mercy) **14.** The entire nation was to be documented by name, not for labor, but to subject them to torture and eventual extermination within a day. (Extermination: complete destruction) **15.** The registration was carried out relentlessly from dawn till dusk and took 40 days to complete. (Registration: official documentation) **16.** The king celebrated, holding banquets before idols, his misguided heart glorifying them while speaking against the true God. (Idols: statues worshipped as gods, Almighty: the all-powerful God) **17.** After the time passed, officials reported that the Jews were too numerous to register. (Officials: government representatives) **18.** Many Jews remained in homes or scattered across regions, making it impossible for the commanders in Egypt to finish the task. (Commanders: military officers) **19.** The king accused them of accepting bribes to help Jews escape, though he eventually accepted the truth. (Bribes: illegal payments) **20.** They proved they had run out of paper and pens, preventing the registration. (Paper: writing material, Pens: writing instruments) **21.** This was a divine act of Providence, offering heavenly help to the Jews. (Providence: divine care, Jews: Israelites)

Chapter 5

1. He summoned Hermon, in charge of the elephants, filled with anger and determined to carry out his vengeful plan. **2.** He ordered Hermon to mix wine and incense for the elephants to drink early the next day, planning to use the enraged animals to execute the Jews. (Hermon: person in charge of elephants) **3.** The king, after giving these orders, went to feast with his friends and army, all who hated the Jews. **4.** Hermon carried out his orders precisely. **5.** Servants bound the hands of the victims that evening, securing them for the night, believing all Jews would perish together. **6.** The heathens thought the Jews were defenseless, as they were bound in chains. **7.** The Jews prayed earnestly to the Almighty, asking their merciful God to save them. **8.** They pleaded for God's miraculous intervention to prevent the death planned for them. **9.** Their urgent prayer reached heaven. **10.** The next morning, Hermon, having prepared the elephants, reported to the king. **11.** God, who grants sleep at His will, made the king fall into a deep slumber. **12.** This divine sleep frustrated the king's plans and halted his cruel resolve. **13.** The Jews, saved from death, praised God and prayed again for His power to defeat their enemies. **14.** As the banquet hour approached, the one in charge woke the king, noting the guests had arrived. **15.** After some effort, he reminded the king that the feast time had passed. **16.** The king listened, then turned back to drinking and ordered the guests to sit. **17.** Once seated, the king encouraged them to enjoy the late banquet. **18.** As the feast continued, the king angrily questioned Hermon about the Jews surviving the day. **19.** Hermon explained he had followed the king's command, and his companions confirmed this. **20.** The king, in even greater cruelty than Phalaris, responded, "They can thank sleep. Prepare the elephants for tomorrow's destruction of the Jews." (Phalaris: a tyrannical king of ancient Sicily) **21.** The guests, pleased with the king's response, left for home. **22.** They did not sleep that night but plotted cruel mockeries for the Jews. **23.** At dawn, Hermon prepared the elephants in the grand colonnade. (Colonnade: a row of columns supporting a roof) **24.** The city crowds gathered, eager for the grim spectacle. **25.** The Jews, trembling with fear, prayed again to God for deliverance. **26.** The sun had not risen, and Hermon, ready, informed the king that his desires would soon be fulfilled. **27.** The king, surprised, asked what this unusual preparation was for. **28.** This was the work of God, who caused the king to forget his plans. **29.** Hermon and his companions pointed to the elephants, prepared as ordered. **30.** The king, confused and filled with anger, threatened Hermon, as God's Providence thwarted his plans. **31.** "If your parents or children were here, they would have fed these wild beasts instead of sacrificing innocent Jews who have served me and my ancestors. (Jews: followers of Judaism; descendants of Judah, Jacob's son) **32.** If not for our friendship and your duties, your life would have been lost in their place." (Forfeit: lost as a penalty) **33.** Hermon, startled by this threat, became visibly distressed, and his expression darkened. (Hermon: official under the king) **34.** The king's friends quietly slipped one by one, dismissing the crowd to their usual activities. **35.** Hearing this, the Jews praised God, the supreme King, for granting them deliverance. (King: referring to God as the ruler of all) **36.** The king hosted another banquet and proclaimed it a time of joy and celebration. (Banquet: formal feast) **37.** Summoning Hermon, he angrily said, "How many times must I order you to handle these people? (Hermon: an official serving the king) **38.** Arm the elephants again for the destruction of the Jews tomorrow!" (Elephants: animals used in ancient warfare) **39.** His relatives, surprised by his inconsistency, remarked, **40.** "O king, why do you test us as if we lack reason? This is the third time you've ordered their destruction and then changed your mind. **41.** Your indecision causes unrest, making the city unstable and prone to chaos." (Chaos: disorder and confusion) **42.** The king, thoughtless like Phalaris (Phalaris: cruel tyrant of Agrigentum), ignored his changing decisions. He vowed to crush the Jews under the elephants and send them to the grave. **43.** He also planned to invade Judea (Judea: region in ancient Israel), destroy its cities, desecrate the temple (Temple: central place of Jewish worship), and stop sacrifices permanently. **44.** His companions, trusting his decision, arranged guards at key points in the city. (Resolve: firm determination) **45.** The elephant master stirred the animals into a frenzy with incense and wine, adorning them with frightening decorations. (Frenzy: extreme excitement or agitation) **46.** At dawn, with crowds filling the hippodrome (Hippodrome: arena for public events), he entered the palace to remind the king of his orders. **47.** Full of rage, the king led the elephants and his forces, eager to witness the Jews' suffering. (Blasphemous: showing disrespect toward God) **48.** The Jews, seeing the elephants and hearing the crowd's roar, **49.** believed their end was near. They wept, embracing each other—fathers holding sons, mothers hugging daughters, and women nursing their infants for what seemed like the last time. (Despair: loss of hope) **50.** Recalling God's past help, they prostrated themselves together, even removing infants from their arms. **51.** They cried out to the Lord of all power, pleading for mercy and deliverance from death. (Mercy: compassion shown to those in need)

Chapter 6

1. Eleazar, a respected and aged priest known for his virtuous life, urged the elders to stop crying out to God and prayed: **2.** "O mighty King, Almighty God, who governs creation with mercy, **3.** look upon Abraham's descendants, the children of Jacob, your sacred inheritance who are suffering unjustly as exiles in a foreign land. (Abraham: the father of the Israelites; Jacob: also called Israel, father of the twelve tribes of Israel) **4.** You defeated Pharaoh and his chariot army when he boasted against you, showing mercy to Israel and overcoming his proud forces. (Pharaoh: ruler of Egypt) **5.** When Sennacherib, the Assyrian king, boasted of his mighty army and threatened your holy city, you destroyed him and revealed your power to many nations. (Sennacherib: king of Assyria; Assyria: an ancient empire) **6.** When three faithful men in Babylon chose the fire over worshipping idols, You sent a miraculous coolness through the flames, protecting them and confounding their enemies.

(Babylon: an ancient city) **7.** You saved Daniel from the lion's den when he was unjustly thrown in due to envy. (Daniel: a prophet of Israel) **8.** When Jonah was trapped in the sea creature, you rescued him to be seen again by his people. (Jonah: a prophet who was swallowed by a sea monster) **9.** O merciful protector, appear quickly to the people of Israel, mocked by the nations who defy Your will. **10.** If our sins in exile have stained our lives, deliver us from our enemies and deliver us from our enemies and, if it be Your will, grant us peace in life or death.**11.** Do not allow idol worshippers to boast of our defeat, saying, 'Their god has not delivered them.' (Idols: false gods) **12.** You, All-Powerful Eternal One, have mercy on us as we face an unjust and untimely death at the hands of lawless men. (Lawless: those who disregard justice) **13.** Let the nations tremble before your power, for you alone can save Jacob's descendants. (Jacob: the patriarch of the twelve tribes of Israel) **14.** The children and their parents cry to you with tears. **15.** Show all nations that you are with us, O Lord, fulfilling your promise to never forsake us, even in enemy lands. **16.** After Eleazar's prayer, the king arrived at the arena with wild animals and his army. (Arena: a place for public events) **17.** The Jews cried out to heaven, causing the valleys to echo, and their sorrow spread throughout the army. **18.** Then, God revealed his presence, and two powerful angels descended, visible only to the enemies, causing fear and confusion. **19.** The angels bound the enemy army with unbreakable chains. **20.** The king was struck with fear, and his strength left him. **21.** The wild animals turned back on the enemy forces, trampling and destroying them. **22.** The king's anger turned to compassion, and he wept over what he had caused. **23.** Seeing the people on the verge of death, he angrily rebuked his advisors, saying, **24.** "You have ruled with cruelty, betraying me, your benefactor, and plotting against the kingdom. (Tyrants: cruel rulers) **25.** Who has gathered those faithful to us and removed them from their homes? **26.** Who has unjustly punished those who have served us loyally and courageously? **27.** Free them and send them home with peace, begging forgiveness for what was done. **28.** Release the children of the Almighty, who has blessed us with prosperity since ancient times!" **29.** As the king spoke, they were freed, narrowly escaping death, and they praised God, their Savior. **30.** The king went to the city, called for a seven-day feast of wine and provisions for the Jews to celebrate their deliverance. **31.** Those who were near death now rejoiced, turning the place of their burial into a banquet hall. **32.** They stopped mourning and praised God, dancing in joy, setting aside all sorrow. **33.** The king invited guests to join in the celebration and gave thanks for their unexpected deliverance. **34.** Those who had condemned the Jews to death now felt shame and their rage was extinguished. **35.** The Jews danced, feasted, and gave thanks, singing psalms of praise to God. (Psalms: sacred songs or hymns) **36.** They made it a public holiday to remember this deliverance for generations, not for indulgence but to honor God's salvation. **37.** They asked the king to allow them to return to their homes. **38.** They were registered from the 25th of Pachon to the 4th of Epiphi, a period of forty days, with the threat to their lives lasting three days. (Pachon and Epiphi: Egyptian months) **39.** During this time, God showed his mercy, keeping them unharmed. **40.** They feasted on the king's provisions until the 14th day and then asked to return home. **41.** The king praised them and sent a letter to every city's leaders, honoring their faith and deliverance.

Chapter 7
1. King Ptolemy Philopator sends strength to the commanders and all those overseeing affairs in Egypt. (Ptolemy Philopator: a king of Egypt) **2.** We and our children are well, as God has guided our actions. **3.** Some of our enemies urged us to punish the Jews in our kingdom severely. **4.** They claimed our affairs wouldn't improve until this was done, accusing the Jews of hating all other people. **5.** They brought the Jews in chains, like traitors, seeking their destruction without investigation, using cruelty worse than Scythians. (Scythians: ancient nomadic people known for their fierceness) **6.** We threatened them but showed mercy, allowing them to live, seeing that God protected them as a father defends his children. **7.** Due to their loyalty to us and our ancestors, we cleared them of all charges. **8.** We sent them home, instructing all not to harm them or speak ill of them for past actions. **9.** If we harm them, our true adversary will be God, the ruler of all, and there will be no escape from His judgment. Farewell. **10.** After receiving the letter, they asked the king to punish those of their own people who had broken God's laws. **11.** They argued that those who violated God's commands for personal gain would never be loyal to the king. **12.** The king agreed, granting them full authority to punish those who broke God's laws in his kingdom. **13.** The priests wished him well, and the people joyfully responded with "Hallelujah!" They left with happiness. (Hallelujah: an expression of praise) **14.** They punished and destroyed every defiled Jew they found, **15.** killing more than three hundred men, seeing their destruction as a celebration of justice. **16.** Having stayed loyal to God and received deliverance, they left the city with garlands, singing hymns and thanking God, the eternal Savior of Israel. **17.** Arriving at Ptolemais (a city known for its roses), they rested for seven days, where the fleet awaited them. (Ptolemais: a coastal city in ancient Palestine) **18.** They enjoyed a feast, as the king generously provided for their journey home. **19.** They returned peacefully, giving thanks and deciding to celebrate these days with joy. **20.** They marked these days as sacred, dedicating the site as a place of prayer. They left unharmed and joyful, under the king's protection, traveling by land, sea, and river to their homes. **21.** They gained more respect and fear from their enemies. No one took their possessions. **22.** Everyone got back their property, and those who had taken it returned it in fear. For God performed great miracles for their salvation. **23.** Blessed be the Redeemer of Israel forever! Amen.

76 – The Book oF Enoch
Chapter 1
1. These are the words of Enoch, who blessed the righteous and elect, **2.** those who will live in the time of tribulation when the wicked are removed. Enoch, a righteous man whose eyes were opened by God, saw a vision of the Holy One in the heavens, revealed by the angels. **3.** From them, he understood all things, but this message was meant for a future generation, not his own. He spoke of the elect: The Holy One will come from His dwelling, **4.** And the Eternal God will tread upon the earth, even on Mount Sinai, [And appear from His camp] And show His might from the highest heavens. (Tread: step; Camp: dwelling; Might: power) **5.** All will be struck with fear, The Watchers will quake, Terror will seize the earth. (Watchers: guardians; Quake: shake; Terror: fear) **6.** The mountains will tremble, The hills will be leveled, And they will melt like wax before fire. (Tremble: shake; Leveled: flattened; Melt: dissolve) **7.** The earth will split apart, And all upon it will perish, For judgment will come upon all men. (Split: tear; Perish: die; Judgment: decision) **8.** But He will bring peace to the righteous, Protect the elect, And show mercy to them. They will belong to God, Be blessed, And prosper. He will help them, Light will shine upon them, And grant peace. (Righteous: just; Mercy: compassion; Prosper: succeed) **9.** He will come with tens of thousands of holy ones, To execute judgment on all, And destroy the ungodly. He will convict all flesh for their wicked deeds, And for the harsh words spoken against Him. (Execute: carry out; Convict: blame; Wicked: evil; Harsh: severe)

Chapter 2
1. Observe everything in the heavens, how the stars and celestial bodies follow their orbits, rising and setting in their proper seasons, never deviating from their appointed order. (Observe: watch; Celestial: heavenly; Deviating: straying) **2.** Look at the earth and consider how everything remains steadfast, from beginning to end, with nothing changing, and all the works of God are evident to you. (Steadfast: unchanging; Works: creations) **3.** Behold the summer and winter, how the earth is filled with water, and clouds, dew, and rain fall upon it. (Behold: see; Dew: moisture; Fall: descend)

Chapter 3
Observe how, in winter, all the trees appear to wither and shed their leaves, except for fourteen trees, which keep their foliage for two to three years until new leaves grow. (Wither: dry up; Foliage: leaves)

Chapter 4
And again, observe the summer days when the sun is directly above the earth. You seek shade to escape the sun's heat, and the earth itself grows unbearably hot, making it impossible to walk on the ground or even on rocks. (Unbearably: too much to endure)

Chapter 5
1. Observe how trees grow green and bear fruit; take note of all His works and understand that the One who lives forever has made them so. (Observe: watch; Bearing: producing) **2.** All His works continue year after year, and their tasks remain unchanged, as God has ordained them. (Tasks: duties; Ordained: decreed) **3.** Similarly, the sea and rivers never change their course, always following God's command. (Course: path) **4.** But you have not remained steadfast or followed the Lord's commandments. You have turned away and spoken proud, harsh words against His greatness. Oh, hard-hearted ones, you will find no peace. (Steadfast: constant; Harsh: severe) **5.** Therefore, your days will be cursed, your years will fade, and your destruction will multiply in eternal cursing, and you will find no mercy. (Execrate: curse; Destruction: ruin) **6.** In those days, your names will be cursed by the righteous, And all who curse will curse through you, And the godless will call down curses upon you. **7.** But the righteous will rejoice, Their sins will be forgiven, Mercy, peace, and patience will be with them, They will have salvation and light. For all sinners, there will be no salvation, A curse will remain upon you. (patience : Forbearance) **8.** But for the elect, there will be light, joy, and peace, They will inherit the earth. (Elect: chosen ones) **9.** Wisdom will be given to the elect, They will live without sin, free from pride or ungodliness, And the wise

will remain humble. (Ungodliness: lack of reverence) 10. They will not sin again, nor die from God's anger, But will live out their days in peace. Their lives will be filled with joy and multiplied in eternal gladness. (Anger: wrath)

Chapter 6

1. When mankind multiplied, beautiful daughters were born to them. The angels, the children of heaven, saw them and lusted after them. They said, "Let us take wives from among the children of men and have children." (Lusted: desired strongly) 2. Semjaza, their leader, said, "I fear you won't agree, and I alone will bear the penalty for this great sin." (Penalty: punishment) 3. They all replied, "Let us swear an oath and bind ourselves by mutual imprecations to carry out this plan." (Imprecations: curses) 4. So they swore and bound themselves by mutual imprecations. Two hundred angels descended during the days of Jared on Mount Hermon, and they named it Mount Hermon because of their oath. (Summit: top) 5. The leaders were Samlazaz, Araklba, Rameel, Kokabiel, Tamlel, Ramlel, Danel, Ezeqeel, Baraqijal, Asael, Armaros, Batarel, Ananel, Zaqiel, Samsapeel, Satarel, Turel, Jomjael, and Sariel. These were their chiefs of tens. (Chiefs: leaders)

Chapter 7

1. The angels took wives for themselves, each choosing one, and began to defile them. They taught them magic, charms, and the use of plants and roots. (Defile: Corrupt; Charms: Spells; Enchantments: Magic) 2. The women became pregnant and gave birth to giants, towering at three thousand ells in height. These giants consumed all that humans had. (Giants: Beasts; Ells: Measure) 3. Unable to support them, humanity was attacked by the giants, who devoured mankind. (Sustain: Endure) 4. The giants sinned against animals—birds, beasts, reptiles, and fish—and even began to eat each other's flesh and drink blood. (Devour: Consume) 5. At last, the earth itself raised an accusation against the lawless giants. (Lawless: Unrighteous; Accusation: Claim)

Chapter 8

1. Azazel taught humanity to make weapons, shields, breastplates, and ornaments. He revealed metals, antimony, cosmetics, and the use of precious stones and dyes. (Forged: Crafted; Antimony: Metallic element; Tinctures: Dyes) 2. This led to widespread godlessness, fornication, and corruption. (Godlessness: Impiety; Fornication: Immorality) 3. Semjaza taught magic, Armaros taught spell-breaking, Baraqijal taught astrology, Kokabel taught constellations, Ezeqeel taught cloud knowledge, Araqiel taught earth signs, Shamsiel taught sun signs, and Sariel taught the moon's course. As humanity perished, their cries reached heaven. (Astrology: Study of stars; Constellations: Star patterns; Enchantments: Spells)

Chapter 9

1. Michael, Uriel, Raphael, and Gabriel looked down from heaven, seeing the earth soaked in blood and full of lawlessness. (Lawlessness: absence of law or order) 2. They said, "The earth, once empty, now cries to heaven in anguish." (Anguish: extreme pain) 3. "The souls of men cry out, 'Present our case to the Most High.'" (Cry out: appeal urgently) 4. They spoke to the Lord: "Lord of lords, King of kings, Your throne lasts forever, and Your name is holy and blessed." (Lasts: continues indefinitely) 5. "You created all things, have power over all, and nothing is hidden from You." (Hidden: kept secret) 6. "You see what Azazel has done, teaching evil on earth and revealing forbidden secrets to men." (Evil: immoral) 7-8. "Semjaza, whom You entrusted with authority, led his followers to corrupt the daughters of men. They defiled themselves and spread sin." (Defiled: corrupted) 9. "These women bore giants, and the earth was filled with blood and injustice." (Giants: monstrous offspring) 10. "Now the souls of the dead cry out, their lamentations rising due to the lawlessness on earth." (Lamentations: passionate mourning) 11. "You know all things before they happen, yet You allow them. You haven't told us how to respond." (Allow: give permission for)

Chapter 10

1. The Most High, the Holy One, spoke and sent Uriel to Lamech's son, Noah, 2. saying, "Tell Noah to hide, for the earth will soon be destroyed by a flood. (Flood: deluge) 3. He and his descendants must survive for future generations." 4. The Lord then commanded Raphael, "Bind Azazel and cast him into the darkness of Dudael, (Dudael: abyss) 5. with rough stones upon him, and cover his face so he cannot see light. He will remain there forever 6. and be cast into the fire on the Day of Judgment. (Judgment: decision) Heal the earth corrupted by the angels, 7. and proclaim its healing so humanity is not lost through the Watchers' secret teachings." (Watchers: angels) 8. The earth is corrupted by Azazel's teachings of sin. (Corrupted: tainted) 9. The Lord told Gabriel, "Punish the wicked and destroy the offspring of the Watchers. Let them fight each other 10. until none are left. Their fathers' requests will not be granted; they seek eternal life but will not find it." (Eternal: endless) 11. The Lord said to Michael, "Bind Semjaza and his followers who have defiled themselves with women. (Defiled: polluted) 12. When their children destroy each other, imprison them for seventy generations in the earth's valleys 13. until the final judgment, where they will be cast into eternal fire and torment." (Torment: agony) 14. Those condemned will remain bound with them forever. (Condemned: doomed) 15. Destroy the spirits of the wicked and the children of the Watchers for their harm to mankind. (Wicked: evil) 16. Erase all evil from the earth and let righteousness and truth grow, bringing blessings and joy forever. (Righteousness: virtue; Truth: fact) 17. The righteous will survive, 18. and their descendants will multiply. They will live in peace throughout their lives, (Descendants: offspring) 19. and the earth will be filled with blessing, planted with fruitful trees and vines that bear abundance. (Abundance: plenty) 20. Cleansed from oppression, unrighteousness, sin, and godlessness, (Oppression: cruelty; Unrighteousness: immorality; Godlessness: atheism) 21. the earth will flourish, and all nations will worship Me. (Flourish: thrive) 22. The earth will be free of sin and punishment, and I will never bring it upon them again." (Sin: wrongdoing; Punishment: penalty)

Chapter 11

1. And in those days I will open the store chambers of blessing which are in the heaven, so as to send (Blessing: gift) 2. them down upon the earth over the work and labour of the children of men. And truth and peace shall be associated together throughout all the days of the world and throughout all the generations of men. (Truth: fact; Peace: harmony)

Chapter 12

1. Before these things, Enoch was hidden, and no one knew where he was (Hidden: concealed) 2. or where he lived, and what had become of him. His activities involved the Watchers, and his days were with the holy ones. (Abode: dwelling; Watchers: angels) 3. And I, Enoch, was blessing the Lord of majesty and the King of the ages, and behold! the Watchers (Majesty: grandeur) 4. called me—Enoch the scribe—and said: "Enoch, scribe of righteousness, go, declare to the Watchers of heaven who left the high, holy eternal place and defiled themselves with women, doing as humans do, and taking wives." (Scribe: writer; Defiled: polluted) 5. "You have caused great destruction on the earth: You shall have no peace or forgiveness (Wrought: caused) 6. for sin. As you delight in your children, you will witness the murder of your loved ones and lament the destruction of your children. You will make endless supplication, but you will find no mercy or peace." (Lament: mourn; Supplication: prayer)

Chapter 13

1. And Enoch went and said: "Azazel, you shall have no peace: a severe sentence has been declared (Peace: calm) 2. against you, to bind you: You will not be tolerated nor have your requests granted, due to the unrighteousness you've taught, and the godlessness and sin you've shown to men." (Unrighteousness: immorality; Godlessness: atheism) 3. Then I spoke to them all together, and fear seized them. They begged me to petition for them to find forgiveness, 4. and to present their petition before the Lord of heaven. From then on, they could not speak with Him nor lift their eyes to heaven due to the shame of their sins for which they were condemned. (Petition: request) 5. Then I wrote out their petition, the prayer for their spirits and deeds, and their request for forgiveness and long life. (Deeds: actions) 6. I went to the waters of Dan, in the land of Dan, south of Hermon, and read their petition until I fell asleep. (Hermon: a mountain range) 7. And behold, a dream came to me, and visions of chastisement fell upon me. A voice commanded me to tell the sons of heaven and reprimand them. (Chastisement: punishment) 8. When I awoke, I went to them, and they were sitting together, weeping in 'Abelsjail, between Lebanon and Seneser, their faces covered. (Weeping: crying) 9. I recounted all the visions I had seen in sleep, speaking words of righteousness and reprimanding the heavenly Watchers. (Righteousness: virtue)

Chapter 14

1. The book of the words of righteousness, and of the reprimand of the eternal Watchers, as commanded by the Holy Great One in that vision. (Reprimand: rebuke) 2. I saw in my sleep what I now speak with fleshly tongue and breath, given to men to understand with the heart. (Tongue: speech) 3. As He created and gave men the power of wisdom, He also gave me the power to reprimand the Watchers, the children of heaven. (Reprimand: rebuke) 4. I wrote your petition, and in my vision, it appeared that your petition will not be granted throughout eternity, for judgment has been passed upon you. (Judgment: decision) 5. You will not ascend into heaven for eternity; your decree has gone forth to bind you on earth forever. (Ascend: rise; Decree: order) 6. You will witness the destruction of your sons, and you will have no pleasure in them; they will fall by the sword. (Destruction: ruin) 7. Your petition for them and for yourselves will not be granted, even though you weep, pray, and speak all the words I have written.

(Petition: request) **8.** The vision showed me clouds inviting me, mist summoning me, and the stars and lightnings hastening me. (Hastening: rushing) **9.** The winds caused me to fly, lifted me upward, and bore me into heaven. (Lifted: raised) **10.** I came close to a crystal wall surrounded by fire, and it terrified me. (Terrified: frightened) **11.** I entered the fire and drew near a large crystal house; its walls were like a tesselated crystal floor. (Tesselated: patterned) **12.** Its ceiling was like the stars and lightning, and fiery cherubim were between them. (Cherubim: angelic beings) **13.** A flaming fire surrounded it, and its portals blazed with fire. (Portals: entrances) **14.** I entered, and it was both hot as fire and cold as ice; fear and trembling overwhelmed me. (Trembling: shaking) **15.** As I quaked, I fell on my face and beheld a vision. (Quaked: shook) **16.** I saw a second house, greater than the first, with a flame-filled portal, surpassing in splendor, magnificence, and size. (Splendor: brilliance) **17.** Its floor was fire, and above were lightning and the stars, and the ceiling was also flaming fire. (Flaming: burning) **18.** I saw a lofty throne, its appearance like crystal, its wheels like the shining sun, with cherubim around it. (Lofty: elevated) **19.** From beneath the throne came streams of flaming fire, too bright for me to look upon. (Streams: currents) **20.** The Great Glory sat upon it, His raiment brighter than the sun, whiter than snow. (Raiment: clothing) **21.** No angel could enter or behold His face due to His magnificence, and no flesh could look at Him. (Magnificence: grandeur) **22.** The flaming fire surrounded Him, and none could approach, though ten thousand times ten thousand stood before Him. (Approach: get near) **23.** He needed no counselor, and the most holy ones near Him never departed, neither by day nor night. (Counselor: advisor) **24.** I had been prostrate on my face, trembling, when the Lord called me with His own mouth, saying: "Come hither, Enoch, and hear my word." (Prostrate: lying face down) **25.** One of the holy ones woke me, made me rise, and approach the door; I bowed my face down. (Woke: roused)

Chapter 15
1. He answered me, and I heard His voice: "Do not fear, Enoch, righteous man and scribe of truth. Come and listen. (Scribe: writer; Truth: accuracy) **2.** Go tell the Watchers of heaven, who sent you to intercede for them: 'You should intercede for mankind, not the other way around. (Intercede: intervene) **3.** Why did you leave the high, holy heaven and defile yourselves with women, taking wives and fathering giants? (Defile: corrupt) **4.** Though you were holy and eternal, you defiled yourselves with human desires, becoming like mortals who die. (Mortals: humans) **5.** I gave humans wives so they could bear children and nothing would be lacking on earth. (Lacking: missing) **6.** But you were spiritual, eternal, and immortal. I did not give you wives, for the spiritual ones of heaven belong in heaven. (Immortal: undying) **7.** Now, the giants born of spirit and flesh will be called evil spirits on earth, their home will be the earth. (Giants: titans) **8.** These spirits, born of both humans and the Watchers, will bring destruction and misery. (Destruction: ruin; Misery: suffering) **9.** They will be evil spirits on earth, causing suffering, conflict, and death. (Evil spirits: demons; Conflict: struggle) **10.** They will not need food but will feel hunger and thirst, bringing harm wherever they go. (Harm: injury) **11.** They will rise up against humans, especially women, because they came from them." (Rise up: rebel)

Chapter 16
1. From the days of the slaughter, destruction, and death of the giants, from the souls of whose flesh the spirits, having gone forth, shall destroy without judgment—so they shall destroy until the great judgment day, when the age is consummated, over the Watchers and the godless, and fully completed. (Slaughter: massacre; Consummation: completion; Judgment: decision; Godless: irreligious) **2.** And now, to the Watchers who sent you to intercede for them, who were once in heaven, (say): "You were in heaven, but the mysteries were not fully revealed to you. You knew worthless ones, and through these, you taught women. By these mysteries, men and women do much evil on earth." (Intercede: intervene; Worthless: futile; Mysteries: secrets; Evil: wickedness) **3.** Tell them: "You have no peace." (Peace: tranquility)

Chapter 17
1. They brought me to a place where those present were like flaming fire, (Flaming: burning) **2-3.** and could appear as men when they wished. They led me to a place of darkness and a mountain whose peak reached the heavens. I saw the luminaries, the treasuries of stars, thunder, and the deepest depths,(Luminaries: lights; Treasuries: storehouses) **4.** where a fiery bow, arrows, a quiver, a fiery sword, and all the lightnings were. They took me to living waters and the fire of the west, which receives the setting sun. (Quiver: container for arrows; Lightnings: flashes of light from storms) **5.** I came to a river of fire flowing like water into the great sea towards the west. (Discharges: releases) **6.** I saw the great rivers, came to the great river and darkness, and went (Rivers: large flowing bodies of water; Darkness: absence of light) **7.** to the place where no flesh walks. I saw the mountains of winter darkness and the place (Flesh: physical body) **8.** from which all the waters of the deep flow, and the mouths of all the rivers and the deep. (Deep: vast body of water, often symbolizing the abyss)

Chapter 18
1. I saw the treasuries of all the winds, how He used them to shape creation (Treasuries: storehouses) **2.** and the earth's foundations. I saw the cornerstone of the earth and the four winds that carry the earth and the heavens. (Corner-stone: foundation stone) **3.** I saw how the winds stretch the heavens, stationed between heaven and earth, these are the pillars of the sky.(Pillars: supports) **4.** I saw the winds of heaven turning and carrying the sun and stars to their setting. **5.** I saw the winds on earth carrying the clouds, and the paths of the angels. (Paths: routes) **6.** At the earth's end, I saw the firmament of heaven above. (Firmament: sky) **7.** I saw a place burning day and night, with seven magnificent mountains: (Magnificent: impressive) **8.** Three east, three south—eastern ones of colored stone, pearl, and jacinth; southern ones of red stone. (Jacinth: a red or orange gemstone) **9.** The middle one reached heaven like God's throne, of alabaster, with a sapphire summit. (Alabaster: fine-grained stone; Summit: peak) **10.** I saw a flaming fire. Beyond these mountains, the heavens were complete. (Flaming: burning) **11.** I saw a deep abyss with columns of heavenly fire, and fire falling, stretching in height and depth. (Abyss: deep void; Columns: vertical supports) **12.** Beyond that abyss was a place with no sky above or earth below, no water or birds—a desolate place. (Waste: desolate; Horrible: terrifying) **13.** I saw seven stars like great burning mountains, (Stars: celestial bodies) **14-15.** and when I asked, the angel said: "This is the end of heaven and earth, a prison for the stars and heavenly hosts. These stars broke the Lord's command by not rising at their appointed times. (Transgressed: violated; Hosts: groups) **16.** He was angry and bound them until their guilt is complete, even for ten thousand years." (Wroth: angry; Guilt: blame)

Chapter 19
1. Uriel said to me: "Here will stand the angels who joined with women, their spirits taking many forms, defiling mankind and leading them to worship demons as gods, until the great judgment day, (Defiling: corrupting; Spirits: beings; Worship: adore) **2.** when they will be judged and end. The women who joined the angels will become sirens." (Sirens: seductive creatures) **3.** I, Enoch, alone saw the vision of the end of all things, and no man shall see as I have seen. (Vision: sight; End: conclusion)

Chapter 20
1-2. These are the names of the holy angels who watch: Uriel, who is over the world and Tartarus. (Tartarus: a deep abyss in Greek mythology) **3.** Raphael, who is over the spirits of men. (Spirits: souls) **4-5.** Raguel, who takes vengeance on the world of the luminaries. (Vengeance: retribution; Luminaries: heavenly bodies) **6.** Michael, who is set over the best part of mankind and over chaos. (Chaos: disorder) **7.** Saraqael, who is over the spirits who sin in the spirit. (Sin: wrongdoing) **8.** Gabriel, who is over Paradise, the serpents, and the Cherubim. (Paradise: Eden; Cherubim: angelic beings) **9.** Remiel, whom God set over those who rise. (Rise: ascend)

Chapter 21
1-2. I went to a chaotic place and saw something horrifying: no heaven above, nor a firmly founded earth, but a place of chaos and horror. (Chaos: disorder; Horror: terror) **3.** There, I saw seven stars of heaven bound together like great mountains, burning with fire. (Stars: celestial bodies; Bound: confined) **4.** I asked, "For what sin are they bound? Why were they cast here?" (Sin: wrongdoing) **5.** Uriel, one of the holy angels, chief over them, answered: "These stars transgressed the Lord's command and are bound here for ten thousand years, until their sins are complete." (Transgressed: violated; Command: order) **6.** I then went to another place, even more horrible, and saw a great fire burning, with the place cleft down to the abyss, full of great descending columns of fire. (Cleft: split; Abyss: deep void) **7.** I could not see its extent or magnitude, nor could I guess its size. (Magnitude: size) **8.** I said, "How fearful and terrible this place is!" (Fearful: frightening) **9.** Uriel, one of the holy angels with me, asked, "Why are you so afraid?" (Affright: fear) **10.** I answered, "Because of this fearful place and the pain I see." (Pain: suffering) **11.** He said, "This is the prison of the angels, where they will be imprisoned forever." (Prison: place of confinement)

Chapter 22
1. I traveled to a mountain of hard rock.(Hard rock: solid) **2.** It had four deep, wide, smooth hollows, dark and eerie to see. (Eerie: strange) **3.** Raphael, a holy angel with me, said, "These hollows are for the souls of the dead." (Hollows: empty spaces) **4.** "They will stay here until judgment day, awaiting their appointed time." (Appointed: assigned) **5.** I saw the spirit of a dead man calling out to heaven. (Spirit: the soul) **6.** I asked Raphael, "Whose voice calls to heaven?" (Call out: shout) **7.** He answered, "This is Abel's spirit, killed by

his brother Cain. He calls for justice until Cain's descendants are destroyed." (Slain: killed; Descendants: offspring) **8.** I asked, "Why are the hollows divided?" (Divided: separated) **9.** Raphael replied, "The divisions separate spirits. One is for the righteous, with a spring of water." (Righteous: morally right) **10.** "Another holds sinners, whose spirits suffer until judgment, as they weren't judged in life." (Sinners: wrongdoers; Judgment: the act of being judged) **11.** "Here, they endure pain until punishment comes, when the wicked are tormented forever." (Endure: suffer; Tormented: caused great suffering) **12.** "A third division is for those wronged, seeking justice for their deaths at the hands of sinners." (Wronged: treated unjustly) **13.** "The last is for the wicked, who lived in transgression and will remain in torment, never revived." (Wicked: evil; Transgression: violation of a law; Revived: brought back to life) **14.** I praised the Lord, saying, "Blessed be the Lord of righteousness, who reigns forever." (Reigns: rules)

Chapter 23

1. From there, I went to a place in the west, at the ends of the earth. (Ends of the earth: farthest points on the earth) **2.** I saw a fire burning without stopping, running continuously day and night. (Continuous: without interruption) **3.** I asked, "What is this fire that never rests?" (Rest: pause) **4.** Raguel, a holy angel with me, answered, "This is the fire in the west that persecutes all the heavenly luminaries." (Persecutes: harasses ; Luminaries: celestial bodies, like stars)

Chapter 24

1. From there, I traveled to another part of the earth, where I saw a range of mountains burning with fire, night and day. (Range: a series of mountains) **2.** I went past it and saw seven stunning mountains, each unique. Their stones were magnificent and beautiful. Three stood in the east, stacked one above the other, and three in the south, separated by deep ravines. (Stunning: extremely impressive; Ravines: deep, narrow valleys) **3.** None of the ravines connected. (Ravines: deep) **4.** The seventh mountain rose in the center, towering above the others, like a throne, surrounded by fragrant trees. (Majestic: grand) **5.** Among them was a tree I had never smelled before. Its fragrance surpassed all others, and its leaves, flowers, and wood never withered. (Withered: dried out) **6.** Its fruit was beautiful, like dates from a palm. I marveled, "How beautiful and fragrant this tree is! Its leaves and blossoms are truly delightful." (Resembling: similar to) **7.** Then Michael, the angel who led them, answered me. (Revered: highly respected; Accompanied: traveled with)

Chapter 25

1. He said to me, "Enoch, why do you ask about the fragrance of the tree and seek the truth?" (Seek: search for) **2.** I replied, "I want to know everything, especially about this tree." (Especially: more than anything) **3.** He answered, "This mountain you see, whose peak is like God's throne, is His throne, where the Holy One, the Eternal King, will sit when He comes to bless the earth." (Peak: top point) **4.** "No mortal can touch this fragrant tree until the great judgment, when God will bring vengeance on all and complete everything forever." (Vengeance: punishment for wrongdoing; Complete: bring to final state) **5.** "Then it will be given to the righteous and holy. Its fruit will feed the elect and be moved to the holy place, the temple of the Eternal King." (Nourish: provide sustenance; Elect: chosen ones) **6.** "They will rejoice, enter the holy place, and its fragrance will fill their bones. They will live long lives, as your ancestors did. In their days, no sorrow, plague, torment, or calamity will touch them." (Rejoice: feel great joy; Plague: widespread disease) **7.** I blessed the God of Glory, the Eternal King, who has prepared such things for the righteous, created them, and promised to give them these blessings. (Blessed: praised; Promised: pledged)

Chapter 26

1. I went to the center of the earth and saw a blessed place with trees whose branches were alive and blooming. (Blooming: producing flowers) **2.** There was a holy mountain, and beneath it to the east, a stream flowed south. (Beneath: below) **3.** To the east, a taller mountain stood, with a deep ravine between it and the first. A stream ran through the ravine. (Ravine: a deep, narrow valley) **4.** To the west, a smaller mountain stood, with a deep, dry ravine between it and the others. (Dry: lacking moisture) **5.** Another dry ravine marked the edge of the three mountains. All the ravines were narrow and rocky, with no trees. (Ravines: deep valleys; Rocky: made of rock) **6.** I marveled at the rocks and ravines, amazed by their appearance. (Marveled: was filled with wonder)

Chapter 27

1. I asked, "What is the purpose of this blessed land full of trees, and this accursed valley between them?" (Accursed: cursed or doomed) **2.** Uriel, one of the holy angels with me, replied, "This accursed valley is for those cursed forever. It is where all those who speak against the Lord, uttering unseemly words and speaking harshly of His glory, will be gathered." (Unseemly: inappropriate; Harshly: severely) **3.** "This is their place of judgment. In the last days, the righteous will witness their judgment, and the merciful will praise the Lord of Glory, the Eternal King." (Witness: see or observe) **4.** "In that day, they will bless Him for the mercy He showed in assigning them their lot." (Lot: portion or fâte) **5.** I then blessed the Lord of Glory, praising and exalting His greatness. (Exalting: praising highly)

Chapter 28

1. I then traveled east, into the heart of the mountain range in the desert. (Heart: center) **2.** I saw a solitary wilderness, full of trees and plants. (Solitary: empty, isolated) **3.** Water gushed from above, flowing like a great river towards the northwest, creating clouds and dew on all sides. (Gushed: flowed out forcefully; Copious: abundant)

Chapter 29

1. I went to another place in the desert, approaching the east side of the mountain range. (Approaching: getting closer to) **2.** There, I saw aromatic trees emitting the fragrance of frankincense and myrrh, resembling almond trees. (fragrant : Aromatic; Emitting: releasing)

Chapter 30

1. I traveled further east and saw another place, a valley full of water. (Valley: lowland) **2.** In the valley, I saw a tree with the color and fragrance of mastic trees. The sides of the valley were lined with fragrant cinnamon. (Mastic: resin; Lined: bordered) **3.** From there, I continued eastward. (Continued: proceeded)

Chapter 31

1. I saw other mountains with groves of trees, from which flowed nectar called sarara and galbanum. (Groves: clusters; Nectar: sweet liquid) **2.** Beyond them, I saw a mountain to the east, at the ends of the earth, covered with aloe trees, all producing stacte like almond trees. (Stacte: resin; Aloe tree) **3.** When burned, it released a fragrance sweeter than any other.(Released: emitted)

Chapter 32

1. Looking north, I saw seven mountains full of nard, fragrant trees, cinnamon, and pepper. (Nard: aromatic plant) **2.** I traveled east, passed the Erythraean Sea, crossed the angel Zotiel, and reached the Garden of Righteousness. (Erythraean: Red Sea) **3.** From afar, I saw many trees, including two large, beautiful ones, and the tree of knowledge, whose fruit gives great wisdom. (Grants: gives) **4.** The tree was like a fir, its leaves like carob, and its fruit like grape clusters. (Carob: edible tree pods) **5.** Its fragrance spread far. (Fragrance: pleasant smell) **6.** I marveled, "How beautiful!" Raphael answered, "This is the tree of wisdom, from which your parents ate, gained wisdom, and realized their nakedness, leading to their expulsion." (Expulsion: being driven out)

Chapter 33

1. I traveled to the ends of the earth and saw great beasts, each different, along with birds of varying beauty, appearance, and voice. (Beasts: large animals) **2.** To the east, I saw the ends of the earth where the heaven rests, with portals opening to the sky. (Portals: openings) **3.** I saw the stars of heaven emerge and counted the portals through which they come, noting their outlets, numbers, names, courses, positions, and times. (Outlets: exits) **4.** Uriel, the holy angel with me, showed me all things and wrote them down, including their names, laws, and groups. (Groups: companies, gatherings)

Chapter 34

1. I went north to the ends of the earth and saw a great and glorious sight. (Sight: vision) **2.** There, I saw three portals of heaven open, through which north winds blow, bringing cold, hail, frost, snow, dew, and rain. (Portals: openings) **3.** One portal sends winds for good, but the other two bring violent winds that cause affliction on the earth. (Affliction: suffering)

Chapter 35

1. I traveled west to the ends of the earth and saw three portals of heaven open, just like those in the east, with the same number of portals and outlets. (Portals: openings; Outlets: exits)

Chapter 36

1. I traveled south to the ends of the earth and saw three portals of heaven open, from which came dew, rain, and wind. (Portals: openings) **2.** Then I went east to the ends of heaven and saw three eastern portals open, with smaller ones above them. (Smaller: tiny) **3.** Through these small portals, the stars pass and move westward along their assigned paths. (Assigned: predetermined) **4.** I continually blessed the Lord of Glory for His great works, shown to angels, spirits, and men, that they might praise His creation and might forever. (Creation: all things made)

Section II.
The Parables

Chapter 37

1. This is the second vision of wisdom, seen by Enoch, son of Jared, and descendant of Adam. (Vision: revelation) **2.** Enoch called out, "Listen, ancient ones, and take heed, you who come after, to the words of the Holy One before the Lord of Spirits." (Heed: pay attention) **3.** "It is right to share this wisdom with the ancients, but even future generations shall not be denied its beginning." (Denied: kept from) **4.** "This wisdom, greater than any before, was given to me by the Lord of Spirits, who granted me eternal life." (Greater: superior) **5.** "I was entrusted with three Parables, and I proclaimed them to all on earth." (Entrusted: given responsibility)

Chapter 38

1. The first Parable: When the righteous appear and sinners are judged, they will be cast off the earth. (Cast off: driven away) **2.** When the Righteous One appears before the righteous, light will shine on the elect. Where will sinners and those who denied the Lord dwell? It would be better if they had never been born. (Elect: chosen ones) **3.** When the secrets of the righteous are revealed, sinners will be judged and the godless driven away. (Godless: those rejecting God) **4.** The powerful will no longer be exalted, and they won't see the holy face of the Lord, whose light will shine on the righteous. (Exalted: lifted up) **5.** Kings and the mighty will perish and be given into the hands of the righteous. (Perish: die) **6.** No one will seek mercy from the Lord, for their life will have ended. (Mercy: forgiveness)

Chapter 39

1. In those days, holy children will descend from heaven and unite with the children of men. Enoch received books of zeal, wrath, disquiet, and expulsion. Mercy will not be shown to them, says the Lord. (Mercy: compassion) **2.** A whirlwind carried me from the earth and set me at the ends of the heavens. (Whirlwind: strong wind) **3.** There, I saw a vision of the dwellings of the holy and resting-places of the righteous. (Dwellings: homes) **4.** I saw their resting places with angels, where they interceded and prayed for mankind. Righteousness flowed before them like water, and mercy fell like dew. This will continue forever. (Interceded: pleaded) **5.** I saw the Elect One of righteousness and faith, dwelling under the wings of the Lord of Spirits. Righteousness will prevail in His days, and the righteous and elect will be countless. (Elect One: chosen one)

6. The righteous will be as strong as fiery lights, their mouths full of blessings, praising the name of the Lord. Righteousness will never fail before Him. (Fiery lights: intense brightness) **7.** I longed to dwell there, for it was my destined place, established by the Lord. (Destined: intended) **8.** I praised and blessed the Lord of Spirits for granting me glory and blessing according to His will. (Glory: honor) **9.** For a long time, I gazed upon that place, blessing and praising Him, saying: "Blessed be He, from the beginning and forever. He knows all that is eternal and what will come. Those who sleep not bless Him, standing before His glory, saying, 'Holy, holy, holy is the Lord of Spirits; He fills the earth with spirits.'" (Eternal: lasting; Sleep not: awake) **10.** I saw all who do not sleep, standing before Him, blessing and saying: "Blessed be Thou, and blessed be the name of the Lord forever." My face changed, for I could no longer behold His glory. (Behold: see)

Chapter 40

1. Then I saw a countless multitude, thousands upon thousands, standing before the Lord of Spirits. (Countless: innumerable) **2.** On four sides of the Lord, I saw four presences, distinct from those who do not sleep. The angel with me revealed their names and showed me hidden things. (Presences: beings) **3.** I heard the voices of these four presences praising the Lord of glory. (Presences: beings) **4.** The first voice blesses the Lord forever. The second voice blesses the Elect One and those who are chosen by the Lord. (Elect One: chosen one) **5.** The third voice prays and intercedes for those on earth, invoking the name of the Lord. (Intercedes: pleads) **6.** The fourth voice defends against Satans, preventing them from accusing the people of earth before the Lord. (Satans: adversaries) **7.** I asked the angel of peace who these four were. The angel said: (Peace: harmony) **8.** The first is Michael, merciful and patient. The second is Raphael, over all the diseases and wounds of humanity. (Merciful: compassionate) **9.** The third is Gabriel, ruler of all powers. The fourth is Phanuel, in charge of repentance and hope for those who inherit eternal life. (Repentance: remorse) **10.** These are the four angels of the Lord, and the four voices I heard. (Angels: messengers)

Chapter 41

1. Afterward, I saw the secrets of the heavens and how the kingdom is divided, and how the deeds of men are weighed. (Deeds: actions) **2.** I saw the dwellings of the elect and holy, and the sinners being cast out, unable to endure the punishment from the Lord of Spirits. (Dwellings: mansions) **3.** I saw the secrets of lightning, thunder, winds, clouds, and dew, how they are distributed to the earth. (Distributed: scattered) **4.** I saw the chambers from which the winds are released—the chamber of hail, mist, and clouds, which cover the earth since the beginning. (Chambers: rooms) **5.** I saw the chambers of the sun and moon, their paths and returns, how one is superior to the other, and how they remain true to their orbits without altering them. (Superior: greater) **6.** The sun follows its course according to the command of the Lord of Spirits, whose name is mighty forever. (Mighty: powerful) **7.** I saw the moon's hidden and visible paths, completing her course by day and night, opposite the sun before the Lord of Spirits. (Opposite: contrary)

Chapter 42

1. Wisdom found no place to dwell, So a dwelling was assigned to her in the heavens. (Dwell: reside) **2.** She went forth to make her home among men, But found no place. So she returned to her seat among the angels. (Forth: out; Dwelling-place: home; Seat: position) **3.** And unrighteousness went forth from her chambers, Seeking whom she did not find, And dwelt with them, Like rain in a desert and dew on thirsty land. (Unrighteousness: wickedness; Chambers: rooms; Dew: moisture)

Chapter 43

1. And I saw other lightnings and the stars of heaven, and how He called them by their names and they listened to Him. (Lightning: flashes; Heed: listened) **2.** They are weighed in a righteous balance by their light, their spaces, their appearing, and their revolution that produces lightning. (Measured: weighed; Proportions: ratios; Revolution: orbit) **3.** They revolve according to the number of angels, and they keep faith with each other. (Loyalty: faith) **4.** I asked the angel who showed me these things: 'What are these?' He answered: 'These are the names of the holy on earth who believe in the Lord of Spirits forever.' (Parabolic: symbolic; Meaning: interpretation)

Chapter 44

Another phenomenon I saw concerning the lightnings: how some stars arise and become lightnings, and cannot return to their original form. (Arise: emerge; Part: return)

Chapter 45

1. This is the second Parable concerning those who deny the name of the dwelling of the holy ones and the Lord of Spirits. (Parable: allegory) **2.** They shall not ascend to heaven, nor walk upon the earth. Such is the fate of sinners who deny the Lord's name, reserved for the day of suffering and tribulation. (Ascend: rise; Tribulation: hardship) **3.** On that day, My Elect One will sit on the throne of glory and judge their works, Their places of rest will be countless, and their souls will grow strong when they see My Elect Ones and those who have called upon My name. (Elect: chosen; Glory: honor; Countless: innumerable) **4.** Then I will make My Elect One dwell among them. (Dwell: reside) **5.** I will transform the heavens into eternal light and blessing, I will make the earth a blessing, and My elect ones will dwell upon it. But sinners and evil-doers shall not walk there. (Transform: change; Eternal: everlasting; Evil-doers: wrongdoers) **6.** I have granted peace to My righteous ones and caused them to dwell before Me, But for sinners, judgement is coming, and I will destroy them from the face of the earth. (Granted: given; Righteous: virtuous; Destroy: annihilate)

Chapter 46

1. I saw One with a head like wool, and with Him another being, with a man's appearance and angelic graciousness. (Graciousness: kindness) **2.** I asked the angel about the Son of Man—who He was, where He came from, and why He went with the Head of Days. (Whence: from where) **3.** The angel replied: This is the Son of Man who has righteousness and reveals hidden treasures, Chosen by the Lord of Spirits, with pre-eminence and eternal uprightness. (Righteousness: justice; Pre-eminence: superiority; Uprightness: moral integrity) **4.** The Son of Man will raise kings from their thrones, Break the reins of the strong, and crush the teeth of sinners. (Raise up: lift; Loosen: release; Reins: control; Break: destroy) **5.** He will remove kings from their thrones, For they failed to praise Him and acknowledge His gift of their kingdoms. (Extol: praise highly; Bestowed: granted) **6.** He will humble the strong and fill them with shame. Darkness will be their dwelling, And worms their bed, with no hope of rising, For they didn't honor the Lord's name. (Dwelling: residence; Worms: decay; Extol: praise highly) **7.** They raised their hands against the Most High, Tread upon the earth, doing deeds of unrighteousness, Relying on riches and false gods, Denying the Lord's name. (Manifest: display; Unrighteousness: wickedness) **8.** They persecute the faithful and those who trust in the Lord's name. (Persecute: harass; Congregations: gatherings; Faithful: devoted ones)

Chapter 47

1. In those days, the prayer of the righteous and the blood of the righteous will ascend from the earth before the Lord of Spirits. (Ascended: risen; Righteous: just, virtuous) **2.** The holy ones in heaven will unite in prayer, praise, thanksgiving, and blessing the name of the Lord of Spirits, for the blood of the righteous shed, that their prayers may not be in vain, and that they may not suffer forever. (Supplicate: plead; In vain: without result; Judgement: justice) **3.** I saw the Head of Days seated on His throne of glory, with the books of the living opened before Him, and all His heavenly host and counselors standing before Him. (Head of Days: ancient one, God; Host: angels; Counselors: advisors) **4.** The hearts of the holy were filled with joy, for the number of the righteous had been offered, their prayer heard, and their blood required before the Lord of Spirits. (Required: demanded; Offered: presented)

Chapter 48

1. I saw an inexhaustible fountain of righteousness surrounded by many fountains of wisdom. The thirsty drank and were filled with wisdom, dwelling with the righteous and elect. (Inexhaustible: endless; Righteous: virtuous) **2.** At that hour, the Son of Man was named before the Lord of Spirits and the Head of Days. (Named: titled) **3.** Before the sun and stars were created, His name was proclaimed before the Lord. (Proclaimed: declared) **4.** He will support the righteous and be the light to the Gentiles, the hope for the troubled heart. (Gentiles: non-Jews; Hope: source of comfort) **5.** All on earth will bow and praise the Lord of Spirits. (Bow: worship) **6.** He was chosen and hidden before creation, and will remain forever. (Hidden: concealed) **7.** The wisdom of the Lord revealed Him to the righteous, preserving them as they despise the world's unrighteousness. They are saved in His name. (Preserving: protecting; Despise: reject) **8.** In those days, the kings and the strong will be humbled and unable to save themselves, given over to My elect. (Humbled: brought low; Affliction: suffering) **9.** They will burn like straw before the holy and sink like lead before the righteous, with no trace left. (Burn: perish; Sink: fall into ruin) **10.** On the day of their affliction, the earth will rest. They will fall and not rise, for they denied the Lord and His Anointed. Blessed be the Lord. (Affliction: hardship; Anointed: chosen)

Chapter 49

1. Wisdom flows like water, and glory will never fade before Him. (Flows: pours; Fade: diminish) **2.** He is mighty in all righteous secrets; unrighteousness will vanish like a shadow. The Elect One stands before the Lord, with glory and might forever. (Mighty: powerful; Vanish: disappear; Forever: eternal) **3.** In Him are wisdom, insight, understanding, might, and the spirits of the righteous dead. (Insight: clarity; Might: strength) **4.** He will judge the hidden, and no lie will stand before Him, for He is the Elect One, chosen by the Lord. (Hidden: secret; Lie: falsehood; Chosen: selected)

Chapter 50

1. In those days, a change will come for the holy and elect; the light of days will shine on them, and glory and honor will be theirs. (Shine: illuminate) **2.** On the day of affliction, when evil is stored up against sinners, the righteous will triumph in the name of the Lord of Spirits. They will witness this victory, repent, and forsake their evil deeds. (Triumph: prevail; Forsake: abandon) **3.** Sinners will have no honor in the name of the Lord, but through His name they will be saved, for His compassion is great. (Sinners: wrongdoers) **4.** The Lord is righteous in judgment, and unrighteousness will not stand in His presence; unrepentant sinners will perish before Him. (Unrighteousness: wrongdoing; Perish: be destroyed) **5.** From now on, I will show no mercy to them, says the Lord of Spirits. (Mercy: compassion)

Chapter 51

1. In those days, the earth will give back what was entrusted to it, and Sheol and hell will return what they have received. (Sheol: realm of the dead; Hell: underworld) **2.** The Elect One shall arise and choose the righteous and holy, for the time to save them has come. (Elect One: chosen figure) **3.** The Elect One will sit on My throne, and His mouth will reveal all the secrets of wisdom and counsel, for the Lord of Spirits has given these to Him and glorified Him. (Reveals: discloses; Glorified: honored) **4.** In those days, the mountains will leap like rams, the hills will skip like lambs, and all the angels in heaven will be filled with joy. (Leap: jump) **5.** The earth will rejoice, the righteous will dwell on it, and the elect will walk upon it. (Rejoice: be glad; Elect: chosen ones)

Chapter 52

1. After those days, in the place where I had seen all the hidden visions (as I was carried off in a whirlwind to the west), my eyes beheld all the secret things of heaven: a mountain of iron, copper, silver, gold, soft metal, and lead. (Whirlwind: powerful wind; Secret things: hidden knowledge) **2.** I asked the angel, "What are these things I've seen in secret?" (Secret: hidden) **3-4.** The angel replied, "These will serve the dominion of His Anointed, to make him powerful and mighty on earth." (Dominion: authority) **5.** The angel of peace then answered, "Wait a little, and all the hidden things surrounding the Lord of Spirits will be revealed to you." (Revealed: disclosed) **6.** These mountains (of iron, copper, silver, gold, soft metal, and lead) will become like wax before the Elect One, as water streaming from above. They will become powerless before His feet. (Elect One: chosen figure; Powerless: weak) **7.** In those days, none will be saved by gold or silver, nor will anyone escape. (Saved: rescued) **8.** There will be no iron for war, no bronze for armor, no tin or lead to be esteemed, as these will be of no use. (Iron: metal used for weapons) **9.** All these things will be destroyed from the earth when the Elect One appears before the Lord of Spirits. (Destroyed: wiped out)

Chapter 53

1. I saw a valley with open mouths; all creatures would bring gifts, but it would never fill. (Tributes: gifts or payments made to show respect) **2.** The wicked oppress and consume others, but they will be destroyed by the Lord and perish forever. (Oppress: to treat someone cruelly) **3.** I saw angels preparing tools of Satan. (Punishment: a penalty for wrongdoing) **4.** I asked the angel of peace, "For whom are these tools?" (Peace: calmness or harmony) **5.** He answered, "For the kings and powerful, to bring their destruction." (Destruction: the action of ruining something) **6.** The Righteous One will reveal His followers' house, and they will no longer be hindered. (Righteous: morally right) **7.** The mountains will bow before His righteousness, and the righteous will rest from the wicked. (Righteousness: the quality of being right; Bow: to bend in respect)

Chapter 54

1. I looked and saw a deep valley with burning fire. **2.** The kings and mighty were cast into this valley. (Cast: thrown or hurled) **3.** I saw iron chains of immense weight being prepared for them. **4.** I asked the angel, "For whom are these chains?" (Chains: strong metal links or ropes for binding) **5.** He said, "For the hosts of Azazel, to be cast into the abyss with rough stones, as commanded by the Lord." (Hosts: large groups or armies; Abyss: a deep or bottomless pit) **6.** Michael, Gabriel, Raphael, and Phanuel will cast them into the furnace on that great day for their unrighteousness in serving Satan and leading others astray. (Furnace: a large chamber for heating or burning; Unrighteousness: behavior not morally right) **7.** Punishment from the Lord will come, opening the chambers of water above and below the earth. (Punishment: a penalty for wrongdoing; Chambers: rooms or compartments) **8.** The waters above (masculine) and below (feminine) will merge. (Masculine: relating to male; Feminine: relating to female; Merge: to combine or unite) **9.** They will destroy all who dwell on earth and under heaven. (Dwell: to live or reside) **10.** When they see their unrighteousness, they will perish by these waters. (Perish: to die or be destroyed)

Chapter 55

1. After that, the Head of Days repented, saying: "In vain have I destroyed all on earth." (Repented: felt remorse or regret) **2.** He swore by His great name: "I will no longer do so, and I will set a sign in the heavens as a pledge of faith between Me and them forever, as long as heaven is above the earth." (Pledge: a promise or guarantee) **3.** "When I desire to act, My chastisement and wrath will remain upon them," says God, the Lord of Spirits. (Chastisement: punishment or correction; Wrath: intense anger) **4.** "You mighty kings on earth will see My Elect One sit on the throne of glory and judge Azazel, his associates, and all his hosts in My name." (Elect One: a chosen or selected individual; Hosts: large groups, often referring to angelic or military forces)

Chapter 56

1. I saw the hosts of the angels of punishment, holding scourges and chains of iron and bronze. (Hosts: large groups or armies; Scourges: tools used for punishment or whipping) **2.** I asked the angel of peace, "To whom are these who hold the scourges going?" (Scourges: tools used for punishment) **3.** He said, "To their elect and beloved ones, to cast them into the chasm of the abyss." (Chasm: a deep or vast opening; Abyss: a deep, bottomless pit) **4.** Then the valley will be filled with the elect, and their days will end, and they will no longer lead others astray. (Elect: those chosen or selected) **5.** In those days, the angels will return, going east to the Parthians and Medes, stirring up the kings to cause unrest. (Parthians: people from ancient Parthia; Medes: ancient Iranian people; Unrest: disturbance or turmoil) **6.** They will rise like lions from their lairs and wolves among flocks, trampling the land of the elect. (Lairs: resting places or dens of animals; Trample: to crush or step heavily on) **7.** But the city of the righteous will hinder their advance, and they will begin to fight among themselves, turning against one another. (Righteous: morally right or justifiable) **8.** In those days, Sheol will open its jaws and swallow them, and their destruction will be complete, as Sheol devours sinners before the elect. (Sheol: the realm of the dead in ancient belief; Devour: to consume or destroy)

Chapter 57

1. I saw a host of wagons with men riding, coming from the east, west, and south. (Host: a large group; Wagons: vehicles for transport) **2.** Their sound was heard, and the holy ones noticed it; the pillars of the earth shook, and the noise spread across the heavens. (Pillars: supports; Shook: moved or trembled) **3.** They will fall and worship the Lord of Spirits. This is the end of the second Parable. (Parable: a story illustrating a lesson)

Chapter 58

1. I began the third Parable about the righteous and elect. (Parable: story) **2.** Blessed are you, righteous and elect, for your reward will be glorious. (Reward: blessing) **3.** The righteous will live in the light of the sun, and the elect in eternal life. Their days will be endless, and the holy without number. (Eternal: forever; Endless: unceasing) **4.** They will seek light, find righteousness with the Lord, and have peace in His name. (Righteousness: morality; Peace: harmony) **5.** The holy in heaven will seek the secrets of righteousness, which shine like the sun, and the darkness will pass. (Secrets: mysteries; Heritage: inheritance) **6.** There will be eternal light, and the darkness destroyed, as the light of uprightness is established forever before the Lord. (Uprightness: integrity; Established: fixed)

Chapter 59

1. In those days, I saw the secrets of the lightning, lights, and the judgments they execute, whether for blessing or curse, as the Lord wills. (Judgments: decisions; Execute: carry out) **2.** I saw the secrets of thunder, how its sound is heard from heaven, and how the judgments on earth are made for well-being or a curse, according to the Lord's word. (Secrets: mysteries; Well-being: good health or happiness) **3.** Then all the secrets of the lights and lightning were revealed to me, showing how they bring blessing and satisfaction. (Satisfaction: contentment)

Chapter 60

1. In the year 500, in the seventh month, on the fourteenth day, I saw a mighty quaking that made heaven tremble, and the host of the Most High and the angels were greatly disturbed. (Quaking: shaking; Host: army) **2.** The Head of Days sat on His throne, surrounded by angels and the righteous. (Throne: seat of power; Righteous: just) **3.** Trembling seized me, and I fell on my face, overwhelmed by fear. (Trembling: shaking; Overwhelmed: overpowered) **4.** Michael sent an angel to raise me, and when I stood, my spirit returned. (Raise: lift up; Spirit: soul) **5.** Michael asked why I was disturbed, reminding me that until this day, God has been merciful and patient with the earth's inhabitants. (Disturbed: unsettled; Merciful: compassionate) **6.** When the day of judgment comes, it will be a covenant for the elect, but for sinners, it will be an inquisition, bringing punishment upon them and their children. (Inquisition: investigation; Covenant: agreement) **7.** On that day, two monsters were separated: Leviathan, the female, into the ocean's abysses, and Behemoth, the male, into the wilderness. (Monsters: creatures; Abysses: deep, vast spaces) **8.** Behemoth dwells in the wilderness east of the garden, where the elect live, and where my grandfather was taken. (Wilderness: desolate land; Elect: chosen) **9.** I asked the angel to show me the might of these monsters and how they were cast into their places. (Might: strength; Cast: thrown) **10.** The angel told me I sought to know what was hidden. (Hidden: concealed) **11.** The angel showed me the mysteries of heaven and earth, including the winds, stars, and thunders, how they are divided, weighed, and how they obey. (Mysteries: secrets; Divided: separated) **12.** The winds, thunders, and lightnings are assigned specific places and work in harmony through the spirit. (Assigned: designated; Harmony: balance) **13.** Thunder and lightning always go together, with the thunder following the lightning's flash. (Following: coming after; Flash: sudden light) **14.** The thunder and lightning are inseparable and controlled by the spirit, which guides them. (Inseparable: unable to be separated; Controlled: directed) **15.** The spirit of the sea is strong and pushes the waters across the earth. (Spirit: force; Strong: powerful) **16.** The spirit of hoar-frost and hail are angels, and the spirit of snow has its own chamber. (Hoar-frost: icy deposits; Chamber: room) **17.** The spirit of mist has its own glorious course, both in light and darkness, in summer and winter. (Glorious: magnificent; Course: path) **18.** The dew has its dwelling at the ends of heaven, connected to the rain, and its course flows in both seasons. (Dwelling: home; Course: path) **19.** The rain angels open their chambers and lead it out, uniting it with the water on earth for nourishment. (Chambers: rooms; Nourishment: sustenance) **20.** These things I saw near the Garden of the Righteous. (Righteous: just) **21.** The angel of peace said these two monsters were prepared according to God's greatness. (Prepared: arranged; Greatness: power)

Chapter 61

1. I saw how long cords were given to the angels, who took wings and flew north. (Cords: ropes; North: direction) **2.** I asked the angel, "Why have they taken the cords and gone?" He replied, "They have gone to measure." (Measure: assess) **3.** The angel said, "These angels bring the measures of the righteous and the ropes of the righteous, that they may stand firm in the name of the Lord forever." (Righteous: just; Stand firm: remain steadfast) **4.** The elect will dwell with the elect, and these measures will strengthen faith and righteousness. (Elect: chosen; Strengthen: support) **5.** These measures will reveal the secrets of the earth, and those destroyed by the desert, beasts, or sea creatures will return on the day of the Elect One. (Measures: standards; Secrets: hidden knowledge) **6.** All in heaven received command and power, and one voice and one light like fire. (Command: instruction; Power: authority) **7.** With their first words, they blessed, praised, and lauded with wisdom. (Lauded: praised; Wisdom: knowledge) **8.** The Lord placed the Elect One on the throne of glory to judge the works of the holy in heaven, weighing their deeds. (Glory: honor; Weighing: assessing) **9.** When He judges their secret ways according to the Lord's righteous judgment, all will speak with one voice, blessing, glorifying, and sanctifying His name. (Sanctifying: consecrating; Judgment: decision) **10-11.** On that day, all the heavenly hosts, angels, and powers on earth and water will raise one voice, glorifying in faith, wisdom, patience, mercy, judgment, peace, and goodness, saying, "Blessed is He, and may the name of the Lord be blessed forever." (Hosts: armies; Glorifying: praising) **12.** All who do not sleep in heaven will bless Him, along with all the holy, elect, and every spirit of light. All flesh will glorify and bless His name forever. (Flesh: human beings; Spirit of light: righteous beings) **13.** Great is the mercy of the Lord, and He is long-suffering, revealing all His works to the righteous in His name. (Mercy: compassion; Long-suffering: patient)

Chapter 62

1. The Lord commanded the kings, the mighty, and those on earth, saying: "Open your eyes and lift up your horns if you can recognize the Elect One." (Horns: power; Recognize: identify) **2.** The Lord seated Him on His throne of glory, and righteousness was poured out on Him. His words slay the sinners, and the unrighteous are destroyed. (Seated: placed; Slay: destroy) **3.** All the kings, mighty, and those who hold the earth will see Him on the throne, judging righteously, with no lies before Him. (Exalted: elevated; Righteously: justly) **4.** Pain will come upon them like a woman in labor, when her child enters the womb and she suffers in bringing forth. (Labor: childbirth) **5.** Some will look at others, terrified and downcast, as they see the Son of Man on His glorious throne. (Downcast: depressed) **6.** The kings, mighty, and all who possess the earth will bless and extol the one who rules over all, who was hidden. (Extol: praise; Possess: own) **7.** From the beginning, the Son of Man was hidden, preserved by the Most High, and revealed to the elect. (Preserved: protected) **8.** The elect and holy congregation shall be gathered, and all the elect will stand before Him. (Congregation: assembly) **9.** The kings and mighty, and those who rule, will fall on their faces, worshiping the Son of Man and seeking mercy. (Supplicate: plead; Petition: request) **10.** The Lord will press them, and they will hastily leave His presence, filled with shame and darkness on their faces. (Press: force; Hastily: quickly) **11.** He will deliver them to the angels for punishment, for oppressing His children and elect. (Deliver: hand over; Oppressing: mistreating) **12.** They will be a spectacle for the righteous and elect, who will rejoice over them as the wrath of the Lord rests upon them, and His sword drinks their blood. (Spectacle: display; Rejoice: celebrate) **13.** The righteous and elect will be saved, never to see the face of sinners and unrighteous again. (Saved: rescued; Unrighteous: unjust) **14.** The Lord will abide with them, and they will eat, lie down, and rise forever. (Abide: remain) **15.** The righteous and elect will rise from the earth, no longer downcast, and be clothed in garments of glory. (Downcast: sad; Garments: robes) **16.** These garments are of life, and they will never grow old, nor will their glory fade before the Lord of Spirits. (Grow old: age; Fade: diminish)

Chapter 63

1. In those days, the mighty and kings will beg the Lord of Spirits for respite from the angels of punishment, hoping to worship and confess their sins. (Implore: beg; Respite: relief) **2.** They will bless and glorify the Lord of Spirits, saying: "Blessed is the Lord of kings, the mighty, the rich, and glory." (Blessed: praised; Glory: honor) **3.** Thy power is magnificent in every secret, and Thy glory is eternal. (Splendid: magnificent; Eternal: never-ending) **4.** We have learned to glorify the Lord of kings, the King over all glory. (Glorify: honor) **5.** They will say: "Would that we had rest to glorify and confess our faith before His glory!" (Rest: relief; Confess: admit) **6.** We long for rest but find none; light has vanished, and darkness is our dwelling place forever. (Dwelling place: home; Obtain: get) **7.** For we did not believe in Him or glorify His name, but hoped in our kingdoms and glory. (Glorify: honor; Sceptre: royal staff) **8.** In our suffering, He does not save us, and we find no relief to confess His works as true, just, and impartial. (Suffering: hardship; Relief: respite) **9.** We pass from His face because of our works, and our sins are counted as righteousness. (Reckoned: counted; Righteousness: moral rightness) **10.** Now they will say: "Our souls are full of unrighteous gain, but it will not stop us from descending into Sheol." (Unrighteous gain: unjust wealth; Sheol: grave or hell) **11.** Their faces will be filled with darkness and shame before the Son of Man, and they will be driven from His presence, with the sword waiting before them. (Darkness: evil; Driven: cast) **12.** The Lord of Spirits spoke: "This is the judgment for the mighty, kings, exalted, and those who possess the earth." (Judgment: divine decision)

Chapter 64

1-2. I saw other hidden forms and heard the angel say: "These are the angels who descended to earth, revealed hidden knowledge to humanity, and led them into sin." (Seduce: lead astray)

Chapter 65

1-2. In those days, Noah saw the earth sinking and its destruction near. He went to the ends of the earth, crying out to his grandfather Enoch. (sinking: falling) **3.** Noah cried three times, "Hear me, hear me, hear me!" I asked him, "Why is the earth in such danger? Should I fear perishing with it?" (bitter: harsh) **4-5.** A great disturbance occurred, a voice from heaven was heard, and I fell to the ground. Enoch came to me and asked, "Why cry with such bitterness?" (disturbance: chaos) **6.** Enoch said, "A command has come from the Lord. The people's destruction is certain because they've learned the secrets of angels, the power of Satan, sorcery, and the making of idols." (ruin: destruction ; sorcery: magic ; witchcraft: spells) **7-8.** They also know how to make silver and soft metals from the earth. Lead and tin come from a hidden fountain, guarded by a powerful angel. (fountain: spring ; pre-eminent: supreme) **9.** Enoch raised me up and said, "I asked the Lord about this turmoil. He answered, 'Their judgment is sealed due to their wickedness, and I will not delay it.'" (turmoil: confusion ; unrighteousness: immorality) **10.** "Because of their sorcery, the earth and its people will be destroyed. There's no repentance for them; they are condemned." (repentance: regret ; condemned: doomed) **11.** "But you, my son, are pure and guiltless in this. The Lord knows your heart and you are not part of their sin." (guiltless: innocent) **12.** "Your name will be among the holy, and your descendants will be rulers, honored, and bring forth a never-ending line of righteous people." (descendants: offspring ; righteous: just)

Chapter 66

1. He showed me the angels of punishment, ready to release the powers of the waters beneath the earth to bring judgment and destruction on all who dwell on the earth. (unleash: release) **2.** The Lord of Spirits commanded the angels to restrain the waters and not let them rise, as they were in charge of the waters. (restrain: hold back) **3.** Then I left Enoch's presence. (presence: company)

Chapter 67

1. In those days, the word of God came to me, saying, "Noah, your lot has come before Me—one of love, uprightness, and no blame. (lot: fate, destiny) **2.** The angels are building a wooden structure. When it's completed, I will protect it, and from it, the seed of life will emerge, ensuring the earth will never be empty. Your descendants will be blessed, fruitful, and multiply in My name." (structure: building ; seed: offspring) **3.** "I will establish your descendants before Me forever, and they shall be fruitful upon the earth." (establish: set, secure) **4.** "I will imprison the angels who acted unrighteously in the fiery valley my grandfather Enoch showed me, in the western mountains filled with gold, silver, and metals." (imprison: confine ; unrighteously: unjustly) **5.** I saw the valley where there was great convulsion and the waters stirred. (convulsion: upheaval) **6.** From the molten metal and the convulsion, sulfuric fumes arose, connected to the waters. The valley burned with fire, where the angels who led mankind astray were punished. (molten: melted ; sulfuric: related to sulfur) **7.** Streams of fire flowed through the valley, punishing the angels who deceived the earth's people. (streams: flowing bodies of water or liquid) **8.** In those days, the waters will heal the body of kings and the mighty, but punish their spirit. Their bodies, full of lust, will suffer as punishment for denying the Lord. (heal: cure ; lust: strong desire) **9.** As their bodies burn, their spirits will undergo eternal change, for no idle word will be spoken before the Lord. (idle: pointless) **10.** The judgment will come because they have followed the lust of the body and rejected the Spirit of the Lord. (rejected: denied) **11.** The waters will change; when the angels are punished, these waters will turn cold. (punished: penalized) **12.** I heard Michael say, "This judgment of the angels is a warning to the kings and mighty of the earth." (warning: caution) **13.** These waters heal the kings' bodies, fulfilling their lust, yet they will not understand that these waters will turn into eternal fire. (lust: craving)

Chapter 68

1. After that, my grandfather Enoch taught me all the secrets in the book of Parables, which had been given to him, and he compiled them into the words of the book. (compiled: assembled) **2.** On that day, Michael spoke to Raphael, saying, "The power of the spirit overwhelms me because of the severity of the judgment on the angels. Who can endure this harsh judgment, before which they melt away?" (overwhelms: controls, affects strongly ; severity: harshness) **3.** Michael continued, "Who can remain unmoved by this judgment that has gone forth, and whose heart is not troubled because of those who led them astray?" (unmoved: unaffected ; troubled: disturbed) **4.** When he stood before the Lord of Spirits, Michael said to Raphael, "I will not defend them before the Lord, for He is angry with them because they act as if they are the Lord." (defend: support, argue for ; act as if: behave like) **5.** "Therefore, all that is hidden will come upon them forever, and neither angel nor man will share in it. They alone will face their judgment for eternity." (share: partake ; eternity: forever)

Chapter 69

1. After this judgment, they will terrify and make the people tremble, for they revealed secrets to those on earth. (Terrify: Frighten) **2.** Behold the names of the angels: Samjaza, Artaqifa, Armen, Kokabel, Turael, Rumjal, Danjal, Neqael, Baraqel, Azazel, Armaros, Batarjal, Busasejal, Hananel, Turel, Simapesiel, Jetrel, Tumael, Turel, Rumael, Azazel. These are the chiefs of the angels, with leaders over hundreds, fifties, and tens. (Chiefs: Leaders; Tens: Groups of ten) **4.** Jeqon led the sons of God astray, bringing them to earth through the daughters of men. (Led astray: Misguided) **5.** Asbeel gave evil counsel to the sons of God, causing them to defile themselves with women. (Defile: Corrupt) **6.** Gadreel showed men the blows of death and led Eve astray, revealing weapons of death, like swords and shields. (Blows: Strikes; Led astray: Misguided) **9.** Penemue taught men the sweet and bitter, secrets of wisdom, and how to write, causing many to sin. (Penemue: Angel who revealed knowledge; Sins: Wrongdoings) **12.** Kasdeja taught wicked smitings—spiritual and physical harm—including causing miscarriages and serpent bites. (Smitings: Strikes or injuries) **14.** Kasbeel showed the oath to the holy ones, and Michael was asked to reveal its hidden name to make those who revealed secrets tremble. (Oath: Sacred promise) **16.** Through the oath, the heavens and earth were formed. (Oath: Sacred promise) **17.** The earth was founded on water, and beautiful waters came from the mountains. (Founded: Established; Waters: Rivers or streams) **18.** The sea was created by the oath, with its boundaries set against the time of anger. (Boundaries: Limits) **20.** The sun, moon, and stars complete their courses, following their appointed paths. (Courses: Paths) **25.** This oath preserves the spirits, ensuring their paths and courses remain intact. (Preserves: Protects) **26.** Great joy filled them as they blessed and glorified because the name of the Son of Man was revealed. (Glorified: Praised) **27.** The Son of Man sat on His throne of glory, judging sinners and destroying those who led the world astray. (Judging: Deciding guilt) **28.** They will be bound in chains and imprisoned, their works vanishing from the earth. (Bound: Tied up; Vanishing: Disappearing) **29.** From now on, no corruption will remain, for the Son of Man has appeared and all evil will pass away before Him. (Corruption: Decay or evil)

Chapter 70

1. After this, his name was exalted before the Son of Man and the Lord of Spirits, above all who live on earth. (Exalted: Elevated) **2.** He ascended on the chariots of the spirit, and his name disappeared among them. (Chariots: Vehicles) **3.** From that moment, I was no longer counted among them. He placed me between the two winds, between the North and the West, (Counted: Included) **4.** where angels measured the destined place for the elect and righteous. There, I saw the first fathers and the righteous who have dwelled there since the beginning. (Destined: Meant; Elect: Chosen; Fathers: Ancestors; Dwelling: Residing)

Chapter 71

1. And after this, my spirit was lifted up, ascending to the heavens, where I saw the holy sons of God. They walked on flames of fire, their garments white, and their faces shone like snow. (Exalted: Elevated) **2.** I saw two streams of fire, glowing like hyacinth, and I fell on my face before the Lord of Spirits. (Hyacinth: A type of gemstone or flower) **3.** The angel Michael took me by the right hand, lifted me up, and led me into all the secrets, showing me the secrets of righteousness. (Righteousness: Moral uprightness) **4.** He showed me the secrets of the ends of heaven, all the chambers of stars, and all the luminaries, from which they proceed before the holy ones. (Luminaries: Sources of light, such as stars or celestial bodies) **5.** He translated my spirit into the highest heaven, where I saw a structure of crystal, with tongues of living fire between them. (Translated: Transferred or elevated) **6.** My spirit saw the girdle around the house of fire, with streams of living fire on its four sides. (Girdle: A belt or encircling structure) **7.** Surrounding were Seraphim, Cherubim, and Ophanim, who never sleep and guard the throne of His glory. (Seraphim: Fiery angels; Cherubim: Angelic beings often associated with guarding sacred places; Ophanim: A type of angelic being in Jewish mysticism) **8.** I saw countless angels—thousands and tens of thousands—encircling the house. Michael, Raphael, Gabriel, Phanuel, and the holy angels above the heavens entered and exited that house. (Countless: Too many to count) **9.** They came out of the house, led by Michael, Gabriel, Raphael, Phanuel, and many holy angels without number. (Led: Guided or directed) **10.** With them came the Head of Days, whose head was white as wool, and His raiment indescribable. (Raiment: Clothing) **11.** I fell on my face, my body relaxed, and my spirit was transfigured; I cried out loudly with the spirit of power, blessing, glorifying, and extolling. (Transfigured: Changed in form or appearance) **12.** These blessings were pleasing before the Head of Days, who came with Michael, Gabriel, Raphael, Phanuel, and thousands of angels without number. **14.** The angel came and greeted me, saying, "This is the Son of Man, born unto righteousness. Righteousness rests upon Him and never forsakes Him." **15.** He declared peace in the name of the world to come, for peace has been from the creation of the world and will be forevermore. (Declared: Announced or proclaimed) **16.** All will walk in His ways, for righteousness never leaves Him. With Him are their dwellings and heritage, and they will never be separated from Him, for all eternity. (Heritage: Inherited rights or possessions) **17.** The Son of Man will have length of days, and the righteous will have peace and an upright way in the name of the Lord of Spirits forever. (Upright: Honest and moral)

Section iii
Chapter 1

1. After some time, my son Methuselah took a wife for his son Lamech, and she bore a son. (Wife: Spouse) **2.** His body was white as snow and red like a rose, his hair white as wool, and his eyes were beautiful. When he opened them, the whole house lit up like the sun. **3.** He rose in the midwife's hands, opened his mouth, and spoke with the Lord of righteousness. (Midwife: Birth assistant) **4.** His father Lamech was afraid and fled to his father Methuselah. (Fled: Ran away) **5.** Lamech said: "I have begotten a son unlike us, resembling the sons of God, with eyes like the sun and a glorious countenance." (Countenance: Appearance) **6.** Lamech feared his son might not be his, but from angels, and asked Methuselah to consult Enoch, who lives among the angels. (Petition: Request) **7.** Methuselah came to me, crying aloud, and I heard his voice. (Cried aloud: Called out) **8.** I asked him, "Why have you come?" (Behold: See) **9.** Methuselah said: "I have come because of great anxiety and a disturbing vision." (Anxiety: Worry; Disturbing: Troubling) **10.** He described the child: his body whiter than snow, redder than a rose, with eyes like the sun, and light filling the house when he opened them. (Described: Told about) **11.** The child opened his mouth and blessed the Lord of heaven. (Blessed: Praised) **12.** Lamech feared he was not his son, but like the angels, and sent Methuselah to seek the truth from me. (Truth: Fact) **13.** I told Methuselah: "The Lord will do a new thing, which I saw in a vision, and I will reveal it to you. In my father Jared's time, some angels transgressed the Lord's word." (Transgressed: Broke; Revealed: Made known) **14.** These angels sinned with women, married them, and fathered children. (Sinned: Wronged) **15.** These children will be giants, not according to the spirit but the flesh, bringing great punishment and cleansing to the earth. (Giants: Large beings) **16.** A great destruction, a deluge, will come, lasting for one year. (Deluge: Flood) **17.** The son born to you will be left on earth, and he and his three sons will be saved when the rest of humanity perishes. (Left: Remained; Perishes: Dies) **18.** Name him Noah, for he and his sons will be saved from the coming destruction caused by sin and unrighteousness. (Unrighteousness: Immorality) **19.** Even more unrighteousness will follow in his time, but a generation of righteousness will arise to destroy sin and bring goodness to the earth. (Unrighteousness: Evil; Righteousness: Morality) **20.** The heavenly tablets reveal that each generation will sin until righteousness prevails and sin is eradicated. (Tablets: Sacred writings; Eradicated: Removed) **21.** Tell Lamech that his son is indeed his son, and this is no lie. (Lie: Falsehood) **22.** Methuselah, upon hearing Enoch's words, returned and named the child Noah, for he will bring comfort after the destruction. (Comfort: Relief)

Chapter 2

1. In those days, Noah saw the earth sinking, and its destruction was near. (Sinking: Falling down) **2.** He went to the ends of the earth and cried out to his grandfather Enoch. (Cried out: Called for help) **3.** Noah said three times with a distressed voice, "Hear me, hear me, hear me." (Distressed: Troubled) **4.** I asked him, "Why is the earth in such trouble? Why is it shaken? Should I perish with it?" (Perish: Die) **5.** Then a great commotion occurred, and a voice from heaven was heard, and I fell to the ground. (Commotion: Disturbance) **6.** Enoch came and stood beside me, saying, "Why are you crying in bitterness?" (Bitterness: Anger or sorrow) **7.** A command from the Lord has gone out, declaring the ruin of the earth. The earth's destruction is because they learned the secrets of the angels and the violence of the Satans. (Ruin: Destruction; Satans: Evil beings) **8.** They have also learned the powers of sorcery, witchcraft, and the making of molten images, and how silver and metals are produced from the earth. (Molten: Melted) **9.** Then my grandfather Enoch took my hand and raised me up, saying, "Go, for I asked the Lord about this commotion on the earth." (Raised: Lifted) **10.** The Lord replied that their judgment is decided because of their unrighteousness, sorceries, and knowledge of evil. The earth and its inhabitants will be destroyed. (Unrighteousness: Immorality; Sorceries: Magic) **11.** They will have no chance of repentance because they revealed hidden things and are condemned. But you, my son, are pure and free from this reproach. (Reproach: Blame) **12.** The Lord will keep you among the holy, and your descendants will be blessed with kingship and honor, producing an endless line of righteous and holy people. (Descendants: Offspring; Righteous: Just) **13.** Enoch showed me the angels of punishment, who are ready to release the powers of the waters beneath the earth to bring judgment and destruction. (Punishment: Retribution; Beneath: Below) **14.** The Lord commanded the angels not to let the waters rise but to hold them back, as they controlled the waters. (Controlled: Managed) **15.** I left the presence of Enoch. (Presence: Company)

Chapter 3

1. In those days, the word of God came to me, saying, "Noah, your lot is before Me, a lot of love and uprightness." (Lot: Fate) **2.** The angels are working, and once their task is done, I will preserve it, and from it will come the seed of life, ensuring the earth will not be empty. (Seed: Offspring; Empty: Without inhabitants) **3.** I will establish your descendants before Me forever, and they shall multiply and prosper in the name of the Lord. (Descendants: Offspring; Prosper: Flourish) **4.** I will imprison the unrighteous angels in a burning valley, shown to me by my grandfather Enoch in the west among mountains of gold, silver, iron, and tin. (Imprison: Confine; Unrighteous: Immoral) **5.** I saw that valley where there was a great disturbance, and the waters convulsed. (Disturbance: Disruption; Convulsed: Shook violently) **6.** From the molten metal and the convulsion, a sulfurous smell arose, linked to the waters, and that valley of the fallen angels burned beneath the earth. (Molten: Melted; Sulfurous: Containing sulfur) **7.** Streams of fire flow through the valley, where the angels who led mankind astray are punished. (Streams: Flowing bodies of water) **8.** These waters will serve kings, the mighty, and those on earth for healing of the body, but as punishment for the spirit. They will suffer in their body for their lustful spirits. (Lustful: Desiring excessive pleasure) **9.** They denied the Lord and see their punishment daily, yet they do not believe in His name. (Punishment: Retribution) **10.** As their physical suffering intensifies, their spirit will change accordingly, for before the Lord, no idle words will be spoken. (Idle: Empty or pointless) **11.** Judgment will come upon them for denying the Spirit of the Lord and indulging in bodily lust. (Indulging: Satisfying desires) **12.** In those days, the waters will change; when the angels are punished in them, the springs will become cold. (Punished: Reprimanded; Springs: Natural water sources) **13.** I heard Michael say, "This judgment is a testimony to the kings and mighty rulers of the earth." (Testimony: Evidence) **14.** These waters serve to heal the kings' bodies, but they will not believe that they will become a fire that burns forever. (Serve: Be useful to; Burn: Destroy by fire)

Chapter 4

1. Afterward, my grandfather Enoch taught me all the hidden wisdom in the book of Parables, which had been entrusted to him. He shared these teachings with me in the words of the book. (Wisdom: knowledge) **2.** On that day, Michael spoke to Raphael, saying, "The power of the spirit fills me with fear because of the severity of the angels' judgement. Who can withstand such a harsh judgement that causes them to melt away?" (Severity: harshness; Judgement: decision) **3.** Michael continued, "Who can remain unshaken by this judgement? Who can ignore the pain caused by the word of judgment passed on those who led others astray?" (Unshaken: unaffected; Astray: misled) **4.** Standing before the Lord of Spirits, Michael said to Raphael, "I will not defend them. The Lord of Spirits is angry with them for acting as though they were the Lord. They will face eternal punishment, and neither angel nor man will share in their fate." (Defend: protect; Eternal: forever) **5.** After this judgement, they will be filled with terror for showing these things to those on earth. (Terror: fear) **6.** The names of the angels are: Samjaza, Artaqifa, Armen, Kokabel, Turael, Rumjal, Danjal, Neqael, Baraqel, Azazel, Armaros, Batarjal, Busasejal, Hananel, Turel, Simapesiel, Jetrel, Tumael, Rumael, and Azazel again. **7.** These are the leaders of the angels, overseeing hundreds, fifties, and tens. (Overseeing: managing) **8.** The first is Jeqon, who led the sons of God astray, bringing them to earth and causing them to sin with the daughters of men. (Astray: off-course; Sin: wrongdoing) **9.** The second is Asbeel, who gave the holy sons of God evil advice, leading them to defile themselves with women. (Defile: corrupt) **10.** The third is Gadreel, who showed mankind the ways of death, led Eve astray, and introduced weapons for war and destruction, which have since plagued the earth. (Plagued: troubled) **11.** The fourth is Penemue, who taught mankind the secrets of wisdom, including writing with ink and paper. This led to sin, as men were not meant to use these tools. By this knowledge, they have fallen from righteousness, and death now claims them. (Righteousness: virtue) **12.** The fifth is Kasdeja, who taught mankind the harmful arts of spirits, demons, and even how to cause miscarriages. He also introduced harmful practices like serpent bites and the heatstroke of midday. (Miscarriages: loss; Heatstroke: illness) **13.** Kasdeja is also the chief of the oath, known as Biqa, which he showed to the holy ones when he dwelt in glory. (Dwelling: living) **14.** This angel asked Michael to reveal the hidden name, so he could pronounce it in an oath, making all who hear it tremble. (Tremble: shake) **15.** The oath, placed in Michael's hands, is powerful and binding. (Binding: obligating) **16.** By this oath, heaven was suspended before the world began. (Suspended: held) **17.** The earth was founded on water, and from the mountains' secret springs, beautiful waters flow eternally. (Springs: sources) **18.** By this oath, the sea was created, with sand set as its boundary, never to cross it. (Boundary: limit) **19.** Through this oath, the deep places of the earth remain still and unchanged forever. (Deep: profound) **20.** Through it, the sun and moon follow their paths without deviation forever. (Deviation: detour) **21.** By this oath, the stars complete their courses, and He calls them by name, and they answer Him eternally. (Courses: paths) **22.** This oath is powerful over them, ensuring their paths remain intact. (Intact: unbroken) **23.** Great joy filled them, and they praised and glorified because the name of the Son of Man was revealed to them. (Glorified: praised; Revealed: disclosed) **24.** He sat on the throne of glory, and judgement was given to Him. He caused the sinners to be wiped from the earth, those who led others astray. (Wiped: erased) **25.** They will be bound with chains and cast into a place of destruction, their works erased from the earth. (Bound: confined; Erased: deleted) **26.** From now on, nothing corruptible will remain, for the Son of Man has appeared and seated Himself on His throne of glory. (Corruptible: decaying) **27.** All evil will be destroyed before Him, and His word will be powerful before the Lord of Spirits. (Destroyed: ruined; Powerful: strong)

77 – The First Epistle of Clement to the Corinthians
Chapter 1
1. Due to the troubles we've faced, dear brothers, we realize we've been slow in addressing the conflicts among you. These quarrels, which are disgraceful and against God's chosen way, have been caused by stubborn individuals, leading to chaos and tarnishing your respected name. (Quarrels: arguments; stubborn: obstinate) **2.** Who among your visitors didn't admire your unwavering faith, praised your patience and devotion to Christ, recognized your hospitality, and acknowledged your sound understanding of the truth? (unwavering: steadfast; hospitality: generosity) **3.** You treated everyone fairly, followed God's laws, honored your leaders, respected the elders, and encouraged the younger members to maintain purity. You instructed women to live with pure consciences, love their husbands, obey them, and manage their homes wisely. (Consciences: moral awareness; purity: holiness)

Chapter 2
1. You were humble, free from pride, eager to give, content with what God provided, listened to His words, and kept His suffering before your eyes. (humble: modest; content: satisfied) **2.** This resulted in deep peace and an unquenchable desire to do good, with the Holy Spirit abundantly poured out on you. (unquenchable: unyielding; abundantly: plentifully) **3.** Filled with wisdom and zeal, you prayed for mercy, asking God if you had sinned unknowingly. (zeal: passion; mercy: compassion) **4.** You worked tirelessly for the salvation of God's people with fear and earnestness in your hearts. (earnestness: sincerity; tirelessly: without rest) **5.** You were sincere, free from malice, and opposed all divisions. (sincere: genuine; malice: ill will) **6.** You mourned others' sins as your own and rejected any bad deeds, always ready for good works. (mourned: grieved; deeds: actions) **7.** Adorned with virtue, you carried out your duties with reverence to God, with His commandments written on your hearts. (adorned: decorated; reverence: deep respect)

Chapter 3
1. All honor and prosperity were given to you, and it fulfilled the scripture: "My beloved ate, grew prosperous, became fat, and rebelled." (prosperous: successful; rebelled: defied) **2.** This led to jealousy, envy, conflict, division, persecution, confusion, war, and captivity. (jealousy: resentment; envy: bitterness) **3.** This stirred people against each other: the lowly against the respected, the foolish against the wise, and the young against the old. (lowly: humble; respected: esteemed) **4.** Righteousness and peace were abandoned as people turned from the fear of the Lord, becoming blind in faith and pursuing the desires of their evil hearts, leading to ungodly jealousy and death. (righteousness: justice; ungodly: immoral)

Chapter 4
1. As it is written: Cain offered the fruits of the earth, and Abel the firstborn of his sheep. (fruits: crops; firstborn: first in birth) **2.** God accepted Abel's offering but not Cain's. (accepted: approved) **3.** Cain became upset, and his face showed it. (Upset: distressed) **4.** God asked Cain why he was upset, saying if he offered correctly, he would be accepted. (Correctly: rightly) **5.** "Your brother will turn to you, and you will rule over him." (rule: dominate) **6.** Cain attacked and killed Abel in the field. (attacked: assaulted) **7.** Jealousy and envy led to brotherly murder. (brotherly: of brothers) **8.** Jealousy caused Jacob to flee from Esau. (flee: escape) **9.** Jealousy persecuted Joseph, leading to his bondage. (persecuted: oppressed; bondage: captivity) **10.** Jealousy forced Moses to flee after being rejected by his people. (forced: compelled) **11.** Aaron and Miriam were cast out due to jealousy. (Cast out: expelled) **12.** Dathan and Abiram were swallowed by the earth for rebelling against Moses. (Swallowed: consumed; rebelling: defying) **13.** Jealousy led David to be persecuted by Saul, despite his victories over the Philistines. (Persecuted: harassed; victories: triumphs).

Chapter 5
1. Now, let's turn to great men closer to our time and consider the noble examples of our generation. (Noble: admirable; generation: era) **2.** Because of jealousy and envy, the greatest Church leaders were persecuted, even to death. (Persecuted: oppressed) **3.** Let us consider the Apostles as examples. (Apostles: early Christian leaders) **4.** Peter, enduring many hardships because of unjust jealousy, went to his place of glory after bearing his testimony. (hardships: difficulties; testimony: witness) **5.** Due to jealousy, Paul showed us the prize of patient endurance: imprisoned, exiled, stoned, and preaching in the East and West. For his faith, he earned a noble reputation. (endurance: persistence; stoned: attacked with stones) **6.** He taught righteousness to the world, and after bearing his testimony before rulers, he departed, leaving a remarkable example of endurance. (righteousness: justice; rulers: authorities)

Chapter 6
1. Many of God's chosen people, like these holy men, endured injustices and sufferings from jealousy, setting a courageous example for us. (chosen: selected; injustices: wrongdoings) **2.** Women, persecuted due to jealousy, suffered cruel insults but reached the goal of faith and received a noble reward despite their physical weakness. (Insults: humiliate; noble: honorable) **3.** Jealousy caused separations between husbands and wives, distorting Adam's words: "This is now bone of my bones and flesh of my flesh." (distorting: twisting) **4.** Jealousy and conflict have overthrown cities and destroyed nations. (Overthrown: toppled; destroyed: ruined)

Chapter 7
1. Dearly beloved, we write these things to warn you and remind ourselves, for the same struggle and contest await us. (beloved: dearly loved; contest: challenge) **2.** Let us reject empty thoughts and follow the glorious teachings passed down to us. (reject: refuse; empty: pointless) **3.** Let us focus on what is good and pleasing to the One who made us. (focus: concentrate) **4.** Let us fix our eyes on the blood of Christ, which, shed for our salvation, secured grace for the world. (secured: guaranteed; salvation: deliverance) **5.** Throughout history, the Lord has made room for repentance for those who turn to Him. (made room: provided opportunity; repentance: remorse) **6.** Noah preached repentance, and those who listened were saved. (preached: proclaimed; listened: heeded) **7.** Jonah preached destruction to Nineveh, but they repented, pleaded for mercy, and received salvation. (pleaded: begged; mercy: compassion)

Chapter 8
1. The ministers of God's grace spoke about repentance through the Holy Spirit. (ministers: servants; grace: favor) **2.** Even the Master of the universe swore an oath about repentance: (Master of the universe: God; swore: made a vow) **3.** "For as I live," says the Lord, "I do not desire the death of the sinner, but rather his repentance." (desire: wish; repentance: remorse) **4.** He also said, "Repent, O house of Israel, for your sins. Though your sins are scarlet, if you turn to Me, I will listen and make you white as snow." (scarlet: red; turn: return) **5.** "Wash yourselves, be clean. Remove your iniquities. Seek justice, defend the oppressed. Though your sins are crimson, I will make them white as snow. If you listen to Me, you will enjoy the earth's blessings; but if you refuse, a sword will devour you." (iniquities: wrongdoings; crimson: deep red; devour: consume) **6.** Since He desires all to experience repentance, He confirmed it by His will. (desires: wants; confirmed: affirmed; will: purpose)

Chapter 9
1. Let us obey His will, present ourselves as beggars of mercy, and turn away from the empty labor that leads to death. (beggars: those seeking; empty: meaningless) **2.** Let us fix our eyes on those who perfectly served His glory. (fix: direct; served: honored) **3.** Consider Enoch, who, found righteous through obedience, was taken up by God and did not experience death. (righteous: just; obedience: compliance; taken up: removed) **4.** Noah, faithful and obedient, preached the world's renewal, and through him, God saved the creatures on the ark. (faithful: loyal; renewal: restoration)

Chapter 10
1. Abraham, called "the friend of God," was found faithful because he obeyed God's commands. (faithful: loyal; commands: instructions) **2.** Through obedience, he left his land, relatives, and father's house to inherit God's

promises. (obedience: compliance; inherit: receive) **3.** God said to him, "Go to a land I will show you. I will make you into a great nation, bless you, and through you, all families of the earth will be blessed." (nation: people; bless: favor) **4.** When Abraham parted from Lot, God said, "Lift your eyes and see the land. I will give it to you and your descendants forever." (parted: separated; descendants: offspring) **5.** "Your descendants will be as numerous as the dust of the earth." (numerous: many) **6.** God said, "Look at the stars; so will your descendants be." Abraham believed, and it was counted as righteousness. (counted: credited; righteousness: virtue) **7.** Through faith and hospitality, God gave Abraham a son in his old age, and through obedience, he offered his son as a sacrifice on the mountain God showed him. (hospitality: generosity; sacrifice: offering)

Chapter 11

1. Lot was saved from Sodom's destruction because of his hospitality and godliness, showing that God protects those who trust in Him but punishes those who stray. (hospitality: kindness to strangers; godliness: piety) **2.** Lot's wife turned into a pillar of salt when she looked back, showing a divided heart, serving as a warning that those who doubt God's power will face judgment. (divided heart: conflicting loyalties; judgment: divine punishment)

Chapter 12

1. Rahab, the prostitute, was saved because of her faith and hospitality. (prostitute: woman who sells sexual services) **2.** When Joshua sent spies to Jericho, the king sought to capture them, but Rahab hid them. (spies: secret agents; Jericho: ancient city) **3.** She misled the king's messengers, sending them in the wrong direction. (misled: deceived; messengers: representatives) **4.** Rahab said to the spies, "I know the Lord is giving this city to you. Please save my family." (save: rescue) **5.** The spies promised safety if she gathered her family inside her house and hung a scarlet thread as a sign. (scarlet thread: red rope, symbol of salvation) **6.** This symbolized redemption through the blood of the Lord. (redemption: salvation; symbolized: represented) **7.** Not only faith, but also prophecy, was seen in Rahab's actions. (prophecy: prediction) **8.** Dearly beloved, you see that not only faith, but also prophecy, was found in this woman. (beloved: dearly loved)

Chapter 13

1. Let us be humble, avoiding arrogance and anger. As the Holy Spirit says: "Let not the wise boast in wisdom, nor the strong in strength, nor the rich in riches, but let him boast in the Lord." (arrogance: pride; boast: brag; strength: power) **2.** Let us seek the Lord, prioritize justice, and remember Jesus' teachings: "Have mercy to receive mercy, forgive to be forgiven, give to receive, and judge as you wish to be judged." (prioritize: put first; mercy: compassion; forgive: pardon) **3.** Let us strengthen ourselves to obey His words with humility. (strengthen: empower; humility: modesty) **4.** "To whom will I look? To the humble, gentle one who fears My words." (fear: reverence)

Chapter 14

1. It is right to obey God rather than follow those who lead through pride and sinful jealousy. (pride: self-importance; jealousy: envy) **2.** Following those who stir division brings great danger and turns us away from what is right. (stir: provoke; division: disagreement) **3.** Let us treat each other with kindness and gentleness, as God has shown us. (kindness: consideration; gentleness: mildness) **4.** "The righteous will live in the land, but wrongdoers will be destroyed." (righteous: virtuous; wrongdoers: evildoers) **5.** "I saw the wicked exalted, but when I passed by, they were gone. Keep integrity and seek righteousness, for there is hope for the peaceful." (exalted: elevated; integrity: honesty; peaceful: calm)

Chapter 15

1. Let us cling to those who pursue peace with godliness, not deceit. (cling: hold fast; pursue: seek; godliness: devotion) **2.** God says, "This people honors Me with their lips, but their heart is far from Me." (honors: praises; lips: speech; heart: inner being) **3.** "They bless with their mouth, but curse with their heart." (bless: speak well of; curse: speak ill of) **4.** "They praise with their mouth, but lie with their tongue, and their heart is not right with Me." (praise: commend; lie: deceive; tongue: speech) **5.** Let deceitful lips be silenced, and those who boast, "Our lips are our own, who is lord over us?" (deceitful: dishonest; boast: brag; lord: master) **6.** "For the suffering of the poor, I will arise and act boldly on their behalf." (suffering: pain; arise: take action; boldly: courageously)

Chapter 16

1. Christ is with the humble, not those who exalt themselves above God's flock. (flock: the community of believers) **2.** Christ, though worthy of arrogance, came in humility, as prophesied by the Holy Spirit. (worthy: deserving; arrogance: pride) **3.** "Who believed our message? He was like a root in dry ground, despised and rejected by men." (root in dry ground: image of a humble, seemingly insignificant beginning) **4.** He bore our sins, suffering for us, though we thought He was in hardship. (bore: carried; sins: wrongdoings) **5.** He was wounded for our sins, bringing us peace through His suffering. (wounded: hurt; peace: reconciliation) **6.** We all went astray, each following our own way. (went astray: strayed; following: pursuing) **7.** The Lord gave Him up to death for our sins; He was silent in His suffering, like a lamb led to slaughter. (gave up: sacrificed; lamb: sacrificial animal) **8.** Who will speak for His generation? His life was taken. (speak for: advocate; generation: people living at the same time) **9.** He died for the sins of my people. (sins: wrongdoings) **10.** He was buried with the wicked, though He did no wrong, and the Lord cleansed Him from His wounds. (buried with the wicked: placed in a tomb with wrongdoers) **11.** A sacrifice for sin brings lasting offspring. (offspring: descendants; sacrifice: atonement) **12.** The Lord desires to free Him, give Him wisdom, and justify Him as a faithful servant. (justify: declare righteous; faithful servant: obedient follower) **13.** He will inherit many because His soul was delivered to death, counted among transgressors. (inherit: receive; transgressors: wrongdoers) **14.** He bore many sins, given up to death for them. (bore: carried; sins: wrongdoings) **15.** "I am a worm, despised by men." (worm: metaphor for being humiliated) **16.** Those who saw Him mocked, saying, "Let God deliver Him if He delights in Him." (mocked: ridiculed; delights in: takes pleasure in) **17.** The Lord was humble, so we too should be humble, as His grace has yoked us. (grace: unmerited favor; yoked: united in purpose)

Chapter 17

1. Let us imitate those who, like Elijah and others, preached Christ's coming with humility. (imitate: copy; preached: proclaimed) **2.** Abraham, called God's friend, humbly said, "I am dust and ashes" before God's glory. (dust and ashes: metaphor for humility and mortality) **3.** Job, righteous and blameless, confessed, "No one is pure from sin." (confessed: admitted; blameless: without fault) **4.** Moses, faithful in God's house, said, "Who am I to be sent?" and "I am slow of speech." He did not speak arrogantly. (faithful: loyal; slow of speech: hesitant in speaking)

Chapter 18

1. David, a man after God's heart, humbly prayed, "Have mercy on me, O God, according to Your great mercy." (man after God's heart: deeply devoted to God; mercy: compassion) **2.** He acknowledged his sin before God: "Against You only have I sinned." (acknowledged: admitted; sin: wrongdoing) **3.** "Wash me clean, for my sin is ever before me." (wash me clean: purify me; ever before me: constantly haunting me) **4.** "You will show me wisdom and cleanse me with hyssop, making me whiter than snow." (hyssop: a plant used in purification rituals; whiter than snow: pure) **5.** "Give me joy, and let the humble rejoice." (humble: modest, not proud; rejoice: celebrate) **6.** "Turn away from my sins and blot out my iniquities." (blot out: erase; iniquities: immoral acts) **7.** "Create in me a clean heart, and renew a right spirit within me." (create: form; renew: refresh) **8.** "Do not cast me away or take Your Spirit from me." (cast away: abandon; Spirit: divine presence) **9.** "Restore my joy and uphold me with a willing spirit." (restore: bring back; uphold: support) **10.** "I will teach sinners Your ways and they will be converted to You." (converted: turned toward; teach: instruct) **11.** "Deliver me from blood guilt, and my tongue will praise You." (blood guilt: responsibility for shedding innocent blood) **12.** "Lord, open my mouth to declare Your praise." (declare: announce; praise: glorify) **13.** "You do not desire sacrifice; a broken spirit is the sacrifice You desire." (sacrifice: offering; broken spirit: a humble heart) **14.** "A broken and humble heart, O God, You will not despise." (despise: reject; broken and humble heart: contrite spirit)

Chapter 19

1. The humility and obedience of great men, whose obedience has benefited us and the generations before us, teaches us to honor God's will. (humility: modesty; obedience: submission to authority) **2.** Let us strive for peace, focusing on God, the Creator, and His gifts of peace and blessings. (strive: make an effort; blessings: gifts of favor) **3.** Let us reflect on His patient will and how free of anger He is toward His creation. (reflect: think deeply; patient will: steady purpose; free of anger: full of mercy)

Chapter 20

1. The heavens obey God's direction in peace. (heavens: sky or universe; obey: follow) **2.** Day and night follow God's order without hindrance. (hindrance: obstacle) **3.** The sun, moon, and stars move in harmony according to God's command. (harmony: balance and agreement) **4.** The earth produces fruit in the seasons set by God, providing for all living things without deviation. (deviation: change or departure from the normal path) **5.** The oceans and underworld obey God's commands, though they remain unexplored. (underworld: subterranean or unknown realms) **6.** The sea stays within its boundaries, as God has commanded. (boundaries: limits; commanded: ordered) **7.** "You shall come this far, and your waves will be contained." (contained: held back, controlled) **8.** The vast ocean and beyond are governed by the same divine laws. (governed: controlled; divine laws:

laws established by God) **9.** The seasons follow in peaceful succession. (succession: sequence or order) **10.** The winds blow at the right time, and fountains never cease to provide life-sustaining water. (cease: stop; life-sustaining: providing what is necessary for life) **11.** All things are ordered by God in peace and harmony, especially for those who seek refuge in His mercy through Jesus Christ. (ordered: arranged; refuge: shelter or protection) **12.** To Him be glory and majesty forever. Amen. (glory: great honor; majesty: grandeur)

Chapter 21
1. Let us not let God's blessings become judgment if we do not live worthy of Him in unity. (blessings: gifts of favor; judgment: consequence for sin; unity: togetherness) **2.** "The Spirit of the Lord is a lamp searching the hidden parts of the heart." (lamp: illuminates, reveals; hidden parts: inner thoughts and emotions) **3.** God is close to us; nothing escapes Him—our thoughts and plans. (escapes: evades) **4.** It is right that we should not abandon His will. (abandon: forsake; His will: God's purpose) **5.** Let us offend foolish men who boast, rather than offend God. (offend: displease; boast: brag) **6.** Let us fear the Lord Jesus Christ, honor our rulers, respect elders, and teach the fear of God to the young. (fear: reverence; honor: give respect; elders: older, wiser individuals) **7.** Let women display purity, affection, moderation, and love for all who fear God in holiness. (purity: cleanliness of mind and body; affection: fondness; moderation: self-control; holiness: being set apart for God) **8.** Let children learn the value of humility, pure love, and the fear of God, which saves those who walk in holiness. (value: importance; humility: modesty; walk in holiness: live a life of devotion to God) **9.** God searches hearts; His breath is in us, and He can take it away at His will. (breath: life force)

Chapter 22
1. Through Christ and the Holy Spirit, we are invited: "Come, children, listen to Me, and I will teach you the fear of the Lord." (invited: called to join; fear of the Lord: reverence for God) **2.** Who desires life and good days? (desires: longs for; good days: happy, fulfilling life) **3.** Keep your tongue from evil and deceit. (evil: immoral actions or speech; deceit: lying) **4.** Turn away from evil, and do good. (turn away from: reject) **5.** Seek peace and pursue it. (seek: search for; pursue: chase or follow) **6.** The Lord's eyes are on the righteous, and His ears hear their prayers; His face is against those who do evil. (righteous: just, morally right; face is against: opposed to) **7.** The righteous cry out, and the Lord delivers them from their troubles. (cry out: call for help; delivers: rescues) **8.** Many are the sufferings of the righteous, but the Lord delivers them from all. "Many are the sufferings of the sinner, but those who hope in the Lord will be surrounded by mercy." (sufferings: hardships; sinners: wrongdoers; hope: trust)

Chapter 23
1. The Father shows mercy to those who fear Him, bestowing blessings on those who approach Him with a sincere heart. (mercy: compassion; bestowing: giving; sincere: genuine) **2.** Let us not be double-minded or indulge in empty thoughts about His gifts. (double-minded: uncertain, wavering; indulge: allow or entertain) **3.** Wretched are those who are double-minded and doubt, saying, "We heard these things in the past, but now we are old and nothing has happened." (wretched: miserable; doubt: uncertainty) **4.** Like a tree's growth, His will will suddenly be fulfilled—quickly and without delay. (fulfilled: brought to completion) **5.** "He will come quickly, and the Lord will come suddenly to His temple." (come quickly: arrive without delay)

Chapter 24
1. God continually shows us the resurrection through the example of Christ, the firstfruit of the dead. (firstfruit: the first in a series, symbolizing the rest) **2.** Let us see the resurrection that comes at the proper time. (proper time: appointed moment) **3.** Day and night show us the resurrection as they follow one another. (show: demonstrate; follow: occur in sequence) **4.** Consider how seeds are sown, decay, and then multiply, showing God's mighty providence. (decay: decompose; providence: care and guidance) **5.** From one seed, fruit is born, symbolizing resurrection. (symbolizing: representing)

Chapter 25
1. Let us consider the marvelous sign that is seen in the eastern regions, namely, in the area around Arabia. (marvelous sign: awe-inspiring event) **2.** There is a bird, known as the phoenix. This bird, being the only one of its kind, lives for five hundred years. When it has reached the end of its life, it makes a coffin out of frankincense, myrrh, and other spices, into which it enters, and so it dies. (coffin: a container for the dead) **3.** But, as the flesh decays, a certain worm is produced, nourished by the moisture of the dead creature. This worm grows wings, and once it becomes strong, it picks up the coffin containing its parent's bones, and carries it from Arabia to Egypt, to a place called the City of the Sun. (nourished: fed; grows wings: develops the ability to fly) **4.** During the day, in front of everyone, it flies to the altar of the Sun and places the coffin there. After doing this, it sets off to return to its homeland. (altar: sacred place for offerings) **5.** The priests then check their records of the times and find that it has arrived exactly at the completion of the five hundred years. (records: documented history or information)

Chapter 26
1. If God can bring about resurrection, as shown even in a bird, how much more can He raise those who serve Him in holiness? (resurrection: rising from the dead; holiness: sacredness) **2.** "You will raise me up, and I will praise You." (raise me up: bring back to life) **3.** Job says, "You will raise this flesh which has endured all these things." (endured: withstood, suffered)

Chapter 27
1. Let our souls be firmly bound to God, who is faithful to His promises and righteous in His judgments. (firmly bound: strongly connected; righteous: just) **2.** He who commands us not to lie will never lie Himself, for nothing is impossible for God except to lie. (commands: instructs; impossible: not able to be done) **3.** Let our faith in Him be ignited, knowing everything is near to Him. (ignited: set aflame, stirred up; near to Him: within His reach or care) **4.** By a word, God created the universe and can destroy it. (created: brought into existence; destroy: bring to an end) **5.** Who can challenge His power? Nothing He decrees will pass away. (decrees: commands or orders; pass away: cease to exist) **6.** All things are in His sight, and nothing escapes His counsel. (sight: vision; counsel: advice or wisdom) **7.** The heavens declare His glory, and day and night proclaim His wisdom. (declare: reveal; proclaim: announce)

Chapter 28
1. Since God sees and hears all, let us fear Him and turn from evil to avoid His judgment. (fear: respect and reverence; judgment: divine decision) **2.** Where can we hide from His powerful hand? (hide: escape; powerful hand: God's strength) **3.** "Where can I go from Your presence? If I ascend to heaven, You are there; if I go to the farthest parts of the earth, You are there." (ascend: rise; presence: near or face-to-face with God) **4.** Where can anyone flee from Him who embraces the entire universe? (flee: escape; embraces: encompasses, includes)

Chapter 29
1. Let us approach God with holiness, lifting pure hands to our merciful Father, who has made us His chosen people. (holiness: purity; merciful: compassionate) **2.** When God scattered the nations, He set boundaries according to the angels, and Jacob became His portion. (scattered: dispersed; boundaries: limits) **3.** "The Lord takes for Himself a nation, as a man gathers the first fruits of his threshing floor." (first fruits: the initial harvest, symbolic of dedication)

Chapter 30
1. As God's special portion, let us live in holiness, avoiding evil speech, drunkenness, arguments, and sinful desires. (special portion: chosen or sacred possession; sinful desires: temptations to act immorally) **2.** God resists the proud but gives grace to the humble. (resists: opposes; grace: unearned favor) **3.** Let us align with those to whom grace is given, living humbly and temperately, and being justified by our actions, not words. (align: agree or match; justified: made right, validated) **4.** "He who speaks much will be heard much. Does the one who speaks freely believe they are righteous?" (speaks freely: talks without restraint; righteous: morally right) **5.** Blessed is the child of a woman who lives a short life. Do not speak excessively. (blessed: fortunate; excessively: beyond what is necessary) **6.** Let our praise be for God, not for ourselves, as God hates those who praise themselves. (praise: admiration or worship) **7.** Let others testify to our good deeds, as was done for our righteous ancestors. (testify: witness or confirm; righteous ancestors: virtuous forebears) **8.** Boldness, arrogance, and recklessness belong to the cursed, while forbearance, humility, and gentleness are with the blessed. (boldness: courage; arrogance: excessive pride; forbearance: patience; gentleness: kindness)

Chapter 31
1. Let us hold fast to His blessings and consider the true ways of blessing, studying the records from the beginning. (hold fast: cling firmly; true ways of blessing: authentic paths to receiving God's favor) **2.** Why was Abraham blessed? Because he lived in righteousness and truth through faith. (righteousness: moral integrity; truth: sincerity; faith: trust in God) **3.** Isaac, with trust, was offered as a willing sacrifice. (trust: faith, belief in God's plan) **4.** Jacob, in humility, left his homeland to serve Laban, from whom came the twelve tribes of Israel. (humility: modesty; served: worked for another; tribes of Israel: the descendants of Jacob, forming the nation of Israel)

Chapter 32
1. Those who examine these examples sincerely will understand the greatness of the blessings God gave them. (sincerely: honestly and earnestly; blessings: divine gifts) **2.** Priests, Levites, and Jesus Himself came from Jacob.

Kings and rulers from Judah are his descendants, and God promised, "Your descendants will be as the stars of heaven." (Levites: a tribe of Israel set apart for religious duties; Judah: one of the twelve tribes, from which kings came; descendants: offspring) **3.** They were glorified not by their own works but by His will. (glorified: honored; His will: God's divine plan) **4.** We, called according to His will in Christ, are justified by faith, not by our actions, wisdom, or works. To Him be the glory forever. Amen. (justified: made right in God's eyes; faith: belief in God's promises)

Chapter 33
1. What must we do? Should we abandon good and love? May it never be! Let us eagerly strive to do every good work. (abandon: give up; eagerly strive: make great effort) **2.** The Creator takes joy in His works. (Creator: God; joy: pleasure, delight) **3.** By His might, He established the heavens and earth, separating them and setting all creatures in place. (might: power; established: created; separating: distinguishing between; creatures: living beings) **4.** As His greatest work, He created man in His own image, male and female. (image: likeness, representation) **5.** After completing His works, He blessed them, saying, "Be fruitful and multiply." (fruitful: productive; multiply: increase in number) **6.** The righteous were adorned with good works. Even the Lord rejoiced in His creation. (adorned: decorated, blessed; rejoiced: took delight in) **7.** Let us conform to His will and work righteousness with all our strength. (conform: align; righteousness: moral integrity) **8.** Since we have this pattern before us, let us diligently conform ourselves to His will and with all our strength, work the work of righteousness. (pattern: example; diligently: with persistent effort)

Chapter 34
1. The diligent worker receives the fruit of his labor with boldness, but the lazy avoids his employer. (diligent: hardworking; fruit of his labor: the results of his work) **2.** Let us be zealous for good works, for all things come from Him. (zealous: enthusiastic, eager; come from: originate with) **3.** He warns: "The Lord's reward is before Him to repay each person according to their works." (reward: recompense for actions; repay: give back) **4.** Let us believe in Him and not be idle or careless. (idle: inactive; careless: without attention) **5.** Our confidence should be in Him; let us observe how angels minister to His will. (confidence: trust, assurance; minister: serve) **6.** As the scripture says, "Ten thousand times ten thousand stood before Him, and they cried, 'Holy, holy, holy is the Lord of hosts.'" (stood before Him: were in His presence; cried: shouted; Lord of hosts: a title for God as ruler of all armies) **7.** Let us unite in one voice, earnestly calling on Him to partake in His great promises. (unite: come together; earnestly: sincerely; partake: take part) **8.** "Eye has not seen, nor ear heard, nor human conceived the great things He has prepared for those who wait for Him." (conceived: imagined; prepared: made ready)

Chapter 35
1. How blessed are God's gifts! (blessed: fortunate, given favor) **2.** Life in immortality, splendor in righteousness, truth, boldness, faith, and temperance are within our reach. (immortality: eternal life; splendor: brilliance, beauty; temperance: self-control) **3.** What rewards are prepared for those who wait for Him? The Creator alone knows their number and beauty. (rewards: blessings, benefits; number: quantity; beauty: magnificence) **4.** Let us strive to be among those who await Him to partake in His gifts. (strive: make great effort; partake: take part) **5.** How? By setting our minds on God through faith, seeking what pleases Him, and living according to His will—avoiding all unrighteousness and malice. (set our minds: focus our thoughts; unrighteousness: immoral acts; malice: desire to harm) **6.** Those who practice such things are hateful to God. (practice: habitually do; hateful: detestable) **7.** As the scripture says, "You declare My statutes but hate instruction and My words." (declare: announce; statutes: laws or commands) **8.** "You associate with thieves and share with adulterers. Your mouth multiplies wickedness." (associate: connect with; adulterers: those who commit infidelity) **9.** "I kept silent, but now I will confront you with your deeds." (confront: challenge; deeds: actions) **10.** "Understand this, you who forget God, lest He seize you like a lion with no one to rescue." (seize: capture; rescue: save) **11.** "The sacrifice of praise will glorify Me, and I will show him the salvation of God." (sacrifice of praise: offering worship; glorify: honor; salvation: deliverance from sin and death)

Chapter 36
1. This is the way of salvation, through Jesus Christ, the High Priest of our offerings, the Guardian and Helper of our weakness. (High Priest: one who intercedes for others; Guardian: protector; Helper: one who assists, especially in times of need) **2.** Through Him, let us look to the heights of heaven; through Him, we see His perfect form as in a mirror. Through Him, the eyes of our hearts were opened, and our minds are lifted to light. Through Him, we taste of immortal knowledge. He, greater than the angels, has inherited a more excellent name. (perfect form: true likeness; opened: enlightened; lifted to light: elevated to understanding; immortal knowledge: eternal wisdom; more excellent name: superior position) **3.** It is written, "Who makes His angels spirits and His ministers a flame of fire." (angels: heavenly messengers; ministers: servants; flame of fire: symbol of power and purity) **4.** Of His Son, God says: "You are My Son; today I have begotten You. Ask of Me, and I will give You the Gentiles as Your inheritance, and the ends of the earth as Your possession." (begotten: created; Gentiles: non-Jews; inheritance: received as a gift or legacy) **5.** Again, He says: "Sit at My right hand, until I make Your enemies a footstool for Your feet." (right hand: place of honor and authority; footstool: symbol of subjugation of enemies) **6.** These enemies are the wicked who resist His will. (wicked: those who oppose God's ways)

Chapter 37
1. Let us earnestly dedicate ourselves to His perfect ordinances. (earnestly: sincerely and with focus; ordinances: divine commands or laws) **2.** Consider the soldiers enlisted under rulers, how diligently and obediently they follow orders. (enlisted: joined the service; diligently: carefully, with effort; obediently: following commands) **3.** Not all are generals or rulers, but each obeys in their rank according to the king's will. (rank: position or status; according to: in line with) **4.** The great cannot exist without the small, and the small without the great. All have their place in the harmony of creation. (harmony: balance, order) **5.** Just as the head cannot function without the feet, nor the feet without the head, all parts of the body work together in unity for preservation. (unity: working together in agreement; preservation: maintenance of life and health)

Chapter 38
1. Let the whole body be saved in Christ Jesus, with each person subject to their neighbor according to grace. (subject to: under the care of; grace: unearned favor or blessing) **2.** The strong should not neglect the weak; the wise should show wisdom through deeds, not words. The humble should let others testify to their character. (neglect: disregard; humble: modest, not prideful; testify: provide evidence, witness) **3.** Let us consider from what substance we were created and how He brought us from darkness and death into His marvelous world. (substance: material or essence; darkness and death: spiritual or physical separation from God; marvelous: wondrous, extraordinary) **4.** Since all things are from Him, we ought to give thanks to Him, to whom be the glory forever. Amen. (ought: should; glory: honor, praise)

Chapter 39
1. Foolish and ignorant people mock us, seeking to exalt themselves. (mock: ridicule; exalt: elevate; self-exaltation: prideful attempt to raise oneself above others) **2.** What power does a mortal man have? What strength does a child of earth possess? (mortal: human, subject to death; child of earth: human being) **3.** As it is written: "There was no form before my eyes; only I heard a breath and a voice." (no form: no visible shape; breath and voice: the sound of God's presence) **4.** Can a mortal be pure in the sight of the Lord? Even He finds fault with some of His angels. (pure: without sin or impurity; fault: deficiency or error) **5.** No, the heavens are not clean in His sight. How then, you who dwell in houses of clay, can you think yourselves clean? (heavens: the sky or spiritual realm; houses of clay: human bodies, fragile and temporary) **6.** He strikes them down like moths, and they perish. (strikes down: brings to ruin; perish: die) **7.** Call out, if anyone listens, or if you see one of the holy angels. Wrath kills the foolish, and envy slays the misguided. (wrath: God's anger; envy: jealousy; misguided: led astray) **8.** I have seen fools whose dwellings were consumed. (consumed: destroyed; dwellings: homes or lives) **9.** Their children will be mocked, and no one will rescue them. The righteous will enjoy what was prepared for them, but the wicked will face trouble. (mocked: ridiculed; rescue: save; righteous: those who live according to God's will)

Chapter 40
1. Since these things are revealed, we must conduct ourselves according to order, doing all as the Master has commanded. (revealed: made known; conduct: behave; order: organization and respect for divine law) **2.** Offerings and services must be performed with care, at fixed times and seasons, not hastily or disorderly. (offering: gift or sacrifice; hastily: carelessly; disorderly: without proper structure) **3.** He has determined where and by whom these services should be performed, according to His will, ensuring piety and acceptance. (determined: decided; piety: devotion; acceptance: pleasing to God) **4.** Those who make offerings at the appointed times are blessed, as they follow the Master's institutions. (appointed times: scheduled moments for worship or sacrifice; blessed: favored by God) **5.** The high priest has his duties, the priests their office, the Levites their ministrations, and the laypeople their responsibilities. (duties: obligations; office: position; ministrations: services; laypeople: non-priestly people)

Chapter 41
1. Let each person give thanks to God with a clear conscience, following the established rules and conducting themselves properly. (clear conscience: without guilt or wrongdoing; established rules: divine commandments; properly: in the correct manner) 2. Not all sacrifices are made everywhere; they are only offered in Jerusalem, and only in the sanctuary, before the altar, by the high priest and appointed ministers after inspecting the victims. (sanctuary: holy place; altar: place of sacrifice; high priest: chief religious leader; appointed ministers: authorized servants) 3. Anyone who deviates from the prescribed order will be subject to death. (deviates: strays from; prescribed order: set procedures or guidelines) 4. The more knowledge we have been given, the greater our accountability, and the greater the danger if we fail to live according to that knowledge. (accountability: responsibility for one's actions; danger: risk of judgment or punishment)

Chapter 42
1. The Apostles received the Gospel from the Lord Jesus Christ, who was sent by God. (Gospel: the message of Christ's teachings and salvation) 2. Christ is from God, and the Apostles are from Christ, following the will of God. (Apostles: Christ's appointed disciples who spread His teachings; will of God: God's divine purpose) 3. Fully assured through the resurrection, they proclaimed the good news of God's kingdom. (fully assured: completely confident; proclaimed: spread the message; good news: the Gospel) 4. They preached everywhere, appointing their first converts as bishops and deacons after testing them by the Spirit. (bishops: church leaders; deacons: church servants; testing them by the Spirit: discerning their faith and qualifications) 5. This was in accordance with ancient writings, as the Scripture says, "I will appoint their bishops in righteousness and their deacons in faith." (ancient writings: the Scriptures; righteousness: moral uprightness; faith: trust in God)

Chapter 43
1. Even Moses, the faithful servant, recorded all commands in the sacred writings as a sign. (faithful servant: devoted follower; sacred writings: holy scriptures; sign: symbol or testimony) 2. When there was a dispute over the priesthood, Moses had the tribal leaders bring rods inscribed with their names, sealed with their rings, and placed in the tabernacle. (priesthood: the office of priest; rods: staffs used as symbols of authority; tabernacle: portable sanctuary) 3. Moses sealed the keys to the tabernacle and locked the doors. (sealed: closed with a sign of authority or security; keys: symbols of access; locked: secured against entry) 4. The tribe whose rod buds would be chosen by God to serve as priests. (buds: sprout or produce new life; chosen: selected by divine will) 5. The next morning, Aaron's rod not only budded but also bore fruit. (bore fruit: produced results or evidence of divine favor) 6. Moses knew what would happen, but he acted this way to avoid disorder and glorify God. (avoid disorder: prevent confusion or chaos; glorify God: honor God through actions)

Chapter 44
1. The Apostles foresaw disagreements over the office of the bishop. (foresaw: predicted; disagreements: disputes or conflicts) 2. They appointed men to this office with succession, so that others would take their place if necessary. Those who serve faithfully should not be removed from their position. (succession: passing on the responsibility to others; faithfully: with dedication and integrity) 3. It is a sin to remove those who have served honorably as bishops. (sin: wrongdoing; honorably: with respect and righteousness) 4. Blessed are the presbyters who have passed away, for their departure was fruitful. (presbyters: church elders; fruitful: bringing good results or rewards) 5. Some have unjustly removed those who lived honorably in their ministry. (Unjustly: without fairness or right reason; lived honorably: performed their duties with integrity)

Chapter 45
1. Be zealous and concerned for the things leading to salvation. (Zealous: eager and passionate; salvation: deliverance from sin and death) 2. You know the scriptures are true and were given through the Holy Spirit. (true: reliable and in accordance with God's will; Holy Spirit: the divine presence and guide) 3. Nothing false or unjust is written in them; righteous men were not removed by holy men. (false: untrue; unjust: unfair; righteous men: those living according to God's will; holy men: those set apart for God's service) 4. Righteous men were persecuted by the lawless: imprisoned, stoned, or slain by the wicked. (persecuted: treated harshly for their beliefs; lawless: those without regard for justice; wicked: evil, immoral people) 5. They endured nobly. (endured: suffered with patience; nobly: with dignity and honor) 6. Was Daniel thrown into the lions' den by those who feared God? (lions' den: place of punishment; feared God: held God in reverence) 7. Or were Shadrach, Meshach, and Abednego thrown into the fiery furnace by those who worshipped the Most High? No, it was wicked men, full of evil, who opposed them. (fiery furnace: place of punishment; wicked men: those who opposed righteousness) 8. Those who endured patiently, trusting in God, received glory and honor, and their names are forever written in God's memorial. Amen. (Endured patiently: withstood suffering without complaint; glory and honor: rewards for faithful service; memorial: lasting remembrance)

1. Therefore, brothers, let us hold fast to such examples. (Hold fast: remain committed to; examples: models to follow) 2. It is written: "Cling to the saints, for those who cling to them will be sanctified." (cling: adhere firmly; saints: holy or devoted people) 3. The Lord says: "You will be guiltless with the innocent, but you will be crooked with the crooked." (Guiltless: free from blame or sin; crooked: morally wrong or deceitful) 4. Let us cling to the righteous and blameless, for they are God's elect. (righteous: morally right; blameless: without fault; elect: chosen by God) 5. Why then are there divisions, strife, and anger among you? (divisions: separations or conflicts; strife: struggle or conflict; anger: intense emotion or rage) 6. Do we not have one God, one Christ, and one calling in Christ? (One God: unified faith in God; one Christ: singular Savior; one calling: shared purpose in Christ) 7. Why tear apart the members of Christ, forgetting we are all one body? (Tear apart: create division; members of Christ: believers who are united in faith; one body: the Church, united in Christ) 8. Jesus said, "Woe to the one who causes one of My elect to stumble... It would be better for him if he had never been born." (Woe: sorrow or judgment; stumble: fall into sin or error; elect: chosen believers) 9. Your divisions have led many astray, causing despair and sorrow. (led astray: caused to wander from the truth; despair: loss of hope; sorrow: deep sadness)

Chapter 47
1. Take up the letter of the blessed Apostle Paul. (letter: epistle; blessed: divinely favored; Apostle Paul: early Christian missionary and writer) 2. What did he write at the beginning of the Gospel? (beginning of the Gospel: the initial spread of the Christian message) 3. He warned you about divisions, even then, among Cephas, Apollos, and himself. (Cephas: Peter, one of the Apostles; Apollos: another early Christian leader; warned: cautioned against) 4. These divisions caused less harm then, as they aligned with respected Apostles. (caused less harm: had a smaller impact; aligned: were in agreement with; respected: esteemed) 5. Now, pay attention to who has led you astray and diminished your love for the brotherhood. (led astray: caused to deviate from the right path; diminished: lessened; brotherhood: fellowship of believers) 6. It is shameful for the Corinthian Church to create division over one or two individuals. (shameful: dishonorable; Corinthian Church: early Christian community in Corinth) 7. This folly dishonors the Name of the Lord and puts you in danger. (folly: foolishness; dishonors: disrespects; danger: risk of judgment or punishment)

Chapter 48
1. Let us quickly root out this division and pray for mercy, reconciliation, and restoration. (root out: eliminate completely; reconciliation: restoring peace; restoration: bringing back to wholeness) 2. This is the gateway to righteousness, as it is written: "Open to me the gates of righteousness." (gateway: entrance; righteousness: moral correctness and purity) 3. The righteous shall enter through this gate. (righteous: those who live according to God's will) 4. The gate of righteousness in Christ is for all who walk in holiness without confusion. (gate: entrance; holiness: purity or set apart for God; confusion: disorder or misunderstanding) 5. Let a man be faithful, wise, diligent, and pure in heart. (faithful: loyal and trustworthy; wise: discerning and understanding; diligent: hardworking; pure in heart: sincere and free from sin) 6. The greater he seems, the more humble he should be, seeking the common good. (humble: modest, not arrogant; common good: the well-being of all)

Chapter 49
1. Let those who love Christ fulfill His commandments. (fulfill: obey or carry out; commandments: divine laws) 2. Who can declare the bond of God's love? (bond: strong connection or tie; God's love: divine love for humanity) 3. Its beauty is beyond description. (beauty: the admirable quality of love; beyond description: too great to explain fully) 4. Love exalts us to heights beyond words. (exalts: lifts up or elevates; heights beyond words: transcends human understanding) 5. Love joins us to God, covers sins, endures all things, and does everything in harmony. Without love, nothing pleases God. (covers sins: forgives wrongdoing; endures all things: perseveres in all circumstances; harmony: peace and order) 6. Jesus, through His love for us, gave His life, blood, and flesh for our salvation. (gave His life: sacrificed Himself for humanity; salvation: deliverance from sin and death)

Chapter 50
1. See how great and marvelous love is, beyond full declaration. (great and marvelous: extraordinary in its qualities; beyond full declaration: too vast to express completely) 2. Only those whom God grants love can truly be in it.

Let us entreat God's mercy to be found blameless in love, apart from factions. (entreat: earnestly ask; mercy: compassion or forgiveness; blameless: without fault; factions: divisions) **3.** It is written: "Enter your room until My anger passes, and I will raise you from your tombs." (anger: divine wrath; raise you from your tombs: resurrection or restoration to life) **4.** Blessed are we if we keep God's commandments in love, for our sins are forgiven through love. (keep commandments: obey divine laws; sins are forgiven: wrongdoing is pardoned) **5.** Blessed are those whose sins are covered and to whom the Lord imputes no sin. (covered: forgiven or hidden from view; imputes no sin: does not hold them accountable for sin) **6.** This blessedness is for those chosen by God through Jesus Christ our Lord. To Him be glory forever. Amen. (blessedness: state of being blessed or favored by God; chosen by God: selected for divine favor; glory: honor or praise)

Chapter 51

1. For all our transgressions, let us pray for forgiveness, and those causing division should seek the common ground of hope. (transgressions: sins, division: separation) **2.** Those who walk in fear and love desire to suffer rather than harm others; they condemn themselves rather than divide the harmony handed down to us. (harm: hurt, condemn: judge) **3.** It is better to confess sins than to harden one's heart, like those who rebelled against Moses. (confess: admit, harden: stiffen) **4.** Their condemnation was clear. (condemnation: judgment) **5.** Pharaoh and his army were drowned in the Red Sea for their hardened hearts, after God's wonders in Egypt. (drowned: submerged, wonders: miracles)

Chapter 52

1. The Master needs nothing, except that we confess our sins. (needs: requires) **2.** David says: "I will confess to the Lord, and it will please Him more than a young calf." (confess: admit) **3.** "Sacrifice to God a sacrifice of praise, and call upon Me in your affliction, and I will deliver you." (affliction: suffering, deliver: rescue) **4.** A sacrifice to God is a broken spirit. (sacrifice: offering, broken: contrite)

Chapter 53

1. You know the sacred scriptures well, dearly beloved, and we write to remind you. (sacred: holy, remind: refresh) **2.** When Moses fasted for forty days, God told him: "The people you brought out of Egypt have made idols." (fasted: abstained, idols: false gods) **3.** The Lord said, "I will destroy them and make you a great nation." (destroy: annihilate, nation: people) **4.** But Moses pleaded: "Forgive them, or blot me out of the book of life." (pleaded: begged, blot: erase) **5.** O mighty love! Moses boldly asks forgiveness or demands to be blotted out with the people. (boldly: courageously, demands: requests)

Chapter 54

1. Who is noble among you, compassionate and filled with love? (noble: honorable, compassionate: kind) **2.** Let him say: "If there is division because of me, let me retire, and let the flock be at peace with its presbyters." (division: discord, retire: step down) **3.** He who does this will gain honor in Christ, and every place will accept him. (gain: receive, honor: respect) **4.** This is the way of those who live as citizens of God's kingdom. (citizens: members, kingdom: realm)

Chapter 55

1. Many kings and rulers, in times of pestilence, offered themselves to die in place of their people, seeking to save them with their own blood. They also left their cities to end divisions. (pestilence: plague, divisions: conflicts) **2.** Many among us have given themselves into bondage to ransom others, using the money earned to feed the needy. (bondage: captivity, ransom: free) **3.** Many women, empowered by God's grace, have done great deeds. (empowered: strengthened, deeds: actions) **4.** The blessed Judith, during a siege, asked the elders for permission to approach the enemy camp. (siege: blockade, permission: approval) **5.** She risked her life out of love for her people, and the Lord delivered Holophernes into her hand. (risked: endangered, delivered: handed) **6.** Esther, with perfect faith, risked her life to save Israel, fasting and praying to the Master, who saw her humility and saved her people. (faith: belief, humility: meekness)

Chapter 56

1. Let us pray for those in transgression, asking for patience and humility to help them yield to God's will, so that His remembrance may be fruitful and complete for them. (transgression: sin, yield: submit) **2.** Let us accept correction, which no one should resent, for it unites us to God's will. (correction: discipline, resent: complain) **3.** As the Holy Word says, "The Lord has chastened me, and not handed me over to death." (chastened: punished, handed over: delivered) **4.** "Whom the Lord loves, He corrects, and He punishes every son He accepts." (punishes: chastises, accepts: receives) **5.** The righteous will correct me in mercy and reprove me, but let not the mercy of sinners anoint my head. (reprove: rebuke, anoint: bless) **6.** "Blessed is the man whom the Lord has reproved; do not refuse the discipline of the Almighty. For He causes pain, but He restores." (reproved: corrected, refuses: rejects) **7.** He strikes, and His hands heal. (strikes: hits, heal: cure) **8.** "Six times He will deliver you from trouble, and at the seventh no evil shall harm you." (deliver: rescue, harm: hurt) **9.** In times of famine, He will deliver you from death, and in times of war, He will protect you from the sword. (famine: hunger, protect: shield) **10.** He will hide you from the scourge of the tongue, and you will not be afraid when evils approach. (scourge: punishment, approach: come) **11.** You will laugh at the unrighteous and wicked, and will not be afraid of wild beasts. (unrighteous: immoral, wicked: evil) **12.** Wild beasts will be at peace with you. (peace: calm) **13.** Then you will know that your house will be at peace, and your dwelling secure. (secure: safe) **14.** Your descendants shall be many, like the abundant grass of the field. (descendants: children, abundant: plentiful) **15.** You will come to the grave like ripe corn gathered at harvest time. (grave: tomb, ripe: mature) **16.** Thus, great protection is given to those whom the Lord corrects, for He is a kind Father who disciplines us to receive mercy. (protection: safety, disciplines: trains)

Chapter 57

1. You who caused the division, humble yourselves before the presbyters, accepting correction that leads to repentance. (division: separation, presbyters: elders) **2.** Put aside arrogance and stubbornness. It is better to be small in Christ's flock than to be honored and cast out from hope. (arrogance: pride, stubbornness: obstinacy) **3.** Wisdom says: "I called you, but you did not obey; I stretched out My hands, but you did not listen." (obey: follow, listen: hear) **4.** Because you made My counsel useless and were disobedient, I will laugh at your destruction when ruin overtakes you suddenly. (counsel: advice, ruin: disaster) **5.** When you call on Me, I will not answer; evil people will seek Me and not find Me. (evil: wicked, seek: search) **6.** They will eat the fruit of their actions, filled with ungodliness, and be destroyed. (fruit: result, ungodliness: wickedness) **7.** But those who listen to Me will live in safety, trusting in hope, and will have no fear of evil. (safety: security, fear: dread)

Chapter 58

1. Let us be obedient to God's holy Name, so we may escape the warnings against disobedience, and live safely trusting in His Name. (obedient: compliant, warnings: cautions) **2.** Receive counsel and have no cause for regret. Those who humbly carry out God's ordinances will be saved through Jesus Christ, to whom be glory forever and ever. Amen. (counsel: advice, regret: sorrow)

Chapter 59

1. If some disobey the words spoken by God through us, let them know they will fall into great danger. (disobey: rebel, danger: peril) **2.** We will be free from this sin and pray that the Creator preserves His elect through Jesus Christ, who called us from darkness to the knowledge of His glory. (sin: wrongdoing, preserves: keeps) **3.** Grant us to set our hope on Your Name, the source of creation, and open our hearts to know You—You who humble the proud, raise the humble, give life, and are the Benefactor of all spirits. You see the depths of hearts, help the needy, and save the lost. Through Your Son, You have instructed, sanctified, and honored us. (humble: lower, raise: lift) **4.** Lord, be our help and protector. Save those in tribulation, have mercy on the humble, heal the ungodly, and strengthen the weak. Let all nations know that You alone are God, and Jesus Christ is Your Son, and we are Your people. (tribulation: suffering, protector: defender)

Chapter 60

1. You, Lord, created the earth and are faithful in all generations, righteous in judgment, and wise in creation. Forgive our sins and wrongdoings. (faithful: loyal, righteous: just) **2.** Do not hold our sins against us, but cleanse us and guide us in holiness and righteousness, pleasing to You and to our rulers. (cleanse: purify, guide: direct) **3.** Let Your face shine upon us for our good, protect us from sin, and deliver us from those who hate us without cause. (shine: glow, deliver: rescue) **4.** Grant peace and unity to all on earth, as You gave to our ancestors when they called on You in faith and truth. (peace: harmony, unity: togetherness)

Chapter 61

1. Lord, You have given authority to rulers through Your incomprehensible power. We submit ourselves to them, seeking Your will, and pray for their health, peace, and stability, that they may govern well. (incomprehensible: unfathomable, submit: surrender) **2.** You, O Master, King of ages, grant glory, honor, and power to men on earth. Direct their decisions in Your will so they may rule in peace and receive Your favor. (grant: bestow, direct: guide) **3.** We praise You, O Lord, through Jesus Christ, our High Priest, for Your eternal glory and majesty. Amen. (praise: honor, majesty: greatness)

Chapter 62

1. We have fully written to you about the essentials of faith, repentance, love, self-control, sobriety, patience, and pleasing God through righteousness and holiness. (essentials: fundamentals, self-control: restraint) **2.** Lay aside malice and seek peace, just as our ancestors did by humbling themselves before God and all men. (Malice: hatred, seek: pursue) **3.** We remind you of these things because we know you are faithful and knowledgeable in the Scriptures. (remind: recall, knowledgeable: versed)

Chapter 63

1. Let us humble ourselves, submit in obedience, and align with our leaders, leaving division behind and seeking truth and peace. (Humble: lower, submit: yield) **2.** Joy will come if you follow this guidance, removing jealousy and anger, and striving for unity in the Holy Spirit. (Guidance: direction, striving: working) **3.** We have sent wise, faithful men to witness between us, showing our deep care for your peace. (Faithful: loyal, care: concern) **4.** Our desire is for you to find peace quickly, as we have always cared for you. (desire: wish, quickly: soon)

Chapter 64

1. May the All-Seeing God, Master of spirits and Lord of all flesh, who chose Jesus Christ and us to be His special people, grant every soul called by His holy Name faith, peace, patience, endurance, self-control, chastity, and sobriety. May they be pleasing to His Name through Jesus Christ, our High Priest and Guardian. To God be glory, majesty, power, and honor, now and forever. Amen. (endurance: perseverance, chastity: purity, pleasing: acceptable)

Chapter 65

1. Send back our messengers, Claudius Ephebus, Valerius Bito, and Fortunatus, in peace and joy, to report the peace and unity we seek. (messengers: envoys, seek: desire) **2.** May the grace of our Lord Jesus Christ be with you and all those called by God, to whom be glory, honor, and dominion forever. Amen. (grace: favor, dominion: rule)

78 – 1 Baruch

1. This is the text written in Babylon by Baruch, son of Neraiah, from the family line of Mahseiah, Zedekiah, Hasadiah, and Hilkiah. **2.** It was written in the fifth year, on the seventh day of the month, when the Chaldeans had captured and burned Jerusalem. (captured: seized) **3.** Baruch read the text of this book aloud to Jeconiah, son of Jehoiakim, king of Judah, and to all the people gathered to listen. (aloud: openly) **4.** The nobles, the king's sons, the elders, and all the people, from the least to the greatest, living by the river Sud in Babylon, heard it. (elders: leaders) **5.** They wept, fasted, and prayed before the Lord upon hearing it. (wept: cried) **6.** They collected as much money as each person could afford. (afford: spare) **7.** They sent it to the priest Jehoiakim, son of Hilkiah, and to the other priests and people in Jerusalem. (sent: delivered) **8.** On the tenth day of Sivan, they gave the silver utensils from the Temple to be sent back to Judah; these were the items made by King Zedekiah of Judah. (utensils: tools) **9.** These had been removed after Nebuchadnezzar, king of Babylon, exiled Jeconiah and the princes, metalworkers, nobles, and common people from Jerusalem. **10.** They wrote that they were sending money for burnt offerings, sin offerings, and incense to be offered on the Lord's altar. (offerings: sacrifices) **11.** They asked for prayers for the long life of Nebuchadnezzar and his son Belshazzar, that they may reign as long as the heavens last. (prayers: requests) **12.** They also prayed that the Lord would grant them strength, open their eyes, and allow them to live under the protection of Nebuchadnezzar and Belshazzar, serving them and gaining their favor. (Favor: approval) **13.** They asked the Lord for forgiveness, as they had sinned against Him, and His anger still had not turned away from them. (forgiveness: pardon) **14.** Finally, they instructed that the booklet be read publicly in the Temple during the feast and other suitable days. (Instructed: directed) **15.** They were to proclaim: "Salvation belongs to the Lord; we bear the shame we deserve, as does Judah and Jerusalem today." (Shame: disgrace) **16.** This shame is upon our kings, princes, priests, prophets, and ancestors. (princes: leaders) **17.** We have sinned against the Lord, (sinned: disobeyed) **18.** Disobeyed Him, and failed to follow His commands. (commands: orders) **19.** Since the day the Lord brought our ancestors out of Egypt until today, we have been disobedient and unfaithful, refusing to listen to His voice. (unfaithful: disloyal) **20.** We are still under the curses and disasters the Lord pronounced through Moses when He brought our ancestors out of Egypt to a land flowing with milk and honey. (curses: punishments) **21.** We have not heeded the prophets He sent us. (heeded: obeyed) **22.** Instead, we followed our evil hearts, serving foreign gods and doing what displeases the Lord our God. (displeases: offends).

79 – 2 Baruch

1. The Lord has carried out the judgment He declared upon us, our leaders, and the people of Israel and Judah. (carried out: executed) **2.** What He did to Jerusalem is unmatched under the heavens, fulfilling what was written in the Law of Moses. (unmatched: unparalleled) **3.** We were reduced to eating the flesh of our own sons and daughters. (reduced: forced) **4.** He delivered us into the hands of surrounding kingdoms, making us a disgrace and a curse among the nations where He scattered us. (disgrace: infamy) **5.** Instead of being rulers, we became slaves because we sinned against the Lord and did not listen to His voice. (slaves: captives) **6.** The Lord's justice is right, but we and our ancestors bear the shame of our actions. (shame: dishonor) **7.** All the disasters the Lord foretold have come upon us. (foretold: predicted) **8.** Yet, we did not seek the Lord's favor by turning from our wicked ways. (favor: kindness) **9.** The Lord saw our misdeeds and has brought disaster upon us, for He is just in all His commands. (misdeeds: wrongdoings) **10.** We have not obeyed His voice nor followed His commandments. (commands: instructions) **11.** Lord, God of Israel, You brought Your people out of Egypt with great power and signs, winning Yourself a name that endures to this day. (signs: miracles) **12.** We have sinned, committed sacrilege, and broken Your precepts, Lord our God. (sacrilege: desecration) **13.** Turn Your anger from us, for we are a small remnant among the nations where You have scattered us. (remnant: small group) **14.** Hear our prayers and deliver us for Your sake, granting us favor with those who deported us. (deported: exiled) **15.** So all the world may know that You are the Lord, for Israel and its descendants bear Your name. (descendants: children) **16.** Look down from Your holy dwelling, listen, and pay attention. (dwellings: sanctuaries) **17.** Open Your eyes, Lord, and see; the dead in Sheol cannot glorify You, (Sheol: the grave) **18.** but those in affliction, weak and hungry, can give You glory, Lord. (affliction: suffering) **19.** We do not rely on our ancestors' merits but seek Your mercy, Lord our God. (merits: virtues) **20.** You sent Your anger and fury upon us, as foretold by Your prophets, saying, (anger: wrath) **21.** "Serve the king of Babylon, and you will remain in the land I gave your ancestors." (ancestors: forefathers) **22.** But if you do not listen and serve the king of Babylon, (listen: obey) **23.** I will silence joy and celebration, and the land of Judah will become a desolate wasteland with no inhabitants. (silence: end) **24.** We did not listen to Your voice, and as You threatened, the bones of our kings and ancestors were desecrated. (threatened: warned) **25.** Their bones were cast out in the heat of the day and the frost of the night, and many died in suffering from famine, sword, and plague. (famine: hunger) **26.** Because of the wickedness of Israel and Judah, You have made the Temple, bearing Your name, what it is today. (wickedness: sinfulness) **27.** Yet, Lord, You have treated us with great mercy, as You promised Moses when He instructed Israel in Your law. (mercy: compassion) **28.** You warned that if we did not listen, we would be scattered among the nations, becoming a tiny remnant. (remnant: small group) **29.** But I knew they would be stubborn, so in their exile, they will come to their senses, (stubborn: obstinate) **30.** acknowledging that I am their Lord, and I will give them a heart to listen. (acknowledging: recognizing) **31.** They will praise me in their exile, remembering My name, (exile: captivity) **32.** and they will stop their stubborn ways, turning from their evil deeds, (evil deeds: wrong actions) **33.** learning from the fate of their ancestors who sinned before the Lord. (fate: consequence) **34.** Then I will bring them back to the land I promised to Abraham, Isaac, and Jacob, and make them prosperous. (prosperous: successful) **35.** I will establish an everlasting covenant with them, so that I will be their God and they will be My people, and I will never again exile Israel from the land I gave them. (everlasting: eternal)

80 – The book of Sirach, or Ecclesiasticus

Chapter 1

1. Wisdom comes from the LORD and stays with Him. (LORD: God) **2.** Who can count eternity, the sand, or raindrops? (Eternity: the eternal) **3.** Who can explore the heavens, earth, or sea? (Heavens: celestial realms, Earth: planet, Sea: vast saltwater) **4.** Wisdom was created before all things; understanding is eternal. (Understanding: deep insight) **5.** Who knows the root and hidden ways of wisdom? (Root: origin, Hidden: secret) **6.** There is one wise and awe-inspiring on His throne. (Throne: royal seat) **7.** It is the LORD; He created and understands wisdom. (LORD: God, Wisdom: divine insight) **8.** He poured wisdom upon His works, according to His generosity. (Generosity: kindness) **9.** Fear of the LORD brings honor, joy, and celebration. (Fear: reverence, LORD: God) **10.** Fear of the LORD refreshes the soul, bringing joy and long life. (Refreshes: revitalizes, Soul: spirit) **11.** He who fears the LORD is blessed, even in death. (Blessed: favored by God) **12.** The foundation of wisdom is the fear of the LORD. (Foundation: base, Wisdom: divine insight) **13.** Wisdom was created with the faithful, and remains with their descendants. (Faithful: loyal followers, Descendants: future generations) **14.** The fullness of wisdom is found in the fear of the LORD. (Fullness: completeness, LORD: God) **15.** Wisdom's house is filled with abundance. (House: dwelling) **16.** Wisdom's crown is fear of the LORD, adorned with peace. (Crown: symbol of honor, Adorned: decorated) **17.** Knowledge and understanding are given to those with wisdom. (Knowledge: information, Understanding: deep insight) **18.** The root of wisdom is fear of the LORD; her results are long life. (Root: origin, Results: outcomes) **19.** Unjust anger leads to ruin. (Unjust: unfair, Ruin: destruction) **20.** A patient person endures and finds contentment. (Contentment: satisfaction) **21.** Wisdom is acknowledged after patiently holding back words. (Acknowledged: recognized, Words: speech) **22.** Wisdom includes prudence, but sinners hate the fear of the LORD. (Prudence: practical wisdom, Sinners: wrongdoers, LORD: God) **23.** Seek wisdom by obeying the commandments, and the LORD will grant it. (Commandments: divine rules, LORD: God) **24.** Fear of the LORD is wisdom and understanding; loyalty pleases Him. (Fear: reverence, LORD: God, Loyalty: faithfulness) **25.** Do not be disloyal or deceitful toward the fear of the LORD. (Deceitful: dishonest, Disloyal: unfaithful) **26.** Do not act hypocritically; mind your words. (Hypocritically: insincerely, Words: speech) **27.** Do not exalt yourself or fall into disgrace. (Exalt: raise in honor, Disgrace: shame) **28.** The LORD will expose your secrets publicly. (Expose: reveal, Secrets: hidden matters, LORD: God) **29.** You approached the fear of the LORD deceitfully. (Deceitfully: dishonestly, Fear of the LORD: reverence for God)

Chapter 2
1. Serving the LORD brings challenges. (LORD: God) **2.** Be sincere, steadfast, and calm in trouble. (Sincere: genuine, Steadfast: unwavering) **3.** Hold onto God, and your future will be great. (Future: what lies ahead) **4.** Accept hardships and remain patient. (Hardships: tough times; Patient: enduring calmly) **5.** Gold is tested in fire, and so are noble people. (Gold: precious metal; Noble: virtuous) **6.** Trust God, and He will help you; hope in Him. (Hope: expectation) **7.** Those who fear the LORD wait for His mercy. (Mercy: compassion) **8.** Trust in the LORD, and your reward is secure. (Reward: outcome of actions) **9.** Hope in the LORD for joy and mercy. (Mercy: compassion) **10.** Has anyone trusted the LORD and been put to shame? (LORD: God) **11.** The LORD is compassionate, forgiving, and saves. (Forgives: pardons) **12.** Woe to those with faint hearts and weak hands. (Faint hearts: lack of courage) **13.** Woe to those who don't trust; they have no refuge. (Refuge: shelter) **14.** Woe to those who have lost hope! (Lost hope: no belief left) **15.** Those who fear the LORD obey His words. (Obey: comply with) **16.** Those who fear the LORD seek to please Him. (Please: satisfy) **17.** Those who fear the LORD humble themselves. (Humble: act modestly) **18.** Let us fall into the LORD's hands, for His mercy is great. (Mercy: compassion; Majesty: greatness)

Chapter 3
1. Children, listen to your father's guidance for a long life. (Father: a male parent) **2.** The LORD honors fathers and confirms a mother's authority. (LORD: God) **3.** Those who honor their father make up for their wrongs. (Honor: to show respect) **4.** Those who respect their mother will prosper. (Respect: to show admiration) **5.** Honoring your father brings children and answered prayers. (Blessed: favored) **6.** Honor your father and follow the LORD for a long life. (LORD: God, Comfort: solace) **7.** He who fears the LORD honors his father and serves his parents. (Fear: reverence, Authorities: those in power) **8.** Honor your father in words and actions for his blessing. (Blessing: prayer for favor) **9.** A father's blessing gives a firm foundation; a mother's curse destroys. (Curse: wish for harm) **10.** Do not boast in your father's shame; it brings no glory. (Boast: to brag, Disgrace: dishonor) **11.** A man's glory is his father's honor, and a mother's disgrace brings shame. (Glory: honor, Disgrace: dishonor) **12.** Care for your father in his old age and do not grieve him. (Sorrowful: filled with sadness) **13.** Be patient with an aging father; do not insult him. (Fades: weakens, Insult: disrespect) **14.** Kindness to a father is remembered, like a sin offering. (Sin offering: atonement) **15.** In times of trouble, your kindness brings relief. (Relief: comfort, Frost: ice) **16.** A blasphemer dishonors his father; cursed is one who angers his mother. (Blasphemer: speaks against God, Cursed: condemned) **17.** Humble yourself, and you will be loved more than a gift-giver. (Humility: being humble, Affairs: matters) **18.** The greater you are, the more humble you should be. (Favor: approval) **19.** God's power is immense; He is glorified by the humble. (Immense: great, Glorified: praised) **20.** Do not seek what you cannot understand or pursue difficult things. (Seek: search for, Pursue: chase) **21.** Focus on what is entrusted to you; hidden matters are not your concern. (Entrusted: given to care, Hidden: concealed) **22.** Do not meddle in things beyond human comprehension. (Meddle: interfere, Comprehension: understanding) **23.** Many are misled by opinions, and false reasoning disturbs their judgment. (Misled: led astray, Judgment: decision-making) **24.** Without the pupil, there is no light; without knowledge, no wisdom. (Pupil: part of the eye, Knowledge: understanding) **25.** A stubborn person will face consequences; one who seeks danger will perish. (Stubborn: unyielding, Perish: die) **26.** A stubborn person suffers sorrow, and a sinner adds sin upon sin. (Sorrow: sadness, Sinner: wrongdoer) **27.** The prideful have no cure; they are the offspring of evil. (Prideful: arrogant, Offspring: children) **28.** A wise person values proverbs, and an attentive ear brings joy to the wise. (Proverbs: wise sayings, Attentive: focused) **29.** Water extinguishes fire, and charity covers sins. (Charity: giving, Sins: wrongdoings) **30.** Kindness is remembered, and when you fall, you will find support. (Kindness: compassion, Support: help)

Chapter 4
1. Do not deprive the poor or make the needy despair. (Deprive: deny someone something they need; Despair: loss of hope) **2.** Do not grieve or anger the hungry and needy. (Grieve: cause sadness; Anger: make upset) **3.** Help the suffering immediately. (Suffering: experiencing hardship) **4.** Do not reject a beggar or the poor in distress. (Reject: turn away; Distress: extreme difficulty) **5.** Do not ignore the needy or give reason to be cursed. (Ignore: pay no attention to; Curse: invoke harm or misfortune) **6.** God will hear the cries of those whom others have cursed. (Cursed: spoken against with ill wishes) **7.** Be kind to the assembly; bow to a ruler. (Assembly: a group of people gathered for a purpose; Bow: show respect by bending forward) **8.** Listen to the poor and greet them kindly. (Greet: give a polite hello) **9.** Rescue the oppressed; do not ignore justice. (Oppressed: those suffering unfair treatment; Justice: fairness or legal rights) **10.** Be like a father to orphans and care for their mother. (Orphan: a child whose parents have died) **11.** Wisdom teaches and guides those who seek her. (Wisdom: knowledge and good judgment) **12.** Those who love wisdom love life and find favor. (Favor: approval or blessings) **13.** Wisdom brings glory, and the Lord blesses those who seek her. (Glory: great honor) **14.** Serving wisdom is serving God; those who love her are loved by the Lord. (Holy One: a title for God) **15.** Obeying wisdom leads to ruling nations. (Obeying: following guidance or rules) **16.** Trusting wisdom leads to possessing her and benefiting future generations. (Descendants: future generations) **17.** Wisdom tests through fear and discipline. (Discipline: training to improve behavior) **18.** Once aligned, wisdom brings happiness and reveals secrets. (Aligned: in harmony or agreement; Secrets: hidden knowledge) **19.** If you fail, wisdom will leave you to be exploited. (Exploited: taken advantage of) **20.** Use your time wisely to avoid evil and shame. (Shame: dishonor or disgrace) **21.** Some shame brings guilt, others respect. (Guilt: responsibility for wrongdoing) **22.** Do not favor anyone to your detriment or be pressured into downfall. (Detriment: harm or damage) **23.** Speak when right, and do not hide wisdom. (Hesitate: delay action) **24.** Wisdom is shown in speech, knowledge in response. (Response: an answer or reply) **25.** Never oppose truth or fight the natural flow. (Oppose: act against) **26.** Be ashamed of ignorance, not faults. (Faults: mistakes or wrongdoings) **27.** Do not abase yourself before the ungodly or refuse respect to rulers. (Ungodly: wicked or immoral) **28.** Fight for truth, and the Lord will fight for you. (Fight: struggle or defend) **29.** Do not speak harshly or be lazy in action. (Harshly: in a rude or severe manner) **30.** Do not be deceitful at work or act like a lion at home. (Deceitful: dishonest or misleading; Lion: a metaphor for being aggressive or domineering) **31.** Do not take with an open hand and give with a closed one. (Close-handed: unwilling to share)

Chapter 5
1. Do not rely on wealth or boast of your power. (Wealth: material riches, Power: control) **2.** Do not trust in your strength to fulfill desires. (Strength: ability, Desires: cravings) **3.** Do not claim, "Who can defeat me?"—the Lord will punish. (Defeat: overcome, Punish: penalty) **4.** Do not question, "Why has this happened?"—the Lord waits. (Happened: occurred, Waits: remains patient) **5.** Do not overestimate forgiveness, adding sin to sin. (Overestimate: overvalue, Sin: wrongdoing) **6.** Do not assume, "His mercy is great; He will forgive my sins." (Mercy: compassion, Sins: offenses) **7.** Mercy and wrath are with Him; the wicked face His anger. (Wrath: anger, Wicked: immoral people) **8.** Do not delay your repentance; His wrath will come suddenly. (Delay: postpone, Repentance: turning away from sin) **9.** Do not trust false wealth; it won't help in the day of judgment. (False: deceitful, Wealth: material riches, Day of judgment: time of reckoning) **10.** Do not be swayed by every influence; be firm in your thoughts. (Swayed: influenced, Firm: stable) **11.** Be steadfast in words and deeds. (Steadfast: loyal, Deeds: actions) **12.** Be quick to listen, slow to speak. (Listen: hear, Speak: respond) **13.** If you know, respond to your neighbor; if not, remain silent. (Neighbor: someone near, Silent: not speaking) **14.** A man's words can bring both respect and shame. (Respect: honor, Shame: disgrace) **15.** Avoid slander; your tongue can cause destruction. (Slander: false speech, Destruction: ruin) **16.** Shame belongs to thieves; reproach to those with deceitful tongues. (Shame: dishonor, Thieves: stealers, Reproach: criticism, Deceitful: dishonest speech)

Chapter 6
1. Avoid harmful speech, whether minor or major, and do not become a foe to a friend. A bad reputation will follow you. "That for the evil man with double tongue!" ("Evil man with double tongue": a deceitful speaker) **2.** Don't let desire consume you, as it can weaken you like fire. ("Desire": craving or longing) **3.** It will ruin your strength, leaving you like a barren tree. ("Barren tree": a lifeless, unproductive tree) **4.** Desire destroys its owner and makes them vulnerable to enemies. ("Foes": enemies or adversaries) **5.** A kind word

creates friends, and gracious speech brings warmth. ("Kind word": gentle speech) **6.** Have many acquaintances, but only one in a thousand is a true confidant. ("Confidant": a trusted friend) **7.** Test your friends before you trust them. ("Test": assess their reliability) **8.** Some friends are only present when it benefits them, but vanish in hardship. ("Trouble": challenging times) **9.** Others will spread rumors and turn against you in conflict. ("Rumors": gossip) **10.** Some are companions in happiness but absent in sorrow. ("Companions": friends) **11.** When life is good, they act as your equal, but avoid you in misfortune. ("Servants": those who serve you) **12.** In your low points, they turn away and refuse to help. ("Turn away": reject) **13.** Stay cautious with friends, and keep your enemies distant. ("Enemies": those who oppose you) **14.** A loyal friend is like a shelter, a true treasure. ("Loyal": faithful) **15.** A faithful friend is priceless and worth more than wealth. ("Priceless": beyond monetary value) **16.** A true friend is like a life-saving remedy, found by those who revere God. ("Life-saving remedy": something that heals) **17.** Those who fear God live with integrity, and their friends reflect that. ("Fear God": reverence for God) **18.** Embrace discipline from youth, and wisdom will come with age. ("Discipline": self-training) **19.** Like a farmer tending the land, approach wisdom and wait for its rewards. ("Farmer": someone who grows crops) **20.** Nurturing wisdom brings little effort, and its fruits will come soon. ("Nurturing": fostering growth) **21.** Wisdom bothers the rebellious, and fools reject it. ("Rebellious": unwilling to follow rules) **22.** The fool cannot bear wisdom and quickly discards it. ("Foolish": lacking judgment) **23.** Discipline, like wisdom, is not accessible to everyone. ("Accessible": easy to attain) **24.** Listen to me, my son, and follow my advice. ("Counsel": guidance) **25.** Walk in wisdom's ways and submit to her guidance. ("Neck": symbol of submission) **26.** Be humble, bear her burdens, and don't resent her discipline. ("Humble": showing modesty) **27.** Pursue wisdom with all your heart, and follow her paths fully. ("Wholeheartedly": fully devoted) **28.** Seek wisdom, and once you find it, hold onto it tightly. ("Hold on tightly": retain something precious) **29.** You will find peace and joy in wisdom, and it will delight you. ("Peace": calm) **30.** Her guidance will elevate you, and her wisdom will be a crown. ("Elevate": raise or lift) **31.** You will wear wisdom like a robe and crown of honor. ("Robe of glory": symbol of greatness) **32.** If you want to learn, you can; apply yourself with a true desire for insight. ("Desire": wish) **33.** Be willing to listen, and wisdom will come to you. ("Willing": ready) **34.** Spend time with the wise; stay near those who are prudent. ("Elders": wise individuals) **35.** Eagerly listen to godly teachings, and don't miss any wise words. ("Eagerly": with enthusiasm) **36.** Seek out wise individuals and learn from them. ("Prudent": wise and cautious) **37.** Reflect on the Lord's teachings, keep His commandments, and He will give you wisdom. ("LORD": a respectfultitle for God)

Chapter 7

1. Do no wrong, and evil will not overtake you (Evil: harm or wrongdoing). **2.** Avoid wickedness, and it will depart from you (Wickedness: moral wrong). **3.** Do not sow injustice, or you will reap it sevenfold (Injustice: unfairness). **4.** Do not seek authority from the LORD, nor honor from the king (Authority: power or control). **5.** Do not boast of your righteousness before the LORD, nor flaunt your wisdom before the king (Boast: to speak with pride). **6.** Do not try to judge if you cannot remove crime, lest you compromise your integrity (Integrity: honesty). **7.** Do no evil before the people, nor disgrace yourself before the assembly (Assembly: gathering). **8.** Do not plan to repeat a sin; even one sin will be punished (Sin: wrong act). **9.** Do not think, "My gifts will be valued; the Most High will accept my offerings" (Gifts: presents or donations). **10.** Be patient in prayer and generous in giving (Generous: willing to give). **11.** Do not mock the distressed; remember the One who exalts and humbles (Exalts: lifts up). **12.** Do not plot against your brother or friend (Plot: plan secretly). **13.** Do not take pleasure in lying, for lies lead to no good (Lying: falsehood). **14.** Do not meddle in the affairs of rulers or repeat your prayers (Meddle: interfere). **15.** Do not despise work, nor farming, ordained by the Most High (Despise: dislike intensely). **16.** Do not see yourself as better than others; remember His wrath is sure (Wrath: anger). **17.** Continually humble your pride; all men face death (Pride: arrogance). **18.** Do not trade a friend for money, nor a brother for gold (Trade: exchange). **19.** Do not reject a wise wife; she is more valuable than coral (Reject: dismiss). **20.** Do not mistreat a faithful servant, nor a worker dedicated to his task (Mistreat: harm). **21.** Value a wise servant as your own self; do not deny him his freedom (Value: regard highly). **22.** Care for your livestock; if they are reliable, keep them (Livestock: animals). **23.** Discipline your sons from their youth (Discipline: teach to follow rules). **24.** Guard your daughters' purity; do not spoil them (Purity: innocence). **25.** Giving your daughter in marriage is a great task; give her to a worthy man (Worthy: deserving). **26.** Do not let your wife become hateful; if there is bitterness, do not trust her (Hateful: full of hate). **27.** Honor your father with all your heart; do not forget the pain your mother endured in childbirth (Endured: suffered through). **28.** Remember your parents' sacrifices; what can you give them in return (Sacrifices: things given up)? **29.** Fear God and honor His priests with all your soul (Fear: respect deeply). **30.** Love your Creator and support His ministers with all your strength (Creator: God). **31.** Honor God and respect the priest; give him the first fruits and offerings (First fruits: first produce). **32.** Extend your hand to the poor, so your blessings may be complete (Extend: offer). **33.** Be generous to the living and kind to the dead (Generous: willing to give). **34.** Mourn with those who weep; do not avoid those in sorrow (Mourn: express grief). **35.** Visit the sick; these actions will earn you love (Earn: receive). **36.** In all you do, remember your final days, and you will not sin (Sin: wrongdoing).

Chapter 8

1. Do not argue with a powerful person, or you may fall under their control. (Influential man: someone with great power) **2.** Avoid quarreling with a wealthy person, as money can corrupt and lead to your downfall. (Wealthy man: a person with much money) **3.** Do not argue with a harsh speaker, as it will only fuel their anger. (Railing speech: harsh, abusive speech) **4.** Stay away from an unruly person, for they may dishonor your ancestors. (Unruly man: a person who is difficult to control) **5.** Do not shame a repentant sinner; we all have our faults. (Repentant sinner: someone seeking forgiveness) **6.** Do not insult the elderly; we will all grow old. (Elderly: older people) **7.** Do not rejoice at a death, for we all must die. (Rejoice: to celebrate) **8.** Respect the wisdom of the wise, as their proverbs teach how to serve rulers. (Proverbs: wise sayings) **9.** Do not dismiss the wisdom of the elderly; it helps in difficult times. (Old men: older generations with life experience) **10.** Do not provoke a sinner, or you may be consumed by their anger. (Sinner: someone who acts immorally) **11.** Do not let the wicked intimidate you, or they will plot against you. (Impious man: someone without reverence for god) **12.** Do not lend to someone stronger than you, or you may lose it. (Lend: to give with the expectation of return) **13.** Do not promise more than you can; be accountable for your debts. (Surety: a person who guarantees another's debt) **14.** Do not argue with a judge, as they decide on their own terms. (Judge: a legal authority) **15.** Do not travel with a ruthless person, as their actions will bring you harm. (Ruthless man: someone without mercy) **16.** Do not provoke a quick-tempered person, especially in dangerous places. (Quick-tempered man: someone easily angered) **17.** Do not take advice from a fool, for they cannot keep secrets. (Fool: a person lacking wisdom) **18.** Do not share secrets with strangers, as you don't know their intentions. (Stranger: someone you don't know well) **19.** Do not open your heart to all, and protect your happiness. (Heart: emotions, feelings)

Chapter 9

1. Do not be envious of your wife, lest she be led to act wrongly. (Wife of your bosom: your closest partner) **2.** Do not let any woman dishonor you. **3.** Avoid getting too close to unfamiliar women, to avoid temptation. (Unfamiliar: unknown or strange) **4.** Stay away from a young woman who sings, lest you fall into her tricks. (Young woman who sings: a girl who entertains) **5.** Do not think badly of a virgin, as it may lead to consequences. (Virgin: an unmarried woman) **6.** Avoid prostitutes, or you may lose your inheritance. (Prostitutes: women who sell their bodies) **7.** Do not linger in the city's streets or public squares. (Public squares: open areas in cities) **8.** Avoid gazing at another's wife—many are ruined by lust. (Lust: intense desire or craving) **9.** Do not eat or drink with a married woman, lest your heart be drawn to her. (Dine: to eat a meal, meet your end: to die or suffer) **10.** Do not abandon old friends, for new ones cannot replace them. New friends are like fresh wine, which improves with age. (Fresh wine: new relationships that improve with time) **11.** Do not envy a sinner's success, for their downfall is unknown. (Sinner: one who does wrong or is morally corrupt) **12.** Do not rejoice in the arrogant's prosperity, for they will face punishment. (Arrogant: overly proud or self-important) **13.** Stay away from those with power to kill, or you will live in fear. Avoid offending them, for they may take your life. (Power to kill: someone with authority to take life, danger: risk of harm) **14.** Understand your neighbors' character and associate with wise people. (Neighbors' character: the nature of those around you) **15.** Spend time with knowledgeable people, and discuss the LORD's teachings. (Knowledgeable: wise or well-informed, LORD: God) **16.** Choose just people for companionship, and let the fear of God be your pride. (Just people: righteous individuals, fear of God: reverence for God) **17.** Skilled craftsmen are respected for their work, but a wise ruler leads best. (Craftsmen: skilled workers, ruler: leader) **18.** A man who speaks harshly is feared, and the reckless are despised. (Harshly: in a severe or cruel manner, recklessly: without thought or care)

Chapter 10

1. A wise ruler brings stability, and a prudent leader ensures good order. (Ruler: a leader or magistrate) **2.** The judge's ministers reflect his decisions, and the city's people mirror their leader. (Minister: a public servant or official)

3. A reckless king destroys his people, but a wise ruler helps the city prosper. (Reckless: careless or irresponsible) **4.** God rules the earth and raises up the right person for each time. (Dominion: control or sovereignty) **5.** Sovereignty over people belongs to God, and He grants majesty to rulers. (Sovereignty: supreme authority or power) **6.** Do not harm your neighbor or walk in arrogance. (Arrogance: excessive pride) **7.** Arrogance and oppression are despised by both God and men. (Oppression: cruel or unjust treatment) **8.** The arrogant bring about shifts in power due to violence. (Violence: extreme force or brutality) **9.** Why be proud, made of dust and ashes? The body decays even in life. (Proud: feeling superior to others) **10.** A small illness can make a doctor laugh, yet even kings may die suddenly. (Illness: a disease or sickness) **11.** When a person dies, corruption follows—decay and worms. (Corruption: decay or moral deterioration) **12.** Pride begins when a person turns their heart away from their Maker. (Hardens: makes less responsive or flexible) **13.** Pride is the source of sin, overflowing with vice; through it, God sends affliction. (Vice: immoral behavior) **14.** God overthrows the proud and lifts up the humble. (Overthrows: removes forcefully) **15.** God removes the proud to establish the humble. (Uproots: removes from the ground) **16.** He lowers their stems and removes their roots. (Stems: the main support of a plant) **17.** God wipes away the memory of the proud from the earth. (Traces: marks or signs) **18.** Insolence and stubborn anger are not fitting for man. (Insolence: rude or disrespectful behavior) **19.** The children of those who fear God are honored. (Fear: reverence or deep respect) **20.** Among brothers, the leader is honored; he who fears God is honored by his people. (Brothers: siblings or close companions) **21.** Whether a tenant, traveler, foreigner, or beggar, the fear of the LORD brings honor. (Tenant: a person renting land or property) **22.** It's wrong to despise a wise poor man or honor a sinner. (Despise: regard with disrespect) **23.** Princes, rulers, and judges are respected, but none more than those who fear God. (Prince: a ruler or monarch) **24.** A wise slave serving free men is not complained about. (Slave: someone bound to serve) **25.** Do not boast of your wisdom, nor in times of need. (Flaunt: show off in an exaggerated manner) **26.** Better a worker with plenty than a boastful person with nothing. (Boastful: given to self-praise) **27.** My son, be humble and value yourself as you deserve. (Humility: modesty or lack of pride) **28.** Who will defend those who condemn themselves? Who will honor those who discredit themselves? (Condemn: express strong disapproval of) **29.** The poor are honored for their wisdom, just as the rich are for their wealth. (Wisdom: the ability to make good judgments) **30.** Honored in poverty, how much more in wealth! Dishonored in wealth, how much more in poverty! (Dishonored: treated with disrespect or contempt)

Chapter 11

1. The poor man's wisdom raises him and places him with rulers. (Rulers: those in positions of power) **2.** Don't praise a man for his appearance; don't despise him for his looks. (Appearance: outward features) **3.** The bee is small but gathers the best harvests. (Bee: a small insect that collects nectar) **4.** Don't mock the poor who worn cloak and their struggles, for God's works are mysterious. (Cloak: a garment worn to provide protection.) **5.** Oppressed people may rise to power, and those least expected may wear a crown. (Oppressed: those suffering hardship) **6.** The high and mighty can fall, and the honored can be defeated by enemies. (High and mighty: powerful individuals) **7.** Don't judge without first investigating the matter. (Investigating: thorough examination) **8.** Don't answer before hearing, and don't interrupt others. (Interrupt: to stop someone from speaking) **9.** Avoid disputes that aren't yours; don't get involved in the proud's quarrels. (Proud: those who are arrogant) **10.** Why worry, my child? Those chasing wealth are rarely blameless, and it's impossible to catch. (Wealth: money or valuable possessions) **11.** Hard work may still fall short of success. **12.** Some are weak and struggling, yet God lifts them up from the dust. **13.** God raises them to the amazement of many. (Astonishment: great surprise) **14.** All things, both good and bad, poverty and riches, come from the Lord. (Poverty: extreme poverty) **15.** Wisdom, understanding, knowledge of affair and love come from the Lord. (Affairs: matters requiring attention) **16.** Sinners are born into darkness, and evil grows with them. (Sinners: those who do wrong) **17.** The righteous remain blessed by God and enjoy lasting success. (Righteous: morally good people) **18.** A miser's riches are his only reward. (Miserly: unwilling to spend money) **19.** He may think he will enjoy his wealth, not realizing death will soon take it from him. **20.** Stay devoted to your duties, my son, and grow old serving them. (Devoted: loyal and dedicated) **21.** Do not envy sinners but trust in the Lord; He can make a poor man wealthy. (Envy: resentment over others' success) **22.** The righteous receive God's blessing, and their hopes are fulfilled in time. (Blessing: favor or approval) **23.** Don't ask, "What more can I enjoy?" **24.** Don't say, "I'm self-sufficient; no harm can come to me." (Self-sufficient: able to manage on your own) **25.** Prosperity makes one forget adversity, and adversity makes one forget prosperity. (Prosperity: wealth or success) **26.** God will repay each man according to his deeds on the day of death. (Repay: to compensate for actions) **27.** A moment of pain can erase past joys, and death reveals the true life lived. **28.** Don't call anyone happy before their death, for their end reveals their true nature. **29.** Be cautious who enters your home, for deceitful people may trap you. (Deceitful: misleading or dishonest) **30.** Though he seems harmless, he will find weaknesses to exploit. (Exploit: to take advantage of for personal gain) **31.** A gossip turns good into evil, setting many fires with a spark. (Gossip: casual, often harmful conversation) **32.** The wicked wait for opportunities to shed blood and steal your best possessions. (Wicked: evil or morally wrong) **33.** Avoid the wicked, for they only bring harm and stain your reputation. (Stain: to tarnish or damage one's character) **34.** A stranger in your home may disrupt your life and alienate you from your own. (Estrange: to cause distance in relationships)

Chapter 12

1. If you do good, remember the one you're doing it for, and your kindness will have an impact. (Kindness: the quality of being friendly, generous, and considerate) **2.** Do good to the righteous, and your reward will come, whether from him or the LORD. (Righteous: morally right or justifiable; LORD: God) **3.** No good comes from comforting the wicked; it's not merciful. (Wicked: morally wrong or evil; Merciful: showing kindness or forgiveness) **4.** Help the good man, reject the sinner, and refresh the humble, not the proud. (Sinner: someone who commits wrong acts; Arrogant: having an exaggerated sense of one's importance) **5.** Don't arm an untrustworthy man, or he'll use the weapons against you. (Arm: to provide with weapons) **6.** For every good you do for him, you'll face double harm. (Harm: physical injury or damage) **7.** The Most High despises sinners and punishes the wicked. (Most High: God; Despises: to feel a strong dislike) **8.** In prosperity, true friends may not be clear; in adversity, an enemy's hostility shows. (Prosperity: state of being successful; Hostility: unfriendly behavior) **9.** In success, enemies are friendly; in trouble, even friends may turn away. **10.** Never trust your enemy, his malice is like rust on bronze. (Malice: the desire to cause harm or pain; Bronze: a metal alloy) **11.** Even if he seems humble, stay cautious; like a polished bronze mirror, rust remains. (Cautious: careful to avoid danger or mistakes) **12.** Keep him away or he may take your place; don't let him sit near you, or he'll demand your seat. **13.** Who feels sorry for a snake charmer after being bitten, or someone who approaches a wild animal? (Snake charmer: a person who controls snakes for entertainment) **14.** It's the same with the companion of the proud man, who shares in his sins. (Proud: having a high opinion of oneself; Companion: a person who accompanies or associates with another) **15.** As long as you stand firm, he'll do nothing; but if you slip, he won't hold back. **16.** An enemy speaks kindly but plans your ruin. Even if he cries, he thirsts for your blood. (Ruin: destruction or downfall; Thirst: strong desire) **17.** When trouble strikes, he'll pretend to help, but secretly harm you. (Strikes: hits or attacks; Pretending: acting as if something is true) **18.** Then he'll nod, clap, and hiss, revealing his true nature. (Nod: a gesture of agreement or understanding; Hiss: a sharp, sibilant sound)

Chapter 13

1. Whoever touches tar stains their hands; those who associate with the wicked adopt their ways. (Tar: a sticky substance; wicked: morally wrong) **2.** Don't take on more than you can carry; avoid associating with those wealthier or more powerful than you. A clay pot cannot go with a metal cauldron; if they collide, the pot will break. (Clay pot: fragile vessel; cauldron: large pot) **3.** The rich boast of wrongdoing, while the poor plead for mercy. (Mercy: compassion or forgiveness) **4.** As long as the rich need you, they will control you, but once you're exhausted, they'll abandon you. (Control: to dominate) **5.** While you have something, the rich speak kindly and win your trust. (Trust: reliance) **6.** When they need something, they flatter you, then leave you in poverty without hesitation. (Flatter: insincere praise) **7.** They deceive you while they benefit, and when done, they disregard you with disdain. (Disdain: contempt) **8.** Be cautious; don't act arrogantly or like a fool. (Arrogant: self-important; fools: lacking wisdom) **9.** If invited by a powerful man, keep your distance—though he may press you to come closer. (Powerful man: influential person) **10.** Don't be too bold, or you may be dismissed; but don't stay too far, or you'll be forgotten. (Dismissed: rejected) **11.** Don't engage too freely in conversation; his words may deceive, testing your responses. (Deceive: mislead) **12.** He will mock you and won't hesitate to harm you or imprison you. (Mock: ridicule; imprison: confine) **13.** Be watchful and avoid violent men. (Watchful: alert) **14.** Every living thing loves its own kind; people seek those like themselves. (Kind: a type of being) **15.** Beings are drawn to their kind, and every person associates with similar people. (Associates: joins) **16.** A wolf does not ally with a lamb, nor the sinner with the just. (Just: righteous) **17.** Can a hyena make peace with a dog? Or can the rich and poor be at peace? (Hyena: wild carnivore; peace: harmony) **18.** Lions hunt wild donkeys; similarly, the poor are preyed upon by the rich. (Preyed upon: exploited) 19. The proud despise humility, and the rich despise the poor. (Despise: look down on) 20. When the rich stumble, their friends help them; when the poor trip, they are pushed down. (Trip: stumble) 21. Many support the rich, even when their words are bad, but the poor are mocked, even when speaking wisely. (Mocked: ridiculed) 22. When the rich speak, all listen in silence, praising them; the poor are ignored or dismissed. (Dismissed: disregarded) 23. Wealth is good if there's no sin, but the proud look down on poverty. (Look down on: scorn) 24. A person's heart changes their expression, for good or evil. (Expression: outward appearance) 25. A cheerful heart shows in a happy face; a troubled heart shows in a schemer's troubled face. (Schemer: deceitful planner)

Chapter 14
1. Blessed is the one whose words cause no sorrow and who regrets no sin. (Blessed: happy, regret: sorrow over past actions) 2. Blessed is the one whose conscience is clear and who retains hope. (Conscience: inner sense of right and wrong) 3. Wealth doesn't suit the lowly, and a miser has no use for gold. (Miser: someone who hoards money) 4. What they deny themselves, others enjoy, and strangers benefit. (Accumulate: gather over time) 5. Who will they share with if they don't even enjoy their own wealth? (Selfish: unwilling to share or give) 6. No one is more stingy than someone who punishes themselves with greed. (Greed: intense desire for wealth or possessions) 7. If they give, it's by mistake, and their greed soon shows. (Greed: excessive desire for material gain) 8. The miser always thinks their portion is too small. (Miser: a person who saves money selfishly) 9. They refuse to help others and bring harm upon themselves. 10. The miser desires bread but serves only stale food. (Eagerly: with great desire, stale: old, not fresh) 11. My child, enjoy what you have and make the most of it. (Child: a term of affection, enjoy: take pleasure in) 12. Remember, death comes without warning, and you don't know when. (Death: end of life, without warning: unexpectedly) 13. Before death, treat your friend well and share with them. (Friend: a close companion) 14. Don't deprive yourself of life's pleasures; seize what's good. (Deprive: take away, opportunity: chance) 15. Will you leave your wealth to others, divided by chance? (Earnings: income, divided by chance: distributed randomly) 16. Give freely, enjoy life, for there are no pleasures after death. (Freely: without hesitation, afterlife: life after death) 17. All flesh grows old like a garment; all must die. (Flesh: the body, ancient: very old) 18. As leaves fall, so generations pass, and others come. (Generations: groups of people born in the same period) 19. All works decay, and what we've done is left behind. (Deeds: actions, decay: rot, left behind: forgotten or passed on) 20. Blessed is the one who meditates on wisdom and reflects on understanding. (Meditates: thinks deeply, reflects: thinks carefully) 21. Blessed is the one who understands wisdom and knows her ways. (Contemplates: thinks about, wisdom: deep understanding) 22. Blessed is the one who seeks wisdom like a scout searching for treasure. (Scout: a person sent to search, treasure: something valuable) 23. Blessed is the one who peers through wisdom's windows and listens at her doors. (Peers: looks closely, windows: openings, metaphor for learning) 24. Blessed is the one who stays near wisdom's house and sets up camp nearby. (House: place of dwelling, camp: temporary dwelling place) 25. Blessed is the one who lives close to wisdom and makes their home there. (Lives: resides, beside: next to) 26. Blessed is the one who builds a nest in her branches and finds shelter there. (Nest: a place of rest, shelter: protection) 27. Blessed is the one who seeks refuge with her, safe from harm, and makes her home. (Refuge: a safe place, sheltered: protected from danger)

Chapter 15
1. Those who fear the LORD will follow His path; those versed in His law will gain wisdom. (Fear: deep respect; versed: skilled) 2. Wisdom will meet him like a loving mother and embrace him like a bride. (Embrace: welcome warmly) 3. She will feed him with understanding and offer him knowledge to drink. (Feed: provide; understanding: comprehension) 4. He will rely on her and not stumble, trusting her without shame. (Rely: depend on; stumble: fall) 5. She will lift him above others, making him eloquent in gatherings. (Lift: raise; eloquent: well-spoken) 6. He will find joy and gain an enduring reputation. (Enduring: lasting) 7. The wicked and proud will not reach or see her. (Wicked: immoral; proud: arrogant) 8. She is far from the impious and ignored by liars. (Impious: disrespectful; liars: deceivers) 9. Praise on a sinner's lips is improper, for God does not honor them. (Improper: inappropriate) 10. The wise man's tongue praises, and the faithful declare it. (Faithful: loyal) 11. Do not say, "God caused me to fall," for He does not do what He hates. 12. Do not claim, "He led me astray," for He has no need of evil men. (Led astray: deceived) 13. The LORD hates wickedness and protects those who fear Him. (Protects: shields) 14. In the beginning, God gave man the freedom to choose. (Freedom: ability to choose) 15. You can follow His commandments if you wish, and loyalty to Him pleases Him. (Loyalty: devotion) 16. Two paths—fire and water—are before you; choose either one. (Paths: choices) 17. Life and death are set before you; you will receive what you choose. (Set before: placed before) 18. The LORD's wisdom is vast, mighty, and all-knowing. (Vast: immense; mighty: powerful) 19. God sees all He created and understands every human act. (Created: made; act: deed) 20. He does not command anyone to sin or empower lies. (Sin: immoral acts; empower: enable)

Chapter 16
1. Do not long for worthless children, nor take pride in wicked offspring. (Worthless: lacking value) 2. Even if many, do not rejoice in them if they lack reverence for the LORD. (Reverence: deep respect) 3. Do not hope for their long life or bright future; one righteous person is worth more than a thousand. It is better to have no children than godless ones. (Godless: without faith in God) 4. A wise person can build a city, but a rebellious people will destroy it. (Desolate: empty) 5. I have seen many such things and heard even more. 6. A sinful group will face fire, and wrath will consume a godless people. (Wrath: intense anger) 7. He did not forgive the rebellious leaders of the past who were powerful. 8. He did not spare the people near Lot, destroyed for their pride. (Pride: arrogance) 9. He did not spare the people destroyed due to their sin. 10. Nor the six hundred thousand soldiers who perished for their wicked hearts. 11. If one stubborn person existed, it would be a miracle if he went unpunished. (Stubborn: determined despite difficulty) 12. His mercy is vast, but so is His punishment; He judges people by their deeds. 13. A criminal won't escape with their stolen goods, and God fulfills the hopes of the righteous. (Criminal: lawbreaker) 14. Those who do good will be rewarded according to their actions. 15. Do not say, "I am hidden from God; who remembers me in heaven? Among so many people, I cannot be known; what am I in the spiritual world?" 16. The heavens, earth, and depths tremble at His visitation. (Visitation: divine judgment) 17. The earth's foundations shake at His mere glance. 18. So why would He care about me? Who would concern themselves with my ways? 19. If I sin, no one will see it; if I am disloyal in secret, who will know? 20. Who tells Him of good deeds, and what should I expect for doing right? 21. These are the thoughts of fools, entertained only by the ignorant. 22. Listen, my child, heed my advice, and pay attention to my words. 23. I speak of wisdom and provide clear knowledge. 24. When God created the world, He assigned each thing its purpose, 25. establishing their tasks for all generations. 26. They would not hunger, tire, or cease from their duties. 27. None should crowd others or disobey His command. 28. The LORD looked upon the earth, filling it with blessings, covering it with life to return to it. (Blessings: divine favor)

Chapter 17
1. The LORD created man from the earth, in His own image. (Man: human being; LORD: God) 2. He gives man a limited lifespan and returns him to the earth. (Limited days: lifespan) 3. He gives man strength and authority over all things on earth. (Authority: control) 4. He instills fear in all creatures, giving man dominion over animals and birds. (Dominion: rule; creatures: living beings) 5. He shapes man's tongue, eyes, and ears, giving him understanding. (Tongue: speech; heart: mind) 6. He fills them with wisdom, showing both good and evil. (Wisdom: insight; knowledge: understanding) 7. He favors their hearts and reveals His glorious works. (Favors: looks with approval) 8. This enables them to speak of His wondrous deeds and praise His holy name. (Wondrous deeds: amazing works) 9. He gave them knowledge, a law of life to inherit. (Law of life: guidance) 10. He made an everlasting covenant with them, revealing His commandments. (Covenant: agreement) 11. Their eyes saw His glory, and their ears heard His voice. (Majestic glory: great splendor) 12. He tells them, "Avoid evil," and gives guidance for others. 13. Their actions are known to Him, and nothing escapes His sight. (Escapes: hides) 14. He places rulers over nations, but Israel is His portion. (Ruler: leader; Israel: God's chosen people) 15. Their deeds are clear to Him, and His eyes are on their ways. (Deeds: actions) 16. Their wickedness is not hidden; their sins are before the LORD. (Wickedness: evil; sins: wrongdoings) 17. A man's goodness is cherished by God, like a signet ring, and his virtue like the apple of His eye. (Virtue: moral excellence) 18. He will repay them, rewarding each as they deserve. (Repay: reward) 19. To the repentant, He provides a way back, encouraging those losing hope. (Repentant: those who regret their wrongs) 20. Return to the LORD, give up sin, and pray to Him. (Abandon: give up) 21. Turn to the Most High and away from sin, hating what He loathes. (Most High: God) 22. Can the dead glorify the Most High as the living who praise Him? (Underworld: realm of the dead) 23. The dead cannot praise; only the living glorify the LORD. (Glorify: honor) 24. How great the mercy of the LORD for those who return to Him! (Mercy: compassion; forgiveness: pardon) 25. Such mercy is rare among men, for no son of man is immortal. (Immortal: eternal) 26. Is anything brighter than the sun? Yet even it can be hidden. How limited

are human thoughts! (Limited: restricted) **27.** God watches over the hosts of heaven, while all men are dust and ashes. (Hosts of the highest heaven: angelic beings)

Chapter 18

1. The Eternal is the judge of all, and only the LORD is just. (Eternal: a title for God) **2.** Who can compare to describing his works or understanding his mighty deeds? (Mighty deeds: powerful actions of God) **3.** Who can measure his majestic power or fully recount his mercies? (Majestic: grand, impressive) **4.** One cannot reduce, increase, or comprehend the wonders of the LORD. (Diminish: reduce) **5.** When a man dies, he is only beginning, and even in rest, he is still in awe. (Awe: wonder and reverence) **6.** What is man's value, and what is the good or evil within him? (Worth: value) **7.** A man's life is important if it lasts a hundred years. (Significant: important) **8.** Like a drop of water or a grain of sand, so are these few years compared to eternity. (Eternity: timeless existence) **9.** This is why the LORD is patient and shows mercy to men. (Mercy: compassion and forgiveness) **10.** He understands the sorrow of death, so he forgives even more. (Sorrowful: full of sadness) **11.** A man may show mercy to others, but the LORD's mercy extends to all. (Mercy: forgiveness and compassion) **12.** He corrects, advises, and teaches like a shepherd guiding his flock. (Shepherd: one who cares for and leads sheep) **13.** Merciful to those who accept his guidance and follow his teachings. (Diligently: with effort and care) **14.** My son, do not spoil your charity with harsh words or reproach. (Reproach: criticism or disapproval) **15.** A kind word, like dew that cools the wind, enhances a gift. (Dew: moisture that cools the air) **16.** Sometimes a kind word is more valuable than the gift itself; both come from a generous heart. (Generous: kind and giving) **17.** Only a fool rebukes before giving; a reluctant gift disappoints. (Reluctant: unwilling) **18.** Think before speaking; prepare a remedy before sickness strikes. (Remedy: solution or cure) **19.** Before judgment, build your inner, and at the reckoning, you will be ransomed. (Ransom: payment for release) **20.** Before you sin, humble yourself; when you sin, repent. (Repent: regret for wrongdoing) **21.** Do not delay forsaking sin or neglect it until distress comes. (Forsaking: abandoning) **22.** Fulfill your vows promptly; do not wait until death. (Vows: promises made to God) **23.** Before making a vow, ensure you can fulfill it; do not test the LORD. (Test: challenge God's will) **24.** Remember wrath and the day of death, when vengeance comes and he hides his face. (Vengeance: punishment for wrongdoing) **25.** Remember hunger in times of plenty, and poverty in times of wealth. (Plenty: abundance) **26.** The weather changes from morning to evening; all things are fleeting before the LORD. (Fleeting: temporary or short-lived) **27.** A wise person is cautious in all things; when sin is abundant, he avoids wrongdoing. (Abundant: present in large quantities) **28.** Those with wisdom should share it, and those who attain it should praise it. (Attain: reach or achieve) **29.** Those trained in wisdom must express it, sharing sound advice like life-giving water. (Sound: reliable or sensible) **30.** Do not pursue your lusts; control your desires. (Lusts: strong, sinful desires) **31.** If you satisfy your lustful desires, they will make you vulnerable to your enemies. (Target: someone or something attacked or harmed) **32.** Do not find joy in fleeting pleasures that lead to lasting poverty. (Fleeting: short-lived) **33.** Do not become a glutton or drunkard with nothing in your purse. (Glutton: someone who eats excessively)

Chapter 19

1. Those who waste their resources gain nothing; those who squander what little they have will lose it all. (Squander: waste recklessly) **2.** Wine and women cloud the mind, and a companion of prostitutes becomes reckless. **3.** Those who trust them without caution lack wisdom and harm themselves. (Caution: care or attention to avoid danger) **4.** Their desires bring decay and destruction upon them. (Decay: decline or deterioration) **5.** Those who delight in evil will encounter it, and those who spread false reports are foolish. (Delight: take pleasure in) **6.** Avoid gossip to prevent being despised. (Gossip: spreading unverified information) **7.** Keep secrets, even from friends and enemies; revealing faults invites blame. (Faults: mistakes or flaws) **8.** Those who hear your flaws will hold it against you and may become your enemy. (Hold it against: resent or blame) **9.** Let what you hear remain in silence; it won't harm you. (Remain: stay or endure without change) **10.** A fool who hears something is like a woman in labor. (Labor: the process of childbirth) **11.** Gossip in a fool's heart is like an arrow in the thigh. (Gossip: idle or malicious talk; Thigh: part of the leg) **12.** Correct your friend—they may not have done wrong, and if they did, help them avoid it again. (Correct: guide or reprimand) **13.** Correct your neighbor—they may not have spoken falsely, and if so, prevent repetition. (Neighbor: a nearby person) **14.** Correct your friend often, as some rumors are false; not everything is true. (Rumors: unverified stories or gossip) **15.** People can slip unintentionally; who hasn't spoken wrongfully? (Slip: make a mistake or error) **16.** Correct your neighbor before breaking ties; this fulfills God's law. (Breaking ties: ending a relationship; Law: divine instruction) **17.** Wisdom begins with fearing the Lord; true wisdom follows His law. (Wisdom: good judgment and knowledge; Lord: God) **18.** Knowledge of evil is not wisdom, nor is the advice of sinners wise. (Sinners: those who commit immoral acts) **19.** Some are shrewd but detestable, while the simple may be sin-free. (Shrewd: clever but deceptive; Simple: innocent or unpretentious) **20.** Some with little understanding fear God, while others with great knowledge break the law. (Understanding: comprehension or insight) **21.** Some use cleverness deceitfully to win judgments. (Deceitfully: dishonestly) **22.** Wicked people appear sorrowful but are deceitful inside. (Wicked: evil or morally wrong) **23.** They act humble, but when unnoticed, they take advantage of others. (Humble: modest or meek) **24.** Weakness may prevent them from sinning, but they will harm others when they can. (Weakness: lack of strength or power) **25.** A person's appearance reveals their character; a wise man is recognized immediately. (Appearance: how someone looks; Character: a person's nature or qualities) **26.** A person's attire, laughter, and walk reveal who they are. (Attire: clothing; Walk: way of moving)

Chapter 20

1. A rebuke may be ill-timed, and sometimes it's wiser to stay silent. (Rebuke: sharp criticism) **2.** Correcting someone is better than losing your temper, as admitting faults avoids disgrace. (Disgrace: loss of honor) **3.** Like a eunuch desiring a virgin, is one who does right only under pressure. (Eunuch: castrated man, Virgin: unmarried woman) **4.** A silent person is seen as wise, while a talkative one is disliked. (Silent: quiet, Disliked: unfavored) **5.** Some remain silent because they have nothing to say, while others wait for the right moment. (Hold their peace: stay quiet) **6.** A wise person speaks at the right time, but a fool speaks at the wrong one. (Boastful: showing pride) **7.** Talkative people are disliked, and those who fake authority are hated. (Excessively: too much) **8.** Some misfortunes lead to success, and some gains end in loss. (Misfortunes: bad luck, Success: desired result) **9.** Some gifts are useless, and others require multiple repayments. (Repay: return) **10.** Fame may bring shame, while obscurity can lead to greatness. (Humiliation: shame, Prominence: importance) **11.** A man may buy cheaply but pay much more later. (Cheaply: low cost) **12.** A wise person gains favor with few words, while fools waste praise. (Favor: approval, Effect: result) **13.** A deceitful gift is worthless, as the giver values it too much. (Deceitful: dishonest) **14.** He gives little, criticizes often, and demands repayment too soon. (Town crier: public announcer, Detestable: deserving hate) **15.** A fool has no true friends and gets no thanks for his generosity. (Generosity: willingness to give) **16.** Those who benefit from him will mock him. (Mocking: making fun of) **17.** A slip of the tongue can bring a quicker downfall than a fall. (Slip of the tongue: accidental words) **18.** Tasteless food is like a poorly timed story, shared by the restless. (Tasteless: lacking flavor) **19.** A proverb from a fool is unwelcome, as it's spoken at the wrong time. (Proverb: wise saying) **20.** A man may lack the means to sin but still remain discontent. (Means: resources, Sin: immoral act) **21.** A man may lose his life due to shame or a fool's intimidation. (Intimidated: made afraid) **22.** A man makes a promise out of shame, gaining an enemy unnecessarily. (Promise: commitment, Enemy: opponent) **23.** A lie stains a person, yet is often spoken by the unruly. (Stain: blemish, Unruly: disobedient) **24.** It's better to be a thief than a habitual liar, though both face disgrace. (Habitual: repeated, Disgrace: loss of honor) **25.** A liar's path leads to dishonor, and his shame remains with him. (Dishonor: loss of respect) **26.** A wise person progresses with his words, while a prudent one pleases the powerful. (Prudent: careful, Powerful: those in charge) **27.** Those who work the land have plenty, while those who please the great have their faults forgiven. (Land: field, Crops: plants) **28.** Gifts and favors blind the eyes, just as a muzzle silences rebuke. (Muzzle: restraint, Rebuke: disapproval) **29.** What value is there in hidden wisdom or treasure? (Wisdom: knowledge, Treasure: valuable items) **30.** It's better to conceal foolishness than hide wisdom. (Conceal: hide, Foolishness: lack of sense)

Chapter 21

1. My child, if you sin, repent sincerely and seek forgiveness for your past wrongs. (Sin: wrongdoing or offense) **2.** Avoid sin like a venomous snake, for its bite destroys souls with lion-like teeth. (Venomous snake: a dangerous snake with poison) **3.** Wrongdoing is a double-edged sword; once it cuts, it cannot heal. (Double-edged sword: a sword with two sharp sides) **4.** Violence and pride destroy wealth, and a proud man's home is ruined. (Pride: excessive self-importance) **5.** A poor man's prayer is heard instantly, and justice is quickly granted. (Justice: fairness, the right treatment) **6.** Those who reject correction walk the sinner's path, but those who fear the LORD repent in their hearts. (Repents: feels regret for past actions) **7.** The boastful are well-known, but the wise know their own faults. (Boastful: showing excessive pride) **8.** Building a house with dishonestly gained money is like collecting stones for your own grave. (Grave: burial place for the dead) **9.** A group of criminals is like dry twigs, ending in a fiery death. (Criminals: wrongdoers) **10.** The path of sinners is smooth, leading to the depths of the underworld. (Underworld: realm of the dead) **11.** One who follows the law controls their impulses, and true fear of the LORD brings wisdom. (Impulses: urges or desires) **12.** The unwise cannot learn, but one kind of cleverness is bitter. (Cleverness: mental sharpness) **13.** A wise person's wisdom overflows like a river, and their advice is like a life-giving spring. (Overflow: to pour out or spill over) **14.** A fool's mind is like a broken jar—unable to hold knowledge. (Fool: a person lacking wisdom) **15.** A wise person accepts wisdom and builds on it, but the foolish mock it and ignore it. (Mockery: ridicule or contempt) **16.** A fool's constant chatter is like an unnecessary burden, but the wise speak with charm. (Chatter: continuous talking) **17.** The prudent are sought for their opinions, and their words are carefully considered. (Prudent: wise and cautious) **18.** Wisdom is like ruins to a fool; they only see it as confusing. (Ruins: collapsed or destroyed structures) **19.** Learning is like heavy chains to a fool, an uncomfortable burden. (Manacle: a metal handcuff or shackles) **20.** A fool laughs loudly, but the wise smile gently. (Laughs: expresses joy with sound) **21.** Learning is like a golden chain to the wise, a bracelet on their arm. (Bracelet: a decorative band worn around the wrist) **22.** The fool enters a home boldly, while the well-mannered person stays outside. (Well-mannered: showing good manners) **23.** A crude person peeks through a doorway, but the cultured person looks down in respect. (Cultured: refined, polite) **24.** It's rude to listen at a door; the well-mannered person would feel ashamed. (Impolite: rude or discourteous) **25.** The wicked speak of what isn't theirs to discuss, while the wise measure their words. (Wicked: morally wrong or evil) **26.** Fools speak their thoughts, but the wise keep their words hidden in their hearts. (Hidden: kept secret) **27.** When a godless person curses their enemy, they curse themselves. (Godless: lacking reverence for God) **28.** A slanderer tarnishes their own reputation and is despised by others. (Slander: false and malicious statements)

Chapter 22

1. A lazy person is like a stone stuck in mud; others mock his disgrace. (Lazy: unwilling to work) **2.** A lazy person is like manure; anyone who touches him washes their hands. (Manure: animal waste) **3.** A rebellious child shames their father; a daughter brings him to poverty. (Rebellious: refusing to obey) **4.** A wise daughter is a blessing to her husband; an unruly one brings sorrow to her father. (Unruly: uncontrollable) **5.** A shameless woman brings shame to her father and husband; both despise her. (Shameless: lacking modesty) **6.** Foolish talk is like a song during mourning; correction is always wise. (Mourning: expressing sorrow for the dead) **7.** Teaching a fool is like fixing a broken pot or waking someone deep in sleep. (Fool: lacking wisdom) **8.** Speaking to a fool is like talking to someone asleep; they won't understand. **9.** Weep for the dead, for their light is gone; weep for the fool, for sense is lost. (Light: symbolizes life or understanding) **10.** Weep for the dead, but the fool's life is worse than death. **11.** Mourning the dead lasts seven days, but the fool's life brings mourning daily. **12.** Avoid foolish people and brutes; they bring trouble. (Brute: a rough person) **13.** Stay away from them to avoid their foolishness. **14.** Nothing is heavier than a fool's name. (Lead: a heavy, dense metal) **15.** Sand, salt, and iron are lighter than a foolish person. **16.** A building with solid beams won't shake in an earthquake; a well-thought plan won't be shaken by fear. (Beams: long pieces of wood) **17.** A decision made with understanding is firm like a polished wall. **18.** Small stones on a hill won't stay in the wind; a weak resolve can't withstand fear. (Resolve: firm determination) **19.** Striking the eye brings tears; piercing the heart exposes pain. **20.** Throwing stones at birds drives them away; insulting a friend breaks the friendship. **21.** Drawing a sword against a friend can be undone. (Sword: a weapon) **22.** Speaking harshly to a friend can be mended, but betrayal destroys friendship. **23.** Be a friend to a poor man, and you will share his prosperity when it comes. (Prosperity: state of being successful) **24.** Abuse often comes before violence, just as the oven smokes before flames. (Flames: burning fire) **25.** There's no shame in helping a friend in need. **26.** Those who harm their friends will be shunned by others. (Shunned: avoided or rejected) **27.** Who will guard my mouth and set a seal on my lips, to prevent sin and destruction? (Guard: protect or watch over)

Chapter 23

1. Lord, Father, and Master of my life, do not let me fall into their hands! (Lord: title for God) **2.** Who will correct my thoughts and discipline my mind so my faults and sins are not overlooked? (Rod: a tool for correction) **3.** Otherwise, my mistakes may increase, and my enemies will rejoice over me. (Enemies: those who oppose) **4.** Lord, Father, and God of my life, do not leave me at their mercy! (God: supreme being) **5.** Do not let me have an arrogant gaze; keep passion from my heart. (Haughty: arrogantly proud) **6.** Do not let desires control me or lead to shameful lusts. (Fleshly: related to the body) **7.** Pay attention, my children, to the guidance I give, for those who follow it will not be enslaved. (Enslaved: controlled, oppressed) **8.** The sinner is trapped by his own words; the proud and arrogant fall because of them. (Sinner: one who sins, Arrogant: excessively proud) **9.** Do not let your mouth become accustomed to swearing or misuse the Holy Name. (Swearing: using offensive language, Holy Name: God's name) **10.** As a servant under constant watch cannot avoid punishment, neither can one who swears by the Holy Name escape sin. (Scrutiny: close examination) **11.** A man who swears often builds guilt; punishment will always follow. If he swears in error, he is guilty; neglecting his duties doubles his sin. Swearing without cause brings suffering. (Guilt: responsibility for wrongdoing) **12.** Some words deserve death; may they never be spoken among Jacob's descendants. Such words are foreign to the devout. (Devout: deeply religious) **13.** Do not let your mouth get used to vulgar speech, for it leads to sin. (Vulgar: crude, unrefined) **14.** Remember your parents among the great, so you do not make a mistake and disgrace your upbringing by wishing you were never born. (Upbringing: the care and education received as a child) **15.** A man who uses foul language will never mature. (Foul: offensive, unclean) **16.** Two men multiply sin, and a third causes wrath: one consumed by passion that burns until it destroys him; (Wrath: intense anger) **17.** the man who is always seeking pleasure until death; (Pleasure: satisfaction, enjoyment) **18.** and the man who dishonors his marriage and thinks, "Who can see me? Darkness hides me." He forgets the eyes of the Most High are always watching. (Dishonors: treats with disrespect, Most High: a title for God) **19.** He fears only human eyes, not realizing that the Lord sees all, even hidden actions. (Observe: watch carefully) **20.** The Lord knows all things, even after they happen. (Knows: has knowledge of) **21.** Such a person will be punished in public; when least expected, he will be caught. (Public square: an open place in a town for public events) **22.** Likewise, the unfaithful woman who bears a child by another man will face punishment. (Unfaithful: not loyal) **23.** First, she disobeyed the Lord's law; second, she wronged her husband; third, she bore children by another. (Adulterous: involving unfaithfulness in marriage) **24.** She will be brought before the assembly, and her punishment will affect her children. (Assembly: a group of people gathered for a purpose) **25.** Her children will not thrive; her descendants will bear no fruit. (Thrive: grow, prosper) **26.** She will leave a cursed memory, and her disgrace will never be erased. (Cursed: condemned, disgrace: dishonor) **27.** All who live on earth will know that nothing is better than the fear of the Lord, and obeying His commandments. (Inhabit: live in, Beneficial: helpful)

Chapter 24

1. Wisdom praises herself and declares her glory before her people. (Wisdom: divine understanding) **2.** In the presence of the Most High, she speaks and shows her worth. (Most High: God) (Hosts: heavenly beings) **3.** "I came from the Most High and covered the earth like mist. (Mist: fine spray) **4.** I dwelled in the heavens, my throne on a cloud. (Heavens: sky or divine realm) **5.** I surrounded the vault of heaven and wandered the abyss. (Vault: sky) (Abyss: deep chasm) **6.** I ruled over the sea, land, and all nations. **7.** I sought a resting place among them. (Inheritance: what is passed down) **8.** The Creator commanded me to settle, choosing Jacob and Israel as my home. (Creator: God) **9.** I was created in the beginning and will last forever. (Ages: long periods) **10.** I served in the holy tent and made Zion my home. (Holy tent: sacred place) (Zion: hill in Jerusalem) **11.** In Jerusalem, the chosen city, I found rest. (Chosen city: Jerusalem) **12.** I rooted myself in the Lord's heritage among His people. (Root: settle) **13.** "I am like a cedar on Lebanon, a cypress on Mount Hermon, (Cedar: large tree) (Lebanon: mountain range) (Cypress: evergreen tree) (Mount Hermon: a mountain) **14.** Like a palm in En-gedi, a rose in Jericho, and an olive tree in the field. (Palm: long-leafed tree) (En-gedi: oasis) (Jericho: ancient city) **15.** Like cinnamon, myrrh, and incense, I offer fragrance in the holy place. (Cinnamon: spice) (Myrrh: resin) (Galbanum: resin) (Incense: burned substance) **16.** I spread my branches like a terebinth, bright and graceful. (Terebinth: tree) **17.** I bear rich fruit like the vine. (Vine: grape-producing plant) **18.** Come, all who desire me, and be filled with my fruit. **19.** You will find me sweeter than honey, more desirable than honeycomb. (Honeycomb: wax storage) **20.** Whoever eats of me will hunger still, and whoever drinks will thirst for more. (Eat: consume) (Drink: partake) **21.** Whoever obeys me will not be ashamed, and those who serve me will not fail. (Obey: follow commands) (Serve: work for) **22.** This is true of the Most High's covenant, the law Moses gave to Israel. (Covenant: sacred agreement) (Moses: prophet) (Inheritance: passed down) (Community of Jacob: Israelites) **23.** It overflows with wisdom, like the Pishon River, and the Tigris in new-fruit season. (Pishon: river in Eden) (Tigris: river in Mesopotamia) **24.** It runs over with understanding, like the Euphrates, and the Jordan during harvest. (Euphrates: river in Mesopotamia) (Jordan: river in Israel) **25.** It sparkles with knowledge, like the Nile, and the Gihon at vintage time. (Nile: river in Egypt) (Gihon: river in Eden) **26.** The first man never fully understood wisdom, nor will the last fathom her. (Fathom: understand) **27.** Her thoughts are deeper than the sea, her counsels beyond the abyss. (Abyss: deep chasm) **28.** I, like a small stream from her, watered a garden. (Rivulet: small stream) **29.** I said, "I will water my plants," and my stream became a river, then a sea. (Drench: soak) **30.** I send my teachings like the dawn, to be known far and wide. (Dawn: first light) **31.** I pour out instruction like prophecy for future generations. (Prophecy: inspired prediction) (Generations: descendants)

Chapter 25

1. I value three things, as they please both the LORD and people: harmony among brethren, kindness between neighbors, and the love between husband and wife. (Brethren: siblings or close companions) **2.** I detest three types of people: an arrogant poor man, a deceitful rich man, and an old man driven by lust. (deceitful: dishonest) **3.** If you don't save when young, how will you manage in old age? **4.** Judgment fits the gray-haired, and good counsel is suitable for elders. **5.** Wisdom, understanding, and prudence to the venerable. (venerable: worthy of respect due to age or character) **6.** The elderly's honor comes from experience, and their glory lies in fearing the LORD. **7.** Nine are blessed, and a tenth I praise: the man who delights in his children and sees his enemies fall. **8.** Blessed is the man with a sensible wife, who works fairly, avoids sinful speech, and serves no inferior. (sinful: wicked, evil) **9.** Fortunate is he who has a good friend and speaks to those who listen. **10.** Wisdom is admirable, but revering the LORD is greater. **11.** The fear of the LORD surpasses all; those who possess it are unmatched. **12.** The worst wounds are of the heart, and a quarrelsome woman causes great trouble. **13.** Pain from enemies and vengeance from foes are the most severe suffering. **14.** A serpent's poison is deadly, but the bitterness of a woman is worse. **15.** I'd rather live with a dragon or lion than with a wicked woman. (dragon: mythical creature; lion: symbol of strength) **16.** Wickedness mars a woman's appearance and makes her hostile like a bear. **17.** A husband sighs bitterly when his wife is troublesome. **18.** Few evils surpass a wicked woman; such women belong with sinners. **19.** A nagging wife burdens a peaceful man like a sandy slope under aged feet. **20.** Don't be deceived by a woman's beauty or greedy for her wealth. **21.** A man who depends on his wife's support lives in shame and disgrace. **22.** An evil wife brings sorrow, weakens her husband, and causes despair. **23.** Sin began with a woman, and death came through her. **24.** Don't allow water to overflow or tolerate a wayward wife. **25.** If she doesn't walk with you, separate from her.

Chapter 26

1. A man with a good wife lives a longer life. (Good: virtuous, moral) **2.** A worthy wife brings her husband joy, making his life peaceful. (Worthy: deserving, commendable) **3.** A noble wife is a precious gift to the one who fears the LORD. (LORD: God of Israel) **4.** Whether rich or poor, he is content and always smiling. (Content: satisfied, at peace) **5.** My heart trembles at three things, and a fourth terrifies me: public false charges, trials before a crowd, and lying testimonies are harder to bear than death. (Testimonies: sworn statements) **6.** A jealous wife causes pain, sorrow, and sharp words that hurt like the other three. (Jealous: envious, distrustful) **7.** A bad wife is like an unbearable yoke; marrying her is like grasping a scorpion. (Yoke: restraining device for animals; Scorpion: stinging arachnid) **8.** A drunk wife angers her husband and shows her shame openly. (Shame: dishonor, disgrace) **9.** An unfaithful wife is known by her bold looks and proud gaze. (Unfaithful: disloyal, untrustworthy) **10.** Keep close watch over an unruly wife, or she might take advantage. (Unruly: disorderly, unmanageable) **11.** If her eyes are bold, do not be surprised if she betrays you. (Betrays: acts disloyally) **12.** Like a thirsty traveler drinks from any water, she welcomes every opportunity for wrongdoing. (Wrongdoing: immoral behavior) **13.** A thoughtful wife brings joy and strengthens her husband. (Thoughtful: considerate, caring) **14.** Her wise words are a gift from the LORD, and her strong virtue is priceless. (Virtue: moral excellence) **15.** A modest wife is a priceless blessing, her purity unmatched. (Modest: humble, chaste) **16.** The beauty of a virtuous wife brightens her home like the sun in the sky. (Virtuous: morally upright) **17.** Her graceful form and radiant face are as lovely as the light of the holy lampstand. (Lampstand: sacred object in temples) **18.** Her steady feet and shapely limbs are like golden columns on silver bases. (Columns: supporting structures) **19.** Three things grieve me, and a fourth horrifies me: a rich man reduced to poverty, respected men disgraced, and those who abandon justice for sin, whom the LORD judges. (Judges: decides, condemns) **20.** It is hard for merchants to stay honest, and shopkeepers often fall into wrongdoing. (Merchants: traders; Wrongdoing: unethical acts)

Chapter 27

1. Many sin for profit, and wealth blinds the mind. (Profit: gain; Blinds: makes unaware) **2.** Sin is wedged between buying and selling. (Wedged: forced into) **3.** Without fearing the Lord, your house will fall. (Fear of the Lord: reverence for God) **4.** A man's flaws show in his speech, like chaff from a sieve. (Chaff: husks of grains) **5.** As a potter's work is tested, so is a man's speech. (Potter: maker of pottery) **6.** A tree's fruit reveals its care, as a man's words show his heart. (Reveals: shows) **7.** Don't praise a man before he speaks, as words test him. (Test: examine) **8.** Seek justice, and you will wear it like a robe. (Seek: pursue; Robe: garment) **9.** Birds stay with their kind, and loyalty comes to the faithful. (Loyalty: faithfulness) **10.** Sin waits for the wicked like a lion for prey. (Lion: predatory animal) **11.** The devout speak wisely, but the wicked are changeable. (Devout: religious; Changeable: fickle) **12.** Limit time with fools and spend it with wise people. (Fools: unwise people) **13.** The wicked speak offensively and laugh in guilt. (Offensively: hurtfully; Guilt: responsibility) **14.** Their speech shocks, and their fights are unbearable. (Shocks: causes fear) **15.** Disputes among the proud lead to violence, and their curses hurt. (Proud: arrogant) **16.** A man who betrays a secret cannot be trusted. (Betrays: reveals dishonestly) **17.** Be loyal to your friend, but don't follow if you betray him. (Loyal: faithful) **18.** Betraying a friend harms more than an enemy. (Betraying: being disloyal) **19.** Once you release a friend, you can't bring him back. (Release: set free) **20.** Don't chase him, for he's gone, like a gazelle escaping a trap. (Gazelle: fast animal) **21.** A wound can heal, but betraying a secret harms deeply. (Wound: injury) **22.** A deceptive man schemes evil, and no one can stop him. (Deceptive: misleading) **23.** He flatters in your presence but twists your words later. (Flatters: praises insincerely) **24.** I hate this with all my heart, and the Lord does too. (Heart: emotions) **25.** Like a stone falling back on the one who throws it, treachery harms both the victim and the betrayer. (Treachery: deceit) **26.** He who digs a pit will fall into it. (Pit: hole) **27.** Those who harm others will face unexpected consequences. (Harm: hurt; Consequences: results) **28.** The proud face mockery, and vengeance waits for them. (Vengeance: revenge) **29.** Those who take pleasure in traps will be caught, and pain will consume them. (Pleasure: enjoyment; Consume: destroy) **30.** Wrath and anger are hated, but sinners cling to them. (Wrath: intense anger)

Chapter 28

1. The wicked will face the LORD's judgment, as He remembers all their wrongs. (LORD: God) **2.** Forgive your neighbor's wrongs, and your own sins will be forgiven when you pray. **3.** Can you hold onto anger and expect healing from the LORD? **4.** How can you deny mercy to others but ask for forgiveness for yourself? **5.** If a human being holds onto wrath, who will forgive their sins? **6.** Reflect on your last days, put aside hatred; remember death and decay, and stop sinning! (Decay: rotting or decomposition) **7.** Think of the commandments, don't hate your neighbor; remember God's covenant and forgive faults. (God: the Most High) **8.** Avoid conflict to lessen your sins; quarrelsome people cause disputes. **9.** Such people break friendships and cause discord among peaceful ones. (Discord: disagreement or conflict) **10.** The more wood, the fiercer the fire; the stronger the anger, the greater the wrath. **11.** Pitch and resin cause fire to flare, and constant quarrels lead to violence. **12.** A small spark can turn into a fire, but if you stop it, it dies out; both actions are in your control! **13.** Cursed are gossips and deceivers, for they destroy peace. (Gossips: rumor-spreaders; Deceivers: dishonest people) **14.** A meddling tongue causes trouble, exiles many, and ruins cities and families. (Exiles: those forced away from home) **15.** A meddling tongue can drive virtuous women from their homes and rob them of their work. (Virtuous: morally good) **16.** Those who listen to it find no peace or rest. **17.** A whip leaves marks, but harsh words can break the spirit. **18.** Many die by the sword, but more by the harm of the tongue. **19.** Blessed is the person who avoids it and is not burdened by its wrath or chains. (Wrath: intense anger) **20.** Its yoke is like iron, and its chains are like bronze! (Yoke: heavy burden) **21.** Its punishment is severe, worse than death itself. **22.** It does not harm the righteous or burn them. (Righteous: morally right) **23.** But those who forsake the LORD will fall victim to it, as it burns uncontrollably within them! It will tear them apart like a lion or panther. (Uncontrollably: unable to be stopped) **24.** Protect your words as you protect your vineyard with thorns. (Vineyard: grapevine field) **25.** Guard your words as carefully as you secure your Gold and Silver. (Gold and Silver: precious metals) **26.** Be careful not to let your tongue slip up and fall into your enemy's trap. (Slip up: make a mistake; Trap: ambush)

Chapter 29

1. A kind person lends to a neighbor and helps others. (Neighbor: a nearby person) **2.** Lend to those in need and repay what you owe. (Repay: return borrowed goods or money) **3.** Be honest, keep your word, and you'll have what you need. (Word: promise) **4.** Borrowers often add burdens to lenders. (Burden: something difficult to carry) **5.** Borrowers flatter the lender but fail to repay, claiming they can't. (Flatter: excessive praise) **6.** Recovering half of the loan is an achievement; failing results in loss and enemies. (Enemies: people who oppose you) **7.** Many avoid lending not out of stinginess, but out of fear of being deceived. (Stingy: unwilling to give) **8.** Be generous to the poor and help them without delay. (Generous: willing to give) **9.** Help the needy as the teachings say, and don't send them away empty. (Teaching: moral lesson) **10.** Use your wealth to help others and don't waste it. (Wealth: money and resources) **11.** Follow God's commands, as it's more valuable than gold. (God: the Most High) **12.** Acts of charity protect you from evil. (Charity: kindness or giving) **13.** Charity is more powerful than a shield or spear, defending you from enemies. (Shield: protection, spear: weapon) **14.** A good person stands by their neighbor, while only the shameless betray trust. (Betray: to deceive or fail someone) **15.** Remember those who risk their lives for you. (Risk: to face danger) **16.** The wicked turn pledges into misfortune, and the ungrateful abandon those who help. (Pledge: promise) **17.** Standing surety ruins many, tossing them into turmoil. (Surety: guaranteeing someone else's debt) **18.** It causes people to be exiled and wander far from home. (Exiled: forced to leave home) **19.** Those who guarantee debts face trouble and legal struggles. (Trouble: difficulties) **20.** Guarantee for others only if you can afford it, and avoid falling into debt. (Afford: to be able to pay) **21.** Life's basic needs are water, bread, clothing, and a home. (Home: place for privacy) **22.** A simple meal at home is better than lavish meals with strangers. (Lavish: extravagant) **23.** Be content with what you have and ignore critics of your home. (Content: satisfied) **24.** It's painful to move from house to house, where you can't speak freely. (Painful: uncomfortable) **25.** Guests receive no thanks and often hear harsh words. (Harsh: unkind) **26.** "Set the table and serve me food, stranger!" (Stranger: unknown person) **27.** "Go away, stranger, my brother needs the room!" **28.** Insults at home and mistreatment by creditors are painful for the sensitive. (Mistreated: treated unfairly)

Chapter 30
1. A loving father corrects his son often, ensuring joy when he matures. (Corrects: disciplines, reproves) **2.** A father who trains his son will benefit and proudly share his achievements. (Trains: teaches, instructs) **3.** A father's education of his son causes envy in his enemies and pride among friends. (Educates: raises, teaches) **4.** After death, a father's legacy remains in a son who resembles him. (Resembles: mirrors, reflects) **5.** A father finds joy in his son's success and has no regrets even in death. **6.** He leaves behind an avenger for his enemies and one to repay his friends' kindness. (Avenger: one who seeks justice) **7.** A father who indulges his son faces constant distress from his outbursts. (Indulges: spoils, pampers) **8.** An untamed colt becomes stubborn; a son unchecked grows unruly. (Colt: young horse) **9.** Pampering a child leads to distress and sorrow. (Pamper: overindulge) **10.** Avoid indulging your child's foolishness, or you will regret it. (Foolishness: silliness, immaturity) **11.** Do not let your child have his way or ignore his wrongs. **12.** Discipline him while young to prevent stubbornness and rebellion. (Rebellion: disobedience) **13.** Discipline your son and make him work hard to avoid future shame. **14.** Better to be strong and poor than rich and frail. **15.** Health is more valuable than gold, and peace of mind more precious than jewels. (Peace of mind: contentment, calm) **16.** A healthy body is the greatest treasure, and a joyful heart is the highest happiness. **17.** Death is preferable to a bitter life, and eternal rest to endless suffering. **18.** Luxuries for someone who cannot enjoy them are like offerings to a grave. (Grave: tomb, burial place) **19.** What is the value of an offering to a lifeless idol? **20.** It's the same for a suffering person who longs for what they cannot have. (Suffering: misery, pain) **21.** Do not dwell on sadness or torment yourself with worry; **22.** A joyful heart is the essence of life, and cheerfulness adds years. **23.** Distract yourself, lift your spirits, and avoid resentment, as worry causes harm. **24.** Envy and anger shorten life, and worry leads to premature aging. **25.** A cheerful person enjoys their food to the fullest.

Chapter 31
1. Watching over wealth harms the body, and caring too much for riches steals rest. (Wealth: accumulation of assets) **2.** Worrying about survival keeps one awake, disturbing sleep more than sickness. (Sickness: illness) **3.** The rich man works to amass wealth, finding rest only in indulgence. (Indulgence: self-gratification) **4.** The poor man works for barely enough, and even in rest, finds himself in need. (Rest: relaxation) **5.** The lover of money will fall into sin, for wealth leads many astray. (Sin: immoral act) **6.** Many have been trapped by gold, even when destruction loomed. (Gold: valuable metal) **7.** Gold is a trap for those who crave it, a snare for the foolish. (Crave: desire intensely) **8.** Blessed is the rich man who is blameless, not seeking gain. (Blameless: without fault) **9.** Who is he, that we may honor him? He has done wonders among his people. (Honor: respect) **10.** Tested by gold, he came out unscathed; he could have sinned but chose not to. (unscathed: unharmed) **11.** His possessions are secure, and his praises are recounted. (praises: admirations) **12.** Do not overindulge when dining with the great, nor complain about the food. (Overindulge: eat too much) **13.** Remember, gluttony is evil; the eye is the most greedy. (Gluttony: excessive eating) **14.** Understand your neighbor's feelings, and be aware of your own dislikes. (Dislikes: things you don't like) **15.** Don't take what your neighbor desires or reach for the same dish. (Reach: extend your hand) **16.** Be a courteous guest, avoiding greed, or you may be scorned. (Courteous: polite) **17.** Stop eating first, as good manners dictate; do not overeat. (Offense: displeasure) **18.** Don't be the first to grab food if many are at the table. (Grab: take quickly) **19.** A well-bred person is content with little; he sleeps soundly. (Well-bred: cultured) **20.** The glutton suffers distress and restlessness; moderation brings peace and clarity. (Distress: discomfort) **21.** If you've overeaten, relief comes after emptying your stomach. (Overeaten: eaten too much) **22.** Listen to my advice; later, you'll see its value. Be moderate to avoid sickness. (avoid: escape) **23.** A generous person is blessed, and his kindness is praised forever. (Generous: giving freely) **24.** A stingy person is publicly criticized, and his selfishness is remembered. (Selfishness: concern only for oneself) **25.** Don't prove strength by drinking wine; it has ruined many. (Strength: power) **26.** As a furnace tests a blacksmith's work, wine reveals the nature of the arrogant. (Blacksmith: metalworker) **27.** Wine brings life when drunk moderately. Can anyone live without it? (Moderation: control) **28.** Enjoy wine at the right time for joy, good cheer, and celebration. (Good cheer: happiness) **29.** Wine consumed in anger brings headaches, bitterness, and shame. (Bitterness: harshness) **30.** Excessive wine weakens the fool, increasing his suffering. (Suffering: pain) **31.** Don't rebuke your neighbor when drinking wine; be gentle and avoid distressing him. (Rebuke: criticize harshly)

Chapter 32
1. If you're chosen to lead a meal, stay humble and serve the guests first. (Meal: a social gathering with food) **2.** After your duties are complete, join them in celebration and earn praise for your hospitality. (Hospitality: the act of being kind to guests) **3.** As an elder, speak wisely, but avoid interrupting the singing. (Elder: an older, respected person) **4.** When wine is served, avoid overtalking or showing off your knowledge. (Wine: fermented beverage made from grapes) **5.** A performance with wine is like a carnelian seal in gold—elegant. (Carnelian: a red gemstone) **6.** Music with wine is like gold with an emerald seal—both enhance the experience. (Emerald: a green gemstone) **7.** Young man, speak only when necessary, after being asked. (Young man: a male youth) **8.** Be concise but meaningful, like the wise who speak little. (Concise: brief in speech) **9.** Don't be too assertive with elders or pressure officials. (Elders: older, respected people) **10.** Modesty's esteem is like lightning before a storm—brief but bright. (Modesty: humility in behavior) **11.** When it's time to leave, don't delay; head home! (Linger: stay longer than needed) **12.** Relax at home and enjoy yourself without sin or pride. (Sin: moral wrongdoing) **13.** Above all, praise your Creator, who blesses you. (Creator: God, the Creator of the universe) **14.** To find God, embrace discipline, and your desires will be fulfilled. (Discipline: self-control or training) **15.** One who studies the law understands it, but the hypocrite falls into its trap. (Hypocrite: someone who pretends to be virtuous) **16.** Those who fear the LORD make wise decisions and gain clarity. (Fear: reverence and respect) **17.** The sinner avoids correction and twists the law for his gain. (Sinner: someone who commits moral wrongdoing) **18.** The thoughtful seek guidance, while the proud ignore it. (Thoughtful: showing careful consideration) **19.** Never act without advice, and you'll have no regrets. (Advice: guidance or recommendations) **20.** Avoid paths with hidden dangers and don't make the same mistake twice. (Hidden dangers: risks not immediately visible) **21.** Even if the road seems clear, be cautious. (Road: a path or route) **22.** Be cautious in all things. (Cautious: being careful to avoid danger) **23.** Stay alert in everything you do to follow the commandments. (Commandments: rules or laws to be followed) **24.** Those who follow the law protect themselves, and those who trust in the LORD will not be ashamed. (Trust: reliance on God for support)

Chapter 33
1. No harm befalls the one who fears the LORD; they are safe in trials. (Trials: difficult experiences) **2.** Those who reject the law lack wisdom and are tossed like a boat in a storm. (Reject: disregard) **3.** The wise trust the LORD's word; His law is a dependable guide. (Guide: a way to follow) **4.** Speak carefully, and your words will be heard; rely on your training. (Training: education or practice) **5.** A fool's mind is always spinning in circles. (Fool: one lacking wisdom) **6.** A fickle friend is like a horse that neighs regardless of the rider. (Fickle: changeable) **7.** Why is one day more important than another when the sun shines on them all? (Important: significant) **8.** The LORD's wisdom makes days and seasons different, and He controls feasts. (Feasts: celebrations) **9.** Some days are holy, others are ordinary. (Holy: sacred) **10.** All men are made from clay, formed from the earth. (Clay: soft, moldable material) **11.** The LORD leads men on different paths by His wisdom. (Paths: directions or ways) **12.** Some are blessed and raised up, others cursed and humbled. (Raised up: exalted) **13.** Like clay in the potter's hands, men are

shaped by their Creator. (Potter: one who molds clay) **14.** Evil contrasts with good, and death with life; sinners oppose the righteous. (Righteous: morally just) **15.** The Most High's works come in pairs, opposites of one another. (Most High: God) **16.** I am the last to keep watch, like a gleaner after the harvest. (Gleaner: one who gathers leftover crops) **17.** By the LORD's blessing, I have progressed like a vintager filling the wine press. (Vintager: a gatherer of grapes) **18.** My labor has been for all who seek wisdom, not just for me. (Labor: work or effort) **19.** Listen, leaders of the people; give ear, rulers of the assembly. (Assembly: a group) **20.** Let no one, not son, wife, brother, or friend, rule over you while you live. (Rule: have control) **21.** While you live, do not give away your wealth or you may plead with others. (Wealth: possessions or money) **22.** It's better that your children plead with you than depend on their generosity. (Generosity: willingness to give) **23.** Keep control of your affairs and protect your reputation. (Affairs: matters or concerns) **24.** When your days end, divide your inheritance. (Inheritance: property or legacy) **25.** Just as an ass bears loads, a servant carries food and correction. (Ass: a type of animal) **26.** A wicked servant faces punishment; a lazy one will seek freedom. (Wicked: evil) **27.** Make them work to avoid mischief; idle hands lead to trouble. (Mischief: harm or trouble) **28.** Keep them working; if rebellious, bind them with chains. (Rebellious: resisting authority) **29.** Never domineer or act unjustly toward anyone. (Domineer: to rule harshly) **30.** If you have only one servant, treat him as an equal, for you have paid with your life's blood. (Equal: of the same worth) **31.** Treat your servant like a brother, for you depend on him as you do your own life. (Depend: rely on) **32.** If you mistreat him and he runs away, where will you search for him? (Mistreat: treat unfairly)

Chapter 34
1. Empty are the hopes of the foolish, and those lifted by dreams are deceived. (Foolish: lacking wisdom) **2.** Believing in dreams is like chasing shadows or the wind. (Chasing the wind: futile pursuit) **3.** Dreams are as distant from reality as a reflection is from the face. (Reflection: an image in a mirror) **4.** Can the unclean make the clean? Can a liar speak truth? (Unclean: morally impure) **5.** Divination, omens, and dreams are false; they reflect only what we expect. (Divination: seeking future knowledge) **6.** Do not trust dreams unless they come from God. (Most High: God) **7.** Many have been led astray by dreams, and those who believed perished. (Astray: misled) **8.** The law is fulfilled, and wisdom comes from the faithful. (Law: divine commandments) **9.** A trained person gains wisdom; a wise person speaks with understanding. (Wise: good judgment) **10.** An untested person knows little, but travel brings resourcefulness. (Resourcefulness: problem-solving skill) **11.** I've seen much and learned more than I can say. (Express: communicate in words) **12.** I faced danger but was saved by my experiences. (Saved: rescued) **13.** Those who fear the LORD are strong, trusting in their Savior. (Savior: rescuer) **14.** Those who fear the LORD are never afraid, for He is their hope. (Hope: confident expectation) **15.** Blessed is the one who fears the LORD! Who is their trust and support? (Blessed: favored by God) **16.** The LORD is their shield, support, refuge, and protector. (Refuge: safe place) **17.** He uplifts their spirits, brightens their eyes, and blesses them with life. (Lift up: encourage) **18.** Gifts from ill-gotten goods are tainted; the unrighteous don't win God's favor. (Ill-gotten: dishonestly gained) **19.** The Most High doesn't accept the offerings of the godless, nor forgive their sins. (Godless: without reverence for God) **20.** The one who sacrifices the poor's possessions is like one who kills a son before his father. (Sacrifices: offerings to God) **21.** Charity's bread is life for the poor; withholding it is like shedding blood. (Charity: voluntary aid) **22.** To deny someone their living is like killing them; withholding wages is shedding blood. (Living: livelihood) **23.** What do they gain if one builds while another destroys? (Tears down: destroys) **24.** If one prays and another curses, whose voice will God hear? (Curses: harmful words) **25.** If a man touches a corpse after bathing, what use is his purification? (Purification: cleansing process) **26.** Similarly, fasting for sins but repeating them is pointless. (Fasting: religious abstinence)

Chapter 35
1. Keeping the law is a great offering; those who follow the commandments make a peace offering. **2.** Charity is like fine flour, and giving alms is a sacrifice of praise. **3.** Avoiding evil pleases the LORD; turning away from injustice is an atonement. **4.** Do not approach the LORD empty-handed; your offerings fulfill the commandments. **5.** The just man's gift enriches the altar and is a pleasing fragrance to the Most High. **6.** The sacrifice of the just is greatly valued and will not be forgotten. **7.** Honor the LORD with a generous heart; do not hold back freewill offerings. **8.** Give cheerfully with each contribution, and bring your tithes with joy. **9.** Give to the Most High as He has given to you, generously according to your means. **10.** The LORD always repays; He will return to you sevenfold. **11.** Do not offer bribes, for He will not accept them. Trust not in ill-gotten gains. **12.** God is just and impartial, showing no favorites. **13.** He may not favor the weak, but He hears the oppressed. **14.** He listens to the orphan's cry and the widow's complaint. **15.** Do not the tears of the widow call out against those who cause them? **16.** The prayer of one who serves God willingly is heard and reaches the heavens. **17.** The humble's prayer pierces the clouds and reaches its goal. **18.** It will not rest until the Most High responds, judges justly, and affirms the right. **19.** God will not delay, like a warrior, He will act. **20.** He will break the backs of the merciless and avenge the proud. **21.** He will destroy the wicked, uprooting them and smashing their scepters. **22.** He will repay each according to their deeds and thoughts. **23.** He will defend His people and bring them joy through His mercy. **24.** His mercy is welcome in times of trouble, like rain in a drought.

Chapter 36
Come to our aid, O God of the universe, and make all nations fear you! **2.** Lift your hand against the heathen, that they may see your power. (heathen: non-believers) **3.** As you used us to reveal your holiness, now use them to reveal your glory. **4.** They will know, as we do, that there is no God but you. **5.** Show new signs and wonders; reveal the strength of your right hand. (wonders: miraculous events) **6.** Stir your anger, pour out wrath, humble the enemy, and scatter the foe. (wrath: intense anger) **7.** Hurry the day and bring about the time. **8.** Crush the heads of hostile rulers. (hostile: aggressive or enemy) **9.** Let raging fire consume the fugitives, and destroy your people's oppressors. (fugitives: people fleeing) **10.** Gather all the tribes of Jacob, that they may inherit the land as in ancient times. **11.** Show mercy to your people, Israel, whom you called your firstborn. (mercy: compassion) **12.** Take pity on your holy city, Jerusalem, your dwelling place. (pity: sorrow for others' suffering) **13.** Fill Zion with your majesty, and your temple with your glory. (majesty: grandeur or splendor) **14.** Recall your mighty deeds of old; fulfill the prophecies spoken in your name. (prophecies: predictions or revelations) **15.** Reward those who have hoped in you, and let your prophets be proven true. **16.** Hear the prayer of your servants, for you are always gracious to your people. (gracious: kind and merciful) **17.** Let it be known to the ends of the earth that you are the eternal God. (eternal: everlasting) **18.** The throat can swallow all kinds of food, but some foods are more pleasant than others. **19.** As the palate tests meat by its flavor, so does a keen mind judge insincere words. (palate: sense of taste) **20.** A deceitful character causes grief, but an experienced man can turn things around. (deceitful: dishonest) **21.** Though any man may marry, one woman is more suitable than another. (suitable: appropriate or fitting) **22.** A woman's beauty lights up her husband's face, for it surpasses all that charms the eye. (surpasses: exceeds or outshines) **23.** If her speech is kind, her husband's life is blessed beyond that of ordinary men. **24.** A wife is her husband's greatest treasure, a helpmate, and a steady support. (helpmate: supportive partner) **25.** A vineyard without a hedge will be overrun; a man without a wife is like a homeless wanderer. (overrun: overtaken or overwhelmed) **26.** Who will trust a band of armed men that moves from city to city? **27.** Or a man who has no home, but sleeps wherever night finds him?

Chapter 37
1. Every friend declares their friendship, but some are friends only in name. **2.** It's a sorrow unto death when your close companion becomes your enemy (sorrow: deep sadness). **3.** "Alas, my friend! Why were you created to deceive the earth?" (deceive: mislead). **4.** A false friend will share your joys, but in trouble, they stay distant. **5.** A true friend will fight alongside you and be your shield against your enemies (shield: protector). **6.** Do not forget your comrade in battle, and don't neglect him when dividing spoils (comrade: companion; spoils: rewards or profits). **7.** Every counselor suggests a way, but some offer their own paths (counselor: advisor). **8.** Be cautious when receiving advice; first, find out what the advisor wants (cautious: careful). **9.** They may say how good your path will be, only to watch your misfortune unfold (misfortune: bad luck). **10.** Avoid seeking advice from those who are hostile; keep your intentions hidden from the envious (hostile: unfriendly; envious: jealous). **11.** Do not speak to a woman about her rival, a coward about war, a merchant about business, a buyer about value, a miser about generosity, a cruel man about mercy, a lazy man about work, a seasonal laborer about harvest, or an idle slave about a great task; ignore their advice (rival: competitor; coward: someone afraid; merchant: business person; miser: someone who hoards money; cruel: unmerciful; lazy: unmotivated; seasonal laborer: temporary worker; idle: inactive). **12.** Instead, associate with a righteous person who keeps the commandments, someone who understands and will care for you if you fall (associate: connect; righteous: virtuous). **13.** Also, listen to your own heart's counsel, for what else can you depend on more? (counsel: advice). **14.** A man's conscience can reveal his situation better than seven watchmen in a high tower (conscience: inner sense of right and wrong; watchmen: guards). **15.** Most importantly, pray to

God to guide you on the path of truth. **16**. Words are the source of all deeds; thoughts precede actions (deeds: actions; precede: come before). **17**. The mind is the root of all behavior, producing four branches (root: foundation). **18**. Good, evil, life, and death—controlled by the tongue (tongue: speech). **19**. A man may be wise and benefit many, yet remain of no use to himself. **20**. Though wise, if his words are rejected, he loses all enjoyment (rejected: dismissed). **21**. When a man's wisdom benefits him, it is reflected in his life (reflected: shown). **22**. When wisdom benefits his people, the effects are lasting (effects: results). **23**. A man's life is limited, but Israel's life is endless (limited: short; endless: eternal). **24**. One who is wise for himself enjoys life fully, and others praise him. **25**. One who is wise for his people earns a legacy of glory, and his name endures (legacy: lasting memory; endures: lasts). **26**. My son, while you are healthy, control your appetite, and avoid what harms you (appetite: desire for food). **27**. Not all food is good for everyone, nor is everything suited to every taste (suited: appropriate). **28**. Do not be drawn to every pleasure, nor indulge in rich foods (drawn: tempted; indulge: overeat or overconsume). **29**. Overeating leads to sickness, and gluttony causes discomfort (gluttony: excessive eating). **30**. Many have died due to lack of self-control, but the moderate person prolongs their life (moderate: balanced; prolongs: lengthens).

Chapter 38

1. Honor the physician, for his role is essential, and God established his profession. **2**. From God comes his wisdom, and the king provides for his sustenance (sustenance: nourishment or support). **3**. His skill sets him apart and grants him access to the powerful. **4**. God makes the earth produce healing herbs, which the wise should not ignore. **5**. Did not a twig sweeten the water to demonstrate His power? **6**. He gives knowledge so people can marvel at His mighty works. **7**. Through this, the doctor eases pain, and the pharmacist prepares medicine. **8**. God's creative work continues unceasingly, healing the earth (unceasingly: without stopping). **9**. My son, when ill, do not delay; pray to God, who will heal you. **10**. Turn from wickedness, act justly, and cleanse your heart from sin (wickedness: evil behavior; justly: in a fair and right way). **11**. Offer your sacrifice and petition sincerely, according to your means (petition: request). **12**. Give the doctor his place, for you need him as well. **13**. There are times when he has the advantage. **14**. He also prays to God for correct diagnosis and successful treatment (diagnosis: identification of a disease). **15**. A sinner defiant toward God will also reject the doctor. **16**. My son, mourn for the dead with tears, wailing, and bitter lament (wailing: loud crying; lament: expression of grief). **17**. Prepare the body and attend the burial as is proper. **18**. Grieve one or two days to avoid gossip, then regain composure (composure: calmness). **19**. Excessive grief can harm health and lead to despair (despair: hopelessness). **20**. Do not dwell on the dead; focus instead on life and its purpose. **21**. The dead will not return, and recalling them offers no benefit. **22**. Remember, their fate is also yours: today for them, tomorrow for you. **23**. Let the memory of the dead fade; strengthen your heart after their passing. **24**. A scribe's work enhances his wisdom (scribe: writer or scholar); free from toil, he grows wise (toil: hard work). **25**. How can one who plows and drives oxen gain learning? **26**. His focus is on furrows and tending cattle (furrows: grooves in the ground for planting). **27**. Likewise, engravers and designers labor tirelessly to craft intricate patterns (engravers: artists who carve or etch; intricate: detailed). **28**. The smith toils near his anvil, enduring heat to shape iron (smith: metalworker; anvil: a heavy block used for shaping metal). **29**. The potter spins his wheel, shaping clay with care and precision. **30**. He molds with his hands, softens with his feet, and watches the kiln's fire (kiln: oven for firing pottery). **31**. All these workers are skilled in their trades, experts in their tasks. **32**. Without them, no city could thrive (thrive: prosper), and they are never in want (want: lack or need). **33**. They do not judge or lead but serve through their craft. **34**. Yet, they preserve God's work, focusing on their skill and purpose.

Chapter 39

1. How different the man who devotes himself to studying the law of the Most High! He learns from ancient wisdom and prophecies. **2**. He treasures the discourses of the wise and seeks deeper understanding of their words. (discourses: discussions) **3**. He explores the meaning of parables and studies the teachings of the sages. (parables: short stories with a moral lesson; sages: wise people) **4**. He attends to great men and has access to rulers. (rulers: leaders) **5**. He travels to foreign lands to understand what is good and evil among men. (foreign: from another country) **6**. His aim is to seek the LORD, ask forgiveness, and pray for understanding. (forgiveness: pardon) **7**. If it pleases the LORD, he will be filled with wisdom and direct his counsel in prayer. (counsel: advice) **8**. He will show the wisdom learned and rejoice in the LORD's covenant. (covenant: agreement) **9**. Many will praise his understanding, and his name will endure forever. (understanding: wisdom) **10**. People will speak of his wisdom and sing his praises in assembly. (assembly: gathering) **11**. While alive, he is rare, and his renown will live on after his death. (renown: fame) **12**. I will present my message clearly, like the full moon shining. **13**. Listen, faithful children: bloom like roses by running waters. (bloom: grow) **14**. Send up the fragrance of incense, and sing praises to the LORD for all he has done. (fragrance: pleasant smell; incense: a substance burned for fragrance) **15**. Proclaim his greatness, singing praises with music and joy. (proclaim: announce) **16**. All the works of God are good; every need is met in its time. **17**. At his word, the waters become still; he speaks, and reservoirs form. (reservoirs: large water stores) **18**. He commands, and nothing can limit his will. **19**. All human works are before him; nothing escapes his eye. **20**. His gaze spans all ages; nothing surprises him. (gaze: look) **21**. Do not question the purpose of things; everything fulfills a need. **22**. His blessing flows like the Nile, enriching the earth. (enriching: making better) **23**. His wrath expels nations and turns fertile land into wasteland. (wrath: anger; expels: drives out; wasteland: desert) **24**. For the virtuous, his paths are straight; for the proud, they are steep. (virtuous: good people; proud: arrogant) **25**. Good things are provided for the good, but the wicked receive both good and evil. (wicked: evil people) **26**. The chief needs of life are water, fire, iron, salt, wheat, milk, honey, wine, oil, and cloth. (chief: main) **27**. For the good, these are blessings, but for the wicked, they turn to evil. **28**. Storms are created to punish, dislodging mountains to satisfy God's anger. (dislodging: moving) **29**. In his storehouse are fire, hail, famine, disease, and beasts to destroy the wicked. (famine: lack of food; disease: sickness; beasts: animals) **30**. They obey his commands, rejoicing in carrying out their tasks. (tasks: duties) **31**. From the beginning, I wrote: God's works are good, and he fills every need. **32**. Do not say one thing is better than another; each serves its purpose in time. **33**. Proclaim with joy the goodness of the LORD. **34**. All his works are good; every need is met in its season. (season: time) **35**. Bless the name of the Holy One with full joy of heart. (Holy One: God)

Chapter 40

1. God has given mankind great anxiety and a heavy burden, from birth to death. **2**. Thoughts, fears, and troubles persist until the day of death. **3**. Whether in wealth or poverty, people face envy, wrath, and suffering. (envy: jealousy; wrath: anger) **4**. From crowns to rags, everyone endures wrath, trouble, and fear, even in sleep. (crowns: royalty; rags: poverty) **5**. Sleep is short and restless, filled with troubled dreams and fears. **6**. Even in dreams, one is pursued, only to awaken and find there was no danger. **7**. This is true for all, but sinners face even greater distress. (sinners: wrongdoers) **8**. Plague, bloodshed, and destruction await the wicked. (plague: disease; bloodshed: killing; wicked: evil people) **9**. For the wicked, these calamities are created by their own actions. (calamities: disasters) **10**. What comes from injustice and corruption will fade, but loyalty endures forever. (injustice: unfairness; corruption: dishonesty) **11**. Wealth gained from wickedness is like a flood that ends suddenly. (wickedness: evil actions; flood: overwhelming water) **12**. The violent do not prosper, their foundations are weak like reeds. (violent: aggressive; foundations: base; reeds: weak plants) **13**. But goodness and justice last forever. (goodness: kindness; justice: fairness) **14**. Wealth and wages make life sweet, but wisdom is better than both. (wages: payment for work) **15**. A child or city can preserve one's name, but wisdom is more valuable. (preserve: keep; wisdom: knowledge) **16**. Sheepfolds and orchards bring health, but a devoted wife is more valuable. (sheepfolds: pens for sheep; orchards: fruit farms) **17**. Wine and music bring joy, but conjugal love is superior. (conjugal: relating to marriage) **18**. The flute and harp bring melody, but a true voice is better. **19**. Charm and beauty delight the eye, but wildflowers surpass them. (charm: attractiveness; surpass: go beyond) **20**. A friend or neighbor may guide, but a prudent wife is better. (prudent: wise) **21**. A brother or helper in times of stress is good, but charity is more valuable. (charity: generosity) **22**. Gold and silver secure one's way, but sound judgment is better. (sound judgment: wise decision-making) **23**. Wealth and strength bring confidence, but the fear of God is better. (fear of God: respect for God) **24**. The fear of God leaves nothing lacking; no other support is needed. **25**. The fear of God is a paradise of blessings, with all glory under its canopy. (paradise: perfect place; canopy: covering) **26**. My son, do not live as a beggar; better to die than to beg. (beggar: person who asks for money) **27**. A life spent depending on others is not truly a life. **28**. The food of others brings discomfort to one who understands. (discomfort: unease) **29**. For the shameless, begging is sweet, but it burns like fire inside. (shameless: lacking shame) **30**. In the mouth of the beggar, begging is sweet, but his soul is consumed with fire. (soul: inner being; consumed: completely taken over)

Chapter 41

1. O death, how bitter for the man at peace, with possessions and pleasures. (possessions: belongings; pleasures: enjoyments) **2.** O death, how welcome to the weak, failing man with no hope or sight. (weak: frail; failing: weakening) **3.** Fear not death; remember, it embraces all, past and future. (embraces: accepts) **4.** God has ordained this for all flesh; why reject the will of the Most High? (ordained: planned; flesh: human beings) **5.** The children of sinners are wicked, and foolish offspring live in wicked homes. (wicked: evil; offspring: children) **6.** The dominion of sinners' children is lost, and reproach follows their descendants. (dominion: rule; reproach: shame; descendants: offspring) **7.** Children curse their wicked father for the disgrace he brings. (curse: speak negatively; disgrace: dishonor) **8.** Woe to you, sinful men, who forsake the law of the Most High. (woe: sorrow; forsake: abandon) **9.** If you have children, calamity will come upon them, and at death, you will be cursed. (calamity: disaster; cursed: condemned) **10.** What is of nothing returns to nothing; so do the godless from void to void. (godless: without God; void: emptiness) **11.** Man's body is fleeting, but a virtuous name lasts forever. (fleeting: short-lived; virtuous: good) **12.** Care for your name; it is worth more than treasures. (treasures: valuables) **13.** Life is short, but a good name lasts for endless days. (endless: without end) **14.** Children, heed my instruction on shame; judge disgrace by my rules. (heed: pay attention to; shame: dishonor; disgrace: shame) **15.** Be ashamed of immorality before parents, falsehood before masters. (immorality: wrong behavior; falsehood: lies; masters: authorities) **16.** Be ashamed of flattery before rulers, crime before the assembly. (flattery: excessive praise; rulers: leaders; crime: wrongdoing) **17.** Be ashamed of disloyalty and broken oaths before friends. (disloyalty: betrayal; oaths: promises) **18.** Be ashamed of theft in your community and overindulgence at meals. (theft: stealing; overindulgence: excessive eating) **19.** Be ashamed of refusing to give when asked, or defrauding others. (defrauding: cheating) **20.** Be ashamed of failing to greet or rebuffing a friend. (rebuffing: rejecting) **21.** Be ashamed of lusting after a married woman or violating a servant girl. (lusting: desiring; violating: mistreating) **22.** Be ashamed of harsh words with friends and insulting gifts. (harsh: unkind; insulting: disrespectful) **23.** Be ashamed of gossip and betraying secrets. (gossip: talking about others; betraying: revealing) **24.** These are the things you should avoid if you want to be favorably seen by all. (favorably: positively)

Chapter 42

1. Do not be ashamed of these things, lest you sin out of human respect. (respect: consideration for others) **2.** Do not be ashamed of the law of the Most High or the judgment on the sinful. (law: rules; judgment: punishment; sinful: wrongdoers) **3.** Do not be ashamed of sharing business or travel expenses, or dividing property. (expenses: costs; dividing: sharing) **4.** Do not be ashamed of using accurate scales and tested measures. (scales: instruments for weighing; measures: units of quantity) **5.** Do not be ashamed of wealth, bargaining with merchants, training children, or disciplining a disloyal servant. (wealth: money and possessions; bargaining: negotiating prices; disloyal: unfaithful) **6.** Do not be ashamed of securing an erring wife or valuables. (erring: mistaken; securing: keeping safe) **7.** Do not be ashamed of keeping a record of deposits or transactions. (deposits: stored money or items; transactions: exchanges) **8.** Do not be ashamed of chastising the foolish or holding the aged accountable for wrongdoing. (chastising: correcting; foolish: unwise; aged: old people; accountable: responsible) **9.** A daughter keeps her father awake with worry over her future, whether unmarried or married. (worry: concern; future: what is to come) **10.** Worry for her safety as an unmarried woman, or for her faithfulness as a wife. (safety: well-being; faithfulness: loyalty) **11.** Watch over her closely to avoid public shame or ridicule. (shame: dishonor; ridicule: mockery) **12.** Do not let her display her beauty or spend time with married women. (display: show; beauty: attractiveness) **13.** Harm to women often comes from women themselves, like moths to garments. (harm: damage; moths: insects that damage fabric) **14.** Better a strict father than an indulgent mother, and a frightened daughter than disgrace. (indulgent: lenient; frightened: scared; disgrace: shame) **15.** I will recall God's works, and describe what I have seen. (recall: remember; works: actions) **16.** The glory of the LORD fills all his works, clear to all like the rising sun. (glory: greatness; clear: obvious) **17.** Even the holy ones fail to recount the wonders of the LORD, though they stand before his glory. (holy ones: saints; recount: tell; wonders: miracles) **18.** God understands the innermost being of all and possesses all knowledge. (innermost: deepest part; possesses: has) **19.** He reveals the past and future, uncovering the deepest secrets. (reveals: makes known; uncovering: revealing) **20.** Nothing escapes God's understanding; no detail is overlooked. (escapes: avoids; detail: small part) **21.** His wisdom is eternal, unchanging, and without need of counsel. (eternal: never-ending; unchanging: constant; counsel: advice) **22.** His works are beautiful, from the smallest spark to the greatest vision. (works: actions; spark: small flame; vision: large view) **23.** The universe endures forever, with each creature preserved for its purpose. (universe: all of creation; endures: lasts; creature: living being) **24.** Each creature is different, yet all are good, none made in vain. (vain: without purpose) **25.** The splendor of God's creation is unmatched, and it is impossible to see enough of it. (splendor: beauty; unmatched: without equal)

Chapter 43

1. The sky, shining like heaven, reveals the glory of God. (glory: greatness) **2.** The sun, resplendent at its rising, is a wondrous work of the Most High. (resplendent: shining brilliantly; wondrous: amazing) **3.** At noon, the sun scorches the earth, unbearable in its fiery heat. (scorches: burns; unbearable: too hot to endure) **4.** Like a furnace, it sets the mountains aflame; its rays consume the land. (furnace: very hot oven; aflame: on fire) **5.** Great is the LORD who commands the sun's path. (path: route or course) **6.** The moon marks time, guiding the seasons and fixed dates. (marks: indicates; fixed: set) **7.** It signals feast days and fixed dates, waning and renewing each month. (waning: decreasing; renewing: starting again) **8.** The moon's renewal each month is a wondrous change. (renewal: restoration; wondrous: amazing) **9.** The stars, adorning the heavens, reflect God's glory. (adorning: decorating; reflect: show) **10.** The stars stay in their place by God's command, never wavering. (wavering: moving back and forth) **11.** The rainbow, a weapon against the flood, shines in the sky. (weapon: protection; flood: great amount of water) **12.** Bless its Maker, for its glory spans the heavens. (spans: stretches across) **13.** His rebuke sends lightning and directs judgment. (rebuke: sharp criticism; directs: guides) **14.** The storehouse opens, and the clouds rush like vultures. (storehouse: place where things are kept; vultures: large birds of prey) **15.** He commands the storm and breaks the hailstones. (hailstones: pieces of ice that fall from the sky) **16.** The thunder of his voice shakes the earth, and mountains quake. (quakes: shake violently) **17.** A word from him drives the winds and storms. (drives: forces) **18.** He sprinkles snow like birds, and it settles like locusts. (sprinkles: scatters; locusts: grasshoppers) **19.** The snow's whiteness blinds the eyes and confuses the mind. (whiteness: being white; blinds: prevents sight; confuses: makes unclear) **20.** He scatters frost like salt, shining like blossoms on thorns. (frost: ice crystals; blossoms: flowers) **21.** The northern winds freeze the ponds, turning waters to ice. (freeze: make cold; ponds: small bodies of water) **22.** The heat scorches the mountains, but the clouds restore the land. (scorches: burns; restore: bring back) **23.** The dew enriches the parched earth, reviving it. (dew: moisture from the air; parched: very dry; reviving: bringing back to life) **24.** His plan calms the deep and plants islands in the sea. (plan: purpose; calms: soothes; islands: land in water) **25.** Those who sail the sea tell of its wonders, filled with God's creatures. (sail: travel by boat; wonders: miracles) **26.** In the sea are wondrous creatures, including the monsters of the deep. (wondrous: amazing; monsters: large, frightening creatures) **27.** All messengers fulfill his will, succeeding at his bidding. (messengers: those who deliver messages; bidding: command) **28.** No more needs to be said: He is all in all! (all in all: everything) **29.** Let us praise him more, for he is greater than all his works. (praise: honor; greater: more powerful) **30.** The LORD's majesty is awe-inspiring, and his power is wonderful. (majesty: grandeur; awe-inspiring: causing wonder) **31.** Lift your voices to glorify the LORD, though you cannot fully praise him. (glorify: honor; fully: completely) **32.** Extol him with renewed strength, and do not tire, for you cannot reach the end. (extol: praise highly; renewed: refreshed; tire: become exhausted) **33.** Who can describe him or praise him fully as he is? (describe: explain; fully: completely) **34.** Many of his works are hidden; we have seen only a few. (hidden: not visible; works: actions) **35.** The LORD made all things and grants wisdom to those who fear him. (grants: gives; wisdom: knowledge; fear: respect)

Chapter 44

1. I will praise the godly men, our ancestors, each in his time. (godly: righteous; ancestors: forefathers) **2.** They shared the glory of the Most High, a portion from ancient times. (portion: share; ancient: very old) **3.** Some were great conquerors, renowned for their might. (conquerors: those who defeat others; renowned: famous) **4.** others were wise counselors or prophets who saw all things. (counselors: advisors; prophets: those who predict the future) **5.** Some were resolute leaders and skilled authors, (resolute: determined; authors: writers) **6.** composers of psalms, or men of wisdom and peace. (composers: creators of music; psalms: religious songs; wisdom: knowledge) **7.** All were glorious in their time, each renowned in his day. (glorious: admirable; renowned: well-known) **8.** Some have left behind a name, their deeds recounted; (deeds: actions; recounted: told) **9.** others are forgotten, as if they never lived. (forgotten: not remembered) **10.** Yet these godly men were remembered for their virtues. (virtues: moral qualities) **11.** Their wealth and heritage remain with their descendants. (wealth: riches; heritage: inheritance) **12.** Through God's covenant, their family and posterity endure.

(covenant: agreement; posterity: future generations) **13.** For all time their legacy remains, their glory never fading. (legacy: what is passed down; fading: disappearing) **14.** Though their bodies are laid to rest, their name lives on. (laid to rest: buried; lives on: continues to exist) **15.** Their wisdom is recalled at gatherings, and their praise proclaimed. (wisdom: knowledge; recalled: remembered; proclaimed: announced) **16.** ENOCH walked with the LORD and was taken up to set an example. (walked with: lived in harmony with; set an example: showed the way) **17.** NOAH, just and perfect, saved the race during devastation, (just: righteous; perfect: complete; race: humanity; devastation: destruction) **18.** and with a sign, the deluge ended, and a lasting covenant was made with him. (deluge: flood; lasting: enduring) **19.** ABRAHAM, father of many nations, kept his glory unstained. (unstained: pure, not spoiled) **20.** He followed God's precepts, and when tested, he was found loyal. (precepts: rules; loyal: faithful) **21.** Because of his faith, God promised his descendants would be numerous, (faith: belief; descendants: children and their children) **22.** that they would inherit the earth, from sea to sea. (inherit: receive as a possession) **23.** For ISAAC, God renewed this promise because of Abraham, his father. (renewed: repeated; promise: commitment)

Chapter 45

1. From Moses, the man favored by all, dear to God and men, (favored: liked; dear: loved) **2.** God honored him and gave him powerful abilities. (honored: respected; abilities: powers) **3.** God performed miracles through him and gave him the commandments. (performed: did; miracles: extraordinary events; commandments: laws) **4.** Due to his trustworthiness and meekness, God chose him above all. (trustworthiness: reliability; meekness: humility) **5.** He heard God's voice, entered the cloud, and received the law to teach Israel. (cloud: divine presence; received: accepted; law: commandments) **6.** His brother Aaron, like Moses in holiness, was chosen as priest. (holiness: purity; priest: religious leader) **7.** God established Aaron's priesthood, crowning him with honor and majesty. (established: set up; priesthood: position as priest; crowning: giving) **8.** Aaron was clothed in splendid robes with pomegranates and bells. (clothed: dressed; splendid: beautiful) **9.** The bells' sound was heard in the sanctuary, and his family was remembered. (sanctuary: holy place; remembered: honored) **10.** His vestments were embroidered with gold, violet, and crimson. (vestments: clothing; embroidered: decorated with stitches) **11.** His breastpiece and ephod, with engraved stones, commemorated the tribes of Israel. (breastpiece: chest adornment; ephod: priestly garment; commemorated: honored) **12.** His turban had a golden diadem, an insignia of holiness, glorious and beautiful. (turban: head covering; diadem: crown; insignia: symbol) **13.** No one could wear these except his descendants, forever. (descendants: children and their children) **14.** Aaron's offering was burned with the daily sacrifices. (offering: gift; burned: consumed by fire) **15.** Moses ordained and anointed Aaron, establishing a lasting covenant. (ordained: made a priest; anointed: consecrated with oil; lasting: enduring) **16.** Aaron was chosen to offer sacrifices and atone for Israel. (atoned: made peace for) **17.** He was given authority to teach God's laws and rituals. (authority: power; rituals: religious ceremonies) **18.** Other men were jealous of him, especially Dathan, Abiram, and Korah. (jealous: envious) **19.** God, angry, destroyed them with fire and a miracle. (destroyed: wiped out; miracle: divine act) **20.** He then increased Aaron's glory and gave him his inheritance. (increased: made greater; inheritance: possessions passed down) **21.** Aaron's offerings, including showbread, were his portion. (showbread: consecrated bread; portion: share) **22.** He had no land, for the Lord was his portion among Israel. (land: territory; portion: share) **23.** Phinehas, Aaron's grandson, showed courage and atoned for Israel. (courage: bravery; atoned: made peace) **24.** God gave Phinehas and his descendants the high priesthood forever. (high priesthood: chief priest's role) **25.** While David's covenant was through one son, Aaron's was for all his descendants. (covenant: agreement) **26.** Bless the Lord, who crowned you with glory, granting wisdom to govern justly. (crowned: gave; glory: honor; granting: giving; govern: rule; justly: fairly)

Chapter 46

1. JOSHUA, son of Nun, a valiant leader and Moses' assistant, saved God's people, defeated enemies, and secured Israel's inheritance (valiant: brave; inheritance: promised land). **2.** His glory shone as he raised his javelin against the city (javelin: spear). **3.** None could withstand him in the LORD's battles (withstand: resist). **4.** By his power, the sun stood still, turning one day into two (stood still: stopped moving). **5.** He called upon God, who answered with hailstones against his enemies (hailstones: large ice). **6.** The LORD destroyed the foes, showing His care for His people's battles (foes: enemies). **7.** Joshua and CALEB, loyal followers of God, opposed the rebels, averting God's wrath (rebels: those who resisted; averting: preventing; wrath: anger). **8.** They alone, of six hundred thousand, entered the promised land (promised land: Canaan). **9.** Caleb, strong even in old age, claimed the summits for his family, proving the rewards of devotion (summits: mountain tops; devotion: faithfulness). **10.** Their inheritance showed God's goodness to those who follow Him (inheritance: received land). **11.** The JUDGES, steadfast and loyal, blessed the nation (steadfast: firm; nation: Israel). **12.** May their bones find life, and their names shine in their descendants (descendants: future generations). **13.** SAMUEL, beloved prophet, judge, and priest, was dedicated to God from birth (dedicated: devoted). **14.** He established the kingdom and anointed rulers for Israel (anointed: blessed with oil). **15.** As a trustworthy prophet, his words proved true (trustworthy: reliable). **16.** He called upon God with a lamb, and the LORD thundered from heaven (thundered: made a loud sound). **17.** God humbled enemy rulers and destroyed the Philistine lords (humbled: defeated; lords: leaders). **18.** In his final days, Samuel declared his honesty before the LORD, unchallenged by any (honesty: truthfulness; unchallenged: not questioned). **19.** Even in death, Samuel's guidance was sought, and his prophecy ended wickedness (guidance: advice; wickedness: evil). **20.** From the grave, he revealed God's will, silencing evil (silencing: stopping).

Chapter 47

1. After him came NATHAN, who served in David's presence (presence: company). **2.** DAVID, like choice fat of offerings, was set apart in Israel (set apart: made special). **3.** He played with lions as with kids and bears like lambs (kids: young goats). **4.** As a youth, he slew the giant, wiping out Israel's shame with a slingstone (slew: killed; slingstone: small rock used in a sling). **5.** He called on God Most High, who strengthened him to defeat the warrior and uplift his people (strengthened: gave power; uplift: raise). **6.** Women sang his praises, calling him greater than tens of thousands (praises: compliments). **7.** With the crown, he subdued enemies and crushed the Philistines (subdued: conquered). **8.** In all deeds, he gave thanks to God in praise (deeds: actions). **9.** He enriched feasts, adding string music before the altar for the psalms (enriched: made better; psalms: sacred songs). **10.** By his song, the sanctuary echoed with praise before dawn (sanctuary: holy place). **11.** The LORD forgave his sins, exalted his strength, and secured his throne in Israel (exalted: lifted high; throne: kingship). **12.** His merits brought a wise son, SOLOMON, who lived in peace (merits: good deeds; peace: calmness). **13.** During Solomon's reign, God made tranquil borders, and he built God's house, a lasting sanctuary (tranquil: peaceful; sanctuary: holy place). **14.** Young and wise, Solomon overflowed with instruction like the Nile (overflowed: was full). **15.** His understanding filled the earth like the sea (understanding: wisdom). **16.** His fame spread, drawing nations to hear his wisdom (fame: reputation). **17.** Through riddles, stories, and answers, he astonished the world (riddles: puzzles; astonished: amazed). **18.** He was honored with the glorious name of Israel (glorious: splendid). **19.** Gold he amassed as iron, and silver as lead (amassed: gathered). **20.** Yet, he succumbed to women, giving them control over him (succumbed: gave in). **21.** This tarnished his name, shamed his legacy, and brought suffering to his domain (tarnished: stained; legacy: reputation; domain: kingdom). **22.** Two kingdoms arose as Ephraim claimed kingship (claimed: took). **23.** Yet, God upheld His mercy, ensuring Jacob's remnant and David's root remained (remnant: small remaining group; root: lineage). **24.** Solomon rested with his fathers, leaving REHOBOAM, unwise and divisive, leading to rebellion (divisive: causing division; rebellion: revolt). **25.** Israel's sin deepened, bringing exile and ruin to Ephraim as they pursued every evil (exile: forced removal; ruin: destruction).

Chapter 48

1. A prophet appeared, blazing like fire, with words like a flaming furnace (blazing: shining brightly; furnace: intense heat). **2.** He shattered their bread staff and reduced them to straits in his zeal (bread staff: food supply; straits: hardship; zeal: passion). **3.** By God's word, he closed the heavens and brought fire three times (closed the heavens: stopped rain). **4.** How awesome are you, ELIJAH! Who equals your glory (glory: greatness)? **5.** By God's will, you raised the dead and restored life from the nether world (nether world: underworld). **6.** You cast kings to destruction and nobles to sickness (nobles: high-ranking people). **7.** You heard God's voice at Sinai and His judgments at Horeb (judgments: decrees). **8.** You anointed kings for vengeance and a prophet as your successor (anointed: appointed; successor: follower). **9.** You ascended in a whirlwind, in a chariot of fiery horses (ascended: rose up; whirlwind: spinning wind). **10.** You are destined to end wrath, restore families, and reestablish Jacob (wrath: anger; reestablish: renew). **11.** Blessed is he who sees you before death (blessed: favored). **12.** O ELIJAH, taken up in the whirlwind (whirlwind: spinning wind)! **13.** ELISHA, filled with a double spirit, performed wonders by his word (double spirit: greater power; wonders: miracles). **14.** He feared no one; flesh revived at his command (revived: came back to life). **15.** In life, he worked marvels; after death, miraculous deeds (marvels: extraordinary acts). **16.** Yet the people did not repent and were scattered across the earth (repent: turn from sin; scattered: dispersed). **17.**

Judah remained, with rulers from David's house—some righteous, others sinful (righteous: virtuous). **18.** HEZEKIAH fortified his city and brought water through rock-cut reservoirs (fortified: strengthened; reservoirs: water storage). **19.** Sennacherib invaded, blaspheming God and terrifying Zion (blaspheming: insulting; Zion: Jerusalem). **20.** In anguish, the people called on the Most High, who saved them through ISAIAH (anguish: deep sorrow). **21.** God struck the Assyrian camp with a plague and delivered them (plague: deadly disease; delivered: rescued). **22.** Hezekiah did what was right, following David's ways under Isaiah's guidance (guidance: leadership). **23.** Isaiah turned back the sun and prolonged Hezekiah's life (prolonged: extended). **24.** With his visions, he comforted Zion's mourners and revealed hidden truths (visions: divine messages; mourners: grievers). **25.** He foretold the future, declaring what would unfold until the end of time (foretold: predicted; unfold: happen).

Chapter 49

1. The name JOSIAH is like blended incense, made lasting by a skilled perfumer. Precious is his memory, like honey to the taste, like music at a banquet (incense: fragrant substance; perfumer: maker of scents; banquet: feast). **2.** For he grieved over our betrayals and destroyed the abominable idols (betrayals: acts of unfaithfulness; abominable: hateful). **3.** He turned to God with his whole heart, and, though times were evil, he practiced virtue (virtue: moral excellence). **4.** Except for David, Hezekiah, and Josiah, they all were wicked; they abandoned the Law of the Most High, these kings of Judah, right to the very end (abandoned: rejected). **5.** So he gave over their power to others, their glory to a foolish foreign nation (glory: honor; foreign: from another land). **6.** Who burned the holy city and left its streets desolate, as JEREMIAH had foretold (desolate: empty and ruined; foretold: predicted). **7.** For they had treated him badly who even in the womb had been made a prophet, to root out, pull down, and destroy, and then to build and to plant (womb: mother's belly; prophet: one who speaks God's will). **8.** EZEKIEL beheld the vision and described the different creatures of the chariot (beheld: saw; vision: divine sight). **9.** He also referred to JOB, who always persevered in the right path (referred: mentioned; persevered: remained steadfast). **10.** Then, too, the TWELVE PROPHETS—may their bones return to life from their resting place!—gave new strength to Jacob and saved him by their faith and hope (resting place: grave; Jacob: Israel). **11.** How can we fittingly praise ZERUBBABEL, who was like a signet ring on God's right hand (fittingly: appropriately; signet ring: symbol of authority)? **12.** And Jeshua, Jozadak's son? In their time they built the house of God; they erected the holy temple, destined for everlasting glory (erected: constructed; everlasting: eternal). **13.** Extolled be the memory of NEHEMIAH! He rebuilt our ruined walls, restored our shattered defenses, and set up gates and bars (extolled: praised; defenses: protective barriers). **14.** Few on earth have been made the equal of ENOCH, for he was taken up bodily (equal: match; bodily: physically). **15.** Was ever a man born like JOSEPH? Even his dead body was provided for (provided for: cared for). **16.** Glorious, too, were SHEM, SETH, and ENOS; but beyond that of any living being was the splendor of ADAM (splendor: magnificence).

Chapter 50

1. Simon the priest, son of Jochanan, was the greatest among his people. During his time, the house of God was renovated, and the temple was reinforced (renovated: restored; reinforced: strengthened). **2.** He built the wall of the temple precincts with powerful turrets (precincts: areas; turrets: towers). **3.** He also dug a large reservoir, as vast as the sea (reservoir: water storage). **4.** He protected his people from brigands and strengthened his city against enemies (brigands: robbers; strengthened: fortified). **5.** He appeared gloriously, like a shining star (gloriously: splendidly). **6.** Like the full moon at a festive time (festive: celebratory). **7.** Like the sun shining on the temple, and the rainbow in the cloudy sky (shining: radiating). **8.** Like spring blossoms, a lily by the stream (blossoms: flowers; stream: flowing water). **9.** Like the trees of Lebanon, and the fire of incense (Lebanon: a region known for its cedar trees; incense: fragrant smoke). **10.** Like a golden vessel studded with precious stones (studied: adorned with). **11.** Like a flourishing olive tree, like a cypress standing tall (flourishing: thriving). **12.** Clad in magnificent robes, he ascended the glorious altar, adding majesty to the sanctuary (clad: dressed; ascended: approached; majesty: grandeur). **13.** As he received the sacrifices, his brethren surrounded him like a garland (brethren: brothers; garland: wreath). **14.** All the sons of Aaron stood around him, offering sacrifices in Israel's presence (sons of Aaron: priests). **15.** After completing the altar services (services: duties). **16.** He offered the wine, pouring it at the foot of the altar as a sweet-smelling odor to God (odor: fragrance). **17.** The priests sounded their trumpets as a reminder before the Most High (reminder: call). **18.** All the people would fall prostrate in worship (prostrate: kneel in reverence). **19.** Hymns echoed as the people prayed, rejoicing in the Merciful One's presence (echoed: resounded; rejoicing: celebrating). **20.** After the services, he would raise his hands to bless Israel, with God's name on his lips (raise: lift). **21.** The people would prostrate again to receive God's blessing (prostrate: bow down). **22.** Bless the God of all, who works wonders and shapes humanity according to His will (wonders: miraculous deeds; shapes: molds). **23.** May He grant joy and peace among us (grant: bestow). **24.** And may His goodness endure in Israel as long as the heavens above (endure: last). **25.** I loathe two nations and one non-people (loathe: detest). **26.** Those of Seir, Philistia, and the degenerate folk of Shechem (degenerate: morally corrupt). **27.** I, Jesus, son of Eleazar, son of Sirach, have written these wise proverbs (proverbs: wise sayings). **28.** Blessed is the man who meditates on these, wise is the man who takes them to heart (meditates: reflects; takes them to heart: fully embraces). **29.** For with the fear of the LORD as his guide, he can face anything (fear of the LORD: reverence for God; guide: direction).

Chapter 51

1. I thank you, O God, my savior, and will make known your name, refuge of my life (refuge: shelter). **2.** You have been my helper against my adversaries, saved me from death, and kept me from the pit (adversaries: enemies; pit: grave). **3.** You delivered me from slander, falsehood, and from those who sought my life (slander: false accusations). **4.** You saved me from flames on every side, from the depths of the nether world (flames: dangers; nether world: realm of the dead). **5.** From deceiving lips and dishonest tongues (deceiving: misleading). **6.** I was near death, my soul nearing the depths of the nether world (soul: inner being). **7.** I searched for help but found no one (searched: looked). **8.** Then I remembered the LORD's mercies; He saves those who take refuge in Him (mercies: kindness; refuge: shelter). **9.** I cried from the earth, from the gates of the nether world (cried: called out). **10.** I called out: O Lord, do not abandon me in times of trouble (abandon: leave). **11.** I will praise your name and pray constantly to you (praise: honor). **12.** The LORD heard me, saved me from every kind of evil, and preserved me (preserved: kept safe). **13.** I thank Him, praise Him, and bless His name (bless: honor). **14.** When I was young and innocent, I sought wisdom (innocent: pure). **15.** She came to me in her beauty, and I will cultivate her to the end (cultivate: nurture). **16.** In a short time, I gained great instruction (instruction: teaching). **17.** I will give my teacher grateful praise for my profit (grateful: thankful; profit: benefit). **18.** I devoted myself to wisdom, always striving for good (devoted: dedicated; striving: working hard). **19.** I was eager for her, never turning back, always extolling her (eager: enthusiastic; extolling: praising). **20.** I purified my hands for her and attained understanding (purified: cleaned; attained: gained). **21.** My whole being was stirred as I learned; I made her my prize possession (stirred: moved; prize possession: cherished possession). **22.** The LORD granted me my lips, and my tongue will declare His praises (granted: gave; declare: speak). **23.** Come to me, you untutored, and lodge in the house of instruction (untutored: uneducated; lodge: stay). **24.** How long will you endure thirst for wisdom? (endure: suffer). **25.** I speak of her: gain wisdom at no cost (gain: acquire). **26.** Submit to her yoke and accept her teaching (submit: yield; yoke: control). **27.** I have labored little but found much (labored: worked). **28.** With a little instruction, you will gain wealth (wealth: success). **29.** Rejoice in God's mercy and praise Him (rejoice: celebrate). **30.** Work at your tasks in due season, and God will give you your reward in time (due season: appropriate time; reward: result).

81 – Jubilees

Chapter 1

1. In the first year after the Israelites' exodus from Egypt, in the third month, on the 16th day, YAHWEH spoke to Moses, saying: "Come up to Me on the mountain, and I will give you two stone tablets containing the Torah and commandments I have written, so that you may teach them." (Torah: the law given by God) **2.** Moses went up the mountain, and YAHWEH's glory rested on Mount Sinai, with a cloud covering it for six days. **3.** On the seventh day, YAHWEH called Moses from the midst of the cloud, and His glory appeared like a blazing fire atop the mountain. **4.** Moses remained on the mountain for forty days and nights, during which YAHWEH taught him the history of the Torah, from its beginning to its end, and the division of all its days. **5.** YAHWEH instructed Moses, saying: "Give your full attention to every word I speak on this mountain. Write them in a book, so that future generations will see how I have not abandoned them, despite the evil they've done in breaking the covenant I made with you today on Mount Sinai." (Covenant: Sacred agreement or promise) **6.** When these things come upon them, they will realize that I am righteous in all My judgments and actions, and they will see that I have truly been with them. **7.** Write down all the words I give you today. I know their rebellious hearts, even before I bring them into the land I promised to their ancestors—Abraham, Isaac, and Jacob—saying, "To your descendants I will give a land flowing with milk and honey." **8.** They will eat, be satisfied, and turn to false gods—gods who cannot save them from their troubles. This will serve as a witness against them, for they will forget My commandments, follow the practices of the nations, and serve their idols. These gods will cause them distress, affliction, and ensnare them. **10.** Many will perish, be taken captive, and fall into the hands of their enemies because they abandoned My laws, My commandments, and the festivals of My covenant. They will disregard My Sabbaths and the holy place I sanctified in their midst—the tabernacle and sanctuary where I set My name to dwell. (Sabbaths: Rest days; Sanctuary: Sacred place of worship) **11.** They will build high places, groves, and graven images, worshiping each his own idol. They will go astray and sacrifice their children to demons and to the works of their misguided hearts. (Graven images: Idols; Demons: Evil spirits) **12.** I will send witnesses to them to testify, but they will not listen. They will kill the witnesses and persecute those who seek the Torah, changing everything to do evil in My sight. (Witnesses: Testifiers of truth; Torah: Divine law) **13.** I will hide My face from them and give them into the hands of the Gentiles for captivity, to be prey and devoured. I will remove them from their land and scatter them among the nations. (Gentiles: Nations outside Israel) **14.** They will forget My Torah, commandments, and judgments, and go astray in the observance of new months, Sabbaths, festivals, jubilees, and ordinances. (Sabbaths: Rest days; Festivals: Sacred observances) **15.** Afterward, they will return to Me from among the Gentiles with all their heart, soul, and strength. I will gather them, and when they seek Me with all their heart, I will be found by them. (Gentiles: Nations; Soul: Inner being) **16.** I will grant them abundant peace with righteousness and will plant them in uprightness. They will be a blessing, not a curse, and they shall be the head, not the tail. (Shalom: Peace; Uprightness: Righteous living) **17.** I will build My sanctuary among them, dwell with them, and be YAHWEH their Sovereign. They will be My people in truth and righteousness. (Sanctuary: Sacred place of worship) **18.** I will not forsake them nor fail them, for I am YAHWEH their Sovereign. (Sovereign: Supreme ruler) **19.** Moses fell on his face and prayed: "O YAHWEH, do not forsake Your people and inheritance. Do not let them wander in error, nor deliver them into the hands of their enemies, the Gentiles, who may lead them to sin." **20.** Let Your mercy be upon Your people, create in them an upright spirit, and let not the spirit of Belial rule over them to accuse them and ensnare them in unrighteous paths, so they may not perish before You. (Belial: Evil spirit or demon) **21.** They are Your people, whom You saved with Your great power from Egypt. Create in them a clean heart and a holy spirit, and let them not be ensnared in their sins from this time onward, forever. (Holy: Sacred or set apart) **22.** YAHWEH said to Moses: "I know their rebelliousness and stubbornness. They will not obey until they confess their sins and the sins of their ancestors." **23.** Then they will return to Me in uprightness, with all their heart and soul. I will circumcise their hearts and the hearts of their descendants, creating in them a holy spirit, and I will cleanse them, so they will never turn away from Me again. (Circumcise: To purify; Holy spirit: Sacred presence) **24.** Their souls will cling to Me and My commandments. They will keep My commandments, and I will be their Father, and they will be My children. **25.** They will be called children of the living YAHWEH, and every angel and spirit will know they are My children, and I am their Father in uprightness and righteousness, and that I love them. (Malak: Angel; Spirit: Inner being) **26.** Write down all these words I declare to you today, from the first to the last, which will take place in the divisions of the days, the Torah, the testimony, the weeks, and the jubilees, until I descend and dwell with them forever. (Testimony: Witness or evidence) **27.** He said to the angel of the presence: "Write for Moses from the beginning of creation until My sanctuary is built among them for all eternity." (Angel of the presence: Divine messenger) **28.** YAHWEH will appear to all eyes, and all will know that I am the Sovereign of Israel, the Father of all the children of Jacob, and the King on Mount Zion forever. Zion and Jerusalem will be holy. (Zion: Sacred hill; Jerusalem: Holy city) **29.** The angel of the presence, who went before Israel's camp, took the tablets with the divisions of the years, from creation to the building of the sanctuary among them for eternity. These tablets detail the creation and renewal of the heavens, the earth, and all creation, until YAHWEH's sanctuary is established in Jerusalem on Mount Zion, renewing all the heavenly bodies for healing, peace, and blessing for Israel's elect. (Elect: Chosen people)

Chapter 2

1. The angel of the presence spoke to Moses, relaying YAHWEH's command: "Record the full account of creation, showing how in six days the Almighty completed His work. On the seventh day, He rested and sanctified it, making it a sign for all generations." (Presence: divine messenger, command: instruction) **2.** "On the first day, He created the heavens, earth, waters, and all spirits that serve before Him—angels of fire, wind, clouds, darkness, snow, hail, thunder, and the spirits of the seasons. He also formed the abyss, night, and day, light and darkness, all according to His divine plan." (Spirits: spiritual beings, Abyss: deep, often meaning the waters or chaos before creation) **3.** "We beheld His works and praised Him, for seven great works were accomplished on the first day." (Beheld: saw, Works: creations, accomplishments) **4.** "On the second day, He made the firmament to divide the waters, with some placed above and others below. This was the only creation of the second day." (Firmament: expanse or sky, Divide: separate) **5.** "On the third day, He gathered the waters to one place, and dry land appeared." (Gathered: collected, Dry land: solid earth) **6.** "The waters obeyed, retreating, and dry land emerged." (Retreated: moved back, Emerged: came forth) **7.** "On this day, He formed the seas, rivers, lakes, plants, fruit trees, and the garden of Eden. These were the four works of the third day." (Formed: created, Seas: large bodies of water) **8.** "On the fourth day, He set the sun, moon, and stars in the firmament to give light, govern day and night, and separate light from darkness." (Set: placed, Govern: rule, Firmament: heavens) **9.** "He appointed the sun as a sign to mark days, Sabbaths, months, feasts, and years." (Appointed: designated, Sign: symbol or marker) **10.** "The sun divides light from darkness, promoting prosperity for all growing things. These were the three creations of the fourth day." (Prosperity: success, flourishing) **11.** "On the fifth day, He created sea creatures, fish, and birds." (Sea creatures: marine life, Fish: aquatic animals, Birds: winged creatures) **12.** "The sun rose to bless them and all growing things on earth. These three kinds were created on the fifth day." (Bless: bring goodness, Growing things: plants and trees) **13.** "On the sixth day, He created land animals, livestock, and all creatures that move on the earth." (Livestock: domesticated animals) **14.** "Finally, He created man—male and female—and gave them dominion over all creation." (Dominion: authority, control) **15.** "These four kinds were created on the sixth day, totaling twenty-two types of creation." (Types: kinds, categories) **16.** "By the end of the sixth day, all works were completed—everything in the heavens, earth, seas, and abyss." (Works: creations, Abyss: deep waters, chaos) **17.** "He gave us the Sabbath, a great sign, commanding us to rest on the seventh day from all work." (Sabbath: day of rest, Sign: symbol) **18.** "The angels of His presence and sanctification were commanded to keep the Sabbath with Him in heaven and on earth." (Sanctification: making holy, Presence: divine being) **19.** "He said, 'I will set apart a people to observe the Sabbath, sanctifying them as My people, just as I have sanctified and blessed the day.'" (Set apart: consecrate, Sanctifying: making holy) **20.** "I have chosen Jacob's descendants to be My people, and I will teach them to keep the Sabbath forever." (Descendants: offspring, Teach: instruct) **21.** "This sign is for them to observe the Sabbath with us, to rest, eat, and bless the Creator. He has sanctified them as a special people." (Observe: keep, Special: unique) **22.** "Their offerings ascend as a sweet aroma before Him daily." (Aroma: scent, ascend: rise) **23.** "There have been twenty-two generations from Adam to Jacob, and twenty-two types of work created in six days, culminating in the seventh day, holy and blessed. This day serves for sanctification and blessing." (Generations: family lines, Culminating: concluding) **24.** "To Jacob's descendants, it was granted to be the blessed and sanctified ones, as He sanctified the Sabbath on the seventh day." (Granted: given, Sanctified: made holy) **25.** "YAHWEH created the heavens and earth in six days, and on the seventh day, He made it holy, commanding that those who work on it or defile it shall die." (Defile: make unclean) **26.** "Instruct the children of Israel to keep the Sabbath, to refrain from work, for it is holier than any other day." (Refrain: abstain, Holier: more sacred) **27.** "Anyone who defiles the Sabbath will surely die, and those who work on it will face eternal death. The children of Israel must observe it forever and never be uprooted from the land." (Uprooted: cast out) **28.** "Whoever keeps the Sabbath will be holy and blessed, like us, forever." (Holy: sacred, Blessed: favored) **29.** "Declare to Israel the law of the Sabbath: they must not forsake it, avoid unseemly work, and not prepare food or carry burdens. It is holier than any jubilee." (Forsake: abandon, Unseemly: inappropriate, Jubilee: year of release) **30.** "This day was kept in heaven before it was revealed to mankind. The Creator sanctified it, but He chose only Israel to observe it on earth." (Revealed: made known) **31.** "He blessed this day above all others, making it holy and splendid." (Splendid: magnificent) **32.** "This law concerning the Sabbath was given to Israel as an eternal decree for all generations." (Decree: command, Eternal: forever)

Chapter 3

1. On the sixth day of the second week, following YAHWEH's command, all the beasts, cattle, birds, and creatures of the earth and water were brought to Adam in their respective kinds. The beasts came on the first day, cattle on the second, birds on the third, land creatures on the fourth, and water creatures on the fifth. **2.** Adam named them according to what he called them, and each creature was given the name he assigned. **3.** Adam observed all these creatures—male and female of each kind—but found no companion to help him. **4.** YAHWEH said, "It is not good for man to be alone; let us make a suitable helper for him." (helper - one who provides support and companionship) **5.** YAHWEH caused Adam to fall into a deep sleep, took one of his ribs, and formed the woman from it. He then closed the place and made the woman from Adam's rib. **6.** When Adam awoke, YAHWEH brought her to him, and he said, "This is bone of my bones, and flesh of my flesh. She shall be called 'wife' because she was taken from me." **7.** Therefore, a man shall leave his parents, cleave to his wife, and they shall become one flesh. **8.** In the first week, Adam was created, and his wife from his rib. In the second week, she was presented to him, and the commandment to remain pure was given: seven days for a male child, fourteen for a female. (pure - clean, holy) **9.** After forty days, Adam was brought into the Garden of Eden to tend it. His wife entered the garden on the eightieth day. **10.** The commandment on childbirth is written: If a woman bears a male, she remains unclean for seven days, followed by thirty-three days of purification. She shall not touch holy things or enter the sanctuary until the days of purification are completed. **11.** If a female is born, the mother remains unclean for fourteen days, followed by sixty-six days of purification, totaling eighty days. **12.** After these eighty days, the woman was brought into the Garden of Eden, which was holier than all the earth, with every tree in it being sacred. **13.** A statute was established for those giving birth, that they must not touch holy things nor enter the sanctuary until the purification is complete. **14.** This is the law and testimony written for Israel, that they may observe it throughout their generations. **15.** In the first week of the first jubilee, Adam and his wife worked in the Garden for seven years. They were instructed in proper care of the garden. **16.** Adam tended the garden, was naked, and unaware of it (unaware: lacked awareness). He protected the garden from animals and birds, gathered fruit, and set aside portions for himself and his wife. **17.** After the completion of seven years, on the seventeenth day of the second month, the serpent approached the woman and said, "Did YAHWEH say you couldn't eat from every tree in the garden?" **18.** She replied, "We can eat from all the trees, except for the one in the middle of the garden. YAHWEH said not to eat or touch it, lest we die." **19.** The serpent contradicted her, "You will not die. YAHWEH knows that your eyes will be opened, and you will become like gods, knowing good and evil." **20.** The woman saw the tree was pleasing to the eye and good for food. She took the fruit, ate it, and gave some to Adam, and he ate it too. **21.** When they ate, they realized they were naked, so they sewed fig leaves together and made aprons to cover themselves. **22.** YAHWEH cursed the serpent and became angry with it forever. **23.** He was also angry with the woman for listening to the serpent and eating the fruit. He said, "I will greatly increase your sorrow and pain in childbirth. You will desire your husband, and he will rule over you." **24.** To Adam, He said, "Because you listened to your wife and ate from the tree I commanded you not to, cursed is the ground because of you. You will toil and sweat to eat, and return to the earth from which you came." (Toil - prolonged and difficult work) **25.** He made garments of skin for Adam and his wife and clothed them before sending them out of the Garden of Eden. **26.** On the day Adam was expelled, he offered incense, galbanum, stacte, and spices to YAHWEH as a sweet aroma. **27.** On that day, the voices of all creatures—beasts, cattle, birds, and walking animals—ceased. They could no longer speak, having once communicated with one language. **28.** YAHWEH cast all living creatures out of the Garden, scattering them according to their kinds and to the places where they belonged. **29.** Only Adam was given the means to cover his shame, unlike the animals. **30.** For this reason, the law is written for all who know the Torah: they must cover their shame and not reveal themselves as others do (reveal; Expose). **31.** On the first day of the fourth month, Adam and his wife left the Garden and settled in the land o f Elda, where they were created. **32.** Adam named his wife Eve. **33.** They had no children until the first jubilee, after which Adam knew her. **34.** Adam worked the land as he had been taught in the Garden of Eden.

Chapter 4
1. In the third week of the second jubilee, she gave birth to Cain, in the fourth to Abel, and in the fifth to Awan. **2.** In the first year of the third jubilee, Cain slew Abel because YAHWEH accepted Abel's sacrifice but not Cain's. (sacrifice :offering made to God). **3.** He killed him in the field, and Abel's blood cried out from the ground to heaven.(cried out: symbolizing divine awareness of wrongdoing)**4.** YAHWEH reproved Cain and made him a fugitive on the earth for killing his brother. (Fugitive - someone fleeing from justice) **5.** It is written on the heavenly tablets, "Cursed is he who kills his neighbor treacherously, and let those who witness it declare, So be it." (heavenly tablets : records of divine decrees). **6.** For this reason, we announce all sin before YAHWEH, on earth and in heaven, in light and darkness (announce; proclaim or make known publicly). **7.** Adam and Eve mourned Abel for four weeks of years, and in the fourth year of the fifth week, they became joyful and had Seth. (four weeks of years : a period of 28 years). **8.** Seth said, "YAHWEH has given us a second seed to replace Abel, whom Cain killed." (Seed - offspring or descendants) **9.** In the sixth week, Seth had a daughter, Azura. **10.** Cain married Awan, his sister, and they had Enoch. He built a city and named it after his son. **11.** In the fifth jubilee, Seth married Azura, and in the fourth year of the sixth week, she bore him Enos. **12.** Enos called on the Name of YAHWEH. (Calling on the Name - an act of worship or dependence) **13.** In the seventh jubilee, Enos married Noam, and she bore him Kenan. **14.** At the close of the eighth jubilee, Kenan married Mualeleth, and she bore him Mahalalel. **15.** In the second week of the tenth jubilee, Mahalalel married Dinah, and she bore him Jared. **16.** In his days, the Watchers descended to teach men uprightness. (Watchers - angels sent to observe and guide) **17.** In the eleventh jubilee, Jared married Baraka, and she bore him Enoch. **18.** Enoch was the first to learn writing, knowledge, and wisdom, and he recorded the signs of heaven. (signs of heaven: divine revelations)**19.** He also testified to men, recounting the jubilees, years, months, and Shabbats. **20.** Enoch had visions of what would happen to men until the Day of Judgment and wrote it down. **21.** In the twelfth jubilee, Enoch married Edna, and she bore him Methuselah. **22.** Enoch was with the angels for six jubilees and recorded everything they showed him. **23.** He testified against the Watchers who had sinned with women, uniting with them to defile themselves.(defile: corrupt)**24.** Enoch was taken by YAHWEH and shown the Garden of Eden, where he wrote down the judgment of the world. **25.** YAHWEH brought the flood upon the earth because of Enoch's testimony against the wickedness of men. **26.** Enoch burned incense before YAHWEH on the Mount. **27.** YAHWEH has four holy places: Eden, the Mount of the East, Mount Sinai, and Mount Zion, which will be sanctified in the new creation. **28.** Methuselah married Edna, and they had Lamech. (Sanctified - set apart as sacred) **29.** In the fifteenth jubilee, Lamech married Betenos, and she bore him Noah, saying, "This one will comfort me for the curse on the earth." **30.** At the close of the nineteenth jubilee, Adam died, and his sons buried him in the land of his creation. **31.** Adam fell short of living a thousand years, as one thousand years is like one day to YAHWEH. **32.** Cain was killed the same year, when his house fell on him, as judgment for killing Abel with a stone. (Judgment - the act of making a decision or punishment) **33.** It was ordained: "With the instrument a man kills, with the same shall he be killed." (Ordained: established by divine law) **34.** In the twenty-fifth jubilee, Noah married Emzara, and they had Shem, Ham, and Japheth.

Chapter 5
1. When the children of men multiplied and daughters were born, the malakim saw them and took wives from among them, bearing giants. (malakim :angels) **2.** Torahlessness increased, corrupting all flesh: men, animals, and creatures on the earth began devouring each other, and evil thoughts filled all men. (Torahlessness - lack of moral or divine law) **3.** YAHWEH saw the earth's corruption, and all flesh had corrupted its ways, doing evil before Him. **4.** He decided to destroy man and all flesh He had created. **5.** Noah found favor in YAHWEH's eyes. **6.** YAHWEH was angry with the angels who had sinned and commanded them to be bound in the depths of the earth. **7.** He commanded that their sons be slain with the sword and removed from the earth. **8.** YAHWEH said, "My spirit will not always abide in man; their days will be 120 years." (Spirit - divine presence or guidance) **9.** He sent a sword among them, causing them to slay each other until they were all destroyed. **10.** Their fathers witnessed their destruction, and they were bound in the depths of the earth until the Day of Judgment. **11.** He destroyed all, judging them for their wickedness. **12.** YAHWEH made all His works new and righteous, ensuring they would not sin again. **13.** The judgment of all is written on the heavenly tablets; those who stray from their path will be judged. **14.** Nothing in heaven, earth, or Sheol (the underworld) escapes judgment, and all deeds are written and engraved. **15.** He will judge the great according to their greatness and the small according to their smallness, each by their deeds. **16.** YAHWEH does not show partiality nor accept gifts; He judges righteously. (Partiality - unfair favor toward one over another) **17.** For Israel, it is written: if they turn to YAHWEH in righteousness, He will forgive their sins and show mercy yearly. **18.** Before the flood, only Noah's person was accepted by YAHWEH for his righteousness, saving his sons from the flood. **19.** YAHWEH decided to destroy everything on earth: men, animals, and birds. **20.** He commanded Noah to build an ark to save himself from the flood. (Righteousness - living according to divine law) **21.** Noah built the ark as YAHWEH commanded, in the twenty-seventh jubilee, fifth week, fifth year (1307 A.M.). **22.** He entered the ark in the sixth year, second month, and stayed there until the seventeenth, when YAHWEH closed it. **23.** YAHWEH opened the seven floodgates of heaven and the fountains of the deep. (Floodgates - barriers that were opened to release water) **24.** The waters fell for 40 days and nights, and the earth was filled with water. **25.** The waters rose 15 cubits above the highest mountains, and the ark floated above the

earth. **26.** The flood prevailed for five months, covering the earth for 150 days. **27.** The ark rested on Mount Lubar, part of the Ararat mountain range. **28.** In the fourth month, the fountains and floodgates closed, and the waters began to recede. (Lubar - a mountain in the Ararat region) **29.** In the seventh month, the abysses opened, and water descended into the depths. **30.** In the tenth month, the mountain tops were visible, and by the first month, the earth became dry. **31.** By the fifth week of the seventh year (1309 A.M.), the waters disappeared, and the earth was dry by the 17th day of the second month. **32.** On the 27th day, Noah opened the ark and released the animals, birds, and all living creatures.

Chapter 6

1. On the first day of the third month, Noah left the ark and built an altar on the mountain. **2.** He made atonement for the earth, offering a kid to cleanse the earth's guilt, as all had been destroyed except for those in the ark. (Atonement - the act of making amends for sin) **3.** He placed fat on the altar, offering an ox, goat, sheep, kids, salt, a turtle dove, and a young dove, with a burnt sacrifice and offerings mingled with oil, wine, and frankincense, creating a pleasing aroma to YAHWEH. **4.** YAHWEH accepted the offering and made a covenant that the earth would never again be destroyed by a flood, and that seasons would never cease. **5.** YAHWEH instructed Noah to multiply and fill the earth, and that the fear of man would be on all creatures. **6.** He gave all beasts, birds, and creatures, as well as the fish of the sea, as food, like the green herbs. **7.** However, they were forbidden to eat flesh with its blood, for the life of all flesh is in the blood, and their blood would be required if shed. **8.** Whoever sheds man's blood, by man shall his blood be shed, for man was made in the image of YAHWEH. **9.** YAHWEH repeated His command to multiply and fill the earth. **10.** Noah and his sons swore to never eat blood and made a covenant with YAHWEH forever, binding their descendants. **11.** YAHWEH instructed that the children of Israel should make a covenant in this month, sprinkling blood as a sign of the covenant. (Covenant - a sacred agreement or promise) **12.** The covenant was written as a testimony to observe forever, forbidding the consumption of blood from any creature. **13.** YAHWEH commanded Israel to refrain from eating blood, so their names and descendants would be preserved before Him. **14.** This law has no end and must be followed through all generations ensuring continuous atonement and forgiveness. **15.** YAHWEH gave Noah and his sons a sign that there would never again be a flood to destroy the earth. **16.** He set His bow in the cloud as a sign of this eternal covenant. **17.** It is ordained that the Feast of Weeks should be celebrated once a year to renew the covenant. **18.** This festival was celebrated in heaven from creation until Noah's time, observed for 26 jubilees and five weeks of years. Noah and his sons continued it for 350 years, but after Noah's death, his sons abandoned it until Abraham's time. **19.** Abraham, Isaac, and Jacob observed it, but in your days, Israel forgot it until you renewed it on this mountain. **20.** YAHWEH commanded Israel to observe this festival yearly as a commandment, one day in the month. (Feast of Weeks - a festival of renewal and thanksgiving) **21.** This is the Feast of Weeks, which is twofold: the Feast of First Fruits and the Feast of Weeks, according to what is written and engraved. **22.** It is written in the first Torah that Israel should observe it in its season and remember its sacrifices. **23.** The first, fourth, seventh, and tenth months are days of remembrance and marking the seasons, written as testimony forever. **24.** Noah ordained these days as feasts for all generations, creating a memorial unto him. **25.** On the first month, Noah was commanded to build the ark, and the earth dried on this day. **26.** On the fourth month, the depths were closed; and on the seventh month, the abysses opened and the waters began to descend. (Abysses - deep waters or caverns of the earth) **27.** By the tenth month, the mountain tops were visible, and Noah was glad. **28.** These feasts were ordained for Noah as perpetual memorials, and they were placed on the heavenly tablets. **29.** Each festival had 13 weeks, passing from one to another, marking their memorials. **30.** The commandment spans 52 weeks, completing the year, as engraved on the heavenly tablets. **31.** This law must be followed every year, without neglect, to maintain the proper order of time. **32.** Israel must observe the years as 364 days, ensuring all seasons and feasts align without disturbance. **33.** If Israel fails to observe this, they will disrupt the seasons, and the years will fall out of order. **34.** If they neglect the ordinances, they will forget the proper path and confuse the months, seasons, Sabbaths, and festivals. **35.** This is written in the heavenly tablets to prevent Israel from adopting pagan practices and celebrating incorrect feasts. (Pagan practices - those of surrounding nations that Israel is warned against following). **36.** The moon will cause confusion, disturbing the seasons and causing a shift in the timing of days. **37.** When Israel disturbs the proper observance, they will make holy days unclean and confuse the sacred and the profane. **38.** I testify that after your death, Israel will forget these laws and disrupt the calendar, eating blood and flesh wrongly. **39.** They will not keep the year at 364 days and will follow false practices, breaking the covenant and forsaking the true festivals. (Covenant; agreement)

Chapter 7

1. In the seventh week of the first year of this Jubilee, Noah planted vines on the mountain where the ark had rested, called Lubar, one of the Ararat Mountains. By the fourth year, the vines bore fruit. **2.** He harvested and made wine from the grapes, storing it until the fifth year, on the first day of the first month. **3.** Noah celebrated the feast with joy, offering a burnt sacrifice to YAHWEH: a young ox, a ram, seven one-year-old sheep, and a goat kid as atonement for himself and his sons. (Atonement: as commanded in covenantal laws established later in Scripture.) **4.** He began with the goat kid, placing its blood on the altar, and laid the fat of the ox, ram, and sheep on it as well. **5.** He offered all the sacrifices mixed with oil, then sprinkled wine on the fire and burned incense, creating a sweet aroma to YAHWEH. **6.** Noah rejoiced and drank the wine with his children, celebrating with joy. (burned Incense: Burning incense is symbolic of prayers rising to heaven.) **7.** As evening fell, Noah went to his tent, became drunk, and lay uncovered in his sleep. **8.** Ham, seeing his father naked, went out and told his brothers. **9.** Shem and Japheth, taking a garment, walked backward and covered Noah's shame without looking at him. **10.** When Noah awoke and realized what Ham had done, he cursed Ham's son, Canaan, declaring him a servant to his brothers. (Shame: a painful feeling of humiliation or distress caused by the consciousness of wrong or foolish behavior.) **11.** Noah then blessed Shem, saying, "May YAHWEH bless Shem, and let Canaan serve him." **12.** "May YAHWEH expand Japheth's territory, and may He dwell in Shem's land, with Canaan as his servant." **13.** Ham, displeased by the curse upon his son, left Noah, taking his children—Cush, Mizraim, Put, and Canaan—with him. (Displeased: feeling upset or unhappy about something.) **14.** Ham built a city and named it after his wife, Ne'elatama'uk. **15.** Japheth, envious of his brother, also built a city and called it after his wife, 'Adataneses. **16.** Shem stayed with Noah and built his city near his father's, naming it after his wife, Sedeqetelebab. (Envious: feeling or showing jealousy of someone's achievements or advantages.) **17.** The three cities were close to Mount Lubar: Sedeqetelebab to the east, Na'eltama'uk to the south, and 'Adataneses to the west. **18.** Shem's sons were Elam, Asshur, Arpachshad (born two years after the flood), Lud, and Aram. **19.** Japheth's sons were Gomer, Magog, Madai, Javan, Tubal, Meshech, and Tiras. These were the sons of Noah. (Flood: a large amount of water covering land that is usually dry.) **20.** In the twenty-eighth Jubilee, Noah began instructing his grandsons on the laws and commandments he knew, urging them to live righteously, respect their bodies, honor their parents, love their neighbors, and avoid sin. (Righteously: in accordance with moral law or justice.) **21.** The flood came upon the earth because of three things: the fornication of the Watchers, who broke the commandments and took wives from the daughters of men, leading to uncleanness. **22.** They fathered sons called the Nephilim, who were different from one another and devoured each other. The Giants killed the Naphil, the Naphil killed the Eljo, and the Eljo killed mankind, with each man killing another. **23.** Everyone turned to evil, shedding much blood, and the earth became filled with wickedness. (Fornication: immoral sexual behavior, often implying adultery or sexual impurity.) **24.** After this, they sinned against the beasts, birds, and all creatures on the earth, shedding even more blood. People's thoughts and desires were filled with evil and vanity continually. **25.** YAHWEH destroyed everything from the earth because of the wickedness of their deeds and the blood they shed. **26.** "We were left, I and you, my sons, and everything that entered the ark with us. But I see that you are not walking in righteousness; you are walking the path of destruction, divided and envious of one another, lacking harmony." (Vanity: emptiness or lack of value, often associated with false pursuits.) **27.** "I see that demons are now seducing you and your children, and I fear that after my death, you will continue to shed human blood and be destroyed from the earth." **28.** "Anyone who sheds the blood of man, or eats the blood of any flesh, shall be destroyed from the earth." **29.** "There will be no man left who eats blood or sheds human blood on the earth. They and their descendants will be condemned and descend into Sheol, the place of darkness, to die a violent death." (Sheol: a temporary holding place for the dead before final judgment, as seen in Jewish eschatology.) **30.** "You must not leave blood on the ground. Wherever blood is shed, cover it, for this is the command I give you, and it is a righteous act for your souls." **31.** "Do not be like those who eat with blood; guard yourselves from eating blood. Cover the blood, as I have been commanded to testify to you and your children, along with all living creatures." **32.** "Do not let the soul be consumed with the flesh, for your blood is your life, and it shall not be required by the one who sheds it on the earth." (Righteous: morally right, just, or virtuous.) **33.** "The earth will not be cleansed of the blood shed upon it, except by the blood of the one who shed it. Only through their blood will the earth be purified throughout all generations." **34.** "Now, my children, listen and do justice and righteousness, so that you may be established in righteousness across the earth, and your praise will be raised up before YAHWEH, my Almighty, who saved me from the floodwaters." **35.** "You will go on to build cities and plant every kind of tree and plant, including fruit-bearing ones," (Justice: the quality of being fair and just.) **36.** "For the first three years, do not harvest the fruit. In the fourth year, the fruit will be considered holy, and the first-fruits must be offered to YAHWEH, the Most High, who created heaven, earth, and all things. Offer wine and oil as the first-fruits, and whatever remains, let the servants of YAHWEH eat at the altar." **37.** "In the fifth year, make a release, letting the land rest, and you shall prosper in all that you plant." **38.** "Enoch, the father of your father, gave these commands to Methuselah, his son, and Methuselah gave them to Lamech, his son. Lamech passed them on to me." (Release: a practice where debts or obligations are forgiven, and the land or people are allowed to rest or reset.) **39.** "Now, I too will command you, my sons, just as Enoch commanded Methuselah. While still living, in the seventh generation, Enoch testified to his son and his grandsons until the day of his death."

Chapter 8
1. In the twenty-ninth jubilee, Arpachshad took a wife named Rasu'eja, the daughter of Susan from Elam, and she bore him a son named Kainam in the third year of this week. **2.** The son grew, and his father taught him to write. Kainam then sought a place where he could establish a city for himself. **3.** He found a writing carved by previous generations on a rock. He read it, transcribed it, and sinned by following it; it taught the ways of the Watchers, who observed the omens of the sun, moon, and stars. (Omens: signs or warnings of future events, often considered supernatural.) **4.** Kainam said nothing about it, fearing Noah's anger if he spoke of it. **5.** In the thirtieth jubilee, Kainam took a wife named Melka, daughter of Madai, and in the fourth year, they had a son named Shelah, as Kainam believed he was sent for a special purpose. **6.** Shelah grew up, married Mu'ak, daughter of Kesed, his father's brother, in the one and thirtieth jubilee. **7.** In the fifth year, Mu'ak bore Shelah a son named Eber. Shelah married Azurad, daughter of Nebrod, in the thirty-second jubilee. **8.** In the sixth year, Azurad gave birth to Peleg, whose name means "division," because in his days, the children of Noah began dividing the earth. (Division: the action of separating or partitioning something into parts.) **9.** They secretly divided the earth among themselves and later informed Noah. **10.** In the beginning of the thirty-third jubilee, the earth was divided into three parts: one for Shem, one for Ham, and one for Japheth, according to their inheritance. **11.** Noah called his sons and they drew near with their children. He divided the earth, and they each took their portion from Noah's writings. **12.** Shem's lot was the middle of the earth, from the mountains of Rafa to the mouth of the river Tina, extending westward, reaching the waters of the abysses and flowing into the great sea. Japheth's portion lay to the north, and Shem's extended to the south. (Abysses: vast, deep, or bottomless spaces or oceans.) **13.** His portion continued to Karaso, towards the south. **14.** It stretched along the great sea and reached the west of the tongue of the Egyptian Sea. **15.** The land turned south toward the mouth of the great sea, extending westward to 'Afra, and to the banks of the river Gihon. **16.** It extended eastward to the Garden of Eden, then southward and eastward, reaching the mountain of Rafa and the bank of the river Tina's mouth. **17.** This portion was allotted to Shem and his descendants, to be their inheritance forever. **18.** Noah rejoiced that this portion was given to Shem and his sons, recalling his earlier prophecy that YAHWEH would dwell in the dwelling of Shem. **19.** Noah recognized that the Garden of Eden was the holiest of holy places, Mount Sinai the center of the desert, and Mount Zion the center of the earth—these three were created as sacred places in alignment with each other. (Sacred: something regarded with reverence and respect, often related to religious or divine significance.) **20.** He blessed the Almighty for giving him the Word, and for YAHWEH's eternal reign. **21.** It was known that Shem and his descendants were given a blessed and eternal portion: the entire land of Eden, the Red Sea region, the eastern lands, India, the mountains of the Red Sea, Bashan, Lebanon, the islands of Kaftur, the mountains of Sanir, Amana, the northern mountains of Asshur, along with Elam, Asshur, Babel, Susan, Ma'edai, Ararat, and the areas beyond the sea north of Asshur's mountains. This vast, blessed land is very good. **22.** For Ham, the second portion was given, extending beyond the Gihon (a river in ancient geography) to the south, towards the right of the Garden of Eden. It stretches to the south and reaches the mountains of fire, going westward to the sea of 'Atel and onward to the sea of Ma'uk (a sea where everything that isn't destroyed falls). **23.** It goes northward to the limits of Gadir, then along the coastline towards the great sea, coming close to the river Gihon, which borders the right side of the Garden of Eden. **24.** This land was designated for Ham to possess forever, with his descendants for all generations. **25.** Japheth's third portion lies beyond the river Tina (an ancient river) to the north, reaching the land of Gog, and extends eastward. **26.** It stretches northward to the mountains of Qelt, then to the sea of Ma'uk, continuing to the east of Gadir, and reaching the waters of the sea. **27.** It moves westward towards Fara, then to 'Aferag, continuing east to the waters of the sea of Me'at (likely a small or specific sea). **28.** It extends to the region of the river Tina, heading north-east to its boundary near the mountain Rafa, and turns northward. **29.** This land, with five great islands and a large northern region, became Japheth's inheritance, to be passed down to his descendants forever. **30.** The land of Japheth is cold, the land of Ham is hot, and the land of Shem has a balanced climate, a blend of both cold and heat.

Chapter 9
1. Ham divided the land among his sons. The first portion for Cush was to the east, then to the west of him, Mizraim received his portion, followed by Put to the west, and Canaan on the sea to the west. **2.** Shem also divided the land among his sons. The first portion for Ham and his descendants was to the east of the Tigris River, extending to the east, including the whole land of India, the coast of the Red Sea, the waters of Dedan, the mountains of Mebri and Ela, the land of Susan, and the area of Pharnak to the Red Sea and the river Tina. **3.** For Asshur, the second portion was given, including all the land of Asshur, Nineveh, Shinar, and the border of India, stretching along the river. (Pharnak: a location in ancient geography; Tina: an ancient river) **4.** Arpachshad received the third portion, which included the land of the Chaldees to the east of the Euphrates River, bordering the Red Sea, it also included the waters of the desert near the tongue of the sea that faces Egypt, as well as the land of Lebanon, Sanir, and 'Amana, up to the Euphrates. **5.** The fourth portion went to Aram, covering all of Mesopotamia between the Tigris and Euphrates Rivers, north of the Chaldees, extending to the border of the mountains of Asshur and the land of 'Arara. **6.** Lud received the fifth portion, including the mountains of Asshur and all the land connected to them, extending to the Great Sea, and reaching the east of Asshur, his brother. ('Arara: an ancient region) **7.** Japheth also divided the land of his inheritance among his sons. **8.** The first portion for Gomer was to the east, from the northern side to the river Tina; and in the north, Magog received all the inner portions of the north until it reached the Sea of Me'at. **9.** Madai's portion lay to the west of his two brothers, including the islands and the coastal areas of these islands. **10.** Javan received the fourth portion, which consisted of every island and the islands near the border of Lud. **11.** For Tubal, the fifth portion was in the middle of the peninsula that approached the border of Lud's portion, extending to the second point and the region beyond it, up to the third. (Me'at: a small or specific body of water in ancient geography) **12.** Meshech's portion, the sixth, included the region beyond the third point, extending to the east of Gadir. **13.** Tiras received the seventh portion, four great islands in the sea, reaching the portion of Ham. The islands of Kamaturi were allocated by lot to the sons of Arpachshad as his inheritance. (Kamaturi: a group of islands) **14.** Thus, Noah's sons divided the land among their descendants in his presence. Noah bound them by an oath, cursing anyone who would try to seize land not assigned to them. **15.** They all agreed, saying, "So be it, so be it," for themselves and their descendants forever, until the Day of Judgment, when YAHWEH ALMIGHTY shall judge them with sword and fire for all the wickedness and sin that have corrupted the earth with transgression, uncleanness, and fornication.

Chapter 10
1. And in the third week of this jubilee, the unclean demons began to lead astray the children of Noah's sons, causing them to err and destroy them. **2.** The sons of Noah came to Noah their father, and told him about the demons that were misleading, blinding, and slaying his grandsons. **3.** Noah prayed before YAHWEH, his Sovereign Ruler, and said, "YAHWEH of the spirits of all flesh, who has shown mercy to me and saved me and my sons from the floodwaters, and who did not cause us to perish as You did the sons of perdition." **4.** "For Your unmerited mercy has been great towards me, and great has been Your mercy to my soul. Let Your mercy be upon my sons, and let wicked spirits not rule over them, lest they destroy them from the earth." **5.** "Bless me and my sons, that we may increase and multiply and fill the earth. You know how Your Watchers, the fathers of these spirits, acted in my day; and concerning these spirits, imprison them and hold them in the place of condemnation, so they do not bring destruction upon the sons of Your servant." (Watchers: fallen angels) **6.** "For these spirits are malignant and created to destroy. Let them not rule over the living spirits; for You alone have dominion over them. Let them not have power over the sons of the righteous forever." **7.** And YAHWEH, our Sovereign Ruler, commanded us to bind them all. **8.** The chief of the spirits, Mastema, came and said, "YAHWEH, Creator, let some of them remain before me, and let them listen to my voice

and obey everything I say. If some are not left to me, I will not be able to execute my will on the sons of men; these spirits are for corruption and leading astray before my judgment, for the wickedness of men is great." (Mastema: a leader of evil spirits) **9.** And YAHWEH replied, "Let one-tenth remain before you, and let the other nine parts descend into the place of condemnation." **10.** "And one of us was commanded to teach Noah all their remedies, for He knew that they would not walk uprightly nor strive for righteousness." (Medicines: healing knowledge) **11.** And we followed His instructions: we bound all the malignant spirits in the place of condemnation, leaving one-tenth of them to be subject to Satan on earth. **12.** "We also explained to Noah all the remedies for their diseases, including their seductions, so that he might heal them with herbs from the earth." **13.** Noah wrote down everything in a book as we instructed him on every kind of remedies, so that the evil spirits would not harm his descendants. **14.** He gave all that he had written to Shem, his eldest son, because he loved him greatly above all his sons. **15.** Noah passed away and was buried on Mount Lubar in the land of Ararat. **16.** He lived for nine hundred and fifty years, completing nineteen jubilees, two weeks, and five years. (Ararat: a mountain range in ancient times) **17.** In his life, Noah excelled the children of men, except for Enoch, because of his righteousness. Enoch's role was ordained as a testimony to future generations, recounting the deeds of mankind until the Day of Judgment. **18.** In the thirty-third jubilee, in the first year of the second week, Peleg took Lomna, the daughter of Sina'ar, as his wife. She bore him a son in the fourth year, and he named him Reu, saying, "The children of men have become evil through their wicked purpose of building a city and a tower in the land of Shinar." **19.** They departed from the land of Ararat to Shinar, where they began building the city and tower, saying, "Let us ascend to heaven by it." **20.** They began to build, and in the fourth week, they made bricks with fire. The bricks served as stone, and the clay used to bind them was asphalt, which came from the sea and fountains of water in Shinar. **21.** They spent forty-three years building it. Its width was 203 bricks, and each brick was one-third the height of a standard brick, with the total height being 5433 cubits and 2 palms. The extent of one wall was thirteen stades, and the other was thirty stades. (Cubit: a unit of length; Stade: an ancient Greek measurement of distance) **22.** YAHWEH said to us, "Behold, they are one people, and this is what they are doing. Nothing will be withheld from them now. Let us go down and confuse their language, so they will not understand one another, and they will be scattered into cities and nations. One purpose will no longer unite them until the Day of Judgment." **23.** YAHWEH descended, and we descended with Him to see the city and the tower the children of men had built. **24.** He confused their language, and they no longer understood one another, causing them to cease building the city and the tower. **25.** That is why the land of Shinar is called Babel, because YAHWEH confused the language of the children of men there, and from there, they were dispersed into their cities, each according to their language and nation. **26.** YAHWEH sent a mighty wind to overthrow the tower upon the earth, between Asshur and Babylon in Shinar. They called it "Overthrow." **27.** In the fourth week of the thirty-fourth jubilee, in the first year, they were dispersed from Shinar. **28.** Ham and his sons went into the land assigned to him, which he acquired in the southern region. **29.** Canaan saw the land of Lebanon to the river of Egypt and found it very good. He chose to dwell in Lebanon, east and west of the Jordan River and the sea, rather than in his inheritance to the west. **30.** Ham, his father, and his brothers Cush and Mizraim warned him, "You have settled in a land that is not yours, and it was not given to us by lot. Do not do this; if you do, you and your descendants will be cursed through sedition. By this act, you and your children will fall and be rooted out forever." **31.** "Do not dwell in Shem's land; for it is his and his sons' by lot." **32.** "Cursed are you and cursed will be your descendants, more than all the sons of Noah, by the curse that we bound ourselves to in an oath before the holy judge and Noah, our father." **33.** But Canaan did not listen to them. He dwelt in Lebanon, from Hamath to the entrance of Egypt, with his sons, and has lived there ever since. **34.** For this reason, the land is called Canaan. **35.** Japheth and his sons went towards the sea and settled in their portion. Madai, however, did not like the land by the sea, so he asked for a portion from Ham, Asshur, and Arpachshad, his wife's brother, and settled in Media, near his wife's family. **36.** He named his dwelling place and the place where his descendants lived "Media," after his father Madai.

Chapter 11

1. In the thirty-fifth jubilee, third week, first year Reu married Ora, daughter of Ur, son of Kesed, and she bore him a son named Seroh in the seventh year of this week (1687 A.M.). **2.** The sons of Noah began to war against each other, taking captives, shedding blood, and building cities with walls and towers. People exalted themselves, founded kingdoms, and went to war—nation against nation, city against city. They acquired weapons, taught their sons to fight, captured cities, and sold slaves. (Slaves: people forced to work without pay) **3.** Ur, son of Kesed, built the city of 'Ara in Chaldea, naming it after himself and his father. (Chaldea: an ancient region in southern Mesopotamia) **4.** They made molten images and worshipped them creating graven and unclean idols.. Malignant spirits led them to sin and uncleanness. (Molten: melted or cast into shape) **5.** The prince Mastema worked hard to spread evil and sent his spirits to commit sin, corruption, and bloodshed on earth. (Mastema: a demon or evil spirit leader) **6.** For this reason, Seroh was named Serug, as everyone turned to sin and transgression. (Transgression: violation of a law or command) **7.** Serug grew up in Ur of the Chaldees, near his father-in-law's family", worshipped idols, and married Melka, daughter of Kaber, in the thirty-sixth jubilee, fifth week, first year (1744 A.M.). **8.** She bore him Nahor in the first year of this week, and Serug taught him the ways of Chaldean divination, interpreting signs of the heavens. (Divination: the practice of seeking knowledge of the future or the unknown) **9.** In the thirty-seventh jubilee, sixth week, first year (1800 A.M.), Nahor took a wife named 'Ijaska, daughter of Nestag from Chaldea. **10.** She bore him Terah in the seventh year of this week (1806 A.M.). Mastema sent ravens and birds to devour the sown seeds, robbing men of their labor. Before they could plough, the ravens ate the seeds. (Plough: farming tool used to till soil) **11.** For this reason, Terah was named so, as the ravens reduced them to poverty, devouring their seeds. (Ravens: large black birds often associated with omens) **12.** The years became barren because of the birds, which consumed all the fruits of the trees. Only with great effort could they save some of the earth's produce. **13.** In the thirty-ninth jubilee, second week, first year (1870 A.M.), Terah married Edna, daughter of Abram, his father's sister. **14.** In the seventh year of this week (1876 A.M.), Edna bore him a son, naming him Abram after his late father. (Abram: the biblical figure who would later become Abraham) **15.** As a child, Abram recognized the errors of the world, realizing how people followed idols and uncleanness. His father taught him writing, and by age 14 years (1890 A.M.), he separated from his father to avoid idol worship. (Weeks of years: a period of seven years) **16.** He prayed to the Creator of all things, asking for salvation from mankind's errors, and that he should not fall into their uncleanness. **17.** When it was time to sow the seeds, the people went out together to protect their crops from ravens. Abram, now fourteen, joined them. **18.** A cloud of ravens appeared to devour the seed, but Abram ran ahead and called to them, "Do not descend; return to where you came from." The ravens turned back. **19.** He commanded the ravens to turn back seventy times that day, and no raven settled to devour the seed across the land where Abram was. (Ravens: large black birds associated with omens) **20.** Everyone who saw him was amazed as the ravens turned back, and Abram's fame spread throughout Chaldea. **21.** People came to him that year to plant their crops, and Abram went with them. They sowed their land, and that year, they harvested enough grain to be satisfied. **22.** In the first year of the fifth week (1891 A.M.), Abram taught those who made tools for oxen. They crafted a vessel above the ground, attached to the plough, to hold the seed. As the plough worked, the seed fell into the earth, no longer feared by ravens. (Oxen: large domesticated animals used for ploughing) **23.** After this, they created similar vessels for all ploughs, and the people sowed and tilled the land as Abram had instructed. They no longer feared the ravens. **24.** After this, they made similar vessels for all the ploughs, and they sowed and tilled the land according to Abram's instructions. They no longer feared the ravens. (Ploughs: farming tools used for tilling the soil)

Chapter 12

1. He said, "Here I am, my son." The son asked, "Why do we worship lifeless idols that offer no help or profit? They mislead the heart and lack any spirit." (Idols: objects of worship made by humans) **2.** "These idols are nothing but dumb forms. Worship YAHWEH, the Sovereign Ruler of heaven, who sends rain and dew, creates all things by His word, and sustains all life." (Dumb: lifeless or mute) **3.** "Why bow to things made by hands that lack life? They are a source of shame to their makers and mislead worshipers. Do not worship them." **4.** His father replied, "I understand, my son, but the people force me to serve these idols." **5.** "If I tell them the truth, they will kill me, for their hearts are bound to their worship. Keep silent, my son, or they may harm you." **6.** Abram shared this with his brothers, which angered them. Afterward, he kept silent to avoid conflict. **9.** In the fortieth jubilee, second week, seventh year, Abram married Sarai, his father's daughter. (Jubilee: a 50-year biblical cycle) **10.** Haran, his brother, married in the third year of the third week. By the seventh year, they had a son named Lot. **11.** Nahor, their other brother, also married around this time. **12.** In Abram's sixtieth year, during the fourth week, he burned the house of idols at night, destroying everything inside. **13.** When the people awoke, they tried to save their gods, but the fire consumed everything. **14.** Haran attempted to save the idols but was consumed by the flames. He died in Ur of the Chaldees and was buried by his father Terah. **15.** Terah left Ur with his family, intending to settle in Canaan. They stopped in Haran, where Abram stayed with him for two weeks of years. (Two weeks of years: 14 years) **16.** In the sixth week, fifth year, Abram observed the stars all night to determine the year's rainfall. **17.** He pondered: "Why search the stars? All their signs are under YAHWEH's control." (Celestial: related to the heavens) **18.** "If YAHWEH wills, He sends rain; if not, He withholds it. Everything is in His hands." **19.** Abram prayed: "YAHWEH Most High, You are my Sovereign Ruler. You created all things, and I choose Your dominion." **20.** "Deliver me from evil spirits that rule men's hearts and prevent me from straying. Establish my descendants forever in Your path." (Dominion: supreme authority) **21.** "Should I return to Ur, where they seek me? Guide me on the right path and protect me from deceit." **22.** YAHWEH's word came: "Leave your country, family, and father's house for a land I will show you. I will make you a great nation." **23.** "I will bless you, make your name great, and all families of the earth will be blessed through you. Those who bless you will be blessed, and those who curse you will be cursed." **24.** "Fear not; I am your Sovereign Ruler, and I will remain with you and your descendants forever." **25.** YAHWEH said, "Open Abram's mouth to understand and speak the language of creation." (Overthrow: the destruction of Babel) **26.** Abram began speaking Hebrew, the tongue of creation. **27.** He transcribed his ancestors' writings in Hebrew and studied them during six rainy months. **28.** In the seventh year of the sixth week, Abram told Terah he planned to leave Haran to explore Canaan. **29.** Terah blessed him: "Go in shalom. May YAHWEH guide, protect, and grant you favor before all people." (Shalom: peace or well-being) **30.** "If you find a good land, take me and Lot with you as your own son. May YAHWEH be with you." **31.** "Leave Nahor with me until your return, and we will join you in shalom."

Chapter 13

1. Abram left Haran with Sarai, his wife, and Lot, his nephew, journeying to Canaan. He reached Asshur, moved to Shechem, and settled near a tall oak. **2.** The land, from Hamath to the oak, was lush and beautiful. **3.** YAHWEH appeared to Abram, saying, "I will give this land to you and your descendants." Abram built an altar and offered a burnt sacrifice. (Burnt sacrifice: an offering completely consumed by fire as worship) **4.** Moving to a mountain between Bethel and Ai, he pitched his tent. **5.** The land was fertile, with vines, figs, pomegranates, and many trees, and water was abundant on the mountains. **6.** Abram praised YAHWEH for bringing him from Ur to this land. (Bountiful: plentiful or abundant) **7.** In the first year, seventh week, Abram built an altar and called on YAHWEH: "You, eternal YAHWEH, are my Sovereign Ruler." **8.** He offered a sacrifice, praying for YAHWEH's guidance. **9.** Abram moved south to Hebron, stayed two years, and then went further south to Bealoth during a famine. (Famine: extreme scarcity of food) **10.** In Egypt, during the third year of the week, Pharaoh took Sarai. **11.** Tanais in Egypt was built seven years after Hebron. **12.** YAHWEH afflicted Pharaoh's house with plagues because of Sarai. (Afflicted: caused pain or suffering) **13.** Abram, already wealthy, gained more possessions after this. **14.** Pharaoh returned Sarai and sent them away. Abram returned to his altar between Bethel and Ai, praising YAHWEH for His peace. (Shalom: peace, harmony, or well-being) **15.** In the forty-first jubilee, Abram sacrificed again, declaring YAHWEH as his Sovereign forever. **16.** Lot parted from Abram and settled in Sodom, where the people were exceedingly sinful. (Exceedingly: to an extreme degree) **17.** Abram grieved Lot's departure, as he had no children. **18.** YAHWEH promised Abram, "Look in all directions; I will give this land to your descendants forever." **19.** Abram's descendants would be as countless as the dust of the earth. (Countless: too many to be counted) **20.** Abram moved to Hebron and dwelled there. That year, Chedorlaomer and other kings attacked Sodom, capturing Lot and his possessions. **21.** A survivor informed Abram, who armed his household to rescue Lot. **22.** Abram gave a tenth of his first fruits to YAHWEH, establishing a law for all generations to give tithes to the priests. (Tithe: a tenth part of income given for religious purposes) **23.** This law ensured joy and provision for the priests. **24.** After rescuing Lot, the king of Sodom offered Abram the recovered goods, but Abram refused, saying, "I will take nothing, so no one can claim they made me rich." (Ordinance: a decree or law established by authority) **25.** Abram only allowed his allies, Aner, Eschol, and Mamre, to take their share of the spoils, dedicating his actions to YAHWEH. **26.** The Torah has no time limit; YAHWEH ordained that every generation must give a tenth of all produce—grain, wine, oil, cattle, and sheep—to Him. (Torah: divine law or instruction) **27.** These offerings were given to His priests for their sustenance, to eat and drink joyfully in His presence. **28.** The king of Sodom bowed before Abram, saying, "Our lord Abram, give us the people you rescued, but keep the goods for yourself." (Booty: goods taken during war) **29.** Abram replied, "I lift my hands to the Most High YAHWEH, vowing not to take anything of yours—not even a thread or sandal strap—so you cannot claim to have made me rich. Only what the young men have eaten and the share of Aner, Eschol, and Mamre will be taken." (Sandal strap: a symbolic term for something trivial or insignificant)

Chapter 14

1. In the fourth year of this week, on the new moon of the third month, YAHWEH spoke to Abram in a vision, saying: "Do not fear, Abram. I am your protector, and your reward will be very great." **2.** Abram replied: "YAHWEH ALMIGHTY, what can You give me since I am childless? My servant, Dammasek Eliezer, the son of my maidservant, will inherit my estate because I have no offspring." **3.** YAHWEH answered: "This man will not be your heir. Instead, a son from your own body will be your heir." (Heir: one who inherits property or position after another's death) **4.** YAHWEH brought Abram outside and said: "Look at the sky and count the stars, if you are able. Your descendants will be just as numerous." **5.** Abram gazed at the stars, and YAHWEH affirmed: "So shall your offspring be." **6.** Abram trusted YAHWEH, and it was credited to him as righteousness. **7.** YAHWEH said: "I am YAHWEH, who brought you out of Ur of the Chaldeans to give you this land to possess forever." **8.** Abram asked: "YAHWEH ALMIGHTY, how can I be sure that I will inherit this land?" **9.** YAHWEH instructed: "Bring a three-year-old heifer, a three-year-old goat, a three-year-old ram, a turtledove, and a pigeon." (Heifer: a young female cow that has not borne a calf) **10.** Abram gathered the specified animals in the middle of the month and stayed at the oak of Mamre near Hebron. He built an altar, sacrificed the animals, poured their blood on the altar, and divided the larger animals, placing the halves opposite each other. The birds, however, were not divided. **11.** When birds of prey descended upon the pieces, Abram drove them away. **12.** As the sun set, Abram fell into a deep sleep, and a heavy and terrifying darkness enveloped him. **13.** YAHWEH revealed: "Your descendants will live as strangers in a foreign land, where they will be enslaved and mistreated for four hundred years. **14.** But I will judge the nation that enslaves them, and afterward, they will leave with great wealth. **15.** You, however, will go to your ancestors in peace and be buried at a ripe old age." (Ripe: fully developed or mature) **16.** YAHWEH added: "In the fourth generation, your descendants will return here, for the sin of the Amorites is not yet complete." **17.** As Abram awoke, he saw a smoking furnace and a blazing torch passing between the divided pieces. **18.** That day, YAHWEH made a covenant with Abram, saying: "To your descendants, I give this land—from the river of Egypt to the great river Euphrates. This includes the land of the Kenites, Kenizzites, Kadmonites, Perizzites, Rephaim, Amorites, Canaanites, Girgashites, and Jebusites." **19.** Abram completed the offerings, including the animals, birds, fruit, and drink offerings, and fire consumed them all. **20.** YAHWEH renewed His covenant with Abram in this month, establishing it as an everlasting ordinance. Abram reaffirmed the festival for future generations. **21.** Abram shared these events with Sarai, fully trusting YAHWEH's promise of offspring, even though Sarai remained barren. **22.** Sarai proposed to Abram: "Take my Egyptian maidservant, Hagar. Perhaps I can have children through her." **23.** Abram agreed, and Sarai gave Hagar to him as a wife. **24.** Hagar conceived and bore a son. Abram named him Ishmael during the fifth year of this week when Abram was eighty-six years old.

Chapter 15

1. In the fifth year of the fourth week of this jubilee [1979 A.M.], during the third month and in its middle, Abram observed the feast of the first fruits of the grain harvest. **2.** On the altar, he offered new sacrifices to YAHWEH: a heifer, a goat, and a sheep as burnt offerings. Alongside these, he presented fruit and drink offerings with frankincense. (Frankincense: aromatic resin used in incense and perfumes) **3.** YAHWEH appeared to Abram and said: **4.** "I am YAHWEH Almighty. Walk blamelessly before Me, and I will establish My covenant with you and you and make your descendants exceedingly numerous." **5.** Abram fell on his face, and YAHWEH continued, saying: **6.** "My covenant is with you, and you will be the father of many nations. **7.** Your name shall no longer be Abram but Abraham, for I have made you the father of many nations. **8.** I will make you exceedingly fruitful, creating nations and kings from your descendants. **9.** I will establish My covenant with you and your seed as an everlasting agreement. I will be your Sovereign Ruler and theirs. **10.** The land of Canaan, where you have lived as a foreigner, will belong to you and your descendants forever, and I will be their Sovereign Ruler." **11.** YAHWEH said further: "As for you, keep My covenant. Circumcise every male among you. **12.** On the eighth day after birth, every male child in your household, whether born there or bought with money, must be circumcised." (Circumcision: the removal of the foreskin as a sign of covenant) **13.** "Both the children of your house and those purchased must be circumcised. This act will serve as a perpetual sign of My covenant with you. **14.** Any uncircumcised male who fails to undergo this on the eighth day will be cut off from his people for breaking My covenant." **15.** YAHWEH said, "Sarai, your wife, will no longer be called Sarai; her name will now be Sarah. (Sarai: my princess; Sarah: princess) **16.** I will bless her and give you a son by her. Through him, nations and kings will come into being." **17.** Abraham fell on his face, rejoicing, and thought: "Will a son be born to a man of one hundred years? And can Sarah, at ninety, give birth?" **18.** Abraham said, "O, that Ishmael might live under Your favor!" **19.** YAHWEH replied: "Indeed, Sarah will bear you a son. Name him Isaac. I will establish My everlasting covenant with him and his descendants. (Isaac: he laughs) **20.** As for Ishmael, I have heard you. I will bless him, make him fruitful, and multiply him greatly. He will father twelve princes and become a great nation. **21.** However, My covenant will be established with Isaac, whom Sarah will bear to you this time next year." **22.** When YAHWEH finished speaking, He departed. **23.** Abraham obeyed YAHWEH's command. He circumcised Ishmael, all the males born in his household, and those purchased with money. **24.** On the same day, Abraham himself and all the males in his house were circumcised. **25.** This law is eternal and must be observed for all generations without delay. The eighth day is fixed, and no exception is allowed. **26.** Any male whose foreskin is not circumcised by the eighth day does not belong to YAHWEH's covenant people. Such a person will be cut off as one who breaks the covenant. **27.** All the angels of the presence and sanctification have been created to honor this covenant, and Yisrael (Israel) has been sanctified to be YAHWEH's chosen people. **28.** Command the children of Yisrael to observe this sign of the covenant for all their generations. They will not be uprooted from the land if they obey (uproot; pull something ot of land). **29.** This command is an eternal covenant for all Yisrael to follow. **30.** YAHWEH did not call Ishmael, his sons, or Esau to Himself, despite being Abraham's descendants. He chose Yisrael alone to be His people. **31.** Among all nations, YAHWEH appointed spirits to lead them, but over Yisrael, He ruled directly as their Sovereign. **32.** YAHWEH will preserve Yisrael, holding them accountable, blessing them, and being their Sovereign forever. **33.** However, the children of Yisrael will stray from this law. Many will fail to circumcise their sons, ignoring this eternal sign. They will become like the Gentiles. **34.** YAHWEH's anger will be fierce against the children of Yisrael, as they have broken His covenant and turned away from His commandments. By provoking Him and speaking blasphemies, they have failed to observe His Torah. Instead, they have conformed to the ways of the Gentiles. Consequently, they will be cast out and expelled from the land. There will be no forgiveness or pardon for the sin of this lasting transgression.(blasphemies ;profane talk.)

Chapter 16

1. In the fourth month, during the new moon, we appeared to Abraham at the oak of Mamre. We spoke with him and announced that Sarah would conceive a son (Mamre ;a notable tree in Canaan Sarah; Abraham's wife). **2.** Sarah laughed when she overheard this promise, as we had spoken these words to Abraham. She was afraid and denied having laughed, but we gently rebuked her. **3.** We told her the name of her son, Yitschaq, which was written and ordained in the heavenly tablets (a spiritual record of divine decrees). **4.** We informed her that at the appointed time, she would conceive and bear a son. **5.** This month, YAHWEH judged Sodom, Gomorrah (two ancient cities), Zeboim, and the entire region of the Jordan. He destroyed them with fire and brimstone for their extreme wickedness, immorality, and impurity (Zeboim; another city of the plain). **6.** YAHWEH's judgment on these cities serves as a warning to places where people have committed similar sins, and their fate will be similar to that of Sodom. **7.** However, Lot (Abraham's nephew) was spared because YAHWEH remembered Abraham and delivered him from the destruction. **8.** Lot, along with his daughters, committed a terrible sin after the destruction, which was wicked than anything since Adam's time. He had relations with his daughters, a sinful act. **9.** It was decreed in the heavenly tablets that Lot's descendants would be removed from the earth and destroyed, for they had defiled themselves. **10.** In this month, Abraham moved from Hebron (a city in Canaan) and settled between Kadesh (a place of refuge) and Shur (a desert region) in the mountains of Gerar (Gerar ;a Philistine territory). **11.** By the middle of the fifth month, Abraham moved again, this time settling at the "Well of the Oath" (a site significant to Abraham's covenant with God). **12.** In the sixth month, YAHWEH visited Sarah as promised and caused her to conceive as He had spoken. **13.** Sarah gave birth to Yitschaq (Isaac) in the third month, on the day YAHWEH had appointed, during the festival of the first fruits (first fruits; harvest offerings). **14.** Abraham circumcised his son on the eighth day, making him the first to be circumcised according to the eternal covenant (covenant ; a sacred bond with God). **15.** In the sixth year of the fourth week, we visited Abraham at the "Well of the Oath" and announced to him that Sarah would have a child, just as we had told her. **16.** Upon our return in the seventh month, we found Sarah pregnant. We blessed them both and told Abraham that he would have six more sons and see them before he died. His name and descendants would be called through Yitschaq . **17.** The descendants of Abraham's other sons would be Gentiles (non-Israelites), but one of Yitschaq's (Isaac's) descendants would be a holy seed, set apart from the Gentiles. **18.** This holy seed would belong to YAHWEH, becoming a kingdom of priests and a holy nation (dedicated to God's service). **19.** We shared this revelation with Sarah, and they both rejoiced greatly. **20.** Abraham built an altar to YAHWEH, who had delivered him and caused him to rejoice during his journey. He celebrated a seven-day festival of joy near the altar at the "Well of the Oath." **21.** During this festival, Abraham constructed booths (temporary shelters) for himself and his servants, being the first to celebrate the Feast of Tabernacles (a festival commemorating God's provision). **22.** Every day during the festival, Abraham brought a burnt offering (sacrifice) of two oxen, two rams, seven sheep, and one goat for sin offerings (atonement for sins). He did this for himself and his descendants. **23.** As a thank offering, Abraham presented seven rams, seven goats, seven sheep, and their fruit and drink offerings. He burned the fat on the altar, offering a pleasing aroma to YAHWEH. **24.** Each morning and evening, he burned fragrant substances such as frankincense, galbanum, stackte (a resin), nard, myrrh, and costum (spices), offering them in equal parts. **25.** Abraham and his household joyfully celebrated this festival, and no uncircumcised person was present, signifying the importance of the covenant with God. **26.** He blessed his Creator for creating him according to His will, knowing that from him would come the righteous plant (a future promise) for future generations and a holy seed to reflect God's image. **27.** He rejoiced and named the festival "The Festival of YAHWEH," a joy that was pleasing to the Most High. **28.** We blessed Abraham and his descendants forever for keeping this festival as commanded in the heavenly tablets. **29.** For this reason, it is ordained in the heavenly tablets that Israel (the descendants of Abraham through Isaac) will celebrate the Feast of Tabernacles (Sukkot) seven days with joy in the seventh month, as a statute forever. **30.** There is no limit to this festival. It is an eternal command for Israel to celebrate it by dwelling in booths setting wreaths on their heads, and taking leafy boughs and willows from the brook (booths; temporary shelters),. **31.** Abraham gathered branches from palm trees and goodly trees, and each day, he walked around the altar seven times, praising YAHWEH for His blessings with joy and gratitude.

Chapter 17

1. In the first year of the fifth week of this jubilee, Yitschaq was weaned, and Abraham held a great banquet in the third month to celebrate his son's weaning. **2.** Ishmael, the son of Hagar, the Egyptian, stood before Abraham, and Abraham rejoiced, blessing YAHWEH for seeing both his sons and not dying childless. **3.** Abraham remembered the promise YAHWEH made when Lot parted from him and rejoiced because YAHWEH had given him descendants to inherit the earth. He blessed the Creator of all things with his full heart. (Descendants: offspring, children) **4.** Sarah saw Ishmael playing and dancing and Abraham rejoicing with great joy. Out of jealousy, she said to Abraham, "Cast out this bondwoman and her son, for the son of the bondwoman will not inherit alongside my son, Yitschaq." **5.** This upset Abraham deeply, as he loved both his maidservant and son, and he did not want to send them away. **6.** But YAHWEH told Abraham, "Do not let it grieve you about the child and the bondwoman. Listen to Sarah and do as she says, for through Yitschaq your name and seed will be called." (Seed: descendants, lineage) **7.** "However, I will make the son of the bondwoman into a great nation because he is your offspring." **8.** Abraham rose early, gave Hagar bread and water, placed them on her and the child's shoulders, and sent them away. **9.** They wandered in the wilderness of Beersheba. When the water ran out and the child became thirsty, Hagar placed him under an olive tree and sat a distance away, not wanting to see her child die, and wept. **10.** Then an angel of YAHWEH appeared to her, asking, "Why are you weeping, Hagar? Get up, take your child, and hold him. YAHWEH has heard your cry and seen the child's suffering." **11.** Hagar opened her eyes, saw a well of water, filled her bottle, gave the child to drink, and then set off toward the wilderness of Paran. **12.** The child grew up to be an archer, and YAHWEH was with him. His mother found him a wife from Egypt, and she bore him a son, naming him Nebaioth. She said, "YAHWEH was close to me when I called to Him." (Archer: someone skilled in shooting arrows) **13.** In the seventh week, first year, on the twelfth day of the month, voices were heard in heaven about Abraham's faithfulness. They praised his unwavering love for YAHWEH and his faithfulness in all trials. **14.** Then Mastema (a being often associated with temptation or opposition in ancient texts) approached YAHWEH and said, "Abraham loves Yitschaq more than anything. Tell him to offer him as a burnt offering, and you will see if he is truly faithful." **15.** YAHWEH knew Abraham's faithfulness, for He had tested him through hardships, famine, wealth, the loss of his wife, circumcision, and the banishment of Ishmael and Hagar. **16.**

In every trial, Abraham remained faithful, his soul patient, and quick to obey. He was truly a lover of YAHWEH (faithful; loyal).

Chapter 18

1. YAHWEH called to Abraham, "Abraham, Abraham!" And Abraham responded, "Here I am (responded; answered)." **2.** YAHWEH instructed him, "Take your beloved son, Yitschaq, the one you love, and go to the high country. There, offer him as a burnt offering on a mountain I will show you." **3.** The next morning, Abraham saddled his donkey, took two young men along with him, and brought Yitschaq. He cut the wood for the burnt offering and set out for the place. After three days, Abraham saw the location from a distance (saddled ; to prepare). **4.** When they reached a well of water, Abraham told his servants, "Stay here with the donkey while the boy and I go ahead. After we worship, we will return to you." **5.** He laid the wood for the offering on Yitschaq's shoulders, took the fire and the knife, and the two of them walked together toward the place. **6.** Yitschaq asked, "Father!" and Abraham replied, "Here I am, my son." Yitschaq said, "We have the fire, the knife, and the wood, but where is the lamb for the burnt offering?" **7.** Abraham answered, "YAHWEH will provide the lamb for the offering, my son." They continued walking together to the mountain (lamb; live sheep before the age of one year). **8.** Upon arriving at the location, Abraham built an altar, arranged the wood, bound Yitschaq, and placed him on the altar. He stretched his hand out to take the knife and sacrifice his son (stretched; tensible). **9.** I stood before them, and before the prince Mastema, and YAHWEH commanded, "Do not harm the boy or do anything to him. Now I know you fear YAHWEH, because you have not withheld your son from Me." **10.** I called out from heaven, "Abraham, Abraham!" He was startled and replied, "Here I am." **11.** I told him, "Do not harm the boy. Now I know you truly fear YAHWEH, and you have not withheld your firstborn son from Me." **12.** Mastema was ashamed, and when Abraham looked up, he saw a ram caught by its horns. He went, took the ram, and offered it as a burnt offering instead of his son. **13.** Abraham named that place "YAHWEH-Jireh" (meaning "YAHWEH will provide"). To this day, people say, "On the mountain of YAHWEH, it will be provided." **14.** YAHWEH then called to Abraham a second time from heaven, saying, "By Myself I have sworn, declares YAHWEH, because you have obeyed and not withheld your son, your only son, I will bless you." **15.** "In blessing, I will bless you, and in multiplying, I will multiply your descendants, as numerous as the stars in the sky and the sand on the shore." **16.** "Your descendants will inherit the cities of their enemies, and through your seed, all the nations of the earth will be blessed, because you obeyed My voice. Go in peace." **17.** Abraham returned to his servants, and they journeyed together to Beersheba, where Abraham settled near the "Well of the Oath." **18.** Abraham celebrated this event every year, holding a seven-day festival called the "Festival of YAHWEH," remembering the peace of his journey. **19.** It is written in the heavenly tablets that the descendants of Israel should observe this seven-day festival with joy.

Chapter 19

1. In the first year of the first week of the forty-second jubilee, Abraham returned to settle near Hebron, which is also known as Kirjath Arba, and lived there for two weeks of years. (Hebron: an ancient city in Canaan; Kirjath Arba: another name for Hebron, meaning "the city of Arba") **2.** In the first year of the third week of this jubilee, Sarah's life was completed, and she passed away in Hebron. **3.** Abraham went to mourn her passing and prepare for her burial. YAHWEH tested him to see if he would remain patient and not be disturbed by the sorrow, and he was found to be steadfast and calm in spirit. (Mourn: to feel or show sorrow; steadfast: resolutely firm or unwavering) **4.** Abraham spoke with the children of Heth, asking them for a burial place, and he did so with a patient heart, making sure his words were respectful and calm. **5.** YAHWEH granted him favor in the eyes of everyone, and Abraham kindly asked the sons of Heth for a plot of land. They agreed to sell him the land of the double cave, located near Mamre (Hebron), for four hundred silver pieces. (Favor: an act of kindness or grace; Mamre: a place near Hebron) **6.** The sons of Heth offered it to him for free, but Abraham insisted on paying the full price, ensuring that the transaction was completed fairly. After paying, he bowed twice before them and buried Sarah in the double cave. (bow: to express respect or submission) **7.** Sarah lived to be 127 years old—two jubilees, four weeks, and one year. These were the total years of her life. **8.** This was Abraham's tenth trial, and he proved to be faithful, remaining patient in spirit throughout. **9.** He did not complain about the rumors circulating in the land regarding YAHWEH's promise of land to him and his descendants. Instead, he humbly asked for a place to bury Sarah, showing that he was truly faithful to YAHWEH. He was honored as YAHWEH's friend in the heavenly records. (Rumors: unverified reports or gossip) **10.** In the fourth year of this period, Abraham sought a wife for his son Yitschaq. Her name was Rebecca, daughter of Bethuel, who was the son of Nahor, Abraham's brother. She was also the sister of Laban. (Rebecca: the wife of Isaac; Nahor: Abraham's brother) **11.** Abraham took a third wife, Keturah, who came from among his household servants, as Hagar had passed away before Sarah. Keturah bore him six sons: Zimram, Jokshan, Medan, Midian, Ishbak, and Shuah. (Keturah: a woman Abraham married after Sarah's death; household servants: servants living within the household) **12.** In the sixth week of the jubilee, in the second year, Rebecca gave birth to twin sons, Yacob and Esau. (Twin: two children born at the same time from the same pregnancy) **13.** Yacob was a quiet and righteous man, while Esau was fierce, a hunter who lived in the field, and covered with hair. Yacob preferred living in tents. (Righteous: morally right or just; tents: portable shelters used by nomadic peoples) **14.** As they grew older, Yacob learned how to write, but Esau focused on being a warrior and a hunter, learning the skills of battle. His actions were always bold and aggressive. (Aggressive: ready or likely to attack or confront) **15.** Abraham favored Yacob, while Yitschaq preferred Esau. **16.** Abraham observed Esau's actions and realized that Yacob was the one through whom his name and lineage would continue. He called Rebecca and gave her instructions regarding Yacob, knowing she loved him more than Esau. (Lineage: descendants or family line) **17.** Abraham spoke to Rebecca, saying: "My daughter, take care of Yacob. He will take my place on earth and be a blessing to all people, bringing honor to the descendants of Shem." (Shem: one of Noah's sons, the ancestor of the Semitic peoples) **18.** "I know that YAHWEH will choose him above all nations to be His people, a special possession for Himself." **19.** "Though Yitschaq loves Esau more than Yacob, I see that you truly love Yacob, and this pleases me." **20.** "Continue showing your kindness to him. Let your love be visible, for he will be a great blessing for us on earth, and for all future generations." (Kindness: the quality of being friendly, generous, and considerate) **21.** "Let your hands be strong, and let your heart rejoice in Yacob, for I love him more than all my sons. He will be blessed forever, and his descendants will fill the earth." (Descendants: children or heirs) **22.** "If a man could count all the grains of sand on the earth, so too would his descendants be as numerous." (Grains of sand: symbolizing countless numbers) **23.** "All the blessings YAHWEH has given to me and my seed will belong to Yacob and his descendants for all time." **24.** "In his descendants, my name will be honored, along with the names of my fathers: Shem, Noah, Enoch, Mahalalel, Enos, Seth, and Adam." **25.** "Through him and his seed, the foundations of heaven will be secured, the earth strengthened, and the stars in the sky renewed." (Foundations: the underlying basis for something; renewed: restored to a better condition) **26.** Abraham called Yacob before Rebecca, kissed him, and blessed him, saying: **27.** "Yacob, my beloved son, whom my soul loves, may YAHWEH bless you from above the heavens. May He give you all the blessings He gave to Adam, Enoch, Noah, and Shem, and all the promises He made to me. May these blessings be with you and your descendants forever." (Beloved: dearly loved or cherished) **28.** "The spirits of Mastema will not have power over you or your descendants to turn you away from YAHWEH, your Sovereign Ruler, forever." **29.** "May YAHWEH be a father to you, and may you be His firstborn son, and the people of the earth will be blessed through you." **30.** "Go in peace, my son." And they both left Abraham's presence and went together. (Peace: a state of tranquility or harmony) **31.** Rebecca loved Yacob deeply, more than Esau. However, Yitschaq continued to love Esau more than Yacob.

Chapter 20

1. In the first year of the seventh week of the forty-second jubilee, Abraham called together Ishmael, his twelve sons, Yitschaq and his two sons, as well as the six sons of Keturah, and their descendants. (Jubilee: 49-year period; descendants: children) **2.** He instructed them to follow the way of YAHWEH, to practice righteousness, and to love one another. They were to act justly with all people, treating others fairly, and walking in the paths of YAHWEH. (Righteousness: moral uprightness) **3.** Abraham commanded that they circumcise their sons according to the covenant YAHWEH had established with them, and that they should not stray from the path of righteousness. They were to avoid fornication and impurity, rejecting sin and uncleanness in their community. (Circumcise: ritual cutting; impurity: moral uncleanness) **4.** He warned that if any woman or young girl committed fornication, they should be burned with fire. Furthermore, they were not to marry women from the daughters of Canaan, as the seed of Canaan would eventually be uprooted from the land. (Fornication: immoral sex; uprooted: removed) **5.** Abraham also spoke of the judgment that befell the giants and the people of Sodom, explaining how their wickedness and immorality led to their destruction due to their fornication and corruption. (Wickedness: evil actions; corruption: moral decay) **6.** He admonished them, saying: "Guard yourselves from fornication and uncleanness, from all forms of sin, so that you do not bring shame upon our name, and so that your descendants are not destroyed by the sword. Let your lineage not become accursed like

Sodom, and your children like the sons of Gomorrah." (Admonish: warn strongly; accursed: doomed) **7.** "I urge you, my children, to love YAHWEH, the God of heaven, and cling to His commandments with all your heart." **8.** "Do not follow their idols, nor adopt their ways of impurity. Do not create for yourselves molten or carved gods, for they are empty and lifeless. They are the work of human hands, and anyone who trusts in them trusts in nothing." (Idols: false gods; molten: cast by heat) **9.** "Instead, serve YAHWEH, the Most High, and worship Him continually. Look to Him with hope, and walk in righteousness before Him. If you do so, He will delight in you, show you mercy, and send rain upon your land in the morning and evening. He will bless your work, your food, your water, the fruit of your womb, your crops, and your livestock." (Righteousness: moral justice; mercy: kindness) **10.** "You will become a blessing to all nations on the earth, and all peoples will desire to be like you. Bless your children in my name, that they may receive the same blessings I have received." (Blessings: divine gifts; desire: wish for) **11.** Abraham gave gifts to Ishmael, to his sons, and to the sons of Keturah, and sent them away from Yitschaq. He entrusted everything to Yitschaq, his son. **12.** Ishmael, his sons, and the sons of Keturah moved away and settled in the region from Paran to the border of Babylon, in all the land facing the desert in the east. (Paran: desert region; Babylon: ancient city) **13.** These groups mixed with each other, and their descendants became known as the Arabs and the Ishmaelites. (Arabs: desert peoples; Ishmaelites: descendants of Ishmael)

Chapter 21

1. In the sixth year of the seventh week of this jubilee, Abraham called his son Yitschaq and commanded him, saying, "I have grown old and do not know the day of my death; I am now filled with the years of my life." (Jubilee: 49-year period; filled: reached full age) **2.** "Behold, I am one hundred seventy-five years old. Throughout my life, I have remembered YAHWEH and have sought with all my heart to do His will, walking uprightly in all His ways." (Uprightly: morally right; ways: conduct) **3.** "My soul has despised idols, and I have given my heart and spirit to observe the will of the One who created me." (Despised: hated; idols: false gods) **4.** "For He is the living YAHWEH, holy and faithful, righteous beyond all, and He shows no partiality nor accepts bribes. YAHWEH executes judgment on those who break His commandments and despise His covenant." (Partiality: favoritism; bribes: gifts to gain favor) **5.** "You, my son, must observe His commandments, ordinances, and judgments, and do not follow the abominations, nor worship graven or molten images." (Abominations: detestable acts; molten: cast metal) **6.** "And eat no blood from animals, cattle, or any bird that flies in the sky." (Blood: life force; cattle: domesticated animals) **7.** "If you offer a peace offering, slaughter it, pour its blood on the altar, and offer all its fat along with fine flour, mixed with oil, and its drink offering. Put everything on the burnt offering altar, a pleasing aroma before YAHWEH." (Peace offering: ritual sacrifice; pleasing: acceptable) **8.** "You must burn the fat from the thank offerings on the altar fire—fat from the belly, the inward parts, the kidneys, loins, and liver, removing them along with the kidneys." (Thank offerings: gratitude sacrifices; inward parts: internal organs) **9.** "Offer all these parts as a pleasing aroma before YAHWEH, along with the meat offering and drink offering, as the bread of offering to YAHWEH." (Meat offering: sacrifice of food; bread: symbol of provision) **10.** "Eat the meat on that day and the next. Do not let the sun set on the second day until it's eaten, and do not leave any for the third day, for it will not be acceptable. If left over, it will cause sin." (Meat: sacrificial food; acceptable: approved) **11.** "On all your offerings, sprinkle salt, and do not let the salt of the covenant be absent in all your sacrifices before YAHWEH." (Covenant: sacred agreement; sprinkle: distribute lightly) **12.** "As for the wood for the offerings, do not bring any other wood to the altar except these: cypress, bay, almond, fir, pine, cedar, savin, fig, olive, myrrh, laurel, or aspalathus." (Wood: fuel for sacrifices; aspalathus: a type of plant) **13.** "These kinds of wood must be tested for their quality. Do not use split, dark, or old wood, for its fragrance is gone." (Fragrance: pleasant scent; old: aged and ineffective) **14.** "Only these kinds of wood should be placed on the altar, as their fragrance will rise to heaven, and no other wood will do." (Fragrance: scent rising; altar: sacrificial place) **15.** "Observe these commandments, my son, so that you may be righteous in all your deeds." (Righteous: morally upright; deeds: actions) **16.** "Always be clean in body. Wash with water before you approach the altar, and wash your hands and feet before drawing near to make offerings. Afterward, wash again." (Clean: free from impurity; wash: cleanse oneself) **17.** "Let no blood stain your clothing or body. Be extremely careful about blood, and cover it with dust if it happens." (Blood: life force; stain: mark of impurity) **18.** "Do not eat any blood, for it is the soul of the animal. Do not accept gifts for the blood of man, for it must not be shed without judgment." (Soul: life essence; gifts: bribes) **19.** "It is the blood of man that causes the earth to sin, and the earth cannot be cleansed of this sin except by the blood of the one who shed it." (Sin: moral wrong; cleansed: made pure) **20.** "Do not accept any gift for the blood of man, but remember that blood for blood is the righteous law. This will keep you accepted by the Almighty YAHWEH, and protect you from evil and death." (Gift: offering; blood for blood: principle of justice) **21.** "I see, my son, that all the works of mankind are sinful and wicked. Their deeds are impure, detestable, and polluted. There is no righteousness among them." (Sinful: morally wrong; polluted: corrupted) **22.** "Beware, my son, that you do not walk in their ways or follow their paths, for this could lead you to sin and death before YAHWEH. He will hide His face from you, give you over to your transgressions, and remove you and your descendants from the land." (Transgressions: sins; remove: expel) **23.** "Turn away from their deeds and uncleanness, and follow the commandments of the Most High YAHWEH. Do His will, and be upright in all things." (Deeds: actions; uncleanness: impurity) **24.** "If you do so, He will bless all your actions and raise up a righteous lineage through all the earth, and my name and yours will be remembered forever." (Lineage: descendants; righteous: just and moral) **25.** "Go in peace, my son. May the Most High YAHWEH, my Sovereign and your Sovereign, strengthen you to do His will. May He bless all your descendants, with righteous blessings, and make you a blessing to the earth." (Sovereign: ruler; blessing: divine favor) **26.** And Yitschaq left his father, rejoicing. (Rejoicing: filled with joy)

Chapter 22

1. In the second year of the forty-fourth jubilee, when Abraham passed away, Isaac and Ishmael came from the "Well of the Oath" to celebrate the Feast of Weeks (Pentecost) with Abraham, their father. Abraham was happy to see both his sons together. (Well of the Oath: sacred site) **2.** Isaac had many possessions in Beersheba, and he often traveled to inspect them before returning to his father. (Beersheba: town in Israel) **3.** During those days, Ishmael visited Abraham, and both sons came together. Isaac offered a burnt offering on the altar that Abraham had built in Hebron. (Hebron: ancient city) **4.** Isaac also made a thank offering and hosted a joyful feast for Ishmael, his brother. Rebekah prepared fresh cakes from the first grains of the harvest, which she gave to Jacob to take to Abraham as a gift. (Thank offering: gratitude sacrifice) **5.** Isaac also sent a special thank offering by Jacob to Abraham, so that Abraham could eat, drink, and bless the Creator of all things before he died. (Special thank offering: sacred gift) **6.** Abraham ate, drank, and praised the Most High YAHWEH, the Creator of heaven and earth, who provided all the rich blessings of the earth for mankind, that they might eat, drink, and bless Him in return. (Most High: supreme God) **7.** "Now I thank You, my Sovereign Lord, for allowing me to see this day. I am 175 years old, an old man with a full life, and my days have been peaceful." (Sovereign Lord: ultimate ruler) **8.** "The sword of my enemies has not overcome me, and You have protected me and my children throughout my life." (Sword: symbol of attack) **9.** "May Your mercy and peace be upon Your servant and his descendants, making them a chosen nation, an inheritance among all the peoples of the earth, for all generations to come." (Mercy: divine compassion) **10.** Abraham then called Jacob and said, "My son, may YAHWEH, the Sovereign Ruler, bless you, strengthen you to do righteousness, and may He choose you and your descendants to be His people forever." (Sovereign Ruler: ultimate authority) **11.** "And you, my son Jacob, come near and kiss me." So Jacob drew near and kissed him, and he said: "Blessed be my son Jacob, and all the sons of YAHWEH Most High, throughout all ages. May YAHWEH give you a seed of righteousness, and may some of your sons be sanctified (made holy) in the midst of the whole earth. May nations serve you, and all nations bow before your descendants." **12.** "Be strong in the presence of men, and exercise authority over all the seed of Seth. Then your ways, and the ways of your sons, will be justified, so that they shall become a kodesh (holy) nation." **13.** "May the Most High YAHWEH give you all the blessings with which He blessed me, and those with which He blessed Noah and Adam. May they rest on the sacred head of your descendants, from generation to generation, forever." (Kodesh: sacred, holy) **14.** "And may He cleanse you from all unrighteousness and impurity, that you may be forgiven for the transgressions you have committed ignorantly. May He strengthen you and bless you." **15.** "And may you inherit the whole earth, and may He renew His covenant with you, so that you may be to Him a nation for His inheritance forever. He will be to you and your descendants an ALMIGHTY in truth and righteousness throughout all the days of the earth." (Transgressions: sins, wrongdoings) **16.** "And you, my son Jacob, remember my words and observe the commandments of Abraham, your father: Separate yourself from the nations, and do not eat with them. Do not follow their works or become their associate, for their works are unclean, and all their ways are polluted, abominable, and impure."

(Abominable: detestable) **17.** "They offer sacrifices to the dead, worship evil spirits, eat over graves, and all their works are vain and empty." **18.** "They have no heart to understand, and their eyes do not see what their works are or how they err in saying to a piece of wood: 'You are my Sovereign Ruler,' and to a stone: 'You are my Sovereign Ruler and my deliverer.'" (Vain: empty, pointless) **19.** "And as for you, my son Jacob, may the Most High YAHWEH help you, and the ALMIGHTY of heaven bless you, and remove you from their impurity and error." **20.** "Beware, my son Jacob, of taking a wife from the daughters of Canaan, for all their seed is to be rooted out of the earth." (Seed: descendants) **21.** "Because of the transgression of Ham, Canaan went astray, and all his descendants shall be destroyed from the earth. None of them will be saved on the day of judgment." **22.** "And as for all idol worshippers and the profane, there shall be no hope for them in the land of the living; they shall have no remembrance on the earth, for they shall descend into Sheol (the grave or underworld), and into the place of condemnation they will go. Just as the children of Sodom were removed from the earth, so will all idolaters be taken away." (Sheol: underworld, grave) **23.** "Do not fear, my son Jacob, and be not dismayed, O son of Abraham! May the Most High YAHWEH preserve you from destruction, and may He deliver you from all paths of error." **24.** "This house I have built for myself, that I might put my name upon it in the earth. It is given to you and your descendants forever, and it will be called the house of Abraham. You will build my house and establish my name before YAHWEH forever; your descendants and your name will stand through all generations." (Path of error: wrong way) **25.** And with that, he stopped giving commands and blessings. **26.** Then the two lay together on one bed. Jacob slept in the arms of Abraham, his grandfather, and kissed him seven times. His heart rejoiced in affection for him. **27.** Abraham blessed him with all his heart and said: "The Most High YAHWEH, the Sovereign Ruler of all, and Creator of all, who brought me from Ur of the Chaldees (ancient Mesopotamia) to give me this land to inherit forever, and to establish a kodesh seed—blessed be the Most High forever." (Chaldees; ancient Mesopotamia) **28.** And he blessed Jacob, saying: "My son, in whom I rejoice with all my heart and affection, may Your unmerited favor and mercy rest upon him and his descendants forever." **29.** "Do not forsake him, nor set him aside from now until the end of time. May Your eyes be open upon him and his seed, to preserve him, bless him, and make him kodesh as a nation for Your inheritance. Bless him with all Your blessings from now on, and renew Your covenant and grace with him and his seed, according to Your will, throughout all generations." (Chaldees: ancient region) **30.** "Bless him and consecrate him as a nation for Your inheritance. Bless him with all Your blessings from now and throughout eternity. Renew Your covenant and Your free unmerited favor with him and his descendants, according to Your good will, for all generations of the earth." (Kodesh: holy, sacred; Unmerited favor: grace, undeserved kindness)

Chapter 23
1. Jacob placed two fingers on his grandfather Abraham's eyes, blessed the ALMIGHTY of gods, covered his face, stretched out his feet, and fell into the sleep of eternity, being gathered to his ancestors. **2.** Meanwhile, Jacob lay in Abraham's bosom, unaware of his death. **3.** When Jacob awoke, he found Abraham's body cold and lifeless. He cried out, "Father, father," but there was no response, and he realized Abraham had passed away. **4.** Jacob ran to his mother Rebekah and told her. She went to Isaac, and together with Jacob, they went to Abraham's house. Jacob held a lamp, and when they entered, they found Abraham lying dead. **5.** Isaac fell on his father's face, weeping and kissing him. **6.** The sounds of mourning filled Abraham's house, and Ishmael arose, joined by all the household, to weep for Abraham with great sorrow. **7.** Isaac and Ishmael buried Abraham in the double cave near Sarah, his wife. They mourned for forty days, as did the entire household, including Isaac, Ishmael, their sons, and the sons of Keturah. The mourning for Abraham ended after this period. **8.** Abraham lived three jubilees and four weeks of years—175 years—and completed his days, being full of years. In earlier times, people lived for nineteen jubilees, but after the Flood, lifespans decreased. (Jubilee: a period of 49 years) **9.** The forefathers lived longer lives, but their days became shorter, and their bodies aged quickly, due to the tribulations and the wickedness of their ways, unlike Abraham, who remained faithful to YAHWEH. **10.** Abraham was perfect in all his deeds with YAHWEH, righteous all his life, but he did not complete four jubilees (a jubilee is 49 years), dying after living to a ripe old age because of the wickedness around him. **11.** Future generations, from that time until the great judgment, will grow old quickly before completing two jubilees. Their knowledge will fade as they age, and their understanding will vanish. (Tribulations: hardships, sufferings) **12.** In those days, if someone lives a jubilee and a half, they will be considered long-lived, but their life will be full of pain, sorrow, and tribulation, with no peace. **13.** Calamities will follow one after another: illness, disasters, wars, famine, death, and every form of suffering. (Calamities: disasters, misfortunes) **14.** These troubles will befall an evil generation that transgresses the earth, engaging in uncleanness, fornication, pollution, and abominations. **15.** People will say, "The forefathers lived many good years, even a thousand, but our lives are only seventy or eighty years, filled with evil, with no peace in this wicked generation." **16.** In this generation, children will accuse their fathers and elders of sin, unrighteousness, and forsaking the covenant of YAHWEH, failing to follow His commandments and Torah. (Torah: the law or teachings of YAHWEH **17.** All have done evil, and their words are full of iniquity. Their works are unclean, polluting the earth with their destruction. **18.** The earth will be destroyed because of their deeds. There will be no vine or oil, for their actions are faithless, and all living things will perish due to mankind's wickedness. **19.** People will fight each other—young against old, poor against rich, lowly against great—over the Torah and the covenant, forgetting the commandments, feasts, months, Sabbaths, and jubilees. **20.** They will resort to war to turn back to the way of righteousness, but much blood will be shed before they return. (Feasts: religious celebrations or festivals) **21.** Those who escape will still not return to righteousness but will exalt deceit and wealth, taking everything from their neighbors. They will misuse the great NAME of YAHWEH, defiling the sacred with their impurity. **22.** A great punishment will fall upon this generation. YAHWEH will give them over to the sword, judgment, captivity, and plunder. **23.** He will send the sinners of the Gentiles against them—merciless, cruel people who will show no respect for the old or young, more wicked and powerful than anyone, and they will oppress Israel, shedding much blood. (Gentiles: non-Jews, people of other nations) **24.** In those days, people will cry out, praying to be saved from the Gentiles' hands, but none will be saved. **25.** The heads of children will be white with gray hair, and even a child of three weeks will seem as old as a man of one hundred. Their stature will be diminished by suffering. **26.** In those days, children will begin to study the laws and seek the commandments, returning to the path of righteousness. (Stature: height, size) **27.** The days will increase, and people will live closer to a thousand years. Their lifespan will extend beyond what it was before. **28.** There will be no old man or one who is dissatisfied with his days. All will be as children and youths, completing their days in peace and joy, with no Satan or evil destroyer among them. **29.** All their days will be full of blessing and healing, and there will be no more evil or suffering. (Satan: adversary, evil spirit) **30.** At that time, YAHWEH will heal His servants. They will rise in great peace, driving out their enemies. The righteous will rejoice and give thanks forever, seeing all their judgments and curses fall upon their enemies. (Healing: restoration, curing) **31.** Their bones will rest in the earth, and their spirits will rejoice, knowing that it is YAHWEH who executes judgment and shows mercy to all who love Him. **32.** "Write these words down, Moses," YAHWEH said, "for they are recorded on the heavenly tablets as a testimony for all generations to come." (Tablets: stone or clay records, often symbolic of divine laws)

Chapter 24
1. After the death of Abraham, YAHWEH blessed Isaac, his son. Isaac left Hebron and settled at the Well of Vision in the first year of the third week [2073 A.M.], staying there for seven years. (Well of Vision: a place associated with spiritual revelations) **2.** In the first year of the fourth week, a famine began in the land [2080 A.M.], which was in addition to the earlier famine that had occurred during Abraham's time. (Famine: a severe shortage of food) **3.** Jacob cooked lentil stew, and Esau came in from the field, famished. Esau said to Jacob, "Let me have some of that red stew." Jacob replied, "First, sell me your birthright, and I'll give you bread and some of the stew." (Lentil stew: a dish made from lentils, a type of legume) **4.** Esau thought to himself, "I am about to die; what good is my birthright to me?" (Birthright: the inheritance and privileges given to the firstborn son) **5.** Esau said to Jacob, "I agree, I will give it to you." Jacob insisted, "Swear to me today." And Esau swore to him, sealing the agreement. (Swear: to make a solemn promise) **6.** Jacob gave Esau bread and lentil stew, and Esau ate until he was satisfied. In doing so, Esau despised his birthright. This is why Esau was called Edom, meaning "red," after the red stew that he traded his birthright for. (Edom: the name Esau received, meaning "red," referencing the stew) **7.** As a result, Jacob became the rightful heir, and Esau lost his status and position of honor. **8.** When the famine ended, Isaac prepared to go to Egypt in the second year of the fourth week. He planned to visit the king of the Philistines, Abimelech, in Gerar. (Gerar: a city in the land of the Philistines) **9.** YAHWEH appeared to Isaac and instructed him, "Do not go to Egypt. Stay in the land I will show you, and sojourn here. I will be with you and bless you." (Sojourn: to stay temporarily in a place) **10.** "I will give you and your descendants all this land. I will keep the oath I swore to your father Abraham, and I will multiply your

descendants like the stars of the sky, giving them all this land." (Descendants: offspring, children, and future generations) **11.** "In your descendants, all the nations of the earth will be blessed, because your father Abraham obeyed My voice and kept My commandments, laws, and statutes. Now obey My voice and live in this land." (Statutes: regulations or decrees; Commandments: divine directives) **12.** Isaac lived in Gerar for three weeks of years. **13.** Abimelech, the king of the Philistines, gave strict orders regarding Isaac and all his possessions, saying, "Anyone who touches Isaac or anything of his shall surely die." (Philistines: an ancient people who lived in the coastal region of the ancient Near East) **14.** Isaac became very wealthy among the Philistines, acquiring many cattle, camels, sheep, and donkeys, as well as a large household. **15.** Isaac sowed crops in the land, and the harvest was plentiful, producing a hundredfold. As a result, Isaac became exceedingly prosperous, which led to the Philistines becoming envious of him. **16.** The Philistines had filled in all the wells that Abraham's servants had dug during Abraham's lifetime after his death, covering them with dirt. **17.** Abimelech told Isaac, "Leave us, for you have become more powerful than we are." Isaac moved out in the first year of the seventh week and settled in the valleys of Gerar. **18.** Isaac's servants dug again the wells that Abraham's servants had dug, and which the Philistines had stopped up after Abraham's death. Isaac renamed the wells after the names his father had given them. **19.** Isaac's servants dug a well in the valley and found fresh water. However, the shepherds of Gerar quarreled with Isaac's shepherds, claiming the water belonged to them. Isaac named the well "Esek," meaning "contention," because of the dispute. (Esek: meaning "contention" or "dispute") **20.** Isaac's servants dug another well, but again there was a quarrel over it. He named this well "Sitnah," which means "enmity." They then dug yet another well, and this time there was no dispute. Isaac named it "Rehoboth," meaning "room," saying, "Now YAHWEH has made room for us, and we shall be fruitful in the land." (Sitnah: meaning "enmity" or hostility; Rehoboth: meaning "broad places" or "room" for expansion) **21.** Isaac then moved to the "Well of the Oath" in the first year of the first week of the forty-fourth jubilee [2108 A.M.]. (Well of the Oath: a place where Isaac swore an oath with Abimelech) **22.** That night, YAHWEH appeared to Isaac and said, "I am YAHWEH, the ALMIGHTY of your father Abraham. Do not be afraid, for I am with you. I will bless you and multiply your descendants like the sand on the seashore for the sake of My servant Abraham." (ALMIGHTY: the all-powerful, supreme God) **23.** Isaac built an altar there, just as his father Abraham had done, and he called upon the NAME of YAHWEH. He offered sacrifices to the ALMIGHTY of Abraham. (NAME: the sacred title of God) **24.** Isaac's servants dug a well there and found fresh water. **25.** Isaac's servants dug another well but did not find water. When they reported this to Isaac, he said, "I have already sworn to the Philistines, and this has been made known to us." **26.** Isaac named the place "The Well of the Oath," because there he had sworn an oath to Abimelech, Ahuzzath, and Phicol, the commander of his army. (Phicol: a military leader of the Philistines) **27.** Isaac realized that he had made the oath under pressure to ensure peace with the Philistines. **28.** Isaac then cursed the Philistines, saying, "Cursed be the Philistines until the day of judgment. May YAHWEH make them an object of reproach, and may they be destroyed by the hands of the nations." (Wrath: intense anger, especially divine anger) **29.** "Whoever survives the sword of the enemy will be judged and rooted out by the righteous nations. The Philistines will remain enemies of my descendants for all generations." **30.** "No remnant will be left, nor anyone to be spared on the day of judgment. The Philistines' seed will be utterly destroyed, and their name and descendants will disappear from the earth." **31.** "Though they rise to heaven, they will be brought down. Though they become strong on the earth, they will be dragged down. Though they hide among the nations, they will be uprooted. Even in Sheol, they will find no peace." (Sheol: the realm of the dead, or the grave) **32.** "If they are captured, those who pursue them will slay them along the way. No name or descendants will remain for them on earth, for they will depart under an eternal curse." (Captivity: the state of being captured or enslaved) **33.** This is what is written and engraved about them on the heavenly tablets, to be executed against them on the Day of Judgment, to root them out from the earth. (Heavenly tablets: divine records or decrees written in

Chapter 25

1. In the second year of this week of the jubilee, Rebecca called her son Jacob and spoke to him, saying, "My son, do not marry a Canaanite woman, as your brother Esau did. He took two wives from the daughters of Canaan, and they have caused me great sorrow because of their wicked deeds. All their actions are full of fornication and lust, and they are far from righteousness." (Fornication: sexual relations outside of marriage; Lust: intense, often immoral desire) **2.** "My son, I love you deeply, and my heart blesses you continually, both day and night, with all my affection." **3.** "Now, my son, listen to my voice and follow the path I recommend. Do not marry a woman from this land, but choose one from the family of my father, from my own kin. If you marry from my father's house, the Most High YAHWEH will bless you, and your descendants will be a righteous generation, a holy seed." (Kodesh: holy or sacred) **4.** Jacob responded to his mother, saying, "Mother, I am only nine weeks old, and I have neither known a woman nor made any engagement to marry. I have not even considered marrying a Canaanite woman." **5.** "I remember what our father Abraham commanded me: not to marry a Canaanite, but to take a wife from the seed of my father's family, from among my kin. **6.** "I have heard that Laban, your brother, has daughters, and I have set my heart on one of them to be my wife." **7.** "For this reason, I have kept myself pure in spirit, guarding against sin and corruption in all my ways. Abraham, our father, gave me many instructions regarding lust and fornication." **8.** "Despite his commandments, my brother Esau has tried for twenty-two years to convince me to marry one of his two wives, but I refused to follow his example." **9.** "I swear to you, mother, that I will never marry a woman from the seed of Canaan, and I will not act wickedly as my brother has done." **10.** "Do not fear, mother; rest assured, I will follow your wishes and walk in righteousness, never corrupting my ways." **11.** At that moment, Rebecca lifted her eyes to heaven, raised her hands, and praised the Most High YAHWEH, who created the heavens and the earth. She thanked Him and gave Him glory. **12.** She said, "Blessed be YAHWEH, the Almighty, and may His holy Name be praised forever, for He has given me Jacob as a pure son and a holy seed. He belongs to You, and his descendants will remain Yours forever, throughout all generations." (Holy Name: the sacred and revered name of YAHWEH) **13.** "Bless him, O YAHWEH, and may the blessing of righteousness be upon my lips so that I may bless him." **14.** As the spirit of righteousness descended into her mouth, Rebecca placed both hands on Jacob's head and said, **15.** "Blessed are You, YAHWEH of righteousness, Sovereign Ruler of all ages. May You bless Jacob above all generations of men. May You guide him in the path of righteousness and reveal righteousness to his descendants." **16.** "May You make his sons numerous in his lifetime, and may they increase according to the number of the months of the year. May their children become countless, as numerous as the stars in the heavens, and their numbers greater than the sands of the sea." (Righteousness: moral purity, justice) **17.** "May You give them this land as You promised to give it to Abraham and his descendants, and may they possess it forever." **18.** "May I see blessed children born to you, my son, during my lifetime. May your seed be holy and blessed in all generations." **19.** "As you have refreshed my spirit with your obedience, the womb that bore you and the affection of your mother bless you. My heart, my breasts, my mouth, and my tongue praise you greatly." **20.** "May you grow and spread across the earth, and may your seed be perfected in the joy of both heaven and earth forever. May your descendants rejoice, and may they find peace on the great Day of Shalom." (Shalom: peace, completeness, wholeness) **21.** "May your name and your descendants endure for all ages. May the Most High YAHWEH be their Sovereign, and may the Almighty of righteousness dwell among them. May His sanctuary be established by them for all generations." **22.** "Blessed is anyone who blesses you, and cursed is anyone who falsely curses you." **23.** Rebecca kissed Jacob and said to him, "May YAHWEH of the world love you as deeply as I do, and may my affection for you be a source of blessing in your life." Then she ceased from her blessings.

Chapter 26

1. In the seventh year of this week, Isaac called his elder son Esau and said, "I am old, my son, my eyes are dim, and I don't know the day of my death." **2.** "Now take your hunting weapons, your quiver, and your bow. Go out to the field, hunt, and prepare me savory meat that I love, and bring it to me so that I may eat and bless you before I die." (Savory: Tasty, flavorful) **3.** But Rebekah overheard Isaac speaking to Esau. **4.** Esau went out early to hunt in the field. **5.** Rebekah called Jacob, her son, and said, "I heard your father speak to Esau, saying, 'Hunt for me and prepare me savory meat, and bring it so that I may eat and bless you before I die.'" **6.** "Now, my son, listen to me: go to your flock and bring me two good goats, and I will make savory meat for your father, as he loves, and you shall bring it to him that he may bless you before he dies." (Savory: Tasty, flavorful) **7.** Jacob replied, "Mother, I fear that he will recognize my voice and touch me. You know that I am smooth, but Esau is hairy. If I deceive him, he will be angry and curse me instead of blessing me." (Deceive: Mislead, trick) **8.** Rebekah said, "Let your curse be on me, my son. Just obey me." **9.** Jacob obeyed, brought the goats, and Rebekah prepared the meat as Isaac liked. **10.** Rebekah took Esau's good clothes and dressed Jacob in them, and put the goats' skins on his hands and neck. **11.** She gave Jacob the meat and bread to take to Isaac. **12.** Jacob went to Isaac and said, "I am your son; I have done as you asked. Please eat and bless me." **13.** Isaac asked, "How did you find it so quickly?" **14.** Jacob answered, "Because the

LORD your God led me to it." **15.** Isaac said, "Come closer so I can feel you and see if you are really Esau." **16.** Jacob approached, and Isaac felt him, saying, "The voice is Jacob's, but the hands are Esau's." Isaac could not recognize him because it was God's will to prevent him from discerning the truth. **17.** Isaac asked, "Are you really Esau?" Jacob replied, "I am." **18.** Isaac said, "Bring it to me so that I may eat and bless you." **19.** Jacob served him the food and wine. **20.** Isaac then said, "Come, kiss me, my son." **21.** Jacob kissed him, and Isaac smelled his clothes. "The scent of my son is like a field the LORD has blessed," he said. **22.** "May the LORD give you the dew of heaven, abundance from the earth, and plenty of grain and oil. Let nations serve you and peoples bow down to you." **23.** "Be ruler over your brothers, and may your mother's sons bow down to you. May all the blessings of Abraham be upon you and your descendants forever. Cursed be those who curse you, and blessed be those who bless you." **24.** As soon as Jacob left, Esau returned from hunting. **25.** Esau prepared savory meat and brought it to his father, saying, "Father, rise and eat so that you may bless me." (Savory: Tasty, flavorful) **26.** Isaac asked, "Who are you?" Esau replied, "I am Esau, your firstborn, and I have done as you commanded." **27.** Isaac was greatly surprised and said, "Who then hunted and brought me food before you came? I have already eaten and blessed him, and he shall be blessed." **28.** When Esau heard this, he cried out loudly and bitterly, "Bless me, too, Father." **29.** Isaac replied, "Your brother came with deceit and took your blessing." (Deceit: Dishonesty or trickery used to gain something) **30.** Esau said, "No wonder his name is Jacob; he has deceived me twice. First, he took my birthright, and now he has taken my blessing." **31.** Esau asked, "Don't you have a blessing for me?" Isaac answered, "I have made him your ruler and given him all your brothers as servants. I have blessed him with plenty of grain, wine, and oil. What can I do for you, my son?" **32.** Esau pleaded, "Is there only one blessing, Father? Bless me too!" **33.** Esau wept loudly. Isaac said, "You will live far from the earth's dew, and far from the heaven's dew. You will live by your sword, and you will serve your brother. But when you grow strong, you will break his yoke from your neck." (Yoke: A wooden frame joining two animals, symbolizing control or burden) **34.** Isaac warned, "You will sin greatly and your descendants will be wiped out from the earth." (Sin: A moral wrong or offense) **35.** Esau harbored anger toward Jacob because of the blessing and said to himself, "When my father dies, I will kill my brother Jacob."

Chapter 27

1. Rebecca was warned in a dream about the words of Esau, her elder son. She called Yacob, her younger son, and said to him, **2.** "Your brother Esau plans to take revenge and kill you." **3.** Rebecca continued, "Obey me, my son. Get up and flee to Haran, to my brother Laban. Stay there for a few days until Esau's anger cools down and he forgets what you have done. Then I will send for you and bring you back." **4.** Yacob replied, "I am not afraid. If he tries to kill me, I will kill him. **5.** Rebecca said, "Do not let me be bereft of both my sons on the same day." (Bereft: deprived of or lacking something.) **6.** Yacob explained, "You know Father is old and his eyesight is failing. If I leave him, he will be upset and may curse me. I will only leave if he sends me." **7.** Rebecca said, "I will speak to him, and he will send you away." **8.** She approached Yitschaq and said, "I am greatly troubled because of Esau's wives, the daughters of Heth. If Yacob also marries a woman from this land, like these, what is the purpose of my life? The daughters of Canaan are wicked." **9.** Yitschaq called Yacob, blessed him, and gave him instructions. **10.** He said, "Do not marry a woman from the daughters of Canaan. Instead, go to Mesopotamia, to the house of Bethuel, your mother's father, and marry one of Laban's daughters." (Mesopotamia: an ancient region between the Tigris and Euphrates rivers.) **11.** Yitschaq prayed, "May YAHWEH bless you, multiply your descendants, and make you a great nation. May He grant you the blessings of Abraham so that you and your offspring inherit this land of promise." **12.** Yitschaq sent Yacob to Mesopotamia, to Laban, the son of Bethuel the Syrian and brother of Rebecca, Yacob's mother. **13.** After Yacob left, Rebecca was deeply sorrowful for her son and wept. **14.** Yitschaq comforted her, saying, "Do not weep for Yacob. He leaves in peace and will return in peace." **15.** He reassured her, "The Most High YAHWEH will protect him from all harm and will remain with him always." **16.** Yitschaq continued, "I am confident that Yacob will prosper in all his ways until he returns safely to us." **17.** "Do not fear for him, my sister. He walks in righteousness, is faithful, and will not perish." **18.** With these words, Yitschaq comforted Rebecca and blessed Yacob. **19.** Yacob left the "Well of the Oath" to travel to Haran during the first year of the second week in the forty-fourth jubilee. He reached Luz, later named Bethel, at the beginning of the first month, [2115 A.M.]. **20.** At evening, he stopped west of the road, took a stone for his pillow, and slept under a tree. (Jubilee: a 50-year period used in biblical timekeeping.) **21.** That night, Yacob dreamed of a ladder that extended from the earth to heaven. Malakim (angels) of YAHWEH were ascending and descending on it, and YAHWEH stood at the top. **22.** YAHWEH spoke, "I am YAHWEH ALMIGHTY, the ALMIGHTY of Abraham and Yitschaq. The land where you sleep will belong to you and your descendants." **23.** "Your descendants will be as numerous as the dust of the earth, spreading to the west, east, north, and south. Through you and your offspring, all the families of the earth will be blessed." **24.** "I will be with you, protect you wherever you go, and bring you back to this land in peace. I will not leave you until I fulfill my promises to you." **25.** Yacob awoke, saying, "This place is truly the house of YAHWEH, and I did not know it." Filled with awe, he declared, "This is none other than the gate of heaven." (Dreadful: inspiring awe or reverence.) **26.** Yacob rose early in the morning, took the stone he had used as a pillow, set it up as a pillar, and poured oil over it. He named the place Bethel, though it had previously been called Luz. **27.** He vowed to YAHWEH, saying, "If YAHWEH protects me, gives me food and clothing, and brings me back safely to my father's house, then He will be my Sovereign Ruler. This stone will mark His house, and I will dedicate a tenth of all He gives me back to Him."

Chapter 28

1. Jacob journeyed onward and arrived in the land of the East, where Laban, his uncle, lived. Jacob stayed with Laban and worked for him for seven years in exchange for his daughter Rachel's hand in marriage. **2.** After the first year of the third week [2122 A.M.], Jacob approached Laban and said, "Give me my wife, for I have fulfilled the seven years of service for her." Laban replied, "I will give you your wife." **3.** Laban then prepared a feast, but instead of Rachel, he gave his elder daughter Leah to Jacob as a wife. He also gave her maidservant, Zilpah, to Jacob. Jacob, unaware, believed Leah was Rachel. **4.** After the wedding night, Jacob discovered that it was Leah, not Rachel, and became angry with Laban. He confronted him, saying, "Why have you done this to me? I worked seven years for Rachel, not Leah. Why have you deceived me?" **5.** Jacob said, "Take your daughter back, and I will leave, for you have done wrong." Jacob loved Rachel more than Leah. Leah's eyes were weak, while Rachel had beautiful eyes and a more graceful form. **6.** Laban answered, "In our land, we cannot marry off the younger daughter before the older. This is a custom that is set in the heavenly books: the elder must be married first. If anyone goes against this rule, they will be held guilty before YAHWEH." **7.** "Tell the children of Israel not to follow this practice—do not give the younger daughter before the elder, for it is a grievous sin." (Grievous sin: A very serious offense, one that brings great disfavor in the sight of YAHWEH.) **8.** Laban then told Jacob, "Let the week-long celebration of Leah's marriage pass, and I will give you Rachel. But you must serve me another seven years." **9.** When the week of Leah's wedding was completed, Laban gave Rachel to Jacob, and Jacob agreed to serve him another seven years as they had arranged. Laban also gave Rachel her maidservant, Bilhah, to assist her. **10.** Thus, Jacob served an additional seven years for Rachel, while Leah was given to him without any further payment. **11.** YAHWEH, seeing that Leah was unloved, opened her womb. She bore Jacob a son, whom she named Reuben, on the fourteenth day of the ninth month, in the first year of the third week [2122 A.M.]. **12.** Meanwhile, Rachel remained barren, as YAHWEH had closed her womb, seeing that Leah was despised while Rachel was loved. (Barren: Unable to conceive or bear children.) **13.** Leah conceived again and bore Jacob a second son, whom she named Simeon, on the twenty-first day of the tenth month, in the third year of that week [2124 A.M.]. **14.** Leah bore Jacob a third son, Levi, in the first month of the new year, the sixth year of that week [2127 A.M.]. **15.** Leah bore a fourth son, whom she named Judah, on the fifteenth day of the third month, in the first year of the fourth week [2129 A.M.]. **16.** Because Leah had borne four sons, Rachel grew jealous of her. She demanded of Jacob, "Give me children, or I will die!" **17.** Jacob replied, "Have I denied you the ability to bear children? Have I forsaken you?" **18.** Rachel, seeing Leah had already had four sons, gave her maidservant Bilhah to Jacob, saying, "Let her bear children on my behalf." **19.** Jacob went in to Bilhah, and she conceived and bore a son. Rachel named him Dan, on the ninth day of the sixth month, in the sixth year of the third week [2127 A.M.]. **20.** When Leah saw that she had stopped bearing children, she became envious of Rachel. She gave her maidservant, Zilpah, to Jacob as a wife, and Zilpah conceived and bore a son. Leah named him Gad, on the twelfth day of the eighth month, in the third year of the fourth week [2131 A.M.] (Maidservant; A woman servant). **21.** Zilpah bore Jacob a second son, whom Leah named Asher, on the second day of the eleventh month, in the fifth year of the fourth week [2133 A.M.]. **22.** Leah then conceived again and bore Jacob a son, whom she named Issachar, on the fourth day of the fifth month, in the fourth year of the fourth week [2132 A.M.]. She entrusted the child to a nurse. **23.** Leah bore Jacob another child—this time a son and a daughter. She named the son Zebulon and the daughter Dinah, on the seventh day of the seventh month, in the sixth year of the fourth week [2134 A.M.]. **24.** YAHWEH finally remembered Rachel and opened her womb. She bore a son, whom she named Joseph, on the new moon of the fourth month, in the sixth year of the fourth week [2134 A.M.]. **25.** When Joseph was born, Jacob said to Laban, "Give me my wives and children, so that I may return to my father Isaac and establish my own household. I have completed the years of service I owed you for your two daughters." **26.** Laban said to Jacob, "Stay with me a little longer. Let me continue paying you for your work by tending my flocks." **27.** They agreed that Jacob would be paid with the lambs and kids born with unique markings: black, spotted, or speckled. These would be Jacob's wages. **28.** Jacob's flock flourished, and many of his sheep were born with the agreed-upon markings. The offspring of these marked sheep resembled their parents, and Jacob's flock grew larger while Laban's remained smaller. **29.** Jacob became very wealthy, owning oxen, sheep, donkeys, camels, and servants. **30.** However, Laban and his sons grew envious of Jacob's success. Laban took back his sheep and began to treat Jacob with hostility, seeking ways to harm him.

Chapter 29

1. After Rachel bore Joseph, Laban went to shear his sheep, which were a three-day journey away. **2.** Jacob saw that Laban was going to shear his sheep, so he called Leah and Rachel to speak kindly to them, telling them to come with him to the land of Canaan. **3.** He explained how he had seen in a dream all that YAHWEH had spoken to him about returning to his father's house. They said, "Wherever you go, we will go with you." **4.** Jacob blessed YAHWEH, the Almighty of Isaac his father, and the Almighty of Abraham his grandfather. He gathered his wives, children, and possessions, crossed the river, and came to the land of Gilead, keeping his intentions hidden from Laban. **5.** In the seventh year of the fourth week [2135 A.M.], Jacob began his journey toward Gilead on the twenty-first day of the first month. Laban pursued and overtook him in the mountains of Gilead on the thirteenth day of the third month. **6.** YAHWEH did not allow Laban to harm Jacob. That night, YAHWEH appeared to Laban in a dream, warning him not to harm Jacob. **7.** Laban spoke to Jacob, and on the fifteenth day of that month, Jacob made a feast for Laban and those who came with him. They swore an oath to not cross the mountain of Gilead with harmful intent. **8.** Jacob set up a heap of stones as a witness to their agreement, and the place was named "The Heap of Witness." **9.** Previously, Gilead was called the land of the Rephaim, a race of giants whose height ranged from seven to ten cubits. (Rephaim: giants; cubits: units of measurement, roughly 18 inches or 45 cm) **10.** Their lands stretched from the children of Ammon to Mount Hermon. Their cities were Karnaim, Ashtaroth, Edrei, Misur, and Beon. (Karnaim, Ashtaroth, Edrei, Misur, Beon: ancient cities of the Rephaim kingdom) **11.** YAHWEH destroyed the Rephaim because of their wickedness. The Amorites replaced them, also a sinful people, and their lifespan was shortened. **12.** Jacob sent Laban away, and he returned to Mesopotamia, while Jacob stayed in Gilead. **13.** Jacob crossed the Jabbok River in the ninth month on the eleventh day. On that day, Esau came to meet him, and they reconciled. Esau left for Seir, while Jacob stayed in tents. (Jabbok: a river; Seir: the mountainous region where Esau settled) **14.** In the first year of the fifth week of this jubilee [2136 A.M.], Jacob crossed the Jordan and settled beyond it, pasturing his flocks from the Sea of the Heap to Bethshan, Dothan, and the Forest of Akrabbim. (Sea of the Heap, Dothan, Forest of Akrabbim: locations where Jacob pastured his flocks) **15.** Jacob sent provisions to his father Isaac, including clothing, food, drink, milk, butter, cheese, and dates from the valley. **16.** He also sent provisions to his mother Rebecca four times a year, during the intervals between planting and harvesting, autumn and the rainy season, and winter and spring, to the tower of Abraham. (Provisions: supplies; intervals: periods between events) **17.** Isaac had returned from the 'Well of the Oath' and moved to the tower of Abraham, where he lived apart from Esau. (Well of the Oath: a location where Abraham swore an oath to Abimelech) **18.** During Jacob's time in Mesopotamia, Esau took Mahalath, the daughter of Ishmael, as his wife. Esau gathered his flocks and moved to Mount Seir, leaving Isaac alone at the 'Well of the Oath.' **19.** Isaac left the 'Well of the Oath' and dwelt in the tower of Abraham on the mountains of Hebron. (Mountains of Hebron: the mountainous region in Canaan, where Abraham and Isaac lived) **20.** Jacob continued to send provisions to his father and mother, who blessed him with all their hearts and souls.

Chapter 30

1. In the first year of the sixth week (2143 A.M.), he went up to Salem, located east of Shechem, in peace during the fourth month. **2.** At that time, Dinah, the daughter of Jacob, was taken into the house of Shechem, son of Hamor, the Hivite prince of the land. Shechem lay with her and defiled her; Dinah was still a young girl, only twelve years old. **3.** Shechem asked his father and Dinah's brothers to arrange for her to become his wife. However, Jacob and his sons were angered because Shechem had defiled their sister. They spoke deceitfully with him and his people, hiding their true intent. (Deceitfully: in a way intended to mislead or deceive.) **4.** Simeon and Levi, Dinah's brothers, went to Shechem unexpectedly and executed judgment by killing all the men they found there. They left no one alive and inflicted great suffering upon them as punishment for dishonoring their sister. **5.** It was ordained in heaven that such defilement of a daughter of Israel would not go unpunished. Judgment required that those responsible be destroyed by the sword to ensure such acts would not occur again. **6.** YAHWEH delivered the men of Shechem into the hands of Jacob's sons so they could execute divine judgment. This established that the daughters of Israel should never be defiled. **7.** Any man in Israel who gives his daughter or sister to a man of the Gentiles will be put to death by stoning because he has brought shame upon Israel. Likewise, the woman involved shall be burned with fire for dishonoring her father's household. (Gentiles: people who are not part of the nation of Israel.) **8.** No adulterer or act of uncleanness should ever be found in Israel. The man who defiles Israel in such a way must be stoned to death as commanded. **9.** This law has no expiration or atonement. Any man who defiles his daughter by giving her to another nation has committed an unpardonable sin and must be rooted out from Israel. **10.** A man who sacrifices his offspring to Moloch (a pagan god) defiles his seed and acts wickedly, and he must be removed from Israel. **11.** Mosheh was instructed to command the children of Israel not to give their daughters to Gentiles or to take Gentile daughters for their sons, as this is detestable to YAHWEH. **12.** The Torah details the deeds of the Shechemites and their defilement of Dinah, emphasizing how Jacob's sons refused to give their sister to an uncircumcised man, seeing it as a disgrace. (Uncircumcised: someone not part of the Abrahamic covenant.) **13.** It is a reproach for Israel to intermarry with Gentiles, as such actions bring impurity and abomination upon the nation. **14.** Israel cannot remain pure if its sons marry Gentile women or its daughters are given to Gentile men. This would bring plagues and curses upon the nation. **15.** Every act of uncleanness or failure to judge those who desecrate the sanctuary of YAHWEH or profane His holy name will bring divine judgment on the entire community. (Profane: to treat something sacred with disrespect.) **16.** Those who commit such sins will not be spared judgment, and their offerings and sacrifices will not be accepted by YAHWEH. **17.** This testimony serves as a warning to Israel, reminding them of the Shechemites' destruction, which was counted as righteousness for Levi and Simeon. **18.** Levi's descendants were chosen for the priesthood because of his zeal in carrying out justice and vengeance for Israel. **19.** Levi's actions were recorded as righteousness on the heavenly tablets, earning blessings for him and his offspring for generations to come. **20.** The righteousness Levi displayed is remembered for a thousand generations, inscribed in heaven as a testament to his faithfulness. **21.** This account was written to instruct Israel to remain obedient to the covenant and avoid sin so they might be recorded as friends of YAHWEH. **22.** Those who break the covenant or commit uncleanness will be recorded as adversaries and erased from the book of life, listed among those destined for destruction. (Adversaries: enemies or opponents.) **23.** The day Simeon and Levi executed judgment on Shechem was recorded in heaven as a righteous act. **24.** They brought their sister Dinah out of Shechem's house and took all the wealth, livestock, and possessions of the city back to Jacob. **25.** Jacob reproached his sons for their actions, fearing retaliation from the neighboring Canaanites and Perizzites. (Reproached: expressed disapproval.) **26.** However, the fear of YAHWEH fell upon the surrounding cities, and they did not pursue Jacob's sons because divine terror had overtaken them.

Chapter 31

1. On the first day of the new month, Jacob gathered all the members of his household and said to them, "Purify yourselves, change your clothes, and let us go up to Bethel. There, I made a vow to the LORD when I fled from my brother Esau. He has been with me and brought me here safely, so let's remove the foreign gods that are among us." **2.** The people removed the foreign gods and the items of idolatry—those in their ears and around their necks. Rachel had stolen her father Laban's idols and handed them all over to Jacob. He burned them, shattered them into pieces, and hid them beneath an oak tree near Shechem. (Idolatry: the worship of false gods) **3.** Jacob then journeyed to Bethel in the seventh month, on the new moon, where he built an altar at the site where he had rested before. He also set up a stone pillar there and sent word to his father Isaac to come and join him for the sacrifice, as well as to his mother Rebecca. (Altar: a place for offering sacrifices) **4.** Isaac responded, "Let my son Jacob come and visit me before I die." (Visit: come to see) **5.** Jacob went to Isaac and Rebecca, taking with him his sons Levi and Judah. He arrived at Isaac's house, the dwelling place of his father Abraham. (Levi and Judah: Jacob's sons, from whom the priestly and royal tribes would descend) **6.** Rebecca, upon hearing that Jacob had arrived, came out of the tower, approached him, kissed him, and embraced him. Her spirit was revived when she learned her son had come home. (Tower: a structure, likely a place of residence or observation; spirit revived: filled with joy and life) **7.** As Rebecca saw Levi and Judah, she recognized them as her grandsons. She embraced and kissed them, blessing them with the words, "In you, the descendants of Abraham will become great, and through you, the earth will be blessed." (Descendants of Abraham: the lineage of Abraham; earth will be blessed: you will bring prosperity and favor to the world) **8.** Jacob went to Isaac in his chamber, where his father lay, with Levi and Judah by his side. He took Isaac's hand, bent down, and kissed him. Isaac wept as he embraced his son, Jacob, and wept upon his neck. (Chamber: a private room or space; bent down: lowered himself to show respect) **9.** The darkness lifted from Isaac's eyes, and he saw Levi and Judah. He asked Jacob, "Are these truly your sons, my son? They resemble you." (Darkness lifted: his sight or awareness returned) **10.** Jacob confirmed, saying, "Yes, these are indeed my sons." (Confirmed: assured Isaac that they were indeed his sons) **11.** Isaac then embraced and kissed both Levi and Judah, blessing them both. (Embraced: showed affection and closeness) **12.** As the spirit of prophecy came upon Isaac, he placed Levi at his right side and Judah at his left. (Spirit of prophecy: divine inspiration to speak the will of God) **13.** Isaac first turned to Levi and began to bless him, saying, "May the Almighty God of all bless you and your descendants for all generations." (Almighty God: a title for God; descendants: your children and future generations) **14.** "May the LORD grant you and your seed greatness and honor, and may you and your descendants be chosen to approach Him and serve in His holy sanctuary, like the angels who stand before Him. May your descendants be great and holy for all generations." (Seed: offspring or descendants; sanctuary: the sacred place where God is worshiped; holy: set apart for God's service) **15.** "Your descendants will be judges, leaders, and rulers over the people of Jacob. They will speak the word of the LORD in righteousness, and they will teach His commandments. They will bring blessings to all the descendants of the beloved." (Rulers: leaders or officials; righteousness) **16.** "Your mother named you Levi, and it was fitting. You will be joined to the LORD and become a companion to all the sons of Jacob. Let the LORD's table be yours, and may you and your descendants partake of it forever. Let your table always be full, and may your provision never fail." (Fitting: appropriate or just) **17.** "All who oppose you will fall before you, and all your enemies will be destroyed. Blessed is anyone who blesses you, and cursed is anyone who curses you." (Oppose: resist or fight against) **18.** Turning to Judah, Isaac said: "May the LORD give you strength to overcome all who hate you. You will be a leader among the sons of Jacob, and your name and the names of your descendants will be known across the earth." (Strength: power and resilience) **19.** "The Gentiles will tremble before you, and all the nations will be afraid. In you, Jacob will find his help, and through you, Israel will be saved." **20.** "When you sit on the throne of justice, bringing peace to all of Israel, you will bring blessings to all the descendants of the beloved. Blessed are those who bless you, and cursed are those who hate or harm you." **21.** Isaac kissed Judah once more, embracing him and rejoicing because he had seen Jacob's sons and confirmed their true identity. (Rejoicing: feeling great happiness and satisfaction) **22.** Isaac rose from between his feet, bowed down before Jacob, and blessed Levi and Judah. They stayed the night with Isaac, eating and drinking with joy. **23.** Jacob made sure his two sons slept, one on his right side and the other on his left. This act was counted to him as righteousness. (Counted as righteousness: regarded as a good or virtuous act) **24.** Jacob shared with Isaac all that had happened, recounting how the LORD had been merciful to him, prospered him, and protected him from harm. **25.** Isaac praised the LORD, the Almighty of his father Abraham, for not withdrawing His mercy and righteousness from Isaac's descendants. (Withdrawing: taking away or holding back) **26.** The next morning, Jacob reminded Isaac of the vow he had made to the LORD, explaining the vision he had seen and how he had prepared for the sacrifice at Bethel, as he had promised. (Vow: solemn promise or pledge) **27.** Isaac, now old, told Jacob, "I cannot accompany you on your journey, for I am too old. Go in peace, my son. I am 165 years old today and can no longer travel. Take your mother with you instead." **28.** Isaac continued, "I know you have come for my sake, and I am blessed to see you alive. May you fulfill the vow you made, and may the LORD who made all things be pleased with your offering." **29.** Isaac said to Rebecca, "Go with Jacob, your son." So, Rebecca, along with her servant Deborah, accompanied Jacob to Bethel. **30.** Jacob reflected on the prayer his father Isaac had prayed over him and his sons, Levi and Judah, and he thanked the LORD, the Almighty of his fathers, Abraham and Isaac. (Reflected: thought deeply) **31.** Jacob rejoiced, saying, "Now I know that I have a secure and eternal hope, and my sons share that hope before the Almighty of all." This was decreed concerning them, and it was recorded on the heavenly tablets as an eternal testimony. **32.** Jacob declared, "Now I am certain that I have an everlasting hope, and that my sons share this hope before the Almighty. This is the decree for them, and it is written as an eternal record in the heavenly tablets, testifying to the blessing that Isaac gave them." (Everlasting hope: a hope that endures forever)

Chapter 32

1. That night, Jacob stayed at Bethel, and Levi had a dream where he was chosen as the priest of the Most High YAHWEH, along with his descendants forever. He awoke and blessed YAHWEH. **2.** Early the next morning, on the fourteenth of the month, Jacob gave a tithe of everything he had, including men, cattle, gold, and all his possessions. **3.** At that time, Rachel became pregnant with her son, Benjamin. Jacob counted his sons, and Levi was given the portion of YAHWEH. His father clothed him with priestly garments. **4.** On the fifteenth of the month, Jacob offered fourteen oxen, twenty-eight rams, forty-nine sheep, seven lambs, and twenty-one goats as burnt offerings on the altar. (Burnt offering: total dedication) **5.** These offerings were part of a vow Jacob made to give a tenth, with fruit and drink offerings as well. (Vow: solemn promise) **6.** After the burnt offerings, Jacob placed incense on the fire and made a thank offering: two oxen, four rams, four sheep, four he-goats, two yearling sheep, and two kids. This was done daily for seven days. (Incense: prayer symbol) **7.** Jacob and his sons, along with their men, joyfully ate together for seven days, blessing and thanking YAHWEH for delivering him from his troubles and fulfilling his vow. **8.** Jacob tithed all the clean animals, making burnt offerings, but he did not give unclean animals to Levi. Instead, he gave him the souls of men. **9.** Levi performed the priestly duties at Bethel before Jacob, being preferred over his ten brothers. Jacob gave his vow and tithed again to YAHWEH, sanctifying it as holy. **10.** This ordinance was written in the heavenly tablets as a Torah for tithing before YAHWEH from year to year, in the chosen place where His Name dwells. (Heavenly tablets: Divine record of commandments) **11.** The ordinance requires that the second tithe be eaten before YAHWEH in the chosen place, and nothing should remain from one year to the next. **12.** In its year, the seed, wine, and oil shall be consumed until the harvest seasons; nothing should remain. (Seed: crops; Wine: new harvest) **13.** Any leftover, old produce is to be considered polluted and must be burned with fire. (Polluted: unclean, ceremonially defiled) **14.** The offerings should be eaten in the sanctuary and not allowed to spoil. (Sanctuary: holy or sacred place) **15.** All tithes from oxen and sheep are holy unto YAHWEH and shall be given to His priests, to be eaten before Him each year. **16.** On the twenty-second day of the month, Jacob decided to build and sanctify the place, making it holy forever for himself and his descendants. (Sanctify: set apart as holy) **17.** YAHWEH appeared to him by night, blessed him, and changed his name from Jacob to Israel. **18.** YAHWEH promised to multiply Israel's descendants, making them kings who will judge all nations and possess the earth forever. **19.** He promised that Israel's seed would inherit the entire earth and judge all nations according to their desires. (Seed: descendants; Inherit: to take possession) **20.** YAHWEH finished speaking, and Jacob watched as He ascended into heaven. (Ascended: went up, rose into the sky) **21.** That night, Jacob saw a vision: an angel descending from heaven with seven tablets, giving them to Jacob. He read them and understood everything that would happen to him and his sons. (Tablets: stone or clay records; Divine messages) **22.** The angel revealed that Jacob should not build the place, but go to the house of his father Abraham and live with Isaac until Isaac's death. (Place: location; Prohibition: command not to do something) **23.** YAHWEH assured him that he would die peacefully in Egypt and be buried with honor in his father's tomb, with Abraham and Isaac. **24.** YAHWEH told Jacob not to fear, for all he saw would come to pass as written, and he should write everything down. **25.** Jacob asked how he could remember all he had seen, and YAHWEH promised to bring everything to his remembrance. (Remembrance: recalling something from memory) **26.** Jacob awoke from his sleep, remembered everything he had seen and read, and wrote down all the words. **27.** Jacob celebrated another day, offering sacrifices as he did before and called the place "Addition" for this day. **28.** It was revealed to Jacob that this day should be added to the seven days of the feast, making it part of the annual celebration. (Addition: extra day added to the festival) **29.** The name "Addition" was recorded as part of the feast days, in accordance with the year's calendar. **30.** On the twenty-third of the month, Deborah, Rebecca's nurse, died. They buried her under the oak near the river, naming it "The river of Deborah" and the oak "The oak of Deborah's mourning." (Mourning: grieving, expressing sorrow) **31.** Rebecca returned to her house, and Jacob sent rams, sheep, and goats with her to prepare a meal for his father Isaac. **32.** Jacob went to the land of Kabratan, where he stayed. (Kabratan: a place name, possibly an ancient location) **33.** Rachel bore a son, whom she named "Son of my sorrow," due to the pain of childbirth, but Jacob called him

Benjamin on the eleventh of the eighth month. (Benjamin: "son of the right hand"; "Son of my sorrow" was Rachel's name for him due to her pain in childbirth) **34.** Rachel died in Ephrath (Bethlehem) and was buried there. Jacob erected a pillar on her grave, near the road. (Ephrath: ancient name for Bethlehem; Pillar: stone monument)

Chapter 33

1. Jacob moved and settled south of Magdaladra'ef. Later, he visited his father Isaac along with Leah, his wife, during the new moon of the tenth month. **2.** Reuben noticed Bilhah, Rachel's servant and Jacob's concubine, bathing privately, and he developed a strong desire for her. **3.** Hiding under the cover of night, Reuben entered Bilhah's house while she was asleep on her bed, and he lay with her. (Concubine: a woman who lives with a man but has lower status than his wife or wives.) **4.** Bilhah woke up to find Reuben lying beside her in bed. She uncovered her covering, grabbed him, and cried out in alarm, realizing that it was Reuben. **5.** Overcome with shame, she let him go, and Reuben fled from the scene. (Shame: a painful feeling of guilt or humiliation caused by one's actions or circumstances.) **6.** Bilhah grieved deeply over this incident but chose not to tell anyone about it. **7.** When Jacob returned and sought to be with her, Bilhah confessed, "I am no longer pure for you, as Reuben defiled me by lying with me while I was asleep. I only realized it after he uncovered me and lay with me." **8.** Jacob became extremely angry with Reuben for this act because it violated his father's dignity and rights. **9.** As a result of Reuben's transgression, Jacob refused to approach Bilhah again. Any man who disrespects his father in this manner commits a grievous sin that is utterly abhorrent to Yahweh. (Transgression: an act that goes against a law or moral code.) **10.** It is commanded and recorded on the heavenly tablets that no man should lie with his father's wife or dishonor his father in this way, for it is unclean. Such an act warrants death for both parties involved because it spreads impurity on the earth. **11.** Yahweh, being holy, does not tolerate any uncleanness in the people He has chosen for Himself. **12.** It is further decreed: "Cursed is the one who lies with his father's wife, for he has dishonored his father's dignity." All the holy ones of Yahweh declared, "So be it, so be it." (Dignity: the state or quality of being worthy of honor or respect.) **13.** Moses was commanded to ensure the children of Israel uphold this law. Such a sin leads to a death penalty and cannot be atoned for. Those who commit this sin must be stoned and eradicated from Yahweh's community. **14.** No one in Israel who commits such an abomination may live even one day longer, as they are unclean and detestable. **15.** Let no one claim that Reuben was spared or forgiven for lying with his father's concubine, as there was no law explicitly revealed at that time condemning such an act. **16.** Until then, the complete ordinances, laws, and judgments had not been made fully known. However, in Moses' time, these laws were revealed as eternal commandments for all generations. **17.** This law is perpetual and cannot be amended. On the same day that this act occurs, those involved must be put to death for their crime. **18.** Moses was instructed to write down these laws for Israel so they might obey them, avoid sinning unto death, and not face destruction or removal from the land Yahweh gave them. **19.** This commandment was given because such acts are detestable, corrupt, and polluting before Yahweh. **20.** There is no sin greater than this fornication, as Israel is a holy nation set apart for Yahweh. They are His inheritance, royal priesthood, and chosen possession. **21.** In the third year of the sixth week (2145 A.M.), Jacob and all his sons relocated to Abraham's house near Isaac and Rebekah. (Relocated: moved to a new place.) **22.** Jacob's sons were Reuben (the firstborn), Simeon, Levi, Judah, Issachar, and Zebulon (from Leah); Joseph and Benjamin (from Rachel); Dan and Naphtali (from Bilhah); Gad and Asher (from Zilpah); and Dinah, his only daughter from Leah. (Inheritance: property or rights passed down from a predecessor.) **23.** When they arrived, they bowed before Isaac and Rebekah. Both parents blessed Jacob and his children. Isaac, especially, was overjoyed to see the sons of his youngest son and gave them his blessings. (Blessings: expressions of divine favor or approval.)

Chapter 34

1. In the sixth year of this week of the forty-fourth jubilee (2148 A.M.), Jacob sent his sons, along with his servants, to pasture their sheep in the fields of Shechem. **2.** Meanwhile, seven kings of the Amorites conspired to attack them, hiding under the trees to ambush and kill them while taking their cattle as plunder. (Plunder: stolen goods, especially during a conflict.) **3.** Jacob, along with Levi, Judah, and Joseph, stayed behind with Isaac, whose spirit was sorrowful, preventing them from leaving him. Benjamin, being the youngest, also remained with his father. (Sorrowful: deeply unhappy or distressed.) **4.** The kings of Taphu, Aresa, Seragan, Selo, Ga'as, Bethoron, and Ma'anisakir, along with those dwelling in the mountains and forests of Canaan, prepared to attack. **5.** Messengers informed Jacob, saying, "The kings of the Amorites have surrounded your sons and taken their herds." **6.** Jacob arose with his three sons, his father's servants, and his own servants. He went to battle with six thousand men armed with swords. **7.** Jacob defeated the Amorite kings at the pastures of Shechem, killing them with the sword. He pursued those who fled and slew them as well. Among the dead were the kings of Aresa, Taphu, Seragan, Selo, Amanisakir, and Ga'as, and he recovered his herds. **8.** Jacob triumphed over them and imposed a tribute, requiring them to provide five kinds of produce from their land. He also constructed the cities of Robel and Tamnatares. (Tribute: a payment made by one ruler or nation to another as a sign of submission or for protection.) **9.** Jacob returned in peace and established peace with the defeated kings, making them his servants until the time he and his sons migrated to Egypt. (Peace: a state of harmony and freedom from conflict.) **10.** In the seventh year of this week (2149 A.M.), Jacob sent Joseph to check on the welfare of his brothers in Shechem. He found them in Dothan. (Welfare: the health, happiness, or fortunes of a person or group.) **11.** Joseph's brothers plotted treacherously against him, planning to kill him but instead sold him to Ishmaelite merchants. These merchants took him to Egypt and sold him to Potiphar, Pharaoh's eunuch and chief cook, who was also a priest in the city of Elew. (Treacherously: in a way that betrays trust or is deceitful.) **12.** Jacob's sons killed a young goat and dipped Joseph's coat in its blood, sending it to their father on the tenth of the seventh month. **13.** Jacob mourned all night upon receiving the blood-stained coat, believing a wild animal had devoured Joseph. He became feverish with grief, and his entire household joined in mourning. (Mourned: expressed sorrow for someone's death.) **14.** Despite his children and Dinah attempting to comfort him, Jacob refused to be consoled for the loss of his son. **15.** On hearing of Joseph's presumed death, Bilhah, Jacob's concubine, died in sorrow while living in Qafratef. Shortly afterward, Dinah also passed away following Joseph's disappearance. **16.** Three deaths occurred in Jacob's family within one month. Bilhah was buried near Rachel's tomb, and Dinah was laid to rest in the same area. **17.** Jacob mourned for Joseph for an entire year, repeatedly saying, "I will go to the grave mourning for my son." (Grave: a burial place for the dead.) **18.** It was ordained for the children of Israel that they afflict themselves annually on the tenth of the seventh month. This day commemorates Jacob's sorrow for Joseph and serves as a day of atonement for sins. A young goat was to be sacrificed on this day. (Atonement: the act of making amends for sin or wrongdoing.) **19.** This day was established for repentance and cleansing from sins, transgressions, and errors, observed once every year. **20.** After Joseph's disappearance, Jacob's sons married. Reuben's wife was Ada; Simeon married Adlba'a, a Canaanite; Levi's wife was Melka of Aram, a descendant of Terah's lineage; Judah's wife was Betasuel, a Canaanite; Issachar's wife was Hezaqa; Zebulon married Ni'iman; Dan's wife was Egla; Naphtali married Rasu'u of Mesopotamia; Gad's wife was Maka; Asher's wife was Ijona; Joseph married Asenath, an Egyptian; and Benjamin's wife was Ijasaka. **21.** Later, Simeon repented for marrying a Canaanite and took a second wife from Mesopotamia, following the example of his brothers. (Repented: expressed regret or remorse for wrongdoing.)

Chapter 35

1. In the first year of the first week of the forty-fifth jubilee [2157 A.M.], Rebecca called her son Jacob and gave him instructions regarding his father and his brother, commanding him to honor both of them throughout his life. **2.** Jacob responded, "I will obey everything you have asked of me, for it will bring me honor and greatness, and it will be pleasing to YAHWEH that I show respect to them." **3.** "And you, mother," Jacob continued, "know that from the day I was born until now, all my deeds and the thoughts of my heart have always been good toward everyone." (Deeds: actions; heart: inner thoughts and feelings) **4.** "How could I not follow your command to honor my father and my brother?" he asked. **5.** "Tell me, mother, if you have seen any wrong in me, and I will turn away from it, and mercy will be shown to me." (Mercy: kindness or compassion) **6.** Rebecca replied, "My son, I have seen no wrong in you. You have always been upright. But let me tell you the truth: I believe I will die this year, for I have seen it in a dream. I will not live beyond 155 years, and I have completed my appointed days." (Upright: morally good or honorable) **7.** Jacob laughed at her words, thinking it impossible, as she was in full health and strength, with no signs of illness. She was still active, walking around, and had no pain or weakness. **8.** Jacob said, "Blessed am I if my life matches the length and strength of yours! But you are joking about your death, for you are in good health." **9.** Rebecca went to Isaac and said, "I have one request: make Esau swear not to harm Jacob or bear any ill will toward him, for you know how Esau has been since his youth—his heart is full of evil. He plans to kill Jacob after your death." **10.** "You know everything Esau has done since Jacob went to Haran: he has abandoned us and treated us poorly. He took your flocks and seized your possessions right in front of us." **11.** "When we asked him to return what was ours, he gave it to us only out of pity, not out of kindness." **12.** "He is bitter toward you because you blessed

Jacob, your righteous and upright son. Jacob has never wronged us, unlike Esau, who has shown nothing but wickedness. Since his return from Haran, Jacob has always honored us and provided for us in all seasons, bringing blessings with joy." (Bitterness: anger or resentment; Wickedness: evil or immoral behavior) **13.** Isaac responded, "I know and see all that Jacob has done for us—how he has honored us with all his heart. But I loved Esau more in the past because he was the firstborn. However, now I love Jacob more, for Esau has done many wicked deeds and shows no righteousness in him. His life is full of unrighteousness and violence." (Unrighteousness: lack of morality or justice) **14.** "I am troubled by his actions, for he and his descendants will be destroyed from the earth. He has forsaken YAHWEH, the Almighty, and followed after his wives' unclean ways and errors." **15.** "You want me to make Esau swear not to harm Jacob, but even if he swears, I know he will not keep his word. He will only do evil." **16.** "But if he desires to kill Jacob, he will be handed over to Jacob, and will not escape his judgment." **17.** "Do not fear for Jacob, for his guardian is powerful, honored, and praised more than the guardian of Esau." (Guardian: protector or caretaker) **18.** Rebecca called Esau and said to him, "I have one request, my son. Promise me that you will fulfill it." **19.** Esau answered, "I will do everything you ask and will not refuse your request." **20.** Rebecca said, "When I die, I ask that you bury me near Sarah, your father's mother, and that you and Jacob love each other and never wish evil on the other. If you do this, you will prosper and be honored in the land, and no enemy will rejoice over you. You will be a blessing and a mercy to all who love you." (Prosper: to succeed or thrive; Honor: to show respect) **21.** Esau replied, "I will do all you ask, and I will bury you next to Sarah as you desire, so that your bones may rest near hers." **22.** "As for Jacob, my brother, I will love him above all others. I have no other brother in the world except him. If I do not love him, who else could I love? We were born together and came from your womb as one." **23.** "I ask that you encourage Jacob to treat me and my sons with kindness, for I know that he will be the king over me and my children. The day your father blessed him, he made him the superior, and me the inferior." (Encourage: to give support or confidence; Superior: higher in rank or importance) **24.** Esau swore, "I will love him and never wish harm upon him, but only good, for all my days." **25.** Esau swore to Rebecca, and she then called Jacob before Esau, repeating the commands she had given Esau to Jacob. **26.** Jacob said, "I will do as you wish; trust me, no evil will come from me or my sons toward Esau. My only desire is to love him." **27.** That night, Rebecca and her sons ate and drank together. The next day, Rebecca died at the age of 155 years—three jubilees, one week, and one year. Esau and Jacob buried her in the double cave, near Sarah, their father's mother.

Chapter 36

1. In the sixth year of this week [2162 A.M.], Isaac called his two sons, Esau and Jacob, and they came to him. He said to them, "My sons, I am about to follow the path of my fathers, to the eternal home where they rest." **2.** "Therefore, bury me near Abraham, my father, in the double cave in the field of Ephron the Hittite, where Abraham purchased a tomb to be buried in. Bury me in the sepulcher that I have dug for myself." **3.** "And this is my command to you, my sons: practice righteousness (Righteousness: moral correctness or just behavior) and integrity on the earth, so that YAHWEH may fulfill all that He promised Abraham and his descendants." (Integrity: the quality of being honest and having strong moral principles). **4.** "And love one another, my sons, as a man loves his own soul. Let each of you seek the welfare of your brother and act together on the earth. Love one another as you love your own soul. As for idols, I command you to reject them, hate them, and never love them, for they deceive those who worship them." **5.** "Remember YAHWEH, the Almighty of Abraham, your father, and how I too worshipped Him and served Him in righteousness (Righteousness: moral correctness or just behavior) and joy, so that He might multiply you and make your descendants as numerous as the stars of heaven, and establish you as a plant of righteousness on the earth, never to be uprooted (Uprooted: removed from its foundation or established place)." **6.** "Now I make you swear a great oath by the magnificent, honored, and mighty name of YAHWEH, who created the heavens and the earth and everything in them, that you will fear Him and worship Him." **7.** "That each of you will love his brother with affection (Affection: a feeling of fondness or love) and righteousness, and that neither will wish evil on the other, from this day forward, so that you may prosper in all your endeavors and not be destroyed." **8.** "If either of you devises (Devises: plans or invents, usually something harmful or evil) evil against your brother, know this: from now on, anyone who plans evil against his brother will fall into his own trap. He will be rooted out of the land of the living, and his descendants will be wiped out from under heaven." **9.** "On the day of judgment, when there is turmoil and anger, with consuming fire as YAHWEH destroyed Sodom, so will He destroy his land, city, and everything he owns. He will be erased from the book of the righteous and will not be found in the book of life, but in the book of destruction. He will face eternal damnation (Damnation: eternal punishment or condemnation), with hatred, wrath, torment, plagues, and disease forever." **10.** "I testify to you, my sons, according to the judgment that will come upon anyone who seeks to harm his brother." **11.** Isaac divided all his possessions between his two sons that day, giving the larger portion to the firstborn, and the tower and all that was around it, along with all that Abraham had at the Well of the Oath. **12.** He said, "I will give this larger portion to the firstborn." **13.** Esau replied, "I have sold my birthright to Jacob. Let it be his. I have no objection to this, for it is his." **14.** Isaac blessed them, saying, "May a blessing rest upon you, my sons, and on your descendants today, for you have given me peace, and my heart is no longer troubled about the birthright, lest you act wickedly because of it." **15.** "May the Most High YAHWEH bless the one who practices righteousness, him and his descendants, forever." **16.** After giving them his final commands and blessings, Isaac rejoiced as they ate and drank together before him. He was glad that they had reconciled, and that their hearts were united. They left his presence, rested that day, and slept. **17.** Isaac lay on his bed that night, rejoicing, and passed away peacefully. He died at the age of 180 years. He lived 25 weeks and 5 years. His two sons, Esau and Jacob, buried him. **18.** Esau went to the land of Edom, to the mountains of Seir, and made his home there. **19.** Jacob settled in the mountains of Hebron, in the tower built by his father Abraham. There, he worshipped YAHWEH with all his heart, following His commandments as He had prescribed for their generations. **20.** Leah, his wife, died in the fourth year of the second week of the forty-fifth jubilee [2167 A.M.]. Jacob buried her in the double cave near Rebecca, his mother, to the left of Sarah, his father's mother. **21.** All of Leah's children and Jacob's sons came to mourn her with him and to comfort him for her passing. He grieved deeply, for he loved her greatly, especially after Rachel, her sister, had died. **22.** Leah was a woman of great integrity (Integrity: the quality of being honest and having strong moral principles) and honor in all her actions. She was kind, peaceful, and upright, and Jacob never heard a harsh word from her. She was gentle, and Jacob cherished her deeply. **23.** Jacob remembered all the good deeds Leah had done during her life, and he mourned her greatly. He loved her with all his heart and soul. **24.** "He remembered all the good deeds she had done throughout her life, and he mourned for her deeply. For he loved her with all his heart and soul." (Mourned: felt deep sorrow or grief)

Chapter 37

1. When Yitshaq, the father of Yacob and Esau, passed away in 2162 A.M., Esau's sons learned that their father had given the elder's portion to Yacob, the younger, and they were furious. (A.M.: era) **2.** They confronted their father, questioning, "Why did your father give the elder's portion to Yacob, passing over you, the elder, while Yacob is the younger?" (Portion: share) **3.** Esau responded, "I sold my birthright to Yacob for a meal of lentils. When my father sent me to hunt, Yacob tricked him, brought him food, and my father blessed him instead of me." (Birthright: inheritance) **4.** "Now, our father made us swear to never harm each other, to live in peace, and show kindness to our brothers, avoiding corruption in our ways." (Swear: vow) **5.** They replied, "We will not make peace with him. We are stronger than him and will destroy him and his sons. If you refuse, we will harm you too." (Harm: damage) **6.** "Let's send for allies from Aram, Philistia, Moab, and Ammon. We'll choose warriors eager for battle and defeat him before he grows strong." (Allies: partners) **7.** Their father warned, "Do not go against him or wage war, lest you fall before him." (Lest: fear) **8.** But they retorted, "You've always yielded to him since your youth. We will not listen to you." (Retorted: replied; Yielded: submitted) **9.** They sent messengers to Aram and 'Aduram, their father's friend, and hired a thousand skilled warriors. (Messengers: couriers) **10.** From Moab, Ammon, Philistia, Edom, and the Horites, they gathered another thousand warriors, and from the Kittim, another thousand strong men of war. (Horites: ancient people; Kittim: people from Cyprus) **11.** They demanded their father lead them, threatening, "Go with us, or we will kill you." (Demanded: insisted; Threatening: warning) **12.** Filled with anger, he was reluctant to lead them but eventually recalled his resentment toward Yacob and forgot the oath he had sworn to never harm him. (Reluctant: unwilling; Resentment: bitterness) **13.** Despite the oath, Yacob remained unaware of the approaching danger as he mourned his wife Leah, until he heard they were coming with four thousand armed men. (Mourned: grieved) **14.** The men of Hebron, who loved Yacob more than Esau, sent word: "Your brother approaches with four thousand men armed with swords and shields." (Hebron: city) **15.** Yacob initially refused to believe it, but when they neared, he sealed the gates of his tower. (Sealed: closed) **16.** From the battlements, he called out to Esau, "Is this your comfort to me in mourning for my wife? You have broken the oath you made to our parents, and now you are condemned." (Battlements: walls) **17.** Esau answered, "No oath among men or beasts is eternal. People constantly plot against each other, seeking to harm and destroy their enemies." (Eternal: everlasting; Plot: scheme) **18.** "You hate me and my descendants, and there is no brotherhood left between us." (Descendants: offspring) **19.** He continued, "Listen: if a boar could change its skin and grow soft bristles like wool, or sprout horns like a stag, then I would keep the bond of brotherhood with you." (Boar: pig; Bristles: hairs; Stag: deer) **20.** "If wolves could make peace with lambs and spare them, I would be at peace with you." (Spare: save) **21.** "If the lion could befriend the ox and plow with him, then I would make peace with you." (Plow: till) **22.** "And when the raven turns white like the dove, then you will know I've loved you and made peace with you. Until then, you and your sons will be cut off, and there will be no peace for you." (Raven: bird; Dove: peaceful bird; Cut off: removed) **23.** Hearing this, Yacob saw the hatred in Esau's heart, knowing Esau was determined to destroy him. He realized Esau was coming with the intent to kill, like a wild boar charging at the spear. (Hatred: dislike; Intent: purpose) **24.** In response, Yacob gathered his people and servants, preparing to defend himself against the threat.(Defend: protect; Threat: danger)

Chapter 38
1. Afterward, Yahudah spoke to his father Yacob, saying: "Bend your bow, father, shoot your arrows, strike down the enemy, and may you have strength, for we will not kill your brother; he is like you, and we will honor him." (Bend: curve) **2.** Yacob bent his bow, shot an arrow, and struck Esau, his brother, in the right breast, killing him. (Breast: chest) **3.** He shot again, hitting 'Adoran the Aramaean in the left breast, knocking him back and killing him. (Aramaean: from Aram) **4.** The sons of Yacob and their servants split into groups and surrounded the enemy. (Servants: attendants) **5.** Yahudah led the south side, with Naphtali and Gad, and fifty men. They killed everyone in their path, leaving no survivors. (Led: guided; Survivors: remaining) **6.** Levi, Dan, and Asher led the east side with fifty men, killing Moabite and Ammonite warriors. (Moabite: from Moab) **7.** Reuben, Issachar, and Zebulon led the north side with fifty men, killing Philistine warriors. (Philistine: from Philistia) **8.** Simeon, Benjamin, and Enoch led the west side with fifty men, killing 400 Edomite and Horite warriors; 600 fled, including four of Esau's sons. They left their father dead on the hill in 'Aduram. (Edomite: from Edom; Horite: ancient group; Stout: strong) **9.** The sons of Yacob chased them to Seir's mountains, buried their brother in 'Aduram, and returned home. (Chased: pursued) **10.** The sons of Yacob pressed the sons of Esau in Seir's mountains, forcing them into servitude. (Pressed: forced; Servitude: slavery) **11.** They sent to Yacob, asking if they should make peace or destroy them. (Inquire: ask) **12.** Yacob replied, commanding peace, and the sons of Esau became his subjects, paying tribute to Yacob and his sons forever. (Tribute: payment) **13.** The sons of Esau continued paying tribute to Yacob until he went to Egypt. (Continued: kept) **14.** The sons of Edom still bear the yoke of servitude imposed by Yacob's twelve sons. (Bear: carry) **15.** These are the kings who reigned in Edom before Israel had a king. (Reigned: ruled) **16.** Bela, son of Beor, ruled in Edom, and his city was Danaba. (Danaba: city name) **17.** Bela died, and Jobab, son of Zara from Boser, succeeded him. (Succeeded: followed) **18.** Jobab died, and 'Asam from Teman succeeded him. (Teman: place name) **19.** 'Asam died, and 'Adath, son of Barad, who killed Midian in Moab, became king, and his city was Avith. (Midian: region; Avith: city name) **20.** 'Adath died, and Salman from 'Amaseqa became king. (Salman: king name) **21.** Salman died, and Saul of Ra'aboth by the river succeeded him. (Ra'aboth: city name) **22.** Saul died, and Ba'elunan, son of Achbor, succeeded him. (Achbor: name) **23.** Ba'elunan died, and 'Adath became king again, with Maitabith, daughter of Matarat, as his wife. (Maitabith: name) **25.** These are the kings who ruled in Edom. (Ruled: governed)

Chapter 39
1. Yacob lived in the land of his father's sojournings, the land of Canaan. (Sojournings: travels) **2.** These are the generations of Yacob. Yoseph was seventeen when he was taken to Egypt, and Potiphar, Pharaoh's eunuch, the chief cook, bought him. (Eunuch: castrated man) **3.** Potiphar made Yoseph overseer of his house, and YAHWEH's blessing came upon the house because of him, prospering all Yoseph did. (Overseer: manager) **4.** Potiphar entrusted everything to Yoseph, recognizing YAHWEH was with him and prospered him. (Entrusted: gave responsibility) **5.** Yoseph was handsome, and his master's wife noticed him. She loved him and asked him to lie with her. (Handsome: good-looking) **6.** But Yoseph refused, remembering YAHWEH's command that no man should commit adultery with another man's wife, a sin punished by death. (Adultery: affair; Punished: penalized) **7.** Yoseph remembered these words and refused her advances. (Advances: proposals) **8.** She persistently asked him for a year, but he refused to listen. (Persistently: constantly) **9.** She then grabbed him to force him into sin, but he left his garment with her and fled. (Garment: clothing) **10.** She falsely accused him to her husband, saying he tried to force her, and when she screamed, he fled, leaving his garment behind. (Falsely: untruthfully) **11.** Potiphar saw the garment, heard her words, and threw Yoseph into prison, the place for the king's prisoners. (Prisoners: captives) **12.** In prison, YAHWEH showed Yoseph favor with the chief guard, who saw that YAHWEH was with him and prospered his work. (Favor: kindness) **13.** The chief guard entrusted everything to Yoseph, knowing YAHWEH perfected his work. (Entrusted: assigned; Perfected: improved) **14.** Yoseph remained in prison for two years. Pharaoh became angry with his two eunuchs, the chief butler and chief baker, and they were imprisoned. (Eunuchs: castrated men) **15.** The chief guard appointed Yoseph to serve the two eunuchs. (Appointed: assigned) **16.** Both the butler and baker had dreams and told Yoseph. (Dreams: visions) **17.** Yoseph interpreted their dreams: the butler was restored, and the baker was executed, just as he had said. (Executed: killed) **18.** The butler forgot Yoseph's help and did not inform Pharaoh of how Yoseph had interpreted his dream. (Informed: notified)

Chapter 40
1. In those days, Pharaoh dreamed two dreams in one night about a coming famine throughout Egypt. He woke and called the dream interpreters and magicians, but they couldn't interpret them. (Magicians: sorcerers) **2.** The chief butler remembered Yoseph and spoke of him to Pharaoh, bringing him from prison to interpret the dreams. (Butler: wine steward) **3.** Yoseph said the two dreams were one: Seven years of plenty would come to Egypt, followed by seven years of severe famine. (Famine: shortage of food) **4.** Yoseph advised Pharaoh to appoint overseers to store food during the seven years of plenty, so the land would survive the famine. (Overseers: managers) **5.** YAHWEH gave Yoseph favor in Pharaoh's eyes, and Pharaoh said, "We cannot find anyone wiser than Yoseph, for YAHWEH's spirit is with him." (Favor: approval) **6.** Pharaoh appointed Yoseph second-in-command over all Egypt, giving him authority and a chariot. (Second-in-command: second in rank) **7.** Pharaoh clothed Yoseph in fine garments, put a gold chain on his neck, and declared him ruler over his house, saying, "Only I will be greater than you." (Fine garments: luxurious clothes; Ruler: leader) **8.** Yoseph ruled Egypt, earning the love and respect of all, as he was humble, just, and did not accept gifts or show favoritism. (Favoritism: bias) **9.** Egypt was at peace because of Yoseph; YAHWEH gave him favor, and Pharaoh's kingdom was orderly without evil. (Orderly: well-managed) **10.** Pharaoh gave Yoseph the name Zaphenath-Paneah and gave him Asenath, the daughter of Potipharah, priest of Heliopolis, as his wife. (Zaphenath-Paneah: Yoseph's Egyptian name; Asenath: his wife's name; Heliopolis: ancient Egyptian city) **11.** Yoseph was thirty years old when he stood before Pharaoh. (Thirty: age of maturity) **12.** In that year, Yitschaq died. As Yoseph had foretold, the seven years of plenty came, and Egypt produced abundantly. (Foretold: predicted) **13.** Yoseph stored food in every city until it could no longer be counted due to its abundance. (Abundance: surplus)

Chapter 41
1. In the 45th jubilee, Judah chose Tamar from Aram as a wife for his firstborn son, Er. (jubilee: period of 50 years, firstborn: eldest) **2.** Er hated Tamar because she wasn't from his mother's family, so he refused to be with her. (hated: despised, refused: declined) **3.** Er's wickedness caused Yahweh to strike him dead. (wickedness: evil, strike: smite) **4.** Judah told Onan to marry Tamar and produce children for his brother. (marry: wed, produce: father) **5.** Onan refused, spilling his seed, which displeased Yahweh, so Yahweh struck him dead too. (refused: declined, seed: semen) **6.** Judah instructed Tamar to remain a widow in her father's house until his youngest son, Shelah, grew up. (instructed: ordered, grew up: matured) **7.** When Shelah matured, Judah's wife, Bedsu'el, refused to let him marry Tamar. (refused: denied, marry: wed) **8.** After Bedsu'el's death, Judah went to Timnah to shear his sheep. (death: passing, shear: cut) **9.** Tamar heard of this, disguised herself with a veil, and waited on Judah's path. (disguised: masked, waited: lingered) **10.** Judah mistook her for a prostitute and asked to sleep with her. (mistook: misidentified, asked: requested) **11.** Tamar requested Judah's ring, necklace, and staff as a pledge until payment was sent. (requested: demanded, pledge: promise) **12.** Judah agreed, slept with her, and Tamar conceived. (agreed: consented, conceived: became pregnant) **13.** Later, Judah sent a goat as payment but couldn't find her. (later: afterward, sent: delivered) **14.** The locals denied any prostitute had been there, so Judah dropped the matter. (locals: people, dropped: ignored) **15.** Three months later, Tamar's pregnancy became known, and Judah ordered her to be burned for immorality. (pregnancy: condition, burned: executed) **16.** As she was brought out, Tamar sent Judah his ring, necklace, and staff, revealing him as the father. (revealing: showing, father: parent) **17.** Judah acknowledged them and admitted Tamar was more righteous than he. (acknowledged: recognized, righteous: just) **18.** Tamar was spared but not given to Shelah. (spared: saved,

given: betrothed) **19.** Tamar later gave birth to twins, Perez and Zerah. (gave birth: bore, twins: brothers) **20.** Judah realized his sin and repented deeply before Yahweh. (realized: recognized, repented: regretted) **21.** Yahweh forgave him after he turned away from his wrongdoing. (forgave: pardoned, wrongdoing: sins) **22.** Yahweh decreed that immorality like this must be punished by burning to cleanse Israel. (decreed: commanded, cleanse: purify) **23.** Judah's repentance ensured his lineage was preserved for future generations. (repentance: regret, lineage: descendants) **24.** Yahweh confirmed Judah's forgiveness through a dream, as he earnestly sought mercy. (confirmed: showed, earnestly: sincerely) **25.** Yahweh instructed Israel to avoid such uncleanness by punishing offenders with fire. (instructed: commanded, uncleanness: impurity) **26.** This law applied to those who sinned with in-laws, turning away Yahweh's wrath. (law: rule, wrath: anger) **27.** Yahweh preserved Judah's family line because his sons had not sinned with Tamar. (preserved: protected, sinned: wronged) **28.** Judah acted according to Abraham's judgment, seeking justice but ultimately showing mercy. (acted: ruled, judgment: fairness)

Chapter 42

1. In the first year of the third week of the 45th jubilee, a famine began, and no rain fell on the earth. (famine: drought, earth: land) **2.** The land became barren, but Egypt had food because Joseph had stored grain during the seven years of plenty. (barren: empty, plenty: abundance) **3.** The Egyptians came to Joseph for food, and he sold it to them from the storehouses in exchange for gold. (sold: traded, storehouses: warehouses) **4.** Jacob heard there was food in Egypt and sent ten of his sons to buy grain, keeping Benjamin behind. (heard: learned, keeping: withholding) **5.** Joseph recognized his brothers, but they did not recognize him. He accused them of being spies. (recognized: identified, accused: charged) **6.** He imprisoned them but later released all except Simeon, whom he detained, sending the others back. (imprisoned: confined, detained: held) **7.** Joseph secretly returned their gold into their sacks, and they did not notice. (secretly: quietly, returned: placed) **8.** He demanded they bring their youngest brother, having learned about their family from their own words. (demanded: required, youngest: little) **9.** The brothers returned to Canaan and told Jacob all that had happened, including Simeon's detainment. (returned: came back, detainment: captivity) **10.** Jacob lamented, saying, "Joseph is gone, Simeon is gone, and now you want to take Benjamin!" (lamented: grieved, gone: lost) **11.** He refused, fearing Benjamin might die, as he was one of Rachel's two sons. (refused: rejected, fearing: dreading) **12.** Jacob was especially hesitant because the gold in their sacks increased his fear. (hesitant: reluctant, increased: heightened) **13.** The famine worsened, affecting all lands except Egypt, where food remained due to Joseph's preparations. (worsened: intensified, preparations: provisions) **14.** The Egyptians ate from their stores during the first year of famine. (ate: consumed, stores: reserves) **15.** When the famine in Canaan grew severe, Jacob told his sons to return for more food. (grew: became, severe: harsh) **16.** The brothers refused to go without Benjamin, per Joseph's demand. (refused: declined, per: according to) **17.** Jacob realized that without Benjamin, they would all starve. (realized: understood, starve: perish) **18.** Reuben offered his two sons as a guarantee for Benjamin's return, but Jacob refused. (offered: pledged, guarantee: assurance) **19.** Judah then promised to take full responsibility, convincing Jacob to let Benjamin go. (promised: vowed, convincing: persuading) **20.** In the second year of the week, on the first day of the month, the brothers went to Egypt with gifts, including honey, almonds, and terebinth nuts. (gifts: presents, including: such as) **21.** Standing before Joseph, they introduced Benjamin. Joseph blessed him, saying, "May Yahweh be kind to you, my son." (introduced: presented, blessed: wished well) **22.** Joseph released Simeon, hosted them in his home, and received their gifts. (released: freed, hosted: entertained) **23.** During the feast, Joseph gave Benjamin a portion seven times larger than the others. (feast: banquet, portion: serving) **24.** They ate, drank, and stayed the night with their donkeys. (ate: dined, stayed: lodged) **25.** Joseph devised a plan to test their hearts, instructing his steward to return their money and place his silver cup in Benjamin's sack. (devised: created, test: examine)

Chapter 43

1. The steward obeyed Joseph's orders: he filled their sacks with food, returned their money, and placed Joseph's silver cup in Benjamin's sack. (obeyed: followed) **2.** Early in the morning, the brothers departed, but Joseph instructed his steward to pursue them, accusing them of stealing his cup. (departed: left, pursue: chase) **3.** The steward caught up with them and relayed Joseph's accusation. (caught up: reached, relayed: conveyed) **4.** The brothers denied it, stating they had returned the money they found earlier and would never steal from Joseph. (denied: rejected, stated: declared) **5.** They vowed that if the cup was found with any of them, that person would die, and the rest would become servants. (vowed: swore, servants: slaves) **6.** The steward replied that only the guilty one would become a servant, and the others could go free. (replied: answered, guilty: wrongdoer) **7.** Starting with the eldest, he searched their sacks and found the cup in Benjamin's. (starting: beginning, searched: examined) **8.** In grief, they tore their clothes, loaded their donkeys, and returned to Joseph's house, bowing before him. (grief: sorrow, tore: ripped) **9.** Joseph accused them of stealing. The brothers, feeling helpless, offered themselves and their animals as servants. (accused: blamed, helpless: powerless) **10.** Joseph insisted that only Benjamin would stay as a servant, while the rest could return home. (insisted: demanded, stay: remain) **11.** Judah pleaded with Joseph, explaining that their father deeply loved Benjamin, especially after losing another son. (pleaded: begged, deeply: greatly) **12.** He said their father would die of sorrow if Benjamin didn't return with them. (die: perish, sorrow: grief) **13.** Judah offered himself as a servant in Benjamin's place, as he had guaranteed the boy's safety. (offered: volunteered, guaranteed: promised) **14.** Moved by their sincerity and unity, Joseph revealed his identity, speaking in Hebrew and weeping. (sincerity: honesty, unity: togetherness) **15.** The brothers were stunned, but Joseph comforted them, saying Yahweh sent him to Egypt to save lives during the famine. (stunned: shocked, comforted: reassured) **16.** He urged them to bring their father and households to Egypt quickly, as five years of famine remained. (urged: insisted, remained: were left) **17.** Joseph assured them not to worry about their possessions, for Yahweh had made him able to provide for them. (assured: promised, possessions: belongings) **18.** He instructed them to tell their father about his position and the blessings Yahweh had given him in Egypt. (instructed: directed, position: role) **19.** Pharaoh supported Joseph, commanding that chariots, supplies, and gifts be sent for their journey. (supported: backed, commanded: ordered) **20.** Joseph sent his father provisions, fine clothing, silver, and donkeys loaded with grain. (provisions: supplies, loaded: filled) **21.** The brothers returned to Jacob, telling him Joseph was alive and ruler over Egypt. (returned: came back, ruler: governor) **22.** Jacob struggled to believe them but revived when he saw the wagons Joseph had sent. (struggled: had difficulty, revived: awakened) **23.** Seeing the evidence, Jacob declared, "Enough! My son Joseph is alive!" (evidence: proof, declared: proclaimed) **24.** He resolved, "I will go to see him before I die." (resolved: decided, see: visit)

Chapter 44

1. Israel (Jacob) left Haran with his family on the 1st of the 3rd month, stopping at the Well of the Oath, where he made a sacrifice to God, the Almighty of his father Isaac, on the 7th. (sacrifice: offering, Almighty: all-powerful) **2.** Jacob remembered his dream at Bethel and was hesitant to go to Egypt. (remembered: recalled, hesitant: reluctant) **3.** While considering sending for Joseph to bring him to Egypt, he stayed for seven days, hoping for divine guidance. (considering: thinking about, guidance: direction) **4.** He celebrated the first-fruits harvest festival with old grain, as there was no new seed in Canaan due to the famine affecting both animals and people. (celebrated: observed, affecting: impacting) **5.** On the 16th, God appeared to Jacob and reassured him not to fear going to Egypt, promising to make him a great nation there, to be with him, and bring him back. (appeared: manifested, reassured: comforted) **6.** God further told him that Joseph would close his eyes at death, and he should not fear going down to Egypt. (close his eyes: die, further: additionally) **7.** Jacob's sons, their children, and their possessions were placed on wagons for the journey. (possessions: belongings, placed: loaded) **8.** Jacob departed from the Well of the Oath on the 16th of the third month, heading to Egypt. (departed: left, heading: traveling) **9.** He sent Judah ahead to Joseph to inspect the Land of Goshen, which Joseph had prepared for them to live near him. (inspect: examine, prepared: arranged) **10.** Goshen was the best land in Egypt, near Joseph and suitable for both the family and their cattle. (suitable: ideal, cattle: livestock) **11.** These are the names of Jacob's sons who went to Egypt: Reuben, Jacob's firstborn, (firstborn: eldest) **12.** Reuben's sons: Enoch, Pallu, Hezron, and Carmi (four). (sons: children, four: 4) **13.** Simeon's sons: Jemuel, Jamin, Ohad, Jachin, Zohar, and Shaul (seven). (sons: children, seven: 7) **14.** Levi's sons: Gershon, Kohath, and Merari (three). (sons: children, three: 3) **15.** Judah's sons: Shela, Perez, and Zerah (three). (sons: children, three: 3) **16.** Issachar's sons: Tola, Phua, Jasub, and Shimron (four). (sons: children, four: 4) **17.** Zebulon's sons: Sered, Elon, and Jahleel (three). (sons: children, three: 3) **18.** These six sons and their one daughter, Dinah, were born to Jacob in Mesopotamia. Including their children, there were 29 souls from Leah's children. (daughter: girl, souls: people) **19.** The sons of Zilpah (Leah's maid) who went with Jacob: Gad and Asher. (maid: servant) **20.** Gad's sons: Ziphion, Haggi, Shuni, Ezbon, Eri, Areli, and Arodi (seven). (sons: children, seven: 7) **21.** Asher's sons: Imnah, Ishvah, Ishvi, Beriah, and Serah (five sons, one daughter). (sons: children, daughter: girl) **22.** Total number of souls from Leah and her maid: 44. (souls: people, maid: servant) **23.** The sons of Rachel:

Joseph and Benjamin. (sons: children) **24.** Before Jacob arrived in Egypt, Joseph had two sons born to him in Egypt by Asenath: Manasseh and Ephraim (two). (sons: children, two: 2) **25.** Benjamin's sons: Bela, Becher, Ashbel, Gera, Naaman, Ehi, Rosh, Muppim, Huppim, and Ard (ten). (sons: children, ten: 10) **26.** Total number of souls from Rachel: 14. (souls: people, total: sum) **27.** The sons of Bilhah (Rachel's maid) who went with Jacob: Dan and Naphtali. (maid: servant) **28.** Dan's sons: Hushim, Samon, Asudi, Ijaka, and Salomon (five). (sons: children, five: 5) **29.** Dan's children died in Egypt, leaving only Hushim. (children: offspring, leaving: remaining) **30.** Naphtali's sons: Jahziel, Guni, Jezer, Shallum, and Iv (five). (sons: children, five: 5) **31.** Iv, born after the famine years, died in Egypt. (born: born later, died: passed away) **32.** Total souls from Rachel's children: 26. (souls: people, total: sum) **33.** In total, 70 souls from Jacob's family went to Egypt, with five dying in Egypt before Joseph, leaving no children. (souls: people, total: sum) **34.** In Canaan, two of Judah's sons, Er and Onan, died without children. The Israelites buried them and they were counted among the 70 nations. (died: passed away, buried: interred)

Chapter 45

1. Israel (Jacob) entered Egypt and settled in the land of Goshen on the 1st of the 4th month, during the second year of the third week of the 45th Jubilee (2172 Anno Mundi.). (settled: dwelled, entered: arrived) **2.** Joseph went to meet his father, Jacob, in Goshen, and they embraced, weeping together. (embraced: hugged, weeping: crying) **3.** Israel said to Joseph, "Now that I have seen you, I can die in peace. Blessed be YAHWEH, the Almighty of Israel, who has shown mercy to me and not withheld His blessings." (die: pass away, mercy: compassion) **4.** "It is enough that I have seen your face while I am still alive. Blessed be YAHWEH, my Sovereign, forever and ever." (enough: sufficient, sovereign: ruler) **5.** Joseph and his brothers ate and drank with their father. Jacob rejoiced, seeing them together, and praised God for preserving him and his twelve sons. (rejoiced: celebrated, preserving: protecting) **6.** Joseph gave his father and brothers land in Goshen and Rameses, the best parts of Egypt, to settle in. Israel was 130 years old when he arrived in Egypt. (gave: provided, best: prime) **7.** Joseph provided for his father, brothers, and their families with enough food during the seven years of famine. (provided: supplied, enough: sufficient) **8.** The famine severely affected Egypt. Joseph acquired all the land of Egypt for Pharaoh in exchange for food, gaining control of the land, people, and cattle. (acquired: gained, severely: greatly) **9.** After the famine, Joseph provided seed and food to the people so they could sow the land in the eighth year, as the Nile had overflowed the land. (provided: gave, overflowed: flooded) **10.** During the seven years of famine, the Nile only irrigated the banks. Now, it flooded, allowing for abundant crops. (irrigated: watered, abundant: plentiful) **11.** The first year of this event was the fourth week of the 45th Jubilee (2178 A.M.), and Egypt's harvest was plentiful. (event: occurrence, plentiful: abundant) **12.** Joseph took one-fifth of the harvest for Pharaoh and allowed the people to keep the rest for food and seed, making it a law in Egypt. (took: collected, allowed: permitted) **13.** Israel lived in Egypt for 17 more years, making his total lifespan 147 years, three jubilees. He died in the 4th year of the 5th week of the 45th Jubilee (2188 A.M.). (lifetime: span, died: passed away) **14.** Before his death, Israel blessed his sons, prophesied what would happen to them in Egypt, and gave Joseph a double portion in the land. (blessed: honored, prophesied: foretold) **15.** Israel passed away, and was buried in the double cave in Hebron, where Abraham had buried his wife Sarah. (passed away: died, buried: interred) **16.** He entrusted his books and the books of his ancestors to his son Levi to preserve and pass down to future generations. (entrusted: gave, preserve: safeguard).

Chapter 46

1. After Yacob (Jacob) died, the children of Yisrael (Israel) grew and became a great nation in Egypt. They were united in heart, helping and loving each other, and they greatly multiplied during Yoseph's (Joseph's) life. (Yisrael: descendants of Jacob, Yoseph: son of Jacob, who ruled in Egypt) **2.** During Yoseph's life, there was no evil or Satan, and all the Egyptians honored the children of Yisrael as long as he lived. (Satan: the adversary, the force of evil) **3.** Yoseph died at 110, having lived seventeen years in Canaan, served ten years, spent three years in prison, and ruled Egypt for eighty years. (Canaan: land promised to Abraham's descendants, Pharaoh: king of Egypt) **4.** Yoseph passed away, as did all his brothers and their generation. **5.** Before his death, Yoseph instructed the children of Yisrael to take his bones when they left Egypt. **6.** Yoseph made them swear to carry his bones, knowing the Egyptians would not bury him in Canaan, because Makamaron (a Canaanite king) had killed the Egyptian king in battle and pursued the Egyptians to the gates of 'Ermon. (Makamaron: king of Canaan, 'Ermon: a location near Canaan) **7.** The new Egyptian king was stronger and stopped Makamaron from entering Egypt, closing the gates, and preventing anyone from leaving or entering. (Pharaoh: king of Egypt) **8.** Yoseph died in the forty-sixth jubilee, in the second year of the sixth week, and was buried in Egypt. All his brothers died afterward. (Jubilee: a 50-year period, marking a time of rest) **9.** In the forty-seventh jubilee, during the second year of the second week, the Egyptian king fought the king of Canaan. The children of Yisrael buried the bones of all the children of Yacob (Jacob), except Yoseph, in the field by the double cave in the mountain. (Yacob: Jacob, a patriarch of the tribes of Israel, double cave: a burial site in Canaan) **10.** Most returned to Egypt, but a few stayed in the mountains of Hebron. Amram (Moses' father) remained with them. (Hebron: a city in Canaan, Amram: father of Moses) **11.** The king of Canaan defeated the Egyptian king and shut Egypt's gates. **12.** The Egyptian king then devised a plan to oppress the children of Yisrael. **13.** He said to the Egyptians, "The children of Yisrael have become too numerous. Let us deal wisely with them before they grow too strong, or they may join our enemies and leave for Canaan." **14.** He appointed taskmasters to force them into slavery, building cities for Pharaoh, including Pithom and Raamses, and repairing Egypt's fortifications. (Pithom, Raamses: cities in Egypt) **15.** The Egyptians harshly oppressed the children of Yisrael, but the more they were mistreated, the more they multiplied. The Egyptians began to despise them.

Chapter 47

1. In the seventh week of the seventh year, during the 47th jubilee, your father left Canaan, and you were born in the fourth week, sixth year, during the 48th jubilee, a time of hardship for Israel. (Canaan: ancient region; jubilee: 49-year period) **2.** Pharaoh, king of Egypt, ordered that all male Israelite infants be thrown into the river. (Pharaoh: title for Egyptian kings) **3.** They cast the infants into the river for seven months, until the day you were born. **4.** Your mother hid you for three months, but was eventually discovered. She made a small ark, sealed it with pitch, and placed it among the reeds by the river. She left you there for seven days, visiting by night to nurse you, while your sister Miriam guarded you by day. (Miriam: Moses' sister) **5.** During that time, Tharmuth, Pharaoh's daughter, came to bathe in the river. She heard your cry and ordered her servants to bring you out. **6.** She took you from the ark and had compassion on you. **7.** Your sister asked her, "Shall I find a Hebrew woman to nurse and care for this child for you?" **8.** Pharaoh's daughter said, "Yes." Miriam went and brought your mother, Jochebed, who was paid to nurse you. (Jochebed: Moses' mother) **9.** When you grew older, they brought you to Pharaoh's daughter, who adopted you. Your father, Amram, taught you to write, and after three weeks, you were brought into the royal court. (Amram: Moses' father) **10.** You spent three weeks at court before leaving and seeing an Egyptian striking an Israelite. You killed the Egyptian and hid him in the sand. **11.** The next day, you found two Israelites fighting and asked the wrongdoer, "Why are you striking your brother?" **12.** The man angrily replied, "Who made you ruler and judge over us? Will you kill me as you did the Egyptian?" You feared and fled, terrified by his words.

Chapter 48

1. In the sixth year of the third week of the forty-ninth jubilee, you left for Midian and stayed there for one year and five weeks, then returned to Egypt in the second week of the second year of the fiftieth jubilee. (Midian: a desert region east of Egypt) **2.** You know what God spoke to you on Mount Sinai and what Prince Mastema planned when you were returning to Egypt. (Mount Sinai: the mountain where Moses received the Ten Commandments; Mastema: a fallen angel or adversary) **3.** Did Mastema not try to kill you and free the Egyptians when he saw you were sent to bring judgment on them? **4.** But I rescued you, and you performed signs and wonders in Egypt against Pharaoh, his family, and his people. (Pharaoh: the ruler of Egypt) **5.** God brought great vengeance for Israel, sending plagues: blood, frogs, lice, dog-flies, boils, cattle deaths, hail, locusts, darkness, and the death of the firstborn, and He burned their idols. (Plagues: calamities sent by God to punish Egypt) **6.** Everything was done through your hand so you could proclaim these events before they happened, speaking to Pharaoh and his people. (Pharaoh: the ruler of Egypt) **7.** Everything you said came to pass, as ten plagues struck Egypt, executing vengeance for Israel. (Plagues: divine punishments) **8.** God did this for Israel, keeping His covenant with Abraham to punish the Egyptians for enslaving His people. (Abraham: the patriarch of Israel) **9.** Prince Mastema opposed you, trying to hand you over to Pharaoh and aiding the Egyptian sorcerers. (Mastema: the evil prince; sorcerers: practitioners of magic) **10.** The sorcerers performed evil acts, but we did not allow them to heal or cure. (Sorcerers: people skilled in magic) **11.** God struck them with painful ulcers, and they could not stand, their powers destroyed, unable to perform a miracle. (Ulcers: painful sores; miracles: supernatural acts) **12.** Despite these signs, Mastema was not shamed, but stirred the Egyptians to pursue you with chariots, horses, and their armies. (Chariots: wheeled vehicles used in battle; armies: military forces) **13.** I stood between the Egyptians and Israel, delivering them, and God parted the sea for Israel to pass through on dry land. (Sea: the Red Sea, through which the Israelites escaped) **14.** Those pursuing Israel were cast into the sea by God, as the Egyptians had cast their children into the river. God took vengeance on them, destroying a million, and for one child thrown into the river, a thousand soldiers were slain. (River: the Nile River, where Egyptian Pharaoh ordered the death of Hebrew infants) **15.** From the fourteenth to the eighteenth day, Mastema was bound behind Israel, unable to accuse them. (Mastema: the evil prince) **16.** On the nineteenth day, we set him free to help the Egyptians pursue Israel. (Egyptians: the people of Egypt, enemies of Israel) **17.** God hardened the Egyptians' hearts, making them stubborn, so His plan to destroy them in the sea would succeed. (Hardened hearts: a biblical expression for stubbornness) **18.** On the fourteenth day, we bound Mastema again to prevent him from accusing Israel when they asked the Egyptians for gold, silver, and bronze vessels, in exchange for the labor they had endured. (Silver, gold, and bronze: precious metals used for trade) **19.** Thus, Israel did not leave Egypt empty-handed. (Egypt: the land of the Egyptians, where Israel was enslaved)

Chapter 49

1. Remember the commandment YAHWEH gave regarding the Passover: celebrate it on the fourteenth day of the first month, slaughter it before evening, and eat it that night, after sunset, on the fifteenth day. (Passover: Jewish festival commemorating the Exodus) **2.** On this night, you ate the Passover in Egypt when the powers of Mastema (Mastema: evil forces or Satan) were unleashed to strike down the firstborn of Egypt, from Pharaoh's son to the captive's child, even the animals. (Pharaoh: king of Egypt) **3.** YAHWEH gave a sign: If a house had the lamb's blood on its doorframe, the destroyer would pass over it, sparing all inside. (Lintels: horizontal beams above doorways) **4.** The powers of YAHWEH obeyed His command and passed over the Israelites, sparing them, their cattle, and even dogs. (Israel: the nation descended from Jacob, also called Israel) **5.** The plague in Egypt was severe; there was no house without death, and mourning filled the land. (Egypt: ancient kingdom in northeastern Africa) **6.** All Israel ate the lamb, drank wine, and praised YAHWEH Almighty, ready to leave Egypt and escape slavery. (YAHWEH: the name of God in the Hebrew Bible) **7.** Remember this day throughout your life, observing it once a year, as commanded. Do not change its date. (Observe: to follow or keep a rule or tradition) **8.** It is an eternal decree, written on heavenly tablets, for Israel to observe the Passover on its fixed day, every year, for all generations. (Heavenly tablets: symbolic or divine records) **9.** Anyone clean who does not observe the Passover by offering a sacrifice, eating and drinking before YAHWEH, will be cut off and bear the guilt. (Ceremonially clean: purified according to religious laws) **10.** Let Israel celebrate the Passover on the fourteenth day of the first month, between the evenings, from the third part of the day to the third part of the night. (Observe: to follow a religious practice) **11.** This is YAHWEH's command: observe it between the evenings. (Evenings: the period between sunset and nightfall) **12.** The lamb should not be slaughtered during daylight but at twilight. Eat it at evening, finishing by the third part of the night, and burn any leftovers by morning. (Twilight: the time just before evening) **13.** Do not cook it in water or eat it raw—roast it over the fire. Eat it quickly, including the head, inwards, and legs, and do not break any bones. No bone of the lamb shall be broken for Israel. (Roast: to cook over an open flame) **14.** YAHWEH commanded Israel to celebrate the Passover on its appointed day and not break any bones, as it is a sacred festival. (Sacred: set apart for religious purpose) **15.** Command Israel to observe the Passover every year at the same time, as it will be a pleasing memorial to YAHWEH. No plague will harm them during the year they follow His command. (Memorial: a celebration to remember) **16.** They must not eat the Passover outside the sanctuary of YAHWEH, but before the sanctuary. All Israel must celebrate it at the appointed time. (Sanctuary: a sacred or holy place) **17.** Anyone who is present on Passover should eat it in the sanctuary before YAHWEH, from twenty years old and up, as it is written. (Ordained: commanded by law or decree) **18.** When Israel enters Canaan and sets up the tabernacle, before the sanctuary is built, they should celebrate the Passover at the tabernacle. (Canaan: the promised land of Israel) **19.** When the house of YAHWEH is built in their land, they will go there and slaughter the Passover at sunset, at the third part of the day. (Inherited land: land given to Israel by God) **20.** They will offer the lamb's blood on the altar's threshold and place its fat on the fire. They will eat the roasted flesh in the court of the sanctified house. (Threshold: the base or entrance of a building) **21.** The Passover should not be celebrated in the cities or elsewhere but only before the tabernacle of YAHWEH, or His house where His name dwells. (Stray: to wander or deviate) **22.** Moses, you must instruct Israel to observe the Passover, as you were commanded. Announce the day every year, the Feast of Unleavened Bread, and daily offerings for seven days of joy before YAHWEH. (Ordinances: established rules or laws) **23.** You celebrated this festival in haste when you left Egypt and reached the wilderness of Shur, finishing it on the shore of the sea. (Shur: a desert region near Egypt, likely on the way to the Red Sea)

Chapter 50

1. After this, I revealed to you the Sabbaths in the desert of Sin, between Elim and Sinai. (Sin: desert region; Elim: oasis; Sinai: mountain) **2.** I shared the Sabbaths of the land on Mount Sinai and the Jubilee years, but the exact year wasn't revealed until you enter the land you will possess. (Mount Sinai: sacred mountain) **3.** The land will observe its Sabbaths while you live in it, and you will recognize the Jubilee year. (Jubilee: year of release) **4.** I set the years, weeks, and Jubilees for you: forty-nine Jubilees have passed from Adam's time, with two more years, and forty more to go before you enter Canaan. (Canaan: promised land; Jordan: river) **5.** The Jubilees will continue until Israel is cleansed of sin and can live in peace, with no evil, and the land will remain pure forever. (Israel: God's chosen people) **6.** I have written down for you the command about the Sabbaths and their related laws. (Sabbaths: day of rest) **7.** Work for six days, but the seventh is the Sabbath of YAHWEH. No work is to be done on it by you, your family, servants, animals, or any visitors. (Sabbath: day of rest) **8.** Anyone who works on the Sabbath will die, including those who work, travel, trade, or carry burdens. (Death penalty: for Sabbath violations) **9.** On the Sabbath, do only what you prepared the day before—eat, drink, rest, and keep the day holy, praising YAHWEH for it. (Holy day: sacred day) **10.** Great honor is given to Israel to celebrate and rest on this festival day, except for offering sacrifices to YAHWEH. (Festival: sacred feast) **11.** The only work allowed on the Sabbath is in the sanctuary, where sacrifices are made continually for Israel's atonement, as commanded. (Atonement: reconciliation with God) **12.** Anyone who works, travels, works the land, lights a fire, rides, or engages in any activity on the Sabbath will die. (Sabbath violations: severe penalties) **13.** Anyone who does these things on the Sabbath will die, and Israel will keep the Sabbaths as instructed in the laws I have given you. (Law: divine command)

82 – Bel and the Dragon

Chapter 1

1. King Astyages died, and Cyrus of Persia took his kingdom. (took: seized) **2.** Daniel spoke with the king and was honored above all his friends. (honored: exalted) **3.** The Babylonians had an idol called Bel, to whom they offered twelve large measures of fine flour, forty sheep, and six vessels of wine every day. (idol: statue, vessels: containers) **4.** The king worshipped Bel daily, but Daniel worshipped only the living God. The king asked why Daniel did not worship Bel. (worshipped: adored) **5.** Daniel answered, "I do not worship idols made by hands, but the living God, who created heaven and earth and rules over all flesh." (flesh: mankind) **6.** The king questioned, "Do you not think Bel is a living god? Do you not see how much he eats and drinks every day?" (living: real, eats: consumes) **7.** Daniel smiled and said, "O king, do not be deceived. Bel is made of clay inside and brass outside. He does not eat or drink." (deceived: misled, inside: interior) **8.** The king became angry and called for his priests, telling them, "If you do not tell me who eats these offerings, you shall die." (angry: furious, offerings: sacrifices) **9.** He added, "But if you can prove that Bel eats them, Daniel will die for blasphemy." Daniel agreed to the king's terms. (prove: show, terms: conditions) **10.** There were seventy priests of Bel, including their wives and children. The king went into the temple with Daniel. (priests: clergy, including: along with) **11.** Bel's priests said, "O king, you set the offerings and seal the door with your signet. If Bel has not eaten them by tomorrow, we will die, or else Daniel will die for lying." (seal: close, lying: deceiving) **12.** They did not worry, for they had made a secret passage under the table to eat the offerings themselves. (secret: hidden, passage: tunnel) **13.** After they left, the king set the food before Bel. Daniel had his servants spread ashes throughout the temple, and the door was sealed with the king's signet. (spread: scatter, ashes: dust) **14.** That night, the priests, with their wives and children, came in as usual and ate the offerings. (usual: normal) **15.** In the morning, the king and Daniel arrived. (arrived: came) **16.** The king asked, "Daniel, are the seals intact?" Daniel replied, "Yes, O king, they are intact." (intact: unbroken) **17.** When the king opened the door, he looked at the table and shouted, "Great is Bel, and there is no deceit in him!" (shouted: exclaimed, deceit: trickery) **18.** Daniel laughed and stopped the king from entering, saying, "Look at the footprints on the floor. Whose are these?" (Footprints: tracks) **19.** The king replied, "I see footprints of men, women, and children." The king was enraged. (enraged: furious) **20.** and he took the priests and their families to the secret entrance where they had eaten the offerings. (Families: households, secret: hidden) **21.** The king had them executed and gave Bel's temple into Daniel's hands, where he destroyed the idol. (executed: killed, destroyed: demolished) **22.** In the same place was a great dragon, worshipped by the Babylonians. (dragon:

serpent) **23.** The king said to Daniel, "Will you also claim this dragon is made of brass? It eats and drinks. You cannot say it is not a living god; therefore, worship it." (claim: say, eats: consumes) **24.** Daniel replied, "I will worship the Lord my God, for He is the living God." (worship: adore) **25.** Daniel asked the king's permission to slay the dragon without sword or staff. The king allowed it. (permission: consent, slay: kill) **26.** Daniel took pitch, fat, and hair, mixed them together, and formed lumps. He fed them to the dragon, which burst open. "These," Daniel said, "are the gods you worship." (pitch: tar, lumps: clumps) **27.** When the Babylonians heard this, they became enraged and conspired against the king, saying, "The king has become a Jew. He destroyed Bel, killed the dragon, and executed the priests." (enraged: furious, conspired: plotted) **28.** They came to the king and demanded, "Hand over Daniel, or we will destroy you and your house." (demanded: ordered, destroy: ruin) **29.** Seeing they were pressing him, the king reluctantly handed Daniel over to them. (pressing: urging, reluctantly: unwillingly) **30.** They cast Daniel into the lions' den, where he remained for six days. (cast: threw) **31.** In the den, there were seven lions, fed daily with two carcasses and two sheep, but they were not fed during Daniel's imprisonment, so they could devour him. (carcasses: bodies, devour: consume) **32.** In Judah, a prophet named Habakkuk had made pottage and was on his way to bring it to the reapers in the field. (pottage: stew, reapers: harvesters) **33.** The angel of the Lord told Habakkuk, "Go, carry this food to Daniel in the lions' den." (food: meal) **34.** Habakkuk replied, "Lord, I have never been to Babylon, and I do not know where the den is." (den: pit) **35.** The angel took him by the crown and, through the power of the Spirit, brought him to Babylon and set him over the den. (crown: head, set: placed) **36.** Habakkuk cried out, "Daniel, take the food that God has sent you." (cried: called) **37.** Daniel replied, "You have remembered me, O God; You have not forsaken those who seek and love You." (forsaken: abandoned) **38.** Daniel ate, and the angel immediately returned Habakkuk to his place. (immediately: instantly) **39.** On the seventh day, the king came to mourn for Daniel. When he reached the den and looked in, he saw Daniel sitting. (Mourn: grieve) **40.** The king cried out, "Great are You, Lord God of Daniel! There is no god but You." (cried: exclaimed, but: except) **41.** The king had Daniel brought out and cast those who had conspired against him into the den, where they were devoured instantly. (cast: threw, devoured: eaten) **42.** The king made a decree that all should honor the God of Daniel. (decree: command).

83 – Prayer of Manasseh

O Lord, Almighty God of our fathers, Abraham, Isaac, and Jacob, who created heaven and earth and all within it; who bound the sea by thy command and sealed the deep with thy glorious name; whom all men fear, for thy power is unbearable, and thy threats to sinners overwhelming. Yet, thy mercy is boundless and thy promise of forgiveness immeasurable. You are compassionate, longsuffering, and merciful, repenting of evil against men. You have promised repentance and forgiveness to sinners. As the God of the just, you offer repentance not to them, but to me, a sinner, who has sinned more than the sands of the sea. My transgressions are many, and I am not worthy to behold the heavens. I am weighed down by my sins and cannot lift my head, for I have provoked your wrath and failed to obey your will. I humbly ask for your grace, acknowledging my iniquities. Forgive me, O Lord, and do not destroy me for my sins. Do not condemn me, but show your mercy, for you are the God of those who repent and will save me according to your great mercy. I will praise you forever, for all the heavens praise you, and yours is the glory forever. Amen. Bound (tied), Sealed (closed), Unbearable (intolerable), Overwhelming (overpowering), Boundless (limitless), Immeasurable (infinite), Compassionate (kind), Longsuffering (patient), Merciful (forgiving), Repenting (feeling regret), Evil (wrongdoing), Forgiveness (absolution), Just (righteous), Transgressions (wrongs), Worthy (deserving), Behold (look upon), Weighed down (burdened), Lift (raise), Provoked (angered), Wrath (anger), Obey (follow), Grace (favor), Acknowledging (admitting), Iniquities (sins), Forgive (pardon), Condemn (judge), Mercy (compassion), Repent (regret), Praise (worship), Forever (eternally),

84 – Psalm 151

1. I was the youngest, tending my father's sheep. (youngest: smallest, tending: caring for) **2.** I played the lyre, crafting music with my hands. (lyre: string instrument, crafting: creating) **3.** Who can tell my story? The Lord hears it Himself. (story: tale, hears: listens to) **4.** God sent an angel to take me from the sheep and anointed me with oil. (anointed: consecrated, oil: olive oil) **5.** My brothers were tall and handsome, but God chose me. (tall: large, handsome: good-looking, chose: selected) **6.** I faced the Philistine, who cursed me by his idols. (faced: confronted, cursed: insulted, idols: false gods) **7.** I took his sword, beheaded him, and brought honor to Israel. (sword: blade, beheaded: decapitated, honor: glory)

85 – The Song of the Three Holy Children

1. They walked in the fire, praising God and blessing the Lord. (praising: worshiping, blessing: adoring) **2.** Azarias stood and prayed, saying: (prayed: petitioned) **3.** Blessed are You, O Lord, God of our fathers, worthy of praise; Your name is glorified forever. (worthy: deserving, glorified: honored) **4.** You are righteous in all Your deeds; Your works are true, Your ways right, and Your judgments just. (righteous: just, works: actions) **5.** You have brought true judgments upon us and Jerusalem, because of our sins. (true: genuine) **6.** We have sinned, departed from You, and committed iniquity. (sinned: wronged, iniquity: wickedness) **7.** We have trespassed, disobeyed Your commandments, and not followed Your ways. (trespassed: violated, followed: obeyed) **8.** Therefore, all that You have done to us is in true judgment. (true: rightful) **9.** You delivered us into the hands of wicked enemies, an unjust king, and the most evil in the world. (wicked: evil, unjust: unfair) **10.** Now we cannot speak; shame and reproach have fallen on Your servants who worship You. (shame: disgrace, reproach: scorn) **11.** Do not abandon us for Your name's sake; do not break Your covenant. (abandon: forsake, covenant: promise) **12.** Let Your mercy not depart from us, for the sake of Abraham, Isaac, and Israel, Your holy ones. (mercy: compassion, depart: leave) **13.** You promised to multiply their descendants as the stars of heaven and the sand by the sea. (multiply: increase, descendants: offspring) **14.** We are fewer than any nation, oppressed because of our sins. (oppressed: persecuted) **15.** There is no prince, prophet, offering, or place to seek mercy before You. (prince: ruler, offering: sacrifice) **16.** Accept us with contrite hearts and humble spirits. (contrite: repentant, humble: modest) **17.** Let our sacrifice be as acceptable as burnt offerings; let us wholly follow You, for those who trust You will not be ashamed. (acceptable: pleasing, trust: rely) **18.** We follow You with all our hearts, fearing You and seeking Your face. (fearing: revering, seeking: pursuing) **19.** Do not shame us, but deal with us in kindness, according to Your mercy. (shame: disgrace, kindness: compassion) **20.** Deliver us by Your marvelous works, and bring glory to Your name, O Lord. (deliver: rescue, marvelous: wondrous) **21.** Let those who harm Your servants be confounded, let their power be broken. (harm: hurt, confounded: confused) **22.** Let them know that You alone are the Lord, glorious over all the earth. (glorious: magnificent) **23.** The king's servants continued to heat the furnace with pitch, naphtha, and wood. (pitch: tar, naphtha: oil) **24.** until the flames rose 49 cubits, burning the Chaldeans near the furnace. (flames: fire, burning: scorching) **25.** But the angel of the Lord came down with Azarias and his companions. (came down: descended) **26.** and extinguished the fire, making the furnace feel like a gentle wind, so that the fire did not touch them. (extinguished: put out, furnace: oven) **27.** Then, as one, they praised, glorified, and blessed God, saying: (praised: worshipped, glorified: honored) **28.** Blessed are You, O Lord, God of our fathers, praised and exalted above all forever. (praised: worshipped, exalted: lifted) **29.** Blessed is Your glorious and holy name, praised and exalted forever. (glorious: magnificent) **30.** Blessed are You in Your holy temple, praised and glorified forever. (temple: sanctuary) **31.** Blessed are You who behold the depths, and sit upon the cherubim, praised above all forever. (behold: see, cherubim: angels) **32.** Blessed are You on the throne of Your kingdom, praised and extolled above all forever. (throne: seat, extolled: praised) **33.** Blessed are You in the heavens, praised and glorified forever. (heavens: skies) **34.** All works of the Lord, bless the Lord; praise and exalt Him above all forever. (works: deeds, praise: worship) **35.** You heavens, bless the Lord; praise and exalt Him above all forever. (heavens: skies) **36.** You angels of the Lord, bless the Lord; praise and exalt Him above all forever. (angels: messengers) **37.** You waters above the heavens, bless the Lord; praise and exalt Him above all forever. (waters: seas) **38.** All powers of the Lord, bless the Lord; praise and exalt Him above all forever. (powers: forces) **39.** Sun and moon, bless the Lord; praise and exalt Him above all forever. (sun: star, moon: satellite) **40.** Stars of heaven, bless the Lord; praise and exalt Him above all forever. (stars: celestial bodies) **41.** All you works of the Lord, bless the Lord; praise and exalt Him above all forever. (works: deeds) **42.** O showers and dew, bless the Lord; exalt Him forever. (showers: rains) **43.** O winds, bless the Lord; exalt Him forever. (winds: breezes) **44.** O fire and heat, bless the Lord; exalt Him forever. (fire: flame, heat: warmth) **47.** O nights and days, bless the Lord; exalt Him forever. (nights: evenings, days: daylight) **48.** O light and darkness, bless the Lord; exalt Him forever. (light: brightness, darkness: night) **50.** O frost and snow, bless the Lord; exalt Him forever. (frost: ice, snow: flakes) **51.** O lightnings and clouds, bless the Lord; exalt Him forever. (lightnings: flashes, clouds: vapor) **52.** Let the earth bless the Lord; exalt Him forever. (earth: land) **53.** O mountains and hills, bless the Lord; exalt Him forever. (mountains: peaks, hills: mounds) **54.** O all that grows on earth, bless the Lord; exalt Him forever. (grows: flourishes) **55.** O sea and rivers, bless the Lord; exalt Him forever. (sea: ocean, rivers: streams) **56.** O fountains, bless the Lord; exalt

Him forever. (fountains: springs) **57.** O whales and all moving in waters, bless the Lord; exalt Him forever. (whales: sea creatures) **58.** O fowls of the air, bless the Lord; exalt Him forever. (fowls: birds) **59.** O beasts and cattle, bless the Lord; exalt Him forever. (beasts: animals, cattle: livestock) **60.** O children of men, bless the Lord; exalt Him forever. (children: descendants) **61.** O Israel, bless the Lord; exalt Him forever. (Israel: people) **62.** O priests of the Lord, bless the Lord; exalt Him forever. (priests: clergy) **63.** O servants of the Lord, bless the Lord; exalt Him forever. (servants: followers) **64.** O spirits and souls of the righteous, bless the Lord; exalt Him forever. (spirits: beings, righteous: virtuous) **65.** O holy and humble of heart, bless the Lord; exalt Him forever. (humble: modest) **66.** O Ananias, Azarias, and Misael, bless the Lord; exalt Him forever—He has rescued us from hell and delivered us from death, from the fire and the flame. (rescued: saved, delivered: freed) **67.** Give thanks to the Lord, for He is good; His mercy endures forever. (thanks: gratitude, endures: lasts) **68.** All who worship the Lord, bless the God of gods, praise Him, and give thanks; His mercy endures forever. (worship: adore, praise: honor).

86 – First Testament of Abraham

Chapter 1
1. Abraham, now old, was called by the Lord: "Abraham, Abraham." He responded, "Here I am." (called: summoned, responded: answered) **2.** The Lord said, "I have chosen you to be a prophet and father of nations. You have yet to see all that God has prepared. Prepare yourself to witness great wonders." (chosen: selected, prepared: arranged) **3.** Abraham replied, "I will do all things according to your word, Lord." (replied: answered)

Chapter 2
1. While Abraham prepared, the Lord sent the archangel Michael. He said, "I've been sent to show you the life to come and the world prepared for the righteous." (righteous: virtuous) **2.** Abraham got ready and followed Michael. (got ready: prepared, followed: accompanied)

Chapter 3
1. They reached a high mountain, and Michael told Abraham, "Look down upon the earth." (reached: arrived, told: said) **2.** Abraham looked and saw the earth as a disk of dust, the sea as a drop of water, and humanity as a swarm of flies. (looked: gazed, swarm: group) **3.** He marveled and praised God for the greatness of His creation. (marveled: wondered, praised: adored)

Chapter 4
1. They arrived at a high place with a gate of fire, where many entered. The brilliance from within shone like the sun. (arrived: reached, brilliance: radiance) **2.** Abraham asked, "What is this place?" Michael replied, "This is the Gate of Righteousness, through which the righteous enter the city of God." (asked: inquired, replied: answered)

Chapter 5
1. They then came to a dark and dreadful place where men were suffering. This was the outer darkness. (Dark: gloomy, dreadful: terrifying) **2.** Abraham wept and asked, "Do all who sin suffer here?" (Wept: cried, suffer: endure) **3.** Michael answered, "These are those who have denied righteousness; they will be tormented until the day of redemption." (Denied: rejected, tormented: tortured)

Chapter 6
1. They came upon a beautiful, light-filled land, where many souls, dressed in shining garments, sang praises to the Lord. (shining: radiant) **2.** Abraham, filled with joy, asked, "Who are these, my Lord?" (filled: overwhelmed, asked: inquired) **3.** Michael answered, "These are those who have kept their garments clean, washed in the blood of the Lamb. They rejoice forever in the Lord's presence." (kept: maintained, rejoice: celebrate)

Chapter 7
1. They reached a place of peace and rest, filled with gardens and flowing waters. Michael said, "This is the rest prepared for the servants of God." (Reached: arrived, rest: repose) **2.** Abraham, filled with joy, asked, "May we remain here?" (filled: overwhelmed, remain: stay) **3.** Michael replied, "You must return to earth for a time, but when your days are fulfilled, you will come here again." (replied: answered, fulfilled: completed)

Chapter 8
1. Abraham returned to his place, living many years, teaching his children and household the ways of the Lord. (returned: went back, teaching: instructing) **2.** As he neared his departure, he called Isaac, blessed him, and gave him all his instructions. (neared: approached, instructions: directions) **3.** Abraham rested with his fathers in peace, full of days and joy, awaiting the resurrection. (rested: rested, awaiting: expecting)

Chapter 9
1. Before his death, Abraham gathered his children and grandchildren, speaking of the visions he had seen and God's promises. (Gathered: assembled, promises: vows) **2.** He instructed them to uphold justice, practice righteousness, and walk humbly with God. He reminded them of the covenant God made with him and his descendants. (Instructed: taught, descendants: heirs) **3.** Abraham's words were full of wisdom and grace, inspiring all who heard him. (Words: teachings, inspiring: motivating)

Chapter 10
1. When the time came, the archangel Michael returned to guide Abraham to his place of rest. (returned: came back, guide: direct) **2.** As Abraham's soul departed, there was great mourning, but peace, as his family knew he was going to be with the Lord. (Departed: left, mourning: grieving) **3.** His family buried him in the cave of Machpelah, beside Sarah, as he had instructed. (Buried: interred, instructed: ordered)

Chapter 11
1. In the afterlife, Abraham was greeted by the righteous souls of Adam, Noah, and Melchizedek, who welcomed him with great joy. (Greeted: welcomed, righteous: virtuous) **2.** They praised God together, rejoicing in the fulfillment of His promises. (Praised: adored, fulfillment: completion) **3.** Abraham was shown the heavenly kingdom, a land of peace and glory where the righteous dwell in God's presence. (Shown: revealed, dwell: reside)

Chapter 12
1. Michael showed Abraham the Book of Life, where the names of the righteous were recorded. Abraham's name shone brightly, marked by his faithful deeds. (Showed: revealed, recorded: written) **2.** The angels proclaimed him a father of many nations, reflecting his impact on generations. (Proclaimed: declared, impact: influence) **3.** Abraham spent his days in the heavenly kingdom, interceding for his descendants and those who walk in righteousness. (Spent: lived, interceding: praying)

Chapter 13
1. On earth, Abraham's memory lived on. Isaac and his descendants carried forward the Abrahamic covenant, living by the laws Abraham had taught them. (Lived on: endured, carried forward: continued) **2.** They became a great nation, as God promised, numerous as the stars and sand. (Numerous: countless) **3.** Through them, the blessings promised to Abraham spread to all nations, fulfilling God's word to him. (Spread: distributed, fulfilling: completing)

Chapter 14
1. In the heavenly realms, Abraham was shown visions of his descendants' future, their trials and victories. (Shown: revealed, trials: struggles) **2.** He saw the coming of a great Deliverer from his lineage, which would bring salvation to all humanity. (Coming: arrival, salvation: deliverance) **3.** Abraham's heart was filled with awe and gratitude for God's unfolding plan. (Filled: overwhelmed, unfolding: developing)

Chapter 15
1. As ages passed, Abraham continued to serve as a patriarch in the heavenly kingdom, a guiding light and intercessor for those who seek righteousness. (Served: acted, intercessor: mediator) **2.** His story, a testament to faith and obedience, inspired generations to seek a closer relationship with God. (Testament: testimony, inspired: motivated) **3.** Thus, Abraham's testament remains a beacon of hope and faith, reminding all of the rewards awaiting the faithful in God's presence. (remains: stands, beacon: guide)

Chapter 16
1. In the heavenly realms, Abraham watched over his descendants with great care. He saw the establishment of Israel, the rise and fall of kings, and God's unwavering love despite the people's disobedience. (watched: observed, unwavering: steadfast) **2.** From paradise, Abraham observed the prophets calling for repentance and righteousness, as he himself had walked. (observed: saw, repentance: remorse) **3.** He rejoiced in moments of revival but wept over the suffering and exile his people endured. (rejoiced: celebrated, endured: suffered)

Chapter 17
1. Abraham saw the great temple in Jerusalem, a symbol of God's presence, with Solomon, his descendant, dedicating it with prayers and sacrifices. (symbol: sign, dedicating: consecrating) **2.** Abraham felt a deep connection to his people, witnessing the fulfillment of God's promises. (felt: experienced, fulfillment: completion) **3.** Yet, he also witnessed the temple's destruction and his people's captivity, which grieved his soul. (destruction: ruin, grieved: saddened)

Chapter 18
1. Abraham was particularly moved by the vision of the coming Messiah, promised through his lineage. (moved: touched, promised: foretold) **2.** He saw the Messiah's humble birth, life of service, profound teachings, and ultimate sacrifice for humanity's sins. (humble: modest, sacrifice: atonement) **3.** This filled Abraham with awe and gratitude, understanding this was the fulfillment of God's promise to bless all nations through his offspring. (awe: wonder, fulfillment: realization)

Chapter 19

1. With the coming of the Messiah, Abraham saw the spread of a new covenant, written on the hearts of all believers, including Gentiles. (spread: expansion, covenant: agreement) **2.** The gospel's spread brought great joy to Abraham, as he saw multitudes from every nation turning to worship God. (spread: dissemination, multitudes: crowds) **3.** He marveled at how the death of the Messiah brought life and hope to all peoples. (marveled: wondered, hope: optimism)

Chapter 20

1. As time passed, Abraham continued as a witness to God's plan, seeing trials and tribulations but also the ultimate victory of the faithful through faith and the Spirit's power. (witness: observer, victory: triumph) **2.** He saw a great multitude from all nations standing before God's throne, praising in redemption. (multitude: crowd, redemption: salvation) **3.** This vision reassured Abraham, confirming the promises God made to him long ago, now beautifully and fully realized. (reassured: comforted, confirmed: affirmed)

87 – The History of Susanna

Set apart from the beginning of DANIEL, be- cause it is not in the Hebrew, as neither the Nar- ration of Bel and the Dragon.

1. A man named Joakim lived in Babylon. **2.** He married Susanna, daughter of Helkias, a beautiful woman who feared the Lord. **3.** Her parents were righteous and taught her the law of Moses. **4.** Joakim was wealthy, with a garden next to his house, and many Jews came to him. **5.** Two elders were appointed as judges, fulfilling the Lord's prophecy about wicked judges from Babylon. (prophecy: prediction) **6.** They visited Joakim's house, and people with legal matters came to them. **7.** At noon, Susanna walked in her husband's garden. **8.** The elders saw her daily and became infatuated. (Infatuated: obsessed) **9.** They ignored their moral judgment and their eyes, avoiding heaven's view. (moral: relating to right and wrong) **10.** Both were troubled by their desires but did not confess them to each other. **11.** They were too ashamed to express their lustful thoughts. (lustful: having strong sexual desire) **12.** They watched her daily, hoping for an opportunity. **13.** One suggested they go home for dinner. **14.** They parted, then returned, confessing their lust and setting a time to find her alone. (Confessing: admitting) **15.** Susanna went to the garden alone with two maids to bathe. **16.** The elders, hidden, watched her. (hidden: concealed) **17.** She asked her maids for oil and bathing supplies, locking the garden doors. (locking: securing) **18.** The maids left through another door to fetch the items, unaware of the elders hiding. (fetch: go and get) **19.** After the maids left, the elders approached and said, **20.** "The garden doors are locked, and we desire you; consent to us." (consent: agree) **21.** "If you refuse, we'll claim you were with a young man and sent your maids away." **22.** Susanna said, "I'm trapped. If I comply, it's death; if not, I can't escape your hands." (comply: obey) **23.** "It's better to fall into your hands and not sin against the Lord." **24.** She cried out, and the elders accused her. (accused: blamed) **25.** One ran and opened the garden doors. (opened: unlocked) **26.** The servants heard the cry and rushed in through a side door. (rushed: hurried) **27.** The elders' story shamed the servants, as such rumors about Susanna had never been heard. (shamed: embarrassed) **28.** The next day, the elders came to Joakim's house to accuse Susanna and seek her death. **29.** They called for Susanna to be brought before them. (called: summoned) **30.** Susanna came with her parents and relatives. **31.** She was beautiful and delicate. (delicate: fragile) **32.** The elders ordered her to be unveiled to gaze at her beauty. (unveiled: uncovered) **33.** Her friends and onlookers wept. (Onlookers: observers) **34.** The elders stood and placed hands on her head. **35.** Susanna, weeping, looked up to heaven, trusting in God. (weeping: crying) **36.** They claimed that she went into the garden with two maids, sent them away, and then slept with a young man. **37.** "We saw them together, but couldn't catch the man, who escaped." **38.** "We asked her who he was, but she refused to tell us." **39.** The assembly believed the elders, condemning her. (assembly: group) **40.** Susanna cried, "O eternal God, you know all secrets. I must die for false accusations." (eternal: lasting forever) **41.** The Lord heard her. **42.** As she was led to death, God raised up a young man named Daniel. (raised: brought up) **43.** He declared, "I am innocent of her blood." (innocent: free from guilt) **44.** The people turned to Daniel and asked what he meant. **45.** Daniel said, "Are you fools, condemning her without truth? (fools: foolish people) **46.** Return to judgment, for the elders are lying." (lying: not telling the truth) **47.** The crowd quickly turned back, and the elders invited Daniel to prove his words. (prove: demonstrate) **48.** Daniel said, "Separate them, and I'll question them." (separate: divide) **49.** The elders were separated, and Daniel addressed one, calling him old in wickedness. (wickedness: evil behavior) **50.** Daniel asked, "Under what tree did you see them together?" **51.** The elder answered, "Under a mastic tree." (mastic: a type of tree) **52.** Daniel replied, "You've lied, and God's angel will cut you in two." (cut: sever) **53.** Daniel then asked the other elder about his testimony. (testimony: statement) **54.** The second elder gave a similar false claim. Daniel exposed the lies of both men. (exposed: revealed) **55.** The assembly condemned the elders, and Susanna was saved from death. (condemned: sentenced) **56.** He put the first elder aside and called the second, saying, "You, descendant of Canaan, not Judah, have been deceived by beauty and corrupted by lust." (deceived: misled) **57.** "You have seduced the daughters of Israel with fear, but the daughter of Judah would not fall for your wickedness." (seduced: attracted or led astray) **58.** "Now, tell me, under what tree did you see them together?" The elder replied, "Under a holm tree." (holm: a type of tree) **59.** Daniel said, "You've also lied, and the angel of God stands with a sword to cut you in two." (sword: weapon) **60.** The assembly cried out, blessing God who saves those who hope in Him. (assembly: group) **61.** The people rose against the two elders, for Daniel exposed their lies. (exposed: revealed) **62.** Following the law of Moses, they did to them as they had planned to do to Susanna: they executed them, and the innocent blood was saved. (Executed: put to death) **63.** Helkias and his wife, along with Joakim and their family, praised God for Susanna, finding no dishonesty in her. (dishonesty: untruthfulness) **64.** From that day, Daniel gained great respect among the people. (respect: admiration)

88 – The Shepherd of Hermas

Vision 1

1. Hermas, a Christian slave, is guided by a radiant lady who instructs him to read a text to the church elders. She tells him he will write two more books, which must also be given to the elders upon completion (radiant: shining brightly).

Vision 2

1. Hermas see the same lady, who reveals herself as the Church. She gives him a small book to copy. Once completed, the book becomes sealed and ascends to heaven, symbolizing its holiness and unchangeable authority.

Vision 3

1. Hermas have a vision of a beast rising from a chasm, symbolizing trials. Guided by the lady, representing faith, he escapes unharmed (chasm: deep opening in the ground).

Vision 4

1. The lady appears as a city on a vast plain, symbolizing the Church. She warns Hermas of coming trials and persecutions but assures him of the Church's ultimate triumph (persecutions: mistreatment due to beliefs).

Vision 5

1. Hermas sees church elders interpreting his visions. They encourage him to remain steadfast in faith and emphasize repentance and adherence to Christ's teachings (steadfast: firmly committed).

Mandate 1

1. Hermas is taught to believe in one God and keep faith, as it shields him from evil and guides him through trials (shields: protects).

Mandate 2

1. Hermas is warned to avoid false prophets and discern true prophecy by observing actions and outcomes.

Mandate 3

1. The mandate highlights simplicity and avoiding hypocrisy, urging Hermas to maintain a pure and truthful heart (hypocrisy: pretending to have moral qualities one does not possess).

Mandate 4

1. Hermas is told to uphold integrity, avoid dishonest gain, and remember that ill-gotten riches bring sorrow (integrity: honesty and strong moral principles).

Mandate 5

1. Patience is emphasized, teaching that enduring trials with joy brings God's favor and is a mark of true faith (enduring: lasting through hardship).

Mandate 6

1. Hermas learn the importance of repentance and forgiving others to receive God's forgiveness (repentance: feeling regret for wrongdoing and seeking to change).

Mandate 7

1. He is warned against fear, which weakens faith, and is encouraged to trust God with confidence (confidence: firm trust or belief).

Mandate 8

1. Hermas is advised to practice chastity and resist lust, as it leads away from righteousness (chastity: purity and self-control, especially regarding desires).

Mandate 9

1. Prayer must be sincere and ceaseless, free of distractions, and offered with unwavering faith (ceaseless: without stopping).

Mandate 10

1. Fasting is explained as a spiritual act of humility and devotion, purifying the soul and bringing it closer to God (humility: modesty and lack of pride).

Similitude 1
1. Hermas see a vineyard with a fence, symbolizing the Law protecting those who follow the Church's teachings (vineyard: a plantation of grapevines).
Similitude 2
1. A mountain of various stones represents the Church, with the faithful forming its structure based on their actions (faithful: loyal believers).
Similitude 3
1. An elderly woman, symbolizing the Church, teaches Hermas about endurance in faith and good deeds (endurance: the ability to remain steadfast through challenges).
Similitude 4
1. Trees reflecting seasons symbolize resurrection and judgment, showing actions determine spiritual outcomes (resurrection: being raised to life after death).
Similitude 5
1. The Lord, as a shepherd, teaches leaders to be just and nurturing, guiding their flock by example (nurturing: caring for and encouraging growth).
Similitude 6
1. A city under construction symbolizes Heaven, built from the deeds of the faithful, urging vigilance and righteousness (vigilance: careful watchfulness).
Similitude 7
1. A great feast represents the eternal reward for the righteous who remain steadfast in faith and deeds (eternal: lasting forever).
Similitude 8
1. A tower being built symbolizes the Church, made of righteous souls, with flawed ones rejected (flawed: having faults or imperfections). **2.** Stones are carefully examined, representing believers' choices strengthening or excluding them from God's Kingdom (examined: inspected or judged closely). **3.** Hermas is taught that actions determine inclusion in the tower or rejection (rejection: being refused or excluded).
Similitude 9
1. A field ready for harvest symbolizes the righteous prepared for salvation, while thorns represent unrepentant sinners (harvest: gathering crops as a metaphor for God's judgment). **2.** The day of salvation comes unexpectedly, urging constant readiness and purity (unexpectedly: without prior warning). **3.** Living righteously ensures inclusion in the harvest (righteously: living in a morally right way).
Similitude 10
1. A tower with ascending seats represents levels of afterlife glory based on faithfulness (ascending: rising upward). **2.** Deeds determine one's place, witnessed by heavenly hosts (hosts: large groups, often referring to angels in this context). **3.** Hermas are exhorted to strive for the highest place through obedience and charity (exhorted: strongly encouraged).
Similitude 11
1. A river of clear water symbolizes the Holy Spirit sanctifying the faithful (sanctifying: making holy or pure). **2.** Trees bearing fruit represent the continuous, fruitful lives of those living by the Spirit (fruitful: productive or beneficial). **3.** The water reflects God's boundless grace for His servants (boundless: limitless or infinite).
Similitude 12
1. A sealed book contains all deeds and is opened only on Judgment Day by the sinless Lamb (sealed: securely closed to prevent access). **2.** The book reveals final destinies; Hermas is warned to remain faithful (destinies: ultimate outcomes or fates). **3.** Righteous deeds ensure inclusion in the book of life (inclusion: being part of something).
Similitude 13
1. A large tree represents Christ, providing rest and sustenance to the faithful (sustenance: nourishment or support). **2.** Its shade and leaves symbolize protection and nourishment from Christ's teachings (nourishment: sustenance needed for growth and health). **3.** Believers must stay close to Christ for guidance and strength (guidance: direction or advice).
Similitude 14
1. A garden of diverse plants symbolizes various gifts and ministries in the Church (ministries: services or functions within the Church). **2.** Each member contributes to the Church's growth, reflecting their unique talents (contributes: adds or gives for a common purpose). **3.** The garden's health depends on proper care, like the Church on its members' stewardship (stewardship: responsibility for managing something).
Similitude 15
1. A banquet with wedding garments symbolizes Heaven, open only to the righteous and prepared (garments: clothing, often symbolic of one's spiritual state). **2.** The garments represent holy living and righteous deeds (righteous: morally right r virtuous). **3.** Vigilance and worthiness ensure participation in the heavenly feast (worthiness: deserving something due to good qualities).

Similitude 16
1. A fortress of shining stones symbolizes faith, offering refuge and joy to the victorious (fortress: a strong and secure place). **2.** Hymns inside reflect the triumph of those overcoming the world (hymns: religious songs of praise). **3.** Hermas is encouraged to live faithfully to enter this fortress (faithfully: with loyalty and devotion).
Similitude 17
1. A race represents the Christian journey, with crowns awarded to those who finish faithfully (crowns: symbols of victory or reward). **2.** The crowns signify eternal life for those persevering in faith and purity (persevering: continuing steadfastly despite difficulty). **3.** Hermas is urged to run with endurance, focusing on the heavenly reward (reward: benefit or prize for effort).
Similitude 18
1. A vine by a spring symbolizes the Church sustained by Christ, the living water (spring: a natural water source). **2.** Its fruitfulness depends on its connection to the spring, like believers on Christ (fruitfulness: being productive and flourishing). **3.** Remaining in Christ allows believers to bear spiritual fruit and gain eternal life (spiritual fruit: qualities reflecting God's character).

The Complete Audio File

Download: Audio File of the Complete 88 Books

Download: Digital 112 Apocrypha Books in PDF Format